$2.64

Loretta Cannon
March 5, 1929

TWELVE CENTURIES OF ENGLISH POETRY AND PROSE

REVISED EDITION

BY

ALPHONSO GERALD NEWCOMER
LATE PROFESSOR OF ENGLISH, STANFORD UNIVERSITY

ALICE E. ANDREWS
ENGLISH DEPARTMENT, CLEVELAND HIGH SCHOOL, ST. PAUL

HOWARD JUDSON HALL
ASSOCIATE PROFESSOR OF ENGLISH, STANFORD UNIVERSITY

SCOTT, FORESMAN & COMPANY
CHICAGO ATLANTA NEW YORK

INTRODUCTION

This book was undertaken in response to the desire, expressed in many quarters, for a large body of standard English literature in an accessible, compact form, to accompany and supplement the manuals of literary history in use. As the project gradually shaped itself in the editors' hands, it took on something like the following threefold purpose:

First, to include, as far as possible, those classics of our literature—the ballads, elegies, and odes, the *L'Allegros* and *Deserted Villages*—which afford the basis for an appreciation of the greatest English writers.

Second, to supplement these with a sufficient number of selections from every period of our literature to provide a perspective and make the volume fairly representative from a historical point of view.

Third, to go somewhat outside of the beaten track, though keeping still to standard literature, and make a liberal addition of selections, especially from the drama and prose, to enliven the collection and widen its human interest.

This comprehensive character is indicated by the title of the volume. A somewhat unusual feature is the inclusion of both poetry and prose. The two forms have not been indiscriminately mingled, but they have been deliberately set side by side in the belief that both will gain by their conjunction. It is scarcely to be denied that at the present time a volume made up wholly of verse gives the impression of a collection of enshrined "classics," meant either to be admired from a distance or studied with tedious minuteness. On the other hand, a miscellaneous collection of unrelieved prose lacks attractiveness by seeming to lack emotional appeal. Putting them together will not only afford the relief of variety, but should lead to a better understanding of both by showing that the difference between them is often more formal than real—that poetry, with all its concern for form, is primarily the medium of the simplest truth and feeling, and that prose, though by preference pedestrian, may at times both soar and sing.

In making the selections, it was considered best to exclude the modern novel, a form of literature that scarcely lends itself to selection at all.* With this exception, pretty much the whole field has been covered, though it is not maintained that every important man or movemen has been represented. The Restoration drama can, for obvious reasons, have no place in these pages; nor should the omissions be regarded with surprise if a volume of confessedly rather elementary purpose fails to include such men as Burton, Browne, Locke, and Newton, voyagers "on strange seas of thought, alone." The endeavor was simply to secure the widest representation consistent with the intended service of the book and compatible with a due regard for both amount and proportion. Inconclusive fragments have been studiously avoided. Here and there, where a specimen of form only was desired—of Surrey's blank verse, for example, or of Thomson's Spenserian manner—this principle has not been adhered to. But apart from such exceptional cases, even where wholes could not be given, enough has still been given, not only to set the reader going, but to take him somewhere.

The order is chronological. The adherence to chronology, however, has not been rigid, either in the order of names or in the order of selections under the names. Prose has usually been separated from verse, and in some periods, lyrics and sonnets have often been placed together. In fact, wherever an unpleasant juxtaposition could be avoided, or a more effective grouping secured, there has been no hesitation to exercise some freedom.

Selections from Old English, from Latin, and from Middle English down to Chaucer, are given in translation. After Chaucer, the original text is followed, but spelling and punctuation are modernized—a course which is almost necessary if a writer like Mandeville is to be read with any ease, and which has every reason to support it in writers of a much later date. To this rule the customary exceptions in poetry are made: Chaucer,

* This rule has been abandoned in the additions from the Post-Victorian Period.

Langland, the Ballads, *Everyman,* and Spenser's artificially archaic *Faerie Queene,* are kept in the original form. Much care has been bestowed upon the text. It is really a matter of somewhat more than curiosity whether, in the poet's fancy, the lowing herd *wind* over the lea, or *winds* over the lea, and he ought by all means to be reported faithfully. At the same time it has seemed equally important in a few instances to correct a manifest and misleading error or to remove an extremely offensive epithet. The instances of such changes are perhaps not a dozen in all.

The notes have been placed at the bottom of the page, primarily for convenience, but also to insure brevity. It will be observed that they serve other purposes than those of a mere glossary. Every care has been taken to make them pertinent and really explanatory, and to avoid unduly distracting the reader's attention or affronting his intelligence. It seemed fair to assume, on the reader's part, the possession of a dictionary and a Bible, and some elementary knowledge of classical mythology. Allusions to matters of very slight relevancy are purposely left unexplained. For example, in such an isolated poem as *Deor's Lament,* it seemed more to the purpose, at least of the present volume, to give a bit of literary comment than to weight down the poem with notes on events in remote Germanic tradition. On the other hand, wherever a note, of whatever nature, seemed absolutely demanded, no pains have been spared to provide it. In the case of selections hitherto not specially edited, this frequently involved great labor, and the editors learned how much easier it is to make an anthology than to equip it for intelligent use.* Finally, there are frequent cross-references within the present volume.

Manifestly many advantages are to be derived from having so much material in a single volume. The book may even be used as a source-book for the study of English history, in a liberal interpretation of that subject. From the Anglo-Saxon period, for example, a sufficient diversity of literature is presented to give body and reality to that far-away time. In a later period, the constantly recurring terms and manners of feudalism and chivalry make that age also historically real, and the archaism of Spenser, as the age passes away, does not appear such a detached, unintelligible phenomenon. The concentric "spheres" of the old Ptolemaic astronomy may be seen revolving about this earth as a center through all the poetry down to Milton, when science steps in with its inexorable logic and man is constrained to take a humbler view of his station in the universe. On the other hand, Utopia may change to Arcadia, and Arcadia to El Dorado, but the dream itself refuses to die. A juster conception of the writers themselves is likewise made possible. Shakespeare is removed from his position of lonely grandeur. Milton, so fallen on evil days, finds ample justification for his poetic complaint in the graphic prose descriptions of Pepys and Evelyn. Johnson is humanized by being presented as the friend of Boswell.

Again, in the detailed study of the literature there is the immense advantage of often having at hand, where each student can see it for himself, the source of an allusion, the echo of a sentiment, or the different play of diverse imaginations about the same theme. One passage of Milton can be set by the side of a similar passage in Caedmon, another can be paralleled in Marlowe, a third in Spenser. The story of the last fight of *The Revenge* can be read first in Raleigh's circumstantial narrative and then in Tennyson's martial ode. Malory's Arthur reappears in Tennyson; Scott's Bonny Dundee in Macaulay's account of the battle of Killiecrankie. If the line in Browning's *Saul* about the "locust-flesh steeped in the pitcher" reminds us of an incident in the life of John the Baptist, we turn with interest to Wyclif's curious version of that story. An unusual word, "brede," occurring in one of Keats's odes, is found to have been used in an ode by Collins, and its literary genealogy can scarcely be doubted. The paths of Addison and Carlyle lie far apart, and yet both appear to have been indebted, the one for a quaint fancy, the other for a striking figure, to the same record of a shipwreck on the frozen shores of Nova Zembla more than three centuries ago. By the discerning teacher

* For instance, one note is still fresh in mind—note 4, page 783—which required the reading of nearly two volumes of Stevenson, to say nothing of the labor spent in searching on the wrong track. Even in such a classic as *Everyman,* there remained obscurities to be cleared up, and apparently no editor had yet hit upon the explanation of so simple a matter as to "take my tappe in my lappe" (page 102, line 801), the meaning of which the editors guessed and subsequently verified by Jamieson's *Scottish Dictionary.* The word "kenns," as used by Scott in *Old Mortality* (see page 544), is not recorded in any of the standard dictionaries, including Jamieson. These examples, which are typical of many others, will serve to show that the preparation of the notes, slight as they may seem, has been no perfunctory or uncritical task.

these cross-references can be multiplied indefinitely and for nearly every cross-reference there will be a decided gain in understanding and appreciation. The student will see what a network a national literature is, and get some conception of the ever increasing enjoyment that attends upon an increasing familiarity with it.

Indeed, it has been one of the chief pleasures in making this compilation to feel that along with the so-called English classics, of finished form and universal content, so much was being gathered which, though less familiar, is scarcely less worthy, and frequently of a more intimate human appeal. It may not be desirable to teach all this matter, nor would it be possible at any one time or place. The important thing is to have it in hand. The teacher is thus given a real freedom of choice and enabled to teach literature, as it should be taught, with the personal touch. For the student, too, there will always remain some tracts of *terra incognita,* with the delight of wandering, of his own free will, along unfrequented paths. To share, for example, in the early Northmen's vague terror of nickers and jotuns, to listen to the words of Alfred-the-Great, to observe the concern of the good bishop of Tarente for the spiritual welfare of the nuns under his charge, to stand by at the birth of the first printed English book and note the aged Caxton's enthusiasm in spite of worn fingers and weary eyes, to join with Jonson in mourning and praising the great fellow-craftsman whom he knew, to watch with Pepys the coronation of the king or hear him piously thank God for the money won at gaming—these are things, it should seem, to arouse the most torpid imagination. If, from excursions of this nature, the student learns that good literature and interesting reading-matter meet, that the one is not confined to exalted odes nor the other to current magazine fiction, a very real service will have been done by widening the scope of this volume.

It is obvious that in pursuing the study of such diverse material, no single method will suffice. Sometimes, as has already been hinted, reading is all that is necessary. But when a writer like Bacon, let us say, or Pope, writes with the deliberate purpose of instruction, his work must be studied with close application and may be analyzed until it yields its last shade of meaning. On the other hand, when Keats sings pathetically of the enduring beauty or art and the transient life of man, or when Browning chants some message of faith and cheer, a minutely analytical or skeptical attitude would be not only futile but fatal. And when the various purposes of instruction, inspiration, and aesthetic delight are combined in one work, as in the supreme example of *Paradise Lost,* the student who hopes to attain to anything like full comprehension must return to it with various methods and in various moods. It is from considerations like these that the teacher must determine his course. One thing, however, cannot be too often repeated. The most successful teacher of literature is he who brings to it a lively sympathy springing from intimate knowledge, assured that method is of minor moment so long as there is the responsive spirit that evokes response.

For ourselves, we would say that while we have divided the labor of preparing both copy and notes, there has been close coöperation at every stage of the work. We owe thanks for suggestions and encouragement to more friends than we may undertake to name. To Dr. Frederick Klaeber, in particular, of the University of Minnesota, we are indebted for advice upon the rendering of certain passages in *Beowulf,* and to Professor Lindsay Todd Damon, of Brown University, for a critical vigilance that has worked to the improvement of almost every page.

1910

A. G. N.
A. E. A.

INTRODUCTION TO THE SECOND EDITION

In preparing a second edition of *Twelve Centuries of English Poetry and Prose,* the editors have had full opportunity to reconsider the entire contents of the book. Down to the post-Victorian period very few changes in authors or selections have seemed necessary. Some slight rearrangements, for the sake of greater clearness, were made in the lyrics of the seventeenth century, and a few poems from that period have been added. The main additions to the volume represent the period from Stevenson to the present time. The editors' task has been to make selections from this period that shall have vivid interest to those for whom the collection is made, and which promise a certain permanence because of their worth. Inevitably, in the ebb and flow of critical ideas, the permanent value of all such selections will, in a few decades, be challenged; we of this generation cannot pass upon the validity of the ideas advanced today or even upon the success of the present experiments in form. But, however posterity may decide, these ideas are set forth vigorously, honestly, and in a style that demands consideration.

In the new edition, headnotes and bibliographies throughout the text introduce each author. The headnotes have two purposes: to give very briefly the main facts of an author's life, especially those most likely to have affected his art; and to furnish a few critical hints that may orient the student, and put him in the way of enjoying the author and of making his own estimate of the author's worth. These critical hints are not designed as a relief to the indifferent or lazy, but as a help to the alert who need only to be directed around hidden pitfalls to solid ground. Brief general introductions have also been prefixed to the literature of each period, setting forth the broad characteristics of the era, and, if possible, the reasons for its trend in ideas and style. A general chronological table, designed to show graphically the social and political backgrounds of English literature, has been made for this edition and will, it is hoped, be useful in fixing in the student's mind the fact that expression through literature is a function of the social organism.

The bibliography is of two kinds. At the end of the volume will be found a general list of the books most serviceable in the field of English literature as a whole. There are also special bibliographical notes incorporated into the headnotes for each author. These cite the most useful biographical and critical books and articles; these lists include standard periodical literature usually found in even small city libraries, and do not exclude references to books that only well-equipped libraries or State circulating libraries contain. The aim throughout is to cite, along with standard criticism, modern or recent criticism that gives the latest fruits of scholarship and well-founded judgment.

There is of course more material in this volume than can be closely studied in the ordinary outline course in the history of English literature; very much more than can be discussed in the classroom. It is hoped, therefore, that the book may be used not wholly as a text, but also as a kind of index, directing the student's reading in the full works of the authors represented in it. To use it blindly as a text demanding complete mastery would be to defeat its intent—to aid students in the enjoyment of a fine art. Mr. George Bernard Shaw, in granting permission to use the extracts from his works appearing in the present volume, made the following pertinent observations concerning the editing of textbooks, and their use:

"By a schoolbook I mean a repulsive volume in which my work appears peppered with references to notes written by some scholastic person to explain that the text means what *he* means, which is usually as nearly as possible the opposite of what *I* mean when it is not too silly to convey any meaning at all. The wretched student, knowing that he will be examined on these notes, finds his preoccupation with them, and the interruption of referring to them so irksome that he acquires a loathing for the author which lasts for a lifetime, and carries with it a loathing for literature in general, even when he has received a certificate of proficiency in it for recollecting the date and place of the author's birth, and giving the names of six of his most eminent contemporaries. . . . ."

Mr. Shaw kindly allows us to use the selections here included provided they are never to be used as an excuse for such an examination paper as this:

"Name the 23 wars referred to. Explain the excessive surtax and state its incidence. What American President is referred to? Name his predecessor and his successor. On what battlefield did Lincoln use the words quoted? Give a brief account of General Grant and Robert E. Lee. Where is Zabern (give latitude and longitude)? Give chapter and verse for the phrase 'humble and contrite heart.' Reconcile the final sentence with the 'Sermon on the Mount.' "

The editors cannot pledge themselves that selections in this book may not be used as instruments of torture, but they would join with Mr. Shaw in horror if they were; for they feel that literature should above all other studies serve for delight.

Since the publication of the first edition, Professor Newcomer has died. The present edition is prepared by the surviving editor, Miss Andrews, and Professor Newcomer's former colleague, Mr. Hall. They are grateful to Nesta Mary Thompson, Ph.D., of La Jolla, California, whose scholarship has been of great assistance in the new compilation; to Carolyn Blain, A.M., of Cupertino, California, for her able help and vigorous judgment; to librarians George Thomas Clark and Nathan Van Patten of Stanford University for many courtesies; and to authors and their representatives, and publishers as follows:

To "A.E." (George William Russell) for "A Summer Night," and for "Promise," from his *Collected Poems.*

To Sir James M. Barrie for the extracts from *Margaret Ogilvy.*

To Robert Bridges for "A Passer-by," "London Snow," "North Wind in October," and "Spring Goeth All in White," all from his *Collected Poems.*

To Gilbert Keith Chesterton for the poems "Elegy in a Country Churchyard," from *The Ballad of St. Barbara,* "The Donkey," from *The Wild Knight;* and for his essay "The Irishman," from *The Uses of Diversity.*

To William Henry Davies for "Clouds," "Days too Short," "In May," and "Dreams of the Sea," all from *The Collected Poems of William H. Davies.*

To Walter de la Mare for "Macbeth," "Nod," "Old Susan," "Silver," and "The Sunken Garden," all from his *Collected Poems.*

To A. T. A. Dobson (as acting for the trustees) for permission to use the poems "Urceus Exit," "Farewell Renown," "In After Days," and "For a Charity Annual," all from the *Complete Poetical Works* of the late Austin Dobson.

To John Drinkwater for "Sunrise on Rydal Water," from *Alton Pools,* and "Symbols," from *Poems 1908-14.*

To Lord Dunsany for "Death and Odysseus," from *Fifty-One Tales,* and "Lord of the Cities," from *The Sword of Welleran;* also for "June," "Thoughts at the Trysting Stile," "A Twilight in Middle March," and "The Lost Ones," all from *Songs of the Fields* by the late Francis Ledwidge.

To John Galsworthy for "Riding in Mist," from *The Inn of Tranquility,* and "The Recruit," from *Tatterdemalion.*

To Wilfrid Wilson Gibson for the Proem from *Fires* and "Hit," from his *Collected Poems.*

To A. C. Gissing for permission to use the extracts from *The Private Papers of Henry Ryecroft,* by the late George Gissing.

To the late Sir Edmund Gosse for "Lying in the Grass," "With a Copy of Herrick," and "Epilogue," from his *Collected Poems.*

To the late Thomas Hardy for the poem "The Darkling Thrush," from *Poems Past and Present,* "The Man he Killed," from *Time's Laughingstocks,* " 'Ah, Are You Digging on My Grave?' " from *Satires of Circumstance,* "Weathers," from *Late Lyrics;* and the extracts from *The Return of the Native.*

To Ralph Hodgson for "Babylon," and "Stupidity Street," from his *Poems.*

To Alfred Edward Housman for " 'Loveliest of Trees,' " "Reveille," " 'On Moonlit Heath,' " and "Bredon Hill," from *A Shropshire Lad.*

To Rudyard Kipling for "Recessional," from *The Five Nations,* "The Ballad of East and West," and "The Ballad of the Bolivar," from *Barrack-Room Ballads.*

To David Herbert Lawrence for "A Baby Asleep After Pain," from *Love Poems and Others,* "Service of all the Dead," from *Amores,* and "Green," from *Look! We Have Come Through!*

To Winifred M. Letts for "The Spires of Oxford" and "The Connaught Rangers," from *The Spires of Oxford and Other Poems.*

To John Masefield for "Sea Fever," "Tewkesbury Road," "Cargoes," and "The 'Wanderer,' " from his *Collected Poems.*

To Wilfrid Meynell for permission to use

"Renouncement," "The Shepherdess," and "A Thrush Before Dawn," from *The Poems of Alice Meynell;* and for "The Hound of Heaven," "To a Snowflake," and " 'In No Strange Land,' " from *The Works of Francis Thompson.*

To Harold Monro for "Real Property," "From an Old House," "Dog," "Thistledown," and "Man Carrying Bale," all from *Real Property.*

To Sir Henry John Newbolt for "Vitaï Lampada," "Drake's Drum," "He Fell Among Thieves," all from *Poems: New and Old.*

To Alfred Noyes for "The Barrel-Organ," and "The Highwayman," from his *Collected Poems.*

To Siegfried Lorraine Sassoon for "Counter-Attack," "The Death Bed," and "The Rear-Guard," from *Counter-Attack and Other Poems,* "A Working Party," from *The Old Huntsman,* and "Aftermath," from *Picture-Show.*

To George Bernard Shaw for the extracts from the Preface to *Heartbreak House.*

To John Collings Squire for "The Three Hills," and "the March," from *Poems,* First Series, and "A Dog's Death," from *Poems,* Second Series.

To James Stephens for "Hate," and "To the Four Courts, Please," from his *Collected Poems.*

To Giles Lytton Strachey for the extract from *Queen Victoria.*

To John Millington Synge for extracts from *The Aran Islands.*

To Herbert George Wells for the extracts from *Men Like Gods.*

To William Butler Yeats for "The Lake Isle of Innisfree," from his *Poetical Works,* and "The Wild Swans at Coole," from *The Wild Swans at Coole.*

To Jonathan Cape, Ltd., for "Clouds," "Days Too Short," "In May," and "Dreams of the Sea" from *The Collected Poems of William H. Davies.*

To Chatto and Windus for the poems "Song" and "Ode," from *Moonlight and Music,* by Arthur O'Shaughnessy.

To Curtis Brown for "A Baby Asleep After Pain," from *Love Poems and Others,* "Service of all the Dead," from *Amores,* and "Green," from *Look! We Have Come Through!* by D. H. Lawrence.

To Dodd, Mead and Company, Inc., for "A Ballad of Heaven," from *Selected Poems* of John Davidson; for "The Soldier," "The Dead," and "The Great Lover," from *Collected Poems* of Rupert Brooke; and for the poems "Elegy in a Country Churchyard," from *The Ballad of Saint Barbara,* "The Donkey," from *The Wild Knight;* and for the essay "The Irishman," from *The Uses of Diversity,* by Gilbert Keith Chesterton.

To Doubleday Doran and Company, Inc., for "The Three Hills," and "The March," from *Poems,* first series, and "A Dog's Death," from *Poems,* second series, by John Collings Squire; and for "Recessional" from *The Five Nations,* "The Ballad of East and West" and "The Ballad of the 'Bolivar' " from *Barrack-Room Ballads* by Rudyard Kipling; and for the selection from Conrad's *The Mirror of the Sea.*

To E. P. Dutton and Company for the extracts from *A Naturalist in La Plata,* by William Henry Hudson; for "The Spires of Oxford" and "The Connaught Rangers," from *The Spires of Oxford and Other Poems,* by Winifred M. Letts; and for "Counter-Attack," "The Death Bed," and "The Rear-Guard," from *Counter-Attack and Other Poems,* "A Working Party," from *The Old Huntsman,* and "Aftermath," from *Picture-Show,* by Siegfried Lorraine Sassoon.

To Harcourt Brace and Company for the extract from *Queen Victoria,* by Giles Lytton Strachey.

To Harper and Brothers, for extracts from *The Return of the Native,* by Thomas Hardy.

To William Heinemann, Ltd., for "Lying in the Grass," "With a copy of Herrick," and "Epilogue," from the *Collected Poems* of the late Sir Edmund Gosse; and for "Riding in Mist," from *The Inn of Tranquility,* and "The Recruit," from *Tatterdemalion,* by John Galsworthy.

To Hodder and Stoughton, Ltd., for the extract from *Margaret Ogilvy,* by Sir James M. Barrie.

To Henry Holt and Company for "Macbeth," "Nod," "Old Susan," "Silver," and "The Sunken Garden," all from the *Collected Poems* of Walter de la Mare.

To Houghton Mifflin Company for "Sunrise on Rydal Water," and "Symbols," from *Poems 1908-14,* by John Drinkwater.

To the Incorporated Society of Authors, Playwrights and Composers for "Sea Fever," "Tewkesbury Road," "Cargoes," and "The 'Wanderer'," from the *Collected Poems* of John Masefield.

To John Lane, The Bodley Head, Ltd., for "A Ballad of Heaven," by John Davidson.

To John W. Luce and Company for extracts

from *The Aran Islands,* by John Millington Synge.

To Alfred A. Knopf for "An Ideal Family," from *The Garden Party and Other Stories,* by Katherine Mansfield.

To The Macmillan Company, N. Y., for "Before," "Clinical," "Apparition," "Invictus," and "Margaritae Sorori," all from *Poems* by W. E. Henley; for "Babylon," and "Stupidity Street," from *Poems,* by Ralph Hodgson; for "Hate," and "To the Four Courts, Please," from *Collected Poems,* by James Stephens; for "The Darkling Thrush," from *Poems Past and Present,* "The Man He Killed," from *Time's Laughingstocks,* " 'Ah, Are You Digging on My Grave?' " from *Satires of Circumstance,* and "Weathers," from *Late Lyrics,* by the late Thomas Hardy; for the Proem from "Fires," and "Hit," from *Collected Poems,* by Wilfrid Gibson; for "A Summer Night," and "Promise," from *Collected Poems* by "A.E."; for "The Lake Isle of Innisfree," from *Poetical Works,* and "The Wild Swans at Coole," from *The Wild Swans at Coole,* by William Butler Yeats; and for the translation representing Cynewulf, from *A History of Early English Literature,* by Stopford A. Brooke.

To Macmillan and Company, Ltd., London, for their concurrence in permissions to use the poems of Hodgson, Stephens, and Hardy, granted by The Macmillan Company of New York; and the poems of Henley granted by Charles Scribner's Sons.

To Methuen Company, Ltd., London, for the extracts from "The Ballad of Reading Gaol," by Oscar Wilde.

To Sir John Murray for "The Spires of Oxford" and "The Connaught Rangers," from *The Spires of Oxford and Other Poems,* by Winifred M. Letts; for "A Passer-by," "London Snow," "North Wind in October," and "Spring Goeth all in White," all from the *Collected Poems* by Robert Bridges; and for "Vitaï Lampada," "Drake's Drum," "He Fell Among Thieves," all from *Poems: New and Old,* by Sir Henry John Newbolt.

To Humphrey Milford, The Oxford University Press, for "Urceus Exit," "Farewell Renown," "In After Days," and "For a Charity Annual" all from the *Complete Poetical Works* of the late Austin Dobson.

To James B. Pinker and Son, agents, for "Initiation," from *The Mirror of the Sea,* by Joseph Conrad; and for the poems "Macbeth," "Nod," "Old Susan," "Silver," and "The Sunken Garden," all from the *Collected Poems* of Walter de la Mare.

To Charles Scribner's Sons for "Juggling Jerry," and "Lucifer in Starlight," from *The Poetical Works of George Meredith,* and the extract from *The Ordeal of Richard Feveral,* by George Meredith; for "Lying in the Grass," "With a Copy of Herrick," and "Epilogue," from the *Collected Poems* of the late Sir Edmund Gosse; for "Before," "Clinical," "Apparition," "Invictus," and "Margaritae Sorori," all from *Poems,* by William E. Henley; for the extracts from *Margaret Ogilvy,* by Sir James M. Barrie; for "The Hound of Heaven," "To a Snowflake," and " 'In No Strange Land,' " from *The Works of Francis Thompson;* for "Riding in Mist," from *The Inn of Tranquility,* and "The Recruit," from *Tatterdemalion,* by John Galsworthy; for the essays "El Dorado," from *Virginibus Puerisque,* and "The Maroon," from *In the South Seas;* and the poems "The Vagabond," " 'The Morning Drum-Call on My Eager Ear,' " "Evensong," and "Requiem," all from *Ballads and Other Poems,* by Robert Louis Stevenson.

To Frederick A. Stokes for "The Barrel-Organ," and "The Highwayman," from the *Collected Poems* of Alfred Noyes.

1928 A. E. A.
H. J. H.

ILLUSTRATIONS

CONTENTS

THE ELIZABETHAN AGE—DRAMA

THE ELIZABETHAN AGE—PROSE

THE SEVENTEENTH CENTURY

CAROLINE LYRICS

EARLY EIGHTEENTH CENTURY

LATER EIGHTEENTH CENTURY

LATE GEORGIAN BALLADS AND LYRICS

THE POST-VICTORIAN PERIOD AND THE EARLY TWENTIETH CENTURY

From a painting by P. Kramen

GEOFFREY CHAUCER

TWELVE CENTURIES OF ENGLISH POETRY AND PROSE

ANGLO-SAXON PERIOD

THE oldest Anglo-Saxon or Old English poetry consists of national legends or sagas brought to Great Britain by Germanic tribes settling there after the Romans had withdrawn. It records the social conditions of a race inured to the presence of ever-threatening death in battle, in seafaring, and in distant wanderings. It is pagan at heart with some mingling of Christian ideas, perhaps inserted by transcribers. This earliest poetry was written down in the Northumbrian dialect. Of the extant Anglo-Saxon verse, however—some 20,000 lines—most is in the tenth century Wessex dialect, and much is purely religious and Christian. For in Alfred's time West-Saxon was the dominant dialect, and into it was transcribed much earlier poetry written in other dialects and thought worthy of preservation.

BEOWULF c [1] 700

Beowulf, now admitted to be the oldest preserved epic of the Teutonic race, is the most important of the group of early national poems mentioned above, all belonging to the times before the unification of England under King Alfred (A.D. 886). Most of them are the work of minstrels, possibly attached to the courts of kings or persons of high rank. Mention of such gleemen is made more than once in *Beowulf* (ll. 90, 1160). The poem, a curious interweaving of heathen and Christian elements, is preserved practically complete in a manuscript of the tenth century, which was not discovered until 1705, and was not published until 1813. Its origin and antiquity are unknown; very likely it grew up during at least a century, and may even be a combination of various lays. Many of the persons and events are found in various Scandinavian records, especially Saxo's *Danish History*. Healfdene, Hrothgar, and Halga are certainly identical with the Danish king Hafdan and his sons Hróarr (Roe) and Helgi.

Is the poem about Beowulf in any sense mythological? Perhaps the latest and best opinion on the subject is that it is not.

[1] *circum:* about

"Undoubtedly one is here on the borderland of myth. But in the actual poem the border is not crossed. Whatever the remote connection of Beowulf the hero with Beowa the god, ... to the poet of the epic its hero is a man, and the monsters are such as folk then believed to haunt sea and lake and moor."—Francis B. Gummere, *The Oldest English Epic*.

"The poem loses nothing of its picturesqueness in being denied its mythology. The fire-drake and Grendel and the she-demon are more terrible when conceived as uncanny and abominable beings whose activities in the world can only be dimly imagined by men than they are when made mere personifications of the forces of nature. Beowulf is no less heroic as a mortal facing with undaunted courage these grisly phantoms of the moor and mere, than as a god subduing the sea or the darkness. And the proud words that he utters in his dying hour are more impressive from the lips of a man than from those of a being who still retains some of the glory of a god about him—'In my home I awaited what time might bring me, held well my own, sought no treacherous feuds, swore no false oaths. In all this I can rejoice, though sick unto death with my wounds.'"—William W. Lawrence, *Pub. Mod. Lang. Association*, June, 1909.

In the construction of the poem note how new sentences and even new subjects begin frequently in the middle of a verse, producing the effect of a continuous narrative. The Anglo-Saxon metrical scheme is timed by accents; each line is divided by a pause into two half-lines, each with two strong stresses. Other technical features are alliteration, one distinguishing mark of Old English verse, as in "Weltering waves, coldest of weathers"; constant repetition or "parallelism" of phrase; and the use of poetic synonyms or "kennings," like *whale-road* for *ocean.*

A recent standard text is that by A. J. Wyatt, new ed. rev., 1914; excellent prose translations are by J. Earle, 1892, and C. B. Tinker, 1902; there are metrical translations by James M. Garnett, 4th ed., 1904; by John Lesslie Hall, 1900; and by Francis B. Gummere, 1909. For discussion, see *Camb. Hist.*

[The Passing of Scyld[1]]

Lo, we have heard of the fame in old time
of the great kings of the Spear-Danes,
how these princes valor displayed.
Oft Scyld, Scef's son, from robber-bands,
from many tribes, their mead-seats took,
filled earls with fear, since first he was
found all forlorn. Howe'er, he won comfort,
waxed great 'neath the welkin, in dignities throve,
until every one of those dwelling near
over the whale-road, was bound to obey him
and pay him tribute: that was a good king.
To him a son was afterward born,
a child in his courts whom God sent
to comfort the people; He felt the dire need
they erst had suffered, how they had princeless
been a long while. Therefore the Lord of Life,
Glory-prince, gave to him worldly honor.
Renowned was Beowulf, widely the glory spread
of Scyld's offspring in the Scanian lands.
So shall a prudent man do good works
with bountiful gifts in his father's hall,
that in his old age still may surround him
willing companions, and when war comes
the people may follow him. By praiseworthy deeds
man shall flourish in every tribe.
Scyld then departed at his fated time,
the very bold one, to the Lord's keeping.
Away to the sea-shore then they bore him,
his dear companions, as himself had bid,
while his words had sway, the Scylding's friend,
the land's loved chief that long had possessed it.
There at the hithe stood the ring-prowed ship,
icy and eager, the prince's vessel.
Then they laid down the beloved chief,
the dispenser of rings, on the ship's bosom—
by the mast laid him. There were treasures many
from far ways, ornaments brought.
I have heard of no comelier keel adorned
with weapons of war and martial weeds,
with glaves and byrnies. On his bosom lay
many treasures which were to go with him,
far depart into the flood's possession.
Not less with gifts, with lordly treasures,
did they provide him, than did those others
who at the beginning sent him forth
alone o'er the wave, a little child.
They set moreover a golden ensign
high o'er his head; let the sea bear him
gave him to ocean. Their mind was sad,
mournful their mood. No man of men,
counselors in hall, heroes 'neath heaven,
can say for sooth who that lading received.

I. [The Building of Heorot]

Then in the towns was Beowulf, the Scyldings'
beloved sovereign, for a long time
famed among nations (his father had passed away,
the prince from his dwelling), till from him in turn sprang
the lofty Healfdene. He ruled while he lived,
old and war-fierce, the glad Scyldings.
From him four children, numbered forth,
sprang in the world, from the head of hosts;
Heorogar and Hrothgar and Halga the good;
and I have heard that Elan[2] was wife
of Ongentheow the Heathoscylfing.
Then was to Hrothgar war-prowess given,

[1] Of the three large sections into which the story of Beowulf falls—the fight with Grendel in Denmark, the fight with Grendel's mother, and the subsequent deeds of Beowulf in Geatland (Sweden)—the first is here given practically entire, and the second in part. It should be noted that the Beowulf mentioned in the opening canto is a Scylding, or Dane; Beowulf the Geat, or Weder-Geat, for whom the poem is named, is not introduced until the fourth canto. The translation is virtually the literal one of Benjamin Thorpe, 1855, relieved of some of its harsher inversions and obscurities and made more consistently rhythmical, also occasionally altered to conform to a more probable interpretation. No attempt is made to preserve the original alliteration.

Certain recurring archaic words are:

atheling, prince
brand, sword
byrnie, corselet
hithe, harbor
jotun, giant
mere, sea, lake
ness, headland
nicker, orken, sea-monster
sark, cuirass
scôp, poet
thane, war-companion, retainer
wyrd, fate

[2] perhaps the fourth child

martial glory, that[1] his dear kinsmen
gladly obeyed him, till his young warriors grew,
a great train of kinsfolk. It ran thro' his mind
that he would give orders for men to make
a hall-building, a mighty mead-house,
which the sons of men should ever hear of;
and therewithin to deal out freely
to young and to old, whatever God gave him,
save the freeman's share and the lives of men.
Then heard I that widely the work was proclaimed
to many a tribe thro' this mid-earth
that a folk-stead was building. Befell him in time,
soon among men, that it was all ready,
of hall-houses greatest; and he, whose word was
law far and wide, named it Heorot.[2]
He belied not his promise, bracelets distributed,
treasures at the feast. The hall arose
high and horn-curved; awaited fierce heat
of hostile flame. Nor was it yet long
when sword-hate 'twixt son- and father-in-law,
after deadly enmity, was to be wakened.[3]
Then the potent guest who in darkness dwelt
with difficulty for a time endured
that he each day heard merriment
loud in the hall. There was sound of the harp,
loud song of the gleeman. The scôp, who could
the origin of men from far back relate,
told how the Almighty wrought the earth,
the plain of bright beauty which water embraces;
in victory exulting set sun and moon,
beams for light to the dwellers on land;
adorned moreover the regions of earth
with boughs and leaves; life eke created
for every kind that liveth and moveth.
Thus the retainers lived in delights,
in blessedness; till one began
to perpetrate crime, a fiend in hell.
Grendel was the grim guest called,
great mark-stepper[4] that held the moors,
the fen and fastness. The sea-monsters' dwelling
the unblest man abode in awhile,
after the Creator had proscribed him.[5]
On Cain's race the eternal Lord
that death avenged, the slaying of Abel;
the Creator joyed not in that feud,
but banished him far from men for his crime.
Thence monstrous births all woke into being,
jotuns, and elves, and orken-creatures,
likewise the giants who for a long space
warred against God: He gave them requital.

II. [The Grim Guest of Heorot]

When night had come he went to visit
the lofty house, to see how the Ring-Danes
after their beer-feast might be faring.
He found therein a band of nobles
asleep after feasting; sorrow they knew not,
misery of men, aught of unhappiness.
Grim and greedy, he was soon ready,
rugged and fierce, and in their rest
took thirty thanes; and thence departed,
in his prey exulting, to his home to go,
with the slaughtered corpses, his quarters to visit.
Then in the morning, at early day,
was Grendel's war-craft manifest:
after that repast was a wail upraised,
a great morning cry. The mighty prince,
the excellent noble, unblithe sat;
the strong thane suffered, sorrow endured,
when they beheld the foeman's traces,
the accursed sprite's. That strife was too strong,
loathsome and tedious. It was no longer
than after one night, again he perpetrated
greater mischief, and scrupled not
at feud and crime; he was too set on them.
Then were those easily found who elsewhere
sought their rest in places of safety,
on beds in the bowers,[6] when it was shown them,
truly declared by a manifest token,
the hall-thane's hate; held themselves after
farther and faster who the fiend escaped.
So Grendel ruled, and warred against right,
alone against all, until empty stood
that best of houses. Great was the while,
twelve winters' tide, the Scyldings' friend
endured his rage, every woe,
ample sorrow. Whence it became
openly known to the children of men,
sadly in songs, that Grendel warred
awhile against Hrothgar, enmity waged,
crime and feud for many years,
strife incessant; peace would not have
with any man of the Danish power,
nor remit for a fee the baleful levy;
nor any wight might hold a hope
for a glorious satisfaction at the murderer's hands.

[1] so that
[2] "The Hart"—probably so named from gable decorations resembling a deer's horns
[3] Hrothgar's son-in-law, Ingeld, tried to avenge upon him the death of his father, and it may have been he who gave the hall to "hostile flame."
[4] roamer of the marches, or land-bounds
[5] That is, Grendel is of the monstrous brood of Cain. The passage is one of the Christian additions to a legend wholly pagan in origin.
[6] apartments used mainly by the women

The fell wretch kept persecuting—
the dark death-shade—the noble and youthful,
oppressed and snared them. All the night
he roamed the mist-moors. Men know not
whither hell-sorcerers wander at times.

Thus many crimes the foe of mankind,
the fell lone-roamer, often accomplished,
cruel injuries. Heorot he held,
seat richly adorned, in the dark nights;
yet might not the gift-throne touch, that treasure,
because of the Lord, nor knew His design.
'Twas great distress to the Scyldings' friend,
grief of spirit; often the wise men
sat in assembly; counsel devised they
what for strong-souled men it were best
to do against the perilous horrors.
Sometimes they promised idolatrous honors
at the temples, prayed in words
that the spirit-slayer aid would afford
against their afflictions.
Such was their custom,
the heathen's hope; hell they remembered,
but the Creator, the Judge of deeds,
they knew not—knew not the Lord God, knew not
how to praise the heavens' Protector,
Glory's Ruler. Woe to him who
thro' cruel malice shall thrust his soul
in the fire's embrace; let him expect not
comfort to find. Well unto him who
after his death-day may seek the Lord,
and win to peace in his Father's bosom.

III. [Beowulf's Resolve]

So Healfdene's son on sorrow brooded;
for all his wisdom the hero could not
avert the evil; that strife was too strong,
loathsome and tedious, that came on the people,
malice-brought misery, greatest of night-woes.
Then Hygelac's thane,[1] a Geatman good,
heard from his home of Grendel's deeds;
he of mankind was strongest in power
in that day of this life, noble and vigorous.
He bade for himself a good wave-rider
to be prepared; said he would go
over the swan-road to seek the war-king,
the prince renowned, since men he had need of.
Dear tho' he was, his prudent liegemen
little blamed him for that voyage,
whetted him rather, and noted the omen.

Then the good chief chose him champions
of the Geat-folk, whomso bravest
he could find, and, fourteen with him,
sought the vessel. Then the hero,
the sea-crafty man, led the way to the shore.
Time passed; the floater was on the waves,
the boat 'neath the hill; the ready warriors
stepped on the prow; the streams surged
the sea 'gainst the sand; the warriors bare
into the bark's bosom bright arms,
a rich war-array. The men shoved out
on the welcome voyage the wooden bark.

Most like to a bird the foamy-necked floater,
impelled by the wind, then flew o'er the waves
till about the same time on the second day
the twisted prow had sailed so far
that the voyagers land descried,
shining ocean-shores, mountains steep,
spacious sea-nesses. Then was the floater
at the end of its voyage. Up thence quickly
the Weders' people stept on the plain;
the sea-wood tied; their mail-shirts shook,
their martial weeds; thanked God that to them
the paths of the waves had been made easy.

When from the wall the Scyldings' warder,
who the sea-shores had to keep,
saw bright shields borne over the gunwale,
war-gear ready, wonder arose
within his mind what those men were.
Hrothgar's thane then went to the shore,
on his horse riding, stoutly shook
the stave in his hands, and formally asked them:

"What are ye of arm-bearing men,
with byrnies protected, who thus come leading
a surgy keel over the water-street,
here o'er the seas? I for this,
placed at the land's end, have kept sea-ward,
that no enemies on the Danes' land
with a ship-force might do injury.
Never more openly hither to come
have shield-men attempted; nay, and ye knew not
surely the pass-word ready of warriors,
permission of kinsmen. Yet ne'er have I seen
earl upon earth more great than is one of you,
or warrior in arms: 'tis no mere retainer
honored in arms, unless his face belies him,
his aspect distinguished. Now your origin
must I know, ere ye farther,
as false spies, into the Danes' land
hence proceed. Now ye dwellers
afar, sea-farers, give ye heed to
my simple thought: best is it quickly
to make known whence your coming is."

IV. [The Mission of the Geats]

Him the chief of them answered then,
the band's war-leader his word-hoard unlocked:
"We are of race of the Geats' nation,

[1] Beowulf; Hygelac was his uncle, and king of the Geats, or Weder-Geats, who lived in Sweden.

and hearth-enjoyers of Hygelac.
Well known to nations was my father,
a noble chieftain, Ecgtheow named;
abode many winters ere he departed
old from his courts; nigh every sage
thro' the wide earth remembers him well.
We in kindness of feeling have come
to seek thy lord, the son of Healfdene,
the folk-defender. Be a kind informant.
We have a great errand to the illustrious
lord of the Danes. Naught shall be secret
whereof my thought is. Thou knowest whether
it be in sooth as we have heard say,
that with the Scyldings I know not what wretch,
a secret ill-doer, in the dark nights
displays thro' terror unheard-of malice,
havoc and slaughter. For this may I teach,
thro' my large mind, counsel to Hrothgar,
how he, wise and good, shall o'ercome the foe,
if ever a change is to befall,
if relief from evil should ever come
and that care-welling calmer grow.
Else he ever after oppression will suffer,
a time of trouble, while standeth there
in its high place the noblest of houses."

Then spake the warder, astride of his horse,
the officer fearless: "Between these two
should a sharp shield-warrior who thinketh well
the difference know—'tween words and works.
This band, I hear, is a friendly one
to the Scyldings' lord. Pass ye on
with weapons and weeds; I will direct you.
Likewise will I give to my fellow-
liegemen orders in honor to keep,
'gainst every foe, your new-tarred ship,
your bark on the sand, till back o'er the water
the vessel with twisted neck shall bear
to the Weder-march the man beloved.
To such a warrior shall it surely be given
the rush of war to escape from whole."

Then they set forth; the vessel still bode
firm in her berth, the wide-bosomed ship,
at anchor fast. A boar's likeness sheen
'bove their cheeks they bore,[1] adorned with gold;
stained and fire-hardened, it held life in ward.
In warlike mood the men hastened on,
descended together, until the well-timbered
hall they might see, adorned all with gold.
Unto earth's dwellers that was the grandest
of houses 'neath heav'n, where the ruler abode;
the light of it shone over many lands.

[1] Boar-images surmounted the helmets.

To them the warrior pointed out clearly
the proud one's court, that they might thither
take their way; then did the warrior
turn his steed and speak these words:
"'Tis time for me to go on my way.
May the all-ruling Father with honor hold you
safe in your fortunes. I will back to the sea,
ward to keep against hostile bands."

V. [The Arrival at Heorot]

The street was stone-paved, the path gave guidance
to the men in a body; the war-byrnie shone,
hard, hand-locked; the ringed iron bright
sang in their gear, as they to the hall
in their arms terrific came striding on.
Their ample shields, their flint-hard bucklers,
the sea-weary set 'gainst the mansion's wall,
then stooped to the benches; their byrnies rang,
the war-gear of men. In a sheaf together
the javelins stood, the seamen's arms,
ash-wood, gray-tipped. These ironclad men
were weaponed well.
Then a proud chief asked
these sons of conflict concerning their lineage:
"Whence do ye bear your plated shields
and gray sarks hither, your visor-helms
and heap of war-shafts? I am Hrothgar's
servant and messenger. Never saw I
strangers so many and proud. I ween
that ye out of pride, of greatness of soul,
and not for exile, have sought Hrothgar."

Him then answered the famed for valor;
the Weders' proud lord, bold 'neath his helmet,
spake words afterward: "We are Hygelac's
table-enjoyers—my name, Beowulf.
I my errand will relate
to the great lord, son of Healfdene,
to thy prince, if he will grant us
graciously to greet him here."

Wulfgar spake (he was lord of the Wendels;
known to many was his spirit,
his valor and wisdom): "I will therefore
ask the Danes' friend, lord of the Scyldings,
mighty prince and ring-distributor,
about thy voyage, as thou requestest,
and make quickly known the answer
that the prince thinks fit to give me."

He then went quickly where Hrothgar sat,
old and gray, among his earls;
the brave chief stood before the shoulders
of the Danes' lord—he knew court-usage.
Wulfgar spake to his friendly lord:
"Hither are borne, come from afar
o'er ocean's course, people of the Geats.

Beowulf these sons of conflict
name their chief. They make petition
that they may hold with thee, my lord,
words of converse. Decree not, Hrothgar,
denial of the boon of answer.
Worthy seem they, in their war-gear,
of earls' esteem—at least the chieftain
who has led the warriors hither."

VI. [Hrothgar's Welcome]

Hrothgar spake, the Scyldings' shield:
"Lo, I knew him when he was a boy.
His old father was named Ecgtheow,
to whom in his home gave Hrethel the Geat
his only daughter. Now his offspring
bold comes hither, has sought a kind friend.
For sea-farers—they who bore gift-treasures
unto the Geats gratuitously—
were wont to say of him, the war-famed,
that he the might of thirty men
has in his hand-grip. Holy God
hath in his mercies sent him to us,
to the West Danes, as I hope,
'gainst Grendel's horror. For his daring,
to the good chief gifts I'll offer.
Be thou speedy, bid these kinsmen,
assembled together, come in to see me.
Say moreover they are welcome
guests to the Danes. [Then to the hall-door
Wulfgar went.] He announced the words:
"My victor-lord, O prince of the East Danes,
bids me tell you he knows your nobleness;
that, boldly striving over the sea-billows,
ye come to him hither welcome guests.
Now ye may go in your war-accoutrements,
'neath martial helm, Hrothgar to see.
Let your battle-boards, spears, and shafts,
here await the council of words."
Arose then the chief, his many men around him,
a brave band of thanes. Some remained there,
held the war-weeds, as the bold one bade them.
They hastened together where the warrior directed,
under Heorot's roof; the valiant one went,
bold 'neath his helmet, till he stood on the dais.
Beowulf spake; his byrnie shone on him,
his war-net sewed by the smith's devices—
"Hail to thee, Hrothgar; I am Hygelac's
kinsman and war-fellow; many great deeds
in my youth have I ventured. To me on my native turf
Grendel's doings became clearly known.
Sea-farers say that this most excellent
house doth stand, for every warrior,
useless and void when the evening light
under heaven's serenity is concealed.
Then, prince Hrothgar, did my people,
the most excellent men, sagacious,
counsel me that I should seek thee,
because they knew the might of my craft.
Themselves beheld—when I came from their snares,
blood-stained from the foes—where five I bound,
the jotun-race ravaged, and slew on the billows
nickers by night; distress I suffered,
avenged the Weders (they had had misery),
crushed the fell foe. And now against Grendel,
that miserable being, will I hold council,
alone with the giant. "Of thee now, therefore,
lord of the bright Danes, Scyldings' protector,
will I make this one petition:
now that I come so far, deny not,
O patron of warriors, friend of people,
that I alone with my band of earls,
with this bold company, may purge Heorot.
I have learned this, that the demon-like being
in his heedlessness recketh not of weapons.
I then will disdain (so may Hygelac,
my liege lord, be to me gracious of mood)
to bear a sword or round yellow shield
into the battle; but shall with the enemy
grip and grapple, and for life contend,
foe against foe. And he whom death taketh
there shall trust in the doom of the Lord.
"I ween that he, if he may prevail,
will fearlessly eat, in the martial hall,
the Geat's people, as oft he has done
the Hrethmen's[1] forces. Thou wilt not need
to shroud my head, for he will have me,
stained with gore, if death shall take me;
will bear off my bloody corse to feast on it;
lonely, will eat it without compunction;
will mark out my moor-mound. Thou wilt not need
care to take for my body's disposal.
If the conflict take me, send to Hygelac
this best of battle-coats shielding my breast,
of vests most excellent; 'tis Hraedla's legacy,
Weland's[2] work. Fate goes aye as it must."

VII. [Hrothgar's Lament]

Hrothgar spake, the Scyldings' shield:
"For battles thou, my friend Beowulf,
and for honor, us hast sought.
Thy father fought in the greatest feud;
he was of Heatholaf the slayer,
with the Wylfings, when the Weder-Geats
for fear of war-feud might not harbor him.
Thence he sought, o'er the rolling waves,

[1] the Danes
[2] the divine smith, or Vulcan, of Northern legend

the South Danes' folk, the noble Scyldings,
when first I ruled the Danish people
and in my youth held spacious realms,
the hoard-burg of heroes. Dead was Heregar,
my elder brother, son of Healfdene—
passed from the living; he was better than I.
Later, that quarrel I settled with money;
over the water's back old treasures
I sent to the Wylfings: he swore to me oaths.
"Sorry am I in my mind to say
to any man what Grendel has wrought me
in Heorot with his hostile designs,
what swift mischiefs done. My courtiers are minished,
my martial band; them fate has off-swept
to the horrors of Grendel. Yet God may easily
turn from his deeds the frenzied spoiler.
Oft have promised the sons of conflict,
with beer drunken, over the ale-cup,
that they in the beer-hall would await
with sharp sword-edges Grendel's warfare.
Then at morning, when the day dawned,
this princely mead-hall was stained with gore,
all the bench-floor with blood besteamed,
the hall with sword-blood: I owned the fewer
of dear, faithful nobles, whom death destroyed.
Sit now to the feast, and joyfully think
of victory for men, as thy mind may incite."
For the sons of the Geats then, all together,
in the beer-hall a bench was cleared.
There the strong-souled went to sit,
proudly rejoicing; a thane did duty,
who bare in his hand the ale-cup bedecked,
poured the bright liquor. Clear rose the glee-man's
song in Heorot. There was joy of warriors,
a noble band of Danes and Weders.

VIII. [Hunferth's Taunt. The Reply]

Hunferth spake, the son of Ecglaf,
who sat at the feet of the Scyldings' lord,
unloosed his malice. To him was the voyage
of the bold sailor, Beowulf, a great displeasure,
because he grudged that another man
should ever 'neath heaven more glories hold
of this middle-earth, than he himself.
"Art thou the Beowulf who strove with Breca
on the wide sea, in a swimming-strife,
where ye from pride tempted the floods,
and, for foolish vaunt, in the deep water
ventured your lives? Nor might any man,
either friend or foe, restrain you from
the perilous voyage, when seaward ye swam
with arms outspread o'er the ocean-stream,
measured the sea-ways, smote with your hands,
o'er the main glided. With winter's fury
the ocean-waves boiled; for a sennight ye toiled
on the water's domain. He conquered thee swimming;
he had more strength. At morningtide then
the sea bore him up to the Heathoraemas,
whence he sought, beloved of his people,
his country dear, the Brondings' land,
his fair, peaceful burg, where a people he owned,
a burg and treasures. All his boast to thee
the son of Beanstan truly fulfilled.
Worse of thee, therefore, now I expect—
though everywhere thou hast excelled in grim war,
in martial exploits—if thou to Grendel
darest near abide for a night-long space."
Beowulf spake, Ecgtheow's son:
"Well, my friend Hunferth, drunken with beer,
a deal hast thou spoken here about Breca,
about his adventure. The sooth I tell,
that I possessed greater endurance at sea,
strength on the waves, than any other.
We two agreed when we were striplings,
and made our boast (we were both as yet
in youthful life), that we on the ocean
would venture our lives; and thus we did.
A naked sword we held in hand
when we swam on the deep, as we meant to defend us
against the whales. Far on the flood-waves
away from me he could not float,
in the sea more swiftly, and from him I would not.
Then we together were in the sea
a five nights' space, till it drove us asunder.
Weltering waves, coldest of tempests,
cloudy night, and the fierce north wind
grimly assaulted us; rough were the billows.
The rage of the sea-fishes was aroused.
Then my body-sark, hard and hand-locked,
afforded me help against my foes;
my braided war-shirt lay on my breast,
with gold adorned. A speckled monster
drew me to bottom, a grim one held me
fast in his grasp. Yet was it granted
that with the point I reached the creature,
with my war-falchion. A deadly blow,
dealt by my hand, destroyed the sea-beast.

IX. [The Queen's Greeting. Glee in Heorot]

"Thus frequently me my hated foes
fiercely threatened; but I served them
with my dear sword as it was fitting.
Not of that gluttony had they joy,

foul destroyers, to sit round the feast
near the sea-bottom and eat my body;
but in the morning, with falchions wounded,
up they lay among the shore-drift,
put to sleep by the sword; so that ne'er after
stopt they the way for ocean-sailors
over the surge. Light came from the east,
God's bright beacon, the seas grew calm,
so that the sea-nesses I might see,
windy walls. Fate often saves
an undoomed man when his valor avails.
"Yes, 'twas my lot with sword to slay
nickers nine. I have heard of no harder
struggle by night 'neath heaven's vault,
nor of man more harried in ocean-streams.
Yet with life I escaped from the grasp of dangers,
aweary of toil. Then the sea bore me,
the flood with its current, the boiling fiords,
to the Finns' land.
"Now never of *thee*
have I heard tell such feats of daring,
such falchion-terrors. Ne'er yet Breca
at game of war, nor either of you,
so valiantly performed a deed
with shining swords (thereof I boast not),
tho' thou of thy brothers wast murderer,
of thy chief kinsmen, wherefore in hell
shalt thou suffer damnation, keen tho' thy wit be.
In sooth I say to thee, son of Ecglaf,
that never had Grendel, the fiendish wretch,
such horrors committed against thy prince,
such harm in Heorot, were thy spirit,
thy mind, as war-fierce as thou supposest.
But he has found that he need not greatly
care for the hatred of your people,
the fell sword-strength of the victor-Scyldings.[1]
He takes a forced pledge, has mercy on none
of the Danish people, but wars at pleasure,
slays and shends you, nor strife expects
from the Spear-Danes. But now of the Geats
the strength and valor shall I unexpectedly
show him in battle. Thereafter may all go
elate to the mead, after the light
of the ether-robed sun on the second day
shines from the south o'er the children of men."[2]
Then was rejoiced the treasure-distributor;

[1] The epithet appears to be ironical. It is noteworthy that Hrothgar takes it all in good part.

[2] "In this speech," says Dr. J. R. C. Hall, "in less than fourscore passionate lines, we have rude and outspoken repartee, proud and unblushing boast, a rapid narrative, Munchausen episodes, flashes of nature, a pagan proverb, a bitter taunt, a reckless insult to the Danish race, a picture of a peaceful time to come."

hoary-locked, war-famed, the bright Danes' lord
trusted in succor; the people's shepherd
from Beowulf heard his steadfast resolve.
There was laughter of men, the din resounded,
words were winsome. Wealhtheow came forth,
Hrothgar's queen; mindful of courtesy,
the gold-adorned greeted the men in the hall.
First then the woman, high-born, handed the
cup to the East-Danes' country's guardian,
bade him be blithe at the beer-drinking,
dear to his people. He gladly partook of
the feast, and the hall-cup, battle-famed king.
Round then went the dame of the Helmings[3]
on every side, among old and young,
costly cups proffered, till came occasion
that she, the high-minded, ring-adorned queen
the mead-cup bore unto Beowulf.
She greeted the lord of the Geats, thanked God,
sagacious in words, that her wish had befallen,
that she in any warrior might trust
for comfort 'gainst crimes. He took the cup,
the warrior fierce, from Wealhtheow's hand,
and then made speech, eager for battle—
Beowulf spake, the son of Ecgtheow:
"I resolved, when I went on the main
with my warrior-band and sat in the seaboat,
that I would wholly accomplish the will
of your people in this, or bow in death,
fast in the foe's grasp. I shall perform
deeds of valor, or look to find
here in this mead-hall my last day."
The Geat's proud speech the woman liked well;
the high-born queen of the people went,
adorned with gold to sit by her lord.
Within the hall then again as before
were bold words spoken—the people's joy,
the victor folk's clamor—up to the moment
when Healfdene's son was fain to go to
his evening rest. He knew that conflict
awaited the monster in the high hall
so soon as they might no longer see
the sun's light, and o'er all murk night,
the shadow-helm of men, came creeping,
dusk under heaven. The company rose.
Hrothgar then paid Beowulf reverence—
one hero the other—and bade him hail,
gave him command of the wine-hall and said:
"Never since hand and shield I could raise,
have I before entrusted to any
the hall of the Danes, save now to thee.
Have now and hold this best of houses;
be mindful of glory, show mighty valor,

[3] name of the queen's family

keep watch for the foe. No wish shall be lacking
if thou from this venture escape with thy life."

X. [Beowulf's Vigil]

Then Hrothgar departed, the Scyldings' protector,
out of the hall with his band of warriors;
the martial leader would seek his consort,
Wealhtheow the queen. The glory of kings
had set against Grendel, as men have heard tell,
a hall-ward; he held a special office
about the Dane-prince, kept guard 'gainst the giant.
But the chief of the Geats well trusted in
his own proud might and the Creator's favor.
He doffed from him then his iron byrnie,
the helm from his head, and gave to a henchman
his sword enchased, choicest of irons,
bade him take charge of the gear of war.
Some words of pride then spake the good chief,
Beowulf the Geat, ere he mounted his bed:
"I count me no feebler in martial vigor
of warlike works than Grendel himself.
Therefore I will not, tho' easy it were,
with sword destroy him or lull him to rest.
'Tis a warfare he knows not—to strike against me
and hew my shield, renowned tho' he be
for hostile works; but we two tonight
shall do without sword, if he dare seek
war without weapon. And afterward God,
the wise, the holy, shall glory doom
to whichever hand it meet to him seemeth."
Then lay down the brave man—the bolster received
the warrior's cheek; and around him many
a seaman keen reclined on his hall-couch.
Not one of them thought that he should thence
seek ever again the home he loved,
the folk or free burg where he was nurtured:
since erst they had heard how far too many
folk of the Danes a bloody death
o'ertook in that wine-hall. But to them the Lord
gave woven victory,[1] to the Weders' people
comfort and succor, so that they all
by the might of one, by his single powers,
their foe overcame. Shown is it truly
that mighty God ruleth the race of men.

[1] This is a characteristic Northern figure, as well as Greek; but it is not Christian. An interesting expansion of it may be found in Gray's poem "The Fatal Sisters."

Now in the murky night came stalking
the shadow-walker. All the warriors
who should defend that pinnacled mansion
slept, save one. To men it was known
that the sinful spoiler, when God willed not,
might not drag them beneath the shade.
Natheless, he, watching in hate for the foe,
in angry mood waited the battle-meeting.

XI. [Grendel's Onslaught]

Then came from the moor, under the mist-hills,
Grendel stalking; he bare God's anger.
The wicked spoiler thought to ensnare
many a man in the lofty hall.
He strode 'neath the clouds until the wine-house,
the gold-hall of men, he readily saw,
richly adorned. Nor was that time
the first that Hrothgar's home he had sought:
but ne'er in his life, before nor since,
found he a bolder man or hall-thanes.
So then to the mansion the man bereft
of joys came journeying; soon with his hands
undid the door, tho' with forged bands fast;
the baleful-minded, angry, burst open
the mansion's mouth. Soon thereafter
the fiend was treading the glittering floor,
paced wroth of mood; from his eyes started
a horrid light, most like to flame.
He in the mansion saw warriors many,
a kindred band, together sleeping,
fellow-warriors. His spirit exulted.
The fell wretch expected that ere day came
he would dissever the life from the body
of each, for in him the hope had risen
of a gluttonous feast. Yet 'twas not his fate
that he might more of the race of men
eat after that night. The mighty kinsman
of Hygelac watched how the wicked spoiler
would proceed with his sudden grasping.
Nor did the monster mean to delay;
for he at the first stroke quickly seized
a sleeping warrior, tore him unawares,
bit his bone-casings, drank his veins' blood,
in great morsels swallowed him. Soon had he
devoured all of the lifeless one,
feet and hands. He stepped up nearer,
took then with his hand the doughty-minded
warrior at rest; with his hand the foe
reached toward him. He instantly grappled
with the evil-minded, and on his arm rested.
Soon as the criminal realized
that in no other man of middle-earth,
of the world's regions, had he found
a stronger hand-grip, his mind grew fearful.
Yet not for that could he sooner escape.

He was bent on flight, would flee to his cavern,
the devil-pack seek; such case had never
in all his life-days befallen before.
Then Hygelac's good kinsman remembered
his evening speech; upright he stood,
and firmly grasped him; his fingers yielded.
The jotun was fleeing; the earl stept further.
The famed one considered whether he might
more widely wheel and thence away
flee to his fen-mound; he knew his fingers' power
in the fierce one's grasp. 'Twas a dire journey
the baleful spoiler made to Heorot.
The princely hall thundered; terror was
on all the Danes, the city-dwellers,
each valiant one, while both the fierce
strong warriors raged; the mansion resounded.
Then was it wonder great that the wine-hall
withstood the war-beasts, nor fell to the ground,
the fair earthly dwelling; yet was it too fast,
within and without, with iron bands,
cunningly forged, though where the fierce ones
fought, I have heard, many a mead-bench,
with gold adorned, from its sill started.
Before that, weened not the Scyldings' sages
that any man ever, in any wise,
in pieces could break it, goodly and bone-decked,
or craftily rive—only the flame's clutch
in smoke could devour it. Startling enough
the noise uprose. Over the North Danes
stood dire terror, on every one
of those who heard from the wall the whoop,
the dread lay sung by God's denier,
the triumphless song of the thrall of hell,
his pain bewailing. He held him fast—
he who of men was strongest of might,
of them who in that day lived this life.

XII. [The Monster Repulsed]

Not for aught would the refuge of earls
leave alive the deadly guest;
the days of his life he counted not useful
to any folk. There many a warrior
of Beowulf's drew his ancient sword;
they would defend the life of their lord,
of the great prince, if so they might.
They knew not, when they entered the strife,
the bold and eager sons of battle,
and thought to hew him on every side
his life to seek, that not the choicest
of irons on earth, no battle-falchion,
could ever touch the wicked scather,
since martial weapons he had forsworn,
every edge whatever. Yet on that day
of this life was his life-parting
wretched to be, and the alien spirit
to travel far into power of fiends.
Then he who before in mirth of mood
(he was God's foe) had perpetrated
many crimes 'gainst the race of men,
found that his body would not avail him,
for him the proud kinsman of Hygelac
had in hand; each was to the other
hateful alive. The fell wretch suffered
bodily pain; a deadly wound
appeared on his shoulder, his sinews started,
his bone-casings burst. To Beowulf was
the war-glory given; Grendel must thence,
death-sick, under his fen-shelters flee,
seek a joyless dwelling; well he knew
that the end of his life was come, his appointed
number of days. For all the Danes,
that fierce fight done, was their wish accomplished.
So he then, the far-come, the wise and strong
of soul, had purified Hrothgar's hall,
saved it from malice; his night's work rejoiced him,
his valor-glories. The Geatish chieftain
had to the East-Danes his boast fulfilled,
had healed, to-wit, the preying sorrow
that they in that country before had suffered
and had to endure for hard necessity,
no small affliction. A manifest token
it was when the warrior laid down the hand—
arm and shoulder, Grendel's whole grappler
together there—'neath the vaulted roof.

XIII. [Joy at Heorot]

Then in the morning, as I have heard tell,
there was many a warrior around the gift hall:
folk-chiefs came, from far and near,
o'er distant ways, the wonder to see,
the tracks of the foe. His taking from life
seemed not grievous to any warrior
who the inglorious one's trail beheld—
how, weary in spirit, o'ercome in the conflict,
death-doomed and fleeing, he bare death-traces
thence away to the nickers' mere.
There was the surge boiling with blood,
the dire swing of waves all commingled;
with clotted blood hot, with sword-gore it welled;
the death-doomed dyed it, when he joyless
laid down his life in his fen-asylum,
his heathen soul. There hell received him.
Thence again turned they, comrades old,
from the joyous journey, and many a younger,
proud from the mere, riding on horses,
warriors on steeds. Then was Beowulf's
glory celebrated. Many oft said
that south or north, between the seas
the wide world over, there was no other

'neath heaven's course who was a better 860
shield-bearer, or one more worthy of power.
Yet found they no fault with their lord beloved,
the joyful Hrothgar: he was their good king.
. . . .
Then was morning light
sent forth and quickened. Many a retainer,
strong in spirit, to the high hall went, 919
to see the rare wonder. The king himself also
from his nuptial bower, guardian of ring-treasures,
with a large troop stept forth, rich in glory,
for virtues famed; and his queen with him
the meadow-path measured with train of maidens.

XIV. [Hrothgar's Gratitude]

Hrothgar spake (he to the hall went,
stood near the threshold, saw the steep roof
shining with gold, and Grendel's hand):
"Now for this sight, to the Almighty thanks!
May it quickly be given! Much ill have I borne,
Grendel's snares; ever can God work 930
wonder on wonder, the King of Glory.
Not long was it since, that I little weened
for woes of mine through all my life,
reparation to know, when, stained with blood,
the best of houses all gory stood;
woe was wide-spread for each of my counselors,
who did not ween that they evermore
from foes could defend the people's landwork,[1]
from devils and phantoms. Now this warrior,
thro' the might of the Lord, has done a deed
which we all together before could not 941
with cunning accomplish. Lo, this may say
whatever woman brought forth this son
among the nations, if yet she lives,
that the ancient Creator was gracious to her
at the birth of her son. Now will I, O Beowulf,
best of warriors, even as a son,
love thee in my heart. Keep henceforth well
our kinship new; no lack shalt thou have
of worldly desires, wherein I have power.
Full often for less have I dealt a reward,
an honor-gift, to a feebler warrior, 952
weaker in conflict. Thou for thyself
hast wrought so well, that thy glory shall live
thro' every age. May the All-wielder
with good reward thee, as now He has done."
Beowulf spake, Ecgtheow's son:
"We with great good will, that arduous work,
that fight, have achieved; we boldly ventured
in war with the monster. The more do I wish
that thou himself mightest have seen, 961
the foe in his trappings, full weary enough.
Him I quickly, with hard and fast fetters,
on his death-bed thought to have bound,

[1] Heorot

that thro' my hand-grips low he should lie,
struggling for life, but his body escaped.
I was not able, the Lord did not will it,
to keep him from going; I held him not firm enough,
the deadly foe; too strong on his feet
the enemy was. Yet his hand he left, 970
for his life's safety, to guard his track,
his arm and shoulder; yet not thereby
did the wretched creature comfort obtain;
nor will he, crime-doer, the longer live
with sins oppressed. For pain has him
in its grip compelling straitly clasped,
in its deadly bonds; there shall he await,
the crime-stained wretch, the Final Doom,
as the Lord of Splendor shall mete it to him."
Then less noisy was Ecglaf's son 980
in vaunting speech of words of war,
after the nobles, thro' might of the hero,
over the high roof had gazed on the hand,
the fingers of the foe, each for himself.[2]
Each finger-nail was firm as steel—
a heathen's hand-spurs and a warrior's—
hideously monstrous. Every one said
that no excellent iron of the bold ones
would be able to touch the demon's hand,
would ever sever the bloody limb. 990

XV. [Feasting and Song]

Then quickly 'twas ordered, that Heorot within
by hand be adorned; many were they,
of men and women, who the wine-house,
the guest-hall, prepared; gold-shimmering shone
the webs on the walls, wondrous sights many
to each and all that gaze upon such.
That splendid dwelling much shattered was,
tho' bound within with bands of iron;
the hinges asunder were rent, the roof
alone was saved all sound, when the monster,
stained with foul deeds, turned him to flight,
hopeless of life. 1002

[The feast is held, gifts are bestowed on the hero, and Hrothgar's minstrel sings a song of a hundred lines about Finn, the king of the Frisians.]

XVII. [The Queen's Speech]

. . . . The lay was sung, 1159
the gleeman's song. Pastime was resumed,
noise rose from the benches, the cup-boys served wine

[2] Beowulf, says Dr. Klaeber, "had placed Grendel's hand (on some projection perhaps) above the door (outside) as high as he could reach," where the nobles, looking from outside "in the direction of the high roof," behold it. Others think that it was hung up within the hall.

from wondrous vessels. Then Wealhtheow came forth
'neath a gold diadem, to where the two good
cousins [1] sat; at peace were they still,
each true to the other; there Hunferth too sat
at the Scylding lord's feet—all had faith in his spirit,
his courage, altho' to his kinsmen he had not
in sword-play been true. [2] Then the Scyldings' queen spake:
"Accept this beaker, my beloved lord, [3]
dispenser of treasure; may'st be joyful,
gold-friend of men! And speak to the Geats
with gentle words! So man shall do.
Be kind toward the Geats, mindful of gifts;
near and far thou now hast safety.
Men have said that thou this warrior
wouldst have for a son. Heorot is purged,
the bright hall of rings; enjoy while thou mayest
the rewards of the many, and to thy sons leave
folk and realm, when thou shalt go forth
to see thy Creator. Well I know that
my gracious Hrothulf will the youth
in honor maintain if thou sooner than he,
O friend of the Scyldings, leavest the world.
I ween that he with good will repay
our offspring dear, if he remembers
all the favors that we for his pleasure
and honor performed when he was a child."
Then she turned to the seat where were her sons,
Hrethric and Hrothmund, and the sons of the heroes,
the youths all together; there sat the noble
Beowulf the Geat, beside the two brothers.

XVIII. [Beowulf Rewarded. Eventide]

The cup was brought him, and friendly greeting
in words was given and twisted gold
kindly proffered—bracelets two,
armor and rings, a collar the largest
of those that on earth I have heard tell of.
Never 'neath heaven have I heard of a better
treasure-hoard of men, since Hama bore off
to the glittering burg the Brosings' necklace, [4]
the jewel and casket (he fled the guileful
hate of Eormenric, chose gain eternal). [5]
Hygelac the Geat wore this collar,
the grandson of Swerting, on his last raid,
when he 'neath his banner the treasure defended,
the slaughter-spoil guarded; fate took him off
when he out of pride sought his own woe,
war with the Frisians; he the jewels conveyed,
the precious stones, over the wave-bowl,
the powerful king; he fell 'neath his shield.
Then into the power of the Franks the king's life
went, and his breast-weeds, went, too, the collar;
warriors inferior plundered the fallen
after the war-lot; the Geat-folk held
the abode of the slain.
The hall resounded.
Wealhtheow spake, before the warrior-band said:
"Use this collar, Beowulf dear,
O youth, with joy, and use this mantle,
these lordly treasures, and thrive thou well;
prove thyself mighty, and be to these boys
gentle in counsels. I will reward thee.
This hast thou achieved, that, far and near,
throughout all time, men will esteem thee,
even so widely as the sea encircles
the windy land-walls. Be while thou livest
a prosperous noble. I grant you well
precious treasures; be thou to my sons
gentle in deeds, thou who hast joy.
Here is each earl to the other true,
mild of mood, to his liege lord faithful;
the thanes are united, the people all ready.
Warriors who have drunken, do as I bid."
To her seat then she went. There was choicest of feasts,
the warriors drank wine; Wyrd they knew not,
calamity grim, as it turned out
for many a man after evening had come
and Hrothgar had to his lodging departed,
the ruler to rest. There guarded the hall
countless warriors, as oft they had done.
They cleared the bench-floor; it soon was o'erspread
with beds and bolsters. A certain beer-bearer,
ready and fated, bent to his rest.
They set at their heads their disks of war,
their shield-wood bright; there on the bench,
over each noble, easy to see,
was his high martial helm, his ringed byrnie
and war-wood stout. It was their custom
that they were ever for war prepared,
at home, in the field, in both alike,
at whatever time to their liege lord
the need befell. 'Twas a ready people.

XIX. [Grendel's Mother]

They sank then to sleep. One sorely paid
for his evening rest, as full oft had happened

[1] Hrothgar, and his nephew, Hrothulf, who must have been older than the king's children (cf. lines 1180 ff.), but who evidently did not remain "true"

[2] He was said to have killed his brothers.

[3] Hrothgar

[4] the famous necklace of Freyja, which Hama stole from Eormenric, the cruel king of the Goths

[5] perhaps entered a monastery (S. Bugge)

since the gold-hall Grendel occupied,
unrighteousness did, until the end came,
death after sins. Then it was seen,
wide-known among men, that still an avenger
lived after the foe, for a long time
after the battle-care—Grendel's mother.
The woman-demon remembered her misery,
she that the watery horrors, the cold streams,
had to inhabit, when Cain became 1261
slayer by sword of his only brother,
his father's son. Then he went forth blood-stained,
by murder marked, fleeing man's joy,
dwelt in the wilderness. Thence awoke many
fated demons; Grendel was one,
the hated fell wolf who at Heorot found
a watchful warrior awaiting the conflict;
and there the monster laid hold of him.
Yet was he mindful of his great strength, 1270
the generous gift that God had given him,
and trusted for help in him the All-wielder,
for comfort and aid; so slew he the fiend,
struck down the hell-spirit. Then humble he made off,
the foe of mankind, to seek his death-home,
of joy deprived. Natheless his mother,
greedy and gloomy, was bent on going
the sorrowful journey, her son's death to avenge.
So came she to Heorot, to where the Ring-Danes 1279
throughout the hall slept. Forthwith there came
to the warriors a change, when in on them rushed
Grendel's mother; the terror was less
by just so much as the force of women is,
the war-dread from woman, than that from a man
when the hilt-bound sword, hammer-beaten,
stained with gore, and doughty of edges,
hews off the head of the boar on the helm.
Then in the hall the hard edge was drawn,
the sword o'er the seats, many a broad shield
raised firm in hand; helms they forgot
and byrnies broad, when the terror seized them.
She was in haste—would out from thence 1292
to save her life, since she was discovered.
One of the nobles she quickly had
with grip fast seized, as she went to fen;
he was to Hrothgar of heroes the dearest
in comradeship beside the two seas,
a mighty shield-warrior, whom she killed,
a hero renowned. (Beowulf was absent,
for another apartment had before been assigned, 1300
after giving of treasures, to the great Geat.)
A cry was in Heorot. She took with its gore
the well known hand;[1] grief had become
renewed in the dwellings. 'Twas no good exchange,
that those on both sides payment must make
with lives of their friends.
Then was the old king,
the hoary war-hero, in stormy mood
when his highest thane, no longer living,
his dearest friend, he knew to be dead.
Quickly to his chamber was Beowulf summoned,
the victor-rich warrior. Together ere day 1311
he went with his earls, the noble champion
with his comrades went where the wise king awaited
whether for him the All-wielder would
after the woe-time a change bring about.
Then along the floor went the warlike man
with his body guard (the hall-wood resounded)
till he the wise prince greeted with words,
the lord of the Ingwins;[2] asked if he had had
according to his wish, an easy night. 1320

XX. [Sorrow for Aeschere. The Monster's Mere]

Hrothgar spake, the Scyldings' protector:
"Ask not after happiness! Grief is renewed
to the folk of the Danes. Dead is Aeschere,
of Yrmenlaf the elder brother,
my confidant and my counselor,
my near attendant when we in war
defended our heads, when hosts contended,
and boar-crests crashed; such should an earl be,
preëminently good, as Aeschere was.
He in Heorot has had for murderer 1330
a ghost-like death-spirit; I know not whether
the fell carrion-gloater her steps back has traced,
made known by her meal. She the feud has avenged,
that thou yester-night didst Grendel slay,
thro' thy fierce nature, with fetter-like grasps,
for that he too long my people diminished
and wrought destruction. He in battle succumbed,
forfeiting life. And now comes another
mighty man-scather to avenge her son—
has from afar warfare established, 1340
as it may seem to many a thane
who mourns in spirit his treasure-giver,
in hard heart-affliction. Now low lies the hand
which once availed you for every desire.
"I have heard it said by the land-dwellers,
by my own subjects, my hall-counselors,
that they have seen a pair of such

[1] Grendel's (see l. 834)
[2] the Danes

mighty march-stalkers holding the moors,
stranger-spirits, whereof the one,
so far as they could certainly know, 1350
was in form of a woman; the other, accurst,
trod an exile's steps in the figure of man
(save that he huger than other men was),
whom in days of yore the dwellers on earth
Grendel named. They know not a father,
whether any was afore-time born
of the dark ghosts. That secret land
they dwell in, wolf-dens, windy nesses,
the perilous fen-path, where the mountain stream
downward flows 'neath the mists of the nesses,
the flood under earth. 'Tis not far thence, 1361
a mile in measure, that the mere stands,
over which hang rustling groves;
a wood fast rooted the water o'ershadows.

"There every night may be seen a dire wonder,
fire in the flood. None so wise lives
of the children of men, who knows the bottom.
Altho' the heath-stepper, wearied by hounds,
the stag strong of horns, seek that holtwood,
driven from far, he will give up his life, 1370
his breath, on the shore, ere he will venture
his head upon it. That is no pleasant place.
Thence surging of waters upward ascends
wan to the welkin, when the wind stirs up
the hateful tempests, till air grows gloomy
and skies shed tears. Again now is counsel
in thee alone! The spot thou yet ken'st not,
the perilous place where thou may'st find
this sinful being. Seek if thou dare.
With riches will I for the strife reward thee,
with ancient treasures, as I before did, 1381
with twisted gold, if thou comest off safe."

XXI. [The Pursuit]

Beowulf spake, Ecgtheow's son:
"Sorrow not, sage man, 'tis better for each
to avenge his friend than greatly to mourn.
Each of us must an end await
of this world's life; let him work who can
high deeds ere death; that will be for the warrior,
when he is lifeless, afterwards best.
Rise, lord of the realm, let us quickly go
to see the course of Grendel's parent. 1391
I promise thee, not to the sea shall she 'scape,
nor to earth's embrace, nor to mountain-wood,
nor to ocean's ground, go whither she will.
This day do thou endurance have
in every woe, as I expect of thee!"

Up leapt the old man then, thanked God,
the mighty Lord, for what the man said.
For Hrothgar then a horse was bridled,
a steed with curled mane. The ruler wise
in state went forth; a troop strode on, 1401
bearing their shields. Tracks there were
along the forest paths widely seen,
her course o'er the ground; she had thither gone
o'er the murky moor. Of their fellow thanes
she bore the best one, soul-bereft,
of those that with Hrothgar defended their home.

Then overpassed these sons of nobles
deep rocky gorges, a narrow road,
strait lonely paths, an unknown way, 1410
precipitous nesses, monster-dens many.
He went in advance, he and a few
of the wary men, to view the plain,
till suddenly he found mountain-trees
overhanging a hoary rock,
a joyless wood; there was water beneath,
gory and troubled. To all the Danes,
friends of the Scyldings, 'twas grievous in mind,
a source of sorrow to many a thane,
pain to each earl, when of Aeschere, 1420
on the sea-shore, the head they found.

The flood boiled with blood, the people looked on
at the hot glowing gore. The horn at times sang
a ready war-song. The band all sat.
They saw in the water a host of the worm-kind,
strange sea-dragons sounding the deep;
in the headland-clefts also, nickers lying,
which in the morning oft-times keep
their sorrowful course upon the sail-road,
worms and wild beasts—they sped away,
bitter and rage-swollen; they heard the sound;
the war-horn singing. The lord of the Geats
with a bolt from his bow took one from life,
from his wave-strife, and left in his vitals 1434
the hard war-shaft; he in the sea was
the slower in swimming, when death took him off.
Quickly on the waves, with hunting-spears
sharply hooked, he was strongly pressed,
felled by force, and drawn up on the headland,
the wonderful swimmer. The men there gazed
on the grisly guest.

Beowulf girt himself 1441
in war-like weeds; for life he feared not;

his warrior-byrnie, woven by hands,
ample and inlaid, must tempt the deep;
it could well his body protect
that battle-grip might not scathe his breast,
the fierce one's wily grasp injure his life.
But the flashing helm guarded his head,
(which with the sea-bottom was to mingle, 1449
and seek the sea-surge) with jewels adorned,
encircled with chains, as in days of yore
the weapon-smith wrought it, wondrously framed,
set with swine-figures, so that thereafter
no brand nor war-sword ever could bite it.
Nor then was that least of powerful aids
which Hrothgar's orator[1] lent him at need:
Hrunting was named the hafted falchion.
'Twas among the foremost of olden treasures;
its edge was iron, tainted with poison, 1459
harden'd with warrior-blood; ne'er in battle
had it failed any of those that brandished it,
who durst to travel the ways of terror,
the perilous trysts. 'Twas not the first time
that it a valorous deed should perform.
Surely Ecglaf's son remembered not,
the mighty in power, what erst he had said,
drunken with wine, when the weapon he lent
to a better sword-warrior. He durst not himself
'mid the strife of the waves adventure his life,
a great deed perform; there lost he his credit
for valorous doing. Not so with the other 1471
when he had prepared himself for battle!

XXII. [The Fight Beneath the Waves]

Beowulf spake, Ecgtheow's son:
"Remember thou now, great son of Healfdene,
sagacious prince, now I am ready to go,
O gold-friend of men, the things we have spoken:
If I should lose my life for thy need,
that thou wouldst ever be to me,
when I am gone, in a father's stead. 1479
Be a guardian thou to my fellow thanes,
to my near comrades, if war take me off.
Also the treasures which thou hast given me,
beloved Hrothgar, to Hygelac send.
By that gold then may the lord of the Geats know,
may Hrethel's son see, when he looks on that treasure,
that I in man's virtue have found one pre-eminent,
a giver of rings, and rejoiced while I might.
And let Hunferth have the ancient relic,
the wondrous war-sword, let the far-famed man
the hard-of-edge have. I with Hrunting 1490
will work me renown, or death shall take me."
After these words the Weder-Geats' lord
with ardor hastened, nor any answer
would he await. The sea-wave received
the warrior-hero. It was a day's space
ere he the bottom could perceive.
Forthwith she found—she who the flood's course
had blood-thirsty held a hundred years,
grim and greedy—that a man from above
was there exploring the realm of strange creatures. 1500
Then at him she grasped, the warrior seized
in her horrible claws. Natheless she crushed not
his unhurt body; the ring-mail guarded him,
so that she might not pierce that war-dress,
the lock-linked sark, with her hostile fingers.
Then when the sea-wolf reached the bottom,
she bore to her dwelling the prince of rings
so that he might not, brave as he was,
his weapons wield; for many strange beings
in the deep oppressed him, many a sea-beast
with its battle-tusks his war-sark broke; 1511
the wretches pursued him. Then the earl found
he was in he knew not what dread hall,
where him no water in aught could scathe,
nor because of the roof could the sudden grip
of the flood reach him; he saw a fire-light,
a brilliant beam brightly shining.
The hero perceived then the wolf of the deeps,
the mighty mere-wife; a powerful onslaught
he made with his falchion, the sword-blow withheld not, 1520
so on her head the ringed brand sang
a horrid war-song. The guest then discovered
how that the battle-beam would not bite,
would not scathe life, but that the edge failed
its lord at his need; erst had it endured
hand-conflicts many, slashed often the helm,
war-garb of the doomed; then was the first time
for the precious gift that its power failed.
Still was he resolute, slacked not his ardor,
of great deeds mindful was Hygelac's kinsman.
Flung he the twisted brand, curiously bound,
the angry champion, that stiff and steel-edged
it lay on the earth; in his strength he trusted,
his powerful hand-grip. So shall man do, 1534
when he in battle thinks of gaining
lasting praise, nor cares for his life.
By the shoulder then seized he (recked not of her malice)
the lord of the war-Geats, Grendel's mother;
the fierce fighter hurled, incensed as he was,

[1] Hunferth (cf. l. 499)

the mortal foe, that she fell to the ground.
She quickly repaid him again in full 1541
with her fierce grasps, and at him caught;
then stumbled he weary, of warriors the strongest,
the active champion, so that he fell.
She pressed down the hall-guest, and drew her dagger,
the broad gleaming blade—would avenge her son,
her only child. On his shoulder lay
the braided breast-net which shielded his life
'gainst point, 'gainst edge, all entrance withstood.
Then would have perished Ecgtheow's son
'neath the wide earth, champion of the Geats,
had not his war-byrnie help afforded, 1552
his battle-net hard, and holy God
awarded the victory. The wise Lord,
Ruler of Heaven, with justice decided it
easily, when he again stood up.

XXIII. [Victory]

Then he saw 'mongst the arms a victorious falchion,
an old jotun-sword, of edges doughty,
the glory of warriors; of weapons 'twas choicest, 1559
save it was greater than any man else
to the game of war could carry forth,
good and gorgeous, the work of giants.
The knotted hilt seized he, the Scyldings' warrior—
fierce and deadly grim, the ringed sword swung;
despairing of life, he angrily struck,
that 'gainst her neck it griped her hard,
her bone-rings [1] brake. Thro' her fated carcass
the falchion passed; on the ground she sank.
The blade was gory, the man joy'd in his work.
The sword-beam shone bright, light rayed within, 1570
even as from heaven serenely shines
the candle of the firmament. He looked down the chamber,
then turned by the wall; his weapon upraised
firm by the hilt Hygelac's thane,
angry and resolute Nor was the edge
to the war-prince useless; for he would forthwith
Grendel requite for the many raids
that he had made upon the West Danes,
and not on one occasion only,
when he Hrothgar's hearth-companions 1580
slew in their rest, sleeping devoured
fifteen men of the folk of the Danes,

[1] vertebrae

and as many others conveyed away,
hateful offerings. He had so repaid him
for that, the fierce champion, that at rest he saw,
weary of contest, Grendel lying
deprived of his life, as he had been scathed by
the conflict at Heorot; the corpse bounded far
when after death he suffered the stroke, 1589
the hard sword-blow, and his head it severed.
Forthwith they saw, the sagacious men,
those who with Hrothgar kept watch on the water,
that the surge of the waves was all commingled,
the deep stained with blood. The grizzly-haired
old men together spake of the hero,
how they of the atheling hoped no more
that, victory-flush'd, he would come to seek
their famous king, since this seemed a sign
that him the sea-wolf had quite destroyed.
The noon-tide [2] came, they left the nesses,
the Scyldings bold; departed home thence
the gold-friend of men. The strangers sat,
sick of mood, and gazed on the mere, 1603
wished but weened not that they their dear lord
himself should see.
Then that sword, the war-blade,
with its battle-gore like bloody icicles,
began to fade. A marvel it was,
how it all melted, most like to ice
when the Father relaxes the bands of the frost,
unwinds the flood-fetters, He who has power
over seasons and times; true Creator is that!
More treasures he took not, the Weder-Geats' lord, 1612
within those dwellings (though many he saw there)
except the head, and the hilt also,
with jewels shining—the blade had all melted,
the drawn brand was burnt, so hot was the blood,
so venomous the demon, who down there had perished.
Afloat soon was he that at strife had awaited
the slaughter of foes; he swam up through the water.
The ocean surges all were cleansed, 1620
the dwellings vast, when the stranger guest
her life-days left and this fleeting existence.
Then came to land the sailor's protector
stoutly swimming, rejoiced in his sea-spoil,
the mighty burden of what he brought with him.
Then toward him they went, with thanks to God,

[2] an apparent admission of the exaggeration in l. 1495, though noon meant formerly the ninth hour of the day, which would bring it near evening

the stout band of thanes, rejoiced in their lord,
because they beheld him safe and sound.
From the vigorous chief both helm and byrnie
were then soon loosed. The sea subsided—
the cloud-shadowed water with death-gore dappled. 1631

Thence forth they went retracing their steps
happy at heart, the high-way measured,
the well-known road. The nobly bold men
up from the sea-shore bore the head,
not without labor for each of them,
the mightily daring. Four undertook
with toil to bear on the battle-spear,
up to the gold-hall, the head of Grendel;
until straightway to the hall they came, 1640
resolute, warlike, four and ten of them,
Geats all marching with their lord.
Proud amid the throng, he trod the meadows.

Then entering came the prince of thanes,
the deed-strong man with glory honored,
the man bold in battle, Hrothgar to greet.
And into the hall, where men were drinking,
Grendel's head by the hair was borne,
a thing of terror to nobles and lady.
'Twas a wonderful sight men looked upon.

XXIV. [Hrothgar's Gratitude and Counsel]

Beowulf spake, Ecgtheow's son: 1651
"Lo, these sea-offerings, son of Healfdene,
lord of the Scyldings, we have joyfully brought,
in token of glory; thou seest them here.
Not easily did I escape with my life,
ventured with pain on the war under water.
Indeed the struggle would have been ended
outright, had not God me shielded.
Not able was I, in the conflict, with Hrunting
aught to accomplish, though that weapon was good; 1660
but the Ruler of men granted to me,
that I saw on the wall, all beautiful hanging,
an old heavy sword (He has often directed
the friendless man), and that weapon I drew.
Then I slew in that strife, as occasion afforded,
the wards of the house. That war-falchion then,
that drawn brand, was burnt, as the blood burst forth,
of strife-blood the hottest. Thence I the hilt
from the foes bore away, avenged the crimes,
the Danes' death-plague, as it was fitting. 1670

"I promise thee now that thou in Heorot
mayest sleep secure with thy warrior-band,
and thy thanes, each one, thanes of thy people,
the tried and the youthful; that thou needest not,
O prince of the Scyldings, fear from that side
life's bane to thy warriors as erst thou didst."

Then the golden hilt, to the aged hero,
the hoar war-leader, in hand was given,
giant-work old; it passed to the keeping
(those devils once fallen) of the lord of the Danes, 1680
wonderful smith-work; when quitted this world
the fierce-hearted creature, God's adversary,
of murder guilty, and his mother also,
it passed to the keeping of the best
of the world-kings that by the two seas,
in Scania-land, treasures dealt.
Then Hrothgar spake; he gazed on the hilt,
old relic whereon was the origin written
of an ancient war, when the flood had slain—
the flowing ocean—the race of the giants;
they had borne them boldly. That was a people
alien from God; them a final reward, 1692
through the rage of the water, the All-wielder gave.
On the mounting, too, of shining gold,
in runic letters, was rightly marked,
was set and said, for whom first was wrought
that choicest of swords, with hilt bound round
and serpentine. Then spake the wise man,
the son of Healfdene (all were silent):

"Lo, this may he say who practices truth
and right 'mong the people, far back all remembers, 1701
a land-warden old, that this earl was
nobly born. Thy fame is exalted,
thro' far and wide ways, Beowulf, my friend,
over every nation. Thou wearest with patience
thy might, and with prudence. I shall show thee my love,
e'en as we two have said: thou shalt be for a comfort
a very long time to thine own people,
a help unto warriors. Not so was Heremod[1]
to Ecgwela's children, the noble Scyldings;
he throve not for their weal, but for their slaughter, 1711
and for a death-plague to the folk of the Danes.
In angry mood slew he his table-sharers,
his nearest friends, till he lonely departed,
the very great prince, from the joys of men.
Tho' him Mighty God, with delights of power,
with strength had exalted, above all men
had advanced him, yet there grew in his heart
a bloodthirsty spirit; he gave no rings
to the Danes, as was custom; joyless continued he, 1720
so that of war he the misery suffered,
long bale to the people. Learn thou from him;
lay hold of man's virtue! For thee have I told this,

[1] a Danish king, banished for cruelty

wise in winters. 'Tis wondrous to say,
how mighty God, to the race of men,
thro' his ample mind, dispenses wisdom,
lands and valor; He has power over all.
Sometimes He lets wander at their own will
the thoughts of a man of race renowned,
in his country gives him the joy of earth,
a shelter-city of men to possess;
thus makes to him subject parts of the world,
ample kingdoms, that he himself may not,
because of his folly, think of his end.
He lives in plenty; no whit deters him
disease or old age, no uneasy care
darkens his soul, nor anywhere strife
breeds hostile hate; but for him the whole world
turns at his will; he the worse knows not—

XXV. [Hrothgar's Counsel Concluded]

until within him a great deal of arrogance
grows and buds, when the guardian sleeps, 1741
the keeper of the soul. Too fast is the sleep,
bound down by cares; very near is the slayer,
who from his arrow-bow wickedly shoots.
Then he in the breast, 'neath the helm, will be stricken
with the bitter shaft; he cannot guard him
from strange evil orders of the Spirit accursed.
Too small seems to him what long he has held;
fierce minded he covets, gives not in his pride
many rich rings; and the future life
he forgets and neglects, because God to him gave,
Ruler of glory, many great dignities.
In the final close at length it chances
that the body-home, inconstant, sinks,
fated falls. Another succeeds,
who without reluctance treasure dispenses,
old wealth of the warrior, terror heeds not.
"From that evil keep thee, Beowulf dear,
best among warriors, and choose thee the better,
counsels eternal. Heed not arrogance,
famous champion! Now is thy might
in flower for awhile; eftsoons will it be
that disease or the sword shall deprive thee of strength,
or the clutch of fire, or rage of flood,
or falchion's grip, or arrow's flight,
or cruel age; or brightness of eyes
shall fail and darken; sudden 'twill be,
that thee, noble warrior, death shall o'erpower.
"Thus I the Ring-Danes half a hundred years
had ruled 'neath the welkin, and saved them in war
from many tribes through this mid-earth,
with spears and swords, so that I counted
that under Heaven I had no foe.
Lo, to me then came a reverse in my realm,
after merriment sadness, since Grendel became
my enemy old, and my assailant.
From that persecution have I constantly borne
great grief of mind. So thanks be to God
the Lord Eternal, that I have lived
till I on that head all clotted with gore,
old conflict ended, might gaze with my eyes.
Go now to thy seat, the banquet enjoy,
O honored in battle; for us two shall be
many treasures in common, when morning shall come."
Glad was the Geat and straightway went
to take his seat, as the sage commanded.
Then as before were the famed for valor,
the sitters at court right handsomely
set feasting afresh. The night-helm grew murky, 1789
dark o'er the vassals; the courtiers all rose;
the grizzly-haired prince would go to his bed,
the aged Scylding; the Geat, exceedingly
famed shield-warrior, desired to rest.
Him, journey-weary, come from afar,
a hall-thane promptly guided forth
who in respect had all things provided
for a thane's need, such as in that day
farers over the sea should have.
The great-hearted rested. High rose the hall
vaulted and gold-hued; therein slept the guest,
until the black raven, blithe-hearted, announced
the joy of heaven. Then came the bright sun
o'er the fields gliding. 1803

[Beowulf returns the sword Hrunting to Hunferth, then goes to the king and announces his intention of returning to his fatherland. The king repeats his thanks and praises.]

XXVI. [The Parting]

. . . .

Then to him gave the warrior's protector,
the son of Healfdene, treasures twelve;
with those gifts bade him his own dear people
in safety to seek, and quickly return. 1869
The king, in birth noble, then kissed the prince,
the lord of the Scyldings the best of thanes;
and round the neck clasped him; tears he shed,
the hoary-headed; chances two
there were to the aged, the second stronger,
whether (or not) they should see each other
again in conference. So dear was the man
that his breast's heaving he could not restrain,
but in his bosom, in heart-bands fast,
for the man beloved his secret longing
burned in his blood. Beowulf thence,
a gold-proud warrior, trod the greensward,
in treasure exulting. The sea-ganger awaited,
at anchor riding, its owner and lord. . . .

c.700

DEOR'S LAMENT

Deor's Lament is one of the poems that may have been brought from the Continent by the Angles in their early migrations. "Its form," says Stopford Brooke, "is remarkable. It has a refrain, and there is no other early English instance of this known to us. It is written in strophes, and one motive, constant throughout, is expressed in the refrain. This dominant cry of passion makes the poem a true lyric, ... the father of all English lyrics . . . . Deor has been deprived of his rewards and lands, and has seen a rival set above his head. It is this whirling down of Fortune's wheel that he mourns in his song, and he compares his fate to that of others who have suffered, so that he may have some comfort. But the comfort is stern like that the Northmen take."

Weland for a woman learned to know exile,
that haughty earl bowed unto hardship,
had for companions sorrow and longing,
the winter's cold sting, woe upon woe,
what time Nithhad laid sore need on him.
Withering sinew-wounds! Ill-starred man!
That was o'erpassed; this may pass also.

On Beadohilde bore not so heavily
her brother's death as the dule in her own heart
when she perceived, past shadow of doubt,
her maidhood departed, and yet could nowise
clearly divine how it might be.
That was o'erpassed; this may pass also.

Of Hild's fate we have heard from many.
Land-bereaved were the Geatish chieftains,
so that sorrow left them sleepless.
That was o'erpassed; this may pass also.

Theodoric kept for thirty winters
in the burg of the Maerings; 'twas known of many.
That was o'erpassed; this may pass also.

Heard have we likewise of Eormanric's mind,
wolfishly tempered; widely enthralled he
the folk of the Goth-realm; he was a grim king.
Many a warrior sat locked in his sorrow,
waiting on woe; wished, how earnestly!
the reign of that king might come to an end.
That was o'erpassed; this may pass also.

. . . .

Now of myself this will I say:
Erewhile I was scôp of the Heodenings,
dear to my lord. Deor my name was.
A many winters I knew good service;
gracious was my lord. But now Heorrenda,
by craft of his singing, succeeds to the land-right
that Guardian of Men erst gave unto me.
That was o'erpassed; this may pass also.

CAEDMON fl.[1] 670

The earliest Christian poet of England was Caedmon, for whose story and name we have to rely upon a prose writer of this early period, Bede, a late contemporary living not far from the scene of Caedmon's life. The simple narrative in Bede's *Ecclesiastical History* (see p. 22) reveals convincingly the poet's kindly, devout nature, picturing for us the man as he lived and sang. The account of his deathbed is of singular beauty. Caedmon is commonly said to have died in 680, in the same year as the Abbess Hilda, though there is no authority for the statement.

A hymn said to be the one composed by Caedmon in his dream still exists in the original Northumbrian form; the West-Saxon version is preserved in Bede's *History*. The most important works commonly assigned to him—though on very uncertain grounds—are *Genesis, Exodus,* and *Daniel*. They are of interest for their possible relation to *Paradise Lost,* which is discussed in Brooke, *Early English Literature*. Also three minor poems have been attributed to him: *The Fall of the Angels; Christ's Harrowing of Hell;* and a fragment on the Temptation. The fragment *Judith,* the finest of all the poems wrongly attributed to Caedmon, was probably written c. 918. The poems show considerable imaginative power and vigor of expression, but lack evidences of literary culture.

"He was the first Englishman—it may be, the first individual of Gothic race—who exchanged the gorgeous images of the old mythology for the chaster beauties of Christian poetry. From the sixth to the twelfth century, he appears to have been the great model, whom all imitated, and few could equal. For upward of five centuries, he was the father of English poetry; and when his body was discovered in the reign of John, it seems to have excited no less reverence than those of the kings and saints by which it was surrounded."
—Guest.

From PARAPHRASE OF THE SCRIPTURES[2]

[The Garden of Eden[3]]

Then beheld our Creator
the beauty of his works and the excellence of his productions,
of the new creatures. Paradise stood
good and spiritual, filled with gifts,
with forward benefits. Fair washed
the genial land the running water,
the well-brook: no clouds as yet

[1] flourished
[2] The translation is the literal one of Thorpe.
[3] from *Genesis,* as is also the following selection

over the ample ground bore rains
lowering with wind; yet with fruits stood
earth adorn'd. Held their onward course
river-streams, four noble ones,
from the new Paradise.
These were parted, by the Lord's might,
all from one (when he this earth created)
water with beauty bright, and sent into the world.

[The Fall of Satan]

The All-powerful had angel tribes,
through might of hand, the holy Lord,
ten established, in whom he trusted well
that they his service would follow,
work his will; therefore gave he them wit,
and shaped them with his hands; the holy Lord.
He had placed them so happily, one he had made so powerful,
so mighty in his mind's thought, he let him sway over so much,
highest after himself in heaven's kingdom. He had made him so fair,
so beauteous was his form in heaven, that came to him from the Lord of hosts,
he was like to the light stars. It was his to work the praise of the Lord,
it was his to hold dear his joys in heaven, and to thank his Lord
for the reward that he had bestow'd on him in that light; then had he let him long possess it;
but he turned it for himself to a worse thing, began to raise war upon him,
against the highest Ruler of heaven, who sitteth in the holy seat.

. . . .

The fiend with all his comrades fell then from heaven above,
through as long as three nights and days,
the angels from heaven into hell, and them all the Lord
transformed to devils, because they his deed and word
would not revere; therefore them in a worse light,
under the earth beneath, Almighty God
had placed triumphless in the swart hell;
there they have at even, immeasurably long,
each of all the fiends, a renewal of fire;
then cometh ere dawn the eastern wind,
frost bitter-cold; ever fire or dart,
some hard torment they must have;
it was wrought for them in punishment.

. . . .

Then spake the haughty king
who of angels erst was brightest,
fairest in heaven:

. . . .

"This narrow place is most unlike
that other that we ere knew,
high in heaven's kingdom, which my master bestow'd on me,
though we it, for the All-powerful, may not possess,
must cede our realm; yet hath he not done rightly
that he hath struck us down to the fiery abyss
of the hot hell, bereft us of heaven's kingdom,
hath it decreed with mankind
to people. That of sorrows is to me the greatest,
that Adam shall, who of earth was wrought,
my strong seat possess,
be to him in delight, and we endure this torment,
misery in this hell. Oh, had I power of my hands,
and might one season be without,
be one winter's space, then with this host I—
But around me lie iron bonds,
presseth this cord of chain: I am powerless!
me have so hard the clasps of hell,
so firmly grasped! Here is a vast fire
above and underneath, never did I see
a loathlier landskip; the flame abateth not,
hot over hell. Me hath the clasping of these rings,
this hard-polish'd band, impeded in my course,
debarr'd me from my way; my feet are bound,
my hands manacled, of these hell-doors are
the ways obstructed, so that with aught I cannot
from these limb-bonds escape."

[The Cloud by Day[1]]

Had the cloud, in its wide embrace,
the earth and firmament above alike divided;
it led the nation-host; quenched was the flame-fire,
with heat heaven-bright. The people were amazed,
of multitudes most joyous, their day-shield's shade
rolled over the clouds. The wise God had
the sun's course with a sail shrouded;
though the mast-ropes men knew not,
nor the sail-cross might they see,
the inhabitants of earth, all the enginery;
how was fastened that greatest of field-houses.

[The Drowning of Pharaoh and His Army]

The folk was affrighted, the flood-dread seized on

[1] from *Exodus*

their sad souls; ocean wailed with death,
the mountain heights were with blood besteamed,
the sea foamed gore, crying was in the waves,
the water full of weapons, a death-mist rose;
the Egyptians were turned back;
trembling they fled, they felt fear;
would that host gladly find their homes;
their vaunt grew sadder; against them as a cloud, rose
the fell rolling of the waves; there came not any
of that host to home, but from behind inclosed them
fate with the wave. Where ways ere lay,
sea raged. Their might was merged,
the streams stood, the storm rose
high to heaven; the loudest army-cry
the hostile uttered; the air above was thickened
with dying voices; blood pervaded the flood,
the shield-walls were riven, shook the firmament
that greatest of sea-deaths: the proud died,
kings in a body; the return prevailed
of the sea at length; their bucklers shone
high over the soldiers; the sea-wall rose,
the proud-ocean-stream, their might in death was
fastly fettered.

BEDE 672-735

Following closely after Caedmon came the English historian and theologian, commonly called "the venerable Bede." Curiously enough, he is the main source for his own biography as well as for that of the poet, for almost all that we know about him is contained in a short autobiographical notice added to his *Ecclesiastical History*. As he himself relates, he was born in the neighborhood of the monastery of Wearmouth and Jarrow; at the age of seven he was given to Abbot Benedict to be educated, and spent the rest of his life in the monastery. "I wholly applied myself to the study of Scripture, and amidst the observance of regular discipline, and the daily care of singing in the church, I always took delight in learning, teaching, and writing." A deacon at nineteen, he was a priest at thirty; his remaining years were devoted to the gathering, preserving, and spreading of knowledge. A beautiful account of his death is contained in a contemporary letter by Cuthbert,[1] afterwards abbot of Wearmouth and Jarrow. His last hours were spent in devotion and teaching; his last work was the dictating of a translation into the vernacular of the Gospel of St. John.

His works, written in Latin, include theology, natural science, grammar, history, even poetry. The most important is the *Ecclesiastical History of the English People,* one of the most valuable and beautiful historical works; it testifies to a feeling for proportion, and a sense of the picturesque and pathetic in the author. The style is clear and unaffected. The history was popular on the Continent as well as in England, and is one of the sources used by Geoffrey of Monmouth in his *History of the Kings of Britain.*

[1] in Brooke's *Early English Literature*

From ECCLESIASTICAL HISTORY

[The Britons Seek Succor from the Romans—The Roman Wall [2]]

From that time,[3] the south part of Britain, destitute of armed soldiers, of martial stores, and of all its active youth, which had been led away by the rashness of the tyrants, never to return, was wholly exposed to rapine, as being totally ignorant of the use of weapons. Whereupon they suffered many years under two very savage foreign nations, the Scots from the west, and the Picts from the north. We call these foreign nations, not on account of their being seated out of Britain, but because they were remote from that part of it which was possessed by the Britons; two inlets of the sea lying between them, one of which runs in far and broad into the land of Britain, from the Eastern Ocean, and the other from the Western, though they do not reach so as to touch one another.

. . . .

On account of the irruption of these nations, the Britons sent messengers to Rome with letters in mournful manner, praying for succors, and promising perpetual subjection, provided that the impending enemy should be driven away. An armed legion was immediately sent them, which, arriving in the island, and engaging the enemy, slew a great multitude of them, drove the rest out of the territories of their allies, and, having delivered them from their cruel oppressors, advised them to build a wall between the two seas across the island, that it might secure them, and keep off the enemy; and thus they returned home with great triumph. The islanders raising the wall, as they had been directed, not of stone, as having no artist capable of such a work, but of sods, made it of no use. However, they drew it for many miles between the two bays or inlets of the seas, which we have spoken of; to the end that where the defense of the water was wanting, they might use the rampart to defend their borders from the irruptions of the enemies. Of which work there erected, that is, of a rampart of extraordinary breadth and height, there

[2] From Book I, Chapter 12. Translation from the Latin, edited by J. A. Giles.

[3] about 400 A.D. onward

are evident remains to be seen at this day. It begins at about two miles' distance from the monastery of Abercurnig, [1] and running westward, ends near the city Alcluith.[2]

But the former enemies, when they perceived that the Roman soldiers were gone, immediately coming by sea, broke into the borders, trampled and overran all places, and like men mowing ripe corn, bore down all before them. Hereupon messengers are again sent to Rome, imploring aid, lest their wretched country should be utterly extirpated, and the name of the Roman province, so long renowned among them, overthrown by the cruelties of barbarous foreigners, might become utterly contemptible. A legion is accordingly sent again, and, arriving unexpectedly in autumn, made great slaughter of the enemy, obliging all those that could escape, to flee beyond the sea; whereas before, they were wont yearly to carry off their booty without any opposition. Then the Romans declared to the Britons that they could not for the future undertake such troublesome expeditions for their sake, advising them rather to handle their weapons like men, and undertake themselves the charge of engaging their enemies, who would not prove too powerful for them, unless they were deterred by cowardice; and, thinking that it might be some help to the allies, whom they were forced to abandon, they built a strong stone wall from sea to sea, in a straight line between the towns that had been there built for fear of the enemy, and not far from the trench of Severus. This famous wall, which is still to be seen, was built at the public and private expense, the Britons also lending their assistance. It is eight feet in breadth, and twelve in height, in a straight line from east to west, as is still visible to beholders. This being finished, they gave that dispirited people good advice, with patterns to furnish them with arms. Besides, they built towers on the sea-coast to the southward, at proper distances, where their ships were, because there also the irruptions of the barbarians were apprehended, and so took leave of their friends, never to return again. . . . .

[A Parable of Man's Life [3]]

The king, hearing these words, answered, that he was both willing and bound to receive the faith which he taught; but that he would confer about it with his principal friends and counselors, to the end that if they also were of his opinion, they might all together be cleansed in Christ the Fountain of life. Paulinus consenting, the king did as he said; for, holding a council with the wise men, he asked of everyone in particular what he thought of the new doctrine, and the new worship that was preached. To which the chief of his own priests, Coifi, immediately answered, "O king, consider what this is which is now preached to us; for I verily declare to you, that the religion which we have hitherto professed has, as far as I can learn, no virtue in it. For none of your people has applied himself more diligently to the worship of our gods than I; and yet there are many who receive greater favors from you, and are more preferred than I, and are more prosperous in all their undertakings. Now if the gods were good for anything, they would rather forward me, who have been more careful to serve them. It remains, therefore, that if upon examination you find those new doctrines, which are now preached to us, better and more efficacious, we immediately receive them without any delay."

Another of the king's chief men, approving of his words and exhortations, presently added: "The present life of man, O king, seems to me, in comparison of that time which is unknown to us, like to the swift flight of a sparrow through the room wherein you sit at supper in winter, with your commanders and ministers, and a good fire in the midst, whilst the storms of rain and snow prevail abroad; the sparrow I say, flying in at one door, and immediately out at another, whilst he is within, is safe from the wintry storm; but after a short space of fair weather, he immediately vanishes out of your sight, into the dark winter from which he had emerged. So this life of man appears for a short space, but of what went before, or what is to follow, we are utterly ignorant. If, therefore, this new doctrine contains something more certain, it seems justly to deserve to be followed." The other elders and king's counselors by Divine inspiration spoke to the same effect. . . . .

[The Story of Caedmon [4]]

In this Abbess's Minster was a certain brother extraordinarily magnified and honored with a divine gift; for he was wont to make fitting

[1] Abercorn, on the south bank of the Firth of Forth
[2] Dumbarton
[3] From Bk. II, Chap. 13. Translation from the Latin, edited by J. A. Giles. This is an incident of the visit of Paulinus, who, in the year 625, during the reign of King Edwin (Eadwine) of Northumbria, came to England as a missionary from Pope Gregory.

[4] Book IV, Chapter 24. Translated from Latin into Anglo-Saxon by Alfred the Great. Modern English translation by Benjamin Thorpe. The "Minster" referred to was the monastery at Whitby, founded by the Abbess Hilda in 658.

songs which conduced to religion and piety; so that whatever he learned through clerks of the holy writings, that he, after a little space, would usually adorn with the greatest sweetness and feeling, and bring forth in the English tongue; and by his songs the minds of many men were often inflamed with contempt for the world, and with desire of heavenly life. And moreover, many others after him, in the English nation, sought to make pious songs; but yet none could do like him, for he had not been taught from men, nor through man, to learn the poetic art; but he was divinely aided, and through God's grace received the art of song. And he therefore never might make aught of leasing [1] or of idle poems, but just those only which conduced to religion, and which it became his pious tongue to sing. The man was placed in worldly life until the time that he was of mature age, and had never learned any poem; and he therefore often in convivial society, when, for the sake of mirth, it was resolved that they all in turn should sing to the harp, when he saw the harp approaching him, then for shame he would rise from the assembly and go home to his house.

When he so on a certain time did, that he left the house of the convivial meeting, and was gone out to the stall of the cattle, the care of which that night had been committed to him—when he there, at proper time, placed his limbs on the bed and slept, then stood some man by him, in a dream, and hailed and greeted him, and named him by his name, saying "Caedmon, sing me something." Then he answered and said "I cannot sing anything, and therefore I went out from this convivial meeting, and retired hither, because I could not." Again he who was speaking with him said, "Yet thou must sing to me" Said he, "What shall I sing?" Said he, "Sing me the origin of things." When he received this answer, then he began forthwith to sing, in praise of God the Creator, the verses and the words which he had never heard, the order of which is this:

"Now must we praise
the Guardian of heaven's kingdom,
the Creator's might,
and his mind's thought;
glorious Father of men!
as of every wonder he,
Lord eternal,
formed the beginning.
He first framed
for the children of earth
the heaven as a roof;
holy Creator!
then mid-earth,
the Guardian of mankind,
the eternal Lord,
afterwards produced;
the earth for men,
Lord Almighty!"

[1] lying

Then he arose from sleep, and had fast in mind all that he sleeping had sung, and to those words forthwith joined many words of song worthy of God in the same measure.

Then came he in the morning to the town-reeve, who was his superior, and said to him what gift he had received; and he forthwith led him to the abbess, and told, and made that known to her. Then she bade all the most learned men and the learners to assemble, and in their presence bade him tell the dream, and sing the poem; that, by the judgment of them all, it might be determined why or whence that was come. Then it seemed to them all, so as it was, that to him, from the Lord himself, a heavenly gift had been given. Then they expounded to him and said some holy history, and words of godly lore; then bade him, if he could, to sing some of them, and turn them into the melody of song. When he had undertaken the thing, then went he home to his house, and came again in the morning, and sang and gave to them, adorned with the best poetry, what had been entrusted to him.

Then began the abbess to make much of and love the grace of God in the man; and she then exhorted and instructed him to forsake worldly life and take to monkhood; and he that well approved. And she received him into the minster with his goods, and associated him with the congregation of those servants of God, and caused him to be taught the series of the Holy History and Gospel; and he, all that he could learn by hearing, meditated with himself, and, as a clean [2] animal, ruminating, turned into the sweetest verse; and his song and his verse were so winsome to hear, that his teachers themselves wrote and learned from his mouth. He first sang of earth's creation, and of the origin of mankind, and all the history of Genesis, which is the first book of Moses, and then of the departure of the people of Israel from the Egyptians' land, and of the entrance of the land of promise, and of many other histories of the canonical books of Holy Writ; and of Christ's incarnation, and of his passion, and of his ascension into heaven; and of the coming of the Holy Ghost, and the doctrine of the Apostles. And also of the terror

[2] in the ceremonial sense (see *Leviticus,* xi)

of the doom to come, and the fear of hell torment, and the sweetness of the heavenly kingdom, he made many poems; and, in like manner, many others of the divine benefits and judgments he made; in all which he earnestly took care to draw men from the love of sins and wicked deeds, and to excite to a love and desire of good deeds; for he was a very pious man, and to regular disciplines [1] humbly subjected; and against those who in otherwise would act, he was inflamed with the heat of great zeal. And he therefore with a fair end his life closed and ended.

For when the time approached of his decease and departure, then was he for fourteen days ere that oppressed and troubled with bodily infirmity; yet so moderately that, during all that time, he could both speak and walk. There was in the neighborhood a house for infirm men, in which it was their custom to bring the infirm, and those who were on the point of departure, and there attend to them together. Then bade he his servant, on the eve of the night that he was going from the world, to prepare him a place in that house, that he might rest; whereupon the servant wondered why he this bade, for it seemed to him that his departure was not so near; yet he did as he said and commanded. And when he there went to bed, and in joyful mood was speaking some things, and joking together with those who were therein previously, then it was over midnight that he asked, whether they had the eucharist [2] within. They answered, "What need is to thee of the eucharist? Thy departure is not so near, now thou thus cheerfully and thus gladly art speaking to us." Again he said, "Bring me nevertheless the eucharist."

When he had it in his hands, he asked, Whether they had all a placid mind and kind, and without any ill-will toward him. Then they all answered, and said, that they knew of no ill-will toward him, but they all were very kindly disposed and they besought him in turn that he would be kindly disposed to them all. Then he answered and said, "My beloved brethren, I am very kindly disposed to you and all God's men." And he thus was strengthening himself with the heavenly viaticum, [3] and preparing himself an entrance into another life. Again he asked, How near it was to the hour that the brethren must rise and teach the people of God, and sing their nocturns. [4] They answered, "It is not far to that." He said, "It is well; let us await the hour." And then he prayed, and signed himself with Christ's cross, and reclined his head on the bolster, and slept for a little space; and so with stillness ended his life. And thus it was, that as he with pure and calm mind and tranquil devotion had served God, that he, in like manner, left the world with as calm a death, and went to His presence; and the tongue that had composed so many holy words in the Creator's praise, he then in like manner its last words closed in His praise, crossing himself, and committing his soul into His hands. Thus it is seen that he was conscious of his own departure, from what we have now heard say.

(finished 731)

[1] penances
[2] host, or consecrated bread
[3] provisions for a journey (in this case the eucharist)
[4] service before daybreak

CYNEWULF fl. 750

Cynewulf was the only Old English vernacular poet known by name of whom undisputed writings remain. Yet little is known about him with any degree of certainty beyond the fact that he was probably a Northumbrian of the eighth century. That he is the author of four well-known poems, preserved in two manuscripts (the *Exeter Book* and the *Vercelli Book*), both of the early eleventh century, is established by the fact that Cynewulf signed some of his poems acrostically by inserting runes which spelled his name. Runes were characters which represented words as well as letters, just as our letter "B" might stand for the words *be* or *bee*. Those used in this passage of which we give a portion are:

ᚳ = C = cēne = keen, bold one
ᚣ = Y = yfel = wretched
ᚾ = N = nyd = need
ᛖ = E = eh = horse
ᚹ = W = wyn = joy
ᚢ = U = ur = our
ᛚ = L = lagu = water
ᚠ = F = feoh = wealth

His poems are: *Christ, The Fates of the Apostles, Juliana,* and *Elene,* his masterpiece, all religious poems, the two latter being legends of saints. According to their testimony Cynewulf was a scholar familiar with Latin and religious literature and gifted with much metrical skill and felicity in the use of traditional poetic language. His work marks an advance over that of Caedmon in that the personal note is emphasized and becomes lyrical; in the descriptions of nature; and in the evidence of a consciousness in art, pointing to foreign literary influences.

Many other works have been attributed to him, the most important being *The Dream of the Rood,* "the choicest blossom of Old English Christian poetry"; the *Phoenix;* and numerous Riddles, a popular form of early literature. The latter were long ascribed to him through a belief that one of them was a charade meaning Cynewulf, a theory refuted by later critics.

RIDDLE II [1]

Who so wary and so wise of the warriors lives,
That he dare declare who doth drive me on my way,
When I start up in my strength! Oft in stormy wrath,
Hugely then I thunder, tear along in gusts,
Fare above the floor of earth, burn the folk-halls down,
Ravage all the rooms! There the reek ariseth
Gray above the gables. Great on earth the din,
And the slaughter-qualm of men. Then I shake the woodland,
Forests rich in fruits; then I fell the trees—
I with water over-vaulted—by the wondrous Powers
Sent upon my way, far and wide to drive along!
On my back I carry that which covered once
All the tribes of Earth's indwellers, spirits and all flesh,
In the sand together! Say who shuts me in,
Or what is my name—I who bear this burden!

Answer: A Storm on Land.

RIDDLE VI

I am all alone, with the iron wounded,
With the sword slashed into, sick of work of battle,
Of the edges weary. Oft I see the slaughter,
Oft the fiercest fighting. Of no comfort ween I—
So that, in the battle-brattling, [2] help may bring itself to me;
Ere I, with the warriors, have been utterly fordone.
But the heritage of hammers [3] hews adown at me,
Stark of edges, sworded-sharp, of the smiths the handiwork,
On me biting in the burgs! Worse the battle is
I must bear for ever! Not one of the Leechkin, [4]
In the fold-stead, could I find out,
Who, with herbs he has, then should heal me of my wound!
But the notching of my edges more and more becomes
Through the deadly strokes of swords, in the daylight, in the night.

Of the Shield.

RIDDLE XV

I a weaponed warrior was! Now in pride bedecks me
A young serving-man all with silver and fine gold,
With the work of waving gyres! [5] Warriors sometimes kiss me;
Sometimes I to strife of battle summon with my calling
Willing war-companions! Whiles, the horse doth carry
Me the march-paths over, or the ocean-stallion
Fares the floods with me, flashing in my jewels.
Often times a bower-maiden, all bedecked with armlets,
Filleth up my bosom; whiles, bereft of covers,
I must, hard and heedless (in the houses) lie!
Then, again, hang I, with adornments fretted,
Winsome on the wall where the warriors drink.
Sometimes the folk-fighters, as a fair thing on warfaring,
On the back of horses bear me; then bedecked with jewels
Shall I puff with wind from a warrior's breast.
Then, again, to glee-feasts I the guests invite
Haughty heroes to the wine—other whiles shall I
With my shouting save from foes what is stolen away,
Make the plundering scather flee. Ask what is my name!

Of the Horn.

From CHRIST [6]

Then the *Courage-hearted* quakes, when the King he hears 797
Speak the words of wrath—Him the wielder of the Heavens—
Speak to those who once on earth but obeyed him weakly,
While as yet their *Yearning pain* and their *Need* most easily
Comfort might discover.

[1] These extracts from Cynewulf's writings are translations by Mr. Stopford Brooke, and have been taken from Mr. Brooke's *History of Early English Literature* by permission of The Macmillan Company.

[2] battle uproar

[3] swords

[4] physicians

[5] circles

[6] The *Christ* is a poem dealing with the Nativity and Ascension of Christ, and the Day of Judgment. The extracts are from the hymn-like passage which presages the Judgment and the poet's dread upon that day, and which closes with a vision of the stormy voyage of life ending in serenity.

. . . .
Gone is then the *Winsomeness*
Of the Earth's adornments! What to *Us* as men belonged
Of the joys of life was locked, long ago, in *Lake-Flood*,[1]
All the *Fee*[2] *on Earth.*
. . . .
Mickle is our need
That in this unfruitful time, ere that fearful Dread,
On our spirit's fairness we should studiously bethink us!
Now most like it is as if we on lake of ocean,
O'er the water cold in our keels are sailing,
And through spacious sea, with our stallions of the Sound,[3]
Forward drive the flood-wood. Fearful is the stream
Of immeasurable surges that we sail on here,
Through this wavering world, through these windy oceans,
O'er the path profound. Perilous our state of life
E'er that we had sailed (our ship) to the shore (at last),
O'er the rough sea-ridges. Then there reached us help,
That to hithe[4] of Healing homeward led us on—
He the Spirit-Son of God! And he dealt us grace,
So that we should be aware, from the vessel's deck,
Where our stallions of the sea we might stay with ropes,
Fast a-riding by their anchors—ancient horses of the waves!
Let us in that haven then all our hope establish,
Which the ruler of the Aether there has roomed for us,
When He climbed to Heaven—Holy in the Highest!

From ELENE[5]

Forth then fared the folk-troop, and a fighting-lay
Sang the Wolf in woodland, wailed a slaughter-rune!
Dewy-feathered, on the foes' track,
Raised the Earn[6] his song.
. . . .
Loud upsang the Raven
Swart, and slaughter-fell. Strode along the war-host;
Blew on high the horn-bearers; heralds of the battle shouted;
Stamped the earth the stallion; and the host assembled
Quickly to the quarrel!
. . . .
Sang the trumpets
Loud before the war-hosts; loved the work the raven;
Dewy-plumed, the earn looked upon the march;
. . . . Song the wolf uplifted,
Ranger of the holt![7] Rose the Terror of the battle!
There was rush of shields together, crush of men together,
Hard hand-swinging there, and of hosts down-dinging,
After that they first encountered flying of the arrows!
On that fated folk, full of hate the hosters[8] grim
Sent the showers of arrows, spears above the yellow shields;
Forth they shot then snakes of battle[9]
Through the surge of furious foes, by the strength of fingers!
Strode the stark[10] in spirit, stroke on stroke they pressed along;
Broke into the wall of boards,[11] plunged the bill[12] therein;
Thronged the bold in battle! There the banner was uplifted;
(Shone) the ensign 'fore the host; victory's song was sung.
Glittered there his javelins, and his golden helm
On the field of fight! Till in death the heathen,
Joyless fell!

THE ANGLO-SAXON CHRONICLE

One of the most important historical documents of the Old English period is the *Anglo-Saxon Chronicle.* Its compilation is usually ascribed to the influence of Alfred. Opening with a summary of early English history, it continued for two centuries and a half after the king's death, "long after the last English king had been slain and the old tongue banished from court and school."—*Camb. Hist.*

[1] the Deluge
[2] property
[3] ships
[4] harbor
[5] The *Elene* is the story of St. Helena, the mother of Constantine the Great, who made a pilgrimage to Jerusalem in search of the Holy Cross. The lines quoted describe the battle in which Constantine is victorious over the Huns. See Brooke's *Early English Literature,* pp. 405-6.

[6] eagle
[7] wood
[8] soldiers, host
[9] darts
[10] firm
[11] shields
[12] sword

As a result of the number of writers engaged in its compilation over so long a period of time, the literary merit of the work is very unequal. Some of the entries merely give the date and statement of events; others are passages of fluent and glowing narrative, especially those of the war-filled years of 911 to 924. The period from 925 to 975 is very bare of entries, most of them being of church matters; yet it is here that the principal poems of the collection are found. From 975 to 1001 the *Chronicle* is of extreme interest, and the annals for 1001 are very full.

The first poem, under the year 937 (see p. 28), is, says Professor Bright, "the most important of the poetic insertions in the Anglo-Saxon Chronicles." It records the victory of Athelstan, son of Edward, grandson of Alfred the Great, and king of the West Saxons and the Mercians, over a combination including Danes from Northumbria and Ireland, Scots, and Welsh. The Danes were headed by Anlaf (or Olaf), the Scots by Constantine.

It is markedly patriotic, showing deep feeling, brilliant lyrical power, and national enthusiasm. The meter is that of the ancient, alliterative rhetorical Anglo-Saxon line.

From THE ANGLO-SAXON CHRONICLE [1]

Anno 409. This year the Goths took the city of Rome by storm, and after this the Romans never ruled in Britain; and this was about eleven hundred and ten years after it had been built. Altogether they ruled in Britain four hundred and seventy years since Caius Julius first sought the land.

Anno 418. This year the Romans collected all the treasures that were in Britain, and some they hid in the earth, so that no one has since been able to find them; and some they carried with them into Gaul.

. . . .

Anno 443. This year the Britons sent over sea to Rome, and begged for help against the Picts; but they had none, because they were themselves warring against Attila, king of the Huns. And then they sent to the Angles, and entreated the like of the athelings [2] of the Angles.

. . . .

Anno 449. This year Martianus and Valentinus succeeded to the empire, and reigned seven years. And in their days Hengist and Horsa, invited by Vortigern, king of the Britons, landed in Britain, on the shore which is called Wippidsfleet; at first in aid of the Britons, but afterwards they fought against them. King Vortigern gave them land in the south-east of this country, on condition that they should fight against the Picts. Then they fought against the Picts, and had the victory wheresoever they came. They then sent to the Angles; desired a larger force to be sent, and caused them to be told the worthlessness of the Britons, and the excellencies of the land. Then they soon sent thither a larger force in aid of the others. At that time there came men from three tribes in Germany; from the Old-Saxons, from the Angles, from the Jutes. From the Jutes came the Kentish-men and the Wightwarians, that is, the tribe which now dwells in Wight, and that race among the West-Saxons which is still called the race of Jutes. From the Old-Saxons came the men of Essex and Sussex and Wessex. From Anglia, which has ever since remained waste betwixt the Jutes and Saxons, came the men of East Anglia, Middle Anglia, Mercia, and all North-humbria. Their leaders were two brothers, Hengist and Horsa: they were the sons of Wihtgils; Wihtgils son of Witta, Witta of Wecta, Wecta of Woden: from this Woden sprang all our royal families, and those of the South-humbrians also. [3]

Anno 455. This year Hengist and Horsa fought against King Vortigern at the place which is called Aegels-threp [4] and his brother Horsa was there slain, and after that Hengist obtained the kingdom, and Aesc his son.

. . . .

Anno 565. This year Ethelbert succeeded to the kingdom of the Kentish-men, and held it fifty-three years. In his days the holy pope Gregory sent us baptism, that was in the two and thirtieth year of his reign; and Columba, a mass-priest, came to the Picts, and converted them to the faith of Christ; they are dwellers by the northern mountains. And their king gave him the island which is called Ii; [5] therein are five hides [6] of land, as men say. There Columba built a monastery, and he was abbot there thirty-seven years, and there he died when he was seventy-two years old. His successors still have the place. The Southern Picts had been baptized long before. Bishop Ninia, who had been instructed at Rome, had preached baptism to them, whose church and his monastery is at Whitherne, consecrated in the name of St. Martin; there he resteth, with many holy men. Now in Ii there must ever be an abbot, and not a bishop; and all the Scottish bishops

[1] from the translation edited by J. A. Giles
[2] princes

[3] The language here appears to be that of a Northern chronicler. The MS. of this portion has been traced to Peterborough.
[4] Aylesford [5] Iona
[6] variously estimated at from 60 to 120 acres

ought to be subject to him because Columba was an abbot and not a bishop.

. . . .

Anno 596. This year Pope Gregory sent Augustine to Britain, with a great many monks, who preached the word of God to the nation of the Angles.

. . . .

Anno 871. . . . . . And about fourteen days after this, King Ethelred and Alfred his brother fought against the army [1] at Basing, and there the Danes obtained the victory. And about two months after this, King Ethelred and Alfred his brother fought against the army at Marden; and they [1] were in two bodies, and they [2] put both to flight, and during a great part of the day were victorious; and there was great slaughter on either hand; but the Danes had possession of the place of carnage; and there Bishop Heahmund was slain, and many good men: and after this battle there came a great army in the summer to Reading. And after this, over Easter, King Ethelred died; and he reigned five years and his body lies at Winburn-minster.

Then Alfred the son of Ethelwulf, his brother, succeeded to the kingdom of the West-Saxons. And about one month after this, King Alfred with a small band fought against the whole army at Wilton, and put them to flight for a good part of the day; but the Danes had possession of the place of carnage. And this year nine general battles were fought against the army in the kingdom south of the Thames, besides which Alfred the king's brother, and single ealdormen, [3] and king's thanes, often times made incursions on them, which were not counted; and within the year nine earls and one king were slain. And that year the West-Saxons made peace with the army.

The Battle of Brunanburh

Anno 937. Here Athelstan the King, ruler of earls,
ring-giver to chieftains, and his brother eke,
Edmund Atheling, [4] lifelong honor
struck out with the edges of swords in battle
at Brunanburh; they cleft the shield-wall [5]
hewed the war-lindens [6] with the leavings of hammers, [7]
these heirs of Edward; for fitting it was
to their noble descent that oft in the battle
'gainst foes one and all the land they should fend,
the hoards and the homes. The enemy fell,
Scot-folk and seamen, [8]
death-doomed they fell; slippery the field
with the blood of men, from sunrise
when at dawn the great star
stole o'er the earth, the bright candle of God
the Eternal Lord, till the noble creation
sank to its seat. There lay many a one
slain by a spear, many a Norseman
shot o'er his shield, many a Scotsman
weary and sated with strife. The men of Wessex
in troops the live-long day
followed on the footsteps of the hostile folk.
From the rear they fiercely struck the fleeing
with the sharp-ground swords. The Mercians did not stint
hard hand-play to any of the heroes
who with Anlaf o'er the wave-welter [9]
in the bosom of boats sought the land,
doomed to fall in the fight. On the field
five young kings lay killed,
put to sleep by swords; and seven, too,
of the earls of Anlaf, and countless warriors
of the seamen and the Scotch; routed was
the Norsemen's king, forced by need
with a little band to the boat's bow.
The galley glided on the waves; the king fled forth
on the fallow flood; so he saved his life.
And so by flight to his northern kinsfolk
came that wise one, Constantine,
gray battle man; boast he durst not
of the strife of swords; shorn of kinsfolk was he,
fallen on the battle-field his friends,
slain were they in strife; and his son, young for war,
left he on the slaughter-spot sore wounded.
Gray-haired hero, hoary traitor,
boast he durst not of the brand-clash; [10]
nor could Anlaf with their armies shattered
laugh that they the better were in battle-work,
in the fight of banners on the battle-field,
in the meeting of the spears, in the mingling of the men,
in the strife of weapons on the slaughter-field
which they played with Edward's heirs.
Departed then the Northmen in the nailèd ships,
a dreary leaving of darts [11] on the dashing sea.
O'er the deep water Dublin they sought,
Ireland again, abashed.
So the brethren both together,

[1] the Danes
[2] Ethelred and Alfred
[3] nobles
[4] prince
[3] the Germanic phalanx, in which the shields were overlapped
[6] shields made of linden wood
[7] swords, hammered out
[8] the Danes
[9] ocean
[10] clashing of swords
[11] the few left alive

King and Atheling, sought their kinsfolk
and West-Saxon land, from war exultant;
left behind to share the slain
the dusky-coated, the dark raven
horny-beaked, and the eagle white behind,
gray-coated, the carrion to consume,
the greedy war-hawk, and that gray beast,
the wolf in the weald.[1] Nor had greater slaughter
ever yet upon this island
e'er before a folk befallen
by sword-edges, say the books,
those old wise ones,[2] since from Eastward hither
Angles and Saxons on advanced,
o'er the waters wide sought the Britons,
warsmiths proud o'ercame the Welsh,
Earls honor-hungry got this homeland.[3]

ALFRED THE GREAT 849-901

What England would have become without Alfred the Great is difficult to imagine. Certain it is that he left a vital impression on many phases of the national life, being military leader, lawgiver, scholar, and saint. "Yet above all I see the grandeur, the freedom, the mildness, the domestic unity, the universal character of the middle ages, condensed into Alfred's glorious institution of the trial by jury."—Coleridge.

He was born at Wantage, the fourth son of King Athelwulf, with three brothers between him and the throne; but as in such troublous times life was likely to be short, he was king at twenty-two. Judging by the many anecdotes about him by several early chroniclers, he must have been a child of singular promise and attraction. At the age of five he was sent to Rome and confirmed by Leo IV. Asser, a Welsh cleric, who became the king's most intimate friend, and assisted him in his study of Latin, tells us: "As he advanced through the years of infancy and youth, his form appeared more comely than that of his brothers; in look, in speech, and in manners he was more graceful than they. His noble nature implanted in him from his cradle a love of wisdom above all things; but, with shame be it spoken, by the unworthy neglect of his parents and nurses, he remained illiterate even till he was twelve years old or more."

His public life began in 866 on the accession of his third brother, when he entered upon his great task of freeing England from the Danes. In 871 he inherited the throne, and after seven more years of conflict had cleared the greater part of the kingdom from the invaders. To remedy the ruin of learning and education wrought by them, Alfred then turned his attention to a revival of learning. He established a school at court, founded other schools and abbeys throughout the kingdom, imported scholars to assist him in the work, and personally set about translating some of the great books of the world into the tongue of his own people. Among these the most important are: *The Pastoral Care* of Pope Gregory, for the benefit of the clergy; the *Universal History* of the Spanish monk Orosius; the *Ecclesiastical History* of Bede; and the *Consolation of Philosophy* by Boethius, a Roman whose work became the most popular philosophical manual of the Middle Ages.

Good material on Alfred will be found in A. Bowker, *Alfred the Great,* 1899; C. Plummer, *The Life and Times of Alfred the Great,* 1902; F. J. Snell, *The Age of Alfred,* 1912.

[1] forest
[2] in apposition with "books"
[3] referring to the Anglo-Saxon conquest of Britain in the fifth century

[OHTHERE'S NARRATIVE[4]]

Ohthere told his lord King Alfred, that he dwelt northmost of all the Northmen. He said that he dwelt in the land to the northward, along the West-Sea; he said, however, that that land is very long north from thence, but it is all waste except in a few places where the Finns here and there dwell, for hunting in the winter, and in the summer for fishing in that sea. He said that he was desirous to try, once on a time, how far that country extended due north, or whether any one lived to the north of the waste. He then went due north along the country, leaving all the way the waste land on the right, and the wide sea on the left, for three days; he was as far north as the whale-hunters go at the farthest. Then he proceeded in his course due north as far as he could sail in another three days; then the land there inclined due east, or the sea into the land, he knew not which, but he knew that he there waited for a west wind, or a little north, and sailed thence eastward along that land as far as he could sail in four days; then he had to wait for a due north wind, because the land there inclined due south, or the sea in on that land, he knew not which; he then sailed along the coast due south, as far as he could sail in five days. There lay a great river[5] up in that land; they then turned up in that river, because they durst not sail on by that river, on account of hostility, because all that country was inhabited on the other side of that river; he had not before met with any land that was inhabited since he came from his own home; but all the way he had waste land on his right,

[4] From the addition made by King Alfred to his translation of Orosius's *History of the World;* modern English translation by Benjamin Thorpe. Ohthere was a Norwegian sailor, who, straying to Alfred's court, was eagerly questioned.
[5] the Dwina

except for fishermen, fowlers, and hunters, all of whom were Finns, and he had constantly a wide sea to the left. The Beormas [1] had well cultivated their country, but they did not dare to enter it; and the Terfinna land [2] was all waste, except where hunters, fishers, or fowlers had taken up their quarters.

The Beormas told him many particulars both of their own land, and of the other lands lying about them; but he knew not what was true, because he did not see it himself; it seemed to him that the Finns and the Beormas spoke nearly one language. He went thither chiefly, in addition to seeing the country, on account of the walruses, because they have very noble bones in their teeth; some of those teeth they brought to the king; and their hides are good for ship-ropes. This whale is much less than other whales, it being not longer than seven ells; but in his own country is the best whale-hunting—there they are eight and forty ells long, and the biggest of them fifty ells long; of these he said that he and five others had killed sixty in two days. He was a very wealthy man in those possessions in which their wealth consists, that is in wild deer. He had at the time he came to the king, six hundred unsold tame deer. These deer they call rein-deer, of which there were six decoy rein-deer, which are very valuable among the Finns, because they catch the wild rein-deer with them.

He was one of the foremost men in that country, yet he had not more than twenty horned cattle, and twenty sheep, and twenty swine, and the little that he ploughed he ploughed with horses. [3] But their wealth consists for the most part in the rent paid them by the Finns. That rent is in skins of animals, and birds' feathers, and whalebone, and in ship-ropes made of whales' hides, and of seals'. Everyone pays according to his birth; the best-born, it is said, pay the skins of fifteen martens and five rein-deers, and one bear's skin, ten ambers [4] of feathers, a bear's or otter's skin kirtle, and two ship-ropes, each sixty ells long, made either of whale-hide or of seal's.

He said that the Northmen's land was very long and narrow; all that his man could either pasture or plough lies by the sea, though that is in some parts very rocky; and to the east are wild mountains, parallel to the cultivated land. The Finns inhabit these mountains, and the cultivated land is broadest to the eastward, and continually narrower the more north. To the east it may be sixty miles broad, or a little broader, and toward the middle thirty, or broader; and northward, he said, where it is narrowest, that it might be three miles broad to the mountain, and the mountain then is in some parts so broad that a man may pass over in two weeks, and in some parts so broad that a man may pass over in six days. Then along this land southwards, on the other side of the mountain, is Sweden; to that land northward, and along that land northward, Cwenland. [5] The Cwenas sometimes make depredations on the Northmen over the mountain, and sometimes the Northmen on them; there are very large fresh meres amongst the mountains, and the Cwenas carry their ships over land into the meres, and thence make depredations on the Northmen; they have very little ships, and very light.

Ohthere said that the shire in which he dwelt is called Halgoland. He said that no one dwelt to the north of him; there is likewise a port to the south of that land, which is called Sciringes-heal; [6] thither, he said, no one could sail in a month, if he landed at night, and every day had a fair wind; and all the while he would sail along the land, and on the starboard will first be Iraland, [7] and then the islands which are between Iraland and this land. [8] Then it is this land until he come to Sciringes-heal, and all the way on the larboard, Norway. To the south of Sciringes-heal, a very great sea runs up into the land, which is broader than any one can see over; and Jutland is opposite on the other side, and then Zealand. This sea runs many miles up in that land. And from Sciringes-heal, he said that he sailed in five days to that port which is called Aet-Haethum, [9] which is between the Wends, and Saxons, and Angles, and belongs to Denmark.

When he sailed thitherward from Sciringes-heal, Denmark was on his left, and on the right a wide sea for three days, and two days before he came to Haethum he had on the right Jutland, Zealand, and many islands. In these lands the Angles dwelt before they came hither to this land. And then for two days he had on his left the islands which belong to Denmark.

[1] a people east of the Dwina
[2] the region between the Gulf of Bothnia and the North Cape
[3] The Anglo-Saxons plowed with oxen.
[4] forty bushels
[5] between the Gulf of Bothnia and the White Sea
[6] in the Gulf of Christiania
[7] Ireland (meaning Scotland; or possibly an error for Iceland)
[8] England
[9] Schleswig

THE ANGLO-NORMAN PERIOD

THE Anglo-Norman period was largely one of transition and amalgamation. With the Norman Conquest, 1066, came a beneficial infusion of the French language and literature, the influence of which was strongly felt in court and castle. The government acquired a distinctly feudal character. The spirit of chivalry found an outlet in the Crusades, and these in turn introduced the broadening civilization and luxury of the East. English youths flocked to Paris to study. The prevailing literature consisted of histories and ecclesiastical writings in Latin, or romances and legends in Norman or Parisian French remodeled by the court singers in England. The native language persisted among the people, under the form of three main dialects—those of the North, the South, and the Midlands; also popular songs in Old English flourished—ballads, riddles, and lyrics.

As the two races intermingled and intermarried, a fusion of their languages, laws, and customs gradually took place, the very name of Norman was forgotten, and the transplanted conquerors became English. By the time when separation from Normandy, 1204, ended French political influence, long poems such as Layamon's *Brut,* or the *Ormulum,* and romances such as *King Horn* and *Havelok the Dane* were written in English, the national language. The poetic forms current at the end of the period showed the same sort of mixture of French and English elements as did the language; Old English alliteration was still used, but it was beginning to give way to hints of the meter and rime in use on the Continent.

GEOFFREY OF MONMOUTH
c. 1100-1154

Though by the twelfth century more details are obtainable about the lives of individuals than in earlier ages, much still remains unknown about Geoffrey of Monmouth, who was born or bred at Monmouth in Wales, received a liberal education from an uncle, and in 1129 is known to have been at Oxford. He was fortunate in having as patrons, Robert, Earl of Gloucester, and Alexander, Bishop of Lincoln. In 1140 he received the archdeaconry of Llandaff "on account of his learning"; but in 1147-8 his two patrons died, and Geoffrey appealed to the Bishop of London, influential with King Stephen. He was ordained priest in 1151, and six months later consecrated bishop of St. Asaph, but apparently never visited his see, dying at Llandaff.

His great work, the *History of the Kings of Britain,* written in Latin in 1135, purports to be an authentic chronicle, the translation of a very old Breton book, which has never been found. Though largely original and chiefly a tissue of legends, it is partly drawn from the earlier histories of Nennius (796) and Bede; moreover it probably borrows much from floating British traditions. King Arthur as a national hero in English literature is Geoffrey's creation. The stories of Lear, Cymbeline, and Sabrina, for which no other sources have so far been found, link him especially with Shakespeare and Milton; but his influence is traceable in a succession of English writers down to modern times—Dryden, Pope, Wordsworth, Tennyson, and others. Considering its immediate and immense popularity, Geoffrey's history would seem to have been, in reality, a response to the growing demand for romance. At any rate, it is the most significant literary product of the twelfth century.

[The Story of King Leir [1]]

After this unhappy fate of Bladud, Leir, his son, was advanced to the throne, and nobly governed his country sixty years. He built upon the river Sore a city, called in the British tongue, Kaerleir, in the Saxon, Leircestre. He was without male issue, but had three daughters, whose names were Gonorilla, Regau, and Cordeilla, of whom he was dotingly fond, but especially of his youngest, Cordeilla. When he began to grow old, he had thoughts of dividing his kingdom among them, and of bestowing them on such husbands as were fit to be advanced to the government with them. But to make trial who was worthy to have the best part of his kingdom, he went to each of them to ask which of them loved him most. The question being proposed, Gonorilla, the eldest, made answer, that she called heaven to witness, she loved him more than her own soul. The father replied, "Since you have preferred my declining age before your own life, I will marry you, my dearest daughter, to whomsoever you shall make choice of, and give with you the third part of my kingdom." Then Regau, the second daughter, willing, after the example of her sister, to prevail upon her father's good nature, answered with an oath, that she could not otherwise express her thoughts, but that she loved him above all creatures. The credulous father upon this made her the same promise that he did to her eldest sister, that is, the choice of a husband, with the third part of his kingdom. But Cordeilla, the youngest, understanding how easily he was satisfied with the flattering expressions of her sisters, was desirous to make trial of his affection after a different manner. "My father," said she, "is there any daughter that can love her father more than duty requires? In my opinion, whoever pretends to it, must disguise her real sentiments under the veil of flattery. I have always loved you as a father, nor do I yet depart from my purposed duty; and if you insist to have something more extorted from me, hear now the greatness of my affection, which I always bear you, and take this for a short answer to all your questions; look how much you have, so much is your value, and so much do I love you." The father, supposing that she spoke this out of the abundance of her heart, was highly provoked, and immediately replied, "Since you have so far despised my old age as not to think me worthy the love that your sisters express for me, you shall have from me the like regard, and shall be excluded from any share with your sisters in my kingdom. Notwithstanding, I do not say but that since you are my daughter, I will marry you to some foreigner, if fortune offers you any such husband; but will never, I do assure you, make it my business to procure so honorable a match for you as for your sisters; because, though I have hitherto loved you more than them, you have in requital thought me less worthy of your affection than they." And, without further delay, after consultation with his nobility, he bestowed his two other daughters upon the dukes of Cornwall and Albania, with half the island at present, but after his death, the inheritance of the whole monarchy of Britain.

It happened after this, that Aganippus, king of the Franks, having heard of the fame of Cordeilla's beauty, forthwith sent his ambassadors to the king to demand her in marriage. The father, retaining yet his anger toward her, made answer, that he was very willing to bestow his daughter, but without either money or territories; because he had already given away his kingdom with all his treasure to his eldest daughters, Gonorilla and Regau. When this was told Aganippus, he, being very much in love with the lady, sent again to King Leir, to tell him, that he had money and territories enough, as he possessed the third part of Gaul, and desired no more than his daughter only, that he might have heirs by her. At last the match was concluded; Cordeilla was sent to Gaul, and married to Aganippus.

A long time after this, when Leir came to be infirm through old age, the two dukes, on whom he had bestowed Britain with his two daughters fostered an insurrection against him, and deprived him of his kingdom, and of all regal authority, which he had hitherto exercised with great power and glory. At length, by mutual agreement, Maglaunus, duke of Albania, one of his sons-in-law, was to allow him a maintenance at his own house, together with sixty soldiers, who were to be kept for state. After two years' stay with his son-in-law, his daughter Gonorilla grudged the number of his men, who began to upraid the ministers of the court with their scanty allowance; and, having spoken to her husband about it, she gave orders that the number of her father's followers should be reduced to thirty, and the rest discharged. The father, resenting this treatment, left Maglaunus, and went to Henuinus, duke of Cornwall, to whom he had married his daughter Regau. Here he met

[1] From the *Historia Britonum Regum,* Book II, Chapters XI-XIV. Translation from the Latin edited by J. A. Giles. Compare with Shakespeare's *King Lear.*

with an honorable reception, but before the year was at an end, a quarrel happened between the two families which raised Regau's indignation; so that she commanded her father to discharge all his attendants but five, and to be contented with their service. This second affliction was insupportable to him, and made him return again to his former daughter, with hopes that the misery of his condition might move in her some sentiments of filial piety, and that he, with his family, might find a subsistence with her. But she, not forgetting her resentment, swore by the gods he should not stay with her, unless he would dismiss his retinue, and be contented with the attendance of one man; and with bitter reproaches she told him how ill his desire of vainglorious pomp suited his age and poverty. When he found that she was by no means to be prevailed upon, he was at last forced to comply, and, dismissing the rest, to take up with one man only. But by this time he began to reflect more sensibly with himself upon the grandeur from which he had fallen, and the miserable state to which he was now reduced, and to enter upon thoughts of going beyond sea to his youngest daughter. Yet he doubted whether he should be able to move her commiseration, because (as was related above) he had treated her so unworthily. However, disdaining to bear any longer such base usage, he took ship for Gaul. In his passage he observed he had only the third place given him among the princes that were with him in the ship, at which, with deep sighs and tears, he burst forth into the following complaint:

"O irreversible decrees of the Fates, that never swerve from your stated course! why did you ever advance me to an unstable felicity, since the punishment of lost happiness is greater than the sense of present misery? The remembrance of the time when vast numbers of men obsequiously attended me in the taking the cities and wasting the enemy's countries, more deeply pierces my heart than the view of my present calamity, which has exposed me to the derision of those who were formerly prostrate at my feet. Oh! the enmity of fortune! Shall I ever again see the day when I may be able to reward those according to their deserts who have forsaken me in my distress? How true was thy answer, Cordeilla, when I asked thee concerning thy love to me, 'As much as you have, so much is your value, and so much do I love you.' While I had anything to give they valued me, being friends, not to me, but to my gifts: they loved me then, but they loved my gifts much more: when my gifts ceased, my friends vanished. But with what face shall I presume to see you, my dearest daughter, since in my anger I married you upon worse terms than your sisters, who, after all the mighty favors they have received from me, suffer me to be in banishment and poverty?"

As he was lamenting his condition in these and the like expressions, he arrived at Karitia,[1] where his daughter was, and waited before the city while he sent a messenger to inform her of the misery he was fallen into, and to desire her relief for a father who suffered both hunger and nakedness. Cordeilla was startled at the news, and wept bitterly, and with tears asked how many men her father had with him. The messenger answered, he had none but one man who had been his armor-bearer, and was staying with him without the town. Then she took what money she thought might be sufficient, and gave it to the messenger, with orders to carry her father to another city, and there give out that he was sick, and to provide for him bathing, clothes, and all other nourishment. She likewise gave orders that he should take into his service forty men, well clothed and accoutered, and that when all things were thus prepared he should notify his arrival to king Aganippus and his daughter. The messenger quickly returning, carried Leir to another city, and there kept him concealed, till he had done everything that Cordeilla had commanded.

As soon as he was provided with his royal apparel, ornaments, and retinue, he sent word to Aganippus and his daughter, that he was driven out of his kingdom of Britain by his sons-in-law, and was come to them to procure their assistance for recovering his dominions. Upon which they, attended with their chief ministers of state and the nobility of the kingdom, went out to meet him, and received him honorably, and gave into his management the whole power of Gaul, till such time as he should be restored to his former dignity.

In the meantime Aganippus sent officers over all Gaul to raise an army, to restore his father-in-law to his kingdom of Britain. Which done, Leir returned to Britain with his son and daughter and the forces which they had raised, where he fought with his sons-in-law and routed them. Having thus reduced the whole kingdom to his power, he died the third year after. Aganippus also died; and Cordeilla, obtaining

[1] Calais

the government of the kingdom, buried her father in a certain vault, which she ordered to be made for him under the river Sore, in Leicester, and which had been built originally[1] under the ground to the honor of the god Janus. And here all the workmen of the city, upon the anniversary solemnity of that festival, used to begin their yearly labors.

[Arthur Makes the Saxons His Tributaries[2]]

After a few days they went to relieve the city Kaerliudcoit, that was besieged by the pagans; which being situated upon a mountain, between two rivers in the province of Lindisia, is called by another name Lindocolinum.[3] As soon as they arrived there with all their forces, they fought with the Saxons, and made a grievous slaughter of them, to the number of six thousand; part of whom were drowned in the rivers, part fell by the hands of the Britons. The rest in a great consternation quitted the siege and fled, but were closely pursued by Arthur, till they came to the wood of Celidon, where they endeavored to form themselves into a body again, and make a stand. And here they again joined battle with the Britons, and made a brave defence, whilst the trees that were in the place secured them against the enemies' arrows. Arthur, seeing this, commanded the trees that were in that part of the wood to be cut down, and the trunks to be placed quite round them, so as to hinder their getting out; resolving to keep them pent up here till he could reduce them by famine. He then commanded his troops to besiege the wood, and continued three days in that place. The Saxons, having now no provisions to sustain them, and being just ready to starve with hunger, begged for leave to go out; in consideration whereof they offered to leave all their gold and silver behind them, and return back to Germany with nothing but their empty ships. They promised also that they would pay him tribute from Germany, and leave hostages with him. Arthur, after consultation about it, granted their petition; allowing them only leave to depart, and retaining all their treasures, as also hostages for payment of the tribute. But as they were under sail on their return home, they repented of their bargain, and tacked about again toward Britain, and went on shore at Totness. No sooner were they landed, than they made an utter devastation of the country as far as the Severn Sea, and put all the peasants to the sword. From thence they pursued their furious march to the town of Bath, and laid siege to it. When the king had intelligence of it, he was beyond measure surprised at their proceedings, and immediately gave orders for the execution of the hostages. And desisting from an attempt which he had entered upon to reduce the Scots and Picts, he marched with the utmost expedition to raise the siege; but labored under very great difficulties, because he had left his nephew Hoel sick at Alclud.[4] At length, having entered the province of Somerset, and beheld how the siege was carried on, he addressed himself to his followers in these words: "Since these impious and detestable Saxons have disdained to keep faith with me, I, to keep faith with God, will endeavor to revenge the blood of my countrymen this day upon them. To arms, soldiers, to arms, and courageously fall upon the perfidious wretches, over whom we shall, with Christ assisting us, undoubtedly obtain victory."

When he had done speaking, St. Dubricius, archbishop of Legions,[5] going to the top of a hill, cried out with a loud voice, "You that have the honor to profess the Christian faith, keep fixed in your minds the love which you owe to your country and fellow subjects, whose sufferings by the treachery of the pagans will be an everlasting reproach to you, if you do not courageously defend them. It is your country which you fight for, and for which you should, when required, voluntarily suffer death; for that itself is victory and the cure of the soul. For he that shall die for his brethren, offers himself a living sacrifice to God, and has Christ for his example, who condescended to lay down his life for his brethren. If therefore any of you shall be killed in this war, that death itself, which is suffered in so glorious a cause, shall be to him for penance and absolution of all his sins." At these words, all of them encouraged with the benediction of the holy prelate, instantly armed themselves, and prepared to obey his orders. Also Arthur himself, having put on a coat of mail suitable to the grandeur of so powerful a king, placed a golden helmet upon his head, on which was engraven the figure of a dragon; and on his shoulders his shield called Priwen; upon which the picture of the blessed Mary, mother of God, was painted, in order to put him frequently in mind of her. Then girding

[1] during the Roman occupation
[2] Book IX, Ch. III, IV.
[3] Lincoln
[4] Dumbarton
[5] the City of Legions (now Newport) in South Wales, where the Roman legions wintered

on his Caliburn,[1] which was an excellent sword made in the isle of Avallon, he graced his right hand with his lance, named Ron, which was hard, broad, and fit for slaughter. After this, having placed his men in order, he boldly attacked the Saxons, who were drawn out in the shape of a wedge, as their manner was. And they, notwithstanding that the Britons fought with great eagerness, made a noble defence all that day; but at length, toward sunsetting, climbed up the next mountain, which served them for a camp: for they desired no larger extent of ground, since they confided very much in their numbers. The next morning Arthur, with his army, went up the mountain, but lost many of his men in the ascent, by the advantage which the Saxons had in their station on the top, from whence they could pour down upon him with much greater speed than he was able to advance against them. Notwithstanding, after a very hard struggle, the Britons gained the summit of the hill and quickly came to a close engagement with the enemy, who again gave them a warm reception, and made a vigorous defence. In this manner was a great part of that day also spent; whereupon Arthur, provoked to see the little advantage he had yet gained and that victory still continued in suspense, drew out his Caliburn, and calling upon the name of the blessed Virgin, rushed forward with great fury into the thickest of the enemy's ranks; of whom (such was the merit of his prayers) not one escaped alive that felt the fury of his sword; neither did he give over the fury of his assault until he had, with his Caliburn alone, killed four hundred and seventy men. The Britons, seeing this, followed their leader in great multitudes, and made slaughter on all sides; so that Colgrin, and Baldulph his brother, and many thousands more fell before them. But Cheldric,[2] in this imminent danger of his men, betook himself to flight.

c. 1135

THE ANCREN RIWLE
(Anchoresses' Rule)
c. 1210

These "Rules and Duties of Monastic Life" were prepared for the guidance of a little society of three nuns who dwelt at Tarente, in Dorsetshire—"gentlewomen, sisters, of one father and of one mother, who had in the bloom of their youth forsaken all the pleasures of the world and become anchoresses." The book consists of eight chapters, the first and last of which deal with the "outward rule," the others with the "inward rule." It is possibly the work of Richard Poor (d. 1237), Bishop of Salisbury, who was a benefactor of the nunnery at Tarente. Very marked is the spirit of charity and tolerance in which it is written. Moreover, it is among the best examples of simple, eloquent prose in English antedating the English Bible. Our translation is that of James Morton.

It is of especial significance because it points to an increased interest in the religious life of women. It stands quite apart from the ordinary prose work of the time by its originality, its personal charm, and its complete sympathy with all that is good in contemporary literature; and is one of the most interesting pieces in the whole Middle English period. It throws much light on the life within an anchorhold, the duties of the inmates, the out-sisters and maids, and their various difficulties, business, domestic, and spiritual. It contains borrowings from the church fathers, and many medieval commonplaces; and it shows considerable acquaintance with animal and plant lore, as well as a delight in allegorical teachings.

From THE ANCREN RIWLE

Do you now ask what rule you anchoresses should observe? Ye should by all means, with all your might and all your strength, keep well the inward rule, and for its sake the outward. The inward rule is always alike. The outward is various, because every one ought so to observe the outward rule as that the body may therewith best serve the inward. All may and ought to observe one rule concerning purity of heart, that is, a clean, unstained conscience, without any reproach of sin that is not remedied by confession. This the body rule effects. This rule is framed not by man's contrivance, but by the command of God. Wherefore, it ever is and shall be the same, without mixture and without change; and all men ought ever invariably to observe it. But the external rule, which I called the handmaid, is of man's contrivance; nor is it instituted for any thing else but to serve the internal law. It ordains fasting, watching, enduring cold, wearing haircloth, and such other hardships as the flesh of many can bear and many cannot. Wherefore, this rule may be changed and varied according to every one's state and circumstances. For some are strong, some are weak, and may very well be excused, and please God with less; some are learned, and some are not, and must work the more, and say their prayers at the stated hours in a different manner; some are old and ill

[1] the famous Excalibur
[2] leader of the Saxons

favored, of whom there is less fear; some are young and lively, and have need to be more on their guard. Every anchoress must, therefore, observe the outward rule according to the advice of her confessor, and do obediently whatever he enjoins and commands her, who knows her state and strength. He may modify the outward rule, as prudence may direct, and as he sees that the inward rule may thus be best kept.

. . . .

When you first arise in the morning bless yourselves with the sign of the cross and say, "In the name of the Father, and of the Son, and of the Holy Ghost, Amen," and begin directly "Creator Spirit, Come," with your eyes and your hands raised up toward heaven, bending forward on your knees upon the bed, and thus say the whole hymn to the end, with the versicle, "Send forth Thy Holy Spirit," and the prayer, "God, who didst teach the hearts of thy faithful people," etc. After this, putting on your shoes and your clothes, say the Paternoster [1] and the Creed, [2] and then, "Jesus Christ, Son of the Living God, have mercy on us! Thou who didst condescend to be born of a virgin, have mercy on us!" Continue saying these words until you be quite dressed. Have these words much in use, and in your mouth as often as ye may, sitting and standing.

. . . .

True anchoresses are compared to birds; for they leave the earth: that is, the love of all earthly things; and through yearning of heart after heavenly things, fly upward toward heaven. And, although they fly high, with high and holy life, yet they hold the head low, through meek humility, as a bird flying boweth down its head, and accounteth all her good deeds and good works nothing worth, and saith, as our Lord taught all his followers, *"Cum omnia bene feceritis, dicite quod servi inutiles estis"*; "When ye have done all well," saith the Lord, "say that ye are unprofitable servants." Fly high, and yet hold the head always low.

The wings that bear them upward are, good principles, which they must move unto good works, as a bird, when it would fly, moveth its wings. Also the true anchoresses, whom we compare to birds—yet not we, but God—spread their wings and make a cross of themselves, as a bird doth when it flieth; that is, in the thoughts of the heart, and the mortification of the flesh, they bear the Lord's cross. Those birds fly well that have little flesh, as the pelican hath, and many feathers. The ostrich, having much flesh, maketh a pretense to fly, and flaps his wings, but his feet always draw to the earth. In like manner, the carnal anchoress, who loveth carnal pleasures, and seeketh her ease, the heaviness of her flesh and its desires deprive her of her power of flying; and though she makes a pretense and much noise with her wings; that is, makes it appear as if she flew, and were a holy anchoress, whoever looks at her narrowly, laughs her to scorn; for her feet, as doth the ostrich's, which are her lusts, draw her to the earth. Such are not like the meagre pelican, nor do they fly aloft, but are birds of the earth, and make their nests on the ground. But God called the good anchoresses birds of heaven, as I said before: *"Vulpes foveas habent et volucres coeli nidos."* "Foxes have their holes, and birds of heaven their nests."

True anchoresses are indeed birds of heaven, that fly aloft, and sit on the green boughs singing merrily; that is, they meditate, enraptured, upon the blessedness of heaven that never fadeth, but is ever green; and sit on this green, singing right merrily; that is, in such meditation they rest in peace and have gladness of heart, as those who sing. A bird, however, sometimes alighteth down on the earth to seek his food for the need of the flesh; but while he sits on the ground he is never secure, and is often turning himself, and always looking cautiously around. Even so, the pious recluse, though she fly ever so high, must at times alight down to the earth in respect of her body—and eat, drink, sleep, work, speak, and hear, when it is necessary, of earthly things. But then, as the bird doth, she must look well to herself, and turn her eyes on every side, lest she be deceived, and be caught in some of the devil's snares, or hurt in any way, while she sits so low.

"The birds," saith our Lord, "have nests"; *"volucres coeli habent nidos."* A nest is hard on the outside with pricking thorns, and is delicate and soft within; even so shall a recluse endure hard and pricking thorns in the flesh; yet so prudently shall she subdue the flesh by labor, that she may say with the Psalmist: *"Fortitudinem meam ad te custodiam"*; that is, "I will keep my strength, O Lord, to thy behoof"; and therefore the pains of the flesh are proportioned to every one's case. The nest shall be hard without and soft

[1] the Lord's Prayer
[2] the Confession of Faith, beginning, "Credo in unum Deum"

within; and the heart sweet. They who are of a bitter or hard heart, and indulgent toward their flesh, make their nest, on the contrary, soft without and thorny within. These are the discontented and fastidious anchoresses; bitter within, when they ought to be sweet; and delicate without, when they ought to be hard. These, in such a nest, may have hard rest, when they consider well. For, from such a nest, they will too late bring forth young birds, which are good works, that they may fly toward heaven. Job calleth a religious house a nest; and saith, as if he were a recluse: *"In nidulo meo moriar";* that is, "I shall die in my nest, and be as dead therein"; for this relates to anchorites; and, to dwell therein until she die; that is, I will never cease, while my soul is in my body, to endure things hard outwardly, as the nest is, and to be soft within.

. . . .

Hear now, as I promised, many kinds of comfort against all temptations, and, with God's grace, thereafter the remedies.

Whosoever leadeth a life of exemplary piety may be certain of being tempted. This is the first comfort. For the higher the tower is, it hath always the more wind. Ye yourselves are the towers, my dear sisters, but fear not while ye are so truly and firmly cemented all of you to one another with the lime of sisterly love. Ye need not fear any devil's blast, except the lime fail; that is to say, except your love for each other be impaired through the enemy. As soon as any of you undoeth her cement, she is soon swept forth; if the other do not hold her she is soon cast down, as a loose stone is from the coping of the tower, down into the deep pitch of some foul sin.

Here is another encouragement which ought greatly to comfort you when ye are tempted. The tower is not attacked, nor the castle, nor the city, after they are taken; even so the warrior of hell attacks, with temptation, none whom he hath in his hand; but he attacketh those whom he hath not. Wherefore, dear sisters, she who is not attacked may fear much lest she be already taken. . . . .

The sixth comfort is, that our Lord, when He suffereth us to be tempted, playeth with us, as the mother with her young darling; she flies from him, and hides herself, and lets him sit alone, and look anxiously around, and call Dame! dame! and weep a while, and then leapeth forth laughing, with outspread arms, and embraceth and kisseth him, and wipeth his eyes. In like manner, our Lord sometimes leaveth us alone, and withdraweth His grace, His comfort, and His support, so that we feel no delight in any good that we do, nor any satisfaction of heart; and yet, at that very time, our dear Father loveth us never the less, but does it for the great love that He hath to us.

. . . .

Ye shall not possess any beast, my dear sisters, except only a cat. An anchoress that hath cattle appears as Martha was, a better housewife than anchoress; nor can she in any wise be Mary, with peacefulness of heart. For then she must think of the cow's fodder, and of the herdsman's hire, flatter the heyward, [1] defend herself when her cattle is shut up in the pinfold, and moreover pay the damage. Christ knoweth, it is an odious thing when people in the town complain of anchoresses' cattle. If, however, any one must needs have a cow, let her take care that she neither annoy nor harm any one, and that her own thoughts be not fixed thereon. An anchoress ought not to have any thing that draweth her heart outward. Carry ye on no traffic. An anchoress that is a buyer and seller selleth her soul to the chapman of hell. Do not take charge of other men's property in your house, nor of their cattle, nor their clothes, neither receive under your care the church vestments, nor the chalice, unless force compel you, or great fear, for oftentimes much harm has come from such care-taking.

Because no man seeth you, nor do ye see any man, ye may be well content with your clothes, be they white, be they black; only see that they be plain, and warm, and well made—skins well tawed; [2] and have as many as you need, for bed, and also for back. Next your flesh ye shall wear no flaxen cloth, except it be of hards [3] and of coarse canvas. Whoso will may have a stamin, [4] and whoso will may be without it. Ye shall sleep in a garment and girt. Wear no iron, nor haircloth, nor hedgehog-skins; and do not beat yourselves therewith, nor with a scourge of leather thongs, nor leaded; and do not with holly nor with briars cause yourselves to bleed without leave of your confessor; and do not, at one time, use too many flagellations. Let your shoes be thick and warm. In summer ye are at liberty to go and sit barefoot, and to wear hose without vamps, [5] and whoso liketh may lie in them. A woman may well enough wear an undersuit of haircloth very well tied with the strapples reaching down to her feet, laced tightly. If ye would dispense with wimples, have warm capes, and over them black veils. She who wishes to be seen, it is no great

[1] a cattle-keeper on a common
[2] prepared with oil, or without tan-liquor
[3] the coarser parts of flax or hemp
[4] a shirt of linsey-woolsey
[5] gaiters

wonder though she adorn herself; but, in the eyes of God, she is more lovely who is unadorned outwardly for his sake. Have neither ring, nor brooch, nor ornamented girdle, nor gloves, nor any such thing that is not proper for you to have.

. . . .

In this book read every day, when ye are at leisure—every day, less or more; for I hope that, if ye read it often, it will be very beneficial to you, through the grace of God, or else I shall have ill employed much of my time. God knows, it would be more agreeable to me to set out on a journey to Rome, than to begin to do it again. And, if ye find that ye do according to what ye read, thank God earnestly; and if ye do not, pray for the grace of God, and diligently endeavor that ye may keep it better, in every point, according to your ability. May the Father, and the Son, and the Holy Ghost, the one Almighty God, keep you under his protection! May he give you joy and comfort, my dear sisters, and for all that ye endure and suffer for him may he never give you a less reward than his entire self. May he be ever exalted from world to world, for ever and ever, Amen.

As often as ye read any thing in this book, greet the Lady with an Ave Mary for him that made this rule, and for him who wrote it, and took pains about it. Moderate enough I am, who ask so little.

c. 1225

PROVERBS OF KING ALFRED[1]

1

Many thanes sat at Seaford,
many bishops, book-learned men,
many proud earls, knights every one.
There was Earl Aelfric, wise in the law;
Alfred also, England's guardian,
England's darling, England's king.
He began, as ye may hear,
to teach them how to lead their lives.
He was king, and he was clerk[2]
well he loved the Lord's work;
wise in word and cautious in deed,
he was the wisest man in England.

2

Thus quoth Alfred, England's comfort:
"Would ye, my people, give ear to your lord,
he would direct you wisely in all things,
how ye might win to worldly honor
and also unite your souls with Christ."

3

Wise were the words King Alfred spake.
"Humbly I rede[3] you, my dear friends,
poor and rich, all you my people,
that ye all fear Christ the Lord,
love him and please him, the Lord of Life.
He is alone good, above all goodness;
He is alone wise, above all wisdom;
He is alone blissful, above all bliss;
He is alone man's mildest Master;
He is alone our Father and Comfort." . . .

4

Thus quoth Alfred:
"The earl and the lord
that heeds the king's word
shall rule o'er his land
with righteous hand;
and the clerk and the knight
shall give judgment aright,
to poor or to rich
it skilleth[4] not which.
For whatso men sow,
the same shall they mow,
and every man's doom
to his own door come." . . .

12

Thus quoth Alfred:
"Small trust may be
in the flowing sea.
Though thou hast treasure
enough and to spare,
both gold and silver,
to nought it shall wear;
to dust it shall drive,
as God is alive.
Many a man for his gold
God's wrath shall behold,
and shall be for his silver
forgot and forlorn.
It were better for him
he had never been born." . . .

14

Thus quoth Alfred:
"If thou hast sorrow,
tell it not to thy foe;
tell it to thy saddle-bow
and ride singing forth.
So will he think,
who knows not thy state,

[1] The proverbs here translated from Middle English, some of them plainly Biblical, were popularly ascribed to King Alfred and were supposed to have been delivered by him to his Witenagemot at Seaford.
[2] scholar
[3] counsel
[4] matters

that not unpleasing
to thee is thy fate.
If thou hast a sorrow
and he knoweth it,
before thee he'll pity,
behind thee will twit.
Thou mightest betray it
to such a one
as would without pity
thou madest more moan.
Hide it deep in thy heart
that it leave no smart;
nor let it be guessed
what is hid in thy breast." . . .

22

Thus quoth Alfred:
"Boast shouldst thou not,
nor chide with a sot;
nor foolishly chatter
and idle tales scatter
at the freeman's board.
Be chary of word.
The wise man can store
few words with great lore.
Soon shot's the fool's bolt;
whence I count him a dolt
who saith all his will
when he should keep still.
For oft tongue breaketh bone,
though herself has none."

CUCKOO SONG

This song, one of the most beautiful Middle English lyrics, belongs to the early years of the period. Its popularity is proved by the existence of music to which it was sung in the first half of the thirteenth century. The manuscript which contains the music adds the following directions in Latin: "This part-song (*rota*) may be sung by four in company. It should not be sung by fewer than three, or at least two, in addition to those who sing the *Foot*. And it should be sung in this manner: One begins, accompanied by those who sing the *Foot*, the rest keeping silent. Then, when he has reached the first note after the cross [a mark on the musical score], another begins; and so on. The first line of the *Foot* one singer repeats as often as necessary, pausing at the end; the other line another man sings, pausing in the middle but not at the end, but immediately beginning again."

The poem shows that a sense of rime, music, and sweetness had arrived, and the lines were settling down into molds of equal length. Moreover, the poet was beginning to enter into the spirit of nature with a glad heart instead of feeling in harmony only with her darker aspects, as was the case in most of the Old English writers.

Summer is y-comen in, [1]
Loudly sing Cuckoo!
Groweth seed and bloweth mead
And springeth wood anew.
Sing Cuckoo!
Loweth after calf the cow,
Bleateth after lamb the ewe,
Buck doth gambol, bullock amble—
Merry sing Cuckoo!
Cuckoo, Cuckoo! Well singest thou
Cuckoo! nor cease thou ever now.

(Foot)

Sing Cuckoo now, sing Cuckoo.
Sing Cuckoo, sing Cuckoo now.

c. 1250

[1] The Middle English version, which has been somewhat modernized above, is as follows:
"Sumer is icumen in,
Lhude sing cuccu!
Groweth sed, and bloweth med,
And springeth the wde nu.
Sing cuccu!"

THE FOURTEENTH CENTURY—AGE OF CHAUCER

BY 1350 was concluded a movement toward national freedom and unity. The English spirit of independence was everywhere manifest; and the power of Parliament modified the "divine right" of kings. The English language, beginning to recover complete ascendancy, supplanted French in the law courts, was heard in the pulpit, and was taught in the school. Not only was literature intended primarily for the people—like Wyclif's translation of the Bible—written in the native tongue, but even writers for court circles used English as a medium of expression; thus Chaucer, choosing the language of the people and the Midland dialect, and abandoning alliteration for meter and rime, became in truth the Father of the English language.

From THE PEARL

This anonymous poem is allegorical; possibly the "pearl" is the poet's daughter. The poem was found in a single manuscript of the late fourteenth or the early fifteenth century with *Cleanness, Patience,* and *Sir Gawayne and the Green Knight,* three other Middle English poems. It is almost positive from similarity in style that the four are by the same author. His identity has not yet been discovered. The works reveal a distinct personality, a knowledge of courtly life, and a familiarity with old English, French, and Latin writers. The main part of *The Pearl* is a paraphrase of the closing chapters of the Apocalypse, and the parable of the vineyard. Another source is Chaucer's *Romance of the Rose,* a translation from an earlier French poem. From the latter and the *Book of Revelation* are derived much of the wealth and brilliancy of the poem. The verse is easy and musical; the poet shows a mastery of descriptive power, a delight in nature, and a wide vocabulary.

The selection here given is translated, because the West Midland dialect of the original presents more difficulties than the East Midland of Chaucer. The poem is a very interesting piece of construction, combining the Romance elements of meter and rime, as employed by Chaucer, with the old Saxon alliteration which the West Midland poets, like Langland, affected. Note also the refrain-like effects. In this translation, the exacting rime-scheme of the original, which permits but three rime sounds in a stanza, has been adhered to in the last three stanzas only.

1

O pearl, for princes' pleasure wrought,[1]
  In lucent gold deftly to set,
Never from orient realms was brought
  Its peer in price, I dare say, yet.
So beautiful, so fresh, so round,
  So smooth its sides, so slender shown,
Whatever gems to judge be found
  I needs must set it apart, alone.
But it is lost! I let it stray
  Down thro' the grass in an arbor-plot.
With love's pain now I pine away,
  Lorn of my pearl without a spot.

2

Since in that spot it slipt from my hand,
  Oft have I lingered there and yearned
For joy that once my sorrows banned
  And all my woes to rapture turned.

[1] The first stanza of the original runs thus:

Perle plesaunte to prynces paye,
  To clanly clos in golde so clere,
Out of oryent I hardyly saye,
  Ne proved I never her precios pere,—
So rounde, so reken in uche a raye,
  So smal, so smothe her sydez were,—
Queresoever I jugged gemmez gaye,
  I sette hyr sengeley in synglere.
Allas! I leste hyr in on erbere;
  Thurgh gresse to grounde hit fro me yot;
I dewyne for-dokked of luf-daungere,
  Of that pryvy perle withouten spot.

Truly my heart with grief is wrung,
And in my breast there dwelleth dole;
Yet never song, methought, was sung
So sweet as through that stillness stole.
O tide of fancies I could not stem!
O fair hue fouled with stain and blot!
O mold, thou marrest a lovely gem,
Mine own, own pearl without a spot. . . . 24

4

Once to that spot I took my way
And passed within the arbor green.
It was mid-August's festal day,
When the corn is cut with sickles keen.
The mound that did my pearl embower
With fair bright herbage was o'erhung,
Ginger and gromwell and gillyflower,
And peonies sprinkled all among.
Yet if that sight was good to see,
Goodlier the fragrance there begot
Where dwells that one so dear to me,
My precious pearl without a spot. 48

5

Then on that spot my hands I wrung,
For I felt the touch of a deadly chill,
And riotous grief in my bosom sprung,
Tho' reason would have curbed my will.
I wailed for my pearl there hid away,
While fiercely warred my doubts withal,
But tho' Christ showed where comfort lay,
My will was still my sorrow's thrall.
I flung me down on that flowery mound,
When so on my brain the fragrance wrought
I sank into a sleep profound,
Above that pearl without a spot. 60

6

Then from that spot my spirit soared.
My senses locked in slumber's spell,
My soul, by grace of God outpoured,
Went questing where his marvels dwell.
I know not where that place may be,
I know 'twas by high cliffs immured,
And that a forest fronted me
Whose radiant slopes my steps allured.
Such splendor scarce might one believe—
The goodly glory wherewith they shone;
No web that mortal hands may weave 71
Has e'er such wondrous beauty known. . . .

9

Yes, beautiful beyond compare,
The vision of that forest-range
Wherein my fortune bade me fare—
No tongue could say how fair, how strange.
I wandered on as one entranced,
No bank so steep as to make me cower;
And the farther I went the brighter danced
The light on grass and tree and flower.
Hedge-rows there were, and paths, and streams
Whose banks were as fine threads of gold,
And I stood on the strand and watched the gleams
Of one that downward in beauty rolled. 108

10

Dear Lord, the beauty of that fair burn!
Its berylline banks were bright as day,
And singing sweetly at every turn
The murmuring waters took their way.
On the bottom were stones a-shimmer with light
As gleams through glass that waver and leap,
Or as twinkling stars on a winter night
That watch in heaven while tired men sleep.
For every pebble there that laved
Seemed like a rare and radiant gem;
Each pool was as with sapphires paved, 119
So lustrous shone the beauty of them. . . .

13

Then longing seized me to explore
The farther margin of that stream,
For fair as was the hither shore
Far fairer did the other seem.
About me earnestly I sought
To find some way to win across,
But all my seeking availed me nought;
There was no ford; I stood at loss.
Methought I must not daunted dwell
In sight of such a blissful goal,
When lo, a strange thing there befell 155
That still more deeply stirred my soul.

14

More wonder still my soul to daze!
I saw beyond that lowly stream
A crystal cliff refulgent raise
Its regal height, and, dazzling, gleam.
And at its foot there sat a child,
A gracious maid, and debonair,
All in a white robe undefiled—
Well had I known her otherwhere.
As glistening gold men use to spin,
So shone that glory the cliff before.
Long did I drink her beauty in, 167
And longed to call to her ever more. . . .

16

But more than my longing was now my fright;
I stood quite still; I durst not call;
With eyes wide open and lips shut tight,
I stood as quiet as hawk in hall.
I weened it was some spectral shape,
I dreaded to think what should ensue

If I should call her and she escape
  And leave me only my plight to rue.
When lo, that gracious, spotless may,[1]
  So delicate, so soft, so slight,
Uprose in all her queenly array,
  A priceless thing in pearls bedight. 192

17

Pearl-dight in royal wise, perdie,
  One might by grace have seen her there,
When all as fresh as a fleur-de-lys
  Adown the margent stepped that fair.
Her robe was white as gleaming snow,
  Unclasped at the sides and closely set
With the loveliest margarites, I trow,
  That ever my eyes looked on yet.
Her sleeves were broad and full, I ween,
  With double braid of pearls made bright.
Her kirtle shone with as goodly sheen, 203
  With precious pearls no less bedight. . . .

20

Pearl-dight, that nature's masterpiece
  Came down the margent, stepping slow;
No gladder man from here to Greece
  When by the stream she stood, I trow.
More near of kin than aunt or niece,
  She made my gladness overflow;
She proffered me speech—O heart's release!—
  In womanly fashion bending low;
Caught off her crown of queenly show
  And welcomed me as a maiden might.
Ah well that I was born to know 239
  And greet that sweet one pearl-bedight!

21

"O pearl," quoth I, "all pearl-bedight,
  Art thou my Pearl, the Pearl I mourn
And long for through the lonely night?
  In weariness my days have worn
Since thou in the grass didst slip from sight.
  Pensive am I, heart-sick, forlorn—
While thou hast won to pure delight
  In Paradise, of sorrow shorn.
What fate has hither my jewel borne
  And left me beggared to moan and cry?
For since we twain asunder were torn,
  A joyless jeweler am I." 252

22

That jewel then, with gems o'erspread,
  Upturned her face and her eyes gray,
Replaced the crown upon her head,
  And thus my longing did allay:
"Oh, sir, thou hast thy tale misread
  To say thy pearl is stolen away,
That is so safely casketed
  Here in this garden bright and gay,
Herein forever to dwell and play
  Where comes not sin nor sorrow's blight.
Such treasury[2] wouldst thou choose, parfay,
  Didst thou thy jewel love aright."[3] 264

1350

[1] maid

WILLIAM LANGLAND?
1332?-1400

One of the many literary mysteries that are met with in the course of English literature is the case of William Langland or Langley, generally accepted as the author of the *Vision of Piers the Plowman*. Little is known about him. One manuscript declares that his father was of gentle birth. From the poem, represented by three greatly differing texts, it is inferred that the poet was born about 1332, was free born, was born in wedlock, and was sent to school; his literary acquirements seem to have been considerable; there are indications that he took minor orders; he speaks of a wife and a daughter; and they lived at Cornhill in London, apparently leading a life of great poverty.

Yet recent critics believe, on account of differences in style, diction, meter, sentence structure, views of social life, and other points, that the poem is the work of perhaps five different individuals; and that the autobiographical facts are not genuine, but merely part of the fiction. They believe that the three texts known as A, B, and C, cannot be by one author even had he been composing and revising them for over thirty years (1362-1399).

This long allegorical poem attacks in the spirit of reform what appear to be outstanding abuses in church, state, and society, and, as Sir Edmund Gosse says, presents "an epitome of the social and political life of England, and particularly of London, seen from within and from below, without regard to what might be thought above and outside the class of workers."

The prologue, of which the first 82 lines are here given, sets the key-note of the poem by a description of the suffering, weakness, and crimes of the contemporary world as seen in a vision. Then in Passus (Chapter) I, of which a few lines are given, is begun a narrative interpretation of his vision. The present text is the B-text as printed by Dr. Skeat.

The most useful edition is that of W. W. Skeat, 2 vols., 1886; further discussion and criticism will be found in Gosse, Guest, Ker (*Med. Lit.*), Scudder, Manly (*Camb. Hist. Lit.*), and H. Monroe, "Chaucer and Langland," *Poetry* 7:297-302.

[2] Compare *Matthew* vi, 21.
[3] A long religious dissertation follows, and the dreamer awakes consoled.

THE VISION OF PIERS THE PLOWMAN

From the PROLOGUE

In a somer seson, whan soft was the sonne,
I shope [1] me in shroudes [2] as I a shepe [3] were,
In habite as an heremite unholy of workes, [4]
Went wyde [5] in this world wondres to here.
Ac [6] on a May mornynge, on Malverne hulles,[7]
Me byfel a ferly, [8] of fairy, [9] me thoughte;
I was wery forwandred [10] and went me to reste
Under a brode banke bi a bornes [11] side,
And as I lay and lened and loked in the wateres,
I slombred in a slepyng, it sweyved [12] so merye.
Thanne gan I to meten [13] a merveilouse swevene, [14]
That I was in a wildernesse, wist I never where;
As I bihelde into the est an hiegh to [15] the sonne,
I seigh [16] a toure [17] on a toft [18] trielich [19] ymaked;
A depe dale binethe, a dongeon [20] there-inne,
With depe dyches and derke and dredful of sight.
A faire felde ful of folke [21] fonde I there bytwene,
Of alle maner of men, the mene and the riche,
Worchyng and wandryng as the worlde asketh.
Some putten hem [22] to the plow, pleyed ful selde,
In settyng [23] and in sowyng swonken [24] ful harde,
And wonnen that wastours with glotonye destruyeth. [25]
And some putten hem to pruyde, apparailed hem there-after,
In contenaunce of clothyng comen disgised. [26]
In prayers and in penance putten hem manye,
Al for love of owre lorde lyveden ful streyte,[27]
In hope forto have hevenriche [28] blisse;
As ancres [29] and heremites that holden hem in here [33] selles,
And coveiten nought in contre to kairen [30] aboute,
For no likerous [31] liflode [32] her [33] lykam [34] to plese.
And somme chosen chaffare; [35] they cheven [36] the bettere,
As it semeth to owre syght that suche men thryveth;
And somme murthes [37] to make as mynstralles conneth, [38]
And geten gold with here [33] glee, giltles, I leve. [39]
Ac iapers [40] and iangelers, [41] Iudas chylderen,
Feynen hem [42] fantasies and foles hem maketh,
And han here witte at wille to worche, yif thei sholde;
That Poule precheth of hem I nel nought preve it here;
Qui turpiloquium loquitur is luciferes hyne. [43]
Bidders [44] and beggeres fast aboute yede, [45]
With her belies and her bagges of bred ful ycrammed;
Fayteden [46] for here fode, foughten atte ale; [47]
In glotonye, god it wote, [48] gon hij [49] to bedde,
And risen with ribaudye [50] tho roberdes knaves; [51]
Slepe and sori sleuthe [52] seweth [53] hem evre. [54]
Pilgrymes and palmers [55] plighted hem togidere
To seke seynt Iames [56] and seyntes in Rome.
Thei went forth in here wey with many wise tales,
And hadden leve to lye al here lyf after.
I seigh somme that seiden thei had ysought seyntes:
To eche a [57] tale that thei tolde here tonge was tempred to lye
More than to sey soth [58] it semed bi here speche.
Heremites on [59] an heep, with hoked staves,
Wenten to Walsyngham, [60] and here wenches after; [61]

[1] arrayed
[2] rough garments
[3] shepherd
[4] not spiritual
[5] abroad
[6] but
[7] hills
[8] wonder
[9] enchantment
[10] weary from wandering
[11] brook's
[12] sounded
[13] to dream
[14] dream
[15] on high toward
[16] saw
[17] the tower of Truth, abode of God the Father
[18] elevated place
[19] cunningly
[20] the "castel of care," abode of Falsehood (Lucifer)
[21] the world
[22] them(selves)
[23] planting
[24] toiled
[25] and won that which wasteful men expend in gluttony.
[26] came strangely garbed
[27] strictly
[28] of the Kingdom of Heaven
[29] anchorites
[30] wander
[31] delicate
[32] livelihood, living
[33] their
[34] body
[35] trade
[36] succeed
[37] mirth
[38] know how
[39] believe
[40] jesters
[41] chatterers
[42] invent for themselves
[43] What Paul preaches about them I will not show here, "for he who speaks slander is Lucifer's servant."
[44] beggars
[45] went
[46] cheated
[47] fought at the ale
[48] knows
[49] they
[50] ribaldry
[51] those robber villains
[52] sloth
[53] pursue
[54] ever
[55] Palmers made it their regular duty to visit shrines
[56] a shrine at Compostella in Galicia
[57] at every
[58] truth
[59] in
[60] shrine of Our Lady of Walsingham (Norfolk) almost more celebrated than Thomas à Becket's
[61] in their train

Grete lobyes [1] and longe, [2] that loth were to swynke, [3]
Clotheden hem in copis [4] to ben knowen fram othere;
And shopen hem [5] heremites here ese to have.
I fonde there Freris, alle the foure ordres, [6]
Preched the peple for profit of hem-selven,
Glosed [7] the gospel as hem good lyked, [8]
For coveitise [9] of copis construed it as thei wolde,
Many of this maistres Freris [10] mowe [11] clothen hem at lykyng,
For here money and marchandise marchen togideres.
For sith [12] charite hath be chapman [13] and chief to shryve lordes, [14]
Many ferlis [15] han fallen in a fewe yeris. [16]
But [17] holychirche and hij holde better togideres,
The most myschief on molde [18] is mountyng wel faste. [19]
There preched a Pardonere [20] as he a prest were,
Broughte forth a bulle [21] with bishopes seles,
And seide that hym-self myghte assoilen [22] hem alle
Of falshed of fastyng, [23] of vowes ybroken.
Lewed [24] men leved [25] hym wel and lyked his wordes,
Comen up knelyng to kissen his bulles;
He bonched [26] hem with his brevet [27] and blered here eyes,
And raughte [28] with his ragman [29] rynges and broches;
Thus they geven here golde, glotones to kepe
. . . . . .
Were the bischop yblissed [30] and worth bothe his eres,
His seel [31] shulde nought be sent to deceyve the peple.
Ac it is naught by [32] the bischop that the boy [33] precheth,
For the parisch prest and the pardonere parten [34] the silver,
That the poraille [35] of the parisch sholde have, yif their nere. [36]
. . . . . .

B text, 1377

From Passus I

What this montaigne bymeneth, [37] and the merke dale,
And the felde ful of folke, I shal yow faire schewe.
A loveli ladi of lere, [38] in lynnen yclothed,
Come down fram a castel and called me faire,
And seide, "Sone, slepestow, [39] sestow [40] this poeple,
How bisi thei ben abouten the mase? [41]
The moste partie of this poeple that passeth on this erthe,
Have thei worschip [42] in this worlde, thei wilne no better;
Of other hevene than here holde thei no tale." [43]
I was aferd of her face theigh [44] she faire were,
And seide, "Mercy, Madame, what is this to mene?"
"The toure up the toft," quod she, "Treuthe is there-inne,
And wolde that ye wroughte as his worde techeth;
For he is fader of feith, fourmed yow alle,
Bothe with fel [45] and with face, and yaf [46] yow fyve wittis
Forto worschip hym ther-with the while that ye ben here."

[1] lubbers
[2] tall
[3] toil
[4] friars' capes
[5] arrayed themselves as
[6] Dominican, Franciscan, Carmelite Augustinian
[7] interpreted
[8] as it pleased them
[9] covetousness
[10] these master friars
[11] may
[12] since
[13] peddler
[14] So worldly were the friars seeking money for hearing confessions and peddling their wares, that they often quarreled with the priests as to which should hear the confession.
[15] wonders
[16] years
[17] unless
[18] earth
[19] will increase rapidly
[20] one commissioned to grant pardons
[21] bull, a Papal mandate
[22] absolve
[23] failure in fasting
[24] ignorant
[25] believed
[26] struck
[27] letter of indulgence
[28] got
[29] bull, with bishop's seals
[30] righteous
[31] seal
[32] not against
[33] i.e., the pardoner

THE BIBLE

One of the most important pieces of literature in the English language is the Bible. Its influence has been evident from early in the eighth century when Bede, on his death bed, made a translation of the Gospel of St. John into Old English. In the time of King Alfred other portions were added; Aelfric (c. 1000) did parts of both testaments; but there was no complete Anglo-Saxon Bible.

During the religious revival of the thirteenth century there were many attempts to translate the Latin Bible into English; but up to 1360 only the Psalter had been finished. In 1382 John

[34] divide
[35] poor
[36] if they (the pardoner and the priest) did not exist
[37] means
[38] face
[39] sleepest thou
[40] seest thou
[41] confused throng
[42] if they have honor
[43] account
[44] though
[45] skin
[46] gave

Wiclif and his fellow workers produced the first complete English Bible. The printed English Bible began with the New Testament of Tyndale, 1525. In 1535 Miles Coverdale in a new translation published the first complete English Bible, including the Apocrypha, which the Church allowed to circulate freely. In 1539 appeared the Great Bible, copies of which were placed in all parish churches. The Geneva Bible, 1560, the work of English refugees in Switzerland, issued in a handy edition, was especially accurate. These various translations naturally represented the popular diction of each period. Notably in 1611, came the authorized King James version, still standard today; it was the result of a careful comparison of all previous versions, including the Hebrew and the Greek, by all the best scholars of the kingdom. Its influence on the English language has been incalculable. No other book has so penetrated and permeated the hearts and speech of the English speaking peoples; it is a racial possession, a racial classic. Its effect can be traced on all the great authors. Its language is dignified and poetic, filled with Saxon simplicity and Hebrew imagery. A later revision (1885), though perhaps closer to the original Hebrew and Greek, lacks the charm of expression of the King James Bible.

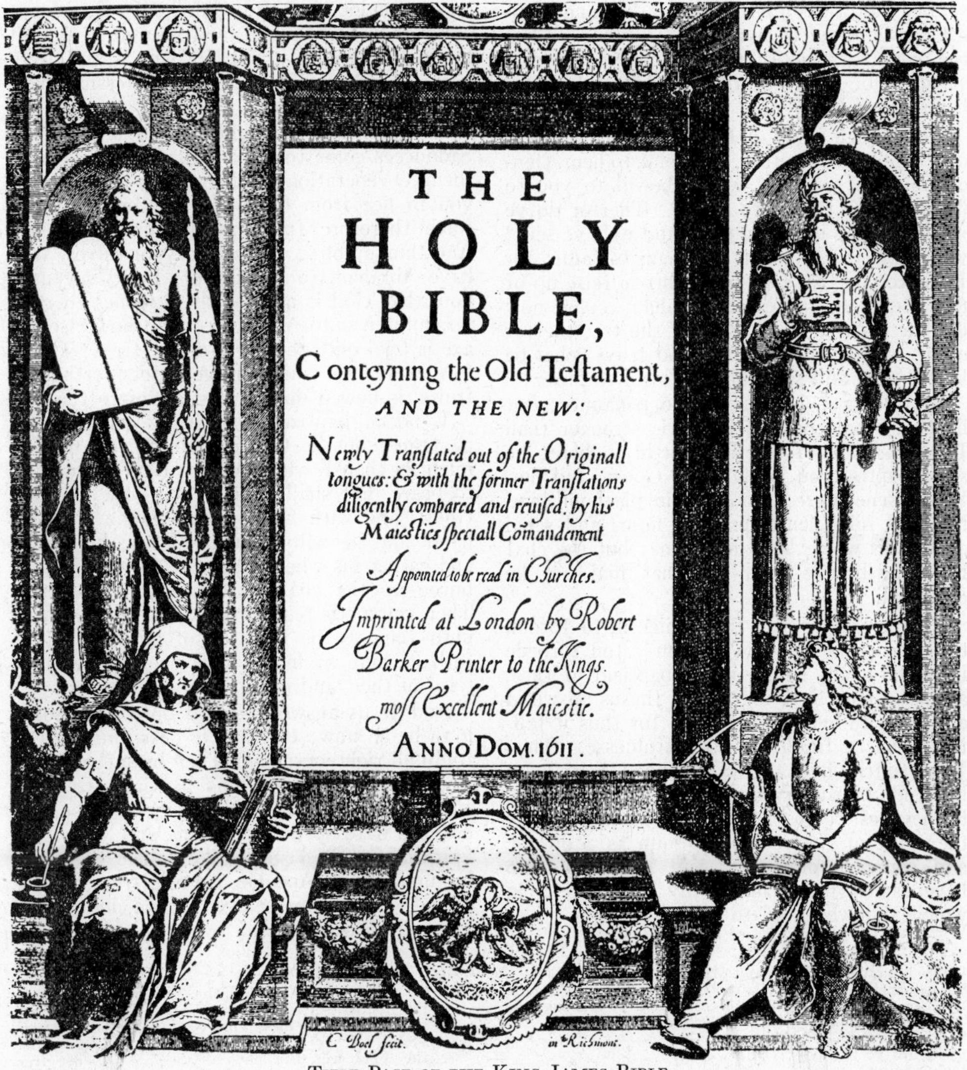

TITLE PAGE OF THE KING JAMES BIBLE

THE WYCLIF BIBLE[1]

Matthew III. The Coming of John the Baptist

In tho daies Joon Baptist cam and prechid in the desert of Judee, and seide, Do ye penaunce, for the kyngdom of hevenes schal nygh. For this is he of whom it is seid bi Isaie the profete, seiynge, A vois of a crier in desert, Make ye redi the weyes of the Lord, make ye right the pathis of hym. And this Joon hadde clothing of camels heris, and a girdil of skyn aboute his leendis, and his mete was hony soukis[2] and hony of the wode. Thanne Jerusalem wente out to hym, and al Judee, and al the countre aboute Jordan, and thei werun waischen of hym in Jordan, and knowlechiden her synnes.

But he sigh many of Farisies and of Saduces comynge to his baptem, and seide to hem, Generaciouns of eddris,[3] who schewid to you to fle fro wrath that is to come? Therfor do ye worthi fruytis of penaunce. And nyle ye seie[4] with ynne you, We han Abraham to fadir; for I seie to you that God is myghti to reise up of thes stones the sones of Abraham. And now the axe is putte to the root of the tre; therfor every tre that makith not good fruyt schal be kutte doun, and schal be cast in to the fire.

I waisch you in watyr in to penaunce; but he that schal come aftir me is stronger than I, whos schoon I am not worthi to bere; he schal baptise you in the Holi Goost, and fier. Whos wenewynge[5] clooth is in his hond, and he schal fulli clense his corn floor, and schal gadere his whete in to his berne; but the chaf he schal brenne with fier that mai not be quenchid.

Thanne Jhesus cam fro Galilee in to Jordan to Joon, to be baptisid of him. Jon forbede hym and seide, I owe to be baptisid of thee, and thou comest to me? But Jhesus answerid and seide to hym, Suffre now; for thus it fallith to us to fulfille alle rightfulnesse. Then Joon suffrid hym. And whanne Jhesus was baptisid, anon he wente up fro the watir; and lo, hevenes weren opened to hym, and he say the spirit of God comynge doun as a dowve, and comynge on him. And lo, a vois fro hevenes, seiynge, This is my loved sone, in whiche I have plesid to me.

c. 1380

[1] only punctuation and capitalization modernized
[2] honey-suckles (Wyclif, translating from the Vulgate, the popular Latin Bible, evidently mistook the meaning of the Latin *locustae*)
[3] adders
[4] will not ye to say
[5] winnowing

THE KING JAMES BIBLE[1]

Matthew III. The Coming of John the Baptist

In those daies came John the Baptist, preaching in the wildernesse of Judea, and saying, Repent yee; for the kingdome of heaven is at hand. For this is he that was spoken of by the Prophet Esaias,[6] saying, The voyce of one crying in the wildernesse, Prepare ye the way of the Lord, make his paths straight. And the same John had his raiment of camels haire, and a leatherne girdle about his loynes, and his meate was locusts[7] and wilde honie. Then went out to him Hierusalem, and all Judea, and all the region round about Jordane. And were baptized of him in Jordane, confessing their sinnes.

But when he saw many of the Pharisees and Sadducees come to his Baptisme, he said unto them, O generation of vipers, who hath warned you to flee from the wrath to come? Bring forth therefore fruits meete for repentance. And thinke not to say within your selves, Wee have Abraham to *our* father; For I say unto you, that God is able of these stones to raise up children unto Abraham. And now also the axe is layd unto the roote of the trees; Therefore every tree which bringeth not foorth good fruite, is hewen downe, and cast into the fire.

I indeed baptize you with water unto repentance; but he that commeth after mee, is mightier than I, whose shooes I am not worthy to beare, hee shall baptize you with the holy Ghost, and with fire. Whose fanne is in his hand, and he will throughly purge his floore, and gather his wheate into the garner; but wil burne up the chaffe with unquenchable fire. Then commeth Jesus from Galilee to Jordane, unto John, to be baptized of him; But John forbade him, saying, I have need to bee baptized of thee, and commest thou to me?

And Jesus answering, said unto him, Suffer it to be so now; for thus it becommeth us to fulfill all righteousnesse. Then he suffered him. And Jesus, when hee was baptized, went up straightway out of the water; and loe, the heavens were opened unto him, and he saw the Spirit of God descending like a dove, and lighting upon him. And loe, a voice from heaven, saying, This is my beloved Soone, in whom I am well pleased.

1611

[6] See *Isaiah* xl, 3.
[7] In the desert countries of the Orient, the flesh of the locust, or grasshopper, has from time immemorial been used for food. See Browning's "Saul," l. 75. Some commentators suggest that the food was the pod of the wild locust tree, sometimes called St. John's bread.

GEOFFREY CHAUCER 1340?-1400

The England of the latter half of the fourteenth century lives for us through the genius of Geoffrey Chaucer. In his works are preserved men and women of most of the important types of the English society of his day, their costumes, their habits, individual peculiarities, and details that transform them into living realities. Thanks to modern research we know enough of his life to understand how he gained his wide knowledge of human nature. In the course of his varied career he may have come into actual contact with some of those he so vividly describes. As a boy he lived in London, where his father was a well-to-do vintner. A little later Geoffrey was a page in the household of Prince Lionel; in 1359 he went with the army of Edward III to France, where he was taken prisoner, the king subscribing £16 toward his ransom. On returning to England he became a valet of the king's chamber, and then collector of customs. Between 1370 and 1380 he was employed on several important diplomatic missions to France, Italy, and Flanders, on one of which he possibly met the great Italian poet Petrarch; the influence of these journeys is seen in his work. He came into lands, was knight of the shire of Kent, married Philippa Roet, sister to John of Gaunt's third wife; and though his fortunes fluctuated at times, he was the recipient of various pensions.

That Chaucer was a student and widely read in French and Latin as well as English literature is proved by his writings. As was customary in medieval and even Elizabethan times, he borrowed profusely from other authors and openly acknowledged his indebtedness; but he had Shakespeare's gift of transforming what he used, making it his own. Coleridge writes, "I take unceasing delight in Chaucer. How exquisitely tender he is, and yet how perfectly free from the least touch of sickly melancholy or morbid drooping! The sympathy of the poet with the subjects of his poetry is particularly remarkable in Shakespeare and Chaucer; but what the first effects by a strong act of imagination and mental metamorphosis, the last does without any effort, merely by the inborn joyousness of his nature. How well we seem to know Chaucer! How absolutely nothing do we know of Shakespeare!"[1]

Chaucer was the first English poet to practice a wide variety of line and stanza forms, and to employ the iambic pentameter; the melody and flexibility of his verse are unequaled by any of his contemporaries; and in the outdoor freshness that breathes through it he is a forerunner of Burns and Wordsworth. Besides the famous *Canterbury Tales,* his works include *Troilus and Criseyde,* his longest single poem, a narrative with so strong an emphasis on character that it has been called a forerunner of the nineteenth century novel; *Parlement of Foules; Hous of Fame; Legend of Good Women;* and many other productions, long and short, prose and verse. There is still much uncertainty as to the actual number of his writings and their dates of composition, numerous Middle English poems having been wrongly included among his works.

[1] See J. L. Lowes, *Convention and Revolt in Poetry,* 1919, ch. 3; also Dryden "On Chaucer" in the present volume, p. 314.

The best edition is that of W. W. Skeat, 6 vols., 1895-97; for handy editions there are Skeat's *Students' Chaucer,* and Pollard's Globe edition, which contains a long and useful introduction. Other valuable books are: J. J. Jusserand, *English Wayfaring Life in the Middle Ages,* 1890 (1903); T. R. Lounsbury. *Studies in Chaucer,* 3 vols; 1891; A. W. Pollard, *Chaucer,* 1893, W. P. Ker, *Epic and Romance,* 1897; F. J. Snell, *The Age of Chaucer,* 1901 (1912); G. K. Root, *The Poetry of Chaucer, a Guide to its Study and Appreciation,* 1906; G. L. Kittredge, *Chaucer and His Poetry,* 1915; J. M. Manly, *Some New Lights on Chaucer,* 1926, an interesting attempt to identify some of the chief characters in the Prologue; R. D. French, *A Chaucer Handbook,* 1927. See also Hazlitt, Lowell, Rossetti (EML).

CHAUCER'S PRONUNCIATION

a long = *ah* as in *father: bathed* [bahth-ed].
a short = *ah* without prolongation, as in *aha: at* [aht].
ai, ay = *ei* as in *day.*
au, aw = *ah'oo* (nearly equal to modern ***ou*** in *house: straunge.*
e long = *ai* as in *pair: bere* [bearë].
e short = *e* as in *ten: hem.*
e final = ë (pronounced as a very light separate syllable, like the final *e* in the German *eine.* So also is *es* of the plural): *soote* [sohtë]. It is regularly elided before a following vowel, before *he, his, him, hire* (her), *here* (their), *hem* (them), and occasionally before other words beginning with *h,* also in *hire, here, oure,* etc.
ea, ee = our long *a; eek* [āke].
ei, ey = *ei* as in *weigh.*
eu, ew = *e* + *u: hewe* [hewë].
i long = *ee* (nearly): *shires* [sheer-es].
i short = *i* in *pin: with.*
o, oo long = *oa* in *oar: roote* [nearly rōtë].
o short = *o* in *coffee.*
oi, oy = *oo'ee* (nearly equal to modern *oi*): *floytinge* [floiting].
ou, ow = our *oo* in *rood* in words that in Mod. Eng. have taken the sound of *ou* in *loud: hous* [hoos].
ou, ow = *oh'oo* in words that now have the ō sound: *soule, knowe* [sōlë, knowë].
u long = French *u* (found only in French words): *vertu* [vehrtü].
u short = *u* in *pull: but.*
c = *k* before *a, o, u,* or any consonant.
= *s* before *e, i, y.*
g = hard in words not of French origin.
g = *j* before *e, i,* in words of French origin.
gh = *ch,* like the German *ch* in *nicht.*

h initial = omitted in unaccented *he, his, him, hire, hem.*
r = trilled.
s = often sharp when final.
= never *sh* or *zh* (*vision* has therefore three syllables, *condicioun* four, etc.).
t = as at present; but final *-tion* = two syllables (si-oon).
th = *th* in *thin* or *th* in *this,* as in Mod. Eng.
w = sometimes *oo* as in *herberw.*

The following may serve to illustrate the approximate pronunciation of a few lines, without attempting Mr. Skeat's finer distinctions. Note that *ë* is a separate syllable lightly pronounced, that *u* equals *u* in *full,* and *ü* is French *u.*

Whan that Ahpreellë with 'is shoorës sohtë
The droocht of March hath persëd toh the rohtë,
And bahthëd evree veyne in swich lecoor
Of which vertü engendred is the floor;
Whan Zephirus aik with 'is swaitë braith
Inspeerëd hath in evry holt and haith
The tendre croopës, and the yungë sunnë
Hath in the Ram 'is halfë coors irunnë,
And smahlë foolës makhen melodeeë
That slaipen al the nicht with ohpen eeë—
So priketh 'em nahtür in her corahgës—
Than longen folk toh gohn on pilgrimahgës,
And palmerz for toh saiken strahwngë strondës,
Toh fernë halwës kooth in sondri londës;
And spesialee, from evree sheerës endë
Of Engëlond, toh Cahwnterberee they wendë,
The hohly blisful marteer for toh saikë,
That hem hath holpen whan that they wair saikë.

CHAUCER'S METER

A large part of Chaucer's work is written in heroic couplets: every two consecutive lines riming, and each line containing five iambic feet, that is, five groups of two syllables each, with the accent on the second syllable of each foot; e. g.,

And bahth'|ed eve'|ry veyn'|in swich'|li cour'|

An extra syllable is often added at the end of the line: e. g.,

Whan that|April|le with|his shou|res soo|te

Sometimes the first foot is shortened to one long syllable: e. g.,

Twen|ty bo|kes clad| in blak| or reed|

THE TEXT

With a few changes, the text of *The Canterbury Tales* printed by Dr. W. W. Skeat in the Clarendon Press Series based on the Ellesmere MS. has been followed. Of six nearly complete manuscripts of the *Tales,* none of which are thought to be of Chaucer's century, the Ellesmere MS. is considered to be, on the whole, the most reliable.

From THE CANTERBURY TALES

The Prologue

Whan that [1] Aprille with his shoures soote [2]
The droghte [3] of Marche hath perced to the roote,
And bathed every veyne [4] in swich licour, [5]
Of which vertu [6] engendred is the flour; [7]
Whan Zephirus [8] eek [9] with his swete breeth
Inspired hath in every holt [10] and heeth
The tendre croppes, [11] and the yonge soone
Hath in the Ram his halfe cours y-ronne, [12]
And smale fowles [13] maken melodye,
That slepen al the night with open yë, [14]
(So priketh hem [15] nature in hir [16] corages; [17])
Than [18] longen [19] folk to goon on pilgrimages,
And palmers for to seken [20] straunge strondes, [21]
To ferne [22] halwes, [23] couthe [24] in sondry londes;
And specially, from every shires ende
Of Engelond, to Caunterbury they wende,
The holy blisful martir [25] for to seke,
That hem hath holpen, whan that they were seke. [26]
  Bifel that, in that sesoun on a day,
In Southwerk at the Tabard [27] as I lay
Redy to wenden on my pilgrimage
To Caunterbury with ful devout corage, [28]
At night was come in-to that hostelrye
Wel [29] nyne and twenty in a compaignye,
Of sondry folk, by aventure [30] y-falle [31]
In felawshipe, and pilgrims were they alle,
That toward Caunterbury wolden ryde;
The chambres and the stables weren wyde,
And wel we weren esed [32] atte beste.
And shortly, whan the sonne was to [33] reste,
So hadde I spoken with hem everichon, [34]
That I was of hir felawshipe anon,
And made forward [35] erly for to ryse,
To take our wey, ther as [36] I yow devyse. [37]
  But natheles, whyl I have tyme and space,
Er that I ferther in this tale pace,

[1] when
[2] sweet showers
[3] drought
[4] vein
[5] such sap
[6] power
[7] flower
[8] the west-wind
[9] also
[10] wood
[11] shoots
[12] when the spring sun has passed through the second, or April, half of his course in that constellation of the zodiac called the Ram, i. e., about April 11
[13] birds
[14] eyes
[15] them
[16] their
[17] hearts
[18] then
[19] indic. pl. of the verb "long"
[20] seek
[21] shores
[22] distant
[23] shrines
[24] known
[25] Thomas à Becket
[26] sick
[27] an inn having for its signboard a tabard (short coat)
[28] heart
[29] full
[30] chance
[31] fallen
[32] made easy; i. e., accommodated in the best manner
[33] at
[34] every one
[35] agreement
[36] where
[37] tell

Me thinketh it acordaunt [1] to resoun,
To telle yow al the condicioun
Of ech of hem, so as it semed me,
And whiche they weren, [2] and of what degree;
And eek in what array [3] that they were inne:
And at a knight than wol I first biginne.
  A Knight there was, and that a worthy man,
That fro the tyme that he first bigan
To ryden out, he loved chivalrye,
Trouthe and honour, fredom [4] and curteisye.
Ful worthy was he in his lordes werre, [5]
And thereto hadde he riden (no man ferre [6])
As wel in cristendom as hethenesse,
And evere honoured for his worthinesse.
At Alisaundre [7] he was, whan it was wonne;
Ful ofte tyme he hadde the bord bigonne [8]
Aboven all naciouns in Pruce. [9]
In Lettow [10] hadde he reysed [11] and in Ruce, [12]
No cristen man so ofte of his degree. [13]
In Gernade [14] at the sege eek hadde he be
Of Algezir, [15] and riden in Belmarye. [16]
At Lyeys [17] was he, and at Satalye [17]
Whan they were wonne; and in the Grete See [18]
At many a noble armee [19] hadde he be.
At mortal batailles hadde he been fiftene,
And foughten for our feith at Tramissene [20]
In listes [21] thryes, and ay slayn his foo.
This ilke [22] worthy knight hadde been also
Somtyme with the lord of Palatye, [23]
Ageyn [24] another hethen in Turkye:
And everemore he hadde a sovereyn prys. [25]
And though that he were worthy, he was wys,
And of his port [26] as meek as is a mayde.
He nevere yet no vileinye [27] ne sayde
In al his lyf, un-to no maner wight.
He was a verray parfit gentil knight.
But for to tellen yow of his array,
His hors [28] were goode, but he was nat gay. [29]
Of fustian [30] he wered a gipoun [31]
Al bismotered [32] with his habergeoun. [33]
For he was late y-come from his viage, [34]
And wente for to doon his pilgrimage. [35]
  With him ther was his sone, a yong Squyer,

[1] according
[2] what sort of people they were
[3] dress
[4] liberality
[5] war
[6] farther
[7] Alexandria (1365)
[8] sat at the head of the table
[9] Prussia
[10] Lithuania (a western province of Russia)
[11] forayed
[12] Russia
[13] rank
[14] Granada
[15] Algeciras
[16] a Moorish kingdom in Africa
[17] a town in Asia Minor
[18] Mediterranean
[19] armed expedition
[20] in Asia Minor
[21] tournaments
[22] same
[23] in Asia Minor
[24] against
[25] high praise
[26] bearing
[27] unbecoming word
[28] horses
[29] gaily dressed
[30] coarse cloth
[31] a short tight-fitting coat
[32] spotted
[33] coat of mail
[34] voyage
[35] in order to give thanks for his safe return

A lovyer, and a lusty bacheler, [36]
With lokkes crulle, [37] as [38] they were leyd in presse.
Of twenty yeer of age he was, I gesse.
Of his stature he was of evene lengthe, [39]
And wonderly delivere, [40] and greet of strengthe.
And he hadde been somtyme in chivachye, [41]
In Flaundres, in Artoys, [42] and Picardye, [42]
And born him wel, as of so litel space, [43]
In hope to stonden in his lady [44] grace.
Embrouded [45] was he, as it were a mede [46]
Al ful of fresshe floures, whyte and rede.
Singinge he was, or floytinge, [47] al the day;
He was as fresh as is the month of May.
Short was his goune, with sleves longe and wyde.
Wel coude he sitte on hors, and faire ryde.
He coulde songes make and wel endyte, [48]
Iuste [49] and eek daunce, and wel purtreye [50] and wryte.
So hote [51] he lovede, that by nightertale [52]
He sleep namore than doth a nightingale.
Curteys he was, lowly, and servisable,
And carf [53] biforn his fader at the table.
  A Yeman hadde he, [54] and servaunts namo [55]
At that tyme, for him liste [56] ryde so;
And he was clad in cote and hood of grene;
A sheef of pecok arwes [57] brighte and kene
Under his belt he bar ful thriftily,
(Wel coude he dresse his takel yemanly: [58]
His arwes drouped noght with fetheres lowe),
And in his hand he bar a mighty bowe.
A not-heed [59] hadde he, with broun visage.
Of wode-craft [60] wel coude [61] he al the usage.
Upon his arm he bar a gay bracer, [62]
And by his syde a swerd and a bokeler, [63]
And on that other syde a gay daggere,
Harneised [64] wel, and sharp as point of spere;
A Cristofre [65] on his brest of silver shene. [66]
An horn he bar, the bawdrik [67] was of grene;
A forster [68] was he, soothly, [69] as I gesse.

[36] an aspirant for knighthood
[37] curly
[38] as if
[39] average height
[40] nimble
[41] military expeditions
[42] an ancient province of France
[43] considering the shortness of the time
[44] lady's
[45] embroidered
[46] meadow
[47] playing the flute
[48] compose
[49] joust (engage in a tournament)
[50] draw
[51] hotly
[52] night-time
[53] carved
[54] the knight
[55] no more
[56] it pleased him
[57] arrows
[58] order his tackle (equipment) in yeomanlike manner
[59] nut-head, a closely cropped head
[60] wood-craft
[61] knew
[62] guard for the arm
[63] shield
[64] equipped
[65] image of St. Christopher
[66] bright
[67] girdle worn over the shoulder
[68] forester
[69] truly

Ther was also a Nonne, a Prioresse,
That of hir smyling was ful simple and coy;
Hir gretteste ooth was but by sëynt Loy; [1]
And she was cleped [2] madame Eglentyne.
Ful wel she song the service divyne,
Entuned in hir nose ful semely;
And Frensh she spak ful faire and fetisly, [3]
After the scole of Stratford atte Bowe, [4]
For Frensh of Paris was to hir unknowe.
At mete wel y-taught was she with-alle;
She leet no morsel from hir lippes falle,
Ne wette hir fingres in hir sauce depe.
Wel coude she carie a morsel, and wel kepe,
That no drope ne fille [5] up-on hir brest.
In curteisye was set full moche hir lest, [6]
Hir over lippe wyped she so clene,
That in hir coppe [7] was no ferthing sene
Of grece, whan she dronken hadde hir draughte.
Ful semely after hir mete she raughte, [8]
And sikerly [9] she was of greet disport, [10]
And ful plesaunt, and amiable of port, [11]
And peyned [12] hir to countrefete [13] chere [14]
Of court, and been estatlich [15] of manere,
And to ben holden digne [16] of reverence.
But, for to speken of hir conscience,
She was so charitable and so pitous, [17]
She wolde wepe, if that she sawe a mous
Caught in a trappe, if it were deed or bledde.
Of smale houndes had she, that she fedde
With rosted flesh, or milk and wastel breed. [18]
But sore weep she if oon of hem were deed,
Or if men smoot it with a yerde [19] smerte; [20]
And al was conscience and tendre herte.
Ful semely hir wimpel [21] pinched [22] was;
Hir nose tretys; [23] hir eyen greye as glas;
Hir mouth ful smal, and ther-to softe and reed;
But sikerly [24] she hadde a fair forheed.
It was almost a spanne brood, I trowe;
For, hardily, [25] she was nat undergrowe.
Ful fetis [26] was hir cloke, as I was war. [27]
Of smal coral aboute hir arm she bar
A peire of bedes, [28] gauded [29] al with grene;
And ther-on heng a broche of gold ful shene,
On which ther was first write a crowned A,
And after, *Amor vincit omnia.* [30]
Another Nonne with hir hadde she,
That was hir Chapeleyne, and Preestes thre.
A Monk ther was, a fair for the maistrye, [31]
An out-rydere, that loevede venerye, [32]
A manly man, to been an abbot able.
Ful many deyntee [33] hors hadde he in stable;
And, whan he rood, men mighte his brydel here
Ginglen in a whistling wynd as clere,
And eek as loude as doth the chapel-belle.
There-as [34] this lord was keper of the celle, [35]
The reule of seint Maure or of seint Beneit, [36]
By-cause that it was old and som-del streit, [37]
This ilke monk leet olde thinges [38] pace, [39]
And held after the newe world the space. [40]
He yaf nat of that text a pulled [41] hen,
That seith, that hunters been nat holy men;
Ne that a monk, whan he is recchelees, [42]
Is likned til a fish that is waterlees;
This is to seyn, a monk out of his cloistre.
But thilke text held he nat worth an oistre.
And I seyde his opinioun was good.
What [43] sholde he studie, and make him-selven wood, [44]
Upon a book in cloistre alwey to poure,
Or swinken [45] with his handes, and laboure,
As Austin bit? [46] How shal the world be served?
Lat Austin have his swink [45] to him reserved.
Therefor he was a pricasour [47] aright;
Grehoundes he hadde, as swifte as fowle in flight;
Of priking and of hunting for the hare
Was al his lust, [48] for no cost wolde he spare.
I seigh [49] his sleves purfiled [50] at the hond
With grys, [51] and that the fyneste of a lond;
And, for to festne his hood under his chin,
He hadde of gold y-wroght a curious pin:
A love-knot in the gretter ende ther was.
His heed was balled, [52] that shoon as any glas,
And eek his face, as he hadde been anoint.
He was a lord ful fat and in good point; [53]
His eyen stepe, [54] and rollinge in his heed,
That stemed as a forneys of a leed, [55]
His botes souple, his hors in greet estat.
Now certeinly he was a fair prelat;

[1] St. Eloy, Loy, or Eligius, patron saint of goldsmiths
[2] named
[3] daintily, exactly
[4] Stratford le Bow, where there was a Benedictine nunnery, and where Anglo-French would be spoken, rather than the Parisian kind
[5] fell
[6] pleasure
[7] cup
[8] reached
[9] surely
[10] good humor
[11] bearing
[12] took pains
[13] imitate
[14] behavior
[15] to be dignified
[16] worthy
[17] compassionate
[18] bread made of the best flour—cakebread
[19] stick
[20] sharply
[21] neck covering
[22] plaited
[23] well proportioned
[24] surely
[25] certainly
[26] well made
[27] aware
[28] a set of beads, a rosary
[29] having the gawdies, or large beads green
[30] "Love conquers all."
[31] a very fine monk indeed
[32] hunting
[33] fine
[34] where
[35] a smaller religious house dependent on a monastery
[36] The oldest forms of monastic discipline were based on the rules of St. Maur and of St. Benet, or Benedict.
[37] somewhat strict
[38] (these rules)
[39] pass
[40] pace, way
[41] plucked (he would not give a straw for that text that—)
[42] wandering or vagrant
[43] why
[44] crazy
[45] work
[46] bids
[47] hard rider
[48] pleasure
[49] saw
[50] bordered
[51] gray fur
[52] bald
[53] *en bon point,* fat
[54] bright
[55] glow like the fire under a caldron

He was nat pale as a for-pyned goost.[1]
A fat swan loved he best of any roost.
His palfrey was as broun as is a berye.
  A Frere[2] there was, a wantown[3] and a merye,
A limitour,[4] a ful solempne[5] man.
In alle the ordres foure[6] is noon that can[7]
So moche of daliaunce and fair langage.
He hadde maad ful many a mariage
Of yonge wommen, at his owne cost.
Un-to his ordre he was a noble post.
Ful wel biloved and famulier was he
With frankeleyns[8] over-al in his contree,
And eek with worthy wommen of the toun;
For he had power of confessioun,
As seyde him-self, more than a curat,
For of his ordre he was licentiat.[9]
Ful swetely herde he confessioun,
And plesaunt was his absolucioun;
He was an esy man to yeve[10] penaunce
Ther-as he wiste to han a good pitaunce;[11]
For unto a povre ordre for to yive[12]
Is signe that a man is wel y-shrive.
For if he[13] yaf, he[14] dorste make avaunt,[15]
He wiste that a man was repentaunt.
For many a man so hard is of his herte,[16]
He may nat wepe al-thogh him sore smerte.[17]
Therfore, in stede of weping and preyeres,
Men moot[18] yeve silver to the povre freres.
His tipet[19] was ay[20] farsed[21] ful of knyves
And pinnes, for to yeven faire wyves.
And certeinly he hadde a mery note;
Wel coude he singe and pleyen on a rote.[22]
Of yeddinges[23] he bar utterly the prys.[24]
His nekke whyt was as the flour-de-lys.[25]
Ther-to he strong was as a champioun.
He knew the tavernes wel in every toun,
And everich hostiler[26] and tappestere[27]
Bet[28] than a lazar[29] or a beggestere;[30]
For un-to swich a worthy man as he
Acorded nat, as by his facultee,[31]
To have with seke[32] lazars aqueyntaunce.

[1] tormented ghost
[2] friar
[3] brisk
[4] one licensed to beg within certain limits
[5] pompous
[6] Dominicans (Black Friars); Franciscans (Gray Friars); Carmelites (White Friars); Augustinians (Austin Friars)
[7] knows
[8] country gentlemen
[9] one licensed to give absolution
[10] give, assign
[11] where he knew he could get a good gift
[12] give
[13] the man
[14] the friar
[15] boast
[16] heart
[17] he suffer sorely
[18] ought to
[19] hood, cowl
[20] ever
[21] stuffed
[22] fiddle
[23] songs
[24] he took the prize
[25] lily
[26] innkeeper
[27] bar maid
[28] better
[29] leper
[30] female beggar
[31] It was unsuitable considering his ability.
[32] sick

It is nat honest,[33] it may nat avaunce[34]
For to delen with no swich poraille,[35]
But al with riche and sellers of vitaille.
And over-al,[36] ther-as[37] profit sholde aryse,
Curteys he was, and lowly of servyse.
Ther nas no man nowher so vertuous.[38]
He was the beste beggere in his hous;
For thogh a widwe hadde noght a sho,[39]
So plesaunt was his *In principio*,[40]
Yet wolde he have a ferthing,[41] er he wente,
His purchas[42] was wel bettre than his rente.[43]
And rage[44] he coude as it were right a whelpe.[45]
In love-dayes[46] ther coude he mochel helpe.
For ther he was nat lyk a cloisterer
With a thredbare cope, as is a povre scoler,
But he was lyk a maister or a pope.
Of double worsted was his semi-cope,[47]
That rounded as a belle out of the presse.
Somwhat he lipsed, for his wantownesse,[48]
To make his English swete up-on his tonge;
And in his harping, whan that he had songe,
His eyen twinkled in his heed aright,
As doon the sterres in the frosty night.
This worthy limitour was cleped Huberd.
  A Marchant was ther with a forked berd,
In mottelee,[49] and hye on horse he sat,
Up-on his heed a Flaundrish bever hat;
His botes clasped faire and fetisly.
His resons[50] he spak ful solempnely,[51]
Sowninge[52] alway thencrees[53] of his winning.
He wolde the see were kept[54] for any thing[55]
Bitwixe Middelburgh and Orewelle.[56]
Wel coude[57] he in eschaunge sheeldes[58] selle.
This worthy man ful wel his wit bisette;[59]
Ther wiste no wight that he was in dette,
So estatly[60] was he of his governaunce,[61]
With his bargaynes, and with his chevisaunce.[62]
For sothe he was a worthy man with-alle,
But sooth to seyn, I noot[63] how men him calle.
  A Clerk[64] ther was of Oxenford also,
That un-to logik hadde longe y-go.[65]

[33] creditable
[34] profit
[35] poor people
[36] everywhere
[37] where
[38] energetic
[39] shoe
[40] *St. John* i, 1, "In the beginning," etc. (the opening of the friar's address)
[41] half a cent
[42] proceeds of his begging
[43] regular income
[44] play
[45] just like a puppy
[46] arbitration days (for settling differences without lawsuit)
[47] short cape
[48] lisped a little out of whimsical jolliness
[49] dress of variegated color
[50] opinions
[51] pompously
[52] proclaiming, sounding
[53] the increase
[54] guarded
[55] at any cost
[56] the first a port in the Netherlands, opposite Harwich in England; the second a town near the mouth of the river Orwell in England
[57] knew how to
[58] French crowns (he was a money-changer)
[59] employed
[60] dignified
[61] management
[62] agreements
[63] ne+wot (know not)
[64] student, scholar
[65] devoted himself

As lene was his hors as is a rake,
And he nas[1] nat right fat, I undertake;[2]
But loked holwe,[3] and ther-to soberly.[4]
Ful thredbar was his overest[5] courtepy,[6]
For he had geten him yet no benefice,[7]
Ne was so worldly for to have office.[8]
For him was levere[9] have at his beddes heed
Twenty bokes, clad in blak or reed,
Of Aristotle and his philosophye,
Than robes riche, or fithele,[10] or gay sautrye.[11]
But al be that he was a philosophre,[12]
Yet hadde he but litel gold in cofre;
But al that he mighte of his frendes hente[13]
On bokes and on lerninge he it spente,
And bisily gan for the soules preye
Of hem that yaf him where-with to scoleye.[14]
Of studie took he most cure[15] and most hede.
Noght o word spak he more than was nede,
And that was seyd in forme and reverence,
And short and quik, and ful of hy sentence.[16]
Sowninge[17] in moral vertu was his speche,
And gladly wolde he lerne, and gladly teche.

A Sergeant of the Lawe,[18] war[19] and wys,
That often hadde been at the parvys,[20]
Ther was also, ful riche of excellence.
Discreet he was, and of greet reverence;[21]
He semed swich, his wordes weren so wyse.
Iustice he was ful often in assyse,[22]
By patente[23] and by pleyn[24] commissioun;
For his science, and for his heigh renoun
Of fees and robes hadde he many oon.
So greet a purchasour[25] was nowher noon.[26]
Al was fee simple[27] to him in effect,
His purchasing mighte nat been infect.[28]
Nowher so bisy a man as he ther nas,
And yet he semed bisier than he was.
In termes hadde he caas and domes alle,[29]
That from the tyme of king William were falle.[30]
Therto he coude endyte, and make a thing,
Ther coude no wight pinche[31] at his wryting;
And every statut coude[32] he pleyn by rote.

[1] ne+was (was not)
[2] affirm
[3] hollow
[4] solemn
[5] outer
[6] coat
[7] ecclesiastical living
[8] secular office
[9] he had rather
[10] fiddle
[11] psaltery, harp
[12] The word meant both philosopher and alchemist.
[13] get
[14] devote himself to study
[15] care
[16] meaning
[17] tending to
[18] king's lawyer
[19] wary
[20] portico (of St. Paul's, where lawyers met for consultation)
[21] exciting much reverence
[22] court of assize
[23] letters patent
[24] full
[25] conveyancer
[26] none
[27] unconditional inheritance
[28] Invalidated (i. e., he could cunningly convey property without entanglements of entail).
[29] In exact words he had all cases and decisions.
[30] had occurred
[31] make an agreement so that none could find fault
[32] knew

He rood but hoomly in a medlee cote
Girt with a ceint[33] of silk, with barres[34] smale;
Of his array telle I no lenger tale.

A Frankeleyn[35] was in his compaignye;
Whyt was his berd,[36] as is the dayesye.[37]
Of his complexioun[38] he was sangwyn.[39]
Wel loved he by the morwe[40] a sop[41] in wyn.
To liven in delyt was evere his wone,[42]
For he was Epicurus[43] owne sone,
That heeld opinioun that pleyn delyt
Was verraily felicitee parfyt.
An housholdere, and that a greet, was he;
Seynt Iulian[44] he was in his contree.
His breed, his ale, was alwey after oon;[45]
A bettre envyned[46] man was no-wher noon.
With-oute bake mete was nevere his hous,
Of fish and flesh, and that so plentevous,
It snewed[47] in his hous of mete and drinke,
Of alle deyntees that men coude thinke.
After the sondry sesons of the yeer,
So chaunged he his mete and his soper.
Ful many a fat partrich hadde he in mewe,[48]
And many a breem[49] and many a luce in stewe.[50]
Wo[51] was his cook but-if[52] his sauce were
Poynaunt and sharp, and redy al his gere.[53]
His table dormant[54] in his halle alway
Stood redy covered al the longe day.
At sessiouns[55] ther was he lord and sire.
Ful ofte tyme he was knight of the shire.[56]
An anlas[57] and a gipser[58] al of silk
Heng at his girdel, whyt as morne milk.
A shirreve hadde he been, and a countour;[59]
Was nowher such a worthy vavasour.[60]

An Haberdassher[61] and a Carpenter,
A Webbe,[62] a Dyere, and a Tapicer,[63]
And they were clothed alle in o liveree,
Of a solempne and greet fraternitee.
Ful fresh and newe hir gere apyked[64] was;
Hir knyves were y-chaped[65] noght with bras,
But al with silver wroght ful clene and weel,
Hir girdles and hir pouches everydeel.
Wel semed ech of hem a fair burgeys,[66]

[33] girdle
[34] bars, or ornaments
[35] country gentleman
[36] beard
[37] daisy
[38] temperament
[39] lively
[40] in the morning
[41] a sort of custard with bread in it
[42] wont, custom
[43] a Greek philosopher, popularly supposed to have considered pleasure the chief good
[44] patron saint of hospitality
[45] of the same quality
[46] provided with wines
[47] snowed; i. e., abounded
[48] coop
[49] bream (a fish)
[50] pond
[51] woe unto his cook
[52] unless
[53] utensils
[54] stationary
[55] meetings of justices of the peace
[56] member of parliament
[57] knife
[58] pouch
[59] auditor
[60] sub-vassal (sub-landholder)
[61] seller of hats
[62] weaver
[63] upholsterer
[64] trimmed
[65] capped (tipped)
[66] citizen

To sitten in a yeldhalle [1] on a deys. [2]
Everich, [3] for the wisdom that he can, [4]
Was shaply [5] for to been an alderman.
For catel [6] hadde they ynogh and rente, [7]
And eek hir wyves wolde it wel assente; [8]
And elles certein were they to blame.
It is ful fair to been y-clept *ma dame,*
And goon [9] to vigilyës [10] al bifore,
And have a mantel roialliche y-bore. [11]
A Cook they hadde with hem for the nones, [12]
To boille chiknes [13] with the mary-bones,
And poudre-marchant [14] tart, [15] and galingale. [16]
Wel coude he knowe [17] a draughte of London ale.
He coude roste, and sethe, [18] and broille, and frye,
Maken mortreux, [19] and wel bake a pye.
But greet harm was it, as it thoughte me,
That on his shine [20] a mormal [21] hadde he;
For blankmanger, [22] that made he with the beste.
A Shipman was ther, woning [23] fer by weste;
For aught I woot, [24] he was of Dertemouthe.
He rood up-on a rouncy, [25] as he couthe, [26]
In a gowne of falding [27] to the knee.
A daggere hanging on a laas [28] hadde he
Aboute his nekke under his arm adoun.
The hote somer had maad his hewe al broun;
And, certeinly, he was a good felawe.
Ful many a draughte of wyn had he y-drawe
From Burdeux-ward, whyl that the chapman [29] sleep.
Of nyce [30] conscience took he no keep. [31]
If that he faught, and hadde the hyer hond,
By water he sente hem hoom to every lond. [32]
But of his craft [33] to rekene wel his tydes,
His stremes and his daungers him bisydes,
His herberwe [34] and his mone, [35] his lodemenage, [36]
Ther nas noon swich from Hulle to Cartage.
Hardy he was, and wys to undertake;
With many a tempest hadde his berd been shake.
He knew wel alle the havenes, as they were,
From Gootlond [37] to the cape of Finistere, [38]
And every cryke in Britayne and in Spayne;
His barge y-cleped was the Maudelayne.
With us ther was a Doctour of Phisyk, [39]
In al this world ne was ther noon him lyk
To speke of phisik and of surgerye;
For he was grounded in astronomye. [40]
He kepte his pacient a ful greet del
In houres, [41] by his magik naturel.
Wel coude he fortunen [42] the ascendent
Of his images [43] for his pacient. [44]
He knew the cause of everich maladye,
Were it of hoot or cold, or moiste, or drye, [45]
And where engendred, and of what humour;
He was a verrey parfit practisour.
The cause y-knowe, and of his harm the rote, [46]
Anon he yaf the seke man his bote. [47]
Ful redy hadde he his apothecaries,
To sende him drogges, and his letuaries. [48]
For ech of hem made other for to winne; [49]
Hir frendschipe nas nat newe to beginne. [50]
Wel knew he the olde Esculapius, [51]
And Deiscorides, and eek Rufus;
Old Ypocras, Haly, and Galien;
Serapion, Razis, and Avicen;
Averrois, Damascien, and Constantyn;
Bernard, and Gatesden, and Gilbertyn.
Of his diete mesurable [52] was he,
For it was of no superfluitee,
But of greet norissing and digestible.
His studie was but litel on the Bible.
In sangwin [53] and in pers [54] he clad was al,
Lyned with taffata [55] and with sendal [55]
And yet he was but esy of dispence; [56]
He kepte that he wan in pestilence.
For gold in phisik is a cordial. [57]
Therfor he lovede gold in special.

[1] guild-hall
[2] dais
[3] everyone
[4] knew (had)
[5] fit
[6] property
[7] income
[8] be glad of it
[9] to go
[10] social gatherings in the church or churchyard
[11] royally carried
[12] occasion
[13] chickens
[14] a seasoning
[15] sharp
[16] the root of sweet cyperus
[17] Well knew he how to distinguish.
[18] boil
[19] chowders
[20] shin
[21] sore
[22] minced capon, cream, sugar, and flour
[23] dwelling
[24] know
[25] common hackney
[26] as well as he could
[27] coarse cloth
[28] cord
[29] merchant
[30] over-scrupulous
[31] heed
[32] made them walk the plank
[33] skill
[34] harbor
[35] moon
[36] pilotage
[37] Jutland, Denmark
[38] on the coast of Spain
[39] medicine
[40] astrology
[41] He treated his patient at favorable astrological times.
[42] forecast
[43] talismans
[44] Figures, or talismans, made when a suitable star was rising above the horizon, (i. e., was in the ascendant) could, it was believed, cause good or evil to a patient.
[45] Diseases were thought to be caused by an excess of one or another of these humors.
[46] the root of all evil
[47] remedy
[48] medicines mixed with confections
[49] The doctor and the druggist each made business for the other.
[50] of recent date
[51] The god of medicine, son of Apollo; the others named in lines 430-434 are all famous physicians and scholars of antiquity and medieval times. Gatisden of Oxford was almost a contemporary of Chaucer.
[52] moderate
[53] reddish
[54] light blue
[55] thin silk
[56] moderate in spending
[57] Gold in medicine was supposed to render it especially efficacious.

A Good Wyf was ther of bisyde Bathe,
But she was som-del deef, and that was scathe.[1]
Of cloth-making she hadde swiche an haunt,[2]
She passed hem of Ypres[3] and of Gaunt.[4]
In al the parisshe wyf ne was ther noon
That to the offring[5] bifore hir sholde goon;
And if ther dide, certeyn, so wrooth was she,
That she was out of alle charitee.
Hir coverchiefs[6] ful fyne were of ground;[7]
I dorste swere they weyeden ten pound[8]
That on a Sonday were upon hir heed.
Hir hosen weren of fyn scarlet reed,
Ful streite y-teyd, and shoes ful moiste[9] and newe.
Bold was hir face, and fair, and reed of hewe.
She was a worthy womman al hir lyve,
Housbondes at chirche-dore[10] she hadde fyve,
Withouten[11] other compaignye in youthe;
But thereof nedeth nat to speke as nouthe.[12]
And thryes hadde she been at Ierusalem;
She hadde passed many a straunge streem;
At Rome she hadde been, and at Boloigne,[13]
In Galice at seint Iame,[14] and at Coloigne.[15]
She coude moche of wandring by the weye.
Gat-tothed[16] was she, soothly for to seye.
Up-on an amblere[17] esily she sat,
Y-wimpled wel, and on hir heed an hat
As brood as is a bokeler[18] or a targe;
A foot-mantel[19] aboute her hipes large,
And on hir feet a paire of spores sharpe.
In felaweschip wel coude she laughe and carpe.[20]
Of remedies of love[21] she knew per-chaunce,
For she coude of that art the olde daunce.

A good man was ther of religioun,
And was a povre Persoun[22] of a toun;
But riche he was of holy thoght and werk.
He was also a lerned man, a clerk,
That Cristes gospel trewely wolde preche;
His parisshens devoutly wolde he teche.
Benigne he was, and wonder diligent,
And in adversitee ful pacient;
And swich he was y-preved[23] ofte sythes.[24]
Ful looth were him to cursen for his tythes,[25]
But rather wolde he yeven, out of doute,
Un-to his povre parisshens aboute
Of his offring,[26] and eek of his substaunce.[27]
He coude in litel thing han suffisaunce.
Wyd was his parisshe, and houses fer a-sonder,
But he ne lafte nat,[28] for reyn ne thonder,
In siknes nor in meschief[29] to visyte
The ferreste[30] in his parisshe, moche and lyte,[31]
Up-on his feet, and in his hand a staf.
This noble ensample to his sheep he yaf,
That first he wroghte, and afterward he taughte;
Out of the gospel he tho[32] wordes caughte;
And this figure he added eek ther-to,
That if gold ruste, what shal yren[33] do?
For if a preest be foul, on whom we truste,
No wonder is a lewed[34] man to ruste;
And shame it is, if a preest take keep,[35]
A [spotted] shepherde and a clene sheep.
Wel oghte a preest ensample for to yive,
By his clennesse, how that his sheep shold live.
He sette nat his benefice to hyre,[36]
And leet his sheep encombred in the myre,
And ran to London, un-to sëynt Poules,
To seken him a chaunterie[37] for soules,
Or with a bretherhed to been withholde,[38]
But dwelte at hoom, and kepte wel his folde,
So that the wolf ne made it nat miscarie;
He was a shepherde and no mercenarie.[39]
And though he holy were, and vertuous,
He was to sinful man nat despitous,[40]
Ne of his speche daungerous[41] ne digne,[42]
But in his teching discreet and benigne.
To drawen folk to heven by fairnesse
By good ensample, this was his bisynesse;
But it were any persone obstinat,
What so he were, of heigh or lowe estat,
Him wolde he snibben[43] sharply for the nones.[44]
A bettre preest, I trowe that nowher non is.
He wayted after no pompe and reverence,
Ne maked him a spyced[45] conscience,
But Cristes lore, and his apostles twelve,
He taughte, but first he folwed it him-selve.

With him ther was a Plowman, was his brother,
That hadde y-lad[46] of dong ful many a fother.[47]
A trewe swinkere[48] and a good was he,

[1] a pity
[2] skill
[3] in West Flanders
[4] Ghent
[5] the ceremony of offering gifts to relics on "Relic-Sunday"
[6] kerchiefs for the head
[7] texture
[8] because ornamented with gold and silver
[9] soft
[10] People were married at the church-porch.
[11] without counting
[12] at present
[13] where there was an image of the Virgin
[14] to the shrine of St. James, in Spain
[15] where according to legend the bones of the Three Wise Men of the East were kept
[16] gap-toothed; i. e., with teeth wide apart
[17] nag
[18] shield
[19] riding skirt
[20] chatter
[21] love-charms
[22] parson
[23] proved
[24] times
[25] He was loath to excommunicate those who would not pay their tithes.
[26] gifts made to him
[27] property
[28] ceased not
[29] trouble
[30] farthest
[31] rich and poor
[32] those
[33] iron
[34] ignorant
[35] notice
[36] He did not sub-let his parish.
[37] a position to sing mass
[38] maintained
[39] hireling
[40] merciless
[41] overbearing
[42] proud
[43] reprove
[44] on occasion
[45] sophisticated
[46] led
[47] load
[48] laborer

Livinge in pees and parfit charitee.
God loved he best with al his hole herte
At alle tymes, thogh him gamed or smerte,[1]
And thanne his neighebour right as him-selve.
He wolde thresshe, and ther-to dyke[2] and delve,
For Cristes sake, for every povre wight,
Withouten hyre,[3] if it lay in his might.
His tythes payed he ful faire and wel,
Bothe of his propre[4] swink and his catel.[5]
In a tabard he rood upon a mere.[6]
Ther was also a Reve[7] and a Millere,
A Somnour[8] and a Pardoner[9] also,
A Maunciple,[10] and my-self; there were namo.[11]
The Miller was a stout carl,[12] for the nones,[13]
Ful big he was of braun, and eek of bones;
That proved wel, for over-al ther[14] he cam,
At wrastling he wolde have alwey the ram.[15]
He was short-sholdred, brood, a thikke knarre,[16]
Ther nas no dore that he nolde heve of harre,[17]
Or breke it, at a renning, with his heed.
His berd as any sowe or fox was reed,
And ther-to brood, as though it were a spade.
Up-on the cop[18] right of his nose he hade
A werte,[19] and ther-on stood a tuft of heres,
Reed as the bristles of a sowes eres;[20]
His nose-thirles[21] blake were and wyde.
A swerd and bokeler bar he by his syde;
His mouth as greet was as a greet forneys.
He was a Ianglere[22] and a goliardeys,[23]
And that was most of sinne and harlotryes.[24]
Wel coude he stelen corn, and tollen thryes;[25]
And yet he hadde a thombe of gold,[26] pardee.
A whyt cote and a blew hood wered he.
A baggepype wel could he blowe and sowne,[27]
And therwithal he broghte us out of towne.
A gentil Maunciple was ther of a temple,[28]
Of which achatours[29] mighte take exemple

[1] whether his luck were good or bad
[2] dig ditches
[3] pay
[4] own
[5] property
[6] mare (then the humble man's steed)
[7] bailiff
[8] a summoner to ecclesiastical courts
[9] one commissioned to grant pardons
[10] a purchaser of food for lawyers at inns of court or for colleges
[11] no more
[12] churl, fellow
[13] for you
[14] everywhere
[15] a customary prize
[16] knotted, thick-set fellow
[17] could not heave off its hinges
[18] tip
[19] wart
[20] ears
[21] nostrils
[22] bold talker
[23] buffoon
[24] ribaldries
[25] take toll three times (instead of once)
[26] worth gold (because with it he tested his flour)
[27] play upon
[28] lawyers' quarters
[29] buyers

For to be wyse in bying of vitaille.
For whether that he payde, or took by taille,[30]
Algate he wayted[31] so in his achat,[32]
That he was ay biforn and in good stat.
Now is nat that of God a full fair grace,
That swich a lewed[33] mannes wit shal pace[34]
The wisdom of an heep of lerned men?
Of maistres hadde he mo[35] than thryes ten,
That were of lawe expert and curious;
Of which ther were a doseyn in that hous,
Worthy to been stiwardes of rente and lond
Of any lord that is in Engelond,
To make him live by his propre good,
In honour dettelees, but he were wood[36]
Or live as scarsly[37] as him list desire;
And able for to helpen al a shire
In any cas that mighte falle or happe;
And yit this maunciple sette hir aller cappe.[38]
The Reve was a sclendre colerik[39] man,
His berd was shave as ny as ever he can.
His heer was by his eres round y-shorn.
His top was dokked[40] lyk a preest biforn.
Ful longe were his legges, and ful lene,
Y-lyk a staf, ther was no calf y-sene.
Wel coude he kepe a gerner[41] and a binne;
Ther was noon auditour coude on him winne.
Wel wiste he, by the droghte, and by the reyn,
The yeldyng of his seed, and of his greyn.
His lordes sheep, his neet,[42] his dayerye,
His swyn, his hors, his stoor,[43] and his pultrye,
Was hoolly in this reves governing,
And by his covenaunt yaf the rekening[44]
Sin[45] that his lord was twenty yeer of age;
Ther coude no man bringe him in arrerage.[46]
Ther nas baillif, ne herde,[47] ne other hyne,[48]
That he ne knew his sleighte and his covyne;[49]
They were adrad of him, as of the deeth.
His woning[50] was ful fair up-on an heeth,
With grene treës shadwed was his place.
He coude bettre than his lord purchace.
Ful riche he was astored prively,
His lord wel coude he plesen subtilly,
To yeve and lene him of his owne good,
And have a thank, and yet a cote, and hood.[51]
In youthe he lerned hadde a good mister;[52]
He was a wel good wrighte, a carpenter.
This reve sat up-on a ful god stot,[53]

[30] tally, i. e., on credit
[31] always he was so careful
[32] purchase
[33] ignorant
[34] surpass
[35] more
[36] crazy
[37] economically
[38] cheated them all
[39] irascible
[40] cut short
[41] granary
[42] cattle
[43] stock
[44] rendered account
[45] since
[46] find him in arrears
[47] herder
[48] servant
[49] whose craft and deceit he did not know
[50] dwelling
[51] lend his lord's own property to him and receive gratitude and interest as well
[52] trade
[53] stallion

That was al pomely[1] grey, and highte Scot.
A long surcote of pers[2] up-on he hade,
And by his syde he bar a rusty blade.
Of Northfolk was this reve, of which I telle,
Bisyde a toun men clepen Baldeswelle.
Tukked[3] he was, as is a frere, aboute,
And evere he rood the hindreste of our route.
  A Somnour was ther with us in that place,
That hadde a fyr-reed cherubinnes face,
For saweceflem[4] he was, with eyen narwe,

. . . . . .

With scalled[5] browes blake, and piled[6] berd;
Of his visage children were aferd.
Ther nas quik-silver, litarge,[7] ne brimstoon,
Boras,[8] ceruce,[7] ne oille of tartre noon,
Ne oynement that wolde clense and byte,
That him mighte helpen of his whelkes[9] whyte,
Ne of the knobbes sittinge on his chekes.
Wel loved he garleek, oynons, and eek lekes,
And for to drinken strong wyn, reed as blood.
Thanne wolde he speke, and crye as he were wood.[10]
And whan that he wel dronken hadde the wyn,
Than wolde he speke no word but Latyn.
A fewe termes hadde he, two or thre,
That he had lerned out of som decree;
No wonder is, he herde it al the day;
And eek ye knowen wel, how that a Iay
Can clepen "Watte,"[11] as well as can the pope.
But who-so coude in other thing him grope,[12]
Thanne hadde he spent al his philosophye;
Ay *"Questio quid iuris"*[13] wolde he crye.
He was a gentil harlot[14] and a kynde;
A bettre felawe sholde men noght fynde.
He wolde suffre for[15] a quart of wyn
A good felawe to have his [wikked sin]
A twelf-month, and excuse him atte fulle;
And prively a finch eek coude he pulle.[16]
And if he fond owher[17] a good felawe,
He wolde techen him to have non awe,
In swich cas, of the erchedeknes curs,[18]
But-if[19] a mannes soule were in his purs;[20]
For in his purs he sholde y-punisshed be.
"Purs is the erchedeknes helle," seyde he.
But wel I woot he lyed right in dede;
Of cursing oghte ech gulty man him drede[21]—
For curs wol slee right as assoilling[22] saveth—
And also war him of a *significavit.*[23]
In daunger[24] hadde he at his owne gyse[25]
The yonge girles[26] of the diocyse,
And knew hir counseil, and was al hir reed.[27]
A gerland hadde he set up-on his heed,
As greet as it were for an ale-stake;[28]
A bokeler hadde he maad him of a cake.
  With him ther rood a gentil Pardoner
Of Rouncivale,[29] his frend and his compeer,
That streight was comen fro the court of Rome.
Ful loude he song, "Com hider, love, to me."
This somnour bar to him a stif burdoun,[30]
Was nevere trompe[31] of half so greet a soun.
This pardoner hadde heer as yelow as wex,
But smothe it heng, as doth a strike of flex;[32]
By ounces[33] henge his lokkes that he hadde,[34]
And ther-with he his shuldres overspradde;
But thinne it lay, by colpons[35] oon and oon;
But hood, for Iolitee, ne wered he noon,
For it was trussed up in his walet.
Him thoughte,[36] he rood al of the newe Iet;[37]
Dischevele, save his cappe, he rood al bare.
Swiche glaringe eyen hadde he as an hare.
A vernicle[38] hadde he sowed on his cappe.
His walet lay biforn him in his lappe,
Bret-ful[39] of pardoun come from Rome al hoot.
A voys he hadde as smal as hath a goot.
No berd hadde he, ne nevere sholde have,
As smothe it was as it were late y-shave;

. . . . . .

But of his craft, fro Berwik unto Ware,[40]
Ne was ther swich another pardoner.
For in his male[41] he hadde a pilwe-beer,[42]
Which that, he seyde, was our lady veyl;[43]
He seyde, he hadde a gobet[44] of the seyl[45]
That sëynt Peter hadde, whan that he wente
Up-on the see, til Iesu Crist him hente.[46]
He hadde a croys[47] of latoun,[48] ful of stones,
And in a glas he hadde pigges bones.
But with thise relikes, whan that he fond
A povre person dwelling up-on lond,[49]
Up-on a day he gat him more moneye

[1] spotted, dappled
[2] blue
[3] His coat was tucked up by means of a girdle.
[4] pimpled
[5] scurfy
[6] plucked (thin)
[7] white lead
[8] borax
[9] blotches
[10] mad
[11] Walter (then a very common name in England)
[12] test
[13] "The question is, What is the law?"
[14] good fellow
[15] in return for
[16] pluck a pigeon for himself
[17] anywhere
[18] excommunication
[19] unless
[20] purse
[21] (reflexive) fear for himself
[22] absolution
[23] writ of excommunication
[24] in his jurisdiction
[25] control
[26] young people of either sex
[27] the adviser of them all
[28] sign-pole of an inn (often a bush hung up in front)
[29] possibly the Hospital of Rouncyvalle, London
[30] accompaniment
[31] trumpet
[32] handful of flax
[33] small portions
[34] such as he had
[35] shreds
[36] It seemed to him.
[37] fashion
[38] a St. Veronica (a cloth bearing a picture of Christ)
[39] brimful
[40] from the north to the south of England
[41] valise
[42] pillow-case
[43] the veil of the Virgin
[44] piece
[45] sail
[46] Caught; see *Matthew,* xiv, 31.
[47] cross
[48] brass
[49] in the country

Than that the person gat in monthes tweye.
And thus with feyned flaterye and Iapes,[1]
He made the person and the peple his apes.
But trewely to tellen, atte laste,
He was in chirche a noble ecclesiaste.
Wel coude he rede a lessoun or a storie,
But alderbest[2] he song an offertorie;
For wel he wiste, whan that song was songe,
He moste preche, and wel affyle[3] his tonge,
To winne silver, as he ful wel coude;
Therefore he song so meriely and loude.
Now have I told you shortly, in a clause,
Thestat, tharray, the nombre, and eek the cause
Why that assembled was this compaignye
In Southwerk, at this gentil hostelrye,
That highte the Tabard, faste by the Belle.
But now is tyme to yow for to telle
How that we baren us that ilke night,
Whan we were in that hostelrye alight.
And after wol I telle of our viage,
And al the remenaunt of our pilgrimage.
But first I pray yow of your curteisye,
That ye narette it nat my vileinye,[4]
Thogh that I pleynly speke in this matere,
To telle yow hir wordes and hir chere;[5]
Ne thogh I speke hir wordes proprely.[6]
For this ye knowen al-so wel as I,
Who-so shal telle a tale after a man,
He moot reherce, as ny[7] as evere he can,
Everich a[8] word, if it be in his charge,[9]
Al[10] speke he never so rudeliche and large;[11]
Or elles he moot telle his tale untrewe;
Or feyne thing, or fynde wordes newe.
He may nat spare, al-thogh he were his brother;
He moot as wel seye o word as another.
Crist spak him-self ful brode in holy writ,
And wel ye woot, no vileinye is it.
Eek Plato seith, who-so that can him rede,[12]
The wordes mote[13] be cosin to the dede.
Also I prey yow to foryeve it me,
Al[14] have I nat set folk in hir degree
Here in this tale, as that they sholde stonde;
My wit is short, ye may wel understonde.
Greet chere[15] made our hoste us everichon,[16]
And to the soper sette he us anon;
And served us with vitaille at the beste.
Strong was the wyn, and wel to drinke us leste.[17]
A semely man our hoste was with-alle
For to han been a marshal in a halle;
A large man he was with eyen stepe,[18]
A fairer burgeys[19] was ther noon in Chepe;[20]
Bold of his speche, and wys, and wel y-taught,
And of manhod him lakkede right naught.
Eek therto he was right a mery man,
And after soper pleyen[21] he bigan,
And spak of mirthe amonges othere thinges,
Whan that we hadde maad our rekeninges;[22]
And seyde thus: "Now, lordinges, trewely
Ye ben to me right welcome hertely;
For by my trouthe, if that I shal nat lye,
I ne saugh[23] this yeer so mery a compaignye
At ones in this herberwe[24] as is now.
Fayn wolde I doon yow mirthe, wiste I how.[25]
And of a mirthe I am right now bithoght,
To doon yow ese,[26] and it shal coste noght.
"Ye goon to Caunterbury; God yow spede,
The blisful martir[27] quyte[28] yow your mede.[29]
And wel I woot, as ye goon by the weye,
Ye shapen[30] yow to talen[31] and to pleye;
For trewely, confort ne mirthe is noon
To ryde by the weye doumb as a stoon;
And therefor wol I maken yow disport,
As I seyde erst, and doon yow som confort.
And if yow lyketh alle, by oon assent,
Now for to stonden at[32] my Iugement,
And for to werken as I shal yow seye,
To-morwe, whan ye ryden by the weye,
Now, by my fader soule, that is deed,
But[33] ye be merye, I wol yeve yow myn heed.
Hold up your hond, withoute more speche."
Our counseil was nat longe for to seche;[34]
Us thoughte it was noght worth to make it wys,[35]
And graunted him with-outen more avys,[36]
And bad him seye his verdit, as him leste.
"Lordinges," quod he, "now herkneth for the beste;
But tak it not, I prey yow, in desdeyn;
This is the poynt, to speken short and pleyn,
That ech of yow, to shorte with our weye,[37]
In this viage, shal telle tales tweye,
To Caunterbury-ward, I mene it so,
And hom-ward he shal tellen othere two,
Of aventures that whylom han bifalle.
And which of yow that bereth him best of alle,

1 tricks
2 best of all
3 file, polish
4 Attribute it not to my ill-breeding.
5 appearance
6 exactly
7 nearly
8 every
9 i.e., in the tale he is repeating
10 although
11 freely
12 Chaucer could not read Greek.
13 must
14 although
15 entertainment
16 every one
17 it pleased
18 bright
19 citizen
20 a market square in London (now a street, Cheapside)
21 to play, jest
22 paid our bills
23 saw not
24 inn
25 give you fun if I knew how
26 give you recreation
27 Thomas à Becket
28 requite (give)
29 reward
30 plan
31 to tell tales
32 by
33 unless
34 seek
35 a matter of deliberation
36 consideration
37 to shorten our way with

That is to seyn, that telleth in this cas
Tales of best sentence and most solas,[1]
Shal han a soper at our aller cost
Here in this place, sitting by this post,
Whan that we come agayn fro Caunterbury.
And for to make yow the more mery,
I wol my-selven gladly with yow ryde,
Right at myn owne cost, and be your gyde.
And who-so wol my Iugement withseye[2]
Shal paye al that we spenden by the weye.
And if ye vouche-sauf that it be so,
Tel me anon, with-outen wordes mo,
And I wol erly shape[3] me therfore."
This thing was graunted, and our othes swore
With ful glad herte, and preyden him also
That he wold vouche-sauf for to do so,
And that he wolde been our governour,
And of our tales Iuge and reportour,
And sette a soper at a certeyn prys;
And we wold reuled been at his devys,[4]
In heigh and lowe; and thus, by oon assent,
We been acorded to his Iugement.
And ther-up-on the wyn was fet[5] anoon;
We dronken, and to reste wente echoon,
With-outen any lenger taryinge.
A-morwe, whan that[6] day bigan to springe,
Up roos our host, and was our aller cok,[7]
And gadrede us togidre, alle in a flok,
And forth we riden, a litel more than pas,[8]
Un-to the watering of seint Thomas.[9]
And there our host bigan his hors areste,
And seyde; "Lordinges, herkneth if yow leste.
Ye woot your forward,[10] and I it yow recorde.[11]
If even-song and morwe-song acorde,
Lat se now who shal telle the firste tale.
As evere mote I drinke wyn or ale,
Who-so be rebel to my Iugement
Shal paye for al that by the weye is spent.
Now draweth cut,[12] er that we ferrer[13] twinne;[14]
He which that hath the shortest shal biginne.
Sire knight," quod he, "my maister and my lord,
Now draweth cut, for that is myn acord.[15]
Cometh neer,"[16] quod he, "my lady prioresse;
And ye, sir clerk, lat be your shamfastnesse,
Ne studieth noght;[17] ley hond to, every man."
Anon to drawen every wight bigan,
And shortly for to tellen, as it was,
Were it by aventure,[18] or sort,[19] or cas,[20]
The sothe[21] is this, the cut fil to the knight,
Of which ful blythe and glad was every wight;
And telle he moste his tale, as was resoun,
By forward and by composicioun,[22]
As ye han herd; what nedeth wordes mo?
And whan this goode man saugh it was so,
As he that wys was and obedient
To kepe his forward by his free assent,
He seyde: "Sin[23] I shal beginne the game,
What, welcome be the cut, a[24] Goddes name!
Now lat us ryde, and herkneth what I seye."
And with that word we riden forth our weye;
And he bigan with right a mery chere[25]
His tale anon, and seyde in this manere.

The Nonne Preestes Tale[26]

Here biginneth the Nonne Preestes Tale of the Cok and Hen, Chauntecleer and Pertelote.

A povre widwe somdel stope[27] in age,
Was whylom[28] dwelling in a narwe[29] cotage,
Bisyde a grove, stondyng in a dale.
This widwe, of which I telle yow my tale,
Sin thilke[30] day that she was last a wyf,
In pacience ladde a ful simple lyf,
For litel was hir catel and hir rent;[31]
By housbondrye, of such as God hir sente,
She fond[32] hir-self, and eek hir doghtren[33] two.
Three large sowes hadde she, and namo,
Three kyn, and eek a sheep that highte[34] Malle.
Ful sooty was hir bour, and eek hir halle,[35]
In which she eet ful many a sclendre meel.
Of poynaunt sauce hir neded[36] never a deel.
No deyntee morsel passed thurgh hir throte;
Hir dyete was accordant to hir cote.
Repleccioun[37] ne made hir nevere syk;
Attempree dyete was al hir phisyk,
And exercyse, and hertes suffisaunce.

[1] amusement
[2] gainsay
[3] prepare
[4] decision
[5] fetched
[6] when
[7] cock of us all (He woke them up.)
[8] faster than a walk
[9] two miles on the way to Canterbury
[10] agreement
[11] remind you of it
[12] lots
[13] further
[14] separate
[15] decision
[16] nearer
[17] don't meditate
[18] chance
[19] fate
[20] accident
[21] truth
[22] contract
[23] since
[24] in
[25] expression
[26] In the Ellesmere MS. this is the twentieth tale. Sir John, the "Nun's Priest," was an escort of Madame Eglentyne; see *Prologue,* 164. His tale is an old one, found in various languages.
[27] advanced
[28] once upon a time
[29] narrow
[30] since that
[31] her property (chattels) and her income
[32] supported
[33] daughters
[34] was called
[35] Bower and hall are terms applicable to a castle; used here humorously of the probably one-room cottage.
[36] (reflexive) she needed
[37] surfeit

The goute lette [1] hir no-thing for to daunce,
Ne poplexye shente [2] nat hir heed;
No wyn ne drank she, neither whyt ne reed;
Hir bord was served most with whyt and blak,
Milk and broun breed, in which she fond no lak,
Seynd [3] bacoun, and somtyme an ey [4] or tweye,
For she was as it were a maner deye. [5]
A yerd she hadde, enclosed al aboute
With stikkes, and a drye dich with-oute,
In which she hadde a cok, hight Chauntecleer,
In al the land of crowing nas [6] his peer.
His vois was merier than the merye orgon [7]
On messe-dayes [8] that in the chirche gon;
Wel sikerer [9] was his crowing in his logge, [10]
Than is a clokke, or an abbey orlogge. [11]
By nature knew he ech ascensioun [12]
Of equinoxial in thilke toun;
For whan degrees fiftene were ascended,
Thanne crew he, that it mighte nat ben amended. [13]
His comb was redder than the fyn coral,
And batailed [14] as it were a castel-wal.
His bile [15] was blak, and as the Ieet [16] it shoon;
Lyk asur were his legges, and his toon; [17]
His nayles whytter than the lilie flour,
And lyk the burned [18] gold was his colour.
This gentil cok hadde in his governaunce
Sevene hennes, for to doon all his plesaunce,
Whiche were his sustres and his paramours,
And wonder lyk to him, as of [19] colours.
Of whiche the faireste hewed on hir throte
Was cleped [20] faire damoysele Pertelote.
Curteys she was, discreet, and debonaire, [21]
And compaignable, and bar hir-self so faire,
Sin thilke day that she was seven night old,
That trewely she hath the herte in hold
Of Chauntecleer loken in every lith, [22]
He loved hir so, that wel him was therwith.
But such a Ioye was it to here hem singe,
Whan that the brighte sonne gan to springe,
In swete accord, "my lief is faren in londe." [23]
For thilke [24] tyme, as I have understonde,

[1] hindered
[2] hurt
[3] singed (broiled)
[4] egg
[5] sort of dairy-woman
[6] was not
[7] organs
[8] mass-days
[9] surer
[10] lodging
[11] horologe, clock
[12] He knew the time every hour of the day (for 15° of the equinoctial arc passed each hour of the twenty-four).
[13] so that it couldn't be improved upon
[14] embattled
[15] bill
[16] jet
[17] toes
[18] burnished
[19] in respect to
[20] named
[21] gracious
[22] locked in every limb
[23] My beloved is gone to the country, gone away.
[24] at that

Bestes and briddes coude speke and singe.
And so bifel, that in a dawenynge,
As Chauntecleer among his wyves alle
Sat on his perche, that was in the halle,
And next him sat this faire Pertelote,
This Chauntecleer gan gronen in his throte,
As man that in his dreem is drecched [25] sore.
And whan that Pertelote thus herde him rore,
She was agast, and seyde, "o herte deere,
What eyleth yow, to grone in this manere?
Ye ben a verray sleper, fy for shame!"
And he answerde and seyde thus, "madame,
I pray yow, that ye take it nat agrief: [26]
By God, me mette [27] I was in swich meschief
Right now, that yet myn herte is sore afright.
Now God," quod he, "my swevene [28] rede [29] aright,
And keep my body out of foul prisoun!
Me mette, how that I romed up and doun
Withinne our yerde, wher as I saugh a beste,
Was lyk an hound, and wolde han maad areste [30]
Upon my body, and wolde han had me deed.
His colour was bitwixe yelwe and reed;
And tipped was his tail, and bothe his eres
With blak, unlyk the remenant of his heres;
His snowte smal, with glowinge eyen tweye.
Yet of his look for fere almost I deye;
This caused me my groning, douteles."
"Avoy!" [31] quod she, "fy on yow, herteles! [32]
Allas!" quod she, "for, by that God above,
Now han ye lost myn herte and al my love;
I can nat love a coward, by my feith.
For certes, what so any womman seith,
We alle desyren, if it mighte be,
To han housbondes hardy, wyse, and free, [33]
And secree, [34] and no nigard, ne no fool,
Ne him that is agast of every tool, [35]
Ne noon avauntour, [36] by that God above!
How dorste ye sayn for shame unto youre love,
That any thing mighte make yow aferd?
Have ye no mannes herte, and han a berd?
Allas! and conne ye been agast of swevenis?
No-thing, God wot, but vanitee, in sweven is.
Swevenes engendren of replecciouns,
And ofte of fume, and of complecciouns, [37]
Whan humours [38] been to [39] habundant in a wight.
Certes this dreem, which ye han met [40] to-night,
Cometh of the grete superfluitee

[25] troubled
[26] amiss
[27] I dreamed
[28] dream
[29] interpret
[30] seizure
[31] away
[32] heartless one
[33] liberal
[34] trusty
[35] weapon
[36] boaster
[37] temperaments
[38] The four causes and classes of disease (see *Prologue*, 420).
[39] too
[40] dreamed

Of youre rede *colera,* [1] pardee,
Which causeth folk to dremen in here [2] dremes
Of arwes, [3] and of fyr with rede lemes, [4]
Of grete bestes, that they wol hem byte,
Of contek, [5] and of whelpes grete and lyte;
Right as the humour of malencolye [6]
Causeth ful many a man, in sleep, to crye,
For fere of blake beres, or boles [7] blake,
Or elles, blake develes wole him take.
Of othere humours coude I telle also,
That werken many a man in sleep ful wo;
But I wol passe as lightly as I can.
“Lo Catoun, [8] which that was so wys a man,
Seyde he nat thus, ne do no fors [9] of dremes?
Now, sire,” quod she, “when we flee fro the bemes,
For Goddes love, as [10] tak som laxatyf;
Up peril of my soule, and of my lyf,
I counseille yow the beste, I wol nat lye,
That both of colere, and of malencolye [6]
Ye purge yow; and for ye shul nat tarie,
Though in this toun is noon apotecarie,
I shal my-self to herbes techen yow,
That shul ben for your hele, and for your prow; [11]
And in our yerd tho herbes shal I fynde,
The whiche han of here propretee, by kynde, [12]
To purgen yow binethe, and eek above.
Forget not this, for Goddes owene love!
Ye been ful colerik of compleccioun.
Ware [13] the sonne in his ascencioun
Ne fynde yow nat repleet of humours hote;
And if it do, I dar wel leye a grote, [14]
That ye shul have a fevere terciane, [15]
Or an agu, that may be youre banc.
A day or two ye shul have digestyves
Of wormes, er ye take your laxatyves,
Of lauriol, centaure, and fumetere, [16]
Or elles of ellebor, [17] that groweth there,
Of catapuce, [18] or of gaytres [19] beryis,
Of erbe yve, growing in our yerd, that mery is;
Pekke hem up right as they growe, and ete hem in.
Be mery, housbond, for your fader kyn!
Dredeth no dreem: I can say yow namore.”
“Madame,” quod he, *“graunt mercy* [20] of your lore.

[1] red cholera (caused by too much bile and blood)
[2] their
[3] arrows
[4] gleams
[5] contest
[6] due to excess of bile
[7] bulls
[8] Dionysius Cato
[9] take no notice
[10] do now (pleonastic)
[11] profit
[12] nature
[13] beware
[14] wager a groat (fourpence)
[15] tertian (every third day)
[16] laurel, centaury, fumitory
[17] hellebore
[18] spurge
[19] dog-wood
[20] great thanks

But natheles, as touching daun [21] Catoun,
That hath of wisdom such a gret renoun,
Though that he bad no dremes for to drede,
By God, men may in olde bokes rede
Of many a man, more of auctoritee
Than evere Catoun was, so moot I thee, [22]
That al the revers [23] seyn of this sentence, [24]
And han wel founden by experience,
That dremes ben significaciouns,
As wel of Ioye as tribulaciouns
That folk enduren in this lyf present.
Ther nedeth make of this noon argument;
The verray preve [25] sheweth it in dede.
Oon of the gretteste auctours that men rede [26]
Seith thus, that whylom two felawes wente
On pilgrimage, in a ful good entente;
And happed so, thay come into a toun,
Where as ther was swich congregacioun
Of peple, and eek so streit [27] of herbergage, [28]
That they ne founde as muche as o cotage,
In which they bothe mighte y-logged be.
Wherfor thay mosten, of necessitee,
As for that night, departen compaignye;
And ech of hem goth to his hostelrye,
And took his logging as it wolde falle.
That oon of hem was logged in a stalle,
Fer [29] in a yerd, with oxen of the plough;
That other man was logged wel y-nough,
As was his aventure, [30] or his fortune,
That us governeth alle as in commune, [31]
And so bifel, that, long er it were day,
This man mette in his bed, ther as he lay,
How that his felawe gan up-on him calle,
And seyde, ‘allas! for in an oxes stalle
This night I shal be mordred ther [32] I lye.
Now help me, dere brother, or I dye;
In alle haste com to me,’ he sayde.
This man out of his sleep for fere abrayde; [33]
But whan that he was wakned of his sleep,
He turned him, and took of this no keep, [34]
Him thoughte [35] his dreem nas but a vanitee.
Thus twyes in his sleping dremed he.
And atte thridde tyme yet his felawe
Cam, as him thoughte, and seide, ‘I am now slawe; [36]
Bihold my bloody woundes, depe and wyde!
Arys up erly in the morwe-tyde, [37]
And at the west gate of the toun,’ quod he,
‘A carte ful of donge ther shaltow see,
In which my body is hid ful prively;

[21] lord, master (Latin *dominus*)
[22] So may I thrive (a strong affirmative; cf. l. 246).
[23] opposite
[24] opinion
[25] proof
[26] Cicero
[27] scant
[28] lodging-places
[29] afar
[30] luck
[31] in general
[32] murdered where
[33] started up
[34] heed
[35] It seemed to him.
[36] slain
[37] morning-time

Do thilke carte arresten [1] boldely.
My gold caused my mordre, sooth to sayn;'
And tolde him every poynt how he was slayn,
With a ful pitous face, pale of hewe.
And truste wel, his dreem he fond ful trewe;
For on the morwe, as sone as it was day,
To his felawes in he took the way;
And whan that he cam to this oxes stalle,
After his felawe he bigan to calle.
The hostiler answerde him anon,
And seyde, 'sire, your felawe is agon,
As sone as day he wente out of the toun.'
This man gan fallen in suspecioun,
Remembring on his dremes that he mette,
And forth he goth, no lenger wolde he lette, [2]
Unto the west gate of the toun, and fond
A dong-carte, as it were to donge lond,
That was arrayed in that same wyse
As ye han herd the dede man devyse; [3]
And with an hardy herte he gan to crye
Vengeaunce and Iustice of this feloyne:
'My felawe mordred is this same night,
And in this carte he lyth gapinge upright.
I crye out on the ministres.' [4] quod he,
'That sholden kepe and reulen this citee;
Harrow! allas! her lyth my felawe slayn!'
What sholde I more un-to this tale sayn?
The peple out-sterte, and caste the cart to
grounde,
And in the middel of the dong they founde
The dede man, that mordred was al newe.
"O blisful God, that art so Iust and trewe!
Lo, how that thou biwreyest [5] mordre alway!
Mordre wol out, that se we day by day.
Mordre is so wlatsom [6] and abhominable
To God, that is so Iust and resonable,
That he ne wol nat suffre it heled [7] be;
Though it abyde a yeer, or two, or three,
Mordre wol out, this [8] my conclusioun.
And right anoon, ministres of that toun
Han hent the carter, and so sore him pyned, [9]
And eek the hostiler so sore engyned, [10]
That thay biknewe [11] hir wikkednesse anoon,
And were an-hanged by the nekke-boon.
"Here may men seen that dremes been to
drede.
And certes, in the same book I rede,
Right in the nexte chapitre after this,
(I gabbe [12] nat, so have I Ioye or blis,)
Two men that wolde han passed over see,
For certeyn cause, in-to a fer contree,

[1] have..stopped
[2] delay
[3] relate
[4] officers
[5] makest known
[6] hateful
[7] hidden
[8] this is
[9] tormented
[10] racked
[11] confessed
[12] lie

If that the wind ne hadde been contrarie,
That made hem in a citee for to tarie,
That stood ful mery upon a haven-syde.
But on a day, agayn [13] the even-tyde,
The wind gan chaunge, and blew right as hem
leste.
Iolif and glad they wente un-to hir reste,
And casten hem [14] ful erly for to saille;
But to that oo [15] man fel a greet mervaille. [16]
That oon of hem, in sleping as he lay,
Him mette a wonder dreem, agayn [13] the day;
Him thoughte a man stood by his beddes syde,
And him comaunded, that he sholde abyde, [17]
And seyde him thus, 'if thou to-morwe
wende,
Thou shalt be dreynt; [18] my tale is at an ende.'
He wook, and tolde his felawe what he mette,
And preyde him his viage for to lette; [19]
As [20] for that day, he preyde him to abyde.
His felawe, that lay by his beddes syde,
Gan for to laughe, and scorned him ful faste.
'No dreem,' quod he, 'may so myn herte
agaste, [21]
That I wol lette [19] for to do my thinges. [22]
I sette not a straw by thy dreminges,
For swevenes been but vanitees and Iapes. [23]
Men dreme al-day [24] of owles or of apes,
And eek of many a mase [25] therwithal;
Men dreme of thing that nevere was ne shal.
But sith [26] I see that thou wolt heer abyde,
And thus for-sleuthen [27] wilfully thy tyde,
God wot it reweth [28] me; and have good day.'
And thus he took his leve, and wente his way.
But er that he hadde halfe his cours y-seyled,
Noot [29] I nat why, ne what mischaunce it
eyled, [30]
But casuelly [31] the shippes botme rente,
And ship and man under the water wente
In sighte of othere shippes it byside,
That with hem seyled at the same tyde.
And therfor, faire Pertelote so dere,
By swiche ensamples olde maistow [32] lere, [33]
That no man sholde been to recchelees [34]
Of dremes, for I sey thee, doutelees,
That many a dreem ful sore is for to drede.
"Lo, in the lyf of seint Kenelm, I rede,
That was Kenulphus sone, the noble king
Of Mercenrike, [35] how Kenelm mette a thing;

[13] toward
[14] planned
[15] one
[16] marvel
[17] tarry
[18] drowned
[19] delay
[20] at least
[21] frighten
[22] business matters
[23] jests
[24] all the time
[25] wild fancy
[26] since
[27] lose through sloth
[28] grieveth
[29] know not
[30] ailed it
[31] accidentally
[32] mayest thou
[33] learn
[34] careless
[35] Mercia

A lyte [1] er he was mordred, on a day,
His mordre in his avisioun [2] he say. [3]
His norice [4] him expouned every del
His swevene, and bad him for to kepe him wel
For [5] traisoun; but he nas but seven yeer old,
And therfore litel tale [6] hath he told [7]
Of any dreem, so holy was his herte.
By God, I hadde levere [8] than my sherte
That ye had rad [9] his legende, as have I.
Dame Pertelote, I sey yow trewely,
Macrobeus, that writ the avisioun [10]
In Affrike of the worthy Cipioun,
Affermeth dremes, and seith that they been
Warning of thinges that men after seen.
And forther-more, I pray yow loketh wel
In the olde testament, of Daniel,
If he held dremes any vanitee.
Reed eek of Ioseph, and ther shul ye see
Wher [11] dremes ben somtyme (I sey nat alle)
Warning of thinges that shul after falle.
Loke of Egipt the king, daun [12] Pharao,
His bakere and his boteler [13] also,
Wher [18] they ne felte noon effect in dremes.
Who so wol seken actes [14] of sondry remes [15]
May rede of dremes many a wonder thing.
"Lo Cresus, which that was of Lyde [16] king,
Mette he nat that he sat upon a tree,
Which signified he sholde anhanged be?
Lo heer Andromacha, Ectores wyf,
That day that Ector sholde lese [17] his lyf,
She dremed on the same night biforn,
How that the lyf of Ector sholde be lorn, [18]
If thilke day he wente in-to bataille;
She warned him, but it mighte nat availle;
He wente for to fighte natheles,
But he was slayn anoon [19] of [20] Achilles.
But thilke tale is al to long to telle,
And eek it is ny [21] day, I may nat dwelle.
Shortly I seye, as for conclusioun,
That I shal han of this avisioun
Adversitee; and I seye forther-more,
That I ne telle of laxatyves no store, [22]
For they ben venimous, [23] I woot it wel;
I hem defye, I love hem nevere a del.
"Now let us speke of mirthe, and stinte al this;
Madame Pertelote, so have I blis, [24]
Of o thing God hath sent me large grace;
For whan I see the beautee of your face,
Ye ben so scarlet-reed about youre yën,
It maketh al my drede for to dyen;
For, also siker [25] as *In principio,*
Mulier est hominis confusio; [26]
Madame, the sentence of this Latin is—
Womman is mannes Ioye and al his blis;

. . . . . .

I am so ful of Ioye and of solas
That I defye bothe sweven and dreem."
And with that word he fley [27] doun fro the beem,
For it was day, and eek his hennes alle;
And with a chuk he gan hem for to calle,
For he had founde a corn, lay in the yerd.
Roial he was, he was namore aferd;

. . . .

He loketh as it were a grim leoun;
And on his toos he rometh up and doun,
Him deyned [28] not to sette his foot to grounde.
He chukketh, whan he hath a corn y-founde,
And to him rennen [29] thanne his wyves alle.
Thus roial, as a prince is in his halle,
Leve I this Chauntecleer in his pasture;
And after wol I telle his aventure.
Whan that the month in which the world bigan,
That highte March, whan God first maked man,
Was complet, and y-passed were also,
Sin March bigan, thritty dayes and two,
Bifel that Chauntecleer, in al his pryde,
His seven wyves walking by his syde,
Caste up his eyen to the brighte sonne,
That in the signe of Taurus hadde y-ronne
Twenty degrees and oon, and somwhat more;
And knew by kynde, and by noon other lore,
That it was pryme, [30] and crew with blisful stevene. [31]
"The sonne," he sayde, "is clomben up on hevene
Fourty degrees and oon, and more, y-wis.
Madame Pertelote, my worldes blis,
Herkneth thise blisful briddes [32] how they singe,
And see the fresshe floures how they springe;
Ful is myn hert of revel and solas."
But sodeinly him fil a sorweful cas; [33]
For evere the latter ende of Ioye is wo.
God woot that worldly Ioye is sone ago; [34]
And if a rethor [35] coude faire endyte, [36]
He in a chronique saufly [37] mighte it write,

[1] little
[2] vision
[3] saw
[4] nurse
[5] for fear of
[6] heed
[7] taken
[8] rather
[9] read
[10] Cicero's *Dream of Scipio,* annotated by the grammarian, Macrobius
[11] whether
[12] lord
[13] butler
[14] the history
[15] realms
[16] Lydia (in Asia Minor)
[17] lose
[18] lost
[19] quickly
[20] by
[21] nigh
[22] set no value upon laxatives
[23] poisonous
[24] as I hope for bliss
[25] sure
[26] In the beginning woman is man's destruction.
[27] flew
[28] He deigned.
[29] run
[30] nine o'clock
[31] voice
[32] birds
[33] fate
[34] gone
[35] rhetorician
[36] relate
[37] safely

As for a sovereyn notabilitee.[1]
Now every wys man, lat him herkne me;
This storie is al-so trewe, I undertake.[2]
As is the book of Launcelot de Lake,[3]
That wommen holde in ful gret reverence.
Now wol I torne agayn to my sentence.
A col-fox,[4] ful of sly iniquitee,
That in the grove hadde woned yeres three,
By heigh imaginacioun forn-cast,[5]
The same night thurgh-out the hegges[6] brast[7]
Into the yerd, ther Chauntecleer the faire
Was wont, and eek his wyves, to repaire;
And in a bed of wortes[8] stille he lay,
Til it was passed undern[9] of the day,
Wayting his tyme on Chauntecleer to falle,
As gladly doon thise homicydes alle,
That in awayt liggen[10] to mordre men.
O false mordrer, lurking in thy den!
O newe Scariot,[11] newe Genilon![12]
False dissimilour,[13] O Greek Sinon,[14]
That broghtest Troye al-outrely[15] to sorwe!
O Chauntecleer, acursed be that morwe,
That thou into that yerd flough fro the bemes!
Thou were ful wel y-warned by thy dremes,
That thilke day was perilous to thee.
But what that God forwot[16] mot nedes be,
After the opinioun of certeyn clerkis.
Witnesse on[17] him, that any perfit clerk is,
That in scole is gret altercacioun
In this matere, and greet disputisoun,
And hath ben of an hundred thousand men.
But I ne can not bulte it to the bren,[18]
As can the holy doctour Augustyn,[19]
Or Boece,[20] or the bishop Bradwardyn,[21]
Whether that Goddes worthy forwiting
Streyneth[22] me nedely for to doon a thing.
(Nedely clepe I simple necessitee);
Or elles, if free choys be graunted me
To do that same thing, or do it noght,
Though God forwot it, er that it was wroght;
Or if his witing streyneth nevere a del
But by necessitee condicionel.[23]
I wol not han to do of swich matere;
My tale is of a cok, as ye may here,
That took his counseil of his wyf, with sorwe,
To walken in the yerd upon that morwe
That he had met the dreem, that I of tolde.
Wommennes counseils been ful ofte colde;[24]
Wommannes counseil broghte us first to wo,
And made Adam fro paradys to go,
Ther as he was ful mery, and wel at ese.
But for I noot,[25] to whom it mighte displese,
If I counseil of wommen wolde blame,
Passe over, for I seyde it in my game.[26]
Rede auctours, wher they trete of swich matere,
And what thay seyn of wommen ye may here.
Thise been the cokkes wordes, and nat myne;
I can noon harme of no womman divyne.
Faire in the sond, to bathe hire merily,
Lyth Pertelote, and all hir sustres by,
Agayn[27] the sonne; and Chauntecleer so free
Song merier than the mermayde in the see;
For Phisiologus[28] seith sikerly,
How that they singen wel and merily.
And so bifel that, as he caste his yë[29]
Among the wortes, on a boterflye,
He was war[30] of this fox that lay ful lowe.
No-thing ne liste him thanne for to crowe,
But cryde anon, "cok, cok," and up he sterte,
As man that was affrayed in his herte.
For naturelly a beest desyreth flee
Fro his contrarie,[31] if he may it see,
Though he never erst had seyn it with his yë.
This Chauntecleer, whan he gan him espye,[32]
He wolde han fled, but that the fox anon
Seyde, "Gentil sire, allas! wher wol ye gon?
Be ye affrayed of me that am your freend?
Now certes, I were worse than a feend,
If I to yow wolde harm or vileinye.
I am nat come your counseil for tespye;
But trewely, the cause of my cominge
Was only for to herkne how that ye singe.
For trewely ye have as mery a stevene,[33]
As eny aungel hath, that is in hevene;
Therwith ye han in musik more felinge
Than hadde Boece, or any that can singe.
My lord your fader (God his soule blesse!)
And eek your moder, of hir gentilesse,
Han in myn hous y-been, to my gret ese;[34]

[1] a thing especially worthy to be known
[2] affirm
[3] a romance of chivalry, obviously false
[4] coal black
[5] pre-ordained, as by Providence or Fate
[6] hedges
[7] burst
[8] herbs
[9] about eleven A.M.
[10] lie
[11] Judas Iscariot
[12] the traitor that caused the defeat of Charlemagne and the death of Roland
[13] deceiver
[14] designer of the wooden horse by which Troy was entered
[15] entirely
[16] foreknows
[17] by
[18] bolt it to the bran; i.e., thoroughly sift the question
[19] St. Augustine
[20] Boethius, a Roman statesman and philosopher of the fifth century, A.D.
[21] Chancellor at Oxford in the fourteenth century
[22] foreknowledge constrains
[23] except by conditional (as opposed to simple or absolute) necessity (the old question whether foreknowledge constitutes foreordination)
[24] baneful
[25] know not
[26] jest
[27] in
[28] Theobaldus's *Physiologus* or "Natural History of Twelve Animals"
[29] eyes
[30] aware
[31] opponent, foe
[32] to espy
[33] voice
[34] To my great pleasure; i.e., the fox had eaten them.

And certes, sire, ful fayn wolde I yow plese.
But for men speke of singing, I wol saye,
So mote I brouke[1] wel myn eyen tweye,
Save yow, I herde nevere man so singe,
As dide your fader in the morweninge;
Certes, it was of herte,[2] al that he song.
And for to make his voys the more strong,
He wolde so peyne him,[3] that with both his yën
He moste winke,[4] so loude he wolde cryen,
And stonden on his tiptoon therwithal,
And strecche forth his nekke long and smal.
And eek he was of swich discrecioun,
That ther nas no man in no regioun
That him in song or wisdom mighte passe.
I have weel rad in daun[5] Burnel the Asse,
Among his vers, how that ther was a cok,
For that a prestes sone yaf him a knok
Upon his leg, whyl he was young and nyce,[6]
He made him for to lese his benefyce.[7]
But certeyn, ther nis no comparisoun
Bitwix the wisdom and discrecioun
Of your fader, and of his subtiltee.
Now singeth, sire, for seinte charitee,
Let se, conne ye your fader countrefete?"
This Chauntecleer his winges gan to bete,
As man that coude his tresoun nat espye,
So was he ravisshed with his flaterye.
Allas! ye lordes, many a fals flatour[8]
Is in your courtes, and many a losengeour,[9]
That plesen yow wel more, by my feith,
Than he that soothfastnesse unto yow seith.
Redeth Ecclesiaste[10] of flaterye;
Beth war, ye lordes, of hir trecherye.
This Chauntecleer stood hye up-on his toos,
Strecching his nekke, and held his eyen cloos,
And gan to crowe loude for the nones;[11]
And daun Russel[12] the foxe sterte up at ones,
And by the gargat[13] hente Chauntecleer,
And on his bak toward the wode him beer,[14]
For yet ne was ther no man that him sewed.[15]
O destinee, that mayst nat ben eschewed!
Allas, that Chauntecleer fleigh fro the bemes!
Allas, his wyf ne roghte[16] nat of dremes!
And on a Friday fil al this meschaunce.
O Venus, that art goddesse of plesaunce,
Sin that thy servant was this Chauntecleer,

. . . .

Why woldestow suffre him on thy day to dye?
O Gaufred, dere mayster soverayn,[17]
That, whan thy worthy king Richard was slayn
With shot, compleynedest his deth so sore,
Why ne hadde I now thy sentence[18] and thy lore,
The Friday for to chide, as diden ye?
(For on a Friday soothly slayn was he.)
Than wolde I shewe yow how that I coude pleyne[19]
For Chauntecleres drede, and for his peyne.
Certes, swich cry ne lamentacioun
Was nevere of ladies maad, whan Ilioun
Was wonne, and Pirrus[20] with his streite[21] swerd,
Whan he hadde hent king Priam by the berd,
And slayn him (as saith us *Eneydos*[22]),
As maden alle the hennes in the clos,[23]
Whan they had seyn of Chauntecleer the sighte.
But sovereynly[24] dame Pertelote shrighte[25]
Ful louder than dide Hasdrubales[26] wyf,
Whan that hir housbond hadde lost his lyf,
And that the Romayns hadde brend Cartage,
She was so ful of torment and of rage,
That wilfully into the fyr she sterte,[27]
And brende[28] hir-selven with a stedfast herte.
O woful hennes, right so cryden ye,
As, whan that Nero brende the citee
Of Rome, cryden senatoures wyves,
For that hir housbondes losten alle hir lyves;
Withouten gilt[29] this Nero hath hem slayn.
Now wol I torne to my tale agayn:
This sely[30] widwe, and eek hir doghtres two,
Herden thise hennes crye and maken wo,
And out at dores sterten thay anoon,
And syen the fox toward the grove goon,
And bar upon his bak the cok away;
And cryden, "Out! harrow! and weylaway!
Ha, ha, the fox!" and after him they ran,
And eek with staves many another man;
Ran Colle our dogge, and Talbot,[31] and Gerland,[31]
And Malkin,[32] with a distaf in hir hand;
Ran cow and calf, and eek the verray hogges
So were they fered for berking of the dogges
And shouting of the men and wimmen eke,
They ronne so, hem thoughte hir herte breke.
They yelleden as feendes doon in helle;
The dokes cryden as men wolde hem quelle;[33]

1 have the use of
2 from his heart
3 strain himself
4 He must shut both eyes.
5 lord (This was an old story.)
6 foolish
7 i.e., by crowing so late that the youth did not awake in time
8 flatterer
9 deceiver
10 *Ecclesiasticus* xii, 10
11 occasion
12 As the ass was called Burnel because he is brown, so the fox was called Russell because he is (usually) red.
13 throat
14 bore
15 followed
16 did not care for
17 Chaucer is making fun of an old writer, Geoffrey de Vinsauf.
18 power of expression
19 complain
20 Pyrrhus
21 drawn
22 the *Aeneid*
23 enclosure
24 surpassingly
25 shrieked
26 a king of Carthage
27 leaped
28 burned
29 guilt
30 pious
31 a dog (?)
32 a servant girl
33 kill

The gees for fere flowen over the trees;
Out of the hyve cam the swarm of bees;
So hidous was the noyse, a! *benedicite!*[1]
Certes, he Iakke Straw,[2] and his meynee,[3]
Ne maden nevere shoutes half so shrille,
Whan that they wolden any Fleming kille,
As thilke day was maad upon the fox.
Of bras thay broghten bemes,[4] and of box,[5]
Of horn, of boon, in whiche they blewe and pouped,[6]
And therwithal thay shryked and they houped;[7]
It semed as that hevene sholde falle.
Now, gode men, I pray yow herkneth alle!
Lo, how fortune turneth sodeinly
The hope and pryde eek of hir enemy!
This cok, that lay upon the foxes bak,
In al his drede, un-to the fox he spak,
And seyde, "sire, if that I were as ye,
Yet sholde I seyn (as wis[8] God helpe me),
Turneth agayn, ye proude cherles alle!
A verray pestilence up-on yow falle!
Now am I come un-to this wodes syde,
Maugree[9] your heed, the cok shal heer abyde;
I wol him ete in feith, and that anon."
The fox answerde, "In feith, it shal be don,"
And as he spak that word, al sodeinly
This cok brak from his mouth deliverly,[10]
And heighe up-on a tree he fleigh anon.
And whan the fox saugh that he was y-gon,
"Allas!" quod he, "O Chauntecleer, allas!
I have to yow," quod he, "y-doon trespas!
In-as-muche as I maked yow aferd,
Whan I yow hente, and broghte out of the yerd;
But, sire, I dide it in no wikke[11] entente;
Com doun, and I shal telle yow what I mente.
I shal seye sooth to yow, God help me so."
"Nay, than," quod he, "I shrewe[12] us bothe two,
And first I shrewe my-self, bothe blood and bones,
If thou bigyle me ofter than ones.
Thou shalt namore, thurgh thy flaterye
Do[13] me to singe and winke with myn yë.
For he that winketh, whan he sholde see,
Al wilfully, God lat him never thee!"[14]
"Nay," quod the fox, "but God yive him meschaunce,
That is so undiscreet of governaunce,
That iangleth[15] whan he sholde holde his pees."
Lo, swich it is for to be recchelees,
And necligent, and truste on flaterye.
But ye that holden this tale a folye,
As of a fox, or of a cok and hen,
Taketh the moralitee therof, good men.
For seint Paul seith, that al that writen is,
To our doctryne[16] it is y-write, y-wis.
Taketh the fruyt, and lat the chaf be stille.
Now, gode God, if that it be thy wille,
As seith my lord, so make us alle good men;
And bringe us to his heighe blisse. Amen.[17]

c. 1386

[1] bless ye
[2] Jack Straw, leader with Wat Tyler in the Peasants' Revolt of 1381; said to have killed "many F l e m i n g s," i.e., Flemish weavers in England, competitors in trade.
[3] followers
[4] horns
[5] wood
[6] made a noise
[7] whooped
[8] certainly
[9] in spite of
[10] quickly
[11] wicked
[12] curse
[13] cause
[14] prosper

FROM THE LEGEND OF GOOD WOMEN

THE STORY OF THISBE OF BABYLON, MARTYR

Incipit Legende Tesba Babilon, Martiris

At Babiloyne whilom fil it[18] thus—
The whiche toun the queene Semyramus[19]
Leet dichen al about, and walles make[20]
Ful hye, of harde tiles wel y-bake:
There were dwellynge in this noble toune
Two lordes, which that were of grete renoune,
And woneden[21] so neigh upon a grene,
That ther nas but a stoon wal hem betwene,
As ofte in grette tounes is the wone.
And sooth to seyn, that o man had a sone,
Of al that londe oon of the lustieste;
That other had a doghtre, the faireste
That esteward in the worlde was tho[22] dwellynge.
The name of everyche[23] gan to other sprynge,[24]
By wommen that were neyghebores aboute;
For in that contre yit, withouten doute,
Máydens ben y-kept for jelousye
Ful streyte,[25] leste they diden somme folye.
This yonge man was cleped Piramus,
And Tesbe highte the maide—Naso[26] seith thus.
And thus by reporte was hir name y-shove,[27]
That as they wex in age, wex hir love.
And certeyn, as by reson of hir age,
Ther myghte have ben betwex hem marïage,
But that hir fadres nold[28] it not assente,
And both in love y-like soore they brente,[29]

[15] chatters
[16] instruction
[17] A sort of benediction; the "my lord" refers probably to the Archbishop of Canterbury.
[18] It happened.
[19] Semiramis, wife of Ninus, the mythical king and founder of Nineveh
[20] caused to be surrounded by ditches and walls
[21] dwelt (*wone* in l. 714 =custom)
[22] then
[23] each
[24] came to the ears of the other
[25] strictly
[26] Ovid (Publius Ovidius Naso) in *Metamorphoses* iv 55, ff., whence this story is taken
[27] Their names were brought forward (literally *pushed*).
[28] would not
[29] burned

That noon of all hir frendes myghte it lette.[1]
But prevely[2] somtyme yit they mette
By sleight, and spoken somme of hir desire,
As wre the glede[3] and hotter is the fire;
Forbeede a love, and it is ten so woode.[4]
 This wal, which that betwixe hem bothe stoode,
Was cloven a-two, right fro the toppe adoun,
Of olde tyme, of his foundacioun.
But yit this clyfte was so narwe and lite[5]
It was nat seene, deere ynogh a myte;[6]
But what is that that love kannat espye?
Ye lovers two, if that I shal nat lye,
Ye founden first this litel narwe clifte,
And with a soune as softe as any shryfte,[7]
They leete hir wordes thurgh the clifte pace,
And tolden, while they stoden in the place,
Al hire compleynt of love, and al hire wo,
At every tyme whan they dorste so.
Upon the o syde of the walle stood he,
And on that other syde stood Tesbe,
The swoote soun of other to receyve.
 And thus here[8] wardeyn wolde they disceyve,
And every day this walle they wolde threete,[9]
And wisshe to God that it were doun y-bete.
Thus wolde they seyn: "Allas, thou wikked walle!
Thurgh thyn envye thow us lettest[10] alle!
Why nyltow cleve,[11] or fallen al a-two?
Or at the leeste, but thow wouldest so,[12]
Yit woldestow but ones let us meete,
Or ones that we myghte kyssen sweete,
Than were we covered[13] of oure cares colde.
But natheles, yit be we to thee holde,[14]
In as muche as thou suffrest for to goon
Our wordes thurgh thy lyme and eke thy stoon;
Yet oghte we with the ben wel apayede."[15]
 And whan these idel wordes weren sayde,
The colde walle they wolden kysse of stoon,
And take hir leve, and forth they wolden goon.
And this was gladly in the evetyde,
Or wonder erly, lest men it espyede.
And longe tyme they wroght in this manere,
Til on a day, whan Phebus[16] gan to clere[17]—
Aurora with the stremes of hire hete[18]
Had dried uppe the dewe of herbes wete—
Unto this clyfte, as it was wont to be,
Come Piramus, and after come Tesbe.

[1] prevent
[2] secretly
[3] cover the glowing coal
[4] ten times as passionate
[5] little
[6] scarcely at all
[7] confession
[8] their
[9] threaten
[10] hinderest
[11] wilt thou not cleave in two
[12] if thou wouldest not do that
[13] recovered
[14] beholden
[15] pleased
[16] Apollo, the sun-god
[17] shine clearly
[18] heat

And plighten trouthe[19] fully in here faye,[20]
That ilke same nyght to steele awaye,
And to begile hire wardeyns everychone,
And forth out of the citee for to gone.
And, for the feeldes ben so broode and wide,
Fór to meete in o place at o tyde
They sette markes, hire metyng sholde bee
Ther[21] kyng Nynus was graven,[22] under a tree—
For olde payens,[23] that ydóles heriede,[24]
Useden tho in feeldes to ben beriede[25]—
And faste by his grave was a welle.
And, shortly of this tale for to telle,
This covenaunt was affermed wonder faste,
And longe hem thoghte that the sonne laste,
That it nere goon[26] under the see adoun.
 This Tesbe hath so greete affeccioun,
And so grete lykynge Piramus to see,
That whan she seigh hire tyme myghte bee,
At nyght she stale[27] awey ful prevely,
With hire face y-wympled subtilly.
For al hire frendes, for to save hire trouthe,
She hath forsake; allas, and that is routhe,[28]
That ever woman wolde be so trewe
To trusten man, but she the bet hym knewe![29]
 And to the tree she goth a ful goode paas,[30]
For love made hir so hardy in this caas;
And by the welle adoun she gan hir dresse,[31]
Allas! than comith a wilde leonesse
Out of the woode, withouten more arreste,[32]
With blody mouth, of strangelynge of a beste,
To drynken of the welle ther as she sat.
And whan that Tesbe had espyed that,
She ryst[33] hir up, with a ful drery herte,
And in a cave with dredful foot she sterte,
For by the moone she saugh it wel withalle.
And as she ranne, hir wympel leet she falle,
And tooke noon hede, so sore she was awhaped,[34]
And eke so glade that she was escaped;
And ther she sytte, and darketh[35] wonder stille.
Whan that this lyonesse hath dronke hire fille,
Aboute the welle gan she for to wynde,[36]
And ryght anon the wympil gan she fynde,
And with hir blody mouth it al to-rente.
Whan this was don, no lenger she ne stente,[37]
But to the woode hir wey than hath she nome.[38]
 And at the laste this Piramus is come,
But al to longe, allas, at home was hee!

[19] troth
[20] faith
[21] where
[22] buried
[23] pagans
[24] worshiped
[25] then used to be buried in fields
[26] were not gone
[27] stole
[28] pity
[29] unless she knew him better
[30] quickly
[31] took her station
[32] delay
[33] riseth
[34] amazed
[35] lies hid
[36] roam
[37] stopped
[38] taken

The moone shone, men myghte wel y-see,
And in his wey, as that he come ful faste,
His eyen to the grounde adoun he caste;
And in the sonde as he behelde adoun,[1]
He seigh the steppes broode of a lyoun;
And in his herte he sodeynly agroos,[2]
And pale he wex, therwith his heer aroos,
And nere he come, and founde the wympel torne.
"Allas," quod he, "the day that I was borne!
This o nyght wol us lovers bothe slee!
How shulde I axen mercy of Tesbee,
Whan I am he that have yow slayne, allas?
My byddyng hath i-slayn yow in this caas!
Allas, to bidde a woman goon by nyghte
In place ther as[3] peril fallen myghte!
And I so slowe! allas, I ne hadde be[4]
Here in this place, a furlong wey or ye![5]
Now what lyon that be in this foreste,
My body mote he renten,[6] or what beste
That wilde is, gnawen mote he now my herte!"
And with that worde he to the wympel sterte,
And kiste it ofte, and wepte on it ful sore;
And seyde, "Wympel, allas! ther nys no more,[7]
But thou shalt feele as wel the blode of me,
As thou hast felt the bledynge of Tesbe."
And with that worde he smot hym to the herte;
The blood out of the wounde as brode sterte
As water, whan the conduyte broken is.
Now Tesbe, which that wyste[8] nat of this,
But syttyng in hire drede, she thoghte thus:
"If it so falle that my Piramus
Be comen hider, and may me nat y-fynde,
He may me holden fals, and eke unkynde."
And oute she comith, and after hym gan espien
Bóthe with hire herte and with hire eyen;
And thoghte, "I wol him tellen of my drede,
Bothe of the lyonesse and al my dede."
And at the laste hire love than hath she founde,
Bétynge with his helis[9] on the grounde,
Al blody; and therwithal abak she sterte,
And lyke the wawes[10] quappe[11] gan hir herte,
And pale as boxe[12] she wax, and in a throwe[13]
Avised hir,[14] and gan him wel to knowe,
That it was Piramus, hire herte dere.
Who koude write which a dedely chere
Hath Tesbe now? and how hire heere[15] she rente?
And how she gan hir-selve to turmente?
And how she lyth and swowneth on the grounde?
And how she wepe of teres ful his wounde?
How medleth[16] she his blood with hir compleynte?
How with his blood hir-selven gan she peynte?
How clippeth[17] she the dede corps? allas!
How doth this woful Tesbe in this cas?
How kysseth she his frosty mouthe so colde?
"Who hath don this? and who hath ben so bolde
To sleen my leefe? O speke, Piramus!
I am thy Tesbe, that thee calleth thus!"
And therwithal she lyfteth up his heed.
This woful man, that was nat fully deed,
whan that he herde the name of Tesbe crien,[18]
On hire he caste his hevy dedely eyen,
And doun agayn, and yeldeth up the goste.
Tesbe rist uppe, withouten noyse or boste,[19]
And saugh hir wympel and his empty shethe,
And eke his swerde, that him hath don to dethe.
Than spake she thus: "Thy woful hande," quod she,
"Is strong ynogh in swiche a werke to me;
For love shal me yive strengthe and hardynesse,
To make my wounde large ynogh, I gesse.
I wole the[20] folowen ded, and I wol be
Felawe and cause eke of thy deeth," quod she.
"And thogh that nothing save the deth only
Myghte the fro me departe[21] trewely,
Thou shal no more departe now fro me
Than fro the deth, for I wol go with the.
"And now, ye wrecched jelouse fadres oure,
Wé, that weren whilome children youre,
We prayen yow, withouten more envye,
That in o grave i-fere[22] we moten lye,
Syn love hath broght us to this pitouse ende.
And ryghtwis[23] God to every lover sende,
That loveth trewely, more prosperite
Than ever hadde Piramus and Tesbe.
And let no gentile woman hire assure,
To putten hire in swiche an áventure.
But God forbede but a woman kan
Ben also trewe and lovynge as a man,
And for my parte I shal anon it kythe!"[24]
And with that worde his swerde she took as swithe,[25]
That warme was of hire loves blood, and hote,
And to the herte she hire-selven smote.
And thus are Tesbe and Piramus ago.[26]

[1] looked down
[2] shuddered
[3] where
[4] that I had not been
[5] a short time before you
[6] may he rend
[7] Nothing remains.
[8] who knew
[9] i.e., still pulsating
[10] waves
[11] flutter
[12] box-wood
[13] moment
[14] considered
[15] hair
[16] mingleth
[17] embraceth
[18] spoken
[19] outcry
[20] thee
[21] separate
[22] together
[23] righteous
[24] show
[25] quickly
[26] gone

Of trewe men I fynde but fewe mo
In al my bookes, save this Piramus,
And therfore have I spoken of hym thus
For it is deyntee to us men to fynde
A man that kan in love be trewe and kynde.
Here may ye seen, what lover so he be,
A woman dar and kan as wel as he.

c. 1385

THE COMPLEYNT OF CHAUCER TO HIS PURSE

To you, my purse, and to noon other wyght
Compleyne I, for ye be my lady dere!
I am so sorry now that ye been light;
For, certes, but ye make me hevy chere,[1]
Me were as leef be leyd upon my bere,[2]
For whiche unto your mercy thus I crye—
Beth[3] hevy ageyn, or elles mot[4] I dye!

Now voucheth sauf[5] this day, or hit[6] be nyght,
That I of you the blisful soun[7] may here,[8]
Or see your colour lyk the sonne bright,
That of yelownesse hadde never pere.[9]
Ye be my lyf! ye be myn hertes stere![10]
Quene of comfort and of good companye!
Beth hevy ageyn, or elles mot I dye!

Now, purse, that be to me my lyves light
And saveour, as doun[11] in this worlde here,
Out of this toun help me throgh your myght,
Syn[12] that ye wole not been my tresorere;[13]
For I am shave as nye as is a frere.[14]
But yet I pray unto your curtesye,
Beth hevy ageyn, or elles mot I dye!

L'Envoye De Chaucer

O conquerour of Brutes Albioun,[15]
Which that by lyne and free eleccioun
Ben verray kyng, this song to you I sende,
And ye that mowen[16] al myn harm amende,
Have mynde upon my supplicacioun!

1399

[1] unless you put on for me a heavy look (with a play on the word *heavy,* which usually in this connection means *sad*)
[2] I would as soon be laid upon my bier
[3] be
[4] must
[5] vouchsafe, grant
[6] before it
[7] sound
[8] hear
[9] peer
[10] helm, guide
[11] down
[12] since
[13] treasurer
[14] shaven as close as a friar (terribly hard pinched)
[15] Henry IV had just been made king. Brutus was a legendary king of England (Albion).
[16] can

From THE TRAVELS OF SIR JOHN MANDEVILLE

This book, which was extremely popular in its day, was accepted then and long after in good faith. We now know it to be mainly a compilation from other books of travel, with additions from almost every possible work of reference—the ancient account of the first crusade by Albert of Aix, eleventh century; the recent itinerary of William of Boldense, 1336; pilgrimage books of the twelfth and thirteenth centuries; the travels of the Franciscan missionary Odoric of Pordenone, 1330; the *Golden Legend;* the *Trésor* of Brunetto Latini; the *Speculum* of Vincent de Beauvais; Caesar, Pliny—ingeniously passed off as a record of original experience. "Mandeville" is probably a fictitious name. The oldest MS. is in French, dated 1371. The English translation from which our selections are taken was made after 1400, and therefore represents the language of the generation succeeding Chaucer. The spelling is modernized.

The work testifies to a wonderful memory, a vast knowledge of current and preceding literature, and genius in combining the materials with such verisimilitude that it was five centuries before any general doubt as to its authenticity or the personality of the author arose. Mandeville appealed to an interest in distant lands and people; he had skillful devices for creating a feeling of reality; and he was familiar with the most recent knowledge of his time. The known facts are: that the author, or authors, of the travels was not an Englishman; that he never visited the places described; that he was a good linguist, and had access to a good library; and that the vast knowledge of literature he displays is hardly compatible with so much travel. The work is the oldest book of English prose that was primarily written and read for entertainment as well as instruction.

Mandeville has been discussed by John Fyvie, *Some Literary Eccentrics,* 1906: P. Hamelius, "Travels of Sir John Mandeville," *Quar. R.* 227:331-52; C. R. Eastman, "History of Natural Science," *Science,* n. s. 24:822-3.

Prologue

Forasmuch as the land beyond the sea, that is to say the Holy Land, that men call the Land of Promission or of Behest,[17] passing all other lands, is the most worthy land, most excellent, and lady and sovereign of all other lands, and is blessed and hallowed of the precious body and blood of our Lord Jesus Christ; in the which land it liked him to take flesh and blood of the Virgin Mary, to environ[18] that holy land with his blessed feet; . . . . and forasmuch as it is long time passed that there was no general passage ne voyage

[17] Land of Promise
[18] go about

over the sea; and many men desire for to hear speak of the Holy Land, and have thereof great solace and comfort;—I, John Mandeville, Knight, albeit I be not worthy, that was born in England, in the town of St. Albans, and passed the sea in the year of our Lord Jesu Christ, 1322, in the day of St. Michael; and hitherto have been long time over the sea, and have seen and gone through many diverse lands, and many provinces and kingdoms and isles; and have passed throughout Turkey, Armenia the little and the great; through Tartary, Persia, Syria, Arabia, Egypt the high and the low; through Libya, Chaldea, and a great part of Ethiopia; through Amazonia, Ind the less and the more,[1] a great part; and throughout many other isles that be about Ind, where dwell many diverse folks, and of diverse manners and laws, and of diverse shapes of men; . . . . I shall tell the way that they shall hold thither. For I have oftentimes passed and ridden that way, with good company of many lords. God be thanked!

And ye shall understand that I have put this book out of Latin into French, and translated it again out of French into English, that every man of my nation may understand it. But lords and knights and other noble and worthy men that con[2] Latin but little, and have been beyond the sea, know and understand if I say truth or no, and if I err in devising,[3] for forgetting or else, that they may redress it and amend it. For things passed out of long time from a man's mind or from his sight, turn soon into forgetting; because that[4] the mind of man ne may not be comprehended ne withholden, for the frailty of mankind.[5]

Of the Cross . . . . of our Lord Jesu Christ

At Constantinople is the cross of our Lord Jesu Christ, and his coat without seams, that is clept *tunica inconsutilis,*[6] and the sponge, and the reed, of the which the Jews gave our Lord eisel[7] and gall, in[8] the cross. And there is one of the nails that Christ was nailed with on the cross. And some men trow that half the cross, that Christ was done on, be in Cyprus, in an abbey of monks, that men call the Hill of the Holy Cross; but it is not so. For that cross, that is in Cyprus, is the cross in the which Dismas the good thief was hanged on. But all men know not that; and that is evil y-done.[9] For for profit of the offering they say that it is the cross of our Lord Jesu Christ.

And ye shall understand that the cross of our Lord was made of four manner of trees, as it is contained in this verse—*In cruce fit palma, cedrus, cypressus, oliva.* For that piece that went upright from the earth to the head was of cypress; and the piece that went overthwart, to the which his hands were nailed, was of palm; and the stock, that stood within the earth, in the which was made the mortise, was of cedar; and the table above his head, that was a foot and an half long, on the which the title was written in Hebrew, Greek, and Latin, that was of olive.

. . . . . .

And the Christian men, that dwell beyond the sea, in Greece, say that the tree of the cross, that we call cypress, was of that tree that Adam ate the apple off; and that find they written. And they say also that their scripture saith that Adam was sick, and said to his son Seth, that he should go to the angel that kept Paradise, that he would send him oil of mercy, for to anoint with his members, that he might have health. And Seth went. But the angel would not let him come in; but said to him, that he might not have the oil of mercy. But he took him three grains of the same tree that his father ate the apple off; and bade him, as soon as his father was dead, that he should put these three grains under his tongue, and grave[10] him so; and so he did. And of these three grains sprang a tree, as the angel said that it should, and bare a fruit, through the which fruit Adam should be saved. And when Seth came again, he found his father near dead. And when he was dead, he did with the grains as the angel bade him; of the which sprung three trees, of the which the cross was made, that bare good fruit and blessed, our Lord Jesu Christ; through whom Adam and all that come of him should be saved and delivered from dread of death without end, but[11] it be their own default. . . . .

. . . . How Roses came first into the World

. . . . And a little from Hebron is the mount of Mamre, of the which the valley taketh his

[1] Mandeville here couples the fabulous land of the Amazons with the actual Lesser and Greater India.

[2] know [3] relating [4] because

[5] Possibly "Sir John" means to give the reader a sly hint here that it is also one of the frailties of mankind to tell big stories.

[6] called "the tunic unsewn"

[7] vinegar

[8] on

[9] old past participle

[10] bury

[11] unless

name. And there is a tree of oak, that the Saracens clepe[1] *Dirpe*, that is of Abraham's time; the which men clepe the Dry Tree. And they say that it hath been there since the beginning of the world, and was some-time green and bare leaves, unto the time that our Lord died on the cross, and then it dried; and so did all the trees that were then in the world. And some say, by their prophecies, that a lord, a prince of the west side of the world, shall win the Land of Promission, that is the Holy Land, with help of Christian men, and he shall do sing[2] a mass under that dry tree; and then the tree shall wax green and bear both fruit and leaves, and through that miracle many Jews and Saracens shall be turned to Christian faith; and therefore they do great worship thereto, and keep it full busily.[3] And, albeit so, that it be dry, nathless[4] yet he[5] beareth great virtue, for certainly he that hath a little thereof upon him, it healeth him of the falling evil, and his horse shall not be afoundered. And many other virtues it hath; wherefore men hold it full precious.

From Hebron men go to Bethlehem in half a day, for it is but five mile; and it is full fair way, by plains and woods full delectable. Bethlehem is a little city, long and narrow and well walled, and in each side enclosed with good ditches; and it was wont to be clept Ephrata, as holy writ saith, *Ecce, audivimus eum in Ephrata*, that is to say, "Lo, we heard him in Ephrata." And toward the east end of the city is a full fair church and a gracious, and it hath many towers, pinnacles, and corners, full strong and curiously made; and within that church be forty-four pillars of marble, great and fair.

And between the city and the church is the field *Floridus*, that is to say, the "field flourished."[6] Forasmuch as a fair maiden was blamed with wrong, and slandered; for which cause she was demned to death, and to be burnt in that place, to the which she was led. And as the fire began to burn about her, she made her prayers to our Lord, that as wisely[7] as she was not guilty of that sin, that he would help her and make it to be known to all men, of his merciful grace. And when she had thus said, she entered into the fire, and anon was the fire quenched and out; and the brands that were burning became red rose-trees, and the brands that were not kindled became white rose-trees, full of roses. And these were the first rose-trees and roses, both white and red, that ever any man saw; and thus was this maiden saved by the grace of God. And therefore is that field clept the field of God flourished, for it was full of roses. . . . .

[1] call
[2] cause to be sung
[3] very attentively
[4] nevertheless
[5] it
[6] in flower
[7] certainly

. . . How the Earth and Sea be of round Form and Shape, by proof of the Star that is clept Antarctic, that is fixed in the South[8]

. . . . In that land, ne in many other beyond that, no man may see the Star Transmontane, that is clept the Star of the Sea, that is unmovable and that is toward the north, that we clepe the Lode-star. But men see another star, the contrary to him, that is toward the south, that is clept Antarctic. And right as the ship-men take their advice here and govern them by the Lode-star, right so do the men beyond those parts by the star of the south, the which star appeareth not to us. And this star that is toward the north, that we clepe the Lode-star, ne appeareth not to them. For which cause men may well perceive that the land and the sea be of round shape and form; for the part of the firmament showeth in one country that showeth not in another country. And men may well prove by experience and subtle compassment of wit, that if a man found passages by ships that would go to search the world, men might go by ship all about the world and above and beneath.

The which thing I prove thus after that I have seen. For I have been toward the parts of Brabant,[9] and beholden the Astrolabe that the star that is clept the Transmontane is fifty-three degrees high; and more farther in Almayne[10] and Bohemia it hath fifty-eight degrees; and more farther toward the parts septentrional[11] it is sixty-two degrees of height and certain minutes; for I myself have measured it by the Astrolabe. Now shall ye know, that against the Transmontane is the tother star that is clept Antarctic, as I have said before. And those two stars ne move never, and by them turneth all the firmament right as doth a wheel that turneth by his axle-tree. So that those stars bear the firmament in two equal parts, so that it hath as much above as it hath beneath. After this I have gone toward the parts meridional, that is, toward the south, and I have found that in Libya men see first the star Antarctic. And so far I have gone more farther in those countries, that I have

[8] an example of the speculations that were rife long before Columbus undertook his voyage
[9] Holland
[10] Germany
[11] north

found that star more high; so that toward the High Libya it is eighteen degrees of height and certain minutes (of the which sixty minutes make a degree). After going by sea and by land toward this country of that I have spoken, and to other isles and lands beyond that country, I have found the Star Antarctic of thirty-three degrees of height and more minutes. And if I had had company and shipping for to go more beyond, I trow well, in certain, that we should have seen all the roundness of the firmament all about.

. . . .

And wit well, that, after that[1] I may perceive and comprehend, the lands of Prester John,[2] Emperor of Ind, be under us. For in going from Scotland or from England toward Jerusalem men go upward always. For our land is in the low part of the earth toward the west, and the land of Prester John is in the low part of the earth toward the east. And they have there the day when we have the night; and also, high to the contrary, they have the night when we have the day. For the earth and the sea be of round form and shape, as I have said before; and that that men go upward to one coast,[3] men go downward to another coast.

Also ye have heard me say that Jerusalem is in the midst of the world. And that may men prove, and show there by a spear, that is pight[4] into the earth, upon the hour of midday, when it is equinox, that showeth no shadow on no side. And that it should be in the midst of the world, David witnesseth it in the Psalter, where he saith, *Deus operatus est salutem in medio terrae.*[5] Then, they that part from those parts of the west for to go toward Jerusalem, as many journeys[6] as they go upward for to go thither, in as many journeys may they go from Jerusalem unto other confines of the superficialty of the earth beyond. And when men go beyond those journeys toward Ind and to the foreign isles, all is environing[7] the roundness of the earth and of the sea under our countries on this half.

And therefore hath it befallen many times of one thing that I have heard counted[8] when I was young, how a worthy man departed sometime from our countries for to go search the world. And so he passed Ind and the isles beyond Ind, where be more than 5000 isles. And so long he went by sea and land, and so environed the world by many seasons, that he found an isle where he heard speak his own language, calling an oxen in the plough such words as men speak to beasts in his own country; whereof he had great marvel, for he knew not how it might be. But I say that he had gone so long by land and by sea, that he had environed all the earth; that he was come again environing, that is to say, going about, unto his own marches,[9] and if he would have passed farther, he would have found his country and his own knowledge. But he turned again from thence, from whence he was come from. And so he lost much painful labor, as himself said a great while after that he was come home. For it befell after, that he went into Norway. And there tempest of the sea took him, and he arrived in an isle. And when he was in that isle, he knew well that it was the isle where he had heard speak his own language before, and the calling of oxen at the plow; and that was possible thing.

But now it seemeth to simple men unlearned, that men ne may not go under the earth, and also that men should fall toward the heaven from under. But that may not be, upon less than[10] we may fall toward heaven from the earth where we be. For from what part of the earth that men dwell, either above or beneath, it seemeth always to them that dwell that they go more right than any other folk. And right as it seemeth to us that they be under us, right so it seemeth to them that we be under them. For if a man might fall from the earth unto the firmament, by greater reason the earth and the sea that be so great and so heavy should fall to the firmament; but that may not be, and therefore saith our Lord God, *Non timeas me, qui suspendi terram ex nihilo!*[11]

And albeit that it be possible thing that men may so environ all the world, natheless, of a thousand persons, one ne might not happen to return into his country. For the greatness of the earth and of the sea, men may go by a thousand and a thousand other ways, that no man could ready him[12] perfectly toward the parts that he came from, but if it were by adventure and hap, or by the grace of God. For the earth is full large and full great, and holds in roundness and about environ,[13] by above and by beneath, 20,425 miles, after the opinion of old wise astronomers; and their sayings I

[1] and know well that, according to what
[2] prester is "presbyter," an elder or priest. This fabulous Christian monarch was supposed to have conquered the Saracens in the East.
[3] and that as men go upward to one region
[4] set
[5] The Lord wrought salvation in the midst of the earth. (See *Psalms,* lxxiv, 12.)
[6] days' travel
[7] they are all the while encircling
[8] recounted
[9] borders
[10] unless
[11] Have no fear of me, who hanged the earth upon nothing. (See *Job,* xxvi, 7.)
[12] direct himself
[13] approximately

reprove nought. But, after my little wit, it seemeth me, saving their reverence, that it is more.

And for to have better understanding I say thus. Be there imagined a figure that hath a great compass. And, about the point of the great compass that is clept the center, be made another little compass. Then after, be the great compass devised by lines in many parts, and that all the lines meet at the center. So that in as many parts as the great compass shall be departed,[1] in as many shall be departed the little, that is about the centre, albeit that the space be less. Now then, be the great compass represented for the firmament, and the little compass represented for the earth. Now then, the firmament is devised by astronomers in twelve signs, and every sign is devised in thirty degrees; that is, 360 degrees that the firmament hath above. Also, be the earth devised in as many parts as the firmament, and let every part answer to a degree of the firmament. And wit it well, that, after the authors of astronomy, 700 furlongs of earth answer to a degree of the firmament, and those be eighty-seven miles and four furlongs. Now be that here multiplied by 360 sithes,[2] and then they be 31,500 miles every[3] of eight furlongs, after[4] miles of our country. So much hath the earth in roundness and of height environ, after mine opinion and mine understanding. . . . .

. . . . Of the Trees that Bear Meal, Honey, Wine, and Venom; and of Other Marvels

. . . . After that isle, in going by sea, men find another isle, good and great, that men clepe Pathen,[5] that is a great kingdom full of fair cities and full of towns. In that land grow trees that grow meal, whereof men make good bread and white and of good savor; and it seemeth as it were of wheat, but it is not allinges[6] of such savor. And there be other trees that bear honey good and sweet, and other trees that bear venom, against the which there is no medicine but one; and that is to take their proper[7] leaves and stamp them and temper them with water and then drink it, and else he shall die; for triacle[8] will not avail, ne none other medicine. Of this venom the Jews had let seek of[9] one of their friends for to empoison all Christianity, as I have heard them say in their confession before their dying; but thanked be Almighty God! they failed of their purpose; but always they[10] make great mortality of people. And other trees there be also that bear wine of noble sentiment.[11] And if you like to hear how the meal cometh out of the trees I shall say you. Men hew the trees with an hatchet, all about the foot of the tree, till that the bark be parted in many parts, and then cometh out thereof a thick liquor, the which they receive in vessels, and dry it at the heat of the sun; and then they have it to a mill to grind and it becometh fair meal and white.[12] And the honey and the wine and the venom be drawn out of other trees in the same manner, and put in vessels for to keep.

In that isle is a dead sea, that is a lake that hath no ground;[13] and if anything fall into that lake it shall never come up again. In that lake grow reeds, that be canes, that they clepe Thaby,[14] that be thirty fathoms long; and of these canes men make fair houses. And there be other canes that be not so long, that grow near the land and have so long roots that endure well a four quarters[15] of a furlong or more; and at the knots of those roots men find precious stones that have great virtues. And he that beareth any of them upon him, iron ne steel may not hurt him, ne draw no blood upon him; and therefore, they that have those stones upon them fight full hardily both upon sea and land, for men may not harm them on no part. And therefore, they that know the manner, and shall fight with them, they shoot to them arrows and quarrels without iron or steel, and so they hurt them and slay them. And also of those canes they make houses and ships and other things, as we have here, making houses and ships of oak or of any other trees. And deem no man that I say it but for a trifle, for I have seen of the canes with mine own eyes, full many times, lying upon the river of that lake, of the which twenty of our fellows ne might not lift up ne bear one to the earth. . . . .

. . . . [Of the] Paradise Terrestrial

. . . . And beyond the land and the isles and the deserts of Prester John's lordship, in going straight toward the east, men find nothing but mountains and rocks, full great. And there is the dark region, where no man may see, neither by day ne by night, as they of the country say.

[1] divided
[2] times
[3] each
[4] according to
[5] Some region of the East Indies; the island described just before this is Java. But India and China are themselves spoken of as islands.
[6] altogether
[7] own
[8] treacle (molasses) in ancient times supposed to be a universal antidote
[9] had caused to be sought by
[10] i.e., the venomous trees
[11] taste
[12] Tapioca is prepared thus from cassava roots.
[13] bottom
[14] bamboos
[15] (perhaps) extend quite one-fourth

And that desert and that place of darkness dure from this coast unto Paradise terrestrial, where that[1] Adam, our foremost[2] father, and Eve were put, that dwelled there but little while; and that is toward the east at the beginning of the earth. But that is not that east that we clepe our east on this half, where the sun riseth to us. For when the sun is east in those parts toward Paradise terrestrial, it is then midnight in our part on this half, for the roundness of the earth, of the which I have touched[3] to you of before. For our Lord God made the earth all round in the mid place of the firmament. And there as[4] mountains and hills be and valleys, that is not but only of[5] Noah's flood, that wasted the soft ground and the tender, and fell down into valleys, and the hard earth and the rocks abide[6] mountains, when the soft earth and tender waxed nesh[7] through the water, and fell and became valleys.

Of Paradise ne can I not speak properly. For I was not there. It is far beyond. And that forthinketh me.[8] And also I was not worthy. But as I have heard say of[9] wise men beyond, I shall tell you with good will.

Paradise terrestrial, as wise men say, is the highest place of earth, that is in all the world. And it is so high that it toucheth nigh to the circle of the moon, there as the moon maketh her turn; for she is so high that the flood of Noah ne might not come to her, that would have covered all the earth of the world all about and above and beneath, save Paradise only alone. And this Paradise is enclosed all about with a wall, and men wit not whereof it is; for the walls be covered all over with moss, as it seemeth. And it seemeth not that the wall is stone of nature, ne of none other thing that the wall is. And that wall stretcheth from the south to the north, and it hath not but one entry that[10] is closed with fire, burning, so that no man that is mortal ne dare not enter.

And in the most high place of Paradise, even in the middle place, is a well that casteth out the four floods that run by divers lands. Of the which the first is clept Pison, or Ganges, that is all one; and it runneth throughout Ind or Emlak, in the which river be many precious stones, and much of lignum aloes[11] and much gravel of gold. And that other river is clept Nilus or Gison, that goeth by Ethiopia and after by Egypt. And that other is clept Tigris, that runneth by Assyria and by Armenia the great. And that other is clept Euphrates, that

[1] where
[2] first
[3] related
[4] wherever
[5] from nothing else than
[6] remain
[7] soft
[8] causes me regret
[9] by
[10] which
[11] a fragrant oriental wood

runneth also by Media and Armenia and by Persia. And men there beyond say, that all the sweet waters of the world, above and beneath, take their beginning of the well of Paradise, and out of that well all waters come and go.

The first river is clept Pison, that is to say in their language, Assembly; for many other rivers meet them there, and go into that river. And some men clepe it Ganges, for a king that was in Ind, that hight[12] Gangeres, and that it ran throughout his land. And that water is in some place clear, and in some place troubled, in some place hot, and in some place cold.

The second river is clept Nilus or Gison; for it is always trouble;[13] and Gison, in the language of Ethiopia, is to say, trouble, and in the language of Egypt also.

The third river, that is clept Tigris, is as much for to say as, fast-running; for he runneth more fast than any of the tother; and also there is a beast, that is clept Tigris, that is fast-running.

The fourth river is clept Euphrates, that is to say, well-bearing; for here grow many goods upon that river, as corn, fruits, and other goods enough plenty.

And ye shall understand that no man that is mortal ne may not approach to that Paradise. For by land no man may go for wild beasts that be in the desert, and for the high mountains and great huge rocks that no man may pass by, for the dark places that be there, and that many. And by the rivers may no man go. For the water runneth so rudely and so sharply, because that it cometh down so outrageously from the high places above, that it runneth in so great waves, that no ship may not row ne sail against it. And the water roareth so, and maketh so huge a noise and so great tempest, that no man may hear other in the ship, though he cried with all the craft that he could in the highest voice that he might. Many great lords have assayed with great will, many times, for to pass by those rivers toward Paradise, with full great companies. But they might not speed on their voyage. And many died for weariness of rowing against those strong waves. And many of them became blind, and many deaf, for the noise of the water. And some were perished and lost within the waves. So that no mortal man may approach to that place, without special grace of God, so that of that place I can say you no more; and therefore I shall hold me still, and return to that that I have seen.

[12] was called
[13] troubled, murky

[Conclusion]

. . . And ye shall understand, if it like you, that at mine home-coming I came to Rome, and showed my life to our holy father the pope, and was assoiled [1] of all that lay in my conscience, of many a diverse grevious point; as men must needs that be in company, dwelling amongst so many a diverse folk of diverse sect and of belief, as I have been. And amongst all I showed him this treatise, that I had made after information of men that knew of things that I had not seen myself, and also of marvels and customs that I had seen myself, as far as God would give me grace; and besought his holy fatherhood that my book might be examined and proved by the advice of his said council. And our holy father, of his special grace, remitted my book to be examined and proved by the advice of his said council. By the which my book was proved for true, insomuch that they showed me a book, that my book was examined by, that comprehended full more, by an hundred part, by the which the *Mappa Mundi* [2] was made after. And so my book (albeit that many men ne list not to give credence to nothing but to that that they see with their eye, ne be the author ne the person never so true) is affirmed and proved by our holy father, in manner and form as I have said.

And I, John Mandeville, knight, abovesaid (although I be unworthy), that departed from our countries and passed the sea, the year of grace a thousand three hundred and twenty-two, that have passed many lands and many isles and countries, and searched many full strange places, and have been in many a full good honorable country, and at many a fair deed of arms (albeit that I did none myself, for mine unable insufficience), now I am come home, mauger myself, to rest, for gouts arthritic that me distrain [3] that define [4] the end of my labor; against my will (God knoweth).

And thus, taking solace in my wretched rest, recording the time past, I have fulfilled these things, and put them written in this book, as it would come into my mind, the year of grace a thousand three hundred and fifty-six, in the thirty-fourth year that I departed from our countries. Wherefore I pray to all the readers and hearers of this book, if it please them, that they would pray to God for me; and I shall pray for them. . . .

c. 1356; English translation after 1400

[1] absolved
[2] Map of the World
[3] afflict
[4] mark

THE FIFTEENTH AND EARLY SIXTEENTH CENTURIES

FOR a century and more after Chaucer, English literature made little progress. It was represented mainly by a few immediate successors and imitators of the great poet, among whom Thomas Hoccleve, or Occleve, and John Lydgate stood first; popular poetry, chiefly ballads; and miracle plays. But various social forces were at work which eventually put an end to medievalism, and opened the era of modernity. Feudalism and the overshadowing power of the Church were passing; the fall of Constantinople, 1453, drove eastern scholars to take refuge in western Europe; the resulting revival of learning (the Renaissance, so-called) in Italy encouraged the creation of fresh art and literature; the introduction of printing (c. 1450) placed knowledge within the reach of all, and linked nation with nation, age with age; and the Reformation added new religious thought.

BALLADS

The popular ballad is a narrative poem without known author, telling of some simple incident of adventure, love, passion, cruelty, or superstition. Some authorities believe that the ballad took form as the joint production of a group of people; others, that it could originate only as the work of an individual. It was meant originally for singing, and was connected with the folk dance. As ballads were handed down orally from generation to generation, they gradually lost their dramatic quality and became narrative in character. The ballad is marked by much repetition of epithets, and by refrains which may be mere "tag" phrases. In England and Scotland it flourished between the fourteenth and sixteenth centuries. In the eighteenth century a conscious interest in this poetry was revived, chiefly through the influence of Bishop Percy and Sir Walter Scott; and many imitations arose (see Chatterton, p. 383). Today versions of the old ballads survive in some parts of the United States, notably among the mountaineers of Kentucky; and a variety of the popular ballad is found among pioneers, frontiersmen, and cowboys.

English and Scottish Ballads, edited by H. C. Sargent and G. L. Kittredge, 1904, a full treatment in introd.; see also F. B. Gummere, *The Beginnings of Poetry,* 1901, and *The Popular Ballad,* 1907; Louise Pound, *Poetic Origins and the Ballad,* 1921; John A. Lomax, *Cowboy Songs,* 1914; W. R. Mackenzie, *The Quest of the Ballad,* 1919; Louise Pound, *American Ballads and Songs,* 1922; J. H. Cox, *Folksongs of the South,* 1925.

ROBIN HOOD AND THE MONK[1]

1

In somer, when the shawes[2] be sheyne,[3]
  And leves be large and long,
Hit is full mery in feyre foreste
  To here the foulys[4] song;

2

To se the dere draw to the dale,
  And leve the hilles hee,
And shadow hem in the levës grene,
  Under the grene-wode tre.

3

Hit befel on Whitsontide,
  Erly in a May mornyng,
The son up feyre can[5] shyne,
  And the briddis mery can syng.

4

"This is a mery mornyng," seid Litull John,
  "Be[6] hym that dyed on tre;
A more mery man then[7] I am one
  Lyves not in Christiantë.

[1] This is one of a group of ballads about Robin Hood and his various adventures. From a MS. of about 1450, though the ballad is probably much earlier.

[2] woods
[3] beautiful
[4] birds'
[5] did
[6] by
[7] than

5

"Pluck up thi hert, my dere mayster,"
Litull John can sey,
"And thynk hit is a full fayre tyme
In a mornyng of May."

6

"Ye, on [1] thyng greves me," seid Robyn,
"And does my hert mych woo;
That I may not no solem day
To mas nor matyns goo.

7

"Hit is a fourtnet and more," seid he,
"Syn I my savyour see; [2]
Today wil I to Notyngham,
With the myght of mylde Marye."

8

Than spake Moche, the mylner sun, [3]
Ever more wel hym betyde!
"Take twelve of thi wyght yemen, [4]
Well weppynd, be thi side.
Such on wolde thi selfe slon, [5]
That twelve dar not abyde." [6]

9

"Of all my mery men," seid Robyn,
"Be my feith I wil non have,
But Litull John shall beyre my bow,
Til that me list [7] to drawe."

10

"Thou shall beyre thin own," seid Litull Jon,
"Maister, and I wyl beyre myne,
And we well shete a peny," [8] seid Litull Jon,
"Under the grene-wode lyne." [9]

11

"I wil not shete a peny," seyd Robyn Hode,
"In feith, Litull John, with the,
But ever for on as [10] thou shetis," seide Robyn,
"In feith I holde [11] the thre."

12

Thus shet thei forth, these yemen too, [12]
Bothe at buske [13] and brome, [14]
Til Litull John wan of his maister
Five shillings to [15] hose and shone. [16]

13

A ferly [17] strife fel them betwene,
As they went bi the wey;
Litull John seid he had won five shillings,
And Robyn Hode seid schortly nay.

14

With that Robyn Hode lyed [18] Litul Jon,
And smote hym with his hande;
Litul Jon waxed wroth therwith,
And pulled out his bright bronde.

15

"Were thou not my maister," seid Litull John,
"Thou shuldis by [19] hit ful sore;
Get the a man wher thou wilt,
For thou getis me no more."

16

Then Robyn goes to Notyngham,
Hym selfe mornyng allone,
And Litull John to mery Scherwode,
The pathes he knew ilkone. [20]

17

Whan Robyn came to Notyngham,
Sertenly withouten layn, [21]
He prayed to God and myld Mary
To bryng hym out save [22] agayn.

18

He gos in to Seynt Mary church,
And kneled down before the rode; [23]
Alle that ever were the church within
Beheld wel Robyn Hode.

19

Beside hym stod a gret-hedid munke,
I pray to God woo [24] he be!
Fful sone he knew gode Robyn,
As sone as he hym se.

20

Out at the durre he ran,
Fful sone and anon;
Alle the gatis of Notyngham
He made to be sparred [25] everychon.

21

"Rise up," he seid, "thou prowde schereff,
Buske [26] the and make the bowne; [27]

[1] one
[2] partook of the sacrament
[3] miller's son
[4] brave yeomen
[5] slay
[6] who would not dare withstand twelve
[7] it pleases me
[8] shoot for a penny
[9] linden
[10] unless for each that
[11] wager
[12] two
[13] bush
[14] broom (heather)
[15] for
[16] shoes
[17] strange
[18] gave the lie to
[19] aby, atone for
[20] each one
[21] lying
[22] safe
[23] rood, cross
[24] unhappy
[25] barred
[26] prepare thee
[27] ready

I have spyed the kynggis felon,
Ffor sothe he is in this town.

22

"I have spyed the false felon,
As he stondis at his masse;
Hit is long [1] of the," seide the munke,
"And [2] ever he fro us passe.

23

"This traytur name is Robyn Hode,
Under the grene-wode lynde;
He robbyt me onys [3] of a hundred pound,
Hit shalle never out of my mynde."

24

Up then rose this prowde shereff,
And radly [4] made hym yare; [5]
Many was the moder son
To the kyrk with hym can fare.

25

In at the durres thei throly [6] thrast,
With staves ful gode wone; [7]
"Alas, alas," seid Robyn Hode,
"Now mysse I Litull John."

26

But Robyn toke out a too-hond sworde,
That hangit down be his kne;
Ther as [8] the schereff and his men stode thyckust,
Thedurwarde wolde he.

27

Thryes thorowout them he ran then
For sothe as I yow sey,
And woundyt mony a moder son,
And twelve he slew that day.

28

His sworde upon the schireff hed
Sertanly he brake in too;
"The smyth that the made," seid Robyn,
"I pray God wyrke hym woo.

29

"Ffor now am I weppynlesse," seid Robyn,
"Alasse! agayn my wylle;
But if [9] I may fle these traytors fro,
I wot thei wil me kyll."

[1] because
[2] if
[3] once
[4] quickly
[5] ready
[6] stoutly
[7] number
[8] where
[9] unless

30

Robyn in to the churchë ran,
Throout hem everilkon, [10]

. . . .

31

Sum [11] fel in swonyng as thei were dede,
And lay stil as any stone;
Non of theym were in her mynde
But only Litull Jon.

32

"Let be your rule," [12] seid Litull Jon,
"For his luf that dyed on tre,
Ye that shulde be dughty men;
Het is gret shame to se.

33

"Oure maister has bene hard bystode [13]
And yet scapyd away;
Pluk up your hertis, and leve this mone,
And harkyn what I shal say.

34

"He has servyd Oure Lady many a day,
And yet wil, securly; [14]
Therfor I trust in hir specialy
No wyckud deth shal he dye.

35

"Therfor be glad," seid Litul John,
"And let this mournyng be;
And I shal be the munkis gyde,
With the myght of mylde Mary.

36

. . . .
"We will go but we too;
And I mete hym," seid Litul John,
. . . .

37

"Loke that ye kepe wel owre tristil-tre, [15]
Under the levys smale,
And spare non of this venyson,
That gose in thys vale."

38

Fforthe then went these yemen too,
Litul John and Moche on fere, [16]

[10] A leaf is missing, some twelve stanzas. Similar gaps occur later.
[11] Robin Hood's men, who have heard of the capture of Robin
[12] folly ? (Some would read *dule* = *grief*.)
[13] pressed
[14] surely
[15] trysting-tree
[16] in company

And lokid on Moch emys hows,[1]
The hye way lay full nere.

39

Litul John stode at a wyndow in the mornyng,
And lokid forth at a stage;[2]
He was war wher the munke came ridyng,
And with hym a litul page.

40

"Be my feith," seid Litul John to Moch,
"I can the tel tithyngus[3] gode;
I se wher the munke cumys rydyng,
I know hym be his wyde hode."

41

They went in to the way, these yemen bothe,
As curtes men and hende;[4]
Thei spyrred[5] tithyngus at[6] the munke,
As they hade bene his frende.[7]

42

"Ffro whens come ye?" seid Litull Jon,
"Tel us tithyngus, I yow pray,
Off a false owtlay, callid Robyn Hode,
Was takyn yisterday.

43

"He robbyt me and my felowes bothe
Of twenti marke[8] in serten;
If that false owtlay be takyn,
Ffor sothe we wolde be fayn."[9]

44

"So did he me," seid the munke,
"Of a hundred pound and more;
I layde furst hande hym apon,
Ye may thonke me therfore."

45

"I pray God thanke you," seid Litull John,
"And we will when we may;
We will go with you, with your leve,
And bryng yow on your way.

46

"Ffor Robyn Hode hase many a wilde felow,
I tell you in certen;
If thei wist ye rode this way,
In feith ye shulde be slayn."

[1] in on Much's uncle's house
[2] from an (upper) story
[3] tidings
[4] civil
[5] asked
[6] of
[7] friends
[8] A mark was 13s. 4d.
[9] glad

47

As thei went talking be the way,
The munke and Litull John,
John toke the munkis horse be the hede,
Fful sone and anon.

48

Johne toke the munkis horse be the hed,
Ffor sothe as I yow say;
So did Much the litull page,
Ffor he shulde not scape away.

49

Be the golett[10] of the hode
John pulled the munke down;
John was nothyng of hym agast,
He lete hym falle on his crown.

50

Litull John was sore agrevyd,
And drew owt his swerde in hye;
This munke saw he shulde be ded,
Lowd mercy can he crye.

51

"He was my maister," seid Litull John,
"That thou haste browght in bale;[11]
Shalle thou never cum at our kyng,
Ffor to telle hym tale."

52

John smote of the munkis hed,
No longer wolde he dwell;
So did Moch the litull page,
Ffor ferd lest he wolde tell.

53

Ther thei beryed hem bothe,
In nouther mosse nor lyng,[12]
And Litull John and Much infere
Bare the letturs to oure kyng.

54

. . . .
He knelid down upon his kne;
"God yow save, my lege lorde,
Jhesus yow save and se!

55

"God yow save, my lege kyng!"
To speke John was full bolde;
He gaf hym the letturs in his hond,
The kyng did hit unfold.

[10] throat-band
[11] harm
[12] neither moss nor heather

56

The kyng red the letturs anon,
And seid, "So mot I the,[1]
Ther was never yoman in mery Inglond
I longut so sore to se.

57

"Wher is the munke that these shuld have brought?"
Oure kyng can say:
"Be my trouth," seid Litull John,
"He dyed after[2] the way."

58

The kyng gaf Moch and Litul Jon
Twenti pound in sertan,
And made theim yemen of the crown,
And bade theim go agayn.

59

He gaf John the seel in hand,
The sheref for to bere,
To bryng Robyn hym to,
And no man do hym dere.[3]

60

John toke his leve at[4] oure kyng,
The sothe as I yow say;
The next way to Notyngham
To take, he yede[5] the way.

61

Whan John came to Notyngham
The gatis were sparred ychon;
John callid up the porter,
He answerid sone anon.

62

"What is the cause," seid Litul Jon,
"Thou sparris the gates so fast?"
"Because of Robyn Hode," seid the porter,
"In depe prison is cast.

63

"John and Moch and Wyll Scathlok,
Ffor sothe as I yow say,
Thei slew oure men upon our wallis,
And sawten[6] us every day."

64

Litull John spyrred after the schereff,
And sone he hym fonde;
He oppyned the kyngus prive seell,
And gaf hym in his honde.

65

Whan the scheref saw the kyngus seell,
He did of[7] his hode anon:
"Wher is the munke that bare the letturs?"
He seid to Litull John.

66

"He[8] is so fayn of[9] hym," seid Litul John,
"Ffor sothe as I yow say,
He has made hym abot of Westmynster,
A lorde of that abbay."

67

The scheref made John gode chere,
And gaf hym wyne of the best;
At nyght thei went to her bedde,
And every man to his rest.

68

When the scheref was on slepe,
Dronken of wyne and ale,
Litul John and Moch for sothe
Toke the way unto the jale.

69

Litul John callid up the jayler,
And bade hym rise anon;
He seyd Robyn Hode had brokyn prison,
And out of hit was gon.

70

The porter rose anon sertan,
As sone as he herd John calle;
Litul John was redy with a swerd,
And bare hym to the walle.

71

"Now wil I be porter," seid Litul John,
"And take the keyes in honde."
He toke the way to Robyn Hode,
And sone he hym unbonde.

72

He gaf hym a gode swerd in his hond,
His hed therwith for to kepe,[10]
And ther as[11] the walle was lowyst
Anon down can thei lepe.

[1] may I thrive
[2] upon
[3] harm
[4] of
[5] went
[6] assault
[7] put off
[8] i.e., the king
[9] pleased with
[10] guard
[11] where

73

Be that the cok began to crow,
  The day began to spryng;
The scheref fond the jaylier ded,
  The comyn [1] bell made he ryng.

74

He made a crye thoroout al the town,
  Wheder he be yoman or knave,
That cowthe bryng hym Robyn Hode,
  His warison [2] he shuld have.

75

"Ffor I dar never," said the scheref,
  "Cum before oure kyng;
Ffor if I do, I wot serten
  Ffor sothe he wil me heng."

76

The scheref made to seke Notyngham,
  Bothe be strete and stye, [3]
And Robyn was in mery Scherwode,
  As light as lef on lynde. [4]

77

Then bespake gode Litull John,
  To Robyn Hode can he say,
"I have done the a gode turn for an evyll,
  Quyte [5] the whan thou may.

78

"I have done the a gode turne," said Litull John,
  "Ffor sothe as I yow say;
I have brought the under grene-wode lyne; [4]
  Ffare wel, and have gode day."

79

"Nay, be my trouth," seid Robyn Hode,
  "So shal hit never be;
I make the maister," seid Robyn Hode,
  "Off alle my men and me."

80

"Nay, be my trouth," seid Litull John,
  "So shalle hit never be;
But lat me be a felow," seid Litull John,
  "No noder kepe I be." [6]

81

Thus John gate Robyn Hod out of prison;
  Sertan withoutyn layn, [7]
Whan his men saw hym hol and sounde,
  Ffor sothe they were full fayne.

82

They filled in wyne, and made hem glad,
  Under the levys smale,
And gete [8] pastes of venyson,
  That gode was with ale.

83

Than worde came to oure kyng
  How Robyn Hode was gon,
And how the scheref of Notyngham
  Durst never loke hym upon.

84

Then bespake oure cumly kyng,
  In an angur hye:
"Litull John hase begyled the schereff,
  In faith so hase he me.

85

"Litul John has begyled us bothe,
  And that full wel I se;
Or ellis the schereff of Notyngham
  Hye hongut [9] shulde he be.

86

"I made hem yemen of the crowne,
  And gaf hem fee [10] with my hond;
I gaf hem grith," [11] seid oure kyng,
  "Thorowout all mery Inglond.

87

"I gaf theym grith," then seid oure kyng;
  "I say, so mot I the,
Ffor sothe soch a yeman as he is on [12]
  In all Inglond ar not thre.

88

"He is trew to his maister," seid our kyng;
  "I sey, be swete Seynt John,
He lovys better Robyn Hode
  Then he dose us ychon.

89

"Robyn Hode is ever bond to hym,
  Bothe in strete and stalle; [13]
Speke no more of this mater," seid our kyng,
  "But John has begyled us alle."

[1] public
[2] reward
[3] alley
[4] linden tree
[5] quit (i.e., clear the debt)
[6] no other care I to be
[7] lying (i.e., truly)
[8] got
[9] hanged
[10] money
[11] security
[12] one
[13] i.e., abroad and at home

90

Thus endys the talkyng of the munke
And Robyn Hode i-wysse;[1]
God, that is ever a crowned kyng,
Bryng us all to his blisse."

MS. c. 1450

THE HUNTING OF THE CHEVIOT[2]

1

The Persë[3] owt[4] off Northombarlonde,
and avowe to God mayd he
That he wold hunte in the mowntayns
off Chyviat within days thre,
In the magger of[5] doughtë Dogles,
and all that ever with him be.

2

The fattiste hartes in all Cheviat
he sayd he wold kyll, and cary them away:
"Be my feth," sayd the dougheti Doglas agayn,
"I wyll let[6] that hontyng yf that I may."

3

Then the Persë owt off Banborowe cam,
with him a myghtee meany,[7]
With fifteen hondrith archares bold off blood
and bone;
the[8] wear chosen owt of shyers[9] thre.

4

This begane on a Monday at morn,
in Cheviat the hillys so he;
The chylde may rue that ys unborn,
it wos the more pittë.

5

The dryvars[10] thorowe the woodës went,
for to reas the dear;
Bomen byckarte[11] uppone the bent[12]
with ther browd aros cleare.[13]

6

Then the wyld[14] thorowe the woodës went,
on every sydë shear;[15]
Greahondës thorowe the grevis[16] glent,[17]
for to kyll thear dear.

7

This begane in Chyviat the hyls abone,[18]
yerly[19] on a Monnyn-day;
Be that[20] it drewe to the oware off none,
a hondrith fat hartës ded ther lay.

8

The blewe a mort[21] uppone the bent,
the semblyde on sydis shear;
To the quyrry[22] then the Persë went,
to se the bryttlynge[23] off the deare.

9

He sayd, "It was the Duglas promys,
this day to met me hear;
But I wyste he wolde faylle, verament;"[24]
a great oth the Persë swear.

10

At the laste a squyar off Northomberlonde
lokyde at his hand full ny;
He was war a the doughetie Doglas commynge,
with him a myghttë meany.

11

Both with spear, bylle,[25] and brande,
yt was a myghtti sight to se;
Hardyar men, both off hart nor hande,
wear not in Cristiantë.

12

The wear twenti hondrith spear-men good,
withoute any feale,[26]
The wear borne along be the watter a Twyde,
yth[27] bowndës of Tividale.

13

"Leave of the brytlyng of the dear," he sayd,
"and to your boys[28] lock ye tayk good hede;
For never sithe ye wear on your mothars borne
had ye never[29] so mickle nede."

14

The dougheti Dogglas on a stede,
he rode alle his men beforne;
His armor glytteryde as dyd a glede;[30]
a boldar barne[31] was never born.

[1] indeed
[2] The ballad commemorates the battle of Otterburn, fought during a Scotch invasion of Northumberland in 1388; it was probably old in 1550. In his *Defense of Poesie,* 1591, Sir Philip Sidney said, "I never heard the old song of Percy and Douglas, that I found not my heart moved more than with a trumpet; and yet it is sung by some blind crowder [ballad singer], with no rougher voice than rude style." There is a later version which is commonly known as "Chevy Chace," praised by Addison in *The Spectator,* 70, 74.
[3] The family of Percy was an old one of northern England.
[4] came out
[5] mauger, in spite of
[6] prevent
[7] band
[8] they
[9] shires
[10] stalkers
[11] skirmished
[12] field
[13] bright
[14] game
[15] several, separate
[16] groves
[17] darted
[18] above
[19] early
[20] by the time
[21] death-note
[22] slaughtered game
[23] cutting up
[24] truly
[25] sword
[26] fail
[27] in the
[28] bows
[29] ever
[30] glowing coal
[31] man

15

"Tell me whos men ye ar," he says,
"or whos men that ye be:
Who gave youe leave to hunte in this Chyviat chays,
in the spyt of myn and of me."

16

The first mane [1] that ever him an answear mayd,
yt was the good lord Persë:
"We wyll not tell the [2] whoys [3] men we ar," he says,
"nor whos men that we be;
But we wyll hounte hear in this chays,
in the spyt of thyne and of the.

17

"The fattiste hartës in all Chyviat
we have kyld, and cast [4] to carry them away."
"Be my troth," sayd the doughetë Dogglas agayn,
"therfor the ton [5] of us shall de [6] this day."

18

Then sayd the doughtë Doglas
unto the lord Persë:
"To kyll alle thes giltles men,
alas, it wear great pittë!

19

"But, Persë, thowe art a lord of lande,
I am a yerle callyd within my contrë;
Let all our men uppone a parti [7] stande,
and do [8] the battell off the and of me."

20

"Nowe Cristes cors [9] on his crowne," [10] sayd the lord Persë,
"who-so-ever ther-to says nay;
Be [11] my troth, doughttë Doglas," he says,
"thow shalt never se that day. [12]

21

"Nethar in Ynglonde, Skottlonde, nar France,
nor for no man of a woman born, [13]
But, and [14] fortune be my chance,
I dar met him, on [15] man for on."

[1] man
[2] thee
[3] whose
[4] intend
[5] one
[6] die
[7] to one side
[8] let us do
[9] curse
[10] head
[11] by
[12] i.e., when I say nay
[13] i.e., will I shrink
[14] if
[15] one

22

Then bespayke a squyar off Northombarlonde,
Richard Wytharyngton was his nam:
"It shall never be told in Sothe-Ynglonde," he says,
"to Kyng Herry the Fourth for sham.

23

"I wat [16] youe byn [17] great lordës twaw,
I am a poor squyar of lande:
I wylle never se my captayne fyght on a fylde,
and stande my selffe and loocke on,
But whylle I may my weppone welde,
I wylle not fayle both hart and hande."

24

That day, that day, that dredfull day!
the first fit [18] here I fynde;
And [19] youe wyll here any mor a [20] the hountyng a the Chyviat,
yet ys ther more behynde.

25

The Ynglyshe men hade ther bowys yebent,
ther hartes wer good yenoughe;
The first off arros that the [21] shote off,
seven skore spear-men the sloughe.

26

Yet byddys [22] the yerle Doglas uppon the bent,
a captayne good yenoughe,
And that was sene verament,
for he wrought hom [23] both woo and wouche. [24]

27

The Dogglas partyd his ost [25] in thre,
lyk a cheffe cheften off pryde;
With suar spears off myghttë tre, [26]
the [21] cum in on every syde:

28

Thrughe our Yngglyshe archery [27]
gave many a wounde fulle wyde;
Many a doughetë [28] the [21] garde [29] to dy,
which ganyde them no pryde.

29

The Ynglyshe men let ther boys be,
and pulde owt brandes that wer brighte;

[16] know
[17] be
[18] division of the song
[19] if
[20] of
[21] they
[22] abides
[23] them
[24] harm
[25] host
[26] wood
[27] archers
[28] doughty man
[29] caused

It was a hevy syght to se
  bryght swordes on basnites [1] lyght.

30

Thorowe ryche male [2] and myneyeple,[3]
  many sterne [4] the strocke done [5] streght;
Many a freyke [6] that was fulle fre, [7]
  ther undar foot dyd lyght.

31

At last the Duglas and the Persë met,
  lyk to captayns of myght and of mayne;
The swapte [8] togethar tylle the both swat, [9]
  with swordes that wear of fyn myllan. [10]

32

Thes worthë freckys for to fyght,
  ther-to [11] the wear fulle fayne, [12]
Tylle the bloode owte off thear basnetes sprente [13]
  as ever dyd heal [14] or rayn.

33

"Yelde the, Persë," sayde the Doglas,
  "and i feth [15] I shalle the brynge
Wher thowe shalte have a yerls wagis [16]
  of Jamy our Skottish kynge.

34

"Thou shalte have thy ransom fre,
  I hight [17] the hear [18] this thinge;
For the manfullyste man yet art thowe
  that ever I conqueryd in filde fight-tynge."

35

"Nay," sayd the lord Persë,
  "I tolde it the beforne,
That I wolde never yeldyde be
  to no man of a woman born."

36

With that ther cam an arrowe hastely,
  forthe off a myghttë wane; [19]
Hit hathe strekene the yerle Duglas
  in at the brest-bane.

[1] helmets
[2] armor
[3] gauntlet
[4] stubborn ones
[5] down
[6] man
[7] noble
[8] smote
[9] sweat
[10] Milan steel
[11] i.e., to fight
[12] glad
[13] sprang
[14] hail
[15] in faith
[16] earl's wages
[17] promise
[18] here
[19] multitude ? (Skeat)

37

Thorowe lyvar and longës [20] bathe [21]
  the sharpe arrowe ys gane,
That never after in all his lyffe-days
  he spayke mo wordës but ane:
That was, "Fyghte ye, my myrry men,
  whyllys ye may,
  for my lyff-days ben gan."

38

The Persë leanyde on his brande,
  and sawe the Duglas de;
He tooke the dede mane by the hande,
  and sayd, "Wo ys me for the!

39

"To have savyde thy lyffe, I wolde have partyde with
  my landes for years thre,
For a better man, of hart nare of hande,
  was nat in all the north contrë."

40

Off all that se [22] a Skottishe knyght,
  was callyd Ser Hewe the Monggombyrry; [23]
He sawe the Duglas to the deth was dyght, [24]
  he spendyd [25] a spear, a trusti tre.

41

He rod uppone a corsiare [26]
  throughe a hondrith archery:
He never stynttyde, [27] nar never blane, [28]
  tylle he cam to the good lord Persë.

42

He set uppone the lorde Persë
  a dynte that was full soare;
With a suar spear of a myghttë tre
  clean thorow the body he the Persë ber, [29]

43

A [30] the tothar syde that a man myght se
  a large cloth-yard and mare:
Towe bettar captayns wear nat in Cristiantë
  then that day slan wear ther.

44

An archar off Northomberlonde
  say [31] slean was the lord Persë;

[20] lungs
[21] both
[22] saw
[23] Montgomery
[24] doomed
[25] spanned, seized
[26] courser
[27] stopped
[28] ceased
[29] pierced
[30] on
[31] saw that

He bar a bende bowe in his hand,
was made off trusti tre.

45

An arow, that a cloth-yarde was lang,
to the harde stele halyde [1] he;
A dynt that was both sad and soar
he sat [2] on Ser Hewe the Monggombyrry.

46

The dynt yt was both sad and sar,
that he of Monggomberry sete;
The swane-fethars that his arrowe bar
with his hart-blood the wear wete.

47

Ther was never a freake [3] wone foot wolde fle,
but still in stour [4] dyd stand,
Heawyng on yche othar, whylle the myghte dre, [5]
with many a balfull brande.

48

This battell begane in Chyviat
an owar before the none,
And when even-songe bell was rang,
the battell was nat half done.

49

The tocke [6] . . . on ethar hande
be the lyght off the mone;
Many hade no strenght for to stande,
in Chyviat the hillys abon.

50

Of fifteen hondrith archars of Ynglonde
went away but seventi and thre;
Of twenti hondrith spear-men of Skotlonde,
but even five and fifti.

51

But all wear slayne Cheviat within;
the hade no strengthe to stand on hy;
The chylde may rue that ys unborne,
it was the mor pittë.

52

Thear was slayne, withe the lord Persë,
Sir Johan of Agerstone,
Ser Rogar, the hinde [7] Hartly,
Ser Wyllyam, the bolde Hearone.

[1] drew [2] set
[3] man
[4] stress of battle
[5] endure
[6] they took (count ?)
[7] gentle

53

Ser Jorg, the worthë Loumle,
a knyghte of great renowen,
Ser Raff, [8] the ryche Rugbe,
with dyntes wear beaten dowene.

54

For Wetharryngton my harte was wo,
that ever he slayne shulde be;
For when both his leggis wear hewyne in to,
yet he knyled and fought on hys kny.

55

Ther was slayne, with the dougheti Duglas,
Ser Hewe the Monggombyrry,
Ser Davy Lwdale, that worthë was,
his sistars son was he.

56

Ser Charles a Murrë [9] in that place,
that never a foot wolde fle;
Ser Hewe Maxwelle, a lorde he was,
with the Doglas dyd he dey.

57

So on the morrowe the mayde them byears [10]
off birch and hasell so gray;
Many wedous, with wepyng tears,
cam to fache ther makys [11] away.

58

Tivydale may carpe off [12] care,
Northombarlond may mayk great mon,
For towe such captayns as slayne wear thear,
on the March-parti [13] shall never be non.

59

Word ys commen to Eddenburrowe,
to Jamy the Skottische kynge,
That dougheti Duglas, lyff-tenant of the Marches,
he lay slean Chyviot within.

60

His handdës dyd he weal [14] and wryng,
he sayd, "Alas, and woe ys me!
Such an othar captayn Skotland within,"
he sayd, "ye-feth shuld never be." [15]

[8] Ralph
[9] Murray
[10] biers
[11] mates
[12] sing of
[13] border side
[14] clench
[15] This lament, contrasted with King Harry's boast that follows, may be taken as an amusing indication of English authorship of the ballad.

61

Worde ys commyn to lovly Londone,
till[1] the fourth Harry our kynge,
That lord Persë, leyff-tenante of the Marchis,
he lay slayne Chyviat within.

62

"God have merci on his solle," sayde Kyng Harry,
"good Lord, yf thy will it be!
I have a hondrith captayns in Ynglonde," he sayd,
"as good as ever was he:
But, Persë, and I brook [2] my lyffe,
thy deth well quyte [3] shall be."

63

As our noble kynge mayd his avowe,
lyke a noble prince of renowen,
For the deth of the lord Persë
he dyde the battell of Hombyll-down;

64

Wher syx and thrittë Skottishe knyghtes
on a day wear beaten down:
Glendale glytteryde on [4] ther armor bryght,
over castille, towar, and town.

65

This was the hontynge off the Cheviat,
that tear [5] begane this spurn, [6]
Old men that knowen the grownde well yenoughe
call it the battell of Otterburn.

66

At Otterburn begane this spurne
uppone a Monnynday;
Ther was the doughtë Doglas slean,
the Persë never went away.

67

Ther was never a tym on the Marche-partës
sen [7] the Doglas and the Persë met,
But yt ys mervele and [8] the rede blude ronne not,
as the reane doys [9] in the stret.

68

Jhesue Crist our balys [10] bete, [11]
and to the blys us brynge!
Thus was the hountynge of the Chivyat:
God send us alle good endyng!

[1] to [2] if I enjoy [3] paid for
[4] in, with (Humbleton is in Glendale district.)
[5] that ere, erewhile [8] if [10] evil
[6] trouble [9] rain does [11] remedy, better
[7] since

SIR PATRICK SPENS [12]

1

The king sits in Dumferling toune, [13]
Drinking the blude-reid wine:
"O whar will I get guid sailor,
To sail this schip of mine?"

2

Up and spak an eldern [14] knicht,
Sat at the kings richt kne:
"Sir Patrick Spence is the best sailor,
That sails upon the se."

3

The king has written a braid [15] letter,
And signd it wi his hand,
And sent it to Sir Patrick Spence,
Was walking on the sand.

4

The first line that Sir Patrick red,
A loud lauch [16] lauched he;
The next line that Sir Patrick red,
The teir blinded his ee.

5

"O wha is this has don this deid,
This ill deid don to me,
To send me out this time o' the yeir,
To sail upon the se!

6

"Mak hast, mak haste, my mirry men all,
Our guid schip sails the morne:"
"O say na sae, my master deir,
For I feir a deadlie storme.

7

"Late, late yestreen I saw the new moone,
Wi the auld moone in hir arme,
And I feir, I feir, my deir master,
That we will cum to harme."

8

O our Scots nobles wer richt laith
To weet their cork-heild schoone;
Bot [17] lang owre [18] a' the play wer playd,
Thair hats they swam aboone. [19]

[12] First made known to the world through the collection of ballads gathered by Bishop Percy in 1765, called the *Reliques of Ancient English poetry;* this ballad may or may not be historical. Cf. with Longfellow's "The Wreck of the Hesperus."

[13] Dunfermline, northwest of Edinburgh, once a royal residence

[14] old [17] but
[15] broad, open [18] before
[16] laugh [19] above

9

O lang, lang may their ladies sit,
  Wi thair fans into their hand,
Or eir they se Sir Patrick Spence
  Cum sailing to the land.

10

O lang, lang may the ladies stand,
  Wi thair gold kems [1] in their hair,
Waiting for thair ain deir lords,
  For they'll se thame na mair.

11

Haf owre, haf owre to Aberdour,
  It's fiftie fadom deip,
And thair lies guid Sir Patrick Spence,
  Wi the Scots lords at his feit.

JOHNIE COCK [2]

1

Up Johnie raise in a May morning,
  Calld for water to wash his hands
And he has calld for his gude gray hunds
  That lay bund in iron bands, bands,
  That lay bund in iron bands.

2

"Ye'll busk, [3] ye'll busk my noble dogs,
  Ye'll busk and mak them boun, [4]
For I'm going to the Braidscaur hill
  To ding [5] the dun [6] deer doun."

3

Johnie's mother has gotten word o that,
  And care-bed she has taen: [7]
"O Johnie, for my benison, [8]
  I beg you'l stay at hame;
For the wine so red, and the well-baken bread,
  My Johnie shall want nane.

4

"There are seven forsters at Pickeram Side,
  At Pickeram where they dwell,
And for a drop of thy heart's bluid
  They wad ride the fords of hell."

[1] combs
[2] This text of the vigorous ballad, called by Professor Child, "a precious specimen of the unspoiled traditional ballad," follows the admirable combination made by Professor F. B. Gummere from various versions.
[3] make ready
[4] ready
[5] strike
[6] dark brown
[7] i.e., is sick with anxiety
[8] blessing

5

But Johnie has cast off the black velvet,
  And put on the Lincoln twine, [9]
And he is on to gude greenwud
  As fast as he could gang.

6

Johnie lookit east, and Johnie lookit west,
  And he lookit aneath the sun,
And there he spied the dun deer sleeping
  Aneath a buss o whun. [10]

7

Johnie shot, and the dun deer lap, [11]
  And she lap wondrous wide,
Until they came to the wan water,
  And he stemd [12] her of her pride.

8

He 'as taen out the little pen-knife,
  'Twas full three quarters [13] long,
And he has taen out of that dun deer
  The liver bot [14] and the tongue.

9

They eat of the flesh, and they drank of the blood,
  And the blood it was so sweet,
Which caused Johnie and his bloody hounds
  To fall in a deep sleep.

10

By then came an old palmer,
  And an ill death may he die!
For he's away to Pickram Side
  As fast as he can drie. [15]

11

"What news, what news?" says the Seven Forsters,
  "What news have ye brought to me?"
"I have noe news," the palmer said,
  "But what I saw with my eye.

12

"As I cam in by Braidisbanks,
  And down among the whuns,
The bonniest youngster eer I saw
  Lay sleepin amang his hunds.

[9] cloth
[10] bush of furze
[11] leaped
[12] stripped
[13] of a yard
[14] as well as
[15] hold out

13

"The shirt that was upon his back
Was o the holland [1] fine;
The doublet [2] which was over that
Was o the Lincoln twine."

14

Up bespake the Seven Forsters,
Up bespake they ane and a':
"O that is Johnie o Cockleys Well,
And near him we will draw."

15

O the first stroke that they gae him,
They struck him off by the knee;
Then up bespake his sister's son:
"O the next'll gar [3] him die!"

16

"O some they count ye well-wight [4] men,
But I do count ye nane;
For you might well ha wakend me,
And askd gin I wad be taen.

17

"The wildest wolf in aw this wood
Wad not ha done so by me;
She'd ha wet her foot ith wan water,
And sprinkled it oer my brae, [5]
And if that wad not ha wakend me,
She wad ha gone and let me be.

18

"O bows of yew, if ye be true,
In London, where ye were bought,
Fingers five, get up belive, [6]
Manhuid shall fail me nought."

19

He has killd the Seven Forsters,
He has killd them all but ane,
And that wan [7] scarce to Pickeram Side,
To carry the bode-words [8] hame.

20

"Is there never a [bird] in a' this wood
That will tell what I can say;
That will go to Cockleys Well,
Tell my mither to fetch me away?"

21

There was a [bird] into that wood,
That carried the tidings away,
And many ae [9] was the well-wight man
At the fetching o Johnie away.

[1] linen [2] waistcoat [3] make [4] very brave [5] brow [6] quick [7] won, made his way [8] message [9] a one

BONNIE GEORGE CAMPBELL

1

High upon Highlands,
and low upon Tay,
Bonnie George Campbell
rade out on a day.

2

Saddled and bridled
and gallant rade he;
Hame cam his guid horse,
but never cam he.

3

Out cam his auld mither
greeting fu' sair, [10]
And out came his bonnie bride
riving [11] her hair .

4

Saddled and bridled
and booted rade he;
Toom [12] hame cam the saddle,
but never cam he.

5

"My meadow lies green,
and my corn is unshorn,
My barn is to build,
and my babe is unborn."

6

Saddled and bridled
and booted rade he;
Toom hame cam the saddle,
but never cam he.

THE WIFE OF USHER'S WELL [13]

1

There lived a wife at Usher's Well,
And a wealthy wife was she;
She had three stout and stalwart sons,
And sent them oer the sea.

2

They hadna been a week from her,
A week but barely ane,
When word came to the carline [14] wife
That her three sons were gane.

3

They hadna been a week from her,
A week but barely three,

[10] weeping full sore [11] tearing [12] empty
[13] taken down by Sir Walter Scott from the recitation of an old woman in West Lothian
[14] old

When word came to the carlin wife
  That her sons she'd never see.

4

"I wish the wind may never cease,
  Nor fashes[1] in the flood,
Till my three sons come hame to me,
  In earthly flesh and blood."

5

It fell about the Martinmass,[2]
  When nights are lang and mirk,[3]
The carlin wife's three sons came hame,
  And their hats were o the birk.[4]

6

It neither grew in syke[5] nor ditch,
  Not yet in ony sheugh,[6]
But at the gates o Paradise,
  That birk grew fair eneugh.

. . . .

7

"Blow up the fire, my maidens!
  Bring water from the well!
For a' my house shall feast this night,
  Since my three sons are well."

8

And she has made to them a bed,
  She's made it large and wide,
And she's ta'en her mantle her about,
  Sat down at the bed-side.

. . . .

9

Up then crew the red, red cock,
  And up and crew the gray;
The eldest to the youngest said,
  " 'Tis time we were away."

10

The cock he hadna craw'd but once,
  And clappd his wings at a',
When the youngest to the eldest said,
  "Brother, we must awa.

11

"The cock doth craw, the day doth daw,
  The channerin[7] worm doth chide;
Gin[8] we be mist out o our place,
  A sair pain we maun bide.

[1] troubles (storms)
[2] November 11
[3] dark
[4] birch
[5] marsh
[6] furrow
[7] fretting
[8] if

12

"Fare ye weel, my mother dear!
  Fareweel to barn[9] and byre![10]
And fare ye weel, the bonny lass
  That kindles my mother's fire!"[11]

KATHARINE JAFFRAY[12]

1

There livd a lass in yonder dale,
  And doun in yonder glen, O,
And Kathrine Jaffray was her name,
  Well known by many men, O.

2

Out came the Laird of Lauderdale,
  Out frae the South Countrie,
All for to court this pretty maid,
  Her bridegroom for to be.

3

He has teld[13] her father and mither baith,
  And a' the rest o her kin,
And has teld the lass hersell,
  And her consent has win.

4

Then came the Laird of Lochinton,
  Out frae the English border,
All for to court this pretty maid,
  Well mounted in good order.

5

He's teld her father and mither baith,
  As I hear sindry say,
But he has nae teld the lass her sell,
  Till on her wedding day.

6

When day was set, and friends were met,
  And married to be,
Lord Lauderdale came to the place,
  The bridal for to see.

7

"O are you come for sport, young man?
  Or are you come for play?
Or are you come for a sight o our bride,
  Just on her wedding day?"

[9] granary
[10] stable
[11] "The beauty of reticence in this last farewell is as delicate as anything in literature."—F. B. Gummere.
[12] Scott's "Lochinvar" is based upon this ballad.
[13] told

8

"I'm nouther come for sport," he says,
  "Nor am I come for play;
But if I had one sight o your bride,
  I'll mount and ride away."

9

There was a glass of the red winé
  Filld up them atween,
And ay she drank to Lauderdale,
  Wha her true-love had been.

10

Then he took her by the milk-white hand,
  And by the grass-green sleeve,
And he mounted her high behind him there,
  At the bridegroom he askt nae leive.

11

Then the blude run down by the Cowden Banks,
  And down by Cowden Braes,
And ay she[1] gard[2] the trumpet sound,
  "O this is foul, foul play!"

12

Now a' ye that in England are,
  Or are in England born,
Come nere to Scotland to court a lass,
  Or else ye'l get the scorn.

13

They haik ye up[3] and settle ye by,[4]
  Till on your wedding day,
And gie ye frogs instead o fish,[5]
  And play ye foul, foul play.

. . . .

THE NUTBROWN MAYDE[6]

. . . .

Be it right or wronge, thes men amonge[7]
  On wymen do complayn,
Affermyng this, how that it is
  A laboure spent in vayn
To love them welle; for never a dele
  They love a man agayn.
For late a man do what he can
  Ther favoure to attayn,
Yet yf a newe do them pursue,
  Ther ferste trew lover than[8]
Laboureth for nought; for from her[9] thought
  He is a banysshed man.

I say not nay, but that alle day
  It is both wreten and said
That woman's feyth is, as who seyth,
  Alle utturly decayde;
But neverthelesse right good witnes
  In this case myght be layde,
That they love trew, and contenewe—
  Recorde the Nutbrown Mayde,
Which, whan her love cam her to prove,
  Tô her to make his mone,
Wolde not departe, for in her hart
  She loved but hym alone.

Than betwen us let us discusse
  What was alle the manere
Between them two: we wille also
  Telle alle the payn in fere[10]
That she was in. Now I begyn,
  So that ye me answere;
Wherfor alle ye that present be,
  I pray you, geve an ere.
I am the knyght; I com by nyght,
  As secrete as I can,
Saying, "Alas! thus stondith the caas,
  I am a banysshed man."

MAYDE

And I your wille for to fulfille
  In this wille not refuse,
Trustyng to shew in wordis fewe
  That men have an ylle use[11]
(To ther own shame) wymen to blame,
  And causelesse them accuse.
Therfor to you I answere now,
  Alle wymen to excuse—
Myn own hart dere, with you what chere?
  I pray you, telle me anon;
For in my mynd, of alle mankynd
  I love but you alon.

---

[1] Perhaps this should be *he,* referring to the Laird of Lochinton.

[2] caused

[3] haul you up

[4] set you aside (lead you on and deceive you)

[5] In the ballad of "Lord Randal," the lord is poisoned with eels (i.e., serpents).

[6] This poem is essentially a little drama, of which the first three stanzas constitute a kind of prologue and the last stanza an epilogue. In the first stanza one speaker propounds the general theme of the fickleness of womankind. In the second stanza, another speaker cites in refutation the story of the Nutbrown Mayde. Then the first speaker proposes that they two enact that story, and he begins by assuming the part of the man who pretended to be outlawed in order to "prove" the maid's love. The second speaker takes the part of the maid, and the dialogue continues regularly in alternate stanzas. It is readily seen that the poem, though for convenience grouped here with the ballads, is of a very different character from the folk-ballads proper, and a product of much less naïve art. Our text is that of the Balliol MS., with some very slight changes of spelling and the regular substitution of MAYDE for the more frequent marginal PUELLA of the manuscript.

[7] all the while

[8] then

[9] their

[10] i-fere, together

[11] evil custom

SQUYRE

It stondith so; a dede is doo
  Wherof gret harme shalle grow:
My destynye ys for to dye
  A shamfulle deth, I trow,
Ore ellis to flee; the on[1] muste be;
  Non other way I know
But to withdraw as an outlawe,
  And take me to my bow.
Wherfor adewe, myn own hart trew!
  Non other rede I can,[2]
For I muste to the grenwode go,
  Alon, a banysshed man.

MAYDE

O Lorde, what is this worldis blis
  That changith as the mone?
The[3] somers day in lusty may
  Is darke beffore the none.
I here you say, Farewelle. Nay, nay,
  We departe[4] not so sone.
Why say ye so? Whether[5] wille ye go?
  Alas, what have ye done?
Alle my welfare to sorrow and care
  Shuld chaunge yf ye were gon;
For in my mynde, of alle mankynd
  I love but you alon.

SQUYRE

I can beleve it shalle you greve,
  And sumwhat you dystreyne,
But afterward your paynes harde,
  Within a day or twayn,
Shalle sone aslake, and ye shalle take
  Conforte to you agayn.
Why should you ought for to take thought?[6]
  Your laboure were in vayn.
And thus I doo, and pray you to,
  As hartely as I can;
For I muste to the grenwode go,
  Alon, a banysshed man.

MAYDE

Now sith[7] that ye have shewed to me
  The secrete of your mynde,
I shalle be playn to you agayn,[8]
  Lyke as ye shalle me fynde.
Sith it is so that ye wille go,
  I will not bide behynde;
Shalle it never be said the Nut Brown Mayde
  Was to here love unkynde.
Make you redy, for so am I,
  Alle though it were anon;[9]
For in my mynd, of alle mankynd
  I love but you alon.

SQUYRE

Yet I you rede to take good hede
  What men wille thynke and say:
Of[10] yong, of olde, hit shalle be told
  That ye be gon away,
Your wanten wille for to fulfille,
  In grenwode you to play,
And that ye myght for your delite
  Ne lengar make delay.
Rather than ye shuld thus for me
  Be called a mysse[11] woman,
Yet wold I to the grenwode go,
  Alon, a banysshed man.

MAYDE

Though it be songe of olde and yonge
  That I shuld be to blame,
Thers be the charge that speke so large
  In hurtyng of my name;
For I wille prove that feythfulle love
  Hit is devoyed of shame,
In your distresse and hevynesse,
  To parte[12] with you the same—
To shewe all tho that do not so
  Trew lovers are they non;
For in my mynd, of all mankynd
  I love but you alon.

SQUYRE

I counsaille you, remembre how
  Hit is no maydyns lawe
Nothyng to doute, but to renne out
  To wode with an outlawe.
For ye muste ther in your hond bere
  A bowe redy to drawe,
And, as a theff, thus must ye leve
  Ever in drede and awe.
Wherby to you gret harm myght grow;
  Yet hade I lever than
That I had to the grenwod go,
  Alon, a banysshed man.

MAYDE

I say not nay, but as ye say,
  Yt is no maydyns lore;
But love may make me to forsake,
  As I have sayd beffore,
To cum on fote, to hunte and shote,
  To get us mete in store;
For so that I your company
  May have, I aske no more.
From which to parte it makyth my harte
  As colde as any ston;
For in my mynde, of alle mankynd
  I love but you alon.

[1] one
[2] No other counsel I know.
[3] variant reading: *my*
[4] part
[5] whither
[6] anxiety
[7] since
[8] in return
[9] at once
[10] by
[11] varient: *ylle* (ill)
[12] share

SQUYRE

For an outlawe this is the lawe,
That men hym take and bynde,
Without pité, hangid to be,
And waver with the wynde.
Yf I had nede, (as God forbede!)
What soccours could ye fynde?
Forsoth, I trow, ye and your bowe
For fere wold draw behynde.
And no mervayle, for littille avayle
Were in your counselle than;
Wherfor I wille to the grenwod go,
Alon, a banysshed man.

MAYDE

Right welle know ye that wymen be
But feeble for to fight;
No womanhede it is indede
To be bolde as a knyght.
Yet in such fere yf that ye were,
With ennemyes day or nyght,
I wold withstond, with bow in honde,
To helpe you with my myght,
And you to save, as wymen have
From deth many [an] one;
For in my mynd, of alle mankynd
I love but you alon.

SQUYRE

Yet take good hede, for ever I drede
That ye could not susteyn
The thorny wayes, the depe valeyes,
The snowe, the froste, the rayn,
The colde, the hete; for drye and wete
We muste logge on the playn,
And, us above, non other roffe
But a brake, bushe, or twayn;
Which sone shuld greve you, I beleve,
And ye wold gladly than
That I had to the grenwode goo,
Alon, a banysshed man.

MAYDE

Sith I have here ben partynere
With you [in] yoye and blisse,
I muste also parte of your woo
Endure, as reason is.
Yet am I sure of on pleasure,
And shortly it is this:
That wher ye be, me semeth, pardé,
I could not fare amysse.
Without more speche I you beseche
That we were shortly gon;
For in my mynd, of alle mankynd
I love but you alon.

SQUYRE

Iff ye go thyder, ye must consider,
Whan ye have luste to dyne,
Ther shalle no mete be for to gete,
Nether bere, ale, ne wyne;
Ne shetes clen, to lay betwen,
Made of threde and twyne;
Non other hous, but levis and boues,
To cover your hede and myne.
Loo, myn hart swete, this ille dyett
Shuld make you pale and wan;
Wherfor I wille to the grenwod go,
Alon, a banysshed man.

MAYDE

Amonge the wilde dere, suche an archere
As men say that ye be
May not faylle of good vytaylle,
Wher is so gret plenté.
And water clere of the rivere
Shalle be fulle swete to me,
With which in hele [1] I shalle right welle
Endure, as ye shalle see.
And, or we go, a bedde or two
I can provide anon;
For in my mynde, of alle mankynd
I love but you alon.

SQUYRE

Loo! yet beffore, ye must do more,
Yf ye wille goo with me:
As, cute your here up by your ere,
Your kyrtyll by your knee,
With bow in honde, for to withstonde
Your enymyes, yf nede be;
And this same nyght, beffore daylight,
To wodewarde wille I flee.
Yff that ye wille alle this fulfille,
Do it as shortly as ye can;
Els wille I to the grenwode go,
Alon, a banysshed man.

MAYDE

I shalle as now [2] do more for you
Than longith to womanhede,
To shorte myn here, a bowe to bere,
To shote in tyme of nede.
O my swete moder, beffore alle oder
For you I have moste drede;
But now, adewe! I must ensue
Wher fortune doth me lede.
Alle this make ye; now lat us flee,
The day commeth fast upon;
For in my mynd, of alle mankynd
I love but you alon.

SQUYRE

Nay, nay, not so; ye shalle not go,
And I shalle telle ye whye:

[1] health [2] now (redundant *as*)

Your appetite is to be light
  Of love, I welle espye;
For like as ye have said to me,
  In likewyse hardely [1]
Ye wolde answere, whosoever it were,
  In way of companye.
It is said of olde, Son whot, sone colde,
  And so is a woman;
For I muste to the grenwode goo,
  Alon, a banysshed man.

MAYDE

Yf ye take hede, it is no nede
  Such wordis to say to me,
For ofte ye prayd, and long assayed,
  Or I you loved, pardé.
And though that I of auncetrye
  A barons doughter be,
Yet have ye proved how I ye loved,
  A squyre of lowe degre,
And ever shalle, what so befalle,
  To dye therefor anon;
For in my mynd, of alle mankynd
  I love but you alon.

SQUYRE

A baron's child to be begiled,
  It were a curséd dede.
To be felowe with an outlawe,
  Almyghty God forbede!
Yet better were, the pore squyer
  Alon to foreste yede, [2]
Than ye shuld say, another day,
  That by my curséd rede
Ye were betrayde. Wherefor, good mayd,
  The best rede that I can,
Ys that I to the grenwod go,
  Alon, a banysshed man.

MAYDE

Whatever befalle, I never shalle
  Of this thyng you outbrayde;
But yf ye go and leve me so,
  Than have ye me betrayde.
Remembre you welle how that ye dele,
  For yf ye be as ye said,
Ye were unkynd to leve me behynd,
  Your love, the Nutbrown Mayde.
Truste [me] truly, that I shalle dye
  Sone after ye be gon;
For in my mynd, of all mankynd
  I love but you alon.

SQUYRE

If that you went, ye shuld repent,
  For in the foreste nowe
I have purveyde [3] me of a mayde
  Whom I love more than you—
Another more fayre than ever ye were,
  I dare it welle avowe;
And of you both, eche wille be wroth
  With other, as I trowe.
It were myn eas to leve [4] in peas,
  So wille I, yf I can;
Wherefore I wille to the grenwod go,
  Alon, a banysshed man.

MAYDE

Though in the wode I understode
  Ye had a paramoure,
Alle this may nought remeve my thought,
  But that I wille be your;
And she shalle fynd me softe and kynd,
  And curteys every oure,
Glad to fulfille alle that she wille
  Comaund me to my powere.
For had ye, loo! an hundredth mo,
  Yet wolde I be that on;
For in my mynd, of alle mankynd
  I love but you alon.

SQUYRE

Myn own der love, I se thee prove
  That ye be kynde and trewe;
Of mayde and wyf, in alle my lyff,
  The best that ever I knew.
Be mery and glade, be no more sade,
  The case is chaunged newe,
For it were rewth that for your trewth
  Ye shuld have cause to rewe.
Be not dysmayde, whatsoever I said
  To you whan I began;
I wille not to the grenwode go;
  I am no banysshed man.

MAYDE

Thes tydingis be more gladder to me
  Than to be made a quene,
Yf I were sure they shuld endure;
  But it is often seen,
When men wille [5] breke promyse, they speke
  The wordis on the splene. [6]
Ye shape som wyle me to begile,
  And stele from me, I wene;
Than were the caas wors than it was,
  And I more woo-begon;
For in my mynd, of alle mankynd
  I love but you alon.

SQUYRE

Ye shalle not nede further to drede;
  I wille not disparage
You, God defende, sith ye descende
  Of so gret a lynage.

[1] assuredly [2] went [3] provided [4] live [5] mean to [6] capriciously

Now understond; to Westmorelond,
  Which is myn herytage,
I wille you bryng, and with a rynge
  By way of maryage
I wille you take, and lady make,
  As shortly as I can;
Than have ye wonne an erles sonne,
  And not a banysshed man.

Here may ye see that women be,
  In love, meke, kynd, and stable;
Latt never man repreve them than
  Or calle them variable,
But rather pray God that we may
  To them be confortable.
God sumtyme provith such as he lovith,
  Yf they be charytable;
For sith men wold that women shuld
  Be meke to them echone,
Moche more aught they to God obey,
  And serve but hym alon.

EVERYMAN

Everyman is the most interesting specimen of a type of medieval drama called Moralities, popular in France as well as in England. The origin of these plays may easily be traced to the service of the Roman Catholic Church. Not only were parts of the service highly dramatic, but also in the Middle Ages Biblical scenes were introduced into the service to impress an unlettered people. As these spectacles became more popular they were transferred to the churchyard, then to the streets, where they were acted upon movable stages. Moreover, they passed from the hands of the clergy to those of the town guilds—a kind of trades-unions—who used them to celebrate special festivals. To these Biblical plays, or Miracle Plays—of which four great cycles, the York, the Wakefield (or Towneley), the Coventry, and the Chester, still survive—a new type, the Moralities, were added. These were allegories in which the characters were personified abstractions, and the main theme was the strife between the powers of good and evil for the soul of man.

The allegory here deals with the end of life. Everyman, summoned by Death, appeals to various life-long companions to accompany him on his pilgrimage to the grave. One by one Fellowship, (Comradeship), Kindred, Strength, Beauty, and the others desert him, and Good-deeds alone is with him, faithful to the end.

This play exists also in Dutch, entitled "Elckerlijk," printed about 1495, and attributed to Petrus Dorlandus. The earliest known English editions date about 1525. From the dates and the almost entire lack of humor in the play, it is most probable that the English form is a free translation from the Dutch. It was very popular in the reign of Henry VIII, and is of impressive power even today in reading and on the stage. In *Everywoman,* by W. Browne, 1911, and in *Intolerance,* 1916, we may see how this type has been revived in modern drama and the moving picture.

Valuable material will be found in Gayley, Pollard, and Chambers.

Here begynneth a treatyse how the hye Fader of Heven sendeth Dethe to somon every creature to come and gyve a counte of theyr lyves in this worlde, and is in maner of a moral playe. [1]

MESSENGER.

I pray you all gyve your audyence,
And here [2] this mater [3] with reverence,
By fygure [4] a morall [5] playe;
The somonynge of Everyman called it is,
That of our lyves and endynge shewes
How transytory we be all daye. [6]
This mater is wonders [7] precyous,
But the entent [8] of it is more gracyous,
And swete to bere awaye.
The story sayth: Man, in the begynnynge
Loke well, and take good heed to the endynge,
Be you never so gay;
Ye thynke synne in the begynnynge full swete,
Whiche in the ende causeth the soule to wepe,
Whan the body lyeth in claye.
Here shall you se how Felawshyp and Jolyte,
Bothe Strengthe, Pleasure and Beaute,
Wyll fade from the [9] as floure in Maye.
For ye shall here, how our heven kynge
Calleth Everyman to a generall rekenynge.
Gyve audyence, and here what he doth saye.

GOD *speketh.*

I perceyve here in my majeste
How that all creatures be to me unkynde,
Lyvynge without drede in worldely prosperyte;
Of ghostly [10] syght the people be so blynde,
Drowned in synne they know me not for theyr God;
In worldely ryches is all theyr mynde.
They fere not my ryghtwysnes, the sharpe rood;
My lawe that I shewed whan I for them dyed
They forgete clene, and shedynge of my blode rede;
I hanged bytwene two, it can not be denyed;
To gete them lyfe I suffred to be deed.
I heled theyr fete; with thornes hurt was my heed;

[1] This text follows the Skot copy in the Britwell Library, as reprinted by W. W. Greg, with capitals and punctuation added.
[2] hear
[3] matter
[4] in form
[5] A Morality
[6] always
[7] wondrously
[8] purpose
[9] thee
[10] spiritual

I coude do no more than I dyde truely.
And nowe I se the people do clene for sake me:
They use [1] the seven deedly synnes dampnable,
As pryde, coveytyse, wrathe, and lechery,
Now in the worlde be made commendable,
And thus they leve of aungelles the hevenly company,
Every man lyveth so after his owne pleasure;
And yet of theyr lyfe they be nothinge sure.
I se, the more that I them forbere,
The worse they be fro yere to yere;
All that lyveth appayreth [2] faste.
Therefore I wyll in all the haste
Have a rekenynge of every mannes persone.
For, and [3] I leve the people thus alone
In theyr lyfe and wycked tempestes,
Veryly they wyll become moche worse than beestes:
For now one wolde by envy another up ete;
Charyte they do all clene forgete.
I hoped well that every man
In my glory shulde make his mansyon,
And thereto I had them all electe;
But now I se, like traytours dejecte,
They thanke me not for the pleasure that I to them ment,
Nor yet for theyr beynge that I them have lent.
I profered the people grete multytude of mercy,
And fewe there be that asketh it hertly; [4]
They be so combred with worldly ryches
That nedes on them I must do justyce,
On every man lyvynge without fere.—
Where arte thou, Deth, thou myghty messengere?

DETHE. Almyghty God, I am here at your wyll,
Your commaundement to fulfyll.

GOD. Go thou to Everyman,
And shewe hym in my name
A pylgrymage he must on hym take,
Which he in no wyse may escape,
And that he brynge with hym a sure rekenynge,
Without delay or ony taryenge.

DETHE. Lorde, I wyll in the worlde go renne [5] over all,
And cruelly out serche bothe grete and small.
Every man wyll I beset that lyveth beestly
Out of Goddes lawes and dredeth not foly.
He that loveth rychesse I wyll stryke with my darte,
His syght to blynde, and fro heven to departe, [6]
Excepte that almes be his good frende,
In hell for to dwell, worlde without ende.
Loo, yonder I se Everyman walkynge,
Full lytell he thynketh on my comynge!
His mynde is on flesshely lustes, and his treasure;
And grete payne it shall cause hym to endure
Before the Lorde, heven kynge.

[EVERYMAN *enters.*]

Everyman, stande styll. Whyder arte thou goynge,
Thus gayly? hast thou thy Maker forgete?

EVERYMAN. Why askest thou?
Woldest thou wete? [7]

DETHE. Ye, syr, I wyll shewe you:
In grete hast I am sende to the
Fro God, out of h's mageste.

EVERYMAN. What, sente to me?

DETHE. Ye, certaynly.
Thoughe thou have forgete hym here,
He thynketh on the in the hevenly spere,
As, or [8] we departe, thou shalte knowe.

EVERYMAN. What desyreth God of me?

DETHE. That shall I shewe thee:
A rekenynge he wyll nedes have,
Without ony lenger respyte.

EVERYMAN. To gyve a rekenynge longer layser [9] I crave;
This blynde mater troubleth my wytte.

DETHE. On the thou must take a longe journey,
Therfore thy boke of counte with the thou brynge,
For turne agayne thou can not by no waye;
And loke thou be sure of thy rekenynge,
For before God thou shalte answere and shewe
Thy many badde dedes and good but a fewe,
How thou hast spente thy lyfe, and in what wyse,
Before the chefe lorde of paradyse.
Have I do [10] we were in that waye,
For, wete thou well, thou shalte make none attournay. [11]

EVERYMAN. Full unredy I am suche rekenynge to gyve.
I knowe the not. What messenger arte thou?

DETHE. I am Dethe, that no man dredeth.
For every man I rest, [12] and no man spareth,
For it is Goddes commaundement
That all to me sholde be obedyent.

EVERYMAN. O Dethe, thou comest whan I had thee leest in mynde!
In thy power it lyeth me to save;
Yet of my good wyl I gyve the, if thou wyl be kynde.
Ye, a thousande pounde shalte thou have,
And dyfferre [13] this matter tyll an other daye.

[1] practice
[2] degenerates
[3] if
[4] heartily
[5] run
[6] separate
[7] know
[8] before
[9] leisure
[10] "have ado," i.e., have done, so we may be on our way
[11] find no intercessor
[12] arrest
[13] defer

DETHE. Everyman, it may not be by no waye.
I set not by [1] golde, sylver, nor rychesse,
Ne by pope, emperour, kynge, duke ne prynces;
For, and I wolde receyve gyftes grete,
All the worlde I myght gete;
But my custome is clene contrary.
I gyve the no respyte, come hens and not tary.

EVERYMAN. Alas! shall I have no lenger respyte?
I may saye Deth geveth no warnynge!
To thynke on the it maketh my herte seke;
For all unredy is my boke of rekenynge.
But, xii yere and I myght have abydynge,
My countynge boke I wolde make so clere,
That my rekenynge I sholde not nede to fere.
Wherfore, Deth, I praye the, for Goddes mercy,
Spare me tyll I be provyded of remedy.

DETHE. The avayleth not to crye, wepe, and praye.
But hast [2] the lyghtly that thou were [3] gone that journaye.
And preve [4] thy frendes, yf thou can.
For, wete thou well, the tyde abydeth no man,
And in the worlde eche lyvynge creature
For Adams synne must dye of nature.

EVERYMAN. Dethe, yf I sholde this pylgrymage take,
And my rekenynge suerly make,
Shewe me, for saynt Charyte,
Sholde I not come agayne shortly?

DETHE. No, Everyman, and thou be ones there,
Thou mayst never more come here,
Trust me veryly.

EVERYMAN. O gracyous God, in the hye sete celestyall,
Have mercy on me in this moost nede.—
Shall I have no company fro this vale terestryall
Of myne acqueynce [5] that way me to lede?

DETHE. Ye, yf ony be son hardy
That wolde go with the and bere the company.
Hye the, that thou were gone to Goddes magnyfycence,
Thy rekenynge to gyve before His presence.
What, wenest thou thy lyve is gyven the
And thy worldely goddes also?

EVERYMAN. I had wende so veryle.

DETHE. Nay, nay, it was but lende the,
For as soone as thou arte go,
Another a whyle shall have it and than go ther fro,
Even as thou hast done.
Everyman, thou arte made! [6] Thou hast thy wyttes fyve,
And here on erthe wyll not amende thy lyve!
For sodeynly I do come.

EVERYMAN. O wretched caytyfe, [7] wheder shall I flee,
That I myght scape this endles sorowe?
Now, gentyll Deth, spare me tyll to morowe,
That I may amende me
With good advysement.

DETHE. Naye, thereto I wyll not consent,
Nor no man wyll I respyte;
But to the herte sodeynly I shall smyte
Without ony advysement.
And now out of thy syght I wyll me hy.
Se thou make the redy shortely,
For thou mayst saye this is the daye
That no man lyvynge may scape awaye.

EVERYMAN. Alas! I may well wepe with syghes depe;
Now have I no maner of company
To helpe me in my journey, and me to kepe;
And also my wrytynge [8] is full unredy.
How shall I do now for to excuse me?
I wolde to God I had never begete! [9]
To my soule a full grete profyte it had be,
For now I fere paynes huge and grete.
The tyme passeth, Lorde, helpe, that all wrought!
For though I mourne it avayleth nought.
The day passeth, and is almoost ago, [10]
I wote not well what for to do.
To whome were I best my complaynt to make?
What and I to Felawshyp therof spake,
And shewed hym of this sodeyne chaunce?
For in hym is all myne affyaunce. [11]
We have in the worlde so many a daye
Be good frendes in sporte and playe.
I se hym yonder certaynely;
I trust that he wyll bere me company,
Therfore to hym wyll I speke to ese my sorowe.
Well mette, good Felawshyp, and good morowe.

FELAWSHYP *speketh:* Everyman, good morowe! By this day,
Syr, why lokest thou so pyteously?
If ony thynge be a mysse I praye the me saye,
That I may helpe to remedy.

EVERYMAN. Ye, good Felawshyp, ye,
I am in greate jeoparde.

FELAWSHYP. My true frende, shewe to me your mynde;
I wyll not forsake the to my lyves ende,
In the waye of good company.

EVERYMAN. That was well spoken, and lovyngly.

FELAWSHYP. Syr, I must nedes knowe your hevynesse,
I have pyte [12] to se you in ony dystresse.

[1] care not for
[2] haste
[3] may be
[4] prove
[5] acquaintance
[6] mad
[7] captive, wretch
[8] (his account)
[9] been born
[10] gone
[11] trust
[12] pity

If ony have you wronged ye shall revenged be,
Thoughe I on the grounde be slayne for the,
Though that I knowe before that I sholde dye.

EVERYMAN. Veryly, Felawshyp, gramercy.[1]

FELAWSHYP. Tusshe! by thy thankes I set not a strawe,
Shewe me your grefe and saye no more.

EVERYMAN. If I my herte sholde to you breke,
And than you to tourne your mynde fro me,
And wolde not me comforte whan ye here me speke,
Than sholde I ten tymes soryer be.

FELAWSHYP. Syr, I saye as I wyll do in dede.

EVERYMAN. Than be you a good frende at nede.
I have founde you true here before.

FELAWSHYP. And so ye shall evermore,
For, in fayth, and thou go to hell
I wyll not forsake the by the waye.

EVERYMAN. Ye speke lyke a good frende, I byleve you well,
I shall deserve it, and I may.

FELAWSHYP. I speke of no deservynge, by this daye,
For he that wyll saye and nothynge do
Is not worthy with good company to go.
Therfore shewe me the grefe of your mynde
As to your frende mooste lovynge and kynde.

EVERYMAN. I shall shewe you how it is:
Commaunded I am to go a journaye,
A long waye, harde and daungerous,
And gyve a strayte counte, without delaye,
Before the hye Juge Adonay.[2]
Wherfore, I pray you, bere me company,
As ye have promysed, in this journaye.

FELAWSHYP. That is mater in dede! Promyse is duty.
But and I sholde take suche a vyage on me,
I knowe it well, it shulde be to my payne;
Also it make me aferde, certayne.
But let us take counsell here as well as we can,
For your wordes wolde fere[3] a strong man.

EVERYMAN. Why, ye sayd, yf I had nede,
Ye wolde me never forsake, quycke[4] ne deed;
Thoughe it were to hell, truely.

FELAWSHYP. So I sayd certaynely.
But such pleasures be[5] set a syde the sothe[6] to saye,
And also, yf we toke suche a journaye,
Whan sholde we come agayne?

EVERYMAN. Naye, never agayne, tyll the daye of dome.[7]

FELAWSHYP. In fayth, than wyll not I come there,
Who hath you these tydynges brought?

EVERYMAN. In dede, Deth was with me here.

FELAWSHYP. Now, by God that all hathe bought,
If Deth were the messenger,
For no man that is lyvynge to daye
I wyll not go that lothe[8] journaye,
Not for the fader that bygate me.

EVERYMAN. Ye promysed other wyse, parde.[9]

FELAWSHYP. I wote well I say[10] so, truely,
And yet yf thou wylte ete, drynke and make good chere
Or haunt to women the lusty company,
I wolde not forsake you, whyle the daye is clere,
Truste me veryly.

EVERYMAN. Ye, therto ye wolde be redy:
To go to myrthe, solas, and playe,
Your mynde wyll soner apply,
Than to bere me company in my longe journaye.

FELAWSHYP. Now, in good fayth, I wyll not that waye;
But, and thou wyll murder, or ony man kyll,
In that I wyll helpe the with a good wyll.

EVERYMAN. Oh, that is a symple[11] advyse in dede!
Gentyll felawe, help me in my necessyte;
We have loved longe, and now I nede!
And now, gentyll Felawshyp, remembre me.

FELAWSHYP. Wheder ye have loved me or no,
By saynt John, I wyll not with the go.

EVERYMAN. Yet I pray the, take the labour and do so moche for me,
To brynge me forwarde, for saynt Charyte,
And comforte me tyll I come without the towne.

FELAWSHYP. Nay, and thou wolde gyve me a newe gowne,
I wyll not a fote with the go;
But and thou had taryed, I wolde not have lefte the so:
And as now, God spede the in thy journaye!
For from the I wyll departe as fast as I maye.

EVERYMAN. Wheder a waye, Felawshyp? wyll thou forsake me?

FELAWSHIP. Ye, by my faye![12] To God I betake[13] the.

EVERYMAN. Farewell, good Fellawshyp! For the my herte is sore!
A dewe for ever, I shall se the no more.

FELAWSHYP. In fayth, Everyman, fare well now at the ende,

[1] great thanks
[2] God
[3] frighten
[4] alive
[5] are (now)
[6] truth
[7] judgment
[8] loathsome
[9] one of the many forms of the oath *pardieu*
[10] said
[11] foolish
[12] faith
[13] commend

For you I wyll remembre that partynge is mournynge.
EVERYMAN. A lacke! shall we thus departe[1] in dede?
A! Lady, helpe! without ony more comforte,
Lo, Felawshyp forsaketh me in my moost nede.
For helpe in this worlde wheder shall I resorte?
Felawshyp here before with me wolde mery make,
And now lytell sorowe for me dooth he take.
It is sayd, in prosperyte men frendes may fynde
Whiche in adversyte be full unkynde.
Now wheder for socoure shall I flee,
Syth that Felawshyp hath forsaken me?
To my kynnesmen I wyll truely,
Prayenge them to helpe me in my necessyte.
I byleve that they wyll do so,
For kynde[2] wyll crepe where it may not go.[3]
I wyll go saye; for yonder I se them go—
Where be ye now, my frendes and kynnesmen?
KYNREDE. Here be we now at your commaundement.
Cosyn, I praye you, shewe us your entent
In ony wyse, and not spare.
COSYN. Ye, Everyman, and to us declare
If ye be dysposed to go ony whyder;
For, wete you well, wyll lyve and dye to gyder.
KYNREDE. In welth and wo we wyll with you holde;
For over his kynne a man may be bolde.
EVERYMAN. Gramercy, my frendes and kynnesmen kynde!
Now shall I shewe you the grefe of my mynde.
I was commaunded by a messenger,
That is a hye kynges chefe offycer;
He bad me go a pylgrymage to my payne,
And, I knowe well, I shall never come agayne.
Also I must gyve a rekenynge strayte;
For I have a grete enemy that hath me in wayte,[4]
Whiche entendeth me for to hynder.
KYNREDE. What a counte is that whiche ye must render?
That wolde I knowe.
EVERYMAN. Of all my workes I must shewe,
How I have lyved, and my dayes spent;
Also of yll dedes that I have used
In my tyme, syth lyfe was me lent,
And of all vertues that I have refused.
Therefore, I praye you, go thyder with me
To helpe to make myn accounte, for saynt Charyte.
COSYN. What, to go thyder! Is that the mater?
Nay, Everyman, I had lever[5] fast[6] brede and water,
All this fyve yere and more.
EVERYMAN. Alas, that ever I was bore,[7]
For now shall I never be mery,
If that you forsake me.
KYNREDE. A! syr, what, ye be a mery man!
Take good herte to you, and make no mone.
But one thynge I warne you, by saynt Anne,
As for me ye shall go alone.
EVERYMAN. My Cosyn, wyll you not with me go?
COSYN. No, by our Lady! I have the crampe in my to:
Trust not to me; for, so God me spede,
I wyll deceyve you in your moost nede.
KYNREDE. It avayleth not us to tyse:[8]
Ye shall have my mayde, with all my herte;
She loveth to go to feestes there to be nyse,[9]
And to daunce, and a brode to sterte,[10]
I wyll gyve her leve to helpe you in that journey,
If that you and she may a gree.
EVERYMAN. Now shewe me the very effecte of your mynde;
Wyll you go with me, or abyde be hynde?
KYNREDE. Abyde behynde! ye[11] that wyll I and I maybe;
Therfore farewell tyll another daye.
EVERYMAN. Howe sholde I be mery or gladde?
For fayre promyses men to me make,
But, whan I have moost nede, they me forsake;
I am deceyved, that maketh me sadde.
COSYN. Cosyn Everyman, farewell now,
For, veryly, I wyll not go with you.
Also of myne owne an unredy rekenynge
I have to accounte, therfore I make taryenge;
Now God kepe the, for now I go.
EVERYMAN. A! Jesus, is all come here to?
Lo, fayre wordes maketh fooles fayne;
They promyse, and nothynge wyll do certayne.
My kynnesmen promysed me faythfully
For to a byde with me stedfastly;
And now fast a waye do they flee;
Even so Felawshyp promysed me.
What frende were best me of to provyde?
I lose my tyme here longer to abyde;
Yet in my mynde a thynge there is—
All my lyfe I have loved ryches;
Yf that my Good now helpe me myght,
He wolde make my herte full lyght;
I wyll speke to hym in this dystresse—
Where arte thou, my Gooddes and Ryches?

[1] separate
[2] nature, kinship
[3] walk (i.e., will do all in its power)
[4] is lying in wait for me
[5] rather
[6] fast on
[7] born
[8] entice
[9] wanton
[10] abroad to run
[11] yea

GOODES. Who calleth me? Everyman? What hast thou haste?
I lye here in corners, trussed and pyled so hye,
And in chestes I am locked so fast,
Also sacked in bagges, thou mayst se with thyn eye,
I can not styre; in packes lowe I lye.
What wolde ye have? Lyghtly me saye.
EVERYMAN. Come hyder, Good, in al the hast thou may,
For of counseyll I must desyre the.
GOODES. Syr, and ye in the worlde have sorowe or adversyte,
That can I helpe you to remedy shortly.
EVERYMAN. It is another dysease that greveth me;
In this worlde it is not, I tell the so,
I am sent for an other way to go,
To gyve a strayte counte generall
Before the hyest Jupyter of all.
And all my lyfe I have had joye and pleasure in the,
Therfore I pray the go with me;
For, paraventure, thou mayst before God almyghty
My rekenynge helpe to clene, and puryfye,
For it is sayd ever amonge[1]
That money maketh all ryght that is wronge.
GOODES. Nay, Everyman, I synge an other songe;
I folowe no man in suche vyages,
For, and I wente with the,
Thou sholdes fare moche the worse for me:
For bycause on me thou dyd set thy mynde,
Thy rekenynge I have made blotted and blynde,
That thyne accounte thou can not make truly;
And that hast thou for the love of me.
EVERYMAN. That wolde greve me full sore,
Whan I sholde come to that ferefull answere.
Up! let us go thyther to gyder.
GOODES. Nay, not so: I am to brytell,[2] I may not endure:
I wyll folowe [no] man one fote be ye sure.
EVERYMAN. Alas, I have the loved, and had grete pleasure
All my lyfe dayes on good and treasure.
GOODES. That is to thy dampnacyon without lesynge,[3]
For my love is contrary to the love everlastynge;
But yf thou had me loved moderately durynge[4]
As to the poore gyve parte of me,
Than sholdest thou not in this dolour be,
Nor in this grete sorowe and care.
EVERYMAN. Lo, now was I deceyved or I was ware,
And all I may wyte[5] my spendynge of tyme.
GOODES. What, wenest thou that I am thyne?
EVERYMAN. I had went[6] so.
GOODES. Naye, Everyman, I saye no:
As for a whyle I was lente the;
A season thou hast had me in prosperyte;
My condycyon is mannes soule to kyll,
If I save one a thousande I do spyll.[7]
Wenest thou that I wyll folowe the?
Nay, fro this worlde not veryle.
EVERYMAN. I had wende otherwyse.
GOODES. Therfore to thy soule Good is a thefe,
For whan thou arte deed, this is my gyse:[8]
Another to deceyve in this same wyse
As I have done the, and all to his soules reprefe.[9]
EVERYMAN. O false Good, cursed thou be,
Thou traytour to God, that hast deceyved me
And caught me in thy snare.
GOODES. Mary,[10] thou brought thy self in care,
Wherof I am gladde;
I must nedes laugh, I can not be sadde.
EVERYMAN. A! Good, thou hast had longe my hertely love;
I gave the that whiche sholde be the Lordes above:
But wylte thou not go with me in dede?
I praye the trouth to saye.
GOODES. No, so God me spede;
Therfore fare well, and have good daye.
EVERYMAN. Oh, to whome shall I make my mone
For to go with me in that hevy journaye?
Fyrst Felawshyp sayd he wolde with me gone;
His wordes were very pleasaunte and gaye,
But afterwarde he lefte me alone.
Than spake I to my kynnesmen all in despayre,
And also they gave me wordes fayre—
They lacked no fayre spekynge;
But all forsake me in the endynge.
Than wente I to my Goodes, that I loved best,
In hope to have comforte, but there had I leest;
For my Goodes sharpely dyd me tell
That he bryngeth many in to hell.
Than of my selfe I was ashamed,
And so I am worthy to be blamed.
Thus may I well my selfe hate.
Of whome shall I now counseyll take?
I thynke that I shall never spede
Tyll that I go to my Good-dede.
But, alas, she is so weke
That she can nother go[11] nor speke.

[1] everywhere
[2] brittle
[3] without lying, i.e., truly
[4] the while
[5] blame to
[6] thought
[7] destroy
[8] custom
[9] reproof
[10] an oath "By the Virgin Mary"
[11] neither walk

Yet wyll I venter on her now.—
My Good-dedes, where be you?
GOOD-DEDES. Here I lye, colde in the grounde;
Thy synnes hath me sore bounde
That I can not stere.[1]
EVERYMAN. O Good-dedes, I stande in fere;
I must you pray of counseyll,
For helpe now sholde come ryght well.
GOOD-DEDES. Everyman, I have understandynge
That ye be somoned a counte to make
Before Myssyas[2] of Jherusalem kynge.
And you do by me[3] that journay with you wyll I take.
EVERYMAN. Therefore I come to you my moone to make.
I pray you that ye wyll go with me.
GOOD-DEDES. I wolde full fayne, but I can not stande veryly.
EVERYMAN. Why, is there ony thynge on you fall?
GOOD-DEDES. Ye, syr, I may thanke you of all.
If ye had parfytely chered[4] me,
Your boke of counte full redy had be.
Loke, the bokes of your workes and dedes eke.
A! se how they lye under the fete,
To your soules hevynes.
EVERYMAN. Our Lord Jesus, helpe me,
For one letter here I can not se.
GOOD-DEDES. There is a blynde rekenynge in tyme of dystress.
EVERYMAN. Good-dedes, I praye you helpe me in this nede,
Or elles I am for ever dampned in dede;
Therfore helpe me to make rekenynge
Before the Redemer of all thynge,
That kynge is, and was, and ever shall.
GOOD-DEDES. Everyman, I am sory of your fall,
And fayne wolde I helpe you, and I were able.
EVERYMAN. Good-dedes, your counseyll I pray you gyve me.
GOOD-DEDES. That shall I do veryly,
Thoughe that on my fete I may not go.
I have a syster that shall with you also,
Called Knowledge, whiche shall with you abyde,
To help you to make that dredefull rekenynge.
KNOWLEDGE. Everyman, I wyll go with the, and be thy gyde,
In thy moost nede to go by thy syde.
EVERYMAN. In good condycyon I am now in every thynge,
And am hole content with this good thynge,
Thanked by[5] God my creature.[6]
GOOD-DEDES. And whan he hath brought you there,
Where thou shalte hele the of thy smarte,
Than go you with your rekenynge and your good dedes togyder,
For to make you joyfull at herte
Before the blessyd Trynyte.
EVERYMAN. My Good-dedes, gramercy;
I am well content certaynly
With your wordes swete.
KNOWLEDGE. Now go we togyder lovyngly
To Confessyon, that clensynge ryvere.
EVERYMAN. For joy I wepe: I wolde we were there;
But, I pray you, gyve me cognycyon[7]
Where dwelleth that holy man Confessyon?
KNOWLEDGE. In the hous of salvacyon;
We shall fynde hym in that place,
That shall us comforte by Goddes grace.—
Lo, this is Confessyon; knele downe, & aske mercy,
For he is in good conceyte[8] with God almyghty.
EVERYMAN. O gloryous fountayne that all unclennes doth claryfy,
Wasshe fro me the spottes of vyce unclene,
That on me no synne may be sene;
I come with Knowlege for my redempcyon,
Redempte with herte and full contrycyon,
For I am commaunded a pylgrymage to take,
And grete accountes before God to make.
Now I praye you, Shryfte,[9] moder of salvacyon,
Helpe my good dedes for my pyteous exclamacyon.
CONFESSYON. I knowe your sorowe well, Everyman:
Bycause with Knowlege ye come to me,
I wyll you comforte as well as I can;
And a precyous jewell I wyll gyve the,
Called penaunce, [voyce] voyder[10] of adversyte;
Therwith shall your body chastysed be
With abstynence and perseveraunce in Goddes servyce:
Here shall you receyve that scourge of me
Whiche is penaunce stronge that ye must endure,
To remembre thy Savyour was scourged for the
With sharpe scourges, and suffred it pacyently;
So must thou, or thou scape that paynful pylgrymage.—
Knowledge, kepe hym in this vyage,
And by that tyme Good-dedes wyll be with the;

[1] stir
[2] Messiah
[3] if you will act by my advice—Pollard. (Or possibly *by* = buy, ransom: if you deliver me.)
[4] entertained
[5] be
[6] creator
[7] information
[8] favor
[9] absolution
[10] expeller (*voyce* is probably an error)

But in ony wyse be seker of mercy,
For your tyme draweth fast; and ye wyll saved be,
Aske God mercy, and he wyll graunte truely:
Whan with the scourge of penaunce man doth hym bynde,
The oyle of forgyvenes than shall he fynde.

EVERYMAN. Thanked be God for his gracyous werke,
For now I wyll my penaunce begyn;
This hath rejoysed and lyghted my herte,
Though the knottes be paynfull and harde within.

KNOWLEDGE. Everyman, loke your penaunce that ye fulfyll,
What payne that ever it to you be;
And Knowledge shall gyve you counseyll at wyll,
How your accounte ye shall make clerely.

EVERYMAN. O eternall God, O hevenly fygure,
O way of ryghtwysnes, O goodly vysyon,
Whiche descended downe in a vyrgyn pure
Because he wolde Everyman redeme,
Whiche Adam forfayted by his dysobedyence,
O blessyd Godheed, electe and hye devyne,
Forgyve my grevous offence;
Here I crye the mercy in this presence;
O ghostly treasure, O raunsomer and redemer!
Of all the worlde, hope and conduyter,[1]
Myrrour of joye, foundatour[2] of mercy,
Whiche enlumyneth heven and erth therby,
Here my clamorous complaynt, though it late be!
Receyve my prayers; unworthy in this hevy lyfe
Though I be, a synner moost abhomynable,
Yet let my name be wryten in Moyses table.[3]
O Mary, praye to the maker of all thynge
Me for to helpe at my endynge,
And save me fro the power of my enemy;
For Deth assayleth me strongly:
And, Lady, that I may by meane of thy prayer
Of your sones glory to be partynere,
By the meanes of his passyon,[4] I it crave;
I beseche you, helpe my soule to save!—
Knowledge, gyve me the scourge of penaunce,
My flesshe therwith shall gyve acqueyntaunce;
I wyll now begyn, yf God gyve me grace.

KNOWLEDGE. Everyman, God gyve you tyme and space;
Thus I bequeth you in the handes of our Savyour;
Now may you make your rekenynge sure.

EVERYMAN. In the name of the holy Trynyte
My body sore punysshyd shall be,
Take this, body, for the synne of the flesshe;
Also thou delytest to go gay and fresshe;
And in the way of dampnacyon thou dyd me brynge;
Therfore suffre now strokes of punysshynge;
Now of penaunce I wyll wade the water clere,
To save me from purgatory, that sharpe fyre.

GOOD-DEDES. I thanke God, now I can walke and go,
And am delyvered of my sykenesse and wo;
Therfore with Everyman I wyll go, and not spare.
His good workes I wyll helpe hym to declare.

KNOWLEDGE. Now, Everyman, be mery and glad;
Your Good-dedes cometh now, ye may not be sad;
Now is your Good-dedes hole and sounde,
Goynge upryght upon the grounde.

EVERYMAN. My herte is lyght, and shalbe evermore;
Now wyll I smyte faster than I dyde before.

GOOD-DEDES. Everyman, pylgryme, my specyall frende,
Blessyd be thou without ende;
For the is preparate the eternall glory.
Ye have me made hole and sounde,
Therfore I will byde by the in every stounde.[5]

EVERYMAN. Welcome, my Good-dedes! Now I here thy voyce
I wepe for very sweteness of love.

KNOWLEDGE. Be no more sad, but ever rejoyce.
God seeth thy lyvynge in his trone above;
Put on this garment to thy behove,[6]
Whiche is wette with your teres,
Or elles before God you may it mysse,
Whan ye to your journeys ende come shall.

EVERYMAN. Gentyll Knowledge, what do ye it call?

KNOWLEDGE. It is a garmente of sorowe,
Fro payne it wyll you borowe;[7]
Contrycyon it is,
That getteth forgyvenes,
He pleasyth God passynge well.

GOOD-DEDES. Everyman, wyll you were it for your hele?[8]

EVERYMAN. Now blessyd be Jesu, Maryes sone,
For now have I on true contrycyon,
And lette us go now without taryenge.—
Good-dedes, have we clere our rekenynge?

GOOD-DEDES. Ye, in dede, I have here.

EVERYMAN. Than I trust we nede not fere.
Now, frendes, let us not parte in twayne.

[1] leader
[2] founder
[3] apparently meaning the Book of Life
[4] death on the cross
[5] hour
[6] profit
[7] redeem
[8] wear it for your healing

KYNDREDE.[1] Nay, Everyman, that wyll we not certayne.
GOOD-DEDES. Yet must thou led[2] with the
Thre persones of grete myght.
EVERYMAN. Who sholde they be?
GOOD-DEDES. Dyscrecyon and Strength they hyght,[3]
And thy Beaute may not abyde behynde.
KNOWLEDGE. Also ye must call to mynde
Your Fyve-wyttes,[4] as for your counseylours.
GOOD-DEDES. You must have them redy at all houres.
EVERYMAN. Howe shall I gette them hyder?
KYNREDE. You must call them all togyder,
And they wyll here you in contynent.[5]
EVERYMAN. My frendes, come hyder, and be present,
Dyscrecyon, Strengthe, my Fyve-wyttes and Beaute.
BEAUTE. Here at your wyll we be all redy.
What wyll ye that we sholde do?
GOOD-DEDES. That ye wolde with Everyman go,
And helpe hym in his pylgrymage.
Advyse you, wyll ye with him or not in that vyage?
STRENGTHE. We wyll brynge hym all thyder
To his helpe and comforte, ye may beleve me.
DYSCRECYON. So wyll we go with hym all togyder.
EVERYMAN. Almyghty God, loved myght thou be;
I gyve the laude[6] that I have hyder brought
Strength, Dyscrecyon, Beaute, & Fyve-wyttes, lacke I nought:
And my Good-dedes, with Knowledge clere,
All be in my company at my wyll here;
I desyre no more to my besynes.
STRENGTHE. And I, Strength, wyll by you stande in dystres,
Though thou wolde in batayle fyght on the ground.
FYVE-WYTTES. And though it were thrugh the worlde rounde,
We wyll not departe for swete ne soure,
BEAUTE. No more wyll I unto dethes houre,
What so ever therof befall.
DYSCRECYON. Everyman, advyse you fyrst of all,
Go with a good advysement and delyberacyon.
We all gyve you vertuous monycyon[7]
That all shall be well.
EVERYMAN. My frendes, harken what I wyll tell;
I praye God rewarde you in his heven spere.
Now herken all that be here,
For I wyll make my testament
Here before you all present;
In almes, halfe my good I wyll gyve with my handes twayne
In the way of charyte with good entent,
And the other halfe styll shall remayne
In queth[8] to be retourned there[9] it ought to be.
This I do in despyte of the fende of hell,
To go quyte out of his perell[10]
Ever after and this daye.
KNOWLEDGE. Everyman, herken what I saye;
Go to presthode I you advyse,
And receyve of him in ony wyse
The holy sacrament and oyntement togyder,
Than shortly se ye tourne agayne hyder,
We wyll all abyde you here.
FYVE-WYTTES. Ye, Everyman, hye you that ye redy were.[11]
There is no Emperour, King, Duke, ne Baron
That of God hath commycyon
As hath the leest preest in the worlde beynge;[12]
For of the blessyd sacramentes pure and benynge
He bereth the keyes, and thereof hath the cure.[13]
For mannes redempcyon it is ever sure
Whiche God for our soules medycyne
Gave us out of his herte with grete payne.
Here in this transytory lyfe, for the and me
The blessyd sacramentes vii there be:
Baptym, confyrmacyon, with preesthode good,
And the sacrament of Goddes precyous flesshe and blod,
Maryage, the holy extreme unccyon[14] and penaunce:
These seven be good to have in remembraunce,
Gracyous sacramentes of hye devynyte.
EVERYMAN. Fayne wolde I receyve that holy body
And mekely to my ghostly fader I wyll go.
FYVE-WYTTES. Everyman, that is the best that ye can do;
God wyll you to salvacyon brynge,
For preesthode excedeth all other thyng
To us holy scrypture they do teche,
And converteth man fro synne, heven to reche;
God hath to them more power gyven
Than to ony aungell that is in heven.
With v wordes he may consecrate
Goddes body in flesshe and blode to make,
And handeleth his Maker bytwene his handes.
The preest byndeth and unbyndeth all bandes
Both in erthe and in heven.

[1] probably error for KNOWLEDGE
[2] lead
[3] are called
[4] the five senses
[5] without delay
[6] praise
[7] admonition
[8] under promise
[9] where
[10] out of his power
[11] haste that ye may be ready
[12] living
[13] care
[14] last anointing

Thou mynystres [1] all the sacramentes seven.
Though we kysse thy fete thou were worthy.
Thou arte surgyon that cureth synne deedly.
No remedy we fynde under God
Bute all onely preesthode.
Everyman, God gave preest that dygnyte
And setteth them in his stede amonge us to be.
Thus be they above aungelles in degree.

KNOWLEDGE. If preestes be good, it is so suerly,
But whan Jesu hanged on the crosse with grete smarte,
There he gave out of his blessyd herte
The same sacrament in grete tourment;
He solde them not to us, that Lorde omnypotent;
Therfore saynt Peter the apostell dothe saye
That Jesus curse hath all they
Whiche God theyr Savyour do by [2] or sell,
Or they for [3] ony money do take or tell. [4]
Synfull preestes gyveth the synners example bad;

. . . .

These be with synne made blynde.

FYVE-WYTTES. I trust to God, no suche may we fynde;
Therfore let us preesthode honour,
And folowe theyr doctryne for our soules socoure.
We be theyr shepe, and they shepeherdes be,
By whome we all be kepte in suerte.
Peas! for yonder I se Everyman come,
Which hath made true satysfaccyon.

GOOD-DEDES. Me thynke, it is he in dede.

EVERYMAN. Now Jesu be your alder spede! [5]
I have receyved the sacrament for my redempcyon,
And than myne extreme unccyon.
Blessyd be all they that counseyled me to take it!
And now frendes, let us go without longer respyte.
I thanke God, that ye have taryed so longe.
Now set eche of you on this rodde [6] your honde,
And shortely folowe me.
I go before there I wolde be. God be your gyde.

STRENGTH. Everyman, we wyll not fro you go
Tyll we have done this vyage longe.

DYSCRECYON. I, Dyscrecyon, wyll byde by you also.

KNOWLEDGE. And though this pylgrymage be never so stronge [7]
I wyll never parte you fro.
Everyman, I wyll be as sure by the
As ever I dyde by Judas Machabee. [8]

EVERYMAN. Alas! I am so faynt I may not stande,
My lymmes under me doth folde.
Frendes, let us not tourne agayne to this lande,
Not for all the worldes golde,
For in to this cave must I crepe,
And tourne to erth and there to slepe.

BEAUTE. What, in to this grave, alas!

EVERYMAN. Ye, there shall ye consume, more, and lesse. [9]

BEAUTE. And what, sholde I smoder here?

EVERYMAN. Ye, by my fayth, and never more appere!
In this worlde lyve no more we shall,
But in heven before the hyest Lorde of all.

BEAUTE. I crosse oute all this! Adewe, by saynt Johan!
I take my tappe [10] in my lappe, and am gone.

EVERYMAN. What, Beaute, whyder wyll ye?

BEAUTE. Peas! I am defe, I loke not behynde me,
Not and thou woldest gyve me all the golde in thy chest.

EVERYMAN. Alas! whereto may I truste?
Beaute gothe fast awaye fro me.
She promysed with me to lyve and dye.

STRENGTHE. Everyman, I wyll the also forsake and denye,
Thy game lyketh [11] me not at all.

EVERYMAN. Why than ye wyll forsake me all!
Swete Strength, tary a lytell space.

STRENGTHE. Nay, syr, by the rode of grace,
I wyll hye me from the fast,
Though thou wepe to [12] thy herte to brast. [13]

EVERYMAN. Ye wolde ever byde by me, ye sayd.

STRENGTHE. Ye, I have you ferre [14] ynoughe conveyde.
Ye be olde ynoughe, I understande,
Your pylgrymage to take on hande.
I repent me, that I hyder came.

EVERYMAN. Strength, you to dysplease I am to blame;
Wyll ye breke promyse that is dette? [15]

STRENGTHE. In fayth, I care not!
Thou arte but a foole to complayne;
You spende your speche, and wast your brayne;
Go, thryst [16] the into the grounde!

[1] administerest
[2] buy
[3] Possibly *they for* should be *therfor*.
[4] count
[5] the help of you all
[6] rood, cross
[7] difficult
[8] Leader of the Jews against the Syrians in the recovery of Jerusalem, 164 B.C.; see I *Maccabees*, iii
[9] high and low alike
[10] bunch of tow (for spinning: an old wives' saying)
[11] pleases
[12] until
[13] burst
[14] far
[15] See l. 248.
[16] thrust

EVERYMAN. I had wende [1] surer I shulde you have founde:
He that trusteth in his Strength,
She hym deceyveth at the length;
Bothe Strength and Beaute forsaketh me,
Yet they promysed me fayre and lovyngly.
DYSCRECION. Everyman, I wyll after Strength be gone;
As for me I wyll leve you alone.
EVERYMAN. Why, Dyscrecyon, wyll ye forsake me?
DYSCRECION. Ye, in fayth, I wyll go frо the;
For whan Strength goth before,
I folowe after ever more.
EVERYMAN. Yet, I pray the, for the love of the Trynyte,
Loke in my grave ones pyteously.
DYSCRECION. Nay, so nye wyll I not come!
Fare well, everychone. [2]
EVERYMAN. Oh, all thynge fayleth, save God alone,
Beaute, Strength, and Dyscrecyon;
For, whan Deth bloweth his blast,
They all renne fro me full fast.
FYVE-WYTTES. Everyman, my leve now of the I take;
I wyll folowe the other, for here I the forsake.
EVERYMAN. Alas, than may I wayle and wepe,
For I toke you for my best frende.
FYVE-WYTTES. I wyll no lenger the kepe;
Now farewell, and there an ende.
EVERYMAN. O Jesu, helpe! all hath forsaken me.
GOOD-DEDES. Nay, Everyman, I wyll byde with the,
I wyll not forsake the in dede;
Thou shalte fynde me a good frende at nede.
EVERYMAN. Gramercy, Good-dedes, now may I true frendes se;
They have forsaken me everychone,
I loved them better than my Good-dedes alone.
Knowledge, wyll ye forsake me also?
KNOWLEDGE. Ye, Everyman, whan ye to deth shall go;
But not yet for no manner of daunger.
EVERYMAN. Gramercy, Knowledge, with all my herte.
KNOWLEDGE. Nay, yet I wyll not from hens [3] departe,
Tyll I se where ye shall be come.
EVERYMAN. Me thynke, alas, that I must be gone
To make my rekenynge and my dettes paye;
For I se my tyme is nye spent awaye.
Take example, all ye that this do here or se,
How they that I love best do forsake me,
Excepte my Good-dedes, that bydeth truely.
GOOD-DEDES. All erthly thynges is but vanyte,
Beaute, Strength, and Dyscrecyon, do man forsake,
Folysshe frendes, and kynnesmen that fayre spake,
All fleeth save Good-dedes and that am I.
EVERYMAN. Have mercy on me, God moost myghty—
And stande by me, thou moder & mayde, holy Mary.
GOOD-DEDES. Fere not, I wyll speke for the.
EVERYMAN. Here I crye, God mercy.
GOOD-DEDES. Shorte [4] our ende and mynysshe [5] our payne;
Let us go and never come agayne.
EVERYMAN. Into thy handes, Lorde, my soule I commende,
Receyve it, Lorde, that it be not lost!
As thou me boughtest, so me defende,
And save me from the fendes boost, [6]
That I may appere with that blessyd hoost
That shall be saved at the day of dome.
In manus tuas, [7] of myghtes moost,
For ever commendo spiritum meum. [8]
KNOWLEDGE. Now hath he suffred that [9] we all shall endure,
The Good-dedes shall make all sure.
Now hath he made endynge,
Me thynketh that I here aungelles synge,
And make grete joy and melody,
Where every mannes soule receyved shall be.
THE AUNGELL. Come excellente electe spouse to Jesu!
Here above thou shalt go,
Bycause of thy synguler vertue.
Now the soule is taken the body fro
Thy rekenynge is crystall clere;
Now shalte thou in to the hevenly spere,
Unto the whiche all ye shall come
That lyveth well before the daye of dome.
DOCTOUR. [10] This morall, men may have in mynde;
Ye herers, take it of worth, olde and yonge,
And forsake Pryde, for he deceyveth you in the ende,
And remembre Beaute, Fyve-wyttes, Strength, and Dyscrecyon,

[1] weened, thought
[2] every one
[3] hence
[4] shorten
[5] diminish
[6] fiend's boast
[7] into Thy hands
[8] I commend my spirit
[9] what
[10] To the Doctor (i. e., learned man, or teacher) is assigned the epilogue, which emphasizes the moral of the play.

They all at the last do Everyman forsake,
Save [1] his Good-dedes there doth he take.
But be ware, and [2] they be small,
Before God he hath no helpe at all.
None excuse may be there for Everyman!
Alas! how shall he do than?
For after dethe amendes may no man make,
For than mercy and pyte doth hym forsake;
If his rekenynge be not clere whan he doth come,
God wyll saye—Ite maledicti, in ignem aeternum. [3]
And he that hath his accounte hole and sounde
Hye in heven he shall be crounde;
Unto whiche place God brynge us all thyder,
That we may lyve body and soule togyder!
Therto helpe the Trynyte!
Amen, saye ye, for saynt Charyte!

Finis

Thus endeth this morall playe of Everyman.

before 1525

[1] only
[2] for if
[3] go, ye accursed, into everlasting fire

WILLIAM CAXTON 1422?-1491

Of significance in the development of our language and literature is the man who not only printed the first book in English, but also introduced the art of printing into the country. Caxton came of an old Kentish family, though nothing definite is known about his parents. After a little early schooling, in 1438 he was apprenticed to Robert Lange, a London mercer, later Lord Mayor. On his master's death Caxton went to Bruges, where in his thirty years of residence he became a man of such importance that in 1465 he was Governor of the English guild of Merchants Adventurers there.

In 1470 he gave up commerce, and entered the household of the Duchess of Burgundy. For her he translated from the French, *The Recuyell of the Histories of Troy,* a popular medieval romance. To supply the demand for this book, the first printed in the English language (at Bruges in Flanders about 1474), he took up there the art of printing. In 1476 he returned to England, set up his press within the ancient precincts of Westminster Abbey, and devoted the rest of his life to supplying the public with books. He was a favorite with Edward IV and Richard III, had many famous friends, and became a man of mark in his own parish before he died.

One of his earliest ventures was a large folio edition of Chaucer's *Canterbury Tales.* In 1483 appeared the most popular of his translations, the *Golden Legend* (a collection of saints' lives). Two years later he perpetuated for English literature the great prose romance, Malory's *Morte Darthur.* His original work, consisting of prefaces and epilogues to his translations, is of interest, especially the preface to the *Eneydos,* 1490, for in it Caxton sets out at length his views and opinions on the English language, its changes and dialects. He did much to fix the literary language of the sixteenth century, and to familiarize the English people with some of the great Latin and French works.

THE RECUYELL OF THE HISTORIES OF TROY [4]

Prologue

When I remember that every man is bounden by the commandment and counsel of the wise man to eschew sloth and idleness, which is mother and nourisher of vices, and ought to put myself unto virtuous occupation and business, then I, having no great change of occupation, following the said counsel took a French book, and read therein many strange and marvelous histories, [5] wherein I had great pleasure and delight, as well for the novelty of the same, as for the fair language of the French, which was in prose so well and compendiously set and written, which methought I understood the sentence [6] and substance of every matter. And for so much of this book was new and late made and drawn into French, and never had seen it in our English tongue, I thought in myself it should be a good business to translate it into our English, to the end that it might be had as well in the royaume [7] of England as in other lands, and also for to pass therewith the time, and thus concluded in myself to begin this said work. And forthwith took pen and ink, and began boldly to run forth as blind Bayard [8] in this present work, which is named "The Recuyell of the Trojan Histories." And afterwards when I remembered myself of my simpleness and unperfectness that I had in both languages, that is to wit in French and in English, for in France was I never, and was born and learned my English in Kent, in the Weald, where I doubt not is spoken as broad and rude English as in any place of England; and have continued by the space of thirty years for the most part in the countries of Brabant, Flanders, Holland, and Zeeland; and thus when all these things came before me, after that [9] I had made and written five or six quires, I fell in despair of this work,

[4] "The collection of the stories of Troy"; the spelling is here modernized.
[5] stories [6] sense [7] realm
[8] A legendary horse in the Charlemagne romances; "As bold as blind Bayard" was an old proverb for recklessness.
[9] after

and purposed no more to have continued therein, and those laid apart, and in two years after labored no more in this work, and was fully in will to have left it, till on a time it fortuned that the right high, excellent, and right virtuous princess, my right redoubted Lady, my Lady Margaret, by the grace of God sister unto the King of England and of France, my sovereign lord, Duchess of Burgundy, of Lotryk, of Brabant, of Limburg, and of Luxemburg, Countess of Flanders, of Artois, and of Burgundy, Palatine of Hainaut, of Holland, of Zeeland, and of Namur, Marquesse of the Holy Empire, Lady of Frisia, of Salins, and of Mechlin, sent for me to speak with her good Grace of divers matters, among the which I let her Highness have knowledge of the foresaid beginning of this work, which [1] anon commanded me to show the said five or six quires to her said Grace; and when she had seen them, anon she found a default in my English, which she commanded me to amend, and moreover commanded me straitly [2] to continue and make an end of the residue then not translated; whose dreadful [3] commandment I durst in no wise disobey, because I am a servant unto her said Grace and receive of her yearly fee and other many good and great benefits (and also hope many more to receive of her Highness), but forthwith went and labored in the said translation after my simple and poor cunning, also [4] nigh as I can follow my author, meekly beseeching the bounteous Highness of my said Lady that of her benevolence list [5] to accept and take in gree [6] this simple and rude work here following; and if there be anything written or said to her pleasure, I shall think my labor well employed, and whereas [7] there is default, that she arette [8] it to the simpleness of my cunning, which is full small in this behalf; and require and pray all them that shall read this said work to correct it, and to hold me excused of the rude and simple translation.

And thus I end my prologue.

Epilogue to Book III

Thus end I this book, which I have translated after mine Author as nigh as God hath given me cunning, to whom be given the laud and praising. And for as much as in the writing of the same my pen is worn, my hand weary and not steadfast, mine eyne dimmed with overmuch looking on the white paper, and my courage not so prone and ready to labor as it hath been, and that age creepeth on me daily and feebleth all the body, and also because I have promised to divers gentlemen and to my friends to address [9] to them as hastily as I might this said book, therefore I have practiced and learned at my great charge and dispense to ordain [10] this said book in print, after the manner and form as ye may here see, and is not written with pen and ink as other books be; to the end that every man may have them at once. For all the books of this story, named "The Recule of the Histories of Troy" thus imprinted as ye here see, were begun in one day and also finished in one day, which book I have presented to my said redoubted Lady, as afore is said. And she hath well accepted it, and largely rewarded me, wherefore I beseech Almighty God to reward her everlasting bliss after this life, praying her said Grace and all them that shall read this book not to disdain the simple and rude work, neither to reply against the saying of the matters touched in this book, though it accord not unto the translation of others which have written it. For divers men have made divers books which in all points accord not, as Dictes, Dares, [11] and Homer. For Dictes and Homer, as Greeks, say and write favorably for the Greeks, and give them more worship than to the Trojans; and Dares writeth otherwise than they do. And also as for the proper names, it is no wonder that they accord not, for some one name in these days have divers equivocations after the countries that they dwell in; but all accord in conclusion the general destruction of that noble city of Troy, and the death of so many noble princes, as kings, dukes, earls, barons, knights, and common people, and the ruin irreparable of that city that never since was reëdified; which may be example to all men during the world how dreadful and jeopardous it is to begin a war, and what harms, losses, and death followeth. Therefore the Apostle saith: "All that is written is written to our doctrine," [12] which doctrine for the common weal I beseech God may be taken in such place and time as shall be most needful in increasing of peace, love, and charity; which grant us He that suffered for the same to be crucified on the rood tree. And say we all Amen for charity!

c. 1474

[1] who
[2] strictly
[3] revered
[4] just as
[5] she please
[6] graciously
[7] where
[8] may she attribute
[9] send
[10] prepare
[11] These were reputed to be authors of Trojan tales which are found only in late Latin and which, though popular in the Middle Ages, have sunk into obscurity.
[12] for our instruction

SIR THOMAS MALORY d. 1471

Little is yet known in detail about the origin and life of the compiler of *Le Morte Darthur.* If, as now seems certain, he was Sir Thomas Malory of Newbold Revill in Warwickshire, he succeeded his father in 1433 or 1434, was a retainer of the last Earl of Warwick, followed him to France, and took part in the famous siege of Rouen, 1449. He tells us that he finished his book in 1470.

Of the hundred books printed by Caxton, this was in every way the most important—in size, in intrinsic literary value, and in the influence it was destined to have upon succeeding literature. Its author compiled it out of the enormous amount of legendary material which had grown up in Western Europe about King Arthur and the Holy Grail. Though he drew mainly from French sources, his structure is original, his imagination vivid, and his narrative style is admirable. The book is of endless interest as a glowing picture of chivalry.

A very pleasing edition is that by A. W. Pollard, 2 vols., 1900. For further discussion see Saintsbury, *Flourishing of Romance;* Ker, *Medieval Literature;* E. C. Dawson, "Morals of the Round Table," *Liv. Age* 267:606-10, giving a picture of life in Malory's day and Tennyson's idealization of it.

From LE MORTE DARTHUR [1]

. . How Arthur Was Chosen King . .

Book I, Chapters IV-VII

And then [King Uther] fell passing [2] sore sick, so that three days and three nights he was speechless: wherefore all the barons made great sorrow, and asked Merlin [3] what counsel were best. There is none other remedy, said Merlin, but God will have his will. But look ye all barons be before King Uther to-morn, and God and I shall make him to speak. So on the morn all the barons with Merlin came before the king; then Merlin said aloud unto King Uther, Sir, shall your son Arthur be king after your days, of this realm with all the appurtenance? Then Uther Pendragon turned him, and said in hearing of them all, I give him God's blessing and mine, and bid him pray for my soul, and righteously and worshipfully that he claim the crown, upon forfeiture of my blessing; and therewith he yielded up the ghost, and then was he interred as longed to a king. Wherefore the queen, fair Igraine, made great sorrow, and all the barons.

Then stood the realm in great jeopardy long while, for every lord that was mighty of men made him strong, and many weened to have been king. Then Merlin went to the Archbishop of Canterbury, and counseled him for to send for all the lords of the realm, and all the gentlemen of arms, that they should to London come by Christmas, upon pain of cursing; and for this cause, that Jesus, that was born on that night, that he would of his great mercy show some miracle, as he was come to be king of mankind, for to show some miracle who should be rightwise king of this realm. So the Archbishop, by the advice of Merlin, sent for all the lords and gentlemen of arms that they should come by Christmas even unto London. And many of them made them clean of their life, [4] that their prayer might be the more acceptable unto God.

So in the greatest church of London, whether it were Paul's [5] or not the French book maketh no mention, all the estates [6] were long or [7] day in the church for to pray. And when matins and the first mass was done, there was seen in the churchyard, against the high altar, a great stone four square, like unto a marble stone, and in midst thereof was like an [8] anvil of steel a foot on high, and therein stuck a fair sword, naked, by the point, and letters there were written in gold about the sword that said thus: —Whoso pulleth out this sword of this stone and anvil, is rightwise king born of all England. Then the people marveled, and told it to the Archbishop. I command, said the Archbishop, that ye keep you within your church, and pray unto God still; that no man touch the sword till the high mass be all done. So when all masses were done all the lords went to behold the stone and the sword. And when they saw the scripture, some assayed; [9] such as would have been king. But none might stir the sword nor move it. He is not here, said the Archbishop, that shall achieve [10] the sword, but doubt not God will make him known. But this is my counsel, said the Archbishop, that we let purvey [11] ten knights, men of good fame, and they to keep this sword. So it was ordained, and then there was made a cry, that every man should assay that would, for to win the sword.

[1] The spelling of the text, as in all the succeeding prose of this volume, is modernized.
[2] exceeding (surpassing)
[3] a magician, Arthur's adviser
[4] were shriven of their sins
[5] The present site of St. Paul's has been occupied by various churches; traditionally, before the Christian Era, a temple of Diana stood on the spot. King Ethelbert erected a cathedral there in 607 and dedicated it to St. Paul. It was burned in 1086. Then was built the old St. Paul's which Malory knew, and which lasted until the great fire of 1666, to be followed by the present structure designed by Sir Christopher Wren, begun in 1675, finished in 1710.
[6] the three estates, clergy, lords, and commons
[7] ere
[8] a kind of
[9] tried
[10] attain
[11] cause to be provided

And upon New Year's Day the barons let make a jousts [1] and a tournament, that all knights that would joust or tourney there might play, and all this was ordained for to keep the lords together and the commons, for the Archbishop trusted that God would make him known that should win the sword. So upon New Years' Day, when the service was done, the barons rode unto the field, some to joust and some to tourney, and so it happened that Sir Ector, that had great livelihood about London, rode unto the jousts, and with him rode Sir Kay his son, and young Arthur that was his nourished [2] brother; and Sir Kay was [3] made knight at All Hallowmass afore.

So as they rode to the jousts-ward, Sir Kay lost his sword, for he had left it at his father's lodging, and so he prayed young Arthur for to ride for his sword. I will well, said Arthur, and rode fast after the sword, and when he came home, the lady and all were out to see the jousting. Then was Arthur wroth, and said to himself, I will ride to the churchyard, and take the sword with me that sticketh in the stone, for my brother Sir Kay shall not be without a sword this day. So when he came to the churchyard, Sir Arthur alit and tied his horse to the stile, and so he went to the tent, and found no knights there, for they were at the jousting; and so he handled the sword by the handles, and lightly and fiercely pulled it out of the stone, and took his horse and rode his way until he came to his brother Sir Kay, and delivered him the sword.

And as soon as Sir Kay saw the sword, he wist [4] well it was the sword of the stone, and so he rode to his father Sir Ector, and said: Sir, lo here is the sword of the stone, wherefore I must be king of this land. When Sir Ector beheld the sword, he returned again and came to the church, and there they alit all three, and went into the church. And anon he made Sir Kay to swear upon a book how he came to that sword. Sir, said Sir Kay, by my brother Arthur, for he brought it to me. How gat ye this sword? said Sir Ector to Arthur. Sir, I will tell you. When I came home for my brother's sword, I found nobody at home to deliver me his sword, and so I thought my brother Sir Kay should not be swordless, and so I came hither eagerly and pulled it out of the stone without any pain. Found ye any knights about this sword? said Sir Ector. Nay, said Arthur. Now, said Sir Ector to Arthur, I understand ye must be king of this land. Wherefore I, said Arthur, and for what cause? Sir, said Ector, for God will have it so, for there should [5] never man have drawn out this sword, but he that shall be rightwise king of this land. Now let me see whether ye can put the sword there as it was, and pull it out again. That is no mastery, [6] said Arthur, and so he put it in the stone, wherewithal Sir Ector assayed to pull out the sword and failed. Now assay, said Sir Ector unto Sir Kay. And anon he pulled at the sword with all his might, but it would not be.

Now shall ye assay, said Sir Ector to Arthur. I will well, said Arthur, and pulled it out easily. And therewithal Sir Ector knelt down to the earth, and Sir Kay. Alas, said Arthur, my own dear father and brother, why kneel ye to me? Nay, nay, my lord Arthur, it is not so; I was never your father nor of your blood, but I wot well ye are of an higher blood than I weened ye were. And then Sir Ector told him all, how he was betaken [7] him for to nourish him, and by whose commandment, and by Merlin's deliverance. Then Arthur made great dole when he understood that Sir Ector was not his father. Sir, said Ector unto Arthur, will ye be my good and gracious lord when ye are king? Else were I to blame, said Arthur, for ye are the man in the world that I am most beholden to, and my good lady and mother your wife, that as well as her own hath fostered me and kept. And if ever it be God's will that I be king as ye say, ye shall desire of me what I may do, and I shall not fail you, God forbid I should fail you. Sir, said Sir Ector, I will ask no more of you, but that ye will make my son, your foster brother, Sir Kay, seneschal of all your lands. That shall be done, said Arthur, and more, by the faith of my body, that never man shall have that office but he, while he and I live.

Therewithal they went unto the Archbishop, and told him how the sword was achieved, and by whom; and on Twelfth-day [8] all the barons came thither, and to assay to take the sword, who that would assay. But there afore them all, there might none take it out but Arthur; wherefore there were many lords wroth, and said it was a great shame unto them all and the realm, to be over governed with a boy of no high blood born, and so they fell out [9] at that time that it was put off till Candlemas, [10] and then all the barons should meet

[1] tilting-match (usually single combat, as distinct from a tourney or tournament)
[2] foster
[3] had been
[4] knew

[5] could
[6] feat
[7] entrusted to
[8] the festival of the Epiphany, twelfth day after Christmas
[9] were so dissatisfied
[10] February 2

there again; but always the ten knights were ordained to watch the sword day and night, and so they set a pavilion over the stone and the sword, and five always watched.

So at Candlemas many more great lords came thither for to have won the sword, but there might none prevail. And right as Arthur did at Christmas, he did at Candlemas, and pulled out the sword easily, whereof the barons were sore aggrieved and put it off in delay till the high feast of Easter. And as Arthur sped [1] before, so did he at Easter, yet there were some of the great lords had indignation that Arthur should be king, and put it off in a delay till the feast of Pentecost. Then the Archbishop of Canterbury by Merlin's providence [2] let purvey then of the best knights that they might get, and such knights as Uther Pendragon loved best and most trusted in his days. And such knights were put about Arthur as Sir Baudwin of Britain, Sir Kay, Sir Ulfius, Sir Brastias. All these with many other were always about Arthur, day and night, till the feast of Pentecost.

And at the feast of Pentecost all manner of men assayed to pull at the sword that would assay, but none might prevail but Arthur, and pulled it out afore all the lords and commons that were there, wherefore all the commons cried at once, We will have Arthur unto our king, we will put him no more in delay, for we all see that it is God's will that he shall be our king, and who that [3] holdeth against it, we will slay him. And therewith all they kneeled at once, both rich and poor, and cried Arthur mercy because they had delayed him so long, and Arthur forgave them, and took the sword between both his hands, and offered it upon the altar, where the Archbishop was, and so was he made knight of [4] the best man that was there. And so anon was the coronation made. And there was he sworn unto his lords and the commons for to be a true king, to stand with true justice from thenceforth the days of this life. . . .

How Arthur by the Mean of Merlin Gat Excalibur His Sword of the Lady of the Lake. Book I, Chapter XXV

Right so the king and he departed, and went unto an hermit that was a good man and a great leech. [5] So the hermit searched all his wounds and gave him good salves; so the king was there three days, and then were his wounds well amended that he might ride and go, [6] and so departed. And as they rode, Arthur said, I have no sword. No force, [7] said Merlin, hereby is a sword that shall be yours, an I may. [8] So they rode till they came to a lake, the which was a fair water and broad, and in the midst of the lake Arthur was ware of an arm clothed in white samite, [9] that held a fair sword in that hand. Lo! said Merlin, yonder is that sword that I spake of. With that they saw a damosel going [10] upon the lake. What damosel is that? said Arthur. That is the Lady of the Lake, said Merlin; and within that lake is a rock, and therein is as fair a place as any on earth, and hichly beseen; [11] and this damosel will come to you anon, and then speak ye fair to her that she will give you that sword. Anon withal came the damosel unto Arthur, and saluted him, and he her again. Damosel, said Arthur, what sword is that, that yonder the arm holdeth above the water? I would it were mine, for I have no sword. Sir Arthur, king, said the damosel, that sword is mine, and if ye will give me a gift when I ask it you, ye shall have it. By my faith, said Arthur, I will give you what gift ye will ask. Well! said the damosel, go ye into yonder barge, and row yourself to the sword, and take it and the scabbard with you, and I will ask my gift when I see my time. So Sir Arthur and Merlin alit and tied their horses to two trees, and so they went into the ship, and when they came to the sword that the hand held, Sir Arthur took it up by the handles, and took it with him, and the arm and the hand went under the water.

And so they came unto the land and rode forth, and then Sir Arthur saw a rich pavilion. What signifieth yonder pavilion? It is the knight's pavilion, said Merlin, that ye fought with last, Sir Pellinore; but he is out, he is not there. He hath ado with a knight of yours that hight [12] Egglame, and they have foughten together, but at the last Egglame fled, and else he had been dead, and he hath chased him even to Carlion, [13] and we shall meet with him anon in the highway. That is well said, said Arthur, now have I a sword, now will I wage battle with him, and be avenged on him. Sir, you shall not so, said Merlin, for the knight is weary of fighting and chasing, so that ye shall have no worship [14] to have ado with him; also he will not be lightly matched of one [15] knight

[1] succeeded
[2] prudence
[3] whoever
[4] by (viz., the Archbishop)
[5] physician
[6] walk
[7] no matter
[8] if I have power
[9] a rich silk fabric
[10] walking
[11] appointed
[12] is called
[13] Carleton-upon-Usk in Wales, one of Arthur's courts
[14] honor
[15] by any

living, and therefore it is my counsel, let him pass, for he shall do you good service in short time, and his sons after his days. Also ye shall see that day in short space, you shall be right glad to give him your sister to wed. When I see him, I will do as ye advise, said Arthur.

Then Sir Arthur looked on the sword, and liked it passing well. Whether liketh [1] you better, said Merlin, the sword or the scabbard? Me liketh better the sword, said Arthur. Ye are more unwise, said Merlin, for the scabbard is worth ten of the swords, for whiles ye have the scabbard upon you, ye shall never lose no blood be ye never so sore wounded, therefore keep well the scabbard always with you. So they rode unto Carlion, and by the way they met with Sir Pellinore; but Merlin had done such a craft, [2] that Pellinore saw not Arthur, and he passed by without any words. I marvel, said Arthur, that the knight would not speak. Sir, said Merlin, he saw you not, for an [3] he had seen you, ye had not lightly departed. So they came unto Carlion, whereof his knights were passing glad. And when they heard of his adventures, they marveled that he would jeopard his person so, alone. But all men of worship said it was merry to be under such a chieftain, that would put his person in adventure as other poor knights did.

How King Arthur Took a Wife, and Wedded Guenever, Daughter to Leodegrance, King of the Land of Cameliard, with Whom He Had the Round Table. Book III, Chapter I, II

In the beginning of Arthur, after he was chosen king by adventure and by grace, for the most part of the barons knew not that he was Uther Pendragon's son, but as Merlin made it openly known, but yet many kings and lords held great war against him for that cause. But well Arthur overcame them all, for [4] the most part the days of his life he was ruled much by the counsel of Merlin. So it fell on a time King Arthur said unto Merlin, My barons will let me have no rest, but needs I must take a wife, and I will none take but by thy counsel and by thine advice. It is well done, said Merlin, that ye take a wife, for a man of your bounty [5] and noblesse should not be without a wife. Now is there any that ye love more than another? Yea, said King Arthur, I love Guenever, the king's daughter, Leodegrance of the land of Cameliard, the which holdeth in his house the Table Round that ye told he had of my father Uther. And this damosel is the most valiant and fairest lady that I know living, or yet that ever I could find. Sir, said Merlin, as of [6] her beauty and fairness she is one of the fairest on live, [7] but, an ye loved her not so well as ye do, I should find you a damosel of beauty and of goodness that should like [8] you and please you, an your heart were not set; but there as a man's heart is set, he will be loth to return. That is truth, said King Arthur. But Merlin warned the king covertly that Guenever was not wholesome for him to take to wife, for he warned him that Launcelot should love her, and she him again; [9] and so he turned his tale to the adventures of the Sangreal.

Then Merlin desired of the king for to have men with him that should enquire of Guenever, and so the king granted him, and Merlin went forth unto King Leodegrance of Cameliard, and told him of the desire of the king that he would have unto his wife Guenever his daughter. That is to me, said King Leodegrance, the best tidings that ever I heard, that so worthy a king of prowess and noblesse will wed my daughter. And as for my lands, I will give him, wist I it might please him, but he hath lands enow, him needeth none, but I shall send him a gift shall please him much more, for I shall give him the Table Round, the which Uther Pendragon gave me, and when it is full complete, there is an hundred knights and fifty. And as for an hundred good knights I have myself, but I fawte [10] fifty, for so many have been slain in my days. And so Leodegrance delivered his daughter Guenever unto Merlin, and the Table Round with the hundred knights, and so they rode freshly, [11] with great royalty, what by water and what by land, till that they came nigh unto London.

When King Arthur heard of the coming of Guenever and the hundred knights with the Table Round, then King Arthur made great joy for her coming, and that rich present, and said openly, This fair lady is passing welcome unto me, for I have loved her long, and therefore there is nothing so lief [12] to me. And these knights with the Round Table please me more than right great riches. And in all haste the king let ordain [13] for the marriage and the coronation in the most honorable wise that could be devised. . . . .

[1] which pleaseth
[2] worked such magic
[3] if
[4] because
[5] prowess
[6] as for
[7] alive
[8] suit
[9] in return
[10] fault (lack)
[11] gaily
[12] dear
[13] ordered preparation

. . . How an Old Man Brought Galahad to the Siege Perilous and Set Him Therein. . . . Book XIII, Chapters I-IV

At the vigil of Pentecost,[1] when all the fellowship of the Round Table were come unto Camelot[2] and there heard their service, and the tables were set ready to[3] the meat, right so entered into the hall a full fair gentlewoman on horseback, that had ridden full fast, for her horse was all besweated. Then she there alit, and came before the king and saluted him; and he said: Damosel, God thee bless. Sir, said she, for God's sake say me where Sir Launcelot is. Yonder ye may see him, said the king. Then she went unto Launcelot and said: Sir Launcelot, I salute you on King Pelles' behalf, and I require you to come on with me hereby into a forest. Then Sir Launcelot asked her with whom she dwelled. I dwell, said she, with King Pelles.[4] What will ye with me? said Launcelot. Ye shall know, said she, when ye come thither. Well, said he, I will gladly go with you. So Sir Launcelot bade his squire saddle his horse and bring his arms; and in all haste he did his commandment. Then came the queen unto Launcelot, and said: Will ye leave us at this high feast? Madam, said the gentlewoman, wit[5] ye well he shall be with you to-morn[6] by dinner time. If I wist, said the queen, that he should not be with us here to-morn he should not go with you by my good will.

Right so departed Sir Launcelot with the gentlewoman, and rode until that he came into a forest and into a great valley, where they saw an abbey of nuns; and there was a squire ready and opened the gates, and so they entered and descended off their horses; and there came a fair fellowship about Sir Launcelot, and welcomed him, and were passing glad of his coming. And then they led him unto the Abbess's chamber and unarmed him; and right so he was ware upon a bed lying two of his cousins, Sir Bors and Sir Lionel, and then he waked them; and when they saw him they made great joy. Sir, said Sir Bors unto Sir Launcelot, what adventure hath brought you hither, for we weened to-morn to have found you at Camelot? As God me help, said Sir Launcelot, a gentlewoman brought me hither, but I know not the cause.

1 Whitsunday (the seventh Sunday after Easter), commemorating the descent of the Holy Spirit upon the Apostles
2 the legendary seat of Arthur's court
3 for
4 "king of the foreign country and cousin nigh unto Joseph of Arimathaea"—Malory
5 know
6 tomorrow morning

In the meanwhile that they thus stood talking together, therein came twelve nuns that brought with them Galahad,[7] the which was passing fair and well made, that unnethe[8] in the world men might not find his match: and all those ladies wept. Sir, said they all, we bring you here this child the which we have nourished, and we pray you to make him a knight; for of a more worthier man's hand may he not receive the order of knighthood. Sir Launcelot beheld the young squire and saw him seemly and demure as a dove, with all manner of good features, that he weened of his age never to have seen so fair a man of form. Then said Sir Launcelot: Cometh this desire of himself? He and all they said yea. Then shall he, said Sir Launcelot, receive the high order of knighthood as[9] to-morn at the reverence[10] of the high feast. That night Sir Launcelot had passing good cheer; and on the morn at the hour of prime,[11] at Galahad's desire, he made him knight and said: God make him a good man, for of beauty faileth you not as any that liveth.

Now fair sir, said Sir Launcelot, will ye come with me unto the court of King Arthur? Nay, said he, I will not go with you as[9] at this time. Then he departed from them and took his two cousins with him, and so they came unto Camelot by the hour of underne[12] on Whitsunday. By that time the king and the queen were gone to the minster to hear their service. Then the king and the queen were passing glad of Sir Bors and Sir Lionel, and so was all the fellowship.

So when the king and all the knights were come from service, the barons espied in the sieges[13] of the Round Table all about, written with golden letters: Here ought to sit he,[14] and he ought to sit here. And thus they went so long till that they came to the Siege Perilous,[15] where they found letters newly written of gold which said: Four hundred winters and four and fifty accomplished after the passion[16] of our Lord Jesu Christ ought this siege to be fulfilled.[17] Then all they said: This is a marvelous thing and an adventurous. In the name of God, said Sir Launcelot; and then accounted the term of the writing[18] from the birth of our Lord unto that day. It seemeth me, said Sir Launcelot, this siege ought to be fulfilled this same day, for this is the feast of Pentecost

7 the son of Launcelot
8 scarcely
9 The word is redundant.
10 observance
11 at the first hour
12 late forenoon
13 seats
14 so-and-so
15 Seat of Peril reserved for the winner of the Grail
16 suffering, crucifixion
17 occupied
18 calculated the time set down in the writing

after the four hundred and four and fifty year; and if it would please all parties, I would none of these letters were seen this day, till he be come that ought to achieve this adventure. Then made they to ordain a cloth of silk, for to cover these letters in the Siege Perilous.

Then the king bade haste unto dinner. Sir, said Sir Kay the Steward, if ye go now unto your meat ye shall break your old custom of your court, for ye have not used on this day to sit at your meat or that [1] ye have seen some adventure. Ye say sooth, said the king, but I had so great joy of Sir Launcelot and of his cousins, which be come to the court whole [2] and sound, so that I bethought me not of mine old custom. So, as they stood speaking, in came a squire and said unto the king: Sir, I bring unto you marvelous tidings. What be they? said the king. Sir, there is here beneath at the river a great stone which I saw fleet [3] above the water, and therein I saw sticking a sword. The king said: I will see that marvel.

So all the knights went with him, and when they came to the river they found there a stone fleeting, as it were of red marble, and therein stuck a fair rich sword, and in the pommel thereof were precious stones wrought with subtil [4] letters of gold. Then the barons read the letters which said in this wise: Never shall man take me hence, but only he by whose side I ought to hang, and he shall be the best knight of the world. When the king had seen the letters, he said unto Sir Launcelot: Fair sir, this sword ought to be yours, for I am sure ye be the best knight of the world. Then Sir Launcelot answered full soberly: Certes, sir, it is not my sword; also, Sir, wit ye well I have no hardiness to set my hand to it, for it longed [5] not to hang by my side. Also, who that assayeth to take the sword and faileth of it, he shall receive a wound by that sword that he shall not be whole [2] long after. And I will that ye wit that this same day shall the adventures of the Sangreal, that is called the Holy Vessel, begin. [6]

Now, fair nephew, said the king unto Sir Gawaine, assay ye, for my love. Sir, he said, save your good grace [7] I shall not do that. Sir, said the king, assay to take the sword and at my commandment. Sir, said Gawaine, your commandment I will obey. And therewith he took up the sword by the handles, but he might not stir it. I thank you, said the king to Sir Gawaine. My lord Sir Gawaine, said Sir Launcelot, now wit ye well this sword shall touch you so sore that ye shall will ye had never set your hand thereto for the best castle of this realm. Sir, he said, I might not withsay mine uncle's will and commandment. But when the king heard this he repented it much, and said unto Sir Percivale that he should assay, for his love. And he said: Gladly, for to bear Sir Gawaine fellowship. And therewith he set his hand on the sword and drew it strongly, but he might not move it. Then were there [no [8]] more that durst be so hardy to set their hands thereto. Now may ye go to your dinner, said Sir Kay unto the king, for a marvelous adventure have ye seen.

So the king and all went unto the court, and every knight knew his own place, and set him therein, and young men that were knights served them. So when they were served, and all sieges fulfilled save only the Siege Perilous, anon there befell a marvelous adventure, that [9] all the doors and windows of the palace shut by themself. Not for then [10] the hall was not greatly darked; and therewith they [were all [8]] abashed both one and other. Then King Arthur spake first and said: By God, fair fellows and lords, we have seen this day marvels, but or [11] night I suppose we shall see greater marvels.

In the meanwhile came in a good old man, and an ancient, clothed all in white, and there was no knight knew from whence he came. And with him he brought a young knight, both on foot, in red arms, without sword or shield, save a scabbard hanging by his side. And these words he said: Peace be with you, fair

[1] ere
[2] hale, well
[3] float
[4] cunning
[5] probably for *longeth*, belongs
[6] "Though the earliest French accounts of the Holy Grail differ in many details, from them all we can make up a story somewhat as follows: Joseph of Arimathaea, after taking Christ's body from the cross, collected his blood in the Grail, a dish or cup which our Lord had used at the Last Supper. Then, because Joseph had buried Christ reverently, he was thrown into prison by the angry Jews, who tried to starve him; but Joseph was solaced and fed by the Grail, miraculously presented to him by Christ in person. Released after forty years, Joseph set out from Jerusalem with his wife and kindred, who, having accepted his faith, were ready to follow him and his sacred vessel to far-off lands. He went through various adventures, principally conversions of heathen, the most important being of the King of Sarras and his people." (Howard Maynadier, *The Arthur of the English Poets.*) After the disappearance of the holy relic (for one account see Tennyson's *Idylls*), the quest of it was a visionary search often undertaken, according to the legends, as a test of purity. It was a wave of fanaticism prompting this search that broke up Arthur's goodly fellowship of knights.

[7] a deprecatory phrase
[8] inserted in the second edition by Caxton's successor, Wynkyn de Worde
[9] in that
[10] nevertheless
[11] ere

lords. Then the old man said unto Arthur: Sir, I bring here a young knight, the which is of king's lineage, and of the kindred of Joseph of Aramathie, whereby the marvels of this court, and of strange realms, shall be fully accomplished. The king was right glad of his words, and said unto the good man: Sir, ye be right welcome, and the young knight with you.

Then the old man made the young man to unarm him, and he was in a coat of red sendal,[1] and bare a mantle upon his shoulder that was furred with ermine, and put that upon him. And the old knight said unto the young knight: Sir, follow me. And anon he led him unto the Siege Perilous, where beside sat Sir Launcelot; and the good man lift up the cloth, and found there letters that said thus: This is the siege of Galahad, the haut[2] prince. Sir, said the old knight, wit ye well that place is yours. And then he set him down surely in that siege. And then he said to the old man: Sir, ye may now go your way, for well have ye done that ye were commanded to do; and recommend me unto my grandsire, King Pelles, and unto my lord Petchere, and say them on my behalf, I shall come and see them as soon as ever I may. So the good man departed; and there met him twenty noble squires, and so took their horses and went their way. Then all the knights of the Table Round marveled greatly of Sir Galahad, that he durst sit there in that Siege Perilous, and was so tender of age; and wist not from whence he came but all only[3] by God; and said: This is he by whom the Sangreal shall be achieved, for there sat never none but he, but he were mischieved.[4]

Then Sir Launcelot beheld his son and had great joy of him. Then Bors told his fellows: Upon pain of my life this young knight shall come unto great worship.[5] This noise was great in all the court, so that it came to the queen. Then she had marvel what knight it might be that durst adventure him to sit in the Siege Perilous. Many said unto the queen he resembled much unto Sir Launcelot. I may well suppose, said the queen, that Sir Launcelot, being won by enchantment, had him of King Pelles' daughter, and his name is Galahad. I would fain see him, said the queen, for he must needs be a noble man, for so is his father, I report me unto[6] all the Table Round. So when the meat was done that the king and all were risen, the king yede[7] unto the Siege Perilous and lift up the cloth, and found there the name of Galahad; and then he shewed it unto Sir Gawaine, and said: Fair nephew, now have we among us Sir Galahad, the good knight that shall worship[8] us all; and upon pain of my life he shall achieve the Sangreal, right as Sir Launcelot had done[9] us to understand. Then came King Arthur unto Galahad and said: Sir, ye be welcome, for ye shall move many good knights to the quest of the Sangreal, and ye shall achieve that never knights might bring to an end. Then the king took him by the hand, and went down from the palace to shew Galahad the adventures of the stone.

[1] thin silk
[2] high
[3] unless it were
[4] harmed
[5] honor
[6] call to witness
[7] went

. . . . How Sir Launcelot Was Tofore the Door of the Chamber Wherein the Holy Sangreal Was. . . . Book XVII. Chapters XIII-XV

Now saith the history, that when Launcelot was come to the water of Mortoise, as it is rehearsed before, he was in great peril, and so he laid him down and slept, and took the adventure that God would send him. So when he was asleep there came a vision unto him and said: Launcelot, arise up and take thine armor, and enter into the first ship that thou shalt find. And when he heard these words he start up and saw great clearness about him. And then he lift up his hand and blessed him,[10] and so took his arms and made him ready; and so by adventure he came by a strand, and found a ship the which was without sail or oar. And as soon as he was within the ship there he felt the most sweetness that ever he felt, and he was fulfilled with all thing that he thought on or desired. Then he said: Fair sweet Father, Jesu Christ, I wot not in what joy I am, for this joy passeth all earthly joys that ever I was in. And so in this joy he laid him down to the ship's board, and slept till day.

And when he awoke he found there a fair bed, and therein lying a gentlewoman dead, the which was Sir Percivale's sister.[11] And as Launcelot devised[12] her, he espied in her right hand a writ, the which he read, the which told him all the adventures that ye have heard tofore, and of what lineage she was come. So

[8] honor
[9] caused
[10] crossed himself
[11] She had given her blood to heal a lady and had made this dying request of her brother: "As soon as I am dead, put me in a boat at the next haven, and let me go as adventure will lead me; and as soon as ye three come to the city of Sarras, there to achieve the Holy Grail, ye shall find me under a tower arrived, and there bury me in the spiritual place."
[12] gazed upon

with this gentlewoman Sir Launcelot was a month and more. If ye would ask how he lived, He that fed the people of Israel with manna in the desert, so was he fed; for every day when he had said his prayers he was sustained with the grace of the Holy Ghost.

So on a night he went to play him by the water side, for he was somewhat weary of the ship. And then he listened and heard an horse come, and one riding upon him. And when he came nigh he seemed a knight. And so he let him pass, and went thereas [1] the ship was; and there he alit, and took the saddle and the bridle and put the horse from him, and went into the ship. And then Launcelot dressed [2] unto him, and said: Ye be welcome. And he answered and saluted him again, [3] and asked him: What is your name? for much my heart giveth [4] unto you. Truly, said he, my name is Launcelot du Lake. Sir, said he, then be ye welcome, for ye were the beginner of me in this world. Ah, said he, are ye Galahad? Yea, forsooth, said he; and so he kneeled down and asked him his blessing, and after took off his helm and kissed him.

And there was great joy between them, for there is no tongue can tell the joy that they made either of other, and many a friendly word spoken between, as kin would, the which is no need here to be rehearsed. And there every each [5] told other of their adventures and marvels that were befallen to them in many journeys sith [6] that they departed from the court. Anon, as Galahad saw the gentlewoman dead in the bed, he knew her well enough, and told great worship of her, that she was the best maid living, and it was great pity of her death. But when Launcelot heard how the marvelous sword was gotten, and who made it, and all the marvels rehearsed afore, then he prayed Galahad, his son, that he would show him the sword, [7] and so he did; and anon he kissed the pommel, and the hilt, and the scabbard. Truly, said Launcelot, never rest knew I of so high adventures done, and so marvelous and strange.

So dwelt Launcelot and Galahad within that ship half a year, and served God daily and nightly with all their power; and often they arrived in isles far from folk, where there repaired none but wild beasts, and there they found many strange adventures and perilous,

[1] where
[2] addressed himself (or simply "went")
[3] in return
[4] goeth out
[5] each one
[6] since
[7] the sword of King David, which had been put by Solomon into this miraculous ship, and which maimed or slew all who attempted to draw it, until Galahad came

which they brought to an end; but for [8] those adventures were with wild beasts, and not in the quest of the Sangreal, therefore the tale maketh here no mention thereof, for it would be too long to tell of all those adventures that befell them.

So after, on a Monday, it befell that they arrived in the edge of a forest tofore a cross; and then saw they a knight armed all in white, and was richly horsed, and led in his right hand a white horse; and so he came to the ship, and saluted the two knights on the High Lord's behalf, and said: Galahad, sir, ye have been long enough with your father, come out of the ship, and start upon this horse, and go where the adventures shall lead thee in the quest of the Sangreal. Then he went to his father and kissed him sweetly, and said: Fair sweet father, I wot not when I shall see you more till I see the body of Jesu Christ. I pray you, said Launcelot, pray ye to the High Father that He hold me in His service. And so he took his horse, and there they heard a voice that said: Think for to do well, for the one shall never see the other before the dreadful day of doom. Now, son Galahad, said Launcelot, syne [9] we shall depart, and never see other, I pray to the High Father to conserve me and you both. Sir, said Galahad, no prayer availeth so much as yours. And therewith Galahad entered into the forest.

And the wind arose, and drove Launcelot more than a month throughout the sea, where he slept but little, but prayed to God that he might see some tidings of the Sangreal. So it befell on a night, at midnight, he arrived afore a castle, on the back side, which was rich and fair, and there was a postern opened toward the sea, and was open without any keeping, save two lions kept the entry; and the moon shone clear. Anon Sir Launcelot heard a voice that said: Launcelot, go out of this ship and enter into the castle, where thou shalt see a great part of thy desire.

Then he ran to his arms, and so armed him, and so went to the gate and saw the lions. Then set he hand to his sword and drew it. Then there came a dwarf suddenly, and smote him on the arm so sore that the sword fell out of his hand. Then heard he a voice say: O man of evil faith and poor belief, wherefore trowest [10] thou more on thy harness than in thy Maker, for He might more avail thee than thine armor, in whose service that thou art set. Then said Launcelot: Fair Father Jesu Christ, I thank thee of Thy great mercy that

[8] because
[9] since
[10] trustest

Thou reprovest me of my misdeed; now see I well that ye hold me for your servant. Then took he again his sword and put it up in his sheath, and made a cross in his forehead, and came to the lions, and they made semblant [1] to do him harm. Notwithstanding he passed by them without hurt, and entered into the castle to the chief fortress, and there were they all at rest.

Then Launcelot entered in so armed, for he found no gate nor door but it was open. And at the last he found a chamber whereof the door was shut, and he set his hand thereto to have opened it, but he might not. Then he enforced him mickle [2] to undo the door. Then he listened and heard a voice which sang so sweetly that it seemed none earthly thing; and him thought the voice said: Joy and honor be to the Father of Heaven. Then Launcelot kneeled down tofore the chamber, for well wist he that there was the Sangreal within that chamber. Then said he: Fair sweet Father, Jesu Christ, if ever I did thing that pleased Thee, Lord for Thy pity never have me not in despite for my sins done aforetime, and that thou show me something of that I seek. And with that he saw the chamber door open, and there came out a great clearness, that the house was as bright as [3] all the torches of the world had been there. So came he to the chamber door, and would have entered. And anon a voice said to him: Flee, Launcelot, and enter not, for thou oughtest not to do it; and if thou enter thou shalt forthink [4] it. Then he withdrew him aback right heavy. [5]

Then looked he up in the middes of the chamber, and saw a table of silver, and the holy vessel, covered with red samite, and many angels about it, whereof one held a candle of wax burning, and the other held a cross, and the ornaments of an altar. And before the holy vessel he saw a good man clothed as a priest. And it seemed that he was at the sacring of the mass. [6] And it seemed to Launcelot that above the priest's hands were three men, whereof the two put the youngest by likeness between the priest's hands; and so he lift it up right high, and it seemed to show so to the people. And then Launcelot marveled not a little, for him thought the priest was so greatly charged of [7] the figure that him seemed that he should fall to the earth. And when he saw none about him that would help him, then came he to the door a great pace, [8] and said: Fair Father Jesu Christ, ne take it for no sin though I help the good man which hath great need of help. Right so entered he into the chamber and came toward the table of silver; and when he came nigh he felt a breath, that him thought it was intermeddled [9] with fire, which smote him so sore in the visage that him thought it brent [10] his visage; and therewith he fell to the earth, and had no power to arise, as he that was so araged, [11] that had lost the power of his body, and his hearing, and his seeing. Then felt he many hands about him, which took him up and bare him out of the chamber door, without any amending of his swoon, and left him there, seeming dead to all people.

So upon the morrow when it was fair day they within were arisen, and found Launcelot lying afore the chamber door. All they marveled how that he came in, and so they looked upon him, and felt his pulse to wit whether there were any life in him; and so they found life in him, but he might not stand nor stir no member that he had. And so they took him by every part of the body, and bare him into a chamber, and laid him in a rich bed, far from all folk; and so he lay four days. Then the one said he was on live, and the other said, Nay. In the name of God, said an old man, for I do you verily to wit he is not dead, but he is so full of life as the mightiest of you all; and therefor I counsel you that he be well kept till God send him life again.

. . . . How Galahad and His Fellows Were Fed of the Holy Sangreal, ... and how Galahad was Made King. Book XVII Chapters XIX-XXII

So departed [Galahad] from thence, and rode five days till that he came to the maimed king. [12] And ever followed Percivale the five days, asking where he had been; and so one told him how the adventures of Logris were achieved. So on a day it befell that they came out of a great forest, and there they met at traverse [13] with Sir Bors, the which rode alone. It is none need to tell if they were glad; and them he saluted, and they yielded him honor and good adventure, [14] and every each told other. Then said Bors: It is more than a year and a half that I ne lay ten times where men dwelled, but in wild forests and in mountains, but God was ever my comfort. Then rode they a great while till that they came to the

1 semblance (made as if)
2 tried hard
3 as if
4 repent
5 sad
6 the communion service
7 burdened with
8 quickly
9 intermingled
10 burnt
11 like one so angry
12 Pelles, who had tried to draw the miraculous sword
13 crossed paths
14 a salutation, *buena ventura,* "good luck"

castle of Carbonek. And when they were entered within the castle King Pelles knew them; then there was great joy, for they wist well by their coming that they had fulfilled the quest of the Sangreal.

Then Eliazar, King Pelles' son, brought tofore them the broken sword wherewith Joseph was stricken through the thigh. Then Bors set his hand thereto, if that he might have soldered it again; but it would not be. Then he took it to Percivale, but he had no more power thereto than he. Now have ye it again, said Percivale to Galahad, for an it be ever achieved by any bodily man ye must do it. And then he took the pieces and set them together, and they seemed that they had never been broken, and as well as it had been first forged. And when they within espied that the adventure of the sword was achieved, then they gave the sword to Bors, for it might not be better set; [1] for he was a good knight and a worthy man.

And a little afore even, the sword arose great and marvelous, and was full of great heat that many men fell for dread. And anon alit a voice among them, and said: They that ought not to sit at the table of Jesu Christ arise, for now shall very [2] knights be fed. So they went thence, all save King Pelles and Eliazar, his son, the which were holy men, and a maid which was his niece; and so these three fellows and they three were there, no more.

Anon they saw knights all armed come in at the hall door, and did off their helms and their arms, and said unto Galahad: Sir, we have hied right much for to be with you at this table where the holy meat shall be departed. [3] Then said he: Ye be welcome, but of whence be ye? So three of them said they were of Gaul, and other three said they were of Ireland, and the other three said they were of Denmark. So as they sat thus there came out a bed of tree, [4] of [5] a chamber, the which four gentlewomen brought; and in the bed lay a good man sick, and a crown of gold upon his head; and there in the middes of the place they set him down, and went again their way. Then he lift up his head, and said: Galahad, Knight, ye be welcome, for much have I desired your coming, for in such pain and in such anguish I have been long. But now I trust to God the term is come that my pain shall be allayed, that I shall pass out of this world so as it was promised me long ago.

Therewith a voice said: There be two among you that be not in the quest of the Sangreal, and therefore depart ye. Then King Pelles and his son departed. And therewithal beseemed them that there came a man, and four angels from heaven, clothed in likeness of a bishop, and had a cross in his hand; and these four angels bare him up in a chair, and set him down before the table of silver whereupon the Sangreal was; and it seemed that he had in middes of his forehead letters the which said: See ye here Joseph, the first bishop of Christendom, the same which Our Lord succored in the city of Sarras in the spiritual place. Then the knights marveled, for that bishop was dead more than three hundred year tofore. O knights, said he, marvel not, for I was sometime [6] an earthly man.

With that they heard the chamber door open, and there they saw angels; and two bare candles of wax, and the third a towel, and the fourth a spear which bled marvelously, and three drops fell within a box which he held with his other hand. And they set the candles upon the table, and the third the towel upon the vessel, and the fourth the holy spear even upright upon the vessel. And then the bishop made semblant as though he would have gone to the sacring of the mass. And then he took an ubbly [7] which was made in likeness of bread. And at the lifting up there came a figure in likeness of a child, and the visage was as red and as bright as any fire, and smote himself into the bread, so that they all saw it that the bread was formed of a fleshly man; and then he put it into the holy vessel again, and then he did that longed [8] to a priest to do to a mass. And then he went to Galahad and kissed him, and bade him go and kiss his fellows: and so he did anon. Now, said he, servants of Jesu Christ, ye shall be fed afore this table with sweetmeats that never knights tasted. And when he had said, he vanished away. And they set them at the table in great dread, and made their prayers.

Then looked they and saw a man come out of the holy vessel, that had all the signs of the passion [9] of Jesu Christ, bleeding all openly, and said: My knights, and my servants, and my true children, which be come out of deadly life into spiritual life, I will now no longer hide me from you, but ye shall see now a part of my secrets and of my hidden things: now hold and receive the high meat which ye have so much desired. Then took he himself the holy vessel and came to Galahad; and he kneeled down, and there he received his Savior, and after him so received all his fellows; and they thought it so sweet that it was marvelous to tell.

[1] placed
[2] true
[3] divided, distributed
[4] wood
[5] from
[6] once
[7] wafer
[8] what belonged
[9] crucifixion

Then said he to Galahad: Son, wotest thou what I hold betwixt my hands? Nay, said he, but if [1] ye will tell me. This is, said he, the holy dish wherein I ate the lamb on Sher-Thursday. [2] And now hast thou seen that thou most desired to see, but yet hast thou not seen it so openly as thou shalt see it in the city of Sarras in the spiritual place. Therefore thou must go hence and bear with thee this holy vessel; for this night it shall depart from the realm of Logris, that it shall never be seen more here. And wotest thou wherefore? For he is not served nor worshiped to his right by them of this land, for they be turned to evil living; therefore I shall disherit them of the honor which I have done them. And therefore go ye three tomorrow unto the sea, where ye shall find your ship ready, and with you take the sword with the strange girdles, and no more with you but Sir Percivale and Sir Bors. Also I will that ye take with you of the blood of this spear for to anoint the maimed king, both his legs and all his body, and he shall have his health.

Sir, said Galahad, why shall not these other fellows go with us? For this cause: for right as I departed [3] my apostles one here and another there, so I will that ye depart; and two of you shall die in my service, but one of you shall come again and tell tidings. Then gave he them his blessing and vanished away. And Galahad went anon to the spear which lay upon the table, and touched the blood with his fingers, and came after to the maimed king and anointed his legs. And therewith he clothed him [4] anon, and start upon his feet out of his bed as an whole man, and thanked Our Lord that He had healed him. . . .

Right so departed Galahad, Percivale and Bors with him; and so they rode three days, and then they came to a rivage, [5] and found the ship whereof the tale speaketh of tofore. And when they came to the board [6] they found in the middes the table of silver which they had left with the maimed king, and the Sangreal which was covered with red samite. Then were they glad to have such things in their fellowship; and so they entered and made great reverence thereto; and Galahad fell in his prayer long time to Our Lord, that at what time he asked, that he should pass out of this world. So much he prayed till a voice said to him: Galahad, thou shalt have they request; and when thou askest the death of thy body thou shalt have it, and then shalt thou find the life of the soul.

Percivale heard this, and prayed him, of [7] fellowship that was between them, to tell him wherefore he asked such things. That shall I tell you, said Galahad; the other day when we saw a part of the adventures of the Sangreal I was in such a joy of heart, that I trow never man was that was earthly. And therefore I wot well, when my body is dead my soul shall be in great joy to see the blessed Trinity every day, and the Majesty of Our Lord, Jesu Christ. So long were they in the ship that they said to Galahad: Sir, in this bed ought ye to lie, for so saith the Scripture. And so he laid him down and slept a great while; and when he awaked he looked afore him and saw the city of Sarras.

And as they would have landed they saw the ship wherein Percivale had put his sister in. Truly, said Percivale, in the name of God, well hath my sister holden us covenant. Then took they out of the ship the table of silver, and he took it to Percivale and to Bors, to go tofore, and Galahad came behind. And right so they went to the city, and at the gate of the city they saw an old man crooked. Then Galahad called him and bade him help to bear this heavy thing. Truly, said the old man, it is ten year ago that I might not go but with crutches. Care thou not, said Galahad, and arise up and shew thy good will. And so he assayed, and found himself as whole as ever he was. Then ran he to the table, and took one part against [8] Galahad. And anon arose there great noise in the city, that a cripple was made whole by knights marvelous that entered into the city. Then anon after, the three knights went to the water, and brought up into the palace Percivale's sister, and buried her as richly as a king's daughter ought to be.

And when the king of the city, which was cleped [9] Estorause, saw the fellowship, he asked them of whence they were, and what thing it was that they had brought upon the table of silver. And they told him the truth of the Sangreal, and the power which that God had set there. Then the king was a tyrant, and was come of the line of paynims, and took them and put them in prison in a deep hole. But as soon as they were there Our Lord sent them the Sangreal, through whose grace they were alway fulfilled while that they were in prison.

So at the year's end it befell that this King Estorause lay sick, and felt that he should die.

[1] unless
[2] the day before Good Friday
[3] parted
[4] himself
[5] shore
[6] aboard
[7] by the
[8] the part opposite
[9] who was called

Then he sent for the three knights, and they came afore him; and he cried them mercy of that he had done to them, and they forgave it him goodly; and he died anon. When the king was dead all the city was dismayed, and wist not who might be their king. Right so as they were in counsel there came a voice among them, and bade them choose the youngest knight of them three to be their king: For he shall well maintain you and all yours. So they made Galahad king by all the assent of the holy city, and else they would have slain him. And when he was come to behold the land, he let make above the table of silver a chest of gold and of precious stones, that hylled [1] the holy vessel. And every day early the three fellows would come afore it, and make their prayers. Now at the year's end, and the self day after Galahad had borne the crown of gold, he arose up early and his fellows, and came to the palace, and saw tofore them the holy vessel, and a man kneeling on his knees in likeness of a bishop, that had about him a great fellowship of angels as it had been Jesu Christ himself; and then he arose and began a mass of Our Lady. And when he came to the sacrament of the mass, and had done, anon he called Galahad, and said to him: Come forth, the servant of Jesu Christ, and thou shalt see that [2] thou hast much desired to see. And then he began to tremble right hard when the deadly [3] flesh began to behold the spiritual things. Then he held up his hands toward heaven and said: Lord, I thank thee, for now I see that that hath been my desire many a day. Now, blessed Lord, would I not longer live, if it might please thee, Lord.

And therewith the good man took Our Lord's body betwixt his hands, and proffered it to Galahad, and he received it right gladly and meekly. Now wotest thou what I am? said the good man. Nay, said Galahad. I am Joseph of Aramathie, the which Our Lord hath sent here to thee to bear thee fellowship; and wotest thou wherefore that he hath sent me more than any other? For thou hast resembled me in two things; in that thou hast seen the marvels of the Sangreal, and in that thou hast been a clean maiden, [4] as I have been and am. And when he had said these words Galahad went to Percivale and kissed him, and commended him to God; and so he went to Sir Bors and kissed him, and commended him to God, and said: Fair lord, salute me to my lord, Sir Launcelot, my father, and as soon as ye see him, bid him

[1] covered
[2] that which
[3] mortal
[4] pure youth

remember of this unstable world.[5] And therewith he kneeled down tofore the table and made his prayers, and then suddenly his soul departed to Jesu Christ, and a great multitude of angels bare his soul up to heaven, that the two fellows might well behold it. Also the two fellows saw come from heaven an hand, but they saw not the body. And then it came right to the Vessel, and took it and the spear, and so bare it up to heaven. Sithen was there never man so hardy to say that he had seen the Sangreal.

How . . . . Mordred Was Slain and Arthur Hurt to the Death . . . Book XXI. Chapters IV-VII

Then were they condescended [6] that King Arthur and Sir Mordred [7] should meet betwixt both their hosts, and every each of them should bring fourteen persons; and they came with this word unto Arthur. Then said he: I am glad that this is done, and so he went into the field. And when Arthur should depart, he warned all his host that an they see any sword drawn: Look ye come on fiercely, and slay that traitor, Sir Mordred, for I in no wise trust him. In likewise Sir Mordred warned his host that: An ye see any sword drawn, look that ye come on fiercely, and so slay all that ever before you standeth; for in no wise I will not trust for this treaty, for I know well my father will be avenged on me. And so they met as their appointment was, and so they were agreed and accorded thoroughly; and wine was fetched, and they drank.

Right soon came an adder out of a little heath bush, and it stung a knight on the foot. And when the knight felt him stung, he looked down and saw the adder, and then he drew his sword to slay the adder, and thought of none other harm. And when the host on both parties saw that sword drawn, then they blew beamous, [8] trumpets, and horns, and shouted grimly. And so both hosts dressed them [9] together. And King Arthur took his horse, and said: Alas this unhappy day! and so rode to his party. And Sir Mordred in likewise.

And never was there seen a more dolefuller battle in no Christian land; for there was but rushing and riding, foining [10] and striking, and many a grim word was there spoken either to other, and many a deadly stroke. But ever

[5] remember the instability of life
[6] agreed
[7] During Arthur's absence, Mordred, his nephew (or son, as he is sometimes called) usurped his throne and gave battle to Arthur upon his return.
[8] beaumes (a kind of trumpet)
[9] prepared to attack
[10] thrusting

King Arthur rode throughout the battle [1] of Sir Mordred many times, and did full nobly as a noble king should, and at all times he fainted never; and Sir Mordred that day put him in devoir, [2] and in great peril. And thus they fought all the long day, and never stinted till the noble knights were laid to the cold earth; and ever they fought still till it was near night, and by that time was there an hundred thousand laid dead upon the down. [3]

Then was Arthur wood [4] wroth out of measure, when he saw his people so slain from him. Then the king looked about him, and then was he ware, of all his host and of all his good knights, were left no more on live but two knights; that one was Sir Lucan the Butler, and his brother Sir Bedivere, and they were full sore wounded. Jesu mercy, said the king, where are all my noble knights become? Alas that ever I should see this doleful day, for now, said Arthur, I am come to mine end. But would to God that I wist where were that traitor Sir Mordred, that hath caused all this mischief.

Then was King Arthur ware where Sir Mordred leaned upon his sword amongst a great heap of dead men. Now give me my spear, said Arthur unto Sir Lucan, for yonder I have espied the traitor that all this woe hath wrought. Sir, let him be, said Sir Lucan, for he is unhappy; [5] and if ye pass this unhappy day ye shall be right well revenged upon him. Good lord, remember ye of your night's dream, and what the spirit of Sir Gawaine told you this night, yet God of his great goodness hath preserved you hitherto. Therefore, for God's sake, my lord, leave off by this, for blessed be God ye have won the field, for here we be three on live, and with Sir Mordred is none on live; and if ye leave off now this wicked day of destiny is past. Tide [6] me death, betide me life, saith the king, now I see him yonder alone he shall never escape mine hands, for at a better avail shall I never have him. God speed you well, said Sir Bedivere.

Then the king gat his spear in both his hands, and ran toward Sir Mordred, crying: Traitor, now is thy death day come. And when Sir Mordred heard Sir Arthur, he ran until him with his sword drawn in his hand. And there King Arthur smote Sir Mordred under the shield, with a foin of his spear, throughout the body, more than a fathom. And when Sir Mordred felt that he had his death wound he thrust himself with the might that he had up to the bur of King Arthur's spear. And right so he smote his father Arthur, with his sword holden in both his hands, on the side of the head, that the sword pierced the helmet and the brain pan, and therewithal Sir Mordred fell stark dead to the earth.

And the noble Arthur fell in a swoon to the earth, and there he swooned ofttimes. And Sir Lucan the Butler and Sir Bedivere ofttimes heaved him up. And so weakly they led him betwixt them both, to a little chapel not far from the seaside. And when the king was there he thought him well eased. Then heard they people cry in the field. Now go thou, Sir Lucan, said the king, and do me to wit [7] what betokens that noise in the field. So Sir Lucan departed, for he was grievously wounded in many places. And so as he yede, [8] he saw and hearkened by the moonlight, how that pillers [9] and robbers were come into the field, to pill and to rob many a full noble knight of brooches, and beads, of many a good ring, and of many a rich jewel; and who that were not dead all out, [10] there they slew them for their harness and their riches. When Sir Lucan understood this work, he came to the king as soon as he might, and told him all what he had heard and seen. Therefore by my rede, [11] said Sir Lucan, it is best that we bring you to some town. I would it were so, said the king, but I may not stand, mine head works so. Ah, Sir Launcelot, said King Arthur, this day have I sore missed thee: alas, that ever I was against thee, for now have I my death, whereof Sir Gawaine me warned in my dream.

Then Sir Lucan took up the king the one part, and Sir Bedivere the other part, and in the lifting the king swooned; and Sir Lucan fell in a swoon with the lift, that the part of his bowels fell out of his body, and therewith the noble knight's heart brast. [12] And when the king awoke, he beheld Sir Lucan, how he lay foaming at the mouth, and part of his bowels lay at his feet. Alas, said the king, this is to me a full heavy sight, to see this noble duke so die for my sake, for he would have holpen me, that had more need of help than I. Alas, he would not complain him, his heart was so set to help me: now Jesu have mercy upon his soul!

Then Sir Bedivere wept for the death of his brother. Leave this mourning and weeping, said the king, for all this will not avail me, for wit thou well an I might live myself, the death of Sir Lucan would grieve me evermore; but my time hieth fast, said the king. Therefore,

[1] ranks
[2] did his best
[3] high plain
[4] madly
[5] of evil omen
[6] befall
[7] let me know
[8] went
[9] pillagers
[10] outright
[11] advice
[12] burst

said Arthur unto Sir Bedivere, take thou Excalabur, my good sword, and go with it to yonder water side, and when thou comest there I charge thee throw my sword in that water, and come again and tell me what thou there seest. My lord, said Bedivere, your commandment shall be done, and lightly bring you word again.

So Sir Bedivere departed, and by the way he beheld that noble sword, that the pommel and the haft was all of precious stones; and then he said to himself: If I throw this rich sword in the water, thereof shall never come good, but harm and loss. And then Sir Bedivere hid Excalibur under a tree. And so, as soon as he might, he came again unto the king, and said he had been at the water, and had thrown the sword in the water. What saw thou there? said the king. Sir, he said, I saw nothing but waves and winds. That is untruly said of thee, said the king, therefore go thou lightly again, and do my commandment; as thou art to me lief and dear, spare not, but throw it in.

Then Sir Bedivere returned again, and took the sword in his hand; and then him thought sin and shame to throw away that noble sword, and so eft [1] he hid the sword, and returned again, and told to the king that he had been at the water, and done his commandment. What saw thou there? said the king. Sir, he said, I saw nothing but the waters wappe and waves wanne. [2] Ah, traitor untrue, said King Arthur, now hast thou betrayed me twice. Who would have weened that, thou that hast been to me so lief and dear? and thou art named a noble knight, and would betray me for the richness of the sword. But now go again lightly, for thy long tarrying putteth me in great jeopardy of my life, for I have taken cold. And but if [3] thou do now as I bid thee, if ever I may see thee I shall slay thee with mine own hands; for thou wouldst for my rich sword see me dead.

Then Sir Bedivere departed, and went to the sword, and lightly took it up, and went to the water side; and there he bound the girdle about the hilts, and then he threw the sword as far into the water as he might; and there came an arm and an hand above the water and met it, and caught it, and so shook it thrice and brandished, and then vanished away the hand with the sword in the water. So Sir Bedivere came again to the king, and told him what he saw. Alas, said the king, help me hence, for I dread me I have tarried over long.

[1] again
[2] lap and ebb (ebb and flow)
[3] unless

Then Sir Bedivere took the king upon his back, and so went with him to that water side. And when they were at the water side, even fast by the bank hoved a little barge with many fair ladies in it, and among them all was a queen, and all they had black hoods, and all they wept and shrieked when they saw King Arthur. Now put me into the barge said the king. And so he did softly; and there received him three queens with great mourning; and so they set them down, and in one of their laps King Arthur laid his head. And then that queen said: Ah, dear brother, why have ye tarried so long from me? alas, this wound on your head hath caught over-much cold. And so then they rowed from the land, and Sir Bedivere beheld all those ladies go from him. Then Sir Bedivere cried: Ah, my lord Arthur, what shall become of me, now ye go from me and leave me here alone among mine enemies? Comfort thyself, said the king, and do as well as thou mayest, for in me is no trust for to trust in; for I will into the vale of Avilion [4] to heal me of my grievous wound: and if thou hear never more of me, pray for my soul. But ever the queens and ladies wept and shrieked, that it was pity to hear.

And as soon as Sir Bedivere had lost the sight of the barge, he wept and wailed, and so took the forest; and so he went all that night, and in the morning he was ware, betwixt two holts hoar, [5] of a chapel and an hermitage. Then was Sir Bedivere glad, and thither he went; and when he came into the chapel, he saw where lay an hermit groveling on all four, there fast by a tomb was new graven. When the hermit saw Sir Bedivere he knew him well, for he was but little tofore Bishop of Canterbury, that Sir Mordred flemed. [6] Sir, said Bedivere, what man is there interred that ye pray so fast for? Fair son, said the hermit, I wot not verily, but by deeming. [7] But this night, at midnight, here came a number of ladies, and brought hither a dead corpse, and prayed me to bury him; and here they offered an hundred tapers, and they gave me an hundred besants. [8] Alas, said Sir Bedivere, that was my lord King Arthur, that here lieth buried in this chapel.

Then Sir Bedivere swooned; and when he awoke he prayed the hermit he might abide with him still there, to live with fasting and prayers. For from hence will I never go, said Sir Bedivere, by my will, but all the days of

[4] or Avalon, the Celtic Land of the Blessed or Earthly Paradise
[5] two gray wooded hills
[6] put to flight
[7] I can only conjecture
[8] a gold coin (named from Byzantium)

my life here to pray for my lord Arthur. Ye are welcome to me, said the hermit, for I know you better than ye ween that I do. Ye are the bold Bedivere, and the full noble duke, Sir Lucan the Butler, was your brother. Then Sir Bedivere told the hermit all as ye have heard tofore. So there bode Sir Bedivere with the hermit that was tofore Bishop of Canterbury, and there Sir Bedivere put upon him poor clothes, and served the hermit full lowly in fasting and in prayers. . . . .

Yet some men say in many parts of England that King Arthur is not dead, but had [1] by the will of our Lord Jesu into another place; and men say that he shall come again, and he shall win the holy cross. I will not say it shall be so, but rather I will say, here in this world he changed his life. But many men say that there is written upon his tomb this verse: *Hic jacet Arthurus, Rex quondam, Rexque futurus.* [2] Thus leave I here Sir Bedivere with the hermit, that dwelled that time in a chapel beside Glastonbury, and there was his hermitage. And so they lived in their prayers, and fastings, and great abstinence. . . . .

finished 1470 1485

[1] taken

[2] *Here lies Arthur, king that was and shall be.*

SIR THOMAS MORE 1478-1535

To gain knowledge of More's charming lovable personality one should read the intimate account of his life written by his son-in-law, William Roper, showing the statesman's affection for his family, his piety, keen sense of justice, and upright conscience. The son of a barrister, he was born in Cheapside, sent early to school, and at fourteen entered Oxford, where he was noted for his scholarship. Though a brilliant lawyer, he still had time for literature, and was intimate with the leading literary men of the day. Devoting himself to public affairs, he became a member of Parliament and stood for the rights of the people, even in opposition to the king and Wolsey. In 1510, when under-sheriff of London, More attracted the notice of Henry VIII; he rose rapidly in favor, was employed on various diplomatic missions, and succeeded Wolsey as Chancellor, being the first layman to hold the office. But as a staunch Catholic he refused to admit the king's right to assume authority over the church and to divorce Katherine. Therefore he resigned his office and retired to live in poverty. This, however, did not satisfy the offended Anne Boleyn; he was accused of treason, imprisoned in the Tower, and finally beheaded.

His best-known production is *Utopia,* a satire on the world as it was in his day, containing his ideas of social and political reform, many of which have since been realized. This book was written and published in Latin in 1516. It was translated by Ralph Robinson in 1551. It is of especial interest as a link in a series of ideal communities from Plato's *Republic* down to modern times (Wells's *Men Like Gods,* p. 858).

Roper's *Life of More* will be found with *Utopia* in the edition by J. R. Lumby, 1888 (1912); in Harvard Classics, vol. 36; and in Bohn's Popular Library. For criticism see Lee; Addison in *The Spectator* 349; R. H. Murray, "Utopian Toleration," *Edin. R.* 219:91-106; "More's Utopia and 400 Years After," *Outl.* 116:359-60.

From UTOPIA [3]

THE EPISTLE

Thomas More to Peter Giles, [4] *sendeth greeting:*

I am almost ashamed, right well-beloved Peter Giles, to send unto you this book of the Utopian commonwealth, well nigh after a year's space, which I am sure you looked for within a month and a half. And no marvel. For you knew well enough that I was already disburdened of all the labor and study belonging to the invention in this work, and that I had no need at all to trouble my brains about the disposition or conveyance of the matter, and therefore had herein nothing else to do but only to rehearse those things which you and I together heard master Raphael [5] tell and declare. Wherefore there was no cause why I should study to set forth the matter with eloquence: forasmuch as his talk could not be fine and eloquent, being first not studied for, but sudden and unpremeditate, and then, as you know, of a man better seen [6] in the Greek language than in the Latin tongue. And my writing, the nigher it should approach to his homely, plain, and simple [7] speech, so much the

[3] The extracts here given are from the second edition of Robinson's translation, 1556. "Utopia" is a word made from the Greek, meaning "nowhere." As the imaginary commonwealth is pictured in such attractive colors, it is easy to regard the first syllable of the name as representing the Greek *eu,* "well," instead of *ou,* "not," and "Utopian" has come to mean "perfect," as well as "visionary."

[4] a friend of More who lived in Antwerp

[5] Raphael Hythloday, the imaginary narrator, whom More professes to have met in Antwerp; his name means "teller of idle tales."

[6] versed

[7] To use two or three words thus for the same idea was a common practice of writers of the time, and especially of translators, who often took this means of giving both the Latin derivative and its Saxon equivalent. More's Latin is much terser than his translator's English.

nigher should it go to the truth, which is the only mark whereunto I do and ought to direct all my travail and study herein.

I grant and confess, friend Peter, myself discharged of so much labor, having all these things ready done to my hand, that almost there was nothing left for me to do. Else either the invention or the disposition of this matter might have required of a wit neither base, neither at all unlearned, both some time and leisure, and also some study. But if it were requisite and necessary that the matter should also have been written eloquently, and not alone truly, of a surety that thing could I have performed by no time nor study. But now seeing all these cares, stays, and lets[1] were taken away, wherein else so much labor and study should have been employed, and that there remained no other thing for me to do but only to write plainly the matter as I heard it spoken, that indeed was a thing light and easy to be done.

Howbeit, to the dispatching of this so little business my other cares and troubles did leave almost less than no leisure. Whiles I do daily bestow my time about law matters, some to plead, some to hear, some as an arbitrator with mine award to determine, some as an umpire or a judge, with my sentence finally to discuss; whiles I go one way to see and visit my friend, another way about mine own private affairs; whiles I spend almost all the day abroad amongst other, and the residue at home among mine own; I leave to myself, I mean to my book, no time. For when I am come home, I must commen[2] with my wife, chat with my children, and talk with my servants. All the which things I reckon and account among business, forasmuch as they must of necessity be done; and done must they needs be, unless a man will be a stranger in his own house. And in any wise a man must so fashion and order his conditions, and so appoint and dispose himself, that he be merry, jocund, and pleasant among them whom either nature hath provided, or chance hath made, or he himself hath chosen, to be the fellows and companions of his life, so that with too much gentle behavior and familiarity he do not mar them, and by too much sufferance of his servants make them his masters.

Among these things now rehearsed stealeth away the day, the month, the year. When do I write then? And all this while have I spoken no word of sleep, neither yet of meat, which among a great number doth waste no less time than doth sleep, wherein almost half the lifetime of man creepeth away. I therefore do win and get only that time which I steal from sleep and meat. Which time because it is very little, and yet somewhat it is, therefore have I once at the last, though it be long first, finished *Utopia,* and have sent it to you, friend Peter, to read and peruse, to the intent that if anything have escaped me, you might put me in remembrance of it. For though in this behalf I do not greatly mistrust myself (which would God I were somewhat in wit and learning as I am not all of the worst and dullest memory) yet have I not so great trust and confidence in it that I think nothing could fall out of my mind.

For John Clement, my boy,[3] who as you know was there present with us, whom I suffer to be away from no talk wherein may be any profit or goodness (for out of this young bladed and new shot up corn, which hath already begun to spring up both in Latin and Greek learning, I look for plentiful increase at length of goodly ripe grain)—he, I say, hath brought me into a great doubt. For whereas Hythloday (unless my memory fail me) said that the bridge of Amaurote, which goeth over the river of Anyder, is five hundred paces, that is to say, half a mile in length, my John sayeth that two hundred of those paces must be plucked away, for that the river containeth there not above three hundred paces in breadth. I pray you heartily, call the matter to your remembrance. For if you agree with him, I also will say as you say, and confess myself deceived. But if you cannot remember the thing, then surely I will write as I have done and as mine own remembrance serveth me. For as I will take good heed that there be in my book nothing false, so if there be anything doubtful, I will rather tell a lie than make a lie; because I had rather be good, than wily.

Howbeit, this matter may easily be remedied if you will take the pains to ask the question of Raphael himself by word of mouth, if he be now with you, or else by your letters. Which you must needs do for another doubt also that hath chanced—through whose fault I cannot tell, whether through mine, or yours, or Raphael's. For neither we remembered to inquire of him, nor he to tell us, in what part of the new world Utopia is situate. The which thing, I had rather have spent no small sum of money than that it should thus have escaped us; as well for that I am ashamed to be ignorant in what sea that island standeth, whereof I write

[1] hindrances [2] commune

[3] He was a tutor in More's household.

so long a treatise, as also because there be with us certain men, and especially one virtuous and godly man, and a professor of divinity, who is exceeding desirous to go unto Utopia; not for a vain and curious desire to see news, [1] but to the intent he may further and increase our religion, which is there already luckily begun. And that he may the better accomplish and perform this his good intent, he is minded to procure that he may be sent thither by the high Bishop; yea, and that he himself may be made Bishop of Utopia; being nothing scrupulous herein, that he must obtain this Bishopric with suit. [2] For he counteth that a godly suit which proceedeth not of the desire of honor or lucre, but only of a godly zeal.

Wherefore I most earnestly desire you, friend Peter, to talk with Hythloday, if you can, face to face, or else to write your letters to him, and so to work in this matter that in this my book there may neither anything be found which is untrue, neither anything be lacking which is true.

And I think verily it shall be well done that you show unto him the book itself. For if I have missed or failed in any point, or if any fault have escaped me, no man can so well correct and amend it as he can; and yet that can he not do unless he peruse and read over my book written. Moreover, by this means shall you perceive whether he be well willing and content that I should undertake to put this work in writing. For if he be minded to publish and put forth his own labors and travels himself, perchance he would be loth, and so would I also, that in publishing the Utopian weal public, [3] I should prevent [4] him, and take from him the flower and grace of the novelty of this his history.

Howbeit, to say the very truth, I am not yet fully determined with myself whether I will put forth my book or no. For the natures of men be so diverse, the fantasies of some so wayward, their minds so unkind, their judgments so corrupt, that they which lead a merry and a jocund life, following their own sensual pleasures and carnal lusts, may seem to be in a much better state or case than they that vex and unquiet themselves with cares and study for the putting forth and publishing of some thing that may be either profit or pleasure to others; which others nevertheless will disdainfully, scornfully, and unkindly accept the same. The most part of all be unlearned. And a great number hath learning in contempt. The rude and barbarous alloweth nothing but that which is very barbarous indeed. If it be one that hath a little smack of learning, he rejecteth as homely gear and common ware whatsoever is not stuffed full of old moth-eaten terms, and that be worn out of use. Some there be that have pleasure only in old rustic antiquities; and some only in their own doings. One is so sour, so crabbed, and so unpleasant, that he can away with [5] no mirth nor sport. Another is so narrow between the shoulders that he can bear no jests nor taunts. Some silly poor souls be so afeard that at every snappish word their nose shall be bitten off, that they stand in no less dread of every quick and sharp word than he that is bitten of a mad dog feareth water. Some be so mutable and wavering that every hour they be in a new mind, saying one thing sitting and another thing standing. Another sort sitteth upon their alebenches, and there among their cups they give judgment of the wits of writers, and with great authority they condemn, even as pleaseth them, every writer according to his writing, in most spiteful manner mocking, louting, and flouting them; being themselves in the mean season safe, and, as sayeth the proverb, out of all danger of gun-shot. For why, [6] they be so smug and smooth that they have not so much as one hair of an honest man whereby one may take hold of them. There be, moreover, some so unkind and ungentle that though they take great pleasure and delectation in the work, yet, for all that, they cannot find in their hearts to love the author thereof, nor to afford him a good word; being much like uncourteous, unthankful, and churlish guests, which, when they have with good and dainty meats well filled their bellies, depart home, giving no thanks to the feast-maker. Go your ways now, and make a costly feast at your own charges for guests so dainty-mouthed, so divers in taste, and besides that of so unkind and unthankful natures.

But nevertheless, friend Peter, do, I pray you, with Hythloday as I willed you before. And as for this matter, I shall be at my liberty afterwards to take new advisement. Howbeit, seeing I have taken great pains and labor in writing the matter, if it may stand with his mind and pleasure, I will, as touching the edition or publishing of the book, follow the counsel and advice of my friends, and specially yours. Thus fare you well, right heartily beloved friend Peter, with your gentle wife; and love me as you have ever done, for I love you better than ever I did.

[1] new things
[2] not scrupling at all to ask for it
[3] commonwealth
[4] anticipate

[5] endure
[6] because

Of the Cities, and Namely of Amaurote [1]
Book II. Chapter II

As for their cities, whoso knoweth one of them, knoweth them all; they be all so like one to another, as farforth as the nature of the place permitteth. I will describe therefore to you one or other of them, for it skilleth [2] not greatly which; but which rather than Amaurote? Of them all this is the worthiest and of most dignity. For the residue 'knowledge it for the head city, because there is the Council-house. Nor to me any of them all is better beloved, as wherein I lived five whole years together.

The city of Amaurote standeth upon the side of a low hill, in fashion almost four square. For the breadth of it beginneth a little beneath the top of the hill, and still continueth by the space of two miles, until it come to the river of Anyder. [3] The length of it, which lieth by the river's side, is somewhat more.

The river of Anyder riseth four and twenty miles above Amaurote out of a little spring. But being increased by other small rivers and brooks that run into it, and among other, two somewhat big ones, before the city it is half a mile broad, and farther, broader. And forty miles beyond the city it falleth into the ocean sea. By all that space that lieth between the sea and the city, and certain miles also above the city, the water ebbeth and floweth six hours together with a swift tide. When the sea floweth in, for the length of thirty miles it filleth all the Anyder with salt water, and driveth back the fresh water of the river. And somewhat farther it changeth the sweetness of the fresh water with saltness. But a little beyond that the river waxeth sweet, and runneth forby [4] the city fresh and pleasant. And when the sea ebbeth and goeth back again, the fresh water followeth it almost even to the very fall into the sea. There goeth a bridge over the river made not of piles or of timber, but of stonework, with gorgeous and substantial arches at that part of the city that is farthest from the sea; to the intent that ships may pass along forby all the side of the city without let.

They have also another river, which indeed is not very great. But it runneth gently and pleasantly. For it riseth even out of the same hill that the city standeth upon, and runneth down a slope through the midst of the city into Anyder. And because it riseth a little without the city, the Amaurotians have inclosed the head spring of it with strong fences and bulwarks, and so have joined it to the city. This is done to the intent that the water should not be stopped, nor turned away, or poisoned, if their enemies should chance to come upon them. From thence the water is derived and conveyed down in canals of brick divers ways into the lower parts of the city. Where that cannot be done, by reason that the place will not suffer it, there they gather the rain-water in great cisterns, which doth them as good service.

The city is compassed about with a high and thick stone wall full of turrets and bulwarks. A dry ditch, but deep, and broad, and overgrown with bushes, briers, and thorns, goeth about three sides or quarters of the city. To the fourth side the river itself serveth for a ditch.

The streets be appointed [5] and set forth very commodious and handsome, both for carriage, [6] and also against the winds. The houses be of fair and gorgeous building, and on the street side they stand joined together in a long row through the whole street without any partition or separation. The streets be twenty foot broad. [7] On the back side of the houses, through the whole length of the street, lie large gardens, inclosed round about with the back part of the streets. Every house hath two doors, one into the street, and a postern door on the back side into the garden. These doors be made with two leaves, never locked nor bolted, so easy to be opened that they will follow the least drawing of a finger, and shut again alone. Whoso will, may go in, for there is nothing within the houses that is private, or any man's own. And every tenth year they change their houses by lot.

They set great store by their gardens. In them they have vineyards, all manner of fruit, herbs, and flowers, so pleasant, so well furnished, and so finely kept, that I never saw thing more fruitful, nor better trimmed in any place. Their study and diligence herein cometh not only of pleasure, but also of a certain strife and contention that is between street and street, concerning the trimming, husbanding, and furnishing of their gardens—every man for his own part. And verily you shall not lightly find in all the city anything that is more commodious, either for the profit of the citizens, or for pleasure. And therefore it may

[1] The name means "dark, unknown."
[2] matters
[3] i.e., waterless
[4] past (German *vorbei*)

[5] arranged
[6] transportation
[7] To More this width seemed generous. Some of the busiest streets of London were, until a recent date, scarcely wider.

seem that the first founder of the city minded nothing so much as these gardens.

For they say that king Utopus himself, even at the first beginning, appointed and drew forth the platform [1] of the city into this fashion and figure that it hath now, but the gallant garnishing, and the beautiful setting forth of it, whereunto he saw that one man's age would not suffice, that he left to his posterity. For their chronicles, which they keep written with all diligent circumspection, containing the history of one thousand seven hundred and sixty years, even from the first conquest of the island, record and witness that the houses in the beginning were very low, and, like homely cottages or poor shepherd houses, made at all adventures [2] of every rude piece of timber that came first to hand, with mud walls, and ridged roofs, thatched over with straw. But now the houses be curiously builded after a gorgeous and gallant sort, with three stories one over another. The outsides of the walls be made either of hard flint, or of plaster, or else of brick, and the inner sides be well strengthened with timber-work. The roofs be plain and flat, covered with a certain kind of plaster that is of no cost, and yet so tempered that no fire can hurt or perish it, and withstandeth the violence of the weather better than any lead. They keep the wind out of their windows with glass, [3] for it is there much used, and somewhere also with fine linen cloth dipped in oil or amber, and that for two commodities. For by this means more light cometh in, and the wind is better kept out.

Of Sciences, Crafts, and Occupations
Book II. Chapter IV

Husbandry is a science common to them all in general, both men and women, wherein they be all expert and cunning. In this they be all instructed even from their youth, partly in their schools with traditions and precepts, and partly in the country nigh the city, brought up [4] as it were in playing, not only beholding the use of it, but, by occasion of exercising their bodies, practicing it also. Besides husbandry, which (as I said) is common to them all, every one of them learneth one or other several [5] and particular science as his own proper craft. That is most commonly either cloth-working in wool or flax, or masonry, or the smith's craft, or the carpenter's science. For there is none other occupation that any number to speak of doth use there.

For [6] their garments, which throughout all the island be of one fashion (saving that there is a difference between the man's garment and the woman's, between the married and the unmarried), and this one continueth for ever more unchanged, seemly and comely to the eye, no let to the moving and wielding of the body, also fit both for winter and summer—as for these garments (I say), every family maketh their own. But of the other aforesaid crafts every man learneth one. And not only the men, but also the women. But the women, as the weaker sort, be put to the easier crafts, as to work wool and flax. The more laborsome sciences be committed to the men. For the most part every man is brought up in his father's craft. For most commonly they be naturally thereto bent and inclined. But if a man's mind stand to any other, he is by adoption put into a family of that occupation which he doth most fantasy. Whom not only his father, but also the magistrates do diligently look to, that he be put to a discreet and an honest householder. Yea, and if any person, when he hath learned one craft, be desirous to learn also another, he is likewise suffered and permitted. When he hath learned both, he occupieth whether he will, [7] unless the city have more need of the one than of the other.

The chief and almost the only office of the Syphogrants [8] is to see and take heed that no man sit idle, but that everyone apply his own craft with earnest diligence; and yet for all that, not to be wearied from early in the morning to late in the evening with continual work, like laboring and toiling beasts. For this is worse than the miserable and wretched condition of bondmen. Which nevertheless is almost everywhere the life of workmen and artificers, saving in Utopia. For they, dividing the day and night into twenty-four just hours, appoint and assign only six of those hours to work, three before noon, upon the which they go straight to dinner; and after dinner, when they have rested two hours, then they work three hours, and upon that they go to supper. [9]

[1] ground-plan
[2] haphazard
[3] Glass windows were introduced into the wealthier houses in England probably in the fourteenth century. Other houses continued to use slat and wicker lattices and panels of horn.
[4] The Latin reads *educti* and should have been translated "led out."
[5] separate
[6] as for
[7] practices whichever he wishes
[8] Officers, two hundred in number, each elected by and ruling over thirty families; the word, like Tranibore and other supposed words of the old Utopian tongue, is meaningless.
[9] In England, in More's time, summer working hours were from 5 a. m. to 7 p. m.

About eight of the clock in the evening (counting one of the clock at the first hour after noon), they go to bed; eight hours they give to sleep. All the void time that is between the hours of work, sleep, and meat, that they be suffered to bestow, every man as he liketh best himself. Not to the intent that they should misspend this time in riot or slothfulness, but, being then licensed [1] from the labor of their own occupations, to bestow the time well and thriftily upon some other science, as shall please them. For it is a solemn custom there to have lectures daily early in the morning, where to be present they only be constrained that be namely chosen and appointed to learning. Howbeit, a great multitude of every sort of people, both men and women, go to hear lectures, some one, and some another, as every man's nature is inclined. Yet, this notwithstanding, if any man had rather bestow this time upon his own occupation (as it chanceth in many whose minds rise not in the contemplation of any science liberal), he is not letted nor prohibited, but is also [2] praised and commended, as profitable to the commonwealth.

After supper they bestow one hour in play, in summer in their gardens, in winter in their common halls, where they dine and sup. There they exercise themselves in music, or else in honest and wholesome communication. Dice-play, and such other foolish and pernicious games, they know not. But they use two games not much unlike the chess. The one is the Battle of Numbers, wherein one number stealeth away another. The other is wherein Vices fight with Virtues, as it were in battle array, or a set field. In the which game is very properly showed, both the strife and discord that vices have among themselves, and again their unity and concord against virtues; and also what vices be repugnant to what virtues—with what power and strength they assail them openly, by what wiles and subtlety they assault them secretly; with what help and aid the virtues resist and overcome the puissance of the vices; by what craft they frustrate their purposes; and finally by what sleight or means the one getteth the victory.

But here, lest you be deceived, one thing you must look more narrowly [3] upon. For seeing they bestow but six hours in work, perchance you may think that the lack of some necessary things hereof may ensue. But this is nothing so. For that small time is not only enough, but also too much, for the store and abundance of all things that be requisite either for the necessity or commodity of life. The which thing you also shall perceive if you weigh and consider with yourselves how great a part of the people in other countries liveth idle. First, almost all women, which be the half of the whole number; or else if the women be somewhere occupied, there most commonly in their stead the men be idle. Besides this, how great and how idle a company is there of priests, and religious men, [4] as they call them. Put thereto all rich men, specially all landed men, which commonly be called gentlemen and noblemen. Take into this number also their servants; I mean all that flock of stout, bragging rush-bucklers. [5] Join to them also sturdy and valiant beggars, cloaking their idle life under the color of some disease or sickness. And truly you shall find them [6] much fewer than you thought, by whose labor all these things are wrought that in men's affairs are now daily used and frequented.

Now consider with yourself, of these few that do work, how few be occupied in necessary works. For where money beareth all the swing, there many vain and superfluous occupations must needs be used to serve only for riotous superfluity and unhonest pleasure. For the same multitude that now is occupied in work, if they were divided into so few occupations as the necessary use of nature requireth, in so great plenty of things as then of necessity would ensue, doubtless the prices would be too little for the artificers to maintain their livings. But if all these that be now busied about unprofitable occupations, with all the whole flock of them that live idly and slothfully, which consume and waste every one of them more of these things that come by other men's labor than two of the workmen themselves do; if all these (I say) were set to profitable occupations, you easily perceive how little time would be enough, yea and too much, to store us with all things that may be requisite either for necessity or for commodity, yea or for pleasure, so that the same pleasure be true and natural.

And this, in Utopia, the thing itself maketh manifest and plain. For there, in all the city, with the whole country or shire adjoining to it, scarcely five hundred persons of all the whole number of men and women, that be neither too old nor too weak to work, be licensed and discharged from labor. Among them be the Syphogrants, who, though they be by the laws

[1] freed
[2] even
[3] closely

[4] men attached to some religious order, monks, etc.
[5] swashbucklers
[6] those

exempt and privileged from labor, yet they exempt not themselves; to the intent that they may the rather by their example provoke others to work. The same vacation from labor do they [1] also enjoy to whom the people, persuaded by the commendation of the priests and secret election of the Syphogrants, have given a perpetual license from labor to learning. But if any one of them prove not according to the expectation and hope of him conceived, he is forthwith plucked back to the company of artificers. And, contrariwise, often it chanceth that a handicraftsman doth so earnestly bestow his vacant and spare hours in learning, and through diligence so profiteth therein, that he is taken from his handy [2] occupation and promoted to the company of the learned. Out of this order of the learned be chosen ambassadors, priests, Tranibores, [3] and finally the prince himself, whom they in their old tongue call Barzanes, and by a newer name, Adamus. [4] The residue of the people being neither idle, nor yet occupied about unprofitable exercises, it may be easily judged in how few hours how much good work by them may be done and dispatched toward those things that I have spoken of.

This commodity they have also above others, that in the most part of necessary occupations they need not so much work as other nations do. For first of all the building or repairing of houses asketh everywhere so many men's continual labor, because that the unthrifty heir suffereth the houses that his father builded in continuance of time to fall in decay. So, that which he might have upholden with little cost, his successor is constrained to build it again anew, to his great charge. Yea, many times also the house that stood one man in [5] much money, another is of so nice and so delicate a mind that he setteth nothing by it. And it being neglected, and therefore shortly falling into ruin, he buildeth up another in another place with no less cost and charge. But among the Utopians, where all things be set in a good order, and the commonwealth in a good stay, [6] it very seldom chanceth that they choose a new plot to build an house upon. And they do not only find speedy and quick remedies for present faults, but also prevent them that be like to fall. And by this means their houses continue and last very long with little labor and small reparations, in so much that this kind of workmen sometimes have almost nothing to do, but that they be commanded to hew timber at home, and to square and trim up stones, to the intent that if any work chance, it may the speedlier rise.

Now, sir, in their apparel, mark (I pray you) how few workmen they need. First of all, whiles they be at work, they be covered homely with leather or skins that will last seven years. When they go forth abroad, they cast upon them a cloak, which hideth the other homely apparel. These cloaks throughout the whole island be all of one color, and that is the natural color of the wool. They therefore do not only spend much less woolen cloth than is spent in other countries, but also the same standeth them in much less cost. But linen cloth is made with less labor, and is therefore had more in use. But in linen cloth only whiteness, in woolen only cleanliness, is regarded. As for the smallness or fineness of the thread, that is nothing passed for. [7] And this is the cause wherefore in other places four or five cloth gowns of divers colors, and as many silk coats, be not enough for one man. Yea, and if he be of the delicate and nice sort, ten be too few; whereas there one garment will serve a man most commonly two years. For why should he desire more? Seeing if he had them, he should not be the better hapt [8] or covered from cold, neither in his apparel any whit the comelier.

Wherefore, seeing they be all exercised in profitable occupations, and that few artificers in the same crafts be sufficient, this is the cause that, plenty of all things being among them, they do sometimes bring forth an innumerable company of people to amend the highways, if any be broken. Many times also, when they have no such work to be occupied about, an open proclamation is made that they shall bestow fewer hours in work. For the magistrates do not exercise their citizens against their wills in unneedful labors. For why, in the institution of that weal public this end is only and chiefly pretended [9] and minded, that what time may possibly be spared from the necessary occupations and affairs of the commonwealth, all that the citizens should withdraw from the bodily service to the free liberty of the mind and garnishing of the same. For herein they suppose the felicity of this life to consist.

[1] those
[2] manual
[3] magistrates, twenty in number, superior to the Syphogrants
[4] or Ademus, "folkless"
[5] cost
[6] state
[7] not at all heeded
[8] wrapped
[9] aimed at

Of Their Journeyings or Traveling Abroad, with Divers Other Matters. . . . . Book II. Chapter VI

But if any be desirous to visit either their friends dwelling in another city, or to see the place itself, they easily obtain license of their Syphogrants and Tranibores, unless there be some profitable let. [1] No man goeth out alone; but a company is sent forth together with their prince's letters, which do testify that they have license to go that journey, and prescribeth also the day of their return. They have a wagon given them, with a common bondman, [2] which driveth the oxen, and taketh charge of them. But unless they have women in their company, they send home the wagon again, as an impediment and a let. And though they carry nothing forth with them, yet in all their journey they lack nothing. For wheresoever they come, they be at home. If they tarry in a place longer than one day, then there every one of them falleth to his own occupation, and be very genteelly entertained of [3] the workmen and companies of the same crafts. If any man of his own head and without leave walk out of his precinct and bounds, taken without the prince's letters, he is brought again for a fugitive or a runaway with great shame and rebuke, and is sharply punished. If he be taken in that fault again, he is punished with bondage.

If any be desirous to walk abroad into the fields, or into the country that belongeth to the same city that he dwelleth in, obtaining the good will of his father, and the consent of his wife, he is not prohibited. But into what part of the country soever he cometh he hath no meat given him until he have wrought out his forenoon's task, or dispatched so much work as there is wont to be wrought before supper. Observing this law and condition, he may go whither he will within the bound of his own city. For he shall be no less profitable to the city than if he were within it.

Now you see how little liberty they have to loiter; how they can have no cloak or pretence to idleness. There be neither wine-taverns, nor ale-houses, nor stews, [4] nor any occasion of vice or wickedness, no lurking corners, no places of wicked counsels or unlawful assemblies. But they be in the present sight and under the eyes of every man. So that of necessity they must either apply [5] their accustomed labors, or else recreate themselves with honest and laudable pastimes. This fashion and trade of life being used among the people, it cannot be chosen but that they must of necessity have store and plenty of all things.

. . . .

They keep at home all the treasure which they have, to be holpen and succored by it either in extreme jeopardies, or in sudden dangers; but especially and chiefly to hire therewith, and that for unreasonable great wages, strange soldiers. For they had rather put strangers in jeopardy than their own countrymen; knowing that for money enough their enemies themselves many times may be bought or sold, or else through treason be set together by the ears among themselves. For this cause they keep an inestimable treasure; but yet not as a treasure; but so they have it, and use it, as in good faith I am ashamed to show, fearing that my words shall not be believed. And this I have more cause to fear, for that I know how difficultly and hardly I myself would have believed another man telling the same if I had not presently seen it with mine own eyes. For it must needs be that how far a thing is dissonant and disagreeing from the guise and trade [6] of the hearers, so far shall it be out of their belief. Howbeit, a wise and indifferent esteemer [7] of things will not greatly marvel, perchance, seeing all their other laws and customs do so much differ from ours, if the use also of gold and silver among them be applied rather to their own fashions than to ours. I mean in that they occupy [8] not money themselves, but keep it for that chance; which as it may happen, so it may be that it shall never come to pass.

In the meantime gold and silver, whereof money is made, they do so use as none of them doth more esteem it than the very nature of the thing deserveth. And then who doth not plainly see how far it is under iron? As without the which men can no better live than without fire and water. Whereas to gold and silver nature hath given no use that we may not well lack if that [9] the folly of men had not set it in higher estimation for the rareness' sake. But of [10] the contrary part, nature, as a most tender and loving mother, hath placed the best and most necessary things open abroad: as the air, the water, and the earth itself; and hath removed and hid farthest from us vain and unprofitable things. Therefore if these metals among them should be fast locked up in some tower, it might be suspected that the prince and the Council (as the people is ever foolishly

[1] business hindrance
[2] Transgressors of the law in Utopia were made slaves and attached to the soil. Each farm had at least two bondmen.
[3] by [4] low resorts [5] ply

[6] manners and practice [7] impartial judge
[8] use [9] if ("that" is redundant) [10] on

imagining) intended by some subtlety to deceive the commons, and to take some profit of it to themselves. Furthermore, if they should make thereof plate and such other finely and cunningly wrought stuff; if at any time they should have occasion to break it, and melt it again, therewith to pay their soldiers wages, they see and perceive very well that men would be loth to part from those things that they once began to have pleasure and delight in.

To remedy all this they have found out a means, which, as it is agreeable to all their other laws and customs, so it is from ours (where gold is so much set by, and so diligently kept) very far discrepant and repugnant; and therefore uncredible, but only to them that be wise. For whereas they eat and drink in earthen and glass vessels, which indeed be curiously and properly[1] made, and yet be of very small value; of gold and silver they make commonly other vessels that serve for vile uses, not only in their common halls, but in every man's private house. Furthermore, of the same metals they make great chains, fetters, and gyves, wherein they tie their bondmen. Finally, whosoever for any offense be infamed,[2] by their ears hang rings of gold; upon their fingers they wear rings of gold, and about their necks chains of gold; and, in conclusion, their heads be tied about with gold. Thus by all means possible they procure to have gold and silver among them in reproach and infamy. And these metals which other nations do so grievously and sorrowfully forego as in a manner their own lives, if they should altogether at once be taken from the Utopians, no man there would think that he had lost the worth of one farthing.

They gather also pearls by the seaside, and diamonds and carbuncles upon certain rocks, and yet they seek not for them; but by chance finding them, they cut and polish them. And therewith they deck their young infants. Which, like as in the first years of their childhood they make much and be fond and proud of such ornaments, so when they be a little more grown in years and discretion, perceiving that none but children do wear such toys and trifles, they lay them away even of their own shamefastness, without any bidding of their parents; even as our children, when they wax big, do cast away nuts, brooches, and puppets. Therefore, these laws and customs, which be so far different from all other nations, how divers fantasies also and minds they do cause, did I never so plainly perceive, as in the ambassadors of the Anemolians.

[1] handsomely [2] disgraced

These ambassadors came to Amaurote whilst I was there. And because they came to entreat of great and weighty matters, those three citizens[3] apiece out of every city were comen thither before them. But all the ambassadors of the next countries which had been there before and knew the fashions and manners of the Utopians, among whom they perceived no honor given to sumptuous apparel, silks to be contemned, gold also to be infamed and reproachful, were wont to come thither in very homely and simple array. But the Anemolians, because they dwell far thence and had very little acquaintance with them, hearing that they were all appareled alike, and that very rudely and homely, thinking them not to have the things which they did not wear, being therefore more proud than wise, determined in the gorgeousness of their apparel to represent very gods, and with the bright shining and glistering of their gay clothing to dazzle the eyes of the silly[4] poor Utopians.

So there came in three ambassadors with one hundred servants all appareled in changeable colors, the most of them in silks, the ambassadors themselves (for at home in their own country they were noblemen) in cloth of gold, with great chains of gold, with gold hanging at their ears, with gold rings upon their fingers, with brooches and aiglets of gold upon their caps, which glistered full of pearls and precious stones; to be short, trimmed and adorned with all those things which among the Utopians were either the punishment of bondmen, or the reproach of infamed persons, or else trifles for young children to play withal.[5] Therefore it would have done a man good at his heart to have seen how proudly they displayed their peacocks' feathers, how much they made of their painted sheaths,[6] and how loftily they set forth and advanced themselves when they compared their gallant apparel with the poor raiment of the Utopians. For all the people were swarmed forth into the streets.

And on the other side it was no less pleasure to consider how much they were deceived, and how far they missed of their purpose, being contrariwise taken than they thought they should have been. For to the eyes of all the Utopians, except very few which had been in other countries for some reasonable cause, all that gorgeousness of apparel seemed shameful and reproachful. In so much that they most reverently saluted the vilest and most abject of them for lords; passing over the ambassadors themselves without any honor,

[3] Utopian delegates mentioned in a previous chapter
[4] simple [5] with [6] coverings

judging them by their wearing of gold chains to be bondmen. Yea, you should have seen children also, that had cast away their pearls and precious stones, when they saw the like sticking on the ambassadors' caps, dig and push their mothers under the sides, saying thus to them: "Look, mother, how great a lubber doth yet wear pearls and precious stones, as though he were a little child still." But the mother, yea and that also in good earnest: "Peace, son," saith she, "I think he be some of the ambassadors' fools." Some found fault at their golden chains, as to no use nor purpose, being so small and weak that a bondman might easily break them, and again so wide and large that, when it pleased him, he might cast them off and run away at liberty whither he would.

But when the ambassadors had been there a day or two and saw so great abundance of gold so lightly esteemed, yea in no less reproach than it was with them in honor; and besides that, more gold in the chains and gyves of one fugitive bondman than all the costly ornaments of them three [1] was worth; they began to abate their courage, and for very shame laid away all that gorgeous array whereof they were so proud; and specially when they had talked familiarly with the Utopians, and had learned all their fashions and opinions. For they marvel that any men be so foolish as to have delight and pleasure in the doubtful glistering of a little trifling stone, which [2] may behold any of the stars, or else the sun itself; or that any man is so mad as to count himself the nobler for the smaller or finer thread of wool, which self-same wool (be it now in never so fine a spun thread) a sheep did once wear; and yet was she all that time no other thing than a sheep. . . . .

These and such like opinions have they conceived, partly by education, being brought up in that commonwealth whose laws and customs be far different from these kinds of folly, and partly by good literature and learning. For though there be not many in every city which be exempt and discharged from all other labors and appointed only to learning, that is to say, such in whom even from their very childhood they have perceived a singular towardness, a fine wit, and a mind apt to good learning; yet all in their childhood be instruct in learning. And the better part of the people, both men and women, throughout all their whole life do bestow in learning those spare hours which we said they have vacant from bodily labors. [3]

In Latin, 1516 English translation, 1551, 1556

[1] any three of them [2] who
[3] It may be worth noting that our word "school" is derived from *schola*, "leisure."

ROGER ASCHAM 1515-1568

One likes to think of Roger Ascham, of whom Carlyle said: "Old Ascham is one of the freshest, truest spirits I have met with; a scholar and writer, yet a genuine man," as the guide of Queen Elizabeth's youthful studies. He came of a good old family, was born at Kirby Wiske, and received his early education from his father. Still young he was placed in the family of Sir Anthony Wingfield and studied under a tutor. At Cambridge he excelled in music and penmanship, and became perhaps the ablest Greek scholar in England, so that in 1548 he was called to court as tutor of the Princess Elizabeth.

In 1545 he received a pension from Henry VIII on account of his *Toxophilus*. When Princess Mary became queen (1553) he was appointed her Latin secretary, and when Elizabeth ascended the throne (1558) he was once more her tutor. Her esteem for him is evident in her words: "I had rather have thrown ten thousand pounds into the sea than have lost my Ascham." But in spite of much royal patronage his life was far from easy; he was in constant financial difficulties, and in continual hot water from his irrepressible love of controversy.

The word *toxophilus* means "a lover of the bow," and the book is in the form of a dialogue between Toxophilus, an archer, and Philologus, a scholar. Two centuries before, at the battle of Crécy, the British yeomen had shown the superiority of the long bow to the equipment of the armed knight, and subsequently archery had been assiduously cultivated, though when Ascham wrote it was, for the purposes of war, gradually giving way to fire-arms. If Ascham was conservative in clinging to this old-time weapon, in another respect he was courageously radical; that is in his employment of the English vernacular for a learned prose treatise. That he was conscious of making a literary departure is manifest in this Preface, and also in the dedication to King Henry which preceded it, where he defended himself for having "written this English matter in the English tongue for Englishmen," although to have written it "either in Latin or Greek had been more easier."

Of equal importance is his *Scholemaster,* on which he worked for five years, and which for a time was accepted as the approved manual of method in teaching. His belief that the interest of the pupil was a better incentive to work than punishment, and that the instruction should be suited to the child's individual ability has come into force again of late years. Though Ascham belongs to the generation preceding the Elizabethans, this last work of his was written and published (posthumously, 1570) well within the Virgin Queen's reign, and the little glimpse behind the curtain which its preface affords may serve both to introduce and to exemplify what Tennyson has so happily called "the spacious times of great Elizabeth."

TOXOPHILUS

From THE FOREWORD

To all Gentlemen and Yeomen of England:

Bias, the wise man, came to Croesus, the rich king, on a time when he was making new ships, purposing to have subdued by water the out isles lying betwixt Greece and Asia Minor. "What news now in Greece?" saith the king to Bias. "None other news but these," saith Bias, "that the isles of Greece have prepared a wonderful company of horsemen to overrun Lydia withal." "There is nothing under heaven," saith the king, "that I would so soon wish, as that they durst be so bold to [1] meet us on the land with horse." "And think you," saith Bias, "that there is anything which they would sooner wish than that you should be so fond [2] to meet them on the water with ships?" And so Croesus, hearing not the true news, but perceiving the wise man's mind and counsel, both gave then over making of his ships, and left also behind him a wonderful example for all commonwealths to follow: that is, evermore to regard and set most by that thing whereunto nature hath made them most apt and use hath made them most fit.

By this matter I mean the shooting in the long bow, for English men. Which thing with all my heart I do wish, and if I were of authority I would counsel, all the gentlemen and yeomen of England not to change it with any other thing, how good soever it seem to be, but that still, according to the old wont of England, youth should use it for the most honest pastime in peace, that men might handle it as a most sure weapon in war. Other strong weapons which both experience doth prove to be good, and the wisdom of the King's Majesty and his Council provides to be had, are not ordained to take away shooting; but that both, not compared together whether [3] should be better than the other, but so joined together that the one should be always an aid and help for the other, might so strengthen the realm on all sides that no kind of enemy, in any kind of weapon, might pass and go beyond us.

For this purpose, I, partly provoked by the counsel of some gentlemen, partly moved by the love which I have always borne toward shooting, have written this little treatise, wherein if I have not satisfied any man, I trust he will the rather be content with my doing, because I am, I suppose, the first which hath said anything in this matter; and few beginnings be perfect, saith wise men. And also because, if I have said amiss, I am content that any man amend it, or if I have said too little, any man that will to add what him pleaseth to it.

My mind is, in profiting and pleasing every man, to hurt or displease no man, intending none other purpose but that youth might be stirred to labor, honest pastime, and virtue, and, as much as lay in me, plucked from idleness, unthrifty games, and vice. Which thing I have labored only in this book, showing how fit shooting is for all kinds of men, how honest a pastime for the mind, how wholesome an exercise for the body, not vile for great men to use, not costly for poor men to sustain, not lurking in holes and corners for ill men at their pleasure to misuse it, but abiding in the open sight and face of the world for good men, if it fault, by their wisdom to correct it. And here I would desire all gentlemen and yeomen to use this pastime in such a mean that the outrageousness of gaming should not hurt the honesty [4] of shooting, which of his own nature is always joined with honesty, yet for men's faults oftentimes blamed unworthily, as all good things have been and evermore shall be.

If any man would blame me, either for taking such a matter in hand, or else for writing it in the English tongue, this answer I may make him, that what the best of the realm think it honest [5] for them to use, I, one of the meanest [6] sort, ought not to suppose it vile for me to write. And though to have written it in another tongue had been both more profitable for my study and also more honest [5] for my name, yet I can think my labor well bestowed if, with a little hindrance of my profit and name, may come any furtherance to the pleasure or commodity of the gentlemen and yeomen of England, for whose sake I took this matter in hand. And as for the Latin or Greek tongue, everything is so excellently done in them that none can do better; in the English tongue, contrary, everything in a manner so meanly, both for the matter and handling, that no man can do worse. For therein the least learned for the most part have been always most ready to write, and they which had least hope in Latin have been most bold in English; when surely every man that is most ready to talk is not most able to write. He that will write well in any tongue must follow this counsel of Aristotle—to speak as the common people do, to think as wise men do; and so should every man understand him, and the judgment of wise men allow [7] him.

[1] as to
[2] foolish
[3] which
[4] good repute
[5] honorable
[6] humblest
[7] approve

Many English writers have not done so, but using strange words, as Latin, French, and Italian, do make all things dark and hard. Once I communed with a man which reasoned the English tongue to be enriched and increased thereby, saying: Who will not praise that feast where a man shall drink at a dinner both wine, ale, and beer? Truly, quoth I, they be all good, every one taken by himself alone, but if you put malmsey and sack, red wine and white, ale and beer, and all in one pot, you shall make a drink neither easy to be known nor yet wholesome for the body. Cicero, in following Isocrates, Plato, and Demosthenes, increased the Latin tongue after another sort. This way [1] because divers men that write do not know, they can neither follow it, because of their ignorancy, nor yet will praise it, for very arrogancy—two faults, seldom the one out of the other's company.

English writers, by diversity of time, have taken diverse matters in hand. In our fathers' time nothing was read but books of feigned chivalry, wherein a man by reading should be led to none other end but only to manslaughter and bawdry. If any man suppose they were good enough to pass the time withal, he is deceived. For surely vain words do work no small thing thereunto of their own nature. These books, as I have heard say, were made the most part in abbeys and monasteries, a very likely and fit fruit of such an idle and blind kind of living. [2]

In our time now, when every man is given to know much rather than to live well, very many do write, but after such a fashion as very many do shoot. Some shooters take in hand stronger bows than they be able to maintain. This thing maketh them sometime to outshoot the mark, sometime to shoot far wide, and perchance hurt some that look on. Other that never learned to shoot, nor yet knoweth good shaft nor bow, will be as busy as the best, but such one commonly plucketh down [3] a side, and crafty archers which be against him will be both glad of him, and also ever ready to lay [4] and bet with him; it were better for such one to sit down than shoot. Other there be which have very good bow and shafts and good knowledge in shooting, but they have been brought up in such evil-favored shooting that they can neither shoot fair nor yet near. If any man will apply these things together, he shall not see the one far differ from the other.

And I also, among all other, in writing this little treatise, have followed some young shooters, which both will begin to shoot for a little money, and also will use to shoot once or twice about the mark for naught afore they begin agood. And therefore did I take this little matter in hand to assay [5] myself, and hereafter, by the grace of God, if the judgment of wise men that look on think that I can do any good, I may perhaps cast my shaft among other for better game.

[The Ways of the Wind] From Book II

The wind is sometimes plain up and down, which is commonly most certain, and requireth least knowledge, wherein a mean shooter with mean gear, [6] if he can shoot home, may make best shift. A side wind tryeth an archer and good gear very much. Sometime it bloweth aloft, sometime hard by the ground; sometime it bloweth by blasts, and sometime it continueth all in one; sometime full side wind, sometime quarter with him and more, and likewise against him, as a man with casting up light grass, or else if he take good heed, shall sensibly learn by experience.

To see the wind with a man his [7] eyes, it is impossible, the nature of it is so fine and subtle; yet this experience of the wind had I once myself, and that was in the great snow that fell four years ago. I rode in the highway betwixt Topcliffe-upon-Swale and Boroughbridge, the way being somewhat trodden before by wayfaring men. The fields on both sides were plain and lay almost yard deep with snow; the night afore had been a little frost, so that the snow was hard and crusted above. That morning the sun shone bright and clear, the wind was whistling aloft, and sharp, according to the time of the year. The snow in the highway lay loose and trodden with horses' feet: so as the wind blew, it took the loose snow with it, and made it so slide upon the snow in the field, which was hard and crusted by reason of the frost over night, that thereby I might see very well the whole nature of the wind as it blew that day. And I had a great delight and pleasure to mark it, which maketh me now far better to remember it.

Sometime the wind would be not past two yards broad, and so it would carry the snow as far as I could see. Another time the snow

[1] Construe after "know."
[2] Ascham is manifestly condemning such romances as Malory's *Le Morte Darthur.* England was at this time Protestant, and the dissolution of the monasteries a recent event.
[3] lowers the score of
[4] wager

[5] try
[6] ordinary equipment
[7] man's (a pedantic form, due to the erroneous idea that the possessive *s* was a contraction of *his*)

would blow over half the field at once. Sometime the snow would tumble softly, by and by it would fly wonderful fast. And this I perceived also, that the wind goeth by streams and not whole together. For I should see one stream within a score [1] of me, then the space of two score no snow would stir, but after so much quantity of ground another stream of snow at the same very time should be carried likewise, but not equally; for the one would stand still when the other flew apace, and so continue, sometime swiftlier, sometime slowlier, sometime broader, sometime narrower, as far as I could see. Nor it flew not straight, but sometime it crooked this way, sometime that way, and sometime it ran round about in a compass. And some time the snow would be lifted clean from the ground up in the air; and by and by it would be all clapped to the ground as though there had been no wind at all; straightway it would rise and fly again.

And—that which was the most marvelous of all—at one time two drifts of snow flew, the one out of the west into the east, the other out of the north into the east. And I saw two winds by reason of the snow, the one cross over the other, as it had been two highways. And again I should hear the wind blow in the air when nothing was stirred at the ground. And when all was still where I rode, not very far from me the snow should be lifted wonderfully. This experience made me more marvel at the nature of the wind, than it made me cunning in the knowledge of the wind; but yet thereby I learned perfectly that it is no marvel at all, although men in a wind lease [2] their length [3] in shooting, seeing so many ways the wind is so variable in blowing.

1544

THE SCHOOLMASTER

From A Preface to the Reader

When the great plague was at London, the year 1563, the Queen's Majesty, Queen Elizabeth, lay at her castle of Windsor; where, upon the tenth day of December, it fortuned that in Sir William Cecil's chamber (her Highness' Principal Secretary), there dined together these personages: Mr. Secretary himself, Sir William Peter, Sir J. Mason, D. Wotton, Sir Richard Sackville, Treasurer of the Exchequer, Sir Walter Mildmay, Chancellor of the Exchequer, Mr. Haddon, Master of Requests, Mr. John Astley, Master of the Jewel House, Mr.

[1] twenty yards
[2] lose
[3] distance between the archer and the target

Bernard Hampton, Mr. Nicasius, and I. Of which number the most part were of her Majesty's most honorable Privy Council, and the rest serving her in very good place. I was glad then, and do rejoice yet to remember, that my chance was so happy to be there that day, in the company of so many wise and good men together as hardly then could have been picked out again out of all England beside.

Mr. Secretary hath this accustomed manner: though his head be never so full of most weighty affairs of the realm, yet at dinner time he doth seem to lay them always aside, and findeth ever fit occasion to talk pleasantly of other matters, but most gladly of some matter of learning; wherein he will courteously hear the mind of the meanest [4] at his table.

Not long after our sitting down, "I have strange news brought me," saith Mr. Secretary, "this morning, that divers scholars of Eton be run away from the school for fear of beating." Whereupon Mr. Secretary took occasion to wish that some more discretion were in many schoolmasters, in using correction, than commonly there is; who many times punish rather the weakness of nature than the fault of the scholar; whereby many scholars, that might else prove well, be driven to hate learning before they know what learning meaneth, and so are made willing to forsake their book and be glad to be put to any other kind of living.

Mr. Peter, as one somewhat severe of nature, said plainly that the rod only [5] was the sword that must keep the school in obedience and the scholar in good order. [6] Mr. Wotton, a man mild of nature, with soft voice and few words, inclined to Mr. Secretary's judgment, and said: "In mine opinion, the schoolhouse should be indeed, as it is called by name, [7] the house of play and pleasure, and not of fear and bondage. And as I do remember, so saith Socrates in one place of Plato. [8] And therefore, if a rod carry the fear of a sword, it is no marvel if those that be fearful of nature choose rather to forsake the play, than to stand always within the fear of a sword in a fond [9] man's handling.

Mr. Mason, after his manner, was very merry with both parties, pleasantly playing both with the shrewd touches [10] of many curst [11] boys, and with the small discretion of many lewd [12] schoolmasters. Mr. Haddon was fully of Mr. Peter's opinion, and said that the best schoolmaster of

[4] humblest
[5] alone
[6] Compare this passage with Johnson, p. 394.
[7] See note on "school," page 129.
[8] i.e., of Plato's works
[9] foolish
[10] mischievous traits
[11] perverse
[12] ignorant

our time was the greatest beater; and named the person. "Though," quoth I, "it was his good fortune to send from his school unto the university one of the best scholars indeed of all our time, yet wise men do think that that came so to pass rather by the great towardness of the scholar than by the great beating of the master; and whether this be true or no, you yourself are best witness." I said somewhat further in the matter how and why young children were sooner allured by love, than driven by beating, to attain good learning; wherein I was the bolder to say my mind because Mr. Secretary courteously provoked me thereunto, or else in such a company, and namely in his presence, my wont is to be more willing to use mine ears than to occupy my tongue. Sir Walter Mildmay, Mr. Astley, and the rest, said very little; only Sir Richard Sackville said nothing at all.

After dinner I went up to read with the Queen's Majesty. We read then together in the Greek tongue, as I well remember, that noble oration of Demosthenes against Aeschines for his false dealing in his embassage to King Philip of Macedonia. Sir Richard Sackville came up soon after, and finding me in her Majesty's privy chamber, he took me by the hand, and carrying me to a window said: "Mr. Ascham, I would not for a good deal of money have been this day absent from dinner, where though I said nothing, yet I gave as good ear, and do consider as well the talk that passed, as anyone did there. Mr. Secretary said very wisely, and most truly, that many young wits be driven to hate learning before they know what learning is. I can be good witness to this myself. For a fond schoolmaster, before I was fully fourteen years old, drave me so, with fear of beating, from all love of learning, as[1] now—when I know what difference it is to have learning, and to have little or none at all—I feel it my greatest grief, and find it my greatest hurt that ever came to me, that it was my so ill chance to light upon so lewd a schoolmaster. But seeing it is but in vain to lament things past, and also wisdom to look to things to come, surely, God willing, if God lend me life, I will make this my mishap some occasion of good hap to little Robert Sackville, my son's son. For whose bringing up I would gladly, if it so please you, use specially your good advice. I hear say you have a son much of his age. We will deal thus together. Point you out a schoolmaster who by your order shall teach my son and yours, and for all the rest I will provide; yea, though they three do cost me a couple of hundred pounds by year. And besides, you shall find me as fast a friend to you and yours as perchance any you have." Which promise the worthy gentleman surely kept with me until his dying day.

[1] that

We had then further talk together of bringing up of children; of the nature of quick and hard wits;[2] of the right choice of a good wit; of fear and love in teaching children. We passed from children and came to young men, namely Gentlemen. We talked of their too much liberty to live as they lust;[3] of their letting loose too soon to overmuch experience of ill, contrary to the good order of many good old commonwealths of the Persians and Greeks; of wit[4] gathered and good fortune gotten by some only by experience, without learning. And lastly, he required of me very earnestly to show what I thought of the common going of English men into Italy.

"But," saith he, "because this place and this time will not suffer so long talk as these good matters require, therefore I pray you, at my request, and at your leisure, put in some order of writing the chief points of this our talk concerning the right order of teaching and honesty of living, for the good bringing up of children and young men. And surely, besides contenting me, you shall both please and profit very many others." I made some excuse by lack of ability and weakness of body. "Well," saith he, "I am not now to learn what you can do. Our dear friend, Mr. Goodrick, whose judgment I could well believe, did once for all satisfy me fully therein. Again, I heard you say not long ago that you may thank Sir John Cheke[5] for all the learning you have. And I know very well myself that you did teach the Queen. And therefore seeing God did so bless you, to make you the scholar of the best master, and also the schoolmaster of the best scholar, that ever were in our time, surely you should please God, benefit your country, and honest[6] your own name, if you would take the pains to impart to others what you learned of such a master, and how ye taught such a scholar. And in uttering the stuff ye received of the one, in declaring the order ye took with the other, ye shall never lack neither matter nor manner, what to write nor how to write, in this kind of argument." I, beginning some further excuse, suddenly was called to come to the Queen.

[2] intellects
[3] like
[4] knowledge
[5] a famous teacher at St. John's, Cambridge, who gave a great impulse to classical learning
[6] honor

The night following I slept little, my head was so full of this our former talk, and I so mindful somewhat to satisfy the honest request of so dear a friend. I thought to prepare some little treatise for a New Year's gift that Christmas. But, as it chanceth to busy builders, so, in building this my poor schoolhouse (the rather because the form of it is somewhat new, and differing from others), the work rose daily higher and wider than I thought it would in the beginning. And though it appear now, and be in very deed, but a small cottage, poor for the stuff and rude for the workmanship, yet in going forward I found the site so good as I was loath to give it over, but the making so costly, outreaching my ability, as many times I wished that some one of those three my dear friends with full purses, Sir Thomas Smith, Mr. Haddon, or Mr. Watson, had had the doing of it. Yet nevertheless I myself, spending gladly that little that I gat at home by good Sir John Cheke, and that that I borrowed abroad of my friend Sturmius, [1] beside somewhat that was left me in reversion by my old masters Plato, Aristotle, and Cicero, I have at last patched it up as I could, and as you see. . . . .

[A Gentle Teacher and Pupil]
From Book I

And one example whether love or fear doth work more in a child for virtue and learning, I will gladly report; which may be heard with some pleasure, and followed with more profit. Before I went into Germany I came to Broadgate in Leicestershire, to take my leave of that noble Lady Jane Grey, to whom I was exceeding much beholden. Her parents, the duke and duchess, with all the household, gentlemen and gentlewomen, were hunting in the park. I found her in her chamber reading "Phaedon Platonis" [2] in Greek, and that with as much delight as some gentlemen would read a merry tale in Bocase. [3] After salutation and duty done, with some other talk, I asked her why she would lose such pastime in the park? Smiling she answered me, "I wis, [4] all their sport in the park is but a shadow to that pleasure that I find in Plato. Alas! good folk, they never felt what true pleasure meant." "And how came you, madam," quoth I, "to this deep knowledge of pleasure, and what did chiefly allure you unto it, seeing, not many women, but very few men, have attained thereunto?" "I will tell you," quoth she; "and tell you a truth which, perchance, ye will marvel at. One of the greatest benefits that ever God gave me is that he sent me so sharp and severe parents and so gentle a schoolmaster. For when I am in presence of either father or mother, whether I speak, keep silence, sit, stand, or go, eat, drink, be merry or sad, be sewing, playing, dancing, or doing anything else, I must do it, as it were, in such weight, measure, and number, even so perfectly as God made the world, or else I am so sharply taunted, so cruelly threatened, yea presently sometimes with pinches, nips, and bobs, [5] and other ways which I will not name for the honor I bear them, so without measure misordered, [6] that I think myself in hell till time come that I must go to Mr. Elmer, who teacheth me so gently, so pleasantly, with such fair allurements to learning, that I think all the time nothing whilst I am with him. And when I am called from him I fall on [7] weeping, because whatsoever I do else but learning, is full of grief, trouble, fear, and whole misliking unto me. And thus my book hath been so much my pleasure, and bringeth daily to me more pleasure and more, that in respect of it all other pleasures, in very deed, be but trifles and troubles unto me."

I remember this talk gladly, both because it is so worthy of memory, and because also it was the last talk that ever I had and the last time that ever I saw that noble and worthy lady.

1570

[1] Johannes von Sturm, 1507-1589, a noted German educator and reformer

[2] Plato's *Phaedo,* on the Immortality of the Soul

[3] Boccaccio

[4] y-wis, certainly

[5] raps

[6] ill disciplined

[7] to (i.e., a-weeping)

THE ELIZABETHAN AGE

THE Elizabethan Age does not actually begin or end with the Virgin Queen. The spirit that characterized the period preceded and survived her by about twenty years. It was during her reign, however, that the greatness of national achievement attained its height. Elizabeth, herself noted for her learning and accomplishments, was surrounded by a group of statesmen, courtiers, poets, and philosophers who made the Court famous for its culture, splendor, and power. The effects of the Renaissance (see Introduction, p. 75) and the Reformation were manifesting themselves in liberal reforms. From the former came a spread of interest in learning and culture; from the latter resulted the independence of the English Church on a safe, conservative basis. The spirit of noble restlessness and curiosity that carried explorers and adventurers to all corners of the globe in search of wealth and conquest was visible also in a sudden developing of scientific investigation. Finally, in the work of the poets, dramatists, and prose writers we find a parallel quickening, an alert interest in the language, an experimentation with the new vehicle of expression around which as yet no tradition had gathered resulting in the two great contributions of the age to literature—song and drama.

POETRY—SONNETS AND LYRICS

After the Wars of the Roses, 1455-1485, England became a power to be reckoned with in European politics. Her increased contact with the kingdoms of the Continent brought her into touch with their intellectual life, which was at least a century in advance of hers; and led her to a fresh interest in the field of poetry, which had remained almost untilled during her social unrest of the fifteenth century. The inspiration was almost wholly foreign; French and Italian models were followed by the courtiers of Henry VIII. As in earlier ages, it was considered a knightly accomplishment to make poetry, and a well-educated man composed poems which circulated in manuscript among his friends. In 1557, for the first time, such poems appeared in print, collected in a book called *Tottel's Miscellany,* which immediately set the fashion for similar collections. Important contributors of this pre-Elizabethan period are Wyatt and Surrey, called by Sidney thirty years later "the two chief lanterns of light to all others that have since employed their pens upon English poesy."

These two introduced the sonnet, which did not reach England until more than three hundred years after its invention in thirteenth-century Italy. The Italian or Petrarchan Sonnet (so named from Petrarch, 1304-1374, a master of the form) is a poem of fourteen lines of five iambic (˘ ′) feet each (pentameter), with a rime scheme more or less fixed, developing a single definite idea or sentiment. The lines are arranged in groups of eight (the octave—*abbaabba*) and six (the sestet—some combination of *cde*). The form was Wyatt's introduction (see p. 137). But the Italian sonnet never ends in a couplet; this innovation was made by Surrey (p. 138), appeared in most sonnets of the time, and was adopted by Shakespeare, who also dropped the division into octave and sestet; the English or Shakespearean sonnet consists of three quatrains and a closing couplet.

Though Wyatt and Surrey had introduced the sonnet, the interest in sonnets in Elizabeth's day sprang from contemporary French influence. A rediscovery of Petrarch through Marot's translations into French two centuries later gave the form its English vogue; and Spenser by his youthful translations (1569) of Marot and Du Bellay (both French poets of the sixteenth century influential in the literary Renaissance in France) became its virtual father.

Sonnet groups, or sequences, usually addressed to some real or imaginary mistress, but sometimes compounded of religious meditation or friendly praise, were a marked feature of Elizabethan verse. Though few Elizabethan sonneteers reached a high level of poetic performance, Sidney was admittedly a prince among them. He was the first Englishman to indicate the lyric capacity of the sonnet. "After Shakespeare's sonnets, Sidney's *Astrophel and Stella* [a sequence of one hundred and ten sonnets which chronicle Sidney's love for Penelope Devereux] offers the most intense and powerful picture of the passion of love in the whole range of our poetry."—F. T. Palgrave. Spenser's mature sonnets may be linked with Sidney's. The *Amoretti* is a series of eighty-eight, recording Spenser's courtship of Elizabeth Boyle, his marriage to whom was the occasion of his *Epithalamion.* The inspirers of most of the other sequences seem more or less imaginary.

The term lyric originally meant a song. By degrees it has assumed a wider meaning, and is now applied to a personal poem of song-like quality revealing the thoughts, sentiments, and emotions of the poet. Yet it must deal with them simply; and it must be neither too narrative nor too descriptive. To the sincerity and passion of Sidney and the artistic seriousness of Spenser is due the prevalence of lyrical poetry in their age. As Schelling says: "In Sidney is struck for the first time unmistakably that individual note, that intense and passionate cry of the poet's very heart, that was thenceforth to be the distinctive mark of the great literature of Elizabeth." The Elizabethan lyric had its origin in the social life of the Court based on the culture of Italy; it is marked by a knowledge and love of the classics, combined with a genuine national spirit; it shows a wide variety of meters and forms; and the contents are equally varied; there are lyrics of love, of death, of religion, of reflection. Among the best are the songs found in the work of the dramatists.

SIR THOMAS WYATT 1503-1542

Wyatt was born in Kent. His early ability for learning brought him his master's degree at Cambridge at the age of seventeen. His short life was filled with the ups and downs characteristic of the age; most of it was spent at court or on royal diplomatic missions which took him to France, Italy, Spain, and the Low Countries. He was also twice imprisoned in the Tower in disgrace, but at the time of his death in Dorset, he was again in high favor. His work was characterized by manliness, independence, and sincerity.

The Lover Having Dreamed of Enjoyment of His Love, Complaineth that the Dream Is not Either Longer or Truer

Unstable dream, according to the place,
Be steadfast once, or else at least be true, [1]
By tasted sweetness make me not to rue
The sudden loss of thy false feigned grace.
By good respect in such a dangerous case
Thou broughtst not her into these tossing seas,
But madest my spirit to live, my care t'en-
crease,
My body in tempest her delight t'embrace.
The body dead, the spirit had his desire;
Painless was the one, the other in delight.
Why then, alas! did it not keep it right,
But thus return to leap into the fire,
And where it was at wish, could not remain?
Such mocks of dreams do turn to deadly pain.

1557

Of His Love That Pricked Her Finger With a Needle

She sat and sewed, that hath done me the
wrong
Whereof I plain, and have done many a day;
And whilst she heard my plaint in piteous
song,
She wished my heart the sampler, [2] that [3] it
lay.
The blind master whom I have served so long,
Grudging to hear that [4] he did hear her say,
Made her own weapon do [5] her finger bleed,
To feel if pricking were so good indeed!

1557

The Lover Complaineth the Unkindness of His Love

My lute, awake, perform the last
Labor that thou and I shall waste,
And end that [6] I have now begun.
And when this song is sung and past,
My lute, be still, for I have done.

As to be heard where ear is none,
As lead to grave [7] in marble stone,
My song may pierce her heart as soon.
Should we then sigh or sing or moan?
No, no, my lute, for I have done.

The rocks do not so cruelly
Repulse the waves continually,
As she my suit and affection;
So that I am past remedy,
Whereby my lute and I have done.

Proud of the spoil that thou hast got
Of simple hearts through Lovës shot,
By whom unkind thou has them won,
Think not he hath his bow forgot,
Although my lute and I have done.

Vengeance shall fall on thy disdain
That makest but game on earnest pain.
Think not alone under the sun
Unquit [8] to cause thy lovers plain, [9]
Although my lute and I have done.

May chance thee lie withered and old
In winter nights that are so cold,
Plaining in vain unto the moon;
Thy wishes then dare not be told.
Care then who list, for I have done.

And then may chance thee to repent
The time that thou hast lost and spent
To cause thy lovers sigh and swoon;
Then shalt thou know beauty but lent,
And wish and want, as I have done.

Now cease, my lute, this is the last
Labor that thou and I shall waste,
And ended is that we begun.
Now is this song both sung and past,
My lute, be still, for I have done.

before 1536 1557

HENRY HOWARD, EARL OF SURREY 1517?-1547

Surrey, son of the earl of Norfolk, showed an early gift for poetry. He was a favorite with Henry VIII, and at fifteen accompanied the king to the French court. In military prowess, scholarship, position at court, poetry, and mastery in chivalric exercises he rivaled Sir Philip Sidney. But his hot temper and pride of race made him many enemies, and brought him into constant trouble; some of his poetry was written while he was a prisoner in the Tower after a quarrel.

[1] This phrase appears to have more rime than reason. Possibly *place = text,* referring to 1 *Cor.,* xv, 58; or—Be true to your place. Cf. Shakespeare's reference to the North Star, *Julius Caesar,* III, 1, 65.
[2] needle-work pattern
[3] as
[4] that which
[5] make
[6] that which
[7] cut, engrave
[8] unrepaid
[9] to complain

Falsely accused of treasonable designs on the throne, he was beheaded at the age of thirty. He excelled in ease, finish, and graceful fancies.

Description of Spring, Wherein Each Thing Renews, Save Only the Lover

The soote [1] season that bud and bloom forth brings
With green hath clad the hill and eke the vale;
The nightingale with feathers new she sings;
The turtle to her make [2] hath told her tale:
Summer is come, for every spray now springs;
The hart hath hung his old head on the pale;
The buck in brake his winter cote he flings;
The fishes flete with new repaired scale;
The adder all her slough away she slings;
The swift swallow pursueth the flies smale;
The busy bee her honey now she mings. [3]
Winter is worn, that was the flowers' bale:
And thus I see among these pleasant things
Each care decays, and yet my sorrow springs.

before 1547 1557

A Praise of His Love, Wherein He Reproveth Them That Compare Their Ladies With His

Give place, ye lovers, here before,
That spent your boasts and brags in vain;
My Lady's beauty passeth more
The best of yours, I dare well sayen,
Than doth the sun the candle light,
Or brightest day the darkest night.

And thereto hath a troth as just
As had Penelope the fair;
For what she saith, ye may it trust
As it by writing sealed were.
And virtues hath she many moe
Than I with pen have skill to show.

I could rehearse, if that I would,
The whole effect [4] of Nature's plaint
When she had lost the perfect mold,
The like to whom she could not paint.
With wringing hands how she did cry,
And what she said, I know it, I.

I know she swore with raging mind,
Her kingdom only set apart,
There was no loss, by law of kind, [5]
That could have gone so near her heart.
And this was chiefly all her pain:
She could not make the like again.

Sith [6] nature thus gave her the praise
To be the chiefest work she wrought,
In faith, methink, some better ways
On your behalf might well be sought,
Than to compare, as ye have done,
To match the candle with the sun.

before 1547 1557

[1] sweet
[2] turtle-dove to her mate
[3] mixes
[4] tenor
[5] nature
[6] since

Departure of Aeneas from Dido [7]

Such great complaints brake forth out of her breast;
Whiles Aeneas full minded to depart,
All things prepared, slept in the poop on high.
To whom in sleep the wonted godhead's form
'Gan aye appear, returning in like shape [8]
As seemed him, and 'gan him thus advise,
Like unto Mercury in voice and hue,
With yellow bush, [9] and comely limbs of youth:
"O goddess' son, in such case canst thou sleep,
Ne yet, bestraught, [10] the dangers dost foresee
That compass thee, nor hear'st the fair winds blow?
Dido in mind rolls vengeance and deceit;
Determ'd to die, swells with unstable ire.
Wilt thou not flee whiles thou hast time of flight?
Straight shalt thou see the seas covered with sails,
The blazing brands the shore all spread with flame,
And if [11] the morrow steal upon thee here.
Come off, have done, set all delay aside;
For full of change these women be alway."
This said, in the dark night he 'gan him hide.
Aeneas, of this sudden vision
Adread, starts up out of his sleep in haste,
Calls up his feres: [12] "Awake, get up, my men!
Aboard your ships, and hoise up sail with speed.
A god me wills, sent from above again,
To haste my flight and wreathen cables cut.
O holy god, whatso thou art, we shall
Follow thee, and all blithe obey thy will.
Be at our hand and friendly us assist;
Address [13] the stars with prosperous influence."
And with that word his glistering sword unsheaths,
With which drawn he the cables cut in twain.
The like desire the rest embraced all.
All things in haste they cast, and forth they whirl;
The shores they leave; with ships the seas are spread:
Cutting the foam by the blue seas they sweep.

1557

[7] from the translation of Vergil's *Aeneid*, Bk. IV
[8] as before
[9] locks
[10] nor yet, distracted
[11] (an if) if
[12] comrades
[13] endue

SIR PHILIP SIDNEY 1554-1586[1]

ASTROPHEL AND STELLA I[2]

Loving in truth, and fain in verse my love to show,
That she, dear she, might take some pleasure of my pain—
Pleasure might cause her read, reading might make her know,
Knowledge might pity win, and pity grace obtain—
I sought fit words to paint the blackest face of woe;
Studying inventions fine, her wits to entertain,
Oft turning others' leaves, to see if thence would flow
Some fresh and fruitful showers upon my sunburn'd brain.
But words came halting forth, wanting Invention's stay;[3]
Invention, Nature's child, fled step-dame Study's blows;
And others' feet still seem'd but strangers in my way.
Thus, great with child to speak, and helpless in my throes,
Biting my truant pen, beating myself for spite;
Fool, said my Muse to me, look in thy heart and write.

1591

ASTROPHEL AND STELLA XXXI

With how sad steps, O Moon, thou climb'st the skies!
How silently, and with how wan a face!
What, may it be that e'en in heavenly place
That busy archer his sharp arrows tries!
Sure, if that long-with-love-acquainted eyes
Can judge of love, thou feel'st a lover's case,
I read it in thy looks; thy languish'd grace,
To me, that feel the like, thy state descries.
Then, e'en of fellowship, O Moon, tell me,
Is constant love deem'd there but want of wit?
Are beauties there as proud as here they be?
Do they above love to be loved, and yet
Those lovers scorn whom that love doth possess?
Do they call virtue, there, ungratefulness?

ASTROPHEL AND STELLA, FIRST SONG

Doubt you to whom my Muse these notes intendeth,
Which now my breast surcharged to music lendeth?
To you, to you, all song of praise is due,
Only in you my song begins and endeth.

Who hath the eyes which marry state with pleasure?
Who keeps the keys of Nature's chiefest treasure?
To you, to you, all song of praise is due,
Only for you the heaven forgat all measure.[4]

Who hath the lips where wit in fairness reigneth?
Who womankind at once both decks and staineth?[5]
To you, to you, all song of praise is due,
Only by you Cupid his crown maintaineth.

Who hath the feet whose step all sweetness planteth?
Who else, for whom Fame worthy trumpets wanteth?
To you, to you, all song of praise is due,
Only to you her scepter Venus granteth.

Who hath the breast whose milk doth patience nourish?
Whose grace is such that when it chides doth cherish?
To you, to you, all song of praise is due,
Only through you the tree of life doth flourish.

Who hath the hand which without stroke subdueth?
Who long-dead beauty with increase reneweth?
To you, to you, all song of praise is due,
Only at you all envy hopeless rueth.[6]

Who hath the hair which, loosest, fastest tieth?
Who makes a man live then glad when he dieth?
To you, to you, all song of praise is due,
Only of you the flatterer never lieth.

Who hath the voice which soul from senses sunders?
Whose force but yours the bolts of beauty thunders?
To you, to you, all song of praise is due,
Only with you not miracles are wonders.[7]

Doubt you to whom my Muse these notes intendeth?
Which now my breast o'ercharged to music lendeth?
To you, to you, all song of praise is due,
Only in you my song begins and endeth.

c. 1581 1591

[1] See p. *224*.
[2] Note that the first sonnet is written in hexameters (six-stressed lines) instead of the usual pentameters (five-stressed).
[3] support

[4] was immeasurably lavish
[5] i.e., by comparison
[6] sorrows
[7] miracles are not wonders

EDMUND SPENSER
1552-1599

Spenser's life, like that of many others dependent on the favor of princes and potentates, was, in spite of his merits, one of hope deferred. His father was a journeyman cloth maker of London, and the boy went to the famous Merchant Tailors' School. At Cambridge he became an excellent scholar in classics and modern languages; and translations from the French, printed anonymously in 1569, but reprinted and acknowledged later, prove him to have been the herald of French influence on Elizabethan sonneteering.

After leaving college he fell in love with a mysterious "Rosalind" whose indifference he mourned in two charming pastoral poems, *The Shepheardes Calender,* 1570, the beginning of his career as a poet, and *Colin Clouts Come Home Again,* 1595. In 1578 he entered the service of the Earl of Leicester, became a close friend of Sir Philip Sidney, and began his *Faerie Queene,* published in 1590-1596. Then he received an appointment in Ireland, and though he rose to a position of great importance and married there, the rest of his life was spent in seeking in vain a position at Court. On several journeys to England he appealed to Elizabeth and also published his poems. His health had been seriously affected by the hardships of an Irish rebellion, during which his house was burned, and his death took place in London, whither he had fled with his family.

Spenser has well been named the Poets' Poet. He excelled all his predecessors in a sense of the capacity of the English language for harmonious combinations of sound—"A silver trumpet Spenser blows," wrote Keats—and it is difficult to overestimate his influence on a long line of successors. His invention of the Spenserian stanza, Chaucer's five-stressed, eight-lined stanza plus an Alexandrine (six-stressed line), has been borrowed by many of them. He represents the tendencies and conventions in literature of the first half of the Elizabethan age; in choosing for his central figures the shepherd and the knight he adopted for his poetry heroes of two widely popular literary forms—the pastoral and the romance. But his merit is more than purely literary; a distinct moral purpose underlies practically all that he wrote. His chief desire was to inspire his contemporaries by ideals of beauty, goodness, and truth.

Spenser's meter was original, yet he was almost always bound by current convention. He was among those who consciously adapted to English verse the conceit of immortality; that is, the claim that poets not only achieve immortality through their verse, but also confer it on those to whom their poetry is addressed.

Good editions are the Cambridge and the Globe. For fuller biography see R. W. Church, (EML). Criticism will be found in G. L. Craik, *Spenser and his Poetry,* 1845; T. Page, *Spenser and Shakespeare,* 1894; W. A. Reed, *Keats and Spenser,* 1897; W. H. Schofield, *Chivalry in English Literature;* J. E. G. de Montmorency, "Red Cross Knight," *Contemp.* 107:659-63; also in Steele, *The Spectator* 540; Johnson, *Rambler* 121; Hazlitt, Rossetti, *Lives,* Dowden, Lee.

AMORETTI XV

Ye tradeful merchants that with weary toil
Do seek most precious things to make your gain,
And both the Indias of their treasures spoil,
What needeth you to seek so far in vain?
For lo, my love doth in herself contain
All this world's riches that may far be found:
If sapphires, lo, her eyes be sapphires plain;
If rubies, lo, her lips be rubies sound;
If pearls, her teeth be pearls, both pure and
    round;
If ivory, her forehead ivory ween;
If gold, her locks are finest gold on ground;
If silver, her fair hands are silver sheen.
But that which fairest is, but few behold—
Her mind adorned with virtues manifold.

AMORETTI XXXVII

What guile is this, that those her golden tresses
She doth attire under a net of gold,
And with sly skill so cunningly them dresses
That which is gold or hair may scarce be told?
Is it that men's frail eyes, which gaze too bold,
She may entangle in that golden snare,
And, being caught, may craftily enfold
Their weaker hearts, which are not well aware?
Take heed, therefore, mine eyes, how ye do stare
Henceforth too rashly on that guileful net,
In which if ever ye entrappèd are,
Out of her bands ye by no means shall get.
Fondness [1] it were for any, being free,
To covet fetters, though they golden be!

AMORETTI LXI

The glorious image of the Maker's beauty,
My sovereign saint, the idol of my thought,
Dare not henceforth, above the bounds of duty,
T' accuse of pride, or rashly blame for ought.
For being, as she is, divinely wrought,
And of the brood of angels heavenly born,
And with the crew of blessed saints upbrought,
Each of which did her with their gifts adorn—
The bud of joy, the blossom of the morn,
The beam of light, whom mortal eyes admire;
What reason is it then but she should scorn
Base things that to her love too bold aspire!
Such heavenly forms ought rather worshipt be
Than dare be loved by men of mean degree.

1595

[1] folly

THE FAERIE QUEENE

The Faerie Queene is an allegory designed to set forth "a gentleman or noble person in virtuous and gentle discipline." The central characters are Gloriana, the queen of an imaginary ("faerie") court, who symbolizes Glory, and her suitor Prince Arthur, who stands for Magnificence (Munificence), "which virtue is the perfection of all the rest." Besides these, the twelve moral virtues were to have been separately represented by twelve knights, each performing deeds and overcoming temptations according to his character. But as the poet's design was never finished, only half these virtues get representation, and the central characters receive rather less prominence than the six several virtues which are set forth in the six completed books. Each of these books, consisting of twelve cantos, is practically a complete story in itself. The first deals with the Knight of the Red Cross, or Holiness, who, clad in the armor of the Christian faith, is sent forth by his Queen as the champion of Una (Truth) to deliver her parents, "who had been by an huge dragon many years shut up in a brazen castle." Beneath the moral allegory may be read also a political one, according to which Gloriana is Queen Elizabeth, Prince Arthur is Lord Leicester, Duessa is Mary Queen of Scots, etc. But after all, the poetry of the poem is worth far more than the elaborate allegory. The language and spelling are deliberately and sometimes falsely archaic. The dedication is that of the 1596 edition.

The Dedication

TO THE MOST HIGH
MIGHTIE, AND MAGNIFICENT EMPRESSE
RENOWMED FOR PIETIE, VERTUE,
AND ALL GRATIOUS GOVERNMENT

ELIZABETH

BY THE GRACE OF GOD
QUEENE OF ENGLAND, FRAUNCE, AND IRELAND,
AND OF VIRGINIA
DEFENDOUR OF THE FAITH, &C.

HER MOST HUMBLE SERVAUNT

EDMUND SPENSER

DOTH IN ALL HUMILITIE
DEDICATE, PRESENT, AND CONSECRATE
THESE HIS LABOURS
TO LIVE WITH THE ETERNITIE
OF HER FAME.

1

Lo I the man, whose Muse whilome [1] did maske,
As time her taught, in lowly Shepheards weeds, [2]
Am now enforst a far unfitter taske,
For trumpets sterne to chaunge mine Oaten reeds,
And sing of Knights and Ladies gentle [3] deeds;
Whose prayses having slept in silence long,
Me, all too meane, the sacred Muse areeds [4]
To blazon broad emongst her learned throng:
Fierce warres and faithfull loves shall moralize my song.

2

Helpe then, O holy Virgin chiefe of nine, [5]
Thy weaker Novice to performe thy will;
Lay forth out of thine everlasting scryne [6]
The antique rolles, which there lye hidden still,
Of Faerie knights and fairest Tanaquill, [7]
Whom that most noble Briton Prince [8] so long
Sought through the world, and suffered so much ill,
That I must rue his undeserved wrong:
O helpe thou my weake wit, and sharpen my dull tong.

3

And thou most dreaded impe [9] of highest Jove,
Faire Venus sonne, that with thy cruell dart
At that good knight so cunningly didst rove,
That glorious fire it kindled in his hart,
Lay now thy deadly Heben [10] bow apart,
And with thy mother milde come to mine ayde;
Come both, and with you bring triumphant Mart, [11]
In loves and gentle jollities arrayd,
After his murdrous spoiles and bloudy rage allayd.

4

And with them eke, O Goddesse heavenly bright,
Mirrour of grace and Majestie divine,
Great Lady of the greatest Isle, whose light

[1] formerly
[2] referring to *The Shepheardes Calender,* a pastoral poem
[3] noble (as distinguished from rustic)
[4] urges
[5] Clio, Muse of History
[6] shrine, chest
[7] the daughter of Oberon: here another name for Gloriana
[8] Prince Arthur
[9] child
[10] ebony
[11] Mars

Like Phoebus lampe [1] throughout the world
doth shine,
Shed thy faire beames into my feeble eyne,
And raise my thoughts, too humble and too
vile,
To thinke of that true glorious type of thine,
The argument of mine afflicted stile: [2]
The which to heare, vouchsafe, O dearest
dred, [3] a-while.

[THE KNIGHT OF THE RED CROSS AND HIS FIGHT WITH THE MONSTER ERROR. THE WILES OF ARCHIMAGO]

From BOOK I, CANTO I

1

A gentle Knight was pricking [4] on the plaine,
Ycladd in mightie armes and silver shielde,
Wherein old dints of deepe wounds did re-
maine,
The cruell markes of many a bloudy fielde;
Yet armes till that time did he never wield:
His angry steede did chide his foming bitt,
As much disdayning to the curbe to yield:
Full jolly [5] knight he seemd, and faire did sitt,
As one for knightly giusts [6] and fierce en-
counters fitt.

2

But on his brest a bloudie Crosse he bore,
The deare remembrance of his dying Lord,
For whose sweete sake that glorious badge he
wore,
And dead as living ever him ador'd:
Upon his shield the like was also scor'd,
For soveraine hope, which in his helpe he had:
Right faithfull true he was in deede and word,
But of his cheere [7] did seeme too solemne sad;
Yet nothing did he dread, but ever was
ydrad. [8]

3

Upon a great adventure he was bond,
That greatest Gloriana to him gave,
That greatest Glorious Queene of Faerie lond,
To winne him worship, [9] and her grace to have,
Which of all earthly things he most did crave;
And ever as he rode, his hart did earne [10]
To prove his puissance in battell brave
Upon his foe, and his new force to learne;
Upon his foe, a Dragon horrible and stearne.

4

A lovely Ladie [11] rode him faire beside,
Upon a lowly Asse more white than snow,
Yet she much whiter, but the same did hide
Under a vele, that wimpled was full low,
And over all a blacke stole she did throw,
As one that inly mournd: so was she sad,
And heavie sat upon her palfrey slow;
Seemed in heart some hidden care she had,
And by her in a line a milke white lambe
she lad. [12]

5

So pure and innocent, as that same lambe,
She was in life and every vertuous lore,
And by descent from Royall lynage came
Of ancient Kings and Queenes, that had of
yore
Their scepters stretcht from East to Westerne
shore,
And all the world in their subjection held;
Till that infernall feend with foule uprore
Forwasted all their land, and them expeld:
Whom to avenge, she had this Knight from
far compeld. [13]

6

Behind her farre away a Dwarfe did lag,
That lasie seemd in being ever last,
Or wearied [14] with bearing of her bag
Of needments at his backe. Thus as they past,
The day with cloudes was suddeine overcast,
And angry Jove an hideous storme of raine
Did poure into his Lemans [15] lap so fast,
That every wight [16] to shrowd [17] it did constrain
And this faire couple eke to shroud them-
selves were fain.

7

Enforst to seeke some covert nigh at hand,
A shadie grove not far away they spide,

[1] the sun
[2] subject of my lowly pen
[3] object of reverence
[4] riding, spurring
[5] handsome
[6] jousts
[7] countenance
[8] dreaded
[9] honor
[10] yearn

[11] Una, personification of Truth
[12] "That lamb we never see again! It was a thought that rose and passed away from the poet's soul; but the image had shown us the character of Una in her simplicity, as if it had been a dove that hung for a moment over her head, and while a voice spoke, disappeared—This is my beloved *daughter*, in whom I am well pleased."—Christopher North.
[13] summoned
[14] Pronounce "wea-ri-ed."
[15] beloved one (the earth)
[16] person
[17] shelter

That promist ayde the tempest to withstand:
Whose loftie trees yclad with sommers pride
Did spred so broad, that heavens light did hide,
Not perceable with power of any starre:
And all within were pathes and alleies wide,
With footing worne, and leading inward farre:
Faire harbour that them seemes; so in they entred arre.

8

And foorth they passe, with pleasure forward led,
Joying to heare the birdes sweete harmony,
Which therein shrouded from the tempest dred,
Seemd in their song to scorne the cruell sky.
Much can [1] they prayse the trees so straight and hy,
The sayling Pine, [2] the Cedar proud and tall,
The vine-prop Elme, the Poplar never dry,
The builder Oake, sole king of forrests all,
The Aspine good for staves, the Cypresse funerall.

9

The Laurell, meed of mightie Conquerours
And Poets sage, the firre that weepeth still,
The Willow worne of forlorne Paramours,
The Eugh [3] obedient to the benders will,
The Birch for shaftes, the Sallow for the mill,
The Mirrhe sweete bleeding in the bitter wound,
The warlike Beech, the Ash for nothing ill,
The fruitful Olive, and the Platane round,
The carver Holme, the Maple seeldom inward sound. [4]

10

Led with delight, they thus beguile the way,
Untill the blustring storme is overblowne;
When weening to returne, whence they did stray,
They cannot finde that path, which first was showne,

[1] did
[2] Cf. *Paradise Lost,* I. 292-294.
[3] yew
[4] "This tree list is, in fact, a great curiosity. It was started by Ovid, *Metam.* x. 90; after whom it appears in Seneca, *Oedipus,* 532; in Lucan, *Phars.* iii. 440; in Statius, *Thebaid,* vi. 98; and in Claudian, *De Raptu Proserpinae,* ii, 107. Statius was followed by Boccaccio, *Tes.* xi. 22-4; *Rom. de la Rose,* 1361; Chaucer (twice); Tasso, *Gier. Lib.* iii, 73; and Spenser. Cf. Vergil, *Aen.* vi. 179."—Skeat, *Chaucer.* A comparison with Chaucer's *Parlement of Foules,* 176-82, is interesting.

The bilder ook, and eek the hardy asshe;
The piler elm, the cofre unto careyne;
The boxtree piper; holm to whippes lasshe;
The sayling firr; the cipres, deth to pleyne;
The sheter ew, the asp for shaftes pleyne;
The olyve of pees, and eek the drunken vyne,
The victor palm, the laurer to deveyne.

But wander too and fro in wayes unknowne,
Furthest from end then, when they neerest weene,
That makes them doubt their wits be not their owne:
So many pathes, so many turnings seene,
That which of them to take, in diverse doubt they been.

11

At last resolving forward still to fare,
Till that some end they finde or in or out,
That path they take, that beaten seemd most bare,
And like to lead the labyrinth about;
Which when by tract [5] they hunted had throughout,
At length it brought them to a hollow cave
Amid the thickest woods. The Champion stout
Eftsoones [6] dismounted from his courser brave,
And to the Dwarfe awhile his needlesse spere he gave.

12

Be well aware, quoth then that Ladie milde,
Least suddaine mischiefe ye too rash provoke:
The danger hid, the place unknowne and wilde,
Breedes dreadfull doubts: Oft fire is without smoke,
And peril without show: therefore your stroke,
Sir Knight, with-hold, till further triall made.
Ah Ladie, (said he) shame were to revoke
The forward footing for an hidden shade:
Vertue gives her selfe light, through darkenesse for to wade. [7]

13

Yea but (quoth she) the perill of this place
I better wot then you, though now too late
To wish you backe returne with foule disgrace,
Yet wisdome warnes, whilest foot is in the gate, [8]
To stay the steppe, ere forced to retrate.
This is the wandring wood, [9] this Errours den,
A monster vile, whom God and man does hate:
Therefore I read [10] beware. Fly, fly (quoth then
The fearefull Dwarfe) this is no place for living men.

14

But full of fire and greedy hardiment,
The youthfull knight could not for ought be staide,
But forth unto the darksome hole he went,
And looked in: his glistring armor made

[5] trace
[6] forthwith
[7] Cf. *Comus,* 373.
[8] way
[9] wood of wandering
[10] counsel

A litle glooming light, much like a shade,
By which he saw the ugly monster plaine,
Halfe like a serpent horribly displaide,
But th'other halfe did womans shape retaine,
Most lothsom, filthie, foule, and full of vile disdaine.[1]

15

And as she lay upon the durtie ground,
Her huge long taile her den all overspred,
Yet was in knots and many boughtes[2] upwound,
Pointed with mortall sting. Of her there bred
A thousand yong ones,[3] which she dayly fed,
Sucking upon her poisnous dugs, eachone
Of sundry shapes, yet all ill favored:
Soone as that uncouth light upon them shone,
Into her mouth they crept, and suddain all were gone.

16

Their dam upstart, out of her den effraide,
And rushed forth, hurling her hideous taile
About her cursed head, whose folds displaid
Were stretcht now forth at length without entraile.[2]
She lookt about, and seeing one in mayle
Armed to point,[4] sought backe to turne againe;
For light she hated as the deadly bale,
Ay wont in desert darknesse to remaine,
Where plain none might her see, nor she see any plaine.

17

Which when the valiant Elfe perceiv'd, he lept
As Lyon fierce upon the flying pray,
And with his trenchand blade her boldly kept
From turning backe, and forced her to stay:
Therewith enrag'd she loudly gan to bray,
And turning fierce, her speckled taile advaunst,
Threatning her angry sting, him to dismay:
Who nought aghast his mightie hand enhaunst:[5]
The stroke down from her head unto her shoulder glaunst.

18

Much daunted with that dint,[6] her sence was dazd,
Yet kindling rage, her selfe she gathered round,
And all attonce her beastly body raizd
With doubled forces high above the ground:
Tho[7] wrapping up her wrethed stern arownd,
Lept fierce upon his shield, and her huge traine
All suddenly about his body wound,
That hand or foot to stirre he strove in vaine:
God helpe the man so wrapt in Errours endlesse traine.

19

His Lady sad to see his sore constraint,
Cride out, Now now Sir knight, shew what ye bee,
Add faith unto your force, and be not faint:
Strangle her, else she sure will strangle thee.
That when he heard, in great perplexitie,
His gall did grate for grief[8] and high disdaine,
And knitting all his force got one hand free,
Wherewith he grypt her gorge with so great paine,[9]
That soone to loose her wicked bands did her constraine.[10]

. . . . . .

27

His Ladie seeing all that chaunst, from farre
Approcht in hast to greet his victorie,
And said, Faire knight, borne under happy starre,
Who see your vanquisht foes before you lye:
Well worthie be you of that Armorie,[11]
Wherein ye have great glory wonne this day,
And proov'd your strength on a strong enimie,
Your first adventure: many such I pray,
And henceforth ever wish that like succeed it may.

28

Then mounted he upon his Steede againe,
And with the Lady backward sought to wend;
That path he kept which beaten was most plaine,
Ne[12] ever would to any by-way bend,
But still did follow one unto the end,
The which at last out of the wood them brought.
So forward on his way (with God to frend)
He passed forth, and new adventure sought;
Long way he travelled, before he heard of ought.

29

At length they chaunst to meet upon the way
An aged Sire,[13] in long blacke weedes yclad,

[1] disgusting vileness
[2] coils
[3] Lies, the children of Error
[4] completely
[5] raised
[6] blow
[7] then

[8] his anger was stirred through pain
[9] effort
[10] Stanzas 20-26 describe, in language made purposely coarse for the sake of the allegory, the monster's foul tactics in self-defense, until from her body the knight "raft her hatefull heade without remorse," and the young ones gorged themselves to death upon her blood.
[11] armor
[12] nor
[13] the enchanter Archimago, or Hypocrisy, who stands for false religion

His feete all bare, his beard all hoarie gray,
And by his belt his booke he hanging had;
Sober he seemde, and very sagely sad,
And to the ground his eyes were lowly bent,
Simple in shew, and voyde of malice bad,
And all the way he prayed, as he went,
And often knockt his brest, as one that did repent.

30

He faire the knight saluted, louting [1] low,
Who faire him quited, [2] as that courteous was:
And after asked him, if he did know
Of straunge adventures, which abroad did pas.
Ah my deare Sonne (quoth he) how should, alas,
Silly [3] old man, that lives in hidden cell,
Bidding his beades [4] all day for his trespas,
Tydings of warre and worldly trouble tell?
With holy father sits [5] not with such things to mell. [6]

31

But if of daunger which hereby doth dwell,
And homebred evil ye desire to heare,
Of a straunge man I can you tidings tell,
That wasteth all this countrey farre and neare.
Of such (said he) I chiefly do inquere,
And shall you well reward to shew the place,
In which that wicked wight his dayes doth weare:
For to all knighthood it is foule disgrace,
That such a cursed creature lives so long a space.

32

Far hence (quoth he) in wastfull wildernesse
His dwelling is, by which no living wight
May ever passe, but thorough [7] great distresse.
Now (sayd the Lady) draweth toward night,
And well I wote, that of your later fight
Ye all forwearied be: for what so strong,
But wanting rest will also want of might?
The Sunne that measures heaven all day long,
At night doth baite [8] his steedes the Ocean waves emong.

33

Then with the Sunne take Sir, your timely rest,
And with new day new worke at once begin:
Untroubled night they say gives counsell best.
Right well Sir knight ye have advised bin,
(Quoth then that aged man;) the way to win
Is wisely to advise: [9] now day is spent;
Therefore with me ye may take up your In
For this same night. The knight was well content:
So with that godly father to his home they went.

34

A little lowly Hermitage it was,
Downe in a dale, hard by a forests side,
Far from resort of people, that did pas
In travell to and froe: a little wyde [10]
There was an holy Chappell edifyde, [11]
Wherein the Hermite dewly wont to say
His holy things each morne and eventyde:
Thereby a Christall streame did gently play,
Which from a sacred fountaine welled forth alway.

35

Arrived there, the little house they fill,
Ne looke for entertainement, where none was:
Rest is their feast, and all things at their will:
The noblest mind the best contentment has.
With faire discourse the evening so they pas:
For that old man of pleasing wordes had store,
And well could file his tongue as smooth as glas,
He told of Saintes and Popes, and evermore
He strowd an *Ave-Mary* after and before.

36

The drouping Night thus creepeth on them fast,
And the sad humour [12] loading their eye liddes,
As messenger of Morpheus on them cast
Sweet slombring deaw, the which to sleepe them biddes.
Unto their lodgings then his guestes he riddes: [13]
Where when all drownd in deadly sleepe he findes,
He to this study goes, and there amiddes
His Magick bookes and artes of sundry kindes,
He seekes out mighty charmes, to trouble sleepy mindes.

37

Then choosing out few words most horrible,
(Let none them read) thereof did verses frame,
With which and other spelles like terrible,
He bad awake blacke Plutoes griesly Dame, [14]
And cursed heaven and spake reprochfull shame
Of highest God, the Lord of life and light;
A bold bad man, that dar'd to call by name
Great Gorgon, [15] Prince of darknesse and dead night,
At which Cocytus quakes, and Styx is put to flight.

[1] bowing
[2] requited
[3] simple
[4] praying his prayers
[5] befits
[6] meddle
[7] except through
[8] feed
[9] consider
[10] distant
[11] built
[12] dew of sleep
[13] dismisses
[14] Proserpine, or Hecate
[15] Cf. *Par. Lost* II, 965.

38

And forth he cald out of deepe darknesse dred
Legions of Sprights,[1] the which like little flyes
Fluttring about his ever damned hed,
Awaite whereto their service he applyes,
To aide his friends, or fray[2] his enimies:
Of those he chose out two, the falsest twoo,
And fittest for to forge true-seeming lyes;
The one of them he gave a message too,
The other by him selfe staide other worke to doo.

39

He making speedy way through spersed[3] ayre,
And through the world of waters wide and deepe,
To Morpheus house doth hastily repaire.
Amid the bowels of the earth full steepe,
And low, where dawning day doth never peepe,
His dwelling is; there Tethys[4] his wet bed
Doth ever wash, and Cynthia[5] still doth steepe
In silver deaw his ever-drouping hed,
Whiles sad Night over him her mantle black doth spred.

40

Whose double gates[6] he findeth locked fast,
The one faire fram'd of burnisht Yvory,
The other all with silver overcast;
And wakeful dogges before them farre do lye,
Watching to banish Care their enimy,
Who oft is wont to trouble gentle Sleepe.
By them the Sprite doth passe in quietly,
And unto Morpheus comes, whom drowned deepe
In drowsie fit he findes: of nothing he takes keepe.[7]

41

And more, to lulle him in his slumber soft,
A trickling streame from high rock tumbling downe,
And ever-drizzling raine upon the loft,
Mixt with a murmuring winde, much like the sowne
Of swarming Bees, did cast him in a swowne:
No other noyse, nor peoples troublous cryes,
As still are wont t'annoy the walled towne,
Might there be heard: but carelesse Quiet lyes,
Wrapt in eternall silence farre from enemyes.[8]

[1] sprites, spirits
[2] affright
[3] widespread
[4] the ocean
[5] the moon
[6] of false and true dreams
[7] care
[8] A stanza not easily matched in literature for adaptation of sound to sense; it has been much admired and imitated. See Thomson's *Castle of Indolence,* I. 3-6; also Tennyson's "The Lotus-Eaters."

42

The messenger approching to him spake,
But his wast wordes returnd to him in vaine:
So sound he slept, that nought mought him awake.
Then rudely he him thrust, and pusht with paine
Whereat he gan to stretch: but he againe
Shooke him so hard, that forced him to speake.
As one then in a dreame, whose dryer[9] braine
Is tost with troubled sights and fancies weake,
He mumbled soft, but would not all his silence breake.

43

The Sprite then gan more boldly him to wake,
And threatned unto him the dreaded name
Of Hecate: whereat he gan to quake,
And lifting up his lumpish head, with blame
Halfe angry asked him, for what he came.
Hither (quoth he) me Archimago sent,
He that the stubborne Sprites can wisely tame,
He bids thee to him send for his intent
A fit false dreame, that can delude the sleepers sent.[10]

44

The God obayde, and, calling forth straight way
A diverse dreame out of his prison darke,
Delivered it to him, and downe did lay
His heavie head, devoide of carefull carke,[11]
Whose sences all were straight benumbed and starke.
He backe returning by the Yvorie dore,
Remounted up as light as chearefull Larke,
And on his litle winges the dreame he bore
In hast unto his Lord, where he him left afore.

45

Who all this while with charmes and hidden artes,
Had made a Lady of that other Spright,
And fram'd of liquid ayre her tender partes
So lively,[12] and so like in all mens sight,
That weaker sence it could have ravisht quight:
The maker selfe, for all his wondrous witt,
Was nigh beguiled with so goodly sight:
Her all in white he clad, and over it
Cast a black stole, most like to seeme for Una fit.

46

Now when that ydle dreame was to him brought,
Unto that Elfin knight he bad him hy,
Where he slept soundly void of evill thought,

[9] feverish
[10] sense
[11] anxious care (characteristic Spenserian tautology)
[12] lifelike

And with false shewes abuse his fantasy,
In sort as he him schooled privily:
And that new creature, borne without her dew,[1]
Full of the makers guile, with usage sly
He taught to imitate that Lady trew,
Whose semblance she did carrie under feigned hew.

. . . . . .

[The knight, deceived by the dream into thinking his lady Una false, flees with the Dwarf, until meeting on the way a Sarazin (Saracen, Pagan), named Sansfoy (Faithless), he slays him, and proceeds in the company of Sansfoy's lady, Duessa (Falsehood), who passes herself off as Fidessa (Faith).]

[Una and the Lion]

From Book I, Canto III

1

Nought is there under heav'ns wide hollownesse,
That moves more deare compassion of mind,
Then beautie brought t' unworthy wretchednesse
Through envies snares, or fortunes freakes unkind.
I, whether lately through her brightnesse blind,
Or through alleageance and fast fealtie,
Which I do owe unto all woman kind,
Feele my heart perst with so great agonie,
When such I see, that all for pittie I could die.

2

And now it is empassioned so deepe,
For fairest Unaes sake, of whom I sing,
That my fraile eyes these lines with teares do steepe,
To thinke how she through guilefull handeling,
Though true as touch,[2] though daughter of a king,
Though faire as ever living wight was faire,
Though nor in word nor deede ill meriting,
Is from her knight divorced in despaire,
And her due loves deriv'd[3] to that vile witches share.

3

Yet she most faithfull Ladie all this while
Forsaken, wofull, solitarie mayd
Far from all peoples prease,[4] as in exile,
In wildernesse and wastfull deserts strayd,
To seeke her knight; who subtilly betrayd
Through that late vision, which th' Enchaunter wrought,
Had her abandond. She of nought affrayd,
Through woods and wastnesse wide him daily sought;
Yet wished tydings none of him unto her brought.

4

One day nigh wearie of the yrkesome way,
From her unhastie beast she did alight,
And on the grasse her daintie limbes did lay
In secret shadow, farre from all mens sight:
From her faire head her fillet she undight,
And laid her stole aside. Her angels face
As the great eye of heaven shyned bright,
And made a sunshine in the shadie place;
Did never mortall eye behold such heavenly grace.

5

It fortuned out of the thickest wood
A ramping Lyon rushed suddainly,
Hunting full greedy after salvage blood;
Soone as the royall virgin he did spy,
With gaping mouth at her ran greedily,
To have attonce devourd her tender corse:
But to the pray when as he drew more ny,
His bloody rage aswaged with remorse,
And with the sight amazd, forgat his furious forse.

6

In stead thereof he kist her wearie feet,
And lickt her lilly hands with fawning tong,
As he her wronged innocence did weet.[5]
O how can beautie maister the most strong,
And simple truth subdue avenging wrong?
Whose yeelded pride and proud submission,
Still dreading death, when she had marked long,
Her hart gan melt in great compassion,
And drizling teares did shed for pure affection.

7

The Lyon Lord of every beast in field,
Quoth she, his princely puissance doth abate,
And mightie proud to humble weake does yield,
Forgetfull of the hungry rage, which late
Him prickt, in pittie of my sad estate:
But he my Lyon, and my noble Lord,
How does he find in cruell hart to hate,
Her that him lov'd, and ever most adord,
As the God of my life? why hath he me abhord?

8

Redounding[6] teares did choke th' end of her plaint,
Which softly ecchoed from the neighbour wood;

[1] unnaturally
[2] as if tested by the touchstone
[3] the love which is her due diverted
[4] press, crowd
[5] wit, know
[6] overflowing

And sad to see her sorrowfull constraint
The kingly beast upon her gazing stood;
With pittie calmd, downe fell his angry mood.
At last in close hart shutting up her paine,
Arose the virgin borne of heavenly brood,
And to her snowy Palfrey got againe,
To seeke her strayed Champion, if she might attaine.

9

The Lyon would not leave her desolate,
But with her went along, as a strong gard
Of her chast person, and a faithfull mate
Of her sad troubles and misfortunes hard:
Still when she slept, he kept both watch and ward,
And when she wakt, he waited diligent,
With humble service to her will prepard:
From her faire eyes he tooke commaundement,
And ever by her lookes conceived her intent.

[Una is overtaken by Archimago, disguised as the Redcross Knight, and accompanies him therefore trustingly. But they are met by Sansloy (Lawless, a brother of Sansfoy) who overcomes both Archimago and the Lion, and takes Una as his prey.]

[The Knight of the Red Cross at the House of Pride]

From Book I, Canto IV

1

Young knight whatever that dost armes professe,
And through long labours huntest after fame,
Beware of fraud, beware of ficklenesse,
In choice, and change of thy deare loved Dame,
Least thou of her beleeve too lightly blame,
And rash misweening doe thy hart remove:
For unto knight there is no greater shame,
Then lightnesse and inconstancie in love;
That doth this Redcrosse knights ensample plainly prove.

2

Who after that he had faire Una lorne,
Through light misdeeming of her loialtie,
And false Duessa in her sted had borne,
Called Fidess', and so supposed to bee;
Long with her traveild, till at last they see
A goodly building, bravely garnished,
The house of mightie Prince it seemd to bee:
And towards it a broad high way that led,
All bare through peoples feet, which thither traveiled.

3

Great troupes of people traveild thitherward
Both day and night, of each degree and place,
But few returned, having scaped hard,
With balefull beggerie, or foule disgrace;
Which ever after in most wretched case,
Like loathsome lazars,[1] by the hedges lay.
Thither Duessa bad him bend his pace:
For she is wearie of the toilesome way,
And also nigh consumed is the lingring day.

4

A stately Pallace built of squared bricke,
Which cunningly was without morter laid,
Whose wals were high, but nothing strong, nor thick,
And golden foile all over them displaid,
That purest skye with brightnesse they dismaid:
High lifted up were many loftie towres,
And goodly galleries farre over laid,
Full of faire windowes and delightful bowres;
And on the top a Diall told the timely howres.

5

It was a goodly heape for to behould,
And spake the praises of the workmans wit;
But full great pittie, that so faire a mould
Did on so weake foundation ever sit:
For on a sandie hill, that still did flit
And fall away, it mounted was full hie,
That every breath of heaven shaked it:
And all the hinder parts, that few could spie,
Were ruinous and old, but painted cunningly.

6

Arrived there, they passed in forth right;
For still to all the gates stood open wide:
Yet charge of them was to a Porter hight[2]
Cald Malvenù,[3] who entrance none denide:
Thence to the hall, which was on every side
With rich array and costly arras dight:
Infinite sorts[4] of people did abide
There waiting long, to win the wished sight
Of her that was the Lady of that Pallace bright.

7

By them they passe, all gazing on them round,
And to the Presence mount; whose glorious vew[5]
Their frayle amazed senses did confound:
In living Princes court none ever knew
Such endlesse richesse, and so sumptuous shew;
Ne Persia selfe, the nourse of pompous pride
Like ever saw. And there a nobel crew

[1] lepers
[2] assigned
[3] Ill-come, opposite of Welcome
[4] throngs
[5] vision of whose glory

Of Lordes and Ladies stood on every side,
Which with their presence faire the place much beautifide.

8

High above all a cloth of State was spred,
And a rich throne, as bright as sunny day,
On which there sate most brave embellished
With royall robes and gorgeous array,
A mayden Queene, that shone as Titans ray,
In glistring gold, and peerelesse pretious stone:
Yet her bright blazing beautie did assay
To dim the brightnesse of her glorious throne,
As envying her selfe, that too exceeding shone.

9

Exceeding shone, like Phoebus fairest childe,[1]
That did presume his fathers firie wayne,
And flaming mouthes of steedes unwonted wilde
Through highest heaven with weaker hand to rayne;
Proud of such glory and advancement vaine,
While flashing beames do daze his feeble eyen,
He leaves the welkin way most beaten plaine,
And rapt with whirling wheeles, inflames the skyen,
With fire not made to burne, but fairely for to shyne.

10

So proud she shyned in her Princely state,
Looking to heaven; for earth she did disdayne:
And sitting high; for lowly she did hate:
Lo underneath her scornefull feete was layne
A dreadfull Dragon with an hideous trayne,
And in her hand she held a mirrhour bright,[2]
Wherein her face she often vewed fayne,
And in her selfe-lov'd semblance tooke delight;
For she was wondrous faire, as any living wight.

11

Of griesly Pluto she the daughter was,
And sad Proserpina the Queene of hell;
Yet did she thinke her pearlesse worth to pas
That parentage, with pride so did she swell;
And thundring Jove, that high in heaven doth dwell,
And wield the world, she claymed for her syre,
Or if that any else did Jove excell:
For to the highest she did still aspyre,
Or if ought higher were then that, did it desyre.

12

And proud Lucifera men did her call,
That made her selfe a Queene, and crowned to be,

[1] Phaethon
[2] Court ladies used to carry mirrors.

Yet rightfull kingdome she had none at all,
Ne heritage of native soveraintie,
But did usurpe with wrong and tyrannie
Upon the scepter, which she now did hold:
Ne ruld her Realmes with lawes, but pollicie,
And strong advizement of six wizards old,[3]
That with their counsels bad her kingdome did uphold.

13

Soone as the Elfin knight in presence came,
And false Duessa seeming Lady faire,
A gentle Husher, Vanitie by name
Made rowme, and passage for them did prepaire:
So goodly brought them to the lowest staire
Of her high throne, where they on humble knee
Making obeyssance, did the cause declare,
Why they were come, her royall state to see,
To prove the wide report of her great Majestee.

14

With loftie eyes, halfe loth to looke so low,
She thanked them in her disdainefull wise;
Ne other grace vouchsafed them to show
Of Princesse worthy, scarse them bad arise.
Her Lordes and Ladies all this while devise
Themselves to setten forth to straungers sight:
Some frounce their curled haire in courtly guise,
Some prancke their ruffes, and others trimly dight
Their gay attire: each others greater pride does spight.

15

Goodly they all that knight do entertaine,
Right glad with him to have increast their crew:
But to Duess' each one himselfe did paine
All kindnesse and faire courtesie to shew;
For in that court whylome her well they knew:
Yet the stout Faerie mongst the middest crowd
Thought all their glorie vaine in knightly vew,
And that great Princesse too exceeding prowd,
That to strange knight no better countenance allowd.

. . . .

[Sansjoy (Joyless, third of the pagan brotherhood) appears, seeking vengeance for the death of Sansfoy, and, secretly encouraged by Duessa, challenges the Knight to combat.]

[3] Pride and her six counselors, Idleness, Gluttony, Lechery, Avarice, Envy, and Wrath, constitute the "seven deadly sins."

[The Combat Between the Knight of the Red Cross and Sansjoy]

From Book I, Canto V

1

The noble hart, that harbours vertuous thought,
And is with child of glorious great intent,
Can never rest, untill it forth have brought
Th' eternall brood of glorie excellent.
Such restlesse passion did all night torment
The flaming corage[1] of that Faery knight,
Devizing, how that doughtie turnament
With greatest honour he atchieven might;
Still did he wake, and still did watch for dawning light.

2

At last the golden Orientall gate,
Of greatest heaven gan to open faire,
And Phoebus fresh, as bridegrome to his mate,
Came dauncing forth, shaking his deawie haire:
And hurls his glistring beams through gloomy aire.
Which when the wakeful Elfe perceiv'd, streightway
He started up, and did him selfe prepaire,
In sunbright armes, and battailous array:
For with that Pagan proud he combat will that day.

3

And forth he comes into the commune hall,
Where earely waite him many a gazing eye,
To weet what end to straunger knights may fall.
There many Minstrales maken melody,
To drive away the dull melancholy,
And many Bardes, that to the trembling chord
Can tune their timely voyces cunningly,
And many Chroniclers that can record
Old loves, and warres for Ladies doen by many a Lord.

4

Soon after comes the cruell Sarazin,
In woven maile all armed warily,
And sternly lookes at him, who not a pin
Does care for looke of living creatures eye.
They bring them wines of Greece and Araby,
And daintie spices fecht from furthest Ynd,
To kindle heat of corage privily:
And in the wine a solemne oth they bynd
T' observe the sacred lawes of armes, that are assynd.

5

At last forth comes that far renowned Queene,
With royall pomp and Princely majestie;
She is ybrought unto a paled greene,[2]
And placed under stately canapee,
The warlike feates of both those knights to see.
On th' other side in all mens open vew
Duessa placed is, and on a tree
Sans-foy his[3] shield is hangd with bloody hew:
Both those the lawrell girlonds[4] to the victor dew.

6

A shrilling trompet sownded from on hye,
And unto battaill bad them selves addresse:
Their shining shieldes about their wrestes they tye,
And burning blades about their heads do blesse,[5]
The instruments of wrath and heavinesse:
With greedy force each other doth assayle,
And strike so fiercely, that they do impresse
Deepe dinted furrowes in the battred mayle;
The yron walles to ward their blowes are weak and fraile.

7

The Sarazin was stout, and wondrous strong,
And heaped blowes like yron hammers great;
For after bloud and vengeance he did long.
The knight was fiers, and full of youthly heat,
And doubled strokes, like dreaded thunders threat:
For all for prayse and honour he did fight.
Both stricken strike, and beaten both do beat,
That from their shields forth flyeth firie light,
And helmets hewen deepe show marks of eithers might.

8

So th' one for wrong, the other strives for right;
As when a Gryfon seized of[6] his pray,
A Dragon fiers encountreth in his flight,
Through widest ayre making his ydle way,
That would his rightfull ravine rend away;
With hideous horror both together smight,
And souce[7] so sore that they the heavens affray:
The wise Soothsayer seeing so sad sight,
Th' amazed vulgar tels[8] of warres and mortall fight.

9

So th' one for wrong, the other strives for right,
And each to deadly shame would drive his foe:

[1] heart

[2] inclosed field [3] Sansfoy's
[4] Both Duessa and shield are the prizes of victory.
[5] brandish [7] swoop (term from falconry)
[6] possessed of [8] prophesies to the amazed people

The cruell steele so greedily doth bight
In tender flesh that streames of bloud down
flow,
With which the armes, that earst so bright
did show,
Into a pure vermillion now are dyde:
Great ruth in all the gazers harts did grow,
Seeing the gored woundes to gape so wyde,
That victory they dare not wish to either
side.

10

At last the Paynim chaunst to cast his eye,
His suddein eye, flaming with wrathful fyre,
Upon his brothers shield, which hong thereby:
Therewith redoubled was his raging yre,
And said, Ah wretched sonne [1] of wofull syre,
Doest thou sit wayling by blacke Stygian lake,
Whilest here thy shield is hangd for victors
hyre,
And sluggish german [2] doest thy forces slake
To after-send his foe, that him may over-
take?

11

Goe captive Elfe, him quickly overtake,
And soone redeeme from his long wandring
woe;
Goe guiltie ghost, to him my message make,
That I his shield have quit [3] from dying foe.
Therewith upon his crest he stroke him so,
That twise he reeled, readie twise to fall;
End of the doubtful battell deemed tho [4]
The lookers on, and lowd to him gan call
The false Duessa, Thine the shield, and I,
and all.

12

Soone as the Faerie heard his Ladie speake,
Out of his swowning dreame he gan awake,
And quickning faith, that earst was woxen
weake,
The creeping deadly cold away did shake:
Tho mov'd with wrath, and shame, and Ladies
sake,
Of all attonce he cast [5] avengd to bee,
And with so' exceeding furie at him strake,
That forced him to stoupe upon his knee;
Had he not stouped so, he should have
cloven bee.

13

And to him said, Goe now proud Miscreant,
Thy selfe thy message doe to german deare;
Alone he wandring thee too long doth want:
Goe say, his foe thy shield with his doth beare.
Therewith his heavie hand he high gan reare,

[1] addressed to his brother
[2] addressed to himself (*german* means *brother*)
[3] redeemed
[4] then
[5] resolved

Him to have slaine; when loe a darkesome
clowd
Upon him fell: he no where doth appeare,
But vanisht is. The Elfe him calls alowd,
But answer none receives: the darkness him
does shrowd.

14

In haste Duessa from her place arose,
And to him running said, O prowest knight,
That ever Ladie to her love did chose,
Let now abate the terror of your might,
And quench the flame of furious despight.
And bloudie vengeance; lo th' infernall
powres,
Covering your foe with cloud of deadly night,
Have borne him hence to Plutoes balefull
bowres.
The conquest yours, I yours, the shield, the
glory yours.

15

Not all so satisfide, with greedie eye
He sought all round about, his thristie [6] blade
To bath in bloud of faithlesse enemy;
Who all that while lay hid in secret shade:
He standes amazed, how he thence should fade.
At last the trumpets Triumph sound on hie,
And running Heralds humble homage made,
Greeting him goodly with new victorie,
And to him brought the shield, the cause of
enmitie.

16

Wherewith he goeth to that soveraine Queene,
And falling her before on lowly knee,
To her makes present of his service seene:
Which she accepts, with thankes, and goodly
gree, [7]
Greatly advauncing [8] his gay chevalree.
So marcheth home, and by her takes the knight,
Whom all the people follow with great glee,
Shouting, and clapping all their hands on
hight,
That all the aire it fils, and flyes to heaven
bright.

17

Home is he brought, and laid in sumptuous
bed:
Where many skilfull leaches him abide,
To salve his hurts, that yet still freshly bled.
In wine and oyle they wash his woundes wide,
And softly can [9] embalme on every side.
And all the while, most heavenly melody
About the bed sweet musicke did divide, [10]
Him to beguile of griefe and agony:
And all the while Duessa wept full bitterly.

[6] thirsty [7] good will [8] lauding [9] did
[10] descant, perform in musical "divisions"

. . . .

[The Knight and the Dwarf escape from the house of Pride, but the Knight is captured by the giant Orgoglio (another impersonator of Pride) and thrown into a dungeon. Meanwhile Una, having escaped from Sansloy, meets the Dwarf, who tells her what has befallen. Just then appears Prince Arthur, seeking the court of the Faerie Queene. He hears their story, fights with Orgoglio, and frees his prisoner. Reunited, the Knight and Una proceed on their way. After further trial in the Cave of Despair, and wholesome discipline at the House of Holiness, they reach the goal of their journey—the wasted kingdom, and the brazen tower where Una's parents are imprisoned by the Dragon. The Knight engages in a desperate conflict with the Dragon, and only on the third day succeeds in conquering him.]

[The Dragon Slain. The Betrothal of Una]

From Book I, Canto XII

1

Behold I see the haven nigh at hand,
To which I meane my wearie course to bend;
Vere the maine shete, and beare up with [1] the land,
The which afore is fairely to be kend,
And seemeth safe from storms that may offend;
There this faire virgin wearie of her way
Must landed be, now at her journeyes end:
There eke my feeble barke a while may stay
Till merry wind and weather call her thence away.

2

Scarsely had Phoebus in the glooming East
Yet harnessed his firie-footed teeme,
Ne reard above the earth his flaming creast;
When the last deadly smoke aloft did steeme
That signe of last outbreathed life did seeme
Unto the watchman on the castle wall,
Who thereby dead that balefull Beast did deeme,
And to his Lord and Ladie lowd gan call,
To tell how he had seene the Dragons fatall fall.

3

Uprose with hastie joy, and feeble speed
That aged Sire, the Lord of all that land,
And looked forth, to weet if true indeede
Those tydings were, as he did understand,
Which whenas true by tryall he out found,
He bad to open wyde his brazen gate,
Which long time had been shut, and out of hond
Proclaymed joy and peace through all his state;
For dead now was their foe which them forrayed late.

4

Then gan triumphant Trompets sound on hie,
That sent to heaven the ecchoed report
Of their new joy, and happie victorie
Gainst him, that had them long opprest with tort, [2]
And fast imprisoned in sieged fort.
Then all the people, as in solemne feast,
To him assembled with one full consort,
Rejoycing at the fall of that great beast,
From whose eternall bondage now they were releast.

5

Forth came that auncient Lord and aged Queene,
Arayd in antique robes downe to the ground,
And sad habiliments right well beseene; [3]
A noble crew about them waited round
Of sage and sober Peres, [4] all gravely gownd;
Whom farre before did march a goodly band
Of tall young men, all hable armes to sownd, [5]
But now they laurell braunches bore in hand;
Glad signe of victorie and peace in all their land.

6

Unto that doughtie Conqueror they came,
And him before themselves prostrating low,
Their Lord and Patrone loud did him proclame,
And at his feet their laurell boughes did throw.
Soone after them all dauncing on a row
The comely virgins came, with girlands dight,
As fresh as flowres in medow greene do grow,
When morning deaw upon their leaves doth light:
And in their hands sweet Timbrels all upheld on hight.

. . . .

17

Then sayd the royall Pere in sober wise;
Deare Sonne, great beene the evils which ye bore
From first to last in your late enterprise,
That I note [6] whether prayse, or pitty more:
For never living man, I weene, so sore
In sea of deadly daungers was distrest;
But since now safe ye seised have the shore,
And well arrived are, (high God be blest)
Let us devize of ease and everlasting rest.

[1] make for

[2] wrong
[3] arrayed
[4] peers, princes
[5] clash, wield
[6] ne wot, know not

18

Ah, dearest Lord, said then that doughty knight,
Of ease or rest I may not yet devize,
For by the faith, which I to armes have plight,
I bounden am streight after this emprize,
As that your daughter can ye well advize,
Backe to returne to that great Faerie Queene,
And her to serve six yeares in warlike wize,
Gainst that proud Paynim king that workes her teene: [1]
Therefore I ought crave pardon, till I there have beene.

19

Unhappie falles that hard necessitie,
(Quoth he) the troubler of my happie peace,
And vowed foe of my felicitie;
Ne I against the same can justly preace: [2]
But since that band ye cannot now release,
Nor doen undo; [3] (for vowes may not be vaine),
Soone as the terms of those six yeares shall cease,
Ye then shall hither backe returne againe,
The marriage to accomplish vowd betwixt you twain.

20

Which for my part I covet to performe,
In sort as through the world I did proclame,
That whoso kild that monster most deforme,
And him in hardy battaile overcame,
Should have mine onely daughter to his Dame,
And of my kingdome heyre apparaunt bee:
Therefore since now to thee perteines the same,
By dew desert of noble chevalree,
Both daughter and eke kingdome, lo, I yield to thee.

. . . .

[Archimago, in a last spiteful effort, comes disguised as a messenger and attempts to prevent the betrothal by producing a letter from Duessa in which she asserts that the Knight is plighted to her. His ruse, however, is exposed.]

36

But they him layd full low in dungeon deepe,
And bound him hand and foote with yron chains
And with continual watch did warely keepe:
Who then would thinke, that by his subtile trains
He could escape fowle death or deadly paines?
Thus when that princes wrath was pacifide,
He gan renew the late forbidden banes, [4]
And to the knight his daughter dear he tyde,
With sacred rites and vowes for ever to abyde.

[1] causes her grief
[2] press
[3] cause to be undone
[4] banns

37

His owne two hands the holy knots did knit,
That none but death for ever can devide;
His owne two hands, for such a turne most fit,
The housling [5] fire did kindle and provide,
And holy water thereon sprinckled wide;
At which the bushy Teade [6] a groome did light,
And sacred lamp in secret chamber hide,
Where it should not be quenched day nor night,
For feare of evill fates, but burnen ever bright.

38

Then gan they sprinckle all the posts with wine,
And made great feast to solemnize that day;
They all perfumde with frankencense divine,
And precious odours fetcht from far away,
That all the house did sweat with great aray:
And all the while sweete Musicke did apply
Her curious skill, the warbling notes to play,
To drive away the dull Melancholy;
The whiles one sung a song of love and jollity.

39

During the which there was an heavenly noise
Heard sound through all the Pallace pleasantly,
Like as it had bene many an Angels voice
Singing before th' eternall Majesty,
In their trinall triplicities [7] on hye;
Yet wist no creature whence that heavenly sweet
Proceeded, yet eachone felt secretly
Himselfe thereby reft of his sences meet,
And ravished with rare impression in his sprite.

40

Great joy was made that day of young and old,
And solemne feast proclaimd throughout the land,
That their exceeding merth may not be told:
Suffice it heare by signes to understand
The usuall joyes at knitting of loves band.
Thrise happy man the knight himselfe did hold,
Possessed of his Ladies hart and hand,
And ever, when his eye did her behold,
His heart did seeme to melt in pleasures manifold.

[5] sacramental
[6] torch
[7] the thrice three orders of the celestial hierarchy: Seraphim, Cherubim, Thrones, Dominions, Virtues, Powers, Princedoms, Archangels, Angels

41

Her joyous presence, and sweet company
In full content he there did long enjoy;
Ne wicked envie, ne vile gealosy,
His deare delights were able to annoy:
Yet swimming in that sea of blissfull joy,
He nought forgot how he whilome had sworne,
In case he could that monstrous beast destroy,
Unto his Faerie Queene backe to returne;
The which he shortly did, and Una left to mourne.

42

Now strike your sailes ye jolly Mariners,
For we be come unto a quiet rode,
Where we must land some of our passengers,
And light this wearie vessell of her lode.
Here she a while may make her safe abode,
Till she repaired have her tackles spent,
And wants supplide. And then againe abroad
On the long voyage whereto she is bent:
Well may she speede and fairely finish her intent.

1590

PROTHALAMION [1]

Calm was the day, and through the trembling air
Sweet-breathing Zephyrus did softly play—
A gentle spirit, that lightly did delay
Hot Titan's beams, which then did glister fair;
When I (whom sullen care,
Through discontent of my long fruitless stay
In princes' court, and expectation vain
Of idle hopes, which still do fly away
Like empty shadows, did afflict my brain)
Walk'd forth to ease my pain
Along the shore of silver-streaming Thames;
Whose rutty [2] bank, the which his river hems,
Was painted all with variable flowers,
And all the meads adorn'd with dainty gems
Fit to deck maidens' bowers,
And crown their paramours
Against the bridal day, which is not long:
Sweet Thames! run softly, till I end my song.

There in a meadow by the river's side
A flock of nymphs I chancèd to espy,
All lovely daughters of the flood thereby,
With goodly greenish locks all loose untied
As each had been a bride;
And each one had a little wicker basket
Made of fine twigs, entrailèd curiously.
In which they gather'd flowers to fill their flasket,
And with fine fingers cropt full feateously [3]
The tender stalks on high.
Of every sort which in that meadow grew
They gather'd some; the violet, pallid blue,
The little daisy that at evening closes,
The virgin lily and the primrose true,
With store of vermeil roses,
To deck their bridegrooms' posies
Against the bridal day, which was not long:
Sweet Thames! run softly, till I end my song.

With that I saw two swans [4] of goodly hue
Come softly swimming down along the Lee; [5]
Two fairer birds I yet did never see;
The snow which doth the top of Pindus strow
Did never whiter show,
Nor Jove himself, when he a swan would be
For love of Leda, whiter did appear;
Yet Leda was (they say) as white as he,
Yet not so white as these, nor nothing near;
So purely white they were
That even the gentle stream, the which them bare,
Seem'd foul to them, and bade his billows spare
To wet their silken feathers, lest they might
Soil their fair plumes with water not so fair,
And mar their beauties bright
That shone as Heaven's light
Against their bridal day, which was not long:
Sweet Thames! run softly, till I end my song.

Eftsoons the nymphs, which now had flowers their fill,
Ran all in haste to see that silver brood
As they came floating on the crystal flood;
Whom when they saw, they stood amazèd still
Their wondering eyes to fill;
Them seem'd they never saw a sight so fair
Of fowls, so lovely, that they sure did deem
Them heavenly born, or to be that same pair

[1] A "Spousall Verse" made in honor of the approaching double marriage of the Ladies Elizabeth and Katherine Somerset in 1596, and apparently celebrating some visit of theirs to Essex House. F. T. Palgrave says of this poem: "Nowhere has Spenser more emphatically displayed himself as the very poet of Beauty: The Renaissance impulse in England is here seen at its highest and purest."

[2] rooty

[3] plucked very dexterously

[4] "The critics blame him because in his *Prothalamion* the subjects of it enter on the Thames as swans and leave it at Temple Gardens as noble damsels; but to those who are grown familiar with his imaginary world such a transformation seems as natural as in the old legend of the Knight of the Swan."—Lowell.

[5] stream

Which through the sky draw Venus' silver team;
For sure they did not seem
To be begot of any earthly seed,
But rather Angels, or of Angels' breed;
Yet were they bred of summer's heat,[1] they say,
In sweetest season, when each flower and weed
The earth did fresh array;
So fresh they seem'd as day,
Ev'n as their bridal day, which was not long:
  Sweet Thames! run softly, till I end my song.

Then forth they all out of their baskets drew
Great store of flowers, the honor of the field,
That to the sense did fragrant odors yield,
All which upon those goodly birds they threw
And all the waves did strew,
That like old Peneus' waters they did seem
When down along by pleasant Tempe's shore
Scatter'd with flowers, through Thessaly they stream,
That they appear, through lilies' plenteous store,
Like a bride's chamber-floor.
Two of those nymphs meanwhile two garlands bound
Of freshest flowers which in that mead they found,
The which presenting all in trim array,
Their snowy foreheads therewithal they crown'd;
Whilst one did sing this lay
Prepared against that day,
Against their bridal day, which was not long:
  Sweet Thames! run softly till I end my song.

"Ye gentle birds! the world's fair ornament,
And Heaven's glory, whom this happy hour
Doth lead unto your lovers' blissful bower,
Joy may you have, and gentle hearts' content
Of your love's couplement;
And let fair Venus, that is queen of love,
With her heart-quelling son upon you smile,
Whose smile, they say, hath virtue to remove
All love's dislike, and friendship's faulty guile
For ever to assoil.
Let endless peace your steadfast hearts accord,
And blessèd plenty wait upon your board;
And let your bed with pleasures chaste abound,
That fruitful issue may to you afford
Which may your foes confound,
And make your joys redound
Upon your bridal day, which is not long:
  Sweet Thames! run softly, till I end my song."

So ended she; and all the rest around
To her redoubled that her undersong,
Which said their bridal day should not be long.
And gentle Echo from the neighbor ground
Their accents did resound.
So forth those joyous birds did pass along
Adown the Lee that to them murmur'd low,
As he would speak but that he lack'd a tongue;
Yet did by signs his glad affection show,
Making his stream run slow.
And all the fowl which in his flood did dwell
'Gan flock about these twain, that did excel
The rest, so far as Cynthia doth shend[2]
The lesser stars. So they, enrangèd well,
Did on those two attend,
And their best service lend
Against their wedding day, which was not long!
  Sweet Thames! run softly, till I end my song.

At length they all to merry London came,
To merry London, my most kindly nurse,
That to me gave this life's first native source,
Though from another place I take my name,
An house of ancient fame.
There when she came whereas[3] those bricky towers
The which on Thames' broad agèd back do ride,
Where now the studious lawyers have their bowers,
There whilom wont the Templar-knights to bide,
Till they decay'd through pride;
Next whereunto there stands a stately place,
Where oft I gainèd gifts and goodly grace
Of that great lord,[4] which therein wont to dwell,
Whose want too well now feels my friendless case;
But ah! here fits not well
Old woes, but joys to tell
Against the bridal day, which is not long:
  Sweet Thames! run softly, till I end my song.

Yet therein now doth lodge a noble peer,[5]
Great England's glory and the world's wide wonder,
Whose dreadful name late through all Spain did thunder,
And Hercules' two pillars standing near

[1] Spenser spelled it Somer's heat (Somerset) and the pun was no doubt regarded as an ornament.

[2] the moon doth shame
[3] where
[4] Lord Leicester, Spenser's patron, whose death left him in "friendless case"
[5] Robert Devereux, second Earl of Essex

Did make to quake and fear.
Fair branch of honor, flower of chivalry!
That fillest England with thy triumphs' fame
Joy have thou of thy noble victory,[1]
And endless happiness of thine own name[2]
That promiseth the same;
That through thy prowess and victorious arms
Thy country may be freed from foreign harms,
And great Elisa's glorious name may ring
Through all the world, fill'd with thy wide
    alarms,
Which some brave Muse may sing
To ages following.
Upon the bridal day, which is not long:
  Sweet Thames! run softly, till I end my song!

From those high towers this noble lord issuing
Like Radiant Hesper, when his golden hair
In th' ocean billows he hath bathèd fair,
Descended to the river's open viewing
With a great train ensuing.
Above the rest were goodly to be seen
Two gentle knights of lovely face and feature,
Beseeming well the bower of any queen,
With gifts of wit and ornaments of nature,
Fit for so goodly stature,
That like the twins of Jove[3] they seem'd in
    sight
Which deck the baldric of the Heavens bright;
They two, forth pacing to the river's side,
Received those two fair brides, their love's
    delight;
Which, at th' appointed tide,
Each one did make his bride
Against their bridal day, which is not long:
  Sweet Thames! run softly till I end my song.

1596

SAMUEL DANIEL 1562-1619

Daniel's career seems to have been devoted chiefly to poetry and social intercourse. He was the son of a musician, was probably born at Taunton, went to Oxford but took no degree, and began publishing in his early twenties. His reputation was assured by 1595, as Spenser testifies in *Colin Clout:*

"And there is a new shepherd late up sprung,
The which doth all afore him far surpass."—

He was tutor to William Herbert, last Earl of Pembroke, Shakespeare's patron; and toward the end of his life was a prominent figure in the court of James I, being master of the queen's revels, for which he wrote many masques.

[1] at Cadiz, 1596

[2] apparently an allusion to the fact that the words *ever* and *heureux* (Fr., "happy") can be seen in the name *Devereux*

[3] Castor and Pollux, who were placed among the stars as the constellation Gemini

Daniel's sonnet sequence *Delia,* 1592, deserves high praise for sweetness of rhythm, delicate imagery, and purity of language. His *Complaint of Rosamond,* 1592, contains stanzas of exquisite pathos. His style is full, easy, and stately, without being very animated or splendid. Other works are *The Civile Wars,* 1595-1609, and *Defence of Rhyme,* 1602-07.

To Delia LI

Care-charmer Sleep, son of the sable Night,
Brother to Death, in silent darkness born.
Relieve my languish, and restore the light;
With dark forgetting of my care return.
And let the day be time enough to mourn
The shipwreck of my ill-adventured youth:
Let waking eyes suffice to wail their scorn,
Without the torment of the night's untruth.
Cease, dreams, the images of day-desires,
To model forth the passions of the morrow;
Never let rising Sun approve you liars,
To add more grief to aggravate my sorrow:
Still let me sleep, embracing clouds in vain,
And never wake to feel the day's disdain.

1592

WILLIAM SHAKESPEARE[4] 1564-1616

" . . . . the Poet paramount,
Whom all the Muses loved, not one alone."

—Longfellow

"Scorn not the sonnet . . . .
. . . . with this key Shakespeare unlocked his heart," said Wordsworth; "the less Shakespeare he," retorted Browning. These opinions represent the endless controversy as to whether Shakespeare's sequence is personal, as Wordsworth felt, or merely conventional, as Browning believed (see Browning's "House"). Most of the sonnets are addressed to some man (possibly either the Earl of Southampton or the Earl of Pembroke, both patrons of the poet), the rest to a woman (some say, Mary Fitton, maid of honor to Queen Elizabeth); but the identity of both is still a secret. The dividing sonnet, 126, is of twelve, not of fourteen lines. Both groups complain that the poet is betrayed by his mistress and his friend. A large portion of the sonnets, however, are full of half abstract and almost impersonal meditation on the joys and sorrows of love. Their real charm lies in the perfection of workmanship, the mastery with which all the elements—diction, verse, thought—have been harmonized and subdued to absolute felicity of poetic expression. Shakespeare's songs, also, are touched with his indefinable magic. However short, they attain perfect lyric form. In them are mingled the emotional quality of music, the simplicity of folk poetry, and the artistic appeal of the inevitable word.

[4] For biography see p. 180.

Sonnet XXIX

When in disgrace with fortune and men's eyes
I all alone beweep my outcast state,
And trouble deaf heaven with my bootless cries,
And look upon myself, and curse my fate;
Wishing me like to one more rich in hope,
Featured like him, like him with friends possest,
Desiring this man's art, and that man's scope,
With what I most enjoy contented least;
Yet in these thoughts myself almost despising,
Haply I think on thee—and then my state,
Like to the lark at break of day arising
From sullen earth, sings hymns at heaven's gate;
For thy sweet love remember'd, such wealth brings
That then I scorn to change my state with kings.

Sonnet XXX

When to the sessions [1] of sweet silent thought
I summon up remembrance of things past,
I sigh the lack of many a thing I sought,
And with old woes new wail my dear time's waste;
Then can I drown an eye, unused to flow,
For precious friends hid in death's dateless night,
And weep afresh love's long-since-cancell'd woe,
And moan the expense [2] of many a vanished sight;
Then can I grieve at grievances foregone,
And heavily from woe to woe tell o'er
The sad account of fore-bemoanèd moan,
Which I new pay as if not paid before:
—But if the while I think on thee, dear Friend,
All losses are restored, and sorrows end.

Sonnet LXIV

When I have seen by Time's fell hand defaced
The rich proud cost of out-worn buried age;
When sometime lofty towers I see down-razed,
And brass eternal slave to mortal rage;
When I have seen the hungry ocean gain
Advantage on the kingdom of the shore,
And the firm soil win of the watery main,
Increasing store with loss, and loss with store;
When I have seen such interchange of state,
Or state itself confounded to decay,
Ruin hath taught me thus to ruminate—
That Time will come and take my Love away:
—This thought is as a death, which cannot choose
But weep to have that which it fears to lose.

[1] legal phraseology
[2] the cost (in grief)

Sonnet LXV

Since brass, nor stone, nor earth, nor boundless sea,
But sad mortality o'ersways their power,
How with this rage shall beauty hold a plea,
Whose action is no stronger than a flower?
Oh, how shall summer's honey breath hold out
Against the wreckful siege of battering days,
When rocks impregnable are not so stout
Nor gates of steel so strong, but time decays?
Oh, fearful meditation! where, alack!
Shall Time's best jewel [3] from Time's chest lie hid?
Or what strong hand can hold his swift foot back,
Or who his spoil of beauty can forbid?
Oh! none, unless this miracle have might,
That in black ink my love may still shine bright.

Sonnet LXXIII

That time of year thou may'st in me behold
When yellow leaves, or none, or few, do hang
Upon those boughs which shake against the cold,
Bare ruin'd choirs, where late the sweet birds sang:
In me thou see'st the twilight of such day
As after sunset fadeth in the west,
Which by and by black night doth take away,
Death's second self, that seals up all in rest.
In me thou see'st the glowing of such fire,
That on the ashes of his youth doth lie
As the death-bed whereon it must expire,
Consumed with that which it was nourish'd by:
—This thou perceiv'st, which makes thy love more strong,
To love that well which thou must leave ere long.

Sonnet LXXIV

But be contented: when that fell arrest
Without all bail [4] shall carry me away,
My life hath in this line some interest,
Which for memorial still with thee shall stay.
When thou reviewest this, thou dost review
The very part was consecrate to thee:
The earth can have but earth, which is his due;
My spirit is thine, the better part of me;
So then thou hast but lost the dregs of life,
The prey of worms, my body being dead,
The coward conquest of a wretch's knife,
Too base of thee to be remembered.
The worth of that is that which it contains,
And that is this, and this with thee remains.

before 1599 1609

[3] i.e., the poet's friend
[4] refusing bail

From As You Like It

Under the greenwood tree
Who loves to lie with me,
And turn [1] his merry note
Unto the sweet bird's throat—
Come hither, come hither, come hither!
Here shall he see
No enemy
But winter and rough weather.

Who doth ambition shun
And loves to live i' the sun,
Seeking the food he eats
And pleased with what he gets—
Come hither, come hither, come hither!
Here shall he see
No enemy
But winter and rough weather.

1599? 1623

From As You Like It

Blow, blow, thou winter wind,
Thou art not so unkind
As man's ingratitude;
Thy tooth is not so keen
Because thou art not seen,
Although thy breath be rude.
Heigh ho! sing heigh ho! unto the green holly:
Most friendship is feigning, most loving mere folly:
Then, heigh ho! the holly!
This life is most jolly.

Freeze, freeze, thou bitter sky,
Thou dost not bite so nigh
As benefits forgot:
Though thou the waters warp,
Thy sting is not so sharp
As friend remember'd not.
Heigh ho! sing heigh ho! unto the green holly:
Most friendship is feigning, most loving mere folly:
Then, heigh ho! the holly
This life is most jolly.

1599? 1623

From Measure for Measure

Take, Oh, take those lips away,
That so sweetly were forsworn;
And those eyes, the break of day,
Lights that do mislead the morn:
But thy kisses bring again,
Bring again,
Seals of love, but sealed in vain,
Sealed in vain!

1604 1623

[1] modulate

From Twelfth Night

Come away, come away, Death,
And in sad cypress let me be laid;
Fly away, fly away, breath;
I am slain by a fair cruel maid.
My shroud of white, stuck all with yew,
O prepare it!
My part of death, no one so true
Did share it.

Not a flower, not a flower sweet
On my black coffin let there be strown;
Not a friend, not a friend greet
My poor corpse, where my bones shall be thrown:
A thousand thousand sighs to save,
Lay me, O where
Sad true lover never find my grave,
To weep there.

1600? 1623

From Hamlet

How should I your true love know
From another one?
By his cockle hat and staff,
And his sandal shoon. [2]

He is dead and gone, lady,
He is dead and gone;
At his head a grass-green turf,
At his heels a stone.

White his shroud as the mountain snow,
Larded [3] with sweet flowers,
Which bewept to the grave did go
With true-love showers.

1602? 1603

From Cymbeline

Hark, hark! the lark at heaven's gate sings,
And Phoebus 'gins arise,
His steeds to water at those springs
On chaliced flowers that lies;
And winking Mary-buds begin
To ope their golden eyes:
With everything that pretty is,
My lady sweet, arise!
Arise, arise!

1610-11 1623

[2] Pilgrims wore cockle shells in their hats in sign of their having crossed the sea to the Holy Land, and lovers not infrequently assumed this disguise in order to carry on love intrigues. Cf. *Romeo and Juliet*, I, v, 99

[3] thickly strewn

MICHAEL DRAYTON
1563-1631

Though some general hints about Drayton's life appear in his writings, almost all that we know of him concerns the making and revision of his poems, at which he worked hard during nearly sixty years. Apparently he came of well-to-do tradespeople, and he says that in his youth he was a page; but nothing is known of his schooling or university training. He was in London in 1591, for his first work, a series of Biblical paraphrases, was published then. In 1593 appeared his *Idea,* clearly modeled upon Spenser's *Shepheardes Calender,* and his first historical poem, the legend of *Peirs Gaveston.* The following year a sonnet sequence, *Ideas Mirrour,* celebrated his passions for a lady whose praises he sang for years. According to Henslow's *Diary,* he was writing for the stage from 1597 to 1602, working alone or collaborating with Chettle, Dekker, and others. His *Poemes Lyrick and Pastorall,* 1606, contains some of his finest productions, the "Ballad of Agincourt" among them. His longest and most famous poem is *Poly-Olbion,* 1613, a description of all England in verse.

Drayton's sonnets are rarely distinguished by poetic elevation. Only in the famous example below did he achieve much success. He borrows ideas and speech from all available sources at home and abroad. Even his sequence title is taken directly from the French model. Yet he inspired many younger men with the ambition to win fame in writing sonnets.

For criticism, see O. Elton, *Michael Drayton: A Critical Study,* 1895 (1905).

Idea LXI

Since there's no help, come let us kiss and part—
Nay I have done, you get no more of me;
And I am glad, yea, glad with all my heart,
That thus so cleanly I myself can free;
Shake hands forever, cancel all our vows,
And when we meet at any time again,
Be it not seen in either of our brows
That we one jot of former love retain.
Now at the last gasp of love's latest breath,
When his pulse failing, passion speechless lies,
When faith is kneeling by his bed of death,
And innocence is closing up his eyes,
—Now if thou would'st, when all have given him over,
From death to life thou might'st him yet recover!

1619

Agincourt[1]

Fair stood the wind for France,
When we our sails advance;
Nor now to prove our chance
Longer will tarry;
But putting to the main,
At Caux, the mouth of Seine,
With all his martial train
Landed King Harry.

And taking many a fort,
Furnished in warlike sort,
Marcheth towards Agincourt
In happy hour;
Skirmishing day by day,
With those that stopped his way,
Where the French general lay
With all his power.

Which,[2] in his height of pride,
King Henry to deride,
His ransom to provide
To the King sending;[3]
Which he neglects the while,
As from a nation vile,
Yet with an angry smile,
Their fall portending.

And turning to his men,
Quoth our brave Henry then:
"Though they to one be ten
Be not amazèd!
Yet have we well begun:
Battles so bravely won
Have ever to the sun
By Fame been raisèd!

"And for myself," quoth he,
"This my full rest[4] shall be:
England ne'er mourn for me,
Nor more esteem me!
Victor I will remain,
Or on this earth lie slain;

[1] In the course of the Hundred Years' War the English won three great victories over the French in the face of enormous odds—Crécy in 1346, Poitiers in 1356, and Agincourt in 1415. The last was won by Henry the Fifth, and so well was the glory of it remembered that after nearly two hundred years Drayton could celebrate it in this ballad, which bids fair to stand as the supreme national ballad of England. Breathless from the first word to the last, rude and rhythmic as the tread of an army, it arouses the martial spirit as few things but its imitations can. High among these stand Longfellow's "Skeleton in Armor" and Tennyson's "Charge of the Light Brigade" (p. 632), both employing the same meter. Cf. also with *Henry V,* Acts III and IV, especially the speeches, III, i, 1-34, and IV, iii, 16-67.

[2] who (the French general)

[3] i.e., sending a message

[4] resolution

Never shall She sustain
  Loss to redeem me!

"Poitiers and Cressy tell,
When most their pride did swell,
Under our swords they fell.
  No less our skill is,
Than when our Grandsire great,
Claiming the regal seat,
By many a warlike feat
  Lopped the French lilies."

The Duke of York so dread
The eager vanward led;
With the main, Henry sped
  Amongst his henchmen:
Exeter had the rear,
A braver man not there!
O Lord, how hot they were
  On the false Frenchmen!

They now to fight are gone;
Armor on armor shone;
Drum now to drum did groan:
  To hear, was wonder;
That, with the cries they make,
The very earth did shake;
Trumpet to trumpet spake;
  Thunder to thunder.

Well it thine age became,
O noble Erpingham,
Which didst the signal aim
  To our hid forces!
When, from a meadow by,
Like a storm suddenly,
The English archery
  Stuck the French horses.

With Spanish yew so strong;
Arrows a cloth-yard long,
That like to serpents stung,
  Piercing the weather.
None from his fellow starts;
But, playing manly parts,
And like true English hearts,
  Stuck close together.

When down their bows they threw,
And forth their bilboes [1] drew,
And on the French they flew:
  Not one was tardy.
Arms were from shoulders sent,
Scalps to the teeth were rent,
Down the French peasants went:
  Our men were hardy.

This while our noble King,
His broad sword brandishing,
Down the French host did ding,
  As to o'erwhelm it;
And many a deep wound lent;
His arms with blood besprent,
And many a cruel dent
  Bruised his helmet.

Gloucester, that duke so good,
Next of the royal blood,
For famous England stood
  With his brave brother;
Clarence, in steel so bright,
Though but a maiden knight,
Yet in that furious fight
  Scarce such another!

Warwick in blood did wade,
Oxford, the foe invade,
And cruel slaughter made,
  Still as they ran up.
Suffolk his axe did ply;
Beaumont and Willoughby
Bare them right doughtily;
  Ferrers and Fanhope.

Upon Saint Crispin's Day
Fought was this noble Fray;
Which Fame did not delay
  To England to carry.
Oh, when shall English men
With such acts fill a pen?
Or England breed again
  Such a King Harry?

1606

[1] swords

GEORGE PEELE 1558?-1597?

Knowledge of Peele's life is hazy. He may have been born in London; his father, a salter, was also clerk of Christ's Hospital; his son, therefore, was a "free scholar" there. He was a noted poet while at Oxford, where he took his M.A. in 1579. His life was one of social gayety and dissipation. He was a successful playwright, his *Arraignment of Paris* being acted before Queen Elizabeth by the Chapel Children in 1581; and an actor, being a member of the Lord Admiral's company, then of the Queen's men. He was intimate with Marlowe, Greene, and Nashe. His dainty, melodious lyrics were popular in literary circles. His works consisted of plays: *The Famous Chronicle of King Edward the First*, 1593, *Old Wives' Tale*, 1595, etc., pageants, and miscellaneous verse.

From the Arraignment of Paris

Oenone

Fair and fair, and twice so fair,
  As fair as any may be,
The fairest shepherd on our green,
  A love for any lady.

Paris

Fair and fair, and twice so fair,
  As fair as any may be;
Thy love is fair for thee alone,
  And for no other lady.

Oenone

My love is fair, my love is gay,
  And fresh as bin the flowers in May,
And of my love my roundelay,
  My merry, merry roundelay,
Concludes with Cupid's curse—
  "They that do change old love for new,
Pray gods they change for worse!"

Ambo Simul[1]

They that do change old love for new,
  Pray gods they change for worse!

Oenone

Fair and fair, and twice so fair,
  As fair as any may be,
The fairest shepherd on our green,
  A love for any lady.

Paris

Fair and fair, and twice so fair,
  As fair as any may be;
Thy love is fair for thee alone,
  And for no other lady.

Oenone

My love can pipe, my love can sing,
My love can many a pretty thing,
And of his lovely praises ring
My merry, merry roundelay.
  Amen to Cupid's curse—
"They that do change old love for new,
Pray gods they change for worse!"

Paris

They that do change old love for new,
  Pray gods they change for worse!

Ambo Simul

Fair and fair, and twice so fair,
  As fair as any may be;
Thy love is fair for thee alone,
  And for no other lady.

acted c. 1581 1584

[1] both together

THOMAS LODGE 1558?-1625

Thomas Lodge had a more highly-flavored career than one expects even of an Elizabethan. He was born either in London or Essex; his father, Lord Mayor of London, had a house in each place. His youth was marked by much restlessness and unhappiness. After leaving Oxford he took up the study of law, but soon abandoned it for literature. Next he tried the army, and then, dissatisfied with that, made voyages to the Canaries and South America.

On his first return to England, 1590, he resumed literature and wrote his best known prose romance *Rosalynde,* which is characterized by many "euphuisms,"[2] and contains some beautiful lyrics; it is based on his Canaries voyage. *Phillis,* a book of forty sonnets, published in 1593, after his second voyage, came between two historical romances: *The History of Robert, Second Duke of Normandy,* and *The Life and Death of William Longbeard.* In 1596 Lodge exchanged Protestantism for Roman Catholicism, and took up medicine, practicing to the end of his life as a prosperous London physician. It is as a lyric poet that he best deserves to be remembered. The "sugared sweetness" of his lyrics gives them rank beside the finest in the language.

Rosalind's Madrigal

Love in my bosom, like a bee,
      Doth suck his sweet;
Now with his wings he plays with me,
      Now with his feet.
   Within mine eyes he makes his nest,
   His bed amidst my tender breast;
   My kisses are his daily feast,
   And yet he robs me of my rest:
      Ah! wanton, will ye?

And if I sleep, then percheth he
      With pretty flight,
And makes his pillow of my knee
      The livelong night.
   Strike I my lute, he tunes the string;
   He music plays if so I sing;
   He lends me every lovely thing,
   Yet cruel he my heart doth sting.
      Whist, wanton, still ye!

Else I with roses every day
      Will whip you hence,
And bind you, when you long to play,
      For your offense;
   I'll shut my eyes to keep you in;
   I'll make you fast it for your sin;
   I'll count your power not worth a pin;
   —Alas! what hereby shall I win,
      If he gainsay me?

[2] See introd., p. 224

What if I beat the wanton boy
With many a rod?
He will repay me with annoy,
Because a god.
Then sit thou safely on my knee,
And let thy bower my bosom be;
Lurk in mine eyes, I like of [1] thee;
O Cupid, so thou pity me,
Spare not, but play thee!

1590

ROBERT SOUTHWELL
1561?-1595

The life of Southwell, illustrative of the religous conflict that permeated the Elizabethan era, was tragic yet ideal, since his lifelong desire for martyrdom was gratified. He was born in Norfolk, came early under the influence of the Jesuits, and went to Douay, then to Paris to study. Determined to join the Society of Jesus, he made his way to Rome after long probation, and was ordained priest in 1584. Next he was sent on a mission to England, where it was treason to be a Catholic priest. After six years of living in disguise, proselytizing and writing religious tracts, he was caught, tortured, imprisoned for over two years, and executed as a traitor at Tyburn.

His poems, written mostly in prison, and published after his death, were popular, and imitations soon abounded. *Saint Peter's Complaint,* his longest poem, 1595, shows the influence of Shakespeare's *Venus and Adonis;* of "The Burning Babe," Ben Jonson said that "so he had written that piece of his, 'The Burning Babe,' he would have been content to destroy many of his." Southwell was a forerunner of the mystical religious poets of the following age—Donne, Herbert, and others. His aim as poet was to prove that virtue or piety was as fit a subject for a poet's pen as the vain, worldly, or sensual topics then in vogue.

The Burning Babe

As I in hoary winter's night
Stood shivering in the snow,
Surprised I was with sudden heat
Which made my heart to glow;
And lifting up a fearful eye
To view what fire was near,
A pretty Babe all burning bright
Did in the air appear,
Who, scorched with excessive heat,
Such floods of tears did shed,
As tho' His floods should quench His flames
Which with His tears were fed.
"Alas!" quoth He, "but newly born
In fiery heats I fry,
Yet none approach to warm their hearts
Or feel my fire but I!
My faultless breast the furnace is,
The fuel, wounding thorns;
Love is the fire and sighs the smoke,
The ashes, shame and scorns;
The fuel Justice layeth on,
And Mercy blows the coals;
The metal in this furnace wrought
Are men's defiled souls;
For which, as now on fire I am
To work them to their good,
So will I melt into a bath
To wash them in my blood."
With this He vanish'd out of sight,
And swiftly shrunk away,
And straight I called unto mind
That it was Christmas-day.

1595

[1] am pleased with

CHRISTOPHER MARLOWE [2]
1564-1593

"That smooth song which was made by Kit Marlowe, now at least fifty years ago; and . . . . an answer to it which was made by Sir Walter Raleigh in his younger days. They were old-fashioned poetry, but choicely good."—Isaac Walton.

The Passionate Shepherd to His Love

Come live with me and be my love,
And we will all the pleasures prove
That valleys, groves, hills and fields,
Woods or steepy mountain yields.

And we will sit upon the rocks,
Seeing the shepherds feed their flocks,
By shallow rivers, to whose falls
Melodious birds sing madrigals.

And I will make thee beds of roses,
And a thousand fragrant posies,
A cap of flowers, and a kirtle
Embroidered all with leaves of myrtle;

A gown made of the finest wool,
Which from our pretty lambs we pull;
Fair linèd slippers for the cold,
With buckles of the purest gold;

A belt of straw and ivy buds
With coral clasps and amber studs:
And if these pleasures may thee move,
Come live with me and be my love.

The shepherd swains shall dance and sing
For thy delight each May-morning:
If these delights thy mind may move,
Then live with me and be my love.

c. 1589 1600

[2] See p. 166.

SIR WALTER RALEIGH[1]
1552?-1618

Neither of the two poems here given as Raleigh's can be ascribed to him with much confidence. The first appeared in *England's Helicon* over the name "Ignoto." The MS. of the second bears the initials "Sr. W. R."

The Nymph's Reply to the Shepherd

If all the world and love were young,
And truth in every shepherd's tongue,
These pretty pleasures might me move
To live with thee and be thy love.

Time drives the flocks from field to fold,
When rivers rage, and rocks grow cold;
And Philomel becometh dumb;
The rest complains of cares to come.

The flowers do fade, and wanton fields
To wayward Winter reckoning yields;
A honey tongue, a heart of gall,
Is fancy's spring, but sorrow's fall.

Thy gowns, thy shoes, thy beds of roses,
Thy cap, thy kirtle, and thy posies,
Soon break, soon wither, soon forgotten,
In folly ripe, in reason rotten.

Thy belt of straw and ivy buds,
Thy coral clasps and amber studs,
All these in me no means can move
To come to thee and be thy love.

But could youth last, and love still breed,
Had joys no date,[2] nor age no need,
Then these delights my mind might move
To live with thee and be thy love.

c. 1589 1600

Pilgrim to Pilgrim

As you came from the holy land
Of Walsinghame,[3]
Met you not with my true love
By the way as you came?

How shall I know your true love,
That have met many one,
As I went to the holy land,
That have come, that have gone?

She is neither white nor brown,
But as the heavens fair;
There is none hath a form so divine
In the earth or the air.

Such a one did I meet, good sir,
Such an angel-like face,
Who like a queen, like a nymph, did appear,
By her gait, by her grace.

She hath left me here all alone,
All alone, as unknown,
Who sometimes did me lead with herself,
And me loved as her own.

What's the cause that she leaves you alone,
And a new way doth take,
Who loved you once as her own,
And her joy did you make?

I have loved her all my youth,
But now old, as you see,
Love likes not the falling fruit
From the withered tree.

Know that Love is a careless child,
And forgets promise past;
He is blind, he is deaf when he list,
And in faith never fast.

His desire is a dureless[4] content,
And a trustless joy;
He is won with a world of despair
And is lost with a toy.[5]

Of womankind such indeed is the love,
Or the word love abusèd,
Under which many childish desires
And conceits are excusèd.

But true love is a durable fire,
In the mind ever burning,
Never sick, never old, never dead,
From itself never turning.

before 1600

THOMAS DEKKER 1570?-1641

There are practically no details known about the life of the first great literary artist of London street life. From Henslow's *Diary* we gather that Dekker was a prolific writer, collaborating with many of the leading dramatists of the day—Webster, Munday, Jonson, Middleton—besides writing independently and revising old plays. His dramas, full of kindly humor, give one a lively

[1] See p. *227*
[2] end
[3] An ancient Priory in Norfolk, with a famous shrine of Our Lady, the object of many pilgrimages until its dissolution in 1538. "A lover growing or grown old, it would seem, has been left in the lurch by the object of his affections. As all the world thronged to Walsingham the lover supposes that she too must have gone that way; and meeting a pilgrim returning from that English Holy Land, asks him if he has seen anything of her runaway ladyship."—J. W. Hales.
[4] unenduring
[5] trifle

impression of city life, the interiors of shops, taverns, and houses. The characters are drawn from life, middle-class citizens and their wives, apprentices, and young aristocrats. The best is his *Shoemakers Holiday,* 1600. He also wrote a great many tracts, moral in purpose, not only of literary interest but invaluable for the information they afford concerning the social life of the times. From these stands out the *Gul's Hornebooke,* 1609, an attack on the gallants and fops of the age. For the sweet sincerity of the songs contained in his plays Dekker ranks high as a lyric poet.

From Patient Grissell

Art thou poor, yet hast thou golden slumbers?
O sweet content!
Art thou rich, yet is thy mind perplexed?
O punishment!
Dost thou laugh to see how fools are vexed
To add to golden numbers golden numbers?
O sweet content, O sweet, O sweet content!

Work apace! apace! apace! apace!
Honest labor bears a lovely face.
Then hey noney, noney, hey noney, noney!

Canst drink the waters of the crispèd spring?
O sweet content!
Swim'st thou in wealth, yet sink'st in thine own tears?
O punishment!
Then he that patiently want's burden bears
No burden bears, but is a king, a king,
O sweet content, O sweet, O sweet content!

Work apace! apace! apace! apace!
Honest labor bears a lovely face.
Then hey noney, noney, hey noney, noney!

1599 1603

THOMAS CAMPION d. 1619

Details of the life of Thomas Campion are so lacking that it would be difficult to reconstruct him as a personality were it not for his writings. He was born in London of well-to-do parents, and studied at Cambridge and Gray's Inn. In 1601 his first collection of English songs, *A Booke of Ayres,* appeared, some of the poems being set to music by Campion himself. The following year he published his *Observations on the Art of English Poesie.* His best work is lyrical; though his life forms a link between the Elizabethans and the Jacobeans,[1] his poetry shows no touch of Jacobean tendencies. In him "euphuism"[2] is restricted to a frequent use of balanced phrase and antithesis. He is also a skilled metrist, producing an infinite variety of cadences and rhythms.

[1] people of James's (Latin *Jacobus*) reign
[2] See page 224

Cherry-Ripe

There is a garden in her face
Where roses and white lilies grow;
A heavenly paradise is that place,
Wherein all pleasant fruits do flow;
There cherries grow that none may buy,
Till "Cherry-Ripe" themselves do cry.

Those cherries fairly do enclose
Of orient pearl a double row,
Which when her lovely laughter shows,
They look like rose-buds fill'd with snow.
Yet them no peer nor prince may buy,
Till "Cherry-Ripe" themselves do cry.

Her eyes like angels watch them still;
Her brows like bended bows do stand,
Threat'ning with piercing frowns to kill
All that attempt with eye or hand
Those sacred cherries to come nigh,
Till "Cherry-Ripe" themselves do cry!

c. 1617

BEN JONSON 1573?-1637 [3]

" . . . . his songs are among the best in the language."—Emerson.

To Celia

Drink to me only with thine eyes,
And I will pledge with mine;
Or leave a kiss but in the cup
And I'll not look for wine.
The thirst that from the soul doth rise
Doth ask a drink divine;
But might I of Jove's nectar sup,
I would not change for thine.

I sent thee late a rosy wreath,
Not so much honoring thee
As giving it a hope that there
It could not wither'd be;
But thou thereon didst only breathe
And sent'st it back to me;
Since when it grows, and smells, I swear,
Not of itself but thee!

1605 1616

The Triumph of Charis

See the chariot at hand here of Love,
Wherein my lady rideth!
Each that draws is a swan or a dove,
And well the car Love guideth.
As she goes, all hearts do duty
Unto her beauty;
And enamor'd, do wish, so they might
But enjoy such a sight,

[3] See page 209.

That they still were to run by her side,
Through swords, through seas, whither she
would ride.

Do but look on her eyes, they do light
All that Love's world compriseth!
Do but look on her hair, it is bright
As Love's star when it riseth!
Do but mark, her forehead smoother
Than words that soothe her;
And from her arched brows, such a grace
Sheds itself through the face
As alone there triumphs to the life
All the gain, all the good, of the elements'
strife.

Have you seen but a bright lily grow,
Before rude hands have touched it?
Have you marked but the fall of the snow
Before the soil hath smutched it?
Have you felt the wool of the beaver?
Or swan's down ever?
Or have smelt o' the bud of the briar?
Or the nard in the fire?
Or have tasted the bag of the bee?
O so white! O so soft! O so sweet is she!

1616? 1631

THE ELIZABETHAN AGE—DRAMA

ELIZABETHAN drama might be considered a thirty-year period of experimentation with scarcely any perceptible progress, and then a sudden flowering in the work of Lyly, Peele, Greene, Lodge, Marlowe, and Shakespeare. Its beginnings lie far back in the crude Miracle Plays and Moralities,[1] popular even in the time of Shakespeare. His phrase "out-herods Herod" (i. e., outrants the Miracle Play character, Herod, *Hamlet* III, ii, 15) refers to the bombast which made these plays enjoyed by the crowd: for despite their religious origin some of them had come to include characters and scenes humorous and realistic that wandered far from Biblical narrative. Such parts, developed into independent plays called Interludes, were common under Henry VIII.

A more fully-developed farce with a thread of plot and low-class characters is *Gammer Gurton's Needle,* acted about the time of Elizabeth's accession. The next step is represented by *Ralph Roister Doister,* a love comedy by Udall about 1550, and *Gorboduc,* a blood-and-thunder tragedy by Sackville and Norton. These three plays betray the influence of ancient Greek and Latin drama; that is, they are arranged in acts and scenes, and observe fairly well classical laws of unity—that of time, which required that the action represented should not exceed one day; that of place, which allowed no change of scene; and that of action, which required one central theme.

The gap still remaining between these plays and the mature Elizabethan drama left much to do: the renouncing of the unities of time and place, the development of a noble and flexible poetic style, a higher conception of the part played by tragedy and comedy in human lives, and a mingling of the two in drama. Just how it was done we cannot tell, but the gap was bridged, as the work of Marlowe testifies.

CHRISTOPHER MARLOWE
1564-1593

We cannot but regret Marlowe's early death when we consider the power and promise shown by his work, and what he did for the drama while he lived. A shoemaker's son, he was born in Canterbury, was educated at Cambridge where he specialized in the classics and acquired a leaning toward atheism, was in London by 1587, and at an early date was dramatist to the Earl of Nottingham's players. Marlowe's heretical opinions had attracted the notice of the authorities, and a warrant of arrest had been issued when he met his death at Deptford by stabbing, as tradition has it, in a drunken brawl.

His first play, *Tamburlaine the Great,* 1590, revolutionized English drama. In it Marlowe, acting as a link between Surrey's mechanical and Shakespeare's flexible blank verse, freed the form from the prevailing restraint and first revealed its poetic capabilities. His second drama, *Dr. Faustus,* is an old medieval legend given a glowing Renaissance setting. The opening scenes of the *Jew of Malta* are full of dramatic energy. *Edward III,* a venture in English historical drama, is the best constructed of all. Other plays were ascribed to him, and he undoubtedly reworked old plays and collaborated on new ones. He also began an extremely beautiful poem, *Hero and Leander,* paraphrasing an ancient Greek poem; but it was left unfinished, and was completed by George Chapman. Shakespeare quoted from it the well-known line:

"Whoever loved that loved not at first sight?"

in *As You Like It,* III, v, 82.

[1] See under Everyman, page 93.

In Marlowe's heroes are summed up the energies and ambitions of his age, the fierce desire to know and do all things; his Faustus is a genuine reincarnation of the Renaissance spirit. His great gift to the drama was in providing it with a heroic mood. But his contribution of a heroic form in his free and swelling blank verse is of almost equal importance. Ellis Fermor comments thus on the three greatest writers of blank verse: "the value of Marlowe's verse is inseparable from the value of the thought; the value of Milton's verse has no relation to the value of the thought; and the value of Shakespeare's verse transcends and includes the value of the thought. Testimonies of Marlowe's eminence as poet and dramatist come from his contemporaries, upon whom his work had much influence, as is clear in Shakespeare's *Richard II* and *The Merchant of Venice.*

Collected works are edited by C. F. T. Brooke, 1910; the plays are also in the Everyman and the Mermaid series. For criticism see essays by Lowell (OED), Dowden (T&S), Symonds, Hazlitt (Eliz.L.); there is an excellent article by A. Compton-Rickett, "Kit Marlowe, Pioneer," in *Liv. Age* 285:348-52; and fascinating recent discoveries are told by J. L. Hotson in *The Death of Christopher Marlowe,* 1925; and "Tracking down a Murderer," *Atlan.* 135:733-41, condensed in *Lit. Dig.* 85:27-8, Je. 13 '25.

From

THE TRAGICAL HISTORY OF DOCTOR FAUSTUS [1]

The Faust legend, which embodies the old fancy of a compact with the Evil One, had its origin in the life of a certain German doctor (i.e., learned man) of evil character, Johann Faustus, who, dying about 1538, was reputed to have been carried off by the Devil. The tales that grew up about his memory were collected in *The History of Dr. Faustus, the Notorious Magician and Master of the Black Art,* published at Frankfort-on-the-Main in 1587. A translation was printed in England and Marlowe immediately dramatized it, 1588; since then the story has appeared in many forms. Marlowe's drama was probably not printed in his lifetime. The editions dated 1604 and 1616 differ in many particulars and certainly neither of them gives us the text as he left it. It is possible that none of the comic scenes, the mingling of which with tragedy came to be one of the characteristics of Elizabethan drama, were from his pen. The extracts given here present only the central tragic theme. The 1616 text is followed with scene numbers inserted to correspond with A. W. Ward's divisions of the 1604 text.

Enter Chorus.

CHORUS. Not marching in the fields of Thrasymene, [2]
Where Mars did mate [3] the warlike Carthagens;
Nor sporting in the dalliance of love,
In courts of kings where state [4] is overturn'd;
Nor in the pomp of proud audacious deeds,
Intends our Muse to vaunt her heavenly verse:
Only this, gentles—we must now perform
The form of Faustus' fortunes, good or bad:
And now to patient judgments we appeal,
And speak for Faustus in his infancy.
Now is he born of parents base of stock,
In Germany, within a town call'd Rhodes: [5]
At riper years, to Wittenberg he went,
Whereas [6] his kinsmen chiefly brought him up.
So much he profits in divinity,
That shortly he was grac'd with doctor's name,
Excelling all, and sweetly can dispute
In th' heavenly matters of theology;
Till swoln with cunning, [7] of a self-conceit,
His waxen wings did mount above his reach, [8]
And, melting, heavens conspir'd his overthrow;
For, falling to a devilish exercise,
And glutted now with learning's golden gifts,
He surfeits upon cursèd necromancy;
Nothing so sweet as magic is to him,
Which he prefers before his chiefest bliss:
And this the man that in his study sits.
[*Exit.*

[SCENE I]

Faustus *discovered in his study*

FAUSTUS. Settle [9] thy studies, Faustus, and begin
To sound the depth of that thou wilt profess: [10]
Having commenc'd, [11] be a divine in show,
Yet level at the end [12] of every art,
And live and die in Aristotle's works.
Sweet Analytics, 'tis thou hast ravish'd me!
Bene disserere est finis logices. [13]
Is, to dispute well, logic's chiefest end?
Affords this art no greater miracle?
Then read no more; thou hast attain'd that end:

[1] A comparison with Goethe's *Faust* is interesting.
[2] The scene of Hannibal's defeat of the Romans, 217 B.C.; Marlowe means that his drama is not to deal, like others, with wars and intrigues.

[3] cope with
[4] statehood, majesty
[5] Roda, near Weimar
[6] where
[7] knowledge
[8] See the story of Icarus.
[9] fix upon
[10] choose for a profession
[11] taken the doctor's degree
[12] aim at the goal (viz., metaphysics)
[13] "To dispute well is the end of logic."

A greater subject fitteth Faustus' wit:
Bid Economy farewell, and Galen [1] come:
Be a physician, Faustus, heap up gold,
And be eterniz'd for some wondrous cure:
Summun bonum medicinae sanitas,
The end of physic is our body's health.
Why, Faustus, hast thou not attain'd that end?
Are not thy bills [2] hung up as monuments,
Whereby whole cities have escap'd the plague,
And thousand desperate maladies been cur'd?
Yet art thou still but Faustus, and a man.
Couldst thou make men to live eternally,
Or, being dead, raise them to life again,
Then this profession were to be esteem'd.
Physic, farewell! Where is Justinian? [3]
[*Reads.*
Si una eademque res legatur duobus, alter rem, alter valorem rei, &c. [4]
A petty case of paltry legacies! [*Reads.*
Exhaereditare filium non potest pater, nisi, &c. [5]
Such is the subject of the institute,
And universal body of the law:
This study fits a mercenary drudge,
Who aims at nothing but external trash;
Too servile and illiberal for me.
When all is done, divinity is best:
Jerome's Bible, [6] Faustus; view it well.
[*Reads.*
Stipendium peccati mors est. Ha! *Stipendium, &c.* The reward of sin is death; that's hard. [*Reads.*
Si peccasse negamus, fallimur, et nulla est in nobis veritas; If we say that we have no sin, we deceive ourselves, and there is no truth in us. Why, then, belike we must sin, and so consequently die:
Aye, we must die an everlasting death.
What doctrine call you this, *Che sera, sera,*
What will be, shall be? Divinity, adieu! [7]
These metaphysics of magicians,
And necromantic books are heavenly;
Lines, circles, scenes, letters, and characters;
Aye, these are those that Faustus most desires.
Oh, what a world of profit and delight,
Of power, of honor, and omnipotence,
Is promis'd to the studious artizan!
All things that move between the quiet poles
Shall be at my command: emperors and kings
Are but obeyed in their several provinces;
But his dominion that exceeds in this,
Stretcheth as far as doth the mind of man;
A sound magician is a demigod;
Here tire, my brains, to gain a deity.

Enter Wagner.

Wagner, commend me to my dearest friends.
The German Valdes and Cornelius;
Request them earnestly to visit me.

WAG. I will, sir. [*Exit.*

FAUST. Their conference [8] will be a greater help to me
Than all my labors, plod I ne'er so fast.

Enter Good Angel *and* Evil Angel.

G. ANG. O Faustus, lay that damnèd book aside,
And gaze not on it, lest it tempt thy soul,
And heap God's heavy wrath upon thy head!
Read, read the Scriptures—that is blasphemy.

E. ANG. Go forward, Faustus, in that famous art [9]
Wherein all Nature's treasure is contain'd:
Be thou on earth as Jove is in the sky,
Lord and commander of these elements.
[*Exeunt* Angels.

FAUST. How am I glutted with conceit of this!
Shall I make spirits fetch me what I please,
Resolve me of [10] all ambiguities,
Perform what desperate enterprise I will?
I'll have them fly to India for gold,
Ransack the ocean for orient pearl,
And search all corners of the new-found world [11]
For pleasant fruits and princely delicates; [12]
I'll have them read me strange philosophy,
And tell the secrets of all foreign kings;
I'll have them wall all Germany with brass,
And make swift Rhine circle fair Wittenberg;
I'll have them fill the public schools with silk,
Wherewith the students shall be bravely clad;
I'll levy soldiers with the coin they bring,
And chase the Prince of Parma [13] from our land,

[1] a famous physician of the second century
[2] prescriptions
[3] a Roman emperor and law-giver
[4] "If one and the same thing be bequeathed to two, one [shall have] the thing, the other its value, etc."
[5] "A father may not disinherit his son, unless, etc."
[6] the Vulgate
[7] Here Faustus turns to his books of magic.
[8] conversation
[9] black art, i.e., magic
[10] interpret for me
[11] America
[12] delicacies
[13] Alexander Farnese, the famous Governor of the Netherlands, who subdued Antwerp in 1585 and later planned at Philip II's orders to invade England

And reign sole king of all the provinces;
Yea, stranger engines for the brunt of war,
Than was the fiery keel at Antwerp-bridge, [1]
I'll make my servile spirits to invent.

Enter Valdes *and* Cornelius.

Come, German Valdes, and Cornelius,
And make me blest with your sage conference.
Valdes, sweet Valdes, and Cornelius,
Know that your words have won me at the last
To practice magic and concealèd arts.
Philosophy is odious and obscure;
Both law and physic are for petty wits:
'Tis magic, magic that hath ravish'd me.
Then, gentle friends, aid me in this attempt;
And I, that have with subtle syllogisms
Gravel'd [2] the pastors of the German church,
And made the flowering pride of Wittenberg
Swarm to my problems, as th' infernal spirits
On sweet Musaeus when he came to hell, [3]
Will be as cunning as Agrippa [4] was,
Whose shadow made all Europe honor him.

VALD. Faustus, these books, thy wit, and our experience,
Shall make all nations to canonize us.
As Indian Moors [5] obey their Spanish lords,
So shall the spirits of every element
Be always serviceable to us three;
Like lions shall they guard us when we please;
Like Almain rutters [6] with their horsemen's staves,
Or Lapland giants, trotting by our sides;
Sometimes like women, or unwedded maids,
Shadowing more beauty in [7] their airy brows
Than have the white breasts of the queen of love:
From Venice shall they drag huge argosies,
And from America the golden fleece
That yearly stuffs old Philip's treasury;
If learnèd Faustus will be resolute.

FAUST. Valdes, as resolute am I in this
As thou to live: therefore object it not. [8]

CORN. The miracles that magic will perform
Will make thee vow to study nothing else.
He that is grounded in astrology,
Enrich'd with tongues, well seen [9] in minerals,
Hath all the principles magic doth require:
Then doubt not, Faustus, but to be renown'd,
And more frequented for this mystery
Than heretofore the Delphian oracle.
The spirits tell me they can dry the sea,
And fetch the treasure of all foreign wrecks,
Yea, all the wealth that our forefathers hid
Within the massy entrails of the earth;
Then tell me, Faustus, what shall we three want?

FAUST. Nothing, Cornelius. Oh, this cheers my soul!
Come, show me some demonstrations magical,
That I may conjure in some bushy grove,
And have these joys in full possession.

VALD. Then haste thee to some solitary grove,
And bear wise Bacon's and Albertus' [10] works,
The Hebrew Psalter, and New Testament;
And whatsoever else is requisite
We will inform thee ere our conference cease.

CORN. Valdes, first let him know the words of art;
And then, all other ceremonies learn'd,
Faustus may try his cunning by himself.

VALD. First I'll instruct thee in the rudiments,
And then wilt thou be perfecter than I.

FAUST. Then come and dine with me, and after meat,
We'll canvass every quiddity [11] thereof;
For, ere I sleep, I'll try what I can do;
This night I'll conjure, though I die therefore. [*Exeunt.*

[SCENE II]

Enter two Scholars.

FIRST SCHOL. I wonder what's become of Faustus, that was wont to make our schools ring with *sic probo*. [12]

SEC. SCHOL. That shall we presently know; here comes his boy.

Enter Wagner.

FIRST SCHOL. How now, sirrah! where's thy master?

WAG. God in heaven knows.

SEC. SCHOL. Why, dost not thou know, then?

WAG. Yes, I know; but that follows not.

FIRST SCHOL. Go to, sirrah! leave your jesting, and tell us where he is.

. . . .

WAG. Truly, my dear brethren, my master is within at dinner, with Valdes and Cornelius, as this wine, if it could speak, would inform your worships: and so, the Lord bless you, preserve you, and keep you, my dear brethren! [*Exit.*

[1] ships set on fire and driven against the Antwerp bridge to burn it down
[2] puzzled
[3] See *Aeneid* VI, 666.
[4] a magician of the time
[5] American Indians
[6] German horsemen
[7] perhaps *in=under*
[8] make it no objection
[9] skilled
[10] Roger Bacon and Albertus Magnus, medieval scholars popularly reputed to have practiced magic
[11] matter
[12] "Thus I prove" (a formula in logical demonstration)

FIRST SCHOL. O Faustus!
Then I fear that which I have long suspected,
That thou art fall'n into that damnèd art
For which they two are infamous through the world.

SEC. SCHOL. Were he a stranger, not allied to me,
The danger of his soul would make me mourn.
But, come, let us go and inform the Rector;
It may be his grave counsel may reclaim him.

FIRST SCHOL. I fear me nothing will reclaim him now.

SEC. SCHOL. Yet let us see what we can do.

[*Exeunt.*

[SCENE III]

Enter Faustus.

FAUST. Now that the gloomy shadow of the night,
Longing to view Orion's drizzling look,[1]
Leaps from th' antarctic world unto the sky,
And dims the welkin with her pitchy breath,
Faustus, begin thine incantations,
And try if devils will obey thy hest,
Seeing thou hast pray'd and sacrific'd to them.
Within this circle is Jehovah's name,
Forward and backward anagrammatiz'd,[2]
Th' abbreviated names of holy saints,
Figures of every adjunct to the heavens,
And characters of signs and erring[3] stars,
By which the spirits are enforc'd to rise:
Then fear not, Faustus, to be resolute,
And try the utmost magic can perform.

[*Thunder.*

Sint mihi dii Acherontis propitii! Valeat numen triplex Jehovae! Ignei, aërii, aquatani spiritus, salvete! Orientis princeps Belzebub, inferni ardentis monarcha, et Demogorgon, propitiamus vos, ut appareat et surgat Mephistophilis Dragon, quod tumeraris: per Jehovam, Gehennam, et consecratam aquam quam nunc spargo, signumque crucis quod nunc facio, et per vota nostra, ipse nunc surgat nobis dicatus Mephistophilis![4]

Enter Mephistophilis.

I charge thee to return, and change thy shape;
Thou art too ugly to attend on me:
Go, and return an old Franciscan friar;
That holy shape becomes a devil best.[5]

[*Exit* Mephistophilis.

I see there's virtue in my heavenly words.
Who would not be proficient in this art?
How pliant is this Mephistophilis,
Full of obedience and humility!
Such is the force of magic and my spells.

Reënter Mephistophilis *like a Franciscan friar.*

MEPH. Now, Faustus, what wouldst thou have me do?

FAUST. I charge thee wait upon me whilst I live,
To do whatever Faustus shall command,
Be it to make the moon drop from her sphere,
Or the ocean to overwhelm the world.

MEPH. I am a servant to great Lucifer,
And may not follow thee without his leave:
No more than he commands must we perform.

FAUST. Did not he charge thee to appear to me?

MEPH. No, I came hither of mine own accord.

FAUST. Did not my conjuring speeches raise thee? speak!

MEPH. That was the cause, but yet *per accidens*;[6]
For, when we hear one rack[7] the name of God,
Abjure the Scriptures and his Savior Christ,
We fly, in hope to get his glorious soul;
Nor will we come, unless he use such means
Whereby he is in danger to be damn'd.
Therefore the shortest cut for conjuring
Is stoutly to abjure all godliness,
And pray devoutly to the prince of hell.

FAUST. So Faustus hath
Already done; and holds this principle,
There is no chief but only Belzebub;
To whom Faustus doth dedicate himself.

---

[1] The rising and setting of the constellation of Orion was said to be accompanied by rain.

[2] written as an anagram

[3] wandering (i.e., planets)

[4] "May the gods of Acheron [river of pain, in Hades], be propitious to me! May the triple name of Jehovah avail! Hail, spirits of fire, air, and water! Beelzebub, prince of the east, monarch of burning hell, and Demogorgon, we propitiate you, that Mephistophilis the Dragon, *quod tumeraris* [text corrupt and untranslatable], may appear and arise: in the name of Jehovah, Gehenna, and the holy water which I now sprinkle, and the sign of the cross which I now make, and in the name of our vows, let Mephistophilis himself at our command, now arise." Beelzebub, etc., were members of the infernal hierarchy, of which Lucifer (Satan) was commonly regarded as chief. Marlowe makes Mephistophilis the servant of Lucifer, to whom he later gives the title of prince of the east, here given to Beelzebub.

[5] a Protestant fling at monasticism

[6] by accident

[7] torture (in anagrams)

This word "damnation" terrifies not me,
For I confound hell in Elysium:[1]
My ghost be with the old philosophers!
But, leaving these vain trifles of men's souls,
Tell me what is that Lucifer thy Lord?

MEPH. Arch-regent and commander of all spirits.

FAUST. Was not that Lucifer an angel once?

MEPH. Yes, Faustus, and most dearly lov'd of God.

FAUST. How comes it, then, that he is prince of devils?

MEPH. Oh, by aspiring pride and insolence;
For which God threw him from the face of heaven.

FAUST. And what are you that live with Lucifer?

MEPH. Unhappy spirits that fell with Lucifer,
Conspired against our God with Lucifer,
And are forever damn'd with Lucifer.

FAUST. Where are you damn'd?

MEPH. In hell.

FAUST. How comes it, then, that thou art out of hell?

MEPH. Why, this is hell, nor am I out of it;[2]
Think'st thou that I, that saw the face of God,
And tasted the eternal joys of heaven,
Am not tormented with ten thousand hells,
In being depriv'd of everlasting bliss?
O Faustus, leave these frivolous demands,
Which strike a terror to my fainting soul!

FAUST. What, is great Mephistophilis so passionate
For being deprivèd of the joys of heaven?
Learn thou of Faustus manly fortitude,
And scorn those joys thou never shalt possess.
Go bear these tidings to great Lucifer:
Seeing Faustus hath incurr'd eternal death
By desperate thoughts against Jove's deity,
Say, he surrenders up to him his soul,
So he will spare him four and twenty years,
Letting him live in all voluptuousness;
Having thee ever to attend on me,
To give me whatsoever I shall ask,
To tell me whatsoever I demand,
To slay mine enemies, and to aid my friends,
And always be obedient to my will.
Go, and return to mighty Lucifer,
And meet me in my study at midnight,
And then resolve me of thy master's mind.

MEPH. I will, Faustus. [*Exit.*

FAUST. Had I as many souls as there be stars,
I'd give them all for Mephistophilis.
By him I'll be great emperor of the world,
And make a bridge thorough the moving air,
To pass the ocean with a band of men;
I'll join the hills that bind the Afric shore,
And make that country continent[3] to Spain,
And both contributary to my crown:
The Emperor shall not live but by my leave,
Nor any potentate of Germany.
Now that I have obtain'd what I desir'd,
I'll live in speculation of this art,
Till Mephistophilis return again. [*Exit.*

. . . .

[SCENE V]

Faustus *discovered in his study.*

FAUST. Now, Faustus,
Must thou needs be damn'd, canst thou not be sav'd.
What boots it, then, to think on God or heaven?
Away with such vain fancies, and despair;
Despair in God, and trust in Belzebub:
Now, go not backward, Faustus, be resolute:
Why waver'st thou? Oh, something soundeth in mine ear,
"Abjure this magic, turn to God again!"
Why, he loves thee not;
The god thou serv'st is thine own appetite,
Wherein is fix'd the love of Belzebub:
To him I'll build an altar and a church,
And offer lukewarm blood of new-born babes.

Enter Good Angel *and* Evil Angel.

E. ANG. Go forward, Faustus, in that famous art.

G. ANG. Sweet Faustus, leave that execrable art.

FAUST. Contrition, prayer, repentance—what of these?

G. ANG. Oh, they are means to bring thee unto heaven.

E. ANG. Rather illusions, fruits of lunacy,
That make men foolish that do use them most.

G. ANG. Sweet Faustus, think of heaven and heavenly things.

E. ANG. No, Faustus; think of honor and of wealth. [*Exeunt* Angels.

FAUST. Wealth!
Why, the signiory[4] of Embden[5] shall be mine.

[1] count hell and Elysium the same
[2] Compare *Par. Lost*, I. 254.

[3] connected
[4] dominion
[5] a town of Hanover, Germany, formerly very prosperous

When Mephistophilis shall stand by me,
What power can hurt me? Faustus, thou art safe.
Cast no more doubts.—Mephistophilis, come,
And bring glad tidings from great Lucifer—
Is't not midnight?—Come, Mephistophilis,
Veni,[1] *veni, Mephistophile!*

Enter Mephistophilis.

Now tell me what saith Lucifer, thy lord?
MEPH. That I shall wait on Faustus whilst he lives,
So he will buy my service with his soul.
FAUST. Already Faustus hath hazarded that for thee.
MEPH. But now thou must bequeath it solemnly,
And write a deed of gift with thine own blood;
For that security craves Lucifer.
If thou deny it, I must back to hell.
FAUST. Stay, Mephistophilis, and tell me, what good will my soul do thy lord?
MEPH. Enlarge his kingdom.
FAUST. Is that the reason why he tempts us thus?
MEPH. *Solamen miseris socios habuisse doloris.*[2]
FAUST. Why, have you any pain that torture others?
MEPH. As great as have the human souls of men.
But tell me, Faustus, shall I have thy soul?
And I will be thy slave, and wait on thee,
And give thee more than thou hast wit to ask.
FAUST. Aye, Mephistophilis, I'll give it thee.
MEPH. Then, Faustus, stab thine arm courageously,
And bind thy soul, that at some certain day
Great Lucifer may claim it as his own;
And then be thou as great as Lucifer.
FAUST. [*Stabbing his arm*] Lo, Mephistophilis, for love of thee,
Faustus hath cut his arm, and with his proper blood
Assures his soul to be great Lucifer's,
Chief lord and regent of perpetual night!
View here this blood that trickles from mine arm,
And let it be propitious for my wish.
MEPH. But, Faustus,
Write it in manner of a deed of gift.
FAUST. [*Writing*] Aye, so I do. But, Mephistophilis,
My blood congeals, and I can write no more.
MEPH. I'll fetch thee fire to dissolve it straight. [*Exit.*
FAUST. What might the staying of my blood portend?
Is it unwilling I should write this bill?
Why streams it not, that I may write afresh?
Faustus gives to thee his soul: Oh, there it stay'd!
Why shouldst thou not? is not thy soul thine own?
Then write again, *Faustus gives to thee his soul.*

Reënter Mephistophilis *with the chafer*[3] *of fire.*

MEPH. See, Faustus, here is fire; set it on.
FAUST. So, now the blood begins to clear again;
Now will I make an end immediately. [*Writes.*
MEPH. What will not I do to obtain his soul? [*Aside.*
FAUST. *Consummatum est;*[4] this bill is ended,
And Faustus hath bequeath'd his soul to Lucifer.
But what is this inscription on mine arm?
Homo, fuge:[5] whither should I fly?
If unto God, he'll throw me down to hell.
My senses are deceiv'd; here's nothing writ—
Oh, yes, I see it plain; even here is writ,
Homo, fuge: yet shall not Faustus fly.
MEPH. I'll fetch him somewhat to delight his mind. [*Aside, and then exit.*

Enter Devils, *giving crowns and rich apparel to* Faustus. *They dance, and then depart.*

Reënter Mephistophilis.

FAUST. What means this show? speak, Mephistophilis.
MEPH. Nothing, Faustus, but to delight thy mind,
And let thee see what magic can perform.
FAUST. But may I raise such spirits when I please?
MEPH. Aye, Faustus, and do greater things than these.
FAUST. Then, Mephistophilis, receive this scroll,
A deed of gift of body and of soul:
But yet conditionally that thou perform
All covenants and articles between us both!
MEPH. Faustus, I swear by hell and Lucifer
To effect all promises between us both!

[1] come
[2] "It is a comfort to the miserable to have associates in their pain."

[3] vessel
[4] "It is done."
[5] "Man, flee!"

FAUST. Then hear me read it, Mephistophilis. [*Reads.*

On these conditions following. First, that Faustus may be a spirit in form and substance. Secondly, that Mephistophilis shall be his servant, and be by him commanded. Thirdly, that Mephistophilis shall do for him, and bring him whatsoever he desires. Fourthly, that he shall be in his chamber or house invisible. Lastly, that he shall appear to the said John Faustus, at all times, in what shape and form soever he please. I, John Faustus, of Wittenberg, Doctor, by these presents, do give both body and soul to Lucifer prince of the east, and his minister Mephistophilis; and furthermore grant unto them, that, four-and-twenty years being expired, and these articles above-written being inviolate, full power to fetch or carry the said John Faustus, body and soul, flesh and blood, into their habitation wheresoever. By me, John Faustus.

MEPH. Speak, Faustus, do you deliver this as your deed?
FAUST. Aye, take it, and the devil give thee good of it!
MEPH. So, now, Faustus, ask me what thou wilt.
FAUST. First I will question with thee about hell.
Tell me, where is the place that men call hell?
MEPH. Under the heavens.
FAUST. Aye, so are all things else; but whereabouts?
MEPH. Within the bowels of these elements,
Where we are tortur'd and remain forever:
Hell hath no limits, nor is circumscrib'd
In one self-place; but where we are is hell,
And where hell is, there must we ever be:
And, to be short, when all the world dissolves,
And every creature shall be purified,
All places shall be hell that are not heaven.
FAUST. I think hell's a fable.
MEPH. Aye, think so still, till experience change thy mind.
FAUST. Why, dost thou think that Faustus shall be damn'd?
MEPH. Aye, of necessity, for here's the scroll
In which thou hast given thy soul to Lucifer.
FAUST. Aye, and body, too; and what of that?
Think'st thou that Faustus is so fond to imagine
That, after this life, there is any pain?
No, these are trifles and mere old wives' tales.
MEPH. But I am an instance to prove the contrary,
For I tell thee I am damn'd and now in hell.

. . . .

Here, take this book, peruse it well:
The iterating of these lines brings gold;
The framing of this circle on the ground
Brings thunder, whirlwinds, storm, and lightning;
Pronounce this thrice devoutly to thyself,
And men in harness[1] shall appear to thee,
Ready to execute what thou command'st.
FAUST. Thanks, Mephistophilis, for this sweet book:
This will I keep as chary as my life. [*Exeunt.*

[SCENE VI]

Enter Faustus, *in his study, and* Mephistophilis.

FAUST. When I behold the heavens, then I repent,
And curse thee, wicked Mephistophilis,
Because thou hast depriv'd me of those joys.
MEPH. 'Twas thine own seeking, Faustus; thank thyself.
But think'st thou heaven is such a glorious thing?
I tell thee, Faustus, it is not half so fair
As thou, or any man that breathes on earth.
FAUST. How prov'st thou that?
MEPH. 'Twas made for man; then he's more excellent.
FAUST. If heaven was made for man, 'twas made for me:
I will renounce this magic and repent.

Enter Good Angel *and* Evil Angel.

G. ANG. Faustus, repent; yet God will pity thee.
E. ANG. Thou art a spirit; God cannot pity thee.
FAUST. Who buzzeth in mine ears I am a spirit?
Be I a devil, yet God may pity me;
Yea, God will pity me, if I repent.
E. ANG. Aye, but Faustus never shall repent.
[*Exeunt* Angels.
FAUST. My heart is harden'd, I cannot repent;
Scarce can I name salvation, faith, or heaven:
Swords, poisons, halters, and envenom'd steel
Are laid before me to despatch myself;

[1] in armor

And long ere this I should have done the deed,
Had not sweet pleasure conquer'd deep despair.
Have not I made blind Homer sing to me
Of Alexander's [1] love and Oenon's [2] death?
And hath not he, that built the walls of Thebes [3]
With ravishing sound of his melodious harp,
Made music with my Mephistophilis?
Why should I die, then, or basely despair?
I am resolv'd; Faustus shall not repent.
Come Mephistophilis, let us dispute again,
And reason of divine astrology.
Speak, are there many spheres above the moon?
Are all celestial bodies but one globe,
As is the substance of this centric [4] earth?

MEPH. As are the elements, such are the heavens,
Even from the moon unto th' empyreal orb, [5]
Mutually folded in each other's spheres,
And jointly move upon one axletree,
Whose termine [6] is term'd the world's wide pole.
Nor are the names of Saturn, Mars, or Jupiter
Feign'd, but are erring [7] stars.

FAUST. But have they all one motion, both *situ et tempore?* [8]

MEPH. All move from east to west in four-and-twenty hours upon the poles of the world; but differ in their motions upon the poles of the zodiac.

FAUST. These slender questions Wagner can decide:
Hath Mephistophilis no greater skill?
Who knows not the double motion of the planets?
That the first is finish'd in a natural day;
The second thus: Saturn in thirty years;
Jupiter in twelve; Mars in four; the Sun,
Venus, and Mercury in a year; the Moon in
twenty-eight days. These are freshmen's
questions. But tell me, hath every sphere a
dominion or *intelligentia?* [9]

MEPH. Aye.

FAUST. How many heavens or spheres are there?

MEPH. Nine; the seven planets, the firmament, and the empyreal heaven. [10]

FAUST. But is there not *coelum igneum et crystallinum?*

MEPH. No, Faustus, they be but fables.

FAUST. Resolve [11] me, then, in this one question; why are not conjunctions, oppositions, aspects, eclipses, all at one time, but in some years we have more, in some less?

MEPH. *Per inaequalem motum respectu totius.* [12]

FAUST. Well, I am answered. Now tell me who made the world?

MEPH. I will not.

FAUST. Sweet Mephistophilis, tell me.

MEPH. Move me not, Faustus.

FAUST. Villain, have not I bound thee to tell me anything?

MEPH. Aye, that is not against our kingdom; this is.
Thou art damned; think thou of hell.

FAUST. Think, Faustus, upon God that made the world.

MEPH. Remember this. [*Exit.*

FAUST. Aye, go, accursèd spirit, to ugly hell!
'Tis thou hast damn'd distressèd Faustus' soul.
Is't not too late?

Reënter Good Angel *and* Evil Angel.

E. ANG. Too late.

G. ANG. Never too late, if Faustus will repent.

E. ANG. If thou repent, devils will tear thee in pieces.

G. ANG. Repent, and they shall never raze thy skin. [*Exeunt* Angels.

FAUST. O Christ, my Savior, my Savior,
Help to save distressèd Faustus' soul!

Enter Lucifer, Belzebub, *and* Mephistophilis.

LUC. Christ cannot save thy soul, for he is just:
There's none but I have interest in the same.

FAUST. Oh, what art thou that look'st so terribly?

LUC. I am Lucifer.
And this is my companion-prince in hell.

FAUST. O Faustus, they are come to fetch thy soul!

BELZ. We are come to tell thee thou dost injure us.

LUC. Thou call'st on Christ, contrary to thy promise.

BELZ. Thou shouldst not think on God.

LUC. Think on the devil.

BELZ. And his dam, too.

---

[1] another name for Paris, whose love for Helen caused the Trojan war
[2] Wife of Paris, who took her own life; see page 616, note 1.
[3] Amphion
[4] central
[5] the sun
[6] terminal
[7] See note 3, page 170
[8] in place and time
[9] sovereign authority and intellect
[10] According to the Ptolmaic system, these were nine concentric spheres, with the earth at the center. A tenth sphere, the "fiery and crystalline heaven" mentioned in the next question, was sometimes added.
[11] free me from doubt
[12] "Because of their unequal motion with respect to the whole."

FAUST. Nor will Faustus henceforth: pardon him for this,
And Faustus vows never to look to heaven.

LUC. So shalt thou show thyself an obedient servant,
And we will highly gratify thee for it.

BELZ. Faustus, we are come from hell in person to show thee some pastime: sit down, and thou shalt behold the Seven Deadly Sins appear to thee in their own proper shapes and likeness.

FAUST. That sight will be as pleasant unto me,
As Paradise was to Adam the first day
Of his creation.

LUC. Talk not of Paradise or creation; but mark the show.—
Go, Mephistophilis, and fetch them in.

Mephistophilis *brings in the* Seven Deadly Sins.

BELZ. Now, Faustus, question them of their names and dispositions.

FAUST. That shall I soon.—What art thou, the first?

PRIDE. I am Pride. I disdain to have any parents. . . . But, fie, what a smell is here? I'll not speak a word more for a king's ransom, unless the ground be perfumed, and covered with cloth of arras.

FAUST. Thou art a proud knave, indeed.—
What art thou, the second?

COVET. I am Covetousness, begotten of an old churl, in a leather bag: and, might I now obtain my wish, this house, you, and all, should turn to gold, that I might lock you safe into my chest: O my sweet gold!

FAUST. And what art thou, the third?

ENVY. I am Envy, begotten of a chimney-sweeper and an oyster-wife. I cannot read, and therefore wish all books burned. I am lean with seeing others eat. Oh, that there would come a famine over all the world, that all might die, and I live alone! then thou shouldst see how fat I'd be. But must thou sit, and I stand? Come down with a vengeance!

FAUST. Out, envious wretch!—But what art thou, the fourth?

WRATH. I am Wrath. I had neither father nor mother: I leapt out of a lion's mouth when I was scarce an hour old; and ever since have run up and down the world with this case of rapiers, wounding myself when I could get none to fight withal. I was born in hell; and look to it, for some of you shall be [1] my father.

[1] must be

FAUST. And what art thou, the fifth?

GLUT. I am Gluttony. My parents are all dead and the devil a penny have they left me, but a small pension, and that buys me thirty meals a day and ten bevers [2]—a small trifle to suffice nature. I come of a royal pedigree: my father was a Gammon of Bacon, and my mother was a Hogshead of Claret-wine; my godfathers were these, Peter Pickled-herring and Martin Martlemas-beef; [3] and my godmother, Oh, she was an ancient gentlewoman; her name was Margery March-beer. [4] Now, Faustus, thou hast heard all my progeny; [5] wilt thou bid me to supper?

FAUST. Not I.

GLUT. Then the devil choke thee!

FAUST. Choke thyself, glutton!—What art thou, the sixth?

SLOTH. Heigho! I am Sloth. I was begotten on a sunny bank. Heigho! I'll not speak a word more for a king's ransom.

. . . .

LUC. Away to hell, away! On, piper!

[*Exeunt the* Sins.

FAUST. Oh, how this sight doth delight my soul!

LUC. Tut, Faustus, in hell is all manner of delight.

FAUST. Oh, might I see hell, and return again safe,
How happy were I then!

LUC. Faustus, thou shalt; at midnight I will send for thee.
Meanwhile peruse this book and view it thoroughly,
And thou shalt turn thyself into what shape thou wilt.

FAUST. Thanks, mighty Lucifer!
This will I keep as chary [6] as my life.

LUC. Now Faustus, farewell.

FAUST. Farewell, great Lucifer.

[*Exeunt* Lucifer *and* Belzebub.

Come, Mephistophilis. [*Exeunt.*

[2] luncheons
[3] beef cured at Martlemas (Nov. 11)
[4] choice beer brewed in March
[5] ancestry
[6] carefully

[In the succeeding scenes are given, partly in relation by the Chorus, partly in action, Faustus' further adventures in the enjoyment of his new power, including a chariot-journey through the stellar heavens, and a ride on the back of a dragon to Rome, where, in disguise, or altogether invisible, he takes huge delight in playing pranks on the Pope and his Cardinals. But at length the twenty-four years of the compact draw to an end.]

[Scene XIII]

Thunder and lightning. Enter Devils *with covered dishes;* Mephistophilis *leads them into* Faustus' *study, then enter* Wagner.

Wag. I think my master means to die shortly; he has made his will, and given me his wealth, his house, his goods, and store of golden plate, besides two thousand ducats ready-coined. I wonder what he means: if death were nigh, he would not frolic thus. He's now at supper with the scholars, where there's such belly-cheer as Wagner in his life ne'er saw the like: and, see where they come! be-like the feast is ended.[1] [*Exit.*

Enter Faustus, Mephistophilis, *and two or three* Scholars

First Schol. Master Doctor Faustus, since our conference about fair ladies, which[2] was the beautifulest in all the world, we have determined with ourselves that Helen of Greece was the admirablest lady that ever lived: therefore, Master Doctor, if you will do us so much favor as to let us see that peerless dame of Greece, whom all the world admires for majesty, we should think ourselves much beholding unto you.

Faust. Gentlemen,
For that[3] I know your friendship is unfeign'd,
It is not Faustus' custom to deny
The just request of those that wish him well:
You shall behold that peerless dame of Greece,
No otherwise for pomp or majesty
Than when Sir Paris cross'd the seas with her
And brought the spoils to rich Dardania.
Be silent, then, for danger is in words.

Music sounds. Mephistophilis *brings in* Helen; *she passeth over the stage.*

Sec. Schol. Was this fair Helen, whose admirèd worth
Made Greece with ten years' war afflict poor Troy?

Third Schol. Too simple is my wit to tell her worth,
Whom all the world admires for majesty.

First Schol. Now we have seen the pride of Nature's work,
We'll take our leaves: and, for this blessèd sight,
Happy and blest be Faustus evermore!

Faust. Gentlemen, farewell: the same wish I to you. [*Exeunt Scholars*

[1] This speech is almost regular blank verse and was probably written as such.
[2] as to which [3] because

Enter an Old Man.

Old Man. O gentle Faustus, leave this damnèd art,
This magic, that will charm thy soul to hell,
And quite bereave thee of salvation!
Though thou hast now offended like a man,
Do not presèver in it like a devil:
Yet, yet thou hast an amiable soul,
If sin by custom grow not into nature;
Then, Faustus, will repentance come too late;
Then thou art banish'd from the sight of heaven:
No mortal can express the pains of hell.
It may be, this my exhortation
Seems harsh and all unpleasant: let it not;
For, gentle son, I speak it not in wrath,
Or envy of thee, but in tender love,
And pity of thy future misery;
And so have hope that this my kind rebuke,
Checking thy body, may amend thy soul.

Faust. Where art thou, Faustus? wretch, what hast thou done?
Hell claims his right, and with a roaring voice
Says, "Faustus, come; thine hour is almost come";
And Faustus now will come to do thee right.

[Mephistophilis *gives him a dagger.*

Old Man. O stay, good Faustus, stay thy desperate steps!
I see an angel hover o'er thy head,
And, with a vial full of precious grace,
Offers to pour the same into thy soul;
Then call for mercy, and avoid despair.

Faust. O friend, I feel
Thy words to comfort my distressèd soul!
Leave me a while to ponder on my sins.

Old Man. Faustus, I leave thee; but with grief of heart,
Fearing the enemy of thy hapless soul. [*Exit.*

Faust. Accursèd Faustus, wretch, what hast thou done?
I do repent; and yet I do despair:
Hell strives with grace for conquest in my breast:
What shall I do to shun the snares of death?

Meph. Thou traitor, Faustus, I arrest thy soul
For disobedience to my sovereign lord:
Revolt, or I'll in piece-meal tear thy flesh.

Faust. I do repent I e'er offended him.
Sweet Mephistophilis, entreat thy lord
To pardon my unjust presumption,
And with my blood again I will confirm
The former vow I made to Lucifer.

Meph. Do it, then, Faustus, with unfeignèd heart,
Lest greater dangers do attend thy drift.

FAUST. Torment, sweet friend, that base and aged man,
That durst dissuade me from thy Lucifer,
With greatest torments that our hell affords.
MEPH. His faith is great; I cannot touch his soul;
But what I may afflict his body with
I will attempt, which is but little worth.
FAUST. One thing, good servant, let me crave of thee,
To glut the longing of my heart's desire—
That I may have unto my paramor
That heavenly Helen which I saw of late,
Whose sweet embraces may extinguish clean
Those thoughts that do dissuade me from my vow,
And keep my oath I made to Lucifer.
MEPH. This, or what else my Faustus shall desire,
Shall be perform'd in twinkling of an eye.

Reënter Helen, *passing over the stage between two Cupids.*

FAUST. Was this the face that launch'd a thousand ships,
And burnt the topless towers of Ilium?[1]
Sweet Helen, make me immortal with a kiss. [*Kisses her.*
Her lips suck forth my soul; see, where it flies.
Come, Helen, come, give me my soul again.
Here will I dwell, for heaven is in these lips,
And all is dross that is not Helena.
I will be Paris, and for love of thee,
Instead of Troy, shall Wittenberg be sack'd;
And I will combat with weak Menelaus,
And wear thy colors on my plumèd crest;
Yea, I will wound Achilles in the heel,
And then return to Helen for a kiss.
Oh, thou art fairer than the evening air
Clad in the beauty of a thousand stars;
Brighter art thou than flaming Jupiter
When he appear'd to hapless Semele;
More lovely than the monarch of the sky
In wanton Arethusa's azur'd arms;
And none but thou shalt be my paramor!
[*Exeunt.*

[SCENE XIV]

Thunder. Enter Lucifer, Belzebub, *and* Mephistophilis.

LUC. Thus from infernal Dis[2] do we ascend
To view the subjects of our monarchy,
Those souls which sin seals the black sons of hell;
'Mong which, as chief, Faustus, we come to thee,
Bringing with us lasting damnation
To wait upon thy soul; the time is come
Which makes it forfeit.
MEPH. And, this gloomy night,
Here, in this room, will wretched Faustus be.
BELZ. And here we'll stay,
To mark him how he doth demean himself.
MEPH. How should he but in desperate lunacy?
Fond worldling, now his heart-blood dries with grief;
His conscience kills it; and his laboring brain
Begets a world of idle fantasies
To over-reach the devil; but all in vain;
His store of pleasures must be sauc'd with pain.
He and his servant Wagner are at hand;
Both come from drawing Faustus' latest will.
See, where they come!

Enter Faustus *and* Wagner.

FAUST. Say, Wagner, thou hast perus'd my will,
How dost thou like it?
WAG. Sir, so wondrous well,
As in all humble duty I do yield
My life and lasting service for your love.
FAUST. Gramercy,[3] Wagner.

Enter Scholars.

Welcome, gentlemen.
[*Exit* Wagner.

FIRST SCHOL. Now, worthy Faustus, methinks your looks are chang'd.
FAUST. O gentlemen!
SEC. SCHOL. What ails Faustus?
FAUST. Ah, my sweet chamber-fellow, had I lived with thee, then had I lived still! but now must die eternally. Look, sirs, comes he not? comes he not?
FIRST SCHOL. O my dear Faustus, what imports this fear?
SEC. SCHOL. Is all our pleasure turn'd to melancholy?
THIRD SCHOL. He is not well with being over-solitary.
SEC. SCHOL. If it be so, we'll have physicians,
And Faustus shall be cur'd.
THIRD SCHOL. 'Tis but a surfeit, sir; fear nothing.
FAUST. A surfeit of deadly sin, that hath damned both body and soul.
SEC. SCHOL. Yet, Faustus, look up to heaven, and remember mercy is infinite.

[1] unsurpassable towers of Troy (These two lines have become a very famous quotation.)
[2] another name for Pluto and his kingdom
[3] great thanks

FAUST. But Faustus' offense can ne'er be pardoned: the serpent that tempted Eve may be saved, but not Faustus. O gentlemen, hear me with patience, and tremble not at my speeches! Though my heart pant and quiver to remember that I have been a student here these thirty years, Oh, would I had never seen Wittenberg, never read book! and what wonders I have done, all Germany can witness, yea, all the world; for which Faustus hath lost both Germany and the world, yea, heaven itself, heaven, the seat of God, the throne of the blessed, the kingdom of joy; and must remain in hell forever, hell, O hell, forever! Sweet friends, what shall become of Faustus, being in hell forever?

SEC. SCHOL. Yet, Faustus, call on God.

FAUST. On God, whom Faustus hath abjured! on God, whom Faustus hath blasphemed! O my God, I would weep! but the devil draws in my tears. Gush forth blood, instead of tears! yea, life and soul! Oh, he stays my tongue! I would lift up my hands; but see they hold 'em, they hold 'em!

ALL. Who, Faustus?

FAUST. Why, Lucifer and Mephistophilis. O gentlemen, I gave them my soul for my cunning!

ALL. Oh, God forbid!

FAUST. God forbade it, indeed; but Faustus hath done it: for the vain pleasure of four-and-twenty years hath Faustus lost eternal joy and felicity. I writ them a bill[1] with mine own blood: the date is expired; this is the time, and he will fetch me.

FIRST SCHOL. Why did not Faustus tell us of this before, that divines might have prayed for thee?

FAUST. Oft have I thought to have done so; but the devil threatened to tear me in pieces, if I named God, to fetch me body and soul, if I once gave ear to divinity: and now 'tis too late. Gentlemen, away, lest you perish with me.

SEC. SCHOL. Oh, what may we do to save Faustus?

FAUST. Talk not of me, but save yourselves, and depart.

THIRD SCHOL. God will strengthen me; I will stay with Faustus.

FIRST SCHOL. Tempt not God, sweet friend; but let us into the next room, and pray for him.

FAUST. Aye, pray for me, pray for me; and what noise soever you hear, come not unto me, for nothing can rescue me.

SEC. SCHOL. Pray thou, and we will pray that God may have mercy upon thee.

FAUST. Gentlemen, farewell: if I live till morning, I'll visit you; if not, Faustus is gone to hell.

ALL. Faustus, farewell. [*Exeunt* Scholars.

MEPH. Aye, Faustus, now thou hast no hope of heaven;
Therefore despair; think only upon hell,
For that must be thy mansion, there to dwell.

FAUST. O thou bewitching fiend, 'twas thy temptation
Hath robb'd me of eternal happiness!

MEPH. I do confess it, Faustus, and rejoice:
'Twas I that, when thou wert i' the way to heaven,
Damm'd up thy passage; when thou took'st the book
To view the Scriptures, then I turn'd the leaves,
And led thine eye.
What, weep'st thou? 'tis too late; despair! Farewell!
Fools that will laugh on earth must weep in hell. [*Exit.*

Enter Good Angel *and* Evil Angel *at several doors.*

G. ANG. O Faustus, if thou hadst given ear to me,
Innumerable joys had follow'd thee!
But thou didst love the world.

E. ANG. Gave ear to me,
And now must taste hell-pains perpetually.

G. ANG. Oh, what will all thy riches, pleasures, pomps,
Avail thee now?

E. ANG. Nothing, but vex thee more,
To want in hell, that had on earth such store.

G. ANG. Oh, thou has lost celestial happiness,
Pleasures unspeakable, bliss without end.
Hadst thou affected[2] sweet divinity,
Hell or the devil had had no power on thee:
Hadst thou kept on that way, Faustus, behold,
[*Music, while a throne descends.*
In what resplendent glory thou hadst sit
In yonder throne, like those bright-shining saints,
And triump'd over hell! That hast thou lost;
And now, poor soul, must thy good angel leave thee:
The jaws of hell are open to receive thee.
[*Exit. The throne ascends.*

[1] bond

[2] applied yourself to

E. ANG. Now, Faustus, let thine eyes with horror stare [*Hell is discovered.*
Into that vast perpetual torture-house:
There are the Furies tossing damnèd souls
On burning forks; there bodies boil in lead;
There are live quarters broiling on the coals,
That ne'er can die; this ever-burning chair
Is for o'er-tortur'd souls to rest them in;
These that are fed with sops [1] of flaming fire
Were gluttons, and lov'd only delicates,
And laugh'd to see the poor starve at their gates:
But yet all these are nothing; thou shalt see
Ten thousand tortures that more horrid be.

FAUST. Oh, I have seen enough to torture me!

E. ANG. Nay, thou must feel them, taste the smart of all:
He that loves pleasure must for pleasure fall:
And so I leave thee, Faustus, till anon;
Then wilt thou tumble in confusion.
[*Exit. Hell disappears. The clock strikes eleven.*

FAUST. O Faustus!
Now hast thou but one bare hour to live,
And then thou must be damn'd perpetually!
Stand still, you ever-moving spheres of heaven,
That time may cease, and midnight never come;
Fair Nature's eye, rise, rise again, and make
Perpetual day; or let this hour be but
A year, a month, a week, a natural day,
That Faustus may repent and save his soul!
O lente, lente currite, noctis equi! [2]
The stars move still, time runs, the clock will strike,
The devil will come, and Faustus must be damn'd.
Oh, I'll leap up to heaven!—Who pulls me down?—
See, where Christ's blood streams in the firmament!
One drop of blood will save me; O my Christ!—
Rend not my heart for naming of my Christ;
Yet will I call on him; O spare me, Lucifer!—
Where is it now? 'tis gone:
And see, a threatening arm, an angry brow!
Mountains and hills, come, come, and fall on me,
And hide me from the heavy wrath of heaven!
No!
Then will I headlong run into the earth:
Gape, earth! Oh, no, it will not harbor me!
You stars that reign'd at my nativity,
Whose influence hath allotted death and hell,
Now draw up Faustus, like a foggy mist,
Into the entrails of yon laboring cloud,
That, when you vomit forth into the air,
My limbs may issue from your smoky mouths;
But let my soul mount and ascend to heaven!
[*The clock strikes the half-hour.*
Oh, half the hour is past! 'twill all be past anon.
Oh, if my soul must suffer for my sin,
Impose some end to my incessant pain;
Let Faustus live in hell a thousand years,
A hundred thousand, and at last be sav'd!
No end is limited to damnèd souls.
Why wert thou not a creature wanting soul?
Or why is this immortal that thou hast?
Oh, Pythagoras' metempsychosis, [3] were that true,
This soul should fly from me, and I be chang'd
Into some brutish beast! all beasts are happy,
For, when they die,
Their souls are soon dissolv'd in elements;
But mine must live, still to be plagu'd in hell.
Curs'd be the parents that engender'd me!
No, Faustus, curse thyself, curse Lucifer
That hath depriv'd thee of the joys of heaven.
[*The clock strikes twelve.*
It strikes, it strikes! Now, body, turn to air,
Or Lucifer will bear thee quick to hell!
O soul, be chang'd into small water-drops,
And fall into the ocean, ne'er be found!

Thunder. Enter Devils.

Oh, mercy, heaven! look not so fierce on me!
Adders and serpents, let me breathe a while!
Ugly hell, gape not! come not, Lucifer!
I'll burn my books!—O Mephistophilis!
[*Exeunt* Devils *with* Faustus.

[SCENE XV]

Enter Scholars.

FIRST SCHOL. Come, gentlemen, let us go visit Faustus,
For such a dreadful night was never seen;
Since first the world's creation did begin,
Such fearful shrieks and cries were never heard:
Pray heaven the doctor have escap'd the danger.

SEC. SCHOL. Oh, help us, heaven! see, here are Faustus' limbs,
All torn asunder by the hand of death!

[1] morsels

[2] "O slowly, slowly run, ye steeds of night."

[3] the theory held by Pythagoras, the Greek philosopher, that the soul, at death, passes into another body

THIRD SCHOL. The devils whom Faustus serv'd have torn him thus;
For, twixt the hours of twelve and one, methought
I heard him shriek and call aloud for help;
At which self time the house seem'd all on fire
With dreadful horror of these damnèd fiends.
SEC. SCHOL. Well, gentlemen, though Faustus' end be such
As every Christian heart laments to think on,
Yet, for he was a scholar once admir'd
For wondrous knowledge in our German schools,
We'll give his mangled limbs due burial;
And all the students, cloth'd in mourning black,
Shall wait upon his heavy[1] funeral.
[*Exeunt.*

Enter Chorus.

CHOR. Cut is the branch that might have grown full straight,
And burnèd is Apollo's laurel-bough,[2]
That sometime grew within this learnèd man.
Faustus is gone: regard his hellish fall,
Whose fiendful fortune may exhort the wise
Only to wonder at unlawful things,
Whose deepness doth entice such forward wits
To practice more than heavenly power permits. [*Exeunt.*
Terminat hora diem; terminat auctor opus.[3]

1604, 1616

WILLIAM SHAKESPEARE
1564-1616

The lack of biographical detail is a matter of regret but is of no real importance as far as Shakespeare and his place in the world of literature are concerned; no additional knowledge could enhance his supreme genius or add to the universal tribute paid to it:

"... the magic of that name
Defies the scythe of time, the torch of flame."
—Byron[4]

Recently-discovered documents, however, some of them bearing the poet's signature, have added to the main facts already known, which are these.

[1] sad
[2] The laurel was sacred to Apollo. Symbolic here for distinction in science or poetry.
[3] "The hour ends the day, the author ends the work."
[4] See also the poem by Jonson, p. 209

William Shakespeare was born of middle-class parents in Stratford-on-Avon, and probably attended the grammar school, which was a good one. He was married at eighteen to Anne Hathaway, a yeoman's daughter eight years his senior, and about 1586, possibly on account of a deer-poaching episode in the park of Sir Thomas Lucy, left Stratford. He was in London the following year, connected with the theater in various capacities, first as actor and hack playwright, then as dramatist and shareholder, prospering greatly and able by 1597 to gratify ambition by buying New Place, the largest house in Stratford. Here he retired to spend the last ten years of his life, dying April 23, supposedly his birthday.

His first printed work was non-dramatic—*Venus and Adonis,* 1593, and *Lucrece,* 1594, long love poems following the popular vogue; the *Sonnets,* too, may have been written early, though not published until 1609. (See p. 156.) His plays may be divided broadly into four groups: first, early plays, *A Midsummer Night's Dream, Romeo and Juliet, Richard III,* and several English chronicle plays; second, plays written after the age of thirty, toward the end of the century, chiefly romantic comedies like *The Merchant of Venice, As You Like It,* and *Twelfth Night;* third, plays of marked maturity belonging to the early sixteen-hundreds, the tragedies of *Julius Caesar, Hamlet, Othello, Macbeth, Lear,* etc.; fourth, late plays of a strangely serene temper, free fancy, and magic touch, especially *Cymbeline, The Winter's Tale,* and *The Tempest.* Shakespeare's thirty-six dramas were not published in a body until the famous "first folio" of 1623.

There is no phase of the drama in which Shakespeare does not excel: he has knowledge of human nature and its presentation; a humor, springing from a tolerant sympathy embracing all the follies and inconsistencies of men, which colors his darkest tragedies as well as his comedies; and the qualities essential to a poet—an imaginative grasp of reality and truth, and a musical interpretation of them. As M. Suddard says: "Shakespeare seems able to pass through all the phases of feeling, without allowing any one phase to be perturbed by the memory of another. . . . . Moreover, he divines beneath the reality an inner and invisible life, deeper causes of outer effects. . . . . His plays have unities, not of time, place, and action, but of psychology, logic, and ethics."

Clark and Wright's Cambridge Shakespeare, 9 vols., is most useful for comprehensive textual and critical study; the Cambridge single volume edition is also excellent; individual plays in good texts are the Temple Shakespeare, Rolfe, Hudson. The most authoritative recent biographies are those by Sir Sidney Lee, new ed., rev. 1916, and by J. Q. Adams, 1923. For critical material we have E. Dowden's *Shakespeare Primer;* A. C. Bradley's *Shakespearean Tragedy;* A. C. Swinburne's *A Study of Shakespeare; Shakespeare's England,* ed. by S. Lee, 2 vols., 1916, containing valuable studies of the period; R. G. Moulton's *Shakespeare as*

From a painting by P. Kramen

WILLIAM SHAKESPEARE

a Dramatic Artist, 1888; essays by Carlyle (HHW), Woodberry (GW;LE), Rossetti (*Lives*), Coleridge, Dowden (TS), Hazlitt (EP), Lowell (AMB), More (Shel. 2), Schofield. Interesting recent material appears in C. W. Wallace, "New Shakespeare Discoveries," *Harp.* 120:489-510; M. Suddard, "Ben Jonson and Shakespeare," *Contemp.* 99:316-28; E. A. Robinson, "Ben Jonson Entertains a Man from Stratford" (in *The Man Against the Sky*); Alfred Noyes, *Tales of the Mermaid Tavern;* G. B. Shaw, "Dark Lady of the Sonnets" (in *Misalliance*).

THE TEMPEST

The Tempest is one of Shakespeare's maturest productions, and is commonly assigned to the year 1610 or 1611. It may have had its origin in the spur given to the imagination by the widespread interest in the newly discovered Bermudas, where, in the year 1609, the vessel of Sir George Somers was wrecked. A romantic play, with elements of both tragedy and comedy, and an included masque (if that be Shakespeare's), and with the characters ranging from a brutish monster through the lowest and highest ranks of men to a creature of the spirit world, it contains perhaps in itself the best epitome of its creator's varied powers.

"The persons in this play," writes Edward Dowden, "while remaining real and living, are conceived in a more abstract way, more as types, than those in any other work of Shakespeare. Prospero is the highest wisdom and moral attainment; Gonzalo is humorous common-sense incarnated; all that is meanest and most despicable appears in the wretched conspirators; Miranda, whose name seems to suggest wonder, is almost an elemental being, framed in the purest and simplest type of womanhood, yet made substantial by contrast with Ariel, who is an unbodied joy, too much a creature of light and air to know human affection or human sorrow; Caliban (the name formed from cannibal) stands at the other extreme, with all the elements in him—appetites, intellect, even imagination—out of which man emerges into early civilization, but with a moral nature that is still gross and malignant. Over all presides Prospero like a providence. And the spirit of reconciliation, of forgiveness, harmonizing the contentions of men, appears in *The Tempest* in the same noble manner that it appears in *The Winter's Tale, Cymbeline,* and *Henry VIII.*"

"Nowhere," says Sidney Lee, "did Shakespeare give rein to his imagination with more imposing effect than in *The Tempest.* As in *A Midsummer Night's Dream,* magical or supernatural agencies are the mainsprings of the plot. But the tone is marked at all points by a solemnity and profundity of thought and sentiment which are lacking in the early comedy. . . . In Prospero, the guiding providence of the romance, who resigns his magic power in the closing scene, traces have been sought of the lineaments of the dramatist himself, who in this play probably bade farewell to the enchanted work of his life."

THE TEMPEST

DRAMATIS PERSONAE

ALONSO, King of Naples
SEBASTIAN, his brother
PROSPERO, the right Duke of Milan
ANTONIO, his brother, the usurping Duke of Milan
FERDINAND, son to the King of Naples
GONZALO, an honest old Counselor
ADRIAN, FRANCISCO } Lords
CALIBAN, a savage and deformed Slave
TRINCULO, a Jester
STEPHANO, a drunken Butler
Master of a ship. Boatswain. Mariners
MIRANDA, daughter to Prospero
ARIEL, an airy Spirit
IRIS, CERES, JUNO, Nymphs, Reapers } presented by Spirits
Other Spirits attending on Prospero

ACT I

SCENE I

On a ship at sea: a tempestuous noise of thunder and lightning heard.

Enter a SHIP-MASTER *and a* BOATSWAIN.

MAST. Boatswain!

BOATS. Here, master; what cheer?

MAST. Good,[1] speak to the mariners. Fall to't, yarely,[2] or we run ourselves aground; bestir, bestir. [*Exit.*

Enter MARINERS.

BOATS. Heigh, my hearts! cheerly, cheerly, my hearts! yare, yare! Take in the topsail. Tend[3] to the master's whistle. Blow, till thou burst thy wind,[4] if room enough![5]

Enter ALONSO, SEBASTIAN, ANTONIO, FERDINAND, GONZALO, *and others.*

ALON. Good boatswain, have care. Where's the master? Play the men.

BOATS. I pray now, keep below.

ANT. Where is the master, boatswain?

BOATS. Do you not hear him? You mar our labor; keep your cabins; you do assist the storm.

[1] good fellow [2] smartly [3] attend
[4] Cf. *Lear,* III, ii, 1; *Pericles,* III, i, 44.
[5] so long as we have sea-room

GON. Nay, good, be patient.

BOATS. When the sea is. Hence! What cares [1] these roarers for the name of king? To cabin. Silence! Trouble us not.

GON. Good, yet remember whom thou hast aboard.

BOATS. None that I more love than myself. You are a counselor; if you can command these elements to silence, and work the peace of the present, [2] we will not hand [3] a rope more; use your authority. If you cannot, give thanks you have lived so long, and make yourself ready in your cabin for the mischance of the hour, if it so hap. Cheerly, good hearts! Out of our way, I say. [*Exit.*

GON. I have great comfort from this fellow; methinks he hath no drowning mark upon him; his complexion is perfect gallows. Stand fast, good Fate, to his hanging; make the rope of his destiny our cable, for our own doth little advantage. [4] If he be not born to be hanged, our case is miserable. [*Exeunt.*

Reënter BOATSWAIN.

Boats. Down with the topmast! yare! lower, lower! Bring her to try [5] with main-course. [6] [*A cry within.*] A plague upon this howling! they are louder than the weather or our office.

Reënter SEBASTIAN, ANTONIO, *and* GONZALO.

Yet again! what do you here? Shall we give o'er, and drown? Have you a mind to sink?

SEB. A pox o' your throat, you bawling, blasphemous, incharitable dog!

BOATS. Work you, then.

ANT. Hang, cur! Hang, you insolent noisemaker. We are less afraid to be drowned than thou art.

GON. I'll warrant him for [7] drowning; though the ship were no stronger than a nutshell.

BOATS. Lay her a-hold, [5] a-hold! Set her two courses off to sea again; lay her off.

Enter MARINERS, *wet.*

MARINERS. All lost! to prayers, to prayers! all lost!

BOATS. What, must our mouths be cold?

GON. The king and prince at prayers. Let's assist them,
For our case is as theirs.

SEB. I'm out of patience.

ANT. We are merely [8] cheated of our lives by drunkards;
This wide-chapped rascal—would thou mightst lie drowning.
The washing of ten tides! [9]

GON. He'll be hanged yet,
Though every drop of water swear against it,
And gape at widest to glut him.

[*A confused noise within:* "Mercy on us!"—
"We split, we split!"—"Farewell my wife and children!"—
"Farewell, brother!"—"We split, we split, we split!"]

ANT. Let's all sink with the king.

SEB. Let's take leave of him. [10]
[*Exeunt* ANT. *and* SEB.

GON. Now would I give a thousand furlongs of sea for an acre of barren ground, long heath, brown furze, anything. The wills above be done! but I would fain die a dry death. [*Exeunt.*

SCENE II

The island. Before PROSPERO'S *cell.*

Enter PROSPERO *and* MIRANDA.

MIR. If by your art, [11] my dearest father, you have
Put the wild waters in this roar, allay them.
The sky, it seems, would pour down stinking pitch,
But that the sea, mounting to the welkin's cheek,
Dashes the fire out. Oh, I have suffered
With those that I saw suffer! A brave [12] vessel,
Who had, no doubt, some noble creature [13] in her,
Dashed all to pieces. Oh, the cry did knock
Against my very heart! Poor souls, they perished!
Had I been any god of power, I would
Have sunk the sea within the earth, or ere [14]
It should the good ship so have swallowed and
The fraughting [15] souls within her.

PROS. Be collected;
No more amazement; tell your piteous heart
There's no harm done.

MIR. Oh, woe the day!

PROS. No harm.
I have done nothing but in care of thee,

[1] Such grammatical freedom is not unusual in Shakespeare and other writers of his time; compare the second line of Ariel's song, I. ii. 397, and the fourth line of "Hark, hark!" *Cymbeline,* II. iii. 24. The "roarers" here are of course the waves, but as the term was also applied to "bullies" we get a lively picture of their rudeness as well as their noise.

[2] Supply "moment."

[3] touch

[4] help (verb)

[5] close to the wind

[6] main sail

[7] against

[8] simply, absolutely

[9] Pirates were hanged at low-water mark and left during the washing of three tides.

[10] bid him farewell

[11] magic (Note the respectful "you" in her address, the familiar "thou" in her father's.)

[12] splendid

[13] collective for "creatures"

[14] sooner than

[15] freight-composing

Of thee, my dear one, thee, my daughter, who
Art ignorant of what thou art, nought knowing
Of whence I am, nor that I am more better
Than Prospero, master of a full poor cell
And thy no greater father.

MIR. More to know
Did never meddle[1] with my thoughts.

PROS. 'Tis time
I should inform thee further. Lend thy hand,
And pluck my magic garment from me. So;
[*Lays down his mantle.*[2]
Lie there, my art. Wipe thou thine eyes; have comfort.
The direful spectacle of the wreck, which touched
The very virtue of compassion in thee,
I have with such provision[3] in mine art
So safely ordered, that there is no soul,
No, not so much perdition as an hair
Betid to any creature in the vessel
Which thou heard'st cry, which thou saw'st sink. Sit down;
For thou must now know further.

MIR. You have often
Begun to tell me what I am; but stopped,
And left me to a bootless inquisition,[4]
Concluding "Stay: not yet."

PROS. The hour's now come;
The very minute bids thee ope thine ear;
Obey, and be attentive. Canst thou remember
A time before we came unto this cell?
I do not think thou canst, for then thou wast not
Out[5] three years old.

MIR. Certainly, sir, I can.

PROS. By what? by any other house or person?
Of anything the image tell me, that
Hath kept with thy remembrance.

MIR. 'Tis far off,
And rather like a dream than an assurance
That my remembrance warrants. Had I not
Four or five women once that tended me?

PROS. Thou hadst, and more, Miranda. But how is it
That this lives in thy mind? What seest thou else
In the dark backward and abysm of time?
If thou remember'st aught ere thou camest here,
How thou camest here thou mayst.

MIR. But that I do not.

PROS. Twelve years since, Miranda, twelve years since,
Thy father was the Duke of Milan, and
A prince of power.

MIR. Sir, are not you my father?

PROS. Thy mother was a piece of virtue, and
She said thou wast my daughter; and thy father
Was Duke of Milan; and his only heir
A princess, no worse issued.[6]

MIR. O the heavens!
What foul play had we, that we came from thence?
Or blessed was't we did?

PROS. Both, both, my girl:
By foul play, as thou say'st, were we heaved thence;
But blessedly holp hither.

MIR. Oh, my heart bleeds
To think o' the teen[7] that I have turned you to,
Which is from[8] my remembrance! Please you, further.

PROS. My brother, and thy uncle, called Antonio—
I pray thee, mark me,—that a brother should
Be so perfidious!—he whom, next thyself,
Of all the world I loved, and to him put
The manage of my state; as at that time
Through all the signories[9] it was the first,
And Prospero the prime duke, being so reputed
In dignity, and for the liberal arts
Without a parallel; those being all my study,
The government I cast upon my brother,
And to my state grew stranger, being transported
And rapt in secret studies. Thy false uncle—
Dost thou attend me?

MIR. Sir, most heedfully.

PROS. Being once perfected how to grant suits,
How to deny them, who to advance, and who
To trash[10] for over-topping,[11] new created
The creatures[12] that were mine, I say, or changed 'em,
Or else new formed 'em; having both the key
Of officer and office, set all hearts i' the state
To what tune pleased his ear; that now he was
The ivy which had hid my princely trunk,
And sucked my verdure out on't.[13] Thou attend'st not.

MIR. Oh, good sir, I do.

PROS. I pray thee, mark me.
I, thus neglecting worldly ends, all dedicated
To closeness[14] and the bettering of my mind

[1] mingle
[2] Prospero wears the mantle only in his capacity as magician.
[3] foresight
[4] vain inquiry
[5] fully
[6] descended
[7] grief
[8] out of
[9] seignories, lordships
[10] check (said of hounds; or it may be a figure from gardening—to "top," lop)
[11] outrunning
[12] followers, lords
[13] out of it
[14] seclusion

With that which, but[1] my being so retired,
O'er-prized all popular rate,[2] in my false brother
Awaked an evil nature; and my trust,
Like a good parent, did beget of him
A falsehood in its contrary, as great
As my trust was; which had indeed no limit,
A confidence sans[3] bound. He being thus lorded,
Not only with what my revenue[4] yielded,
But what my power might else exact, like one
Who having into truth, by telling of it,
Made such a sinner of his memory,
To credit his own lie,[5] he did believe
He was indeed the duke; out o' the[6] substitution,
And executing the outward face of royalty,
With all prerogative—hence his ambition growing—
Dost thou hear?

MIR. Your tale, sir, would cure deafness.

PROS. To have no screen between this part he played
And him he played it for, he needs will be
Absolute Milan.[7] Me, poor man, my library
Was dukedom large enough; of temporal royalties
He thinks me now incapable; confederates,
So dry he was for sway, wi' the King of Naples
To give him annual tribute, do him homage,
Subject his coronet to his crown, and bend
The dukedom, yet unbowed—alas, poor Milan!—
To most ignoble stooping.

MIR. O the heavens!

PROS. Mark his condition,[8] and the event;[9] then tell me
If this might be a brother.

MIR. I should sin
To think but[10] nobly of my grandmother;
Good wombs have borne bad sons.

PROS. Now the condition.
This King of Naples, being an enemy
To me inveterate, hearkens my brother's suit;
Which was, that he, in lieu o' the premises[11]
Of homage and I know not how much tribute,
Should presently[12] extirpate me and mine
Out of the dukedom, and confer fair Milan,
With all the honors, on my brother. Whereon,
A treacherous army levied, one midnight
Fated to the purpose, did Antonio open
The gates of Milan; and, i' the dead of darkness,
The ministers for the purpose hurried thence
Me and thy crying self.

MIR. Alack, for pity!
I, not remembering how I cried out then,
Will cry it o'er again; it is a hint
That wrings mine eyes to't.

PROS. Hear a little further,
And then I'll bring thee to the present business
Which now's upon's; without the which, this story
Were most impertinent.[13]

MIR. Wherefore did they not
That hour destroy us?

PROS. Well demanded, wench;[14]
My tale provokes that question. Dear, they durst not,
So dear the love my people bore me; nor set
A mark so bloody on the business; but
With colors fairer painted their foul ends.
In few,[15] they hurried us aboard a bark,
Bore us some leagues to sea; where they prepared
A rotten carcass of a butt, not rigged,
Nor tackle, sail, nor mast; the very rats
Instinctively have quit it. There they hoist us,
To cry to the sea that roared to us; to sigh
To the winds, whose pity, sighing back again,
Did us but loving wrong.

MIR. Alack, what trouble
Was I then to you!

PROS. Oh, a cherubin
Thou wast that did preserve me. Thou didst smile,
Infused with a fortitude from heaven,
When I have decked[16] the sea with drops full salt,
Under my burthen groaned; which raised in me
An undergoing stomach,[17] to bear up
Against what should ensue.

MIR. How came we ashore?

PROS. By Providence divine.
Some food we had, and some fresh water, that
A noble Neapolitan, Gonzalo,
Out of his charity, who being then appointed
Master of this design, did give us, with
Rich garments, linens, stuffs, and necessaries,
Which since have steaded[18] much; so, of his gentleness,
Knowing I loved my books, he furnished me
From mine own library with volumes that
I prize above my dukedom.

[1] except
[2] out-valued all popular esteem (was better than any popularity, except that it enforced seclusion)
[3] without
[4] Pronounce *reven'ue.*
[5] like one who has told an untruth until his false memory makes it seem truth (Perhaps *into* should be *unto.*)
[6] in consequence of the
[7] Duke of Milan (So Cleopatra is called *Egypt,* etc.)
[8] terms of confederation
[9] outcome
[10] otherwise than
[11] in return for the guarantees
[12] at once
[13] not pertinent
[14] girl (with none of the modern contemptuous sense)
[15] in brief
[16] sprinkled
[17] an enduring courage
[18] aided

MIR. Would I might
But ever see that man!
PROS. Now I arise; [*Resumes his mantle.*
Sit still, and hear the last of our sea-sorrow.
Here in this island we arrived; and here
Have I, thy schoolmaster, made thee more profit
Than other princess [1] can, that have more time
For vainer hours, and tutors not so careful.
MIR. Heavens thank you for't! And now, I pray you, sir,
For still 'tis beating in my mind, your reason
For raising this sea-storm?
PROS. Know thus far forth.
By accident most strange, bountiful Fortune,
Now my dear lady, hath mine enemies
Brought to this shore; and by my prescience
I find my zenith doth depend upon
A most auspicious star, whose influence
If now I court not, but omit, my fortunes
Will ever after droop. Here cease more questions.
Thou art inclined to sleep; 'tis a good dullness,
And give it way; I know thou canst not choose.
[MIRANDA *sleeps.*
Come away, servant, come. I am ready now.
Approach, my Ariel, come.

Enter ARIEL.

ARI. All hail, great master! grave sir, hail! I come
To answer thy best pleasure; be't to fly,
To swim, to dive into the fire, to ride
On the curled clouds, to thy strong bidding task
Ariel and all his quality. [2]
PROS. Hast thou, spirit,
Performed to point the tempest that I bade thee?
ARI. To every article.
I boarded the king's ship; now on the beak,
Now in the waist, the deck, in every cabin,
I flamed amazement. Sometime I'ld divide,
And burn in many places; on the topmast,
The yards, and bowsprit, would I flame distinctly, [3]
Then meet and join. Jove's lightnings, the precursors
O' the dreadful thunder-claps, more momentary
And sight-outrunning were not; the fire and cracks
Of sulphurous roaring the most mighty Neptune
Seem to besiege, and make his bold waves tremble,
Yea, his dread trident shake.
PROS. My brave spirit!
Who was so firm, so constant, that this coil [4]
Would not infect his reason?
ARI. Not a soul
But felt a fever of the mad, and played
Some tricks of desperation. All but mariners
Plunged in the foaming brine, and quit the vessel,
Then all afire with me. The king's son, Ferdinand,
With hair up-staring—then like reeds, not hair—
Was the first man that leaped; cried, "Hell is empty,
And all the devils are here."
PROS. Why, that's my spirit!
But was not this nigh shore?
ARI. Close by, my master.
PROS. But are they, Ariel, safe?
ARI. Not a hair perished;
On their sustaining garments not a blemish,
But fresher than before; and, as thou badest me,
In troops I have dispersed them 'bout the isle.
The king's son have I landed by himself;
Whom I left cooling of the air with sighs
In an odd angle of the isle, and sitting,
His arms in this sad knot.
PROS. Of the king's ship,
The mariners, say how thou hast disposed,
And all the rest o' the fleet.
ARI. Safely in harbor
Is the king's ship; in the deep nook, where once
Thou call'dst me up at midnight to fetch dew
From the still-vexed Bermoothes, [5] there she's hid.
The mariners all under hatches stowed;
Who, with a charm joined to their suffered labor,
I have left asleep; and for the rest o' the fleet,
Which I dispersed, they all have met again,
And are upon the Mediterranean flote, [6]
Bound sadly home for Naples;
Supposing that they saw their king's ship wrecked,
And his great person perish.
PROS. Ariel, thy charge
Exactly is performed; but there's more work.
What is the time o' the day?
ARI. Past the mid season.
PROS. At least two glasses. The time 'twixt six and now
Must by us both be spent most preciously.
ARI. Is there more toil? Since thou dost give me pains,
Let me remember thee what thou hast promised,
Which is not yet performed me.
PROS. How now? moody?
What is't thou canst demand?
ARI. My liberty.

[1] princesses
[2] associates
[3] separately
[4] turmoil
[5] the ever-tempestuous Bermudas (See introductory note.)
[6] flood, sea

PROS. Before the time be out? No more!
ARI. I prithee,
Remember I have done thee worthy service;
Told thee no lies, made thee no mistakings, served
Without or grudge or grumblings; thou didst promise
To bate me a full year.
PROS. Dost thou forget
From what a torment I did free thee?
ARI. No.
PROS. Thou dost, and think'st it much to tread the ooze
Of the salt deep,
To run upon the sharp wind of the north,
To do me business in the veins o' the earth
When it is baked with frost.
ARI. I do not, sir.
PROS. Thou liest, malignant thing! Hast thou forgot
The foul witch Sycorax, who with age and envy
Was grown into a hoop? Hast thou forgot her?
ARI. No, sir.
PROS. Thou hast. Where was she born? speak; tell me.
ARI. Sir, in Argier.[1]
PROS. Oh, was she so? I must
Once in a month recount what thou hast been,
Which thou forget'st. This damned witch Sycorax,
For mischiefs manifold, and sorceries terrible
To enter human hearing, from Argier,
Thou know'st, was banished; for one thing she did
They would not take her life. Is not this true?
ARI. Aye, sir.
PROS. This blue-eyed[2] hag was hither brought with child,
And here was left by the sailors. Thou, my slave,
As thou report'st thyself, wast then her servant;
And, for[3] thou wast a spirit too delicate
To act her earthy and abhorred commands,
Refusing her grand hests, she did confine thee,
By help of her more potent ministers,
And in her most unmitigable rage,
Into a cloven pine; within which rift
Imprisoned thou didst painfully remain
A dozen years; within which space she died,
And left thee there; where thou didst vent thy groans
As fast as mill-wheels strike. Then was this island—
Save for the son that she did litter here,
A freckled whelp hag-born—not honored with
A human shape.

[1] Algiers
[2] with blue-circled eyes
[3] because

ARI. Yes, Caliban, her son.
PROS. Dull thing, I say so; he, that Caliban,
Whom now I keep in service. Thou best know'st
What torment I did find thee in; thy groans
Did make wolves howl, and penetrate the breasts
Of ever-angry bears; it was a torment
To lay upon the damned, which Sycorax
Could not again undo; it was mine art,
When I arrived and heard thee, that made gape
The pine, and let thee out.
ARI. I thank thee, master.
PROS. If thou more murmur'st, I will rend an oak,
And peg thee in his knotty entrails, till
Thou hast howled away twelve winters.
ARI. Pardon, master;
I will be correspondent to command,
And do my spiriting gently.
PROS. Do so; and after two days
I will discharge thee.
ARI. That's my noble master!
What shall I do? say what; what shall I do?
PROS. Go make thyself like a nymph o' the sea; be subject
To no sight but thine and mine; invisible
To every eyeball else. Go take this shape,
And hither come in't; go hence with diligence!
[*Exit* ARIEL.
Awake, dear heart, awake! thou hast slept well;
Awake!
MIR. The strangeness of your story put
Heaviness in me.
PROS. Shake it off. Come on;
We'll visit Caliban my slave, who never
Yields us kind answer.
MIR. 'Tis a villain, sir,
I do not love to look on.
PROS. But, as 'tis,
We cannot miss[4] him; he does make our fire,
Fetch in our wood, and serves in offices
That profit us. What, ho! slave! Caliban!
Thou earth, thou! speak.
CAL. [*Within*] There's wood enough within.
PROS. Come forth, I say! there's other business for thee.
Come, thou tortoise! when?

Reënter ARIEL *like a water-nymph.*

Fine apparition! My quaint[5] Ariel,
Hark in thine ear.
ARI. My lord, it shall be done. [*Exit.*
PROS. Thou poisonous slave, got by the devil himself
Upon thy wicked dam, come forth!

[4] do without
[5] dainty

Enter CALIBAN.

CAL. As wicked dew as e'er my mother brushed
With raven's feather from unwholesome fen
Drop on you both! A south-west blow on ye
And blister you all o'er!

PROS. For this, be sure, tonight thou shalt have cramps,
Side-stitches that shall pen thy breath up; urchins [1]
Shall, for that vast of night that [2] they may work,
All exercise on thee; thou shalt be pinched
As thick as honeycomb, each pinch more stinging
Than bees that made 'em.

CAL. I must eat my dinner.
This island's mine, by Sycorax my mother,
Which thou takest from me. When thou camest first,
Thou strokedst me, and madest much of me; wouldst give me
Water with berries in't; [3] and teach me how
To name the bigger light, and how the less,
That burn by day and night; and then I loved thee,
And showed thee all the qualities o' th' isle,
The fresh springs, brine-pits, barren places and fertile;
Cursed be I that did so! All the charms
Of Sycorax, toads, beetles, bats, light on you!
For I am all the subjects that you have,
Which [4] first was mine own king; and here you sty me
In this hard rock, whiles you do keep from me
The rest o' th' island.

PROS. Thou most lying slave,
Whom stripes may move, not kindness! I have used thee,
Filth as thou art, with human care; and lodged thee
In mine own cell, till thou didst seek to violate
The honor of my child.

CAL. O ho, O ho! would't had been done!
Thou didst prevent me; I had peopled else
This isle with Calibans.

PROS. Abhorred slave,
Which any print of goodness wilt not take,
Being capable of all ill! I pitied thee,
Took pains to make thee speak, taught thee each hour
One thing or other; when thou didst not, savage,
Know thine own meaning, but wouldst gabble like
A thing most brutish, I endowed thy purposes
With words that made them known. But thy vile race, [5]
Though thou didst learn, had that in't which good natures
Could not abide to be with; therefore wast thou
Deservedly confined into this rock,
Who hadst deserved more than a prison.

CAL. You taught me language; and my profit on't
Is, I know how to curse. The red plague rid [6] you
For learning me your language!

PROS. Hag-seed, hence!
Fetch us in fuel; and be quick, thou'rt best,
To answer [7] other business. Shrug'st thou, malice?
If thou neglect'st, or dost unwillingly
What I command, I'll rack thee with old cramps,
Fill all thy bones with aches, [8] make thee roar,
That beasts shall tremble at thy din.

CAL. No, pray thee,
[*Aside*] I must obey; his art is of such power,
It would control my dam's god, Setebos, [9]
And make a vassal of him.

PROS. So, slave, hence! [*Exit* CALIBAN.

Reënter ARIEL, *invisible, playing and singing;* FERDINAND *following.*

ARIEL'S *song.*

Come unto these yellow sands,
And then take hands;
Courtsied when you have and kissed
The wild waves whist; [10]
Foot it featly here and there;
And, sweet sprites, the burthen bear. [11]
Hark, hark!
BURTHEN [*dispersedly*]. Bow-wow.
ARI. The watch dogs bark;
BURTHEN [*dispersedly*]. Bow-wow.
ARI. Hark, hark! I hear
The strain of strutting chanticleer
Cry, Cock-a-diddle-dow.

FER. Where should this music be? i' th' air or th' earth?

[1] goblins
[2] that waste and void of night wherein
[3] Coffee was at this time hardly known in England. In William Strachey's account of the shipwreck of Sir George Somers, the men are said to have made a pleasant drink of an infusion of berries of the cedar.
[4] who (Antecedent is I.)

[5] nature
[6] destroy
[7] perform
[8] Pronounced *aitches* or *atches;* the ch was pronounced like *k* only in the verb; compare *bake, batch, break, breach.*
[9] a Patagonian diety
[10] into silence
[11] take up the refrain

It sounds no more; and, sure, it waits upon
Some god o' th' island. Sitting on a bank,
Weeping again the king my father's wreck,
This music crept by me upon the waters,
Allaying both their fury and my passion [1]
With its sweet air; thence I have followed it,
Or it hath drawn me rather. But 'tis gone.
No, it begins again.

ARIEL *sings.*

Full fathom five thy father lies;
Of his bones are coral [2] made;
Those are pearls that were his eyes;
Nothing of him that doth fade,
But doth suffer a sea-change
Into something rich and strange.
Sea-nymphs hourly ring his knell;
BURTHEN. Ding-dong.

ARI. Hark! now I hear them—Ding-dong, bell.
FER. The ditty does remember [3] my drowned father.
This is no mortal business, nor no sound
That the earth owes [4]—I hear it now above me.
PROS. The fringed curtains of thine eye advance, [5]
And say what thou seest yond.
MIR. What is't? a spirit?
Lord, how it looks about! Believe me, sir,
It carries a brave [6] form. But 'tis a spirit.
PROS. No, wench; it eats and sleeps and hath such senses
As we have, such. This gallant which thou seest
Was in the wreck; and, but he's something stained
With grief, that's beauty's canker, thou mightst call him
A goodly person; he hath lost his fellows,
And strays about to find 'em.
MIR. I might call him
A thing divine; for nothing natural
I ever saw so noble.
PROS. [*Aside*] It goes on, I see,
As my soul prompts it. Spirit, fine spirit! I'll free thee
Within two days for this.
FER. Most sure the goddess
On whom these airs attend! Vouchsafe my prayer
May know if you remain upon this island;
And that you will some good instruction give
How I may bear me here; my prime request,
Which I do last pronounce, is, O you wonder!

[1] suffering (from Latin *patior*)
[2] perhaps used collectively (But see note on I. i. 17.)
[3] commemorate
[4] owns
[5] raise
[6] fine

If you be maid or no?
MIR. No wonder, sir;
But certainly a maid.
FER. My language! Heavens!
I am the best of them that speak this speech,
Were I but where 'tis spoken.
PROS. How? the best?
What wert thou, if the King of Naples heard thee?
FER. A single [7] thing, as I am now, that wonders
To hear thee speak of Naples. [8] He does hear me;
And that he does I weep; myself am Naples,
Who with mine eyes, never since at ebb, beheld
The king my father wrecked.
MIR. Alack, for mercy!
FER. Yes, faith, and all his lords; the Duke of Milan
And his brave son [9] being twain.
PROS. [*Aside*] The Duke of Milan
And his more braver daughter could control [10] thee,
If now 'twere fit to do it. At the first sight
They have changed eyes. Delicate Ariel,
I'll set thee free for this. [*To* FER.] A word, good sir;
I fear you have done yourself some wrong; [11] a word.
MIR. Why speaks my father so ungently? This
Is the third man that e'er I saw; the first
That e'er I sighed for; pity move my father
To be inclined my way!
FER. Oh, if a virgin,
And your affection not gone forth, I'll make you
The queen of Naples.
PROS. Soft, sir! one word more.
[*Aside*] They are both in either's powers; but this swift business
I must uneasy [12] make, lest too light winning
Make the prize light. [*To* FER.] One word more; I charge thee
That thou attend me. Thou dost here usurp
The name thou owest [13] not; and hast put thyself
Upon this island as a spy, to win it
From me, the lord on't.
FER. No, as I am a man.
MIR. There's nothing ill can dwell in such a temple;

[7] solitary; also, miserable
[8] See note 7, p. 184.
[9] possibly an oversight, for no such character appears
[10] confute
[11] made a mistake
[12] difficult
[13] ownest

If the ill spirit have so fair a house,
Good things will strive to dwell with't.
PROS. Follow me.
Speak not you for him; he's a traitor. Come;
I'll manacle thy neck and feet together;
Sea-water shalt thou drink; thy food shall be
The fresh-brook mussels, withered roots, and husks
Wherein the acorn cradled. Follow.
FER. No;
I will resist such entertainment till
Mine enemy has more power.
[*Draws, and is charmed from moving.*
MIR. O dear father,
Make not too rash a trial of him, for
He's gentle, and not fearful.[1]
PROS. What! I say,
My foot my tutor? Put thy sword up, traitor;
Who makest a show, but darest not strike, thy conscience
Is so possessed with guilt. Come from thy ward;[2]
For I can here disarm thee with this stick
And make thy weapon drop.
MIR. Beseech you, father.
PROS. Hence! hang not on my garments.
MIR. Sir, have pity;
I'll be his surety.
PROS. Silence! One word more
Shall make me chide thee, if not hate thee. What!
An advocate for an impostor! hush!
Thou think'st there is no more such shapes as he,
Having seen but him and Caliban; foolish wench!
To[3] the most of men this is a Caliban,
And they to him are angels.
MIR. My affections
Are, then, most humble; I have no ambition
To see a goodlier man.
PROS. Come on; obey;
Thy nerves[4] are in their infancy again,
And have no vigor in them,
FER. So they are.
My spirits, as in a dream, are all bound up.
My father's loss, the weakness which I feel,
The wreck of all my friends, nor[5] this man's threats,
To whom I am subdued, are but light to me,
Might I but through my prison once a day
Behold this maid; all corners else o' th' earth
Let liberty make use of; space enough
Have I in such a prison.
PROS. [*Aside*] It works. [*To* FER.] Come on.
Thou hast done well, fine Ariel! [*To* FER.] Follow me.
[*To* ARI.] Hark what thou else shalt do me.
MIR. Be of comfort;
My father's of a better nature, sir,
Than he appears by speech; this is unwonted
Which now came from him.
PROS. Thou shalt be as free
As mountain winds; but then exactly do
All points of my command.
ARI. To the syllable.
PROS. Come, follow. Speak not for him.
[*Exeunt.*

ACT II

SCENE I

Another part of the island.

Enter ALONSO, SEBASTIAN, ANTONIO, GONZALO, ADRIAN, FRANCISCO, *and others.*

GON. Beseech you, sir, be merry; you have cause,
So have we all, of joy; for our escape
Is much beyond our loss. Our hint[6] of woe
Is common; every day, some sailor's wife,
The masters of some merchant,[7] and the merchant,
Have just our theme of woe; but for the miracle,
I mean our preservation, few in millions
Can speak like us; then wisely, good sir, weigh
Our sorrow with our comfort.
ALON. Prithee, peace.
SEB.[8] He receives comfort like cold porridge.
ANT. The visitor[9] will not give him o'er so.
SEB. Look, he's winding up the watch of his wit; by and by it will strike.
GON. Sir—
SEB. One; tell.[10]
GON. When every grief is entertained that's offered,
Comes to the entertainer—
SEB. A dollar.
GON. Dolor comes to him, indeed; you have spoken truer than you purposed.

[1] mild and harmless (or possibly, high-spirited and not afraid)
[2] posture of defense
[3] compared to
[4] sinews
[5] used, by confusion of construction, for "and"

[6] occasion
[7] vessel
[8] The conversation of Sebastian and Antonio takes place aside.
[9] comforter (Gonzalo; the word was used of parish visitors of the sick.)
[10] keep count

SEB. You have taken it wiselier than I meant you should.

GON. Therefore, my lord—

ANT. Fie, what a spendthrift is he of his tongue!

ALON. I prithee, spare.

GON. Well, I have done; but yet—

SEB. He will be talking.

ANT. Which, of he or Adrian, for a good wager, first begins to crow?

SEB. The old cock.

ANT. The cockerel.

SEB. Done. The wager?

ANT. A laughter.

SEB. A match!

ADR. Though this island seem to be desert—

SEB. Ha, ha, ha! So, you're paid.

ADR. Uninhabitable, and almost inaccessible—

SEB. Yet—

ADR. Yet—

ANT. He could not miss't.[1]

ADR. It must needs be of subtle, tender, and delicate temperance.[2]

ANT. Temperance[3] was a delicate wench.

SEB. Aye, and a subtle; as he most learnedly delivered.

ADR. The air breathes upon us here most sweetly.

SEB. As if it had lungs, and rotten ones.

ANT. Or as 'twere perfumed by a fen.

GON. Here is everything advantageous to life.

ANT. True; save means to live.

SEB. Of that there's none, or little.

GON. How lush and lusty the grass looks! how green!

ANT. The ground, indeed, is tawny.

SEB. With an eye[4] of green in't.

ANT. He misses not much.

SEB. No; he doth but mistake the truth totally.

GON. But the rarity of it is—which is indeed almost beyond credit—

SEB. As many vouched rarities are.

GON. That our garments, being, as they were, drenched in the sea, hold, notwithstanding, their freshness and glosses, being rather new-dyed than stained with salt water.

ANT. If but one of his pockets could speak, would it not say he lies?

SEB. Aye, or very falsely pocket up his report.

GON. Methinks our garments are now as fresh as when we put them on first in Afric, at the marriage of the king's fair daughter Claribel to the King of Tunis.

SEB. 'Twas a sweet marriage, and we prosper well in our return.

ADR. Tunis was never graced before with such a paragon to[5] their queen.

GON. Not since widow Dido's time.

ANT. Widow! A pox o' that! How came that widow in? widow Dido!

SEB. What if he had said "widower Aeneas," too? Good Lord, how you take it!

ADR. "Widow Dido" said you? You make me study of that; she was of Carthage, not of Tunis.

GON. This Tunis, sir, was Carthage.

ADR. Carthage?

GON. I assure you, Carthage.

ANT. His word is more than the miraculous harp.[6]

SEB. He hath raised the wall, and houses, too.

ANT. What impossible matter will he make easy next?

SEB. I think he will carry this island home in his pocket, and give it his son for an apple.

ANT. And, sowing the kernels of it in the sea, bring forth more islands.

GON. Aye.

ANT. Why, in good time.

GON. Sir, we were talking that our garments seem now as fresh as when we were at Tunis at the marriage of your daughter, who is now queen.

ANT. And the rarest that e'er came there.

SEB. Bate,[7] I beseech you, widow Dido.

ANT. Oh, widow Dido! Aye, widow Dido.

GON. Is not, sir, my doublet as fresh as the first day I wore it? I mean, in a sort.

ANT. That sort was well fished for.

GON. When I wore it at your daughter's marriage?

ALON. You cram these words into mine ears against
The stomach of my sense. Would I had never
Married my daughter there! For, coming thence,
My son is lost, and, in my rate,[8] she, too,
Who is so far from Italy removed
I ne'er again shall see her. O thou mine heir
Of Naples and of Milan, what strange fish
Hath made his meal on thee?

FRAN. Sir, he may live;
I saw him beat the surges under him,
And ride upon their backs; he trod the water,
Whose enmity be flung aside, and breasted
The surge most swoln that met him; his bold head

[1] i.e., not fail to say just what you anticipated
[2] temperature
[3] a proper name among the Puritans
[4] tinge
[5] for
[6] Amphion's harp, which raised the walls of Thebes
[7] except
[8] opinion

'Bove the contentious waves he kept, and oared
Himself with his good arms in lusty stroke
To the shore, that o'er his [1] wave-worn basis bowed,
As stooping to relieve him; I not doubt
He came alive to land.

ALON. No, no, he's gone.

SEB. Sir, you may thank yourself for this great loss,
That would not bless our Europe with your daughter,
But rather lose her to an African;
Where she, at least, is banished from your eye
Who [2] hath cause to wet the grief on't. [3]

ALON. Prithee, peace.

SEB. You were kneeled to, and importuned otherwise,
By all of us; and the fair soul herself
Weighed [4] between loathness and obedience, at
Which end o' the beam should [5] bow. We have lost your son,
I fear, forever; Milan and Naples have
Mo widows in them of this business' making
Than we bring men to comfort them;
The fault's your own.

ALON. So is the dear'st [6] o' the loss.

GON. My lord Sebastian,
The truth you speak doth lack some gentleness,
And time [7] to speak it in; you rub the sore,
When you should bring the plaster.

SEB. Very well.

ANT. And most chirurgeonly. [8]

GON. It is foul weather in us all, good sir,
When you are cloudy.

SEB. Foul weather?

ANT. Very foul.

GON. Had I plantation [9] of this isle, my lord—

ANT. He'ld sow't with nettle-seed.

SEB. Or docks, or mallows.

GON. And were the king on't, what would I do?

SEB. 'Scape being drunk for want of wine.

GON. I' the commonwealth I would by contraries
Execute all things; for no kind of traffic
Would I admit; no name of magistrate;
Letters [10] should not be known; riches, poverty,
And use of service, [11] none; contract, succession,
Bourn, bound of land, tilth, vineyard, none;
No use of metal, corn, or wine, or oil;
No occupation; all men idle, all;
And women, too, but innocent and pure;
No sovereignty—

SEB. Yet he would be king on't.

ANT. The latter end of his commonwealth forgets the beginning.

GON. All things in common nature should produce
Without sweat or endeavor; treason, felony,
Sword, pike, knife, gun, or need of any engine, [12]
Would I not have; but nature should bring forth,
Of it own kind, [13] all foison, [14] all abundance,
To feed my innocent people.

. . . .

I would with such perfection govern, sir,
To excel the golden age.

SEB. 'Save his majesty!

ANT. Long live Gonzalo!

GON. And—do you mark me, sir?

ALON. Prithee, no more; thou dost talk nothing to me.

GON. I do well believe your highness; and did it to minister occasion to these gentlemen, who are of such sensible [15] and nimble lungs that they always use to laugh at nothing.

ANT. 'Twas you we laughed at.

GON. Who in this kind of merry fooling am nothing to you; so you may continue, and laugh at nothing still.

ANT. What a blow was there given!

SEB. An [16] it had not fallen flat-long. [17]

GON. You are gentlemen of brave mettle; you would lift the moon out of her sphere, if she would continue in it five weeks without changing.

Enter ARIEL *(invisible), playing solemn music.*

SEB. We would so, and then go a bat-fowling. [18]

ANT. Nay, good my lord, be not angry.

GON. No, I warrant you; I will not adventure my discretion so weakly. Will you laugh me asleep, for I am very heavy?

ANT. Go sleep, and hear us. [19]

[*All sleep except* ALON., SEB., *and* ANT.

ALON. What, all so soon asleep! I wish mine eyes
Would, with themselves, shut up my thoughts; I find
They are inclined to do so.

[1] its
[2] which
[3] to weep over it
[4] balanced
[5] Supply "she."
[6] heaviest
[7] Supply "proper."
[8] surgeon-like
[9] colonization
[10] literature
[11] practice of servitude
[12] of war
[13] spontaneously
[14] plenty
[15] sensitive
[16] if
[17] flatwise
[18] catching birds at night by beating the bushes
[19] This passage is obscure. Perhaps it is a colloquial inversion for "Hear us, and go to sleep."

SEB. Please you, sir,
Do not omit [1] the heavy offer of it;
It seldom visits sorrow; when it doth,
It is a comforter.
ANT. We two, my lord,
Will guard your person while you take your rest,
And watch your safety.
ALON. Thank you.—Wondrous heavy.
[ALONSO *sleeps*. *Exit* ARIEL.
SEB. What a strange drowsiness possesses them!
ANT. It is the quality o' the climate.
SEB. Why
Doth it not then our eyelids sink? I find not
Myself disposed to sleep.
ANT. Nor I; my spirits are nimble.
They fell together all, as by consent;
They dropped, as by a thunder-stroke. What might,
Worthy Sebastian?—Oh, what might?—No more—
And yet methinks I see it in thy face,
What thou shouldst be; the occasion speaks [2] thee; and
My strong imagination sees a crown
Dropping upon thy head.
SEB. What, art thou waking?
ANT. Do you not hear me speak?
SEB. I do; and surely
It is a sleepy language, and thou speak'st
Out of thy sleep. What is it thou didst say?
This is a strange repose, to be asleep
With eyes wide open; standing, speaking, moving,
And yet so fast asleep.
ANT. Noble Sebastian,
Thou let'st thy fortune sleep—die, rather; wink'st
Whiles thou art waking.
SEB. Thou dost snore distinctly; [3]
There's meaning in thy snores.
ANT. I am more serious than my custom; you
Must be so, too, if heed me; which to do
Trebles thee o'er. [4]
SEB. Well, I am standing water.
ANT. I'll teach you how to flow.
SEB. Do so; to ebb
Hereditary sloth instructs me.
ANT. Oh,
If you but knew how you the purpose cherish
Whiles thus you mock it! how, in stripping it,
You more invest it! [5] Ebbing men, indeed,
Most often do so near the bottom run
By their own fear or sloth.
SEB. Prithee, say on;
The setting of thine eye and cheek proclaim
A matter from thee; and a birth, indeed,
Which throes [6] thee much to yield. [7]
ANT. Thus, sir:
Although this lord of weak remembrance, this,
Who shall be of as little memory
When he is earthed, hath here almost persuaded—
For he's a spirit of persuasion, only
Professes [8] to persuade—the king his son's alive,
'Tis as impossible that he's undrowned
As he that sleeps here swims.
SEB. I have no hope
That he's undrowned.
ANT. Oh, out of that "no hope"
What great hope have you! No hope that way is
Another way so high a hope that even
Ambition cannot pierce a wink beyond,
But doubt [9] discovery there. Will you grant with me
That Ferdinand is drowned?
SEB. He's gone.
ANT. Then, tell me,
Who's the next heir of Naples?
SEB. Claribel.
ANT. She that is queen of Tunis; she that dwells
Ten leagues beyond man's life; she that from Naples
Can have no note, unless the sun were post—
The man i' the moon's too slow—till new-born chins
Be rough and razorable; she that from whom [10]
We all were sea-swallowed, though some cast again,
And by that destiny, to perform an act
Whereof what's past is prologue; what to come,
In yours and my discharge.
SEB. What stuff is this! How say you?
'Tis true, my brother's daughter's queen of Tunis;
So is she heir of Naples; 'twixt which regions
There is some space.
ANT. A space whose every cubit
Seems to cry out, "How shall that Claribel
Measure us [11] back to Naples? Keep in Tunis,

[1] let pass
[2] invites
[3] significantly
[4] will treble thy fortunes
[5] more alluringly clothe it
[6] pains
[7] bring forth
[8] his sole profession is
[9] but must doubt (the possibility of)
[10] Supply "coming."
[11] traverse us (the cubits)

And let Sebastian wake." Say, this were death
That now hath seized them; why, they were no worse
Than now they are. There be that can rule Naples
As well as he that sleeps; lords that can prate
As amply and unnecessarily
As this Gonzalo; I myself could make
A chough of as deep chat.[1] Oh, that you bore
The mind that I do! what a sleep were this
For your advancement! Do you understand me?

SEB. Methinks I do.

ANT. And how does your content
Tender[2] your own good fortune?

SEB. I remember
You did supplant your brother Prospero.

ANT. True;
And look how well my garments sit upon me;
Much feater than before. My brother's servants
Were then my fellows; now they are my men.

SEB. But, for your conscience?

ANT. Aye, sir; where lies that? If 'twere a kibe,[3]
'Twould put me to my slipper; but I feel not
This deity in my bosom; twenty consciences,
That stand 'twixt me and Milan, candied be they,
And melt, ere they molest! Here lies your brother,
No better than the earth he lies upon,
If he were that which now he's like, that's dead;
Whom I, with this obedient steel, three inches of it,
Can lay to bed forever; whiles you, doing thus,
To the perpetual wink for aye might put
This ancient morsel, this Sir Prudence, who
Should not upbraid our course. For all the rest,
They'll take suggestion as a cat laps milk;
They'll tell the clock[4] to any business that
We say befits the hour.

SEB. Thy case, dear friend,
Shall be my precedent; as thou got'st Milan,
I'll come by Naples. Draw thy sword; one stroke
Shall free thee from the tribute which thou payest;
And I the king shall love thee.

ANT. Draw together;
And when I rear my hand, do you the like,
To fall it on Gonzalo.

SEB. Oh, but one word.
[*They talk apart.*

Reënter ARIEL *(invisible).*

ARI. My master through his art foresees the danger
That you, his friend, are in; and sends me forth—
For else his project dies—to keep them living.
[*Sings in* GONZALO'S *ear.*

While you here do snoring lie,
Open-eyed conspiracy
His time doth take.
If of life you keep a care,
Shake off slumber, and beware;
Awake, awake!

ANT. Then let us both be sudden.

GON. Now, good angels
Preserve the king! [*They awake.*

ALON. Why, how now? Ho, awake!—Why are you drawn?
Wherefore this ghastly looking?

GON. What's the matter?

SEB. Whiles we stood here securing your repose,
Even now, we heard a hollow burst of bellowing
Like bulls, or rather lions. Didn't not wake you?
It struck mine ear most terribly.

ALON. I heard nothing.

ANT. Oh, 'twas a din to fright a monster's ear,
To make an earthquake! Sure, it was the roar
Of a whole herd of lions.

ALON. Heard you this, Gonzalo?

GON. Upon mine honor, sir, I heard a humming,
And that a strange one, too, which did awake me;
I shaked you, sir, and cried; as mine eyes opened,
I saw their weapons drawn—there was a noise,
That's verily. 'Tis best we stand upon our guard,
Or that we quit this place; let's draw our weapons.

ALON. Lead off this ground; and let's make further search
For my poor son.

GON. Heavens keep him from these beasts!
For he is, sure, i' th' island.

ALON. Lead away.

ARI. Prospero my lord shall know what I have done;
So, king, go safely on to seek thy son. [*Exeunt.*

[1] a jackdaw talk as deeply
[2] regard
[3] heel-sore
[4] count time (make the hour fit)

Scene II

Another part of the island.

Enter Caliban *with a burden of wood. A noise of thunder heard.*

Cal. All the infections that the sun sucks up
From bogs, fens, flats, on Prosper fall, and make him
By inch-meal [1] a disease! His spirits hear me,
And yet I needs must curse. But they'll nor pinch,
Fright me with urchin-shows, pitch me i' the mire,
Nor lead me, like a firebrand, in the dark
Out of my way, unless he bid 'em. But
For every trifle are they set upon me;
Sometime like apes, that mow and chatter at me,
And after bite me; then like hedgehogs, which
Lie tumbling in my barefoot way, and mount 11
Their pricks at my footfall; sometime am I
All wound with adders, who with cloven tongues
Do hiss me into madness.

Enter Trinculo.

Lo, now, lo!
Here comes a spirit of his, and to torment me
For bringing wood in slowly. I'll fall flat;
Perchance he will not mind me. 17

Trin. Here's neither bush nor shrub, to bear off any weather at all, and another storm brewing; I hear it sing i' the wind; yond same black cloud, yond huge one, looks like a foul bombard [2] that would shed his liquor. If it should thunder as it did before, I know not where to hide my head; yond same cloud cannot choose but fall by pailfuls. What have we here? a man or a fish? dead or alive? A fish. He smells like a fish; a very ancient and fish-like smell; a kind of not of the newest Poor-John. [3] A strange fish! Were I in England now, as once I was, and had but this fish painted, not a holiday fool there but would give a piece of silver; there would this monster make [4] a man; any strange beast there makes a man; when they will not give a doit [5] to relieve a lame beggar, they will lay out ten to see a dead Indian. Legged like a man! and his fins like arms! Warm o' my troth! I do now let loose my opinion; hold it no longer; this is no fish, but an islander, that hath lately suffered by a thunderbolt. [*Thunder.*] Alas, the storm is come again! my best way is to creep under his gaberdine; [6] there is no other shelter hereabout; misery acquaints a man with strange bed-fellows. I will here shroud till the dregs of the storm be past 45

Enter Stephano, *singing; a bottle in his hand.*

Ste. I shall no more to sea, to sea,
Here shall I die a-shore—
This is a very scurvy tune to sing at a man's funeral; well, here's my comfort. [*Drinks.*

[*Sings.*
The master, the swabber, the boatswain, and I,
The gunner, and his mate, 51
Loved Moll, Meg, and Marian, and Margery,
But none of us cared for Kate;
For she had a tongue with a tang,
Would cry to a sailor, Go hang!
She loved not the savor of tar nor of pitch—
Then, to sea, boys, and let her go hang!

This is a scurvy tune, too; but here's my comfort. [*Drinks.*

Cal. Do not torment me—Oh! 60

Ste. What's the matter? Have we devils here? Do you put tricks upon 's with salvages and men of Ind, ha? I have not escaped drowning, to be afeard now of your four legs; for it hath been said, "As proper a man as ever went on four legs cannot make him give ground;" and it shall be said so again, while Stephano breathes at nostrils.

Cal The spirit torments me—Oh! 69

Ste. This is some monster of the isle with four legs, who hath got, as I take it, an ague. Where the devil should he learn [7] our language? I will give him some relief, if it be but for that. If I can recover him, and keep him tame, and get to Naples with him, he's a present for any emperor that ever trod on neat's leather.

Cal. Do not torment me, prithee; I'll bring my wood home faster. 78

Ste. He's in his fit now, and does not talk after the wisest. He shall taste of my bottle; if he have never drunk wine afore, it will go near to remove his fit. If I can recover him, and keep him tame, I will not take [8] too much for him; he shall pay for him that hath him, and that soundly. 85

Cal. Thou dost me yet but little hurt; thou wilt anon, I know it by thy trembling; now Prosper works upon thee.

Ste. Come on your ways; open your mouth; here is that which will give language to you, cat; [9] open your mouth; this will shake your shaking, I can tell you, and that soundly; you

[1] piece-meal
[2] large leathern liquor-vessel
[3] salted hake
[4] used punningly: "to make the fortune of"
[5] a small Dutch coin
[6] long cloak
[7] can he have learned
[8] cannot ask
[9] Proverb: "Good liquor will make a cat speak."

cannot tell who's your friend; open your chaps again. 94

TRIN. I should know that voice; it should be—but he is drowned; and these are devils—Oh, defend me!

STE. Four legs and two voices—a most delicate monster! His forward voice, now, is to speak well of his friend; his backward voice is to utter foul speeches and to detract. If all the wine in my bottle will recover him, I will help his ague. Come—Amen! I will pour some in thy other mouth.

TRIN. Stephano! 105

STE. Doth thy other mouth call me? Mercy, mercy! This is a devil, and no monster; I will leave him; I have no long spoon.[1]

TRIN. Stephano! If thou beest Stephano, touch me, and speak to me; for I am Trinculo—be not afeard—thy good friend Trinculo.

STE. If thou beest Trinculo, come forth; I'll pull thee by the lesser legs; if any be Trinculo's legs, these are they. Thou art very Trinculo indeed! How camest thou to be the siege of this moon-calf?[2] Can he vent[3] Trinculos? 117

TRIN. I took him to be killed with a thunder-stroke. But art thou not drowned, Stephano? I hope, now, thou art not drowned. Is the storm overblown? I hid me under the dead moon-calf's gaberdine for fear of the storm. And art thou living, Stephano? O Stephano, two Neapolitans scaped!

STE. Prithee, do not turn me about; my stomach is not constant.

CAL. [*Aside*] These be fine things, an if they be not sprites. 127
That's a brave god, and bears celestial liquor;
I will kneel to him.

STE. How didst thou scape? How camest thou hither? Swear, by this bottle, how thou camest hither. I escaped upon a butt of sack, which the sailors heaved o'erboard, by this bottle! which I made of the bark of a tree with mine own hands, since I was cast ashore.

CAL. I'll swear, upon that bottle, to be thy true subject; for the liquor is not earthly. 137

STE. Here; swear, then, how thou escapedst.

TRIN. Swum ashore, man, like a duck. I can swim like a duck, I'll be sworn.

STE. Here, kiss the book. Though thou canst swim like a duck, thou art made like a goose.

TRIN. O Stephano, hast any more of this?

STE. The whole butt, man; my cellar is in a rock by the sea-side, where my wine is hid. How now, moon-calf! How does thine ague?

CAL. Hast thou not dropped from heaven?

STE. Out o' the moon, I do assure thee; I was the man i' the moon when time was. 149

CAL. I have seen thee in her, and I do adore thee; my mistress showed me thee, and thy dog, and thy bush.

STE. Come, swear to that; kiss the book; I will furnish it anon with new contents; swear.

TRIN. By this good light, this is a very shallow monster! I afeard of him! A very weak monster! The man i' the moon! A most poor credulous monster! Well drawn,[4] monster, in good sooth! 159

CAL. I will show thee every fertile inch o' th' island; and I will kiss thy foot; I prithee, be my god.

TRIN. By this light, a most perfidious and drunken monster! When's god's asleep, he'll rob his bottle.

CAL. I'll kiss thy foot; I'll swear myself thy subject.

STE. Come on, then; down, and swear.

TRIN. I shall laugh myself to death at this puppy-headed monster. A most scurvy monster! I could find it in my heart to beat him— 171

STE. Come, kiss.

TRIN. But that the poor monster's in drink. An abominable monster!

CAL. I'll show thee the best springs; I'll pluck thee berries;
I'll fish for thee, and get thee wood enough.
A plague upon the tyrant that I serve!
I'll bear him no more sticks, but follow thee,
Thou wondrous man.

TRIN. A most ridiculous monster, to make a wonder of a poor drunkard! 181

CAL. I prithee, let me bring thee where crabs[5] grow;
And I with my long nails will dig thee pignuts;[6]
Show thee a jay's nest, and instruct thee how
To snare the nimble marmoset; I'll bring thee
To clustering filberts, and sometimes I'll get thee
Young scamels[7] from the rock. Wilt thou go with me?

STE. I prithee, now, lead the way, without any more talking. Trinculo, the king and all our company else being drowned, we will inherit here. Here, bear my bottle; fellow Trinculo, we'll fill him by and by again. 192

CAL. [*sings drunkenly.*]
Farewell, master; farewell, farewell!

[1] Proverb: "He must have a long spoon that would eat with the devil."
[2] the offscum of this monstrosity
[3] spawn
[4] well drunk, well drained
[5] crab apples
[6] edible roots
[7] meaning unknown (possibly for sea-mell, sea-mew)

TRIN. A howling monster; a drunken monster.
CAL. No more dams I'll make for fish;
Nor fetch in firing
At requiring;
Nor scrape trencher, nor wash dish.
'Ban, 'Ban, Cacaliban
Has a new master;—get a new man.
Freedom, hey-day! Hey-day, freedom! Freedom, hey-day, freedom!
STE. O brave monster! Lead the way.
[*Exeunt.*

ACT III

SCENE I

Before Prospero's cell.

Enter FERDINAND, *bearing a log.*

FER. There be some sports are painful, and their labor
Delight in them sets off; [1] some kinds of baseness [2]
Are nobly undergone, and most poor matters
Point to rich ends. This my mean task
Would be as heavy to me as odious, but
The mistress which I serve quickens what's dead,
And makes my labors pleasures. Oh, she is
Ten times more gentle than her father's crabbed,
And he's composed of harshness. I must remove
Some thousands of these logs, and pile them up,
Upon a sore injunction; [3] my sweet mistress
Weeps when she sees me work, and says, such baseness
Had never like executor. I forget;
But these sweet thoughts do even refresh my labors,
Most busy lest, [4] when I do it.

Enter MIRANDA; *and* PROSPERO, *at a distance, unseen.*

MIR. Alas, now, pray you,
Work not so hard; I would the lightning had
Burnt up those logs that you are enjoined to pile!
Pray, set it down, and rest you; when this burns,
'Twill weep for having wearied you. My father
Is hard at study; pray, now, rest yourself;
He's safe for these three hours.

FER. O most dear mistress,
The sun will set before I shall discharge
What I must strive to do.

MIR. If you'll sit down,
I'll bear your logs the while; pray, give me that;
I'll carry it to the pile.

FER. No, precious creature;
I had rather crack my sinews, break my back,
Than you should such dishonor undergo,
While I sit lazy by.

MIR. It would become me
As well as it does you; and I should do it
With much more ease, for my good will is to it,
And yours it is against.

PROS. Poor worm, thou art infected!
This visitation [5] shows it.

MIR. You look wearily.

FER. No, noble mistress; 'tis fresh morning with me
When you are by at night. I do beseech you—
Chiefly that I might set it in my prayers—
What is your name?

MIR. Miranda.—O my father,
I have broke your hest to say so!

FER. Admired Miranda!
Indeed the top of admiration! worth
What's dearest to the world! Full many a lady
I have eyed with best regard, and many a time
The harmony of their tongues hath into bondage
Brought my too diligent ear; for several virtues
Have I liked several women; never any
With so full soul, but some defect in her
Did quarrel with the noblest grace she owed
And put it to the foil. [6] But you, O you,
So perfect and so peerless, are created
Of every creature's best!

MIR. I do not know
One of my sex; no woman's face remember,
Save, from my glass, mine own; nor have I seen
More that I may call men than you, good friend,
And my dear father. How features are abroad,
I am skilless [7] of; but, by my modesty,
The jewel in my dower, I would not wish
Any companion in the world but you;
Nor can imagination form a shape,
Besides yourself, to like of. But I prattle
Something too wildly, and my father's precepts
I therein do forget.

[1] This sentence yields various meanings, according as "labor" is subject or object, and according as "sets off" means "heightens" or "offsets."
[2] menial work
[3] behest
[4] Another very obscure passage; the later Folios read *least,* Theobald surmises *busyless,* Holt *busiest.*
[5] visit
[6] disadvantage
[7] ignorant

FER. I am, in my condition,
A prince, Miranda; I do think, a king;
I would, not so!—and would no more endure
This wooden slavery than to suffer
The flesh-fly blow my mouth. Hear my soul speak:
The very instant that I saw you, did
My heart fly to your service; there resides,
To make me slave to it; and for your sake
Am I this patient log-man.
MIR. Do you love me?
FER. O heaven, O earth, bear witness to this sound,
And crown what I profess with kind event,[1]
If I speak true! If hollowly, invert
What best is boded me to mischief! I,
Beyond all limit of what else i' the world
Do love, prize, honor you.
MIR. I am a fool
To weep at what I am glad of.
PROS. Fair encounter
Of two most rare affections! Heavens rain grace
On that which breeds between 'em!
FER. Wherefore weep you?
MIR. At mine unworthiness, that dare not offer
What I desire to give; and much less take
What I shall die to want.[2] But this is trifling;
And all the more it seeks to hide itself,
The bigger bulk it shows. Hence, bashful cunning!
And prompt me, plain and holy innocence!
I am your wife, if you will marry me;
If not, I'll die your maid. To be your fellow
You may deny me; but I'll be your servant,
Whether you will or no.
FER. My mistress, dearest;
And I thus humble ever.
MIR. My husband, then?
FER. Aye, with a heart as willing
As bondage e'er of freedom; here's my hand.
MIR. And mine, with my heart in't; and now farewell
Till half an hour hence.
FER. A thousand thousand!
[*Exeunt* FER. *and* MIR. *severally*.
PROS. So glad of this as they I cannot be,
Who are surprised withal; but my rejoicing
At nothing can be more. I'll to my book;
For yet, ere supper-time, must I perform
Much business appertaining.
[*Exit*

[1] outcome
[2] lack

SCENE II

Another part of the island.

Enter CALIBAN, STEPHANO, *and* TRINCULO.

STE. Tell not me—when the butt is out, we will drink water; not a drop before; therefore bear up, and board 'em.[3] Servant-monster, drink to me.

TRIN. Servant-monster! the folly of this island! They say there's but five upon this isle; we are three of them; if th' other two be brained like us, the state totters.

STE. Drink, servant-monster, when I bid thee; thy eyes are almost set[4] in thy head.

TRIN. Where should they be set else? He were a brave monster indeed, if they were set in his tail.

STE. My man-monster hath drowned his tongue in sack. For my part, the sea cannot drown me; I swam, ere I could recover the shore, five-and-thirty leagues off and on. By this light, thou shalt be my lieutenant, monster, or my standard.[5]

TRIN. Your lieutenant, if you list; he's no standard.

STE. We'll not run, Monsieur Monster.

TRIN. Nor go neither; but you'll lie, like dogs, and yet say nothing neither.

STE. Moon-calf, speak once in thy life, if thou beest a good moon-calf.

CAL. How does thy honor? Let me lick thy shoe. I'll not serve him, he is not valiant.

TRIN. Thou liest, most ignorant monster; I am in case to justle[6] a constable. Why, thou deboshed[7] fish, thou, was there ever man a coward that hath drunk so much sack as I today? Wilt thou tell a monstrous lie, being but half a fish and half a monster?

CAL. Lo, how he mocks me! Wilt thou let him, my lord?

TRIN. "Lord," quoth he! That a monster should be such a natural![8]

CAL. Lo, lo, again! Bite him to death, I prithee.

STE. Trinculo, keep a good tongue in your head; if you prove a mutineer—the next tree! The poor monster's my subject, and he shall not suffer indignity.

CAL. I thank my noble lord. Wilt thou be pleased to hearken once again to the suit I made to thee?

STE. Marry, will I; kneel and repeat it; I will stand, and so shall Trinculo.

[3] sail up and attack them (the cups)
[4] fixed
[5] standard-bearer
[6] in trim to jostle
[7] debauched
[8] simpleton

Enter ARIEL *(invisible)*

CAL. As I told thee before, I am subject to a tyrant, a sorcerer, that by his cunning hath cheated me of the island.

ARI. Thou liest.

CAL. Thou liest, thou jesting monkey, thou;
I would my valiant master would destroy thee!
I do not lie.

STE. Trinculo, if you trouble him any more in 's tale, by this hand, I will supplant some of your teeth.

TRIN. Why, I said nothing.

STE. Mum, then, and no more. Proceed.

CAL. I say, by sorcery he got this isle;
From me he got it. If thy greatness will
Revenge it on him—for I know thou darest,
But this thing dare not—

STE. That's most certain.

CAL. Thou shalt be lord of it, and I'll serve thee.

STE. How now shall this be compassed? Canst thou bring me to the party?

CAL. Yea, yea, my lord; I'll yield him thee asleep,
Where thou mayst knock a nail into his head.

ARI. Thou liest; thou canst not.

CAL. What a pied ninny's [1] this! Thou scurvy patch! [2]
I do beseech thy greatness, give him blows,
And take his bottle from him. When that's gone,
He shall drink naught but brine; for I'll not show him
Where the quick freshes are.

STE. Trinculo, run into no further danger; interrupt the monster one word further, and, by this hand, I'll turn my mercy out o' doors, and make a stock-fish [3] of thee.

TRIN. Why, what did I? I did nothing. I'll go farther off.

STE. Didst thou not say he lied?

ARI. Thou liest.

STE. Do I so? Take thou that. [*Beats him.*] As you like this, give me the lie another time.

TRIN. I did not give the lie. Out o' your wits, and hearing, too? A pox o' your bottle! This can sack and drinking do. A murrain on your monster, and the devil take your fingers!

CAL. Ha, ha, ha!

STE. Now, forward with your tale.—Prithee, stand farther off.

CAL. Beat him enough; after a little time, I'll beat him, too.

STE. Stand farther.—Come, proceed.

CAL. Why, as I told thee, 'tis a custom with him
I' th' afternoon to sleep; there thou mayst brain him,
Having first seized his books; or with a log
Batter his skull, or paunch him with a stake,
Or cut his wezand [4] with thy knife. Remember
First to possess his books; for without them
He's but a sot, as I am, nor hath not
One spirit to command; they all do hate him
As rootedly as I. Burn but his books.
He has brave utensils—for so he calls them—
Which, when he has a house, he'll deck withal.
And that [5] most deeply to consider is
The beauty of his daughter; he himself
Calls her a nonpareil. I never saw a woman,
But only Sycorax my dam and she;
But she as far surpasseth Sycorax
As great'st does least.

STE. Is it so brave a lass?

CAL. Aye, lord; she will become thy bed, I warrant,
And bring thee forth brave brood.

STE. Monster, I will kill this man; his daughter and I will be king and queen—save our graces!—and Trinculo and thyself shall be viceroys. Dost thou like the plot, Trinculo?

TRIN. Excellent.

STE. Give me thy hand; I am sorry I beat thee; but, while thou livest, keep a good tongue in thy head.

CAL. Within this half hour will he be asleep.
Wilt thou destroy him then?

STE. Aye, on mine honor.

ARI. This will I tell my master.

CAL. Thou makest me merry; I am full of pleasure;
Let us be jocund; will you troll the catch [6]
You taught me but while-ere?

STE. At thy request, monster, I will do reason, any reason.—Come on, Trinculo, let us sing. [*Sings.*

Flout 'em and scout 'em,
And scout 'em and flout 'em;
Thought is free.

CAL. That's not the tune.

[ARIEL *plays the tune on a tabor and pipe.*

STE. What is this same?

TRIN. This is the tune of our catch, played by the picture of Nobody. [7]

STE. If thou beest a man, show thyself in thy likeness; if thou beest a devil, take't as thou list.

[1] motley-coated fool
[2] fool
[3] dried cod (which was beaten before being cooked)
[4] wind-pipe
[5] that which
[6] part-song
[7] alluding to a print (of merely head, legs, and arms) prefixed to an old comedy

TRIN. Oh, forgive me my sins!
STE. He that dies pays all debts; I defy thee. Mercy upon us!
CAL. Art thou afeard?
STE. No, monster, not I.
CAL. Be not afeard; the isle is full of noises,
Sounds and sweet airs, that give delight, and hurt not.
Sometimes a thousand twangling instruments
Will hum about mine ears; and sometime voices,
That, if I then had waked after long sleep,
Will make me sleep again; and then, in dreaming,
The clouds methought would open, and show riches
Ready to drop upon me; that, when I waked,
I cried to dream again.
STE. This will prove a brave kingdom to me, where
I shall have my music for nothing.
CAL. When Prospero is destroyed.
STE. That shall be by and by; I remember the story.
TRIN. The sound is going away; let's follow it, and after do our work.
STE. Lead, monster; we'll follow. I would I could see this taborer; he lays it on.
TRIN. Wilt come? I'll follow, Stephano.
[*Exeunt.*

SCENE III

Another part of the island.

Enter ALONSO, SEBASTIAN, ANTONIO, GONZALO, ADRIAN, FRANCISCO, *and others.*

GON. By'r lakin,[1] I can go no farther, sir;
My old bones ache; here's a maze trod, indeed,
Through forth-rights and meanders! By your patience,
I needs must rest me.
ALON. Old lord, I cannot blame thee,
Who am myself attached[2] with weariness,
To the dulling of my spirits; sit down, and rest.
Even here I will put off my hope, and keep it
No longer for[3] my flatterer; he is drowned
Whom thus we stray to find; and the sea mocks
Our frustrate search on land. Well, let him go.
ANT. [*Aside to* SEB.] I am right glad that he's so out of hope.
Do not, for one repulse, forego the purpose
That you resolved to effect.
SEB. [*Aside to* ANT.] The next advantage
Will we take thoroughly.

[1] ladykin (little lady, the Virgin Mary)
[2] attacked
[3] as

ANT. [*Aside to* SEB.] Let it be tonight;
For, now they are oppressed with travel, they
Will not, nor cannot, use such vigilance
As when they are fresh.
SEB. [*Aside to* ANT.] I say, tonight; no more. [*Solemn and strange music.*
ALON. What harmony is this? My good friends, hark!
GON. Marvelous sweet music!

Enter PROSPERO *above (invisible). Enter several strange* SHAPES, *bringing in a banquet; they dance about it with gentle actions of salutations; and, inviting the King, etc., to eat, they depart.*

ALON. Give us kind keepers, heavens!
What were these?
SEB. A living drollery.[4] Now I will believe
That there are unicorns; that in Arabia
There is one tree, the phoenix' throne; one phoenix
At this hour reigning there.
ANT. I'll believe both;
And what does else want credit,[5] come to me,
And I'll be sworn 'tis true; travelers ne'er did lie,
Though fools at home condemn 'em.
GON. If in Naples
I should report this now, would they believe me?
If I should say, I saw such islanders—
For, certes, these are people of the island—
Who, though they are of monstrous shape, yet, note,
Their manners are more gentle-kind than of
Our human generation you shall find
Many, nay, almost any.
PROS. [*Aside*] Honest lord,
Thou hast said well; for some of you there present
Are worse than devils.
ALON. I cannot too much muse[6]
Such shapes, such gesture, and such sound, expressing—
Although they want the use of tongue—a kind
Of excellent dumb discourse.
PROS. [*Aside*] Praise in departing.[7]
FRAN. They vanished strangely.
SEB. No matter, since
They have left their viands behind; for we have stomachs.—
Will't please you taste of what is here?

[4] puppet show
[5] whatever else is incredible
[6] wonder at
[7] Proverb: "Save your praises till you go."

ALON. Not I.
GON. Faith, sir, you need not fear. When we were boys,
Who would believe that there were mountaineers
Dew-lapped like bulls, whose throats had hanging at 'em
Wallets of flesh? Or that there were such men
Whose heads stood in their breasts? Which now we find
Each putter-out of five for one [1] will bring us
Good warrant of.
ALON. I will stand to, and feed,
Although my last; no matter, since I feel
The best is past. Brother, my lord the duke,
Stand to, and do as we.

Thunder and lightning. Enter ARIEL, *like a harpy; claps his wings upon the table; and, with a quaint device, the banquet vanishes.*

ARI. You are three men of sin, whom Destiny—
That hath to [2] instrument this lower world
And what is in't—the never-surfeited sea
Hath caused to belch up you; and on this island,
Where man doth not inhabit—you 'mongst men
Being most unfit to live. I have made you mad;
And even with such-like valor men hang and drown
Their proper selves.
[ALON., SEB., *etc., draw their swords.*
You fools! I and my fellows
Are ministers of Fate; the elements,
Of whom your swords are tempered, may as well
Wound the loud winds, or with bemocked-at stabs
Kill the still-closing waters, as diminish
One dowle [3] that's in my plume; my fellow-ministers
Are like invulnerable. If you could hurt,
Your swords are now too massy for your strengths,
And will not be uplifted. But remember—
For that's my business to you—that you three
From Milan did supplant good Prospero;
Exposed unto the sea, which hath requit it,
Him and his innocent child; for which foul deed
The powers, delaying, not forgetting, have
Incensed the seas and shores, yea, all the creatures,
Against your peace. Thee of thy son, Alonso,
They have bereft; and do pronounce by me:
Lingering perdition—worse than any death
Can be at once—shall step by step attend
You and your ways; whose wraths to guard you from—
Which here, in this most desolate isle, else falls
Upon your heads—is nothing but [4] heart-sorrow
And a clear life ensuing.

He vanishes in thunder; then, to soft music, enter the SHAPES *again and dance, with mocks and mows, and carrying out the table.*

PROS. Bravely the figure of this harpy hast thou
Performed, my Ariel; a grace it had, devouring.
Of my instruction hast thou nothing bated
In what thou hadst to say; so, with good life
And observation strange, [5] my meaner ministers
Their several kinds [6] have done. My high charms work,
And these mine enemies are all knit up
In their distractions; they now are in my power;
And in these fits I leave them, while I visit
Young Ferdinand—whom [7] they suppose is drowned—
And his and mine loved darling.
[*Exit above.*
GON. I' the name of something holy, sir, why stand you
In this strange stare?
ALON. Oh, it is monstrous, monstrous!
Methought the billows spoke, and told me of it;
The winds did sing it to me; and the thunder,
That deep and dreadful organ-pipe, pronounced
The name of Prosper; it did bass my trespass.
Therefore my son i' th' ooze is bedded; and
I'll seek him deeper than e'er plummet sounded,
And with him there lie mudded.
[*Exit.*
SEB. But one fiend at a time,
I'll fight their legions o'er.
ANT. I'll be thy second.
[*Exeunt* SEB. *and* ANT.
GON. All three of them are desperate; their great guilt,
Like poison given to work a great time after,

[1] referring to travelers going on a perilous journey, who sometimes made over their property on condition that if they returned safe it should be restored to them two, three, or even five fold
[2] for
[3] filament of down
[4] nothing will avail but
[5] rare observance
[6] appropriate functions
[7] for "who"

Now 'gins to bite the spirits. I do beseech you,
That are of suppler joints, follow them swiftly,
And hinder them from what this ecstasy [1]
May now provoke them to.

ADR. Follow, I pray you. [*Exeunt.*

ACT IV

SCENE I

Before Prospero's cell.

Enter PROSPERO, FERDINAND, *and* MIRANDA.

PROS. If I have too austerely punished you,
Your compensation makes amends; for I
Have given you here a third [2] of mine own life,
Or that for which I live; who once again
I tender to thy hand. All thy vexations
Were but my trials of thy love, and thou
Hast strangely stood the test; here, afore Heaven,
I ratify this my rich gift. O Ferdinand,
Do not smile at me that I boast her off,
For thou shalt find she will outstrip all praise
And make it halt behind her.

FER. I do believe it [3]
Against an oracle.

PROS. Then, as my gift, and thine own acquisition
Worthily purchased, take my daughter; but
If thou dost break her virgin-knot [4] before
All sanctimonious ceremonies may
With full and holy rite be ministered,
No sweet aspersions [5] shall the heavens let fall
To make this contract grow; but barren hate,
Sour-eyed disdain and discord shall bestrew
The union of your bed with weeds so loathly
That you shall hate it both; therefore take heed,
As Hymen's lamps shall light you. [6]

FER. As I hope
For quiet days, fair issue, and long life,
With such love as 'tis now, the murkiest den,
The most opportune place, the strong'st suggestion
Our worser genius can, shall never melt
Mine honor into lust, to take away
The edge of that day's celebration
When I shall think, or [7] Phoebus' steeds are foundered,
Or Night kept chained below.

PROS. Fairly spoke.
Sit, then, and talk with her; she is thine own.
What, Ariel! my industrious servant, Ariel!

Enter ARIEL.

ARI. What would my potent master? Here I am.

PROS. Thou and thy meaner fellows your last service
Did worthily perform; and I must use you
In such another trick. Go bring the rabble,
O'er whom I give thee power, here to this place.
Incite them to quick motion; for I must
Bestow upon the eyes of this young couple
Some vanity [8] of mine art; it is my promise,
And they expect it from me.

ARI. Presently? [9]

PROS. Aye, with a twink.

ARI. Before you can say "come," and "go,"
And breathe twice, and cry, "so, so,"
Each one, tripping on his toe,
Will be here with mop [10] and mow.
Do you love me, master? No?

PROS. Dearly, my delicate Ariel. Do not approach
Till thou dost hear me call.

ARI. Well, I conceive. [*Exit.*

PROS. Look thou be true; do not give dalliance
Too much the rein. The strongest oaths are straw
To the fire i' the blood; be more abstemious,
Or else, good night your vow!

FER. I warrant you, sir;
The white cold virgin snow upon my heart
Abates the ardor of my liver. [11]

PROS. Well.
Now come, my Ariel! Bring a corollary, [12]
Rather than want a spirit; appear, and pertly! [13]
No tongue! all eyes! be silent. [*Soft music.*

Enter IRIS.

IRIS. Ceres, most bounteous lady, thy rich leas
Of wheat, rye, barley, vetches, oats, and pease;
Thy turfy mountains, where live nibbling sheep,
And flat meads thatched with stover, [14] them to keep;
Thy banks with pioned and twilled [15] brims,
Which spongy April at thy hest betrims,

[1] madness
[2] Commonly taken to mean that he himself and his dukedom (or his wife) are the two other thirds; but some editors read *thread*.
[3] Supply "and should."
[4] girdle worn as mark of maidenhood
[5] sprinkling
[6] as you hoped to be blessed by the god of marriage
[7] either
[8] illusion
[9] at once
[10] grimace (about the same as "mow")
[11] then regarded as the seat of passion
[12] surplusage
[13] nimbly
[14] coarse hay
[15] peonied and reedy (?)

To make cold nymphs chaste crowns; and thy broom-groves,
Whose shadow the dismissed bachelor loves,
Being lass-lorn; thy pole-clipt [1] vineyard;
And thy sea-marge, sterile and rocky-hard,
Where thou thyself dost air;—the queen o' the sky, [2]
Whose watery arch and messenger am I,
Bids thee leave these; and with her sovereign grace,
Here, on this grass-plot, in this very place,
To come and sport—her peacocks fly amain;
Approach, rich Ceres, her to entertain.

Enter CERES.

CER. Hail, many-colored messenger, that ne'er
Dost disobey the wife of Jupiter;
Who, with thy saffron wings, upon my flowers
Diffusest honey-drops, refreshing showers;
And with each end of thy blue bow dost crown
My bosky [3] acres and my unshrubbed down, [4]
Rich scarf to my proud earth—why hath thy queen
Summoned me hither, to this short-grassed green?

IRIS. A contract of true love to celebrate;
And some donation freely to estate [5]
On the blest lovers.

CER. Tell me, heavenly bow,
If Venus or her son, as thou dost know,
Do now attend the queen? Since they did plot
The means that dusky Dis [6] my daughter got,
Her and her blind boy's scandaled company
I have forsworn.

IRIS. Of her society.
Be not afraid; I met her deity
Cutting the clouds toward Paphos, and her son
Dove-drawn with her. Here thought they to have done
Some wanton charm upon this man and maid,
Whose vows are, that no bed-right shall be paid
Till Hymen's torch be lighted. But in vain;
Mar's hot minion [7] is returned again;
Her waspish-headed son has broke his arrows,
Swears he will shoot no more, but play with sparrows,
And be a boy right out.

CER. High'st queen of state,
Great Juno, comes; I know her by her gait.

Enter JUNO.

JUNO. How does my bounteous sister? Go with me
To bless this twain, that they may prosperous be,
And honored in their issue. [*They sing.*

JUNO. Honor, riches, marriage-blessing,
Long continuance, and increasing,
Hourly joys be still upon you!
Juno sings her blessings on you.

CER. Earth's increase, foison [8] plenty,
Barns and garners never empty;
Vines with clustering bunches growing;
Plants with goodly burthen bowing;
Spring come to you at the farthest
In the very end of harvest!
Scarcity and want shall shun you;
Ceres' blessing so is on you.

FER. This is a most majestic vision, and
Harmonious charmingly. May I be bold
To think these spirits?

PROS. Spirits, which by mine art
I have from their confines called to enact
My present fancies.

FER. Let me live here ever;
So rare a wondered father and a wise
Makes this place Paradise.

[JUNO *and* CERES *whisper, and send* IRIS *on employment.*

PROS. Sweet, now, silence!
Juno and Ceres whisper seriously;
There's something else to do; hush and be mute,
Or else our spell is marred.

IRIS. You nymphs, called Naiads, of the winding brooks,
With your sedged crowns and ever-harmless looks,
Leave your crisp [9] channels, and on this green land
Answer your summons; Juno does command.
Come, temperate nymphs, and help to celebrate
A contract of true love; be not too late.

Enter certain NYMPHS.

You sunburned sicklemen, of August weary,
Come hither from the furrow, and be merry.
Make holiday; your rye-straw hats put on,
And these fresh nymphs encounter every one
In country footing. [10]

Enter certain REAPERS, *properly habited; they join with the* NYMPHS *in a graceful dance; toward the end whereof* PROSPERO *starts suddenly, and speaks; after which, to a strange, hollow, and confused noise, they heavily vanish.*

PROS. [*Aside.*] I had forgot that foul conspiracy

[1] pole-entwined
[2] Juno
[3] woody
[4] cleared slopes
[5] bestow
[6] Pluto (who carried off Proserpina)
[7] darling (Venus)
[8] abundance
[9] waveleted
[10] dancing

Of the beast Caliban and his confederates
Against my life; the minute of their plot
Is almost come. [*To the* SPIRITS.] Well done! avoid;[1] no more!

FER. This is strange; your father's in some passion
That works him strongly.

MIR. Never till this day
Saw I him touched with anger so distempered.

PROS. You do look, my son, in a moved sort.
As if you were dismayed; be cheerful, sir.
Our revels now are ended. These our actors,
As I foretold you, were all spirits, and
Are melted into air, into thin air.
And, like the baseless fabric of this vision,
The cloud-capped towers, the gorgeous palaces,
The solemn temples, the great globe itself,
Yea, all which it inherit, shall dissolve,
And, like this insubstantial pageant faded,
Leave not a rack[2] behind. We are such stuff
As dreams are made on;[3] and our little life
Is rounded with a sleep. Sir, I am vexed;
Bear with my weakness; my old brain is troubled.
Be not disturbed with my infirmity;
If you be pleased, retire into my cell,
And there repose; a turn or two I'll walk,
To still my beating mind.

FER. MIR. We wish you peace. [*Exeunt.*

PROS. Come with a thought.[4] I thank thee, Ariel; come.

Enter ARIEL.

ARI. Thy thoughts I cleave to. What's thy pleasure?

PROS. Spirit,
We must prepare to meet with[5] Caliban.

ARI. Aye, my commander; when I presented Ceres,
I thought to have told thee of it; but I feared
Lest I might anger thee.

PROS. Say again, where didst thou leave these varlets?

ARI. I told you, sir, they were red-hot with drinking;
So full of valor that they smote the air
For breathing in their faces; beat the ground
For kissing of their feet; yet always bending
Toward their project. Then I beat my tabor;
At which, like unbacked[6] colts, they pricked their ears,
Advanced their eyelids, lifted up their noses
As they smelt music. So I charmed their ears,
That, calf-like, they my lowing followed through
Toothed briars, sharp furzes, pricking goss,[7] and thorns,
Which entered their frail shins; at last I left them
I' the filthy-mantled pool beyond your cell,
There dancing up to the chins, that the foul lake
O'erstunk their feet.

PROS. This was well done, my bird.
Thy shape invisible retain thou still.
The trumpery in my house, go bring it hither,
For stale[8] to catch these thieves.

ARI. I go, I go. [*Exit.*

PROS. A devil, a born devil, on whose nature
Nurture can never stick; on whom my pains,
Humanely taken, all, all lost, quite lost;
And as with age his body uglier grows,
So his mind cankers. I will plague them all,
Even to roaring.

Reënter ARIEL, *loaden with glistering apparel, etc.*

Come, hang them on this line.[9]

PROSPERO *and* ARIEL *remain, invisible.*

Enter CALIBAN, STEPHANO, *and* TRINCULO, *all wet.*

CAL. Pray you, tread softly, that the blind mole may not hear a foot fall; we now are near his cell.

STE. Monster, your fairy, which you say is a harmless fairy, has done little better than played the Jack with us.

TRIN. Monster, my nose is in great indignation.

STE. So is mine. Do you hear, monster? If I should take a displeasure against you, look you—

TRIN. Thou wert but a lost monster.

CAL. Good my lord, give me thy favor still.
Be patient, for the prize I'll bring thee to
Shall hoodwink[10] this mischance; therefore speak softly.
All's hushed as midnight yet.

TRIN. Aye, but to lose our bottles in the pool—

STE. There is not only disgrace and dishonor in that, monster, but an infinite loss.

TRIN. That's more to me than my wetting; yet this is your harmless fairy, monster.

STE. I will fetch off my bottle, though I be o'er ears for my labor.

CAL. Prithee, my king, be quiet. See'st thou here,
This is the mouth o' the cell; no noise, and enter.
Do that good mischief which may make this island

[1] depart
[2] shred of vapor
[3] of
[4] quick as thought
[5] meet, frustrate
[6] unridden
[7] gorse
[8] decoy
[9] lime-tree, linden
[10] blind you to

Thine own forever, and I, thy Caliban,
For aye thy foot-licker.

STE. Give me thy hand. I do begin to have bloody thoughts.

TRIN. O King Stephano! O peer! O worthy Stephano! Look what a wardrobe here is for thee!

CAL. Let it alone, thou fool; it is but trash.

TRIN. Oh, ho, monster! we know what belongs to a frippery.[1] O King Stephano!

STE. Put off that gown, Trinculo; by this hand, I'll have that gown.

TRIN. Thy grace shall have it.

CAL. The dropsy drown this fool! what do you mean
To dote thus on such luggage? Let's alone,[2]
And do the murder first; if he awake,
From toe to crown he'll fill our skins with pinches,
Make us strange stuff.

STE. Be you quiet, monster. Mistress line, is not this my jerkin? Now is the jerkin under the line; now, jerkin, you are like to lose your hair, and prove a bald jerkin.[3]

TRIN. Do, do; we steal by line and level,[4] an't like your grace.

STE. I thank thee for that jest; here's a garment for't; wit shall not go unrewarded while I am king of this country. "Steal by line and level" is an excellent pass of pate;[5] there's another garment for't.

TRIN. Monster, come, put some lime[6] upon your fingers, and away with the rest.

CAL. I will have none on't; we shall lose our time,
And all be turned to barnacles, or to apes
With foreheads villainous low.

STE. Monster, lay-to your fingers; help to bear this away where my hogshead of wine is, or I'll turn you out of my kingdom; go to, carry this.

TRIN. And this.

STE. Aye, and this.

A noise of hunters heard. Enter divers SPIRITS, *in shape of dogs and hounds, hunting them about;* PROSPERO *and* ARIEL *setting them on.*

PROS. Hey, Mountain, hey!

ARI. Silver! there it goes, Silver!

PROS. Fury, Fury! there, Tyrant, there! hark, hark!

[CAL., STE., *and* TRIN. *are driven out.*
Go charge my goblins that they grind their joints
With dry convulsions; shorten up their sinews
With aged cramps; and more pinch-spotted make them
Than pard or cat o' mountain.

ARI. Hark, they roar!

PROS. Let them be hunted soundly. At this hour
Lie at my mercy all mine enemies.
Shortly shall all my labors end, and thou
Shalt have the air at freedom; for a little
Follow, and do me service. [*Exeunt.*

ACT V

SCENE I

Before the cell of PROSPERO.

Enter PROSPERO *in his magic robes, and* ARIEL.

PROS. Now does my project gather to a head;
My charms crack[7] not, my spirits obey, and time
Goes upright with his carriage.[8] How's the day?

ARI. On the sixth hour; at which time, my lord,
You said our work should cease.

PROS. I did say so,
When first I raised the tempest. Say, my spirit,
How fares the king and 's followers?

ARI. Confined together
In the same fashion as you gave in charge,
Just as you left them; all prisoners, sir,
In the line-grove[9] which weather-fends your cell;
They cannot budge till your release. The king,
His brother, and yours, abide all three distracted,
And the remainder mourning over them,
Brimful of sorrow and dismay; but chiefly
Him that you termed, sir, "The good old lord, Gonzalo";
His tears run down his beard, like winter's drops
From eaves of reeds. Your charm so strongly works 'em,
That if you now beheld them, your affections
Would become tender.

PROS. Dost thou think so, spirit?

ARI. Mine would, sir, were I human.

PROS. And mine shall.
Hast thou, which art but air, a touch, a feeling
Of their afflictions, and shall not myself,

[1] old-clothes shop
[2] Supply "go" (*Alone* may be an error for *along;* or read, with Rowe and other editors, "let't alone.").
[3] Perhaps this alludes to the frequent loss of hair from fevers contracted in crossing the Line, or equator.
[4] by rule [5] thrust of wit [6] bird-lime

[7] break, fail
[8] carries all through well
[9] See note 9, p. 203.

One of their kind, that relish all as sharply,[1]
Passion[2] as they, be kindlier moved than thou art?
Though with their high wrongs[3] I am struck to the quick,
Yet with my nobler reason 'gainst my fury
Do I take part. The rarer action is
In virtue than in vengeance; they being penitent,
The sole drift of my purpose doth extend
Not a frown further. Go release them, Ariel;
My charms I'll break, their senses I'll restore,
And they shall be themselves.

ARI. I'll fetch them, sir. [*Exit.*

PROS. Ye elves of hills, brooks, standing lakes, and groves;
And ye that on the sands with printless foot
Do chase the ebbing Neptune, and do fly him
When he comes back; you demi-puppets that
By moonshine do the green sour ringlets[4] make,
Whereof the ewe not bites; and you whose pastime
Is to make midnight mushrooms, that rejoice
To hear the solemn curfew; by whose aid—
Weak masters though ye be—I have bedimmed
The noontide sun, called forth the mutinous winds,
And 'twixt the green sea and the azured vault
Set roaring war; to the dread rattling thunder
Have I given fire, and rifted Jove's stout oak
With his own bolt; the strong-based promontory
Have I made shake, and by the spurs plucked up
The pine and cedar; graves at my command
Have waked their sleepers, oped, and let 'em forth
By my so potent art. But this rough magic
I here abjure; and, when I have required
Some heavenly music—which even now I do—
To work mine end upon their senses, that
This airy charm is for, I'll break my staff,
Bury it certain fathoms in the earth,
And deeper than did ever plummet sound
I'll drown my book. [*Solemn music.*

Reënter ARIEL *before; then* ALONSO, *with a frantic gesture, attended by* GONZALO; SEBASTIAN *and* ANTONIO *in like manner, attended by* ADRIAN *and* FRANCISCO; *they all enter the circle which* PROSPERO *had made, and there stand charmed; which* PROSPERO *observing, speaks.*

A solemn air, and the best comforter
To an unsettled fancy, cure thy brains,
Now useless, boiled within thy skull! There stand,
For you are spell-stopped.
Holy Gonzalo, honorable man,
Mine eyes, even sociable to[5] the show of thine,
Fall fellowly drops. The charm dissolves apace;
And as the morning steals upon the night
Melting the darkness, so their rising senses
Begin to chase the ignorant fumes that mantle
Their clearer reason. O good Gonzalo,
My true preserver, and a loyal sir
To him thou follow'st! I will pay thy graces
Home[6] both in word and deed. Most cruelly
Didst thou, Alonzo, use me and my daughter;
Thy brother was a furtherer in the act.
Thou art pinched for't now, Sebastian. Flesh and blood,
You, brother mine, that entertained ambition,
Expelled remorse and nature; who, with Sebastian—
Whose inward pinches therefore are most strong—
Would here have killed your king; I do forgive thee,
Unnatural though thou art. Their understanding
Begins to swell; and the approaching tide
Will shortly fill the reasonable shore,[7]
That now lies foul and muddy. Not one of them
That yet looks on me, or would know me. Ariel,
Fetch me the hat and rapier in my cell.
I will discase me, and myself present
As I was sometime Milan. Quickly, spirit;
Thou shalt ere long be free.

ARIEL *sings and helps to attire him.*

Where the bee sucks, there suck I;
In a cowslip's bell I lie;
There I couch when owls do cry.
On the bat's back I do fly
After summer merrily.
Merrily, merrily shall I live now
Under the blossom that hangs on the bough.

PROS. Why, that's my dainty Ariel! I shall miss thee;
But yet thou shalt have freedom; so, so, so.
To the king's ship, invisible as thou art;
There shalt thou find the mariners asleep
Under the hatches; the master and the boatswain
Being awake, enforce them to this place,
And presently, I prithee.

ARI. I drink the air before me, and return
Or ere your pulse twice beat. [*Exit.*

GON. All torment, trouble, wonder, and amazement

[1] feel quite as keenly
[2] have passions
[3] crimes
[4] of grass ("fairy rings")
[5] sympathetic with
[6] fully
[7] shore of reason

Inhabits here; some heavenly power guide us
Out of this fearful country!
PROS. Behold, sir king,
The wronged Duke of Milan, Prospero;
For more assurance that a living prince
Does now speak to thee, I embrace thy body;
And to thee and thy company I bid
A hearty welcome.
ALON. Whether thou be'st he or no,
Or some enchanted trifle to abuse [1] me,
As late I have been, I not know. Thy pulse
Beats, as of flesh and blood; and, since I saw thee,
The affliction of my mind amends, with which,
I fear, a madness held me. This must crave—
An if this be at all—a most strange story.
Thy dukedom I resign, and do entreat
Thou pardon me my wrongs. But how should Prospero
Be living and be here?
PROS. First, noble friend,
Let me embrace thine age, whose honor cannot
Be measured or confined.
GON. Whether this be
Or be not, I'll not swear.
PROS. You do yet taste
Some subtilties [2] o' the isle, that will not let you
Believe things certain. Welcome, my friends all!
[*Aside to* SEB. *and* ANT.] But you, my brace of lords, were I so minded,
I here could pluck his highness' frown upon you,
And justify [3] you traitors; at this time
I will tell no tales.
SEB. [*Aside*] The devil speaks in him.
PROS. No.
For you, most wicked sir, whom to call brother
Would even infect my mouth, I do forgive
Thy rankest fault—all of them; and require
My dukedom of thee, which perforce, I know,
Thou must restore.
ALON. If thou be'st Prospero,
Give us particulars of thy preservation;
How thou hast met us here, who three hours since
Were wrecked upon this shore; where I have lost—
How sharp the point of this remembrance is!—
My dear son Ferdinand.
PROS. I am woe for't, sir.
ALON. Irreparable is the loss; and patience
Says it is past her cure.
PROS. I rather think
You have not sought her help, of whose soft grace
For the like loss I have her sovereign aid,
And rest myself content.

[1] deceive [2] strange concoctions [3] prove

ALON. You the like loss!
PROS. As great to me as late; and, supportable
To make the dear loss, have I means much weaker
Than you may call to comfort you, for I
Have lost my daughter.
ALON. A daughter?
O heavens, that they were living both in Naples,
The king and queen there! That they were, I wish
Myself were mudded in that oozy bed
Where my son lies. When did you lose your daughter?
PROS. In this last tempest. I perceive, these lords
At this encounter do so much admire, [4]
That they devour their reason, and scarce think
Their eyes do offices of truth, their words
Are natural breath; but, howsoe'er you have
Been justled from your senses, know for certain
That I am Prospero, and that very duke
Which was thrust forth of Milan, who most strangely
Upon this shore, where you were wrecked, was landed,
To be the lord on't. No more yet of this;
For 'tis a chronicle of day by day,
Not a relation for a breakfast, nor
Befitting this first meeting. Welcome, sir;
This cell's my court; here have I few attendants,
And subjects none abroad. Pray you, look in.
My dukedom since you have given me again,
I will requite you with as good a thing;
At least bring forth a wonder, to content ye
As much as me my dukedom.

Here PROSPERO *discovers* FERDINAND *and* MIRANDA *playing at chess.*

MIR. Sweet lord, you play me false.
FER. No, my dear'st love,
I would not for the world.
MIR. Yes, [5] for a score of kingdoms you should [6] wrangle,
And I would call it fair play.
ALON. If this prove
A vision of the island, one dear son
Shall I twice lose.
SEB. A most high miracle!
FER. Though the seas threaten, they are merciful;
I have cursed them without cause. [*Kneels.*
ALON. Now all the blessings
Of a glad father compass thee about!
Arise, and say how thou camest here.

[4] wonder [6] might
[5] Supply "but what then?"

MIR. Oh, wonder!
How many goodly creatures are there here!
How beauteous mankind is! O brave new world,
That has such people in't!
PROS. 'Tis new to thee.
ALON. What is this maid with whom thou wast at play?
Your eld'st acquaintance cannot be three hours.
Is she the goddess that hath severed us,
And brought us thus together?
FER. Sir, she is mortal;
But by immortal Providence she's mine.
I chose her when I could not ask my father
For his advice, nor thought I had one. She
Is daughter to this famous Duke of Milan,
Of whom so often I have heard renown,
But never saw before; of whom I have
Received a second life; and second father
This lady makes him to me.
ALON. I am hers;
But, oh, how oddly will it sound that I
Must ask my child forgiveness!
PROS. There, sir, stop;
Let us not burthen our remembrances with
A heaviness that's gone.
GON. I have inly wept,
Or should have spoke ere this. Look down, you gods,
And on this couple drop a blessed crown!
For it is you that have chalked forth the way
Which brought us hither.
ALON. I say, Amen, Gonzalo!
GON. Was Milan thrust from Milan, that his issue
Should become kings of Naples? Oh, rejoice
Beyond a common joy! and set it down
With gold on lasting pillars. In one voyage
Did Claribel her husband find at Tunis,
And Ferdinand, her brother, found a wife
Where he himself was lost, Prospero his dukedom
In a poor isle, and all of us ourselves
When no man was his own.
ALON. [*To* FER. *and* MIR.] Give me your hands.
Let grief and sorrow still embrace his heart
That doth not wish you joy!
GON. Be it so! Amen!

Reënter ARIEL *with the* MASTER *and* BOATSWAIN *amazedly following.*

Oh, look, sir, look, sir! here is more of us;
I prophesied, if a gallows were on land,
This fellow could not drown. Now, blasphemy,
That swear'st grace o'erboard, not an oath on shore?
Hast thou no mouth by land? What is the news?
BOATS. The best news is, that we have safely found
Our king and company; the next, our ship—
Which, but three glasses since, we gave out split—[1]
Is tight and yare and bravely rigged, as when
We first put out to sea.
ARI. [*Aside to* PROS.] Sir, all this service
Have I done since I went.
PROS. [*Aside to* ARI.] My tricksy spirit!
ALON. These are not natural events; they strengthen
From strange to stranger. Say, how came you hither?
BOATS. If I did think, sir, I were well awake,
I'ld strive to tell you. We were dead of sleep,
And—how we know not—all clapped under hatches;
Where, but even now, with strange and several noises
Of roaring, shrieking, howling, jingling chains,
And mo diversity of sounds, all horrible,
We were awaked; straightway, at liberty;
Where we, in all her trim, freshly beheld
Our royal, good, and gallant ship; our master
Capering to eye her;—on a trice, so please you,
Even in a dream, were we divided from them,
And were brought moping hither.
ARI. [*Aside to* PROS.] Was't well done?
PROS. [*Aside to* ARI.] Bravely, my diligence. Thou shalt be free.
ALON. This is as strange a maze as e'er men trod;
And there is in this business more than nature
Was ever conduct[2] of. Some oracle
Must rectify our knowledge.
PROS. Sir, my liege,
Do not infest[3] your mind with beating on
The strangeness of this business; at picked leisure
Which shall be shortly, single I'll resolve you,[4]
Which to you shall seem probable, of every
These happened accidents; till when, be cheerful,
And think of each thing well. [*Aside to* ARI.] Come hither, spirit;
Set Caliban and his companions free;
Untie the spell. [*Exit* ARIEL.] How fares my gracious sir?
There are yet missing of your company
Some few odd lads that you remember not.

Reënter ARIEL, *driving in* CALIBAN, STEPHANO, *and* TRINCULO, *in their stolen apparel.*

STE. Every man shift for all the rest, and

[1] declared wrecked
[2] conductor
[3] trouble
[4] give you explanation

let no man take care for himself; [1] for all is but fortune.—Coragio, bully-monster, coragio!

TRIN. If these be true spies which I wear in my head, here's a goodly sight.

CAL. O Setebos, these be brave spirits indeed!
How fine my master is! I am afraid
He will chastise me.

SEB. Ha, ha!
What things are these, my lord Antonio?
Will money buy 'em?

ANT. Very like; one of them
Is a plain fish, and, no doubt, marketable.

PROS. Mark but the badges [2] of these men, my lords,
Then say if they be true. This misshapen knave,
His mother was a witch; and one so strong
That could control the moon, make flows and ebbs,
And deal in her command, [3] without her power.
These three have robbed me; and this demi-devil—
For he's a bastard one—had plotted with them
To take my life. Two of these fellows you
Must know and own; this thing of darkness I
Acknowledge mine.

CAL. I shall be pinched to death.

ALON. Is not this Stephano, my drunken butler?

SEB. He is drunk now. Where had he wine?

ALON. And Trinculo is reeling ripe. Where should they
Find this grand liquor that hath gilded 'em?—
How camest thou in this pickle?

TRIN. I have been in such a pickle since I saw you last, that, I fear me, will never out of my bones; I shall not fear fly-blowing.

SEB. Why, how now, Stephano!

STE. Oh, touch me not—I am not Stephano, but a cramp.

PROS. You'ld be king o' the isle, sirrah?

STE. I should have been a sore one, then.

ALON. This is a strange thing as e'er I looked on.

[*Pointing to* CALIBAN.

PROS. He is as disproportioned in his manners
As in his shape. Go, sirrah, to my cell;
Take with you your companions; as you look
To have my pardon, trim it handsomely.

CAL. Aye, that I will; and I'll be wise hereafter,
And seek for grace. What a thrice-double ass
Was I, to take this drunkard for a god,
And worship this dull fool!

PROS. Go to; away!

ALON. Hence, and bestow your luggage where you found it.

SEB. Or stole it, rather.

[*Exeunt* CAL., STE., *and* TRIN.

PROS. Sir, I invite your Highness and your train
To my poor cell, where you shall take your rest
For this one night; which, part of it, I'll waste
With such discourse as, I not doubt, shall make it
Go quick away—the story of my life,
And the particular accidents gone by
Since I came to this isle. And in the morn
I'll bring you to your ship, and so to Naples,
Where I have hope to see the nuptial
Of these our dear-beloved solemnized;
And thence retire me to my Milan, where
Every third thought shall be my grave.

ALON. I long
To hear the story of your life, which must
Take [4] the ear strangely.

PROS. I'll deliver all;
And promise you calm seas, auspicious gales,
And sail so expeditious, that shall catch
Your royal fleet far off. [*Aside to* ARI.] My Ariel, chick,
That is thy charge; then to the elements
Be free, and fare thou well! Please you, draw near.

[*Exeunt.*

Epilogue [5]

Spoken by PROSPERO.

Now my charms are all o'erthrown,
And what strength I have's mine own,
Which is most faint. Now, 'tis true,
I must be here confined by you,
Or sent to Naples. Let me not,
Since I have my dukedom got,
And pardoned the deceiver, dwell
In this bare island by your spell;
But release me from my bands
With the help of your good hands.
Gentle breath of yours my sails
Must fill, or else my project fails,
Which was to please. Now I want [6]
Spirits to enforce, art to enchant;
And my ending is despair,
Unless I be relieved by prayer,
Which pierces so, that it assaults
Mercy itself, and frees all faults.
As you from crimes would pardoned be,
Let your indulgence set me free.

c. 1610 1623

[1] a drunkenly distorted speech
[2] i.e., the stolen apparel
[3] act in the moon's place(?)
[4] captivate
[5] probably not written by Shakespeare
[6] lack

BEN JONSON 1573?-1635

Of all Shakespeare's contemporaries none was more English to the backbone than "Rare Ben Jonson." Though of Border descent, he was born in Westminster, and received a good early education; whether he attended any university is not known. He ran away from his trade of bricklaying to fight in Flanders, but in 1597 was a player and playwright in London. He is known to have killed a fellow-actor in a duel, but suffered only imprisonment. His first plays were satirical comedies, chief among them being *Every Man Out of His Humor,* in which Shakespeare is said to have acted at the Globe Theater in 1598. His first tragedy, *Sejanus,* was acted by Shakespeare's company in 1603.

Jonson's most prosperous period began with the accession of James I in 1603; he received a pension of £200, and succeeded Drayton as poet laureate. He was also producing a succession of comedies, tragedies, masques, entertainments, satires, and minor writings. He was acquainted with nearly all the remarkable men of his times, and in his later days the young poets gathered about him as the dominant literary figure of the age. Under Charles I his fortunes declined so that at the end of his life he was appealing to the Duke of Newcastle for aid, and died in poverty. He was buried in Westminster Abbey.

His great defect was an inability to portray character as Shakespeare did. Instead, he set forth "humors," a word used with a special sense in Elizabethan days, with him meaning a personal peculiarity, a ruling passion, a whim; and by their means he aimed particularly to satirize in realistic comedy the follies of his day. A master of classical learning as well as of scenic effects, plot, and action, he could skillfully combine realism with the classical methods of dramatic workmanship. He has long been thought to be heavy to dullness, but, as L. Woolf pointed out recently, "The only defense of Jonson which is necessary is to tell people to read him." His Masques show him to be a poet; *Volpone, The Silent Woman,* and *The Alchemist* will stand with any comedies written in English, except Shakespeare's; *Conversations,* records of a visit to Drummond of Hawthornden, a Scotch poet, indicate that he is a critic of high rank, a first-rate prose writer, an original thinker, and a great character. "He could afford to do without genius."

Jonson's individual plays, three vols., Mermaid Series. Biography and criticism: J. A. Symonds's *Ben Jonson,* 1886, and *Shakespeare's Predecessors;* A. C. Swinburne's *A Study of Ben Jonson,* 1889; G. G. Smith (EML); there are also essays by Hazlitt and Carlyle *(Historical Sketches of Notable Persons and Events in the Reigns of James I and Charles I);* L. Woolf, "Rare Ben Jonson," *Liv. Age* 318:281-2; and Suddard, Robinson, and Noyes (see bibliographical material under Shakespeare on pp. 180-1).

TO THE MEMORY OF MY BELOVED MASTER WILLIAM SHAKESPEARE AND WHAT HE HATH LEFT US [1]

To draw no envy, Shakespeare, on thy name,
Am I thus ample [2] to thy book and fame;
While I confess thy writings to be such,
As neither man, nor Muse, can praise too much.
'Tis true, and all men's suffrage. [3] But these ways
Were not the paths I meant unto thy praise;
For silliest ignorance on these may light,
Which, when it sounds at best, but echoes right;
Or blind affection, which doth ne'er advance
The truth, but gropes, and urgeth all by chance;
Or crafty malice might pretend this praise,
And think to ruin, where it seemed to raise.

. . . .

But thou art proof against them, and, indeed,
Above the ill fortune of them, or the need.
I therefore will begin: Soul of the age!
The applause! delight! the wonder of our stage!
My Shakespeare rise! I will not lodge thee by
Chaucer, or Spenser, or bid Beaumont lie
A little farther off, to make thee room;
Thou art a monument without a tomb,
And art alive still, while thy book doth live,
And we have wits to read, and praise to give.
That I not mix thee so, my brain excuses,
I mean with great, but disproportioned Muses;

[1] Written after Shakespeare's death, which took place in April, 1616. Beaumont (see p. 215) died in March and was buried in Westminster Abbey beside Chaucer and Spenser, where twenty-one years later Jonson himself was to lie. Shakespeare, however, was buried at Stratford. Lines 19-21 refer to the following "Epitaph on Shakespeare" which was written by William Basse:

"Renowned Spenser, lie a thought more nigh
To learned Chaucer; and, rare Beaumont, lie
A little nearer Spenser, to make room
For Shakespeare in your threefold, fourfold tomb.
To lodge all four in one bed make a shift,
For until doomsday hardly will a fifth,
Betwixt this day and that, by fates be slain,
For whom your curtains need be drawn again.
But if precedency in death doth bar
A fourth place in your sacred sepulcher,
Under this sable marble of thine own,
Sleep, rare tragedian, Shakespeare, sleep alone.
Thy unmolested peace, in an unshared cave,
Possess as lord, not tenant, of thy grave;
That unto us, and others, it may be
Honor hereafter to be laid by thee."

The tenor of Jonson's praise appears to be that other English poets, though great, are "disproportioned," that is, inferior to Shakespeare; his peers are to be found only among the ancients, though he himself knew little about them.

[2] liberal

[3] verdict

For if I thought my judgment were of years,[1]
I should commit thee surely with thy peers,
And tell how far thou didst our Lyly outshine,
Or sporting Kyd, or Marlowe's mighty line.
And though thou hadst small Latin and less Greek,
From thence to honor thee, I will not seek[2]
For names; but call forth thund'ring Aeschylus,
Euripides, and Sophocles to us,
Pacuvius, Accius, him of Cordova dead,[3]
To live again, to hear thy buskin[4] tread,
And shake a stage; or when thy socks[5] were on,
Leave thee alone for the comparison
Of all, that insolent Greece, or haughty Rome
Sent forth, or since did from their ashes come.
Triumph, my Britain, thou hast one to show,
To whom all scenes of Europe homage owe.
He was not of an age, but for all time!
And all the Muses still were in their prime,
When, like Apollo, he came forth to warm
Our ears, or like a Mercury to charm!
Nature herself was proud of his designs,
And joyed to wear the dressing of his lines!
Which were so richly spun, and woven so fit,
As, since, she will vouchsafe no other wit.
The merry Greek, tart Aristophanes,
Neat Terence, witty Plautus, now not please;
But antiquated and deserted lie,
As they were not of nature's family.
Yet must I not give nature all; thy art,
My gentle Shakespeare, must enjoy a part.
For though the poet's matter nature be,
His art doth give the fashion; and, that he
Who casts to write a living line, must sweat,
(Such as thine are) and strike the second heat
Upon the Muses' anvil; turn the same,
And himself with it, that he thinks to frame;
Or for the laurel, he may gain a scorn;
For a good poet's made as well as born.
And such wert thou! Look how the father's face
Lives in his issue; even so the race
Of Shakespeare's mind and manners brightly shines
In his well turnèd and true filèd lines;
In each of which he seems to shake a lance,
As brandished at the eyes of ignorance.
Sweet Swan of Avon! what a sight it were
To see thee in our water yet appear,
And make those flights upon the banks of Thames,
That so did take Eliza,[6] and our James!
But stay, I see thee in the hemisphere
Advanced, and made a constellation there!
Shine forth, thou Star of Poets, and with rage
Or influence, chide or cheer the drooping stage,
Which, since thy flight from hence, hath mourned like night,
And despairs day, but for thy volume's light.

1616 1623

[1] mature
[2] will not be at a loss
[3] Roman tragic poets (the Cordovan is Seneca).
[4] a high boot worn by ancient tragic actors; figurative for "tragedy"
[5] a low shoe worn by ancient comedians; hence "comedy"
[6] captivate Queen Elizabeth

From VOLPONE; OR, THE FOX

THE ARGUMENT[7]

Volpone, childless, rich, feigns sick, despairs,
Offers his state to hopes of several heirs,
Lies languishing. His parasite receives
Presents of all, assures, deludes; then weaves
Other cross plots, which ope themselves, are told.
New tricks for safety are sought; they thrive; when bold,
Each tempts the other again, and all are sold.

ACT I

SCENE I

A Room in VOLPONE'S *House.*

Enter VOLPONE *and* MOSCA.

VOLPONE. Good-morning to the day; and next, my gold!
Open the shrine, that I may see my saint.
[MOSCA *withdraws the curtain, and discovers piles of gold, plate, jewels, etc.*
Hail the world's soul, and mine! more glad than is
The teeming earth to see the longed-for sun
Peep through the horns of the celestial Ram[8]
Am I, to view thy splendor darkening his;
That lying here, amongst my other hoards,
Show'st like a flame by night, or like the day
Struck out of chaos, when all darkness fled
Unto the center. O thou son of Sol,
But brighter than thy father, let me kiss,
With adoration, thee, and every relic
Of sacred treasure in this blessed room.
Well did wise poets, by thy glorious name,
Title that age which they would have the best;

[7] This Argument—which is in the form of an acrostic, the initial letters of the seven lines spelling the title—gives in condensed form the plot of the play. The purpose is to present instructively some of the worst passions of men, especially avarice. Volpō'ne, the rich, hypocritical old "fox," assisted by his parasite, Mosca ("fly"), amuses himself with deluding those who hope to become his heirs, namely, the advocate Voltore ("vulture"), Corbaccio ("old raven"), etc.; but all come to grief in the end. The selection here printed constitutes the major portion of Act I.
[8] the first sign of the zodiac, ascendant at the vernal equinox

Thou being the best of things; and far transcending
All style of joy, in children, parents, friends,
Or any other waking dream on earth.
Thy looks when they to Venus did ascribe,
They should have given her twenty thousand Cupids;
Such are thy beauties and our loves! Dear saint,
Riches, the dumb god, that giv'st all men tongues,
That canst do naught, and yet mak'st men do all things;
The price of souls; even hell, with thee to boot,
Is made worth heaven. Thou art virtue, fame,
Honor, and all things else. Who can get thee,
He shall be noble, valiant, honest, wise—

Mos. And what he will, sir. Riches are in fortune
A greater good than wisdom is in nature.

Volp. True, my beloved Mosca. Yet I glory
More in the cunning purchase of my wealth
Than in the glad possession, since I gain
No common way; I use no trade, no venture;
I wound no earth with plowshares, fat no beasts
To feed the shambles; have no mills for iron,
Oil, corn, or men, to grind them into powder;
I blow no subtle glass, expose no ships
To threat'nings of the furrow-faced sea;
I turn no monies in the public bank,
Nor usure private.[1] . . . .
. . . What should I do,
But cocker up[2] my genius, and live free
To all delights my fortune calls me to?
I have no wife, no parent, child, ally,
To give my substance to; but whom I make
Must be my heir; and this makes men observe me.
This draws new clients daily to my house,
Women and men, of every sex and age,
That bring me presents, send me plate, coin, jewels,
With hope that when I die (which they expect
Each greedy minute) it shall then return
Tenfold upon them; whilst some, covetous
Above the rest, seek to engross me whole,
And counter-work the one unto the other,
Contend in gifts, as they would seem in love.
All which I suffer, playing with their hopes,
And am content to coin them into profit,
And look upon their kindness, and take more,
And look on that; still bearing them in hand,[3]
Letting the cherry knock against their lips,
And draw it by their mouths, and back again.—
How now! . . . .

[1] practice no private usury
[2] pamper
[3] leading them on

[*Knocking without.*

Who's that? . . Look, Mosca. . . .

Mos. 'Tis Signior Voltore, the advocate;
I know him by his knock.

Volp. Fetch me my gown,
My furs, and night-caps; say my couch is changing,
And let him entertain himself awhile
Without i' the gallery. [*Exit* Mosca.] Now, now my clients
Begin their visitation! Vulture, kite,
Raven, and gorcrow, all my birds of prey,
That think me turning carcass, now they come;
I am not for them yet.

Reënter Mosca, *with the gown, etc.*

How now! the news?

Mos. A piece of plate, sir.

Volp. Of what bigness?

Mos. Huge,
Massy, and antique, with your name inscribed,
And arms engraven.

Volp. Good! and not a fox
Stretched on the earth, with fine delusive sleights,
Mocking a gaping crow? Ha, Mosca!

Mos. Sharp, sir.

Volp. Give me my furs.

[*Puts on his sick dress.*

Why dost thou laugh so, man?

Mos. I cannot choose, sir, when I apprehend
What thoughts he has without now, as he walks:
That this might be the last gift he should give;
That this would fetch you; if you died today,
And gave him all, what he should be tomorrow;
What large return would come of all his ventures;
How he should worshiped be, and reverenced;
Ride with his furs, and foot-cloths; waited on
By herds of fools and clients; have clear way
Made for his mule, as lettered as himself;
Be called the great and learned advocate;
And then concludes, there's naught impossible.

Volp. Yes, to be learned, Mosca.

Mos. Oh, no; rich
Implies it. Hood an ass with reverend purple,
So you can hide his two ambitious ears,
And he shall pass for a cathedral doctor.[4]

Volp. My caps, my caps, good Mosca. Fetch him in.

Mos. Stay, sir; your ointment for your eyes.

Volp. That's true.
Dispatch, dispatch. I long to have possession
Of my new present.

[4] learned man worthy to occupy the seat (*cathedra*) of authority

Mos. That, and thousands more,
I hope to see you lord of.
VOLP. Thanks, kind Mosca.
Mos. And that, when I am lost in blended dust,
And hundreds such as I am, in succession—
VOLP. Nay, that were too much, Mosca.
Mos. You shall live
Still to delude these harpies.
VOLP. Loving Mosca.
'Tis well; my pillow now, and let him enter.
[*Exit* MOSCA.
Now, my feigned cough, my phthisic, and my gout,
My apoplexy, palsy, and catarrhs,
Help, with your forced functions, this my posture,
Wherein, this three year, I have milked their hopes.
He comes; I hear him—Uh! [*Coughing.*] uh! uh! uh! O——

Reënter MOSCA, *introducing* VOLTORE *with a piece of plate.*

Mos. You still are what you were, sir. Only you,
Of all the rest, are he [1] commands his love,
And you do wisely to preserve it thus,
With early visitation, and kind notes [2]
Of your good meaning to him, which, I know,
Cannot but come most grateful. Patron! Sir!
Here's Signior Voltore is come——
VOLP. [*Faintly.*] What say you?
Mos. Sir, Signior Voltore is come this morning
To visit you.
VOLP. I thank him.
Mos. And hath brought
A piece of antique plate, bought of St. Mark, [3]
With which he here presents you.
VOLP. He is welcome.
Pray him to come more often.
Mos. Yes.
VOLT. What says he?
Mos. He thanks you, and desires you to see him often.
VOLP. Mosca.
Mos. My patron!
VOLP. Bring him near, where is he?
I long to feel his hand.
Mos. The plate is here, sir.
VOLT. How fare you, sir?
VOLP. I thank you, Signior Voltore;
Where is the plate? Mine eyes are bad.
VOLT. [*putting it into his hands.*] I'm sorry
To see you still thus weak.

[1] he that
[2] tokens
[3] the great square and mart of Venice

Mos. That he's not weaker. [*Aside.*
VOLP. You are too munificent.
VOLT. No, sir; would to heaven,
I could as well give health to you, as that plate!
VOLP. You give, sir, what you can; I thank you. Your love
Hath taste in this, and shall not be unanswered;
I pray you see me often.
VOLT. Yes, I shall, sir.
VOLP. Be not far from me.
Mos. Do you observe that, sir?
VOLP. Hearken unto me still; it will concern you.
Mos. You are a happy man, sir; know your good.
VOLP. I cannot now last long——
Mos. You are his heir, sir.
VOLT. Am I?
VOLP. I feel me going. Uh! uh! uh! uh!
I'm sailing to my port, Uh! uh! uh! uh!
And I am glad I am so near my haven.
Mos. Alas, kind gentleman! Well, we must all go——
VOLT. But, Mosca——
Mos. Age will conquer.
VOLT. Pray thee, hear me;
Am I inscribed his heir for certain?
Mos. Are you!
I do beseech you, sir, you will vouchsafe
To write me in your family. [4] All my hopes
Depend upon your worship; I am lost
Except the rising sun do shine on me.
VOLT. It shall both shine, and warm thee, Mosca.
Mos. Sir,
I am a man that hath not done your love
All the worst offices; here I wear your keys,
See all your coffers and your caskets locked,
Keep the poor inventory of your jewels,
Your plate, and monies; am your steward, sir,
Husband your goods here.
VOLT. But am I sole heir?
Mos. Without a partner, sir; confirmed this morning;
The wax is warm yet, and the ink scarce dry
Upon the parchment.
VOLT. Happy, happy me!
By what good chance, sweet Mosca?
Mos. Your desert, sir;
I know no second cause.
VOLT. Thy modesty
Is not to know it; [5] well, we shall requite it.
Mos. He ever liked your course, sir; that first took him.

[4] engage me as your servant
[5] It is your modesty that speaks thus.

I oft have heard him say how he admired
Men of your large profession, that could speak
To every cause, and things mere contraries,
Till they were hoarse again, yet all be law;
That, with most quick agility, could turn,
And return; make knots, and undo them;
Give forked counsel; take provoking [1] gold
On either hand, and put it up; [2] these men,
He knew, would thrive with their humility.
And, for his part, he thought he should be blest
To have his heir of such a suffering spirit,
So wise, so grave, of so perplexed a tongue,
And loud withal, that would not wag, nor scarce
Lie still, without a fee; when every word
Your worship but lets fall, is a chequin! [3]
[*Knocking without.*
Who's that? One knocks; I would not have you seen, sir.
And yet—pretend you came, and went in haste;
I'll fashion an excuse—and, gentle sir,
When you do come to swim in golden lard,
Up to the arms in honey, that your chin
Is borne up stiff with fatness of the flood,
Think on your vassal; but remember me;
I have not been your worst of clients.
VOLT. Mosca!—
MOS. When will you have your inventory brought, sir?
Or see a copy of the will?—Anon! [4]—
I'll bring them to you, sir. Away, begone,
Put business in your face. [*Exit* VOLTORE.
VOLP. [*Springing up.*] Excellent Mosca!
Come hither, let me kiss thee.
MOS. Keep you still, sir.
Here is Corbaccio.
VOLP. Set the plate away;
The vulture's gone, and the old raven's come.
MOS. Betake you to your silence, and your sleep.
Stand there and multiply. [*Putting the plate to the rest.*] Now we shall see
A wretch who is indeed more impotent
Than this can feign to be; yet hopes to hop
Over his grave.

Enter CORBACCIO.

Signior Corbaccio!
You're very welcome, sir.
CORB. How does your patron?
MOS. Troth, as he did, sir, no amends.
CORB. What! mends he?
MOS. No, sir; he's rather worse.
CORB. That's well. Where is he?
MOS. Upon his couch, sir, newly fall'n asleep.

[1] alluring [2] pouch it
[3] sequin; an Italian coin worth about $2.25
[4] at once (addressed to the one knocking)

CORB. Does he sleep well?
MOS. No wink, sir, all this night,
Nor yesterday; but slumbers.
CORB. Good! he should take
Some counsel of physicians. I have brought him
An opiate here, from mine own doctor.
MOS. He will not hear of drugs.
CORB. Why? I myself
Stood by while it was made, saw all the ingredients;
And know it cannot but most gently work;
My life for his, 'tis but to make him sleep.
VOLP. Aye, his last sleep, if he would take it.
[*Aside.*
MOS. Sir,
He has no faith in physic.
CORB. Say you, say you?
MOS. He has no faith in physic; he does think
Most of your doctors are the greater danger,
And worse disease, to escape. I often have
Heard him protest that your [5] physician
Should never be his heir.
CORB. Not I his heir?
MOS. Not your physician, sir
CORB. Oh, no, no, no.
I do not mean it.
MOS. No, sir, nor their fees
He cannot brook; he says they flay a man
Before they kill him.
CORB. Right, I do conceive you.
MOS. And then they do it by experiment;
For which the law not only doth absolve them,
But gives them great reward; and he is loath
To hire his death so.
CORB. It is true, they kill
With as much license as a judge.
MOS. Nay, more;
For he but kills, sir, where the law condemns,
And these can kill him, too.
CORB. Aye, or me;
Or any man. How does his apoplex?
Is that strong on him still?
MOS. Most violent.
His speech is broken, and his eyes are set,
His face drawn longer than 'twas wont——
CORB. How! how!
Stronger than he was wont?
MOS. No, sir; his face
Drawn longer than 'twas wont.
CORB. Oh, good!
MOS. His mouth
Is ever gaping, and his eyelids hang.
CORB. Good.
MOS. A freezing numbness stiffens all his joints,

[5] a

And makes the color of his flesh like lead.
CORB. 'Tis good.
MOS. His pulse beats slow and dull.
CORB. Good symptoms still.
MOS. And from his brain——
CORB. I conceive you; good.
MOS. Flows a cold sweat, with a continual rheum,
Forth the resolved[1] corners of his eyes.
CORB. Is't possible? Yet I am better, ha!
How does he with the swimming of his head?
MOS. Oh, sir, 'tis past the scotomy;[2] he now
Hath lost his feeling, and hath left to snort;[3]
You hardly can perceive him, that he breathes.
CORB. Excellent, excellent! sure I shall outlast him;
This makes me young again, a score of years.
MOS. I was a-coming for you, sir.
CORB. Has he made his will?
What has he given me?
MOS. No, sir.
CORB. Nothing! ha?
MOS. He has not made his will, sir.
CORB. Oh, oh, oh!
What then did Voltore, the lawyer, here?
MOS. He smelt a carcass, sir, when he but heard
My master was about his testament;
As I did urge him to it for your good——
CORB. He came unto him, did he? I thought so.
MOS. Yes, and presented him this piece of plate.
CORB. To be his heir?
MOS. I do not know, sir.
CORB. True;
I know it, too.
MOS. By your own scale,[4] sir. [*Aside.*
CORB. Well,
I shall prevent him yet. See, Mosca, look,
Here I have brought a bag of bright chequines,
Will quite weigh down his plate.
MOS. [*Taking the bag.*] Yea, marry, sir.
This is true physic, this your sacred medicine;
No talk of opiates to[5] this great elixir!
CORB. 'Tis aurum palpabile, if not potabile.[6]
MOS. It shall be ministered to him in his bowl.
CORB. Aye, do, do, do.
MOS. Most blessed cordial!
This will recover him.
CORB. Yes, do, do, do.
MOS. I think it were not best, sir.
CORB. What?
MOS. To recover him.
CORB. Oh, no, no, no; by no means.
MOS. Why, sir, this
Will work some strange effect, if he but feel it.
CORB. 'Tis true, therefore forbear; I'll take my venture;
Give me it again.
MOS. At no hand;[7] pardon me;
You shall not do yourself that wrong, sir. I
Will so advise you, you shall have it all.
CORB. How?
MOS. All, sir; 'tis your right, your own; no man
Can claim a part; 'tis yours without a rival,
Decreed by destiny.
CORB. How, how, good Mosca?
MOS. I'll tell you, sir. This fit he shall recover.
CORB. I do conceive you.
MOS. And on first advantage
Of his gained sense, will I re-importune him
Unto the making of his testament;
And show him this. [*Pointing to the money.*
CORB. Good, good.
MOS. 'Tis better yet,
If you will hear, sir.
CORB. Yes, with all my heart.
MOS. Now would I counsel you, make home with speed;
There, frame a will; whereto you shall inscribe
My master your sole heir.
CORB. And disinherit
My son!
MOS. Oh, sir, the better; for that color[8]
Shall make it much more taking.
CORB. Oh, but color?
MOS. This will, sir, you shall send it unto me.
Now, when I come to inforce, as I will do,
Your cares, your watchings, and your many prayers,
Your more than many gifts, your this day's present,
And last, produce your will; where, without thought,
Or least regard, unto your proper issue,
A son so brave, and highly meriting,
The stream of your diverted love hath thrown you
Upon my master, and made him your heir;
He cannot be so stupid, or stone-dead,
But out of conscience and mere gratitude——

[1] relaxed
[2] dizziness
[3] ceased to snore
[4] judging him by yourself
[5] compared to
[6] Gold that can be felt, though not drunk (potable gold was believed to have medicinal value).
[7] by no means
[8] pretense

CORB. He must pronounce me his?
MOS. 'Tis true.
CORB. This plot
Did I think on before.
MOS. I do believe it.
CORB. Do you not believe it?
MOS. Yes, sir.
CORB. Mine own project.
MOS. Which, when he hath done, sir——
CORB. Published me his heir?
MOS. And you so certain to survive him——
CORB. Aye.
MOS. Being so lusty a man——
CORB. 'Tis true.
MOS. Yes, sir——
CORB. I thought on that, too. See, how he should be
The very organ to express my thoughts!
MOS. You have not only done yourself a good——
CORB. But multiplied it on my son.
MOS. 'Tis right, sir.
CORB. Still, my invention.
MOS. 'Las, sir! heaven knows,
It hath been all my study, all my care
(I e'en grow gray withal), how to work things——
CORB. I do conceive, sweet Mosca.
MOS. You are he
For whom I labor here.
CORB. Aye, do, do, do;
I'll straight about it. [*Going.*
MOS. Rook go with you, raven![1] [*Aside.*
CORB. I know thee honest.
MOS. You do lie, sir!
CORB. And——
MOS. Your knowledge is no better than your ears, sir.
CORB. I do not doubt to be a father to thee.
MOS. Nor I to gull[2] my brother of his blessing.
CORB. I may have my youth restored to me, why not?
MOS. Your worship is a precious ass!
CORB. What sayest thou?
MOS. I do desire your worship to make haste, sir.
CORB. 'Tis done, 'tis done; I go. [*Exit.*
VOLP. [*Leaping from his couch.*] Oh, I shall burst!
Let out my sides, let out my sides——
MOS. Contain
Your flux[3] of laughter, sir; you know this hope
Is such a bait, it covers any hook.
VOLP. Oh, but thy working, and thy placing it!
I cannot hold; good rascal, let me kiss thee;
I never knew thee in so rare a humor.
MOS. Alas, sir, I but do as I am taught;
Follow your grave instructions; give them words;
Pour oil into their ears, and send them hence.
VOLP. 'Tis true, 'tis true. What a rare punishment
Is avarice to itself!

1605

[1] may cheat pursue you, cheat!
[2] cheat
[3] flow

BEAUMONT and FLETCHER
1584-1613 1579-1625

The names of Beaumont and Fletcher, like those of Wyatt and Surrey, are always linked because of their intimate connection in friendship and in literary production. Both men came of better families than most of the dramatists. John Fletcher was the son of a clergyman, and may have studied at Cambridge. Francis Beaumont, whose father was a judge, attended Oxford for a time. They became friends in London about 1607 and lived together "on the Bank-side near the Play-house," sharing nearly all things in common and collaborating in a number of plays until Beaumont's early death.

Their plays, romantic comedies, fall far short of Shakespeare's in loftiness of treatment. Moreover, they indicate the change that was coming into the drama; the moral tone is lower, the language is less refined, vice is no longer mainly an element of comedy, as in the plays of Shakespeare and his contemporaries, but is accepted as a necessary part of life—hence of realism in drama—and frequently comes out triumphant. Yet the construction is good, the plots are rich in action, and the characters pleasingly lifelike. It is not always easy to distinguish the respective parts of the two authors in these plays, the best of which are *Philaster,* c. 1608, *The Maid's Tragedy,* c. 1610, and *A King and No King,* 1611. Beaumont's share in their collaboration outweighs Fletcher's in quantity and quality; he had a firmer hand, a statelier manner, his decision was more solid, and his verse was more musical. Fletcher excelled in brilliant dialogue and sprightly repartee; he sought by various devices to give greater freedom to the movement of blank verse. He wrote some fifteen independent plays and collaborated in many more after his friend died. He is at his best in his comedies, especially *The Wild Goose Chase,* 1621. *The Faithful Shepherdess,* 1609, a beautiful pastoral drama, is a forerunner of Jonson's fragment, *The Sad Shepherd,* 1637, and Milton's *Comus.*

Besides G. C. Macaulay's *Francis Beaumont, A Critical Study,* 1883, there are essays by Swinburne, Lowell (OED), More (Shel. 10), and Hazlitt (DLAE).

From THE KNIGHT OF THE BURNING PESTLE[1]

INDUCTION

Several GENTLEMEN *sitting on Stools upon the Stage. The* CITIZEN, *his* WIFE, *and* RALPH *sitting below among the audience.*

Enter SPEAKER OF THE PROLOGUE.

S. OF PROL. "From all that's near the court, from all that's great,
Within the compass of the city-walls,
We now have brought our scene——"

CITIZEN *leaps on the Stage.*

CIT. Hold your peace, goodman boy!

S. OF PROL. What do you mean, sir?

CIT. That you have no good meaning. This seven years[2] there hath been plays at this house, I have observed it, you have still[3] girds at citizens; and now you call your play "The London Merchant." Down with your title, boy! down with your title!

S. OF PROL. Are you a member of the noble city?

CIT. I am.

S. OF PROL. And a freeman?[4]

CIT. Yea, and a grocer.

S. OF PROL. So, grocer, then, by your sweet favor, we intend no abuse to the city.

CIT. No, sir! yes, sir. If you were not resolved to play the Jacks,[5] what need you study for new subjects, purposely to abuse your betters? Why could not you be contented, as well as others, with "The Legend of Whittington," or "The Life and Death of Sir Thomas Gresham, with the building of the Royal Exchange," or "The story of Queen Eleanor, with the rearing of London Bridge upon woolsacks?"[6]

S. OF PROL. You seem to be an understanding man. What would you have us do, sir?

CIT. Why, present something notably in honor of the commons[7] of the city.

S. OF PROL. Why, what do you say to "The Life and Death of fat Drake, or the Repairing of Fleet Sewers?"

CIT. I do not like that; but I will have a citizen, and he shall be of my own trade.

S. OF PROL. Oh, you should have told us your mind a month since; our play is ready to begin now.

CIT. 'Tis all one for that; I will have a grocer, and he shall do admirable things.

S. OF PROL. What will you have him do?

CIT. Marry, I will have him——

WIFE. [*Below.*] Husband, husband!

RALPH, [*Below.*] Peace, mistress.

WIFE. [*Below.*] Hold thy peace, Ralph; I know what I do, I warrant ye.—Husband, husband!

CIT. What sayest thou, cony?[8]

WIFE. [*Below.*] Let him kill a lion with a pestle, husband! Let him kill a lion with a pestle!

CIT. So he shall.—I'll have him kill a lion with a pestle.

WIFE. [*Below.*] Husband! shall I come up, husband?

CIT. Aye, cony.—Ralph, help your mistress this way.—Pray, gentlemen, make her a little room.—I pray you, sir, lend me your hand to help up my wife. I thank you, sir.—So.

[WIFE *comes on the Stage.*

WIFE. By your leave, gentlemen all; I'm something troublesome. I'm a stranger here; I was ne'er at one of these plays, as they say, before; but I should have seen "Jane Shore" once; and my husband hath promised me, any time this twelvemonth, to carry me to "The Bold Beauchamps," but in truth he did not. I pray you, bear with me.

CIT. Boy, let my wife and I have a couple of stools, and then begin; and let the grocer do rare things. [*Stools are brought.*

S. OF PROL. But, sir, we have never a boy to play him; every one hath a part already.

WIFE. Husband, husband, for God's sake, let Ralph play him! Beshrew me, if I do not think he will go beyond them all.

CIT. Well remembered, wife.—Come up,

[1] This play was written and acted about 1611. Like Shakespeare's *A Midsummer Night's Dream,* it is made up of two diverse elements—a romantic comedy and a burlesque. From the latter are given a few scenes of the burlesque, which can easily be detached from the main plot. It must be understood that it was the custom of theaters to admit gallants and others who liked to be conspicuous, and who were willing to pay an extra sixpence, to seats, on the stage, where they often abused their privilege by indulging in audible criticism of the play and players. The authors of the present drama ingeniously staged that custom as a part of their own play and took the opportunity to satirize both the taste and understanding of their dunce-critics. Furthermore, they wove in a burlesque upon the romantic extravagance of knight-errantry, presenting in Ralph, the grocer's apprentice, another Don Quixote, like him whose immortal deeds had been given to the world's laughter but a few years before.

[2] Supply "that."

[3] always

[4] one invested with full citizen's rights

[5] play the knave (cf. *The Tempest,* IV, i, 199.)

[6] These are titles of old plays, more or less distorted; the reference to London Bridge is a jesting addition. The title proposed five lines farther down is of course a jest.

[7] ordinary citizens

[8] rabbit (a term of endearment)

Ralph.—I'll tell you, gentlemen; let them but lend him a suit of reparel and necessaries,[1] and, by gad, if any of them all put him to shame, I'll be hanged.

[RALPH *comes on the Stage.*

WIFE. I pray you, youth, let him have a suit of reparel!—I'll be sworn, gentlemen, my husband tells you true; he will act you sometimes at our house, that all the neighbors cry out on him; he will fetch you up a couraging[2] part so in the garret, that we are all as feared, I warrant you, that we quake again. We'll fear[3] our children with him; if they be never so unruly, do but cry, "Ralph comes, Ralph comes!" to them, and they'll be as quiet as lambs.—Hold up thy head, Ralph; show the gentlemen what thou can'st do; speak a huffing[4] part; I warrant you, the gentlemen will accept of it.

CIT. Do, Ralph, do.

RALPH. "By Heaven, methinks, it were an easy leap
To pluck bright honor from the pale-faced moon;
Or dive into the bottom of the sea,
Where never fathom-line touched any ground,
And pluck up drowned honor from the lake of hell."[5]

CIT. How say you, gentlemen, is it not as I told you?

WIFE. Nay, gentlemen, he hath played before, my husband says, Mucedorus,[6] before the wardens of our company.

CIT. Aye, and he should have played Jeronimo[6] with a shoemaker for a wager.

S. OF PROL. He shall have a suit of apparel, if he will go in.

CIT. In, Ralph; in, Ralph; and set out the grocery in their kind,[7] if thou lovest me.

[*Exit* RALPH.

WIFE. I warrant, our Ralph will look finely when he's dressed.

S. OF PROL. But what will you have it called?

CIT. "The Grocer's Honor."

S. OF PROL. Methinks "The Knight of the Burning Pestle" were better.

WIFE. I'll be sworn, husband, that's as good a name as can be.

CIT. Let it be so.—Begin, begin; my wife and I will sit down.

[1] The grocer means to say "apparel and accessories."
[2] valiant
[3] scare
[4] swaggering
[5] Hotspur's speech in *1 Henry IV*, I, iii, somewhat distorted
[6] a character in an Elizabethan comedy
[7] proper garb

S. OF PROL. I pray you, do.

CIT. What stately music have you? You have shawms?

S. OF PROL. Shawms! no.

CIT. No! I'm a thief, if my mind did not give[8] me so. Ralph plays a stately part, and he must needs have shawms. I'll be at the charge of them myself, rather than we'll be without them.

S. OF PROL. So you are like to be.

CIT. Why, and so I will be; there's two shillings—[*Gives money.*]—let's have the waits[9] of Southwark; they are as rare fellows as any are in England, and that will fetch them all o'er the water[10] with a vengeance, as if they were mad.

S. OF PROL. You shall have them. Will you sit down, then?

CIT. Aye.—Come, wife.

WIFE. Sit you merry all, gentlemen; I'm bold to sit amongst you for my ease.

[CITIZEN *and* WIFE *sit down.*

S. OF PROL. "From all that's near the court, from all that's great,
Within the compass of the city-walls,
We now have brought our scene. Fly far from hence
All private taxes,[11] immodest phrases,
Whatever may but show like vicious!
For wicked mirth never true pleasure brings,
But honest minds are pleased with honest things."—

Thus much for that we do; but for Ralph's part you must answer for yourself.

CIT. Take you no care for Ralph; he'll discharge himself, I warrant you.

[*Exit* SPEAKER OF PROLOGUE.

WIFE. I' faith, gentlemen, I'll give my word for Ralph.

ACT I

SCENE III

A Grocer's Shop.

Enter RALPH, *as a Grocer, reading "Palmerin of England,"*[12] *with* TIM *and* GEORGE.

[WIFE. Oh, husband, husband, now, now! there's Ralph, there's Ralph.

CIT. Peace, fool! let Ralph alone.—Hark you, Ralph; do not strain yourself too much at the first.—Peace!—Begin, Ralph.]

RALPH. [*Reads.*] Then Palmerin and Trineus, snatching their lances from their dwarfs,

[8] tell
[9] professional carolers
[10] the Thames
[11] personal hits
[12] a Spanish romance then lately translated

and clasping their helmets, galloped amain after the giant; and Palmerin, having gotten a sight of him, came posting amain, saying, "Stay, traitorous thief! for thou mayst not so carry away her, that is worth the greatest lord in the world"; and, with these words, gave him a blow on the shoulder, that he struck him besides[1] his elephant. And Trineus, coming to the knight that had Agricola behind him, set him soon besides his horse, with his neck broken in the fall; so that the princess, getting out of the throng, between joy and grief, said, "All happy knight, the mirror of all such as follow arms, now may I be well assured of the love thou bearest me."—I wonder why the kings do not raise an army of fourteen or fifteen hundred thousand men, as big as the army that the Prince of Portigo brought against Rosicleer,[2] and destroy these giants; they do much hurt to wandering damsels, that go in quest of their knights.

[WIFE. Faith, husband, and Ralph says true; for they say the King of Portugal cannot sit at his meat, but the giants and the ettins[3] will come and snatch it from him.

CIT. Hold thy tongue.—On, Ralph!]

RALPH. And certainly those knights are much to be commended, who, neglecting their possessions, wander with a squire and a dwarf through the deserts to relieve poor ladies.

[WIFE. Aye, by my faith, are they, Ralph; let 'em say what they will, they are indeed. Our knights neglect their possessions well enough, but they do not the rest.] . . .

RALPH. But what brave spirit could be content to sit in his shop, with a flappet[4] of wood, and a blue apron before him, selling mithridatum and dragon's-water[5] to visited[6] houses, that might pursue feats of arms, and, through his noble achievements, procure such a famous history to be written of his heroic prowess?

[CIT. Well said, Ralph; some more of those words, Ralph.

WIFE. They go finely, by my troth.]

RALPH. Why should not I, then, pursue this course, both for the credit of myself and our company? For amongst all the worthy books of achievements, I do not call to mind that I yet read of a grocer-errant; I will be the said knight.—Have you heard of any that hath wandered unfurnished of his squire and dwarf? My elder prentice Tim shall be my trusty squire, and little George my dwarf. Hence, my blue apron! Yet, in remembrance of my former trade, upon my shield shall be portrayed a Burning Pestle, and I will be called the Knight of the Burning Pestle.

[WIFE. Nay, I dare swear thou wilt not forget thy old trade; thou wert ever meek.]

RALPH. Tim!

TIM. Anon.

RALPH. My beloved squire, and George my dwarf, I charge you that from henceforth you never call me by any other name but "the right courteous and valiant Knight of the Burning Pestle"; and that you never call any female by the name of a woman or wench, but "fair lady," if she have her desires; if not, "distressed damsel"; that you call all forests and heaths "deserts," and all horses "palfreys."

[WIFE. This is very fine, faith.—Do the gentlemen like Ralph, think you, husband?

CIT. Aye, I warrant thee; the players would give all the shoes in their shop for him.]

RALPH. My beloved squire Tim, stand out. Admit this were a desert, and over it a knight-errant pricking,[7] and I should bid you inquire of his intents, what would you say?

TIM. Sir, my master sent me to know whither you are riding?

RALPH. No, thus: "Fair sir, the right courteous and valiant Knight of the Burning Pestle commanded me to inquire upon what adventure you are bound, whether to relieve some distressed damsel, or otherwise."

[CIT. Scurvy blockhead, cannot remember!

WIFE. I' faith, and Ralph told him on't before; all the gentlemen heard him.—Did he not, gentlemen? Did not Ralph tell him on't?]

GEORGE. Right courteous and valiant Knight of the Burning Pestle, here is a distressed damsel to have a halfpenny-worth of pepper.

[WIFE. That's a good boy! see, the little boy can hit it; by my troth, it's a fine child.]

RALPH. Relieve her, with all courteous language. Now shut up shop; no more my prentices, but my trusty squire and dwarf. I must bespeak[8] my shield and arming pestle.

[*Exeunt* TIM *and* GEORGE.

[CIT. Go thy ways, Ralph! As I'm a true man, thou art the best on 'em all.

WIFE. Ralph, Ralph!

RALPH. What say you, mistress?

WIFE. I prithee, come again quickly, sweet Ralph.

RALPH. By and by.][9] [*Exit.*

. . . .

[In the main plot, Jasper Merrythought has

[1] by the side of (struck him off his elephant)
[2] a character in another Spanish romance
[3] giants
[4] small piece (here pestle)
[5] popular medicines of the time
[6] plague-stricken
[7] riding
[8] order
[9] immediately

been dismissed by his employer for falling in love with his employer's daughter. His father takes his part, but his mother is incensed, and, taking her younger son, Michael, and her money and jewels, she leaves her home, and the two are wandering in Waltham Forest, when Ralph comes on the scene.]

ACT II

SCENE II

Waltham Forest.

Enter MISTRESS MERRYTHOUGHT *and* MICHAEL.

MIST. MER. Come, Michael; art thou not weary, boy?

MICH. No, forsooth, mother, not I.

MIST. MER. Where be we now, child?

MICH. Indeed, forsooth, mother, I cannot tell, unless we be at Mile-End. Is not all the world Mile-End, mother?

MIST. MER. No, Michael, not all the world, boy; but I can assure thee, Michael, Mile-End is a goodly matter. There has been a pitch-field,[1] my child, between the naughty Spaniels and the Englishmen; and the Spaniels ran away, Michael, and the Englishmen followed; my neighbor Coxstone was there, boy, and killed them all with a birding-piece.

MICH. Mother, forsooth—

MIST. MER. What says my white boy?[2]

MICH. Shall not my father go with us, too?

MIST. MER. No, Michael, let thy father go snick-up;[3] . . let him stay at home, and sing for his supper, boy. Come, child, sit down, and I'll show my boy fine knacks, indeed. [*They sit down; and she takes out a casket.*] Look here, Michael; here's a ring, and here's a brooch, and here's a bracelet, and here's two rings more, and here's money and gold by the eye,[4] my boy.

MICH. Shall I have all this, mother?

MIST. MER. Aye, Michael, thou shalt have all, Michael.

[CIT. How likest thou this, wench?

WIFE. I cannot tell; I would have Ralph, George; I'll see no more else, indeed, la; and I pray you, let the youths understand so much by word of mouth; for, I tell you truly, I'm afraid o' my boy. Come, come, George, let's be merry and wise; the child's a fatherless child; and say they should put him into a strait pair of gaskins,[5] 'twere worse than knot-grass;[6] he would never grow after it.]

[1] pitched battle (possibly a mock battle, for the Spanish never fought the English there)
[2] dear boy
[3] go hang
[4] galore
[5] breeches
[6] supposed, when taken as an infusion, to retard growth

Enter RALPH, TIM, *and* GEORGE.

[CIT. Here's Ralph, here's Ralph!

WIFE. How do you do, Ralph? You are welcome, Ralph, as I may say; it's a good boy, hold up thy head and be not afraid; we are thy friends, Ralph; the gentlemen will praise thee, Ralph, if thou playest thy part with audacity. Begin, Ralph, a' God's name!]

RALPH. My trusty squire, unlace my helm; give me my hat. Where are we, or what desert may this be?

GEORGE. Mirror of knighthood, this is, as I take it, the perilous Waltham-down; in whose bottom stands the enchanted valley.

MIST. MER. Oh, Michael, we are betrayed, we are betrayed! Here be giants! Fly, boy! fly, boy, fly!

[*Exit with* MICHAEL, *leaving the casket.*

RALPH. Lace on my helm again. What noise is this?
A gentle lady, flying the embrace
Of some uncourteous knight! I will relieve her.
Go, squire, and say, the Knight, that wears this Pestle
In honor of all ladies, swears revenge
Upon that recreant coward that pursues her;
Go, comfort her, and that same gentle squire
That bears her company.

TIM. I go, brave knight. [*Exit.*

RALPH. My trusty dwarf and friend, reach me my shield;
And hold it while I swear. First, by my knighthood;
Then by the soul of Amadis de Gaul,[7]
My famous ancestor; then by my sword
The beauteous Brionella girt about me;
By this bright burning Pestle, of mine honor
The living trophy; and by all respect
Due to distressèd damsels; here I vow
Never to end the quest of this fair lady
And that forsaken squire till by my valor
I gain their liberty!

GEORGE. Heaven bless the knight
That thus relieves poor errant gentlewomen!

[*Exeunt.*

[WIFE. Aye, marry, Ralph, this has some savor in't; I would see the proudest of them all offer to carry his books after him. But, George, I will not have him go away so soon; I shall be sick if he go away, that I shall. Call Ralph again, George, call Ralph again; I prithee, sweetheart, let him come fight before me, and let's ha' some drums and some trumpets, and let him kill all that comes near him, an[8] thou lov'st me, George!

[7] a hero of medieval romance, "Knight of the Burning Sword"
[8] if

CIT. Peace a little, bird; he shall kill them all, an they were twenty more on 'em than there are.]

. . . .

[Jasper enters and, finding the casket, carries it off.]

SCENE III

Another part of the Forest.

Enter RALPH *and* GEORGE.

[WIFE. But here comes Ralph, George; thou shalt hear him speak as he were an emperal.]

RALPH. Comes not sir squire again?

GEORGE. Right courteous knight,
Your squire doth come, and with him comes the lady,
And the Squire of Damsels, as I take it.

Enter TIM, MISTRESS MERRYTHOUGHT, *and* MICHAEL.

RALPH. Madam, if any service or devoir[1]
Of a poor errant knight may right your wrongs,
Command it; I am prest[2] to give you succor;
For to that holy end I bear my armor.

MIST. MER. Alas, sir, I am a poor gentlewoman, and I have lost my money in this forest.

RALPH. Desert, you would say, lady; and not lost
Whilst I have sword and lance. Dry up your tears,
Which ill befit the beauty of that face,
And tell the story, if I may request it,
Of your disastrous fortune.

MIST. MER. Out, alas! I left a thousand pound, a thousand pound, e'en all the money I had laid up for this youth, upon the sight of your mastership, you looked so grim, and, as I may say it, saving your presence, more like a giant than a mortal man.

RALPH. I am as you are, lady; so are they;
All mortal. But why weeps this gentle squire?

MIST. MER. Has he not cause to weep, do you think, when he hath lost his inheritance?

RALPH. Young hope of valor, weep not; I am here
That will confound thy foe, and pay it dear
Upon his coward head, that dares deny
Distressèd squires and ladies equity.
I have but one horse, on which shall ride
The fair lady behind me, and before
This courteous squire; fortune will give us more
Upon our next adventure. Fairly speed
Beside us, squire and dwarf, to do us need!
[*Exeunt.*

[CIT. Did not I tell you, Nell, what your man would do? By the faith of my body, wench, for clean action and good delivery, they may all cast their caps at him.

WIFE. And so they may, i' faith; for I dare speak it boldly, the twelve companies[3] of London cannot match him, timber for timber. Well, George, an he be not inveigled by some of these paltry players, I ha' much marvel; but, George, we ha' done our parts, if the boy have any grace to be thankful.

CIT. Yes, I warrant thee, duckling.]

. . . .

[Ralph encounters Jasper, who knocks him down with his own pestle, whereupon Ralph and his party seek shelter at the Bell Inn.]

SCENE VI

Before the Bell-Inn, Waltham.

Enter RALPH, MISTRESS MERRYTHOUGHT, MICHAEL, TIM, *and* GEORGE

[WIFE. Oh, husband, here's Ralph again!—Stay, Ralph, let me speak with thee. How dost thou, Ralph? Art thou not shrewdly hurt? The foul great lungies[4] laid unmercifully on thee. There's some sugar-candy for thee. Proceed; thou shalt have another bout with him.

CIT. If Ralph had him at the fencing-school, if he did not make a puppy of him, and drive him up and down the school, he should ne'er come in my shop more.]

MIST. MER. Truly, Master Knight of the Burning Pestle, I am weary.

MICH. Indeed, la, mother, and I am very hungry.

RALPH. Take comfort, gentle dame, and your fair squire;
For in this desert there must needs be placed
Many strong castles held by courteous knights;
And till I bring you safe to one of those,
I swear by this my order ne'er to leave you.

. . . .

GEORGE. I would we had a mess of pottage and a pot of drink, squire, and were going to bed!

TIM. Why, we are at Waltham-town's end, and that's the Bell-Inn.

GEORGE. Take courage, valiant knight, damsel, and squire!
I have discovered, not a stone's cast off,
An ancient castle, held by the old knight
Of the most holy order of the Bell,
Who gives to all knights-errant entertain.
There plenty is of food, and all prepared
By the white hands of his own lady dear.
He hath three squires that welcome all his guests;

[1] duty
[2] ready

[3] licensed companies of players
[4] lubbers

The first, hight [1] Chamberlino, who will see
Our beds prepared, and bring us snowy sheets,
Where never footman stretched his buttered hams; [2]
The second, hight Tapstero, who will see
Our pots full fillèd, and no froth therein;
The third, a gentle squire, Ostlero hight,
Who will our palfreys slick with wisps of straw,
And in the manger put them oats enough,
And never grease their teeth with candle-snuff. [3]

[WIFE. That same dwarf's a pretty boy, but the squire's a groutnol. [4]]

RALPH. Knock at the gates, my squire, with stately lance.

[TIM *knocks at the door.*

Enter TAPSTER.

TAP. Who's there?—You're welcome, gentlemen; will you see a room?

GEORGE. Right courteous and valiant Knight of the Burning Pestle, this is the Squire Tapstero.

RALPH. Fair Squire Tapstero, I a wandering knight,
Hight of the Burning Pestle, in the quest
Of this fair lady's casket and wrought purse,
Losing myself in this vast wilderness,
Am to this castle well by fortune brought;
Where, hearing of the goodly entertain
Your knight of holy order of the Bell
Gives to all damsels and all errant knights,
I thought to knock, and now am bold to enter.

TAP. An't please you see a chamber, you are very welcome. [*Exeunt.*

[WIFE. George, I would have something done, and I cannot tell what it is.

CIT. What is it, Nell?

WIFE. Why, George, shall Ralph beat nobody again? Prithee, sweetheart, let him.

CIT. So he shall, Nell; and if I join with him, we'll knock them all.]

ACT III

SCENE II

A Room in the Bell-Inn, Waltham.

Enter MISTRESS MERRYTHOUGHT, RALPH, MICHAEL, TIM, GEORGE, HOST, *and* TAPSTER.

[WIFE. Oh, Ralph! how dost thou, Ralph? How has thou slept tonight? Has the knight used thee well?

CIT. Peace, Nell; let Ralph alone.]

TAP. Master, the reckoning is not paid.

RALPH. Right courteous knight, who, for the order's sake
Which thou has ta'en, hang'st out the holy Bell,
As I this flaming Pestle bear about,
We render thanks to your puissant self,
Your beauteous lady, and your gentle squires,
For thus refreshing of our wearied limbs,
Stiffened with hard achievements in wild desert.

TAP. Sir, there is twelve shillings to pay.

RALPH. Thou merry Squire Tapstero, thanks to thee
For comforting our souls with double jug;
And, if adventurous fortune prick thee forth,
Thou jovial squire, to follow feats of arms,
Take heed thou tender [5] every lady's cause,
Every true knight, and every damsel fair;
But spill the blood of treacherous Saracens,
And false enchanters that with magic spells
Have done to death full many a noble knight.

HOST. Thou valiant Knight of the Burning Pestle, give ear to me; there is twelve shillings to pay, and, as I am a true knight, I will not bate a penny.

[WIFE. George, I prithee, tell me, must Ralph pay twelve shillings now?

CIT. No, Nell, no; nothing but the old knight is merry with Ralph.

WIFE. Oh, is't nothing else? Ralph will be as merry as he.]

RALPH. Sir Knight, this mirth of yours becomes you well;
But, to requite this liberal courtesy,
If any of your squires will follow arms,
He shall receive from my heroic hand
A knighthood, by the virtue of this Pestle.

HOST. Fair knight, I thank you for your noble offer.
Therefore, gentle knight,
Twelve shillings you must pay, or I must cap [6] you.

[WIFE. Look, George! did not I tell thee as much? The knight of the Bell is in earnest. Ralph shall not be beholding to him; give him his money, George, and let him go snick-up. [7]

CIT. Cap Ralph! no.—Hold your hand, Sir Knight of the Bell; there's your money. [*Gives money.*] Have you anything to say to Ralph now? Cap Ralph!

WIFE. I would you should know it, Ralph has friends that will not suffer him to be capt for ten times so much, and ten times to the end of that.—Now take thy course, Ralph.]

MIST. MER. Come, Michael; thou and I will go home to thy father; he hath enough left to keep us a day or two, and we'll set our fellows

[1] called
[2] Footmen anointed their calves with grease.
[3] a trick to prevent horses from eating
[4] blockhead
[5] cherish
[6] arrest
[7] go hang

abroad to cry our purse and our casket. Shall we, Michael?

MICH. Aye, I pray, mother; in truth, my feet are full of chilblains with traveling.

[WIFE. Faith, and those chilblains are a foul trouble. Mistress Merrythought, when your youth comes home, let him rub all the soles of his feet, and his heels, and his ankles, with a mouse-skin; or, if none of your people can catch a mouse, when he goes to bed let him roll his feet in the warm embers, and, I warrant you, he shall be well. . . . .]

MIST. MER. Master Knight of the Burning Pestle, my son Michael and I bid you farewell; I thank your worship heartily for your kindness.

RALPH. Farewell, fair lady, and your tender squire.
If pricking through these deserts I do hear
Of any traitorous knight, who through his guile
Hath light upon your casket and your purse,
I will despoil him of them, and restore them.

MIST. MER. I thank your worship.

[*Exit with* MICHAEL.

RALPH. Dwarf, bear my shield; squire, elevate my lance;—
And now farewell, you Knight of holy Bell.

[CIT. Aye, aye, Ralph, all is paid.]

RALPH. But yet, before I go, speak, worthy knight,
If aught you do of sad adventures know,
Where errant knight may through his prowess win
Eternal fame, and free some gentle souls
From endless bonds of steel and lingering pain.

HOST. Sirrah, go to Nick the barber, and bid him prepare himself, as I told you before, quickly.

TAP. I am gone, sir. [*Exit.*

HOST. Sir Knight, this wilderness affordeth none
But the great venture, where full many a knight
Hath tried his prowess, and come off with shame;
And where I would not have you lose your life
Against no man, but furious fiend of hell.

RALPH. Speak on, Sir Knight; tell what he is and where;
For here I vow, upon my blazing badge,
Never to blaze [1] a day in quietness,
But bread and water will I only eat,
And the green herb and rock shall be my couch,
Till I have quelled that man, or beast, or fiend,
That works such damage to all errant knights.

HOST. Not far from hence, near to a craggy cliff,
At the north end of this distressèd town,
There doth stand a lowly house,
Ruggedly builded, and in it a cave
In which an ugly giant now doth won, [2]
Ycleped [3] Barbarossa; in his hand
He shakes a naked lance of purest steel,
With sleeves turned up; and him before he wears
A motley garment, to preserve his clothes
From blood of those knights which he massacres
And ladies gent; [4] without his door doth hang
A copper basin on a prickant [5] spear;
At which no sooner gentle knights can knock,
But the shrill sound fierce Barbarossa hears,
And rushing forth, brings in the errant knight,
And sets him down in an enchanted chair;
Then with an engine, [6] which he hath prepared,
With forty teeth, he claws his courtly crown;
Next makes him wink, and underneath his chin
He plants a brazen piece of mighty bord, [7]
And knocks his bullets [8] round about his cheeks;
Whilst with his fingers, and an instrument
With which he snaps his hair off, he doth fill
The wretch's ears with a most hideous noise.
Thus every knight-adventurer he doth trim,
And now no creature dares encounter him.

RALPH In God's name, I will fight with him. Kind sir,
Go but before me to this dismal cave,
Where this huge giant Barbarossa dwells,
And, by that virtue that brave Rosicleer
That damnèd brood of ugly giants slew,
And Palmerin Frannarco overthrew,
I doubt not but to curb this traitor foul,
And to the devil send his guilty soul.

HOST. Brave-sprighted knight, thus far I will perform
This your request; I'll bring you within sight
Of this most loathsome place, inhabited
By a more loathsome man; but dare not stay,
For his main force swoops all he sees away.

RALPH. Saint George, set on before!
March, squire and page. [*Exeunt.*

[WIFE. George, dost think Ralph will confound the giant?

CIT. I hold my cap to a farthing he does; why, Nell, I saw him wrestle with the great Dutchman, and hurl him.

WIFE. Faith, and that Dutchman was a goodly man, if all things were answerable [9] to his bigness. And yet they say there was a Scotchman higher than he, and that they two and a knight met, and saw one another for nothing. . . .]

[1] shine

[2] dwell
[3] called
[4] gentle, courteous
[5] pointing upward
[6] instrument
[7] broad rim (i.e., a barber's basin)
[8] soap-balls (soap bubbles, lather)
[9] in proportion

SCENE IV

Before a Barber's Shop, Waltham.

Enter RALPH, HOST, TIM, *and* GEORGE.

[WIFE. Oh, Ralph's here, George!—God send thee good luck, Ralph!]

HOST. Puissant knight, yonder his mansion is.
Lo, where the spear and copper basin are!
Behold that string, on which hangs many a tooth,
Drawn from the gentle jaw of wandering knights![1]
I dare not stay to sound; he will appear. [*Exit.*

RALPH. Oh, faint not, heart! Susan, my lady dear,
The cobbler's maid in Milk-street, for whose sake
I take these arms, oh, let the thought of thee
Carry thy knight through all adventurous deeds;
And, in the honor of thy beauteous self,
May I destroy this monster Barbarossa!—
Knock, squire, upon the basin, till it break
With the shrill strokes, or till the giant speak.
[TIM *knocks upon the basin.*

Enter BARBER

[WIFE. Oh, George, the giant, the giant!—Now, Ralph, for thy life!]

BAR. What fond[2] unknowing wight is this, that dares
So rudely knock at Barbarossa's cell,
Where no man comes but leaves his fleece behind?

RALPH. I, traitorous caitiff, who am sent by fate
To punish all the sad enormities
Thou has committed against ladies gent
And errant knights. Traitor to God and men,
Prepare thyself; this is the dismal hour
Appointed for thee to give strict account
Of all thy beastly treacherous villanies.

BAR. Fool-hardy knight, full soon thou shalt aby[3]
This fond reproach; thy body will I bang;
[*Takes down his pole.*
And lo, upon that string thy teeth shall hang!
Prepare thyself, for dead soon shalt thou be.

RALPH. Saint George for me! [*They fight.*

BAR. Gargantua[4] for me!

[WIFE. To him, Ralph, to him! hold up the giant; set out thy leg before, Ralph!

CIT. Falsify a blow, Ralph, falsify a blow! the giant lies open on the left side.

WIFE. Bear't off, bear't off still! there, boy!—Oh, Ralph's almost down, Ralph's almost down!]

RALPH. Susan, inspire me! now have up again.

[WIFE. Up, up, up, up, up! so, Ralph! down with him, down with him, Ralph!

CIT. Fetch him o'er the hip, boy!

[RALPH *knocks down the* BARBER.

WIFE. There, boy! kill, kill, kill, kill, kill, Ralph!

CIT. No, Ralph; get all out of him first.]

RALPH. Presumptuous man, see to what desperate end
Thy treachery hath brought thee! The just gods,
Who never prosper those that do despise them,
For all the villanies which thou has done
To knights and ladies, now have paid thee home
By my stiff arm, a knight adventurous.
But say, vile wretch, before I send thy soul
To sad Avernus (whither it must go),
What captive holdst thou in thy sable cave?

BAR. Go in, and free them all; thou hast the day.

RALPH. Go, squire and dwarf, search in this dreadful cave,
And free the wretched prisoners from their bonds.

. . . . .

[*Exeunt* TIM *and* GEORGE, *who presently reënter.*

[CIT. Cony, I can tell thee, the gentlemen like Ralph.

WIFE. Aye, George, I see it well enough.—Gentlemen, I thank you all heartily for gracing my man Ralph; and I promise you, you shall see him oftener.]

BAR. Mercy, great knight! I do recant my ill,
And henceforth never gentle blood will spill.

RALPH. I give thee mercy; but yet shalt thou swear
Upon my Burning Pestle, to perform
Thy promise utterèd.

BAR. I swear and kiss. [*Kisses the Pestle.*

RALPH. Depart, then, and amend.

[*Exit* BARBER.

Come, squire and dwarf; the sun grows toward his set,
And we have many more adventures yet.

[*Exeunt.*

[CIT. Now Ralph is in this humor, I know he would ha' beaten all the boys in the house, if they had been set on him.

WIFE. Aye, George, but it is well as it is. I warrant you, the gentlemen do consider what it is to overthrow a giant.]

c. 1611

[1] Barbers were also surgeons and dentists.
[2] foolish [3] pay for
[4] a giant in Rabelais's satire

THE ELIZABETHAN AGE—PROSE

ELIZABETHAN prose begins, about the time that Spenser's early poems were preluding the true Elizabethan poetry, with the work of John Lyly. He produced two mild society romances, *Euphues, or the Anatomy of Wit,* 1579, and *Euphues and his England,* 1580. These are so characterized by excessive verbal balance, antithesis, alliteration, rime, and endless fantastic similes drawn from mythical nature, that he established a style known to this day as "euphuism," imitated by many of his contemporaries, and ridiculed by Shakespeare in *Love's Labor's Lost.*

Besides such romances, a prevalent form of prose literature was the scholastic treatise. Sidney represented both types; the first in his half-chivalresque, half-pastoral tale of *Arcadia,* and the second in his *Defence of Poesie.* Lodge's *Rosalynde,* upon which Shakespeare based the plot of *As You Like It,* is a purely pastoral romance. In addition there were numerous travelers' chronicles, essays, and tracts or pamphlets, serious, satirical, or humorous, on a great variety of subjects. The writers of the day had not yet discarded a belief that Latin was the only dignified language for serious literature; not only did it have a marked influence on the style of Elizabethan prose, but it was used by Bacon and others a hundred years after More employed it for his *Utopia* (see p. 120). The "Authorized Version" or King James Bible (see p. 46), 1611, which may be regarded as the first masterpiece of modern prose, possibly did more than anything else, not excepting even the drama, to establish the vernacular as the common literary medium.

SIR PHILIP SIDNEY 1554-1586

Possibly the most charming personality of the Elizabethan Age, certainly the one that seems best to embody its ideals of chivalry and culture, is Sir Philip Sidney, beloved of all who knew him—

> ". . . . . Sidney, as he fought
> And as he fell and as he lived and loved
> Sublimely mild, a Spirit without spot."
> —Shelley, *Adonais.*

Fortune smiled on him from the first. Born at Penhurst, eldest son of Sir Henry Sidney, he was honored by having Philip II of Spain and the Earl of Bedford as godfathers. From childhood he was a lover of learning, writing letters in French and Latin at eleven. On account of the plague he left Oxford in 1571 without a degree, and traveled on the Continent for two years, a member of the most distinguished circles. Returning to England, he was a general favorite at Court, was in touch with all great men of learning, was one of the founders of the literary club, the "Areopagus," and showed his interest in the drama by his *Defence of Poesie* or *Apologie for Poetry,* 1595, containing some of the best prose since Ascham's *Schoolmaster.* He also wrote his sonnet sequence *Astrophel and Stella,* which ranks even higher than his two prose works.

Like many of his contemporaries, he was a victim of Elizabeth's caprice; his prose romance *Arcadia* was written during a period of banishment, the result of her displeasure at several acts of independence. He was also refused permission to join various expeditions of discovery and colonization. Finally she gratified his desire for active service by appointing him Governor of Flushing, in Flanders, where, he was soon after mortally wounded at the Battle of Zutphen, the scene of his famous act of renunciation, when he gave his last drop of water to a dying soldier with the words: "Thy necessity is yet greater than mine." He was a patriotic and religious man, possessing political sagacity, high poetic and oratorical gifts, and excelling in manly sports.

An interesting appreciation is the *Life of Sir Philip Sidney* by Fulke Greville (Lord Brooke), a contemporary and friend; modern essays are by Lee (GE), and Hazlitt (DLAE).

From THE COUNTESS OF PEMBROKE'S ARCADIA [1]

To My Dear Lady and Sister, the Countess of Pembroke:

Here now have you, most dear, and most worthy to be most dear, Lady, this idle work of mine, which, I fear, like the spider's web, will be thought fitter to be swept away than worn to any other purpose. For my part, in very truth, as the cruel fathers among the Greeks were wont to do to the babes they would not foster, I could well find in my heart to cast out in some desert of forgetfulness this child, which I am loath to father. But you desired me to do it; and your desire, to my heart, is an absolute commandment. Now it is done only for you, only to you. If you keep it to yourself, or to such friends as will weigh errors in the balance of good will, I hope, for the father's sake, it will be pardoned, perchance made much of, though in itself it have deformities; for, indeed, for severer eyes it is not, being but a trifle, and that triflingly handled. Your dear self can best witness the manner, being done in loose sheets of paper, most of it in your presence, the rest by sheets sent unto you as fast as they were done. In sum, a young head, not so well stayed [2] as I would it were, and shall be when God will, having many, many fancies begotten in it, if it had not been in some way delivered, would have grown a monster, and more sorry I might be that they came in than that they gat out. But his chief safety shall be the not walking abroad, and his chief protection the bearing the livery of your name, which, if my good will do not deceive me, is worthy to be a sanctuary for a greater offender. This say I because I know thy virtue so; and this say I because I know it may be ever so, or, to say better, because it will be ever so. Read it then, at your idle times, and the follies your good judgment will find in it blame not, but laugh at; and so, looking for no better stuff than, as in a haberdasher's shop, glasses or feathers, you will continue to love the writer, who doth exceedingly love you, and most, most heartily prays you may long live to be a principal ornament to the family of the Sidneys.

Your loving brother,

PHILIP SIDNEY

From BOOK I

It was in the time that the earth begins to put on her new apparel against the approach of her lover, and that the sun running a most even course becomes an indifferent arbiter between the night and the day, when the hopeless shepherd Strephon was come to the sands which lie against the island of Cithera, [3] where, viewing the place with a heavy kind of delight, and sometimes casting his eyes to the isleward, he called his friendly rival the pastor [4] Claius unto him; and, setting first down in his darkened countenance a doleful copy of what he would speak, [5]

"O my Claius," said he, "hither we are now come to pay the rent for which we are so called unto by overbusy remembrance; remembrance, restless remembrance, which claims not only this duty of us, but for it will have us forget ourselves. I pray you, when we were amid our flock, and that, [6] of other shepherds, some were running after their sheep, strayed beyond their bounds, some delighting their eyes with seeing them nibble upon the short and sweet grass, some medicining their sick ewes, some setting a bell for an ensign of a sheepish squadron, some with more leisure inventing new games for exercising their bodies, and sporting their wits—did remembrance grant us an holiday, either for pastime or devotion, nay, either for necessary food or natural rest, but that still it forced our thoughts to work upon this place, where we last—alas, that the word 'last' should so long last—did grace our eyes upon her ever-flourishing beauty; did it not still cry within us: 'Ah, you base-minded wretches! Are your thoughts so deeply bemired in the trade of ordinary worldlings, as, for respect of gain some paltry

1 Sidney did not mean to "walk abroad" into print with his book. This will partly explain the loose style in which it is written. But Elizabethan prose in general was much inferior to Elizabethan poetry. The brief selection given here lacks narrative interest, but will exemplify the curious style known as "euphuism" and also give a glimpse of that Arcadia which has been idealized in poetry and romance into an imaginary paradise of the simple, natural life.

2 steadied

3 As the native isle of Aphrodite, this is a fitting place for Urania, the "heavenly," to depart to. It lies south of Greece, and Arcadia is a region of Greece; but in Arcadian romances geography matters little.

4 shepherd

5 a good example of the "conceits" which marked the prose and often the poetry of this period

6 when

wool may yield you, to let so much time pass without knowing perfectly her estate, especially in so troublesome a season; to leave that shore unsaluted from whence you may see to the island where she dwelleth; to leave those steps unkissed wherein Urania printed the farewell of all beauty?'

"Well, then, remembrance commanded, we obeyed, and here we find that as our remembrance came ever clothed unto us in the form of this place, so this place gives new heat to the fever of our languishing remembrance. Yonder, my Claius, Urania alighted; the very horse methought bewailed to be so disburdened; and as for thee, poor Claius, when thou wentest to help her down, I saw reverence and desire so divide thee that thou didst at one instant both blush and quake, and instead of bearing her wert ready to fall down thyself. There she sate vouchsafing[1] my cloak (then most gorgeous) under her; at yonder rising of the ground she turned herself, looking back toward her wonted abode, and because of her parting, bearing much sorrow in her eyes, the lightsomeness whereof had yet so natural a cheerfulness as it made even sorrow seem to smile; at the turning she spake to us all, opening the cherry of her lips, and, Lord! how greedily mine ears did feed upon the sweet words she uttered! And here she laid her hand over thine eyes, when she saw the tears springing in them, as if she would conceal them from other[2] and yet herself feel some of thy sorrow. But woe is me! yonder, yonder did she put her foot into the boat, at that instant, as it were, dividing her heavenly beauty between the earth and the sea. But when she was embarked, did you not mark how the winds whistled, and the seas danced for joy, how the sails did swell with pride, and all because they had Urania? O Urania, blessed be thou, Urania, the sweetest fairness and fairest sweetness!"

With that word his voice brake so with sobbing that he could say no further; and Claius thus answered, "Alas, my Strephon," said he, "what needs this score to reckon up only our losses? What doubt is there but that the sight of this place doth call our thoughts to appear at the court of affection, held by that racking steward Remembrance? As well may sheep forget to fear when they spy wolves, as we can miss such fancies, when we see any place made happy by her treading. Who can choose that saw her but think where she stayed, where she walked, where she turned, where she spoke? But what is all this? Truly no more but, as this place served us to think of those things, so those things serve as places to call to memory more excellent matters. No, no, let us think with consideration, and consider with acknowledging, and acknowledge with admiration, and admire with love, and love with joy in the midst of all woes; let us in such sort think, I say, that our poor eyes were so enriched as to behold, and our low hearts so exalted as to love, a maid who is such, that as the greatest thing the world can show is her beauty, so the least thing that may be praised in her is her beauty. Certainly, as her eyelids are more pleasant to behold than two white kids climbing up a fair tree, and browsing on his tenderest branches, and yet are nothing compared to the day-shining stars contained in them; and as her breath is more sweet than a gentle southwest wind, which comes creeping over flowery fields and shadowed waters in the extreme heat of summer, and yet is nothing compared to the honey-flowing speech that breath doth carry—no more all that our eyes can see of her—though when they have seen her, what else they shall ever see is but dry stubble after clover-grass—is to be matched with the flock of unspeakable virtues laid up delightfully in that best builded fold.

"But, indeed, as we can better consider the sun's beauty by marking how he gilds these waters and mountains than by looking upon his own face, too glorious for our weak eyes; so it may be our conceits—not able to bear her sun-staining excellency—will better weigh it by her works upon some meaner subject employed. And, alas, who can better witness that than we, whose experience is grounded upon feeling? Hath not the only[3] love of her made us, being silly ignorant shepherds, raise up our thoughts above the ordinary level of the world, so as great clerks[4] do not disdain our conference?[5] Hath not the desire to seem worthy in her eyes made us, when others were sleeping, to sit viewing the course of the heavens; when others were running at base,[6] to run over learned writings; when others mark their sheep, we to mark ourselves? Hath not she thrown reason upon our desires, and, as it were, given eyes unto Cupid? Hath in any, but in her, love-fellowship maintained friendship between rivals, and beauty taught the beholders chastity?"

. . . .

[1] allowing
[2] others
[3] mere
[4] scholars
[5] conversation
[6] prisoner's base

[The shepherds rescue the shipwrecked Musidorus and undertake to lead him to the home of a hospitable man in their native country of Arcadia.]

So that the third day after, in the time that the morning did strow roses and violets in the heavenly floor against the coming of the sun, the nightingales, striving one with the other which could in most dainty variety recount their wrong-caused sorrow, made them put off their sleep; and, rising from under a tree, which that night had been their pavilion, they went on their journey, which by-and-by welcomed Musidorus' eyes with delightful prospects. There were hills which garnished their proud heights with stately trees; humble valleys whose base estate seemed comforted with the refreshing of silver rivers; meadows enameled with all sorts of eye-pleasing flowers; thickets which, being lined with most pleasant shade, were witnessed so to, by the cheerful disposition of many well-tuned birds; each pasture stored with sheep, feeding with sober security, while the pretty lambs, with bleating oratory, craved the dam's comfort; here a shepherd's boy piping, as though he should never be old; there a young shepherdess knitting, and withal singing; and it seemed that her voice comforted her hands to work, and her hands kept time to her voice-music.

As for the houses of the country—for many houses came under their eye—they were all scattered, no two being one by the other, and yet not so far off as that it barred mutual succor; a show, as it were, of an accompanable [1] solitariness, and of a civil wildness.

"I pray you," said Musidorus, then first unsealing his long-silent lips, "what countries be these we pass through, which are so diverse in show, the one wanting no store, the other having no store but of want?"

"The country," answered Claius, "where you were cast ashore, and now are passed through, is Laconia, not so poor by the barrenness of the soil—though in itself not passing fertile—as by a civil war, which being these two years within the bowels of that estate, between the gentlemen and the peasants—by them named Helots—hath in this sort, as it were, disfigured the face of nature and made it so unhospitable as now you have found it; the towns neither of the one side nor the other willingly opening their gates to strangers, nor strangers willingly entering, for fear of being mistaken. But this country where now you set your foot, is Arcadia; and even hard by is the house of Kalander, whither we lead you. This country being thus decked with peace, and the child of peace, good husbandry, these houses you see so scattered are of men, as we two are, that live upon the commodity of their sheep, and therefore, in the division of the Arcadian estate, are termed shepherds—a happy people, wanting little because they desire not much."

1590

[1] companionable

SIR WALTER RALEIGH
1552?-1618

Raleigh was born in Devon, and probably acquired his passion for the sea from boyhood contact with sailors. He spent three years at Oxford, but in 1569 was seeking adventure as a volunteer in the Huguenot army in France. In 1578 he was helping his half brother, Sir Humphrey Gilbert, to fit out a fleet of discovery. He saw some military service in Ireland, where he visited Spenser, but his heart was set on voyages of discovery.

Unfortunately he came into favor with Queen Elizabeth—according to the famous legend by spreading his cloak for her to walk on—and, as was her wont with favorites, she would not permit him to leave the country; he was, however, able to distinguish himself in various engagements with the Spanish Armada, 1588. Then he fell into disgrace for preferring a maid of honor to her majesty, and being out of favor could do as he pleased. Accordingly, 1595, he sailed in search of El Dorado, explored the Orinoco, and mapped the coast of Guiana. On the accession of James I, who believed that Raleigh had opposed his claim to the throne, the unfortunate man was deprived of honors and estates, imprisoned for thirteen years, and only released that he might search for rich mines in the new world. The voyage was a failure; Raleigh was accused of treason, imprisoned, and beheaded. He was writing poetry most of his life, but only about thirty songs survive (p. 163). He is best known perhaps for his prose writings: *The Discovery of Guiana*, 1596; and a *History of the World*, 1614, written in the Tower.

"A shining and violent specimen of the Elizabethan adventurous type," Sir Edmund Gosse calls him; the very mirror and summary of Elizabethan qualities—soldier, admiral, explorer, colonizer, courtier, poet, historian, scientist, freethinker according to *The Nation*, it is not surprising that a third modern writer, Mr. Tupper, should find many points of resemblance between Sir Walter Raleigh and Theodore Roosevelt.

Kingsley's *Westward Ho!*, much of which is based on Raleigh's account of his voyages, offers a picturesque narrative of the period. See also Lee, "Raleigh in 1918," *Nation* 107:505-6; E. Gosse, "Tercentenary of Sir Walter Raleigh's Death," *Fortn.* 110:715-23; F. Tupper, "Raleigh and Roosevelt," *Nation* 108:344-5.

THE LAST FIGHT OF THE REVENGE[1]

The Lord Thomas Howard, with six of her Majesty's ships, six victualers of London, the bark *Raleigh,* and two or three pinnaces, riding at anchor near unto Flores, one of the westerly islands of the Azores, the last of August in the afternoon, had intelligence by one Captain Middleton, of the approach of the Spanish Armada.[2] Which Middleton, being in a very good sailer, had kept them company three days before, of good purpose both to discover their forces the more, as also to give advice to my Lord Thomas of their approach.

He had no sooner delivered the news but the fleet was in sight. Many of our ships' companies were on shore in the island, some providing ballast for their ships, others filling of water and refreshing themselves from the land with such things as they could either for money or by force recover.[3] By reason whereof our ships being all pestered, and rummaging every thing out of order,[4] very light for want of ballast, and that which was most to our disadvantage, the one half of the men of every ship sick and utterly unserviceable. For in the *Revenge* there were ninety diseased; in the *Bonaventure,* not so many in health as could handle her mainsail—for had not twenty men been taken out of a bark of Sir George Cary's, his being commanded to be sunk, and those appointed to her, she had hardly ever recovered[5] England. The rest, for the most part, were in little better state.

The names of her Majesty's ships were these, as followeth: The *Defiance,* which was Admiral, the *Revenge,* Vice Admiral, the *Bonaventure,* commanded by Captain Crosse, the *Lion,* by George Fenner, the *Foresight,* by Thomas Vavisour, and the *Crane,* by Duffield; the *Foresight* and the *Crane* being but small ships only—the other were of middle size. The rest, besides the bark *Raleigh,* commanded by Captain Thin, were victualers, and of small force or none.

The Spanish fleet, having shrouded their approach by reason of the island, were now so soon at hand as[6] our ships had scarce time to weigh their anchors, but some of them were driven to let slip their cables and set sail. Sir Richard Grenville was the last weighed, to recover the men that were upon the island, which otherwise had been lost. The Lord Thomas with the rest very hardly recovered the wind, which Sir Richard Grenville not being able to do, was persuaded[7] by the master and others to cut[8] his mainsail and cast[9] about, and to trust to the sailing of his ship; for the squadron of Seville were on his weather bow. But Sir Richard utterly refused to turn from the enemy, alleging that he would rather choose to die, than to dishonor himself, his country, and her Majesty's ship, persuading his company that he would pass through the two squadrons in despite of them, and enforce those of Seville to give him way. Which he performed upon divers of the foremost, who, as the mariners term it, sprang their luff,[10] and fell under the lee of the *Revenge.* But the other course had been the better, and might right well have been answered in so great an impossibility of prevailing. Notwithstanding out of the greatness of his mind he could not be persuaded.[11]

In the meanwhile, as he attended those which were nearest him, the great *San Philip,* being in the wind of him, and coming toward him, becalmed his sails in such sort as the ship could neither weigh nor feel the helm; so huge and high carged[12] was the Spanish ship, being of a thousand and five hundred tons; who afterlaid the *Revenge* aboard.[13] When he was thus bereft of his sails, the ships that were under his lee, luffing up, also laid him aboard; of which the next was the admiral of the Biscayans, a very mighty and puissant ship commanded by Brittan Dona. The said *Philip* carried three tier of ordnance on a side, and eleven pieces in every tier. She shot[14] eight forthright out of her chase,[15] besides those of her stern ports.

[1] In the fall of 1591 a small fleet of English vessels lay at the Azores to intercept the Spanish treasure-ships from the Indies. On the appearance of the Spanish war-vessels sent to convoy the treasure-ships, the English vessels took to flight, with the exception of the *Revenge* commanded by Sir Richard Grenville, Vice Admiral of the fleet. The story of the fight of the *Revenge* was written by Raleigh, a cousin of Grenville's, and published anonymously in 1591; it was included, eight years later, in Hakluyt's *Voyages.* Bacon also celebrated the fight as "a defeat exceeding a victory," "memorable even beyond credit and to the hight of some heroical fable," in which "the ship for the span of fifteen hours sat like a stag amongst hounds at the bay, and was sieged and fought with in turn by fifteen great ships of Spain." See also Froude's essay on *England's Forgotten Worthies,* and Tennyson's ballad, "The Revenge" (p. 634).

[2] armada=fleet; armado=single warship

[3] obtain

[4] i.e., were all cumbered, and badly stowed. The syntax of this sentence, as of others that follow, is very faulty. Cf. note on the style of the preceding selection.

[5] regained

[6] that [7] advised [8] shift [9] turn

[10] kept close to the wind by means of the helm

[11] He was a fierce man, "of nature very severe," who in his day had the reputation of eating the wine-glasses after he drank the wine.

[12] or *cargued* (a nautical term of uncertain meaning, possibly high-carved or built)

[13] came alongside of (from behind)

[14] could shoot [15] fore-deck

After the *Revenge* was entangled with this *Philip*, four other boarded her, two on her larboard, and two on her starboard. The fight thus beginning at three of the clock in the afternoon continued very terrible all that evening. But the great *San Philip*, having received the lower tier of the *Revenge*, discharged with crossbar shot, shifted herself with all diligence from her sides, utterly misliking her first entertainment. Some say that the ship foundered, but we cannot report it for truth, unless we were assured.

The Spanish ships were filled with companies of soldiers, in some two hundred besides the mariners, in some five, in others eight hundred. In ours there were none at all, besides the mariners, but the servants of the commanders and some few voluntary gentlemen only.

After many interchanged volleys of great ordnance and small shot, the Spaniards deliberated to enter the *Revenge*, and made divers attempts, hoping to force her by the multitudes of their armed soldiers and musketeers, but were still repulsed again and again, and at all times beaten back into their own ships or into the seas. In the beginning of the fight, the *George Noble* of London, having received some shot through her by the armados, fell under the lee of the *Revenge*, and asked Sir Richard what he would command him, being but one of the victualers and of small force. Sir Richard bade him save himself, and leave him to his fortune.

After the fight had thus without intermission continued while the day lasted and some hours of the night, many of our men were slain and hurt, and one of the great galleons of the Armada and the admiral of the Hulks [1] both sunk, and in many other of the Spanish ships great slaughter was made. Some write that Sir Richard was very dangerously hurt almost in the beginning of the fight, and lay speechless for a time ere he recovered. But two of the *Revenge's* own company brought home in a ship of lime from the islands, examined by some of the Lords and others, affirmed that he was never so wounded as that he forsook the upper deck, till an hour before midnight; and then being shot into the body with a musket, as he was a-dressing [2] was again shot into the head, and withal his chirurgeon [3] wounded to death. This agreeth also with an examination, taken by Sir Francis Godolphin, of four other mariners of the same ship being returned, which examination the said Sir Francis sent unto master William Killigrew, of her Majesty's Privy Chamber.

But to return to the fight, the Spanish ships which attempted to board the *Revenge*, as they were wounded and beaten off, so always others came in their places, she having never less than two mighty galleons by her sides and aboard her. So that ere the morning from three of the clock the day before, there had fifteen several armados assailed her; and all so ill approved their entertainment, as they were by the break of day far more willing to hearken to a composition [4] than hastily to make any more assaults or entries. But as the day increased, so our men decreased; and as the light grew more and more, by so much more grew our discomforts. For none appeared in sight but enemies, saving one small ship called the *Pilgrim*, commanded by Jacob Whiddon, who hovered all night to see the success; [5] but in the morning, bearing with the *Revenge*, was hunted like a hare among many ravenous hounds, but escaped.

All the powder of the *Revenge* to the last barrel was now spent, all her pikes broken, forty of her best men slain, and the most part of the rest hurt. In the beginning of the fight she had but one hundred free from sickness, and fourscore and ten sick, laid in hold upon the ballast. A small troop to man such a ship, and a weak garrison to resist so mighty an army! By those hundred all was sustained, the volleys, boardings, and enterings of fifteen ships of war, besides those which beat her at large. On the contrary, the Spanish were always supplied with soldiers brought from every squadron, all manner of arms and powder at will. Unto ours there remained no comfort at all, no hope, no supply either of ships, men, or weapons; the masts all beaten overboard, all her tackle cut asunder, her upper work altogether razed; and, in effect, evened she was with the water, but [6] the very foundation or bottom of a ship, nothing being left overhead either for flight or defense.

Sir Richard finding himself in this distress, and unable any longer to make resistance, having endured in this fifteen hours' fight the assault of fifteen several armados, all by turns aboard him, and by estimation eight hundred shot of great artillery, besides many assaults and entries, and that himself and the ship must needs be possessed by the enemy, who were now cast in a ring round about him, the *Revenge* not able to move one way or other but as she

[1] heavy ships
[2] having the wound dressed
[3] also his surgeon

[4] agreement, terms
[5] outcome
[6] nothing but

was moved by the waves and billows of the sea—commanded the master gunner, whom he knew to be a most resolute man, to split and sink the ship, that thereby nothing might remain of glory or victory to the Spaniards, seeing in so many hours' fight, and with so great a navy, they were not able to take her, having had fifteen hours' time, fifteen thousand men, and fifty and three sail of men-of-war to perform it withal; and persuaded the company, or as many as he could induce, to yield themselves unto God, and to the mercy of none else, but, as they had, like valiant resolute men, repulsed so many enemies, they should not now shorten the honor of their nation by prolonging their own lives for a few hours or a few days.

The master gunner readily condescended,[1] and divers others. But the Captain and the Master were of another opinion and besought Sir Richard to have care of them, alleging that the Spaniard would be as ready to entertain a composition as they were willing to offer the same, and that there being divers sufficient and valiant men yet living, and whose wounds were not mortal, they might do their country and prince acceptable service hereafter. And (that where Sir Richard had alleged that the Spaniards should never glory to have taken one ship of her Majesty's, seeing that they had so long and so notably defended themselves) they answered that the ship had six foot of water in hold, three shot under water which were so weakly stopped as, with the first working of the sea, she must needs sink, and was besides so crushed and bruised as she could never be removed out of the place.

And as the matter was thus in dispute, and Sir Richard refusing to hearken to any of those reasons, the Master of the *Revenge* (while the Captain won unto him the greater party) was conveyed aboard the *General Don Alfonso Bassan.* Who finding none over hasty to enter the *Revenge* again, doubting lest Sir Richard would have blown them up and himself, and perceiving by the report of the Master of the *Revenge* his dangerous disposition, yielded that all their lives should be saved, the company sent for England, and the better sort to pay such reasonable ransom as their estate would bear, and in the mean season to be free from galley or imprisonment. To this he so much the rather condescended, as well, as I have said, for fear of further loss and mischief to themselves, as also for the desire he had to recover Sir Richard Grenville; whom for his notable valor he seemed greatly to honor and admire.

[1] agreed

When this answer was returned, and that safety of life was promised, the common sort being now at the end of their peril, the most drew back from Sir Richard and the gunner, being no hard matter to dissuade men from death to life. The master gunner finding himself and Sir Richard thus prevented and mastered by the greater number, would have slain himself with a sword had he not been by force withheld and locked into his cabin. Then the *General* sent many boats aboard the *Revenge,* and divers of our men, fearing Sir Richard's disposition, stole away aboard the *General* and other ships. Sir Richard, thus overmatched, was sent unto by Alfonso Bassan to remove out of the *Revenge,* the ship being marvelous unsavory, filled with blood and bodies of dead and wounded men like a slaughter-house. Sir Richard answered that he might do with his body what he list,[2] for he esteemed it not; and as he was carried out of the ship he swoonded,[3] and reviving again desired the company to pray for him. The General used Sir Richard with all humanity, and left nothing unattempted that tended to his recovery, highly commending his valor and worthiness, and greatly bewailed the danger wherein he was, being unto them a rare spectacle, and a resolution seldom approved,[4] to see one ship turn toward so many enemies, to endure the charge and boarding of so many huge armados, and to resist and repel the assaults and entries of so many soldiers. All which, and more, is confirmed by a Spanish captain of the same Armada, and a present actor in the fight, who, being severed from the rest in a storm, was by the *Lion of London,* a small ship, taken, and is now prisoner in London.

The General Commander of the Armada was Don Alfonso Bassan, brother to the Marquis of Santa Cruce. The Admiral of the Biscayan squadron was Brittan Dona; of the squadron of Seville, Marquis of Arumburch. The Hulks and Fly-boats[5] were commanded by Luis Cutino. There were slain and drowned in this fight well near two thousand of the enemies, and two especial Commanders, Don Luis de Sant John, and Don George de Prunaria de Malaga, as the Spanish Captain confesseth, besides divers others of special account, whereof as yet report is not made.

The admiral of the Hulks and the *Ascension* of Seville were both sunk by the side of the *Revenge;* one other recovered the road of Saint Michaels, and sunk also there; a fourth ran

[2] pleased [3] swooned [4] experienced
[5] Dutch boats that had been impressed into the Spanish service

herself with the shore to save her men. Sir Richard died, as it is said, the second or third day aboard the *General,* and was by them greatly bewailed. What became of his body, whether it was buried in the sea or on the land we know not. The comfort that remaineth to his friends is, that he hath ended his life honorably in respect of the reputation won to his nation and country, and of the same to his posterity, and that, being dead, he hath not outlived his own honor.[1]

1591 1591

FRANCIS BACON 1561-1626

One of the most endlessly fruitful subjects for controversy is a man whom Pope called "the wisest, brightest, meanest of mankind," and of whom Ben Jonson said, "The fear of every man that heard him speak was lest he should make an end." In his aims and career Bacon was not unlike Sir Thomas More. He was the son of Sir Nicholas Bacon, a high official at Court, and was born at York House, a famous residence in the Strand, London. As a boy he was eager to defend Protestantism against its enemies, improve the government of his country, and create a new system of philosophy. At twelve he entered Cambridge; at eighteen he was left by his father's sudden death to make his own career; and at thirty he uttered what Paul Kaufman calls "his famous and splendidly audacious words: 'I have taken all knowledge to be my province.'" In spite of the fact that his father was lord keeper and his uncle, Lord Burleigh, treasurer under Elizabeth, Bacon never obtained from the Queen the preferment he was constantly seeking. Under James I, however, he rose step by step to the peerage as Baron Verulam, and to the chancellorship in 1618. But at the height of his power he was accused of accepting bribes, was imprisoned, heavily fined, and finally banished from Court. He retired to devote himself to writing, and died from a chill caught while stuffing a fowl with snow in order to prove the preservative properties of cold.

[1] The account of his death by another contemoprary, Jan Huyghen van Linschoten, runs thus: "He was borne into the ship called the *Saint Paul,* wherein was the Admiral of the Fleet, Don Alonso de Barsan. There his wounds were dressed by the Spanish surgeons, but Don Alonso himself would neither see him nor speak with him. All the rest of the captains and gentlemen went to visit him and to comfort him in his hard fortune, wondering at his courage and stout heart, for that he shewed not any sign of faintness nor changing of color. But feeling the hour of death to approach, he spake these words in Spanish, and said: 'Here die I, Richard Grenville, with a joyful and quiet mind, for that I have ended my life as a true soldier ought to do that hath fought for his country, queen, religion, and honor, whereby my soul most joyful departeth out of this body, and shall always leave behind it an everlasting fame of a valiant and true soldier that hath done his duty as he was bound to do.'"

He was a brilliant lawyer, an ardent philosopher and scientist, and his numerous writings form a noble monument. Because of the *Novum Organum,* 1620, written in Latin, he is often called the founder of the inductive system of philosophy, though he merely simplified a method already in vogue. In English he wrote the *Advancement of Learning,* 1605; the *New Atlantis,* 1624, the picture of an ideal state resembling More's *Utopia* (see p. 120); and the *Essays,* his most enduring literary work, dealing with a wide range of themes, touching closely on life and filled with shrewd truth. It is a matter of interest that Bacon is seriously believed by a few critics to be the only possible author of Shakespeare's dramas; the proof was supposedly found in a cipher said to be hidden in the plays.

The *Essays,* edited by A. S. West, are in the Pitt Press Series, also in Temple, Cassell, etc. R. W. Church's *Bacon* (EML) is a good biography; there are essays, too, by Macaulay, Lee, Hazlitt (DLAE); recent articles of interest are: H. B. C. Pollard, "Bacon after 300 Years," *Liv. Age* 329:677-81, showing Bacon's modernity; F. J. C. Hearnshaw, "Bacon as Historian," *Contemp.* 123: 606-14, a worthwhile discussion of one phase of Bacon's work; Sydenham of Combe, "Shakespeare —and Bacon," *19th Cent.* 93:80-9, an interesting paper on the Bacon-Shakespeare controversy.

ESSAYS[2]

Of Studies

Studies serve for delight, for ornament, and for ability. Their chief use for delight is in privateness and retiring; for ornament, is in discourse; and for ability, is in the judgment and disposition of business. For expert men can execute, and perhaps judge of particulars, one by one; but the general counsels, and the plots and marshaling of affairs, come best from those that are learned. To spend too much time in studies is sloth; to use them too much for ornament is affectation; to make judgment wholly by their rules is the humor of a scholar. They perfect nature, and are perfected by experience; for natural abilities are like natural plants, that need pruning by study; and studies themselves do give forth directions too much at large, except they be bounded in[3] by experience. Crafty men[4] contemn studies, simple men admire[5] them, and

[2] The first edition of Bacon's *Essays* (ten in number) was printed in 1597; revised and enlarged editions appeared in 1612 and 1625. The first two essays given here were in the first edition, the next two in the second, the last two in the third; but all follow the text of the third. The spelling is modernized, the paragraphing not; as the essays consist often of detached thoughts, a change of thought may be expected at any point.

[3] checked

[4] craftsmen, men of practical skill (much like "expert men" above)

[5] wonder at

wise men use them; for they teach not their own use; but that is a wisdom without [1] them, and above them, won by observation. Read not to contradict and confute; nor to believe and take for granted; nor to find talk and discourse; but to weigh and consider. Some books are to be tasted, [2] others to be swallowed, and some few to be chewed and digested; that is, some books are to be read only in parts; others to be read, but not curiously; and some few to be read wholly, and with diligence and attention. Some books also may be read by deputy, and extracts made of them by others; but that would be only in the less important arguments, and the meaner sort of books; else distilled books are like common distilled waters, flashy [3] things. Reading maketh a full man; conference [4] a ready man; and writing an exact man. And therefore, if a man write little, he had need have a great memory; if he confer little, he had need have a present wit; and if he read little, he had need have much cunning, to seem to know that [5] he doth not. Histories make men wise; poets witty; [6] the mathematics subtle; natural philosophy deep; moral grave; logic and rhetoric able to contend. *Abeunt studia in mores.* [7] Nay, there is no stond [8] or impediment in the wit but may be wrought out [9] by fit studies; like as diseases of the body may have appropriate exercises. Bowling is good for the stone [10] and reins; shooting [11] for the lungs and breast; gentle walking for the stomach; riding for the head; and the like. So if a man's wit be wandering, let him study the mathematics; for in demonstrations, if his wit be called away never so little, he must begin again. If his wit be not apt to distinguish or find differences, let him study the Schoolmen, [12] for they are *cymini sectores.* If he be not apt to beat over matters, and to call up one thing to prove and illustrate another, let him study the lawyers' cases. So every defect of the mind may have a special receipt.

1597

[1] outside of
[2] Of the six sentences beginning here Macaulay said, "We do not believe Thucydides himself has anywhere compressed so much thought in so small a space."
[3] insipid
[4] conversation
[5] that which
[6] imaginative
[7] "Studies are transmuted into character."
[8] stand, obstacle
[9] removed
[10] gravel (a disease of the kidneys, or reins)
[11] archery
[12] medieval theologians, who were "splitters of cumin-seeds," hair-splitters

Of Discourse

Some in their discourse [13] desire rather commendation of wit, in being able to hold all arguments, than of judgment, in discerning what is true; as if it were a praise to know what might be said, and not what should be thought. Some have certain common places and themes wherein they are good, and want variety; which kind of poverty is for the most part tedious, and when it is once perceived, ridiculous. The honorablest part of talk is to give the occasion; and again to moderate and pass to somewhat else; for then a man leads the dance. It is good, in discourse and speech of conversation, to vary and intermingle speech of the present occasion with arguments, tales with reasons, asking of questions with telling of opinions, and jest with earnest; for it is a dull thing to tire, and, as we say now, to jade anything too far. As for jest, there be certain things which ought to be privileged from it; namely, religion, matters of state, great persons, any man's present business of importance, and any case that deserveth pity. Yet there be some that think their wits have been asleep, except they dart out somewhat that is piquant, and to the quick. That is a vein which would [14] be bridled;

Parce, puer, stimulis, et fortius utere loris. [15]

And generally, men ought to find the difference between saltness and bitterness. Certainly, he that hath a satirical vein, as he maketh others afraid of his wit, so he had need be afraid of others' memory. He that questioneth much shall learn much, and content much; but especially if he apply [16] his questions to the skill of the persons whom he asketh; for he shall give them occasion to please themselves in speaking, and himself shall continually gather knowledge. But let his questions not be troublesome; for that is fit for a poser. [17] And let him be sure to leave other men their turns to speak. Nay, if there be any that would reign and take up all the time, let him find means to take them off, and to bring others on; as musicians use to do with those that dance too long galliards. [18] If you dissemble sometimes your knowledge of that you are thought to know, you shall be thought another time to know that you know not. Speech of a man's self ought to be seldom, and well chosen. I knew one was wont to say in scorn, *He must*

[13] conversation
[14] should
[15] "Spare the whip, boy, and hold more firmly the reins," Ovid, *Met.* ii, 127.
[16] adapt
[17] examiner
[18] a lively French dance for two

needs be a wise man, he speaks so much of himself; and there is but one case wherein a man may commend himself with good grace; and that is in commending virtue in another; especially if it be such a virtue whereunto himself pretendeth. Speech of touch toward others should be sparingly used; for discourse ought to be as a field, without coming home to any man. I knew two noblemen, of the west part of England, whereof the one was given to scoff, but kept ever royal cheer in his house; the other would ask of those that had been at the other's table, *Tell truly, was there never a flout or dry*[1] *blow given?* To which the guest would answer, *Such and such a thing passed.* The lord would say, *I thought he would mar a good dinner.* Discretion of speech is more than eloquence; and to speak agreeably to him with whom we deal is more than to speak in good words or in good order. A good continued speech, without a good speech of interlocution, shows slowness; and a good reply or second speech, without a good settled speech, showeth shallowness and weakness. As we see in beasts, that those that are weakest in the course are yet nimblest in the turn; as it is betwixt the greyhound and the hare. To use too many circumstances ere one come to the matter is wearisome; to use none at all is blunt.

1597

Of Friendship

It had been hard for him[2] that spake it to have put more truth and untruth together in few words, than in that speech, *Whosoever is delighted in solitude is either a wild beast or a god.* For it is most true that a natural and secret hatred and aversation toward[3] society in any man hath somewhat of the savage beast; but it is most untrue that it should have any character at all of the divine nature; except it proceed, not out of a pleasure in solitude, but out of a love and desire to sequester a man's self for higher conversation—such as is found to have been falsely and feignedly in some of the heathen; as Epimenides the Candian, Numa the Roman, Empedocles the Sicilian, and Apollonius of Tyana;[4] and truly and really in divers of the ancient hermits and holy fathers of the church. But little do men perceive what solitude is, and how far it extendeth. For a crowd is not company; and faces are but a gallery of pictures; and talk but a tinkling cymbal, where there is no love. The Latin adage meeteth[5] with it a little: *Magna civitas, magna solitudo;*[6] because in a great town friends are scattered; so that there is not that fellowship, for the most part, which is in less neighborhoods. But we may go further, and affirm most truly that it is a mere[7] and miserable solitude to want true friends; without which the world is but a wilderness; and even in this sense also of solitude, whosoever in the frame of his nature and affections is unfit for friendship, he taketh it of the beast, and not from humanity.

A principal fruit of friendship is the ease and discharge of the fullness and swellings of the heart, which passions of all kinds do cause and induce. We know diseases of stoppings and suffocations are the most dangerous in the body; and it is not much otherwise in the mind; you may take sarza[8] to open the liver, steel to open the spleen, flowers[9] of sulphur for the lungs, castoreum for the brain; but no receipt openeth the heart but a true friend; to whom you may impart griefs, joys, fears, hopes, suspicions, counsels, and whatsoever lieth upon the heart to oppress it, in a kind of civil shrift or confession.

It is a strange thing to observe how high a rate great kings and monarchs do set upon this fruit of friendship whereof we speak; so great, as[10] they purchase it many times at the hazard of their own safety and greatness. For princes, in regard of the distance of their fortune from that of their subjects and servants, cannot gather this fruit, except (to make themselves capable thereof) they raise some persons to be as it were companions and almost equals to themselves, which many times sorteth to[11] inconvenience. The modern languages give unto such persons the name of favorites, or privadoes; as if it were matter of grace or conversation. But the Roman name attaineth the true use and cause thereof, naming them *participes curarum;*[12] for it is that which tieth the knot. And we see plainly that this hath been done, not by weak and passionate princes only, but by the wisest and most politic that ever reigned; who have oftentimes joined to themselves some of their servants; whom both themselves have called friends, and allowed others likewise to call them in the same manner; using the word which is received between private men.

[1] hard
[2] Aristotle, *Politics, i. 2*
[3] aversion for
[4] Epimenides, the Cretan poet, was said to have slept in a cave for fifty-seven years; Numa was instructed by the Muse Egeria in a sacred grove; Empedocles surrounded himself with mystery; Apollonius was a religious recluse.
[5] agrees
[6] "A great town is a great solitude."
[7] pure, complete
[8] sarsaparilla
[9] flower (i.e., flour, ed. 1639)
[10] that
[11] results in
[12] "partners of cares"

L. Sylla, when he commanded Rome, raised Pompey (after surnamed the Great) to that height, that Pompey vaunted himself for Sylla's over-match. For when he had carried the consulship for a friend of his[1] against the pursuit of Sylla, and that Sylla did a little resent thereat and began to speak great, Pompey turned upon him again, and in effect bade him be quiet; *for that more men adored the sun rising than the sun setting.* With Julius Caesar, Decimus Brutus had obtained that interest, as[2] he set him down in his testament for heir in remainder after his nephew. And this was the man that had power with him to draw him forth to his death. For when Caesar would have discharged the senate, in regard of some ill presages, and specially a dream of Calpurnia, this man lifted him gently by the arm out of his chair, telling him he hoped he would not dismiss the senate till his wife had dreamt a better dream. And it seemeth his favor was so great, as Antonius, in a letter which is recited *verbatim* in one of Cicero's Philippics, calleth him *venefica, witch,* as if he had enchanted Caesar. Augustus raised Agrippa (though of mean birth) to that height, as when he consulted with Maecenas about the marriage of his daughter Julia, Maecenas took the liberty to tell him *that he must either marry his daughter to Agrippa, or take away his life; there was no third way, he had made him so great.* With Tiberius Caesar, Sejanus had ascended to that height, as they two were termed and reckoned as a pair of friends. Tiberius in a letter to him saith, *Haec pro amicitiâ nostrâ non occultavi;*[3] and the whole senate dedicated an altar to Friendship, as to a goddess, in respect of the great dearness of friendship between them two. The like or more was between Septimius Severus and Plautianus. For he forced his eldest son to marry the daughter of Plautianus; and would often maintain Plautianus in doing affronts to his son; and did write also in a letter to the senate, by these words: *I love the man so well, as I wish he may over-live me.* Now if these princes had been as a Trajan or a Marcus Aurelius, a man might have thought that this had proceeded of an abundant goodness of nature; but being men so wise, of such strength and severity of mind, and so extreme lovers of themselves, as all these were, it proveth most plainly that they found their own felicity (though as great as ever happened to mortal men) but as an half-piece,[4] except they might have a friend to make it entire; and yet, which is more, they were princes that had wives, sons, nephews; and yet all these could not supply the comfort of friendship.

It is not to be forgotten what Comineus observeth of his first master, Duke Charles the Hardy; namely, that he would communicate his secrets with none; and least of all, those secrets which troubled him most. Whereupon he goeth on and saith that toward his latter time that *closeness did impair and a little perish his understanding.* Surely Comineus might have made the same judgment also, if it had pleased him, of his second master, Louis the Eleventh, whose closeness was indeed his tormentor. The parable of Pythagoras is dark, but true; *Cor ne edito: Eat not the heart.* Certainly, if a man would give it a hard phrase, those that want friends to open themselves unto are cannibals of their own hearts. But one thing is most admirable[5] (wherewith I will conclude this first fruit of friendship), which is, that this communicating of a man's self to his friend works two contrary effects; for it redoubleth joys, and cutteth griefs in halves. For there is no man that imparteth his joys to his friend, but he joyeth the more; and no man that imparteth his griefs to his friend, but he grieveth the less. So that it is, in truth, of[6] operation upon a man's mind, of like virtue as the alchemists use[7] to attribute to their stone[8] for man's body; that it worketh all[9] contrary effects, but still to the good and benefit of nature. But yet without praying in aid of[10] alchemists, there is a manifest image of this in the ordinary course of nature. For in bodies, union strengtheneth and cherisheth any natural action; and on the other side weakeneth and dulleth any violent impression; and even so is it of minds.

The second fruit of friendship is healthful and sovereign for the understanding, as the first is for the affections.[11] For friendship maketh indeed a fair day in the affections, from storm and tempests; but it maketh daylight in the understanding, out of darkness and confusion of thoughts. Neither is this to be understood only of faithful counsel, which a man receiveth from his friend; but before you come to that, certain it is that whosoever hath his mind fraught with many thoughts, his wits and understanding do clarify and break up, in the

[1] Lepidus
[2] such interest that
[3] "Because of our friendship I have not concealed this."
[4] a half-coin (which sometimes circulated)
[5] remarkable
[6] in its
[7] are wont
[8] the "philosopher's stone"
[9] wholly
[10] calling upon (a legal term)
[11] feelings

communicating and discoursing with another; he tosseth his thoughts more easily; he marshaleth them more orderly; he seeth how they look when they are turned into words. Finally, he waxeth wiser than himself; and that more by an hour's discourse than by a day's meditation. It was well said of Themistocles to the king of Persia *that speech was like cloth of Arras opened and put abroad, whereby the imagery doth appear in figure; whereas in thoughts they lie but as in packs.* Neither is this second fruit of friendship, in opening the understanding, restrained only to such friends as are able to give a man counsel (they indeed are best); but even without that, a man learneth of himself, and bringeth his own thoughts to light, and whetteth his wits as against a stone, which itself cuts not. In a word, a man were better relate[1] himself to a statue or picture than to suffer his thoughts to pass in smother.

Add now, to make this second fruit of friendship complete, that other point which lieth more open and falleth within vulgar[2] observation; which is faithful counsel from a friend. Heraclitus saith well in one of his enigmas, *Dry light is ever the best.* And certain it is that the light that a man receiveth by counsel from another is drier and purer than that which cometh from his own understanding and judgment, which is ever infused and drenched in his affections and customs. So as[3] there is as much difference between the counsel that a friend giveth, and that a man giveth himself, as there is between the counsel of a friend and of a flatterer. For there is no such flatterer as is a man's self; and there is no such remedy against flattery of a man's self as the liberty of a friend. Counsel is of two sorts: the one concerning manners, the other concerning business. For the first, the best preservative to keep the mind in health is the faithful admonition of a friend. The calling of a man's self to a strict account is a medicine, sometime too piercing and corrosive. Reading good books of morality is a little flat and dead. Observing our faults in others is sometimes improper for our case. But the best recipe (best, I say, to work, and best to take) is the admonition of a friend. It is a strange thing to behold what gross errors and extreme absurdities many (especially of the greater sort) do commit, for want of a friend to tell them of them; to the great damage both of their fame and fortune; for, as St. James saith,[4] they are as men *that look sometimes into a glass, and presently forget their own shape and favor.*[5] As for business, a man may think, if he will, that two eyes see no more than one; or that a gamester seeth always more than a looker-on; or that a man in anger is as wise as he that hath said over the four and twenty letters;[6] or that a musket may be shot off as well upon the arm as upon a rest; and such other fond and high imaginations, to think himself all in all. But when all is done, the help of good counsel is that which setteth business straight. And if any man think that he will take counsel, but it shall be by pieces; asking counsel in one business of one man, and in another business of another man; it is well (that is to say, better perhaps than if he asked none at all); but he runneth two dangers: one, that he shall not be faithfully counseled; for it is a rare thing, except it be from a perfect and entire friend, to have counsel given, but such as shall be bowed and crooked to some ends which he hath that giveth it. The other, that he shall have counsel given, hurtful and unsafe (though with good meaning) and mixed partly of mischief and partly of remedy; even as if you would call a physician that is thought good for the cure of the disease you complain of, but is unacquainted with your body; and therefore may put you in way for a present cure, but overthroweth your health in some other kind; and so cure the disease and kill the patient. But a friend that is wholly acquainted with a man's estate will beware, by furthering any present business, how he dasheth upon other inconvenience. And therefore rest not upon scattered counsels; they will rather distract and mislead, than settle and direct.

After these two noble fruits of friendship (peace in the affections, and support of the judgment) followeth the last fruit, which is like the pomegranate, full of many kernels; I mean aid and bearing a part in all actions and occasions. Here the best way to represent to life the manifold use of friendship is to cast[7] and see how many things there are which a man cannot do himself; and then it will appear that it was a sparing speech of the ancients, to say *that a friend is another himself;* for that a friend is far more than himself. Men have their time,[8] and die many times in desire of[9] some things which they principally take to heart; the bestowing of a child,[10] the

[1] unbosom
[2] common
[3] so that
[4] *Epistle* i, 23

[5] features
[6] The number in the Greek alphabet, as also in the English when J and U were not differentiated from I and V.
[7] consider
[8] appointed time
[9] often die while still desiring
[10] in marriage

finishing of a work, or the like. If a man have a true friend, he may rest almost secure that the care of those things will continue after him. So that a man hath, as it were, two lives in his desires. A man hath a body, and that body is confined to a place; but where friendship is, all offices of life are as it were granted to him and his deputy. For he may exercise them by his friend. How many things are there which a man cannot, with any face or comeliness, say or do himself? A man can scarce allege his own merits with modesty, much less extol them; a man cannot sometimes brook to supplicate or beg; and a number of the like. But all these things are graceful in a friend's mouth, which are blushing in a man's own. So again, a man's person hath many proper relations which he cannot put off. A man cannot speak to his son but as a father, to his wife but as a husband, to his enemy but upon terms; whereas a friend may speak as the case requires, and not as it sorteth with the person. But to enumerate these things were endless; I have given the rule, where a man cannot fitly play his own part; if he have not a friend he may quit the stage.

1612

Of Riches

I cannot call riches better than the baggage of virtue. The Roman word is better, *impedimenta.* For as the baggage is to an army, so is riches to virtue. It cannot be spared nor left behind, but it hindereth the march; yea, and the care of it sometimes loseth or disturbeth the victory. Of great riches there is no real use, except it be in the distribution; the rest is but conceit.[1] So saith Solomon, *Where much is, there are many to consume it; and what hath the owner but the sight of it with his eyes?* The personal fruition[2] in any man cannot reach to feel great riches; there is a custody of them, or a power of dole and donative[3] of them, or a fame of them, but no solid use to the owner. Do you not see what feigned prices are set upon little stones[4] and rarities? And what works of ostentation are undertaken, because there might seem to be some use of great riches? But then you will say, they may be of use to buy men out of dangers or troubles. As Solomon saith, *Riches are as a strong hold, in the imagination of the rich man.* But this is excellently expressed, that it is in imagination, and not always in fact. For certainly great riches have sold more men than they have bought out. Seek not proud riches, but such as thou mayest get justly, use soberly, distribute cheerfully, and leave contentedly. Yet have no abstract nor friarly contempt of them. But distinguish, as Cicero saith well of Rabirius Posthumus, *In studio rei amplificandae apparebat, non avaritiae praedam, sed instrumentum bonitati quaeri.*[5] Harken also to Solomon, and beware of hasty gathering of riches: *Qui festinat ad divitias, non erit insons.*[6] The poets feign that when Plutus (which is Riches) is sent from Jupiter, he limps and goes slowly; but when he is sent from Pluto, he runs and is swift of foot. Meaning that riches gotten by good means and just labor pace slowly; but when they come by the death of others (as by the course of inheritance, testaments, and the like), they come tumbling upon a man. But it might be applied likewise to Pluto, taking him for the devil. For when riches come from the devil (as by fraud and oppression and unjust means) they come upon[7] speed. The ways to enrich are many, and most of them foul. Parsimony is one of the best, and yet is not innocent; for it withholdeth men from works of liberality and charity. The improvement of the ground is the most natural obtaining of riches; for it is our great mother's blessing, the earth's; but it is slow. And yet where men of great wealth do stoop to husbandry, it multiplieth riches exceedingly. I knew a nobleman in England, that had the greatest audits of any man in my time; a great grazier, a great sheepmaster, a great timber man, a great collier, a great corn-master, a great lead-man, and so of iron, and a number of the like points of husbandry. So as[8] the earth seemed a sea to him, in respect of the perpetual importation. It was truly observed by one, that himself came very hardly to a little riches, and very easily to great riches. For when a man's stock is come to that, that he can expect[9] the prime of markets, and overcome[10] those bargains which for their greatness are few men's money, and be partner in the industries of younger men, he cannot but increase mainly.[11] The gains of ordinary trades and vocations are honest, and furthered by two things chiefly: by diligence, and by a good name for good and fair dealing. But the gains of bargains are of a more doubtful nature, when men shall wait upon[12] others' necessity, broke[13] by servants and instruments to draw them on, put

[1] fancy
[2] enjoyment
[3] distribution and gift
[4] Cf. *Utopia*, p. 128.

[5] "In his endeavor to increase his wealth, it was evident that he sought not what should be a mere prey for avarice, but an instrument of good."
[6] "Who hastens to become rich shall not be innocent."
[7] with
[8] so that
[9] wait for
[10] command
[11] greatly
[12] must watch for
[13] negotiate

off others cunningly that would be better chapmen,[1] and the like practices, which are crafty and naught.[2] As for the chopping[3] of bargains, when a man buys not to hold but to sell over again, that commonly grindeth double, both upon the seller and upon the buyer. Sharings do greatly enrich, if the hands be well chosen that are trusted. Usury is the certainest means of gain, though one of the worst; as that whereby a man doth eat his bread *in sudore vultus alieni,*[4] and besides, doth plow upon Sundays. But yet certain though it be, it hath flaws; for that[5] the scriveners and brokers do value[6] unsound men to serve their own turn. The fortune in being the first in an invention or in a privilege doth cause sometimes a wonderful overgrowth in riches; as it was with the first sugar man in the Canaries. Therefore if a man can play the true logician, to have as well judgment as invention, he may do great matters; especially if the times be fit. He that resteth upon gains certain shall hardly[7] grow to great riches; and he that puts all upon adventures doth oftentimes break and come to poverty; it is good therefore to guard adventures with certainties that may uphold losses. Monopolies, and coemption[8] of wares for resale, where they are not restrained,[9] are great means to enrich; especially if the party have intelligence what things are like to come into request, and so store himself beforehand. Riches gotten by service, though it be of the best rise,[10] yet when they are gotten by flattery, feeding humors,[11] and other servile conditions, they may be placed amongst the worst. As for fishing for testaments and executorships (as Tacitus saith of Seneca, *testamenta et orbos tamquam indagine capi*[12]), it is yet worse, by how much men submit themselves to meaner persons than in service. Believe not much them that seem to despise riches; for they despise them that[13] despair of them; and none worse when they come to them. Be not penny-wise; riches have wings, and sometimes they fly away of themselves, sometimes they must be set flying to bring in more. Men leave their riches either to their kindred, or to the public; and moderate portions prosper best in both. A great state left to an heir, is as a lure to all the birds of prey round about to seize on him, if he be not the better stablished in years and judgment. Likewise glorious[14] gifts and foundations are like *sacrifices without salt;* and but the painted sepulchers of alms, which soon will putrefy and corrupt inwardly.[15] Therefore measure not thine advancements by quantity, but frame them by measure; and defer not charities till death; for, certainly, if a man weigh it rightly, he that doth so is rather liberal of another man's than of his own.

1612

[1] buyers
[2] bad
[3] bartering, dealing in
[4] "in the sweat of another man's face"
[5] because
[6] represent them as financially sound (so as to get a commission on the loan)
[7] with difficulty
[8] cornering
[9] i. e., by law
[10] source
[11] catering to whims
[12] "He took wills and wardships as with a net."
[13] who (antecedent *they*)
[14] vain-glorious

Of Revenge

Revenge is a kind of wild justice; which the more man's nature runs to, the more ought law to weed it out. For as for the first wrong, it doth but offend the law; but the revenge of that wrong putteth the law out of office.[16] Certainly, in taking revenge, a man is but even with his enemy; but in passing it over, he is superior, for it is a prince's part to pardon. And Solomon, I am sure, saith, *It is the glory of a man to pass by an offense.* That which is past is gone and irrevocable, and wise men have enough to do with things present and to come; therefore they do but trifle with themselves, that labor in past matters. There is no man doth a wrong for the wrong's sake; but thereby to purchase himself profit, or pleasure, or honor, or the like. Therefore, why should I be angry with a man for loving himself better than me? And if any man should do wrong merely out of ill-nature, why, yet it is but like the thorn or briar, which prick and scratch because they can do no other. The most tolerable sort of revenge is for those wrongs which there is no law to remedy; but then let a man take heed the revenge be such as there is no law to punish; else a man's enemy is still before hand, and it is two for one. Some, when they take revenge, are desirous the party should know whence it cometh. This is the more generous. For the delight seemeth to be not so much in doing the hurt as in making the party repent. But base and crafty cowards are like the arrow that flieth in the dark. Cosmus, duke of Florence, had a desperate saying against perfidious or neglecting friends, as if those wrongs were unpardonable: *You shall read* (saith he) *that we are commanded to forgive our enemies; but you never read that we are commanded to forgive our friends.* But yet the spirit of Job was in a better tune: *Shall we* (saith he) *take good at God's hands, and not be content to take evil also?* And so of friends in a proportion. This is certain, that a man that studieth revenge, keeps his own wounds green, which otherwise would heal and do well. Public revenges are

[15] See *Mark* ix, 49; *Matthew* xxiii, 27.
[16] i.e., by assuming its function

for the most part fortunate;[1] as that for the death of Caesar, for the death of Pertinax, for the death of Henry the Third of France, and many more. But in private revenges it is not so. Nay rather, vindictive persons live the life of witches; who, as they are michievous, so end they infortunate.

1625

Of Gardens

God Almighty first planted a garden. And indeed it is the purest of human pleasures. It is the greatest refreshment to the spirits of man, without which buildings and palaces are but gross handiworks; and a man shall ever see that when ages grow to civility and elegancy, men come to build stately sooner than to garden finely; as if gardening were the greater perfection. I do hold it,[2] in the royal ordering of gardens, there ought to be gardens for all the months in the year; in which severally things of beauty may be then in season.[3] For December, and January, and the latter part of November, you must take such things as are green all winter: holly; ivy; bays; juniper; cypress trees; yew; pine-apple trees,[4] fir trees; rosemary; lavender; periwinkle, the white, the purple and the blue; germander; flags; orange trees; lemon trees; and myrtles, if they be stoved;[5] and sweet marjoram, warm set.[6] There followeth, for the latter part of January and February, the mezereon tree,[7] which then blossoms; crocus vernus,[8] both the yellow and the gray; primroses; anemones; the early tulippa; hyacinthus orientalis; chamaïris;[9] fritellaria. For March, there come violets, specially the single blue, which are the earliest; the yellow daffodil; the daisy; the almond tree in blossom; the peach tree in blossom; the cornelian tree in blossom; sweet-briar. In April follow the double white violet; the wall-flower; the stock-gilliflower; the cowslip; flower-delices,[10] and lilies of all natures; rosemary-flowers; the tulippa; the double peony; the pale daffodil; the French honeysuckle; the cherry tree in blossom; the damson and plum trees in blossom; the white thorn in leaf; the lilac tree. In May and June come pinks of all sorts, specially the blush-pink; roses of all kinds, except the musk, which comes later; honeysuckles; strawberries; bugloss; columbine; the French marigold; flos Africanus;[11] cherry tree in fruit; ribes;[12] figs in fruit; rasps;[13] vine-flowers; lavender in flowers; the sweet satyrian,[14] with the white flower; herba muscaria;[15] lilium convallium; the apple tree in blossom. In July come gilliflowers of all varieties; musk-roses; the lime tree in blossom; early pears and plums in fruit; jennetings;[16] codlins. In August come plums of all sorts in fruit; pears; apricocks; berberries; filberds; musk-melons; monkshoods, of all colors. In September come grapes; apples; poppies of all colors; peaches; melocotones;[17] nectarines; cornelians; wardens;[18] quinces. In October and the beginning of November come services;[19] medlars; bullaces;[20] roses cut or removed to come late; hollyhocks; and such like. These particulars are for the climate of London; but my meaning is perceived, that you may have *ver perpetuum*,[21] as the place affords.

And because the breath of flowers is far sweeter in the air (where it comes and goes like the warbling of music) than in the hand, therefore nothing is more fit for that delight than to know what be the flowers and plants that do best perfume the air. Roses, damask and red, are fast[22] flowers of their smells; so that you may walk by a whole row of them and find nothing of their sweetness; yea though it be in a morning's dew. Bays likewise yield no smell as they grow. Rosemary little, nor sweet marjoram. That which above all others yields the sweetest smell in the air is the violet, specially the white double violet, which comes twice a year, about the middle of April and about Bartholomew-tide.[23] Next to that is the muskrose. Then the strawberry-leaves dying, which [yield] a most excellent cordial smell. Then the flower of the vines;[24] it is a little dust, like the dust of a bent,[25] which grows upon the cluster in the first coming forth. Then sweet-briar. Then wall-flowers, which are very delightful to be set under a parlor or lower chamber window. Then pinks and gilliflowers, specially the matted pink and clove gilliflower. Then the flowers of the lime tree. Then the honeysuckles, so they be somewhat afar off. Of bean-flowers I speak not, because they are field flowers. But those which perfume the air most delightfully, not passed by as the rest, but being trodden upon and crushed, are three; that is, burnet, wild-thyme, and watermints. Therefore you are to set whole alleys[26] of them to have the pleasure when you walk or tread.

. . . .

1625

[1] of good result
[2] maintain
[3] Cf. *The Winter's Tale*, IV. iv, 72 ff.
[4] pines (cones being called pine-apples)
[5] kept in a hot-house
[6] warmly placed
[7] a shrub-laurel
[8] spring crocus
[9] dwarf iris
[10] fleur-de-lis
[11] African marigold
[12] currants
[13] raspberries
[14] orchis
[15] grape hyacinth
[16] early apples
[17] variety of peach
[18] late pears
[19] sorb, mountain-ash, rowan
[20] a plum
[21] "perpetual spring"
[22] frugal
[23] August 24
[24] grapes
[25] grass-stalk or rush
[26] paths

THE SEVENTEENTH CENTURY

THE high ideals, the vigor of imagination, and the enthusiasm for action which we associate with Elizabeth's reign lasted on into the seventeenth century. But early in the reign of the Stuarts, hints of decline are visible. Under James I began the political tyranny based upon "divine right" of kings, and the religious tyranny culminating in persecutions which, gaining strength under Charles I, finally led to the Civil War and the supremacy of Puritanism under the Commonwealth.

The poetry of the period covering the reign of Charles, a time of bitter struggle between the Royalists and the Puritans, mirrors the time closely. On one hand was the Court circle, light-heartedly indulging in dissipation and extravagance of all kinds, indifferent to the terrible political and religious conflict impending. On the other hand were the Puritans, their eyes fixed on the future life, working in direct opposition to the intellectual freedom and curiosity which had marked the great minds of Elizabeth's day. "As a result of this split between the sacred and the secular world in poetry as elsewhere," says Schelling, "the age of Charles I produced the purest of our poetical worshipers of beauty as it produced the most saintly and rhapsodic of English devotional poets."

CAROLINE LYRICS

The Caroline (Latin *Carolus,* Charles) Poets may be divided into several groups. One, sometimes referred to as the "Sacred Poets," consisted of Herbert, Crashaw, Vaughan, and others, of whom Donne was the direct forerunner. Of these Herbert is the most distinctly sacred, and has always been the most widely read; Crashaw, a Catholic, ranks high for fluent verse and flashes of poetic fire. These poets are markedly "metaphysical"; that is, they show a strong tendency to get "beyond nature" in both substance and manner; their work is highly fantastic; the distortion of simple ideas and the hiding of them under quaint images and phrases are characteristic of their poetry as it is of "euphuistic" prose (Cf. p. *226,* 14, r.). Another group, the "Cavalier Poets," was composed of writers in a light vein, Herrick, Carew, Suckling, Lovelace, and Waller, producing charming lyrics, witty, graceful, nonchalant, pointed. Their themes were for the most part amatory praises of their mistress's cheeks, envy of her girdle, or complaints of her inconstance, the idea often being pursued with such conceits as that of Lovelace—that his Ellinda's glove is a snowy farm with five tenements—or of Suckling that

> "Her feet beneath her petticoat
> Like little mice stole in and out."

Herrick was the real prince of this Cavalier tribe.

JOHN DONNE 1573-1631

Donne began his career as a fashionable gentleman of means, early noted for his wit and his poetry; he ended it as a famous preacher under James I. He attended Oxford and Cambridge, inherited a fortune, saw foreign service under the Earl of Essex, and was private secretary to the Lord Keeper. Unfortunately he ruined his prospects by a romantic runaway marriage with his master's niece, and was reduced to poverty for a time, but was prospering as a lawyer when the king offered him a living if he would enter the Church. After long hesitation Donne accepted, was ordained, became Dean of St. Paul's and died just before his promotion to a bishopric, his life shortened by devout austerity.

Though Donne was writing secular verse in Elizabeth's days, he broke away from the prevailing conventions of sonneteering and pastoral poetry; avoiding classical allusions and similes from nature, he drew from science and divinity such new and striking figures that he created a vogue, and thus became the founder of the Metaphysical School. Despite his involved fancy, his favorite themes of Love and Death sometimes reveal the rapt vision, melancholy passion, and power that make him notable.

Biography and criticism: Walton, *Life of Dr. John Donne;* E. Gosse, *The Life and Letters of John Donne,* 2 vols., 1889; "John Donne," *Contemp.* 127:669-71.

DEATH

Death, be not proud, though some have callèd thee
Mighty and dreadful, for thou art not so;
For those whom thou think'st thou dost overthrow
Die not, poor Death; nor yet canst thou kill me.
From Rest and Sleep, which but thy picture be,
Much pleasure; then from thee much more must flow;
And soonest our best men with thee do go—
Rest of their bones and souls' delivery!
Thou'rt slave to fate, chance, kings, and desperate men,[1]
And dost with poison, war, and sickness dwell;
And poppy or charms can make us sleep as well
And better than thy stroke. Why swell'st thou then?
One short sleep past, we wake eternally,
And Death shall be no more. Death, thou shalt die!

1633

[1] Cf. with Dunsany's *Death and Odysseus,* p. 855.

THE FUNERAL

Whoever comes to shroud me, do not harm
Nor question much
That subtle wreath of hair about mine arm;
The mystery, the sign you must not touch,
For 'tis my outward soul,
Viceroy to that which, unto heav'n being gone,
Will leave this to control
And keep these limbs, her provinces, from dissolution.

For if the sinewy thread[2] my brain lets fall
Through every part
Can tie those parts, and make me one of all;
Those hairs, which upward grew, and strength and art
Have from a better brain,
Can better do't; except she meant that I
By this should know my pain,
As prisoners then are manacled, when they're condemned to die.

Whate'er she meant by't, bury it with me,
For since I am
Love's martyr, it might breed idolatry
If into other hands these reliques came.
As 'twas humility
T' afford to it all that a soul can do,
So 'tis some bravery
That, since you[3] would have none of me, I bury some of you.

1633

A VALEDICTION FORBIDDING MOURNING[4]

As virtuous men pass mildly away,
And whisper to their souls to go,
Whilst some of their sad friends do say,
"Now his breath goes," and some say, "No";

So let us melt and make no noise,
No tear-floods nor sigh-tempests move;
'T were profanation of our joys
To tell the laity our love.

Moving of th' earth brings harms and fears;
Men reckon what it did and meant;
But trepidation of the spheres,
Though greater far, is innocent.

Dull sublunary[5] lovers' love
Whose soul is sense, cannot admit

[2] the spinal cord, and nerves
[3] addressed to the *she* of ll. 14, 17
[4] Said by Walton to have been given by Donne to his wife when he was about to accompany an embassy from James I to Henry IV of France; during this journey Donne was twice visited by an apparition of his wife carrying a dead child. He later learned that their child had been born dead at the hour of her first appearance to him.
[5] earthly

Of absence, 'cause it doth remove
  The thing which elemented it.

But we, by a love so far refined
  That ourselves know not what it is,
Inter-assurèd of the mind,
  Care less eyes, lips, and hands to miss.

Our two souls therefore, which are one,
  Though I must go, endure not yet
A breach, but an expansion,
  Like gold to airy thinness beat.

If they be two, they are two so
  As stiff twin compasses are two.
Thy soul, the fixt foot, makes no show
  To move, but doth if th' other do;

And though it in the center sit,
  Yet when the other far doth roam,
It leans and hearkens after it,
  And grows erect as that comes home.

Such wilt thou be to me, who must,
  Like th'other foot, obliquely run;
Thy firmness makes my circle just,
  And makes me end where I begun.

1611? 1633

GEORGE HERBERT
1593-1633

Herbert is one of several men of the period who felt personally the conflict between the worldly and the religious life, abandoning one for the other. He came of very good family, received his early education at home from his mother, was then sent to Westminster School, and later to Cambridge. Appointed official orator for the university, his duties brought him into close relations with the Court, where he became a favorite with James I. But an early leaning toward the Church revived, and after a period of meditation in the country and a romantic marriage following a four days' courtship, he accepted the living of Bemerton, Wiltshire, was ordained, and spent the three years before his death in devoting himself to faithful service to his church and parish.

He is best known for his religious poems, contained in *The Temple,* 1633, which are limited in subject-matter, but show sincere piety and religious fervor. His constructive ability is one of his best artistic gifts. His fondness for fantastic conceits, full of quaint and unexpected imagery, is more than counterbalanced by the sweetness of his faith and the rare poetic quality of his imagination.

An interesting and intimate account of his life is that by Izaak Walton, a friend and contemporary.

VIRTUE

1

Sweet day, so cool, so calm, so bright,
  The bridal of the earth and sky!
The dew shall weep thy fall tonight;
  For thou must die.

2

Sweet rose, whose hue, angry and brave,
  Bids the rash gazer wipe his eye,
Thy root is ever in its grave,
  And thou must die.

3

Sweet spring, full of sweet days and roses,
  A box where sweets compacted lie,
My music shows ye have your closes,
  And all must die.

4

Only a sweet and virtuous soul,
  Like seasoned timber, never gives;
But though the whole world turn to coal,
  Then chiefly lives.

1633

THE COLLAR

I struck the board, and cried, "No more!
    I will abroad.
What? Shall I ever sigh and pine?
My lines and life are free, free as the road,
Loose as the wind, as large as store.[1]
    Shall I be still in suit?
Have I no harvest but a thorn
To let me blood, and not restore
What I have lost with cordial fruit?
    Sure there was wine
Before my sighs did dry it. There was corn
    Before my tears did drown it.
Is the year only lost to me?
    Have I no bays to crown it?
No flowers, no garlands gay? All blasted?
    All wasted?
Not so, my heart! But there is fruit,
    And thou hast hands.
  Recover all thy sigh-blown age
On double pleasures. Leave thy cold dispute
Of what is fit and not. Forsake thy cage,
    Thy rope of sands,
Which petty thoughts have made, and made to thee
Good cable, to enforce and draw,
    And be thy law,
While thou didst wink[2] and wouldst not see.
    Away! Take heed!
    I will abroad.

[1] abundance
[2] purposely shut the eyes

Call in thy death's head there. Tie up thy fears.
He that forbears
To suit and serve his need
Deserves his load."
But as I raved and grew more fierce and wild
At every word,
Methought I heard one calling, "Child!"
And I replied, "My Lord."

1633

THE PULLEY

When God at first made man,
Having a glass of blessings standing by,
"Let us," said He, "pour on him all we can.
Let the world's riches, which dispersèd lie,
Contract into a span."

So strength first made a way,
Then beauty flowed, then wisdom, honor, pleasure.
When almost all was out, God made a stay,
Perceiving that alone of all his treasure
Rest in the bottom lay.

"For if I should," said He,
"Bestow this jewel also on my creature,
He would adore my gifts instead of me,
And rest in Nature, not the God of Nature.
So both should losers be.

Yet let him keep the rest,
But keep them with repining restlessness.
Let him be rich and weary, that at least,
If goodness lead him not, yet weariness
May toss him to my breast."

1633

RICHARD CRASHAW 1613-1650

Though his father was a Protestant divine, Crashaw early leaned toward the Roman Catholic religion. Influenced by Herbert's *Temple,* he began writing religious poetry at the age of twenty (published in 1646 under the title of *Steps to the Temple*). And when, in 1644, during the Civil Wars, he was forcibly ejected from a fellowship at Cambridge, he escaped to France and joined the Roman Catholic Church. He was for a time in the service of Cardinal Palotta at Rome, and died a canon of the Basilica Church of Our Lady of Loretto. He excelled in languages, music, and painting. He is a follower of Donne in the use of conceits, and at times his verse is confused from excess of eloquence and imagery; but at its best it flows with musical ease, pervaded by a note of spiritual exaltation.

Criticism: C. Spender, "Life and Works," *Contemp.* 116:210-115; C. Falls, "Divine Poet," *19th Cent.* 93:225-33.

IN THE HOLY NATIVITY OF OUR LORD GOD

A Hymn as Sung by the Shepherds

The Hymn

Chorus

Come, we shepherds, whose blest sight
Hath met Love's noon in Nature's night;
Come, lift we up our loftier song,
And wake the sun that lies too long.

To all our world of well-stolen joy
He slept; and dreamt of no such thing
While we found out heaven's fairer eye,
And kissed the cradle of our King.
Tell him he rises now too late
To show us aught worth looking at.

Tell him we now can show him more
Than he e'er showed to mortal sight;
Than he himself e'er saw before,
Which to be seen needs not his light.
Tell him, Tityrus, where th'hast been,
Tell him, Thyrsis, what th'hast seen.

TITYRUS. Gloomy night embraced the place
Where the noble Infant lay.
The Babe looked up and showed his face;
In spite of darkness, it was day.
It was Thy day, Sweet! and did rise,
Not from the east but from Thine eyes.

Chorus: It was Thy day, Sweet, etc.

THYRSIS. Winter chid aloud, and sent
The angry North to wage his wars.
The North forgot his fierce intent,
And left perfumes instead of scars.
By those sweet eyes' persuasive powers.
Where he meant frost, he scattered flowers.

Chorus: By those sweet eyes', etc.

BOTH. We saw Thee in Thy balmy nest,
Young dawn of our eternal day!
We saw Thine eyes break from their east,
And chase the trembling shades away.
We saw Thee; and we blessed the sight,
We saw Thee by Thine Own sweet light.

Chorus: We saw Thee, etc.

TITYRUS. Poor world, said I, what wilt thou do
To entertain this starry Stranger?
Is this the best thou canst bestow?
A cold, and not too cleanly, manger?
Contend, the powers of heaven and earth,
To fit a bed for this huge birth?

Chorus: Contend the powers, etc.

THYRSIS. Proud world, said I, cease your contest,
And let the mighty Babe alone.
The phoenix builds the phoenix' nest,
Love's architecture is his own.
The Babe whose birth embraves [1] this morn,
Made His Own bed ere He was born.

Chorus: The Babe whose, etc.

TITYRUS. I saw the curled drops, soft and slow,
Come hovering o'er the place's head;
Offering their whitest sheets of snow
To furnish the fair Infant's bed;
Forbear, said I; be not too bold,
Your fleece is white, but 'tis too cold.

Chorus: Forbear, said I, etc.

THYRSIS. I saw the obsequious Seraphims
Their rosy fleece [2] of fire bestow,
For well they now can spare their wing,
Since heaven itself lies here below.
Well done, said I; but are you sure
Your down so warm, will pass for pure?

Chorus: Well done, said I, etc.

TITYRUS. No, no! your king's not yet to seek
Where to repose His royal head;
See, see, how soon His new-bloomed cheek
'Twixt's mother's breasts is gone to bed.
Sweet choice, said we! no way but so
Not to lie cold, yet sleep in snow.

Chorus: Sweet choice, said we, etc.

BOTH. We saw Thee in Thy balmy nest,
Bright dawn of our eternal day!
We saw Thine eyes break from their east,
And chase the trembling shades away.
We saw Thee; and we blessed the sight,
We saw Thee by Thine Own sweet light.

Chorus: We saw Thee, etc.

Full Chorus

Welcome, all wonders in one sight!
Eternity, shut in a span!
Summer in winter, day in night!
Heaven in earth, and God in man!
Great, little One! whose all-embracing birth
Lifts earth to heaven, stoops heaven to earth.
Welcome, though not to gold nor silk,
To more than Caesar's birthright is;
Two sister-seas of virgin-milk,
With many a rarely tempered kiss,
That breathes at once both maid and mother,
Warms in the one, cools in the other.

[1] makes illustrious [2] down of feathers, not wool

Welcome, though not to those gay flies, [3]
Gilded i'th'beams of earthly kings;
Slippery souls in smiling eyes:
But to poor shepherds, home-spun things;
Whose wealth's their flock; whose wit, to be
Well-read in their simplicity.
Yet when young April's husband-showers
Shall bless the fruitful Maia's [4] bed,
We'll bring the firstborn of her flowers
To kiss Thy feet, and crown Thy head.
To Thee, dread Lamb! Whose love must keep
The Shepherds, more than they their sheep.
To Thee, meek Majesty! soft King
Of simple Graces and sweet Loves:
Each of us his lamb will bring,
Each his pair of silver doves:
Till burnt at last in fire of Thy fair eyes,
Ourselves become our own best sacrifice.

1646-1652

HENRY VAUGHAN
1622-1695

Henry Vaughan, who called himself the "Silurist" [5] to express his intimate love of the Welsh mountains and valleys, led a quiet, uneventful life, untouched by contemporary stress and strife. He was born in Wales and, except for a few years when he was at Oxford and studying medicine, he passed his life practicing as a physician in his native place and died there. His *Poems,* 1646, were of a secular nature, a record of London days, showing the influence of Jonson and Donne. But *Silex Scintillans,* a collection published in 1650, after a severe illness, showed a revolution in his nature that brought forth sacred and philosophical poems, clearly influenced by George Herbert. They are remote, timeless, mysterious; they show an intimate and religious feeling for nature, a brooding over man's relations to the unseen and the eternal, and a simplicity of expression pointing forward to Wordsworth.

Discussed in Dowden (T&S); E. Lyttelton, "Henry Vaughan and Optimism," *Contemp.* 109: 462-9; "Poetry of Henry Vaughan," *Liv. Age* 286: 672-7; "Henry Vaughan: Silurist," by J. Vaughan, *19th Cent.* 67:492-504, a good account of what is known of his life and works.

THE RETREAT [6]

Happy those early days, when I
Shined in my angel infancy!
Before I understood this place
Appointed for my second race,
Or taught my soul to fancy ought
But a white, celestial thought;

[3] courtiers
[4] May
[5] The Silures were ancient inhabitants of southern Wales.
[6] Cf. Wordsworth's "Intimations of Immortality," p. 461.

When yet I had not walked above
A mile or two from my first love,
And looking back—at that short space—
Could see a glimpse of His bright face;
When on some gilded cloud or flower
My gazing soul would dwell an hour,
And in those weaker glories spy
Some shadows of eternity;
Before I taught my tongue to wound
My conscience with a sinful sound,
Or had the black art to dispense
A several sin to every sense,
But felt through all this fleshly dress
Bright shoots of everlastingness.
O how I long to travel back,
And tread again that ancient track!
That I might once more reach that plain,
Where first I left my glorious train;
From whence the enlightened spirit sees
That shady city of palm trees.
But ah! my soul with too much stay
Is drunk, and staggers in the way!
Some men a forward motion love,
But I by backward steps would move;
And when this dust falls to the urn,
In that state I came, return.

1650

From THE WORLD

I saw Eternity the other night,
Like a great ring of pure and endless light,
All calm, as it was bright;
And round beneath it Time in hours, days, years,
Driven by the spheres
Like a cast shadow moved; in which the world
And all her train were hurled.

1650

ROBERT HERRICK
1591-1674

In strong contrast to Herbert and his voluntary resignation of a worldly life is Herrick. In his little country parish in Devonshire he seemed ever to regret the social and convivial life of London, where he was born and where, after leaving Cambridge, he had associated with Jonson and the leading literary men of the age. Ejected from his living during the Commonwealth for his royalist devotion, he returned immediately to London, delighted at his release from a "long and dreary banishment." Yet the pictures he draws in his poems of his country household with his maid Prue and his various pet animals are full of idyllic charm and happiness. In 1662, after the Restoration, his living was returned to him and he died in his Devonshire parish.

His single volume, *Hesperides,* 1648, is a collection of poems (including his religious verse, "Noble Numbers"), which vary greatly in length and subject. Some of the most spirited lyrics and songs were written in his early London days. He was a disciple of the great lyrists of antiquity, and inherited through Jonson a touch of the Elizabethan spirit. His work is pervaded by pastoral simplicity, perennial romance, and a pagan joy of life tinged with regret for fleeting youth, love, and beauty—under the hem of his cassock the cloven foot of Pan is often visible.

For criticism see Swinburne (SPP).

CORINNA'S GOING A-MAYING [1]

Get up, get up for shame, the blooming morn
Upon her wings presents the god unshorn.
See how Aurora throws her fair,
Fresh-quilted colors through the air;
Get up, sweet slug-a-bed, and see
The dew bespangling herb and tree.
Each flower has wept and bowed toward the east
Above an hour since; yet you not dressed,
Nay! not so much as out of bed?
When all the birds have matins said
And sung their thankful hymns, 'tis sin,
Nay, profanation, to keep in,
When as a thousand virgins on this day
Spring, sooner than the lark, to fetch in May.

Rise and put on your foliage, and be seen
To come forth, like the springtime, fresh and green,
And sweet as Flora. Take no care
For jewels for your gown or hair.
Fear not, the leaves will strew
Gems in abundance upon you.
Besides, the childhood of the day has kept,
Against you come, some orient pearls unwept;
Come and receive them while the light
Hangs on the dew-locks of the night;
And Titan on the eastern hill
Retires himself, or else stands still
Till you come forth. Wash, dress, be brief in praying:
Few beads are best when once we go a-Maying.

Come, my Corinna, come; and, coming, mark
How each field turns a street, each street, a park
Made green and trimmed with trees; see how
Devotion gives each house a bough
Or branch; each porch, each door ere this
An ark, a tabernacle is,
Made up of white-thorn, neatly interwove;

[1] The "god unshorn" of line 2 is Titan with all his beams; "May" (14) is hawthorne and other May blossoms; "beads" (28) are prayers; "green-gown" (51) is a tumble on the grass.

As if here were those cooler shades of love.
Can such delights be in the street
And open fields and we not see't?
Come, we'll abroad; and let's obey
The proclamation made for May;
And sin no more, as we have done, by staying;
But, my Corinna, come, let's go a-Maying.

There's not a budding boy or girl this day
But is got up, and gone to bring in May.
A deal of youth, ere this, is come
Back, and with white-thorn laden, home.
Some have despatched their cakes and cream
Before that we have left to dream;
And some have wept, and wooed, and plighted troth,
And chose their priest, ere we can cast off sloth.
Many a green-gown has been given;
Many a kiss, both odd and even;
Many a glance, too, has been sent
From out the eye, love's firmament;
Many a jest told of the keys betraying
This night, and locks picked, yet we're not a-Maying.

Come, let us go while we are in our prime;
And take the harmless folly of the time.
We shall grow old apace, and die
Before we know our liberty.
Our life is short, and our days run
As fast away as does the sun;
And, as a vapor or a drop of rain,
Once lost, can never be found again;
So when or you or I are made
A fable, song, or fleeting shade,
All love, all liking, all delight
Lies drowned with us in endless night.
Then while time serves, and we are but decaying,
Come, my Corinna, come, let's go a-Maying.

1648

TO THE VIRGINS TO MAKE MUCH OF TIME

1

Gather ye rosebuds while ye may,
Old time is still a-flying;
And this same flower that smiles today,
Tomorrow will be dying.

2

The glorious lamp of heaven, the sun,
The higher he's a-getting,
The sooner will his race be run,
And nearer he's to setting.

3

That age is best which is the first,
When youth and blood are warmer;
But being spent, the worse and worst
Times still succeed the former.

4

Then be not coy, but use your time,
And while ye may, go marry;
For, having lost but once your prime,
You may forever tarry.

1648

TO ELECTRA

1

I dare not ask a kiss,
I dare not beg a smile,
Lest having that or this,
I might grow proud the while.

2

No, no, the utmost share
Of my desire shall be
Only to kiss that air
That lately kissèd thee.

1648

HOW ROSES CAME RED

1

Roses at first were white,
Till they could not agree
Whether my Sapho's breast
Or they more white should be.

2

But being vanquished quite,
A blush their cheeks bespread;
Since which, believe the rest,
The roses first came red.

1648

THOMAS CAREW 1598?-1639?

Carew had the usual Cavalier background of good family. After attending Oxford for a time he entered the Court circle, changing from one position to another, and making various journeys to the Continent. Finally he entered the household of Charles I, where he was highly esteemed for his wit and ability. He was associated with most of the eminent literary men of his time, wrote an elaborate masque (*Coelum Britannicum*, 1634), lyrics, and society verse, (*Poems*, 1640).

Carew stands next to Herrick among the Caroline lyrists. The poems of both show the persistence of the Elizabethan lyric spirit in the seventeenth century: Herrick carries on the delicate, spontaneous, simple charm of pure lyricism; Carew the light, complimentary, amatory tone of the world of fashion. His verse is melodious, highly polished, full of fancy, yet almost free from the usual conceits and affections.

SONG

1

Ask me no more where Jove bestows,
When June is past, the fading rose,
For in your beauty's orient deep
These flowers, as in their causes, sleep.

2

Ask me no more whither do stray
The golden atoms of the day,
For, in pure love, heaven did prepare
Those powders to enrich your hair.

3

Ask me no more whither doth haste
The nightingale when May is past,
For in your sweet dividing [1] throat
She winters and keeps warm her note.

4

Ask me no more where those stars light
That downward fall in dead of night,
For in your eyes they sit, and there
Fixèd become as in their sphere. [2]

5

Ask me no more if east or west
The phoenix builds her spicy nest,
For unto you at last she flies,
And in your fragrant bosom dies.

1640

SIR JOHN SUCKLING
1609-1642

The short life of Suckling probably duplicates that of many contemporary Cavaliers; it was marked by good family, college education, large private fortune, Continental travel, and prodigality at Court. He gained the king's favor by raising troops for the Scottish campaign; later, during the conflict between Charles I and the Puritans, he was involved in a royalist plot to secure the army for the king, had to flee from parliamentary arrest, and died in Paris. As a lyric poet he waged war upon unreality and love-lorn fancies. He excels in impetuous movement of verse, and tunefulness, and perfect accord of theme and rhythm. *Fragmenta Aurea*, 1646, is a collection of poems, plays, and miscellaneous verse.

[1] "Dividing" means singing floridly.
[2] See note 4 on page 279.

SONG from AGLAURA

1

Why so pale and wan, fond lover?
Prithee, why so pale?
Will, when looking well can't move her,
Looking ill prevail?
Prithee, why so pale?

2

Why so dull and mute, young sinner?
Prithee, why so mute?
Will, when speaking well can't win her,
Saying nothing do't?
Prithee, why so mute?

3

Quit, quit for shame! This will not move;
This cannot take her.
If of herself she will not love,
Nothing can make her;
The devil take her!

1637 *1638*

RICHARD LOVELACE
1618-1658

The contrast offered by the life of Lovelace to that of Sidney, both endowed with personal beauty, charm, intellect, aristocratic background, and opportunities, is typical of the difference between morals and manners under Elizabeth and Charles II respectively. Sidney, representing an age of ideals, even today stands for the type of perfect gentleman; Lovelace, representative of an age of self-indulgence, is all too typical of the fickle lover and prodigal Cavalier adventurer. Devoting himself to the fluctuating Stuart fortunes, he passed his life in a series of ups and downs; now a favorite at Court, now seeing active military service with the royalist army, now living on his estates in Kent, now a Parliamentary prisoner, until, his fortune dissipated, he died in London in utter destitution. Among his poems (*Lucasta*, 1649), most of which abound in faults of taste and fantastic extravagances, he left two or three songs which deserve enduring fame; in simplicity, chivalrous feeling, and nobility of thought they touch perfection.

TO LUCASTA. GOING TO THE WARS

1

Tell me not, sweet, I am unkind,
That from the nunnery
Of thy chaste breast and quiet mind
To war and arms I fly.

2

True, a new mistress now I chase,
The first foe in the field;

And with a stronger faith embrace
A sword, a horse, a shield.

3

Yet this inconstancy is such
As you, too, shall adore;
I could not love thee, dear, so much,
Loved I not honor more.

1649

TO ALTHEA, FROM PRISON[1]

1

When Love with unconfinèd wings
Hovers within my gates,
And my divine Althea brings
To whisper at the grates;
When I lie tangled in her hair
And fettered to her eye,
The birds that wanton in the air
Know no such liberty.

2

When flowing cups run swiftly round
With no allaying Thames,
Our careless heads with roses bound,
Our hearts with loyal flames;
When thirsty grief in wine we steep,
When healths and drafts go free—
Fishes that tipple in the deep
Know no such liberty.

3

When, like committed linnets, I
With shriller throat shall sing
The sweetness, mercy, majesty,
And glories of my King;
When I shall voice aloud how good
He is, how great should be,
Enlargèd winds, that curl the flood,
Know no such liberty.

4

Stone walls do not a prison make,
Nor iron bars a cage;
Minds innocent and quiet take
That for an hermitage;
If I have freedom in my love
And in my soul am free,
Angels alone, that soar above,
Enjoy such liberty.

1649

[1] Lovelace, the gallant cavalier and poet, was, for his devotion to King Charles, twice behind bars—a "committed" song-bird. In line 7, the original reading is "gods," but the emendation "birds" is too plausible to be dismissed, especially in view of the sequence—birds, fishes, winds, angels. In stanza 2, "allaying" means diluting.

EDMUND WALLER 1606-1687

Waller's life was curiously eventful for one who desired only to enjoy his wealth and social position in peace. Born at Beaconsfield, the family estate, he was educated at Eton and Cambridge, and when very young sat in the House of Parliament, where he shone as a fluent speaker. He inherited a large fortune and married an heiress. He at first favored the popular party; but at heart he was a courtier, and by 1643 he was involved in a royalist plot that ended in his arrest, imprisonment, and exile. In 1651 his sentence was revoked and he returned from France. He was a great favorite at the Courts of Charles II and James II, but the last ten years of his life were spent on his estate, where he died. Waller stood apart from the characteristic fashions of his time; he had no taste for elaborate or fantastic metaphors. Dryden claims that Waller "first made writing easily an art." His conscious efforts to simplify the couplet, keep it within fixed bounds, and regulate its prevailing "ragged rime," carried it a step further toward systematic coherence and conciseness. His *Poems,* 1645, show a consistent smoothness of rhythm, and a polished simplicity of diction.

Criticism in Johnson's *Lives;* R. Aldington, "Note on Waller's Poems," *Liv. Age* 312:179-81; W. W. Gay, "Origin of Waller's Couplets," *No. Am.* 191:227-39

GO, LOVELY ROSE

1

Go, lovely Rose!
Tell her that wastes her time and me,
That now she knows,
When I resemble her to thee,
How sweet and fair she seems to be.

2

Tell her that's young,
And shuns to have her graces spied,
That hadst thou sprung
In deserts, where no men abide,
Thou must have uncommended died.

3

Small is the worth
Of beauty from the light retired;
Bid her come forth,
Suffer herself to be desired,
And not blush so to be admired.

4

Then die! that she
The common fate of all things rare
May read in thee;

How small a part of time they share
That are so wondrous sweet and fair.

1645

ON A GIRDLE

1

That which her slender waist confined,
Shall now my joyful temples bind;
No monarch but would give his crown,
His arms might do what this has done.

2

It was my heaven's extremest sphere,
The pale which held that lovely deer.
My joy, my grief, my hope, my love,
Did all within this circle move.

3

A narrow compass! and yet there
Dwelt all that's good, and all that's fair;
Give me but what this ribband bound,
Take all the rest the sun goes round.

1645

JOHN MILTON 1608-1674

The name of John Milton stands preëminent in the Puritan literature of this divided age, representing both its prose and its poetry, lyric and epic. In influence upon the lyric poets following him he was second only to Spenser. Tennyson calls him the "God-gifted organ-voice of England," while Longfellow compares his music to that of the sea:

". . . . . in majestic cadence rise and fall
The mighty undulations of thy song,
O sightless bard."

Milton was born in Cheapside. His father was a scrivener (public writer) skilled in music. The boy early showed literary talent: "My father destined me from a child to the pursuits of literature; and from twelve years of age, I hardly ever left my studies, or went to bed before midnight." On leaving Cambridge in 1632 he spent six years in the country at Horton, Buckinghamshire, studying and producing most of his lyric poetry: "L'Allegro" and "Il Penseroso," remarkable for their sustained lyric grace; *Comus,* half masque, half lyrical drama; and "Lycidas," the first of the three or four great elegies, including Shelley's "Adonais" and Tennyson's *In Memoriam,* which enrich our literature. He then traveled on the Continent for two years, welcomed as a scholar by many famous people.

Hearing of civil strife in England, he returned ("I thought it base to be traveling for amusement abroad while my fellow citizens were fighting for liberty at home"), and before long he was writing for the Puritan cause. His work at this time was almost entirely prose (see p. 283). In spite of approaching blindness (see sonnets, p. 258, 259) he served through the Protectorate. After the Restoration forced him into retirement he lived out his life in seclusion, dictating to his daughters his great epic poems, *Paradise Lost,* 1667, *Paradise Regained,* and the stern scriptural drama, *Samson Agonistes,* 1671.

Milton's few sonnets bridge the gap of twenty years between his two chief poetic periods, the lyric and the epic. In both lyric and epic he is a master of musical harmony and rhythm. In the former the dominant quality is richness; in the latter, it is sublimity. In his epic verse, splendor of diction, stateliness of style, vast sweep of imagination, and exaltation of mood, form a fit accompaniment to his great purpose announced in *Paradise Lost*—"to justify the ways of God to man."

Milton's Poetical Works, edited by D. Masson, 3 volumes, are in the Cambridge edition; D. Masson's *Life of John Milton,* 6 volumes, is authoritative; for more concise material consult lives by R. Garnett (GW); M. Pattison (EML); and Masterman's *Age of Milton;* early essays by Addison, *The Spectator,* 262, 265; Johnson, Macaulay, Carlyle; later by Arnold, Dowden, Masson, Woodberry, etc.; R. S. Stevenson, "Milton and the Puritans," *No. Am.* 214:825-32, a good article; G. Sampson, "Macaulay and Milton," *Edin R.* 242:165-78; A. H. M. Sime, "Milton and Music," *Contemp.* 115:337-40.

ON THE MORNING OF CHRIST'S NATIVITY

This is the month, and this the happy morn,
Wherein the Son of heaven's eternal King,
Of wedded maid and virgin mother born,
Our great redemption from above did bring;
For so the holy sages [1] once did sing,
That he our deadly forfeit [2] should release,
And with his Father work us a perpetual peace.

That glorious form, that light unsufferable,
And that far-beaming blaze of majesty,
Wherewith he wont [3] at heaven's high council-table
To sit the midst of Trinal Unity,
He laid aside; and here with us to be,
Forsook the courts of everlasting day,
And chose with us a darksome house of mortal clay.

Say, heavenly muse, shall not thy sacred vein
Afford a present to the infant God?
Hast thou no verse, no hymn, or solemn strain,
To welcome him to this his new abode,
Now while the heaven, by the sun's team untrod,
Hath took no print of the approaching light,

[1] the Old Testament prophets
[2] penalty for sin
[3] was wont

From a painting by Thomas Faed

JOHN MILTON

And all the spangled host keep watch in squadrons bright?

See how from far upon the eastern road
The star-led wizards [1] haste with odors sweet!
O run, prevent [2] them with thy humble ode,
And lay it lowly at his blessed feet;
Have thou the honor first thy Lord to greet
And join thy voice unto the angel choir,
From out his secret altar touched with hallowed fire.

THE HYMN

It was the winter wild,
While the heaven-born child
All meanly wrapped in the rude manger lies;
Nature, in awe to him,
Had doffed her gaudy trim,
With her great Master so to sympathize.
It was no season then for her
To wanton with the sun, her lusty paramour.

Only with speeches fair
She woos the gentle air
To hide her guilty front with innocent snow,
And on her naked shame,
Pollute with sinful blame,
The saintly veil of maiden white to throw;
Confounded, that her Maker's eyes
Should look so near upon her foul deformities.

But he, her fears to cease,
Sent down the meek-eyed Peace.
She, crowned with olive green, came softly sliding
Down through the turning sphere, [3]
His ready harbinger [4]
With turtle [5] wing the amorous clouds dividing;
And waving wide her myrtle wand,
She strikes a universal peace through sea and land.

No war, or battle's sound,
Was heard the world around;
The idle spear and shield were high uphung;
The hookèd [6] chariot stood
Unstained with hostile blood;
The trumpet spake not to the armèd throng;
And kings sat still with awful [7] eye,
As if they surely knew their sovran Lord was by.

But peaceful was the night
Wherein the Prince of Light
His reign of peace upon the earth began.
The winds, with wonder whist, [8]
Smoothly the waters kissed,
Whispering new joys to the mild ocean,
Who now hath quite forgot to rave,
While birds of calm sit brooding on the charmèd wave.

The stars, with deep amaze,
Stand fixed in steadfast gaze,
Bending one way their precious influence,
And will not take their flight,
For all the morning light,
Or Lucifer [9] that often warned them thence;
But in their glimmering orbs did glow,
Until their Lord himself bespake and bid them go.

And though the shady gloom
Had given day her room,
The sun himself withheld his wonted speed,
And hid his head for shame,
As [10] his inferior flame
The new-enlightened world no more should need;
He saw a greater Sun appear
Than his bright throne or burning axletree could bear.

The shepherds on the lawn, [11]
Or ere the point of dawn,
Sat simply chatting in a rustic row;
Full little thought they than [12]
That the mighty Pan [13]
Was kindly come to live with them below;
Perhaps their loves, or else their sheep,
Was all that did their silly [14] thoughts so busy keep.

When such music sweet
Their hearts and ears did greet
As never was by mortal finger strook, [15]
Divinely-warbled voice
Answering the stringèd noise,
As all their souls in blissful rapture took;
The air, such pleasure loath to lose,
With thousand echoes still prolongs each heavenly close.

Nature, that heard such sound
Beneath the hollow round

[1] Wise Men from the East
[2] anticipate
[3] See note to *Par. Lost,* II, 1030.
[4] forerunner
[5] turtle-dove
[6] The axles of ancient war-chariots were armed with scythes.
[7] full of awe
[8] stilled
[9] the morning star
[10] as if
[11] green pasture-land
[12] then
[13] god of shepherds; here Christ, as Good Shepherd
[14] from the same root as the German *selig,* holy; here, innocent
[15] struck

Of Cynthia's seat [1] the airy region thrilling,
Now was almost won
To think her part was done,
And that her reign had here its last fulfilling.
She knew such harmony alone
Could hold all heaven and earth in happier union.

At last surrounds their sight
A globe of circular light,
That with long beams the shamefaced night arrayed;
The helmèd cherubim
And sworded seraphim
Are seen in glittering ranks with wings displayed,
Harping in loud and solemn choir,
With unexpressive [2] notes, to heaven's newborn heir.

Such music (as 'tis said)
Before was never made,
But when of old the sons of morning sung, [3]
While the Creator great
His constellations set,
And the well-balanced world on hinges hung,
And cast the dark foundations deep,
And bid the weltering waves their oozy channel keep.

Ring out, ye crystal spheres!
Once bless our human ears
(If ye have power to touch our senses so),
And let your silver chime
Move in melodious time;
And let the bass of heaven's deep organ blow;
And with your ninefold [4] harmony
Make up full consort to the angelic symphony.

For if such holy song
Enwrap our fancy long,
Time will run back and fetch the age of gold;
And speckled Vanity
Will sicken soon and die,
And leprous Sin will melt from earthly mold;
And Hell itself will pass away,
And leave her dolorous mansions to the peering day.

Yea, Truth and Justice then
Will down return to men,
Orbed in a rainbow; and, like glories wearing,
Mercy will sit between,
Throned in celestial sheen,
With radiant feet the tissued clouds down steering;
And Heaven, as at some festival,
Will open wide the gates of her high palace hall.

But wisest Fate says no,
This must not yet be so;
The Babe yet lies in smiling infancy
That on the bitter cross
Must redeem our loss,
So both himself and us to glorify.
Yet first, to those ychained in sleep,
The wakeful trump of doom must thunder through the deep, [5]

With such a horrid clang
As on Mount Sinai rang, [6]
While the red fire and smoldering clouds outbrake.
The aged earth, aghast
With terror of that blast, [7]
Shall from the surface to the center shake,
When, at the world's last session,
The dreadful Judge in middle air shall spread his throne.

And then at last our bliss
Full and perfect is, [8]
But now begins; for from this happy day
The old Dragon under ground,
In straiter limits bound,
Not half so far casts his usurpèd sway;
And wroth to see his kingdom fail,
Swinges [9] the scaly horror of his folded tail.

The oracles are dumb; [10]
No voice or hideous hum
Runs through the archèd roof in words deceiving.
Apollo from his shrine
Can no more divine,
With hollow shriek the steep of Delphos leaving.
No nightly trance, or breathèd spell,
Inspires the pale-eyed priest from the prophetic cell.

The lonely mountains o'er,
And the resounding shore,

[1] the moon's sphere
[2] inexpressible
[3] "When the morning stars sang together." *Job*, xxxviii, 7.
[4] See note on page 279. The spheres were sometimes held to be only nine in number.
[5] The universe; (cf. *Par. Lost*, I, i. 177.)
[6] when God gave Moses the ten commandments
[7] Cf. l. 156.
[8] will be
[9] lashes
[10] Christ's coming is conceived as putting to naught the heathen divinities.

A voice of weeping heard and loud lament;
From haunted spring, and dale
Edged with poplar pale,
The parting Genius [1] is with sighing sent;
With flower-inwoven tresses torn,
The Nymphs in twilight shade of tangled thickets mourn.

In consecrated earth,
And on the holy hearth,
The Lars and Lemures [2] moan with midnight plaint;
In urns and altars round,
A drear and dying sound
Affrights the flamens [3] at their service quaint;
And the chill marble seems to sweat,
While each peculiar power forgoes his wonted seat.

Peor [4] and Baälim [4]
Forsake their temples dim,
With that twice-battered god of Palestine; [5]
And moonèd Ashtaroth, [6]
Heaven's queen and mother both,
Now sits not girt with tapers' holy shine;
The Libyc Hammon [7] shrinks his horn;
In vain the Tyrian maids their wounded Thammuz [8] mourn.

And sullen Moloch, [9] fled,
Hath left in shadows dread
His burning idol all of blackest hue;
In vain with cymbals' ring
They call the grisly king,
In dismal dance about the furnace blue;
The brutish gods of Nile as fast,
Isis [10] and Orus [11] and the dog Anubis, [12] haste.

Nor is Osiris seen
In Memphian grove or green,
Trampling the unshowered grass with lowings loud;
Nor can he be at rest
Within his sacred chest; [13]
Naught but profoundest Hell can be his shroud;
In vain, with timbreled anthems dark,
The sable-stolèd sorcerers bear his worshiped ark.

He feels from Juda's land
The dreaded Infant's hand;
The rays of Bethlehem blind his dusky eyn;
Nor all the gods beside
Longer dare abide,
Not Typhon [14] huge ending in snaky twine.
Our Babe, to show his Godhead true,
Can in his swaddling bands control the damnèd crew.

So when the sun in bed,
Curtained with cloudy red,
Pillows his chin upon an orient wave,
The flocking shadows pale
Troop to the infernal jail,
Each fettered ghost slips to his several grave,
And the yellow-skirted fays
Fly after the night-steeds, leaving their moon-loved maze.

But see! the Virgin blest
Hath laid her Babe to rest.
Time is our tedious song should here have ending;
Heaven's youngest-teemèd [15] star
Hath fixed her polished car,
Her sleeping Lord with handmaid lamp attending;
And all about the courtly stable
Bright-harnessed angels sit in order serviceable.

1629 1645

ON SHAKESPEARE

What needs my Shakespeare for his honored bones
The labor of an age in pilèd stones?
Or that his hallowed reliques should be hid
Under a star-ypointing [16] pyramid?
Dear son of memory, great heir of fame,
What need'st thou such weak witness of thy name?
Thou in our wonder and astonishment
Hast built thyself a livelong monument.
For whilst to the shame of slow-endeavoring art,
Thy easy numbers flow, and that each heart
Hath from the leaves of thy unvalued [17] book

[1] singular of *genii*—spirits
[2] spirits of the departed (to whom sacrifices would no longer be made)
[3] Roman priests
[4] Phoenician divinities
[5] Dagon (*I Samuel,* v, 1-4)
[6] Phoenician goddess of the moon
[7] the Egyptian horned god Ammon
[8] Adonis, a god of the Syrians, who, having been slain by a wild boar, was said to die every year and revive again
[9] Chief god of the Phoenicians; (his image was of brass and filled with fire and into his arms children were thrown to be sacrificed.)
[10] wife of Osiris, the god of the Nile, who is below confused with the bull-god Apis
[11] their son
[12] an Egyptian divinity in the form of a dog
[13] He was captured by being lured to enter a chest.
[14] a mythological, snake-like monster
[15] born (the Star of Bethlehem)
[16] The form has no warrant, but the meaning is clear.
[17] invaluable

Those Delphic[1] lines with deep impression took;
Then thou, our fancy of itself bereaving,
Dost make us marble with too much conceiving;[2]
And so sepulchered in such pomp dost lie,
That kings for such a tomb would wish to die.

1630 *1632*

L'ALLEGRO[3]

Hence, loathèd Melancholy,
Of Cerberus[4] and blackest Midnight born
In Stygian cave forlorn,
'Mongst horrid shapes and shrieks and sights unholy!
Find out some uncouth[5] cell,
Where brooding darkness spreads his jealous wings,
And the night-raven sings;
There under ebon shades and low-browed rocks,
As ragged as thy locks,
In dark Cimmerian[6] desert ever dwell.
But come, thou Goddess fair and free,
In heaven yclept Euphrosyne,
And by men heart-easing Mirth;
Whom lovely Venus, at a birth,
With two sister Graces[7] more,
To ivy-crownèd Bacchus bore;
Or whether (as some sager[8] sing)
The frolic wind that breathes the spring,
Zephyr, with Aurora playing,
As he met her once a-Maying,
There on beds of violets blue
And fresh-blown roses washed in dew,
Filled her with thee, a daughter fair,
So buxom,[9] blithe, and debonair.
Haste thee, nymph, and bring with thee
Jest, and youthful Jollity,
Quips and cranks[10] and wanton wiles,
Nods and becks[11] and wreathèd smiles,
Such as hang on Hebe's[12] cheek,
And love to live in dimple sleek;
Sport that wrinkled Care derides,
And Laughter holding both his sides.
Come, and trip it as you go,
On the light fantastic toe;
And in thy right hand lead with thee
The mountain-nymph, sweet Liberty;
And if I give thee honor due,
Mirth, admit me of thy crew,
To live with her, and live with thee,
In unreprovèd pleasures free.
To hear the lark begin his flight,
And singing, startle the dull night,
From his watch-tower in the skies,
Till the dappled dawn doth rise;
Then to come[13] in spite of sorrow,
And at my window bid good-morrow,
Through the sweet-briar or the vine,
Or the twisted eglantine;[14]
While the cock, with lively din,
Scatters the rear of darkness thin;
And to the stack, or the barn-door,
Stoutly struts his dames before.
Oft listening how the hounds and horn
Cheerly rouse the slumbering morn,
From the side of some hoar hill,
Through the high wood echoing shrill;
Sometime walking, not unseen,
By hedge-row elms, on hillocks green,
Right against the eastern gate
Where the great sun begins his state,
Robed in flames and amber light,
The clouds in thousand liveries dight;[15]
While the plowman, near at hand,
Whistles o'er the furrowed land,
And the milkmaid singeth blithe,
And the mower whets his scythe,
And every shepherd tells his tale[16]
Under the hawthorn in the dale.
Straight mine eye hath caught new pleasures,
Whilst the landskip round it measures;
Russet lawns and fallows[17] gray,
Where the nibbling flocks do stray;
Mountains on whose barren breast
The laboring clouds do often rest;
Meadows trim, with daisies pied,
Shallow brooks and rivers wide;
Towers and battlements it sees
Bosomed high in tufted trees,
Where perhaps some beauty lies,
The cynosure[18] of neighboring eyes.
Hard by, a cottage chimney smokes
From betwixt two aged oaks,
Where Corydon and Thyrsis[19] met
Are at their savory dinner set
Of herbs and other country messes,
Which the neat-handed Phillis[19] dresses;
And then in haste her bower she leaves,
With Thestylis[19] to bind the sheaves;
Or, if the earlier season lead,

[1] oracular, wise
[2] The thought is not very clear, but cf. lines 7, 8, and *Il Penseroso,* 42.
[3] The Cheerful Man
[4] the three-headed dog that guarded the entrance to Hades
[5] unknown
[6] The Cimmerians of fable lived beyond the ocean streams, out of reach of the sun.
[7] Aglaia and Thalia, goddesses of festive joy
[8] more sagely (The mythology that follows is Milton's own invention.)
[9] lithe, lively
[10] odd turns of speech
[11] beckonings
[12] daughter of Jupiter and Juno; goddess of youth
[13] i.e., arise and go (to the window)
[14] honeysuckle
[15] decked
[16] counts his sheep
[17] untilled land
[18] center of observation
[19] common names of rustics in pastoral poetry

To the tanned haycock in the mead.
Sometimes, with secure delight,
The upland hamlets will invite,
When the merry bells ring round,
And the jocund rebecks [1] sound
To many a youth and many a maid
Dancing in the checkered shade;
And young and old come forth to play
On a sunshine holiday,
Till the livelong daylight fail.
Then to the spicy nut-brown ale,
With stories told of many a feat,
How Faery Mab the junkets eat.
She [2] was pinched and pulled, she said;
And he, by Friar's [3] lantern led,
Tells how the drudging goblin [4] sweat
To earn his cream-bowl duly set,
When in one night, ere glimpse of morn,
His shadowy flail hath threshed the corn
That ten day-laborers could not end;
Then lies him down, the lubber fiend,
And, stretched out all the chimney's
    length,
Basks at the fire his hairy strength,
And crop-full out of doors he flings,
Ere the first cock his matin rings.
Thus done the tales, to bed they creep,
By whispering winds soon lulled asleep.
Towered cities please us then,
And the busy hum of men,
Where throngs of knights and barons bold,
In weeds [5] of peace high triumphs [6] hold,
With store of ladies, whose bright eyes
Rain influence, and judge the prize
Of wit or arms, while both contend
To win her grace whom all commend.
There let Hymen [7] oft appear
In saffron robe, with taper clear,
And pomp and feast and revelry,
With mask [8] and antique pageantry;
Such sights as youthful poets dream
On summer eves by haunted stream.
Then to the well-trod stage anon,
If Jonson's learnèd sock [9] be on,
Or sweetest Shakespeare, Fancy's child,
Warble his native wood-notes wild.
And ever, against eating cares,
Lap me in soft Lydian [10] airs,
Married to immortal verse,
Such as the meeting soul may pierce,
In notes with many a winding bout [11]
Of linkèd sweetness long drawn out,
With wanton heed [12] and giddy cunning,
The melting voice through mazes running,
Untwisting all the chains that tie
The hidden soul of harmony;
That Orpheus' self [13] may heave his head
From golden slumber on a bed
Of heaped Elysian flowers, and hear
Such strains as would have won the ear
Of Pluto to have quite set free
His half-regained Eurydice.
These delights if thou canst give,
Mirth, with thee I mean to live.

1634 1645

IL PENSEROSO [14]

Hence, vain deluding Joys,
    The brood of Folly without father bred!
How little you bested, [15]
    Or fill the fixèd mind with all your toys!
Dwell in some idle brain,
    And fancies fond [16] with gaudy shapes pos-
        sess, [17]
As thick and numberless
    As the gay motes that people the sunbeams,
Or likest hovering dreams,
    The fickle pensioners of Morpheus' train. [18]
But hail, thou Goddess sage and holy,
Hail, divinest Melancholy!
Whose saintly visage is too bright
To hit the sense of human sight,
And therefore to our weaker view
O'erlaid with black, staid Wisdom's hue;
Black, but such as in esteem
Prince Memnon's sister [19] might beseem,
Or that starred Ethiop queen [20] that strove
To set her beauty's praise above
The sea nymphs, and their powers offended.
Yet thou art higher far descended:
Thee bright-haired Vesta [21] long of yore
To solitary Saturn bore;
His daughter she (in Saturn's reign
Such mixture was not held a stain).
Oft in glimmering bowers and glades

[1] instruments like violins
[2] one of the story-tellers. (For the pranks of Faery Mab, see *Romeo and Juliet,* I, iv, 53, ff.)
[3] Will-o'-the-wisp
[4] Robin Goodfellow, the mischievous fairy; people placed a bowl of cream at the door to insure his help, and to prevent his mischief.
[5] dress
[6] processions, shows, revels
[7] the god of marriage
[8] a form of entertainment
[9] low-heeled shoe, symbol of comedy
[10] one of the three moods of Grecian music
[11] turn
[12] freedom and care combined
[13] Stones and trees and beasts followed his music and by it he even drew his wife Eurydice forth from Hades, but lost her because he looked back to see whether she were coming.
[14] The Thoughtful Man
[15] bestead (profit)
[16] foolish
[17] captivate
[18] followers of the god of dreams
[19] Memnon was king of the Ethiopians at the time of the Trojan wars.
[20] Cassiopeia was carried by Perseus to heaven, where she became a constellation.
[21] Goddess of the hearth or of fire, possibly signifying genius; the genealogy is Milton's invention.

He met her, and in secret shades
Of woody Ida's[1] inmost grove,
Whilst yet there was no fear of Jove.
Come, pensive Nun, devout and pure,
Sober, steadfast, and demure,
All in a robe of darkest grain,[2]
Flowing with majestic train,
And sable stole[3] of cypress lawn[4]
Over thy decent[5] shoulders drawn.
Come, but keep thy wonted state,
With even step, and musing gait,
And looks commercing with the skies,
Thy rapt soul sitting in thine eyes.
There, held in holy passion still,
Forget thyself to marble, till
With a sad leaden downward cast
Thou fix them on the earth as fast.
And join with thee calm Peace, and Quiet,
Spare Fast, that oft with gods doth diet,
And hears the Muses in a ring
Aye round about Jove's altar sing;
And add to these retired Leisure,
That in trim gardens takes his pleasure;
But first, and chiefest, with thee bring
Him that yon soars on golden wing,
Guiding the fiery-wheelèd throne,
The cherub Contemplation;[6]
And the mute Silence hist[7] along,
'Less Philomel will deign a song,
In her sweetest, saddest plight,
Smoothing the rugged brow of Night,
While Cynthia checks her dragon yoke[8]
Gently o'er the accustomed[9] oak;
Sweet bird, that shunn'st the noise of folly,
Most musical, most melancholy!
Thee, chauntress, oft the woods among,
I woo, to hear thy even-song;
And missing thee, I walk unseen
On the dry smooth-shaven green,
To behold the wandering moon,
Riding near her highest noon,
Like one that had been led astray
Through the heaven's wide pathless way,
And oft, as if her head she bowed,
Stooping through a fleecy cloud.
Oft, on a plat of rising ground,
I hear the far-off curfew[10] sound,
Over some wide-watered shore,
Swinging slow with sullen roar;
Or if the air will not permit,
Some still removèd place will fit,
Where glowing embers through the room
Teach light to counterfeit a gloom,
Far from all resort of mirth,
Save the cricket on the hearth,
Or a bellman's drowsy charm[11]
To bless the doors from nightly harm.
Or let my lamp at midnight hour
Be seen in some high, lonely tower,
Where I may oft out-watch the Bear[12]
With thrice-great Hermes;[13] or unsphere
The spirit of Plato, to unfold
What worlds or what vast regions hold
The immortal mind that hath forsook
Her mansion in this fleshly nook;
And[14] of those demons that are found
In fire, air, flood, or underground,
Whose power hath a true consent[15]
With planet or with element.
Sometime let gorgeous Tragedy
In sceptered pall[16] come sweeping by,
Presenting Thebes,[17] or Pelops'[18] line,
Or the tale of Troy divine,[19]
Or what (though rare) of later age
Ennobled hath the buskined stage.[20]
But, O sad virgin! that thy power
Might raise Musaeus[21] from his bower;
Or bid the soul of Orpheus[22] sing
Such notes as, warbled to the string,
Drew iron tears down Pluto's cheek,
And made Hell grant what love did seek;
Or call up him that left half-told
The story of Cambuscan bold,[23]
Of Camball, and of Algarsife,
And who had Canace to wife,
That owned the virtuous[24] ring and glass,
And of the wondrous horse of brass
On which the Tartar king did ride!
And if aught else great bards beside
In sage and solemn tunes have sung,
Of turneys, and of trophies hung,
Of forests, and enchantments drear,
Where more is meant than meets the ear.[25]

[1] Mt. Ida in Crete, the ancient kingdom of Saturn, from which he was driven by his son Jupiter
[2] dye
[3] robe
[4] a thin texture
[5] seemly, modest
[6] The name is Milton's, but cf. *Ezekiel* x.
[7] lead hushed
[8] Cynthia (Diana, goddess of the moon) was not drawn by dragons; Ceres, goddess of harvests, was. But see *Cymbeline*, II, ii, 48: "Swift, swift, you dragons of the night."
[9] frequented (by Philomel, the nightingale)
[10] a bell rung in olden times at eight o'clock as a signal that fires were to be covered and lights put out
[11] The night watchman's hourly cry often ended with a benediction.
[12] the constellation of the Great Dipper which remains in the heavens all night
[13] i e., read the works of Hermes Trismegistus (thrice great), a mythical learned king of Egypt
[14] Supply "to tell"
[15] *con-sentio*, agreement
[16] mantle of state
[17] Aeschylus's *Seven Against Thebes*
[18] Sophocles's *Electra*
[19] Homer's *Iliad*
[20] Shakespeare? The buskin was the high-heeled shoe symbolical of tragedy.
[21] son of Orpheus
[22] See note 13, p. 253.
[23] References in ll. 110-115 are all to Chaucer's "Squiere's Tale."
[24] powerful
[25] Spenser?

Thus, Night, oft see me in thy pale career,
Till civil-suited Morn appear,
Not tricked and frounced [1] as she was wont
With the Attic boy [2] to hunt,
But kerchieft in a comely cloud,
While rocking winds are piping loud,
Or ushered with a shower still,
When the gust hath blown his fill,
Ending on the rustling leaves,
With minute-drops from off the eaves.
And when the sun begins to fling
His flaring beams, me, Goddess, bring
To archèd walks of twilight groves,
And shadows brown, that Sylvan [3] loves,
Of pine, or monumental oak,
Where the rude axe with heavèd stroke
Was never heard the nymphs to daunt,
Or fright them from their hallowed haunt.
There in close covert by some brook,
Where no profaner eye may look,
Hide me from day's garish eye,
While the bee with honeyed thigh,
That at her flowery work doth sing,
And the waters murmuring,
With such consort as they keep,
Entice the dewy-feathered Sleep;
And let some strange mysterious dream
Wave at his [4] wings in airy stream
Of lively portraiture displayed,
Softly on my eyelids laid; [5]
And as I wake, [6] sweet music breathe
Above, about, or underneath,
Sent by some spirit to mortals good,
Or the unseen Genius of the wood.
But let my due feet never fail
To walk the studious cloister's pale, [7]
And love the high embowèd [8] roof,
With antique pillars massy proof, [9]
And storied [10] windows richly dight,
Casting a dim religious light.
There let the pealing organ blow,
To the full-voiced choir below,
In service high and anthems clear,
As may with sweetness, through mine ear,
Dissolve me into ecstasies,
And bring all Heaven before mine eyes.
And may at last my weary age
Find out the peaceful hermitage,
The hairy gown, and mossy cell,
Where I may sit and rightly spell [11]
Of every star that heaven doth shew,
And every herb that sips the dew,
Till old experience do attain
To something like prophetic strain.
These pleasures, Melancholy, give,
And I with thee will choose to live.

1634 1645

[1] curled
[2] Cephalus, beloved by Aurora
[3] Sylvanus, a forest god
[4] Sleep's
[5] modifies "dream"
[6] Supply "let."
[7] limits
[8] vaulted
[9] of massive strength
[10] painted to represent stories
[11] construe, study

LYCIDAS [12]

Yet once more, [13] O ye laurels, [14] and once more,
Ye myrtles [14] brown, with ivy [14] never sere,
I come to pluck your berries harsh and crude,
And with forced fingers rude
Shatter your leaves before the mellowing year.
Bitter constraint and sad occasion dear
Compels me to disturb your season due;
For Lycidas is dead, dead ere his prime,
Young Lycidas, and hath not left his peer.
Who would not sing for Lycidas? He knew
Himself to sing, and build the lofty rime.
He must not float upon his watery bier
Unwept, and welter [15] to the parching wind,
Without the meed of some melodious tear.
  Begin then, Sisters of the sacred well [16]
That from beneath the seat of Jove doth spring,
Begin, and somewhat loudly sweep the string.
Hence with denial vain and coy excuse;
So may some gentle Muse
With lucky words favor my destined urn,
And as he passes turn,
And bid fair peace to be my sable shroud.
  For we were nursed upon the self-same hill, [17]
Fed the same flock, by fountain, shade, and rill;
Together both, ere the high lawns [18] appeared
Under the opening eyelids of the morn,
We drove a-field, and both together heard
What time the gray-fly [19] winds her sultry horn,
Battening [20] our flocks with the fresh dews of night,
Oft till the star that rose at evening, bright,
Toward heaven's descent had sloped his westering wheel.

[12] This elegy was written in memory of Edward King, a fellow student of Milton's at Cambridge, who was drowned off the Welsh coast, August, 1637. The sad event and the poet's sorrow are poetically set forth in the pastoral guise of one shepherd mourning for another. The fact, moreover, that King was destined for the Church enabled Milton to introduce St. Peter, and voice, through him, a Puritanic denunciation of the corruption among the clergy.
[13] Milton apparently had written nothing for three years.
[14] symbols of the poet's rewards
[15] toss, roll
[16] the Pierian spring at the foot of Mt. Olympus, Jove's seat; the birthplace of the nine muses
[17] i. e., at the same college
[18] pastures
[19] the trumpet fly that makes a sharp hissing sound at noon
[20] fattening

Meanwhile the rural ditties were not mute,
Tempered to the oaten flute;
Rough Satyrs danced, and Fauns with cloven heel
From the glad sound would not be absent long;
And old Damoetas [1] loved to hear our song.
But, Oh, the heavy change, now thou art gone,
Now thou art gone, and never must return!
Thee, Shepherd, thee the woods and desert caves,
With wild thyme and the gadding vine o'er-grown,
And all their echoes, mourn.
The willows and the hazel copses green
Shall now no more be seen,
Fanning their joyous leaves to thy soft lays.
As killing as the canker to the rose,
Or taint-worm to the weanling [2] herds that graze,
Or frost to flowers, that their gay wardrobe wear,
When first the white-thorn blows;
Such, Lycidas, thy loss to shepherd's ear.
Where were ye, Nymphs, when the remorseless deep
Closed o'er the head of your loved Lycidas?
For neither were ye playing on the steep
Where your old bards, the famous Druids, lie,
Nor on the shaggy top of Mona [3] high,
Nor yet where Deva [4] spreads her wizard stream.
Aye me, I fondly dream!
Had ye been there—for what could that have done?
What could the Muse [5] herself that Orpheus bore,
The Muse herself, for her enchanting son,
Whom universal nature did lament,
When, by the rout that made the hideous roar,
His gory visage down the stream was sent,
Down the swift Hebrus to the Lesbian shore? [6]
Alas! what boots it with uncessant care
To tend the homely, slighted, shepherd's trade, [7]
And strictly meditate the thankless Muse?
Were it not better done, as others use,
To sport with Amaryllis in the shade,
Or with the tangles of Neaera's hair? [8]
Fame is the spur that the clear spirit doth raise
(That last infirmity of noble mind)
To scorn delights and live laborious days;
But the fair guerdon [9] when we hope to find,
And think to burst out into sudden blaze,
Comes the blind Fury [10] with the abhorrèd shears,
And slits the thin-spun life. "But not the praise,"
Phoebus [11] replied, and touched my trembling ears;
"Fame is no plant that grows on mortal soil,
Nor in the glistering foil
Set off to the world, nor in broad rumor lies;
But lives and spreads aloft by those pure eyes
And perfect witness of all-judging Jove;
As he pronounces lastly on each deed,
Of so much fame in heaven expect thy meed."
O fountain Arethuse, [12] and thou honored flood,
Smooth-sliding Mincius, [13] crowned with vocal reeds,
That strain I heard was of a higher mood.
But now my oat proceeds,
And listens to the herald [14] of the sea,
That came in Neptune's plea. [15]
He asked the waves, and asked the felon winds,
What hard mishap hath doomed this gentle swain?
And questioned every gust of rugged wings
That blows from off each beakèd promontory.
They knew not of his story;
And sage Hippotades [16] their answer brings,
That not a blast was from his dungeon strayed;
The air was calm, and on the level brine
Sleek Panope [17] with all her sisters played.
It was that fatal and perfidious bark,
Built in the eclipse, [18] and rigged with curses dark,
That sunk so low that sacred head of thine.
Next Camus, [19] reverend sire, went footing slow,
His mantle hairy, and his bonnet sedge, [20]
Inwrought with figures dim, and on the edge
Like to that sanguine flower [21] inscribed with woe.

[1] a pastoral disguise, doubtless, for some friend or tutor
[2] young
[3] Anglesey, an island county of N. Wales, which was also a seat of the Druids
[4] the River Dee, of legendary associations
[5] Calliope
[6] Orpheus, having angered the Thracian Bacchantes, was torn into pieces by them.
[7] poetry
[8] i.e., live for pleasure (The names are imaginary.)
[9] reward
[10] Atropos, the third Fate, cuts the thread of life.
[11] Apollo, god of wisdom, music, and poetry
[12] sung of by Theocritus, a pastoral poet of Sicily; invoked here because of this association
[13] a river of which Vergil sang; near his home, Mantua.
[14] Triton, son of Neptune
[15] to inquire in the name of Neptune, god of ocean
[16] Aeolus, god of the winds, son of Hippotas
[17] one of the Nereids, or sea-nymphs
[18] For this superstition, cf. *Macbeth,* IV, i, 28.
[19] the river Cam, that flows past Cambridge
[20] a rush-like reed which has on the edges of its leaf peculiar letter-like characters
[21] the hyacinth, which was said to have the Greek words *ai ai* (alas) on its petals

"Ah! who hath reft," quoth he, "my dearest pledge?"[1]
Last came, and last did go,
The pilot[2] of the Galilean lake;
Two massy keys he bore of metals twain
(The golden opes, the iron shuts amain).
He shook his mitered[3] locks, and stern bespake:[4]
"How well could I have spared for thee, young swain,
Enow of such as for their bellies' sake,
Creep and intrude and climb into the fold!
Of other care they little reckoning make
Than how to scramble at the shearers' feast,
And shove away the worthy bidden guest.
Blind mouths![5] that scarce themselves know how to hold
A sheep-hook, or have learnt aught else the least
That to the faithful herdman's art belongs!
What recks[6] it them? What need they? They are sped;[7]
And when they list, their lean and flashy songs
Grate on their scrannel[8] pipes of wretched straw;
The hungry sheep look up, and are not fed,
But swoln with wind and the rank mist[9] they draw,
Rot inwardly, and foul contagion spread;
Besides what the grim wolf[10] with privy paw
Daily devours apace, and nothing said.
But that two-handed engine[11] at the door
Stands read to smite once, and smite no more."
  Return, Alpheus;[12] the dread voice is past
That shrunk thy streams; return, Sicilian Muse,[13]
And call the vales, and bid them hither cast
Their bells and flowrets of a thousand hues.
Ye valleys low, where the mild whispers use[14]
Of shades and wanton winds and gushing brooks,
On whose fresh lap the swart star[15] sparely[16] looks,
Throw hither all your quaint enameled eyes,
That on the green turf suck the honeyed showers,
And purple all the ground with vernal flowers.
Bring the rathe[17] primrose that forsaken dies,
The tufted crow-toe,[18] and pale jessamine,
The white pink, and the pansy freaked with jet,
The glowing violet,
The musk-rose, and the well-attired woodbine,
With cowslips wan that hang the pensive head,
And every flower that sad embroidery wears;
Bid amaranthus[19] all his beauty shed,
And daffodillies fill their cups with tears,
To strew the laureate hearse[20] where Lycid lies.
For so to interpose a little ease,
Let our frail thoughts dally with false surmise,
Aye me! whilst thee the shores and sounding seas
Wash far away, where'er thy bones are hurled;
Whether beyond the stormy Hebrides,[21]
Where thou perhaps under the whelming tide
Visit'st the bottom of the monstrous world;[22]
Or whether thou, to our moist vows denied,
Sleep'st by the fable of Bellerus old,
Where the great vision of the guarded mount[23]
Looks toward Namancos[24] and Bayona's[25] hold.
Look homeward, Angel, now, and melt with ruth;
And O ye dolphins,[26] waft the hapless youth.
  Weep no more, woeful shepherds, weep no more,
For Lycidas, your sorrow, is not dead,
Sunk though he be beneath the watery floor.
So sinks the day-star in the ocean bed,
And yet anon repairs his drooping head,
And tricks[27] his beams, and with new-spangled ore
Flames in the forehead of the morning sky;
So Lycidas sunk low, but mounted high,
Through the dear might of Him that walked the waves,
Where, other groves and other streams along,
With nectar pure his oozy locks he laves,
And hears the unexpressive[28] nuptial song,
In the blest kingdoms meek of joy and love.
There entertain him all the saints above,
In solemn troops and sweet societies,
That sing, and singing in their glory move,

[1] offspring [2] Peter, *Matthew*, xiv, 22-33; xvi, 18-19
[3] The miter was the bishop's official headdress.
[4] spoke out
[5] See Ruskin's comment on this passage in his *Sesame and Lilies*.
[6] concerns [7] cared for
[8] lean, thin, therefore harsh (Flashy means tasteless.)
[9] false teachings
[10] Milton's hostile characterization of the Church of Rome.
[11] perhaps the two Houses of Parliament
[12] The river god who pursued Arethusa and was made one with her in the fountain of Arethusa; cf. l. 85.
[13] the muse of pastoral poetry
[14] dwell [15] dog-star [16] sparingly
[17] early [18] purple hyacinth
[19] an imaginary flower that never fades
[20] garlanded bier
[21] islands north of Scotland
[22] world of monsters (the sea)
[23] Fable of Bellerus=fabled Bellerus; he is sometimes said to have been a Cornish giant. At the western end of Cornwall is a rock called the Giant's Chair; and near Land's End is a rock called St. Michael's Mount, said to be guarded by the archangel himself.
[24] in Spain
[25] near Namancos; both found on ancient maps
[26] Dolphins rescued Arion the Greek poet when jealous sailors, coveting his treasures, threw him overboard.
[27] arranges [28] inexpressible

And wipe the tears forever from his eyes.
Now, Lycidas, the shepherds weep no more;
Henceforth thou art the Genius of the shore,
In thy large recompense,[1] and shalt be good
To all that wander in that perilous flood.

Thus sang the uncouth[2] swain to the oaks and rills,
While the still morn went out with sandals gray;
He touched the tender stops of various quills,
With eager thought warbling his Doric[3] lay;
And now the sun had stretched out all the hills,
And now was dropped into the western bay.
At last he rose, and twitched his mantle blue;
Tomorrow to fresh woods and pastures new.

1637 1638

SONNETS

When the Assault Was Intended to the City[4]

Captain, or colonel, or knight in arms,
Whose chance on these defenseless doors[5] may seize,
If ever deed of honor did thee please,
Guard them, and him within protect from harms.
He can requite thee; for he knows the charms
That call[6] fame on such gentle acts as these,
And he can spread thy name o'er lands and seas,
Whatever clime the sun's bright circle warms.
Lift not thy spear against the Muses' bower;
The great Emathian conqueror[7] bid spare
The house of Pindarus,[8] when temple and tower
Went to the ground; and the repeated air[9]
Of sad Electra's poet had the power
To save the Athenian walls from ruin bare.

1642 1645

To the Lord General Cromwell

Cromwell, our chief of men, who through a cloud
Not of war only, but detractions[10] rude,
Guided by faith and matchless fortitude,
To peace and truth thy glorious way hast plowed,
And on the neck of crownèd Fortune proud
Hast reared God's trophies, and his work pursued,
While Darwen stream,[11] with blood of Scots imbrued,
And Dunbar field, resounds thy praises loud,
And Worcester's laureate wreath. Yet much remains
To conquer still; peace hath her victories
No less renowned than war; new foes arise,
Threatening to bind our souls with secular chains.[12]
Help us to save free conscience from the paw
Of hireling wolves, whose gospel is their maw.

May, 1652 1694

On the Late Massacre in Piedmont[13]

Avenge, O Lord, thy slaughtered saints, whose bones
Lie scattered on the Alpine mountains cold;
Even them who kept thy truth so pure of old,
When all our fathers worshiped stocks and stones,
Forget not. In thy book record their groans
Who were thy sheep, and in their ancient fold
Slain by the bloody Piedmontese, that rolled
Mother with infant down the rocks. Their moans
The vales redoubled to the hills, and they
To heaven. Their martyred blood and ashes sow
O'er all the Italian fields, where still doth sway
The triple tyrant; that from these may grow
A hundred-fold, who, having learnt thy way,
Early may fly the Babylonian woe.

1655 1673

On His Blindness

When I consider how my light is spent
Ere half my days, in this dark world and wide,
And that one talent which is death to hide
Lodged with me useless, though my soul more bent

[1] as thy great reward
[2] unknown
[3] pastoral
[4] when Charles I advanced upon London, which was largely Puritan
[5] of Milton's home
[6] call forth
[7] Alexander the Great; Emathia, part of Macedonia
[8] The home of Pindar, the Grecian lyric poet, was ordered saved when Thebes was destroyed, B.C. 333.
[9] After the taking of Athens by the Lacedemonians in B.C. 404, the singing of part of Euripides's drama *Electra* moved the conquerors to spare the city.
[10] proceeding from Presbyterian opponents
[11] At the Darwen, Cromwell defeated the Scotch in 1648; at Dunbar in 1650; at Worcester he defeated Charles I, in 1651.
[12] i. e., state control of religion
[13] the Protestant Vaudois, or Waldenses, in southern France were practically crushed out in 1655 because of their refusal to accept the state religion. They were an ancient sect, originating in 1170; see line 3. In line 12 there is an allusion to the triple tiara of the Pope; in line 14, to the doom of the mystical Babylon of *Revelation* xvii and xviii.

To serve therewith my Maker, and present
My true account, lest he returning chide;
"Doth God exact day labor, light denied?"
I fondly [1] ask. But Patience, to prevent
That murmur, soon replies, "God doth not need
Either man's work or his own gifts. Who best
Bear his mild yoke, they serve him best. His state
Is kingly; thousands at his bidding speed,
And post o'er land and ocean without rest;
They also serve who only stand and wait."
after 1652 1673

To Cyriack Skinner

Cyriack, this three years' day these eyes, though clear
To outward view, of blemish or of spot,
Bereft of light, their seeing have forgot;
Nor to their idle orbs doth sight appear
Of sun or moon or star throughout the year,
Or man or woman. Yet I argue not
Against Heaven's hand or will, nor bate a jot
Of heart or hope, but still bear up and steer
Right onward. What supports me, dost thou ask?
The conscience, [2] friend, to have lost them overplied
In liberty's defense, [3] my noble task,
Of which all Europe talks from side to side.
This thought might lead me through the world's vain mask
Content, though blind, had I no better guide.
1655 1694

From PARADISE LOST

Book I

THE ARGUMENT

This First Book proposes, first, in brief, the whole subject: Man's disobedience, and the loss thereupon of Paradise, wherein he was placed; then touches the prime cause of his fall—the Serpent, or rather Satan in the Serpent, who, revolting from God and drawing to his side many legions of Angels, was by the command of God driven out of Heaven with all his crew into the great Deep. Which action passed over, the Poem hastens into the midst of things; presenting Satan with his Angels now fallen into Hell—described here, not in the Center [4] (for heaven and earth may be supposed as yet not made, certainly not yet accursed) but in a place of utter darkness fitliest called Chaos. Here Satan with his angels lying on the burning lake, thunderstruck and astonished, after a certain space recovers, as from confusion; calls up him who, next in order and dignity, lay by him; they confer of their miserable fall. Satan awakens all his legions, who lay till then in the same manner confounded. They rise; their numbers, array of battle, their chief leaders named, according to the idols known afterwards in Canaan and the countries adjoining. To these Satan directs his speech, comforts them with hope yet of regaining Heaven, but tells them lastly of a new world and new kind of creature to be created, according to an ancient prophecy or report in Heaven; for that Angels were long before this visible creation was the opinion of many ancient Fathers. To find out the truth of this prophecy, and what to determine thereon, he refers to a full council. What his associates thence attempt. Pandemonium, the palace of Satan, rises, suddenly built out of the Deep; the infernal Peers there sit in council.

[1] foolishly
[2] consciousness
[3] He wrote the answer to Salmasius (the *Defensio pro Populo Anglicano*) in the face of warning from physicians that he would become blind unless he gave up work.
[4] Earth; see note on l. 74.

Of Man's first disobedience, and the fruit
Of that forbidden tree, whose mortal taste
Brought death into the world, and all our woe,
With loss of Eden, [5] till one greater Man
Restore us, and regain the blissful seat,
Sing, Heavenly Muse, [6] that on the secret [7] top
Of Oreb, [8] or of Sinai, didst inspire
That shepherd who first taught the chosen seed [9]
In the beginning [10] how the Heavens and Earth
Rose out of Chaos; or, if Sion [11] hill
Delight thee more, and Siloa's brook that flowed
Fast [12] by the oracle of God, I thence
Invoke thy aid to my adventurous song,
That with no middle flight intends to soar
Above the Aonian mount, [13] while it pursues
Things unattempted yet in prose or rime.
And chiefly thou, O spirit, that dost prefer
Before all temples the upright heart and pure,
Instruct me, for thou know'st; thou from the first
Wast present, and, with mighty wings outspread
Dove-like sat'st brooding on the vast abyss,
And mad'st it pregnant. What in me is dark
Illumine, what is low raise and support;
That to the highth of this great argument [14]
I may assert eternal providence,
And justify the ways of God to men.
Say first—for Heaven hides nothing from thy view,

[5] "And the Lord God planted a garden eastward in Eden."—*Genesis* ii, 8. Strictly, therefore, Eden is the region, Paradise the garden.
[6] See VII, 1-12, p. 282.
[7] hidden (Cowper), retired (Landor)
[8] Horeb, or Sinai, whereon god spoke to Moses from the burning bush
[9] *Deuteronomy* x, 15
[10] modifies "rose"
[11] Zion, in Jerusalem
[12] close, (by the Temple)
[13] Helicon (fig. for Grecian poetry)
[14] theme

Nor the deep tract of Hell—say first what cause
Moved our grand parents, in that happy state,
Favored of Heaven so highly, to fall off
From their Creator, and transgress his will
For one restraint, lords of the world besides.
Who first seduced them to that foul revolt?
The infernal serpent; he it was, whose guile,
Stirred up with envy and revenge, deceived
The mother of mankind, what time his pride
Had cast him out from Heaven,[1] with all his host
Of rebel angels, by whose aid, aspiring
To set himself in glory above his peers,
He trusted to have equaled the Most High,
If he opposed; and with ambitious aim
Against the throne and monarchy[2] of God
Raised impious war in Heaven, and battle proud,
With vain attempt. Him the Almighty Power
Hurled headlong flaming from the ethereal sky,
With hideous ruin and combustion, down
To bottomless perdition; there to dwell
In adamantine chains and penal fire,
Who durst defy the Omnipotent to arms.
Nine times the space that measures day and night
To mortal men, he with his horrid crew
Lay vanquished, rolling in the fiery gulf,
Confounded, though immortal. But his doom
Reserved him to more wrath; for now the thought
Both of lost happiness and lasting pain
Torments him; round he throws his baleful eyes,
That witnessed[3] huge affliction and dismay,
Mixed with obdurate pride and steadfast hate.
At once, as far as Angels ken, he views
The dismal situation waste and wild:
A dungeon horrible on all sides round
As one great furnace flamed; yet from those flames
No light; but rather darkness visible
Served only to discover[4] sights of woe,
Regions of sorrow, doleful shades, where peace
And rest can never dwell, hope never comes
That comes to all; but torture without end
Still urges,[5] and a fiery deluge, fed
With ever-burning sulphur unconsumed.
Such place Eternal Justice had prepared
For those rebellious; here their prison ordained
In utter[6] darkness, and their portion set,
As far removed from God and light of Heaven
As from the center thrice to the utmost pole.[7]
Oh, how unlike the place from whence they fell!
There the companions of his fall, o'erwhelmed
With floods and whirlwinds of tempestuous fire,
He soon discerns; and, weltering by his side,
One next himself in power, and next in crime,
Long after known in Palestine, and named
Beëlzebub. To whom the arch-enemy,
And thence in Heaven called Satan,[8] with bold words
Breaking the horrid silence, thus began:
"If thou beest he—but oh, how fallen! how changed
From him, who in the happy realms of light,
Clothed with transcendent brightness, didst outshine
Myriads, though bright!—if he whom mutual league,
United thoughts and counsels, equal hope
And hazard in the glorious enterprise,
Joined with me once, now misery hath joined
In equal ruin—into what pit thou seest
From what highth fallen:[9] so much the stronger proved
He with his thunder; and till then who knew
The force of those dire arms? Yet not for those,
Nor what the potent Victor in his rage
Can else inflict, do I repent, or change,
Though changed in outward luster, that fixed mind,
And high disdain from sense of injured merit,
That with the Mightiest raised me to contend,
And to the fierce contention brought along
Innumerable force of Spirits armed,
That durst dislike his reign, and, me preferring,
His utmost power with adverse power opposed
In dubious battle on the plains of Heaven,
And shook his throne. What though the field be lost?
All is not lost: the unconquerable will,
And study of revenge, immortal hate,
And courage never to submit or yield,
And what is else not to be overcome;
That glory never shall his wrath or might
Extort from me. To bow and sue for grace
With suppliant knee, and deify his power
Who, from the terror of this arm, so late
Doubted his empire[10]—that were low indeed;

[1] Cf. Caedmon's account, p. 20.
[2] single rule
[3] bore witness to (within himself)
[4] reveal
[5] presses (a Latinism)
[6] outer
[7] According to the Ptolemaic system, the earth is the center of the physical universe. The utmost, or outmost, pole would be the outer boundary, the firmament. Milton, while disposed to accept the new Copernican theory, clung to the old system for poetic purposes.
[8] i.e., Adversary
[9] an exclamatory sentence without regular construction
[10] sovereignty

That were an ignominy and shame beneath
This downfall; since by fate the strength of gods
And this empyreal substance cannot fail;
Since, through experience of this great event,
In arms not worse, in foresight much advanced,
We may with more successful hope resolve
To wage by force or guile eternal war,
Irreconcilable to our grand Foe,
Who now triumphs and in the excess of joy
Sole reigning holds the tyranny of Heaven."
  So spake the apostate Angel, though in pain,
Vaunting aloud, but racked with deep despair;
And him thus answered soon his bold compeer:
  "O prince! O chief of many throned powers
That led the embattled Seraphim [1] to war
Under thy conduct, and, in dreadful deeds
Fearless, endangered Heaven's perpetual King,
And put to proof his high supremacy,
Whether upheld by strength, or chance, or fate!
Too well I see and rue the dire event
That with sad overthrow and foul defeat
Hath lost us Heaven, and all this mighty host
In horrible destruction laid thus low,
As far as gods and heavenly essences
Can perish; for the mind and spirit remains
Invincible, and vigor soon returns,
Though all our glory extinct, and happy state
Here swallowed up in endless misery.
But what if he our Conqueror (whom I now
Of force [2] believe almighty, since no less
Than such could have o'erpowered such force as ours)
Have left us this our spirit and strength entire,
Strongly to suffer and support our pains,
That we may so suffice his vengeful ire,
Or do him mightier service as his thralls
By right of war, whate'er his business be,
Here in the heart of Hell to work in fire,
Or do his errands in the gloomy deep?
What can it then avail, though yet we feel
Strength undiminished, or eternal being
To undergo eternal punishment?"
  Whereto with speedy words the Arch-Fiend replied:
"Fallen Cherub, to be weak is miserable,
Doing or suffering; but of this be sure—
To do aught good never will be our task,
But ever to do ill our sole delight,
As being the contrary to his high will
Whom we resist. If then his providence
Out of our evil seek to bring forth good,
Our labor must be to pervert that end,
And out of good still to find means of evil;
Which ofttimes may succeed so as perhaps
Shall grieve him, if I fail not, and disturb
His inmost counsels from their destined aim.
But see! the angry Victor hath recalled
His ministers of vengeance and pursuit
Back to the gates of Heaven; the sulphurous hail,
Shot after us in storm, o'erblown hath laid
The fiery surge that from the precipice
Of Heaven received us falling; and the thunder,
Winged with red lightning and impetuous rage,
Perhaps hath spent his shafts, and ceases now
To bellow through the vast and boundless Deep. [3]
Let us not slip the occasion, whether scorn
Or satiate fury yield it from our Foe.
Seest thou yon dreary plain, forlorn and wild,
The seat of desolation, void of light,
Save what the glimmering of these livid flames
Casts pale and dreadful? Thither let us tend [4]
From off the tossing of these fiery waves;
There rest, if any rest can harbor there;
And, reassembling our afflicted [5] powers,
Consult how we may henceforth most offend
Our Enemy, our own loss how repair,
How overcome this dire calamity,
What reinforcement we may gain from hope,
If not what resolution from despair,"
  Thus Satan, talking to his nearest mate,
With head uplift above the wave, and eyes
That sparkling blazed; his other parts besides,
Prone on the flood, extended long and large,
Lay floating many a rood, in bulk as huge
As whom the fables name of monstrous size, [6]
Titanian, or Earth-born, that warred on Jove,
Briareos or Typhon, whom the den
By ancient Tarsus held, or that sea-beast
Leviathan, [7] which God of all his works
Created hugest that swim the ocean-stream.
Him, haply slumbering on the Norway foam,
The pilot of some small night-foundered skiff
Deeming some island, oft, as seamen tell,
With fixed anchor in his scaly rind,
Moors by his side under the lee, while night
Invests the sea, and wished morn delays.
So stretched out huge in length the Arch-Fiend lay,
Chained [8] on the burning lake; nor ever thence

[1] See p. 153, note 7. [2] perforce

[3] Even above the resonance to be felt everywhere through Milton's verse this line rises with a resonance of its own.

[4] make our way (a Latinism)

[5] beaten down (a Latinism)

[6] The Titans were the children of Uranus and Gaea (Heaven and Earth). Briareos and Typhon were giants, sometimes said to have been imprisoned beneath mountains, thus representing the forces of earthquake and volcano.

[7] *Psalms* civ, 26 [8] *II Peter* ii, 4

Had[1] risen or heaved his head, but that the will
And high permission of all-ruling Heaven
Left him at large to his own dark designs,
That with reiterated crimes he might
Heap on himself damnation, while he sought
Evil to others, and enraged might see
How all his malice served but to bring forth
Infinite goodness, grace, and mercy, shewn
On Man by him seduced; but on himself
Treble confusion, wrath, and vengeance poured.
  Forthwith upright he rears from off the pool
His mighty stature; on each hand the flames
Driven backward slope their pointing spires, and, rolled
In billows, leave i' the midst a horrid vale.
Then with expanded wings he steers his flight
Aloft, incumbent on the dusky air,
That felt unusual weight; till on dry land
He lights—if it were land that ever burned
With solid, as the lake with liquid fire,
And such appeared in hue, as when the force
Of subterranean wind transports a hill
Torn from Pelorus,[2] or the shattered side
Of thundering Aetna, whose combustible
And fueled entrails thence conceiving fire,
Sublimed[3] with mineral fury, aid the winds,
And leave a singed bottom all involved
With stench and smoke; such resting found the sole
Of unblest feet. Him followed his next mate,
Both glorying to have scaped the Stygian flood
As gods, and by their own recovered strength,
Not by the sufferance of supernal power.
  "Is this the region, this the soil, the clime,"
Said then the lost Archangel, "this the seat
That we must change for Heaven? this mournful gloom
For that celestial light? Be it so, since he
Who now is sovran can dispose and bid
What shall be right; farthest from him is best,
Whom reason hath equaled, force hath made supreme
Above his equals. Farewell, happy fields,
Where joy forever dwells! Hail, horrors! hail,
Infernal world! and thou, profoundest Hell,
Receive thy new possessor, one who brings
A mind not to be changed by place or time.
The mind is its own place, and in itself
Can make a Heaven of Hell, a Hell of Heaven.[4]
What matter where, if I be still the same,
And what I should be, all but[5] less than he
Whom thunder hath made greater? Here at least
We shall be free; the Almighty hath not built
Here for his envy, will not drive us hence;
Here we may reign secure, and in my choice
To reign is worth ambition, though in Hell;
Better to reign in Hell, than serve in Heaven.
But wherefore let we then our faithful friends,
The associates and copartners of our loss,
Lie thus astonished on the oblivious pool,
And call them not to share with us their part
In this unhappy mansion, or once more
With rallied arms to try what may be yet
Regained in Heaven, or what more lost in Hell?"
  So Satan spake; and him Beëlzebub
Thus answered: "Leader of those armies bright
Which but the Omnipotent none could have foiled?
If once they hear that voice, their liveliest pledge
Of hope in fears and dangers—heard so oft
In worst extremes, and on the perilous edge
Of battle when it raged, in all assaults
Their surest signal—they will soon resume
New courage and revive, though now they lie
Groveling and prostrate on yon lake of fire,
As we erewhile, astounded and amazed;
No wonder, fallen such a pernicious highth!"
  He scarce had ceased when the superior Fiend
Was moving toward the shore; his ponderous shield,
Ethereal temper,[6] massy, large, and round,
Behind him cast. The broad circumference
Hung on his shoulders like the moon, whose orb
Through optic glass the Tuscan artist[7] views
At evening from the top of Fesole,[8]
Or in Valdarno,[9] to descry new lands,
Rivers, or mountains, in her spotty globe.
His spear—to equal which the tallest pine
Hewn on Norwegian hills, to be the mast
Of some great ammiral,[10] were but a wand—
He walked with, to support uneasy steps
Over the burning marl, not like those steps
On heaven's azure; and the torrid clime
Smote on him sore besides, vaulted with fire.
Natheless he so endured, till on the beach
Of that inflamed sea he stood, and called
His legions, Angel forms, who lay entranced,
Thick as autumnal leaves that strow the brooks
In Vallombrosa,[11] where the Etrurian shades
High over-arched embower; or scattered sedge
Afloat, when with fierce winds Orion[12] armed

[1] would have
[2] a Sicilian cape, now Faro
[3] sublimated
[4] Cf. p. 171, l. 77.
[5] only
[6] of ethereal temper
[7] scientist (though possibly referring to Galileo as a maker of telescopes)
[8] a hill above Florence
[9] valley of the Arno
[10] admiral's flagship
[11] in Tuscany (Etruria)
[12] a Greek hunter; then a constellation supposed to bring tempests

Hath vexed the Red-Sea coast, whose waves o'erthrew
Busiris [1] and his Memphian chivalry,
While with perfidious hatred they pursued
The sojourners of Goshen, [2] who beheld
From the safe shore their floating carcasses
And broken chariot-wheels; so thick bestrown,
Abject and lost, lay these, covering the flood,
Under amazement of their hideous change.
He called so loud that all the hollow deep
Of Hell resounded: "Princes, Potentates,
Warriors, the flower of Heaven—once yours, now lost,
If such astonishment as this can seize
Eternal Spirits! Or have ye chosen this place
After the toil of battle to repose
Your wearied virtue, for the ease you find
To slumber here, as in the vales of Heaven?
Or in this abject posture have ye sworn
To adore the Conqueror, who now beholds
Cherub and Seraph rolling in the flood
With scattered arms and ensigns, till anon
His swift pursuers from Heaven-gates discern
The advantage, and descending tread us down
Thus drooping, or with linked thunderbolts
Transfix us to the bottom of this gulf?
Awake, arise, or be forever fallen!"
They heard, and were abashed, and up they sprung
Upon the wing, as when men wont to watch,
On duty sleeping found by whom they dread,
Rouse and bestir themselves ere well awake.
Nor did they not perceive the evil plight
In which they were, or the fierce pains not feel;
Yet to their General's voice they soon obeyed
Innumerable. As when the potent rod
Of Amram's son, [3] in Egypt's evil day,
Waved round the coast, up called a pitchy cloud
Of locusts, warping on the eastern wind,
That o'er the realm of impious Pharaoh hung
Like night, and darkened all the land of Nile;
So numberless were those bad Angels seen
Hovering on wing under the cope of Hell,
'Twixt upper, nether, and surrounding fires;
Till, as a signal given, the uplifted spear
Of their great Sultan waving to direct
Their course, in even balance down they light
On the firm brimstone, and fill all the plain;
A multitude like which the populous North
Poured never from her frozen loins, to pass
Rhene or the Danaw, when her barbarous sons [4]
Came like a deluge on the South, and spread
Beneath Gibraltar to the Libyan sands.
Forthwith, from every squadron and each band,
The heads and leaders thither haste where stood
Their great Commander; godlike shapes, and forms
Excelling human, Princely Dignities,
And powers that erst in Heaven sat on thrones;
Though of their names in Heavenly records now
Be no memorial, blotted out and rased
By their rebellion from the Books of Life. [5]
Nor had they yet among the sons of Eve
Got them new names, till, wandering o'er the Earth,
Through God's high sufferance for the trial of man,
By falsities and lies the greatest part
Of mankind they corrupted to forsake
God their Creator, and the invisible
Glory of him that made them, to transform
Oft to the image of a brute, adorned
With gay religions [6] full of pomp and gold,
And devils to adore for deities;
Then were they known to men by various names,
And various idols through the heathen world.
Say, Muse, their names then known, who first, who last,
Roused from the slumber on that fiery couch,
At their great Emperor's call, as next in worth
Came singly where he stood on the bare strand,
While the promiscuous crowd stood yet aloof.
The chief were those who, from the pit of Hell
Roaming to seek their prey on Earth, durst fix
Their seats, long after, next the seat of God,
Their altars by his altar, gods adored
Among the nations round, and durst abide
Jehovah thundering out of Sion, throned
Between the Cherubim; yea, often placed
Within his sanctuary itself their shrines,
Abominations; and with cursed things
His holy rites and solemn feasts profaned,
And with their darkness durst affront [7] his light.
First Moloch, horrid king, besmeared with blood
Of human sacrifice, and parents' tears,
Though, for the noise of drums and timbrels loud,
Their children's cries unheard that passed through fire [8]
To his grim idol. Him the Ammonite

[1] one of the Pharaohs; used here for the Pharaoh of the time of the Exodus
[2] *Exodus* xii, 26, xiv, 22-28
[3] Moses
[4] Vandals from the Rhine and Danube, 429 A.D.

[5] Three lines of infinite sadness; conversely, Dante does not allow the name of Christ to be spoken in his Inferno.
[6] rites [7] confront [8] *Jeremiah* xxxii, 35

Worshiped in Rabba and her watery plain,
In Argob and in Basan, to the stream
Of utmost Arnon. Nor content with such
Audacious neighborhood, the wisest [1] heart
Of Solomon he led by fraud to build
His temple right against the temple of God
On that opprobrious hill, [2] and made his grove
The pleasant valley of Hinnom, [3] Tophet thence
And black Gehenna called, the type of Hell.
Next Chemos, the obscene dread of Moab's sons,
From Aroar to Nebo and the wild
Of southmost Abarim; in Hesebon
And Horonaim, Seon's realm, beyond
The flowery dale of Sibma clad with vines,
And Elealè to the Asphaltic pool.[4]
Peor his other name, when he enticed
Israel in Sittim, on their march from Nile,
To do him wanton rites, which cost them woe. [5]
Yet thence his lustful orgies he enlarged
Even to that hill of scandal, by the grove
Of Moloch homicide, lust hard by hate,
Till good Josiah drove them thence to Hell. [6]
With these came they who, from the bordering flood
Of old Euphrates to the brook that parts
Egypt from Syrian ground, had general names
Of Baalim and Ashtaroth [7]—those male,
These feminine. For Spirits, when they please,
Can either sex assume, or both; so soft
And uncompounded is their essence pure,
Not tied or manacled with joint or limb,
Nor founded on the brittle strength of bones,
Like cumbrous flesh; but, in what shape they choose,
Dilated or condensed, bright or obscure,
Can execute their aery purposes,
And works of love or enmity fulfill.
For those the race of Israel oft forsook
Their living Strength, and unfrequented left
His righteous altar, bowing lowly down
To bestial gods; for which their heads as low
Bowed down in battle, sunk before the spear
Of despicable foes. With these in troop
Came Astoreth, whom the Phoenicians called
Astarte, Queen of Heaven, with crescent horns;
To whose bright image nightly by the moon
Sidonian virgins paid their vows and songs;
In Sion also not unsung, where stood
Her temple on the offensive mountain, built
By that uxorious king whose heart, though large,
Beguiled by fair idolatresses, fell [8]

[1] most wise
[2] *II Kings* xxiii, 13
[3] *Jer.* vii, 31
[4] Dead Sea
[5] *Numb.* xxv, 9
[6] *II Kings* xxiii
[7] Phoenician deities; singular forms are Baal and Astoreth.
[8] *I Kings* xi, 4

To idols foul. Thammuz [9] came next behind,
Whose annual wound in Lebanon allured
The Syrian damsels to lament his fate
In amorous ditties all a summer's day,
While smooth Adonis [10] from his native rock
Ran purple to the sea, supposed with blood
Of Thammuz yearly wounded. The love-tale
Infected Sion's daughters with like heat,
Whose wanton passions in the sacred porch
Ezekiel saw, when, by the vision led,
His eye surveyed the dark idolatries
Of alienated Judah. Next came one
Who mourned in earnest, when the captive ark
Maimed his brute image, head and hands lopt off
In his own temple, on the grunsel-edge, [11]
Where he fell flat, and shamed his worshipers.
Dagon [12] his name, sea-monster, upward man
And downward fish; yet had his temple high
Reared in Azotus, dreaded through the coast
Of Palestine, in Gath and Ascalon,
And Accaron and Gaza's frontier bounds.
Him followed Rimmon, whose delightful seat
Was fair Damascus, on the fertile banks
Of Abbana and Pharphar, lucid streams.
He also against the house of God was bold.
A leper once he lost, and gained a king, [13]
Ahaz, his sottish conqueror, whom he drew
God's altar to disparage and displace
For one of Syrian mode, whereon to burn
His odious offerings, and adore the gods
Whom he had vanquished. After these appeared
A crew who, under names of old renown,
Osiris, Isis, Orus, and their train,
With monstrous shapes and sorceries abused
Fanatic Egypt and her priests, to seek
Their wandering gods disguised in brutish forms
Rather than human. Nor did Israel scape
The infection, when their borrowed gold composed
The calf in Oreb, [14] and the rebel king [15]
Doubled that sin in Bethel and in Dan,
Likening his Maker to the grazed ox—
Jehovah, who, in one night, when he passed
From Egypt marching, equaled with one stroke
Both her first-born and all her bleating gods. [16]
Belial [17] came last, than whom a spirit more lewd
Fell not from Heaven, or more gross to love

[9] identified with the Greek Adonis
[10] a Phoenician stream, tinged red by soil from the Libanus mountains
[11] ground-sill
[12] God of the Philistines: *I Sam.* v, 4
[13] *II Kings* v
[14] *Exod.* xii, 35; xxxii, 4
[15] *I Kings* xii, 28
[16] *Exod.* xii, 29
[17] "wickedness" (*II Cor.* vi, 15; personified by Milton)

Vice for itself. To him no temple stood
Or altar smoked; yet who more oft than he
In temples and at altars, when the priest
Turns atheist, as did Eli's sons, [1] who filled
With lust and violence the house of God?
In courts and palaces he also reigns, [2]
And in luxurious cities, where the noise
Of riot ascends above their loftiest towers,
And injury and outrage; and when night
Darkens the streets, then wander forth the sons
Of Belial, flown with insolence and wine.
Witness the streets of Sodom, and that night
In Gibeah, when the hospitable door
Exposed a matron, to avoid worse rape.
These were the prime in order and in might;
The rest were long to tell, though far renowned
The Ionian [3] gods—of [4] Javan's issue held
Gods, yet confessed later [5] than Heaven and Earth,
Their boasted parents—Titan, Heaven's first-born,
With his enormous brood, and birthright seized
By younger Saturn; he from mightier Jove,
His own and Rhea's son, like measure found;
So Jove usurping reigned. These, first in Crete
And Ida known, thence on the snowy top
Of cold Olympus ruled the middle air,
Their highest Heaven; or on the Delphian cliff,
Or in Dodona, and through all the bounds
Of Doric land; or who with Saturn old
Fled over Adria to the Hesperian [6] fields,
And o'er the Celtic roamed the utmost isles.
All these and more came flocking; but with looks
Downcast and damp, yet such wherein appeared
Obscure some glimpse of joy, to have found their Chief
Not in despair, to have found themselves not lost
In loss itself; which on his countenance cast
Like doubtful hue. But he, his wonted pride
Soon recollecting, with high words that bore
Semblance of worth, not substance, gently raised
Their fainting courage, and dispelled their fears.
Then straight commands that at the warlike sound
Of trumpets loud and clarions, be upreared
His mighty standard. That proud honor claimed
Azazel as his right, a Cherub tall;
Who forthwith from the glittering staff unfurled
The imperial ensign, which, full high advanced,
Shone like a meteor streaming to the wind,
With gems and golden luster rich emblazed,
Seraphic arms and trophies; all the while
Sonorous metal blowing martial sounds;
At which the universal host up-sent
A shout that tore Hell's concave, and beyond
Frighted the reign of Chaos and old Night.
All in a moment through the gloom were seen
Ten thousand banners rise into the air,
With orient colors waving; with them rose
A forest huge of spears; and thronging helms
Appeared, and serried shields in thick array
Of depth immeasurable. Anon they move
In perfect phalanx to the Dorian mood [7]
Of flutes and soft recorders [8]—such as raised
To highth of noblest temper heroes old
Arming to battle, and instead of rage
Deliberate valor breathed, firm and unmoved
With dread of death to flight or foul retreat;
Nor wanting power to mitigate and swage, [9]
With solemn touches, troubled thoughts, and chase
Anguish and doubt and fear and sorrow and pain
From mortal or immortal minds. Thus they,
Breathing united force with fixed thought,
Moved on in silence to soft pipes that charmed
Their painful steps o'er the burnt soil; and now
Advanced in view they stand, a horrid front
Of dreadful length and dazzling arms, in guise
Of warriors old, with ordered spear and shield,
Awaiting what command their mighty Chief
Had to impose. He through the armed files
Darts his experienced eye, and soon traverse
The whole battalion views—their order due,
Their visages and stature as of gods;
Their number last he sums. And now his heart
Distends with pride, and hardening in his strength
Glories; for never, since created man, [10]
Met such embodied force as, named with these,
Could merit more than that small infantry [11]
Warred on by cranes; though all the giant brood
Of Phlegra [12] with the heroic race were joined
That fought at Thebes and Ilium, on each side
Mixed with auxiliar gods; and what resounds
In fable or romance of Uther's son, [13]
Begirt with British and Armoric knights;
And all who since, [14] baptized or infidel,

[1] *I Samuel* ii, 12
[2] Perhaps alluding to conditions in England under Charles II; cf. VII, 32, p. 283.
[3] Grecian (a name traceable to Javan, Noah's grandson)
[4] by
[5] referring to the successive dynasties
[6] western, Italian
[7] a grave harmony, employed by the Spartans
[8] flageolets
[9] assuage
[10] since the creation of man (a Latinism)
[11] the pigmies; *Iliad* III, 6
[12] in Thrace
[13] King Arthur
[14] as described in French and Italian medieval romances

Jousted in Aspramont, or Montalban,
Damasco, or Marocco, or Trebisond;
Or whom Biserta sent from Afric shore
When Charlemain with all his peerage fell
By Fontarabbia.[1] Thus far these beyond
Compare of mortal prowess, yet observed[2]
Their dread commander. He, above the rest
In shape and gesture proudly eminent,
Stood like a tower; his form had yet not lost
All her original brightness, nor appeared
Less than Archangel ruined, and the excess
Of glory obscured; as when the sun new-risen
Looks through the horizontal misty air
Shorn of his beams, or from behind the moon,
In dim eclipse, disastrous twilight sheds
On half the nations, and with fear of change
Perplexes monarchs. Darkened so, yet shone
Above them all the Archangel; but his face
Deep scars of thunder had intrenched, and care
Sat on his faded cheek, but under brows
Of dauntless courage, and considerate pride
Waiting revenge. Cruel his eye, but cast
Signs of remorse and passion, to behold
The fellows of his crime, the followers rather
(Far other once beheld in bliss), condemned
Forever now to have their lot in pain;
Millions of Spirits for his fault amerced[3]
Of Heaven, and from eternal splendors flung
For his revolt; yet faithful how[4] they stood,
Their glory withered: as when Heaven's fire
Hath scathed the forest oaks or mountain pines,
With singed top their stately growth, though bare,
Stands on the blasted heath. He now prepared
To speak; whereat their doubled ranks they bend
From wing to wing, and half enclose him round
With all his peers; attention held them mute.
Thrice he assayed, and thrice, in spite of scorn,
Tears, such as Angels weep, burst forth. At last
Words interwove with sighs found out their way:
"O myriads of Immortal Spirits! O powers
Matchless, but with the Almighty!—and that strife
Was not inglorious, though the event[5] was dire,
As this place testifies, and this dire change,
Hateful to utter. But what power of mind,
Foreseeing or presaging, from the depth
Of knowledge past or present, could have feared
How such united force of gods, how such
As stood like these, could ever know repulse?
For who can yet believe, though after loss,
That all these puissant legions, whose exile
Hath emptied Heaven, shall fail to reascend,
Self-raised, and repossess their native seat?
For me, be witness all the host of Heaven,
If counsels different, or danger shunned
By me, have lost our hopes. But he who reigns
Monarch in Heaven, till then as one secure
Sat on his throne, upheld by old repute,
Consent or custom, and his regal state
Put forth at full, but still his strength concealed;
Which tempted our attempt,[6] and wrought our fall.
Henceforth his might we know, and know our own
So as not either to provoke, or dread
New war provoked. Our better part remains
To work in close design, by fraud or guile,
What force effected not; that he no less
At length from us may find, who overcomes
By force hath overcome but half his foe.
Space may produce new worlds; whereof so rife
There went a fame in Heaven that he ere long
Intended to create, and therein plant
A generation whom his choice regard
Should favor equal to the Sons of Heaven.
Thither, if but to pry, shall be perhaps
Our first eruption; thither or elsewhere;
For this infernal pit shall never hold
Celestial Spirits in bondage, nor the Abyss
Long under darkness cover. But these thoughts,
Full counsel must mature. Peace is despaired,
For who can think submission? War, then, war
Open or understood, must be resolved."
He spake; and, to confirm his words, out-flew
Millions of flaming swords, drawn from the thighs
Of mighty Cherubim; the sudden blaze
Far round illumined Hell. Highly they raged
Against the Highest, and fierce with grasped arms
Clashed on their sounding shields the din of war,
Hurling defiance toward the vault of Heaven.

[1] Fontarabbia, in northern Spain (perhaps purposely substituted for the pass of Roncesvalles, where, according to tradition, Charlemagne's rear guard was cut to pieces, though Charlemagne did not fall)
[2] these (though) thus far beyond compare of mortal prowess, yet observed (reverenced)
[3] deprived
[4] follows "behold," l. 605
[5] issue
[6] This word-play was severely condemned by Landor. Compare ll. 606, 666-667.

There stood a hill not far, whose grisly[1] top
Belched fire and rolling smoke; the rest entire
Shone with a glossy scurf, undoubted sign
That in his womb was hid metallic ore,
The work of sulphur.[2] Thither, winged with speed,
A numerous brigade hastened; as when bands
Of pioneers, with spade and pickaxe armed,
Forerun the royal camp, to trench a field,
Or cast a rampart. Mammon led them on,
Mammon, the least erected Spirit that fell
From Heaven, for even in Heaven his looks and thoughts
Were always downward bent, admiring more
The riches of Heaven's pavement, trodden gold,
Than aught divine or holy else enjoyed
In vision beatific. By him first
Men also, and by his suggestion taught,
Ransacked the Center,[3] and with impious hands
Rifled the bowels of their mother Earth
For treasures better hid. Soon had his crew
Opened into the hill a spacious wound,
And digged out ribs of gold. Let none admire[4]
That riches grow in Hell; that soil may best
Deserve the precious bane. And here let those
Who boast in mortal things, and wondering tell
Of Babel, and the works of Memphian kings,
Learn how their greatest monuments of fame,
And strength, and art, are easily outdone
By Spirits reprobate, and in an hour
What in an age they, with incessant toil
And hands innumerable, scarce perform.
Nigh on the plain, in many cells prepared,
That underneath had veins of liquid fire
Sluiced from the lake, a second multitude
With wondrous art founded[5] the massy ore,
Severing each kind, and scummed the bullion[6] dross.
A third as soon had formed within the ground
A various mold, and from the boiling cells
By strange conveyance filled each hollow nook:
As in an organ, from one blast of wind,
To many a row of pipes the sound-board breathes.
Anon out of the earth a fabric huge
Rose like an exhalation, with the sound
Of dulcet symphonies and voices sweet—
Built like a temple, where pilasters round
Were set, and Doric pillars overlaid
With golden architrave; nor did there want
Cornice or frieze, with bossy[7] sculptures graven;
The roof was fretted gold. Not Babylon,
Nor great Alcairo,[8] such magnificence
Equaled in all their glories, to enshrine
Belus or Serapis their gods, or seat
Their kings, when Egypt with Assyria strove
In wealth and luxury. The ascending pile
Stood fixed her stately highth, and straight the doors,
Opening their brazen folds, discover, wide
Within, her ample spaces o'er the smooth
And level pavement; from the arched roof,
Pendent by subtle magic, many a row
Of starry lamps and blazing cressets, fed
With naphtha and asphaltus, yielded light
As from a sky. The hasty multitude
Admiring entered, and the work some praise,
And some the architect. His hand was known
In Heaven by many a towered structure high,
Where sceptered Angels held their residence,
And sat as Princes, whom the supreme King
Exalted to such power, and gave to rule,
Each in his hierarchy, the Orders bright.
Nor was his name unheard or unadored
In ancient Greece; and in Ausonian[9] land
Men called him Mulciber;[10] and how he fell
From Heaven they fabled, thrown by angry Jove
Sheer o'er the crystal battlements; from morn
To noon he fell, from noon to dewy eve,
A summer's day; and with the setting sun
Dropped from the zenith, like a falling star,
On Lemnos, the Aegaean isle. Thus they relate,
Erring; for he with this rebellious rout
Fell long before; nor aught availed him now
To have built in Heaven high towers; nor did he scape
By all his engines,[11] but was headlong sent
With his industrious crew to build in Hell.
Meanwhile the winged heralds, by command
Of sovran power, with awful ceremony
And trumpet's sound, throughout the host proclaim
A solemn council forthwith to be held
At Pandemonium,[12] the high capital
Of Satan and his peers. Their summons called
From every band and squared regiment
By place or choice the worthiest; they anon
With hundreds and with thousands trooping came
Attended. All access was thronged; the gates
And porches wide, but chief the spacious hall
(Though like a covered field, where champions bold

[1] terrifying
[2] an early chemical theory
[3] Cf. l. 74.
[4] wonder
[5] melted
[6] base ore (used adjectively)
[7] in high relief
[8] Cairo
[9] Italian
[10] Vulcan
[11] contrivances
[12] "Hall of all Demons" (a word coined by Milton after the model of *Pantheon*)

Wont [1] ride in armed, and at the Soldan's [2] chair
Defied the best of Panim chivalry
To mortal combat, or career with lance)
Thick swarmed, both on the ground and in the air,
Brushed with the hiss of rustling wings. As bees
In springtime, when the Sun with Taurus rides,
Pour forth their populous youth about the hive
In clusters; they among fresh dews and flowers
Fly to and fro, or on the smoothed plank,
The suburb of their straw-built citadel,
New rubbed with balm, expatiate and confer [3]
Their state-affairs. So thick the aery crowd
Swarmed and were straitened, [4] till, the signal given,
Behold a wonder; they but now who seemed
In bigness to surpass Earth's giant sons,
Now less than smallest dwarfs, in narrow room
Throng numberless, like that pygmean race [5]
Beyond the Indian mount; or fairy elves,
Whose midnight revels, by a forest-side
Or fountain, some belated peasant sees,
Or dreams he sees, while overhead the Moon
Sits arbitress, and nearer to the Earth
Wheels her pale course; they, on their mirth and dance
Intent, with jocund music charm his ear;
At once with joy and fear his heart rebounds.
Thus incorporeal Spirits to smallest forms
Reduced their shapes immense, and were at large,
Though without number still, amidst the hall
Of that infernal court. But far within,
And in their own dimensions like themselves,
The great Seraphic Lords and Cherubim
In close recess and secret conclave sat,
A thousand demi-gods on golden seats,
Frequent and full. [6] After short silence then,
And summons read, the great consult [7] began.

Book II

THE ARGUMENT

The consulation begun. Satan debates whether another battle be [is] to be hazarded for the recovery of Heaven; some advise it, others dissuade. A third proposal is preferred, mentioned before by Satan, to search the truth of that prophecy or tradition in Heaven concerning another world, and another kind of creature, equal, or not much inferior, to themselves, about this time to be created. Their doubt who shall be sent on this difficult search: Satan, their chief, undertakes alone the voyage; is honored and applauded. The council thus ended, the rest betake them several ways and to several employments, as their inclinations lead them, to entertain the time till Satan return. He passes on his journey to Hell-gates, finds them shut, and who sat there to guard them; by whom at length they are opened, and discover to him the great gulf between Hell and Heaven; with what difficulty he passes through, directed by Chaos, the Power of that place, to the sight of this new World which he sought.

[1] used to
[2] Sultan's
[3] walk about and discuss
[4] contracted
[5] Cf. l. 575.
[6] close and all occupied
[7] a noun, like "compare," l. 588

High on a throne of royal state, which far
Outshone the wealth of Ormus [8] and of Ind,
Or where the gorgeous East with richest hand
Showers on her kings barbaric pearl and gold,
Satan exalted sat, [9] by merit raised
To that bad eminence; and, from despair
Thus high uplifted beyond hope, aspires
Beyond thus high, insatiate to pursue
Vain war with Heaven; and, by success [10] untaught,
His proud imaginations thus displayed:—
"Powers and Dominions, deities of Heaven!
For since no deep within her gulf can hold
Immortal vigor, though oppressed and fallen,
I give not Heaven for lost: from this descent
Celestial Virtues rising will appear
More glorious and more dread than from no fall,
And trust themselves to fear no second fate.
Me though just right, and the fixed laws of Heaven,
Did first create your leader, next, free choice,
With what besides, in council or in fight,
Hath been achieved of merit, yet this loss,
Thus far at least recovered, hath much more
Established in a safe, unenvied throne,
Yielded with full consent. The happier state
In Heaven, which follows dignity, might draw
Envy from each inferior; but who here
Will envy whom the highest place exposes
Foremost to stand against the Thunderer's aim,
Your bulwark, and condemns to greatest share
Of endless pain? Where there is then no good
For which to strive, no strife can grow up there

[8] an eastern island, once a diamond mart
[9] The imagery and language of this famous periodic opening evidently owe something to *The Faerie Queene,* I, iv, st. 8. The "barbaric gold" is from *Aeneid* II, 504.
[10] result

From faction; for none sure will claim in Hell
Precedence, none whose portion is so small
Of present pain that with ambitious mind
Will covet more. With this advantage then
To union, and firm faith, and firm accord,
More than can be in Heaven, we now return
To claim our just inheritance of old,
Surer to prosper than prosperity
Could have assured us; and by what best way,
Whether of open war or covert guile,
We now debate; who can advise may speak."
He ceased; and next him Moloch, sceptered king,
Stood up, the strongest and the fiercest Spirit
That fought in Heaven, now fiercer by despair.
His trust was with the Eternal to be deemed
Equal in strength, and rather than be less
Cared not to be at all; with that care lost
Went all his fear; of God, or Hell, or worse,
He recked not, and these words thereafter spake:
"My sentence[1] is for open war. Of wiles,
More unexpert, I boast not: them let those
Contrive who need, or when they need; not now.
For while they sit contriving, shall the rest—
Millions that stand in arms, and longing wait
The signal to ascend—sit lingering here,
Heaven's fugitives, and for their dwelling-place
Accept this dark opprobrious den of shame,
The prison of his tyranny who reigns
By our delay? No! Let us rather choose,
Armed with Hell-flames and fury, all at once
O'er Heaven's high towers to force resistless way,
Turning our tortures into horrid arms
Against the Torturer; when to meet the noise
Of his almighty engine he shall hear
Infernal thunder, and for lightning see
Black fire and horror shot with equal rage
Among his Angels, and his throne itself
Mixed with Tartarean sulphur and strange fire,
His own invented torments. But perhaps
The way seems difficult and steep to scale
With upright wing against a higher foe.
Let such bethink them, if the sleepy drench
Of that forgetful lake benumb not still,
That in our proper motion[2] we ascend
Up to our native seat; descent and fall
To us is adverse. Who but felt of late,
When the fierce foe hung on our broken rear
Insulting, and pursued us through the deep,
With what compulsion and laborious flight
We sunk thus low? The ascent is easy then;

[1] judgment
[2] Being of ethereal nature they would naturally rise.

The event is feared! Should we again provoke
Our stronger,[3] some worse way his wrath may find
To our destruction—if there be in Hell
Fear to be worse destroyed! What can be worse
Than to dwell here, driven out from bliss, condemned
In this abhorred deep to utter woe;
Where pain of unextinguishable fire
Must exercise us, without hope of end.
The vassals of his anger, when the scourge
Inexorably, and the torturing hour,
Calls us to penance? More destroyed than thus,
We should be quite abolished, and expire.
What fear we then? What doubt we to incense
His utmost ire? Which, to the highth enraged,
Will either quite consume us, and reduce
To nothing this essential[4]—happier far
Than miserable to have eternal being!—
Or if our substance be indeed divine,
And cannot cease to be, we are at worst
On this side nothing; and by proof we feel
Our power sufficient to disturb his Heaven,
And with perpetual inroads to alarm,
Though inaccessible, his fatal throne;
Which, if not victory, is yet revenge."
He ended frowning, and his look denounced
Desperate revenge, and battle dangerous
To less than gods. On the other side up rose
Belial, in act more graceful and humane;
A fairer person lost not Heaven; he seemed
For dignity composed, and high exploit.
But all was false and hollow; though his tongue
Dropped manna,[5] and could make the worse appear
The better reason, to perplex and dash
Maturest counsels; for his thoughts were low,
To vice industrious, but to nobler deeds
Timorous and slothful; yet he pleased the ear;
And with persuasive accent thus began:
"I should be much for open war, O Peers,
As not behind in hate, if what was urged
Main reason to persuade immediate war
Did not dissuade me most, and seem to cast
Ominous conjecture on the whole success;
When he who most excels in fact[6] of arms,
In what he counsels and in what excels
Mistrustful, grounds his courage on despair
And utter dissolution, as the scope
Of all his aim, after some dire revenge.

[3] superior (put as an imaginary argument)
[4] essence
[5] a sweet gum, exuding from shrubs (not the Biblical manna)
[6] feat

First, what revenge? The towers of Heaven are filled
With armed watch, that render all access
Impregnable: oft on the bordering deep
Encamp their legions, or with obscure wing
Scout far and wide into the realm of Night,
Scorning surprise. Or could we break our way
By force, and at our heels all Hell should rise
With blackest insurrection, to confound
Heaven's purest light, yet our great Enemy
All incorruptible, would on his throne
Sit unpolluted, and the ethereal mold,
Incapable of stain, would soon expel
Her mischief, and purge off the baser fire,
Victorious. Thus repulsed, our final hope
Is flat despair. We must exasperate
The Almighty Victor to spend all his rage;
And that must end us, that must be our cure—
To be no more. Sad cure! For who would lose,
Though full of pain, this intellectual being,
Those thoughts that wander through eternity,
To perish rather, swallowed up and lost
In the wide womb of uncreated Night,
Devoid of sense and motion? And who knows,
Let this be good,[1] whether our angry foe
Can give it, or will ever? How he can
Is doubtful; that he never will is sure.
Will he, so wise, let loose at once his ire,
Belike through impotence, or unaware,
To give his enemies their wish, and end
Them in his anger, whom his anger saves
To punish endless? 'Wherefore cease we then?'
Say they who counsel war; 'we are decreed,
Reserved, and destined to eternal woe; 161
Whatever doing, what can we suffer more,
What can we suffer worse?' Is this then worst,
Thus sitting, thus consulting, thus in arms?
What when we fled amain, pursued and struck
With Heaven's afflicting thunder, and besought
The deep to shelter us? This Hell then seemed
A refuge from those wounds. Or when we lay
Chained on the burning lake? That sure was worse.
What if the breath that kindled those grim fires,
Awaked, should blow them into sevenfold rage,
And plunge us in the flames; or from above
Should intermitted vengeance arm again
His red right hand to plague us? What if all
Her stores were opened, and this firmament
Of Hell should spout her cataracts of fire,
Impendent horrors, threatening hideous fall
One day upon our heads; while we perhaps
Designing or exhorting glorious war,
Caught in a fiery tempest, shall be hurled,

[1] supposing annihilation good

Each on his rock transfixed, the sport and prey
Of racking whirlwinds, or forever sunk
Under yon boiling ocean, wrapped in chains;
There to converse with everlasting groans,
Unrespited, unpitied, unreprieved,
Ages of hopeless end! This would be worse.
War therefore, open or concealed, alike
My voice dissuades: for what can[2] force or guile
With him, or who deceive his mind, whose eye
Views all things at one view? He from Heaven's highth
All these our motions vain sees and derides;
Not more almighty to resist our might
Than wise to frustrate all our plots and wiles.
Shall we then live thus vile, the race of Heaven
Thus trampled, thus expelled to suffer here
Chains and these torments? Better these than worse,
By my advice; since fate inevitable
Subdues us, and omnipotent decree,
The Victor's will. To suffer, as to do,
Our strength is equal, nor the law unjust
That so ordains; this[3] was at first resolved,
If we were wise, against so great a foe
Contending, and so doubtful what might fall.
I laugh, when those who at the spear are bold
And venturous, if that fail them, shrink, and fear
What yet they know must follow—to endure
Exile, or ignominy, or bonds, or pain,
The sentence of their conqueror. This is now
Our doom; which if we can sustain and bear,
Our Supreme Foe in time may much remit
His anger, and perhaps, thus far removed,
Not mind us not offending, satisfied
With what is punished; whence these raging fires
Will slacken, if his breath stir not their flames.
Our purer essence then will overcome
Their noxious vapor, or, inured, not feel;
Or, changed at length, and to the place conformed
In temper and in nature, will receive
Familiar the fierce heat; and, void of pain,
This horror will grow mild, this darkness light;
Besides what hope the never-ending flight
Of future days may bring, what chance, what change
Worth waiting—since our present lot appears
For happy[4] though but ill, for ill not worst,
If we procure not to ourselves more woe."
Thus Belial, with words clothed in reason's garb,

[2] avails
[3] viz., to abide the issue
[4] in respect to happiness

Counseled ignoble ease, and peaceful sloth,
Not peace; and after him thus Mammon spake:
"Either to disenthrone the King of Heaven
We war, if war be best, or to regain
Our own right lost. Him to unthrone we then
May hope, when everlasting Fate shall yield
To fickle Chance, and Chaos judge the strife.
The former, vain to hope, argues as vain
The latter; for what place can be for us
Within Heaven's bound, unless Heaven's Lord Supreme
We overpower? Suppose he should relent,
And publish grace to all, on promise made
Of new subjection; with what eyes could we
Stand in his presence, humble, and receive
Strict laws imposed, to celebrate his throne
With warbled hymns, and to his Godhead sing
Forced Hallelujahs; while he lordly sits
Our envied sovereign, and his altar breathes
Ambrosial odors and ambrosial flowers,
Our servile offerings? This must be our task
In Heaven, this our delight. How wearisome
Eternity so spent in worship paid
To whom we hate! Let us not then pursue—
By force impossible, by leave obtained
Unacceptable [1]—though in Heaven, our state
Of splendid vassalage; but rather seek
Our own good from ourselves, and from our own [2]
Live to ourselves, though in this vast recess,
Free, and to none accountable, preferring
Hard liberty before the easy yoke
Of servile pomp. Our greatness will appear
Then most conspicuous, when great things of small,
Useful of hurtful, prosperous of adverse,
We can create, and in what place soe'er
Thrive under evil, and work ease out of pain
Through labor and endurance. This deep world
Of darkness do we dread? How oft amidst
Thick clouds and dark doth Heaven's all-ruling Sire
Choose to reside, his glory unobscured,
And with the majesty of darkness round
Covers his throne, from whence deep thunders roar,
Mustering their rage, and Heaven resembles Hell!
As he our darkness, cannot we his light
Imitate when we please? This desert soil
Wants not her hidden luster, gems and gold;
Nor want we skill or art, from whence to raise
Magnificence; and what can Heaven show more?
Our torments also may in length of time
Become our elements, these piercing fires
As soft as now severe, our temper changed
Into their temper; which must needs remove
The sensible [3] of pain. All things invite
To peaceful counsels, and the settled state
Of order, how in safety best we may
Compose our present evils, with regard
Of what we are and where, dismissing quite
All thoughts of war. Ye have what I advise."
He scarce had finished, when such murmur filled
The assembly, as when hollow rocks retain
The sound of blustering winds, which all night long
Had roused the sea, now with hoarse cadence lull
Seafaring men o'erwatched, whose bark by chance,
Or pinnace, anchors in a craggy bay
After the tempest. Such applause was heard
As Mammon ended, and his sentence pleased,
Advising peace; for such another field
They dreaded worse than Hell; so much the fear
Of thunder and the sword of Michaël
Wrought still within them; and no less desire
To found this nether empire, which might rise,
By policy, and long process [4] of time,
In emulation opposite to Heaven.
Which when Beëlzebub perceived, than whom,
Satan except, none higher sat, with grave
Aspect he rose, and in his rising seemed
A pillar of state; deep on his front engraven
Deliberation sat and public care;
And princely counsel in his face yet shone,
Majestic, though in ruin. Sage he stood,
With Atlantean [5] shoulders fit to bear
The weight of mightiest monarchies; his look
Drew audience and attention still as night
Or summer's noontide air, while thus he spake:
"Thrones and Imperial Powers, Offspring of Heaven,
Ethereal Virtues! Or these titles now
Must we renounce, and, changing style, [6] be called
Princes of Hell? For so the popular vote
Inclines—here to continue, and build up here
A growing empire; doubtless! while we dream,
And know not that the King of Heaven hath doomed
This place our dungeon—not our safe retreat
Beyond his potent arm, to live exempt
From Heaven's high jurisdiction, in new league

[1] unac′ceptable
[2] resources
[3] sense
[4] process′
[5] Atlas-like
[6] appellation

Banded against his throne, but to remain
In strictest bondage, though thus far removed,
Under the inevitable curb, reserved [1]
His captive multitude. For he, be sure,
In highth or depth, still first and last will reign
Sole king, and of his kingdom lose no part
By our revolt, but over Hell extend
His empire, and with iron scepter rule
Us here, as with his golden those in Heaven.
What [2] sit we then projecting peace and war?
War hath determined us, and foiled with loss
Irreparable; terms of peace yet none
Vouchsafed or sought; for what peace will be given
To us enslaved, but custody severe,
And stripes, and arbitrary punishment
Inflicted? And what peace can we return,
But, to [3] our power, hostility and hate,
Untamed reluctance, and revenge, though slow,
Yet ever plotting how the Conqueror least
May reap his conquest, and may least rejoice
In doing what we most in suffering feel?
Nor will occasion want, nor shall we need
With dangerous expedition to invade
Heaven, whose high walls fear no assault or siege,
Or ambush from the Deep. What if we find
Some easier enterprise? There is a place
(If ancient and prophetic fame in Heaven
Err not), another World, the happy seat
Of some new race called Man, about this time
To be created like to us, though less
In power and excellence, but favored more
Of him who rules above; so was his will
Pronounced among the gods, and by an oath
That shook Heaven's whole circumference, confirmed.
Thither let us bend all our thoughts, to learn
What creatures there inhabit, of what mold
Or substance, how endued, and what their power,
And where their weakness; how attempted [4] best,
By force or subtlety. Though Heaven be shut,
And Heaven's high Arbitrator sit secure
In his own strength, this place may lie exposed,
The utmost border of his kingdom, left
To their defense who hold it; here, perhaps,
Some advantageous act may be achieved
By sudden onset; either with Hell-fire
To waste his whole creation, or possess
All as our own, and drive, as we were driven,
The puny [5] habitants; or if not drive,

[1] reserved for (A Latinism; cf. *arrive,* 409.)
[2] why
[3] to the extent of
[4] assailed
[5] from French *puis né,* later born

Seduce them to our party, [6] that their God
May prove their foe, and with repenting hand
Abolish his own works. This would surpass
Common revenge, and interrupt his joy
In our confusion, and our joy upraise
In his disturbance; when his darling sons,
Hurled headlong to partake with us, shall curse
Their frail original, and faded bliss—
Faded so soon! Advise if this be worth
Attempting, or to sit in darkness here
Hatching vain empires." Thus Beëlzebub
Pleaded his devilish counsel, first devised
By Satan, and in part proposed; for whence,
But from the author of all ill, could spring
So deep a malice, to confound the race
Of Mankind in one root, and Earth with Hell
To mingle and involve, done all to spite
The great Creator? But their spite still serves
His glory to augment. The bold design
Pleased highly those Infernal States, [7] and joy
Sparkled in all their eyes; with full assent
They vote. Whereat his speech he thus renews:
"Well have ye judged, well ended long debate,
Synod of gods! and, like to what ye are,
Great things resolved; which from the lowest deep
Will once more lift us up, in spite of fate,
Nearer our ancient seat—perhaps in view
Of those bright confines, whence, with neighboring arms
And opportune excursion, we may chance
Reënter Heaven; or else in some mild zone
Dwell not unvisited of Heaven's fair light,
Secure, and at the brightening orient beam
Purge off this gloom; the soft delicious air,
To heal the scar of these corrosive fires,
Shall breathe her balm. But first, whom shall we send
In search of this new world? whom shall we find
Sufficient? who shall tempt with wandering feet
The dark, unbottomed, infinite Abyss,
And through the palpable obscure [8] find out
His uncouth way, or spread his aery flight,
Upborne with indefatigable wings
Over the vast abrupt, [8] ere he arrive [9]
The happy isle? What strength, what art, can then
Suffice, or what evasion bear him safe
Through the strict senteries and stations thick
Of Angels watching round? Here he had need [10]

[6] side
[7] lords
[8] adjective used as noun
[9] arrive at
[10] would have need of

All circumspection, and we now no less[1]
Choice in our suffrage; for on whom we send,
The weight of all, and our last hope, relies."
This said, he sat; and expectation held
His look suspense, awaiting who appeared
To second, or oppose, or undertake
The perilous attempt; but all sat mute,
Pondering the danger with deep thoughts; and each
In other's countenance read his own dismay,
Astonished. None among the choice and prime
Of those Heaven-warring champions could be found
So hardy as to proffer or accept,
Alone, the dreadful voyage; till at last
Satan, whom now transcendent glory raised
Above his fellows, with monarchal pride
Conscious of highest worth, unmoved thus spake:
"O Progeny of Heaven! Empyreal Thrones!
With reason hath deep silence and demur
Seized us, though undismayed. Long is the way
And hard, that out of Hell leads up to Light;
Our prison strong, this huge convex of fire,
Outrageous to devour, immures us round
Ninefold; and gates of burning adamant,
Barred over us, prohibit all egress.
These passed, if any pass, the void profound
Of unessential[2] Night receives him next,
Wide-gaping, and with utter loss of being
Threatens him, plunged in that abortive[3] gulf.
If thence he scape into whatever world,
Or unknown region, what remains him less
Than unknown dangers and as hard escape?
But I should ill become this throne, O Peers,
And this imperial sovereignty, adorned
With splendor, armed with power, if aught proposed
And judged of public moment, in the shape
Of difficulty or danger, could deter
Me from attempting. Wherefore do I assume
These royalties, and not refuse to reign,
Refusing[4] to accept as great a share
Of hazard as of honor, due alike
To him who reigns, and so much to him due
Of hazard more, as he above the rest
High honored sits? Go therefore, mighty Powers,
Terror of Heaven, though fallen; intend[5] at home,
While here shall be our home, what best may ease
The present misery, and render Hell
More tolerable; if there be cure or charm
To respite, or deceive, or slack the pain
Of this ill mansion; intermit no watch
Against a wakeful foe, while I abroad
Through all the coasts of dark destruction seek
Deliverance for us all; this enterprise
None shall partake with me." Thus saying, rose
The Monarch, and prevented all reply;
Prudent, lest, from his resolution raised,[6]
Others among the chief might offer now
(Certain to be refused) what erst they feared,
And, so refused, might in opinion stand
His rivals, winning cheap the high repute
Which he through hazard huge must earn. But they
Dreaded not more the adventure than his voice
Forbidding; and at once with him they rose.
Their rising all at once was as the sound
Of thunder heard remote. Toward him they bend
With awful reverence prone; and as a god
Extol him equal to the Highest in Heaven.
Nor failed they to express how much they praised
That for the general safety he despised
His own; for neither do the Spirits damned
Lose all their virtue—lest bad men should[7] boast
Their spacious deeds on Earth, which glory excites,
Or close ambition varnished o'er with zeal.
Thus they their doubtful consultations dark
Ended, rejoicing in their matchless Chief;
As when from mountain-tops the dusky clouds
Ascending, while the North-wind sleeps, o'erspread
Heaven's cheerful face, the louring element
Scowls o'er the darkened landskip snow or shower;
If chance the radiant sun with farewell sweet
Extend his evening beam, the fields revive,
The birds their notes renew, and bleating herds
Attest their joy, that hill and valley rings.
Oh, shame to men! Devil with devil damned
Firm concord holds; men only disagree
Of creatures rational, though under hope
Of heavenly grace; and, God proclaiming peace,
Yet live in hatred, enmity, and strife
Among themselves, and levy cruel wars,
Wasting the Earth, each other to destroy.
As if (which might induce us to accord)
Man had not hellish foes enow besides,
That day and night for his destruction wait!
The Stygian council thus dissolved; and forth
In order came the grand Infernal Peers;

[1] Supply "need."
[2] without substance
[3] destructive (bringing to naught)
[4] if I refuse
[5] consider
[6] taking courage
[7] as a warning lest bad men should, etc.

Midst came their mighty Paramount, and seemed
Alone [1] the antagonist of Heaven, nor less
Than Hell's dread Emperor, with pomp supreme,
And god-like imitated state; him round
A globe of fiery Seraphim enclosed
With bright emblazonry, and horrent [2] arms,
Then of their session ended they bid cry
With trumpet's regal sound the great result.
Toward the four winds four speedy Cherubim
Put to their mouths the sounding alchymy, [3]
By herald's voice explained; the hollow Abyss
Heard far and wide, and all the host of Hell
With deafening shout returned them loud acclaim.
Thence more at ease their minds, and somewhat raised
By false presumptuous hope, the ranged powers
Disband; and, wandering, each his several way
Pursues, as inclination or sad choice
Leads him perplexed, where he may likeliest find
Truce to his restless thoughts, and entertain
The irkesome hours, till his great Chief return.
Part on the plain, or in the air sublime, [4]
Upon the wing or in swift race contend,
As at the Olympian games or Pythian fields;
Part curb their fiery steeds, or shun the goal [5]
With rapid wheels, or fronted [6] brigades [7] form:
As when, to warn proud cities, war appears
Waged in the troubled sky, and armies rush
To battle in the clouds; before each van
Prick forth the aery knights, and couch their spears,
Till thickest legions close; with feats of arms
From either end of Heaven the welkin burns.
Others, with vast Typhoean [8] rage more fell,
Rend up both rocks and hills, and ride the air
In whirlwind; Hell scarce holds the wild uproar;
As when Alcides [9] from Oechalia crowned
With conquest, felt the envenomed robe, and tore
Through pain up by the roots Thessalian pines,
And Lichas from the top of Oeta threw
Into the Euboic sea. Others, more mild,
Retreated in a silent valley, sing
With notes angelical to many a harp
Their own heroic deeds and hapless fall

[1] in himself
[2] bristling
[3] metallic compound
[4] uplifted
[5] avoid striking the column that marks the turning point (description taken from the ancient Grecian national games, the Olympian, Pythian, etc.)
[6] confronting
[7] brig'ades
[8] See Book I. 199.
[9] Hercules (referring to the story of the revenge of Nessus)

By doom of battle; and complain that Fate
Free Virtue should enthrall to Force or Chance.
Their song was partial, but the harmony
(What could it less when Spirits immortal sing?)
Suspended Hell, and took with ravishment
The thronging audience. In discourse more sweet
(For eloquence the soul, song charms the sense)
Others apart sat on a hill retired,
In thoughts more elevate, and reasoned high
Of providence, foreknowledge, will, and fate,
Fixed fate, free will, foreknowledge absolute;
And found no end, in wandering mazes lost.
Of good and evil much they argued then,
Of happiness and final misery,
Passion and apathy, and glory and shame,
Vain wisdom all, and false philosophy!
Yet with a pleasing sorcery could charm
Pain for a while or anguish, and excite
Fallacious hope, or arm the obdured breast
With stubborn patience as with triple steel.
Another part, in squadrons and gross bands,
On bold adventure to discover wide
That dismal world, if any clime perhaps
Might yield them easier habitation, bend
Four ways their flying march, along the banks
Of four infernal rivers that disgorge
Into the burning lake their baleful streams:
Abhorred Styx, the flood of deadly hate;
Sad Acheron of sorrow, black and deep;
Cocytus, named of lamentation loud
Heard on the rueful stream; fierce Phlegethon,
Whose waves of torrent fire inflame with rage.
Far off from these a slow and silent stream,
Lethe, the river of oblivion, rolls
Her watery labyrinth, whereof who drinks
Forthwith his former state and being forgets,
Forgets both joy and grief, pleasure and pain.
Beyond this flood a frozen continent
Lies dark and wild, beat with perpetual storms
Of whirlwind and dire hail, which on firm land
Thaws not, but gathers heap, and ruin seems
Of ancient pile; [10] all else deep snow and ice,
A gulf profound as that Serbonian bog [11]
Betwixt Damiata and Mount Casius old,
Where armies whole have sunk; the parching air
Burns frore, [12] and cold performs the effect of fire.
Thither, by harpy-footed Furies haled,
At certain revolutions all the damned
Are brought; and feel by turns the bitter change
Of fierce extremes, extremes by change more fierce,
From beds of raging fire to starve [13] in ice

[10] masonry
[11] Herodotus II, 6; III, 5
[12] frosty
[13] freeze

Their soft ethereal warmth, and there to pine
Immovable, infixed, and frozen round
Periods of time; thence hurried back to fire.
They ferry over this Lethean sound
Both to and fro, their sorrow to augment,
And wish and struggle, as they pass to reach
The tempting stream, with one small drop to lose
In sweet forgetfulness all pain and woe,
All in one moment, and so near the brink;
But Fate withstands, and, to oppose the attempt
Medusa with Gorgonian terror guards
The ford, and of itself the water flies
All taste of living wight, as once it fled
The lip of Tantalus. Thus roving on
In confused march forlorn, the adventurous bands,
With shuddering horror pale, and eyes aghast,
Viewed first their lamentable lot, and found
No rest. Through many a dark and dreary vale
They passed, and many a region dolorous,
O'er many a frozen, many a fiery Alp,[1]
Rocks, caves, lakes, fens, bogs, dens, and shades of death—
A universe of death, which God by curse
Created evil, for evil only good;
Where all life dies, death lives, and Nature breeds,
Perverse, all monstrous, all prodigious things,
Abominable, inutterable, and worse
Than fables yet have feigned, or fear conceived,
Gorgons, and Hydras, and Chimaeras dire.
  Meanwhile the Adversary of God and Man,
Satan, with thoughts inflamed of highest design,
Puts on swift wings, and toward the gates of Hell
Explores his solitary flight; sometimes
He scours the right hand coast, sometimes the left;
Now shaves with level wing the deep, then soars
Up to the fiery concave towering high.
As when far off at sea a fleet descried
Hangs in the clouds, by equinoctial winds
Close sailing from Bengala, or the isles
Of Ternate and Tidore,[2] whence merchants bring
Their spicy drugs; they on the trading flood,
Through the wide Ethiopian[3] to the Cape,
Ply stemming nightly toward the pole; so seemed
Far off the flying Fiend. At last appear
Hell-bounds, high reaching to the horrid roof,
And thrice threefold the gates; three folds were brass,
Three iron, three of adamantine rock
Impenetrable, impaled with circling fire,
Yet unconsumed. Before the gates there sat
On either side a formidable Shape.
The one seemed woman to the waist, and fair,
But ended foul in many a scaly fold
Voluminous and vast, a serpent armed
With mortal sting. About her middle round
A cry of Hell-hounds never-ceasing barked
With wide Cerberean[4] mouths full loud, and rung
A hideous peal; yet, when they list, would creep
If aught disturbed their noise, into her womb,
And kennel there, yet there still barked and howled
Within unseen. Far less abhorred than these
Vexed Scylla, bathing in the sea that parts
Calabria from the hoarse Trinacrian shore;[5]
Nor uglier follow the night hag, when, called
In secret, riding through the air she comes,
Lured with the smell of infant blood, to dance
With Lapland witches, while the laboring moon
Eclipses at their charms. The other Shape—
If shape it might be called that shape had none
Distinguishable in member, joint, or limb;
Or substance might be called that shadow seemed,
For each seemed either—black it stood as Night,
Fierce as ten furies, terrible as Hell,
And shook a dreadful dart; what seemed his head
The likeness of a kingly crown had on.
Satan was now at hand, and from his seat
The monster moving onward came as fast,
With horrid strides; Hell trembled as he strode.
The undaunted Fiend what this might be admired—[6]
Admired, not feared—God and his Son except,
Created thing naught valued he nor shunned—
And with disdainful look thus first began:
  "Whence and what art thou, execrable Shape,
That dar'st, though grim and terrible, advance
Thy miscreated front athwart my way
To yonder gates? Through them I mean to pass,
That be assured, without leave asked of thee.

[1] mount
[2] two of the Molucca islands
[3] Indian Ocean
[4] like those of Cerberus, the three-headed monster that guarded Hades
[5] Through Circe's jealousy, says Ovid, the lower part of Scylla's body was transformed into barking dogs; whereupon, throwing herself into the sea, she was changed into a rock. The next simile is drawn from Scandinavian superstition.
[6] wondered

Retire; or taste thy folly, and learn by proof,
Hell-born, not to contend with Spirits of Heaven."
To whom the Goblin, full of wrath, replied:
"Art thou that Traitor-Angel, art thou he
Who first broke peace in Heaven and faith, till then
Unbroken, and in proud rebellious arms
Drew after him the third part of Heaven's sons,
Conjured against the Highest, for which both thou
And they, outcast from God, are here condemned
To waste eternal days in woe and pain?
And reckon'st thou thyself with Spirits of Heaven,
Hell-doomed, and breath'st defiance here and scorn,
Where I reign king, and, to enrage thee more,
Thy king and lord? Back to thy punishment,
False fugitive, and to thy speed add wings,
Lest with a whip of scorpions I pursue
Thy lingering, or with one stroke of this dart
Strange horror seize thee, and pangs unfelt before."
  So spake the grisly Terror, and in shape,
So speaking and so threatening, grew tenfold
More dreadful and deform. On the other side,
Incensed with indignation, Satan stood
Unterrified, and like a comet burned,
That fires the length of Ophiuchus huge [1]
In the arctic sky, and from his horrid hair
Shakes pestilence and war. Each at the head
Leveled his deadly aim; their fatal hands
No second stroke intend; and such a frown
Each cast at the other, as when two black clouds,
With Heaven's artillery fraught, come rattling on
Over the Caspian, then stand front to front
Hovering a space, till winds the signal blow
To join their dark encounter in mid-air—
So frowned the mighty combatants, that Hell
Grew darker at their frown; so matched they stood;
For never but once more was either like
To meet so great a foe. And now great deeds
Had been achieved, whereof all Hell had rung,
Had not the snaky Sorceress that sat
Fast by Hell-gate and kept the fatal key,
Risen, and with hideous outcry rushed between.
  "O father, what intends thy hand," she cried,
"Against thy only son? What fury, O son,
Possesses thee to bend that mortal dart
Against thy father's head? and know'st for whom?
For him who sits above, and laughs the while
At thee ordained his drudge, to execute
Whate'er his wrath, which he calls justice, bids—
His wrath, which one day will destroy ye both!"
  She spake, and at her words the hellish Pest
Forbore. Then these to her Satan returned:
  "So strange thy outcry, and thy words so strange
Thou interposest, that my sudden hand,
Prevented, spares to tell thee yet by deeds
What it intends, till first I know of thee
What thing thou art, thus double-formed, and why,
In this infernal vale first met, thou call'st
Me father, and that phantasm call'st my son.
I know thee not, nor ever saw till now
Sight more detestable than him and thee."
  To whom thus the Portress of Hell-gate replied:
"Hast thou forgot me then, and do I seem
Now in thine eye so foul, once deemed so fair
In Heaven, when at the assembly, and in sight
Of all the Seraphim with thee combined
In bold conspiracy against Heaven's King,
All on a sudden miserable pain
Surprised thee; dim thine eyes, and dizzy swum
In darkness, while thy head flames thick and fast
Threw forth, till on the left side opening wide,
Likest to thee in shape and countenance bright,
Then shining heavenly fair, a goddess armed,
Out of thy head I sprung? [2] Amazement seized
All the host of Heaven. Back they recoiled afraid
At first, and called me *Sin,* and for a sign
Portentous held me; but, familiar grown,
I pleased, and with attractive graces won
The most averse; thee chiefly, who full oft
Thyself in me thy perfect image viewing
Becam'st enamoured; and such joy thou took'st
With me in secret, that my womb conceived
A growing burden. Meanwhile war arose,
And fields were fought in Heaven; wherein remained
(For what could else?) to our Almighty Foe
Clear victory, to our part loss and rout
Through all the Empyrean. Down they fell,
Driven headlong from the pitch of Heaven, down
Into this deep; and in the general fall
I also. At which time this powerful key
Into my hands was given, with charge to keep
These gates forever shut, which none can pass
Without my opening. Pensive here I sat

[1] a northern constellation

[2] Milton draws from pagan myths with especial freedom in describing his evil characters and scenes.

Alone; but long I sat not, till my womb,
Pregnant by thee, and now excessive grown,
Prodigious motion felt and rueful throes.
At last this odious offspring whom thou seest,
Thine own begotten, breaking violent way,
Tore through my entrails, that, with fear and pain
Distorted, all my nether shape thus grew
Transformed; but he, my inbred enemy,
Forth issued, brandishing his fatal dart,
Made to destroy. I fled, and cried out *Death!*
Hell trembled at the hideous name, and sighed
From all her caves, and back resounded *Death!*
I fled; but he pursued (though more, it seems,
Inflamed with lust than rage) and, swifter far,
Me overtook, his mother, all dismayed,
And, in embraces forcible and foul
Engendering with me, of that rape begot
These yelling monsters, that with ceaseless cry
Surround me, as thou saw'st, hourly conceived
And hourly born, with sorrow infinite
To me; for, when they list, into the womb
That bred them they return, and howl, and gnaw
My bowels, their repast; then, bursting forth
Afresh, with conscious terrors vex me round,
That rest or intermission none I find.
Before mine eyes in opposition sits
Grim Death, my son and foe, who sets them on,
And me, his parent, would full soon devour
For want of other prey, but that he knows
His end with mine involved, and knows that I
Should prove a bitter morsel, and his bane,
Whenever that shall be; so Fate pronounced.
But thou, O father, I forewarn thee, shun
His deadly arrow; neither vainly hope
To be invulnerable in those bright arms,
Though tempered heavenly; for that mortal dint,[1]
Save he who reigns above, none can resist."
She finished; and the subtle Fiend his lore
Soon learned, now milder, and thus answered smooth:
"Dear daughter—since thou claim'st me for thy sire,
And my fair son here show'st me, the dear pledge
Of dalliance had with thee in Heaven, and joys
Then sweet, now sad to mention, through dire change
Befallen us unforeseen, unthought of—know,
I come no enemy, but to set free
From out this dark and dismal house of pain
Both him and thee, and all the Heavenly host
Of Spirits that, in our just pretenses [2] armed,
Fell with us from on high. From them I go
This uncouth errand sole, and one for all
Myself expose, with lonely steps to tread
The unfounded Deep, and through the void immense
To search with wandering quest a place foretold
Should be—and by concurring signs, ere now
Created vast and round—a place of bliss
In the purlieus of Heaven; and therein placed
A race of upstart creatures, to supply
Perhaps our vacant room, though more removed,
Lest Heaven, surcharged with potent multitude,
Might hap to move new broils. Be this, or aught
Than this more secret, now designed, I haste
To know; and, this once known, shall soon return,
And bring ye to the place where thou and Death
Shall dwell at ease, and up and down unseen
Wing silently the buxom [3] air, embalmed
With odors. There ye shall be fed and filled
Immeasurably; all things shall be your prey."
He ceased; for both seemed highly pleased, and Death
Grinned horrible a ghastly smile, to hear
His famine should be filled, and blessed his maw
Destined to that good hour. No less rejoiced
His mother bad, and thus bespake her sire:
"The key of this infernal pit, by due
And by command of Heaven's all-powerful King,
I keep, by him forbidden to unlock
These adamantine gates; against all force
Death ready stands to interpose his dart,
Fearless to be o'ermatched by living might.
But what owe I to his commands above,
Who hates me, and hath hither thrust me down
Into this gloom of Tartarus profound,
To sit in hateful office here confined,
Inhabitant of Heaven and Heavenly-born,
Here in perpetual agony and pain,
With terrors and with clamors compassed round
Of mine own brood, that on my bowels feed?
Thou art my father, thou my author, thou
My being gav'st me; whom should I obey
But thee? whom follow? Thou wilt bring me soon
To that new world of light and bliss, among
The gods who live at ease, where I shall reign
At thy right hand voluptuous, as beseems
Thy daughter and thy darling, without end."
Thus saying, from her side the fatal key,

[1] blow [2] claims

[3] yielding

Sad instrument of all our woe, she took;
And, toward the gate rolling her bestial train,
Forthwith the huge portcullis high up-drew,
Which but herself not all the Stygian Powers
Could once have moved; then in the keyhole turns
The intricate wards, and every bolt and bar
Of massy iron or solid rock with ease
Unfastens. On a sudden open fly,
With impetuous recoil and jarring sound,
The infernal doors, and on their hinges grate
Harsh thunder, that the lowest bottom shook
Of Erebus.[1] She opened; but to shut
Excelled her power. The gates wide open stood,
That with extended wings a bannered host,
Under spread ensigns marching, might pass through
With horse and chariots ranked in loose array;
So wide they stood, and like a furnace-mouth
Cast forth redounding smoke and ruddy flame.
Before their eyes in sudden view appear
The secrets of the hoary Deep, a dark
Illimitable ocean, without bound,
Without dimension; where length, breadth, and highth,
And time, and place, are lost; where eldest Night
And Chaos, ancestors of Nature, hold
Eternal anarchy, amidst the noise
Of endless wars, and by confusion stand.
For Hot, Cold, Moist, and Dry, four champions fierce,
Strive here for mastery, and to battle bring
Their embryon[2] atoms; they around the flag
Of each his faction, in their several clans,
Light-armed or heavy, sharp, smooth, swift or slow,
Swarm populous, unnumbered as the sands
Of Barca or Cyrene's torrid soil,
Levied to side with warring winds, and poise
Their lighter wings. To whom these most adhere,
He rules a moment; Chaos umpire sits,
And by decision more embroils the fray
By which he reigns; next him, high arbiter,
Chance governs all. Into this wild Abyss,
The womb of nature, and perhaps her grave,
Of neither sea, nor shore, nor air, nor fire,
But all these in their pregnant causes mixed
Confusedly, and which thus must ever fight,
Unless the Almighty Maker them ordain
His dark materials to create more worlds—
Into this wild Abyss the wary fiend
Stood on the brink of Hell and looked awhile,
Pondering his voyage; for no narrow frith
He had to cross. Nor was his ear less pealed
With noises loud and ruinous (to compare
Great things with small) than when Bellona[3] storms
With all her battering engines, bent to rase
Some capital city; or less than if this frame
Of Heaven were falling, and these elements
In mutiny had from her axle torn
The steadfast Earth. At last his sail-broad vans
He spreads for flight, and in the surging smoke
Uplifted spurns the ground; thence many a league,
As in a cloudy chair, ascending rides
Audacious; but, that seat soon failing, meets
A vast vacuity; all unawares,
Fluttering his pennons vain, plumb-down he drops
Ten thousand fathom deep, and to this hour
Down had been falling, had not by ill chance
The strong rebuff of some tumultuous cloud,
Instinct with fire and niter, hurried him
As many miles aloft. That fury stayed—
Quenched in a boggy Syrtis,[4] neither sea,
Nor good dry land—nigh foundered, on he fares,
Treading the crude consistence, half on foot,
Half flying; behooves him[5] now both oar and sail.
As when a gryphon through the wilderness
With winged course, o'er hill or moory dale,
Pursues the Arimaspian,[6] who by stealth
Had from his wakeful custody purloined
The guarded gold; so eagerly the Fiend
O'er bog or steep, through strait, rough, dense, or rare,
With head, hands, wings, or feet, pursues his way,
And swims, or sinks, or wades, or creeps, or flies.
At length a universal hubbub wild
Of stunning sounds and voices all confused,
Borne through the hollow dark, assaults his ear
With loudest vehemence. Thither he plies
Undaunted, to meet there whatever Power
Or Spirit of the nethermost Abyss
Might in that noise reside, of whom to ask
Which way the nearest coast of darkness lies
Bordering on light; when straight behold the throne
Of Chaos, and his dark pavilion spread
Wide on the wasteful Deep! With him enthroned
Sat sable-vested Night, eldest of things,
The consort of his reign; and by them stood

[1] "Darkness," the Virgilian name for hell
[2] rudimentary
[3] Roman goddess of war [4] quicksand [5] needs he
[6] "It is said the Arimaspians, a one-eyed people, steal gold from the griffins."—Herodotus III, 116.

Orcus and Ades, and the dreaded name
Of Demogorgan;[1] Rumor next, and Chance,
And Tumult, and Confusion, all embroiled,
And Discord with a thousand various mouths.
To whom Satan, turning boldly, thus: "Ye Powers
And Spirits of this nethermost Abyss,
Chaos and ancient Night, I come no spy,
With purpose to explore or to disturb
The secrets of your realm; but, by constraint
Wandering this darksome desert, as my way
Lies through your spacious empire up to light,
Alone and without guide, half lost, I seek
What readiest path leads where your gloomy bounds
Confine with[2] Heaven; or if some other place,
From your dominion won, the Ethereal King
Possesses lately, thither to arrive
I travel this profound. Direct my course;
Directed, no mean recompense it brings
To your behoof, if I that region lost,
All usurpation thence expelled, reduce
To her original darkness and your sway
(Which is my present journey), and once more
Erect the standard there of ancient Night.
Yours be the advantage all, mine the revenge!"
Thus Satan; and him thus the Anarch[3] old,
With faltering speech and visage incomposed,
Answered: "I know thee, stranger, who thou art;
That mighty leading Angel, who of late
Made head against Heaven's King, though overthrown.
I saw and heard; for such a numerous host
Fled not in silence through the frighted deep,
With ruin upon ruin, rout on rout,
Confusion worse confounded; and Heaven-gates
Poured out by millions her victorious bands,
Pursuing. I upon my frontiers here
Keep residence; if all I can will serve
That little which is left so to defend,
Encroached on still through our intestine broils
Weakening the scepter of old Night; first Hell,
Your dungeon, stretching far and wide beneath;
Now lately Heaven and Earth, another world
Hung o'er my realm, linked in a golden chain
To that side Heaven from whence your legions fell.
If that way be your walk, you have not far;
So much the nearer danger. Go, and speed!
Havoc, and spoil, and ruin, are my gain."
He ceased; and Satan stayed not to reply,
But, glad that now his sea should find a shore,
With fresh alacrity and force renewed
Springs upward like a pyramid of fire
Into the wild expanse, and through the shock
Of fighting elements, on all sides round
Environed, wins his way; harder beset
And more endangered, than when Argo passed
Through Bosporus betwixt the justling rocks;
Or when Ulysses on the larboard shunned
Charybdis, and by the other whirlpool steered.
So he with difficulty and labor hard
Moved on; with difficulty and labor he;
But, he once passed, soon after, when Man fell,
Strange alteration! Sin and Death amain,
Following his track (such was the will of Heaven)
Paved after him a broad and beaten way
Over the dark Abyss, whose boiling gulf
Tamely endured a bridge of wondrous length,
From Hell continued, reaching the utmost orb
Of this frail World;[4] by which the Spirits perverse
With easy intercourse pass to and fro
To tempt or punish mortals, except whom
God and good Angels guard by special grace.
But now at last the sacred influence[5]
Of light appears, and from the walls of Heaven
Shoots far into the bosom of dim Night
A glimmering dawn. Here Nature first begins
Her farthest verge, and Chaos to retire,
As from her outmost works, a broken foe,
With tumult less and with less hostile din;
That[6] Satan with less toil, and now with ease,
Wafts on the calmer wave by dubious light,
And, like a weather-beaten vessel, holds
Gladly the port, though shrouds and tackle torn;
Or in the emptier waste, resembling air,
Weighs his spread wings, at leisure to behold
Far off the empyreal Heaven, extended wide
In circuit, undetermined square or round,
With opal towers, and battlements adorned
Of living sapphire, once his native seat;
And, fast by, hanging in a golden chain,
This pendent World, in bigness as a star
Of smallest magnitude close by the moon.
Thither, full fraught with mischievous revenge,
Accurst, and in a cursed hour, he hies.

[1] Names of rather vague significance, sufficiently defined in 969; it is said that the name of Demogorgon was never uttered until a Christian writer of the fourth century broke the spell.

[2] border on

[3] word first used by Milton

[4] By world is meant the starry universe with the earth at the center. The Ptolemaic theory held the universe to consist of ten concentric transparent, revolving spheres, each carrying with it its own body—Moon, Mercury, Venus, Sun, Mars, Jupiter, Saturn, Fixed Stars, with finally the Crystalline Sphere, and the Primum Mobile ("first movable," primary source of motion). From their revolutions came, according to Pythagoras, the "music of the spheres."

[5] perhaps literally "inflow"

[6] so that

From Book III

[Invocation to Light][1]

Hail, holy Light, offspring of Heaven first-born!
Or of the eternal coeternal beam,
May I express thee unblamed? Since God is light,
And never but in unapproached light
Dwelt from eternity—dwelt then in thee,
Bright effluence of bright essence increate![2]
Or hear'st thou rather[3] pure Ethereal stream,
Whose fountain who shall tell? Before the Sun,
Before the Heavens, thou wert, and at the voice
Of God, as with a mantle, didst invest
The rising World of waters dark and deep,
Won from the void and formless Infinite!
Thee I revisit now with bolder wing,
Escaped the Stygian Pool, though long detained
In that obscure sojourn, while in my flight,
Through utter and through middle darkness borne,
With other notes than to the Orphean lyre
I sung of Chaos and eternal Night,
Taught by the Heavenly Muse to venture down
The dark descent, and up to re-ascend,
Though hard and rare. Thee I revisit safe,
And feel thy sovereign vital lamp; but thou
Revisit'st not these eyes, that roll in vain
To find thy piercing ray, and find no dawn;
So thick a drop serene[4] hath quenched their orbs
Or dim suffusion veiled. Yet not the more
Cease I to wander where the Muses haunt
Clear spring, or shady grove, or sunny hill,
Smit with the love of sacred song; but chief
Thee, Sion, and the flowery brooks beneath,
That wash thy hallowed feet, and warbling flow,
Nightly I visit. Nor sometimes forget
Those other two equaled with me in fate,
So were I[5] equaled with them in renown,
Blind Thamyris and blind Maeonides,[6]
And Tiresias and Phineus, prophets old.
Then feed on thoughts that voluntary move
Harmonious numbers; as the wakeful bird
Sings darkling, and, in shadiest covert hid,
Tunes her nocturnal note. Thus with the year
Seasons return; but not to me returns
Day, or the sweet approach of even or morn
Or sight of vernal bloom, or summer's rose,
Or flocks, or herds, or human face divine;
But cloud instead and ever-during dark
Surrounds me, from the cheerful ways of men
Cut off, and, for the book of knowledge fair,
Presented with a universal blank
Of Nature's works, to me expunged and rased,
And wisdom at one entrance quite shut out.
So much the rather thou, Celestial Light,
Shine inward, and the mind through all her powers
Irradiate; there plant eyes; all mist from thence
Purge and disperse, that I may see and tell
Of things invisible to mortal sight.

. . . .

[1] Milton speaks here in his own person; it is to be remembered that he was blind (Cf. line 23).
[2] uncreated
[3] wouldst rather be called
[4] the *gutta serena,* supposed cause of blindness
[5] would I were so
[6] Homer, who mentions Thamyris as another blind bard

From Book IV

[Satan in Sight of Eden][7]

. . . . .

Sometimes toward Eden, which now in his view
Lay pleasant, his grieved look he fixes sad;
Sometimes toward Heaven and the full-blazing sun,
Which now sat high in his meridian tower;
Then, much revolving, thus in sighs began:
"O thou that, with surpassing glory crowned,
Look'st from thy sole dominion like the god
Of this new World—at whose sight all the stars
Hide their diminished heads—to thee I call,
But with no friendly voice, and add thy name,
O Sun, to tell thee how I hate thy beams,
That bring to my remembrance from what state
I fell, how glorious once above thy sphere,
Till pride and worse ambition threw me down,
Warring in Heaven against Heaven's matchless King!
Ah, wherefore? He deserved no such return
From me, whom he created what I was
In that bright eminence, and with his good
Upbraided none; nor was his service hard.
What could be less than to afford him praise,
The easiest recompense, and pay him thanks,
How due? Yet all his good proved ill in me,
And wrought but malice. Lifted up so high,
Isdained[8] subjection, and thought one step higher
Would set me highest, and in a moment quit
The debt immense of endless gratitude,
So burdensome, still paying, still to owe;
Forgetful what from him I still received;
And understood not that a grateful mind
By owing owes not, but still pays, at once

[7] Satan has just alighted upon Mount Niphates, in Armenia
[8] disdained

Indebted and discharged—what burden then?
Oh, had his powerful destiny ordained
Me some inferior Angel, I had stood
Then happy; no unbounded hope had raised
Ambition. Yet why not? Some other Power
As great might have aspired, and me, though mean,
Drawn to his part. But other Powers as great
Fell not, but stand unshaken, from within
Or from without to all temptations armed!
Hadst thou the same free will and power to stand?
Thou hadst. Whom hast thou then, or what, to accuse,
But Heaven's free love dealt equally to all?
Be then his love accursed, since, love or hate,
To me alike it deals eternal woe.
Nay, cursed be thou; since against his thy will
Chose freely what it now so justly rues.
Me miserable! which way shall I fly
Infinite wrath and infinite despair?
Which way I fly is Hell; myself am Hell; [1]
And, in the lowest deep, a lower deep
Still threatening to devour me opens wide,
To which the Hell I suffer seems a Heaven.
Oh, then, at last relent! Is there no place
Left for repentance, none for pardon left?
None left but by submission; and that word
Disdain forbids me, and my dread of shame
Among the Spirits beneath, whom I seduced
With other promises and other vaunts
Than to submit, boasting I could subdue
The Omnipotent. Aye me! they little know
How dearly I abide that boast so vain,
Under what torments inwardly I groan.
While they adore me on the throne of Hell,
With diadem and scepter high advanced,
The lower still I fall, only supreme
In misery. Such joy ambition finds!
But say I could repent, and could obtain,
By act of grace, my former state; how soon
Would highth recall high thoughts, how soon unsay
What feigned submission swore! Ease would recant
Vows made in pain, as violent and void
(For never can true reconcilement grow
Where wounds of deadly hate have pierced so deep);
Which would but lead me to a worse relapse
And heavier fall. So should I purchase dear
Short intermission, bought with double smart.
This knows my Punisher; therefore as far
From granting he, as I from begging, peace.
All hope excluded thus, behold, instead
Of us, outcast, exiled, his new delight,
Mankind, created, and for him this World!
So farewell hope, and, with hope, farewell fear,
Farewell remorse! All good to me is lost;
Evil, be thou my Good. By thee at least
Divided empire with Heaven's King I hold,
By thee, and more than half perhaps will reign;
As Man ere long, and this new World, shall know."

. . . .

From Book IV
[Evening in Paradise]

. . . .

Now came still Evening on, and Twilight gray
Had in her sober livery all things clad;
Silence accompanied; for beast and bird,
They to their grassy couch, these to their nests
Were slunk, all but the wakeful nightingale.
She all night long her amorous descant sung;
Silence was pleased. Now glowed the firmament
With living sapphires; Hesperus, that led
The starry host, rode brightest, till the Moon,
Rising in clouded majesty, at length
Apparent queen, unveiled her peerless light,
And o'er the dark her silver mantle threw;
When Adam thus to Eve: "Fair consort, the hour
Of night, and all things now retired to rest,
Mind us of like repose; since God hath set
Labor and rest, as day and night, to men
Successive, and the timely dew of sleep,
Now falling with soft slumberous weight, inclines
Our eyelids. Other creatures all day long
Rove idle, unemployed, and less need rest;
Man hath his daily work of body or mind
Appointed, which declares his dignity,
And the regard of Heaven on all his ways;
While other animals unactive range,
And of their doings God takes no account.
Tomorrow, ere fresh morning streak the east
With first approach of light, we must be risen,
And at our pleasant labor, to reform
Yon flowery arbors, yonder alleys green,
Our walk at noon, with branches overgrown,
That mock our scant manuring, and require
More hands than ours to lop their wanton growth.
Those blossoms also, and those dropping gums,
That lie bestrewn, unsightly and unsmooth,
Ask riddance, if we mean to tread with ease.
Meanwhile, as Nature wills, Night bids us rest."

[1] Cf. Marlowe's *Faustus* p. 171, l. 77; p. 173, ll. 125-6.

From Book V

[The Morning Hymn of Adam and Eve]

. . . .

"These are thy glorious works, Parent of good,
Almighty! thine this universal frame,
Thus wondrous fair; thyself how wondrous then!
Unspeakable! who sitt'st above these heavens
To us invisible, or dimly seen
In these thy lowest works; yet these declare
Thy goodness beyond thought, and power divine.
Speak, ye who best can tell, ye Sons of Light,
Angels—for ye behold him, and with songs
And choral symphonies, day without night,
Circle his throne rejoicing—ye in Heaven;
On Earth join, all ye creatures, to extol
Him first, him last, him midst, and without end.
Fairest of Stars, last in the train of Night,
If better thou belong not to the Dawn,
Sure pledge of day, that crown'st the smiling morn
With thy bright circlet, praise him in thy sphere
While day arises, that sweet hour of prime.
Thou Sun, of this great World both eye and soul,
Acknowledge him thy greater; sound his praise
In thy eternal course, both when thou climb'st,
And when high noon hast gained, and when thou fall'st.
Moon, that now meet'st the orient Sun, now fliest,
With the fixed Stars, fixed in their orb that flies;[1]
And ye five other wandering Fires, that move
In mystic dance, not without song, resound
His praise who out of Darkness called up Light.
Air, and ye Elements, the eldest birth,
Of Nature's womb, that in quaternion[2] run
Perpetual circle, multiform, and mix
And nourish all things, let your ceaseless change
Vary to our great Maker still new praise.
Ye Mists and Exhalations, that now rise
From hill or steaming lake, dusky or gray,
Till the sun paint your fleecy skirts with gold,
In honor to the World's Great Author rise;
Whether to deck with clouds the uncolored sky,
Or wet the thirsty earth with falling showers,
Rising or falling, still advance his praise.
His praise, ye Winds, that from four quarters blow,
Breathe soft or loud; and wave your tops, ye Pines,
With every Plant, in sign of worship wave.
Fountains, and ye that warble as ye flow,
Melodious murmurs, warbling tune his praise.
Join voices, all ye living Souls. Ye Birds
That, singing, up to Heaven-gate ascend,
Bear on your wings and in your notes his praise.
Ye that in waters glide, and ye that walk
The earth, and stately tread, or lowly creep,
Witness if *I* be silent, morn or even,
To hill or valley, fountain, or fresh shade,
Made vocal by my song, and taught his praise.
Hail, universal Lord! Be bounteous still
To give us only good; and, if the night
Have gathered aught of evil, or concealed,
Disperse it, as now light dispels the dark.

. . . .

[1] See note 4, p. 279.

[2] In their fourfold character of Earth, Water, Air, and Fire. See II, 898.

From Book VII

[Invocation to Urania]

Descend from Heaven, Urania, by that name
If rightly thou art called,[3] whose voice divine
Following, above the Olympian hill I soar,
Above the flight of Pegasean wing!
The meaning, not the name, I call; for thou
Nor of the Muses nine, nor on the top
Of old Olympus dwell'st; but, heavenly-born,
Before the hills appeared or fountain flowed,
Thou with Eternal Wisdom didst converse,
Wisdom thy sister, and with her didst play
In presence of the Almighty Father, pleased
With thy celestial song. Up led by thee,
Into the Heaven of Heavens I have presumed,
An earthly guest, and drawn empyreal air,
Thy tempering. With like safety guided down,
Return me to my native element;
Lest, from this flying steed unreined (as once
Bellerophon,[4] though from a lower clime)
Dismounted, on the Aleian field I fall,
Erroneous there to wander and forlorn.
Half yet remains unsung, but narrower bound
Within the visible Diurnal Sphere.
Standing on Earth, not rapt above the pole,
More safe I sing with mortal voice, unchanged
To hoarse or mute, though fallen on evil days,
On evil days though fallen, and evil tongues,
In darkness, and with dangers compassed round,
And solitude; yet not alone, while thou
Visit'st my slumbers nightly, or when Morn

[3] Milton declares that the Urania whom he invokes is not the pagan muse of that name, but a loftier Christian muse, the "heavenly one."

[4] Bellerophon, the fabled rider of Pegasus, tried to mount to heaven upon him, but was thrown for his presumption and doomed to wander in the Aleian ("wandering") field.

Purples the East. Still govern thou my song,
Urania, and fit audience find, though few.
But drive far off the barbarous dissonance
Of Bacchus and his revelers, the race
Of that wild rout that tore the Thracian bard [1]
In Rhodope, where woods and rocks had ears,
To rapture, till the savage clamor drowned
Both harp and voice; nor could the Muse defend
Her son. So fail not thou who thee implores;
For thou art heavenly, she an empty dream.

. . . .

From Book XII

[The Expulsion from Paradise]

. . . .

He [2] ended, and they both descend the hill.
Descended, Adam to the bower where Eve
Lay sleeping ran before, but found her waked;
And thus with words not sad she him received:
"Whence thou return'st and whither went'st I know;
For God is also in sleep, and dreams advise,
Which he hath sent propitious, some great good
Presaging, since, with sorrow and heart's distress
Wearied, I fell asleep. But now lead on;
In me is no delay; with thee to go
Is to stay here; without thee here to stay
Is to go hence unwilling; thou to me
Art all things under Heaven, all places thou,
Who for my willful crime art banished hence.
This further consolation yet secure
I carry hence; though all by me is lost,
Such favor I unworthy am vouchsafed,
By me the Promised Seed shall all restore."
So spake our mother Eve; and Adam heard
Well pleased, but answered not; for now too nigh
The Archangel stood, and from the other hill
To their fixed station, all in bright array,
The Cherubim descended, on the ground
Gliding, meteorous, as evening mist
Risen from a river o'er the marish glides,
And gathers ground fast at the laborer's heel
Homeward returning. High in front advanced,
The brandished sword of God before them blazed,
Fierce as a comet; which with torrid heat,
And vapor as the Libyan air adust, [3]
Began to parch that temperate clime; whereat
In either hand the hastening Angel caught
Our lingering parents, and to the eastern gate
Led them direct, and down the cliff as fast
To the subjected [4] plain—then disappeared.
They, looking back, all the eastern side beheld
Of Paradise, so late their happy seat,
Waved over by that flaming brand; the gate
With dreadful faces thronged and fiery arms.
Some natural tears they dropped, but wiped them soon;
The world was all before them, where to choose
Their place of rest, and Providence their guide.
They, hand in hand, with wandering steps and slow,
Through Eden [5] took their solitary way.

1600-67 *1667*

[1] Orpheus offended the Thracian Bacchantes and was torn to pieces by them. Milton, blind, and, since the Restoration, reviled as a Puritan, had "fallen on evil days" and might even fear from the dissolute courtiers of Charles a fate not unlike that of Orpheus.

[2] Michael, the angel delegated to lead them forth

[3] scorched

ON EDUCATION

To Master Samuel Hartlib: [6]

I am long since persuaded, Master Hartlib, that to say or do aught worth memory and imitation, no purpose or respect should sooner move us than simply the love of God and of mankind. . . . I will not resist, therefore, whatever it is either of divine or human obligement that you lay upon me; but will forthwith set down in writing, as you request me, that voluntary idea, which hath long in silence presented itself to me, of a better education, in extent and comprehension far more large, and yet of time far shorter and of attainment far more certain, than hath been yet in practice. Brief I shall endeavor to be; for that which I have to say assuredly this nation hath extreme need should be done sooner than spoken. . . .

The end, then, of learning is, to repair the ruins of our first parents by regaining to know God aright, and out of that knowledge to love him, to imitate him, to be like him, as we may the nearest by possessing our souls of true virtue, [7] which, being united to the heavenly grace of faith, makes up the highest perfection. But because our understanding cannot in this body found itself but on sensible things, [8] nor arrive so clearly to the knowledge of God and things invisible as by orderly conning over the visible and inferior creature, the same method is necessarily to be followed in all discreet teaching. And seeing every nation affords not

[4] underlying

[5] See note 5, p. 259.

[6] Hartlib was a Pole, settled in England, who had had some discussions with Milton on the subject of education. The slight omissions made here from the beginning of the tractate are made with the purpose of enabling the reader to get more rapidly into the subject.

[7] which we may most readily do by putting our souls in possession of true virtue

[8] things perceived by the senses

experience and tradition enough for all kinds of learning, therefore we are chiefly taught the languages of those people who have at any time been most industrious after wisdom; so that language is but the instrument conveying to us things useful to be known. And though a linguist should pride himself to have all the tongues that Babel cleft the world into, yet if he have not studied the solid things in them as well as the words and lexicons, he were nothing so much to be esteemed a learned man as any yeoman or tradesman competently wise in his mother-dialect only. Hence appear the many mistakes which have made learning generally so unpleasing and so unsuccessful. First, we do amiss to spend seven or eight years merely in scraping together so much miserable Latin and Greek as might be learned otherwise easily and delightfully in one year. And that which casts our proficiency therein so much behind is our time lost partly in too oft idle vacancies given both to schools and universities; partly in a preposterous exaction, forcing the empty wits of children to compose themes, verses, and orations, which are the acts of ripest judgment, and the final work of a head filled by long reading and observing with elegant maxims and copious invention. These are not matters to be wrung from poor striplings, like blood out of the nose, or the plucking of untimely fruit; besides the ill habit which they get of wretched barbarizing against the Latin and Greek idiom with their untutored Anglicisms, odious to be read, yet not to be avoided without a well-continued and judicious conversing among pure authors, digested, which they scarce taste. Whereas, if after some preparatory grounds of speech by their certain forms got into memory they were led to the praxis [1] thereof in some chosen short book lessoned thoroughly to them, they might then forthwith proceed to learn the substance of good things and arts in due order, which would bring the whole language quickly into their power. . . .

I shall detain you now no longer in the demonstration of what we should not do, but straight conduct you to a hillside, where I will point you out the right path of a virtuous and noble education; laborious indeed at the first ascent, but else so smooth, so green, so full of goodly prospect and melodious sounds on every side, that the harp of Orpheus was not more charming. I doubt not but ye shall have more ado to drive our dullest and laziest youth, our stocks and stubs, from the infinite desire of such a happy nurture, than we have now to hale and drag our choicest and hopefulest wits to that asinine feast of sow-thistles and brambles which is commonly set before them as all the food and entertainment of their tenderest and most docile age. I call, therefore, a complete and generous education that which fits a man to perform justly, skillfully, and magnanimously all the offices, both private and public, of peace and war. And how all this may be done between twelve and one-and-twenty, less time than is now bestowed in pure trifling at grammar and sophistry, is to be thus ordered:

First, to find out a spacious house and ground about it fit for an academy, and big enough to lodge a hundred and fifty persons, whereof twenty or thereabout may be attendants, all under the government of one who shall be thought of desert sufficient, and ability either to do all, or wisely to direct and oversee it done. This place should be at once both school and university, not needing a remove to any other house of scholarship, except it be some peculiar college of law or physic where [2] they mean to be practitioners; but as for those general studies which take up all our time from Lilly [3] to the commencing, as they term it, master of art, it should be absolute. [4] After this pattern as many edifices may be converted to this use as shall be needful in every city throughout this land, which would tend much to the increase of learning and civility [5] everywhere. This number, less or more, thus collected, to the convenience [6] of a foot-company or interchangeably two troops of cavalry, should divide their day's work into three parts as it lies orderly—their studies, their exercise, and their diet.

For their studies: first, they should begin with the chief and necessary rules of some good grammar, either that now used, or any better; and while this is doing, their speech is to be fashioned to a distinct and clear pronunciation, as near as may be to the Italian, especially in the vowels. For we Englishmen, being far northerly, do not open our mouths in the cold air wide enough to grace a southern tongue, but are observed by all other nations to speak exceeding close and inward; so that to smatter Latin with an English mouth is as ill a hearing as law French. Next, to make them expert in the usefulest points of grammar, and withal to season them and win them early to the love of virtue and true labor,

[1] practical exercises

[2] some special college . . . . in case that
[3] the author of a Latin grammar which was once a standard textbook
[4] complete in itself
[5] civilization
[6] collective number

ere any flattering seducement or vain principle seize them wandering, some easy and delightful book of education should be read to them, whereof the Greeks have store, as Cebes, Plutarch, and other Socratic discourses; but in Latin we have none of classic authority extant, except the two or three first books of Quintilian and some select pieces elsewhere. But here the main skill and groundwork will be to temper [1] them such lectures and explanations upon every opportunity as may lead and draw them in willing obedience, inflamed with the study of learning and the admiration of virtue, stirred up with high hopes of living to be brave men and worthy patriots, dear to God and famous to all ages; that they may despise and scorn all their childish and ill-taught qualities, to delight in manly and liberal exercises; which he who hath the art and proper eloquence to catch them with, what with mild and effectual persuasions, and what with the intimation of some fear, if need be, [2] but chiefly by his own example, might in a short space gain them to an incredible diligence and courage, infusing into their young breasts such an ingenuous and noble ardor as would not fail to make many of them renowned and matchless men. At the same time, some other hour of the day might be taught them the rules of arithmetic, and, soon after, the elements of geometry, even playing, as the old manner was. After evening repast till bed-time their thoughts would be best taken up in the easy grounds of religion and the story of Scripture. The next step would be to the authors of agriculture, Cato, Varro, and Columella, for the matter is most easy; and if the language is difficult, so much the better; it is not a difficulty above their years. And here will be an occasion of inciting and enabling them hereafter to improve the tillage of their country, to recover the bad soil, and to remedy the waste that is made of good; for this was one of Hercules' praises.

Ere half these authors be read (which will soon be, with plying hard and daily) they cannot choose but be masters of any ordinary prose; so that it will be then seasonable for them to learn in any modern author the use of the globes and all the maps, first with the old names and then with the new; or they might be then capable to read any compendious method of natural philosophy; and, at the same time, might be entering into the Greek tongue, after the same manner as was before prescribed in the Latin; whereby the difficulties of grammar being soon overcome, all the historical physiology of Aristotle and Theophrastus are open before them, and, as I may say, under contribution. The like access will be to Vitruvius, to Seneca's *Natural Questions,* to Mela, Celsus, Pliny, or Solinus. And having thus past the principles of arithmetic, geometry, astronomy, and geography, with a general compact of physics, they may descend in mathematics to the instrumental science of trigonometry, and from thence to fortification, architecture, enginery, or navigation. And in natural philosophy they may proceed leisurely from the history of meteors, minerals, plants, and living creatures, as far as anatomy. Then also in course might be read to them out of some not tedious writer the institution of physic; [3] that they may know the tempers, the humors, the seasons, and how to manage a crudity, [4] which he who can wisely and timely do is not only a great physician to himself and to his friends, but also may at some time or other save an army by this frugal and expenseless means only, and not let the healthy and stout bodies of young men rot away under him for want of this discipline, which is a great pity, and no less a shame to the commander. To set forward all these proceedings in nature and mathematics, what hinders but that they may procure, as oft as shall be needful, the helpful experiences of hunters, fowlers, fishermen, shepherds, gardeners, apothecaries; and in the other sciences, architects, engineers, mariners, anatomists, who, doubtless, would be ready, some for reward and some to favor such a hopeful seminary. And this will give them such a real tincture of natural knowledge as they shall never forget, but daily augment with delight. [5]

. . . .

These are the studies wherein our noble and our gentle youth ought to bestow their time in a disciplinary way from twelve to one-and-twenty, unless they rely more upon their ancestors dead than upon themselves living. In which methodical course it is so supposed they must proceed by the steady pace of learning onward, as at convenient times for memory's sake to retire back into the middleward, and sometimes into the rear of what they have been taught, until they have confirmed and solidly united the whole body of their perfected knowledge, like the last embattling of a Roman legion. Now will be worth the seeing what

[1] intermingle
[2] Compare this with Ascham's *Schoolmaster,* p. 130 and Boswell's *Johnson,* pp. 394, 395.

[3] the elements of physiology and medicine
[4] indigestion
[5] At this point Milton takes up, in rapid succession, ethics, politics, theology, history, logic, and poetry.

exercises and recreations may best agree and become these studies.

The course of study hitherto briefly described is, what [1] I can guess by reading, likest to those ancient and famous schools of Pythagoras, Plato, Isocrates, Aristotle, and such others, out of which were bred such a number of renowned philosophers, orators, historians, poets, and princes all over Greece, Italy, and Asia, besides the flourishing studies of Cyrene and Alexandria. But herein it shall exceed them, and supply a defect as great as that which Plato noted in the commonweath of Sparta. Whereas that city trained up their youth most for war, and these in their academies and Lycaeum [2] all for the gown, [3] this institution of breeding which I here delineate shall be equally good both for peace and war. Therefore, about an hour and a half ere they eat at noon should be allowed them for exercise, and due rest afterwards; but the time for this may be enlarged at pleasure, according as their rising in the morning shall be early.

The exercise which I commend first is the exact use of their weapon, to guard, and to strike safely with edge or point; this will keep them healthy, nimble, strong, and well in breath; is also the likeliest means to make them grow large and tall, and to inspire them with a gallant and fearless courage, which being tempered with seasonable lectures and precepts to make them of true fortitude and patience, will turn into a native and heroic valor, and make them hate the cowardice of doing wrong. They must be also practiced in all the locks and grips of wrestling, wherein Englishmen were wont to excel, as need may often be in fight to tug, to grapple, and to close. And this, perhaps, will be enough wherein to prove and heat their single strength. The interim of unsweating themselves regularly, and convenient rest before meat, may both with profit and delight be taken up in recreating and composing their travailed spirits with the solemn and divine harmonies of music heard or learned, either whilst the skillful organist plies his grave and fancied descant in lofty fugues, or the whole symphony with artful and unimaginable touches adorn and grace the well-studied chords of some choice composer; sometimes the lute or soft organ-stop, waiting on [4] elegant voices either to religious, martial, or civil ditties, which, if wise men and prophets be not extremely out, [5] have a great power over dispositions and manners to smooth and make them gentle from rustic harshness and distempered passions. The like also would not be unexpedient after meat, to assist and cherish nature in her first concoction, [6] and send their minds back to study in good tune and satisfaction. Where having followed it close under vigilant eyes till about two hours before supper, they are, by a sudden alarm or watchword, to be called out to their military motions, under sky or covert, according to the season, as was the Roman wont; first on foot, then, as their age permits, on horseback to all the art of cavalry; that having in sport, but with much exactness and daily muster, served out the rudiments of their soldiership in all the skill of embattling, marching, encamping, fortifying, besieging, and battering, with all the helps of ancient and modern stratagems, tactics, and warlike maxims, they may, as it were out of a long war, come forth renowned and perfect commanders in the service of their country. They would not then, if they were trusted with fair and hopeful armies, suffer them for want of just and wise discipline to shed away from about them like sick feathers, though they be never so oft supplied; they would not suffer their empty and unrecruitable [7] colonels of twenty men in a company to quaff out or convey into secret hoards the wages of a delusive list [8] and miserable remnant; yet in the meanwhile to be overmastered with a score or two of drunkards, the only soldiery left about them, or else to comply with all rapines and violences. No, certainly, if they knew aught of that knowledge that belongs to good men or good governors they would not suffer these things.

But to return to our own institute; besides these constant exercises at home, there is another opportunity of gaining experience to be won from pleasure itself abroad. In those vernal seasons of the year, when the air is calm and pleasant, it were an injury and sullenness against nature not to go out and see her riches and partake in her rejoicing with heaven and earth. I should not, therefore, be a persuader to them of studying much then, after two or three years that they have well laid their grounds, but to ride out in companies with prudent and staid guides to all the quarters of the land, learning and observing all places of strength, all commodities of building and of

[1] so far as
[2] the exercise ground and grove of Athens, where Aristotle taught
[3] philosophy
[4] accompanying
[5] mistaken
[6] digestion
[7] incapable of recruiting their forces ("Quaff out" in the next line appears to mean "spend for drink.")
[8] "stuffed pay-roll"

soil for towns and tillage, harbors, and ports for trade; sometimes taking sea as far as to our navy, to learn there also what they can in the practical knowledge of sailing and of sea-fight. These ways would try all their peculiar gifts of nature, and if there were any secret excellence among them, would fetch it out and give it fair opportunities to advance itself by, which could not but mightily redound to the good of this nation, and bring into fashion again those old admired virtues and excellencies, with far more advantage now in this purity of Christian knowledge. Nor shall we then need the monsieurs of Paris to take our hopeful youth into their slight and prodigal custodies, and send them over back again transformed into mimics, apes, and kickshaws.[1] But if they desire to see other countries at three or four and twenty years of age, not to learn principles, but to enlarge experience and make wise observation, they will by that time be such as shall deserve the regard and honor of all men where they pass, and the society and friendship of those in all places who are best and most eminent. And perhaps then other nations will be glad to visit us for their breeding, or else to imitate us in their own country.

Now, lastly, for their diet there cannot be much to say, save only that it would be best in the same house; for much time else would be lost abroad, and many ill habits got; and that it should be plain, healthful, and moderate I suppose is out of controversy.

Thus, Mr. Hartlib, you have a general view in writing, as your desire was, of that which at several times I had discoursed with you concerning the best and noblest way of education; not beginning, as some have done, from the cradle, which yet might be worth many considerations, if brevity had not been my scope. Many other circumstances also I could have mentioned, but this, to such as have the worth in them to make trial, for light and direction may be enough. Only I believe that this is not a bow for every man to shoot in that counts himself a teacher, but will require sinews almost equal to those which Homer gave Ulysses;[2] yet I am withal persuaded that it may prove much more easy in the assay[3] than it now seems at distance, and much more illustrious; howbeit not more difficult than I imagine, and that imagination presents me with nothing but very happy and very possible according to best wishes, if God have so decreed, and this age have spirit and capacity enough to apprehend.[4]

[1] triflers

[2] referring to the bow which none of the suitors could draw, but with which Ulysses slew them on his return

[3] trial

From AREOPAGITICA[5]

A SPEECH FOR THE LIBERTY OF UNLICENSED PRINTING, TO THE PARLIAMENT OF ENGLAND

. . . . . .

If ye be thus resolved, as it were injury to think ye were not, I know not what should withhold me from presenting ye with a fit instance wherein to show both that love of truth which ye eminently profess, and that uprightness of your judgment which is not wont to be partial to yourselves; by judging over again that Order which ye have ordained *to regulate Printing: That no book, pamphlet, or paper shall be henceforth printed, unless the same be first approved and licensed by such,* or at least one of such, as shall be thereto appointed. For that part which preserves justly every man's copy[6] to himself, or provides for the poor, I touch not, only wish they be not made pretenses to abuse and persecute honest and painful[7] men, who offend not in either of these particulars. But that other clause of Licensing Books, which we thought had died with his brother quadragesimal and matrimonial[8] when the prelates expired, I shall now attend with such a homily as shall lay before ye, first, the inventors of it to be those whom ye will be loath to own; next, what is to be thought in general of reading, whatever sort the books be; and that this Order avails nothing to the suppressing of scandalous, seditious, and libelous books, which were mainly intended to be suppressed. Last, that it will be primely to the discouragement of all learning, and the stop of Truth, not only by disexercising and blunting our abilities in what we know already, but by hindering and cropping the discovery that might be yet further made both in religious and civil Wisdom.

[4] This sentence is a good example of Milton's awkwardness in prose, in which he said he had but the use of his "left hand."

[5] The title is taken from that of a speech by the Greek orator, Isocrates, addressed to the Great Council of Athens, which was called the Areopagus because it held its meetings on the Areopagus, or "Hill of Ares" ("Mars' Hill," where Paul preached: *Acts* xvii, 22). The tract was written late in 1644. Parliament, in its long struggle with Charles, had brought about many changes, the Westminster Assembly even going so far as practically to abolish prelacy, or episcopacy, and establish Presbyterianism. But an ordinance had been enacted in 1643 reëstablishing the censorship of the press. Milton pleads to have this revoked; and his opening words (here omitted) praise Parliament for its professed willingness to "obey the voice of reason."

[6] copyright

[7] painstaking

[8] orders concerning the keeping of Lent, and marriage

I deny not, but that it is of greatest concernment in the Church and Commonwealth, to have a vigilant eye how books demean themselves as well as men; and thereafter to confine, imprison, and do sharpest justice on them as malefactors. For books are not absolutely dead things, but do contain a potency of life in them to be as active as that soul was whose progeny they are; nay, they do preserve as in a vial the purest efficacy and extraction of that living intellect that bred them. I know they are as lively, and as vigorously productive, as those fabulous dragon's teeth; [1] and being sown up and down, may chance to spring up armed men. And yet, on the other hand, unless wariness be used, as good almost kill a man as kill a good book. Who kills a man kills a reasonable creature, God's image; but he who destroys a good book, kills reason itself, kills the image of God, as it were in the eye. [2] Many a man lives, a burden to the earth; but a good book is the precious life-blood of a master spirit, embalmed and treasured up on purpose to a life beyond life. 'Tis true, no age can restore a life, whereof perhaps there is no great loss; and revolutions of ages do not oft recover the loss of a rejected truth, for the want of which whole nations fare the worse. We should be wary therefore what persecution we raise against the living labors of public men, how we spill that seasoned life of man, preserved and stored up in books; since we see a kind of homicide may be thus committed, sometimes a martyrdom, and if it extend to the whole impression, [3] a kind of massacre, whereof the execution ends not in the slaying of an elemental life, but strikes at that ethereal and fifth essence, [4] the breath of reason itself, slays an immortality rather than a life. But lest I should be condemned of introducing license, while I oppose licensing, I refuse not the pains to be so much historical, as will serve to show what hath been done by ancient and famous commonweaths against this disorder, till the very time that this project of licensing crept out of the Inquisition, was catched up by our prelates, and hath caught some of our presbyters.

. . . .

I conceive, therefore, that when God did enlarge the universal diet of man's body, saving ever the rules of temperance, He then also, as before, left arbitrary the dieting and repasting of our minds; as wherein every mature man might have to exercise his own leading capacity. How great a virtue is temperance, how much of moment through the whole life of man! Yet God commits the managing so great a trust without particular law or prescription, wholly to the demeanor of every grown man. And, therefore, when He himself tabled [5] the Jews from heaven, that omer [6] which was every man's daily portion of manna, is computed to have been more than might have well sufficed the heartiest feeder thrice as many meals. For those actions which enter into a man, rather than issue out of him, and therefore defile not, God uses not to captivate under a perpetual childhood of prescription, but trusts him with the gift of reason to be his own chooser; there were but little work left for preaching, if law and compulsion should grow so fast upon those things which heretofore were governed only by exhortation. Solomon informs us that much reading is a weariness to the flesh; but neither he nor other inspired author tells us that such or such reading is unlawful. Yet certainly, had God thought good to limit us herein, it had been much more expedient to have told us what was unlawful, than what was wearisome. As for the burning of those Ephesian books [7] by St. Paul's converts; 'tis replied the books were magic, the Syriac so renders them. It was a private act, a voluntary act, and leaves us to a voluntary imitation. The men in remorse burnt those books which were their own; the magistrate by this example is not appointed. These men practiced the books, another might perhaps have read them in some sort usefully. Good and evil we know in the field of this world grow up together almost inseparably; and the knowledge of good is so involved and interwoven with the knowledge of evil, and in so many cunning resemblances hardly to be discerned, that those confused seeds which were imposed upon Psyche as an incessant labor to cull out and sort asunder, were not more intermixed. It was from out the rind of one apple tasted that the knowledge of good and evil, as two twins cleaving together, leaped forth into the world. And perhaps this is that doom which Adam fell into of knowing good and evil, that is to say of knowing good by evil. As, therefore, the state of man now is, what wisdom can there be to choose, what continence to forbear without the knowledge of evil? He that can apprehend and

[1] sown by Cadmus of Thebes
[2] The reason of man is, as it were, the eye of his divine nature.
[3] edition
[4] Aristotle's fifth element: "quintessence," ether, or spirit

[5] fed (*Exodus*, xvi, 16)
[6] about one-tenth of a bushel
[7] *Acts*, xix, 19

consider vice with all her baits and seeming pleasures, and yet abstain, and yet distinguish, and yet prefer that which is truly better, he is the true warfaring Christian. I cannot praise a fugitive and cloistered virtue, unexercised and unbreathed, that never sallies out and sees her adversary, but slinks out of the race, where that immortal garland is to be run for, not without dust and heat.[1] Assuredly we bring not innocence into the world, we bring impurity much rather; that which purifies us is trial, and trial is by what is contrary. That virtue therefore which is but a youngling in the contemplation of evil, and knows not the utmost that vice promises to her followers, and rejects it, is but a blank virtue, not a pure; her whiteness is but an excremental[2] whiteness; which was the reason why our sage and serious poet Spenser, whom I dare be known to think a better teacher than Scotus or Aquinas,[3] describing true temperance under the person of Guion,[4] brings him in with his palmer through the cave of Mammon, and the bower of earthly bliss, that he might see and know, and yet abstain. Since, therefore, the knowledge and survey of vice is in this world so necessary to the constituting of human virtue, and the scanning of error to the confirmation of truth, how can we more safely, and with less danger scout into the regions of sin and falsity than by reading all manner of tractates and hearing all manner of reason? And this is the benefit which may be had of books promiscuously read.

. . . .

1644 1644

IZAAK WALTON
1593-1683

Living far beyond the allotted span of man, witnessing the reigns of five monarchs and the Commonwealth, yet reflecting in his writings little of what passed in the political world, Izaak Walton represents seventeenth century prose by works of two very different types—an open-air classic on angling, and some of the first real biographies in our literature. He was born in Staffordshire, was apprenticed in London, probably to an ironmonger, and by 1614 owned half a shop in Fleet Street. After the Royalist defeat at Marston Moor in 1644 he thought it wise to retire from active business; for he was such a known Cavalier sympathizer that he had even been entrusted by Charles II with a royal jewel, later restored to the king in exile.

[1] This is one—but only one—of the noble sentiments so nobly expressed, which make the *Areopagitica* one of the prized documents in our literature.
[2] surface
[3] scholastic philosophers
[4] *The Faerie Queene,* Bk. II

Though of humble origin, Walton was the friend of many famous men, most of them learned divines and prelates. After 1662 he lived in the palace of George Morley, Bishop of Winchester, but much of his time was spent with his friend Cotton in a little fishing cottage on the river Dove in Staffordshire. His writings reveal his kindly, humorous, pious disposition, and his love of music and nature. His best-known work, *The Complete Angler,* 1653, is in the form of a dialogue, chiefly between a fisherman, *Piscator,* and a scholar-hunter *Venator.* Besides this he wrote, over a period of forty years, a volume of five brief lives—Donne, Herbert, Hooker, Wotton, and Sanderson—one of Johnson's favorite books. "*Dr. Donne's Life,* he said, was the most perfect of them all."—Boswell.

The Complete Angler is in Cassell, the *Lives* in Morley's Universal Library; critical material appears in W. S. Landor, *Imaginary Conversations;* A. Lang; Lowell; L. Powys' "Isaac Walton," *Forum* 68:1052-7; J. Vaughan, "Plant Lore of *The Complete Angler,*" *Scrib. M.* 70:720-8.

THE COMPLETE ANGLER
From Chapter IV

. . . Of the Trout, and how to fish for Him. And of the Milkmaid's Song

Venator. Trust me, master, I see now it is a harder matter to catch a trout than a chub; for I have put on patience and followed you these two hours and not seen a fish stir, neither at your minnow nor your worm.

Piscator. Well, scholar, you must endure worse luck some time, or you will never make a good angler. But what say you now? There is a trout now, and a good one, too, if I can but hold him, and two or three turns more will tire him. Now you see he lies still, and the sleight is to land him. Reach me that landing-net; so, sir, now he is mine own. What say you now? Is not this worth all my labor and your patience?

Ven. On my word, master, this is a gallant trout; what shall we do with him?

Pisc. Marry, e'en eat him to supper. We'll go to my hostess, from whence we came; she told me, as I was going out of door, that my brother Peter, a good angler and a cheerful companion, had sent word that he would lodge there tonight, and bring a friend with him. My hostess has two beds, and I know you and I may have the best; we'll rejoice with my brother Peter and his friend, tell tales or sing ballads or make a catch[5] or find some harmless sport to content us and pass away a little time, without offense to God or man.

[5] a singing "round"

Ven. A match,[1] good master, let's go to that house; for the linen looks white and smells of lavender, and I long to lie in a pair of sheets that smell so. Let's be going, good master, for I am hungry again with fishing.

Pisc. Nay, stay a little, good scholar. I caught my last trout with a worm; now I will put on a minnow and try a quarter of an hour about yonder trees for another, and so walk toward our lodging. Look you, scholar, thereabout we shall have a bite presently or not at all. Have with you, sir! o' my word I have hold of him. Oh! it is a great logger-headed chub; come hang him upon that willow twig and let's be going. But turn out of the way a little, good scholar, toward yonder high honeysuckle hedge; there we'll sit and sing whilst this shower falls so gently upon the teeming earth and gives yet a sweeter smell to the lovely flowers that adorn these verdant meadows.

Look! Under that broad beech tree I sat down when I was last this way a-fishing. And the birds in the adjoining grove seemed to have a friendly contention with an echo, whose dead voice seemed to live in a hollow tree near to the brow of that primrose hill. There I sat viewing the silver streams glide silently toward their center, the tempestuous sea; yet sometimes opposed by rugged roots and pebblestones, which broke their waves and turned them into foam. And sometimes I beguiled time by viewing the harmless lambs; some leaping securely in the cool shade whilst others sported themselves in the cheerful sun; and saw others craving comfort from the swollen udders of their bleating dams. As I thus sat, these and other sights had so fully possessed my soul with content that I thought, as the poet hath happily expressed it,

I was for that time lifted above earth,
And possessed joys not promised in my birth.

As I left this place and entered into the next field a second pleasure entertained me; 'twas a handsome milkmaid that had not yet attained so much age and wisdom as to load her mind with any fears of many things that will never be, as too many men too often do. But she cast away all care, and sang like a nightingale; her voice was good, and the ditty fitted for it; it was that smooth song which was made by Kit Marlow, now at least fifty years ago; and the milkmaid's mother sang an answer to it which was made by Sir Walter Raleigh in his younger days.

[1] a bargain

They were old-fashioned poetry but choicely good, I think much better than the strong lines that are now in fashion in this critical age. Look yonder! on my word, yonder they both be a-milking again. I will give her the chub, and persuade them to sing those two songs to us.

God speed you, good woman! I have been a-fishing and am going to Bleak Hall to my bed, and having caught more fish than will sup myself and my friend, I will bestow this upon you and your daughter, for I use to sell none.

Milk-W. Marry, God requite you, sir, and we'll eat it cheerfully; and if you come this way a-fishing two months hence, a[2] grace of God, I'll give you a syllabub of new verjuice,[3] in a new-made haycock, for it, and my Maudlin shall sing you one of her best ballads; for she and I both love all anglers, they be such honest, civil, quiet men; in the meantime will you drink a draft of red cow's milk? you shall have it freely.

Pisc. No, I thank you; but, I pray, do us a courtesy that shall stand[4] you and your daughter in nothing, and yet we will think ourselves still something in your debt; it is but to sing us a song that was sung by your daughter when I last passed over this meadow, about eight or nine days since.

Milk-W. What song was it, I pray? Was it "Come, Shepherds, deck your heads," or "As at noon Dulcina rested," or "Phillida flouts me," or "Chevy Chace," or "Johnny Armstrong," or "Troy Town"?

Pisc. No, it is none of those; it is a song that your daughter sang the first part and you sang the answer to it.

Milk-W. Oh, I know it now. I learned the first part in my golden age, when I was about the age of my poor daughter; and the latter part, which indeed fits me best now, but two or three years ago, when the cares of the world began to take hold of me; but you shall, God willing, hear them both, and sung as well as we can, for we both love anglers. Come, Maudlin, sing the first part to the gentlemen with a merry heart, and I'll sing the second when you have done.

THE MILKMAID'S SONG

Come live with me and be my love, etc.[5]

Ven. Trust me, master, it is a choice song, and sweetly sung by honest Maudlin. I now see it was not without cause that our good

[2] by the
[3] whipped cream and grape-juice
[4] cost
[5] For this song, see p. 162.

Queen Elizabeth did so often wish herself a milkmaid all the month of May, because they are not troubled with fears and cares, but sing sweetly all the day and sleep securely all the night; and without doubt, honest, innocent, pretty Maudlin does so. I'll bestow Sir Thomas Overbury's milkmaid's wish upon her: that she may die in the spring, and being dead may have good store of flowers stuck round about her winding-sheet.[1]

. . . .

From Chapter XXI

[A Sermon on Content]

. . . .

Piscator. Let me tell you, scholar, that Diogenes walked on a day, with his friend, to see a country fair; where he saw ribbons and looking-glasses and nut-crackers and fiddles and hobby-horses and many other gimcracks; and, having observed them, and all the other finnimbruns[2] that make a complete country fair, he said to his friend, "Lord how many things are there in this world of which Diogenes hath no need!" And truly it is so, or might be so, with very many who vex and toil themselves to get what they have no need of. Can any man charge God that He hath not given him enough to make his life happy? No, doubtless, for nature is content with a little. And yet you shall hardly meet with a man that complains not of some want; though he, indeed, wants nothing but his will; it may be nothing but his will of his poor neighbor for not worshiping or not flattering him. And thus, when we might be happy and quiet, we create trouble to ourselves. I have heard of a man that was angry with himself because he was no taller; and of a woman that broke her looking-glass because it would not show her face to be as young and handsome as her next neighbor's was. And I knew another to whom God had given health and plenty, but a wife that nature had made peevish and her husband's riches had made purse-proud; and must, because she was rich and for no other virtue, sit in the highest pew in the church; which being denied her, she engaged her husband into a contention for it, and at last into a law-suit with a dogged neighbor who was as rich as he, and had a wife as peevish and purse-proud as the other; and this law-suit begot higher oppositions, and actionable[3] words, and more vexations and law-suits; for you must remember that both were rich and must, therefore, have their wills. Well, this willful, purse-proud law-suit lasted during the life of the first husband; after which his wife vext and chid, and chid and vext till she also chid and vext herself into her grave; and so the wealth of these poor rich people was curst into a punishment, because they wanted meek and thankful hearts; for those only can make us happy. I knew a man that had health and riches and several houses, all beautiful and ready furnished, and would often trouble himself and family to be removing from one house to another; and being asked by a friend why he removed so often from one house to another, replied, it was to find content in some one of them. But his friend, knowing his temper, told him, if he would find content in any of his houses, he must leave himself behind him; for content will never dwell but in a meek and quiet soul. And this may appear, if we read and consider what our Savior says in St. Matthew's Gospel; for He there says: "Blessed be the merciful, for they shall obtain mercy. Blessed be the pure in heart, for they shall see God. Blessed be the poor in spirit, for theirs is the kingdom of heaven." And, "Blessed be the meek, for they shall possess the earth." Not that the meek shall not also obtain mercy and see God and be comforted and at last come to the kingdom of heaven; but in the meantime he, and he only, possesses the earth as he goes toward that kingdom of heaven, by being humble and cheerful and content with what his good God has allotted him. He has no turbulent, repining, vexatious thoughts that he deserves better; nor is vext when he sees others possessed of more honor or more riches than his wise God has allotted for his share; but he possesses what he has with a meek and contented quietness, such a quietness as makes his very dreams pleasing, both to God and himself.

My honest scholar, all this is told to incline you to thankfulness; and to incline you the more, let me tell you, that though the prophet David was guilty of murder and, indeed, of many other of the most deadly sins, yet he was said to be a man after God's own heart, because he abounded more with thankfulness than any other that is mentioned in holy Scripture, as may appear in his book of Psalms; where there is such a commixture of his confessing of his sins and unworthiness,

[1] The mother then sings the answer. See p. 163. Overbury's milkmaid is one of the most famous of his "Characters," a species of literary portrait much affected in the seventeenth century.

[2] Walton appears to have coined this word. It is found only here.

[3] affording cause for legal action

and such thankfulness for God's pardon and mercies as did make him to be accounted, even by God Himself, to be a man after His own heart. And let us, in that, labor to be as like him as we can; let not the blessings we receive daily from God make us not to value or not praise Him because they be common; let us not forget to praise Him for the innocent mirth and pleasure we have met with since we met together. What would a blind man give to see the pleasant rivers and meadows and flowers and fountains that we have met with since we met together? I have been told that if a man that was born blind could obtain to have his sight for but only one hour during his whole life, and should, at the first opening of his eyes, fix his sight upon the sun when it was in its full glory, either at the rising or setting of it, he would be so transported and amazed, and so admire the glory of it, that he would not willingly turn his eyes from that first ravishing object to behold all the other various beauties this world could present to him. And this, and many other like blessings, we enjoy daily. And for most of them, because they be so common, most men forget to pay their praises; but let not us, because it is a sacrifice so pleasing to Him that made that sun and us, and still protects us, and gives us flowers and showers, and stomachs and meat, and content and leisure to go a-fishing.

. . . .

1653

JOHN BUNYAN 1628-1688

John Bunyan, born near Bedford, and twenty years younger than Milton, represents in origin, life, and works a totally different aspect of Puritanism. His father was a tinker, and the boy was taken early from a very simple education to follow the same trade. At sixteen he became a soldier in the parliamentary army and fought in the Civil War. Returning home in 1647 he married a girl as poor as himself, her only dowry two pious books which changed Bunyan's life after a long spiritual conflict well described in *Grace Abounding,* 1666.

He joined the Nonconformist church, began preaching, and soon was famous. With the Restoration of 1660 it became illegal to conduct any but the Episcopal form of worship; Bunyan, refusing to obey the law, spent the next twelve years in prison, earning his living by making tagged laces, preaching whenever possible, and writing much; his chief companions were the Bible and Foxe's *Book of Martyrs.* In 1672 he was released and granted a license to preach. *Pilgrim's Progress,* an allegory of the soul that through its underlying intensity and reality has been as true for thousands of readers as it was for Bunyan, was published in 1678. In well-drawn contrast to it, two years later appeared the *Life and Death of Mr. Badman;* in 1680, the *Holy War.*

Pilgrim's Progress "as a portrait of rough English country-town life in the days of Charles II [is] unapproached save by the tales of Defoe," and like them may be considered a forerunner of the novel. Bunyan took the simple facts of his life and wove from them a tapestry picturing the life of his day and the various classes of men and women with whom he came into contact. In a truer sense than even Milton's magnificent epics of Paradise is this work in home-spun prose the great literary record of English Puritanism. Milton's poems were conscious literary productions, dealing with sacred history; their appeal, largely, artistic, is limited. Bunyan's book presents concrete problems of everyday life, and speaks straight to the hearts of all people, simple and learned alike.

"The *Pilgrim's Progress* is composed in the lowest style of English without slang or false grammar. If you were to polish it, you would at once destroy the reality of the vision. For works of imagination should be written in very plain language; the more purely imaginative they are the more necessary it is to be plain."—Coleridge.

Biography: Froude (EML) and Venables, (GW). Besides essays by Coleridge, Dowden, Macaulay, Lang, More (Shel. 6), there are articles by L. Powys, "Bunyan, the Bible, and Bedfordshire," *No. Am.* 217:232-8, a readable presentation of Bunyan's personality; and, most interesting, W. E. Beet, *"Pilgrim's Progress* as a History Source Book," *Liv. Age* 321:1103-7.

From THE PILGRIM'S PROGRESS [1]

[CHRISTIAN FLEES FROM THE CITY OF DESTRUCTION]

As I walked through the wilderness of this world, I lighted on a certain place where was a den, [2] and I laid me down in that place to sleep; and as I slept I dreamed a dream. I dreamed, and behold, I saw a man clothed with rags standing in a certain place with his face from his own house, a book in his hand and a great burden upon his back. I looked and saw him open the book and read therein; and as he read he wept and trembled; and not being able longer to contain, he brake out with a lamentable cry, saying, "What shall I do?"

I saw also that he looked this way and that way, as if he would run; yet he stood still, because, as I perceived, he could not tell which way to go. I looked then, and saw a man

[1] "The Pilgrim's Progress from This World to That which is to come: Delivered under the Similitude of a Dream, wherein is Discovered the manner of his setting out, his Dangerous Journey, and safe Arrival at the Desired Country" is the title of the first edition, 1678, from which this text is taken.

[2] Bedford Jail

named Evangelist coming to him, and [he] asked, "Wherefore dost thou cry?"

He answered, "Sir, I perceive by the book in my hand that I am condemned to die, and after that to come to judgment; and I find that I am not willing to do the first nor able to do the second."

Then said Evangelist, "Why not willing to die, since this life is attended with so many evils?" The man answered, "Because I fear that this burden that is upon my back will sink me lower than the grave, and I shall fall into Tophet.[1] And, sir, if I be not fit to go to prison I am not fit (I am sure) to go to judgment, and from thence to execution; and the thoughts of these things make me cry."

Then said Evangelist, "If this be thy condition why standest thou still?" He answered, "Because I know not whither to go." Then he gave him a parchment roll, and there was written within, "Fly from the wrath to come."

The man therefore read it, and, looking upon Evangelist very carefully, said, "Whither must I fly?" Then said Evangelist, pointing with his finger over a very wide field, " Do you see yonder wicket gate?" The man said, "No." Then said the other, "Do you see yonder shining light?" He said, "I think I do." Then said Evangelist, "Keep that light in your eye, and go up directly thereto, so shalt thou see the gate; at which when thou knockest, it shall be told thee what thou shalt do."

So I saw in my dream that the man began to run. Now he had not run far from his own door but his wife and children, perceiving it, began to cry after him to return; but the man put his fingers in his ears and ran on, crying, "Life! life! eternal life!" So he looked not behind him, but fled toward the middle of the plain.

The neighbors also came out to see him run; and as he ran, some mocked, others threatened, and some cried after him to return. Now among those that did so, there were two that were resolved to fetch him back by force. The name of the one was Obstinate and the name of the other Pliable. Now by this time the man was got a good distance from them; but, however, they were resolved to pursue him, which they did, and in a little time overtook him. Then said the man, "Neighbors, wherefore are you come?" They said, "To persuade you to go back with us." But he said, "That can by no means be. You dwell," said he, "in the City of Destruction (the place also where I was born); I see it to be so; and dying there, sooner or later, you will sink lower than the grave, into a place that burns with fire and brimstone; be content, good neighbors, and go along with me."

What, said Obstinate, and leave our friends and our comforts behind us!

Yes, said Christian (for that was his name), because that all is not worthy to be compared with a little of that that I am seeking to enjoy; and if you will go along with me you shall fare as I myself; for there, where I go, is enough and to spare. Come away and prove my words.

Obst. What are the things you seek, since you leave all the world to find them?

Chr. I seek an inheritance, incorruptible, undefiled, and that fadeth not away; and it is laid up in heaven, and fast there, to be bestowed, at the time appointed, on them that diligently seek it. Read it so, if you will, in my book.

Obst. Tush, said Obstinate, away with your book; will you go back with us or no?

Chr. No, not I, said the other, because I have laid my hand to the plow.

Obst. Come then, neighbor Pliable, let us turn again, and go home without him; there is a company of these craz'd-headed coxcombs that when they take a fancy by the end, are wiser in their own eyes than seven men that can render a reason.

Then said Pliable, Don't revile; if what the good Christian says is true, the things he looks after are better than ours. My heart inclines to go with my neighbor.

Obst. What, more fools still! Be ruled by me, and go back; who knows whither such a brain-sick fellow will lead you? Go back, go back and be wise.

Chr. Come with me, neighbor Pliable; there are such things to be had which I spoke of, and many more glories besides. If you believe not me read here in this book; and for the truth of what is expressed therein, behold, all is confirmed by the blood of Him that made it.

Pli. Well, neighbor Obstinate, said Pliable, I begin to come to a point; I intend to go along with this good man, and to cast in my lot with him; but, my good companion, do you know the way to this desired place?

Chr. I am directed by a man whose name is Evangelist to speed me to a little gate that is before us, where we shall receive instruction about the way.

Pli. Come then, good neighbor, let us be going. Then they went both together.

Obst. And I will go back to my place, said

[1] hell

Obstinate; I will be no companion of such misled, fantastical fellows.

Now I saw in my dream that when Obstinate was gone back, Christian and Pliable went talking over the plain; and thus they began their discourse.

Chr. Come, neighbor Pliable, how do you do? I am glad you are persuaded to go along with me; and had even Obstinate himself but felt what I have felt of the powers and terrors of what is yet unseen, he would not thus lightly have given us the back.

Pli. Come, neighbor Christian, since there is none but us two here, tell me now further what the things are and how to be enjoyed, whither we are going.

Chr. I can better conceive of them with my mind than speak of them with my tongue; but yet, since you are desirous to know, I will read of them in my book.

Pli. And do you think that the words of your book are certainly true?

Chr. Yes, verily; for it was made by Him that cannot lie.

Pli. Well said; what things are they?

Chr. There is an endless kingdom to be inhabited, and everlasting life to be given us that we may inhabit that kingdom forever.

Pli. Well said; and what else?

Chr. There are crowns of glory to be given us, and garments that will make us shine like the sun in the firmament of heaven.

Pli. This is excellent; and what else?

Chr. There shall be no more crying nor sorrow; for he that is owner of the place will wipe all tears from our eyes.

Pli. And what company shall we have there?

Chr. There we shall be with seraphims and cherubims, creatures that will dazzle your eyes to look on them. There also you shall meet with thousands and ten thousands that have gone before us to that place; none of them are hurtful, but loving and holy; every one walking in the sight of God, and standing in his presence with acceptance forever. In a word, there we shall see the elders with their golden crowns; there we shall see the holy virgins with their golden harps; there we shall see men that by the world were cut in pieces, burned in flames, eaten of beasts, drowned in the seas, for the love that they bare to the Lord of the place, all well, and clothed with immortality as with a garment.

Pli. The hearing of this is enough to ravish one's heart. But are these things to be enjoyed? How shall we get to be sharers hereof?

Chr. The Lord, the governor of that country, hath recorded that in this book; the substance of which is, If we be truly willing to have it He will bestow it upon us freely.

Pli. Well, my good companion, glad am I to hear of these things; come on, let us mend our pace.

Chr. I cannot go so fast as I would by reason of this burden that is upon my back.

Now I saw in my dream that, just as they had ended this talk, they drew near to a very miry slough that was in the midst of the plain; and they, being heedless, did both fall suddenly into the bog. The name of the slough was Despond. Here, therefore, they wallowed for a time, being grievously bedaubed with the dirt; and Christian, because of the burden that was on his back, began to sink in the mire.

Pli. Then said Pliable, Ah, neighbor Christian, where are you now?

Chr. Truly, said Christian, I do not know.

Pli. At that Pliable began to be offended, and angerly said to his fellow, Is this the happiness you have told me all this while of? If we have such ill speed at our first setting out what may we expect 'twixt this and our journey's end? May I get out again with my life, you shall possess the brave country alone for me. And with that he gave a desperate struggle or two, and got out of the mire on that side of the slough which was next to his own house; so away he went, and Christian saw him no more.

Wherefore Christian was left to tumble in the Slough of Despond alone; but still he endeavored to struggle to that side of the slough that was still farther from his own house, and next to the wicket gate; the which he did, but could not get out because of the burden that was upon his back. But I beheld in my dream that a man came to him whose name was Help, and asked him what he did there.

Chr. Sir, said Christian, I was directed this way by a man called Evangelist, who directed me also to yonder gate, that I might escape the wrath to come. And as I was going thither I fell in here.

Help. But why did you not look for the steps?

Chr. Fear followed me so hard that I fled the next [1] way and fell in.

Help. Give me thy hand.

So he gave him his hand, and he drew him out, and set him upon sound ground, and bid him go on his way. [2] . . . .

[1] nearest

[2] Christian passes through the gate, where he gets instructions for his journey; visits the House of the Interpreter; loses his burden at the foot of the Cross; receives a Roll from three Shining Ones; and after falling in with Formalist and Hypocrisy, comes to the Hill of Difficulty.

[The Hill of Difficulty and the Sinful Sleep]

. . . .

I beheld then that they all went on till they came to the foot of an hill, at the bottom of which was a spring. There was also in the same place two other ways besides that which came straight from the gate; one turned to the left hand and the other to the right at the bottom of the hill; but the narrow way lay right up the hill, and the name of the going up the side of the hill is called Difficulty. Christian now went to the spring and drank thereof to refresh himself, and then began to go up the hill, saying,

This hill, though high, I covet to ascend;
The difficulty will not me offend;
For I perceive the way to life lies here.
Come, pluck up, Heart, let's neither faint nor fear;
Better, though difficult, the right way to go,
Than wrong, though easy, where the end is woe.

The other two also came to the foot of the hill. But when they saw that the hill was steep and high, and that there was two other ways to go; and supposing also that these two ways might meet again with that up which Christian went, on the other side of the hill; therefore they were resolved to go in those ways. Now the name of one of those ways was Danger, and the name of the other Destruction. So the one took the way which is called Danger, which led him into a great wood; and the other took directly up the way to Destruction, which led him into a wide field, full of dark mountains, where he stumbled and fell, and rose no more.

I looked then after Christian to see him go up the hill, where I perceived he fell from running to going,[1] and from going to clambering upon his hands and his knees, because of the steepness of the place. Now about the midway to the top of the hill was a pleasant arbor made by the Lord of the hill for the refreshment of weary travelers. Thither, therefore, Christian got, where also he sat down to rest him. Then he pulled his Roll out of his bosom, and read therein to his comfort; he also now began afresh to take a review of the coat or garment that was given him as he stood by the cross. Thus pleasing himself awhile he at last fell into a slumber, and thence into a fast sleep which detained him in that place until it was almost night; and in his sleep his Roll fell out of his hand. Now as he was sleeping, there came one to him and awaked him, saying, "Go to the ant, thou sluggard; consider her ways, and be wise." And with that, Christian suddenly started up and sped him on his way, and went apace till he came to the top of the hill.

[1] walking

Now when he was got up to the top of the hill there came two men running against him amain; the name of the one was Timorous and the name of the other Mistrust; to whom Christian said, sirs, what's the matter? You run the wrong way. Timorous answered, that they were going to the City of Zion, and had got up that difficult place; but, said he, the farther we go the more danger we meet with; wherefore we turned and are going back again.

Yes, said Mistrust, for just before us lie a couple of lions in the way, whether sleeping or waking we know not; and we could not think, if we came within reach, but they would presently pull us in pieces.

Chr. Then said Christian, You make me afraid; but whither shall I fly to be safe? If I go back to mine own country, that is prepared for fire and brimstone, and I shall certainly perish there. If I can get to the Celestial City I am sure to be in safety there. I must venture. To go back is nothing but death; to go forward is fear of death, and life everlasting beyond it; I will yet go forward. So Mistrust and Timorous ran down the hill, and Christian went on his way. But thinking again of what he had heard from the men, he felt in his bosom for his Roll that he might read therein and be comforted; but he felt, and found it not.

Then was Christian in great distress, and knew not what to do; for he wanted that which used to relieve him and that which should have been his pass into the Celestial City. Here, therefore, he began to be much perplexed, and knew not what to do. At last he bethought himself that he had slept in the arbor that is on the side of the hill; and falling down upon his knees he asked God forgiveness for that his foolish fact,[2] and then went back to look for his Roll. But all the way he went back, who can sufficiently set forth the sorrow of Christian's heart? Sometimes he sighed, sometimes he wept, and oftentimes he chid himself for being so foolish to fall asleep in that place which was erected only for a little refreshment from his weariness. Thus, therefore, he went back, carefully looking on this side and on that all the way as he went, if happily he might find his Roll that had been his comfort so many times in his journey. He went thus till he came again

[2] deed

within sight of the arbor where he sat and slept; but that sight renewed his sorrow the more by bringing again, even afresh, his evil of sleeping into his mind. Thus, therefore, he now went on bewailing his sinful sleep, saying, Oh, wretched man that I am, that I should sleep in the daytime! that I should sleep in the midst of difficulty! that I should so indulge the flesh as to use that rest for ease to my flesh which the Lord of the hill hath erected only for the relief of the spirits of pilgrims! How many steps have I taken in vain! Thus it happened to Israel; for their sin they were sent back again by the way of the Red Sea; and I am made to tread those steps with sorrow which I might have trod with delight, had it not been for this sinful sleep. How far might I have been on my way by this time! I am made to tread those steps thrice over which I needed not to have trod but once; yea, now also I am like to be benighted, for the day is almost spent. Oh, that I had not slept!

Now by this time he was come to the arbor again, where for a while he sat down and wept; but at last (as Providence would have it), looking sorrowfully down under the settle, there he espied his Roll, the which he with trembling and haste catched up and put it into his bosom. But who can tell how joyful this man was when he had gotten his Roll again? For this Roll was the assurance of his life, and acceptance at the desired haven. Therefore he laid it up in his bosom, gave thanks to God for directing his eye to the place where it lay, and with joy and tears betook himself again to his journey. But oh, how nimbly now did he go up the rest of the hill! Yet before he got up the sun went down upon Christian; and this made him again recall the vanity of his sleeping to his remembrance; and thus he again began to condole with himself: Ah, thou sinful sleep! how for thy sake am I like to be benighted in my journey! I must walk without the sun, darkness must cover the path of my feet, and I must hear the noise of doleful creatures because of my sinful sleep! Now also he remembered the story that Mistrust and Timorous told him of how they were frighted with the sight of the lions. Then said Christian to himself again, These beasts range in the night for their prey; and if they should meet with me in the dark how should I shift them, how should I escape being by them torn in pieces? Thus he went on his way. But while he was thus bewailing his unhappy miscarriage, he lift up his eyes, and behold, there was a very stately Palace before him, the name whereof was Beautiful, and it stood just by the highway-side.

. . . .

1678

SAMUEL PEPYS 1633-1703

Of value as social historical documents, throwing light on many phases of life after the Restoration—court society, the theater, music, literature, science, public events—and of interest as revealing two very different personalities and their reaction to the life about them, are two diaries which have become classics in their way—those of Pepys and Evelyn.

Unfortunately, Pepys's eyesight began to fail while he was still a comparatively young man; hence his *Diary* covers only ten years of his life, 1660-1670. It belongs to what may be called unconscious literature. It was not intended for publication, is reckless in grammar, unconcerned for style, oblivious of any sort of propriety, yet famous for its portrayal of an interesting man in an interesting period. It was written in an original shorthand and was not published until 1825.

Its author, after the usual education, early showed a good business mind and executive ability. He became a clerk in the navy department, prospered financially, and rose to positions of great importance. At the height of his fame he was secretary of the Admiralty, "a very able and energetic official, [who] came at a critical period, when an approach to the modern system of organization was being introduced." An ardent royalist, he came into intimate connection with court life and all the most notable people of his time. In 1689, after the flight of James II, he was accused of giving information to the French, deprived of his offices and imprisoned; but being released on a plea of ill-health, retired from public life.

Samuel Pepys and the World He Lived In, by Henry B. Wheatley, is an authoritative work; the essay in R. L. Stevenson's *Familiar Studies* is good; and Gamaliel Bradford's *Soul of Samuel Pepys,* 1924, is an interesting example of recent biography.

From His DIARY

[Pepys Appointed Secretary to the Generals of the Fleet. The Return of King Charles]

Jan. 1, 1660 (Lord's day). This morning (we living lately in the garret) I rose, put on my suit with great skirts, having not lately worn any other clothes but them. Went to Mr. Gunning's chapel at Exeter House, where he made a very good sermon. Dined at home in the garret, where my wife dressed the remains of a turkey, and in the doing of it she burned her hand. I stayed at home all the afternoon, looking over my accounts; then went with my wife to my father's and in going observed the great posts which the City have set up at the Conduit in Fleet Street.

Mar. 5th. To Westminster by water, only seeing Mr. Pinkney at his own house, where he showed me how he had always kept the lion and unicorn, in the back of his chimney, bright in expectation of the King's coming again. At home I found Mr. Hunt, who told me how the Parliament had voted that the Covenant [1] be printed and hung in churches again. Great hopes of the King's coming again.

6th. . . . . Everybody now drinks the King's health without any fear, whereas before it was very private that a man dare do it. . . . .

22nd. To Westminster, and received my warrant of Mr. Blackburne to be secretary to the two Generals of the Fleet. . . . .

23rd. My Lord,[2] Captain Isham, Mr. Thomas, John Crewe, W. Howe, and I to the Tower, where the barges stayed for us; my Lord and the Captain in one, and W. Howe and I, &c., in the other, to the Long Reach, where the *Swiftsure* lay at anchor; (in our way we saw the great breach which the late high water had made, to the loss of many £1000 to the people about Limehouse). Soon as my Lord on board, the guns went off bravely from the ships. And a little while after comes the Vice-Admiral Lawson, and seemed very respectful to my Lord, and so did the rest of the commanders of the frigates that were thereabouts. I to the cabin allotted for me, which was the best that any had that belonged to my Lord. We were late writing of orders, for the getting of ships ready, &c. . . . .

May 1. . . . Today I hear they were very merry at Deal,[3] setting up the King's flag upon one of their maypoles, and drinking his health upon their knees in the streets, and firing the guns, which the soldiers of the castle threatened, but durst not oppose.

2nd. In the morning at a breakfast of radishes in the Purser's cabin. After that, to writing till dinner. At which time comes Dunne from London, with letters that tell us the welcome news of the Parliament's votes yesterday, which will be remembered for the happiest May-day that hath been many a year to England. The King's letter was read in the House, wherein he submits himself and all things to them, as to an Act of Oblivion to all, unless they shall please to except any. . . .

May 29th. . . . . Abroad to shore with my Lord (which he offered me of himself, saying that I had a great deal of work to do this month, which was very true.) On shore we took horses, my Lord and Mr. Edward, Mr. Hetly and I, and three or four servants, and had a great deal of pleasure in riding. . . . . At last we came upon a very high cliff by the seaside, and rode under it, we having laid great wagers, I and Dr. Matthews, that it was not so high as Pauls,[4] my Lord and Mr. Hetly, that it was. But we riding under it, my Lord made a pretty good measure of it with two sticks, and found it to be not above thirty-five yards high, and Paul's is reckoned to be about ninety. From thence toward the barge again, and in our way found the people of Deal going to make a bonfire for joy of the day, it being the King's birthday, and had some guns which they did fire at my Lord's coming by. For which I did give twenty shillings among them to drink. While we were on the top of the cliff, we saw and heard our guns in the fleet go off for the same joy. And it being a pretty fair day, we could see above twenty miles into France. Being returned on board, my Lord called for Mr. Shepley's book of Paul's, by which we were confirmed in our wager. . . . . This day, it is thought, the King do enter the City of London.

30th. . . . . All this morning making up my accounts, in which I counted that I had made myself now worth about £80, at which my heart was glad, and blessed God.

[Matters Personal and Domestic]

Oct. 13th. I went out to Charing Cross, to see Major-General Harrison [5] hanged, drawn, and quartered; which was done there, he looking as cheerful as any man could do in that condition. He was presently cut down, and his head and heart shown to the people, at which there was great shouts of joy. It is said that he said that he was sure to come shortly at the right hand of Christ to judge them that now had judged him; and that his wife do expect his coming again. Thus it was my chance to see the King beheaded at

[1] The Scottish "Covenant with God," a declaration of resistance to the Roman Church; the next year it was ordered to be publicly burnt.

[2] Sir Edward Montagu, whose service Pepys had entered, and who, as admiral and general, was appointed to convey Charles II from Holland to England

[3] a port near Dover

[4] St. Paul's Cathedral, London

[5] He had served under Cromwell, and had signed the warrant for the execution of Charles I.

Whitehall, and to see the first blood shed in revenge for the blood of the King at Charing Cross. From thence to my Lord's, and took Captain Cuttance and Mr. Sheply to the Sun Tavern, and did give them some oysters. After that I went by water home, where I was angry with my wife for her things lying about, and in my passion kicked the little fine basket which I bought her in Holland, and broke it, which troubled me after I had done it. Within all the afternoon setting up shelves in my study. At night to bed.

Nov. 22nd. This morning come the carpenters to make me a door at the other side of my house, going into the entry, which I was much pleased with. At noon, my wife and I walked to the Old Exchange, and there she bought her a white whisk [1] and put it on, and I a pair of gloves, and so we took coach for Whitehall to Mr. Fox's, where we found Mrs. Fox within, and an alderman of London paying £1000 or £1400 in gold upon the table for the King, which was the most gold that ever I saw together in my life. Mr. Fox come in presently and did receive us with a great deal of respect; and then did take my wife and I to the Queen's presence-chamber, where he got my wife placed behind the Queen's chair, and I got into the crowd, and by and by the Queen and the two Princesses come to dinner. The Queen a very little, plain, old woman, [2] and nothing more in her presence in any respect nor garb than any ordinary woman. The Princess of Orange I had often seen before. The Princess Henrietta is very pretty, but much below my expectation; and her dressing of herself with her hair frizzed short up to her ears, did make her seem so much the less to me. But my wife standing near her with two or three black patches on, and well dressed, did seem to me much handsomer than she. . . . .

Feb. 27th, 1661. I called for a dish of fish, which we had for dinner, this being the first day of Lent; and I do intend to try whether I can keep it or no. . . . .

28th. I took boat at Whitehall for Redriffe but in my way overtook Captain Cuttance and Tiddiman in a boat and so ashore with them at Queenhithe, and so to a tavern with them to a barrel of oysters, and so away. Capt. Cuttance and I walked from Redriffe to Deptford, and there we dined, and notwithstanding my resolution, yet for want of other victuals, I did eat flesh this Lent, but am resolved to eat as little as I can.

[1] neckerchief

[2] Henrietta Maria, mother of Charles; the princesses mentioned were two of her daughters.

[The Coronation of Charles II]

Apr. 23rd. Coronation Day. About four I rose and got to the Abbey, where I followed Sir J. Denham, the Surveyor, with some company that he was leading in. And with much ado, by the favor of Mr. Cooper, his man, did get up into a great scaffold across the north end of the Abbey, where with a great deal of patience I sat from past four till eleven before the King come in. And a great pleasure it was to see the Abbey raised in the middle, all covered with red, and a throne (that is a chair) and foot-stool on the top of it; and all the officers of all kinds, so much as the very fiddlers, in red vests.

At last comes in the Dean and Prebends of Westminster, with the Bishops (many of them in cloth-of-gold copes), and after them the Nobility, all in their Parliament robes, which was a most magnificent sight. Then the Duke and the King with a scepter (carried by my Lord Sandwich) and sword and wand before him, and the crown, too. The King in his robes, bare-headed, which was very fine. And after all had placed themselves, there was a sermon and the service; and then in the Choir at the high altar, the King passed through all the ceremonies of the Coronation, which to my great grief I and most in the Abbey could not see. The crown being put upon his head, a great shout began, and he come forth to the throne, and there passed more ceremonies; as taking the oath, and having things read to him by the Bishop; and his Lords (who put on their caps as soon as the King put on his crown) and bishops come, and kneeled before him. And three times the King at Arms [3] went to the three open places on the scaffold, and proclaimed, that if any one could show any reason why Charles Stewart should not be King of England, that now he should come and speak. And a General Pardon also was read by the Lord Chancellor, and medals flung up and down by my Lord Cornwallis, of silver, but I could not come by any. But so great a noise that I could make but little of the music; and indeed, it was lost to everybody.

I went out a little while before the King had done all his ceremonies, and went round the Abbey to Westminster Hall, all the way within rails, and 10,000 people, with the ground covered with blue cloth; and scaffolds all the way. Into the Hall I got, where it was very fine with hangings and scaffolds one upon another full of brave ladies; and my wife in one

[3] the Garter King-at-Arms, head of the heralds

little one, on the right hand. Here I stayed walking up and down, and at last, upon one of the side stalls I stood and saw the King come in with all the persons (but the soldiers) that were yesterday in the cavalcade; and a most pleasant sight it was to see them in their several robes. And the King come in with his crown on, and his scepter in his hand, under a canopy borne up by six silver staves, carried by Barons of the Cinque Ports, [1] and little bells at every end.

And after a long time, he got up to the farther end, and all set themselves down at their several tables; and that was also a brave sight; and the King's first course carried up by the Knights of the Bath. And many fine ceremonies there was of the herald's leading up people before him, and bowing; and my Lord of Albemarle's going to the kitchen and eat a bit of the first dish that was to go to the King's table. But, above all, was these three Lords, Northumberland, and Suffolk, and the Duke of Ormond, coming before the courses on horseback, and staying so all dinner-time, and at last to bring up [2][Dymock] the King's champion, all in armor on horseback, with his spear and target carried before him. And a herald proclaims, that if any dare deny Charles Stewart to be lawful King of England, here was a champion that would fight with him; and with these words, the champion flings down his gauntlet, and all this he do three times in his going up toward the King's table. At last when he is come, the King drinks to him, and then sends him the cup, which is of gold, and he drinks it off, and then rides back again with the cup in his hand. I went from table to table to see the bishops and all others at their dinner, and was infinitely pleased with it. And at the Lord's table, I met with William Howe, and he spoke to my Lord for me, and he did give me four rabbits and a pullet, and so I got it and Mr. Creed and I got Mr. Minshell to give us some bread, and so we at a stall eat it, as everybody else did what they could get. I took a great deal of pleasure to go up and down, and look upon the ladies, and to hear the music of all sorts, but above all, the twenty-four violins.

About six at night they had dined, and I went up to my wife. And strange it is to think, that these two days have held up fair till now that all is done, and the King gone out of the Hall; and then it fell a-raining and thundering and lightening as I have not seen it do for some years, which people did take great notice of; God's blessing of the work of these two days, which is a foolery to take too much notice of such things. I observed little disorder in all this, only the King's footmen had got hold of the canopy, and would keep it from the Barons of the Cinque Ports, which they endeavored to force from them again, but could not do it till my Lord Duke of Albemarle caused it to be put into Sir R. Pye's hand till tomorrow to be decided.

At Mr. Bowyer's; a great deal of company, some I knew, other I did not. Here we stayed upon the leads [3] and below till it was late, expecting to see the fireworks, but they were not performed tonight; only the City had a light like a glory round about it with bonfires. At last I went to King Street, and there sent Crockford to my father's and my house, to tell them I could not come home tonight because of the dirt, and a coach could not be had. And so I took my wife and Mrs. Frankleyn (who I proffered the civility of lying with my wife at Mrs. Hunt's tonight) to Axe Yard, in which at the farther end there were three great bonfires, and a great many great gallants, men and women; and they laid hold of us, and would have us drink the King's health upon our knees, kneeling upon a faggot, which we all did, they drinking to us one after another; which we thought a strange frolic; but these gallants continued thus a great while, and I wondered to see how the ladies did tipple. At last I sent my wife and her bedfellow to bed, and Mr. Hunt and I went in with Mr. Thornbury (who did give the company all their wine, he being yeoman of the winecellar to the King) to his home; and there, with his wife and two of his sisters and some gallant sparks that were there, we drank the King's health, and nothing else, till one of the gentlemen fell down stark drunk, and there lay; and I went to my Lord's pretty well. . . . .

Thus did the day end with joy everywhere; and blessed be God, I have not heard of any mischance to anybody through it all, but only to Sergt. Glynne, whose horse fell upon him yesterday, and is like to kill him, which people do please themselves to see how just God is to punish the rogue at such a time as this; he being now one of the King's Sergeants, and rode in the cavalcade with Maynard, to whom people wish the same fortune. [4] There was also

[1] the five English Channel ports, Hastings, Sandwich, Dover, Romney, Hythe

[2] This ceremony is no longer observed.

[3] roof (of sheets of lead)

[4] Both men had served Cromwell during the Protectorate, but unscrupulously transferred their allegiance to Charles at the time of the Restoration.

this night in King Street, a woman had her eye put out by a boy's flinging a firebrand into the coach. Now, after all this, I can say that, besides the pleasure of the sight of these glorious things, I may now shut my eyes against any other objects, nor for the future trouble myself to see things of state and show as being sure never to see the like again in this world.

24th. . . . . At night, set myself to write down these three days' diary, and while I am about it, I hear the noise of the chambers, and other things of the fireworks, which are now playing upon the Thames before the King; and I wish myself with them, being sorry not to see them.

1660-1 1825

JOHN EVELYN 1620-1706

John Evelyn, "a good man in difficult times," a favorite of Charles II, traveler, and member of the Royal Society of London, was a man of real culture and wide intellectual interests. He lived a much more retired life than Pepys, though the two possessed in common one quality invaluable to a diarist—that of curiosity. He seems to have shrunk from contact with public events, and consistently avoided strife. As a boy he refused to go to Eton, and he took no university degree; he joined the king's army in 1642, but apparently did not see action. Much of his time was spent in traveling on the Continent, or on the family estate at Wotton, gardening and studying. He was frequently at Court after the Restoration and held minor offices, but took no part in political intrigues. After the Revolution of 1688 he lived in retirement until his death, a recognized authority on architecture and landscape gardening.

His *Diary* extends from 1640 to 1706, covering a much longer period than that of Pepys. Austin Dobson says of it: "If it does not, like the Diary of Pepys, disclose the inner character of the writer, it nevertheless possesses a distinctive interest. Its entries have the precise value of veracious statements; it is a magazine—a mine, Scott called it—of contemporary memories of a definite kind." It "is the commentary of a man who sits quietly by, watching a turbulent world which wrings nothing more from him than an occasional complaint at its strange contrariety. And it is the diary, too, of a mind equally at peace with itself."—Hale Bellot.

Recent articles are by Hale Bellot, "John Evelyn, 1620-1706," *Contemp.* 114:201-7, a picture of the diarist's personality; and H. Chartres Biron, "An Adventuring Diarist," *Liv. Age* 307:160-9.

From His DIARY

The Restoration of Charles II

May 29, 1660. This day his Majesty Charles II came to London after a sad and long exile and calamitous suffering both of the King and Church, being 17 years. This was also his birthday, and with a triumph of above 20,000 horse and foot, brandishing their swords and shouting with inexpressible joy; the ways strewed with flowers, the bells ringing, the streets hung with tapestry, fountains running with wine; the Mayor, Aldermen, and all the Companies [1] in their liveries, chains of gold and banners; Lords and Nobles clad in cloth of silver, gold, and velvet; the windows and balconies all set with ladies; trumpets, music, and myriads of people flocking, even so far as from Rochester, so as they were seven hours in passing the City, even from 2 in the afternoon till 9 at night.

I stood in the Strand and beheld it, and blessed God. And all this was done without one drop of blood shed, and by that very army which rebelled against him; but it was the Lord's doing, for such a Restoration was never mentioned in any history, ancient or modern, since the return of the Jews from the Babylonish captivity; nor so joyful a day and so bright ever seen in this nation, this happening when to expect or effect it was past all human policy.

July 6. His Majesty began first to *touch for the evil*,[2] according to custom, thus: his Majesty sitting under his State [3] in the Banqueting-House, the chirurgeons cause the sick to be brought or led to the throne, where they kneeling, the King strokes their faces or cheeks with both his hands at once, at which instant a chaplain in his formalities says, "He put his hands upon them and he healed them." This is said to every one in particular. When they have been all touched they come up again in the same order, and the other chaplain kneeling, and having angel gold [4] strung on white ribbon on his arm, delivers them one by one to his Majesty, who puts them about the necks of the touched as they pass, whilst the first chaplain repeats, "That is the true light who came into the world." Then follows an epistle (as at first a gospel) with the liturgy, prayers for the sick, with some alteration, lastly the blessing; and then the Lord Chamberlain and Comptroller of the Household bring a basin, ewer, and towel, for his Majesty to wash. . . . .

Jan. 30, 1661. Was the first solemn fast and day of humiliation to deplore the sins which so

[1] the Livery Companies, or Guilds, established in the fourteenth century as a part of the city government to protect members of the various crafts.

[2] The scrofula was familiarly known as "the king's evil," from the superstition that it could be healed by the royal touch.

[3] canopy of state

[4] gold coin (bearing the figure of an angel)

long had provoked God against this afflicted church and people, ordered by Parliament to be annually celebrated to expiate the guilt of the execrable murder of the late King.

This day (Oh, the stupendous and inscrutable judgments of God!) were the carcasses of those arch rebels, Cromwell, Bradshaw, the judge who condemned his Majesty, and Ireton, son-in-law to the Usurper, dragged out of their superb tombs in Westminster among the kings, to Tyburn, and hanged on the gallows there from 9 in the morning till 6 at night, and then buried under that fatal and ignominious monument in a deep pit; thousands of people who had seen them in all their pride being spectators. Look back at October 22, 1658, [Oliver's funeral] and be astonished! and fear God and honor the King; but meddle not with them who are given to change!

Nov. 11. I was so idle as to go see a play called *Love and Honor.*—Dined at Arundel House; and that evening discoursed with his Majesty about shipping, in which he was exceeding skillful.

26. I saw *Hamlet, Prince of Denmark* played, but now the old plays began to disgust this refined age, since his Majesty's being so long abroad.

Dec. 14. I saw otter hunting with the King, and killed one.

23. I heard an Italian play and sing to the guitar with extraordinary skill before the Duke.

Jan. 6, 1662. This evening, according to custom, his Majesty opened the revels of that night by throwing the dice himself in the privy chamber, where was a table set on purpose, and lost his £100. (The year before he won £1500.) The ladies also played very deep. I came away when the Duke of Ormond had won about £1000, and left them still at *passage,*[1] *cards,* etc. At other tables, both there and at the Groom-porter's,[2] observing the wicked folly and monstrous excess of passion amongst some losers; sorry I am that such a wretched custom as play to that excess should be countenanced in a Court which ought to be an example of virtue to the rest of the kingdom.

[The Great Plague]

Aug. 2, 1665. A solemn fast through England to deprecate God's displeasure against the land by pestilence and war; our Doctor preaching on 26 *Levit.* 41, 42, that the means to obtain remission of punishment was not to repine at it, but humbly submit to it.

28. The contagion still increasing and growing now all about us, I sent my wife and whole family (two or three necessary servants excepted) to my brother's at Wotton, being resolved to stay at my house myself and to look after my charge, trusting in the providence and goodness of God.

Sept. 7. Came home, there perishing near 10,000 poor creatures weekly; however, I went all along the City and suburbs from Kent Street to St. James's, a dismal passage, and dangerous to see so many coffins exposed in the streets, now thin of people; the shops shut up, and all in mournful silence, as not knowing whose turn might be next. I went to the Duke of Albemarle for a pest-ship, to wait on our infected men, who were not a few.

Dec. 31. Now blessed be God for his extraordinary mercies and preservation of me this year, when thousands and ten thousands perished and were swept away on each side of me, there dying in our parish this year 406 of the pestilence!

[The Great Fire]

Sept. 2, 1666. This fatal night about ten, began that deplorable fire near Fish Street in London.

3. I had public prayers at home. The fire continuing, after dinner I took coach with my wife and son, and went to the Bankside in Southwark where we beheld the dismal spectacle, the whole City in dreadful flames near the water side; all the houses from the Bridge, all Thames Street, and upward toward Cheapside, down to the Three Cranes, were now consumed; and so returned exceeding astonished what would become of the rest.

The fire having continued all this night (if I may call that night which was light as day for ten miles round about, after a dreadful manner) when conspiring with a fierce eastern wind in a very dry season; I went on foot to the same place, and saw the whole south part of the City burning from Cheapside to the Thames, and all along Cornhill (for it likewise kindled back against the wind as well as forward), Tower Street, Fenchurch Street, Gracious Street, and so along to Baynard's Castle, and was now taking hold of St. Paul's Church, to which the scaffolds contributed exceedingly. The conflagration was so universal, and the people so astonished, that from the beginning, I know not by what despondency or fate, they hardly stirred to quench it, so that there was nothing heard or seen but crying out and lamentation, running about like distracted creatures, without at all attempting to save even

[1] a game of dice [2] the royal director of games

their goods; such a strange consternation there was upon them, so as it burned both in breadth and length, the churches, public halls, Exchange, hospitals, monuments, and ornaments, leaping after a prodigious manner from house to house and street to street, at great distances one from the other; for the heat with a long set of fair and warm weather had even ignited the air and prepared the materials to conceive the fire, which devoured after an incredible manner houses, furniture, and everything. Here we saw the Thames covered with goods floating, all the barges and boats laden with what some had time and courage to save, as, on the other side, the carts, etc., carrying out to the fields, which for many miles were strewed with movables of all sorts, and tents erecting to shelter both people and what goods they could get away. Oh, the miserable and calamitous spectacle! such as haply the world had not seen the like since the foundation of it, nor be outdone, till the universal conflagration of it. All the sky was of a fiery aspect, like the top of a burning oven, and the light seen above 40 miles round about for many nights. God grant mine eyes may never behold the like, who now saw above 10,000 houses all in one flame; the noise and cracking and thunder of the impetuous flames, and shrieking of women and children, the hurry of people, the fall of towers, houses, and churches, was like an hideous storm, and the air all about so hot and inflamed that at the last one was not able to approach it, so that they were forced to stand still and let the flames burn on, which they did for near two miles in length and one in breadth. The clouds, also, of smoke were dismal, and reached, upon computation, near 50 miles in length. Thus I left it this afternoon burning, a resemblance of Sodom, or the last day. It forcibly called to my mind that passage—*non enim hic habemus stabilem civitatem;* [1] the ruins resembling the picture of Troy. London was, but is no more. Thus I returned home.

[The Death of Cowley]

Aug. 1, 1667. I received the sad news of Abraham Cowley's death, that incomparable poet and virtuous man, my very dear friend, and was greatly deplored.

3. Went to Mr. Cowley's funeral, whose corpse lay at Wallingford House, and was thence conveyed to Westminster Abbey in a hearse with six horses and all funeral decency, near an hundred coaches of noblemen and persons of quality following; among these all the wits [2] of the town, divers bishops and clergymen. He was interred next Geoffrey Chaucer and near to Spenser. A goodly monument has been since erected to his memory.

[Popular Pastimes]

June 16, 1670. I went with some friends to the Bear Garden, where was cock-fighting, dog-fighting, bear- and bull-baiting, it being a famous day for all these butcherly sports, or rather barbarous cruelties. The bulls did exceeding well, but the Irish wolf-dog exceeded, which was a tall greyhound, a stately creature indeed, who beat a cruel mastiff. One of the bulls tossed a dog full into a *lady's lap,* as she sat in one of the boxes at a considerable height from the arena. Two poor dogs were killed, and so all ended with the ape on horseback, and I most heartily weary of the rude and dirty pastime, which I had not seen, I think, in twenty years before.

[The Death of Charles II]

Feb. 4, 1685. I went to London, hearing his Majesty had been the Monday before (2 Feb.) surprised in his bedchamber with an apoplectic fit. On Thursday hopes of recovery were signified in the public Gazette, but that day, about noon, the physicians thought him feverish. . . . . He passed Thursday night with great difficulty, when, complaining of a pain in his side, they drew two ounces more of blood from him; this was by 6 in the morning on Friday, and it gave him relief, but it did not continue, for being now in much pain, and struggling for breath, he lay dozing, and after some conflicts, the physicians despairing of him, he gave up the ghost at half an hour after eleven in the morning, being 6 Feb. 1685, in the 36th year of his reign, and 54th of his age. . . . .

Thus died King Charles II, of a vigorous and robust constitution, and in all appearance promising a long life. He was a Prince of many virtues, and many great imperfections; debonair, easy of access, not bloody nor cruel; his countenance fierce, his voice great, proper of person, every motion became him; a lover of the sea, and skillful in shipping; not affecting other studies, yet he had a laboratory and knew of many empirical [3] medicines, and the easier mechanical mathematics; he loved planting and building, and brought in a politer way of living, which passed to luxury and intolerable expense. He had a particular talent in telling a story

[1] "For we have no abiding city."

[2] men of culture

[3] approved by unscientific observation

and facetious passages, of which he had innumerable; this made some buffoons and vicious wretches too presumptuous and familiar, not worthy the favor they abused. He took delight in having a number of little spaniels follow him and lie in his bedchamber.

. . . .

Certainly never had king more glorious opportunities to have made himself, his people, and all Europe happy, and prevented innumerable mischiefs, had not his too easy nature resigned him to be managed by crafty men, and some abandoned and profane wretches who corrupted his otherwise sufficient parts, disciplined as he had been by many afflictions during his banishment, which gave him much experience and knowledge of men and things; but those wicked creatures took him off from all application becoming so great a king. The history of his reign will certainly be the most wonderful for the variety of matter and accidents, above any extant in former ages; the sad tragical death of his father, his banishment and hardships, his miraculous restoration, conspiracies against him, parliaments, wars, plagues, fires, comets, revolutions abroad happening in his time, with a thousand other particulars. He was ever kind to me, and very gracious upon all occasions, and therefore I cannot, without ingratitude, but deplore his loss, which for many respects, as well as duty, I do with all my soul.

. . . .

I can never forget the inexpressible luxury and profaneness, gaming and all dissoluteness, and as it were total forgetfulness of God (it being Sunday evening) which this day se'nnight I was witness of, the King sitting and toying with his concubines, Portsmouth, Cleaveland, and Mazarine, etc., a French boy singing love songs, in that glorious gallery, whilst about twenty of the great courtiers and other dissolute persons were at basset[1] round a large table, a bank of at least 2000 in gold before them; upon which two gentlemen who were with me made reflections with astonishment. Six days after was all in the dust! . . . .

1660-85 1818

JOHN DRYDEN 1631-1700

The most important writer of his time, representing court, university, and theater circles was John Dryden, Historiographer Royal and Poet Laureate. A reigning figure at Will's Coffee House,[2] he was almost as much of an autocrat in London letters as Ben Jonson, three quarters of a century earlier, or Samuel Johnson, three quarters of a century later; indeed, the period is often called the Age of Dryden.

Dryden came of a good Norfolk family of Puritan sympathies. After leaving Cambridge he found employment in London and began writing occasional verse. His elegy mourning Cromwell's death did not deter him from celebrating the Restoration in *Astraea Redux,* 1660. His first important poem, *Annus Mirabilis,* 1666, chronicled the year of the Great Fire of London and the Dutch War. By this time he was recognized as a poet, was intimate with the great writers of the day, and had married Lady Elizabeth Howard. For the next fifteen years he turned his attention to drama, producing his *Essay of Dramatic Poesy,* 1668, and nearly a score of plays, among them *All for Love,* 1678, his finest play, a tragedy modeled on Shakespeare's *Antony and Cleopatra,* but showing his adherence to the classicism of the French stage. He began writing his tragedies in heroic couplets, a form which his experiments helped largely to perfect; but later returned to the native English blank-verse freedom.

In 1681 Dryden turned once more to poetry, but in a new vein. *Absalom and Achitophel,* a political satire, was a fine example of masculine insight and vigor of expression. He was now a consummate master of style and had found in satire, in which he outranks even Pope in forthright vigor and incisiveness of phrase, his best literary field. It was followed, after his becoming Catholic on the accession of James II, by the *Hind and the Panther,* 1687, a religious allegory in defense of the Catholic Church. Dryden has been severely criticized for changing his political opinions and his religion in order to keep in favor with the party in power, but he remained a devout Catholic and was content at the end of his life to suffer for his convictions.

Losing all his offices in the Revolution of 1688, the poet again began writing for the stage, but, when Congreve threatened to supplant him in popularity, he took up translation. The *Fables,* published in 1700, the last year of Dryden's life, were metrical translations, or rather paraphrases, of stories from Homer, Ovid, Boccaccio, and Chaucer.

Besides ranking as a notable poet and dramatist, Dryden heralded the "classical" school of the following century; he believed in a poetry regulated by the intellect rather than by the emotions. Moreover, he has been recognized as a leader in if not the founder of modern English criticism and modern English prose; in fact, the latter has not changed fundamentally since Dryden's day. Not only did he produce a considerable body of critical literature—the Preface to the *Fables* (p. 314) is an excellent example—but he imparted precision, clearness, and regularity to the written prose, which, after Malory's day, had wandered into a maze of "euphuism" and involved construction borrowed from the Latin.

[1] a game at cards
[2] See Macaulay, *Hist. of England,* p. 584.

Dryden's works come in the Cambridge Edition. Besides R. Garnett's *Age of Dryden,* and G. Saintsbury (EML), consult Johnson's *Lives,* Lowell, Hazlitt, Rossetti, Macaulay, Masson, Swinburne, and T. S. Eliot, *Homage to John Dryden,* 1924.

From ABSALOM AND ACHITOPHEL[1]

. . . . The inhabitants of old Jerusalem[2]
Were Jebusites;[3] the town so called from them,
And theirs the native right.
But when the chosen people[4] grew more strong,
The rightful cause at length became the wrong;
And every loss the men of Jebus bore,
They still were thought God's enemies the more.
Thus worn and weakened, well or ill content,
Submit they must to David's[5] government.
Impoverished and deprived of all command,
Their taxes doubled as they lost their land;
And, what was harder yet to flesh and blood,
Their gods disgraced, and burnt like common wood.
This set the heathen priesthood in a flame,
For priests of all religions are the same.
Of whatso'er descent their godhead be,
Stock, stone, or other homely pedigree,
In his defense his servants are as bold
As if he had been born of beaten gold.
The Jewish Rabbins,[6] though their enemies,
In this conclude them honest men and wise;
For 'twas their duty, all the learned think,
To espouse his cause by whom they eat and drink.
From hence began that Plot,[7] the nation's curse,
Bad in itself, but represented worse,
Raised in extremes, and in extremes decried,
With oaths affirmed, with dying vows denied,
Not weighed or winnowed by the multitude,
But swallowed in the mass, unchewed and crude.
Some truth there was, but dashed and brewed with lies
To please the fools and puzzle all the wise;
Succeeding times did equal folly call
Believing nothing or believing all.
The Egyptian[8] rights the Jebusites embraced,
Where gods were recommended by their taste;
Such savory deities must needs be good
As served at once for worship and for food.[9]
By force they could not introduce these gods,
For ten to one in former days was odds.
So fraud was used, the sacrificer's trade;
Fools are more hard to conquer than persuade.
Their busy teachers mingled with the Jews
And raked for converts even the court and stews;
Which Hebrew priests the more unkindly took,
Because the fleece accompanies the flock.
Some thought they God's anointed meant to slay
By guns, invented since full many a day.
Our author swears it not; but who can know
How far the Devil and Jebusites may go?
This plot, which failed for want of common sense,
Had yet a deep and dangerous consequence;
For as, when raging fevers boil the blood,
The standing lake soon floats into a flood,
And every hostile humor which before
Slept quiet in its channels bubbles o'er;
So several factions from this first ferment
Work up to foam and threat the government.
Some by their friends, more by themselves thought wise,
Opposed the power to which they could not rise.
Some had in courts been great and, thrown from thence,
Like fiends were hardened in impenitence.
Some of their Monarch's fatal mercy grown
From pardoned rebels kinsmen to the throne
Were raised in power and public office high;
Strong bands, if bands ungrateful men could tie.
Of these the false Achitophel was first,
A name to all succeeding ages curst;
For close designs and crooked counsels fit,
Sagacious, bold, and turbulent of wit,
Restless, unfixed in principles and place,
In power unpleased, impatient of disgrace;
A fiery soul, which working out its way,
Fretted the pigmy body to decay
And o'er-informed[10] the tenement of clay.
A daring pilot in extremity,
Pleased with the danger, when the waves went high,

[1] This, the first of Dryden's satires, was directed against the Earl of Shaftesbury (Achitophel) and the opponents of the Court. The strong excitement aroused by the "Popish Plot," an alleged attempt to strengthen Roman Catholic power in England by the murder of Charles II, had impelled Shaftesbury, a Whig, to endeavor to secure the succession to the Protestant Duke of Monmouth (Absalom), thus preventing the Catholic Duke of York from ascending the throne. Charles II, who was secretly a Catholic, and was receiving aid from France, waited a favorable moment; then, aided by the Tories, he recalled his brother, the Duke of York, and threw Shaftesbury into prison on the charge of high treason. The poem appeared November 17, 1681. Shaftesbury's case was to come up November 24.

[2] London

[3] Roman Catholics

[4] used ironically of the Puritans

[5] Charles II's

[6] dignitaries of the Church of England

[7] the Popish Plot

[8] French

[9] a reference to the doctrine of transubstantiation

[10] filled to excess

He sought the storms; but, for a calm unfit,
Would steer too nigh the sands to boast his wit.
Great wits are sure to madness near allied
And thin partitions do their bounds divide;
Else, why should he, with wealth and honor blest,
Refuse his age the needful hours of rest?
Punish a body which he could not please,
Bankrupt of life, yet prodigal of ease?
And all to leave what with his toil he won
To that unfeathered two-legged thing, a son,
Got while his soul did huddled notions try,
And born a shapeless lump, like anarchy.[1]
In friendship false, implacable in hate,
Resolved to ruin or to rule the state;
To compass this the triple bond[2] he broke,
The pillars of the public safety shook,
And fitted Israel[3] for a foreign yoke;[4]
Then, seized with fear, yet still affecting fame,
Usurped a patriot's all-atoning name.
So easy still it proves in factious times
With public zeal to cancel private crimes.
How safe is treason and how sacred ill,
Where none can sin against the people's will,
Where crowds can wink and no offense be known,
Since in another's guilt they find their own!
Yet fame deserved no enemy can grudge;
The statesman we abhor, but praise the judge.
In Israel's court ne'er sat an Abbethdin[5]
With more discerning eyes or hands more clean,
Unbribed, unsought, the wretched to redress,
Swift of despatch and easy of access.
Oh! had he been content to serve the crown
With virtues only proper to the gown,
Or had the rankness of the soil been freed
From cockle that oppressed the noble seed,
David for him his tuneful harp had strung
And Heaven had wanted[6] one immortal song.
But wild ambition loves to slide, not stand,
And Fortune's ice prefers to Virtue's land.
Achitophel, grown weary to possess
A lawful fame and lazy happiness,
Disdained the golden fruit to gather free
And lent the crowd his arm to shake the tree.
Now, manifest of crimes contrived long since,
He stood at bold defiance with his Prince,
Held up the buckler of the people's cause
Against the crown, and skulked behind the laws.
The wished occasion of the Plot he takes;
Some circumstances finds, but more he makes;
By buzzing emissaries fills the ears
Of listening crowds with jealousies and fears
Of arbitrary counsels brought to light,
And proves the King himself a Jebusite.
Weak arguments! which yet he knew full well
Were strong with people easy to rebel.
For governed by the moon, the giddy Jews
Tread the same track when she the prime renews;
And once in twenty years, their scribes record,
By natural instinct they change their lord.
Achitophel still wants a chief, and none
Was found so fit as warlike Absalon.
Not that he wished his greatness to create,
For politicians neither love nor hate;
But, for he knew his title not allowed
Would keep him still depending on the crowd,
That kingly power, thus ebbing out, might be
Drawn to the dregs of a democracy.
Him he attempts with studied arts to please
And sheds his venom in such words as these:

. . . .

He said, and this advice[7] above the rest
With Absalom's mild nature suited best;
Unblamed of life (ambition set aside),
Not stained with cruelty nor puffed with pride,
How happy had he been, if Destiny
Had higher placed his birth or not so high!
His kingly virtues might have claimed a throne
And blessed all other countries but his own;
But charming greatness since so few refuse,
'Tis juster to lament him than accuse.
Strong were his hopes a rival to remove,
With blandishments to gain the public love,
To head the faction while their zeal was hot,
And popularly prosecute the plot.
To further this, Achitophel unites
The malcontents of all the Israelites,
Whose differing parties he could wisely join
For several ends to serve the same design;
The best, (and of the princes some were such)
Who thought the power of monarchy too much;
Mistaken men and patriots in their hearts,
Not wicked, but seduced by impious arts;
By these the springs of property were bent
And wound so high they cracked the government.
The next for interest sought to embroil the state
To sell their duty at a dearer rate,
And make their Jewish markets of the throne;
Pretending public good to serve their own.

[1] Shaftsbury's son was a weakling.
[2] the alliance of England, Holland, and Sweden, broken by the alliance in 1670 of England and France against Holland
[3] England
[4] that of France
[5] Chief judge of the Jewish court; Shaftesbury had been Lord Chancellor in 1672-3.
[6] lacked (Dryden is referring to his own poem.)
[7] Achitophel has been urging Absalom to advance his cause by securing possession of the person of the king.

Others thought kings an useless heavy load,
Who cost too much and did too little good.
These were for laying honest David by
On principles of pure good husbandry.
With them joined all the haranguers of the throng
That thought to get preferment by the tongue.
Who follow next a double danger bring,
Not only hating David, but the King;
The Solymaean rout [1] well versed of old
In godly faction and in treason bold,
Cowering and quaking at a conqueror's sword,
But lofty to a lawful prince restored,
Saw with disdain an Ethnic [2] plot begun
And scorned by Jebusites to be outdone.
Hot Levites [3] headed these; who pulled before
From the ark, which in the Judges' days [4] they bore,
Resumed their cant, and with a zealous cry
Pursued their old beloved theocracy,
Where Sanhedrin and priest enslaved the nation
And justified their spoils by inspiration;
For who so fit for reign as Aaron's race,
If once dominion they could found in grace?
These led the pack; though not of surest scent,
Yet deepest mouthed against the government.
A numerous host of dreaming saints succeed
Of the true old enthusiastic breed;
'Gainst form and order they their power employ,
Nothing to build and all things to destroy.
But far more numerous was the herd of such
Who think too little and who talk too much.
These out of mere instinct, they knew not why,
Adored their fathers' God and property,
And by the same blind benefit of Fate
The Devil and the Jebusite did hate;
Born to be saved even in their own despite,
Because they could not help believing right.
Such were the tools; but a whole Hydra more
Remains of sprouting heads too long to score.
Some of their chiefs were princes of the land;
In the first rank of these did Zimri [5] stand,
A man so various that he seemed to be
Not one, but all mankind's epitome;
Stiff in opinions, always in the wrong,
Was everything by starts and nothing long;
But in the course of one revolving moon
Was chemist, fiddler, statesman, and buffoon;
Then all for women, painting, riming, drinking,
Besides ten thousand freaks that died in thinking.
Blest madman, who could every hour employ
With something new to wish or to enjoy!
Railing and praising were his usual themes,
And both, to show his judgment, in extremes;
So over violent or over civil
That every man with him was God or Devil.
In squandering wealth was his peculiar art;
Nothing went unrewarded but desert.
Beggared by fools whom still he found too late,
He had his jest, and they had his estate.
He laughed himself from Court; then sought relief
By forming parties, but could ne'er be chief;
For, spite of him, the weight of business fell
On Absalom and wise Achitophel.
Thus wicked but in will, of means bereft,
He left not faction, but of that was left.

. . . .

1681 1681

MAC FLECKNOE [6]

All human things are subject to decay
And, when Fate summons, monarchs must obey.
This Flecknoe found, who, like Augustus, [7] young
Was called to empire and had governed long,
In prose and verse was owned without dispute
Through all the realms of Nonsense absolute.
This aged prince, now flourishing in peace
And blest with issue of a large increase,
Worn out with business, did at length debate
To settle the succession of the state;
And pondering which of all his sons was fit
To reign and wage immortal war with wit,
Cried: "'Tis resolved, for Nature pleads that he
Should only rule who most resembles me,
Shadwell alone my perfect image bears,
Mature in dullness from his tender years;
Shadwell alone of all my sons is he
Who stands confirmed in full stupidity.
The rest to some faint meaning make pretense,
But Shadwell never deviates into sense.
Some beams of wit on other souls may fall,
Strike through and make a lucid interval;
But Shadwell's genuine night admits no ray,
His rising fogs prevail upon the day.

[1] the London populace (Jerusalem=Hierosolyma)
[2] Gentile (i.e., the Popish Plot)
[3] Presbyterian ministers deprived of their office by the act of Uniformity
[4] the days of the Commonwealth, when (l. 523) the clergy were unusually prominent in affairs of state
[5] The Duke of Buckingham, favorite, and former minister, of Charles II; he had ridiculed Dryden.

[6] "Son of Flecknoe." Dryden is satirizing Thomas Shadwell, a rival dramatist and personal enemy, by making him the son of a very dull poet, Flecknoe, who had died several years before the date of this poem, 1682, at an advanced age.
[7] successor of Caesar at the age of eighteen, and virtual emperor at thirty-two

Besides, his goodly fabric [1] fills the eye
And seems designed for thoughtless majesty,
Thoughtless as monarch oaks that shade the plain
And, spread in solemn state, supinely reign.
Heywood and Shirley [2] were but types of thee,
Thou last great prophet of tautology.
Even I, a dunce of more renown than they,
Was sent before but to prepare thy way,
And coarsely clad in Norwich drugget [3] came
To teach the nations in thy greater name.
My warbling lute, the lute I whilom strung,
When to King John of Portugal [4] I sung,
Was but the prelude to that glorious day
When thou on silver Thames didst cut thy way
With well-timed oars before the royal barge,
Swelled with the pride of thy celestial charge, [5]
And, big with hymn, commander of an host;
The like was ne'er in Epsom blankets tost. [6]
Methinks I see the new Arion [7] sail,
The lute still trembling underneath thy nail.
At thy well-sharpened thumb from shore to shore
The treble squeaks for fear, the basses roar;
Echoes from Private-alley Shadwell call,
And Shadwell they resound from Aston-hall.
About thy boat the little fishes throng
As at the morning toast that floats along.
Sometimes, as prince of thy harmonious band,
Thou wieldst thy papers in thy threshing hand.
St. André's feet [8] ne'er kept more equal time,
Not even the feet of thy own 'Psyche's' [9] rime;
Though they in number as in sense excel,
So just, so like tautology, they fell,
That, pale with envy, Singleton [10] forswore
The lute and sword which he in triumph bore,
And vowed he ne'er would act Villerius [11] more."
Here stopped the good old sire and wept for joy,
In silent raptures of the hopeful boy.
All arguments, but most his plays, persuade
That for anointed dullness he was made.
  Close to the walls which fair Augusta [12] bind
(The fair Augusta much to fears [13] inclined)

[1] Shadwell was corpulent.
[2] contemporary dramatists
[3] rough woolen cloth
[4] Flecknoe had visited the court of Lisbon.
[5] The precise occasion of this is unknown, but Shadwell was proficient in music.
[6] a familiar form of punishment, with an allusion to the title of Shadwell's play *Epsom Wells*
[7] a Grecian musician who, when thrown into the sea, was saved by the dolphins
[8] a French dancing master
[9] an opera by Shadwell
[10] a singer
[11] the principal character in one of Davenant's plays
[12] London
[13] of Popish and other plots

An ancient fabric raised to inform the sight
There stood of yore, and Barbican it hight;
A watch-tower once, but now, so fate ordains,
Of all the pile an empty name remains;

. . . . . .

Near these a Nursery [14] erects its head
Where queens are formed and future heroes bred,
Where unfledged actors learn to laugh and cry,
Where infant trulls their tender voices try,
And little Maximins [15] the gods defy.
Great Fletcher [16] never treads in buskins [17] here,
Nor greater Jonson dares in socks [18] appear;
But gentle Simkin just reception finds
Amidst this monument of vanished minds;
Pure clinches [19] the suburban muse affords
And Panton waging harmless war with words.
Here Flecknoe, as a place to fame well known,
Ambitiously designed his Shadwell's throne.
For ancient Dekker prophesied long since
That in this pile should reign a mighty prince,
Born for a scourge of wit and flail of sense,
To whom true dullness should some "Psyches" [20] owe,
But worlds of "Misers" [21] from his pen should flow;
"Humorists" [21] and Hypocrites it should produce,
Whole Raymond families and tribes of Bruce. [22]
  Now empress Fame had published the renown
Of Shadwell's coronation through the town.
Roused by report of fame, the nations meet
From near Bunhill and distant Watling-street.
No Persian carpets spread the imperial way,
But scattered limbs of mangled poets lay;
From dusty shops neglected authors come,

. . . . . .

Much Heywood, Shirley, Ogleby [23] there lay,
But loads of Shadwell almost choked the way.
Bilked stationers for yeomen [24] stood prepared
And Herringman [25] was captain of the guard.
The hoary prince [26] in majesty appeared,
High on a throne of his own labors reared.
At his right hand our young Ascanius [27] sate,

[14] a school for training boys and girls for the stage
[15] character in Dryden's *Tyrannic Love,* who defies the gods
[16] Fletcher, Jonson, and Dekker: see. pp. 215, 209, 163. Simkin, "a stupid clown" in a farce, Panton a punster.
[17] high-heeled shoes worn by tragedians, hence "tragedy"
[18] low shoes worn by comic actors, hence "comedy"
[19] puns
[20] See note 9.
[21] a play by Shadwell
[22] characters in his plays
[23] an inferior poet
[24] defrauded booksellers as guardsmen
[25] Shadwell's publisher
[26] Flecknoe
[27] Shadwell (Ascanius was the son of Aeneas, the mythical founder of Rome).

Rome's other hope and pillar of the state.
His brows thick fogs instead of glories grace,
And lambent dullness played around his face.
As Hannibal did to the altars come,
Sworn by his sire a mortal foe to Rome;[1]
So Shadwell swore, nor should his vow be vain,
That he till death true dullness would maintain;
And, in his father's right and realm's defense,
Ne'er to have peace with wit nor truce with sense.
The king himself the sacred unction made,
As king by office and as priest by trade.
In his sinister[2] hand, instead of ball,
He placed a mighty mug of potent ale;
"Love's Kingdom"[3] to his right he did convey,
At once his scepter and his rule of sway;
Whose righteous lore the prince had practiced young
And from whose loins recorded "Psyche" sprung.
His temples, last, with poppies[4] were o'erspread,
That nodding seemed to consecrate his head.
Just at that point of time, if fame not lie,
On his left hand twelve reverend owls did fly.
So Romulus, 'tis sung, by Tiber's brook,
Presage of sway from twice six vultures took.
The admiring throng loud acclamations make
And omens of his future empire take.
The sire then shook the honors of his head,
And from his brows damps of oblivion shed
Full on the filial dullness. Long he stood,
Repelling from his breast the raging god;
At length burst out in this prophetic mood:
"Heavens bless my son! from Ireland let him reign
To far Barbadoes on the western main;
Of his dominion may no end be known
And greater than his father's be his throne;
Beyond 'Love's Kingdom' let him stretch his pen!"
He paused, and all the people cried "Amen."
Then thus continued he: "My son, advance
Still in new impudence, new ignorance.
Success let others teach, learn thou from me
Pangs without birth and fruitless industry.
Let 'Virtuosos'[5] in five years be writ,
Yet not one thought accuse thy toil of wit.
Let gentle George[6] in triumph tread the stage,
Make Dorimant betray, and Loveit rage;
Let Cully, Cockwood, Fopling, charm the pit,
And in their folly show the writer's wit.
Yet still thy fools shall stand in thy defense
And justify their author's want of sense.
Let them be all by thy own model made
Of dullness and desire no foreign aid,
That they to future ages may be known,
Not copies drawn, but issue of thy own.
Nay, let thy men of wit, too, be the same,
All full of thee and differing but in name.
But let no alien Sedley[7] interpose
To lard with wit thy hungry Epsom prose.
And when false flowers of rhetoric thou wouldst cull,
Trust nature, do not labor to be dull;
But write thy best and top,[8] and in each line
Sir Formal's[9] oratory will be thine.
Sir Formal, though unsought, attends thy quill
And does thy northern dedications fill.[10]
Nor let false friends seduce thy mind to fame
By arrogating Jonson's hostile name;[11]
Let father Flecknoe fire thy mind with praise
And uncle Ogleby[12] thy envy raise.
Thou art my blood, where Jonson has no part.
What share have we in nature or in art?
Where did his wit on learning fix a brand
And rail at arts he did not understand?
Where made he love in Prince Nicander's[13] vein
Or swept the dust in Psyche's humble strain?

. . . .

Promised a play and dwindled to a farce?
When did his muse from Fletcher[14] scenes purloin,
As thou whole Etherege[15] dost transfuse to thine?
But so transfused as oil on waters flow,
His always floats above, thine sinks below.
This is thy province, this thy wondrous way,
New humors to invent for each new play;
This is that boasted bias of thy mind,
By which one way to dullness 'tis inclined,
Which makes thy writings lean on one side still,
And, in all changes, that way bends thy will.
Nor let thy mountain belly make pretense
Of likeness; thine's a tympany[16] of sense.
A tun of man[17] in thy large bulk is writ,

[1] Livy, Book xxi
[2] left
[3] a play by Flecknoe
[4] "Perhaps in allusion to Shadwell's frequent use of opium, as well as to his dullness." (Scott).
[5] a play by Shadwell
[6] Etherege, a comic dramatist; Dorimant, etc., are characters in his plays.
[7] writer of the prologue to Shadwell's *Epsom Wells*
[8] excel
[9] a character in Shadwell's *Virtuoso*
[10] Shadwell dedicated much of his work to the Duke of Newcastle.
[11] i.e., by comparing him with Jonson, who was quite his contrary (See also l. 193.)
[12] an inferior poet
[13] a character in Shadwell's *Psyche*
[14] See note 16, p. 307.
[15] See note 6.
[16] dropsy
[17] Cf. *I Henry IV*, II, iv, 493.

But sure thou'rt but a kilderkin [1] of wit.
Like mine, thy gentle numbers feebly creep;
Thy tragic Muse gives smiles, thy comic sleep.
With whate'er gall thou setst thyself to write,
Thy inoffensive satires never bite;
In thy felonious heart though venom lies,
It does but touch thy Irish [2] pen, and dies,
Thy genius calls thee not to purchase fame
In keen Iambics, [3] but mild Anagram.
Leave writing plays, and choose for thy command
Some peaceful province in Acrostic land.
There thou mayest wings display and altars raise,
And torture one poor word ten thousand ways;
Or, if thou wouldst thy different talents suit,
Set thy own songs, and sing them to thy lute."
He said, but his last words were scarcely heard,
For Bruce and Longville [4] had a trap prepared,
And down they sent the yet declaiming bard.
Sinking, he left his drugget robe behind,
Borne upward by a subterranean wind.
The mantle fell to the young prophet's part
With double portion of his father's art.

1682 1682

A SONG FOR ST. CECELIA'S DAY [5]

NOVEMBER 22, 1687

1

From harmony, from heavenly harmony
This universal frame began;
When Nature underneath a heap
Of jarring atoms lay,
And could not heave her head,
The tuneful voice was heard from high,
Arise, ye more than dead.

Then cold and hot and moist and dry
In order to their stations leap,
And Music's power obey.
From harmony, from heavenly harmony
This universal frame began;
From harmony to harmony
Through all the compass of the notes it ran,
The diapason [6] closing full in Man.

2

What passion cannot music raise and quell?
When Jubal [7] struck the chorded shell,
His listening brethren stood around,
And, wondering, on their faces fell
To worship that celestial sound;
Less than a god they thought there could not dwell
Within the hollow of that shell
That spoke so sweetly, and so well.
What passion cannot music raise and quell?

3

The trumpet's loud clangor
Excites us to arms
With shrill notes of anger
And mortal alarms.
The double, double, double beat
Of the thundering drum
Cries, hark! the foes come;
Charge, charge, 'tis too late to retreat.

4

The soft complaining flute
In dying notes discovers
The woes of hopeless lovers,
Whose dirge is whispered by the warbling lute.

5

Sharp violins proclaim
Their jealous pangs and desperation,
Fury, frantic indignation,
Depth of pains and height of passion,
For the fair, disdainful dame.

6

But oh! what art can teach,
What human voice can reach
The sacred organ's praise?
Notes inspiring holy love,
Notes that wing their heavenly ways
To mend the choirs above.

7

Orpheus could lead the savage race,
And trees unrooted left their place,
Sequacious of [8] the lyre;
But bright Cecilia raised the wonder higher:
When to her organ vocal breath was given,
An angel heard, and straight appeared
Mistaking earth for heaven.

[1] small barrel
[2] Shadwell was not Irish and insisted that he had never been in Ireland more than a few hours.
[3] Iambics were the standard verse-form of satire in classical poetry.
[4] characters in Shadwell's plays
[5] St. Cecilia, as patroness of music, is commonly represented in paintings with a harp or organ, and Dryden makes her the inventor of the latter. Public festivals in her honor were held annually in London at this period. Compare the following Ode, and also Pope's, p. 333.
[6] a chord including all tones
[7] "the father of all such as handle the harp or organ" *Genesis* iv, 21
[8] following

GRAND CHORUS

As from the power of sacred lays
The spheres began to move,
And sung the great Creator's praise
To all the blessed above;
So when the last and dreadful hour
This crumbling pageant shall devour,
The trumpet shall be heard on high,
The dead shall live, the living die,
And Music shall untune the sky.

1687 *1687*

ALEXANDER'S FEAST; OR, THE POWER OF MUSIC

A Song in Honor of St. Cecilia's Day: 1697

1

'Twas at the royal feast for Persia won
By Philip's warlike son [1]—
Aloft in awful state
The godlike hero sate
On his imperial throne;
His valiant peers were placed around,
Their brows with roses and with myrtles bound
(So should desert in arms be crowned);
The lovely Thais by his side
Sat like a blooming Eastern bride,
In flower of youth and beauty's pride.
Happy, happy, happy pair!
None but the brave,
None but the brave,
None but the brave deserves the fair.

CHORUS

Happy, happy, happy pair!
None but the brave,
None but the brave,
None but the brave deserves the fair.

2

Timotheus [2] placed on high
Amid the tuneful choir,
With flying fingers touched the lyre;
The trembling notes ascend the sky,
And heavenly joys inspire.
The song began from [3] Jove,
Who left his blissful seats above,
(Such is the power of mighty love).
A dragon's fiery form belied the god;
Sublime on radiant spires he rode
When he to fair Olympia [4] pressed;
And while he sought her snowy breast,
Then round her slender waist he curled,
And stamped an image of himself, a sovereign of the world.
The listening crowd admire the lofty sound;
A present deity! they shout around;
A present deity! the vaulted roofs rebound.
With ravished ears
The monarch hears,
Assumes the god,
Affects to nod,
And seems to shake the spheres.

CHORUS

With ravished ears
The monarch hears,
Assumes the god,
Affects to nod,
And seems to shake the spheres.

3

The praise of Bacchus then the sweet musician sung,
Of Bacchus ever fair and ever young.
The jolly god in triumph comes;
Sound the trumpets, beat the drums;
Flushed with a purple grace
He shows his honest face.
Now give the hautboys [5] breath; he comes, he comes.
Bacchus, ever fair and young,
Drinking joys did first ordain;
Bacchus' blessings are a treasure,
Drinking is the soldier's pleasure;
Rich the treasure,
Sweet the pleasure,
Sweet is pleasure after pain.

CHORUS

Bacchus' blessings are a treasure,
Drinking is the soldier's pleasure;
Rich the treasure,
Sweet the pleasure,
Sweet is pleasure after pain.

4

Soothed with the sound the king grew vain;
Fought all his battles o'er again;
And thrice he routed all his foes, and thrice he slew the slain.
The master saw the madness rise,
His glowing cheeks, his ardent eyes;
And while he heaven and earth defied,
Changed his hand, and checked his pride.
He chose a mournful Muse
Soft pity to infuse;

[1] Alexander the Great conquered Persia in 331 B.C.
[2] musician to Alexander
[3] sang first of
[4] Alexander's mother
[5] oboes

He sung Darius[1] great and good,
By too severe a fate
Fallen, fallen, fallen, fallen,
Fallen from his high estate,
And weltering in his blood;
Deserted at his utmost need
By those his former bounty fed;
On the bare earth exposed he lies,
With not a friend to close his eyes.

With downcast looks the joyless victor sate,
Revolving in his altered soul
The various turns of chance below;
And now and then a sigh he stole,
And tears began to flow.

CHORUS

Revolving in his altered soul
The various turns of chance below;
And now and then a sigh he stole,
And tears began to flow.

5

The mighty master smiled to see
That love was in the next degree;
'Twas but a kindred-sound to move,
For pity melts the mind to love.
Softly sweet, in Lydian[2] measures,
Soon he soothed his soul to pleasures,
War, he sung, is toil and trouble,
Honor but an empty bubble;
Never ending, still beginning,
Fighting still, and still destroying;
If the world be worth thy winning,
Think, oh, think it worth enjoying.
Lovely Thais sits beside thee,
Take the good the gods provide thee.

The many rend the skies with loud applause;
So Love was crowned, but Music won the cause.
The prince, unable to conceal his pain,
Gazed on the fair
Who caused his care,
And sighed and looked, sighed and looked,
Sighed and looked, and sighed again;
At length, with love and wine at once oppressed,
The vanquished victor sunk upon her breast.

CHORUS

The prince, unable to conceal his pain,
Gazed on the fair
Who caused his care,
And sighed and looked, sighed and looked,
Sighed and looked, and sighed again;
At length, with love and wine at once oppressed,
The vanquished victor sunk upon her breast.

[1] King of the Persians
[2] a soft, pathetic mode of Grecian music

6

Now strike the golden lyre again,
A louder yet, and yet a louder strain.
Break his bands of sleep asunder,
And rouse him, like a rattling peal of thunder.
Hark, hark, the horrid sound
Has raised up his head;
As awaked from the dead,
And amazed, he stares around.
Revenge, revenge, Timotheus cries,
See the Furies[3] arise;
See the snakes that they rear,
How they hiss in their hair,
And the sparkles that flash from their eyes!
Behold a ghastly band,
Each a torch in his hand!
Those are Grecian ghosts, that in battle were slain,
And unburied remain
Inglorious on the plain.
Give the vengeance due
To the valiant crew.
Behold how they toss their torches on high,
How they point to the Persian abodes
And glittering temples of their hostile gods.
The princes applaud with a furious joy;
And the king seized a flambeau with zeal to destroy.
Thais led the way
To light him to his prey,
And, like another Helen, fired another Troy.

CHORUS

And the king seized a flambeau with zeal to destroy.
Thais led the way
To light him to his prey,
And, like another Helen, fired another Troy.

7

Thus, long ago,
Ere heaving bellows learned to blow,
While organs yet were mute,
Timotheus, to his breathing flute
And sounding lyre,
Could swell the soul to rage, or kindle soft desire.
At last divine Cecilia came,
Inventress of the vocal frame;
The sweet enthusiast from her sacred store
Enlarged the former narrow bounds,
And added length to solemn sounds,
With Nature's mother-wit, and arts unknown before.
Let old Timotheus yield the prize,

[3] the Eumenides, avenging spirits

Or both divide the crown;
He raised a mortal to the skies;
She drew an angel down.

GRAND CHORUS

At last divine Cecilia came,
Inventress of the vocal frame;
The sweet enthusiast from her sacred store
Enlarged the former narrow bounds,
And added length to solemn sounds,
With Nature's mother-wit, and arts unknown before.
Let old Timotheus yield the prize,
Or both divide the crown;
He raised a mortal to the skies;
She drew an angel down.

1697 1697

LINES PRINTED UNDER THE ENGRAVED PORTRAIT OF MILTON

Three poets,[1] in three distant ages born,
Greece, Italy, and England did adorn.
The first in loftiness of thought surpassed,
The next in majesty, in both the last;
The force of nature could no farther go;
To make a third she joined the former two.

1688 1688

SONG From THE INDIAN EMPEROR

Ah fading joy! how quickly art thou past!
Yet we thy ruin haste.
As if the cares of human life were few,
We seek out new;
And follow fate, that does too fast pursue.

See, how on every bough the birds express,
In their sweet notes, their happiness.
They all enjoy, and nothing spare;
But on their mother nature lay their care.
Why then should man, the lord of all below,
Such troubles choose to know,
As none of all his subjects undergo?
Hark, hark, the waters—fall, fall, fall,
And with a murmuring sound
Dash, dash, upon the ground,
To gentle slumbers call.

1665

SONG OF THAMESIS[2]

Old father Ocean calls my tide,
Come away, come away;
The barks upon the billows ride,
The master will not stay;
The merry boatswain from his side
His whistle takes, to check and chide
The lingering lads' delay,
And all the crew aloud has cried,
Come away, come away.

See, the god of seas attends thee,
Nymphs divine, a beauteous train;
All the calmer gales befriend thee,
In thy passage o'er the main;
Every maid her locks is binding,
Every Triton's horn is winding;
Welcome to the wat'ry plain!

1685

[1] Homer, Vergil, Milton

[2] From the opera *Albion and Albanius*, 1685; Thamesis is the River God Thames, addressing Albanius, who represents the Duke of York (afterwards James II). The latter, in 1679, had been compelled to retire to Brussels, in temporary exile, until the excitement against the Roman Catholics, created by the "Popish plot," should die away. The flattery of James is evident; but the song has a haunting beauty which sets it apart from mere eulogy.

SONG From CLEOMENES

No, no, poor suff'ring heart, no change endeavor;
Choose to sustain the smart, rather than leave her.
My ravished eyes behold such charms about her,
I can die with her, but not live without her;
One tender sigh of hers to see me languish,
Will more than pay the price of my past anguish.
Beware, O cruel fair, how you smile on me;
'Twas a kind look of yours that has undone me.

Love has in store for me one happy minute,
And she will end my pain who did begin it.
Then, no day void of bliss or pleasure leaving,
Ages shall slide away without perceiving;
Cupid shall guard the door, the more to please us,
And keep out Time and Death, when they would seize us;
Time and Death shall depart, and say in flying,
Love has found out a way to live by dying.

1692 1692

THE SECULAR MASQUE

Enter JANUS.[3]

JANUS

Chronos, Chronos,[4] mend thy pace;
An hundred times the rolling sun
Around the radiant belt has run
In his revolving race.
Behold, behold, the goal in sight;
Spread thy fans, and wing thy flight.

[3] anciently the highest divinity, who presided over the beginnings of things

[4] the god of time; ruler of the world before Zeus

Enter CHRONOS, *with a scythe in his hand and a globe on his back, which he sets down at his entrance.*

CHRONOS

Weary, weary of my weight,
Let me, let me drop my freight
  And leave the world behind.
    I could not bear,
    Another year,
  The load of human kind.

Enter MOMUS,[1] *laughing.*

MOMUS

Ha! ha! ha! ha! ha! ha! well hast thou done
    To lay down thy pack,
    And lighten thy back.
The world was a fool e'er since it begun;
And since neither Janus, nor Chronos, nor I
    Can hinder the crimes
    Or mend the bad times,
  'Tis better to laugh than to cry.

Chorus of all three.

  'Tis better to laugh than to cry.

JANUS

Since Momus comes to laugh below,
    Old Time, begin the show,
That he may see, in every scene,
What changes in this age have been.

CHRONOS

Then, goddess of the silver bow, begin.
  (*Horns, or hunting music within.*)

Enter DIANA.

DIANA

With horns and with hounds I waken the day,
And hie to my woodland-walks away;
I tuck up my robe, and am buskined [2] soon,
And tie to my forehead a wexing [3] moon.
I course the fleet stag, unkennel the fox,
And chase the wild goats o'er summits of rocks,
With shouting and hooting we pierce through the sky,
And Echo turns hunter, and doubles the cry.

Chorus of all.

With shouting and hooting we pierce through the sky,
And Echo turns hunter and doubles the cry.

JANUS

Then our age was in its prime;

CHRONOS

Free from rage;

DIANA

  And free from crime.

MOMUS

A very merry, dancing, drinking,
Laughing, quaffing, and unthinking time.

Chorus of all.

Then our age was in its prime,
Free from rage and free from crime,
A very merry, dancing, drinking,
Laughing, quaffing, and unthinking time.

Dance of DIANA'S *attendants.*

Enter MARS.

MARS

Inspire [4] the vocal brass, inspire;
The world is past its infant age;
    Arms and honor,
    Arms and honor,
Set the martial mind on fire,
  And kindle manly rage.
    Mars has looked the sky to red,
  And Peace, the lazy god, is fled.
  Plenty, peace, and pleasure fly;
    The sprightly green
  In woodland-walks no more is seen;
The sprightly green has drunk the Tyrian [5] dye.

Chorus of all.

  Plenty, peace, and pleasure fly;
    The sprightly green
  In woodland-walks no more is seen;
The sprightly green has drunk the Tyrian dye.

MARS

Sound the trumpet, beat the drum;
  Through all the world around
  Sound a reveille, [6] sound, sound,
The warrior god is come.

Chorus of all.

Sound the trumpet, beat the drum;
  Through all the world around
  Sound a reveille, sound, sound,
The warrior god is come.

[1] the personification of mockery
[2] booted
[3] waxing, crescent
[4] breathe into, blow
[5] purple
[6] morning call

MOMUS

Thy sword within the scabbard keep,
And let mankind agree;
Better the world were fast asleep
Than kept awake by thee.
The fools are only thinner,
With all our cost and care;
But neither side a winner,
For things are as they were.

Chorus of all.

The fools are only thinner,
With all our cost and care;
But neither side a winner,
For things are as they were.

Enter VENUS

Calms appear when storms are past;
Love will have his hour at last;
Nature is my kindly care;
Mars destroys, and I repair;
Take me, take me while you may,
Venus comes not every day.

Chorus of all.

Take her, take her while you may,
Venus comes not every day.

CHRONOS

The world was then so light
I scarcely felt the weight;
Joy ruled the day, and Love the night.
But, since the Queen of Pleasure left the ground,
I faint, I lag,
And feebly drag
The ponderous orb around.

MOMUS

All, all of a piece throughout;
(*Pointing to Diana.*
Thy chase had a beast in view,
(*To Mars.*
Thy wars brought nothing about,
(*To Venus.*
Thy lovers were all untrue.

JANUS

'Tis well an old age is out.

CHRONOS

And time to begin a new.

Chorus of all.

All, all of a piece throughout;
Thy chase had a beast in view,
Thy wars brought nothing about,
Thy lovers were all untrue.
'Tis well an old age is out,
And time to begin a new.
(*Dance of huntsmen, nymphs, warriors, and lovers.*)

1700 1700

[ON CHAUCER]

From the PREFACE TO THE FABLES [1]

. . . .

It remains that I say somewhat of Chaucer in particular.

In the first place, as he is the father of English poetry, so I hold him in the same degree of veneration as the Grecians held Homer or the Romans Vergil. He is a perpetual fountain of good sense, learned in all sciences, and therefore speaks properly on all subjects. As he knew what to say, so he knows also when to leave off; a continence which is practiced by few writers, and scarcely by any of the ancients excepting Vergil and Horace. One of our late great poets [2] is sunk in his reputation because he could never forgive any conceit which came in his way, but swept, like a dragnet, great and small. There was plenty enough, but the dishes were ill sorted; whole pyramids of sweetmeats for boys and women, but little of solid meat for men. All this proceeded, not from any want of knowledge, but of judgment. Neither did he want that in discerning the beauties and faults of other poets, but only indulged himself in the luxury of writing; and perhaps knew it was a fault but hoped the reader would not find it. For this reason, though he must always be thought a great poet, he is no longer esteemed a good writer; and for ten impressions [3] which his works have had in so many successive years, yet at present a hundred books are scarcely purchased once a twelvemonth; for, as my last Lord Rochester said, though somewhat profanely, "Not being of God, he could not stand."

Chaucer followed nature everywhere, but was never so bold to go beyond her, and there is a great difference of being *poeta* and *nimis poeta*,[4] if we believe Catullus, as much as betwixt a modest behavior and affectation. The verse of Chaucer, I confess, is not harmonious to us; but 'tis like the eloquence of one whom

[1] This particular selection is characterized by Mr. George Saintsbury as "forcible without the slightest effort, eloquent without declamation, graceful yet thoroughly manly."

[2] Abraham Cowley, who could not "forgive" (i.e., give up, forego) strained fancies and distorted forms of expression; see Evelyn on Cowley, p. 302.

[3] new printings

[4] "Overmuch a poet" (said by Martial, not Catullus)

Tacitus commends, it was *auribus istius temporis accommodata.* [1] They who lived with him, and some time after him, thought it musical; and it continues so, even in our judgment, if compared with the numbers of Lydgate and Gower, his contemporaries; there is the rude sweetness of a Scotch tune in it, which is natural and pleasing though not perfect. 'Tis true I cannot go so far as he who published the last edition of him, [2] for he would make us believe the fault is in our ears, and that there were really ten syllables in a verse where we find but nine; but this opinion is not worth confuting; 'tis so gross and obvious an error that common sense (which is a rule in everything but matters of faith and revelation) must convince the reader that equality of numbers [3] in every verse which we call heroic [4] was either not known or not always practiced in Chaucer's age. It were an easy matter to produce some thousands of his verses which are lame for want of half a foot and sometimes a whole one, and which no pronunciation can make otherwise. [5] We can only say that he lived in the infancy of our poetry, and that nothing is brought to perfection at the first. We must be children before we grow men. There was an Ennius, and in process of time a Lucilius and a Lucretius, before Vergil and Horace; even after Chaucer there was a Spenser, a Harrington, a Fairfax, before Waller and Denham were in being, and our numbers were in their nonage till these last appeared. [6]

. . . .

He must have been a man of a most wonderful comprehensive nature, because, as it has been truly observed of him, he has taken into the compass of his *Canterbury Tales* the various manners and humors (as we now call them) of the whole English nation in his age. Not a single character has escaped him. All his pilgrims are severally distinguished from each other, and not only in their inclinations but in their very physiognomies and persons. Baptista Porta [7] could not have described their natures better than by the marks which the poet gives them.

The matter and manner of their tales and of their telling are so suited to their different educations, humors, and callings that each of them would be improper in any other mouth. Even the grave and serious characters are distinguished by their several sorts of gravity; their discourses are such as belong to their age, their calling, and their breeding, such as are becoming of them and of them only. Some of his persons are vicious and some virtuous; some are unlearned, or (as Chaucer calls them) lewd, and some are learned. Even the ribaldry of the low characters is different; the Reeve, the Miller, and the Cook are several men, and distinguished from each other as much as the mincing Lady Prioress and the broad-speaking, gap-toothed Wife of Bath. But enough of this; there is such a variety of game springing up before me that I am distracted in my choice and know not which to follow. It is sufficient to say, according to the proverb, that here is God's plenty. We have our forefathers and great-grand-dames all before us as they were in Chaucer's days; their general characters are still remaining in mankind, and even in England, though they are called by other names than those of monks and friars and canons and lady abbesses and nuns; for mankind is ever the same, and nothing lost out of nature though everything is altered. . . . .

1700

1 "Suited to the ears of that time."
2 that of Thomas Speght, 1597-1602
3 measures
4 the iambic pentameter couplet (See p. 135.)
5 Dryden did not understand Chaucer's pronunciation nor sufficiently allow for imperfections in the manuscripts.
6 Posterity has not sustained this verdict.
7 a Neapolitan physiognomist

EARLY EIGHTEENTH CENTURY

THE early eighteenth century held that over-enthusiasm in religion and politics had well-nigh wrecked England in the seventeenth century. It therefore took decorum as its watchword. Social institutions and forms, and standards in art, were weighed, estimated, and revalued, and new standards were set up.

Because of this attitude, literature took notably two directions—that of the periodical essay gently or severely critical of society in the broad sense; and satire, both in prose and verse, directed to about the same ends. Men, manners and customs, government, philosophy, art, and religion were objects of satirical comment and controversy. Prose developed rapidly. With small exceptions, notably in the case of Dryden, seventeenth century prose had borne traces of the medieval both in matter and style. From Charles II to Anne it took an immense stride toward our present prose manner. Because it aimed to make men understand their everyday problems, it became simple, direct, nervous, the language that men actually spoke.

In Pope, English verse satire reaches perfection of form. It is formal, self-conscious, polished, full of antithesis, filed, trimmed, and garnished, for the sake of emphasis and epigram. It abounds in fancy and wit, and appeals to the intellect through the finish of its workmanship; but not to the imagination through largeness of ideas. In a word, the Age of Pope following the Age of Dryden, turns aside from the prevailing romantic course of English literature to pursue for a century the literary manner of the Greeks and Romans.

SIR RICHARD STEELE
1672-1729

Steele and Addison, in a partnership as famous as that of Wyatt and Surrey, or Beaumont and Fletcher, are distinguished for giving the periodical essay, a literary form originated by Defoe, a definite character and place in literature. What Steel originated and stimulated, Addison developed and perfected. Simple, frank, lovable, weak Dick Steele (portrayed in Thackeray's *Henry Esmond*) was born in Dublin, but educated at Charterhouse, where his enthusiastic devotion to Addison began, and at Oxford, gaining reputation as a scholar but no degree. He was a soldier for ten years, a gay man about town, a frequenter of the coffee houses (note 2, p. 317), master of a good income, yet always in debt from extravagance.

Unpopular in the army for his religious attitude he took to comedy and produced *The Funeral,* 1701, and *The Tender Husband,* 1705. After seriously wounding an adversary in a duel he opposed the practice, notably in two plays, *The Lying Lover,* 1703, and *The Conscious Lovers,* 1722. In 1709 he established the *Tatler,* a Whig, penny tri-weekly, to which Swift and Addison contributed; it ended abruptly at the rise of the Tories in 1711; two months later the *Spectator* replaced it, and Sir Roger de Coverley, created by Steele, developed by Addison, came into being. The paper was non-political, choosing its topics from a wide variety of interests, and rose at once to popularity. But Steele, a true Irishman, could not preserve neutrality and was in constant hot water until the Whigs returned to power with George I. He was elected to Parliament and knighted; but his noteworthy friendship with Addison was broken by a political controversy and never healed.

Steele's comedies are light, yet helped to raise the morals of the stage and substitute the comedy of sentiment (drama distinctly moral in tone, presenting everyday people triumphing over vice and wickedness through homely virtue) for that of brutal licentiousness. As an essayist he excelled; he was important as a painter of domesticity, and he was unusual in his day in offering respectful homage to women.

See *The Sir Roger de Coverley Papers,* ed. by Abbott in Lake English Classics for an excellent discussion of Steele's time. G. A. Aitken's *Life of Richard Steele,* 2 vols., 1889, and W. J. Courthope's *Addison* (EML) are good. See also Johnson, Macaulay, Thackeray, *English Humorists* and *Henry Esmond,* etc.; A. Quiller-Couch, "Bicentenary of Addison," *Liv. Age* 302:210-13; and an estimate of Addison's place in literature, "First of Lay Preachers," *Liv. Age* 283:798-802.

[PROSPECTUS]

The Tatler, No. 1. Tuesday, April 12, 1709

Quicquid agunt homines——
nostri est farrago libelli.
Juv. *Sat.* i. 85, 86.

Whate'er men do, or say, or think, or dream,
Our motley Paper seizes for its theme.

Though the other papers, which are published for the use of the good people of England,[1] have certainly very wholesome effects, and are laudable in their particular kinds, they do not seem to come up to the main design of such narrations, which, I humbly presume, should be principally intended for the use of politic persons who are so public-spirited as to neglect their own affairs to look into transactions of state. Now these gentlemen, for the most part, being persons of strong zeal and weak intellects, it is both a charitable and necessary work to offer something whereby such worthy and well-affected members of the commonwealth may be instructed, after their reading, what to think; which shall be the end and purpose of this my paper, wherein I shall, from time to time, report and consider all matters of what kind soever that shall occur to me, and publish such my advices and reflections every Tuesday, Thursday, and Saturday in the week, for the convenience of the post. I resolve to have something which may be of entertainment to the fair sex, in honor of whom I have invented the title of this paper. I therefore earnestly desire all persons, without distinction, to take it in for the present *gratis,* and hereafter at the price of one penny, forbidding all hawkers to take more for it at their peril. And I desire all persons to consider, that I am at a very great charge for proper materials for this work, as well as that, before I resolved upon it, I had settled a correspondence in all parts of the known and knowing world. And forasmuch as this globe is not trodden upon by mere drudges of business only, but that men of spirit and genius are justly to be esteemed as considerable agents in it, we shall not, upon a dearth of news, present you with musty foreign edicts and dull proclamations, but shall divide our relation of the passages which occur in action or discourse throughout this town, as well as elsewhere, under such dates of places as may prepare you for the matter you are to expect in the following manner.

All accounts of gallantry, pleasure, and entertainment shall be under the article of White's Chocolate-house;[2] poetry, under that of Will's Coffee-house; learning, under the title of Grecian; foreign and domestic news you will have from St. James's Coffee-house; and what else I have to offer on any other subject shall be dated from my own apartment.

I once more desire my reader to consider, that as I cannot keep an ingenious man to go daily to Will's under two-pence each day, merely for his charges; to White's under sixpence; nor to the Grecian, without allowing him some plain Spanish,[3] to be as able as others at the learned table; and that a good observer cannot speak with even Kidney[4] at St. James's without clean linen; I say, these considerations will, I hope, make all persons willing to comply with my humble request (when my *gratis* stock is exhausted) of a penny apiece; especially since they are sure of some proper amusement, and that it is impossible for me to want means to entertain them, having, besides the force of my own parts, the power of divination, and that I can, by casting a figure,[5] tell you all that will happen before it comes to pass.

But this last faculty I shall use very sparingly, and speak but of few things until they are passed, for fear of divulging matters which may offend our superiors.

[1] Newspapers had been published for nearly a century. Steele proposed in *The Tatler* to publish periodical essays, stories, etc., which should provide moral tone as well as information.

[2] The public coffee and chocolate houses of London were used as headquarters for the meetings of clubs. White's and St. James's were frequented by statesmen and men of fashion; Will's was a rendezvous for men of letters, and The Grecian for lawyers and scholars. See also p. 584.

[3] probably wine (which, according to *The Tatler,* No. 252, "heightens conversation")

[4] a waiter

[5] horoscope

MEMORIES

The Tatler, No. 181. Tuesday, June 6, 1710

—— Dies, ni fallor, adest, quem semper ascerbum,
Semper honoratum, sic dii voluistis habebo.
Verg. Aen. v, 49.

And now the rising day renews the year,
A day forever sad, forever dear.

There are those among mankind who can enjoy no relish of their being except the world is made acquainted with all that relates to them, and think everything lost that passes unobserved; but others find a solid delight in stealing by the crowd, and modeling their life after such a manner as is as much above the approbation as the practice of the vulgar. Life being too short to give instances great enough of true friendship or good will, some sages have thought it pious to preserve a certain reverence for the *Manes* [1] of their deceased friends; and have withdrawn themselves from the rest of the world at certain seasons, to commemorate in their own thoughts such of their acquaintance who have gone before them out of this life. And indeed, when we are advanced in years, there is not a more pleasing entertainment than to recollect in a gloomy moment the many we have parted with, that have been dear and agreeable to us, and to cast a melancholy thought or two after those with whom, perhaps, we have indulged ourselves in whole nights of mirth and jollity. With such inclinations in my heart I went to my closet [2] yesterday in the evening, and resolved to be sorrowful; upon which occasion I could not but look with disdain upon myself, that though all the reasons which I had to lament the loss of many of my friends are now as forcible as at the moment of their departure, yet did not my heart swell with the same sorrow which I felt at that time; but I could, without tears, reflect upon many pleasing adventures I have had with some who have long been blended with common earth.

Though it is by the benefit of nature that length of time thus blots out the violence of afflictions; yet, with tempers too much given to pleasure, it is almost necessary to revive the old places of grief in our memory, and ponder step by step on past life, to lead the mind into that sobriety of thought which poises the heart and makes it beat with due time, without being quickened with desire or retarded with despair, from its proper and equal motion. When we wind up a clock that is out of order to make it go well for the future, we do not immediately set the hand to the present instant, but we make it strike the round of all its hours before it can recover the regularity of its time. Such, thought I, shall be my method this evening; and since it is that day of the year which I dedicate to the memory of such in another life as I much delighted in when living, an hour or two shall be sacred to sorrow and their memory while I run over all the melancholy circumstances of this kind which have occurred to me in my whole life. The first sense of sorrow I ever knew was upon the death of my father, at which time I was not quite five years of age; but was rather amazed at what all the house meant, than possessed with a real understanding why nobody was willing to play with me. I remember I went into the room where his body lay, and my mother sat weeping alone by it. I had my battledore in my hand, and fell a-beating the coffin and calling papa; for, I know not how, I had some slight idea that he was locked up there. My mother catched me in her arms, and, transported beyond all patience [3] of the silent grief she was before in, she almost smothered me in her embraces; and told me, in a flood of tears, papa could not hear me, and would play with me no more, for they were going to put him under ground, whence he could never come to us again. She was a very beautiful woman, of a noble spirit, and there was a dignity in her grief amidst all the wildness of her transport which, methought, struck me with an instinct of sorrow that, before I was sensible of what it was to grieve, seized my very soul, and has made pity the weakness of my heart ever since. The mind in infancy is, methinks, like the body in embryo, and receives impressions so forcible that they are as hard to be removed by reason as any mark with which a child is born is to be taken away by any future application. Hence it is, that good-nature in me is no merit; but having been so frequently overwhelmed with her tears before I knew the cause of any affliction, or could draw defenses from my own judgment, I imbibed commiseration, remorse, and an unmanly gentleness of mind which has since insnared me into ten thousand calamities; from whence I can reap no advantage, except it be that, in such a humor as I am now in, I can the better indulge myself in the softnesses of humanity, and enjoy that sweet anxiety which arises from the memory of past afflictions.

[1] spirits [2] private room [3] endurance

We that are very old are better able to remember things which befell us in our distant youth than the passages of later days. For this reason it is that the companions of my strong and vigorous years present themselves more immediately to me in this office of sorrow. Untimely and unhappy deaths are what we are most apt to lament; so little are we able to make it indifferent when a thing happens, though we know it must happen. Thus we groan under life, and bewail those who are relieved from it. Every object that returns to our imagination raises different passions, according to the circumstances of their departure. Who can have lived in an army, and in a serious hour reflect upon the many gay and agreeable men that might long have flourished in the arts of peace, and not join with the imprecations of the fatherless and widow on the tyrant to whose ambition they fell sacrifices? But gallant men who are cut off by the sword move rather our veneration than our pity; and we gather relief enough from their own contempt of death, to make that no evil which was approached with so much cheerfulness, and attended with so much honor. But when we turn our thoughts from the great parts of life on such occasions, and instead of lamenting those who stood ready to give death to those from whom they had the fortune to receive it; I say, when we let our thoughts wander from such noble objects, and consider the havoc which is made among the tender and the innocent, pity enters with an unmixed softness and possesses all our souls at once.

Here (were there words to express such sentiments with proper tenderness) I should record the beauty, innocence, and untimely death of the first object my eyes ever beheld with love. The beauteous virgin! How ignorantly did she charm, how carelessly excel! O Death! thou hast right to the bold, to the ambitious, to the high, and to the haughty; but why this cruelty to the humble, to the meek, to the undiscerning, to the thoughtless? Nor age, nor business, nor distress can erase the dear image from my imagination. In the same week I saw her dressed for a ball and in a shroud. How ill did the habit of death become the pretty trifler! I still behold the smiling earth——A large train of disasters were coming on to my memory when my servant knocked at my closet-door, and interrupted me with a letter, attended with a hamper of wine of the same sort with that which is to be put to sale, on Thursday next, at Garraway's Coffee-house. [1] Upon the receipt of it I sent for three of my friends. We are so intimate that we can be company in whatever state of mind we meet, and can entertain each other without expecting always to rejoice. The wine we found to be generous and warming, but with such an heat as moved us rather to be cheerful than frolicsome. It revived the spirits without firing the blood. We commended it until two of the clock this morning; and having today met a little before dinner, [2] we found that though we drank two bottles a man, we had much more reason to recollect than forget what had passed the night before.

[THE CLUB]

The Spectator, No. 2, Friday, March 2, 1711

—Ast alii sex
Et plures uno conclamant ore—
Juv. *Sat.* vii, 167.
Six more at least join their consenting voice.

The first of our society is a gentleman of Worcestershire, of ancient descent, a baronet, his name Sir Roger de Coverley. His great grandfather was inventor of that famous country-dance which is called after him. All who know that shire are very well acquainted with the parts and merits of Sir Roger. He is a gentleman that is very singular in his behavior, but his singularities proceed from his good sense, and are contradictions to the manners of the world only as he thinks the world is in the wrong. However, this humor creates him no enemies, for he does nothing with sourness or obstinacy; and his being unconfined to modes and forms makes him but the readier and more capable to please and oblige all who know him. When he is in town, he lives in Soho Square. [3] It is said he keeps himself a bachelor by reason he was crossed in love by a perverse, beautiful widow of the next county to him. Before this disappointment Sir Roger was what you call a fine gentleman, had often supped with my Lord Rochester [4] and Sir George Etherege, [5] fought a duel upon his first coming to town, and kicked bully Dawson [6] in a public coffee-house for calling him youngster. But being ill-used by the above-mentioned widow he was very serious for a year and a

[1] This was a place where periodical auctions were held, and lotteries conducted.
[2] The fashionable dinner hour was four o'clock.
[3] then a fashionable part of London
[4] a favorite of Charles II
[5] a Restoration dramatist
[6] a notorious character of the time

half; and though, his temper being naturally jovial, he at last got over it, he grew careless of himself, and never dressed afterwards. He continues to wear a coat and doublet of the same cut that were in fashion at the time of his repulse, which, in his merry humors, he tells us has been in and out twelve times since he first wore it. . . . He is now in his fifty-sixth year, cheerful, gay, and hearty; keeps a good house both in town and country; a great lover of mankind; but there is such a mirthful cast in his behavior that he is rather beloved than esteemed.

His tenants grow rich, his servants look satisfied, all the young women profess love to him, and the young men are glad of his company. When he comes into a house he calls the servants by their names, and talks all the way upstairs to a visit. I must not omit that Sir Roger is a justice of the quorum; [1] that he fills the chair at a quarter-session with great abilities, and, three months ago, gained universal applause by explaining a passage in the game act.

The gentleman next in esteem and authority among us is another bachelor, who is a member of the Inner Temple; [2] a man of great probity, wit, and understanding; but he has chosen his place of residence rather to obey the direction of an old humorsome father than in pursuit of his own inclinations. He was placed there to study the laws of the land, and is the most learned of any of the house in those of the stage. Aristotle and Longinus [3] are much better understood by him than Littleton or Coke.[4] The father sends up every post questions relating to marriage-articles, leases, and tenures in the neighborhood; all which questions he agrees with [5] an attorney to answer and take care of in the lump. He is studying the passions themselves, when he should be inquiring into the debates among men which arise from them. He knows the argument of each of the orations of Demosthenes and Tully, [6] but not one case in the reports of our own courts. No one ever took him for a fool; but none, except his intimate friends, know he has a great deal of wit. This turn makes him at once both disinterested and agreeable. As few of his thoughts are drawn from business, they are most of them fit for conversation. His taste of books is a little too just for the age he lives in; he has read all, but approves of very few. His familiarity with the customs, manners, actions, and writings of the ancients, makes him a very delicate observer of what occurs to him in the present world. He is an excellent critic, and the time of the play is his hour of business; exactly at five he passes through New-Inn, [7] crosses through Russel-court, and takes a turn at Will's till the play begins; he has his shoes rubbed and his periwig powdered at the barber's as you go into the Rose. [8] It is for the good of the audience when he is at the play, for the actors have an ambition to please him.

The person of next consideration is Sir Andrew Freeport, a merchant of great eminence in the city of London; a person of indefatigable industry, strong reason, and great experience. His notions of trade are noble and generous, and (as every rich man has usually some sly way of jesting which would make no great figure were he not a rich man) he calls the sea the British Common. He is acquainted with commerce in all its parts; and will tell you that it is a stupid and barbarous way to extend dominion by arms; for true power is to be got by arts and industry. He will often argue that if this part of our trade were well cultivated we should gain from one nation; and if another, from another. I have heard him prove that diligence makes more lasting acquisitions than valor, and that sloth has ruined more nations than the sword. He abounds in several frugal maxims, among which the greatest favorite is, "A penny saved is a penny got." A general trader of good sense is pleasanter company than a general scholar; and Sir Andrew having a natural unaffected eloquence, the perspicuity of his discourse gives the same pleasure that wit would in another man. He has made his fortune himself; and says that England may be richer than other kingdoms by as plain methods as he himself is richer than other men; though at the same time I can say this of him, that there is not a point in the compass but blows home a ship in which he is an owner.

Next to Sir Andrew in the club-room sits Captain Sentry, a gentleman of great courage, good understanding, but invincible modesty. He is one of those that deserve very well, but are very awkward at putting their talents within the observation of such as should take notice of them. He was some years a captain, and behaved himself with great gallantry in several engagements and at several sieges; but

[1] Justices of the peace presided over the criminal courts or quarter sessions. Those chosen to sit with the higher court which met twice a year were called "justices of the quorum."

[2] one of the four great colleges of law in London

[3] ancient Greek philosophers and critics

[4] great English lawyers of the 15th and 16th centuries, respectively

[5] engages

[6] Cicero

[7] of one of the law colleges

[8] a dissolute tavern-resort

having a small estate of his own, and being next heir to Sir Roger, he has quitted a way of life in which no man can rise suitably to his merit who is not something of a courtier as well as a soldier. I have heard him often lament that in a profession where merit is placed in so conspicuous a view, impudence should get the better of modesty. When he has talked to this purpose, I never heard him make a sour expression, but frankly confess that he left the world because he was not fit for it. A strict honesty and an even regular behavior are in themselves obstacles to him that must press through crowds who endeavor at the same end with himself, the favor of a commander. He will, however, in his way of talk, excuse generals for not disposing according to men's desert, or inquiring into it; for, says he, that great man who has a mind to help me has as many to break through to come at me as I have to come at him; therefore, he will conclude that a man who would make a figure, especially in a military way, must get over all false modesty, and assist his patron against the importunity of other pretenders by a proper assurance in his own vindication. He says it is a civil cowardice to be backward in asserting what you ought to expect, as it is a military fear to be slow in attacking when it is your duty. With this candor does the gentleman speak of himself and others. The same frankness runs through all his conversation. The military part of his life has furnished him with many adventures, in the relation of which he is very agreeable to the company; for he is never overbearing, though accustomed to command men in the utmost degree below him; nor ever too obsequious from an habit of obeying men highly above him.

But that our society may not appear a set of humorists,[1] unacquainted with the gallantries and pleasures of the age, we have among us the gallant Will Honeycomb, a gentleman who, according to his years, should be in the decline of his life; but having ever been very careful of his person, and always had a very easy fortune, time has made but very little impression, either by wrinkles on his forehead or traces in his brain. His person is well turned and of a good height. He is very ready at that sort of discourse with which men usually entertain women. He has all his life dressed very well; and remembers habits[2] as others do men. He can smile when one speaks to him, and laughs easily. He knows the history of every mode, and can inform you from which of the French king's wenches our wives and daughters had this manner of curling their hair, that way of placing their hoods; whose frailty was covered by such a sort of petticoat; and whose vanity to show her foot made that part of the dress so short in such a year. In a word, all his conversation and knowledge has been in the female world. As other men of his age will take notice to you what such a minister said upon such and such an occasion, he will tell you, when the Duke of Monmouth danced at Court such a woman was then smitten, another was taken with him at the head of his troop in the park. In all these important relations he has ever about the same time received a kind glance, or a blow of a fan, from some celebrated beauty, mother of the present Lord Such-a-one. If you speak of a young commoner that said a lively thing in the house, he starts up, "He has good blood in his veins; Tom Mirabel begot him; the rogue cheated me in that affair; that young fellow's mother used me more like a dog than any woman I ever made advances to." This way of talking of his very much enlivens the conversation among us of a more sedate turn; and I find there is not one of the company but myself, who rarely speak at all, but speaks of him as of that sort of man who is usually called a well-bred, fine gentleman. To conclude his character, where women are not concerned he is an honest worthy man.

I cannot tell whether I am to account him whom I am next to speak of as one of our company, for he visits us but seldom; but when he does, it adds to every man else a new enjoyment of himself. He is a clergyman, a very philosophic man, of general learning, great sanctity of life, and the most exact good breeding. He has had the misfortune to be of a very weak constitution and, consequently, cannot accept of such cares and business as preferments in his function would oblige him to; he is, therefore, among the divines what a chamber-counselor is among lawyers. The probity of his mind and the integrity of his life create him followers, as being eloquent or loud advances others. He seldom introduces the subject he speaks upon; but we are so far gone in years that he observes, when he is among us, an earnestness to have him fall on some divine topic, which he always treats with much authority, as one who has no interest in this world, as one who is hastening to the object of all his wishes, and conceives hope from his decays and infirmities. These are my ordinary companions.

[1] queer fellows [2] costumes

JOSEPH ADDISON 1672-1719

Every sentence Addison wrote "seems to reflect the image of a courtly, well-bred man of the town, polite, traveled, learned, and possessed, beyond all else, of an inexhaustible gift of shrewd, yet humorous observation of men and things."—Law. And it is easy to believe that the life of such a man would be serene, successful, comparatively uneventful in contrast to that of Steele. Addison received an excellent training at good schools, and at Oxford soon attracted attention by his classical scholarship. Taking his place among professional writers in London, he won by his political poems a traveling pension to fit himself for diplomacy. He spent four years on the Continent, studying, observing, and writing. On his return he obtained official positions; his poem the "Campaign," 1704, on the Battle of Blenheim, raised him to the post of under-secretary of state.

His time of greatest literary activity was from 1710 to 1714. He joined Steele in the *Spectator,* contributing two hundred and seventy-four papers out of five hundred and fifty-five; his great success is Sir Roger de Coverley, who, though originated by Steele, really incarnates Addison's kindly tenderness. In 1713 was produced Addison's tragedy *Cato,* immediately popular for its political significance but held in greater regard for its moral sentiments. In 1716 he married the Countess of Warwick, an old friend, and was made secretary of state; but being in failing health he soon retired on a pension.

Addison was a creator, says the *Living Age:* "he created an English style, the pleasantest we ever possessed." More than any other man of his age he aroused a general taste for literature and things of the mind. Moreover, he was a literary as well as a political diplomat; he assumed unity with his reader, omitting abuse, contempt, or superiority. "Never, perhaps, was there a more illustrious instance of a great mind descending to minds of low estate. It may be said of Addison that 'he stooped to conquer.'" Despite the pleasing urbanity of his style the material of the *Spectator* shows somewhat faded when compared with the more brilliant and penetrating criticism of life and society of recent essayists.

[SIR ROGER AT CHURCH]

The Spectator, No. 112. Monday, July 9, 1711

Αθανάτους μὲν πρῶτα θεούς, νόμῳ ὡς διάκειται,
Τίμα Pythag.

First, in obedience to thy country's rites,
Worship the immortal gods.

I am always very well pleased with a country Sunday, and think, if keeping holy the seventh day were only a human institution, it would be the best method that could have been thought of for the polishing and civilizing of mankind. It is certain the country people would soon degenerate into a kind of savages and barbarians, were there not such frequent returns of a stated time in which the whole village meet together with their best faces, and in their cleanliest habits, to converse with one another upon indifferent subjects, hear their duties explained to them, and join together in adoration of the Supreme Being. Sunday clears away the rust of the whole week, not only as it refreshes in their minds the notions of religion, but as it puts both the sexes upon appearing in their most agreeable forms, and exerting all such qualities as are apt to give them a figure in the eye of the village. A country fellow distinguishes himself as much in the churchyard as a citizen does upon the 'Change, the whole parish-politics being generally discussed in that place either after sermon or before the bell rings.

My friend Sir Roger, being a good churchman, has beautified the inside of his church with several texts of his own choosing. He has likewise given a handsome pulpit-cloth, and railed in the communion-table at his own expense. He has often told me that at his coming to his estate he found his parishioners very irregular; and that in order to make them kneel and join in the responses he gave every one of them a hassock and a common prayer-book; and at the same time employed an itinerant singing-master, who goes about the country for that purpose, to instruct them rightly in the tunes of the psalms; upon which they now very much value themselves, and indeed outdo most of the country churches that I have ever heard.

As Sir Roger is landlord to the whole congregation, he keeps them in very good order, and will suffer nobody to sleep in it besides himself; for if by chance he has been surprised into a short nap at sermon, upon recovering out of it he stands up and looks about him, and if he sees anybody else nodding either wakes them himself or sends his servant to them. Several other of the old knight's peculiarities break out upon these occasions. Sometimes he will be lengthening out a verse in the singing psalms half a minute after the rest of the congregation have done with it; sometimes when he is pleased with the matter of his devotion, he pronounces Amen three or four times to the same prayer; and sometimes stands up when everybody else is upon their knees, to count the congregation or see if any of his tenants are missing.

I was yesterday very much surprised to hear my old friend in the midst of the service calling out to one John Matthews to mind what he was about, and not disturb the congregation. This John Matthews it seems is remarkable for being an idle fellow, and at that time was kicking his heels for his diversion. This authority of the knight, though exerted in that odd manner which accompanies him in all circumstances of life, has a very good effect upon the parish, who are not polite [1] enough to see anything ridiculous in his behavior; besides that the general good sense and worthiness of his character make his friends observe these little singularities as foils that rather set off than blemish his good qualities.

As soon as the sermon is finished, nobody presumes to stir till Sir Roger is gone out of the church. The knight walks down from his seat in the chancel between a double row of his tenants that stand bowing to him on each side; and every now and then inquires how such an one's wife, or mother, or son, or father do, whom he does not see at church; which is understood as a secret reprimand to the person that is absent.

The chaplain has often told me that upon a catechising day, when Sir Roger has been pleased with a boy than answers well, he has ordered a Bible to be given him next day for his encouragement; and sometimes accompanies it with a flitch of bacon to his mother. Sir Roger has likewise added five pounds a year to the clerk's place; and, that he may encourage the young fellows to make themselves perfect in the church service, has promised upon the death of the present incumbent, who is very old, to bestow it according to merit.

The fair understanding between Sir Roger and his chaplain, and their mutual concurrence in doing good, is the more remarkable because the very next village is famous for the differences and contentions that rise between the parson and the squire, who live in a perpetual state of war. The parson is always preaching at the squire; and the squire, to be revenged on the parson, never comes to church. The squire has made all his tenants atheists and tithe-stealers; [2] while the parson instructs them every Sunday in the dignity of his order, and insinuates to them almost in every sermon that he is a better man than his patron. In short, matters are come to such an extremity that the squire has not said his prayers either in public or private this half year; and that the parson threatens him, if he does not mend his manners, to pray for him in the face of the whole congregation.

Feuds of this nature, though too frequent in the country, are very fatal to the ordinary people; who are so used to be dazzled with riches that they pay as much deference to the understanding of a man of an estate as of a man of learning; and are very hardly brought to regard any truth, how important soever it may be, that is preached to them, when they know there are several men of five hundred a year who do not believe it.

[1] polished

[2] those who do not pay their church tax

[NED SOFTLY]

The Tatler, No. 163. Tuesday, April 25, 1710

Idem inficeto est inficetior rure,
Simul poemata attigit; neque idem unquam
Aequè est beatus, ac poema cum scribit:
Tam gaudet in se, tamque se ipse miratur.
Nimirum idem omnes fallimur; neque est quisquam
Quem non in aliquâ re videre Suffenum
Possis——

Catul. *de Suffeno,* xx, 14.

Suffenus has no more wit than a mere clown when he attempts to write verses, and yet he is never happier than when he is scribbling; so much does he admire himself and his compositions. And, indeed, this is the foible of every one of us, for there is no man living who is not a Suffenus in one thing or other.

I yesterday came hither [3] about two hours before the company generally make their appearance, with a design to read over all the newspapers; but, upon my sitting down, I was accosted by Ned Softly, who saw me from a corner in the other end of the room, where I found he had been writing something. "Mr. Bickerstaff," [4] says he, "I observe by a late Paper of yours that you and I are just of a humor; for you must know, of all impertinences there is nothing which I so much hate as news. I never read a Gazette [5] in my life; and never trouble my head about our armies, whether they win or lose, or in what part of the world they lie encamped." Without giving me time to reply he drew a paper of verses out of his pocket, telling me that he had something which would entertain me more agreeably; and that he would desire my judgment upon every line, for that we had

[3] Will's Coffee-House

[4] the assumed name of the editor of *The Tatler* which Steele had chosen

[5] the official court newspaper

time enough before us until the company came in.

Ned Softly is a very pretty poet, and a great admirer of easy lines. Waller [1] is his favorite; and as that admirable writer has the best and worst verses of any among our great English poets, Ned Softly has got all the bad ones without book; which he repeats upon occasion, to show his reading and garnish his conversation. Ned is indeed a true English reader, incapable of relishing the great and masterly strokes of this art; but wonderfully pleased with the little Gothic [2] ornaments of epigrammatical conceits, turns, points, and quibbles which are so frequent in the most admired of our English poets, and practiced by those who want genius and strength to represent, after the manner of the ancients, simplicity in its natural beauty and perfection.

Finding myself unavoidably engaged in such a conversation, I was resolved to turn my pain into a pleasure, and to divert myself as well as I could with so very odd a fellow. "You must understand," says Ned, "that the sonnet I am going to read to you was written upon a lady who showed me some verses of her own making and is, perhaps, the best poet of our age. But you shall hear it."

Upon which he began to read as follows:

To Mira on Her Incomparable Poems

When dressed in laurel wreaths you shine,
  And tune your soft melodious notes,
You seem a sister of the Nine,
  Or Phoebus' self in petticoats.

I fancy, when your song you sing,
  (Your song you sing with so much art)
Your pen was plucked from Cupid's wing;
  For, ah! it wounds me like his dart.

"Why," says I, "this is a little nosegay of conceits, a very lump of salt; every verse has something in it that piques; and then the *dart* in the last line is certainly as pretty a sting in the tail of an epigram, for so I think you critics call it, as ever entered into the thought of a poet." "Dear Mr. Bickerstaff," says he, shaking me by the hand, "everybody knows you to be a judge of these things; and to tell you truly I read over Roscommon's translation of Horace's *Art of Poetry* three several times before I sat down to write the sonnet which I have shown you. But you shall hear it again, and pray observe every line of it; for not one of them shall pass without your approbation.

When dressed in laurel wreaths you shine,

That is," says he, "when you have your garland on; when you are writing verses." To which I replied, "I know your meaning; a metaphor!" "The same," said he, and went on.

"And tune your soft melodious notes,

Pray observe the gliding of that verse; there is scarce a consonant in it; I took care to make it run upon liquids. Give me your opinion of it." "Truly," said I, "I think it as good as the former." "I am very glad to hear you say so," says he; "but mind the next.

You seem a sister of the Nine,

That is," says he, "you seem a sister of the Muses; for, if you look into ancient authors you will find it was their opinion that there were nine of them." "I remember it very well," said I; "but pray proceed."

"Or Phoebus' self in petticoats.

Phoebus," says he, "was the god of poetry. These little instances, Mr. Bickerstaff, show a gentleman's reading. Then, to take off from the air of learning which Phoebus and the Muses had given to this first stanza, you may observe how it falls all of a sudden into the familiar, 'in petticoats'!

Or Phoebus' self in petticoats."

"Let us now," says I, "enter upon the second stanza; I find the first line is still a continuation of the metaphor,

I fancy when your song you sing."

"It is very right," says he, "but pray observe the turn of words in those two lines. I was a whole hour in adjusting of them, and have still a doubt upon me, whether in the second line it should be 'Your song you sing'; or, 'You sing your song.' You shall hear them both:

I fancy when your song you sing,
  (Your song you sing with so much art)
or
I fancy, when your song you sing,
  (You sing your song with so much art.)"

"Truly," said I, "the turn is so natural either way that you have made me almost

[1] a very popular poet of the 17th century (p. 247)
[2] used contemptuously, as equivalent to quaint or in bad taste

giddy with it." "Dear sir," said he, grasping me by the hand, "you have a great deal of patience; but pray what do you think of the next verse?

Your pen was plucked from Cupid's wing."

"Think!" says I; "I think you have made Cupid look like a little goose." "That was my meaning," says he; "I think the ridicule is well enough hit off. But we come now to the last, which sums up the whole matter.

For, ah! it wounds me like his dart.

Pray how do you like that *Ah!* doth it not make a pretty figure in that place? *Ah!*——it looks as if I felt the dart, and cried out as being pricked with it.

For, ah! it wounds me like his dart.

"My friend Dick Easy," continued he, "assured me, he would rather have written that *Ah!* than to have been the author of the *Aeneid*. He indeed objected that I made Mira's pen like a quill in one of the lines and like a dart in the other. But as to that——" "Oh! as to that," says I, "it is but supposing Cupid to be like a porcupine, and his quills and darts will be the same thing." He was going to embrace me for the hint; but half a dozen critics coming into the room, whose faces he did not like, he conveyed the sonnet into his pocket, and whispered me in the ear, he would show it me again as soon as his man had written it over fair.

FROZEN WORDS

The Tatler, No. 254. Thursday, November 23, 1710

Splendidè mendax——.

Hor. *2 Od.*, iii, 35.

Gloriously false——.

There are no books which I more delight in than in travels, especially those that describe remote countries and give the writer an opportunity of showing his parts without incurring any danger of being examined or contradicted. Among all the authors of this kind, our renowned countryman, Sir John Mandeville, [1] has distinguished himself by the copiousness of his invention and the greatness of his genius. The second to Sir John I take to have been Ferdinand Mendez Pinto, [2] a person of infinite adventure and unbounded imagination. One reads the voyages of these two great wits with as much astonishment as the travels of Ulysses in Homer, or of the Red-Cross Knight in Spenser. All is enchanted ground and fairyland.

I have got into my hands, by great chance, several manuscripts of these two eminent authors, which are filled with greater wonders than any of those they have communicated to the public; and indeed, were they not so well attested, they would appear altogether improbable. I am apt to think the ingenious authors did not publish them with the rest of their works lest they should pass for fictions and fables; a caution not unnecessary when the reputation of their veracity was not yet established in the world. But as this reason has now no further weight, I shall make the public a present of these curious pieces at such times as I shall find myself unprovided with other subjects.

The present paper I intend to fill with an extract from Sir John's Journal, in which that learned and worthy knight gives an account of the freezing and thawing of several short speeches which he made in the territories of Nova Zembla. [3] I need not inform my reader that the author of "Hudibras" [4] alludes to this strange quality in that cold climate, when, speaking of abstracted notions clothed in a visible shape, he adds that apt simile,

Like words congealed in northern air."

Not to keep my reader any longer in suspense, the relation, put into modern language, is as follows:

"We were separated by a storm in the latitude of seventy-three, insomuch that only the ship which I was in, with a Dutch and French vessel, got safe into a creek of Nova Zembla. We landed in order to refit our vessels and store ourselves with provisions. The crew of each vessel made themselves a cabin of turf and wood, at some distance from each other, to fence themselves against the inclemencies of the weather, which was severe beyond imagination. We soon observed that in talking to one another we lost several of our words, and could not hear one another at above two yards distance, and that, too, when we sat very near the fire. After much perplexity I found that our words froze in the air before they

[1] See p. 68.

[2] a Portuguese adventurer and writer of the sixteenth century, now generally believed to have been veracious

[3] An island in the Arctic Ocean; the journal of William Barentz, a Dutch navigator who was shipwrecked there in 1596, may have afforded Addison a hint for this fancy.

[4] a poem satirizing the Puritans, by Samuel Butler

could reach the ears of the persons to whom they were spoken. I was soon confirmed in this conjecture when, upon the increase of the cold, the whole company grew dumb, or rather deaf; for every man was sensible, as we afterwards found, that he spoke as well as ever; but the sounds no sooner took air than they were condensed and lost. It was now a miserable spectacle to see us nodding and gaping at one another, every man talking, and no man heard. One might observe a seaman that could hail a ship at a league's distance beckoning with his hand, straining his lungs, and tearing his throat; but all in vain.

"—— Nec vox nec verba sequuntur.

"Nor voice, nor words ensued.

"We continued here three weeks in this dismal plight. At length, upon a turn of wind, the air about us began to thaw. Our cabin was immediately filled with a dry clattering sound which I afterwards found to be the crackling of consonants that broke above our heads, and were often mixed with a gentle hissing which I imputed to the letter *s* that occurs so frequently in the English tongue. I soon after felt a breeze of whispers rushing by my ear; for those, being of a soft and gentle substance, immediately liquefied in the warm wind that blew across our cabin. These were soon followed by syllables and short words, and at length by entire sentences that melted sooner or later as they were more or less congealed; so that we now heard everything that had been *spoken* during the whole three weeks that we had been *silent*, if I may use that expression. It was now very early in the morning, and yet, to my surprise, I heard somebody say, 'Sir John, it is midnight, and time for the ship's crew to go to bed.' This I knew to be the pilot's voice; and upon recollecting myself, I concluded that he had spoken these words to me some days before, though I could not hear them until the present thaw. My reader will easily imagine how the whole crew was amazed to hear every man talking and see no man opening his mouth. In the midst of this great surprise we were all in we heard a volley of oaths and curses, lasting for a long while, and uttered in a very hoarse voice which I knew belonged to the boatswain, who was a very choleric fellow, and had taken his opportunity of cursing and swearing at me when he thought I could not hear him; for I had several times given him the strappado [1] on that account, as I did not fail to repeat it for these his pious soliloquies when I got him on shipboard.

"I must not omit the names of several beauties in Wapping [2] which were heard every now and then in the midst of a long sigh that accompanied them; as, 'Dear Kate!' 'Pretty Mrs. Peggy!' 'When shall I see my Sue again!' This betrayed several amours which had been concealed until that time, and furnished us with a great deal of mirth in our return to England.

"When this confusion of voices was pretty well over, though I was afraid to offer at speaking as fearing I should not be heard, I proposed a visit to the Dutch cabin, which lay about a mile farther up in the country. My crew were extremely rejoiced to find they had again recovered their hearing; though every man uttered his voice with the same apprehensions that I had done,

"—— Et timidè verba intermissa retentat.

"And tried his tongue, his silence softly broke.

"At about half-a-mile's distance from our cabin we heard the groanings of a bear, which at first startled us; but, upon inquiry, we were informed by some of our company that he was dead and now lay in salt, having been killed upon that very spot about a fortnight before, in the time of the frost. Not far from the same place we were likewise entertained with some posthumous snarls and barkings of a fox.

"We at length arrived at the little Dutch settlement; and upon entering the room, found it filled with sighs that smelt of brandy, and several other unsavory sounds that were altogether inarticulate. My valet, who was an Irishman, fell into so great a rage at what he heard that he drew his sword; but not knowing where to lay the blame he put it up again. We were stunned with these confused noises, but did not hear a single word until about half-an-hour after; which I ascribed to the harsh and obdurate sounds of that language, which wanted more time than ours to melt and become audible.

"After having here met with a very hearty welcome we went to the cabin of the French who, to make amends for their three weeks' silence, were talking and disputing with greater rapidity and confusion than I ever heard in an assembly, even of that nation. Their language, as I found, upon the first giving of the weather

[1] a severe form of military punishment

[2] a quarter of London along the Thames frequented by seamen

fell asunder and dissolved. I was here convinced of an error into which I had before fallen; for I fancied that for the freezing of the sound, it was necessary for it to be wrapped up and, as it were, preserved in breath; but I found my mistake when I heard the sound of a kit [1] playing a minuet over our heads. I asked the occasion of it; upon which one of the company told me that it would play there above a week longer; 'for,' says he, 'finding ourselves bereft of speech, we prevailed upon one of the company who had his musical instrument about him, to play to us from morning to night; all which time was employed in dancing in order to dissipate our chagrin, and *tuer le temps*.'" [2]

Here Sir John gives very good philosophical reason why the kit could not be heard during the frost; but as they are something prolix, I pass them over in silence, and shall only observe that the honorable author seems, by his quotations, to have been well versed in the ancient poets, which perhaps raised his fancy above the ordinary pitch of historians, and very much contributed to the embellishment of his writings.

[A COQUETTE'S HEART]

The Spectator, No. 281. Tuesday, January 22, 1712

Pectoribus inhians spirantia consulit exta.
Verg. *Aen.*, ii, 64.

Anxious the reeking entrails he consults.

Having already given an account of the dissection of a beau's head, with the several discoveries made on that occasion, I shall here, according to my promise, enter upon the dissection of a coquette's heart, and communicate to the public such particularities as we observed in that curious piece of anatomy.

I should perhaps have waived this undertaking, had not I been put in mind of my promise by several of my unknown correspondents who are very importunate with me to make an example of the coquette, as I have already done of the beau. It is, therefore, in compliance with the request of friends that I have looked over the minutes of my former dream in order to give the public an exact relation of it, which I shall enter upon without further preface.

Our operator, before he engaged in this visionary dissection, told us that there was nothing in his art more difficult than to lay open the heart of a coquette, by reason of the many labyrinths and recesses which are to be found in it, and which do not appear in the heart of any other animal.

He desired us first of all to observe the pericardium, or outward case of the heart, which we did very attentively; and by the help of our glasses discerned in it millions of little scars, which seemed to have been occasioned by the points of innumerable darts and arrows that, from time to time, had glanced upon the outward coat; though we could not discover the smallest orifice by which any of them had entered and pierced the inward substance.

Every smatterer in anatomy knows that this pericardium, or case of the heart, contains in it a thin reddish liquor, supposed to be bred from the vapors which exhale out of the heart and, being stopped here, are condensed into this watery substance. Upon examining this liquor we found that it had in it all the qualities of that spirit which is made use of in the thermometer to show the change of weather.

Nor must I here omit an experiment one of the company assured us he himself had made with this liquor, which he found in great quantity about the heart of a coquette whom he had formerly dissected. He affirmed to us that he had actually inclosed it in a small tube made after the manner of a weather-glass; but that instead of acquainting him with the variations of the atmosphere it showed him the qualities of those persons who entered the room where it stood. He affirmed also that it rose at the approach of a plume of feathers, an embroidered coat, or a pair of fringed gloves; and that it fell as soon as an ill-shaped periwig, a clumsy pair of shoes, or an unfashionable coat came into his house. Nay, he proceeded so far as to assure us that upon his laughing aloud when he stood by it, the liquor mounted very sensibly, and immediately sunk again upon his looking serious. In short, he told us that he knew very well by this invention whenever he had a man of sense or a coxcomb in his room.

Having cleared away the pericardium, or the case, and liquor above-mentioned, we came to the heart itself. The outward surface of it was extremely slippery, and the mucro, or point, so very cold, withal, that upon endeavoring to take hold of it, it glided through the fingers like a smooth piece of ice.

The fibers were turned and twisted in a more intricate and perplexed manner than they are usually found in other hearts; insomuch that the whole heart was wound up together like a Gordian knot, and must have had very irregular

[1] a small fiddle [2] kill time

and unequal motions while it was employed in its vital function.

One thing we thought very observable, namely, that upon examining all the vessels which came into it or issued out of it, we could not discover any communication that it had with the tongue.

We could not but take notice likewise that several of those little nerves in the heart which are affected by the sentiments of love, hatred, and other passions, did not descend to this before us from the brain, but from the muscles which lie about the eye.

Upon weighing the heart in my hand I found it to be extremely light, and consequently very hollow, which I did not wonder at when, upon looking into the inside of it, I saw multitudes of cells and cavities running one within another, as our historians describe the apartments of Rosamond's bower. [1] Several of these little hollows were stuffed with innumerable sorts of trifles which I shall forbear giving any particular account of, and shall, therefore, only take notice of what lay first and uppermost, which, upon our unfolding it and applying our microscopes to it, appeared to be a flame-colored hood.

We are informed that the lady of this heart, when living, received the addresses of several who made love to her, and did not only give each of them encouragement but made everyone she conversed with believe that she regarded him with an eye of kindness; for which reason we expected to have seen the impression of multitudes of faces among the several plaits and foldings of the heart; but to our great surprise not a single print of this nature discovered itself till we came into the very core and center of it. We there observed a little figure which, upon applying our glasses to it, appeared dressed in a very fantastic manner. The more I looked upon it, the more I thought I had seen the face before, but could not possibly recollect either the place or time; when at length one of the company who had examined this figure more nicely than the rest, showed us plainly by the make of its face and the several turns of its features that the little idol which was thus lodged in the very middle of the heart was the deceased beau, whose head I gave some account of in my last Tuesday's paper.

As soon as we had finished our dissection, we resolved to make an experiment of the heart, not being able to determine among ourselves the nature of its substance, which differed in so many particulars from that in the heart of other females. Accordingly, we laid it into a pan of burning coals, when we observed in it a certain salamandrine quality that made it capable of living in the midst of fire and flame without being consumed or so much as singed.

As we were admiring this strange phenomenon, and standing round the heart in a circle, it gave a most prodigious sigh, or rather crack, and dispersed all at once in smoke and vapor. This imaginary noise, which methought was louder than the burst of a cannon, produced such a violent shake in my brain that it dissipated the fumes of sleep, and left me in an instant broad awake.

[1] Henry II, it was said, built a labyrinth to conceal the abode of "Fair Rosamond."

[THE VISION OF MIRZA]

The Spectator, No. 159. Saturday, September 1, 1711

—Omnem, quae nunc obducta tuenti
Mortales hebetat visus tibi, et humida circum
Caligat, nubem eripiam—

Verg. *Aen.*, ii, 604.

The cloud, which, intercepting the clear light,
Hangs o'er thy eyes, and blunts thy mortal sight,
I will remove—

When I was at Grand Cairo, I picked up several Oriental manuscripts which I have still by me. Among others I met with one entitled The Visions of Mirza, which I have read over with great pleasure. I intend to give it to the public when I have no other entertainment for them; and shall begin with the first vision which I have translated word for word, as follows:

"On the fifth day of the moon which, according to the custom of my forefathers, I always keep holy, after having washed myself and offered up my morning devotions, I ascended the high hills of Bagdad in order to pass the rest of the day in meditation and prayer. As I was here airing myself on the tops of the mountains, I fell into a profound contemplation on the vanity of human life; and passing from one thought to another, 'Surely,' said I, 'man is but a shadow, and life a dream.' Whilst I was thus musing I cast my eyes toward the summit of a rock that was not far from me, where I discovered one in the habit of a shepherd, with a musical instrument in his hand. As I looked upon him he applied it to his lips, and began to play upon it. The sound of it was exceedingly sweet, and wrought into a variety of tunes that were inexpressibly melodious, and altogether different from anything I had ever heard. They put me in mind of those heavenly airs that are played to the departed souls of good men upon their first arrival in Paradise, to wear out the impressions of their last agonies, and qualify them for the pleasures of that happy place. My heart melted away in secret raptures.

"I had been often told that the rock before me was the haunt of a Genius; [1] and that several had been entertained with music who had passed by it, but never heard that the musician had before made himself visible. When he had raised my thoughts by those transporting airs which he played to taste the pleasures of his conversation, as I looked upon him like one astonished he beckoned to me, and by the waving of his hand directed me to approach the place where he sat. I drew near with that reverence which is due to a superior nature; and as my heart was entirely subdued by the captivating strains I had heard, I fell down at his feet and wept. The Genius smiled upon me with a look of compassion and affability that familiarized him to my imagination, and at once dispelled all the fears and apprehensions with which I approached him. He lifted me from the ground and, taking me by the hand, 'Mirza,' said he, 'I have heard thee in thy soliloquies; follow me.'

"He then led me to the highest pinnacle of the rock and, placing me on the top of it, 'Cast thy eyes eastward,' said he, 'and tell me what thou seest.' 'I see,' said I, 'a huge valley, and a prodigious tide of water rolling through it' 'The valley that thou seest,' said he, 'is the Vale of Misery, and the tide of water that thou seest is part of the great Tide of Eternity.' 'What is the reason,' said I, 'that the tide I see rises out of a thick mist at one end and again loses itself in a thick mist at the other?' 'What thou seest,' said he, 'is that portion of eternity which is called time, measured out by the sun, and reaching from the beginning of the world to its consummation. Examine now,' said he, 'this sea that is bounded with darkness at both ends, and tell me what thou discoverest in it.' 'I see a bridge,' said I, 'standing in the midst of the tide.' 'The bridge thou seest,' said he, 'is Human Life; consider it attentively.' Upon a more leisurely survey of it, I found that it consisted of three score and ten entire arches, with several broken arches which, added to those that were entire, made up the number about a hundred. As I was counting the arches, the Genius told me that this bridge consisted at first of a thousand arches; but that a great flood swept away the rest, and left the bridge in the ruinous condition I now beheld it. 'But tell me further,' said he, 'what thou discoverest on it.' 'I see multitudes of people passing over it,' said I, 'and a black cloud hanging on each end of it.' As I looked more attentively, I saw several of the passengers dropping through the bridge into the great tide that flowed underneath it; and upon further examination, perceived there were innumerable trapdoors that lay concealed in the bridge, which the passengers no sooner trod upon but they fell through them into the tide, and immediately disappeared. These hidden pitfalls were set very thick at the entrance of the bridge, so that throngs of people no sooner broke through the cloud but many of them fell into them. They grew thinner toward the middle, but multiplied and lay closer together toward the end of the arches that were entire.

"There were indeed some persons, but their number was very small, that continued a kind of hobbling march on the broken arches, but fell through one after another, being quite tired and spent with so long a walk.

"I passed some time in the contemplation of this wonderful structure and the great variety of objects which it presented. My heart was filled with a deep melancholy to see several dropping unexpectedly in the midst of mirth and jollity, and catching at everything that stood by them to save themselves. Some were looking up toward the heavens in a thoughtful posture, and in the midst of a speculation stumbled and fell out of sight. Multitudes were very busy in the pursuit of bubbles that glittered in their eyes and danced before them; but often when they thought themselves within the reach of them, their footing failed and down they sunk. In this confusion of objects I observed some who ran to and fro upon the bridge thrusting several persons on trapdoors which did not seem to lie in their way, and which they might have escaped had they not been thus forced upon them.

"The Genius seeing me indulge myself on this melancholy prospect, told me I had dwelt long enough upon it. 'Take thine eyes off the bridge,' said he, 'and tell me if thou yet seest anything thou dost not comprehend.' Upon looking up, 'What mean,' said I, 'those great flights of birds that are perpetually hovering about the bridge, and settling upon it from

[1] spirit

time to time? I see vultures, harpies, ravens, cormorants, and among many other feathered creatures several little winged boys that perch in great numbers upon the middle arches.' 'These,' said the Genius, 'are Envy, Avarice, Superstition, Despair, Love, with the like cares and passions that infest human life.'

"I here fetched a deep sigh. 'Alas,' said I, 'Man was made in vain! how is he given away to misery and mortality! tortured in life, and swallowed up in death!' The Genius being moved with compassion toward me, bid me quit so uncomfortable a prospect. 'Look no more,' said he, 'on man in the first stage of his existence, in his setting out for eternity; but cast thine eye on that thick mist into which the tide bears the several generations of mortals that fall into it. I directed my sight as I was ordered, and (whether or no the good Genius strengthened it with any supernatural force, or dissipated part of the mist that was before too thick for the eye to penetrate) I saw the valley opening at the farther end, and spreading forth into an immense ocean that had a huge rock of adamant running through the midst of it and dividing it into two equal parts. The clouds still rested on one half of it, insomuch that I could discover nothing in it; but the other appeared to me a vast ocean planted with innumerable islands that were covered with fruits and flowers, and interwoven with a thousand little shining seas that ran among them. I could see persons dressed in glorious habits with garlands upon their heads, passing among the trees, lying down by the sides of fountains, or resting on beds of flowers; and could hear a confused harmony of singing birds, falling waters, human voices, and musical instruments. Gladness grew in me upon the discovery of so delightful a scene. I wished for the wings of an eagle that I might fly away to those happy seats; but the Genius told me there was no passage to them except through the gates of death that I saw opening every moment upon the bridge. 'The islands,' said he, 'that lie so fresh and green before thee, and with which the whole face of the ocean appears spotted as far as thou canst see, are more in number than the sands on the seashore; there are myriads of islands behind those which thou here discoverest, reaching farther than thine eye or even thine imagination can extend itself. These are the mansions of good men after death who, according to the degree and kinds of virtue in which they excelled, are distributed among these several islands, which abound with pleasures of different kinds and degrees suitable to the relishes and perfections of those who are settled in them; every island is a paradise accommodated to its respective inhabitants. Are not these, O Mirza, habitations worth contending for? Does life appear miserable that gives thee opportunities of earning such a reward? Is death to be feared that will convey thee to so happy an existence? Think not man was made in vain, who has such an eternity reserved for him.' I gazed with inexpressible pleasure on these happy islands. At length, said I, 'Show me now, I beseech thee, the secrets that lie hid under those dark clouds which cover the ocean on the other side of the rock of adamant.' The Genius making me no answer, I turned me about to address myself to him a second time, but I found that he had left me; I then turned again to the vision which I had been so long contemplating; but instead of the rolling tide, the arched bridge, and the happy islands, I saw nothing but the long hollow valley of Bagdad, with oxen, sheep, and camels grazing upon the sides of it."

MATTHEW PRIOR 1664-1721

Matthew Prior, like others of the period, combined the diplomatist with the man of letters. He says himself that he was only a poet "by accident"; yet some modern critics feel that he inherited from Shakespeare, through Fletcher, Herrick, and Dryden the note of pure lyricism later revived by Burns and Blake. It is none too usual for a person of his obscure origin to rise to a position of political eminence, for he was taken from school to keep accounts in the wine shop of his uncle. There Lord Dorset found the boy reading Horace, and sent him back to school; and from that time his advancement was steady.

After leaving college he held one important office after another. From 1690 to 1715 his life is a part of English diplomatic history; at The Hague and at Paris he was actual plenipotentiary, in favor with Anne, William, and Louis XIV. On the death of Anne he was impeached and imprisoned, but was released. He made a good sum of money in 1718 by publishing a folio edition of his *Poems*, first appearing in 1709, and was presented with Down Hall in Essex by Lord Harley. Here Prior spent the rest of his life in delightful retirement.

His nature was kindly and lovable, attracting many friends. Though involved in political struggle, he preserved a tone of lighthearted gaiety, shrewd worldly wisdom, and friendly tolerance uncommon in his contemporaries; and his ideas were noticeably modern and in advance of his age.

Further material on Prior will be found in Johnson, Thackeray, and E. S. Roscoe's extremely interesting article, "Diplomatist and Poet," *Edin. R.* 218:151-62.

TO A CHILD OF QUALITY FIVE YEARS OLD

Lords, knights, and 'squires, the numerous band,
That wear the fair Miss Mary's fetters,
Were summoned by her high command
To show their passions by their letters.

My pen among the rest I took,
Lest those bright eyes that cannot read
Should dart their kindling fires, and look
The power they have to be obeyed.

Nor quality, nor reputation
Forbid me yet my flame to tell,
Dear Five-years-old befriends my passion,
And I may write till she can spell.

For while she makes her silk-worms beds
With all the tender things I swear,
Whilst all the house my passion reads
In papers round her baby's hair,

She may receive and own my flame,
For, though the strictest prudes should know it,
She'll pass for a most virtuous dame
And I for an unhappy poet.

Then, too, alas! when she shall tear
The lines some younger rival sends,
She'll give me leave to write, I fear,
And we shall still continue friends.

For, as our different ages move,
'Tis so ordained (would Fate but mend it!)
That I shall be past making love
When she begins to comprehend it.

1704 1704

A SIMILE

Dear Thomas, didst thou never pop
Thy head into a tinman's shop?
There, Thomas, didst thou never see
('Tis but by way of simile)
A squirrel spend his little rage
In jumping round a rolling cage?
The cage, as either side turned up,
Striking a ring of bells a-top?

Moved in the orb, pleased with the chimes
The foolish creature thinks he climbs;
But here or there, turn wood or wire,
He never gets two inches higher.

So fares it with those merry blades
That frisk it under Pindus' [1] shades.
In noble songs and lofty odes,
They tread on stars and talk with gods;
Still dancing in an airy round,
Still pleased with their own verses' sound;
Brought back, how fast soe'er they go,
Always aspiring, always low.

1707

AN ODE

The merchant, to secure his treasure,
Conveys it in a borrowed name.
Euphelia serves to grace my measure,
But Cloe is my real flame.

My softest verse, my darling lyre,
Upon Euphelia's toilet lay;
When Cloe noted [2] her desire
That I should sing, that I should play.

My lyre I tune, my voice I raise;
But with my numbers [3] mix my sighs.
And whilst I sing Euphelia's praise,
I fix my soul on Cloe's eyes.

Fair Cloe blushed; Euphelia frowned;
I sung and gazed; I played and trembled;
And Venus to the Loves around
Remarked, how ill we all dissembled.

1709

A BETTER ANSWER [4]

Dear Cloe, how blubbered is that pretty face!
Thy cheek all on fire, and thy hair all uncurled;
Prythee quit this caprice, and (as old Falstaff says [5])
Let us e'en talk a little like folks of this world.

How canst thou presume thou hast leave to destroy
The beauties which Venus but lent to thy keeping?
Those looks were designed to inspire love and joy;
More ord'nary eyes may serve people for weeping.

To be vexed at a trifle or two that I writ,
Your judgment at once and my passion you wrong;
You take that for fact which will scarce be found wit.
Odds life! Must one swear to the truth of a song?

[1] a mountain in Greece sacred to the Muses

[2] denoted, expressed [3] verses

[4] This poem was preceded by one called "An Answer to Cloe Jealous." (Prior's "Cloe," perhaps for distinction, has no *h* in her name.)

[5] See II *Henry IV,* V, iii, 101.

What I speak, my fair Cloe, and what I write, shows
The difference there is betwixt Nature and Art;
I court others in verse, but I love thee in prose;
And they have my whimsies, but thou hast my heart.

The god of us verse-men (you know, Child), the sun,
How after his journeys he sets up his rest;
If at morning o'er earth 'tis his fancy to run,
At night he declines on his Thetis's breast.

So when I am wearied with wandering all day,
To thee, my delight, in the evening I come;
No matter what beauties I saw in my way,
They were but my visits, but thou art my home.

Then finish, dear Cloe, this pastoral war,
And let us, like Horace and Lydia,[1] agree;
For thou art a girl so much brighter than her,
As he was a poet sublimer than me.

1718

JOHN GAY 1685-1732

In disposition Gay showed great contrast to Prior. By nature he was lazy and dilatory; despondent at lack of success and humiliated by his dependence on patrons, he relieved his feelings by bitter satire which antagonized those who might have aided him. Yet he really got more out of life than he or his friends would admit. After being a shop-keeper's apprentice he became the friend of great writers, the companion of nobles, was well known for his work, and made a very good income which he squandered in wild speculations. When his health failed, the kindly Duke and Duchess of Queensbury cherished him to the end of his life.

From 1708 to 1728 he produced a good deal of varied work. His best known poems are *Shepherd's Week,* 1714, abounding with interesting folklore and closely studied rural pictures; *Trivia, or the Art of Walking the Streets of London,* 1716, containing much detail of street life under Anne; *Fables,* 1727, written for Prince William; and the *Beggar's Opera,* 1728, the fore-runner of Gilbert and Sullivan's *Pinafore.* This burlesque opera, which made him famous, caricatured the fashionable life of his day through scenes laid in Newgate prison and treated in the spirit of Hogarth, the great satirical artist of Gay's time. It slashed Walpole and other high politicians; and challenged the Italian school of opera then in favor. It was popular in England and on the Continent; was the first recorded opera sung in America, 1750; and was successfully revived in England and America in 1920.

Early essays on Gay are by Johnson, Thackeray, Hazlitt, etc. For more recent material see *Lit. Dig.* 68:28-9, Jan. 22, '21; and A. N. Meyer, *Bookm.* 52:521-4.

[1] Horace addressed many of his odes to "Lydia."

From FABLES

XLIV. The Hound and the Huntsman

Impertinence at first is borne
With heedless slight, or smiles of scorn;
Teased into wrath, what patience bears
The noisy fool who perseveres?

The morning wakes, the Huntsman sounds,
At once rush forth the joyful hounds.
They seek the wood with eager pace,
Through bush, through brier, explore the chase.
Now scattered wide, they try the plain,
And snuff the dewy turf in vain.
What care, what industry, what pains!
What universal silence reigns!

Ringwood, a dog of little fame,
Young, pert, and ignorant of game,
At once displays his babbling throat;
The pack, regardless of the note,
Pursue the scent; with louder strain
He still persists to vex the train.

The Huntsman to the clamor flies;
The smacking lash he smartly plies.
His ribs all welked,[2] with howling tone
The puppy thus expressed his moan:

"I know the music of my tongue
Long since the pack with envy stung.
What will not spite?[3] These bitter smarts
I owe to my superior parts."

"When puppies prate," the Huntsman cried,
"They show both ignorance and pride;
Fools may our scorn, not envy, raise,
For envy is a kind of praise.
Had not thy forward noisy tongue
Proclaimed thee always in the wrong,
Thou might'st have mingled with the rest,
And ne'er thy foolish nose confest.
But fools, to talking ever prone,
Are sure to make their follies known."

1727

XLV. The Poet and the Rose

I hate the man who builds his name
On ruins of another's fame.
Thus prudes, by characters o'erthrown,
Imagine that they raise their own.
Thus scribblers, covetous of praise,
Think slander can transplant the bays.

[2] covered with ridges [3] Supply "do."

Beauties and bards have equal pride,
With both all rivals are decried.
Who praises Lesbia's eyes and feature,
Must call her sister awkward creature;
For the kind flattery's sure to charm,
When we some other nymph disarm.

As in the cool of early day
A Poet sought the sweets of May,
The garden's fragrant breath ascends,
And every stalk with odor bends.
A rose he plucked, he gazed, admired,
Thus singing as the Muse inspired:

"Go Rose, my Chloe's bosom grace;
How happy should I prove,
Might I supply that envied place
With never-fading love!
There, Phoenix-like, beneath her eye,
Involved in fragrance, burn and die!

"Know, hapless flower, that thou shall find
More fragrant roses there;
I see thy withering head reclined
With envy and despair!
One common fate we both must prove;
You die with envy, I with love."

"Spare your comparisons," replied
An angry Rose who grew beside.
"Of all mankind you should not flout us;
What can a Poet do without us?
In every love-song roses bloom;
We lend you color and perfume.
Does it to Chloe's charms conduce,
To found her praise on our abuse?
Must we, to flatter her, be made
To wither, envy, pine, and fade?"

1727

ALEXANDER POPE 1688-1744

Pope's parents, middle-class Catholics comfortably off, did not find London, in the year their son was born, a very congenial place. That was the year of "the glorious Revolution" when almost all Londoners upheld the banner of William III just as much because it was anti-Catholic as because it promised political freedom. Later, when Pope grew up, he was debarred from Oxford and Cambridge because of the oath required of students to uphold the Church of England. We may see him more justly if we remember that his life was, as he tells us, "one long disease." Physical deformity added to religious discrimination helped to distort his sensitive nature so that his relations to individuals and society became unnatural. He seemed obsessed with the idea that all men were his enemies, for sooner or later he quarreled with all his friends, and even exposed them in his writings to public ridicule.

Pope perfected the English heroic couplet, making a "closed" couplet forming a complete grammatical unit, with the sense usually finished in the second line, and formulated rules for writing it. It is interesting to note in this verse form the cycle of change from Chaucer and Waller through Pope to Keats. Dryden and Pope are the two great English verse satirists. Though Dryden excelled in imagination and invention, and even in depth and vigor of satire—for Dryden flays where Pope stings—Pope went beyond his master in perfection of artifice, polish and, above all, wit. In his age, the only age in English poetry where mere "style" was considered the preëminent virtue, Pope was easily chief. Aside from the works quoted from below, he is best known for *The Dunciad,* 1728, and for his translation of Homer, 1715-26, which was so popular that it brought him a comfortable fortune. With his death at Twickenham on the Thames, and that of Swift that soon followed, the supreme satirists of the English tongue had passed away.

W. J. Courthope, *Life of A. Pope,* 1889; Sir L. Stephen (EML). Criticism: J. Warton's *Essay on the Writings and Genius of Pope,* 1756-1782, questions Pope's right to be called poet; but see S. Johnson, Lowell, and Stephen (HL), Vol. I; G. K. Chesterton, "Pope and the Art of Satire," *Varied Types,* 1921; F. S. Thackeray, "Is the Present Neglect of Pope Merited," *19th Cent.* 74:865-71, and P. E. More, "Pope as a Poet," *Nation,* 90:647-50. Austin Dobson's poem, "A Dialogue to the Memory of Alexander Pope," 1888, is witty, sympathetic.

ODE ON ST. CECILIA'S DAY [1]

1

Descend, ye Nine! descend and sing;
The breathing instruments inspire,
Wake into voice each silent string,
And sweep the sounding lyre!
In a sadly-pleasing strain
Let the warbling lute complain;
Let the loud trumpet sound
Till the roofs all around
The shrill echoes rebound;
While in more lengthened notes and slow,

[1] This ode, composed when Pope was but twenty years of age, is interesting chiefly for comparison with the odes written by Dryden for similar occasions. Pope has drawn freely upon classical mythology—the nine Muses, Morpheus, god of dreams, the voyage of the Argonauts with Orpheus drawing the trees of Mt. Pelion down to the sea by the sweetness of his strain, and especially the sad story of Orpheus's descent into Hades to win back his lost Eurydice only to lose her again and wander forlorn until the jealous and enraged Bacchantes stoned him to death and threw his limbs into the Hebrus. It is pointed out by Mr. W. J. Courthope that Dryden, by weaving in history instead of legend, secured greater human interest.

The deep, majestic, solemn organs blow.
Hark! the numbers soft and clear,
Gently steal upon the ear;
Now louder, and yet louder rise
And fill with spreading sounds the skies;
Exulting in triumph now swell the bold notes,
In broken air, trembling, the wild music floats;
Till, by degrees, remote and small,
The strains decay,
And melt away,
In a dying, dying fall.

2

By music, minds an equal temper know,
Nor swell too high nor sink too low.
If in the breast tumultuous joys arise,
Music her soft, assuasive voice applies;
Or, when the soul is pressed with cares,
Exalts her in enlivening airs.
Warriors she fires with animated sounds;
Pours balm into the bleeding lover's wounds;
Melancholy lifts her head,
Morpheus rouses from his bed,
Sloth unfolds her arms and wakes,
Listening Envy drops her snakes;
Intestine war no more our passions wage,
And giddy factions hear away their rage.

3

But when our country's cause provokes to arms,
How martial music every bosom warms!
So when the first bold vessel dared the seas,
High on the stern the Thracian raised his strain,
While Argo saw her kindred trees
Descend from Pelion to the main.
Transported demi-gods stood round,
And men grew heroes at the sound,
Inflamed with glory's charms.
Each chief his sevenfold shield displayed,
And half unsheathed the shining blade,
And seas, and rocks, and skies rebound,
To arms, to arms, to arms!

4

But when through all th' infernal bounds
Which flaming Phlegethon surrounds,
Love, strong as Death, the poet led
To the pale nations of the dead,
What sounds were heard,
What scenes appeared,
O'er all the dreary coasts!
Dreadful gleams,
Dismal screams,
Fires that glow,
Shrieks of woe,
Sullen moans,
Hollow groans,
And cries of tortured ghosts!
But hark! he strikes the golden lyre;
And see! the tortured ghosts respire,
See, shady forms advance!
Thy stone, O Sisyphus, stands still,
Ixion rests upon his wheel,
And the pale specters dance!
The Furies sink upon their iron beds,
And snakes uncurled hang listening round their heads.

5

By the streams that ever flow,
By the fragrant winds that blow
O'er th' Elysian flowers;
By those happy souls who dwell
In yellow meads of asphodel
Or amaranthine bowers;
By the hero's armed shades,
Glittering through the gloomy glades,
By the youths that died for love,
Wandering in the myrtle grove,
Restore, restore Eurydice to life;
Oh, take the husband, or return the wife!

He sung, and hell consented
To hear the poet's prayer;
Stern Proserpine relented,
And gave him back the fair.
Thus song could prevail
O'er death, and o'er hell,
A conquest how hard and how glorious!
Though fate had fast bound her
With Styx nine times round her,
Yet music and love were victorious.

6

But soon, too soon, the lover turns his eyes;
Again she falls, again she dies, she dies;
How wilt thou now the fatal sisters [1] move?
No crime was thine, if 'tis no crime to love.
Now under hanging mountains,
Beside the fall of fountains,
Or where Hebrus wanders,
Rolling in meanders,
All alone,
Unheard, unknown,
He makes his moan;
And calls her ghost.
For ever, ever, ever lost!
Now with Furies surrounded,
Despairing, confounded,
He trembles, he glows,

[1] the three Fates

Amidst Rhodope's[1] snows;
See, wild as the winds, o'er the desert he flies;
Hark! Haemus[1] resounds with the Bacchanals' cries—
Ah see, he dies!
Yet even in death Eurydice he sung,
Eurydice still trembled on his tongue,
Eurydice the woods,
Eurydice the floods,
Eurydice the rocks, and hollow mountains rung.

7

Music the fiercest grief can charm,
And fate's severest rage disarm;
Music can soften pain to ease,
And make despair and madness please;
Our joys below it can improve,
And antedate the bliss above.
This the divine Cecilia found,
And to her Maker's praise confined the sound.
When the full organ joins the tuneful choir,
Th' immortal powers incline their ear,
Borne on the swelling notes our souls aspire,
While solemn airs improve the sacred fire;
And angels lean from heaven to hear.
Of Orpheus now no more let poets tell,
To bright Cecilia greater power is given;
His numbers raised a shade from hell,
Hers lift the soul to heaven.

1708

From AN ESSAY ON CRITICISM

'Tis hard to say if greater want of skill
Appear in writing or in judging ill;
But, of the two, less dangerous is th' offense
To tire our patience than mislead our sense.
Some few in that, but numbers err in this,
Ten censure wrong for one who writes amiss;
A fool might once himself alone expose,
Now one in verse makes many more in prose.
'Tis with our judgments as our watches, none
Go just alike, yet each believes his own.
In poets as true genius is but rare,
True taste as seldom is the critic's share;
Both must alike from heaven derive their light,
These born to judge, as well as those to write.
Let such teach others, who themselves excel,
And censure freely who have written well.
Authors are partial to their wit, 'tis true,
But are not critics to their judgment, too?
Yet if we look more closely we shall find
Most have the seeds of judgment in their mind;
Nature affords at least a glimmering light;
The lines, though touched but faintly, are drawn right.
But as the slightest sketch, if justly traced,
Is by ill-coloring but the more disgraced,
So by false learning is good sense defaced.

. . . .

First follow nature and your judgment frame
By her just standard, which is still the same.
Unerring Nature, still divinely bright,
One clear, unchanged, and universal light,
Life, force, and beauty, must to all impart,
At once the source, and end, and test of Art.
Art from that fund each just supply provides,
Works without show, and without pomp presides;
In some fair body thus th' informing[2] soul
With spirits feeds, with vigor fills the whole,
Each motion guides, and every nerve sustains;
Itself unseen, but in th' effects remains.
Some, to whom Heaven in wit[3] has been profuse,
Want as much more to turn it to its use;
For wit and judgment often are at strife,
Though meant each other's aid, like man and wife.
'Tis more to guide, than spur the Muse's steed;
Restrain his fury, than provoke his speed;
The wingèd courser, like a generous horse,
Shows most true mettle when you check his course.
Those rules of old discovered, not devised,
Are nature still, but nature methodized;
Nature, like liberty, is but restrained
By the same laws which first herself ordained.
Hear how learn'd Greece her useful rules indites,
When to repress and when indulge our flights;
High on Parnassus' top[4] her sons she showed,
And pointed out those arduous paths they trod;
Held from afar, aloft, th' immortal prize,
And urged the rest by equal steps to rise.
Just precepts thus from great examples given,
She drew from them what they derived from Heaven.
The generous critic fanned the poet's fire,
And taught the world with reason to admire.
Then Criticism the Muse's handmaid proved,
To dress her charms and make her more beloved;
But following wits from that intention strayed,
Who could not win the mistress, wooed the maid;

[1] a mountain of Thrace

[2] animating

[3] This word has here the rather special 18th century meaning of brilliancy of intellect, talent.

[4] the abode of Apollo and the Muses; figurative for the heights of poetic fame

Against the poets their own arms they turned,
Sure to hate most the men from whom they learned.
So modern 'pothecaries, taught the art
By doctor's bills [1] to play the doctor's part,
Bold in the practice of mistaken rules,
Prescribe, apply, and call their masters fools.
Some on the leaves of ancient authors prey,
Nor time nor moths e'er spoiled so much as they.
Some dryly plain without invention's aid,
Write dull receipts how poems may be made;
These leave the sense, their learning to display,
And those explain the meaning quite away.

You then whose judgment the right course would steer,
Know well each ancient's proper character;
His fable, [2] subject, scope in every page;
Religion, country, genius of his age.
Without all these at once before your eyes,
Cavil you may, but never criticise.
Be Homer's works your study and delight,
Read them by day, and meditate by night;
Thence form your judgment, thence your maxims bring,
And trace the Muses upward to their spring.
Still with itself compared, his text peruse;
And let your comment be the Mantuan Muse. [3]

When first young Maro [3] in his boundless mind
A work t' outlast immortal Rome designed,
Perhaps he seemed above the critic's law,
And but from nature's fountains scorned to draw;
But when t' examine every part he came,
Nature and Homer were, he found, the same.
Convinced, amazed, he checks the bold design;
And rules as strict his labored work confine,
As if the Stagirite [4] o'erlooked each line.
Learn hence for ancient rules a just esteem;
To copy nature is to copy them.

Some beauties yet no precepts can declare,
For there's a happiness as well as care.
Music resembles poetry, in each
Are nameless graces which no methods teach,
And which a master-hand alone can reach.
If, where the rules not far enough extend,
(Since rules were made but to promote their end)
Some lucky license answer to the full
Th' intent proposed, that license is a rule.
Thus Pegasus, [5] a nearer way to take,
May boldly deviate from the common track.
Great wits sometimes may gloriously offend,
And rise to faults true critics dare not mend; [6]
From vulgar bounds with grave disorder part,
And snatch grace beyond the reach of art,
Which, without passing through the judgment, gains
The heart, and all its end at once attains.
In prospects thus, some objects please our eyes,
Which out of nature's common order rise,
The shapeless rock, or hanging precipice.
But though the ancients thus their rules invade,
(As kings dispense with laws themselves have made)
Moderns beware! Or if you must offend
Against the precept, ne'er transgress its end;
Let it be seldom, and compelled by need;
And have, at least, their precedent to plead.
The critic else proceeds without remorse,
Seizes your fame and puts his laws in force.

I know there are to whose presumptuous thoughts
Those freer beauties, even in them, seem faults.
Some figures monstrous and misshaped appear,
Considered singly, or beheld too near,
Which, but proportioned to their light or place,
Due distance reconciles to form and grace.
A prudent chief not always must display
His powers in equal ranks and fair array,
But with th' occasion and the place comply,
Conceal his force, nay, seem sometimes to fly.
Those oft are stratagems which errors seem,
Nor is it Homer nods, but we that dream.

. . . .

Of all the causes which conspire to blind
Man's erring judgment, and misguide the mind,
What the weak head with strongest bias rules,
Is pride, the never-failing vice of fools.
Whatever nature has in worth denied,
She gives in large recruits of needful pride;
For as in bodies, thus in souls, we find
What wants in blood and spirits, swelled with wind.
Pride, where wit fails, steps in to our defense,
And fills up all the mighty void of sense.
If once right reason drives that cloud away,
Truth breaks upon us with resistless day.
Trust not yourself; but your defects to know,
Make use of every friend—and every foe.

A little learning is a dangerous thing;
Drink deep, or taste not the Pierian spring. [7]
There, shallow drafts intoxicate the brain,
And drinking largely sobers us again.
Fired at first sight with what the Muse imparts,
In fearless youth we tempt [8] the heights of arts,

[1] prescriptions
[2] story, plot
[3] Vergil
[4] Aristotle, the foremost critic of ancient times
[5] the winged horse of the Muses
[6] Pope, in the 1743 ed., placed ll. 152-3 after l. 160.
[7] at the foot of Mt. Olympus, reputed birthplace of the Muses
[8] attempt

While from the bounded level of our mind
Short views we take, nor see the lengths behind;
But more advanced, behold with strange surprise
New distant scenes of endless science rise!
So pleased at first the towering Alps we try,
Mount o'er the vales, and seem to tread the sky,
Th' eternal snows appear already past,
And the first clouds and mountains seem the last;
But, those attained, we tremble to survey
The growing labors of the lengthened way,
Th' increasing prospect tires our wandering eyes,
Hills peep o'er hills, and Alps on Alps arise!

A perfect judge will read each work of wit
With the same spirit that its author writ;
Survey the whole, nor seek slight faults to find
Where nature moves, and rapture warms the mind;
Nor lose, for that malignant dull delight,
The generous pleasure to be charmed with wit.
But in such lays as neither ebb nor flow,
Correctly cold, and regularly low,
That shunning faults, one quiet tenor keep,
We cannot blame indeed—but we may sleep.
In wit, as nature, what affects our hearts
Is not th' exactness of peculiar parts;
'Tis not a lip, or eye, we beauty call,
But the joint force and full result of all.
Thus when we view some well-proportioned dome,
(The world's just wonder, and even thine, O Rome!)
No single parts unequally surprise,
All comes united to th' admiring eyes;
No monstrous height, or breadth, or length appear;
The whole at once is bold and regular.

Whoever thinks a faultless piece to see,
Thinks what ne'er was, nor is, nor e'er shall be.
In every work regard the writer's end,
Since none can compass more than they intend;
And if the means be just, the conduct true,
Applause, in spite of trivial faults, is due.
As men of breeding, sometimes men of wit,
T' avoid great errors, must the less commit;
Neglect the rules each verbal critic lays,
For not to know some trifles is a praise.
Most critics, fond of some subservient art,
Still make the whole depend upon a part;
They talk of principles, but notions prize,
And all to one loved folly sacrifice.

Once on a time, La Mancha's knight,[1] they say,
A certain bard encountering on the way,
Discoursed in terms as just, with looks as sage,
As e'er could Dennis,[2] of the Grecian stage;
Concluding all were desperate sots and fools,
Who durst depart from Aristotle's rules.
Our author, happy in a judge so nice,
Produced his play, and begged the knight's advice;
Made him observe the subject, and the plot,
The manners, passions, unities,[3] what not?
All which, exact to rule, were brought about,
Were but a combat in the lists left out.
"What! leave the combat out?" exclaims the knight;
Yes, or we must renounce the Stagirite.[4]
"Not so, by heaven!" (he answers in a rage),
"Knights, squires, and steeds must enter on the stage."
So vast a throng the stage can ne'er contain.
"Then build a new, or act it in a plain."

Thus critics, of less judgment than caprice,
Curious not knowing, not exact but nice,[5]
Form short ideas; and offend in arts,
(As most in manners) by a love to parts.

Some to conceit alone[6] their taste confine,
And glittering thoughts struck out at every line;
Pleased with a work where nothing's just or fit;
One glaring chaos and wild heap of wit.
Poets like painters, thus unskilled to trace
The naked nature and the living grace,
With gold and jewels cover every part,
And hide with ornaments their want of art.
True wit is nature to advantage dressed,
What oft was thought, but ne'er so well expressed;
Something, whose truth convinced at sight we find,
That gives us back the image of our mind.
As shades more sweetly recommend the light,
So modest plainness sets off sprightly wit.
For works may have more wit than does them good,
As bodies perish through excess of blood.

Others for language all their care express,
And value books, as women men, for dress;
Their praise is still—the style is excellent;

[1] Don Quixote (in a spurious addition to Cervantes's work)
[2] John Dennis, a critic of the time, the author of unsuccessful tragedies
[3] Aristotle's three "unities" of time, place, and action
[4] See note 4, p. 336.
[5] discriminating
[6] extravagant fancy

The sense they humbly take upon content.[1]
Words are like leaves; and where they most abound,
Much fruit of sense beneath is rarely found:
False eloquence, like the prismatic glass,
Its gaudy colors spreads on every place;
The face of nature we no more survey,
All glares alike, without distinction gay.
But true expression, like th' unchanging sun,
Clears and improves whate'er it shines upon,
It gilds all objects, but it alters none.
Expression is the dress of thought, and still
Appears more decent, as more suitable;
A vile conceit in pompous words expressed,
Is like a clown in regal purple dressed:
For different styles with different subjects sort,
As several garbs with country, town, and court.
Some by old words to fame have made pretense,
Ancients in phrase, mere moderns in their sense;
Such labored nothings, in so strange a style,
Amaze th' unlearned, and make the learnèd smile.
Unlucky, as Fungoso[2] in the play,
These sparks with awkward vanity display
What the fine gentleman wore yesterday;
And but so mimic ancient wits at best,
As apes our grandsires in their doublets drest.
In words, as fashions, the same rule will hold;
Alike fantastic if too new, or old.
Be not the first by whom the new are tried,
Nor yet the last to lay the old aside.

. . . .

1709 *1711*

THE RAPE OF THE LOCK[3]

Canto I

What dire offense from amorous causes springs,
What mighty contests rise from trivial things,
I sing.—This verse to Caryll, Muse! is due;
This, e'en Belinda may vouchsafe to view.
Slight is the subject, but not so the praise,
If she inspire, and he approve my lays.
Say what strange motive, Goddess! could compel
A well-bred lord t' assault a gentle belle?
Oh, say what stranger cause, yet unexplored,
Could make a gentle belle reject a lord?
In tasks so bold, can little men engage,
And in soft bosoms dwells such mighty rage?
Sol through white curtains shot a timorous ray,
And oped those eyes that must eclipse the day.
Now lap-dogs give themselves the rousing shake,
And sleepless lovers, just at twelve, awake.
Thrice rung the bell, the slipper knocked the ground,[4]
And the pressed watch[5] returned a silver sound.
Belinda still her downy pillow pressed,
Her guardian sylph prolonged the balmy rest;
'Twas he had summoned to her silent bed
The morning dream that hovered o'er her head;
A youth more glittering than a birth-night beau[6]
(That e'en in slumber caused her cheek to glow)
Seemed to her ear his winning lips to lay,
And thus in whispers said, or seemed to say:
"Fairest of mortals, thou distinguished care
Of thousand bright inhabitants of air!
If e'er one vision touched thy infant thought,
Of all the nurse and all the priest have taught,
Of airy elves by moonlight shadows seen,
The silver token,[7] and the circled green,
Or virgins visited by angel powers,
With golden crowns and wreaths of heavenly flowers;
Hear and believe! thy own importance know,
Nor bound thy narrow views to things below.
Some secret truths, from learnèd pride concealed,
To maids alone and children are revealed.
What though no credit doubting wits may give?
The fair and innocent shall still believe.
Know, then, unnumbered spirits round thee fly,
The light militia of the lower sky.
These, though unseen, are ever on the wing,
Hang o'er the box,[8] and hover round the Ring.[9]
Think what an equipage thou hast in air,
And view with scorn two pages and a chair.[10]

[1] on trust

[2] a character in Jonson's *Every Man Out of His Humor* who vainly tries to keep up with court fashions

[3] This mock-heroic, or, as Pope styled it, "heroi-comical poem," was published first in 1712 and in the present enlarged form in 1714. The subject, proposed to Pope by one Mr. Caryll, was suggested by a trifling feud that had arisen between two families because Lord Petre, a dapper little baron, had cut a lock from the head of Miss Arabella Fermor ("Belinda"). The opening is in imitation of classic epics, more especially of Vergil's *Aeneid*. The chief addition in the later form is the machinery of sylphs, gnomes, nymphs, and salamanders—spirits inhabiting air, earth, water, and fire, respectively. Dr. Johnson pronounced the poem "the most airy, the most ingenious, and the most delightful" of all the author's compositions, and De Quincey went so far as to declare it "the most exquisite monument of playful fancy that universal literature offers."

[4] summoning the lady's maid

[5] a striking-watch

[6] one befitting the royal birthday ball

[7] silver pieces dropped by fairies into the shoes of tidy maids

[8] at the theater

[9] a fashionable promenade and drive in Hyde Park

[10] sedan-chair

As now your own, our beings were of old,
And once enclosed in woman's beauteous mold;
Thence, by a soft transition, we repair
From earthly vehicles to these of air.
Think not, when woman's transient breath is fled,
That all her vanities at once are dead;
Succeeding vanities she still regards,
And though she plays no more, o'erlooks the cards.
Her joy in gilded chariots, when alive,
And love of omber, [1] after death survive.
For when the fair in all their pride expire,
To their first elements their souls retire:
The sprites of fiery termagants in flame
Mount up, and take a salamander's name.
Soft yielding minds to water glide away,
And sip, with nymphs, their elemental tea. [2]
The graver prude sinks downward to a gnome,
In search of mischief still on earth to roam.
The light coquettes in sylphs aloft repair,
And sport and flutter in the fields of air.
"Know further yet: whoever fair and chaste
Rejects mankind, is by some sylph embraced;
For spirits, freed from mortal laws, with ease
Assume what sexes and what shapes they please.
What guards the purity of melting maids,
In courtly balls, and midnight masquerades,
Safe from the treacherous friend, the daring spark, [3]
The glance by day, the whisper in the dark,
When kind occasion prompts their warm desires,
When music softens, and when dancing fires?
'Tis but their sylph, the wise celestials know,
Though honor is the word with men below.
Some nymphs there are, too conscious of their face,
For life predestined to the gnomes' embrace.
These swell their prospects and exalt their pride
When offers are disdained, and love denied;
Then gay ideas crowd the vacant brain,
While peers, and dukes, and all their sweeping train,
And garters, stars, and coronets appear,
And in soft sounds 'Your Grace' salutes their ear.
'Tis these that early taint the female soul,
Instruct the eyes of young coquettes to roll,
Teach infant cheeks a bidden blush to know.
And little hearts to flutter at a beau.

[1] a game of cards
[2] in Pope's time pronounced "tay"
[3] gallant

"Oft when the world imagine women stray,
The sylphs through mystic mazes guide their way,
Through all the giddy circle they pursue,
And old impertinence expel by new.
What tender maid but must a victim fall
To one man's treat, but for another's ball?
When Florio speaks, what virgin could withstand,
If gentle Damon did not squeeze her hand?
With varying vanities from every part,
They shift the moving toyshop of their heart;
Where wigs with wigs, with sword-knots sword-knots strive,
Beaux banish beaux, and coaches coaches drive.
This erring mortals levity may call;
Oh, blind to truth! the sylphs contrive it all.
"Of these am I, who thy protection claim,
A watchful sprite, and Ariel is my name.
Late, as I ranged the crystal wilds of air,
In the clear mirror of thy ruling star
I saw, alas! some dread event impend,
Ere to the main [4] this morning sun descend,
But Heaven reveals not what, or how, or where.
Warned by the sylph, O pious maid, beware!
This to disclose is all thy guardian can:
Beware of all, but most beware of man!"
He said; when Shock, who thought she slept too long,
Leaped up, and waked his mistress with his tongue.
'Twas then, Belinda, if report say true,
Thy eyes first opened on a billet-doux;
Wounds, charms, and ardors were no sooner read,
But all the vision vanished from thy head.
And now, unveiled, the toilet stands displayed,
Each silver vase in mystic order laid.
First, robed in white, the nymph intent adores,
With head uncovered, the cosmetic powers.
A heavenly image in the glass appears,
To that she bends, to that her eyes she rears;
Th' inferior priestess at her altar's side,
Trembling begins the sacred rites of pride.
Unnumbered treasures ope at once, and here
The various offerings of the world appear;
From each she nicely culls with curious toil,
And decks the goddess with the glittering spoil.
This casket India's glowing gems unlocks,
And all Arabia breathes from yonder box.
The tortoise here and elephant unite,
Transformed to combs, the speckled, and the white.

[4] sea

Here files of pins extend their shining rows,
Puffs, powders, patches, bibles, billets-doux.
Now awful beauty puts on all its arms;
The fair each moment rises in her charms.
Repairs her smiles, awakens every grace,
And calls forth all the wonders of her face;
Sees by degrees a purer blush arise,
And keener lightnings quicken in her eyes.
The busy sylphs surround their darling care,
These set the head,[1] and those divide the hair,
Some fold the sleeve, whilst others plait the gown;
And Betty's praised for labors not her own.

Canto II

Not with more glories, in th' ethereal plain,
The sun first rises o'er the purpled main,
Than, issuing forth, the rival of his beams
Launched on the bosom of the silver Thames.
Fair nymphs, and well-dressed youths around her shone,
But every eye was fixed on her alone.
On her white breast a sparkling cross she wore,
Which Jews might kiss, and infidels adore.
Her lively looks a sprightly mind disclose,
Quick as her eyes, and as unfixed as those;
Favors to none, to all she smiles extends;
Oft she rejects, but never once offends.
Bright as the sun, her eyes the gazers strike,
And, like the sun, they shine on all alike.
Yet graceful ease, and sweetness void of pride,
Might hide her faults, if belles had faults to hide;
If to her share some female errors fall,
Look on her face, and you'll forget 'em all.
This nymph, to the destruction of mankind,
Nourished two locks, which graceful hung behind
In equal curls, and well conspired to deck
With shining ringlets the smooth ivory neck.
Love in these labyrinths his slaves detains,
And mighty hearts are held in slender chains.
With hairy springes, we the birds betray,
Slight lines of hair surprise the finny prey,
Fair tresses man's imperial race ensnare,
And beauty draws us with a single hair.
Th' adventurous baron the bright locks admired;
He saw, he wished, and to the prize aspired.
Resolved to win, he meditates the way,
By force to ravish, or by fraud betray;
For when success a lover's toil attends,
Few ask if fraud or force attained his ends.
For this, ere Phoebus rose, he had implored
Propitious Heaven, and every power adored,
But chiefly Love; to Love an altar built
Of twelve vast French romances,[2] neatly gilt.
There lay three garters, half a pair of gloves,
And all the trophies of his former loves;
With tender billets-doux he lights the pyre,
And breathes three amorous sighs to raise the fire.
Then prostrate falls, and begs with ardent eyes
Soon to obtain, and long possess the prize.
The powers gave ear, and granted half his prayer;
The rest the winds dispersed in empty air.
But now secure the painted vessel glides,
The sunbeams trembling on the floating tides;
While melting music steals upon the sky,
And softened sounds along the waters die;
Smooth flow the waves, the zephyrs gently play,
Belinda smiled, and all the world was gay.
All but the sylph—with careful thoughts oppressed,
Th' impending woe sat heavy on his breast.
He summons straight his denizens of air;
The lucid squadrons round the sails repair;
Soft o'er the shrouds aërial whispers breathe,
That seemed but zephyrs to the train beneath.
Some to the sun their insect wings unfold,
Waft on the breeze, or sink in clouds of gold;
Transparent forms, too fine for mortal sight,
Their fluid bodies half dissolved in light.
Loose to the wind their airy garments flew,
Thin glittering textures of the filmy dew,[3]
Dipt in the richest tincture of the skies,
Where light disports in ever-mingling dyes,
While every beam new transient colors flings,
Colors that change whene'er they wave their wings.
Amid the circle, on the gilded mast,
Superior, by the head, was Ariel placed;
His purple pinions opening to the sun,
He raised his azure wand, and thus begun:
"Ye sylphs and sylphids, to your chief give ear!
Fays, fairies, genii, elves, and demons, hear!
Ye know the spheres, and various tasks assigned
By laws eternal to th' aërial kind.
Some in the fields of purest ether play,
And bask and whiten in the blaze of day.
Some guide the course of wandering orbs on high,
Or roll the planets through the boundless sky.
Some less refined, beneath the moon's pale light
Pursue the stars that shoot athwart the night,

[1] head-dress

[2] ponderous romances, like Mlle. de Scudéry's *Le Grand Cyrus* and *Clélie*, then in vogue

[3] gossamer (once supposed to be a product of dew)

Or suck the mists in grosser air below,
Or dip their pinions in the painted bow,
Or brew fierce tempests on the wintry main,
Or o'er the glebe distill the kindly rain;
Others on earth o'er human race preside,
Watch all their ways, and all their actions guide.
Of these the chief the care of nations own,
And guard with arms divine the British throne.
"Our humbler province is to tend the fair,
Not a less pleasing, though less glorious care;
To save the powder from too rude a gale,
Nor let th' imprisoned essences exhale;
To draw fresh colors from the vernal flowers;
To steal from rainbows, ere they drop in showers,
A brighter wash; to curl their waving hairs,
Assist their blushes, and inspire their airs;
Nay, oft in dreams, invention we bestow,
To change a flounce or add a furbelow.
"This day, black omens threat the brightest fair
That e'er deserved a watchful spirit's care;
Some dire disaster, or by force, or sleight;
But what, or where, the fates have wrapped in night.
Whether the nymph shall break Diana's law,
Or some frail china jar receive a flaw;
Or stain her honor or her new brocade;
Forget her prayers or miss a masquerade;
Or lose her heart, or necklace, at a ball;
Or whether Heaven has doomed that Shock must fall.
Haste, then, ye spirits! to your charge repair;
The fluttering fan be Zephyretta's care;
The drops [1] to thee, Brillante, we consign;
And, Momentilla, let the watch be thine;
Do thou, Crispissa, tend her favorite lock;
Ariel himself shall be the guard of Shock.

. . . .

"Whatever spirit, careless of his charge,
His post neglects, or leaves the fair at large,
Shall feel sharp vengeance soon o'ertake his sins,
Be stopped in vials, or transfixed with pins;
Or plunged in lakes of bitter washes lie,
Or wedged whole ages in a bodkin's eye;
Gums and pomatums shall his flight restrain,
While clogged he beats his silken wings in vain;
Or alum styptics with contracting power
Shrinks his thin essence like a rivelled [2] flower;
Or, as Ixion fixed, the wretch shall feel
The giddy motion of the whirling mill, [3]
In fumes of burning chocolate shall glow,
And tremble at the sea that froths below!"

[1] ear-rings [2] shriveled [3] chocolate-mill

He spoke; the spirits from the sails descend;
Some, orb in orb, around the nymph extend;
Some thrid the mazy ringlets of her hair;
Some hang upon the pendants of her ear;
With beating hearts the dire event they wait,
Anxious and trembling for the birth of fate.

Canto III

Close by those meads, forever crowned with flowers,
Where Thames with pride surveys his rising towers,
There stands a structure of majestic frame [4]
Which from the neighboring Hampton takes its name.
Here Britain's statesmen oft the fall foredoom
Of foreign tyrants and of nymphs at home;
Here thou, great Anna! whom three realms obey,
Dost sometimes counsel take—and sometimes tea.
Hither the heroes and nymphs resort
To taste awhile the pleasures of a court;
In various talk th' instructive hours they passed,
Who gave the ball, or paid the visit last;
One speaks the glory of the British Queen,
And one describes a charming Indian screen;
A third interprets motions, looks, and eyes;
At every word a reputation dies.
Snuff or the fan supply each pause of chat,
With singing, laughing, ogling, and all that.
Meanwhile, declining from the noon of day,
The sun obliquely shoots his burning ray;
The hungry judges soon the sentence sign,
And wretches hang that jurymen may dine;
The merchant from th' Exchange returns in peace,
And the long labors of the toilet cease.
Belinda now, whom thirst of fame invites,
Burns to encounter two adventurous knights,
At omber singly to decide their doom;
And swells her breast with conquests yet to come.
Straight the three bands prepare in arms to join,
Each band the number of the sacred nine. [5]
Soon as she spreads her hand, th' aërial guard
Descend, and sit on each important card;
First, Ariel perched upon a Matadore, [6]

[4] Hampton Court, at times a royal residence
[5] Each player holds nine cards.
[6] The three best cards—Spadillio, ace of spades; Manillio, a trump; and Basto, ace of clubs—were each called a Matadore (Spanish for the slayer in a bull-fight).

Then each, according to the rank they bore;
For sylphs, yet mindful of their ancient race,
Are, as when women, wondrous fond of place.
  Behold, four kings in majesty revered,
With hoary whiskers and a forky beard;
And four fair queens whose hands sustain a flower,
The expressive emblem of their softer power;
Four knaves in garbs succinct, a trusty band,
Caps on their heads, and halberds in their hand;
And parti-colored troops, a shining train,
Draw forth to combat on the velvet plain.
  The skilful nymph reviews her force with care.
"Let spades be trumps!" she said, and trumps they were.
  Now move to war her sable Matadores,
In show like leaders of the swarthy Moors.
Spadillio first, unconquerable lord!
Led off two captive trumps and swept the board.
As many more Manillio forced to yield
And marched a victor from the verdant field.
Him Basto followed, but his fate more hard
Gained but one trump and one plebeian card.
With his broad saber next, a chief in years,
The hoary majesty of spades appears,
Puts forth one manly leg, to sight revealed,
The rest his many-colored robe concealed.
The rebel knave, who dares his prince engage,
Proves the just victim of his royal rage.
E'en mighty Pam,[1] that kings and queens o'erthrew,
And mowed down armies in the fights of Loo,
Sad chance of war! now destitute of aid,
Falls undistinguished by the victor spade!
  Thus far both armies to Belinda yield;
Now to the baron fate inclines the field.
His warlike Amazon her host invades,
The imperial consort of the crown of spades;
The club's black tyrant first her victim died,
Spite of his haughty mien and barbarous pride.
What boots the regal circle on his head,
His giant limbs in state unwieldly spread,
That long behind he trails his pompous robe,
And, of all monarchs, only grasps the globe?
  The baron now his diamonds pours apace;
Th' embroidered king who shows but half his face,
And his refulgent queen, with powers combined,
Of broken troops an easy conquest find.
Clubs, diamonds, hearts, in wild disorder seen,
With throngs promiscuous strew the level green.
Thus when dispersed a routed army runs,
Of Asia's troops, and Afric's sable sons,
With like confusion different nations fly,
Of various habit, and of various dye,
The pierced battalions disunited fall
In heaps on heaps; one fate o'erwhelms them all.
  The knave of diamonds tries his wily arts,
And wins (O shameful chance!) the queen of hearts.
At this the blood the virgin's cheek forsook,
A livid paleness spreads o'er all her look;
She sees, and trembles at th' approaching ill,
Just in the jaws of ruin, and codille.[2]
And now (as oft in some distempered state)
On one nice trick depends the general fate.
An ace of hearts steps forth; the king unseen
Lurked in her hand, and mourned his captive queen;
He springs to vengeance with an eager pace,
And falls like thunder on the prostrate ace.
The nymph exulting fills with shouts the sky;
The walls, the woods, and long canals reply.
  O thoughtless mortals! ever blind to fate,
Too soon dejected, and too soon elate.
Sudden, these honors shall be snatched away,
And cursed forever this victorious day.
  For lo! the board with cups and spoons is crowned,
The berries[3] crackle, and the mill turns round;
On shining altars of Japan[4] they raise
The silver lamp; the fiery spirits blaze;
From silver spouts the grateful liquors glide,
While China's earth receives the smoking tide;
At once they gratify their scent and taste,
And frequent cups prolong the rich repast.
Straight hover round the fair her airy band;
Some, as she sipped, the fuming liquor fanned,
Some o'er her lap their careful plumes displayed,
Trembling, and conscious of the rich brocade.
Coffee (which makes the politician wise,
And see through all things with his half-shut eyes)
Sent up in vapors to the baron's brain
New stratagems the radiant lock to gain.
Ah, cease, rash youth! desist ere 'tis too late,
Fear the just gods, and think of Scylla's[5] fate!
Changed to a bird, and sent to flit in air,
She dearly pays for Nisus' injured hair!
  But when to mischief mortals bend their will,
How soon they find fit instruments of ill!
Just then Clarissa drew with tempting grace
A two-edged weapon from her shining case;
So ladies in romance assist their knight,

[1] knave of clubs, the highest card in the game of Loo

[2] a term signifying defeat of the lone hand, who loses the pool

[3] coffee berries

[4] japanned tables

[5] King Nisus's daughter, who betrayed her father by sending the enemy one of his hairs

Present the spear, and arm him for the fight.
He takes the gift with reverence, and extends
The little engine on his fingers' ends;
This just behind Belinda's neck he spread,
As o'er the fragrant steams she bends her head.
Swift to the lock a thousand sprites repair,
A thousand wings, by turns, blow back the hair;
And thrice they twitched the diamond in her ear;
Thrice she looked back, and thrice the foe drew near.
Just in that instant, anxious Ariel sought
The close recesses of the virgin's thought;
As on the nosegay in her breast reclined,
He watched th' ideas rising in her mind,
Sudden he viewed, in spite of all her art,
An earthly lover lurking at her heart.
Amazed, confused, he found his power expired,
Resigned to fate, and with a sigh retired.
The peer now spreads the glittering forfex [1] wide,
T' inclose the lock; now joins it, to divide.
E'en then, before the fatal engine closed,
A wretched sylph too fondly interposed;
Fate urged the shears, and cut the sylph in twain,
(But airy substance soon unites again). [2]
The meeting points the sacred hair dissever
From the fair head, forever, and forever!
Then flashed the living lightning from her eyes,
And screams of horror rend th' affrighted skies.
Not louder shrieks to pitying Heaven are cast
When husbands, or when lap-dogs, breathe their last;
Or when rich China vessels, fallen from high,
In glittering dust and painted fragments lie!
"Let wreaths of triumph now my temples twine,"
The victor cried; "the glorious prize is mine!
While fish in streams, or birds delight in air,
Or in a coach and six the British fair,
As long as Atalantis [3] shall be read,
Or the small pillow grace a lady's bed,
While visits shall be paid on solemn days,
When numerous waxlights in bright order blaze,
While nymphs take treats, or assignations give,
So long my honor, name, and praise shall live!
What Time would spare, from steel receives its date, [4]
And monuments, like men, submit to fate!
Steel could the labor of the gods destroy,
And strike to dust th' imperial towers of Troy;
Steel could the works of mortal pride confound,
And hew triumphal arches to the ground.
What wonder then, fair nymph! thy hairs should feel
The conquering force of unresisted steel?"

Canto IV

But anxious cares the pensive nymph oppressed,
And secret passions labored in her breast.
Not youthful kings in battle seized alive,
Not scornful virgins who their charms survive,
Not ardent lovers robbed of all their bliss,
Not ancient ladies when refused a kiss,
Not tyrants fierce that unrepenting die,
Not Cynthia [5] when her manteau's pinned awry
E'er felt such rage, resentment, and despair
As thou, sad virgin, for thy ravished hair.
For, that sad moment, when the sylphs withdrew
And Ariel weeping from Belinda flew,
Umbriel, a dusky, melancholy sprite
As ever sullied the fair face of light,
Down to the central earth, his proper scene,
Repaired to search the gloomy cave of Spleen.[6]
Swift on his sooty pinions flits the gnome,
And in a vapor reached the dismal dome.
No cheerful breeze this sullen region knows,
The dreaded east is all the wind that blows.
Here in a grotto, sheltered close from air,
And screened in shades from day's detested glare,
She sighs forever on her pensive bed,
Pain at her side, and Megrim [7] at her head.
Two handmaids wait [8] the throne, alike in place,
But differing far in figure and in face.
Here stood Ill-nature like an ancient maid,
Her wrinkled form in black and white arrayed;
With store of prayers for mornings, nights, and noons
Her hand is filled; her bosom with lampoons.
There Affectation, with a sickly mien,
Shows in her cheek the roses of eighteen,
Practiced to lisp, and hang the head aside,
Faints into airs, and languishes with pride,
On the rich quilt sinks with becoming woe,
Wrapped in a gown for sickness, and for show.
The fair ones feel such maladies as these
When each new night-dress gives a new disease.
A constant vapor o'er the palace flies;

[1] shears (Latin)
[2] a parody of *Paradise Lost,* vi., 330
[3] a scandalous novel of the time by Mrs. Manley
[4] fatal day

[5] any frivolous society woman
[6] ill humor
[7] low spirits
[8] Supply "at."

Strange phantoms rising as the mists arise;
Dreadful as hermit's dreams in haunted shades,
Or bright as visions of expiring maids.
Now glaring fiends, and snakes on rolling spires,
Pale specters, gaping tombs, and purple fires;
Now lakes of liquid gold, Elysian scenes,
And crystal domes, and angels in machines.[1]
  Unnumbered throngs on every side are seen,
Of bodies changed to various forms by Spleen.
Here living tea-pots stand, one arm held out,
One bent; the handle this, and that the spout.
A pipkin there, like Homer's tripod, walks;[2]
Here sighs a jar, and there a goose-pie talks.

. . . .

  Safe past the gnome through this fantastic band,
A branch of healing spleenwort in his hand.
Then thus addressed the power: "Hail, wayward queen!
Who rule the sex, to fifty from fifteen;
Parent of vapors and of female wit,
Who give th' hysteric or poetic fit;
On various tempers act by various ways,
Make some take physic, others scribble plays;
Who cause the proud their visits to delay,
And send the godly in a pet to pray.
A nymph there is that all thy power disdains,
And thousands more in equal mirth maintains.
But oh! if e'er thy gnome could spoil a grace,
Or raise a pimple on a beauteous face,
Like citron-waters matrons' cheeks inflame,
Or change complexions at a losing game.

. . . .

Hear me, and touch Belinda with chagrin,
That single act gives half the world the spleen."
  The goddess with a discontented air
Seems to reject him, though she grants his prayer.
A wondrous bag with both her hands she binds,
Like that where once Ulysses held the winds;[3]
There she collects the force of female lungs,
Sighs, sobs, and passions, and the war of tongues.
A vial next she fills with fainting fears,
Soft sorrows, melting griefs, and flowing tears.
The gnome rejoicing bears her gifts away,
Spreads his black wings and slowly mounts to day.
  Sunk in Thalestris'[4] arms the nymph he found,
Her eyes dejected and her hair unbound.
Full o'er their heads the swelling bag he rent,
And all the furies issued at the vent.
Belinda burns with more than mortal ire,
And fierce Thalestris fans the rising fire.
"O wretched maid!" she spread her hands and cried,
(While Hampton's echoes, "Wretched maid!" replied)
"Was it for this you took such constant care
The bodkin, comb, and essence to prepare?
For this your locks in paper durance bound?
For this with torturing irons wreathed around?
For this with fillets strained your tender head,
And bravely bore the double loads of lead?[5]
Gods! shall the ravisher display your hair,
While the fops envy, and the ladies stare!
Honor forbid! at whose unrivaled shrine
Ease, pleasure, virtue, all our sex resign.
Methinks already I your tears survey,
Already hear the horrid things they say,
Already see you a degraded toast,
And all your honor in a whisper lost!
How shall I, then, your helpless fame defend?
'Twill then be infamy to seem your friend!
And shall this prize, th' inestimable prize,
Exposed through crystal to the gazing eyes,
And heightened by the diamond's circling rays,
On that rapacious hand forever blaze?
Sooner shall grass in Hyde Park Circus[6] grow,
And wits take lodgings in the sound of Bow;[7]
Sooner let earth, air, sea to chaos fall,
Men, monkeys, lap dogs, parrots perish all!"
  She said; then raging to Sir Plume repairs,
And bids her beau demand the precious hairs
(Sir Plume, of amber snuffbox justly vain,
And the nice conduct of a clouded[8] cane).
With earnest eyes, and round unthinking face,
He first the snuffbox opened, then the case,
And thus broke out—"My lord, why, what the devil?
Zounds! Damn the lock! 'Fore Gad, you must be civil!
Plague on't! 'tis past a jest—nay prithee, pox!
Give her the hair," he spoke, and rapped his box.
"It grieves me much," replied the peer again,
"Who speaks so well should ever speak in vain.
But by this lock, this sacred lock, I swear
(Which never more shall join its parted hair;
Which never more its honors shall renew,
Clipped from the lovely head where late it grew)
That while my nostrils draw the vital air

[1] stage devices
[2] *Iliad*, xviii, 373
[3] *Odyssey* x, 20
[4] for Mrs. Morley, a sister of Sir George Brown, the "Sir Plume" of line 121
[5] leaded curl-papers
[6] the "Ring" mentioned in I, 44
[7] Bow Bells, the bells of St. Mary-le-Bow in the cockney and hack-writer center of London
[8] mottled

This hand, which won it, shall forever wear."
He spoke, and speaking, in proud triumph spread
The long-contended honors of her head.
But Umbriel, hateful gnome! forbears not so;
He breaks the vial whence the sorrows flow.
Then see! The nymph in beauteous grief appears,
Her eyes half languishing, half drowned in tears;
On her heaved bosom hung her drooping head,
Which, with a sigh, she raised; and thus she said:
"Forever cursed be this detested day
Which snatched my best, my favorite curl away!
Happy! ah, ten times happy had I been
If Hampton Court these eyes had never seen!
Yet am not I the first mistaken maid,
By love of courts to numerous ills betrayed.
Oh, had I rather unadmired remained
In some lone isle or distant northern land;
Where the gilt chariot never marks the way,
Where none learn ombер, none e'er taste bohea![1]
There kept my charms concealed from mortal eye,
Like roses that in deserts bloom and die.
What moved my mind with youthful lords to roam?
Oh, had I stayed, and said my prayers at home!
'Twas this the morning omens seemed to tell;
Thrice from my trembling hand the patch-box[2] fell;
The tottering china shook without a wind;
Nay, Poll sat mute, and Shock was most unkind!
A sylph, too, warned me of the threats of fate,
In mystic visions, now believed too late!
See the poor remnants of these slighted hairs!
My hands shall rend what e'en thy rapine spares;
These in two sable ringlets taught to break,
Once gave new beauties to the snowy neck;
The sister lock now sits uncouth, alone,
And in its fellow's fate foresees its own;
Uncurled it hangs, the fatal shears demands,
And tempts once more thy sacrilegious hands.
Oh, hadst thou, cruel! been content to seize
Hairs less in sight, or any hairs but these!"

Canto V

She said; the pitying audience melt in tears.
But Fate and Jove had stopped the baron's ears.
In vain Thalestris with reproach assails,
For who can move when fair Belinda fails?
Not half so fixed the Trojan[3] could remain
While Anna begged and Dido raged in vain.
Then grave Clarissa graceful waved her fan;
Silence ensued, and thus the nymph began:
"Say, why are beauties praised and honored most,
The wise man's passion, and the vain man's toast?
Why decked with all that land and sea afford,
Why angels called, and angel-like adored?
Why round our coaches crowd the white-gloved beaux,
Why bows the side-box from its inmost rows?
How vain are all these glories, all our pains,
Unless good sense preserve what beauty gains;
That men may say, when we the front-box grace,
'Behold the first in virtue as in face!'
Oh! if to dance all night, and dress all day
Charmed the smallpox, or chased old age away,
Who would not scorn what housewife's cares produce,
Or who would learn one earthly thing of use?
To patch, nay ogle, might become a saint,
Nor could it sure be such a sin to paint.
But since, alas! frail beauty must decay;
Curled or uncurled, since locks will turn to gray;
Since painted or not painted, all shall fade,
And she who scorns a man must die a maid;
What then remains but well our power to use,
And keep good humor still whate'er we lose?
And trust me, dear! good humor can prevail
When airs, and flights, and screams, and scolding fail.
Beauties in vain their pretty eyes may roll;
Charms strike the sight, but merit wins the soul."
So spoke the dame, but no applause ensued;
Belinda frowned, Thalestris called her prude.
"To arms, to arms!" the fierce virago cries,
And swift as lightning to the combat flies.
All side in parties, and begin th' attack;
Fans clap, silks rustle, and tough whalebones crack;
Heroes' and heroines' shouts confus'dly rise,
And bass and treble voices strike the skies.
No common weapons in their hands are found,
Like gods they fight, nor dread a mortal wound.
So when bold Homer makes the gods engage,
And heavenly breasts with human passions rage;

[1] a kind of black tea

[2] for face-patches

[3] Aeneas when repelling Dido's love and the entreaties of her sister Anna (*Aeneid* iv, 440)

'Gainst Pallas,[1] Mars,[2] Latona,[2] Hermes[1] arms;
And all Olympus rings with loud alarms;
Jove's thunder roars, Heaven trembles all around,
Blue Neptune storms, the bellowing deeps resound;
Earth shakes her nodding towers, the ground gives way,
And the pale ghosts start at the flash of day!
Triumphant Umbriel on a sconce's[3] height
Clapped his glad wings, and sat to view the fight;
Propped on their bodkin spears, the sprites survey
The growing combat, or assist the fray.
While through the press enraged Thalestris flies,
And scatters death around from both her eyes,
A beau and witling perished in the throng,
One died in metaphor, and one in song.
"O cruel nymph! a living death I bear,"
Cried Dapperwit, and sunk beside his chair.
A mournful glance Sir Fopling upward cast,
"Those eyes are made so killing"—was his last.
Thus on Maeander's flowery margin lies
Th' expiring swan, and as he sings he dies.[4]
When bold Sir Plume had drawn Clarissa down,
Chloe stepped in and killed him with a frown;
She smiled to see the doughty hero slain,
But, at her smile, the beau revived again.
Now Jove suspends his golden scales in air,
Weighs the men's wits against the lady's hair;
The doubtful beam long nods from side to side;
At length the wits mount up, the hairs subside.
See, fierce Belinda on the Baron flies
With more than usual lightning in her eyes;
Nor feared the chief th' unequal fight to try,
Who sought no more than on his foe to die.
But this bold lord with manly strength endued,
She with one finger and a thumb subdued;
Just where the breath of life his nostrils drew,
A charge of snuff the wily virgin threw;
The gnomes direct, to every atom just,
The pungent grains of titillating dust.
Sudden, with starting tears each eye o'erflows,
And the high dome reëchoes to his nose.
"Now meet thy fate," incensed Belinda cried,
And drew a deadly bodkin from her side.
(The same, his ancient personage to deck,
Her great great grandsire wore about his neck
In three seal-rings; which after, melted down,
Formed a vast buckle for his widow's gown;
Her infant grandame's whistle next it grew,
The bells she jingled, and the whistle blew;
Then in a bodkin graced her mother's hairs,
Which long she wore, and now Belinda wears.)
"Boast not my fall," he cried, "insulting foe!
Thou by some other shalt be laid as low;
Nor think to die dejects my lofty mind;
All that I dread is leaving you behind!
Rather than so, ah, let me still survive,
And burn in Cupid's flames—but burn alive."
"Restore the lock!" she cries; and all around
"Restore the lock!" the vaulted roofs rebound.
Not fierce Othello in so loud a strain
Roared for the handkerchief that caused his pain.
But see how oft ambitious aims are crossed,
And chiefs contend till all the prize is lost!
The lock, obtained with guilt, and kept with pain,
In every place is sought, but sought in vain:
With such a prize no mortal must be blessed,
So Heaven decrees! With Heaven who can contest?
Some thought it mounted to the lunar sphere,
Since all things lost on earth are treasured there.
There heroes' wits are kept in ponderous vases,
And beaux' in snuffboxes and tweezer cases;
There broken vows and death-bed alms are found,
And lovers' hearts with ends of riband bound,
The courtier's promises, and sick man's prayers,
The smiles of harlots, and the tears of heirs,
Cages for gnats, and chains to yoke a flea,
Dried butterflies, and tomes of casuistry.
But trust the Muse—she saw it upward rise,
Though marked by none but quick, poetic eyes;
(So Rome's great founder[5] to the heavens withdrew,
To Proculus alone confessed in view)
A sudden star, it shot through liquid air
And drew behind a radiant trail of hair.
Not Berenice's locks[6] first rose so bright,
The heavens bespangling with disheveled light.
The sylphs behold it kindling as it flies,
And pleased pursue its progress through the skies.
This the beau monde shall from the Mall[7] survey,
And hail with music its propitious ray.

[1] aider of the Greeks
[2] aider of the Trojans
[3] chandelier's
[4] Ovid's *Epistles*, vii, 1, 2
[5] Romulus, carried to heaven by Mars, afterwards appeared to Proculus in great glory.
[6] "Berenice's Hair," a group of seven stars in the constellation Leo
[7] a fashionable walk in St. James's Park

This the blest lover shall for Venus take,
And send up vows from Rosamonda's lake.[1]
This Partridge[2] soon shall view in cloudless skies,
When next he looks through Galileo's eyes;
And hence th' egregious wizard shall foredoom
The fate of Louis and the fall of Rome.
Then cease, bright nymph! to mourn thy ravished hair,
Which adds new glory to the shining sphere!
Not all the tresses that fair head can boast
Shall draw such envy as the lock you lost.
For, after all the murders of your eye,
When, after millions slain, yourself shall die;
When those fair suns shall set, as set they must,
And all those tresses shall be laid in dust;
This lock the Muse shall consecrate to fame,
And 'midst the stars inscribe Belinda's name.

1712, 1713 *1712, 1714*

From AN ESSAY ON MAN

Epistle I

Awake, my St. John![3] Leave all meaner things
To low ambition and the pride of kings.
Let us, since life can little more supply
Than just to look about us and to die,
Expatiate free o'er all this scene of man;
A mighty maze! but not without a plan;
A wild, where weeds and flowers promiscuous shoot;
Or garden, tempting with forbidden fruit.
Together let us beat this ample field,
Try what the open, what the covert yield;
The latent tracts, the giddy heights explore
Of all who blindly creep or sightless soar;
Eye nature's walks, shoot folly as it flies,
And catch the manners living as they rise;
Laugh where we must, be candid where we can;
But vindicate the ways of God to man.

I

Say first, of God above or man below,
What can we reason, but from what we know?
Of man, what see we but his station here
From which to reason or to which refer?
Through worlds unnumbered though the God be known,
'Tis ours to trace him only in our own.
He, who through vast immensity can pierce,
See worlds on worlds compose one universe,
Observe how system into system runs,
What other planets circle other suns,
What varied being peoples every star,
May tell why Heaven has made us as we are.
But of this frame the bearings, and the ties,
The strong connections, nice dependencies,
Gradations just, has thy pervading soul
Looked through? Or can a part contain the whole?
Is the great chain that draws all to agree,
And drawn supports, upheld by God, or thee?

II

Presumptuous man! The reason wouldst thou find,
Why formed so weak, so little, and so blind?
First, if thou canst, the harder reason guess,
Why formed no weaker, blinder, and no less?
Ask of thy mother earth why oaks are made
Taller or stronger than the weeds they shade?
Or ask of yonder argent fields above
Why Jove's satellites are less than Jove.
Of systems possible, if 'tis confessed
That wisdom infinite must form the best,
Where all must full or not coherent be,
And all that rises, rise in due degree;
Then in the scale of reasoning life, 'tis plain,
There must be, somewhere, such a rank as man;
And all the question (wrangle e'er so long)
Is only this—if God has placed him wrong?
Respecting man, whatever wrong we call,
May, must be right, as relative to all.
In human works, though labored on with pain,
A thousand movements scarce one purpose gain;
In God's, one single can its end produce;
Yet serves to second, too, some other use.
So man, who here seems principal alone,
Perhaps acts second to some sphere unknown,
Touches some wheel, or verges to some goal;
'Tis but a part we see, and not a whole.
When the proud steed shall know why man restrains
His fiery course, or drives him o'er the plains;
When the dull ox, why now he breaks the clod,
Is now a victim, and now Egypt's god;[4]
Then shall man's pride and dullness comprehend
His actions', passions', being's use and end;
Why doing, suffering, checked, impelled; and why
This hour a slave, the next a deity.
Then say not man's imperfect, Heaven in fault;
Say, rather, man's as perfect as he ought;
His knowledge measured to his state and place,

[1] in St. James's Park
[2] an almanac-maker of the time who yearly prophesied disaster
[3] Henry St. John, Lord Bolingbroke, a politician and philosopher to whom Pope was indebted for the substance of this poem; the name is usually pronounced *sin jun.*
[4] Apis, the sacred bull of Egypt

His time a moment, and a point his space.
If to be perfect in a certain sphere,
What matter, soon or late, or here or there?
The blest today is as completely so
As who began a thousand years ago.

III

Heaven from all creatures hides the book of fate,
All but the page prescribed, their present state;
From brutes[1] what men, from men what spirits know;
Or who could suffer being here below?
The lamb thy riot dooms to bleed today,
Had he thy reason, would he skip and play?
Pleased to the last, he crops the flowery food,
And licks the hand just raised to shed his blood.
Oh, blindness to the future! kindly given,
That each may fill the circle marked by Heaven,
Who sees with equal eye, as God of all,
A hero perish, or a sparrow fall,
Atoms or systems into ruin hurled,
And now a bubble burst, and now a world.
  Hope humbly then; with trembling pinions soar;
Wait the great teacher Death; and God adore.
What future bliss, he gives not thee to know,
But gives that hope to be thy blessing now.
Hope springs eternal in the human breast;
Man never is, but always to be blest.
The soul, uneasy and confined from home,
Rests and expatiates in a life to come.
  Lo, the poor Indian! whose untutored mind
Sees God in clouds, or hears him in the wind;
His soul, proud science never taught to stray
Far as the solar walk, or milky way;
Yet simple nature to his hope has given,
Behind the cloud-topped hill, an humbler Heaven;
Some safer world in depths of woods embraced,
Some happier island in the watery waste,
Where slaves once more their native land behold,
No fiends torment, no Christians thirst for gold.
To be, contents his natural desire,
He asks no angel's wing, no seraph's fire;
But thinks, admitted to that equal sky,
His faithful dog shall bear him company.

[1] Supply "heaven hides." Pope's verse is full of such ellipses.

IV

Go, wiser thou! and in thy scale of sense
Weigh thy opinion against Providence;
Call imperfection what thou fanciest such,
Say, "Here he gives too little, there too much";
Destroy all creatures for thy sport or gust,[2]
Yet cry, "If man's unhappy, God's unjust";
If man alone engross not Heaven's high care,
Alone made perfect here, immortal there,
Snatch from his hand the balance and the rod,
Re-judge his justice, be the god of God.
In pride, in reasoning pride, our error lies;
All quit their sphere, and rush into the skies.
Pride still is aiming at the blest abodes,
Men would be angels, angels would be gods.
Aspiring to be gods, if angels fell,
Aspiring to be angels, men rebel;
And who but wishes to invert the laws
Of order, sins against the Eternal Cause.

V

Ask for what end the heavenly bodies shine,
Earth for whose use? Pride answers, "'Tis for mine.
For me kind nature wakes her genial power,
Suckles each herb, and spreads out every flower;
Annual for me, the grape, the rose renew
The juice nectareous, and the balmy dew;
For me, the mine a thousand treasures brings;
For me, health gushes from a thousand springs;
Seas roll to waft me, suns to light me rise;
My footstool earth, my canopy the skies."
  But errs not Nature from this gracious end,
From burning suns when livid deaths descend,
When earthquakes swallow, or when tempests sweep
Towns to one grave, whole nations to the deep?
No ('tis replied), the first Almighty Cause
Acts not by partial, but by general laws;
Th' exceptions few; some change, since all began
And what created perfect?—Why then man?
If the great end be human happiness,
Then nature deviates; and can man do less?
As much that end a constant course requires
Of showers and sunshine, as of man's desires;
As much eternal springs and cloudless skies,
As men forever temperate, calm, and wise.
If plagues or earthquakes break not Heaven's design,
Why then a Borgia,[3] or a Cataline?[4]

[2] delight
[3] Cesare Borgia, a notorious criminal and tyrant, son of Pope Alexander VI
[4] Roman conspirator

Who knows but He, whose hand the lightning forms,
Who heaves old ocean, and who wings the storms;
Pours fierce ambition in a Caesar's mind,
Or turns young Ammon [1] loose to scourge mankind?
From pride, from pride, our very reasoning springs.
Account for moral, as for natural things.
Why charge we Heaven in those, in these acquit?
In both, to reason right is to submit.
  Better for us, perhaps, it might appear,
Were there all harmony, all virtue here;
That never air or ocean felt the wind;
That never passion discomposed the mind.
But all subsists by elemental strife;
And passions are the elements of life.
The general order, since the whole began,
Is kept in nature, and is kept in man.

VI

What would this man? Now upward will he soar,
And little less than angel, would be more;
Now looking downward, just as grieved appears
To want the strength of bulls, the fur of bears.
Made for his use all creatures if he call,
Say what their use, had he the powers of all?
Nature to these, without profusion, kind,
The proper organs, proper powers assigned;
Each seeming want compensated, of course,
Here with degrees of swiftness, there of force;
All in exact proportion to the state;
Nothing to add, and nothing to abate.
Each beast, each insect, happy in its own;
Is Heaven unkind to man, and man alone?
Shall he alone, whom rational we call,
Be pleased with nothing, if not blessed with all?
  The bliss of man (could pride that blessing find)
Is not to act or think beyond mankind;
No powers of body or of soul to share,
But what his nature and his state can bear.
Why has not man a microscopic eye?
For this plain reason, man is not a fly.
Say what the use, were finer optics given,
T' inspect a mite, not comprehend the heaven?
Or touch, if tremblingly alive all o'er,
To smart and agonize at every pore?
Or, quick effluvia darting through the brain,
Die of a rose in aromatic pain?

[1] Alexander the Great, who was flatteringly styled the son of Jupiter Ammon

If nature thundered in his opening ears,
And stunned him with the music of the spheres, [2]
How would he wish that Heaven had left him still
The whispering zephyr and the purling rill!
Who finds not Providence all good and wise,
Alike in what it gives, and what denies?

VII

Far as creation's ample range extends,
The scale of sensual, mental powers ascends.
Mark how it mounts to man's imperial race
From the green myriads in the peopled grass;
What modes of sight betwixt each wide extreme,
The mole's dim curtain, and the lynx's beam;
Of smell, the headlong lioness between
And hound sagacious on the tainted green;
Of hearing, from the life that fills the flood,
To that which warbles through the vernal wood;
The spider's touch, how exquisitely fine!
Feels at each thread, and lives along the line;
In the nice bee, what sense so subtly true
From poisonous herbs extracts the healing dew.
How instinct varies in the groveling swine,
Compared, half-reasoning elephant, with thine!
'Twixt that and reason, what a nice barrier,
Forever separate, yet forever near!
Remembrance and reflection how allied;
What thin partitions sense from thought divide;
And middle natures, how they long to join,
Yet never pass th' insuperable line!
Without this just gradation, could they be
Subjected, these to those, or all to thee?
The powers of all subdued by thee alone,
Is not thy reason all these powers in one?

VIII

See, through this air, this ocean, and this earth
All matter quick, [3] and bursting into birth.
Above, how high progressive life may go!
Around, how wide! how deep extend below!
Vast chain of being! which from God began,
Natures ethereal, human, angel, man,
Beast, bird, fish, insect, what no eye can see,
No glass can reach; from infinite to thee,

[2] Music, too fine or too mighty for mortal ears, supposed to be made by the revolution of the concentric spheres which, according to the old Ptolemaic system composed the universe; see note 10 on *Doctor Faustus*, p. 174.

[3] alive

From thee to nothing.—On superior powers
Were we to press, inferior might[1] on ours;
Or in the full creation leave a void,
Where, one step broken, the great scale's destroyed:
From nature's chain whatever link you strike,
Tenth, or ten thousandth, breaks the chain alike.
  And if each system in gradation roll
Alike essential to th' amazing whole,
The least confusion but in one, not all
That system only but the whole must fall.
Let earth unbalanced from her orbit fly,
Planets and suns run lawless through the sky;
Let ruling angels from their spheres be hurled,
Being on being wrecked, and world on world;
Heaven's whole foundations to their center nod,
And nature tremble to the throne of God.
All this dread order break—for whom? For thee?
Vile worm!—Oh, madness! pride! impiety!

IX

What if the foot, ordained the dust to tread,
Or hand to toil, aspired to be the head?
What if the head, the eye, or ear repined
To serve mere engines to the ruling mind?
Just as absurd for any part to claim
To be another, in this general frame;[2]
Just as absurd, to mourn the tasks or pains
The great directing Mind of all ordains.
  All are but parts of one stupendous whole,
Whose body nature is, and God the soul;
That, changed through all, and yet in all the same;
Great in the earth, as in th' ethereal frame;
Warms in the sun, refreshes in the breeze,
Glows in the stars, and blossoms in the trees,
Lives through all life, extends through all extent,
Spreads undivided, operates unspent;
Breathes in our soul, informs our mortal part,
As full, as perfect, in a hair as heart;
As full, as perfect, in vile man that mourns,
As the rapt seraph that adores and burns.
To him no high, no low, no great, no small;
He fills, he bounds, connects, and equals all.

X

Cease then, nor order imperfection name;
Our proper bliss depends on what we blame.
Know thy own point: this kind, this due degree
Of blindness, weakness, Heaven bestows on thee.
Submit. In this, or any other sphere,
Secure to be as blest as thou canst bear;
Safe in the hand of one disposing Power,
Or in the natal, or the mortal hour.
All nature is but art, unknown to thee;
All chance, direction, which thou canst not see;
All discord, harmony not understood;
All partial evil, universal good;
And, spite of pride, in erring reason's spite,
One truth is clear, whatever is, is right.

[1] Supply "press."
[2] universe

EPISTLE II

I

Know then thyself, presume not God to scan:
The proper study of mankind is man.
Placed on this isthmus of a middle state,
A being darkly wise and rudely great;
With too much knowledge for the sceptic side,
With too much weakness for the stoic's pride,
He hangs between; in doubt to act, or rest;
In doubt to deem himself a god or beast;
In doubt his mind or body to prefer;
Born but to die, and reasoning but to err;
Alike in ignorance, his reason such,
Whether he thinks too little or too much:
Chaos of thought and passion, all confused;
Still by himself abused, or disabused;
Created half to rise, and half to fall;
Great lord of all things, yet a prey to all;
Sole judge of truth, in endless error hurled;
The glory, jest, and riddle of the world!
  Go, wondrous creature; mount where science guides,
Go, measure earth, weigh air, and state the tides;
Instruct the planets in what orbs to run,
Correct old Time, and regulate the sun;[3]
Go, soar with Plato to th' empyreal sphere,[4]
To the first good, first perfect, and first fair;
Or tread the mazy round his followers trod,
And quitting sense call imitating God;
As eastern priests in giddy circles run,[5]
And turn their heads to imitate the sun.
Go, teach Eternal Wisdom how to rule—
Then drop into thyself, and be a fool!
  Superior beings, when of late they saw
A mortal man unfold all nature's law,

[3] alluding to the reformation of the calendar, which had fallen some twelve days behind the sun—a reformation then already generally adopted in Europe, though not in England till 1751
[4] Compare note on I, 202. (Bolingbroke held Plato in contempt.)
[5] the dancing dervishes

Admired such wisdom in an earthly shape,
And showed a Newton, as we show an ape.
  Could he, whose rules the rapid comet bind,
Describe or fix one movement of his mind?
Who saw its fires here rise, and there descend,
Explain his own beginning or his end?
Alas! what wonder! Man's superior part
Unchecked may rise, and climb from art to art;
But when his own great work is but begun,
What reason weaves, by passion is undone.
  Trace science, then, with modesty thy guide;
First strip off all her equipage of pride;
Deduct what is but vanity or dress,
Or learning's luxury, or idleness,
Or tricks to show the stretch of human brain,
Mere curious pleasure, or ingenious pain;
Expunge the whole, or lop th' excrescent parts
Of all our vices have created arts;
Then see how little the remaining sum,
Which served the past, and must the times to come!

II

  Two principles in human nature reign;
Self-love to urge, and reason to restrain;
Nor this a good, nor that a bad we call,
Each works its end to move or govern all;
And to their proper operation still
Ascribe all good; to their improper, ill.
  Self-love, the spring of motion, acts[1] the soul;
Reason's comparing balance rules the whole.
Man, but for that, no action could attend,
And, but for this, were active to no end;
Fixed like a plant on his peculiar spot,
To draw nutrition, propagate, and rot;
Or, meteor-like, flame lawless through the void,
Destroying others, by himself destroyed.
  Most strength the moving principle requires;
Active its task, it prompts, impels, inspires;
Sedate and quiet, the comparing[2] lies,
Formed but to check, deliberate, and advise.
Self-love still stronger, as its objects nigh,
Reason's at distance and in prospect lie;
That sees immediate good by present sense;
Reason, the future and the consequence.
Thicker than arguments, temptations throng,
At best more watchful this, but that more strong.
The action of the stronger to suspend,
Reason still use, to reason still attend.
Attention, habit and experience gains;
Each strengthens reason, and self-love restrains.
  Let subtle schoolmen teach these friends to fight,
More studious to divide than to unite;
And grace and virtue, sense and reason split,
With all the rash dexterity of wit.
Wits, just like fools, at war about a name,
Have full as oft no meaning, or the same.
Self-love and reason to one end aspire,
Pain their aversion, pleasure their desire;
But greedy that, its object would devour,
This taste the honey, and not wound the flower;
Pleasure, or wrong or rightly understood,
Our greatest evil or our greatest good.

III

Modes of self-love the passions we may call;
'Tis real good, or seeming, moves them all.
But since not every good we can divide,
And reason bids us for our own provide,
Passions, though selfish, if their means be fair,
List under reason, and deserve her care;
Those that imparted, court a nobler aim,
Exalt their kind, and take some virtue's name.
  In lazy apathy let stoics boast
Their virtue fixed. 'Tis fixed as in a frost;
Contracted all, retiring to the breast;
But strength of mind is exercise, not rest.
The rising tempest puts in act the soul,
Parts it may ravage, but preserves the whole.
On life's vast ocean diversely we sail,
Reason the card,[3] but passion is the gale;
Nor God alone in the still calm we find,
He mounts the storm, and walks upon the wind.
  Passions, like elements, though born to fight,
Yet, mixed and softened, in his work unite.
These 'tis enough to temper and employ;
But what composes man, can man destroy?
Suffice that reason keep to nature's road,
Subject, compound them, follow her and God.
Love, hope, and joy, fair pleasure's smiling train,
Hate, fear, and grief, the family of pain,
These mixed with art, and to due bounds confined,
Make and maintain the balance of the mind:
The lights and shades, whose well-accorded strife
Gives all the strength and color of our life.
  Pleasures are ever in our hands or eyes,
And when in act they cease, in prospect rise;
Present to grasp, and future still to find,
The whole employ of body and of mind.

[1] actuates, moves

[2] Supply "principle."

[3] compass

All spread their charms, but charm not all alike;
On different senses different objects strike;
Hence different passions more or less inflame,
As strong or weak the organs of the frame;
And hence one master-passion in the breast,
Like Aaron's serpent, swallows up the rest.
As man, perhaps, the moment of his breath,
Receives the lurking principle of death;
The young disease, that must subdue at length,
Grows with his growth, and strengthens with his strength;
So, cast and mingled with his very frame,
The mind's disease, its ruling passion, came;
Each vital humor which should feed the whole,
Soon flows to this, in body and in soul;
Whatever warms the heart, or fills the head,
As the mind opens, and its functions spread,
Imagination plies her dangerous art,
And pours it all upon the peccant part.
Nature its mother, habit is its nurse;
Wit, spirit, faculties, but make it worse;
Reason itself but gives it edge and power;
As Heaven's blest beam turns vinegar more sour.
We, wretched subjects, though to lawful sway,
In this weak queen some favorite still obey;
Ah! if she lend not arms as well as rules,
What can she more than tell us we are fools?
Teach us to mourn our nature, not to mend;
A sharp accuser, but a helpless friend!
Or from a judge turn pleader, to persuade
The choice we make, or justify it made;
Proud of an easy conquest all along,
She but removes weak passions for the strong.
So, when small humors gather to a gout,
The doctor fancies he has driven them out.
Yes, nature's road must ever be preferred;
Reason is here no guide, but still a guard;
'Tis hers to rectify, not overthrow,
And treat this passion more as friend than foe.
A mightier power the strong direction sends,
And several men impels to several ends;
Like varying winds by other passions tossed,
This drives them constant to a certain coast.
Let power or knowledge, gold or glory, please,
Or (oft more strong than all) the love of ease;
Through life 'tis followed, even at life's expense;
The merchant's toil, the sage's indolence,
The monk's humility, the hero's pride,
All, all alike find reason on their side.
Th' Eternal Art, educing good from ill,
Grafts on this passion our best principle;
'Tis thus the mercury of man is fixed,
Strong grows the virtue with his nature mixed;
The dross cements what else were too refined,
And in one interest body acts with mind.
As fruits, ungrateful to the planter's care,
On savage stocks inserted, learn to bear,
The surest virtues thus from passions shoot,
Wild nature's vigor working at the root.
What crops of wit and honesty appear
From spleen, from obstinacy, hate, or fear!
See anger, zeal and fortitude supply;
Even avarice, prudence; sloth, philosophy;
Lust, through some certain strainers well refined,
Is gentle love, and charms all womankind;
Envy, to which th' ignoble mind's a slave,
Is emulation in the learned or brave;
Nor virtue, male or female, can we name,
But what will grow on pride, or grow on shame.
Thus nature gives us (let it check our pride)
The virtue nearest to our vice allied;
Reason the bias turns to good from ill,
And Nero reigns a Titus, if he will.[1]
The fiery soul abhorred in Catiline,
In Decius charms, in Curtius is divine;[2]
The same ambition can destroy or save,
And makes a patriot as it makes a knave.

IV

This light and darkness in our chaos joined,
What shall divide? The God within the mind.
Extremes in nature equal ends produce,
In man they join to some mysterious use;
Though each by turns the other's bound invade,
As, in some well-wrought picture, light and shade,
And oft so mix, the difference is too nice
Where ends the virtue, or begins the vice.
Fools! who from hence into the notion fall,
That vice or virtue there is none at all.
If white and black blend, soften, and unite
A thousand ways, is there no black or white?
Ask your own heart, and nothing is so plain;
'Tis to mistake them costs the time and pain.

V

Vice is a monster of so frightful mien,
As to be hated needs but to be seen;
Yet seen too oft, familiar with her face,

[1] i.e., the tyrant turns benefactor

[2] Decius voluntarily rushed into death because of a vision assuring victory to the side whose general should fall. Curtius is alleged to have made a similar self-sacrifice, leaping into a chasm in the Roman forum.

We first endure, then pity, then embrace.
But where th' extreme of vice, was ne'er agreed.
Ask "where's the north?" at York 'tis on the Tweed;
In Scotland, at the Orcades; and there,
At Greenland, Zembla, or the Lord knows where.
No creature owns it in the first degree,
But thinks his neighbor further gone than he;
Even those who dwell beneath its very zone,
Or never feel the rage, or never own;
What happier natures shrink at with affright
The hard inhabitant contends is right.

VI

Virtuous and vicious every man must be;
Few in th' extreme, but all in the degree;
The rogue and fool by fits is fair and wise;
And even the best, by fits, what they despise.
'Tis but by parts we follow good or ill;
For, vice or virtue, self directs it still;
Each individual seeks a several goal;
But Heaven's great view is one, and that the whole.
That counterworks each folly and caprice;
That disappoints th' effect of every vice;
That, happy frailties to all ranks applied,
Shame to the virgin, to the matron pride,
Fear to the statesman, rashness to the chief,
To kings presumption, and to crowds belief;
That, virtue's ends from vanity can raise,
Which seeks no interest, no reward but praise;
And build on wants, and on defects of mind,
The joy, the peace, the glory of mankind.
  Heaven, forming each on other to depend,
A master, or a servant, or a friend,
Bids each on other for assistance call,
Till one man's weakness grows the strength of all.
Wants, frailties, passions, closer still ally
The common interest, or endear the tie.
To these we owe true friendship, love sincere,
Each home-felt joy that life inherits here;
Yet from the same we learn, in its decline,
Those joys, those loves, those interests to resign;
Taught half by reason, half by mere decay,
To welcome death, and calmly pass away.
  Whate'er the passion—knowledge, fame, or pelf—
Not one will change his neighbor with himself.
The learned is happy nature to explore,
The fool is happy that he knows no more;
The rich is happy in the plenty given,
The poor contents him with the care of Heaven.
See the blind beggar dance, the cripple sing,
The sot a hero, lunatic a king;
The starving chemist[1] in his golden views
Supremely blest, the poet in his Muse.
  See some strange comfort every state attend,
And pride bestowed on all, a common friend;
See some fit passion every age supply,
Hope travels through, nor quits us when we die.
  Behold the child, by Nature's kindly law,
Pleased with a rattle, tickled with a straw;
Some livelier plaything gives his youth delight,
A little louder, but as empty quite;
Scarfs, garters,[2] gold, amuse his riper stage;
And beads and prayer-books are the toys of age.
Pleased with this bauble still, as that before;
Till tired he sleeps, and life's poor play is o'er.
  Meanwhile Opinion gilds, with varying rays,
Those painted clouds that beautify our days;
Each want of happiness by hope supplied,
And each vacuity of sense by pride.
These build as fast as knowledge can destroy;
In Folly's cup still laughs the bubble joy;
One prospect lost, another still we gain;
And not a vanity is given in vain;
Even mean self-love becomes, by force divine,
The scale to measure others' wants by thine.
See, and confess, one comfort still must rise;
'Tis this—though man's a fool, yet God is wise!

1732 1733

THE UNIVERSAL PRAYER

Father of all! in every age,
  In every clime adored,
By saint, by savage, and by sage,
  Jehovah, Jove, or Lord!

Thou Great First Cause, least understood,
  Who all my sense confined
To know but this, that Thou art good,
  And that myself am blind;

Yet gave me, in this dark estate,
  To see the good from ill;
And binding nature fast in fate,
  Left free the human will.

What conscience dictates to be done,
  Or warns me not to do,
This, teach me more than hell to shun,
  That, more than heaven pursue.

[1] alchemist
[2] the badge of the highest order of the English knighthood

What blessings Thy free bounty gives,
Let me not cast away;
For God is paid when man receives;
T' enjoy is to obey.

Yet not to earth's contracted span
Thy goodness let me bound,
Or think Thee Lord alone of man,
When thousand worlds are round.

Let not this weak, unknowing hand
Presume Thy bolts to throw,
And deal damnation round the land,
On each I judge Thy foe.

If I am right, Thy grace impart,
Still in the right to stay;
If I am wrong, oh! teach my heart
To find that better way.

Save me alike from foolish pride
Or impious discontent,
At aught Thy wisdom has denied,
Or aught Thy goodness lent.

Teach me to feel another's woe,
To hide the fault I see;
That mercy I to others show,
That mercy show to me.

Mean though I am, not wholly so,
Since quickened by Thy breath;
Oh, lead me wheresoe'er I go,
Through this day's life or death.

This day, be bread and peace my lot;
All else beneath the sun,
Thou know'st if best bestowed or not,
And let Thy will be done.

To Thee, whose temple is all space,
Whose altar earth, sea, skies,
One chorus let all being raise,
All nature's incense rise!

1738

DANIEL DEFOE
1661-1731

With Defoe begins the modern journalistic essay written upon the spur of the moment for its immediate importance. Its inventor, besides being a journalist, was a publicist, a novelist, and a politician. His parents, middle-class Dissenters living in London, gave him a practical education in English and the modern languages. After unsuccessful attempts at business he became engaged in politics, and spent the remainder of his life, whether in poverty or affluence, amid the excitement of party strife. He was a Whig and an ardent though not always dignified reformer. For example, he trapped some thick-wits of the High Church party into publicly endorsing as sound reasoning his anonymous ironical tract, *The Shortest Way with the Dissenters.* In this he had suggested extreme penalties, even death, for these disturbers of Church and State. When the trick was discovered, its author was fined, imprisoned, and set in the pillory. Here, however, he was surrounded by an admiring crowd of Dissenters who threw him flowers, and bought and sang his "Hymn to the Pillory," composed and printed, with journalistic forethought, for the occasion.

Defoe's literary life was extraordinarily active. From 1704 to 1713 he wrote, almost unaided, the *Review,* an essay-newspaper. Some three hundred and sixty books, poems, essays, novels, tracts, histories upon religious, economic, moral, and current social topics are also accredited to him. His work as a pioneer novelist is seen in such books as *Moll Flanders,* 1722, and *Roxanna,* 1724. His notable *Journal of the Plague Year,* 1722, though largely a transcript of fact, contains elements of realistic fiction; and his tale of adventure, *Robinson Crusoe,* 1719, now in the third century of its popularity, is very likely the most widely known book, save the Bible, in the English language.

Defoe lived at a time of great social ferment, when political power was passing from the monarchy into the hands of the mass of voting freeholders. To these particularly he appealed in his political tracts, for he wrote in everyday language, as a plain citizen to other plain citizens. Moreover, although he used many methods of modern "yellow" journalism, in subject-matter, style, and even demagogic appeal, Defoe must be credited with opening to English readers the delight of the commonplace with its infinite possibilities. For especially the same rather literal-minded middle-class people who could understand his political tracts eagerly read his fiction. It was as simple in style as Bunyan's and more modern; and so full of realistic touches that it fairly achieved verisimilitude—the appearance of truth in what is actually the writer's own creation. It is also true that Defoe's journalistic, periodical essays (i.e., published weekly or from day to day) developed taste for writings on current and familiar topics and led the way to the more urbane and polished periodical essays of Steele and Addison.

There is no complete edition of Defoe. His *Romances and Narratives* with notable introductions by G. A. Aitken are in 16 vols. Lond. 1895-6. Biography: W. Minto (EML). Criticism: see W. L. Phelps; "Two Hundred Years of Defoe," *Liv. Age,* 301:619-24; Edith Wyatt, "The Author of *Robinson Crusoe,*" *No. Am.* 198:87-99, a vivid estimate; J. Masefield, "Defoe," *Fortn.* 91:65-73, analytic but unsympathetic.

From ROBINSON CRUSOE

[The Castaway [1]]

Chapter IV

THE VOYAGE TO GUINEA

. . . . Had I continued in the station I was now in, I had room for all the happy things to have yet befallen me for which my father so earnestly recommended a quiet, retired life, and of which he had so sensibly described the middle station of life to be full. But other things attended [2] me, and I was still to be the willful agent of all my own miseries, and particularly to increase my fault and double the reflections upon myself which in my future sorrows I should have leisure to make. All these miscarriages were procured by my apparent obstinate adherence to my foolish inclinations of wandering abroad, and pursuing that inclination in contradiction to the clearest views of doing myself good in a fair and plain pursuit of those prospects and those measures of life which Nature and Providence concurred to present me with and to make my duty.

As I had once done thus in my breaking away from my parents, so I could not be content now, but I must go and leave the happy view [3] I had of being a rich and thriving man in my new plantation, only to pursue a rash and immoderate desire of rising faster than the nature of the thing admitted; and thus I cast myself down again into the deepest gulf of human misery that ever man fell into, or perhaps could be consistent with life and a state of health in the world.

To come, then, by the just degrees to the particulars of this part of my story. You may suppose that having now lived almost four years in the Brazils, and beginning to thrive and prosper very well upon my plantation, I had not only learned the language but had contracted acquaintance and friendship among my fellow-planters, as well as among the merchants at St. Salvador, which was our port, and that in my discourses among them I had frequently given them an account of my two voyages to the coast of Guinea, the manner of trading with the negroes there, and how easy it was to purchase upon the coast for trifles—such as beads, toys, knives, scissors, hatchets, bits of glass, and the like—not only gold-dust, Guinea grains, [4] elephants' teeth, etc., but negroes, for the service of the Brazils, in great numbers.

They listened always very attentively to my discourses on these heads, but especially to that part which related to the buying negroes; which was a trade, at that time, not only not far entered into but, as far as it was, had been carried on by the *assiento,* or permission, of the kings of Spain and Portugal, and engrossed in the public [5] so that few negroes were brought, and those excessive dear.

It happened, being in company with some merchants and planters of my acquaintance, and talking of those things very earnestly, three of them came to me the next morning, and told me they had been musing very much upon what I had discoursed with them of, the last night, and they came to make a secret proposal to me. And, after enjoining me secrecy, they told me that they had a mind to fit out a ship to go to Guinea; that they had all plantations as well as I, and were straitened for nothing so much as servants; that as it was a trade that could not be carried on because they could not publicly sell the negroes when they came home, so they desired to make but one voyage, to bring the negroes on shore privately, and divide them among their own plantations; and, in a word, the question was whether I would go their supercargo in the ship to manage the trading part upon the coast of Guinea. And they offered me that I should have my equal share of the negroes without providing any part of the stock.

This was a fair proposal, it must be confessed, had it been made to any one that had not had a settlement and plantation of his own to look after, which was in a fair way of coming to be very considerable, and with a good stock upon it. But for me, that was thus entered and established, and had nothing to do but go on as I had begun for three or four years more, and to have sent for the other hundred pounds from England; and who, in that time and with that little addition, could scarce have failed of being worth three or four thousand pounds sterling, and that increasing, too—for me to think of such a voyage was the most preposterous thing that ever man in such circumstances could be guilty of.

[1] Crusoe, having run away to sea at the age of nineteen and been wrecked on the English coast, had next embarked on a trading vessel to the coast of Guinea. Upon a third voyage he was captured by the Moors. Escaping, after two years of slavery, he was picked up by a Portuguese vessel and taken to the Brazils. There he set up as a planter and sent back to England for half of the two hundred pounds he had saved from his first venture.

[2] awaited

[3] prospect

[4] aromatic seeds (used for spicing liquor)

[5] held as a state monopoly (Possibly some word like "stock" has been omitted.)

But I, that was born to be my own destroyer, could no more resist the offer than I could restrain my first rambling designs when my father's good counsel was lost upon me. In a word, I told them I would go with all my heart if they would undertake to look after my plantation in my absence, and would dispose of it to such as I should direct if I miscarried. This they all engaged to do, and entered into writings or covenants to do so; and I made a formal will, disposing of my plantation and effects in case of my death; making the captain of the ship that had saved my life, as before, my universal heir, but obliging him to dispose of my effects as I had directed in my will, one half of the produce being to himself, and the other to be shipped to England.

In short, I took all possible caution to preserve my effects and keep up my plantation. Had I used half as much prudence to have looked into my own interest, and have made a judgment of what I ought to have done and not to have done, I had certainly never gone away from so prosperous an undertaking, leaving all the probable views of a thriving circumstance, and gone upon a voyage to sea, attended with all its common hazards, to say nothing of the reasons I had to expect particular misfortune to myself.

But I was hurried on, and obeyed blindly the dictates of my fancy rather than my reason. And accordingly, the ship being fitted out and the cargo furnished and all things done as by agreement by my partners in the voyage, I went on board in an evil hour, the [first] of [September 1659], being the same day eight year that I went from my father and mother at Hull, in order to act the rebel to their authority, and the fool to my own interest.

Chapter V

THE SHIPWRECK

Our ship was about 120 tons burthen; carried six guns and fourteen men besides the master, his boy, and myself. We had on board no large cargo of goods, except of such toys as were fit for our trade with the negroes—such as beads, bits of glass, shells, and odd trifles, especially little looking-glasses, knives, scissors, hatchets, and the like.

The same day I went on board we set sail, standing away to the northward upon our own coast, with design to stretch over for the African coast when they [1] came about ten or twelve degrees of northern latitude; which, it seems, was the manner of their course in those days. We had very good weather, only excessive hot, all the way upon our own coast till we came the height of [2] Cape St. Augustino; [3] from whence, keeping farther off at sea, we lost sight of land, and steered as if we were bound for the isle Fernando de Noronha, holding our course N.E. by N., and leaving those isles on the east. In this course we passed the line in about twelve days' time, and were, by our last observation, in 7° 22′ northern latitude when a violent tornado, or hurricane, took us quite out of our knowledge. It began from the south-east, came about to the north-west, and then settled into the north-east, from whence it blew in such a terrible manner that for twelve days together we could do nothing but drive, and, scudding away before it, let it carry us wherever fate and the fury of the winds directed; and during these twelve days I need not say that I expected every day to be swallowed up; nor, indeed, did any in the ship expect to save their lives.

In this distress we had, besides the terror of the storm, one of our men died of the calenture, [4] and one man and the boy washed overboard. About the twelfth day, the weather abating a little, the master made an observation as well as he could, and found that he was in about 11 degrees north latitude, but that he was 22 degrees of longitude difference west from Cape St. Augustino; so that he found he was gotten upon the coast of Guiana, or the north part of Brazil beyond the river Amazon, toward that of the river Orinoco, commonly called the Great River, and began to consult with me what course he should take, for the ship was leaky and very much disabled, and he was going directly back to the coast of Brazil.

I was positively against that; and looking over the charts of the seacoast of America with him, we concluded there was no inhabited country for us to have recourse to till we came within the circle of the Caribbee Islands, and therefore resolved to stand away for Barbadoes; which by keeping off at sea, to avoid the indraft of the Bay or Gulf of Mexico, we might easily perform, as we hoped, in about fifteen days' sail; whereas we could not possibly make our voyage to the coast of Africa without some assistance both to our ship and to ourselves.

[1] This change of subject need not surprise. Defoe's syntax is often very loose.

[2] reached the lattitude of

[3] Cape São Agostinhos, about four degrees north of São Salvador (Bahia)

[4] a delirious fever

With this design we changed our course, and steered away N.W. by W. in order to reach some of our English islands, where I hoped for relief; but our voyage was otherwise determined; for being in the latitude of 12 degrees 18 minutes a second storm came upon us, which carried us away with the same impetuosity westward, and drove us so out of the very way of all human commerce that had all our lives been saved as to the sea, we were rather in danger of being devoured by savages than ever returning to our own country.

In this distress, the wind still blowing very hard, one of our men early in the morning cried out, "Land!" and we had no sooner ran out of the cabin to look out, in hopes of seeing whereabouts in the world we were, but the ship struck upon a sand, and in a moment, her motion being so stopped, the sea broke over her in such a manner that we expected we should all have perished immediately; and we were immediately driven into our close quarters to shelter us from the very foam and spray of the sea.

It is not easy for anyone who has not been in the like condition, to describe or conceive the consternation of men in such circumstances. We knew nothing where we were or upon what land it was we were driven, whether an island or the main, whether inhabited or not inhabited; and as the rage of the wind was still great, though rather less than at first, we could not so much as hope to have the ship hold many minutes without breaking in pieces, unless the winds, by a kind of miracle, should turn immediately about. In a word, we sat looking one upon another, and expecting death every moment, and every man acting accordingly, as preparing for another world; for there was little or nothing more for us to do in this. That which was our present comfort, and all the comfort we had, was that, contrary to our expectation, the ship did not break yet, and that the master said the wind began to abate.

Now, though we thought that the wind did a little abate, yet the ship having thus struck upon the sand, and sticking too fast for us to expect her getting off, we were in a dreadful condition indeed, and had nothing to do but to think of saving our lives as well as we could. We had a boat at our stern just before the storm, but she was first staved by dashing against the ship's rudder, and in the next place she broke away, and either sunk or was driven off to sea, so there was no hope from her. We had another boat on board, but how to get off into the sea was a doubtful thing. However, there was no room to debate, for we fancied the ship would break in pieces every minute, and some told us she was actually broken already.

In this distress the mate of our vessel lays hold of the boat, and with the help of the rest of the men they got her slung over the ship's side; and getting all into her, let go; and committed ourselves, being eleven in number, to God's mercy and the wild sea; for though the storm was abated considerably, yet the sea went dreadful high upon the shore, and might well be called *den wild zee*, as the Dutch call the sea in a storm.

And now our case was very dismal indeed, for we all saw plainly that the sea went so high that the boat could not live, and that we should be inevitably drowned. As to making sail, we had none; nor, if we had, could we have done anything with it. So we worked at the oar toward the land, though with heavy hearts, like men going to execution; for we all knew that when the boat came nearer the shore she would be dashed in a thousand pieces by the breach of the sea. However, we committed our souls to God in the most earnest manner; and the wind driving us toward the shore, we hastened our destruction with our own hands, pulling as well as we could toward land.

What the shore was, whether rock or sand, whether steep or shoal, we knew not; the only hope that could rationally give us the least shadow of expectation was if we might happen into some bay or gulf, or the mouth of some river, where by great chance we might have run our boat in, or got under the lee of the land, and perhaps made smooth water. But there was nothing of this appeared; but as we made nearer and nearer the shore the land looked more frightful than the sea.

After we had rowed, or rather driven, about a league and a half, as we reckoned it, a raging wave, mountain-like, came rolling astern of us, and plainly bade us expect the *coup de grâce.* [1] In a word, it took us with such a fury that it overset the boat at once; and separating us, as well from the boat as from one another, gave us not time hardly to say, "O God!" for we were all swallowed up in a moment.

Nothing can describe the confusion of thought which I felt when I sunk into the water; for though I swam very well, yet I could not deliver myself from the waves so as to draw breath till that wave having driven me, or rather carried me, a vast way on toward

[1] finishing stroke

the shore, and having spent itself, went back and left me upon the land almost dry, but half dead with the water I took in. I had so much presence of mind, as well as breath, left that seeing myself nearer the mainland than I expected, I got upon my feet and endeavored to make on toward the land as fast as I could, before another wave should return and take me up again. But I soon found it was impossible to avoid it; for I saw the sea come after me as high as a great hill, and as furious as an enemy, which I had no means or strength to contend with. My business was to hold my breath, and raise myself upon the water if I could; and so, by swimming, to preserve my breathing and pilot myself toward the shore, if possible; my greatest concern now being that the sea, as it would carry me a great way toward the shore when it came on, might not carry me back again with it when it gave back toward the sea.

The wave that came upon me again, buried me at once twenty or thirty feet deep in its own body, and I could feel myself carried with a mighty force and swiftness toward the shore a very great way; but I held my breath, and assisted myself to swim still forward with all my might. I was ready to burst with holding my breath when, as I felt myself rising up, so, to my immediate relief, I found my head and hands shoot out above the surface of the water; and though it was not two seconds of time that I could keep myself so, yet it relieved me greatly, gave me breath and new courage. I was covered again with water a good while, but not so long but I held it out; and finding the water had spent itself, and began to return, I struck forward against the return of the waves, and felt ground again with my feet. I stood still a few moments to recover breath, and till the water went from me, and then took to my heels and ran with what strength I had farther toward the shore. But neither would this deliver me from the fury of the sea, which came pouring in after me again, and twice more I was lifted up by the waves and carried forward as before, the shore being very flat.

The last time of these two had well near been fatal to me; for the sea, having hurried me along as before, landed me, or rather dashed me, against a piece of a rock, and that with such force as it left me senseless, and indeed helpless as to my own deliverance; for the blow taking my side and breast, beat the breath as it were quite out of my body; and had it returned again immediately I must have been strangled in the water. But I recovered a little before the return of the waves, and seeing I should be covered again with the water, I resolved to hold fast by a piece of the rock, and so hold my breath, if possible, till the wave went back. Now as the waves were not so high as at first, being near land, I held my hold till the wave abated, and then fetched another run which brought me so near the shore that the next wave, though it went over me, yet did not so swallow me up as to carry me away, and the next run I took I got to the mainland where, to my great comfort, I clambered up the cliffs of the shore, and sat me down upon the grass, free from danger, and quite out of the reach of the water.

I was now landed and safe on shore, and began to look up and thank God that my life was saved in a case wherein there was some minutes before scarce any room to hope. I believe it is impossible to express to the life what the ecstasies and transports of the soul are when it is so saved, as I may say, out of the very grave; and I do not wonder now at that custom, namely, that when a malefactor who has the halter about his neck, is tied up, and just going to be turned off, and has a reprieve brought to him—I say, I do not wonder that they bring a surgeon with it, to let him blood [1] that very moment they tell him of it, that the surprise may not drive the animal spirits from the heart and overwhelm him;

"For sudden joys, like griefs, confound at first."

I walked about on the shore, lifting up my hands, and my whole being, as I may say, wrapt up in the contemplation of my deliverance, making a thousand gestures and motions which I cannot describe, reflecting upon all my comrades that were drowned, and that there should not be one soul saved but myself; for, as for them, I never saw them afterwards, or any sign of them except three of their hats, one cap, and two shoes that were not fellows.

I cast my eyes to the stranded vessel, when the breach and froth of the sea being so big, I could hardly see it, it lay so far off, and considered, Lord! how was it possible I could get on shore?

After I had solaced my mind with the comfortable part of my condition, I began to look round me to see what kind of place I was in, and what was next to be done, and I soon found my comforts abate, and that, in a word, I had a dreadful deliverance; for I was wet,

[1] i. e., bleed him

had no clothes to shift me, nor anything either to eat or drink to comfort me, neither did I see any prospect before me but that of perishing with hunger or being devoured by wild beasts; and that which was particularly afflicting to me was that I had no weapon either to hunt and kill any creature for my sustenance or to defend myself against any other creature that might desire to kill me for theirs. In a word, I had nothing about me but a knife, a tobacco-pipe, and a little tobacco in a box. This was all my provision; and this threw me into terrible agonies of mind, that for a while I ran about like a madman. Night coming upon me, I began, with a heavy heart, to consider what would be my lot if there were any ravenous beasts in that country, seeing at night they always come abroad for their prey.

All the remedy that offered to my thoughts at that time was to get up into a thick bushy tree like a fir, but thorny, which grew near me, and where I resolved to sit all night, and consider the next day what death I should die, for as yet I saw no prospect of life. I walked about a furlong from the shore to see if I could find any fresh water to drink, which I did, to my great joy; and having drank, and put a little tobacco in my mouth to prevent hunger, I went to the tree, and getting up into it, endeavored to place myself so as that if I should sleep I might not fall; and having cut me a short stick, like a truncheon, for my defense, I took up my lodging, and having been excessively fatigued, I fell fast asleep, and slept as comfortably as, I believe, few could have done in my condition, and found myself the most refreshed with it that I think I ever was on such an occasion.

1719, 1720

JONATHAN SWIFT
1667-1745

"The greatest genius of his age," said Addison; and modern judgment adds the verdict that Swift was one of the greatest satirists of all time. Swift's father was business manager of King's Inns, an association of lawyers in Dublin. He died before his son was born, leaving the lad to be brought up by his mother, and by uncles who little understood his gloomy nature. From youth he had attacks of the heart or nerve centers which may have caused the lunacy in which he died.

After graduating from Trinity College, Dublin, he spent the happiest years of his life in England as secretary to Sir William Temple, the great Whig statesman. He had literary ambitions and knew his own power, but meeting no encouragement he took orders in the English Church and was given livings in Ireland. Though a Tory at heart, he was nominally a Whig and sought preferment in the Church through Whig friends in office in London. They could do little for him because he was the reputed author of *The Tale of a Tub*, a satire upon the Church, and on this basis Queen Anne refused to give him a bishopric. When, therefore, the Tories came to office, inclination and interest led him to join them: he was made Dean of St. Patrick's in Dublin, where he died.

Swift was a master of plain prose, and within its limits was strikingly inventive. His diction is of the tersest and most trenchant, recalling his definition of style, "proper words in proper places." For whole volumes he borrowed not a single idea. Says Sir Walter Scott: "No word drops from Gulliver's pen in vain. Where his work ceases for a moment to satirize the vices of mankind in general, it becomes a stricture upon the parties, politics, and court of Britain; where it abandons that subject of censure, it presents a lively picture of the vices and follies of the fashionable world, or of the vain pursuits of philosophy, while the parts of the narrative which refer to the traveler's own adventures form a humorous and striking parody of the manner of old voyagers."

His severest satires are revolting, and some of his verses are scurrilous, it may be the product of a diseased brain. Yet Swift was a philanthropist, too, and some of his most venemous attacks, directed against the oppressors of the Irish people, brought such relief to the poor in Dublin that they would have defended their Dean to the death.

Swift's books, poems, tracts, and pamphlets number nearly one hundred and fifty. He is chiefly known for *The Tale of a Tub*, 1704; *The Drapier Letters* (Irish tracts), 1724-5; *The Travels of Lemuel Gulliver*, 1726.

Biographies: Sir H. Craik, 1882; J. Forster, vol. I, 1875; Stephen (EML), 1882. Criticism: Thackeray; articles by E. Boyd, *Harp.* 150:584-94, and P. E. More, *Nation* 101:171-73, are attempts to solve some of the enigmas of Swift's life.

GULLIVER'S TRAVELS[1]

From PART I. A VOYAGE TO LILLIPUT

CHAPTER I

My father had a small estate in Nottinghamshire; I was the third of five sons. He sent me to Emmanuel College in Cambridge at fourteen years old, where I resided three years, and applied myself close to my studies; but the charge of maintaining me, although I had a very scanty allowance, being too great for a

[1] Of Part I, the Voyage to Lilliput, Sir Walter Scott says: "The satire is here leveled against the court and ministry of George I. In some points the parallel is very closely drawn, as where the parties in the church and state are described, and the mode in which offices and marks of distinction are conferred in the Lilliputian court."

narrow fortune I was bound apprentice to Mr. James Bates, an eminent surgeon in London, with whom I continued four years; and my father now and then sending me small sums of money, I laid them out in learning navigation and other parts of the mathematics useful to those who intend to travel, as I always believed it would be, some time or other, my fortune to do. When I left Mr. Bates I went down to my father; where, by the assistance of him and my uncle John and some other relations, I got forty pounds, and a promise of thirty pounds a year to maintain me at Leyden. There I studied physic two years and seven months, knowing it would be useful in long voyages.

Soon after my return from Leyden I was recommended by my good master, Mr. Bates, to be surgeon to *The Swallow,* Captain Abraham Pannell, commander; with whom I continued three years and a half, making a voyage or two into the Levant [1] and some other parts. When I came back I resolved to settle in London; to which Mr. Bates, my master, encouraged me, and by him I was recommended to several patients. I took part of a small house in the Old Jewry; [2] and being advised to alter my condition, I married Mrs. [3] Mary Burton, second daughter to Mr. Edmund Burton, hosier in Newgate Street, with whom I received four hundred pounds for a portion.

But my good master, Bates, dying in two years after, and I having few friends, my business began to fail; for my conscience would not suffer me to imitate the bad practice of too many among my brethren. Having, therefore, consulted with my wife and some of my acquaintance, I determined to go again to sea. I was surgeon successively in two ships, and made several voyages, for six years, to the East and West Indies, by which I got some addition to my fortune. My hours of leisure I spent in reading the best authors, ancient and modern, being always provided with a good number of books; and, when I was ashore, in observing the manners and dispositions of the people, as well as learning their language, wherein I had a great facility by the strength of my memory.

The last of these voyages not proving very fortunate, I grew weary of the sea, and intended to stay at home with my wife and family. I removed from the Old Jewry to Fetter Lane, and from thence to Wapping, hoping to get business among the sailors; but it would not turn to account. After three years' expectation that things would mend, I accepted an advantageous offer from Captain William Prichard, master of *The Antelope,* who was making a voyage to the South Sea. We set sail from Bristol, May 4, 1699; and our voyage at first was very prosperous.

It would not be proper, for some reasons, to trouble the reader with the particulars of our adventures in those seas. Let it suffice to inform him that, in our passage from thence to the East Indies, we were driven by a violent storm to the northwest of Van Diemen's Land. By an observation we found ourselves in the latitude of 30 degrees 2 minutes south. Twelve of our crew were dead by immoderate labor and ill food; the rest were in a very weak condition.

On the fifth of November, which was the beginning of summer in those parts, the weather being very hazy, the seamen spied a rock within half a cable's length of the ship; but the wind was so strong that we were driven directly upon it, and immediately split. Six of the crew, of whom I was one, having let down the boat into the sea, made a shift to get clear of the ship and the rock. We rowed, by my computation, about three leagues, till we were able to work no longer, being already spent with labor while we were in the ship. We, therefore, trusted ourselves to the mercy of the waves; and in about half an hour the boat was overset by a sudden flurry from the north. What became of my companions in the boat, as well as of those who escaped on the rock or were left in the vessel, I cannot tell, but conclude they were all lost.

For my own part I swam as fortune directed me, and was pushed forward by wind and tide. I often let my legs drop, and could feel no bottom; but when I was almost gone, and able to struggle no longer, I found myself within my depth; and by this time the storm was much abated.

The declivity was so small that I walked near a mile before I got to the shore, which I conjectured was about eight o'clock in the evening. I then advanced forward near half a mile, but could not discover any sign of houses or inhabitants; at least, I was in so weak a condition that I did not observe them. I was extremely tired, and with that and the heat of the weather and about half a pint of brandy that I drank as I left the ship, I found myself much inclined to sleep. I lay down on

[1] the Orient, especially the east coast of the Mediterranean

[2] a street in the heart of London

[3] Mistress was a title then given to both married and unmarried women.

the grass, which was very short and soft, where I slept sounder than ever I remembered to have done in my life, and, as I reckoned, above nine hours; for when I awaked it was just daylight. I attempted to rise, but was not able to stir; for as I happened to lie on my back, I found my arms and legs were strongly fastened on each side to the ground; and my hair, which was long and thick, tied down in the same manner. I likewise felt several slender ligatures across my body, from my armpits to my thighs. I could only look upward; the sun began to grow hot, and the light offended my eyes.

I heard a confused noise about me; but, in the posture I lay, could see nothing except the sky. In a little time I felt something alive on my left leg, which, advancing gently forward over my breast, came almost up to my chin; when, bending my eyes downward as much as I could, I perceived it to be a human creature not six inches high, with a bow and arrow in his hands and a quiver at his back. In the meantime I felt at least forty more of the same kind (as I conjectured) following the first.

I was in the utmost astonishment, and roared so loud that they all ran back in a fright; and some of them, as I was afterwards told, were hurt with the falls they got by leaping from my sides upon the ground. However, they soon returned, and one of them who ventured so far as to get a full sight of my face, lifting up his hands and eyes by way of admiration, cried out in a shrill but distinct voice—*Hekinah degul!* The others repeated the same words several times, but I then knew not what they meant.

I lay all this while, as the reader may believe, in great uneasiness. At length, struggling to get loose, I had the fortune to break the strings and wrench out the pegs that fastened my left arm to the ground; for by lifting it up to my face, I discovered the methods they had taken to bind me, and at the same time, with a violent pull which gave me excessive pain, I a little loosened the strings that tied down my hair on the left side, so that I was just able to turn my head about two inches.

But the creatures ran off a second time, befor I could seize them; whereupon there was a great shout in a very shrill accent, and after it ceased I heard one of them cry aloud, *Tolgo phonac;* when, in an instant, I felt above an hundred arrows discharged on my left hand, which pricked me like so many needles; and besides, they shot another flight into the air, as we do bombs in Europe, whereof many, I suppose, fell on my body (though I felt them not) and some on my face, which I immediately covered with my left hand.

When this shower of arrows was over I fell a-groaning with grief and pain, and then striving again to get loose, they discharged another volley larger than the first, and some of them attempted with spears to stick me in the sides; but by good luck I had on me a buff jerkin,[1] which they could not pierce. I thought it the most prudent method to lie still, and my design was to continue so till night when, my left hand being already loose, I could easily free myself; and as for the inhabitants, I had reason to believe I might be a match for the greatest armies they could bring against me, if they were all of the same size with him that I saw.

But fortune disposed otherwise of me. When the people observed I was quiet, they discharged no more arrows; but by the noise I heard, I knew their numbers increased; and about four yards from me, over against my right ear, I heard a knocking for above an hour, like that of people at work; when, turning my head that way as well as the pegs and strings would permit me, I saw a stage erected about a foot and a half from the ground, capable of holding four of the inhabitants, with two or three ladders to mount it; from whence one of them, who seemed to be a person of quality, made me a long speech, whereof I understood not one syllable.

But I should have mentioned that before the principal person began his oration, he cried out three times, *Langro dehul san* (these words, and the former, were afterwards repeated and explained to me). Whereupon immediately about fifty of the inhabitants came and cut the strings that fastened the left side of my head, which gave me the liberty of turning it to the right and of observing the person and gesture of him that was to speak. He appeared to be of a middle age, and taller than any of the other three who attended him, whereof one was a page that held up his train, and seemed to be somewhat longer than my middle finger; the other two stood one on each side to support him. He acted every part of an orator, and I could observe many periods[2] of threatenings and others of promises, pity, and kindness.

I answered in a few words, but in the most submissive manner, lifting up my left hand and both my eyes to the sun, as calling him for a witness; and being almost famished with hunger, having not eaten a morsel for some

[1] leather waistcoat [2] sentences

hours before I left the ship, I found the demands of nature so strong upon me that I could not forbear showing my impatience (perhaps against the strict rules of decency) by putting my finger frequently to my mouth to signify that I wanted food. The *hurgo* (for so they call a great lord, as I afterwards learned) understood me very well. He descended from the stage, and commanded that several ladders should be applied to my sides; on which above an hundred of the inhabitants mounted, and walked toward my mouth, laden with baskets full of meat which had been provided and sent thither by the king's orders, upon the first intelligence he received of me.

I observed there was the flesh of several animals, but could not distinguish them by the taste. There were shoulders, legs, and loins shaped like those of mutton, and very well dressed, but smaller than the wings of a lark. I ate them by two or three at a mouthful, and took three loaves at a time, about the bigness of musket bullets. They supplied me as they could, showing a thousand marks of wonder and astonishment at my bulk and appetite. I then made another sign that I wanted drink.

They found by my eating that a small quantity would not suffice me; and being a most ingenious people they slung up, with great dexterity, one of their largest hogsheads, then rolled it toward my hand, and beat out the top. I drank it off at a draft; which I might well do, for it did not hold half a pint, and tasted like a small[1] wine of Burgundy, but much more delicious. They brought me a second hogshead, which I drank in the same manner, and made signs for more; but they had none to give me.

When I had performed these wonders, they shouted for joy and danced upon my breast, repeating, several times, as they did at first, *Hekinah degul.* They made me a sign that I should throw down the two hogsheads, but first warning the people below to stand out of the way, crying aloud, *Borach mivola;* and when they saw the vessels in the air, there was an universal shout of *Hekinah degul.*

I confess I was often tempted, while they were passing backward and forward on my body, to seize forty or fifty of the first that came in my reach and dash them against the ground. But the remembrance of what I had felt, which probably might not be the worst they could do, and the promise of honor I made them—for so I interpreted my submissive behavior—soon drove out these imaginations. Besides, I now considered myself as bound by the laws of hospitality to a people who had treated me with so much expense and magnificence. However, in my thoughts I could not sufficiently wonder at the intrepidity of these diminutive mortals who durst venture to mount and walk upon my body while one of my hands was at liberty, without trembling at the very sight of so prodigious a creature as I must appear to them.

After some time, when they observed that I made no more demands for meat, there appeared before me a person of high rank from his imperial majesty. His excellency, having mounted on the small of my right leg, advanced forward up to my face, with about a dozen of his retinue; and, producing his credentials under the signet-royal, which he applied close to my eyes, spoke about ten minutes, without any signs of anger but with a kind of determinate resolution, often pointing forward, which, as I afterwards found, was toward the capital city, about half a mile distant, whither it was agreed by his majesty in council that I must be conveyed. I answered in a few words, but to no purpose, and made a sign with my hand that was loose, putting it to the other (but over his excellency's head, for fear of hurting him or his train) and then to my own head and body, to signify that I desired my liberty.

It appeared that he understood me well enough, for he shook his head by way of disapprobation, and held his hands in a posture to show that I must be carried as a prisoner. However, he made other signs to let me understand that I should have meat and drink enough, and very good treatment. Whereupon I once more thought of attempting to break my bonds; but again, when I felt the smart of their arrows upon my face and hands, which were all in blisters and many of the darts still sticking in them, and observing, likewise, that the number of my enemies increased, I gave tokens to let them know that they might do with me what they pleased. Upon this the *hurgo* and his train withdrew with much civility, and cheerful countenances.

Soon after, I heard a general shout, with frequent repetitions of the words, *Peplom selan,* and I felt great numbers of people on my left side relaxing the cords to such a degree that I was able to turn upon my right, and so get a little ease. But, before this, they had daubed my face and both my hands with a sort of ointment, very pleasant to the smell, which, in a few minutes, removed all the smart

[1] weak

of their arrows. These circumstances, added to the refreshment I had received by their victuals and drink, which were very nourishing, disposed me to sleep. I slept about eight hours, as I was afterwards assured; and it was no wonder, for the physicians, by the emperor's order, had mingled a sleepy potion in the hogsheads of wine.

It seems that upon the first moment I was discovered sleeping on the ground, after my landing, the emperor had early notice of it by an express; and determined in council that I should be tied in the manner I have related (which was done in the night, while I slept), that plenty of meat and drink should be sent to me, and a machine prepared to carry me to the capital city.

This resolution, perhaps, may appear very bold and dangerous, and I am confident would not be imitated by any prince in Europe on the like occasion. However, in my opinion it was extremely prudent, as well as generous; for, supposing these people had endeavored to kill me with their spears and arrows while I was asleep, I should certainly have awaked with the first sense of smart, which might so far have roused my rage and strength as to have enabled me to break the strings wherewith I was tied; after which, as they were not able to make resistance, so they could expect no mercy.

These people are most excellent mathematicians, and arrived to a great perfection in mechanics, by the countenance and encouragement of the emperor, who is a renowned patron of learning. This prince hath several machines fixed on wheels for the carriage of trees and other great weights. He often builds his largest men-of-war, whereof some are nine foot long, in the woods where the timber grows, and has them carried on these engines three or four hundred yards to the sea.[1] Five hundred carpenters and engineers were immediately set at work to prepare the greatest engine they had. It was a frame of wood raised three inches from the ground, about seven feet long and four wide, moving upon twenty-two wheels. The shout I heard was upon the arrival of this engine, which, it seems, set out in four hours after my landing. It was brought parallel to me as I lay. But the principal difficulty was to raise and place me in this vehicle.

Eighty poles, each of one foot high, were erected for this purpose, and very strong cords, of the bigness of packthread, were fastened by hooks to many bandages which the workmen had girt round my neck, my hands, my body, and my legs. Nine hundred of the strongest men were employed to draw up these cords by many pulleys fastened on the poles; thus in less than three hours I was raised and slung into the engine, and there tied fast.

All this I was told; for while the whole operation was performing I lay in a profound sleep, by the force of that soporiferous medicine infused into my liquor. Fifteen hundred of the emperor's largest horses, each about four inches and a half high, were employed to draw me toward the metropolis, which, as I said, was half a mile distant.

About four hours after we began our journey I awaked, by a very ridiculous accident; for the carriage being stopped a while to adjust something that was out of order, two or three of the young natives had the curiosity to see how I looked when I was asleep. They climbed up into the engine, and advancing very softly to my face, one of them, an officer in the guards, put the sharp end of his half-pike a good way up into my left nostril, which tickled my nose like a straw and made me sneeze violently; whereupon they stole off, unperceived, and it was three weeks before I knew the cause of my awaking so suddenly.

We made a long march the remaining part of that day, and rested at night with five hundred guards on each side of me, half with torches and half with bows and arrows ready to shoot me if I should offer to stir. The next morning, at sunrise, we continued our march, and arrived within two hundred yards of the city gates about noon. The emperor and all his court came out to meet us; but his great officers would by no means suffer his majesty to endanger his person by mounting on my body.

At the place where the carriage stopped there stood an ancient temple, esteemed to be the largest in the whole kingdom; which, having been polluted some years before by an unnatural murder, was, according to the zeal of those people, looked upon as profane, and therefore had been applied to common use, and all the ornaments and furniture carried away. In this edifice it was determined I should lodge. The great gate, fronting to the north, was about four feet high and almost two feet wide, through which I could easily creep. On each side of the gate was a small window not above six inches from the ground; into that on the left side the king's smith conveyed four

[1] Swift has been admired for the correctness of his figures. Compare the length of these men-of-war with the height of the Lilliputians.

score and eleven chains, like those that hang to a lady's watch in Europe and almost as large, which were locked to my left leg with six-and-thirty padlocks.

Over against this temple, on the other side of the great highway, at twenty feet distance, there was a turret at least five feet high. Here the emperor ascended, with many principal lords of his court, to have an opportunity of viewing me, as I was told, for I could not see them. It was reckoned that above an hundred thousand inhabitants came out of the town upon the same errand; and in spite of my guards, I believe there could not be fewer than ten thousand, at several times, who mounted my body by the help of ladders. But a proclamation was soon issued to forbid it upon pain of death.

When the workmen found it was impossible for me to break loose they cut all the strings that bound me; whereupon I rose up, with as melancholy a disposition as ever I had in my life. But the noise and astonishment of the people at seeing me rise and walk, are not to be expressed. The chains that held my left leg were about two yards long, and gave me not only the liberty of walking backward and forward in a semicircle but, being fixed within four inches of the gate, allowed me to creep in and lie at my full length in the temple.

Chapter II

When I found myself on my feet I looked about me, and must confess I never beheld a more entertaining prospect. The country around appeared like a continued garden, and the enclosed fields, which were generally forty foot square, resembled so many beds of flowers. These fields were intermingled with woods of half a stang,[1] and the tallest trees, as I could judge, appeared to be seven foot high. I viewed the town on my left hand, which looked like the painted scene of a city in a theater.

. . . .

The emperor was already descended from the tower and advancing on horseback toward me, which had like to have cost him dear; for the beast, though very well trained, yet wholly unused to such a sight, which appeared as if a mountain moved before him, reared up on his hinder feet. But that prince, who is an excellent horseman, kept his seat till his attendants ran in and held the bridle while his majesty had time to dismount.

When he alighted he surveyed me round with great admiration, but kept without the length of my chain. He ordered his cooks and butlers, who were already prepared, to give me victuals and drink, which they pushed forward in a sort of vehicles upon wheels till I could reach them. I took these vehicles, and soon emptied them all; twenty of them were filled with meat and ten with liquor; each of the former afforded me two or three good mouthfuls; and I emptied the liquor of ten vessels, which was contained in earthen vials, into one vehicle, drinking it off at a draft; and so I did with the rest. The empress and young princes of the blood of both sexes, attended by many ladies, sat at some distance in their chairs;[2] but upon the accident that happened to the emperor's horse they alighted, and came near his person, which I am now going to describe. He is taller by almost the breadth of my nail than any of his court, which alone is enough to strike an awe into the beholders. His features are strong and masculine, with an Austrian lip and arched nose, his complexion olive, his countenance erect, his body and limbs well proportioned, all his motions graceful, and his deportment majestic. He was then past his prime, being twenty-eight years and three-quarters old, of which he had reigned about seven in great felicity, and generally victorious. For the better convenience of beholding him I lay on my side, so that my face was parallel to his, and he stood but three yards off. However, I have had him, since, many times in my hand, and therefore cannot be deceived in the description.

His dress was very plain and simple, and the fashion of it between the Asiatic and the European; but he had on his head a light helmet of gold, adorned with jewels and a plume on the crest. He held his sword drawn in his hand, to defend himself if I should happen to break loose; it was almost three inches long; the hilt and scabbard were gold enriched with diamonds. His voice was shrill, but very clear and articulate, and I could distinctly hear it when I stood up.

The ladies and courtiers were all most magnificently clad; so that the spot they stood upon seemed to resemble a petticoat spread on the ground, embroidered with figures of gold and silver. His imperial majesty spoke often to me, and I returned answers, but neither of us could understand a syllable. There were several of his priests and lawyers present (as I conjectured by their habits[3]), who were

[1] half a rood (one-eighth of an acre)

[2] sedan-chairs

[3] costumes

commanded to address themselves to me; and I spoke to them in as many languages as I had the least smattering of, which were High and Low Dutch, Latin, French, Spanish, Italian, and Lingua Franca; [1] but all to no purpose.

After about two hours the court retired, and I was left with a strong guard to prevent the impertinence and probably the malice of the rabble, who were very impatient to crowd about me as near as they durst; and some of them had the impudence to shoot their arrows at me as I sat on the ground by the door of my house, whereof one very narrowly missed my left eye. But the colonel ordered six of the ring-leaders to be seized, and thought no punishment so proper as to deliver them bound into my hands; which some of his soldiers accordingly did, pushing them forward with the butt-ends of their pikes into my reach. I took them all in my right hand, put five of them into my coat-pocket; and as to the sixth, I made a countenance as if I would eat him alive. The poor man squalled terribly, and the colonel and his officers were in much pain, especially when they saw me take out my penknife; but I soon put them out of fear, for, looking mildly, and immediately cutting the strings he was bound with, I set him gently on the ground, and away he ran. I treated the rest in the same manner, taking them one by one out of my pocket; and I observed both the soldiers and people were highly obliged at this mark of my clemency, which was represented very much to my advantage at court.

Toward night I got with some difficulty into my house, where I lay on the ground, and continued to do so about a fortnight, during which time the emperor gave orders to have a bed prepared for me. Six hundred beds of the common measure were brought in carriages and worked up in my house; an hundred and fifty of their beds, sewn together, made up the breadth and length; and these were four double, which, however, kept me but very indifferently from the hardness of the floor, that was of smooth stone. By the same computation they provided me with sheets, blankets, and coverlets, tolerable enough for one who had been so long inured to hardships as I.

As the news of my arrival spread through the kingdom, it brought prodigious numbers of rich, idle, and curious people to see me; so that the villages were almost emptied; and great neglect of tillage and household affairs must have ensued if his imperial majesty had not provided, by several proclamations and orders of state, against this inconveniency. He directed that those who had already beheld me should return home, and not presume to come within fifty yards of my house without license from court; whereby the secretaries of state got considerable fees.

In the meantime the emperor held frequent councils to debate what course should be taken with me; and I was afterwards assured by a particular friend, a person of great quality, who was looked upon to be as much in the secret as any, that the court was under many difficulties concerning me. They apprehended my breaking loose; that my diet would be very expensive, and might cause a famine. Sometimes they determined to starve me, or at least to shoot me in the face and hands with poisoned arrows, which would soon dispatch me; but again they considered that the stench of so large a carcass might produce a plague in the metropolis, and probably spread through the whole kingdom.

In the midst of these consultations several officers of the army went to the door of the great council-chamber and, two of them being admitted, gave an account of my behavior to the six criminals above-mentioned, which made so favorable an impression in the breast of his majesty and the whole board in my behalf, that an imperial commission was issued out, obliging all the villages nine hundred yards round the city to deliver in, every morning, six beeves, forty sheep, and other victuals for my sustenance; together with a proportionable quantity of bread and wine, and other liquors; for the due payment of which his majesty gave assignments upon his treasury. For this prince lives chiefly upon his own demesnes, [2] seldom, except upon great occasions, raising any subsidies upon his subjects, who are bound to attend him in his wars at their own expense. An establishment was also made of six hundred persons to be my domestics, who had board-wages allowed for their maintenance, and tents built for them very conveniently on each side of my door.

It was likewise ordered that three hundred tailors should make me a suit of clothes, after the fashion of the country; that six of his majesty's greatest scholars should be employed to instruct me in their language; and, lastly, that the emperor's horses, and those of the nobility and troops of guards, should be frequently exercised in my sight, to accustom themselves to me.

[1] a commercial jargon compounded then chiefly of Italian and Oriental languages

[2] income

All these orders were duly put in execution, and in about three weeks I made a great progress in learning their language; during which time the emperor frequently honored me with his visits, and was pleased to assist my masters in teaching me. We began already to converse together in some sort; and the first words I learnt were to express my desire that he would please to give me liberty, which I every day repeated on my knees. His answer, as I could apprehend it, was that this must be a work of time, not to be thought on without the advice of his council, and that first I must *lumos kelmin pesso desmar lon emposo;* that is, swear a peace with him and his kingdom; however, that I should be used with all kindness; and he advised me to acquire by my patience and discreet behavior, the good opinion of himself and his subjects.

He desired I would not take it ill if he gave orders to certain proper officers to search me; for probably I might carry about me several weapons which must needs be dangerous things if they answered the bulk of so prodigious a person. I said his majesty should be satisfied, for I was ready to strip myself and turn up my pockets before him. This I delivered, part in words and part in signs.

He replied that by the laws of the kingdom I must be searched by two of his officers; that he knew this could not be done without my consent and assistance; that he had so good an opinion of my generosity and justice as to trust their persons in my hands; that whatever they took from me should be returned when I left the country, or paid for at the rate which I should set upon them. I took up the two officers in my hands, put them first into my coat-pockets, and then into every other pocket about me except my two fobs and another secret pocket I had no mind should be searched, wherein I had some little necessaries that were of no consequence to any but myself. In one of my fobs there was a silver watch, and in the other a small quantity of gold in a purse.

These gentlemen, having pen, ink, and paper about them, made an exact inventory of everything they saw; and when they had done, desired I would set them down that they might deliver it to the emperor. This inventory I afterwards translated into English, and is word for word as follows: [1]

Imprimis, [2] In the right coat-pocket of the great man-mountain (for so I interpret the words *quinbus flestrin*), after the strictest search, we found only one great piece of coarse cloth, large enough to be a foot-cloth for your majesty's chief room of state. In the left pocket we saw a huge silver chest, with a cover of the same metal, which we the searchers were not able to lift. We desired it should be opened, and one of us stepping into it found himself up to the mid-leg in a sort of dust, some part whereof flying up to our faces set us both a-sneezing for several times together. In his right waistcoat pocket we found a prodigious bundle of white thin substances folded one over another, about the bigness of three men, tied with a strong cable, and marked with black figures; which we humbly conceive to be writings, every letter almost half as large as the palm of our hands. In the left there was a sort of engine, from the back of which were extended twenty long poles resembling the palisadoes before your majesty's court; wherewith we conjecture the man-mountain combs his head, for we did not always trouble him with questions because we found it a great difficulty to make him understand us. In the large pocket on the right side of his middle cover (so I translate the word *ranfu-lo,* by which they meant my breeches) we saw a hollow pillar of iron, about the length of a man, fastened to a strong piece of timber larger than the pillar; and upon one side of the pillar were huge pieces of iron sticking out, cut into strange figures, which we know not what to make of. In the left pocket, another engine of the same kind. In the smaller pocket on the right side were several round flat pieces of white and red metal, of different bulk; some of the white, which seemed to be silver, were so large and heavy that my comrade and I could hardly lift them. In the left pocket were two black pillars irregularly shaped; we could not without difficulty reach the top of them as we stood at the bottom of his pocket. One of them was covered, and seemed all of a piece; but at the upper end of the other there appeared a white round substance about twice the bigness of our heads. Within each of these was enclosed a prodigious plate of steel which, by our orders, we obliged him to show us because we apprehended they might be dangerous engines. He took them out of their cases, and told us that in his own country his practice was to shave his beard with one of these, and to cut his meat with the other. There were two pockets which we could not enter; these he called his fobs. Out of the right fob hung

[1] This report may possibly satirize the reports of the Committees of Secrecy (of which Walpole was head) organized to unearth Jacobite plots.

[2] first

a great silver chain, with a wonderful kind of engine at the bottom. We directed him to draw out whatever was fastened to that chain, which appeared to be a globe, half silver and half of some transparent metal; for on the transparent side we saw certain strange figures, circularly drawn, and thought we could touch them till we found our fingers stopped by that lucid substance. He put this engine to our ears, which made an incessant noise like that of a water-mill; and we conjecture it is either some unknown animal, or the god that he worships; but we are more inclined to the latter opinion because he assured us (if we understood him right, for he expressed himself very imperfectly) that he seldom did anything without consulting it. He called it his oracle, and said it pointed out the time for every action of his life. From the left fob he took out a net almost large enough for a fisherman, but contrived to open and shut like a purse, and served him for the same use; we found therein several massy pieces of yellow metal which, if they be real gold, must be of immense value.

Having thus, in obedience to your majesty's commands, diligently searched all his pockets, we observed a girdle about his waist made of the hide of some prodigious animal, from which, on the left side, hung a sword of the length of five men; and on the right, a bag, or pouch, divided into two cells, each cell capable of holding three of your majesty's subjects. In one of these cells were several globes, or balls, of a most ponderous metal, about the bigness of our heads, and required a strong hand to lift them; the other cell contained a heap of certain black grains, but of no great bulk or weight, for we could hold about fifty of them in the palms of our hands.

This is an exact inventory of what we found about the body of the man-mountain, who used us with great civility and due respect to your majesty's commission. Signed and sealed, on the fourth day of the eighty-ninth moon of your majesty's auspicious reign.

Clefren Freloc
Marsi Freloc

When this inventory was read over to the emperor he directed me, although in very gentle terms, to deliver up the several particulars.

He first called for my scimitar, which I took out, scabbard and all. In the meantime he ordered three thousand of his choicest troops (who then attended him) to surround me at a distance, with their bows and arrows just ready to discharge; but I did not observe it, for mine eyes were wholly fixed upon his majesty. He then desired me to draw my scimitar, which, although it had got some rust by the sea-water, was in most parts exceeding bright. I did so, and immediately all the troops gave a shout between terror and surprise; for the sun shone clear, and the reflection dazzled their eyes as I waved the scimitar to and fro in my hand. His majesty, who is a most magnanimous prince, was less daunted than I could expect; he ordered me to return it into the scabbard and cast it on the ground, as gently as I could, about six foot from the end of my chain.

The next thing he demanded was one of the hollow iron pillars, by which he meant my pocket-pistols. I drew it out, and at his desire, as well as I could, expressed to him the use of it; and charging it only with powder, which, by the closeness of my pouch, happened to escape wetting in the sea (an inconvenience against which all prudent mariners take special care to provide), I first cautioned the emperor not to be afraid, and then I let it off in the air.

The astonishment here was much greater than at the sight of my scimitar. Hundreds fell down as if they had been struck dead; and even the emperor, although he stood his ground, could not recover himself in some time.

I delivered up both my pistols in the same manner as I had done my scimitar, and then my pouch of powder and bullets, begging him that the former might be kept from the fire, for it would kindle with the smallest spark, and blow up his imperial palace into the air.

I likewise delivered up my watch, which the emperor was very curious to see, and commanded two of his tallest yeomen of the guards to bear it on a pole upon their shoulders, as draymen in England do a barrel of ale. He was amazed at the continual noise it made and the motion of the minutehand, which he could easily discern (for their sight is much more acute than ours), and asked the opinions of his learned men about it, which were various and remote, as the reader may well imagine without my repeating; although, indeed, I could not very perfectly understand them.

I then gave up my silver and copper money, my purse with nine large pieces of gold and some smaller ones; my knife and razor, my comb and silver snuff-box, my handkerchief and journal-book. My scimitar, pistols, and pouch were conveyed in carriages to his majesty's stores; but the rest of my goods were returned to me.

I had, as I before observed, one private pocket which escaped their search, wherein there was a pair of spectacles (which I sometimes use for the weakness of mine eyes), a pocket perspective,[1] and several other little conveniences; which being of no consequence to the emperor, I did not think myself bound in honor to discover; and I apprehended they might be lost or spoiled if I ventured them out of my possession.

Chapter III

My gentleness and good behavior had gained so far on the emperor and his court, and indeed upon the army and people in general, that I began to conceive hopes of getting my liberty in a short time. I took all possible methods to cultivate this favorable disposition. The natives came by degrees to be less apprehensive of any danger from me. I would sometimes lie down and let five or six of them dance on my hand; and at last the boys and girls would venture to come and play at hide-and-seek in my hair. I had now made a good progress in understanding and speaking their language.

The emperor had a mind, one day, to entertain me with several of the country shows, wherein they exceed all nations I have known, both for dexterity and magnificence. I was diverted with none so much as that of the rope-dancers, performed upon a slender white thread, extended about two feet, and twelve inches from the ground. Upon which I shall desire liberty, with the reader's patience, to enlarge a little.

This diversion is only practiced by those persons who are candidates for great employments and high favor at court. They are trained in this art from their youth, and are not always of noble birth or liberal education. When a great office is vacant, either by death or disgrace (which often happens), five or six of those candidates petition the emperor to entertain his majesty and the court with a dance on the rope; and whoever jumps the highest, without falling, succeeds in the office. Very often the chief ministers themselves are commanded to show their skill, and to convince the emperor that they have not lost their faculty. Flimnap,[2] the treasurer, is allowed to cut a caper on the strait rope, at least an inch higher than any other lord in the whole empire. I have seen him do the somersault several times together upon a trencher, fixed on a rope which is no thicker than a common packthread in England. My friend Reldresal, principal secretary for private affairs, is, in my opinion, if I am not partial, the second after the treasurer; the rest of the great officers are much upon a par.

These diversions are often attended with fatal accidents, whereof great numbers are on record. I myself have seen two or three candidates break a limb. But the danger is much greater when the ministers themselves are commanded to show their dexterity; for, by contending to excel themselves and their fellows, they strain so far that there is hardly one of them who hath not received a fall, and some of them two or three. I was assured that a year or two before my arrival, Flimnap would have infallibly broke[3] his neck if one of the king's cushions, that accidently lay on the ground, had not weakened the force of his fall.[4]

There is likewise another diversion, which is only shown before the emperor and empress and first minister upon particular occasions. The emperor lays on the table three fine silken threads, of six inches long; one is purple, the other yellow, and the third white.[5] These threads are proposed as prizes for those persons whom the emperor hath a mind to distinguish by a peculiar mark of his favor. The ceremony is performed in his majesty's great chamber of state, where the candidates are to undergo a trial of dexterity very different from the former, and such as I have not observed the least resemblance of in any other country of the old or the new world.

The emperor holds a stick in his hands, both ends parallel to the horizon, while the candidates, advancing one by one, sometimes leap over the stick, sometimes creep under it backward and forward several times, according as the stick is advanced or depressed. Sometimes the emperor holds one end of the stick, and his first minister the other; sometimes the minister has it entirely to himself. Whoever performs his part with most agility and holds out the longest in leaping and creeping is rewarded

[1] telescope

[2] Flimnap stands for Sir Robert Walpole, at that time Lord of the Treasury, who, when Swift was a Whig—before 1710—had failed to aid Swift to gain promotion.

[3] The preterit form for the participle was freely used in the eighteenth century. Note also p. 369, l. 17, r., "these kind of feats."

[4] In 1717 Walpole was dismissed from office, but was probably saved from disastrous consequences through the influence of the Duchess of Kendal, favorite of George I.

[5] In some editions these colors are given as blue, red, and green, the colors of the badges of the Orders of the Garter, Bath, and Thistle. The second named order, says Walpole's biographer, William Coxe, was revived by Walpole as "a cheap means of gratifying his political adherents."

with the purple colored silk; the yellow is given to the next, and the white to the third, which they all wear girt twice round about the middle; and you see few great persons about this court who are not adorned with one of these girdles.

The horses of the army and those of the royal stables having been daily led before me, were no longer shy, but would come up to my very feet without starting. The riders would leap them over my hand as I held it on the ground; and one of the emperor's huntsmen, upon a large courser, took my foot, shoe and all, which was indeed a prodigious leap.

I had the good fortune to divert the emperor one day after a very extraordinary manner. I desired he would order several sticks of two feet high, and the thickness of an ordinary cane, to be brought me; whereupon his majesty commanded the master of his woods to give directions accordingly; and the next morning six woodmen arrived with as many carriages, drawn by eight horses to each.

I took nine of these sticks, and fixing them firmly in the ground in a quadrangular figure, two foot and a half square, I took four other sticks and tied them parallel at each corner, about two foot from the ground; then I fastened my handkerchief to the nine sticks that stood erect, and extended it on all sides, till it was as tight as the top of a drum; and the four parallel sticks, rising about five inches higher than the handkerchief, served as ledges on each side.

When I had finished my work I desired the emperor to let a troop of his best horse, twenty-four in number, come and exercise upon this plain. His majesty approved of the proposal, and I took them up one by one in my hands, ready mounted and armed, with the proper officers to exercise them. As soon as they got into order they divided into two parties, performed mock skirmishes, discharged blunt arrows, drew their swords, fled and pursued, attacked and retired, and, in short, discovered the best military discipline I ever beheld. The parallel sticks secured them and their horses from falling over the stage; and the emperor was so much delighted that he ordered this entertainment to be repeated several days, and once was pleased to be lifted up and give the word of command; and, with great difficulty, persuaded even the empress herself to let me hold her in her close chair within two yards of the stage, from whence she was able to take a full view of the whole performance.

It was my good fortune that no ill accident happened in these entertainments; only once a fiery horse that belonged to one of the captains, pawing with his hoof, struck a hole in my handkerchief, and his foot slipping he overthrew his rider and himself; but I immediately relieved them both, and covering the hole with one hand, I set down the troop with the other in the same manner as I took them up. The horse that fell was strained in the left shoulder, but the rider got no hurt, and I repaired my handkerchief as well as I could; however, I would not trust to the strength of it any more in such dangerous enterprises.

About two or three days before I was set at liberty, as I was entertaining the court with these kind of feats, there arrived an express to inform his majesty that some of his subjects, riding near the place where I was first taken up, had seen a great black substance lying on the ground, very oddly shaped, extending its edges round as wide as his majesty's bedchamber, and rising up in the middle as high as a man; that it was no living creature, as they at first apprehended, for it lay on the grass without motion; and some of them had walked round it several times; that by mounting upon each other's shoulders they had got to the top, which was flat and even, and, stamping upon it, they found it was hollow within; that they humbly conceived it might be something belonging to the man-mountain; and if his majesty pleased, they would undertake to bring it with only five horses.

I presently knew what they meant, and was glad at heart to receive this intelligence. It seems upon my first reaching the shore after our shipwreck, I was in such confusion that before I came to the place where I went to sleep, my hat, which I had fastened with a string to my head while I was rowing, and had stuck on all the time I was swimming, fell off after I came to land; the string, as I conjecture, breaking by some accident which I never observed, but thought my hat had been lost at sea. I entreated his imperial majesty to give orders it might be brought to me as soon as possible, describing to him the use and nature of it; and the next day the wagoners arrived with it, but not in a very good condition; they had bored two holes in the brim within an inch and a half of the edge, and fastened two hooks in the holes; these hooks were tied by a long cord to the harness, and thus my hat was dragged along for above half an English mile; but the ground in that country being extremely smooth and level, it received less damage than I expected.

Two days after this adventure the emperor, having ordered that part of the army which quarters in and about his metropolis to be in readiness, took a fancy of diverting himself in a very singular manner.[1] He desired I would stand like a colossus, with my legs as far asunder as I conveniently could. He then commanded his general (who was an old, experienced leader and a great patron of mine) to draw up the troops in close order and march them under me; the foot by twenty-four in a breast and the horse by sixteen, with drums beating, colors flying, and pikes advanced. This body consisted of three thousand foot and a thousand horse.

. . . .

I had sent so many memorials and petitions for my liberty that his majesty at length mentioned the matter, first in the cabinet, and then in a full council; where it was opposed by none except Skyresh Bolgolam, who was pleased, without any provocation, to be my mortal enemy. But it was carried against him by the whole board, and confirmed by the emperor. That minister was *galbet,* or admiral of the realm, very much in his master's confidence, and a person well versed in affairs but of a morose and sour complexion. However, he was at length persuaded to comply; but prevailed that the articles and conditions upon which I should be set free, and to which I must swear, should be drawn up by himself.

These articles were brought to me by Skyresh Bolgolam in person, attended by two under-secretaries and several persons of distinction. After they were read I was demanded to swear to the performance of them, first in the manner of my own country, and afterwards in the method prescribed by their laws; which was to hold my right foot in my left hand, and to place the middle finger of my right hand on the crown of my head, and my thumb on the tip of my right ear.

But because the reader may be curious to have some idea of the style and manner of expression peculiar to that people, as well as to know the articles upon which I recovered my liberty, I have made a translation of the whole instrument, word for word, as near as I was able, which I here offer to the public.

Golbasto Momaren Evlame Gurdilo Shefin Mully Ully Gue, most mighty Emperor of Lilliput, delight and terror of the universe, whose dominions extend five thousand *blustrugs* (about twelve miles in circumference) to the extremities of the globe; monarch of all monarchs, taller than the sons of men; whose feet press down to the center, and whose head strikes against the sun; at whose nod the princes of the earth shake their knees; pleasant as the spring, comfortable as the summer, fruitful as autumn, dreadful as winter. His most sublime Majesty proposeth to the Man-mountain, lately arrived to our celestial dominions, the following articles, which by a solemn oath he shall be obliged to perform.

First. The Man-mountain shall not depart from our dominions without our license under our great seal.

2d. He shall not presume to come into our metropolis without our express order; at which time the inhabitants shall have two hours' warning to keep within their doors.

3d. The said Man-mountain shall confine his walks to our principal high roads, and not to walk or lie down in a meadow or field of corn.

4th. As he walks the said roads, he shall take the utmost care not to trample upon the bodies of any of our loving subjects, their horses or carriages, nor take any of our said subjects into his hands without their own consent.

5th. If an express requires extraordinary dispatch, the Man-mountain shall be obliged to carry in his pocket the messenger and horse a six-days' journey once in every moon, and return the said messenger back (if so required) safe to our imperial presence.

6th. He shall be our ally against our enemies in the island of Blefuscu, and do his utmost to destroy their fleet which is now preparing to invade us.

7th. That the said Man-mountain shall at his times of leisure be aiding and assisting to our workmen in helping to raise certain great stones toward covering the wall of the principal park, and other our royal buildings.

8th. That the said Man-mountain shall, in two moons' time, deliver in an exact survey of the circumference of our dominions, by a computation of his own paces round the coast.

Lastly. That upon his solemn oath to observe all the above articles, the said Man-mountain shall have a daily allowance of meat and drink sufficient for the support of 1724 of our subjects, with free access to our royal person, and other marks of our favor. Given at our palace at Belfalorac the twelfth day of the ninety-first moon of our reign.

[1] George I was especially fond of reviews.

I swore and subscribed to these articles with great cheerfulness and content, although some of them were not as honorable as I could have wished; which proceeded wholly from the malice of Skyresh Bolgolam the high admiral. Whereupon my chains were immediately unlocked, and I was at full liberty; the Emperor himself in person did me the honor to be by at the whole ceremony. I made my acknowledgements by prostrating myself at his majesty's feet; but he commanded me to rise; and after many gracious expressions, which to avoid the censure of vanity I shall not repeat, he added that he hoped I should prove a useful servant, and well deserve all the favors he had already conferred upon me, or might do for the future.

The reader may please to observe that in the last article for the recovery of my liberty the emperor stipulates to allow me a quantity of meat and drink sufficient for the support of 1724 Lilliputians. Some time after, asking a friend at court how they came to fix on that determined number, he told me that his majesty's mathematicians having taken the height of my body by the help of a quadrant, and finding it to exceed theirs in the proportion of twelve to one, they concluded, from the similarity of their bodies, that mine must contain at least 1724 of theirs, and consequently would require as much food as was necessary to support that number of Lilliputians. By which the reader may conceive an idea of the ingenuity of that people, as well as the prudent and exact economy of so great a prince.

1726

JAMES THOMSON
1700-1748

While the "classic" vogue in English poetry was at its height, and during Pope's life, a new interest was rising in nature as a theme for poets. This appears notably in Thomson, often felt to be in this respect the forerunner of English romanticism. He was born in the Lowlands, son of a Scotch minister, spent four years at Edinburgh University, and then sought his fortune in London as a writer. He was of mild and affable disposition, made and held friendships among his helpful patrons, and lived a life of comfort in days when literature was not self-supporting. Among his friends were Pope, Lyttleton, and Shenstone.

The *Seasons,* beginning with "Winter," 1726, appeared in parts at intervals of about a year until 1730. The separate poems were immediately popular, were often reprinted, and some six editions of the whole work were published before Thomson died, the later editions being considerably enlarged. He was the author of several plays. It is significant that his work was chiefly in blank verse, a form that had been discarded since Milton; and that "The Castle of Indolence," a graceful poem written in the year he died, revived the Spenserian stanza, an essentially romantic form.

Joseph Warton, one of Thomson's earliest critics, said in 1756, "His descriptions have a distinctness and truth which are utterly wanting to those of poets who have only copied from each other and have never looked abroad on the objects themselves"; and one of his latest critics, G. C. Macaulay, 1908, says "he looked at nature with his own eyes and not through the medium of books, and he combined a singular keenness and accuracy of observation with the imagination of an artist."

Biographies: D. G. Tovey, in Aldine edition of Thomson's poems, 1897; G. C. Macaulay (EML), 1908. Criticism: Johnson, Rossetti, Hazlitt, More (Shel. 5).

From THE SEASONS [1]

SPRING

Come, gentle Spring, ethereal mildness, come;
And from the bosom of yon dropping cloud,
While music wakes around, veiled in a shower
Of shadowing roses, on our plains descend.
  O Hertford, fitted or to shine in courts
With unaffected grace, or walk the plain
With innocence and meditation joined
In soft assemblage, listen to my song,
Which thy own season paints; when nature all
Is blooming, and benevolent, like thee.
  And see where surly Winter passes off,
Far to the north, and calls his ruffian blasts.
His blasts obey, and quit the howling hill,
The shattered forest, and the ravaged vale;
While softer gales succeed, at whose kind touch,
Dissolving snows in livid torrents lost,
The mountains lift their green heads to the sky.
  As yet the trembling year is unconfirmed,
And winter oft at eve resumes the breeze,
Chills the pale morn, and bids his driving sleets
Deform the day delightless; so that scarce
The bittern knows his time, with bill ingulfed,
To shake the sounding marsh; or from the shore
The plovers when to scatter o'er the heath,
And sing their wild notes to the listening waste.
  At last from Aries rolls the bounteous sun, [2]

[1] Of the four sections of this poem, "Spring" was published last, in 1728; the Countess of Hertford, to whom it is dedicated, was a patroness of poetry whose interest in the author had been aroused by the publication of the preceding parts.

[2] passing from Aries, the first sign of the zodiac, to Taurus, the second (April 20)

And the bright Bull receives him. Then no more
The expansive atmosphere is cramped with cold;
But, full of life and vivifying soul,
Lifts the light clouds sublime, and spreads them thin,
Fleecy, and white, o'er all-surrounding Heaven.
Forth fly the tepid airs; and unconfined,
Unbinding earth, the moving softness strays.
Joyous the impatient husbandman perceives
Relenting Nature, and his lusty steers
Drives from their stalls, to where the well-used plow
Lies in the furrow, loosened from the frost.
There, unrefusing, to the harnessed yoke
They lend their shoulder, and begin their toil,
Cheered by the simple song and soaring lark.
Meanwhile incumbent o'er the shining share [1]
The Master leans, removes the obstructing clay,
Winds [2] the whole work, and sidelong lays the glebe.
White, through the neighboring fields the sower stalks,
With measured step; and, liberal, throws the grain
Into the faithful bosom of the ground;
The harrow follows harsh, and shuts the scene.
Be gracious, Heaven! for now laborious man
Has done his part. Ye fostering breezes, blow!
Ye softening dews, ye tender showers descend!
And temper all, thou world-reviving sun,
Into the perfect year! Nor ye who live
In luxury and ease, in pomp and pride,
Think these last themes unworthy of your ear:
Such themes as these the rural Maro [3] sung
To wide-imperial Rome, in the full height
Of elegance and taste, by Greece refined.
In ancient times the sacred plow employed
The kings and awful fathers of mankind;
And some, [4] with whom compared your insect tribes
Are but the beings of a summer's day,
Have held the scale of empire, ruled the storm
Of mighty war; then, with victorious hand,
Disdaining little delicacies, seized
The plow, and, greatly independent, scorned
All the vile stores corruption can bestow.

. . . .

As rising from the vegetable world
My theme ascends, with equal wing ascend,
My panting Muse; and hark, how loud the woods
Invite you forth in all your gayest trim.
Lend me your song, ye nightingales! O pour
The mazy-running soul of melody
Into my varied verse! while I deduce
From the first note the hollow cuckoo sings,
The symphony of spring, and touch a theme
Unknown to fame—the passion of the groves.
When first the soul of Love is sent abroad,
Warm through the vital air, and on the heart
Harmonious seizes, the gay troops begin,
In gallant thought, to plume the painted wing;
And try again the long-forgotten strain,
At first faint-warbled. But no sooner grows
The soft infusion prevalent and wide,
Than, all alive, at once their joy o'erflows
In music unconfined. Up-springs the lark,
Shrill-voiced and loud, the messenger of morn.
Ere yet the shadows fly, he mounted sings
Amid the dawning clouds, and from their haunts
Calls up the tuneful nations. Every copse
Deep-tangled, tree irregular, and bush
Bending with dewy moisture o'er the heads
Of the coy quiristers [5] that lodge within,
Are prodigal of harmony. The thrush
And wood-lark, o'er the kind-contending throng
Superior heard, run through the sweetest length
Of notes; when listening Philomela [6] deigns
To let them joy, and purposes, in thought
Elate, to make her night excel their day.
The black-bird whistles from the thorny brake;
The mellow bull-finch answers from the grove;
Nor are the linnets, o'er the flowering furze
Poured out [7] profusely, silent. Joined to these,
Innumerous [8] songsters, in the freshening shade
Of new-sprung leaves, their modulations mix
Mellifluous. The jay, the rook, the daw,
And each harsh pipe, discordant heard alone,
Aid the full concert; while the stock-dove breathes
A melancholy murmur through the whole.
'Tis Love creates their melody, and all
This waste of music is the voice of Love.

. . . .

1728

From THE CASTLE OF INDOLENCE [9]

1

O mortal man, who livest here by toil,
Do not complain of this thy hard estate;

[1] plowshare
[2] directs
[3] Vergil, in his *Georgics*
[4] e. g., Cincinnatus
[5] choristers
[6] the nightingale
[7] spread about
[8] innumerable
[9] "This poem being writ in the manner of Spenser, the obsolete words, and the simplicity of diction in some of the lines, which borders on the ludicrous, were necessary to make the imitation more perfect." (Thomson's note) The influence of *The Castle of Indolence* upon Tennyson's "The Lotus Eaters" (p. 616) should be noted.

That like an emmet thou must ever moil [1]
Is a sad sentence of an ancient date; [2]
And certes, there is for it reason great;
For, though sometimes it makes thee weep
and wail,
And curse thy star, and early drudge and late;
Withouten that would come a heavier bale;
Loose life, unruly passions, and diseases pale.

2

In lowly dale, fast by a river's side
With woody hill o'er hill encompassed round,
A most enchanting wizard did abide,
Than whom a fiend more fell is nowhere found.
It was, I ween, a lovely spot of ground;
And there a season atween June and May,
Half prankt [3] with spring, with summer half
imbrowned,
A listless climate made, where, sooth to say,
No living wight could work, ne carèd even
for play.

3

Was naught around but images of rest;
Sleep-soothing groves, and quiet lawns between;
And flowery beds, that slumbrous influence
kest, [4]
From poppies breathed; and beds of pleasant
green,
Where never yet was creeping creature seen.
Meantime unnumbered glittering streamlets
played,
And hurlèd everywhere their waters sheen;
That as they bickered through the sunny glade,
Though restless still themselves, a lulling
murmur made.

4

Joined to the prattle of the purling rills,
Were heard the lowing herds along the vale,
And flocks loud-bleating from the distant hills,
And vacant [5] shepherds piping in the dale;
And now and then sweet Philomel would wail,
Or stock-doves plain [6] amid the forest deep,
That drowsy rustled to the sighing gale;
And still a coil [7] the grasshopper did keep;
Yet all the sounds yblent [8] inclinèd all to
sleep.

5

Full in the passage of the vale, above,
A sable, silent, solemn forest stood;
Where naught but shadowy forms was seen to
move,
As Idless [9] fancied in her dreaming mood.
And up the hills, on either side, a wood
Of blackening pines, aye waving to and fro,
Sent forth a sleepy horror through the blood;
And where this valley winded out below,
The murmuring main was heard, and scarcely heard, to flow.

6

A pleasing land of drowsy-hed [10] it was:
Of dreams that wave before the half-shut eye;
And of gay castles in the clouds that pass,
Forever flushing round a summer sky.
There eke the soft delights that witchingly
Instill a wanton sweetness through the breast,
And the calm pleasures always hovered nigh;
But whate'er smackt of noyance, or unrest,
Was far, far off expelled from this delicious
nest.

7

The landskip such, inspiring perfect ease,
Where INDOLENCE (for so the wizard hight [11])
Close-hid his castle mid embowering trees,
That half shut out the beams of Phoebus bright,
And made a kind of checkered day and night.
Meanwhile, unceasing, at the massy gate,
Beneath a spacious palm, the wicked wight
Was placed; and to his lute, of cruel fate
And labor harsh, complained, lamenting
man's estate.

8

Thither continual pilgrims crowded still,
From all the roads of earth that pass there by:
For, as they chanced to breathe on neighboring hill,
The freshness of this valley smote their eye,
And drew them ever and anon more nigh;
Till clustering round the enchanter false they
hung,
Ymolten [12] with his syren melody;
While o'er the enfeebling lute his hand he
flung,
And to the trembling chords these tempting
verses sung:

9

"Behold! ye pilgrims of this earth, behold!
See all but man with unearned pleasure gay.
See her bright robes the butterfly unfold,
Broke from her wintry tomb in prime of May!
What youthful bride can equal her array?
Who can with her for easy pleasure vie?
From mead to mead with gentle wing to stray,
From flower to flower on balmy gales to fly,
Is all she has to do beneath the radiant sky.

[1] labor
[2] *Genesis* iii, 19
[3] adorned
[4] cast
[5] care-free
[6] mourn
[7] a noise, a stir
[8] blended
[9] idleness
[10] drowsiness
[11] was named
[12] melted

10

"Behold the merry minstrels of the morn,
The swarming songsters of the careless grove;
Ten thousand throats that, from the flowering
 thorn,
Hymn their good God, and carol sweet of love,
Such grateful kindly raptures them emove!
They neither plow, nor sow; ne, fit for flail,
E'er to the barn the nodding sheaves they
 drove;
Yet theirs each harvest dancing in the gale,
 Whatever crowns the hill, or smiles along
 the vale.

11

"Outcast of Nature, man! the wretched thrall
Of bitter-dropping sweat, of sweltry[1] pain,
Of cares that eat away thy heart with gall,
And of the vices, an inhuman train,
That all proceed from savage thirst of gain:
For when hard-hearted Interest first began
To poison earth, Astraea[2] left the plain;
Guile, Violence, and Murder seized on man,
 And, for soft milky streams, with blood the
 rivers ran.

12

"Come, ye who still the cumbrous load of life
Push hard uphill; but as the farthest steep
You trust to gain, and put an end to strife,
Down thunders back the stone with mighty
 sweep,
And hurls your labors to the valley deep,
Forever vain. Come, and, withouten fee,
I in oblivion will your sorrows steep,
Your cares, your toils; will steep you in a sea
 Of full delight. O come, ye weary wights,
 to me!"

. . . .

1736-48 1748

RULE, BRITANNIA

From ALFRED, A MASQUE

1

When Britain first, at Heaven's command,
 Arose from out the azure main,
This was the charter of the land,
 And guardian angels sang this strain:
 Rule, Britannia, rule the waves,
 Britons never will be slaves.

2

The nations not so blest as thee,
 Must in their turns to tyrants fall,
Whilst thou shalt flourish great and free,
 The dread and envy of them all.
 Rule, Britannia, rule the waves,
 Britons never will be slaves.

3

Still more majestic shalt thou rise,
 More dreadful from each foreign stroke;
As the loud blast that tears the skies
 Serves but to root thy native oak.
 Rule, Britannia, rule the waves,
 Britons never will be slaves.

4

Thee haughty tyrants ne'er shall tame;
 All their attempts to bend thee down
Will but arouse thy generous flame,
 But work their woe and thy renown.
 Rule, Britannia, rule the waves,
 Britons never will be slaves.

5

To thee belongs the rural reign;
 Thy cities shall with commerce shine;
All thine shall be the subject main,
 And every shore it circles thine.
 Rule, Britannia, rule the waves,
 Britons never will be slaves.

6

The Muses, still with freedom found,
 Shall to thy happy coast repair;
Blest isle, with matchless beauty crowned,
 And manly hearts to guard the fair!
 Rule, Britannia, rule the waves,
 Britons never will be slaves.

1740

[1] sultry
[2] the goddess of justice, who in the golden age lived among men

LATER EIGHTEENTH CENTURY

IN THE later eighteenth century, poetry tends to leave man and "the town." Nature not only becomes a background for human emotions, but is a theme for its own sake. Its grand and gloomy aspects fill Macpherson's *Ossian;* its moods of gayety or sadness are seen in Chatterton; its apparent sympathy with man's emotions is found in Burns. This later poetry of the century shows less of satire, more of lyric tenderness, than that of the first half; it takes increased interest in the sufferings of the masses, as is seen in Goldsmith, Gray, and Burns; real peasants begin to figure as its characters. On the whole, however, the poetical field yields but a scanty harvest. In prose fiction the century sees the real birth of the modern English novel in Richardson and Fielding; and also the appearance of the "Gothic" novel, a type of fiction with its scenes laid in medieval times, with an atmosphere of the supernatural, and often with a background of Gothic architecture, well illustrated by Walpole's *Castle of Otranto* and Ann Radcliffe's *Mysteries of Udolpho.* In expository prose, Johnson, Gibbon, and Burke show the development of the oratorical tendency perhaps to its climax. As a whole, the period is one of transition from the classic to the romantic manner, with now and then, as in Burns, some rumblings of the coming social revolution.

WILLIAM COLLINS
1721-1759

Collins is often associated in criticism with his more famous contemporary, Thomas Gray, since the work of the two poets has many characteristics in common. He was the son of a wealthy tradesman and mayor of the town of Chichester, where he was born and died. After attending school at Winchester College he went to Oxford, where he took his bachelor's degree in 1743. For a while after this he lived in London a life of dissipation that undermined his health and led to the violent insanity in which he died.

Collins's offering to poetry is small. His *Persian Eclogues,* 1742, his *Odes,* 1746, and his *Ode on the Popular Superstitions of the Highlands,* unfinished, and published long after his death, make up the list. The significance of the man lies in the difference between his work and that of any of his contemporaries; though in simplicity and delicacy of imagination he most resembles Gray, and like him he forms a link between the poetry of his day and the poetry that was to come.

Biography and criticism: *Poems,* with Memoir by William Moy Thomas, 1894; *Poems,* ed. W. C. Bronson, Boston, 1898; also Johnson, Hazlitt, Swinburne.

A SONG FROM SHAKESPEARE'S CYMBELINE [1]

1

To fair Fidele's grassy tomb
  Soft maids and village hinds [2] shall bring
Each opening sweet, of earliest bloom,
  And rifle all the breathing spring.

[1] This song, which flows almost like an improvisation, Collins constructed from the scene in *Cymbeline* IV, ii, 215-229, in which Guiderius and Arviragus speak over the body of their sister Imogen, who is disguised as Fidele and whom they suppose to be dead:

Gui. Why, he but sleeps.
If he be gone, he'll make his grave a bed;
With female fairies will his tomb be haunted,
And worms will not come to thee.
Arv. With fairest flowers
Whilst summer lasts and I live here, Fidele,
I'll sweeten thy sad grave; thou shalt not lack
The flower that's like thy face, pale primrose, nor
The azured harebell, like thy veins, no, nor
The leaf of eglantine, whom not to slander,
Out-sweetened not thy breath. The ruddock would,
With charitable bill, . . . bring thee all this;
Yea, and furred moss besides, when flowers are none,
To winter-ground thy corse.

[2] rustics, peasants

2

No wailing ghost shall dare appear,
  To vex with shrieks this quiet grove;
But shepherd lads assemble here,
  And melting virgins own their love.

3

No withered witch shall here be seen,
  No goblins lead their nightly crew;
The female fays shall haunt the green,
  And dress thy grave with pearly dew.

4

The redbreast oft at evening hours
  Shall kindly lend his little aid,
With hoary moss, and gathered flowers
  To deck the ground where thou art laid.

5

When howling winds, and beating rain,
  In tempests shake the silvan cell,
Or midst the chase on every plain,
  The tender thought on thee shall dwell.

6

Each lonely scene shall thee restore,
  For thee the tear be duly shed;
Beloved, till life could charm no more;
  And mourned, till Pity's self be dead.

1744

ODE [1]

1

How sleep the brave who sink to rest
By all their country's wishes blest!
When Spring, with dewy fingers cold,
Returns to deck their hallowed mold,
She there shall dress a sweeter sod
Than Fancy's feet have ever trod.

2

By fairy hands their knell is rung,
By forms unseen their dirge is sung;
There Honor comes, a pilgrim gray,
To bless the turf that wraps their clay;
And Freedom shall awhile repair,
To dwell a weeping hermit there!

1746 *1746*

[1] "Written," says Collins, "in the beginning of the year 1746." The British troops had lately suffered losses in the War of the Austrian Succession, e. g., at Fontenoy in 1745, and Falkirk, January, 1746.

ODE TO EVENING [2]

1

If ought of oaten stop, [3] or pastoral song,
May hope, chaste Eve, to soothe thy modest ear,
  Like thy own solemn springs,
  Thy springs and dying gales,

2

O nymph reserved, while now the bright-haired sun
Sits in yon western tent, whose cloudy skirts,
  With brede [4] ethereal wove,
  O'erhang his wavy bed:

3

Now air is hushed, save where the weak-eyed bat,
With short shrill shriek, flits by on leathern wing,
  Or where the beetle winds
  His small but sullen horn,

4

As oft he rises 'midst the twilight path,
Against the pilgrim borne in heedless hum:
  Now teach me, maid composed,
  To breathe some softened strain,

5

Whose numbers, stealing through thy darkening vale
May not unseemly with its stillness suit,
  As, musing slow, I hail
  Thy genial loved return!

6

For when thy folding-star [5] arising shows
His paly circlet, at his warning lamp
  The fragrant Hours, and elves
  Who slept in flowers the day,

7

And many a nymph who wreathes her brows with sedge,
And sheds the freshening dew, and, lovelier still,
  The pensive Pleasures sweet,
  Prepare thy shadowy car.

[2] "Although less popular than 'the Deserted Village' and Gray's 'Elegy,' the 'Ode to Evening' is yet like them in embodying in exquisite form sights, sounds, and feelings of such permanent beauty that age cannot wither them nor custom stale." —W. C. Bronson.

[3] musical pipe

[4] embroidery

[5] marking the time for folding the flocks

8

Then lead, calm votaress, where some sheety lake
Cheers the lone heath, or some time-hallowed pile
Or upland fallows gray
Reflect its last cool gleam.

9

But when chill blustering winds, or driving rain,
Forbid my willing feet, be mine the hut
That from the mountain's side
Views wilds, and swelling floods,

10

And hamlets brown, and dim-discovered spires,
And hears their simple bell, and marks o'er all
Thy dewy fingers draw
The gradual dusky veil.

11

While Spring shall pour his showers, as oft he wont,
And bathe thy breathing tresses, meekest Eve;
While Summer loves to sport
Beneath thy lingering light;

12

While sallow Autumn fills thy lap with leaves;
Or Winter, yelling through the troublous air,
Affrights thy shrinking train,
And rudely rends thy robes;

13

So long, sure-found beneath the sylvan shed,
Shall Fancy, Friendship, Science, rose-lipped Health,
Thy gentlest influence own,
And hymn thy favorite name!

1746

THOMAS GRAY
1716-1771

Thomas Gray, scholar and antiquarian, shares with Burns preëminence among British poets of the eighteenth century. He was born in London. He was of delicate health, and, because of the irascible temper of his father, he was obliged to rely upon his mother's help in his education at Eton and at Cambridge. After a considerable tour upon the Continent as guest of his friend Horace Walpole, son of the prime minister, he returned to Cambridge and spent the remainder of his life as a private student in the libraries. Just before his death there, he was appointed professor of history.

Gray's life of quiet, steady scholarship made him one of the most erudite men of his age. His intellectual curiosity seems to have been unbounded. Interest in natural scenery, antiquities, and botany led him on walking tours through England; linguistics and architecture, into scholarly research. Having exhausted the stores of classical literature, he turned to the Norse and Anglo-Saxon languages, and found in their records the inspiration of some of his most significant poetry, especially that which looked forward to the romantic age. Gray was a transition poet. His most popular poem, the "Elegy," years in the making and polishing, though romantic in temper and form, is classical in restraint and intellectuality. It lives by the universality of its theme, by the sympathy and humanity of its treatment, and by the delicacy of its art.

The best recent editions: Gosse, 4 vols. 1884, and J. Bradshaw, Aldine edition, with Life, Notes, and Bibliography, 1891. Gray's letters, admirably edited by D. C. Tovey, 3 vols. 1900-12. Biography: Gosse (EML). Criticism: M. Arnold, Intro. to Gray's poems, Ward (EP), vol. III; Johnson; A. C. Benson, *Liv. Age,* 291:761-2, opposes Arnold's views; G. Bradford, "Bare Souls," *Harp.* 148:734-44, an interesting analysis; P. E. More, *Nation,* 96:592-5, speaks of the loneliness of Gray's life.

ELEGY WRITTEN IN A COUNTRY CHURCHYARD

1

The curfew tolls the knell of parting day,
The lowing herd wind slowly o'er the lea,
The plowman homeward plods his weary way,
And leaves the world to darkness and to me.

2

Now fades the glimmering landscape on the sight,
And all the air a solemn stillness holds,
Save where the beetle wheels his droning flight,
And drowsy tinklings lull the distant folds;

3

Save that from yonder ivy-mantled tower
The moping owl does to the moon complain
Of such as, wandering near her secret bower,
Molest her ancient solitary reign.

4

Beneath those rugged elms, that yew-tree's shade,
Where heaves the turf in many a moldering heap,
Each in his narrow cell forever laid,
The rude forefathers of the hamlet sleep.

5

The breezy call of incense-breathing morn,
The swallow twittering from the straw-built shed,

The cock's shrill clarion, or the echoing horn,
No more shall rouse them from their lowly bed.

6

For them no more the blazing hearth shall burn,
Or busy housewife ply her evening care;
No children run to lisp their sire's return,
Or climb his knees the envied kiss to share.

7

Oft did the harvest to their sickle yield,
Their furrow oft the stubborn glebe has broke;
How jocund did they drive their team afield!
How bowed the woods beneath their sturdy stroke!

8

Let not ambition mock their useful toil,
Their homely joys, and destiny obscure;
Nor grandeur hear with a disdainful smile,
The short and simple annals of the poor.

9

The boast of heraldry, the pomp of power,
And all that beauty, all that wealth e'er gave,
Awaits alike th' inevitable hour. [1]
The paths of glory lead but to the grave.

10

Nor you, ye proud, impute to these the fault,
If memory o'er their tomb no trophies raise,
Where through the long-drawn aisle and fretted vault
The pealing anthem swells the note of praise.

11

Can storied urn [2] or animated bust
Back to its mansion call the fleeting breath?
Can honor's voice provoke [3] the silent dust,
Or flattery soothe the dull cold ear of death?

12

Perhaps in this neglected spot is laid
Some heart once pregnant with celestial fire;
Hands that the rod of empire might have swayed,
Or waked to ecstasy the living lyre.

13

But knowledge to their eyes her ample page
Rich with the spoils of time did ne'er unroll;
Chill penury repressed their noble rage,
And froze the genial [4] current of the soul.

14

Full many a gem of purest ray serene
The dark unfathomed caves of ocean bear;

[1] subject of "awaits"
[2] a burial urn, pictorially decorated
[3] call forth
[4] natural

Full many a flower is born to blush unseen,
And waste its sweetness on the desert air.

15

Some village Hampden, [5] that with dauntless breast
The little tyrant of his fields withstood;
Some mute inglorious Milton here may rest,
Some Cromwell guiltless of his country's blood. [6]

16

Th' applause of listening senates to command,
The threats of pain and ruin to despise,
To scatter plenty o'er a smiling land,
And read their history in a nation's eyes,

17

Their lot forbade; nor circumscribed alone
Their growing virtues, but their crimes confined;
Forbade to wade through slaughter to a throne,
And shut the gates of mercy on mankind,

18

The struggling pangs of conscious truth to hide,
To quench the blushes of ingenuous shame,
Or heap the shrine of luxury and pride
With incense kindled at the Muse's flame. [7]

19

Far [8] from the madding crowd's ignoble strife, [9]
Their sober wishes never learned to stray;
Along the cool sequestered vale of life
They kept the noiseless tenor of their way.

20

Yet even these bones from insult to protect,
Some frail memorial still erected nigh,
With uncouth rimes and shapeless sculpture decked,
Implores the passing tribute of a sigh.

21

Their name, their years, spelt by th' unlettered Muse, [10]
The place of fame and elegy supply;
And many a holy text around she strews,
That teach the rustic moralist to die.

22

For who to dumb forgetfulness a prey,
This pleasing anxious being e'er resigned,

[5] a Puritan leader who resisted Charles I
[6] Until a comparatively recent time Cromwell was very generally regarded as a man who sacrificed everything to his own inordinate ambition. In the first draft of this stanza, Gray had written the names of Romans—Cato, Tully (Cicero), Caesar.
[7] i.e., write flattering verses to win favor
[8] i.e., being far
[9] "Far from the madding worldlings harsh discords."—Drummond of Hawthornden, 1585-1649
[10] untaught poet

Left the warm precincts of the cheerful day,
  Nor cast one longing lingering look behind?

23

On some fond breast the parting soul relies,
  Some pious drops the closing eye requires;
Even from the tomb the voice of nature cries,
  Even in our ashes live their wonted fires.

24

For thee, who mindful of th' unhonored dead
  Dost in these lines their artless tale relate;
If chance, [1] by lonely contemplation led,
  Some kindred spirit shall inquire thy fate,

25

Haply some hoary-headed swain may say,
  "Oft have we seen him at the peep of dawn
Brushing with hasty steps the dews away
  To meet the sun upon the upland lawn.

26

"There at the foot of yonder nodding beech
  That wreathes its old fantastic roots so high,
His listless length at noontide would he stretch,
  And pore upon the brook that babbles by.

27

"Hard by yon wood, now smiling as in scorn,
  Muttering his wayward fancies he would rove,
Now drooping, woeful wan, like one forlorn,
  Or crazed with care, or crossed in hopeless love.

28

"One morn I missed him on the customed hill,
  Along the heath and near his favorite tree;
Another came; nor yet beside the rill,
  Nor up the lawn, nor at the wood was he;

29

"The next with dirges due in sad array
  Slow through the church-way path we saw him borne.
Approach and read (for thou canst read) the lay,
  Graved on the stone beneath yon aged thorn."

THE EPITAPH

30

Here rests his head upon the lap of earth
  A youth to fortune and to fame unknown.
Fair science frowned not on his humble birth,
  And melancholy marked him for her own.

31

Large was his bounty, and his soul sincere,
  Heaven did a recompense as largely send:
He gave to misery all he had, a tear,
  He gained from Heaven ('twas all he wished) a friend.

[1] perchance

32

No further seek his merits to disclose,
  Or draw his frailties from their dread abode,
(There they alike in trembling hope repose)
  The bosom of his Father and his God.

1742-50 1751

THE PROGRESS OF POESY

A Pindaric Ode [2]

I. 1. Strophe

Awake, Aeolian lyre, awake,
And give to rapture all thy trembling strings.
From Helicon's harmonious springs
A thousand rills their mazy progress take;
The laughing flowers, that round them blow,
Drink life and fragrance as they flow.
Now the rich stream of music winds along,
Deep, majestic, smooth, and strong,
Through verdant vales, and Ceres' golden reign;
Now rolling down the steep amain,
Headlong, impetuous, see it pour;
The rocks and nodding groves rebellow to the roar.

I. 2. Antistrophe

Oh! sovereign of the willing soul,
Parent of sweet and solemn-breathing airs,
Enchanting shell! [3] the sullen cares,
And frantic passions hear thy soft control.
On Thracia's hills the Lord of War [4]
Has curbed the fury of his car,
And dropped his thirsty lance at thy command.
Perching on the sceptered hand
Of Jove, the magic lulls the feathered king [5]
With ruffled plumes, and flagging wing:
Quenched in dark clouds of slumber lie
The terror of his beak, and lightnings of his eye.

[2] The odes of Pindar, the most renowned lyric poet of ancient Greece, were mostly constructed in triads, groups of three stanzas, each containing a strophe, antistrophe, and epode, or turn, counter-turn, and after-song. In meter and rime-scheme the three parts respectively are exactly alike in any one Pindaric ode. The livelier odes were written in the so-called Aeolian mode, in contrast to the graver Dorian mode and the more tender Lydian measures. Gray has borrowed freely from Pindar, even translating a portion of the first Pythian Ode. The following is a condensation of Gray's notes to his own poem: I. 1. The various sources of poetry, which gives life and luster to all it touches.—I. 2. Power of harmony to calm the turbulent sallies of the soul.—I. 3. Power of harmony to produce all the graces of motion in the body. II. 1. Poetry given to mankind to compensate the real and imaginary ills of life.—II. 2. Extensive influence of poetic genius over the remotest and most uncivilized nations.—II. 3. Progress of Poetry from Greece to Italy, and from Italy to England.—III. 1. 2. 3. Shakespeare, Milton, Dryden.

[3] the lyre, said to have been made by Hermes from a tortoise shell

[4] Mars

[5] Jove's eagle

I. 3. Epode

Thee the voice, the dance obey,
Tempered to thy warbled lay.
O'er Idalia's velvet-green [1]
The rosy-crownèd Loves are seen
On Cytherea's day
With antic Sports, and blue-eyed Pleasures,
Frisking light in frolic measures;
Now pursuing, now retreating,
Now in circling troops they meet;
To brisk notes in cadence beating
Glance their many-twinkling feet.
Slow-melting strains their queen's approach declare;
Where'er she turns the Graces homage pay.
With arms sublime, [2] that float upon the air,
In gliding state she wins her easy way.
O'er her warm cheek, and rising bosom, move
The bloom of young desire, and purple light of love.

II. 1. Strophe

Man's feeble race what ills await,
Labor and penury, the racks of pain,
Disease, and sorrow's weeping train,
And death, sad refuge from the storms of fate!
The fond [3] complaint, my song, disprove,
And justify the laws of Jove.
Say, has he given in vain the heavenly Muse?
Night, and all her sickly dews,
Her specters wan, and birds of boding cry,
He gives to range the dreary sky;
Till down the eastern cliffs afar
Hyperion's march they spy, and glittering shafts of war.

II. 2. Antistrophe

In climes beyond the solar road,
Where shaggy forms o'er ice-built mountains roam,
The Muse has broke the twilight-gloom
To cheer the shivering native's dull abode.
And oft, beneath the odorous shade
Of Chili's boundless forests laid,
She deigns to hear the savage youth repeat
In loose numbers wildly sweet
Their feather-cinctured chiefs, and dusky loves.
Her track, where'er the goddess roves,
Glory pursue, and generous shame,
Th' unconquerable mind, and freedom's holy flame.

II. 3. Epode

Woods, that wave o'er Delphi's steep,
Isles, that crown th' Aegean deep,
Fields, that cool Ilissus laves,
Or where Maeander's amber waves
In lingering labyrinths creep,

[1] in Cyprus, sacred to Venus (Cytherea)
[2] uplifted
[3] foolish

How do your tuneful echoes languish,
Mute, but to the voice of anguish?
Where each old poetic mountain
Inspiration breathed around;
Every shade and hallowed fountain
Murmured deep a solemn sound;
Till the sad Nine in Greece's evil hour
Left their Parnassus for the Latian plains.
Alike they scorn the pomp of tyrant-power,
And coward vice that revels in her chains.
When Latium had her lofty spirit lost,
They sought, O Albion! next, thy sea-encircled coast.

III. 1. Strophe

Far from the sun and summer-gale,
In thy green lap was nature's darling laid,
What time, where lucid Avon strayed,
To him the mighty mother did unveil
Her awful face: the dauntless child
Stretched forth his little arms, and smiled.
This pencil take (she said) whose colors clear
Richly paint the vernal year;
Thine too these golden keys, immortal boy!
This can unlock the gates of joy;
Of horror that, and thrilling fears,
Or ope the sacred source of sympathetic tears.

III. 2. Antistrophe

Nor second he, that rode sublime
Upon the seraph-wings of ecstasy,
The secrets of th' abyss to spy.
He passed the flaming bounds of place and time;
The living throne, the sapphire-blaze, [4]
Where angels tremble while they gaze,
He saw; but blasted with excess of light,
Closed his eyes in endless night.
Behold, where Dryden's less presumptuous car,
Wide o'er the fields of glory bear
Two coursers of ethereal race, [5]
With necks in thunder clothed, [6] and long-resounding pace.

III. 3. Epode

Hark, his hands the lyre explore!
Bright-eyed Fancy hovering o'er
Scatters from her pictured urn
Thoughts that breathe, and words that burn.
But ah! 'tis heard no more—
O lyre divine, what daring spirit
Wakes thee now? Though he inherit
Nor the pride, nor ample pinion
That the Theban Eagle [7] bear,

[4] *Ezekiel* i, 26
[5] "Meant to express the stately march and sounding energy of Dryden's rimes." (Gray)
[6] *Job* xxxix, 19.
[7] Pindar

Sailing with supreme dominion
Through the azure deep of air;
Yet oft before his infant eyes would run
Such forms as glitter in the Muse's ray
With orient hues, unborrowed of the sun.
Yet shall he mount, and keep his distant way
Beyond the limits of a vulgar fate,
Beneath the good how far—but far above the
great.

1754 *1757*

JAMES MACPHERSON
1738-1796

Macpherson was of humble parentage but had some training at Aberdeen University and was schoolmaster in the parish of his birth, Ruthven, Invernesshire, Scotland. His early poems, based he said, on traditional Celtic stories, pleased some Scotch men of letters who saw them. They urged him to seek more material and make more translations. Aided financially, he made a search through the Highlands and within a few months produced an epic which, he said, was translated from the work of Ossian, an ancient Celtic hero.

Most scholars think the epic a forgery either by Macpherson or by Scotch Gaelic scholars, companions of Macpherson in the search. Some of its parts seem genuine Celtic remains. The publication, especially of *Fingal*, 1762, and *Temora*, 1763, aroused immediate controversy; but Macpherson's friends stood by him, and even procured government sinecures that made him wealthy.

Conscious that his work was not in the prevailing mood of the time, Macpherson adopted, like Walpole and Chatterton, the ruse of finding ancient manuscripts. Unfortunately he carried the deception too far. Nevertheless the poems manifest the genuine Celtic tenderness, melancholy, and love of nature. Matthew Arnold says that there is "in the book a residue with the very soul of the Celtic genius in it," and that the poem "has the proud distinction of having brought this soul of the Celtic genius into contact with the nations of modern Europe, and enriched all our poetry by it." To an age hungry for romance it became life-giving food. It solaced Goethe; Napoleon carried a copy in his campaigns; its influence on German romance is incalculable. As to its style, those who are familiar with the poetry of the Old Testament, known to every Scotch boy of Macpherson's time, will easily see one source of the rhythmic prose.

Biographies: T. B. Saunders, *Life and Letters of James Macpherson*, . . 1895; J. S. Smart, *J. Macpherson, an Episode in Literature*, 1905. Criticism: G. M. Fraser, *Quar.* 245:331-45, expressing the theory that the real forgery was made by friends of Macpherson.

From "OSSIAN"

OINA-MORUL [1]

As flies the inconstant sun, over Larmon's grassy hill, so pass the tales of old, along my soul by night! When bards are removed to their place; when harps are hung in Selma's hall; [2] then comes a voice to Ossian, and awakes his soul! It is the voice of years that are gone! They roll before me, with all their deeds! I seize the tales as they pass, and pour them forth in song. Nor a troubled stream is the song of the king, it is like the rising of music from Lutha of the strings. Lutha of many strings, not silent are thy streamy rocks, when the white hands of Malvina move upon the harp! Light of the shadowy thoughts, that fly across my soul, daughter of Toscar of helmets, wilt thou not hear the song? We call back, maid of Lutha, the years that have rolled away!

It was in the days of the king, while yet my locks were young, that I marked Con-cathlin, [3]on high, from ocean's nightly wave. My course was toward the isle of Fuärfed, woody dweller of seas! Fingal had sent me to the aid of Mal-orchol, king of Fuärfed wild; for war was around him, and our fathers had met at the feast.

In Col-coiled, I bound my sails; I sent my sword to Mal-orchol of shells. [4] He knew the signal of Albion, and his joy arose. He came from his own high hall, and seized my hand in grief. "Why comes the race of heroes to a falling king? Ton-thormod of many spears is the chief of wavy Sar-dronlo. He saw and loved my daughter, white-bosomed Oina-morul. He sought; I denied the maid; for our fathers had been foes. He came, with battle, to Fuärfed; my people are rolled away. Why comes the race of heroes to a falling king?"

"I come not," I said, "to look, like a boy, on the strife. Fingal remembers Mal-orchol, and his hall for strangers. From his waves, the warrior descended on thy woody isle. Thou wert no cloud before him. Thy feast was spread with songs. For this my sword shall rise; and thy foes perhaps may fail. Our

[1] In the poem here given, Ossian, addressing his daughter-in-law Malvina, "maid of Lutha," relates a generous deed of his youthful days. Sent by his father to the assistance of the king of Fuärfed, he defeated the foe, Ton-thormod, and was promised the king's daughter, Oina-morul. But discovering that she loved Ton-thormod, he yielded his claim and brought about a reconciliation of the foes. The rather excessive punctuation of the piece is meant to emphasize its rhythmical character.

[2] the royal residence of Fingal

[3] a star, perhaps the pole star

[4] See note 3, page 379.

friends are not forgot in their danger, though distant is our land."

"Descendant of the daring Trenmor, thy words are like the voice of Cruth-loda,[1] when he speaks, from his parting cloud, strong dweller of the sky! Many have rejoiced at my feast; but they all have forgot Mal-orchol. I have looked toward all the winds; but no white sails were seen. But steel resounds in my hall; and not the joyful shells. Come to my dwelling, race of heroes; dark-skirted night is near. Hear the voice of songs, from the maid of Fuärfed wild."

We went. On the harp arose the white hands of Oina-morul. She waked her own sad tale, from every trembling string. I stood in silence; for bright in her locks was the daughter of many isles! Her eyes were two stars, looking forward through a rushing shower. The mariner marks them on high, and blesses the lovely beams. With morning we rushed to battle, to Tormul's resounding stream. The foe moved to the sound of Ton-thormod's bossy shield. From wing to wing the strife was mixed. I met Ton-thormod in flight. Wide flew his broken steel. I seized the king in war. I gave his hand, bound fast with thongs, to Mal-orchol, the giver of shells. Joy rose at the feast of Fuärfed, for the foe had failed. Ton-thormod turned his face away, from Oina-morul of isles!

"Son of Fingal," began Mal-orchol, "not forgot shalt thou pass from me. A light shall dwell in thy ship, Oina-morul of slow-rolling eyes. She shall kindle gladness, along thy mighty soul. Nor unheeded shall the maid move in Selma, through the dwelling of kings!"

In the hall I lay in night. Mine eyes were half-closed in sleep. Soft music came to mine ear: it was like the rising breeze, that whirls, at first, the thistle's beard; then flies, dark shadowy, over the grass. It was the maid of Fuärfed wild! She raised the nightly song; she knew that my soul was a stream, that flowed at pleasant sounds. "Who looks," she said, "from his rock on ocean's closing mist? His long locks, like the raven's wing, are wandering on the blast. Stately are his steps in grief! The tears are in his eyes! His manly breast is heaving over his bursting soul! Retire, I am distant far; a wanderer in lands unknown. Though the race of kings are around me, yet my soul is dark. Why have our fathers been foes, Ton-thormod, love of maids?"

"Soft voice of the streamy isle," I said, "why dost thou mourn by night? The race of daring Trenmor are not the dark in soul. Thou shalt not wander, by streams unknown, blue-eyed Oina-morul! Within this bosom is a voice; it comes not to other ears; it bids Ossian hear the hapless, in their hour of woe. Retire, soft singer by night! Ton-thormod shall not mourn on his rock!"

With morning I loosed the king. I gave the long-haired maid. Mal-orchol heard my words, in the midst of his echoing halls. "King of Fuärfed wild, why should Ton-thormod mourn? He is of the race of heroes, and a flame in war. Your fathers have been foes, but now their dim ghosts rejoice in death. They stretch their hands of mist to the same shell in Loda.[2] Forget their rage, ye warriors; it was the cloud of other years."

Such were the deeds of Ossian, while yet his locks were young; though loveliness, with a robe of beams, clothed the daughter of many isles. We call back, maid of Lutha, the years that have rolled away!

1762

From CARTHON

[OSSIAN'S ADDRESS TO THE SUN]

. . . .

O thou that rollest above, round as the shield of my fathers! Whence are thy beams, O sun! thy everlasting light! Thou comest forth, in thy awful beauty; the stars hide themselves in the sky; the moon, cold and pale, sinks in the western wave. But thou thyself movest alone; who can be a companion of thy course? The oaks of the mountains fall; the mountains themselves decay with years; the ocean shrinks and grows again; the moon herself is lost in heaven; but thou art forever the same; rejoicing in the brightness of thy course. When the world is dark with tempests; when thunder rolls, and lightning flies; thou lookest in thy beauty from the clouds, and laughest at the storm. But to Ossian, thou lookest in vain; for he beholds thy beams no more; whether thy yellow hair flows on the eastern clouds, or thou tremblest at the gates of the west. But thou art, perhaps, like me, for a season; thy years will have an end. Thou shalt sleep in thy clouds, careless of the voice of the morning. Exult then, O sun! in the strength of thy youth: age is dark and unlovely; it is like the glimmering light of the moon, when it shines through broken clouds, and the mist is on the hills; the blast of the north is on the plain, the traveler shrinks in the midst of his journey.

1762

[1] Odin

[2] the Hall of Odin

THOMAS CHATTERTON
1752-1770

Wordsworth's lines:

". . . . Chatterton, the marvelous boy,
The sleepless soul that perished in his pride."

characterize one of the most tragic personalities of English literature. Through his early death English literature lost a poet whose genius might have placed him above any of his contemporaries. The lad was born at Bristol after the death of his father, a bookish, antiquarian schoolmaster. Even before Chatterton could read he seemed to have been absorbing the spirit of the medieval, especially from the architecture, glass, effigies and monuments of the parish church of St. Mary Redcliffe, where his uncle was custodian. From his fourteenth year he composed poetry imitating the form and spirit of the Middle Ages. He chose his vocabulary from word lists compiled mostly from Chaucer and he passed off the poems on the public as the work of Rowley, an imaginary monk of the fourteenth century. Escaping from an irksome apprenticeship to a Bristol lawyer, he went to London, began writing for papers and magazines, and was meeting with fair success when, in a moment of despondency, he took poison. He had been too proud to beg, too shy to demand his pay for his work.

Chatterton's "Rowley poems" do not reflect the poetical fashion of his own time for he has the same eager delight in beauty, in love for the past, and in expressing these, that characterizes the work of Spenser and his contemporaries. His verse, with that of Gray, Collins, and Macpherson, encouraged coming poets to look at life afresh, and to assess its values in new terms.

Recent editions: W. W. Skeat, 2 vols. 1891, and Sir S. Lee, 2 vols. 1906-9, the former with biography, and introduction to the "Rowley poems." Biographies: C. E. Russell, *Chatterton: The Marvelous Boy,* 1908; J. H. Ingram, *The True Chatterton,* 1910. Criticism: Interesting reviews of the foregoing, *Cur. Lit.* 44:505-9 and 49:448-9; *Nation,* 86:378-9; see also Hazlitt.

EPITAPH ON ROBERT CANYNGE [1]

Thys Morneygne Starre of Radcleves rysynge Raie,
A True Man, Good of Mynde, and Canynge hyghte, [2]
Benethe thys Stone lies moltrynge ynto Claie,
Untylle the darke Tombe sheene an aeterne Lyghte.
Thyrde from hys Loyns the present Canynge came; [3]
Houton [4] are wordes for to telle his doe; [5]
For aie shall lyve hys Heaven-recorded Name,
Ne shalle ytte die whanne Tyme shall be ne moe; [6]
Whan Mychael's Trompe shalle sounde to rize the Soulle,
He'lle wynge toe heaven with kynne, and happie be their dolle. [7]

1777

AN EXCELENTE BALADE OF CHARITIE
(As Written by the Good Priest Thomas Rowley, 1464)

1

In Virgo now the sultry sun did sheene,
And hot upon the meads did cast his ray;
The apple reddened from its paly green,
And the soft pear did bend the leafy spray;
The pied chelandry [8] sang the livelong day;
'Twas now the pride, the manhood of the year,
And eke the ground was decked in its most deft aumere. [9]

2

The sun was gleaming in the midst of day,
Dead-still the air, and eke the welkin blue,
When from the sea arose in drear array
A heap of clouds of sable sullen hue,
The which full fast unto the woodland drew,
Hiding at once the sunnès festive face,
And the black tempest swelled, and gathered up apace.

3

Beneath a holm, [10] fast by a pathway-side,
Which did unto Saint Godwin's convent lead,
A hapless pilgrim moaning did abide,
Poor in his view, ungentle in his weed, [11]
Long brimful of the miseries of need.
Where from the hailstorm could the beggar fly?
He had no houses there, nor any convent nigh.

[1] William Canning, an actual mayor of Bristol in the time of Edward IV, who with his grandfather rebuilt the beautiful church of St. Mary Redcliffe ("Radcleves rysynge Raie"); it does not appear that the great-grandfather, Robert, had any share in it. William Canning was said by Chatterton to have been Rowley's patron.

[2] named

[3] The selections are from the "Rowley poems." In all here given (except the "Epitaph," which is left unaltered) the spelling and some words are modernized, in accordance with Professor Skeat's edition, the better to show what genuine powers the youthful poet possessed. Chatterton wrote after this fashion:

"In Virgyne the sweltrie sun gan sheene,
And hotte upon the mees did caste his raie;
The apple rodded from its palie greene," etc.

This Spenserian manner, as in the poetry of Thomson a generation earlier, is in marked contrast to the prevailing classicism of the age.

[4] hollow
[5] deeds
[6] no more
[7] their dole (lot)
[8] goldfinch
[9] misused for "apparel"; properly, "a purse"
[10] holm oak (holly)
[11] rustic in his dress

4

Look in his gloomèd face, his sprite there scan;
How woe-begone, how withered, dwindled, dead!
Haste to thy church-glebe-house, accursèd man!
Haste to thy shroud, thy only sleeping bed.
Cold as the clay which will grow on thy head
Are Charity and Love among high elves;
For knights and barons live for pleasure and themselves.

5

The gathered storm is ripe; the big drops fall,
The sun-burnt meadows smoke, and drink the rain;
The coming ghastness [1] doth the cattle 'pall, [2]
And the full flocks are driving o'er the plain;
Dashed from the clouds, the waters fly again;
The welkin opes; the yellow lightning flies,
And the hot fiery steam in the wide flashings dies.

6

List! Now the thunder's rattling noisy sound
Moves slowly on, and then full-swollen clangs,
Shakes the high spire, and lost, expended, drowned,
Still on the frighted ear of terror hangs;
The winds are up; the lofty elm tree swangs;
Again the lightning, and the thunder pours,
And the full clouds are burst at once in stony showers.

7

Spurring his palfrey o'er the watery plain,
The Abbot of Saint Godwin's convent came;
His chapournette [3] was drenchèd with the rain,
His painted girdle met with mickle shame;
He aynewarde told his bederoll [4] at the same;
The storm increases, and he drew aside,
With the poor alms-craver near to the holm to bide.

8

His cope was all of Lincoln cloth so fine,
With a gold button fastened near his chin,
His autremete [5] was edged with golden twine,
And his shoe's peak a noble's might have been;
Full well it shewèd he thought cost no sin.
The trammels of his palfrey pleased his sight,
For the horse-milliner his head with roses dight. [6]

9

"An alms, sir priest!" the drooping pilgrim said,
"Oh! let me wait within your convent-door,
Till the sun shineth high above our head,
And the loud tempest of the air is o'er.
Helpless and old am I, alas! and poor.

[1] for "ghastliness" [3] small round hat
[2] appall
[4] backward told his beads, i.e., cursed (Chatterton)
[5] loose white robe [6] arrayed

No house, no friend, nor money in my pouch,
All that I call my own is this my silver crouche." [7]

10

"Varlet!" replied the Abbot, "cease your din;
This is no season alms and prayers to give,
My porter never lets a beggar in;
None touch my ring who not in honor live."
And now the sun with the black clouds did strive,
And shot upon the ground his glaring ray;
The Abbot spurred his steed, and eftsoons rode away.

11

Once more the sky was black, the thunder rolled,
Fast running o'er the plain a priest was seen;
Not dight full proud, nor buttoned up in gold,
His cope and jape [8] were gray, and eke were clean;
A Limitor [9] he was of order seen;
And from the pathway-side then turnèd he,
Where the poor beggar lay beneath the holman tree.

12

"An alms, sir priest!" the drooping pilgrim said,
"For sweet Saint Mary and your order's sake."
The Limitor then loosened his pouch-thread,
And did thereout a groat of silver take;
The needy pilgrim did for gladness shake,
"Here, take this silver, it may ease thy care,
We are God's stewards all, naught of our own we bear.

13

"But ah! unhappy pilgrim, learn of me.
Scarce any give a rentroll to their lord;
Here take my semicope, [10] thou'rt bare, I see,
'Tis thine; the saints will give me my reward."
He left the pilgrim, and his way aborde. [11]
Virgin and holy Saints, who sit in gloure, [12]
Or give the mighty will, or give the good man power!

1770 *1777*

From BATTLE OF HASTINGS [13]

17

And now Duke William marèshall'd his band,
And stretched his army out, a goodly row.

[7] cross
[8] a short surplice (?)
[9] licensed begging friar
[10] short cape
[11] for "pursued"
[12] for "glory"
[13] There are two versions of this poem, one of which Chatterton admitted to be his own. The other, from which the stanzas above are taken, he declared to be Rowley's. There are seventy-two stanzas in all, but the battle is not ended.

First did a rank of arcublastries[1] stand,
Next those on horseback drew th' ascending
flo;[2]
Brave champions, each well learnèd in the bow,
Their asenglave[3] across their horses tied;
Or[4] with the loverds[5] squires behind did go,
Or waited, squire-like, at the horse's side.
When thus Duke William to a monk did say:
"Prepare thyself with speed, to Harold haste
away.

18

"Tell him from me one of these three to take;
That he to me do homage for this land,
Or me his heir, when he deceaseth, make,
Or to the judgment of Christ's vicar[6] stand."
He said; the monk departed out of hand,
And to King Harold did this message bear,
Who said: "Tell thou the duke, at his likand,[7]
If he can get the crown, he may it wear."
He said; and drove the monk out of his sight,
And with his brothers roused each man to
bloody fight.

19

A standard made of silk and jewels rare,
Wherein all colors, wrought about in bighes,[8]
An armèd knight was seen death-doing there,
Under this motto—"He conquers or he dies."[9]
This standard rich, endazzling mortal eyes,
Was borne near Harold at the Kenters' head,
Who charged his brothers for the great em-
prise,
That straight the hest[10] for battle should be
spread.
To every earl and knight the word is given,
And cries *"a guerre!"*[11] and slogans shake
the vaulted heaven.

20

As when the earth,[12] torn by convulsions dire,
In realms of darkness hid from human sight;
The warring force of water, air, and fire,
Bursts from the regions of eternal night,
Through the dark caverns seeks the realms of
light;
Some lofty mountain, by its fury torn,
Dreadfully moves, and causes great affright;
Now here, now there, majestic nods the
bourne,[13]
And awful shakes, moved by th' almighty
force;

[1] crossbow-men [4] either [7] pleasure
[2] arrow [5] lords [8] jewels
[3] lance? (Skeat) [6] the Pope
[9] King Harold's banner at the battle of Hastings bore the design of a fighting man.
[10] command [11] "To battle!"
[12] sentence grammatically defective
[13] for "cliff"

Whole woods and forests nod, and rivers
change their course.

21

So did the men of war at once advance,
Linked man to man, appeared one body light;
Above, a wood, y-formed of bill and lance,
That nodded in the air, most strange to sight;
Hard as the iron were the men of might,
No need of slogans to enrouse their mind;
Each shooting spear made ready for the fight,
More fierce than falling rocks, more swift than
wind;
With solemn step, by echo made more dire,
One single body all, they marched, their eyes
on fire.

22

And now the gray-eyed morn with violets drest,
Shaking the dewdrops on the flowery meads,
Fled with her rosy radiance to the west.
Forth from the eastern gate the fiery steeds
Of the bright sun awaiting spirits leads.[14]
The sun, in fiery pomp enthroned on high,
Swifter than thought along his journey
gledes,[15]
And scatters night's remains from out the sky.
He saw the armies make for bloody fray,
And stopped his driving steeds, and hid his
lightsome ray.

23

King Harold high in air majestic raised
His mighty arm, decked with a manchyn[16]
rare;
With even hand a mighty javelin peised,[17]
Then furious sent it whistling through the air.
It struck the helmet of the Sieur de Beer.
In vain did brass or iron stop its way;
Above his eyes it came, the bones did tear,
Piercing quite through, before it did allay.[18]
He tumbled, screeching with his horrid pain,
His hollow cuishes[19] rang upon the bloody
plain.

24

This William saw, and, sounding Roland's song,
He bent his iron interwoven bow,
Making both ends to meet with might full
strong;
From out of mortal's sight shot up the flo.
Then swift as falling stars to earth below,
It slanted down on Alfwold's painted shield,
Quite through the silver-bordured cross did go,
Nor lost its force, but stuck into the field;

[14] singular verb wrongly used for sake of rime
[15] for "glides" [18] for "stop"
[16] sleeve [19] armor for the thighs
[17] poised

The Normans, like their sovereign, did prepare,
And shot ten thousand floes uprising in the air.

25

As when a flight of cranes that take their way
In household armies through the archèd sky,
Alike [1] the cause, or company or prey,
If that perchance some boggy fen is nigh,
Soon as the muddy nation [2] they espy,
In one black cloud they to the earth descend;
Fierce as the falling thunderbolt they fly,
In vain do reeds the speckled folk defend;
So prone to heavy blow the arrows fell,
And pierced through brass, and sent many to heaven or hell.

26

Aelan Adelfred, of the stow [3] of Leigh,
Felt a dire arrow burning in his breast;
Before he died, he sent his spear away,
Then sank to glory and eternal rest.
Neville, a Norman of all Normans best,
Through the joint cuishè did the javelin feel,
As he on horseback for the fight addressed,
And saw his blood come smoking o'er the steel;
He sent the avenging flo into the air,
And turned his horse's head, and did to leech repair.

27

And now the javelins, barbed with deathès wings,
Hurled from the English hands by force aderne, [4]
Whizz drear along, and songs of terror sings,
Such songs as always closed in life eterne.
Hurled by such strength along the air they burn,
Not to be quenchèd but in Normans' blood.
Where'er they came, they were of life forlorn,
And always followed by a purple flood.
Like clouds the Norman arrows did descend,
Like clouds of carnage full, in purple drops did end.

1777

[1] whatever
[2] frogs (a manifest 18th century paraphrase)
[3] place
[4] cruel

SAMUEL JOHNSON 1709-1784

The most striking personality among English writers of his day was Samuel Johnson. Boswell's biography makes his huge bulk, commanding voice, and formidable manner in discussion almost as well known to us as the traits of our living friends. Johnson was reared among books, for his father was a bookseller of Litchfield, and he read voraciously and without discrimination. Encouraged by a friend who promised him help, he entered Oxford as a commoner (pensioner) where he spent possibly three years, but took no degree. Failing as a schoolmaster, he set out in 1737 to make a living as a writer in London.

For years he toiled upon Cave's *Gentleman's Magazine* and in any honest literary employment, and at length undertook to make a dictionary of the English language upon a scale and plan never before attempted. This work, appearing in 1755, gained him great reputation. He had written *The Rambler,* 1750-52, and this was followed by *The Idler,* 1758-60, both periodicals in the manner of *The Spectator.* His edition of Shakespeare came out in 1765, and his *Lives of the English Poets,* 1779, 1781. He died in London.

Johnson's tenacious memory, good sense, and keen repartee made him the most prominent figure in the famous Literary Club which included Goldsmith, Burke, Gibbon, Boswell, Sheridan, Garrick, Percy, and others better known in politics and society than in literature. A Tory in politics and a stern conservative in art, he despised the newly-developing romantic tendencies, was unsympathetic with Gray, and contemptuous of Macpherson. But when his prejudices were not at stake his literary judgments were solid and penetrating. His firmly conservative views of social conditions were clear-cut, and often served as props for a society already shaken by the coming revolution. His style is ever clear, though his studied circumlocutions and erudite vocabulary annoy as well as amuse the modern reader.

Biographies: Aside from Boswell's, many times reprinted, Stephen (EML) and F. Grant (GW) are most useful. Criticism: Macaulay on Johnson and Boswell, and Carlyle's penetrating comment give contrasting views; see also Sir W. Raleigh, *Six Essays on Johnson,* 1910; C. B. Tinker, *Johnson and Mme. D'Arblay,* 1911; J. Bailey, *Dr. Johnson and his Circle,* 1913; C. H. Clark, *No. Am.* 222:321-30, gives the disagreeable side of Johnson's personality. See also Stephen.

From the PLAN OF AN ENGLISH DICTIONARY [5]

To the Right Honorable Philip Dormer, Earl of Chesterfield, One of His Majesty's Principal Secretaries of State

My Lord,

When first I undertook to write an English Dictionary, I had no expectation of any higher patronage than that of the proprietors of the copy, nor prospect of any other advantage than

[5] Johnson's ponderous diction may have been in some measure due to his labors in the field of lexicography, though doubtless much more to his habit of thinking in general and abstract terms. It was jestingly said in his time that he used hard words in the *Rambler* papers on purpose to make his forthcoming Dictionary indispensable. Yet the diction confers a not unpleasing dignity upon the wisdom it clothes; and it grew simpler with time, as is shown by the admirable style of his *Lives of the Poets.*

the price of my labor. I knew that the work in which I engaged is generally considered as drudgery for the blind, as the proper toil of artless industry; a task that requires neither the light of learning, nor the activity of genius, but may be successfully performed without any higher quality than that of bearing burthens with dull patience, and beating the track of the alphabet with sluggish resolution.

Whether this opinion, so long transmitted, and so widely propagated, had its beginning from truth and Nature or from accident and prejudice; whether it be decreed by the authority of reason or the tyranny of ignorance, that of all the candidates for literary praise, the unhappy lexicographer holds the lowest place, neither vanity nor interest incited me to inquire. It appeared that the province allotted me was, of all the regions of learning, generally confessed to be the least delightful, that it was believed to produce neither fruit nor flowers; and that, after a long and laborious cultivation, not even the barren laurel[1] had been found upon it.

Yet on this province, my Lord, I entered, with the pleasing hope that, as it was low, it likewise would be safe. I was drawn forward with the prospect of employment which, though not splendid, would be useful; and which, though it could not make my life envied, would keep it innocent; which would awaken no passion, engage me in no contention, nor throw in my way any temptation to disturb the quiet of others by censure, or my own by flattery.

I had read, indeed, of times in which princes and statesmen thought it part of their honor to promote the improvement of their native tongues; and in which dictionaries were written under the protection of greatness. To the patrons of such undertakings I willingly paid the homage of believing that they, who were thus solicitous for the perpetuity of their language, had reason to expect that their actions would be celebrated by posterity, and that the eloquence which they promoted would be employed in their praise. But I consider such acts of beneficence as prodigies, recorded rather to raise wonder than expectation; and content with the terms that I had stipulated, had not suffered my imagination to flatter me with any other encouragement, when I found that my design had been thought by your Lordship of importance sufficient to attract your favor.

How far this unexpected distinction can be rated among the happy incidents of life, I am not yet able to determine. Its first effect has been to make me anxious lest it should fix the attention of the public too much upon me, and, as it once happened to an epic poet of France,[2] by raising the reputation of the attempt, obstruct the reception of the work. I imagine what the world will expect from a scheme prosecuted under your Lordship's influence; and I know that expectation, when her wings are once expanded, easily reaches heights which performance never will attain; and when she has mounted the summit of perfection, derides her follower, who dies in the pursuit.

Not therefore to raise expectation, but to repress it, I here lay before your Lordship the Plan of my undertaking, that more may not be demanded than I intend; and that, before it is too far advanced to be thrown into a new method, I may be advertised of its defects or superfluities. Such informations I may justly hope, from the emulation with which those who desire the praise of elegance or discernment must contend in the promotion of a design that you, my Lord, have not thought unworthy to share your attention with treaties and with wars.

. . . .

[Then follows the plan, with many details of vocabulary, orthography, pronunciation, etc.]

When I survey the Plan which I have laid before you, I cannot, my Lord, but confess that I am frighted at its extent, and, like the soldiers of Caesar, look on Britain as a new world which it is almost madness to invade. But I hope that though I should not complete the conquest, I shall at least discover the coast, civilize part of the inhabitants, and make it easy for some other adventurer to proceed farther, to reduce them wholly to subjection, and settle them under laws.

We are taught by the great Roman orator that every man should propose to himself the highest degree of excellence, but that he may stop with honor at the second or third. Though, therefore, my performance should fall below the excellence of other dictionaries, I may obtain, at least, the praise of having endeavored well; nor shall I think it any reproach to my diligence that I have retired, without a triumph, from a contest with united academies and long successions of learned compilers. I cannot hope, in the warmest moments, to preserve so much caution through so long a work, as not often to sink into negligence, or to obtain so much knowledge of all its parts as not frequently to fail by ignorance. I expect that

[1] The actual laurel is not barren, whatever he thought of the triumphs it symbolizes.

[2] Chapelain's *La Pucelle,* heralded for many years, was coldly received after publication.

sometimes the desire of accuracy will urge me to superfluities, and sometimes the fear of prolixity betray me to omissions; that in the extent of such variety I shall be often bewildered, and in the mazes of such intricacy be frequently entangled; that in one part refinement will be subtilized beyond exactness, and evidence dilated in another beyond perspicuity. Yet I do not despair of approbation from those who, knowing the uncertainty of conjecture, the scantiness of knowledge, the fallibility of memory, and the unsteadiness of attention, can compare the causes of error with the means of avoiding it, and the extent of art with the capacity of man; and whatever be the event of my endeavors, I shall not easily regret an attempt which has procured me the honor of appearing thus publicly,

My Lord,
Your Lordship's most obedient,
and most humble servant,
SAM. JOHNSON

1747

LETTER TO LORD CHESTERFIELD[1]
(Feb. 7, 1755)

To the Right Honorable the Earl of Chesterfield

MY LORD:

I have been lately informed by the proprietor of the *World*, that two papers, in which my Dictionary is recommended to the public, were written by your Lordship. To be so distinguished is an honor which, being very little accustomed to favors from the great, I know not well how to receive, or in what terms to acknowledge.

When, upon some slight encouragement, I first visited your Lordship, I was overpowered, like the rest of mankind, by the enchantment of your address, and could not forbear to wish that I might boast myself *Le vainqueur du vainqueur de la terre;*[2]—that I might obtain that regard for which I saw the world contending; but I found my attendance so little encouraged that neither pride nor modesty would suffer me to continue it. When I had once addressed your Lordship in public, I had exhausted all the art of pleasing which a retired and uncourtly scholar can possess. I had done all that I could; and no man is well pleased to have his all neglected, be it ever so little.

Seven years, my Lord, have now passed since I waited in your outward room, or was repulsed from your door; during which time I have been pushing on my work through difficulties, of which it is useless to complain, and have brought it, at last, to the verge of publication without one act of assistance, one word of encouragement, or one smile of favor. Such treatment I did not expect, for I never had a Patron before.

The shepherd in Vergil grew at last acquainted with Love, and found him a native of the rocks.[3]

Is not a Patron, my Lord, one who looks with unconcern on a man struggling for life in the water, and when he has reached ground, encumbers him with help? The notice which you have been pleased to take of my labors, had it been early, had been kind; but it has been delayed till I am indifferent, and cannot enjoy it; till I am solitary, and cannot impart it; till I am known, and do not want it. I hope it is no very cynical asperity not to confess obligations where no benefit has been received, or to be unwilling that the Public should consider me as owing that to a Patron, which Providence has enabled me to do for myself.

Having carried on my work thus far with so little obligation to any favorer of learning, I shall not be disappointed though I should conclude it, if less be possible, with less; for I have been long wakened from that dream of hope, in which I once boasted myself with so much exultation,

My Lord,
Your Lordship's most humble,
Most obedient servant,
SAM. JOHNSON

From the PREFACE TO THE ENGLISH DICTIONARY, 1755

. . . .

In hope of giving longevity to that which its own nature forbids to be immortal, I have devoted this book, the labor of years, to the

[1] "Johnson told me," says Boswell, "that there never was any particular incident which produced a quarrel between Lord Chesterfield and him; but that his Lordship's continued neglect was the reason why he resolved to have no connection with him. When the Dictionary was upon the eve of publication, Lord Chesterfield, who, it is said, had flattered himself with expectations that Johnson would dedicate the work to him, attempted . . . to conciliate him, by writing two papers in *The World* in recommendation of the work." "Upon which," commented Johnson, "I wrote him a letter expressed in civil terms, but such as might show him that I did not mind what he said or wrote, and that I had done with him." Boswell later obtained a copy of this celebrated letter, and gave it to the world. Carlyle, in his essay on *Boswell's Life of Johnson,* speaks of it as "that far-famed Blast of Doom, proclaiming into the ear of Lord Chesterfield, and, through him, of the listening world, that patronage should be no more."

[2] "The conqueror of the conqueror of the world" (Boileau)

[3] *Eclogue* VIII, 43

honor of my country, that we may no longer yield the palm of philology, without a contest, to the nations of the Continent. The chief glory of every people arises from its authors; whether I shall add anything by my own writings to the reputation of English literature, must be left to time. Much of my life has been lost under the pressure of disease; much has been trifled away; [1] and much has always been spent in provision for the day that was passing over me; but I shall not think my employment useless or ignoble, if by my assistance foreign nations and distant ages gain access to the propagators of knowledge, and understand the teachers of truth; if my labors afford light to the repositories of science, and add celebrity to Bacon, to Hooker, to Milton, and to Boyle. [2]

When I am animated by this wish, I look with pleasure on my book, however defective, and deliver it to the world with the spirit of a man that has endeavored well. That it will immediately become popular I have not promised to myself. A few wild blunders and risible absurdities, from which no work of such multiplicity was ever free, may for a time furnish folly with laughter and harden ignorance into contempt; [3] but useful diligence will at last prevail, and there never can be wanting some who distinguish desert; who will consider that no dictionary of a living tongue ever can be perfect, since, while it is hastening to publication, some words are budding, and some falling away; that a whole life cannot be spent upon syntax and etymology, and that even a whole life would not be sufficient; that he, whose design includes whatever language can express, must often speak of what he does not understand; that a writer will sometimes be hurried by eagerness to the end, and sometimes faint with weariness under a task which Scaliger [4] compares to the labors of the anvil and the mine; that what is obvious is not always known, and what is known is not always present; that sudden fits of inadvertency will surprise vigilance, slight avocations will seduce attention, and casual eclipses of the mind will darken learning; and that the writer shall often in vain trace his memory, at the moment of need, for that which yesterday he knew with intuitive readiness, and which will come uncalled into his thoughts tomorrow.

In this work, when it shall be found that much is omitted, let it not be forgotten that much likewise is performed; and though no book was ever spared out of tenderness to the author, and the world is little solicitous to know whence proceed the faults of that which it condemns, yet it may gratify curiosity to inform it that the *English Dictionary* was written with little assistance of the learned, and without any patronage of the great; not in the soft obscurities of retirement, or under the shelter of academic bowers, but amidst inconvenience and distraction, in sickness and in sorrow. [5] It may repress the triumph of malignant criticism to observe, that if our language is not here fully displayed, I have only failed in an attempt which no human powers have hitherto completed. If the lexicons of ancient tongues, now immutably fixed, and comprised in a few volumes, be yet, after the toil of successive ages, inadequate and delusive; if the aggregated knowledge and coöperating diligence of the Italian academicians did not secure them from the censure of Beni; [6] if the embodied critics of France, when fifty years had been spent upon their work, were obliged to change its economy, [7] and give their second edition another form, I may surely be contented without the praise of perfection, which, if I could obtain, in this gloom of solitude, what would it avail me? I have protracted my work till most of those whom I wished to please have sunk into the grave, and success and miscarriage are empty sounds; I therefore dismiss it with frigid tranquillity, having little to fear or hope from censure or from praise.

1755

From the PREFACE TO AN EDITION OF SHAKESPEARE'S PLAYS

. . . .

The poet, of whose works I have undertaken the revision, may now begin to assume the dignity of an ancient, and claim the privilege of

[1] Boswell reports Johnson as saying: "I have been trying to cure my laziness all my life, and could not do it."

[2] Robert Boyle, the natural philosopher, 1627-1691

[3] Johnson spoke prophetically. Among amusing entries, some of course intentional, Boswell has noted the following:

Lexicographer. A writer of dictionaries, a harmless drudge.

Pension. An allowance made to anyone without an equivalent. In England it is generally understood to mean pay given to a state hireling for treason to his country.

Oats. A grain which in England is generally given to horses, but in Scotland supports the people.

Network. Anything reticulated or decussated at equal distances, with interstices between the intersections.

[4] a European scholar of the 16th century

[5] Johnson's wife died March 17, 1752, and the anniversary of her death he spent "in prayer and self-examination."

[6] He objected to their basing their lexicon on Tuscan usage.

[7] system

established fame and prescriptive veneration. He has long outlived his century, the term commonly fixed as the test of literary merit. Whatever advantages he might once derive from personal allusions, local customs, or temporary opinions, have for many years been lost; and every topic of merriment, or motive of sorrow, which the modes of artificial life afforded him, now only obscure the scenes which they once illuminated. The effects of favor and competition are at an end; the tradition of his friendships and his enmities has perished; his works support no opinion with arguments, nor supply any faction with invectives; they can neither indulge vanity nor gratify malignity; but are read without any other reason than the desire of pleasure, and are therefore praised only as pleasure is obtained; yet, thus unassisted by interest or passion, they have passed through variations of taste and changes of manners, and, as they devolved from one generation to another, have received new honors at every transmission.

But because human judgment, though it be gradually gaining upon certainty, never becomes infallible, and approbation, though long continued, may yet be only the approbation of prejudice or fashion, it is proper to inquire by what peculiarities of excellence Shakespeare has gained and kept the favor of his countrymen.

Nothing can please many, and please long, but just representations of general nature. Particular manners can be known to few, and therefore few only can judge how nearly they are copied. The irregular combinations of fanciful invention may delight awhile, by that novelty of which the common satiety of life sends us all in quest; but the pleasures of sudden wonder are soon exhausted, and the mind can only repose on the stability of truth.

Shakespeare is, above all writers, at least above all modern writers, the poet of nature; the poet that holds up to his readers a faithful mirror of manners and of life. His characters are not modified by the customs of particular places, unpracticed by the rest of the world; by the peculiarities of studies or professions which can operate but upon small numbers; or by the accidents of transient fashions or temporary opinions: they are the genuine progeny of common humanity, such as the world will always supply and observation will always find. His persons act and speak by the influence of those general passions and principles by which all minds are agitated, and the whole system of life is continued in motion. In the writings of other poets a character is too often an individual; in those of Shakespeare it is commonly a species.

It is from this wide extension of design that so much instruction is derived. It is this which fills the plays of Shakespeare with practical axioms and domestic wisdom. It was said of Euripides that every verse was a precept; and it may be said of Shakespeare, that from his works may be collected a system of civil and economical prudence. Yet his real power is not shown in the splendor of particular passages, but by the progress of his fable[1] and the tenor of his dialogue; and he that tries to recommend him by select quotations, will succeed like the pedant in Hierocles[2] who, when he offered his house to sale, carried a brick in his pocket as a specimen.

It will not easily be imagined how much Shakespeare excels in accommodating his sentiments to real life, but by comparing him with other authors. It was observed of the ancient schools of declamation that the more diligently they were frequented, the more was the student disqualified for the world, because he found nothing there which he should ever meet in any other place. The same remark may be applied to every stage but that of Shakespeare. The theater, when it is under any other direction, is peopled by such characters as were never seen, conversing in a language which was never heard, upon topics which will never arise in the commerce of mankind. But the dialogue of this author is often so evidently determined by the incident which produces it, and is pursued with so much ease and simplicity, that it seems scarcely to claim the merit of fiction, but to have been gleaned by diligent selection out of common conversation and common occurrences.

Upon every other stage the universal agent is love, by whose power all good and evil is distributed, and every action quickened or retarded. To bring a lover, a lady, and a rival into a fable; to entangle them in contradictory obligations, perplex them with oppositions of interest, and harass them with violence of desires inconsistent with each other; to make them meet in rapture, and part in agony; to fill their mouths with hyperbolical joy and outrageous sorrow; to distress them as nothing human ever was distressed; to deliver them as nothing human ever was delivered—is the business of a modern dramatist. For this, probability is violated, life is misrepresented, and

[1] story, plot
[2] an Alexandrian philosopher to whom were attributed certain jests which Johnson once translated

language is depraved. But love is only one of many passions; and as it has no great influence upon the sum of life, it has little operation in the dramas of a poet who caught his ideas from the living world and exhibited only what he saw before him. He knew that any other passion, as it was regular or exorbitant, was a cause of happiness or calamity.

Characters thus ample and general were not easily discriminated and preserved, yet perhaps no poet ever kept his personages more distinct from each other. I will not say with Pope that every speech may be assigned to the proper speaker, because many speeches there are which have nothing characteristical; but, perhaps, though some may be equally adapted to every person, it will be difficult to find that any can be properly transferred from the present possessor to any other claimant. The choice is right, when there is reason for choice.

Other dramatists can only gain attention by hyperbolical or aggravated characters, by fabulous and unexampled excellence or depravity, as the writers of barbarous romances invigorated the reader by a giant and a dwarf; and he that should form his expectations of human affairs from the play, or from the tale, would be equally deceived. Shakespeare has no heroes; his scenes are occupied only by men, who act and speak as the reader thinks that he should himself have spoken or acted on the same occasion: even where the agency is supernatural, the dialogue is level with life. Other writers disguise the most natural passions and most frequent incidents; so that he who contemplates them in the book will not know them in the world: Shakespeare approximates the remote, and familiarizes the wonderful; the event which he represents will not happen, but, if it were possible, its effects would probably be such as he has assigned; and it may be said that he has not only shown human nature as it acts in real exigencies, but as it would be found in trials to which it cannot be exposed.

This therefore is the praise of Shakespeare, that his drama is the mirror of life; that he who has mazed his imagination in following the phantoms which other writers raise up before him, may here be cured of his delirious ecstasies by reading human sentiments in human language, by scenes from which a hermit may estimate the transactions of the world, and a confessor predict the progress of the passions.

. . . .

1765-68

From the LIVES OF THE ENGLISH POETS

[THE CHARACTER OF ADDISON]

. . . .

The end of this useful life was now approaching. Addison had for some time been oppressed by shortness of breath, which was now aggravated by a dropsy; and, finding his danger pressing, he prepared to die conformably to his own precepts and professions.

During this lingering decay he sent, as Pope relates, a message by the Earl of Warwick [1] to Mr. Gay, [2] desiring to see him. Gay, who had not visited him for some time before, obeyed the summons, and found himself received with great kindness. The purpose for which the interview had been solicited was then discovered: Addison told him that he had injured him; but that, if he recovered, he would recompense him. What the injury was he did not explain, nor did Gay ever know; but supposed that some preferment designed for him had, by Addison's intervention, been withheld.

Lord Warwick was a young man of very irregular life, and perhaps of loose opinions. Addison, for whom he did not want respect, had very diligently endeavored to reclaim him; but his arguments and expostulations had no effect. One experiment, however, remained to be tried; when he found his life near its end, he directed the young lord to be called; and when he desired, with great tenderness, to hear his last injunctions, told him, "I have sent for you that you may see how a Christian can die." What effect this awful scene had on the earl I know not; he likewise died himself in a short time.

In Tickell's [3] excellent elegy on his friend are these lines:

He taught us how to live; and oh! too high
The price of knowledge, taught us how to die.

In which he alludes, as he told Dr. Young, [4] to this moving interview.

Having given directions to Mr. Tickell for the publication of his works, and dedicated them on his death-bed to his friend Mr. Craggs, he died June 17, 1719, at Holland House, leaving no child but a daughter.

Of his virtue it is a sufficient testimony that the resentment of party has transmitted no charge of any crime. He was not one of those who are praised only after death; for his merit was so generally acknowledged that Swift, having observed that his election passed

[1] Addison's step-son
[2] John Gay, the poet
[3] Thomas Tickell, a contributor to the *Spectator*
[4] Edward Young, the poet

without a contest, adds, that if he had proposed himself for king he would hardly have been refused.[1]

His zeal for his party did not extinguish his kindness for the merit of his opponents: when he was Secretary in Ireland he refused to intermit his acquaintance with Swift.[2]

Of his habits, or external manners, nothing is so often mentioned as that timorous or sullen taciturnity, which his friends called modesty by too mild a name. Steele mentions with great tenderness "that remarkable bashfulness, which is a cloak that hides and muffles merit"; and tells us that "his abilities were covered only by modesty, which doubles the beauties which are seen, and gives credit and esteem to all that are concealed." Chesterfield affirms that "Addison was the most timorous and awkward man that he ever saw." And Addison, speaking of his own deficiency in conversation, used to say of himself that with respect to intellectual wealth, "he could draw bills for a thousand pounds though he had not a guinea in his pocket."

That he wanted current coin for ready payment, and by that want was often obstructed and distressed; that he was oppressed by an improper and ungraceful timidity, every testimony concurs to prove; but Chesterfield's representation is doubtless hyperbolical. That man cannot be supposed very unexpert in the arts of conversation and practice of life, who, without fortune or alliance, by his usefulness and dexterity, became Secretary of State; and who died at forty-seven, after having not only stood long in the highest rank of wit and literature, but filled one of the most important offices of State.

The time in which he lived had reason to lament his obstinacy of silence; for "he was," says Steele, "above all men in that talent called humor, and enjoyed it in such perfection that I have often reflected, after a night spent with him apart from all the world, that I had had the pleasure of conversing with an intimate acquaintance of Terence and Catullus, who had all their wit and nature, heightened with humor more exquisite and delightful than any other man ever possessed." This is the fondness of a friend; let us hear what is told us by a rival. "Addison's conversation," says Pope, "had something in it more charming than I have found in any other man. But this was only when familiar; before strangers, or perhaps a single stranger, he preserved his dignity by a stiff silence."

This modesty was by no means inconsistent with a very high opinion of his own merit. He demanded to be the first name in modern wit;[3] and, with Steele to echo him, used to depreciate Dryden, whom Pope and Congreve defended against them. There is no reason to doubt that he suffered too much pain from the prevalence of Pope's poetical reputation; nor is it without strong reason suspected that by some disingenuous acts he endeavored to obstruct it; Pope was not the only man whom he insidiously injured, though the only man of whom he could be afraid.

His own powers were such as might have satisfied him with conscious excellence. Of very extensive learning he has indeed given no proofs. He seems to have had small acquaintance with the sciences, and to have read little except Latin and French; but of the Latin poets his *Dialogue on Medals* shows that he had perused the works with great diligence and skill. The abundance of his own mind left him little need of adventitious sentiments; his wit always could suggest what the occasion demanded. He had read with critical eyes the important volume of human life, and knew the heart of man from the depths of stratagem to the surface of affectation.

What he knew he could easily communicate. "This," says Steele, "was particular in this writer, that when he had taken his resolution, or made his plan what he designed to write, he would walk about a room and dictate it into language with as much freedom and ease as anyone could write it down, and attend to the coherence and grammar of what he dictated."

Pope, who can be less suspected of favoring his memory, declares that he wrote very fluently, but was slow and scrupulous in correcting; that many of his *Spectators* were written very fast, and sent immediately to the press; and that it seemed to be for his advantage not to have time for much revisal.

"He would alter," says Pope, "anything to please his friends, before publication; but would not retouch his pieces afterwards; and I believe not one word in *Cato,* to which I made an objection, was suffered to stand."

The last line of *Cato* is Pope's, having been originally written

> And, oh! 'twas this that ended Cato's life.

Pope might have made more objections to the

[1] Addison was elected to Parliament in 1708.

[2] Addison, a Whig, and Swift, a Tory, took opposite sides in political controversy.

[3] used in the 18th century sense of "polite learning"

six concluding lines.[1] In the first couplet the words "From hence" are improper; and the second line is taken from Dryden's *Vergil.* Of the next couplet, the first verse, being included in the second, is therefore useless; and in the third "discord" is made to produce "strife."[2]

Of the course of Addison's familiar day, before his marriage, Pope has given a detail. He had in the house with him Budgell, and perhaps Philips. His chief companions were Steele, Budgell, Philips, Carey, Davenant, and Colonel Brett. With one or other of these he always breakfasted. He studied all morning; then dined at a tavern, and went afterwards to Button's.

Button had been a servant in the Countess of Warwick's family, who, under the patronage of Addison, kept a coffee-house on the south side of Russell Street, about two doors from Covent Garden. Here it was that the wits of that time used to assemble. It is said that when Addison suffered any vexation from the countess, he withdrew the company from Button's house.[3]

From the coffee-house he went again to a tavern, where he often sat late, and drank too much wine. In the bottle, discontent seeks for comfort, cowardice for courage, and bashfulness for confidence. It is not unlikely that Addison was first seduced to excess by the manumission which he obtained from the servile timidity of his sober hours. He that feels oppression from the presence of those to whom he knows himself superior, will desire to set loose his powers of conversation; and who, that ever asked succor from Bacchus, was able to preserve himself from being enslaved by his auxiliary?

Among those friends it was that Addison displayed the elegance of his colloquial accomplishments, which may easily be supposed such as Pope represents them. The remark of Mandeville,[4] who, when he had passed an evening in his company, declared that he was a parson in a tie-wig,[5] can detract little from his character; he was always reserved to strangers, and was not incited to uncommon freedom by a character like that of Mandeville.

From any minute knowledge of his familiar manners, the intervention of sixty years has now debarred us. Steele once promised Congreve and the public a complete description of his character; but the promises of authors are like the vows of lovers. Steele thought no more on his design, or thought on it with anxiety that at last disgusted him, and left his friend in the hands of Tickell.

One slight lineament of his character Swift has preserved. It was his practice when he found any man invincibly wrong, to flatter his opinions by acquiescence, and sink him yet deeper in absurdity. This artifice of mischief was admired by Stella;[6] and Swift seems to approve her admiration.

His works will supply some information. It appears from his various pictures of the world that, with all his bashfulness, he had conversed with many distinct classes of men, had surveyed their ways with very diligent observation, and marked with great acuteness the effects of different modes of life. He was a man in whose presence nothing reprehensible was out of danger; quick in discerning whatever was wrong or ridiculous, and not unwilling to expose it. There are, says Steele, in his writings many oblique strokes upon some of the wittiest men of the age. His delight was more to excite merriment than detestation, and he detects follies rather than crimes.

If any judgment be made, from his books, of his moral character, nothing will be found but purity and excellence. Knowledge of mankind, indeed, less extensive than that of Addison, will show that to write, and to live, are very different. Many who praise virtue do no more than praise it. Yet it is reasonable to believe that Addison's professions and practice were at no great variance since, amidst that storm of faction in which most of his life was passed, though his station made him conspicuous, and his activity made him formidable, the character given him by his friends was never contradicted by his enemies. Of those with whom interest or opinion united him, he had not only the esteem, but the kindness; and of others, whom the violence of opposition drove against him, though he might lose the love, he retained the reverence.

It is justly observed by Tickell that he employed wit on the side of virtue and religion. He not only made the proper use of wit himself, but taught it to others; and from his time it has been generally subservient to the cause of reason and of truth. He has dissipated the prejudice that had long connected gaiety with

[1] "From hence let fierce contending nations know
What dire effects from civil discord flow.
'Tis this that shakes our country with alarms,
And gives up Rome a prey to Roman arms,
Produces fraud, and cruelty, and strife,
And robs the guilty world of Cato's life."

[2] The rather trivial verbal criticism is characteristic of the time.

[3] Addison married the countess in 1716.

[4] Bernard Mandeville, a poet and somewhat of a cynic

[5] i. e., in the latest court-fashion (tie-wigs having just come in; moreover, the learned professions affected the loose, flowing wigs)

[6] Esther Johnson, a woman beloved by Swift

vice, and easiness of manners with laxity of principles. He has restored virtue to its dignity, and taught innocence not to be ashamed. This is an elevation of literary character, *above all Greek, above all Roman fame.* [1] No greater felicity can genius attain than that of having purified intellectual pleasure, separated mirth from indecency, and wit from licentiousness; of having taught a succession of writers to bring elegance and gaiety to the aid of goodness; and, if I may use expressions yet more awful, of having *turned many to righteousness.* [2]

. . . .

1779

JAMES BOSWELL 1740-1795

Modern biography, which aims so to depict character as to enable the reader to see the subject as he appeared to his living friends, was begun by Boswell. He was the son of an old-fashioned Scotch judge and landed proprietor. Although he studied for awhile at Edinburgh and was admitted to the bar, his indolent and convivial habits and his fondness for society, especially that of famous persons, long interfered with his following any serious calling. He spent much time in London. There his lively conversation and buoyant spirit lifted Johnson from many a fit of melancholy and made the younger man a welcome companion. His *Journal of a Tour to the Hebrides with Dr. Johnson,* 1785, gained him recognition, and his *Life of Dr. Johnson,* 1791, made him famous.

In this book, Johnson's conversation, whims, weaknesses, virtues, and faults are exhibited as in a photograph. Its apparent artlessness, its carelessness of the reputation of the author or of Johnson himself, and the naïve faith of the writer that his whole task was to record Johnson's life and not comment on it, give the book some of the qualities of a realistic novel and make it one of the clearest and completest biographical portraits ever drawn. The work was immediately popular, and not a decade has passed since but has seen one or two new editions.

Macaulay's and Carlyle's essays taken together excellently introduce the subject. Recent research by Professor Tinker shows Boswell in new and interesting situations. See *Young Boswell,* Boston, 1922, and *Letters of James Boswell,* 2 vols., Oxford, 1924; also his articles in *Atlan.* 127:577-83, 129: 22-9, 157-66, 356-61, especially the last; also Margery Bailey, *The Hypochondriack,* 2 vols., 1928. P. Bicknell, *Dial* 38:141-44, analyzes the elements of Boswell's success; L. Strachey, *New Rep.* 41:283-5, vigorously characterizes Boswell on the basis of the new evidence.

[1] quoted from Pope, "To Augustus"
[2] *Daniel,* xii, 3

From THE LIFE OF SAMUEL JOHNSON, LL.D.

[JOHNSON AT SCHOOL]

. . . .

He was first taught to read English by Dame Oliver, a widow, who kept a school for young children in Lichfield. He told me she could read the black letter, and asked him to borrow for her, from his father, a Bible in that character. When he was going to Oxford she came to take leave of him, brought him, in the simplicity of her kindness, a present of gingerbread, and said he was the best scholar she ever had. He delighted in mentioning this early compliment; adding, with a smile, that "this was as high a proof of his merit as he could conceive." His next instructor in English was a master whom, when he spoke of him to me, he familiarly called Tom Brown, who, said he, "published a spelling book, and dedicated it to the Universe; but I fear no copy of it can now be had."

He began to learn Latin with Mr. Hawkins, usher, or undermaster, of Lichfield school—"a man," said he, "very skillful in his little way." With him he continued two years, and then rose to be under the care of Mr. Hunter, the head master, who, according to his account, "was very severe, and wrongheadedly severe. He used," said he, "to beat us unmercifully; and he did not distinguish between ignorance and negligence; for he would beat a boy equally for not knowing a thing, as for neglecting to know it. He would ask a boy a question, and if he did not answer it, he would beat him, without considering whether he had an opportunity of knowing how to answer it. For instance, he would call up a boy and ask him Latin for a candlestick, which the boy could not expect to be asked. Now, sir, if a boy could answer every question, there would be no need of a master to teach him."

However, . . . Johnson was very sensible how much he owed to Mr. Hunter. Mr. Langton one day asked him how he had acquired so accurate a knowledge of Latin, in which I believe he was exceeded by no man of his time; he said, "My master whipped me very well. Without that, sir, I should have done nothing." He told Mr. Langton that while Hunter was flogging his boys unmercifully, he used to say, "And this I do to save you from the gallows." Johnson, upon all occasions, expressed his approbation of enforcing instruction by means of the rod. "I would rather," said he, "have the rod to be the general terror to all, [3] to make

[3] Cf. with Ascham, p. 132, and Milton, p. 285.

them learn, than tell a child, if you do thus, or thus, you will be more esteemed than your brothers or sisters. The rod produces an effect which terminates in itself. A child is afraid of being whipped, and gets his task, and there's an end on't; whereas, by exciting emulation and comparisons of superiority, you lay the foundation of lasting mischief; you make brothers and sisters hate each other."

. . . .

That superiority over his fellows which he maintained with so much dignity in his march through life, was not assumed from vanity and ostentation, but was the natural and constant effect of those extraordinary powers of mind, of which he could not but be conscious by comparison; the intellectual difference, which in other cases of comparison of characters is often a matter of undecided contest, being as clear in his case as the superiority of stature in some men above others. Johnson did not strut or stand on tiptoe; he only did not stoop. From his earliest years his superiority was perceived and acknowledged. He was from the beginning *anax andrōn,* a king of men. His schoolfellow, Mr. Hector, has obligingly furnished me with many particulars of his boyish days; and assured me that he never knew him corrected at school but for talking and diverting other boys from their business. He seemed to learn by intuition; for though indolence and procrastination were inherent in his constitution, whenever he made an exertion he did more than anyone else. In short, he is a memorable instance of what has been often observed, that the boy is the man in miniature; and that the distinguishing characteristics of each individual are the same through the whole course of life. His favorites used to receive very liberal assistance from him; and such was the submission and deference with which he was treated, such the desire to obtain his regard, that three of the boys, of whom Mr. Hector was sometimes one, used to come in the morning as his humble attendants, and carry him to school. One in the middle stooped while he sat upon his back, and one on each side supported him, and thus he was borne triumphant. Such a proof of the early predominance of intellectual vigor is very remarkable, and does honor to human nature.

[Johnson's Friends, 1752-53 [1]]

His acquaintance with Bennet Langton, Esq., of Langton, in Lincolnshire, another much valued friend, commenced soon after the conclusion of his *Rambler;* which that gentleman, then a youth, had read with so much admiration that he came to London chiefly with the view of endeavoring to be introduced to its author. By a fortunate chance he happened to take lodgings in a house where Mr. Levet [2] frequently visited; and having mentioned his wish to his landlady, she introduced him to Mr. Levet, who readily obtained Johnson's permission to bring Mr. Langton to him; as, indeed, Johnson, during the whole course of his life, had no shyness, real or affected, but was easy of access to all who were properly recommended, and even wished to see numbers at his *levee,* as his morning circle of company might, with strict propriety, be called. Mr. Langton was exceedingly surprised when the sage first appeared. He had not received the smallest intimation of his figure, dress, or manner. From perusing his writings, he fancied he should see a decent, well-dressed, in short, a remarkably decorous philosopher. Instead of which, down from his bed-chamber, about noon, came, as newly risen, a huge uncouth figure, with a little dark wig which scarcely covered his head, and his clothes hanging loose about him. But his conversation was so rich, so animated, and so forcible, and his religious and political notions so congenial with those in which Langton had been educated, that he conceived for him that veneration and attachment which he ever preserved.

. . . .

One night when Beauclerk [3] and Langton had supped at a tavern in London, and sat till about three in the morning, it came into their heads to go and knock up Johnson, and see if they could prevail on him to join them in a ramble. They rapped violently at the door of his chambers in the Temple, till at last he appeared in his shirt, with his little black wig on the top of his head instead of a nightcap, and a poker in his hand, imagining, probably, that some ruffians were coming to attack him. When he discovered who they were, and was told their errand, he smiled, and with great good humor agreed to their proposal: "What, is it you, you dogs! I'll have a frisk with you." He was soon dressed, and they sallied forth together into Covent-Garden, where the greengrocers and fruiterers were beginning to arrange their hampers, just come in from the country. Johnson made some attempts to help

[1] These dates indicate the period of Johnson's life concerning which the particular records are made. See any edition of Boswell's *Johnson.*

[2] a surgeon, an odd character, inmate of Dr. Johnson's house

[3] a gentleman of elegant tastes but rather free manners and opinions

them; but the honest gardeners stared so at his figure and manner and odd interference that he soon saw his services were not relished. They then repaired to one of the neighboring taverns, and made a bowl of that liquor called *Bishop,*[1] which Johnson had always liked; while, in joyous contempt of sleep, from which he had been roused, he repeated the festive lines,

Short, O short, then be thy reign,
And give us to the world again!

They did not stay long, but walked down to the Thames, took a boat, and rowed to Billingsgate. Beauclerk and Johnson were so well pleased with their amusement that they resolved to persevere in dissipation for the rest of the day; but Langton deserted them, being engaged to breakfast with some young ladies. Johnson scolded him for "leaving his social friends, to go and sit with a set of wretched *un-idea'd* girls." Garrick, being told of this ramble, said to him smartly, "I heard of your frolic t'other night. You'll be in the *Chronicle.*" Upon which Johnson afterwards observed, "*He* durst not do such a thing. His *wife* would not *let* him!"

He entered upon this year, 1753, with his usual piety, as appears from the following prayer, which I transcribed from that part of his diary which he burned a few days before his death:

"Jan. 1, 1753, N. S.,[2] which I shall use for the future.

"Almighty GOD, who has continued my life to this day, grant that, by the assistance of thy Holy Spirit, I may improve the time which thou shalt grant me, to my eternal salvation. Make me to remember, to thy glory, thy judgments and thy mercies. Make me so to consider the loss of my wife, whom thou hast taken from me, that it may dispose me by thy grace, to lead the residue of my life in thy fear. Grant this, O LORD, for JESUS CHRIST'S sake. Amen."

. . . .

[JOHNSON AND GOLDSMITH, 1773]

He and Mr. Langton and I went together to THE CLUB,[3] where we found Mr. Burke, Mr. Garrick, and some other members, and amongst them our friend Goldsmith, who sat silently brooding over Johnson's reprimand to him after dinner.[4] Johnson perceived this, and said aside to some of us, "I'll make Goldsmith forgive me;" and then called to him in a loud voice, "Dr. Goldsmith—something passed today where you and I dined. I ask your pardon." Goldsmith answered placidly, "It must be much from you, sir, that I take ill." And so at once the difference was over, and they were on as easy terms as ever, and Goldsmith rattled away as usual.

In our way to the club tonight, when I regretted that Goldsmith would, upon every occasion, endeavor to shine, by which he often exposed himself, Mr. Langton observed that he was not like Addison, who was content with the fame of his writings, and did not aim also at excellency in conversation, for which he found himself unfit; and that he said to a lady who complained of his having talked little in company, "Madam, I have but nine-pence in ready money, but I can draw for a thousand pounds." I observed that Goldsmith had a great deal of gold in his cabinet, but not content with that, was always taking out his purse. JOHNSON. "Yes, sir, and that so often an empty purse!"

Goldsmith's incessant desire of being conspicuous in company was the occasion of his sometimes appearing to such disadvantage as one should hardly have supposed possible in a man of his genius. When his literary reputation had risen deservedly high, and his society was much courted, he became very jealous of the extraordinary attention which was everywhere paid to Johnson. One evening, in a circle of wits, he found fault with me for talking of Johnson as entitled to the honor of unquestionable superiority. "Sir," said he, "you are for making a monarchy of what should be a republic."

He was still more mortified, when talking in a company with fluent vivacity, and, as he flattered himself, to the admiration of all who were present, a German who sat next him, and perceived Johnson rolling himself as if about to speak, suddenly stopped him, saying, "stay, stay—Toctor Shonson is going to say something." This was, no doubt, very provoking, especially to one so irritable as Goldsmith, who frequently mentioned it with strong expressions of indignation.

It may also be observed that Goldsmith was sometimes content to be treated with an easy familiarity, but upon occasions would be consequential and important. An instance of this

[1] mulled wine, oranges, and sugar
[2] New Style; this refers to the change to the Gregorian calendar, which was adopted in England in 1752, when the dates between September 2nd and 14th were omitted.
[3] the Literary Club
[4] After one of Johnson's long discourses, Goldsmith had begged that somebody else might be heard; whereupon Johnson called him impertinent.

occurred in a small particular. Johnson had a way of contracting the names of his friends: as Beauclerk, Beau; Boswell, Bozzy; Langton, Lanky; Murphy, Mur; Sheridan,[1] Sherry. I remember one day, when Tom Davies[2] was telling that Dr. Johnson said, "We are all in labor for a name to *Goldy's* play," Goldsmith seemed displeased that such a liberty should be taken with his name, and said, "I have often desired him not to call me *Goldy*." Tom was remarkably attentive to the most minute circumstance about Johnson. I recollect his telling me once, on my arrival in London, "Sir, our great friend has made an improvement on his appellation of old Mr. Sheridan. He calls him now *Sherry derry*."

. . . .

[CRITICAL OPINIONS]

. . . .

1775. Johnson was in high spirits this evening at the club, and talked with great animation and success. He attacked Swift, as he used to do upon all occasions. "The *Tale of a Tub* is so much superior to his other writings that one can hardly believe he was the author of it; there is in it such a vigor of mind, such a swarm of thoughts, so much of nature, and art, and life." I wondered to hear him say of *Gulliver's Travels,* "When once you have thought of big men and little men, it is very easy to do all the rest." I endeavored to make a stand for Swift, and tried to rouse those who were much more able to defend him; but in vain. Johnson at last, of his own accord, allowed very great merit to the inventory of articles found in the pocket of "the Man Mountain," particularly the description of his watch, which it was conjectured was HIS GOD, as he consulted it upon all occasions. He observed that "Swift put his name to but two things (after he had a name to put), *The Plan for the Improvement of the English Language* and the last *Drapier's Letter.*" . . .

1775. . . . . Next day I dined with Johnson at Mr. Thrale's. He attacked Gray, calling him "a dull fellow." BOSWELL: "I understand he was reserved, and might appear dull in company; but surely he was not dull in poetry." JOHNSON: "Sir, he was dull in company, dull in his closet, dull everywhere. He was dull in a new way, and that made many people think him GREAT. He was a mechanical poet." He then repeated some ludicrous lines, which have escaped my memory, and said, "Is not that GREAT, like his Odes?" Mrs. Thrale maintained that his Odes were melodious; upon which he exclaimed,

"Weave the warp, and weave the woof";

I added, in a solemn tone,

"The winding-sheet of Edward's race.

There is a good line."—"Aye," said he, "and the next line is a good one," pronouncing it contemptuously,

"Give ample verge and room enough.

No, sir, there are but two good stanzas in Gray's poetry, which are in his 'Elegy in a Country Churchyard.' " He then repeated the stanza,

"For who to dumb forgetfulness a prey," etc.,

mistaking one word; for instead of *precincts* he said *confines*. He added, "The other stanza I forget." . . . .

1776. . . . Talking of *The Spectator,* he said, "It is wonderful that there is such a proportion of bad papers in the half of the work which was not written by Addison; for there was all the world to write that half, yet not a half of that half is good." . . . .

[TALK AT THE CLUB, 1778]

. . . .

On Friday, April 3, I dined with him in London, in a company where were present several eminent men, whom I shall not name, but distinguish their parts in the conversation by different letters.[3]

F. "I have been looking at this famous antique marble dog of Mr. Jennings,[4] valued at a thousand guineas, said to be Alcibiades's dog." JOHNSON. "His tail then must be docked. That was the mark of Alcibiades's dog." E. "A thousand guineas! The representation of no animal whatever is worth so much. At this rate a dead dog would indeed be better than a living lion." JOHNSON. "Sir, it is not the worth of the thing, but of the skill in forming it, which is so highly estimated. Everything that enlarges the sphere of

[1] Thomas Sheridan, father of the dramatist

[2] a bookseller and publisher who published a pirated edition of Johnson's writings but was forgiven

[3] "It appears by the books of the Club, that the company on that evening consisted of Dr. Johnson, president, Mr. Burke, Mr. Boswell, Dr. George Fordyce, Mr. Gibbon, Sir Joshua Reynolds, Lord Upper Ossory, and Mr. R. B. Sheridan. In Mr. Boswell's account the letter E. no doubt stands for Edmund Burke; F., in allusion to his family name of Fitzpatrick, probably means Lord Upper Ossory; but the appropriation of the other letters is very difficult."—Croker

[4] Henry C. Jennings, a collector of antiques; the marble dog was at this date an object of great curiosity in London. Johnson had in mind the story in Plutarch's *Lives:* "Alcibiades had a dog of uncommon size and beauty, which cost him seventy minae, and yet his tail, which was his principal ornament, he caused to be cut off."

human powers, that shows man he can do what he thought he could not do, is valuable. The first man who balanced a straw upon his nose; Johnson, who rode upon three horses at a time; in short, all such men deserved the applause of mankind, not on account of the use of what they did, but of the dexterity which they exhibited." BOSWELL. "Yet a misapplication of time and assiduity is not to be encouraged. Addison, in one of his *Spectators,* commends the judgment of a king, who as a suitable reward to a man that by long perseverance had attained to the art of throwing a barley-corn through the eye of a needle, gave him a bushel of barley." JOHNSON. "He must have been a king of Scotland, where barley is scarce." F. "One of the most remarkable antique figures of an animal is the boar at Florence." JOHNSON. "The first boar that is well made in marble, should be preserved as a wonder. When men arrive at a facility of making boars well, then the workmanship is not of such value, but they should however be preserved as examples, and as a greater security for the restoration of the art, should it be lost." . .

E. "From the experience which I have had —and I have had a great deal—I have learnt to think *better* of mankind." JOHNSON. "From my experience I have found them worse in commercial dealings, more disposed to cheat than I had any notion of; but more disposed to do one another good than I had conceived." J. "Less just and more beneficent." JOHNSON. "And really it is wonderful, considering how much attention is necessary for men to take care of themselves and ward off immediate evils which press upon them, it is wonderful how much they do for others. As it is said of the greatest liar that he tells more truth than falsehood; so it may be said of the worst man that he does more good than evil." BOSWELL. "Perhaps from experience men may be found *happier* than we suppose." JOHNSON. "No, sir; the more we enquire we shall find men the less happy." P. "As to thinking better or worse of mankind from experience, some cunning people will not be satisfied unless they have put men to the test, as they think. There is a very good story told of Sir Godfrey Kneller, [1] in his character of a justice of the peace. A gentleman brought his servant before him, upon an accusation of having stolen some money from him; but it having come out that he had laid it purposely in the servant's way in order to try his honesty, Sir Godfrey sent the master to prison." JOHNSON. "To resist temptation once is not a sufficient proof of honesty. If a servant, indeed, were to resist the continued temptation of silver lying in a window, as some people let it lie, when he is sure his master does not know how much there is of it, he would give a strong proof of honesty. But this is a proof to which you have no right to put a man. You know, humanly speaking, there is a certain degree of temptation which will overcome any virtue. Now, in so far as you approach temptation to a man, you do him an injury; and, if he is overcome, you share his guilt." . . .

[1] portrait painter to Charles II and William III

[JOHNSON'S CHARACTER]

. . . .

The character of Samuel Johnson has, I trust, been so developed in the course of this work, that they who have honored it with a perusal may be considered as well acquainted with him. As, however, it may be expected that I should collect into one view the capital and distinguishing features of this extraordinary man, I shall endeavor to acquit myself of that part of my biographical undertaking, however difficult it may be to do that which many of my readers will do better for themselves.

His figure was large and well formed, and his countenance of the cast of an ancient statue; yet his appearance was rendered strange and somewhat uncouth, by convulsive cramps, by the scars of that distemper [2] which it was once imagined the royal touch could cure, and by a slovenly mode of dress. He had the use only of one eye; yet so much does mind govern, and even supply the deficiency of organs, that his visual perceptions, as far as they extended, were uncommonly quick and accurate. So morbid was his temperament [3] that he never knew the natural joy of a free and vigorous use of his limbs; when he walked, it was like the struggling gait of one in fetters; when he rode, he had no command or direction of his horse, but was carried as if in a balloon. That with his constitution and habits of life he should have lived seventy-five years is a proof that an inherent *vivida vis*[4] is a powerful preservative of the human frame.

Man is, in general, made up of contradictory qualities; and these will ever show themselves in strange succession where a consistency, in appearance at least, if not in reality, has not been attained by long habits of philosophical discipline. In proportion to the native vigor of

[2] Scrofula, or King's Evil; on the "royal touch," see Evelyn's *Diary,* July 6, 1660 (p. 300).

[3] so sickly was his constitution

[4] living force, spiritual energy

the mind, the contradictory qualities will be the more prominent, and more difficult to be adjusted; and, therefore, we are not to wonder that Johnson exhibited an eminent example of this remark which I have made upon human nature. At different times he seemed a different man, in some respects; not, however, in any great or essential article upon which he had fully employed his mind and settled certain principles of duty, but only in his manners, and in the display of argument and fancy in his talk. He was prone to superstition, but not to credulity. Though his imagination might incline him to a belief of the marvelous and the mysterious, his vigorous reason examined the evidence with jealousy. He was a sincere and zealous Christian, of high Church of England and monarchical principles, which he would not tamely suffer to be questioned; and had, perhaps, at an early period, narrowed his mind somewhat too much, both as to religion and politics. His being impressed with the danger of extreme latitude in either, though he was of a very independent spirit, occasioned his appearing somewhat unfavorable to the prevalence of that noble freedom of sentiment which is the best possession of man. Nor can it be denied that he had many prejudices; which, however, frequently suggested many of his pointed sayings, that rather show a playfulness of fancy than any settled malignity. He was steady and inflexible in maintaining the obligations of religion and morality; both from a regard for the order of society, and from a veneration for the Great Source of all order; correct, nay, stern in his taste; hard to please and easily offended; impetuous and irritable in his temper, but of a most humane and benevolent heart, which showed itself not only in a most liberal charity, as far as his circumstances would allow, but in a thousand instances of active benevolence. He was afflicted with a bodily disease, which made him often restless and fretful; and with a constitutional melancholy, the clouds of which darkened the brightness of his fancy, and gave a gloomy cast to his whole course of thinking. We, therefore, ought not to wonder at his sallies of impatience and passion at any time; especially when provoked by obtrusive ignorance, or presuming petulance; and allowance must be made for his uttering hasty and satirical sallies even against his best friends. And, surely, when it is considered that "amidst sickness and sorrow" he exerted his faculties in so many works for the benefit of mankind, and particularly that he achieved the great and admirable *Dictionary* of our language, we must be astonished at his resolution. The solemn text, "Of him to whom much is given much will be required," seems to have been ever present to his mind, in a rigorous sense, and to have made him dissatisfied with his labors and acts of goodness, however comparatively great; so that the unavoidable consciousness of his superiority was, in that respect, a cause of disquiet. He suffered so much from this, and from the gloom which perpetually haunted him and made solitude frightful, that it may be said of him, "If in this life only he had hope, he was of all men most miserable."

He loved praise, when it was brought to him; but was too proud to seek for it. He was somewhat susceptible of flattery. As he was general and unconfined in his studies, he cannot be considered as master of any one particular science; but he had accumulated a vast and various collection of learning and knowledge, which was so arranged in his mind as to be ever in readiness to be brought forth. But his superiority over other learned men consisted chiefly in what may be called the art of thinking, the art of using his mind; a certain continual power of seizing the useful substance of all that he knew, and exhibiting it in a clear and forcible manner; so that knowledge, which we often see to be no better than lumber in men of dull understanding, was, in him, true, evident, and actual wisdom. His moral precepts are practical; for they are drawn from an intimate acquaintance with human nature. His maxims carry conviction; for they are founded on the basis of common sense and a very attentive and minute survey of real life. His mind was so full of imagery that he might have been perpetually a poet; yet it is remarkable that however rich his prose is in this respect, his poetical pieces, in general, have not much of that splendor, but are rather distinguished by strong sentiment and acute observation, conveyed in harmonious and energetic verse, particularly in heroic couplets.

Though usually grave, and even awful in his deportment, he possessed uncommon and peculiar powers of wit and humor; he frequently indulged himself in colloquial pleasantry; and the heartiest merriment was often enjoyed in his company; with this great advantage that, as it was entirely free from any poisonous tincture of vice or impiety, it was salutary to those who shared in it. He had accustomed himself to such accuracy in his common conversation that he at all times expressed his thoughts with great force and an elegant choice of language, the effect of which was aided by his having a loud voice, and a slow, deliberate utterance. In him were united a most logical head with a most fertile imagination, which gave him an extraordinary advantage in arguing; for he could reason close or wide, as he saw best for the moment. Exulting in his intellectual strength and dexterity, he could, when he pleased, be the greatest sophist that ever contended in the lists of declamation; and from a spirit of contradiction and a delight in showing his powers, he would often maintain the wrong side with equal warmth and ingenuity; so that, when there was an audience, his real opinions could seldom be gathered from his talk; though when he was in company with a single friend he would discuss a subject with genuine fairness; but he was too conscientious to make error permanent and pernicious by deliberately writing it; and, in all his numerous works, he earnestly inculcated what appeared to him to be the truth; his piety being constant, and the ruling principle of all his conduct.

Such was SAMUEL JOHNSON, a man whose talents, acquirements, and virtues were so extraordinary, that the more his character is considered, the more he will be regarded by the present age, and by posterity, with admiration and reverence.

1791

OLIVER GOLDSMITH
1728-1774

Goldsmith, probably best-beloved of all eighteenth century English men of letters, essayist, novelist, dramatist, and miscellaneous writer, was born in Ireland (exact place uncertain), where his father was a country parson of the established Church. The family could not afford this younger son a gentleman's education, but the lad went to Trinity College, Dublin, as a sizar, and partly worked his way by performing manual labor. Not much better off for the degree he received in 1749, he led for the next seven years a wandering life, the despair of his relatives. During this time he studied medicine, and somehow managed to gain the title doctor of medicine; and also made the "grand tour" of Europe, penniless and afoot. At length he settled in London, where he spent the last eighteen years of his life as a writer.

As a literary journeyman he produced all sorts of hack work, journals, biographies, histories, essays, and reviews. From this slavery he was slowly emerging when he died. *The Traveler* appeared in 1764, and at intervals of two years successively, *The Vicar of Wakefield, The Good-Natured Man,* and the *Deserted Village.* One year before his death came, *She Stoops to Conquer* still played to delighted audiences. Though Goldsmith as a child of his generation uses Pope's verse forms, and shows little sympathy with romanticism, his kindliness, humanity, and compassion separate him from his contemporaries. His work as a whole rings true and holds no drop of cynicism. No clearer prose than his has been written. His critical opinions were probably influenced by Johnson who was his staunch friend and wrote of him, "He was a very great man."

Biographies: W. Black (EML); A. Dobson; F. F. Moore, 1910. Interesting reviews of Moore's life, *Nation* 92:194-5, *Dial* 50:472-4; see also *Cur. Lit.* 51:94-6, and E. Clarke, "Oliver Goldsmith as a Medical Man," *19th Cent.* 75:821-31; Macaulay, Thackeray, Rossetti.

From THE CITIZEN OF THE WORLD [1]

LETTER I

To Mr. ——, Merchant in London

Amsterdam

Sir—Yours of the 13th instant, covering two bills, one on Messrs. R. and D., value £478 10s., and the other on Mr. —, value £285, duly came to hand, the former of which met with honor, but the other has been trifled with, and I am afraid will be returned protested.

The bearer of this is my friend, therefore let him be yours. He is a native of Honan in China, and one who did me signal services, when he was a mandarin, and I a factor, at Canton. By frequently conversing with the English there, he has learned the language, though entirely a stranger to their manners and customs. I am told he is a philosopher; I am sure he is an honest man; that to you will be his best recommendation, next to the consideration of his being the friend of, sir,

Yours, etc.

LETTER II

From Lien Chi Altangi to ——, Merchant in Amsterdam

London

Friend of my Heart—May the wings of peace rest upon thy dwelling, and the shield of conscience preserve thee from vice and misery! For all thy favors accept my gratitude and esteem, the only tributes a poor philosophic wanderer can return. Sure, fortune is resolved to make me unhappy, when she gives others a power of testifying their friendship by actions,

[1] These "Chinese Letters," as they were commonly called, 123 in number, were written for *The Public Ledger* in 1760 and 1761. The source of their popularity lay in the amusing social satire obtained by viewing the customs of one country through the eyes of a citizen of another. Lien Chi Altangi is of course fictitious, as are the other Chinese characters mentioned.

and leaves me only words to express the sincerity of mine.

I am perfectly sensible of the delicacy with which you endeavor to lessen your own merit and my obligations. By calling your late instances of friendship only a return for former favors, you would induce me to impute to your justice what I owe to your generosity.

The services I did you at Canton, justice, humanity, and my office bade me perform; those you have done me since my arrival at Amsterdam, no laws obliged you to, no justice required. Even half your favors would have been greater than my most sanguine expectations.

The sum of money, therefore, which you privately conveyed into my baggage when I was leaving Holland, and which I was ignorant of till my arrival in London, I must beg leave to return. You have been bred a merchant, and I a scholar; you consequently love money better than I. You can find pleasure in superfluity; I am perfectly content with what is sufficient. Take therefore what is yours; it may give you some pleasure, even though you have no occasion to use it; my happiness it cannot improve, for I have already all that I want.

My passage by sea from Rotterdam to England was more painful to me than all the journeys I ever made on land. I have traversed the immeasurable wilds of Mogul Tartary; felt all the rigors of Siberian skies; I have had my repose a hundred times disturbed by invading savages, and have seen, without shrinking, the desert sands rise like a troubled ocean all around me. Against these calamities I was armed with resolution; but in my passage to England, though nothing occurred that gave the mariners any uneasiness, to one who was never at sea before, all was a subject of astonishment and terror. To find the land disappear—to see our ship mount the waves, swift as an arrow from the Tartar bow—to hear the wind howling through the cordage—to feel a sickness which depresses even the spirits of the brave—these were unexpected distresses, and consequently assaulted me, unprepared to receive them.

You men of Europe think nothing of a voyage by sea. With us of China a man who has been from sight of land is regarded upon his return with admiration. I have known some provinces where there is not even a name for the ocean. What a strange people, therefore, am I got amongst, who have founded an empire on this unstable element, who build cities upon billows that rise higher than the mountains of Tipartala,[1] and make the deep more formidable than the wildest tempest!

Such accounts as these, I must confess, were my first motives for seeing England. These induced me to undertake a journey of seven hundred painful days, in order to examine its opulence, buildings, sciences, arts, and manufactures, on the spot. Judge, then, my disappointment on entering London, to see no signs of that opulence so much talked of abroad. Wherever I turn I am presented with a gloomy solemnity in the houses, the streets, and the inhabitants; none of that beautiful gilding which makes a principal ornament in Chinese architecture. The streets of Nankin are sometimes strewed with gold leaf; very different are those of London; in the midst of their pavement a great lazy puddle moves muddily along; heavy-laden machines, with wheels of unwieldy thickness, crowd up every passage; so that a stranger, instead of finding time for observation, is often happy if he has time to escape from being crushed to pieces.

The houses borrow very few ornaments from architecture; their chief decoration seems to be a paltry piece of painting hung out at their doors or windows,[2] at once a proof of their indigence and vanity; their vanity, in each having one of those pictures exposed to public view; and their indigence, in being unable to get them better painted. In this respect the fancy of their painters is also deplorable. Could you believe it? I have seen five black lions and three blue boars in less than the circuit of half a mile; and yet you know that animals of these colors are nowhere to be found, except in the wild imaginations of Europe.

From these circumstances in their buildings and from the dismal looks of the inhabitants, I am induced to conclude that the nation is actually poor; and that, like the Persians, they make a splendid figure everywhere but at home. The proverb of Xixofou is that a man's riches may be seen in his eyes; if we judge of the English by this rule, there is not a poorer nation under the sun.

I have been here but two days, so will not be hasty in my decisions. Such letters as I shall write to Fipsihi in Moscow I beg you will endeavor to forward with all diligence; I shall send them open, in order that you may take copies or translations, as you are equally versed in the Dutch and Chinese languages. Dear

[1] unidentified

[2] House or door signs were formerly extensively used in London in place of numbers.

friend, think of my absence with regret, as I sincerely regret yours; even while I write I lament our separation. Farewell.

Letter III

From Lien Chi Altangi to the care of Fipsihi, resident in Moscow; to be forwarded by the Russian caravan to Fum Hoam, First President of the Ceremonial Academy at Pekin, in China

Think not, O thou guide of my youth, that absence can impair my respect, or interposing trackless deserts blot your reverend figure from my memory. The farther I travel I feel the pain of separation with stronger force; those ties that bind me to my native country and you are still unbroken. By every remove I only drag a greater length of chain.

Could I find aught worth transmitting from so remote a region as this to which I have wandered, I should gladly send it; but instead of this you must be contented with a renewal of my former professions, and an imperfect account of a people with whom I am as yet but superficially acquainted. The remarks of a man who has been but three days in the country can only be those obvious circumstances which force themselves upon the imagination. I consider myself here as a newly created being introduced into a new world. Every object strikes with wonder and surprise. The imagination, still unsated, seems the only active principle of the mind. The most trifling occurrences give pleasure till the gloss of novelty is worn away. When I have ceased to wonder, I may possibly grow wise; I may then call the reasoning principle to my aid, and compare those objects with each other which were before examined without reflection.

Behold me, then, in London, gazing at the strangers, and they at me. It seems they find somewhat absurd in my figure; and had I never been from home it is possible I might find an infinite fund of ridicule in theirs. But by long traveling I am taught to laugh at folly alone, and to find nothing truly ridiculous but villainy and vice.

When I had just quitted my native country and crossed the Chinese wall, I fancied every deviation from the customs and manners of China was a departing from nature. I smiled at the blue lips and red foreheads of the Tonguese;[1] and could hardly contain when I saw the Daures[2] dress their heads with horns. The Ostiacs[3] powdered with red earth, and the Calmuck[4] beauties tricked out in all the finery of sheepskin, appeared highly ridiculous. But I soon perceived that the ridicule lay not in them but in me; that I falsely condemned others for absurdity because they happened to differ from a standard originally founded in prejudice or partiality.

I find no pleasure, therefore, in taxing the English with departing from nature in their external appearance, which is all I yet know of their character. It is possible they only endeavor to improve her simple plan, since every extravagance in dress proceeds from a desire of becoming more beautiful than nature made us; and this is so harmless a vanity that I not only pardon but approve it. A desire to be more excellent than others is what actually makes us so; and as thousands find a livelihood in society by such appetites, none but the ignorant inveigh against them.

You are not insensible, most reverend Fum Hoam, what numberless trades, even among the Chinese, subsist by the harmless pride of each other. Your nose-borers, feet-swathers, teeth-stainers, eyebrow-pluckers, would all want bread, should their neighbors want vanity. These vanities, however, employ much fewer hands in China than in England; and a fine gentleman or a fine lady here, dressed up to the fashion, seems scarcely to have a single limb that does not suffer some distortions from art.

To make a fine gentleman several trades are required, but chiefly a barber. You have undoubtedly heard of the Jewish champion[5] whose strength lay in his hair. One would think that the English were for placing all wisdom there. To appear wise, nothing more is requisite here than for a man to borrow hair from the heads of all his neighbors, and clap it like a bush on his own. The distributors of law and physic stick on such quantities that it is almost impossible, even in idea, to distinguish between the head and the hair.

Those whom I have now been describing affect the gravity of the lion; those I am going to describe more resemble the pert vivacity of smaller animals. The barber, who is still master of the ceremonies, cuts their hair close to the crown; and then, with a composition of meal and hog's-lard, plasters the whole in such a manner as to make it impossible to distinguish whether the patient wears a cap or a

[1] the Tunguses, Mongolians of eastern Siberia
[2] the Daurians in Manchuria
[3] a tribe of western Siberia
[4] western Mongols
[5] Samson (*Judges* xvi, 17)

plaster; but, to make the picture more perfectly striking, conceive the tail of some beast, a greyhound's tail, or a pig's tail, for instance, appended to the back of the head, and reaching down to the place where tails in other animals are generally seen to begin; thus betailed and bepowdered, the man of taste fancies he improves in beauty, dresses up his hard-featured face in smiles, and attempts to look hideously tender. Thus equipped he is qualified to make love, and hopes for success more from the powder on the outside of his head than the sentiments within.

Yet when I consider what sort of a creature the fine lady is to whom he is supposed to pay his addresses, it is not strange to find him thus equipped in order to please. She is herself every whit as fond of powder, and tails, and hog's lard, as he. To speak my secret sentiments, most reverend Fum, the ladies here are horridly ugly; I can hardly endure the sight of them; they no way resemble the beauties of China; the Europeans have a quite different idea of beauty from us. When I reflect on the small-footed perfections of an Eastern beauty, how is it possible I should have eyes for a woman whose feet are ten inches long? I shall never forget the beauties of my native city of Nangfew. How very broad their faces! how very short their noses! how very little their eyes! how very thin their lips! how very black their teeth! the snow on the tops of Bao[1] is not fairer than their cheeks; and their eyebrows are small as the line by the pencil of Quamsi. Here a lady with such perfections would be frightful. Dutch and Chinese beauties, indeed, have some resemblance, but English women are entirely different; red cheeks, big eyes, and teeth of a most odious whiteness, are not only seen here, but wished for; and then they have such masculine feet, as actually serve *some* for walking!

Yet, uncivil as nature has been, they seem resolved to outdo her in unkindness; they use white powder, blue powder, and black powder for their hair, and a red powder for the face on some particular occasions.

They like to have the face of various colors as among the Tartars of Koreki,[1] frequently sticking on, with spittle, little black patches on every part of it, except on the tip of the nose, which I have never seen with a patch. You'll have a better idea of their manner of placing these spots when I have finished a map of an English face patched up to the fashion, which shall shortly be sent to increase your curious collection of paintings, medals, and monsters.

But what surprises more than all the rest is what I have just now been credibly informed of by one of this country. "Most ladies here," says he, "have two faces; one face to sleep in, and another to show in company. The first is generally reserved for the husband and family at home; the other put on to please strangers abroad. The family face is often indifferent enough, but the outdoor one looks something better; this is always made at the toilet, where the looking-glass and toad-eater[2] sit in council, and settle the complexion of the day."

I cannot ascertain the truth of this remark; however, it is actually certain that they wear more clothes within doors than without; and I have seen a lady who seemed to shudder at a breeze in her own apartment, appear half naked in the streets. Farewell.

Letter IV

To the Same

The English seem as silent as the Japanese, yet vainer than the inhabitants of Siam. Upon my arrival I attributed that reserve to modesty, which, I now find, has its origin in pride. Condescend to address them first, and you are sure of their acquaintance; stoop to flattery, and you conciliate their friendship and esteem. They bear hunger, cold, fatigue, and all the miseries of life, without shrinking; danger only calls forth their fortitude; they even exult in calamity; but contempt is what they cannot bear. An Englishman fears contempt more than death; he often flies to death as a refuge from its pressure, and dies when he fancies the world has ceased to esteem him.

Pride seems the source not only of their national vices, but of their national virtues also. An Englishman is taught to love his king as his friend, but to acknowledge no other master than the laws which himself has contributed to enact. He despises those nations who, that one may be free, are all content to be slaves; who first lift a tyrant into terror, and then shrink under his power as if delegated from Heaven. Liberty is echoed in all their assemblies; and thousands might be found ready to offer up their lives for the sound, though perhaps not one of all the number understands its meaning. The lowest mechanic, however, looks upon it as his duty to be a watchful guardian of his country's freedom, and often uses a language that might seem

[1] These places have never been identified; they are possibly inventions.

[2] flattering attendant

haughty even in the mouth of the great emperor who traces his ancestry to the Moon.

A few days ago, passing by one of their prisons, I could not avoid stopping, in order to listen to a dialogue which I thought might afford me some entertainment. The conversation was carried on between a debtor through the grate of his prison, a porter who had stopped to rest his burden, and a soldier at the window. The subject was upon a threatened invasion from France, and each seemed extremely anxious to rescue his country from the impending danger. "For my part," cries the prisoner, "the greatest of my apprehensions is for our freedom; if the French should conquer, what would become of English liberty? My dear friends, liberty is the Englishman's prerogative; we must preserve that at the expense of our lives; of that the French shall never deprive us. It is not to be expected that men who are slaves themselves would preserve our freedom should they happen to conquer." "Aye, slaves," cries the porter, "they are all slaves, fit only to carry burdens, every one of them. Before I would stoop to slavery may this be my poison (and he held the goblet in his hand), may this be my poison—but I would sooner list for a soldier."

The soldier, taking the goblet from his friend, with much awe fervently cried out, "It is not so much our liberties as our religion that would suffer by such a change; aye, our religion, my lads. May the devil sink me into flames (such was the solemnity of his adjuration), if the French should come over, but our religion would be utterly undone!" So saying, instead of a libation, he applied the goblet to his lips, and confirmed his sentiments with a ceremony of the most persevering devotion.

In short, every man here pretends to be a politician; even the fair sex are sometimes found to mix the severity of national altercation with the blandishments of love, and often become conquerors by more weapons of destruction than their eyes.

This universal passion for politics is gratified by daily gazettes, as with us in China. But as in ours the emperor endeavors to instruct his people, in theirs the people endeavor to instruct the administration. You must not, however, imagine that they who compile these papers have any actual knowledge of the politics or the government of a state; they only collect their materials from the oracle of some coffee-house, which oracle has himself gathered them the night before from a beau at a gaming-table, who has pillaged his knowledge from a great man's porter, who has had his information from the great man's gentleman,[1] who has invented the whole story for his own amusement the night preceding.

The English, in general, seem fonder of gaining the esteem than the love of those they converse with. This gives a formality to their amusements. Their gayest conversations have something too wise for innocent relaxation; though in company you are seldom disgusted with the absurdity of a fool, you are seldom lifted into rapture by those strokes of vivacity which give instant though not permanent pleasure.

What they want, however, in gaity, they make up in politeness. You smile at hearing me praise the English for their politeness; you who have heard very different accounts from the missionaries at Pekin, who have seen such a different behavior in their merchants and seamen at home. But I must still repeat it, the English seem more polite than any of their neighbors; their great art in this respect lies in endeavoring, while they oblige, to lessen the force of the favor. Other countries are fond of obliging a stranger; but seem desirous that he should be sensible of the obligation. The English confer their kindness with an appearance of indifference, and give away benefits with an air as if they despised them.

Walking, a few days ago, between an English and a French man, into the suburbs of the city, we were overtaken by a heavy shower of rain. I was unprepared; but they had each large coats which defended them from what seemed to me a perfect inundation. The Englishman, seeing me shrink from the weather, accosted me thus: "Pshaw, man, what dost shrink at? Here, take this coat; I don't want it; I find it no way useful to me; I had as lief be without it." The Frenchman began to show his politeness in turn. "My dear friend," cries he, "why won't you oblige me by making use of my coat? You see how well it defends me from the rain; I should not choose to part with it to others, but to such a friend as you I could even part with my skin to do him service."

From such minute instances as these, most reverend Fum Hoam, I am sensible your sagacity will collect instruction. The volume of nature is the book of knowledge; and he becomes most wise who makes the most judicious selection.

Farewell.

1760

[1] valet

THE DESERTED VILLAGE[1]

Sweet Auburn![2] loveliest village of the plain,
Where health and plenty cheered the laboring swain,
Where smiling spring its earliest visit paid,
And parting summer's lingering blooms delayed;
Dear lovely bowers of innocence and ease,
Seats of my youth, when every sport could please,
How often have I loitered o'er thy green,
Where humble happiness endeared each scene!
How often have I paused on every charm,
The sheltered cot, the cultivated farm,
The never-failing brook, the busy mill,
The decent church that topped the neighboring hill,
The hawthorn bush, with seats beneath the shade,
For talking age and whispering lovers made!
How often have I blessed the coming day,
When toil remitting lent its turn to play,
And all the village train, from labor free,
Led up their sports beneath the spreading tree,
While many a pastime circled in the shade,
The young contending as the old surveyed;
And many a gambol frolicked o'er the ground,
And sleights of art and feats of strength went round!
And still, as each repeated pleasure tired,
Succeeding sports the mirthful band inspired;
The dancing pair that simply sought renown
By holding out to tire each other down;
The swain mistrustless of his smutted face,
While secret laughter tittered round the place;
The bashful virgin's sidelong looks of love,
The matron's glance that would those looks reprove.
These were thy charms, sweet village! Sports like these,
With sweet succession, taught even toil to please;
These round thy bowers their cheerful influence shed;
These were thy charms—but all these charms are fled.

Sweet smiling village, loveliest of the lawn,
Thy sports are fled, and all thy charms withdrawn;
Amidst thy bowers the tyrant's[3] hand is seen,
And desolation saddens all thy green;
One only master grasps the whole domain,
And half a tillage stints thy smiling plain.
No more thy glassy brook reflects the day,
But choked with sedges, works its weedy way;
Along thy glades, a solitary guest,
The hollow-sounding bittern guards its nest;
Amidst thy desert walks the lapwing flies,
And tires their echoes with unvaried cries.
Sunk are thy bowers in shapeless ruin all,
And the long grass o'ertops the moldering wall;
And trembling, shrinking from the spoiler's hand,
Far, far away, thy children leave the land.

Ill fares the land, to hastening ills a prey,
Where wealth accumulates, and men decay.
Princes and lords may flourish, or may fade—
A breath can make them, as a breath has made—
But a bold peasantry, their country's pride,
When once destroyed, can never be supplied.

A time there was, ere England's griefs began,
When every rood of ground maintained its man;
For him light labor spread her wholesome store,
Just gave what life required, but gave no more;
His best companions, innocence and health,
And his best riches ignorance of wealth.

But times are altered; trade's unfeeling train
Usurp the land, and dispossess the swain.
Along the lawn, where scattered hamlets rose,
Unwieldy wealth and cumbrous pomp repose;
And every want to luxury allied,
And every pang that folly pays to pride.
Those gentle hours that plenty bade to bloom,
Those calm desires that asked but little room,
Those healthful sports that graced the peaceful scene,
Lived in each look, and brightened all the green;
These, far departing, seek a kinder shore,
And rural mirth and manners are no more.

Sweet Auburn! parent of the blissful hour,
Thy glades forlorn confess the tyrant's power.
Here, as I take my solitary rounds
Amidst thy tangling walks and ruined grounds,

[1] This poem was inspired by Goldsmith's conviction that Ireland was being steadily depopulated. In the letter in which he inscribed the poem to Sir Joshua Reynolds, he wrote: "In regretting the depopulation of the country, I inveigh against the increase of our luxuries; and here also I expect a shout of modern politicians against me. For twenty or thirty years past, it has been the fashion to consider luxury as one of the greatest national advantages. Still, I must continue to think those luxuries prejudicial to states by which so many vices are introduced, and so many kingdoms have been undone."

[2] probably Lissoy, where Goldsmith spent his childhood

[3] a certain English landlord who evicted many tenants

And, many a year elapsed, return to view
Where once the cottage stood, the hawthorn grew,
Remembrance wakes with all her busy train,
Swells at my breast, and turns the past to pain.

In all my wanderings round this world of care,
In all my griefs—and God has given my share—
I still had hopes, my latest hours to crown,
Amidst these humble bowers to lay me down;
To husband out life's taper at the close,
And keep the flame from wasting by repose.
I still had hopes, for pride attends us still,
Amidst the swains to show my book-learned skill,
Around my fire an evening group to draw,
And tell of all I felt, and all I saw;
And, as a hare whom hounds and horns pursue
Pants to the place from whence at first he flew,
I still had hopes, my long vexations past,
Here to return—and die at home at last.

O blest retirement, friend to life's decline,
Retreats from care, that never must be mine,
How blest is he who crowns, in shades like these,
A youth of labor with an age of ease;
Who quits a world where strong temptations try,
And, since 'tis hard to combat, learns to fly!
For him no wretches, born to work and weep,
Explore the mine, or tempt the dangerous deep;
Nor surly porter stands, in guilty state,
To spurn imploring famine from the gate;
But on he moves to meet his latter end,
Angels around befriending virtue's friend;
Sinks to the grave with unperceived decay,
While resignation gently slopes the way;
And, all his prospects brightening to the last,
His heaven commences, ere the world be past!

Sweet was the sound, when oft at evening's close
Up yonder hill the village murmer rose;
There, as I passed with careless steps and slow,
The mingling notes came softened from below;
The swain responsive as the milkmaid sung,
The sober herd that lowed to meet their young;
The noisy geese that gabbled o'er the pool,
The playful children just let loose from school;
The watchdog's voice that bayed the whispering wind,
And the loud laugh that spoke the vacant mind;
These all in sweet confusion sought the shade,
And filled each pause the nightingale had made.
But now the sounds of population fail,
No cheerful murmurs fluctuate in the gale,
No busy steps the grass-grown footway tread,
For all the bloomy flush of life is fled.
All but yon widowed, solitary thing,
That feebly bends beside the plashy spring;
She, wretched matron—forced in age, for bread,
To strip the brook with mantling cresses spread,
To pick her wintry fagot from the thorn,
To seek her nightly shed, and weep till morn—
She only left of all the harmless train,
The sad historian of the pensive plain!

Near yonder copse, where once the garden smiled,
And still where many a garden flower grows wild;
There, where a few torn shrubs the place disclose,
The village preacher's modest mansion rose.
A man he was to all the country dear, [1]
And passing [2] rich with forty pounds a year;
Remote from towns he ran his godly race,
Nor e'er had changed, nor wished to change his place;
Unpracticed he to fawn, or seek for power,
By doctrines fashioned to the varying hour;
Far other aims his heart had learned to prize,
More skilled to raise the wretched than to rise.
His house was known to all the vagrant train,
He chid their wanderings, but relieved their pain;
The long-remembered beggar was his guest,
Whose beard descending swept his aged breast;
The ruined spendthrift, now no longer proud,
Claimed kindred there, and had his claims allowed;
The broken soldier, kindly bade to stay,
Sat by his fire, and talked the night away,
Wept o'er his wounds, or, tales of sorrow done,
Shouldered his crutch and showed how fields were won.
Pleased with his guests, the good man learned to glow,
And quite forgot their vices in their woe;
Careless their merits or their faults to scan,
His pity gave ere charity began.

Thus to relieve the wretched was his pride,
And e'en his failings leaned to virtue's side;
But in his duty, prompt at every call,
He watched and wept, he prayed and felt for all;
And, as a bird each fond endearment tries
To tempt its new-fledged offspring to the skies,

[1] a description drawn from the poet's father or brother
[2] surpassingly

He tried each art, reproved each dull delay,
Allured to brighter worlds, and led the way.

Beside the bed where parting life was laid,
And sorrow, guilt, and pain, by turns dismayed,
The reverend champion stood.[1] At his control
Despair and anguish fled the struggling soul;
Comfort came down the trembling wretch to raise,
And his last faltering accents whispered praise.

At church, with meek and unaffected grace,
His looks adorned the venerable place;
Truth from his lips prevailed with double sway,
And fools who came to scoff remained to pray.
The service past, around the pious man,
With steady zeal, each honest rustic ran;
E'en children followed, with endearing wile,
And plucked his gown, to share the good man's smile.
His ready smile a parent's warmth expressed,
Their welfare pleased him, and their cares distressed;
To them his heart, his love, his griefs were given,
But all his serious thoughts had rest in heaven.
As some tall cliff that lifts its awful form,
Swells from the vale, and midway leaves the storm,
Though round its breast the rolling clouds are spread,
Eternal sunshine settles on its head.

Beside yon straggling fence that skirts the way
With blossomed furze unprofitably gay—
There, in his noisy mansion, skilled to rule,
The village master[2] taught his little school.
A man severe he was, and stern to view,
I knew him well, and every truant knew;
Well had the boding tremblers learned to trace
The day's disasters in his morning face;
Full well they laughed with counterfeited glee
At all his jokes, for many a joke had he;
Full well the busy whisper, circling round,
Conveyed the dismal tidings when he frowned.
Yet he was kind, or if severe in aught,
The love he bore to learning was in fault.
The village all declared how much he knew;
'Twas certain he could write, and cipher, too;
Lands he could measure, terms and tides presage,
And even the story ran that he could gauge.[3]
In arguing, too, the parson owned his skill,
For e'en though vanquished, he could argue still;

[1] a striking metaphor, taken from the tourney
[2] Probably Thomas Byrne, Goldsmith's teacher, was the model for this portrait.
[3] estimate the capacity of casks

While words of learnèd length and thundering sound
Amazed the gazing rustics ranged around,
And still they gazed, and still the wonder grew
That one small head could carry all he knew.
But past is all his fame. The very spot,
Where many a time he triumphed, is forgot.

Near yonder thorn that lifts its head on high,
Where once the sign-post caught the passing eye,
Low lies that house where nut-brown drafts inspired,
Where gray-beard mirth and smiling toil retired,
Where village statesmen talked with looks profound,
And news much older than their ale went round.
Imagination fondly stoops to trace
The parlor splendors of that festive place;
The white-washed wall, the nicely sanded floor,
The varnished clock that clicked behind the door,
The chest contrived a double debt to pay,
A bed by night, a chest of drawers by day;
The pictures placed for ornament and use,
The twelve good rules,[4] the royal game of goose;
The hearth, except when winter chilled the day,
With aspen boughs and flowers and fennel gay;
While broken tea-cups, wisely kept for show,
Ranged o'er the chimney, glistened in a row.

Vain transitory splendors! Could not all
Reprieve the tottering mansion from its fall?
Obscure it sinks, nor shall it more impart
An hour's importance to the poor man's heart.
Thither no more the peasant shall repair
To sweet oblivion of his daily care;
No more the farmer's news, the barber's tale,
No more the woodman's ballad shall prevail;
No more the smith his dusky brow shall clear,
Relax his ponderous strength and lean to hear;
The host himself no longer shall be found
Careful to see the mantling bliss go round;
Nor the coy maid, half-willing to be pressed,
Shall kiss the cup to pass it to the rest.

Yes! let the rich deride, the proud disdain
These simple blessings of the lowly train;
To me more dear, congenial to my heart,
One native charm, than all the gloss of art.
Spontaneous joys, where nature has its play,

[4] "Urge no healths," "Pick no quarrels," etc., commonly hung in public houses, and attributed to Charles I; the game mentioned in this line was played with counters and dice.

The soul adopts, and owns their first-born sway;
Lightly they frolic o'er the vacant mind,
Unenvied, unmolested, unconfined.
But the long pomp, the midnight masquerade,
With all the freaks of wanton wealth arrayed,
In these, ere triflers half their wish obtain,
The toiling pleasure sickens into pain;
And, even while fashion's brightest arts decoy,
The heart, distrusting, asks if this be joy.

Ye friends to truth, ye statesmen who survey
The rich man's joys increase, the poor's decay,
'Tis yours to judge how wide the limits stand
Between a splendid and a happy land.
Proud swells the tide with loads of freighted ore,
And shouting Folly hails them from her shore;
Hoards even beyond the miser's wish abound,
And rich men flock from all the world around.
Yet count our gains. This wealth is but a name
That leaves our useful products still the same.
Not so the loss. The man of wealth and pride
Takes up a place that many poor supplied;
Space for his lake, his park's extended bounds,
Space for his horses, equipage, and hounds;
The robe that wraps his limbs in silken sloth
Has robbed the neighboring fields of half their growth;
His seat, where solitary sports are seen,
Indignant spurns the cottage from the green;
Around the world each needful product flies,
For all the luxuries the world supplies;
While thus the land, adorned for pleasures, all
In barren splendor, feebly waits the fall.

As some fair female, unadorned and plain,
Secure to please while youth confirms her reign,
Slights every borrowed charm that dress supplies,
Nor shares with art the triumph of her eyes;
But when those charms are past, for charms are frail,
When time advances, and when lovers fail,
She then shines forth, solicitous to bless,
In all the glaring impotence of dress;
Thus fares the land by luxury betrayed,
In nature's simplest charms at first arrayed,
But verging to decline, its splendors rise,
Its vistas strike, its palaces surprise;
While, scourged by famine, from the smiling land
The mournful peasant leads his humble band;
And while he sinks, without one arm to save,
The country blooms—a garden and a grave.

Where then, ah! where shall poverty reside,
To 'scape the pressure of contiguous pride?
If to some common's fenceless limits strayed,
He drives his flock to pick the scanty blade,
Those fenceless fields the sons of wealth divide;
And e'en the bare-worn common is denied.

If to the city sped—what waits him there?
To see profusion that he must not share;
To see ten thousand baneful arts combined
To pamper luxury and thin mankind;
To see each joy the sons of pleasure know,
Extorted from his fellow-creature's woe.
Here, while the courtier glitters in brocade,
There, the pale artist [1] plies the sickly trade;
Here, while the proud their long-drawn pomps display,
There, the black gibbet glooms beside the way.
The dome where pleasure holds her midnight reign,
Here, richly decked, admits the gorgeous train;
Tumultuous grandeur crowds the blazing square,
The rattling chariots clash, the torches glare.
Sure scenes like these no troubles e'er annoy;
Sure these denote one universal joy!
Are these thy serious thoughts?—Ah! turn thine eyes
Where the poor houseless, shivering female lies.
She once, perhaps, in village plenty blessed,
Has wept at tales of innocence distressed;
Her modest looks the cottage might adorn,
Sweet as the primrose peeps beneath the thorn;
Now lost to all; her friends, her virtue fled,
Near her betrayer's door she lays her head—
And, pinched with cold, and shrinking from the shower,
With heavy heart deplores that luckless hour,
When idly first, ambitious of the town,
She left her wheel and robes of country brown.

Do thine, sweet Auburn! thine the loveliest train,
Do thy fair tribes participate her pain?
E'en now, perhaps, by cold and hunger led,
At proud men's doors they ask a little bread.

Ah, no! To distant climes, a dreary scene,
Where half the convex world intrudes between,
Through torrid tracts with fainting steps they go,
Where wild Altama [2] murmurs to their woe.
Far different there from all that charmed before,
The various terrors of that horrid shore;
Those blazing suns that dart a downward ray,
And fiercely shed intolerable day;
Those matted woods where birds forget to sing;
But silent bats in drowsy clusters cling;
Those poisonous fields with rank luxuriance crowned,
Where the dark scorpion gathers death around;

[1] artisan
[2] the Altamaha, a river of Georgia

Where at each step the stranger fears to wake
The rattling terrors of the vengeful snake;
Where crouching tigers[1] wait their hapless prey,
And savage men more murderous still than they;
While oft in whirls the mad tornado flies,
Mingling the ravaged landscape with the skies.
Far different these from every former scene,
The cooling brook, the grassy-vested green,
The breezy covert of the warbling grove,
That only sheltered thefts of harmless love.

Good Heaven! what sorrows gloomed that parting day
That called them from their native walks away;
When the poor exiles, every pleasure past,
Hung round the bowers, and fondly looked their last—
And took a long farewell, and wished in vain
For seats like these beyond the western main—
And, shuddering still to face the distant deep,
Returned and wept, and still returned to weep.
The good old sire the first prepared to go
To new-found worlds, and wept for others' woe;
But for himself, in conscious virtue brave,
He only wished for worlds beyond the grave.
His lovely daughter, lovelier in her tears,
The fond companion of his helpless years,
Silent went next, neglectful of her charms,
And left a lover's for a father's arms.
With louder plaints the mother spoke her woes,
And blessed the cot where every pleasure rose,
And kissed her thoughtless babes with many a tear,
And clasped them close, in sorrow doubly dear;
Whilst her fond husband strove to lend relief
In all the silent manliness of grief.

O luxury! thou cursed by Heaven's decree,
How ill exchanged are things like these for thee!
How do thy potions, with insidious joy,
Diffuse their pleasures only to destroy!
Kingdoms, by thee to sickly greatness grown,
Boast of a florid vigor not their own.
At every draft more large and large they grow,
A bloated mass of rank unwieldy woe;
Till, sapped their strength, and every part unsound,
Down, down they sink, and spread a ruin round.

Even now the devastation is begun
And half the business of destruction done;
Even now, methinks, as pondering here I stand,
I see the rural virtues leave the land.
Down where yon anchoring vessel spreads the sail
That idly waiting flaps with every gale,
Downward they move, a melancholy band,
Pass from the shore, and darken all the strand.
Contented toil, and hospitable care,
And kind connubial tenderness are there,
And piety with wishes placed above,
And steady loyalty, and faithful love.
And thou, sweet Poetry, thou loveliest maid,
Still first to fly where sensual joys invade;
Unfit, in these degenerate times of shame,
To catch the heart, or strike for honest fame;
Dear charming nymph, neglected and decried,
My shame in crowds, my solitary pride;
Thou source of all my bliss and all my woe,
Thou found'st me poor at first, and keep'st me so;
Thou guide, by which the nobler arts excel,
Thou nurse of every virtue, fare thee well!
Farewell; and oh! where'er thy voice be tried,
On Torno's[2] cliffs, or Pambamarca's[3] side,
Whether where equinoctial fervors glow,
Or winter wraps the polar world in snow,
Still let thy voice, prevailing over time,
Redress the rigors of the inclement clime;
Aid slighted truth with thy persuasive strain;
Teach erring man to spurn the rage of gain;
Teach him, that states of native strength possessed,
Though very poor, may still be very blest;
That trade's proud empire hastes to swift decay,
As ocean sweeps the labored mole away;
While self-dependent power can time defy,
As rocks resist the billows and the sky.

1770

THE HAUNCH OF VENISON

A Poetical Epistle to Lord Clare

Thanks, my Lord, for your venison, for finer or fatter
Never ranged in a forest, or smoked in a platter;
The haunch was a picture for painters to study—
The fat was so white, and the lean was so ruddy;
Though my stomach was sharp, I could scarce help regretting
To spoil such a delicate picture by eating;
I had thoughts in my chambers to place it in view,

[1] Here Goldsmith's imagination played him false, unless tigers may stand for panthers.

[2] the Tornea, a river in Sweden

[3] a mountain peak in Ecuador

To be shown to my friends as a piece of virtù;
As in some Irish houses, where things are so-so,
One gammon of bacon hangs up for a show;—
But, for eating a rasher of what they take pride in,
They'd as soon think of eating the pan it is fried in.
But hold—let me pause—don't I hear you pronounce
This tale of the bacon a damnable bounce?[1]
Well, suppose it a bounce; sure a poet may try,
By a bounce now and then, to get courage to fly.
But, my Lord, it's no bounce. I protest in my turn
It's a truth—and your Lordship may ask Mr. Byrne.[2]
  To go on with my tale: as I gazed on the haunch,
I thought of a friend that was trusty and staunch;
So I cut it, and sent it to Reynolds[3] undrest,
To paint it or eat it, just as he liked best.
Of the neck and the breast I had next to dispose—
'Twas a neck and a breast that might rival Monroe's[4]—
But in parting with these I was puzzled again,
With the how, and the who, and the where, and the when.
There's Howard, and Coley, and H—rth, and Hiff,
I think they love venison—I know they love beef.
There's my countryman Higgins—oh! let him alone,
For making a blunder, or picking a bone.
But, hang it!—to poets who seldom can eat,
Your very good mutton's a very good treat;
Such dainties to them, their health it might hurt;
It's like sending them ruffles when wanting a shirt.
While thus I debated, in reverie centered,
An acquaintance, a friend, as he called himself, entered;
An under-bred, fine-spoken fellow was he,
And he smiled as he looked at the venison and me.
"What have we got here?—Why this is good eating!
Your own, I suppose—or is it in waiting?"
"Why, whose should it be?" cried I with a flounce;
"I get these things often"—but that was a bounce.
"Some lords, my acquaintance, that settle the nation,
Are pleased to be kind—but I hate ostentation."
"If that be the case, then," cried he, very gay,
"I'm glad I have taken this house in my way.
Tomorrow you take a poor dinner with me;
No words—I insist on't—precisely at three;
We'll have Johnson, and Burke; all the wits will be there;
My acquaintance is slight, or I'd ask my Lord Clare.
And now that I think on't, as I am a sinner!
We wanted this venison to make out the dinner.
What say you—a pasty? It shall, and it must,
And my wife, little Kitty, is famous for crust.
Here, porter! This venison with me to Mile-end;[5]
No stirring—I beg—my dear friend—my dear friend!"
Thus, snatching his hat, he brushed off like the wind,
And the porter and eatables followed behind.
  Left alone to reflect, having emptied my shelf,
And "nobody with me at sea but myself,"
Though I could not help thinking my gentleman hasty,
Yet Johnson, and Burke, and a good venison pasty,
Were things that I never disliked in my life,
Though clogged with a coxcomb, and Kitty his wife.
So next day, in due splendor to make my approach,
I drove to his door in my own hackney-coach.
  When come to the place where we all were to dine
(A chair-lumbered closet, just twelve feet by nine),
My friend bade me welcome, but struck me quite dumb
With tidings that Johnson and Burke would not come.
"For I knew it," he cried; "both eternally fail,
The one with his speeches, and t'other with Thrale.[6]
But no matter, I'll warrant we'll make up the party
With two full as clever and ten times as hearty.
The one is a Scotchman, the other a Jew;

[1] impudent falsehood
[2] Lord Clare's nephew
[3] Sir Joshua Reynolds
[4] Dorothy Monroe, a celebrated beauty
[5] in East London, where the poorer classes lived
[6] Mrs. Thrale, Dr. Johnson's friend

They're both of them merry, and authors like you;
The one writes the 'Snarler', the other the 'Scourge';
Some think he writes 'Cinna'—he owns to 'Panurge'."[1]
While thus he described them by trade and by name,
They entered, and dinner was served as they came.
  At the top a fried liver and bacon were seen;
At the bottom was tripe, in a swingeing[2] tureen;
At the sides there was spinach and pudding made hot;
In the middle a place where the pasty—was not.
Now, my Lord, as for tripe, it's my utter aversion,
And your bacon I hate like a Turk or a Persian;
So there I sat stuck, like a horse in a pound,
While the bacon and liver went merrily round.
But what vexed me most was that d—d Scottish rogue,
With his long-winded speeches, his smiles, and his brogue.
And, "Madam," quoth he, "may this bit be my poison,
A prettier dinner I never set eyes on;
Pray a slice of your liver, though may I be curst,
But I've eat of your tripe till I'm ready to burst."
"The tripe!" quoth the Jew, with his chocolate cheek,
"I could dine on this tripe seven days in a week.
I like these here dinners so pretty and small;
But your friend there, the doctor, eats nothing at all."
"Oho!" quoth my friend, "he'll come on in a trice;
He's keeping a corner for something that's nice.
There's a pasty."—"A pasty!" repeated the Jew;
"I don't care if I keep a corner for't, too."
"What the de'il, mon, a pasty!" reëchoed the Scot;
"Though splitting, I'll still keep a corner for that."
"We'll all keep a corner," the lady cried out;
"We'll all keep a corner," was echoed about.

[1] These were signatures to contemporary letters addressed to the *Public Advertiser* in support of the government.

[2] immense

While thus we resolved, and the pasty delayed,
With looks that quite petrified, entered the maid;
A visage so sad, and so pale with affright,
Waked Priam in drawing his curtains by night.[3]
But we quickly found out—for who could mistake her—
That she came with some terrible news from the baker.
And so it fell out, for that negligent sloven
Had shut out the pasty on shutting his oven.
Sad Philomel thus—but let similes drop;
And now that I think on't, the story may stop.
  To be plain, my good Lord, it's but labor misplaced
To send such good verses to one of your taste;
You've got an odd something—a kind of discerning,
A relish, a taste—sickened over by learning;[4]
At least, it's your temper, as very well known,
That you think very slightly of all that's your own.
So, perhaps, in your habits of thinking amiss,
You may make a mistake, and think slightly of this.

1771 *1776*

From RETALIATION[5]

Of old, when Scarron[6] his companions invited,
Each guest brought his dish, and the feast was united;
If our landlord supplies us with beef and with fish,
Let each guest bring himself—and he brings the best dish.

[3] See *II Henry IV*, I, i, 72.

[4] See *Hamlet*, III, i, 85.

[5] Goldsmith, because of his vanity and frequently empty talk, was the occasion of much diversion among his friends, and sometimes a butt of ridicule. At a gathering at St. James's coffee-house, he desired to try with David Garrick, the actor, his skill at epigram, and each was to write the other's epitaph. Garrick immediately composed the well-known couplet:

"Here lies Nolly Goldsmith, for shortness called Noll,
Who wrote like an angel, but talked like poor Poll."

Goldsmith took his time to reply, and the result was "Retaliation," a poem which he left unfinished, and which was published after his death. The characters whom he imagines gathered about the table are Thomas Barnard, Dean of Derry; Edmund Burke, with William Burke, a kinsman, and Richard, a younger brother; Richard Cumberland, the dramatist; John Douglas, a Scotch canon; David Garrick; John Ridge and Tom Hickey, two Irish lawyers; Sir Joshua Reynolds, the painter; and himself. A kindlier satire—if satire it may be called—has scarcely been written.

[6] a French burlesque poet

Our Dean shall be venison, just fresh from the plains;
Our Burke shall be tongue, with the garnish of brains;
Our Will shall be wild-fowl of excellent flavor,
And Dick with his pepper shall heighten the savor;
Our Cumberland's sweetbread its place shall obtain,
And Douglas is pudding, substantial and plain;
Our Garrick's a salad; for in him we see
Oil, vinegar, sugar, and saltness agree.
To make out the dinner, full certain I am
That Ridge is anchovy, and Reynolds is lamb,
That Hickey's a capon, and, by the same rule,
Magnanimous Goldsmith a gooseberry fool. [1]
At a dinner so various, at such a repast,
Who'd not be a glutton, and stick to the last?
Here, waiter, more wine! Let me sit while I'm able,
Till all my companions sink under the table;
Then, with chaos and blunders encircling my head,
Let me ponder, and tell what I think of the dead.

Here lies the good Dean, reunited to earth,
Who mixed reason with pleasure, and wisdom with mirth.
If he had any faults, he has left us in doubt—
At least, in six weeks I could not find 'em out;
Yet some have declared, and it can't be denied 'em,
That sly-boots was cursedly cunning to hide 'em.

Here lies our good Edmund, whose genius was such,
We scarcely can praise it, or blame it too much;
Who, born for the universe, narrowed his mind,
And to party gave up what was meant for mankind.
Though fraught with all learning, yet straining his throat
To persuade Tommy Townshend [2] to lend him a vote;
Who, too deep for his hearers, still went on refining,
And thought of convincing while they thought of dining.
Though equal to all things, for all things unfit,
Too nice for a statesman, too proud for a wit;
For a patriot too cool; for a drudge, disobedient,
And too fond of the right to pursue the expedient.
In short, 'twas his fate, unemployed or in place, sir,
To eat mutton cold, and cut blocks with a razor.

. . . . . .

Here Cumberland lies, having acted his parts,
The Terence [3] of England, the mender of hearts;
A flattering painter, who made it his care
To draw men as they ought to be, not as they are.
His gallants are all faultless, his women divine,
And comedy wonders at being so fine;
Like a tragedy queen he has dizened her out,
Or rather like tragedy giving a rout. [4]
His fools have their follies so lost in a crowd
Of virtues and feelings that folly grows proud;
And coxcombs, alike in their failings alone,
Adopting his portraits, are pleased with their own.
Say, where has our poet this malady caught,
Or wherefore his characters thus without fault?
Say, was it that, vainly directing his view
To find out men's virtues, and finding them few,
Quite sick of pursuing each troublesome elf,
He grew lazy at last, and drew from himself.

. . . . . .

Here lies David Garrick, describe me who can
An abridgment of all that was pleasant in man;
As an actor, confessed without rival to shine;
As a wit, if not first, in the very first line;
Yet, with talents like these, and an excellent heart,
The man had his failings, a dupe to his art.
Like an ill-judging beauty, his colors he spread,
And beplastered with rouge his own natural red.
On the stage he was natural, simple, affecting;
'Twas only that when he was off he was acting.
With no reason on earth to go out of his way,
He turned and he varied full ten times a day:
Though secure of our hearts, yet confoundedly sick,
If they were not his own by finessing and trick;
He cast off his friends as a huntsman his pack,
For he knew when he pleased he could whistle them back.
Of praise a mere glutton, he swallowed what came,

[1] a dish of crushed gooseberries
[2] an M. P., afterwards Lord Sydney
[3] a Roman comic writer
[4] gay party

And the puff of a dunce, he mistook it for
    fame;
'Till his relish grown callous, almost to dis-
    ease,
Who peppered the highest was surest to please.
But let us be candid, and speak out our mind;
If dunces applauded, he paid them in kind.
Ye Kenricks, ye Kellys, and Woodfalls so
    grave,[1]
What a commerce was yours, while you got and
    you gave!
How did Grub Street[2] reëcho the shouts that
    you raised,
While he was be-Rosciused[3] and you were be-
    praised!
But peace to his spirit, wherever it flies,
To act as an angel and mix with the skies:
Those poets who owe their best fame to his
    skill
Shall still be his flatterers, go where he will,
Old Shakespeare receive him with praise and
    with love,
And Beaumonts and Bens[4] be his Kellys above.

. . . .

Here Reynolds is laid, and, to tell you my
    mind,
He has not left a wiser or better behind;
His pencil was striking, resistless, and grand;
His manners were gentle, complying, and
    bland;
Still born to improve us in every part,
His pencil our faces, his manners our heart.
To coxcombs averse, yet most civilly steering;
When they judged without skill, he was still
    hard of hearing;
When they talked of their Raphaels, Correg-
    gios, and stuff,
He shifted his trumpet, and only took snuff.
By flattery unspoiled—[5]

1774 1774

EDWARD GIBBON 1737-1794

Partly because of the universal interest in the subject, but more because of the treatment given the matter, the *History of the Decline and Fall of the Roman Empire* stands as the most famous English historical writing of the eighteenth century. Gibbon was born at Putney of a family intrenched in conservative politics. He studied for some fourteen months at Oxford and then went to Lausanne, Switzerland, where he perfected himself in languages, and later wrote most of his history. While sojourning in Rome in 1764, as he "sat musing amid the ruins of the Capitol" the idea of the history came to him. Twelve years later the first volume was published, and twelve years later still, the sixth and last. Although Gibbon's life was that of a scholar, he was an active officer in the Hampshire militia for years, and sat in Parliament with the conservatives as his father and grandfather had done.

Much criticism of the history was aroused and still continues because of its unsympathetic treatment of the rise of Christianity, for Gibbon's attitude was that of the skeptical French philosophers of the day. Of Gibbon's style many contradictory opinions have been expressed, for though it is clear and sustained it is sometimes pompous when it should be simple. At its best it represents the height of eighteenth century dignity. The structure that he has reared from his varied materials is massive, dignified, and unified.

Woodrow Wilson says of him: "If we continue Gibbon in his fame, it will be for love of his art, not for worship of his scholarship. We, some of us, nowadays, know the period of which he wrote better even than he did; but which one of us shall build so admirable a monument to ourselves, as artists, out of what we know? The scholar finds his immortality in the form he gives to his work. It is a hard saying, but the truth is inexorable: be an artist, or prepare for oblivion."

Biography: J. C. Morison (EML). Criticism: Stephen; A. H. T. Clarke, "The Genius of Gibbon," *19th Cent.* 68:512-21, 672-85, 882-97, sketches the author's scholarship; J. F. Rhodes, "Gibbon and His Work," *Scrib.* 45:724-36, is a discriminating, comprehensive criticism by a historian.

[THE FALL OF CONSTANTINOPLE[6]]

. . . .

After a siege of forty days the fate of Constantinople could no longer be averted. The diminutive garrison was exhausted by a double attack; the fortifications, which had stood for ages against hostile violence, were dismantled on all sides by the Ottoman cannon; many breaches were opened; and near the gate of St. Romanus, four towers had been leveled with the ground. For the payment of his feeble and mutinous troops, Constantine was compelled to despoil the churches, with the promise

[1] dramatists and critics of the time
[2] hackwriterdom
[3] Roscius was the greatest Roman comic actor.
[4] "Rare Ben" Jonson
[5] Here Death took the pen from the poet's hand before he could write his own epitaph.

[6] From *The Decline and Fall of the Roman Empire,* chapter lxviii; long after Rome had fallen before the incursions of the barbarians, Constantinople, the capital of the Eastern Empire, "the decrepit daughter of ancient Rome, alone remained standing, and for ten centuries, like a rocky island, defied the fury of the waves." (Victor Duruy.) The last Christian emperor was a Greek, Constantine Palaeol'ogus. When the city was finally besieged, in 1453, by the Ottoman Turks under Mahomet II, the defense was conducted by an alliance of Greeks, Venetians, and Genoese, sadly divided by their own religious differences. Their foremost general was Justiniani, a Genoese nobleman.

of a fourfold restitution; and his sacrilege offered a new reproach to the enemies of the union. A spirit of discord impaired the remnant of the Christian strength; the Genoese and Venetian auxiliaries asserted the pre-eminence of their respective service; and Justiniani and the great Duke, whose ambition was not extinguished by the common danger, accused each other of treachery and cowardice.

During the siege of Constantinople the words of peace and capitulation had been sometimes pronounced; and several embassies had passed between the camp and the city. The Greek emperor was humbled by adversity, and would have yielded to any terms compatible with religion and royalty. The Turkish sultan was desirous of sparing the blood of his soldiers; still more desirous of securing for his own use the Byzantine treasures; and he accomplished a sacred duty in presenting to the *Gabours* [1] the choice of circumcision, of tribute, or of death. The avarice of Mahomet might have been satisfied with an annual sum of one hundred thousand ducats; but his ambition grasped the capital of the East; to the prince he offered a rich equivalent, to the people a free toleration or a safe departure; but, after some fruitless treaty, he declared his resolution of finding either a throne or a grave under the walls of Constantinople. A sense of honor and the fear of universal reproach forbade Palaeologus to resign the city into the hands of the Ottomans; and he determined to abide the last extremities of war. Several days were employed by the sultan in the preparations of the assault; and a respite was granted by his favorite science of astrology, which had fixed on the twenty-ninth of May as the fortunate and fatal hour. On the evening of the twenty-seventh, he issued his final orders; assembled in his presence the military chiefs; and dispersed his heralds through the camp to proclaim the duty and motives of the perilous enterprise. Fear is the first principle of a despotic government; and his menaces were expressed in the Oriental style, that the fugitives and deserters, had they the wings of a bird, should not escape from his inexorable justice. The greatest part of his bashaws [2] and Janizaries [3] were the offspring of Christian parents; but the glories of the Turkish name were perpetuated by successive adoption; and, in the gradual change of individuals, the spirit of a legion, a regiment, or an *oda* [4] is kept alive by imitation and discipline. In this holy warfare the Moslems were exhorted to purify their minds with prayer, their bodies with seven ablutions; and to abstain from food till the close of the ensuing day. A crowd of dervishes visited the tents to instil the desire of martyrdom and the assurance of spending an immortal youth amidst the rivers and gardens of paradise and in the embraces of the black-eyed virgins. [5] Yet Mahomet principally trusted to the efficacy of temporal and visible rewards. A double pay was promised to the victorious troops. "The city and the buildings," said Mahomet, "are mine; but I resign to your valor the captives and the spoil, the treasures of gold and beauty; be rich and be happy. Many are the provinces of my empire: the intrepid soldier who first ascends the walls of Constantinople shall be rewarded with the government of the fairest and most wealthy; and my gratitude shall accumulate his honors and fortunes above the measure of his own hopes." Such various and potent motives diffused among the Turks a general ardor, regardless of life and impatient for action; the camp reëchoed with the Moslem shouts of "God is God, there is but one God, and Mahomet is the apostle of God"; and the sea and land, from Galata [6] to the seven towers, [7] were illuminated by the blaze of their nocturnal fires.

Far different was the state of the Christians; who with loud and impotent complaints, deplored the guilt, or the punishment, of their sins. The celestial image of the Virgin had been exposed in solemn procession; but their divine patroness was deaf to their entreaties; they accused the obstinacy of the emperor for refusing a timely surrender; anticipated the horrors of their fate; and sighed for the repose and security of Turkish servitude. The noblest of the Greeks, and the bravest of the allies, were summoned to the palace, to prepare them, on the evening of the twenty-eighth, for the duties and dangers of the general assault. The last speech of Palaeologus was the funeral oration of the Roman Empire. He promised, he conjured, and he vainly attempted to infuse the hope which was extinguished in his own mind. In this world all was comfortless and gloomy; and neither the gospel nor the church have proposed any conspicuous recompense to the heroes who fall in the service of their country. But the example of their prince and the confinement of a siege had armed these warriors with the courage of despair; and the pathetic scene is described by

[1] giaours, "infidels" [2] ministers and generals
[3] Ottoman infantry, especially the Sultan's bodyguard
[4] company

[5] houris, nymphs of the Mohammedan Paradise
[6] northern suburb of Constantinople [7] southern gate

the feelings of the historian Phranza,[1] who was himself present at this mournful assembly. They wept, they embraced; regardless of their families and fortunes, they devoted their lives; and each commander, departing to his station, maintained all night a vigilant and anxious watch on the rampart. The emperor and some faithful companions entered the dome of St. Sophia, which in a few hours was to be converted into a mosque; and devoutly received, with tears and prayers, the sacrament of the holy communion. He reposed some moments in the palace, which resounded with cries and lamentations; solicited the pardon of all whom he might have injured; and mounted on horseback to visit the guards and explore the motions of the enemy. The distress and fall of the last Constantine are more glorious than the long prosperity of the Byzantine Caesars.[2]

In the confusion of darkness an assailant may sometimes succeed; but in this great and general attack, the military judgment and astrological knowledge of Mahomet advised him to expect the morning, the memorable twenty-ninth of May, in the fourteen hundred and fifty-third year of the Christian era. The preceding night had been strenuously employed; the troops, the cannon, and the fascines[3] were advanced to the edge of the ditch, which, in many parts, presented a smooth and level passage to the breach; and his fourscore galleys almost touched, with the prows and their scaling-ladders, the less defensible walls of the harbor. Under pain of death, silence was enjoined; but the physical laws of motion and sound are not obedient to discipline or fear; each individual might suppress his voice and measure his footsteps, but the march and labor of thousands must inevitably produce a strange confusion of dissonant clamors which reached the ears of the watchmen of the towers. At daybreak, without the customary signal of the morning gun, the Turks assaulted the city by sea and land; and the similitude of a twined or twisted thread has been applied to the closeness and continuity of their line of attack. The foremost ranks consisted of the refuse of the host, a voluntary crowd, who fought without order or command; of the feebleness of age or childhood, of peasants and vagrants, and of all who had joined the camp in the blind hope of plunder and martyrdom. The common impulse drove them onward to the wall; the most audacious to climb were instantly precipitated; and not a dart, not a bullet, of the Christians was idly wasted on the accumulated throng. But their strength and ammunition were exhausted in this laborious defense; the ditch was filled with the bodies of the slain; they supported the footsteps of their companions; and of this devoted vanguard the death was more serviceable than the life. Under their respective bashaws and sanjaks,[4] the troops of Anatolia and Romania were successively led to the charge; their progress was various and doubtful; but, after a conflict of two hours, the Greeks still maintained and improved their advantage; and the voice of the emperor was heard, encouraging his soldiers to achieve, by a last effort, the deliverance of their country. In that fatal moment the Janizaries arose, fresh, vigorous, and invincible. The sultan, himself, on horseback, with an iron mace in his hand, was the spectator and judge of their valor; he was surrounded by ten thousand of his domestic troops, whom he reserved for the decisive occasion; and the tide of battle was directed and impelled by his voice and eye. His numerous ministers of justice were posted behind the line, to urge, to restrain, and to punish; and, if danger was in the front, shame and inevitable death were in the rear of the fugitives. The cries of fear and of pain were drowned in the martial music of drums, trumpets, and attaballs;[5] and experience has proved that the mechanical operation of sounds, by quickening the circulation of the blood and spirits, will act on the human machine more forcibly than the eloquence of reason and honor. From the lines, the galleys, and the bridge, the Ottoman artillery thundered on all sides; and the camp and city, the Greeks and the Turks, were involved in a cloud of smoke which could only be dispelled by the final deliverance or destruction of the Roman empire. The single combats of the heroes of history or fable amuse our fancy and engage our affections; the skillful evolutions of war may inform the mind, and improve a necessary though pernicious science. But in the uniform and odious pictures of a general assault, all is blood, and horror, and confusion; nor shall I strive, at the distance of three centuries and a thousand miles, to delineate a scene of which there could be no spectators, and of which the actors themselves were incapable of forming any just or adequate idea.

The immediate loss of Constantinople may be ascribed to the bullet, or arrow, which pierced

[1] chamberlain of Palaeologus
[2] i. e., the Emperors of the East
[3] bundles of sticks for filling ditches
[4] provincial governors
[5] kettle-drums

the gauntlet of John Justiniani. The sight of his blood, and the exquisite pain, appalled the courage of the chief, whose arms and counsels were the firmest rampart of the city. As he withdrew from his station in quest of a surgeon, his flight was perceived and stopped by the indefatigable emperor. "Your wound," exclaimed Palaeologus, "is slight; the danger is pressing; your presence is necessary; and whither will you retire?" "I will retire," said the trembling Genoese, "by the same road which God has opened to the Turks"; and at these words he hastily passed through one of the breaches of the inner wall. By this pusillanimous act he stained the honors of a military life; and the few days which he survived in Galata, or the isle of Chios, were embittered by his own and the public reproach. His example was imitated by the greatest part of the Latin auxiliaries, and the defense began to slacken when the attack was pressed with redoubled vigor. The number of the Ottomans was fifty, perhaps a hundred, times superior to that of the Christians; the double walls were reduced by the cannon to a heap of ruins; in a circuit of several miles, some places must be found more easy of access or more feebly guarded; and if the besiegers could penetrate in a single point, the whole city was irrecoverably lost. The first who deserved the sultan's reward was Hassan, the Janizary, of gigantic stature and strength. With his scimitar in one hand and his buckler in the other he ascended the outward fortification; of the thirty Janizaries who were emulous of his valor, eighteen perished in the bold adventure. Hassan and his twelve companions had reached the summit; the giant was precipitated from the rampart; he rose on one knee, and was again oppressed by a shower of darts and stones. But his success had proved that the achievement was possible: the walls and towers were instantly covered with a swarm of Turks; and the Greeks, now driven from the vantage ground, were overwhelmed by increasing multitudes. Amidst these multitudes, the emperor, who accomplished all the duties of a general and a soldier, was long seen, and finally lost. The nobles who fought round his person sustained, till their last breath, the honorable names of Palaeologus and Cantacuzene.[1] His mournful exclamation was heard, "Cannot there be found a Christian to cut off my head?" and his last fear was that of falling alive into the hands of the infidels. The prudent despair of Constantine cast away the purple; amidst the tumult, he fell by an unknown hand, and his body was buried under a mountain of the slain. After his death, resistance and order were no more; the Greeks fled toward the city; and many were pressed and stifled in the narrow pass of the gate of St. Romanus. The victorious Turks rushed through the breaches of the inner wall; and, as they advanced into the streets, they were soon joined by their brethren who had forced the gate Phenar on the side of the harbor. In the first heat of the pursuit, about two thousand Christians were put to the sword; but avarice soon prevailed over cruelty; and the victors acknowledged that they should immediately have given quarter if the valor of the emperor and his chosen bands had not prepared them for a similar opposition in every part of the capital. It was thus, after a siege of fifty-three days, that Constantinople, which had defied the power of Chosroes,[2] the Chagan,[3] and the caliphs,[4] was irretrievably subdued by the arms of Mahomet the Second. Her empire only had been subverted by the Latins; her religion was trampled in the dust by the Moslem conquerors.

. . . .

1788

[1] the names of several Byzantine emperors

[2] a Persian king, who in the seventh century besieged Constantinople for ten years

[3] title of the king of the Avars, ally of Chosroes

[4] Ottoman sovereigns

GILBERT WHITE 1720-1793

Gilbert White came of a family in comfortable circumstances, many of whose members were clergymen. He was born and he died at Selborne in Hampshire, a region of salubrious climate abounding in a variety of plant and animal life. After receiving his bachelor's degree at Oriel College, Oxford, he became a fellow of the college and later its dean. Official duties and several church livings he held did not prevent his traveling on horseback over the whole southern part of England during his middle life, and engaging in a copious correspondence with gentlemen who, like him, had an interest in natural history.

The publication of *The Natural History of Selborne,* 1789, illustrates the growth of scientific curiosity, during that generation, among gentlemen without scientific training, whose tastes dictated their avocations. Out of such natural history grew modern science. White's book, however, is prized not so much for its scientific value as for its style, exactly suited to the subject in hand, intimate, quiet, and sometimes a bit humorous; and for its revelation of a distinct, attractive personality. The book has gone through scores of editions and printings, and its aged tortoise, like Stevenson's donkey, "Modesto," has taken its place in the fauna of English literature.

The Life and Letters of Gilbert White by R. Holt-White, 1901, presents an intimate view of the naturalist; C. S. Brooks, "The Shrine of Gilbert White," *Cent.* 107 :696-700, describes White's home as it is today.

From THE NATURAL HISTORY OF SELBORNE

Selborne,[1] Nov. 20, 1773[2]

To the Honorable Daines Barrington

Dear Sir,

In obedience to your injunctions I sit down to give you some account of the house martin or martlet; and if my monography of this little domestic and familiar bird should happen to meet with your approbation, I may probably soon extend my inquiries to the rest of the British *Hirundines*—the swallow, the swift, and the bank martin.

A few house martins begin to appear about the 16th of April; usually some few days later than the swallow. For some time after they appear the *Hirundines* in general pay no attention to the business of nidification, but play and sport about either to recruit from the fatigue of their journey, if they do migrate at all, or else that their blood may recover its true tone and texture after it has been so long benumbed by the severities of winter. About the middle of May, if the weather be fine, the martin begins to think in earnest of providing a mansion for its family. The crust or shell of this nest seems to be formed of such dirt or loam as comes most readily to hand, and is tempered and wrought together with little bits of broken straws to render it tough and tenacious. As this bird often builds against a perpendicular wall without any projecting ledge under, it requires its utmost efforts to get the first foundation firmly fixed, so that it may safely carry the superstructure. On this occasion the bird not only clings with its claws, but partly supports itself by strongly inclining its tail against the wall, making that a fulcrum; and thus steadied, it works and plasters the materials into the face of the brick or stone. But then, that this work may not, while it is soft and green, pull itself down by its own weight, the provident architect has prudence and forbearance enough not to advance her work too fast; but by building only in the morning, and by dedicating the rest of the day to food and amusement, gives it sufficient time to dry and harden. About half an inch seems to be a sufficient layer for a day. Thus careful workmen when they build mud walls (informed at first perhaps by this little bird) raise but a moderate layer at a time, and then desist; lest the work should become top-heavy, and so be ruined by its own weight. By this method in about ten or twelve days is formed an hemispheric nest with a small aperture toward the top, strong, compact, and warm; and perfectly fitted for all the purposes for which it was intended. But then nothing is more common than for the house sparrow, as soon as the shell is finished, to seize on it as its own, to eject the owner, and to line it after its own manner.

After so much labor is bestowed in erecting a mansion, as Nature seldom works in vain, martins will breed on for several years together in the same nest, where it happens to be well sheltered and secure from the injuries of weather. The shell or crust of the nest is a sort of rustic-work full of knobs and protuberances on the outside; nor is the inside of those that I have examined smoothed with any exactness at all, but is rendered soft and warm, and fit for incubation, by a lining of small straws, grasses, and feathers; and sometimes by a bed of moss interwoven with wool. In this nest the hen lays from three to five white eggs.

. . . .

As the young of small birds presently arrive at their *hēlikia*, or full growth, they soon become impatient of confinement, and sit all day with their heads out at the orifice, where the dams, by clinging to the nest, supply them with food from morning to night. For a time the young are fed on the wing by their parents; but the feat is done by so quick and almost imperceptible a sleight, that a person must have attended very exactly to their motions before he would be able to perceive it.

As soon as the young are able to shift for themselves, the dams immediately turn their thoughts to the business of a second brood; while the first flight, shaken off and rejected by their nurses, congregate in great flocks, and are the birds that are seen clustering and hovering on sunny mornings and evenings round towers and steeples, and on the roofs of churches and houses. These congregatings usually begin to take place about the first week in August; and, therefore, we may conclude that by that time the first flight is pretty well over. The young of this species do not quit their abodes all together, but the more forward

[1] a beautiful village in a beautiful country eminently suited for the purpose of White in making it the center of a life's work of zoölogical research. —Wheatley

[2] Letter XVI (or LV)

birds get abroad some days before the rest. These, approaching the eaves of buildings, and playing about before them, make people think that several old ones attend one nest. They are often capricious in fixing on a nesting-place, beginning many edifices, and leaving them unfinished; but when once a nest is completed in a sheltered place, it serves for several seasons. Those which breed in a ready-finished house get the start, in hatching, of those that build new, by ten days or a fortnight. These industrious artificers are at their labors in the long days before four in the morning. When they fix their materials, they plaster them on with their chins, moving their heads with a quick vibratory motion. They dip and wash as they fly, sometimes, in very hot weather, but not so frequently as swallows. It has been observed that martins usually build to a northeast or northwest aspect that the heat of the sun may not crack and destroy their nests; but instances are also remembered where they bred for many years in a vast abundance in a hot stifled innyard, against a wall facing to the south.

Birds in general are wise in their choice of situation; but in this neighborhood, every summer, is seen a strong proof to the contrary at a house without eaves, in an exposed district, where some martins build year by year in the corners of the windows. But, as the corners of these windows (which face to the southeast and southwest) are too shallow, the nests are washed down every hard rain; and yet these birds drudge on to no purpose from summer to summer without changing their aspect or house. It is a piteous sight to see them laboring when half their nest is washed away, and bringing dirt—*"generis lapsi sarcire ruinas."*[1] Thus is instinct a most wonderful unequal faculty, in some instances so much above reason, in other respects so far below it! Martins love to frequent towns, especially if there are great lakes and rivers at hand; nay, they even affect the close air of London. And I have not only seen them nesting in the Borough[2] but even in the Strand and Fleet Street; but then it was obvious from the dinginess of their aspect that their feathers partook of the filth of that sooty atmosphere. Martins are by far the least agile of the four species; their wings and tails are short, and therefore they are not capable of such surprising turns, and quick and glancing evolutions as the swallow. Accordingly they make use of a placid easy motion in a middle region of the air, seldom mounting to any great height, and never sweeping long together over the surface of the ground or water. They do not wander far for food, but affect sheltered districts, over some lake, or under some hanging wood, or in some hollow vale, especially in windy weather. They breed the latest of all the swallow kind; in 1772 they had nestlings on to October the 21st, and are never without unfledged young as late as Michaelmas.[3]

As the summer declines, the congregating flocks increase in numbers daily, by the constant accession of the second broods; till at last they swarm in myriads upon myriads round the villages on the Thames, darkening the face of the sky as they frequent the aits[4] of that river where they roost. They retire (the bulk of them, I mean) in vast flocks, together, about the beginning of October; but have appeared of late years in a considerable flight in this neighborhood, for one day or two, as late as November the 3rd and 6th after they were supposed to have been gone for more than a fortnight. They therefore withdraw with us the latest of any species. Unless these birds are very short-lived indeed, or unless they do not return to the district where they are bred, they must undergo vast devastations somehow, and somewhere; for the birds that return yearly bear no manner of proportion to the birds that retire.

House martins are distinguished from their congeners by having their legs covered with soft downy feathers down to their toes. They are no songsters; but twitter in a pretty inward soft manner in their nests. During the time of breeding they are often greatly molested with fleas.

Selborne, April 21, 1780[5]

Dear Sir,

The old Sussex tortoise that I have mentioned to you so often, is become my property. I dug it out of its winter dormitory in March last, when it was enough awakened to express its resentment by hissing; and, packing it in a box with earth, carried it eighty miles in post chaises. The rattle and hurry of the journey so perfectly roused it that when I turned it out on a border, it walked twice down to the bottom of my garden. However, in the evening, the weather being cold, it buried itself in the loose mold, and continues still concealed.

[1] "to repair the wreck of the fallen house." Vergil, *Georgics* iv, 249

[2] a street extending north from London Bridge

[3] Sept. 29

[4] islets

[5] Letter L (or XCII)

As it will be under my eye, I shall now have an opportunity of enlarging my observations on its mode of life and propensities; and perceive already that, toward the time of coming forth, it opens a breathing place in the ground near its head, requiring, I conclude, a freer respiration as it becomes more alive. This creature not only goes under the earth from the middle of November to the middle of April, but sleeps great part of the summer; for it goes to bed in the longest days at four in the afternoon, and often does not stir in the morning till late. Besides, it retires to rest for every shower; and does not move at all in wet days.

When one reflects on the state of this strange being, it is a matter of wonder to find that Providence should bestow such a profusion of days, such a seeming waste of longevity, on a reptile that appears to relish it so little as to squander more than two-thirds of its existence in a joyless stupor, and be lost to all sensation for months together in the profoundest of slumbers.

While I was writing this letter, a moist and warm afternoon, with the thermometer at 50, brought forth troops of shell-snails; and, at the same juncture, the tortoise heaved up the mold and put out its head; and the next morning came forth, as it were raised from the dead; and walked about till four in the afternoon. This was a curious coincidence! a very amusing occurrence! to see such a similarity of feeling between the two *phereoikoi!* for so the Greeks call both the shell-snail and the tortoise. . . .

More Particulars Respecting the Old Family Tortoise [1]

Because we call this creature an abject reptile, we are too apt to undervalue his abilities, and depreciate his powers of instinct. Yet he is, as Mr. Pope says of his lord, [2]

> Much too wise to walk into a well;

and has so much discernment as not to fall down a haha; [3] but to stop and withdraw from the brink with the readiest precaution.

Though he loves warm weather he avoids the hot sun; because his thick shell, when once heated, would, as the poet says of solid armor, "scald with safety." He therefore spends the more sultry hours under the umbrella of a large cabbage leaf, or amidst the waving forests of an asparagus bed.

But as he avoids heat in the summer, so, in the decline of the year, he improves the faint autumnal beams, by getting within the reflection of a fruit-wall; and, though he never has read that planes inclining to the horizon receive a greater share of warmth, he inclines his shell by tilting it against the wall, to collect and admit every feeble ray.

Pitiable seems the condition of this poor embarrassed reptile; to be cased in a suit of ponderous armor, which he cannot lay aside; to be imprisoned, as it were, within his own shell, must preclude, we should suppose, all activity and disposition for enterprise. Yet there is a season of the year (usually the beginning of June) when his exertions are remarkable. He then walks on tiptoe, and is stirring by five in the morning; and, traversing the garden, examines every wicket and interstice in the fences, through which he will escape if possible; and often has eluded the care of the gardener, and wandered to some distant field. . . .

1789

[1] from *The Antiquities of Selborne*
[2] *Imitations of Horace,* II, ii, 191
[3] a hedge in a ditch

EDMUND BURKE 1729-1797

Little is known of the early life of Edmund Burke, essayist, orator, statesman, and philosopher. From his Protestant father, who was a lawyer, and his Catholic mother, respectively, he inherited conservatism and warmth of emotion, traits of character which were counterbalancing forces in him throughout his life. After graduating from Trinity College of his native city, Dublin, he went to London, where he spent years in wide reading. Politicians saw his ability and gave him a seat in Parliament. There he remained twenty-eight years, several times reëlected for various constituencies.

Among English philosophers of his time, Burke stands preëminent. In his outlook he saw humanity as a whole and had a brooding care for all its accumulated inheritance. Such minds love order, justice, and the continuity of institutions. This is why Burke sympathized with the American Revolution, fought, as he felt, to save ancestral, traditional rights of English citizens in both England and America; and why he opposed with passionate vehemence the French Revolution because, in his mind, it cast the fruits of civilization into the melting-pot and endangered the real liberties of all humanity. The principles of statesmanship that he advocated saved England from violent revolution at the end of the eighteenth century.

Burke's style, at times simple and direct, rises upon occasion to an impassioned eloquence that carries greater conviction than the more rotund oratory of Webster. High among the works of Burke stand his speech on American taxation, 1774, and that upon conciliation the following year; *Reflections on the Revolution in France,* 1790, shows his ideas on the fundamental constitution of all civilized society; and the "Letter to a Noble Lord," 1795, justifies his own career as a statesman. Financial difficulties and personal bereavement clouded Burke's last years, which ended on his estate at Beaconsfield.

Biography: Morley (EML), and *Edmund Burke, a Historical Study,* 1893. Criticism: Woodrow Wilson, "E. Burke and the French Revolution," *Cent.* 62:784-92, a clear analysis; "Burke on Bolshevism," A. V. Dicey, *19th Cent.* 84:274-87, an application of Burke's principles to present conditions.

From the SPEECH AT BRISTOL, 1780 [1]

. . . .

Since you have suffered me to trouble you so much on this subject, permit me, gentlemen, to detain you a little longer. I am indeed most solicitous to give you perfect satisfaction. I find there are some of a better and softer nature than the persons with whom I have supposed myself in debate, who neither think ill of the Act of Relief nor by any means desire the repeal; yet who, not accusing but lamenting what was done, on account of the consequences, have frequently expressed their wish that the late Act had never been made. Some of this description, and persons of worth, I have met with in this city. They conceive that the prejudices, whatever they might be, of a large part of the people ought not to have been shocked; that their opinions ought to have been previously taken, and much attended to; and that thereby the late horrid scenes might have been prevented.

I confess my notions are widely different, and I never was less sorry for any action of my life. I like the bill the better on account of the events of all kinds that followed it. It relieved the real sufferers; it strengthened the state; and, by the disorders that ensued, we had clear evidence that there lurked a temper somewhere which ought not to be fostered by the laws. No ill consequences whatever could be attributed to the Act itself. We knew beforehand, or we were poorly instructed, that toleration is odious to the intolerant; freedom to oppressors; property to robbers; and all kinds and degrees of prosperity to the envious. We knew that all these kinds of men would gladly gratify their evil dispositions under the sanction of law and religion if they could; if they could not, yet, to make way to their objects, they would do their utmost to subvert all religion and all law. This we certainly knew; but, knowing this, is there any reason, because thieves break in and steal, and thus bring detriment to you, and draw ruin on themselves, that I am to be sorry that you are in the possession of shops, and of warehouses, and of wholesome laws to protect them? Are you to build no houses because desperate men may pull them down upon their own heads? Or, if a malignant wretch will cut his own throat because he sees you give alms to the necessitous and deserving, shall his destruction be attributed to your charity, and not to his own deplorable madness? If we repent of our good actions, what, I pray you, is left for our faults and follies? It is not the beneficence of the laws, it is the unnatural temper, which beneficence can fret and sour, that is to be lamented. It is this temper which, by all rational means ought to be sweetened and corrected. If froward men should refuse this cure, can they vitiate anything but themselves? Does evil so react upon good as not only to retard its motion, but to change its nature? If it can so operate, then good men will always be in the power of the bad; and virtue, by a dreadful reverse of order, must lie under perpetual subjection and bondage to vice.

As to the opinion of the people, which some think, in such cases, is to be implicitly obeyed. —Nearly two years' tranquillity which followed the Act, and its instant imitation in Ireland, proved abundantly that the late horrible spirit was, in a great measure, the effect of insidious art, and perverse industry, and gross misrepresentation. But suppose that the dislike had been much more deliberate and much more general than I am persuaded it was. When we know that the opinions of even the greatest multitudes are the standard of rectitude, I shall think myself obliged to make those opinions the masters of my conscience; but if it may be doubted whether Omnipotence itself is competent to alter the essential constitution of right and wrong, sure I am that such *things* as they and I are possessed of no such power. No man carries further than I do the policy of making government pleasing to the people; but the wildest range of this politic complaisance is confined within the limits of justice. I would not only consult the interest of the people, but I would cheerfully gratify their humors. We are all

[1] In 1699 a most tyrannical law against Roman Catholics had been passed. The abolition of this law in 1778, by the Act of Relief, aroused some fanatical opposition expressed in cries of "No Popery" and in the Lord George Gordon riots. Burke is defending before his constituents his support of the repeal. Sir Samuel Romilly called the entire speech "perhaps the first piece of oratory in our language."

a sort of children that must be soothed and managed. I think I am not austere or formal in my nature. I would bear, I would even, myself, play my part in any innocent buffooneries to divert them; but I never will act the tyrant for their amusement. If they will mix malice in their sports, I shall never consent to throw them any living, sentient creature whatsoever, no, not so much as a kitling, to torment.

"But, if I profess all this impolitic stubbornness, I may chance never to be elected into Parliament." It is certainly not pleasing to be put out of the public service; but I wish to be a member of Parliament to have my share of doing good and resisting evil. It would therefore be absurd to renounce my objects in order to obtain my seat. I deceive myself indeed most grossly if I had not much rather pass the remainder of my life hidden in the recesses of the deepest obscurity, feeding my mind even with the visions and imaginations of such things, than to be placed on the most splendid throne of the universe, tantalized with a denial of the practice of all which can make the greatest situation any other than the greatest curse. Gentlemen, I have had my day. I can never sufficiently express my gratitude to you for having set me in a place wherein I could lend the slightest help to great and laudable designs. If I have had my share in any measure giving quiet to private property and private conscience; if by my vote I have aided in securing to families the best possession, peace; if I have joined in reconciling kings to their subjects, and subjects to their prince; if I have assisted to loosen the foreign holdings of the citizen, and taught him to look for his protection to the laws of his country, and for his comfort to the goodwill of his countrymen; if I have thus taken my part with the best of men in the best of their actions, I can shut the book—I might wish to read a page or two more, but this is enough for my measure—I have not lived in vain.

And now, gentlemen, on this serious day, when I come, as it were, to make up my account with you, let me take to myself some degree of honest pride on the nature of the charges that are against me. I do not here stand before you accused of venality, or of neglect of duty. It is not said that, in the long period of my service, I have in a single instance sacrificed the slightest of your interests to my ambition, or to my fortune. It is not alleged that, to gratify any anger or revenge of my own or of my party, I have had a share in wronging or oppressing any description of men, or any one man in any description. No! the charges against me are all of one kind: that I have pushed the principles of general justice and benevolence too far, further than a cautious policy would warrant, and further than the opinions of many would go along with me. In every accident which may happen through life—in pain, in sorrow, in depression and distress—I will call to mind this accusation, and be comforted. . . . .

From REFLECTIONS ON THE REVOLUTION IN FRANCE [1]

. . . .

Yielding to reasons, at least as forcible as those which were so delicately urged in the compliment on the new year, [2] the king of France will probably endeavor to forget these events and that compliment. But history, who keeps a durable record of all our acts, and exercises her awful censure over the proceedings of all sorts of sovereigns, will not forget either those events, or the era of this liberal refinement [3] in the intercourse of mankind. History will record that on the morning of the 6th of October, 1789, the king and queen of France, after a day of confusion, alarm, dismay, and slaughter, lay down, under the pledged security of public faith, to indulge nature in a few hours of respite, and troubled, melancholy repose. From this sleep the queen was first startled by the voice of the sentinel at her door, who cried out to her to save herself by flight—that this was the last proof of fidelity he could give—that they were upon him; and he was dead. Instantly he was cut down. A band of cruel ruffians and assassins, reeking with his blood, rushed into the chamber of the queen, and pierced with a hundred strokes of bayonets and poniards the bed, from whence this persecuted woman had but just time to fly almost naked, and, through ways unknown to the murderers, had escaped to refuge at the feet of a king and husband, not secure of his own life for a moment.

This king, to say no more of him, and this queen, and their infant children, (who once would have been the pride and hope of a great and generous people) were then forced to

[1] These reflections grew out of a correspondence which Burke had with "a very young gentleman of Paris," and they retain the tone of a personal letter. They were published in 1790.

[2] An address from the Assembly had been presented to the King and Queen Jan. 3, 1790, felicitating them upon the new year and begging them to forget the past in view of the good they might do in the future.

[3] Spoken sarcastically; see beginning of third paragraph.

abandon the sanctuary of the most splendid palace in the world, which they left swimming in blood, polluted by massacre, and strewed with scattered limbs and mutilated carcasses. Thence they were conducted into the capital of their kingdom. Two had been selected from the unprovoked, unresisted, promiscuous slaughter which was made of the gentlemen of birth and family who composed the king's body guard. These two gentlemen, with all the parade of an execution of justice, were cruelly and publicly dragged to the block, and beheaded in the great court of the palace. Their heads were stuck upon spears, and led the procession; whilst the royal captives who followed in the train were slowly moved along, amidst the horrid yells, and shrilling screams, and frantic dances, and infamous contumelies, and all the unutterable abominations of the furies of hell, in the abused shape of the vilest of women. After they had been made to taste, drop by drop, more than the bitterness of death, in the slow torture of a journey of twelve miles, protracted to six hours, they were, under a guard, composed of those very soldiers who had thus conducted them through this famous triumph, lodged in one of the old palaces of Paris now converted into a bastile for kings.

Is this a triumph to be consecrated at altars? to be commemorated with grateful thanksgiving? to be offered to the divine humanity with fervent prayer and enthusiastic ejaculation? These Theban and Thracian orgies,[1] acted in France, and applauded only in the Old Jewry,[2] I assure you, kindle prophetic enthusiasm in the minds but of very few people in this kingdom: although a saint and apostle, who may have revelations of his own, and who has so completely vanquished all the mean superstitions of the heart, may incline to think it pious and decorous to compare it with the entrance into the world of the Prince of Peace, proclaimed in a holy temple by a venerable sage, and not long before not worse announced by the voice of angels to the quiet innocence of shepherds.

At first I was at a loss to account for this fit of unguarded transport. I knew, indeed, that the sufferings of monarchs make a delicious repast to some sort of palates. There were reflections which might serve to keep this appetite within some bounds of temperance. But when I took one circumstance into my consideration, I was obliged to confess that much allowance ought to be made for the society, and that the temptation was too strong for common discretion; I mean the circumstance of the Io Paean[3] of the triumph, the animating cry which called "for *all* the BISHOPS to be hanged on the lamp posts," might well have brought forth a burst of enthusiasm on the foreseen consequences of this happy day. I allow to so much enthusiasm some little deviation from prudence. I allow this prophet to break forth into hymns of joy and thanksgiving on an event which appears like the precursor of the Millennium, and the projected fifth monarchy,[4] in the destruction of all church establishments. There was, however, (as in all human affairs there is) in the midst of this joy, something to exercise the patience of these worthy gentlemen, and to try the long-suffering of their faith. The actual murder of the king and queen, and their child, was wanting to the other auspicious circumstances of this *"beautiful day."* The actual murder of the bishops, though called for by so many holy ejaculations, was also wanting. A group of regicide and sacrilegious slaughter, was indeed boldly sketched, but it was only sketched. It unhappily was left unfinished, in this great history-piece of the massacre of innocents. What hardy pencil of a great master, from the school of the rights of men,[5] will finish it, is to be seen hereafter. The age has not yet the complete benefit of that diffusion of knowledge that has undermined superstition and error; and the king of France wants another object or two to consign to oblivion, in consideration of all the good which is to arise from his own sufferings, and the patriotic crimes of an enlightened age.

Although this work of our new light and knowledge did not go to the length that in all probability it was intended it should be carried, yet I must think that such treatment of any human creatures must be shocking to any but those who are made for accomplishing revolutions. But I cannot stop here. Influenced by the inborn feelings of my nature, and not being illuminated by a single ray of this new sprung modern light, I confess to you, sir, that the exalted rank of the persons suffering, and particularly the sex, the beauty,

[1] Bacchanalian orgies of ancient Greece

[2] a London street, where Dr. Richard Price, of the Revolution Society, had preached a sermon in approbation of the Revolution in France

[3] ancient shout of victory

[4] the dream of a Puritan sect of Cromwell's time of establishing a monarchy rivaling ancient Assyria, Persia, Macedonia, and Rome

[5] Ironically alluding to the philosophers who upheld revolutionary doctrines in the name of humanity; Burke's extreme conservatism on this subject must not be forgotten.

and the amiable qualities of the descendant of so many kings and emperors, with the tender age of royal infants, insensible only through infancy and innocence of the cruel outrages to which their parents were exposed, instead of being a subject of exultation, adds not a little to my sensibility on that most melancholy occasion.

I hear that the august person who was the principal object of our preacher's triumph, though he supported himself, felt much on that shameful occasion. As a man it became him to feel for his wife and his children, and the faithful guards of his person that were massacred in cold blood about him; as a prince it became him to feel for the strange and frightful transformation of his civilized subjects, and to be more grieved for them than solicitous for himself. It derogates little from his fortitude, while it adds infinitely to the honor of his humanity. I am very sorry to say it, very sorry indeed, that such personages are in a situation in which it is not becoming in us to praise the virtues of the great.

I hear, and I rejoice to hear, that the great lady, the other object of the triumph, has borne that day, (one is interested that beings made for suffering should suffer well) and that she bears all the succeeding days, that she bears the imprisonment of her husband, and her captivity, and the exile of her friends, and the insulting adulation of addresses, and the whole weight of her accumulated wrongs with a serene patience, in a manner suited to her rank and race, and becoming the offspring of a sovereign [1] distinguished for her piety and her courage; that, like her, she has lofty sentiments; that she feels with the dignity of a Roman matron; that in the last extremity she will save herself from the last disgrace; [2] and that, if she must fall, she will fall by no ignoble hand.

It is now sixteen or seventeen years since I saw the queen of France, then the dauphiness, at Versailles; and surely never lighted on this orb, which she hardly seemed to touch, a more delightful vision. I saw her just above the horizon, decorating and cheering the elevated sphere she just began to move in—glittering like the morning star, full of life, and splendor, and joy. Oh! what a revolution! and what a heart must I have to contemplate without emotion that elevation and that fall! Little did I dream when she added titles of veneration to those of enthusiastic, distant, respectful love that she should ever be obliged to carry the sharp antidote against disgrace concealed in that bosom; little did I dream that I should have lived to see such disasters fallen upon her in a nation of gallant men, in a nation of men of honor, and of cavaliers. I thought ten thousands swords must have leaped from their scabbards to avenge even a look that threatened her with insult. But the age of chivalry is gone. That of sophisters, economists, and calculators, has succeeded; and the glory of Europe is extinguished forever. Never, never more shall we behold that generous loyalty to rank and sex, that proud submission, that dignified obedience, that subordination of the heart, which kept alive, even in servitude itself, the spirit of an exalted freedom. The unbought grace of life, the cheap defense of nations, the nurse of manly sentiment and heroic enterprise is gone! It is gone, that sensibility of principle, that chastity of honor, which felt a stain like a wound, which inspired courage whilst it mitigated ferocity, which ennobled whatever it touched, and under which vice itself lost half its evil by losing all its grossness.

This mixed system of opinion and sentiment had its origin in the ancient chivalry; and the principle, though varied in its appearance by the varying state of human affairs, subsisted and influenced through a long succession of generations, even to the time we live in. If it should ever be totally extinguished, the loss I fear will be great. It is this which has given its character to modern Europe. It is this which has distinguished it under all its forms of government, and distinguished it to its advantage, from the states of Asia, and possibly from those states which flourished in the most brilliant periods of the antique world. It was this which, without confounding ranks, had produced a noble equality, and handed it down through all the gradations of social life. It was this opinion which mitigated kings into companions, and raised private men to be fellows with kings. Without force or opposition, it subdued the fierceness of pride and power; it obliged sovereigns to submit to the soft collar of social esteem, compelled stern authority to submit to elegance, and gave a dominating vanquisher of laws to be subdued by manners.

But now all is to be changed. All the pleasing illusions which made power gentle and obedience liberal, which harmonized the different shades of life, and which, by a bland assimilation, incorporated into politics the sentiments which beautify and soften private society, are to be dissolved by this new conquering empire of light and reason. All the

[1] Maria Theresa [2] by poison, self-administered

decent drapery of life is to be rudely torn off. All the superadded ideas, furnished from the wardrobe of a moral imagination, which the heart owns, and the understanding ratifies as necessary to cover the defects of our naked, shivering nature, and to raise it to dignity in our own estimation, are to be exploded as a ridiculous, absurd, and antiquated fashion.

On this scheme of things, a king is but a man, a queen is but a woman; a woman is but an animal, and an animal not of the highest order. All homage paid to the sex in general as such, and without distinct views, is to be regarded as romance and folly. Regicide, and parricide, and sacrilege are but fictions of superstition, corrupting jurisprudence by destroying its simplicity. The murder of a king, or a queen, or a bishop, or a father, are only common homicide; and if the people are by any chance, or in any way, gainers by it, a sort of homicide much the most pardonable, and into which we ought not to make too severe a scrutiny.

On the scheme of this barbarous philosophy, which is the offspring of cold hearts and muddy understandings, and which is as void of solid wisdom as it is destitute of all taste and elegance, laws are to be supported only by their own terrors, and by the concern which each individual may find in them from his own private speculations, or can spare to them from his own private interests. In the groves of *their* academy,[1] at the end of every vista, you see nothing but the gallows. Nothing is left which engages the affections on the part of the commonwealth. On the principles of this mechanic philosophy, our institutions can never be embodied, if I may use the expression, in persons; so as to create in us love, veneration, admiration, or attachment. But that sort of reason which banishes the affections is incapable of filling their place. These public affections, combined with manners, are required sometimes as supplements, sometimes as correctives, always as aids to law. The precept given by a wise man, as well as a great critic, for the construction of poems, is equally true as to states:—*Non satis est pulchra esse poemata, dulcia sunto.* [2] There ought to be a system of manners in every nation, which a well-formed mind would be disposed to relish. To make us love our country, our country ought to be lovely. . . . .

1790

[1] The Athenian philosophers taught while walking in the groves of the Academe. See p. 591.

[2] "It is not enough that poems be beautiful, they must have sweetness." Horace, *Ars Poetica,* 99

WILLIAM COWPER
1731-1800

It is not commonly remembered that Cowper, translator and writer of hymns, was the most popular English poet of his day. He was born in Hertfordshire. His father was a chaplain of George II, and the family, because of its intellectual ability, had for generations maintained itself on terms of equality with the aristocracy. Cowper himself was trained in the law, and after the usual study was called to the bar. But timidity of disposition, working upon weakness of constitution, preyed upon him so that when a place requiring examination at the bar of the House of Lords opened to him, he became temporarily insane. He was obliged to retire to the country where recurrences of his malady sometimes took place, but where he found friends and companions who solicitously cared for him until his death in Norfolk.

An intensely religious nature is shown in Cowper's hymns, some of which are still in use; and there is no doubt that the high moral tone of his poetry helped to make it popular when it was first written. In endures for its quiet, sympathetic realism, its intimate, restful sketches of the country almost photographic in detail, and unlike the set canvases of Thomson. The realism is selective, not indiscriminate, and reveals to us in its pictures the kindly personality of the author.

Cowper's Correspondence, 4 vols., Thomas Wright, 1904, reveals a charming personality. Biography: Smith (EML). Criticism: Hazlitt; Rossetti; Stephen (HL 2), "Cowper and Rosseau"; More (Shel 3), a clear analysis of Cowper's religious state; G. Bradford, "Diversions of a Lost Soul," *Atlan.* 134:361-70, vivid, interesting.

From OLNEY HYMNS

XXXV. LIGHT SHINING OUT OF DARKNESS

1

God moves in a mysterious way
His wonders to perform;
He plants his footsteps in the sea,
And rides upon the storm.

2

Deep in unfathomable mines
Of never-failing skill
He treasures up his bright designs,
And works his sovereign will.

3

Ye fearful saints, fresh courage take,
The clouds ye so much dread
Are big with mercy, and shall break
In blessings on your head.

4

Judge not the Lord by feeble sense,
But trust him for his grace:

Behind a frowning providence
  He hides a smiling face.

5

His purposes will ripen fast,
  Unfolding every hour;
The bud may have a bitter taste,
  But sweet will be the flower.

6

Blind unbelief is sure to err,
  And scan his work in vain:
God is his own interpreter,
  And he will make it plain.

1779

ON THE LOSS OF THE ROYAL GEORGE [1]

1

Toll for the brave!
  The brave that are no more!
All sunk beneath the wave,
  Fast by their native shore!

2

Eight hundred of the brave,
  Whose courage well was tried,
Had made the vessel heel,
  And laid her on her side.

3

A land breeze shook the shrouds,
  And she was overset;
Down went the Royal George,
  With all her crew complete.

4

Toll for the brave!
  Brave Kempenfelt is gone;
His last sea fight is fought;
  His work of glory done.

5

It was not in the battle;
  No tempest gave the shock;
She sprang no fatal leak;
  She ran upon no rock.

6

His sword was in its sheath;
  His fingers held the pen
When Kempenfelt went down
  With twice four hundred men.

7

Weigh the vessel up,
  Once dreaded by our foes!
And mingle with our cup
  The tear that England owes.

8

Her timbers yet are sound,
  And she may float again,
Full charged with England's thunder,
  And plow the distant main.

9

But Kempenfelt is gone,
  His victories are o'er;
And he and his eight hundred
  Shall plow the wave no more.

1782 1803

[1] A man-of-war which, in 1782, while undergoing repairs, turned over, filled, and sank with Admiral Kempenfelt and over eight hundred men on board; this poem takes a place among the great poems written about the British navy, like Campbell's "Ye Mariners of England" and Tennyson's "The Revenge."

THE JACKDAW [2]

1

There is a bird, who, by his coat,
And by the hoarseness of his note,
  Might be supposed a crow;
A great frequenter of the church,
Where bishop-like he finds a perch,
  And dormitory, too.

2

Above the steeple shines a plate
That turns and turns, to indicate
  From what point blows the weather;
Look up—your brains begin to swim,
'Tis in the clouds—that pleases him;
  He chooses it the rather.

3

Fond of the speculative height,
Thither he wings his airy flight,
  And thence securely sees
The bustle and the raree-show [3]
That occupy mankind below,
  Secure and at his ease.

4

You think, no doubt, he sits and muses
On future broken bones and bruises,
  If he should chance to fall.
No; not a single thought like that
Employs his philosophic pate,
  Or troubles it at all.

5

He sees that this great roundabout,
The world, with all its motley rout,
  Church, army, physic, law,
Its customs, and its businesses,
Is no concern at all of his,
  And says—what says he?—"Caw."

[2] translated from the Latin of Cowper's teacher, Vincent Bourne

[3] a show that can be carried about in a box

6

Thrice happy bird! I, too, have seen
Much of the vanities of men;
  And, sick of having seen 'em,
Would cheerfully these limbs resign
For such a pair of wings as thine,
  And such a head between 'em.

1782

ON THE RECEIPT OF MY MOTHER'S PICTURE, OUT OF NORFOLK; THE GIFT OF MY COUSIN, ANN BODHAM

Oh, that those lips had language! Life has passed
With me but roughly since I heard thee last.
Those lips are thine—thy own sweet smile I see,
The same that oft in childhood solaced me;
Voice only fails, else how distinct they say,
"Grieve not, my child, chase all thy fears away!"
The meek intelligence of those dear eyes
(Blest be the art that can immortalize,
The art that baffles Time's tyrannic claim
To quench it) here shines on me, still the same.

Faithful remembrancer of one so dear,
O welcome guest, though unexpected here!
Who bidst me honor with an artless song,
Affectionate, a mother lost so long,
I will obey, not willingly alone,
But gladly, as the precept were her own.
And, while that face renews my filial grief,
Fancy shall weave a charm for my relief,
Shall steep me in Elysian reverie,
A momentary dream that thou art she.

My mother! when I learned that thou wast dead,
Say, wast thou conscious of the tears I shed?
Hovered thy spirit o'er thy sorrowing son,
Wretch even then, life's journey just begun?
Perhaps thou gavest me, though unfelt, a kiss;
Perhaps a tear, if souls can weep in bliss—
Ah, that maternal smile! It answers—Yes.
I heard the bell tolled on thy burial day,
I saw the hearse that bore thee slow away,
And, turning from my nursery window, drew
A long, long sigh, and wept a last adieu!
But was it such?—It was.—Where thou art gone,
Adieus and farewells are a sound unknown.
May I but meet thee on that peaceful shore,
The parting word shall pass my lips no more!
Thy maidens, grieved themselves at my concern,
Oft gave me promise of thy quick return.
What ardently I wished I long believed,
And, disappointed still, was still deceived.
By expectation every day beguiled,
Dupe of *tomorrow* even from a child.
Thus many a sad tomorrow came and went,
Till, all my stock of infant sorrow spent,
I learned at last submission to my lot;
But, though I less deplored thee, ne'er forgot.

Where once we dwelt our name is heard no more,
Children not thine have trod my nursery floor;
And where the gardener, Robin, day by day,
Drew me to school along the public way,
Delighted with my bauble coach, and wrapped
In scarlet mantle warm, and velvet capped,
'Tis now become a history little known
That once we called the pastoral house our own.
Short-lived possession! But the record fair
That memory keeps, of all thy kindness there,
Still outlives many a storm that has effaced
A thousand other themes less deeply traced.
Thy nightly visits to my chamber made,
That thou might'st know me safe and warmly laid;
Thy morning bounties ere I left my home,
The biscuit, or confectionery plum;
The fragrant waters on my cheeks bestowed
By thy own hand, till fresh they shone and glowed;
All this, and more endearing still than all,
Thy constant flow of love that knew no fall,
Ne'er roughened by those cataracts and brakes
That humor, interposed, too often makes;
All this still legible in memory's page,
And still to be so to my latest age,
Adds joy to duty, makes me glad to pay
Such honors to thee as my numbers may;
Perhaps a frail memorial, but sincere,
Not scorned in heaven, though little noticed here.

Could Time, his flight reversed, restore the hours
When, playing with thy vesture's tissued flowers,
The violet, the pink, and jessamine,
I pricked them into paper with a pin
(And thou wast happier than myself the while,
Wouldst softly speak, and stroke my head and smile),
Could those few pleasant days again appear,
Might one wish bring them, would I wish them here?
I would not trust my heart—the dear delight
Seems so to be desired, perhaps I might—
But no—what here we call our life is such
So little to be loved, and thou so much,

That I should ill requite thee to constrain
Thy unbound spirit into bonds again.

Thou, as a gallant bark from Albion's coast
(The storms all weathered and the ocean crossed)
Shoots into port at some well-havened isle,
Where spices breathe, and brighter seasons smile,
There sits quiescent on the floods that show
Her beauteous form reflected clear below,
While airs impregnated with incense play
Around her, fanning light her streamers gay;
So thou, with sails how swift! hast reached the shore,
"Where tempests never beat nor billows roar,"
And thy loved consort on the dangerous tide
Of life long since has anchored by thy side.
But me, scarce hoping to attain that rest,
Always from port withheld, always distressed—
Me howling blasts drive devious, tempest tost,
Sails ripped, seams opening wide, and compass lost,
And day by day some current's thwarting force
Sets me more distant from a prosperous course.
Yet, oh, the thought that thou art safe, and he!
That thought is joy, arrive what may to me.
My boast is not that I deduce my birth
From loins enthroned, and rulers of the earth;
But higher far my proud pretensions rise—
The son of parents passed into the skies!
And now, farewell. Time unrevoked has run
His wonted course, yet what I wished is done.
By contemplation's help, not sought in vain,
I seem to have lived my childhood o'er again;
To have renewed the joys that once were mine,
Without the sin of violating thine.
And, while the wings of Fancy still are free
And I can view this mimic show of thee,
Time has but half succeeded in his theft—
Thyself removed, thy power to soothe me left.

1785 1798

TO MRS UNWIN [1]

Mary! I want a lyre with other strings,
Such aid from heaven as some have feigned they drew,
An eloquence scarce given to mortals, new
And undebased by praise of meaner things,
That, ere through age or woe I shed my wings,
I may record thy worth with honor due,
In verse as musical as thou art true,
And that immortalizes whom it sings.
But thou hast little need. There is a book
By seraphs writ with beams of heavenly light,
On which the eyes of God not rarely look,
A chronicle of actions just and bright;
There all thy deeds, my faithful Mary, shine,
And, since thou own'st that praise, I spare thee mine.

1815

[1] the friend and constant companion of Cowper for thirty-four years

THE CASTAWAY [2]

1

Obscurest night involved the sky,
The Atlantic billows roared,
When such a destined wretch as I,
Washed headlong from on board,
Of friends, of hope, of all bereft,
His floating home forever left.

2

No braver chief could Albion boast
Than he with whom he went,
Nor ever ship left Albion's coast
With warmer wishes sent.
He loved them both, but both in vain,
Nor him beheld, nor her again.

3

Not long beneath the whelming brine,
Expert to swim, he lay;
Nor soon he felt his strength decline,
Or courage die away;
But waged with death a lasting strife,
Supported by despair of life.

4

He shouted; nor his friends had failed
To check the vessel's course,
But so the furious blast prevailed
That, pitiless perforce,
They left their outcast mate behind,
And scudded still before the wind.

5

Some succor yet they could afford;
And such as storms allow,
The cask, the coop, the floated cord,
Delayed not to bestow;
But he, they knew, nor ship nor shore,
Whate'er they gave, should visit more.

6

Nor, cruel as it seemed, could he
Their haste himself condemn,
Aware that flight, in such a sea,
Alone could rescue them;
Yet bitter felt it still to die
Deserted, and his friends so nigh.

[2] The last poem that Cowper wrote; founded on an incident in Admiral Anson's *Voyages*. It portrays imaginatively his own melancholy condition.

7

He long survives who lives an hour
  In ocean, self-upheld;
And so long he, with unspent power,
  His destiny repelled;
And ever, as the minutes flew,
Entreated help, or cried "Adieu!"

8

At length, his transient respite past,
  His comrades, who before
Had heard his voice in every blast,
  Could catch the sound no more;
For then, by toil subdued, he drank
The stifling wave, and then he sank.

9

No poet wept him; but the page
  Of narrative sincere,
That tells his name, his worth, his age
  Is wet with Anson's tear.
And tears by bards or heroes shed
Alike immortalize the dead.

10

I therefore purpose not, or dream,
  Descanting on his fate,
To give the melancholy theme
  A more enduring date:
But misery still delights to trace
Its semblance in another's case.

11

No voice divine the storm allayed,
  No light propitious shone,
When, snatched from all effectual aid,
  We perished, each alone;
But I beneath a rougher sea,
And whelmed in deeper gulfs than he.

1799 1803

GEORGE CRABBE 1754-1832

Crabbe was born in the seacoast village of Aldborough, Suffolk, son of a petty customs officer. His early years were hard and he had little schooling, for the family means were but slender. He was early apprenticed to an Aldborough apothecary and, after medical training, became a physician; but his practice was so poor that at times he was forced to day labor. At length he went to London, urged by the idea that he could make a living by writing. There he failed at first, and in despair appealed personally to Burke, who took him to his own home and, with Johnson, gave him encouragement. Opportunity to write developed his talent. He was advised to take orders, was given livings by influential friends, spent his life as a faithful and efficient clergyman, and died at Trowbridge, Wiltshire.

Crabbe used the material that he knew best. *The Village,* 1783, *The Borough,* 1810, and *Tales of the Hall,* 1819, celebrate his youthful haunts. The truth-telling quality was rare in the verse of his day, but he described men and situations such as he knew in his own parish with all its crime, lust, and brutality, and there is often the fascination of the horrible in his lines. His method is stark realism cast in the form, and often in the diction, of the eighteenth century. His realism was a needed protest against such doctrines as those of Rousseau, that the simplest life is the purest and noblest; it was also the voice of good sense raised against the conventional hypocrisy concerning the joys of the "shepherd swains" that had trailed through poetry for so many generations. Crabbe, then, must be regarded as a transition poet, whose ideas were mainly those of the Romantic Age, but who conformed in verse and diction to the school of Dryden and Pope.

Biographies: Ainger (EML), Kebbel (GW). Criticism: Hazlitt; Saintsbury; Woodberry; Stephen (HL 2); P. E. More, "A Plea for Crabbe," *Atlan.* 88:850-57, an excellent summary; *Liv. Age,* 247:179-183.

From THE BOROUGH[1]

LETTER I

"Describe the Borough."—Though our idle tribe
May love description, can we so describe
That you shall fairly streets and buildings trace,
And all that gives distinction to a place?
This cannot be; yet, moved by your request,
A part I paint—let fancy form the rest.

Cities and towns, the various haunts of men,
Require the pencil; they defy the pen.
Could he who sang so well the Grecian fleet,[2]
So well have sung of alley, lane, or street?
Can measured lines these various buildings show,
The Town-Hall Turning, or the Prospect Row?
Can I the seats of wealth and want explore,
And lengthen out my lays from door to door?

Then, let thy fancy aid me.—I repair
From this tall mansion of our last-year's mayor,
Till we the outskirts of the Borough reach,
And these half-buried buildings next the beach;
Where hang at open doors the net and cork,
While squalid sea-dames mend the meshy work;

[1] This poem was inscribed to the Duke of Rutland, to whom Crabbe had been chaplain, and takes the form of letters from a resident of a seaport to the owner of an inland countryseat. Crabbe's reputation, however, was established by *The Village* in 1783.

[2] Homer, *Iliad* II.

Till comes the hour, when, fishing through the tide,
The weary husband throws his freight aside—
A living mass, which now demands the wife,
The alternate labors of their humble life.

Can scenes like these withdraw thee from thy wood,
Thy upland forest, or thy valley's flood?
Seek, then, thy garden's shrubby bound, and look,
As it steals by, upon the bordering brook:
That winding streamlet, limpid, lingering, slow,
Where the reeds whisper when the zephyrs blow;
Where in the midst, upon her throne of green,
Sits the large lily as the water's queen;
And makes the current, forced awhile to stay,
Murmur and bubble as it shoots away;
Draw then the strongest contrast to that stream,
And our broad river will before thee seem.

With ceaseless motion comes and goes the tide;
Flowing, it fills the channel vast and wide;
Then back to sea, with strong majestic sweep
It rolls, in ebb yet terrible and deep;
Here sampire-banks and salt-wort bound the flood;
There stakes and sea-weeds, withering on the mud;
And, higher up, a ridge of all things base,
Which some strong tide has rolled upon the place.

Thy gentle river boasts its pigmy boat,
Urged on by pains, half grounded, half afloat;
While at her stern an angler takes his stand,
And marks the fish he purposes to land,
From that clear space, where, in the cheerful ray
Of the warm sun, the scaly people play.

Far other craft our prouder river shows—
Hoys, pinks, and sloops, brigs, brigantines, and snows:
Nor angler we on our wide stream descry,
But one poor dredger where his oysters lie.
He, cold and wet, and driving with the tide,
Beats his weak arms against his tarry side,
Then drains the remnant of diluted gin,
To aid the warmth that languishes within;
Renewing oft his poor attempts to beat
His tingling fingers into gathering heat.

He shall again be seen when evening comes,
And social parties crowd their favorite rooms;
Where on the table pipes and papers lie,
The steaming bowl or foaming tankard by.
'Tis then, with all these comforts spread around,
They hear the painful dredger's welcome sound;
And few themselves the savory boon deny,
The food that feeds, the living luxury.

Yon is our quay! Those smaller hoys from town,
Its various wares, for country-use, bring down;
Those laden wagons, in return, impart
The country-produce to the city mart;
Hark to the clamor in that miry road,
Bounded and narrowed by yon vessel's load;
The lumbering wealth she empties round the place,
Package, and parcel, hogshead, chest, and case;
While the loud seaman and the angry hind,
Mingling in business, bellow to the wind.

Near these a crew amphibious, in the docks,
Rear, for the sea, those castles on the stocks.
See the long keel, which soon the waves must hide;
See the strong ribs which form the roomy side;
Bolts yielding slowly to the sturdiest stroke,
And planks which curve and crackle in the smoke.
Around the whole rise cloudy wreaths, and far
Bear the warm pungence of o'er-boiling tar.

Dabbling on shore half-naked sea-boys crowd,
Swim round a ship, or swing upon the shroud;
Or, in a boat purloined, with paddles play,
And grow familiar with the watery way.
Young though they be, they feel whose sons they are;
They know what British seamen do and dare;
Proud of that fame, they raise and they enjoy
The rustic wonder of the village boy.

. . . . .

Turn to the watery world!—But who to thee
(A wonder yet unviewed) shall paint—the sea?
Various and vast, sublime in all its forms,
When lulled by zephyrs, or when roused by storms;
Its colors changing, when from clouds and sun
Shades after shades upon the surface run;
Embrowned and horrid[1] now, and now serene,
In limpid blue, and evanescent green;
And oft the foggy banks on ocean lie,
Lift the fair sail, and cheat the experienced eye.

Be it the summer noon—a sandy space
The ebbing tide has left upon its place;
Then just the hot and stony beach above,

[1] rough

Light twinkling streams in bright confusion move
(For heated thus, the warmer air ascends,
And with the cooler in its fall contends);
Then the broad bosom of the ocean keeps
An equal motion, swelling as it sleeps,
Then slowly sinking; curling to the strand,
Faint, lazy waves o'ercreep the ridgy sand,
Or tap the tarry boat with gentle blow,
And back return in silence, smooth and slow.
Ships in the calm seem anchored; for they glide
On the still sea, urged solely by the tide;
Art thou not present, this calm scene before,
Where all beside is pebbly length of shore
And far as eye can reach, it can discern no more?

Yet sometimes comes a ruffling cloud to make
The quiet surface of the ocean shake;
As an awakened giant with a frown
Might show his wrath, and then to sleep sink down.

View now the winter storm, above, one cloud,
Black and unbroken, all the skies o'ershroud.
The unwieldy porpoise through the day before
Had rolled in view of boding men on shore;
And sometimes hid, and sometimes showed, his form,
Dark as the cloud, and furious as the storm.

All where the eye delights, yet dreads, to roam,
The breaking billows cast the flying foam
Upon the billows rising—all the deep
Is restless change; the waves so swelled and steep,
Breaking and sinking, and the sunken swells,
Nor one, one moment, in its station dwells.
But, nearer land, you may the billows trace,
As if contending in their watery chase;
May watch the mightiest till the shoal they reach,
Then break and hurry to their utmost stretch;
Curled as they come, they strike with furious force,
And then, reflowing, take their grating course,
Raking the rounded flints, which ages past
Rolled by their rage, and shall to ages last.

Far off, the petrel in the troubled way
Swims with her brood, or flutters in the spray;
She rises often, often drops again,
And sports at ease on the tempestuous main.

High o'er the restless deep, above the reach
Of gunner's hope, vast flights of wild ducks stretch;
Far as the eye can glance on either side,
In a broad space and level line they glide;
All in their wedge-like figures from the north,
Day after day, flight after flight, go forth.

Inshore their passage tribes of sea gulls urge,
And drop for prey within the sweeping surge;
Oft in the rough opposing blast they fly
Far back, then turn, and all their force apply,
While to the storm they give their weak complaining cry;
Or clap the sleek white pinion to the breast,
And in the restless ocean dip for rest.

Darkness begins to reign; the louder wind
Appalls the weak and awes the firmer mind;
But frights not him, whom evening and the spray
In part conceal—yon prowler on his way.
Lo! he has something seen; he runs apace,
As if he feared companion in the chase;
He sees his prize, and now he turns again,
Slowly and sorrowing—"Was your search in vain?"
Gruffly he answers, "'Tis a sorry sight!
A seaman's body; there'll be more tonight!"

Hark to those sounds! they're from distress at sea;
How quick they come! What terrors may there be!
Yes, 'tis a driven vessel. I discern
Lights, signs of terror, gleaming from the stern;
Others beheld them too, and from the town
In various parties seamen hurry down;
Their wives pursue, and damsels urged by dread,
Lest men so dear be into danger led;
Their head the gown has hooded, and their call
In this sad night is piercing like the squall;
They feel their kinds of power, and when they meet,
Chide, fondle, weep, dare, threaten, or entreat.

See, one poor girl, all terror and alarm,
Has fondly seized upon her lover's arm;
"Thou shalt not venture"; and he answers, "No!
I will not"—still she cries, "Thou shalt not go."

No need of this; not here the stoutest boat
Can through such breakers, o'er such billows float;

Yet may they view these lights upon the beach,
Which yield them hope, whom help can never reach.

From parted clouds the moon her radiance throws
On the wild waves, and all the danger shows;
But shows them beaming in her shining vest,
Terrific splendor! gloom in glory dressed!
This for a moment, and then clouds again
Hide every beam, and fear and darkness reign.

But hear we now those sounds? Do lights appear?
I see them not! The storm alone I hear.
And lo! the sailors homeward take their way;
Man must endure—let us submit and pray.

Such are our winter views; but night comes on—
Now business sleeps, and daily cares are gone;
Now parties form, and some their friends assist
To waste the idle hours at sober whist;
The tavern's pleasure or the concert's charm
Unnumbered moments of their sting disarm;
Playbills and open doors a crowd invite,
To pass off one dread portion of the night;
And show and song and luxury combined
Lift off from man this burthen of mankind.

Others adventurous walk abroad and meet
Returning parties pacing through the street;
When various voices, in the dying day,
Hum in our walks, and greet us in our way;
When tavern lights flit on from room to room,
And guide the tippling sailor, staggering home.
There as we pass, the jingling bells betray
How business rises with the closing day.
Now walking silent, by the river's side,
The ear perceives the rippling of the tide;
Or measured cadence of the lads who tow
Some entered hoy, to fix her in her row;
Or hollow sound, which from the parish-bell
To some departed spirit bids farewell!

Thus shall you something of our BOROUGH know.
Far as a verse, with Fancy's aid, can show;
Of sea or river, of a quay or street,
The best description must be incomplete;
But when a happier theme succeeds, and when
Men are our subjects and the deeds of men;
Then may we find the Muse in happier style,
And we may sometimes sigh and sometimes smile.

1810

WILLIAM BLAKE
1757-1827

Blake, artist and mystic, sprang from the home of a middle-class London tradesman. Talent in drawing made him highly successful as an engraver and illustrator. His finest achievements were such imaginative decorations and illustrations as *Paradise Lost* and Young's *Night Thoughts* suggested. The original, symbolic quality of these creations, not of the earth earthy, makes his paintings and engravings sought today at high prices.

From youth he had visions, to him perfectly natural, that many would now class as hallucination—fields full of angels, and trees full of wings. His poetry tends with his increasing years more and more toward the shadowy, until to many people it swings quite over the line into insanity. It is an extreme example of romantic mysticism. Some critics, however, find in it a symbolism that makes it the voice of prophecy or the utterance of an intuitive psychologist. We need not stumble over these problems; we can love Blake's lyrics for their own sake, for their fresh, intense beauty.

Blake is best known for his *Songs of Innocence,* 1789, and *Songs of Experience,* 1794. His work as an artist dwindled during his later years, and he died in poverty in London.

Critical and biographical: S. F. Damon, *William Blake, his Philosophy and Symbols,* 1924; More (Shel. 4); "Resurrected Art of William Blake." *Lit. Dig.* 56:25-6, Jan. 12, '18; M. Sherwood, "William Blake and Catharine," *No. Am.* 202:576-91; "Poetry of William Blake," *Liv. Age* 312:102-6; A. Bertram, "Blake: an Aesthetic Approach," *19th C.* 99:442-9.

SONG

1

How sweet I roamed from field to field,
And tasted all the summer's pride,
Till I the Prince of Love beheld,
Who in the sunny beams did glide.

2

He showed me lilies for my hair,
And blushing roses for my brow;
And led me through his gardens fair
Where all his golden pleasures grow.

3

With sweet May-dews my wings were wet,
And Phoebus fired my vocal rage;
He caught me in his silken net,
And shut me in his golden cage.

4

He loves to sit and hear me sing,
Then, laughing, sports and plays with me;
Then stretches out my golden wing,
And mocks my loss of liberty.

1783

TO THE MUSES

1

Whether on Ida's[1] shady brow,
Or in the chambers of the East,
The chambers of the sun, that now
From ancient melody have ceased;

2

Whether in heaven ye wander fair,
Or the green corners of the earth,
Or the blue regions of the air
Where the melodious winds have birth;

3

Whether on crystal rocks ye rove,
Beneath the bosom of the sea
Wandering in many a coral grove,
Fair Nine, forsaking poetry!

4

How have you left the ancient love
That bards of old enjoyed in you!
The languid strings do scarcely move,
The sound is forced, the notes are few.

1783

INTRODUCTION TO SONGS OF INNOCENCE

1

Piping down the valleys wild,
Piping songs of pleasant glee,
On a cloud I saw a child,
And he, laughing, said to me:

2

"Pipe a song about a lamb!"
So I piped with merry cheer.
"Piper, pipe that song again."
So I piped: he wept to hear.

3

"Drop thy pipe, thy happy pipe;
Sing thy songs of happy cheer."
So I sang the same again,
While he wept with joy to hear.

4

"Piper, sit thee down and write
In a book, that all may read."
So he vanished from my sight;
And I plucked a hollow reed,

5

And I made a rural pen,
And I stained the water clear,
And I wrote my happy songs
Every child may joy to hear.

1789

[1] A mountain of the Troad; also one in Crete; Helicon, in Boeotia, is more properly the mountain of the Muses.

THE TIGER[2]

1

Tiger, tiger, burning bright
In the forest of the night,
What immortal hand or eye
Could frame thy fearful symmetry?

2

In what distant deeps or skies
Burnt the fire of thine eyes?
On what wings dare he aspire?
What the hand dare seize the fire?

3

And what shoulder, and what art,
Could twist the sinews of thy heart?
When thy heart began to beat,
What dread hand forged thy dread feet?

4

What the hammer? What the chain?
In what furnace was thy brain?
What the anvil? What dread grasp
Dared its deadly terrors clasp?

5

When the stars threw down their spears,
And watered heaven with their tears,
Did he smile his work to see?
Did he who made the lamb make thee?

6

Tiger, tiger, burning bright
In the forest of the night,
What immortal hand or eye
Dare frame thy fearful symmetry?

1794

AH, SUNFLOWER

1

Ah, sunflower! weary of time,
Who countest the steps of the Sun;
Seeking after that sweet golden clime
Where the traveler's journey is done;

2

Where the Youth, pined away with desire,
And the pale Virgin, shrouded in snow,
Arise from their graves, and aspire
Where my Sunflower wishes to go!

1794

SCOTTISH LYRICS

Native Scottish music and poetry were for a long time eclipsed by the popularity of English and foreign modes, but they never died out completely, and during the eighteenth century, considerable Scotch poetry of real value was written. Even during the "Queen Anne" period of English literature Scotch poetry had retained romantic qualities like those of Elizabethan English poetry.

[2] The Text is that of Malkin, 1806.

In fact, the romantic spirit never was extinguished in the parts of Great Britain remote from the cities and the universities. Some of the new Scotch poetry gave Burns models both in matter and in form.

Robert Fergusson, 1750-1774, the most important of the poets here chosen, was born in Edinburgh and died there. He studied at the University, but lived a rather irregular and convivial life, supporting himself by a clerkship. He published his poems in 1773. Burns freely acknowledged his indebtedness to Fergusson, which is seen, for example, in "The Cotter's Saturday Night," prompted by Fergusson's "Farmer's Ingle."

Lady Anne Lindsay, 1750-1825, born in Fifeshire, daughter of the Earl of Balcarres, had in her early years the advantages of the literary and professional society of Edinburgh. She married Andrew Barnard, lived in South Africa, and later came to London, where she was again in the society of literary people. "Auld Robin Gray" she wrote at the age of twenty-one.

Isobel Pagan, who died about the age of eighty, in 1821, was a peasant woman of Ayrshire living in poverty, and locally popular for her singing of songs and ballads, and for her vituperative wit. A book of her poems was published in Glasgow about 1805.

Caroline (Baroness) Nairne, 1766-1845, daughter of a Perthshire gentleman, and wife of Major William Murray Nairne, afterwards Baron, contributed a good many songs and ballads, under an assumed name, to collections of Scottish songs. Her life was spent in Scotland.

ROBERT FERGUSSON

Elegy on the Death of Scots Music [1]

1

On Scotia's plains, in days of yore,
When lads and lasses tartan wore,
Saft music rang on ilka [2] shore,
    In hamely weid; [3]
But harmony is now no more,
    And music dead.

2

Round her the feathered choir would wing,
Sae bonnily she wont to sing,
And sleely [4] wake the sleeping string,
    Their sang to lead,
Sweet as the zephyrs o' the spring;
    But now she's dead.

3

Mourn, ilka nymph and ilka swain,
Ilk sunny hill and dowie [5] glen;
Let weeping streams and Naiads drain
    Their fountain head;
Let Echo swell the dolefu' strain,
    Sin' music's dead.

4

Whan the saft vernal breezes ca'
The gray-haired winter's fogs awa',
Naebody than is heard to blaw,
    Near hill or mead,
On chaunter [6] or on aiten straw, [7]
    Sin' music's dead.

5

Nae lasses now, on simmer days,
Will lilt [8] at bleaching o' their claes;
Nae herds [9] on Yarrow's bonny braes, [10]
    Or banks o' Tweed,
Delight to chaunt their hameil [11] lays,
    Sin' music's dead.

6

At glomin now the bagpipe's dumb,
Whan weary owsen [12] hameward come;
Sae sweetly as it won't to bum, [13]
    And pibrochs, [14] skreed; [15]
We never hear its weirlike [16] hum,
    For music's dead.

7

Macgibbon's [17] gane. Ah! wae's my heart!
The man in music maist expert,
Wha cou'd sweet melody impart,
    And tune the reed
Wi' sic a slee and pawky [18] art;
    But now he's dead.

8

Ilk carline [19] now may grunt and grane,
Ilk bonny lassie make great mane;
Sin' he's awa, I trow there's nane
    Can fill his stead;
The blythest sangster on the plain,
    Alack, is dead!

9

Now foreign sonnets bear the gree, [20]
And crabbit [21] queer variety
O' sounds fresh sprung frae Italy,
    A bastard breed!
Unlike that saft-tongued melody
    Whilk [22] now lies dead.

[1] As a matter of fact at the time this poem was written the revival of Scotch poetry had begun.
[2] every
[3] homely garb
[4] skillfully
[5] gloomy
[6] finger-pipe (of a bag-pipe)
[7] oaten reed
[8] sing cheerily
[9] shepherds
[10] slopes
[11] homely
[12] oxen
[13] drone
[14] martial tunes
[15] quaver forth
[16] warlike
[17] Wm. Macgibbon, a musician of Edinburgh
[18] cunning
[19] old woman
[20] victory
[21] crabbed
[22] which

10

Cou'd lav'rocks [1] at the dawning day,
Cou'd linties chirming [2] frae the spray,
Or todling burns [3] that smoothly play
O'er gowden [4] bed,
Compare wi' *Birks of Invermay?* [5]
But now they're dead.

11

O Scotland! that cou'd yence [6] afford
To bang the pith [7] o' Roman sword,
Winna your sons, wi' joint accord,
To battle speed,
And fight till Music be restored,
Whilk now lies dead!

c. 1773

LADY ANNE LINDSAY

Auld Robin Gray

1

When the sheep are in the fauld, and the kye at hame,
And a' the warld to rest are gane,
The waes o' my heart fa' in showers frae my e'e
While my gudeman lies sound by me.

2

Young Jamie lo'ed me weel, and sought me for his bride;
But saving a croun he had naething else beside;
To make the croun a pund, young Jamie gaed to sea;
And the croun and the pund were baith for me.

3

He hadna been awa' a week but only twa,
When my father brak his arm, and the cow was stown [8] awa';
My mother she fell sick—and my Jamie at the sea—
And auld Robin Gray came a-courtin' me.

4

My father couldna work, and my mother couldna spin;
I toiled day and night, but their bread I couldna win;
Auld Rob maintained them baith, and wi' tears in his e'e
Said, "Jennie, for their sakes, Oh, marry me!"

5

My heart it said nay; I looked for Jamie back;
But the wind it blew high, and the ship it was a wrack;
His ship it was a wrack—why didna Jamie dee?
Or why do I live to cry, Wae's me!

[1] sky-larks [2] linnets chirping [3] loitering brooks [4] golden [5] popular song [6] once [7] surpass the might [8] stolen

6

My father urged me sair. My mother didna speak;
But she looked in my face till my heart was like to break.
They gi'ed him my hand, though my heart was in the sea;
Sae auld Robin Gray he was gudeman to me.

7

I hadna been a wife a week but only four,
When mournfu' as I sat on the stane at the door,
I saw my Jamie's wraith—for I couldna think it he,
Till he said, "I'm come hame to marry thee."

8

O sair, sair did we greet, [9] and mickle [10] say of a';
We took but ae kiss, and I bade him gang awa';
I wish that I were dead, but I'm no like to dee;
And why was I born to say, Wae's me!

9

I gang like a ghaist, and I carena to spin;
I daurna think on Jamie, for that wad be a sin;
But I'll do my best a gude wife aye to be,
For auld Robin Gray he is kind unto me.

1771

ISOBEL PAGAN

Ca' the Yowes

1

As I gaed down the water side,
There I met my shepherd lad,
He rowed [11] me sweetly in his plaid,
And he ca'd me his dearie.

Ca' the yowes [12] to the knowes, [13]
Ca' them where the heather grows,
Ca' them where the burnie rows, [14]
My bonnie dearie.

2

"Will ye gang down the water side,
And see the waves sae sweetly glide
Beneath the hazels spreading wide?
The moon it shines fu' clearly."

Ca' the yowes, etc.

3

"I was bred up at nae sic school,
My shepherd lad, to play the fool;
And a' the day to sit in dool, [15]
And naebody to see me."

[9] cry [10] much [11] rolled [12] ewes [13] knolls [14] brook flows [15] sorrow

4

"Ye shall get gowns and ribbons meet,
Cauf-leather shoon upon your feet,
And in my arms ye'se [1] lie and sleep,
And ye shall be my dearie."

5

"If ye'll but stand to what ye've said,
I'se gang wi' you, my shepherd lad;
And ye may row me in your plaid,
And I shall be your dearie."

6

"While waters wimple to the sea,
While day blinks in the lift [2] sae hie,
Till clay-cauld death shall blin' my e'e,
Ye aye shall be my dearie."

c. 1787 1853

LADY NAIRNE

The Land o' the Leal

I'm wearin' awa', John,
Like snaw-wreaths in thaw, John,
I'm wearin' awa'
To the land o' the leal. [3]
There's nae sorrow there, John,
There's neither cauld nor care, John,
The day is aye fair
In the land o' the leal.

Our bonnie bairn's there, John,
She was baith gude and fair, John;
And oh! we grudged her sair
To the land o' the leal.
But sorrow's sel' wears past, John,
And joy's a-coming fast, John,
The joy that's aye to last
In the land o' the leal.

Sae dear that joy was bought, John,
Sae free the battle fought, John,
That sinfu' man e'er brought
To the land o' the leal.
Oh, dry your glistening e'e, John!
My saul langs to be free, John,
And angels beckon me
To the land o' the leal.

Oh, haud [4] ye leal and true, John!
Your day it's wearin' through, John,
And I'll welcome you
To the land o' the leal.
Now fare-ye-weel, my ain John,
This warld's cares are vain, John,
We'll meet, and we'll be fain, [5]
In the land o' the leal.

1798 1821-24

[1] ye shall [2] sky [3] loyal, faithful [4] hold [5] happy

ROBERT BURNS
1759-1796

If we can imagine an Arkansas farmer or an Idaho cowboy appearing some winter in Boston with a thin volume of verses to his credit, written in local dialect and printed at the county seat, and see him entertained and patronized by the élite of the city and of Harvard, we can perhaps figure Burns, the somewhat radical peasant that he was, greeted in conservative, learned Edinburgh with its university atmosphere, in 1787. Born on a rented farm at Ayr, with but a few months' schooling all told, he was already bent by the plow and the sickle. His country-printed verses, eagerly bought by his neighbors, had reached the city, and society and culture looked in wonder on their maker. His new friends helped him in the publication of further poems, and procured for him a petty customs office in his home district. But unfortunately he had become dissipated, and his reputation for sobriety, the heritage, as Carlyle says, of every Scotch youth, was gone. The idle, high and low, interfered with his work on the farm that the sale of his books had furnished him, and led him further into company where his wit livened parties made for eating and drinking. His personal affairs went from bad to worse, he contracted consumption, and he died in the sordid town of Dumfries.

Such is the personal tragedy of Burns. But the two collections of his verse, 1786 and 1793, place him almost among the leading half dozen British poets. In his poetry we find an outstanding, complex personality comparable with Johnson or Byron. The fun, the tenderness, and the pathos of his nature are revealed in his lyrics. His satires voice the fiercely passionate soul chafing against hypocrisy and caste, and against intrenched social privilege.

Individual though Burns was, his poetry is in accord with the romantic tendencies of his time. It is simple, it leans hard upon Nature, it expresses the natural emotions of men, and it sets forth the democratic ideals of its time—liberty, fraternity, equality. The ideas he sets forth are few in number; yet Burns is a poet of all time. Matthew Arnold says of him, ". . . . in 'Tam O'Shanter,' or still more in that puissant and splendid production, 'The Jolly Beggars,' his world may be what it will, his poetic genius triumphs over it. In the world of the 'Jolly Beggars' there is more than hideousness and squalor, there is bestiality; yet the piece is a superb poetic success. It has a breadth, truth, and power which make the famous scene in Auerbach's cellar, of Goethe's *Faust*, seem artificial and tame beside it, and which are only matched by Shakespeare and Aristophanes…"

Biography and criticism: Shairp (EML); Blackie (GW); Carlyle's *Essay*, sympathetic, illuminating; Hazlitt; Rossetti; Stevenson; Lang; "Robert Burns, Can English People Understand Him?" Charles Lowe, *19th Cent.* 93:850-59, discusses the language of Burns.

THE COTTER'S SATURDAY NIGHT [1]

INSCRIBED TO ROBERT AIKEN, ESQ.

Let not Ambition mock their useful toil,
  Their homely joys, and destiny obscure;
Nor Grandeur hear, with a disdainful smile,
  The short and simple annals of the poor.
GRAY

1

My loved, my honored, much respected friend!
No mercenary bard his homage pays;
With honest pride, I scorn each selfish end—
My dearest meed, a friend's esteem and praise.[2]
To you I sing, in simple Scottish lays,
The lowly train in life's sequestered scene,
The native feelings strong, the guileless ways,
What Aiken in a cottage would have been;
  Ah! though his worth unknown, far happier there, I ween!

2

November chill blaws loud wi' angry sugh; [3]
The short'ning winter day is near a close;
The miry beasts retreating frae the pleugh;
The black'ning trains o' craws to their repose;
The toil-worn cotter [4] frae his labor goes—
This night his weekly moil [5] is at an end—
Collects his spades, his mattocks, and his hoes,
Hoping the morn in ease and rest to spend,
  And weary, o'er the moor, his course does hameward bend.

3

At length his lonely cot appears in view,
Beneath the shelter of an aged tree;
Th' expectant wee-things, toddlin, stacher [6] through
To meet their dad, wi' flichterin [7] noise an' glee.
His wee-bit ingle, [8] blinkin bonilie,
His clean hearth-stane, his thrifty wifie's smile,
The lisping infant prattling on his knee,
Does a' his weary kiaugh [9] and care beguile,
  And makes him quite forget his labor and his toil.

4

Belyve, [10] the elder bairns come drappin in,
At service out, amang the farmers roun';
Some ca' [11] the pleugh, some herd, some tentie [12] rin
A cannie [13] errand to a neibor town.
Their eldest hope, their Jenny, woman-grown,
In youthfu' bloom, love sparkling in her e'e,
Comes hame, perhaps to shew a braw [14] new gown,
Or deposite her sair-won penny-fee,
  To help her parents dear, if they in hardship be.

5

With joy unfeigned, brothers and sisters meet,
And each for other's weelfare kindly spiers; [15]
The social hours, swift-winged, unnoticed fleet;
Each tells the uncos [16] that he sees or hears.
The parents, partial, eye their hopeful years;
Anticipation forward points the view;
The mother, wi' her needle an' her sheers,
Gars [17] auld claes look amaist as weel's the new;
  The father mixes a' wi' admonition due.

6

Their master's an' their mistress's command
The younkers a' are warnèd to obey;
An' mind their labors wi' an eydent [18] hand,
An' ne'er, though out o' sight, to jauk or play;
"And oh! be sure to fear the Lord alway,
And mind your duty, duly, morn an' night;
Lest in temptation's path ye gang astray,
Implore His counsel and assisting might:
  They never sought in vain that sought the Lord aright!"

7

But hark! a rap comes gently to the door;
Jenny, wha kens the meaning o' the same,
Tells how a neibor lad cam o'er the moor,
To do some errands, and convoy her hame.
The wily mother sees the conscious flame
Sparkle in Jenny's e'e, and flush her cheek;

[1] Of this poem, Gilbert Burns, Robert's brother, writes: "Robert had frequently remarked to me that he thought there was something peculiarly venerable in the phrase, 'Let us worship God,' used by a decent, sober head of a family, introducing family worship. To this sentiment of the author, the world is indebted for 'The Cotter's Saturday Night.' The cotter is an exact copy of my father, in his manners, his family devotion, and exhortations; yet the other parts of the description do not apply to our family. None of us were 'at service out among the farmers roun'. Instead of our depositing our 'sairwon penny-fee' with our parents, my father labored hard, and lived with the most rigid economy, that he might be able to keep his children at home." Mr. J. L. Robertson, commenting on the fact that more than half the poem is in English, says: "An unusually elevated or serious train of thought in the mind of a Scottish peasant seems to demand for its expression the use of a speech which one may describe as Sabbath Scotch." Most readers feel that Burns loses power when he writes in English.

[2] Aiken was not only a patron but a genuine friend of Burns.

[3] sough (sigh)

[4] cottager

[5] labor

[6] stagger

[7] fluttering

[8] fire-place or fire

[9] anxiety

[10] by and by

[11] drive

[12] heedful

[13] careful

[14] handsome

[15] inquires

[16] strange things

[17] makes; see also in *Margaret Ogilvy*, p. 786.

[18] diligent

Wi' heart-struck, anxious care, inquires his name,
While Jenny hafflins [1] is afraid to speak;
Weel pleased the mother hears it's nae wild worthless rake.

8

Wi' kindly welcome Jenny brings him ben, [2]
A strappin youth; he takes the mother's eye;
Blythe Jenny sees the visit's no ill taen;
The father cracks [3] of horses, pleughs, and kye.
The youngster's artless heart o'erflows wi' joy,
But blate [4] and laithfu', [5] scarce can weel behave;
The mother, wi' a woman's wiles, can spy
What makes the youth sae bashfu' and sae grave,
Weel-pleased to think her bairn's respected like the lave. [6]

9

O happy love! where love like this is found!
O heart-felt raptures! bliss beyond compare!
I've pacèd much this weary, mortal round,
And sage experience bids me this declare—
"If Heaven a draft of heavenly pleasure spare,
One cordial in this melancholy vale,
'Tis when a youthful, loving, modest pair
In other's arms breathe out the tender tale,
Beneath the milk-white thorn that scents the evening gale."

10

Is there, in human form, that bears a heart,
A wretch! a villain! lost to love and truth!
That can, with studied, sly, ensnaring art,
Betray sweet Jenny's unsuspecting youth?
Curse on his perjured arts! dissembling smooth!
Are honor, virtue, conscience, all exiled?
Is there no pity, no relenting ruth,
Points to the parents fondling o'er their child;
Then paints the ruined maid, and their distraction wild?

11

But now the supper crowns their simple board,
The halesome parritch, chief of Scotia's food;
The sowpe [7] their only hawkie [8] does afford,
That yont [9] the hallan [10] snugly chows her cood;
The dame brings forth, in complimental mood,
To grace the lad, her weel-hain'd kebbuck, [11] fell; [12]
An' aft he's prest, an' aft he ca's it guid:
The frugal wifie, garrulous, will tell
How 'twas a towmond auld, sin' lint was i' the bell. [13]

12

The cheerfu' supper done, wi' serious face,
They round the ingle form a circle wide;
The sire turns o'er, with patriarchal grace,
The big ha' [14] Bible, ance his father's pride;
His bonnet rev'rently is laid aside,
His lyart haffets [15] wearing thin and bare;
Those strains that once did sweet in Zion glide,
He wales [16] a portion with judicious care;
And "Let us worship God!" he says with solemn air.

13

They chant their artless notes in simple guise,
They tune their hearts, by far the noblest aim;
Perhaps "Dundee's" wild, warbling measures rise,
Or plaintive "Martyrs," worthy of the name;
Or noble "Elgin" beets [17] the heavenward flame,
The sweetest far of Scotia's holy lays.
Compared with these, Italian trills are tame:
The tickled ears no heartfelt raptures raise;
Nae unison hae they with our Creator's praise.

14

The priest-like father reads the sacred page,
How Abram was the friend of God on high;
Or Moses bade eternal warfare wage
With Amalek's ungracious progeny;
Or how the royal bard [18] did groaning lie
Beneath the stroke of Heaven's avenging ire;
Or Job's pathetic plaint, and wailing cry;
Or rapt Isaiah's wild, seraphic fire;
Or other holy seers that tune the sacred lyre.

15

Perhaps the Christian volume is the theme,
How guiltless blood for guilty man was shed;
How He, who bore in heaven the second name,
Had not on earth whereon to lay His head;
How His first followers and servants sped;
The precepts sage they wrote to many a land;
How he, [19] who lone in Patmos banished,
Saw in the sun a mighty angel stand,
And heard great Bab'lon's doom pronounced by Heaven's command.

16

Then kneeling down to Heaven's Eternal King,
The saint, the father, and the husband prays:

[1] partly
[2] into the parlor
[3] talks
[4] shamefaced
[5] bashful
[6] rest
[7] sup, portion (of milk)
[8] cow
[9] beyond
[10] partition
[11] well saved cheese
[12] biting
[13] a twelve-month old, since flax was in flower
[14] hall (In ancient usage, the "hall" was the general assembly room of the house, as opposed to the private "bowers.")
[15] gray temples
[16] chooses
[17] adds fuel to, fans
[18] David
[19] John

Hope "springs exulting on triumphant wing,"[1]
That thus they all shall meet in future days,
There ever bask in uncreated rays,
No more to sigh, or shed the bitter tear,
Together hymning their Creator's praise,
In such society, yet still more dear,
While circling Time moves round in an eternal sphere.

17

Compared with this, how poor Religion's pride
In all the pomp of method and of art,
When men display to congregations wide
Devotion's ev'ry grace, except the heart!
The Pow'r, incensed, the pageant will desert,
The pompous strain, the sacerdotal stole;
But haply, in some cottage far apart,
May hear, well-pleased, the language of the soul,
And in His Book of Life the inmates poor enroll.

18

Then homeward all take off their sev'ral way;
The youngling cottagers retire to rest;
The parent-pair their secret homage pay,
And proffer up to Heaven the warm request,
That He who stills the raven's clam'rous nest,
And decks the lily fair in flow'ry pride,
Would, in the way His wisdom sees the best,
For them and for their little ones provide;
But chiefly, in their hearts with grace divine preside.

19

From scenes like these old Scotia's grandeur springs,
That makes her loved at home, revered abroad:
Princes and lords are but the breath of kings,
"An honest man's the noblest work of God";[2]
And certes, in fair Virtue's heavenly road,
The cottage leaves the palace far behind;
What is a lordling's pomp? A cumbrous load,
Disguising oft the wretch of human kind,
Studied in arts of hell, in wickedness refined!

20

O Scotia! my dear, my native soil!
For whom my warmest wish to Heaven is sent,
Long may thy hardy sons of rustic toil
Be blest with health, and peace, and sweet content!
And oh! may Heaven their simple lives prevent
From luxury's contagion, weak and vile!
Then, howe'er crowns and coronets be rent,
A virtuous populace may rise the while,

[1] Pope, *Winsdor Forest,* 112
[2] Pope, *Essay on Man,* iv, 248

And stand a wall of fire around their much-loved isle.

21

O Thou! who poured the patriotic tide
That streamed through Wallace's undaunted heart,
Who dared to nobly stem tyrannic pride,
Or nobly die, the second glorious part—
(The patriot's God peculiarly thou art,
His friend, inspirer, guardian, and reward!)
O never, never Scotia's realm desert,
But still the patriot, and the patriot-bard,
In bright succession raise, her ornament and guard!

c. 1785 1786

ADDRESS TO THE DEIL[3]

O Prince! O chief of many thronèd pow'rs
That led th' embattled seraphim to war.

MILTON

1

O THOU! whatever title suit thee—
Auld Hornie, Satan, Nick, or Clootie[4]—
Wha in yon cavern grim an' sootie,
Closed under hatches,
Spairges[5] about the brunstane[6] cootie,
To scaud[7] poor wretches!

2

Hear me, auld Hangie,[8] for a wee,
An' let poor damnèd bodies be;
I'm sure sma' pleasure it can gie,
E'en to a deil,
To skelp[9] an' scaud poor dogs like me,
An' hear us squeel!

3

Great is thy pow'r an' great thy fame;
Far kenned an' noted is thy name;

[3] "The humorous satire of the piece is at the expense of popular Scottish Calvinism."—J. L. Robertson.

[4] from *cloot,* one of the divisions of a cloven hoof

[5] "*Spairges* is the best Scots word in its place I ever met with. The deil is not standing flinging the liquid brimstone on his friends with a ladle, but we see him standing at a large boiling vat, with something like a golf-bat, striking the liquid this way and that way aslant, with all his might, making it fly through the whole apartment, while the inmates are winking and holding up their arms to defend their faces." (James Hogg.) This interpretation admirably fits the word *spairges* (Latin, *spargere,* to sprinkle; English, *asperge, asperse*); if it is correct, the word *cootie,* which properly means a wooden kitchen dish of any size from a ladle to a small tub, is used rather boldly for the contents of the cootie.

[6] brimstone
[7] scald
[8] hangman
[9] slap

An' though yon lowin[1] heugh's[2] thy hame,
Thou travels far;
An' faith! thou's neither lag[3] nor lame,
Nor blate[4] nor scaur.[5]

4

Whyles,[6] rangin like a roarin lion,
For prey a' holes and corners tryin;
Whyles, on the strong-winged tempest flyin,
Tirlin[7] the kirks;
Whyles, in the human bosom pryin,
Unseen thou lurks.

5

I've heard my rev'rend graunie say,
In lanely[8] glens ye like to stray;
Or where auld ruined castles gray
Nod to the moon,
Ye fright the nightly wand'rer's way
Wi' eldritch[9] croon.[10]

6

When twilight did my graunie summon
To say her pray'rs, douce[11] honest woman!
Aft yont[12] the dyke she's heard you bummin,[13]
Wi' eerie[9] drone;
Or, rustlin, through the boortress[14] comin,
Wi' heavy groan.

7

Ae dreary, windy, winter night,
The stars shot down wi' sklentin[15] light,
Wi' you mysel I gat a fright
Ayont[12] the lough;[16]
Ye like a rash-buss[17] stood in sight,
Wi' waving sough.

8

The cudgel in my nieve[18] did shake,
Each bristled hair stood like a stake,
When wi' an eldritch, stoor[19] "Quaick, quaick."
Amang the springs,
Awa ye squatter'd[20] like a drake,
On whistlin wings.

9

Let warlocks[21] grim, an' withered hags,
Tell how wi' you, on ragweed nags,
They skim the muirs[22] an' dizzy crags,
Wi' wicked speed;
And in kirk-yards renew their leagues,
Owre howket[23] dead.

10

Thence, countra wives wi' toil and pain
May plunge an' plunge the kirn[24] in vain;
For oh! the yellow treasure's ta'en
By witchin skill;
An' dawtet,[25] twal-pint[26] hawkie's[27] gaen
As yell's[28] the bill.[29]

11

Thence, mystic knots make great abuse
On young guidmen, fond, keen, an' crouse;[30]
When the best wark-lume i' the house,
By cantrip[31] wit,
Is instant made no worth a louse,
Just at the bit.[32]

12

When thowes dissolve the snawy hoord,
An' float the jinglin icy boord,
Then water-kelpies[33] haunt the foord,
By your direction,
An' 'nighted trav'lers are allured
To their destruction.

13

And aft your moss-traversing spunkies[34]
Decoy the wight that late an' drunk is.
The bleezin,[35] curst, mischievous monkies
Delude his eyes,
Till in some miry slough he sunk is,
Ne'er mair to rise.

14

When Masons' mystic word an' grip
In storms an' tempests raise you up,
Some cock or cat your rage maun stop,
Or, strange to tell!
The youngest brither ye wad whip
Aff straught to hell.

15

Lang syne,[36] in Eden's bonie[37] yard,
When youthfu' lovers first were paired,
An' all the soul of love they shared,
The raptured hour,
Sweet on the fragrant flow'ry swaird,
In shady bow'r;

16

Then you, ye auld snick[38]-drawing dog!
Ye cam to Paradise incog,

[1] blazing
[2] pit
[3] slow
[4] bashful
[5] timid
[6] sometimes
[7] unroofing
[8] lonely
[9] ghostly
[10] moan
[11] grave
[12] beyond
[13] buzzing
[14] elder bushes
[15] slanting
[16] lake
[17] bush of rushes
[18] fist
[19] harsh
[20] fluttered
[21] wizards
[22] moors
[23] dug up
[24] churn
[25] doted on, dear
[26] twelve pint
[27] cow
[28] dry as
[29] bull
[30] spirited
[31] magic
[32] nick of time
[33] spirits
[34] will-o'-the-wisps
[35] blazing
[36] since
[37] This spelling represents the broad Scotch pronunciation rather better than *bonny*.
[38] latch

An' played on man a cursèd brogue,[1]
(Black be your fa'![2])
An' gied the infant warld a shog,[3]
'Maist ruined a'.

17

D'ye mind that day when, in a bizz,[4]
Wi' reeket duds, an' reestet gizz,[5]
Ye did present your smoutie phiz
'Mang better folk,
An' sklented on the man of Uz[6]
Your spitefu' joke?

18

An' how ye gat him i' your thrall,
An' brak him out o' house an hal',
While scabs and blotches did him gall
Wi' bitter claw;
An' lows'd[7] his ill-tongued wicked scaul',[8]
Was warst ava?

19

But a' your doings to rehearse,
Your wily snares an' fechtin[9] fierce,
Sin' that day Michael did you pierce,[10]
Down to this time,
Wad ding a Lallan[11] tongue, or Erse,[12]
In prose or rime.

20

An' now, auld Cloots,[13] I ken ye're thinkin
A certain bardie's rantin, drinkin,
Some luckless hour will send him linkin[14]
To your black pit;
But faith! he'll turn a corner jinkin,[15]
An' cheat you yet.

21

But fare you weel, auld Nickie-ben!
O wad ye tak a thought an' men'!
Ye aiblins[16] might—I dinna ken—
Still hae a stake:
I'm wae[17] to think upo' yon den,
Ev'n for your sake!

1785 *1786*

ADDRESS TO THE UNCO GUID[18] OR THE RIGIDLY RIGHTEOUS

My son, these maxims make a rule,
An' lump them aye thegither;
The *Rigid Righteous* is a fool,
The *Rigid Wise anither:*
The cleanest corn that e'er was dight[19]
May hae some pyles o' caff[20] in;
So ne'er a fellow creature slight
For random fits o' daffin.[21]

SOLOMON—Eccles. vii, 16

1

O ye wha are sae guid yoursel',
Sae pious and sae holy,
Ye've nought to do but mark and tell
Your neibors' fauts and folly!
Whase life is like a weel-gaun[22] mill,
Supplied wi' store o' water;
The heapet happer's ebbing still,
An' still the clap[23] plays clatter.

2

Hear me, ye venerable core,[24]
As counsel for poor mortals
That frequent pass douce[25] Wisdom's door
For glaiket[26] Folly's portals;
I, for their thoughtless, careless sakes,
Would here propone[27] defenses—
Their donsie[28] tricks, their black mistakes,
Their failings and mischances.

3

Ye see your state wi' theirs compared,
And shudder at the niffer;[29]
But cast a moment's fair regard,
What makes the mighty differ?[30]
Discount what scant occasion gave,
That purity ye pride in;
And (what's aft mair than a' the lave)
Your better art o' hidin.

4

Think, when your castigated pulse
Gies now and then a wallop,
What ragings must his veins convulse
That still eternal gallop!
Wi' wind and tide, fair i' your tail,
Right on ye scud your sea-way;
But in the teeth o' baith to sail,
It makes an unco lee-way.

5

See Social Life and Glee sit down,
All joyous and unthinking,
Till, quite transmugrified,[31] they're grown
Debauchery and Drinking:

[1] trick
[2] lot
[3] shock
[4] bustle
[5] smoked garments and singed face
[6] shot (literally, squinted) at Job
[7] loosed
[8] scold
[9] fighting
[10] *Par. Lost* vi, 325
[11] baffle a lowland
[12] Gaelic
[13] hoofs (Satan)
[14] tripping
[15] dodging
[16] perhaps
[17] sad
[18] The word *unco* (*uncouth,* "unknown") is used both as adjective, meaning "unusual, strange," and as adverb, meaning "extremely, wonderfully."
[19] dressed, winnowed
[20] grains of chaff
[21] merriment
[22] well-going
[23] clapper
[24] corps, company
[25] grave
[26] giddy
[27] propose
[28] mischievous
[29] exchange
[30] difference
[31] transformed

Oh, would they stay to calculate
  Th' eternal consequences;
Or—your more dreaded hell to state—
  Damnation of expenses!

. . . .

7

Then gently scan your brother man,
  Still gentler sister woman;
Though they may gang a kennin [1] wrang,
  To step aside is human;
One point must still be greatly dark—
  The moving *Why* they do it;
And just as lamely can ye mark,
  How far perhaps they rue it.

8

Who made the heart, 'tis He alone
  Decidedly can try us;
He knows each chord, its various tone,
  Each spring, its various bias:
Then at the balance let's be mute,
  We never can adjust it;
What's *done* we partly may compute,
  But know not what's *resisted.*

c. 1786 *1787*

TO A MOUSE

ON TURNING HER UP IN HER NEST WITH THE PLOW, NOVEMBER, 1785

1

Wee, sleekit, [2] cowrin', tim'rous beastie,
Oh, what a panic's in thy breastie!
Thou need na start awa sae hasty
    Wi' bickering [3] brattle! [4]
I wad be laith to rin an' chase thee
    Wi' murd'rin pattle! [5]

2

I'm truly sorry man's dominion
Has broken nature's social union,
An' justifies that ill opinion
    Which makes thee startle
At me, thy poor, earth-born companion,
    An' fellow-mortal!

3

I doubt na, whyles, [6] but thou may thieve;
What then? poor beastie, thou maun live!
A daimen [7] icker [8] in a thrave [9]
    'S a sma' request;
I'll get a blessin wi' the lave, [10]
    An' never miss't!

4

Thy wee bit housie, too, in ruin!
It's silly wa's the win's are strewin!
An' naething, now, to big [11] a new ane,
    O' foggage [12] green!
An' bleak December's winds ensuin,
    Baith snell [13] an' keen!

5

Thou saw the fields laid bare and waste,
An' weary winter comin' fast,
An' cozie here, beneath the blast,
    Thou thought to dwell,
Till crash! the cruel coulter [14] past
    Out through thy cell.

6

That wee bit heap o' leaves an' stibble
Has cost thee mony a weary nibble!
Now thou's turned out, for a' thy trouble,
    But [15] house or hald, [16]
To thole [17] the winter's sleety dribble
    An' cranreuch [18] cauld!

7

But, mousie, thou art no thy lane [19]
In proving foresight may be vain;
The best laid schemes o' mice an' men
    Gang aft a-gley, [20]
An' lea'e us nought but grief an' pain,
    For promised joy.

8

Still, thou art blest compared wi' me;
The present only toucheth thee;
But och! I backward cast my e'e
    On prospects drear!
An' forward, though I canna see,
    I guess an' fear!

1785 *1786*

TO A LOUSE

ON SEEING ONE ON A LADY'S BONNET AT CHURCH

1

Ha! whaur ye gaun, ye crowlin [21] ferlie? [22]
Your impudence protects you sairly; [23]
I canna say but ye strunt [24] rarely,
    Owre gauze and lace;
Though, faith! I fear ye dine but sparely
    On sic a place.

2

Ye ugly, creepin', blastit [25] wonner, [26]
Detested, shunned by saunt an' sinner,

[1] a little
[2] sleek
[3] hastening
[4] scamper
[5] plow-staff, or scraper
[6] sometimes
[7] occasional
[8] head of grain
[9] twenty-four sheaves
[10] rest
[11] build
[12] herbage
[13] sharp
[14] plow
[15] without
[16] abode
[17] endure
[18] hoar-frost
[19] alone
[20] awry
[21] crawling
[22] wonder
[23] greatly
[24] strut
[25] blasted, "confounded"
[26] marvel

How daur ye set your fit [1] upon her—
Sae fine a lady?
Gae somewhere else and seek your dinner
On some poor body.

3

Swith! [2] in some beggar's haffet [3] squattle; [4]
There ye may creep, and sprawl, and sprattle, [5]
Wi' ither kindred, jumping cattle,
In shoals and nations;
Whaur horn [6] nor bane [7] ne'er daur unsettle
Your thick plantations.

4

Now haud [8] you there, ye're out o' sight,
Below the fatt'rels, [9] snug and tight;
Na, faith ye yet! ye'll no be right
Till ye've got on it—
The vera tapmost, tow'rin height
O' Miss's bonnet.

5

My sooth! [10] right bauld ye set your nose out,
As plump an' gray as ony grozet. [11]
Oh, for some rank, mercurial rozet, [12]
Or fell, red smeddum, [13]
I'd gie you sic a hearty dose o't,
Wad dress your droddum. [14]

6

I wad na been surprised to spy
You on an auld wife's flainen toy; [15]
Or aiblin's some bit duddie [16] boy,
On's wyliecoat; [17]
But Miss's fine Lunardi! [18] fye!
How daur ye do't?

7

O Jenny, dinna toss your head,
An' set your beauties a' abread!
Ye little ken what cursed speed
The blastie's makin!
Thae winks an' finger-ends, I dread,
Are notice takin!

8

Oh, wad some power the giftie gie us
To see oursels as ithers see us!
It wad frae mony a blunder free us,
An' foolish notion.
What airs in dress an' gait wad lea'e us,
An' ev'n devotion!

1786

[1] foot
[2] quick
[3] temple
[4] sprawl
[5] struggle
[6] horn-comb
[7] poison
[8] hold
[9] ribbon-ends
[10] truth
[11] gooseberry
[12] resin
[13] powder
[14] back
[15] flannel cap
[16] ragged
[17] flannel vest
[18] a bonnet

TO A MOUNTAIN DAISY

ON TURNING ONE DOWN WITH THE PLOW, IN APRIL, 1786

Wee, modest, crimson-tippèd flow'r,
Thou's met me in an evil hour;
For I maun [19] crush amang the stoure [20]
Thy slender stem:
To spare thee now is past my pow'r,
Thou bonie gem.

2

Alas! it's no thy neibor sweet,
The bonie lark, companion meet,
Bending thee 'mang the dewy weet
Wi' spreckled breast,
When upward-springing, blythe, to greet
The purpling east.

3

Cauld blew the bitter-biting north
Upon thy early, humble birth;
Yet cheerfully thou glinted forth
Amid the storm,
Scarce reared above the parent-earth
Thy tender form.

4

The flaunting flow'rs our gardens yield,
High shelt'ring woods an' wa's [21] maun shield;
But thou, beneath the random bield [22]
O' clod or stane,
Adorns the histie [23] stibble field
Unseen, alane.

5

There, in thy scanty mantle clad,
Thy snawie bosom sun-ward spread,
Thou lifts thy unassuming head
In humble guise;
But now the share uptears thy bed,
And low thou lies!

6

Such is the fate of artless maid,
Sweet flow'ret of the rural shade!
By love's simplicity betray'd,
And guileless trust;
Till she, like thee, all soiled, is laid
Low i' the dust.

7

Such is the fate of simple bard,
On life's rough ocean luckless starred!
Unskillful he to note the card [24]
Of prudent lore,

[19] must
[20] flying dust
[21] walls
[22] shelter
[23] barren
[24] compass-card

Till billows rage, and gales blow hard,
And whelm him o'er!

8

Such fate to suffering Worth is giv'n,
Who long with wants and woes has striv'n,
By human pride or cunning driv'n
To mis'ry's brink;
Till wrenched of ev'ry stay but Heaven,
He ruined sink!

9

Ev'n thou who mourn'st the Daisy's fate,
That fate is thine—no distant date;
Stern Ruin's plow-share drives elate,
Full on thy bloom,
Till crushed beneath the furrow's weight
Shall be thy doom!

1786 1786

TAM O' SHANTER

A TALE

Of Brownyis and of Bogillis full is this Buke.
—Gawin Douglas

When chapman [1] billies[2] leave the street,
And drouthy [3] neibors neibors meet,
As market-days are wearing late,
And folk begin to tak the gate;
While we sit bousin [4] at the nappy, [5]
An' getting fou [6] and unco [7] happy,
We think na on the lang Scots miles,
The mosses, waters, slaps, [8] and stiles
That lie between us and our hame,
Whare sits our sulky, sullen dame,
Gathering her brows like gathering storm,
Nursing her wrath to keep it warm.

This truth fand [9] honest Tam o' Shanter,
As he frae Ayr ae night did canter
(Auld Ayr, wham ne'er a town surpasses
For honest men and bonie lasses).

O Tam! had'st thou but been sae wise
As taen thy ain wife Kate's advice!
She tauld thee weel thou was a skellum, [10]
A bletherin, [11] blusterin, drunken blellum; [12]
That frae November till October,
Ae market-day thou was na sober;
That ilka melder [13] wi' the miller,
Thou sat as lang as thou had siller;
That ev'ry naig was ca'd [14] a shoe on,
The smith and thee gat roarin fou on;
That at the Lord's house, ev'n on Sunday,
Thou drank wi' Kirkton Jean till Monday.
She prophesied that, late or soon,
Thou would be found, deep drowned in Doon,
Or catched wi' warlocks [15] in the mirk [16]
By Alloway's auld, haunted kirk.

Ah, gentle dames! it gars me greet [17]
To think how mony counsels sweet,
How mony lengthened, sage advices,
The husband frae the wife despises!

But to our tale:—Ae market night,
Tam had got planted unco right,
Fast by an ingle, bleezin finely,
Wi' reamin swats [18] that drank divinely;
And at his elbow, Souter [19] Johnie,
His ancient, trusty, drouthy crony—
Tam lo'ed him like a vera brither;
They had been fou for weeks thegither.
The night drave on wi' sangs and clatter,
And aye the ale was growing better;
The landlady and Tam grew gracious,
Wi' secret favors, sweet and precious;
The souter tauld his queerest stories,
The landlord's laugh was ready chorus;
The storm without might rair and rustle,
Tam did na mind the storm a whistle.

Care, mad to see a man sae happy,
E'en drowned himsel amang the nappy:
As bees flee hame wi' lades o' treasure,
The minutes winged their way wi' pleasure;
Kings may be blest, but Tam was glorious,
O'er a' the ills o' life victorious!

But pleasures are like poppies spread,
You seize the flow'r, its bloom is shed;
Or like the snow falls [20] in the river,
A moment white—then melts forever;
Or like the borealis race,
That flit ere you can point their place;
Or like the rainbow's lovely form
Evanishing amid the storm.—
Nae man can tether time or tide:
The hour approaches Tam maun ride;
That hour, o' night's black arch the key-stane,
That dreary hour he mounts his beast in;
And sic a night he taks the road in,
As ne'er poor sinner was abroad in.

The wind blew as 'twad blawn its last;
The rattling show'rs rose on the blast;

[1] pedlar
[2] fellows
[3] thirsty
[4] drinking
[5] ale
[6] full
[7] very
[8] gap in a fence
[9] found
[10] rascal
[11] idly-talking
[12] babbler
[13] every grinding of corn
[14] driven

[15] wizards
[16] dark
[17] make me weep
[18] frothing ales
[19] shoemaker
[20] supply "that"

The speedy gleams the darkness swallowed;
Loud, deep, and lang the thunder bellowed:
That night, a child might understand,
The Deil had business on his hand.

Weel-mounted on his gray mare, Meg—
A better never lifted leg—
Tam skelpit [1] on through dub [2] and mire,
Despising wind, and rain, and fire;
Whiles holding fast his gude blue bonnet,
Whiles crooning o'er some auld Scots sonnet,
Whiles glow'rin round wi' prudent cares
Lest bogles catch him unawares.
Kirk-Alloway was drawing nigh,
Where ghaists and houlets [3] nightly cry.

By this time he was cross the ford
Whare in the snaw the chapman smoored; [4]
And past the birks [5] and meikle [6] stane
Whare drucken Charlie brak's neck-bane;
And through the whins, [7] and by the cairn [8]
Whare hunters fand the murdered bairn;
And near the thorn, aboon the well,
Whare Mungo's mither hanged hersel.
Before him Doon pours all his floods;
The doubling storm roars through the woods,
The lightnings flash from pole to pole,
Near and more near the thunders roll;
When, glimmering through the groaning trees,
Kirk-Alloway seemed in a bleeze, [9]
Through ilka bore [10] the beams were glancing,
And loud resounded mirth and dancing.

Inspiring bold John Barleycorn!
What dangers thou canst make us scorn!
Wi' tippenny, [11] we fear nae evil;
Wi' usquabae, [12] we'll face the devil!
The swats sae reamed in Tammie's noddle,
Fair play, he cared na deils a boddle. [13]
But Maggie stood, right sair astonished,
Till, by the heel and hand admonished,
She ventured forward on the light;
And, wow! Tam saw an unco [14] sight!

Warlocks and witches in a dance;
Nae cotillion brent [15] new frae France,
But hornpipes, jigs, strathspeys, and reels [16]
Put life and mettle in their heels.
A winnock-bunker [17] in the east,
There sat Auld Nick, in shape o' beast;
A towzie tyke, [18] black, grim, and large,
To gie them music was his charge;
He screwed the pipes and gart them skirl [19]
Till roof and rafters a' did dirl. [20]
Coffins stood round, like open presses,
That shawed the dead in their last dresses;
And by some devilish cantraip [21] sleight
Each in its cauld hand held a light,
By which heroic Tam was able
To note upon the haly table
A murderer's banes in gibbet-airns;
Twa span-lang, wee, unchristened bairns;
A thief, new-cutted frae the rape, [22]
Wi' his last gasp his gab [23] did gape;
Five tomahawks, wi' blude red-rusted;
Five scymitars, wi' murder crusted;
A garter, which a babe had strangled;
A knife, a father's throat had mangled,
Whom his ain son o' life bereft,
The gray hairs yet to stack to the heft;
Wi' mair o' horrible and awfu',
Which ev'n to name wad be unlawfu'.

As Tammie glowered, [24] amazed, and curious,
The mirth and fun grew fast and furious;
The piper loud and louder blew,
The dancers quick and quicker flew;
They reeled, they set, they crossed, they cleekit [25]
Till ilka carlin [26] swat [27] and reekit, [28]
And coost [29] her duddies [30] to the wark, [31]
And linket [32] at it in her sark! [33]

Now, Tam, O Tam; had thae been queans [34]
A' plump and strapping in their teens!
Their sarks, instead o' creeshie [35] flannen,
Been snaw-white seventeen hunder linen! [36]
Thir [37] breeks o' mine, my only pair,
That ance were plush, o' gude blue hair,
I wad hae gien them aff my hurdies [38]
For ae blink o' the bonie burdies! [39]
But withered beldams, auld and droll,
Rigwoodie [40] hags wad spean [41] a foal,
Lowping [42] an' flinging on a crummock, [43]
I wonder dina turn thy stomach.

But Tam kenned what was what fu' brawlie: [44]
There was ae winsome wench and walie [45]
That night enlisted in the core [46]
(Lang after kenned on Carrick shore:

[1] hurried
[2] puddle
[3] owls
[4] smothered
[5] birches
[6] great
[7] furze
[8] heap of stones
[9] a blaze
[10] chink
[11] two-penny ale
[12] whisky
[13] a small coin
[14] strange
[15] bright (new)
[16] all Scottish dances
[17] window-seat
[18] shaggy cur
[19] made them shriek
[20] rattle
[21] magic
[22] rope
[23] mouth
[24] stared
[25] joined hands
[26] old woman
[27] sweated
[28] steamed
[29] cast off
[30] clothes
[31] work
[32] tripped
[33] smock
[34] girls
[35] greasy
[36] very fine woven linen, 1700 threads to the yard
[37] these
[38] hips
[39] lasses
[40] bony
[41] that would wean (by disgust)
[42] leaping
[43] staff
[44] well
[45] goodly
[46] company

For mony a beast to dead she shot,
And perished mony a bonie boat,
And shook baith meikle corn and bear,[1]
And kept the country-side in fear);
Her cutty sark, o' Paisley harn,[2]
That while a lassie she had worn,
In longitude though sorely scanty
It was her best, and she was vauntie.[3]
Ah! little kenned thy reverend grannie,
That sark she coft[4] for her wee Nannie,
Wi' twa pund Scots[5] ('twas a' her riches),
Wad ever graced a dance of witches!

But here my Muse her wing maun cow'r,
Sic flights are far beyond her pow'r;
To sing how Nannie lap and flang
(A souple jade she was and strang),
And how Tam stood like one bewitched,
And thought his very een[6] enriched;
Even Satan glowered and fidged[7] fu' fain,
And hotched[8] and blew wi' might and main;
Till first ae caper, syne[9] anither,
Tam tint[10] his reason a' thegither
And roars out, "Weel done, Cutty-sark!"
And in an instant all was dark.
And scarcely had he Maggie rallied,
When out the hellish legion sallied.

As bees bizz out wi' angry fyke,[11]
When plundering herds assail their byke;[12]
As open pussie's[13] mortal foes,
When, pop! she starts before their nose;
As eager runs the market-crowd,
When "Catch the thief!" resounds aloud;
So Maggie runs, the witches follow,
Wi' mony an eldritch[14] skriech and hollo.

Ah, Tam! Ah, Tam! thou'll get thy fairin![15]
In hell they'll roast thee like a herrin!
In vain thy Kate awaits thy comin!
Kate soon will be a woefu' woman!
Now, do thy speedy utmost, Meg,
And win the key-stane of the brig;[16]
There, at them thou thy tail may toss,
A running stream they dare na cross.
But ere the key-stane she could make,
The fient[17] a tail she had to shake!
For Nannie, far before the rest,
Hard upon noble Maggie prest,
And flew at Tam Wi' furious ettle;[18]
But little wist she Maggie's mettle—
Ae spring brought aff her master hale,
But left behind her ain gray tail:
The carlin claught her by the rump,
And left poor Maggie scarce a stump.

Now, wha this tale o' truth shall read,
Ilk man, and mother's son, take heed:
Whene'er to drink you are inclined,
Or cutty-sarks run in your mind,
Think, ye may buy the joys owre dear;
Remember Tam o' Shanter's mare.

1790 1791

GREEN GROW THE RASHES

There's nought but care on ev'ry han',
In ev'ry hour that passes, oh;
What signifies the life o' man,
An 'twere na for the lasses, oh.
Chor.—Green grow the rashes,[19] oh;
Green grow the rashes, oh;
The sweetest hours that e'er I spend
Are spent among the lasses, oh.

The war'ly[20] race may riches chase,
An' riches still may fly them, oh;
An' though at last they catch them fast,
Their hearts can ne'er enjoy them, oh.
Green grow, etc.

But gie me a cannie[21] hour at e'en,
My arms about my dearie, oh;
An' war'ly cares, an' war'ly men,
May a' gae tapsalterrie,[22] oh!
Green grow, etc.

For you sae douce,[23] ye sneer at this;
Ye're nought but senseless asses, oh;
The wisest man the warl' e'er saw,
He dearly loved the lasses, oh.
Green grow, etc.

Auld Nature swears, the lovely dears
Her noblest work she classes, oh;
Her prentice han' she tried on man,
An' then she made the lasses, oh.
Green grow, etc.

1786 1787

AULD LANG SYNE

Should auld acquaintance be forgot,
And never brought to min'?
Should auld acquaintance be forgot
And auld lang syne![24]

[1] barley
[2] short skirt, of Paisley yarn
[3] proud
[4] bought
[5] A pound Scots is one shilling, eight pence—about forty cents.
[6] eyes
[7] fidgeted
[8] squirmed
[9] then
[10] lost
[11] fuss
[12] hive
[13] the hare's
[14] ghostly
[15] reward
[16] bridge
[17] devil
[18] intent
[19] rushes
[20] worldly
[21] quiet
[22] topsy-turvey
[23] grave
[24] old long since (old times)

Chorus—For auld lang syne, my dear,
For auld lang syne,
We'll take a cup o' kindness yet
For auld lang syne.

And surely ye'll be your pint-stowp![1]
And surely I'll be mine!
And we'll tak a cup o' kindness yet,
For auld lang syne.
For auld, etc.

We twa hae run about the braes,[2]
And pu'd the gowans[3] fine;
But we've wandered mony a weary fit,[4]
Sin' auld lang syne.
For auld, etc.

We twa hae paidled i' the burn,[5]
From mornin' sun till dine;[6]
But seas between us braid[7] hae roared
Sin' auld lang syne.
For auld, etc.

And there's a hand, my trusty fier![8]
And gie's a hand o' thine!
And we'll tak a right guid-willie waught,[9]
For auld lang syne.
For auld, etc.

1788 *1796*

JOHN ANDERSON MY JO

John Anderson my jo,[10] John,
When we were first acquent,
Your locks were like the raven
Your bonie brow was brent;[11]
But now your brow is beld,[12] John,
Your locks are like the snaw;
But blessings on your frosty pow,[13]
John Anderson my jo.

John Anderson my jo, John,
We clamb the hill thegither;
And mony a canty[14] day, John,
We've had wi' ane anither;
Now we maun totter down, John,
And hand in hand we'll go,
And sleep thegither at the foot,
John Anderson my jo.

1790

WHISTLE O'ER THE LAVE O'T

First when Maggie was my care,
Heaven, I thought, was in her air,
Now we're married—speir[15] nae mair,
But whistle o'er the lave[16] o't!
Meg was meek, and Meg was mild,
Sweet and harmless as a child—
Wiser men than me's beguiled;
Whistle o'er the lave o't!

How we live, my Meg and me,
How we love, and how we gree,
I care na by how few may see—
Whistle o'er the lave o't!
Wha I wish were maggot's meat,
Dished up in her winding-sheet,
I could write—but Meg maun see't—
Whistle o'er the lave o't!

1789

TO MARY IN HEAVEN[17]

Thou ling'ring star, with less'ning ray,
That lov'st to greet the early morn,
Again thou usher'st in the day
My Mary from my soul was torn.
O Mary! dear departed shade!
Where is thy place of blissful rest?
See'st thou thy lover lowly laid?
Hear'st thou the groans that rend his breast?

That sacred hour can I forget,
Can I forget the hallowed grove,
Where by the winding Ayr we met
To live one day of parting love?
Eternity will not efface
Those records dear of transports past,
Thy image at our last embrace—
Ah! little thought we 'twas our last!

Ayr, gurgling, kissed his pebbled shore,
O'erhung with wild woods, thick'ning green;
The fragrant birch and hawthorn hoar
Twined amorous round the raptured scene;
The flowers sprang wanton to be prest,
The birds sang love on every spray,
Till too, too soon the glowing west
Proclaimed the speed of wingèd day.

Still o'er these scenes my mem'ry wakes,
And fondly broods with miser care!
Time but th' impression stronger makes,
As streams their channels deeper wear.
My Mary, dear departed shade!
Where is thy place of blissful rest?
See'st thou thy lover lowly laid?
Hear'st thou the groans that rend his breast?

1789 *1790*

[1] be good for (stand for) your three-pint measure
[2] slopes
[3] daisies
[4] foot
[5] brook
[6] dinner-time
[7] broad
[8] comrade
[9] hearty draught
[10] sweetheart (joy)
[11] smooth
[12] bald
[13] head
[14] merry
[15] ask
[16] rest
[17] Mary Campbell, died 1786; Burns's "Highland Mary"

MY HEART'S IN THE HIGHLANDS

Farewell to the Highlands, farewell to the North,
The birthplace of valor, the country of worth;
Wherever I wander, wherever I rove,
The hills of the Highlands forever I love.
My heart's in the Highlands, my heart is not here;
My heart's in the Highlands, a-chasing the deer;
A-chasing the wild deer, and following the roe,
My heart's in the Highlands wherever I go.

Farewell to the mountains, high-covered with snow;
Farewell to the straths[1] and green valleys below;
Farewell to the forests and wild-hanging woods,
Farewell to the torrents and loud-pouring floods.

My heart's in the Highlands, my heart is not here;
My heart's in the Highlands, a-chasing the deer;
A-chasing the wild deer, and following the roe,
My heart's in the Highlands wherever I go.

1790

THE BANKS O' DOON

Ye flowery banks o' bonie Doon,
How can ye blume sae fair?
How can ye chant, ye little birds,
And I sae fu' o' care?

Thou'll break my heart, thou bonie bird
That sings upon the bough;
Thou minds me o' the happy days
When my fause luve was true.

Thou'll break my heart, thou bonie bird
That sings beside thy mate;
For sae I sat, and sae I sang,
And wist na o' my fate.

Aft hae I roved by bonie Doon
To see the woodbine twine,
And ilka bird sang o' its luve,
And sae did I o' mine.

Wi' lightsome heart I pu'd a rose,
Frae aff its thorny tree;
And my fause luver staw[2] my rose
But left the thorn wi' me.

1791 1808

AFTON WATER

Flow gently, sweet Afton, among thy green braes,[3]
Flow gently, I'll sing thee a song in thy praise;
My Mary's asleep by thy murmuring stream,
Flow gently, sweet Afton, disturb not her dream.

Thou stock-dove whose echo resounds through the glen,
Ye wild whistling blackbirds in yon thorny den,
Thou green-crested lapwing, thy screaming forbear,
I charge you, disturb not my slumbering fair.

How lofty, sweet Afton, thy neighboring hills,
Far marked with the courses of clear, winding rills;
There daily I wander as noon rises high,
My flocks and my Mary's sweet cot in my eye.

How pleasant thy banks and green valleys below,
Where wild in the woodlands the primroses blow;
There oft, as mild Evening weeps over the lea,
The sweet-scented birk[4] shades my Mary and me.

Thy crystal stream, Afton, how lovely it glides,
And winds by the cot where my Mary resides;
How wanton thy waters her snowy feet lave,
As gathering sweet flow'rets she stems thy clear wave.

Flow gently, sweet Afton, among thy green braes,
Flow gently, sweet river, the theme of my lays;
My Mary's asleep by thy murmuring stream,
Flow gently, sweet Afton, disturb not her dream.

1792

HIGHLAND MARY

Ye banks, and braes, and streams around
The castle o' Montgomery,
Green be your woods, and fair your flowers,
Your waters never drumlie![5]
Their simmer first unfald[6] her robes,

[1] broad vales

[2] stole
[3] hills, slopes
[4] birch
[5] muddy
[6] i.e., may summer unfold

And there the langest tarry;
For there I took the last fareweel
O' my sweet Highland Mary.

How sweetly bloomed the gay green birk,
How rich the hawthorn's blossom,
As underneath their fragrant shade
I clasped her to my bosom!
The golden hours on angel wings,
Flew o'er me and my dearie;
For dear to me as light and life,
Was my sweet Highland Mary.

Wi' monie a vow, and locked embrace,
Our parting was fu' tender;
And, pledging aft to meet again,
We tore oursels asunder;
But oh, fell death's untimely frost,
That nipt my flower sae early!
Now green's the sod, and cauld's the clay,
That wraps my Highland Mary!

Oh, pale, pale now, those rosy lips
I aft hae kissed sae fondly!
And closed for aye the sparkling glance
That dwelt on me sae kindly!
And mold'ring now in silent dust,
That heart that lo'ed me dearly!
But still within my bosom's core
Shall live my Highland Mary.

1792 *1799*

BANNOCKBURN

Robert Bruce's Address to His Army

Scots, wha hae wi' Wallace bled,
Scots, wham Bruce has aften led;
Welcome to your gory bed,
Or to victory!

Now's the day, and now's the hour;
See the front o' battle lour;
See approach proud Edward's power—
Chains and slavery!

Wha will be a traitor knave?
Wha can fill a coward's grave?
Wha sae base as be a slave?
Let him turn and flee!

Wha for Scotland's king and law
Freedom's sword will strongly draw,
Freeman stand or freeman fa',
Let him follow me!

By oppression's woes and pains!
By your sons in servile chains!
We will drain our dearest veins,
But they shall be free!

Lay the proud usurpers low!
Tyrants fall in every foe!
Liberty's in every blow!—
Let us do or die!

1793 *1794*

CONTENTED WI' LITTLE AND CANTIE WI' MAIR

Contented wi' little, and cantie [1] wi' mair,
Whene'er I forgather [2] wi' Sorrow and Care
I gie them a skelp [3] as their creeping alang,
Wi' a cog [4] o' gude swats [5] and an auld Scottish sang.

I whiles claw [6] the elbow o' troublesome Thought;
But man is a soger, and life is a faught;
My mirth and gude humor are coin in my pouch,
And my freedom's my lairdship nae monarch dare touch.

A towmond [7] o' trouble, should that be my fa',[8]
A night o' gude fellowship sowthers [9] it a';
When at the blithe end of our journey at last,
Wha the deil ever thinks o' the road he has past?

Blind Chance, let her snapper and stoyte [10] on her way;
Be't to me, be't frae me, e'en let the jade gae;
Come ease or come travail, come pleasure or pain,
My warst word is "Welcome, and welcome again!"

1794 *1799*

A MAN'S A MAN FOR A' THAT

Is there, [11] for honest poverty,
That hings his head, an' a' that?
The coward slave, we pass him by,
We dare be poor for a' that!
For a' that, an' a' that,
Our toils obscure, an' a' that;
The rank is but the guinea's stamp;
The man's the gowd [12] for a' that.

What though on hamely fare we dine,
Wear hodden-gray, [13] an' a' that;
Gie fools their silks, and knaves their wine,
A man's a man for a' that.
For a' that, an' a' that,

[1] merry
[2] meet
[3] slap
[4] cup
[5] ale
[6] scratch
[7] twelve-month
[8] lot
[9] solders, mends
[10] stumble and stagger
[11] supply "a man"
[12] gold
[13] coarse cloth

Their tinsel show, an' a' that;
The honest man, though e'er sae poor,
Is king o' men for a' that.
Ye see yon birkie,[1] ca'd a lord,
Wha struts, an' stares, an' a' that;
Though hundreds worship at his word,
He's but a coof[2] for a' that.
For a' that, an a' that,
His riband, star, an' a' that,
The man o' independent mind,
He looks and laughs at a' that.

A prince can mak a belted knight,
A marquis, duke, an' a' that;
But an honest man's aboon his might,
Guid faith, he mauna fa'[3] that!
For a' that, an' a' that,
Their dignities, an' a' that,
The pith o' sense, an' pride o' worth,
Are higher rank than a' that.

Then let us pray that come it may,
As come it will for a' that,
That sense and worth, o'er a' the earth,
May bear the gree,[4] an' a' that.
For a' that, an' a' that,
It's coming yet for a' that,
That man to man, the warld o'er,
Shall brothers be for a' that.

1794 1795

[1] fellow
[2] fool
[3] may not accomplish
[4] prize

OH, WERT THOU IN THE CAULD BLAST

Oh, wert thou in the cauld blast,
On yonder lea, on yonder lea,
My plaidie to the angry airt,[5]
I'd shelter thee, I'd shelter thee.
Or did misfortune's bitter storms
Around thee blaw, around thee blaw,
Thy bield[6] should be my bosom,
To share it a', to share it a'.

Or were I in the wildest waste,
Sae black and bare, sae black and bare,
The desert were a paradise,
If thou wert there, if thou wert there.
Or were I monarch o' the globe,
Wi' thee to reign, wi' thee to reign,
The brightest jewel in my crown
Wad be my queen, wad be my queen.

1796 1800

[5] to the windy quarter
[6] shelter

THE ROMANTIC REVIVAL

As literary forces, classicism and romanticism tend to counterbalance each other. They represent the ebb and flow of ideas and forms from conservatism to liberalism, from conformity to revolt. The terms classic and classicism are pretty well understood. In literature they refer to the writings of the Greeks and the Romans and especially to those of Homer, Vergil, and Cicero or to any writings governed especially by the Greek and Latin qualities of clearness, restraint, and intellectuality. In English literature the classic authors were used as models from the Restoration until about the close of the eighteenth century. Then, for many reasons, the pendulum paused in its swing toward the classic and turned back. The era that followed is called romantic.

Romantic literature, wherever it appears, is easily recognized. It emphasizes the individual and his emotions; it is impatient of curb or law. It exalts rather than restrains the feelings. "Romance is, in wide range, the control and combination of facts by imagination and hope."[1] It does not accept as final such an interpretation of the physical world as may appear reasonable to the intellect, but, with Wordsworth, interprets the external world by the experiences of the soul.

In the period of English literature now before us, some of the outward signs of the romantic are as follows. Nature takes a prominent place both as an object of pleasure to man and an inspiration and guide to his higher and deeper spiritual emotions. Indeed, a "return to nature" was the dream of many idealists inspired by Rousseau's saying that man was born free but finds himself everywhere in chains. Another sign of the romantic spirit in the England of 1798-1832 is the echo of the rallying cry of the French Revolutionists—"Liberty, fraternity, equality." Still another sign is the use of medieval subjects and the treating of them in the medieval manner with full scope for the play of the elemental passions of love, fear, revenge, and hate. Romantic literature shows more openly the medieval qualities of aspiration and enthusiasm than does the classic. It is content if it suggests answers to the deepest problems of existence where classicism demands cool definitions. English literature as a whole has been prevailingly romantic; for although under the spell of classicism from Johnson to Dryden, it returned to a spirit akin to the Elizabethan.

[1] F. B. Gummere, *Atlan.* 120:490 ff.

WILLIAM WORDSWORTH
1770-1850

With Wordsworth and the English Lake Country more than with any other person or place we associate the romantic revival of English poetry dating from the close of the eighteenth century. Travelers were only then discovering the beauty of the region. In the year before Wordsworth's birth Gray had been charmed with its mountains and waters. At its northwest border, at Cockermouth, Wordsworth was born, son of the legal and business agent of a large estate, and its forests, streams, and moors became his playground. It was the region in which he settled in manhood, the scene of his greatest poetical activity, and of his death.

Before his years at Cambridge, Wordsworth had written some verse, and in 1795 had published two poems in the conventional style of the time. But after his meeting with Coleridge in that same year his poetical manner wholly changed, became simple and direct. Indeed, for both poets their friendship was most profitable; only during the next ten years, those of its closest intimacy, did either do his best work. Their joint volume, *Lyrical Ballads,* 1798, struck a new note which at first was misunderstood and derided. In the preface to a second edition, 1800, Wordsworth set forth his principles of poetry. This essay-preface defends the choice of "Humble and rustic life . . . because, in that condition, the essential passions of the heart . . . . speak a plainer and more emphatic language." Henceforth, Wordsworth was the champion of the new school and the target of its enemies. The essay voiced universal principles of poetry that had been neglected for a century and a half but have been followed ever since, consciously or unconsciously.

Simple subjects simply developed form but a small part of Wordsworth's harvest from nature; for in nature he observed and experienced a power that molds human character and develops it to its highest levels, a force that cheers, admonishes, and exalts the soul. This is the sincere belief, sometimes miscalled the philosophy, of Wordsworth.

Wordsworth did not confine his poetry to nature but set himself to criticize society at large. Unfortunately for his artistic fame he lacked, like many reformers, the faculty of objective self-criticism; large tracts of his work are arid, unimaginative. But there is a faultlessness in some of his lyrics that defies criticism, and this we may perfectly enjoy. As Arnold says,

> He laid us as we lay at birth
> On the cool flowery lap of earth.

The outstanding biography of Wordsworth is G. M. Harper's, 2 vols., 1916; see also E. Legouis's *Early Life of Wordsworth,* revised ed.; *Letters of the Wordsworth Family,* 3 vols., 1907; *Journals of Dorothy Wordsworth,* 2 vols., 1904; Coleridge; Arnold. Criticism: Payne; Rossetti; Swinburne; Dowden; More (Shel. 7), etc.; G. M. Harper, "Rousseau, Godwin, and Wordsworth," *Atlan.* 109:639-50; same, "Wordsworth at Blois," *Nation* 96:354-5; same, "Did Wordsworth Defy the Guillotine?" *Quart.* 248:254-64.

DEAR NATIVE REGIONS [1]

Dear native regions, I foretell,
From what I feel at this farewell,
That, wheresoe'er my steps may tend,
And whensoe'er my course shall end,
If in that hour a single tie
Survive of local sympathy,
My soul will cast the backward view,
The longing look alone on you.

Thus, while the sun sinks down to rest
Far in the regions of the west,
Though to the vale no parting beam
Be given, not one memorial gleam,
A lingering light he fondly throws
On the dear hills where first he rose.

1786 1815

WE ARE SEVEN [2]

—A simple Child,
That lightly draws its breath,
And feels its life in every limb,
What should it know of death?

I met a little cottage Girl;
She was eight years old, she said;
Her hair was thick with many a curl
That clustered round her head.

She had a rustic, woodland air,
And she was wildly clad;
Her eyes were fair, and very fair;
—Her beauty made me glad.

"Sisters and brothers, little Maid,
How many may you be?"
"How many? Seven in all," she said
And wondering looked at me.

[1] Wordsworth thought it worth while to print this "extract from the conclusion of a poem" which was written, at the age of sixteen, just before he left school at Hawkshead. It both reveals his strong local attachment and anticipates his reliance upon what became for him a chief source of poetic inspiration, namely, "emotion recollected in tranquility."

[2] This, and the two poems that follow it, were among those contributed by Wordsworth to the joint volume of *Lyrical Ballads* which he and Coleridge published in 1798. This poem was written to show "the obscurity and perplexity which in childhood attend our notion of death, or rather our utter inability to admit that notion." The capitalization in this and the following poems is Wordsworth's own and was regarded by him as significant.

"And where are they? I pray you tell."
She answered, "Seven are we;
And two of us at Conway dwell,
And two are gone to sea.

"Two of us in the churchyard lie,
My sister and my brother;
And, in the churchyard cottage, I
Dwell near them with my mother."

"You say that two at Conway dwell,
And two are gone to sea.
Yet ye are seven! I pray you tell,
Sweet Maid, how this may be."

Then did the little Maid reply,
"Seven boys and girls are we;
Two of us in the churchyard lie,
Beneath the churchyard tree."

"You run about, my little Maid,
Your limbs they are alive;
If two are in the churchyard laid,
Then ye are only five."

"Their graves are green, they may be seen,"
The little Maid replied,
"Twelve steps or more from my mother's door,
And they are side by side.

"My stockings there I often knit,
My kerchief there I hem;
And there upon the ground I sit,
And sing a song to them.

"And often after sunset, Sir,
When it is light and fair,
I take my little porringer,
And eat my supper there.

"The first that died was sister Jane;
In bed she moaning lay,
Till God released her of her pain;
And then she went away.

"So in the churchyard she was laid;
And, when the grass was dry,
Together round her grave we played,
My brother John and I.

"And when the ground was white with snow,
And I could run and slide,
My brother John was forced to go,
And he lies by her side."

"How many are you, then," said I,
"If they two are in heaven?"
Quick was the little Maid's reply,
"O master! we are seven."

"But they are dead; those two are dead!
Their spirits are in heaven!"
'Twas throwing words away; for still
The little Maid would have her will,
And said, "Nay, we are seven!"

1798 1800

LINES WRITTEN IN EARLY SPRING [1]

I heard a thousand blended notes,
While in a grove I sat reclined,
In that sweet mood when pleasant thoughts
Bring sad thoughts to the mind.

To her fair works did nature link
The human soul that through me ran;
And much it grieved my heart to think
What man has made of man.

Through primrose tufts, in that green bower,
The periwinkle trailed its wreaths;
And 'tis my faith that every flower
Enjoys the air it breathes.

The birds around me hopped and played,
Their thoughts I cannot measure—
But the least motion which they made
It seemed a thrill of pleasure.

The budding twigs spread out their fan,
To catch the breezy air;
And I must think, do all I can,
That there was pleasure there.

If this belief from heaven be sent,
If such be nature's holy plan,
Have I not reason to lament
What man has made of man?

1798 1798

LINES COMPOSED A FEW MILES ABOVE TINTERN ABBEY, ON REVISITING THE BANKS OF THE WYE DURING A TOUR, JULY 13, 1798. [2]

Five years have past; five summers, with the length
Of five long winters! and again I hear

[1] This is one of the earliest and most definite expressions of Wordsworth's faith in the real oneness of man and nature, and of his sorrow over man's having fallen away from that faith.

[2] Note by Wordsworth: "I have not ventured to call this poem an Ode; but it was written with a hope that in the transitions, and the impassioned music of the versification, would be found the principal requisites of that species of composition." Professor Dowden remarks upon the four stages of the poet's growth to be found described in the poem: First, animal enjoyment of nature in boyhood; second, passion for beauty and sublimity; third, perception of nature's tranquilizing and elevating influence on the spirit; and fourth, deep communion with a spiritual presence; stages which he further describes as the periods of the blood, of the senses, of the imagination, and of the soul.

These waters, rolling from their mountain-springs
With a soft inland murmur.[1]—Once again
Do I behold these steep and lofty cliffs,
That on a wild secluded scene impress
Thoughts of more deep seclusion; and connect
The landscape with the quiet of the sky.
The day is come when I again repose
Here, under this dark sycamore, and view
These plots of cottage-ground, these orchard-tufts,
Which at this season, with their unripe fruits,
Are clad in one green hue, and lose themselves
'Mid groves and copses. Once again I see
These hedgerows, hardly hedgerows, little lines
Of sportive wood run wild: these pastoral farms,
Green to the very door; and wreaths of smoke
Sent up, in silence, from among the trees!
With some uncertain notice, as might seem
Of vagrant dwellers in the houseless woods,
Or of some Hermit's cave, where by his fire
The Hermit sits alone.
These beauteous forms,
Through a long absence, have not been to me
As is a landscape to a blind man's eye:
But oft, in lonely rooms, and 'mid the din
Of towns and cities, I have owed to them,
In hours of weariness, sensations sweet,
Felt in the blood, and felt along the heart;
And passing even into my purer mind
With tranquil restoration—feelings, too,
Of unremembered pleasure: such, perhaps,
As have no slight or trivial influence
On that best portion of a good man's life,
His little, nameless, unremembered acts
Of kindness and of love. Nor less, I trust,
To them I may have owed another gift,
Of aspect more sublime; that blessed mood
In which the burthen of the mystery,
In which the heavy and the weary weight
Of all this unintelligible world
Is lightened—that serene and blessed mood
In which the affections gently lead us on—
Until, the breath of this corporeal frame
And even the motion of our human blood
Almost suspended, we are laid asleep
In body, and become a living soul:
While with an eye made quiet by the power
Of harmony, and the deep power of joy,
We see into the life of things.
If this
Be but a vain belief, yet, oh! how oft—
In darkness and amid the many shapes
Of joyless daylight; when the fretful stir
Unprofitable, and the fever of the world,
Have hung upon the beatings of my heart—
How oft, in spirit, have I turned to thee,
O silvan Wye! thou wanderer through the woods,
How often has my spirit turned to thee!
And now, with gleams of half-extinguished thought,
With many recognitions dim and faint,
And somewhat of a sad perplexity,
The picture of the mind revives again:
While here I stand, not only with the sense
Of present pleasure, but with pleasing thoughts
That in this moment there is life and food
For future years. And so I dare to hope,
Though changed, no doubt, from what I was when first
I came among these hills; when like a roe
I bounded o'er the mountains, by the sides
Of the deep rivers, and the lonely streams,
Wherever nature led: more like a man
Flying from something that he dreads than one
Who sought the thing he loved. For nature then
(The coarser pleasures of my boyish days,
And their glad animal movements all gone by)
To me was all in all.—I cannot paint
What then I was. The sounding cataract
Haunted me like a passion: the tall rock,
The mountain, and the deep and gloomy wood,
Their colors and their forms, were then to me
An appetite; a feeling and a love
That had no need of a remoter charm,
By thought supplied, nor any interest
Unborrowed from the eye.—That time is past,
And all its aching joys are now no more,
And all its dizzy raptures. Not for this
Faint I, nor mourn nor murmur; other gifts
Have followed; for such loss, I would believe,
Abundant recompense. For I have learned
To look on nature, not as in the hour
Of thoughtless youth; but hearing oftentimes
The still, sad music of humanity,
Nor harsh nor grating, though of ample power
To chasten and subdue. And I have felt
A presence that disturbs me with the joy
Of elevated thoughts; a sense sublime
Of something far more deeply interfused,
Whose dwelling is the light of setting suns,
And the round ocean and the living air,
And the blue sky, and in the mind of man;
A motion and a spirit that impels
All thinking things, all objects of all thought,
And rolls through all things. Therefore am I still
A lover of the meadows and the woods,

[1] For the effect of the tides on the Wye nearer its mouth, see Tennyson's *In Memoriam*, XIX.

And mountains; and of all that we behold
From this green earth; of all the mighty world
Of eye, and ear—both what they half create,
And what perceive; well pleased to recognize
In nature and the language of the sense,
The anchor of my purest thoughts, the nurse,
The guide, the guardian of my heart, and soul
Of all my moral being.
Nor perchance,
If I were not thus taught, should I the more
Suffer my genial spirits to decay;
For thou art with me here upon the banks
Of this fair river; thou my dearest Friend,
My dear, dear Friend; and in thy voice I catch
The language of my former heart, and read
My former pleasures in the shooting lights
Of thy wild eyes. Oh! yet a little while
May I behold in thee what I was once,
My dear, dear Sister! and this prayer I make,
Knowing that Nature never did betray
The heart that loved her; 'tis her privilege,
Through all the years of this our life, to lead
From joy to joy; for she can so inform [1]
The mind that is within us, so impress
With quietness and beauty, and so feed
With lofty thoughts, that neither evil tongues,
Rash judgments, nor the sneers of selfish men,
Nor greetings where no kindness is, nor all
The dreary intercourse of daily life
Shall e'er prevail against us, or disturb
Our cheerful faith that all which we behold
Is full of blessings. Therefore let the moon
Shine on thee in thy solitary walk;
And let the misty mountain-winds be free
To blow against thee; and, in after years,
When these wild ecstasies shall be matured
Into a sober pleasure; when thy mind
Shall be a mansion for all lovely forms,
Thy memory be as a dwelling-place
For all sweet sounds and harmonies; oh! then,
If solitude, or fear, or pain, or grief,
Should be thy portion, with what healing thoughts
Of tender joy wilt thou remember me,
And these my exhortations! Nor, perchance—
If I should be where I no more can hear
Thy voice, nor catch from thy wild eyes these gleams
Of past existence—wilt thou then forget
That on the banks of this delightful stream
We stood together; and that I, so long
A worshiper of Nature, hither came
Unwearied in that service: rather say
With warmer love—oh! with far deeper zeal
Of holier love. Nor wilt thou then forget
That after many wanderings, many years
Of absence, these steep woods and lofty cliffs,
And this green pastoral landscape, were to me
More dear, both for themselves and for thy sake!

1798 *1798*

STRANGE FITS OF PASSION HAVE I KNOWN [2]

Strange fits of passion have I known;
And I will dare to tell,
But in the Lover's ear alone,
What once to me befell.

When she I loved looked every day
Fresh as a rose in June,
I to her cottage bent my way
Beneath an evening moon.

Upon the moon I fixed my eye,
All over the wide lea;
With quickening pace my horse drew nigh
Those paths so dear to me.

And now we reached the orchard plot;
And, as we climbed the hill,
The sinking moon to Lucy's cot
Came near, and nearer still.

In one of those sweet dreams I slept,
Kind Nature's gentlest boon!
And all the while my eyes I kept
On the descending moon.

My horse moved on; hoof after hoof
He raised, and never stopped;
When down behind the cottage roof,
At once, the bright moon dropped.

What fond and wayward thoughts will slide
Into a Lover's head!
"O mercy!" to myself I cried,
"If Lucy should be dead!"

1799 1800

SHE DWELT AMONG THE UNTRODDEN WAYS

She dwelt among the untrodden ways
Beside the springs of Dove, [3]

[1] give form to, animate

[2] The five poems which follow, upon an unknown and perhaps imaginary Lucy, were written in Germany in the winter of 1799-1800. Without titles, or any ornament beyond two or three of the simplest figures, they convey their emotion with absolute directness, exemplifying that poetry which, in moments of deepest feeling, is the natural language of man. The fifth poem appears to sum up the preceding four; in its two brief stanzas it presents the two opposing and inscrutable mysteries of life and death, and leaves them to the imagination without comment.

[3] The name of several streams in England; this one is probably in Yorkshire.

A Maid whom there were none to praise
And very few to love:

A violet by a mossy stone
Half hidden from the eye!
—Fair as a star, when only one
Is shining in the sky.

She lived unknown, and few could know
When Lucy ceased to be;
But she is in her grave, and, oh,
The difference to me!

1799 1800

I TRAVELED AMONG UNKNOWN MEN

I traveled among unknown men,
In lands beyond the sea;
Nor, England! did I know till then
What love I bore to thee.

'Tis past, that melancholy dream!
Nor will I quit thy shore
A second time; for still I seem
To love thee more and more.

Among thy mountains did I feel
The joy of my desire;
And she I cherished turned her wheel
Beside an English fire.

Thy mornings showed, thy nights concealed
The bowers where Lucy played;
And thine, too, is the last green field
That Lucy's eyes surveyed.

1799 1807

THREE YEARS SHE GREW IN SUN AND SHOWER

Three years she grew in sun and shower,
Then Nature said, "A lovelier flower
On earth was never sown;
This Child I to myself will take;
She shall be mine, and I will make
A Lady of my own.

"Myself will to my darling be
Both law and impulse: and with me
The Girl, in rock and plain,
In earth and heaven, in glade and bower,
Shall feel an overseeing power
To kindle or restrain.

"She shall be sportive as the fawn
That wild with glee across the lawn,
Or up the mountain springs;
And hers shall be the breathing balm,
And hers the silence and the calm
Of mute insensate things.

"The floating clouds their state shall lend
To her; for her the willow bend;
Nor shall she fail to see,
Even in the motions of the Storm,
Grace that shall mold the Maiden's form
By silent sympathy.

"The stars of midnight shall be dear
To her; and she shall lean her ear
In many a secret place
Where rivulets dance their wayward round,
And beauty born of murmuring sound
Shall pass into her face.

"And vital feelings of delight
Shall rear her form to stately height,
Her virgin bosom swell;
Such thoughts to Lucy I will give
While she and I together live
Here in this happy dell."

Thus Nature spake.—The work was done—
How soon my Lucy's race was run!
She died, and left to me
This heath, this calm and quiet scene;
The memory of what has been,
And never more will be.

1799 1800

A SLUMBER DID MY SPIRIT SEAL

A Slumber did my spirit seal;
I had no human fears.
She seemed a thing that could not feel
The touch of earthly years.

No motion has she now, no force;
She neither hears nor sees;
Rolled round in earth's diurnal course,
With rocks, and stones, and trees.

1799 1800

LUCY GRAY

OR, SOLITUDE

Oft I had heard of Lucy Gray:
And, when I crossed the wild,
I chanced to see at break of day
The solitary Child.

No mate, no comrade Lucy knew;
She dwelt on a wide moor
—The sweetest thing that ever grew
Beside a human door!

You yet may spy the fawn at play,
The hare upon the green;
But the sweet face of Lucy Gray
Will never more be seen.

"Tonight will be a stormy night—
You to the town must go;
And take a lantern, Child, to light
Your mother through the snow."

"That, Father! will I gladly do:
'Tis scarcely afternoon—
The minster-clock has just struck two,
And yonder is the moon!"

At this the Father raised his hook,
And snapped a fagot-band;
He plied his work—and Lucy took
The lantern in her hand.

Not blither is the mountain roe;
With many a wanton stroke
Her feet disperse the powdery snow,
That rises up like smoke.

The storm came on before its time:
She wandered up and down;
And many a hill did Lucy climb,
But never reached the town.

The wretched parents all that night
Went shouting far and wide;
But there was neither sound nor sight
To serve them for a guide.

At daybreak on a hill they stood,
That overlooked the moor;
And thence they saw the bridge of wood,
A furlong from their door.

They wept—and, turning homeward, cried,
"In heaven we all shall meet;"
—When in the snow the mother spied
The print of Lucy's feet.

Then downward from the steep hill's edge
They tracked the footmarks small;
And through the broken hawthorn hedge,
And by the long stone-wall;

And then an open field they crossed:
The marks were still the same;
They tracked them on, nor ever lost;
And to the bridge they came.

They followed from the snowy bank
Those footmarks, one by one,
Into the middle of the plank—
And farther there were none!

—Yet some maintain that to this day
She is a living child;
That you may see sweet Lucy Gray
Upon the lonesome wild.

O'er rough and smooth she trips along,
And never looks behind;
And sings a solitary song
That whistles in the wind.

1799 1800

THE PRELUDE; OR, GROWTH OF A POET'S MIND

From Book I. Childhood

Fair seed-time had my soul, and I grew up
Fostered alike by beauty and by fear:
Much favored in my birthplace, and no less
In that beloved Vale[1] to which erelong
We were transplanted—there were we let loose
For sports of wider range. Ere I had told
Ten birthdays, when among the mountain slopes
Frost, and the breath of frosty wind, had snapped
The last autumnal crocus, 'twas my joy
With store of springes o'er my shoulder hung
To range the open heights where woodcocks run
Along the smooth green turf. Through half the night,
Scudding away from snare to snare, I plied
That anxious visitation—moon and stars
Were shining o'er my head. I was alone,
And seemed to be a trouble to the peace
That dwelt among them. Sometimes it befell
In these night wanderings, that a strong desire
O'erpowered my better reason, and the bird
Which was the captive of another's toil
Became my prey; and when the deed was done
I heard among the solitary hills
Low breathings coming after me, and sounds
Of undistinguishable motion, steps
Almost as silent as the turf they trod.

Nor less, when spring had warmed the cultured Vale,
Moved we as plunderers where the mother-bird
Had in high places built her lodge; though mean
Our object and inglorious, yet the end
Was not ignoble. Oh! when I have hung
Above the raven's nest, by knots of grass
And half-inch fissures in the slippery rock
But ill sustained, and almost—so it seemed—
Suspended by the blast that blew amain,
Shouldering the naked crag, oh, at that time
While on the perilous ridge I hung alone,
With what strange utterance did the loud dry wind

[1] Esthwaite, Lancashire, where, at the village of Hawkshead, Wordsworth attended school

Blow through my ear! The sky seemed not a sky
Of earth—and with what motion moved the clouds!

Dust as we are, the immortal spirit grows
Like harmony in music; there is a dark
Inscrutable workmanship that reconciles
Discordant elements, makes them cling together
In one society. How strange that all
The terrors, pains, and early miseries,
Regrets, vexations, lassitudes interfused
Within my mind, should e'er have borne a part,
And that a needful part, in making up
The calm existence that is mine when I
Am worthy of myself! Praise to the end!
Thanks to the means which Nature deigned to employ;
Whether her fearless visitings, or those
That came with soft alarm, like hurtless light
Opening the peaceful clouds; or she would use
Severer interventions, ministry
More palpable, as best might suit her aim.

One summer evening—led by her—I found
A little boat tied to a willow tree
Within a rocky cave, its usual home.
Straight I unloosed her chain, and stepping in
Pushed from the shore. It was an act of stealth
And troubled pleasure, nor without the voice
Of mountain echoes did my boat move on,
Leaving behind her still, on either side,
Small circles glittering idly in the moon
Until they melted all into one track
Of sparkling light. But now, like one who rows,
Proud of his skill, to reach a chosen point
With an unswerving line, I fixed my view
Upon the summit of a craggy ridge,
The horizon's utmost boundary; far above
Was nothing but the stars and the gray sky.
She was an elfin pinnace; lustily
I dipped my oars into the silent lake,
And, as I rose upon the stroke, my boat
Went heaving through the water like a swan;
When, from behind that craggy steep till then
The horizon's bound, a huge peak, black and huge,
As if with voluntary power instinct,
Upreared its head. I struck and struck again,
And growing still in stature the grim shape
Towered up between me and the stars, and still,
For so it seemed, with purpose of its own
And measured motion like a living thing,
Strode after me. With trembling oars I turned,
And through the silent water stole my way
Back to the covert of the willow tree;
There in her mooring-place I left my bark—
And through the meadows homeward went, in grave
And serious mood; but after I had seen
That spectacle, for many days, my brain
Worked with a dim and undetermined sense
Of unknown modes of being; o'er my thoughts
There hung a darkness, call it solitude
Or blank desertion. No familiar shapes
Remained, no pleasant images of trees,
Of sea or sky, no colors of green fields;
But huge and mighty forms, that do not live
Like living men, moved slowly through the mind
By day, and were a trouble to my dreams.

Wisdom and Spirit of the universe!
Thou Soul that art the eternity of thought
That givest to forms and images a breath
And everlasting motion, not in vain
By day or starlight thus from my first dawn
Of childhood didst thou intertwine for me
The passions that build up our human soul;
Not with the mean and vulgar works of man,
But with high objects, with enduring things—
With life and nature—purifying thus
The elements of feeling and of thought,
And sanctifying, by such discipline,
Both pain and fear, until we recognize
A grandeur in the beatings of the heart.
Nor was this fellowship vouchsafed to me
With stinted kindness. In November days,
When vapors rolling down the valley made
A lonely scene more lonesome, among woods
At noon and 'mid the calm of summer nights,
When, by the margin of the trembling lake,
Beneath the gloomy hills homeward I went
In solitude, such intercourse was mine;
Mine was it in the fields both day and night,
And by the waters, all the summer long.

And in the frosty season, when the sun
Was set, and visible for many a mile
The cottage windows blazed through twilight gloom,
I heeded not their summons: happy time
It was indeed for all of us—for me
It was a time of rapture! Clear and loud
The village clock tolled six—I wheeled about,
Proud and exulting like an untired horse
That cares not for his home. All shod with steel,
We hissed along the polished ice in games
Confederate, imitative of the chase
And woodland pleasures—the resounding horn,
The pack loud chiming, and the hunted hare.
So through the darkness and the cold we flew,
And not a voice was idle; with the din

Smitten, the precipices rang aloud;
The leafless trees and every icy crag
Tinkled like iron; while far distant hills
Into the tumult sent an alien sound
Of melancholy not unnoticed, while the stars
Eastward were sparkling clear, and in the west
The orange sky of evening died away.
Not seldom from the uproar I retired
Into a silent bay, or sportively
Glanced sideway, leaving the tumultous throng,
To cut across the reflex of a star
That fled, and flying still before me, gleamed
Upon the glassy plain; and oftentimes,
When we had given our bodies to the wind,
And all the shadowy banks on either side
Came sweeping through the darkness, spinning still
The rapid line of motion, then at once
Have I, reclining back upon my heels,
Stopped short; yet still the solitary cliffs
Wheeled by me—even as if the earth had rolled
With visible motion her diurnal round!
Behind me did they stretch in solemn train,
Feebler and feebler, and I stood and watched
Till all was tranquil as a dreamless sleep.

Ye Presences of Nature in the sky
And on the earth! Ye Visions of the hills!
And Souls of lonely places! Can I think
A vulgar hope was yours when ye employed
Such ministry, when ye, through many a year
Haunting me thus among my boyish sports,
On caves and trees, upon the woods and hills,
Impressed upon all forms the characters
Of danger or desire; and thus did make
The surface of the universal earth,
With triumph and delight, with hope and fear,
Work like a sea?
Not uselessly employed,
Might I pursue this theme through every change
Of exercise and play, to which the year
Did summon us in his delightful round.

From Book V

There was a Boy; ye knew him well, ye cliffs
And islands of Winander! [1] Many a time
At evening, when the earliest stars began
To move along the edges of the hills,
Rising or setting, would he stand alone
Beneath the trees or by the glimmering lake,
And there, with fingers interwoven, both hands
Pressed closely palm to palm, and to his mouth
Uplifted, he, as through an instrument,
Blew mimic hootings to the silent owls,
That they might answer him; and they would shout
Across the watery vale, and shout again,
Responsive to his call, with quivering peals,
And long halloos and screams, and echoes loud,
Redoubled and redoubled, concourse wild
Of jocund din; and, when a lengthened pause
Of silence came and baffled his best skill,
Then sometimes, in that silence while he hung
Listening, a gentle shock of mild surprise
Has carried far into his heart the voice
Of mountain torrents; or the visible scene
Would enter unawares into his mind,
With all its solemn imagery, its rocks,
Its woods, and that uncertain heaven, received
Into the bosom of the steady lake.

This Boy was taken from his mates, and died
In childhood, ere he was full twelve years old.
Fair is the spot, most beautiful the vale
Where he was born; the grassy churchyard hangs
Upon a slope above the village school,
And through that churchyard when my way has led
On summer evenings, I believe that there
A long half hour together I have stood
Mute, looking at the grave in which he lies!

1799-1805 1850

[1] Winandermere, now Windermere, is a lake bordering Westmoreland.

MY HEART LEAPS UP WHEN I BEHOLD

My heart leaps up when I behold
A rainbow in the sky.
So was it when my life began;
So is it now I am a man;
So be it when I shall grow old,
Or let me die!
The Child is father of the Man;
And I could wish my days to be
Bound each to each by natural piety. [2]

1802 1807

THE SOLITARY REAPER

Behold her, single in the field,
Yon solitary Highland Lass!
Reaping and singing by herself;
Stop here, or gently pass!
Alone she cuts and binds the grain,
And sings a melancholy strain;
O listen; for the Vale profound
Is overflowing with the sound.

No Nightingale did ever chaunt
More welcome notes to weary bands

[2] religious regard for nature

Of travelers in some shady haunt,
Among Arabian sands.
A voice so thrilling ne'er was heard
In springtime from the Cuckoo-bird,
Breaking the silence of the seas
Among the farthest Hebrides.

Will no one tell me what she sings?—
Perhaps the plaintive numbers flow
For old, unhappy, far-off things,
And battles long ago.
Or is it some more humble lay,
Familiar matter of today?
Some natural sorrow, loss, or pain
That has been, and may be again?

Whate'er the theme, the Maiden sang
As if her song could have no ending;
I saw her singing at her work,
And o'er the sickle bending,
I listened, motionless and still;
And, as I mounted up the hill,
The music in my heart I bore,
Long after it was heard no more.

1803-1805 1807

TO THE CUCKOO

O blithe New-comer! I have heard,
I hear thee and rejoice.
O Cuckoo! shall I call thee Bird,
Or but a wandering Voice?

While I am lying on the grass
Thy twofold shout I hear,
From hill to hill it seems to pass,
At once far off, and near.

Though babbling only to the Vale,
Of sunshine and of flowers,
Thou bringest unto me a tale
Of visionary hours.

Thrice welcome, darling of the Spring!
Even yet thou art to me
No bird, but an invisible thing,
A voice, a mystery;

The same whom in my schoolboy days
I listened to; that Cry
Which made me look a thousand ways
In bush, and tree, and sky.

To seek thee did I often rove
Through woods and on the green;
And thou wert still a hope, a love,
Still longed for, never seen.

And I can listen to thee yet;
Can lie upon the plain
And listen till I do beget
That golden time again.

O blessed Bird! The earth we pace
Again appears to be
An unsubstantial, faery place
That is fit home for Thee.

1802 1807

SHE WAS A PHANTOM OF DELIGHT[1]

She was a Phantom of delight
When first she gleamed upon my sight;
A lovely Apparition sent
To be a moment's ornament;
Her eyes as stars of Twilight fair;
Like Twilight's, too, her dusky hair;
But all things else about her drawn
From Maytime and the cheerful dawn;
A dancing Shape, an Image gay,
To haunt, to startle, and way-lay.

I saw her upon nearer view,
A Spirit, yet a Woman, too!
Her household motions light and free,
And steps of virgin liberty;
A countenance in which did meet
Sweet records, promises as sweet;
A Creature not too bright or good
For human nature's daily food;
For transient sorrows, simple wiles,
Praise, blame, love, kisses, tears, and smiles.

And now I see with eye serene
The very pulse of the machine;
A Being breathing thoughtful breath,
A Traveler between life and death;
The reason firm, the temperate will,
Endurance, foresight, strength, and skill;
A perfect Woman, nobly planned,
To warm, to comfort, and command;
And yet a Spirit still, and bright
With something of angelic light.

1804 1807

I WANDERED LONELY AS A CLOUD

I wandered lonely as a cloud
That floats on high o'er vales and hills,
When all at once I saw a crowd,
A host, of golden daffodils
Beside the lake, beneath the trees,
Fluttering and dancing in the breeze.

Continuous as the stars that shine
And twinkle on the milky way,
They stretched in never-ending line
Along the margin of a bay—

[1] written of Mrs. Wordsworth

Ten thousand saw I at a glance,
Tossing their heads in sprightly dance.

The waves beside them danced; but they
Out-did the sparkling waves in glee:
A poet could not but be gay
In such a jocund company.
I gazed—and gazed—but little thought
What wealth the show to me had brought.

For oft, when on my couch I lie
In vacant or in pensive mood,
They flash upon that inward eye
Which is the bliss of solitude;
And then my heart with pleasure fills,
And dances with the daffodils.

1804 1807

ODE TO DUTY

Stern Daughter of the Voice of God!
O Duty! if that name thou love
Who art a light to guide, a rod
To check the erring, and reprove;
Thou, who art victory and law
When empty terrors overawe:
From vain temptations dost set free:
And calm'st the weary strife of frail humanity!

There are who ask not if thine eye
Be on them; who, in love and truth,
Where no misgiving is, rely
Upon the genial sense of youth:
Glad Hearts! without reproach or blot
Who do thy work, and know it not—
Oh! if through confidence misplaced
They fail, thy saving arms, dread Power! around them cast.

Serene will be our days and bright,
And happy will our nature be,
When love is an unerring light,
And joy its own security.
And they a blissful course may hold
Even now, who, not unwisely bold,
Live in the spirit of this creed;
Yet seek thy firm support, according to their need.

I, loving freedom, and untried,
No sport of every random gust,
Yet being to myself a guide,
Too blindly have reposed my trust:
And oft, when in my heart was heard
Thy timely mandate, I deferred
The task, in smoother walks to stray;
But thee I now would serve more strictly, if I may.

Through no disturbance of my soul,
Or strong compunction in me wrought,
I supplicate for thy control;
But in the quietness of thought:
Me this unchartered freedom tires;
I feel the weight of chance desires;
My hopes no more must change their name,
I long for a repose that ever is the same.

Stern Lawgiver! yet thou dost wear
The Godhead's most benignant grace;
Nor know we anything so fair
As is the smile upon thy face:
Flowers laugh before thee on their beds
And fragrance in thy footing treads;
Thou dost preserve the stars from wrong;
And the most ancient heavens, through Thee, are fresh and strong.

To humbler functions, awful Power!
I call thee: I myself commend
Unto thy guidance from this hour;
Oh, let my weakness have an end!
Give unto me, made lowly wise,
The spirit of self-sacrifice;
The confidence of reason give;
And in the light of truth thy Bondman let me live!

1805 1807

TO A SKYLARK

1805

Up with me! up with me into the clouds!
For thy song, Lark, is strong;
Up with me, up with me into the clouds!
Singing, singing,
With clouds and sky about thee ringing,
Lift me, guide me till I find
That spot which seems so to thy mind!

I have walked through wildernesses dreary,
And today my heart is weary;
Had I now the wings of a Faery,
Up to thee would I fly.
There is madness about thee, and joy divine
In that song of thine;
Lift me, guide me, high and high
To thy banqueting place in the sky.

Joyous as morning,
Thou art laughing and scorning;
Thou hast a nest for thy love and thy rest,
And, though little troubled with sloth,
Drunken Lark! thou would'st be loth
To be such a traveler as I.
Happy, happy Liver,
With a soul as strong as a mountain river

Pouring out praise to the Almighty Giver,
Joy and jollity be with us both!

Alas! my journey, rugged and uneven,
Through prickly moors or dusty ways must wind;
But hearing thee, or others of thy kind,
As full of gladness and as free of heaven,
I, with my fate contented, will plod on,
And hope for higher raptures, when life's day is done.

1807

TO A SKYLARK
1825

Ethereal minstrel! pilgrim of the sky!
Dost thou despise the earth where cares abound?
Or, while the wings aspire, are heart and eye
Both with thy nest upon the dewy ground?
Thy nest which thou canst drop into at will,
Those quivering wings composed, that music still!

Leave to the nightingale her shady wood;
A privacy of glorious light is thine;
Whence thou dost pour upon the world a flood
Of harmony, with instinct more divine;
Type of the wise who soar, but never roam;
True to the kindred points of Heaven and Home!

1827

ODE
INTIMATIONS OF IMMORTALITY FROM RECOLLECTIONS OF EARLY CHILDHOOD [1]

I

There was a time when meadow, grove, and stream,
The earth, and every common sight,
To me did seem
Appareled in celestial light,
The glory and the freshness of a dream.
It is not now as it hath been of yore—
Turn wheresoe'er I may,
By night or day,
The things which I have seen I now can see no more.

II

The Rainbow comes and goes,
And lovely is the Rose;
The Moon doth with delight
Look round her when the heavens are bare;
Waters on a starry night
Are beautiful and fair;
The sunshine is a glorious birth;
But yet I know, where'er I go,
That there hath past away a glory from the earth.

III

Now, while the birds thus sing a joyous song,
And while the young lambs bound
As to the tabor's sound,
To me alone there came a thought of grief;
A timely utterance gave that though relief,
And I again am strong.
The cataracts blow their trumpets from the steep;
No more shall grief of mine the season wrong;
I hear the Echoes through the mountains throng,
The Winds come to me from the fields of sleep,
And all the earth is gay;
Land and sea
Give themselves up to jollity,
And with the heart of May
Doth every Beast keep holiday—
Thou Child of Joy,
Shout round me, let me hear thy shouts, thou happy Shepherd-boy!

IV

Ye blessèd Creatures, I have heard the call
Ye to each other make; I see
The heavens laugh with you in your jubilee;
My heart is at your festival,
My head hath its coronal,
The fullness of your bliss I feel—I feel it all.
Oh, evil day! If I were sullen
While Earth herself is adorning,
This sweet May morning;
And the Children are culling
On every side,
In a thousand valleys far and wide,
Fresh flowers; while the sun shines warm,
And the Babe leaps up on his Mother's arm—
I hear, I hear, with joy I hear!
But there's a Tree, of many, one,
A single Field which I have looked upon,
Both of them speak of something that is gone:
The Pansy at my feet

[1] "To that dream-like vividness and splendor which invest objects of sight in childhood, every one, I believe, if he would look back, could bear testimony, and I need not dwell upon it here; but, having in the poem regarded it as presumptive evidence of a prior state of existence, I think it right to protest against a conclusion which has given pain to some good and pious persons, that I meant to inculcate such a belief. It is far too shadowy a notion to be recommended to faith, as more than an element in our instincts of immortality. . . . A preëxistent state has entered into the popular creeds of many nations; and, among all persons acquainted with classic literature, is known as an ingredient in Platonic philosophy."—Extract from Wordsworth's note. Compare Henry Vaughan's "The Retreat," p. 243.

Doth the same tale repeat:
Whither is fled the visionary gleam?
Where is it now, the glory and the dream?

V

Our birth is but a sleep and a forgetting:
The Soul that rises with us, our life's Star,
Hath had elsewhere its setting,
And cometh from afar:
Not in entire forgetfulness,
And not in utter nakedness,
But trailing clouds of glory do we come
From God, who is our home:
Heaven lies about us in our infancy!
Shades of the prison house begin to close
Upon the growing Boy,
But he beholds the light, and whence it flows,
He sees it in his joy;
The Youth, who daily farther from the east
Must travel, still is Nature's Priest,
And by the vision splendid
Is on his way attended;
At length the Man perceives it die away
And fade into the light of common day.

VI

Earth fills her lap with pleasures of her own;
Yearnings she hath in her own natural kind,
And, even with something of a Mother's mind,
And no unworthy aim,
The homely Nurse doth all she can
To make her Foster-child, her Inmate Man,
Forget the glories he hath known,
And that imperial palace whence he came.

VII

Behold the Child among his new-born blisses,
A six year's Darling of a pigmy size!
See, where 'mid work of his own hand he lies,
Fretted by sallies of his mother's kisses,
With light upon him from his father's eyes!
See, at his feet, some little plan or chart,
Some fragment from his dream of human life,
Shaped by himself with newly-learnèd art;
A wedding or a festival,
A mourning or a funeral;
And this hath now his heart,
And unto this he frames his song.
Then will he fit his tongue
To dialogues of business, love, or strife;
But it will not be long
Ere this be thrown aside,
And with new joy and pride
The little Actor cons another part;
Filling from time to time his "humorous[1] stage"

[1] in Jonson's sense (p. 209) following a bent, here the chief trait of the type he is mimicking

With all the Persons, down to palsied Age,
That Life brings with her in her equipage;
As if his whole vocation
Were endless imitation.

VIII

Thou, whose exterior semblance doth belie
Thy Soul's immensity;
Thou best Philosopher, who yet dost keep
Thy heritage, thou Eye among the blind,
That, deaf and silent, read'st the eternal deep,
Haunted forever by the eternal mind—
Mighty Prophet! Seer blest!
On whom those truths do rest
Which we are toiling all our lives to find,
In darkness lost, the darkness of the grave;
Thou, over whom thy Immortality
Broods like the Day, a Master o'er a Slave,
A Presence which is not to be put by;
Thou little Child, yet glorious in the might
Of heaven-born freedom on thy being's height,
Why with such earnest pains dost thou provoke
The years to bring the inevitable yoke,
Thus blindly with thy blessedness at strife?
Full soon thy Soul shall have her earthly freight,
And custom lie upon thee with a weight,
Heavy as frost, and deep almost as life!

IX

O joy! that in our embers
Is something that doth live,
That nature yet remembers
What was so fugitive!
The thought of our past years in me doth breed
Perpetual benediction; not indeed
For that which is most worthy to be blest—
Delight and liberty, the simple creed
Of Childhood, whether busy or at rest,
With new-fledged hope still fluttering in his breast—
Not for these I raise
The song of thanks and praise;
But for those obstinate questionings
Of sense and outward things,
Fallings from us, vanishings;
Blank misgivings of a Creature
Moving about in worlds not realized,
High instincts before which our mortal Nature
Did tremble like a guilty Thing surprised:
But for those first affections,
Those shadowy recollections,
Which, be they what they may,
Are yet the fountain light of all our day,
Are yet a master light of all our seeing;
Uphold us, cherish, and have power to make
Our noisy years seem moments in the being

Of the eternal Silence: truths that wake,
To perish never;
Which neither listlessness, nor mad endeavor,
Nor Man nor Boy,
Nor all that is at enmity with joy,
Can utterly abolish or destroy!
Hence in a season of calm weather
Though inland far we be,
Our Souls have sight of that immortal sea
Which brought us hither,
Can in a moment travel thither,
And see the Children sport upon the shore,
And hear the mighty waters rolling evermore.

X

Then sing, ye Birds, sing, sing a joyous song!
And let the young Lambs bound
As to the tabor's sound!
We in thought will join your throng,
Ye that pipe and ye that play,
Ye that through your hearts today
Feel the gladness of the May!
What though the radiance which was once so bright
Be now forever taken from my sight,
Though nothing can bring back the hour
Of splendor in the grass, of glory in the flower;
We will grieve not, rather find
Strength in what remains behind;
In the primal sympathy
Which having been must ever be;
In the soothing thoughts that spring
Out of human suffering;
In the faith that looks through death,
In years that bring the philosophic mind.

XI

And O ye Fountains, Meadows, Hills, and Groves,
Forebode not any severing of our loves!
Yet in my heart of hearts I feel your might;
I only have relinquished one delight
To live beneath your more habitual sway.
I love the Brooks which down their channels fret,
Even more than when I tripped lightly as they;
The innocent brightness of a new-born Day
Is lovely yet;
The Clouds that gather round the setting sun
Do take a sober coloring from an eye
That hath kept watch o'er man's mortality;
Another race hath been, and other palms are won.
Thanks to the human heart by which we live,
Thanks to its tenderness, its joys, and fears,
To me the meanest flower that blows can give
Thoughts that do often lie too deep for tears.

1803-06 1807

COMPOSED UPON WESTMINISTER BRIDGE, SEPTEMBER 3, 1802

Earth has not anything to show more fair;
Dull would he be of soul who could pass by
A sight so touching in its majesty.
This City now doth, like a garment, wear
The beauty of the morning; silent, bare,
Ships, towers, domes, theaters, and temples lie
Open unto the fields, and to the sky;
All bright and glittering in the smokeless air.
Never did sun more beautifully steep
In his first splendor, valley, rock, or hill;
Ne'er saw I, never felt, a calm so deep!
The river glideth at his own sweet will;
Dear God! the very houses seem asleep,
And all that mighty heart is lying still!

1807

IT IS A BEAUTEOUS EVENING, CALM AND FREE

It is a beauteous evening, calm and free,
The holy time is quiet as a Nun
Breathless with adoration; the broad sun
Is sinking down in its tranquillity;
The gentleness of heaven broods o'er the sea.
Listen! the mighty Being is awake,
And doth with his eternal motion make
A sound like thunder—everlastingly.
Dear Child! [1] dear Girl! that walkest with me here,
If thou appear untouched by solemn thought,
Thy nature is not therefore less divine—
Thou liest in Abraham's bosom [2] all the year,
And worship'st at the Temple's inner shrine,
God being with thee when we know it not.

1802 1807

ON THE EXTINCTION OF THE VENETIAN REPUBLIC [3]

Once did She hold the gorgeous east in fee,
And was the safeguard of the west; the worth
Of Venice did not fall below her birth,
Venice, the eldest Child of Liberty.
She was a maiden City, bright and free;
No guile seduced, no force could violate;
And when she took unto herself a Mate,
She must espouse the everlasting Sea. [4]
And what if she had seen those glories fade,
Those titles vanish, and that strength decay;
Yet shall some tribute of regret be paid

[1] Wordsworth's daughter, Caroline
[2] See *Luke* xvi, 22
[3] Venice threw off the yoke of the Eastern Empire as early as 809 and remained a republic or an oligarchy until conquered by Napoleon in 1797. At one time she had extensive possessions and colonies in the Levant.
[4] The ancient Doges (rulers) annually, on Ascension Day, threw a ring into the Adriatic in formal token of this espousal of Venice to the Sea.

When her long life hath reached its final day:
Men are we, and must grieve when even the
Shade
Of that which once was great, is passed away.

1802 1807

LONDON, 1802 [1]

Milton! thou should'st be living at this hour:
England hath need of thee; she is a fen
Of stagnant waters: altar, sword, and pen,
Fireside, the heroic wealth of hall and bower,
Have forfeited their ancient English dower
Of inward happiness. We are selfish men;
Oh! raise us up, return to us again;
And give us manners, virtue, freedom, power.
Thy soul was like a Star, and dwelt apart:
Thou hadst a voice whose sound was like the
sea:
Pure as the naked heavens, majestic, free,
So didst thou travel on life's common way,
In cheerful godliness; and yet thy heart
The lowliest duties on herself did lay.

1807

THE WORLD IS TOO MUCH WITH US

The world is too much with us; late and soon,
Getting and spending, we lay waste our powers:
Little we see in Nature that is ours;
We have given our hearts away, a sordid boon!
The Sea that bares her bosom to the moon;
The winds that will be howling at all hours,
And are up-gathered now like sleeping flowers;
For this, for everything, we are out of tune;
It moves us not.—Great God! I'd rather be
A Pagan suckled in a creed outworn;
So might I, standing on this pleasant lea,
Have glimpses that would make me less for-
lorn;
Have sight of Proteus rising from the sea;
Or hear old Triton blow his wreathèd horn.

1807

AFTERTHOUGHT [2]

I thought of Thee, my partner and my guide,
As being past away.—Vain sympathies!
For, backward, Duddon, as I cast my eyes,
I see what was, and is, and will abide;
Still glides the Stream, and shall forever glide;
The Form remains, the Function never dies;
While we, the brave, the mighty, and the wise,
We Men, who in our morn of youth defied
The elements, must vanish—be it so!
Enough, if something from our hands have
power
To live, and act, and serve the future hour;
And if, as toward the silent tomb we go,
Through love, through hope, and faith's tran-
scendant dower,
We feel that we are greater than we know.

1820

[1] written in despondency over the inert attitude of England toward the hopes and ideals of the revolutionists and the opponents of Napoleon

[2] the conclusion of a series of sonnets to the river Duddon

SAMUEL TAYLOR COLERIDGE
1772-1834

Through his fascinating conversation and personality, as well as through his writings, Coleridge was one of the leading figures in the advancement of English literature and criticism during the first quarter of the nineteenth century. He was an admirable lecturer, an essayist, critic, journalist, and philosopher. He was early sent from his father's home, that of a schoolmaster-clergyman of aristocratic connections, to the "Blue-Coat" School (Christ's Hospital), in London. There one of his companions was Lamb, who tells of Coleridge's rare and enthusiastic love for Greek literature. Already, and even more at Cambridge, later, he was known as a wide reader and a brilliant talker, and became the center of discussions among students upon social, political, and philosophical topics. His meeting with Wordsworth, 1795, stimulated his most notable poetical work which fell off only when the friendship waned. In middle life Coleridge fell into ill health, took opium, and was at times incapacitated by its use. Among his notable works are "The Ancient Mariner," "Christabel," 1816, *Biographia Literaria*, 1817, and *Poetical and Dramatic Works*, 1828. His *Notes and Lectures on Shakespere* were published after his death.

Sympathetic as Coleridge and Wordsworth were, the basic differences in their poetry are clearly seen in even a casual reading of "The Ancient Mariner" and "Tintern Abby"; both published in *Lyrical Ballads*, 1798. The one makes of airy nothing the habitation for the most enduring of pictures. The other turns his mind inward and shows the relation between what the senses bring to us and the inner reality. Of the writing of the *Lyrical Ballads*, Coleridge, in the fourteenth chapter of *Biographia Literaria*, says:

"During the first year that Mr. Wordsworth and I were neighbors, our conversations turned frequently on the two cardinal points of poetry, the power of exciting the sympathy of the reader by a faithful adherence to the truth of nature, and the power of giving the interest of novelty by the modifying colors of the imagination. The sudden charm which accidents of light and shade, which moonlight or sunset, diffused over a known and familiar landscape, appeared to represent the practicability of combining both. These are the poetry of nature. The thought suggested itself (to which of us I do not recollect) that a series of poems might be composed of two sorts. In the one, the incidents and agents were to be, in part at least, supernatural; and the excellence aimed at was to consist in the interesting of the affections by the dramatic truth of such emotions as would naturally accompany such situations, supposing them real. And real in this sense they have been to every human being who, from whatever source of delusion, has at any time believed himself under supernatural agency. For the second class, subjects were to be chosen from ordinary life; the characters and incidents were to be such as will be found in every village and its vicinity where there is a meditative and feeling mind to seek after them, or to notice them when they present themselves.

"In this idea originated the plan of the *Lyrical Ballads;* in which it was agreed that my endeavors should be directed to persons and characters supernatural, or at least romantic; yet so as to transfer from our inward nature a human interest and a semblance of truth sufficient to procure for these shadows of imagination that willing suspension of disbelief for the moment, which constitutes poetic faith. Mr. Wordsworth, on the other hand, was to propose to himself as his object, to give the charm of novelty to things of everyday, and to excite a feeling analogous to the supernatural, by awakening the mind's attention from the lethargy of custom, and directing it to the loveliness and the wonders of the world before us; an inexhaustible treasure, but for which, in consequence of the film of familiarity and selfish solicitude, we have eyes, yet see not, ears that hear not, and hearts that neither feel nor understand. With this view I wrote *The Ancient Mariner.*"

The most important recent comment on Coleridge is J. L. Lowes' *The Road to Xanadu,* 2 vols. 1927, an inquiry into the sources of Coleridge's most famous poems. Biography: Traill (EML). Criticism: Hazlitt; Saintsbury; Stephen; Woodberry; Payne.

KUBLA KHAN [1]

In Xanadu [2] did Kubla Khan [3]
A stately pleasure-dome decree:
Where Alph, the sacred river, ran
Through caverns measureless to man
  Down to a sunless sea.
So twice five miles of fertile ground
With walls and towers were girdled round:
And here were gardens bright with sinuous rills,
Where blossomed many an incense-bearing tree;
And here were forests ancient as the hills,
Enfolding sunny spots of greenery.

But oh! that deep romantic chasm which slanted
Down the green hill athwart a cedarn cover!
A savage place! as holy and enchanted
As e'er beneath a waning moon was haunted
By woman wailing for her demon-lover!
And from this chasm, with ceaseless turmoil seething,
As if this earth in fast, thick pants were breathing,
A mighty fountain momently was forced:
Amid whose swift half-intermitted burst,
Huge fragments vaulted like rebounding hail,
Or chaffy grain beneath the thresher's flail:
And 'mid these dancing rocks at once and ever
It flung up momently the sacred river.
Five miles meandering with a mazy motion
Through wood and dale the sacred river ran,
Then reached the caverns measureless to man,
And sank in tumult to a lifeless ocean:
And 'mid this tumult Kubla heard from far
Ancestral voices prophesying war!

  The shadow of the dome of pleasure
  Floated midway on the waves;
  Where was heard the mingled measure
  From the fountain and the caves.
It was a miracle of rare device,
A sunny pleasure-dome with caves of ice!

  A damsel with a dulcimer
  In a vision once I saw:
  It was an Abyssinian maid,
  And on her dulcimer she played,
  Singing of Mount Abora.
  Could I revive within me
  Her symphony and song,
To such a deep delight 'twould win me,
That with music loud and long,
I would build that dome in air,
That sunny dome! those caves of ice!
And all who heard should see them there,
And all should cry, "Beware! Beware!
His flashing eyes, his floating hair!
Weave a circle round him thrice,
And close your eyes with holy dread,
For he on honey-dew hath fed,
And drunk the milk of Paradise."

c. 1798 1816

[1] Coleridge says this poem was composed when he had fallen asleep just after reading from Marco Polo in *Purchas's Pilgrimage* how "In Xandu did Cublai Can build a stately palace," etc. Immediately upon awakening he wrote down the poem as it stands. There was much more, but the interruption of "a person on business from Porlock" erased this forever from his memory. Charles Lamb spoke of the poem as "a vision which he [Coleridge] repeats so enchantingly that it irradiates and brings heaven and elysian bowers into my parlor when he sings or says it."

[2] a region in Tartary

[3] Kubla the Cham, or Emperor, Cf.
. . . . "the destined walls
Of "Cambalu, seat of Cathaian Can."—*Par. Lost,* xi, 388.

THE RIME OF THE ANCIENT MARINER[1]

IN SEVEN PARTS

ARGUMENT

How a Ship having passed the Line was driven by storms to the cold country toward the South Pole; and how from thence she made her course to the Tropical Latitude of the Great Pacific Ocean; and of the strange things that befell; and in what manner the Ancyent Marinere came back to his own country.

PART I

An ancient Mariner meeteth three Gallants bidden to a wedding-feast, and detaineth one.

It is an ancient Mariner,
And he stoppeth one of three.
"By thy long gray beard and glittering eye,
Now wherefore stopp'st thou me?

The Bridegroom's doors are opened wide,
And I am next of kin;
The guests are met, the feast is set:
May'st hear the merry din."

He holds him with his skinny hand,
"There was a ship," quoth he.
"Hold off! unhand me, graybeard loon!"
Eftsoons[2] his hand dropt he.

The Wedding-Guest is spell-bound by the eye of the old sea-faring man, and constrained to hear his tale.

He holds him with his glittering eye;
The Wedding-Guest stood still,
And listens like a three years' child:
The Mariner hath his will.

The Wedding-Guest sat on a stone:
He cannot choose but hear;
And thus spake on that ancient man,
The bright-eyed Mariner.

The Mariner tells how the ship sailed southward with a good wind and fair weather till it reached the Line.

"The ship was cheered, the harbor cleared,
Merrily did we drop
Below the kirk, below the hill,
Below the lighthouse top.

The Sun came up upon the left,
Out of the sea came he!
And he shone bright, and on the right
Went down into the sea.

Higher and higher every day,
Till over the mast at noon—"
The Wedding-Guest here beat his breast,
For he heard the loud bassoon.

The Wedding-Guest heareth the bridal music; but the Mariner continueth his tale.

The bride hath paced into the hall;
Red as a rose is she;
Nodding their heads before her goes
The merry minstrelsy.

The Wedding-Guest he beat his breast,
Yet he cannot choose but hear;
And thus spake on that ancient man,
The bright-eyed Mariner.

The ship driven by a storm toward the south pole.

"And now the Storm-Blast came, and he
Was tyrannous and strong:
He struck with his o'ertaking wings,
And chased us south along.

With sloping masts and dipping prow,
As who pursued with yell and blow
Still treads the shadow of his foe,
And forward bends his head,
The ship drove fast, loud roared the blast,
And southward aye we fled.

And now there came both mist and snow,
And it grew wondrous cold:
And ice, mast-high, came floating by,
As green as emerald.

The land of ice, and of fearful sounds, where no living thing was to be seen;

And through the drifts the snowy clifts
Did send a dismal sheen:
Nor shapes of men nor beasts we ken—
The ice was all between.

[1] The poem is here given in the revised text of 1829. As first printed in the *Lyrical Ballads*, the diction and spelling were considerably more archaic, as the Argument, which was not retained in the later edition, shows. Wordsworth gives the following information: "Much the greatest part of the story was Mr. Coleridge's invention, but certain parts I suggested; for example, some crime was to be committed which should bring upon the Old Navigator, as Coleridge afterward delighted to call him, the spectral persecution, as a consequence of that crime and his own wanderings. I had been reading in Shelvocke's *Voyages* a day or two before, that, while doubling Cape Horn, they frequently saw albatrosses in that latitude, the largest sort of sea-fowl, some extending their wings twelve or thirteen feet. 'Suppose,' said I, 'you represent him as having killed one of these birds on entering the South Sea, and that the tutelary spirits of these regions take upon them to avenge the crime.' The incident was thought fit for the purpose and adopted accordingly." Wordsworth also furnished several lines of the poem, especially 15-16, 226-227.

[2] at once

The ice was here, the ice was there,
The ice was all around:
It cracked and growled, and roared and howled,
Like voices in a swound![1]

Till a great sea-bird called the Albatross, came through the snow-fog, and was received with great joy and hospitality.

At length did cross an Albatross,
Through the fog it came;
As if it had been a Christian soul,
We hailed it in God's name.

It ate the food it ne'er had eat,[2]
And round and round it flew.
The ice did split with a thunder-fit;
The helmsman steered us through!

And lo! the Albatross proveth a bird of good omen, and followeth the ship as it returned northward, through fog and floating ice.

And a good south wind sprung up behind;
The Albatross did follow,
And every day, for food or play,
Came to the mariners' hollo!

In mist or cloud, on mast or shroud,
It perched for vespers nine;[3]
Whiles all the night, through fog-smoke white
Glimmered the white moon-shine."

The ancient Mariner inhospitably killeth the pious bird of good omen.

"God save thee, ancient Mariner,
From the fiends that plague thee thus!—
Why look'st thou so?"—"With my crossbow
I shot the Albatross."

PART II

"The Sun now rose upon the right:
Out of the sea came he,
Still hid in mist, and on the left
Went down into the sea.

And the good south wind still blew behind,
But no sweet bird did follow,
Nor any day, for food or play,
Came to the mariners' hollo!

His shipmates cry out against the ancient Mariner, for killing the bird of good luck.

And I had done a hellish thing,
And it would work 'em woe;
For all averred, I had killed the bird
That made the breeze to blow.
'Ah, wretch!' said they, 'the bird to slay,
That made the breeze to blow!'

But when the fog cleared off they justify the same, and thus make themselves accomplices in the crime.

Nor dim nor red, like God's own head,
The glorious Sun uprist:[4]
Then all averred, I had killed the bird
That brought the fog and mist.
' 'Twas right,' said they, 'such birds to slay,
That bring the fog and mist.'

The fair breeze continues; the ship enters the Pacific Ocean and sails northward, even till it reaches the Line.

The fair breeze blew, the white foam flew,
The furrow followed free;
We were the first that ever burst
Into that silent sea.

The ship hath been suddenly becalmed.

Down dropt the breeze, the sails dropt down,
'Twas sad as sad could be;
And we did speak only to break
The silence of the sea!

All in a hot and copper sky,
The bloody Sun, at noon,
Right up above the mast did stand,
No bigger than the Moon.

Day after day, day after day,
We stuck, nor breath nor motion;
As idle as a painted ship
Upon a painted ocean.

And the Albatross begins to be avenged.

Water, water, everywhere,
And all the boards did shrink;
Water, water, everywhere,
Nor any drop to drink.

The very deep did rot—O Christ!
That ever this should be!
Yea, slimy things did crawl with legs
Upon the slimy sea.

About, about, in reel and rout
The death-fires danced at night;
The water, like a witch's oils,
Burnt green, and blue, and white.

A spirit had followed them; one of the invisible inhabitants of this planet, neither departed souls nor angels; concerning whom the learned Jew Josephus and the Platonic Constantinopolitan, Michael Psellus, may be consulted. They are very numerous, and there is no climate or element without one or more.

And some in dreams assurèd were
Of the spirit that plagued us so;
Nine fathom deep he had followed us
From the land of mist and snow.

[1] swoon, dream
[2] "The mariners gave it biscuit-worms" (1798 ed.)
[3] nine evenings
[4] properly a present tense; cf p. 66 note 33

The shipmates in their sore distress would fain throw the whole guilt on the ancient Mariner; in sign whereof they hang the dead sea-bird round his neck.

And every tongue, through utter drought,
Was withered at the root;
We could not speak no more than if
We had been choked with soot.

Ah! well-a-day! what evil looks
Had I from old and young!
Instead of the cross, the Albatross
About my neck was hung."

PART III

"There passed a weary time. Each throat
Was parched, and glazed each eye.
A weary time! a weary time!
How glazed each weary eye!—
When looking westward, I beheld
A something in the sky.

The ancient Mariner beholdeth a sign in the element afar off.

At first it seemed a little speck,
And then it seemed a mist;
It moved, and moved, and took at last
A certain shape, I wist.[1]

A speck, a mist, a shape, I wist!
And still it neared and neared:
As if it dodged a water-sprite,
It plunged and tacked and veered.

At its nearer approach, it seemeth him to be a ship; and at a dear ransom he freeth his speech from the bonds of thirst.

With throats unslaked, with black lips baked,
We could nor laugh nor wail;
Through utter drought all dumb we stood!
I bit my arm, I sucked the blood,
And cried, 'A sail! a sail!'

With throats unslaked, with black lips baked,
Agape they heard me call:
Gramercy![2] they for joy did grin,
And all at once their breath drew in,
As they were drinking all.

A flash of joy;

'See! see!' I cried, 'she tacks no more!
Hither to work us weal,
Without a breeze, without a tide,
She steadies with upright keel!'

And horror follows. For can it be a ship *that comes onward without wind or tide?*

The western wave was all a-flame,
The day was well-nigh done!
Almost upon the western wave
Rested the broad bright Sun;
When that strange shape drove suddenly
Betwixt us and the Sun.

And straight the Sun was flecked with bars,
(Heaven's Mother send us grace!),
As if through a dungeon-grate he peered,
With broad and burning face.

It seemeth him but the skeleton of a ship.

Alas! (thought I, and my heart beat loud)
How fast she nears and nears!
Are those *her* sails that glance in the Sun
Like restless gossameres?

Are those *her* ribs through which the Sun
Did peer, as through a grate?
And is that Woman all her crew?
Is that a Death? and are there two?
Is Death that Woman's mate?

And its ribs are seen as bars on the face of the setting Sun. The Specter-Woman and her Death-mate, and no other on board the skeleton-ship.

Her lips were red, her looks were free,
Her locks were yellow as gold;
Her skin was as white as leprosy,
The Nightmare Life-in-Death was she,
Who thicks man's blood with cold.

Like vessel, like crew!

The naked hulk alongside came,
And the twain were casting dice;
'The game is done! I've won! I've won!'
Quoth she, and whistles thrice.

Death and Life-in-Death have diced for the ship's crew, and she (the latter) winneth the ancient Mariner.

The Sun's rim dips; the stars rush out.
At one stride comes the dark;
With far-heard whisper, o'er the sea,
Off shot the specter-bark.

No twilight within the courts of the Sun.

We listened and looked sideways up!
Fear at my heart, as at a cup,
My life-blood seemed to sip!
The stars were dim, and thick the night,
The steersman's face by his lamp gleamed white;
From the sails the dew did drip—
Till clomb above the eastern bar
The hornèd Moon, with one bright star
Within the nether tip.

At the rising of the Moon,

[1] I knew (but apparently confused in form and meaning with the old participial adverb *y-wis*, "surely")

[2] great thanks

One after another

One after one, by the star-dogged Moon,
Too quick for groan or sigh,
Each turned his face with a ghastly pang,
And cursed me with his eye.

His shipmates drop down dead.

Four times fifty living men
(And I heard nor sigh nor groan),
With heavy thump, a lifeless lump,
They dropped down one by one.

But Life-in-Death begins her work on the ancient Mariner.

The souls did from their bodies fly—
They fled to bliss or woe!
And every soul, it passed me by,
Like the whizz of my crossbow!"

PART IV

The Wedding-Guest feareth that a Spirit is talking to him:

"I fear thee, ancient Mariner!
I fear thy skinny hand!
And thou art long, and lank, and brown,
As is the ribbed sea-sand.

But the ancient Mariner assureth him of his bodily life, and proceedeth to relate his horrible penance.

I fear thee and thy glittering eye,
And thy skinny hand, so brown"—
"Fear not, fear not, thou Wedding-Guest!
This body dropt not down.

Alone, alone, all, all alone,
Alone on a wide, wide sea!
And never a saint took pity on
My soul in agony.

He despiseth the creatures of the calm,

The many men, so beautiful!
And they all dead did lie;
And a thousand thousand slimy things
Lived on; and so did I.

And envieth that they should live and so many lie dead,

I looked upon the rotting sea,
And drew my eyes away;
I looked upon the rotting deck,
And there the dead men lay.

I looked to Heaven, and tried to pray;
But or ever a prayer had gusht,
A wicked whisper came, and made
My heart as dry as dust.

I closed my lids, and kept them close,
And the balls like pulses beat;
For the sky and the sea, and the sea and the sky
Lay like a load on my weary eye,
And the dead were at my feet.

But the curse liveth for him in the eye of the dead men.

The cold sweat melted from their limbs,
Nor rot nor reek did they:
The look with which they looked on me
Had never passed away.

An orphan's curse would drag to hell
A spirit from on high;
But oh! more horrible than that
Is a curse in a dead man's eye!
Seven days, seven nights, I saw that curse
And yet I could not die.

In his loneliness and fixedness he yearneth toward the journeying Moon, and the stars that still sojourn, yet still move onward; and everywhere the blue sky belongs to them, and is their appointed rest and their native country and their own natural homes, which they enter unannounced, as lords that are certainly expected and yet there is a silent joy at their arrival.

The moving Moon went up the sky,
And nowhere did abide;
Softly she was going up,
And a star or two beside—

Her beams bemocked the sultry main,
Like April hoarfrost spread;
But where the ship's huge shadow lay,
The charmèd water burnt alway
A still and awful red.

By the light of the Moon he beholdeth God's creatures of the great calm,

Beyond the shadow of the ship,
I watched the water-snakes;
They moved in tracks of shining white,
And when they reared, the elfish light
Fell off in hoary flakes.

Their beauty and their happiness.

Within the shadow of the ship
I watched their rich attire:
Blue, glossy green, and velvet black
They coiled and swam; and every track
Was a flash of golden fire.

He blesseth them in his heart.

O happy living things! no tongue
Their beauty might declare:
A spring of love gushed from my heart,
And I blessed them unaware:
Sure my kind saint took pity on me,
And I blessed them unaware.

The spell begins to break.

The selfsame moment I could pray;
And from my neck so free
The Albatross fell off, and sank
Like lead into the sea."

PART V

"Oh, sleep! it is a gentle thing,
Beloved from pole to pole!
To Mary Queen the praise be given!
She sent the gentle sleep from Heaven,
That slid into my soul.

By grace of the holy Mother, the ancient Mariner is refreshed with rain.

The silly[1] buckets on the deck,
That had so long remained,
I dreamt that they were filled with dew;
And when I awoke, it rained.

My lips were wet, my throat was cold,
My garments all were dank;
Sure I had drunken in my dreams,
And still my body drank.

I moved, and could not feel my limbs.
I was so light—almost
I thought that I had died in sleep,
And was a blessed ghost.

He heareth sounds, and seeth strange sights and commotions in the sky and the element.

And soon I heard a roaring wind;
It did not come anear:
But with its sound it shook the sails,
That were so thin and sear.

The upper air burst into life!
And a hundred fire-flags sheen;
To and fro they were hurried about!
And to and fro, and in and out,
The wan stars danced between.

And the coming wind did roar more loud,
And the sails did sigh like sedge;
And the rain poured down from one black cloud;
The Moon was at its edge.

The thick black cloud was cleft, and still
The Moon was at its side;
Like waters shot from some high crag,
The lightning fell with never a jag,
A river steep and wide.

[1] Perhaps "useless"; but the original meaning "blessed" will fit very well.

The bodies of the ship's crew are inspired, and the ship moves on.

The loud wind never reached the ship,
Yet now the ship moved on!
Beneath the lightning and the Moon
The dead men gave a groan.

They groaned, they stirred, they all uprose,
Nor spake, nor moved their eyes;
It had been strange, even in a dream,
To have seen those dead men rise.

The helmsman steered, the ship moved on;
Yet never a breeze up-blew.
The mariners all 'gan work the ropes,
Where they were wont to do;
They raised their limbs like lifeless tools—
We were a ghastly crew.

The body of my brother's son
Stood by me, knee to knee:
The body and I pulled at one rope
But he said naught to me."

"I fear thee, ancient Mariner!"
"Be calm, thou Wedding-Guest!
'Twas not those souls that fled in pain,
Which to their corses came again,
But a troop of spirits blest:

But not by the souls of the men, nor by demons of earth or middle air, but by a blessed troop of angelic spirits, sent down by the invocation of the guardian saint.

For when it dawned—they dropped their arms,
And clustered round the mast;
Sweet sounds rose slowly through their mouths,
And from their bodies passed.

Around, around, flew each sweet sound;
Then darted to the Sun;
Slowly the sounds came back again,
Now mixed, now one by one.

Sometimes a-dropping from the sky
I heard the skylark sing;
Sometimes all little birds that are,
How they seemed to fill the sea and air
With their sweet jargoning!

And now 'twas like all instruments,
Now like a lonely flute;
And now it is an angel's song,
That makes the heavens be mute.

It ceased; yet still the sails made on
A pleasant noise till noon,
A noise like of a hidden brook
In the leafy month of June,
That to the sleeping woods all night
Singeth a quiet tune.

Till noon we quietly sailed on,
Yet never a breeze did breathe:
Slowly and smoothly went the ship,
Moved onward from beneath.

The lonesome Spirit from the south pole carries on the ship as far as the Line, in obedience to the angelic troop, but still requireth vengeance.

Under the keel nine fathom deep,
From the land of mist and snow,
The spirit slid; and it was he
That made the ship to go.
The sails at noon left off their tune,
And the ship stood still also.

The Sun, right up above the mast,
Had fixed her to the ocean;
But in a minute she 'gan stir,
With a short, uneasy motion—
Backwards and forwards half her length
With a short, uneasy motion.

Then, like a pawing horse let go,
She made a sudden bound:
It flung the blood into my head,
And I fell down in a swound.

How long in that same fit I lay,
I have not to declare;
But ere my living life returned,
I heard and in my soul discerned
Two voices in the air.

The Polar Spirit's fellow demons, the invisible inhabitants of the element, take part in his wrong; and two of them relate, one to the other, that penance long and heavy for the ancient Mariner hath been accorded to the Polar Spirit, who returneth southward.

'Is it he?' quoth one, 'Is this the man?
By Him who died on cross,
With his cruel bow he laid full low
The harmless Albatross.

The spirit who bideth by himself
In the land of mist and snow,
He loved the bird that loved the man
Who shot him with his bow.'

The other was a softer voice,
As soft as honey-dew:
Quoth he, 'The man hath penance done
And penance more will do'."

PART VI

First Voice

" 'But tell me, tell me! speak again,
Thy soft response renewing—
What makes that ship drive on so fast?
What is the Ocean doing?'

Second Voice

'Still as a slave before his lord,
The Ocean hath no blast;
His great bright eye most silently
Up to the Moon is cast—

If he may know which way to go;
For she guides him smooth or grim.
See, brother, see! how graciously
She looketh down on him.'

First Voice

The Mariner hath been cast into a trance; for the angelic power causeth the vessel to drive northward faster than human life could endure.

'But why drives on that ship so fast,
Without or wave or wind?'

Second Voice

'The air is cut away before,
And closes from behind.

Fly, brother, fly! more high, more high,
Or we shall be belated:
For slow and slow that ship will go,
When the Mariner's trance is abated.'

The supernatural motion is retarded; the Mariner awakes, and his penance begins anew.

I woke, and we were sailing on
As in a gentle weather:
'Twas night, calm night, the Moon was high,
The dead men stood together.

All stood together on the deck,
For a charnal-dungeon fitter:
All fixed on me their stony eyes,
That in the Moon did glitter.

The pang, the curse, with which they died,
Had never passed away:
I could not draw my eyes from theirs,
Nor turn them up to pray.

The curse is finally expiated.

And now this spell was snapt: once more
I viewed the ocean green,

And looked far forth, yet little saw
Of what had else been seen—

Like one that on a lonesome road
Doth walk in fear and dread,
And having once turned round, walks on,
And turns no more his head;
Because he knows a frightful fiend
Doth close behind him tread.

But soon there breathed a wind on me,
Nor sound nor motion made:
Its path was not upon the sea,
In ripple or in shade.

It raised my hair, it fanned my cheek
Like a meadow-gale of spring—
It mingled strangely with my fears,
Yet it felt like a welcoming.

Swiftly, swiftly flew the ship,
Yet she sailed softly too:
Sweetly, sweetly blew the breeze—
On me alone it blew.

And the ancient Mariner beholdeth his native country.

Oh! dream of joy! is this indeed
The lighthouse top I see?
Is this the hill? Is this the kirk?
Is this mine own countree?

We drifted o'er the harbor-bar,
And I with sobs did pray—
'O let me be awake, my God!
Or let me sleep alway.'

The harbor-bay was clear as glass,
So smoothly it was strewn!
And on the bay the moonlight lay,
And the shadow of the Moon.

The rock shone bright, the kirk no less,
That stands above the rock:
The moonlight steeped in silentness
The steady weathercock.

The angelic spirits leave the dead bodies,

And the bay was white with silent light,
Till rising from the same,
Full many shapes, that shadows were,
In crimson colors came.

And appear in their own forms of light.

A little distance from the prow
Those crimson shadows were:
I turned my eyes upon the deck—
Oh, Christ! what saw I there!

Each corse lay flat, lifeless and flat,
And, by the holy rood![1]
A man all light, a seraph-man,
On every corse there stood.

This seraph-band, each waved his hand:
It was a heavenly sight!
They stood as signals to the land,
Each one a lovely light;

This seraph-band, each waved his hand;
No voice did they impart—
No voice; but oh! the silence sank
Like music on my heart.

But soon I heard the dash of oars,
I heard the Pilot's cheer:
My head was turned perforce away,
And I saw a boat appear.

The Pilot, and the Pilot's boy,
I heard them coming fast:
Dear Lord in Heaven! it was a joy
The dead men could not blast.

I saw a third—I heard his voice:
It is the Hermit good!
He singeth loud his godly hymns
That he makes in the wood.
He'll shrieve my soul, he'll wash away
The Albatross's blood."

PART VII

The Hermit of the wood

"This Hermit good lives in that wood
Which slopes down to the sea.
How loudly his sweet voice he rears!
He loves to talk with marineres
That come from a far countree.

He kneels at morn, and noon, and eve—
He hath a cushion plump:
It is the moss that wholly hides
The rotted old oak-stump.

The skiff-boat neared; I heard them talk,
'Why, this is strange, I trow!
Where are those lights so many and fair,
That signal made but now?'

[1] cross

Approacheth the ship with wonder.

'Strange, by my faith!' the Hermit said—
'And they answered not our cheer!
The planks look warped! and see those sails,
How thin they are and sear!
I never saw aught like to them,
Unless perchance it were

Brown skeletons of leaves that lag
My forest-brook along;
When the ivy-tod [1] is heavy with snow,
And the owlet whoops to the wolf below
That eats the she-wolf's young.'

'Dear Lord! it hath a fiendish look'—
The Pilot made reply,
'I am a-feared'—'Push on, push on!'
Said the Hermit cheerily.

The boat came closer to the ship,
But I nor spake nor stirred;
The boat came close beneath the ship,
And straight a sound was heard.

The ship suddenly sinketh.

Under the water it rumbled on,
Still louder and more dread:
It reached the ship, it split the bay;
The ship went down like lead.

Stunned by that loud and dreadful sound,
Which sky and ocean smote,
Like one that hath been seven days drowned
My body lay afloat;
But swift as dreams, myself I found
Within the Pilot's boat.

The ancient Mariner is saved in the Pilot's boat.

Upon the whirl, where sank the ship,
The boat spun round and round;
And all was still, save that the hill
Was telling of the sound.

I moved my lips—the Pilot shrieked
And fell down in a fit;
The holy Hermit raised his eyes
And prayed where he did sit.

I took the oars; the Pilot's boy,
Who now doth crazy go,
Laughed loud and long, and all the while
His eyes went to and fro.
'Ha! ha!' quoth he, 'full plain I see,
The Devil knows how to row.'

And now, all in my own countree,
I stood on the firm land!
The Hermit stepped forth from the boat,
And scarcely he could stand.

The ancient Mariner earnestly entreateth the Hermit to shrieve him; and the penance of life falls on him.

'O shrieve me, shrieve me, holy man!'
The Hermit crossed his brow.
'Say quick,' quoth he, 'I bid thee say—
What manner of man art thou?'

Forthwith this frame of mine was wrenched
With a woeful agony,
Which forced me to begin my tale;
And then it left me free.

And ever and anon throughout his future life an agony constraineth him to travel from land to land,

Since then, at an uncertain hour,
That agony returns:
And till my ghastly tale is told,
This heart within me burns.

I pass, like night, from land to land;
I have strange power of speech;
That moment that his face I see,
I know the man that must hear me—
To him my tale I teach.

What loud uproar bursts from that door!
The wedding-guests are there:
But in the garden-bower the bride
And bride-maids singing are:
And hark the little vesper bell,
Which biddeth me to prayer!

O Wedding-Guest! this soul hath been
Alone on a wide wide sea:
So lonely 'twas, that God himself
Scarce seemèd there to be.

O sweeter than the marriage-feast,
'Tis sweeter far to me,
To walk together to the kirk,
With a goodly company!—

[1] ivy-bush

And to teach, by his own example, love and reverence to all things that God made and loveth.

To walk together to the kirk,
And all together pray.
While each to his great Father
 bends,
Old men, and babes, and loving
 friends
And youths and maidens gay!

Farewell, farewell! but this I tell
To thee, thou Wedding-Guest!
He prayeth well, who loveth well,
Both man and bird and beast.

He prayeth best, who loveth best
All things both great and small;
For the dear God who loveth us,
He made and loveth all."

The Mariner, whose eye is bright,
Whose beard with age is hoar,
Is gone; and now the Wedding-
 Guest
Turned from the bridegroom's
 door.

He went like one that hath been
 stunned,
And is of sense forlorn:
A sadder and a wiser man,
He rose the morrow morn.

1797-8 1798

CHRISTABEL[1]

Part the First

'Tis the middle of night by the castle clock,
And the owls have awakened the crowing cock,
To—whit!—Tu—whoo!
And hark, again! the crowing cock,
How drowsily it crew.

Sir Leoline, the baron rich,
Hath a toothless mastiff, which
From her kennel beneath the rock
Maketh answer to the clock,
Four for the quarters, and twelve for the hour;
Ever and aye, by shine and shower,
Sixteen short howls, not over loud;
Some say, she sees my lady's shroud.

Is the night chilly and dark?
The night is chilly, but not dark.
The thin gray cloud is spread on high,
It covers but not hides the sky.
The moon is behind, and at the full;
And yet she looks both small and dull.
The night is chill, the cloud is gray;
'Tis a month before the month of May,
And the Spring comes slowly up this way.

The lovely lady, Christabel,
Whom her father loves so well,
What makes her in the woods so late,
A furlong from the castle gate?
She had dreams all yesternight
Of her own betrothèd knight;
And she in the midnight wood will pray
For the weal of her lover that's far away.

She stole along, she nothing spoke,
The sighs she heaved were soft and low,
And naught was green upon the oak
But moss and rarest mistletoe:
She kneels beneath the huge oak tree,
And in silence prayeth she.

The lady sprang up suddenly,
The lovely lady, Christabel!
It moaned as near, as near can be,
But what it is she cannot tell—
On the other side it seems to be,
Of the huge, broad-breasted, old oak tree.

The night is chill; the forest bare;
Is it the wind that moaneth bleak?
There is not wind enough in the air
To move away the ringlet curl
From the lovely lady's cheek—
There is not wind enough to twirl
The one red leaf, the last of its clan,
That dances as often as dance it can,
Hanging so light, and hanging so high,
On the topmost twig that looks up at the sky.

Hush, beating heart of Christabel!
Jesu, Maria, shield her well!
She folded her arms beneath her cloak,
And stole to the other side of the oak.
 What sees she there?

There she sees a damsel bright,
Dressed in a silken robe of white,
That shadowy in the moonlight shone;
The neck that made the white robe wan,
Her stately neck, and arms were bare;
Her blue-veined feet unsandaled were,
And wildly glittered here and there
The gems entangled in her hair.
I guess 'twas frightful there to see
A lady so richly clad as she—
Beautiful exceedingly!

[1] A second part was added, in 1816, though "three parts yet to come" were never written; the first part circulated in manuscript and had considerable influence, especially in the matter of form, on Scott and other poets.

"Mary mother, save me now!"
Said Christabel, "And who art thou?"
The lady strange made answer meet,
And her voice was faint and sweet:
"Have pity on my sore distress,
I scarce can speak for weariness:
Stretch forth thy hand, and have no fear!"
Said Christabel, "How camest thou here?"
And the lady, whose voice was faint and sweet,
Did thus pursue her answer meet:

"My sire is of a noble line,
And my name is Geraldine:
Five warriors seized me yestermorn,
Me, even me, a maid forlorn:
They choked my cries with force and fright,
And tied me on a palfrey white.
The palfrey was as fleet as wind,
And they rode furiously behind.
They spurred amain, their steeds were white:
And once we crossed the shade of night.
As sure as Heaven shall rescue me,
I have no thought what men they be;
Nor do I know how long it is
(For I have lain entranced I wis)
Since one, the tallest of the five,
Took me from the palfrey's back,
A weary woman, scarce alive.
Some muttered words his comrades spoke:
He placed me underneath this oak;
He swore they would return with haste;
Whither they went I cannot tell—
I thought I heard, some minutes past,
Sounds as of a castle bell.
Stretch forth thy hand"—thus ended she—
"And help a wretched maid to flee."

Then Christabel stretched forth her hand,
And comforted fair Geraldine:
"Oh, well, bright dame, may you command
The service of Sir Leoline;
And gladly our stout chivalry
Will he send forth, and friends withal,
To guide and guard you safe and free
Home to your noble father's hall."

She rose: and forth with steps they past
That strove to be, and were not, fast.
Her gracious stars the lady blest,
And thus spake on sweet Christabel:
"All our household are at rest,
The hall as silent as the cell;
Sir Leoline is weak in health,
And may not well awakened be,
But we will move as if in stealth,
And I beseech your courtesy,
This night, to share your couch with me."

They crossed the moat, and Christabel
Took the key that fitted well;
A little door she opened straight,
All in the middle of the gate;
The gate that was ironed within and without,
Where an army in battle array had marched
out.
The lady sank, belike through pain,
And Christabel with might and main
Lifted her up, a weary weight,
Over the threshold of the gate.
Then the lady rose again,
And moved, as she were not in pain.[1]

So, free from danger, free from fear,
They crossed the court; right glad they were.
And Christabel devoutly cried
To the lady by her side,
"Praise we the Virgin all divine
Who hath rescued thee from thy distress!"
"Alas, alas!" said Geraldine,
"I cannot speak for weariness."
So, free from danger, free from fear,
They crossed the court: right glad they were.

Outside her kennel, the mastiff old
Lay fast asleep, in moonshine cold.
The mastiff old did not awake,
Yet she an angry moan did make!
And what can ail the mastiff bitch?
Never till now she uttered yell
Beneath the eye of Christabel.
Perhaps it is the owlet's scritch;
For what can ail the mastiff bitch?

They passed the hall that echoes, still,
Pass as lightly as you will!
The brands were flat, the brands were dying,
Amid their own white ashes lying;
But when the lady passed, there came
A tongue of light, a fit of flame;
And Christabel saw the lady's eye,
And nothing else saw she thereby,
Save the boss of the shield of Sir Leoline tall,
Which hung in a murky old niche in the wall.
"Oh, softly tread," said Christabel,
"My father seldom sleepeth well."

Sweet Christabel her feet doth bare,
And, jealous of the listening air
They steal their way from stair to stair,
Now in glimmer, and now in gloom,
And now they pass the Baron's room
As still as death, with stifled breath!
And now have reached her chamber door;

[1] Thresholds were often blessed to keep out evil spirits. The malign character of the supernatural Geraldine is clearly hinted at here and in the lines that follow.

And now doth Geraldine press down
The rushes of the chamber floor.

The moon shines dim in the open air,
And not a moonbeam enters here.
But they without its light can see
The chamber carved so curiously,
Carved with figures strange and sweet,
All made out of the carver's brain,
For a lady's chamber meet;
The lamp with two-fold silver chain
Is fastened to an angel's feet.

The silver lamp burns dead and dim;
But Christabel the lamp will trim.
She trimmed the lamp, and made it bright,
And left it swinging to and fro,
While Geraldine, in wretched plight,
Sank down upon the floor below.

"O weary lady, Geraldine,
I pray you, drink this cordial wine!
It is a wine of virtuous powers;
My mother made it of wild flowers."

"And will your mother pity me,
Who am a maiden most forlorn?"
Christabel answered—"Woe is me!
She died the hour that I was born.
I have heard the gray-haired friar tell
How on her deathbed she did say
That she should hear the castle-bell
Strike twelve upon my wedding day.
O mother dear! that thou wert here!"
"I would," said Geraldine, "she were!"
But soon with altered voice, said she—
"Off, wandering mother! Peak and pine! [1]
I have power to bid thee flee."
Alas! what ails poor Geraldine?
Why stares she with unsettled eye?
Can she the bodiless dead espy?
And why with hollow voice cries she,
"Off, woman, off! this hour is mine—
Though thou her guardian spirit be,
Off, woman, off! 'tis given to me."

Then Christabel knelt by the lady's side,
And raised to heaven her eyes so blue—
"Alas!" said she, "this ghastly ride—
Dear lady! it hath wildered you!"
The lady wiped her moist cold brow,
And faintly said, "'Tis over now!"

Again the wild-flower wine she drank:
Her fair large eyes 'gan glitter bright,
And from the floor whereon she sank,
The lofty lady stood upright:
She was most beautiful to see,
Like a lady of a far countree.

And thus the lofty lady spake—
"All they who live in the upper sky
Do love you, holy Christabel!
And you love them, and for their sake
And for the good which me befell
Even I in my degree will try,
Fair maiden, to requite you well.
But now unrobe yourself; for I
Must pray, ere yet in bed I lie."

Quoth Christabel, "So let it be!"
And as the lady bade, did she.
Her gentle limbs did she undress,
And lay down in her loveliness.

But through her brain of weal and woe
So many thoughts moved to and fro,
That vain it were her lids to close;
So halfway from the bed she rose,
And on her elbow did recline
To look at the lady Geraldine.

Beneath the lamp the lady bowed,
And slowly rolled her eyes around;
Then drawing in her breath aloud,
Like one that shuddered, she unbound
The cincture from beneath her breast:
Her silken robe and inner vest,
Dropped to her feet, and full in view,
Behold! her bosom and half her side—
A sight to dream of, not to tell!
O shield her! shield sweet Christabel!

Yet Geraldine nor speaks nor stirs;
Ah! what a stricken look was hers!
Deep from within she seems halfway
To lift some weight with sick assay,
And eyes the maid and seeks delay;
Then suddenly, as one defied,
Collects herself in scorn and pride,
And lay down by the maiden's side!—
And in her arms the maid she took,
Ah, welladay!
And with low voice and doleful look
These words did say:
"In the touch of this bosom there worketh a spell
Which is lord of thy utterance, Christabel!
Thou knowest tonight, and wilt know tomorrow,
This mark of my shame, this seal of my sorrow;
But vainly thou warrest,
For this is alone in
Thy power to declare,
That in the dim forest
Thou heard'st a low moaning,

[1] Cf. *Macbeth* I, iii, 23.

And found'st a bright lady, surpassingly fair;
And didst bring her home with thee in love and in charity,
To shield her and shelter her from the damp air."

THE CONCLUSION TO PART THE FIRST

It was a lovely sight to see
The lady Christabel, when she
Was praying at the old oak tree.
Amid the jagged shadows
Of mossy leafless boughs,
Kneeling in the moonlight,
To make her gentle vows;
Her slender palms together prest,
Heaving sometimes on her breast;
Her face resigned to bliss or bale—
Her face, oh, call it fair not pale,
And both blue eyes more bright than clear,
Each about to have a tear.

With open eyes (ah, woe is me!)
Asleep, and dreaming fearfully,
Fearfully dreaming, yet, I wis,
Dreaming that alone, which is—
O sorrow and shame! Can this be she,
The lady who knelt at the old oak tree?
And lo! the worker of these harms,
That holds the maiden in her arms,
Seems to slumber still and mild,
As a mother with her child.

A star hath set, a star hath risen,
O Geraldine! since arms of thine
Have been the lovely lady's prison.
O Geraldine! one hour was thine—
Thou'st had thy will! By tairn and rill,
The night-birds all that hour were still,
But now they are jubilant anew,
From cliff and tower, tu—whoo! tu—whoo!
Tu—whoo! tu—whoo! from wood and fell!

And see! the lady Christabel
Gathers herself from out her trance;
Her limbs relax, her countenance
Grows sad and soft; the smooth thin lids
Close o'er her eyes! and tears she sheds—
Large tears that leave the lashes bright!
And oft the while she seems to smile
As infants at a sudden light!

Yea, she doth smile, and she doth weep,
Like a youthful hermitess,
Beauteous in a wilderness,
Who, praying always, prays in sleep.
And if she move unquietly,
Perchance 'tis but the blood so free
Comes back and tingles in her feet.
No doubt she hath a vision sweet.
What if her guardian spirit 'twere?
What if she knew her mother near?
But this she knows, in joys and woes,
That saints will aid if men will call:
For the blue sky bends over all!

1797 1816

FRANCE: AN ODE [1]

I

Ye Clouds! that far above me float and pause,
Whose pathless march no mortal may control!
Ye Ocean Waves! that, wheresoe'er ye roll,
Yield homage only to eternal laws!
Ye Woods! that listen to the night-bird's singing,
Midway the smooth and perilous slope reclined,
Save when your own imperious branches swinging
Have made a solemn music of the wind!
Where, like a man beloved of God,
Through glooms which never woodman trod,
How oft, pursuing fancies holy,
My moonlight way o'er flowering weeds I wound,
Inspired beyond the guess of folly,
By each rude shape and wild unconquerable sound!
O ye loud Waves! and O ye Forests high!
And O ye Clouds that far above me soared!
Thou rising Sun! Thou blue rejoicing Sky!
Yea, everything that is and will be free!
Bear witness for me, wheresoe'er ye be,
With what deep worship I have still adored
The spirit of divinest Liberty.

II

When France in wrath her giant limbs upreared,
And with that oath which smote air, earth, and sea,
Stamped her strong foot and said she would be free,
Bear witness for me, how I hoped and feared!
With what a joy my lofty gratulation
Unawed I sang, amid a slavish band:
And when to whelm the disenchanted nation,
Like fiends embattled by a wizard's wand,
The Monarchs marched in evil day,
And Britain joined the dire array;
Though dear her shores and circling ocean,
Though many friendships, many youthful loves
Had swoln the patriot emotion

[1] This was called forth by the French invasion of Switzerland.

And flung a magic light o'er all her hills and groves;
Yet still my voice, unaltered, sang defeat
To all that braved the tyrant-quelling lance,
And shame too long delayed and vain retreat!
For ne'er, O Liberty! with partial aim
I dimmed thy light or damped thy holy flame;
But blessed the paeans of delivered France,
And hung my head and wept at Britain's name.

III

"And what," I said, "though Blasphemy's loud scream
With that sweet music of deliverance strove!
Though all the fierce and drunken passions wove
A dance more wild than e'er was maniac's dream![1]
Ye storms that round the dawning east assembled,
The Sun[2] was rising, though ye hid his light!"
And when to soothe my soul, that hoped and trembled,
The dissonance ceased, and all seemed calm and bright;
When France her front, deep scarred and gory,
Concealed with clustering wreaths of glory;
When, insupportably advancing,
Her arm made mockery of the warrior's ramp;
While timid looks of fury glancing,
Domestic treason, crushed beneath her fatal stamp,
Writhed like a wounded dragon in his gore;
Then I reproached my fears that would not flee;
"And soon," I said, "shall Wisdom teach her lore
In the low huts of them that toil and groan;
And, conquering by her happiness alone,
Shall France compel the nations to be free,
Till Love and Joy look round, and call the earth their own."

IV

Forgive me, Freedom! O forgive those dreams!
I hear thy voice, I hear thy loud lament,
From bleak Helvetia's[3] icy caverns sent—
I hear thy groans upon her blood-stained streams!
Heroes that for your peaceful country perished,
And ye, that fleeing, spot your mountain snows
With bleeding wounds; forgive me, that I cherished
One thought that ever blessed your cruel foes!
To scatter rage and traitorous guilt
Where Peace her jealous home had built;
A patriot race to disinherit
Of all that made their stormy wilds so dear;
And with inexpiable spirit
To taint the bloodless freedom of the mountaineer—
O France, that mockest Heaven, adulterous, blind,
And patriot only in pernicious toils!
Are these thy boasts, Champion of human kind?
To mix with Kings in the low lust of sway,
Yell in the hunt, and share the murderous prey;
To insult the shrine of Liberty with spoils
From freemen torn; to tempt and to betray?

V

The Sensual and the Dark rebel in vain,
Slaves by their own compulsion! In mad game
They burst their manacles and wear the name
Of Freedom, graven on a heavier chain!
O Liberty! with profitless endeavor
Have I pursued thee, many a weary hour;
But thou nor swell'st the victor's strain nor ever
Didst breathe thy soul in forms of human power.
Alike from all, howe'er they praise thee,
(Nor prayer, nor boastful name delays thee)
Alike from Priestcraft's harpy minions,
And factious Blasphemy's obscener slaves,
Thou speedest on thy subtle pinions,
The guide of homeless winds, and playmate of the waves!
And there I felt thee!—on that sea cliff's verge,
Whose pines, scarce traveled by the breeze above,
Had made one murmur with the distant surge!
Yes, while I stood and gazed, my temples bare,
And shot my being through earth, sea, and air,
Possessing all things with intensest love,
O Liberty! my spirit felt thee there.

1798 1798

HYMN BEFORE SUNRISE IN THE VALE OF CHAMOUNI[4]

Hast thou a charm to stay the morning star
In his steep course? So long he seems to pause
On thy bald awful head, O sovran Blanc!

[1] alluding to the excesses that attended the French Revolution
[2] Liberty
[3] Switzerland's

[4] This poem, resembling in style Macpherson's "Ossian," (p. 381), has been perhaps unduly admired. Coleridge never was at Chamouni; his immediate model was a poem by the German poetess Frederike Brun.

The Arve and Arveiron at thy base
Rave ceaselessly; but thou, most awful Form!
Risest from forth thy silent sea of pines,
How silently! Around thee and above,
Deep is the air and dark, substantial, black,
An ebon mass: methinks thou piercest it
As with a wedge! But when I look again,
It is thine own calm home, thy crystal shrine,
Thy habitation from eternity!
O dread and silent Mount! I gazed upon thee,
Till thou, still present to the bodily sense,
Didst vanish from my thought: entranced in prayer
I worshiped the Invisible alone.

Yet, like some sweet beguiling melody,
So sweet we know not we are listening to it,
Thou, the meanwhile, wast blending with my Thought,
Yea, with my Life and Life's own secret joy:
Till the dilating Soul, enrapt, transfused,
Into the mighty vision passing—there
As in her natural form, swelled vast to Heaven!

Awake, my soul! Not only passive praise
Thou owest! Not alone these swelling tears,
Mute thanks and secret ecstasy! Awake,
Voice of sweet song! Awake, my heart, awake!
Green vales and icy cliffs, all join my Hymn.

Thou first and chief, sole sovereign of the Vale!
Or struggling with the darkness all the night,
And visited all night by troops of stars,
Or when they climb the sky or when they sink:
Companion of the morning star at dawn,
Thyself Earth's rosy star, and of the dawn
Co-herald: wake, O wake, and utter praise!
Who sank thy sunless pillars deep in Earth?
Who filled thy countenance with rosy light?
Who made thee parent of perpetual streams?

And you, ye five wild torrents fiercely glad!
Who called you forth from night and utter death,
From dark and icy caverns called you forth,
Down those precipitous, black, jagged rocks,
Forever shattered and the same forever?
Who gave you your invulnerable life,
Your strength, your speed, your fury, and your joy,
Unceasing thunder and eternal foam?
And who commanded (and the silence came),
Here let the billows stiffen, and have rest?
Ye Ice-falls! ye that from the mountain's brow
Adown enormous ravines slope amain—
Torrents, methinks, that heard a mighty voice,
And stopped at once amid their maddest plunge!
Motionless torrents! silent cataracts!
Who made you glorious as the Gates of Heaven
Beneath the keen full moon? Who bade the sun
Clothe you with rainbows? Who, with living flowers
Of loveliest blue, spread garlands at your feet?—
God! let the torrents, like a shout of nations,
Answer! and let the ice-plains echo, God!
God! sing ye meadow streams with gladsome voice!
Ye pine groves, with your soft and soul-like sounds!
And they, too, have a voice, yon piles of snow,
And in their perilous fall shall thunder, God!

Ye living flowers that skirt the eternal frost!
Ye wild goats sporting round the eagle's nest!
Ye eagles, playmates of the mountain storm!
Ye lightnings, the dread arrows of the clouds!
Ye signs and wonders of the element!
Utter forth God, and fill the hills with praise!

Thou, too, hoar Mount! with the sky-pointing peaks,
Oft from whose feet the avalanche, unheard,
Shoots downward, glittering through the pure serene
Into the depth of clouds that veil thy breast—
Thou, too, again, stupendous Mountain! thou
That as I raise my head, awhile bowed low
In adoration, upward from thy base
Slow traveling with dim eyes suffused with tears,
Solemnly seemest, like a vapory cloud,
To rise before me—Rise, O ever rise,
Rise like a cloud of incense from the Earth!
Thou kingly Spirit throned among the hills,
Thou dread ambassador from Earth to Heaven,
Great Hierarch! tell thou the silent sky,
And tell the stars, and tell yon rising sun
Earth, with her thousand voices, praises God.

1802 1802

THE KNIGHT'S TOMB

Where is the grave of Sir Arthur O'Kellyn?
Where may the grave of that good man be?—
By the side of a spring, on the breast of Helvellyn,[1]
Under the twigs of a young birch tree!

[1] a mountain in Cumberland

The oak that in summer was sweet to hear,
And rustled its leaves in the fall of the year,
And whistled and roared in the winter alone,
Is gone—and the birch in its stead is grown.
The Knight's bones are dust,
And his good sword rust—
His soul is with the saints, I trust.

1817? 1834

SONG

From ZAPOLYA, ACT II, SCENE I

A sunny shaft did I behold,
From sky to earth it slanted;
And poised therein a bird so bold—
Sweet bird, thou wert enchanted!

He sunk, he rose, he twinkled, he trolled
Within that shaft of sunny mist;
His eyes of fire, his beak of gold,
All else of amethyst!

And thus he sang: Adieu! adieu!
Love's dreams prove seldom true.
The blossoms they make no delay;
The sparkling dewdrops will not stay.
Sweet month of May,
We must away;
Far, far away!
Today! today!

1815 1817

YOUTH AND AGE [1]

Verse, a breeze mid blossoms straying,
Where Hope clung feeding, like a bee—
Both were mine! Life went a-maying
With Nature, Hope, and Poesy,
When I was young!

When I was young?—Ah, woeful When!
Ah! for the change 'twixt Now and Then!
This breathing house not built with hands,
This body that does me grievous wrong,
O'er aery cliffs and glittering sands,
How lightly *then* it flashed along—
Like those trim skiffs, unknown of yore,
On winding lakes and rivers wide,
That ask no aid of sail or oar,
That fear no spite of wind or tide!
Nought cared this body for wind or weather
When Youth and I lived in't together.

Flowers are lovely; Love is flower-like;
Friendship is a sheltering tree;
Oh! the joys, that came down shower-like,
Of Friendship, Love, and Liberty,
Ere I was old!
Ere I was old? Ah, woeful Ere,
Which tells me, Youth's no longer here!
O Youth! for years so many and sweet,
'Tis known, that Thou and I were one,
I'll think it but a fond conceit—
It cannot be that Thou art gone!
Thy vesper-bell hath not yet tolled—
And thou wert aye a masker bold!
What strange disguise hast now put on,
To *make believe* that thou art gone?
I see these locks in silvery slips,
This drooping gait, this altered size:
But Springtide blossoms on thy lips,
And tears take sunshine from thine eyes!
Life is but thought; so think I will
That Youth and I are housemates still.

Dewdrops are the gems of morning,
But the tears of mournful eve!
Where no hope is, life's a warning
That only serves to make us grieve,
When we are old:
That only serves to make us grieve
With oft and tedious taking-leave,
Like some poor nigh-related guest,
That may not rudely be dismist;
Yet hath outstayed his welcome while,
And tells the jest without the smile.

1823-32 1834

[1] A first rough draft of this poem was called "Area Spontanea," and the whole still reads like a musical improvisation.

WORK WITHOUT HOPE [2]

All Nature seems at work. Slugs leave their lair—
The bees are stirring—birds are on the wing—
And Winter slumbering in the open air,
Wears on his smiling face a dream of Spring!
And I the while, the sole unbusy thing,
Nor honey make, nor pair, nor build, nor sing.

Yet well I ken the banks where amaranths blow,
Have traced the fount whence streams of nectar flow.
Bloom, O ye amaranths! bloom for whom ye may,
For me ye bloom not! Glide, rich streams, away!
With lips unbrightened, wreathless brow, I stroll.
And would you learn the spells that drowse my soul?
Work without Hope draws nectar in a sieve,
And Hope without an object cannot live.

1825 1828

[2] the mournful *Ay de mi* (*alas!*) of a man confronted by age and sickness, and looking back over a life of defeated hopes and wasted opportunities

SIR WALTER SCOTT 1771-1832

The death of Scott is often taken to mark the end of the early nineteenth century romantic period, as the publication of the *Lyrical Ballads* marks its beginning. Born and reared in the society of Edinburgh, and with two years at the university, Scott had a taste for literature; as a youth he had spent much time riding and walking through the border land, and had collected ballads and songs from the old singers, which he afterwards published. Until 1815 he was chiefly a poet, producing *The Lay of the Last Minstrel,* 1805; *Marmion,* 1808; *The Lady of the Lake,* 1810. Then *Waverley* opened a new vein.

The immediate and vast popularity of his novels, and his personal ambition to found a family and to be known to posterity as "Scott of Abbotsford," tempted him into a publishing enterprise that failed and left him, six years before his death, with a debt of £120,000. This he resolutely set himself to write off. Before the stroke that preceded his death at Abbotsford he had actually earned one third of this amount and fifteen years later, the last penny was paid by royalties.

The spirit of romance gained from his background and experiences pervades Scott's work, and is seen to great advantage in his poems. In these his imagination seems stimulated rather than restrained by their historical setting. Vigorous, headlong narrative is his forte. He follows his theme with the spirit of a Roosevelt, and leaves with the reader the sense of abundant resources untouched. The possession of tireless energy is the first and last impression given by Scott's narratives. His lyric poetry, though full of grace and tenderness, is quite different from Burns's, for Scott is impersonal, almost objective.

Scott's inborn romanticism was greatly stimulated by his antiquarian pursuits, which confirmed in him an attitude of mind that looked toward the past. His Tory sympathies also led him to magnify the virtues of a social order that had faded away. The stirring life of the Scotch border from medieval days down to those of his immediate ancestors first filled his imagination and then became the subject of his serious study. All this enabled him, when Byron's more passionate narrative poetry eclipsed his own, to take up the writing of prose fiction and reach eminent success in the historical romance, a practically new field in his day.

Biography: Lockhart, Scott's son-in-law, in his *Memoirs of Scott,* 2 vols. 1837-8, produced one of the famous literary biographies of the century; Hutton (EML); Yonge (GW). Criticism: Carlyle, a little unsympathetic; Hazlitt; Saintsbury; Stephen; Lang; Woodberry, Swinburne; Jenks, *In the Days of Scott.* Interesting recent comment: V. Rendall's "Scott and the Waverley Novels," *19th Cent.* 96:531-6; T. Seccombe's "Scott: Waverley," *Liv. Age* 282:485-91; B. Croce, "Walter Scott: an Italian Estimate," *Liv. Age* 317:99-103, and *Dial* 75:325-31.

LOCHINVAR [1]

From MARMION, CANTO V

Oh! young Lochinvar is come out of the west,
Through all the wide Border his steed was the best;
And save his good broadsword he weapons had none.
He rode all unarmed and he rode all alone.
So faithful in love and so dauntless in war,
There never was knight like the young Lochinvar. 6

He stayed not for brake and he stopped not for stone,
He swam the Eske river where ford there was none,
But ere he alighted at Netherby gate
The bride had consented, the gallant came late:
For a laggard in love and a dastard in war
Was to wed the fair Ellen of brave Lochinvar.

So boldly he entered the Netherby Hall, 13
Among bridesmen, and kinsmen, and brothers, and all.
Then spoke the bride's father, his hand on his sword—
For the poor craven bridegroom said never a word—
"Oh! come ye in peace here, or come ye in war,
Or to dance at our bridal, young Lord Lochinvar?" 18

"I long wooed your daughter, my suit you denied;
Love swells like the Solway, [2] but ebbs like its tide—
And now am I come, with this lost love of mine
To lead but one measure, drink one cup of wine.
There are maidens in Scotland more lovely by far,
That would gladly be bride to the young Lochinvar." 24

The bride kissed the goblet; the knight took it up,
He quaffed off the wine, and he threw down the cup.
She looked down to blush, and she looked up to sigh,
With a smile on her lips and a tear in her eye.

[1] Compare "Katharine Jaffray," p. 88, upon which Scott "in a very slight degree" founded the present ballad.

[2] Solway Firth is noted for its swift tides.

He took her soft hand ere her mother could bar—
"Now tread we a measure!" said young Lochinvar.

So stately his form, and so lovely her face,
That never a hall such a galliard[1] did grace;
While her mother did fret, and her father did fume,
And the bridegroom stood dangling his bonnet[2] and plume;
And the bride-maidens whispered "'Twere better by far
To have matched our fair cousin with young Lochinvar."

One touch to her hand and one word in her ear,
When they reached the hall door, and the charger stood near;
So light to the croup the fair lady he swung,
So light to the saddle before her he sprung!
"She is won! We are gone, over bank, bush, and scaur;[3]
They'll have fleet steeds that follow," quoth young Lochinvar.

There was mounting 'mong Graemes of the Netherby clan;
Forsters, Fenwicks, and Musgraves, they rode and they ran:
There was racing and chasing on Cannobie Lee,
But the lost bride of Netherby ne'er did they see.
So daring in love and so dauntless in war,
Have ye e'er heard of gallant like young Lochinvar?

1806-8 1808

SOLDIER, REST!

From The Lady of the Lake, Canto I

Soldier, rest! thy warfare o'er,
Sleep the sleep that knows not breaking!
Dream of battled fields no more,
Days of danger, nights of waking.
In our isle's enchanted hall
Hands unseen thy couch are strewing,
Fairy strains of music fall,
Every sense in slumber dewing.
Soldier, rest! thy warfare o'er,
Dream of fighting fields no more;
Sleep the sleep that knows not breaking,
Morn of toil, nor night of waking.

No rude sound shall reach thine ear,
Armor's clang, or war-steel champing,
Trump nor pibroch summon here
Mustering clan or squadron tramping.
Yet the lark's shrill fife may come
At the daybreak from the fallow,
And the bittern sound his drum,
Booming from the sedgy shallow.
Ruder sounds shall none be near,
Guards nor warders challenge here,
Here's no war-steed's neigh and champing,
Shouting clans or squadrons stamping.

Hunstman, rest! thy chase is done;
While our slumbrous spells assail ye,
Dream not, with the rising sun,
Bugles here shall sound reveillé.
Sleep! the deer is in his den;
Sleep! thy hounds are by thee lying:
Sleep! nor dream in yonder glen
How thy gallant steed lay dying.
Hunstman, rest! thy chase is done;
Think not of the rising sun,
For at dawning to assail ye
Here no bugles sound reveillé.

1809-10 1810

CORONACH[4]

From The Lady of the Lake, Canto III

He is gone on the mountain,
He is lost to the forest,
Like a summer-dried fountain,
When our need was the sorest.
The font, reappearing,
From the raindrops shall borrow,
But to us comes no cheering,
To Duncan no morrow!

The hand of the reaper
Takes the ears that are hoary,
But the voice of the weeper
Wails manhood in glory.
The autumn winds rushing
Waft the leaves that are searest,
But our flower was in flushing
When blighting was nearest.

Fleet foot on the correi,[5]
Sage counsel in cumber,[6]
Red hand in the foray,
How sound is thy slumber!
Like the dew on the mountain,
Like the foam on the river,
Like the bubble on the fountain,
Thou art gone, and forever!

1809-10 1810

[1] a brisk dance [2] cap [3] cliff

[4] a Highland dirge [5] a hollow hillside, resort of game [6] trouble

THE BATTLE OF BEAL' AN DUINE [1]

From The Lady of the Lake, Canto VI

[Introduction]

The Chieftain reared his form on high,
And fever's fire was in his eye;
But ghastly, pale, and livid streaks
Checkered his swarthy brow and cheeks.
—"Hark, Minstrel! I have heard thee play,
With measure bold, on festal day,
In yon lone isle—again where ne'er
Shall harper play, or warrior hear!—
That stirring air that peals on high,
O'er Dermid's race [2] our victory.
Strike it!—and then—for well thou canst—
Free from thy minstrel spirit glanced,
Fling me the picture of the fight,
When met my clan the Saxon [3] might.
I'll listen, till my fancy hears
The clang of swords, the crash of spears!
These grates, these walls, shall vanish then,
For the fair field of fighting men,
And my free spirit burst away
As if it soared from battle fray."
The trembling Bard with awe obeyed—
Slow on the harp his hand he laid;
But soon remembrance of the sight
He witnessed from the mountain's height,
With what old Bertram [4] told at night,
Awakened the full power of song,
And bore him in career along—
As shallop launched on river's tide,
That slow and fearful leaves the side,
But, when it feels the middle stream,
Drives downward swift as lightning's beam.

[The Battle]

"The Minstrel came once more to view
The eastern ridge of Benvenue,
For ere he parted, he would say
Farewell to lovely Loch Achray—
Where shall he find in foreign land,
So lone a lake, so sweet a strand!—
There is no breeze upon the fern,
No ripple on the lake,
Upon her aerie nods the erne, [5]
The deer has sought the brake;
The small birds will not sing aloud,
The springing trout lies still,
So darkly glooms yon thunder cloud,
That swathes, as with a purple shroud,
Benledi's distant hill.
Is it the thunder's solemn sound
That mutters deep and dread,
Or echoes from the groaning ground
The warrior's measured tread?
Is it the lightning's quivering glance
That on the thicket streams,
Or do they flash on spear and lance
The sun's retiring beams?—
I see the dagger-crest of Mar, [6]
I see the Moray's [6] silver star,
Wave o'er the cloud of Saxon war,
That up the lake comes winding far!
To hero bourne [7] for battle-strife,
Or bard of martial lay,
'Twere worth ten years of peaceful life,
One glance at their array!

"Their light-armed archers far and near
Surveyed the tangled ground,
Their center ranks, with pike and spear,
A twilight forest frowned,
Their barded [8] horsemen, in the rear,
The stern battalia [9] crowned.
No cymbal clashed, no clarion rang,
Still were the pipe and drum;
Save heavy tread, and armor's clang,
The sullen march was dumb.
There breathed no wind their crests to shake,
Or wave their flags abroad;
Scarce the frail aspen seemed to quake,
That shadowed o'er their road.
Their vaward [10] scouts no tidings bring,
Can rouse no lurking foe,
Nor spy a trace of living thing,
Save when they stirred the roe;
The host moves, like a deep-sea wave,
Where rise no rocks its pride to brave,
High-swelling, dark, and slow.
The lake is passed, and now they gain
A narrow and a broken plain,
Before the Trossachs' [11] rugged jaws:
And here the horse and spearmen pause,
While, to explore the dangerous glen,
Dive through the pass the archer-men.

"At once there rose so wild a yell
Within that dark and narrow dell,
As all the fiends from heaven that fell
Had pealed the banner-cry of hell!
Forth from the pass in tumult driven,
Like chaff before the wind of heaven,
The archery appear:

[1] Roderick Dhu, a marauding chieftain of the Highland Clan-Alpine, having been wounded in combat with the disguised King of Scotland, lies dying in prison, while the Minstrel, Allan-bane, recites to him the story of the conflict between his clan and the forces of the king. The Minstrel's tale begins at line 369; he speaks of himself in the third person.

[2] the Campbells

[3] Lowland

[4] one of the king's men

[5] eagle

[6] a Lowland leader

[7] prepared

[8] armed with plate-armor

[9] battle array

[10] vanward

[11] the rough mountains and pass in the Highlands between Lochs Katrine and Achray

For life! for life! their flight they ply—
And shriek, and shout, and battle-cry,
And plaids and bonnets waving high,
And broadswords flashing to the sky,
Are maddening in the rear.
Onward they drive, in dreadful race,
Pursuers and pursued;
Before that tide of flight and chase,
How shall it keep its rooted place,
The spearmen's twilight wood?
'Down, down,' cried Mar, 'your lances down!
Bear back both friend and foe!'
Like reeds before the tempest's frown,
That serried grove of lances brown
At once lay leveled low;
And closely shouldering side to side,
The bristling ranks the onset bide.
'We'll quell the savage mountaineer,
As their Tinchel [1] cows the game!
They come as fleet as forest deer,
We'll drive them back as tame.'

"Bearing before them, in their course,
The relics of the archer force,
Like wave with crest of sparkling foam,
Right onward did Clan-Alpine come.
Above the tide, each broadsword bright
Was brandishing like beam of light,
Each targe was dark below;
And with the ocean's mighty swing,
When heaving to the tempest's wing,
They hurled them on the foe.
I heard the lance's shivering crash,
As when the whirlwind rends the ash;
I heard the broadsword's deadly clang,
As if an hundred anvils rang!
But Moray wheeled his rearward rank
Of horsemen on Clan-Alpine's flank,
'My banner-man, advance!
I see,' he cried, 'their column shake.
Now, gallants! for your ladies' sake,
Upon them with the lance!'
The horsemen dashed among the rout,
As deer break through the broom;
Their steeds are stout, their swords are out,
They soon make lightsome room.
Clan-Alpine's best are backward borne—
Where, where was Roderick then!
One blast upon his bugle horn
Were worth a thousand men.
And refluent through the pass of fear
The battle's tide was poured;
Vanished the Saxon's struggling spear,
Vanished the mountain-sword.
As Bracklinn's chasm, so black and steep,
Receives her roaring linn, [2]
As the dark caverns of the deep
Suck the wild whirlpool in,
So did the deep and darksome pass
Devour the battle's mingled mass:
None linger now upon the plain,
Save those who ne'er shall fight again.

"Now westward rolls the battle's din,
That deep and doubling pass within.
Minstrel, away! the work of fate
Is bearing on: its issue wait,
Where the rude Trossachs' dread defile
Opens on Katrine's lake and isle.
Gray Benvenue I soon repassed,
Loch Katrine lay beneath me cast.
The sun is set; the clouds are met,
The lowering scowl of heaven
An inky hue of livid blue
To the deep lake has given;
Strange gusts of wind from the mountain glen
Swept o'er the lake, then sunk again.
I heeded not the eddying surge,
Mine eye but saw the Trossachs' gorge,
Mine ear but heard the sullen sound,
Which like an earthquake shook the ground,
And spoke the stern and desperate strife
That parts not but with parting life,
Seeming, to minstrel ear, to toll
The dirge of many a passing soul.
Nearer it comes—the dim-wood glen
The martial flood disgorged again,
But not in mingled tide;
The plaided warriors of the North
High on the mountain thunder forth
And overhang its side;
While by the lake below appears
The dark'ning cloud of Saxon spears.
At weary bay each shattered band,
Eying their foemen, sternly stand;
Their banners stream like tattered sail
That flings its fragments to the gale,
And broken arms and disarray
Marked the fell havoc of the day.

"Viewing the mountain's ridge askance,
The Saxon stood in sullen trance,
Till Moray pointed with his lance,
And cried—'Behold yon isle!
See! none are left to guard its strand,
But women weak, that wring the hand:
'Tis there of yore the robber band
Their booty wont to pile.
My purse, with bonnet-pieces store, [3]
To him will [4] swim a bow-shot o'er,
And loose a shallop from the shore.

[1] hunters surrounding game
[2] waterfall
[3] gold coins (stamped with the king's head) in plenty
[4] who will

Lightly we'll tame the war-wolf then,
Lords of his mate, and brood, and den.'
Forth from the ranks of spearman sprung,
On earth his casque and corslet rung,
  He plunged him in the wave;
All saw the deed—the purpose knew,
And to their clamors Benvenue
  A mingled echo gave;
The Saxon's shout, their mate to cheer,
The helpless females scream for fear,
And yells for rage the mountaineer.
'Twas then, as by the outcry riven,
Poured down at once the lowering heaven;
A whirlwind swept Loch Katrine's breast,
Her billows reared their snowy crest.
Well for the swimmer swelled they high,
To mar the Highland marksman's eye;
For round him showered, 'mid rain and hail,
The vengeful arrows of the Gael; [1]
In vain.—He nears the isle—and lo!
His hand is on a shallop's bow.
Just then a flash of lightning came,
It tinged the waves and strand with flame;
I marked Duncraggan's widowed dame, [2]
Behind an oak I saw her stand,
A naked dirk gleamed in her hand;
It darkened—but, amid the moan
Of waves, I heard a dying groan.
Another flash!—the spearman floats
A weltering corse beside the boats,
And the stern matron o'er him stood,
Her hand and dagger streaming blood.

"'Revenge! revenge!' the Saxons cried,
The Gaels' exulting shout replied.
Despite the elemental rage,
Again they hurried to engage;
But, ere they closed in desperate fight,
Bloody with spurring came a knight,
Sprung from his horse, and from a crag,
Waved 'twixt the hosts a milk-white flag.
Clarion and trumpet by his side
Rung forth a truce-note high and wide,
While, in the Monarch's name, afar
A herald's voice forbade the war,
For Bothwell's lord, [3] and Roderick bold,
Were both, he said, in captive hold."

But here the lay made sudden stand,
The harp escaped the Minstrel's hand!
Oft had he stolen a glance, to spy
How Roderick brooked his minstrelsy:

[1] Highlander
[2] widow of the Duncan mourned for in the "Coronach" on p. 482.
[3] Douglas, an exile, to whom Roderick Dhu had given shelter

At first, the Chieftain, to the chime,
With lifted hand kept feeble time;
That motion ceased—yet feeling strong
Varied his look as changed the song;
At length, no more his deafened ear
The minstrel melody can hear;
His face grows sharp—his hands are clenched
As if some pang his heart-strings wrenched;
Set are his teeth, his fading eye
Is sternly fixed on vacancy;
Thus, motionless and moanless, drew
His parting breath, stout Roderick Dhu!
Old Allan-bane looked on aghast
While grim and still his spirit passed;
But when he saw that life was fled,
He poured his wailing o'er the dead.

1809-10 1810

JOCK OF HAZELDEAN

"Why weep ye by the tide, ladie?
  Why weep ye by the tide?
I'll wed ye to my youngest son,
  And ye sall be his bride:
And ye sall be his bride, ladie,
  Sae comely to be seen"—
But aye she loot the tears down fa'
  For Jock of Hazeldean.

"Now let this wilfu' grief be done,
  And dry that cheek so pale;
Young Frank is chief of Errington
  And lord of Langley-dale;
His step is first in peaceful ha',
  His sword in battle keen"—
But aye she loot the tears down fa'
  For Jock of Hazeldean.

"A chain of gold ye sall not lack,
  Nor braid to bind your hair;
Nor mettled hound, nor managed [4] hawk,
  Nor palfrey fresh and fair;
And you, the foremost o' them a',
  Shall ride our forest queen"—
But aye she loot the tears down fa'
  For Jock of Hazeldean.

The kirk was decked at morning-tide,
  The tapers glimmered fair;
The priest and bridegroom wait the bride,
  And dame and knight are there.
They sought her baith by bower and ha';
  The ladie was not seen!
She's o'er the Border and awa'
  Wi' Jock of Hazeldean.

1816 1816

[4] trained

PROUD MAISIE

From The Heart of Midlothian

Proud Maisie is in the wood,
  Walking so early;
Sweet Robin sits on the bush,
  Singing so rarely.

"Tell me, thou bonny bird,
  When shall I marry me?"
"When six braw [1] gentlemen
  Kirkward shall carry ye."

"Who makes the bridal bed,
  Birdie, say truly?"
"The gray-headed sexton
  That delves the grave duly.

"The glowworm o'er grave and stone
  Shall light thee steady;
The owl from the steeple sing
  'Welcome, proud lady.'"

1818

COUNTY GUY

From Quentin Durward

Ah! County Guy, the hour is nigh,
  The sun has left the lea,
The orange flower perfumes the bower,
  The breeze is on the sea.
The lark, his lay who thrilled all day,
  Sits hushed his partner nigh:
Breeze, bird, and flower confess the hour,
  But where is County Guy?

The village maid steals through the shade
  Her shepherd's suit to hear;
To beauty shy by lattice high,
  Sings high-born Cavalier.
The star of love, all stars above,
  Now reigns o'er earth and sky;
And high and low the influence know—
  But where is County Guy?

1821 1823

BONNY DUNDEE [2]

To the lords of Convention 'twas Claver'se who spoke,
"Ere the King's crown shall fall there are crowns to be broke;
So let each Cavalier who loves honor and me,
Come follow the bonnet of Bonny Dundee.
  Come fill up my cup, come fill up my can,
  Come saddle your horses and call up your men;
  Come open the West Port and let me gang free,
  And it's room for the bonnets of Bonny Dundee!"

Dundee he is mounted, he rides up the street,
The bells are run backward, [3] the drums they are beat;
But the Provost, [4] douce [5] man, said, "Just e'en let him be,
The Gude Town is weel quit of that deil of Dundee."
  Come fill up my cup, etc.

As he rode down the sanctified bends of the Bow, [6]
Ilk carline [7] was flyting [8] and shaking her pow; [9]
But the young plants of grace they looked couthia and slee, [10]
Thinking, luck to thy bonnet, thou Bonny Dundee!
  Come fill up my cup, etc.

With sour-featured Whigs the Grassmarket [11] was crammed
As if half the West had set tryst to be hanged;
There was spite in each look, there was fear in each e'e,
As they watched for the bonnets of Bonny Dundee.
  Come fill up my cup, etc.

These cowls of Kilmarnock [12] had spits and had spears,
And lang-hafted gullies [13] to kill Cavaliers;
But they shrunk to close-heads [14] and the causeway was free,
At the toss of the bonnet of Bonny Dundee.
  Come fill up my cup, etc.

He spurred to the foot of the proud Castle rock, [15]
And with the gay Gordon he gallantly spoke;

[1] brave, fine
[2] John Graham of Claverhouse, Viscount Dundee, in support of James II, withstood the Scotch Covenanters, defied the Convention, or Scotch Parliament, which had accepted King William, and marched out of Edinburgh with a few faithful followers in 1689, thus creating the "Jacobite" party. He met the government forces at Killiecrankie and defeated them, but was killed in the battle. See Macaulay's account of that battle in the present volume, p. 586.

[3] reversing the chimes (as an alarm)
[4] mayor
[5] sedate
[6] windings of Bow Street
[7] each old woman
[8] scolding
[9] head
[10] gracious and sly
[11] the place of execution (see *Midlothian*, chap. II)
[12] hoods made at Kilmarnock (here used for the wearers, Presbyterians)
[13] knives
[14] blind alleys
[15] the site of Edinburgh Castle, then held by the Duke of Gordon

"Let Mons Meg[1] and her marrows[2] speak
twa words or three,
For the love of the bonnet of Bonny Dundee."
Come fill up my cup, etc.

The Gordon demands of him which way he
goes—
"Where'er shall direct me the shade of Montrose![3]
Your Grace in short space shall hear tidings
of me,
Or that low lies the bonnet of Bonny Dundee.
Come fill up my cup, etc.

"There are hills beyond Pentland and lands
beyond Forth,
If there's lords in the Lowlands, there's chiefs
in the North;
There are wild duniewassals[4] three thousand
times three,
Will cry *hoigh!* for the bonnet of Bonny
Dundee.
Come fill up my cup, etc.

"There's brass on the target of barkened[5]
bull-hide;
There's steel in the scabbard that dangles
beside;
The brass shall be burnished, the steel shall
flash free
At a toss of the bonnet of Bonny Dundee.
Come fill up my cup, etc.

"Away to the hills, to the caves, to the rocks—
Ere I own an usurper, I'll couch with the fox;
And tremble, false Whigs, in the midst of your
glee,
You have not seen the last of my bonnet and
me!"
Come fill up my cup, etc.

He waved his proud hand and the trumpets
were blown,
The kettle-drums clashed and the horsemen
rode on,
Till on Ravelston's cliffs and on Clermiston's lea
Died away the wild war-notes of Bonny Dundee.

Come fill up my cup, come fill up my can,
Come saddle the horses and call up the men,
Come open your gates and let me gae free,
For it's up with the bonnets of Bonny
Dundee!

1825 1830

[1] nickname of a cannon
[2] mates
[3] a royalist executed in 1650
[4] men of minor degree
[5] tanned

HERE'S A HEALTH TO KING CHARLES

From Woodstock

Bring the bowl which you boast,
Fill it up to the brim;
'Tis to him we love most,
And to all who love him.
Brave gallants, stand up,
And avaunt ye, base carles!
Were there death in the cup,
Here's a health to King Charles.

Though he wanders through dangers,
Unaided, unknown,
Dependent on strangers,
Estranged from his own;
Though 'tis under our breath,
Amidst forfeits and perils,
Here's to honor and faith,
And a health to King Charles!

Let such honors abound
As the time can afford,
The knee on the ground,
And the hand on the sword;
But the time shall come round
When, 'mid Lords, Dukes, and Earls,
The loud trumpet shall sound,
Here's a health to King Charles.

1826

LORD BYRON
1788-1824

From his birth in London until his death in the Greek war for independence at Missolonghi, Byron's career was notorious for turbulence of temper and passions. His was the most marked personality in English letters since Johnson. After his mother had lost her fortune by her husband's gambling, she lived in retirement with her son until, at the age of ten, he inherited the estates and title of a great-uncle. The young nobleman's spectacular career at Harrow and Cambridge ended with a master's degree in 1808. His *Hours of Idleness,* 1807, having drawn savage criticism from the *Edinburgh Review,* he retorted with a scurrilous satire, *English Bards and Scotch Reviewers,* 1809. Henceforth he was a marked man. After a prolonged tour of Europe, which included the Levant and the Balkans, the scene of many of his future poems, he began in London, a career of markedly riotous living that made him notorious. He married in 1815, but the next year his wife left him and, socially ostracized, he left England, and lived thereafter mostly in Italy.

Byron's chief works are his loose chronicle-narrative poems, partly autobiographical, *Childe Harold,* 1812-1818, and *Don Juan,* 1819-1824; *Manfred,* 1817; *Cain,* 1821; and *The Vision of Judgment,* 1822. Byron is unsurpassed in English poetry for the power with which he depicts scenes and facts, and for the cynical and masterful assurance of his satire. His popularity was as wide as it was sudden: "I awoke one morning and found myself famous," he recorded after the publication of *Childe Harold*. His manner contrasts with that of the finer lyrics of Keats and Wordsworth. His virile qualities, his hatred of hypocrisy, and his vigor will often serve to relieve the reader weary of the sometimes overwrought sensitiveness of Byron's contemporaries.

Biography: Nichol (EML); Noel (GW). See also: Macaulay, Arnold (penetrating), Hazlitt, Rossetti, Swinburne, Lang, Woodberry, More.

Notable recent criticism and biography: Mayne, 2 vols. 1913; Drinkwater's *Pilgrim of Eternity*, 1925. See also: Tinker's "Assault upon the Poets," *Yale Rev.* ns, 14:625-44; K. F. Gerould's "Men, Women and the Byron-Complex," *Atlan.* 130:289-95; C. F. Lawrence's "Personality of Byron," *Edin. Rev.* 239:342-57.

From ENGLISH BARDS AND SCOTCH REVIEWERS [1]

When Vice triumphant holds her sov'reign sway,
Obeyed by all who nought beside obey;
When Folly, frequent harbinger of crime,
Bedecks her cap with bells of every clime;
When knaves and fools combined o'er all prevail,
And weigh their Justice in a Golden Scale;
E'en then the boldest start from public sneers,
Afraid of Shame, unknown to other fears,
More darkly sin, by Satire kept in awe,
And shrink from Ridicule, though not from Law.

Such is the force of Wit! but not belong
To me the arrows of satiric song;
The royal vices of our age demand
A keener weapon, and a mightier hand.
Still there are follies, e'en for me to chase,
And yield at least amusement in the race:
Laugh when I laugh, I seek no other fame,
The cry is up, and scribblers are my game.
Speed, Pegasus!—ye strains of great and small,
Ode! Epic! Elegy!—have at you all!
I, too, can scrawl, and once upon a time
I poured along the town a flood of rime,
A schoolboy freak, unworthy praise or blame;
I printed—older children do the same.
'Tis pleasant, sure, to see one's name in print;
A Book's a Book, although there's nothing in't.
Not that a title's sounding charm can save
Or scrawl or scribbler from an equal grave:
This Lamb [2] must own, since his patrician name
Failed to preserve the spurious farce from shame.

No matter, George continues still to write,
Though now the name is veiled from public sight.
Moved by the great example, I pursue
The self-same road, but make my own review:
Not seek great Jeffrey's, yet like him will be
Self-constituted judge of poesy.

A man must serve his time to every trade
Save censure—critics all are ready made.
Take hackneyed jokes from Miller, [3] got by rote,
With just enough of learning to misquote;
A mind well skilled to find or forge a fault;
A turn for punning—call it Attic salt; [4]
To Jeffrey go, be silent and discreet,
His pay is just ten sterling pounds per sheet;
Fear not to lie, 'twill seem a *sharper* hit;
Shrink not from blasphemy, 'twill pass for wit;
Care not for feelings—pass your proper jest,
And stand a Critic, hated yet caressed.

And shall we own such judgment? No—as soon
Seek roses in December—ice in June;
Hope constancy in wind, or corn in chaff,
Believe a woman or an epitaph,
Or any other thing that's false, before
You trust in Critics, who themselves are sore;
Or yield one single thought to be misled
By Jeffrey's heart, or Lamb's Boeotian head [5]
To these young tyrants, by themselves misplaced,
Combined usurpers on the Throne of Taste;
To these, when authors bend in humble awe,
And hail their voice as Truth, their word as Law;
While these are Censors, 'twould be sin to spare;
While such are Critics, why should I forbear?

. . . .

Behold! in various throngs the scribbling crew,
For notice eager, pass in long review:
Each spurs his jaded Pegasus apace,

[1] Although Byron was stung into making this retort by the *Edinburgh Review's* reception of his *Hours of Idleness*, he had before planned a satirical poem upon contemporary English poets. In later years he regretted his severity, and especially his treatment of Francis Jeffrey, the editor of the journal, whom he had wrongly suspected of writing the offending article.

[2] George (son of Sir Peniston) Lamb, author of an unsuccessful farce

[3] "Joe" Miller, an 18th century actor and the reputed author of a famous compilation of jests.

[4] wit

[5] The Boeotians were proverbial for dullness.

And Rime and Blank maintain an equal race;
Sonnets on sonnets crowd, and ode on ode;
And Tales of Terror [1] jostle on the road;
Immeasurable measures move along; [2]
For simpering Folly loves a varied song,
To strange, mysterious Dullness still the friend,
Admires the strain she cannot comprehend.
Thus Lays of Minstrels—may they be the last!—
On half-strung harps whine mournful to the blast,
While mountain spirits prate to river sprites,
That dames may listen to the sound at nights;
And goblin brats, of Gilpin Horner's brood, [3]
Decoy young Border-nobles through the wood,
And skip at every step, Lord knows how high,
And frighten foolish babes, the Lord knows why;
While high-born ladies in their magic cell,
Forbidding knights to read who cannot spell,
Despatch a courier to a wizard's grave,
And fight with honest men to shield a knave.

Next view in state, proud prancing on his roan,
The golden-crested haughty Marmion,
Now forging scrolls, now foremost in the fight,
Not quite a felon, yet but half a knight.
The gibbet or the field prepared to grace—
A mighty mixture of the great and base.
And think'st thou, Scott! by vain conceit perchance,
On public taste to foist thy stale romance,
Though Murray with his Miller [4] may combine
To yield thy muse just half-a-crown per line?
No! when the sons of song descend to trade,
Their bays are sear, their former laurels fade;
Let such forego the poet's sacred name,
Who rack their brains for lucre, not for fame:
Still for stern Mammon may they toil in vain!
And sadly gaze on gold they cannot gain!
Such be their meed, such still the just reward
Of prostituted Muse and hireling bard!
For this we spurn Apollo's venal son, [5]
And bid a long "goodnight to Marmion." [6]

These are the themes that claim our plaudits now;
These are the bards to whom the Muse must bow;
While Milton, Dryden, Pope, alike forgot,
Resign their hallowed bays to Walter Scott.

[1] by "Monk" Lewis
[2] This is a sneer at the new anapestic meters.
[3] Scott's *Lay of the Last Minstrel,* 1805, grew out of a suggestion for a ballad derived from an absurd old Border legend of Gilpin Horner.
[4] publishers
[5] i.e., this bought Orpheus (Scott)
[6] *Marmion,* line 869

The time has been, when yet the Muse was young,
When Homer swept the lyre, and Maro [7] sung,
An epic [8] scarce ten centuries could claim,
While awe-struck nations hailed the magic name:
The work of each immortal bard appears
The single wonder of a thousand years.
Empires have moldered from the face of earth,
Tongues have expired with those who gave them birth,
Without the glory such a strain can give,
As even in ruin bids the language live.
Not so with us, though minor bards, content.
On one great work a life of labor spent:
With eagle pinion soaring to the skies,
Behold the Ballad-monger Southey rise!
To him let Camoens, Milton, Tasso yield,
Whose annual strains, like armies, take the field. [9]
First in the ranks see Joan of Arc advance,
The scourge of England and the boast of France!
Though burnt by wicked Bedford [10] for a witch
Behold her statue placed in Glory's niche:
Her fetters burst, and just released from prison,
A virgin Phoenix from her ashes risen.
Next see tremendous Thalaba come on,
Arabia's monstrous, wild, and wondrous son;
Domdaniel's [11] dread destroyer, who o'erthrew
More mad magicians than the world e'er knew.
Immortal Hero! All thy foes o'ercome,
Forever reign—the rival of Tom Thumb! [12]
Since startled meter fled before thy face,
Well wert thou doomed the last of all thy race!
Well might triumphant Genii bear thee hence,
Illustrious conqueror of common sense!
Now, last and greatest, Madoc spreads his sails,
Cacique [13] in Mexico, and Prince in Wales;
Tells us strange tales, as other travelers do,
More old than Mandeville's, [14] and not so true.
Oh, Southey! Southey! cease thy varied song!
A bard may chant too often and too long;
As thou art strong in verse, in mercy spare!
A fourth, alas! were more than we could bear.
But if, in spite of all the world can say,
Thou still wilt verseward plod thy weary way;
If still in Berkley-Ballads, most uncivil,

[7] Virgil
[8] object of "claim"
[9] Southey's *Joan of Arc,* 1796; *Thalaba the Destroyer,* 1801; *Madoc* (in two parts: *Madoc in Wales, Madoc in Aztlan*), 1805
[10] John Plantagenet, the general of the English forces in France
[11] in Arabian tales, a cavern where magicians were schooled
[12] the hero of a farce by Fielding
[13] chieftain
[14] See p. 68.

Thou wilt devote old women to the devil,[1]
The babe unborn thy dread intent may rue:
"God help thee, Southey," and thy readers, too.

Next comes the dull disciple of thy school,
That mild apostate from poetic rule,
The simple Wordsworth, framer of a lay
As soft as evening in his favorite May,
Who warns his friend[2] to shake off toil and
trouble,
And quit his books, for fear of growing double;
Who, both by precept[3] and example, shows
That prose is verse, and verse is merely prose.
Convincing all, by demonstration plain:
Poetic souls delight in prose insane;
And Christmas stories tortured into rime
Contain the essence of the true sublime.
Thus, when he tells the tale of Betty Foy,
The idiot mother of "an idiot boy,"
A moon-struck, silly lad, who lost his way,
And, like his bard, confounded night with day;
So close on each pathetic part he dwells,
And each adventure so sublimely tells,
That all who view the "idiot in his glory"
Conceive the bard the hero of the story.

Shall gentle Coleridge pass unnoticed here,
To turgid Ode and tumid stanza dear?
Though themes of innocence amuse him best,
Yet still Obscurity's a welcome guest.
If Inspiration should her aid refuse
To him who takes a Pixy for a muse,[4]
Yet none in lofty numbers can surpass
The bard who soars to elegize an ass;
So well the subject suits his noble mind,
He brays, the Laureate of the long-eared kind.

. . . . .

1807-9 1809

MAID OF ATHENS, ERE WE PART

Ζωη μου, σας αγαπω[5]

Maid of Athens, ere we part,
Give, oh, give me back my heart!
Or, since that has left my breast,
Keep it now, and take the rest!
Hear my vow before I go,
Ζωη μου, σας αγαπω.

By those tresses unconfined,
Wooed by each Aegean wind;
By those lids whose jetty fringe
Kiss thy soft cheeks' blooming tinge;
By those wild eyes like the roe,
Ζωη μου, σας αγαπω.

By that lip I long to taste;
By that zone-encircled waist;
By all the token-flowers that tell
What words can never speak so well;
By love's alternate joy and woe,
Ζωη μου, σας αγαπω.

Maid of Athens! I am gone:
Think of me, sweet! when alone.
Though I fly to Istambol,[6]
Athens holds my heart and soul;
Can I cease to love thee? No!
Ζωη μου, σας αγαπω.

1810 *1812*

SHE WALKS IN BEAUTY

She walks in beauty, like the night
Of cloudless climes and starry skies;
And all that's best of dark and bright
Meet in her aspect and her eyes:
Thus mellowed to that tender light
Which heaven to gaudy day denies.

One shade the more, one ray the less,
Had half impaired the nameless grace
Which waves in every raven tress,
Or softly lightens o'er her face;
Where thoughts serenely sweet express
How pure, how dear, their dwelling place.

And on that cheek, and o'er that brow,
So soft, so calm, yet eloquent,
The smiles that win, the tints that glow,
But tell of days in goodness spent,
A mind at peace with all below,
A heart whose love is innocent!

1814 *1815*

THE DESTRUCTION OF SENNACHERIB[7]

The Assyrian came down like the wolf on the
fold,
And his cohorts were gleaming in purple and
gold;
And the sheen of their spears was like stars on
the sea,
When the blue wave rolls nightly on deep
Galilee.

Like the leaves of the forest when summer is
green,
That host with their banners at sunset were
seen;
Like the leaves of the forest when autumn hath
blown,

[1] In Southey's ballad, "The Old Woman of Berkeley," the old woman is carried off by the Devil.
[2] in "The Tables Turned"
[3] in his preface to *Lyrical Ballads*
[4] in *Songs of the Pixies,* containing "Lines to a Young Ass"
[5] "My life; I love you."
[6] Constantinople
[7] *2 Kings,* xix, 35

That host on the morrow lay withered and strown.

For the Angel of Death spread his wings on the blast,
And breathed in the face of the foe as he passed;
And the eyes of the sleepers waxed deadly and chill,
And their hearts but once heaved, and forever grew still!

And there lay the steed with his nostril all wide,
But through it there rolled not the breath of his pride;
And the foam of his gasping lay white on the turf,
And cold as the spray of the rock-beating surf.

And there lay the rider distorted and pale,
With the dew on his brow, and the rust on his mail:
And the tents were all silent, the banners alone,
The lances unlifted, the trumpet unblown.

And the widows of Ashur are loud in their wail,
And the idols are broke in the temple of Baal;
And the might of the Gentile, unsmote by the sword,
Hath melted like snow in the glance of the Lord!

1815 *1815*

SO WE'LL GO NO MORE A-ROVING

So we'll go no more a-roving
So late into the night,
Though the heart be still as loving,
And the moon be still as bright.

For the sword outwears its sheath,
And the soul wears out the breast,
And the heart must pause to breathe,
And love itself have rest.

Though the night was made for loving,
And the day returns too soon,
Yet we'll go no more a-roving
By the light of the moon.

1817 1830

STANZAS WRITTEN ON THE ROAD BETWEEN FLORENCE AND PISA

Oh, talk not to me of a name great in story;
The days of our youth are the days of our glory;
And the myrtle and ivy of sweet two-and-twenty
Are worth all your laurels, though ever so plenty.

What are garlands and crowns to the brow that is wrinkled?
'Tis but as a dead flower with May-dew besprinkled.
Then away with all such from the head that is hoary!
What care I for the wreaths that can *only* give glory!

Oh, Fame!—if I e'er took delight in thy praises,
'Twas less for the sake of thy high-sounding phrases,
Than to see the bright eyes of the dear one discover
She thought that I was not unworthy to love her.

There chiefly I sought thee, *there* only I found thee;
Her glance was the best of the rays that surround thee;
When it sparkled o'er aught that was bright in my story,
I knew it was love, and I felt it was glory.

1821 1830

TO THOMAS MOORE[1]

My boat is on the shore,
And my bark is on the sea;
But, before I go, Tom Moore,
Here's a double health to thee!

Here's a sigh to those who love me,
And a smile to those who hate;
And, whatever sky's above me,
Here's a heart for every fate.

Though the ocean roar around me,
Yet it still shall bear me on;
Though a desert should surround me,
It hath springs that may be won.

Were't the last drop in the well,
As I gasped upon the brink,
Ere my fainting spirit fell,
'Tis to thee that I would drink.

With that water, as this wine,
The libation I would pour
Should be—peace with thine and mine,
And a health to thee, Tom Moore.

1817 1821

[1] The first stanza of this poem was written in 1816, when Byron left England for the last time.

SONNET ON CHILLON

Eternal Spirit of the chainless Mind!
Brightest in dungeons, Liberty! thou art,
For there thy habitation is the heart—
The heart which love of thee alone can bind;
And when thy sons to fetters are consigned—
To fetters, and the damp vault's dayless gloom,
Their country conquers with their martyrdom,
And Freedom's fame finds wings on every wind.
Chillon! [1] thy prison is a holy place,
And thy sad floor an altar—for 'twas trod,
Until his very steps have left a trace
Worn, as if thy cold pavement were a sod,
By Bonnivard! May none those marks efface!
For they appeal from tyranny to God.

1816 1816

THE PRISONER OF CHILLON [2]

My hair is gray, but not with years,
  Nor grew it white
  In a single night,
As men's have grown from sudden fears;
My limbs are bowed, though not with toil,
  But rusted with a vile repose,
For they have been a dungeon's spoil,
  And mine has been the fate of those
To whom the goodly earth and air
Are banned and barred—forbidden fare;
But this was for my father's faith
I suffered chains and courted death;
That father perished at the stake
For tenets he would not forsake;
And for the same his lineal race
In darkness found a dwelling place;
We were seven—who now are one,
  Six in youth, and one in age,
Finished as they had begun,
  Proud of Persecution's rage;
One in fire, and two in field
Their belief with blood have sealed,
Dying as their father died,
For the God their foes denied;
Three were in a dungeon cast,
Of whom this wreck is left the last.

[1] This French word has no very marked accent on either syllable. Byron usually accents the first.

[2] François de Bonnivard was a republican of Geneva who resisted the domination of the Duke of Savoy and was imprisoned for six years (1530-1536) in the castle of Chillon, on the Lake of Geneva (Leman). When the castle was captured by his republican friends, he was released. Byron has greatly idealized the character and has invented the circumstance of the imprisonment and death of the brothers. The poem was composed in two days. Of it Dr. F. I. Carpenter writes: "There is very little action; there is very little ornament; the narrative evolves from within, and is presented with high dramatic fidelity, and with subtle gradation and progression. The situation in itself is bare and simple; the art with which the poet develops it is masterly. Who else, except Dante perhaps, as in the Ugolino episode [*Inferno* 33], could do so much with so little?"

There are seven pillars of Gothic mold,
In Chillon's dungeons deep and old,
There are seven columns, massy and gray,
Dim with a dull imprisoned ray,
A sunbeam which hath lost its way
And through the crevice and the cleft
Of the thick wall is fallen and left;
Creeping o'er the floor so damp,
Like a marsh's meteor lamp:
And in each pillar there is a ring,
  And in each ring there is a chain;
That iron is a cankering thing,
  For in these limbs its teeth remain,
With marks that will not wear away
Till I have done with this new day,
Which now is painful to these eyes
Which have not seen the sun so rise
For years—I cannot count them o'er,
I lost their long and heavy score,
When my last brother drooped and died,
And I lay living by his side.

They chained us each to a column stone,
And we were three—yet, each alone;
We could not move a single pace,
We could not see each other's face
But with that pale and livid light
That made us strangers in our sight:
And thus together—yet apart,
Fettered in hand, but joined in heart,
'Twas still some solace, in the dearth
Of the pure elements of earth,
To harken to each other's speech,
And each turn comforter to each
With some new hope, or legend old,
Or song heroically bold;
But even these at length grew cold.
Our voices took a dreary tone,
An echo of the dungeon stone,
  A grating sound, not full and free
  As they of yore were wont to be;
  It might be fancy, but to me
They never sounded like our own.

I was the eldest of the three,
  And to uphold and cheer the rest
  I ought to do—and did, my best—
And each did well in his degree.
  The youngest, whom my father loved
Because our mother's brow was given
To him, with eyes as blue as heaven—
  For him my soul was sorely moved;
And truly might it be distressed
To see such bird in such a nest;
For he was beautiful as day—
  (When day was beautiful to me
  As to young eagles, being free)—

A polar day, which will not see
A sunset till its summer's gone,
Its sleepless summer of long light,
The snow-clad offspring of the sun:
And thus he was as pure and bright,
And in his natural spirit gay,
With tears for nought but others' ills,
And then they flowed like mountain rills,
Unless he could assuage the woe
Which he abhorred to view below.

The other was as pure of mind,
But formed to combat with his kind;
Strong in his frame, and of a mood
Which 'gainst the world in war had stood,
And perished in the foremost rank
With joy: but not in chains to pine:
His spirit withered with their clank,
I saw it silently decline—
And so perchance in sooth did mine:
But yet I forced it on to cheer
Those relics of a home so dear.
He was a hunter of the hills,
Had followed there the deer and wolf;
To him this dungeon was a gulf,
And fettered feet the worst of ills.

Lake Leman lies by Chillon's walls:
A thousand feet in depth below
Its massy waters meet and flow;
Thus much the fathom-line was sent
From Chillon's snow-white battlement,
Which round about the wave enthralls:
A double dungeon wall and wave
Have made—and like a living grave.
Below the surface of the lake,
The dark vault lies wherein we lay:
We heard it ripple night and day,
Sounding o'er our heads it knocked;
And I have felt the winter's spray
Wash through the bars when winds were high
And wanton in the happy sky;
And then the very rock hath rocked,
And I have felt it shake, unshocked,
Because I could have smiled to see
The death that would have set me free.

I said my nearer brother pined,
I said his mighty heart declined,
He loathed and put away his food;
It was not that 'twas coarse and rude,
For we were used to hunter's fare,
And for the like had little care:
The milk drawn from the mountain goat
Was changed for water from the moat,
Our bread was such as captives' tears
Have moistened many a thousand years,
Since man first pent his fellow men
Like brutes within an iron den;
But what were these to us or him?
These wasted not his heart or limb;
My brother's soul was of that mold
Which in a palace had grown cold,
Had his free breathing been denied
The range of the steep mountain's side;
But why delay the truth?—He died.
I saw, and could not hold his head,
Nor reach his dying hand—nor dead—
Though hard I strove, but strove in vain
To rend and gnash my bonds in twain.
He died, and they unlocked his chain,
And scooped for him a shallow grave
Even from the cold earth of our cave.
I begged them as a boon to lay
His corse in dust whereon the day
Might shine—it was a foolish thought,
But then within my brain it wrought,
That even in death his freeborn breast
In such a dungeon could not rest.
I might have spared my idle prayer—
They coldly laughed, and laid him there:
The flat and turfless earth above
The being we so much did love;
His empty chain above it leant,
Such murder's fitting monument!

But he, the favorite and the flower,
Most cherished since his natal hour,
His mother's image in fair face,
The infant love of all his race,
His martyred father's dearest thought,
My latest care, for whom I sought
To hoard my life that his might be
Less wretched now, and one day free;
He, too, who yet had held untired
A spirit natural or inspired—
He, too, was struck, and day by day
Was withered on the stalk away.
Oh, God! It is a fearful thing
To see the human soul take wing
In any shape, in any mood:
I've seen it rushing forth in blood,
I've seen it on the breaking ocean
Strive with a swoln, convulsive motion,
I've seen the sick and ghastly bed
Of Sin delirious with its dread.
But these were horrors—this was woe
Unmixed with such—but sure and slow:
He faded, and so calm and meek,
So softly worn, so sweetly weak,
So tearless, yet so tender, kind,
And grieved for those he left behind;
With all the while a cheek whose bloom
Was as a mockery of the tomb,

Whose tints as gently sunk away
As a departing rainbow's ray;
An eye of most transparent light,
That almost made the dungeon bright;
And not a word of murmur, not
A groan o'er his untimely lot—
A little talk of better days,
A little hope my own to raise,
For I was sunk in silence—lost
In this last loss, of all the most;
And then the sighs he would suppress
Of fainting nature's feebleness,
More slowly drawn, grew less and less:
I listened, but I could not hear;
I called, for I was wild with fear:
I knew 'twas hopeless, but my dread
Would not be thus admonishèd;
I called, and thought I heard a sound—
I burst my chain with one strong bound,
And rushed to him—I found him not,
I only stirred in this black spot,
I only lived, *I* only drew
The accursèd breath of dungeon-dew;
The last, the sole, the dearest link
Between me and the eternal brink,
Which bound me to my failing race,
Was broken in this fatal place.
One on the earth, and one beneath:
My brothers—both had ceased to breathe.
I took that hand which lay so still,
Alas! my own was full as chill;
I had not strength to stir, or strive,
But felt that I was still alive—
A frantic feeling, when we know
That what we love shall ne'er be so.
I know not why
I could not die,
I had no earthly hope—but faith,
And that forbade a selfish death.

What next befell me then and there
I know not well—I never knew—
First came the loss of light, and air,
And then of darkness, too:
I had no thought, no feeling—none—
Among the stones I stood a stone,
And was scarce conscious what I wist,
As shrubless crags within the mist;
For all was blank, and bleak, and gray;
It was not night, it was not day;
It was not even the dungeon-light,
So hateful to my heavy sight,
But vacancy absorbing space,
And fixedness without a place;
There were no stars, no earth, no time,
No check, no change, no good, no crime,
But silence, and a stirless breath
Which neither was of life nor death;
A sea of stagnant idleness,
Blind, boundless, mute, and motionless!

A light broke in upon my brain—
It was the carol of a bird;
It ceased, and then it came again,
The sweetest song ear ever heard,
And mine was thankful till my eyes
Ran over with the glad surprise,
And they that moment could not see
I was the mate of misery;
But then by dull degrees came back
My senses to their wonted track;
I saw the dungeon walls and floor
Close slowly round me as before,
I saw the glimmer of the sun
Creeping as it before had done,
But through the crevice where it came
That bird was perched, as fond and tame,
And tamer than upon the tree;
A lovely bird, with azure wings,
And song that said a thousand things,
And seemed to say them all for me!

I never saw its like before,
I ne'er shall see its likeness more:
It seemed like me to want a mate,
But was not half so desolate,
And it was come to love me when
None lived to love me so again,
And cheering from my dungeon's brink,
Had brought me back to feel and think.
I know not if it late were free,
Or broke its cage to perch on mine,
But knowing well captivity,
Sweet bird! I could not wish for thine!
Or if it were, in wingèd guise,
A visitant from Paradise;
For—Heaven forgive that thought! the while
Which made me both to weep and smile—
I sometimes deemed that it might be
My brother's soul come down to me;
But then at last away it flew,
And then 'twas mortal, well I knew,
For he would never thus have flown,
And left me twice so doubly lone,
Lone as the corse within its shroud,
Lone as a solitary cloud—
A single cloud on a sunny day,
While all the rest of heaven is clear,
A frown upon the atmosphere,
That hath no business to appear
When skies are blue, and earth is gay.

A kind of change came in my fate,
My keepers grew compassionate;

I know not what had made them so,
They were inured to sights of woe,
But so it was; my broken chain
With links unfastened did remain,
And it was liberty to stride
Along my cell from side to side,
And up and down, and then athwart,
And tread it over every part;
And round the pillars one by one,
Returning where my walk begun,
Avoiding only, as I trod,
My brothers' graves without a sod;
For if I thought with heedless tread
My step profaned their lowly bed,
My breath came gaspingly and thick,
And my crushed heart fell blind and sick.

I made a footing in the wall,
  It was not therefrom to escape,
For I had buried one and all
  Who loved me in a human shape;
And the whole earth would henceforth be
A wider prison unto me:
No child, no sire, no kin had I,
No partner in my misery;
I thought of this, and I was glad,
For thought of them had made me mad;
But I was curious to ascend
To my barred windows, and to bend
Once more, upon the mountains high,
The quiet of a loving eye.

I saw them, and they were the same,
They were not changed like me in frame;
I saw their thousand years of snow
On high—their wide, long lake below,
And the blue Rhone in fullest flow;
I heard the torrents leap and gush
O'er channeled rock and broken bush;
I saw the white-walled, distant town,
And whiter sails go skimming down;
And then there was a little isle,
Which in my very face did smile,
  The only one in view;
A small green isle, it seemed no more,
Scarce broader than my dungeon floor,
But in it there were three tall trees,
And o'er it blew the mountain breeze,
And by it there were waters flowing,
And on it there were young flowers growing,
  Of gentle breath and hue.
The fish swam by the castle wall,
And they seemed joyous each and all;
The eagle rode the rising blast,
Methought he never flew so fast
As then to me he seemed to fly;
And then new tears came in my eye,
And I felt troubled—and would fain
I had not left my recent chain;
And when I did descend again,
The darkness of my dim abode
Fell on me as a heavy load;
It was as is a new-dug grave,
Closing o'er one we sought to save—
And yet my glance, too much opprest,
Had almost need of such a rest.

It might be months, or years, or days,
  I kept no count, I took no note,
I had no hope my eyes to raise,
  And clear them of their dreary mote;
At last men came to set me free;
  I asked not why, and recked not where;
It was at length the same to me,
Fettered or fetterless to be,
  I learned to love despair.
And thus when they appeared at last,
And all my bonds aside were cast,
These heavy walls to me had grown
A hermitage—and all my own!
And half I felt as they were come
To tear me from a second home:
With spiders I had friendship made,
And watched them in their sullen trade,
Had seen the mice by moonlight play,
And why should I feel less than they?
We were all inmates of one place,
And I, the monarch of each race,
Had power to kill—yet, strange to tell!
In quiet we had learned to dwell;
My very chains and I grew friends,
So much a long communion tends
To make us what we are:—even I
Regained my freedom with a sigh.

1816 1816

From CHILDE HAROLD

Waterloo. From Canto III [1]

21

There was a sound of revelry by night,
And Belgium's capital had gathered then
Her Beauty and her Chivalry, and bright
The lamps shone o'er fair women and brave men;
A thousand hearts beat happily; and when
Music arose with its voluptuous swell,
Soft eyes looked love to eyes which spake again,
And all went merry as a marriage bell;
  But hush! hark! a deep sound strikes like a rising knell!

[1] Three days before the battle of Waterloo, on the eve of the battle of Quatre-Bras, the Duchess of Richmond gave a ball in Brussels, which was attended by Wellington and other British officers.

22

Did ye not hear it?—No; 'twas but the wind,
Or the car rattling o'er the stony street;
On with the dance! let joy be unconfined;
No sleep till morn, when Youth and Pleasure meet
To chase the glowing Hours with flying feet—
But hark!—that heavy sound breaks in once more,
As if the clouds its echo would repeat;
And nearer, clearer, deadlier than before!
Arm! Arm! it is—it is—the cannon's opening roar!

23

Within a windowed niche of that high hall
Sat Brunswick's fated chieftain; [1] he did hear
That sound the first amidst the festival,
And caught its tone with Death's prophetic ear;
And when they smiled because he deemed it near,
His heart more truly knew that peal too well
Which stretched his father on a bloody bier,
And roused the vengeance blood alone could quell;
He rushed into the field, and, foremost fighting, fell.

24

Ah! then and there was hurrying to and fro,
And gathering tears, and tremblings of distress,
And cheeks all pale, which but an hour ago
Blushed at the praise of their own loveliness;
And there were sudden partings, such as press
The life from out young hearts, and choking sighs
Which ne'er might be repeated; who could guess
If ever more should meet those mutual eyes,
Since upon night so sweet such awful morn could rise!

25

And there was mounting in hot haste: the steed,
The mustering squadron, and the clattering car,
Went pouring forward with impetuous speed,
And swiftly forming in the ranks of war;
And the deep thunder peal on peal afar;
And near, the beat of the alarming drum
Roused up the soldier ere the morning star;
While thronged the citizens with terror dumb,
Or whispering, with white lips—"The foe, they come! they come!"

26

And wild and high the "Cameron's gathering" rose!
The war-note of Lochiel, [2] which Albyn's [3] hills
Have heard, and heard, too, have her Saxon [4] foes:—
How in the noon of night that pibroch thrills,
Savage and shrill! But with the breath which fills
Their mountain-pipe, so fill the mountaineers
With the fierce native daring which instills
The stirring memory of a thousand years,
And Evan's, Donald's fame rings in each clansman's ears!

27

And Ardennes [5] waves above them her green leaves,
Dewy with nature's teardrops as they pass,
Grieving, if aught inanimate e'er grieves,
Over the unreturning brave—alas!
Ere evening to be trodden like the grass
Which now beneath them, but above shall grow
In its next verdure, when this fiery mass
Of living valor, rolling on the foe
And burning with high hope, shall molder cold and low.

28

Last noon beheld them full of lusty life,
Last eve in Beauty's circle proudly gay,
The midnight brought the signal-sound of strife,
The morn the marshaling in arms—the day
Battle's magnificently stern array!
The thunder-clouds close o'er it, which when rent
The earth is covered thick with other clay,
Which her own clay shall cover, heaped and pent,
Rider and horse—friend, foe—in one red burial blent!

NIGHT ON LAKE LEMAN. From CANTO III

85

Clear, placid Leman! [6] thy contrasted lake,
With the wild world I dwelt in, is a thing
Which warns me, with its stillness, to forsake
Earth's troubled waters for a purer spring.
This quiet sail is as a noiseless wing
To waft me from distraction; once I loved
Torn ocean's roar, but thy soft murmuring
Sounds sweet as if a sister's voice reproved,
That I with stern delights should e'er have been so moved.

[1] The Duke of Brunswick, nephew of George III; his father was killed at Auerstädt in 1806.

[2] Donald Cameron of Lochiel, chief of the Cameron clan

[3] Scotland's

[4] Lowland and English (Sir Evan Cameron fought against Cromwell.)

[5] a forest, properly Soignies

[6] the Lake of Geneva (Latin *Lemannus*)

86

It is the hush of night, and all between
Thy margin and the mountains, dusk, yet clear,
Mellowed and mingling, yet distinctly seen,
Save darkened Jura, whose capped heights appear
Precipitously steep; and drawing near,
There breathes a living fragrance from the shore,
Of flowers yet fresh with childhood; on the ear
Drops the light drip of the suspended oar,
Or chirps the grasshopper one good-night carol more;

87

He is an evening reveler, who makes
His life an infancy, and sings his fill;
At intervals, some bird from out the brakes
Starts into voice a moment, then is still.
There seems a floating whisper on the hill,
But that is fancy, for the starlight dews
All silently their tears of love instill,
Weeping themselves away, till they infuse
Deep into nature's breast the spirit of her hues.

88

Ye stars! which are the poetry of heaven!
If in your bright leaves we would read the fate
Of men and empires—'tis to be forgiven
That in our aspirations to be great,
Our destinies o'erleap their mortal state,
And claim a kindred with you; for ye are
A beauty and a mystery, and create
In us such love and reverence from afar
That fortune, fame, power, life, have named themselves a star.

89

All heaven and earth are still—though not in sleep,
But breathless, as we grow when feeling most;
And silent, as we stand in thoughts too deep—
All heaven and earth are still. From the high host
Of stars to the lulled lake and mountain coast,
All is concentered in a life intense,
Where not a beam, nor air, nor leaf is lost,
But hath a part of being, and a sense
Of that which is of all Creator and defense.

90

Then stirs the feeling infinite, so felt
In solitude, where we are *least* alone;
A truth which through our being then doth melt,
And purifies from self: it is a tone,
The soul and source of music, which makes known
Eternal harmony, and sheds a charm
Like to the fabled Cytherea's zone,[1]
Binding all things with beauty—'twould disarm
The specter Death, had he substantial power to harm.

91

Not vainly did the early Persian make
His altar the high places, and the peak
Of earth-o'ergazing mountains, and thus take
A fit and unwalled temple, there to seek
The Spirit, in whose honor shrines are weak,
Upreared of human hands. Come, and compare
Columns and idol dwellings, Goth or Greek,
With Nature's realms of worship, earth and air,
Nor fix on fond abodes to circumscribe thy prayer!

92

The sky is changed!—and such a change! O night,
And storm, and darkness, ye are wondrous strong,
Yet lovely in your strength as is the light
Of a dark eye in woman! Far along,
From peak to peak, the rattling crags among,
Leaps the live thunder! Not from one lone cloud,
But every mountain now hath found a tongue,
And Jura answers, through her misty shroud,
Back to the joyous Alps who call to her aloud!

93

And this is in the night: most glorious night!
Thou wert not sent for slumber! Let me be
A sharer in thy fierce and far delight—
A portion of the tempest and of thee!
How the lit lake shines, a phosphoric sea,
And the big rain comes dancing to the earth!
And now again 'tis black—and now the glee
Of the loud hills shakes with its mountain-mirth,
As if they did rejoice o'er a young earthquake's birth.

94

Now, where the swift Rhone cleaves his way between
Heights which appear as lovers who have parted
In hate, whose mining depths so intervene,
That they can meet no more though broken-hearted;
Though in their souls, which thus each other thwarted,
Love was the very root of the fond rage

[1] the cestus (girdle) of Venus, which inspired Love

Which blighted their life's bloom, and then departed:
Itself expired, but leaving them an age
Of years all winters—war within themselves to wage.

95

Now, where the quick Rhone thus hath cleft his way,
The mightiest of the storms hath ta'en his stand:
For here, not one, but many, make their play,
And fling their thunderbolts from hand to hand,
Flashing and cast around; of all the band,
The brightest through these parted hills hath forked
His lightnings—as if he did understand
That in such gaps as desolation worked,
There the hot shaft should blast whatever therein lurked.

96

Sky, mountains, river, winds, lake, lightnings! ye
With night, and clouds, and thunder, and a soul
To make these felt and feeling, well may be
Things that have made me watchful; the far roll
Of your departing voices is the knoll
Of what in me is sleepless—if I rest.
But where of ye, O tempests! is the goal?
Are ye like those within the human breast?
Or do ye find, at length, like eagles, some high nest?

97

Could I embody and unbosom now
That which is most within me—could I wreak
My thoughts upon expression, and thus throw
Soul, heart, mind, passions, feelings, strong or weak,
All that I would have sought, and all I seek,
Bear, know, feel, and yet breathe—into *one* word,
And that one word were Lightning, I would speak;
But as it is I live and die unheard,
With a most voiceless thought, sheathing it as a sword.

98

The morn is up again, the dewy morn,
With breath all incense, and with cheek all bloom,
Laughing the clouds away with playful scorn,
And living as if earth contained no tomb—
And glowing into day. We may resume
The march of our existence: and thus I,
Still on thy shores, fair Leman! may find room
And food for meditation, nor pass by
Much that may give us pause if pondered fittingly.

1816 1816

VENICE. From CANTO IV

1

I stood in Venice, on the Bridge of Sighs;[1]
A palace and a prison on each hand:
I saw from out the wave her structures rise
As from the stroke of the enchanter's wand:
A thousand years their cloudy wings expand
Around me,[2] and a dying glory smiles
O'er the far times, when many a subject land
Looked to the winged Lion's[3] marble piles,
Where Venice sat in state, throned on her hundred isles!

2

She looks a sea Cybele, fresh from ocean,
Rising with her tiara of proud towers[4]
At airy distance, with majestic motion,
A ruler of the waters and their powers;
And such she was—her daughters had their dowers
From spoils of nations, and the exhaustless East
Poured in her lap all gems in sparkling showers.
In purple was she robed, and of her feast
Monarchs partook, and deemed their dignity increased.

3

In Venice Tasso's echoes are no more,[5]
And silent rows the songless gondolier;
Her palaces are crumbling to the shore,
And music meets not always now the ear:
Those days are gone—but Beauty still is here.
States fall, arts fade—but Nature doth not die,
Nor yet forget how Venice once was dear,
The pleasant place of all festivity,
The revel of the earth, the masque of Italy!

4

But unto us she hath a spell beyond
Her name in story, and her long array
Of mighty shadows, whose dim forms despond
Above the dogeless city's vanished sway;
Ours is a trophy which will not decay
With the Rialto;[6] Shylock and the Moor,[7]

[1] the gallery spanning the canal between the ducal palace and the prison
[2] See note on Wordsworth's sonnet, p. 463.
[3] The Lion of St. Mark, surmounting one of the two pillars in the square in front of the palace; it was also the standard of the republic; see st. 14.
[4] As represented in ancient art, the goddess Cybele wore a turreted crown.
[5] Stanzas of Tasso's *Jerusalem Delivered* were once sung by the gondoliers.
[6] here evidently meaning the bridge of the Rialto across the Grand Canal
[7] Othello

And Pierre,[1] cannot be swept or worn away—
The keystones of the arch! though all were o'er,
For us repeopled were the solitary shore.

5

The beings of the mind are not of clay;
Essentially immortal, they create
And multiply in us a brighter ray
And more beloved existence: that which Fate
Prohibits to dull life, in this our state
Of mortal bondage, by these spirits supplied,
First exiles, then replaces what we hate;
Watering the heart whose early flowers have died,
And with a fresher growth replenishing the void.

. . . .

13

Before St. Mark still glow his Steeds of brass,
Their gilded collars glittering in the sun;
But is not Doria's menace come to pass?[2]
Are they not *bridled?*—Venice, lost and won,
Her thirteen hundred years of freedom done,
Sinks, like a seaweed, into whence she rose!
Better be whelmed beneath the waves, and shun,
Even in destruction's depth, her foreign foes,
From whom submission wrings an infamous repose.

14

In youth she was all glory, a new Tyre,
Her very byword sprung from victory,
The "Planter of the Lion," which through fire
And blood she bore o'er subject earth and sea;
Though making many slaves, herself still free,
And Europe's bulwark 'gainst the Ottomite;—
Witness Troy's rival, Candia![3] Vouch it, ye
Immortal waves that saw Lepanto's fight![4]
For ye are names no time nor tyranny can blight.

15

Statues of glass—all shivered—the long file
Of her dead Doges are declined to dust;
But where they dwelt, the vast and sumptuous pile
Bespeaks the pageant of their splendid trust;
Their scepter broken, and their sword in rust,
Have yielded to the stranger: empty halls,
Thin streets, and foreign aspects, such as must
Too oft remind her who and what enthralls,
Have flung a desolate cloud o'er Venice' lovely walls.

16

When Athens' armies fell at Syracuse,
And fettered thousands bore the yoke of war,
Redemption rose up in the Attic Muse,[5]
Her voice their only ransom from afar;
See! as they chant the tragic hymn, the car
Of the o'ermastered victor stops, the reins
Fall from his hands, his idle scimitar
Starts from its belt—he rends his captive's chains,
And bids him thank the bard for freedom and his strains.

17

Thus, Venice, if no stronger claim were thine,
Were all thy proud historic deeds forgot,
Thy choral memory of the Bard divine,
Thy love of Tasso, should have cut the knot
Which ties thee to thy tyrants; and thy lot
Is shameful to the nations—most of all,
Albion! to thee: the Ocean queen should not
Abandon ocean's children; in the fall
Of Venice, think of thine, despite thy watery wall.

18

I loved her from my boyhood; she to me
Was as a fairy city of the heart,
Rising like water-columns from the sea,
Of joy the sojourn, and of wealth the mart;
And Otway, Radcliffe,[6] Schiller,[7] Shakespeare's art,
Had stamped her image in me, and even so,
Although I found her thus, we did not part,
Perchance even dearer in her day of woe,
Than when she was a boast, a marvel, and a show.

ROME. From CANTO IV

78

O Rome! My country! City of the soul!
The orphans of the heart must turn to thee,
Lone mother of dead empires! and control
In their shut breasts their petty misery.
What are our woes and sufferance? Come and see
The cypress, hear the owl, and plod your way
O'er steps of broken thrones and temples, Ye!
Whose agonies are evils of a day—
A world is at our feet as fragile as our clay.

[1] a character in Otway's *Venice Preserved*
[2] This Genoese admiral once threatened to put a bridle on the bronze steeds that adorn St. Mark's.
[3] Crete, once possessed by Venice, but lost again to the Turks
[4] the battle of Lepanto, 1571, a victory over the Turks in which Venice took a leading part
[5] It is said that the Athenian prisoners who could recite Euripides were set free. Cf. page 258.
[6] in *The Mysteries of Udolpho*
[7] in *The Ghost-Seer*

79

The Niobe of nations![1] there she stands,
Childless and crownless, in her voiceless woe;
An empty urn within her withered hands,
Whose holy dust was scattered long ago;
The Scipios' tomb contains no ashes now;
The very sepulchers lie tenantless
Of their heroic dwellers: dost thou flow,
Old Tiber! through a marble wilderness?
Rise, with thy yellow waves, and mantle her distress.

80

The Goth, the Christian, Time, War, Flood, and Fire
Have dealt upon the seven-hilled city's pride;
She saw her glories star by star expire,
And up the steep, barbarian monarchs ride
Where the car climbed the Capitol; far and wide
Temple and tower went down, nor left a site:
Chaos of ruins! Who shall trace the void,
O'er the dim fragments cast a lunar light,
And say, "here was, or is," where all is doubly night?

81

The double night of ages, and of her,
Night's daughter, Ignorance, hath wrapped and wrap
All round us; we but feel our way to err:
The Ocean hath his chart, the stars their map,
And Knowledge spreads them on her ample lap;
But Rome is as the desert, where we steer
Stumbling o'er recollections; now we clap
Our hands, and cry "Eureka!" "It is clear"—
When but some false mirage of ruin rises near.

82

Alas! the lofty city! and, alas,
The trebly hundred triumphs; and the day
When Brutus made the dagger's edge surpass
The Conqueror's sword in bearing fame away!
Alas, for Tully's[2] voice, and Virgil's lay,
And Livy's pictured page—but these shall be
Her resurrection; all beside—decay.
Alas, for Earth, for never shall we see
That brightness in her eye she bore when Rome was free!

. . . .

96

Can tyrants but by tyrants conquered be,
And freedom find no champion, and no child
Such as Columbia saw arise when she
Sprung forth a Pallas, armed and undefiled?
Or must such minds be nourished in the wild,
Deep in the unpruned forest, 'midst the roar
Of cataracts, where nursing Nature smiled
On infant Washington? Has earth no more
Such seeds within her breast, or Europe no such shore?

97

But France got drunk with blood to vomit crime;
And fatal have her Saturnalia been
To freedom's cause, in every age and clime;
Because the deadly days which we have seen,
And vile Ambition that built up between
Man and his hopes an adamantine wall,
And the base pageant last upon the scene,[3]
Are grown the pretext for the eternal thrall
Which nips life's tree, and dooms man's worst—his second fall.

98

Yet, Freedom! yet thy banner, torn but flying,
Streams like the thunderstorm *against* the wind;
Thy trumpet voice, though broken now and dying,
The loudest still the tempest leaves behind;
Thy tree hath lost its blossoms, and the rind,
Chopped by the axe, looks rough and little worth,
But the sap lasts—and still the seed we find
Sown deep, even in the bosom of the North;
So shall a better spring less bitter fruit bring forth.

THE COLISEUM. From CANTO IV

139

And here the buzz of eager nations ran
In murmured pity, or loud-roared applause,
As man was slaughtered by his fellow-man,
And wherefore slaughtered? wherefore, but because
Such were the bloody Circus' genial laws,
And the imperial pleasure. Wherefore not?
What matters where we fall to fill the maws
Of worms—on battle-plains or listed spot?
Both are but theaters where the chief actors rot.

140

I see before me the gladiator lie.[4]
He leans upon his hand—his manly brow

[1] The twelve children of Niobe were slain by Apollo. They are the subject of a famous ancient group of statuary.

[2] Cicero's

[3] the Congress of Vienna, the "Holy Alliance" (which Wellington refused to enter), and the Second Treaty of Paris, according to E. H. Coleridge

[4] suggested by the statue of the Dying Gaul, once supposed to represent a dying gladiator

Consents to death, but conquers agony,
And his drooped head sinks gradually low—
And through his side the last drops, ebbing slow
From the red gash, fall heavy, one by one,
Like the first of a thundershower; and now
The arena swims around him—he is gone
Ere ceased the inhuman shout which hailed the wretch who won.

141

He heard it, but he heeded not—his eyes
Were with his heart, and that was far away:
He recked not of the life he lost, nor prize,
But where his rude hut by the Danube lay,
There were his young barbarians all at play,
There was their Dacian mother—he, their sire,
Butchered to make a Roman holiday—
All this rushed with his blood—Shall he expire,
And unavenged? Arise! ye Goths, and glut your ire!

142

But here, where murder breathed her bloody steam:
And here, where buzzing nations choked the ways,
And roared or murmured like a mountain stream
Dashing or winding as its torrent strays:
Here, where the Roman millions' blame or praise
Was death or life, the playthings of a crowd,
My voice sounds much—and fall the stars' faint rays
On the arena void—seats crushed, walls bowed—
And galleries, where my steps seem echoes strangely loud.

143

A ruin—yet what ruin! From its mass
Walls, palaces, half-cities, have been reared;
Yet oft the enormous skeleton ye pass,
And marvel where the spoil could have appeared.
Hath it indeed been plundered, or but cleared?
Alas! developed, opens the decay,
When the colossal fabric's form is neared:
It will not bear the brightness of the day,
Which streams too much on all years, man, have left away.

144

But when the rising moon begins to climb
Its topmost arch, and gently pauses there;
When the stars twinkle through the loops of time,
And the low night-breeze waves along the air
The garland-forest, which the gray walls wear,
Like laurels on the bald, first Caesar's head; [1]
When the light shines serene but doth not glare,
Then in this magic circle raise the dead:
Heroes have trod this spot—'tis on their dust ye tread.

145

"While stands the Coliseum, Rome shall stand;
When falls the Coliseum, Rome shall fall;
And when Rome falls—the World." From our own land
Thus spake the pilgrims o'er this mighty wall
In Saxon times, which we are wont to call
Ancient; and these three mortal things are still
On their foundations, and unaltered all;
Rome and her Ruin past Redemption's skill,
The World, the same wide den—of thieves, or what ye will.

The Ocean. From Canto IV

178

There is a pleasure in the pathless woods,
There is a rapture on the lonely shore,
There is society, where none intrudes,
By the deep sea, and music in its roar:
I love not man the less, but Nature more,
From these our interviews, in which I steal
From all I may be, or have been before,
To mingle with the Universe, and feel
What I can ne'er express, yet cannot all conceal.

179

Roll on, thou deep and dark blue Ocean—roll!
Ten thousand fleets sweep over thee in vain;
Man marks the earth with ruin—his control
Stops with the shore; upon the watery plain
The wrecks are all thy deed, nor doth remain
A shadow of man's ravage, save his own,
When, for a moment, like a drop of rain,
He sinks into thy depths with bubbling groan,
Without a grave, unknelled, uncoffined, and unknown.

180

His steps are not upon thy paths—thy fields
Are not a spoil for him—thou dost arise
And shake him from thee; the vile strength he wields
For earth's destruction thou dost all despise,
Spurning him from thy bosom to the skies,
And send'st him, shivering in thy playful spray
And howling, to his gods, where haply lies
His petty hope in some near port or bay,

[1] Caesar was glad to cover his baldness with the wreath of laurel which the senate decreed he should wear.

And dashest him again to earth—there let
him lay.[1]

181

The armaments which thunderstrike the walls
Of rock-built cities, bidding nations quake,
And monarchs tremble in their capitals,
The oak leviathans, whose huge ribs make
Their clay creator the vain title take
Of lord of thee, and arbiter of war—
These are thy toys, and, as the snowy flake,
They melt into thy yeast of waves, which mar
Alike the Armada's pride or spoils of Trafalgar.

182

Thy shores are empires, changed in all save thee—
Assyria, Greece, Rome, Carthage, what are they?
Thy waters washed them power while they were free,
And many a tyrant since; their shores obey
The stranger, slave, or savage; their decay
Has dried up realms to deserts: not so thou—
Unchangeable, save to thy wild waves' play,
Time writes no wrinkle on thine azure brow:
Such as creation's dawn beheld, thou rollest now.

183

Thou glorious mirror where the Almighty's form
Glasses itself in tempests; in all time—
Calm or convulsed, in breeze or gale or storm,
Icing the pole, or in the torrid clime
Dark-heaving—boundless, endless, and sublime,
The image of eternity, the throne
Of the Invisible; even from out thy slime
The monsters of the deep are made; each zone
Obeys thee; thou goest forth, dread, fathomless, alone.

184

And I have loved thee, Ocean! and my joy
Of youthful sports was on thy breast to be
Borne, like thy bubbles, onward; from a boy
I wantoned with thy breakers—they to me
Were a delight; and if the freshening sea
Made them a terror—'twas a pleasing fear,
For I was as it were a child of thee,
And trusted to thy billows far and near,
And laid my hand upon thy mane—as I do here.

1817 *1818*

[1] This grammatical error, occurring in so lofty a passage, is perhaps the most famous in our literature. It is quite characteristic of Byron's negligence or indifference.

From DON JUAN

THE SHIPWRECK. From CANTO II[2]

38

But now there came a flash of hope once more;
Day broke, and the wind lulled: the masts were gone,
The leak increased; shoals round her, but no shore,
The vessel swam, yet still she held her own.
They tried the pumps again, and though before
Their desperate efforts seemed all useless grown,
A glimpse of sunshine set some hands to bale—
The stronger pumped, the weaker thrummed[3] a sail.

39

Under the vessel's keel the sail was past,
And for the moment it had some effect.
But with a leak, and not a stick of mast,
Nor rag of canvas, what could they expect?
But still 'tis best to struggle to the last,
'Tis never too late to be wholly wrecked:
And though 'tis true that man can only die once,
'Tis not so pleasant in the Gulf of Lyons.

40

There winds and waves had hurled them, and from thence,
Without their will, they carried them away;
For they were forced with steering to dispense,
And never had as yet a quiet day
On which they might repose, or even commence
A jurymast, or rudder, or could say
The ship would swim an hour, which, by good luck,
Still swam—though not exactly like a duck.

41

The wind, in fact, perhaps was rather less,
But the ship labored so, they scarce could hope
To weather out much longer; the distress
Was also great with which they had to cope
For want of water, and their solid mess
Was scant enough: in vain the telescope
Was used—nor sail nor shore appeared in sight,
Nought but the heavy sea, and coming night.

42

Again the weather threatened—again blew
A gale, and in the fore and after hold
Water appeared; yet, though the people knew
All this, the most were patient, and some bold,

[2] Don Juan, with his servants and his tutor Pedrillo, meets with shipwreck in the Mediterranean.

[3] wove in bits of rope-yarn (usually done to prevent chafing)

Until the chains and leathers were worn through
Of all our pumps—a wreck complete she rolled,
At mercy of the waves, whose mercies are
Like human beings' during civil war.

43

Then came the carpenter, at last, with tears
In his rough eyes, and told the captain he
Could do no more: he was a man in years,
And long had voyaged through many a stormy sea,
And if he wept at length, they were not fears
That made his eyelids as a woman's be,
But he, poor fellow, had a wife and children—
Two things for dying people quite bewildering.

44

The ship was evidently settling now
Fast by the head; and, all distinction gone,
Some went to prayers again, and made a vow
Of candles to their saints—but there were none
To pay them with; and some looked o'er the bow;
Some hoisted out the boats; and there was one
That begged Pedrillo for an absolution,
Who told him to be damned—in his confusion.

45

Some lashed them in their hammocks; some put on
Their best clothes, as if going to a fair;
Some cursed the day on which they saw the Sun,
And gnashed their teeth, and, howling, tore their hair;
And others went on as they had begun,
Getting the boats out, being well aware
That a tight boat will live in a rough sea,
Unless with breakers close beneath her lee.

46

The worst of all was, that in their condition,
Having been several days in great distress,
'Twas difficult to get out such provision
As now might render their long suffering less:
Men, even when dying, dislike inanition;
Their stock was damaged by the weather's stress:
Two casks of biscuit and a keg of butter
Were all that could be thrown into the cutter.

47

But in the longboat they contrived to stow
Some pounds of bread, though injured by the wet;
Water, a twenty-gallon cask or so;
Six flasks of wine; and they contrived to get
A portion of their beef up from below,
And with a piece of pork, moreover, met,
But scarce enough to serve them for a luncheon—
Then there was rum, eight gallons in a puncheon.

48

The other boats, the yawl and pinnace, had
Been stove in the beginning of the gale;
And the longboat's condition was but bad,
As there were but two blankets for a sail,
And one oar for a mast, which a young lad
Threw in by good luck over the ship's rail;
And two boats could not hold, far less be stored,
To save one half the people then on board.

49

'Twas twilight, and the sunless day went down
Over the waste of waters; like a veil
Which, if withdrawn, would but disclose the frown
Of one whose hate is masked but to assail.
Thus to their hopeless eyes the night was shown,
And grimly darkled o'er the faces pale,
And the dim desolate deep. Twelve days had Fear
Been their familiar, and now Death was here.

50

Some trial had been making at a raft,
With little hope in such a rolling sea,
A sort of thing at which one would have laughed
If any laughter at such times could be,
Unless with people who too much have quaffed,
And have a kind of wild and horrid glee,
Half epileptical, and half hysterical—
Their preservation would have been a miracle.

51

At half-past eight o'clock, booms, hencoops, spars,
And all things, for a chance, had been cast loose
That still could keep afloat the struggling tars,
For yet they strove, although of no great use:
There was no light in heaven but a few stars,
The boats put off o'ercrowded with their crews;
She gave a heel, and then a lurch to port,
And, going down head-foremost—sunk, in short.

52

Then rose from sea to sky the wild farewell—
Then shrieked the timid, and stood still the brave—

Then some leaped overboard with dreadful yell,
  As eager to anticipate their grave;
And the sea yawned around her like a hell,
  And down she sucked with her the whirling wave,
Like one who grapples with his enemy,
And strives to strangle him before he die.

53

And first one universal shriek there rushed,
  Louder than the loud ocean, like a crash
Of echoing thunder; and then all was hushed,
  Save the wild wind and the remorseless dash
Of billows; but at intervals there gushed,
  Accompanied with a convulsive splash,
A solitary shriek, the bubbling cry
Of some strong swimmer in his agony.

1818-19 1819

The Isles of Greece. From Canto III[1]

78

And now they were diverted by their suite,
  Dwarfs, dancing girls, black eunuchs, and a poet,
Which made their new establishment complete;
  The last was of great fame, and liked to show it;
His verses rarely wanted their due feet—
  And for his theme—he seldom sung below it,
He being paid to satirize or flatter,
As the psalm says, "inditing a good matter."

79

He praised the present, and abused the past,
  Reversing the good custom of old days,
An Eastern anti-jacobin, [2] at last
  He turned, preferring pudding to *no* praise [3]—
For some few years his lot had been o'ercast
  By his seeming independent in his lays,
But now he sung the Sultan and the Pasha
With truth like Southey, and with verse like Crashaw. [4]

80

He was a man who had seen many changes,
  And always changed as true as any needle;
His polar star being one which rather ranges,
  And not the fixed—he knew the way to wheedle;
So vile he 'scaped the doom which oft avenges;
  And being fluent (save indeed when feed ill),
He lied with such a fervor of intention—
There was no doubt he earned his laureate pension.

. . . .

85

Thus, usually, when he was asked to sing,
  He gave the different nations something national;
'Twas all the same to him—"God save the King,"
  Or, "Ça ira," [5] according to the fashion all.
His muse made increment of anything,
  From the high lyric down to the low rational;
If Pindar [6] sang horse races, what should hinder
Himself from being as pliable as Pindar.

86

In France, for instance, he would write a chanson;
  In England a six canto quarto tale;
In Spain he'd make a ballad or romance on
  The last war—much the same in Portugal;
In Germany, the Pegasus he'd prance on
  Would be old Goethe's (see what says De Stael [7]);
In Italy he'd ape the "Trecentisti"; [8]
In Greece, he'd sing some sort of hymn like this t'ye:

The isles of Greece, the isles of Greece!
  Where burning Sappho loved and sung,
Where grew the arts of war and peace—
  Where Delos [9] rose, and Phoebus sprung!
Eternal summer gilds them yet,
But all, except their sun, is set.

The Scian and the Teian muse, [10]
  The hero's harp, the lover's lute,
Have found the fame your shores refuse:
  Their place of birth alone is mute
To sounds which echo farther west
Than your sires' "Islands of the Blest." [11]

The mountains look on Marathon—
  And Marathon looks on the sea;
And musing there an hour alone,
  I dreamed that Greece might still be free;

[1] Juan and Haidée, the daughter of Lambro, a pirate, and lord of one of the Grecian isles, hold a feast in Lambro's halls during his absence.
[2] anti-revolutionary, anti-democratic
[3] see Pope *The Dunciad*, l. 52
[4] Southey, as poet laureate, flattered royalty. The name of Crashaw serves chiefly for a rime.
[5] a song of the French revolutionists "It will succeed"
[6] an ancient Greek poet who composed songs in honor of the victors in the national games, for which he was doubtless well remunerated
[7] Madame de Staël had lately written a book on Germany.
[8] writers in the Italian style of the 14th century
[9] the birth-place of Phoebus Apollo
[10] Homer was sometimes said to have been born on the isle of Chios (Italian name, Scio). Anacreon was born at Teios in Asia Minor.
[11] the fabled Western Isles, lying somewhere in the Atlantic

For standing on the Persians' grave,
I could not deem myself a slave.

A king sat on the rocky brow
Which looks o'er sea-born Salamis;
And ships, by thousands, lay below,
And men in nations—all were his!
He counted them at break of day—
And when the sun set, where were they?

And where are they? And where art thou,
My country? On thy voiceless shore
The heroic lay is tuneless now—
The heroic bosom beats no more!
And must thy lyre, so long divine,
Degenerate into hands like mine?

'Tis something, in the dearth of fame,
Though linked among a fettered race,
To feel at least a patriot's shame,
Even as I sing, suffuse my face;
For what is left the poet here?
For Greeks a blush—for Greece a tear.

Must *we* but weep o'er days more blest?
Must *we* but blush?—Our fathers bled.
Earth! render back from out thy breast
A remnant of our Spartan dead!
Of the three hundred grant but three,
To make a new Thermopylae!

What, silent still? and silent all?
Ah! no—the voices of the dead
Sound like a distant torrent's fall,
And answer, "Let one living head,
But one arise—we come, we come!"
'Tis but the living who are dumb.

In vain—in vain: strike other chords;
Fill high the cup with Samian wine!
Leave battles to the Turkish hordes,
And shed the blood of Scio's vine!
Hark! rising to the ignoble call—
How answers each bold Bacchanal!

You have the Pyrrhic dance [1] as yet;
Where is the Pyrrhic phalanx [2] gone?
Of two such lessons, why forget
The nobler and the manlier one?
You have the letters Cadmus [3] gave—
Think ye he meant them for a slave?

Fill high the bowl with Samian wine!
We will not think of themes like these!
It made Anacreon's song divine;
He served—but served Polycrates [4]—
A tyrant; but our masters then
Were still, at least, our countrymen.

The tyrant of the Chersonese [5]
Was freedom's best and bravest friend;
That tyrant was Miltiades!
Oh! that the present hour would lend
Another despot of the kind!
Such chains as his were sure to bind.

Fill high the bowl with Samian wine!
On Suli's rock, and Parga's shore, [6]
Exists the remnant of a line
Such as the Doric mothers bore;
And there, perhaps, some seed is sown,
The Heracleidan [7] blood might own.

Trust not for freedom to the Franks—
They have a king who buys and sells;
In native swords and native ranks,
The only hope of courage dwells:
But Turkish force, and Latin fraud,
Would break your shield, however broad.

Fill high the bowl with Samian wine!
Our virgins dance beneath the shade—
I see their glorious black eyes shine;
But gazing on each glowing maid,
My own the burning teardrop laves,
To think such breasts must suckle slaves.

Place me on Sunium's [8] marbled steep,
Where nothing, save the waves and I,
May hear our mutual murmurs sweep;
There, swan-like, let me sing and die:
A land of slaves shall ne'er be mine—
Dash down yon cup of Samian wine!

87

Thus sung, or would, or could, or should have sung,
The modern Greek, in tolerable verse;
If not like Orpheus quite, when Greece was young,
Yet in these times he might have done much worse:
His strain displayed some feeling—right or wrong;
And feeling, in a poet, is the source
Of others' feeling; but they are such liars,
And take all colors—like the hands of dyers. [9]

[1] a war-dance
[2] as employed by the great general, Pyrrhus
[3] Cadmus was said to have introduced the Greek alphabet from Phoenicia.
[4] tyrant (ruler) of Samos, who gave refuge to Anacreon
[5] a Thracian peninsula
[6] in western Greece
[7] i.e., ancient Greek
[8] the southernmost promontory of Attica
[9] Shakespeare: Sonnet 111

88

But words are things, and a small drop of ink,
Falling like dew upon a thought, produces
That which makes thousands, perhaps millions, think;
'Tis strange, the shortest letter which man uses
Instead of speech, may form a lasting link
Of ages; to what straits old Time reduces
Frail man when paper—even a rag like this,
Survives himself, his tomb, and all that's his!

. . . .

101

T' our tale.—The feast was over, the slaves gone,
The dwarfs and dancing girls had all retired:
The Arab lore and poet's song were done,
And every sound of revelry expired;
The lady and her lover, left alone,
The rosy flood of twilight's sky admired;
Ave Maria! o'er the earth and sea,
That heavenliest hour of Heaven is worthiest thee!

102

Ave Maria! blessed be the hour!
The time, the clime, the spot, where I so oft
Have felt that moment in its fullest power
Sink o'er the earth so beautiful and soft,
While swung the deep bell in the distant tower,
Or the faint dying day-hymn stole aloft,
And not a breath crept through the rosy air,
And yet the forest leaves seemed stirred with prayer.

103

Ave Maria! 'tis the hour of prayer!
Ave Maria! 'tis the hour of love!
Ave Maria! may our spirits dare
Look up to thine and to thy Son's above!
Ave Maria! Oh, that face so fair!
Those downcast eyes beneath the Almighty dove—
What though 'tis but a pictured image?—strike—
That painting is no idol,—'tis too like.

104

Some kinder casuists are pleased to say,
In nameless print—that I have no devotion;
But set those persons down with me to pray,
And you shall see who has the properest notion
Of getting into heaven the shortest way;
My altars are the mountains and the ocean,
Earth, air, stars—all that springs from the great Whole,
Who hath produced, and will receive the soul.

105

Sweet hour of twilight!—in the solitude
Of the pine forest, and the silent shore
Which bounds Ravenna's immemorial wood,
Rooted where once the Adrian [1] wave flowed o'er,
To where the last Caesarean fortress stood,
Evergreen forest! which Boccaccio's lore
And Dryden's lay made haunted ground to me, [2]
How have I loved the twilight hour and thee!

106

The shrill cicalas, [3] people of the pine,
Making their summer lives one ceaseless song,
Were the sole echoes, save my steed's and mine,
And vesper bell's that rose the boughs along;
The specter huntsman of Onesti's line,
His hell-dogs, and their chase, and the fair throng
Which learned from this example not to fly
From a true lover—shadowed my mind's eye.

107

O Hesperus! [4] thou bringest all good things—
Home to the weary, to the hungry cheer,
To the young bird the parent's brooding wings,
The welcome stall to the o'erlabored steer;
Whate'er of peace about our hearthstone clings,
Whate'er our household gods protect of dear,
Are gathered round us by thy look of rest;
Thou bring'st the child, too, to the mother's breast.

108

Soft hour! which wakes the wish and melts the heart
Of those who sail the seas, on the first day
When they from their sweet friends are torn apart;
Or fills with love the pilgrim on his way
As the far bell of vesper makes him start,
Seeming to weep the dying day's decay.
Is this a fancy which our reason scorns?
Ah! surely, nothing dies but something mourns!

1819 *1821*

[1] the Adriatic

[2] Dryden's "Theodore and Honoria" is a translation from Boccaccio, an Italian story-teller of the fourteenth century, of the tale of a specter huntsman who haunted this region. Byron lived for some time at Ravenna and frequently rode in the adjoining forest. In Boccaccio's *Decameron,* the tale is the eighth story told upon the fifth day. In this story, Anastasio de gli Honesti—Byron writes it Onesti in stanza 106 above—a specter horseman, perpetually hunts and with the aid of his hounds perpetually seizes a specter lady who has refused his love.

[3] or, cicadas, a general term for insects, like crickets or grasshoppers, that make a chirping noise

[4] the evening star

PERCY BYSSHE SHELLEY
1792-1822

Shelley was the grandson of a wealthy, conservative country baronet to whose estates he was heir presumptive. An unfortunate early marriage with Harriet Westbrook, whom he deserted, and his subsequent elopement with Mary, daughter of the radical publicist and reformer, William Godwin, brought estrangement from his family. The rest of his life he spent abroad, mostly in Italy, where he was frequently in touch with Byron and other Englishmen of advanced ideas. He was drowned while yachting in the Gulf of Spezia. His first prominent poem was *Queen Mab,* 1813. *The Cenci,* 1819, is a powerful tragedy of medieval Italy. *Prometheus Unbound,* 1820, and *Adonais,* 1821, contain some of his greatest poetry.

During Shelley's boyhood the abstract theories underlying the revolutionary cry of "Liberty, Fraternity, and Equality" found ready acceptance by his generous nature. He wholly rejected the social theorems of the social class in which he was born, and filled his mind with Utopian dreams of perfect freedom. As a propagandist and reformer, he first attracted notice: he was promptly expelled from Oxford when he wrote a tract defending atheism; and he made some public attempts in the cause of Irish reform. Shelley's acknowledged "passion for reforming the world" never forsook him. His doctrines did not countenance physical violence, for, as Mrs. Shelley points out, he felt that "evil is . . . . an accident that might be expelled"; and, further, that "mankind only had to will that there should be no evil, and there would be none." In his relations to society, Shelley revealed a singular innocent benevolence of spirit and a warm zeal to serve mankind, but he also showed a mind incapable of understanding the complexity of social problems or the deep rooting of social prejudices. All of Shelley's critics have noticed the wide gap between his sincere desire to uplift humanity and what he accomplished in that direction. Matthew Arnold characterizes him as "a beautiful *and ineffectual* angel, beating in the void his luminous wings in vain."

It is as a lyric poet that Shelley makes his most notable appeal. Although Byron and Scott, with their more popular verse obscured him in his own day, the next generation gave him full recognition. The unflagging energy of his imagination is almost other-worldly.

Biography: J. A. Symonds (EML), Sharp (GW), W. E. Peck, *Shelley, His Life and Work,* 2 vols., 1927; André Maurois' *Ariel,* 1924, imaginative and illuminating. Criticism: Rossetti, Dowden, Stephen, Lang, Payne, More (Shel. 7), Woodberry. Notable criticism is M. Arnold's "Shelley," *19th C.* 23:23-39, same in Essays; Francis Thompson's *Shelley,* 1909. See also: A. Symons, "Poetry of Shelley," *Atlan.* 100:347-56; G. Slaughter, "Poet's Heritage," *No. Am.* 218:97-108; R. M. Lovett, "Ethical Paradox in Shelley," *New. Rep.* 31:204-6.

ALASTOR, OR THE SPIRIT OF SOLITUDE[1]

Nondum amabam, et amare amabam, quærebam quid amarem, amans amare.[2]—*Confes. St. August.*

Preface

The poem entitled "Alastor" may be considered as allegorical of one of the most interesting situations of the human mind. It represents a youth of uncorrupted feelings and adventurous genius led forth by an imagination inflamed and purified through familarity with all that is excellent and majestic, to the contemplation of the universe. He drinks deep of the fountains of knowledge, and is still insatiate. The magnificence and beauty of the external world sinks profoundly into the frame of his conceptions, and affords to their modifications a variety not to be exhausted. So long as it is possible for his desires to point toward objects thus infinite and unmeasured, he is joyous, and tranquil, and self-possessed. But the period arrives when these objects cease to suffice. His mind is at length suddenly awakened and thirsts for intercourse with an intelligence similar to itself. He images to himself the Being whom he loves. Conversant with speculations of the sublimest and most perfect natures, the vision in which he embodies his own imaginations unites all of wonderful, or wise, or beautiful, which the poet, the philospher, or the lover, could depicture. The intellectual faculties, the imagination, the functions of sense, have their respective requisitions on the sympathy of corresponding powers in other human beings. The Poet is represented as uniting these requisitions, and attaching them to a single image. He seeks in vain for a prototype of his conception. Blasted by his disappointment, he descends to an untimely grave.

The picture is not barren of instruction to actual men. The Poet's self-centered seclusion

[1] The word *Alastor* means, strictly, avenging spirit which is treated here as a spirit of evil, or a spirit leading to disaster; it must not be mistaken for the name of the hero of the poem. In the introduction (lines 1-49) Shelley speaks in his own person; but the Poet whose history he then proceeds to relate bears very markedly his own traits, and the whole must be considered as largely a spiritual autobiography. It is difficult to resist calling attention to some of the features of this impressive poem; to its quiet mastery of theme and sustained poetic power; to its blank-verse harmonies subtler than rimes; to the graphic descriptions, as in lines 239-369, whence Bryant, Poe, and Tennyson have mani festly all drawn inspiration; to occasional lines of an impelling swiftness (612, 613), or occasional phrases of startling strength (676, 681); to the fervent exaltation of self-sacrifice in the prayer that one life might answer for all, and the pangs of death be henceforth banished from the world (609-624); or to the unapproachable beauty of the description of slow-coming death itself—a euthanasia in which life passes away like a strain of music or like an "exhalation." There can be no higher conception of poetry than is implicit in these things.

[2] Not yet did I love, yet I yearned to love; I sought what I might love, yearning to love. "In this vain pursuit of ideal loveliness," said Mrs. Shelley, "is the deeper meaning of 'Alastor' to be found."

was avenged by the furies of an irresistible passion pursuing him to speedy ruin. But that Power which strikes the luminaries of the world with sudden darkness and extinction, by awakening them to too exquisite a perception of its influences, dooms to a slow and poisonous decay those meaner spirits that dare to abjure its dominion. Their destiny is more abject and inglorious as their delinquency is more contemptible and pernicious. They who, deluded by no generous error, instigated by no sacred thirst of doubtful knowledge, duped by no illustrious superstition, loving nothing on this earth, and cherishing no hopes beyond, yet keep aloof from sympathies with their kind, rejoicing neither in human joy nor mourning with human grief; these, and such as they, have their apportioned curse. They languish because none feel with them their common nature. They are morally dead. They are neither friends, nor lovers, nor fathers, nor citizens of the world, nor benefactors of their country. Among those who attempt to exist without human sympathy, the pure and tenderhearted perish through the intensity and passion of their search after its communities, when the vacancy of their spirit suddenly makes itself felt. All else, selfish, blind, and torpid, are those unforeseeing multitudes who constitute, together with their own, the lasting misery and loneliness of the world. Those who love not their fellow-beings live unfruitful lives, and prepare for their old age a miserable grave.

"The good die first,
And those whose hearts are dry as summer dust,
Burn to the socket!. . . ."

December 14, 1815

Earth, ocean, air, belovèd brotherhood!
If our great Mother has imbued my soul
With aught of natural piety [1] to feel
Your love, and recompense the boon with mine;
If dewy morn, and odorous noon, and even
With sunset and its gorgeous ministers,
And solemn midnight's tingling silentness;
If autumn's hollow sighs in the sere wood,
And winter robing with pure snow and crowns
Of starry ice the gray grass and bare boughs;
If spring's voluptuous pantings when she breathes
Her first sweet kisses—have been dear to me;
If no bright bird, insect, or gentle beast
I consciously have injured, but still loved
And cherished these my kindred; then forgive
This boast, belovèd brethren, and withdraw
No portion of your wonted favor now!

Mother of this unfathomable world!
Favor my solemn song, for I have loved
Thee ever, and thee only; I have watched
Thy shadow, and the darkness of thy steps,
And my heart ever gazes on the depth
Of thy deep mysteries. I have made my bed
In charnels and on coffins, [2] where black death
Keeps record of the trophies won from thee,
Hoping to still these obstinate questionings [3]
Of thee and thine, by forcing some lone ghost,
Thy messenger, to render up the tale
Of what we are. In lone and silent hours,
When night makes a weird sound of its own stillness,
Like an inspired and desperate alchemist
Staking his very life on some dark hope,
Have I mixed awful talk and asking looks
With my most innocent love, until strange tears
Uniting with those breathless kisses, made
Such magic as compels the charmèd night
To render up thy charge: and though ne'er yet
Thou hast unveiled thy inmost sanctuary,
Enough from incommunicable dream,
And twilight phantasms, and deep noonday thought,
Has shone within me, that serenely now
And moveless, as a long-forgotten lyre
Suspended in the solitary dome
Of some mysterious and deserted fane,
I wait thy breath, Great Parent, that my strain
May modulate with murmurs of the air,
And motions of the forests and the sea,
And voice of living beings, and woven hymns
Of night and day, and the deep heart of man.

There was a Poet whose untimely tomb
No human hands with pious reverence reared,
But the charmed eddies of autumnal winds
Built o'er his moldering bones a pyramid
Of moldering leaves in the waste wilderness.
A lovely youth—no mourning maiden decked
With weeping flowers, or votive cypress wreath,
The lone couch of his everlasting sleep—
Gentle, and brave, and generous—no lorn bard
Breathed o'er his dark fate one melodious sigh;
He lived, he died, he sung, in solitude.
Strangers have wept to hear his passionate notes,
And virgins, as unknown he passed, have pined
And wasted for fond love of his wild eyes.
The fire of those soft orbs has ceased to burn,
And Silence, too, enamored of that voice,
Locks its mute music in her rugged cell.

By solemn vision and bright silver dream
His infancy was nurtured. Every sight

[1] Wordsworth's phrase; see his "My Heart Leaps Up," p. 458.

[2] According to Hogg, Shelley had actually done this.

[3] Wordsworth's "Ode . . . Immortality," (p. 462) line 142

And sound from the vast earth and ambient air
Sent to his heart its choicest impulses,
The fountains of divine philosophy
Fled not his thirsting lips, and all of great,
Or good, or lovely, which the sacred past
In truth or fable consecrates, he felt
And knew. When early youth had passed he left
His cold fireside and alienated home
To seek strange truths in undiscovered lands.
Many a wide waste and tangled wilderness
Has lured his fearless steps; and he has bought
With his sweet voice and eyes, from savage men,
His rest and food. Nature's most secret steps
He like her shadow has pursued, where'er
The red volcano overcanopies
Its fields of snow and pinnacles of ice
With burning smoke, or where bitumen lakes
On black bare pointed islets ever beat
With sluggish surge, or where the secret caves
Rugged and dark, winding among the springs
Of fire and poison, inaccessible
To avarice or pride, their starry domes
Of diamond and of gold expand above
Numberless and immeasurable halls,
Frequent with crystal column, and clear shrines
Of pearl, and thrones radiant with chrysolite.
Nor had that scene of ampler majesty
Than gems or gold, the varying roof of heaven
And the green earth, lost in his heart its claims
To love and wonder; he would linger long
In lonesome vales, making the wild his home,
Until the doves and squirrels would partake
From his innocuous hand his bloodless food,
Lured by the gentle meaning of his looks,
And the wild antelope, that starts whene'er
The dry leaf rustles in the brake, suspend
Her timid steps to gaze upon a form
More graceful than her own.

His wandering step,
Obedient to high thoughts, has visited
The awful ruins of the days of old:
Athens, and Tyre, and Balbec, and the waste
Where stood Jerusalem, the fallen towers
Of Babylon, the eternal pyramids,
Memphis and Thebes, and whatsoe'er of strange
Sculptured on alabaster obelisk,
Or jasper tomb, or mutilated sphinx,
Dark Aethiopia in her desert hills
Conceals. Among the ruined temples there,
Stupendous columns, and wild images
Of more than man, where marble demons watch
The Zodiac's brazen mystery,[1] and dead men
Hang their mute thoughts on the mute walls around,
He lingered, poring on memorials
Of the world's youth, through the long burning day
Gazed on those speechless shapes, nor, when the moon
Filled the mysterious halls with floating shades
Suspended he that task, but ever gazed
And gazed, till meaning on his vacant mind
Flashed like strong inspiration, and he saw
The thrilling secrets of the birth of time.

Meanwhile an Arab maiden brought his food,
Her daily portion, from her father's tent,
And spread her matting for his couch, and stole
From duties and repose to tend his steps—
Enamored, yet not daring for deep awe
To speak her love—and watched his nightly sleep,
Sleepless herself, to gaze upon his lips
Parted in slumber, whence the regular breath
Of innocent dreams arose: then, when red morn
Made paler the pale moon, to her cold home
Wildered, and wan, and panting, she returned.

The Poet wandering on, through Arabie
And Persia, and the wild Carmanian waste,[2]
And o'er the aërial mountains which pour down
Indus and Oxus from their icy caves,
In joy and exultation held his way;
Till in the vale of Cashmire,[3] far within
Its loneliest dell, where odorous plants entwine
Beneath the hollow rocks a natural bower,
Beside a sparkling rivulet he stretched
His languid limbs. A vision on his sleep
There came, a dream of hopes that never yet
Had flushed his cheek. He dreamed a veilèd maid
Sat near him, talking in low solemn tones.
Her voice was like the voice of his own soul
Heard in the calm of thought; its music long,
Like woven sounds of streams and breezes, held
His inmost sense suspended in its web
Of many-colored woof and shifting hues.
Knowledge and truth and virtue were her theme,
And lofty hopes of divine liberty,
Thoughts the most dear to him, and poesy,
Herself a poet. Soon the solemn mood
Of her pure mind kindled through all her frame
A permeating fire: wild numbers then
She raised, with voice stifled in tremulous sobs
Subdued by its own pathos: her fair hands

[1] figures on the temple of Denderah in Upper Egypt

[2] the desert of Kirman, Persia

[3] in central Asia; poetically regarded as an earthly paradise

Were bare alone, sweeping from some strange harp
Strange symphony, and in their branching veins
The eloquent blood told an ineffable tale.
The beating of her heart was heard to fill
The pauses of her music, and her breath
Tumultuously accorded with those fits
Of intermitted song. Sudden she rose,
As if her heart impatiently endured
Its bursting burthen. At the sound he turned,
And saw by the warm light of their own life
Her glowing limbs beneath the sinuous veil
Of woven wind, her outspread arms now bare,
Her dark locks floating in the breath of night,
Her beamy bending eyes, her parted lips
Outstretched, and pale, and quivering eagerly.
His strong heart sunk and sickened with excess
Of love. He reared his shuddering limbs and quelled
His gasping breath, and spread his arms to meet
Her panting bosom—she drew back awhile,
Then, yielding to the irresistible joy,
With frantic gesture and short breathless cry
Folded his frame in her dissolving arms.
Now blackness veiled his dizzy eyes, and night
Involved and swallowed up the vision; sleep,
Like a dark flood suspended in its course,
Rolled back its impulse on his vacant brain.

Roused by the shock he started from his trance—
The cold white light of morning, the blue moon
Low in the west, the clear and garish hills,
The distinct valley and the vacant woods,
Spread round him where he stood. Whither have fled
The hues of heaven that canopied his bower
Of yesternight? The sounds that soothed his sleep,
The mystery and the majesty of Earth,
The joy, the exultation? His wan eyes
Gazed on the empty scene as vacantly
As ocean's moon looks on the moon in heaven.
The spirit of sweet human love has sent
A vision to the sleep of him who spurned
Her choicest gifts. He eagerly pursues
Beyond the realms of dream that fleeting shade;
He overleaps the bounds. Alas! alas!
Were limbs, and breath, and being intertwined
Thus treacherously? Lost, lost, forever lost,
In the wide pathless desert of dim sleep,
That beautiful shape! Does the dark gate of death
Conduct to thy mysterious paradise,
O Sleep? Does the bright arch of rainbow clouds,
And pendent mountains seen in the calm lake,
Lead only to a black and watery depth,
While death's blue vault, with loathliest vapors hung,
Where every shade which the foul grave exhales
Hides its dead eye from the detested day,
Conducts, O Sleep, to thy delightful realms?
This doubt with sudden tide flowed on his heart;
The insatiate hope which it awakened stung
His brain even like despair.

While daylight held
The sky, the Poet kept mute conference
With his still soul. At night the passion came,
Like the fierce fiend of a distempered dream,
And shook him from his rest, and led him forth
Into the darkness.—As an eagle, grasped
In folds of the green serpent, feels her breast
Burn with the poison, and precipitates
Through night and day, tempest, and calm, and cloud,
Frantic with dizzying anguish, her blind flight
O'er the wide aëry wilderness: thus driven
By the bright shadow of that lovely dream,
Beneath the cold glare of the desolate night,
Through tangled swamps and deep precipitous dells,
Startling with careless step the moonlight snake,
He fled. Red morning dawned upon his flight,
Shedding the mockery of its vital hues
Upon his cheek of death. He wandered on
Till vast Aornos [1] seen from Petra's steep,
Hung o'er the low horizon like a cloud;
Through Balk, and where the desolated tombs
Of Parthian kings scatter to every wind
Their wasting dust, wildly he wandered on,
Day after day, a weary waste of hours,
Bearing within his life the brooding care
That ever fed on its decaying flame.
And now his limbs were lean; his scattered hair
Sered by the autumn of strange suffering
Sung dirges in the wind: his listless hand
Hung like dead bone within its withered skin;
Life, and the luster that consumed it, shone
As in a furnace burning secretly
From his dark eyes alone. The cottagers,
Who minstered with human charity
His human wants, beheld with wondering awe
Their fleeting visitant. The mountaineer,
Encountering on some dizzy precipice
That spectral form, deemed that the Spirit of wind
With lightning eyes, and eager breath, and feet
Disturbing not the drifted snow, had paused
In its career. The infant would conceal
His troubled visage in his mother's robe

[1] Aornos was a city in Bactria (Balk).

In terror at the glare of those wild eyes,
To remember their strange light in many a dream
Of after-times; but youthful maidens, taught
By nature, would interpret half the woe
That wasted him, would call him with false names
Brother, and friend, would press his pallid hand
At parting, and watch, dim through tears, the path
Of his departure from their father's door.

At length upon the lone Chorasmian shore [1]
He paused, a wide and melancholy waste
Of putrid marshes. A strong impulse urged
His steps to the seashore. A swan was there,
Beside a sluggish stream among the reeds.
It rose as he approached, and with strong wings
Scaling the upward sky, bent its bright course
High over the immeasurable main.
His eyes pursued its flight.—"Thou hast a home,
Beautiful bird; thou voyagest to thine home,
Where thy sweet mate will twine her downy neck
With thine, and welcome thy return with eyes
Bright in the luster of their own fond joy.
And what am I that I should linger here,
With voice far sweeter than thy dying notes,
Spirit more vast than thine, frame more attuned
To beauty, wasting these surpassing powers
In the deaf air, to the blind earth, and heaven
That echoes not my thoughts?" A gloomy smile
Of desperate hope wrinkled his quivering lips.
For sleep, he knew, kept most relentlessly
Its precious charge, and silent death exposed,
Faithless perhaps as sleep, a shadowy lure,
With doubtful smile mocking its own strange charms.

Startled by his own thoughts he looked around.
There was no fair fiend near him, not a sight
Or sound of awe but in his own deep mind.
A little shallop floating near the shore
Caught the impatient wandering of his gaze.
It had been long abandoned, for its sides
Gaped wide with many a rift, and its frail joints
Swayed with the undulations of the tide.
A restless impulse urged him to embark
And meet lone Death on the drear ocean's waste;
For well he knew that mighty shadow loves
The slimy caverns of the populous deep.

[1] the Aral Sea; apparently meant for the Caspian (Woodberry)

The day was fair and sunny, sea and sky
Drank its inspiring radiance, and the wind
Swept strongly from the shore, blackening the waves.
Following his eager soul, the wanderer
Leaped in the boat, he spread his cloak aloft
On the bare mast, and took his lonely seat,
And felt the boat speed o'er the tranquil sea
Like a torn cloud before the hurricane.

As one that in a silver vision floats
Obedient to the sweep of odorous winds
Upon resplendent clouds, so rapidly
Along the dark and ruffled waters fled
The straining boat. A whirlwind swept it on,
With fierce gusts and precipitating force,
Through the white ridges of the chafèd sea.
The waves arose. Higher and higher still
Their fierce necks writhed beneath the tempest's scourge
Like serpents struggling in a vulture's grasp.
Calm and rejoicing in the fearful war
Of wave ruining on wave, and blast on blast
Descending, and black flood on whirlpool driven
With dark obliterating course, he sat:
As if their genii were the ministers
Appointed to conduct him to the light
Of those belovèd eyes, the Poet sat
Holding the steady helm. Evening came on,
The beams of sunset hung their rainbow hues
High 'mid the shifting domes of sheeted spray
That canopied his path o'er the waste deep;
Twilight, ascending slowly from the east,
Entwined in duskier wreaths her braided locks
O'er the fair front and radiant eyes of day;
Night followed, clad with stars. On every side
More horribly the multitudinous streams
Of ocean's mountainous waste to mutual war
Rushed in dark tumult thundering, as to mock
The calm and spangled sky. The little boat
Still fled before the storm; still fled, like foam
Down the steep cataract of a wintry river;
Now pausing on the edge of the riven wave;
Now leaving far behind the bursting mass
That fell, convulsing ocean. Safely fled—
As if that frail and wasted human form,
Had been an elemental god.

At midnight
The moon arose: and lo! the ethereal cliffs
Of Caucasus, whose icy summits shone
Among the stars like sunlight, and around
Whose caverned base the whirlpools and the waves
Bursting and eddying irresistibly
Rage and resound forever.—Who shall save?—
The boat fled on—the boiling torrent drove—

The crags closed round with black and jagged arms,
The shattered mountains overhung the sea,
And faster still, beyond all human speed,
Suspended on the sweep of the smooth wave,
The little boat was driven. A cavern there
Yawned, and amid its slant and winding depths
Ingulfed the rushing sea.—The boat fled on
With unrelaxing speed. "Vision and Love!"
The Poet cried aloud, "I have beheld
The path of thy departure. Sleep and death
Shall not divide us long!"

The boat pursued
The windings of the cavern. Daylight shone
At length upon that gloomy river's flow;
Now, where the fiercest war among the waves
Is calm, on the unfathomable stream
The boat moved slowly. Where the mountain, riven,
Exposed those black depths to the azure sky,
Ere yet the flood's enormous volume fell
Even to the base of Caucasus, with sound
That shook the everlasting rocks, the mass
Filled with one whirlpool all that ample chasm;
Stair above stair the eddying water rose,
Circling immeasurably fast, and laved
With alternating dash the gnarlèd roots
Of mighty trees that stretched their giant arms
In darkness over it. I' the midst was left,
Reflecting, yet distorting every cloud,
A pool of treacherous and tremendous calm.
Seized by the sway of the ascending stream,
With dizzy swiftness, round, and round, and round,
Ridge after ridge the straining boat arose,
Till on the verge of the extremest curve,
Where, through an opening of the rocky bank,
The waters overflow, and a smooth spot
Of glassy quiet mid those battling tides
Is left, the boat paused shuddering. Shall it sink
Down the abyss? Shall the reverting stress
Of that resistless gulf embosom it?
Now shall it fall? A wandering stream of wind,
Breathed from the west, has caught the expanded sail,
And, lo! with gentle motion, between banks
Of mossy slope, and on a placid stream,
Beneath a woven grove it sails, and hark!
The ghastly torrent mingles its far roar
With the breeze murmuring in the musical woods.
Where the embowering trees recede and leave
A little space of green expanse, the cove
Is closed by meeting banks, whose yellow flowers
Forever gaze on their own drooping eyes,
Reflected in the crystal calm. The wave
Of the boat's motion marred their pensive task,
Which nought but vagrant bird, or wanton wind,
Or falling spear-grass, or their own decay
Had e'er disturbed before. The Poet longed
To deck with their bright hues his withered hair,
But on his heart its solitude returned,
And he forebore. Not the strong impulse hid
In those flushed cheeks, bent eyes, and shadowy frame
Had yet performed its ministry: it hung
Upon his life, as lightning in a cloud
Gleams, hovering ere it vanish, ere the floods
Of night close over it.

The noonday sun
Now shone upon the forest, one vast mass
Of mingling shade, whose brown magnificence
A narrow vale embosoms. There, huge caves,
Scooped in the dark base of their aëry rocks,
Mocking its moans, respond and roar forever.
The meeting boughs and implicated leaves
Wove twilight o'er the Poet's path, as led
By love, or dream, or god, or mightier Death,
He sought in Nature's dearest haunt some bank,
Her cradle, and his sepulcher. More dark
And dark the shades accumulate. The oak,
Expanding its immense and knotty arms,
Embraces the light beech. The pyramids
Of the tall cedar overarching frame
Most solemn domes within, and far below,
Like clouds suspended in an emerald sky,
The ash and acacia floating hang
Tremulous and pale. Like restless serpents, clothed
In rainbow and in fire, the parasites,
Starred with ten thousand blossoms, flow around
The gray trunks, and, as gamesome infants' eyes,
With gentle meanings, and most innocent wiles,
Fold their beams round the hearts of those that love,
These twine their tendrils with the wedded boughs
Uniting their close union; the woven leaves
Make network of the dark blue light of day,
And the night's noontide clearness, mutable
As shapes in the weird clouds. Soft mossy lawns
Beneath these canopies extend their swells,
Fragrant with perfumed herbs, and eyed with blooms
Minute yet beautiful. One darkest glen
Sends from its woods of musk rose, twined with jasmine,
A soul-dissolving odor, to invite
To some more lovely mystery. Through the dell,
Silence and Twilight here, twin-sisters, keep

Their noonday watch, and sail among the shades,
Like vaporous shapes half seen; beyond, a well,
Dark, gleaming, and of most translucent wave,
Images all the woven boughs above,
And each depending leaf, and every speck
Of azure sky, darting between their chasms;
Nor aught else in the liquid mirror laves
Its portraiture, but some inconstant star
Between one foliaged lattice twinkling fair,
Or painted bird, sleeping beneath the moon,
Or gorgeous insect floating motionless,
Unconscious of the day, ere yet his wings
Have spread their glories to the gaze of noon.

Hither the Poet came. His eyes beheld
Their own wan light through the reflected lines
Of his thin hair, distinct in the dark depth
Of that still fountain; as the human heart,
Gazing in dreams over the gloomy grave,
Sees its own treacherous likeness there. He heard
The motion of the leaves, the grass that sprung
Startled and glanced and trembled even to feel
An unaccustomed presence, and the sound
Of the sweet brook that from the secret springs
Of that dark fountain rose. A Spirit seemed
To stand beside him—clothed in no bright robes
Of shadowy silver or enshrining light,
Borrowed from aught the visible world affords
Of grace, or majesty, or mystery—
But undulating woods, and silent well,
And leaping rivulet, and evening gloom
Now deepening the dark shades, for speech assuming,
Held commune with him, as if he and it
Were all that was; only—when his regard
Was raised by intense pensiveness—two eyes,
Two starry eyes, hung in the gloom of thought,
And seemed with their serene and azure smiles
To beckon him.

Obedient to the light
That shone within his soul, he went, pursuing
The windings of the dell. The rivulet
Wanton and wild, through many a green ravine
Beneath the forest flowed. Sometimes it fell
Among the moss with hollow harmony
Dark and profound. Now on the polished stones
It danced, like childhood laughing as it went:
Then through the plain in tranquil wanderings crept,
Reflecting every herb and drooping bud
That overhung its quietness. "O stream!
Whose source is inaccessibly profound,
Whither do thy mysterious waters tend?
Thou imagest my life. Thy darksome stillness,
Thy dazzling waves, thy loud and hollow gulfs,
Thy searchless fountain, and invisible course
Have each their type in me; and the wide sky,
And measureless ocean may declare as soon
What oozy cavern or what wandering cloud
Contains thy waters, as the universe
Tell where these living thoughts reside, when stretched
Upon thy flowers my bloodless limbs shall waste
I' the passing wind!"

Beside the grassy shore
Of the small stream he went; he did impress
On the green moss his tremulous step that caught
Strong shuddering from his burning limbs. As one
Roused by some joyous madness from the couch
Of fever, he did move; yet not like him
Forgetful of the grave, where, when the flame
Of his frail exultation shall be spent,
He must descend. With rapid steps he went
Beneath the shade of trees, beside the flow
Of the wild babbling rivulet; and now
The forest's solemn canopies were changed
For the uniform and lightsome evening sky.
Gray rocks did peep from the spare moss, and stemmed
The struggling brook; tall spires of windlestrae[1]
Threw their thin shadows down the rugged slope,
And nought but gnarled roots of ancient pines
Branchless and blasted, clenched with grasping roots
The unwilling soil. A gradual change was here,
Yet ghastly. For, as fast years flow away,
The smooth brow gathers, and the hair grows thin
And white, and where irradiate dewy eyes
Had shone, gleam stony orbs—so from his steps
Bright flowers departed, and the beautiful shade
Of the green groves, with all their odorous winds
And musical motions. Calm, he still pursued
The stream that with a larger volume now
Rolled through the labyrinthine dell, and there
Fretted a path through its descending curves
With its wintry speed. On every side now rose
Rocks, which, in unimaginable forms,
Lifted their black and barren pinnacles
In the light of evening, and, its precipice
Obscuring the ravine, disclosed above,
Mid toppling stones, black gulfs and yawning caves,
Whose windings gave ten thousand various tongues
To the loud stream. Lo! where the pass expands

[1] withered grass stalks

Its stony jaws, the abrupt mountain breaks,
And seems, with its accumulated crags,
To overhang the world: for wide expand
Beneath the wan stars and descending moon
Islanded seas, blue mountains, mighty streams,
Dim tracts and vast, robed in the lustrous gloom
Of leaden colored even, and fiery hills
Mingling their flames with twilight on the verge
Of the remote horizon. The near scene,
In naked and severe simplicity,
Made contrast with the universe. A pine,
Rock-rooted, stretched athwart the vacancy
Its swinging boughs, to each inconstant blast
Yielding one only response, at each pause
In most familiar cadence, with the howl,
The thunder and the hiss of homeless streams
Mingling its solemn song, whilst the broad river,
Foaming and hurrying o'er its rugged path,
Fell into that immeasurable void
Scattering its waters to the passing winds.

Yet the gray precipice and solemn pine
And torrent were not all—one silent nook
Was there. Even on the edge of that vast mountain,
Upheld by knotty roots and fallen rocks,
It overlooked in its serenity
The dark earth, and the bending vault of stars.
It was a tranquil spot that seemed to smile
Even in the lap of horror. Ivy clasped
The fissured stones with its entwining arms,
And did embower with leaves forever green,
And berries dark, the smooth and even space
Of its inviolated floor, and here
The children of the autumnal whirlwind bore,
In wanton sport, those bright leaves, whose decay,
Red, yellow, or ethereally pale,
Rivals the pride of summer. 'Tis the haunt
Of every gentle wind whose breath can teach
The wilds to love tranquillity. One step,
One human step alone, has ever broken
The stillness of its solitude—one voice
Alone inspired its echoes—even that voice
Which hither came, floating among the winds,
And led the loveliest among human forms
To make their wild haunts the depository
Of all the grace and beauty that endued
Its motions, render up its majesty,
Scatter its music on the unfeeling storm,
And to the damp leaves and blue cavern mold,
Nurses of rainbow flowers and branching moss,
Commit the colors of that varying cheek,
That snowy breast, those dark and drooping eyes.

The dim and hornèd moon hung low, and poured
A sea of luster on the horizon's verge
That overflowed its mountains. Yellow mist
Filled the unbounded atmosphere, and drank
Wan moonlight even to fullness: not a star
Shone, not a sound was heard; the very winds,
Danger's grim playmates, on that precipice
Slept, clasped in his embrace. O storm of Death!
Whose sightless speed divides this sullen night:
And thou, colossal Skeleton, that, still
Guiding its irresistible career
In thy devastating omnipotence,
Art king of this frail world! [1] from the red field
Of slaughter, from the reeking hospital,
The patriot's sacred couch, the snowy bed
Of innocence, the scaffold, and the throne,
A mighty voice invokes thee. Ruin calls
His brother Death. A rare and regal prey
He hath prepared, prowling around the world;
Glutted with which thou mayst repose, and men
Go to their graves like flowers or creeping worms,
Nor ever more offer at thy dark shrine
The unheeded tribute of a broken heart.

When on the threshold of the green recess
The wanderer's footsteps fell, he knew that death
Was on him. Yet a little, ere it fled,
Did he resign his high and holy soul
To images of the majestic past,
That paused within his passive being now,
Like winds that bear sweet music, when they breathe
Through some dim latticed chamber. He did place
His pale lean hand upon the rugged trunk
Of the old pine. Upon an ivied stone
Reclined his languid head, his limbs did rest,
Diffused and motionless, on the smooth brink
Of that obscurest chasm—and thus he lay,
Surrendering to their final impulses
The hovering powers of life. Hope and despair,
The torturers, slept; no mortal pain or fear
Marred his repose, the influxes of sense,
And his own being unalloyed by pain,
Yet feebler and more feeble, calmly fed
The stream of thought, till he lay breathing there
At peace, and faintly smiling—his last sight
Was the great moon, which o'er the western line
Of the wide world her mighty horn suspended,
With whose dun beams in woven darkness seemed
To mingle. Now upon the jaggèd hills

[1] *Par. Lost* II, 1030. X, 597-600.

It rests, and still as the divided frame
Of the vast meteor sunk, the Poet's blood,
That ever beat in mystic sympathy
With nature's ebb and flow, grew feebler still:
And when two lessening points of light alone
Gleamed through the darkness, the alternate gasp
Of his faint respiration scarce did stir
The stagnate night—till the minutest ray
Was quenched, the pulse yet lingered in his heart.
It paused—it fluttered. But when heaven remained
Utterly black, the murky shades involved
An image, silent, cold, and motionless
As their own voiceless earth and vacant air.
Even as a vapor fed with golden beams
That ministered on sunlight, ere the west
Eclipses it, was now that wondrous frame—
No sense, no motion, no divinity—
A fragile lute, on whose harmonious strings
The breath of heaven did wander—a bright stream
Once fed with many-voiced waves—a dream
Of youth, which night and time have quenched forever,
Still, dark, and dry, and unremembered now.

Oh, for Medea's wondrous alchemy, [1]
Which wheresoe'er it fell made the earth gleam
With bright flowers, and the wintry boughs exhale
From vernal blooms fresh fragrance! Oh, that God,
Profuse of poisons, would concede the chalice
Which but one living man [2] has drained, who now
Vessel of deathless wrath, a slave that feels
No proud exemption in the blighting curse
He bears, over the world wanders forever,
Lone as incarnate death! Oh, that the dream [3]
Of dark magician in his visioned cave,
Raking the cinders of a crucible
For life and power, even when his feeble hand
Shakes in its last decay, were the true law
Of this so lovely world! But thou art fled
Like some frail exhalation; which the dawn
Robes in its golden beams—ah! thou hast fled!
The brave, the gentle, and the beautiful,
The child of grace and genius. Heartless things
Are done and said i' the world, and many worms
And beasts and men live on, and mighty Earth,

[1] magic decoction (For example of Medea's witchcraft, see the story of Jason.)
[2] Ahasuerus, the legendary Wandering Jew, said to have been condemned by Christ, for his insolence, to wander till Christ's second coming
[3] i.e., immortal youth

From sea and mountain, city and wilderness,
In vesper low or joyous orison,
Lifts still its solemn voice—but thou art fled;
Thou canst no longer know or love the shapes
Of this phantasmal scene, who have to thee
Been purest ministers, who are, alas!
Now thou art not. Upon those pallid lips
So sweet even in their silence, on those eyes
That image sleep in death, upon that form
Yet safe from the worm's outrage, let no tear
Be shed—not even in thought. Nor, when those hues
Are gone, and those divinest lineaments,
Worn by the senseless wind, shall live alone
In the frail pauses of this simple strain,
Let not high verse, mourning the memory
Of that which is no more, or painting's woe
Or sculpture, speak in feeble imagery
Their own cold powers. Art and eloquence,
And all the shows o' the world are frail and vain
To weep a loss that turns their lights to shade.
It is a woe too "deep for tears," [4] when all
Is reft at once, when some surpassing Spirit,
Whose light adorned the world around it, leaves
Those who remain behind, not sobs or groans,
The passionate tumult of a clinging hope;
But pale despair and cold tranquillity,
Nature's vast frame, the web of human things,
Birth and the grave, that are not as they were.

1815 *1816*

OZYMANDIAS

I met a traveler from an antique land
Who said: "Two vast and trunkless legs of stone
Stand in the desert. Near them, on the sand,
Half sunk, a shattered visage lies, whose frown,
And wrinkled lip, and sneer of cold command,
Tell that its sculptor well those passions read
Which yet survive, stamped on these lifeless things,
The hand that mocked them and the heart that fed. [5]
And on the pedestal these words appear—
'My name is Ozymandias, king of kings.
Look on my works, ye mighty, and despair!'
Nothing beside remains. Round the decay
Of that colossal wreck, boundless and bare
The lone and level sands stretch far away."

1817 *1818*

[4] Wordsworth's "Ode . . . Immortality," last line p. 463
[5] That is, they survived both him who imaged them and him who nursed them.

ODE TO THE WEST WIND [1]

I

O wild West Wind, thou breath of Autumn's being,
Thou, from whose unseen presence the leaves dead
Are driven, like ghosts from an enchanter fleeing,

Yellow, and black, and pale, and hectic red,
Pestilence-stricken multitudes: O thou,
Who chariotest to their dark wintry bed

The wingèd seeds, where they lie cold and low,
Each like a corpse within its grave, until
Thine azure sister of the spring shall blow

Her clarion o'er the dreaming earth, and fill
(Driving sweet buds like flocks to feed in air)
With living hues and odors plain and hill;

Wild Spirit, which art moving everywhere;
Destroyer and preserver; hear, O hear!

II

Thou on whose stream, 'mid the steep sky's commotion,
Loose clouds like earth's decaying leaves are shed,
Shook from the tangled boughs of Heaven and Ocean,

Angels of rain and lightning; there are spread
On the blue surface of thine airy surge,
Like the bright hair uplifted from the head

Of some fierce Maenad, [2] even from the dim verge
Of the horizon to the zenith's height,
The locks of the approaching storm. Thou dirge

Of the dying year, to which this closing [3] night
Will be the dome of a vast sepulcher,
Vaulted with all thy congregated might

[1] Note by Shelley: "This poem was conceived and chiefly written in a wood that skirts the Arno, near Florence. . . The phenomenon alluded to at the conclusion of the third stanza is well known to naturalists. The vegetation at the bottom of the sea, of rivers, and of lakes, sympathizes with that of the land in the change of seasons, and is consequently influenced by the winds which announce it."

The poem has something of the impetuosity of the wind—a breathless swiftness which seems almost to scorn rime, and which is characteristic of many of Shelley's longer poems. Characteristically, too, it breathes his intense "passion for reforming the world," the combination of which with lyric delicacy, as here, is exceedingly rare.

[2] a frenzied priestess of Bacchus

[3] closing in

Of vapors from whose solid atmosphere
Black rain, and fire, and hail will burst; O hear!

III

Thou who didst waken from his summer dreams
The blue Mediterranean, where he lay,
Lulled by the coil of his crystàlline streams,

Beside a pumice isle in Baiae's bay, [4]
And saw in sleep old palaces and towers
Quivering within the wave's intenser day,

All overgrown with azure moss and flowers
So sweet, the sense faints picturing them! Thou
For whose path the Atlantic's level powers

Cleave themselves into chasms, while far below
The sea-blooms and the oozy woods which wear
The sapless foliage of the ocean, know

Thy voice, and suddenly grow gray with fear,
And tremble and despoil themselves: O hear!

IV

If I were a dead leaf thou mightest bear;
If I were a swift cloud to fly with thee;
A wave to pant beneath thy power, and share

The impulse of thy strength, only less free
Than thou, O uncontrollable! If even
I were as in my boyhood, and could be

The comrade of thy wanderings over heaven,
As then, when to outstrip thy skyey speed
Scarce seemed a vision; I would ne'er have striven

As thus with thee in prayer in my sore need.
Oh, lift me as a wave, a leaf, a cloud!
I fall upon the thorns of life! I bleed!

A heavy weight of hours has claimed and bowed
One too like thee tameless, and swift, and proud.

V

Make me thy lyre, even as the forest is:
What if my leaves are falling like its own!
The tumult of thy mighty harmonies

Will take from both a deep, autumnal tone,
Sweet though in sadness. Be thou, spirit fierce,
My spirit! Be thou me, impetuous one!

[4] near Naples, the site of many ruins of ancient luxury

Drive my dead thoughts over the universe
Like withered leaves to quicken a new birth!
And, by the incantation of this verse,

Scatter, as from an unextinguished hearth,
Ashes and sparks, my words among mankind!
Be through my lips to unawakened earth

The trumpet of a prophecy! O Wind,
If Winter comes, can Spring be far behind?

1819 1820

THE INDIAN SERENADE

I arise from dreams of thee
In the first sweet sleep of night,
When the winds are breathing low,
And the stars are shining bright;
I arise from dreams of thee,
And a spirit in my feet
Hath led me—who knows how?
To thy chamber window, sweet!

The wandering airs, they faint
On the dark, the silent stream;
The champak[1] odors fail
Like sweet thoughts in a dream;
The nightingale's complaint,
It dies upon her heart,
As I must die on thine,
Oh, belovèd as thou art!

Oh, lift me from the grass!
I die! I faint! I fail!
Let thy love in kisses rain
On my lips and eyelids pale.
My cheek is cold and white, alas!
My heart beats loud and fast,
Oh, press it close to thine again,
Where it will break at last.

1819 1822

From PROMETHEUS UNBOUND

[Song[2]]

Life of life! thy lips enkindle
With their love the breath between them;
And thy smiles before they dwindle
Make the cold air fire; then screen them
In those looks, where whoso gazes
Faints, entangled in their mazes.

Child of Light! thy limbs are burning
Through the vest which seems to hide them;
As the radiant lines of morning
Through the clouds, ere they divide them;
And this atmosphere divinest
Shrouds thee wheresoe'er thou shinest.

Fair are others; none beholds thee,
But thy voice sounds low and tender
Like the fairest, for it folds thee
From the sight, that liquid splendor,
And all feel, yet see thee never,
As I feel now, lost forever.

Lamp of Earth! where'er thou movest
Its dim shapes are clad with brightness,
And the souls of whom thou lovest
Walk upon the winds with lightness,
Till they fail, as I am failing,
Dizzy, lost, yet unbewailing!

[Asia's Response]

My soul is an enchanted boat,
Which, like a sleeping swan, doth float
Upon the silver waves of thy sweet singing;
And thine doth like an angel sit
Beside a helm conducting it,
Whilst all the winds with melody are ringing.
It seems to float ever, forever,
Upon the many-winding river,
Between mountains, woods, abysses,
A paradise of wildernesses!
Till, like one in slumber bound,
Borne to the ocean, I float down, around,
Into a sea profound of ever-spreading sound.

Meanwhile thy spirit lifts its pinions
In music's most serene dominions;
Catching the winds that fan that happy heaven.
And we sail on, away, afar,
Without a course, without a star,
But by the instinct of sweet music driven;
Till through Elysian garden islets
By thee, most beautiful of pilots,
Where never mortal pinnace glided,
The boat of my desire is guided;
Realms where the air we breathe is love,
Which in the winds on the waves doth move,
Harmonizing this earth with what we feel above.

We have passed Age's icy caves,
And Manhood's dark and tossing waves,
And Youth's smooth ocean, smiling to betray;
Beyond the glassy gulfs we flee
Of shadow-peopled Infancy,

[1] an Indian tree of the Magnolia family
[2] This is the song of an unseen spirit to *Asia*, who is the dramatic embodiment of the spirit of love working through all nature.

Through Death and Birth, to a diviner day;[1]
A paradise of vaulted bowers
Lit by downward-gazing flowers,
And watery paths that wind between
Wildernesses calm and green,
Peopled by shapes too bright to see,
And rest, having beheld; somewhat like thee;
Which walk upon the sea, and chant melodiously!

1818-19 1820

THE CLOUD

I bring fresh showers for the thirsting flowers
From the seas and the streams;
I bear light shade for the leaves when laid
In their noonday dreams.
From my wings are shaken the dews that waken
The sweet buds every one,
When rocked to rest on their mother's breast,
As she dances about the sun.
I wield the flail of the lashing hail,
And whiten the green plains under,
And then again I dissolve it in rain,
And laugh as I pass in thunder.

I sift the snow on the mountains below,
And their great pines groan aghast;
And all the night 'tis my pillow white,
While I sleep in the arms of the blast.
Sublime on the towers of my skyey bowers,
Lightning my pilot sits;
In a cavern under is fettered the thunder,
It struggles and howls at fits;
Over earth and ocean, with gentle motion,
This pilot is guiding me,
Lured by the love of the genii that move
In the depths of the purple sea;
Over the rills, and the crags, and the hills,
Over the lakes and the plains,
Wherever he dream, under mountain or stream,
The spirit he loves remains;
And I all the while bask in heaven's blue smile,
Whilst he is dissolving in rains.

The sanguine sunrise, with his meteor eyes,
And his burning plumes outspread,
Leaps on the back of my sailing rack
When the morning star shines dead,
As on the jag of a mountain crag,
Which an earthquake rocks and swings,
An eagle alit one moment may sit
In the light of its golden wings.
And when sunset may breathe, from the lit sea beneath,
Its ardors of rest and of love,
And the crimson pall of eve may fall
From the depth of heaven above,
With wings folded I rest, on mine airy nest,
As still as a brooding dove.

That orbèd maiden with white fire laden,
Whom mortals call the moon,
Glides glimmering o'er my fleece-like floor,
By the midnight breezes strewn;
And wherever the beat of her unseen feet,
Which only the angels hear,
May have broken the woof of my tent's thin roof,
The stars peep behind her and peer;
And I laugh to see them whirl and flee,
Like a swarm of golden bees,
When I widen the rent in my wind-built tent,
Till the calm rivers, lakes, and seas,
Like strips of the sky fallen through me on high,
Are each paved with the moon and these.

I bind the sun's throne with a burning zone,
And the moon's with a girdle of pearl;
The volcanoes are dim, and the stars reel and swim,
When the whirlwinds my banner unfurl.
From cape to cape, with a bridge-like shape,
Over a torrent sea,
Sunbeam-proof, I hang like a roof—
The mountains its columns be.
The triumphal arch through which I march
With hurricane, fire, and snow,
When the powers of the air are chained to my chair,
Is the million-colored bow;
The sphere-fire above its soft colors wove,
While the moist earth was laughing below.

I am the daughter of earth and water,
And the nursling of the sky;
I pass through the pores of the ocean and shores;
I change, but I cannot die.
For after the rain when with never a stain
The pavilion of heaven is bare,
And the winds and sunbeams with their convex gleams
Build up the blue dome of air,
I silently laugh at my own cenotaph,[2]
And out of the caverns of rain,
Like a child from the womb, like a ghost from the tomb,
I arise and unbuild it again.

1820 1820

[1] In imagination reversing the course of nature, she passes back through the portals of earthly being to the spirit's condition of primordial immortality; see Wordsworth's note, p. 461.

[2] an empty tomb

TO A SKYLARK

Hail to thee, blithe spirit!
Bird thou never wert,
That from heaven, or near it,
Pourest thy full heart
In profuse strains of unpremeditated art.

Higher still and higher
From the earth thou springest
Like a cloud of fire;
The blue deep thou wingest,
And singing still dost soar, and soaring ever singest.

In the golden lightning
Of the sunken sun,
O'er which clouds are brightning,
Thou dost float and run;
Like an unbodied joy whose race is just begun.

The pale purple even
Melts around thy flight;
Like a star of heaven
In the broad daylight
Thou are unseen, but yet I hear thy shrill delight,

Keen as are the arrows
Of that silver sphere,
Whose intense lamp narrows
In the white dawn clear,
Until we hardly see, we feel that it is there.

All the earth and air
With thy voice is loud,
As, when night is bare,
From one lonely cloud
The moon rains out her beams, and heaven is overflowed.

What thou art we know not;
What is most like thee?
From rainbow clouds there flow not
Drops so bright to see,
As from thy presence showers a rain of melody.

Like a poet hidden
In the light of thought,
Singing hymns unbidden,
Till the world is wrought
To sympathy with hopes and fears it heeded not:

Like a highborn maiden
In a palace tower,
Soothing her love-laden
Soul in secret hour
With music sweet as love, which overflows her bower:

Like a glowworm golden
In a dell of dew,
Scattering unbeholden
Its aërial hue
Among the flowers and grass, which screen it from the view:

Like a rose embowered
In its own green leaves,
By warm winds deflowered,
Till the scent it gives
Makes faint with too much sweet those heavy-winged thieves:

Sound of vernal showers
On the twinkling grass,
Rain-awakened flowers,
All that ever was
Joyous, and clear, and fresh, thy music doth surpass.

Teach us, sprite or bird,
What sweet thoughts are thine:
I have never heard
Praise of love or wine
That panted forth a flood of rapture so divine.

Chorus Hymeneal,
Or triumphal chant,
Matched with thine would be all
But an empty vaunt,
A thing wherein we feel there is some hidden want.

What objects are the fountains
Of thy happy strain?
What fields, or waves, or mountains?
What shapes of sky or plain?
What love of thine own kind? what ignorance of pain?

With thy clear keen joyance
Languor cannot be:
Shadow of annoyance
Never came near thee:
Thou lovest, but ne'er knew love's sad satiety.

Waking or asleep,
Thou of death must deem
Things more true and deep
Than we mortals dream,
Or how could thy notes flow in such a crystal stream?

We look before and after,
And pine for what is not;
Our sincerest laughter

With some pain is fraught;
Our sweetest songs are those that tell of saddest thought.

Yet if we could scorn
Hate, and pride, and fear;
If we were things born
Not to shed a tear,
I know not how thy joy we ever should come near.

Better than all measures
Of delightful sound,
Better than all treasures
That in books are found,
Thy skill to poet were, thou scorner of the ground!

Teach me half the gladness
That thy brain must know,
Such harmonious madness
From my lips would flow,
The world should listen then, as I am listening now.

1820 1820

From ADONAIS[1]

[The Grave of Keats]

49

Go thou to Rome—at once the paradise,
The grave, the city, and the wilderness;
And where its wrecks like shattered mountains rise,
And flowering weeds, and fragrant copses dress
The bones of Desolation's nakedness,
Pass, till the Spirit of the spot shall lead
Thy footsteps to a slope of green access
Where, like an infant's smile, over the dead
A light of laughing flowers along the grass is spread.

[1] "John Keats died at Rome of a consumption, in his twenty-fourth [twenty-sixth] year, on the [22d] day of [February], 1821; and was buried in the romantic and lonely cemetery of the Protestants in that city, under the pyramid which is the tomb of Cestius and the massy walls and towers, now moldering and desolate, which formed the circuit of ancient Rome. The cemetery is an open space among the ruins, covered in winter with violets and daisies. It might make one in love with death to think that one should be buried in so sweet a place."—From Shelley's Preface. "Adonais" is of course a poetical name for Keats. The elegy was the outcome of Shelley's noble indignation over a death which he somewhat mistakenly supposed was immediately due to the savage criticism of Keats's reviewers—"Wretched men," as he characterized them, who "know not what they do," murderers who had "spoken daggers but used none." The especially beautiful concluding stanzas, which are given here, are almost purely personal; Shelley is communing with himself, and thinking of his own troubled life.

50

And gray walls molder round, on which dull Time
Feeds, like slow fire upon a hoary brand;
And one keen pyramid with wedge sublime,
Pavilioning the dust of him who planned
This refuge for his memory, doth stand
Like flame transformed to marble; and beneath,
A field is spread, on which a newer band
Have pitched in heaven's smile their camp of death
Welcoming him we lose with scarce extinguished breath.

51

Here pause: these graves are all too young as yet
To have outgrown the sorrow which consigned
Its charge to each; and if the seal is set,
Here, on one fountain of a mourning mind,
Break it not thou! too surely shalt thou find
Thine own well full, if thou returnest home,
Of tears and gall. From the world's bitter wind
Seek shelter in the shadow of the tomb.
What Adonais is, why fear we to become?

52

The One remains, the many change and pass;
Heaven's light forever shines, Earth's shadows fly;
Life, like a dome of many-colored glass,
Stains the white radiance of Eternity
Until Death tramples it to fragments.—Die,
If thou wouldst be with that which thou dost seek!
Follow where all is fled!—Rome's azure sky,
Flowers, ruins, statues, music, words, are weak,
The glory they transfuse with fitting truth to speak.

53

Why linger, why turn back, why shrink, my Heart?
Thy hopes are gone before: from all things here
They have departed: thou shouldst now depart!
A light is past from the revolving year,
And man, and woman; and what still is dear
Attracts to crush, repels to make thee wither.
The soft sky smiles—the low wind whispers near;
'Tis Adonais calls! oh, hasten thither,
No more let life divide what Death can join together.

54

That Light whose smile kindles the Universe,
That Beauty in which all things work and move,

That Benediction which the eclipsing Curse
Of birth can quench not, that sustaining Love
Which through the web of being blindly wove
By man and beast and earth and air and sea,
Burns bright or dim, as each are mirrors of
The fire for which all thirst; now beams on me,
Consuming the last clouds of cold mortality.

55

The breath whose might I have invoked in song
Descends on me; my spirit's bark is driven
Far from the shore, far from the trembling throng
Whose sails were never to the tempest given;
The massy earth and spherèd skies are riven!
I am borne darkly, fearfully, afar;
Whilst burning through the inmost veil of Heaven,
The soul of Adonais, like a star,
Beacons from the abode where the Eternal are.

1821 1821

From HELLAS[1]

Chorus

The world's great age begins anew,
The golden years return,
The earth doth like a snake renew
Her winter weeds[2] outworn:
Heaven smiles, and faiths and empires[3] gleam
Like wrecks of a dissolving dream.

A brighter Hellas rears its mountains
From waves serener far;
A new Peneus rolls his fountains
Against the morning star.
Where fairer Tempes bloom, there sleep
Young Cyclads on a sunnier deep.

A loftier Argo cleaves the main,
Fraught with a later prize;
Another Orpheus sings again,
And loves, and weeps, and dies.
A new Ulysses leaves once more
Calypso for his native shore.

[1] Shelley's drama of the modern Greeks' struggle for independence concludes with this Chorus, prophesying the return of that Golden Age when Saturn was fabled to have reigned over a universe of peace and love. Of the fulfillment of this prophecy Shelley had at times an ardent hope, which reaches perhaps its highest expression in this Chorus (with which compare Byron's "Isles of Greece"), and at other times a profound despair, which can easily be read in some of the lyrics that are given on subsequent pages.

[2] robes

[3] creeds and monarchies (to which, as such, Shelley was devotedly hostile)

Oh, write no more the tale of Troy,[4]
If earth death's scroll must be!
Nor mix with Laian rage the joy
Which dawns upon the free:
Although a subtler Sphinx renew
Riddles of death Thebes never knew.

Another Athens shall arise,
And to remoter time
Bequeath, like sunset to the skies,
The splendor of its prime;
And leave, if nought so bright may live,
All earth can take or Heaven can give.

Saturn and love their long repose
Shall burst, more bright and good
Than all who fell,[5] than One who rose,[6]
Than many unsubdued;[7]
Not gold, not blood, their altar dowers,
But votive tears and symbol flowers.

Oh, cease! must hate and death return?
Cease! must men kill and die?
Cease! Drain not to its dregs the urn
Of bitter prophecy.
The world is weary of the past,
Oh, might it die or rest at last!

1821 1822

TO ———

Music, when soft voices die,
Vibrates in the memory;
Odors, when sweet violets sicken,
Live within the sense they quicken.

Rose leaves, when the rose is dead,
Are heaped for the belovèd's bed;
And so thy thoughts, when thou art gone,
Love itself shall slumber on.

1821 1824

TO ———

One word is too often profaned
For me to profane it,
One feeling too falsely disdained
For thee to disdain it;
One hope is too like despair
For prudence to smother,
And pity from thee more dear
Than that from another.

I can give not what men call love,
But wilt thou accept not

[4] The more or less historic Trojan War, and the woes of the Theban house of Laius and his son Oedipus, belong of course to a time succeeding the Golden Age of fable.

[5] pagan gods

[6] Christ

[7] objects of heathen idolatry

The worship the heart lifts above
And the heavens reject not—
The desire of the moth for the star,
Of the night for the morrow,
The devotion to something afar
From the sphere of our sorrow?

1821 1824

A LAMENT

O world! O life! O time!
On whose last steps I climb,
Trembling at that where I had stood before;
When will return the glory of your prime?
No more—oh, never more!

Out of the day and night
A joy has taken flight;
Fresh spring, and summer, and winter hoar,
Move my faint heart with grief, but with delight
No more—oh, never more!

1821 1824

WHEN THE LAMP IS SHATTERED

When the lamp is shattered,
The light in the dust lies dead—
When the cloud is scattered,
The rainbow's glory is shed.
When the lute is broken,
Sweet tones are remembered not;
When the lips have spoken,
Loved accents are soon forgot.

As music and splendor
Survive not the lamp and the lute,
The heart's echoes render
No song when the spirit is mute—
No song but sad dirges,
Like the wind through a ruined cell,
Or the mournful surges
That ring the dead seaman's knell.

When hearts have once mingled,
Love first leaves the well-built nest;
The weak one is singled
To endure what it once possessed.
O Love! who bewailest
The frailty of all things here,
Why choose you the frailest
For your cradle, your home, and your bier?

Its passions will rock thee
As the storms rock the ravens on high;
Bright reason will mock thee,
Like the sun from a wintry sky.
From thy nest every rafter
Will rot, and thine eagle home
Leave thee naked to laughter,
When leaves fall and cold winds come.

1822 1824

A DIRGE

Rough wind, that moanest loud
Grief too sad for song;
Wild wind, when sullen cloud
Knells all the night long;
Sad storm, whose tears are vain,
Bare woods, whose branches strain,
Deep caves and dreary main,
Wail, for the world's wrong!

1822 1824

JOHN KEATS 1795-1821

Keats, often grouped, in time, with Byron and Shelley, was youngest and shortest lived of the three. He was born in London. His parents, ambitious working people, gave him such school advantages as they could afford, and apprenticed him to a surgeon; but before he had finished his term he came into contact with literature that fired his imagination and awakened his genius. Leigh Hunt, poet and liberal journalist, and Hazlitt, also of the liberal group, encouraged and helped him. His first book of poems, chiefly because it was patronized by liberals, was savagely reviewed by Lockhart, son-in-law of Scott, in the Tory *Edinburgh Review*. The criticism was personal and scurrilous, and unfair in almost every particular. Keats was wounded but not daunted; for he set immediately at work upon a new volume, *Endymion,* published the following year, 1818. Two years later came his final volume including "Lamia," "The Eve of St. Agnes," "Hyperion," and most of the odes and sonnets that we associate oftenest with his name. Within a year he died of consumption at Rome.

The memory of Keats will always carry conjectures of what longer life might have brought from one who in so brief space had written poetry destined to last with the English language. Exquisite joy in all that delights the senses, the passionate yearning to express this, and frequently, perfect workmanship, are the enduring characteristics of Keats. His influence is to be seen throughout the following generation of poets; and particularly through Tennyson, whose early work, especially, was strongly affected by Keats.

Biographies: Rossetti (GW); notable, recent, Colvin (EML), 1917, and Amy Lowell, 2 vols. 1925 (reviewed, with criticism by C. B. Tinker, *Sat. Rev. of Lit.* 1:521-22; C. Aiken, *Dial* 78: 475-90; S. C. Chew, *No. Am.* 221:545-55). Criticism: Arnold, Payne, Rossetti, Swinburne, More (Shel. 4), Woodberry. See also G. Bradford, "Bare Souls," *Harp.* 149:259-70.

From ENDYMION

PROEM. From BOOK I

A thing of beauty is a joy forever:
Its loveliness increases; it will never
Pass into nothingness; but still will keep
A bower quiet for us, and a sleep
Full of sweet dreams, and health, and quiet breathing.
Therefore, on every morrow,[1] are we wreathing
A flowery band to bind us to the earth,
Spite of despondence, of the inhuman dearth
Of noble natures, of the gloomy days,
Of all the unhealthy and o'er-darkened ways
Made for our searching; yes, in spite of all,
Some shape of beauty moves away the pall
From our dark spirits. Such the sun, the moon,
Trees old and young, sprouting a shady boon
For simple sheep; and such are daffodils
With the green world they live in; and clear rills
That for themselves a cooling covert make
'Gainst the hot season; the mid-forest brake,
Rich with a sprinkling of fair musk rose blooms:
And such, too, is the grandeur of the dooms[2]
We have imagined for the mighty dead;
All lovely tales that we have heard or read:
An endless fountain of immortal drink,
Pouring unto us from the heaven's brink.

Nor do we merely feel these essences
For one short hour; no, even as the trees
That whisper round a temple become soon
Dear as the temple's self, so does the moon,
The passion poesy, glories infinite,
Haunt us till they become a cheering light
Unto our souls, and bound to us so fast,
That, whether there be shine, or gloom o'ercast,
They alway must be with us, or we die.

Therefore, 'tis with full happiness that I
Will trace the story of Endymion.
The very music of the name has gone
Into my being, and each pleasant scene
Is growing fresh before me as the green
Of our own valleys: so I will begin,
Now while I cannot hear the city's din;
Now while the early budders are just new,
And run in mazes of the youngest hue
About old forests; while the willow trails
Its delicate amber; and the dairy pails
Bring home increase of milk. And, as the year
Grows lush in juicy stalks, I'll smoothly steer
My little boat, for many quiet hours,
With streams that deepen freshly into bowers.
Many and many a verse I hope to write,
Before the daisies, vermeil rimmed and white,
Hide in deep herbage; and ere yet the bees
Hum about globes of clover and sweet peas,
I must be near the middle of my story.
Oh, may no wintry season, bare and hoary,
See it half finished: but let Autumn bold,
With universal tinge of sober gold,
Be all about me when I make an end.
And now at once, adventuresome, I send
My herald thought into a wilderness:
There let its trumpet blow, and quickly dress
My uncertain path with green, that I may speed
Easily onward, thorough[3] flowers and weed.

. . . .

1817 1818

[1] morning
[2] destinies

THE EVE OF ST. AGNES

1

St. Agnes' Eve[4]—Ah, bitter chill it was!
The owl, for all his feathers, was a-cold;
The hare limped trembling through the frozen grass,
And silent was the flock in woolly fold:
Numb were the Beadsman's fingers, while he told
His rosary, and while his frosted breath,
Like pious incense from a censer old,
Seemed taking flight for heaven, without a death,
Past the sweet Virgin's picture, while his prayer he saith.

2

His prayer he saith, this patient, holy man;
Then takes his lamp, and riseth from his knees,
And back returneth, meager, barefoot, wan,
Along the chapel aisle by slow degrees:
The sculptured dead, on each side, seem to freeze,
Imprisoned in black, purgatorial rails:
Knights, ladies, praying in dumb orat'ries,
He passeth by; and his weak spirit fails
To think how they may ache in icy hoods and mails.

3

Northward he turneth through a little door,
And scarce three steps, ere Music's golden tongue
Flattered to tears this aged man and poor;
But no—already had his deathbell rung;
The joys of all his life were said and sung:
His was harsh penance on St. Agnes' Eve.
Another way he went, and soon among

[3] through
[4] the night preceding Jan. 21

Rough ashes sat he for his soul's reprieve,
And all night kept awake, for sinners' sake to grieve.

4

That ancient Beadsman heard the prelude soft;
And so it chanced, for many a door was wide,
From hurry to and fro. Soon, up aloft,
The silver, snarling trumpets 'gan to chide:
The level chambers, ready with their pride,
Were glowing to receive a thousand guests:
The carvèd angels, ever eager-eyed,
Stared, where upon their heads the cornice rests,
With hair blown back, and wings put cross-wise on their breasts.

5

At length burst in the argent revelry,
With plume, tiara, and all rich array,
Numerous as shadows, haunting fairily
The brain, new stuffed, in youth, with triumphs gay
Of old romance. These let us wish away,
And turn, sole-thoughted, to one Lady there,
Whose heart had brooded, all that wintry day,
On love, and winged St. Agnes' saintly care,
As she had heard old dames full many times declare.

6

They told her how, upon St. Agnes' Eve,
Young virgins might have visions of delight,
And soft adorings from their loves receive
Upon the honeyed middle of the night,
If ceremonies due they did aright;
As, supperless to bed they must retire,
And couch supine their beauties, lily white;
Nor look behind, nor sideways, but require
Of heaven with upward eyes for all that they desire.

7

Full of this whim was thoughtful Madeline;
The music, yearning like a god in pain,
She scarcely heard: her maiden eyes divine,
Fixed on the floor, saw many a sweeping train [1]
Pass by—she heeded not at all: in vain
Came many a tiptoe, amorous cavalier,
And back retired; not cooled by high disdain,
But she saw not: her heart was otherwhere:
She sighed for Agnes' dreams, the sweetest of the year.

8

She danced along with vague, regardless eyes,
Anxious her lips, her breathing quick and short:

[1] i.e., of robes—Keats

The hallowed hour was near at hand; she sighs
Amid the timbrels, and the thronged resort
Of whisperers in anger, or in sport;
'Mid looks of love, defiance, hate, and scorn,
Hoodwinked [2] with fairy fancy; all amort, [3]
Save to St. Agnes and her lambs unshorn, [4]
And all the bliss to be before tomorrow morn.

9

So, purposing each moment to retire,
She lingered still. Meantime, across the moors,
Had come young Porphyro, with heart on fire
For Madeline. Beside the portal doors,
Buttressed from moonlight, stands he, and implores
All saints to give him sight of Madeline,
But for one moment in the tedious hours,
That he might gaze and worship all unseen;
Perchance speak, kneel, touch, kiss—in sooth such things have been.

10

He ventures in: let no buzzed whisper tell:
All eyes be muffled, or a hundred swords
Will storm his heart, Love's feverous citadel:
For him, those chambers held barbarian hordes,
Hyena foemen, and hot-blooded lords,
Whose very dogs would execrations howl
Against his lineage: not one breast affords
Him any mercy, in that mansion foul,
Save one old beldame, weak in body and in soul.

11

Ah, happy chance! The aged creature came,
Shuffling along with ivory-headed wand,
To where he stood, hid from the torch's flame
Behind a broad hall-pillar, far beyond
The sound of merriment and chorus bland:
He startled her; but soon she knew his face,
And grasped his fingers in her palsied hand,
Saying, "Mercy, Porphyro! hie thee from this place;
They are all here tonight, the whole blood-thirsty race!

12

"Get hence! get hence! There's dwarfish Hildebrand;
He had a fever late, and in the fit
He cursèd thee and thine, both house and land:
Then there's that old Lord Maurice, not a whit

[2] blinded (to all else)
[3] dead
[4] St. Agnes was a Roman Virgin who suffered martyrdom. At Mass, on the day sacred to her, while the *Agnus Dei* (Lamb of God) was chanted, two lambs were dedicated to her, and afterwards shorn and the wool woven (stanza 13).

More tame for his gray hairs—Alas me! flit!
Flit like a ghost away."—"Ah, Gossip [1] dear,
We're safe enough; here in this armchair sit,
And tell me how"—"Good Saints! not here, not here;
Follow me, child, or else these stones will be thy bier."

13

He followed through a lowly archèd way,
Brushing the cobwebs with his lofty plume;
And as she muttered "Well-a—well-a-day!"
He found him in a little moonlight room,
Pale, latticed, chill, and silent as a tomb.
"Now tell me where is Madeline," said he,
"O tell me, Angela, by the holy loom
Which none but secret sisterhood may see,
When they St. Agnes' wool are weaving piously."

14

"St. Agnes! Ah! it is St. Agnes' Eve—
Yet men will murder upon holy days:
Thou must hold water in a witch's sieve,
And be liege-lord of all the Elves and Fays,
To venture so: it fills me with amaze
To see thee, Porphyro!—St. Agnes' Eve!
God's help! my lady fair the conjurer plays
This very night; good angels her deceive!
But let me laugh awhile, I've mickle time to grieve."

15

Feebly she laugheth in the languid moon,
While Porphyro upon her face doth look,
Like puzzled urchin on an aged crone
Who keepeth closed a wond'rous riddle-book,
As spectacled she sits in chimney nook.
But soon his eyes grew brilliant, when she told
His lady's purpose; and he scarce could brook [2]
Tears, at the thought of those enchantments cold,
And Madeline asleep in lap of legends old.

16

Sudden a thought came like a full-blown rose,
Flushing his brow, and in his painèd heart
Made purple riot: then doth he propose
A stratagem, that makes the beldame start:
"A cruel man and impious thou art:
Sweet lady, let her pray, and sleep, and dream
Alone with her good angels, far apart
From wicked men like thee. Go, go!—I deem
Thou canst not surely be the same that thou didst seem."

[1] elderly woman, trusted servant, nurse
[2] misused for "check"

17

"I will not harm her, by all saints I swear,"
Quoth Porphyro: "Oh, may I ne'er find grace
When my weak voice shall whisper its last prayer,
If one of her soft ringlets I displace,
Or look with ruffian passion in her face:
Good Angela, believe me by these tears;
Or I will, even in a moment's space,
Awake, with horrid shout, my foeman's ears,
And beard them, though they be more fanged than wolves and bears."

18

"Ah! why wilt thou affright a feeble soul?
A poor, weak, palsy-stricken churchyard thing,
Whose passing-bell may ere the midnight toll;
Whose prayers for thee, each morn and evening,
Were never missed." Thus plaining, doth she bring
A gentler speech from burning Porphyro;
So woeful, and of such deep sorrowing,
That Angela gives promise she will do
Whatever he shall wish, betide her weal or woe.

19

Which was, to lead him, in close secrecy,
Even to Madeline's chamber, and there hide
Him in a closet, of such privacy
That he might see her beauty unespied,
And win perhaps that night a peerless bride,
While legioned fairies paced the coverlet,
And pale enchantment held her sleepy-eyed.
Never on such a night have lovers met,
Since Merlin paid his demon all the monstrous debt. [3]

20

"It shall be as thou wishest," said the dame;
"All cates [4] and dainties shall be storèd there
Quickly on this feast-night: by the tambour frame [5]
Her own lute thou wilt see; no time to spare,
For I am slow and feeble, and scare dare
On such a catering trust my dizzy head.
Wait here, my child, with patience; kneel in prayer
The while: Ah! thou must needs the lady wed,
Or may I never leave my grave among the dead."

[3] Merlin, the famous wizard, became himself a victim of magic. See Tennyson's "Merlin and Vivien."
[4] delicacies
[5] an embroidery frame which was shaped like a tambour, a kind of drum

21

So saying, she hobbled off with her busy fear.
The lover's endless minutes slowly passed;
The dame returned, and whispered in his ear
To follow her; with aged eyes aghast
From fright of dim espial. Safe at last,
Through many a dusky gallery, they gain
The maiden's chamber, silken, hushed, and
chaste;
Where Porphyro took covert, pleased amain.
His poor guide hurried back with agues in
her brain.

22

Her faltering hand upon the balustrade,
Old Angela was feeling for the stair,
When Madeline, St. Agnes' charmèd maid,
Rose, like a missioned spirit, unaware:
With silver taper's light, and pious care,
She turned, and down the aged gossip led
To a safe level matting. Now prepare,
Young Porphyro, for gazing on that bed;
She comes, she comes again, like ringdove
frayed and fled.

23

Out went the taper as she hurried in;
Its little smoke, in pallid moonshine, died:
She closed the door, she panted, all akin
To spirits of the air, and visions wide:
No uttered syllable, or woe betide!
But to her heart, her heart was voluble,
Paining with eloquence her balmy side;
As though a tongueless nightingale should
swell
Her throat in vain, and die, heart-stifled, in
her dell.

24

A casement high and triple arched there was,
All garlanded with carven imageries
Of fruits, and flowers, and bunches of knot-
grass,
And diamonded with panes of quaint device,
Innumerable of stains and splendid dyes
As are the tiger-moth's deep-damasked wings;
And in the midst, 'mong thousand heraldries,
And twilight saints, and dim emblazonings,
A shielded scutcheon blushed with blood of
queens and kings

25

Full on this casement shone the wintry moon,
And threw warm gules [1] on Madeline's fair
breast,
As down she knelt for heaven's grace and
boon;
Rose-bloom fell on her hands, together prest,
And on her silver cross soft amethyst,
And on her hair a glory, like a saint.
She seemed a splendid angel, newly drest,
Save wings, for heaven—Porphyro grew faint:
She knelt, so pure a thing, so free from mor-
tal taint.

[1] red color (a heraldic term)

26

Anon his heart revives: her vespers done,
Of all its wreathèd pearls her hair she frees;
Unclasps her warmèd jewels one by one;
Loosens her fragrant bodice; by degrees
Her rich attire creeps rustling to her knees;
Half-hidden, like a mermaid in seaweed,
Pensive awhile she dreams awake, and sees,
In fancy, fair St. Agnes in her bed,
But dares not look behind, or all the charm
is fled.

27

Soon, trembling in her soft and chilly nest,
In sort of wakeful swoon, perplexed she lay,
Until the poppied warmth of sleep oppressed
Her soothèd limbs, and soul fatigued away;
Flown, like a thought, until the morrow-day;
Blissfully havened both from joy and pain;
Clasped like a missal [2] where swart paynims
pray;
Blinded alike from sunshine and from rain,
As though a rose should shut, and be a bud
again.

28

Stol'n to this paradise, and so entranced,
Porphyro gazed upon her empty dress,
And listened to her breathing, if it chanced
To wake into a slumberous tenderness;
Which when he heard, that minute did he
bless,
And breathed himself: then from the closet
crept,
Noiseless as fear in a wide wilderness,
And over the hushed carpet, silent, stepped,
And 'tween the curtains peeped, where, lo!
how fast she slept.

29

Then by the bed-side, where the faded moon
Made a dim, silver twilight, soft he set
A table, and, half-anguished, threw thereon
A cloth of woven crimson, gold, and jet:—
Oh, for some drowsy Morphean amulet!

[2] Mass-book (which pagans would have no occasion to unclasp); or, a prayer-book with margins adorned with pictures of converted heathen praying—*Century Readings.*

The boisterous, midnight, festive clarion,
The kettledrum, and far-heard clarinet,
Affray his ears, though but in dying tone:—
The hall door shuts again, and all the noise is gone.

30

And still she slept an azure-lidded sleep,
In blanchèd linen, smooth, and lavendered,
While he from forth the closet brought a heap
Of candied apple, quince, and plum, and gourd;
With jellies soother[1] than the creamy curd,
And lucent sirups, tinct with cinnamon;
Manna and dates, in argosy transferred
From Fez; and spicèd dainties, every one,
From silken Samarcand to cedared Lebanon.

31

These delicates he heaped with glowing hand
On golden dishes and in baskets bright
Of wreathèd silver: sumptuous they stand
In the retired quiet of the night,
Filling the chilly room with perfume light.—
"And now, my love, my seraph fair, awake!
Thou art my heaven, and I thine eremite;
Open thine eyes, for meek St. Agnes' sake,
Or I shall drowse beside thee, so my soul doth ache."

32

Thus whispering, his warm, unnervèd arm
Sank in her pillow. Shaded was her dream
By the dusk curtains:—'twas a midnight charm
Impossible to melt as icèd stream:
The lustrous salvers in the moonlight gleam:
Broad golden fringe upon the carpet lies:
It seemed he never, never could redeem
From such a steadfast spell his lady's eyes;
So mused awhile, entoiled in woofèd phantasies.

33

Awakening up, he took her hollow lute,—
Tumultuous,—and, in chords that tenderest be,
He played an ancient ditty, long since mute,
In Provence called, "La Belle Dame sans Merci";[2]
Close to her ear touching the melody;—
Wherewith disturbed, she uttered a soft moan:
He ceased—she panted quick—and suddenly
Her blue, affrayèd eyes wide open shone:
Upon his knees he sank, pale as smooth-sculptured stone.

[1] apparently used here for "smoother"
[2] "The Beautiful Lady without Pity."

34

Her eyes were open, but she still beheld,
Now wide awake, the vision of her sleep:
There was a painful change, that nigh expelled
The blisses of her dream so pure and deep,
At which fair Madeline began to weep,
And moan forth witless words with many a sigh;
While still her gaze on Porphyro would keep;
Who knelt, with joinèd hands and piteous eye,
Fearing to move or speak, she looked so dreamingly.

35

"Ah, Porphyro!" said she, "but even now
Thy voice was at sweet tremble in mine ear,
Made tunable with every sweetest vow;
And those sad eyes were spiritual and clear;
How changed thou art; how pallid, chill, and drear!
Give me that voice again, my Porphyro,
Those looks immortal, those complainings dear!
Oh, leave me not in this eternal woe,
For if thou diest, my Love, I know not where to go."

36

Beyond a mortal man impassioned far
At these voluptuous accents, he arose,
Ethereal, flushed, and like a throbbing star
Seen mid the sapphire heaven's deep repose;
Into her dream he melted, as the rose
Blendeth its odor with the violet—
Solution sweet; meantime the frost-wind blows
Like love's alarum, pattering the sharp sleet
Against the windowpanes; St. Agnes' moon hath set.

37

'Tis dark: quick pattereth the flaw-blown sleet.
"This is no dream, my bride, my Madeline!"
'Tis dark: the icèd gusts still rave and beat:
"No dream, alas! alas! and woe is mine!
Porphyro will leave me here to fade and pine.
Cruel! what traitor could thee hither bring?
I curse not, for my heart is lost in thine,
Though thou forsakest a deceivèd thing—
A dove forlorn and lost with sick unprunèd wing."

38

"My Madeline! sweet dreamer! lovely bride!
Say, may I be for aye thy vassal blest?
Thy beauty's shield, heart-shaped and vermeil dyed?
Ah, silver shrine, here will I take my rest

After so many hours of toil and quest,
A famished pilgrim—saved by miracle.
Though I have found, I will not rob thy nest
Saving of thy sweet self; if thou think'st well
To trust, fair Madeline, to no rude infidel.

39

"Hark! 'tis an elfin-storm from fairyland,
Of haggard seeming, but a boon indeed:
Arise—arise! the morning is at hand;—
The bloated wassailers will never heed—
Let us away, my love, with happy speed;
There are no ears to hear, or eyes to see—
Drowned all in Rhenish and the sleepy mead.
Awake! arise; my love, and fearless be,
For o'er the southern moors I have a home for thee."

40

She hurried at his words, beset with fears,
For there were sleeping dragons all around,
At glaring watch, perhaps, with ready spears—
Down the wide stairs a darkling way they found—
In all the house was heard no human sound.
A chain-drooped lamp was flickering by each door;
The arras, rich with horseman, hawk, and hound,
Fluttered in the besieging wind's uproar;
And the long carpets rose along the gusty floor.

41

They glide, like phantoms, into the wide hall;
Like phantoms, to the iron porch, they glide;
Where lay the Porter, in uneasy sprawl,
With a huge, empty flagon by his side:
The wakeful bloodhound rose, and shook his hide,
But his sagacious eye an inmate owns:
By one and one, the bolts full easy slide:—
The chains lie silent on the footworn stones;—
The key turns, and the door upon its hinges groans.

42

And they are gone: aye, ages long ago
These lovers fled away into the storm.
That night the Baron dreamt of many a woe,
And all his warrior-guests, with shade and form
Of witch, and demon, and large coffin-worm,
Were long be-nightmared. Angela the old
Died palsy-twitched, with meager face deform;
The Beadsman, after thousand aves told,
For aye unsought-for, slept among his ashes cold.

1819 1820

ODE TO A NIGHTINGALE

My heart aches, and a drowsy numbness pains
My sense, as though of hemlock I had drunk,
Or emptied some dull opiate to the drains
One minute past, and Lethe-wards had sunk:
'Tis not through envy of thy happy lot,
But being too happy in thine happiness—
That thou, light-wingèd Dryad of the trees,
In some melodious plot
Of beechen green, and shadows numberless,
Singest of summer in full-throated ease.

Oh, for a draught of vintage that hath been
Cooled a long age in the deep-delvèd earth,
Tasting of Flora and the country green,
Dance, and Provençal song,[1] and sunburnt mirth!
Oh, for a beaker full of the warm South,
Full of the true, the blushful Hippocrene,[2]
With beaded bubbles winking at the brim,
And purple-stainèd mouth;
That I might drink, and leave the world unseen,
And with thee fade away into the forest dim:—

Fade far away, dissolve, and quite forget
What thou among the leaves hast never known,
The weariness, the fever, and the fret
Here, where men sit and hear each other groan;
Where palsy shakes a few, sad, last gray hairs,
Where youth grows pale, and specter-thin, and dies;
Where but to think is to be full of sorrow
And leaden-eyed despairs;
Where Beauty cannot keep her lustrous eyes,
Or new Love pine at them beyond tomorrow.

Away! away! for I will fly to thee,
Not charioted by Bacchus and his pards,[3]
But on the viewless wings of Poesy,
Though the dull brain perplexes and retards:
Already with thee! tender is the night,
And haply the Queen-Moon is on her throne,

[1] of southern France, the home of the troubadours
[2] a fountain of the Muses on Mt. Helicon
[3] The sources of Keats's classical knowledge are interesting. The suggestion for this particular metaphor came, doubtless, from Titian's painting of Ariadne (with Bacchus and his leopards) which was brought to England in 1806, and of which Keats must at least have seen a print, for he describes it in his "Sleep and Poetry," line 335. The painting was put in the National Gallery in 1826.

Clustered around by all her starry Fays;
But here there is no light
Save what from heaven is with the breezes blown
Through verdurous glooms and winding mossy ways.

I cannot see what flowers are at my feet,
Nor what soft incense hangs upon the boughs,
But, in embalmèd[1] darkness, guess each sweet
Wherewith the seasonable month endows
The grass, the thicket, and the fruit-tree wild;
White hawthorn, and the pastoral eglantine;
Fast fading violets covered up in leaves;
And mid-May's eldest child,
The coming musk rose, full of dewy wine,
The murmurous haunt of flies on summer eves.

Darkling I listen; and, for[2] many a time
I have been half in love with easeful Death,
Called him soft names in many a musèd rime,
To take into the air my quiet breath;
Now more than ever seems it rich to die,
To cease upon the midnight with no pain,
While thou art pouring forth thy soul abroad
In such an ecstasy!
Still wouldst thou sing, and I have ears in vain—
To thy high requiem become a sod.

Thou wast not born for death, immortal Bird!
No hungry generations tread thee down;
The voice I hear this passing night was heard
In ancient days by emperor and clown:
Perhaps the self-same song that found a path
Through the sad heart of Ruth, when, sick for home,
She stood in tears amid the alien corn;[3]
The same that ofttimes hath
Charmed magic casements, opening on the foam
Of perilous seas, in fairy lands forlorn.

Forlorn! The very word is like a bell
To toll me back from thee to my sole self!
Adieu! the fancy cannot cheat so well
As she is famed to do, deceiving elf.
Adieu! adieu! thy plaintive anthem fades
Past the near meadows, over the still stream,
Up the hillside; and now 'tis buried deep
In the next valley-glades.
Was it a vision, or a waking dream?
Fled is that music:—do I wake or sleep?

1819 1820

[1] balmy
[2] inasmuch as, while
[3] *Ruth,* ii

ODE ON A GRECIAN URN[4]

Thou still unravished bride of quietness,
Thou foster-child of silence and slow time,
Silvan historian,[5] who canst thus express
A flowery tale more sweetly than our rime:
What leaf-fringed legend haunts about thy shape
Of deities or mortals, or of both,
In Tempe or the dales of Arcady?
What men or gods are these? What maidens loath?
What mad pursuit? What struggle to escape?
What pipes and timbrels? What wild ecstasy?

Heard melodies are sweet, but those unheard
Are sweeter; therefore, ye soft pipes, play on;
Not to the sensual ear, but, more endeared,
Pipe to the spirit ditties of no tone:
Fair youth, beneath the trees, thou canst not leave
Thy song, nor ever can those trees be bare;
Bold Lover, never, never canst thou kiss,
Though winning near the goal—yet, do not grieve;
She cannot fade, though thou hast not thy bliss,
Forever wilt thou love, and she be fair!

Ah, happy, happy boughs! that cannot shed
Your leaves, nor ever bid the Spring adieu;
And, happy melodist, unwearièd,
Forever piping songs forever new;
More happy love! more happy, happy love!
Forever warm and still to be enjoyed,
Forever panting, and forever young;
All breathing human passion far above,
That leaves a heart high-sorrowful and cloyed,
A burning forehead, and a parching tongue.

Who are these coming to the sacrifice?
To what green altar, O mysterious priest,
Lead'st thou that heifer lowing at the skies,
And all her silken flanks with garlands dressed?
What little town by river or seashore,
Or mountain-built with peaceful citadel,

[4] "There is some reason for thinking that the particular urn which inspired this beautiful poem is a somewhat weather-beaten work in marble still preserved in the garden of Holland House, and figured in Piranesi's *Vasi e Candelabri.*"—H. B. Forman.
[5] historian of silvan scenes

Is emptied of this folk, this pious morn?
And, little town, thy streets for evermore
Will silent be; and not a soul to tell
Why thou art desolate, can e'er return.

O Attic shape; Fair attitude! with brede [1]
Of marble men and maidens overwrought,
With forest branches and the trodden weed;
Thou, silent form, dost tease us out of thought [2]
As doth eternity. Cold Pastoral!
When old age shall this generation waste,
Thou shalt remain, in midst of other woe
Than ours, a friend to man, to whom thou say'st,
"Beauty is truth, truth beauty"—that is all
Ye know on earth, and all ye need to know.

1819 1820

ODE ON MELANCHOLY

No, no, go not to Lethe, neither twist
Wolf's-bane, tight-rooted, for its poisonous wine;
Nor suffer thy pale forehead to be kissed
By nightshade, ruby grape of Proserpine;
Make not your rosary of yewberries,
Nor let the beetle, nor the death-moth be
Your mournful Psyche,[3] nor the downy owl
A partner in your sorrow's mysteries;
For shade to shade will come too drowsily,
And drown the wakeful anguish of the soul.

But when the melancholy fit shall fall
Sudden from heaven like a weeping cloud,
That fosters the droop-headed flowers all,
And hides the green hill in an April shroud;
Then glut thy sorrow on a morning rose,
Or on the rainbow of the salt sand-wave,
Or on the wealth of globèd peonies;
Or if thy mistress some rich anger shows,
Emprison her soft hand, and let her rave,
And feed deep, deep upon her peerless eyes.

She dwells with Beauty—Beauty that must die;
And Joy, whose hand is ever at his lips
Bidding adieu; and aching Pleasure nigh,
Turning to poison while the bee-mouth sips.
Aye, in the very temple of Delight
Veiled Melancholy has her sovran shrine,
Though seen of none save him whose strenuous tongue
Can burst Joy's grape against his palate fine:
His soul shall taste the sadness of her might,
And be among her cloudy trophies hung.

1819 1820

TO AUTUMN

Season of mists and mellow fruitfulness,
Close bosom-friend of the maturing sun;
Conspiring with him how to load and bless
With fruit the vines that round the thatch-eaves run;
To bend with apples the mossed cottage-trees
And fill all fruit with ripeness to the core;
To swell the gourd, and plump the hazel shells
With a sweet kernel; to set budding more,
And still more, later flowers for the bees,
Until they think warm days will never cease,
For Summer has o'er-brimmed their clammy cells.

Who hath not seen thee oft amid thy store?
Sometimes whoever seeks abroad may find
Thee sitting careless on a granary floor,
Thy hair soft-lifted by the winnowing wind;
Or on a half-reaped furrow sound asleep,
Drowsed with the fume of poppies, while thy hook
Spares the next swath and all its twinèd flowers.
And sometimes like a gleaner thou dost keep
Steady thy laden head across a brook;
Or by a cider-press, with patient look,
Thou watchest the last oozings hours by hours.

Where are the songs of Spring? Aye, where are they?
Think not of them, thou hast thy music too,—
While barrèd clouds bloom the soft-dying day,
And touch the stubble-plains with rosy hue;
Then in a wailful choir the small gnats mourn
Among the river sallows, borne aloft
Or sinking as the light wind lives or dies;
And full-grown lambs loud bleat from hilly bourn;
Hedge-crickets sing; and now with treble soft
The red-breast whistles from a garden-croft;
And gathering swallows twitter in the skies.

1819 1820

[1] embroidery (Cf. Collins's "Ode to Evening," line 7, p. 376.)
[2] draw us from our anxieties
[3] Psyche, the soul, was conventionally symbolized by the butterfly.

LINES ON THE MERMAID TAVERN [1]

Souls of Poets dead and gone,
What Elysium have ye known,
Happy field or mossy cavern,
Choicer than the Mermaid Tavern?
Have ye tippled drink more fine
Than mine host's Canary wine?
Or are fruits of Paradise
Sweeter than those dainty pies
Of venison? O generous food!
Dressed as though bold Robin Hood
Would, with his maid Marian,
Sup and bowse from horn and can.

I have heard that on a day
Mine host's signboard flew away,
Nobody knew whither, till
An astrologer's old quill
To a sheepskin gave the story,
Said he saw you in your glory,
Underneath a new old sign
Sipping beverage divine,
And pledging with contented smack
The Mermaid in the zodiac.

Souls of Poets dead and gone,
What Elysium have ye known,
Happy field or mossy cavern,
Choicer than the Mermaid Tavern?
1818 1820

IN A DREAR-NIGHTED DECEMBER

In a drear-nighted December,
Too happy, happy tree,
Thy branches ne'er remember
Their green felicity:
The north cannot undo them,
With a sleety whistle through them;
Nor frozen thawings glue them
From budding at the prime.

In a drear-nighted December,
Too happy, happy brook,
Thy bubblings ne'er remember
Apollo's summer look;
But with a sweet forgetting,
They stay their crystal fretting,
Never, never petting [2]
About the frozen time.

Ah! would 'twere so with many
A gentle girl and boy!
But were there ever any
Writhed not at passèd joy?
To know the change and feel it,
When there is none to heal it,
Nor numbèd sense to steel it,
Was never said in rime.
c. 1811 1829

[1] The Mermaid Tavern was a favorite resort of Shakespeare, Jonson, and their friends.

[2] in a pet (temper)

LA BELLE DAME SANS MERCI [3]

Oh, what can ail thee, knight-at-arms,
Alone and palely loitering?
The sedge has withered from the lake,
And no birds sing.

Oh, what can ail thee, knight-at-arms,
So haggard and so woebegone?
The squirrel's granary is full,
And the harvest's done.

I see a lily on thy brow,
With anguish moist and fever dew;
And on thy cheeks a fading rose
Fast withereth, too.—

I met a lady in the meads,
Full beautiful—a faëry's child;
Her hair was long, her foot was light,
And her eyes were wild.

I made a garland for her head,
And bracelets too, and fragrant zone;
She looked at me as she did love,
And made sweet moan.

I set her on my pacing steed,
And nothing else saw, all day long.
For sidelong would she bend, and sing
A faëry's song.

She found me roots of relish sweet,
And honey wild, and manna dew;
And sure in language strange she said,
"I love thee true."

She took me to her elfin grot,
And there she wept, and sighed full sore;
And there I shut her wild, wild eyes
With kisses four.

And there she lullèd me asleep,
And there I dreamed, ah, woe betide!

[3] "The Fair Lady without Pity." Cf. "The Eve of St. Agnes," st. 33. Keats obtained the title from an old French poem, a translation of which was once attributed to Chaucer. There are two versions of Keats's poem, but the second is hardly an improvement over the first, which is the more familiar, and which is given here. The reply of the knight begins at the fourth stanza. The story has some resemblance to that of Tannhäuser and the Venusberg.

The latest dream I ever dreamt
  On the cold hill's side.

I saw pale kings, and princes, too,
  Pale warriors, death-pale were they all;
They cried, "La Belle Dame sans Merci
  Hath thee in thrall!"

I saw their starved lips in the gloam
  With horrid warning gapèd wide—
And I awoke, and found me here,
  On the cold hill's side.

And this is why I sojourn here,
  Alone and palely loitering,
Though the sedge is withered from the lake
  And no birds sing.

1819 1820

ON FIRST LOOKING INTO CHAPMAN'S HOMER [1]

Much have I traveled in the realms of gold,
And many goodly states and kingdoms seen;
Round many western islands have I been
Which bards in fealty to Apollo hold.
Oft of one wide expanse had I been told
That deep-browed Homer ruled as his demesne;
Yet did I never breathe its pure serene
Till I heard Chapman speak out loud and bold:
Then felt I like some watcher of the skies
When a new planet swims into his ken;
Or like stout Cortez when with eagle eyes
He stared at the Pacific—and all his men
Looked at each other with a wild surmise—
Silent, upon a peak in Darien.

1816 1817

ON THE GRASSHOPPER AND CRICKET [2]

The poetry of earth is never dead:
When all the birds are faint with the hot sun,
And hide in cooling trees, a voice will run
From hedge to hedge about the new-mown
  mead;
That is the Grasshopper's—he takes the lead
In summer luxury—he has never done
With his delights; for when tired out with fun
He rests at ease beneath some pleasant weed.
The poetry of earth is ceasing never:
On a lone winter evening when the frost
Has wrought a silence, from the stove there
  shrills
The Cricket's song, in warmth increasing ever,
And seems to one in drowsiness half lost,
The Grasshopper's among some grassy hills.

1816 1817

ON SEEING THE ELGIN MARBLES [3]

My spirit is too weak—mortality
Weighs heavily on me like unwilling sleep,
And each imagined pinnacle and steep
Of godlike hardship tells me I must die
Like a sick Eagle looking at the sky.
Yet 'tis a gentle luxury to weep
That I have not the cloudy winds to keep,
Fresh for the opening of the morning's eye.
Such dim-conceivèd glories of the brain
Bring round the heart an undescribable feud;
So do these wonders a most dizzy pain,
That mingles Grecian grandeur with the rude
Wasting of old Time—with a billowy main—
A sun—a shadow of a magnitude.

1817 1817

ON THE SEA

It keeps eternal whisperings around
Desolate shores, and with its mighty swell
Gluts twice ten thousand caverns, till the spell
Of Hecate [4] leaves them their old shadowy
  sound.
Often 'tis in such gentle temper found,
That scarcely will the very smallest shell
Be moved for days from where it sometime
  fell,
When last the winds of heaven were unbound.
O ye! who have your eyeballs vexed and
  tired,
Feast them upon the wideness of the Sea;
O ye! whose ears are dinned with uproar
  rude,
Or fed too much with cloying melody—
Sit ye near some old cavern's mouth, and brood
Until ye start, as if the sea-nymphs choired!

1817 1817

WHEN I HAVE FEARS THAT I MAY CEASE TO BE

When I have fears that I may cease to be
Before my pen has gleaned my teeming brain,
Before high-pilèd books, in charactery,
Hold like rich garners the full ripened grain;
When I behold, upon the night's starred face,
Huge cloudy symbols of a high romance,
And think that I may never live to trace

[1] This sonnet of discovery was written after Keats had spent a night with a friend reading in Chapman's translation of Homer. Keats could not read Greek, and had to content himself mainly with "western islands" of poetry and romance. It should be noted that it was not Cortez, but Balboa, who discovered the Pacific.

[2] Written in a friendly competition with Leigh Hunt; see Hunt's sonnet, p. 537.

[3] These marbles are mainly sculptures from the Parthenon which were transferred from Athens to London by Lord Elgin in 1803.

[4] the moon

Their shadows, with the magic hand of chance;
And when I feel, fair creature of an hour!
That I shall never look upon thee more,
Never have relish in the faëry power
Of unreflecting love!—then on the shore
Of the wide world I stand alone, and think
Till Love and Fame to nothingness do sink.

1818 1848

BRIGHT STAR! WOULD I WERE STEADFAST AS THOU ART[1]

Bright star! would I were steadfast as thou art—
Not in lone splendor hung aloft the night,
And watching, with eternal lids apart,
Like nature's patient, sleepless Eremite,
The moving waters at their priestlike task
Of pure ablution round earth's human shores,
Or gazing on the new, soft-fallen mask
Of snow upon the mountains and the moors—
No—yet still steadfast, still unchangeable,
Pillowed upon my fair love's ripening breast,
To feel forever its soft fall and swell,
Awake for ever in a sweet unrest,
Still, still to hear her tender-taken breath,
And so live ever—or else swoon to death.

1819 1846

LATE GEORGIAN BALLADS AND LYRICS

Under this general title are given here some minor poems of the reigns of George Third and George Fourth, though one or two are really post-Georgian. Hunt's "Abou ben Adhem," for instance, is as late as 1844; but Hunt was himself a contemporary of Shelley and Keats. The poems have been selected partly for their real value as shown by their continued popularity, and partly to illustrate the character and range of the minor verse of the period.

ROBERT SOUTHEY, 1774-1843, son of a Bristol tradesman, was educated at Westminster School and at Oxford, came under the influence of Coleridge, and was one of the group of liberals including Wordsworth, devoted to freer ways in literature and society. In 1803 he settled in the "lake country" at Keswick, where eventually he died. Here Southey entered upon a toilsome life as a man of letters, editing literary works, writing histories, essays, biographies, and poems, and "feeding many mouths from one inkstand." He became poet laureate in 1813. Although he wrote many long poems, as, for example, *Thalaba,* 1801, and *The Curse of Kehama,* 1810, Southey will be remembered longest for a few lyrics.

[1] This sonnet was composed on the Dorsetshire coast just as Keats was sailing for Italy the autumn before his death. It was written in a copy of Shakespeare's poems on a blank page facing "A Lover's Complaint."

THE BATTLE OF BLENHEIM[2]

It was a summer evening;
Old Kaspar's work was done,
And he before his cottage door
Was sitting in the sun;
And by him sported on the green
His little grandchild Wilhelmine.

She saw her brother Peterkin
Roll something large and round,
Which he beside the rivulet
In playing there had found.
He came to ask what he had found,
That was so large, and smooth, and round.

Old Kaspar took it from the boy,
Who stood expectant by;
And then the old man shook his head,
And with a natural sigh,
"'Tis some poor fellow's skull," said he,
"Who fell in the great victory.

"I find them in the garden,
For there's many here about;
And often, when I go to plow,
The plowshare turns them out;
For many thousand men," said he,
"Were slain in that great victory."

"Now tell us what 'twas all about,"
Young Peterkin, he cries;
And little Wilhelmine looks up
With wonder-waiting eyes;
"Now tell us all about the war,
And what they fought each other for."

"It was the English," Kaspar cried,
"Who put the French to rout;
But what they fought each other for,
I could not well make out;
But everybody said," quoth he,
"That 'twas a famous victory.

"My father lived at Blenheim then,
Yon little stream hard by;
They burnt his dwelling to the ground,
And he was forced to fly;
So with his wife and child he fled,
Nor had he where to rest his head.

"With fire and sword the country round
Was wasted far and wide,
And many a childing mother then,
And new-born baby, died;

[2] At Blenheim, in Bavaria, in 1704, the British and their German allies, under the Duke of Marlborough and the Austrian Prince Eugene, defeated the French and Bavarians with great loss.

But things like that, you know, must be
At every famous victory.

"They say it was a shocking sight
After the field was won;
For many thousand bodies here
Lay rotting in the sun;
But things like that, you know, must be
After a famous victory.

"Great praise the Duke of Marlboro' won,
And our good Prince Eugene."
"Why, 'twas a very wicked thing!"
Said little Wilhelmine.
"Nay, nay, my little girl," quoth he;
"It was a famous victory.

"And everybody praised the Duke
Who this great fight did win."
"But what good came of it at last?"
Quoth little Peterkin,
"Why, that I cannot tell," said he;
"But 'twas a famous victory."

1798 1798

THOMAS CAMPBELL, 1777-1844, was born in the family of a Scotch overseas trader of Glasgow who lost his fortune in the American Revolution. The son was educated at Glasgow University and had the advantage of travel in Germany. He settled in London. Events of his time led him to compose battle poetry, opportune and sometimes of more than temporary popularity. But most of his poetry is too much mingled with rhetoric to stand the test of time. *Pleasures of Hope*, 1799, and *Gertrude of Wyoming* were widely read in their day.

Ye Mariners of England

A Naval Ode [1]

Ye mariners of England!
That guard our native seas;
Whose flag has braved a thousand years,
The battle and the breeze!
Your glorious standard launch again
To match another foe!
And sweep through the deep
While the stormy winds do blow;
While the battle rages loud and long,
And the stormy winds do blow.

The spirits of your fathers
Shall start from every wave—
For the deck it was their field of fame,
And Ocean was their grave.
Where Blake and mighty Nelson fell,
Your manly hearts shall glow,
As ye sweep through the deep
While the stormy winds do blow;
While the battle rages loud and long,
And the stormy winds do blow.

Britannia needs no bulwarks,
No towers along the steep;
Her march is o'er the mountain waves,
Her home is on the deep,
With thunders from her native oak,
She quells the floods below—
As they roar on the shore
When the stormy winds do blow;
When the battle rages loud and long,
And the stormy winds do blow.

The meteor flag of England
Shall yet terrific burn,
Till danger's troubled night depart,
And the star of peace return.
Then, then, ye ocean warriors!
Our song and feast shall flow
To the fame of your name,
When the storm has ceased to blow;
When the fiery fight is heard no more,
And the storm has ceased to blow.

1800 1801

Hohenlinden [2]

On Linden, when the sun was low,
All bloodless lay the untrodden snow,
And dark as winter was the flow
Of Iser, rolling rapidly.

But Linden saw another sight,
When the drum beat at dead of night,
Commanding fires of death to light
The darkness of her scenery.

By torch and trumpet fast arrayed,
Each horseman drew his battle blade,
And furious every charger neighed,
To join the dreadful revelry.

Then shook the hills with thunder riven,
Then rushed the steed to battle driven,

[1] This poem was written, it is said, in 1800, on the prospect of a war with Russia (see line 5); but it must have undergone some later revision, for Nelson (line 15) fell at Trafalgar in 1805. Admiral Robert Blake died at sea in 1657.

[2] At the Bavarian village of Hohenlinden, not far from Munich, the Austrian army (referred to in this poem as the "Hun") was defeated by the French (the "Frank") in December, 1800. Campbell was not present at the battle, as a pleasing tradition relates, but he was on the Continent at the time and saw at least one skirmish. Scott greatly admired this ballad, though the author himself spoke somewhat contemptuously of its "drum and trumpet lines."

And louder than the bolts of heaven
Far flashed the red artillery.

But redder yet that light shall glow
On Linden's hills of stained snow,
And bloodier yet the torrent flow
Of Iser, rolling rapidly.

'Tis morn, but scarce yon level sun
Can pierce the war clouds, rolling dun,
Where furious Frank and fiery Hun
Shout in their sulphurous canopy.

The combat deepens. On, ye brave
Who rush to glory, or the grave!
Wave, Munich! all thy banners wave,
And charge with all thy chivalry!

Few, few, shall part where many meet!
The snow shall be their winding-sheet,
And every turf beneath their feet
Shall be a soldier's sepulcher.

1801 1802

CHARLES WOLFE, 1791-1823, clergyman of the established Church, was educated at Trinity College, Dublin, and spent his entire life in his native Ireland. He wrote few poems, and is remembered solely by the poem here printed, which during the entire nineteenth century was most popular.

The Burial of Sir John Moore [1]

Not a drum was heard, not a funeral note,
  As his corse to the rampart we hurried;
Not a soldier discharged his farewell shot
  O'er the grave where our hero we buried.

We buried him darkly, at dead of night,
  The sods with our bayonets turning;
By the struggling moonbeam's misty light,
  And the lantern dimly burning.

No useless coffin enclosed his breast,
  Not in sheet or in shroud we wound him,
But he lay like a warrior taking his rest,
  With his martial cloak around him.

Few and short were the prayers we said,
  And we spoke not a word of sorrow;
But we steadfastly gazed on the face that was dead,
  And we bitterly thought of the morrow.

[1] Sir John Moore, a British general, was killed at Corunna in January, 1809, just as the British troops, retreating from the French, were about to embark, though he lived long enough to hear that the French were beaten back. He was buried at night in the citadel.

We thought, as we hollowed his narrow bed
  And smoothed down his lonely pillow,
That the foe and the stranger would tread o'er his head,
  And we far away on the billow!

Lightly they'll talk of the spirit that's gone,
  And o'er his cold ashes upbraid him;
But little he'll reck, if they let him sleep on
  In the grave where a Briton has laid him.

But half of our weary task was done
  When the clock struck the note for retiring;
And we heard the distant and random gun
  Of the enemy sullenly firing.

Slowly and sadly we laid him down,
  From the field of his fame fresh and gory;
We carved not a line, and we raised not a stone,
  But we left him alone with his glory.

1816 1816

THOMAS MOORE, 1779-1852, son of a small tradesman of Dublin and educated at Trinity College there, spent his life chiefly in England. His most notable friendship was with Byron, who made him his literary executor and biographer. He composed many songs that were immediately popular because of their sentimentality and their musical quality. A large number of them voiced the pathos and melancholy generally attributed to the Irish race. *Lalla Rookh*, 1817, Moore's longest poetical tale, and his *Irish Melodies*, produced at intervals from 1807 to 1834, are his best known works.

The Harp that Once Through Tara's Halls [2]

The harp that once through Tara's halls
    The soul of music shed,
Now hangs as mute on Tara's walls
    As if that soul were fled.
So sleeps the pride of former days,
    So glory's thrill is o'er,
And hearts that once beat high for praise
    Now feel that pulse no more!

No more to chiefs and ladies bright
    The harp of Tara swells;
The chord alone that breaks at night
    Its tale of ruin tells.
Thus Freedom now so seldom wakes,
    The only throb she gives
Is when some heart indignant breaks,
    To show that still she lives.

1808

[2] Tara Hill, some twenty miles from Dublin, is said to have been the seat of the ancient kings of Ireland.

The Minstrel Boy

The Minstrel Boy to the war is gone,
 In the ranks of death you'll find him;
His father's sword he has girded on,
 And his wild harp slung behind him.—
"Land of song!" said the warrior-bard,
 "Though all the world betrays thee,
One sword at least thy rights shall guard,
 One faithful harp shall praise thee!"

The Minstrel fell!—but the foeman's chain
 Could not bring his proud soul under;
The harp he loved ne'er spoke again,
 For he tore its cords asunder;
And said, "No chains shall sully thee,
 Thou soul of love and bravery!
Thy songs were made for the brave and free,
 They shall never sound in slavery!"

1813

Oft in the Stilly Night
(Scotch Air)

Oft, in the stilly night,
 Ere Slumber's chain has bound me,
Fond Memory brings the light
 Of other days around me;
  The smiles, the tears,
  Of boyhood's years,
 The words of love then spoken;
  The eyes that shone,
  Now dimmed and gone,
 The cheerful hearts now broken!
Thus, in the stilly night,
 Ere Slumber's chain has bound me,
Sad Memory brings the light
 Of other days around me.

When I remember all
 The friends, so linked together,
I've seen around me fall,
 Like leaves in wintry weather;
  I feel like one
  Who treads alone
 Some banquet hall deserted,
  Whose lights are fled,
  Whose garlands dead,
 And all but he departed!
Thus, in the stilly night,
 Ere Slumber's chain has bound me,
Sad Memory brings the light
 Of other days around me.

1815

CHARLES LAMB [1]

The Old Familiar Faces

I have had playmates, I have had companions,
In my days of childhood, in my joyful school-days—
All, all are gone, the old familiar faces.

I have been laughing, I have been carousing,
Drinking late, sitting late, with my bosom cronies—
All, all are gone, the old familiar faces.

I loved a love once, fairest among women;
Closed are her doors on me, I must not see her—
All, all are gone, the old familiar faces.

I have a friend, a kinder friend has no man;
Like an ingrate, I left my friend abruptly;
Left him, to muse on the old familiar faces.

Ghost-like I paced round the haunts of my childhood,
Earth seemed a desert I was bound to traverse,
Seeking to find the old familiar faces.

Friend of my bosom, thou more than a brother,
Why wert not thou born in my father's dwelling?
So might we talk of the old familiar faces—

How some they have died, and some they have left me,
And some are taken from me; all are departed;
All, all are gone, the old familiar faces.

1798 1798

WALTER SAVAGE LANDOR [2]

Rose Aylmer [3]

Ah, what avails the sceptered race,
 Ah, what the form divine!
What every virtue, every grace!
 Rose Aylmer, all were thine.

Rose Aylmer, whom these wakeful eyes
 May weep, but never see,
A night of memories and of sighs
 I consecrate to thee.

1806

LEIGH HUNT, 1784-1859, born in Middlesex, spent most of the active part of his life as a liberal journalist in London at a time when social and political rancor were intense. For an article criticizing the personal character of the Prince Regent, Hunt was fined and for two years imprisoned. This circumstance brought him into the notice of Byron and Shelley with whom, and Keats, he was more or less associated as long as they lived. As a critic of catholic tastes he was influential in defending new tendencies in literature against conservative criticism. His best poetry is graceful, delicate, and varied.

[1] See p. 545.

[2] See p. 553.

[3] Rose, a daughter of Baron Aylmer, and a youthful companion of Landor, died in India in 1800.

To the Grasshopper and the Cricket [1]

Green little vaulter in the sunny grass,
Catching your heart up at the feel of June,
Sole voice that's heard amidst the lazy noon,
When even the bees lag at the summoning brass;
And you, warm little housekeeper, who class
With those who think the candles come too soon,
Loving the fire, and with your tricksome tune
Nick the glad silent moments as they pass;
O sweet and tiny cousins, that belong,
One to the fields, the other to the hearth,
Both have your sunshine; both, though small, are strong
At your clear hearts; and both seem given to earth
To ring in thoughtful ears this natural song—
Indoors and out, summer and winter, mirth.

1816 1817

Rondeau [2]

Jenny kissed me when we met,
  Jumping from the chair she sat in;
Time, you thief, who love to get
  Sweets into your list, put that in:
Say I'm weary, say I'm sad,
  Say that health and wealth have missed me,
Say I'm growing old, but add,
  Jenny kissed me.

1838 1838

Abou Ben Adhem

Abou Ben Adhem—may his tribe increase!—
Awoke one night from a deep dream of peace,
And saw, within the moonlight in his room,
Making it rich, and like a lily in bloom,
An angel writing in a book of gold:
Exceeding peace had made Ben Adhem bold,
And to the presence in the room he said,
"What writest thou?"—The vision raised its head,
And, with a look made of all sweet accord,
Answered, "The names of those who love the Lord."
"And is mine one?" said Abou. "Nay, not so,"
Replied the angel. Abou spoke more low,
But cheerly still; and said, "I pray thee, then,
Write me as one that loves his fellow men." [3]
The angel wrote, and vanished. The next night
It came again, with a great wakening light,
And showed the names whom love of God had blessed—
And lo! Ben Adhem's name led all the rest.

1834 1838

[1] written in competition with Keats, whose sonnet may be seen on p. 532.

[2] The "Jenny" of the rondeau is said to have been Jane Welsh Carlyle, who was overjoyed when Hunt, a near neighbor, brought in the news of the success of one of Carlyle's books.

[3] This line is carved on Hunt's monument in Kensal Green Cemetery.

WINTHROP MACKWORTH PRAED, 1802-1839, born in a favored social group and educated at Trinity College, Cambridge, where at first he was known as a liberal, soon became conservative in opinions and entered parliament opposed to reform. He was successful in debate, but delicate health and an early death from consumption cut short his career. Praed's most characteristic verse is full of lightness and humor, and a delicacy of touch, which makes him easily foremost among contemporary English writers of *vers de société*.

From Letters From Teignmouth

I—Our Ball [4]

You'll come to our ball;—since we parted
  I've thought of you more than I'll say;
Indeed, I was half broken-hearted
  For a week, when they took you away.
Fond fancy brought back to my slumbers
  Our walks on the Ness and the Den,
And echoed the musical numbers
  Which you used to sing to me then.
I know the romance, since it's over,
  'Twere idle, or worse, to recall;—
I know you're a terrible rover;
  But, Clarence, you'll come to our Ball!

It's only a year since, at College,
  You put on your cap and your gown;
But, Clarence, you're grown out of knowledge,
  And changed from the spur to the crown;
The voice that was best when it faltered,
  Is fuller and firmer in tone:
And the smile that should never have altered—
  Dear Clarence—it is not your own;
Your cravat was badly selected,

[4] Teignmouth is a watering place in Devonshire. The various places named belong to the locality. The Ness is a promontory. The Den is a promenade formed by a sand bank between the town and the sea. Haldon is a range of hills; Shaldon, a village just across the river Teign; Dawlish, another seaside resort three miles away. As for the other allusions, Sir Thomas Lawrence was a famous portrait painter of that date (1829); National Schools (line 38) had lately been established at various places by a national society for the education of the poor; "Captain Rock" was a fictitious name signed to public notices by one of the Irish insurgents of 1822; "Hock" is a kind of wine—Hochheimer; a "Blue" is a "bluestocking"—a woman affecting literature and politics.

Your coat don't become you at all;
And why is your hair so neglected?
You must have it curled for our Ball.

I've often been out upon Haldon
To look for a covey with Pup;
I've often been over to Shaldon
To see how your boat is laid up.
In spite of the terrors of Aunty,
I've ridden the filly you broke;
And I've studied your sweet little Dante
In the shade of your favorite oak.
When I sat in July to Sir Lawrence,
I sat in your love of a shawl;
And I'll wear what you brought me from Florence,
Perhaps, if you'll come to our Ball.

You'll find us all changed since you vanished;
We've set up a National School;
And waltzing is utterly banished;
And Ellen has married a fool;
The Major is going to travel;
Miss Hyacinth threatens a rout;
The walk is laid down with fresh gravel;
Papa is laid up with the gout;
And Jane has gone on with her easels,
And Anne has gone off with Sir Paul;
And Fanny is sick with the measles,
And I'll tell you the rest at the Ball.

You'll meet all your beauties—the Lily,
And the Fairy of Willowbrook Farm,
And Lucy, who made me so silly
At Dawlish, by taking your arm;
Miss Manners, who always abused you
For talking so much about Hock;
And her sister, who often amused you
By raving of rebels and Rock;
And something which surely would answer,
An heiress quite fresh from Bengal—
So, though you were seldom a dancer,
You'll dance, just for once, at our Ball.

But out on the world!—from the flowers
It shuts out the sunshine of truth;
It blights the green leaves in the bowers,
It makes an old age of our youth;
And the flow of our feeling, once in it,
Like a streamlet beginning to freeze,
Though it cannot turn ice in a minute,
Grows harder by sudden degrees.
Time treads o'er the graves of affection;
Sweet honey is turned into gall;
Perhaps you have no recollection
That ever you danced at our Ball.

You once could be pleased with our ballads—
Today you have critical ears;
You once could be charmed with our salads—
Alas! you've been dining with Peers;
You trifled and flirted with many;
You've forgotten the when and the how;
There was one you liked better than any—
Perhaps you've forgotten her now.
But of those you remember most newly,
Of those who delight or enthrall,
None love you a quarter so truly
As some you will find at our Ball.

They tell me you've many who flatter
Because of your wit and your song;
They tell me (and what does it matter?)
You like to be praised by the throng;
They tell me you're shadowed with laurel,
They tell me you're loved by a Blue;
They tell me you're sadly immoral—
Dear Clarence, that cannot be true!
But to me you are still what I found you
Before you grew clever and tall;
And you'll think of the spell that once bound you;
And you'll come—WON'T you come—to our Ball?

1829 1844

THOMAS LOVELL BEDDOES, 1803-1849, son of a Clifton physician, was educated at Oxford where he was conspicuous for his liberal views on society and politics. These principles he carried with him to Germany where he went to study anatomy and medicine, and he was so outspoken in their defense that he lost academic preferment there, and was even obliged to retire for a while to Switzerland. He died at Basle. His best poetry is found in his lyrics, which, as Saintsbury says, are "of the most exquisite fancy and music, such as since the seventeenth century none but Blake and Coleridge had given."

Dream-Pedlary [1]

If there were dreams to sell,
What would you buy?
Some cost a passing bell;
Some a light sigh
That shakes from Life's fresh crown
Only a rose leaf down.
If there were dreams to sell,
Merry and sad to tell,
And the crier rang the bell,
What would you buy?

A cottage lone and still,
With bowers nigh,
Shadowy, my woes to still
Until I die.

[1] This poem is somewhat obscure, but to paraphrase it into perfect lucidity would be to destroy an element of its charm.

Such pearl from Life's fresh crown
Fain would I shake me down;
Were dreams to have at will,
This would best heal my ill,
This would I buy.

But there were dreams to sell,
Ill didst thou buy;
Life is a dream, they tell,
Waking, to die.
Dreaming a dream to prize
Is wishing ghosts to rise;
And, if I had the spell
To call the buried well,
Which one would I?

If there are ghosts to raise,
What shall I call,
Out of hell's murky haze,
Heaven's blue pall?
Raise my loved, long-lost boy
To lead me to his joy—
There are no ghosts to raise;
Out of death lead no ways;
Vain is the call.

Know'st thou not ghosts to sue,
No love thou hast.
Else lie, as I will do,
And breathe thy last.
So out of Life's fresh crown
Fall like a rose leaf down.
Thus are the ghosts to woo;
Thus are all dreams made true,
Ever to last!

c. 1825 1851

THOMAS HOOD, 1798-1845, came into literature by way of journalism, especially in his poetry through his work upon the *London Magazine*. He wrote both serious and comic verse, but his pathos seems likely to outlast his humor. The grim story of "Eugene Aram" shows power usually found only in the great poets.

The Deathbed

We watched her breathing through the night,
Her breathing soft and low,
As in her breast the wave of life
Kept heaving to and fro.

So silently we seemed to speak,
So slowly moved about,
As we had lent her half our powers
To eke her living out.

Our very hopes belied our fears,
Our fears our hopes belied—
We thought her dying when she slept,
And sleeping when she died.

For when the morn came dim and sad,
And chill with early showers,
Her quiet eyelids closed—she had
Another morn than ours.

1831

The Song of the Shirt

With fingers weary and worn,
With eyelids heavy and red,
A woman sat, in unwomanly rags,
Plying her needle and thread—
Stitch! stitch! stitch!
In poverty, hunger, and dirt,
And still with a voice of dolorous pitch
She sang the "Song of the Shirt."

"Work! work! work!
While the cock is crowing aloof!
And work—work—work,
Till the stars shine through the roof!
It's oh! to be a slave
Along with the barbarous Turk,
Where woman has never a soul to save,
If this is Christian work!

"Work—work—work
Till the brain begins to swim;
Work—work—work
Till the eyes are heavy and dim!
Seam, and gusset, and band,
Band, and gusset, and seam,
Till over the buttons I fall asleep,
And sew them on in a dream!

"Oh, men, with Sisters dear!
Oh, men, with Mothers and Wives!
It is not linen you're wearing out,
But human creatures' lives!
Stitch—stitch—stitch,
In poverty, hunger, and dirt,
Sewing at once, with a double thread,
A Shroud as well as a Shirt.

"But why do I talk of Death?
That Phantom of grisly bone,
I hardly fear its terrible shape,
It seems so like my own—
It seems so like my own,
Because of the fasts I keep;
O God! that bread should be so dear
And flesh and blood so cheap!

"Work—work—work!
My labor never flags.

And what are its wages? A bed of straw,
  A crust of bread—and rags.
That shattered roof—this naked floor—
  A table—a broken chair—
And a wall so blank, my shadow I thank
  For sometimes falling there!

"Work—work—work!
  From weary chime to chime,
Work—work—work,
  As prisoners work for crime!
Band, and gusset, and seam,
  Seam, and gusset, and band,
Till the heart is sick, and the brain benumbed,
  As well as the weary hand.

"Work—work—work,
  In the dull December light,
And work—work—work,
  When the weather is warm and bright—
While underneath the eaves
  The brooding swallows cling
As if to show me their sunny backs
  And twit me with the spring.

"Oh! but to breathe the breath
  Of the cowslip and primrose sweet—
With the sky above my head,
  And the grass beneath my feet;
For only one short hour
  To feel as I used to feel,
Before I knew the woes of want
  And the walk that costs a meal.

"Oh! but for one short hour!
  A respite however brief!
No blessed leisure for Love or Hope,
  But only time for Grief!
A little weeping would ease my heart,
  But in their briny bed
My tears must stop, for every drop
  Hinders needle and thread!"

With fingers weary and worn,
  With eyelids heavy and red,
A woman sat, in unwomanly rags,
  Plying her needle and thread—
Stitch! stitch! stitch!
  In poverty, hunger, and dirt,
And still with a voice of dolorous pitch—
Would that its tone could reach the Rich!—
  She sang this "Song of the Shirt!"

1843 1843

ROBERT STEPHEN HAWKER, 1803-1875, was an antiquarian clergyman settled in Cornwall. He is best known for his lyrics of local color, most of them associated with a seacoast celebrated for its dangers and its romantic history.

The Song of the Western Men [1]

A good sword and a trusty hand!
  A merry heart and true!
King James's men shall understand
  What Cornish lads can do.

And have they fixed the where and when?
  And shall Trelawny die?
Here's twenty thousand Cornish men
  Will know the reason why!

Out spake their captain brave and bold,
  A merry wight was he:
"If London Tower were Michael's hold,
  We'll set Trelawny free!

"We'll cross the Tamar, land to land,
  The Severn is no stay,
With 'one and all,' and hand in hand,
  And who shall bid us nay?

"And when we come to London Wall,
  A pleasant sight to view,
Come forth! come forth, ye cowards all,
  Here's men as good as you!

"Trelawny he's in keep and hold.
  Trelawny he may die;
But here's twenty thousand Cornish bold,
  Will know the reason why!"

1825 1826

The Silent Tower of Bottreau [2]

Tintadgel bells ring o'er the tide,
The boy leans on his vessel side;
He hears that sound, and dreams of home
Soothe the wild orphan of the foam.

[1] In 1688, Sir Jonathan Trelawny, a native of Cornwall, was, with six other bishops, thrown into the Tower of London for resisting James the Second's Declaration of Indulgence. He was soon released. It was long supposed that this ballad, which was first printed anonymously, dated from that time. The refrain is ancient, but the ballad was written by Hawker in 1825. The Tamar and Severn (lines 13 and 14) are rivers of southwestern England. Michael (line 11) is the archangel to whom was given the task of defeating Satan and consigning him to hell.

[2] "The rugged heights that line the seashore in the neighborhood of Tintadgel Castle and Church [on the coast of Cornwall] are crested with towers. Among these, that of Bottreau, or, as it is now written, Boscastle, is without bells. The silence of this wild and lonely churchyard on festive or solemn occasions is not a little striking. On inquiry I was told that the bells were once shipped for this church, but that when the vessel was within sight of the tower the blasphemy of her captain was punished in the manner related. The bells, they told me, still lie in the bay, and announce by strange sounds the approach of a storm."—R. S. Hawker.

"Come to thy God in time!"
Thus saith their pealing chime;
Youth, manhood, old age past,
"Come to thy God at last."

But why are Bottreau's echoes still?
Her tower stands proudly on the hill;
Yet the strange chough that home hath found,
The lamb lies sleeping on the ground.
"Come to thy God in time!"
Should be her answering chime;
"Come to thy God at last!"
Should echo on the blast.

The ship rode down with courses free,
The daughter of a distant sea;
Her sheet was loose, her anchor stored,
The merry Bottreau bells on board.
"Come to thy God in time!"
Rung out Tintadgel chime;
Youth, manhood, old age past,
"Come to thy God at last!"

The pilot heard his native bells
Hang on the breeze in fitful swells;
"Thank God," with reverent brow he cried,
"We make the shore with evening's tide."
"Come to thy God in time!"
It was his marriage chime:
Youth, manhood, old age past,
His bell must ring at last.

"Thank God, thou whining knave, on land,
But thank, at sea, the steersman's hand,"
The captain's voice above the gale:
"Thank the good ship and ready sail."
"Come to thy God in time!"
Sad grew the boding chime:
"Come to thy God at last!"
Boomed heavy on the blast.

Uprose that sea! as if it heard
The mighty Master's signal-word.
What thrills the captain's whitening lip?
The death groans of his sinking ship.
"Come to thy God in time!"
Swung deep the funeral chime:
Grace, mercy, kindness past,
"Come to thy God at last!"

Long did the rescued pilot tell—
When gray hairs o'er his forehead fell,
While those around would hear and weep—
That fearful judgment of the deep,
"Come to thy God in time!"
He read his native chime:
Youth, manhood, old age past,
His bell rung out at last.

Still when the storm of Bottreau's waves
Is wakening in his weedy caves,
Those bells, that sullen surges hide,
Peal their deep notes beneath the tide:
"Come to thy God in time!"
Thus saith the ocean chime:
Storm, billow, whirlwind past,
"Come to thy God at last!"

1831 *1832*

SIR WALTER SCOTT [1] 1771-1832

From OLD MORTALITY [2]

CHAPTER I. PRELIMINARY

"Most readers," says the manuscript of Mr. Pattieson, "must have witnessed with delight the joyous burst which attends the dismissing of a village school on a fine summer evening. The buoyant spirit of childhood, repressed with so much difficulty during the tedious hours of discipline, may then be seen to explode, as it were, in shout, and song, and frolic, as the little urchins join in groups on their playground, and arrange their matches of sport for the evening. But there is one individual who partakes of the relief afforded by the moment of dismission, whose feelings are not so obvious to the eye of the spectator, or so apt to receive his sympathy. I mean the teacher himself, who, stunned with the hum and suffocated with the closeness of his schoolroom, has spent the whole day (himself against a host) in controlling petulance, exciting indifference to action, striving to enlighten stupidity, and laboring to soften obstinacy; and whose very powers of intellect have been confounded by hearing the same dull lesson repeated a hundred times by rote, and only varied by the various blunders of the reciters. Even the flowers of classic genius, with which his solitary fancy is most gratified, have been rendered degraded in his imagination, by their connection with tears, with errors, and with punishment; so that the *Eclogues* of Virgil and *Odes* of Horace are

[1] For biographical note see p. 481.

[2] *Old Mortality* is a story of the rising of the Scotch Covenanters about 1677-9 against the English church and throne. Scott had once met, in the churchyard of Dunnottar, one Robert Paterson, familiarly known as "Old Mortality," and he chooses to make him responsible for the substance of the tale. It is one of the *Tales of My Landlord;* and the Landlord of Wallace Inn, Mr. Cleishbottom the schoolmaster, and the manuscript of his assistant, the frail Mr. Pattieson, are all a part of the fictitious background.

each inseparably allied in association with the sullen figure and monotonous recitation of some blubbering schoolboy. If to these mental distresses are added a delicate frame of body, and a mind ambitious of some higher distinction than that of being the tyrant of childhood, the reader may have some slight conception of the relief which a solitary walk, in the cool of a fine summer evening, affords to the head which has ached, and the nerves which have been shattered, for so many hours, in plying the irksome task of public instruction.

"To me these evening strolls have been the happiest hours of an unhappy life; and if any gentle reader shall hereafter find pleasure in perusing these lucubrations, I am not unwilling he should know that the plan of them has been usually traced in those moments when relief from toil and clamor, combined with the quiet scenery around me, has disposed my mind to the task of composition.

"My chief haunt in these hours of golden leisure, is the banks of the small stream which, winding through a 'lone vale of green bracken,' passes in front of the village schoolhouse of Gandercleugh. For the first quarter of a mile, perhaps, I may be disturbed from my meditations, in order to return the scrape, or doffed bonnet, of such stragglers among my pupils as fish for trouts or minnows in the little brook, or seek rushes and wild flowers by its margin. But beyond the space I have mentioned the juvenile anglers do not, after sunset, voluntarily extend their excursions. The cause is, that farther up the narrow valley, and in a recess which seems scooped out of the side of the steep heathy bank, there is a deserted burial ground, which the little cowards are fearful of approaching in the twilight. To me, however, the place has an inexpressible charm. It has been long the favorite termination of my walks, and, if my kind patron forgets not his promise, will (and probably at no very distant day) be my final resting place after my mortal pilgrimage.

"It is a spot which possesses all the solemnity of feeling attached to a burial ground, without exciting those of a more unpleasing description. Having been very little used for many years, the few hillocks which rise above the level plain are covered with the same short velvet turf. The monuments, of which there are not above seven or eight, are half sunk in the ground, and overgrown with moss. No newly-erected tomb disturbs the sober serenity of our reflections by reminding us of recent calamity, and no rank-springing grass forces upon our imagination the recollection that it owes its dark luxuriance to the foul and festering remnants of mortality which ferment beneath. The daisy which sprinkles the sod, and the harebell which hangs over it, derive their pure nourishment from the dew of heaven, and their growth impresses us with no degrading or disgusting recollections. Death has indeed been here, and its traces are before us; but they are softened and deprived of their horror by our distance from the period when they have been first impressed. Those who sleep beneath are only connected with us by the reflection that they have once been what we now are, and that, as their relics are now identified with their mother earth, ours shall, at some future period, undergo the same transformation.

"Yet, although the moss has been collected on the most modern of these humble tombs during four generations of mankind, the memory of some of those who sleep beneath them is still held in reverent remembrance. It is true that upon the largest and, to an antiquary, the most interesting monument of the group, which bears the effigies of a doughty knight in his hood of mail with his shield hanging on his breast, the armorial bearings are defaced by time, and a few worn-out letters may be read, at the pleasure of the decipherer, *Dns. Johan ---de Hamel,* --- or *Johan---de Lamel* ---. And it is also true that of another tomb, richly sculptured with an ornamental cross, miter, and pastoral staff,[1] tradition can only aver that a certain nameless bishop lies interred there. But upon other two stones which lie beside, may still be read in rude prose, and ruder rime, the history of those who sleep beneath them. They belong, we are assured by the epitaph, to the class of persecuted Presbyterians who afforded a melancholy subject for history in the times of Charles II and his successor. In returning from the battle of Pentland Hills, a party of the insurgents had been attacked in this glen by a small detachment of the King's troops, and three or four either killed in the skirmish, or shot after being made prisoners, as rebels taken with arms in their hands. The peasantry continued to attach to the tombs of those victims of prelacy an honor which they do not render to more splendid mausoleums; and when they point them out to their sons and narrate the fate of the sufferers, usually conclude by exhorting them to be ready, should times call for it, to resist to the death in the cause of civil and religious liberty, like their brave forefathers.

[1] The cross, miter, and staff symbolized a bishop's office.

"Although I am far from venerating the peculiar tenets asserted by those who call themselves the followers of those men, and whose intolerance and narrow-minded bigotry are at least as conspicuous as their devotional zeal, yet it is without depreciating the memory of those sufferers, many of whom united the independent sentiments of a Hampden [1] with the suffering zeal of a Hooper or Latimer. [2] On the other hand, it would be unjust to forget that many even of those who had been most active in crushing what they conceived the rebellious and seditious spirit of those unhappy wanderers, displayed themselves, when called upon to suffer for their political and religious opinions, the same daring and devoted zeal, tinctured, in their case, with chivalrous loyalty, as in the former with republican enthusiasm. It has often been remarked of the Scottish character that the stubbornness with which it is molded shows most to advantage in adversity, when it seems akin to the native sycamore of their hills which scorns to be biased in its mode of growth, even by the influence of the prevailing wind, but, shooting its branches with equal boldness in every direction, shows no weather side to the storm, and may be broken, but can never be bended. It must be understood that I speak of my countrymen as they fall under my own observation. When in foreign countries, I have been informed that they are more docile. But it is time to return from this digression.

"One summer evening, as in a stroll, such as I have described, I approached this deserted mansion of the dead, I was somewhat surprised to hear sounds distinct from those which usually soothe its solitude, the gentle chiding, namely, of the brook, and the sighing of the wind in the boughs of three gigantic ash trees, which mark the cemetery. The clink of a hammer was, on this occasion, distinctly heard; and I entertained some alarm that a march-dike, long meditated by the two proprietors whose estates were divided by my favorite brook, was about to be drawn up the glen in order to substitute its rectilinear deformity for the graceful winding of the natural boundary. As I approached I was agreeably undeceived. An old man was seated upon the monument of the slaughtered Presbyterians, and busily employed in deepening with his chisel the letters of the inscription, which, announcing, in scriptural language, the promised blessings of futurity to be the lot of the slain, anathematised the murderers with corresponding violence. A blue bonnet of unusual dimensions covered the gray hairs of the pious workman. His dress was a large old-fashioned coat of the coarse cloth called hodden gray, usually worn by the elder peasants, with waistcoat and breeches of the same; and the whole suit, though still in decent repair, had obviously seen a train of long service. Strong clouted shoes, studded with hobnails, and gramoches, or leggins, made of thick black cloth, completed his equipment. Beside him, fed among the graves a pony, the companion of his journey, whose extreme whiteness, as well as its projecting bones and hollow eyes indicated its antiquity. It was harnessed in the most simple manner, with a pair of branks [3] a hair tether, or halter, and a sunk, or cushion of straw, instead of bridle and saddle. A canvas pouch hung around the neck of the animal, for the purpose, probably, of containing the rider's tools, and anything else he might have occasion to carry with him. Although I had never seen the old man before, yet from the singularity of his employment, and the style of his equipage, I had no difficulty in recognizing a religious itinerant whom I had often heard talked of, and who was known in various parts of Scotland by the title of Old Mortality.

"Where this man was born, or what was his real name, I have never been able to learn; nor are the motives which made him desert his home, and adopt the erratic mode of life which he pursued, known to me except very generally. According to the belief of most people, he was a native of either the county of Dumfries or Galloway, and lineally descended from some of those champions of the Covenant whose deeds and sufferings were his favorite theme. He is said to have held, at one period of his life, a small moorland farm; but, whether from pecuniary losses or domestic misfortune, he had long renounced that and every other gainful calling. In the language of Scripture, he left his house, his home, and his kindred, and wandered about until the day of his death, a period of nearly thirty years.

"During this long pilgrimage, the pious enthusiast regulated his circuit so as annually to visit the graves of the unfortunate Covenanters, who suffered by the sword, or by the executioner, during the reigns of the two last monarchs of the Stewart line. These are most numerous in the western districts of Ayr, Galloway, and Dumfries; but they are also to be found in other parts of Scotland, wherever the fugitives had sought, or fallen, or suffered by

[1] John Hampden, who refused to pay taxes levied by Charles I

[2] John Hooper and Bishop Latimer were both burned for heresy in 1555.

[3] bits

military or civil execution. Their tombs are often apart from all human habitation, in the remote moors and wilds to which the wanderers had fled for concealment. But wherever they existed, Old Mortality was sure to visit them when his annual round brought them within his reach. In the most lonely recesses of the mountains, the moor-fowl shooter has been often surprised to find him busied in cleaning the moss from the gray stones, renewing with his chisel the half-defaced inscriptions, and repairing the emblems of death with which these simple monuments are usually adorned. Motives of the most sincere though fanciful devotion induced the old man to dedicate so many years of existence to perform this tribute to the memory of the deceased warriors of the church. He considered himself as fulfilling a sacred duty, while renewing to the eyes of posterity the decaying emblems of the zeal and sufferings of their forefathers, and thereby trimming, as it were, the beacon light which was to warn future generations to defend their religion even unto blood.

"In all his wanderings the old pilgrim never seemed to need, or was known to accept, pecuniary assistance. It is true his wants were very few; for wherever he went he found ready quarters in the house of some Cameronian [1] of his own sect, or of some other religious person. The hospitality which was reverentially paid to him he always acknowledged by repairing the gravestones (if there existed any) belonging to the family or ancestors of his host. As the wanderer was usually to be seen bent on this pious task within the precincts of some country churchyard, or reclined on the solitary tombstone among the heath, disturbing the plover and the blackcock with the clink of his chisel and mallet, with his old white pony grazing by his side, he acquired from his converse among the dead the popular appellation of Old Mortality.

"The character of such a man could have in it little connection even with innocent gaiety. Yet, among those of his own religious persuasion, he is reported to have been cheerful. The descendants of persecutors, or those whom he supposed guilty of entertaining similar tenets, and the scoffers at religion by whom he was sometimes assailed, he usually termed the generation of vipers. [2] Conversing with others, he was grave and sententious, not without a cast of severity. But he is said never to have been observed to give way to violent passion, excepting upon one occasion when a mischievous truant boy defaced with a stone the nose of a cherub's face which the old man was engaged in retouching. I am in general a sparer of the rod, notwithstanding the maxim of Solomon, for which schoolboys have little reason to thank his memory; but on this occasion I deemed it proper to show that I did not hate the child.—But I must return to the circumstances attending my first interview with this interesting enthusiast.

"In accosting Old Mortality I did not fail to pay respect to his years and his principles, beginning my address by a respectful apology for interrupting his labors. The old man intermitted the operation of the chisel, took off his spectacles and wiped them, then replacing them on his nose, acknowledged my courtesy by a suitable return. Encouraged by his affability I intruded upon him some questions concerning the sufferers on whose monument he was now employed. To talk of the exploits of the Covenanters was the delight, as to repair their monuments was the business, of his life. He was profuse in the communication of all the minute information which he had collected concerning them, their wars, and their wanderings. One would almost have supposed he must have been their contemporary, and have actually beheld the passages which he related, so much had he indentified his feelings and opinions with theirs, and so much had his narratives the circumstantiality of an eyewitness.

" 'We,' he said, in a tone of exultation—'*we* are the only true whigs. Carnel men have assumed that triumphant appellation, following him whose kingdom is of this world. Which of them would sit six hours on a wet hillside to hear a godly sermon? I trow an hour o't wad staw [3] them. They are ne'er a hair better than them that shamena to take upon themsells the persecuting name of bludethirsty tories. Self-seekers all of them, strivers after wealth, power, and worldly ambition, and forgetters alike of what has been dreed [4] and done by the mighty men who stood in the gap in the great day of wrath. Nae wonder they dread the accomplishment of what was spoken by the mouth of the worthy Mr. Peden [5] (that precious servant of the Lord, none of whose words fell to the ground), that the French monzies [6] sall rise as fast in the glens of Ayr, and the kenns [7] of Galloway, as ever the Highlandmen did in 1677. And now they are gripping to the bow and to the spear,

[1] an austere sect of Presbyterians
[2] *Matthew* iii, 7.

[3] disgust [4] suffered
[5] Alexander Peden, an eloquent minister who was supposed to have prophetic gifts
[6] monsieurs (referring to a possible French invasion)
[7] from Gaelic *ceann,* head, headland, mountain

when they suld be mourning for a sinfu' land and a broken covenant.'

"Soothing the old man by letting his peculiar opinions pass without contradiction, and anxious to prolong conversation with so singular a character, I prevailed upon him to accept that hospitality which Mr. Cleishbotham is always willing to extend to those who need it. In our way to the schoolmaster's house we called at the Wallace Inn, where I was pretty certain I should find my patron about that hour of the evening. After a courteous interchange of civilities, Old Mortality was with difficulty prevailed upon to join his host in a single glass of liquor, and that on condition that he should be permitted to name the pledge, which he prefaced with a grace of about five minutes, and then, with bonnet doffed and eyes uplifted, drank to the memory of those heroes of the Kirk [1] who had first uplifted her banner upon the mountains. As no persuasion could prevail on him to extend his conviviality to a second cup, my patron accompanied him home, and accommodated him in the Prophet's Chamber, as it is his pleasure to call the closet which holds a spare bed, and which is frequently a place of retreat for the poor traveler.

"The next day I took leave of Old Mortality, who seemed affected by the unusual attention with which I had cultivated his acquaintance and listened to his conversation. After he had mounted, not without difficulty, the old white pony, he took me by the hand and said, 'The blessing of our Master be with you, young man! My hours are like the ears of the latter harvest, and your days are yet in the spring; and yet you may be gathered into the garner of mortality before me, for the sickle of death cuts down the green as oft as the ripe, and there is a color in your cheek that, like the bud of the rose, serveth oft to hide the worm of corruption. Wherefore labor as one who knoweth not when his master calleth. And if it be my lot to return to this village after ye are gane hame to your ain place, these alud withered hands will frame a stane of memorial, that your name may not perish from among the people.'

"I thanked Old Mortality for his kind intentions in my behalf, and heaved a sigh, not, I think, of regret so much as of resignation, to think of the chance that I might soon require his good offices. But though, in all human probability, he did not err in supposing that my span of life may be abridged in youth, he had over-estimated the period of his own pilgrimage on earth. It is now some years since he has been missed in all his usual haunts, while moss, lichen, and deer-hair, are fast covering those stones, to cleanse which had been the business of his life. About the beginning of this century he closed his mortal toils, being found on the highway near Lockerby, in Dumfries-shire, exhausted and just expiring. The old white pony, the companion of all his wanderings, was standing by the side of his dying master. There was found about his person a sum of money sufficient for his decent interment, which serves to show that his death was in no ways hastened by violence or by want. The common people still regard his memory with great respect; and many are of opinion that the stones which he repaired will not again require the assistance of the chisel. They even assert that on the tombs where the manner of the martyrs' murder is recorded, their names have remained indelibly legible since the death of Old Mortality, while those of the persecutors, sculptured on the same monuments, have been entirely defaced. It is hardly necessary to say that this is a fond imagination, and that, since the time of the pious pilgrim, the monuments which were the objects of his care are hastening, like all earthly memorials, into ruin or decay."

. . . .

1816

[6] the Scotch, or Presbyterian Church

CHARLES LAMB 1775-1834

Lamb, child of London and its life-long devotee, was born in the Inner Temple. Training that his parents were too poor to afford him he received at Christ's Hospital School where he stayed from his eighth to his fifteenth year, and where Coleridge was a fellow pupil. An impediment in his speech closed to him a scholarship in one of the universities, and he spent the remainder of his active life as a clerk, first in the South Sea House, and afterwards for thirty-three years in the counting room of the East India Company. In 1825 he was generously pensioned.

His first literary success was in *Tales from Shakespeare,* written with his sister Mary, 1807. This was followed shortly by *Specimens from the Dramatic Poets,* which established him as one of the ablest critics of his time.

Domestic tragedy in the insanity of his sister, who killed her mother, gripped him from young manhood and limited his literary efforts. Lamb, himself, suffered mild attacks of insanity almost until his death. But the *Essays of Elia,* 1820, 1825, 1833, ebullient in their humor, optimistic in their outlook, show how an unconquerable spirit may triumph over its environment. These essays we do not read to enlarge our intellectual bounds, but to quicken our emotions; they bring us not a schoolmaster, but a friend. In them Lamb carries on from Addison the discursive type of essay, makes it more personal, and at the same time makes himself a living companion of the reader. Well as we know Lamb through anecdotes, we know him better through these essays.

Biography: Ainger (EML). Criticism: Hazlitt, Swinburne, More (Shel. 2 and 4). Of Interest: "Lamb and the Fools of Shakespeare," G. Bradford, *Cent.* 109:73-82; "Lamb and the Periodical Essay," H. T. Baker, *No. Am.* 215:519-28.

From ESSAYS OF ELIA [1]

DREAM-CHILDREN: A REVERIE

Children love to listen to stories about their elders, when *they* were children; to stretch their imagination to the conception of a traditionary great-uncle, or grandame, whom they never saw. It was in this spirit that my little ones crept about me the other evening to hear about their great-grandmother Field, who lived in a great house in Norfolk (a hundred times bigger than that in which they and papa lived) which had been the scene (so at least it was generally believed in that part of the country) of the tragic incidents which they had lately become familiar with from the ballad of the *Children in the Wood.* Certain it is that the whole story of the children and their cruel uncle was to be seen fairly carved out in wood upon the chimney piece of the great hall, the whole story down to the robin redbreasts; till a foolish rich person pulled it down to set up a marble one of modern invention in its stead, with no story upon it. Here Alice put out one of her dear mother's looks, too tender to be called upbraiding. Then I went on to say how religious and how good their great-grandmother Field was, how beloved and respected by everybody, though she was not indeed the mistress of this great house, but had only the charge of it (and yet in some respects she might be said to be the mistress of it, too) committed to her by the owner, who preferred living in a newer and more fashionable mansion which he had purchased somewhere in the adjoining county; but still she lived in it in a manner as if it had been her own, and kept up the dignity of the great house in a sort while she lived, which afterwards came to decay, and was nearly pulled down, and all its old ornaments stripped and carried away to the owner's other house, where they were set up, and looked as awkward as if some one were to carry away the old tombs they had seen lately at the Abbey, [2] and stick them up in Lady C.'s tawdry gilt drawing-room. Here John smiled, as much as to say, "that would be foolish indeed." And then I told how, when she came to die, her funeral was attended by a concourse of all the poor, and some of the gentry, too, of the neighborhood for many miles round, to show their respect for her memory, because she had been such a good and religious woman; so good indeed that she knew all the Psaltery by heart, aye, and a great part of the Testament besides. Here little Alice spread her hands. Then I told what a tall, upright, graceful person their great-grandmother Field once was; and how in her youth she was esteemed the best dancer—here Alice's little right foot played an involuntary movement, till, upon my looking grave, it desisted—the best dancer, I was saying, in the county, till a cruel disease, called a cancer, came, and bowed her down with pain; but it could never bend her good spirits, or make them stoop, but they were still upright, because she was so good and religious. Then I told how she was used to sleep by herself in a lone chamber of the great lone house; and how she believed that an apparition of two infants was to be seen at midnight gliding up and down the great staircase near where she slept, but she said, "those innocents would do her no harm"; and how frightened I used to be, though in those days I had my maid to sleep with me, because I was never half so good or religious as she—and yet I never saw the infants. Here John expanded all his eyebrows and tried to look courageous. Then I told how good she was to all her grandchildren, having us to the great house in the holidays, where I in particular used to spend many hours by myself, in gazing upon the old busts of the Twelve Caesars, that had been Emperors of Rome, till the old marble heads would seem to live again, or I to be turned into marble with them; how I never could be tired with roaming about that huge mansion, with its vast empty rooms, with their worn-out hangings, fluttering tapestry, and carved oaken panels, with the gilding almost rubbed out—sometimes in the spacious

[1] "Elia," the signature under which Lamb published his essays in the *London Magazine,* was the name of an Italian clerk at the South-Sea House where Lamb had been employed nearly thirty years before. The essay entitled "Dream-Children" was written some time after the death of his brother John, late in the year 1821, when he and his sister Mary ("Bridget Elia") were left alone. "Alice W——n" or "Alice Winterton" may have stood, in part at least, for one Ann Simmons (later Mrs. Bartrum) for whom Lamb seems to have felt some attachment. The "great house in Norfolk" was a manor house in Hertfordshire where his grandmother, Mary Field, had for many years been housekeeper.

[2] Lamb was fond of visiting Westminster Abbey, and he wrote an essay in protest against the charge for admittance which had lately been imposed.

old-fashioned gardens, which I had almost to myself, unless when now and then a solitary gardening man would cross me—and how the nectarines and peaches hung upon the walls, without my ever offering to pluck them, because they were forbidden fruit, unless now and then—and because I had more pleasure in strolling about among the old melancholy-looking yew trees, or the firs, and picking up the red berries, and the fir apples, which were good for nothing but to look at—or in lying about upon the fresh grass with all the fine garden smells around me—or basking in the orangery till I could almost fancy myself ripening, too, along with the oranges and the limes in that grateful warmth—or in watching the dace that darted to and fro in the fish pond at the bottom of the garden, with here and there a great sulky pike hanging midway down the water in silent state, as if it mocked at their impertinent friskings—I had more pleasure in these busy-idle diversions than in all the sweet flavors of peaches, nectarines, oranges, and such-like common baits of children. Here John slyly deposited back upon the plate a bunch of grapes which, not unobserved by Alice, he had meditated dividing with her, and both seemed willing to relinquish them for the present as irrelevant. Then, in somewhat a more heightened tone, I told how, though their great-grandmother Field loved all her grandchildren, yet in an especial manner she might be said to love their uncle, John L——, because he was so handsome and spirited a youth, and a king to the rest of us; and instead of moping about in solitary corners, like some of us, he would mount the most mettlesome horse he could get, when but an imp no bigger than themselves, and make it carry him half over the county in a morning, and join the hunters when there were any out —and yet he loved the old, great house and gardens, too, but had too much spirit to be always pent up within their boundaries—and how their uncle grew up to man's estate as brave as he was handsome, to the admiration of everybody, but of their great-grandmother Field most especially; and how he used to carry me upon his back when I was a lame-footed boy—for he was a good bit older than me—many a mile when I could not walk for pain;—and how in after life he became lame-footed, too, and I did not always (I fear) make allowances enough for him when he was impatient and in pain, nor remember sufficiently how considerate he had been to me when I was lame-footed; and how when he died, though he had not been dead an hour, it seemed as if he had died a great while ago, such a distance there is betwixt life and death; and how I bore his death as I thought pretty well at first, but afterwards it haunted and haunted me; and though I did not cry or take it to heart as some do, and as I think he would have done if I had died, yet I missed him all day long, and knew not till then how much I had loved him. I missed his kindness, and I missed his crossness, and wished him to be alive again, to be quarreling with him (for we quarreled sometimes) rather than not have him again, and was as uneasy without him as he their poor uncle must have been when the doctor took off his limb. Here the children fell a crying, and asked if their little mourning which they had on was not for uncle John, and they looked up, and prayed me not to go on about their uncle, but to tell them some stories about their pretty, dead mother. Then I told how for seven long years, in hope sometimes, sometimes in despair, yet persisting ever, I courted the fair Alice W——n; and, as much as children could understand, I explained to them what coyness, and difficulty, and denial, meant in maidens—when suddenly, turning to Alice, the soul of the first Alice looked out at her eyes with such a reality of re-presentment, that I became in doubt which of them stood there before me, or whose that bright hair was; and while I stood gazing, both the children gradually grew fainter to my view, receding, and still receding, till nothing at last but two mournful features were seen in the uttermost distance, which, without speech, strangely impressed upon me the effects of speech: "We are not of Alice, nor of thee, nor are we children at all. The children of Alice call Bartrum father. We are nothing; less than nothing, and dreams. We are only what might have been, and must wait upon the tedious shores of Lethe millions of ages before we have existence and a name"——and immediately awaking, I found myself quietly seated in my bachelor armchair, where I had fallen asleep, with the faithful Bridget unchanged by my side—but John L. (or James Elia) was gone forever.

1822 1822

A Dissertation Upon Roast Pig

Mankind, says a Chinese manuscript,[1] which my friend M. was obliging enough to read and explain to me, for the first seventy thousand ages ate their meat raw, clawing or biting it

[1] The manuscript, and the Chinese names (except that of Confucius the great philosopher), are fictitious, but the tradition itself, which Lamb obtained from the traveler Thomas Manning, is an ancient one.

from the living animal, just as they do in Abyssinia to this day. This period is not obscurely hinted at by their great Confucius in the second chapter of his Mundane Mutations, where he designates a kind of golden age by the term Chofang, literally the Cooks' Holiday. The manuscript goes on to say that the art of roasting, or rather broiling (which I take to be the elder brother), was accidentally discovered in the manner following. The swineherd, Ho-ti, having gone out into the woods one morning, as his manner was, to collect mast for his hogs, left his cottage in the care of his eldest son, Bo-bo, a great lubberly boy, who being fond of playing with fire, as younkers of his age commonly are, let some sparks escape into a bundle of straw, which kindling quickly, spread the conflagration over every part of their poor mansion till it was reduced to ashes. Together with the cottage (a sorry antediluvian makeshift of a building, you may think it), what was of much more importance, a fine litter of new-farrowed pigs, no less than nine in number, perished. China pigs have been esteemed a luxury all over the East, from the remotest periods that we read of. Bo-bo was in the utmost consternation, as you may think, not so much for the sake of the tenement, which his father and he could easily build up again with a few dry branches, and the labor of an hour or two, at any time, as for the loss of the pigs. While he was thinking what he should say to his father, and wringing his hands over the smoking remnants of one of those untimely sufferers, an odor assailed his nostrils, unlike any scent which he had before experienced. What could it proceed from? Not from the burnt cottage—he had smelt that smell before—indeed this was by no means the first accident of the kind which had occurred through the negligence of this unlucky young firebrand. Much less did it resemble that of any known herb, weed, or flower. A premonitory moistening at the same time overflowed his nether lip. He knew not what to think. He next stooped down to feel the pig, if there were any signs of life in it. He burnt his fingers, and to cool them he applied them in his booby fashion to his mouth. Some of the crumbs of the scorched skin had come away with his fingers, and for the first time in his life (in the world's life indeed, for before him no man had known it) he tasted—crackling![1] Again he felt and fumbled at the pig. It did not burn him so much now; still he licked his fingers from a sort of habit. The truth at length broke into his slow understanding, that it was the pig that smelt so, and the pig that tasted so delicious; and, surrendering himself up to the new-born pleasure, he fell to tearing up whole handfuls of the scorched skin with the flesh next it, and was cramming it down his throat in his beastly fashion, when his sire entered amid the smoking rafters, armed with retributory cudgel, and finding how affairs stood, began to rain blows upon the young rogue's shoulders, as thick as hailstones, which Bo-do heeded not any more than if they had been flies. The tickling pleasure which he experienced in his lower regions, had rendered him quite callous to any inconveniences he might feel in those remote quarters. His father might lay on, but he could not beat him from his pig till he had fairly made an end of it, when, becoming a little more sensible of his situation, something like the following dialogue ensued.

"You graceless whelp, what have you got there devouring? Is it not enough that you have burnt me down three houses with your dog's tricks, and be hanged to you! but you must be eating fire, and I know not what—what have you got there, I say?"

"O father, the pig, the pig! do come and taste how nice the burnt pig eats."

The ears of Ho-ti tingled with horror. He cursed his son, and he cursed himself, that ever he should beget a son that should eat burnt pig.

Bo-bo, whose scent was wonderfully sharpened since morning, soon raked out another pig, and fairly rendering it asunder, thrust the lesser half by main force into the fists of Ho-ti, still shouting out, "Eat, eat, eat, the burnt pig, Father; only taste—O Lord!"—with such-like barbarous ejaculations, cramming all the while as if he would choke.

Ho-ti trembled in every joint while he grasped the abominable thing, wavering whether he should not put his son to death for an unnatural young monster, when the crackling scorching his fingers as it had done his son's, and applying the same remedy to them, he in his turn tasted some of its flavor which, make what sour mouths he would for a pretense, proved not altogether displeasing to him. In conclusion (for the manuscript here is a little tedious) both father and son fairly sat down to the mess, and never left off till they had despatched all that remained of the litter.

Bo-bo was strictly enjoined not to let the secret escape, for the neighbors would certainly have stoned them for a couple of abominable wretches, who could think of improving upon the good meat which God had sent them.

[1] the crisp skin of roast pork

Nevertheless, strange stories got about. It was observed that Ho-ti's cottage was burnt down now more frequently than ever. Nothing but fires from this time forward. Some would break out in broad day, others in the night-time. As often as the sow farrowed, so sure was the house of Ho-ti to be in a blaze; and Ho-ti himself, which was the more remarkable, instead of chastising his son, seemed to grow more indulgent to him than ever. At length they were watched, the terrible mystery discovered, and father and son summoned to take their trial at Pekin, then an inconsiderable assize town. Evidence was given, the obnoxious food itself produced in court, and verdict about to be pronounced, when the foreman of the jury begged that some of the burnt pig, of which the culprits stood accused, might be handed into the box. He handled it, and they all handled it; and burning their fingers as Bo-bo and his father had done before them, and nature prompting to each of them the same remedy, against the face of all the facts, and the clearest charge which judge had ever given—to the surprise of the whole court, townsfolk, strangers, reporters, and all present—without leaving the box, or any manner of consultation whatever, they brought in a simultaneous verdict of Not Guilty.

The judge, who was a shrewd fellow, winked at the manifest iniquity of the decision; and when the court was dismissed, went privily, and bought up all the pigs that could be had for love or money. In a few days his lordship's town house was observed to be on fire. The thing took wing, and now there was nothing to be seen but fires in every direction. Fuel and pigs grew enormously dear all over the district. The insurance offices one and all shut up shop. People built slighter and slighter every day, until it was feared that the very science of architecture would in no long time be lost to the world. Thus this custom of firing houses continued, till in process of time, says my manuscript, a sage arose, like our Locke, [1] who made a discovery that the flesh of swine, or indeed of any other animal, might be cooked (burnt, as they called it) without the necessity of consuming a whole house to dress it. Then first began the rude form of a gridiron. Roasting by the string, or spit, came in a century or two later, I forget in whose dynasty. By such slow degrees, concludes the manuscript, do the most useful and seemingly the most obvious arts make their way among mankind.

[1] John Locke, b. 1632, a British philosopher, one of the most celebrated thinkers of modern times

Without placing too implicit faith in the account above given, it must be agreed that if a worthy pretext for so dangerous an experiment as setting houses on fire (especially in these days) could be assigned in favor of any culinary object, that pretext and excuse might be found in ROAST PIG.

Of all the delicacies in the whole *mundus edibilis,* [2] I will maintain it to be the most delicate—*princeps obsoniorum.* [3]

I speak not of your grown porkers—things between pig and pork—those hobbydehoys [4]—but a young and tender suckling—under a moon old—guiltless as yet of the sty—with no original speck of the *amor immunditiae,* [5] the hereditary failing of the first parent, yet manifest—his voice as yet not broken, but something between a childish treble and a grumble—the mild forerunner, or *praeludium,* of a grunt.

He must be roasted. I am not ignorant that our ancestors ate them seethed, or boiled—but what a sacrifice of the exterior tegument!

There is no flavor comparable, I will contend, to that of the crisp, tawny, well-watched, not over-roasted, crackling, as it is well called—the very teeth are invited to their share of the pleasure at this banquet in overcoming the coy, brittle resistance—with the adhesive oleaginous—Oh, call it not fat! but an indefinable sweetness growing up to it—the tender blossoming of fat—fat cropped in the bud—taken in the shoot—in the first innocence—the cream and quintessence of the child-pig's yet pure food—the lean, no lean, but a kind of animal manna—or, rather, fat and lean (if it must be so) so blended and running into each other that both together make but one ambrosian result, or common substance.

Behold him, while he is "doing"—it seemeth rather a refreshing warmth than a scorching heat that he is so passive to. How equably he twirleth round the string!—Now he is just done. To see the extreme sensibility of that tender age, he hath wept out his pretty eyes,—radiant jellies—shooting stars [6]—

See him in the dish, his second cradle, how meek he lieth! Wouldst thou have had this innocent grow up to the grossness and indocility which too often accompany maturer swinehood? Ten to one he would have proved a glutton, a sloven, an obstinate disagreeable animal—wallowing in all manner of filthy conversation.

[2] world of edibles
[3] chief of tidbits
[4] youths at the awkward age
[5] love of dirt
[6] Ancient superstition regarded certain jelly-like fungi as fallen shooting-stars. Compare, moreover, Cornwall's "Out, vile jelly" (*King Lear,* III, vii, 83).

From these sins he is happily snatched away—

Ere sin could blight or sorrow fade,
Death came with timely care [1]—

his memory is odoriferous—no clown curseth, while his stomach half rejecteth, the rank bacon—no coalheaver bolteth him in reeking sausages—he hath a fair sepulcher in the grateful stomach of the judicious epicure—and for such a tomb might be content to die.

He is the best of sapors.[2] Pineapple is great. She is indeed almost too transcendent—a delight, if not sinful, yet so like to sinning that really a tender-conscienced person would do well to pause—too ravishing for mortal taste, she woundeth and excoriateth the lips that approach her—like lovers' kisses, she biteth—she is a pleasure bordering on pain from the fierceness and insanity of her relish—but she stoppeth at the palate—she meddleth not with the appetite—and the coarsest hunger might barter her consistently for a mutton chop.

Pig—let me speak his praise—is no less provocative of the appetite, than he is satisfactory to the criticalness of the censorious palate. The strong man may batten on him, and the weakling refuseth not his mild juices.

Unlike to mankind's mixed characters, a bundle of virtues and vices, inexplicably intertwisted and not to be unraveled without hazard, he is—good throughout. No part of him is better or worse than another. He helpeth, as far as his little means extend, all around. He is the least envious of banquets. He is all neighbors' fare.

I am one of those who freely and ungrudgingly impart a share of the good things of this life which fall to their lot (few as mine are in this kind) to a friend. I protest I take as great an interest in my friend's pleasures, his relishes, and proper satisfactions, as in mine own. "Presents," I often say, "endear absents." Hares, pheasants, partridges, snipes, barn-door chickens (those "tame villatic [3] fowl"), capons, plovers, brawn,[4] barrels of oysters, I dispense as freely as I receive them. I love to taste them, as it were, upon the tongue of my friend. But a stop must be put somewhere. One would not, like Lear, "give everything."[5] I make my stand upon [6] pig. Methinks it is an ingratitude to the Giver of all good flavors, to extra-domiciliate, or send out of the house slightingly (under pretext of friendship, or I know not what) a blessing so particularly adapted, predestined, I may say, to my individual palate—it argues an insensibility.

I remember a touch of conscience in this kind at school. My good old aunt, who never parted from me at the end of a holiday without stuffing a sweetmeat, or some nice thing, into my pocket, had dismissed me one evening with a smoking plum cake, fresh from the oven. In my way to school (it was over London Bridge) a gray-headed, old beggar saluted me (I have no doubt at this time of day that he was a counterfeit). I had no pence to console him with, and in the vanity of self-denial, and the very coxcombry of charity, schoolboy-like, I made him a present of—the whole cake! I walked on a little, buoyed up, as one is on such occasions, with a sweet soothing of self-satisfaction; but before I had got to the end of the bridge, my better feelings returned, and I burst into tears, thinking how ungrateful I had been to my good aunt, to go and give her good gift away to a stranger that I had never seen before, and who might be a bad man for aught I knew; and then I thought of the pleasure my aunt would be taking in thinking that I—I myself and not another—would eat her nice cake—and what should I say to her the next time I saw her—how naughty I was to part with her pretty present!—and the odor of that spicy cake came back upon my recollection, and the pleasure and the curiosity I had taken in seeing her make it, and her joy when she had sent it to the oven, and how disappointed she would feel that I had never had a bit of it in my mouth at last—and I blamed my impertinent spirit of alms-giving, and out-of-place hypocrisy of goodness; and above all, I wished never to see the face again of that insidious, good-for-nothing, old gray impostor.

Our ancestors were nice [7] in their method of sacrificing these tender victims. We read of pigs whipped to death with something of a shock, as we hear of any other obsolete custom. The age of discipline is gone by, or it would be curious to inquire (in a philosophical light merely) what effect this process might have toward intenerating and dulcifying a substance naturally so mild and dulcet as the flesh of young pigs. It looks like refining a violet. Yet we should be cautious, while we condemn the inhumanity, how we censure the wisdom of the practice. It might impart a gusto—

I remember an hypothesis, argued upon by the young students when I was at St. Omer's,[8]

[1] Coleridge: "Epitaph on an Infant."
[2] savors
[3] farmyard (Milton: *Samson Agonistes*, line 1695)
[4] pickled boar's flesh
[5] *King Lear*, II, iv, 253
[6] halt at
[7] particular
[8] a Jesuit college (Lamb was never a student there)

and maintained with much learning and pleasantry on both sides, "Whether, supposing that the flavor of a pig who obtained his death by whipping *(per flagellationem extremam)* superadded a pleasure upon the palate of a man more intense than any possible suffering we can conceive in the animal, is man justified in using that method of putting the animal to death?" I forget the decision.

His sauce should be considered. Decidedly a few bread crumbs, done up with his liver and brains, and a dash of mild sage. But banish, dear Mrs. Cook, I beseech you, the whole onion tribe. Barbecue your whole hogs to your palate, steep them in shalots, stuff them out with plantations of the rank and guilty garlic; you cannot poison them, or make them stronger than they are—but consider, he is a weakling—a flower.

1822

From THE LAST ESSAYS OF ELIA

Old China

I have an almost feminine partiality for old china. When I go to see any great house, I inquire for the china closet, and next for the picture gallery. I cannot defend the order of preference, but by saying that we have all some taste or other of too ancient a date to admit of our remembering distinctly that it was an acquired one. I can call to mind the first play and the first exhibition that I was taken to; but I am not conscious of a time when china jars and saucers were introduced into my imagination.

I had no repugnance then—why should I now have?—to those little, lawless, azure-tinctured grotesques that, under the notion of men and women, float about, uncircumscribed by any element, in that world before perspective—a china teacup.

I like to see my old friends—whom distance cannot diminish—figuring up in the air (so they appear to our optics) yet on *terra firma*, still—for so we must in courtesy interpret that speck of deeper blue which the decorous artist, to prevent absurdity, has made to spring up beneath their sandals.

I love the men with women's faces, and the women, if possible, with still more womanish expressions.

Here is a young and courtly Mandarin handing tea to a lady from a salver—two miles off. See how distance seems to set off respect! And here the same lady, or another—for likeness is identity on teacups—is stepping into a little fairy boat, moored on the hither side of this calm garden river, with a dainty mincing foot, which in a right [1] angle of incidence (as angles go in our world) must infallibly land her in the midst of a flowery mead—a furlong off on the other side of the same strange stream!

Farther on—if far or near can be predicated of their world—see horses, trees, pagodas, dancing the hays. [2]

Here—a cow and rabbit couchant and coextensive—so objects show, seen through the lucid atmosphere of fine Cathay. [3]

I was pointing out to my cousin last evening, over our Hyson [4] (which we are old-fashioned enough to drink unmixed still of an afternoon), some of these *speciosa miracula* [5] upon a set of extraordinary, old blue china (a recent purchase) which we were now for the first time using; and could not help remarking how favorable circumstances had been to us of late years, that we could afford to please the eye sometimes with trifles of this sort—when a passing sentiment seemed to overshade the brows of my companion. I am quick at detecting these summer clouds in Bridget. [6]

"I wish the good old times would come again," she said, "when we were not quite so rich. I do not mean that I want to be poor; but there was a middle state"—so she was pleased to ramble on—"in which I am sure we were a great deal happier. A purchase is but a purchase, now that you have money enough and to spare. Formerly it used to be a triumph. When we coveted a cheap luxury (and, oh! how much ado I had to get you to consent in those times!) we were used to have a debate two or three days before, and to weigh the *for* and *against*, and think what we might spare it out of, and what saving we could hit upon that should be an equivalent. A thing was worth buying then when we felt the money that we paid for it.

"Do you remember the brown suit, which you made to hang upon you till all your friends cried shame upon you, it grew so threadbare—and all because of that folio Beaumont and Fletcher [7] which you dragged home late at night from Barker's in Covent Garden? [8] Do you remember how we eyed it for weeks before we could make up our minds to the purchase, and had not come to a determination till it was near ten o'clock of the Saturday night, when you set

[1] properly calculated
[2] an old English dance
[3] Chinese Tartary (used loosely for China)
[4] green tea
[5] radiant wonders
[6] See introductory note on "Elia."
[7] This particular volume, with notes in it by Coleridge, is now in the British Museum.
[8] a square in the heart of London, best known for its fruit and flower markets

off from Islington,[1] fearing you should be too late—and when the old bookseller with some grumbling opened his shop, and by the twinkling taper (for he was setting bedward) lighted out the relic from his dusty treasures—and when you lugged it home, wishing it were twice as cumbersome—and when you presented it to me—and when we were exploring the perfectness of it (collating, you called it)—and while I was repairing some of the loose leaves with paste which your impatience would not suffer to be left till daybreak—was there no pleasure in being a poor man? Or can those neat, black clothes which you wear now, and are so careful to keep brushed, since we have become rich and finical, give you half the honest vanity with which you flaunted it about in that overworn suit—your old corbeau[2]—for four or five weeks longer than you should have done, to pacify your conscience for the mighty sum of fifteen—or sixteen shillings was it?—a great affair we thought it then—which you had lavished on the old folio. Now you can afford to buy any book that pleases you, but I do not see that you ever bring me home any nice old purchases now.

"When you came home with twenty apologies for laying out a less number of shillings upon that print after Lionardo,[3] which we christened the 'Lady Blanche'; when you looked at the purchase, and thought of the money—and thought of the money, and looked again at the picture—was there no pleasure in being a poor man? Now, you have nothing to do but to walk into Colnaghi's, and buy a wilderness[4] of Lionardos. Yet do you?

"Then, do you remember our pleasant walks to Enfield, and Potter's Bar, and Waltham,[5] when we had a holiday—holidays and all other fun are gone now we are rich—and the little handbasket in which I used to deposit our day's fare of savory, cold lamb and salad—and how you would pry about at noontide for some decent house where we might go in and produce our store—only paying for the ale that you must call for—and speculate upon the looks of the landlady, and whether she was likely to allow us a table-cloth—and wish for such another honest hostess as Izaak Walton has described many a one on the pleasant banks of the Lea, when he went a-fishing—and sometimes they would prove obliging enough, and sometimes they would look grudgingly upon us—but we had cheerful looks still for one another, and would eat our plain food savorily, scarcely grudging Piscator[6] his Trout Hall? Now, when we go out a day's pleasuring, which is seldom moreover, we *ride* part of the way—and go into a fine inn, and order the best of dinners, never debating the expense—which, after all, never has half the relish of those chance country snaps, when we were at the mercy of uncertain usage, and a precarious welcome.

"You are too proud to see a play anywhere now but in the pit. Do you remember where it was we used to sit when we saw the *Battle of Hexam* and the *Surrender of Calais*,[7] and Bannister[8] and Mrs. Bland in the *Children in the Wood*[9]—when we squeezed out our shilling apiece to sit three or four times in a season in the one-shilling gallery—where you felt all the time that you ought not to have brought me—and more strongly I felt obligation to you for having brought me—and the pleasure was the better for a little shame—and when the curtain drew up, what cared we for our place in the house, or what mattered it where we were sitting when our thoughts were with Rosalind in Arden, or with Viola at the court of Illyria?[10] You used to say that the gallery was the best place of all for enjoying a play socially—that the relish of such exhibitions must be in proportion to the infrequency of going—that the company we met there, not being in general readers of plays, were obliged to attend the more, and did attend, to what was going on on the stage—because a word lost would have been a chasm which it was impossible for them to fill up. With such reflections we consoled our pride then—and I appeal to you, whether, as a woman, I met generally with less attention and accommodation than I have done since in more expensive situations in the house? The getting in, indeed, and the crowding up those inconvenient staircases was bad enough—but there was still a law of civility to women recognized to quite as great an extent as we ever found in the other passages—and how a little difficulty overcome heightened the snug seat and the play, afterwards! Now we can only pay our money, and walk in. You cannot see, you say, in the galleries, now. I am sure we saw, and heard, too, well enough then—but sight and all, I think, is gone with our poverty.

"There was pleasure in eating strawberries, before they became quite common—in the first dish of peas, while they were yet dear—to have them for a nice supper, a treat. What treat

[1] in northern London [2] black coat
[3] Leonardo da Vinci, the Italian painter
[4] *Merchant of Venice,* III, i, 128
[5] London suburbs
[6] See Walton's *The Complete Angler,* p. 289.
[7] plays by George Colman the younger
[8] John Bannister, a pupil of Garrick
[9] a comedy by Thomas Morton
[10] in *As You Like It* and *Twelfth Night*

can we have now? If we were to treat ourselves now—that is, to have dainties a little above our means, it would be selfish and wicked. It is the very little more that we allow ourselves, beyond what the actual poor can get at, that makes what I call a treat—when two people, living together as we have done, now and then indulge themselves in a cheap luxury which both like; while each apologizes, and is willing to take both halves of the blame to his single share. I see no harm in people making much of themselves, in that sense of the word. It may give them a hint how to make much of others. But now—what I mean by the word—we never do make much of ourselves. None but the poor can do it. I do not mean the veriest poor of all, but persons as we were, just above poverty.

"I know what you were going to say, that it is mighty pleasant at the end of the year to make all meet—and much ado we used to have every thirty-first night of December to account for our exceedings—many a long face did you make over your puzzled accounts, and in contriving to make it out how we had spent so much—or that we had not spent so much—or that it was impossible we should spend so much next year—and still we found our slender capital decreasing—but then, betwixt ways, and projects, and compromises of one sort or another, and talk of curtailing this charge, and doing without that for the future—and the hope that youth brings, and laughing spirits (in which you were never poor till now), we pocketed up our loss, and in conclusion, with 'lusty brimmers' (as you used to quote it out of 'hearty, cheerful Mr. Cotton,'[1] as you called him) we used to welcome in the 'coming guest.' Now we have no reckoning at all at the end of the old year—no flattering promises about the new year doing better for us."

Bridget is so sparing of her speech on most occasions, that when she gets into a rhetorical vein, I am careful how I interrupt it. I could not help, however, smiling at the phantom of wealth which her dear imagination had conjured up out of a clear income of poor —— hundred pounds a year. "It is true we were happier when we were poorer, but we were also younger, my cousin. I am afraid we must put up with the excess, for if we were to shake the superflux into the sea, we should not much mend ourselves. That we had much to struggle with, as we grew up together, we have reason to be most thankful. It strengthened, and knit our compact closer. We could never have been what we have been to each other if we had always had the sufficiency which you now complain of. The resisting power—those natural dilations of the youthful spirit, which circumstances cannot straiten—with us are long since passed away. Competence to age is supplementary youth; a sorry supplement indeed, but I fear the best that is to be had. We must ride, where we formerly walked; live better, and lie softer—and shall be wise to do so—than we had means to do in those good old days you speak of. Yet could those days return—could you and I once more walk our thirty miles aday—could Bannister and Mrs. Bland again be young, and you and I be young to see them—could the good old one-shilling gallery days return—they are dreams, my cousin, now—but could you and I at this moment, instead of this quiet argument, by our well-carpeted fireside, sitting on this luxurious sofa—be once more struggling up those inconvenient staircases, pushed about, and squeezed, and elbowed by the poorest rabble of poor, gallery scramblers—could I once more hear those anxious shrieks of yours—and the delicious 'Thank God, we are safe,' which always followed when the topmost stair, conquered, let in the first light of the whole cheerful theater down beneath us—I know not the fathom line that ever touched a descent so deep as I would be willing to bury more wealth in than Croesus[2] had, or the great Jew R——[3] is supposed to have, to purchase it.

"And now do just look at that merry, little, Chinese waiter holding an umbrella, big enough for a bed tester,[4] over the head of that pretty, insipid, half-Madonna-ish chit of a lady in that very blue summerhouse."

1823

[1] Charles Cotton: "The New Year"

WALTER SAVAGE LANDOR
1775-1864

Landor, born of an ancient Warwickshire family, was for nearly seventy years one of the most picturesque figures of English literature. Both Eton and Oxford he was obliged to leave at the request of the authorities. All through life he found himself at war with the things that are, and in continual quarrels, often of his own seeking; for, though capable of the tenderest affection, he was violent of temper and expression.

Landor's foremost works include his *Poems,* 1795; *Gebir,* a poetic tale, 1798, and *Imaginary Conversations,* which appeared in series from 1824 for almost thirty years. One basis of his work is his absolute knowledge of the classics. He is said to have used Latin, both in prose

[2] King of Lydia
[3] Rothschild
[4] bed canopy

and poetry, as effectively as English. He lived in a world of books, of hero-worship, and of the great spirits of all the ages. These he recreates before us in his imaginary conversations involving sometimes the ancients alone, sometimes the dead and the living. Through intense realization of the personalities that appear before him, Landor develops the dramatic moments of their experiences in rhythmic language, plastic as clay, severe yet brilliant, passionate yet restrained, fitting every mood of life. And in so doing he reaches a new boundary in the development of English prose.

Biography: Colvin (EML). Criticism: Lowell, Saintsbury, Swinburne, Dowden, Payne, Woodberry. Interesting and suggestive: Field, "Last Days of W. S. Landor," *Atlan.* 17:385-95, 540-51, 684-705; "W. S. Landor," C. Spender, *Liv. Age* 296:738-43; "Landor's Llanthony" [a Welsh estate that Landor attempted to improve], S. Wheeler, *19th Cent.* 89:445-56; "Poetry of Landor," A. Symons, *Atlan.* 97:808-16.

From IMAGINARY CONVERSATIONS

METELLUS AND MARIUS [1]

METELLUS. Well met, Caius Marius! My orders are to find instantly a centurion who shall mount the walls; one capable of observation, acute in remark, prompt, calm, active, intrepid. The Numantians are sacrificing to the gods in secrecy; they have sounded the horn once only, —and hoarsely and low and mournfully.

MARIUS. Was that ladder I see yonder among the caper bushes and purple lilies, under where the fig tree grows out of the rampart, left for me?

METELLUS. Even so, wert thou willing. Wouldst thou mount it?

MARIUS. Rejoicingly. If none are below or near, may I explore the state of things by entering the city?

METELLUS. Use thy discretion in that.

What seest thou? Wouldst thou leap down? Lift the ladder.

MARIUS. Are there spikes in it where it sticks in the turf? I should slip else.

[1] The siege and capture, in 132 B.C., of the Numantians, struggling with 8,000 men against the whole power of Rome, was one of the stages in the disgraceful third Punic war, which was conducted by Scipio Africanus the Younger. Caius Caecilius Metellus, the tribune, was a comparatively unimportant personage. Marius, the centurion, of obscure birth, rose later to be seven times consul. Plutarch tells us that Scipio had marked the youth's good qualities, and when asked who should succeed himself in case of accident, had touched the shoulder of Marius, saying, "Perhaps this man"; which saying "raised the hopes of Marius like a divine oracle." On this slight historical foundation Landor constructs his dramatic scene. The Numantians, in all probability, had no regular walls; and Appian says that some of them preferred surrender to death and were led in a Roman Triumph.

METELLUS. How! bravest of our centurions, art even though afraid? Seest thou anyone by?

MARIUS. Aye; some hundreds close beneath me.

METELLUS. Retire, then. Hasten back; I will protect thy descent.

MARIUS. May I speak, O Metellus, without an offense to discipline?

METELLUS. Say.

MARIUS. Listen! Dost thou not hear?

METELLUS. Shame on thee! alight, alight! my shield shall cover thee.

MARIUS. There is a murmur like the hum of bees in the bean field of Cereaté; [2] for the sun is hot, and the ground is thirsty. When will it have drunk up for me the blood that has run, and is yet oozing on it, from those fresh bodies!

METELLUS. How! We have not fought for many days; what bodies, then, are fresh ones?

MARIUS. Close beneath the wall are those of infants and of girls; in the middle of the road are youths, emaciated; some either unwounded or wounded months ago; some on their spears, others on their swords; no few have received in mutual death the last interchange of friendship; their daggers unite them, hilt to hilt, bosom to bosom.

METELLUS. Mark rather the living—what are they about?

MARIUS. About the sacrifice, which portends them, I conjecture, but little good—it burns sullenly and slowly. The victim will lie upon the pyre till morning, and still be unconsumed, unless they bring more fuel.

I will leap down and walk on cautiously, and return with tidings if death should spare me.

Never was any race of mortals so unmilitary as these Numantians; no watch, no stations, no palisades across the streets.

METELLUS. Did they want, then, all the wood for the altar?

MARIUS. It appears so—I will return anon.

METELLUS. The gods speed thee, my brave, honest Marius!

MARIUS (*returned*). The ladder should have been better spiked for that slippery ground. I am down again safe, however. Here a man may walk securely, and without picking his steps.

METELLUS. Tell me, Caius, what thou sawest.

MARIUS. The streets of Numantia.

METELLUS. Doubtless; but what else?

MARIUS. The temples and markets and places of exercise and fountains.

[2] the rustic home of Marius's childhood, near Arpinum

METELLUS. Art thou crazed, centurion? What more? Speak plainly, at once, and briefly.

MARIUS. I beheld, then, all Numantia.

METELLUS. Has terror maddened thee? Hast thou descried nothing of the inhabitants but those carcasses under the ramparts?

MARIUS. Those, O Metellus, lie scattered, although not indeed far asunder. The greater part of the soldiers and citizens—of the fathers, husbands, widows, wives, espoused—were assembled together.

METELLUS. About the altar?

MARIUS. Upon it.

METELLUS. So busy and earnest in devotion! But how all upon it?

MARIUS. It blazed under them, and over them, and round about them.

METELLUS. Immortal gods! Art thou sane, Caius Marius? Thy visage is scorched; thy speech may wander after such an enterprise; thy shield burns my hand.

MARIUS. I thought it had cooled again. Why, truly, it seems hot; I now feel it.

METELLUS. Wipe off those embers.

MARIUS. 'Twere better; there will be none opposite to shake them upon, for some time.

The funereal horn, that sounded with such feebleness, sounded not so from the faint heart of him who blew it. Him I saw; him only of the living. Should I say it? There was another; there was one child whom its parent could not kill, could not part from. She had hidden it in her robe, I suspect; and when the fire had reached it, either it shrieked or she did. For suddenly a cry pierced through the crackling pinewood, and something of round in figure fell from brand to brand until it reached the pavement at the feet of him who had blown the horn. I rushed toward him, for I wanted to hear the whole story, and felt the pressure of time. Condemn not my weakness, O Caecilius! I wished an enemy to live an hour longer; for my orders were to explore and bring intelligence. When I gazed on him, in height almost gigantic, I wondered not that the blast of his trumpet was so weak; rather did I wonder that famine, whose hand had indented every limb and feature, had left him any voice articulate. I rushed toward him, however, ere my eyes had measured either his form or strength. He held the child against me, and staggered under it.

"Behold," he exclaimed, "the glorious ornament of a Roman triumph!"

I stood horror-stricken; when suddenly drops, as of rain, pattered down from the pyre. I looked; and many were the precious stones, many were the amulets and rings and bracelets and other barbaric ornaments, unknown to me in form or purpose, that tinkled on the hardened and black branches, from mothers and wives and betrothed maids; and some, too, I can imagine, from robuster arms —things of joyance, won in battle. The crowd of incumbent bodies was so dense and heavy that neither the fire nor the smoke could penetrate upward from among them; and they sank, whole and at once, into the smoldering cavern eaten out below. He at whose neck hung the trumpet felt this, and started.

"There is yet room," he cried, "and there is strength enough yet, both in the element and in me."

He extended his withered arms, he thrust forward the gaunt links of his throat, and upon gnarled knees that smote each other audibly, tottered into the civic[1] fire. It—like some hungry and strangest beast on the innermost wild of Africa, pierced, broken, prostrate, motionless, gazed at by its hunter in the impatience of glory, in the delight of awe—panted once more, and seized him.

I have seen within this hour, O Metellus, what Rome in the cycle of her triumphs will never see, that the Sun in his eternal course can never show her, what the Earth has borne but now, and must never rear again for her, what Victory herself has envied her—a Numantian.

METELLUS. We shall feast tomorrow. Hope, Caius Marius, to become a tribune; trust in fortune.

MARIUS. Auguries are surer; surest of all is perseverance.

METELLUS. I hope the wine has not grown vapid in my tent; I have kept it waiting, and must now report to Scipio the intelligence of our discovery. Come after me, Caius.

MARIUS (*alone*). The tribune is the discoverer! The centurion is the scout! Caius Marius must enter more Numantias. Light-hearted Caecilius, thou mayest perhaps hereafter, and not with humbled but with exulting pride, take orders from this hand. If Scipio's words are fate, and to me they sound so, the portals of the Capitol may shake before my chariot, as my horses plunge back at the applauses of the people, and Jove in his high domicile[2] may welcome the citizen of Arpinum.

1829

[1] citizens' (perhaps after the analogy of the "civic" crown, conferred for distinction)

[2] the Temple of Jupiter, whither the leader of a Triumph went to offer sacrifice

Leofric and Godiva [1]

Godiva. There is a dearth in the land, my sweet Leofric! Remember how many weeks of drought we have had, even in the deep pastures of Leicestershire; and how many Sundays we have heard the same prayers for rain, and supplications that it would please the Lord in his mercy to turn aside his anger from the poor, pining cattle. You, my dear husband, have imprisoned more than one malefactor for leaving his dead ox in the public way; and other hinds [2] have fled before you out of the traces, in which they, and their sons and their daughters, and haply their old fathers and mothers, were dragging the abandoned wain homeward. Although we were accompanied by many brave spearmen and skilful archers, it was perilous to pass the creatures which the farm-yard dogs, driven from the hearth by the poverty of their masters, were tearing and devouring; while others, bitten and lamed, filled the air either with long and deep howls or sharp and quick barkings, as they struggled with hunger and feebleness, or were exasperated by heat and pain. Nor could the thyme from the heath, nor the bruised branches of the fir tree, extinguish or abate the foul odor.

Leofric. And now, Godiva, my darling, thou art afraid we should be eaten up before we enter the gates of Coventry; or perchance that in the gardens there are no roses to greet thee, no sweet herbs for thy mat and pillow.

Godiva. Leofric, I have no such fears. This is the month of roses; I find them everywhere since my blessed marriage. They, and all other sweet herbs, I know not why, seem to greet me wherever I look at them, as though they knew and expected me. Surely they cannot feel that I am fond of them.

Leofric. O light, laughing simpleton! But what wouldst thou? I came not hither to pray; and yet if praying would satisfy thee, or remove the drought, I would ride up straightway to Saint Michael's and pray until morning.

Godiva. I would do the same, O Leofric! but God hath turned away his ear from holier lips than mine. Would my own dear husband hear me, if I implored him for what is easier to accomplish—what he can do like God?

Leofric. How! What is it?

Godiva. I would not in the first hurry of your wrath, appeal to you, my loving Lord, in behalf of these unhappy men who have offended you.

Leofric. Unhappy! Is that all?

Godiva. Unhappy they must surely be, to have offended you so grievously. What a soft air breathes over us! how quiet and serene and still an evening! how calm are the heavens and the earth!—Shall none enjoy them; not even we, my Leofric? The sun is ready to set; let it never set, O Leofric, on your anger. These are not my words; they are better than mine. [3] Should they lose their virtue from my unworthiness in uttering them?

Leofric. Godiva, wouldst thou plead to me for rebels?

Godiva. They have, then, drawn the sword against you? Indeed, I knew it not.

Leofric. They have omitted to send me my dues, established by my ancestors, well knowing of our nuptials, and of the charges and festivities they require, and that in a season of such scarcity my own lands are insufficient.

Godiva. If they were starving, as they said they were——

Leofric. Must I starve, too? Is it not enough to lose my vassals?

Godiva. Enough! O God! Too much! Too much! May you never lose them! Give them life, peace, comfort, contentment. There are those among them who kissed me in my infancy, and who blessed me at the baptismal font. Leofric, Leofric! the first old man I meet I shall think is one of those; and I shall think on the blessing he gave me, and—ah me! —on the blessing I bring back to him. My heart will bleed, will burst; and he will weep at it! He will weep, poor soul, for the wife of a cruel lord who denounces vengeance on him, who carries death into his family!

Leofric. We must hold solemn festivals.

Godiva. We must, indeed.

Leofric. Well, then?

Godiva. Is the clamorousness that succeeds the death of God's dumb creatures, are crowded halls, are slaughtered cattle, festivals—are maddening songs, and giddy dances, and hireling praises from parti-colored coats? Can the voice of a minstrel tell us better things of ourselves than our own internal one might tell us; or can his breath make our breath softer in sleep? Oh, my beloved! let everything be a joyance to us; it will, if we will. Sad is the day, and worse must follow, when we hear the blackbird in the garden, and do not throb with joy. But, Leofric, the high festival is strown by the servant of God upon the heart of man.

[1] According to legend, Leofric, Earl of Mercia in the 11th century, acceded to his wife's plea that he remit a certain burdensome tax on the people, on the harsh condition that she ride through the street naked at noonday. She fulfilled the condition with modesty, owing to her luxuriant hair.

[2] peasants

[3] *Ephesians*, iv, 26

It is gladness, it is thanksgiving; it is the orphan, the starveling, pressed to the bosom, and bidden as its first commandment to remember its benefactor. We will hold this festival; the guests are ready; we may keep it up for weeks, and months, and years together, and always be the happier and the richer for it. The beverage of this feast, O Leofric, is sweeter than bee or flower or vine can give us; [1] it flows from heaven; and in heaven will it abundantly be poured out again to him who pours it out here unsparingly.

LEOFRIC. Thou art wild.

GODIVA. I have, indeed, lost myself. Some power, some good, kind Power melts me—body and soul and voice—into tenderness and love. O my husband, we must obey it. Look upon me! look upon me! lift your sweet eyes from the ground! I will not cease to supplicate; I dare not.

LEOFRIC. We may think upon it.

GODIVA. Never say that! What! think upon goodness when you can be good? Let not the infants cry for sustenance! The mother of our blessed Lord will hear them; us never, never afterwards.

LEOFRIC. Here comes the Bishop; we are but one mile from the walls. Why dismountest thou? No bishop can expect it. Godiva! my honor and rank among men are humbled by this. Earl Godwin will hear of it. Up! up! the Bishop hath seen it; he urgeth his horse onward. Dost thou not hear him now upon the solid turf behind thee?

GODIVA. Never, no, never will I rise, O Leofric, until you remit this most impious tax —this tax on hard labor, on hard life.

LEOFRIC. Turn round; look how the fat nag canters, as to the tune of a sinner's psalm, slow and hard-breathing. What reason or right can the people have to complain while their bishop's steed is so sleek and well caparisoned? Inclination to change, desire to abolish old usages. Up! up! For shame! They shall smart for it, idlers! Sir Bishop, I must blush for my young bride.

GODIVA. My husband, my husband! Will you pardon the city?

LEOFRIC. Sir Bishop! I could not think you would have seen her in this plight. Will I pardon? Yea, Godiva, by the holy rood, will I pardon the city, when thou ridest naked at noontide through the streets!

GODIVA. Oh, my dear, cruel Leofric, where is the heart you gave me? It was not so. Can mine have hardened it?

[1] honey, nectar, and wine

BISHOP. Earl, thou abashest thy spouse; she turneth pale, and weepeth. Lady Godiva, peace be with thee.

Godiva. Thanks, holy man! Peace will be with me when peace is with your city. Did you hear my Lord's cruel word?

BISHOP. I did, lady.

GODIVA. Will you remember it, and pray against it?

BISHOP. Wilt *thou* forget it, daughter?

GODIVA. I am not offended.

BISHOP. Angel of peace and purity!

GODIVA. But treasure it up in your heart; deem it an incense, good only when it is consumed and spent, ascending with prayer and sacrifice. And, now, what was it?

BISHOP. Christ save us! that he will pardon the city when thou ridest naked through the streets at noon.

GODIVA. Did he not swear an oath?

BISHOP. He sware by the holy rood.

GODIVA. My Redeemer, thou hast heard it! Save the city!

LEOFRIC. We are now upon the beginning of the pavement; these are the suburbs. Let us think of feasting; we may pray afterwards; tomorrow we shall rest.

GODIVA. No judgments, then, tomorrow, Leofric?

LEOFRIC. None—we will carouse.

GODIVA. The saints of heaven have given me strength and confidence; my prayers are heard; the heart of my beloved is now softened.

LEOFRIC (*aside*). Aye, aye—they shall smart, though.

GODIVA. Say, dearest Leofric, is there indeed no other hope, no other mediation?

LEOFRIC. I have sworn. Besides, thou hast made me redden and turn my face away from thee, and all the knaves have seen it; this adds to the city's crime.

GODIVA. I have blushed, too, Leofric, and was not rash nor obdurate.

LEOFRIC. But thou, my sweetest, art given to blushing; there is no conquering it in thee. I wish thou hadst not alighted so hastily and roughly; it hath shaken down a sheaf of thy hair. Take heed thou sit not upon it, lest it anguish thee. Well done! It mingleth now sweetly with the cloth of gold upon the saddle, running here and there, as if it had life and faculties and business, and were working thereupon some newer and cunninger device. O my beauteous Eve! there is a Paradise about thee! the world is refreshed as thou movest and breathest on it. I cannot see or think of evil where thou art. I could throw my arms even here about thee. No signs for me! no shaking of sunbeams! no reproof or frown or wonderment —I *will* say it—now, then, for worse—I could close with my kisses thy half-open lips, aye, and those lovely and loving eyes, before the people.

GODIVA. Tomorrow you shall kiss me, and they shall bless you for it. I shall be very pale, for tonight I must fast and pray.

LEOFRIC. I do not hear thee; the voices of the folk are so loud under this archway.

GODIVA (*to herself*). God help them! good kind souls! I hope they will not crowd about me so tomorrow. O Leofric! could my name be forgotten, and yours alone remembered! But perhaps my innocence may save me from reproach; and how many as innocent are in fear and famine! No eye will open on me but fresh from tears. What a young mother for so large a family! Shall my youth harm me? Under God's hand it gives me courage. Ah! when will the morning come? Ah! when will the noon be over?

1829

THOMAS DE QUINCEY
1785-1859

Born at Manchester of cultured and wealthy parents who gave him every intellectual opportunity as a child, De Quincey was steeped in the classics, read voraciously, and amassed a fund of miscellaneous information unsurpassed in his day. As a child he was a dreamer. In youth he wandered at times from his home, ill, and in dire necessity. His guardians finally sent him to Oxford where he remained five years, though shyness prevented him from qualifying for a degree or a fellowship.

Unfortunately he was advised to relieve the pains of neuralgia by the use of opium, the disastrous effects of which even physicians did not then know, and he became a life-long victim. For periods of years he so modified the amounts of opium that he took that he was able to write effectively. For other long periods he was under the complete influence of the drug. Its effect was to intensify the natural dreaminess of his imagination and his distaste for regular habits. His first work to attract attention was *Confessions of an English Opium Eater,* 1821, written when he supposed that he had conquered the habit. Late in life he revised his *Confessions,* but the early text of 1821-1822 is, from a rhetorical point of view, generally the superior and is here retained.

In his *Confessions,* De Quincey made an almost unique contribution to the literature of the world. To English literature he has made, moreover, the important contribution of a style known as "impassioned prose." De Quincey's style, like Landor's, is founded upon the classics, but it is ruled by his own romantic disposition. It is sometimes restrained, but is more often discursive, expanded, desultory, following the whim of the author's mind rather than the demands of the subject. No one has ever had a finer ear for the sound of language, and no writer of English prose has equaled him in such sustained melody as that of the "Dream Fugue" of *The English Mail Coach,* or *Joan of Arc.* Almost all his works, which consist of autobiography, essays, criticism, reviews, appeared first in magazine form. These pieces he collected and edited a few years before his death, which occurred at Edinburgh.

Biography: Masson (EML). Criticism: Stephen (HL 1); Saintsbury; H. M. Paull, *Fortn.* 118:152-62.

From CONFESSIONS OF AN ENGLISH OPIUM EATER [1]

THE PAINS OF OPIUM

. . . .

I now pass to what is the main subject of these latter confessions, to the history and journal of what took place in my dreams; for these were the immediate and proximate cause of my acutest suffering.

The first notice I had of any important change going on in this part of my physical economy, was from the re-awakening of a state of eye generally incident to childhood, or exalted states of irritability. I know not whether my reader is aware that many children, perhaps most, have a power of painting, as it were, upon the darkness, all sorts of phantoms; in some that power is simply a mechanic affection of the eye; others have a voluntary or semi-voluntary power to dismiss or to summon them; or as a child once said to me when I questioned him on this matter, "I can tell them to go, and they go; but sometimes they come when I don't tell them to come." Whereupon I told him that he had almost as unlimited a command over apparitions as a Roman centurion over his soldiers. In the middle of 1817, I think it was, that this faculty became positively distressing

[1] De Quincey says: "*The Opium Confessions* were written with some slight secondary purpose of exposing the specific power of opium upon the faculty of dreaming, but much more with the purpose of displaying the faculty itself." And again: "The machinery for dreaming planted in the human brain was not planted for nothing. That faculty, in alliance with the mystery of darkness, is the one great tube through which man communicates with the shadowy. And the dreaming organ, in connection with the heart, the eye, and the ear, compose the magnificent apparatus which forces the infinite into the chambers of the human brain, and throws dark reflections from eternities below all life upon the mirrors of that mysterious *camera obscura*—the sleeping mind."

to me: at night, when I lay awake in bed, vast processions passed along in mournful pomp; friezes of never-ending stories, that to my feelings were as sad and solemn as if they were stories drawn from times before Oedipus or Priam—before Tyre—before Memphis.[1] And, at the same time, a corresponding change took place in my dreams; a theater seemed suddenly opened and lighted up within my brain, which presented nightly spectacles of more than earthly splendor. And the four following facts may be mentioned, as noticeable at this time:

1. That as the creative state of the eye increased, a sympathy seemed to arise between the waking and the dreaming states of the brain in one point—that whatsoever I happened to call up and to trace by a voluntary act upon the darkness was very apt to transfer itself to my dreams; so that I feared to exercise this faculty; for, as Midas turned all things to gold that yet baffled his hopes and defrauded his human desires, so whatsoever things capable of being visually represented I did but think of in the darkness, immediately shaped themselves into phantoms of the eye; and, by a process apparently no less inevitable, when thus once traced in faint and visionary colors, like writings in sympathetic ink, they were drawn out by the fierce chemistry of my dreams into insufferable splendor that fretted my heart.

2. For this and all other changes in my dreams were accompanied by deep-seated anxiety and gloomy melancholy, such as are wholly incommunicable by words. I seemed every night to descend, not metaphorically but literally to descend, into chasms and sunless abysses, depths below depths, from which it seemed hopeless that I could ever re-ascend. Nor did I, by waking, feel that I *had* re-ascended. This I do not dwell upon; because the state of gloom which attended these gorgeous spectacles, amounting at last to utter darkness, as of some suicidal despondency, cannot be approached by words.

3. The sense of space and, in the end, the sense of time were both powerfully affected. Buildings, landscapes, etc., were exhibited in proportions so vast as the bodily eye is not fitted to receive. Space swelled, and was amplified to an extent of unutterable infinity. This, however, did not disturb me so much as the vast expansion of time; I sometimes seemed to have lived for seventy or a hundred years in one night; nay, sometimes had feelings representative of a millennium passed in that time, or, however,[2] of a duration far beyond the limits of any human experience.

4. The minutest incidents of childhood, or forgotten scenes of later years, were often revived; I could not be said to recollect them; for if I had been told of them when waking, I should not have been able to acknowledge them as parts of my past experience. But placed as they were before me in dreams, like intuitions, and clothed in all their evanescent circumstances and accompanying feelings, I *recognized* them instantaneously. I was once told by a near relative of mine, that having in her childhood fallen into a river, and being on the very verge of death but for the critical assistance which reached her, she saw in a moment her whole life, in its minutest incidents, arrayed before her simultaneously as in a mirror; and she had a faculty developed as suddenly for comprehending the whole and every part. This, from some opium experiences of mine, I can believe; I have, indeed, seen the same thing asserted twice in modern books, and accompanied by a remark which I am convinced is true—viz., that the dread book of account, which the Scriptures speak of,[3] is, in fact, the mind itself of each individual. Of this, at least, I feel assured, that there is no such thing as *forgetting* possible to the mind; a thousand accidents may and will interpose a veil between our present consciousness and the secret inscriptions on the mind; accidents of the same sort will also rend away this veil; but alike, whether veiled or unveiled, the inscription remains forever; just as the stars seem to withdraw before the common light of day, whereas, in fact, we all know that it is the light which is drawn over them as a veil, and that they are waiting to be revealed when the obscuring daylight shall have withdrawn.

Having noticed these four facts as memorably distinguishing my dreams from those of health, I shall now cite a case illustrative of the first fact; and shall then cite any others that I remember, either in their chronological order, or any other that may give them more effect as pictures to the reader.

I had been in youth, and even since, for occasional amusement, a great reader of Livy, whom I confess that I prefer, both for style and matter, to any other of the Roman historians; and I had often felt as most solemn and appalling sounds, and most emphatically representative of the majesty of the Roman people, the two words so often occurring in Livy—*Consul Romanus;*

[1] Greece, Phoenicia, Egypt; they form a climax of antiquity.

[2] at any rate

[3] *Revelation*, xx, 12

especially when the consul is introduced in his military character. I mean to say that the words king—sultan—regent, etc., or any other titles of those who embody in their own persons the collective majesty of a great people, had less power over my reverential feelings. I had also, though no great reader of history, made myself minutely and critically familiar with one period of English history—viz., the period of the Parliamentary War—having been attracted by the moral grandeur of some who figured in that day, and by the many interesting memoirs which survive those unquiet times. Both these parts of my lighter reading, having furnished me often with matter of reflection, now furnished me with matter for my dreams. Often I used to see, after painting upon the blank darkness a sort of rehearsal whilst waking, a crowd of ladies, and perhaps a festival, and dances. And I heard it said, or I said to myself, "These are English ladies from the unhappy times of Charles I. These are the wives and the daughters of those who met in peace, and sat at the same tables, and were allied by marriage or by blood; and yet, after a certain day in August, 1642,[1] never smiled upon each other again, nor met but in the field of battle; and at Marston Moor, at Newbury, or at Naseby, cut asunder all ties of love by the cruel saber, and washed away in blood the memory of ancient friendship." The ladies danced, and looked as lovely as the court of George IV. Yet I knew, even in my dreams, that they had been in the grave for nearly two centuries. This pageant would suddenly dissolve; and at a clapping of hands, would be heard the heart-quaking sound of *Consul Romanus;* and immediately came "sweeping by," in gorgeous paludaments,[2] Paulus or Marius,[3] girt round by a company of centurions, with the crimson tunic hoisted on a spear,[4] and followed by the *alalagmos*[5] of the Roman legions.

. . . .

And now came a tremendous change, which, unfolding itself slowly like a scroll, through many months, promised an abiding torment; and, in fact, it never left me until the winding up of my case. Hitherto the human face had mixed often in my dreams, but not despotically, nor with any special power of tormenting. But now that which I have called the tyranny of the human face began to unfold itself. Perhaps some part of my London life might be answerable for this. Be that as it may, now it was that upon the rocking waters of the ocean the human face began to appear; the sea appeared paved with innumerable faces, upturned to the heavens; faces imploring, wrathful, despairing, surged upward by thousands, by myriads, by generations, by centuries:—my agitation was infinite—my mind tossed and surged with the ocean.

May, 1818.

The Malay[6] has been a fearful enemy for months. I have been every night, through his means, transported into Asiatic scenes. I know not whether others share in my feelings on this point; but I have often thought that if I were compelled to forego England, and to live in China, and among Chinese manners and modes of life and scenery, I should go mad. The causes of my horror lie deep; and some of them must be common to others. Southern Asia, in general, is the seat of awful images and associations. As the cradle of the human race, it would alone have a dim and reverential feeling connected with it. But there are other reasons. No man can pretend that the wild barbarous, and capricious superstitions of Africa, or of savage tribes elsewhere, affect him in the way that he is affected by the ancient, monumental, cruel, and elaborate religions of Indostan, etc. The mere antiquity of Asiatic things, of their institutions, histories, modes of faith, etc., is so impressive that to me the vast age of the race and name overpowers the sense of youth in the individual. A young Chinese seems to me an antediluvian man renewed. Even Englishmen, though not bred in any knowledge of such institutions, cannot but shudder at the mystic sublimity of *castes* that have flowed apart, and refused to mix, through such immemorial tracts of time; nor can any man fail to be awed by the names of the Ganges, or the Euphrates. It contributes much to these feelings, that Southern Asia is, and has been for thousands of years, the part of the earth most swarming with human life; the great *officina gentium.*[7] Man is a weed in those regions. The vast empires, also, in which the enormous population of Asia has always been cast give a further sublimity to the feelings associated with all oriental names or images. In China, over and above what it has in common with the

[1] Charles's standard was raised, giving the signal for civil war, August 22, 1642.
[2] military cloaks
[3] For this latter Consul, see note to Landor's "Metellus and Marius," p. 554.
[4] a signal of battle
[5] "A word expressing collectively the gathering of the Roman war cries—*Alála, Alála.*"—De Quincey.
[6] A Malay, as related in an earlier part of the *Confessions,* once knocked at De Quincey's door.
[7] laboratory of nations

rest of Southern Asia, I am terrified by the modes of life, by the manners, and the barrier of utter abhorrence, and want of sympathy, placed between us by feelings deeper than I can analyse. I could sooner live with lunatics, or brute animals. All this, and much more than I can say, or have time to say, the reader must enter into before he can comprehend the unimaginable horror which these dreams of oriental imagery and mythological tortures, impressed upon me. Under the connecting feeling of tropical heat and vertical sunlights, I brought together all creatures, birds, beasts, reptiles, all trees and plants, usages and appearances, that are found in all tropical regions, and assembled them together in China or Indostan. From kindred feelings, I soon brought Egypt and all her gods under the same law. I was stared at, hooted at, grinned at, chattered at, by monkeys, by paroquets, by cockatoos. I ran into pagodas—and was fixed for centuries, at the summit, or in secret rooms; I was the idol; I was the priest; I was worshiped; I was sacrificed. I fled from the wrath of Brama through all the forests of Asia; Vishnu hated me; Seeva laid wait for me.[1] I came suddenly upon Isis and Osiris; I had done a deed, they said, which the ibis and the crocodile trembled at. I was buried, for a thousand years, in stone coffins, with mummies and sphinxes, in narrow chambers at the heart of eternal pyramids. I was kissed with cancerous kisses by crocodiles; and laid, confounded with all unutterable slimy things, amongst reeds and Nilotic mud.

I thus give the reader some slight abstraction of my oriental dreams, which always filled me with such amazement at the monstrous scenery, that horror seemed absorbed, for a while, in sheer astonishment. Sooner or later came a reflux of feeling that swallowed up the astonishment, and left me, not so much in terror as in hatred and abomination of what I saw. Over every form, and threat, and punishment, and dim, sightless incarceration brooded a sense of eternity and infinity that drove me into an oppression as of madness. Into these dreams only, it was, with one or two slight exceptions, that any circumstances of physical horror entered. All before had been moral and spiritual terrors. But here the main agents were ugly birds, or snakes, or crocodiles; especially the last. The cursed crocodile became to me the object of more horror than almost all the rest. I was compelled to live with him; and (as was always the case, almost, in my dreams) for centuries. I escaped sometimes, and found myself in Chinese houses, with cane tables, etc. All the feet of the tables, sofas, etc., soon became instinct with life; the abominable head of the crocodile, and his leering eyes, looked out at me, multiplied into a thousand repetitions; and I stood loathing and fascinated. And so often did this hideous reptile haunt my dreams, that many times the very same dream was broken up in the very same way; I heard gentle voices speaking to me (I hear everything when I am sleeping), and instantly I awoke; it was broad noon; and my children were standing, hand in hand, at my bedside; come to show me their colored shoes, or new frocks, or to let me see them dressed for going out. I protest that so awful was the transition from the damned crocodile, and the other unutterable monsters and abortions of my dreams, to the sight of innocent *human* natures and of infancy, that in the mighty and sudden revulsion of mind, I wept, and could not forbear it, as I kissed their faces.

. . . . .

1821-2

From SUSPIRIA DE PROFUNDIS[2]

Levana and Our Ladies of Sorrow

Oftentimes at Oxford I saw Levana in my dreams. I knew her by her Roman symbols. Who is Levana? Reader, that do not pretend to have leisure for very much scholarship, you will not be angry with me for telling you. Levana was the Roman goddess that performed for the new-born infant the earliest office of ennobling kindness—typical, by its mode, of that grandeur which belongs to man everywhere, and of that benignity in powers invisible which even in Pagan worlds sometimes descends to sustain it. At the very moment of birth, just as the infant tasted for the first time the atmosphere of our troubled planet, it was laid on the

[1] Brahma the creator, Vishnu the preserver, and Siva the destroyer, constitute the great triad of Hindu mythology. Osiris the creator, and Isis, his sister and wife, were Egyptian deities, and the ibis and crocodile were regarded as sacred animals.

[2] *Suspiria de Profundis* (Sighs from the Depths) is the title under which De Quincey began in 1845 to publish a series of articles which were to have closed with a crowning succession of "some twenty or twenty-five dreams and noon-day visions." Most of the articles were either never written or were destroyed. Of "Levana," one of the earliest, Professor Masson has said that "it is a permanent addition to the mythology of the human race," typifying as it does "the varieties and degrees of misery that there are in the world." As for De Quincey's own education through initiation into these several degrees of sorrow, it is to be remembered that in childhood he lost by death his father and two sisters, in youth he ran away from an uncongenial school and wandered like an outcast in Wales and London, and in manhood his body, intellect, and will became enslaved to opium.

ground. *That* might bear different interpretations. But immediately, lest so grand a creature should grovel there for more than one instant, either the paternal hand, as proxy for the goddess Levana, or some near kinsman, as proxy for the father, raised it upright, bade it look erect as the king of all this world, and presented its forehead to the stars, saying, perhaps, in his heart, "Behold what is greater than yourselves!" This symbolic act represented the function of Levana. And that mysterious lady, who never revealed her face—except to me in dreams—but always acted by delegation, had her name from the Latin verb—as still it is the Italian verb—*levare,* to raise aloft.

This is the explanation of Levana, and hence it has arisen that some people have understood by Levana the tutelary power that controls the education of the nursery. She, that would not suffer at his birth even a prefigurative or mimic degradation for her awful ward, far less could be supposed to suffer the real degradation attaching to the non-development of his powers. She therefore watches over human education. Now the word *edŭco* with the penultimate short, was derived—by a process often exemplified in the crystallization of languages—from the word *edūco* with the penultimate long. Whatsoever *educes,* or developes, *educates.* By the education of Levana, therefore, is meant—not the poor machinery that moves by spelling-books and grammars, but that mighty system of central forces hidden in the deep bosom of human life, which by passion, by strife, by temptation, by the energies of resistance, works forever upon children—resting not day or night, any more than the mighty wheel of day and night themselves, whose moments, like restless spokes, are glimmering forever as they revolve.

If, then, *these* are the ministries by which Levana works, how profoundly must she reverence the agencies of grief! But you, reader, think that children generally are not liable to grief such as mine. There are two senses in the word *generally*—the sense of Euclid, where it means *universally* (or in the whole extent of the *genus*), and a foolish sense of this word, where it means usually. Now, I am far from saying that children universally are capable of grief like mine. But there are more than you ever heard of who die of grief in this island of ours. I will tell you a common case. The rules of Eton require that a boy on the *foundation* [1] should be there twelve years; he is superannuated at eighteen, consequently he must come at six. Children torn away from mothers and sisters at that age not unfrequently die. I speak of what I know. The complaint is not entered by the registrar as grief; but *that* it is. Grief of that sort, and at that age, has killed more than ever have been counted amongst its martyrs.

Therefore it is that Levana often communes with the powers that shake man's heart; therefore it is that she dotes upon grief. "These ladies," said I softly to myself, on seeing the ministers with whom Levana was conversing, "these are the Sorrows; and they are three in number, as the *Graces* are three, who dress man's life with beauty; the *Parcae* [2] are three, who weave the dark arras of man's life in their mysterious loom, always with colors sad in part, sometimes angry with tragic crimson and black; the *Furies* are three, who visit with retributions called from the other side of the grave offenses that walk upon this; and once even the *Muses* were but three, who fit the harp, the trumpet, or the lute to the great burdens of man's impassioned creations. These are the Sorrows, all three of whom I know." The last words I say now; but in Oxford I said, "One of whom I know, and the others too surely I *shall* know." For already, in my fervent youth, I saw—dimly relieved upon the dark background of my dreams—the imperfect lineaments of the awful sisters. These sisters—by what name shall we call them? If I say simply, "The Sorrows," there will be a chance of mistaking the term; it might be understood of individual sorrow—separate cases of sorrow—whereas I want a term expressing the mighty abstractions that incarnate themselves in all individual sufferings of man's heart; and I wish to have these abstractions presented as impersonations, that is, as clothed with human attributes of life, and with functions pointing to flesh. Let us call them, therefore, *Our Ladies of Sorrow.*

I know them thoroughly, and have walked in all their kingdoms. Three sisters they are, of one mysterious household; and their paths are wide apart; but of their dominion there is no end. Them I saw often conversing with Levana, and sometimes about myself. Do they talk, then? Oh, no! Mighty phantoms like these disdain the infirmities of language. They may utter voices through the organs of man when they dwell in human hearts, but amongst themselves is no voice nor sound; eternal silence reigns in *their* kingdoms. *They* spoke not, as *they* talked with Levana; *they* whis-

[1] a scholarship provided by the endowment

[2] Fates

pered not; *they* sang not; though oftentimes methought they *might* have sung; for I upon earth had heard their mysteries oftentimes deciphered by harp and timbrel, by dulcimer and organ. Like God, whose servants they are, they utter their pleasure, not by sounds that perish, or by words that go astray, but by signs in heaven, by changes on earth, by pulses in secret rivers, heraldries painted on darkness, and hieroglyphics written on the tablets of the brain. *They* wheeled in mazes; I spelled the steps. *They* telegraphed [1] from afar; I read the signals. *They* conspired together; and on the mirrors of darkness *my* eye traced the plots. *Theirs* were the symbols; *mine* are the words.

What is it the sisters are? What is it that they do? Let me describe their form, and their presence; if form it were that still fluctuated in its outline, or presence it were that forever advanced to the front, or forever receded amongst shades.

The eldest of the three is named *Mater Lachrymarum*—Our Lady of Tears. She it is that night and day raves and moans, calling for vanished faces. She stood in Rama, where a voice was heard of lamentation—Rachel weeping for her children, and refusing to be comforted. [2] She it was that stood in Bethlehem on the night when Herod's sword swept its nurseries of Innocents, and the little feet were stiffened forever, which, heard at times as they tottered along floors overhead, woke pulses of love in household hearts that were not unmarked in heaven.

Her eyes are sweet and subtle, wild and sleepy, by turns; oftentimes rising to the clouds, oftentimes challenging the heavens. She wears a diadem round her head. And I knew by childish memories that she could go abroad upon the winds, when she heard the sobbing of litanies or the thundering of organs, and when she beheld the mustering of summer clouds. This sister, the eldest, it is that carries keys more than papal [3] at her girdle, which open every cottage and every palace. She, to my knowledge, sat all last summer by the bedside of the blind beggar, him that so often and so gladly I talked with, whose pious daughter, eight years old, with the sunny countenance, resisted the temptations of play and village mirth to travel all day long on dusty roads with her afflicted father. For this did God send her a great reward. In the springtime of the year, and whilst yet her own spring was budding, He recalled her to himself. But her blind father mourns forever over *her;* still he dreams at midnight that the little guiding hand is locked within his own; and still he wakens to a darkness that is *now* within a second and a deeper darkness. This *Mater Lachrymarum* also has been sitting all this winter of 1844-5 within the bedchamber of the Czar, [4] bringing before his eyes a daughter (not less pious) that vanished to God not less suddenly, and left behind her a darkness not less profound. By the power of the keys it is that Our Lady of Tears glides a ghostly intruder into the chambers of sleepless men, sleepless women, sleepless children, from Ganges to Nile, from Nile to Mississippi. And her, because she is the first-born of her house, and has the widest empire, let us honor with the title of "Madonna!"

The second sister is called *Mater Suspiriorum*—Our Lady of Sighs. She never scales the clouds, nor walks abroad upon the winds. She wears no diadem. And her eyes, if they were ever seen, would be neither sweet nor subtle; no man could read their story; they would be found filled with perishing dreams, and with wrecks of forgotten delirium. But she raises not her eyes; her head, on which sits a dilapidated turban, droops forever, forever fastens on the dust. She weeps not. She groans not. But she sighs inaudibly at intervals. Her sister, Madonna, is oftentimes stormy and frantic, raging in the highest against heaven, and demanding back her darlings. But Our Lady of Sighs never clamors, never defies, dreams not of rebellious aspirations. She is humble to abjectness. Hers is the meekness that belongs to the hopeless. Murmur she may, but it is in her sleep. Whisper she may, but it is to herself in the twilight. Mutter she does at times, but it is in solitary places that are desolate as she is desolate, in ruined cities, and when the sun has gone down to his rest. This sister is the visitor of the Pariah, [5] of the Jew, of the bondsman to the oar in the Mediterranean galleys; and of the English criminal in Norfolk Island, [6] blotted out from the books of remembrance in sweet far-off England; of the baffled penitent reverting his eyes forever upon a solitary grave, which to him seems the altar overthrown of some past and bloody sacrifice, on which altar no oblations can now be availing, whether toward pardon that he might implore, or toward reparation that he might attempt. Every slave that at noonday looks up

[1] The word was formerly used of various methods of signaling, as by beacon fires.
[2] *Jeremiah,* xxxi, 15; *Matthew,* ii, 16-18.
[3] St. Peter's keys, emblem of papal power; cf. Milton's "Lycidas," l. 110.
[4] Nicholas I, whose daughter Alexandra had died
[5] social outcast (Hindu term)
[6] a penal colony in the south Pacific, 1825-1845

to the tropical sun with timid reproach, as he points with one hand to the earth, our general mother, but for *him* a stepmother—as he points with the other hand to the Bible, our general teacher, but against *him* sealed and sequestered —every woman sitting in darkness, without love to shelter her head, or hope to illumine her solitude, because the heaven-born instincts kindling in her nature germs of holy affections which God implanted in her womanly bosom, having been stifled by social necessities, now burn sullenly to waste, like sepulchral lamps amongst the ancients; every nun defrauded of her unreturning May-time by wicked kinsman, whom God will judge; every captive in every dungeon; all that are betrayed and all that are rejected; outcasts by traditionary law, and children of *hereditary* disgrace—all these walk with Our Lady of Sighs. She also carries a key; but she needs it little. For her kingdom is chiefly amongst the tents of Shem,[1] and the houseless vagrant of every clime. Yet in the very highest ranks of man she finds chapels of her own; and even in glorious England there are some that, to the world, carry their heads as proudly as the reindeer, who yet secretly have received her mark upon their foreheads.

But the third sister, who is also the youngest ——! Hush, whisper whilst we talk of her! Her kingdom is not large, or else no flesh should live; but within that kingdom all power is hers. Her head, turreted like that of Cybele,[2] rises almost beyond the reach of sight. She droops not; and her eyes rising so high might be hidden by distance; but, being what they are, they cannot be hidden; through the treble veil of crape which she wears, the fierce light of a blazing misery, that rests not for matins or for vespers, for noon of day or noon of night, for ebbing or for flowing tide, may be read from the very ground. She is the defier of God. She also is the mother of lunacies, and the suggestress of suicides. Deep lie the roots of her power; but narrow is the nation that she rules. For she can approach only those in whom a profound nature has been upheaved by central convulsions; in whom the heart trembles, and the brain rocks under conspiracies of tempest from without and tempest from within. Madonna moves with uncertain steps, fast or slow, but still with tragic grace. Our Lady of Sighs creeps timidly and stealthily. But this youngest sister moves with incalculable motions, bounding, and with tiger's leaps. She carries no key; for, though coming rarely amongst men, she storms all doors at which she is permitted to enter at all. And *her* name is *Mater Tenebrarum*—Our Lady of Darkness.

These were the *Semnai Theai,* or Sublime Goddesses, these were the *Eumenides*[3] or Gracious Ladies (so called by antiquity in shuddering propitiation), of my Oxford dreams. Madonna spoke. She spoke by her mysterious hand. Touching my head, she beckoned to Our Lady of Sighs; and *what* she spoke, translated out of the signs which—except in dreams—no man reads, was this:

"Lo! here is he whom in childhood I dedicated to my altars. This is he that once I made my darling. Him I led astray, him I beguiled, and from heaven I stole away his young heart to mine. Through me did he become idolatrous; and through me it was, by languishing desires, that he worshiped the worm, and prayed to the wormy grave. Holy was the grave to him; lovely was its darkness; saintly its corruption. Him, this young idolator, I have seasoned for thee, dear gentle Sister of Sighs! Do thou take him now to *thy* heart, and season him for our dreadful sister. And thou"—turning to the *Mater Tenebrarum,* she said—"wicked sister, that temptest and hatest, do thou take him from *her*. See that thy scepter lie heavy on his head. Suffer not woman and her tenderness to sit near him in his darkness. Banish the frailties of hope, wither the relenting of love, scorch the fountains of tears, curse him as only thou canst curse. So shall he be accomplished[4] in the furnace, so shall he see the things that ought *not* to be seen, sights that are abominable, and secrets that are unutterable. So shall he read elder truths, sad truths, grand truths, fearful truths. So shall he rise again *before* he dies, and so shall our commission be accomplished which from God we had—to plague his heart until we had unfolded the capacities of his spirit."

1845

Savannah-la-Mar[5]

God smote Savannah-la-Mar, and in one night, by earthquake, removed her, with all her towers standing and population sleeping, from the steadfast foundations of the shore to the coral floors of ocean. And God said—"Pompeii did I bury and conceal from men through seventeen centuries; this city I will bury, but

[1] son of Noah, reputed ancestor of the Semitic races, for example, the Hebrews and Arabs, *Genesis* ix, 27
[2] See note 4 on *Childe Harold,* IV, 2, p. 498.

[3] a euphemistic name for the Furies
[4] perfected
[5] "Plain (of) the Sea"—a fanciful name adopted by De Quincey for this vision of a sunken city; the "Dark Interpreter" mentioned here gives name to another of the Suspiria papers.

not conceal. She shall be a monument to men of my mysterious anger, set in azure light through generations to come; for I will enshrine her in a crystal dome of my tropic seas." This city, therefore, like a mighty galleon with all her apparel mounted, streamers flying, and tackling perfect, seems floating along the noiseless depths of ocean; and oftentimes in glassy calms, through the translucid atmosphere of water that now stretches like an air-woven awning above the silent encampment, mariners from every clime look down into her courts and terraces, count her gates, and number the spires of her churches. She is one ample cemetery, and *has* been for many a year; but, in the mighty calms that brood for weeks over tropic latitudes, she fascinates the eye with a *Fata-Morgana*[1] revelation, as of human life still subsisting in submarine asylums sacred from the storms that torment our upper air.

Thither, lured by the loveliness of cerulean depths, by the peace of human dwellings privileged from molestation, by the gleam of marble altars sleeping in everlasting sanctity, oftentimes in dreams did I and the Dark Interpreter cleave the watery veil that divided us from her streets. We looked into the belfries, where the pendulous bells were waiting in vain for the summons which should awaken their marriage peals; together we touched the mighty organ-keys that sang no *jubilates*[2] for the ear of heaven, that sang no requiems for the ear of human sorrow; together we searched the silent nurseries where the children were all asleep, and had been asleep through five generations. "They are waiting for the heavenly dawn," whispered the Interpreter to himself: "and, when that comes, the bells and organs will utter a *jubilate* repeated by the echoes of Paradise." Then, turning to me, he said—"This is sad, this is piteous; but less would not have sufficed for the purpose of God. Look here. Put into a Roman clepsydra[3] one hundred drops of water; let these run out as the sands in an hourglass, every drop measuring the hundredth part of a second, so that each shall represent but the three-hundred-and-sixty-thousandth part of an hour. Now count the drops as they race along; and, when the fiftieth of the hundred is passing, behold! forty-nine are not, because already they have perished, and fifty are not, because they are yet to come. You see, therefore, how narrow, how incalculably narrow, is the true and actual present. Of that time which we call the present, hardly a hundredth part but belongs either to a past which has fled, or to a future which is still on the wing. It has perished, or it is not born. It was, or it is not. Yet even this approximation to the truth is infinitely false. For again subdivide that solitary drop, which only was found to represent the present, into a lower series of similar fractions, and the actual present which you arrest measures now but the thirty-sixmillionth of an hour; and so by infinite declensions the true and very present, in which only we live and enjoy, will vanish into a mote of a mote, distinguishable only by a heavenly vision. Therefore the present, which only man possesses, offers less capacity for his footing than the slenderest film that ever spider twisted from her womb. Therefore, also, even this incalculable shadow from the narrowest pencil of moonlight is more transitory than geometry can measure, or thought of angel can overtake. The time which *is* contracts into a mathematic point; and even that point perishes a thousand times before we can utter its birth. All is finite in the present; and even that finite is infinite in its velocity of flight toward death. But in God there is nothing finite; but in God there is nothing transitory; but in God there *can* be nothing that tends to death. Therefore, it follows that for God there can be no present. The future is the present of God, and to the future it is that he sacrifices the human present. Therefore it is that he works by earthquake. Therefore it is that he works by grief. Oh, deep is the plowing of earthquake! Oh, deep"—and his voice swelled like a *sanctus*[4] rising from the choir of a cathedral—"Oh, deep is the plowing of grief. But oftentimes less would not suffice for the agriculture of God. Upon a night of earthquake he builds a thousand years of pleasant habitations for man. Upon the sorrow of an infant he raises, oftentimes, from human intellects glorious vintages that could not else have been. Less than these fierce plowshares would not have stirred the stubborn soil. The one is needed for Earth, our planet—for Earth itself as the dwelling-place of man; but the other is needed yet oftener for God's mightiest instrument—yes" (and he looked solemnly at myself), "is needed for the mysterious children of the earth!"

1845

[1] here "mirage-like"; from the *fata morgana* of the Sicilian coast—a phenomenon attributed to Morgan le Fay, or Morgana the Fairy

[2] hymns of rejoicing (specifically the 100th *Psalm*)

[3] water clock

[4] the anthem "Holy, Holy, Holy"

From JOAN OF ARC [1]

What is to be thought of *her?* What is to be thought of the poor shepherd girl from the hills and forests of Lorraine, that—like the Hebrew shepherd boy from the hills and forests of Judea—rose suddenly out of the quiet, out of the safety, out of the religious inspiration, rooted in deep pastoral solitudes, to a station in the van of armies, and to the more perilous station at the right hand of kings? The Hebrew boy inaugurated his patriotic mission by an *act,* by a victorious *act,* such as no man could deny. [2] But so did the girl of Lorraine, if we read her story as it was read by those who saw her nearest. Adverse armies bore witness to the boy as no pretender; but so they did to the gentle girl. Judged by the voices of all who saw them *from a station of good will,* both were found true and loyal to any promises involved in their first acts. Enemies it was that made the difference between their subsequent fortunes. The boy rose to a splendor and a noonday prosperity, both personal and public, that rang through the records of his people, and became a byword among his posterity for a thousand years, until the scepter was departing from Judah. [3] The poor forsaken girl, on the contrary, drank not herself from that cup of rest which she had secured for France. She never sang together with the songs that rose in her native Domrémy as echoes to the departing steps of invaders. She mingled not in the festal dances at Vaucouleurs [4] which celebrated in rapture the redemption of France. No! for her voice was then silent; no! for her feet were dust. Pure, innocent, noble-hearted girl! whom, from earliest youth, ever I believed in as full of truth and self-sacrifice, this was among the strongest pledges for *thy* truth, that never once—no, not for a moment of weakness—didst thou revel in the vision of coronets and honor from man. Coronets for thee! Oh, no! Honors, if they come when all is over, are for those that share thy blood. Daughter of Domrémy, when the gratitude of thy king shall awaken, thou wilt be sleeping the sleep of the dead. Call her, king of France, but she will not hear thee. Cite her by the apparitors [5] to come and receive a robe of honor, but she will be found *en contumace.* [6] When the thunders of universal France, as even yet may happen, [7] shall proclaim the grandeur of the poor shepherd girl that gave up all for her country, thy ear, young shepherd girl, will have been deaf for five centuries. To suffer and to do, that was thy portion in this life, that was thy destiny; and not for a moment was it hidden from thyself. Life, thou saidst, is short; and the sleep which is in the grave is long; let me use that life, so transitory, for the glory of those heavenly dreams destined to comfort the sleep which is so long! This pure creature—pure from every suspicion of even a visionary self-interest, even as she was pure in senses more obvious—never once did this holy child, as regarded herself, relax from her belief in the darkness that was traveling to meet her. She might not prefigure the very manner of her death; she saw not in vision, perhaps, the aërial altitude of the fiery scaffold, the spectators without end, on every road, pouring into Rouen [8] as to a coronation, the surging smoke, the volleying flames, the hostile faces all around, the pitying eye that lurked but here and there, until nature and imperishable truth broke loose from artificial restraints—these might not be apparent through the mists of the hurrying future. But the voice that called her to death, *that* she heard forever.

Great was the throne of France, even in those days, and great was he that sat upon it; but well Joanna knew that not the throne, nor he that sat upon it, was for *her;* but, on the contrary, that she was for *them;* not she by them, but they by her, should rise from the dust. Gorgeous were the lilies of France, [9] and for centuries had the privilege to spread their beauty over land and sea, until, in another century, the wrath of God and man combined to wither them; but well Joanna knew, early at Domrémy she had read that bitter truth, that the lilies of France would decorate no garland for *her.* Flower nor bud, bell nor blosson, would ever bloom for *her!*

. . . .

Bishop of Beauvais! [10] thy victim died in fire upon a scaffold—thou upon a down bed. But. for the departing minutes of life, both are oftentimes alike. At the farewell crisis, when the gates of death are opening, and flesh is resting from its struggles, oftentimes the tortured and the torturer have the same truce from

[1] De Quincey's venture into this particular field of history, in his time obscure and acrimoniously debated, was inspired by Michelet's *Histoire de France,* then (1847) appearing, and his avowed object was to do justice to the maligned Maid, defending her even against her own countrymen. The body of his article, which is narrative and argumentative, is here omitted, only the introduction and conclusion being given.

[2] the killing of Goliath, *I Samuel,* xvii

[3] *Genesis,* xlix, 10

[4] a village near Domrémy

[5] court summoners

[6] a legal term signifying failure to appear in court

[7] Joan was in 1920 canonized by the Church

[8] place of Joan's martyrdom

[9] the fleur-de-lis

[10] The presiding judge at Joan's trial; he had played traitor to the French and abetted the English.

carnal torment; both sink together into sleep; together both sometimes kindle into dreams. When the mortal mists were gathering fast upon you two, bishop and shepherd girl—when the pavilions of life were closing up their shadowy curtains about you—let us try, through the gigantic glooms, to decipher the flying features of your separate visions.

The shepherd girl that had delivered France —she, from her dungeon, she, from her baiting at the stake, she, from her duel with fire, as she entered her last dream—saw Domrémy, saw the fountain of Domrémy, saw the pomp of forests in which her childhood had wandered. That Easter festival which man had denied to her languishing heart—that resurrection of springtime which the darkness of dungeons had intercepted from *her*, hungering after the glorious liberty of forests—were by God given back into her hands as jewels that had been stolen from her by robbers. With those, perhaps (for the minutes of dreams can stretch into ages), was given back to her by God the bliss of childhood. By special privilege for *her* might be created, in this farewell dream, a second childhood, innocent as the first; but not, like *that*, sad with the gloom of a fearful mission in the rear. This mission had now been fulfilled. The storm was weathered; the skirts even of that mighty storm were drawing off. The blood that she was to reckon for had been exacted; the tears that she was to shed in secret had been paid to the last. The hatred to herself in all eyes had been faced steadily, had been suffered, had been survived. And in her last fight upon the scaffold she had triumphed gloriously; victoriously she had tasted the stings of death. For all, except this comfort from her farewell dream, she had died—died amid the tears of ten thousand enemies—died amid the drums and trumpets of armies—died amid peals redoubling upon peals, volleys upon volleys, from the saluting clarions of martyrs.[1]

Bishop of Beauvais! because the guilt-burdened man is in dreams haunted and waylaid by the most frightful of his crimes, and because upon that fluctuating mirror—rising (like the mocking mirrors of mirage in Arabian deserts) from the fens of death—most of all are reflected the sweet countenances which the man has laid in ruins; therefore I know, Bishop, that you also, entering your final dream, saw Domrémy. That fountain, of which the witnesses spoke so much, showed itself to your eyes in pure morning dews; but neither dews, nor the holy dawn, could cleanse away the bright spots of innocent blood upon its surface. By the fountain, Bishop, you saw a woman seated, that hid her face. But, as you draw near, the woman raises her wasted features. Would Domrémy know them again for the features of her child? Ah, but you know them, Bishop, well! Oh, mercy! What a groan was *that* which the servants, waiting outside the bishop's dream at his bedside, heard from his laboring heart, as at this moment he turned away from the fountain and the woman, seeking rest in the forests afar off. Yet not *so* to escape the woman, whom once again he must behold before he dies. In the forests to which he prays for pity, will he find a respite? What a tumult, what a gathering of feet is there! In glades where only wild deer should run, armies and nations are assembling; towering in the fluctuating crowd are phantoms that belong to departed hours. There is the great English Prince, Regent of France. There is my Lord of Winchester, the princely cardinal, that died and made no sign.[2] There is the Bishop of Beauvais, clinging to the shelter of thickets. What building is that which hands so rapidly are raising? Is it a martyr's scaffold? Will they burn the child of Domrémy a second time? No; it is a tribunal that rises to the clouds; and two nations stand around it, waiting for a trial. Shall my Lord of Beauvais sit again upon the judgment seat, and again number the hours for the innocent? Ah, no! He is the prisoner at the bar. Already all is waiting: the mighty audience is gathered, the court is hurrying to their seats, the witnesses are arrayed, the trumpets are sounding, the judge is taking his place. Oh, but this is sudden! My Lord, have you no counsel? "Counsel I have none; in heaven above, or on earth beneath, counselor there is none now that would take a brief from *me*; all are silent." Is it, indeed, come to this? Alas! the time is short, the tumult is wondrous, the crowd stretches away into infinity; but yet I will search in it for somebody to take your brief; I know of somebody that will be your counsel. Who is this that cometh from Domrémy? Who is she in bloody coronation robes from Rheims?[3] Who is she that cometh with blackened flesh from walking the furnaces of Rouen? This is she, the shepherd girl, counselor that had none for herself, whom I choose, Bishop, for yours. She it is, I engage, that shall take my lord's brief. She it is, Bishop, that would plead for you; yes, Bishop, *she*—when heaven and earth are silent.

1847

[1] Contrast with the last scene of Shaw's *Saint Joan*.

[2] See Shakespeare's *2 Henry VI*, III, iii.

[3] Joan was present at the coronation of Charles VII at Rheims—a coronation made possible by her own martial exploits.

THE VICTORIAN AGE

THE Victorian age was an age of peace. England, victor in the wars following the French Revolution, was busy with colonial expansion, commerce, and the application to life of new discoveries in science. The romantic spirit remained, but modified by a sobering sense of the responsibilities the new freedom entailed. Prose, keeping pace with the developing social consciousness, became more realistic in the novel, and more comprehensive as applied to religious discussion, scientific inquiry, and artistic appreciation. Poetry, at first following the manner of Keats, soon developed new types, and showed new richness and strength of imagination. Both poetry and prose quickened as the social interests expanded, and the minds of men were aroused by the significance of what science was revealing. Socially, the age was one of decorum that took its key from the wholesome life of the Court. In literary expansion and activity the age is comparable with that of Elizabeth.

THOMAS CARLYLE 1795-1881

Carlyle, the lay prophet of his age, son of a Scotch stone mason, was born in Dumfriesshire, and died in Chelsea, London. His parents, realizing his mental gifts, sought to educate him for the Scotch church. In his fifteenth year he went to Edinburgh where as a student he lived a life of such extreme economy that he was never afterwards really well. Feeling no call to preach, he supported himself for a while by teaching and journeyman writing. He early married a brilliant Scotch woman, on the whole fortunately, and turned to literature.

His first work to attract wide attention was *Sartor Resartus* (1833-1834, published in *Frazer's Magazine*. It is a spiritual autobiography showing the philosophical doubts through which he had labored. The book is written in a style figurative, whimsical, allegorical, and gnarled, marked on every page by wrestlings of the spirit.

Courage, sincerity, endurance are the simple virtues that Carlyle preaches. His moral tonics have often been curative for despondent youth. The spirit of praise to him who strives manfully runs through all Carlyle's work, *Heroes and Hero Worship,* 1841; *The French Revolution,* 1837, and even through his *History of Friedrich the Great,* 1858-1865. Like Macaulay, Carlyle seizes upon the graphic and dramatic moments of history or biography, though nothing can be more different than the style of the two men. In his perverse dislike of democracy and "progress," and in his stimulating sense of the value of the unseen, he is also the absolute opposite of Macaulay.

Biographies: Nichol (EML), Garnett (GW), Froude, 4 vols. 1882-1884, most comprehensive. Criticism: Lowell, Dowden, Stephen, More (Shel. 1); Bliss Perry, *Carlyle, How to Know Him,* 1915, is exceedingly useful. M. D. Conway's "Thomas Carlyle," *Harp.* 62:888-912, condensed, interesting; S. K. Phelps's "Two More of our Invisible Hosts," *19th Cent.* 99:759-65, a visit to Carlyle's house, a vivacious picture. Of interest, *Letters of C. E. Norton,* 2 vols. 1913; also *Scrib. M.* 53:500-11.

From SARTOR RESARTUS—BOOK II

CHAPTER IX

THE EVERLASTING YEA [1]

"Temptations in the Wilderness!" [2] exclaims Teufelsdröckh: "Have we not all to be tried with such? Not so easily can the old Adam, lodged in us by birth, be dispossessed. Our Life is compassed round with Necessity; yet is the meaning of Life itself no other than Freedom, than Voluntary Force; thus have

[1] *Sartor Resartus,* or "The Tailor Re-Tailored," is nominally a work on clothes; in reality, it is a philosophy, or rather gospel, of life. Carlyle poses as the editor merely, professing to have received the work from a certain German Professor "Teufelsdröckh" of the University of "Weissnichtwo." In the Second Book he assumes to give the physical and spiritual biography of the author as culled from imaginary "Paper-bags"—bundles of loose documents—sent him by a friend of Teufelsdröckh's. The Professor, afflicted with personal sorrows, and beset by religious and speculative doubts, has set forth on a world pilgrimage. In his mental struggle he passes from the "Everlasting No," a period of doubt and denial, through the "Center of Indifference" to the "Everlasting Yea."

[2] See *Luke,* iv, 1, 2.

we a warfare; in the beginning, especially, a hard-fought battle. For the God-given mandate, *Work Thou in Welldoing,* lies mysteriously written, in Promethean, [1] Prophetic Characters, in our hearts; and leaves us no rest, night or day, till it be deciphered and obeyed; till it burn forth in our conduct, a visible, acted Gospel of Freedom. And as the clay-given mandate, *Eat thou and be filled,* at the same time persuasively proclaims itself through every nerve—must there not be a confusion, a contest, before the better influence can become the upper?

"To me nothing seems more natural than that the Son of Man—when such God-given mandate first prophetically stirs within him, and the Clay must now be vanquished or vanquish—should be carried of the spirit into grim Solitudes, and there fronting the Tempter do grimmest battle with him; defiantly setting him at naught, till he yield and fly. Name it as we choose; with or without visible Devil, whether in the natural Desert of rocks and sands, or in the populous moral Desert of selfishness and baseness—to such Temptation are we all called. Unhappy if we art not! Unhappy if we are but Half-men, in whom that divine handwriting has never blazed forth, all-subduing, in true sun-splendor; but quivers dubiously amid meaner lights; or smolders, in dull pain, in darkness, under earthly vapors! Our Wilderness is the Wide World in an Atheistic Century; our Forty Days are long years of suffering and fasting; nevertheless, to these also comes an end. Yes, to me also was given, if not Victory, yet the consciousness of Battle, and the resolve to persevere therein while life or faculty is left. To me also, entangled in the enchanted forests, demon-peopled, doleful of sight and of sound, it was given, after weariest wanderings, to work out my way into the higher sunlit slopes—of that Mountain which has no summit, or whose summit is in Heaven only!"

He says elsewhere, under a less ambitious figure; as figures are, once for all, natural to him: "Has not thy Life been that of most sufficient men (*tüchtigen Männer*) thou hast known in this generation? An outflush of foolish young Enthusiasm, like the first fallow crop, wherein are as many weeds as valuable herbs; this all parched away, under the Droughts of practical and spiritual Unbelief, as Disappointment, in thought and act, often repeated gave rise to Doubt, and Doubt gradually settled into Denial! If I have had a second crop, and now see the perennial greensward, and sit under umbrageous cedars, which defy all Drought, (and Doubt); herein, too, be the Heavens praised, I am not without examples, and even exemplars."

[1] The name Prometheus, fabled defender of man against Jupiter's tyranny, means "forethought."

So that, for Teufelsdröckh also, there has been a "glorious revolution"; these mad, shadow-hunting and shadow-hunted Pilgrimings of his were but some purifying "Temptation in the Wilderness," before his apostolic work (such as it was) could begin; which Temptation is now happily over, and the Devil once more worsted! Was "that high moment in the *Rue de l'Enfer,*" [2] then, properly, the turning point of the battle; when the Fiend said, *Worship me, or be torn in shreds,* and was answered valiantly with an *Apage Satana?* [3]—Singular Teufelsdröckh, would thou hadst told thy singular story in plain words! But it is fruitless to look there, in those Paper-bags, for such. Nothing but innuendoes, figurative crotchets; a typical Shadow, fitfully wavering, prophetico-satiric; no clear logical Picture. "How paint to the sensual eye," asks he once, "what passes in the Holy-of-Holies of Man's Soul; in what words, known to these profane times, speak even afar off of the unspeakable?" We ask in turn: Why perplex these times, profane as they are, with needless obscurity, by omission and by commission? Not mystical only is our Professor, but whimsical; and involves himself, now more than ever, in eye-bewildering *chiaroscuro.* [4] Successive glimpses, here faithfully imparted, our more gifted readers must endeavor to combine for their own behoof.

He says: "The hot Harmattan-wind [5] had raged itself out; its howl went silent within me, and the long-deafened soul could now hear. I paused in my wild wanderings; and sat me down to wait, and consider; for it was as if the hour of change drew nigh. I seemed to surrender, to renounce utterly, and say: Fly, then, false shadows of Hope; I will chase you no more, I will believe you no more. And ye, too, haggard specters of Fear, I care not for you; ye, too, are all shadows and a lie. Let me rest here; for I am way-weary and life-weary; I will rest here, were it but to die; to die or to

[2] Described in a previous chapter as a "dirty little" street in the French Capital where fresh courage had suddenly come to him; this passage Carlyle admitted to be autobiographical, and the street was Leith Walk, Edinburgh.

[3] "Get thee hence, Satan." *Matthew,* iv, 10.

[4] light and shade

[5] a withering wind of Africa; here figurative for doubt

live is alike to me; alike insignificant." And again: "Here, then, as I lay in that CENTER OF INDIFFERENCE; cast, doubtless by benignant upper Influence, into a healing sleep, the heavy dreams rolled gradually away, and I awoke to a new Heaven and a new Earth. The first, preliminary, moral Act, Annihilation of Self (*Selbst-tödtung*), had been happily accomplished; and my mind's eyes were now unsealed, and its hands ungyved."

Might we not also conjecture that the following passage refers to his Locality, during this same "healing sleep"; that his Pilgrim-staff lies cast aside here on "the high table-land"; and indeed that the repose is already taking wholesome effect on him? If it were not that the tone, in some parts, has more of riancy,[1] even of levity, than we could have expected! However, in Teufelsdröckh, there is always the strangest Dualism; light dancing, with guitar music, will be going on in the fore-court, while by fits from within comes the faint whimpering of woe and wail. We transcribe the piece entire:

"Beautiful it was to sit there, as in my skyey Tent, musing and meditating; on the high table-land, in front of the Mountains; over me, as roof, the azure Dome, and around me, for walls, four azure flowing curtains—namely, of the Four azure Winds, on whose bottom fringes also I have seen gilding. And then to fancy the fair Castles that stood sheltered in these Mountain hollows; with their green flower lawns, and white dames and damosels, lovely enough; or better still, the straw-roofed Cottages, wherein stood many a Mother baking bread, with her children round her:—all hidden and protectingly folded-up in the valley folds; yet there and alive, as sure as if I beheld them. Or to see, as well as fancy, the nine Towns and Villages that lay round my mountain-seat, which in still weather were wont to speak to me (by their steeple bells) with metal tongue; and, in almost all weather, proclaimed their vitality by repeated Smoke clouds; whereon, as on a culinary horologe, I might read the hour of the day. For it was the smoke of cookery, as kind housewives at morning, midday, eventide, were boiling their husbands' kettles; and ever a blue pillar rose up into the air, successively or simultaneously, from each of the nine, saying, as plainly as smoke could say: Such and such a meal is getting ready here. Not uninteresting! For you have the whole Borough, with all its love makings and scandal mongeries, contentions and contentments, as in miniature, and could cover it all with your hat. If, in my wide Wayfarings, I had learned to look into the business of the World in its details, here perhaps was the place for combining it into general propositions, and deducing inferences therefrom.

[1] laughing gayety

"Often also could I see the black Tempest marching in anger through the Distance: round some Schreckhorn,[2] as yet grim-blue, would the eddying vapor gather, and there tumultuously eddy, and flow down like a mad witch's hair, till, after a space, it vanished, and, in the clear sunbeam, your Schreckhorn stood smiling grim-white, for the vapor had held snow. How thou fermentest and elaboratest in thy great fermenting vat and laboratory of an Atmosphere, of a World, O Nature! Or what is Nature? Ha! why do I not name thee GOD? Art thou not the 'Living Garment of God?' O Heavens, is it, in very deed, HE then that ever speaks through thee; that lives and loves in thee, that lives and loves in me?

"Fore-shadows, call them rather fore-splendors, of that Truth, and Beginning of Truths, fell mysteriously over my soul. Sweeter than Dayspring to the Shipwrecked in Nova Zembla;[3] ah, like the mother's voice to her little child that strays bewildered, weeping, in unknown tumults; like soft streamings of celestial music to my too-exasperated heart, came that Evangel. The Universe is not dead and demoniacal, a charnel house with specters; but godlike, and my Father's!

"With other eyes, too, could I now look upon my fellow man; with an infinite love, an infinite Pity. Poor, wandering, wayward man! Art thou not tired, and beaten with stripes, even as I am? Ever, whether thou bear the royal mantle or the beggar's gabardine, art thou not so weary, so heavy-laden; and thy Bed of Rest is but a Grave. Oh, my Brother, my Brother, why cannot I shelter thee in my bosom, and wipe away all tears from thy eyes! Truly, the din of many-voiced Life, which in this solitude, with the mind's organ, I could hear, was no longer a maddening discord, but a melting one; like inarticulate cries and sobbings of a dumb creature, which in the ear of Heaven are prayers. The poor Earth, with her poor joys, was now my needy Mother, not my cruel Stepdame. Man, with his so mad Wants

[2] "peak of terror"

[3] Carlyle got the suggestion for his comparison from the journal of William Barentz, a Dutch navigator who was shipwrecked in the winter of 1596 on these Arctic islands, where the sun returns only after weeks of darkness. Compare the third note on Addison's paper on "Frozen Words," p. 325.

and so mean Endeavors, had become the dearer to me; and even for his sufferings and his sins, I now first named him brother. Thus was I standing in the porch of that *'Sanctuary of Sorrow'*; by strange, steep ways, had I, too, been guided thither; and ere long its sacred gates would open, and the *'Divine Depth of Sorrow'* lie disclosed to me."

The Professor says, he here first got eye on the Knot that had been strangling him, and straightway could unfasten it, and was free. "A vain interminable controversy," writes he, "touching what is at present called Origin of Evil, or some such thing, arises in every soul, since the beginning of the world; and in every soul that would pass from idle Suffering into actual Endeavoring, must first be put an end to. The most, in our time, have to go content with a simple, incomplete enough Suppression of this controversy; to a few, some Solution of it is indispensable. In every new era, too, such Solution comes out in different terms; and ever the Solution of the last era has become obsolete, and is found unserviceable. For it is man's nature to change his Dialect from century to century; he cannot help it though he would. The authentic *Church-Catechism* of our present century has not yet fallen into my hands; meanwhile, for my own private behoof, I attempt to elucidate the matter so. Man's Unhappiness, as I construe, comes of his Greatness; it is because there is an Infinite in him, which with all his cunning he cannot quite bury under the Finite. Will the whole finance Ministers and Upholsterers and Confectioners of modern Europe undertake, in joint-stock company, to make one Shoeblack HAPPY? They cannot accomplish it, above an hour or two; for the Shoeblack also has a Soul quite other than his stomach; and would require, if you consider it, for his permanent satisfaction and saturation, simply this allotment, no more, and no less: *God's infinite Universe altogether to himself*, therein to enjoy infinitely, and fill every wish as fast as it rose. Oceans of Hochheimer,[1] a Throat like that of Ophiuchus[2]—speak not of them; to the infinite Shoeblack they are as nothing. No sooner is your ocean filled, than he grumbles that it might have been of better vintage. Try him with half of a Universe, of an Omnipotence, he sets to quarreling with the proprietor of the other half, and declares himself the most maltreated of men. Always there is a black spot in our sunshine; it is even, as I said, the *Shadow of Ourselves*.

[1] a wine

[2] See *Par. Lost,* II, 708.

"But the whim we have of Happiness is somewhat thus. By certain valuations, and averages, of our own striking, we come upon some sort of average terrestrial lot; this we fancy belongs to us by nature, and of indefeasible right. It is simple payment of our wages, of our deserts; requires neither thanks nor complaint—only such *overplus* as there may be do we account Happiness; and *deficit* again is Misery. Now consider that we have the valuation of our own deserts ourselves, and what a fund of Self-conceit there is in each of us—do you wonder that the balance should so often dip the wrong way, and many a Blockhead cry: See there, what a payment; was ever worthy gentleman so used!—I tell thee, blockhead, it all comes of thy Vanity; of what thou *fanciest* those same deserts of thine to be. Fancy that thou deservest to be hanged (as is most likely), thou wilt feel it happiness to be only shot: fancy that thou deservest to be hanged in a hair halter, it will be a luxury to die in hemp.

"So true it is, what I then said, that *the Fraction of Life can be increased in value not so much by increasing your Numerator as by lessening your Denominator*. Nay, unless my algebra deceive me, *Unity*, itself, divided by *Zero* will give *Infinity*. Make thy claim of wages a zero, then; thou hast the world under thy feet. Well did the Wisest of our time[3] write: 'It is only with Renunciation *(Entsagen)* that Life, properly speaking, can be said to begin.'

"I asked myself: What is this that, ever since earliest years, thou hast been fretting and fuming, and lamenting and self-tormenting, on account of? Say it in a word: is it not because thou art not HAPPY? Because the THOU (sweet gentleman) is not sufficiently honored, nourished, soft-bedded, and lovingly cared-for? Foolish soul! What Act of Legislature was there that *thou* shouldst be Happy? A little while ago thou hadst no right to *be* at all. What if thou wert born and predestined not to be Happy, but to be Unhappy! Art thou nothing other than a Vulture, then, that fliest through the Universe seeking after somewhat to *eat;* and shrieking dolefully because carrion enough is not given thee? Close thy *Byron;*[4] open thy *Goethe.*"

"*Es leuchtet mir ein,* I see a glimpse of it!" cries he elsewhere; "there is in man a HIGHER than Love of Happiness; he can do without happiness, and instead thereof find Blessedness! Was it not to preach forth this same

[3] Goethe

[4] Byron's verse is full of his grievances.

HIGHER that sages and martyrs, the Poet and the Priest, in all times, have spoken and suffered; bearing testimony, through life and through death, of the Godlike that is in Man, and how in the Godlike only has he strength and Freedom? Which God-inspired Doctrine art thou also honored to be taught; O Heavens! and broken with manifold, merciful Afflictions, even till thou become contrite, and learn it! O thank thy Destiny for these; thankfully bear what yet remain: thou hadst need of them; the Self in thee needed to be annihilated. By benignant fever-paroxysms is Life rooting out the deep-seated, chronic Disease, and triumphs over Death. On the roaring billows of Time, thou art not engulfed, but borne aloft into the azure of Eternity. Love not Pleasure; love God. This is the EVERLASTING YEA, wherein all contradiction is solved; wherein whoso walks and works, it is well with him."

. . . .

From BOOK III, CHAPTER VIII

NATURAL SUPERNATURALISM

. . . .

"But deepest of all illusory Appearances, for hiding Wonder, as for many other ends, are your two grand, fundamental, world-enveloping Appearances, SPACE and TIME. These, as spun and woven for us from before Birth itself, to clothe our celestial ME for dwelling here, and yet to blind it—lie all-embracing as the universal canvas, or warp and woof, whereby all minor Illusions in this Phantasm Existence, weave and paint themselves. In vain, while here on Earth, shall you endeavor to strip them off; you can, at best, but rend them asunder for moments, and look through.

"Fortunatus[1] had a wishing Hat, which when he put on, and wished himself anywhere, behold he was There. By this means had Fortunatus triumphed over Space, he had annihilated Space; for him there was no Where, but all was Here. Were a Hatter to establish himself in the Wahngasse of Weissnichtwo,[2] and make felts of this sort for all mankind, what a world we should have of it! Still stranger, should, on the opposite side of the street, another Hatter establish himself; and, as his fellow craftsman made Space-annihilating Hats, make Time-annihilating! Of both would I purchase, were it with my last groschen;[3] but chiefly of this latter. To clap on your felt, and, simply by wishing that you were Any*where,* straightway to be *There!* Next to clap on your other felt, and simply by wishing that you were Any*when,* straightway to be *Then!* This were indeed the grander; shooting at will from the Fire-Creation of the World to its Fire-Consummation; here historically present in the First Century, conversing face to face with Paul and Seneca;[4] there prophetically in the Thirty-first, conversing also face to face with other Pauls and Senecas, who as yet stand hidden in the depth of that late time!

"Or thinkest thou, it were impossible, unimaginable? Is the Past annihilated, then, or only past; is the Future non-extant, or only future? Those mystic faculties of thine, Memory and Hope, already answer; already through those mystic avenues, thou the Earth-blinded summonest both Past and Future, and communest with them, though as yet darkly, and with mute beckonings. The curtains of Yesterday drop down, the curtains of Tomorrow roll up; but Yesterday and Tomorrow both *are.* Pierce through the Time-Element, glance into the Eternal. Believe what thou findest written in the sanctuaries of Man's Soul, even as all Thinkers, in all ages, have devoutly read it there—that Time and Space are not God, but creations of God; that with God as it is a universal HERE, so is it an everlasting NOW.

"And seest thou therein any glimpse of IMMORTALITY?—O Heaven! Is the white tomb of our loved one, who died from our arms, and had to be left behind us there, which rises in the distance like a pale, mournfully receding Milestone, to tell how many toilsome, uncheered miles we have journeyed on alone—but a pale spectral Illusion! Is the lost Friend still mysteriously Here, even as we are Here mysteriously with God!—Know of a truth that only the Time-shadows have perished, or are perishable; that the real Being of whatever was, and whatever is, and whatever will be, is even now and forever. This, should it unhappily seem new, thou mayst ponder at thy leisure; for the next twenty years, or the next twenty centuries—believe it thou must; understand it thou canst not.

"That the Thought-forms, Space and Time, wherein, once for all, we are sent into this Earth to live, should condition and determine our whole Practical reasonings, conceptions, and imagings or imaginings—seems altogether fit, just, and unavoidable. But that they

[1] the hero of a popular legend
[2] "Dream-lane of Know-not-where"; see note 1, p. 568.
[3] a very small silver coin of Germany, now obsolete
[4] Certain spurious letters have come down to us which were said to have passed between Paul and Seneca

should, furthermore, usurp such sway over pure, spiritual Meditation, and blind us to the wonder everywhere lying close on us, seems nowise so. Admit Space and Time to their due rank as Forms of Thought; nay, even, if thou wilt, to their quite undue rank of Realities; and consider, then, with thyself how their thin disguises hide from us the brightest God-effulgences! Thus, were it not miraculous, could I stretch forth my hand and clutch the Sun? Yet thou seest me daily stretch forth my hand, and therewith clutch many a thing, and swing it hither and thither. Art thou a grown baby, then, to fancy that the Miracle lies in miles of distance, or in pounds avoirdupois of weight; and not to see that the true inexplicable God-revealing miracle lies in this, that I can stretch forth my hand at all; that I have free Force to clutch aught therewith? Innumerable other of this sort are the deceptions, and wonder-hiding stupefactions, which Space practices on us.

"Still worse is it with regard to Time. Your grand anti-magician, and universal wonder-hider, is this same lying Time. Had we but the Time-annihilating Hat to put on for once only, we should see ourselves in a World of Miracles wherein all fabled or authentic Thaumaturgy and feats of Magic, were outdone. But unhappily we have not such a Hat; and man, poor fool that he is, can seldom and scantily help himself without one.

"Were it not wonderful, for instance, had Orpheus, or Amphion, built the walls of Thebes by the mere sound of his Lyre?[1] Yet tell me, Who built these walls of Weissnichtwo; summoning out all the sandstone rocks to dance along from the *Stein-bruch*[2] (now a huge Troglodyte Chasm with frightful, green-mantled pools); and shape themselves into Doric and Ionic pillars, squared ashlar houses, and noble streets? Was it not the still higher Orpheus, or Orpheuses, who, in past centuries, by the divine Music of Wisdom, succeeded in civilizing man? Our highest Orpheus walked in Judea, eighteen hundred years ago; his sphere-melody,[3] flowing in wild native tones, took captive the ravished souls of men; and, being of a truth sphere-melody, still flows and sounds, though now with thousandfold accomplishments, and rich symphonies, through all our hearts; and modulates, and divinely leads them. Is that a wonder, which happens in two hours; and does it cease to be wonderful if happening in two million? Not only was Thebes built by the music of an Orpheus; but without the music of some inspired Orpheus was no city ever built, no work that man glories in ever done.

"Sweep away the Illusion of Time; glance, if thou have eyes, from the near moving-cause, to its far-distant Mover. The stroke that came transmitted through a whole galaxy of elastic balls, was it less a stroke than if the last ball only had been struck, and sent flying? Oh, could I (with the Time-annihilating Hat) transport thee direct from the Beginnings to the Endings, how were thy eyesight unsealed, and thy heart set flaming in the Light-sea of celestial wonder! Then sawest thou that this fair Universe, were it in the meanest province thereof, is in very deed the star-domed City of God; that through every star, through every grass blade, and most through every Living Soul, the glory of a present God still beams. But Nature, which is the Time-vesture of God, and reveals Him to the wise, hides Him from the foolish.

"Again, could anything be more miraculous than an actual authentic Ghost? The English Johnson longed all his life to see one; but could not, though he went to Cock Lane,[4] and thence to the church vaults and tapped on coffins. Foolish Doctor! Did he never, with the mind's eye as well as with the body's, look round him into that full tide of human Life he so loved; did he never so much as look into Himself? The good Doctor was a Ghost, as actual and authentic as heart could wish; well-nigh a million of Ghosts were traveling the streets by his side. Once more I say, sweep away the illusion of Time; compress the three-score years into three minutes: what else was he, what else are we? Are we not Spirits that are shaped into a body, into an Appearance; and that fade away again into air, and Invisibility? This is no metaphor, it is a simple scientific *fact;* we start out of Nothingness, take figure, and are Apparitions; round us, as round the veriest specter, is Eternity; and to eternity minutes are as years and aeons. Come there not tones of Love and Faith, as from celestial harp strings, like the Song of beatified Souls? And again, do not we squeak and gibber[5] (in our discordant, screech-owlish debatings and recriminatings); and glide bodeful, and feeble, and fearful; or uproar (*poltern*) and revel in our mad Dance of the Dead—till the scent of the morning air[6] summons us to our still Home; and dreamy Night becomes awake and Day? Where now is Alexander of

[1] An ancient tradition; cf. p. 253, note 13.

[2] stone-quarry

[3] See p. 349, note 2.

[4] The "Cock Lane Ghost" was a notorious imposture perpetrated in London in 1762.

[5] *Hamlet,* I, v, 58.

[6] *Hamlet,* I, v, 58.

Macedon? Does the steel Host that yelled in fierce battle shouts, at Issus and Arbela, remain behind him; or have they all vanished utterly, even as perturbed Goblins must? Napoleon, too, and his Moscow Retreats and Austerlitz Campaigns! Was it all other than the veriest Specter-hunt; which has now, with its howling tumult that made night hideous, flitted away? Ghosts! There are nigh a thousand million walking the Earth openly at noontide; some half-hundred have vanished from it, some half-hundred have arisen in it, ere thy watch ticks once.

"O Heaven, it is mysterious, it is awful to consider that we not only carry each a future Ghost within him; but are, in very deed, Ghosts! These Limbs, whence had we them; this stormy Force; this lifeblood with its burning passion? They are dust and shadow; a Shadow-system gathered round our ME; wherein through some moments or years, the Divine Essence is to be revealed in the Flesh. That warrior on his strong war horse, fire flashes through his eyes; force dwells in his arm and heart; but warrior and war horse are a vision; a revealed Force, nothing more. Stately they tread the Earth, as if it were a firm substance. Fool! The Earth is but a film; it cracks in twain, and warrior and war horse sink beyond plummet's sounding. Plummet's? Fantasy herself will not follow them. A little while ago they were not; a little while and they are not, their very ashes are not.

"So has it been from the beginning, so will it be to the end. Generation after generation takes to itself the Form of a Body; and forth-issuing from Cimmerian Night, [1] on Heaven's mission APPEARS. What Force and Fire is in each he expends; one grinding in the mill of Industry; one hunter-like climbing the giddy Alpine heights of Science; one madly dashed in pieces on the rocks of Strife, in war with his fellow:—and then the Heaven-sent is recalled; his earthly Vesture falls away, and soon even to Sense becomes a Vanished Shadow. Thus, like some wild-flaming, wild-thundering train of Heaven's Artillery, does this mysterious MANKIND thunder and flame, in long-drawn, quick-succeeding grandeur, through the unknown Deep. Thus, like a God-created, fire-breathing Spirit-host, we emerge from the Inane; haste stormfully across the astonished Earth; then plunge again into the Inane. Earth's mountains are leveled, and her seas filled up, in our passage. Can the Earth, which is but dead and a vision, resist Spirits which have reality and are alive? On the hardest adamant some footprint of us is stamped-in; the last Rear of the host will read traces of the earliest Van. But whence?—O Heaven, whither? Sense knows not; Faith knows not; only that it is through Mystery to Mystery, from God and to God.

"We are such stuff
As Dreams are made on, and our little Life
Is rounded with a sleep!" [2]

1833-4

[1] Cimmeria was a fabled country of perpetual darkness.

From THE FRENCH REVOLUTION

[UPRISING OF THE POPULACE. STORMING OF THE BASTILLE.] From VOLUME I, BOOK V, CHAPTERS IV-VI [3]

So hangs it, dubious, fateful, in the sultry days of July. It is the passionate, printed *advice* of M. Marat [4] to abstain, of all things, from violence. Nevertheless the hungry poor are already burning Town Barriers, [5] where tribute on eatables is levied; getting clamorous for food.

The twelfth July morning is Sunday: the streets are all placarded with an enormous-sized *De part le Roi,* [6] "inviting peaceable citizens to remain within doors," [7] to feel no alarm, to gather in no crowd. Why so? What mean these "placards of enormous size?" Above all, what means this clatter of military; dragoons, hussars, rattling in from all points of the compass toward the Place Louis Quinze, [8] with a staid gravity of face, though saluted with mere nicknames, hootings, and even missiles? Besenval [9] is with them. Swiss Guards

[2] *The Tempest,* IV, i, 156.

[3] The immediate cause of the French Revolution was a deficiency of revenue and the oppressive taxation of the people—the Commonalty, or Third Estate—to the exemption of the two other Estates, the Nobility and the Clergy. Necker, a Genevese statesman, who was Director General of Finance, convened the States-General, or legislative assemblies, at Versailles in May, 1789. As they failed to come to an agreement, the Third Estate resolved itself into a National Assembly with the object of forming a Constitution. Such in brief was the situation when this narrative opens—the King and his court at Versailles, just outside of Paris, hopelessly at odds with the National Assembly, and the starving populace in Paris and all of France beginning to clamor for bread.

[4] Jean Paul Marat, at one time the Prince d'Artois's horse-leech (horse doctor); one of the earliest inciters to revolution, and a leader of the Jacobin party after it was formed

[5] city gates

[6] an order *de part le roi,* "by the authority of the king"

[7] Words thus quoted by Carlyle are taken from various memoirs and contemporary documents.

[8] "Square of Louis XV"; a noted square west of the Tuileries, or royal residence; now the Place de la Concorde

[9] then Commandant of Paris

of his are already in the Champs Elysées,[1] with four pieces of artillery.

Have the destroyers descended on us,[2] then? From the Bridge of Sèvres to utmost Vincennes, from Saint-Denis to the Champ-de-Mars, we are begirt! Alarm of the vague unknown is in every heart. The Palais Royal[3] has become a place of awestruck interjections, silent shakings of the head. One can fancy with what dolorous sound the noontide cannon (which the Sun fires at crossing of his meridian) went off there; bodeful, like an inarticulate voice of doom. Are these troops verily come out "against Brigands"? Where are the Brigands? What mystery is in the wind?—Hark! a human voice reporting articulately the Job's-news:[4] *Necker, People's Minister, Savior of France, is dismissed.* Impossible, incredible! Treasonous to the public peace! Such a voice ought to be choked in the waterworks—had not the newsbringer quickly fled. Nevertheless, friends, make of it what ye will, the news is true. Necker is gone. Necker hies northward incessantly, in obedient secrecy, since yesternight. We have a new Ministry: Broglie the War-god;[5] Aristocrat Breteuil; Foulon who said the people might eat grass!

Rumor, therefore, shall arise; in the Palais Royal, and in broad France. Paleness sits on every face: confused tremor and fremescence,[6] waxing into thunder-peals, of Fury stirred on by Fear.

But see Camille Desmoulins, from the Café de Foy, rushing out, sibylline[7] in face, his hair streaming, in each hand a pistol! He springs to a table; the Police satellites are eying him; alive they shall not take him, not they alive him alive. This time he speaks without stammering: Friends! Shall we die like hunted hares? Like sheep hounded into their pinfold, bleating for mercy, where is no mercy but only a whetted knife? The hour is come; the supreme hour of Frenchman and Man; when Oppressors are to try conclusions with Oppressed; and the word is, swift Death or Deliverance forever. Let such hour be *well-come!* Us, meseems, one cry only befits: To Arms! Let universal Paris, universal France, as with the throat of the whirlwind, sound only: To arms!—"To arms!" yell responsive the innumerable voices; like one great voice, as of a Demon yelling from the air; for all faces wax fire-eyed, all hearts burn up into madness. In such, or fitter words, does Camille evoke the Elemental Powers, in this great moment. Friends, continues Camille, some rallying sign! Cockades; green ones—the color of Hope! As with the flight of locusts, these green tree-leaves; green ribands from the neighboring shops; all green things are snatched, and made cockades of. Camille descends from his table; "stifled with embraces, wetted with tears"; has a bit of green ribbon handed him; sticks it in his hat. And now to Curtius' Image-shop there; to the Boulevards; to the four winds, and rest not till France be on fire!

France, so long shaken and wind-parched, is probably at the right inflammable point. As for poor Curtius who, one grieves to think, might be but imperfectly paid—he cannot make two words about his images. The Wax-bust of Necker, the Wax-bust of D'Orléans, helpers of France; these, covered with crape, as in funeral procession, or after the manner of suppliants appealing to Heaven, to Earth, and Tartarus itself, a mixed multitude bears off. For a sign! As indeed man, with his singular imaginative faculties, can do little or nothing without signs; thus Turks look to their Prophet's Banner; also Osier *Mannikins*[8] have been burnt, and Necker's Portrait has erewhile figured, aloft on its perch.

In this manner march they, a mixed, continually increasing multitude; armed with axes, staves, and miscellanea; grim, many-sounding, through the streets. Be all Theaters shut; let all dancing on planked floor, or on the natural greensward, cease! Instead of a Christian Sabbath, and feast of *guinguette*[9] tabernacles, it shall be a Sorcerer's Sabbath;[10] and Paris, gone rabid, dance—with the Fiend for piper!

. . . .

Raging multitudes surround the Hôtel-de-Ville,[11] crying: Arms! Orders! The Six-and-twenty Town Councilors, with their long gowns, have ducked under (into the ravaging chaos), shall never emerge more. Besenval is painfully wriggling himself out, to the Champ-de-Mars;[12]

[1] an avenue and public park extending westward from the Place de la Concorde
[2] Carlyle speaks from the point of view of the Parisian populace, or revolutionists, whom he later calls by the collective name of "Patriotism."
[3] A palace, with galleries and gardens, built by Cardinal Richelieu in the heart of Paris; at this time it was occupied by the Duc d'Orléans (Philippe Égalité), one of the nobles who had joined the Commons, and its cafés were the resort of the more violent democrats.
[4] disheartening news
[5] i. e., Minister of War
[6] from Latin *fremo,* to growl
[7] like the ancient Sibyl, or inspired prophetess
[8] images of Guy Fawkes, for example
[9] tea-garden
[10] assembly of witches or wizards
[11] the Town Hall, which became the rallying place of the democratic party
[12] a military field, south of the Seine

he must sit there "in the cruelest uncertainty!" Courier after courier may dash off for Versailles; but will bring back no answer, can hardly bring himself back. For the roads are all blocked with batteries and pickets, with floods of carriages arrested for examination; such was Broglie's one, sole order; the Oeil-de-Boeuf,[1] hearing in the distance such mad-din, which sounded almost like invasion, will before all things keep its own head whole. A new Ministry with, as it were, but one foot in the stirrup, cannot take leaps. Mad Paris is abandoned altogether to itself.

What a Paris, when the darkness fell! A European metropolitan City hurled suddenly forth from its old combinations and arrangements; to crash tumultuously together, seeking new. Use and wont will now no longer direct any man; each man with what of originality he has, must begin thinking; or following those that think. Seven hundred thousand individuals, on the sudden, find all their old paths, old ways of acting and deciding, vanish from under their feet. And so there go they, with clangor and terror, they know not as yet whether running, swimming, or flying—headlong into the New Era. With clangor and terror—from above, Broglie, the war god, impends, preternatural, with his red-hot cannon-balls; and from below a preternatural Brigand-world menaces with dirk and firebrand—madness rules the hour.

Happily, in place of the submerged Twenty-six, the Electoral Club is gathering; has declared itself a "Provisional Municipality." On the morrow, it will get Provost Flesselles, with an Echevin or two,[2] to give help in many things. For the present it decrees one most essential thing: that forthwith a "Parisian Militia" shall be enrolled. Depart, ye heads of Districts, to labor in this great work; while we here, in Permanent Committee, sit alert. Let fencible[3] men, each party in its own range of streets, keep watch and ward, all night. Let Paris court a little fever-sleep; confused by such fever-dreams, of "violent motions at the Palais Royal"—or from time to time start awake, and look out, palpitating, in its nightcap, at the clash of discordant, mutually-unintelligible Patrols; on the gleam of distant Barriers, going up all too ruddy toward the vault of Night.

[1] the hall of the king's counselors, at Versailles, only a few miles from Paris
[2] the Provost of Merchants, with his municipal magistrates
[3] capable of defending

On Monday, the huge City has awoke, not to its week-day industry—to what a different one! The working man has become a fighting man; has one want only—that of arms. The industry of all crafts has paused—except it be the smith's, fiercely hammering pikes; and, in a faint degree, the kitchener's, cooking offhand victuals, for *bouche va toujours*.[4] Women, too, are sewing cockades—not now of *green*, which being d'Artois[5] color, the Hôtel-de-Ville has had to interfere in it; but of *red* and *blue*, our old Paris colors. These, once based on a ground of constitutional white, are the famed TRICOLOR—which (if Prophecy err not) "will go round the world."

All shops, unless it be the Bakers' and Vintners', are shut. Paris is in the streets—rushing, foaming like some Venice wineglass into which you had dropped poison. The tocsin, by order, is pealing madly from all steeples. Arms, ye Elector Municipals; thou Flesselles with thy Echevins, give us arms! Flesselles gives what he can; fallacious, perhaps insidious promises of arms from Charleville; order to seek arms here, order to seek them there. The new Municipals give what they can; some three hundred and sixty indifferent firelocks, the equipment of the City-watch—"a man in wooden shoes, and without coat, directly clutches one of them, and mounts guard." Also as hinted, an order to all Smiths to make pikes with their whole soul.

Heads of Districts are in fervent consultation; subordinate Patriotism roams distracted, ravenous for arms. Hitherto at the Hôtel-de-Ville was only such modicum of indifferent firelocks as we have seen. At the so-called Arsenal, there lies nothing but rust, rubbish, and saltpeter—overlooked, too, by the guns of the Bastille. His Majesty's Repository, what they call *Garde-Meuble*, is forced and ransacked; tapestries enough, and gauderies; but of serviceable fighting-gear small stock! Two silver-mounted cannons there are; an ancient gift from his Majesty of Siam to Louis Fourteenth; gilt sword of the Good Henri;[6] antique chivalry arms and armor. These, and such as these, a necessitous Patriotism snatches greedily, for want of better. The Siamese cannons go trundling, on an errand they were not meant for. Among the indifferent firelocks are seen tourney lances; the princely helm and hauberk glittering amid ill-hatted

[4] "Eating must go on."
[5] Monseigneur d'Artois was an unpopular adherent of the king.
[6] Henry of Navarre

heads—as in a time when all times and their possessions are suddenly sent jumbling!

. . . . .

In such circumstances, the Aristocrat, the unpatriotic rich man is packing up for departure. But he shall not get departed. A wooden-shod force has seized all Barriers, burnt or not: all that enters, all that seeks to issue, is stopped there, and dragged to the Hôtel-de-Ville—coaches, tumbrils,[1] plate, furniture, "many meal-sacks," in time even "flocks and herds" encumber the Place de Grève.[2]

And so it roars, and rages, and brays: drums beating, steeples pealing; criers rushing with hand-bells: "Oyez,[3] oyez, All men to their Districts to be enrolled!" The Districts have met in gardens, open squares; are getting marshaled into volunteer troops. No red-hot ball has yet fallen from Besenval's Camp; on the contrary, Deserters with their arms are continually dropping in; nay, now, joy of joys, at two in the afternoon, the Gardes Françaises,[4] being ordered to Saint-Denis, and flatly declining, have come over in a body! It is a fact worth many. Three thousand six hundred of the best fighting men, with complete accouterment; with cannoneers even, and cannon! Their officers are left standing alone; could not so much as succeed in "spiking the guns." The very Swiss, it may now be hoped, Château-Vieux[5] and the others, will have doubts about fighting.

Our Parisian Militia—which some think it were better to name National Guard—is prospering as heart could wish. It promised to be forty-eight thousand, but will in few hours double and quadruple that number: invincible, if we had only arms!

But see, the promised Charleville Boxes, marked *Artillerie!* Here then are arms enough? —Conceive the blank face of Patriotism, when it found them filled with rags, foul linen, candle ends, and bits of wood! Provost of the Merchants, how is this? Neither at the Chartreux Convent, whither we were sent with signed order, is there or ever was there any weapon of war. Nay here, in this Seine Boat, safe under tarpaulins (had not the nose of Patriotism been of the finest), are "five thousand-weight of gunpowder"; not coming *in,* but surreptitiously going *out!* What meanest thou, Flesselles? 'Tis a ticklish game, that of "amusing" us. Cat plays with captive mouse: but mouse with enraged cat, with enraged National Tiger?

Meanwhile, the faster, O ye black-aproned Smiths, smite; with strong arm and willing heart. This man and that, all stroke from head to heel, shall thunder alternating, and ply the great forge-hammer, till stithy reel and ring again; while ever and anon, overhead, booms the alarm cannon—for the City has now got gunpowder. Pikes are fabricated; fifty thousand of them, in six-and-thirty hours; judge whether the Black-aproned have been idle. Dig trenches, unpave the streets, ye others, assiduous, man and maid; cram the earth in barrel-barricades, at each of them a volunteer sentry; pile the whinstones in window sills and upper rooms. Have scalding pitch, at least boiling water ready, ye weak old women, to pour it and dash it on Royal-Allemand,[6] with your skinny arms: your shrill curses along with it will not be wanting!—Patrols of the new-born National Guard, bearing torches, scour the streets all that night; which otherwise are vacant, yet illuminated in every window by order. Strange looking; like some naphtha-lighted City of the Dead, with here and there a flight of perturbed Ghosts.

O poor mortals, how ye make this Earth bitter for each other; this fearful and wonderful Life fearful and horrible; and Satan has his place in all hearts! Such agonies and ragings and wailings ye have, and have had, in all times:—to be buried all, in so deep silence; and the salt sea is not swollen with your tears.

Great meanwhile is the moment, when tidings of Freedom reach us; when the long-enthralled soul, from amid its chains and squalid stagnancy, arises, were it still only in blindness and bewilderment, and swears by Him that made it, that it will be *free!* Free? Understand that well, it is the deep commandment, dimmer or clearer, of our whole being, to be *free.* Freedom is the one purport, wisely aimed at or unwisely, of all man's struggles, toilings, and sufferings in this Earth. Yes, supreme is such a moment (if thou have known it); first vision as of a flame-girt Sinai,[7] in this our waste pilgrimage—which thenceforth wants not its pillar of cloud by day, and pillar of fire by night![8] Something it is, even—nay, something considerable, when the chains have grown *corrosive,* poisonous—to be free "from oppression by our fellow-man." Forward, ye maddened sons of France; be it toward this destiny or

[1] two-wheeled carts
[2] now the Place de l'Hôtel-de-Ville
[3] "Hear ye!"
[4] French Guards, chief regiment of the French army
[5] a regiment of Swiss troops
[6] a regiment of German troops
[7] the mountain on which the law was given to Moses, *Exodus,* xix
[8] *Exodus,* xiii, 21

toward that! Around you is but starvation, falsehood, corruption, and the clam of death. Where ye are is no abiding.

Imagination may, imperfectly, figure how Commandant Besenval, in the Champ-de-Mars, has worn out these sorrowful hours. Insurrection raging all round; his men melting away! From Versailles, to the most pressing messages, comes no answer; or once only some vague word of answer which is worse than none. A Council of Officers can decide merely that there is no decision. Colonels inform him, "weeping," that they do not think their men will fight. Cruel uncertainty is here: war-god Broglie sits yonder, inaccessible in his Olympus; does not descend terror-clad, does not produce his whiff of grapeshot; [1] sends no orders.

Truly, in the Château [2] of Versailles all seems mystery; in the Town of Versailles, were we there, all is rumor, alarm, and indignation. An august National Assembly sits, to appearance, menaced with death; endeavoring to defy death. It has resolved "that Necker carries with him the regrets of the Nation." It has sent solemn Deputation over to the Château, with entreaty to have these troops withdrawn. In vain; his Majesty, with a singular composure, invites us to be busy rather with our own duty, making the Constitution! . . . .

So at Versailles. But at Paris, agitated Besenval, before retiring for the night, has stepped over to old M. de Sombreuil of the *Hôtel des Invalides* [3] hard by. M. de Sombreuil has, what is a great secret, some eight-and-twenty-thousand stand of muskets deposited in his cellars there; but no trust in the temper of his Invalides. This day, for example, he sent twenty of the fellows down to unscrew those muskets; lest sedition might snatch at them. But scarcely, in six hours, had the twenty unscrewed twenty gun-locks, or dogsheads (*chiens*) of locks—each Invalide his dogshead! If ordered to fire, they would, he imagines, turn their cannon against himself.

Unfortunate old military gentlemen, it is your hour, not of glory! Old Marquis de Launay, too, of the Bastille, has pulled up his drawbridges long since, "and retired into his interior"; with sentries walking on his battlements, under the midnight sky, aloft over the glare of illuminated Paris—whom a National Patrol passing that way, takes the liberty of firing at; "seven shots toward twelve at night," which do not take effect. This was the 13th day of July, 1789; a worse day, many said, than the last 13th was, when only hail fell out of Heaven, not madness rose out of Tophet, [4] ruining worse than crops!

. . . . .

But . . . . a new, Fourteenth morning dawns. Under all roofs of this distracted City is the nodus [5] of a drama, not untragical, crowding toward solution. The bustlings and preparings, the tremors and menaces; the tears that fell from old eyes! This day, my sons, ye shall quit [6] you like men. By the memory of your fathers' wrongs, by the hope of your children's rights! Tyranny impends in red wrath: help for you is none, if not in your own right hands. This day ye must do or die.

From earliest light, a sleepless Permanent Committee has heard the old cry, now waxing almost frantic, mutinous: Arms! Arms! Provost Flesselles, or what traitors there are among you, may think of those Charleville Boxes. A hundred-and-fifty-thousand of us; and but the third man furnished with so much as a pike! Arms are the one thing needful: with arms we are an unconquerable, man-defying National Guard; without arms, a rabble to be whiffed with grapeshot.

Happily the word has arisen—for no secret can be kept—that there lie muskets at the *Hôtel des Invalides*. Thither will we; King's Procureur [7] M. Ethys de Corny, and whatsoever of authority a Permanent Committee can lend, shall go with us. Besenval's Camp is there; perhaps he will not fire on us; if he kill us, we shall but die.

Alas, poor Besenval, with his troops melting away in that manner, has not the smallest humor to fire! At five o'clock this morning, as he lay dreaming, oblivious in the *École Militaire,* [8] a "figure" stood suddenly at his bedside; "with face rather handsome; eyes inflamed, speech rapid and curt, air audacious"; such a figure drew Priam's curtains! [9] The message and monition of the figure was that resistance would be hopeless; that if blood flowed, woe to him who shed it. Thus spoke the figure—and vanished. "Withal there was a kind of eloquence that struck one." Besenval admits

[1] Broglie had boasted that he would settle the Third Estate with a "whiff of grapeshot" (*salve de canons*). Six years later the whiff was delivered by Napoleon, and the Revolution ended. See the next to the last chapter of Carlyle's *History*.

[2] the residence of the king

[3] an establishment for disabled soldiers, not far from the Champs de Mars

[4] Hell

[5] "knot," tangle, plot

[6] acquit, conduct

[7] attorney

[8] Military School; by the Champs de Mars

[9] Cf. Goldsmith's "The Haunch of Venison," l. 110, p. 411, and note.

that he should have arrested him, but did not. Who this figure with inflamed eyes, with speech rapid and curt, might be? Besenval knows, but mentions not. Camille Desmoulins? Pythagorean Marquis Valadi,[1] inflamed with "violent motions all night at the Palais Royal?" Fame names him "Young M. Meillar"; then shuts her lips about him forever.

In any case, behold, about nine in the morning, our National Volunteers rolling in long, wide flood, south-westward to the *Hôtel des Invalides*; in search of the one thing needful. King's Procureur M. Ethys de Corny and officials are there; the Curé of Saint-Ètienne du Mont marches, unpacific, at the head of his militant Parish; the Clerks of the Basoche[2] in red coats, we see marching, now Volunteers of the Basoche; the Volunteers of the Palais Royal—National Volunteers, numerable by tens of thousands; of one heart and mind. The King's muskets are the Nation's; think, old M. de Sombreuil, how, in this extremity, thou wilt refuse them! Old M. de Sombreuil would fain hold parley, send couriers; but it skills[3] not. The walls are scaled, no Invalide firing a shot; the gates must be flung open. Patriotism rushes in, tumultuous, from grunsel[4] up to ridge-tile, through all rooms and passages; rummaging distractedly for arms. What cellar, or what cranny can escape it? The arms are found; all safe there; lying packed in straw—apparently with a view to being burnt! More ravenous than famishing lions over dead prey, the multitude, with clangor and vociferation, pounces on them; struggling, dashing, clutching:—to the jamming-up, to the pressure, fracture, and probable extinction of the weaker Patriot. And so, with such protracted crash of deafening, most discordant, Orchestra-music, the Scene is changed; and eight-and-twenty thousand sufficient firelocks are on the shoulders of as many National Guards, lifted thereby out of darkness into fiery light.

Let Besenval look at the glitter of these muskets, as they flash by. Gardes Françaises, it is said, have cannon leveled on him; ready to open, if need were, from the other side of the River. Motionless sits he; "astonished," one may flatter oneself, "at the proud bearing (*fière contenance*) of the Parisians."—And now to the Bastille, ye intrepid Parisians! There grapeshot still threatens; thither all men's thoughts and steps are now tending.

[1] another of the nobles who had joined the people
[2] a collective term for "the Law"
[3] avails
[4] groundsill

Old De Launay, as we hinted, withdrew "into his interior" soon after midnight of Sunday. He remains there ever since, hampered, as all military gentlemen now are, in the saddest conflict of uncertainties. The Hôtel-de-Ville "invites" him to admit National Soldiers, which is a soft name for surrendering. On the other hand, His Majesty's orders were precise. His garrison is but eighty-two old Invalides, reinforced by thirty-two young Swiss; his walls indeed are nine feet thick, he has cannon and powder; but, alas, only one day's provision of victuals. The city, too, is French, the poor garrison mostly French. Rigorous, old De Launay, think what thou wilt do!

All morning, since nine, there has been a cry everywhere: To the Bastille! Repeated "deputations of citizens" have been here, passionate for arms; whom De Launay has got dismissed by soft speeches through portholes. Toward noon, Elector Thuriot de la Rosière gains admittance; finds De Launay indisposed for surrender; nay, disposed for blowing up the place rather. Thuriot mounts with him to the battlements; heaps of paving-stones, old iron, and missiles lie piled; cannon all duly leveled; in every embrasure a cannon—only drawn back a little! But outward, behold, O Thuriot, how the multitude flows on, welling through every street; tocsin furiously pealing, all drums beating the *générale;*[5] the Suburb Saint-Antoine rolling hitherward wholly, as one man![6] such vision (spectral yet real) thou, O Thuriot, as from thy Mount of Vision, beholdest in this moment; prophetic of what other Phantasmagories, and loud-gibbering, Spectral Realities, which thou yet beholdest not, but shalt! *"Que voulez-vous?"*[7] said De Launay, turning pale at the sight, with an air of reproach, almost of menace. "Monsieur," said Thuriot, rising into the moral sublime, "what mean *you?* Consider if I could not precipitate *both* of us from this height"—say only a hundred feet, exclusive of the walled ditch! Whereupon De Launay fell silent. Thuriot shows himself from some pinnacle, to comfort the multitude becoming suspicious, fremescent; then descends; departs with protest; with warning addressed also to the Invalides—on whom, however, it produces but a mixed, indistinct impression. The old heads are none of the clearest; besides, it is said, De Launay has been profuse of beverages (*prodigua des*

[5] the signal for assembling, or of alarm
[6] The Faubourg St. Antoine, or east side of Paris, much like the east side of London, is mainly a residence of the lower classes.
[7] "What do you want? What do you mean?"

buissons). They think they will not fire—if not fired on, if they can help it; but must, on the whole, be ruled considerably by circumstances.

Woe to thee, De Launay, in such an hour, if thou canst not, taking some one firm decision, *rule* circumstances! Soft speeches will not serve; hard grapeshot is questionable; but hovering between the two is *un*questionable. Ever wilder swells the tide of men; their infinite hum waxing ever louder, into imprecations, perhaps into crackle of stray musketry,—which latter, on walls nine feet thick, cannot do execution. The Outer Drawbridge has been lowered for Thuriot; new *deputation of citizens* (it is the third, and noisiest of all) penetrates that way into the Outer Court: soft speeches producing no clearance of these, De Launay gives fire; pulls up his Drawbridge. A slight sputter—which has *kindled* the too combustible chaos—made it a roaring fire-chaos! Bursts forth Insurrection, at sight of its own blood (for there were deaths by that sputter of fire), into endless rolling explosion of musketry, distraction, execration—and overhead, from the Fortress, let one great gun, with its grapeshot, go booming, to show what we *could* do. The Bastille is besieged!

On, then, all Frenchmen that have hearts in your bodies! Roar with all your throats of cartilage and metal, ye Sons of Liberty; stir spasmodically whatsoever of utmost faculty is in you, soul, body, or spirit; for it is the hour! Smite, thou Louis Tournay, cartwright of the Marais,[1] old soldier of the Regiment Dauphiné; smite at that Outer Drawbridge chain, though the fiery hail whistles round thee! Never, over nave or felloe, did thy axe strike such a stroke. Down with it, man; down with it to Orcus;[2] let the whole accursed Edifice sink thither, and Tyranny be swallowed up forever! Mounted, some say, on the roof of the guardroom, some "on bayonets stuck into joints of the wall," Louis Tournay smites, brave Aubin Bonnemère (also an old soldier) seconding him; the chain yields, breaks; the huge drawbridge slams down, thundering (*avec fracas*). Glorious; and yet, alas, it is still but the outworks. The Eight grim Towers, with their Invalide musketry, their paving stones and cannon-mouths, still soar aloft intact—Ditch yawning impassable, stone-faced; the inner Drawbridge with its *back* toward us; the Bastille is still to take!

To describe this siege of the Bastille (thought to be one of the most important in History) perhaps transcends the talent of mortals. Could one but, after infinite reading, get to understand so much as the plan of the building! But there is open Esplanade, at the end of the Rue Saint-Antoine; there are such Forecourts, *Cour Avancée, Cour de l'Orme,* arched Gateway (where Louis Tournay now fights); then new drawbridges, dormant-bridges, rampart-bastions, and the grim Eight Towers; a labyrinthic Mass, high-frowning there, of all ages from twenty years to four hundred and twenty—beleaguered, in this its last hour, as we said, by mere Chaos come again! Ordnance of all calibers; throats of all capacities; men of all plans, every man his own engineer—seldom since the war of Pygmies and Cranes[3] was there seen so anomalous a thing. Half-pay Elie is home for a suit of regimentals;[4] no one would heed him in colored clothes. Half-pay Hulin is haranguing Gardes Françaises in the Place de Grève. Frantic Patriots pick up the grapeshots; bear them, still hot (or seemingly so), to the Hôtel-de-Ville—Paris, you perceive, is to be burnt! Flesselles is "pale to the very lips," for the roar of the multitude grows deep. Paris wholly has got to the acme of its frenzy; whirled all ways by panic madness. At every street-barricade there whirls simmering a minor whirlpool—strengthening the barricade, since God knows what is coming; and all minor whirlpools play distractedly into that grand Fire-Maelstrom[5] which is lashing round the Bastille.

And so it lashes and it roars. Cholat the wine-merchant has become an impromptu cannoneer. See Georget, of the Marine Service, fresh from Brest,[6] ply the King of Siam's cannon. Singular (if we were not used to the like)—Georget lay, last night, taking his ease at his inn;[7] the King of Siam's cannon also lay, knowing nothing of *him,* for a hundred years. Yet now, at the right instant, they have got together, and discourse eloquent music. For, hearing what was toward, Georget sprang from the Brest Diligence,[8] and ran. Gardes Françaises also will be here, with real artillery; were not the walls so thick! Upward from the Esplanade, horizontally from all neighboring roofs and windows, flashes one irregular deluge of musketry, without effect.

[1] a manufacturing quarter of Paris
[2] Hades

[3] An ancient fable; see *Iliad,* III, 5.
[4] Carlyle is here merely reporting a glimpse of Elie as he gets it from some record. He has earlier described these two captains, Elie and Hulin, as "both with an air of half-pay."
[5] maelstrom, whirlpool
[6] the principal naval port of France
[7] "Shall I not take mine ease in mine inn?" *1 Henry IV,* III, iii, 93
[8] stage-coach

The Invalides lie flat, firing comparatively at their ease from behind stone; hardly through portholes show the tip of a nose. We fall, shot; and make no impression!

Let conflagration rage; of whatsoever is combustible! Guardrooms are burnt, Invalides mess-rooms. A distracted "Peruke-maker with two fiery torches" is for burning "the saltpeters of the Arsenal"—had not a woman run screaming; had not a Patriot, with some tincture of Natural Philosophy, [1] instantly struck the wind out of him (butt of musket on pit of stomach), overturned barrels, and stayed the devouring element. A young, beautiful lady, seized escaping in these Outer Courts, and thought falsely to be De Launay's daughter, shall be burnt in De Launay's sight; she lies swooned on a paillasse; [2] but again a Patriot, it is brave Aubin Bonnemère, the old soldier, dashes in and rescues her. Straw is burnt; three cartloads of it, hauled thither, go up in white smoke; almost to the choking of Patriotism itself; so that Elie had, with singed brows, to drag back one cart; and Réole the "gigantic haberdasher" another. Smoke as of Tophet; confusion as of Babel; noise as of the Crack of Doom!

Blood flows; the aliment of new madness. The wounded are carried into houses of the Rue Cerisaie; the dying leave their last mandate not to yield till the accursed Stronghold fall. And yet, alas, how fall? The walls are so thick! Deputations, three in number, arrive from the Hôtel-de-Ville; Abbé Fauchat (who was of one) can say with what almost superhuman courage of benevolence. These wave their Town-flag in the arched Gateway; and stand, rolling their drum; but to no purpose. In such Crack of Doom, De Launay cannot hear them, dare not believe them: they return, with justified rage, the whew of lead still singing in their ears. What to do? The Firemen are here, squirting with their fire pumps on the Invalides cannon, to wet the touchholes; they unfortunately cannot squirt so high; but produce only clouds of spray. Individuals of classical knowledge propose *catapults*. Santerre, the sonorous Brewer of the Suburb Saint-Antoine, advises rather that the place be fired, by a "mixture of phosphorus and oil-of-turpentine spouted up through forcing pumps"—O Spinola-Santerre, [3] hast thou the mixture *ready*? Every man his own engineer! And still the fire-deluge abates not; even women are firing, and Turks; at least one woman (with her sweetheart) and one Turk. Gardes Françaises have come; real cannon, real cannoneers. Usher [4] Maillard is busy; half-pay Elie, half-pay Hulin rage in the midst of thousands.

How the great Bastille Clock ticks (inaudible) in its Inner Court there, at its ease, hour after hour; as if nothing special, for it or the world, were passing! It tolled One when the firing began; and is now pointing toward Five, and still the firing slakes not. Far down, in their vaults, the seven Prisoners hear muffled din as of earthquakes; their Turnkeys answer vaguely.

Woe to thee, De Launay, with thy poor hundred Invalides! Broglie is distant, and his ears heavy: Besenval hears, but can send no help. One poor troop of Hussars has crept, reconnoitering, cautiously along the Quais, as far as the Pont Neuf. [5] "We are come to join you," said the captain; for the crowd seems shoreless. A large-headed dwarfish individual of smoke-bleared aspect, shambles forward, opening his blue lips, for there is sense in him; and croaks: "Alight then, and give up your arms!" The Hussar-Captain is too happy to be escorted to the Barriers, and dismissed on parole. Who the squat individual was? Men answer, it is M. Marat, author of the excellent pacific *Avis au Peuple!* [6] Great, truly, O thou remarkable Dog-leech, is this thy day of emergence and new birth: and yet this same day come four years——But let the curtains of the Future hang. [7]

What shall De Launay do? One thing only De Launay could have done; what he said he would do. Fancy him sitting, from the first, with lighted taper, within arm's length of the Powder-Magazine; motionless, like old Roman Senator, or Bronze Lamp-holder; coldly apprising Thuriot, and all men, by a slight motion of his eye, what his resolution was. Harmless he sat there, while unharmed; but the King's Fortress, meanwhile, could, might, would, or should, in nowise be surrendered, save to the King's Messenger. One old man's life is worthless, so it be lost with honor; but think, ye brawling *canaille,* [8] how will it be when a whole Bastille springs skyward! In such statuesque, taper-holding attitude, one fancies De Launay might have left Thuriot, the red Clerks of the Basoche, Curé of Saint Stephen, and all the tag-rag-and-bobtail of the world to work their will.

[1] some knowledge of physics
[2] straw mattress
[3] General Spinola in 1625 took the fortress of Breda in Holland.

[4] *huissier,* constable
[5] "New Bridge"
[6] "Advice to the People"
[7] He was assassinated by Charlotte Corday, July 13, 1793.
[8] rabble

And yet, withal, he could not do it. Hast thou considered how each man's heart is so tremulously responsive to the hearts of all men; hast thou noted how omnipotent is the very sound of many men? How their shriek of indignation palsies the strong soul; their howl of contumely withers with unfelt pangs? The Ritter Gluck [1] confessed that the ground-tone of the noblest passage, in one of his noblest Operas, was the voice of the Populace he had heard at Vienna, crying to their Kaiser: Bread! Bread! Great is the combined voice of men; the utterance of their *instincts,* which are truer than their *thoughts*—it is the greatest a man encounters among the sounds and shadows which make up this World of Time. He who can resist that, has his footing somewhere *beyond* Time. De Launay could not do it. Distracted, he hovers between two; hopes in the middle of despair; surrenders not his Fortress; declares that he will blow it up, seizes torches to blow it up, and does not blow it. Unhappy old De Launay, it is the death-agony of thy Bastille and thee! Jail, Jailoring, and Jailor, all three, such as they may have been, must finish.

For four hours now has the World-Bedlam roared; call it the World-Chimaera, blowing fire! The poor Invalides have sunk under their battlements, or rise only with reversed muskets; they have made a white flag of napkins: go beating the *chamade,* [2] or seeming to beat, for one can hear nothing. The very Swiss at the Portcullis look weary of firing; disheartened in the fire-deluge; a porthole at the drawbridge is opened, as by one that would speak. See Huissier Maillard, the shifty man! On his plank, swinging over the abyss of that stone Ditch; plank resting on parapet, balanced by weight of Patriots—he hovers perilous; such a Dove toward such an ark! Deftly, thou shifty Usher; one man already fell; and lies smashed, far down there, against the masonry; Usher Maillard falls not; deftly, unerring, he walks with outspread palm. The Swiss holds a paper through his porthole; the shifty Usher snatches it, and returns. Terms of surrender: Pardon, immunity to all! Are they accepted?—*"Foi d' officier,* On the word of an officer," answers half-pay Hulin—or half-pay Elie, for men do not agree on it, "they are!" Sinks the drawbridge—Usher Maillard bolting it when down; rushes-in the living deluge; the Bastille is fallen! *Victoire! La Bastille est prise!* [2]

1837

[1] Of Germany: a *ritter* is a knight.
[2] parley, a signal for a parley
[3] "Victory! The Bastille is taken!"

THOMAS BABINGTON, LORD MACAULAY 1800-1859

At a single stride Macaulay stepped into public notice with the appearance in 1825 of his essay upon Milton published in the *Edinburgh Review.* Such everyday convincingness, such brilliancy, and such eloquence marked an advance in prose style that had made little progress since Johnson's time, and revealed a rarely-gifted intellect. Macaulay was born in a Leicestershire family of comfortable circumstances and interested in social betterment. He was graduated from Cambridge and held a fellowship there. Then family reverses came, and obliged him to write for a living. He became deeply interested in public affairs and in 1830 entered Parliament. There his eloquence, his prodigious memory, his convincingness in debate made him valuable for the reforms which he supported, and from then nearly until his death he was in public office or connected with public affairs.

Following his *Lays of Ancient Rome,* 1842, and his *Essays,* 1843, came his greatest work, the *History of England* (vol. I, 1848), which was still unfinished at his death. Macaulay's style has been criticized as artificial, self-conscious, and oratorical, but it is brilliant, vivid, crystal-clear, enthralling the mind. The chief point against his history is that, as the trained scholar is aware, the facts of social developments are more complex, sinuous, and difficult of correct explanation than Macaulay makes them to be. With him all is black or white. But never before was history made so picturesque, dramatic, alluring.

Biography: Morison (EML); Trevelyan (2 vols., standard, authorized). Criticism: Stephen (HL 3); Macaulay's value as a historian is discussed in *Dial* 49:225, 277-8, 454; see also W. R. Thayer's "Macaulay Fifty Years After," *No Am.* 190:735-52.

THE HISTORY OF ENGLAND

London [in 1685.] From Chapter III

. . . .

Whoever examines the maps of London which were published toward the close of the reign of Charles the Second will see that only the nucleus of the present capital then existed. The town did not, as now, fade by imperceptible degrees into the country. No long avenues of villas, embowered in lilacs and laburnums, extended from the great center of wealth and civilization almost to the boundaries of Middlesex and far into the heart of Kent and Surrey. In the east, no part of the immense line of warehouses and artificial lakes which now stretches from the Tower to Blackwall had even been projected. On the west, scarcely one of those stately piles of building which are inhabited by the noble and wealthy was in existence; and Chelsea, which is now peopled by more than forty thousand human beings, was a quiet country village with about a thousand inhabitants. On the north, cattle fed, and sportsmen wandered with dogs and guns over the site of the borough of Marylebone, [1] and over far the greater part of the space now covered by the boroughs of Finsbury and of the Tower Hamlets. Islington was almost a solitude; and poets loved to contrast its silence and repose with the din and turmoil of the monster London. [2] On the south the capital is now connected with its suburb by several bridges, not inferior in magnificence and solidity to the noblest works of the Caesars. In 1685, a single line of irregular arches, overhung by piles of mean and crazy houses, and garnished, after a fashion worthy of the naked barbarians of Dahomy, [3] with scores of moldering heads, impeded the navigation of the river.

. . . .

He who then rambled to what is now the gayest and most crowded part of Regent Street [4] found himself in a solitude, and was sometimes so fortunate as to have a shot at a woodcock. On the north the Oxford road ran between hedges. Three or four hundred yards to the south were the garden walls of a few great houses which were considered as quite out of town. On the west was a meadow renowned for a spring from which, long afterwards, Conduit Street was named. On the east was a field not to be passed without a shudder by any Londoner of that age. There, as in a place far from the haunts of men, had been dug, twenty years before, when the great plague was raging, a pit into which the dead-carts had nightly shot corpses by scores. It was popularly believed that the earth was deeply tainted with infection, and could not be disturbed without imminent risk to human life. No foundations were laid there till two generations had passed without any return of the pestilence, and till the ghastly spot had long been surrounded by buildings.

We should greatly err if we were to suppose that any of the streets and squares then bore the same aspect as at present. The great majority of the houses, indeed, have since that time been wholly, or in great part, rebuilt. If the most fashionable parts of the capital could be placed before us, such as they then were, we should be disgusted by their squalid appearance, and poisoned by their noisome atmosphere. In Covent Garden [5] a filthy and noisy market was held close to the dwellings of the great. Fruit women screamed, carters fought, cabbage stalks and rotten apples accumulated in heaps at the thresholds of the Countess of Berkshire and of the Bishop of Durham.

The center of Lincoln's Inn Fields [6] was an open space where the rabble congregated every evening, within a few yards of Cardigan House and Winchester House, to hear mountebanks harangue, to see bears dance, and to set dogs at oxen. Rubbish was shot [7] in every part of the area. Horses were exercised there. The beggars were as noisy and importunate as in the worst governed cities of the Continent. A Lincoln's Inn mumper [8] was a proverb. The whole fraternity knew the arms and liveries of every charitably disposed grandee in the neighborhood, and as soon as his lordship's coach and six appeared, came hopping and crawling in crowds to persecute him. These disorders lasted, in spite of many accidents, and of some legal proceedings, till, in the reign of George the Second, Sir Joseph Jekyll, Master of the Rolls, was knocked down and nearly killed in the middle of the square. Then at length palisades were set up, and a pleasant garden laid out.

Saint James's Square [9] was a receptacle for all the offal and cinders, for all the dead cats and dead dogs of Westminster. [10] At one time a cudgel player [11] kept the ring there. At another time an impudent squatter settled himself there, and built a shed for rubbish under the windows of the gilded saloons in which the first magnates of the realm, Norfolk, Ormond, Kent, and Pembroke, gave banquets and balls. It was not till these nuisances had lasted through a whole generation, and till much had been written about them, that the inhabitants applied to Parliament for permission to put up rails, and to plant trees.

When such was the state of the region inhabited by the most luxurious portion of society, we may easily believe that the great body of the population suffered what would now be considered as insupportable grievances. The pavement was detestable; all foreigners cried shame upon it. The drainage was so bad that in rainy weather the gutters soon became torrents. Several facetious poets have commemorated the fury with which these black rivulets

[1] popularly pronounced Marlibun, or Maribun
[2] Cf. Cowley: "Discourse of Solitude."
[3] in Africa: a description of the old London Bridge
[4] a fashionable shopping district in West London
[5] north of the Strand; a fruit and flower market
[6] the largest of London's squares, surrounded by lawyers' offices and ancient mansions
[7] dumped
[8] beggar and impostor
[9] the site of the most aristocratic mansions and clubs
[10] the portion of London which was once the city of Westminster; the site of the Government houses
[11] one skilled in contests with cudgels or staves

roared down Snow Hill and Ludgate Hill, bearing to Fleet Ditch a vast tribute of animal and vegetable filth from the stalls of butchers and greengrocers. This flood was profusely thrown to right and left by coaches and carts. To keep as far from the carriage road as possible was therefore the wish of every pedestrian. The mild and timid gave the wall. The bold and athletic took it. If two roisterers met, they cocked their hats in each other's faces, and pushed each other about till the weaker was shoved toward the kennel.[1] If he was a mere bully he sneaked off, muttering that he should find a time. If he was pugnacious, the encounter probably ended in a duel behind Montague House.[2]

The houses were not numbered. There would indeed have been little advantage in numbering them; for of the coachmen, chairmen,[3] porters, and errand boys of London, a very small proportion could read. It was necessary to use marks which the most ignorant could understand. The shops were therefore distinguished by painted or sculptured signs, which gave a gay and grotesque aspect to the streets. The walk from Charing Cross to Whitechapel lay through an endless succession of Saracens' Heads, Royal Oaks, Blue Bears, and Golden Lambs, which disappeared when they were no longer required for the direction of the common people.

When the evening closed in, the difficulty and danger of walking about London became serious indeed. The garret windows were opened, and pails were emptied, with little regard to those who were passing below. Falls, bruises, and broken bones were of constant occurrence. For, till the last year of the reign of Charles the Second, most of the streets were left in profound darkness. Thieves and robbers plied their trade with impunity; yet they were hardly so terrible to peaceable citizens as another class of ruffians. It was a favorite amusement of dissolute young gentlemen to swagger by night about the town, breaking windows, upsetting sedans, beating quiet men, and offering rude caresses to pretty women. Several dynasties of these tyrants had, since the Restoration, domineered over the streets. The Muns and Tityre Tus had given place to the Hectors, and the Hectors had been recently succeeded by the Scourers. At a later period rose the Nicker, the Hawcubite, and the yet more dreaded name of Mohawk. The machinery for keeping the peace was utterly contemptible. There was an act of Common Council which provided that more than a thousand watchmen should be constantly on the alert in the city, from sunset to sunrise, and that every inhabitant should take his turn of duty. But this Act was negligently executed. Few of those who were summoned left their homes; and those few generally found it more agreeable to tipple in alehouses than to pace the streets. . . . .

[1] gutter
[2] in Whitehall, the region of the Government offices
[3] sedan-chair bearers

THE [LONDON] COFFEE HOUSES. From CHAPTER III

The coffee house must not be dismissed with a cursory mention. It might indeed at that time have been not improperly called a most important political institution. No Parliament had sat for years. The municipal council of the city had ceased to speak the sense of the citizens. Public meetings, harangues, resolutions, and the rest of the modern machinery of agitation had not yet come into fashion. Nothing resembling the modern newspaper existed. In such circumstances the coffee houses were the chief organs through which the public opinion of the metropolis vented itself.

The first of these establishments had been set up, in the time of the Commonwealth, by a Turkey merchant, who had acquired among the Mahometans a taste for their favorite beverage. The convenience of being able to make appointments in any part of the town, and of being able to pass evenings socially at a very small charge, was so great that the fashion spread fast. Every man of the upper or middle class went daily to his coffee house to learn the news and to discuss it. Every coffee house had one or more orators to whose eloquence the crowd listened with admiration, and who soon became, what the journalists of our own time have been called, a fourth Estate of the realm. The court had long seen with uneasiness the growth of this new power in the state. An attempt had been made, during Danby's[4] administration, to close the coffee houses. But men of all parties missed their usual places of resort so much that there was an universal outcry. The government did not venture, in opposition to a feeling so strong and general, to enforce a regulation of which the legality might well be questioned. Since that time ten years had elapsed, and during those years the number and influence of the coffee houses had been constantly increasing. Foreigners remarked that the coffee house was that which especially distinguished London from all other cities; that

[4] Thomas Osborn, Lord Treasurer under Charles II

the coffee house was the Londoner's home, and that those who wished to find a gentleman commonly asked, not whether he lived in Fleet Street or Chancery Lane, but whether he frequented the Grecian or the Rainbow. Nobody was excluded from these places who laid down his penny at the bar. Yet every rank and profession, and every shade of religious and political opinion, had its own headquarters. There were houses near Saint James's Park where fops congregated, their heads and shoulders covered with black or flaxen wigs, not less ample than those which are now worn by the Chancellor and by the Speaker of the House of Commons. The wig came from Paris; and so did the rest of the fine gentleman's ornaments, his embroidered coat, his fringed gloves, and the tassel which upheld his pantaloons. The conversation was in that dialect which, long after it had ceased to be spoken in fashionable circles, continued, in the mouth of Lord Foppington,[1] to excite the mirth of theaters. The atmosphere was like that of a perfumer's shop. Tobacco in any other form than that of richly scented snuff was held in abomination. If any clown, ignorant of the usages of the house, called for a pipe, the sneers of the whole assembly and the short answers of the waiters soon convinced him that he had better go somewhere else. Nor, indeed, would he have had far to go. For, in general, the coffee rooms reeked with tobacco like a guardroom; and strangers sometimes expressed their surprise that so many people should leave their own firesides to sit in the midst of eternal fog and stench. Nowhere was the smoking more constant than at Will's. That celebrated house, situated between Covent Garden and Bow Street, was sacred to polite letters. There the talk was about poetical justice and the unities of place and time. There was a faction for Perrault and the moderns, a faction for Boileau and the ancients.[2] One group debated whether *Paradise Lost* ought not to have been in rime. To another an envious poetaster demonstrated that *Venice Preserved*[3] ought to have been hooted from the stage. Under no roof was a greater variety of figures to be seen. There were Earls in stars and garters, clergymen in cassocks and bands, pert Templars,[4] sheepish lads from the universities, translators and index makers in ragged coats of frieze. The great press was to get near the chair where John Dryden sat. In winter that chair was always in the warmest nook by the fire; in summer it stood in the balcony. To bow to the Laureate, and to hear his opinion of Racine's last tragedy or of Bossu's treatise on epic poetry, was thought a privilege. A pinch from his snuffbox was an honor sufficient to turn the head of a young enthusiast. There were coffee houses where the first medical men might be consulted. Doctor John Radcliffe, who, in the year 1685, rose to the largest practice in London, came daily, at the hour when the Exchange was full, from his house in Bow Street, then a fashionable part of the capital, to Garraway's, and was to be found, surrounded by surgeons and apothecaries, at a particular table. There were Puritan coffee houses where no oath was heard, and where lank-haired men discussed election and reprobation through their noses; Jew coffee houses where dark-eyed money changers from Venice and from Amsterdam greeted each other; and Popish coffee houses where, as good Protestants believed, Jesuits planned, over their cups, another great fire, and cast silver bullets to shoot the King.

These gregarious habits had no small share in forming the character of the Londoner of that age. He was, indeed, a different being from the rustic Englishman. There was not then the intercourse which now exists between the two classes. Only very great men were in the habit of dividing the year between town and country. Few esquires came to the capital thrice in their lives. Nor was it yet the practice of all citizens in easy circumstances to breathe the fresh air of the fields and woods during some weeks of every summer. A cockney in a rural village, was stared at as much as if he had intruded into a Kraal of Hottentots. On the other hand, when the Lord of a Lincolnshire or Shropshire manor appeared in Fleet Street, he was as easily distinguished from the resident population as a Turk or a Lascar. His dress, his gait, his accent, the manner in which he stared at the shops, stumbled into the gutters, ran against the porters, and stood under the water spouts, marked him out as an excellent subject for the operations of swindlers and banterers. Bullies jostled him into the kennel. Hackney coachmen splashed him from head to foot. Thieves explored with perfect security the huge pockets of his horseman's coat, while he stood entranced by the splendor of the Lord Mayor's show.

[1] A character in Vanbrugh's *The Relapse*; as an example of the dialect Macaulay gives the word Lord, pronounced Lard.
[2] Between Perrault and Boileau, two members of the French Academy, arose about 1687 a famous quarrel over the respective merits of modern and ancient literature.
[3] by Thomas Otway, a contemporary with Dryden.
[4] students or lawyers residing in the Temple

Moneydroppers,[1] sore from the cart's tail,[2] introduced themselves to him, and appeared to him the most honest, friendly gentlemen that he had ever seen. Painted women, the refuse of Lewkner Lane and Whetstone Park, passed themselves on him for countesses and maids of honor. If he asked his way to Saint James's,[3] his informants sent him to Mile End.[4] If he went into a shop, he was instantly discerned to be a fit purchaser of everything that nobody else would buy, of secondhand embroidery, copper rings, and watches that would not go. If he rambled into any fashionable coffee house, he became a mark for the insolent derision of fops and the grave waggery of Templars. Enraged and mortified, he soon returned to his mansion, and there, in the homage of his tenants, and the conversation of his boon companions, found consolation for the vexations and humiliations which he had undergone. There he was once more a great man, and saw nothing above himself except when at the assizes he took his seat on the bench near the Judge, or when at the muster of the militia he saluted the Lord Lieutenant. . . . .

[The Battle of Killiecrankie.] From Chapter XIII[5]

. . . . . .

While these things were passing in the Parliament House, the civil war in the Highlands, having been during a few weeks suspended, broke forth again more violently than before. Since the splendor of the House of Argyle[6] had been eclipsed, no Gaelic chief could vie in power with the Marquess of Athol. The district from which he took his title, and of which he might almost be called the sovereign, was in extent larger than an ordinary county, and was more fertile, more diligently cultivated, and more thickly peopled than the greater part of the Highlands. The men who followed his banner were supposed to be not less numerous than all the Macdonalds and Macleans united, and were, in strength and courage, inferior to no tribe in the mountains. But the clan had been made insignificant by the insignificance of the chief. The Marquess was the falsest, the most fickle, the most pusillanimous of mankind. Already, in the short space of six months, he had been several times a Jacobite, and several times a Williamite. Both Jacobites and Williamites regarded him with contempt and distrust, which respect for his immense power prevented them from fully expressing. After repeatedly vowing fidelity to both parties, and repeatedly betraying both, he began to think that he should best provide for his safety by abdicating the functions both of a peer and of a chieftain, by absenting himself both from the Parliament House at Edinburgh and from his castle in the mountains, and by quitting the country to which he was bound by every tie of duty and honor at the very crisis of her fate. While all Scotland was waiting with impatience and anxiety to see in which army his numerous retainers would be arrayed, he stole away to England, settled himself at Bath, and pretended to drink the waters. His principality, left without a head, was divided against itself. The general leaning of the Athol men was towards King James. For they had been employed by him, only four years before, as the ministers of his vengeance against the House of Argyle. They had garrisoned Inverary; they had ravaged Lorn; they had demolished houses, cut down fruit trees, burned fishing boats, broken millstones, hanged Campbells, and were therefore not likely to be pleased by the prospect of MacCallum More's[7] restoration. One word from the Marquess would have sent two thousand claymores[8] to the Jacobite side. But that word he would not speak; and the consequence was that the conduct of his followers was as irresolute and inconsistent as his own.

While they were waiting for some indication of his wishes, they were called to arms at once by two leaders, either of whom might, with some show of reason, claim to be considered as the representative of the absent chief. Lord Murray, the Marquess's eldest son, who was married to a daughter of the Duke of Hamilton, declared for King William. Stewart of Ballenach, the Marquess's confidential agent, declared for King James. The people knew not which summons to obey. He

[1] confidence men who drop money and pretend to find it for the purposes of fraud

[2] Offenders were tied to the end of a cart and whipped through the streets.

[3] in West London

[4] in East London

[5] The events here described took place in July, 1689, during the English Revolution. James the Second had lately been deposed, but the success of the party of William was still in doubt. In Scotland, William was supported by the parliament at Edinburgh and had a body of troops commanded by General Mackay. On the other hand, John Graham of Claverhouse, Viscount Dundee, had gathered about him his own Lowland adherents and a considerable force of Highland clansmen who supported James. Compare Scott's poem, "Bonny Dundee," p. 486.

[6] The Campbells—the last Earl of Argyle had been executed for participating in Monmouth's rising against James.

[7] a name given to the Dukes and Earls of Argyle who were Campbells

[8] broadswords

whose authority would have been held in profound reverence, had plighted faith to both sides, and had then run away for fear of being under the necessity of joining either; nor was it very easy to say whether the place which he had left vacant belonged to his steward or to his heir apparent.

The most important military post in Athol was Blair Castle. The house which now bears that name is not distinguished by any striking peculiarity from other country seats of the aristocracy. The old building was a lofty tower of rude architecture which commanded a vale watered by the Garry. The walls would have offered very little resistance to a battering train, but were quite strong enough to keep the herdsmen of the Grampians [1] in awe. About five miles south of this stronghold, the valley of the Garry contracts itself into the celebrated glen of Killiecrankie. At present a highway as smooth as any road in Middlesex [2] ascends gently from the low country to the summit of the defile. White villas peep from the birch forest; and on a fine summer day, there is scarcely a turn of the pass at which may not be seen some angler casting his fly on the foam of the river, some artist sketching a pinnacle of rock, or some party of pleasure banqueting on the turf in the fretwork of shade and sunshine. But in the days of William the Third, Killiecrankie was mentioned with horror by the peaceful and industrious inhabitants of the Perthshire lowlands. It was deemed the most perilous of all those dark ravines through which the marauders of the hills were wont to sally forth. The sound, so musical to modern ears, of the river brawling round the mossy rocks and among the smooth pebbles, the masses of gray crag and verdure worthy of the pencil of Wilson, [3] the fantastic peaks bathed, at sunrise and sunset, with light rich as that which glows on the canvas of Claude, [4] suggested to our ancestors thoughts of murderous ambuscades and of bodies stripped, gashed, and abandoned to the birds of prey. The only path was narrow and rugged; a horse could with difficulty be led up; two men could hardly walk abreast; and in some places, the way ran so close by the precipice that the traveler had great need of a steady eye and foot. Many years later, the first Duke of Athol constructed a road up which it was just possible to drag his coach. But even that road was so steep and so straight that a handful of resolute men might have defended it against an army; nor did any Saxon [5] consider a visit to Killiecrankie as a pleasure, till experience had taught the English Government that the weapons by which the Celtic clans could be most effectually subdued were the pickaxe and the spade.

The country which lay just above this pass was now the theater of a war such as the Highlands had not often witnessed. Men wearing the same tartan, and attached to the same lord, were arrayed against each other. The name of the absent chief was used, with some show of reason, on both sides. Ballenach, at the head of a body of vassals who considered him as the representative of the Marquess, occupied Blair Castle. Murray, with twelve hundred followers, appeared before the walls and demanded to be admitted into the mansion of his family, the mansion which would one day be his own. The garrison refused to open the gates. Messages were sent off by the besiegers to Edinburgh, and by the besieged to Lochaber. [6] In both places the tidings produced great agitation. Mackay and Dundee agreed in thinking that the crisis required prompt and strenuous exertion. On the fate of Blair Castle probably depended the fate of all Athol. On the fate of Athol might depend the fate of Scotland. Mackay hastened northward, and ordered his troops to assemble in the low country of Perthshire. Some of them were quartered at such a distance that they did not arrive in time. He soon, however, had with him the three Scotch regiments which had served in Holland, and which bore the names of their Colonels, Mackay himself, Balfour, and Ramsay. There was also a gallant regiment of infantry from England, then called Hastings's, but now known as the thirteenth of the line. With these old troops were joined two regiments newly levied in the Lowlands. One of them was commanded by Lord Kenmore; the other, which had been raised on the Border, and which is still styled the King's Own Borderers, by Lord Leven. Two troops of horse, Lord Annandale's and Lord Belhaven's, probably made up the army to the number of above three thousand men. Belhaven rode at the head of his troop; but Annandale, the most factious of all Montgomery's followers, preferred the Club and the Parliament House to the field. [7]

[1] a mountain system in Scotland
[2] an English county which then included a great part of the metropolis of London
[3] Richard Wilson, English landscape painter
[4] Claude Lorrain, French landscape painter

[5] an Englishman or Lowlander, as opposed to the Highlanders, who are Celts
[6] Mackay was at Edinburgh, Dundee in the district of Lochaber.
[7] Sir James Montgomery, a malcontent scheming for office, had formed a club at Edinburgh to concert plans of secret opposition to the king.

Dundee, meanwhile, had summoned all the clans which acknowledged his commission, to assemble for an expedition into Athol. His exertions were strenuously seconded by Lochiel.[1] The fiery crosses[2] were sent again in all haste through Appin and Ardnamurchan, up Glenmore, and along Loch Leven. But the call was so unexpected, and the time allowed was so short, that the muster was not a very full one. The whole number of broadswords seems to have been under three thousand. With this force, such as it was, Dundee set forth. On his march he was joined by succors which had just arrived from Ulster. They consisted of little more than three hundred Irish foot, ill armed, ill clothed, and ill disciplined. Their commander was an officer named Cannon, who had seen service in the Netherlands, and who might perhaps have acquitted himself well in a subordinate post and in the regular army, but who was altogether unequal to the part now assigned him. He had already loitered among the Hebrides so long that some ships which had been sent with him, and which were laden with stores, had been taken by English cruisers. He and his soldiers had with difficulty escaped the same fate. Incompetent as he was, he bore a commission which gave him military rank in Scotland next to Dundee.

The disappointment was severe. In truth James would have done better to withhold all assistance from the Highlanders than to mock them by sending them, instead of the well appointed army which they had asked and expected, a rabble contemptible in numbers and appearance. It was now evident that whatever was done for his cause in Scotland must be done by Scottish hands.

While Mackay from one side, and Dundee from the other, were advancing toward Blair Castle, important events had taken place there. Murray's adherents soon began to waver in their fidelity to him. They had an old antipathy to Whigs; for they considered the name of Whig as synonymous with the name of Campbell. They saw arrayed against them a large number of their kinsmen, commanded by a gentleman who was supposed to possess the confidence of the Marquess. The besieging army therefore melted rapidly away. Many returned home on the plea that, as their neighborhood was about to be the seat of war, they must place their families and cattle in security. Others more ingenuously declared that they would not fight in such a quarrel. One large body went to a brook, filled their bonnets with water, drank a health to King James, and then dispersed. Their zeal for King James, however, did not induce them to join the standard of his general. They lurked among the rocks and thickets which overhang the Garry, in the hope that there would soon be a battle, and that, whatever might be the event, there would be fugitives and corpses to plunder.

Murray was in a strait. His force had dwindled to three or four hundred men: even in those men he could put little trust; and the Macdonalds and Camerons were advancing fast. He therefore raised the siege of Blair Castle and retired with a few followers into the defile of Killiecrankie. There he was soon joined by a detachment of two hundred fusileers whom Mackay had sent forward to secure the pass. The main body of the Lowland army speedily followed.

Early in the morning of Saturday the twenty-seventh of July, Dundee arrived at Blair Castle. There he learned that Mackay's troops were already in the ravine of Killiecrankie. It was necessary to come to a prompt decision. A council of war was held. The Saxon officers were generally against hazarding a battle. The Celtic chiefs were of a different opinion. Glengarry[3] and Lochiel were now both of a mind. "Fight, my Lord," said Lochiel with his usual energy; "fight immediately. Fight, if you have only one to three. Our men are in heart. Their only fear is that the enemy should escape. Give them their way; and be assured that they will either perish or gain a complete victory. But if you restrain them, if you force them to remain on the defensive, I answer for nothing. If we do not fight, we had better break up and retire to our mountains."

Dundee's countenance brightened. "You hear, gentlemen," he said to his Lowland officers, "you hear the opinion of one who understands Highland war better than any of us." No voice was raised on the other side. It was determined to fight; and the confederated clans in high spirits set forward to encounter the enemy.

The enemy meanwhile had made his way up the pass. The ascent had been long and toilsome; for even the foot had to climb by twos and threes; and the baggage horses, twelve hundred in number, could mount only one at a time. No wheeled carriage had ever been tugged up that arduous path. The head of the column had emerged and was on the table-land while the rearguard was still in the plain be-

[1] Sir Ewan Cameron of Lochiel
[2] the signal for gathering
[3] Macdonald of Glengarry, another Highland chieftain

low. At length the passage was effected; and the troops found themselves in a valley of no great extent. Their right was flanked by a rising ground, their left by the Garry. Wearied with the morning's work, they threw themselves on the grass to take some rest and refreshment.

Early in the afternoon, they were roused by an alarm that the Highlanders were approaching. Regiment after regiment started up and got into order. In a little while the summit of an ascent which was about a musket shot before them was covered with bonnets and plaids. Dundee [1] rode forward for the purpose of surveying the force with which he was to contend, and then drew up his own men with as much skill as their peculiar character permitted him to exert. It was desirable to keep the clans distinct. Each tribe, large or small, formed a column separated from the next column by a wide interval. One of these battalions might contain seven hundred men, while another consisted of only a hundred and twenty. Lochiel had represented that it was impossible to mix men of different tribes without destroying all that constituted the peculiar strength of a Highland army.

On the right, close to the Garry, were the Macleans. Nearest to them were Cannon and his Irish foot. Next stood the Macdonalds of Clanronald, commanded by the guardian of their young prince. On their left were other bands of Macdonalds. At the head of one large battalion towered the stately form of Glengarry, who bore in his hand the royal standard of King James the Seventh. [2] Still farther to the left were the cavalry, a small squadron consisting of some Jacobite gentlemen who had fled from the Lowlands to the mountains and of about forty of Dundee's old troopers. The horses had been ill fed and ill tended among the Grampians, and looked miserably lean and feeble. Beyond them was Lochiel with his Camerons. On the extreme left, the men of Skye were marshaled by Macdonald of Sleat.

In the Highlands, as in all countries where war has not become a science, men thought it the most important duty of a commander to set an example of personal courage and of bodily exertion. Lochiel was especially renowned for his physical prowess. His clansmen looked big with pride when they related how he had himself broken hostile ranks and hewn down tall warriors. He probably owed quite as much of his influence to these achievements as to the high qualities which, if fortune had placed him in the English Parliament or at the French court, would have made him one of the foremost men of his age. He had the sense, however, to perceive how erroneous was the notion which his country men had formed. He knew that to give and to take blows was not the business of a general. He knew with how much difficulty Dundee had been able to keep together, during a few days, an army composed of several clans; and he knew that what Dundee had effected with difficulty Cannon would not be able to effect at all. The life on which so much depended must not be sacrificed to a barbarous prejudice. Lochiel therefore adjured Dundee not to run into any unnecessary danger. "Your Lordship's business," he said, "is to overlook everything, and to issue your commands. Our business is to execute those commands bravely and promptly." Dundee answered with calm magnanimity that there was much weight in what his friend Sir Ewan had urged, but that no general could effect anything great without possessing the confidence of his men. "I must establish my character for courage. Your people expect to see their leaders in the thickest of the battle; and today they shall see me there. I promise you, on my honor, that in future fights I will take more care of myself."

Meanwhile a fire of musketry was kept up on both sides, but more skillfully and more steadily by the regular soldiers than by the mountaineers. The space between the armies was one cloud of smoke. Not a few Highlanders dropped; and the clans grew impatient. The sun, however, was low in the west before Dundee gave the order to prepare for action. His men raised a great shout. The enemy probably exhausted by the toil of the day, returned a feeble and wavering cheer. "We shall do it now," said Lochiel; "that is not the cry of men who are going to win." He had walked through all his ranks, had addressed a few words to every Cameron, and had taken from every Cameron a promise to conquer or die.

It was past seven o'clock. Dundee gave the word. The Highlanders dropped their plaids. The few who were so luxurious as to wear rude socks of untanned hide spurned them away. It was long remembered in Lochaber that Lochiel took off what probably was the only pair of shoes in his clan, and charged barefoot at the head of his men. The whole

[1] Here the narrative returns abruptly to the Jacobite army.
[2] James Second of England was James Seventh of Scotland.

line advanced firing. The enemy returned the fire and did much execution. When only a small space was left between the armies, the Highlanders suddenly flung away their firelocks, drew their broadswords, and rushed forward with a fearful yell. The Lowlanders prepared to receive the shock; but this was then a long and awkward process, and the soldiers were still fumbling with the muzzles of their guns and the handles of their bayonets when the whole flood of Macleans, Macdonalds, and Camerons came down. In two minutes the battle was lost and won. The ranks of Balfour's regiment broke. He was cloven down while struggling in the press. Ramsey's men turned their backs and dropped their arms. Mackay's own foot were swept away by the furious onset of the Camerons. His brother and nephew exerted themselves in vain to rally the men. The former was laid dead on the ground by a stroke from a claymore. The latter, with eight wounds on his body, made his way through the tumult and carnage to his uncle's side. Even in that extremity Mackay retained all his self-possession. He had still one hope. A charge of horse might recover the day—for of horse the bravest Highlanders were supposed to stand in awe. But he called on the horse in vain. Belhaven indeed behaved like a gallant gentleman; but his troopers, appalled by the rout of the infantry, galloped off in disorder; Annandale's men followed—all was over; and the mingled torrent of redcoats and tartans went raving down the valley to the gorge of Killiecrankie.

Mackay, accompanied by one trusty servant, spurred bravely through the thickest of the claymores and targets, and reached a point from which he had a view of the field. His whole army had disappeared, with the exception of some Borderers whom Leven had kept together, and of the English regiment, which had poured a murderous fire into the Celtic ranks, and which still kept unbroken order. All the men that could be collected were only a few hundreds. The general made haste to lead them across the Garry, and having put that river between them and the enemy, paused for a moment to meditate on his situation.

He could hardly understand how the conquerors could be so unwise as to allow him even that moment for deliberation. They might with ease have killed or taken all who were with him before the night closed in. But the energy of the Celtic warriors had spent itself in one furious rush and one short struggle. The pass was choked by the twelve hundred beasts of burden which carried the provisions and baggage of the vanquished army. Such a booty was irresistibly tempting to men who were impelled to war quite as much by the desire of rapine as by the desire of glory. It is probable that few even of the chiefs were disposed to leave so rich a prize for the sake of King James. Dundee himself might at that moment have been unable to persuade his followers to quit the heaps of spoil, and to complete the great work of the day; and Dundee was no more.

At the beginning of the action he had taken his place in front of his little band of cavalry. He bade them follow him, and rode forward. But it seemed to be decreed that, on that day, the Lowland Scotch should in both armies appear to disadvantage. The horse hesitated. Dundee turned round, stood up in his stirrups, and, waving his hat, invited them to come on. As he lifted his arm, his cuirass rose, and exposed the lower part of his left side. A musketball struck him; his horse sprang forward and plunged into a cloud of smoke and dust which hid from both armies the fall of the victorious general. A person named Johnstone was near him and caught him as he sank down from the saddle. "How goes the day?" said Dundee. "Well for King James"; answered Johnstone: "but I am sorry for Your Lordship." "If it is well for him," answered the dying man, "it matters the less for me." He never spoke again; but when, half an hour later, Lord Dunfermline and some other friends came to the spot, they thought that they could still discern some faint remains of life. The body, wrapped in two plaids, was carried to the Castle of Blair.

. . . .

1848-60

JOHN HENRY, CARDINAL NEWMAN 1801-1890

It is not as a great personality or as the most notable theologian of his times, though he was both, but as a master of style that Newman comes into English literature. He was born in London of a wealthy commercial family, received his bachelor's degree at Oxford where also he obtained a fellowship at Oriel College, and in 1824 took orders in the English Church. He was a brilliant preacher and became a leader in the "Oxford movement" to awaken the spirituality of the Church; but as an inquirer into the basic history of Christianity he found himself drawn irresistibly to the Church of Rome. This he entered in 1845; he soon became a priest, and was made a cardinal in 1879. In the controversy that followed this change of faith, Newman so clearly showed his sincerity of conscience and his honesty in conduct that he retained the affectionate regard of his former associates, some of whom were his stout opponents. His *Apologia pro Vita Sua*, 1864, is an account of his intellectual and spiritual conflicts, and an answer to his critics.

Luminous is the word that fits Newman's style. His subject and style glow in their own light. Simplicity, dignity, unfettered ease in diction reveal, moreover, a personality of grace and benignity. His work shows what Bacon terms a "full" man, one who has but to select from vast resources of mind and spirit what his unerring judgment directs.

Biographies: R. Hutton, 1891; W. P. Ward, 2 vols. 1912. Criticism: More (Shel. 8); especially L. Strachey in *Eminent Victorians* (Cardinal Manning), 1924; also J. J. Daly, "John Henry Newman as a Man of Letters," *Bookm.* 51:209-11.

From SITE OF A UNIVERSITY[1]

If we would know what a University is, considered in its elementary idea, we must betake ourselves to the first and most celebrated home of European literature and source of European civilization, to the bright and beautiful Athens —Athens, whose schools drew to her bosom, and then sent back again to the business of life the youth of the Western World for a long thousand years. Seated on the verge of the continent, the city seemed hardly suited for the duties of a central metropolis of knowledge; yet, what it lost in convenience of approach, it gained in its neighborhood to the traditions of the mysterious East, and in the loveliness of the region in which it lay. Hither, then, as to a sort of ideal land, where all archetypes of the great and the fair were found in substantial being, and all departments of truth explored, and all diversities of intellectual power exhibited, where taste and philosophy were majestically enthroned as in a royal court, where there was no sovereignty but that of mind, and no nobility but that of genius, where professors were rulers, and princes did homage, hither flocked continually from the very corners of the *orbis terrarum*,[2] the many-tongued generation, just rising, or just risen into manhood, in order to gain wisdom.

Pisistratus[3] had in an early age discovered and nursed the infant genius of his people, and Cimon, after the Persian war,[4] had given it a home. That war had established the naval supremacy of Athens; she had become an imperial state; and the Ionians,[5] bound to her by the double chain of kindred and of subjection, were importing into her both their merchandise and their civilization. The arts and philosophy of the Asiatic coast were easily carried across the sea, and there was Cimon, as I have said, with his ample fortune, ready to receive them with due honors. Not content with patronizing their professors, he built the first of those noble porticoes,[6] of which we hear so much in Athens, and he formed the groves, which in process of time became the celebrated Academy. Planting is one of the most graceful, as in Athens it was one of the most beneficent, of employments. Cimon took in hand the wild wood, pruned and dressed it, and laid it out with handsome walks and welcome fountains. Nor, while hospitable to the authors of the city's civilization, was he ungrateful to the instruments of her prosperity. His trees extended their cool, umbrageous branches over the merchants, who assembled in the Agora,[7] for many generations.

Those merchants certainly had deserved that act of bounty; for all the while their ships had been carrying forth the intellectual fame of Athens to the western world. Then commenced what may be called her University existence. Pericles, who succeeded Cimon both in the government and in the patronage of art, is said by Plutarch to have entertained the idea of making Athens the capital of federated Greece. In this he failed, but his encouragement of such men as Phidias[8] and Anaxagoras[9] led the way to her acquiring a far more lasting sovereignty over a far wider empire. Little understanding the sources of her own greatness, Athens would go to war; peace is the interest of a seat of commerce and the arts; but to war she went; yet to her, whether peace or war, it

[1] From *The Rise and Progress of Universities*, originally published in 1854. Newman's large purpose, in this and his related works, of setting forth an ideal of University life and training, cannot be conveyed in an extract; but the present selection may afford some hint of it, besides exemplifying the author's imagination and rhetoric in their more gracious aspects.

[2] the world

[3] a ruler of Athens in the sixth Century, B. C., who established the groves and gymnasium known as the Lyceum, and who is said to have commissioned a body of scholars to collect and write down the poems of Homer

[4] B. C. 500-449. Cimon, having signally defeated the Persians in 466 B. C., made liberal use of his spoils in adorning Athens.

[5] Greeks of Asia Minor

[6] Porches, or independent covered walks, often built in magnificent style, and used as outdoor resorts for conversation, study, or pleasure; in the Academy, mentioned just below, Plato taught for nearly fifty years.

[7] the Market, or Exchange

[8] sculptor of the frieze of the Parthenon, etc.

[9] a philosopher

mattered not. The political power of Athens waned and disappeared; kingdoms rose and fell; centuries rolled away—they did but bring fresh triumphs to the city of the poet and the sage. There at length the swarthy Moor and Spaniard were seen to meet the blue-eyed Gaul; and the Cappadocian, late subject of Mithridates, gazed without alarm at the haughty conquering Roman.[1] Revolution after revolution passed over the face of Europe, as well as of Greece, but still she was there—Athens, the city of mind—as radiant, as splendid, as delicate, as young, as ever she had been.

Many a more fruitful coast or isle is washed by the blue Aegean, many a spot is there more beautiful or sublime to see, many a territory more ample; but there was one charm in Attica which, in the same perfection, was nowhere else. The deep pastures of Arcadia, the plain of Argos, the Thessalian vale, these had not the gift; Boeotia, which lay to its immediate north, was notorious for its very want of it. The heavy atmosphere of that Boeotia might be good for vegetation, but it was associated in popular belief with the dullness of the Boeotian intellect.[2] On the contrary, the special purity, elasticity, clearness and salubrity of the air of Attica, fit concomitant and emblem of its genius, did that for it which earth did not:—it brought out every bright hue and tender shade of the landscape over which it was spread, and would have illuminated the face of even a more bare and rugged country.

A confined triangle, perhaps fifty miles its greatest length, and thirty its greatest breadth; two elevated rocky barriers, meeting at an angle; three prominent mountains, commanding the plain,—(Parnes, Pentelicus, and Hymettus) an unsatisfactory soil; some streams, not always full;—such is about the report which the agent of a London company would have made of Attica. He would report that the climate was mild; the hills were limestone; there was plenty of good marble; more pasture land than at first survey might have been expected, sufficient certainly for sheep and goats; fisheries productive; silver mines once, but long since worked out; figs fair; oil first-rate; olives in profusion. But what he would not think of noting down, was, that the olive tree was so choice in nature and so noble in shape that it excited a religious veneration; and that it took so kindly to the light soil, as to expand into woods upon the open plain, and to climb up and fringe the hills. He would not think of writing word to his employers, how that clear air, of which I have spoken, brought out, yet blended and subdued, the colors on the marble, till they had a softness and harmony, for all their richness, which in a picture looks exaggerated, yet is after all within the truth. He would not tell how that same delicate and brilliant atmosphere freshened up the pale olive, till the olive forgot its monotony, and its cheek glowed like the arbutus[3] or beech of the Umbrian hills.[4] He would say nothing of the thyme and the thousand fragrant herbs which carpeted Hymettus; he would hear nothing of the hum of its bees; nor take much account of the rare flavor of its honey, since Gozo and Minorca[5] were sufficient for the English demand. He would look over the Aegean from the height he had ascended; he would follow with his eye the chain of islands which, starting from the Sunian headland, seemed to offer the fabled divinities of Attica, when they would visit their Ionian cousins, a sort of viaduct thereto across the sea; but that fancy would not occur to him, nor any admiration of the dark violet billows with their white edges down below; nor of those graceful, fan-like jets of silver upon the rocks, which slowly rise aloft like water spirits from the deep, then shiver, and break, and spread, and shroud themselves, and disappear in a soft mist of foam; nor of the gentle, incessant heaving and panting of the whole liquid plain; nor of the long waves, keeping steady time, like a line of soldiery as they resound upon the hollow shore—he would not deign to notice that restless living element at all except to bless his stars that he was not upon it.[6] Nor the distinct details, nor the refined coloring, nor the graceful outline and roseate golden hue of the jutting crags, nor the bold shadows cast from Otus or Laurium by the declining sun—our agent of a mercantile firm would not value these matters even at a low figure. Rather we must turn for the sympathy we seek to yon pilgrim student, come from a semi-barbarous land to that small corner of the earth as to a shrine, where he might take his fill of gazing on those emblems and coruscations of invisible, unoriginate[7] perfection. It was the stranger from a remote

[1] After the death of Mithridates, a powerful enemy of the Romans, Cappadocia passed into Roman control. The significance of the passage is that Athens was at the center of the great conflicts of races—of the South against the North, and the East against the West.

[2] "As the nimble Attics would say, a glorious climate for eels, but a bad air for brains."—B. L. Gildersleeve. Yet Pindar was a Boeotian.

[3] strawberry-tree, madroña

[4] in Italy

[5] islands in the Mediterranean

[6] The Aegean is famous for squalls.

[7] not originated, self-existing, divine

province, from Britain or from Mauritania, who in a scene so different from that of his chilly, woody swamps, or of his fiery, choking sands, learned at once what a real University must be, by coming to understand the sort of country which was its suitable home.

Nor was this all that a University required, and found in Athens. No one, even there, could live on poetry. If the students at that famous place had nothing better than bright hues and soothing sounds, they would not have been able or disposed to turn their residence there to much account. Of course they must have the means of living, nay, in a certain sense, of enjoyment, if Athens was to be an Alma Mater [1] at the time, or to remain afterwards a pleasant thought in their memory. And so they had. Be it recollected Athens was a port, and a mart of trade, perhaps the first in Greece; and this was very much to the point, when a number of strangers were ever flocking to it, whose combat was to be with intellectual, not physical difficulties, and who claimed to have their bodily wants supplied, that they might be at leisure to set about furnishing their minds. Now, barren as was the soil of Attica, and bare the face of the country, yet it had only too many resources for an elegant, nay, luxurious abode there. So abundant were the imports of the place, that it was a common saying that the productions, which were found singly elsewhere, were brought all together in Athens. Corn and wine, the staple of subsistence in such a climate, came from the isles of the Aegean; fine wool and carpeting from Asia Minor; slaves, as now, from the Euxine, and timber, too; and iron and brass from the coasts of the Mediterranean. The Athenian did not condescend to manufactures himself, but encouraged them in others; and a population of foreigners caught at the lucrative occupation both for home consumption and for exportation. Their cloth, and other textures for dress and furniture, and their hardware—for instance, armor—were in great request. Labor was cheap; stone and marble in plenty; and the taste and skill, which at first were devoted to public buildings, as temples and porticos, were in course of time applied to the mansions of public men. If nature did much for Athens, it is undeniable that art did much more.

Here some one will interrupt me with the remark: "By the bye, where are we, and whither are we going? What has all this to do with a University? At least what has it to do with education? It is instructive doubtless; but still how much has it to do with your subject?" Now I beg to assure the reader that I am most conscientiously employed upon my subject; and I should have thought every one would have seen this. However, since the objection is made, I may be allowed to pause awhile, and show distinctly the drift of what I have been saying, before I go further. What has this to do with my subject? Why, the question of the site is the very first that comes into consideration, when a *Studium Generale* [2] is contemplated; for that site should be a liberal and a noble one; who will deny it? All authorities agree in this, and very little reflection will be sufficient to make it clear. I recollect a conversation I once had on this very subject with a very eminent man. [3] I was a youth of eighteen, and was leaving my University for the Long Vacation, when I found myself in company in a public conveyance with a middle-aged person, whose face was strange to me. However, it was the great academical luminary of the day, whom afterwards I knew very well. Luckily for me, I did not suspect it; and luckily, too, it was a fancy of his, as his friends knew, to make himself on easy terms especially with stage-coach companions. So, what with my flippancy and his condescension, I managed to hear many things which were novel to me at the time; and one point which he was strong upon, and was evidently fond of urging, was the material pomp and circumstance which should environ a great seat of learning. He considered it was worth the consideration of the government, whether Oxford should not stand in a domain of its own. An ample range, say four miles in diameter, should be turned into wood and meadow, and the University should be approached on all sides by a magnificent park, with fine trees in groups and groves and avenues, and with glimpses and views of the fair city, as the traveler drew near it. There is nothing surely absurd in the idea, though it would cost a round sum to realize it. What has a better claim to the purest and fairest possessions of nature, than the seat of wisdom? So thought my coach companion; and he did but express the tradition of ages and the instinct of mankind.

For instance, take the great University of Paris. That famous school engrossed as its territory the whole south bank of the Seine,

[1] fostering mother

[2] School of Universal Learning

[3] Probably Dr. Edward Copleston (1776-1849), Provost of Oriel College, where Newman later became a Fellow; it was he who raised Oriel to a position of leadership at Oxford.

and occupied one half, and that the pleasanter half, of the city. King Louis had the island pretty well as his own—it was scarcely more than a fortification; and the north of the river was given over to the nobles and citizens to do what they could with its marshes; but the eligible south, rising from the stream, which swept around its base, to the fair summit of St. Genevieve with its broad meadows, its vineyards and its gardens, and with the sacred elevation of Montmartre [1] confronting it, all this was the inheritance of the University. There was that pleasant Pratum, [2] stretching along the river's bank, in which the students for centuries took their recreation, which Alcuin [3] seems to mention in his farewell verses to Paris, and which has given a name to the great Abbey of St. Germain-des-Prés. [4] For long years it was devoted to the purposes of innocent and healthy enjoyment; but evil times came on the University; disorder arose within its precincts, and the fair meadow became the scene of party brawls; heresy stalked through Europe, and Germany and England no longer sending their contingent of students, a heavy debt was the consequence to the academical body. To let their land was the only resource left to them; buildings rose upon it, and spread along the green sod, and the country at length became town. Great was the grief and indignation of the doctors and masters, when this catastrophe occurred. "A wretched sight," said the Proctor of the German Nation, [5] "a wretched sight, to witness the sale of that ancient manor, whither the Muses were wont to wander for retirement and pleasure. Whither shall the youthful student now betake himself, what relief will he find for his eyes, wearied with intense reading, now that the pleasant stream is taken from him?" Two centuries and more have passed since this complaint was uttered; and time has shown that the outward calamity, which it recorded, was but the emblem of the great moral revolution which was to follow; till the institution itself has followed its green meadows, into the region of things which once were and now are not. [6]

. . . .

1854

[1] "Mount of Martyrs," north of the Seine, so named from the tradition that St. Denis, Bishop of Paris, suffered martyrdom there
[2] Latin for "meadow"; French *pré*
[3] Charlemagne's superintendent of education
[4] founded about 542 and dedicated to St. Germain
[5] the Dean of the resident German students
[6] During the French Revolution, the Faculties of the University were abolished and its organization destroyed. In Newman's time it was only a member of the National University of France, but in 1896 it was again the University of Paris.

CHARLES DICKENS 1812-1870

The most popular of all nineteenth century novelists was born near Portsmouth. His father, a naval clerk, the original of "Mr. Micawber," was always in straits, and the son acquired small schooling except in making his own way in the world and observing the seamy side of life that sometimes led the family into courts and even debtors' prisons. He was a lawyer's clerk, a reporter, and at length one of the regular staff of the *Morning Chronicle.*

Experiences in lower and middle-class London gave him the material for the crowded world of his narratives and sketches, beginning with *Pickwick,* 1836-7, and continuing through a score of books, notable among which are *Oliver Twist,* 1837-8; *Dombey and Son,* 1846-8; *David Copperfield,* 1849-50; *A Tale of Two Cities,* 1859. Money from sales, royalties, lectures, and readings poured into Dickens's hands from England and America in such profusion as never before enriched a writer of fiction. He yielded to the temptation to overwork, and died suddenly at his home at Gadshill, near London.

Popularity in material, style, and pitch is the key to Dickens's success. He writes for the average intelligence, psychology, and morality. Abundant grotesquerie, inventiveness, largeness of heart, degenerating at times into sentimentality, fill his pages. He uses the reporter's method of description and caricature, rather than analysis, and his works are replete with broadly-painted pictures of goodness, virtue, and vice. He is the cinema of the nineteenth century. But the wholesomeness of his entertaining novels and essays has been the delight of more readers than have followed any other English author.

Biographies: Forster, 3 vols., Ward (EML), Marzials (GW). Criticism: Lang, More (Shel. 5); G. K. Chesterton, *Liv. Age* 312:480-85; G. Santayana, *Dial* 71:537-49; E. Boyd, *Harp.* 151: 96-104; M. A. de Wolfe Howe, "With Dickens in America," *Harp.* 144: 708-22, 145:110-20.

A CHRISTMAS TREE [7]

I have been looking on, this evening, at a merry company of children assembled round that pretty German toy, a Christmas Tree. The tree was planted in the middle of a great round table, and towered high above their heads. It was brilliantly lighted by a multitude of little tapers; and everywhere sparkled and glittered with bright objects. There were rosy-cheeked dolls, hiding behind the green leaves; and there were real watches (with movable hands, at least, and an endless capacity of being wound up) dangling from innumerable twigs; there were French-polished tables, chairs, bedsteads, wardrobes, eight-day clocks,

[7] contributed by Dickens to *Household Words,* Dec. 21, 1850

and various other articles of domestic furniture (wonderfully made, in tin, at Wolverhampton [1]) perched among the boughs, as if in preparation for some fairy housekeeping; there were jolly, broad-faced, little men, much more agreeable in appearance than many real men—and no wonder, for their heads took off, and showed them to be full of sugarplums; there were fiddles and drums; there were tambourines, books, work boxes, paint boxes, sweetmeat boxes, peep-show boxes, and all kinds of boxes; there were trinkets for the elder girls, far brighter than any grown-up gold and jewels; there were baskets and pincushions in all devices; there were guns, swords, and banners; there were witches standing in enchanted rings of pasteboard, to tell fortunes; there were teetotums, humming tops, needle cases, pen wipers, smelling bottles, conversation cards, bouquet holders; real fruit, made artificially dazzling with goldleaf; imitation apples, pears, and walnuts, crammed with surprises; in short, as a pretty child before me delightedly whispered to another pretty child, her bosom friend, "There was everything, and more." This motley collection of odd objects, clustering on the tree like magic fruit, and flashing back the bright looks directed toward it from every side—some of the diamond-eyes admiring it were hardly on a level with the table, and a few were languishing in timid wonder on the bosoms of pretty mothers, aunts, and nurses—made a lively realization of the fancies of childhood; and set me thinking how all the trees that grow and all the things that come into existence on the earth, have their wild adornments at that well-remembered time.

Being now at home again, and alone, the only person in the house awake, my thoughts are drawn back, by a fascination which I do not care to resist, to my own childhood. I begin to consider, what do we all remember best upon the branches of the Christmas Tree of our own young Christmas days, by which we climbed to real life.

Straight, in the middle of the room, cramped in the freedom of its growth by no encircling walls or soon-reached ceiling, a shadowy tree arises; and, looking up into the dreamy brightness of its top—for I observe in this tree the singular property that it appears to grow downward toward the earth—I look into my youngest Christmas recollections!

All toys, at first I find. Up yonder, among the green holly and red berries, is the Tumbler with his hands in his pockets, who wouldn't lie down, but whenever he was put upon the floor persisted in rolling his fat body about until he rolled himself still, and brought those lobster eyes of his to bear upon me—when I affected to laugh very much, but in my heart of hearts was extremely doubtful of him. Close beside him is that infernal snuffbox, out of which there sprang a demoniacal Counselor in a black gown, with an obnoxious head of hair, and a red cloth mouth, wide open, who was not to be endured on any terms, but could not be put away either; for he used suddenly, in a highly magnified state, to fly out of Mammoth Snuffboxes in dreams, when least expected. Nor is the frog with cobbler's wax on his tail, far off; for there was no knowing where he wouldn't jump; and when he flew over the candle, and came upon one's hand with that spotted back—red on a green ground—he was horrible. The cardboard lady in a blue-silk skirt, who was stood up against the candlestick to dance, and whom I see on the same branch, was milder, and was beautiful; but I can't say as much for the larger cardboard man, who used to be hung against the wall and pulled by a string; there was a sinister expression in that nose of his; and when he got his legs round his neck (which he very often did) he was ghastly, and not a creature to be alone with.

When did that dreadful Mask first look at me? Who put it on, and why was I so frightened that the sight of it is an era in my life? It is not a hideous visage in itself; it is even meant to be droll; why then were its stolid features so intolerable? Surely not because it hid the wearer's face. An apron would have done as much; and though I should have preferred even the apron away, it would not have been absolutely insupportable, like the mask. Was it the immovability of the mask? The doll's face was immovable, but I was not afraid of her. Perhaps that fixed and set change coming over a real face, infused into my quickened heart some remote suggestion and dread of the universal change that is to come on every face, and make it still? Nothing reconciled me to it. No drummers, from whom proceeded a melancholy chirping on the turning of a handle; no regiment of soldiers, with a mute band, taken out of a box, and fitted, one by one, upon a stiff and lazy little set of lazy-tongs; [2] no old woman, made of wires and a brown-paper composition, cutting up a pie for two small

[1] in Staffordshire; a center for the manufacture of hardware

[2] scissors-like, extensible tongs, commonly used for picking up objects at a distance

children, could give me a permanent comfort, for a long time. Nor was it any satisfaction to be shown the Mask, and see that it was made of paper, or to have it locked up and be assured that no one wore it. The mere recollection of that fixed face, the mere knowledge of its existence anywhere, was sufficient to awake me in the night all perspiration and horror, with, "Oh, I know it's coming! Oh, the mask!"

I never wondered what the dear, old donkey with the panniers—there he is!—was made of, then! His hide was real to the touch, I recollect. And the great black horse with the round red spots all over him—the horse that I could even get upon—I never wondered what had brought him to that strange condition, or thought that such a horse was not commonly seen at Newmarket.[1] The four horses of no color, next to him, that went into the wagon of cheeses, and could be taken out and stabled under the piano, appear to have bits of fur-tippet for their tails, and other bits for their manes, and to stand on pegs instead of legs; but it was not so when they were brought home for a Christmas present. They were all right, then; neither was their harness unceremoniously nailed into their chests, as appears to be the case now. The tinkling works of the music-cart, I *did* find out to be made of quill tooth-picks and wire; and I always thought that little tumbler in his shirt sleeves, perpetually swarming up one side of a wooden frame, and coming down, head foremost, on the other, rather a weak-minded person—though good-natured; but the Jacob's Ladder,[2] next him, made of little squares of red wood, that went flapping and clattering over one another, each developing a different picture, and the whole enlivened by small bells, was a mighty marvel and a great delight.

Ah! The doll's house!—of which I was not proprietor, but where I visited. I don't admire the Houses of Parliament half so much as that stone-fronted mansion with real glass windows, and door-steps, and a real balcony—greener than I ever see now, except at watering-places; and even they afford but a poor imitation. And though it *did* open all at once, the entire house-front (which was a blow, I admit, as cancelling the fiction of a staircase), it was but to shut it up again, and I could believe. Even open, there were three distinct rooms in it: a sitting-room and bedroom, elegantly furnished, and best of all, a kitchen, with uncommonly soft fire irons, a plentiful assortment of diminutive utensils—oh, the warming pan!—and a tin man-cook in profile, who was always going to fry two fish. What Barmecide justice[3] have I done to the noble feasts wherein the set of wooden platters figured, each with its own peculiar delicacy, as a ham or turkey, glued tight on to it, and garnished with something green, which I recollect as moss! Could all the Temperance Societies of these later days, united, give me such a tea-drinking as I have had through the means of yonder little set of blue crockery, which really would hold liquid (it ran out of the small wooden cask, I recollect, and tasted of matches), and which made tea, nectar. And if the two legs of the ineffectual little sugar tongs did tumble over one another, and want purpose, like Punch's[4] hands, what does it matter? And if I did once shriek out, as a poisoned child, and strike the fashionable company with consternation, by reason of having drunk a little teaspoon, inadvertently dissolved in too hot tea, I was never the worse for it, except by a powder!

Upon the next branches of the tree, lower down, hard by the green roller and miniature gardening tools, how thick the books begin to hang. Thin books, in themselves, at first, but many of them, and with deliciously smooth covers of bright red or green. What fat black letters to begin with! "A was an archer, and shot at a frog." Of course he was. He was an apple pie also, and there he is! He was a good many things in his time, was A, and so were most of his friends, except X, who had so little versatility, that I never knew him to get beyond Xerxes or Xantippe—like Y, who was always confined to a Yacht or a Yew tree; and Z condemned forever to be a Zebra or a Zany. But now, the very tree itself changes, and becomes a bean-stalk—the marvelous bean-stalk up which Jack climbed to the Giant's house! And now, those dreadfully interesting, double-headed giants, with their clubs over their shoulders, begin to stride along the boughs in a perfect throng, dragging knights and ladies home for dinner by the hair of their heads. And Jack—how noble, with his sword of sharpness, and his shoes of swiftness! Again those old meditations come upon me as I gaze up at him; and I debate within myself whether there was more than one Jack (which I am loth to believe possible), or only one genuine, original, admirable Jack, who achieved all the recorded exploits.

Good for Christmas time is the ruddy color

[1] Newmarket Heath, where annual horse races are held
[2] name taken from *Genesis,* xxviii, 12

[3] In the story of the "Barber's Sixth Brother" in the *Arabian Nights,* a rich Barmecide sets before a starving man a service of empty dishes.
[4] the masculine puppet of a Punch and Judy show

of the cloak, in which—the tree making a forest of itself for her to trip through, with her basket—Little Red Riding-Hood comes to me one Christmas Eve to give me information of the cruelty and treachery of that dissembling wolf who ate her grandmother, without making any impression on his appetite, and then ate her, after making that ferocious joke about his teeth. She was my first love. I felt that if I could have married Little Red Riding-Hood, I should have known perfect bliss. But, it was not to be; and there was nothing for it but to look out the Wolf in the Noah's Ark there, and put him late in the procession on the table, as a monster who was to be degraded. Oh, the wonderful Noah's Ark! It was not found seaworthy when put in a washing tub, and the animals were crammed in at the roof, and needed to have their legs well shaken down before they could be got in, even there—and then, ten to one but they began to tumble out at the door, which was but imperfectly fastened with a wire latch—but what was *that* against it! Consider the noble fly, a size or two smaller than the elephant: the ladybird, the butterfly—all triumphs of art! Consider the goose whose feet were so small, and whose balance was so indifferent, that he usually tumbled forward, and knocked down all the animal creation. Consider Noah and his family, like idiotic tobacco-stoppers; [1] and how the leopard stuck to warm little fingers; and how the tails of the larger animals used gradually to resolve themselves into frayed bits of string!

Hush! Again a forest, and somebody up in a tree—not Robin Hood, not Valentine, not the Yellow Dwarf (I have passed him and all Mother Bunch's wonders, [2] without mention), but an Eastern King with a glittering scimitar and turban. By Allah! Two Eastern Kings, for I see another looking over his shoulder! Down upon the grass, at the tree's foot, lies the full length of a coal-black Giant, stretched asleep, with his head in a lady's lap; and near them is a glass box, fastened with four locks of shining steel, in which he keeps the lady prisoner when he is awake. I see the four keys at his girdle, now. The lady makes signs to the two kings in the tree, who softly descend. It is the setting-in of the bright Arabian Nights.

Oh, now all common things become uncommon and enchanted to me. All lamps are wonderful; all rings are talismans. Common flowerpots are full of treasure, with a little earth scattered on the top; trees are for Ali Baba to hide in; beefsteaks are to throw down into the Valley of Diamonds, that the precious stones may stick to them, and be carried by the eagles to their nests, whence the traders, with loud cries, will scare them. Tarts are made according to the recipe of the Vizier's son of Bussorah, who turned pastry-cook after he was set down in his drawers at the gate of Damascus; cobblers are all Mustaphas, and in the habit of sewing up people cut into four pieces, to whom they are taken blindfold.

[1] plugs used to compress tobacco in a pipe
[2] in *Mother Bunch's Fairy Tales*

Any iron ring let into stone is the entrance to a cave which only waits for the magician, and the little fire, and the necromancy that will make the earth shake. All the dates imported come from the same tree as that unlucky date with whose shell the merchant knocked out the eye of the genie's invisible son. All olives are of the stock of that fresh fruit, concerning which the Commander of the Faithful overheard the boy conduct the fictitious trial of the fraudulent olive merchant; all apples are akin to the apple purchased (with two others) from the Sultan's gardener for three sequins, and which the tall, black slave stole from the child. All dogs are associated with the dog, really a transformed man, who jumped upon the baker's counter, and put his paw on the piece of bad money. All rice recalls the rice which the awful lady, who was a ghoul, could only peck by grains, because of her nightly feasts in the burial place. My very rocking-horse—there he is, with his nostrils turned completely inside-out, indicative of Blood!—should have a peg in his neck, by virtue thereof to fly away with me, as the wooden horse did with the Prince of Persia, in the sight of all his father's court.

Yes, on every object that I recognize among those upper branches of my Christmas Tree, I see this fairy light! When I wake in bed, at daybreak, on the cold, dark, winter mornings, the white snow dimly beheld, outside, through the frost on the windowpane, I hear Dinarzade. "Sister, sister, if you are yet awake, I pray you finish the history of the Young King of the Black Islands." Scheherazade replies, "If my lord the Sultan will suffer me to live another day, sister, I will not only finish that, but tell you a more wonderful story yet." Then, the gracious Sultan goes out, giving no orders for the execution, and we all three breathe again. [3]

[3] The stories of the *Arabian Nights* were professedly related on successive nights by Scheherazade to her sister, in order to interest the Sultan, whom she had wedded, and so prevent him from carrying out his practice of beheading his bride the day after the wedding.

At this height of my tree I begin to see, cowering among the leaves—it may be born of turkey, or of pudding, or mince pie, or of these many fancies, jumbled with Robinson Crusoe on his desert island, Philip Quarll among the monkeys,[1] Sandford and Merton[2] with Mr. Barlow, Mother Bunch, and the mask—or it may be the result of indigestion, assisted by imagination and over-doctoring—a prodigious nightmare. It is so exceedingly indistinct that I don't know why it's frightful—but I know it is. I can only make out that it is an immense array of shapeless things, which appear to be planted on a vast exaggeration of the lazy-tongs that used to bear the toy soldiers, and to be slowly coming close to my eyes, and receding to an immeasurable distance. When it comes closest, it is worst. In connection with it I descry remembrances of winter nights incredibly long; of being sent early to bed, as a punishment for some small offense, and waking in two hours with a sensation of having been asleep two nights; of the leaden hopelessness of morning ever dawning; and the oppression of a weight of remorse.

And now I see a wonderful row of little lights rise smoothly out of the ground, before a vast green curtain. Now a bell rings—a magic bell, which still sounds in my ears unlike all other bells—and music plays, amidst a buzz of voices, and a fragrant smell of orange-peel and oil. Anon, the magic bell commands the music to cease, and the great green curtain rolls itself up majestically, and The Play begins! The devoted dog of Montargis avenges the death of his master, foully murdered in the Forest of Bondy;[3] and a humorous Peasant with a red nose and a very little hat whom I take from this hour forth to my bosom as a friend (I think he was a Waiter or an Hostler at a village Inn, but many years have passed since he and I have met), remarks that the sassigassity of that dog is indeed surprising; and evermore this jocular conceit will live in my remembrance fresh and unfading, overtopping all possible jokes, until the end of time. Or now I learn with bitter tears how poor Jane Shore, dressed all in white, and with her brown hair hanging down, went starving through the streets;[4] or how George Barnwell killed the worthiest uncle that ever man had, and was afterwards so sorry for it that he ought to have been let off.[5] Comes swift to comfort me, the Pantomime—stupendous Phenomenon!—when clowns are shot from loaded mortars into the great chandelier, bright constellation that it is; when Harlequins, covered all over with scales of pure gold, twist and sparkle, like amazing fish; when Pantaloon (whom I deem it no irreverence to compare in my own mind to my grandfather) puts red-hot pokers in his pocket, and cries, "Here's somebody coming!" or taxes the Clown with petty larceny, by saying, "Now, I sawed you do it!" when Everything is capable, with the greatest ease, of being changed into Anything; and "Nothing is, but thinking makes it so." Now, too, I perceive my first experience of the dreary sensation—often to return in after-life—of being unable, next day, to get back to the dull, settled world; of wanting to live forever in the bright atmosphere I have quitted; of doting on the little Fairy, with the wand like a celestial Barber's Pole, and pining for a fairy immortality along with her. Ah, she comes back in many shapes, as my eye wanders down the branches of my Christmas Tree, and goes as often, and has never yet stayed by me!

Out of this delight springs the toy-theater—there it is, with its familiar proscenium,[6] and ladies in feathers, in the boxes!—and all its attendant occupation with paste and glue, and gum, and water colors, in the getting-up of *The Miller and His Men,*[7] and *Elizabeth, or the Exile of Siberia.*[8] In spite of a few besetting accidents and failures (particularly an unreasonable disposition in the respectable Kelmar, and some others, to become faint in the legs, and double up, at exciting points of the drama), a teeming world of fancies so suggestive and all-embracing that, far below it on my Christmas Tree, I see dark, dirty, real Theaters in the daytime, adorned with these associations as with the freshest garlands of the rarest flowers, and charming me yet.

[1] a castaway, like Robinson Crusoe, who was solaced on his desert island by a monkey

[2] The heroes of a juvenile book by Thomas Day, popular in the days of Dickens—Mr. Barlow was the boys' instructor.

[3] Aubrey de Montdidier was murdered in 1371 in the forest of Bondy (or of Montargis) and avenged by his dog, which attracted such suspicion to the slayer that the king finally required the slayer to fight with the dog. The story has been dramatized.

[4] In a tragedy (founded on fact) by Nicholas Rowe; see the ballad "Jane Shore" in Percy's *Reliques.*

[5] *George Barnwell, or The London Merchant,* by George Lillo; founded on another ballad.

[6] stage-curtain and its framework

[7] originally a popular melodrama by Isaac Pocock, first played at Covent Garden in 1813; a gang of bandits, disguised as millers, try to carry off the daughter of Kelmar, an old cottager.

[8] Taken from a French novel published by Madame Cottin in 1806; Elizabeth walks from Siberia to Russia to get the Czar's pardon for her exiled family.

But hark! The Waits[1] are playing, and they break my childish sleep! What images do I associate with the Christmas music as I see them set forth on the Christmas Tree? Known before all the others, keeping far apart from all the others, they gather round my little bed. An angel, speaking to a group of shepherds in a field; some travelers, with eyes uplifted, following a star; a baby in a manger; a child in a spacious temple, talking with grave men; a solemn figure, with a mild and beautiful face, raising a dead girl by the hand; again, near a city gate, calling back the son of a widow, on his bier, to life; a crowd of people looking through the opened roof of a chamber where he sits, and letting down a sick person on a bed, with ropes; the same, in a tempest, walking on the water to a ship; again, on a seashore, teaching a great multitude; again, with a child upon his knee, and other children round; again, restoring sight to the blind, speech to the dumb, hearing to the deaf, health to the sick, strength to the lame, knowledge to the ignorant; again, dying upon a Cross, watched by armed soldiers, a thick darkness coming on, the earth beginning to shake, and only one voice heard, "Forgive them, for they know not what they do."

Still, on the lower and maturer branches of the Tree, Christmas associations cluster thick. School-books shut up; Ovid and Virgil silenced; the Rule of Three,[2] with its cool impertinent inquiries, long disposed of; Terence and Plautus acted no more, in an arena of huddled desks and forms, all chipped, and notched, and inked; cricket-bats, stumps,[3] and balls, left higher up, with the smell of trodden grass and the softened noise of shouts in the evening air; the tree is still fresh, still gay. If I no more come home at Christmas time, there will be boys and girls (thank Heaven!) while the world lasts; and they do! Yonder they dance and play upon the branches of my Tree, God bless them, merrily, and my heart dances and plays, too!

And I come home at Christmas. We all do, or we all should. We all come home, or ought to come home, for a short holiday—the longer, the better—from the great boarding-school where we are forever working at our arithmetical slates, to take, and give a rest. As to going a visiting, where can we not go, if we will; where have we not been, when we would; starting our fancy from our Christmas Tree!

Away into the winter prospect. There are many such upon the tree! On, by low-lying, misty grounds, through fens and fogs, up long hills, winding dark as caverns between thick plantations, almost shutting out the sparkling stars; so, out on broad heights, until we stop at last, with sudden silence, at an avenue. The gate bell has a deep, half-awful sound in the frosty air; the gate swings open on its hinges; and as we drive up to a great house, the glancing lights grow larger in the windows, and the opposing rows of trees seem to fall solemnly back on either side to give us place. At intervals, all day, a frightened hare has shot across this whitened turf; or the distant clatter of a herd of deer trampling the hard frost, has, for the minute, crushed the silence, too. Their watchful eyes beneath the fern may be shining now, if we could see them, like the icy dewdrops on the leaves; but they are still, and all is still. And so, the lights growing larger, and the trees falling back before us, and closing up again behind us, as if to forbid retreat, we come to the house.

There is probably a smell of roasted chestnuts and other good comfortable things all the time, for we are telling Winter Stories—Ghost stories, or more shame for us—round the Christmas fire; and we have never stirred, except to draw a little nearer to it. But, no matter for that. We come to the house, and it is an old house, full of great chimneys where wood is burnt on ancient dogs upon the hearth, and grim portraits (some of them with grim legends, too) lower distrustfully from the oaken panels of the walls. We are a middle-aged nobleman, and we make a generous supper with our host and hostess and their guests—it being Christmas time, and the old house full of company—and then we go to bed. Our room is a very old room. It is hung with tapestry. We don't like the portrait of a cavalier in green, over the fireplace. There are great, black beams in the ceiling, and there is a great, black bedstead, supported at the foot by two, great, black figures who seem to have come off a couple of tombs in the old baronial church in the park for our particular accommodation. But we are not a superstitious nobleman and we don't mind. Well! we dismiss our servant, lock the door, and sit before the fire in our dressing gown, musing about a great many things. At length we go to bed. Well! we can't sleep. We toss and tumble, and can't sleep. The embers on the

[1] street musicians who sing from house to house on Christmas Eve
[2] the rule of arithmetical "proportion"
[3] the three posts constituting a wicket, in the game of cricket

hearth burn fitfully and make the room look ghostly. We can't help peeping out over the counterpane, at the two black figures and the cavalier—that wicked-looking cavalier—in green. In the flickering light they seem to advance and retire; which, though we are not by any means a superstitious nobleman, is not agreeable. Well! we get nervous—more and more nervous. We say, "This is very foolish, but we can't stand this; we'll pretend to be ill, and knock up somebody." Well! we are just going to do it, when the locked door opens, and there comes in a young woman, deadly pale, and with long, fair hair, who glides to the fire, and sits down in the chair we have left there, wringing her hands. Then, we notice that her clothes are wet. Our tongue cleaves to the roof of our mouth, and we can't speak; but, we observe her accurately. Her clothes are wet; her long hair is dabbled with moist mud; she is dressed in the fashion of two hundred years ago; and she has at her girdle a bunch of rusty keys. Well! there she sits, and we can't even faint, we are in such a state about it. Presently she gets up, and tries all the locks in the room with the rusty keys, which won't fit one of them; then, she fixes her eyes on the portrait of the cavalier in green, and says, in a low, terrible voice, "The stags know it!" After that, she wrings her hands again, passes the bedside, and goes out at the door. We hurry on our dressing gown, seize our pistols (we always travel with pistols), and are following, when we find the door locked. We turn the key, look out into the dark gallery; no one there. We wander away, and try to find our servant. Can't be done. We pace the gallery till daybreak; then return to our deserted room, fall asleep, and are awakened by our servant (nothing ever haunts him) and the shining sun. Well! we make a wretched breakfast, and all the company say we look queer. After breakfast, we go over the house with our host, and then we take him to the portrait of the cavalier in green, and then it all comes out. He was false to a young housekeeper once attached to that family, and famous for her beauty, who drowned herself in a pond, and whose body was discovered, after a long time, because the stags refused to drink of the water. Since which, it has been whispered that she traverses the house at midnight (but goes especially to that room where the cavalier in green was wont to sleep) trying the old locks with the rusty keys. Well! we tell our host of what we have seen, and a shade comes over his features, and he begs it may be hushed up; and so it is. But, it's all true; and we said so, before we died (we are dead now) to many responsible people.

There is no end to the old houses, with resounding galleries, and dismal state bedchambers, and haunted wings shut up for many years, through which we may ramble, with an agreeable creeping up our back, and encounter any number of ghosts, but (it is worthy of remark, perhaps) reducible to a very few general types and classes; for ghosts have little originality, and "walk" in a beaten track. Thus it comes to pass that a certain room in a certain old hall, where a certain bad lord, baronet, knight, or gentleman shot himself, has certain planks in the floor from which the blood *will not* be taken out. You may scrape and scrape, as the present owner has done, or plane and plane, as his father did, or scrub and scrub, as his grandfather did, or burn and burn with strong acids, as his great-grandfather did, but, there the blood will still be—no redder and no paler—no more and no less—always just the same. Thus, in such another house there is a haunted door that never will keep open; or another door that never will keep shut; or a haunted sound of a spinning wheel, or a hammer, or a footstep, or a cry, or a sigh, or a horse's tramp, or the rattling of a chain. Or else there is a turret-clock which, at the midnight hour, strikes thirteen when the head of the family is going to die; or a shadowy, immovable black carriage which at such a time is always seen by somebody, waiting near the great gates in the stable yard. Or thus, it came to pass how Lady Mary went to pay a visit at a large, wild house in the Scottish Highlands, and, being fatigued with her long journey, retired to bed early, and innocently said, next morning, at the breakfast table, "How odd, to have so late a party last night, in this remote place, and not to tell me of it, before I went to bed!" Then, every one asked Lady Mary what she meant? Then, Lady Mary replied, "Why, all night long, the carriages were driving round and round the terrace, underneath my window!" Then, the owner of the house turned pale, and so did his Lady, and Charles Macdoodle of Macdoodle signed to Lady Mary to say no more, and every one was silent. After breakfast, Charles Macdoodle told Lady Mary that it was a tradition in the family that those rumbling carriages on the terrace betokened death. And so it proved, for, two months afterwards, the Lady of the mansion died. And Lady Mary, who was a Maid of Honor at Court, often told this story to the old Queen Charlotte; by this token that the old King always said, "Eh, eh? What, what? Ghosts, ghosts? No such thing, no such thing!" And never left off saying so, until he went to bed.

Or, a friend of somebody's whom most of us know, when he was a young man at college had a particular friend with whom he made the compact that, if it were possible for the spirit to return to this earth after its separation from the body, he of the twain who first died should reappear to the other. In course of time, this compact was forgotten by our friend; the two young men having progressed in life, and taken diverging paths that were wide asunder. But one night, many years afterwards, our friend being in the north of England, and staying for the night in an inn, on the Yorkshire Moors, happened to look out of bed; and there, in the moonlight, leaning on a bureau near the window, steadfastly regarding him, saw his old college friend! The appearance being solemnly addressed, replied, in a kind of whisper, but very audibly, "Do not come near me. I am dead. I am here to redeem my promise. I come from another world, but may not disclose its secrets!" Then, the whole form becoming paler, melted, as it were, into the moonlight, and faded away.

Or, there was the daughter of the first occupier of the picturesque Elizabethan house, so famous in our neighbourhood. You have heard about her? No! Why, *She* went out one summer evening at twilight, when she was a beautiful girl, just seventeen years of age, to gather flowers in the garden; and presently came running, terrified, into the hall to her father, saying, "Oh, dear father, I have met myself!" He took her in his arms, and told her it was fancy, but she said, "Oh, no! I met myself in the broad walk, and I was pale and gathering withered flowers, and I turned my head, and held them up!" And, that night, she died; and a picture of her story was begun, though never finished, and they say it is somewhere in the house to this day, with its face to the wall.

Or, the uncle of my brother's wife was riding home on horseback, one mellow evening at sunset, when, in a green lane close to his own house, he saw a man standing before him, in the very center of the narrow way. "Why does that man in the cloak stand there!" he thought. "Does he want me to ride over him?" But the figure never moved. He felt a strange sensation at seeing it so still, but slackened his trot and rode forward. When he was so close to it, as almost to touch it with his stirrup, his horse shied, and the figure glided up the bank, in a curious, unearthly manner—backward, and without seeming to use its feet—and was gone. The uncle of my brother's wife, exclaiming, "Good Heaven! It's my cousin Harry, from Bombay!" put spurs to his horse, which was suddenly in a profuse sweat, and, wondering at such strange behavior, dashed round to the front of his house. There, he saw the same figure, just passing in at the long, French window of the drawing-room, opening on the ground. He threw his bridle to a servant, and hastened in after it. His sister was sitting there, alone. "Alice, where's my cousin Harry?" "Your cousin Harry, John?" "Yes. From Bombay. I met him in the lane just now, and saw him enter here, this instant." Not a creature had been seen by any one; and in that hour and minute, as it afterwards appeared, this cousin died in India.

Or, it was a certain, sensible, old, maiden lady, who died at ninety-nine, and retained her faculties to the last, who really did see the Orphan Boy; a story which has often been incorrectly told, but, of which the real truth is this—because it is, in fact, a story belonging to our family—and she was a connection of our family. When she was about forty years of age, and still an uncommonly fine woman (her lover died young, which was the reason why she never married, though she had many offers), she went to stay at a place in Kent which her brother, an Indian-Merchant, had newly bought. There was a story that this place had once been held in trust by the guardian of a young boy; who was himself the next heir, and who killed the young boy by harsh and cruel treatment. She knew nothing of that. It has been said that there was a Cage in her bedroom in which the guardian used to put the boy. There was no such thing. There was only a closet. She went to bed, made no alarm whatever in the night, and in the morning said composedly to her maid when she came in, "Who is the pretty, forlorn-looking child who has been peeping out of that closet all night?" The maid replied by giving a loud scream, and instantly decamping. She was surprised; but she was a woman of remarkable strength of mind, and she dressed herself and went downstairs, and closeted herself with her brother. "Now, Walter," she said, "I have been disturbed all night by a pretty, forlorn-looking boy, who has been constantly peeping out of that closet in my room, which I can't open. This is some trick." "I am afraid not, Charlotte," said he, "for it is the legend of the house. It is the Orphan Boy. What did he do?" "He opened the door softly," said she, "and peeped out. Sometimes he came a step or two into the room. Then I called to him, to encourage him, and he shrunk, and shuddered, and crept in again, and shut the door." "The closet has no communication, Charlotte," said her brother, "with any other part of the house, and it's nailed up." This was undeniably true, and it took two carpenters a whole forenoon to get it open for examination. Then she was satisfied that she had seen the Orphan Boy. But the wild and terrible part of the story is that he was also seen by three of her brother's sons in succession, who all died young. On the occasion of each child being taken ill, he came home in a heat, twelve hours before, and said, oh, Mamma, he had been playing under a particular oak tree, in a certain meadow, with a strange boy—a pretty, forlorn-looking boy, who was very timid, and made signs! From fatal experience, the parents came to know that this was the Orphan Boy, and that the course of that child whom he chose for his little playmate was surely run.

Legion is the name of the German castles where we sit up alone to wait for the Specter—where we are shown into a room, made comparatively cheerful for our reception—where we glance round at the shadows thrown on the blank walls by the crackling fire—where we feel very lonely when the village innkeeper and his pretty daughter have retired, after laying down a fresh store of wood upon the hearth, and setting forth on the small table such supper-cheer as a cold roast capon, bread, grapes, and a flask of old Rhine wine—where the reverberating doors close on their retreat, one after another, like so many peals of sullen thunder—and where, about the small hours of the night, we come into the knowledge of divers supernatural mysteries. Legion is the name of the haunted German students, in whose society we draw yet nearer to the fire, while the schoolboy in the corner opens his eyes wide and round, and flies off the footstool he has chosen for his seat when the door accidentally blows open. Vast is the crop of such fruit, shining on our Christmas Tree; in blossom, almost at the very top; ripening all down the boughs!

Among the later toys and fancies hanging there—as idle often and less pure—be the image once associated with the sweet old Waits, the softened music in the night, ever unalterable! Encircled by the social thoughts of Christmas time, still let the benignant figure of my childhood stand unchanged! In every cheerful image and suggestion that the season brings, may the bright star that rested above the poor roof be the star of all the Christian World! A moment's pause, O vanishing tree, of which the lower boughs are dark to me as yet, and let me look once more! I know there are blank spaces on thy branches, where eyes that I have loved have shone and smiled; from which they are departed. But, far above, I see the raiser of the dead girl, and the Widow's Son; and God is good! If Age be hiding for me in the unseen portion of thy downward growth, oh may I, with a gray head, turn a child's heart to that figure yet, and a child's trustfulness and confidence!

Now the tree is decorated with bright merriment, and song, and dance, and cheerfulness. And they are welcome. Innocent and welcome be they ever held, beneath the branches of the Christmas Tree, which cast no gloomy shadow! But, as it sinks into the ground, I hear a whisper going through the leaves. "This, in commemoration of the law of love and kindness, mercy, and compassion. This, in remembrance of Me!"

1850 1850

WILLIAM MAKEPEACE THACKERAY
1811-1863

Thackeray was born in Calcutta, where his father was an employee of the East India Company. He received good training in English schools, and was for three years at Cambridge. Unwise use of an inheritance falling to him about the time when he was ready for active life thrust him out upon the world. He was illustrator, caricaturist, and writer for London periodicals for more than ten years before he wrote his first noteworthy novel, *Vanity Fair,* 1847-1848. *Pendennis,* 1849-1850, and its sequel, *The Newcomes,* 1854-1855, constitute a solid portrait of nineteenth century England. In *Esmond,* 1852, he produced a notable historical novel. He was also a successful lecturer and a critic of eighteenth century literature.

Thackeray is essentially a satirist. This does not mean that he hated mankind as Swift did, or that he saw only the unpleasant side of life. But he did see the hollowness of the society with which he was most familiar, that of the upper middle classes and the aristocracy, and his sense of justice as well as his humor directed many a telling blow at sham and hypocrisy. On the other hand, his Colonel Newcome, one of the most noble characters in English fiction, is Thackeray's tribute to simple-hearted, high-minded honor and fortitude. Thackeray follows Fielding in realism, but his singular gracefulness of style is his own.

Biographies: Trollope (EML), Merivale and Marzials (GW), Ritchie (Anne Thackeray) *Thackeray and his Daughter,* 1924, Criticism: Lang, Macaulay; more recent: "Thackeray, a New Interpretation," M. P. Wilcocks, *Liv. Age* 306:776-83; "Thackeray and Real Men," H. van Dyke, *Harp.* 140:172-8; "Founding of Main Street, Letters of Thackeray," S. T. Williams, *No. Am.,* 216:248-53.

From THE ENGLISH HUMORISTS OF THE EIGHTEENTH CENTURY[1]

GOLDSMITH

Jeté sur cette boule,
  Laid chétif et souffrant;
Etouffé dans la foule,
  Faute d'être assez grand:

Une plainte touchante
  De ma bouche sortit.
Le bon Dieu me dit: Chante,
  Chante, pauvre petit!

Chanter, ou je m'abuse,
  Est ma tâche ici-bas.
Tous ceux qu'ainsi j'amuse,
  Ne m'aimeront-ils pas?[2]

In those charming lines of Béranger, one may fancy described the career, the sufferings, the genius, the gentle nature of Goldsmith, and the esteem in which we hold him. Who, of the millions whom he has amused, doesn't love him? To be the most beloved of English writers, what a title that is for a man! A wild youth, wayward, but full of tenderness and affection, quits the country village where his boyhood has been passed in happy musing, in idle shelter, in fond longing to see the great world out of doors, and achieve name and fortune: and after years of dire struggle, and neglect and poverty, his heart turning back as fondly to his native place as it had longed eagerly for change when sheltered there, he writes a book and a poem, full of the recollections and feelings of home. He paints the friends and scenes of his youth, and peoples Auburn and Wakefield[3] with remembrances of Lissoy. Wander he must, but he carries away a home relic with him, and dies with it on his breast. His nature is truant; in repose it longs for change, as on the journey it looks back for friends and quiet. He passes today in building an air castle for tomorrow, or in writing yesterday's elegy; and he would fly away this hour, but that a cage and necessity keep him. What is the charm of his verse, of his style and humor? His sweet regrets, his delicate compassion, his soft smile, his tremulous sympathy, the weakness which he owns? Your love for him is half pity. You come hot and tired from the day's battle, and this sweet minstrel sings to you. Who could harm the kind vagrant harper? Whom did he ever hurt? He carries no weapon, save the harp on which he plays to you; and with which he delights great and humble, young and old, the captains in the tents, or the soldiers round the fire, or the women and children in the villages, at whose porches he stops and sings his simple songs of love and beauty. With that sweet story of the "Vicar of Wakefield" he has found entry into every castle and every hamlet in Europe. Not one of us, however busy or hard, but once or twice in our lives has passed an evening with him, and undergone the charm of his delightful music.

Goldsmith's father was no doubt the good Doctor Primrose,[4] whom we all of us know. Swift was yet alive, when the little Oliver was born at Pallas, or Pallasmore, in the county of Longford, in Ireland. In 1730, two years after the child's birth, Charles Goldsmith removed his family to Lissoy, in the county Westmeath, that sweet "Auburn" which every person who hears me has seen in fancy. Here the kind parson brought up his eight children; and loving all the world, as his son says, fancied all the world loved him. He had a crowd of poor dependants besides those hungry children. He kept an open table; round which sat flatterers and poor friends, who laughed at the honest rector's many jokes, and ate the produce of his seventy acres of farm. Those who have seen an Irish house in the present day can fancy that one of Lissoy. The old beggar still has his allotted corner by the kitchen turf;[5] the maimed old soldier still gets

[1] These papers, six in number, were prepared by Thackeray as lectures and were delivered in England in 1851, and in America in the winter of 1852-53. The first lecture dealt with Swift, the last with Sterne and Goldsmith.

[2] Béranger (1780-1851) was a kind of French Burns, a writer of songs beloved by the people. The lines may be translated somewhat freely thus:

Flung into life,
  Dwarfed, ugly, in pain;
Nigh crushed in the strife
  Where I struggle in vain;

What wonder, should spring
  To my lips my dole?
God said to me, "Sing!
  Sing, poor little soul!"

So my task here below
  Is a-singing to rove;
If pleasure I sow,
  Shall I not reap love?

[3] The scenes respectively of the poem and the romance on which Goldsmith's literary reputation chiefly rests; compare "The Deserted Village" and the notes thereon, p. 405.

[4] the "Vicar of Wakefield"

[5] peat

his potatoes and buttermilk; the poor cottier [1] still asks his honor's charity, and prays God bless his reverence for the sixpence; the ragged pensioner still takes his place by right and sufferance. There's still a crowd in the kitchen, and a crowd round the parlor table, profusion, confusion, kindness, poverty. If an Irishman comes to London to make his fortune, he has a half dozen of Irish dependants who take a percentage of his earnings. The good Charles Goldsmith left but little provision for his hungry race when death summoned him; and one of his daughters being engaged to a squire of rather superior dignity, Charles Goldsmith impoverished the rest of his family to provide the girl with a dowry.

The smallpox which scourged all Europe at that time, and ravaged the roses off the cheeks of half the world, fell foul of poor little Oliver's face, when the child was eight years old, and left him scarred and disfigured for his life. An old woman in his father's village taught him his letters, and pronounced him a dunce. Paddy Byrne, the hedge schoolmaster, [2] took him in hand; and from Paddy Byrne he was transmitted to a clergyman at Elphin. When a child was sent to school in those days, the classic phrase was that he was placed under Mr. So-and-so's *ferule*. Poor little ancestors! It is hard to think how ruthlessly you were birched; and how much of needless whipping and tears our small forefathers had to undergo! A relative—kind uncle Contarine—took the main charge of little Noll, who went through his school days righteously doing as little work as he could: robbing orchards, playing at ball, and making his pocket money fly about whenever fortune sent it to him. Everybody knows the story of that famous "Mistake of a Night," when the young schoolboy, provided with a guinea and a nag, rode up to the "best house" in Ardagh, called for the landlord's company over a bottle of wine at supper, and for a hot cake for breakfast in the morning; and found, when he asked for the bill, that the best house was Squire Featherstone's, and not the inn for which he mistook it. [3] Who does not know every story about Goldsmith? That is a delightful and fantastic picture of the child dancing and capering about in the kitchen at home, when the old fiddler gibed at him for his ugliness, and called him Aesop; [4] and little Noll made his repartee of "Heralds proclaim aloud this saying—See Aesop dancing and his monkey playing." One can fancy a queer pitiful look of humor and appeal upon that little scarred face—the funny little dancing figure, the funny little brogue. In his life, and his writings, which are the honest expression of it, he is constantly bewailing that homely face and person; anon he surveys them in the glass ruefully; and presently assumes the most comical dignity. He likes to deck out his little person in splendor and fine colors. He presented himself to be examined for ordination in a pair of scarlet breeches, and said honestly that he did not like to go into the Church because he was fond of colored clothes. When he tried to practice as a doctor, he got by hook or by crook a black velvet suit, and looked as big and grand as he could, and kept his hat over a patch on the old coat: in better days he bloomed out in plum color, in blue silk, and in new velvet. For some of those splendors the heirs and assignees of Mr. Filby, the tailor, have never been paid to this day; perhaps the kind tailor and his creditor have met and settled their little account in Hades.

They showed until lately a window at Trinity College, Dublin, on which the name of O. Goldsmith was engraved with a diamond. Whose diamond was it? Not the young sizar's, [5] who made but a poor figure in that place of learning. He was idle, penniless, and fond of pleasure: he learned his way early to the pawnbroker's shop. He wrote ballads, they say, for the street singers, who paid him a crown for a poem; and his pleasure was to steal out at night and hear his verses sung. He was chastised by his tutor for giving a dance in his rooms, and took the box on the ear so much to heart that he packed up his all, pawned his books and little property, and disappeared from college and family. He said he intended to go to America, but when his money was spent, the young prodigal came home ruefully, and the good folks there killed their calf—it was but a lean one—and welcomed him back.

After college he hung about his mother's house, and lived for some years the life of a buckeen [6]—passed a month with this relation and that, a year with one patron, a great deal of time at the public house. Tired of this life, it was resolved that he should go to London, and study at the Temple; [7] but he got no farther on the road to London and the woolsack [8] than Dublin, where he gambled away the

[1] a peasant renting and cultivating a small holding
[2] Open air schools, held by hedge sides, were once common in Ireland.
[3] This joke was played on Goldsmith, and he worked it into the plot of *She Stoops to Conquer*.
[4] This traditionary Greek writer of fables is represented to have been deformed.
[5] student given free rations, usually for menial work
[6] an idle younger son of the poorer aristocracy
[7] quarters occupied by students of law
[8] cushion, hence office, of the Lord High Chancellor

fifty pounds given to him for his outfit, and whence he returned to the indefatigable forgiveness of home. Then he determined to be a doctor, and uncle Contarine helped him to a couple of years at Edinburgh. Then from Edinburgh he felt that he ought to hear the famous professors of Leyden and Paris, and wrote most amusing pompous letters to his uncle about the great Farheim, Du Petit, and Duhamel du Monceau, whose lectures he proposed to follow. If uncle Contarine believed those letters—if Oliver's mother believed that story which the youth related of his going to Cork, with the purpose of embarking for America, of his having paid his passage money, and having sent his kit on board; of the anonymous captain sailing away with Oliver's valuable luggage in a nameless ship, never to return; if uncle Contarine and the mother at Ballymahon, believed his stories, they must have been a very simple pair; as it was a very simple rogue indeed who cheated them. When the lad, after failing in his clerical examination, after failing in his plan for studying the law, took leave of these projects and of his parents, and set out for Edinburgh, he saw mother, and uncle, and lazy Ballymahon, and green native turf, and sparkling river for the last time. He was never to look on old Ireland more, and only in fancy revisit her.

"But me not destined such delights to share
My prime of life in wandering spent and care,
Impelled, with steps unceasing to pursue
Some fleeting good that mocks me with the view;
That like the circle bounding earth and skies
Allures from far, yet, as I follow, flies:
My fortune leads to traverse realms alone,
And find no spot of all the world my own." [1]

I spoke in a former lecture of that high courage which enabled Fielding, [2] in spite of disease, remorse, and poverty, always to retain a cheerful spirit and to keep his manly benevolence and love of truth intact, as if these treasures had been confided to him for the public benefit, and he was accountable to posterity for their honorable employ; and a constancy equally happy and admirable I think was shown by Goldsmith, whose sweet and friendly nature bloomed kindly always in the midst of a life's storm, and rain, and bitter weather. The poor fellow was never so friendless but he could befriend some one; never so pinched and wretched but he could give of his crust, and speak his word of compassion. If he had but his flute left, he could give that, and make the children happy in the dreary London court. He could give the coals in that queer coal scuttle we read of to his poor neighbor; he could give away his blankets in college to the poor widow, and warm himself as he best might in the feathers; he could pawn his coat to save his landlord from gaol; when he was a school usher he spent his earnings in treats for the boys, and the good-natured schoolmaster's wife said justly that she ought to keep Mr. Goldsmith's money as well as the young gentlemen's. When he met his pupils in later life, nothing would satisfy the Doctor but he must treat them still. "Have you seen the print of me after Sir Joshua Reynolds?" [3] he asked of one of his old pupils. "Not seen it? Not bought it? Sure, Jack, if your picture had been published, I'd not have been without it half an hour." His purse and his heart were everybody's, and his friends', as much as his own. When he was at the height of his reputation, and the Earl of Northumberland, going as Lord Lieutenant to Ireland, asked if he could be of any service to Doctor Goldsmith, Goldsmith recommended his brother, and not himself, to the great man. "My patrons," he gallantly said, "are the booksellers, and I want no others." Hard patrons they were, and hard work he did; but he did not complain, much. If in his early writings some bitter words escaped him, some allusions to neglect and poverty, he withdrew these expressions when his works were republished, and better days seemed to open for him; and he did not care to complain that printer or publisher had overlooked his merit, or left him poor. The Court face was turned from honest Oliver, the Court patronized Beattie; [4] the fashion did not shine on him—fashion adored Sterne. [5] Fashion pronounced Kelly [6] to be the great writer of comedy of his day. A little —not ill-humor, but plaintiveness—a little betrayal of wounded pride which he showed render him not the less amiable. The author of the *Vicar of Wakefield* had a right to protest when Newbery [7] kept back the manuscript for two years; had a right to be a little peevish with Sterne; a little angry when Colman's [8] actors declined their parts in his delightful comedy, when the manager refused to have a

[1] Goldsmith's *The Traveler,* lines 23-30
[2] Henry Fielding, the novelist

[3] Reynolds painted his portrait, and it was engraved in mezzotint by Marchi in 1770.
[4] James Beattie, a Scottish poet
[5] Laurence Sterne, author of *Tristram Shandy*
[6] Hugh Kelly, author of *False Delicacy,* which was produced at Drury Lane just before Goldsmith's *The Good-Natured Man*
[7] a publisher
[8] George Colman the elder, a dramatist and manager, who brought out Goldsmith's *She Stoops to Conquer* only after much urging by Dr. Johnson and his friends

scene painted for it, and pronounced its damnation before hearing. He had not the great public with him; but he had the noble Johnson, and the admirable Reynolds, and the great Gibbon, and the great Burke, and the great Fox—friends and admirers illustrious indeed, as famous as those who, fifty years before, sat round Pope's table.

Nobody knows, and I dare say Goldsmith's buoyant temper kept no account of, all the pains which he endured during the early period of his literary career. Should any man of letters in our day have to bear up against such, Heaven grant he may come out of the period of misfortune with such a pure, kind heart as that which Goldsmith obstinately bore in his breast. The insults to which he had to submit are shocking to read of—slander, contumely, vulgar satire, brutal malignity perverting his commonest motives and actions; he had his share of these, and one's anger is roused at reading of them, as it is at seeing a woman insulted or a child assaulted, at the notion that a creature so very gentle and weak, and full of love, should have had to suffer so. And he had worse than insult to undergo—to own to fault and deprecate the anger of ruffians. There is a letter of his extant to one Griffiths, a bookseller, in which poor Goldsmith is forced to confess that certain books sent by Griffiths are in the hands of a friend from whom Goldsmith had been forced to borrow money. "He was wild, sir," Johnson said, speaking of Goldsmith to Boswell, with his great, wise benevolence and noble mercifulness of heart—"Dr. Goldsmith was wild, sir; but he is so no more." Ah! if we pity the good and weak man who suffers undeservedly, let us deal very gently with him from whom misery extorts not only tears, but shame; let us think humbly and charitably of the human nature that suffers so sadly and falls so low. Whose turn may it be tomorrow? What weak heart, confident before trial, may not succumb under temptation invincible? Cover the good man who has been vanquished—cover his face and pass on.

For the last half-dozen years of his life, Goldsmith was far removed from the pressure of any ignoble necessity: and in the receipt, indeed, of a pretty large income from the booksellers, his patrons. Had he lived but a few years more, his public fame would have been as great as his private reputation, and he might have enjoyed alive a part of that esteem which his country has ever since paid to the vivid and versatile genius who has touched on almost every subject of literature, and touched nothing that he did not adorn. Except in rare instances, a man is known in our profession, and esteemed as a skillful workman, years before the lucky hit which trebles his usual gains, and stamps him a popular author. In the strength of his age, and the dawn of his reputation, having for backers and friends the most illustrious literary men of his time, fame and prosperity might have been in store for Goldsmith, had fate so willed it, and at forty-six, had not sudden disease carried him off. I say prosperity rather than competence, for it is probable that no sum could have put order into his affairs, or sufficed for his irreclaimable habits of dissipation. It must be remembered that he owed £2,000 when he died. "Was ever poet," Johnson asked, "so trusted before?" As has been the case with many another good fellow of his nation, his life was tracked and his substance wasted by crowds of hungry beggars and lazy dependants. If they came at a lucky time (and be sure they knew his affairs better than he did himself, and watched his pay day), he gave them of his money: if they begged on empty-purse days, he gave them his promissory bills; or he treated them to a tavern where he had credit; or he obliged them with an order upon honest Mr. Filby for coats, for which he paid as long as he could earn, and until the shears of Filby were to cut for him no more. Staggering under a load of debt and labor, tracked by bailiffs and reproachful creditors, running from a hundred poor dependants, whose appealing looks were perhaps the hardest of all pains for him to bear, devising fevered plans for the morrow, new histories, new comedies, all sorts of new literary schemes, flying from all these into seclusion, and out of seclusion into pleasure—at last, at five-and-forty, death seized him and closed his career. I have been many a time in the chambers in the Temple which were his, and passed up the staircase, which Johnson and Burke and Reynolds trod to see their friend, their poet, their kind Goldsmith—the stair on which the poor women sat weeping bitterly when they heard that the greatest and most generous of all men was dead within the black oak door. Ah! it was a different lot from that for which the poor fellow sighed when he wrote with heart yearning for home those most charming of all fond verses, in which he fancies he revisits Auburn—

"Here, as I take my solitary rounds,
Amidst thy tangling walks and ruined grounds,
And, many a year elapsed, return to view
Where once the cottage stood, the hawthorn grew,

Remembrance wakes, with all her busy train,
Swells at my breast, and turns the past to pain. . . . "[1]

In these verses, I need not say with what melody, with what touching truth, with what exquisite beauty of comparison—as indeed in hundreds more pages of the writings of this honest soul—the whole character of the man is told—his humble confession of faults and weakness; his pleasant little vanity, and desire that his village should admire him; his simple scheme of good in which everybody was to be happy—no beggar was to be refused his dinner—nobody in fact was to work much, and he to be the harmless chief of the Utopia,[2] and the monarch of the Irish Yvetot.[3] He would have told again, and without fear of their failing, those famous jokes which had hung fire in London;[4] he would have talked of his great friends of the Club—of my Lord Clare and my Lord Bishop, my Lord Nugent—sure he knew them intimately, and was hand and glove with some of the best men in town—and he would have spoken of Johnson and of Burke, and of Sir Joshua who had painted him—and he would have told wonderful sly stories of Ranelagh and the Pantheon,[5] and the masquerades of Madame Cornelys;[6] and he would have toasted, with a sigh, the Jessamy Bride[7]—the lovely Mary Horneck.

The figure of that charming, young lady forms one of the prettiest recollections of Goldsmith's life. She and her beautiful sister, who married Bunbury, the graceful and humorous amateur artist of those days, when Gillray[8] had but just begun to try his powers, were among the kindest and dearest of Goldsmith's many friends, cheered and pitied him, traveled abroad with him, made him welcome at their home, and gave him many a pleasant holiday. He bought his finest clothes to figure at their country house at Barton—he wrote them droll verses. They loved him, laughed at him, played him tricks, and made him happy. He asked for a loan from Garrick,[9] and Garrick kindly supplied him, to enable him to go to Barton; but there were to be no more holidays and only one brief struggle more for poor Goldsmith. A lock of his hair was taken from the coffin and given to the Jessamy Bride. She lived quite into our time. Hazlitt[10] saw her an old lady, but beautiful still, in Northcote's[11] painting room, who told the eager critic how proud she always was that Goldsmith had admired her. The younger Colman[12] has left a touching reminiscence of him (vol. i, 63, 64):

"I was only five years old," he says, "when Goldsmith took me on his knee one evening whilst he was drinking coffee with my father, and began to play with me, which amiable act I returned, with the ingratitude of a peevish brat, by giving him a very smart slap on the face; it must have been a tingler, for it left the marks of my spiteful paw on his cheek. This infantile outrage was followed by summary justice, and I was locked up by my indignant father in an adjoining room to undergo solitary imprisonment in the dark. Here I began to howl and scream most abominably, which was no bad step towards my liberation, since those who were not inclined to pity me might be likely to set me free for the purpose of abating a nuisance.

"At length a generous friend appeared to extricate me from jeopardy, and that generous friend was no other than the man I had so wantonly molested by assault and battery—it was the tender-hearted Doctor himself, with a lighted candle in his hand and a smile upon his countenance, which was still partially red from the effects of my petulance. I sulked and sobbed as he fondled and soothed, till I began to brighten. Goldsmith seized the propitious moment of returning good humor, when he put down the candle and began to conjure. He placed three hats, which happened to be in the room, and a shilling under each. The shillings, he told me, were England, France, and Spain. 'Hey presto cockalorum!' cried the Doctor, and lo, on uncovering the shillings, which had been dispersed each beneath a separate hat, they were all found congregated under one. I was no politician at five years old, and therefore might not have wondered at the sudden revolution which brought England, France, and

[1] Thackeray's quotation here from "The Deserted Village" extends through thirty lines more, for which see p. 405, ll. 83-112.

[2] See p. 120.

[3] A little town in Normandy whose lords were once called kings—Beranger wrote a ballad on the subject, which Thackeray translated:

There was a king of Yvetot,
Of whom renown hath little said.
Who let all thoughts of glory go,
And dawdled half his days abed;
And every night, as night came round,
By Jenny with a nightcap crowned,
Slept very sound.
Sing ho, ho, ho! and he, he, he!
That's the kind of king for me. Etc.

[4] Compare p. 396.

[5] London pleasure resorts of that time

[6] conductress of a public place for social gatherings

[7] Goldsmith's pet name for his young girl friend

[8] James Gillray, a caricaturist

[9] David Garrick, the actor

[10] William Hazlitt, the essayist

[11] James Northcote, of the Royal Academy

[12] George Colman, a dramatist, son of the Colman mentioned above

Spain all under one crown; but as also I was no conjurer, it amazed me beyond measure. . . . From that time, whenever the Doctor came to visit my father, 'I plucked his gown to share the good man's smile'; a game at romps constantly ensued, and we were always cordial friends and merry playfellows. Our unequal companionship varied somewhat as to sports as I grew older; but it did not last long; my senior playmate died in his forty-fifth year, when I had attained my eleventh. . . . In all the numerous accounts of his virtues and foibles, his genius and absurdities, his knowledge of nature and ignorance of the world, his 'compassion for another's woe' was always predominant; and my trivial story of his humoring a froward child weighs but as a feather in the recorded scale of his benevolence."

Think of him reckless, thriftless, vain, if you like—but merciful, gentle, generous, full of love and pity. He passes out of our life, and goes to render his account beyond it. Think of the poor pensioners weeping at his grave; think of the noble spirits that admired and deplored him; think of the righteous pen that wrote his epitaph—and of the wonderful and unanimous response of affection with which the world has paid back the love he gave it. His humor delighting us still; his song fresh and beautiful as when first he charmed with it; his words in all our mouths; his very weaknesses beloved and familiar—his benevolent spirit seems still to smile upon us; to do gentle kindnesses; to succor with sweet charity; to soothe, caress, and forgive; to plead with the fortunate for the unhappy and the poor.

His name is the last in the list of those men of humor who have formed the themes of the discourses which you have heard so kindly.

1851 1851

From ROUNDABOUT PAPERS [1]

De Juventute [2]

Our last paper of this veracious and roundabout series related to a period which can only be historical to a great number of readers of this magazine. Four I saw at the station today with orange-covered books in their hands, who can but have known George IV [3] by books, and statues, and pictures. Elderly gentlemen were in their prime, old men in their middle age, when he reigned over us. His image remains on coins; on a picture or two hanging here and there in a club or old-fashioned dining room; on horseback, as at Trafalgar Square, for example, where I defy any monarch to look more uncomfortable. He turns up in sundry memoirs and histories which may have been published in Mr. Massey's [4] *History;* in the *Buckingham and Grenville Correspondence;* and gentlemen who have accused a certain writer of disloyalty are referred to those volumes to see whether the picture drawn of George is overcharged. Charon [5] has paddled him off; he has mingled with the crowded republic of the dead. His effigy smiles from a canvas or two. Breechless he bestrides his steed in Trafalgar Square. I believe he still wears his robes at Madame Tussaud's [6] (Madame herself having quitted Baker Street and life, and found him she modeled t'other side the Stygian stream). On the head of a five-shilling piece we still occasionally come upon him, with St. George, the dragon slayer, on the other side of the coin. [7] Ah me! did this George slay many dragons? Was he a brave, heroic champion, and rescuer of virgins? Well! Well! Have you and I overcome all the dragons that assail *us?* Come alive and victorious out of all the caverns which we have entered in life, and succored, at risk of life and limb, all poor distressed persons in whose naked limbs the dragon Poverty is about to fasten his fangs, whom the dragon Crime is poisoning with his horrible breath, and about to crunch up and devour? O my royal liege! O my gracious prince and warrior! *You* a champion to fight that monster? Your feeble spear ever pierce that slimy paunch or plated back? See how the flames come gurgling out of his red-hot, brazen throat! What a roar! Nearer and nearer he trails, with eyes flaming like the lamps of a railroad engine. How he squeals, rushing out through the darkness of his tunnel! Now he is near. Now he is *here.* And now—what?—lance, shield, knight, feathers, horse, and all? Oh, horror, horror! Next day, round the monster's cave there lie a few bones more. You, who wish to keep yours in

[1] In emulation of *Household Words,* which Dickens had made so successful in the fifties, *The Cornhill Magazine* was founded in 1860 and Thackeray was engaged to edit it. The "Roundabout Papers" were his regular contribution for three years. The magazine bore an orange cover.

[2] "Upon Youth"

[3] died 1830

[4] William Massey, author of a history of George III's reign; Grenville's *Memoirs of the Court of George IV* had just been published (1859). Thackeray's lectures on *The Four Georges* had been delivered about five years before.

[5] ferryman of the river Styx

[6] the proprietress of a famous show place containing wax effigies of various celebrities

[7] St. George is a great Christian hero of the middle ages, and legendary slayer of the dragon (the devil), whereby he delivered the virgin Sabra (the Church); adopted as the patron saint of England.

your skins, be thankful that you are not called upon to go out and fight dragons. Be grateful that they don't sally out and swallow you. Keep a wise distance from their caves, lest you pay too dearly for approaching them. Remember that years passed, and whole districts were ravaged, before the warrior came who was able to cope with the devouring monster. When that knight does make his appearance, with all my heart let us go out and welcome him with our best songs, huzzas, and laurel wreaths, and eagerly recognize his valor and victory. But he comes only seldom. Countless knights were slain before St. George won the battle. In the battle of life are we all going to try for the honors of championship? If we can do our duty, if we can keep our place pretty honorably through the combat, let us say *Laus Deo!* [1] at the end of it, as the firing ceases, and the night falls over the field.

The old were middle-aged, the elderly were in their prime, then, thirty years since, when yon royal George was still fighting the dragon. As for you, my pretty lass, with your saucy hat and golden tresses tumbled in your net, and you, my spruce young gentleman in your mandarin's cap (the young folks at the country-place where I am staying are so attired), your parents were unknown to each other, and wore short frocks and short jackets, at the date of this five-shilling piece. Only today I met a dogcart crammed with children—children with moustaches and mandarin caps—children with saucy hats and hair nets—children in short frocks and knickerbockers (surely the prettiest boy's dress that has appeared these hundred years)—children from twenty years of age to six; and father, with mother by his side, driving in front—and on father's countenance I saw that very laugh which I remember perfectly in the time when this crown piece was coined—in *his* time, in King George's time, when we were schoolboys seated on the same form. The smile was just as broad, as bright, as jolly, as I remember it in the past—unforgotten, though not seen or thought of, for how many decades of years, and quite and instantly familiar, though so long out of sight.

Any contemporary of that coin who takes it up and reads the inscription round the laureled head, "Georgius IV Britanniarum Rex. Fid. Def. [2] 1823," if he will but look steadily at the round, and utter the proper incantation, [3] I dare say may conjure back his life there. Look well, my elderly friend, and tell me what you see? First, I see a sultan, with hair, beautiful hair, and a crown of laurels round his head, and his name is Georgius Rex. Fid. Def., and so on. Now the sultan has disappeared; and what is it that I see? A boy—a boy in a jacket. He is at a desk; he has great books before him, Latin and Greek books and dictionaries. Yes, but behind the great books, which he pretends to read, is a little one, with pictures, which he is really reading. It is—yes, I can read now—it is the *Heart of Midlothian*, by the author of *Waverly*—or, no, it is *Life in London, or the Adventures of Corinthian Tom, Jeremiah Hawthorn, and their friend Bob Logic*, by Pierce Egan; and it has pictures—oh! such funny pictures! As he reads there comes behind the boy, a man, a dervish in a black gown, like a woman, and a black, square cap, and he has a book in each hand, and he seizes the boy who is reading the picture book, and lays his head upon one of his books, and smacks it with the other. The boy makes faces, and so that picture disappears.

Now the boy has grown bigger. *He* has got on a black gown and cap, something like the dervish. He is at a table, with ever so many bottles on it, and fruit, and tobacco; and other young dervishes come in. They seem as if they were singing. To them enters an old moollah; he takes down their names, and orders them all to go to bed. What is this? A carriage, with four beautiful horses all galloping—a man in red is blowing a trumpet. Many young men are on the carriage—one of them is driving the horses. Surely they won't drive into that—? —ah! they have all disappeared. And now I see one of the young men alone. He is walking in a street—a dark street—presently a light comes to a window. There is the shadow of a lady who passes. He stands there till the light goes out. Now he is in a room scribbling on a piece of paper, and kissing a miniature every now and then. There seem to be lines each pretty much of a length. I can read *heart, smart, dart; Mary, fairy; Cupid, stupid; true, you;* and never mind what more. Bah! it is bosh. Now see, he has got a gown on again, and a wig of white hair on his head, and he is sitting with other dervishes in a great room full of them, and on a throne in the

[1] "Praise God"

[2] "King of Britain, Defender of the Faith"

[3] This word suggests to Thackeray's fancy the oriental terms in which he proceeds to describe the vision. The king is a "sultan." The conjurer who reviews his own past life sees himself as a schoolboy under the instruction of a gowned "dervish"; later, as a college youth in cap and gown he is himself a "dervish," disciplined by an old proctor perhaps ("moollah," judge, priest); and so on.

middle is an old Sultan in scarlet, sitting before a desk, and he wears a wig, too—and the young man gets up and speaks to him. And now what is here? He is in a room with ever so many children, and the miniature hanging up. Can it be a likeness of that woman who is sitting before that copper urn with a silver vase in her hand, from which she is pouring hot liquor into cups? Was *she* ever a fairy? She is as fat as a hippopotamus now. He is sitting on a divan by the fire. He has a paper on his knees. Read the name. It is the *Superfine Review.* It inclines to think that Mr. Dickens is not a true gentleman, that Mr. Thackeray is not a true gentleman, and that when the one is pert and the other arch, we, the gentlemen of the *Superfine Review,* think, and think rightly, that we have some cause to be indignant. The great cause why modern humor and modern sentimentalism repel us is that they are unwarrantably familiar. Now, Mr. Sterne, the *Superfine Review* thinks, "was a true sentimentalist, because he was *above all things* a true gentleman." The flattering inference is obvious; let us be thankful for an elegant moralist watching over us, and learn, if not too old, to imitate his high-bred politeness and catch his unobtrusive grace. If we are unwarrantably familiar we know who is not. If we repel by pertness we know who never does. If our language offends we know whose is always modest. O pity! The vision has disappeared off the silver, the images of youth and the past are vanishing away! We who have lived before railways were made belong to another world. In how many hours could the Prince of Wales drive from Brighton to London, with a light carriage built expressly, and relays of horses longing to gallop the next stage? Do you remember Sir Somebody, the coachman of the Age, who took our half-crown so affably? It was only yesterday; but what a gulf between now and then! Then was the old world. Stagecoaches, more or less swift, riding horses, pack horses, highwaymen, knights in armor, Norman invaders, Roman legions, Druids, Ancient Britons painted blue, and so forth—all these belong to the old period. I will concede a halt in the midst of it, and allow that gunpowder and printing tended to modernize the world. But your railroad starts the new era, and we of a certain age belong to the new time and the old one. We are of the time of chivalry as well as the Black Prince [1] or Sir Walter Manny. [2] We are of the age of steam. We have stepped out of the old world on to "Brunel's" vast deck, [3] and across the waters *ingens patet tellus.* [4] Toward what new continent are we wending; to what new laws, new manners, new politics, vast new expanses of liberties unknown as yet, or only surmised? I used to know a man who had invented a flying machine. "Sir," he would say, "give me but five hundred pounds, and I will make it. It is so simple of construction that I tremble daily lest some other person should light upon and patent my discovery." Perhaps faith was wanting; perhaps the five hundred pounds. He is dead, and somebody else must make the flying machine. But that will only be a step forward on the journey already begun since we quitted the old world. There it lies on the other side of yonder embankments. You young folks have never seen it; and Waterloo [5] is to you no more than Agincourt, [6] and George IV than Sardanapalus. [7] We elderly people have lived in that pre-railroad world which has passed into limbo and vanished from under us. I tell you it was firm under our feet once, and not long ago. They have raised those railroad embankments up, and shut off the old world that was behind them. Climb up that bank on which the irons are laid, and look to the other side—it is gone. There is no other side. Try and catch yesterday. Where is it? Here is a *Times* newspaper, dated Monday 26th, and this is Tuesday 27th. Suppose you deny there was such a day as yesterday.

We who lived before railways, and survive out of the ancient world, are like Father Noah and his family out of the Ark. The children will gather round and say to us patriarchs, "Tell us, grandpapa, about the old world." And we shall mumble our old stories; and we shall drop off one by one; and there will be fewer and fewer of us, and these very old and feeble. There will be but ten pre-railroadites left; then three—then two—then one—then, Oh! if the hippopotamus had the least sensibility (of which I cannot trace any signs either in his hide or his face) I think he would go down to the bottom of his tank, and never come up again. Does he not see that he belongs to bygone ages, and that his great hulking barrel of a body is out of place in these times? What has he in common with the brisk young life surrounding him? In the watches of the night, when the keepers are asleep, when the birds

[1] the son of Edward III; hero of Poitiers, 1356
[2] a soldier of Edward III

[3] the steamship *Great Eastern,* designed by I. K. Brunel, 1858
[4] "a great world looms"
[5] fought 1815
[6] fought 1415
[7] Assyrian king; died 626 B.C.

are on one leg, when even the little armadillo is quiet, and the monkeys have ceased their chatter—he, I mean the hippopotamus, and the elephant, and the long-necked giraffe, perhaps, may lay their heads together and have a colloquy about the great, silent, antediluvian world which they remember, where mighty monsters floundered through the ooze, crocodiles basked on the banks, and dragons darted out of the caves and waters before men were made to slay them. We who lived before railroads are antediluvians—we must pass away. We are growing scarcer every day; and old—old—very old relics of the times when George was still fighting the Dragon.

. . . .

1860-63

ALFRED, LORD TENNYSON
1809-1892

The most popular of the Victorian poets was born in a country rectory at Somersby, Lincolnshire. He was one of a large and gifted family, all schooled at home by their father, a man of strong character and excellent scholarship, who himself prepared three of his sons, all poets, for Cambridge. In this stimulating atmosphere of high thought, mutual sacrifice, and ambition, there was time for wide reading, sport, and roaming the countryside with its rich farms, streams, and seashore. At Cambridge Tennyson was one of a group of ambitious men, most of whom later attained prominence in literature and public life. In the years that followed he disciplined himself by intense, systematic study, with poetry always his goal.

Tennyson's *Poems,* published in 1833, met severe criticism, and for nine years he published nothing, but bent more firmly to his task of self-discipline. After his volume of 1842, containing "Ulysses," there was no doubt of his high place among the poets of the day; and 1850 saw the publication of *In Memoriam,* and Tennyson's appointment to the laureateship. Forty years more of fruitful life followed, marked chiefly by the *Idylls of the King,* 1858-1888. When he died at his home in Surrey he had been before the British public for two generations.

More exactly and fully than any other poet, Tennyson represents the Victorian Age, one of the greatest epochs in the political, social, industrial, intellectual, and artistic development of England; he reflects its faiths and doubts, its defects and its aspirations. In the richness of his pictures he follows Keats, but exercises greater restraint. The effects he produces are like those seen in rich paintings of historical or legendary themes—balanced, dignified, dramatic, and in splendor of detail often approaching the gorgeous.

Best edition: *Works,* edited by Hallam, Lord Tennyson, 1898-9, 1907, 1913. Standard biography: *Memoir* (same editor), 2 vols. 1897: Lyall (EML); see also *Tennyson and His Friends* (same editor), 1911; T. R. Lounsbury, *Life and Times of Tennyson from 1809 to 1850,* 1915. Criticism: Walker, *The Age of Tennyson*; Dowden, Swinburne, Stephen, More (Shel. 7), Payne, R. M. Alden *Alfred Tennyson, How to Know Him,* 1917; H. G. Nicolson, *Tennyson: Aspects of His Life, Character, and Poetry,* 1923; see also Lockhart's attack, *Quar.* 49:81 ff; recent: E. Wilson, "Pope and Tennyson," *New Rep.* 44: 96-97; H. *Warren,* "The Real Tennyson," *19th Cent.* 94: 507-19; F. J. C. Hearnshaw, "Tennyson Twenty-five Years After," *Liv. Age* 295:503-6; "Tennyson as a Minor Poet," *Lit. Dig.* 48:619-20.

THE LADY OF SHALOTT [1]

PART I

On either side the river lie
Long fields of barley and of rye,
That clothe the wold and meet the sky;
And through the field the road runs by
        To many-towered Camelot; [2]
And up and down the people go,
Gazing where the lilies blow
Round an island there below,
        The island of Shalott.

Willows whiten, aspens quiver,
Little breezes dusk and shiver
Through the wave that runs forever
By the island in the river
        Flowing down to Camelot.
Four gray walls, and four gray towers,
Overlook a space of flowers,
And the silent isle imbowers
        The Lady of Shalott.

By the margin, willow-veiled,
Slide the heavy barges trailed
By slow horses; and unhailed
The shallop flitteth silken-sailed
        Skimming down to Camelot.
But who hath seen her wave her hand?
Or at the casement seen her stand?
Or is she known in all the land,
        The Lady of Shalott?

Only reapers, reaping early
In among the bearded barley,
Hear a song that echoes cheerly
From the river winding clearly,
        Down to towered Camelot;
And by the moon the reaper weary,
Piling sheaves in uplands airy,

[1] This is, with some variations, essentially the story of Elaine, "the lily maid of Astolat," which is told at greater length and with more detail in the *Idylls of the King.* It is Tennyson's earliest venture into the Arthurian field.

[2] the place of Arthur's court

Listening, whispers "'Tis the fairy
Lady of Shalott."

PART II

There she weaves by night and day
A magic web with colors gay.
She has heard a whisper say,
A curse is on her if she stay
To look down to Camelot.
She knows not what the curse may be,
And so she weaveth steadily,
And little other care hath she,
The Lady of Shalott.

And moving through a mirror clear
That hangs before her all the year,
Shadows of the world appear.
There she sees the highway near,
Winding down to Camelot;
There the river eddy whirls,
And there the surly village-churls,
And the red cloaks of market girls,
Pass onward from Shalott.

Sometimes a troop of damsels glad,
An abbot on an ambling pad,
Sometimes a curly shepherd-lad,
Or long-haired page in crimson clad,
Goes by to towered Camelot;
And sometimes through the mirror blue
The knights come riding two and two:
She hath no loyal knight and true,
The Lady of Shalott.

But in her web she still delights
To weave the mirror's magic sights,
For often through the silent nights
A funeral, with plumes and lights
And music, went to Camelot;
Or when the moon was overhead,
Came two young lovers lately wed:
"I am half sick of shadows," said
The Lady of Shalott.[1]

PART III

A bow shot from her bower eaves,
He rode between the barley sheaves,
The sun came dazzling through the leaves,
And flamed upon the brazen greaves
Of bold Sir Lancelot.
A red-cross knight forever kneeled
To a lady in his shield,
That sparkled on the yellow field,
Beside remote Shalott.

[1] In these lines, says Tennyson's son, is to be found the key to the poem. The allegory then, if one be desired, is not hard to trace.

The gemmy bridle glittered free,
Like to some branch of stars we see
Hung in the golden Galaxy.[2]
The bridle bells rang merrily
As he rode down to Camelot;
And from his blazoned baldric slung,
A mighty silver bugle hung,
And as he rode his armor rung,
Beside remote Shalott.

All in the blue, unclouded weather
Thick-jeweled shone the saddle leather,
The helmet and the helmet feather
Burned like one burning flame together,
As he rode down to Camelot;
As often through the purple night,
Below the starry clusters bright,
Some bearded meteor, trailing light,
Moves over still Shalott.

His broad clear brow in sunlight glowed;
On burnished hooves his warhorse trode;
From underneath his helmet flowed
His coal-black curls as on he rode,
As he rode down to Camelot.
From the bank and from the river
He flashed into the crystal mirror,
"Tirra lirra," by the river
Sang Sir Lancelot.

She left the web, she left the loom,
She made three paces through the room,
She saw the water lily bloom,
She saw the helmet and the plume,
She looked down to Camelot.
Out flew the web and floated wide;
The mirror cracked from side to side;
"The curse is come upon me," cried
The Lady of Shalott.

PART IV

In the stormy, east wind straining,
The pale yellow woods were waning,
The broad stream in his banks complaining,
Heavily the low sky raining
Over towered Camelot;
Down she came and found a boat
Beneath a willow left afloat,
And round about the prow she wrote
The Lady of Shalott.

And down the river's dim expanse
Like some bold seër in a trance,
Seeing all his own mischance—
With a glassy countenance
Did she look to Camelot.

[2] the Milky Way

And at the closing of the day
She loosed the chain, and down she lay;
The broad stream bore her far away;
The Lady of Shalott.

Lying, robed in snowy white
That loosely flew to left and right—
The leaves upon her falling light—
Through the noises of the night
She floated down to Camelot;
And as the boat-head wound along
The willowy hills and fields among,
They heard her singing her last song,
The Lady of Shalott.

Heard a carol, mournful, holy,
Chanted loudly, chanted lowly,
Till her blood was frozen slowly,
And her eyes were darkened wholly,
Turned to towered Camelot.
For ere she reached upon the tide
The first house by the waterside,
Singing in her song, she died,
The Lady of Shalott.

Under tower and balcony,
By garden wall and gallery,
A gleaming shape she floated by,
Dead-pale, between the houses high,
Silent into Camelot.
Out upon the wharfs they came,
Knight and burgher, lord and dame,
And round the prow they read her name,
The Lady of Shalott.

Who is this? And what is here?
And in the lighted palace near
Died the sound of royal cheer,
And they crossed themselves for fear,
All the knights at Camelot:
But Lancelot mused a little space;
He said, "She has a lovely face;
God in his mercy lend her grace,
The Lady of Shalott."

1833-42

OENONE [1]

There lies a vale in Ida, lovelier
Than all the valleys of Ionian hills.
The swimming vapor slopes athwart the glen,
Puts forth an arm, and creeps from pine to pine,
And loiters, slowly drawn. On either hand
The lawns and meadow-ledges midway down
Hang rich in flowers, and far below them roars
The long brook falling through the cloven ravine
In cataract after cataract to the sea.
Behind the valley topmost Gargarus
Stands up and takes the morning; but in front
The gorges, opening wide apart, reveal
Troas and Ilion's columned citadel,
The crown of Troas.

Hither came at noon
Mournful Oenone, wandering forlorn
Of Paris, once her playmate on the hills.
Her cheek had lost the rose, and round her neck
Floated her hair or seemed to float in rest.
She, leaning on a fragment twined with vine,
Sang to the stillness, till the mountain shade
Sloped downward to her seat from the upper cliff.

"O mother Ida, many fountained Ida,
Dear mother Ida, harken ere I die.
For now the noonday quiet holds the hill;
The grasshopper is silent in the grass;
The lizard, with his shadow on the stone,
Rests like a shadow, and the winds are dead.
The purple flower droops, the golden bee
Is lily-cradled; I alone awake.
My eyes are full of tears, my heart of love,
My heart is breaking and my eyes are dim,
And I am all aweary of my life.

"O mother Ida, many-fountained Ida,
Dear mother Ida, harken ere I die.
Hear me, O earth, hear me, O hills, O caves
That house the cold crowned snake! O mountain brooks,
I am the daughter of a River-God,
Hear me, for I will speak, and build up all
My sorrow with my song, as yonder walls
Rose slowly to a music slowly breathed,[2]
A cloud that gathered shape; for it may be
That, while I speak of it, a little while
My heart may wander from its deeper woe.

"O mother Ida, many-fountained Ida,
Dear mother Ida, harken ere I die.
I waited underneath the dawning hills;
Aloft the mountain lawn was dewy-dark,
And dewy-dark aloft the mountain pine.
Beautiful Paris, evil-hearted Paris,
Leading a jet-black goat, white-horned, white-hooved,
Came up from reedy Simois all alone.

"O mother Ida, harken ere I die.
Far off the torrent called me from the cleft;

[1] Oenone, a nymph of Mt. Ida in the Troad, early the beloved of the shepherd Paris, mourns his desertion of her, and relates the story of the famous "Judgment of Paris" which led to the Trojan war.

[2] According to a legend in Ovid, the walls of Troy rose to the music of Apollo's lyre.

Far up the solitary morning smote
The streaks of virgin snow. With down-dropped eyes
I sat alone; white-breasted, like a star
Fronting the dawn, he moved; a leopard skin
Drooped from his shoulder, but his sunny hair
Clustered about his temples like a God's;
And his cheek brightened as the foam-bow brightens
When the wind blows the foam, and all my heart
Went forth to embrace him coming ere he came.

"Dear mother Ida, harken ere I die.
He smiled, and opening out his milk-white palm
Disclosed a fruit of pure Hesperian gold,
That smelt ambrosially, and while I looked
And listened, the full-flowing river of speech
Came down upon my heart:
'My own Oenone,
Beautiful-browed Oenone, my own soul,
Behold this fruit, whose gleaming rind in-graven
"For the most fair," would seem to award it thine,
As lovelier than whatever Oread[1] haunt
The knolls of Ida, loveliest in all grace
Of movement, and the charm of married brows.'

"Dear mother Ida, harken ere I die.
He pressed the blossom of his lips to mine,
And added, 'This was cast upon the board,
When all the full-faced presence of the Gods
Ranged in the halls of Peleus;[2] whereupon
Rose feud, with question unto whom 'twere due;
But light-foot Iris[3] brought it yester-eve,
Delivering, that to me, by common voice
Elected umpire, Herè comes today,
Pallas and Aphrodite,[4] claiming each
This meed of fairest. Thou, within the cave
Behind yon whispering tuft of oldest pine,
Mayst well behold them unbeheld, unheard
Hear all, and see thy Paris judge of Gods.'

"Dear mother Ida, harken ere I die.
It was the deep midnoon; one silvery cloud
Had lost his way between the piny sides
Of this long glen. Then to the bower they came,
Naked they came to that smooth-swarded bower,
And at their feet the crocus brake like fire,
Violet, amaracus, and asphodel,
Lotus, and lilies; and a wind arose,
And overhead the wandering ivy and vine,
This way and that, in many a wild festoon
Ran riot, garlanding the gnarlèd boughs
With bunch and berry and flower through and through.

"O mother Ida, harken ere I die.
On the tree tops a crested peacock[5] lit,
And o'er him flowed a golden cloud, and leaned
Upon him, slowly dropping fragrant dew.
Then first I heard the voice of her to whom
Coming through heaven, like a light that grows
Larger and clearer, with one mind the Gods
Rise up for reverence. She to Paris made
Proffer of royal power, ample rule
Unquestioned, overflowing revenue
Wherewith to embellish state, 'from many a vale
And river-sundered champaign clothed with corn,
Or labored mine undrainable of ore.
Honor,' she said, 'and homage, tax and toll,
From many an inland town and haven large,
Mast-thronged beneath her shadowing citadel
In glassy bays among her tallest towers.'

"O mother Ida, harken ere I die.
Still she spake on and still she spake of power,
'Which in all action is the end of all;
Power fitted to the season; wisdom-bred
And throned of wisdom—from all neighbor crowns
Alliance and allegiance, till thy hand
Fail from the scepter-staff. Such boon from me,
From me, heaven's queen, Paris, to thee, king-born,
A shepherd all thy life but yet king-born,[6]
Should come most welcome, seeing men, in power
Only, are likest Gods, who have attained
Rest in a happy place and quiet seats
Above the thunder, with undying bliss
In knowledge of their own supremacy.'

"Dear mother Ida, harken ere I die.
She ceased, and Paris held the costly fruit
Out at arm's length, so much the thought of power
Flattered his spirit; but Pallas where she stood
Somewhat apart, her clear and barèd limbs
O'erthwarted with the brazen-headed spear
Upon her pearly shoulder leaning cold,
The while, above, her full and earnest eye

[1] mountain nymph
[2] the husband of the sea-nymph Thetis, and the father of Achilles
[3] the messenger of the gods
[4] Juno, Minerva, and Venus
[5] sacred to Juno
[6] Paris was the son of Priam of Troy; he had been left exposed on the mountain-side because of the prophecy that he would bring ruin to Troy.

Over her snow-cold breast and angry cheek
Kept watch, waiting decision, made reply:
'Self-reverence, self-knowledge, self-control,
These three alone lead life to sovereign power.
Yet not for power (power of herself
Would come uncalled for) but to live by law,
Acting the law we live by without fear;
And, because right is right, to follow right
Were wisdom in the scorn of consequence.'

"Dear mother Ida, harken ere I die.
Again she said: 'I woo thee not with gifts.
Sequel of guerdon could not alter me
To fairer. Judge thou me by what I am,
So shalt thou find me fairest.
Yet, indeed,
If gazing on divinity disrobed
Thy mortal eyes are frail to judge of fair,
Unbiased by self-profit, oh, rest thee sure
That I shall love thee well and cleave to thee,
So that my vigor, wedded to thy blood,
Shall strike within thy pulses, like a God's,
To push thee forward through a life of shocks,
Dangers, and deeds, until endurance grow
Sinewed with action, and the full-grown will,
Circled through all experiences, pure law,
Commeasure perfect freedom.' [1]
"Here she ceased,
And Paris pondered and I cried, 'O Paris,
Give it to Pallas!' but he heard me not,
Or hearing would not hear me, woe is me!

"O mother Ida, many-fountained Ida,
Dear mother Ida, harken ere I die.
Idalian Aphrodite beautiful,
Fresh as the foam, new-bathed in Paphian wells, [2]
With rosy slender fingers backward drew [3]
From her warm brows and bosom her deep hair
Ambrosial, golden round her lucid throat
And shoulder; from the violets her light foot
Shone rosy-white, and o'er her rounded form
Between the shadows of the vine-bunches
Floated the glowing sunlights, as she moved.

"Dear mother Ida, harken ere I die.
She with a subtle smile in her mild eyes,
The herald of her triumph, drawing nigh
Half-whispered in his ear, 'I promise thee
The fairest and most loving wife in Greece.'
She spoke and laughed; I shut my sight for fear;
But when I looked, Paris had raised his arm,
And I beheld great Herè's angry eyes,
As she withdrew into the golden cloud,
And I was left alone within the bower;
And from that time to this I am alone,
And I shall be alone until I die.

"Yet, mother Ida, harken ere I die.
Fairest—why fairest wife? Am I not fair?
My love hath told me so a thousand times.
Methinks I must be fair, for yesterday,
When I passed by, a wild and wanton pard,
Eyed like the evening star, with playful tail
Crouched fawning in the weed. Most loving is she?
Ah me, my mountain shepherd, that my arms
Were wound about thee, and my hot lips pressed
Close, close to thine in that quick-falling dew
Of fruitful kisses, thick as autumn rains
Flash in the pools of whirling Simois!

"O mother, hear me yet before I die.
They came, they cut away my tallest pines,
My tall dark pines that plumed the craggy ledge
High over the blue gorge, and all between
The snowy peak and snow-white cataract
Fostered the callow eaglet—from beneath
Whose thick mysterious boughs in the dark morn
The panther's roar came muffled, while I sat
Low in the valley. Never, never more
Shall lone Oenone see the morning mist
Sweep through them; never see them overlaid
With narrow moonlit slips of silver cloud,
Between the low stream and the trembling stars.

"O mother, hear me yet before I die.
I wish that somewhere in the ruined folds,
Among the fragments tumbled from the glens,
Or the dry thickets, I could meet with her,
The Abominable, [4] that uninvited came
Into the fair Peleïan banquet hall,
And cast the golden fruit upon the board,
And bred this change; that I might speak my mind,
And tell her to her face how much I hate
Her presence, hated both of Gods and men.

"O mother, hear me yet before I die.
Hath he not sworn his love a thousand times,
In this green valley, under this green hill,
Even on this hand, and sitting on this stone?
Sealed it with kisses; watered it with tears?
O happy tears, and how unlike to these!
O happy heaven, how canst thou see my face?

[1] The will, tried and perfected by experience until it is redeemed from all temptation to lawlessness, attains—and only then—to perfect freedom.

[2] Idalia and Paphos, in Cyprus, were places where Venus was especially worshiped.

[3] Note the marked delaying effect of four trochaic words in an iambic line.

[4] Eris, or "Strife"; whence the apple was called the "Apple of Discord"

O happy earth, how canst thou bear my weight?
O death, death, death, thou ever-floating cloud,
There are enough unhappy on this earth,
Pass by the happy souls that love to live;
I pray thee, pass before my light of life,
And shadow all my soul, that I may die.
Thou weighest heavy on the heart within,
Weigh heavy on my eyelids; let me die.

"O mother, hear me yet before I die.
I will not die alone,[1] for fiery thoughts
Do shape themselves within me, more and more,
Whereof I catch the issue, as I hear
Dead sounds at night come from the inmost hills,
Like footsteps upon wool. I dimly see
My far-off, doubtful purpose, as a mother
Conjectures of the features of her child
Ere it is born. Her child!—a shudder comes
Across me: never child be born of me,
Unblest, to vex me with his father's eyes!

"O mother, hear me yet before I die.
Hear me, O earth. I will not die alone,
Lest their shrill happy laughter come to me
Walking the cold and starless road of death
Uncomforted, leaving my ancient love
With the Greek woman. I will rise and go
Down into Troy, and ere the stars come forth
Talk with the wild Cassandra,[2] for she says
A fire dances before her, and a sound
Rings ever in her ears of armèd men.
What this may be I know not, but I know
That wheresoe'er I am by night and day,
All earth and air seem only burning fire."

1833-42

THE LOTUS-EATERS[3]

"Courage!" he said, and pointed toward the land,
"This mounting wave will roll us shoreward soon."
In the afternon they came unto a land
In which it seemèd always afternoon.
All round the coast the languid air did swoon,
Breathing like one that hath a weary dream.
Full-faced above the valley stood the moon;
And, like a downward smoke, the slender stream
Along the cliff to fall and pause and fall did seem.

A land of streams! some, like a downward smoke,
Slow-dropping veils of thinnest lawn, did go;
And some through wavering lights and shadows broke,
Rolling a slumbrous sheet of foam below.
They saw the gleaming river seaward flow
From the inner land; far off, three mountain-tops,
Three silent pinnacles of aged snow,
Stood sunset-flushed; and, dewed with showery drops,
Up-clomb the shadowy pine above the woven copse.

The charmèd sunset lingered low adown
In the red West; through mountain clefts the dale
Was seen far inland, and the yellow down
Bordered with palm, and many a winding vale
And meadow, set with slender galingale;[4]
A land where all things always seemed the same!
And round about the keel with faces pale,
Dark faces pale against that rosy flame,
The mild-eyed, melancholy Lotus-eaters came.

Branches they bore of that enchanted stem,
Laden with flower and fruit, whereof they gave
To each, but whoso did receive of them
And taste, to him the gushing of the wave
Far, far away did seem to mourn and rave
On alien shores; and if his fellow spake,
His voice was thin, as voices from the grave;
And deep-asleep he seemed, yet all awake,
And music in his ears his beating heart did make.

They sat them down upon the yellow sand,
Between the sun and moon upon the shore;
And sweet it was to dream of Fatherland,
Of child, and wife, and slave; but evermore
Most weary seemed the sea, weary the oar,
Weary the wandering fields of barren foam.
Then some one said, "We will return no more";
And all at once they sang, "Our island home
Is far beyond the wave; we will no longer roam."

1833-42

[1] "The Death of Oenone," a late poem of Tennyson's, describes her death on the funeral pyre of Paris.
[2] sister of Paris, and a prophetess
[3] This poem is founded on the story told by Ulysses (*Odyssey* IX, 83-97) of himself and his men arriving at the land of the lotus and partaking of the "flowery food" which caused forgetfulness of home. These five Spenserian stanzas, which are followed in the original by a long "Choric Song," contain some distinct echoes of Thomson's *Castle of Indolence*, which see (p. 372).
[4] a tall sedge

SAINT AGNES' EVE

Deep on the convent roof the snows
  Are sparkling to the moon;
My breath to heaven like vapor goes;
  May my soul follow soon!
The shadows of the convent towers
  Slant down the snowy sward,
Still creeping with the creeping hours
  That lead me to my lord.
Make Thou my spirit pure and clear
  As are the frosty skies,
Or this first snowdrop of the year
  That in my bosom lies.

As these white robes are soiled and dark,
  To yonder shining ground;
As this pale taper's earthly spark,
  To yonder argent round;
So shows my soul before the Lamb,
  My spirit before Thee;
So in mine earthly house I am,
  To that I hope to be.
Break up the heavens, O Lord! and far,
  Through all yon starlight keen,
Draw me, thy bride, a glittering star,
  In raiment white and clean.

He lifts me to the golden doors;
  The flashes come and go;
All heaven bursts her starry floors,
  And strows her lights below,
And deepens on and up! The gates
  Roll back, and far within
For me the Heavenly Bridegroom waits,
  To make me pure of sin.
The Sabbaths of eternity,
  One Sabbath deep and wide—
A light upon the shining sea—
  The Bridegroom with his bride!

1837

SIR GALAHAD [1]

My good blade carves the casques of men,
  My tough lance thrusteth sure,
My strength is as the strength of ten,
  Because my heart is pure.
The shattering trumpet shrilleth high,
  The hard brands shiver on the steel,
The splintered spear-shafts crack and fly,
  The horse and rider reel;
They reel, they roll in clanging lists,
  And when the tide of combat stands,
Perfume and flowers fall in showers,
  That lightly rain from ladies' hands.

How sweet are looks that ladies bend
  On whom their favors fall!
For them I battle till the end,
  To save from shame and thrall;
But all my heart is drawn above,
  My knees are bowed in crypt [2] and shrine;
I never felt the kiss of love,
  Nor maiden's hand in mine.
More bounteous aspects on me beam,
  Me mightier transports move and thrill;
So keep I fair through faith and prayer
  A virgin heart in work and will.

When down the stormy crescent goes,
  A light before me swims,
Between dark stems the forest glows,
  I hear a noise of hymns.
Then by some secret shrine I ride;
  I hear a voice, but none are there;
The stalls are void, the doors are wide,
  The tapers burning fair.
Fair gleams the snowy altar-cloth,
  The silver vessels sparkle clean,
The shrill bell rings, the censer swings,
  And solemn chants resound between.

Sometimes on lonely mountain-meres
  I find a magic bark.
I leap on board; no helmsman steers;
  I float till all is dark.
A gentle sound, an awful light!
  Three angels bear the Holy Grail;
With folded feet, in stoles of white,
  On sleeping wings they sail.
Ah, blessed vision! blood of God!
  My spirit beats her mortal bars,
As down dark tides the glory slides,
  And starlike mingles with the stars.

When on my goodly charger borne
  Through dreaming towns I go,
The cock crows ere the Christmas morn, [3]
  The streets are dumb with snow.
The tempest crackles on the leads,
  And, ringing, springs from brand and mail;
But o'er the dark a glory spreads,
  And gilds the driving hail.
I leave the plain, I climb the height;
  No branchy thicket shelter yields;
But blessed forms in whistling storms
  Fly o'er waste fens and windy fields.

A maiden knight—to me is given
  Such hope, I know not fear;

[1] See Malory's account on pages 110-117.

[2] vault, cell

[3] Cf. Hamlet, I, i, 158.

I yearn to breathe the airs of heaven
  That often meet me here.
I muse on joy that will not cease,
  Pure spaces clothed in living beams,
Pure lilies of eternal peace,
  Whose odors haunt my dreams;
And, stricken by an angel's hand,
  This mortal armor that I wear,
This weight and size, this heart and eyes,
  Are touched, are turned to finest air.

The clouds are broken in the sky,
  And through the mountain walls
A rolling organ-harmony
  Swells up and shakes and falls.
Then move the trees, the copses nod,
  Wings flutter, voices hover clear:
"O just and faithful knight of God!
  Ride on! The prize is near."
So pass I hostel, hall, and grange;
  By bridge and ford, by park and pale,
All-armed I ride, whate'er betide,
  Until I find the Holy Grail.

1842

THE BEGGAR MAID [1]

Her arms across her breast she laid;
  She was more fair than words can say;
Barefooted came the beggar maid
  Before the king Cophetua.
In robe and crown the king stepped down
  To meet and greet her on her way;
"It is no wonder," said the lords,
  "She is more beautiful than day."

As shines the moon in clouded skies,
  She in her poor attire was seen;
One praised her ankles, one her eyes,
  One her dark hair and lovesome mien.
So sweet a face, such angel grace,
  In all that land had never been.
Cophetua sware a royal oath:
  "This beggar maid shall be my queen!"

1842

YOU ASK ME, WHY, THOUGH ILL AT EASE

You ask me, why, though ill at ease,
  Within this region I subsist,
  Whose spirits falter in the mist,
And languish for the purple seas.

It is the land that freemen till,
  That sober-suited Freedom chose,
  The land, where girt with friends or foes
A man may speak the thing he will;

A land of settled government,
  A land of just and old renown,
  Where Freedom slowly broadens down [2]
From precedent to precedent;

Where faction seldom gathers head,
  But, by degrees to fullness wrought,
  The strength of some diffusive thought
Hath time and space to work and spread.

Should banded unions persecute
  Opinion, and induce a time
  When single thought is civil crime,
And individual freedom mute,

Though power should make from land to land
  The name of Britain trebly great—
  Though every channel of the State
Should fill and choke with golden sand—

Yet waft me from the harbor mouth,
  Wild wind! I seek a warmer sky,
  And I will see before I die
The palms and temples of the South.

1842

OF OLD SAT FREEDOM ON THE HEIGHTS

Of old sat Freedom on the heights,
  The thunders breaking at her feet;
Above her shook the starry lights;
  She heard the torrents meet.

There in her place she did rejoice,
  Self-gathered in her prophet mind,
But fragments of her mighty voice
  Came rolling on the wind.

Then stepped she down through town and field
  To mingle with the human race,
And part by part to men revealed
  The fullness of her face—

Grave mother of majestic works,
  From her isle-altar gazing down,
Who, Godlike, grasps the triple forks, [3]
  And, king-like, wears the crown.

Her open eyes desire the truth.
  The wisdom of a thousand years

[1] founded on an old ballad, which may be read in Percy's *Reliques*

[2] The original reading, "broadens slowly down," which was changed for the sake of euphony, gave a more correct emphasis.

[3] Jove's thunderbolt

Is in them. May perpetual youth
 Keep dry their light from tears;

That her fair form may stand and shine,
 Make bright our days and light our dreams,
Turning to scorn with lips divine
 The falsehood of extremes!

1842

MORTE D'ARTHUR [1]

So all day long the noise of battle rolled
Among the mountains by the winter sea,
Until King Arthur's Table, man by man,
Had fallen in Lyonesse [2] about their lord,
King Arthur; then, because his wound was deep,
The bold Sir Bedivere uplifted him,
Sir Bedivere, the last of all his knights,
And bore him to a chapel nigh the field,
A broken chancel with a broken cross,
That stood on a dark strait of barren land.
On one side lay the ocean, and on one
Lay a great water, and the moon was full.

 Then spake King Arthur to Sir Bedivere:
"The sequel of today unsolders all
The goodliest fellowship of famous knights
Whereof this world holds record. Such a sleep
They sleep—the men I loved. I think that we
Shall never more, at any future time,
Delight our souls with talk of knightly deeds,
Walking about the gardens and the halls
Of Camelot, [3] as in the days that were.
I perish by this people which I made—
Though Merlin [4] sware that I should come again
To rule once more—but let what will be, be.
I am so deeply smitten through the helm
That without help I cannot last till morn.
Thou therefore take my brand Excalibur,
Which was my pride; for thou rememberest how
In those old days, one summer noon, an arm
Rose up from out the bosom of the lake,
Clothed in white samite, mystic, wonderful,
Holding the sword—and how I rowed across
And took it, and have worn it, like a king; [5]
And, wheresoever I am sung or told
In aftertime, this also shall be known.
But now delay not; take Excalibur,
And fling him far into the middle mere; [6]
Watch what thou seest, and lightly [7] bring me word."

 To him replied the bold Sir Bedivere:
"It is not meet, Sir King, to leave thee thus,
Aidless, alone, and smitten through the helm.
A little thing may harm a wounded man.
Yet I thy hest will all perform at full,
Watch what I see, and lightly bring thee word."

 So saying, from the ruined shrine he stepped
And in the moon athwart the place of tombs,
Where lay the mighty bones of ancient men,
Old knights, and over them the sea-wind sang
Shrill, chill, with flakes of foam. He, stepping down
By zigzag paths and juts of pointed rock,
Came on the shining levels of the lake.

 There drew he forth the brand Excalibur,
And o'er him, drawing it, the winter moon,
Brightening the skirts of a long cloud, ran forth
And sparkled keen with frost against the hilt;
For all the haft twinkled with diamond sparks,
Myriads of topaz lights, and jacinth work
Of subtlest jewelry. He gazed so long
That both his eyes were dazzled as he stood,
This way and that dividing the swift mind,
In act to throw; but at the last it seemed
Better to leave Excalibur concealed
There in the many-knotted water-flags
That whistled stiff and dry about the marge.
So strode he back slow to the wounded king.

 Then spake King Arthur to Sir Bedivere:
"Hast thou performed my mission which I gave?
What is it thou has seen, or what hast heard?"

 And answer made the bold Sir Bedivere:
"I heard the ripple washing in the reeds,
And the wild water lapping on the crag."

 To whom replied King Arthur, faint and pale:
"Thou hast betrayed thy nature and thy name,
Not rendering true answer, as beseemed
Thy fealty, nor like a noble knight;
For surer sign had followed, either hand,
Or voice, or else a motion of the mere.
This is a shameful thing for men to lie.
Yet now, I charge thee, quickly go again
As thou art lief [8] and dear, and do the thing

[1] See Malory's account on p. 106. This fragment was the germ of the *Idylls of the King*. It was written in 1835, and was incorporated in the "Passing of Arthur" when that was published in 1869.
[2] supposed to have been in Cornwall
[3] the capital of Arthur
[4] See pages 106-107, etc.
[5] See pages 108-109.
[6] into the mid-lake
[7] quickly
[8] beloved

I bade thee, watch, and lightly bring me word."

Then went Sir Bedivere the second time
Across the ridge, and paced beside the mere,
Counting the dewy pebbles, fixed in thought;
But when he saw the wonder of the hilt,
How curiously and strangely chased, he smote
His palms together, and he cried aloud:
"And if indeed I cast the brand away,
Surely a precious thing, one worthy note,
Should thus be lost forever from the earth,
Which might have pleased the eyes of many men.
What good should follow this, if this were done?
What harm, undone? Deep harm to disobey,
Seeing obedience is the bond of rule.
Were it well to obey then, if a king demand
An act unprofitable, against himself?
The king is sick, and knows not what he does.
What record, or what relic of my lord
Should be to aftertime, but empty breath
And rumors of a doubt? But were this kept,
Stored in some treasure house of mighty kings,
Some one might show it at a joust of arms,
Saying, 'King Arthur's sword, Excalibur,
Wrought by the lonely maiden of the lake;
Nine years she wrought it, sitting in the deeps
Upon the hidden bases of the hills.'
So might some old man speak in the aftertime
To all the people, winning reverence;
But now much honor and much fame were lost."

So spake he, clouded with his own conceit,[1]
And hid Excalibur the second time,
And so strode back slow to the wounded king.

Then spoke King Arthur, breathing heavily:
"What is it thou hast seen, or what hast heard?"

And answer made the bold Sir Bedivere:
"I heard the water lapping on the crag,
And the long ripple washing in the reeds."

To whom replied King Arthur, much in wrath:
"Ah, miserable and unkind, untrue,
Unknightly, traitor-hearted! Woe is me!
Authority forgets a dying king,
Laid widowed of the power in his eye
That bowed the will. I see thee what thou art,
For thou, the latest-left of all my knights,
In whom should meet the offices of all,
Thou wouldst betray me for the precious hilt;

[1] fancy

Either from lust of gold, or like a girl
Valuing the giddy pleasure of the eyes.
Yet, for[2] a man may fail in duty twice,
And the third time may prosper, get thee hence;
But, if thou spare to fling Excalibur,
I will arise and slay thee with my hands."

Then quickly rose Sir Bedivere, and ran,
And, leaping down the ridges lightly, plunged
Among the bulrush-beds, and clutched the sword,
And strongly wheeled and threw it. The great brand
Made lightnings in the splendor of the moon,
And flashing round and round, and whirled in an arch,
Shot like a streamer of the northern morn,
Seen where the moving isles of winter shock
By night, with noises of the northern sea.
So flashed and fell the brand Excalibur;
But ere he dipped the surface, rose an arm
Clothed in white samite, mystic, wonderful,
And caught him by the hilt, and brandished him
Three times, and drew him under in the mere.
And lightly went the other to the king.

Then spoke King Arthur, drawing thicker breath:
"Now I see by thine eyes that this is done.
Speak out; what is it thou hast heard, or seen?"

And answer made the bold Sir Bedivere:
"Sir King, I closed mine eyelids, lest the gems
Should blind my purpose, for I never saw,
Nor shall see, here or elsewhere, till I die,
Not though I live three lives of mortal men,
So great a miracle as yonder hilt.
Then with both hands I flung him, wheeling him;
But when I looked again, behold an arm,
Clothed in white samite, mystic, wonderful,
That caught him by the hilt, and branished him
Three times, and drew him under in the mere."

And answer made King Arthur, breathing hard:
"My end draws nigh; 'tis time that I were gone.
Make broad thy shoulders to receive my weight,
And bear me to the margin; yet I fear
My wound hath taken cold, and I shall die."
So saying, from the pavement he half rose,

[2] because

Slowly, with pain, reclining on his arm,
And looking wistfully with wide blue eyes
As in a picture. Him Sir Bedivere
Remorsefully regarded through his tears,
And would have spoken, but he found not words;
Then took with care, and kneeling on one knee,
O'er both his shoulders drew the languid hands,
And rising bore him through the place of tombs.

But, as he walked, King Arthur panted hard,
Like one that feels a nightmare on his bed
When all the house is mute. So sighed the king,
Muttering and murmuring at his ear, "Quick, quick!
I fear it is too late and I shall die."
But the other swiftly strode from ridge to ridge,
Clothed with his breath, and looking, as he walked,
Larger than human on the frozen hills.
He heard the deep behind him, and a cry
Before. His own thought drove him like a goad.
Dry clashed his harness in the icy caves
And barren chasms, and all to left and right
The bare black cliff clanged round him, as he based
His feet on juts of slippery crag that rang
Sharp-smitten with the dint of armèd heels—
And on a sudden, lo! the level lake,
And the long glories of the winter moon.

Then saw they how there hove a dusky barge,
Dark as a funeral scarf from stem to stern,
Beneath them; and descending they were ware
That all the decks were dense with stately forms
Black-stoled, black-hooded, like a dream—by these,
Three queens with crowns of gold—and from them rose
A cry that shivered to the tingling stars,
And, as it were one voice, an agony
Of lamentation, like a wind that shrills
All night in a waste land, where no one comes,
Or hath come, since the making of the world.

Then murmured Arthur, "Place me in the barge."
And to the barge they came. There those three queens
Put forth their hands, and took the king, and wept.
But she that rose the tallest of them all,
And fairest, laid his head upon her lap,
And loosed his shattered casque, and chafed his hands,
And called him by his name, complaining loud,
And dropping bitter tears against his brow
Striped with dark blood; for all his face was white
And colorless, and like the withered moon
Smote by the fresh beam of the springing east;
And all his greaves and cuisses dashed with drops
Of onset; and the light and lustrous curls—
That made his forehead like a rising sun
High from the dais-throne—were parched with dust;
Or, clotted into points and hanging loose,
Mixed with the knightly growth that fringed his lips.
So like a shattered column lay the king;
Not like that Arthur who, with lance in rest,
From spur to plume a star of tournament,
Shot through the lists at Camelot, and charged
Before the eyes of ladies and of kings.

Then loudly cried the bold Sir Bedivere:
"Ah! my Lord Arthur, whither shall I go?
Where shall I hide my forehead and my eyes?
For now I see the good old times are dead,
When every morning brought a noble chance,
And every chance brought out a noble knight.
Such times have not been since the light that led
The holy Elders with the gift of myrrh.
But now the whole Round Table is dissolved
Which was an image of the mighty world;
And I, the last, go forth companionless,
And the days darken round me, and the years,
Among new men, strange faces, other minds."

And slowly answered Arthur from the barge:
"The old order changeth, yielding place to new,
And God fulfills himself in many ways,
Lest one good custom should corrupt the world.
Comfort thyself; what comfort is in me?
I have lived my life, and that which I have done
May He within himself make pure! But thou,
If thou shouldst never see my face again,
Pray for my soul. More things are wrought by prayer
Than this world dreams of. Wherefore, let thy voice
Rise like a fountain for me night and day.
For what are men better than sheep or goats
That nourish a blind life within the brain,
If, knowing God, they lift not hands of prayer

Both for themselves and those who call them
friend?
For so the whole round earth is every way
Bound by gold chains about the feet of God.[1]
But now farewell. I am going a long way
With these thou seest—if indeed I go—
For all my mind is clouded with a doubt—
To the island-valley of Avilion;[2]
Where falls not hail, or rain, or any snow,
Nor ever wind blows loudly, but it lies
Deep-meadowed, happy, fair with orchard lawns
And bowery hollows crowned with summer sea,
Where I will heal me of my grievous wound."

So said he, and the barge with oar and sail
Moved from the brink, like some full-breasted
swan
That, fluting a wild carol ere her death,
Ruffles her pure cold plume, and takes the flood
With swarthy webs. Long stood Sir Bedivere
Revolving many memories, till the hull
Looked one black dot against the verge of
dawn,
And on the mere the wailing died away.

1835 1842

ULYSSES[3]

It little profits that an idle king,
By this still hearth, among these barren crags,
Matched with an aged wife, I mete and dole
Unequal laws unto a savage race
That hoard, and sleep, and feed, and know
not me.
I cannot rest from travel; I will drink
Life to the lees. All times I have enjoyed
Greatly, have suffered greatly, both with those
That loved me, and alone; on shore, and when
Through scudding drifts the rainy Hyades[4]
Vexed the dim sea. I am become a name;
For, always roaming with a hungry heart,
Much have I seen and known—cities of men,
And manners, climates, councils, governments,
Myself not least, but honored of them all—
And drunk delight of battle with my peers,
Far on the ringing plains of windy Troy.
I am a part of all that I have met;
Yet all experience is an arch wherethrough
Gleams that untraveled world whose margin
fades
For ever and for ever when I move.
How dull it is to pause, to make an end,
To rust unburnished, not to shine in use!
As though to breathe were life! Life piled on
life
Were all too little, and of one to me
Little remains; but every hour is saved
From that eternal silence, something more,
A bringer of new things: and vile it were
For some three suns to store and hoard myself,
And this gray spirit yearning in desire
To follow knowledge like a sinking star,
Beyond the utmost bound of human thought.

This is my son, mine own Telemachus,
To whom I leave the scepter and the isle—
Well-loved of me, discerning to fulfill
This labor, by slow prudence to make mild
A rugged people, and through soft degrees
Subdue them to the useful and the good.
Most blameless is he, centered in the sphere
Of common duties, decent not to fail
In offices of tenderness, and pay
Meet adoration to my household gods,
When I am gone. He works his work, I mine.

There lies the port; the vessel puffs her sail;
There gloom the dark, broad seas. My mariners.
Souls that have toiled, and wrought, and
thought with me—
That ever with a frolic welcome took
The thunder and the sunshine, and opposed
Free hearts, free foreheads—you and I are old;
Old age hath yet his honor and his toil.
Death closes all. But something ere the end,
Some work of noble note may yet be done,
Not unbecoming men that strove with Gods.
The lights begin to twinkle from the rocks;
The long day wanes; the slow moon climbs;
the deep
Moans round with many voices.[5] Come, my
friends,
'Tis not too late to seek a newer world.
Push off, and sitting well in order smite
The sounding furrows; for my purpose holds
To sail beyond the sunset, and the baths
Of all the western stars, until I die.
It may be that the gulfs will wash us down;

[1] Cf. *Paradise Lost,* II, 1051 (p. 279).
[2] the earthly paradise of medieval romance, corresponding to the Grecian Isles of the Blest
[3] The germ of the poem is found, not in the *Odyssey,* but in the story which Dante makes Ulysses tell of his adventures (*Inferno,* XXVI, 91 ff.). It was written shortly after the death of Tennyson's friend, Arthur Hallam (see *In Memoriam*), and voiced, said Tennyson, his "feelings about the need of going forward and braving the struggle of life, more simply than anything in *In Memoriam.*" (*Memoir,* I, 196.) It is an admirable complement to "The Lotus-Eaters." Of lines 62-64 Carlyle said: "These lines do not make me weep, but there is in me what would fill whole Lachrymatories as I read."
[4] Stars in the constellation Taurus, supposed to be harbingers of rain; see *Aeneid,* I, 744.
[5] Successive heavy monosyllables, long vowels, and full pauses, combine to make this a passage of remarkable weight and slowness.

It may be we shall touch the Happy Isles,[1]
And see the great Achilles, whom we knew.
Though much is taken, much abides; and though
We are not now that strength which in old days
Moved earth and heaven, that which we are, we are—
One equal temper of heroic hearts,
Made weak by time and fate, but strong in will
To strive, to seek, to find, and not to yield.

1842

LOCKSLEY HALL[2]

Comrades, leave me here a little, while as yet 'tis early morn;
Leave me here, and when you want me, sound upon the bugle horn.

'Tis the place, and all around it, as of old, the curlews call,
Dreary gleams about the moorland flying over Locksley Hall;

Locksley Hall, that in the distance overlooks the sandy tracts,
And the hollow ocean-ridges roaring into cataracts.

Many a night from yonder, ivied casement, ere I went to rest,
Did I look on great Orion sloping slowly to the west.

Many a night I saw the Pleiads, rising through the mellow shade,
Glitter like a swarm of fireflies tangled in a silver braid.

Here about the beach I wandered, nourishing a youth sublime
With the fairy tales of science, and the long result of time;

When the centuries behind me like a fruitful land reposed;
When I clung to all the present for the promise that it closed;[3]

When I dipped into the future far as human eye could see,
Saw the vision of the world and all the wonder that would be.—

In the spring a fuller crimson comes upon the robin's breast;
In the spring the wanton lapwing gets himself another crest;

In the spring a livelier iris changes on the burnished dove;
In the spring a young man's fancy lightly turns to thoughts of love.

Then her cheek was pale and thinner than should be for one so young,
And her eyes on all my motions with a mute observance hung.

And I said, "My cousin Amy, speak, and speak the truth to me,
Trust me, cousin, all the current of my being sets to thee."

On her pallid cheek and forehead came a color and a light,
As I have seen the rosy red flushing in the northern night.

And she turned—her bosom shaken with a sudden storm of sighs—
All the spirit deeply dawning in the dark of hazel eyes—

Saying, "I have hid my feelings, fearing they should do me wrong";
Saying, "Dost thou love me, cousin?" weeping, "I have loved thee long."

Love took up the glass of Time, and turned it in his glowing hands;
Every moment, lightly shaken, ran itself in golden sands.

Love took up the harp of Life, and smote on all the chords with might;
Smote the chord of Self, that, trembling, passed in music out of sight.

Many a morning on the moorland did we hear the copses ring,
And her whisper thronged my pulses with the fullness of the spring.

Many an evening by the waters did we watch the stately ships,
And our spirits rushed together at the touching of the lips.

O my cousin, shallow-hearted! O my Amy, mine no more!
O the dreary, dreary moorland! O the barren, barren shore!

Falser than all fancy fathoms, falser than all songs have sung,

[1] Compare note on "Morte D'Arthur," l. 259.

[2] This was intended to be a purely dramatic poem, giving expression to the conflicting and somewhat morbid feelings characteristic perhaps of introspective youth at any time, but with particular reference both to contemporary social conditions in England (it was published in 1842), and to the fresh spur given to imagination by the discoveries in science and mechanics. Some forty years later, Tennyson wrote a sequel, "Locksley Hall Sixty Years After."

[3] enclosed

Puppet to a father's threat, and servile to a shrewish tongue!

Is it well to wish thee happy; having known me—to decline
On a range of lower feelings and a narrower heart than mine?

Yet it shall be; thou shalt lower to his level day by day,
What is fine within thee growing coarse to sympathize with clay.

As the husband is, the wife is; thou art mated with a clown,
And the grossness of his nature will have weight to drag thee down.

He will hold thee, when his passion shall have spent its novel force,
Something better than his dog, a little dearer than his horse.

What is this? His eyes are heavy; think not they are glazed with wine.
Go to him, it is thy duty; kiss him, take his hand in thine.

It may be my lord is weary, that his brain is overwrought;
Soothe him with thy finer fancies, touch him with thy lighter thought.

He will answer to the purpose, easy things to understand—
Better thou were dead before me, though I slew thee with my hand!

Better thou and I were lying, hidden from the heart's disgrace,
Rolled in one another's arms, and silent in a last embrace.

Cursed be the social wants that sin against the strength of youth!
Cursed be the social lies that warp us from the living truth!
Cursed be the sickly forms that err from honest nature's rule!
Cursed be the gold that gilds the straightened forehead of the fool!
Well—'tis well that I should bluster!—Hadst thou less unworthy proved—
Would to God—for I had loved thee more than ever wife was loved.
Am I mad that I should cherish that which bears but bitter fruit?

I will pluck it from my bosom, though my heart be at the root.

Never, though my mortal summers to such length of years should come
As the many-wintered crow that leads the clanging rookery home.

Where is comfort? In division of the records of the mind?

Can I part her from herself, and love her, as I knew her, kind?

I remember one that perished;[1] sweetly did she speak and move;

Such a one do I remember, whom to look at was to love.

Can I think of her as dead, and love her for the love she bore?
No—she never loved me truly; love is love forevermore.

Comfort? Comfort scorned of devils! This is truth the poet sings,
That a sorrow's crown of sorrow is remembering happier things.[2]

Drug thy memories, lest thou learn it, lest thy heart be put to proof,
In the dead unhappy night, and when the rain is on the roof.

Like a dog, he hunts in dreams, and thou art staring at the wall,
Where the dying night-lamp flickers, and the shadows rise and fall.

Then a hand shall pass before thee, pointing to his drunken sleep,
To the widowed marriage-pillows, to the tears that thou wilt weep.

Thou shalt hear the "Never, never," whispered by the phantom years,
And a song from out the distance in the ringing of thine ears;

And an eye shall vex thee, looking ancient kindness on thy pain.
Turn thee, turn thee on thy pillow; get thee to thy rest again.

Nay, but Nature brings thee solace; for a tender voice will cry.
'Tis a purer life than thine, a lip to drain thy trouble dry.

Baby lips will laugh me down; my latest rival brings thee rest.
Baby fingers, waxen touches, press me from the mother's breast.

[1] i.e., she has lost the personality which I remember
[2] Dante: *Inferno*, V, 121; the thought may be traced to many writers—to Pindar, among the earliest.

Oh, the child, too, clothes the father with a dearness not his due.
Half is thine and half is his; it will be worthy of the two.

Oh, I see thee old and formal, fitted to thy petty part,
With a little hoard of maxims preaching down a daughter's heart.

"They were dangerous guides, the feelings—she herself was not exempt—
Truly, she herself had suffered" [1]—Perish in thy self-contempt!

Overlive it—lower yet—be happy! Wherefore should I care?
I myself must mix with action, lest I wither by despair.

What is that which I should turn to, lighting upon days like these?
Every door is barred with gold, and opens but to golden keys.

Every gate is thronged with suitors, all the markets overflow.
I have but an angry fancy; what is that which I should do?

I had been content to perish, falling on the foeman's ground,
When the ranks are rolled in vapor, and the winds are laid with sound.

But the jingling of the guinea helps the hurt that Honor feels,
And the nations do but murmur, snarling at each other's heels.

Can I but relive in sadness? I will turn that earlier page.
Hide me from my deep emotion, O thou wondrous Mother-Age! [2]

Make me feel the wild pulsation that I felt before the strife,
When I heard my days before me, and the tumult of my life;

Yearning for the large excitement that the coming years would yield,
Eager-hearted as a boy when first he leaves his father's field,

And at night along the dusky highway, near and nearer drawn,
Sees in heaven the light of London flaring like a dreary dawn;

And his spirit leaps within him to be gone before him then,
Underneath the light he looks at, in among the throngs of men;

Men, my brothers, men the workers, ever reaping something new;
That which they have done but earnest of the things that they shall do.

For I dipped into the future, far as human eye could see,
Saw the Vision of the world, and all the wonder that would be;

Saw the heavens fill with commerce, argosies of magic sails,
Pilots of the purple twilight, dropping down with costly bales; [3]

Heard the heavens fill with shouting, and there rained a ghastly dew
From the nations' airy navies grappling in the central blue;

Far along the world-wide whisper of the south wind rushing warm,
With the standards of the peoples plunging through the thunderstorm;

Till the war drum throbbed no longer, and the battle flags were furled
In the Parliament of man, the Federation of the world.

There the common sense of most shall hold a fretful realm in awe,
And the kindly earth shall slumber, lapped [4] in universal law.

So I triumphed ere my passion sweeping through me left my dry,
Left me with the palsied heart, and left me with the jaundiced eye;

Eye, to which all order festers, all things here are out of joint. [5]
Science moves, but slowly, slowly, creeping on from point to point;

Slowly comes a hungry people, as a lion, creeping nigher,

[1] Amy is imagined to be talking to her daughter, at some future time, of her own early life.

[2] Cf. line 185.

[3] Tennyson had a rare faculty for putting the hopes and achievements of science into poetic language. It is interesting, however, to observe at what a cautious distance he placed the realization of this seemingly extravagant prophecy.

[4] wrapped

[5] He of the "jaundiced eye" scoffs at science and is suspicious of democratic and socialistic tendencies. The weak point in Tennyson's picture is the connection of this large pessimism with the purely personal disappointment of his hero. It may not be altogether unreal, but it is undramatic.

Glares at one that nods and winks behind a slowly-dying fire.

Yet I doubt not through the ages one increasing purpose runs,
And the thoughts of men are widened with the process of the suns.

What is that to him that reaps not harvest of his youthful joys,
Though the deep heart of existence beat forever like a boy's?

Knowledge comes, but wisdom lingers, and I linger on the shore,
And the individual withers, and the world is more and more.[1]

Knowledge comes, but wisdom lingers, and he bears a laden breast,
Full of sad experience, moving toward the stillness of his rest.

Hark, my merry comrades call me, sounding on the bugle horn,
They to whom my foolish passion were a target for their scorn.

Shall it not be scorn to me to harp on such a moldered string?
I am shamed through all my nature to have loved so slight a thing.

Weakness to be wroth with weakness! Woman's pleasure, woman's pain—
Nature made them blinder motions [2] bounded in a shallower brain.

Woman is the lesser man, and all thy passions, matched with mine,
Are as moonlight unto sunlight, and as water unto wine—

Here at least, where nature sickens, nothing. [3] Ah, for some retreat
Deep in yonder shining Orient, where my life began to beat,

Where in wild Mahratta-battle [4] fell my father evil-starred;
I was left a trampled orphan, and a selfish uncle's ward.

Or to burst all links of habit—there to wander far away,
On from island unto island at the gateways of the day.

Larger constellations burning, mellow moons and happy skies,
Breadths of tropic shade and palms in cluster, knots of Paradise. [5]

Never comes the trader, never floats an European flag,
Slides the bird o'er lustrous woodland, swings the trailer from the crag;

Droops the heavy-blossomed bower, hangs the heavy-fruited tree—
Summer isles of Eden lying in dark-purple spheres of sea.

There methinks would be enjoyment more than in this march of mind,
In the steamship, in the railway, in the thoughts that shake mankind.

There the passions cramped no longer shall have scope and breathing space;
I will take some savage woman, she shall rear my dusky race.

Iron-jointed, supple-sinewed, they shall dive, and they shall run,
Catch the wild goat by the hair, and hurl their lances in the sun;

Whistle back the parrot's call, and leap the rainbows of the brooks,
Not with blinded eyesight poring over miserable books—

Fool, again the dream, the fancy! But I *know* my words are wild,
But I count the gray barbarian lower than the Christian child.

I, to herd with narrow foreheads, vacant of our glorious gains,
Like a beast with lower pleasures, like a beast with lower pains!

Mated with a squalid savage—what to me were sun or clime!
I the heir of all the ages, in the foremost files of time—

I that rather held it better men should perish one by one,
Than that earth should stand at gaze like Joshua's moon in Ajalon! [6]

Not in vain the distance beacons. Forward, forward let us range,
Let the great world spin forever down the ringing grooves of change. [7]

[1] Looms forever larger by contrast. Cf. *In Memoriam,* lv.
[2] beings
[3] Implying that the inferiority of woman may be the result of the conventions of a false civilization; compare *The Princess.*
[4] The British have had many conflicts with the warlike Mahrattas of India.
[5] See *Par. Lost,* iv, 242.
[6] *Joshua,* x, 13
[7] Tennyson drew this figure from the railway, then new, under the false impression that the car wheels ran in grooves.

Through the shadow of the globe we sweep into the younger day;
Better fifty years of Europe than a cycle of Cathay.

Mother-Age—for mine I knew not—help me as when life begun;
Rift the hills, and roll the waters, flash the lightnings, weigh the sun.

Oh, I see the crescent promise of my spirit hath not set.
Ancient founts of inspiration well through all my fancy yet.

Howsoever these things be, a long farewell to Locksley Hall!
Now for me the woods may wither, now for me the rooftree fall.

Comes a vapor from the margin, blackening over heath and holt,
Cramming all the blast before it, in its breast a thunderbolt.

Let it fall on Locksley Hall, with rain or hail, or fire or snow;
For the mighty wind arises, roaring seaward, and I go.

1842

A FAREWELL

Flow down, cold rivulet, to the sea,
Thy tribute wave deliver;
No more by thee my steps shall be,
Forever and forever.

Flow, softly flow, by lawn and lea,
A rivulet, then a river;
Nowhere by thee my steps shall be,
Forever and forever.

But here will sigh thine alder tree,
And here thine aspen shiver;
And here by thee will hum the bee,
Forever and forever.

A thousand suns will stream on thee,
A thousand moons will quiver;
But not by thee my steps shall be,
Forever and forever.

1842

BREAK, BREAK, BREAK [1]

Break, break, break,
On thy cold gray stones, O Sea!
And I would that my tongue could utter
The thoughts that arise in me.

Oh, well for the fisherman's boy
That he shouts with his sister at play!
Oh, well for the sailor lad
That he sings in his boat on the bay!

And the stately ships go on
To their haven under the hill;
But, oh, for the touch of a vanished hand,
And the sound of a voice that is still!

Break, break, break,
At the foot of thy crags, O Sea!
But the tender grace of a day that is dead
Will never come back to me.

1842

SONGS from THE PRINCESS

Sweet and Low

Sweet and low, sweet and low,
Wind of the western sea,
Low, low, breathe and blow,
Wind of the western sea!
Over the rolling waters go,
Come from the dying moon, and blow,
Blow him again to me;
While my little one, while my pretty one, sleeps.

Sleep and rest, sleep and rest,
Father will come to thee soon;
Rest, rest, on mother's breast,
Father will come to thee soon;
Father will come to his babe in the nest,
Silver sails all out of the west
Under the silver moon;
Sleep, my little one, sleep, my pretty one, sleep.

1850

The Splendor Falls [2]

The splendor falls on castle walls
And snowy summits old in story;
The long light shakes across the lakes,
And the wild cataract leaps in glory.
Blow, bugle, blow, set the wild echoes flying,
Blow, bugle; answer, echoes, dying, dying, dying.

Oh, hark, oh, hear! how thin and clear,
And thinner, clearer, farther going!
Oh, sweet and far from cliff and scar
The horns of Elfland faintly blowing!
Blow, let us hear the purple glens replying,
Blow, bugle; answer, echoes, dying, dying, dying.

O love, they die in yon rich sky,
They faint on hill or field or river;

[1] These lines were written in memory of Arthur Hallam, and might well have been included among the poems of *In Memoriam* had they not been cast in a different meter.

[2] This song was inspired by the echoes at the Lakes of Killarney.

Our echoes roll from soul to soul,
  And grow forever and forever.
Blow, bugle, blow, set the wild echoes flying,
And answer, echoes, answer, dying, dying,
    dying.

1848 1850

Tears, Idle Tears

  Tears, idle tears, I know not what they mean,
Tears from the depth of some divine despair
Rise in the heart, and gather to the eyes,
In looking on the happy autumn fields,
And thinking of the days that are no more.

  Fresh as the first beam glittering on a sail,
That brings our friends up from the under-
    world,
Sad as the last which reddens over one
That sinks with all we love below the verge;
So sad, so fresh, the days that are no more.

  Ah, sad and strange as in dark summer
    dawns
The earliest pipe of half-awakened birds
To dying ears, when unto dying eyes
The casement slowly grows a glimmering
    square;
So sad, so strange, the days that are no more.

  Dear as remembered kisses after death,
And sweet as those by hopeless fancy feigned
On lips that are for others; deep as love,
Deep as first love, and wild with all regret;
O Death in Life, the days that are no more!

1847

From IN MEMORIAM [1]

I

I held it the truth, with him [2] who sings
  To one clear harp in divers tones,
  That men may rise on stepping-stones
Of their dead selves to higher things.

But who shall so forecast the years
  And find in loss a gain to match?
  Or reach a hand through time to catch
The far-off interest of tears?

Let Love clasp Grief lest both be drowned,
  Let darkness keep her raven gloss. [3]
  Ah, sweeter to be drunk with loss,
To dance with Death, to beat the ground,

Than that the Victor Hours should scorn
  The long [4] result of love, and boast,
  "Behold the man that loved and lost,
But all he was is overworn."

. . . . . .

XXVII

I envy not in any moods
  The captive void of noble rage,
  The linnet born within the cage,
That never knew the summer woods;

I envy not the beast that takes
  His license in the field of time,
  Unfettered by the sense of crime,
To whom a conscience never wakes;

Nor, what may count itself as blest,
  The heart that never plighted troth
  But stagnates in the weeds of sloth;
Nor any want-begotten rest. [5]

I hold it true, whate'er befall;
  I feel it, when I sorrow most;
  'Tis better to have loved and lost
Than never to have loved at all.

. . . . . .

LIV

Oh, yet we trust that somehow good
  Will be the final goal of ill,
  To pangs of nature, sins of will,
Defects of doubt, and taints of blood;

That nothing walks with aimless feet;
  That not one life shall be destroyed,
  Or cast as rubbish to the void,
When God hath made the pile complete;

That not a worm is cloven in vain;
  That not a moth with vain desire
  Is shriveled in a fruitless fire,
Or but subserves another's gain.

Behold, we know not anything;
  I can but trust that good shall fall
  At last—far off—at last, to all,
And every winter change to spring.

So runs my dream; but what am I?
  An infant crying in the night;
  An infant crying for the light,
And with no language but a cry.

[1] Tennyson's friend, Arthur Henry Hallam, died at Vienna in 1833. The short poems written in his memory at various times and in various moods, Tennyson arranged and published in the year 1850. The earlier poems are chiefly personal in nature; the later treat some of the larger problems of human life and destiny thrust on Tennyson by personal bereavement and the unrest produced by the changes taking place in the realms of religious and scientific thought.

[2] Goethe, says Tennyson.

[3] Cf. Milton's "Comus," 251.

[4] Used poetically for "ultimate"; Cf. "Locksley Hall," l. 12.

[5] content due to mere want of higher faculties

LV

The wish, that of the living whole
No life may fail beyond the grave,
Derives it not from what we have
The likest God within the soul?

Are God and Nature then at strife,
That Nature lends such evil dreams?
So careful of the type she seems,
So careless of the single life,

That I, considering everywhere
Her secret meaning in her deeds,
And finding that of fifty seeds
She often brings but one to bear,

I falter where I firmly trod,
And falling with my weight of cares
Upon the great world's altar-stairs
That slope through darkness up to God,

I stretch lame hands of faith, and grope,
And gather dust and chaff, and call
To what I feel is Lord of all,
And faintly trust the larger hope.

LVI

"So careful of the type?" but no,
From scarpèd cliff and quarried stone [1]
She cries, "A thousand types are gone;
I care for nothing, all shall go.

"Thou makest thine appeal to me:
I bring to life, I bring to death;
The spirit does but mean the breath.
I know no more." And he, shall he,

Man, her last work, who seemed so fair,
Such splendid purpose in his eyes,
Who rolled the psalm to wintry skies,
Who built him fanes of fruitless prayer,

Who trusted God was love indeed
And love Creation's final law—
Though Nature, red in tooth and claw
With ravine, shrieked against his creed—

Who loved, who suffered countless ills,
Who battled for the True, the Just,
Be blown about the desert dust,
Or sealed within the iron hills?

No more? A monster then, a dream,
A discord. Dragons of the prime,
That tear each other in their slime,
Were mellow music matched with him.

O life as futile, then, as frail!
Oh, for thy voice to soothe and bless!
What hope of answer, or redress?
Behind the veil, behind the veil.

[1] which shows fossil remains of extinct forms

LVII

Peace; come away. The song of woe
Is after all an earthly song.
Peace; come away: we do him wrong
To sing so wildly; let us go.

Come; let us go: your cheeks are pale;
But half my life I leave behind. [2]
Methinks my friend is richly shrined; [3]
But I shall pass, my work will fail.

Yet in these ears, till hearing dies,
One set slow bell will seem to toll
The passing of the sweetest soul
That ever looked with human eyes.

I hear it now, and o'er and o'er,
Eternal greetings to the dead;
And "Ave, Ave, Ave," said,
"Adieu, adieu," forevermore.

LVIII

In those sad words I took farewell.
Like echoes in sepulchral halls,
As drop by drop the water falls
In vaults and catacombs, they fell;

And, falling, idly broke the peace
Of hearts that beat from day to day,
Half-conscious [4] of their dying clay,
And those cold crypts where they shall cease.

The high Muse answered: "Wherefore grieve
Thy brethren with a fruitless tear?
Abide a little longer here,
And thou shalt take a nobler leave."

. . . . .

CIV

The time draws near the birth of Christ; [5]
The moon is hid, the night is still;
A single church below the hill
Is pealing, folded in the mist.

A single peal of bells below,
That wakens at this hour of rest
A single murmur in the breast,
That these are not the bells I know.

Like strangers' voices here they sound,
In lands where not a memory strays,
Nor landmark breathes of other days,
But all is new unhallowed ground.

. . . . . .

[2] in the grave
[3] in these poems
[4] only half-conscious
[5] This is the third Christmas described in the poem. Tennyson had removed to a new home.

CVI

Ring out, wild bells, to the wild sky,
  The flying cloud, the frosty light:
  The year is dying in the night;
Ring out, wild bells, and let him die.

Ring out the old, ring in the new,
  Ring, happy bells, across the snow:
  The year is going, let him go;
Ring out the false, ring in the true.

Ring out the grief that saps the mind,
  For those that here we see no more;
  Ring out the feud of rich and poor;
Ring in redress to all mankind.

Ring out a slowly dying cause,
  And ancient forms of party strife;
  Ring in the nobler modes of life,
With sweeter manners, purer laws.

Ring out the want, the care, the sin,
  The faithless coldness of the times;
  Ring out, ring out my mournful rimes,
But ring the fuller minstrel in.

Ring out false pride in place and blood,
  The civic slander and the spite;
  Ring in the love of truth and right,
Ring in the common love of good.

Ring out old shapes of foul disease;
  Ring out the narrowing lust of gold;
  Ring out the thousand wars of old,
Ring in the thousand years of peace.

Ring in the valiant man and free,
  The larger heart, the kindlier hand;
  Ring out the darkness of the land,
Ring in the Christ that is to be.

. . . .

CXV

Now fades the last long streak of snow,
  Now burgeons every maze of quick [1]
  About the flowering squares, [2] and thick
By ashen roots the violets blow.

Now rings the woodland loud and long,
  The distance takes a lovelier hue,
  And drowned in yonder living blue
The lark becomes a sightless song.

Now dance the lights on lawn and lea,
  The flocks are whiter down the vale,
  And milkier every milky sail
On winding stream or distant sea;

Where now the seamew pipes, or dives
  In yonder greening gleam, and fly
  The happy birds that change their sky
To build and brood, that live their lives

From land to land; and in my breast
  Spring wakens, too, and my regret
  Becomes an April violet,
And buds and blossoms like the rest.

CXVI

Is it, then, regret for buried time
  That keenlier in sweet April wakes,
  And meets the year, and gives and takes
The colors of the crescent prime? [3]

Not all: the songs, the stirring air,
  The life re-orient out of dust,
  Cry through the sense to hearten trust
In that which made the world so fair.

Not all regret: the face will shine
  Upon me, while I muse alone,
  And that dear voice, I once have known,
Still speak to me of me and mine.

Yet loss of sorrow lives in me
  For days of happy commune dead.
  Less yearning for the friendship fled
Than some strong bond which is to be.

CXVII

O days and hours, your work is this,
  To hold me from my proper place,
  A little while from his embrace,
For fuller gain of after bliss;

That out of distance might ensue
  Desire of nearness doubly sweet,
  And unto meeting, when we meet,
Delight a hundredfold accrue,

For every grain of sand that runs, [4]
  And every span of shade that steals,
  And every kiss of toothèd wheels,
And all the courses of the suns.

CXVIII

Contemplate all this work of Time,
  The giant laboring in his youth;
  Nor dream of human love and truth,
As dying Nature's earth and lime;

But trust that those we call the dead
  Are breathers of an ampler day
  For ever nobler ends. They say
The solid earth whereon we tread

In tracts of fluent heat began,
  And grew to seeming-random forms,

[1] hedge (especially hawthorn)
[2] fields
[3] increasing Spring
[4] This stanza describes the various means of measuring time.

The seeming prey of cyclic[1] storms,
Till at the last arose the man;

Who throve and branched from clime to clime,
The herald of a higher race,
And of himself in higher place,
If so he type[2] this work of time

Within himself, from more to more;
Or, crowned with attributes of woe
Like glories, move his course, and show
That life is not as idle ore,

But iron dug from central gloom,
And heated hot with burning fears,
And dipped in baths of hissing tears,
And battered with the shocks of doom

To shape and use. Arise and fly
The reeling Faun, the sensual feast;
Move upward, working out the beast,
And let the ape and tiger die.

. . . . .

CXXV

Whatever I have said or sung,
Some bitter notes my harp would give,
Yea, though there often seemed to live
A contradiction on the tongue.

Yet Hope had never lost her youth,
She did but look through dimmer eyes;
Or Love but played with gracious lies,
Because he felt so fixed in truth;

And if the song were full of care,
He breathed the spirit of the song;
And if the words were sweet and strong
He set his royal signet there;

Abiding with me till I sail
To seek thee on the mystic deeps,
And this electric force, that keeps
A thousand pulses dancing, fail.

CXXVI

Love is and was my lord and king,
And in his presence I attend
To hear the tidings of my friend,
Which every hour his couriers bring.

Love is and was my king and lord,
And will be, though as yet I keep
Within the court on earth, and sleep
Encompassed by his faithful guard,

And hear at times a sentinel
Who moves about from place to place,
And whispers to the worlds of space,
In the deep night, that all is well.

[1] periodic (in a large sense)
[2] represent (properly)

CXXVII

And all is well, though faith and form
Be sundered in the night of fear;
Well roars the storm to those that hear
A deeper voice across the storm,

Proclaiming social truth shall spread,
And justice, even though thrice again
The red fool-fury of the Seine
Should pile her barricades with dead.[3]

But ill for him that wears a crown,
And him, the lazar, in his rags!
They tremble, the sustaining crags;
The spires of ice are toppled down,

And molten up, and roar in flood;
The fortress crashes from on high,
The brute earth lightens to the sky,
And the great Aeon sinks in blood,

And compassed by the fires of hell;
While thou, dear spirit, happy star,
O'erlook'st the tumult from afar,
And smilest, knowing all is well.

. . . . .

1833-50 1850

IN THE VALLEY OF CAUTERETZ[4]

All along the valley, stream that flashest white,
Deepening thy voice with the deepening of the night,
All along the valley, where thy waters flow,
I walked with one I loved two and thirty years ago.
All along the valley, while I walked today,
The two and thirty years were a mist that rolls away;
For all along the valley, down thy rocky bed,
Thy living voice to me was as the voice of the dead,
And all along the valley, by rock and cave and tree,
The voice of the dead was a living voice to me.

1861 1864

IN THE GARDEN AT SWAINSTON[5]

Nightingales warbled without,
Within was weeping for thee;
Shadows of three dead men

[3] There was a violent revolution in France in 1830, resulting in the overthrow of Charles X.
[4] In 1861, Tennyson revisited this valley in the French Pyrenees which he had visited with Hallam in 1830.
[5] The home of Sir John Simeon in the Isle of Wight, where Tennyson also lived in the latter part of his life; Sir John died in 1870. The other two friends referred to were Arthur Hallam (see preceding poems) and Henry Lushington (d. 1855), to whom Tennyson had dedicated *The Princess*. All three, by a curious coincidence, died abroad.

Walked in the garden with me,
Shadows of three dead men, and thou wast one of the three.

Nightingales sang in his woods,
The Master was far away;
Nightingales warbled and sang
Of a passion that lasts but a day;
Still in the house in his coffin the Prince of courtesy lay.

Two dead men have I known
In courtesy like to thee;
Two dead men have I loved
With a love that ever will be;
Three dead men have I loved, and thou art last of the three.

1870 1874

SONG from MAUD [1]

Come into the garden, Maud,
For the black bat, night, has flown,
Come into the garden, Maud,
I am here at the gate alone;
And the woodbine spices are wafted abroad,
And the musk of the rose is blown.

For a breeze of morning moves,
And the planet of love is on high,
Beginning to faint in the light that she loves
On a bed of daffodil sky,
To faint in the light of the sun she loves,
To faint in his light, and to die.

All night have the roses heard
The flute, violin, bassoon;
All night has the casement jessamine stirred
To the dancers dancing in tune;
Till a silence fell with the waking bird,
And a hush with the setting moon.

I said to the lily, "There is but one,
With whom she has heart to be gay.
When will the dancers leave her alone?
She is weary of dance and play."
Now half to the setting moon are gone,
And half to the rising day;
Low on the sand and loud on the stone
The last wheel echoes away.

I said to the rose, "The brief night goes
In babble and revel and wine.
O young lord-lover, what sighs are those,
For one that will never be thine?
But mine, but mine," so I sware to the rose,
"For ever and ever, mine."

And the soul of the rose went into my blood,
As the music clashed in the Hall;
And long by the garden lake I stood,
For I heard your rivulet fall
From the lake to the meadow and on to the wood,
Our wood, that is dearer than all;

From the meadow your walks have left so sweet
That whenever a March wind sighs
He sets the jewel-print of your feet
In violets blue as your eyes,
To the woody hollows in which we meet
And the valleys of Paradise.

The slender acacia would not shake
One long milk-bloom on the tree;
The white lake-blossom fell into the lake
As the pimpernel dozed on the lea;
But the rose was awake all night for your sake,
Knowing your promise to me;
The lilies and roses were all awake,
They sighed for the dawn and thee.

Queen rose of the rosebud garden of girls,
Come hither, the dances are done,
In gloss of satin and glimmer of pearls,
Queen lily and rose in one;
Shine out, little head, sunning over with curls,
To the flowers, and be their sun.

There has fallen a splendid tear
From the passion flower at the gate,
She is coming, my dove, my dear;
She is coming, my life, my fate.
The red rose cries, "She is near, she is near";
And the white rose weeps, "She is late";
The larkspur listens, "I hear, I hear";
And the lily whispers, "I wait."

She is coming, my own, my sweet;
Were it ever so airy a tread,
My heart would hear her and beat,
Were it earth in an earthy bed;
My dust would hear her and beat,
Had I lain for a century dead,
Would start and tremble under her feet,
And blossom in purple and red.

1855

THE CHARGE OF THE LIGHT BRIGADE [2]

Half a league, half a league,
Half a league onward,
All in the valley of Death
Rode the six hundred.

[1] There is a distinct echo in this song of *The Song of Solomon;* cf. chapters v and vi.

[2] This fatal charge, due to a misunderstanding of orders, was made at Balaklava, in the Crimea, in 1854. Less than one-third of the brigade returned alive.

"Forward the Light Brigade!
Charge for the guns!" he said.
Into the valley of Death
Rode the six hundred.

"Forward, the Light Brigade!"
Was there a man dismayed?
Not though the soldier knew
Some one had blundered.
Theirs not to make reply,
Theirs not to reason why,
Theirs but to do and die.
Into the valley of Death
Rode the six hundred.

Cannon to right of them,
Cannon to left of them,
Cannon in front of them
Volleyed and thundered;
Stormed at with shot and shell,
Boldly they rode and well,
Into the jaws of Death,
Into the mouth of hell
Rode the six hundred.

Flashed all their sabers bare,
Flashed as they turned in air
Sabring the gunners there,
Charging an army, while
All the world wondered.
Plunged in the battery-smoke
Right through the line they broke;
Cossack and Russian
Reeled from the saber stroke
Shattered and sundered.
Then they rode back, but not,
Not the six hundred.

Cannon to right of them,
Cannon to left of them,
Cannon behind them
Volleyed and thundered;
Stormed at with shot and shell,
While horse and hero fell,
They that had fought so well
Came through the jaws of Death,
Back from the mouth of hell,
All that was left of them,
Left of six hundred.

When can their glory fade?
Oh, the wild charge they made!
All the world wondered.
Honor the charge they made!
Honor the Light Brigade,
Noble six hundred!

1854 1854

THE CAPTAIN

A LEGEND OF THE NAVY

He that only rules by terror
Doeth grievous wrong.
Deep as hell I count his error.
Let him hear my song.
Brave the captain was; the seamen
Made a gallant crew,
Gallant sons of English freemen,
Sailors bold and true.
But they hated his oppression;
Stern he was and rash,
So for every light transgression
Doomed them to the lash.
Day by day more harsh and cruel
Seemed the Captain's mood.
Secret wrath like smothered fuel
Burnt in each man's blood.
Yet he hoped to purchase glory,
Hoped to make the name
Of his vessel great in story,
Wheresoe'er he came.
So they passed by capes and islands,
Many a harbor mouth,
Sailing under palmy highlands
Far within the south.
On a day when they were going
O'er the lone expanse,
In the north, her canvas flowing,
Rose a ship of France.
Then the Captain's color heightened,
Joyful came his speech;
But a cloudy gladness lightened
In the eyes of each.
"Chase," he said; the ship flew forward,
And the wind did blow;
Stately, lightly, went she norward,
Till she neared the foe.
Then they looked at him they hated,
Had what they desired;
Mute with folded arms they waited—
Not a gun was fired.
But they heard the foeman's thunder
Roaring out their doom;
All the air was torn in sunder,
Crashing went the boom,
Spars were splintered, decks were shattered,
Bullets fell like rain;
Over mast and deck were scattered
Blood and brains of men.
Spars were splintered; decks were broken;
Every mother's son—
Down they dropped—no word was spoken—
Each beside his gun.

On the decks as they were lying,
Were their faces grim.
In their blood, as they lay dying,
Did they smile on him.
Those in whom he had reliance
For his noble name
With one smile of still defiance
Sold him unto shame.
Shame and wrath his heart confounded,
Pale he turned and red,
Till himself was deadly wounded
Falling on the dead.
Dismal error! fearful slaughter!
Years have wandered by;
Side by side beneath the water
Crew and Captain lie;
There the sunlit ocean tosses
O'er them moldering,
And the lonely seabird crosses
With one waft of the wing.

1865

THE REVENGE[1]

A BALLAD OF THE FLEET

I

At Flores in the Azores Sir Richard Grenville lay,
And a pinnace, like a fluttered bird, came flying from far away;
"Spanish ships of war at sea! we have sighted fifty-three!"
Then sware Lord Thomas Howard: "'Fore God I am no coward;
But I cannot meet them here, for my ships are out of gear,
And the half my men are sick. I must fly, but follow quick.
We are six ships of the line;[2] can we fight with fifty-three?"

II

Then spake Sir Richard Grenville: "I know you are no coward;
You fly them for a moment to fight with them again.
But I've ninety men and more that are lying sick ashore.
I should count myself the coward if I left them, my Lord Howard,
To these Inquisition dogs and the devildoms of Spain."

III

So Lord Howard passed away with five ships of war that day,
Till he melted like a cloud in the silent summer heaven;
But Sir Richard bore in hand all his sick men from the land
Very carefully and slow,
Men of Bideford in Devon,
And we laid them on the ballast down below:
For we brought them all aboard,
And they blessed him in their pain, that they were not left to Spain,
To the thumb-screw and the stake, for the glory of the Lord.

IV

He had only a hundred seamen to work the ship, and to fight,
And he sailed away from Flores till the Spaniard came in sight,
With his huge sea-castles heaving upon the weather bow.
"Shall we fight or shall we fly?
Good Sir Richard, tell us now,
For to fight is but to die!
There'll be little of us left by the time this sun be set."
And Sir Richard said again: "We be all good English men.
Let us bang these dogs of Seville, the children of the devil,
For I never turned my back upon Don or devil yet."

V

Sir Richard spoke and he laughed, and we roared a hurrah, and so
The little Revenge ran on sheer into the heart of the foe,
With her hundred fighters on deck, and her ninety sick below;
For half of their fleet to the right and half to the left were seen,
And the little Revenge ran on through the long sea-lane between.

VI

Thousands of their soldiers looked down from their decks and laughed,
Thousands of their seamen made mock at the mad little craft
Running on and on, till delayed
By their mountain-like San Philip that, of fifteen hundred tons,
And up-shadowing high above us with her yawning tiers of guns,
Took the breath from our sails, and we stayed.

[1] See Sir Walter Raleigh's account, p. 228.
[2] i. e., ships of the fighting line, the old term for battleships

VII

And while now the great San Philip hung
above us like a cloud
Whence the thunderbolt will fall
Long and loud,
Four galleons drew away
From the Spanish fleet that day,
And two upon the larboard and two upon the
starboard lay,
And the battle-thunder broke from them all.

VIII

But anon the great San Philip, she bethought
herself and went,
Having that within her womb that had left her
ill content;
And the rest they came aboard us, and they
fought us hand to hand,
For a dozen times they came with their pikes
and musqueteers,
And a dozen times we shook 'em off as a dog
that shakes his ears
When he leaps from the water to the land.

IX

And the sun went down, and the stars came
out far over the summer sea,
But never a moment ceased the fight of the
one and the fifty-three.
Ship after ship, the whole night long, their
high-built galleons came,
Ship after ship, the whole night long, with her
battle-thunder and flame;
Ship after ship, the whole night long, drew
back with her dead and her shame.
For some were sunk and many were shattered,
and so could fight no more—
God of battles, was ever a battle like this in
the world before?

X

For he said, "Fight on! fight on!"
Though his vessel was all but a wreck;
And it chanced that, when half of the short
summer night was gone,
With a grisly wound to be dressed he had left
the deck,
But a bullet struck him that was dressing it
suddenly dead,
And himself he was wounded again in the side
and the head,
And he said, "Fight on! fight on!"

XI

And the night went down, and the sun smiled
out far over the summer sea,
And the Spanish fleet with broken sides lay
round us all in a ring;
But they dared not touch us again, for they
feared that we still could sting,
So they watched what the end would be.
And we had not fought them in vain,
But in perilous plight were we,
Seeing forty of our poor hundred were slain,
And half of the rest of us maimed for life
In the crash of the cannonades and the des-
perate strife.
And the sick men down in the hold were most
of them stark and cold,
And the pikes were all broken or bent, and the
powder was all of it spent;
And the masts and the rigging were lying over
the side;
But Sir Richard cried in his English pride:
"We have fought such a fight for a day and
a night
As may never be fought again!
We have won great glory, my men!
And a day less or more
At sea or ashore,
We die—does it matter when?
Sink me the ship, Master Gunner—sink her,
split her in twain!
Fall into the hands of God, not into the hands
of Spain!"

XII

And the gunner said, "Aye, aye," but the sea-
men made reply:
"We have children, we have wives,
And the Lord hath spared our lives.
We will make the Spaniard promise, if we
yield, to let us go;
We shall live to fight again and to strike an-
other blow."
And the lion there lay dying, and they yielded
to the foe.

XIII

And the stately Spanish men to their flagship
bore him then,
Where they laid him by the mast, old Sir
Richard caught at last,
And they praised him to his face with their
courtly foreign grace;
But he rose upon their decks, and he cried:
"I have fought for Queen and Faith like a
valiant man and true;
I have only done my duty as a man is bound
to do.
With a joyful spirit I, Sir Richard Grenville,
die!"
And he fell upon their decks, and he died.

XIV

And they stared at the dead that had been so valiant and true,
And had holden the power and glory of Spain so cheap
That he dared her with one little ship and his English few;
Was he devil or man? He was devil for aught they knew,
But they sank his body with honor down into the deep.
And they manned the Revenge with a swarthier, alien crew,
And away she sailed with her loss and longed for her own;
When a wind from the lands they had ruined awoke from sleep,
And the water began to heave and the weather to moan,
And or ever that evening ended a great gale blew,
And a wave like the wave that is raised by an earthquake grew,
Till it smote on their hulls and their sails and their masts and their flags,
And the whole sea plunged and fell on the shot-shattered navy of Spain,
And the little Revenge herself went down by the island crags
To be lost evermore in the main.

1878 1878

NORTHERN FARMER[1]

OLD STYLE

I

Wheer 'asta beän saw long and meä liggin' 'ere aloän?
Noorse? thoort nowt o' a noorse; whoy, Doctor 's abeän an' agoän;
Says that I moänt 'a naw moor aäle, but I beänt a fool;
Git ma my aäle, fur I beänt a-gawin' to breäk my rule.

II

Doctors, they knaws nowt, fur a says what 's nawways true;
Naw soort o' koind o' use to saäy the things that a do.
I 've 'ed my point o' aäle ivry noight sin' I beän 'ere.
An' I've 'ed my quart ivry market-noight for foorty year.

III

Parson 's a beän loikewoise, an' a sittin' ere o' my bed.
"The Amoighty 's a taäkin o' you[2] to 'issén, my friend," a said,
An' a towd ma my sins, an' 's toithe were due, an' I gied it in hond;
I done moy duty boy 'um, as I 'a done boy the lond.

IV

Larn'd a ma' beä. I reckons I 'annot sa mooch to larn.
But a cast oop, thot a did, 'bout Bessy Marris's barne.
Thaw a knaws I hallus voäted wi' Squoire an' choorch an' staäte,
An' i' the woost o' toimes I wur niver agin the raäte.

V

An' I hallus coom'd to 's choorch afoor moy Sally wur deäd,
An' 'eärd 'um a bummin' awaäy loike a buzzard-clock[3] ower my 'ead,
An' I niver knaw'd whot a meän'd but I thowt a 'ad summut to saäy,
An' I thowt a said whot a owt to 'a said, an' I coom'd awaäy.

VI

Bessy Marris's barne! tha knaws she laäid it to meä.
Mowt a beän, mayhap, for she wur a bad un, sheä.
'Siver, I kep 'um, I kep 'um, my lass, tha mun understond;
I done moy duty boy 'um, as I 'a done boy the lond.

VII

But Parson a cooms an' a goäs, an' a says it eäsy an' freä:
"The Amoighty 's a taäkin o' you to 'issén, my friend," says 'eä.
I weänt saäy men be loiars, thaw summun said it in 'aäste;
But 'e reäds wonn sarmin a weeäk, an' I 'a stubb'd Thurnaby waäste.

[1] Note that in this dialect poem an *a* pronounced very lightly represents *thou,* as in "'asta" (hast thou), or *he,* as in "a says"; or it is a mere prefix to a participle, as in "a beän," "a sittin'"; or, pronounced broadly, it may stand for *have,* as in "as I 'a done." Further, toithe = tithe; barne = bairn; raäte = church-rate, or tax; 'siver = howsoever; stubbed = grubbed; boggle = bogle (ghost); raäved and rembled = tore out and removed; 'soize = assizes; yows = ewes; 'aäpoth = half-penny-worth; sewer-loy = surely; atta = art thou; hallus i' the owd taäle = always urging the same thing. The rest of the notes are Tennyson's.

[2] *ou* as in *hour*

[3] cockchafer

VIII

D' ya moind the waäste, my lass? naw, naw, tha was not born then;
Theer wur a boggle in it, I often 'eärd 'um mysén;
Moäst loike a butter-bump,[1] fur I 'eärd 'um about an' about,
But I stubb'd 'um oop wi' the lot, an' raäved an' rembled 'um out.

IX

Keäper's it wur; fo' they fun 'um theer a-laäid of 'is faäce
Down i' the woild 'enemies[2] afoor I coom'd to the plaäce.
Noäks or Thimbleby—toäner[3] 'ed shot 'um as deäd as a naäil.
Noäks wur 'ang'd for it oop at 'soize—but git ma my aäle.

X

Dubbut looök at the waäste; theer warn't not feeäd for a cow;
Nowt at all but bracken an' fuzz, an' looök at it now—
Warn't worth nowt a haäcre, an' now theer 's lots o' feeäd,
Fourscooe[4] yows upon it, an' some on it down i' seeäd.[5]

XI

Nobbut a bit on it 's left, an' I meän'd to 'a stubb'd it at fall,
Done it ta-year I meän'd, an' runn'd plow thruff it an' all,
If Godamoighty an' parson 'ud nobbut let ma aloän,—
Meä, wi' haäte hoonderd haäcre o' Squoire's, an' lond o' my oän.

XII

Do Godamoighty knaw what a's doing a-taäkin' o' meä?
I beänt wonn as saws 'ere a beän an yonder a peä;
An' Squoire 'ull be sa mad an' all—a' dear, a' dear!
And I 'a managed for Squoire coom Michael-mas thutty year.

XIII

A mowt 'a taäen owd Joänes, as 'ant not a 'aäpoth o' sense,
Or a mowt a' taäen young Robins—a niver mended a fence;

[1] bittern
[2] anemones
[3] one or other
[4] *ou* as in *hour*
[5] clover

But Godamoighty a moost taäke meä an' taäke ma now,
Wi' aäf the cows to cauve an' Thurnaby hoälms to plow!

XIV

Looök 'ow quoloty smoiles when they seeäs ma a passin' boy,
Says to thessén, naw doubt, "What a man a beä sewer-loy!"
Fur they knaws what I beän to Squoire sin' fust a coom'd to the 'All;
I done moy duty by Squoire an' I done moy duty boy hall.

XV

Squoire 's i' Lunnon, an' summun I reckons 'ull 'a to wroite,
For whoä 's to howd the lond ater meä thot muddles ma quoit;
Sartin-sewer I beä thot a weänt niver give it to Joänes,
Naw, nor a moänt to Robins—a niver rembles the stoäns.

XVI

But summun 'ull come ater meä mayhap wi' 'is kittle o' steäm
Huzzin' an' maäzin' the blessed feälds wi' the divil's oän teäm.
Sin' I mun doy I mun doy, thaw loife they says is sweet,
But sin' I mun doy I mun doy, for I couldn abeär to see it.

XVII

What atta stannin' theer fur, an' doesn bring ma the aäle?
Doctor 's a 'toättler, lass, an a's hallus i' the owd taäle;
I weänt breäk rules fur Doctor, a knaws naw moor nor a floy;
Git ma my aäle, I tell tha, an' if I mun doy I mun doy.

1864

RIZPAH[6]

17—

I

Wailing, wailing, wailing, the wind over land and sea—
And Willy's voice in the wind, "O mother, come out to me!"

[6] Founded on a story related in a penny magazine and on the fact that criminals were often denied Christian burial. The title is taken from the narrative in *2 Samuel*, xxi, 1-14.

Why should he call me tonight, when he knows that I cannot go?
For the downs are as bright as day, and the full moon stares at the snow.

II

We should be seen, my dear; they would spy us out of the town.
The loud black nights for us, and the storm rushing over the down,
When I cannot see my own hand, but am led by the creak of the chain,[1]
And grovel and grope for my son till I find myself drenched with the rain.

III

Anything fallen again? Nay—what was there left to fall?
I have taken them home, I have numbered the bones, I have hidden them all.
What am I saying—and what are *you?* Do you come as a spy?
Falls? What falls! Who knows? As the tree falls so must it lie.

IV

Who let her in? How long has she been? You—what have you heard?
Why did you sit so quiet? You never have spoken a word.
Oh—to pray with me—yes—a lady—none of their spies—
But the night has crept into my heart, and begun to darken my eyes.

V

Ah—you that have lived so soft, what should *you* know of the night,
The blast and the burning shame and the bitter frost and the fright?
I have done it, while you were asleep—you were only made for the day.
I have gathered my baby together—and now you may go your way.

VI

Nay—for it's kind of you, madam, to sit by an old dying wife.
But say nothing hard of my boy, I have only an hour of life.
I kissed my boy in the prison, before he went out to die.
"They dared me to do it," he said, and he never has told me a lie.
I whipped him for robbing an orchard once when he was but a child—
"The farmer dared me to do it," he said; he was always so wild—
And idle—and couldn't be idle—my Willy—he never could rest.
The king should have made him a soldier, he would have been one of his best.

VII

But he lived with a lot of wild mates, and they never would let him be good;
They swore that he dare not rob the mail, and he swore that he would;
And he took no life, but he took one purse, and when all was done
He flung it among his fellows—"I'll none of it," said my son.

VIII

I came into court to the judge and the lawyers. I told them my tale,
God's own truth—but they killed him, they killed him for robbing the mail.
They hanged him in chains for a show—we had always borne a good name—
To be hanged for a thief—and then put away—isn't that enough shame?
Dust to dust—low down—let us hide! But they set him so high
That all the ships of the world could stare at him, passing by.
God 'll pardon the hell-black raven and horrible fowls of the air,
But not the black heart of the lawyer who killed him and hanged him there.

IX

And the jailer forced me away. I had bid him my last good-by;
They had fastened the door of his cell. "O mother!" I heard him cry.
I couldn't get back though I tried, he had something further to say,
And now I never shall know it. The jailer forced me away.

X

Then since I couldn't but hear that cry of my boy that was dead,
They seized me and shut me up: they fastened me down on my bed.
"Mother, O mother!"—he called in the dark to me year after year—
They beat me for that, they beat me—you know that I couldn't but hear;
And then at the last they found I had grown so stupid and still

[1] See line 35.

They let me abroad again—but the creatures
had worked their will.

XI

Flesh of my flesh was gone, but bone of my
bone was left—
I stole them all from the lawyers—and you,
will you call it a theft?—
My baby, the bones that had sucked me, the
bones that had laughed and had cried—
Theirs? Oh, no! They are mine—not theirs—
they had moved in my side.

XII

Do you think I was scared by the bones? I
kissed 'em, I buried 'em all—
I can't dig deep, I am old—in the night by the
churchyard wall.
My Willy 'll rise up whole when the trumpet
of judgment 'll sound,
But I charge you never to say that I laid him
in holy ground.

XIII

They would scratch him up—they would hang
him again on the cursèd tree.
Sin? Oh, yes, we are sinners, I know—let all
that be,
And read me a Bible verse of the Lord's good-
will toward men—
"Full of compassion and mercy, the Lord"—
let me hear it again;
"Full of compassion and mercy—long-suffer-
ing." Yes, oh, yes!
For the lawyer is born but to murder—the
Saviour lives but to bless.
He'll never put on the black cap except for
the worst of the worst,
And the first may be last—I have heard it in
church—and the last may be first.
Suffering—O long-suffering—yes, as the Lord
must know,
Year after year in the mist and the wind and
the shower and the snow.

XIV

Heard, have you? what? They have told you
he never repented his sin.
How do they know it? Are *they* his mother?
Are *you* of his kin?
Heard! Have you ever heard, when the storm
on the downs began,
The wind that'll wail like a child and the sea
that'll moan like a man?

XV

Election, Election, and Reprobation—it's all
very well.
But I go tonight to my boy, and I shall not
find him in hell.
For I cared so much for my boy that the Lord
has looked into my care,
And He means me I'm sure to be happy with
Willy, I know not where.

XVI

And if *he* be lost—but to save *my* soul, that is
all your desire—
Do you think that I care for *my* soul if my boy
be gone to the fire?
I have been with God in the dark—go, go, you
may leave me alone—
You never have borne a child—you are just as
hard as a stone.

XVII

Madam, I beg your pardon! I think that you
mean to be kind,
But I cannot hear what you say for my Willy's
voice in the wind —
The snow and the sky so bright—he used but
to call in the dark,
And he calls to me now from the church and
not from the gibbet—for hark!
Nay—you can hear it yourself—it is coming—
shaking the walls—
Willy—the moon's in a cloud——Good-night.
I am going. He calls.

1880

MILTON

(ALCAICS) [1]

O mighty-mouthed inventor of harmonies,
O skilled to sing of Time or Eternity,
God-gifted organ-voice of England,
Milton, a name to resound for ages:
Whose Titan angels, Gabriel, Abdiel,
Starred from Jehovah's gorgeous armories,
Tower, as the deep-domed empyrean
Rings to the roar of an angel onset!
Me rather all that bowery loneliness,
The brooks of Eden mazily murmuring,
And bloom profuse and cedar arches
Charm, as a wanderer out in ocean,
Where some refulgent sunset of India
Streams o'er a rich ambrosial ocean isle,
And crimson-hued the stately palm-woods
Whisper in odorous heights of even.

1863

[1] This poem is one of Tennyson's experiments in the quantitative meter of the classics. The two styles of Milton here described may be found in many passages of *Paradise Lost:* see especially, for the "angel onset," Book VI, 96 ff., and for the "bowery loneliness," IV, 214 ff.

TO DANTE

(Written at the Request of the Florentines) [1]

King, that hast reigned six hundred years, and grown
In power, and ever growest, since thine own
Fair Florence honoring thy nativity,
Thy Florence now the crown of Italy,
Hath sought the tribute of a verse from me,
I, wearing but the garland of a day,
Cast at thy feet one flower that fades away.

1865

TO VIRGIL

(written at the request of the mantuans for the nineteenth centenary of virgil's death)

Roman Virgil, thou that singest
  Ilion's lofty temples robed in fire,
Ilion falling, Rome arising,
  wars, and filial faith, and Dido's pyre;

Landscape-lover, lord of language
  more than he that sang the "Works and Days," [2]
All the chosen coin of fancy
  flashing out from many a golden phrase;

Thou that singest wheat and woodland,
  tilth and vineyard, hive and horse and herd;
All the charm of all the Muses
  often flowering in a lonely word;

Poet of the happy Tityrus [3]
  piping underneath his beechen bowers;
Poet of the poet-satyr
  whom the laughing shepherd bound with flowers; [4]

Chanter of the Pollio, [5] glorying
  in the blissful years again to be,
Summers of the snakeless meadow,
  unlaborious earth and oarless sea;

Thou that seest Universal
  Nature moved by Universal Mind;
Thou majestic in thy sadness
  at the doubtful doom of human kind;

Light among the vanished ages;
  star that gildest yet this phantom shore;
Golden branch amid the shadows,
  kings and realms that pass to rise no more;

Now thy Forum roars no longer,
  fallen every purple Caesar's dome—
Though thine ocean-roll of rhythm
  sound forever of Imperial Rome—

Now the Rome of slaves hath perished,
  and the Rome of freemen holds her place,
I, from out the Northern Island
  sundered once from all the human race,

I salute thee, Mantovano,
  I that loved thee since my day began,
Wielder of the stateliest measure
  ever molded by the lips of man.

1882 1882

"FRATER AVE ATQUE VALE" [6]

Row us out from Desenzano, to your Sirmione row!
So they rowed, and there we landed—"O venusta Sirmio!"
There to me through all the groves of olive in the summer glow,
There beneath the Roman ruin where the purple flowers grow,
Came that "Ave atque Vale" of the Poet's hopeless woe,
Tenderest of Roman poets nineteen hundred years ago,
"Frater Ave atque Vale"—as we wandered to and fro
Gazing at the Lydian laughter of the Garda Lake below
Sweet Catullus's all-but-island, olive-silvery Sirmio!

1880 1883

FLOWER IN THE CRANNIED WALL

Flower in the crannied wall,
I pluck you out of the crannies,
I hold you here, root and all, in my hand,
Little flower—but *if* I could understand
What you are, root and all, and all in all,
I should know what God and man is.

1869

[1] for a festival on the six hundredth anniversary of the birth of Dante, 1865

[2] Hesiod

[3] a shepherd piper in Vergil's first Eclogue

[4] Eclogue sixth

[5] title of the fourth Eclogue, which is prophetic of a golden age

[6] In these words, "Hail, brother, and farewell," the Roman poet Catullus lamented the death of his brother (*Carmina* 101, 10). Catullus had a villa on the peninsula of Sermione—"venusta (beautiful) Sirmio"—in Lake Garda, northern Italy. The last two lines of this little poem, which reproduces so well the soft music of Catullus's verse, are modeled upon lines in his thirty-first song. Catullus used the word "Lydian" in the belief that the Etruscans, who anciently had settlements near the Lake of Garda, were of Lydian origin.

WAGES

Glory of warrior, glory of orator, glory of song,
Paid with a voice flying by to be lost on an endless sea—
Glory of Virtue, to fight, to struggle, to right the wrong—
Nay, but she aimed not at glory, no lover of glory she:
Give her the glory of going on, and still to be.

The wages of sin is death; if the wages of Virtue be dust,
Would she have heart to endure for the life of the worm and the fly?
She desires no isles of the blest, no quiet seats of the just,
To rest in a golden grove, or to bask in a summer sky;
Give her the wages of going on, and not to die.

1868 1868

BY AN EVOLUTIONIST

The Lord let the house of a brute to the soul of a man,
And the man said, "Am I your debtor?"
And the Lord—"Not yet; but make it as clean as you can,
And then I will let you a better."

I

If my body come from brutes, my soul uncertain or a fable,
Why not bask amid the senses while the sun of morning shines,
I, the finer brute rejoicing in my hounds, and in my stable,
Youth and health, and birth and wealth, and choice of women and of wines?

II

What hast thou done for me, grim Old Age, save breaking my bones on the rack?
Would I had passed in the morning that looks so bright from afar!

OLD AGE

Done for thee? Starved the wild beast that was linked with thee eighty years back.
Less weight now for the ladder of heaven that hangs on a star.

I

If my body come from brutes, though somewhat finer than their own,
I am heir, and this my kingdom. Shall the royal voice be mute?
No, but if the rebel subject seek to drag me from the throne,
Hold the scepter, Human Soul, and rule thy province of the brute.

II

I have climbed to the snows of Age, and I gaze at a field in the Past,
Where I sank with the body at times in the sloughs of a low desire,
But I hear no yelp of the beast, and the Man is quiet at last
As he stands on the heights of his life with a glimpse of a height that is higher.

1889

VASTNESS

Many a hearth upon our dark globe sighs after many a vanished face,
Many a planet by many a sun may roll with the dust of a vanished race.

Raving politics, never at rest—as this poor earth's pale history runs—
What is it all but a trouble of ants in the gleam of a million million of suns?

Lies upon this side, lies upon that side, truthless violence mourned by the wise,
Thousands of voices drowning his own in a popular torrent of lies upon lies;

Stately purposes, valor in battle, glorious annals of army and fleet,
Death for the right cause, death for the wrong cause, trumpets of victory, groans of defeat;

Innocence seethed in her mother's milk, and Charity setting the martyr aflame;
Thraldom who walks with the banner of Freedom, and recks not to ruin a realm in her name.

Faith at her zenith, or all but lost in the gloom of doubts that darken the schools;
Craft with a bunch of all-heal in her hand, followed up by her vassal legion of fools;

Trade flying over a thousand seas with her spice and her vintage, her silk and her corn;
Desolate offing, sailorless harbors, famishing populace, wharves forlorn;

Star of the morning, Hope in the sunrise; gloom of the evening, Life at a close;
Pleasure who flaunts on her wide downway with her flying robe and her poisoned rose;

Pain that has crawled from the corpse of Pleasure, a worm which writhes all day, and at night

Stirs up again in the heart of the sleeper, and stings him back to the curse of the light;

Wealth with his wines and his wedded harlots; honest Poverty, bare to the bone;
Opulent Avarice, lean as Poverty; Flattery gilding the rift in a throne;

Fame blowing out from her golden trumpet a jubilant challenge to Time and to Fate;
Slander, her shadow, sowing the nettle on all the laureled graves of the great;

Love for the maiden, crowned with marriage, no regrets for aught that has been,
Household happiness, gracious children, debtless competence, golden mean;

National hatreds of whole generations, and pigmy spites of the village spire;
Vows that will last to the last death-ruckle, and vows that are snapped in a moment of fire;

He that has lived for the lust of the minute, and died in the doing it, flesh without mind;
He that has nailed all flesh to the Cross, till self died out in love of his kind;

Spring and Summer and Autumn and Winter, and all these old revolutions of earth;
All new-old revolutions of Empire—change of the tide—what is all of it worth?

What the philosophies, all the sciences, poesy, varying voices of prayer,
All that is noblest, all that is basest, all that is filthy with all that is fair?

What is it all, if we all of us end but in being our own corpse-coffins at last?
Swallowed in Vastness, lost in Silence, drowned in the deeps of a meaningless Past?

What but a murmur of gnats in the gloom, or a moment's anger of bees in their hive?—

. . . .

Peace, let it be! for I loved him, and love him for ever; the dead are not dead but alive.

1885 *1885*

CROSSING THE BAR [1]

Sunset and evening star,
And one clear call for me!
And may there be no moaning of the bar,
When I put out to sea,

But such a tide as moving seems asleep,
Too full for sound and foam,
When that which drew from out the boundless deep
Turns again home.

Twilight and evening bell,
And after that the dark!
And may there be no sadness of farewell,
When I embark;

For though from out our bourne of Time and Place
The flood may bear me far,
I hope to see my Pilot face to face
When I have crossed the bar.

1889 *1892*

[1] written in Tennyson's eighty-first year

ROBERT BROWNING 1812-1889

From childhood Robert Browning was possessed of most of the advantages that wealth and culture afford. He was born in London, son of a retired business man who wrote verse as a pastime, and who took great interest in his son's instruction in art and literature. Nearly all of his formal education he received through tutors. The reading of Shelley seems to have turned him definitely toward poetry. After ten years of writing, partly dramatic, that drew little attention, Browning published, in 1842, his *Dramatic Lyrics,* the first of his works to gain public favor. This was also the year of Tennyson's first decided success. From this time until his death in Venice, Browning was constantly increasing in public favor. In 1846 he married the poetess, Elizabeth Barrett, and until her death lived in Florence. After that he lived in London, mingling freely in its brilliant intellectual and artistic society. His greatest single work is *The Ring and the Book,* 1868.

Browning was a psychological observer. His greatest interest may be described as curiosity in the functioning of mind and soul in given circumstances. This is the underlying reason for his undeviating devotion to dramatic lyrics and monologues, the new types of poetry that he and Tennyson, quite independently, gave to the world in the same year. These pieces are not the masking of the author under different disguises, but are objective dramatic studies.

Courage, abounding and incurable optimism, faith in the inherent goodness and beneficence of the universe are the basal forces in the stimulating and invigorating personality that shines through Browning's poetry. His strength and swiftness express a nature too abounding in life to tarry for complete or conventional phrase.

Biographies: Chesterton (EML), Sharp (GW). Criticism: Dowden, Stephen, Payne, More (Shel. 3), Woodberry. Browning's obscurity is partly a myth, but the following are useful: Alexandra Orr's *Handbook to the Works of Browning,* 1902; W. L. Phelps's *Browning: How to Know Him,* 1915; Edward Berdoe's *Browning Cyclopædia,* 1897. Recent criticism: F. T. Russell, *One*

Word More on Browning, 1927; "Who Reads Robert Browning?" *Liv. Age* 304:96-98; "Optimism of Robert Browning," P. Littell, *New Rep.* 2:330; "Robert Browning," W. L. Phelps, *Cent.* 84: 118-27; D. Figgis, *No. Am.* 195:577-93; H. A. Clarke, *Browning and His Century,* reviewed in *Dial* 54:294-6.

From PIPPA PASSES

NEW YEAR'S HYMN

All service ranks the same with God:
If now, as formerly he trod
Paradise, his presence fills
Our earth, each only as God wills
Can work—God's puppets, best and worst,
Are we; there is no last nor first.

Say not "a small event!" Why "small"?
Costs it more pain that this, ye call
A "great event," should come to pass,
Than that? Untwine me from the mass
Of deeds which make up life, one deed
Power shall fall short in or exceed!

SONG

The year's at the spring
And day's at the morn;
Morning's at seven;
The hillside's dew-pearled;

The lark's on the wing;
The snail's on the thorn;
God's in his heaven—
All's right with the world!

1841

CAVALIER TUNES [1]

I. MARCHING ALONG

Kentish Sir Byng stood for his King,
Bidding the crop-headed Parliament swing.
And, pressing [2] a troop unable to stoop
And see the rogues flourish and honest folk droop,
Marched them along, fifty-score strong,
Great-hearted gentlemen, singing this song.

God for King Charles! Pym and such carles
To the Devil that prompts 'em their treasonous parles! [3]
Cavaliers, up! Lips from the cup,
Hands from the pasty, nor bite take, nor sup,
Till you're—
CHORUS.—Marching along, fifty-score strong,
Great-hearted gentlemen, singing this song!

Hampden to hell, and his obsequies' knell
Serve [4] Hazelrig, Fiennes, and young Harry, as well!
England, good cheer! Rupert is near!
Kentish and loyalists, keep we not here,
CHO.—Marching along, fifty-score strong,
Great-hearted gentlemen, singing this song?

Then, God for King Charles! Pym and his snarls
To the Devil that pricks on such pestilent carles!
Hold by the right, you double your might;
So, onward to Nottingham, [5] fresh for the fight,
CHO.—March we along, fifty-score strong,
Great-hearted gentlemen, singing this song!

II. GIVE A ROUSE

King Charles, and who'll do him right now?
King Charles, and who's ripe for fight now?
Give a rouse: here's, in hell's despite now,
King Charles!

Who gave me the goods that went since?
Who raised me the house that sank once?
Who helped me to gold I spent since?
Who found me in wine you drank once?

CHO.—King Charles, and who'll do him right now?
King Charles, and who's ripe for fight now?
Give a rouse: here's, in hell's despite now,
King Charles!

To whom used my boy George quaff else,
By the old fool's side that begot him?
For whom did he cheer and laugh else,
While Noll's [6] damned troopers shot him?
CHO.—King Charles, and who'll do him right now?
King Charles, and who's ripe for fight now?
Give a rouse: here's, in hell's despite now,
King Charles!

[1] These songs are meant to portray the spirit of the adherents of Charles I, and their hatred of the Puritans, or Roundheads. The Byngs of Kent are famous in the annals of British warfare. Pym, a leader of the Long Parliament, Hazelrig (or Hesilrige), Fiennes (Lord Say), and Sir Henry Vane the Younger, were all important figures in the rebellion against Charles. Prince Rupert was a nephew of Charles, and a celebrated cavalry leader.

[2] impressing, enlisting

[3] parleys, debates

[4] may it serve

[5] The standard of Charles was raised there in 1642, marking the beginning of the Civil War.

[6] Oliver's (i. e., Cromwell's)

III. BOOT AND SADDLE

Boot, saddle, to horse, and away!
Rescue my castle before the hot day
Brightens to blue from its silvery gray.
  Cho.—Boot, saddle, to horse, and away!

Ride past the suburbs, asleep as you'd say;
Many's the friend there, will listen and pray
"God's luck to gallants that strike up the lay—
  Cho.—Boot, saddle, to horse, and away!"

Forty miles off, like a roebuck at bay,
Flouts Castle Brancepeth the Roundheads' array:
Who laughs, "Good fellows ere this, by my fay,
  Cho.—Boot, saddle, to horse, and away?"

Who? My wife Gertrude; that, honest and gay,
Laughs when you talk of surrendering, "Nay!
I've better counselors; what counsel they?
  Cho.—Boot, saddle, to horse, and away!"

1842

INCIDENT OF THE FRENCH CAMP

You know, we French stormed Ratisbon.[1]
  A mile or so away,
On a little mound, Napoleon
  Stood on our storming-day;
With neck out-thrust, you fancy how,
  Legs wide, arms locked behind,
As if to balance the prone brow
  Oppressive with its mind.

Just as perhaps he mused "My plans
  That soar, to earth may fall,
Let once my army-leader Lannes
  Waver at yonder wall"—
Out 'twixt the battery smokes there flew
  A rider, bound on bound
Full-galloping; nor bridle drew
  Until he reached the mound.

Then off there flung in smiling joy,
  And held himself erect
By just his horse's mane, a boy:
  You hardly could suspect—
(So tight he kept his lips compressed,
  Scarce any blood came through)
You looked twice ere you saw his breast
  Was all but shot in two.

"Well," cried he, "Emperor, by God's grace
  We've got you Ratisbon!
The Marshal's in the market-place,
  And you'll be there anon
To see your flag-bird flap his vans
  Where I, to heart's desire,
Perched him!" The chief's eye flashed; his plans
  Soared up again like fire.

The chief's eye flashed; but presently
  Softened itself, as sheathes
A film the mother-eagle's eye
  When her bruised eaglet breathes;
"You're wounded!" "Nay," the soldier's pride
  Touched to the quick, he said:
"I'm killed, Sire!" And, his chief beside,
  Smiling, the boy fell dead.

1842

[1] a Bavarian town stormed by Napoleon in 1809

MY LAST DUCHESS [2]

FERRARA

That's my last Duchess painted on the wall,
Looking as if she were alive. I call
That piece a wonder, now: Frà Pandolf's hands
Worked busily a day, and there she stands.
Will't please you sit and look at her? I said
"Frà Pandolf" by design, for never read
Strangers like you that pictured countenance,
The depth and passion of its earnest glance,
But to myself they turned (since none puts by
The curtain I have drawn for you, but I)
And seemed as they would ask me, if they durst,
How such a glance came there; so, not the first
Are you to turn and ask thus. Sir, 'twas not
Her husband's presence only, called that spot
Of joy into the Duchess' cheek: perhaps
Frà Pandolf chanced to say, "Her mantle laps
Over my lady's wrist too much," or "Paint
Must never hope to reproduce the faint
Half-flush that dies along her throat." Such stuff
Was courtesy, she thought, and cause enough
For calling up that spot of joy. She had
A heart—how shall I say?—too soon made glad,
Too easily impressed: she liked whate'er
She looked on, and her looks went everywhere.
Sir, 'twas all one! My favor at her breast,

[2] A Duke of Ferrara stands before a portrait of his deceased Duchess, talking coolly with the envoy of a Count whose daughter he seeks to marry. The poem is a study in the heartless jealousy of supreme selfishness; also, by implication, of the charming, joyous nature of the Duchess. The nature of the commands (line 45) which such a man might give, living at the time of the Italian Renaissance, may be left to the imagination, as Browning leaves it. The artists mentioned (lines 3, 56) are imaginary.

The dropping of the daylight in the West,
The bough of cherries some officious fool
Broke in the orchard for her, the white mule
She rode with round the terrace—all and each
Would draw from her alike the approving speech,
Or blush, at least. She thanked men—good! but thanked
Somehow—I know not how—as if she ranked
My gift of a nine-hundred-years-old name
With anybody's gift. Who'd stoop to blame
This sort of trifling? Even had you skill
In speech—which I have not—to make your will
Quite clear to such an one, and say, "Just this
Or that in you disgusts me; here you miss,
Or there exceed the mark"—and if she let
Herself be lessoned so, nor plainly set
Her wits to yours, forsooth, and made excuse,
—E'en then would be some stooping; and I choose
Never to stoop. Oh, sir, she smiled, no doubt,
Whene'er I passed her; but who passed without
Much the same smile? This grew; I gave commands;
Then all smiles stopped together. There she stands
As if alive. Will't please you rise? We'll meet
The company below, then. I repeat,
The Count your master's known munificence
Is ample warrant that no just pretense
Of mine for dowry will be disallowed;
Though his fair daughter's self, as I avowed
At starting, is my object. Nay, we'll go
Together down, sir. Notice Neptune, though,
Taming a sea-horse, thought a rarity,
Which Claus of Innsbruck cast in bronze for me!

1842

IN A GONDOLA [1]

He sings

I send my heart up to thee, all my heart
  In this my singing.
For the stars help me, and the sea bears part;
  The very night is clinging
Closer to Venice' streets to leave one space
  Above me, whence thy face
May light my joyous heart to thee its dwelling place.

[1] Written for a picture, "The Serenade," by Daniel Maclise. The characters are imaginary. So also are the pictures mentioned in lines 183-202, though the painters are well known. Haste-thee-Luke was a nickname for the Neapolitan, Luca Giordano. Castelfranco is Giorgione. Tizian we know best as Titian, and his "Ser" (Sir) would be the portrait of an Italian gentleman.

She speaks

Say after me, and try to say
My very words, as if each word
Came from you of your own accord,
In your own voice, in your own way:
"This woman's heart and soul and brain
Are mine as much as this gold chain
She bids me wear; which" (say again)
"I choose to make by cherishing
A precious thing, or choose to fling
Over the boat-side, ring by ring."
And yet once more say . . . no word more!
Since words are only words. Give o'er!

Unless you call me, all the same,
Familiarly by my pet name,
Which if the Three should hear you call,
And me reply to, would proclaim
At once our secret to them all.
Ask of me, too, command me, blame—
Do, break down the partition-wall
'Twixt us, the daylight world beholds
Curtained in dusk and splendid folds!
What's left but—all of me to take?
I am the Three's: prevent them, slake
Your thirst! 'Tis said, the Arab sage,
In practicing with gems, can loose
Their subtle spirit in his cruce
And leave but ashes: so, sweet mage,
Leave them my ashes when thy use
Sucks out my soul, thy heritage!

He sings

Past we glide, and past, and past!
  What's that poor Agnese doing
Where they make the shutters fast?
  Gray Zanobi's just a-wooing
To his couch the purchased bride:
  Past we glide!

Past we glide, and past, and past!
  Why's the Pucci Palace flaring
Like a beacon to the blast?
  Guests by hundreds, not one caring
If the dear host's neck were wried;
  Past we glide!

She sings

The moth's kiss, first!
Kiss me as if you made believe
You were not sure, this eve,
How my face, your flower, had pursed
Its petals up; so, here and there
You brush it, till I grow aware
Who wants me, and wide ope I burst.

The bee's kiss, now!
Kiss me as if you entered gay

My heart at some noonday,
A bud that dares not disallow
The claim, so all is rendered up,
And passively its shattered cup
Over your head to sleep I bow.

He sings

What are we two?
I am a Jew,
And carry thee, farther than friends can pursue,
To a feast of our tribe;
Where they need thee to bribe
The devil that blasts them unless he imbibe
Thy . . . . Scatter the vision forever! And now,
As of old, I am I, thou art thou!
Say again, what we are?
The sprite of a star,
I lure thee above where the destinies bar
My plumes their full play
Till a ruddier ray
Than my pale one announce there is withering away
Some . . . . Scatter the vision forever! And now,
As of old, I am I, thou art thou!

He muses

Oh, which were best, to roam or rest?
The land's lap or the water's breast?
To sleep on yellow millet-sheaves,
Or swim in lucid shallows just
Eluding water-lily leaves,
An inch from Death's black fingers, thrust
To lock you, whom release he must;
Which life were best on Summer eves?

He speaks, musing

Lie back; could thought of mine improve you?
From this shoulder let there spring
A wing; from this, another wing;
Wings, not legs and feet, shall move you!
Snow-white must they spring, to blend
With your flesh, but I intend
They shall deepen to the end,
Broader, into burning gold,
Till both wings crescent-wise enfold
Your perfect self, from 'neath your feet
To o'er your head, where, lo, they meet
As if a million sword-blades hurled
Defiance from you to the world!

Rescue me thou, the only real!
And scare away this mad ideal
That came, nor motions to depart!
Thanks! Now, stay ever as thou art!

Still he muses

What if the Three should catch at last
Thy serenader? While there's cast
Paul's cloak about my head, and fast
Gian pinions me, Himself has past
His stylet through my back; I reel;
And . . . . is it thou I feel?

They trail me, these three godless knaves,
Past every church that saints and saves,
Nor stop till, where the cold sea raves
By Lido's [1] wet accursèd graves,
They scoop mine, roll me to its brink,
And . . . . on thy breast I sink!

She replies, musing

Dip your arm o'er the boat-side, elbow-deep,
As I do: thus: were death so unlike sleep,
Caught this way? Death's to fear from flame or steel,
Or poison doubtless; but from water—feel!
Go find the bottom! Would you stay me? There!
Now pluck a great blade of that ribbon-grass
To plait in where the foolish jewel was,
I flung away: since you have praised my hair,
'Tis proper to be choice in what I wear.

He speaks

Row home? Must we row home? Too surely
Know I where its front's demurely
Over the Giudecca [2] piled;
Window just with window mating,
Door on door exactly waiting,
All's the set face of a child.
But behind it, where's a trace
Of the staidness and reserve,
And formal lines without a curve,
In the same child's playing-face?
No two windows look one way
O'er the small sea-water thread
Below them. Ah, the autumn day
I, passing, saw you overhead!
First, out a cloud of curtain blew,
Then a sweet cry, and last came you—
To catch your lory [3] that must needs
Escape just then, of all times then,
To peck a tall plant's fleecy seeds,
And make me happiest of men.
I scarce could breathe to see you reach
So far back o'er the balcony
To catch him ere he climbed too high
Above you in the Smyrna peach,
That quick the round smooth cord of gold,

[1] A long sandy bar lying off Venice—there is a Jewish cemetery there.
[2] a Venetian canal
[3] a kind of parrot

This coiled hair on your head, unrolled,
Fell down you like a gorgeous snake
The Roman girls were wont, of old,
When Rome there was, for coolness' sake
To let lie curling o'er their bosoms.
Dear lory, may his beak retain
Ever its delicate rose stain
As if the wounded lotus-blossoms
Had marked their thief to know again!

Stay longer yet, for others' sake
Than mine! What should your chamber do?
—With all its rarities that ache
In silence while day lasts, but wake
At nighttime and their life renew,
Suspended just to pleasure you
Who brought against their will together
These objects, and, while day lasts, weave
Around them such a magic tether
That dumb they look: Your harp, believe,
With all the sensitive tight strings
Which dare not speak, now to itself
Breathes slumberously, as if some elf
Went in and out the chords,[1] his wings
Make murmur wheresoe'er they graze,
As an angel may, between the maze
Of midnight palace-pillars, on
And on, to sow God's plagues, have gone
Through guilty glorious Babylon.
And while such murmurs flow, the nymph
Bends o'er the harp-top from her shell
As the dry limpet for the lymph
Come with a tune he knows so well.
And how your statues' hearts must swell!
And how your pictures must descend
To see each other, friend with friend!
Oh, could you take them by surprise,
You'd find Schidone's eager Duke
Doing the quaintest courtesies
To that prim saint by Haste-thee-Luke!
And, deeper into her rock den,
Bold Castelfranco's Magdalen
You'd find retreated from the ken
Of that robed counsel-keeping Ser—
As if the Tizian thinks of her,
And is not, rather, gravely bent
On seeing for himself what toys
Are these,[1] his progeny invent,
What litter now the board employs
Whereon he signed a document
That got him murdered! Each enjoys
Its night so well, you cannot break
The sport up, so, indeed must make
More stay with me, for others' sake.

[1] Supply "which" before "his."

She speaks

Tomorrow, if a harp string, say,
Is used to tie the jasmine back
That overfloods my room with sweets,
Contrive your Zorzi somehow meets
My Zanze! If the ribbon's black,
The Three are watching: keep away!

Your gondola—let Zorzi wreathe
A mesh of water-weeds about
Its prow, as if he unaware
Had struck some quay or bridge-foot stair!
That I may throw a paper out
As you and he go underneath.

There's Zanze's vigilant taper; safe are we.
Only one minute more tonight with me?
Resume your past self of a month ago!
Be you the bashful gallant, I will be
The lady with the colder breast than snow.
Now bow you, as becomes, nor touch my hand
More than I touch yours when I step to land,
And say, "All thanks, Siora!"—
Heart to heart
And lips to lips! Yet once more, ere we part,
Clasp me and make me thine, as mine thou art!
[*He is surprised, and stabbed.*]

He speaks

It was ordained to be so, sweet!—and best
Comes now, beneath thine eyes, upon thy breast.
Still kiss me! Care not for the cowards! Care
Only to put aside thy beauteous hair
My blood will hurt! The Three, I do not scorn
To death, because they never lived: but I
Have lived indeed, and so—yet one more kiss
—can die!

1842

THE PIED PIPER OF HAMELIN[2]

A CHILD'S STORY

I

Hamelin Town's in Brunswick,
By famous Hanover city;
The river Weser, deep and wide,
Washes its wall on the southern side;
A pleasanter spot you never spied;
But when begins my ditty,
Almost five hundred years ago,

[2] This poem was written by Browning to amuse the little son of the actor, William Macready, and furnish him a subject for drawings. The legend is an old one. John Fiske is disposed to identify it with various myths: "Goethe's Erlking is none other than the Piper of Hamelin. And the piper, in turn, is the classic Hermes or Orpheus. . . . . His wonderful pipe is the horn of Oberon, the lyre of Apollo (who, like the piper, was a rat-killer), the harp stolen by Jack when he climbed the bean-stalk to the ogre's castle."

To see the townsfolk suffer so
From vermin was a pity.

II

Rats!
They fought the dogs and killed the cats,
And bit the babies in the cradles,
And ate the cheeses out of the vats,
And licked the soup from the cooks' own ladles,
Split open the kegs of salted sprats,
Made nests inside men's Sunday hats,
And even spoiled the women's chats
By drowning their speaking
With shrieking and squeaking
In fifty different sharps and flats.

III

At last the people in a body
To the Town Hall came flocking.
"'Tis clear," cried they, "our Mayor's a noddy;
And as for our Corporation—shocking
To think we buy gowns lined with ermine
For dolts that can't or won't determine
What's best to rid us of our vermin!
You hope, because you're old and obese,
To find in the furry civic robe ease?
Rouse up, sirs! Give your brains a racking
To find the remedy we're lacking,
Or, sure as fate, we'll send you packing!"
At this the Mayor and Corporation
Quaked with a mighty consternation.

IV

An hour they sat in council;
At length the Mayor broke the silence:
"For a guilder [1] I'd my ermine gown sell,
I wish I were a mile hence!
It's easy to bid one rack one's brain—
I'm sure my poor head aches again,
I've scratched it so, and all in vain.
Oh, for a trap, a trap, a trap!"
Just as he said this, what should hap
At the chamber door but a gentle tap?
"Bless us," cried the Mayor, "what's that?"
(With the Corporation as he sat,
Looking little though wondrous fat;
Nor brighter was his eye, nor moister
Than a too-long-opened oyster,
Save when at noon his paunch grew mutinous
For a plate of turtle, green and glutinous)
"Only a scraping of shoes on the mat?
Anything like the sound of a rat
Makes my heart go pit-a-pat!"

[1] a dutch coin, worth forty cents

V

"Come in!"—the Mayor cried, looking bigger;
And in did come the strangest figure!
His queer long coat from heel to head
Was half of yellow and half of red,
And he himself was tall and thin,
With sharp blue eyes, each like a pin,
And light loose hair, yet swarthy skin,
No tuft on cheek nor beard on chin,
But lips where smiles went out and in;
There was no guessing his kith and kin;
And nobody could enough admire
The tall man and his quaint attire.
Quoth one: "It's as my great-grandsire,
Starting up at the Trump of Doom's tone,
Had walked this way from his painted tombstone!"

VI

He advanced to the council-table:
And, "Please your honors," said he, "I'm able,
By means of a secret charm, to draw
All creatures living beneath the sun,
That creep or swim or fly or run,
After me so as you never saw!
And I chiefly use my charm
On creatures that do people harm,
The mole and toad and newt and viper;
And people call me the Pied Piper."
(And here they noticed round his neck
A scarf of red and yellow stripe,
To match with his coat of the self-same check;
And at the scarf's end hung a pipe;
And his fingers, they noticed, were ever straying
As if impatient to be playing
Upon this pipe, as low it dangled
Over his vesture so old-fangled.)
"Yet," said he, "poor piper as I am,
In Tartary I freed the Cham,
Last June, from his huge swarms of gnats;
I eased in Asia the Nizam
Of a monstrous brood of vampire-bats;
And as for what your brain bewilders,
If I can rid your town of rats
Will you give me a thousand guilders?"
"One? Fifty thousand!"—was the exclamation
Of the astonished Mayor and Corporation.

VII

Into the street the Piper stept,
Smiling first a little smile,
As if he knew what magic slept
In his quiet pipe the while;
Then, like a musical adept,
To blow the pipe his lips he wrinkled,
And green and blue his sharp eyes twinkled,
Like a candle flame where salt is sprinkled;

And ere three shrill notes the pipe uttered,
You heard as if an army muttered;
And the muttering grew to a grumbling;
And the grumbling grew to a mighty rumbling;
And out of the houses the rats came tumbling.
Great rats, small rats, lean rats, brawny rats,
Brown rats, black rats, gray rats, tawny rats,
Grave old plodders, gay young friskers,
  Fathers, mothers, uncles, cousins,
Cocking tails and pricking whiskers,
  Families by tens and dozens,
Brothers, sisters, husbands, wives—
Followed the Piper for their lives.
From street to street he piped advancing,
And step for step they followed dancing,
Until they came to the river Weser,
Wherein all plunged and perished!
—Save one who, stout as Julius Caesar,
Swam across and lived to carry
(As he, the manuscript he cherished[1])
To Rat-land home his commentary;
Which was, "At the first shrill notes of the pipe,
I heard a sound as of scraping tripe,
And putting apples, wondrous ripe,
Into a cider-press's gripe:
And a moving away of pickle-tub-boards,
And a leaving ajar of conserve-cupboards,
And a drawing the corks of train-oil-flasks,
And a breaking the hoops of butter-casks:
And it seemed as if a voice
(Sweeter far than by harp or by psaltery
Is breathed) called out, "O rats, rejoice!
The world is grown to one vast dry-saltery!
So munch on, crunch on, take your nuncheon,[2]
Breakfast, supper, dinner, luncheon!'
And just as a bulky sugar puncheon,
All ready staved, like a great sun shone
Glorious scarce an inch before me,
Just as methought it said, 'Come, bore me!'
—I found the Weser rolling o'er me."

VIII

You should have heard the Hamelin people
Ringing the bells till they rocked the steeple.
"Go," cried the Mayor, "and get long poles,
Poke out the nests and block up the holes!
Consult with carpenters and builders,
And leave in our town not even a trace
Of the rats!"—when, suddenly, up the face
Of the Piper perked in the market-place,
With a, "First, if you please, my thousand guilders!"

[1] This happened in Egypt, according to Plutarch, who tells the story.
[2] about the same as "luncheon"

IX

A thousand guilders! The Mayor looked blue;
So did the Corporation, too.
For council dinners made rare havoc
With Claret, Moselle, Vin-de-Grave, Hock;
And half the money would replenish
Their cellar's biggest butt with Rhenish.
To pay this sum to a wandering fellow
With a gypsy coat of red and yellow!
"Beside," quoth the Mayor with a knowing wink
"Our business was done at the river's brink;
We saw with our eyes the vermin sink,
And what's dead can't come to life, I think.
So, friend, we're not the folks to shrink
From the duty of giving you something for drink,
And a matter of money to put in your poke;
But as for the guilders, what we spoke
Of them, as you very well know, was in joke.
Beside, our losses have made us thrifty.
A thousand guilders! Come, take fifty!"

X

The Piper's face fell, and he cried,
"No trifling! I can't wait! Beside,
I've promised to visit by dinner time
Bagdad, and accept the prime
Of the Head-Cook's pottage, all he's rich in,
For having left, in the Caliph's kitchen,
Of a nest of scorpions no survivor:
With him I proved no bargain driver,
With you, don't think I'll bate a stiver!
And folks who put me in a passion
May find me pipe after another fashion."

XI

"How?" cried the Mayor, "d'ye think I brook
Being worse treated than a Cook?
Insulted by a lazy ribald
With idle pipe and vesture piebald?
You threaten us, fellow? Do your worst,
Blow your pipe there till you burst!"

XII

Once more he stepped into the street,
  And to his lips again
Laid his long pipe of smooth straight cane;
  And ere he blew three notes (such sweet
Soft notes as yet musician's cunning
  Never gave the enraptured air)
There was a rustling that seemed like a bustling
Of merry crowds justling at pitching and hustling;
Small feet were pattering, wooden shoes clattering,

Little hands clapping and little tongues chattering,
And, like fowls in a farmyard when barley is scattering,
Out came the children running.
All the little boys and girls,
With rosy cheeks and flaxen curls,
And sparkling eyes and teeth like pearls,
Tripping and skipping, ran merrily after
The wonderful music with shouting and laughter.

XIII

The Mayor was dumb, and the Council stood
As if they were changed into blocks of wood,
Unable to move a step, or cry
To the children merrily skipping by,
—Could only follow with the eye
That joyous crowd at the Piper's back.
But the Mayor was on the rack,
And the wretched Council's bosoms beat,
As the Piper turned from the High Street
To where the Weser rolled its waters
Right in the way of their sons and daughters!
However, he turned from South to West,
And to Koppelberg Hill his steps addressed,
And after him the children pressed;
Great was the joy in every breast.
"He never can cross that mighty top!
He's forced to let the piping drop,
And we shall see our children stop!"
When, lo, as they reached the mountain-side,
A wondrous portal opened wide,
As if a cavern was suddenly hollowed;
And the Piper advanced and the children followed,
And when all were in to the very last,
The door in the mountain-side shut fast.
Did I say all? No! One was lame,
And could not dance the whole of the way;
And in after years if you would blame
His sadness, he was used to say—
"It's dull in our town since my playmates left!
I can't forget that I'm bereft
Of all the pleasant sights they see,
Which the Piper also promised me.
For he led us, he said, to a joyous land,
Joining the town and just at hand,
Where waters gushed and fruit-trees grew
And flowers put forth a fairer hue,
And everything was strange and new;
The sparrows were brighter than peacocks here,
And their dogs outran our fallow deer,
And honey-bees had lost their stings,
And horses were born with eagles' wings;
And just as I became assured
My lame foot would be speedily cured,
The music stopped and I stood still,
And found myself outside the hill,
Left alone against my will,
To go now limping as before,
And never hear of that country more!"

XIV

Alas, alas for Hamelin!
There came into many a burgher's pate
A text which says that heaven's gate
Opes to the rich at as easy rate
As the needle's eye takes a camel in!
The Mayor sent East, West, North, and South,
To offer the Piper, by word of mouth,
Wherever it was men's lot to find him,
Silver and gold to his heart's content,
If he'd only return the way he went,
And bring the children behind him.
But when they saw 'twas a lost endeavor,
And Piper and dancers were gone forever,
They made a decree that lawyers never
Should think their records dated duly
If, after the day of the month and year,
These words did not as well appear,
"And so long after what happened here
On the Twenty-second of July,
Thirteen hundred and seventy-six."
And the better in memory to fix
The place of the children's last retreat,
They called it, the Pied Piper's Street—
Where anyone playing on pipe or tabor
Was sure for the future to lose his labor.
Nor suffered they hostelry or tavern
To shock with mirth a street so solemn;
But opposite the place of the cavern
They wrote the story on a column.
And on the great church-window painted
The same, to make the world acquainted
How their children were stolen away,
And there it stands to this very day.
And I must not omit to say
That in Transylvania there's a tribe
Of alien people who ascribe
The outlandish ways and dress
On which their neighbors lay such stress,
To their fathers and mothers having risen
Out of some subterraneous prison
Into which they were trepanned[1]
Long time ago in a mighty band
Out of Hamelin town in Brunswick land,
But how or why, they don't understand.

XV

So, Willy, let me and you be wipers
Of scores out with all men—especially pipers!
And, whether they pipe us free from rats or from mice,
If we've promised them aught, let us keep our promise!

1842

[1] ensnared

HOW THEY BROUGHT THE GOOD NEWS FROM GHENT TO AIX [1]

I sprang to the stirrup, and Joris, and he;
I galloped, Dirck galloped, we galloped all three;
"Good speed!" cried the watch, as the gate-bolts undrew;
"Speed!" echoed the wall to us galloping through;
Behind shut the postern, the lights sank to rest,
And into the midnight we galloped abreast.

Not a word to each other; we kept the great pace
Neck by neck, stride by stride, never changing our place;
I turned in my saddle and made its girths tight,
Then shortened each stirrup, and set the pique [2] right,
Rebuckled the cheek-strap, chained slacker the bit,
Nor galloped less steadily Roland a whit.

'Twas moonset at starting; but while we drew near
Lokeren, the cocks crew and twilight dawned clear;
At Boom, a great yellow star came out to see;
At Düffeld, 'twas morning as plain as could be;
And from Mecheln church steeple we heard the half-chime,
So Joris broke silence with, "Yet there is time!"

At Aershot, up leaped of a sudden the sun,
And against him the cattle stood black every one,
To stare through the mist at us galloping past,
And I saw my stout galloper Roland at last,
With resolute shoulders, each butting away
The haze, as some bluff river headland its spray;

And his low head and crest, just one sharp ear bent back
For my voice, and the other pricked out on his track;
And one eye's black intelligence—ever that glance
O'er its white edge at me, his own master, askance!
And the thick, heavy spume-flakes which aye and anon
His fierce lips shook upward in galloping on.

By Hasselt, Dirck groaned; and cried Joris, "Stay spur!
Your Roos galloped bravely, the fault's not in her.
We'll remember at Aix"—for one heard the quick wheeze
Of her chest, saw the stretched neck and staggering knees,
And sunk tail, and horrible heave of the flank,
As down on her haunches she shuddered and sank.

So, we were left galloping, Joris and I,
Past Looz and past Tongres, no cloud in the sky;
The broad sun above laughed a pitiless laugh,
'Neath our feet broke the brittle, bright stubble like chaff;
Till over by Dalhem a dome spire sprang white,
And "Gallop," gasped Joris, "for Aix is in sight!"

"How they'll greet us!"—and all in a moment his roan
Rolled neck and croup over, lay dead as a stone;
And there was my Roland to bear the whole weight
Of the news which alone could save Aix from her fate,
With his nostrils like pits full of blood to the brim,
And with circles of red for his eye-sockets' rim.

Then I cast loose my buff coat, each holster let fall,
Shook off both my jack-boots, let go belt and all,
Stood up in the stirrup, leaned, patted his ear,
Called my Roland his pet name, my horse without peer;
Clapped my hands, laughed and sang, any noise, bad or good,
Till at length into Aix Roland galloped and stood.

And all I remember is—friends flocking round
As I sat with his head 'twixt my knees on the ground;
And no voice but was praising this Roland of mine,
As I poured down his throat our last measure of wine,
Which (the burgesses voted by common consent)
Was no more than his due who brought good news from Ghent.

1845

[1] This poem has no historical foundation. It suggests comparison with Longfellow's "Paul Revere's Ride," which was written later. Ghent (*g* hard) is in Belgium, and Aix-la-Chapelle in Prussia, about ninety miles distant.

[2] peak, pommel

THE LOST LEADER[1]

Just for a handful of silver he left us,
Just for a riband to stick in his coat—
Found the one gift of which fortune bereft us,
Lost all the others she lets us devote;
They, with the gold to give, doled him out silver,
So much was theirs who so little allowed:
How all our copper had gone[2] for his service!
Rags—were they purple,[3] his heart had been proud!
We that had loved him so, followed him, honored him,
Lived in his mild and magnificent eye,
Learned his great language, caught his clear accents,
Made him our pattern to live and to die!
Shakespeare was of us, Milton was for us,
Burns, Shelley, were with us—they watch from their graves!
He alone breaks from the van and the freemen,
He alone sinks to the rear and the slaves!
We shall march prospering—not through his presence;
Songs may inspirit us—not from his lyre;
Deeds will be done—while he boasts his quiescence,
Still bidding crouch whom the rest bade aspire:
Blot out his name, then, record one lost soul more,
One task more declined, one more footpath untrod,
One more devils'-triumph and sorrow for angels,
One wrong more to man, one more insult to God!
Life's night begins: let him never come back to us!
There would be doubt, hesitation, and pain,
Forced praise on our part—the glimmer of twilight,
Never glad, confident morning again!
Best fight on well,[4] for we taught him—strike gallantly,
Menace our heart ere we master his own;
Then let him receive the new knowledge and wait us,
Pardoned in heaven, the first by the throne!

1845

[1] This poem was suggested by Wordsworth's change from very radical views to conservatism and Toryism. Browning later apologized for its great injustice to Wordsworth—it was the effusion of "hasty youth," and was, moreover, not intended as an exact characterization. Compare Browning's poem, "Why I am a Liberal" (p. 675). Whittier's poem, "Ichabod," on the supposed defection of Daniel Webster from party principles, is written in a similar strain.

[2] would have gone (gladly)

[3] had they been royal robes (spoken in sarcasm)

HOME-THOUGHTS, FROM ABROAD

Oh, to be in England
Now that April's there,
And whoever wakes in England
Sees, some morning, unaware,
That the lowest boughs and the brushwood sheaf
Round the elm-tree bole are in tiny leaf,
While the chaffinch sings on the orchard bough
In England—now!

And after April, when May follows,
And the whitethroat builds, and all the swallows!
Hark, where my blossomed pear tree in the hedge
Leans to the field and scatters on the clover
Blossoms and dewdrops—at the bent spray's edge—
That's the wise thrush; he sings each song twice over,
Lest you should think he never could recapture
The first fine careless rapture!
And though the fields look rough with hoary dew,
All will be gay when noontide wakes anew
The buttercups, the little children's dower—
Far brighter than this gaudy melon-flower!

1845

HOME-THOUGHTS, FROM THE SEA

Nobly, nobly Cape Saint Vincent to the northwest died away;[5]
Sunset ran, one glorious blood-red, reeking into Cadiz Bay;
Bluish 'mid the burning water, full in face Trafalgar lay;
In the dimmest northeast distance dawned Gibraltar grand and gray;
"Here and here did England help me; how can I help England?"—say,
Whoso turns as I, this evening, turn to God to praise and pray,
While Jove's planet rises yonder, silent over Africa.

1845

[4] i. e., against us

[5] The scene is that of Nelson's great victory.

THE BOY AND THE ANGEL[1]

Morning, evening, noon, and night,
"Praise God!" sang Theocrite.

Then to his poor trade he turned,
Whereby the daily meal was earned.

Hard he labored, long and well;
O'er his work the boy's curls fell.

But ever, at each period,
He stopped and sang, "Praise God!"

Then back again his curls he threw,
And cheerful turned to work anew.

Said Blaise, the listening monk, "Well done;
I doubt not thou art heard, my son:

"As well as if thy voice today
Were praising God, the Pope's great way.

"This Easter Day, the Pope at Rome
Praises God from Peter's dome."

Said Theocrite, "Would God that I
Might praise him that great way, and die!"

Night passed, day shone,
And Theocrite was gone.

With God a day endures alway,
A thousand years are but a day.

God said in heaven, "Nor day nor night
Now brings the voice of my delight."

Then Gabriel, like a rainbow's birth,
Spread his wings and sank to earth;

Entered, in flesh, the empty cell,
Lived there, and played the craftsman well;

And morning, evening, noon, and night,
Praised God in place of Theocrite.

And from a boy, to youth he grew:
The man put off the stripling's hue:

The man matured and fell away
Into the season of decay:

And ever o'er the trade he bent,
And ever lived on earth content.

(He did God's will; to him, all one
If on the earth or in the sun.)

God said "A praise is in mine ear;
There is no doubt in it, no fear:

"So sing old worlds, and so
New worlds that from my footstool go.

"Clearer loves sound other ways:
I miss my little human praise."

Then forth sprang Gabriel's wings, off fell
The flesh disguise, remained the cell.

'Twas Easter Day: he flew to Rome,
And paused above St. Peter's dome.

In the tiring-room close by
The great outer gallery,

With his holy vestments dight,[2]
Stood the new Pope, Theocrite;

And all his past career
Came back upon him clear,

Since when, a boy, he plied his trade,
Till on his life the sickness weighed;

And in his cell, when death drew near,
An angel in a dream brought cheer:

And rising from the sickness drear,
He grew a priest, and now stood here.

To the East with praise he turned,
And on his sight the angel burned.

"I bore thee from thy craftsmen's cell,
And set thee here; I did not well.

"Vainly I left my angel-sphere,
Vain was thy dream of many a year.

"Thy voice's praise seemed weak; it dropped—
Creation's chorus stopped!

"Go back and praise again
The early way, while I remain.

"With that weak voice of our disdain,
Take up creation's pausing strain.

"Back to the cell and poor employ;
Resume the craftsman and the boy!"

Theocrite grew old at home;
A new Pope dwelt in Peter's dome.

One vanished as the other died:
They sought God side by side.

1845

[1] This legend is a pure invention in the medieval spirit. The moral is the same as that of the "New Year's Hymn" from *Pippa Passes* above. Or, in the words of Emerson,
"There is no great and no small
To the Soul that maketh all."

[2] arrayed

SAUL[1]

I

Said Abner,[2] "At last thou art come! Ere I tell, ere thou speak,
Kiss my cheek, wish me well!" Then I wished it, and did kiss his cheek.
And he: "Since the king, O my friend, for thy countenance sent,
Neither drunken nor eaten have we; nor until from his tent
Thou return with the joyful assurance the king liveth yet,
Shall our lip with the honey be bright, with the water be wet,
For out of the black mid-tent's silence, a space of three days,
Not a sound hath escaped to thy servants, of prayer nor of praise,
To betoken that Saul and the Spirit have ended their strife,
And that, faint in his triumph, the monarch sinks back upon life.

II

"Yet now my heart leaps, O beloved! God's child with his dew
On thy gracious gold hair, and those lilies still living and blue
Just broken to twine round thy harp strings, as if no wild heat
Were now raging to torture the desert!"

III

Then I, as was meet,
Knelt down to the God of my fathers, and rose on my feet,
And ran o'er the sand burnt to powder. The tent was unlooped;
I pulled up the spear that obstructed, and under I stooped;
Hands and knees on the slippery grass patch, all withered and gone,
That extends to the second enclosure, I groped my way on
Till I felt where the foldskirts fly open. Then once more I prayed,
And opened the foldskirts and entered, and was not afraid
But spoke, "Here is David, thy servant!" And no voice replied.
At the first I saw naught but the blackness: but soon I descried
A something more black than the blackness—the vast, the upright,
Main prop which sustains the pavilion: and slow into sight
Grew a figure against it, gigantic and blackest of all.
Then a sunbeam that burst through the tent-roof, showed Saul.

IV

He stood as erect as that tent prop, both arms stretched out wide
On the great cross-support in the center, that goes to each side;
He relaxed not a muscle, but hung there as, caught in his pangs
And waiting his change, the king-serpent all heavily hangs,
Far away from his kind, in the pine, till deliverance come
With the springtime[3]—so agonized Saul, drear and stark, blind and dumb.

V

Then I tuned my harp—took off the lilies we twine round its chords
Lest they snap 'neath the stress of the noontide—those sunbeams like swords!
And I first played the tune all our sheep know, as, one after one,
So docile they come to the pen door till folding be done.
They are white and untorn by the bushes, for lo, they have fed
Where the long grasses stifle the water within the stream's bed;
And now one after one seeks its lodging, as star follows star
Into eve and the blue far above us—so blue and so far!

VI

—Then the tune for which quails on the corn land will each leave his mate
To fly after the player; then, what makes the crickets elate
Till for boldness they fight one another; and then, what has weight

[1] In *1 Samuel,* xvi, 14-23, David, the shepherd boy, is summoned to play on his harp and drive away the evil spirit which troubles Saul. Browning has availed himself of the theme to set forth, in majestic anapests, the range and power of the various kinds of music. He thence passes to a view of the boundlessness of spiritual influence, and rises in the end to a vision of the ultimate oneness of human sympathy and love with divine. A. J. George writes: "The severity, sweetness, and beauty of the closing scene where David returns to his simple task of tending his flocks, when all nature is alive with the new impulse and pronounces the benediction on his efforts, is not surpassed by anything in our literature."

[2] The captain of Saul's host; David is the speaker throughout.

[3] through the sloughing of his old skin

To set the quick jerboa[1] a-musing outside his sand house—
There are none such as he for a wonder, half bird and half mouse!
God made all the creatures and gave them our love and our fear,
To give sign, we and they are his children, one family here.

VII

Then I played the help-tune of our reapers, their wine-song, when hand
Grasps at hand, eye lights eye in good friendship, and great hearts expand
And grow one in the sense of this world's life.—And then, the last song
When the dead man is praised on his journey—"Bear, bear him along,
With his few faults shut up like dead flowerets! Are balm seeds not here
To console us? The land has none left such as he on the bier.
Oh, would we might keep thee, my brother!"—And then, the glad chaunt
Of the marriage—first go the young maidens, next, she whom we vaunt
As the beauty, the pride of our dwelling.—And then, the grand march
Wherein man runs to man to assist him and buttress an arch
Naught can break; who shall harm them, our friends? Then, the chorus intoned
As the Levites go up to the altar in glory enthroned.
But I stopped here; for here in the darkness Saul groaned.

VIII

And I paused, held my breath in such silence, and listened apart:
And the tent shook, for mighty Saul shuddered; and sparkles 'gan dart
From the jewels that woke in his turban, at once, with a start.
All its lordly male-sapphires,[2] and rubies courageous at heart.
So the head: but the body still moved not, still hung there erect.
And I bent once again to my playing, pursued it unchecked,
As I sang:—

IX

"Oh, our manhood's prime vigor! No spirit feels waste,
Not a muscle is stopped in its playing nor sinew unbraced.
Oh, the wild joys of living! the leaping from rock up to rock,
The strong rending of boughs from the fir tree, the cool silver shock
Of the plunge in a pool's living water, the hunt of the bear,
And the sultriness showing the lion is couched in his lair.
And the meal, the rich dates yellowed over with gold dust divine,
And the locust flesh[3] steeped in the pitcher, the full draught of wine,
And the sleep in the dried river-channel where bulrushes tell
That the water was wont to go warbling so softly and well.
How good is man's life, the mere living! How fit to employ
All the heart and the soul and the senses forever in joy!
Hast thou loved the white locks of thy father, whose sword thou didst guard
When he trusted thee forth with the armies, for glorious reward?
Didst thou see the thin hands of thy mother held up as men sung
The low song of the nearly-departed, and hear her faint tongue
Joining in while it could to the witness, 'Let one more attest
I have lived, seen God's hand through a lifetime, and all was for best?'
Then they sung through their tears in strong triumph, not much, but the rest.
And thy brothers, the help and the contest, the working whence grew
Such result as, from seething grape bundles, the spirit strained true;
And the friends of thy boyhood—that boyhood of wonder and hope,
Present promise and wealth of the future beyond the eye's scope—
Till lo, thou art grown to a monarch: a people is thine;
And all gifts, which the world offers singly, on one head combine!
On one head, all the beauty and strength, love and rage (like the throe
That, a-work in the rock, helps its labor and lets the gold go)
High ambition and deeds which surpass it, fame crowning them—all

[1] a small rodent with long hind legs, with which it can spring like a hopping bird
[2] sapphires of superior hardness and brilliancy
[3] The meat of John the Baptist in the wilderness; see page 46 and the note on Wyclif's mistranslation.

Brought to blaze on the head of one creature—King Saul!"

X

And lo, with that leap of my spirit—heart, hand, harp, and voice,
Each lifting Saul's name out of sorrow, each bidding rejoice
Saul's fame in the light it was made for—as when, dare I say,
The Lord's army, in rapture of service, strains through its array,[1]
And upsoareth the cherubim chariot—"Saul!" cried I, and stopped,
And waited the thing that should follow. Then Saul, who hung propped
By the tent's cross-support in the center, was struck by his name.
Have ye seen when Spring's arrowy summons goes right to the aim,
And some mountain, the last to withstand her, that held (he alone,
While the vale laughed in freedom and flowers) on a broad bust of stone
A year's snow bound about for a breastplate,—leaves grasp of the sheet?
Fold on fold all at once it crowds thunderously down to his feet,
And there fronts you, stark, black, but alive yet, your mountain of old,
With his rents, the successive bequeathings of ages untold—
Yea, each harm got in fighting your battles, each furrow and scar
Of his head thrust 'twixt you and the tempest—all hail, there they are!
—Now again to be softened with verdure, again hold the nest
Of the dove, tempt the goat and its young to the green on his crest
For their food in the ardors of summer. One long shudder thrilled
All the tent till the very air tingled, then sank and was stilled
At the King's self left standing before me, released and aware.
What was gone, what remained? All to traverse 'twixt hope and despair.
Death was past, life not come: so he waited. Awhile his right hand
Held the brow, helped the eyes left too vacant forthwith to remand
To their place what new objects should enter: 'twas Saul as before.
I looked up and dared gaze at those eyes, nor was hurt any more
Than by slow pallid sunsets in autumn, ye watch from the shore,
At their sad level gaze o'er the ocean—a sun's slow decline
Over hills which, resolved[2] in stern silence, o'erlap and entwine
Base with base to knit strength more intensely: so, arm folded arm
O'er the chest whose slow heavings subsided.

XI

What spell or what charm
(For awhile there was trouble within me), what next should I urge
To sustain him where song had restored him? Song filled to the verge
His cup with the wine of this life, pressing all that it yields
Of mere fruitage, the strength and the beauty: beyond, on what fields,
Glean a vintage more potent and perfect to brighten the eye
And bring blood to the lip, and commend them the cup they put by?
He saith, "It is good"; still he drinks not: he lets me praise life,
Gives assent, yet would die for his own part.

XII

Then fancies grew rife
Which had come long ago on the pasture, when round me the sheep
Fed in silence—above, the one eagle wheeled slow as in sleep;
And I lay in my hollow and mused on the world that might lie
'Neath his ken, though I saw but the strip 'twixt the hill and the sky:
And I laughed—"Since my days are ordained to be passed with my flocks,
Let me people at least, with my fancies, the plains and the rocks,
Dream the life I am never to mix with, and image the show
Of mankind as they live in those fashions I hardly shall know!
Schemes of life, its best rules and right uses, the courage that gains,
And the prudence that keeps what men strive for." And now these old trains
Of vague thought came again; I grew surer; so, once more the string
Of my harp made response to my spirit, as thus—

[1] See *Ezekiel*, x.

[2] separated in outline

XIII

"Yea, my King,"
I began—"thou dost well in rejecting mere comforts that spring
From the mere mortal life held in common by man and by brute:
In our flesh grows the branch of this life, in our soul it bears fruit.
Thou hast marked the slow rise of the tree—how its stem trembled first
Till it passed the kid's lip, the stag's antler; then safely outburst
The fan-branches all round; and thou mindest when these, too, in turn,
Broke a-bloom and the palm tree seemed perfect: yet more was to learn,
E'en the good that comes in with the palm-fruit. Our dates shall we slight,
When their juice brings a cure for all sorrow? or care for the plight
Of the palm's self whose slow growth produced them? Not so! Stem and branch
Shall decay, nor be known in their place, while the palm-wine shall stanch
Every wound of man's spirit in winter. I pour thee such wine,
Leave the flesh to the fate it was fit for! the spirit be thine!
By the spirit, when age shall o'ercome thee, thou still shalt enjoy
More indeed than at first, when inconscious, the life of a boy.
Crush that life, and behold its wine running! Each deed thou hast done
Dies, revives, goes to work in the world! Until e'en as the sun
Looking down on the earth, though clouds spoil him, though tempests efface,
Can find nothing his own deed produced not, must everywhere trace
The results of his past summer-prime—so each ray of thy will,
Every flash of thy passion and prowess, long over, shall thrill
Thy whole people, the countless, with ardor, till they, too, give forth
A like cheer to their sons, who in turn, fill the South and North
With the radiance thy deed was the germ of. Carouse in the past!
But the license of age has its limit; thou diest at last:
As the lion when age dims his eyeball, the rose at her height,
So with man—so his power and his beauty forever take flight.
No! Again a long draught of my soul-wine! Look forth o'er the years!
Thou hast done now with eyes for the actual; begin with the seer's!
Is Saul dead? In the depth of the vale make his tomb—bid arise
A gray mountain of marble heaped four-square, till, built to the skies,
Let it mark where the great First King[1] slumbers: whose fame would ye know?
Up above see the rock's naked face, where the record shall go
In great characters cut by the scribe.—Such was Saul, so he did;
With the sages directing the work, by the populace chid—
For not half, they'll affirm, is comprised there! Which fault to amend,
In the grove with his kind grows the cedar, whereon they shall spend
(See, in tablets 'tis level before them) their praise, and record
With the gold of the graver, Saul's story—the statesman's great word
Side by side with the poet's sweet comment. The river's a-wave
With smooth paper-reeds grazing each other when prophet-winds[2] rave:
So the pen gives unborn generations their due and their part
In thy being! Then, first of the mighty, thank God that thou art!"

XIV

And behold while I sang . . . . but O Thou who didst grant me that day,
And before it not seldom hast granted thy help to essay,
Carry on and complete an adventure—my shield and my sword
In that act where my soul was thy servant, thy word was my word—
Still be with me, who then at the summit of human endeavor
And scaling the highest man's thought could, gazed hopeless as ever
On the new stretch of heaven above me—till, mighty to save,
Just one lift of thy hand cleared that distance—God's throne from man's grave!
Let me tell out my tale to its ending—my voice to my heart
Which can scarce dare believe in what marvels last night I took part,
As this morning I gather the fragments, alone with my sheep,

[1] of Israel
[2] Even the river reeds, made into papyrus, will record divine prophecy.

And still fear lest the terrible glory evanish like sleep!
For I wake in the gray, dewy covert, while Hebron[1] upheaves
The dawn, struggling with night, on his shoulder, and Kidron retrieves
Slow the damage of yesterday's sunshine.[2]

XV

I say then,—my song
While I sang thus, assuring the monarch, and ever more strong
Made a proffer of good to console him—he slowly resumed
His old motions and habitudes kingly. The right hand replumed
His black locks to their wonted composure, adjusted the swathes
Of his turban, and see—the huge sweat that his countenance bathes,
He wipes off with the robe; and he girds now his loins as of yore,
And feels slow for the armlets of price, with the clasp set before.
He is Saul, ye remember in glory—ere error had bent
The broad brow from the daily communion; and still, though much spent
Be the life and the bearing that front you, the same God did choose
To receive what a man may waste, desecrate, never quite lose.
So sank he along by the tent prop till, stayed by the pile
Of his armor and war cloak and garments, he leaned there awhile,
And sat out my singing—one arm round the tent prop, to raise
His bent head, and the other hung slack—till I touched on the praise
I foresaw from all men in all time, to the man patient there;
And thus ended, the harp falling forward. Then first I was 'ware
That he sat, as I say, with my head just above his vast knees
Which were thrust out on each side around me, like oak roots which please
To encircle a lamb when it slumbers. I looked up to know
If the best I could do had brought solace; he spoke not, but slow
Lifted up the hand slack at his side, till he laid it with care
Soft and grave, but in mild settled will, on my brow: through my hair
The large fingers were pushed, and he bent back my head, with kind power—
All my face back, intent to peruse it, as men do a flower.
Thus held he me there with his great eyes that scrutinized mine—
And oh, all my heart how it loved him! But where was the sign?
I yearned—"Could I help thee, my father, inventing a bliss,
I would add, to that life of the past, both the future and this;
I would give thee new life altogether, as good, ages hence,
As this moment—had love but the warrant, love's heart to dispense!"

XVI

Then the truth came upon me. No harp more—no song more! outbroke—

XVII

"I have gone the whole round of creation: I saw and I spoke;
I, a work of God's hand for that purpose, received in my brain
And pronounced on the rest of his handwork—returned him again
His creation's approval or censure: I spoke as I saw;
I report, as a man may of God's work—all's love, yet all's law.
Now I lay down the judgeship he lent me. Each faculty tasked
To perceive him, has gained an abyss, where a dewdrop was asked.
Have I knowledge? Confounded it shrivels at Wisdom laid bare.
Have I forethought? How purblind, how blank to the Infinite Care!
Do I task any faculty highest, to image success?
I but open my eyes—and perfection, no more and no less,
In the kind I imagined, full-fronts me, and God is seen God
In the star, in the stone, in the flesh, in the soul and the clod.
And thus looking within and around me, I ever renew
(With that stoop of the soul which in bending upraises it, too)
The submission of man's nothing-perfect to God's all-complete,

[1] the city which became for a time David's royal residence

[2] The Kidron is a nearly dry watercourse at the foot of Mt. Olivet. In dry countries, small streams are always perceptibly fuller at morning than at night.

As by each new obeisance in spirit, I climb to his feet.
Yet with all this abounding experience, this deity known,
I shall dare to discover some province, some gift of my own.
There's a faculty pleasant to exercise, hard to hoodwink,
I am fain to keep still in abeyance (I laugh as I think)
Lest, insisting to claim and parade in it, wot ye, I worst
E'en the Giver in one gift.—Behold, I could love if I durst!
But I sink the pretension as fearing a man may o'ertake
God's own speed in the one way of love: I abstain for love's sake.
—What, my soul? See thus far and no farther? When doors great and small,
Nine-and-ninety flew ope at our touch, should the hundredth appall?
In the least things have faith, yet distrust in the greatest of all?
Do I find love so full in my nature, God's ultimate gift,
That I doubt His own love can compete with it? Here, the parts shift?
Here, the creature surpass the Creator—the end, what Began?
Would I fain in my impotent yearning do all for this man,
And dare doubt He alone shall not help him, who yet alone can?
Would it ever have entered my mind, the bare will, much less power,
To bestow on this Saul what I sang of, the marvelous dower
Of the life he was gifted and filled with? To make such a soul,
Such a body, and then such an earth for insphering the whole?
And doth it not enter my mind (as my warm tears attest)
These good things being given, to go on, and give one more, the best?
Aye, to save and redeem and restore him, maintain at the height
This perfection—succeed with life's dayspring, death's minute of night?
Interpose at the difficult minute, snatch Saul the mistake,
Saul the failure, the ruin he seems now—and bid him awake
From the dream, the probation, the prelude, to find himself set
Clear and safe in new light and new life—a new harmony yet
To be run, and continued, and ended—who knows?—or endure!
The man taught enough by life's dream, of the rest to make sure;
By the pain-throb, triumphantly winning intensified bliss,
And the next world's reward and repose, by the struggles in this.

XVIII

"I believe it! 'Tis thou, God, that givest, 'tis I who receive:
In the first is the last, in thy will is my power to believe.
All's one gift: thou canst grant it moreover, as prompt to my prayer
As I breathe out this breath, as I open these arms to the air.
From thy will stream the worlds, life and nature, thy dread Sabaoth.[1]
I will? The mere atoms despise me! Why am I not loath
To look that, even that in the face, too? Why is it I dare
Think but lightly of such impuissance? What stops my despair?
This—'tis not what man Does which exalts him, but what man Would do!
See the King—I would help him but cannot, the wishes fall through.
Could I wrestle to raise him from sorrow, grow poor to enrich,
To fill up his life, starve my own out, I would—knowing which,
I know that my service is perfect. Oh, speak through me now!
Would I suffer for him that I love? So wouldst thou—so wilt thou!
So shall crown thee the topmost, ineffablest, uttermost crown—
And thy love fill infinitude wholly, nor leave up nor down
One spot for the creature to stand in! It is by no breath,
Turn of eye, wave of hand, that salvation joins issue with death!
As thy Love is discovered almighty, almighty be proved
Thy power, that exists with and for it, of being Beloved!
He who did most, shall bear most; the strongest shall stand the most weak.
'Tis the weakness in strength, that I cry for! my flesh, that I seek

[1] the armies of the Lord

In the Godhead! I seek and I find it. O Saul, it shall be
A Face like my face that receives thee; a Man like to me
Thou shalt love and be loved by, forever: a Hand like this hand
Shall throw open the gates of new life to thee! See the Christ stand!"

XIX

I know not too well how I found my way home in the night.
There were witnesses, cohorts about me, to left and to right,
Angels, powers, the unuttered, unseen, the alive, the aware.
I repressed, I got through them as hardly, as strugglingly there,
As a runner beset by the populace famished for news—
Life or death. The whole earth was awakened, hell loosed with her crews;
And the stars of night beat with emotion, and tingled and shot
Out in fire the strong pain of pent knowledge: but I fainted not,
For the Hand still impelled me at once and supported, suppressed
All the tumult, and quenched it with quiet, and holy behest,
Till the rapture was shut in itself, and the earth sank to rest.
Anon at the dawn, all that trouble had withered from earth—
Not so much, but I saw it die out in the day's tender birth;
In the gathered intensity brought to the gray of the hills;
In the shuddering forests' held breath; in the sudden wind-thrills;
In the startled wild beasts that bore off, each with eye sidling still
Though averted with wonder and dread; in the birds stiff and chill
That rose heavily as I approached them, made stupid with awe;
E'en the serpent that slid away silent—he felt the new law.
The same stared in the white humid faces upturned by the flowers;
The same worked in the heart of the cedar and moved the vine bowers:
And the little brooks witnessing murmured, persistent and low,
With their obstinate, all but hushed voices—"E'en so, it is so!"

1845-55

EVELYN HOPE

Beautiful Evelyn Hope is dead!
  Sit and watch by her side an hour.
That is her bookshelf, this her bed;
  She plucked that piece of geranium flower,
Beginning to die, too, in the glass;
  Little has yet been changed, I think;
The shutters are shut, no light may pass
  Save two long rays through the hinge's chink.

Sixteen years old when she died!
  Perhaps she had scarcely heard my name;
It was not her time to love; beside,
  Her life had many a hope and aim,
Duties enough and little cares,
  And now was quiet, now astir,
Till God's hand beckoned unawares—
  And the sweet white brow is all of her.

Is it too late then, Evelyn Hope?
  What, your soul was pure and true,
The good stars met in your horoscope,
  Made you of spirit, fire, and dew—
And, just because I was thrice as old
  And our paths in the world diverged so wide,
Each was naught to each, must I be told?
  We were fellow mortals, naught beside?

No, indeed! for God above
  Is great to grant, as mighty to make,
And creates the love to reward the love:
  I claim you still, for my own love's sake!
Delayed it may be for more lives yet,
  Through worlds I shall traverse, not a few:
Much is to learn, much to forget
  Ere the time be come for taking you.

But the time will come—at last it will,
  When, Evelyn Hope, what meant (I shall say)
In the lower earth, in the years long still,
  That body and soul so pure and gay?
Why your hair was amber, I shall divine,
  And your mouth of your own geranium's red—
And what you would do with me, in fine,
  In the new life come in the old one's stead.

I have lived (I shall say) so much since then,
  Given up myself so many times,
Gained me the gains of various men,
  Ransacked the ages, spoiled the climes;
Yet one thing, one, in my soul's full scope,
  Either I missed or itself missed me:
And I want and find you, Evelyn Hope!
  What is the issue? Let us see!

I loved you, Evelyn, all the while!
  My heart seemed full as it could hold;

There was place and to spare for the frank young smile,
And the red young mouth, and the hair's young gold.
So, hush—I will give you this leaf to keep:
See, I shut it inside the sweet cold hand!
There, that is our secret; go to sleep!
You will wake, and remember, and understand.

1855

FRA LIPPO LIPPI [1]

I am poor brother Lippo, by your leave!
You need not clap your torches to my face.
Zooks, what's to blame? You think you see a monk!
What, 'tis past midnight, and you go the rounds,
And here you catch me at an alley's end
Where sportive ladies leave their doors ajar?
The Carmine's my cloister; hunt it up,
Do—harry out, if you must show your zeal,
Whatever rat, there, haps on his wrong hole,
And nip each softling of a wee white mouse,
Weke, weke, that's crept to keep him company!
Aha, you know your betters! Then, you'll take
Your hand away that's fiddling on my throat,
And please to know me likewise. Who am I?
Why, one, sir, who is lodging with a friend
Three streets off—he's a certain . . . . how d'ye call?
Master—a . . . . Cosimo of the Medici,
In the house that caps the corner. Boh! you were best!
Remember and tell me, the day you're hanged,
How you affected such a gullet's gripe!
But you, sir, it concerns you that your knaves
Pick up a manner [2] nor discredit you.
Zooks, are we pilchards, [3] that they sweep the streets
And count fair prize what comes into their net?
He's Judas to a tittle, that man is!
Just such a face! Why, sir, you make amends.
Lord, I'm not angry! Bid your hang-dogs go
Drink out this quarter-florin to the health
Of the munificent House that harbors me
(And many more beside, lads! more beside!)
And all's come square again. I'd like his face—
His, elbowing on his comrade in the door
With the pike and lantern—for the slave that holds
John Baptist's head a-dangle by the hair
With one hand ("Look you, now," as who should say)
And his weapon in the other, yet unwiped!
It's not your chance to have a bit of chalk,
A wood-coal or the like? Or you should see!
Yes, I'm the painter, since you style me so.
What, brother Lippo's doings, up and down,
You know them and they take you? Like enough!
I saw the proper twinkle in your eye—
'Tell you, I liked your looks at very first.
Let's sit and set things straight now, hip to haunch.
Here's spring come, and the nights one makes up bands
To roam the town and sing out carnival,
And I've been three weeks shut within my mew,
A-painting for the great man, saints and saints
And saints again. I could not paint all night—
Ouf! I leaned out of window for fresh air.
There came a hurry of feet and little feet,
A sweep of lute strings, laughs, and whifts of song—
Flower o' the broom,
Take away love, and our earth is a tomb!
Flower o' the quince,
I let Lisa go, and what good in life since?
Flower o' the thyme—and so on. Round they went. [4]
Scarce had they turned the corner when a titter
Like the skipping of rabbits by moonlight—three slim shapes,
And a face that looked up . . . zooks, sir, flesh and blood,
That's all I'm made of! Into shreds it went,
Curtain and counterpane and coverlet,
All the bed furniture—a dozen knots,
There was a ladder! Down I let myself,

[1] This, like, "My Last Duchess," is among Browning's best dramatic monologues. It portrays admirably that period of the Italian Renaissance when men were growing more keenly awake to the charm of physical life, and society began to break through the restraints to which it had long submitted. In painting, the new spirit was manifested in the change from religious and symbolical subjects—haloed saints and choiring angels—to portraits and scenes from human life and the world of nature, or to religious pictures thoroughly humanized. The poem was suggested by a picture, the "Coronation of the Virgin" (described in lines 347 ff.), which is in the Academy of Fine Arts at Florence; the incidents of the life of Fra Filippo Lippi (1406?-1469) were obtained from Vasari's *Lives of the Painters.* He was first a monk, but he broke away from the Carmine, or Carmelite monastery, and came under the patronage of Cosimo de' Medici the Elder, the great banker, patron of art and literature, and practical ruler of the Florentine Republic. It is said that his patron once shut him up in his palace to keep him at work on some frescoes he was painting. Browning invents for him an evening of freedom from this captivity. Fra Lippo, stealing home, is caught by the watchman.

[2] mend a little

[3] Mediterranean sardines

[4] i. e., took up the song in turn

Hands and feet, scrambling somehow, and so dropped,
And after them. I came up with the fun
Hard by Saint Laurence,[1] hail fellow, well met—
Flower o' the rose,
If I've been merry, what matter who knows?
And so as I was stealing back again
To get to bed and have a bit of sleep
Ere I rise up tomorrow and go to work
On Jerome[2] knocking at his poor old breast
With his great round stone to subdue the flesh,
You snap me of the sudden. Ah, I see!
Though your eye twinkles still, you shake your head—
Mine's shaved—a monk, you say—the sting's in that!
If Master Cosimo announced himself,
Mum's the word naturally; but a monk!
Come, what am I a beast for? Tell us, now!
I was a baby when my mother died
And father died and left me in the street.
I starved there, God knows how, a year or two
On fig skins, melon parings, rinds and shucks,
Refuse and rubbish. One fine frosty day,
My stomach being empty as your hat,
The wind doubled me up and down I went.
Old Aunt Lapaccia trussed me with one hand,
(Its fellow was a stinger as I knew)
And so along the wall, over the bridge,
By the straight cut to the convent. Six words there,
While I stood munching my first bread that month:
"So, boy, you're minded," quoth the good fat father,
Wiping his own mouth—'twas refection time—
"To quit this very miserable world?
Will you renounce" . . . "the mouthful of bread?" thought I;
By no means! Brief, they made a monk of me;
I did renounce the world, its pride and greed,
Palace, farm, villa, shop, and banking house,
Trash, such as these poor devils of Medici
Have given their hearts to—all at eight years old.
Well, sir, I found in time, you may be sure,
'Twas not for nothing—the good bellyful,
The warm serge, and the rope that goes all round,
And day-long, blessed idleness beside!
"Let's see what the urchin's fit for"—that came next.
Not overmuch their way, I must confess.
Such a to-do! They tried me with their books;
Lord, they'd have taught me Latin in pure waste!
Flower o' the clove,
All the the Latin I construe is "amo," I love!
But, mind you, when a boy starves in the streets
Eight years together, as my fortune was,
Watching folk's faces to know who will fling
The bit of half-stripped grape-bunch he desires,
And who will curse or kick him for his pains—
Which gentleman processional[3] and fine,
Holding a candle to the Sacrament,
Will wink and let him lift a plate and catch
The droppings of the wax to sell again,
Or holla for the Eight[4] and have him whipped—
How say I?—nay, which dog bites, which lets drop
His bone from the heap of offal in the street—
Why, soul and sense of him grow sharp alike,
He learns the look of things, and none the less
For admonition from the hunger pinch.
I had a store of such remarks, be sure,
Which, after I found leisure, turned to use.
I drew men's faces on my copy books,
Scrawled them within the antiphonary's[5] marge,
Joined legs and arms to the long music-notes,
Found eyes and nose and chin for A's and B's,
And made a string of pictures of the world
Betwixt the ins and outs of verb and noun,
On the wall, the bench, the door. The monks looked black.
"Nay," quoth the Prior, "turn him out, d'ye say?
In no wise. Lose a crow and catch a lark.
What if at last we get our man of parts,
We Carmelites, like those Camaldolese[6]
And Preaching Friars,[7] to do our church up fine
And put the front on it that ought to be!"
And hereupon he bade me daub away.
Thank you! my head being crammed, the walls a blank,
Never was such prompt disemburdening.
First, every sort of monk, the black and white,[8]
I drew them, fat and lean; then, folk at church,
From good old gossips waiting to confess
Their cribs[9] of barrel droppings, candle ends—
To the breathless fellow at the altar foot,
Fresh from his murder, safe and sitting there
With the little children round him in a row
Of admiration, half for his beard and half

[1] the Church of San Lorenzo
[2] St. Jerome, one of the early church fathers

[3] taking part in a religious procession (as at one of the sacraments)
[4] the city magistrates
[5] a book of antiphons, or responsive songs
[6] a monastic order founded by St. Romuald at Camaldoli, near Florence
[7] Dominicans
[8] The Dominicans wore black, the Carmelites white.
[9] pilferings

For that white anger of his victim's son
Shaking a fist at him with one fierce arm,
Signing himself with the other because of Christ
(Whose sad face on the cross sees only this
After the passion of a thousand years)
Till some poor girl, her apron o'er her head,
(Which the intense eyes looked through) came at eve
On tiptoe, said a word, dropped in a loaf,
Her pair of earrings and a bunch of flowers
(The brute took growling), prayed, and so was gone.
I painted all, then cried " 'Tis ask and have;
Choose, for more's ready!"—laid the ladder flat,
And showed my covered bit of cloister wall.
The monks closed in a circle and praised loud
Till checked, taught what to see and not to see,
Being simple bodies—"That's the very man!
Look at the boy who stoops to pat the dog!
That woman's like the Prior's niece who comes
To care about his asthma; it's the life!"
But there my triumph's straw-fire flared and funked;
Their betters took their turn to see and say;
The Prior and the learned pulled a face
And stopped all that in no time. "How? what's here?
Quite from the mark of painting, bless us all!
Faces, arms, legs, and bodies like the true
As much as pea and pea! It's devil's game!
Your business is not to catch men with show,
With homage to the perishable clay,
But lift them over it, ignore it all,
Make them forget there's such a thing as flesh.
Your business is to paint the souls of men—
Man's soul, and it's a fire, smoke . . . no, it's not . . .
It's vapor done up like a new-born babe—
(In that shape when you die it leaves your mouth[1])
It's . . . well, what matters talking, it's the soul!
Give us no more of body than shows soul!
Here's Giotto[2] with his Saint a-praising God,
That sets us praising—why not stop with him?
Why put all thoughts of praise out of our head
With wonder at lines, colors, and what not?
Paint the soul, never mind the legs and arms!
Rub all out, try at it a second time.
Oh, that white, smallish female with the breasts,
She's just my niece . . . Herodias,[3] I would say—
Who went and danced and got men's heads cut off!
Have it all out!" Now, is this sense, I ask?
A fine way to paint soul, by painting body
So ill, the eye can't stop there, must go further
And can't fare worse! Thus, yellow does for white
When what you put for yellow's simply black,
And any sort of meaning looks intense
When all beside itself means and looks naught.
Why can't a painter lift each foot in turn,
Left foot and right foot, go a double step,
Make his flesh liker and his soul more like,
Both in their order? Take the prettiest face,
The Prior's niece . . . patron-saint—is it so pretty
You can't discover if it means hope, fear,
Sorrow, or joy? Won't beauty go with these?
Suppose I've made her eyes all right and blue,
Can't I take breath and try to add life's flash,
And then add soul and heighten them three-fold?
Or say there's beauty with no soul at all—
(I never saw it—put the case the same—)
If you get simple beauty and naught else,
You get about the best thing God invents;
That's somewhat: and you'll find the soul you have missed,
Within yourself, when you return him thanks.
"Rub all out!" Well, well, there's my life, in short,
And so the thing has gone on ever since.
I'm grown a man no doubt, I've broken bounds:
You should not take a fellow eight years old
And make him swear to never kiss the girls.
I'm my own master, paint now as I please—
Having a friend, you see, in the Corner-house!
Lord, it's fast holding by the rings in front—
Those great rings serve more purposes than just
To plant a flag in, or tie up a horse!
And yet the old schooling sticks, the old grave eyes
Are peeping o'er my shoulder as I work.
The heads shake still—"It's art's decline, my son!
You're not of the true painters, great and old;
Brother Angelico's[4] the man, you'll find;

[1] frequently represented so in early paintings, e. g., in the "Triumph of Death," ascribed to Orcagna, in the Campo Santo of Pisa

[2] Sometimes called "the father of modern Italian art"; he flourished at the beginning of the 14th century.

[3] It was not Herodias, but her daughter, Salome, who danced before Herod and obtained the head of John the Baptist. See *Matthew*, 14.

[4] Fra Angelico (1387-1415), who painted in the earlier manner; famous for his paintings of angels; cf. what Ruskin says, p. 730.

Brother Lorenzo [1] stands his single peer:
Fag on at flesh, you'll never make the third!"
Flower o' the pine,
You keep your mistr . . . manners, and I'll stick to mine!
I'm not the third, then: bless us, they must know!
Don't you think they're the likeliest to know,
They with their Latin? So, I swallow my rage,
Clench my teeth, suck my lips in tight, and paint
To please them—sometimes do and sometimes don't;
For, doing most, there's pretty sure to come
A turn, some warm eve finds me at my saints—
A laugh, a cry, the business of the world—
(Flower o' the peach,
Death for us all, and his own life for each!)
And my whole soul revolves, the cup runs over,
The world and life's too big to pass for a dream,
And I do these wild things in sheer despite,
And play the fooleries you catch me at,
In pure rage! The old mill-horse, out at grass
After hard years, throws up his stiff heels so,
Although the miller does not preach to him
The only good of grass is to make chaff.
What would men have? Do they like grass or no—
May they or mayn't they? All I want's the thing
Settled forever one way. As it is,
You tell too many lies and hurt yourself;
You don't like what you only like too much,
You do like what, if given you at your word,
You find abundantly detestable.
For me, I think I speak as I was taught;
I always see the garden and God there
A-making man's wife: and, my lesson learned,
The value and significance of flesh,
I can't unlearn ten minutes afterwards.

You understand me; I'm a beast, I know.
But see, now—why, I see as certainly
As that the morning star's about to shine,
What will hap some day. We've a youngster here
Comes to our convent, studies what I do,
Slouches and stares and lets no atom drop:
His name is Guidi [2]—he'll not mind the monks—
They call him Hulking Tom, he lets them talk—
He picks my practice up—he'll paint apace.
I hope so—though I never live so long,
I know what's sure to follow. You be judge!
You speak no Latin more than I, belike;
However, you're my man, you've seen the world—
The beauty and the wonder and the power,
The shapes of things, their colors, lights and shades,
Changes, surprises—and God made it all!
For what? Do you feel thankful, aye or no,
For this fair town's face, yonder river's line,
The mountain round it and the sky above,
Much more the figures of man, woman, child,
These are the frame to? What's it all about?
To be passed over, despised? or dwelt upon,
Wondered at? Oh, this last of course!—you say.
But why not do as well as say,—paint these
Just as they are, careless what comes of it?
God's work—paint anyone, and count it crime
To let a truth slip. Don't object, "His works
Are here already; nature is complete:
Suppose you reproduce her—which you can't—
There's no advantage! You must beat her, then."
For, don't you mark? we're made so that we love
First when we see them painted, things we have passed
Perhaps a hundred times nor cared to see;
And so they are better, painted—better to us,
Which is the same thing. Art was given for that;
God uses us to help each other so,
Lending our minds out. Have you noticed, now,
Your cullion's [3] hanging face? A bit of chalk,
And trust me but you should, though! How much more,
If I drew higher things with the same truth!
That were to take the Prior's pulpit-place,
Interpret God to all of you! Oh, oh,
It makes me mad to see what men shall do
And we in our graves! This world's no blot for us,
Nor blank; it means intensely, and means good:
To find its meaning is my meat and drink.
"Aye, but you don't so instigate to prayer!"
Strikes in the Prior: "When your meaning's plain
It does not say to folk—remember matins,
Or, mind you fast next Friday!" Why, for this,
What need of art at all? A skull and bones,
Two bits of stick nailed crosswise, or, what's best,

[1] Lorenzo Monaco, another contemporary painter

[2] Tommaso Guidi, better known as Masaccio (i. e. Tommasaccio, "Careless Tom"), the great pioneer of the Renaissance period, was the master of Filippo Lippi, not the pupil.

[3] rascal's

A bell to chime the hour with, does as well.
I painted a Saint Laurence [1] six months since
At Prato, [2] splashed the fresco in fine style:
"How looks my painting, now the scaffold's down?"
I ask a brother. "Hugely," he returns,
"Already not one phiz of your three slaves
Who turn the Deacon off his toasted side,
But's scratched and prodded to our heart's content,
The pious people have so eased their own
With coming to say prayers there in a rage:
We get on fast to see the bricks beneath.
Expect another job this time next year,
For pity and religion grow i' the crowd—
Your painting serves its purpose!" Hang the fools!

—That is—you'll not mistake an idle word
Spoke in a huff by a poor monk, God wot,
Tasting the air this spicy night which turns
The unaccustomed head like Chianti [3] wine!
Oh, the church knows! Don't misreport me, now!
It's natural a poor monk out of bounds
Should have his apt word to excuse himself:
And harken how I plot to make amends.
I have bethought me; I shall paint a piece
. . . . There's for you! [4] Give me six months, then go, see
Something in Sant' Ambrogio's! [5] Bless the nuns!
They want a cast o' my office. [6] I shall paint
God in the midst, Madonna and her babe,
Ringed by a bowery, flowery, angel brood,
Lilies and vestments and white faces, sweet
As puff on puff of grated orris root
When ladies crowd to Church at midsummer.
And then i' the front, of course a saint or two—
Saint John, [7] because he saves the Florentines.
Saint Ambrose, who puts down in black and white
The convent's friends and gives them a long day,
And Job, I must have him there past mistake,
The man of Uz (and Us without the z,
Painters who need his patience). Well, all these
Secured at their devotion, up shall come
Out of a corner when you least expect,
As one by a dark stair into a great light,
Music and talking, who but Lippo! I!—
Mazed, motionless, and moonstruck—I'm the man!
Back I shrink—what is this I see and hear?
I, caught up with my monk's things by mistake,
My old serge gown and rope that goes all round,
I, in this presence, this pure company!
Where's a hole, where's a corner for escape?
Then steps a sweet angelic slip of a thing
Forward, puts out a soft palm—"Not so fast!"
—Addresses the celestial presence, "Nay—
He made you and devised you, after all.
Though he's none of you! Could Saint John, there, draw—
His camel-hair [8] make up a painting brush?
We come to brother Lippo for all that,
Iste perfecit opus!" [9] So, all smile—
I shuffle sideways with my blushing face
Under the cover of a hundred wings
Thrown like a spread of kirtles when you're gay
And play hot cockles, all the doors being shut,
Till, wholly unexpected, in there pops
The hot-head husband! Thus I scuttle off
To some safe bench behind, not letting go
The palm of her, the little, lily thing
That spoke the good word for me in the nick,
Like the Prior's niece . . . Saint Lucy, I would say,
And so all's saved for me, and for the church
A pretty picture gained. Go, six months hence!
Your hand, sir, and good-by; no lights, no lights!
The street's hushed, and I know my own way back,
Don't fear me! There's the gray beginning. Zooks!

1855

UP AT A VILLA—DOWN IN THE CITY

(AS DISTINGUISHED BY AN ITALIAN PERSON OF QUALITY)

Had I but plenty of money, money enough and to spare,
The house for me, no doubt, were a house in the city-square;
Ah, such a life, such a life as one leads at the window there!

Something to see, by Bacchus, something to hear, at least!
There, the whole day long, one's life is a perfect feast;

[1] a Christian martyr of the 3d century who was roasted alive on a gridiron, or iron chair
[2] a town near Florence
[3] a famous vineyard region near Florence
[4] giving them money
[5] St. Ambrose's, a Florentine convent
[6] a stroke of my skill
[7] the patron saint of Florence

[8] See page 46 (*Matthew*, iii, 4).
[9] "This is he who made it" is the inscription on a scroll in the painting described, indicating the portrait of Lippi.

While up at a villa one lives, I maintain it, no more than a beast.

Well now, look at our villa! stuck like the horn of a bull
Just on a mountain edge as bare as the creature's skull,
Save a mere shag of a bush with hardly a leaf to pull—
I scratch my own, sometimes, to see if the hair's turned wool.

But the city, oh, the city—the square with the houses! Why,
They are stone-faced, white as a curd, there's something to take the eye!
Houses in four straight lines, not a single front awry;
You watch who crosses and gossips, who saunters, who hurries by;
Green blinds, as a matter of course, to draw when the sun gets high;
And the shops with fanciful signs which are painted properly.

What of a villa? Though winter be over in March by rights,
'Tis May, perhaps, ere the snow shall have withered well off the heights:
You've the brown plowed land before, where the oxen steam and wheeze,
And the hills over-smoked behind by the faint gray olive trees.

Is it better in May, I ask you? You've summer all at once;
In a day he leaps complete with a few strong April suns.
'Mid the sharp, short, emerald wheat, scarce risen three fingers well,
The wild tulip, at end of its tube, blows out its great red bell
Like a thin, clear bubble of blood, for the children to pick and sell.

Is it ever hot in the square? There's a fountain to spout and splash!
In the shade it sings and springs; in the shine such foambows flash
On the horses with curling fish tails, that prance and paddle and pash
Round the lady atop in her conch—fifty gazers do not abash,
Though all that she wears is some weeds round her waist in a sort of sash.

All the year long at the villa, nothing to see though you linger,
Except yon cypress that points like death's lean, lifted forefinger.
Some think fireflies pretty, when they mix i' the corn and mingle,
Or thrid the stinking hemp till the stalks of it seem a-tingle.
Late August or early September, the stunning cicala is shrill,
And the bees keep their tiresome whine round the resinous firs on the hill.
Enough of the seasons—I spare you the months of the fever and chill.

Ere you open your eyes in the city, the blessed church bells begin;
No sooner the bells leave off than the diligence rattles in;
You get the pick of the news, and it costs you never a pin.
By and by there's the traveling doctor gives pills, lets blood, draws teeth;
Or the Pulcinello[1] trumpet breaks up the market beneath.
At the post office such a scene-picture—the new play, piping hot!
And a notice how, only this morning, three liberal thieves were shot.[2]
Above it, behold the Archbishop's most fatherly of rebukes,
And beneath, with his crown and his lion, some little new law of the Duke's!
Or a sonnet with flowery marge, to the Reverend Don So-and-so,
Who is Dante, Boccaccio, Petrarca, Saint Jerome, and Cicero.
"And moreover," (the sonnet goes riming,) "the skirts of Saint Paul has reached,
Having preached us those six Lent-lectures more unctuous than ever he preached."
Noon strikes—here sweeps the procession! our Lady borne smiling and smart 52
With a pink gauze gown all spangles, and seven swords stuck in her heart!
Bang-whang-whang goes the drum, *tootle-te-tootle* the fife;
No keeping one's haunches still; it's the greatest pleasure in life.

But bless you, it's dear—it's dear! fowls, wine, at double the rate.
They have clapped a new tax upon salt, and what oil pays passing the gate
It's a horror to think of. And so, the villa for me, not the city!
Beggars can scarcely be choosers: but still—ah, the pity, the pity!

[1] English "Punch" (Punch and Judy show)
[2] There is a subtle irony in making this soulless civilian betray his childish contempt for the liberal or republican party.

Look, two and two go the priests, then the monks with cowls and sandals.
And the penitents dressed in white shirts, a-holding the yellow candles;
One, he carries a flag up straight, and another a cross with handles,
And the Duke's guard brings up the rear, for the better prevention of scandals.
Bang-whang-whang goes the drum, *tootle-te tootle* the fife.
Oh, a day in the city-square, there is no such pleasure in life!

1855

MEMORABILIA [1]

Ah, did you once see Shelley plain,
And did he stop and speak to you,
And did you speak to him again?
How strange it seems and new!

But you were living before that,
And also you are living after;
And the memory I started at—
My starting moves your laughter!

I crossed a moor, with a name of its own
And a certain use in the world no doubt,
Yet a hand's breadth of it shines alone
'Mid the blank miles round about:

For there I picked up on the heather
And there I put inside my breast
A molted feather, an eagle feather!
Well, I forget the rest.

1855

POPULARITY

Stand still, true poet that you are! [2]
I know you; let me try and draw you.
Some night you'll fail us; when afar
You rise, remember one man saw you,
Knew you, and named a star!

My star, God's glowworm! Why extend
That loving hand of his which leads you,
Yet locks you safe from end to end
Of this dark world, unless he needs you,
Just saves your light to spend?

His clenched hand shall unclose at last,
I know, and let out all the beauty:
My poet holds the future fast,
Accepts the coming ages' duty,
Their present for this past.

That day the earth's feast-master's brow
Shall clear, to God the chalice raising;
"Others give best at first, but thou
Forever set'st our table praising,
Keep'st the good wine till now!"

Meantime, I'll draw you as you stand,
With few or none to watch and wonder:
I'll say—a fisher, on the sand
By Tyre the old, with ocean plunder,
A netful, brought to land.

Who has not heard how Tyrian shells
Enclosed the blue, that dye of dyes
Whereof one drop worked miracles,
And colored like Astarte's [3] eyes
Raw silk the merchant sells?

And each bystander of them all
Could criticize, and quote tradition
How depths of blue sublimed some pall [4]—
To get which, pricked a king's ambition;
Worth scepter, crown and ball. [5]

Yet there's the dye, in that rough mesh,
The sea has only just o'er-whispered!
Live whelks, each lip's beard dripping fresh,
As if they still the water's lisp heard
Through foam the rock-weeds thresh.

Enough to furnish Solomon
Such hangings for his cedar house,
That, when gold-robed he took the throne
In that abyss of blue, the Spouse [6]
Might swear his presence shone.

Most like the center spike of gold
Which burns deep in the bluebell's womb
What time, with ardors manifold,
The bee goes singing to her groom,
Drunken and overbold.

Mere conchs! not fit for warp or woof!
Till cunning come to pound and squeeze
And clarify—refine to proof
The liquor filtered by degrees,
While the world stands aloof.

[1] Once, in a bookstore, Browning overheard some one mention the fact that he had once seen Shelley. Browning was a youthful admirer of Shelley, having received from certain volumes of him and Keats—a chance-found "eagle feather," as it were—some of his earliest inspiration. On Keats, see the next poem.

[2] This poet is not necessarily Keats, but Keats is a type of the great man who, missing popularity in his own life, dies obscurely—like the ancient, obscure discoverer of the murex, the fish whose precious purple dyes made the fortune of many a mere trader or artisan who came after him. (Without intimating for a moment that Tennyson was a mere artisan, it may be freely acknowledged that much of his popularity, in which at this time, 1855, he quite exceeded Browning, was due to qualities which he derived from Keats.)

[3] the Syrian Aphrodite (Venus)

[4] coronation robe

[5] the golden orb borne with the scepter as emblem of sovereignty

[6] *The Song of Solomon,* v, i.

And there's the extract, flasked and fine,
  And priced and salable at last!
And Hobbs, Nobbs, Stokes, and Nokes combine
  To paint the future from the past,
Put blue into their line.[1]

Hobbs hints blue—straight he turtle eats;
  Nobbs prints blue—claret crowns his cup;
Nokes outdares Stokes in azure feats—
  Both gorge. Who fished the murex up?
What porridge had John Keats?

1855

THE PATRIOT[2]

AN OLD STORY.

It was roses, roses, all the way,
  With myrtle mixed in my path like mad:
The house roofs seemed to heave and sway,
  The church spires flamed, such flags they had,
A year ago on this very day.

The air broke into a mist with bells,
  The old walls rocked with the crowd and cries.
Had I said, "Good folk, mere noise repels—
  But give me your sun from yonder skies!"
They had answered, "And afterwards, what else?"

Alack, it was I who leaped at the sun
  To give it my loving friends to keep!
Naught man could do, have I left undone:
  And you see my harvest, what I reap
This very day, now a year is run.

There's nobody on the house-tops now—
  Just a palsied few at the windows set;
For the best of the sight is, all allow,
  At the Shambles' Gate—or, better yet,
By the very scaffold's foot, I trow.

I go in the rain, and, more than needs,
  A rope cuts both my wrists behind;
And I think, by the feel, my forehead bleeds,
  For they fling, whoever has a mind,
Stones at me for my year's misdeeds.

Thus I entered, and thus I go!
  In triumphs, people have dropped down dead.
"Paid by the world, what dost thou owe
  Me?"—God might question; now instead,
'Tis God shall repay; I am safer so.

1855

[1] i. e., aspire to popularity in literature
[2] The poem is purely dramatic, not historical.

"CHILDE ROLAND TO THE DARK TOWER CAME"[3]

My first thought was, he lied in every word,
  That hoary cripple, with malicious eye
  Askance to watch the working of his lie
On mine, and mouth scarce able to afford
Suppression of the glee that pursed and scored
  Its edge, at one more victim gained thereby.

What else should he be set for, with his staff?
  What, save to waylay with his lies, ensnare
  All travelers who might find him posted there,
And ask the road? I guessed what skull-like laugh
Would break, what crutch 'gin write my epitaph
  For pastime in the dusty thoroughfare,

If at his counsel I should turn aside
  Into that ominous tract which, all agree,
  Hides the Dark Tower. Yet acquiescingly
I did turn as he pointed: neither pride
Nor hope rekindling at the end descried,
  So much as gladness that some end might be.

For, what with my whole world-wide wandering,
  What with my search drawn out through years, my hope
  Dwindled into a ghost not fit to cope
With that obstreperous joy success would bring—
I hardly tried now to rebuke the spring
  My heart made, finding failure in its scope.

As when a sick man very near to death
  Seems dead indeed, and feels begin and end
  The tears, and takes the farewell of each friend,
And hears one bid the other go, draw breath
Freelier outside—("Since all is o'er," he saith,
  "And the blow fallen no grieving can amend";)

While some discuss if near the other graves
  Be room enough for this, and when a day
  Suits best for carrying the corpse away,
With care about the banners, scarves, and staves:
And still the man hears all, and only craves
  He may not shame such tender love and stay.

[3] The title is a line of Edgar's song, *King Lear,* III, iv, 187. "Childe" is an old title for a youth of noble birth. There has been much discussion over the question whether the knight's pilgrimage, which is here so vividly and yet so mystically portrayed, is allegorical or not. Doubtless there is no elaborate allegory in it, though there may well be a moral—something like constancy to an ideal, Browning admitted.

Thus, I had so long suffered in this quest,
Heard failure prophesied so oft, been writ
So many times among "The Band"—to wit
The knights who to the Dark Tower's search addressed
Their steps—that just to fail as they, seemed best,
And all the doubt was now—should I be fit?

So, quiet as despair, I turned from him,
That hateful cripple, out of his highway
Into the path he pointed. All the day
Had been a dreary one at best, and dim
Was settling to its close, yet shot one grim
Red leer to see the plain catch its estray.

For mark! No sooner was I fairly found
Pledged to the plain, after a pace or two,
Than, pausing to throw backward a last view
O'er the safe road, 'twas gone; gray plain all round;
Nothing but plain to the horizon's bound.
I might go on; naught else remained to do.

So, on I went. I think I never saw
Such starved ignoble nature; nothing throve:
For flowers—as well expect a cedar grove!
But cockle, spurge, according to their law
Might propagate their kind, with none to awe,
You'd think; a burr had been a treasure trove.

No! penury, inertness, and grimace,
In some strange sort, were the land's portion. "See
Or shut your eyes," said Nature peevishly,
"It nothing skills; [1] I cannot help my case;
'Tis the Last Judgment's fire must cure this place,
Calcine its clods and set my prisoners free."

If there pushed any ragged thistle stalk
Above its mates, the head was chopped; the bents [2]
Were jealous else. What made those holes and rents
In the dock's harsh swarth leaves, bruised as to balk
All hope of greenness? 'Tis a brute must walk
Pashing their life out, with a brute's intents.

As for the grass, it grew as scant as hair
In leprosy; thin dry blades pricked the mud
Which underneath looked kneaded up with blood.
One stiff, blind horse, his every bone a-stare,
Stood stupefied, however he came there;
Thrust out past service from the devil's stud!

[1] avails nothing
[2] grass stalks

Alive? He might be dead for aught I know,
With that red, gaunt, and colloped [3] neck a-strain,
And shut eyes underneath the rusty mane;
Seldom went such grotesqueness with such woe;
I never saw a brute I hated so;
He must be wicked to deserve such pain.

I shut my eyes and turned them on my heart.
As a man calls for wine before he fights,
I asked one draught of earlier, happier sights,
Ere fitly I could hope to play my part.
Think first, fight afterwards—the soldier's art:
One taste of the old time sets all to rights.

Not it! I fancied Cuthbert's reddening face
Beneath its garniture of curly gold,
Dear fellow, till I almost felt him fold
An arm in mine to fix me to the place,
That way he used. Alas, one night's disgrace!
Out went my heart's new fire and left it cold.

Giles then, the soul of honor—there he stands
Frank as ten years ago when knighted first.
What honest man should dare (he said) he durst.
Good—but the scene shifts—faugh! what hangman hands
Pin to his breast a parchment? His own bands
Read it. Poor traitor, spit upon and curst!

Better this present than a past like that;
Back therefore to my darkening path again!
No sound, no sight as far as eye could strain.
Will the night send a howlet or a bat?
I asked: when something on the dismal flat
Came to arrest my thoughts and change their train.

A sudden little river crossed my path
As unexpected as a serpent comes.
No sluggish tide congenial to the glooms;
This, as it frothed by, might have been a bath
For the fiend's glowing hoof—to see the wrath
Of its black eddy bespate [4] with flakes and spumes..

So petty, yet so spiteful! All along,
Low scrubby alders kneeled down over it;
Drenched willows flung them headlong in a fit
Of mute despair, a suicidal throng:
The river which had done them all the wrong,
Whate'er that was, rolled by, deterred no whit.

[3] ridged
[4] That is, bespit, bespattered; from the archaic *bespete*. The rather unusual diction employed throughout the poem helps to heighten its grotesque character.

Which, while I forded—good saints, how I feared
To set my foot upon a dead man's cheek,
Each step, or feel the spear I thrust to seek
For hollows, tangled in his hair or beard!
—It may have been a water rat I speared,
But, ugh, it sounded like a baby's shriek.

Glad was I when I reached the other bank.
Now for a better country. Vain presage!
Who were the strugglers, what war did they wage,
Whose savage trample thus could pad the dank
Soil to a plash? Toads in a poisoned tank,
Or wild cats in a red-hot iron cage—

The fight must so have seemed in that fell cirque.
What penned them there, with all the plain to choose?
No footprint leading to that horrid mews,
None out of it. Mad brewage set to work
Their brains, no doubt, like galley slaves the Turk
Pits for his pastime, Christians against Jews.

And more than that—a furlong on—why, there!
What bad use was that engine for, that wheel,
Or brake, not wheel—that harrow fit to reel
Men's bodies out like silk? With all the air
Of Tophet's[1] tool, on earth left unaware,
Or brought to sharpen its rusty teeth of steel.

Then came a bit of stubbed ground, once a wood,
Next a marsh, it would seem, and now mere earth
Desperate and done with (so a fool finds mirth,
Makes a thing and then mars it, till his mood
Changes and off he goes); within a rood—
Bog, clay and rubble, sand, and stark black dearth.

Now blotches rankling, colored gay and grim,
Now patches where some leanness of the soil's
Broke into moss or substances like boils;
Then came some palsied oak, a cleft in him
Like a distorted mouth that splits its rim
Gaping at death, and dies while it recoils.

And just as far as ever from the end!
Naught in the distance but the evening, naught
To point my footstep farther! At the thought,
A great black bird, Apollyon's[2] bosom friend,
Sailed past, nor beat his wide wing dragon-penned[3]
That brushed my cap—perchance the guide I sought.

For, looking up, aware I somehow grew,
'Spite of the dusk, the plain had given place
All round to mountains—with such name to grace
Mere ugly heights and heaps now stolen in view.
How thus they had surprised me—solve it, you!
How to get from them was no clearer case.

Yet half I seemed to recognize some trick
Of mischief happened to me, God knows when—
In a bad dream, perhaps. Here ended, then,
Progress this way. When, in the very nick
Of giving up, one time more, came a click
As when a trap shuts—you're inside the den!

Burningly it came on me all at once,
This was the place! Those two hills on the right,
Crouched like two bulls locked horn in horn in fight;
While to the left, a tall scalped mountain . . . Dunce,
Dotard, a-dozing at the very nonce,[4]
After a life spent training for the sight!

What in the midst lay but the Tower itself?
The round, squat turret, blind as the fool's heart,
Built of brown stone, without a counterpart
In the whole world. The tempest's mocking elf
Points to the shipman thus the unseen shelf
He strikes on, only when the timbers start.

Not see? Because of night, perhaps?—Why, day
Came back again for that! Before it left,
The dying sunset kindled through a cleft:
The hills, like giants at a hunting, lay,
Chin upon hand, to see the game at bay,
"Now stab and end the creature—to the heft!"

Not hear? When noise was everything! It tolled
Increasing like a bell. Names in my ears,
Of all the lost adventurers my peers,—
How such a one was strong, and such was bold,
And such was fortunate, yet each of old
Lost, lost! One moment knelled the woe of years.

[1] hell's

[2] Satan's
[3] with pinions like a dragon's
[4] critical moment

There they stood, ranged along the hillsides, met
To view the last of me, a living frame
For one more picture! In a sheet of flame
I saw them and I knew them all. And yet
Dauntless the slug-horn [1] to my lips I set,
And blew: *"Childe Roland to the Dark Tower came."*

1855

RABBI BEN EZRA [2]

Grow old along with me!
The best is yet to be,
The last of life, for which the first was made:
Our times are in his hand
Who saith, "A whole I planned,
Youth shows but half; trust God; see all, nor be afraid!"

Not that, amassing flowers,
Youth sighed, "Which rose make ours,
Which lily leave and then as best recall?"
Not that, admiring stars,
It yearned, "Nor Jove, nor Mars;
Mine be some figured flame which blends, transcends them all!"

Not for such hopes and fears [3]
Annulling youth's brief years,
Do I remonstrate: folly wide the mark!
Rather I prize the doubt [4]
Low kinds exist without,
Finished and finite clods, untroubled by a spark.

Poor vaunt of life indeed,
Were man but formed to feed
On joy, to solely seek and find and feast:
Such feasting ended, then
As sure an end to men:
Irks care [5] the crop-full bird? Frets doubt the maw-crammed beast?

Rejoice we are allied
To that which doth provide
And not partake, effect and not receive!
A spark disturbs our clod;
Nearer we hold of God
Who gives, than of his tribes that take, I must believe.

Then, welcome each rebuff
That turns earth's smoothness rough,
Each sting that bids nor sit nor stand but go!
Be our joys three parts pain!
Strive, and hold cheap the strain;
Learn, nor account the pang; dare, never grudge the throe!

For thence—a paradox
Which comforts while it mocks—
Shall life succeed in that it seems to fail:
What I aspired to be,
And was not, comforts me;
A brute I might have been, but would not sink i' the scale.

What is he but a brute
Whose flesh has soul to suit,
Whose spirit works lest arms and legs want play?
To man, propose this test—
Thy body at its best,
How far can that project thy soul on its lone way?

Yet gifts should prove their use:
I own the Past profuse
Of power each side, perfection every turn:
Eyes, ears took in their dole,
Brain treasured up the whole;
Should not the heart beat once "How good to live and learn?"

Not once beat "Praise be thine!
I see the whole design,
I, who saw power, see now Love, perfect, too;
Perfect I call thy plan:
Thanks that I was a man!
Maker, remake, complete—I trust what thou shalt do!"

For pleasant is this flesh;
Our soul, in its rose-mesh
Pulled ever to the earth, still yearns for rest.
Would we some prize might hold
To match those manifold
Possessions of the brute—gain most, as we did best!

Let us not always say,
"Spite of this flesh today
I strove, made head, gained ground upon the whole!"
As the bird wings and sings,
Let us cry, "All good things
Are ours, nor soul helps flesh more, now, than flesh helps soul!"

[1] Not properly the name of a horn, if the word is a corruption of "slogan." It was thus misused by Chatterton frequently, and Browning may have obtained it from that source.

[2] There was a certain Rabbi, Ben Ezra (cr Abenezra, or Ibn Ezra), who was a great scholar and theologian of the twelfth century. He was born at Toledo and traveled widely, dwelling at Rome, London, in Palestine, and elsewhere. Of his sayings in this poem, many express Browning's philosophy though some are taken from the Rabbi's own writings.

[3] i. e., such as those just mentioned, which seem to make youth ineffectual

[4] Supply "that." This is exactly the thought which Tennyson had already expressed in *In Memoriam*, xxvii.

[5] subject of "irks"

Therefore I summon age
To grant youth's heritage,
Life's struggle having so far reached its term:
Thence shall I pass, approved
A man, for aye removed
From the developed brute; a God though in the germ.

And I shall thereupon
Take rest, ere I be gone
Once more on my adventure brave and new:
Fearless and unperplexed,
When I wage battle next,
What weapons to select, what armor to indue.[1]

Youth ended, I shall try
My gain or loss thereby;
Leave the fire ashes, what survives is gold.
And I shall weigh the same,
Give life its praise or blame:
Young, all lay in dispute; I shall know, being old.

For note, when evening shuts,
A certain moment cuts
The deed off, calls the glory from the gray:
A whisper from the west
Shoots—"Add this to the rest,
Take it and try its worth; here dies another day."

So, still within this life,
Though lifted o'er its strife,
Let me discern, compare, pronounce at last,
"This rage was right i' the main,
That acquiescence vain;
The Future I may face now I have proved the Past."

For more is not reserved
To man, with soul just nerved
To act tomorrow what he learns today:
Here, work enough to watch
The Master work, and catch
Hints of the proper craft, tricks of the tool's true play.

As it was better, youth
Should strive, through acts uncouth,
Toward making, than repose on aught found made:
So, better, age, exempt
From strife, should know, than tempt
Further. Thou waitedst age; wait death, nor be afraid!

Enough now, if the Right
And Good and Infinite
Be named here, as thou callest thy hand thine own,
With knowledge absolute,
Subject to no dispute
From fools that crowded youth, nor let thee feel alone.

Be there, for once and all,
Severed great minds from small,
Announced to each his station in the Past!
Was I,[2] the world arraigned,
Were they,[2] my soul disdained,
Right? Let age speak the truth and give us peace at last!

Now, who shall arbitrate?
Ten men love what I hate,
Shun what I follow, slight what I receive;
Ten, who in ears and eyes
Match me; we all surmise,
They this thing, and I that: whom shall my soul believe?

Not on the vulgar mass
Called "work" must sentence pass,
Things done, that took the eye and had the price;
O'er which, from level stand,
The low world laid its hand,
Found straightway to its mind, could value in a trice:

But all, the world's coarse thumb
And finger failed to plumb,
So passed in making up the main account;
All instincts immature,
All purposes unsure,
That weighed not as his work, yet swelled the man's amount;

Thoughts hardly to be packed
Into a narrow act,
Fancies that broke through language and escaped;
All I could never be,
All, men ignored in me,
This, I was worth to God, whose wheel the pitcher shaped.

Aye, note that Potter's wheel,
That metaphor! and feel
Why time spins fast, why passive lies our clay—
Thou, to whom fools propound,
When the wine makes its round,
"Since life fleets, all is change; the past gone, seize today!"[3]

[1] put on

[2] supply "whom"

[3] Both the figure and the philosophy here obviously suggest Omar Khayyàm, though both are very much older.

Fool! All that is, at all,
Lasts ever, past recall;
Earth changes, but thy soul and God stand
sure:
What entered into thee,
That was, is, and shall be:
Time's wheel runs back or stops; Potter and
clay endure.

He fixed thee 'mid this dance
Of plastic [1] circumstance,
This present, thou, forsooth, would fain arrest;
Machinery just meant
To give thy soul its bent,
Try thee and turn thee forth, sufficiently
impressed. [2]

What though the earlier grooves,
Which ran the laughing loves
Around thy base, no longer pause and press?
What though, about thy rim,
Skull-things in order grim
Grow out, in graver mood, obey the sterner
stress?

Look not thou down, but up!
To uses of a cup,
The festal board, lamp's flash, and trumpet's
peal,
The new wine's foaming flow,
The Master's lips aglow!
Thou, heaven's consummate cup, what needst
thou with earth's wheel?

But I need, now as then,
Thee, God, who moldest men;
And since, not even while the whirl was worst,
Did I—to the wheel of life
With shapes and colors rife,
Bound dizzily—mistake my end, to slake thy
thirst:

So, take and use thy work:
Amend what flaws may lurk,
What strain o' the stuff, what warpings past
the aim!
My times be in thy hand!
Perfect the cup as planned!
Let age approve of youth, and death complete
the same!

1864

PROSPICE [3]

Fear death?—To feel the fog in my throat,
The mist in my face,
When the snows begin, and the blasts denote
I am nearing the place,
The power of the night, the press of the storm,
The post of the foe;
Where he stands, the Arch Fear in a visible
form,
Yet the strong man must go:
For the journey is done and the summit
attained,
And the barriers fall,
Though a battle's to fight ere the guerdon be
gained,
The reward of it all.
I was ever a fighter, so—one fight more,
The best and the last!
I would hate that death bandaged my eyes,
and forbore,
And bade me creep past.
No! Let me taste the whole of it, fare like my
peers,
The heroes of old,
Bear the brunt, in a minute pay glad life's
arrears
Of pain, darkness, and cold.
For sudden the worst turns the best to the
brave,
The black minute's at end,
And the elements' rage, the fiend-voices that
rave,
Shall dwindle, shall blend,
Shall change, shall become first a peace out of
pain,
Then a light, then thy breast,
O thou soul of my soul! I shall clasp thee
again,
And with God be the rest!

1861 1864

[1] shaping [2] molded and figured

[3] This poem was written in 1861, shortly after Mrs. Browning's death. The title means "Look forward."

HERVÉ RIEL [4]

I

On the sea and at the Hogue, sixteen hundred
ninety-two,
Did the English fight the French—woe to
France!
And, the thirty-first of May, helter-skelter
through the blue,
Like a crowd of frightened porpoises [5] a shoal
of sharks pursue,
Came crowding ship on ship to Saint Malo
on the Rance,
With the English fleet in view.

[4] The victory of La Hogue was won off the north coast of Normandy by the British and Dutch Allies against Louis XIV. Hervé Riel, a Breton sailor from the village of Croisic, saved many of the fleeing French vessels by piloting them through the shallows at the mouth of the river Rance to the roadstead at St. Malo.

[5] Supply "which."

II

'Twas the squadron that escaped, with the victor in full chase;
First and foremost of the drove, in his great ship, Damfreville;
Close on him fled, great and small,
Twenty-two good ships in all;
And they signaled to the place
"Help the winners of a race!
Get us guidance, give us harbor, take us quick—or, quicker still,
Here's the English can and will!"

III

Then the pilots of the place put out brisk and leaped on board;
"Why what hope or chance have ships like these to pass?" laughed they;
"Rocks to starboard, rocks to port, all the passage scarred and scored,
Shall the *Formidable* here with her twelve and eighty guns
Think to make the river mouth by the single narrow way,
Trust to enter where 'tis ticklish for a craft of twenty tons,
And with flow at full beside?
Now, 'tis slackest ebb of tide.
Reach the mooring? Rather say,
While rock stands or water runs,
Not a ship will leave the bay!"

IV

Then was called a council straight.
Brief and bitter the debate:
"Here's the English at our heels; would you have them take in tow
All that's left us of the fleet, linked together stern and bow,
For a prize to Plymouth Sound?
Better run the ships aground!"
(Ended Damfreville his speech).
"Not a minute more to wait!
Let the Captains all and each
Shove ashore, then blow up, burn the vessels on the beach!
France must undergo her fate."

V

"Give the word!" But no such word
Was ever spoke or heard;
For up stood, for out stepped, for in struck amid all these
—A Captain? A Lieutenant? A Mate—first, second, third?
No such man of mark, and meet
With his betters to compete!
But a simple Breton sailor pressed by Tourville for the fleet,
A poor, coasting pilot he, Hervé Riel the Croisickese.

VI

And "What mockery or malice have we here?" cries Hervé Riel:
"Are you mad, you Malouins? Are you cowards, fools, or rogues?
Talk to me of rocks and shoals, me who took the soundings, tell
On my fingers every bank, every shallow, every swell,
'Twixt the offing here and Grève where the river disembogues?
Are you bought by English gold? Is it love the lying's for?
Morn and eve, night and day,
Have I piloted your bay,
Entered free and anchored fast at the foot of Solidor.
Burn the fleet and ruin France? That were worse than fifty Hogues!
Sirs, they know I speak the truth! Sirs, believe me there's a way!
Only let me lead the line,
Have the biggest ship to steer,
Get this *Formidable* clear,
Make the others follow mine.
And I lead them, most and least, by a passage I know well,
Right to Solidor past Grève,
And there lay them safe and sound:
And if one ship misbehave,
Keel so much as grate the ground,
Why I've nothing but my life—here's my head!" cries Hervé Riel.

VII

Not a minute more to wait.
"Steer us in, then, small and great!
Take the helm, lead the line, save the squadron!" cried its chief.
Captains, give the sailor place!
He is Admiral, in brief.
Still the north wind, by God's grace!
See the noble fellow's face
As the big ship, with a bound,
Clears the entry like a hound,
Keeps the passage as its inch of way were the wide sea's profound!
See, safe through shoal and rock,
How they follow in a flock,
Not a ship that misbehaves, not a keel that grates the ground,
Not a spar that comes to grief!

The peril, see, is past,
All are harbored to the last,
And just as Hervé Riel hollas "Anchor!"—sure as fate,
Up the English come—too late!

VIII

So, the storm subsides to calm;
They see the green trees wave
On the heights o'erlooking Grève.
Hearts that bled are stanched with balm.
"Just our rapture to enhance,
Let the English rake the bay,
Gnash their teeth and glare askance
As they cannonade away!
'Neath rampired Solidor pleasant riding on the Rance!"
How hope succeeds despair on each captain's countenance!
Out burst all with one accord,
"This is Paradise for Hell!
Let France, let France's King
Thank the man that did the thing!"
What a shout, and all one word,
"Hervé Riel!"
As he stepped in front once more,
Not a symptom of surprise
In the frank, blue, Breton eyes,
Just the same man as before.

IX

Then said Damfreville, "My friend,
I must speak out at the end,
Though I find the speaking hard.
Praise is deeper than the lips:
You have saved the King his ships,
You must name your own reward.
'Faith, our sun was near eclipse!
Demand whate'er you will,
France remains your debtor still.
Ask to heart's content and have! or my name's not Damfreville."

X

Then a beam of fun outbroke
On the bearded mouth that spoke,
As the honest heart laughed through
Those frank eyes of Breton blue:
"Since I needs must say my say,
Since on board the duty's done,
And from Malo Roads to Croisic Point, what is it but a run?—
Since 'tis ask and have, I may—
Since the others go ashore—
Come! A good whole holiday!
Leave to go and see my wife, whom I call the Belle Aurore!"
That he asked and that he got—nothing more.

XI

Name and deed alike are lost:
Not a pillar nor a post
In his Croisic keeps alive the feat as it befell;
Not a head in white and black
On a single fishing smack,
In memory of the man but for whom had gone to wrack
All that France saved from the fight whence England bore the bell.[1]
Go to Paris: rank on rank
Search the heroes flung pell-mell
On the Louvre,[2] face and flank;
You shall look long enough ere you come to Hervé Riel.
So, for better and for worse,
Hervé Riel, accept my verse!
In my verse, Hervé Riel, do thou once more
Save the squadron, honor France, love thy wife, the Belle Aurore!

1871 1871

WANTING IS—WHAT?

Wanting is—what?
Summer redundant,
Blueness abundant,
—Where is the blot?
Beamy the world, yet a blank all the same,
—Framework which waits for a picture to frame.
What of the leafage, what of the flower?
Roses embowering with naught they embower!
Come then, complete incompletion, O comer,
Pant through the blueness, perfect the summer!
Breathe but one breath
Rose-beauty above,
And all that was death
Grows life, grows love,
Grows love!

1883

WHY I AM A LIBERAL

"Why?" Because all I haply can and do,
All that I am now, all I hope to be—
Whence comes it save from fortune setting free
Body and soul the purpose to pursue,
God traced for both. If fetters not a few,
Of prejudice, convention, fall from me,
These shall I bid men—each in his degree
Also God-guided—bear, and gayly, too?

[1] had the victory
[2] an ancient royal palace, now mainly an art-gallery, adorned with the statues of eminent Frenchmen

But little do or can the best of us;
That little is achieved through Liberty.
Who, then, dares hold, emancipated thus,
His fellow shall continue bound? Not I,
Who live, love, labor freely, nor discuss
A brother's right to freedom. That is "Why."
1885

EPILOGUE [1]

At the midnight in the silence of the sleep-time,
When you set your fancies free,
Will they pass to where—by death, fools think, imprisoned—
Low he lies who once so loved you, whom you loved
—Pity me?

Oh, to love so, be so loved, yet so mistaken!
What had I on earth to do
With the slothful, with the mawkish, the unmanly?
Like the aimless, helpless, hopeless, did I drivel
—Being—who?

One who never turned his back but marched breast forward,
Never doubted clouds would break,
Never dreamed, though right were worsted, wrong would triumph,
Held we fall to rise, are baffled to fight better,
Sleep to wake.

No, at noonday in the bustle of man's work-time
Greet the unseen with a cheer!
Bid him forward, breast and back as either should be,
"Strive and thrive!" cry "Speed—fight on, fare ever
There as here!"

1899

ELIZABETH BARRETT BROWNING 1806-1861

When Wordsworth died in 1850, many English people felt that Elizabeth Barrett should be appointed laureate. She was popular, and she represented the English ideals of the time. She had passed a joyous childhood in her Durham home and in a later home in Buckinghamshire. Her delight at eight in reading Homer in Greek did not keep her from dolls and ponies and gardening. At fifteen, however, she received a severe physical injury; and family misfortune and bereavements brought her to an invalid's life. Even this narrow existence did not cut her off from wide reading in many languages, and the writing of translations, reviews, articles, and poems. A common interest in poetry brought her and Browning together. Their marriage and removal to Florence followed in 1846. For a time the new life almost restored her to normal health. Their home, "Casa Guidi," was the meeting place for distinguished Americans and English people.

During her lifetime Mrs. Browning was better known and more generally esteemed as a poet than her husband. Her popular poem, the versified novel, *Aurora Leigh,* 1856, expressed what she considered her best ideas on literature and art. Much of her poetry was occasional, called forth by the Italian struggles for liberty going on around her. Although recognizing her passion for great ideals, modern critics and readers value most her lyric poetry, at its best in the selections here given. The strict form of the sonnet curbed her unfortunate tendencies toward diffuseness and carelessness.

Anne (Thackeray) Ritchie, *Records of Tennyson, Ruskin, and the Brownings,* 1892; R. W. Gilder, "A Romance of the Nineteenth Century," *Cent.* 70:918-27.

SONNETS FROM THE PORTUGUESE [2]

I

I thought once how Theocritus had sung [3]
Of the sweet years, the dear and wished-for years,
Who each one in a gracious hand appears
To bear a gift for mortals, old or young:
And, as I mused it in his antique tongue,
I saw, in gradual vision through my tears,
The sweet, sad years, the melancholy years,
Those of my own life, who by turns had flung
A shadow across me. Straightway I was 'ware,
So weeping, how a mystic Shape did move
Behind me, and drew me backward by the hair;
And a voice said in mastery, while I strove—
"Guess now who holds thee?"—"Death," I said. But, there,
The silver answer rang—"Not Death, but Love."

III

Unlike are we, unlike, O princely Heart!
Unlike our uses and our destinies.
Our ministering two angels look surprise

[1] This is the Epilogue to *Asolando,* which was published at London on the day when Browning died at Venice.

[2] These Sonnets, forty-four in number, were written by Miss Barrett during the time of Mr. Browning's courtship, but were not shown to him until after their marriage in 1846. The title under which they were published 1850, was adopted as a disguise. To understand them aright, it must be remembered that Miss Barrett was in middle life and had long been an invalid. F. G. Kenyon, in his edition of Mrs. Browning's *Letters,* writes: "With the single exception of Rossetti, no modern English poet has written of love with such genius, such beauty, and such sincerity, as the two who gave the most beautiful example of it in their own lives."

[3] *Idyls,* xv, 104

On one another, as they strike athwart
Their wings in passing. Thou, bethink thee, art
A guest for queens to social pageantries,
With gages from a hundred brighter eyes
Than tears even can make mine, to play thy part
Of chief musician. What hast *thou* to do
With looking from the lattice-lights at me,
A poor, tired, wandering singer, singing through
The dark, and leaning up a cypress tree?
The chrism[1] is on thine head—on mine, the dew—
And Death must dig the level where these agree.

IV

Thou hast thy calling to some palace floor,
Most gracious singer of high poems, where
The dancers will break footing, from the care
Of watching up thy pregnant lips for more.
And dost thou lift this house's latch too poor
For hand of thine? And canst thou think and bear
To let thy music drop here unaware
In folds of golden fullness at my door?
Look up and see the casement broken in,
The bats and owlets builders in the roof!
My cricket chirps against thy mandolin.
Hush, call no echo up in further proof
Of desolation! There's a voice within
That weeps—as thou must sing—alone, aloof.

XIV

If thou must love me, let it be for nought
Except for love's sake only. Do not say
"I love her for her smile—her look—her way
Of speaking gently—for a trick of thought
That falls in well with mine, and certes brought
A sense of pleasant ease on such a day"—
For these things in themselves, Belovèd, may
Be changed, or change for thee—and love, so wrought,
May be unwrought so. Neither love me for
Thine own dear pity's wiping my cheeks dry—
A creature might forget to weep, who bore
Thy comfort long, and lose thy love thereby!
But love me for love's sake, that evermore
Thou may'st love on, through love's eternity.

XXII

When our two souls stand up erect and strong,
Face to face, silent, drawing nigh and nigher,
Until the lengthening wings break into fire
At either curvèd point—what bitter wrong
Can the earth do to us, that we should not long
Be here contented? Think. In mounting higher,
The angels would press on us and aspire
To drop some golden orb of perfect song
Into our deep, dear silence. Let us stay
Rather on earth, Belovèd—where the unfit
Contrarious moods of men recoil away
And isolate pure spirits, and permit
A place to stand and love in for a day,
With darkness and the death-hour rounding it.

XLIII

How do I love thee? Let me count the ways.
I love thee to the depth and breadth and height
My soul can reach, when feeling out of sight
For the ends of Being and ideal Grace.
I love thee to the level of everyday's
Most quiet need, by sun and candle light.
I love thee freely, as men strive for Right;
I love thee purely, as they turn from Praise.
I love thee with the passion put to use
In my old griefs, and with my childhood's faith.
I love thee with a love I seemed to lose
With my lost saints—I love thee with the breath,
Smiles, tears, of all my life!—and, if God choose,
I shall but love thee better after death.

1850

[1] the sacred ointment; here figurative for poetic consecration

EDWARD FITZGERALD
1809-1883

Though of Irish extraction, Fitzgerald was born near Woodbridge in Suffolk, and educated at Cambridge where he received his bachelor's degree in 1830. At the university he was in the group with the Tennysons, Spedding, and others of fame in their later lives. He spent his entire life in the country for, though not unsocial, he had an extreme distaste for the conventionalities of formal society.

The Persian quatrains of Omar (p. 678) came to his attention through a student of Oriental languages. They appealed to his emotional nature and to his rather dark view of life, and he made a translation of them, published in 1859. The five-shilling book attracted few readers and at length made its way to the penny-box outside the publisher's shop. A passer-by bought a copy and showed it to Rossetti, who showed it to Swinburne, and Fitzgerald's literary fame was made.

It must be remembered that Fitzgerald is more author than translator of the quatrains. His practice, like that of all very free translators, was to get the spirit of the original and then write unhampered by its form or minute details. Omar's quatrains are short, epigrammatic poems, virtually independent of each other. From among them Fitzgerald selected freely. The number of quatrains in the first edition was seventy-five; in the second, one hundred ten; and in the third and later editions, one hundred one. Each new edition Fitzgerald worked over with fastidious care. The fourth is followed below. Of Fitzgerald's quatrains, half are translations of particular quatrains from Omar; about half are combinations of Omar's quatrains; a few reproduce old Persian quatrains; and a few are probably of Fitzgerald's own invention. The whole may then be considered as an English poem founded upon such ideas of the Rubàiyàt as are not incompatible with English thought.

Biography: Benson (EML). Criticism: More (Shel. 1); Gamaliel Bradford, *Bare Souls;* for an appreciation, *Nation* 88: 322-3; see also "Poetry, Time, and Edward Fitzgerald," W. B. Blake, *Dial* 46:177-180.

RUBÀIYÀT OF OMAR KHAYYÀM [1]

I

Wake! For the Sun, who scattered into flight
The Stars before him from the Field of Night,
Drives Night along with them from Heaven and strikes
The Sultàn's Turret with a Shaft of Light. [2]

II

Before the phantom of False morning died, [3]
Methought a Voice within the Tavern cried,
"When all the Temple is prepared within,
Why nods the drowsy Worshiper outside?"

III

And, as the Cock crew, those who stood before
The Tavern shouted—"Open then the Door!
You know how little while we have to stay,
And, once departed, may return no more."

IV

Now the New Year [4] reviving old desires,
The thoughtful Soul to solitude retires,
Where the WHITE HAND OF MOSES on the Bough
Puts out, [5] and Jesus from the Ground suspires. [6]

V

Iram indeed is gone with all his Rose,
And Jamshyd's Seven-ringed Cup where no one knows;
But still a Ruby kindles in the Vine,
And many a Garden by the Water blows. [7]

VI

And David's lips are locked; but in divine
High-piping Pehleví, [8] with "Wine! Wine! Wine!
Red Wine!"—the Nightingale cries to the Rose
That sallow cheek of hers to incarnadine.

VII

Come, fill the Cup, and in the fire of Spring
Your Winter-Garment of Repentance fling:
The Bird of Time has but a little way
To flutter—and the Bird is on the Wing.

VIII

Whether at Naishàpùr or Babylon,
Whether the Cup with sweet or bitter run,
The Wine of Life keeps oozing drop by drop,
The Leaves of Life keep falling one by one.

IX

Each Morn a thousand Roses brings, you say;
Yes, but where leaves the Rose of Yesterday?
And this first Summer month that brings the Rose
Shall take Jamshyd and Kaikobàd away.

X

Well, let it take them! What have we to do
With Kaikobàd the Great, or Kaikhosrù?
Let Zàl and Rustum bluster as they will,
Or Hàtim call to Supper—heed not you.

[1] Omar Khayyàm (i. e., Omar the Tent-maker) was a Persian astronomer and poet of the 12th century, who dwelt at Naishàpùr. *Rubàiyàt* is a Persian word, the plural of *rubài,* which signifies "a quatrain."

Two widely divergent views are held of the philosophy of the Rubaiyat, the one regarding it as wholly materialistic, raising questions of the "Two Worlds" only to dismiss them and take refuge in the pleasures of sense—an Epicurean philosophy of "Eat, drink, and be merry." The other regards it as an example of Oriental mysticism, employing Wine and the like as poetic symbols of deity. Fitzgerald held firmly to the former view, content, however, "to believe that, while the wine Omar celebrates is simply the juice of the grape, he bragged more than he drank of it, in very defiance perhaps of that spiritual wine which left its votaries sunk in hypocrisy or disgust."

[2] The opening stanza of the first edition is considerably more daring in its imagery, drawing one of its figures from the practice, in the desert, of flinging a stone into the cup as a signal "To Horse!"—

Awake for Morning in the Bowl of Night
Has flung the Stone that puts the Stars to Flight:
And, Lo, the Hunter of the East has caught
The Sultan's Turret in a Noose of Light.

[3] "False dawn" precedes the real dawn about an hour; "a well known phenomenon in the East." (This note, and many that follow, are condensed from Fitzgerald's notes.)

[4] the Vernal equinox

[5] See *Exodus,* iv, 6; a strong figure for the miracle of spring blossoms.

[6] "According to the Persians, the healing power of Jesus resided in his breath."

[7] Iram was an ancient garden, planted by King Shaddàd. Jamshyd was a legendary king of Persia's golden age; his seven-ringed cup was "typical of the seven heavens, etc., and was a divining cup." Other kings and heroes are mentioned in quatrains x and xviii. Hàtim was "a well known type of oriental generosity." For Zàl and Rustum, see Arnold's poem of "Sohrab and Rustum," p. 690.

[8] an ancient literary language of Persia

XI

With me along the strip of Herbage strown
That just divides the desert from the sown,
Where name of Slave and Sultàn is forgot—
And peace to Màhmùd [1] on his golden Throne!

XII

A Book of Verses underneath the Bough,
A Jug of Wine, a Loaf of Bread—and Thou
Beside me singing in the Wilderness—
Oh, Wilderness were Paradise enow!

XIII

Some for the Glories of This World; and some
Sigh for the Prophet's Paradise to come;
Ah, take the Cash, and let the Credit go,
Nor heed the rumble of a distant Drum! [2]

XIV

Look to the blowing Rose about us—"Lo,
Laughing," she says, "into the world I blow,
At once the silken tassel of my Purse
Tear, and its Treasure on the Garden throw."

XV

And those who husbanded the Golden Grain,
And those who flung it to the winds like Rain,
Alike to no such aureate Earth are turned
As, buried once, Men want dug up again.

XVI

The Worldly Hope Men set their Hearts upon
Turns Ashes—or it prospers; and anon,
Like Snow upon the Desert's dusty Face,
Lighting a little hour or two—was gone.

XVII

Think, in this battered Caravanserai [3]
Whose Portals are alternate Night and Day,
How Sultàn after Sultàn with his Pomp
Abode his destined Hour, and went his way.

XVIII

They say the Lion and the Lizard keep
The Courts [4] where Jamshyd gloried and drank deep;
And Bahràm, that great Hunter—the Wild Ass
Stamps o'er his Head, but cannot break his Sleep.

XIX

I sometimes think that never blows so red
The Rose as where some buried Caesar [5] bled;
That every Hyacinth the Garden wears
Dropped in her Lap from some Once lovely Head.

[1] See quatrain LX.
[2] "Beaten outside a palace."
[3] inn
[4] Persepolis
[5] emperor

XX

And this reviving Herb whose tender Green
Fledges the River-Lip on which we lean—
Ah, lean upon it lightly! for who knows
From what once lovely Lip it springs unseen!

XXI

Ah, my Belovèd, fill the Cup that clears
TODAY of past Regrets and future Fears;
Tomorrow!—Why, Tomorrow I may be
Myself with Yesterday's Seven thousand Years. [6]

XXII

For some we loved, the loveliest and the best
That from his Vintage rolling Time hath prest,
Have drunk their Cup a Round or two before,
And one by one crept silently to rest.

XXIII

And we that now make merry in the Room
They left, and Summer dresses in new bloom,
Ourselves must we beneath the Couch of Earth
Descend—ourselves to make a Couch—for whom?

XXIV

Ah, make the most of what we yet may spend,
Before we too into the Dust descend;
Dust into Dust, and under Dust to lie,
Sans [7] Wine, sans Song, sans Singer, and—sans End!

XXV

Alike for those who for TODAY prepare,
And those that after TOMORROW stare,
A Muezzin [8] from the Tower of Darkness cries,
"Fools! your Reward is neither Here nor There."

XXVI

Why, all the Saints and Sages who discussed
Of the Two Worlds so wisely—they are thrust
Like foolish Prophets forth; their Words to Scorn
Are scattered, and their Mouths are stopped with Dust.

XXVII

Myself when young did eagerly frequent
Doctor and Saint, and heard great argument
About it and about; but evermore
Came out by the same door where in I went.

XXVIII

With them the seed of Wisdom did I sow,
And with mine own hand wrought to make it grow;

[6] "A thousand years to each planet."
[7] without
[8] a summoner to prayer

And this was all the Harvest that I reaped—
"I came like Water, and like Wind I go."

XXIX

Into this Universe, and *Why* not knowing
Nor *Whence,* like Water willy-nilly flowing;
And out of it, as Wind along the Waste,
I know not *Whither,* willy-nilly blowing.

XXX

What, without asking, hither hurried *Whence?*
And, without asking, *Whither* hurried hence!
Oh, many a Cup of this forbidden Wine
Must drown the memory of that insolence!

XXXI

Up from Earth's Center through the Seventh Gate
I rose, and on the Throne of Saturn [1] sate,
And many a Knot Unraveled by the Road;
But not the Master-knot of Human Fate.

XXXII

There was the Door to which I found no Key;
There was the Veil through which I might not see:
Some little talk awhile of ME *and* THEE [2]
There was—and then no more of THEE and ME.

XXXIII

Earth could not answer; nor the Seas that mourn
In flowing Purple, of their Lord forlorn;
Nor rolling Heaven, with all his Signs revealed
And hidden by the sleeve of Night and Morn.

XXXIV

Then of the THEE IN ME who works behind
The Veil, I lifted up my hands to find
A Lamp amid the Darkness; and I heard,
As from Without—"THE ME WITHIN THEE BLIND!"

XXXV

Then to the Lip of this poor earthen Urn
I leaned, the Secret of my Life to learn:
And Lip to Lip it murmured—"While you live,
Drink!—for, once dead, you never shall return."

[1] "Lord of the Seventh Heaven"
[2] "Some dividual existence or personality distinct from the whole."

XXXVI

I think the Vessel, that with fugitive
Articulation answered, once did live,
And drink; and Ah! the passive Lip I kissed,
How many Kisses might it take—and give!

XXXVII

For I remember stopping by the way
To watch a Potter thumping his wet Clay;
And with its all-obliterated Tongue
It murmured—"Gently, Brother, gently, pray!"

XXXVIII

And has not such a Story from of Old
Down Man's successive generations rolled
Of such a clod of saturated Earth
Cast by the Maker into Human mold?

XXXIX

And not a drop that from our Cups we throw
For Earth to drink of, but may steal below
To quench the fire of Anguish in some Eye
There hidden—far beneath, and long ago.

XL

As then the Tulip for her morning sup
Of Heavenly Vintage from the soil looks up,
Do you devoutly do the like, till Heaven
To Earth invert you—like an empty Cup.

XLI

Perplexed no more with Human or Divine,
Tomorrow's tangle to the winds resign,
And lose your fingers in the tresses of
The Cypress-slender Minister of Wine.

XLII

And if the Wine you drink, the Lip you press,
End in what All begins and ends in—Yes;
Think then you are TODAY what YESTERDAY
You were—TOMORROW you shall not be less.

XLIII

So when the Angel of the darker Drink
At last shall find you by the river brink,
And, offering his Cup invite your Soul
Forth to your Lips to quaff—you shall not shrink.

XLIV

Why, if the Soul can fling the Dust aside,
And naked on the Air of Heaven ride,
Were't not a Shame—were't not a Shame for him
In this clay carcass crippled to abide?

XLV

'Tis but a Tent where takes his one day's rest
A Sultàn to the realm of Death addrest;

The Sultàn rises, and the dark Ferràsh[1]
Strikes, and prepares it for another Guest.

XLVI

And fear not lest Existence closing your
Account, and mine, should know the like no more;
The Eternal Sàki[2] from that Bowl has poured
Millions of Bubbles like us, and will pour.

XLVII

When You and I behind the Veil are past,
Oh, but the long, long while the World shall last,
Which of our Coming and Departure heeds
As the Sea's self should heed a pebble-cast.

XLVIII

A Moment's Halt—a momentary taste
Of BEING from the Well amid the Waste—
And Lo!—the phantom Caravan has reached
The NOTHING it set out from—oh, make haste!

XLIX

Would you that spangle of Existence spend
About THE SECRET—quick about it, Friend!
A Hair perhaps divides the False and True—
And upon what, prithee, does life depend?

L

A Hair perhaps divides the False and True;
Yes; and a single Alif[3] were the clue;
Could you but find it—to the Treasure-house,
And peradventure to THE MASTER, too;

LI

Whose secret Presence, through Creation's veins
Running Quicksilver-like eludes your pains;
Taking all shapes from Màh to Màhi;[4] and
They change and perish all—but He remains;

LII

A moment guessed—then back behind the Fold
Immersed of Darkness round the Drama rolled
Which, for the Pastime of Eternity,
He doth Himself contrive, enact, behold.

LIII

But if in vain, down on the stubborn floor
Of Earth, and up to Heaven's unopening door,

[1] attendant
[2] wine-bearer
[3] the letter *a*, often represented by a slight mark like an apostrophe, the presence or absence of which could change the meaning of a word
[4] from fish to moon

You gaze TODAY, while You are You—how then
TOMORROW, You when shall be You no more?

LIV

Waste not your Hour, nor in vain pursuit
Of This and That endeavor and dispute;
Better be jocund with the fruitful Grape
Than sadden after none, or bitter, Fruit.

LV

You know, my Friends, with what a brave Carouse
I made a Second Marriage in my house;
Divorced old barren Reason from my Bed,
And took the Daughter of the Vine to Spouse.

LVI

For "IS" and "IS-NOT" though with rule and Line,
And "UP-AND-DOWN" by Logic I define,
Of all that one should care to fathom, I
Was never deep in anything but—Wine.

LVII

Ah, but my Computations, People say,
Reduced the Year to better reckoning?[5]—Nay,
'Twas only striking from the Calendar
Unborn Tomorrow, and dead Yesterday.

LVIII

And lately, by the Tavern Door agape,
Came shining through the Dusk an Angel Shape
Bearing a Vessel on his shoulder; and
He bid me taste of it; and t'was—the Grape!

LIX

The Grape that can with Logic absolute
The Two-and-Seventy jarring Sects[6] confute:
The sovereign Alchemist that in a trice
Life's leaden metal into Gold Transmute;

LX

The mighty Mahmùd, Allah-breathing Lord,[7]
That all the misbelieving and black Horde
Of Fears and Sorrows that infest the Soul
Scatters before him with his whirlwind Sword.

LXI

Why, be this Juice the growth of God, who dare
Blaspheme the twisted tendril as a Snare?

[5] Omar assisted in reforming the calendar.
[6] "The seventy-two religions supposed to divide the world."
[7] "Alluding to Sultan Mahmùd's conquest of India and its dark people." By "Allah-breathing" is meant that the Sultan was a Mohammedan, or worshiper of Allah.

A Blessing, we should use it, should we not?
And if a Curse—why, then, Who set it there?

LXII

I must abjure the Balm of Life, I must,
Scared by some After-reckoning ta'en on trust,
Or lured with Hope of some Diviner Drink,
To fill the Cup—when crumbled into Dust!

LXIII

Oh, threats of Hell and Hopes of Paradise!
One thing at least is certain—*This* Life flies;
One thing is certain and the rest is Lies;
The Flower that once has blown forever dies.

LXIV

Strange, is it not? that of the myriads who
Before us passed the door of Darkness through,
Not one returns to tell us of the Road,
Which to discover we must travel, too.

LXV

The Revelations of Devout and Learned
Who rose before us, and as Prophets burned,
Are all but Stories, which, awoke from Sleep
They told their comrades, and to Sleep returned.

LXVI

I sent my Soul through the Invisible,
Some letter of that After-life to spell:
And by and by my Soul returned to me,
And answered "I, Myself, am Heaven and Hell:"[1]

LXVII

Heaven but the Vision of fulfilled Desire,
And Hell the Shadow from a Soul on fire,
Cast on the Darkness into which Ourselves,
So late emerged from, shall so soon expire.

LXVIII

We are no other than a moving row
Of Magic Shadow-shapes that come and go
Round with the Sun-illuminated Lantern[2] held
In Midnight by the Master of the Show;

LXIX

But helpless Pieces of the Game He plays
Upon this Checkerboard of Nights and Days;
Hither and thither moves, and checks, and slays,
And one by one back in the Closet lays.

LXX

The Ball no question makes of Ayes and Noes,
But Here or There as strikes the Player goes;
And He that tossed you down into the Field,
He knows about it all—HE knows—HE knows!

LXXI

The Moving Finger writes; and, having writ,
Moves on; nor all your Piety nor Wit
Shall lure it back to cancel half a Line,
Nor all your Tears wash out a Word of it.

LXXII

And that inverted Bowl they call the Sky,
Whereunder, crawling, cooped we live and die,
Lift not your hands to *It* for help—for It
As impotently moves as you or I.

LXXIII

With Earth's first Clay they did the Last Man knead,
And there of the Last Harvest sowed the Seed:
And the first Morning of Creation wrote
What the Last Dawn of Reckoning shall read.

LXXIV

YESTERDAY *This* Day's Madness did prepare;
TOMORROW's Silence, Triumph, or Despair:
Drink! for you know not whence you came, nor why:
Drink! for you know not why you go, nor where.

LXXV

I tell you this—When, started from the Goal,
Over the flaming shoulders of the foal
Of Heaven Parwin and Mushtari[3] they flung,
In my predestined Plot of Dust and Soul.

LXXVI

The Vine had struck a fiber: which about
If clings my Being—let the Dervish[4] flout;
Of my Base metal may be filed a Key,
That shall unlock the Door he howls without.

LXXVII

And this I know: whether the one True Light
Kindle to Love, or Wrath consume me quite,
One Flash of It within the Tavern caught
Better than in the Temple lost outright.

LXXVIII

What! out of senseless Nothing to provoke
A conscious Something to resent the yoke
Of unpermitted Pleasure, under pain
Of Everlasting Penalties, if broke!

LXXIX

What! from his helpless Creature be repaid
Pure Gold for what he lent him dross-allayed—
Sue for a Debt we never did contract,
And cannot answer—Oh, the sorry trade!

[1] Cf. *Faustus*, Sc. III, 77, p. 171; also *Par. Lost* I, 254, p. 262.
[2] i. e., the earth
[3] the Pleiads and Jupiter
[4] a Mohammedan devotee

LXXX

Oh, Thou, who didst with pitfall and with gin
Beset the Road I was to wander in,
Thou wilt not with Predestined Evil round
Enmesh, and then impute my Fall to Sin!

LXXXI

Oh Thou, who Man of baser Earth didst make,
And e'en with Paradise devise the Snake:
For all the Sin wherewith the Face of Man
Is blackened—Man's forgiveness give—and take!

. . . .

LXXXII

As under cover of departing Day
Slunk hunger-stricken Ramazàn[1] away,
Once more within the Potter's house alone
I stood, surrounded by the Shapes of Clay.

LXXXIII

Shapes of all Sorts and Sizes, great and small,
That stood along the floor and by the wall;
And some loquacious Vessels were; and some
Listened perhaps, but never talked at all.

LXXXIV

Said one among them—"Surely not in vain
My substance of the common Earth was ta'en
And to this Figure molded, to be broke,
Or trampled back to shapeless Earth again."

LXXXV

Then said a Second—"Ne'er a peevish Boy
Would break the Bowl from which he drank in joy;
And He that with his hand the Vessel made
Will surely not in after Wrath destroy."

LXXXVI

After a momentary silence spake
Some Vessel of a more ungainly Make:
"They sneer at me for leaning all awry;
What! did the Hand then of the Potter shake?"

LXXXVII

Whereat some one of the loquacious Lot—
I think a Sùfi[2] pipkin—waxing hot—
"All this of Pot and Potter—Tell me then,
Who is the Potter, pray, and who the Pot?"

LXXXVIII

"Why," said another, "Some there are who tell
Of one who threatens he will toss to Hell
The luckless Pots he marred in making—Pish!
He's a Good Fellow, and 'twill all be well."

LXXXIX

"Well," murmured one, "Let whoso make or buy,
My Clay with long Oblivion is gone dry:
But fill me with the old familiar Juice,
Methinks I might recover by and by."

XC

So while the Vessels one by one were speaking,
The little Moon[3] looked in that all were seeking;
And then they jogged each other, "Brother! Brother!
Now for the Porter's shoulder-knot[4] a-creaking!"

. . . .

XCI

Ah, with the Grape my fading Life provide,
And wash the Body whence the Life has died,
And lay me, shrouded in the living Leaf,
By some not unfrequented Garden-side.

XCII

That ev'n my buried Ashes such a snare
Of Vintage shall fling up into the Air
As not a True Believer passing by
But shall be overtaken unaware.

XCIII

Indeed the Idols I have loved so long
Have done my credit in this World much wrong:
Have drowned my Glory in a shallow Cup,
And sold my Reputation for a Song.

XCIV

Indeed, indeed, Repentance oft before
I swore—but was I sober when I swore?
And then, and then came Spring, and rose-in-hand
My thread-bare Penitence apieces tore.

XCV

And much as Wine has played the Infidel,
And robbed me of my Robe of Honor—Well,
I wonder often what the Vintners buy
One half so precious as the stuff they sell.

[1] the month of fasting, during which no food is taken between sunrise and sunset
[2] The allusion here is to a sect of oriental mystics who held a pantheistic doctrine.
[3] marking the new month and the end of the fast
[4] a shoulder-strap in which the jars of wine were slung

XCVI

Yet, ah, that Spring should vanish with the Rose!
That Youth's sweet-scented manuscript should close!
The Nightingale that in the branches sang,
Ah, whence, and whither flown again, who knows!

XCVII

Would but the Desert of the Fountain yield,
One glimpse—if dimly, yet indeed, revealed,
To which the fainting Traveler might spring,
As springs the trampled herbage of the field.

XCVIII

Would but some Wingèd Angel, ere too late,
Arrest the yet unfolded Roll of Fate,
And make the stern Recorder otherwise
Enregister, or quite obliterate!

XCIX

Ah, Love! could you and I with Him conspire
To grasp this sorry Scheme of Things Entire,
Would not we shatter it to bits—and then
Remold it nearer to the Heart's Desire!

. . . . . .

C

Yon rising Moon that looks for us again—
How oft hereafter will she wax and wane;
How oft hereafter, rising, look for us
Through this same Garden—and for *one* in vain!

CI

And when, like her, oh Sàki, you shall pass
Among the Guests Star-scattered on the Grass,
And in your joyous errand reach the spot
Where I made One—turn down an empty Glass!

TAMAM [1]

1873-79

[1] "The end."

ARTHUR HUGH CLOUGH
1819-1861

Clough is often coupled with Arnold because of the general similarity of their lives, their attitude toward their own time, and the tone of their poetry. The two were close personal friends, and Arnold's "Thyrsis" in memory of Clough is one of the noblest elegies of the century.

Clough was born at Liverpool, was, like Arnold, educated at Rugby and Oxford, and was likewise for a while a fellow of Oriel. Both felt that the world in which they had been born was slipping beneath them. In the poignant attachment they felt toward this vanishing world there is more of struggle in Arnold, and more of resignation in Clough. The verse of Clough has not the finish of Tennyson's and Arnold's, but in it we hear a sincere voice, undaunted, though shaken by the intellectual conflicts of the time.

Clough made a prolonged visit to America, where he was on the friendliest terms with Lowell and the Cambridge-Boston group of literary men. He died in Florence, Italy, while on a tour of southern Europe.

Criticism: S. A. Brooke, *Four Victorian Poets: a Study of Clough, Arnold, Rossetti, Morris,* 1908.

IN A LECTURE ROOM

Away, haunt thou not me,
Thou vain Philosophy!
Little hast thou bestead,
Save to perplex the head,
And leave the spirit dead.
Unto thy broken cisterns wherefore go,
While from the secret treasure-depths below,
Fed by the skyey shower,
And clouds that sink and rest on hilltops high,
Wisdom at once, and Power,
Are welling, bubbling forth, unseen, incessantly?
Why labor at the dull mechanic oar,
When the fresh breeze is blowing,
And the strong current flowing,
Right onward to the Eternal Shore?

1840 1849

QUA CURSUM VENTUS [2]

As ships, becalmed at eve, that lay
With canvas drooping, side by side,
Two towers of sail at dawn of day
Are scarce long leagues apart descried;

When fell the night, upsprung the breeze,
And all the darkling hours they plied,
Nor dreamt but each the self-same seas
By each was cleaving, side by side:

E'en so, but why the tale reveal
Of those, whom year by year unchanged,
Brief absence joined anew to feel,
Astounded, soul from soul estranged?

At dead of night their sails were filled,
And onward each rejoicing steered—
Ah, neither blame, for neither willed,
Or wist, what first with dawn appeared!

To veer, how vain! On, onward strain,
Brave barks! In light, in darkness, too,

[2] "As the wind (directs) the course." The poem expresses in metaphor the divergence of men's creeds.

Through winds and tides one compass guides—
  To that, and your own selves, be true.

But O blithe breeze! and O great seas,
  Though ne'er, that earliest parting past,
On your wide plain they join again,
  Together lead them home at last.

One port, methought, alike they sought,
  One purpose hold where'er they fare—
O bounding breeze, O rushing seas!
  At last, at last, unite them there!

1849

SAY NOT THE STRUGGLE NOUGHT AVAILETH

Say not the struggle nought availeth,
  The labor and the wounds are vain,
The enemy faints not, nor faileth,
  And as things have been they remain.

If hopes were dupes, fears may be liars;
  It may be, in yon smoke concealed,
Your comrades chase e'en now the fliers,
  And, but for you, possess the field.

For while the tired waves, vainly breaking,
  Seem here no painful inch to gain,
Far back, through creeks and inlets making,
  Comes silent, flooding in, the main.[1]

And not by eastern windows only,
  When daylight comes, comes in the light,
In front, the sun climbs slow, how slowly,
  But westward, look, the land is bright.

1849 1862

ITE DOMUM SATURAE, VENIT HESPERUS[2]

The skies have sunk, and hid the upper snow
(Home, Rose, and home, Provence and La Palie[3]),
The rainy clouds are filing fast below,
And wet will be the path, and wet shall we.
Home, Rose, and home, Provence and La Palie.

Ah dear, and where is he, a year agone,
Who stepped beside and cheered us on and on?
My sweetheart wanders far away from me,
In foreign land or on a foreign sea,
Home, Rose, and home, Provence and La Palie.

The lightning zigzags shoot across the sky
(Home, Rose, and home, Provence and La Palie),
And through the vale the rains go sweeping by;
Ah me, and when in shelter shall we be?
Home, Rose, and home, Provence and La Palie.

Cold, dreary cold, the stormy winds feel they
O'er foreign lands and foreign seas that stray
(Home, Rose, and home, Provence and La Palie).
And doth he e'er, I wonder, bring to mind
The pleasant huts and herds he left behind?
And doth he sometimes in his slumbering see
The feeding kine, and doth he think of me,
My sweetheart wandering wheresoe'er it be?
Home, Rose, and home, Provence and La Palie.

The thunder bellows far from snow to snow
(Home, Rose, and home, Provence and La Palie),
And loud and louder roars the flood below.
Heigho! but soon in shelter shall we be:
Home, Rose, and home, Provence and La Palie.

Or shall he find before his term be sped
Some comelier maid that he shall wish to wed?
(Home, Rose, and home, Provence and La Palie.)
For weary is work, and weary day by day
To have your comfort miles on miles away.
Home, Rose, and home, Provence and La Palie.

Or may it be that I shall find my mate,
And he returning see himself too late?
For work we must, and what we see, we see,
And God He knows, and what must be, must be,
When sweethearts wander far away from me.
Home, Rose, and home, Provence and La Palie.

The sky behind is brightening up anew
(Home, Rose, and home, Provence and La Palie),
The rain is ending, and our journey, too:
Heigho! aha! for here at home are we—
In, Rose, and in, Provence and La Palie.

1862

ALL IS WELL

Whate'er you dream, with doubt possessed,
Keep, keep it snug within your breast,
And lay you down and take your rest;
Forget in sleep the doubt and pain,
And when you wake, to work again.

[1] "Perhaps Clough's greatest title to poetic fame is this exquisite and exquisitely expressed image of the rising tide."—George Saintsbury. See also Tennyson's "Crossing the Bar," st. 2, p. 642.

[2] "Go home, now that you have fed; evening comes."—Vergil, *Eclog.* x, 77.

[3] "The Pale One"—a name of obvious significance, like "Blanche" or "Brindle"

The wind it blows, the vessel goes,
And where and whither, no one knows.

'Twill all be well: no need of care;
Though how it will, and when, and where,
We cannot see, and can't declare.
In spite of dreams, in spite of thought,
'Tis not in vain, and not for nought,
The wind it blows, the ship it goes,
Though where and whither, no one knows.

1869

MATTHEW ARNOLD 1822-1888

Arnold, foremost literary critic of the nineteenth century, was a son of the most famous master of Rugby School, Thomas Arnold. He was born at Laleham Rectory, on the Thames, was trained at Rugby and Oxford, and received a fellowship at Oriel College. After a short experience in teaching he became secretary of the Marquis of Lansdowne, a prominent English politician. In 1851 he was appointed an inspector of the English schools, and it was in the midst of the arduous tasks of his official position, which he retained for thirty-five years, that he produced his literary work. He died suddenly at Liverpool while on a journey.

Although Arnold was a critic of literature, he was more—a critic of the basis of all literature, life. He questioned the spirit and ideals and attainments of whole societies and peoples, especially those of his own race. He examined their judgments, prejudices, attitudes of mind. He became the "apostle of sweetness and light," that is, of a temperate and intelligent basis for whatever people think and feel. He was the enemy of smugness. He irritated and rather amazed the self-complacent British or American middle-class citizen of his time. And the principles upon which he based his criticism of society and art are as good for one age as for another.

Moreover, he placed criticism on a higher plane than it had before known in England, raising it above a fault-finding estimate of art, and defining it as a disinterested endeavor to know and to propagate the best that is known and thought in the world. His most noteworthy critical works are *On Translating Homer,* 1861; *The Study of Celtic Literature,* 1867; *Culture and Anarchy,* 1869, and his *Essays in Criticism,* 1865-1888.

His prose, with its characteristic bantering humor, abounds in formulas, is insistent and argumentative, but invites to vigorous thinking. Arnold's poetry lacks the abounding optimism of Browning's; it is diffused with a sadness and regret rising from a loss of religious certainty; it is governed by an emotional and intellectual restraint which raises its value but limits its quantity. But though small in amount Arnold's verse is nearly all of distinction in fineness of workmanship.

Biography: Paul (EML). Criticism: Rossetti, Stephen, Payne, Woodberry, Brownell; recent: S. T. Williams, "A Century of Matthew Arnold," *No. Am.* 217:107-16; same, "The Founding of Main Street—The Letters of Matthew Arnold," *No. Am.* 216:411-16; Sir M. E. Salder, "Matthew Arnold," *19th Cent.* 93:199-207, 366-377.

THE FORSAKEN MERMAN[1]

Come, dear children, let us away;
Down and away below!
Now my brothers call from the bay,
Now the great winds shoreward blow,
Now the salt tides seaward flow;
Now the wild white horses[2] play,
Champ and chafe and toss in the spray.
Children dear, let us away!
This way, this way!

Call her once before you go—
Call once yet!
In a voice that she will know:
"Margaret! Margaret!"
Children's voices should be dear
(Call once more) to a mother's ear;
Children's voices, wild with pain—
Surely she will come again!
Call her once and come away;
This way, this way!
"Mother dear, we cannot stay!
The wild white horses foam and fret."
Margaret! Margaret!

Come, dear children, come away down;
Call no more!
One last look at the white-walled town,
And the little, gray church on the windy shore,
Then come down!
She will not come though you call all day;
Come away, come away!

Children dear, was it yesterday
We heard the sweet bells over the bay?
In the caverns where we lay,
Through the surf and through the swell,
The far-off sound of a silver bell?
Sand-strewn caverns, cool and deep,
Where the winds are all asleep;
Where the spent lights quiver and gleam,
Where the salt weed sways in the stream,
Where the sea beasts, ranged all round,
Feed in the ooze of their pasture ground;
Where the sea snakes coil and twine,
Dry their mail and bask in the brine;
Where great whales come sailing by,
Sail and sail, with unshut eye,
Round the world forever and aye?

[1] This poem is based on a legend which is found in the literature of various nations
[2] the breakers

When did music come this way?
Children dear, was it yesterday?

Children dear, was it yesterday
(Call yet once) that she went away?
Once she sat with you and me,
On a red gold throne in the heart of the sea,
And the youngest sat on her knee.
She combed its bright hair, and she tended it well,
When down swung the sound of a far-off bell.
She sighed, she looked up through the clear green sea;
She said: "I must go, for my kinsfolk pray
In the little gray church on the shore today.
'Twill be Easter-time in the world—ah me!
And I lose my poor soul, Merman! here with thee."
I said: "Go up, dear heart, through the waves;
Say thy prayer, and come back to the kind sea-caves!"
She smiled, she went up through the surf in the bay.
Children dear, was it yesterday?

Children dear, were we long alone?
"The sea grows stormy, the little ones moan;
Long prayers," I said, "in the world they say;
Come!" I said; and we rose through the surf in the bay.
We went up the beach, by the sandy down
Where the sea-stocks bloom, to the white-walled town;
Through the narrow paved streets, where all was still,
To the little gray church on the windy hill.
From the church came a murmur of folk at their prayers,
But we stood without in the cold blowing airs.
We climbed on the graves, on the stones worn with rains,
And we gazed up the aisle through the small leaded panes.
She sat by the pillar; we saw her clear;
"Margaret, hist! come quick, we are here!
Dear heart," I said, "we are long alone;
The sea grows stormy, the little ones moan."
But, ah, she gave me never a look,
For her eyes were sealed to the holy book!
Loud prays the priest; shut stands the door.
Come away, children, call no more!
Come away, come down, call no more!

Down, down, down!
Down to the depths of the sea!
She sits at her wheel in the humming town,
Singing most joyfully.
Hark what she sings: "O joy, O joy,
For the humming street, and the child with its toy!
For the priest, and the bell, and the holy well;
For the wheel where I spun,
And the blessed light of the sun!"
And so she sings her fill,
Singing most joyfully,
Till the spindle drops from her hand,
And the whizzing wheel stands still.
She steals to the window, and looks at the sand,
And over the sand at the sea;
And her eyes are set in a stare;
And anon there breaks a sigh,
And anon there drops a tear,
From a sorrow-clouded eye,
And a heart sorrow-laden,
A long, long sigh;
For the cold strange eyes of a little Mermaiden
And the gleam of her golden hair.

Come away, away children;
Come children, come down!
The hoarse wind blows coldly;
Lights shine in the town.
She will start from her slumber
When gusts shake the door;
She will hear the winds howling,
Will hear the waves roar.
We shall see, while above us
The waves roar and whirl,
A ceiling of amber,
A pavement of pearl.
Singing: "Here came a mortal,
But faithless was she!
And alone dwell forever
The kings of the sea."

But, children, at midnight,
When soft the winds blow,
When clear falls the moonlight,
When spring tides are low;
When sweet airs come seaward
From heaths starred with broom,
And high rocks throw mildly
On the blanched sands a gloom;
Up the still, glistening beaches,
Up the creeks we will hie,
Over banks of bright seaweed
The ebb tide leaves dry.
We will gaze, from the sand-hills,

At the white, sleeping town;
At the church on the hillside—
And then come back down,
Singing: "There dwells a loved one,
But cruel is she!
She left lonely forever
The kings of the sea."

1849

TO A FRIEND [1]

Who prop, thou ask'st, in these bad days, my
mind?
He much, the old man, who, clearest-souled of
men,
Saw the wide prospect, and the Asian fen,
And Tmolus hill, and Smyrna bay, though blind.
Much he, whose friendship I not long since won,
That halting slave, who in Nicopolis
Taught Arrian, when Vespasian's brutal son
Cleared Rome of what most shamed him. But
be his
My special thanks, whose even-balanced soul,
From first youth tested up to extreme old age,
Business could not make dull, nor passion wild;
Who saw life steadily, and saw it whole;
The mellow glory of the Attic stage,
Singer of sweet Colonus, and its child.

1849

SHAKESPEARE

Others abide our question. Thou art free.
We ask and ask—Thou smilest and art still,
Out-topping knowledge. For the loftiest hill,
Who to the stars uncrowns his majesty,
Planting his steadfast footsteps in the sea,
Making the heaven of heavens his dwelling-
place,
Spares but the cloudy border of his base
To the foiled searching of mortality;
And thou, who didst the stars and sunbeams
know,
Self-schooled, self-scanned, self-honored, self-
secure,
Didst tread on earth unguessed at.—Better so!
All pains the immortal spirit must endure,
All weakness which impairs, all griefs which
bow,
Find their sole speech in that victorious brow.

1849

AUSTERITY OF POETRY

That son of Italy who tried to blow, [2]
Ere Dante came, the trump of sacred song,
In his light youth amid a festal throng
Sat with his bride to see a public show.
Fair was the bride, and on her front did glow
Youth like a star; and what to youth belong—
Gay raiment, sparkling gauds, elation strong.
A prop gave way! Crash fell a platform! Lo,
'Mid struggling sufferers, hurt to death, she
lay!
Shuddering, they drew her garments off—and
found
A robe of sackcloth next the smooth, white skin.
Such, poets, is your bride, the Muse! young,
gay,
Radiant, adorned outside; a hidden ground
Of thought and of austerity within.

1849

MEMORIAL VERSES

APRIL, 1850

Goethe in Weimar sleeps, and Greece,
Long since, saw Byron's struggle cease.
But one such death remained to come;
The last poetic voice is dumb—
We stand today by Wordsworth's tomb.

When Byron's eyes were shut in death,
We bowed our head and held our breath.
He taught us little; but our soul
Had *felt* him like the thunder's roll.
With shivering heart the strife we saw
Of passion with eternal law;
And yet with reverential awe
We watched the fount of fiery life
Which served for that Titanic strife.

When Goethe's death was told, we said:
Sunk, then, is Europe's sagest head.
Physician of the iron age,
Goethe has done his pilgrimage.
He took the suffering human race,

[1] This sonnet gives expression to Arnold's steady reliance, for mental and moral support, upon the great poets and philosophers—his constant recourse to "the best that is known and thought in the world." The three "props" mentioned here are Homer, the blind bard whom the city of Smyrna in Asia Minor claimed as her son; Epictetus, the lame philosopher who had been a slave, and who, when Domitian banished the philosophers from Rome, went to Nicopolis in Greece and taught his Stoic principles to Arrian; and Sophocles, the Athenian dramatist, author of *Oedipus at Colonus* and other tragedies. Arnold explains the third line by pointing out that the name Europe means "the wide prospect," and Asia probably means "marshy." The twelfth line has passed into familiar quotation.

[2] Jacopone da Todi, who was, says Gaspary, a "true type of the medieval Christian ascetic." According to the record, he was turned by the incident which Arnold relates from a life of gayety to one of rigorous, self-imposed penances.

He read each wound, each weakness clear;
And struck his finger on the place,
And said: *Thou ailest here, and here!*
He looked on Europe's dying hour
Of fitful dream and feverish power;
His eye plunged down the weltering strife,
The turmoil of expiring life—
He said: *The end is everywhere,*
Art still has truth, take refuge there!
And he was happy, if to know
Causes of things, and far below
His feet to see the lurid flow
Of terror, and insane distress,
And headlong fate, be happiness.

And Wordsworth!—Ah, pale ghosts, rejoice!
For never has such soothing voice
Been to your shadowy world conveyed,
Since erst, at morn, some wandering shade
Heard the clear song of Orpheus come
Through Hades, and the mournful gloom.
Wordsworth has gone from us—and ye,
Ah, may ye feel his voice as we!
He, too, upon a wintry clime
Had fallen—on this iron time
Of doubts, disputes, distractions, fears.
He found us when the age had bound
Our souls in its benumbing round;
He spoke, and loosed our heart in tears.
He laid us as we lay at birth
On the cool flowery lap of earth,
Smiles broke from us and we had ease;
The hills were round us, and the breeze
Went o'er the sun-lit fields again;
Our foreheads felt the wind and rain.
Our youth returned; for there was shed
On spirits that had long been dead,
Spirits dried up and closely furled,
The freshness of the early world.

Ah! since dark days still bring to light
Man's prudence and man's fiery might,
Time may restore us in his course
Goethe's sage mind and Byron's force;
But where will Europe's latter hour
Again find Wordsworth's healing power?
Others will teach us how to dare,
And against fear our breast to steel;
Others will strengthen us to bear—
But who, ah! who will make us feel?
The cloud of mortal destiny,
Others will front it fearlessly—
But who, like him, will put it by?

Keep fresh the grass upon his grave,
O Rotha, [1] with thy living wave!
Sing him thy best! for few or none
Hears thy voice right, now he is gone.

1850

[1] the stream which flows past the churchyard of Grasmere where Wordsworth is buried

SELF-DEPENDENCE

Weary of myself, and sick of asking
What I am, and what I ought to be,
At this vessel's prow I stand, which bears me
Forward, forward, o'er the starlit sea.

And a look of passionate desire
O'er the sea and to the stars I send:
"Ye who from my childhood up have calmed me,
Calm me, ah, compose me to the end!

"Ah, once more," I cried, "ye stars, ye waters,
On my heart your mighty charm renew;
Still, still let me, as I gaze upon you,
Feel my soul becoming vast like you!"

From the intense, clear, star-sown vault of heaven,
Over the lit sea's unquiet way,
In the rustling night-air came the answer:
"Wouldst thou *be* as these are? *Live* as they.

"Unaffrighted by the silence round them,
Undistracted by the sights they see,
These demand not that the things without them
Yield them love, amusement, sympathy.

"And with joy the stars perform their shining,
And the sea its long, moon-silvered roll;
For self-poised they live, nor pine with noting
All the fever of some differing soul.

"Bounded by themselves, and unregardful
In what state God's other works may be,
In their own tasks all their powers pouring,
These attain the mighty life you see."

O air-born voice! long since, severely clear,
A cry like thine in mine own heart I hear:
"Resolve to be thyself; and know that he,
Who finds himself, loses his misery!"

1852

LINES WRITTEN IN KENSINGTON GARDENS [2]

In this lone, open glade I lie,
Screened by deep boughs on either hand;
And at its end, to stay the eye,
Those black-crowned, red-boled pine trees stand!

[2] an extensive London park

Birds here make song, each bird has his,
Across the girdling city's hum.
How green under the boughs it is!
How thick the tremulous sheep-cries come!

Sometimes a child will cross the glade
To take his nurse his broken toy;
Sometimes a thrush flit overhead
Deep in her unknown day's employ.

Here at my feet what wonders pass,
What endless, active life is here!
What blowing daisies, fragrant grass!
An air-stirred forest, fresh and clear.

Scarce fresher is the mountain-sod
Where the tired angler lies, stretched out,
And, eased of basket and of rod,
Counts his day's spoil, the spotted trout.

In the huge world, which roars hard by,
Be others happy if they can!
But in my helpless cradle I
Was breathed on by the rural Pan.[1]

I, on men's impious uproar hurled,
Think often, as I hear them rave,
That peace has left the upper world
And now keeps only in the grave.

Yet here is peace for-ever new!
When I who watch them am away,
Still all things in this glade go through
The changes of their quiet day.

Then to their happy rest they pass!
The flowers upclose, the birds are fed,
The night comes down upon the grass,
The child sleeps warmly in his bed.

Calm soul of all things! make it mine
To feel, amid the city's jar,
That there abides a peace of thine,
Man did not make, and cannot mar.

The will to neither strive nor cry,
The power to feel with others give!
Calm, calm me more! nor let me die
Before I have begun to live.

1852

REQUIESCAT[2]

Strew on her roses, roses,
  And never a spray of yew!
In quiet she reposes;
  Ah, would that I did, too!

Her mirth the world required;
  She bathed it in smiles of glee.
But her heart was tired, tired,
  And now they let her be.

Her life was turning, turning,
  In mazes of heat and sound.
But for peace her soul was yearning,
  And now peace laps her round.

Her cabined, ample spirit,
  It fluttered and failed for breath.
Tonight it doth inherit
  The vasty hall of death.

1853

SOHRAB AND RUSTUM[3]

And the first gray of morning filled the east,
And the fog rose out of the Oxus stream.[4]
But all the Tartar camp along the stream
Was hushed, and still the men were plunged in sleep;
Sohrab alone, he slept not; all night long
He had lain wakeful, tossing on his bed;
But when the gray dawn stole into his tent,
He rose, and clad himself, and girt his sword,
And took his horseman's cloak, and left his tent,
And went abroad into the cold, wet fog,
Through the dim camp to Peran-Wisa's[5] tent.
  Through the black Tartar tents he passed, which stood
Clustering like beehives on the low, flat strand
Of Oxus, where the summer-floods o'erflow
When the sun melts the snows in high Pamere;
Through the black tents he passed, o'er that low strand,
And to a hillock came, a little back
From the stream's brink—the spot where first a boat,
Crossing the stream in summer, scrapes the land.
The men of former times had crowned the top
With a clay fort; but that was fallen, and now
The Tartars built there Peran-Wisa's tent,

[1] Arnold was born at Laleham in the Thames valley, and grew up amid country scenes.

[2] "May she rest."

[3] Founded on a story in the Persian epic, *Shah Nameh,* or "Book of Kings." Rustum is the great legendary warrior-hero of Iran, or Persia. In the Turanian, or Tartar land, which is ruled over by Afrasiab, an enemy of the Persians, Rustum's son Sohrab has grown up without ever having seen his father; nor does the father know of the existence of his son, having been told that the child born to him was a girl. The rest of the tragic tale may be left to tell itself in the simple and dignified language which Arnold, in professed imitation of the Homeric poems, has chosen.

[4] now the Amu-Daria, flowing from the plateau of Pamir, in central Asia, to the Aral Sea

[5] a Turanian chieftain

A dome of laths, and o'er it felts were spread.
And Sohrab came there, and went in, and stood
Upon the thick piled [1] carpets in the tent,
And found the old man sleeping on his bed
Of rugs and felts, and near him lay his arms.
And Peran-Wisa heard him, though the step
Was dulled; for he slept light, an old man's sleep;
And he rose quickly on one arm, and said:
"Who art thou? for it is not yet clear dawn.
Speak! is there news, or any night alarm?"
But Sohrab came to the bedside, and said:
"Thou know'st me, Peran-Wisa! it is I.
The sun is not yet risen, and the foe
Sleep; but I sleep not; all night long I lie
Tossing and wakeful, and I come to thee.
For so did King Afrasiab bid me seek
Thy counsel, and to heed thee as thy son,
In Samarcand, before the army marched;
And I will tell thee what my heart desires.
Thou know'st if, since from Ader-baijan [2] first
I came among the Tartars and bore arms,
I have still served Afrasiab well, and shown,
At my boy's years, the courage of a man.
This, too, thou know'st, that while I still bear on
The conquering Tartar ensigns through the world,
And beat the Persians back on every field,
I seek one man, one man, and one alone—
Rustum, my father; who I hoped should greet,
Should one day greet, upon some well-fought field,
His not unworthy, not inglorious son.
So I long hoped, but him I never find.
Come then, hear now, and grant me what I ask.
Let the two armies rest today; but I
Will challenge forth the bravest Persian lords
To meet me, man to man; if I prevail,
Rustum will surely hear it; if I fall—
Old man, the dead need no one, claim no kin.
Dim is the rumor of a common fight,
Where host meets host, and many names are sunk;
But of a single combat fame speaks clear."
He spoke; and Peran-Wisa took the hand
Of the young man in his, and sighed, and said:
"O Sohrab, an unquiet heart is thine!
Canst thou not rest among the Tartar chiefs,
And share the battle's common chance with us
Who love thee, but must press forever first,
In single fight incurring single risk,
To find a father thou hast never seen?
That were far best, my son, to stay with us
Unmurmuring; in our tents, while it is war,
And when 'tis truce, then in Afrasiab's towns.
But, if this one desire indeed rules all,
To seek out Rustum—seek him not through fight!
Seek him in peace, and carry to his arms,
O Sohrab, carry an unwounded son!
But far hence seek him, for he is not here.
For now it is not as when I was young,
When Rustum was in front of every fray;
But now he keeps apart, and sits at home,
In Seistan, [3] with Zal, his father old.
Whether that his own mighty strength at last
Feels the abhorred approaches of old age,
Or in some quarrel with the Persian King.
There go!—Thou wilt not? Yet my heart forebodes
Danger or death awaits thee on this field.
Fain would I know thee safe and well, though lost
To us! Fain therefore send thee hence, in peace
To seek thy father, not seek single fights
In vain;—but who can keep the lion's cub
From ravening, and who govern Rustum's son?
Go, I will grant thee what thy heart desires."
So said he, and dropped Sohrab's hand, and left
His bed, and the warm rugs whereon he lay;
And o'er his chilly limbs his woolen coat
He passed, and tied his sandals on his feet,
And threw a white cloak round him, and he took
In his right hand a ruler's staff, no sword;
And on his head he set his sheepskin cap,
Black, glossy, curled, the fleece of Kara-Kul; [4]
And raised the curtain of his tent, and called
His herald to his side, and went abroad.
The sun by this had risen, and cleared the fog
From the broad Oxus and the glittering sands.
And from their tents the Tartar horsemen filed
Into the open plain; so Haman bade—
Haman, who next to Peran-Wisa ruled
The host, and still was in his lusty prime.
From their black tents, long files of horse, they streamed;
As when some gray November morn the files,
In marching order spread, of long-necked cranes
Stream over Casbin and the southern slopes
Of Elburz, from the Aralian estuaries,
Or some frore [5] Caspian reed-bed, southward bound
For the warm Persian seaboard—so they streamed.
The Tartars of the Oxus, the King's guard,
First, with black sheepskin caps and with long spears;

[1] from "pile"—fur, or hair-like nap
[2] a northerly province of Persia
[3] three syllables, *Se-is-tan;* in eastern Persia
[4] a town in Bokhara
[5] See *Par. Lost,* ii, 595.

Large men, large steeds; who from Bokhara come
And Khiva, and ferment the milk of mares.[1]
Next, the more temperate Toorkmuns of the south,
The Tukas, and the lances of Salore,
And those from Attruck and the Caspian sands;
Light men and on light steeds, who only drink
The acrid milk of camels, and their wells.
And then a swarm of wandering horse, who came
From far and a more doubtful service owned;
The Tartars of Ferghana, from the banks
Of the Jaxartes, men with scanty beards
And close-set skullcaps; and those wilder hordes
Who roam o'er Kipchak and the northern waste,
Kalmucks and unkempt Kuzzaks, tribes who stray
Nearest the Pole, and wandering Kirghizzes,
Who come on shaggy ponies from Pamere;
These all filed out from camp into the plain.
And on the other side the Persians formed;—
First a light cloud of horse, Tartars they seemed,
The Ilyats of Khorassan; and behind,
The royal troops of Persia, horse and foot,
Marshaled battalions bright in burnished steel.
But Peran-Wisa with his herald came,
Threading the Tartar squadrons to the front,
And with his staff kept back the foremost ranks.
And when Ferood, who led the Persians, saw
That Peran-Wisa kept the Tartars back,
He took his spear, and to the front he came,
And checked his ranks, and fixed them where they stood.
And the old Tartar came upon the sand
Betwixt the silent hosts, and spake, and said:
"Ferood, and ye, Persians and Tartars, hear!
Let there be truce between the hosts today.
But choose a champion from the Persian lords
To fight our champion Sohrab, man to man."
As, in the country, on a morn in June,
When the dew glistens on the pearlèd ears,
A shiver runs through the deep corn for joy—
So, when they heard what Peran-Wisa said,
A thrill through all the Tartar squadron ran
Of pride and hope for Sohrab, whom they loved.
But as a troop of peddlers, from Cabool,
Cross underneath the Indian Caucasus,
That vast, sky-neighboring mountain of milk snow;
Crossing so high, that, as they mount, they pass
Long flocks of traveling birds dead on the snow,
Choked by the air, and scarce can they themselves
Slake their parched throats with sugared mulberries—
In single file they move, and stop their breath,
For fear they should dislodge the o'erhanging snows—
So the pale Persians held their breath with fear.
And to Ferood his brother chiefs came up
To counsel; Gudurz and Zoarrah came,
And Feraburz, who ruled the Persian host
Second, and was the uncle of the King;
These came and counseled, and then Gudurz said:
"Ferood, shame bids us take their challenge up,
Yet champion have we none to match this youth.
He has the wild stag's foot, the lion's heart.
But Rustum came last night; aloof he sits
And sullen, and has pitched his tents apart.
Him will I seek, and carry to his ear
The Tartar challenge, and this young man's name.
Haply he will forget his wrath, and fight.[2]
Stand forth the while, and take their challenge up."
So spake he; and Ferood stood forth and cried:
"Old man, be it agreed as thou hast said!
Let Sohrab arm, and we will find a man."
He spake: and Peran-Wisa turned, and strode
Back through the opening squadrons to his tent.
But through the anxious Persians Gudurz ran,
And crossed the camp which lay behind, and reached,
Out on the sands beyond it, Rustum's tents.
Of scarlet cloth they were, and glittering gay,
Just pitched; the high pavilion in the midst
Was Rustum's, and his men lay camped around.
And Gudurz entered Rustum's tent, and found
Rustum; his morning meal was done, but still
The table stood before him, charged with food—
A side of roasted sheep, and cakes of bread,
And dark green melons; and there Rustum sat
Listless, and held a falcon on his wrist,
And played with it; but Gudurz came and stood
Before him; and he looked, and saw him stand,
And with a cry sprang up and dropped the bird,
And greeted Gudurz with both hands, and said:
"Welcome! These eyes could see no better sight.
What news? But sit down first, and eat and drink."

[1] making the drink called kumiss

[2] This is a distinct echo of the *Iliad*.

But Gudurz stood in the tent door, and said:
"Not now! a time will come to eat and drink,
But not today; today has other needs.
The armies are drawn out, and stand at gaze;
For from the Tartars is a challenge brought
To pick a champion from the Persian lords
To fight their champion—and thou know'st his name—
Sohrab men call him, but his birth is hid.
O Rustum, like thy might is this young man's!
He has the wild stag's foot, the lion's heart;
And he is young, and Iran's chiefs are old,
Or else too weak; and all eyes turn to thee.
Come down and help us, Rustum, or we lose!"
He spoke; but Rustum answered with a smile:
"Go to! if Iran's chiefs are old, then I
Am older; if the young are weak, the King
Errs strangely; for the King, for Kai Khosroo,
Himself is young, and honors younger men,
And lets the aged molder to their graves.
Rustum he loves no more, but loves the young—
The young may rise at Sohrab's vaunts, not I.
For what care I, though all speak Sohrab's fame?
For would that I myself had such a son,
And not that one, slight helpless girl I have—
A son so famed, so brave, to send to war,
And I to tarry with the snow-haired Zal,[1]
My father, whom the robber Afghans vex,
And clip his borders short, and drive his herds,
And he has none to guard his weak old age.
There would I go, and hang my armor up,
And with my great name fence that weak old man,
And spend the goodly treasures I have got,
And rest my age, and hear of Sohrab's fame,
And leave to death the hosts of thankless kings,
And with these slaughterous hands draw sword no more."
He spoke and smiled; and Gudurz made reply:
"What then, O Rustum, will men say to this,
When Sohrab dares our bravest forth, and seeks
Thee most of all, and thou, whom most he seeks,
Hidest thy face? Take heed lest men should say:
Like some old miser, Rustum hoards his fame,
And shuns to peril it with younger men."
And greatly moved, then Rustum made reply:
"O Gudurz, wherefore dost thou say such words?

[1] Zal was born with white hair, and on that account had been cast out to die, but was fostered by a marvelous bird, the simburg, or roc. Cf. l. 679.

Thou knowest better words than this to say.
What is one more, one less, obscure or famed,
Valiant or craven, young or old, to me?
Are not they mortal, am not I myself?
But who for men of nought would do great deeds?
Come, thou shalt see how Rustum hoards his fame!
But I will fight unknown, and in plain arms;
Let not men say of Rustum, he was matched
In single fight with any mortal man."
He spoke, and frowned; and Gudurz turned, and ran
Back quickly through the camp in fear and joy—
Fear at his wrath, but joy that Rustum came.
But Rustum strode to his tent-door, and called
His followers in, and bade them bring his arms,
And clad himself in steel; the arms he chose
Were plain, and on his shield was no device,
Only his helm was rich, inlaid with gold,
And, from the fluted spine atop, a plume
Of horsehair waved, a scarlet horsehair plume.
So armed, he issued forth; and Ruksh, his horse,
Followed him like a faithful hound at heel—
Ruksh, whose renown was noised through all the earth,
The horse whom Rustum on a foray once
Did in Bokhara by the river find
A colt beneath its dam, and drove him home,
And reared him; a bright bay, with lofty crest,
Dight with a saddle-cloth of broidered green
Crusted with gold, and on the ground were worked
All beasts of chase, all beasts which hunters know.
So followed, Rustum left his tents, and crossed
The camp, and to the Persian host appeared.
And all the Persians knew him, and with shouts
Hailed; but the Tartars knew not who he was.
And dear as the wet diver to the eyes
Of his pale wife who waits and weeps on shore,
By sandy Bahrein, in the Persian Gulf,
Plunging all day in the blue waves, at night,
Having made up his tale of precious pearls,
Rejoins her in their hut upon the sands—
So dear to the pale Persians Rustum came.
And Rustum to the Persian front advanced,
And Sohrab armed in Haman's tent, and came.
And as afield the reapers cut a swath
Down through the middle of a rich man's corn,
And on each side are squares of standing corn,
And in the midst a stubble, short and bare—
So on each side were squares of men, with spears
Bristling, and in the midst, the open sand.

And Rustum came upon the sand, and cast
His eyes toward the Tartar tents, and saw
Sohrab come forth, and eyed him as he came.
  As some rich woman, on a winter's morn,
Eyes through her silken curtains the poor drudge
Who with numb, blackened fingers makes her fire—
At cockcrow, on a starlit winter's morn,
When the frost flowers the whitened window-panes—
And wonders how she lives, and what the thoughts
Of that poor drudge may be; so Rustum eyed
The unknown adventurous youth, who from afar
Came seeking Rustum, and defying forth
All the most valiant chiefs; long he perused
His spirited air, and wondered who he was.
For very young he seemed, tenderly reared;
Like some young cypress, tall, and dark, and straight,[1]
Which in a queen's secluded garden throws
Its slight, dark shadow on the moonlit turf,
By midnight, to a bubbling fountain's sound—
So slender Sohrab seemed, so softly reared.
And a deep pity entered Rustum's soul
As he beheld him coming; and he stood,
And beckoned to him with his hand, and said:
  "O thou young man, the air of Heaven is soft,
And warm, and pleasant; but the grave is cold!
Heaven's air is better than the cold, dead grave.
Behold me! I am vast, and clad in iron,
And tried; and I have stood on many a field
Of blood, and I have fought with many a foe—
Never was that field lost, or that foe saved.
O Sohrab, wherefore wilt thou rush on death?
Be governed! Quit the Tartar host, and come
To Iran, and be as my son to me,
And fight beneath my banner till I die!
There are no youths in Iran brave as thou."
  So he spake, mildly; Sohrab heard his voice,
The mighty voice of Rustum, and he saw
His giant figure planted on the sand,
Sole, like some single tower, which a chief
Hath builded on the waste in former years
Against the robbers; and he saw that head,
Streaked with its first gray hairs—hope filled his soul,
And he ran forward and embraced his knees,
And clasped his hand within his own, and said:
  "Oh, by thy father's head! By thine own soul!
Art thou not Rustum? Speak! Art thou not he?"

[1] For this oriental figure, compare the *Rubàiyàt* st. xli.

  But Rustum eyed askance the kneeling youth,
And turned away, and spake to his own soul:
  "Ah, me, I muse what this young fox may mean!
False, wily, boastful, are these Tartar boys.
For if I now confess this thing he asks,
And hide it not, but say: *Rustum is here!*
He will not yield indeed, nor quit our foes,
But he will find some pretext not to fight,
And praise my fame, and proffer courteous gifts,
A belt or sword perhaps, and go his way.
And on a feast-tide, in Afrasiab's hall,
In Samarcand, he will arise and cry:
'I challenged once, when the two armies camped
Beside the Oxus, all the Persian lords
To cope with me in single fight; but they
Shrank, only Rustum dared; then he and I
Changed gifts, and went on equal terms away.'
So will he speak, perhaps, while men applaud;
Then were the chiefs of Iran shamed through me."
  And then he turned, and sternly spake aloud:
"Rise! Wherefore dost thou vainly question thus
Of Rustum? I am here, whom thou hast called
By challenge forth; make good thy vaunt, or yield!
Is it with Rustum only thou wouldst fight?
Rash boy, men look on Rustum's face and flee!
For well I know, that did great Rustum stand
Before thy face this day, and were revealed,
There would be then no talk of fighting more.
But being what I am, I tell thee this—
Do thou record it in thine inmost soul:
Either thou shalt renounce thy vaunt and yield,
Or else thy bones shall strew this sand, till winds
Bleach them, or Oxus with his summer-floods,
Oxus in summer wash them all away."
  He spoke; and Sohrab answered, on his feet:
"Art thou so fierce? Thou wilt not fright me so!
I am no girl, to be made pale by words.
Yet this thou hast said well, did Rustum stand
Here on this field, there were no fighting then.
But Rustum is far hence, and we stand here.
Begin! Thou art more vast, more dread than I,
And thou art proved, I know, and I am young—
But yet success sways with the breath of Heaven.
And though thou thinkest that thou knowest sure
Thy victory, yet thou canst not surely know,

For we are all, like swimmers in the sea,
Poised on the top of a huge wave of fate,
Which hangs uncertain to which side to fall.
And whether it will heave us up to land,
Or whether it will roll us out to sea,
Back out to sea, to the deep waves of death,
We know not, and no search will make us know;
Only the event will teach us in its hour."
He spoke and Rustum answered not, but hurled
His spear; down from the shoulder, down it came,
As on some partridge in the corn a hawk,
That long has towered in the airy clouds,
Drops like a plummet; Sohrab saw it come,
And sprang aside, quick as a flash; the spear
Hissed, and went quivering down into the sand,
Which it sent flying wide—then Sohrab threw
In turn, and full struck Rustum's shield; sharp rang,
The iron plates rang sharp, but turned the spear.
And Rustum seized his club, which none but he
Could wield; an unlopped trunk it was, and huge,
Still rough—like those which men in treeless plains
To build them boats fish from the flooded rivers,
Hyphasis or Hydaspes, when, high up
By their dark springs, the wind in wintertime
Hath made in Himalayan forests wrack,
And strewn the channels with torn boughs—so huge
The club which Rustum lifted now, and struck
One stroke; but again Sohrab sprang aside,
Lithe as the glancing snake, and the club came
Thundering to earth, and leaped from Rustum's hand.
And Rustum followed his own blow, and fell
To his knees, and with his fingers clutched the sand;
And now might Sohrab have unsheathed his sword,
And pierced the mighty Rustum while he lay
Dizzy, and on his knees, and choked with sand;
But he looked on and smiled, nor bared his sword
But courteously drew back, and spoke, and said:
"Thou strik'st too hard! That club of thine will float
Upon the summer-floods, and not my bones.
But rise, and be not wroth! not wroth am I;
No, when I see thee, wrath forsakes my soul.
Thou say'st thou art not Rustum; be it so!
Who art thou then, that canst so touch my soul?
Boy as I am, I have seen battles, too—
Have waded [1] foremost in their bloody waves,
And heard their hollow roar of dying men;
But never was my heart thus touched before.
Are they from Heaven, these softenings of the heart?
O thou old warrior, let us yield to Heaven!
Come, plant we here in earth our angry spears,
And make a truce, and sit upon this sand,
And pledge each other in red wine, like friends,
And thou shalt talk to me of Rustum's deeds.
There are enough foes in the Persian host,
Whom I may meet, and strike, and feel no pang;
Champions enough Afrasiab has, whom thou
Mayst fight; fight *them,* when they confront thy spear!
But oh, let there be peace 'twixt thee and me!"
He ceased, but while he spake, Rustum had risen,
And stood erect, trembling with rage; his club
He left to lie, but had regained his spear,
Whose fiery point now in his mailed right hand
Blazed bright and baleful, like that autumn-star,
The baleful sign of fevers; dust had soiled
His stately crest, and dimmed his glittering arms.
His breast heaved, his lips foamed, and twice his voice
Was choked with rage; at last these words broke way:
"Girl! nimble with thy feet, not with thy hands!
Curled minion, dancer, coiner of sweet words!
Fight, let me hear thy hateful voice no more!
Thou art not in Afrasiab's gardens now
With Tartar girls, with whom thou art wont to dance;
But on the Oxus-sands, and in the dance
Of battle and with me, who make no play
Of war; I fight it out, and hand to hand.
Speak not to me of truce, and pledge, and wine!
Remember all thy valor; try thy feints
And cunning! All the pity I had is gone;
Because thou hast shamed me before both the hosts
With thy light skipping tricks, and thy girl's wiles."
He spoke, and Sohrab kindled at his taunts,
And he, too, drew his sword; at once they rushed

[1] The word originally meant only "walked"; with the change in meaning grew up the hyperbole of "seas of blood," "bloody waves," etc.

Together, as two eagles on one prey
Come rushing down together from the clouds,
One from the east, one from the west; their shields
Dashed with a clang together, and a din
Rose, such as that the sinewy woodcutters
Make often in the forest's heart at morn,
Of hewing axes, crashing trees—such blows
Rustum and Sohrab on each other hailed.
And you would say that sun and stars took part
In that unnatural conflict; for a cloud
Grew suddenly in Heaven, and darked the sun
Over the fighters' heads; and a wind rose
Under their feet, and moaning swept the plain,
And in a sandy whirlwind wrapped the pair.
In gloom they twain were wrapped, and they alone;
For both the on-looking hosts on either hand
Stood in broad daylight, and the sky was pure,
And the sun sparkled on the Oxus stream.
But in the gloom they fought, with bloodshot eyes
And laboring breath; first Rustum struck the shield
Which Sohrab held stiff out; the steel-spiked spear
Rent the tough plates, but failed to reach the skin,
And Rustum plucked it back with angry groan.
Then Sohrab with his sword smote Rustum's helm,
Nor clove its steel quite through; but all the crest
He shore away, and that proud horsehair plume,
Never till now defiled, sank to the dust;
And Rustum bowed his head; but then the gloom
Grew blacker, thunder rumbled in the air,
And lightnings rent the cloud; and Ruksh, the horse,
Who stood at hand, uttered a dreadful cry—
No horse's cry was that, most like a roar
Of some pained desert lion, who all day
Hath trailed the hunter's javelin in his side,
And comes at night to die upon the sand.
The two hosts heard that cry, and quaked for fear,
And Oxus curdled as it crossed his stream.
But Sohrab heard, and quailed not, but rushed on,
And struck again; and again Rustum bowed
His head; but this time all the blade, like glass,
Sprang in a thousand shivers on the helm,
And in the hand the hilt remained alone.
Then Rustum raised his head; his dreadful eyes
Glared, and he shook on high his menacing spear,
And shouted, *Rustum!*—Sohrab heard that shout,
And shrank amazed; back he recoiled one step,
And scanned with blinking eyes the advancing form;
And then he stood bewildered; and he dropped
His covering shield, and the spear pierced his side.
He reeled, and staggering back, sank to the ground,
And then the gloom dispersed, and the wind fell,
And the bright sun broke forth, and melted all
The cloud; and the two armies saw the pair—
Saw Rustum standing, safe upon his feet,
And Sohrab, wounded, on the bloody sand.

Then, with a bitter smile, Rustum began:
"Sohrab, thou thoughtest in thy mind to kill
A Persian lord this day, and strip his corpse,
And bear thy trophies to Afrasiab's tent.
Or else that the great Rustum would come down
Himself to fight, and that thy wiles would move
His heart to take a gift, and let thee go.
And then that all the Tartar host would praise
Thy courage or thy craft, and spread thy fame,
To glad thy father in his weak old age.
Fool, thou art slain, and by an unknown man!
Dearer to the red jackals shalt thou be
Than to thy friends, and to thy father old."

And, with a fearless mien, Sohrab replied:
"Unknown thou art; yet thy fierce vaunt is vain.
Thou dost not slay me, proud and boastful man!
No! Rustum slays me, and this filial heart.
For were I matched with ten such men as thee,
And I were that which till today I was,
They should be lying here, I standing there.
But that belovèd name unnerved my arm—
That name, and something, I confess, in thee,
Which troubles all my heart, and made my shield
Fall; and thy spear transfixed an unarmed foe.
And now thou boastest, and insult'st my fate.
But hear thou this, fierce man, tremble to hear
The mighty Rustum shall avenge my death!
My father, whom I seek through all the world,
He shall avenge my death, and punish thee!"

As when some hunter in the spring hath found
A breeding eagle sitting on her nest,
Upon the craggy isle of a hill-lake,
And pierced her with an arrow as she rose,

And followed her to find her where she fell
Far off;—anon her mate comes winging back
From hunting, and a great way off descries
His huddling young left sole; at that, he checks
His pinion, and with short uneasy sweeps
Circles above his aerie, with loud screams
Chiding his mate back to her nest; but she
Lies dying, with the arrow in her side,
In some far, stony gorge out of his ken,
A heap of fluttering feathers—never more
Shall the lake glass her, flying over it;
Never the black and dripping precipices
Echo her stormy scream as she sails by—
As that poor bird flies home, nor knows his loss,
So Rustum knew not his own loss, but stood
Over his dying son, and knew him not.
But, with a cool incredulous voice, he said:
"What prate is this of fathers and revenge?
The mighty Rustum never had a son."
And, with a failing voice, Sohrab replied:
"Ah, yes, he had! and that lost son am I.
Surely the news will one day reach his ear,
Reach Rustum, where he sits, and tarries long,
Somewhere, I know not where, but far from here,
And pierce him like a stab, and make him leap
To arms, and cry for vengeance upon thee.
Fierce man, bethink thee, for an only son!
What will that grief, what will that vengeance be?
Oh, could I live, till I that grief had seen!
Yet him I pity not so much, but her,
My mother, who in Ader-baijan dwells
With that old king, her father, who grows gray
With age, and rules over the valiant Koords.
Her most I pity, who no more will see
Sohrab returning from the Tartar camp,
With spoils and honor, when the war is done.
But a dark rumor will be bruited up,
From tribe to tribe, until it reach her ear;
And then will that defenseless woman learn
That Sohrab will rejoice her sight no more,
But that in battle with a nameless foe,
By the far-distant Oxus, he is slain."
He spoke; and as he ceased, he wept aloud,
Thinking of her he left, and his own death.
He spoke; but Rustum listened, plunged in thought.
Nor did he yet believe it was his son
Who spoke, although he called back names he knew;
For he had had sure tidings that the babe,
Which was in Ader-baijan born to him,
Had been a puny girl, no boy at all—
So that sad mother sent him word, for fear
Rustum should seek the boy, to train in arms.
And so he deemed that either Sohrab took,
By a false boast, the style of Rustum's son;
Or that men gave it him, to swell his fame.
So deemed he; yet he listened, plunged in thought.
And his soul set to grief, as the vast tide
Of the bright, rocking Ocean sets to shore
At the full moon; tears gathered in his eyes;
For he remembered his own early youth,
And all its bounding rapture; as, at dawn,
The shepherd from his moutain-lodge descries
A far, bright city, smitten by the sun,
Through many rolling clouds—so Rustum saw
His youth; saw Sohrab's mother, in her bloom;
And that old king, her father, who loved well
His wandering guest, and gave him his fair child
With joy; and all the pleasant life they led,
They three, in that long-distant summer-time—
The castle, and the dewy woods, and hunt
And hound, and morn on those delightful hills
In Ader-baijan. And he saw that Youth,
Of age and looks to be his own dear son,
Piteous and lovely, lying on the sand,
Like some rich hyacinth which by the scythe
Of an unskillful gardener has been cut,
Mowing the garden grassplots near its bed,
And lies, a fragrant tower of purple bloom,
On the mown, dying grass—so Sohrab lay,
Lovely in death, upon the common sand.
And Rustum gazed on him with grief, and said:
"O Sohrab, thou indeed art such a son
Whom Rustum, wert thou his, might well have loved.
Yet here thou errest, Sohrab, or else men
Have told thee false—thou art not Rustum's son.
For Rustum had no son; one child he had—
But one—a girl; who with her mother now
Plies some light, female task, nor dreams of us—
Of us she dreams not, nor of wounds, nor war."
But Sohrab answered him in a wrath; for now
The anguish of the deep-fixed spear grew fierce,
And he desired to draw forth the steel,
And let the blood flow free, and so to die—
But first he would convince his stubborn foe;
And, rising sternly on one arm, he said:
"Man, who art thou who dost deny my words?
Truth sits upon the lips of dying men,
And falsehood, while I lived, was far from mine.
I tell thee, pricked upon this arm I bear
That seal which Rustum to my mother gave,

That she might prick it on the babe she bore."
He spoke; and all the blood left Rustum's cheeks,
And his knees tottered, and he smote his hand
Against his breast, his heavy, mailèd hand,
That the hard iron corslet clanked aloud;
And to his heart he pressed the other hand,
And in a hollow voice he spake, and said:
"Sohrab, that were a proof which could not lie!
If thou show this, then art thou Rustum's son."
Then, with weak hasty fingers, Sohrab loosed
His belt, and near the shoulder bared his arm,
And showed a sign in faint vermilion points
Pricked; as a cunning workman, in Pekin,
Pricks with vermilion some clear porcelain vase,
An emperor's gift—at early morn he paints,
And all day long, and, when night comes, the lamp
Lights up his studious forehead and thin hands—
So delicately pricked the sign appeared
On Sohrab's arm, the sign of Rustum's seal.
It was that griffin, which of old reared Zal,
Rustum's great father, whom they left to die,
A helpless babe, among the mountain-rocks;
Him that kind creature found, and reared, and loved—
Then Rustum took it for his glorious sign.
And Sohrab bared that image on his arm,
And himself scanned it long with mournful eyes,
And then he touched it with his hand and said:
"How say'st thou? Is that sign the proper sign
Of Rustum's son, or of some other man's?"
He spoke; but Rustum gazed, and gazed, and stood
Speechless; and then he uttered one sharp cry:
O boy—thy father!—and his voice choked there.
And then a dark cloud passed before his eyes,
And his head swam, and he sank down to earth.
But Sohrab crawled to where he lay, and cast
His arms about his neck, and kissed his lips,
And with fond, faltering fingers stroked his cheeks,
Trying to call him back to life; and life
Came back to Rustum, and he oped his eyes,
And they stood wide with horror; and he seized
In both his hands the dust which lay around,
And threw it on his head, and smirched his hair—
His hair, and face, and beard, and glittering arms;
And strong, convulsive groanings shook his breast,
And his sobs choked him; and he clutched his sword,
To draw it, and forever let life out.
But Sohrab saw his thought, and held his hands,
And with a soothing voice he spake, and said:
"Father, forbear! for I but meet today
The doom which at my birth was written down
In Heaven, and thou art Heaven's unconscious hand.
Surely my heart cried out that it was thou,
When first I saw thee; and thy heart spoke, too,
I know it! But fate trod those promptings down
Under its iron heel; fate, fate engaged
The strife, and hurled me on my father's spear.
But let us speak no more of this! I find
My father; let me feel that I have found!
Come, sit beside me on this sand, and take
My head betwixt thy hands, and kiss my cheeks,
And wash them with thy tears, and say: *My son!*
Quick! quick! for numbered are my sands of life,
And swift; for like the lightning to this field
I came, and like the wind I go away—
Sudden, and swift, and like a passing wind.
But it was writ in Heaven that this should be."
So said he, and his voice released the heart
Of Rustum, and his tears broke forth; he cast
His arms round his son's neck, and wept aloud,
And kissed him. And awe fell on both the hosts,
When they saw Rustum's grief; and Ruksh, the horse,
With his head bowing to the ground and mane
Sweeping the dust, came near, and in mute woe
First to the one, then to the other moved
His head, as if inquiring what their grief
Might mean; and from his dark, compassionate eyes,
The big, warm tears rolled down, and caked the sand.[1]
But Rustum chid him with stern voice, and said:
"Ruksh, now thou grievest; but, O Ruksh, thy feet
Should first have rotted on their nimble joints,
Or ere they brought thy master to this field!"
But Sohrab looked upon the horse and said:
"Is this, then, Ruksh? How often, in past days,

[1] Compare the action of the horse of Achilles, *Iliad,* xix, end.

My mother told me of thee, thou brave steed,
My terrible father's terrible horse! and said,
That I should one day find thy lord and thee.
Come, let me lay my hand upon thy mane!
O Ruksh, thou art more fortunate than I;
For thou hast gone where I shall never go,
And snuffed the breezes of my father's home,
And thou hast trod the sands of Seistan,
And seen the River of Helmund, and the Lake
Of Zirrah; and the aged Zal himself
Has often stroked thy neck, and given thee food,
Corn in a golden platter soaked with wine,
And said: *O Ruksh! bear Rustum well!*—but I
Have never known my grandsire's furrowed face,
Nor seen his lofty house in Seistan,
Nor slaked my thirst at the clear Helmund stream;
But lodged among my father's foes, and seen
Afrasiab's cities only, Samarcand,
Bokhara, and lone Khiva in the waste,
And the black Toorkmun tents; and only drunk
The desert rivers, Moorghab and Tejend,
Kohik, and where the Kalmuks feed their sheep,
The northern Sir; and this great Oxus stream,
The yellow Oxus, by whose brink I die."
Then, with a heavy groan, Rustum bewailed:
"Oh, that its waves were flowing over me!
Oh, that I saw its grains of yellow silt
Roll tumbling in the current o'er my head!"
But with a grave mild voice, Sohrab replied:
"Desire not that, my father! thou must live.
For some are born to do great deeds, and live,
As some are born to be obscured, and die.
Do thou the deeds I die too young to do,
And reap a second glory in thine age;
Thou art my father, and thy gain is mine.
But come! thou seest this great host of men
Which follow me; I pray thee, slay not these!
Let me entreat for them; what have they done?
They followed me, my hope, my fame, my star.
Let them all cross the Oxus back in peace.
But me thou must bear hence, not send with them,
But carry me with thee to Seistan,
And place me on a bed, and mourn for me,
Thou, and the snow-haired Zal, and all thy friends.
And thou must lay me in that lovely earth,
And heap a stately mound above my bones,
And plant a far-seen pillar over all.
That so the passing horseman on the waste
May see my tomb a great way off, and cry:
Sohrab, the mighty Rustum's son, lies there,
Whom his great father did in ignorance kill!
And I be not forgotten in my grave."
And with a mournful voice, Rustum replied:
"Fear not! as thou hast said, Sohrab, my son,
So shall it be; for I will burn my tents,
And quit the host, and bear thee hence with me,
And carry thee away to Seistan,
And place thee on a bed, and mourn for thee,
With the snow-headed Zal, and all my friends,
And I will lay thee in that lovely earth,
And heap a stately mound above thy bones,
And plant a far-seen pillar over all,
And men shall not forget thee in thy grave.
And I will spare thy host; yea, let them go!
Let them all cross the Oxus back in peace!
What should I do with slaying any more?
For would that all that I have ever slain
Might be once more alive; my bitterest foes,
And they who were called champions in their time,
And through whose death I won that fame I have—
And I were nothing but a common man,
A poor, mean soldier, and without renown,
So thou mightest live, too, my son, my son!
Or rather would that I, even I myself,
Might now be lying on this bloody sand,
Near death, and by an ignorant stroke of thine,
Not thou of mine; and I might die, not thou;
And I, not thou, be borne to Seistan;
And Zal might weep above my grave, not thine;
And say: *O son, I weep thee not too sore,*
For willingly, I know, thou met'st thine end!
But now in blood and battles was my youth,
And full of blood and battles is my age,
And I shall never end this life of blood."
Then at the point of death, Sohrab replied:
"A life of blood indeed, thou dreadful man!
But thou shalt yet have peace; only not now,
Not yet! But thou shalt have it on that day,
When thou shalt sail in a high-masted ship,
Thou and the other peers of Kai Khosroo,
Returning home over the salt blue sea,
From laying thy dear master in his grave."
And Rustum gazed in Sohrab's face, and said:
"Soon be that day, my son, and deep that sea!
Till then, if fate so wills, let me endure."
He spoke; and Sohrab smiled on him, and took
The spear, and drew it from his side, and eased
His wound's imperious anguish; but the blood
Came welling from the open gash, and life
Flowed with the stream—all down his cold white side

The crimson torrent ran, dim now and soiled,
Like the soiled tissue of white violets
Left, freshly gathered, on their native bank,
By children whom their nurses call with haste
Indoors from the sun's eye; his head drooped low,
His limbs grew slack; motionless, white, he lay—
White, with eyes closed; only when heavy gasps,
Deep, heavy gasps quivering through all his frame,
Convulsed him back to life, he opened them,
And fixed them feebly on his father's face;
Till now all strength was ebbed, and from his limbs
Unwillingly the spirit fled away,
Regretting the warm mansion which it left,
And youth, and bloom, and this delightful world.
  So, on the bloody sand, Sohrab lay dead;
And the great Rustum drew his horseman's cloak
Down o'er his face, and sat by his dead son.
As those black granite pillars, once high-reared
By Jemshid [1] in Persepolis, to bear
His house, now 'mid their broken flights of steps
Lie prone, enormous, down the mountain side—
So in the sand lay Rustum by his son.
  And night came down over the solemn waste,
And the two gazing hosts, and that sole pair,
And darkened all; and a cold fog, with night,
Crept from the Oxus. Soon a hum arose
As of a great assembly loosed, and fires
Began to twinkle through the fog; for now
Both armies moved to camp, and took their meal;
The Persians took it on the open sands
Southward, the Tartars by the river marge;
And Rustum and his son were left alone.
  But the majestic river floated on,
Out of the mist and hum of that low land,
Into the frosty starlight, and there moved,
Rejoicing, through the hushed Chorasmian waste,
Under the solitary moon;—he flowed
Right for the polar star, past Orgunjè, [2]
Brimming, and bright, and large; then sands begin
To hem his watery march, and dam his streams,
And split his currents; that for many a league
The shorn and parceled Oxus strains along
Through beds of sand and matted rushy isles—
Oxus, forgetting the bright speed he had
In his high mountain-cradle in Pamere,
A foiled, circuitous wanderer—till at last
The longed-for dash of waves is heard, and wide
His luminous home of waters opens, bright
And tranquil, from whose floor the new-bathed stars
Emerge, and shine upon the Aral Sea.

1853

PHILOMELA [3]

Hark! ah, the nightingale—
The tawny-throated!
Hark, from that moonlit cedar what a burst!
What triumph! hark!—what pain!

O wanderer from a Grecian shore,
Still, after many years, in distant lands,
Still nourishing in thy bewildered brain
That wild, unquenched, deep-sunken, old-world pain—
Say, will it never heal?
And can this fragrant lawn
With its cool trees, and night,
And the sweet, tranquil Thames,
And moonshine, and the dew,
To thy racked heart and brain
Afford no balm?

Dost thou tonight behold,
Here, through the moonlight on this English grass,
The unfriendly palace in the Thracian wild?
Dost thou again peruse
With hot cheeks and seared eyes
The too clear web, and thy dumb sister's shame?
Dost thou once more assay
Thy flight, and feel come over thee,
Poor fugitive, the feathery change
Once more, and once more seem to make resound
With love and hate, triumph and agony,
Lone Daulis, and the high Cephissian vale?

Listen, Eugenia—
How thick the bursts come crowding through the leaves!
Again—thou hearest?
Eternal passion!
Eternal pain!

1853

[1] Or Jamshid; a mythical king of Persia; Persepolis is noted for its ruins of ancient grandeur.
[2] a village near Khiva

[3] See the familiar story of Philomela and Procne in Greek mythology. The poem is evidently addressed to a friend, "Eugenia."

KAISER DEAD

April 6, 1887

What, Kaiser dead? The heavy news
Posthaste to Cobham [1] calls the Muse,
From where in Farringford [2] she brews
The ode sublime,
Or with Pen-bryn's bold bard [3] pursues
A rival rime.

Kai's bracelet tail, Kai's busy feet,
Were known to all the village-street.
"What, poor Kai dead?" say all I meet;
"A loss indeed!"
Oh, for the croon pathetic, sweet,
Of Robin's reed! [4]

Six years ago I brought him down,
A baby dog, from London town;
Round his small throat of black and brown
A ribbon blue,
And vouched by glorious renown
A dachshound true.

His mother, most majestic dame,
Of blood unmixed, from Potsdam [5] came;
And Kaiser's race we deemed the same—
No lineage higher.
And so he bore the imperial name.
But, ah, his sire!

Soon, soon the days conviction bring.
The collie hair, the collie swing,
The tail's indomitable ring,
The eye's unrest—
The case was clear; a mongrel thing
Kai stood confest.

But all those virtues, which commend
The humbler sort who serve and tend,
Were thine in store, thou faithful friend.
What sense, what cheer!
To us, declining toward our end,
A mate how dear!

For Max, thy brother dog, began
To flag, and feel his narrowing span.
And cold, besides, his blue blood ran,
Since, 'gainst the classes,
He heard, of late, the Grand Old Man
Incite the Masses. [6]

Yes, Max and we grew slow and sad;
But Kai, a tireless shepherd-lad,
Teeming with plans, alert, and glad
In work or play,
Like sunshine went and came, and bade
Live out the day!

Still, still I see the figure smart—
Trophy in mouth, agog to start,
Then, home returned, once more depart;
Or pressed together
Against thy mistress, loving heart,
In winter weather.

I see the tail, like bracelet twirled,
In moments of disgrace uncurled,
Then at a pardoning word refurled,
A conquering sign;
Crying, "Come on, and range the world,
And never pine."

Thine eye was bright, thy coat it shone;
Thou hadst thine errands, off and on;
In joy thy last morn flew; anon,
A fit! All's over;
And thou art gone where Geist [7] hath gone,
And Toss, and Rover.

Poor Max, with downcast, reverent head,
Regards his brother's form outspread;
Full well Max knows the friend is dead
Whose cordial talk,
And jokes, in doggish language said,
Beguiled his walk.

And Glory, stretched at Burwood gate,
Thy passing by doth vainly wait;
And jealous Jock, thy only hate,
The chiel from Skye,
Lets from his shaggy Highland pate
Thy memory die.

Well, fetch his graven collar fine,
And rub the steel, and make it shine,
And leave it round thy neck to twine,
Kai, in thy grave.
There of thy master keep that sign,
And this plain stave.

1887 *1890*

DOVER BEACH [8]

The sea is calm tonight,
The tide is full, the moon lies fair
Upon the straits;—on the French coast the light
Gleams and is gone; the cliffs of England stand,
Glimmering and vast, out in the tranquil bay.
Come to the window, sweet is the night air!

[1] in Surrey, where Arnold was then living
[2] Tennyson's home on the Isle of Wight
[3] Sir Lewis Morris lived at Penbryn, in Wales.
[4] Adapted from Burns's "Poor Mailie's Elegy," which Arnold is imitating.
[5] a residence of the German emperor
[6] This is a mild thrust at Gladstone and his Home Rule Bill.
[7] mourned in a previous elegy, "Geist's Grave"
[8] Another expression of Arnold's Stoic creed; see note on his sonnet "To a Friend," p. 688.

Only, from the long line of spray
Where the sea meets the moon-blanched land,
Listen! you hear the grating roar
Of pebbles which the waves draw back, and fling,
At their return, up the high strand,
Begin, and cease, and then again begin,
With tremulous cadence slow, and bring
The eternal note of sadness in.

Sophocles long ago
Heard it on the Aegean, and it brought
Into his mind the turbid ebb and flow
Of human misery; we
Find also in the sound a thought,
Hearing it by this distant northern sea.

The Sea of Faith
Was once, too, at the full, and round earth's shore
Lay like the folds of a bright girdle furled.
But now I only hear
Its melancholy, long, withdrawing roar,
Retreating, to the breath
Of the night wind, down the vast edges drear
And naked shingles of the world.

Ah, love, let us be true
To one another; for the world, which seems
To lie before us like a land of dreams,
So various, so beautiful, so new,
Hath really neither joy, nor love, nor light,
Nor certitude, nor peace, nor help for pain;
And we are here as on a darkling plain
Swept with confused alarms of struggle and flight,
Where ignorant armies clash by night.

1867

THE LAST WORD

Creep into thy narrow bed,
Creep, and let no more be said!
Vain thy onset! all stands fast.
Thou thyself must break at last.

Let the long contention cease!
Geese are swans, and swans are geese.
Let them have it how they will!
Thou art tired; best be still.

They out-talked thee, hissed thee, tore thee?
Better men fared thus before thee;
Fired their ringing shot and passed,
Hotly charged—and sank at last.

Charge once more, then, and be dumb!
Let the victors, when they come,
When the forts of folly fall,
Find thy body by the wall!

1867

CULTURE AND HUMAN PERFECTION[1]

The disparagers of culture make its motive curiosity; sometimes, indeed, they make its motive mere exclusiveness and vanity. The culture which is supposed to plume itself on a smattering of Greek and Latin is a culture which is begotten by nothing so intellectual as curiosity; it is valued either out of sheer vanity and ignorance, or else as an engine of social and class distinction, separating its holder, like a badge or title, from other people who have not got it. No serious man would call this *culture,* or attach any value to it, as culture, at all. To find the real ground for the very different estimate which serious people will set upon culture, we must find some motive for culture in the terms of which may lie a real ambiguity; and such a motive the word *curiosity* gives us.

I have before now pointed out that we English do not, like the foreigners, use this word in a good sense as well as in a bad sense. With us the word is always used in a somewhat disapproving sense. A liberal and intelligent eagerness about the things of the mind may be meant by a foreigner when he speaks of curiosity, but with us the word always conveys a certain notion of frivolous and unedifying activity. In the *Quarterly Review,* some little time ago, was an estimate of the celebrated French critic, M. Sainte-Beuve, and a very inadequate estimate it, in my judgment, was. And its inadequacy consisted chiefly in this: that in our English way it left out of sight the double sense really involved in the word *curiosity,* thinking enough was said to stamp M. Sainte-Beuve with blame if it was said that he was impelled in his operations as a critic by curiosity, and omitting either to perceive that M. Sainte-Beuve himself, and many other people with him, would consider that this was praiseworthy and not blameworthy, or to point out why it ought really to be accounted worthy of blame and not of praise. For, as there is a curiosity about intellectual matters which is futile and merely a disease, so there is certainly a curiosity,—a desire after the things of the mind simply for their own sakes and for the pleasure of seeing them as they are,—which is, in an intelligent being, natural and laudable. Nay, and the very desire to see things as they are[2] implies a balance and regulation of mind which is not often attained without fruitful

[1] From the first chapter of *Culture and Anarchy,* 1867, entitled "Sweetness and Light."

[2] This phrase, derived from Wordsworth, has been given wide currency by Arnold. See Wordsworth's "Essay" supplementary to the Preface in the 1815 edition of his poems.

effort, and which is the very opposite of the blind and diseased impulse of mind which is what we mean to blame when we blame curiosity. Montesquieu[1] says: "The first motive which ought to impel us to study is the desire to augment the excellence of our nature, and to render an intelligent being yet more intelligent." This is the true ground to assign for the genuine, scientific passion, however manifested, and for culture, viewed simply as a fruit of this passion; and it is a worthy ground, even though we let the term *curiosity* stand to describe it.

But there is of culture another view, in which not solely the scientific passion, the sheer desire to see things as they are, natural and proper in an intelligent being, appears as the ground of it. There is a view in which all the love of our neighbor, the impulses toward action, help, and beneficence, the desire for removing human error, clearing human confusion, and diminishing human misery, the noble aspiration to leave the world better and happier than we found it,—motives eminently such as are called social—come in as part of the grounds of culture, and the main and preëminent part. Culture is, then, properly described, not as having its origin in curiosity, but as having its origin in the love of perfection; it is *a study of perfection.* It moves by the force, not merely or primarily of the scientific passion for pure knowledge, but also of the moral and social passion for doing good. As, in the first view of it, we took for its worthy motto Montesquieu's words, "To render an intelligent being yet more intelligent!" so, in the second view of it, there is no better motto which it can have than these words of Bishop Wilson:[2] "To make reason and the will of God prevail!"

Only, whereas the passion for doing good is apt to be over-hasty in determining what reason and the will of God say, because its turn is for acting rather than thinking, and it wants to be beginning to act; and whereas it is apt to take its own conceptions, which proceed from its own state of development and share in all the imperfections and immaturities of this, for a basis of action; what distinguishes culture is, that it is possessed by the scientific passion, as well as by the passion of doing good; that it demands worthy notions of reason and the will of God, and does not readily suffer its own crude conceptions to substitute themselves for them. And knowing that no action or institution can be salutary and stable which is not based on reason and the will of God, it is not so bent on acting and instituting, even with the great aim of diminishing human error and misery ever before its thoughts, but that it can remember that acting and instituting are of little use, unless we know how and what we ought to act and to institute.

This culture is more interesting and more far-reaching than that other, which is founded solely on the scientific passion for knowing. But it needs times of faith and ardor, times when the intellectual horizon is opening and widening all round us, to flourish in. And is not the close and bounded intellectual horizon within which we have long lived and moved now lifting up, and are not new lights finding free passage to shine in upon us? For a long time there was no passage for them to make their way in upon us, and then it was of no use to think of adapting the world's action to them. Where was the hope of making reason and the will of God prevail among people who had a routine which they had christened reason and the will of God, in which they were inextricably bound, and beyond which they had no power of looking? But now the iron force of adhesion to the old routine—social, political, religious,—has wonderfully yielded; the iron force of exclusion of all which is new has wonderfully yielded. The danger now is, not that people should obstinately refuse to allow anything but their old routine to pass for reason and the will of God, but either that they should allow some novelty or other to pass for these too easily, or else that they should underrate the importance of them altogether, and think it enough to follow action for its own sake, without troubling themselves to make reason and the will of God prevail therein. Now, then, is the moment for culture to be of service, culture which believes in making reason and the will of God prevail; believes in perfection; is the study and pursuit of perfection; and is no longer debarred, by a rigid invincible exclusion of whatever is new, from getting acceptance for its ideas, simply because they are new.

The moment this view of culture is seized, the moment it is regarded not solely as the endeavor to see things as they are, to draw toward a knowledge of the universal order which seems to be intended and aimed at in the world, and which it is a man's happiness to go along with or his misery to go counter to,—to learn, in short, the will of God—the moment, I say, culture is considered not

[1] a French writer of the 18th century, author of the celebrated philosophical work *The Spirit of the Laws*

[2] Thomas Wilson, Bishop of the Isle of Man (d. 1765)

merely as the endeavor to *see* and *learn* this, but as the endeavor, also, to make it *prevail,* the moral, social, and beneficent character of culture becomes manifest. The mere endeavor to see and learn the truth for our own personal satisfaction is indeed a commencement for making it prevail, a preparing the way for this, which always serves this, and is wrongly, therefore, stamped with blame absolutely in itself and not only in its caricature and degeneration. But perhaps it has got stamped with blame and disparaged with the dubious title of curiosity because, in comparison with this wider endeavor of such great and plain utility, it looks selfish, petty, and unprofitable.

And religion, the greatest and most important of the efforts by which the human race has manifested its impulse to perfect itself—religion, that voice of the deepest human experience—does not only enjoin and sanction the aim which is the great aim of culture, the aim of setting ourselves to ascertain what perfection is, and to make it prevail; but also, in determining generally in what human perfection consists, religion comes to a conclusion identical with that which culture—culture seeking the determination of this question through *all* the voices of human experience which have been heard upon it, of art, science, poetry, philosophy, history, as well as of religion, in order to give a greater fullness and certainty to its solution—likewise reaches. Religion says: *The kingdom of God is within you;* and culture, in like manner, places human perfection in an *internal* condition, in the growth and predominance of our humanity proper, as distinguished from our animality. It places it in the ever-increasing efficacy and in the general harmonious expansion of those gifts of thought and feeling which make the peculiar dignity, wealth, and happiness of human nature. As I have said on a former occasion: "It is in making endless additions to itself, in the endless expansion of its powers, in endless growth in wisdom and beauty, that the spirit of the human race finds its ideal. To reach this ideal, culture is an indispensable aid, and that is the true value of culture." Not a having and a resting, but a growing and a becoming, is the character of perfection as culture conceives it; and here, too, it coincides with religion.

. . . . . .

But the point of view of culture, keeping the mark of human perfection simply and broadly in view, and not assigning to this perfection, as religion or utilitarianism assigns to it, a special and limited character, this point of view, I say, of culture is best given by these words of Epictetus[1]: "It is a sign of ἀφυια," says he—that is, of a nature not finely tempered—"to give yourselves up to things which relate to the body; to make, for instance, a great fuss about exercise, a great fuss about eating, a great fuss about drinking, a great fuss about walking, a great fuss about riding. All these things ought to be done merely by the way; the formation of the spirit and character must be our real concern." This is admirable; and, indeed, the Greek word εὐφυια, a finely tempered nature, gives exactly the notion of perfection as culture brings us to conceive it: a harmonious perfection, a perfection in which the characters of beauty and intelligence are both present, which unites "the two noblest of things"—as Swift, who of one of the two, at any rate, had himself all too little, most happily calls them in his *Battle of the Books*—"the two noblest of things, *sweetness and light.*"[2] The εὐφυής[3] is the man who tends toward sweetness and light; the ἀφυής[4] on the other hand, is our Philistine.[5] The immense spiritual significance of the Greeks is due to their having been inspired with this central and happy idea of the essential character of human perfection; and Mr. Bright's[6] misconception of culture, as a smattering of Greek and Latin, comes itself, after all, from this wonderful significance of the Greeks having affected the very machinery of our education, and is in itself a kind of homage to it.

In thus making sweetness and light to be characters of perfection, culture is of like spirit with poetry, follows one law with poetry. Far more than on our freedom, our population, and our industrialism, many amongst us rely upon our religious organizations to save us. I have called religion a yet more important manifestation of human nature than poetry, because it has worked on a broader scale for perfection, and with greater masses of men. But the idea of beauty and of a human nature perfect on all its sides, which is

[1] See note on Arnold's sonnet "To a Friend," p. 688.

[2] Swift derived the words from the labor of the bees that fill their hives "with honey and wax, thus furnishing mankind with the two noblest of things, sweetness and light." The terms stand for spiritual beauty and intellectual illumination.

[3] "Well endowed by nature."

[4] "Ill endowed by nature."

[5] Arnold's name for the middle class of English society, whose defect he declares to be narrowness.

[6] John Bright, a Liberal statesman, who had scoffed at Arnold's gospel of culture.

the dominant idea of poetry, is a true and invaluable idea, though it has not yet had the success that the idea of conquering the obvious faults of our animality, and of a human nature perfect on the moral side—which is the dominant idea of religion—has been enabled to have; and it is destined, adding to itself the religious idea of a devout energy, to transform and govern the other.

The best art and poetry of the Greeks, in which religion and poetry are one, in which the idea of beauty and of a human nature perfect on all sides adds to itself a religious and devout energy, and works in the strength of that, is on this account of such surpassing interest and instructiveness for us, though it was—as having regard to the human race in general, and, indeed, having regard to the Greeks themselves, we must own—a premature attempt, an attempt which for success needed the moral and religious fiber in humanity to be more braced and developed than it had yet been. But Greece did not err in having the idea of beauty, harmony, and complete human perfection, so present and paramount. It is impossible to have this idea too present and paramount; only, the moral fiber must be braced, too. And we, because we have braced the moral fiber, are not on that account in the right way, if at the same time the idea of beauty, harmony, and complete human perfection is wanting or misapprehended amongst us.

. . . .

1867 1867-68

NATURAL MAGIC IN CELTIC LITERATURE[1]

. . . . . .

The Celt's quick feeling for what is noble and distinguished gave his poetry style; his indomitable personality gave it pride and passion; his sensibility and nervous exaltation gave it a better gift still, the gift of rendering with wonderful felicity the magical charm of nature. The forest solitude, the bubbling spring, the wild flowers, are everywhere in romance. They have a mysterious life and grace there; they are Nature's own children, and utter her secret in a way which makes them something quite different from the woods, waters, and plants of Greek and Latin poetry. Now of this delicate magic, Celtic romance is so preëminent a mistress, that it seems impossible to believe the power did not come into romance from the Celts. Magic is just the word for it—the magic of nature; not merely the beauty of nature—that the Greeks and Latins had; not merely an honest smack of the soil, a faithful realism—that the Germans had; but the intimate life of Nature, her weird power and her fairy charm. As the Saxon names of places, with the pleasant wholesome smack of the soil in them—Weathersfield, Thaxted, Shalford—are to the Celtic names of places, with their penetrating, lofty beauty—Velindra, Tyntagel, Caernarvon—so is the homely realism of German and Norse nature to the fairy-like loveliness of Celtic nature. Gwydion wants a wife for his pupil: "Well," says Math, "we will seek, I and thou, by charms and illusions, to form a wife for him out of flowers. So they took the blossoms of the oak, and the blossoms of the broom, and the blossoms of the meadow-sweet, and produced from them a maiden, the fairest and most graceful that man ever saw. And they baptized her, and gave her the name of Flower-Aspect."[2] Celtic romance is full of exquisite touches like that, showing the delicacy of the Celt's feeling in these matters, and how deeply Nature lets him come into her secrets. The quick dropping of blood is called "faster than the fall of the dewdrop from the blade of reed-grass upon the earth, when the dew of June is at the heaviest." And thus is Olwen described: "More yellow was her hair than the flower of the broom, and her skin was whiter than the foam of the wave, and fairer were her hands and her fingers than the blossoms of the wood-anemony amidst the spray of the meadow fountains." For loveliness it would be hard to beat that; and for magical clearness and nearness take the following:

"And in the evening Peredur entered a valley, and at the head of the valley he came to a hermit's cell, and the hermit welcomed him gladly, and there he spent the night. And in the morning he arose, and when he went forth, behold! a shower of snow had fallen the night before, and a hawk had killed a wild-fowl in front of the cell. And the noise of the horse scared the hawk away, and a raven alighted upon the bird. And Peredur stood and compared the blackness of the raven and the whiteness of the snow, and the redness of the blood, to the hair of the lady whom best he loved, which was blacker than the raven, and to her skin, which was whiter than the snow, and to

[1] From *On the Study of Celtic Literature,* 1866; The Celtic race is represented mainly by the Welsh, the Irish, and the Highland Scotch.

[2] This and the following quotations are taken from the Welsh *Mabinogion,* translated by Lady Charlotte Guest.

her two cheeks, which were redder than the blood upon the snow appeared to be."

And this, which is perhaps less striking, is not less beautiful:

"And early in the day Geraint and Enid left the wood, and they came to an open country, with meadows on one hand and mowers mowing the meadows. And there was a river before them, and the horses bent down and drank the water. And they went up out of the river by a steep bank, and there they met a slender stripling with a satchel about his neck; and he had a small blue pitcher in his hand, and a bowl on the mouth of the pitcher."

And here the landscape, up to this point so Greek in its clear beauty, is suddenly magicalized by the romance touch:

"And they saw a tall tree by the side of the river, one half of which was in flames from the root to the top, and the other half was green and in full leaf."

Magic is the word to insist upon—a magically vivid and near interpretation of nature; since it is this which constitutes the special charm and power of the effect I am calling attention to, and it is for this that the Celt's sensibility gives him a peculiar aptitude.

. . . .

1865-6 1866

WORDSWORTH [1]

. . . . . .

"But turn we," as Wordsworth says, "from these bold, bad men," the haunters of Social Science Congresses. And let us be on our guard, too, against the exhibitors and extollers of a "scientific system of thought" in Wordsworth's poetry. The poetry will never be seen aright while they thus exhibit it. The cause of its greatness is simple, and may be told quite simply. Wordsworth's poetry is great because of the extraordinary power with which Wordsworth feels the joy offered to us in nature, the joy offered to us in the simple primary affections and duties; and because of the extraordinary power with which, in case after case, he shows us this joy, and renders it so as to make us share it.

The source of joy from which he thus draws is the truest and most unfailing source of joy accessible to man. It is also accessible universally. Wordsworth brings us word, therefore, according to his own strong and characteristic line, he brings us word

"Of joy in widest commonality spread." [2]

Here is an immense advantage for a poet. Wordsworth tells of what all seek, and tells of it at its truest and best source, and yet a source where all may go and draw from it.

Nevertheless, we are not to suppose that everything is precious which Wordsworth, standing even at this perennial and beautiful source, may give us. Wordsworthians are apt to talk as if it must be. They will speak with the same reverence of "The Sailor's Mother," for example, as of "Lucy Gray." They do their master harm by such lack of discrimination. "Lucy Gray" is a beautiful success; "The Sailor's Mother" is a failure. [3] To give aright what he wishes to give, to interpret and render successfully, is not always within Wordsworth's own command. It is within no poet's command; here is the part of the Muse, the inspiration, the God, the "not ourselves." [4] In Wordsworth's case, the accident, for so it may almost be called, of inspiration is of peculiar importance. No poet, perhaps, is so evidently filled with a new and sacred energy when the inspiration is upon him; no poet, when it fails him, is so left "weak as is a breaking wave." [5] I remember hearing him say that "Goethe's poetry was not inevitable [6] enough." The remark is striking and true; no line in Goethe, as Goethe said himself, but its maker knew well how it came there. Wordsworth is right, Goethe's poetry is not inevitable; not inevitable enough. But Wordsworth's poetry, when he is at his best, is inevitable, as inevitable as Nature herself. It might seem that Nature not only gave him the matter for his poem, but wrote his poem for him. He has no style. He was too conversant with Milton not to catch at times his master's manner, and he has fine Miltonic lines; but he has no assured, poetic style of his own, like Milton. When he seeks to have a style, he falls into ponderosity and pomposity. In the *Excursion* we have his style, as an artistic product of his own creation; and although Jeffrey [7] completely failed to recognize Wordsworth's real greatness, he was yet not wrong in saying of the *Excursion*, as a work of poetic

[1] From the Preface to *The Poems of Wordsworth,* chosen and edited by Arnold (1879). In the passage just preceding, Arnold deprecates the attempt to make Wordsworth sponsor for any complete philosophical or social system, such, for instance, as a Social Science congress might dryly and dismally quote and discuss.

[2] "The Recluse," line 771

[3] Swinburne thought otherwise. See his *Miscellanies.*

[4] Arnold elsewhere speaks of deity as the "tendency not ourselves that makes for righteousness."

[5] from "The Poet's Epitaph," l. 58

[6] i.e., spontaneous

[7] Francis Jeffrey, editor of the *Edinburgh Review,* 1803-29

style, "This will never do." And yet magical as is that power, which Wordsworth has not, of assured and possessed poetic style, he has something which is an equivalent for it.

Every one who has any sense for these things feels the subtle turn, the heightening, which is given to a poet's verse by his genius for style. We can feel it in the

"After life's fitful fever, he sleeps well"[1]

of Shakespeare; in the

". . . . though fallen on evil days,
On evil days though fallen, and evil tongues"[2]—

of Milton. It is the incomparable charm of Milton's power of poetic style which gives such worth to *Paradise Regained,* and makes a great poem of a work in which Milton's imagination does not soar high. Wordsworth has in constant possession, and at command, no style of this kind; but he had too poetic a nature, and had read the great poets too well, not to catch, as I have already remarked, something of it occasionally. We find it not only in his Miltonic lines; we find it in such a phrase as this, where the manner is his own, not Milton's—

". . . . the fierce confederate storm
Of sorrow barricadoed evermore
Within the walls of cities";[3]

although even here, perhaps, the power of style, which is undeniable, is more properly that of eloquent prose than the subtle heightening and change wrought by genuine poetic style. It is style, again, and the elevation given by style, which chiefly makes the effectiveness of "Laodamia." Still, the right sort of verse to choose from Wordsworth, if we are to seize his true and most characteristic form of expression, is a line like this from "Michael,"

"And never lifted up a single stone."

There is nothing subtle in it, no heightening, no study of poetic style, strictly so-called, at all; yet it is expression of the highest and most truly expressive kind.

Wordsworth owed much to Burns, and a style of perfect plainness, relying for effect solely on the weight and force of that which with entire fidelity it utters, Burns could show him:

"The poor inhabitant below
Was quick to learn and wise to know
And keenly felt the friendly glow
And softer flame;
But thoughtless follies laid him low
And stained his name."[4]

[1] *Macbeth,* III, ii, 23
[2] *Par. Lost,* vii, 25
[3] "The Recluse," ll. 831-833
[4] "A Bard's Epitaph," st. 4

Every one will be conscious of a likeness here to Wordsworth; and if Wordsworth did great things with this nobly plain manner, we must remember, what indeed he himself would always have been forward to acknowledge, that Burns used it before him.

Still, Wordsworth's use of it has something unique and unmatchable. Nature, herself, seems, I say, to take the pen out of his hand, and to write for him with her own bare, sheer, penetrating power. This arises from two causes; from the profound sincereness with which Wordsworth feels his subject, and also from the profoundly sincere and natural character of his subject itself. He can and will treat such a subject with nothing but the most plain, first-hand, almost austere naturalness. His expression may often be called bald, as, for instance, in the poem of "Resolution and Independence"; but it is bald as the bare mountain tops are bald, with a baldness which is full of grandeur.

Wherever we meet with the successful balance, in Wordsworth, of profound truth of subject with profound truth of execution, he is unique. His best poems are those which most perfectly exhibit this balance. I have a warm admiration for "Laodamia" and for the great "Ode"; but if I am to tell the very truth, I find "Laodamia" not wholly free from something artificial, and the great "Ode" not wholly free from something declamatory. If I had to pick out poems of a kind most perfectly to show Wordsworth's unique power, I should rather choose poems such as "Michael," "The Fountain," "The Highland Reaper." And poems with the peculiar and unique beauty which distinguishes these, Wordsworth produced in considerable number; besides very many other poems of which the worth, although not so rare as the worth of these, is still exceedingly high.

On the whole, then, as I said at the beginning, not only is Wordsworth eminent by reason of the goodness of his best work, but he is eminent also by reason of the great body of good work which he has left to us. With the ancients I will not compare him. In many respects the ancients are far above us, and yet there is something that we demand which they can never give. Leaving the ancients, let us come to the poets and poetry of Christendom. Dante, Shakespeare, Molière, Milton, Goethe are altogether larger and more splendid luminaries in the poetical heaven than Wordsworth. But I know not where else, among the moderns, we are to find his superiors. . . . He is one of the very chief glories of English

Poetry; and by nothing is England so glorious as by her poetry. Let us lay aside every weight which hinders our getting him recognized as this, and let our one study be to bring to pass, as widely as possible and as truly as possible, his own word concerning his poems: "They will coöperate with the benign tendencies in human nature and society, and will, in their degree, be efficacious in making men wiser, better, and happier."[1]

. . . .

1879

JAMES ANTHONY FROUDE
1818-1894

As one of the great literary historians of his century, Froude stands with Macaulay and Carlyle. He was born at Tartington in Devonshire, and his scholastic training was at Oxford where he was chosen a fellow of Oriel. He became a constant writer for reviews and magazines, and his varied life included diplomatic experience, editorship of *Frazer's Magazine* and the Regius professorship of history at Oxford. He died at his home in Devon.

In the use he made of the materials of history, Froude followed Carlyle, whom he acknowledged as his master. Both used original documents that furnished the minute details of events and relationships. Imagination enabled them to produce, from these, pictures that strike the eye of the reader and fix a scene or situation forever in the memory.

Although Froude was Carlyle's disciple in methods, his style bears little resemblance to his master's. His manner is easy, simple, fluent, and direct, a model of finished narrative expression. His general plan of narration, moreover, is so orderly that complex social movements appear plain, and events march without confusion.

Acting as literary executor of Carlyle, Froude produced his biography of the essayist, which is probably his best known work. It is characterized by the same excellencies that mark his historical writings, and the same defects. The portrait he drew of Carlyle and his wife is unforgettable, yet a portrait that many of their friends were unable to recognize. The fact seems to be, that Froude was prone to begin any historical investigation with a preconceived notion of what conclusions should be drawn from it, and to use only such documents and records in the writing as bore proof to his point of view. Froude's defense against the attacks of his critics was that history is not a science, not a body of facts concerning which absolute truth may be found, but a series of records and events capable of only approximate interpretation.

Biography and criticism: Paul, *Life of J. A. Froude,* 1905; Stephen.

[1] in a letter to Lady Beaumont, May 21, 1807

[THE] SAILING OF THE [SPANISH] ARMADA[2]

. . . .

The weather moderating, the fleet was again collected in the Bay of Ferrol[3] by the 6th-16th[4] of July. All repairs were completed by the 11th-21st, and the next day, 12th-22nd, the Armada took leave of Spain for the last time.

The scene as the fleet passed out of the harbor must have been singularly beautiful. It was a treacherous interval of real summer. The early sun was lighting the long chain of the Galician mountains, marking with shadows the cleft defiles, and shining softly on the white walls and vineyards of Coruña. The wind was light, and falling toward a calm; the great galleons drifted slowly with the tide on the purple water, the long streamers trailing from the trucks, the red crosses, the emblem of the crusade, showing bright upon the hanging sails. The fruit boats were bringing off the last fresh supplies, and the pinnaces hastening to the ships with the last loiterers on shore. Out of thirty thousand men who that morning stood upon the decks of the proud Armada, twenty thousand and more were never again to see the hills of Spain. Of the remnant who in two short months crept back ragged and torn, all but a few hundred returned only to die.

The Spaniards, though a great people, were usually over conscious of their greatness, and boasted too loudly of their fame and prowess:

[2] The story of the spectacular but ill-fated expedition of the Spanish Armada has often been told, but by no one perhaps more graphically than by Froude. His first account of the episode is in his *History of England,* 1856-1870, from which has been taken this description of the sailing of the Armada. Later in life, after much additional research, Froude wrote and published *The Spanish Story of the Armada,* 1892. About the same time he was appointed to a lectureship at Oxford, where he delivered some lectures on the subject which were published after his death (*English Seamen in the XVIth Century,* 1895). From these the second selection has been taken. In the summer of 1588, Philip II of Spain, who was trying to restore the Catholic faith through the Protestant countries of Europe, fitted out his "Invincible Armada" with the purpose of invading England. His great Admiral, Santa Cruz, had just died, and the expedition was given into the command of the Duke of Medina Sidonia, a wealthy nobleman of little experience and less ability, who ought to have been allowed to remain at home among his orange groves. His instructions were to effect a junction with the Duke of Parma, a general in the Spanish service in the Low Countries, and to assist the latter in transplanting his army to the English shores. The obvious tactics for the English were to cripple and if possible defeat the fleet as it sailed through the English Channel. The fleet started from Lisbon on the 29th of May, but was delayed on the route six weeks by bad weather.

[3] off northwestern Spain

[4] The first date is Old Style; see note on p. 350.

but among the soldiers and sailors of the doomed expedition against England, the national vainglory was singularly silent. They were the flower of the country, culled and chosen over the entire Peninsula, and they were going with a modest nobility upon a service which they knew to be dangerous, but which they believed to be peculiarly sacred. Every one, seaman, officer, and soldier, had confessed and communicated before he went on board. Gambling, swearing, profane language of all kinds had been peremptorily forbidden. Private quarrels and differences had been made up or suspended. . . . . In every vessel, and in the whole fleet, the strictest order was prescribed and observed. Medina Sidonia led the way in the *San Martin,* showing lights at night, and firing guns when the weather was hazy. Mount's Bay [1] was to be the next place of rendezvous if they were again separated.

On the first evening the wind dropped to a calm. The morning after, the 13th-23rd, a fair, fresh breeze came up from the south and southwest; the ships ran flowingly before it; and in two days and nights they had crossed the bay, [2] and were off Ushant. [3] The fastest of the pinnaces was dispatched from thence to Parma, with a letter bidding him expect the Duke's immediate coming.

But they had now entered the latitude of the storms which through the whole season had raged round the English shore. The same night a southwest gale overtook them. They lay to, not daring to run farther. The four galleys, unable to keep the sea, were driven in upon the French coast, and wrecked. The *Santa Aña,* a galleon of eight hundred tons, went down, carrying with her ninety seamen, three hundred soldiers, and fifty thousand ducats in gold. The weather was believed to be under the peculiar care of God, and this first misfortune was of evil omen for the future. The storm lasted two days, and then the sky cleared, and again gathering into order they proceeded on their way. On the 19th-29th they were in the mouth of the Channel. At daybreak on the morning of the 20th-30th the Lizard was under their lee, and an English fishing boat was hanging near them, counting their numbers. They gave chase, but the boat shot away down wind and disappeared. They captured another an hour or two later, from which they learned the English fleet was in

[1] on the English coast of Cornwall, between Land's End on the west and Lizard Head on the east

[2] of Biscay

[3] an island off the extreme northwestern coast of France

Plymouth, and Medina Sidonia called a council of war to consider whether they should go in, and fall upon it while at anchor. Philip's orders, however, were peremptory that they should turn neither right nor left, and make straight for Margate roads [4] and Parma. The Duke was unenterprising, and consciously unequal to his work; and already bending under his responsibilities, he hesitated to add to them.

Had he decided otherwise it would have made no difference, for the opportunity was not allowed him. Long before the Spaniards saw the Lizard they had themselves been seen, and on the evening of the 19th-29th, the beacons along the coast had told England that the hour of its trial was come.

1856-70

DEFEAT OF THE ARMADA

In the gallery at Madrid there is a picture, painted by Titian, representing the Genius of Spain coming to the delivery of the afflicted Bride of Christ. Titian was dead, but the temper of the age survived, and in the study of that great picture you will see the spirit in which the Spanish nation had set out for the conquest of England. The scene is the seashore. The Church, a naked Andromeda [5] with disheveled hair, fastened to the trunk of an ancient disbranched tree. The cross lies at her feet, the cup overturned, the serpents of heresy biting at her from behind with uplifted crests. Coming on before a leading breeze is the sea monster, the Moslem fleet, eager for their prey, while in front is Perseus, the Genius of Spain, banner in hand, with the legions of the faithful laying not raiment before him, but shield and helmet, the apparel of war for the Lady of Nations to clothe herself with strength and smite her foes.

In the Armada the crusading enthusiasm had reached its point and focus. England was the stake to which the Virgin, the daughter of Sion, was bound in captivity. Perseus had come at last in the person of the Duke of Medina Sidonia, and with him all that was best and brightest in the countrymen of Cervantes, [6] to break her bonds and replace her on her throne. They had sailed into the Channel

[4] Just north of Dover, opposite Calais; vessels sailing up the English Channel and through Dover Strait would round the North Foreland and Margate to pass into the Thames. The passage of the fleet up the Channel was virtually a running fight, beginning at Plymouth and lasting for a week.

[5] Andromeda, according to the Greek legend, was exposed to be devoured by a sea-monster, but was rescued by Perseus.

[6] creator of Don Quixote, the half-mad knight-errant

in pious hope, with the blessed banner waving over their heads.

To be the executor of the decrees of Providence is a lofty ambition, but men in a state of high emotion overlook the precautions which are not to be dispensed with even on the sublimest of errands. Don Quixote, when he set out to redress the wrongs of humanity, forgot that a change of linen might be necessary, and that he must take money with him to pay his hotel bills. Philip II, in sending the Armada to England, and confident in supernatural protection, imagined an unresisted triumphal procession. He forgot that contractors might be rascals, that water four months in the casks in a hot climate turned putrid, and that putrid water would poison his ships' companies, though his crews were companies of angels. He forgot that the servants of the Evil One might fight for their mistress, after all, and that he must send adequate supplies of powder, and, worst forgetfulness of all, that a great naval expedition required a leader who understood his business. Perseus, in the shape of the Duke of Medina Sidonia, after a week of disastrous battles, found himself at the end of it in an exposed roadstead, [1] where he ought never to have been, nine-tenths of his provisions thrown overboard as unfit for food, his ammunition exhausted by the unforeseen demands upon it, the seamen and soldiers harassed and dispirited, officers the whole week without sleep, and the enemy, who had hunted him from Plymouth to Calais, anchored within half a league of him.

Still, after all his misadventures, he had brought the fleet, if not to the North Foreland, [2] yet within a few miles of it, and to outward appearance not materially injured. Two of the galleons had been taken; a third, the *Santa Aña,* had strayed; and his galleys had left him, being found too weak for the channel sea, but the great armament had reached its destination substantially uninjured so far as English eyes could see. Hundreds of men had been killed and hundreds more wounded, and the spirit of the rest had been shaken. But the loss of life could only be conjectured on board the English fleet. The English admiral [3] could only see that the Duke was now in touch with Parma. Parma, they knew, had an army at Dunkirk [4] with him, which was to cross to England. He had been collecting men, barges, and transports all the winter and spring, and the backward state of Parma's preparations could not be anticipated, still less relied upon. The Calais anchorage was unsafe; but at that season of the year, especially after a wet summer, the weather usually settled; and to attack the Spaniards in a French port might be dangerous for many reasons. It was uncertain after the day of the Barricades [5] whether the Duke of Guise or Henry of Valois was master of France, and a violation of the neutrality laws might easily at that moment bring Guise and France into the field on the Spaniards' side. It was, no doubt, with some such expectation that the Duke and his advisers had chosen Calais as the point at which to bring up. It was now Saturday, the 7th of August. The governor of the town came off in the evening to the *San Martin.* He expressed surprise to see the Spanish fleet in so exposed a position, but he was profuse in his offers of service. Anything which the Duke required should be provided,especially every facility for communicating with Dunkirk and Parma. The Duke thanked him, said that he supposed Parma to be already embarked with his troops, ready for the passage, and that his own stay in the roads would be but brief. On Monday morning at latest he expected that the attempt to cross would be made. The governor took his leave, and the Duke, relieved from his anxieties, was left to a peaceful night. He was disturbed on the Sunday morning by an express from Parma informing him that, so far from being embarked, the army could not be ready for a fortnight. The barges were not in condition for sea. The troops were in camp. The arms and stores were on the quays at Dunkirk. As for the fly-boats [6] and ammunition which the Duke had asked for, he had none to spare. He had himself looked to be supplied from the Armada. He promised to use his best expedition, but the Duke, meanwhile, must see to the safety of the fleet.

Unwelcome news to a harassed landsman thrust into the position of an admiral and eager to be rid of his responsibilities. If by evil fortune the northwester should come down upon him, with the shoals and sandbanks close under his lee, he would be in a bad way. Nor was the view behind him calculated for comfort. There lay the enemy almost within gunshot, who, though scarcely more than half his

[1] Calais Roads
[2] See last note of preceding selection.
[3] Lord Charles Howard; Sir Frances Drake, vice admiral, commanded a second division of the British fleet; Sir Henry Seymour, a third. Among the commanders of squadrons were Sir John Hawkins and Sir Martin Frobisher.

[4] a port twenty miles east of Calais
[5] May 12, when the Duke of Guise entered Paris in an attempt to depose Henry III
[6] gunboats worked with oars

numbers, had hunted him like a pack of bloodhounds, and, worse than all, in double strength; for the Thames squadron—three Queen's ships and thirty London adventurers—under Lord H. Seymour and Sir John Hawkins, had crossed in the night. There they were between him and Cape Grisnez,[1] and the reinforcements meant plainly enough that mischief was in the wind.

After a week so trying the Spanish crews would have been glad of a Sunday's rest if they could have had it; but the rough handling which they had gone through had thrown everything into disorder. The sick and wounded had to be cared for, torn rigging looked to, splintered timbers mended, decks scoured, and guns and arms cleaned up and put to rights. And so it was that no rest could be allowed; so much had to be done, and so busy was every one, that the usual rations were not served out and the Sunday was kept as a fast. In the afternoon the stewards went ashore for fresh meat and vegetables. They came back with their boats loaded, and the prospect seemed a little less gloomy. Suddenly, as the Duke and a group of officers were watching the English fleet from the *San Martin's* poop deck, a small smart pinnace, carrying a gun in her bow, shot out from Howard's lines, bore down on the *San Martin*, sailed round her, sending in a shot or two as she passed, and went off unhurt. The Spanish officers could not help admiring such airy impertinence. Hugo de Moncada[2] sent a ball after the pinnace, which went through her mainsail, but did no damage, and the pinnace again disappeared behind the English ships.

So a Spanish officer describes the scene. The English story says nothing of the pinnace, but she doubtless came and went as the Spaniard says, and for sufficient purpose. The English, too, were in straits, though the Duke did not dream of it. You will remember that the last supplies which the Queen had allowed to the fleet had been issued in the middle of June. They were to serve for a month, and the contractors were forbidden to prepare more. The Queen had clung to her hope that her differences with Philip were to be settled by the Commission at Ostend;[3] and she feared that if Drake and Howard were too well furnished they would venture some fresh rash stroke on the coast of Spain, which might mar the negotiations. Their month's provisions had been stretched to serve for six weeks, and when the Armada appeared but two full days' rations remained. On these they had fought their way up Channel. Something had been brought out by private exertion on the Dorsetshire coast, and Seymour had, perhaps, brought a little more. But they were still in extremity. The contractors had warned the Government that they could provide nothing without notice, and notice had not been given. The adventurers were in better state, having been equipped by private owners. But the Queen's ships in a day or two more must either go home or their crews would be starving. They had been on reduced rations for near two months. Worse than that, they were still poisoned by the sour beer. The Queen had changed her mind so often, now ordering the fleet to prepare for sea, then recalling her instructions and paying off the men, that those whom Howard had with him had been enlisted in haste, had come on board as they were, and their clothes were hanging in rags on them. The fighting and the sight of the flying Spaniards were meat and drink, and clothing, too, and had made them careless of all else. There was no fear of mutiny; but there was a limit to the toughest endurance. If the Armada was left undisturbed, a long struggle might be still before them. The enemy would recover from its flurry, and Parma would come out from Dunkirk. To attack them directly in French waters might lead to perilous complications, while delay meant famine. The Spanish fleet had to be started from the roads in some way. Done it must be, and done immediately.

Then, on that same Sunday afternoon a memorable council of war was held in the *Ark's*[4] main cabin. Howard, Drake, Seymour, Hawkins, Martin Frobisher, and two or three others met to consult, knowing that on them at that moment the liberties of England were depending. Their resolution was taken promptly. There was no time for talk. After nightfall a strong flood tide would be setting up along shore to the Spanish anchorage. They would try what could be done with fire ships, and the excursion of the pinnace, which was taken for bravado, was probably for a survey of the Armada's exact position. Meantime eight useless vessels were coated with pitch—hulls, spars, and rigging. Pitch was poured on the decks and over the sides, and parties were told off to steer them to their destination and then fire and leave them.

[1] eighteen miles S.W. of Calais
[2] commander of the Duke's flagship, and "captain-general of the four galleasses" (large galleys, with masts and oars), according to the State Records
[3] a conference between commissioners of Elizabeth and Parma, trying to arrange terms of peace
[4] the *Ark Raleigh,* Howard's flagship

The hours stole on, and twilight passed into dark. The night was without a moon. The Duke paced his deck late with uneasy sense of danger. He observed lights moving up and down the English lines, and imagining that the *endemoniada gente*—the infernal devils—might be up to mischief, ordered a sharp lookout. A faint westerly air was curling the water, and toward midnight the watchers on board the galleons made out dimly several ships which seemed to be drifting down upon them. Their experience since the action off Plymouth had been so strange and unlooked for that anything unintelligible which the English did was alarming.

The phantom forms drew nearer, and were almost among them when they broke into a blaze from water line to truck, and the two fleets were seen by the lurid light of the conflagration; the anchorage, the walls and windows of Calais, and the sea shining red as far as eye could reach, as if the ocean itself was burning. Among the dangers which they might have to encounter, English fireworks had been especially dreaded by the Spaniards. Fire ships —a fit device of heretics—had worked havoc among the Spanish troops, when the bridge was blown up at Antwerp.[1] They imagined that similar infernal machines were approaching the Armada. A capable commander would have sent a few launches to grapple the burning hulks, which of course were now deserted, and tow them out of harm's way. Spanish sailors were not cowards, and would not have flinched from duty because it might be dangerous; but the Duke and Diego Florez[2] lost their heads again. A signal gun from the *San Martin* ordered the whole fleet to slip their cables and stand out to sea.

Orders given in panic are doubly unwise, for they spread the terror in which they originate. The danger from the fire ships was chiefly from the effect on the imagination, for they appear to have drifted by and done no real injury. And it speaks well for the seamanship and courage of the Spaniards that they were able, crowded together as they were, at midnight, and in sudden alarm, to set their canvas and clear out without running into one another. They buoyed their cables, expecting to return for them at daylight, and with only a single accident, to be mentioned directly, they executed successfully a really difficult maneuver.

The Duke was delighted with himself. The fire ships burned harmlessly out. He had baffled the inventions of the *endemoniada gente*.

[1] three years previously
[2] the Duke's nautical adviser

He brought up a league outside the harbor, and supposed that the whole Armada had done the same. Unluckily for himself, he found it at daylight divided into two bodies. The *San Martin* with forty of the best appointed of the galleons were riding together at their anchors. The rest, two-thirds of the whole, having no second anchors ready, and inexperienced in Channel tides and currents, had been lying to. The west wind was blowing up. Without seeing where they were going they had drifted to leeward and were two leagues off, toward Gravelines, dangerously near the shore. The Duke was too ignorant to realize the full peril of his situation. He signaled to them to return and join him. As the wind and the tide stood it was impossible. He proposed to follow them. The pilots told him that if he did the whole fleet might be lost on the banks. Toward the land the look of things was not more encouraging.

One accident only had happened the night before. The *Capitana* galleass, with Don Hugo de Moncada and eight hundred men on board, had fouled her helm in a cable in getting under way and had become unmanageable. The galley slaves disobeyed orders, or else Don Hugo was as incompetent as his commander-in-chief. The galleass had gone on the sands, and as the tide ebbed had fallen over on her side. Howard, seeing her condition, had followed her in the *Ark* with four or five other of the Queen's ships, and was furiously attacking her with his boats careless of neutrality laws. Howard's theory was, as he said, to pluck the feathers one by one from the Spaniard's wing, and here was a feather worth picking up. The galleass was the most splendid vessel of her kind afloat, Don Hugo one of the greatest of Spanish grandees.

Howard was making a double mistake. He took the galleass at last after three hours' fighting. Don Hugo was killed by a musket ball. The vessel was plundered and Howard's men took possession, meaning to carry her away when the tide rose. The French authorities ordered him off, threatening to fire upon him; and after wasting the forenoon, he was obliged at last to leave her where she lay. Worse than this, he had lost three precious hours, and had lost along with them, in the opinion of the Prince of Parma, the honors of the great day.

Drake and Hawkins knew better than to waste time plucking single feathers. The fire ships had been more effective than they could have dared to hope. The enemy was broken up. The Duke was shorn of half his strength, and the Lord had delivered him into their hand. He had got under way, still signaling wildly, and uncertain in which direction to turn. His uncertainties were ended for him by seeing Drake bear down upon him with the whole English fleet, save those which were loitering about the galleass. The English had now the advantage of numbers. The superiority of their guns he knew already, and their greater speed allowed him no hope to escape a battle. Forty ships alone were left to him to defend the banner of the crusade and the honor of Castile; but those forty were the largest and most powerfully armed and manned that he had, and on board them were Oquendo, De Leyva, Recalde, Bretandona, the best officers in the Spanish navy next to the lost Don Pedro.[1]

It was now or never for England. The scene of the action which was to decide the future of Europe was between Calais and Dunkirk, a few miles off shore, and within sight of Parma's camp. There was no more maneuvering for the weather gage, no more fighting at long range. Drake dashed straight upon his prey as the falcon stoops upon its quarry. A chance had fallen to him which might never return; not for the vain distinction of carrying prizes into English ports, not for the ray of honor which would fall on him if he could carry off the sacred banner itself and hang it in the Abbey at Westminster, but a chance so to handle the Armada that it should never be seen again in English waters, and deal such a blow on Philip that the Spanish Empire should reel with it. The English ships had the same superiority over the galleons which steamers have now over sailing vessels. They had twice the speed; they could lie two points nearer to the wind. Sweeping around them at cable's length, crowding them in one upon the other, yet never once giving them a chance to grapple, they hurled in their cataracts of round shot. Short as was the powder supply, there was no sparing it that morning. The hours went on, and still the battle raged, if battle it could be called where the blows were all dealt on one side and the suffering was all on the other. Never on sea or land did the Spaniards show themselves worthier of their great name than on that day. But from the first they could do nothing. It was said afterwards in Spain that the Duke showed the white feather, that he charged his pilot to keep him out of harm's way, that he shut himself up in his cabin, buried in woolpacks, and so on. The Duke had faults enough, but poltroonery was not one of them. He, who till he entered the English Channel had never been in action on sea or land, found himself, as he said, in the midst of the most furious engagement recorded in the history of the world. As to being out of harm's way, the standard at his masthead drew the hottest of the fire upon him. The *San Martin's* timbers were of oak and a foot thick, but the shot, he said, went through them enough to shatter a rock. Her deck was a slaughterhouse; half his company were killed or wounded, and no more would have been heard or seen of the *San Martin* or her commander had not Oquendo and De Leyva pushed in to the rescue and enabled him to creep away under their cover. He himself saw nothing more of the action after this. The smoke, he said, was so thick that he could make out nothing, even from his masthead. But all round it was but a repetition of the same scene. The Spanish shot flew high, as before, above the low English hulls, and they were themselves helpless butts to the English guns. And it is noticeable and supremely creditable to them that not a single galleon struck her colors. One of them, after a long duel with an Englishman, was on the point of sinking. An English officer, admiring the courage which the Spaniards had shown, ran out upon his bowsprit, told them that they had done all which became men, and urged them to surrender and save their lives. For answer they cursed the English as cowards and chickens because they refused to close. The officer was shot. His fall brought a last broadside on them, which finished the work. They went down, and the water closed over them. Rather death to the soldiers of the Cross than surrender to a heretic.

The deadly hail rained on. In some ships blood was seen streaming out of the scupper holes. Yet there was no yielding; all ranks showed equal heroism. The priests went up and down in the midst of the carnage, holding the crucifix before the eyes of the dying. At midday Howard came up to claim a second share in a victory which was no longer doubtful. Toward the afternoon the Spanish fire slackened. Their powder was gone, and they could make no return to the cannonade which was still overwhelming them. They admitted freely afterwards that if the attack had been continued but two hours more they must all have struck or gone ashore. But the English magazines were empty also; the last cartridge was shot away, and the battle ended from mere inability to keep it up. It had been fought on

[1] taken captive by Drake in the first action at Plymouth

both sides with peculiar determination. In the English there was the accumulated resentment of thirty years of menace to their country and their creed, with the enemy in tangible shape at last to be caught and grappled with; in the Spanish, the sense that if their cause had not brought them the help they looked for from above, the honor and faith of Castile should not suffer in their hands.

It was over. The English drew off, regretting that their thrifty mistress had limited their means of fighting for her, and so obliged them to leave their work half done. When the cannon ceased the wind rose, the smoke rolled away, and in the level light of the sunset they could see the results of the action.

A galleon in Recalde's squadron was sinking with all hands. The *San Philip* and the *San Matteo* were drifting dismasted toward the Dutch coast, where they were afterwards wrecked. Those which were left with canvas still showing were crawling slowly after their comrades who had not been engaged, the spars and rigging so cut up that they could scarce bear their sails. The loss of life could only be conjectured, but it had been obviously terrible. The nor'wester was blowing up and was pressing the wounded ships upon the shoals, from which, if it held, it seemed impossible in their crippled state they would be able to work off.

In this condition Drake left them for the night, not to rest, but from any quarter to collect, if he could, more food and powder. The snake had been scotched, but not killed.[1] More than half the great fleet were far away, untouched by shot, perhaps able to fight a second battle if they recovered heart. To follow, to drive them on the banks if the wind held, or into the North Sea, anywhere so that he left them no chance of joining hands with Parma again, and to use the time before they had rallied from his blows, that was the present necessity. His own poor fellows were famished and in rags; but neither he nor they had leisure to think of themselves. There was but one thought in the whole of them, to be again in chase of the flying foe. Howard was resolute as Drake. All that was possible was swiftly done. Seymour and the Thames squadron were to stay in the straits and watch Parma. From every obtainable source food and powder were collected for the rest—far short in both ways of what ought to have been, but, as Drake said, "we were resolved to put on a brag and go on as if we needed nothing." Before dawn the admiral and he were again off on the chase.

[1] *Macbeth,* III, ii, 13

The brag was unneeded. What man could do had been done, and the rest was left to the elements. Never again could Spanish seamen be brought to face the English guns with Medina Sidonia to lead them. They had a fool at their head. The Invisible Powers in whom they had been taught to trust had deserted them. Their confidence was gone and their spirit broken. Drearily the morning broke on the Duke and his consorts the day after the battle. The Armada had collected in the night. The nor'wester had freshened to a gale, and they were laboring heavily along, making fatal leeway toward the shoals.

It was St. Lawrence's Day, Philip's patron saint, whose shoulder bone he had lately added to the treasures of the Escurial;[2] but St. Lawrence was as heedless as St. Dominic.[3] The *San Martin* had but six fathoms under her. Those nearer to the land signaled five, and right before them they could see the brown foam of the breakers curling over the sands, while on their weather beam, a mile distant and clinging to them like the shadow of death, were the English ships which had pursued them from Plymouth like the dogs of the Furies. The Spanish sailors and soldiers had been without food since the evening when they anchored at Calais. All Sunday they had been at work, no rest allowed them to eat. On the Sunday night they had been stirred out of their sleep by the fire ships. Monday they had been fighting, and Monday night committing their dead to the sea. Now they seemed advancing directly upon inevitable destruction. As the wind stood there was still room for them to wear and thus escape the banks, but they would then have to face the enemy, who seemed only refraining from attacking them because while they continued on their present course the winds and waves would finish the work without help from man. Recalde, De Leyva, Oquendo, and other officers were sent for to the *San Martin* to consult. Oquendo came last. "Ah, Señor Oquendo," said the Duke as the heroic Biscayan stepped on board, "que haremos?" (what shall we do?) "Let your Excellency bid load the guns again," was Oquendo's gallant answer. It could not be. De Leyva himself said that the men would not fight the English again. Florez advised surrender. The Duke wavered. It was said that a boat was actually lowered to go off to Howard and make terms, and that Oquendo swore that if the boat left

[2] the palace of Philip II

[3] referring to a disastrous engagement five days before on St. Dominic's Day, Aug. 4

the *San Martin* on such an errand he would fling Florez into the sea. Oquendo's advice would have, perhaps, been the safest if the Duke could have taken it. There were still seventy ships in the Armada little hurt. The English were "bragging", as Drake said, and in no condition themselves for another serious engagement. But the temper of the entire fleet made a courageous course impossible. There was but one Oquendo. Discipline was gone. The soldiers in their desperation had taken the command out of the hands of the seamen. Officers and men alike abandoned hope, and, with no human prospect of salvation left to them, they flung themselves on their knees upon the decks and prayed the Almighty to have pity on them. But two weeks were gone since they had knelt on those same decks on the first sight of the English shore to thank Him for having brought them so far on an enterprise so glorious. Two weeks; and what weeks! Wrecked, torn by cannon shot, ten thousand of them dead or dying—for this was the estimated loss by battle—the survivors could now but pray to be delivered from a miserable death by the elements. In cyclones the wind often changes suddenly back from northwest to west, from west to south. At that moment, as if in answer to their petition, one of these sudden shifts of wind saved them from the immediate peril. The gale backed round to S.S.W., and ceased to press them on the shoals. They could ease their sheets, draw off into open water, and steer a course up the middle of the North Sea.

So only that they went north, Drake was content to leave them unmolested. Once away into the high latitudes they might go where they would. Neither Howard nor he, in the low state of their own magazines, desired any unnecessary fighting. If the Armada turned back they must close with it. If it held its present course they must follow it till they could be assured it would communicate no more for that summer with the Prince of Parma. Drake thought they would perhaps make for the Baltic or some port in Norway. They would meet no hospitable reception from either Swedes or Danes, but they would probably try. One only imminent danger remained to be provided against. If they turned into the Forth, it was still possible for the Spaniards to redeem their defeat, and even yet shake Elizabeth's throne. Among the many plans which had been formed for the invasion of England, a landing in Scotland had long been the favorite. Guise had always preferred Scotland when it was intended that Guise should be the leader. Santa Cruz had been in close correspondence with Guise on this very subject, and many officers in the Armada must have been acquainted with Santa Cruz's views. The Scotch Catholic nobles were still savage at Mary Stuart's execution, and had the Armada anchored in Leith Roads [1] with twenty thousand men, half a million ducats, and a Santa Cruz at its head, it might have kindled a blaze at that moment from John o'Groat's Land [2] to the Border.

But no such purpose occurred to the Duke of Medina Sidonia. He probably knew nothing at all of Scotland or its parties. Among the many deficiencies which he had pleaded to Philip as unfitting him for the command, he had said that Santa Cruz had acquaintances among the English and Scotch peers. He had himself none. The small information which he had of anything did not go beyond his orange gardens and his tunny fishing. His chief merit was that he was conscious of his incapacity; and, detesting a service into which he had been fooled by a hysterical nun, [3] his only anxiety was to carry home the still considerable fleet which had been trusted to him without further loss. Beyond Scotland and the Scotch isles there was the open ocean, and in the open ocean there were no sandbanks and no English guns. Thus, with all sail set, he went on before the wind. Drake and Howard attended him till they had seen him past the Forth, and knew then that there was no more to fear. It was time to see to the wants of their own poor fellows, who had endured so patiently and fought so magnificently. On the 13th day of August they saw the last of the Armada, turned back, and made their way to the Thames. [4]

. . . .

1895

THOMAS HENRY HUXLEY
1825-1895

Huxley, one of the foremost English scientists of his century, was born at Ealing, London, son of a schoolmaster. His early study was without purpose, but relatives who were physicians turned him to medicine, and, after taking courses at the Medical School of Charing Cross Hospital and the University of London, he was graduated a physician in 1846. In that year he obtained a place in a marine scientific expedition that lasted four

[1] on the Firth of Forth, near Edinburgh
[2] the northwestern extremity of Scotland
[3] A nun at Lisbon had told the wavering Duke that "Our Lady had sent her to promise him success."
[4] The remainder of the narrative is the story of the disasters that attended the Spanish in their voyage around Scotland and Ireland. Many died from exposure, scanty food, and poisonous water; many were wrecked; even of those who reached Spain alive, few ever rallied from the experience.

years, during which he made discoveries of the utmost importance in anatomy. These corroborated theories of Darwin published in 1849 in *The Origin of Species,* and gave the initial impetus to present laboratory methods in biology.

Huxley's fruitful life is marked especially by the publication of *Evidence as to Man's Place in Nature,* 1863; *Lay Sermons, Addresses, and Reviews,* 1870; and *Anatomy of Vertebrated Animals,* 1871. He was constantly delivering public addresses, and was a member of many royal commissions. Before his death, at Eastbourne, he had received the most distinguished scientific honors.

Huxley's gift to modern biology lay as much in the convincing explanation he made of facts as in his discoveries themselves. He was a born expositor and controversialist. He explained Darwin's theories—though he did not accept them all—more convincingly than did Darwin himself, and it is as a master of lucid exposition that he has a place in English literature. If it be held that no writing that lacks imagination can be veritable art, it may also be maintained that the clear statement and arrangement of facts requires a kind of constructive imagination that is one of the highest powers of intellect. For clearness of exposition Huxley certainly has few or no superiors.

Criticism: Stephen; More (Shel. 8); "Thomas Henry Huxley," J. S. Huxley, *New Rep.* 43:36-38; E. Clodd, *Cent.* 110:33-41; "Agnostic Defeat," G. K. Chesterton, *Liv. Age* 272:777-83.

ON A PIECE OF CHALK [1]

If a well were to be sunk at our feet in the midst of the city of Norwich, the diggers would very soon find themselves at work in that white substance, almost too soft to be called rock, with which we are all familiar as "chalk." Not only here, but over the whole county of Norfolk, the well-sinker might carry his shaft down many hundred feet without coming to the end of the chalk; and, on the seacoast, where the waves have pared away the face of the land which breasts them, the scarped faces of the high cliffs are often wholly formed of the same material. Northward, the chalk may be followed as far as Yorkshire; on the south coast it appears abruptly in the picturesque western bays of Dorset, and breaks into the Needles [2] of the Isle of Wight; while on the shores of Kent it supplies that long line of white cliffs to which England owes her name of Albion. [3]

[1] A lecture delivered to the working men of Norwich, England, and printed in *Macmillan's Magazine,* 1868; now in *Lay Sermons, Addresses and Reviews.* Some changes have here been made in paragraphing and punctuation, for the system of paragraphing employed in Huxley's works as they are ordinarily printed not infrequently has an obscuring effect.

[2] three white rocks rising abruptly from the sea to the height of 100 feet

[3] Latin *albus,* "white"

Were the thin soil which covers it all washed away, a curved band of white chalk, here broader and there narrower, might be followed diagonally across England from Lulworth in Dorset to Flamborough Head in Yorkshire—a distance of over two hundred and eighty miles as the crow flies. From this band to the North Sea, on the east, and the Channel, on the south, the chalk is largely hidden by other deposits; but, except in the Weald [4] of Kent and Sussex, it enters into the very foundation of all the southeastern counties.

Attaining, as it does in some places, a thickness of more than a thousand feet, the English chalk must be admitted to be a mass of considerable magnitude. Nevertheless, it covers but an insignificant portion of the whole area occupied by the chalk formation of the globe, which has precisely the same general characters as ours, and is found in detached patches, some less and others more extensive than the English. Chalk occurs in northwest Ireland; it stretches over a large part of France—the chalk which underlies Paris being, in fact, a continuation of that of the London basin; runs through Denmark and Central Europe, and extends southward to North Africa; while eastward, it appears in the Crimea and in Syria, and may be traced as far as the shores of the Sea of Aral, in Central Asia. If all the points at which true chalk occurs were circumscribed, they would lie within an irregular oval about three thousand miles in long diameter, the area of which would be as great as that of Europe, and would many times exceed that of the largest existing inland sea—the Mediterranean.

Thus the chalk is no unimportant element in the masonry of the earth's crust, and it impresses a peculiar stamp, varying with the conditions to which it is exposed, on the scenery of the districts in which it occurs. The undulating downs and rounded coombs, [5] covered with sweet-grassed turf, of our inland chalk country, have a peacefully domestic and mutton-suggesting prettiness, but can hardly be called either grand or beautiful. But on our southern coasts, the wall-sided cliffs, many hundred feet high, with vast needles and pinnacles standing out in the sea, sharp and solitary enough to serve as perches for the wary cormorant, confer a wonderful beauty and grandeur upon the chalk headlands. And in the East, chalk has its share in the formation of some of the most

[4] This name for the region is old: Anglo-Saxon *weald* (German *Wald*) means "forest." Compare Caxton's account of his birth, p. 104.

[5] or combs; bowl-shaped valleys

venerable of mountain ranges, such as the Lebanon.

What is this wide-spread component of the surface of the earth—and whence did it come?

You may think this no very hopeful inquiry. You may not unnaturally suppose that the attempt to solve such problems as these can lead to no result, save that of entangling the inquirer in vague speculations, incapable of refutation and of verification. If such were really the case, I should have selected some other subject than a "piece of chalk" for my discourse. But in truth, after much deliberation, I have been unable to think of any topic which would so well enable me to lead you to see how solid is the foundation upon which some of the most startling conclusions of physical science rest. A great chapter in the history of the world is written in the chalk. Few passages in the history of man can be supported by such an overwhelming mass of direct and indirect evidence as that which testifies to the truth of the fragment of the history of the globe which I hope to enable you to read, with your own eyes, tonight.

Let me add that few chapters of human history have a more profound significance for ourselves. I weigh my words well when I assert that the man who should know the true history of the bit of chalk which every carpenter carries about in his breeches pocket, though ignorant of all other history, is likely, if he will think his knowledge out to its ultimate results, to have a truer, and therefore a better, conception of this wonderful universe, and of man's relation to it, than the most learned student who is deep read in the records of humanity and ignorant of those of Nature. The language of the chalk is not hard to learn, not nearly so hard as Latin, if you only want to get at the broad features of the story it has to tell; and I propose that we now set to work to spell that story out together.

. . . .

[In the intervening portion of his address Huxley sets forth the following facts:

First. Chemically, chalk consists of carbonic acid and quicklime. Under the microscope it is seen to be made up of granules in which are imbedded numerous calcareous skeletons known as *Globigerinae.*

Second. The bed of the North Atlantic, between Ireland and Newfoundland, is found to be a vast plain of deep-sea mud which is substantially chalk, deposited there by multitudes of organisms (*Globigerinae*), which in life have the power of separating from the ocean the small proportion of carbonate of lime which is dissolved in seawater, and of building that substance into skeletons for themselves.

Third. The living *Globigerinae* are exclusively marine animals, and this, along with other evidence, compels the conclusion that the chalk beds of the dry land are the dried mud of an ancient deep sea.

Fourth. The thickness of the chalk bed and the character of its fossil remains prove that the period of deposit—the cretaceous epoch—was of great duration.]

Thus not only is it certain that the chalk is the mud of an ancient sea-bottom; but it is no less certain that the chalk sea existed during an extremely long period, though we may not be prepared to give a precise estimate of the length of that period in years. The relative duration is clear, though the absolute duration may not be definable. The attempt to affix any precise date to the period at which the chalk sea began, or ended, its existence, is baffled by difficulties of the same kind. But the relative age of the cretaceous epoch may be determined with as great ease and certainty as the long duration of that epoch.

You will have heard of the interesting discoveries recently made in various parts of Western Europe of flint implements, obviously worked into shape by human hands, under circumstances which show conclusively that man is a very ancient denizen of these regions. It has been proved that the old populations of Europe, whose existence has been revealed to us in this way, consisted of savages, such as the Eskimos are now; that, in the country which is now France, they hunted the reindeer, and were familiar with the ways of the mammoth and the bison. The physical geography of France was in those days different from what it is now—the river Somme, for instance, having cut its bed a hundred feet deeper between that time and this; and it is probable that the climate was more like that of Canada or Siberia than that of Western Europe.

The existence of these people is forgotten even in the traditions of the oldest historical nations. The name and fame of them had utterly vanished until a few years back; and the amount of physical change which has been effected since their day renders it more than probable that, venerable as are some of the historical nations, the workers of the chipped flints of Hoxne [1] or of Amiens [2] are to them, as they are to us, in point of antiquity.

[1] in Suffolk, England, where an important discovery of flint implements was made in 1797

[2] in northern France

But if we assign to these hoar relics of long-vanished generations of men the greatest age that can possibly be claimed for them, they are not older than the drift, or boulder clay, which, in comparison with the chalk, is but a very juvenile deposit. You need go no farther than your own seaboard for evidence of this fact. At one of the most charming spots on the coast of Norfolk, Cromer, you will see the boulder clay forming a vast mass, which lies upon the chalk, and must consequently have come into existence after it. Huge boulders of chalk are, in fact, included in the clay, and have evidently been brought to the position they now occupy by the same agency as that which has planted blocks of syenite from Norway side by side with them.

The chalk, then, is certainly older than the boulder clay. If you ask how much, I will again take you no farther than the same spot upon your own coasts for evidence. I have spoken of the boulder clay and drift as resting upon the chalk. That is not strictly true. Interposed between the chalk and the drift is a comparatively insignificant layer, containing vegetable matter. But that layer tells a wonderful history. It is full of stumps of trees standing as they grew. Fir trees are there with their cones, and hazel bushes with their nuts; there stand the stools [1] of oak and yew trees, beeches and alders. Hence this stratum is appropriately called the "forest-bed."

It is obvious that the chalk must have been upheaved and converted into dry land before the timber trees could grow upon it. As the boles of some of these trees are from two to three feet in diameter, it is no less clear that the dry land thus formed remained in the same condition for long ages. And not only do the remains of stately oaks and well-grown firs testify to the duration of this condition of things, but additional evidence to the same effect is afforded by the abundant remains of elephants, rhinoceroses, hippopotamuses and other great wild beasts, which it has yielded to the zealous search of such men as the Rev. Mr. Gunn. [2] When you look at such a collection as he has formed, and bethink you that these elephantine bones did veritably carry their owners about, and these great grinders crunch, in the dark woods of which the forest-bed is now the only trace, it is impossible not to feel that they are as good evidence of the lapse of time as the annual rings of the tree stumps.

Thus there is a writing upon the walls of cliffs at Cromer, and whoso runs may read it. It tells us, with an authority which cannot be impeached, that the ancient sea-bed of the chalk sea was raised up, and remained dry land until it was covered with forest, stocked with the great game whose spoils have rejoiced your geologist. How long it remained in that condition cannot be said; but "the whirligig of time brought its revenges" [3] in those days as in these. That dry land, with the bones and teeth of generations of long-lived elephants hidden away among the gnarled roots and dry leaves of its ancient trees, sank gradually to the bottom of the icy sea, which covered it with huge masses of drift and boulder clay. Sea beasts, such as the walrus, now restricted to the extreme north, paddled about where birds had twittered among the topmost twigs of the fir trees. How long this state of things endured we know not, but at length it came to an end. The upheaved glacial mud hardened into the soil of modern Norfolk. Forests grew once more, the wolf and the beaver replaced the reindeer and the elephant; and at length what we call the history of England dawned.

Thus you have, within the limits of your own county, proof that the chalk can justly claim a very much greater antiquity than even the oldest physical traces of mankind. But we may go further and demonstrate, by evidence of the same authority as that which testifies to the existence of the father of men, that the chalk is vastly older than Adam himself.

The Book of Genesis informs us that Adam, immediately upon his creation, and before the appearance of Eve, was placed in the Garden of Eden. The problem of the geographical position of Eden has greatly vexed the spirits of the learned in such matters, but there is one point respecting which, so far as I know, no commentator has ever raised a doubt. This is, that of the four rivers which are said to run out of it, Euphrates and Hiddekel are identical with the rivers now known by the names of Euphrates and Tigris. But the whole country in which these mighty rivers take their origin, and through which they run, is composed of rocks which are either of the same age as the chalk, or of later date. So that the chalk must not only have been formed, but, after its formation, the time required for the deposit of these later rocks, and for their upheaval into dry land, must have elapsed before the smallest brook which feeds the swift stream of "the great river, the river of Babylon," [4] began to flow.

[1] stumps
[2] Robert Campbell Gunn, 1808-1881, British naturalist
[3] *Twelfth Night,* V, i, 384
[4] *Genesis,* xv. 18

Thus evidence which cannot be rebutted, and which need not be strengthened, though if time permitted I might indefinitely increase its quantity, compels you to believe that the earth, from the time of the chalk to the present day, has been the theater of a series of changes as vast in their amount as they were slow in their progress. The area on which we stand has been first sea and then land, for at least four alternations; and has remained in each of these conditions for a period of great length. Nor have these wonderful metamorphoses of sea into land, and of land into sea, been confined to one corner of England. During the chalk period, or "cretaceous epoch," not one of the present great physical features of the globe was in existence. Our great mountain ranges, Pyrenees, Alps, Himalayas, Andes, have all been upheaved since the chalk was deposited, and the cretaceous sea flowed over the sites of Sinai and Ararat. All this is certain, because rocks of cretaceous, or still later date, have shared in the elevatory movements which gave rise to these mountain chains; and may be found perched up, in some cases, many thousand feet high upon their flanks. An evidence of equal cogency demonstrates that, though in Norfolk the forest-bed rests directly upon the chalk, yet it does so, not because the period at which the forest grew immediately followed that at which the chalk was formed, but because an immense lapse of time, represented elsewhere by thousands of feet of rock, is not indicated at Cromer.

I must ask you to believe that there is no less conclusive proof that a still more prolonged succession of similar changes occurred before the chalk was deposited. Nor have we any reason to think that the first term in the series of these changes is known. The oldest sea beds preserved to us are sands, and mud, and pebbles, the wear and tear of rocks which were formed in still older oceans.

But, great as is the magnitude of these physical changes of the world, they have been accompanied by a no less striking series of modifications in its living inhabitants. All the great classes of animals, beasts of the field, fowls of the air, creeping things, and things which dwell in the waters, flourished upon the globe long ages before the chalk was deposited. Very few, however, if any, of these ancient forms of animal life were identical with those which now live. Certainly not one of the higher animals was of the same species as any of those now in existence. The beasts of the field, in the days before the chalk, were not our beasts of the field, nor the fowls of the air such as those which the eye of man has seen flying, unless his antiquity dates infinitely further back than we at present surmise. If we could be carried back into those times, we should be as one suddenly set down in Australia before it was colonized. We should see mammals, birds, reptiles, fishes, insects, snails, and the like, clearly recognizable as such, and yet not one of them would be just the same as those with which we are familiar, and many would be extremely different.

From that time to the present, the population of the world has undergone slow and gradual, but incessant changes. There has been no grand catastrophe—no destroyer has swept away the forms of life of one period and replaced them by a totally new creation; but one species has vanished and another has taken its place; creatures of one type of structure have diminished, those of another have increased, as time has passed on. And thus, while the differences between the living creatures of the time before the chalk and those of the present day appear startling if placed side by side, we are led from one to the other by the most gradual progress if we follow the course of Nature through the whole series of those relics of her operations which she has left behind.

And it is by the population of the chalk sea that the ancient and the modern inhabitants of the world are most completely connected. The groups which are dying out flourish side by side with the groups which are now the dominant forms of life. Thus the chalk contains remains of those strange flying and swimming reptiles, the pterodactyl, the ichthyosaurus, and the plesiosaurus, which are found in no later deposits, but abounded in preceding ages. The chambered shells called ammonites and belemnites, which are so characteristic of the period preceding the cretaceous, in like manner die with it. But amongst these fading remainders of a previous state of things are some very modern forms of life, looking like Yankee peddlers among a tribe of Red Indians. Crocodiles of modern type appear; bony fishes, many of them very similar to existing species, almost supplant the forms of fish which predominate in more ancient seas; and many kinds of living shellfish first become known to us in the chalk. The vegetation acquires a modern aspect. A few living animals are not even distinguishable as species from those which existed at that remote epoch. The *Globigerina* of the present day, for example, is not different specifically from that of the chalk; and the same may be said of many other *Foraminifera*. I think it probable that critical and unprejudiced examination will show that more than one species of much higher animals have had a similar longevity; but the only example which I can at present give confidently is the snake's-head lamp-shell (*Terebratulina caput serpentis*), which lives in our English seas and abounded (as *Terebratulina striata* of authors) in the chalk.

The longest line of human ancestry must hide its diminished head [1] before the pedigree of this insignificant shell-fish. We Englishmen are proud to have an ancestor who was present at the Battle of Hastings. [2] The ancestors of *Terebratulina caput serpentis* may have been present at a battle of *Ichthyosauria* in that part of the sea which, when the chalk was forming, flowed over the site of Hastings. While all around has changed, this *Terebratulina* has peacefully propagated its species from generation to generation, and stands, to this day, as a living testimony to the continuity of the present with the past history of the globe.

Up to this moment I have stated, so far as I know, nothing but well-authenticated facts, and the immediate conclusions which they force upon the mind. But the mind is so constituted that it does not willingly rest in facts and immediate causes, but seeks always after a knowledge of the remoter links in the chain of causation. Taking the many changes of any given spot of the earth's surface, from sea to land and from land to sea, as an established fact, we cannot refrain from asking ourselves how these changes have occurred. And when we have explained them—as they must be explained—by the alternate slow movements of elevation and depression which have affected the crust of the earth, we go still further back and ask, Why these movements?

I am not certain that anyone can give you a satisfactory answer to that question. Assuredly I cannot. All that can be said, for certain, is that such movements are part of the ordinary course of nature, inasmuch as they are going on at the present time. Direct proof may be given that some parts of the land of the northern hemisphere are at this moment insensibly rising and others insensibly sinking; and there is indirect, but perfectly satisfactory, proof that an enormous area now covered by the Pacific has been deepened thousands of feet since the present inhabitants of that sea came into existence. Thus there is not a shadow of a reason for believing that the physical changes of the globe in past times have been effected by other than natural causes. Is there any more reason for believing that the concomitant modifications in the forms of the living inhabitants of the globe have been brought about in other ways?

Before attempting to answer this question, let us try to form a distinct mental picture of what has happened in some special case. The crocodiles are animals which, as a group, have a very vast antiquity. They abounded ages before the chalk was deposited; they throng the rivers in warm climates at the present day. There is a difference in the form of the joints of the backbone, and in some minor particulars, between the crocodiles of the present epoch and those which lived before the chalk; but in the cretaceous epoch, as I have already mentioned, the crocodiles had assumed the modern type of structure. Notwithstanding this, the crocodiles of the chalk are not identically the same as those which lived in the times called "older tertiary," which succeeded the cretaceous epoch, and the crocodiles of the older tertiaries are not identical with those of the newer tertiaries nor are these identical with existing forms. (I leave open the question whether particular species may have lived on from epoch to epoch.) Thus each epoch has had its peculiar crocodiles; though all, since the chalk, have belonged to the modern type, and differ simply in their proportions, and in such structural particulars as are discernible only to trained eyes.

How is the existence of this long succession of different species of crocodiles to be accounted for? Only two suppositions seem to be open to us—either each species of crocodile has been specially created, or it has arisen out of some preëxisting form by the operation of natural causes. Choose your hypothesis; I have chosen mine. I can find no warranty for believing in the distinct creation of a score of successive species of crocodiles in the course of countless ages of time. Science gives no countenance to such a wild fancy; nor can even the perverse ingenuity of a commentator pretend to discover this sense in the simple words in which the writer of Genesis records the proceedings of the fifth and sixth days of the Creation. On the other hand, I see no good reason for doubting the necessary alternative, that all these varied species have been evolved from preëxisting crocodilian forms, by the operation of causes as completely a part of the common order of nature as those which have effected

[1] *Paradise Lost*, IV, 35, p. 280.
[2] the Norman Conquest, 1066

the changes of the inorganic world. Few will venture to affirm that the reasoning which applies to crocodiles loses its force among other animals, or among plants. If one series of species has come into existence by the operation of natural causes, it seems folly to deny that all may have arisen in the same way.

A small beginning has led us to a great ending. If I were to put the bit of chalk with which we started into the hot but obscure flame of burning hydrogen, it would presently shine like the sun. It seems to me that this physical metamorphosis is no false image of what has been the result of our subjecting it to a jet of fervent, though nowise brilliant, thought tonight. It has become luminous, and its clear rays penetrating the abyss of the remote past have brought within our ken some stages of the evolution of the earth. And in the shifting "without haste, but without rest" [1] of the land and sea, as in the endless variation of the forms assumed by living beings, we have observed nothing but the natural product of the forces originally possessed by the substance of the universe.

1868

JOHN RUSKIN 1819-1900

One destined to devote his life to art criticism could scarcely be more favorably situated as a child than was Ruskin. His father, a cultivated and artistically inclined business man, gave the boy every advantage of books, tutors, and travel. Close touch with Continental art, especially the painting and architecture of Italy, furnished Ruskin the foundation of his artistic creeds. His criticism, beginning with *Modern Painters,* 1843, the year he received his master's degree from Oxford, and including *Seven Lamps of Architecture,* 1849, and *Stones of Venice,* 1851-1853, occupied some twenty years.

During the time his conviction had been deepening: that art and morality are interdependent, that beauty in a person's surroundings is requisite to his morality, and that art can be produced only in a moral environment. From 1860 he labored for thirty years in disseminating these doctrines in lectures and in books. *Unto this Last,* 1862, and *Crown of Wild Olives,* 1866, are discussions of economic and social ethics. Upon Utopian schemes for coöperation among toilers, and bettering the conditions in which they worked, he lavished a large fortune, and so overtaxed his brain that he spent the last ten years of his life partly in mental obscurity. He is often grouped with Arnold and Carlyle as a critic-prophet of his age. He put forth his ideas with an almost religious fervor in rich, rhythmic prose, replete with such imagination as Tennyson and Morris wrought into verse.

Biography: F. Harrison (EML). Criticism: Anne (Thackeray) Ritchie, *Records of Tennyson, Ruskin,* etc.; Benson, A. C., *Ruskin, a Study in Personality,* 1911; Stephen; see also "Ruskin, a Centenary View," R. Roberts, *Nation* 108:563-65; "Ruskin Centenary," *Liv. Age* 300:678-87; "A Girl's Friendship with Ruskin," ed. L. Huxley, *Atlan.* 138:776-88, 139:88-101.

From THE SEVEN LAMPS OF ARCHITECTURE [2]

The Lamp of Memory

Among the hours of his life to which the writer looks back with peculiar gratitude as having been marked by more than ordinary fullness of joy or clearness of teaching, is one passed, now some years ago, near time of sunset, among the broken masses of pine forest which skirt the course of the Ain, above the village of Champagnole, in the Jura. [3] It is a spot which has all the solemnity, with none of the savageness, of the Alps; where there is a sense of a great power beginning to be manifested in the earth, and of a deep and majestic concord in the rise of the long, low lines of piny hills; the first utterance of those mighty mountain symphonies, soon to be more loudly lifted and wildly broken along the battlements of the Alps. But their strength is as yet restrained; and the far-reaching ridges of pastoral mountain succeed each other, like the long and sighing swell which moves over quiet waters from some far-off, stormy sea. And there is a deep tenderness pervading that vast monotony. The destructive forces and the stern expression of the central ranges are alike withdrawn. No frost-plowed, dust-encumbered paths of ancient glacier fret the soft Jura pastures; no splintered heaps of ruin break the fair ranks of her forests; no pale, defiled, or furious rivers rend their rude and changeful ways among her rocks. Patiently, eddy by eddy, the clear green streams wind along their well-known beds; and under the dark quietness of the undisturbed pines there

[1] *"Ohne Hast, aber ohne Rast."*—Goethe.

[2] The seven "Lamps" are Sacrifice, Truth, Power, Beauty, Life, Memory, and Obedience. The word "lamp" is used in allusion to the story of Aladdin's magic lamp; and the book was written, said Ruskin, "to show that certain right states of temper and moral feeling were the magic powers by which all good architecture, without exception, had been produced." The selection here given illustrates Ruskin's early exuberant style.

[3] a chain of mountains in eastern France

spring up, year by year, such company of joyful flowers as I know not the like of among all the blessings of the earth. It was springtime, too; and all were coming forth in clusters crowded for very love; there was room enough for all, but they crushed their leaves into all manner of strange shapes only to be nearer each other. There was the wood anemone, star after star, closing every now and then into nebulae; and there was the oxalis, troop by troop, like virginal processions of the *Mois de Marie*,[1] the dark vertical clefts in the limestone choked up with them as with heavy snow, and touched with ivy on the edges—ivy as light and lovely as the vine; and, ever and anon, a blue gush of violets, and cowslip bells in sunny places; and in the more open ground the vetch and comfrey, and mezereon, and the small sapphire buds of the Polygala Alpina,[2] and the wild strawberry, just a blossom or two all showered amidst the golden softness of deep, warm, amber-colored moss. I came out presently on the edge of the ravine; the solemn murmur of its waters rose suddenly from beneath, mixed with the singing of the thrushes among the pine boughs; and on the opposite side of the valley, walled all along as it was by gray cliffs of limestone, there was a hawk sailing slowly off their brow, touching them nearly with his wings, and with the shadows of the pines flickering upon his plumage from above; but with the fall of a hundred fathoms under his breast, and the curling pools of the green river gliding and glittering dizzily beneath him, their foam globes moving with him as he flew. It would be difficult to conceive a scene less dependent upon any other interest than that of its own secluded and serious beauty; but the writer well remembers the sudden blankness and chill which were cast upon it when he endeavored, in order more strictly to arrive at the sources of its impressiveness, to imagine it, for a moment, a scene in some aboriginal forest of the New Continent. The flowers in an instant lost their light, the river its music; the hills became oppressively desolate; a heaviness in the boughs of the darkened forest showed how much of their former power had been dependent upon a life which was not theirs, how much of the glory of the imperishable, or continually renewed, creation is reflected from things more precious in their memories than it, in its renewing. Those ever-springing flowers and ever-flowing streams had been dyed by the deep colors of human endurance, valor, and virtue; and the crests of the sable hills that rose against the evening sky received a deeper worship, because their far shadows fell eastward over the iron wall of Joux,[3] and the four-square keep of Granson.[4]

It is as the centralization and protectress of this sacred influence, that Architecture is to be regarded by us with the most serious thought. We may live without her, and worship without her, but we cannot remember without her. How cold is all history, how lifeless all imagery, compared to that which the living nation writes, and the uncorrupted marble bears! How many pages of doubtful record might we not often spare, for a few stones left one upon another! The ambition of the old Babel builders was well directed for this world[5]—there are but two strong conquerors of the forgetfulness of men, Poetry and Architecture; and the latter in some sort includes the former, and is mightier in its reality; it is well to have, not only what men have thought and felt, but what their hands have handled, and their strength wrought, and their eyes beheld, all the days of their life. The age of Homer is surrounded with darkness, his very personality with doubt. Not so that of Pericles.[6] And the day is coming when we shall confess that we have learned more of Greece out of the crumbled fragments of her sculpture than even from her sweet singers or soldier historians. And if indeed there be any profit in our knowledge of the past, or any joy in the thought of being remembered hereafter, which can give strength to present exertion, or patience to present endurance, there are two duties respecting national architecture whose importance it is impossible to overrate; the first, to render the architecture of the day historical; and the second, to preserve, as the most precious of inheritances, that of past ages.

It is in the first of these two directions that Memory may truly be said to be the Sixth Lamp of Architecture; for it is in becoming memorial or monumental that a true perfection is attained by civil and domestic buildings; and this partly as they are, with such a view, built in a more stable manner, and partly as their decorations are consequently animated by a metaphorical or historical meaning.

[1] "Mary's Month"; in honor of the Virgin

[2] a milkwort

[3] In the Fort de Joux, Mirabeau, the French orator, was once imprisoned; and Toussaint L'Ouverture, the Haitian revolutionist, died there.

[4] A village and castle on the Lake of Neuchâtel, Switzerland; a Swiss garrison was treacherously put to death there by Charles the Bold in 1476 and gloriously avenged by the Swiss army.

[5] See *Genesis*, xi, 4.

[6] It was during the ascendancy of Pericles that the Parthenon was built.

As regards domestic buildings, there must always be a certain limitation to views of this kind in the power, as well as in the hearts, of men; still I cannot but think it an evil sign of a people when their houses are built to last for one generation only. There is a sanctity in a good man's house which cannot be renewed in every tenement that rises on its ruins; and I believe that good men would generally feel this; and that having spent their lives happily and honorably, they would be grieved, at the close of them, to think that the place of their earthly abode, which had seen, and seemed almost to sympathize in, all their honor, their gladness, or their suffering—that this, with all the record it bare of them, and of all material things that they had loved and ruled over, and set the stamp of themselves upon—was to be swept away, as soon as there was room made for them in the grave; that no respect was to be shown to it, no affection felt for it, no good to be drawn from it by their children; that though there was a monument in the church, there was no warm monument in the heart and house to them; that all that they ever treasured was despised, and the places that had sheltered and comforted them were dragged down to the dust. I say that a good man would fear this; and that, far more, a good son, a noble descendant, would fear doing it to his father's house. I say that if men lived like men indeed, their houses would be temples—temples which we should hardly dare to injure, and in which it would make us holy to be permitted to live; and there must be a strange dissolution of natural affection, a strange unthankfulness for all that homes have given and parents taught, a strange consciousness that we have been unfaithful to our father's honor, or that our own lives are not such as would make our dwellings sacred to our children, when each man would fain build to himself, and build for the little revolution of his own life only. And I look upon those pitiful concretions of lime and clay which spring up in mildewed forwardness, out of the kneaded fields about our capital—upon those thin, tottering, foundationless shells of splintered wood and imitated stone—upon those gloomy rows of formalized minuteness, alike without difference and without fellowship, as solitary as similar—not merely with the careless disgust of an offended eye, not merely with sorrow for a desecrated landscape, but with a painful foreboding that the roots of our national greatness must be deeply cankered when they are thus loosely struck in their native ground; that those comfortless and unhonored dwellings are the signs of a great and spreading spirit of popular discontent; that they mark the time when every man's aim is to be in some more elevated sphere than his natural one, and every man's past life is his habitual scorn; when men build in the hope of leaving the palaces they have built, and live in the hope of forgetting the years that they have lived; when the comfort, the peace, the religion of home have ceased to be felt, and the crowded tenements of a struggling and restless population differ only from the tents of the Arab or the Gipsy by their less healthy openness to the air of heaven, and less happy choice of their spot of earth; by their sacrifice of liberty without the gain of rest, and of stability without the luxury of change.

This is no slight, no consequenceless evil; it is ominous, infectious, and fecund of other fault and misfortune. When men do not love their hearths, nor reverence their thresholds, it is a sign that they have dishonored both, and that they have never acknowledged the true universality of that Christian worship which was indeed to supersede the idolatry, but not the piety, of the pagan. Our God is a household God, as well as a heavenly one; He has an altar in every man's dwelling; let men look to it when they rend it lightly and pour out its ashes. It is not a question of mere ocular delight, it is no question of intellectual pride, or of cultivated and critical fancy, how, and with what aspect of durability and of completeness, the domestic buildings of a nation shall be raised. It is one of those moral duties, not with more impunity to be neglected because the perception of them depends on a finely toned and balanced conscientiousness, to build our dwellings with care, and patience, and fondness, and diligent completion, and with a view to their duration at least for such a period as, in the ordinary course of national revolutions, might be supposed likely to extend to the entire alteration of the direction of local interests. This at the least; but it would be better if, in every possible instance, men built their own houses on a scale commensurate rather with their condition at the commencement, than their attainments at the termination, of their worldly career; and built them to stand as long as human work at its strongest can be hoped to stand; recording to their children what they have been, and from what, if so it had been permitted them, they had risen. And when houses are thus built, we may have that true domestic architecture, the beginning of all other, which does not disdain to treat with respect and thoughtfulness the small habitation as well as the large, and which invests with the dignity of contented manhood the narrowness of worldly circumstance.

. . . .

1849

From THE STONES OF VENICE

Volume II, Chapter I[1]—The Throne

In the olden days of traveling, now to return no more, in which distance could not be vanquished without toil, but in which that toil was rewarded, partly by the power of deliberate survey of the countries through which the journey lay, and partly by the happiness of the evening hours, when from the top of the last hill he had surmounted, the traveler beheld the quiet village where he was to rest, scattered among the meadows beside its valley stream; or, from the long hoped for turn in the dusty perspective of the causeway, saw, for the first time, the towers of some famed city, faint in the rays of sunset—hours of peaceful and thoughtful pleasure, for which the rush of the arrival in the railway station is perhaps not always, or to all men, an equivalent,—in those days, I say, when there was something more to be anticipated and remembered in the first aspect of each successive halting-place, than a new arrangement of glass roofing and iron girder, there were few moments of which the recollection was more fondly cherished by the traveler, than that which, as I endeavored to describe in the close of the last chapter, brought him within sight of Venice, as his gondola shot into the open lagoon from the canal of Mestre. Not but that the aspect of the city itself was generally the source of some slight disappointment, for, seen in this direction, its buildings are far less characteristic than those of the other great towns of Italy; but this inferiority was partly disguised by distance, and more than atoned for by the strange rising of its walls and towers out of the midst, as it seemed, of the deep sea, for it was impossible that the mind or the eye could at once comprehend the shallowness of the vast sheet of water which stretched away in leagues of rippling luster to the north and south, or trace the narrow line of islets bounding it to the east. The salt breeze, the white moaning sea birds, the masses of black weed separating and disappearing gradually, in knots of heaving shoal, under the advance of the steady tide, all proclaimed it to be indeed the ocean on whose bosom the great city rested so calmly; not such blue, soft, lake-like ocean as bathes the Neapolitan promontories, or sleeps beneath the marble rocks of Genoa, but a sea with the bleak power of our own northern waves, yet subdued into a strange spacious rest, and changed from its angry pallor into a field of burnished gold, as the sun declined behind the belfry tower of the lonely island church, fitly named "St. George of the Seaweed." As the boat drew nearer to the city, the coast which the traveler had just left sank behind him into one long, low, sad-colored line, tufted irregularly with brushwood and willows; but at what seemed its northern extremity, the hills of Arqua rose in a dark cluster of purple pyramids, balanced on the bright mirage of the lagoon; two or three smooth surges of inferior hill extended themselves about their roots, and beyond these, beginning with the craggy peaks above Vicenza, the chain of the Alps girded the whole horizon to the north—a wall of jagged blue, here and there showing through its clefts a wilderness of misty precipices, fading far back into the recesses of Cadore, and itself rising and breaking away eastward, where the sun struck opposite upon its snow into mighty fragments of peaked light, standing up behind the barred clouds of evening, one after another, countless, the crown of the Adrian Sea, until the eye turned back from pursuing them, to rest upon the nearer burning of the campaniles[2] of Murano, and on the great city, where it magnified itself along the waves, as the quick silent pacing of the gondola drew nearer and nearer. And at last, when its walls were reached, and the outmost of its untrodden streets was entered, not through towered gate or guarded rampart, but as a deep inlet between two rocks of coral in the Indian sea; when first upon the traveler's sight opened the long ranges of columned palaces,—each with its black boat moored at the portal,—each with its image cast down beneath its feet upon that green pavement which every breeze broke into new fantasies of rich tessellation; when first, at the extremity of the bright vista, the shadowy Rialto threw its colossal curve slowly forth from behind the palace of the Camerlenghi;[3] that strange curve, so delicate,

[1] In this "faithful view of the site of the Venetian Throne," we have both an illustration of Ruskin's descriptive and narrative powers, and an expression of the deep religious convictions which informed his earlier writings. In the selection that follows will be found his defense and praise of Gothic art, together with his central social theory.

[2] bell-towers (Murano, an island north of Venice)

[3] The Bridge of the Rialto, across the Grand Canal, consists of a single marble arch 74 feet in span and 32 feet in height.

so adamantine, strong as a mountain cavern, graceful as a bow just bent; when first, before its moonlike circumference was all risen, the gondolier's cry, "Ah! Stalii,"[1] struck sharp upon the ear, and the prow turned aside under the mighty cornices that half met over the narrow canal, where the plash of the water followed close and loud, ringing along the marble by the boat's side; and when at last that boat darted forth upon the breadth of silver sea, across which the front of the Ducal Palace, flushed with its sanguine veins, looks to the snowy dome of Our Lady of Salvation,[2] it was no marvel that the mind should be so deeply entranced by the visionary charm of a scene so beautiful and so strange, as to forget the darker truths of its history and its being. Well might it seem that such a city had owed her existence rather to the rod of the enchanter than the fear of the fugitive; that the waters which encircled her had been chosen for the mirror of her state, rather than the shelter of her nakedness; and that all which in nature was wild or merciless—Time and Decay, as well as the waves and tempests—had been won to adorn her instead of to destroy, and might still spare, for ages to come, that beauty which seemed to have fixed for its throne the sands of the hourglass as well as of the sea.

And although the last, few, eventful years, fraught with change to the face of the whole earth, have been more fatal in their influence on Venice than the five hundred that preceded them; though the noble landscape of approach to her can now be seen no more, or seen only by a glance, as the engine slackens its rushing on the iron line; and though many of her palaces are forever defaced, and many in desecrated ruins, there is still so much of magic in her aspect that the hurried traveler, who must leave her before the wonder of that first aspect has been worn away, may still be led to forget the humility of her origin, and to shut his eyes to the depth of her desolation. They, at least, are little to be envied, in whose hearts the great charities of the imagination lie dead, and for whom the fancy has no power to repress the importunity of painful impressions, or to raise what is ignoble, and disguise what is discordant, in a scene so rich in its remembrances, so surpassing in its beauty. But for this work of the imagination there must be no permission during the task which is before us.

[1] indicating that the gondolier meant to turn to the right

[2] the church of Santa Maria della Salute, on the right side of the mouth of the Grand Canal

The impotent feelings of romance, so singularly characteristic of this century, may indeed gild, but never save, the remains of those mightier ages to which they are attached like climbing flowers; and they must be torn away from the magnificent fragments, if we would see them as they stood in their own strength. Those feelings, always as fruitless as they are fond, are in Venice not only incapable of protecting, but even of discerning, the objects to which they ought to have been attached. The Venice of modern fiction and drama is a thing of yesterday, a mere efflorescence of decay, a stage dream which the first ray of daylight must dissipate into dust. No prisoner, whose name is worth remembering, or whose sorrow deserved sympathy, ever crossed that "Bridge of Sighs," which is the center of the Byronic ideal of Venice;[3] no great merchant of Venice ever saw that Rialto under which the traveler now passes with breathless interest; the statue which Byron makes Faliero address as one of his great ancestors was erected to a soldier of fortune a hundred and fifty years after Faliero's death;[4] and the most conspicuous parts of the city have been so entirely altered in the course of the last three centuries, that if Henry Dandolo or Francis Foscari[5] could be summoned from their tombs, and stood each on the deck of his galley at the entrance of the Grand Canal, that renowned entrance, the painter's favorite subject, the novelist's favorite scene, where the water first narrows by the steps of the Church of La Salute,—the mighty Doges would not know in what part of the world they stood, would literally not recognize one stone of the great city, for whose sake, and by whose ingratitude, their gray hairs had been brought down with bitterness to the grave. The remains of *their* Venice lie hidden behind the cumbrous masses which were the delight of the nation in its dotage; hidden in many a grass-grown court, and silent pathway, and lightless canal, where the slow waves have sapped their foundations for five hundred years, and must soon prevail over them for ever. It must be our task[6] to glean and gather them forth, and restore out of them some faint image of the lost city; more gorgeous a thousandfold than that which now exists, yet not created in the day-dream of the prince, nor by the ostentation of the noble, but built

[3] See *Childe Harold*, IV, i.

[4] See *Marino Faliero*, III, i, 36.

[5] Early Doges of Venice; the one was blinded by the Byzantine emperor, the other compelled to abdicate.

[6] i. e., Ruskin's task, in this intended work on Venetian architecture and sculpture

by iron hands and patient hearts, contending against the adversity of nature and the fury of man, so that its wonderfulness cannot be grasped by the indolence of imagination, but only after frank inquiry into the true nature of that wild and solitary scene, whose restless tides and trembling sands did indeed shelter the birth of the city, but long denied her dominion.

When the eye falls casually on a map of Europe, there is no feature by which it is more likely to be arrested than the strange sweeping loop formed by the junction of the Alps and Apennines, and enclosing the great basin of Lombardy. This return of the mountain chain upon itself causes a vast difference in the character of the distribution of its débris on its opposite sides. The rock fragments and sediment which the torrents on the other side of the Alps bear into the plains are distributed over a vast extent of country, and, though here and there lodged in beds of enormous thickness, soon permit the firm substrata to appear from underneath them; but all the torrents which descend from the southern side of the high Alps, and from the northern slope of the Apennines, meet concentrically in the recess or mountain bay which the two ridges enclose; every fragment which thunder breaks out of their battlements, and every grain of dust which the summer rain washes from their pastures, is at last laid at rest in the blue sweep of the Lombardic plain; and that plain must have risen within its rocky barriers as a cup fills with wine, but for two contrary influences which continually depress, or disperse from its surface, the accumulation of the ruins of ages.

I will not tax the reader's faith in modern science by insisting on the singular depression of the surface of Lombardy, which appears for many centuries to have taken place steadily and continually; the main fact with which we have to do is the gradual transport, by the Po and its great collateral rivers, of vast masses of the finer sediment to the sea. The character of the Lombardic plain is most strikingly expressed by the ancient walls of its cities, composed for the most part of large rounded Alpine pebbles alternating with narrow courses of brick; and was curiously illustrated in 1848, by the ramparts of these same pebbles thrown up four or five feet high round every field, to check the Austrian cavalry in the battle under the walls of Verona. The finer dust among which these pebbles are dispersed is taken up by the rivers, fed into continual strength by the Alpine snow, so that, however pure their waters may be when they issue from the lakes at the foot of the great chain, they become of the color and opacity of clay before they reach the Adriatic; the sediment which they bear is at once thrown down as they enter the sea, forming a vast belt of low land along the eastern coast of Italy. The powerful stream of the Po of course builds forward the fastest; on each side of it, north and south, there is a tract of marsh, fed by more feeble streams, and less liable to rapid change than the delta of the central river. In one of these tracts is built RAVENNA, and in the other VENICE.

What circumstances directed the peculiar arrangement of this great belt of sediment in the earliest times, it is not here the place to inquire. It is enough for us to know that from the mouths of the Adige to those of the Piave there stretches, at a variable distance of from three to five miles from the actual shore, a bank of sand, divided into long islands by narrow channels of sea. The space between this bank and the true shore consists of the sedimentary deposits from these and other rivers, a great plain of calcareous mud,[1] covered, in the neighborhood of Venice, by the sea at high water, to the depth in most places of a foot or a foot and a half, and nearly everywhere exposed at low tide, but divided by an intricate network of narrow and winding channels, from which the sea never retires. In some places, according to the run of the currents, the land has risen into marshy islets, consolidated, some by art, and some by time, into ground firm enough to be built upon, or fruitful enough to be cultivated. In others, on the contrary, it has not reached the sea level; so that, at the average low water, shallow lakelets glitter among its irregularly exposed fields of seaweed. In the midst of the largest of these, increased in importance by the confluence of several large, river channels toward one of the openings in the sea bank, the city of Venice itself is built, on a crowded cluster of islands; the various plots of higher ground which appear to the north and south of this central cluster, have at different periods been also thickly inhabited, and now bear, according to their size, the remains of cities, villages, or isolated convents and churches, scattered among spaces of open ground, partly waste and encumbered by ruins, partly under cultivation for the supply of the metropolis.

The average rise and fall of the tide is about three feet (varying considerably with the

[1] Compare what Huxley says on the chalk formation of Europe, pp. 716, 717.

seasons); but this fall, on so flat a shore, is enough to cause continual movement in the waters, and in the main canals to produce a reflux which frequently runs like a mill stream. At high water no land is visible for many miles to the north or south of Venice, except in the form of small islands crowned with towers or gleaming with villages. There is a channel, some three miles wide, between the city and the mainland, and some mile and a half wide between it and the sandy breakwater called the Lido, which divides the lagoon from the Adriatic, but which is so low as hardly to disturb the impression of the city's having been built in the midst of the ocean, although the secret of its true position is partly, yet not painfully, betrayed by the clusters of piles set to mark the deep-water channels, which undulate far away in spotty chains like the studded backs of huge sea-snakes, and by the quick glittering of the crisped and crowded waves that flicker and dance before the strong winds upon the uplifted level of the shallow sea. But the scene is widely different at low tide. A fall of eighteen or twenty inches is enough to show ground over the greater part of the lagoon; and at the complete ebb the city is seen standing in the midst of a dark plain of seaweed, of gloomy green, except only where the larger branches of the Brenta and its associated streams converge toward the port of the Lido. Through this salt and somber plain the gondola and the fishing boat advance by tortuous channels, seldom more than four or five feet deep, and often so choked with slime that the heavier keels furrow the bottom till their crossing tracks are seen through the clear sea water like the ruts upon a wintry road, and the oar leaves blue gashes upon the ground at every stroke, or is entangled among the thick weed that fringes the banks with the weight of its sullen waves, leaning to and fro upon the uncertain sway of the exhausted tide. The scene is often profoundly oppressive, even at this day, when every plot of higher ground bears some fragment of fair building. But in order to know what it was once, let the traveler follow in his boat at evening the windings of some unfrequented channel far into the midst of the melancholy plain; let him remove, in his imagination, the brightness of the great city that still extends itself in the distance, and the walls and towers from the islands that are near; and so wait, until the bright investiture and sweet warmth of the sunset are withdrawn from the waters, and the black desert of their shore lies in its nakedness beneath the night, pathless, comfortless, infirm, lost in dark languor and fearful silence, except where the salt runlets plash into the tideless pools, or the sea birds flit from their margins with a questioning cry; and he will be enabled to enter in some sort into the horror of heart with which this solitude was anciently chosen by man for his habitation. They little thought, who first drove the stakes into the sand, and strewed the ocean reeds for their rest, that their children were to be the princes of that ocean, and their palaces its pride; and yet, in the great natural laws that rule that sorrowful wilderness, let it be remembered what strange preparation had been made for the things which no human imagination could have foretold, and how the whole existence and fortune of the Venetian nation were anticipated or compelled, by the setting of those bars and doors to the rivers and the sea. Had deeper currents divided their islands, hostile navies would again and again have reduced the rising city into servitude; had stronger surges beaten their shores, all the richness and refinement of the Venetian architecture must have been exchanged for the walls and bulwarks of an ordinary seaport. Had there been no tide, as in other parts of the Mediterranean, the narrow canals of the city would have become noisome, and the marsh in which it was built pestiferous. Had the tide been only a foot or eighteen inches higher in its rise, the water-access to the doors of the palaces would have been impossible; even as it is, there is sometimes a little difficulty, at the ebb, in landing without setting foot upon the lower and slippery steps; and the highest tides sometimes enter the courtyards, and overflow the entrance halls. Eighteen inches more of difference between the level of the flood and ebb would have rendered the doorsteps of every palace, at low water, a treacherous mass of weeds and limpets, and the entire system of water-carriage for the higher classes, in their easy and daily intercourse, must have been done away with. The streets of the city would have been widened, its network of canals filled up, and all the peculiar character of the place and the people destroyed.

The reader may perhaps have felt some pain in the contrast between this faithful view of the site of the Venetian Throne, and the romantic conception of it which we ordinarily form; but this pain, if he have felt it, ought to be more than counterbalanced by the value of the instance thus afforded to us at once of the inscrutableness and the wisdom of the ways of God. If, two thousand years ago, we had been permitted to watch the slow settling of the slime of those turbid rivers into the polluted sea, and the gaining upon its deep and fresh waters of the lifeless, impassable, unvoyageable plain, how little could we have understood the purpose with which those islands were shaped out of the void, and the torpid waters enclosed with their desolate walls of sand! How little could we have known, any more than of what now seems to us most distressful, dark, and objectless, the glorious aim which was then in the mind of Him in whose hand are all the corners of the earth! How little imagined that in the laws which were stretching forth the gloomy margins of those fruitless banks, and feeding the bitter grass among their shallows, there was indeed a preparation, and *the only preparation possible*, for the founding of a city which was to be set like a golden clasp on the girdle of the earth, to write her history on the white scrolls of the sea surges, and to word it in their thunder, and to gather and give forth, in world-wide pulsation, the glory of the West and of the East, from the burning heart of her Fortitude and Splendor.

[The Medieval and the Modern Workman]

From Volume II, Chapter VI

. . . . . .

Now, in the make and nature of every man, however rude or simple, whom we employ in manual labor, there are some powers for better things—some tardy imagination, torpid capacity of emotion, tottering steps of thought, there are, even at the worst; and in most cases it is all our own fault that they *are* tardy or torpid. But they cannot be strengthened, unless we are content to take them in their feebleness, and unless we prize and honor them in their imperfection above the best and most perfect manual skill. And this is what we have to do with all our laborers; to look for the *thoughtful* part of them, and get that out of them, whatever we lose for it, whatever faults and errors we are obliged to take with it. For the best that is in them cannot manifest itself, but in company with much error. Understand this clearly: you can teach a man to draw a straight line, and to cut one; to strike a curved line, and to carve it; and to copy and carve any number of given lines or forms with admirable speed and perfect precision; and you find his work perfect of its kind. But if you ask him to think about any of those forms, to consider if he cannot find any better in his own head, he stops; his execution becomes hesitating; he thinks, and ten to one he thinks wrong; ten to one he makes a mistake in the first touch he gives to his work as a thinking being. But you have made a man of him for all that. He was only a machine before, an animated tool.

And observe, you are put to stern choice in this matter. You must either make a tool of the creature, or a man of him. You cannot make both. Men were not intended to work with the accuracy of tools, to be precise and perfect in all their actions. If you will have that precision out of them, and make their fingers measure degrees like cogwheels, and their arms strike curves like compasses, you must unhumanize them. All the energy of their spirits must be given to make cogs and compasses of themselves. All their attention and strength must go to the accomplishment of the mean act. The eye of the soul must be bent upon the finger point, and the soul's force must fill all the invisible nerves that guide it, ten hours a day, that it may not err from its steely precision, and so soul and sight be worn away, and the whole human being be lost at last—a heap of sawdust, so far as its intellectual work in this world is concerned; saved only by its Heart, which cannot go into the form of cogs and compasses, but expands, after the ten hours are over, into fireside humanity. On the other hand, if you will make a man of the working creature, you cannot make a tool. Let him but begin to imagine, to think, to try to do anything worth doing; and the engine-turned precision is lost at once. Out come all his roughness, all his dullness, all his incapability; shame upon shame, failure upon failure, pause after pause. But out comes the whole majesty of him, also; and we know the height of it only when we see the clouds settling upon him. And, whether the clouds be bright or dark, there will be transfiguration behind and within them.

And now, reader, look around this English room of yours, about which you have been proud so often, because the work of it was so good and strong, and the ornaments of it so finished. Examine again all those accurate moldings, and perfect polishings, and unerring adjustments of the seasoned wood and tempered steel. Many a time you have exulted over them, and thought how great England was, because her slightest work was done so thoroughly. Alas! if read rightly, these perfectnesses are signs of a slavery in our England a thousand times more bitter and more degrading than that of the scourged African, or helot [1]

[1] state-owned Spartan slave, attached to the soil

Greek. Men may be beaten, chained, tormented, yoked like cattle, slaughtered like summer flies, and yet remain in one sense, and the best sense, free. But to smother their souls within them, to blight and hew into rotting pollards the suckling branches of their human intelligence, to make the flesh and skin which, after the worm's work on it, is to see God,[1] into leathern thongs to yoke machinery with—this it is to be slave masters indeed; and there might be more freedom in England, though her feudal lords' lightest words were worth men's lives, and though the blood of the vexed husbandman dropped in the furrows of her fields, than there is while the animation of her multitudes is sent like fuel to feed the factory smoke, and the strength of them is given daily to be wasted into the fineness of a web, or racked into the exactness of a line.

And, on the other hand, go forth again to gaze upon the old cathedral front, where you have smiled so often at the fantastic ignorance of the old sculptures; examine once more those ugly goblins, and formless monsters, and stern statues, anatomiless and rigid; but do not mock at them, for they are signs of the life and liberty of every workman who struck the stone; a freedom of thought, and rank in scale of being, such as no laws, no charters, no charities can secure; but which it must be the first aim of all Europe at this day to regain for her children.

Let me not be thought to speak wildly or extravagantly. It is, verily, this degradation of the operative into a machine which, more than any other evil of the times, is leading the mass of the nations everywhere into vain, incoherent, destructive struggling for a freedom of which they cannot explain the nature to themselves. Their universal outcry against wealth, and against nobility, is not forced from them either by the pressure of the famine, or the sting of mortified pride. These do much, and have done much in all ages; but the foundations of society were never yet shaken as they are at this day. It is not that men are ill fed, but that they have no pleasure in the work by which they make their bread, and therefore look to wealth as the only means of pleasure. It is not that men are pained by the scorn of the upper classes, but they cannot endure their own; for they feel that the kind of labor to which they are condemned is verily a degrading one, and makes them less than men. Never had the upper classes so much sympathy with the lower, or charity for them, as they have at this day, and yet never were they so much hated by them; for, of old, the separation between the noble and the poor was merely a wall built by law; now it is a veritable difference in level of standing, a precipice between upper and lower grounds in the field of humanity, and there is pestilential air at the bottom of it. I know not if a day is ever to come when the nature of right freedom will be understood, and when men will see that to obey another man, to labor for him, yield reverence to him or to his place, is not slavery. It is often the best kind of liberty—liberty from care. The man who says to one, Go, and he goeth, and to another, Come, and he cometh,[2] has, in most cases, more sense of restraint and difficulty than the man who obeys him. The movements of the one are hindered by the burden on his shoulder; of the other, by the bridle on his lips—there is no way by which the burden may be lightened; but we need not suffer from the bridle if we do not champ at it. To yield reverence to another, to hold ourselves and our lives at his disposal, is not slavery; often it is the noblest state in which a man can live in this world. There is, indeed, a reverence which is servile, that is to say irrational or selfish; but there is also noble reverence, that is to say, reasonable and loving. And a man is never so noble as when he is reverent in this kind; nay, even if the feeling pass the bounds of mere reason, so that it be loving, a man is raised by it. Which had, in reality, most of the serf nature in him—the Irish peasant who was lying in wait yesterday for his landlord, with his musket muzzle thrust through the ragged hedge; or that old mountain servant, who 200 years ago, at Inverkeithing, gave up his own life and the lives of his seven sons for his chief?—as each fell, calling forth his brother to the death, "Another for Hector!"[3] And therefore, in all ages and all countries, reverence has been paid and sacrifice made by men to each other, not only without complaint, but rejoicingly; and famine, and peril, and sword, and all evil, and all shame, have been borne willingly in the causes of masters and kings; for all these gifts of the heart ennobled the men who gave, not less than the men who received, them, and nature prompted, and God rewarded the sacrifice. But to feel their souls withering within them, unthanked, to find their whole being sunk into an unrecognized abyss, to be counted off into a heap of mechanism, numbered with its wheels, and weighed with

[1] See *Job,* xix, 26

[2] See *Matthew,* viii, 9.

[3] See the Preface to Scott's *The Fair Maid of Perth.*

its hammer strokes—this nature bade not—this God blesses not—this humanity for no long time is able to endure.

We have much studied and much perfected, of late, the great civilized invention of the division of labor; only we give it a false name. It is not, truly speaking, the labor that is divided; but the men; divided into mere segments of men—broken into small fragments and crumbs of life; so that all the little piece of intelligence that is left in a man is not enough to make a pin, or a nail, but exhausts itself in making the point of a pin or the head of a nail. Now it is a good and desirable thing, truly, to make many pins in a day; but if we could only see with what crystal sand their points were polished—sand of human soul, much to be magnified before it can be discerned for what it is—we should think there might be some loss in it also. And the great cry that rises from all our manufacturing cities, louder than their furnace blast, is all in very deed for this—that we manufacture everything there except men; we blanch cotton, and strengthen steel, and refine sugar, and shape pottery; but to brighten, to strengthen, to refine, or to form a single living spirit, never enters into our estimate of advantages. And all the evil to which that cry is urging our myriads can be met only in one way: not by teaching nor preaching, for to teach them is but to show them their misery, and to preach to them, if we do nothing more than preach, is to mock at it. It can be met only by a right understanding, on the part of all classes, of what kinds of labor are good for men, raising them, and making them happy; by a determined sacrifice of such convenience, or beauty, or cheapness as is to be got only by the degradation of the workman; and by equally determined demand for the products and results of healthy and ennobling labor.

. . . .

1851-53

From MODERN PAINTERS

Part IV, Chapter VI

Of the True Ideal—First, Purist

Having thus glanced at the principal modes in which the imagination works for evil, we must rapidly note also the principal directions in which its operation is admissible, even in changing, or strangely combining what is brought within its sphere.

For hitherto we have spoken as if every change wilfully wrought by the imagination was an error; apparently implying that its only proper work was to summon up the memories of past events, and the anticipations of future ones, under aspects which would bear the sternest tests of historical investigation or abstract reasoning. And in general this is, indeed, its noblest work. Nevertheless, it has also permissible functions peculiarly its own, and certain rights of feigning, and adorning, and fancifully arranging, inalienable from its nature. Everything that is natural is, within certain limits, right; and we must take care not, in over-severity, to deprive ourselves of any refreshing or animating power ordained to be in us for our help.

(A) It was noted in speaking above of the Angelican [1] or passionate ideal, that there was a certain virtue in it dependent on the expression of its loving enthusiasm.

(B) In speaking of the pursuit of beauty as one of the characteristics of the highest art, it was also said that there were certain ways of showing this beauty by gathering together, without altering, the finest forms, and marking them by gentle emphasis.

(C) And in speaking of the true uses of imagination it was said that we might be allowed to create for ourselves, in innocent play, fairies and naiads and other such fictitious creatures.

Now this loving enthusiasm which seeks for a beauty fit to be the object of eternal love; this inventive skill which kindly displays what exists around us in the world; and this playful energy of thought which delights in various conditions of the impossible, are three forms of idealism more or less connected with the three tendencies of the artistical mind which I had occasion to explain in the chapter on the Nature of Gothic, in the *Stones of Venice.* It was there pointed out, that, the things around us containing mixed good and evil, certain men chose the good and left the evil (thence properly called Purists); others received both good and evil together (thence properly called Naturalists); and others had a tendency to choose the evil and leave the good, whom, for convenience' sake, I termed Sensualists. I do not mean to say that painters of fairies and naiads must belong to this last and lowest class, or habitually choose the evil and leave the good; but there is, nevertheless, a strange connection between the reinless play of the imagination, and a sense of the presence of

[1] so named by Ruskin because Fra Angelico, 1387-1455, famous for his paintings of angels, was "the central master of the school"

evil, which is usually more or less developed in those creations of the imagination to which we properly attach the word *Grotesque*.

For this reason, we shall find it convenient to arrange what we have to note respecting true idealism under the three heads—

A. Purist Idealism.
B. Naturalist Idealism.
C. Grotesque Idealism.

A. Purist Idealism—It results from the unwillingness of men whose dispositions are more than ordinarily tender and holy, to contemplate the various forms of definite evil which necessarily occur in the daily aspects of the world around them. They shrink from them as from pollution, and endeavor to create for themselves an imaginary state in which pain and imperfection either do not exist, or exist in some edgeless and enfeebled condition.

As, however, pain and imperfection are, by eternal laws, bound up with existence, so far as it is visible to us, the endeavor to cast them away invariably indicates a comparative childishness of mind, and produces a childish form of art. In general, the effort is most successful when it is most naïve, and when the ignorance of the draftsman is in some frank proportion to his innocence. For instance, one of the modes of treatment, the most conducive to this ideal expression, is simply drawing everything without shadows, as if the sun were everywhere at once. This, in the present state of our knowledge, we could not do with grace, because we could not do it without fear or shame. But an artist of the thirteenth century did it with no disturbance of conscience,—knowing no better, or rather, in some sense, we might say, knowing no worse. It is, however, evident, at the first thought, that all representations of nature without evil must either be ideals of a future world, or be false ideals, if they are understood to be representations of facts. They can only be classed among the branches of the true ideal, in so far as they are understood to be nothing more than expressions of the painter's personal affections or hopes.

Let us take one or two instances in order clearly to explain our meaning.

The life of Angelico was almost entirely spent in the endeavor to imagine the beings belonging to another world. By purity of life, habitual elevation of thought, and natural sweetness of disposition, he was enabled to express the sacred affections upon the human countenance as no one ever did before or since. In order to effect clearer distinction between heavenly beings and those of this world, he represents the former as clothed in draperies of the purest colors, crowned with glories of burnished gold, and entirely shadowless. With exquisite choice of gesture, and disposition of folds of drapery, this mode of treatment gives perhaps the best idea of spiritual beings which the human mind is capable of forming. It is, therefore, a true ideal; but the mode in which it is arrived at—being so far mechanical and contradictory of the appearances of nature—necessarily precludes those who practice it from being complete masters of their art. It is always childish, but beautiful in its childishness.

The works of our own Stothard [1] are examples of the operation of another mind, singular in gentleness and purity, upon mere worldly subject. It seems as if Stothard could not conceive wickedness, coarseness, or baseness; every one of his figures looks as if it had been copied from some creature who had never harbored an unkind thought, or permitted itself in an ignoble action. With this intense love of mental purity is joined, in Stothard, a love of mere physical smoothness and softness, so that he lived in a universe of soft grass and stainless fountains, tender trees, and stones at which no foot could stumble.

All this is very beautiful, and may sometimes urge us to an endeavor to make the world itself more like the conception of the painter. At least, in the midst of its malice, misery, and baseness, it is often a relief to glance at the graceful shadows, and take, for momentary companionship, creatures full only of love, gladness, and honor. But the perfect truth will at last vindicate itself against the partial truth; the help which we can gain from the unsubstantial vision will be only like that which we may sometimes receive, in weariness, from the scent of a flower or the passing of a breeze. For all firm aid, and steady use, we must look to harder realities; and, as far as the painter himself is regarded, we can only receive such work as the sign of an amiable imbecility. It is indeed ideal; but ideal as a fair dream is in the dawn of morning, before the faculties are astir. The apparent completeness of grace can never be attained without much definite falsification as well as omission; stones, over which we cannot stumble, must be ill-drawn stones; trees, which are all gentleness and softness, cannot be trees of wood; nor companies without evil in them, companies of flesh and

[1] Thomas Stothard, 1755-1834, is best known, perhaps, for his painting of the "Canterbury Pilgrims."

blood. The habit of falsification (with whatever aim) begins always in dullness and ends always in incapacity: nothing can be more pitiable than any endeavor by Stothard to express facts beyond his own sphere of soft pathos or graceful mirth, and nothing more unwise than the aim at a similar ideality by any painter who has power to render a sincerer truth.

I remember another interesting example of ideality on this same root, but belonging to another branch of it, in the works of a young German painter, which I saw some time ago in a London drawing-room. He had been traveling in Italy, and had brought home a portfolio of sketches remarkable alike for their fidelity and purity. Every one was a laborious and accurate study of some particular spot. Every cottage, every cliff, every tree, at the site chosen, had been drawn; and drawn with palpable sincerity of portraiture, and yet in such a spirit that it was impossible to conceive that any sin or misery had ever entered into one of the scenes he had represented; and the volcanic horrors of Radicofani,[1] the pestilent gloom of the Pontines,[2] and the boundless despondency of the Campagna[3] became, under his hand, only various appearances of Paradise.

It was very interesting to observe the minute emendations or omissions by which this was effected. To set the tiles the slightest degree more in order upon a cottage roof; to insist upon the vine leaves at the window, and let the shadow which fell from them naturally conceal the rent in the wall; to draw all the flowers in the foreground, and miss the weeds; to draw all the folds of the white clouds, and miss those of the black ones; to mark the graceful branches of the trees, and, in one way or another, beguile the eye from those which were ungainly; to give every peasant-girl whose face was visible the expression of an angel, and every one whose back was turned the bearing of a princess; finally to give a general look of light, clear organization, and serene vitality to every feature in the landscape—such were his artifices, and such his delights. It was impossible not to sympathize deeply with the spirit of such a painter; and it was just cause for gratitude to be permitted to travel, as it were, through Italy with such a friend. But his work had, nevertheless, its stern limitations and marks of everlasting inferiority. Always soothing and pathetic, it could never be sublime, never perfectly nor entrancingly beautiful; for the narrow spirit of correction could not cast itself fully into any scene; the calm cheerfulness which shrank from the shadow of the cypress, and the distortion of the olive, could not enter into the brightness of the sky that they pierced, nor the softness of the bloom that they bore. For every sorrow that his heart turned from, he lost a consolation; for every fear which he dared not confront, he lost a portion of his hardiness; the unsceptered sweep of the storm-clouds, the fair freedom of glancing shower and flickering sunbeam, sank into sweet rectitudes and decent formalisms; and, before eyes that refused to be dazzled or darkened, the hours of sunset wreathed their rays unheeded, and the mists of the Apennines spread their blue veils in vain.

To this inherent shortcoming and narrowness of reach the further defect was added, that this work gave no useful representation of the state of facts in the country which it pretended to contemplate. It was not only wanting in all the higher elements of beauty, but wholly unavailable for instruction of any kind beyond that which exists in pleasurableness of pure emotion. And considering what cost of labor was devoted to the series of drawings, it could not but be matter for grave blame, as well as for partial contempt, that a man of amiable feelings and considerable intellectual power should thus expend his life in the declaration of his own petty pieties and pleasant reveries, leaving the burden of human sorrow unwitnessed, and the power of God's judgments unconfessed; and, while poor Italy lay wounded and moaning at his feet, pass by, in priestly calm, lest the whiteness of his decent vesture should be spotted with unhallowed blood.

Of several other forms of Purism I shall have to speak hereafter, more especially of that exhibited in the landscapes of the early religious painters; but these examples are enough, for the present, to show the general principle that the purest ideal, though in some measure true, in so far as it springs from the true longings of an earnest mind, is yet necessarily in many things deficient or blamable, and *always* an indication of some degree of weakness in the mind pursuing it. But, on the other hand, it is to be noted that entire scorn of this purist ideal is the sign of a far greater weakness. Multitudes of petty artists, incapable of any

[1] a town in the province of Siena, Italy, situated on a hill at the foot of a basaltic rock
[2] a marshy region in central Italy
[3] The Roman Campagna. In his preface to the second edition of the first volume of *Modern Painters,* Ruskin has a remarkable description of this "wild and wasted plain."

noble sensation whatever, but acquainted, in a dim way, with the technicalities of the schools, mock at the art whose depths they cannot fathom, and whose motives they cannot comprehend, but of which they can easily detect the imperfections, and deride the simplicities. Thus poor, fumigatory Fuseli,[1] with an art composed of the tinsel of the stage and the panics of the nursery, speaks contemptuously of the name of Angelico as "dearer to sanctity than to art." And a large portion of the resistance to the noble pre-Raphaelite movement of our own days [2] has been offered by men who suppose the entire function of the artist in this world to consist in laying on color with a large brush, and surrounding dashes of flake white with bituminous brown; men whose entire capacities of brain, soul, and sympathy, applied industriously to the end of their lives, would not enable them, at last, to paint so much as one of the leaves of the nettles, at the bottom of Hunt's picture of the Light of the World. [3]

It is finally to be remembered, therefore, that Purism is always noble when it is *instinctive*. It is not the greatest thing that can be done, but it is probably the greatest thing that the man who does it can do, provided it comes from his heart. True, it is a sign of weakness, but it is not in our choice whether we will be weak or strong; and there is a certain strength which can only be made perfect in weakness. If he is working in humility, fear of evil, desire of beauty, and sincere purity of purpose and thought, he will produce good and helpful things; but he must be much on his guard against supposing himself to be greater than his fellows, because he has shut himself into this calm and cloistered sphere. His only safety lies in knowing himself to be, on the contrary, *less* than his fellows, and in always striving, so far as he can find it in his heart, to extend his delicate narrowness toward the great naturalist ideal. The whole group of modern German purists have lost themselves, because they founded their work not on humility, nor on religion, but on small self-conceit. Incapable of understanding the great Venetians, or any other masters of true, imaginative power, and having fed what mind they had with weak poetry and false philosophy, they thought themselves the best and greatest of artistic mankind, and expected to found a new school of painting in pious plagiarism and delicate pride. It is difficult at first to decide which is the more worthless, the spiritual affectation of the petty German, or the composition and chiaroscuro of the petty Englishman; on the whole, however, the latter have lightest weight, for the pseudo-religious painter must, at all events, pass much of his time in meditation upon solemn subjects, and in examining venerable models; and may sometimes even cast a little useful reflected light, or touch the heart with a pleasant echo.

1856

[1] A Swiss-English painter and art critic, 1741-1825; he had a powerful but ill-regulated fancy, being both a fantastic designer and a reckless colorist. Perhaps Ruskin means something like this by calling him "fumigatory," but his meaning is not clear.

[2] The movement led by Rossetti, Millais, and Hunt. Holman Hunt's well-known "Light of the World" (at Keble College, Oxford) represents Christ, a lantern in his hand, knocking at a door.

[3] "Not that the pre-Raphaelite is a purist movement, it is stern naturalist; but its unfortunate opposers, who neither know what nature is, nor what purism is, have mistaken the simple nature for morbid purism, and therefore cried out against it."—Ruskin's note.

DANTE GABRIEL ROSSETTI
1828-1882

Rossetti was a successful artist as well as a poet, the son of an Italian poet and artist, a political refugee living in London. There Rossetti was born, one of three members of the family who became eminent in verse. His academic training at King's College School was followed by the study of art at the Royal Academy. His young manhood was occupied with both painting and poetry, though later years brought forth only poetry.

In painting he produced the best-known pictures of the pre-Raphaelite school, characterized, in his view, by a truth to nature abandoned by the followers of Raphael. These are marked by their brilliancy of color, and by the symbolism that shows through an abundance of detail. In this respect they carry out the principles of Ruskin who was in sympathy with the school as a whole, and who greatly befriended Rossetti. Among his best known pictures are "Meeting of Dante and Beatrice" and "Dante's Dream."

In poetry Rossetti carries out the same principles that underlie his pictures. He often seems to conceive his poems first as paintings, and as closely as possible to represent colors and forms in his use of words.

Rossetti's life was made dark two years after his marriage by the death of his wife, whom he had made famous in his paintings. Great mental depression following this loss, and an unduly severe criticism of his poems by Robert Buchanan, produced insomnia which he attempted to relieve by using chloral. He became a victim of the drug and his last years were unhappy, though his mind seems to have been clear to the end.

Biography: A. C. Benson (EML), Knight (GW). Criticism: E. L. Cary, *The Rossettis,* 1907, Payne; *Pre-Raphaelitism and the Pre-Raphaelite Brotherhood,* Holman Hunt, 2 vols., 1905; "The Rossettis," F. J. Mather, Jr., *Bookm.* 49:139-47.

THE BLESSED DAMOZEL [1]

The blessed damozel leaned out
  From the gold bar of Heaven;
Her eyes were deeper than the depth
  Of waters stilled at even;
She had three lilies in her hand,
  And the stars in her hair were seven.

Her robe, ungirt from clasp to hem,
  No wrought flowers did adorn,
But a white rose of Mary's gift,
  For service meetly worn;
Her hair that lay along her back
  Was yellow like ripe corn.

Herseemed she scarce had been a day
  One of God's choristers;
The wonder was not yet quite gone
  From that still look of hers;
Albeit, to them she left, her day
  Had counted as ten years.

(To one, it is ten years of years.
  . . . Yet now, and in this place,
Surely she leaned o'er me—her hair
  Fell all about my face. . . .
Nothing: the autumn fall of leaves.
  The whole year sets apace.)

It was the rampart of God's house
  That she was standing on;
By God built over the sheer depth
  The which is Space begun;
So high, that looking downward thence
  She scarce could see the sun.

It lies in Heaven, across the flood
  Of ether, as a bridge.
Beneath, the tides of day and night
  With flames and darkness ridge
The void, as low as where this earth
  Spins like a fretful midge.

Around her, lovers, newly met
  'Mid deathless love's acclaims,
Spoke evermore among themselves
  Their heart-remembered names;
And the souls mounting up to God
  Went by her like thin flames.

And still she bowed herself and stooped
  Out of the circling charm;
Until her bosom must have made
  The bar she leaned on warm,
And the lilies lay as if asleep
  Along her bended arm.

From the fixed place of Heaven she saw
  Time like a pulse shake fierce
Through all the worlds. Her gaze still strove
  Within the gulf to pierce
Its path; and now she spoke as when
  The stars sang in their spheres.

The sun was gone now; the curled moon
  Was like a little feather
Fluttering far down the gulf; and now
  She spoke through the still weather.
Her voice was like the voice the stars
  Had when they sang together.

(Ah sweet! Even now, in that bird's song,
  Strove not her accents there,
Fain to be hearkened? When those bells
  Possessed the midday air,
Strove not her steps to reach my side
  Down all the echoing stair?)

"I wish that he were come to me,
  For he will come," she said.
"Have I not prayed in Heaven?—On earth,
  Lord, Lord, has he not prayed?
Are not two prayers a perfect strength?
  And shall I feel afraid?

"When round his head the aureole clings,
  And he is clothed in white,
I'll take his hand and go with him
  To the deep wells of light;
As unto a stream we will step down,
  And bathe there in God's sight.

"We two will stand beside that shrine,
  Occult, withheld, untrod,
Whose lamps are stirred continually
  With prayer sent up to God;
And see our old prayers, granted, melt
  Each like a little cloud.

"We two will lie i' the shadow of
  That living mystic tree
Within whose secret growth the Dove [2]
  Is sometimes felt to be,
While every leaf that His plumes touch
  Saith His Name audibly.

[1] Slight in substance as this poem is, it has two unusual sources of charm—a very definite pictorial character which stamps it as the work of a poet who was also a painter, and a mystical quality springing from an imagination that dared to portray earthly love in heavenly surroundings. Those who are interested in sources may consult Vergil, *Eclogue* v. 56; and Petrarch, Sonnets *In Morte di Madonna Laura* (to Laura in death), 74.

[2] The Dove typifies the third member of the Trinity, the Holy Spirit.

"And I myself will teach to him,
  I myself, lying so,
The songs I sing here; which his voice
  Shall pause in, hushed and slow,
And find some knowledge at each pause,
  Or some new thing to know."

(Alas! We two, we two, thou say'st!
  Yea, one wast thou with me
That once of old. But shall God lift
  To endless unity
The soul whose likeness with thy soul
  Was but its love for thee?)

"We two," she said, "will seek the groves
  Where the lady Mary is,
With her five handmaidens, whose names
  Are five sweet symphonies,
Cecily, Gertrude, Magdalen,
  Margaret, and Rosalys.

"Circlewise sit they, with bound locks
  And foreheads garlanded;
Into the fine cloth white like flame
  Weaving the golden thread,
To fashion the birth-robes for them
  Who are just born, being dead.

"He shall fear, haply, and be dumb;
  Then will I lay my cheek
To his, and tell about our love,
  Not once abashed or weak;
And the dear Mother will approve
  My pride, and let me speak.

"Herself shall bring us, hand in hand,
  To Him round whom all souls
Kneel, the clear-ranged unnumbered heads
  Bowed with their aureoles;
And angels meeting us shall sing
  To their citherns and citoles.

"There will I ask of Christ the Lord
  Thus much for him and me:—
Only to live as once on earth
  With Love, only to be,
As then awhile, forever now
  Together, I and he."

She gazed and listened and then said,
  Less sad of speech than mild—
"All this is when he comes." She ceased.
  The light thrilled toward her, filled
With angels in strong, level flight.
  Her eyes prayed, and she smiled.

(I saw her smile.) But soon their path
  Was vague in distant spheres:
And then she cast her arms along
  The golden barriers,
And laid her face between her hands,
  And wept. (I heard her tears.)

1850

SISTER HELEN[1]

"Why did you melt your waxen man,
    Sister Helen?
Today is the third since you began."
"The time was long, yet the time ran,
    Little brother."
  (O Mother, Mary Mother,
Three days today, between Hell and Heaven!)

"But if you have done your work aright,
    Sister Helen,
You'll let me play, for you said I might."
"Be very still in your play tonight,
    Little Brother."
  (O Mother, Mary Mother,
Third night, tonight, between Hell and Heaven!)

"You said it must melt ere vesper-bell,
    Sister Helen;
If now it be molten, all is well."
"Even so,—nay, peace! you cannot tell,
    Little brother."
  (O Mother, Mary Mother,
Oh, what is this, between Hell and Heaven?)

"Oh, the waxen knave was plump today,
    Sister Helen;
How like dead folk he has dropped away!"
"Nay now, of the dead what can you say,
    Little brother?"
  (O Mother, Mary Mother,
What of the dead, between Hell and Heaven?)

"See, see, the sunken pile of wood,
    Sister Helen,
Shines through the thinned wax red as blood!"
"Nay, now, when looked you yet on blood,
    Little brother?"
  (O Mother, Mary Mother,
How pale she is, between Hell and Heaven!)

[1] This ballad is founded on an old superstition. Holinshed, for example, tells a story of an attempt upon the life of King Duffe—how certain soldiers breaking into a house, "found one of the witches roasting upon a wooden broach an image of wax at the fire, resembling in each feature the king's person, . . . by which means it should have come to pass that when the wax was once clean consumed, the death of the king should immediately follow."

"Now close your eyes, for they're sick and sore,
Sister Helen,
And I'll play without the gallery door."
"Aye, let me rest,—I'll lie on the floor,
Little brother."
(O Mother, Mary Mother,
What rest tonight, between Hell and Heaven?)

"Here high up in the balcony,
Sister Helen,
The moon flies face to face with me."
"Aye, look and say whatever you see,
Little brother."
(O Mother, Mary Mother,
What sight tonight, between Hell and Heaven?)

"Outside it's merry in the wind's wake,
Sister Helen;
In the shaken trees the chill stars shake."
"Hush, heard you a horse-tread as you spake,
Little brother?"
(O Mother, Mary Mother,
What sound tonight, between Hell and Heaven?)

"I hear a horse-tread, and I see,
Sister Helen,
Three horsemen that ride terribly."
"Little brother, whence come the three,
Little brother?"
(O Mother, Mary Mother,
Whence should they come, between Hell and Heaven?)

"They come by the hill-verge from Boyne Bar,
Sister Helen,
And one draws nigh, but two are afar."
"Look, look, do you know them who they are,
Little brother?"
(O Mother, Mary Mother,
Who should they be, between Hell and Heaven?)

"Oh, it's Keith of Eastholm rides so fast,
Sister Helen,
For I know the white mane on the blast."
"The hour has come, has come at last,
Little brother!"
(O Mother, Mary Mother,
Her hour at last, between Hell and Heaven?)

"He has made a sign and called Halloo!
Sister Helen,
And he says that he would speak with you."
"Oh, tell him I fear the frozen dew,
Little brother."
(O Mother, Mary Mother,
Why laughs she thus, between Hell and Heaven?)

"The wind is loud, but I hear him cry,
Sister Helen,
That Keith of Ewern's like to die."
"And he and thou, and thou and I,
Little brother."
(O Mother, Mary Mother,
And they and we, between Hell and Heaven!)

"Three days ago, on his marriage morn,
Sister Helen,
He sickened, and lies since then forlorn."
"For bridegroom's side is the bride a thorn,
Little brother?"
(O Mother, Mary Mother,
Cold bridal cheer, between Hell and Heaven!)

"Three days and nights he has lain abed,
Sister Helen,
And he prays in torment to be dead."
"The thing may chance, if he have prayed,
Little brother!"
(O Mother, Mary Mother,
If we have prayed, between Hell and Heaven!)

"But he has not ceased to cry today,
Sister Helen,
That you should take your curse away."
"*My* prayer was heard,—he need but pray,
Little brother!"
(O Mother, Mary Mother,
Shall God not hear, between Hell and Heaven?)

"But he says, till you take back your ban,
Sister Helen,
His soul would pass, yet never can."
"Nay then, shall I slay a living man,
Little brother?"
(O Mother, Mary Mother,
A living soul, between Hell and Heaven!)

"But he calls forever on your name,
Sister Helen,
And says that he melts before a flame."
"My heart for his pleasure fared the same,
Little brother."
(O Mother, Mary Mother,
Fire at the heart, between Hell and Heaven!)

"Here's Keith of Westholm riding fast,
Sister Helen,
For I know the white plume on the blast."

"The hour, the sweet hour I forecast,
Little brother!"
(O Mother, Mary Mother,
Is the hour sweet, between Hell and Heaven?)

"He stops to speak, and he stills his horse,
Sister Helen;
But his words are drowned in the wind's course."
"Nay hear, nay hear, you must hear perforce,
Little brother!"
(O Mother, Mary Mother,
What word now heard, between Hell and Heaven?)

"Oh, he says that Keith of Ewern's cry,
Sister Helen,
Is ever to see you ere he die."
"In all that his soul sees, there am I,
Little brother!"
(O Mother, Mary Mother,
The soul's one sight, between Hell and Heaven!)

"He sends a ring and a broken coin,
Sister Helen,
And bids you mind the banks of Boyne."
"What else he broke will he ever join,
Little brother?"
(O Mother, Mary Mother,
No, never joined, between Hell and Heaven!)

"He yields you these and craves full fain,
Sister Helen,
You pardon him in his mortal pain."
"What else he took will he give again,
Little brother?"
(O Mother, Mary Mother,
Not twice to give, between Hell and Heaven!)

"He calls your name in an agony,
Sister Helen,
That even dead love must weep to see."
"Hate, born of love, is blind as he,
Little brother!"
(O Mother, Mary Mother,
Love turned to hate, between Hell and Heaven!)

"Oh, it's Keith of Keith now that rides fast,
Sister Helen,
For I know the white hair on the blast."
"The short, short hour will soon be past,
Little brother!"
(O Mother, Mary Mother,
Will soon be past, between Hell and Heaven!)

"He looks at me and he tries to speak,
Sister Helen,
But oh! his voice is sad and weak!"
"What here should the mighty baron seek,
Little brother?"
(O Mother, Mary Mother,
Is this the end, between Hell and Heaven?)

"Oh his son still cries, if you forgive,
Sister Helen,
The body dies, but the soul shall live."
"Fire shall forgive me as I forgive,
Little brother!"
(O Mother, Mary Mother,
As she forgives, between Hell and Heaven!)

"Oh he prays you, as his heart would rive,
Sister Helen,
To save his dear son's soul alive."
"Fire cannot slay it, it shall thrive,
Little brother!"
(O Mother, Mary Mother,
Alas, alas, between Hell and Heaven!)

"He cries to you, kneeling in the road,
Sister Helen,
To go with him for the love of God!"
"The way is long to his son's abode,
Little brother."
(O Mother, Mary Mother,
The way is long, between Hell and Heaven!)

"A lady's here, by a dark steed brought,
Sister Helen,
So darkly clad, I saw her not."
"See her now or never see aught,
Little brother!"
(O Mother, Mary Mother,
What more to see, between Hell and Heaven?)

"Her hood falls back, and the moon shines fair,
Sister Helen,
On the Lady of Ewern's golden hair."
"Blest hour of my power and her despair,
Little brother!"
(O Mother, Mary Mother,
Hour blest and banned, between Hell and Heaven?)

"Pale, pale her cheeks, that in pride did glow,
Sister Helen,
'Neath the bridal wreath three days ago."
"One morn for pride and three days for woe,
Little brother!"
(O Mother, Mary Mother,
Three days, three nights, between Hell and Heaven!)

"Her clasped hands stretch from her bending
head,
Sister Helen;
With the loud wind's wail her sobs are wed."
"What wedding-strains hath her bridal bed,
Little brother?"
(O Mother, Mary Mother,
What strain but death's, between Hell and
Heaven!)

"She may not speak, she sinks in a swoon,
Sister Helen,
She lifts her lips and gasps on the moon."
"Oh! might I but hear her soul's blithe tune,
Little brother!"
(O Mother, Mary Mother,
Her woe's dumb cry, between Hell and
Heaven!)

"They've caught her to Westholm's saddle-
bow,
Sister Helen,
And her moonlit hair gleams white in its flow."
"Let it turn whiter than winter snow,
Little brother!"
(O Mother, Mary Mother,
Woe-withered gold, between Hell and Heaven!)

"O Sister Helen, you heard the bell,
Sister Helen!
More loud than the vesper chime it fell."
"No vesper chime, but a dying knell,
Little brother!"
(O Mother, Mary Mother,
His dying knell, between Hell and Heaven!)

"Alas! but I fear the heavy sound,
Sister Helen;
Is it in the sky or in the ground?"
"Say, have they turned their horses round,
Little brother?"
(O Mother, Mary Mother,
What would she more, between Hell and
Heaven?)

"They have raised the old man from his knee,
Sister Helen,
And they ride in silence hastily."
"More fast the naked soul doth flee,
Little brother!"
(O Mother, Mary Mother,
The naked soul, between Hell and Heaven!)

"Flank to flank are the three steeds gone,
Sister Helen,
But the lady's dark steed goes alone."
"And lonely her bridegroom's soul hath flown,
Little brother."
(O Mother, Mary Mother,
The lonely ghost, between Hell and Heaven!)

"Oh the wind is sad in the iron chill,
Sister Helen,
And weary sad they look by the hill."
"But he and I are sadder still,
Little brother!"
(O Mother, Mary Mother,
Most sad of all, between Hell and Heaven!)

"See, see, the wax has dropped from its place,
Sister Helen,
And the flames are winning up apace!"
"Yet here they burn but for a space,
Little brother!"
(O Mother, Mary Mother,
Here for a space, between Hell and Heaven!)

"Ah! what white thing at the door has crossed,
Sister Helen?
Ah! what is this that sighs in the frost?"
"A soul that's lost as mine is lost,
Little brother!"
(O Mother, Mary Mother,
Lost, lost, all lost, between Hell and Heaven!)

1853-70

LA BELLA DONNA [1]

She wept, sweet lady,
And said in weeping:
"What spell is keeping
The stars so steady?
Why does the power
Of the sun's noon-hour
To sleep so move me?
And the moon in heaven,
Stained where she passes
As a worn-out glass is,—
Why walks she above me?

"Stars, moon, and sun, too,
I'm tired of either
And all together!
Whom speak they unto
That I should listen?
For very surely,
Though my arms and shoulders
Dazzle beholders,
And my eyes glisten,
All's nothing, purely!

[1] This is a translation, by Rossetti, of an Italian song (probably also written by him) found in his poem, *A Last Confession.* Though apparently little more than a skillful exercise in rime, it has a quality and portrays a mood not common in our literature.

What are words said for
At all about them,
If he they are made for
Can do without them?"

She laughed, sweet lady,
And said in laughing:
"His hand clings half in
My own already!
Oh! do you love me?
Oh! speak of passion
In no new fashion,
But the old sayings
You once said of me.

"You said: 'As summer,
Through boughs grown brittle,
Comes back a little
Ere frosts benumb her—
So bring'st thou to me
All leaves and flowers,
Though autumn's gloomy
Today in the bowers.'

"Oh! does he love me,
When my voice teaches
The very speeches
He then spoke of me?
Alas! what flavor
Still with me lingers—"
(But she laughed as my kisses
Glowed in her fingers
With love's old blisses)
"Oh! what one favor
Remains to woo him,
Whose whole poor savor
Belongs not to him?"

1870

THE WOODSPURGE

The wind flapped loose, the wind was still,
Shaken out dead from tree and hill:
I had walked on at the wind's will,—
I sat now, for the wind was still.

Between my knees my forehead was—
My lips, drawn in, said not Alas!
My hair was over in the grass,
My naked ears heard the day pass.

My eyes, wide open, had the run
Of some ten weeds to fix upon;
Among those few, out of the sun,
The woodspurge flowered, three cups in one.

From perfect grief there need not be
Wisdom or even memory:
One thing then learned remains to me,
The woodspurge has a cup of three.

1870

THE SONG OF THE BOWER

Say, is it day, is it dusk in thy bower,
Thou whom I long for, who longest for me?
Oh! be it light, be it night, 'tis Love's hour,
Love's that is fettered as Love's that is free.
Free love has leaped to that innermost chamber,
Oh! the last time, and the hundred before:
Fettered Love, motionless, can but remember,
Yet something that sighs from him passes the door.

Nay, but my heart when it flies to thy bower,
What does it find there that knows it again?
There it must droop like a shower-beaten flower.
Red at the rent core and dark with the rain.
Ah! yet what shelter is still shed above it—
What waters still image its leaves torn apart?
Thy soul is the shade that clings round it to love it,
And tears are its mirror deep down in thy heart.

What were my prize, could I enter the bower,
This day, tomorrow, at eve or at morn?
Large, lovely arms and a neck like a tower,
Bosom then heaving that now lies forlorn.
Kindled with love-breath (the sun's kiss is colder!),
Thy sweetness all near me, so distant today;
My hand round thy neck and thy hand on my shoulder,
My mouth to thy mouth as the world melts away.

What is it that keeps me afar from thy bower—
My spirit, my body, so fain to be there?
Waters engulfing or fires that devour?—
Earth heaped against me or death in the air?
Nay, but in day-dreams, for terror, for pity,
The trees wave their heads with an omen to tell;
Nay, but in night-dreams, throughout the dark city,
The hours, clashed together, lose count in the bell.

Shall I not one day remember thy bower,
One day when all days are one day to me?—
Thinking, "I stirred not, and yet had the power,"
Yearning, "Ah, God, if again it might be!"

Peace, peace! such a small lamp illumes, on this highway,
So dimly so few steps in front of my feet—
Yet shows me that her way is parted from my way. . . .
Out of sight, beyond light, at what goal may we meet?

1870

THE CLOUD CONFINES

The day is dark and the night
To him that would search their heart;
No lips of cloud that will part
Nor morning song in the light:
Only, gazing alone,
To him wild shadows are shown,
Deep under deep unknown
And height above unknown height.
Still we say as we go—
"Strange to think by the way,
Whatever there is to know,
That shall we know one day."

The Past is over and fled;
Named new, we name it the old;
Thereof some tale hath been told,
But no word comes from the dead;
Whether at all they be,
Or whether as bond or free,
Or whether they too were we,
Or by what spell they have sped.
Still we say as we go—
"Strange to think by the way,
Whatever there is to know,
That shall we know one day."

What of the heart of hate
That beats in thy breast, O Time?
Red strife from the furthest prime,
And anguish of fierce debate;
War that shatters her slain,
And peace that grinds them as grain,
And eyes fixed ever in vain
On the pitiless eyes of Fate.
Still we say as we go,—
"Strange to think by the way,
Whatever there is to know,
That shall we know one day."

What of the heart of love
That bleeds in thy breast, O Man?
Thy kisses snatched 'neath the ban
Of fangs that mock them above;
Thy bells prolonged unto knells,
Thy hope that a breath dispels,
Thy bitter forlorn farewells
And the empty echoes thereof?
Still we say as we go—
"Strange to think by the way,
Whatever there is to know,
That shall we know one day."

The sky leans dumb on the sea,
Aweary with all its wings;
And oh! the song the sea sings
Is dark everlastingly.
Our past is clean forgot,
Our present is and is not,
Our future's a sealed seedplot,
And what betwixt them are we?—
We who say as we go—
"Strange to think by the way,
Whatever there is to know,
That shall we know one day."

1872

From THE HOUSE OF LIFE[1]

THE SONNET

A Sonnet is a moment's monument—
Memorial from the Soul's eternity
To one dead deathless hour. Look that it be,
Whether for lustral rite or dire portent,
Of its own arduous fullness reverent:
Carve it in ivory or in ebony,
As Day or Night may rule; and let Time see
Its flowering crest impearled and orient.
A Sonnet is a coin. Its face reveals
The Soul,—its converse, to what Power 'tis due:—
Whether for tribute to the august appeals
Of Life, or dower in Love's high retinue,
It serve; or 'mid the dark wharf's cavernous breath,
In Charon's palm it pay the toll to Death.

IV. LOVESIGHT

When do I see thee most, beloved one?
When in the light the spirits of mine eyes
Before thy face, their altar, solemnize
The worship of that Love through thee made known?
Or when in the dusk hours (we two alone)
Close-kissed and eloquent of still replies
Thy twilight-hidden, glimmering visage lies,
And my soul only sees thy soul its own?

[1] The "house of life" was the first of the twelve divisions of the heavens made by old astrologers in casting the horoscope of a man's destiny. This series of a hundred and one sonnets is a faithful record, drawn from Rossetti's own inward experience, "of the mysterious conjunctions and oppositions wrought by Love, Change, and Fate in the House of Life."

O love, my love! If I no more should see
Thyself, nor on the earth the shadow of thee,
Nor image of thine eyes in any spring—
How then should sound upon Life's darkening slope
The ground-whirl of the perished leaves of Hope,
The wind of Death's imperishable wing?

XIX. Silent Noon

Your hands lie open in the long fresh grass,
The finger-points look through like rosy blooms;
Your eyes smile peace. The pasture gleams and glooms
'Neath billowing skies that scatter and amass.
All round our nest, far as the eye can pass,
Are golden kingcup-fields with silver edge
Where the cow-parsley skirts the hawthorn hedge.
'Tis visible silence, still as the hourglass.
Deep in the sun-searched growths the dragon fly
Hangs like a blue thread loosened from the sky:—
So this wing'd hour is dropped to us from above.
Oh! clasp we to our hearts, for deathless dower,
This close-companioned, inarticulate hour
When twofold silence was the song of love.

XLIX—LII. Willowwood

I

I sat with Love upon a woodside well,
Leaning across the water, I and he;
Nor ever did he speak nor looked at me,
But touched his lute wherein was audible
The certain secret thing he had to tell:
Only our mirrored eyes met silently
In the low wave; and that sound came to be
The passionate voice I knew; and my tears fell.
And at their fall, his eyes beneath grew hers;
And with his foot and with his wing-feathers
He swept the spring that watered my heart's drouth.
Then the dark ripples spread to waving hair,
And as I stooped, her own lips rising there
Bubbled with brimming kisses at my mouth.

II

And now Love sang. But his was such a song,
So meshed with half-remembrance hard to free,
As souls disused in death's sterility
May sing when the new birthday tarries long.
And I was made aware of a dumb throng
That stood aloof, one form by every tree,
All mournful forms, for each was I or she,
The shades of those our days that had no tongue.
They looked on us, and knew us and were known;
While fast together, alive from the abyss,
Clung the soul-wrung implacable close kiss;
And pity of self through all made broken moan
Which said, "For once, for once, for once alone!"
And still Love sang, and what he sang was this:—

III

"O ye, all ye that walk in Willowwood,
That walk with hollow faces burning white;
What fathom-depth of soul-struck widowhood,
What long, what longer hours, one life-long night,
Ere ye again, who so in vain have wooed
Your last hope lost, who so in vain invite
Your lips to that their unforgotten food,
Ere ye, ere ye again shall see the light!
Alas! the bitter banks in Willowwood,
With tear-spurge wan, with blood-wort burning red:
Alas! if ever such a pillow could
Steep deep the soul in sleep till she were dead—
Better all life forget her than this thing,
That Willowwood should hold her wandering!"

IV

So sang he: and as meeting rose and rose
Together cling through the wind's wellaway[1]
Nor change at once, yet near the end of day
The leaves drop loosened where the heart-stain glows—
So when the song died did the kiss unclose;
And her face fell back drowned, and was as gray
As its gray eyes; and if it ever may
Meet mine again I know not if Love knows.
Only I know that I leaned low and drank
A long draught from the water where she sank,
Her breath and all her tears and all her soul;
And as I leaned, I know I felt Love's face
Pressed on my neck with moan of pity and grace,
Till both our heads were in his aureole.

LXV. Known in Vain

As two whose love, first foolish, widening scope,
Knows suddenly, to music high and soft,
The Holy of holies; who because they scoffed
Are now amazed with shame, nor dare to cope
With the whole truth aloud, lest heaven should ope;

[1] an archaic expression of grief

Yet, at their meetings, laugh not as they
laughed
In speech; nor speak, at length; but sitting oft
Together, within hopeless sight of hope
For hours are silent:—so it happeneth
When Work and Will awake too late, to gaze
After their life sailed by, and hold their breath.
Ah! who shall dare to search through what sad
maze
Thenceforth their incommunicable ways
Follow the desultory feet of Death?

LXVI. The Heart of the Night

From child to youth; from youth to arduous
man;
From lethargy to fever of the heart;
From faithful life to dream-dowered days
apart;
From trust to doubt; from doubt to brink of
ban—
Thus much of change in one swift cycle ran
Till now. Alas, the soul!—how soon must she
Accept her primal immortality—
The flesh resume its dust whence it began?
O Lord of work and peace! O Lord of life!
O Lord, the awful Lord of will! Though late,
Even yet renew this soul with duteous breath:
That when the peace is garnered in from strife,
The work retrieved, the will regenerate,
This soul may see thy face, O Lord of death!

LXVII. The Landmark

Was *that* the landmark? What—the foolish
well
Whose wave, low down, I did not stoop to
drink,
But sat and flung the pebbles from its brink
In sport to send its imaged skies pell-mell
(And mine own image, had I noted well!)—
Was that my point of turning?—I had thought
The stations of my course should rise unsought,
As altar-stone or ensigned citadel.
But lo! the path is missed, I must go back,
And thirst to drink when next I reach the
spring
Which once I stained, which since may have
grown black.
Yet though no light be left nor bird now sing
As here I turn, I'll thank God, hastening,
That the same goal is still on the same track.

LXX. The Hill Summit

This feast-day of the sun, his altar there
In the broad west has blazed for vesper-song;
And I have loitered in the vale too long
And gaze now a belated worshiper.
Yet may I not forget that I was 'ware,
So journeying, of his face at intervals
Transfigured where the fringed horizon falls,—
A fiery bush with coruscating hair.
And now that I have climbed and won this
height,
I must tread downward through the sloping
shade
And travel the bewildered tracks till night.
Yet for this hour I still may here be stayed
And see the gold air and the silver fade
And the last bird fly into the last light.

LXXIX. The Monochord [1]

Is it this sky's vast vault or ocean's sound
That is Life's self and draws my life from me,
And by instinct ineffable decree
Holds my breath quailing on the bitter bound?
Nay, is it Life or Death, thus thunder-crowned,
That 'mid the tide of all emergency
Now notes my separate wave, and to what sea
Its difficult eddies labor in the ground?
Oh! what is this that knows the road I came,
The flame turned cloud, the cloud returned to
flame,
The lifted shifted steeps and all the way?—
That draws round me at last this wind-warm
space,
And in regenerate rapture turns my face
Upon the devious coverts of dismay?

1870-81

CHRISTINA ROSSETTI
1830-1894

Christina Rossetti was two years younger than her brother, Dante Gabriel. She was educated in the home circle, and her entire life was spent in domestic seclusion. Her native genius responded to the stimulating influences of her brothers and their friends and she began early to write poems for periodicals produced by members of their artistic group. Her *Goblin Market and Other Poems* appeared in 1862, *The Prince's Progress* four years later, and *Pageant and Other Poems* in 1881.

Many critics have placed Miss Rossetti foremost among the English women poets of the nineteenth century. It is with Mrs. Browning that she comes into closest rivalry. Her range of subjects is narrower than Mrs. Browning's and more carefully wrought, with a clearness of image like that found in her brother's work both as poet

[1] a musical instrument of one string, hence, unity, harmony: here apparently used to symbolize the ultimate merging of separate lives into one Life

and painter. Her religious poems are most characteristic of her; their rare quality gives her a place with the foremost religious poets of the seventeenth century, Herbert and Crashaw.

Criticism: More (Shel. 3); "Character of C. Rossetti," F. M. Hueffer, *Fortn.* 95:422-29, an able estimate; "Santa Christina," K. Tynan, *Liv. Age* 272:431-36, an interesting personal appreciation.

GOBLIN MARKET[1]

Morning and evening
Maids heard the goblins cry:
"Come buy our orchard fruits,
Come buy, come buy:
Apples and quinces,
Lemons and oranges,
Plump unpecked cherries,
Melons and raspberries,
Bloom-down-cheeked peaches,
Swart-headed mulberries,
Wild free-born cranberries,
Crab apples, dewberries,
Pineapples, blackberries,
Apricots, strawberries—
All ripe together
In summer weather—
Morns that pass by,
Fair eves that fly;
Come buy, come buy:
Our grapes fresh from the vine,
Pomegranates full and fine,
Dates and sharp bullaces,
Rare pears and greengages,
Damsons and bilberries,
Taste them and try:
Currants and gooseberries,
Bright-fire-like barberries,
Figs to fill your mouth,
Citrons from the South,
Sweet to tongue and sound to eye;
Come buy, come buy."

Evening by evening
Among the brook-side rushes,
Laura bowed her head to hear,
Lizzie veiled her blushes:
Crouching close together
In the cooling weather,
With clasping arms and cautioning lips,
With tingling cheeks and finger tips.
"Lie close," Laura said,
Pricking up her golden head:
"We must not look at goblin men,
We must not buy their fruits:
Who knows upon what soil they fed
Their hungry, thirsty roots?"
"Come buy," call the goblins
Hobbling down the glen.
"Oh," cried Lizzie, "Laura, Laura,
You should not peep at goblin men."
Lizzie covered up her eyes,
Covered close lest they should look;
Laura reared her glossy head,
And whispered like the restless brook:
"Look, Lizzie, look, Lizzie,
Down the glen tramp little men.
One hauls a basket,
One bears a plate,
One lugs a golden dish
Of many pounds' weight
How fair the vine must grow
Whose grapes are so luscious;
How warm the wind must blow
Through those fruit bushes."
"No," said Lizzie; "No, no, no;
Their offers should not charm us,
Their evil gifts would harm us."
She thrust a dimpled finger
In each ear, shut eyes and ran:
Curious Laura chose to linger
Wondering at each merchant man.
One had a cat's face,
One whisked a tail,
One tramped at a rat's pace,
One crawled like a snail,
One like a wombat[2] prowled obtuse and furry,
One like a ratel[3] tumbled hurry skurry.
She heard a voice like voice of doves
Cooing all together:
They sounded kind and full of loves
In the pleasant weather.

Laura stretched her gleaming neck
Like a rush-imbedded swan,
Like a lily from the beck,[4]
Like a moonlit poplar branch,
Like a vessel at the launch
When its last restraint is gone.

Backward up the mossy glen
Turned and trooped the goblin men,

[1] Of this poem, William M. Rossetti, Christina's brother, writes: "I have more than once heard Christina say that she did not mean anything profound by this fairy tale—it is not a moral apologue consistently carried out in detail. Still the incidents are . . . suggestive, and different minds may be likely to read different messages into them." He remarks further that the central point of the story, read merely as a story, is often missed. Lizzie's service to her sister lies in procuring for her a *second* taste of the goblin fruits, such as those who have once tasted them ever afterwards long for, and pine away with longing, but which the goblins themselves will not voluntarily accord.

[2] an Australian marsupial, something like a small bear
[3] a honey-badger; a nocturnal animal
[4] brook; see Shelley's "To A Skylark"

With their shrill repeated cry,
"Come buy, come buy."
When they reached where Laura was
They stood stock still upon the moss,
Leering at each other,
Brother with queer brother;
Signaling each other,
Brother with sly brother.
One set his basket down,
One reared his plate;
One began to weave a crown
Of tendrils, leaves, and rough nuts brown
(Men sell not such in any town);
One heaved the golden weight
Of dish and fruit to offer her:
"Come buy, come buy," was still their cry.
Laura stared but did not stir,
Longed but had no money.
The whisk-tailed merchant bade her taste
In tones as smooth as honey,
The cat-faced purred,
The rat-paced spoke a word
Of welcome, and the snail-paced even was heard;
One parrot-voiced and jolly
Cried "Pretty Goblin" still for "Pretty Polly";
One whistled like a bird.

But sweet-tooth Laura spoke in haste:
"Good Folk, I have no coin;
To take were to purloin:
I have no copper in my purse,
I have no silver either,
And all my gold is on the furze
That shakes in windy weather
Above the rusty heather."
"You have much gold upon your head,"
They answered all together:
"Buy from us with a golden curl."
She clipped a precious golden lock,
She dropped a tear more rare than pearl,
Then sucked their fruit globes fair or red.
Sweeter than honey from the rock,
Stronger than man-rejoicing wine,
Clearer than water flowed that juice;
She never tasted such before,
How should it cloy with length of use?
She sucked and sucked and sucked the more
Fruits which that unknown orchard bore;
She sucked until her lips were sore;
Then flung the emptied rinds away
But gathered up one kernel stone,
And knew not was it night or day
As she turned home alone.

Lizzie met her at the gate
Full of wise upbraidings:
"Dear, you should not stay so late,
Twilight is not good for maidens;
Should not loiter in the glen
In the haunts of goblin men.
Do you not remember Jeanie,
How she met them in the moonlight,
Took their gifts both choice and many,
Ate their fruits and wore their flowers
Plucked from bowers
Where summer ripens at all hours?
But ever in the moonlight
She pined and pined away;
Sought them by night and day,
Found them no more, but dwindled and grew gray;
Then fell with the first snow,
While to this day no grass will grow
Where she lies low:
I planted daisies there a year ago
That never blow.
You should not loiter so."
"Nay, hush," said Laura,
"Nay, hush, my sister:
I ate and ate my fill,
Yet my mouth waters still:
Tomorrow night I will
Buy more"; and kissed her.
"Have done with sorrow;
I'll bring you plums tomorrow
Fresh on their mother twigs,
Cherries worth getting;
You cannot think what figs
My teeth have met in,
What melons icy-cold
Piled on a dish of gold
Too huge for me to hold,
What peaches with a velvet nap,
Pellucid grapes without one seed:
Odorous indeed must be the mead
Whereon they grow, and pure the wave they drink
With lilies at the brink,
And sugar-sweet their sap."

Golden head by golden head,
Like two pigeons in one nest
Folded in each other's wings,
They lay down in their curtained bed:
Like two blossoms on one stem,
Like two flakes of new-fallen snow,
Like two wands of ivory
Tipped with gold for awful kings.
Moon and stars gazed in at them,
Wind sang to them lullaby,
Lumbering owls forebore to fly,
Not a bat flapped to and fro
Round their nest:
Cheek to cheek and breast to breast
Locked together in one nest.

Early in the morning
When the first cock crowed his warning,
Neat like bees, as sweet and busy,
Laura rose with Lizzie;
Fetched in honey, milked the cows,
Aired and set to rights the house,
Kneaded cakes of whitest wheat,
Cakes for dainty mouths to eat,
Next churned butter, whipped up cream,
Fed their poultry, sat and sewed;
Talked as modest maidens should:
Lizzie with an open heart,
Laura in an absent dream,
One content, one sick in part;
One warbling for the mere bright day's delight,
One longing for the night.

At length slow evening came:
They went with pitchers to the reedy brook;
Lizzie most placid in her look,
Laura most like a leaping flame.
They drew the gurgling water from its deep.
Lizzie plucked purple and rich golden flags,
Then turning homeward said: "The sunset flushes
Those farthest, loftiest crags;
Come, Laura, not another maiden lags.
No willful squirrel wags,
The beasts and birds are fast asleep."

But Laura loitered still among the rushes,
And said the bank was steep,
And said the hour was early still,
The dew not fallen, the wind not chill;
Listening ever, but not catching
The customary cry,
"Come buy, come buy,"
With its iterated jingle
Of sugar-baited words:
Not for all her watching
Once discerning even one goblin
Racing, whisking, tumbling, hobbling—
Let alone the herds
That used to tramp along the glen,
In groups or single,
Of brisk fruit-merchant men.

Till Lizzie urged, "O Laura, come;
I hear the fruit-call, but I dare not look:
You should not loiter longer at this brook;
Come with me home.
The stairs rise, the moon bends her arc,
Each glowworm winks her spark,
Let us go home before the night grows dark;
For clouds may gather
Though this is summer weather,
Put out the lights and drench us through;
Then if we lost our way what should we do?"

Laura turned cold as stone
To find her sister heard that cry alone,
That goblin cry,
"Come buy our fruits, come buy."
Must she then buy no more such dainty fruit?
Must she no more such succous pasture [1] find,
Gone deaf and blind?
Her tree of life drooped from the root:
She said not one word in her heart's sore ache:
But peering through the dimness, nought discerning,
Trudged home, her pitcher dripping all the way;
So crept to bed, and lay
Silent till Lizzie slept;
Then sat up in a passionate yearning,
And gnashed her teeth for balked desire, and wept
As if her heart would break.

Day after day, night after night,
Laura kept watch in vain
In sullen silence of exceeding pain.
She never caught again the goblin cry,
"Come buy, come buy";
She never spied the goblin men
Hawking their fruits along the glen:
But when the noon waxed bright
Her hair grew thin and gray;
She dwindled, as the fair full moon doth turn
To swift decay and burn
Her fire away.

One day remembering her kernel-stone
She set it by a wall that faced the south;
Dewed it with tears, hoped for a root,
Watched for a waxing shoot,
But there came none.
It never saw the sun,
It never felt the trickling moisture run:
While with sunk eyes and faded mouth
She dreamed of melons, as a traveler sees
False waves in desert drouth
With shade of leaf-crowned trees,
And burns the thirstier in the sandful breeze.

She no more swept the house,
Tended the fowls or cows,
Fetched honey, kneaded cakes of wheat,
Brought water from the brook;
But sat down listless in the chimney nook
And would not eat.

Tender Lizzie could not bear
To watch her sister's cankerous care,
Yet not to share.

[1] juicy feasting

She night and morning
Caught the goblin's cry:
"Come buy our orchard fruits,
Come buy, come buy":—
Beside the brook, along the glen,
She heard the tramp of goblin men,
The voice and stir
Poor Laura could not hear;
Longed to buy fruit to comfort her,
But feared to pay too dear.
She thought of Jeanie in her grave,
Who should have been a bride;
But who for joys brides hope to have
Fell sick and died
In her gay prime,
In earliest winter time,
With the first glazing rime
With the first snowfall of crisp winter time.

Till Laura dwindling
Seemed knocking at Death's door.
Then Lizzie weighed no more
Better and worse;
But put a silver penny in her purse,
Kissed Laura, crossed the heath with clumps
of furze
At twilight, halted by the brook:
And for the first time in her life
Began to listen and look.

Laughed every goblin
When they spied her peeping:
Came toward her hobbling,
Flying, running, leaping,
Puffing and blowing,
Chuckling, clapping, crowing,
Clucking and gobbling,
Mopping and mowing,[1]
Full of airs and graces.
Pulling wry faces,
Demure grimaces,
Cat-like and rat-like,
Ratel- and wombat-like,
Snail-paced in a hurry,
Parrot-voiced and whistler,
Helter skelter, hurry skurry,
Chattering like magpies,
Fluttering like pigeons,
Gliding like fishes—
Hugged her and kissed her,
Squeezed and caressed her,
Stretched up their dishes,
Panniers and plates:
"Look at our apples
Russet and dun,
Bob at our cherries,
Bite at our peaches,
Citrons and dates,
Grapes for the asking,
Pears red with basking
Out in the sun,
Plums on their twigs;
Pluck them and suck them—
Pomegranates, figs."

"Good folk," said Lizzie,
Mindful of Jeanie,
"Give me much and many":
Held out her apron,
Tossed them her penny.
"Nay, take a seat with us,
Honor and eat with us,"
They answered, grinning:
"Our feast is but beginning.
Night yet is early,
Warm and dew-pearly,
Wakeful and starry:
Such fruits as these
No man can carry;
Half their bloom would fly,
Half their dew would dry,
Half their flavor would pass by.
Sit down and feast with us,
Be welcome guest with us,
Cheer you and rest with us."—
"Thank you," said Lizzie, "But one waits
At home alone for me:
So without further parleying,
If you will not sell me any
Of your fruits though much and many,
Give me back my silver penny
I tossed you for a fee."—
They began to scratch their pates,
No longer wagging, purring,
But visibly demurring,
Grunting and snarling.
One called her proud,
Cross-grained, uncivil;
Their tones waxed loud,
Their looks were evil.
Lashing their tails
They trod and hustled her,
Elbowed and jostled her,
Clawed with their nails,
Barking, mewing, hissing, mocking,
Tore her gown and soiled her stocking,
Twitched her hair out by the roots,
Stamped upon her tender feet,
Held her hands and squeezed their fruits
Against her mouth to make her eat.

White and golden Lizzie stood,
Like a lily in a flood,—

[1] See *The Tempest,* IV, i, 47, and note 10, p. 201.

Like a rock of blue-veined stone
Lashed by tides obstreperously—
Like a beacon left alone
In a hoary, roaring sea,
Sending up a golden fire,—
Like a fruit-crowned orange tree
White with blossoms honey-sweet
Sore beset by wasp and bee—
Like a royal virgin town
Topped with gilded dome and spire
Close beleaguered by a fleet
Mad to tug her standard down.

One may lead a horse to water,
Twenty cannot make him drink.
Though the goblins cuffed and caught her,
Coaxed and fought her,
Bullied and besought her,
Scratched her, pinched her black as ink,
Kicked and knocked her,
Mauled and mocked her,
Lizzie uttered not a word;
Would not open lip from lip
Lest they should cram a mouthful in:
But laughed in heart to feel the drip
Of juice that siruped all her face,
And lodged in dimples of her chin,
And streaked her neck which quaked like curd.
At last the evil people,
Worn out by her resistance,
Flung back her penny, kicked their fruit
Along whichever road they took,
Not leaving root or stone or shoot;
Some writhed into the ground,
Some dived into the brook
With ring and ripple,
Some scudded on the gale without a sound,
Some vanished in the distance.

In a smart, ache, tingle,
Lizzie went her way;
Knew not was it night or day;
Sprang up the bank, tore through the furze,
Threaded copse and dingle,
And heard her penny jingle
Bouncing in her purse—
Its bounce was music to her ear.
She ran and ran
As if she feared some goblin man
Dogged her with gibe or curse
Or something worse;
But not one goblin skurried after,
Nor was she pricked by fear;
The kind heart made her windy-paced
That urged her home quite out of breath with
haste
And inward laughter.

She cried, "Laura," up the garden,
"Did you miss me?
Come and kiss me.
Never mind my bruises,
Hug me, kiss me, suck my juices
Squeezed from goblin fruits for you,
Goblin pulp and goblin dew.
Eat me, drink me, love me;
Laura, make much of me;
For your sake I have braved the glen
And had to do with goblin merchant men."

Laura started from her chair,
Flung her arms up in the air,
Clutched her hair:
"Lizzie, Lizzie, have you tasted
For my sake the fruit forbidden?
Must your light like mine be hidden,
Your young life like mine be wasted,
Undone in mine undoing,
And ruined in my ruin,
Thirsty, cankered, goblin-ridden?"
She clung about her sister,
Kissed and kissed and kissed her.
Tears once again
Refreshed her shrunken eyes,
Dropping like rain
After long sultry drouth;
Shaking with aguish fear, and pain,
She kissed and kissed her with a hungry mouth.

Her lips began to scorch,
That juice was wormwood to her tongue,
She loathed the feast:
Writhing as one possessed she leaped and sung,
Rent all her robe, and wrung
Her hands in lamentable haste,
And beat her breast.
Her locks streamed like the torch
Borne by a racer at full speed,
Or like the mane of horses in their flight,
Or like an eagle when she stems the light
Straight toward the sun,
Or like a caged thing freed,
Or like a flying flag when armies run.

Swift fire spread through her veins, knocked
at her heart,
Met the fire smoldering there
And overbore its lesser flame;
She gorged on bitterness without a name:
Ah, fool, to choose such part
Of soul-consuming care!
Sense failed in the mortal strife:
Like the watchtower of a town
Which an earthquake shatters down,
Like a lightning-stricken mast,

Like a wind-uprooted tree
Spun about,
Like a foam-topped waterspout
Cast down headlong in the sea,
She fell at last;
Pleasure past and anguish past.
Is it death or is it life?

Life out of death.
That night long, Lizzie watched by her,
Counted her pulse's flagging stir,
Felt for her breath,
Held water to her lips, and cooled her face
With tears and fanning leaves.
But when the first birds chirped about their eaves,
And early reapers plodded to the place
Of golden sheaves,
And dew-wet grass
Bowed in the morning winds so brisk to pass,
And new buds with new day
Opened of cup-like lilies on the stream,
Laura awoke as from a dream,
Laughed in the innocent old way,
Hugged Lizzie but not twice or thrice;
Her gleaming locks showed not one thread of gray,
Her breath was sweet as May,
And light danced in her eyes.

Days, weeks, months, years
Afterwards, when both were wives
With children of their own;
Their mother-hearts beset with fears,
Their lives bound up in tender lives;
Laura would call the little ones
And tell them of her early prime,
Those pleasant days long gone
Of not-returning time:
Would talk about the haunted glen,
The wicked, quaint fruit-merchant men,
Their fruits like honey to the throat
But poison in the blood—
Men sell not such in any town—
Would tell them how her sister stood
In deadly peril to do her good,
And win the fiery antidote:
Then joining hands to little hands
Would bid them cling together—
"For there is no friend like a sister
In calm or stormy weather;
To cheer one on the tedious way,
To fetch one if one goes astray,
To lift one if one totters down,
To strengthen whilst one stands."

1862

THE THREE ENEMIES

THE FLESH

"Sweet, thou art pale."
"More pale to see,
Christ hung upon the cruel tree
And bore His Father's wrath for me."

"Sweet, thou art sad."
"Beneath a rod
More heavy, Christ for my sake trod
The winepress of the wrath of God."

"Sweet, thou art weary."
"Not so Christ;
Whose mighty love of me sufficed
For Strength, Salvation, Eucharist."

"Sweet, thou art footsore."
"If I bleed,
His feet have bled; yea in my need
His Heart once bled for mine indeed."

THE WORLD

"Sweet, thou art young."
"So He was young
Who for my sake in silence hung
Upon the Cross with Passion wrung."

"Look, thou art fair."
"He was more fair
Than men, Who deigned for me to wear
A visage marred beyond compare."

"And thou hast riches."
"Daily bread—
All else is His: Who, living, dead,
For me lacked where to lay His Head."

"And life is sweet."
"It was not so
To Him, Whose Cup did overflow
With mine unutterable woe."

THE DEVIL

"Thou drinkest deep."
"When Christ would sup
He drained the dregs from out my cup;
So how should I be lifted up?"

"Thou shalt win Glory."
"In the skies,
Lord Jesus, cover up mine eyes
Lest they should look on vanities."

"Thou shalt have knowledge."
"Helpless dust!
In Thee, O Lord, I put my trust;
Answer Thou for me, Wise and Just."

"And Might"—
"Get thee behind me. Lord,
Who hast redeemed and not abhorred
My soul, oh, keep it by Thy Word."

1851 1862

AN APPLE GATHERING

I plucked pink blossoms from mine apple tree
And wore them all that evening in my hair:
Then in due season when I went to see
I found no apples there.

With dangling basket all along the grass
As I had come I went the selfsame track:
My neighbors mocked me while they saw me pass
So empty-handed back.

Lilian and Lilias smiled in trudging by,
Their heaped-up basket teased me like a jeer;
Sweet-voiced they sang beneath the sunset sky,
Their mother's home was near.

Plump Gertrude passed me with her basket full,
A stronger hand than hers helped it along;
A voice talked with her through the shadows cool
More sweet to me than song.

Ah Willie, Willie, was my love less worth
Than apples with their green leaves piled above?
I counted rosiest apples on the earth
Of far less worth than love.

So once it was with me you stooped to talk
Laughing and listening in this very lane;
To think that by this way we used to walk
We shall not walk again!

I let my neighbors pass me, ones and twos
And groups; the latest said the night grew chill,
And hastened: but I loitered; while the dews
Fell fast I loitered still.

1857 1861

MONNA INNOMINATA[1]

1

Come back to me, who wait and watch for you:—
Or come not yet, for it is over then,
And long it is before you come again,
So far between my pleasures are, and few.
While, when you come not, what I do I do
Thinking "Now when he comes," my sweetest "when."
For one man is my world of all the men
This wide world holds; O love, my world is you.
Howbeit, to meet you grows almost a pang
Because the pang of parting comes so soon;
My hope hangs waning, waxing, like a moon
Between the heavenly days on which we meet:
Ah me, but where are now the songs I sang
When life was sweet because you called them sweet?

2

I wish I could remember that first day,
First hour, first moment of your meeting me,
If bright or dim the season—it might be
Summer or Winter for aught I can say;
So unrecorded did it slip away,
So blind was I to see and to foresee,
So dull to mark the budding of my tree
That would not blossom yet for many a May.
If only I could recollect it, such
A day of days! I let it come and go
As traceless as a thaw of bygone snow;
It seemed to mean so little, meant so much;
If only now I could recall that touch,
First touch of hand in hand—Did one but know!

11

Many in aftertimes will say of you
"He loved her"—while of me what will they say?
Not that I loved you more than just in play,
For fashion's sake as idle women do.
Even let them prate; who know not what we knew
Of love and parting in exceeding pain,
Of parting hopeless here to meet again,
Hopeless on earth, and heaven is out of view.
But by my heart of love laid bare to you,
My love that you can make not void nor vain,
Love that foregoes you but to claim anew
Beyond this passage of the gate of death,
I charge you at the Judgment make it plain
My love of you was life and not a breath.

1881

UPHILL

Does the road wind uphill all the way?
Yes, to the very end.
Will the day's journey take the whole long day?
From morn to night, my friend.

But is there for the night a resting-place?
A roof for when the slow dark hours begin.

[1] "Lady Unnamed"; a series of fourteen sonnets in which the personal utterance, as in Mrs. Browning's *Sonnets from the Portuguese,* is disguised by the title.

May not the darkness hide it from my face?
  You cannot miss that inn.

Shall I meet other wayfarers at night?
  Those who have gone before.
Then must I knock, or call when just in sight?
  They will not keep you standing at that door.

Shall I find comfort, travel-sore and weak?
  Of labor you shall find the sum.
Will there be beds for me and all who seek?
  Yea, beds for all who come.

1861 1861

WILLIAM MORRIS 1834-1896

Morris was one of the most interesting of nineteenth century poets in the variety of his social and artistic interests and the courage and vigor with which he followed them. He was born in London, and his education was conventional and tending toward the Anglican ministry until he found, at Oxford, that his tastes were inclined toward art. Burne-Jones and other kindred spirits there stimulated Morris's latent interest in medieval art and architecture so strongly that he left Oxford without a degree, to become architect, painter, decorator, printer, and a patron of and worker in many kinds of handicraft.

His object was, like Ruskin's, to bring back into modern life the spirit that animated medieval art. Through writing and lecturing he sought to arouse in the public a taste for what was truly artistic, especially in domestic architecture, decoration, and furnishings. He worked to instill into tradesmen an enthusiasm for their crafts like that which inspired the artisans of the medieval guilds to design and execute beautiful objects of handicraft. To some degree his efforts in promoting good art succeeded, for he brought into vogue, in an age of hideous architecture and ornamentation, a taste for the simple, practical, and artistic.

Morris's literary work is sometimes classic in scene and subject, though more often medieval; but whether of the ancient times or the middle ages, it is medieval in spirit and action, and illuminated with the colors of romance.

Amidst the distracting occupations of his artistic propaganda, during forty years, Morris was writing: masterpieces of metrical romance such as *The Defence of Guenevere,* 1858, *The Life and Death of Jason,* 1867, *The Earthly Paradise,* 1868-70; translations such as the *Odyssey,* 1887, *Beowulf,* 1895, and notably the Icelandic *Volsunga Saga,* 1870; and prose romances including *The Roots of the Mountains,* 1890, and *The Water of the Wondrous Isles,* 1897. His work, whether medieval or classic in theme, expresses the spirit, action, and color of romance. He often follows Chaucer in plan and form, but with an elemental boldness and spontaneity at once ancient and modern.

Biography: A. Noyes (EML). Criticism: More (Shel. 7); Payne; J. Drinkwater, *William Morris, a Critical Study,* 1912; E. L. Cary, *William Morris, Poet, Craftsman, Socialist,* 1902. See also, "Literary Work of W. Morris," P. E. More, *Nation* 88:243-6.

THE GILLIFLOWER OF GOLD

A golden gilliflower today
I wore upon my helm alway,
And won the prize of this tourney.
  Hah! hah! la belle jaune giroflée.[1]

However well Sir Giles might sit,
His sun was weak to wither it;
Lord Miles's blood was dew on it.
  Hah! hah! la belle jaune giroflée—

Although my spear in splinters flew
From John's steel coat, my eye was true;
I wheeled about, and cried for you,
  Hah; hah; la belle jaune giroflée—

Yea, do not doubt my heart was good,
Though my sword flew like rotten wood,
To shout, although I scarcely stood,
  Hah! hah! la belle jaune giroflée.

My hand was steady, too, to take
My axe from round my neck, and break
John's steel coat up for my love's sake.
  Hah! hah! la belle jaune giroflée.

When I stood in my tent again,
Arming afresh, I felt a pain
Take hold of me, I was so fain—
  Hah! hah! la belle jaune giroflée—

To hear: *"Honneur aux fils des preux!"*[2]
Right in my ears again, and shew
The gilliflower blossomed new.
  Hah! hah! la belle jaune giroflée.

The Sieur Guillaume against me came,
His tabard bore three points of flame
From a red heart; with little blame[3]—
  Hah! hah! la belle jaune giroflée—

Our tough spears crackled up like straw;
He was the first to turn and draw
His sword, that had nor speck nor flaw;
  Hah! hah! la belle jaune giroflée.

But I felt weaker than a maid,
And my brain, dizzied and afraid,
Within my helm a fierce tune played,
  Hah! hah! la belle jaune giroflée,

Until I thought of your dear head,
Bowed to the gilliflower bed,
The yellow flowers stained with red;
  Hah! hah! la belle jaune giroflée,

[1] Hah! hah! the beautiful yellow gilliflower!
[2] Honor to the sons of the brave!
[3] hurt

Crash! how the swords met; *"giroflée!"*
The fierce tune in my helm would play,
"La belle! la belle jaune giroflée!"
Hah! hah! la belle jaune giroflée.

Once more the great swords met again.
"La belle! la belle!" but who fell then?
Le Sieur Guillaume, who struck down ten;
Hah! hah! la belle jaune giroflée.

And as with mazed and unarmed face,
Toward my own crown and the Queen's place,
They led me at a gentle pace—
Hah! hah! la belle jaune giroflée,—

I almost saw your quiet head
Bowed o'er the gilliflower bed,
The yellow flowers stained with red,
Hah! hah! la belle jaune giroflée.

1858

THE SAILING OF THE SWORD

Across the empty garden-beds,
When the Sword went out to sea,
I scarcely saw my sisters' heads
Bowed each beside a tree.
I could not see the castle leads,
When the Sword went out to sea.

Alicia wore a scarlet gown,
When the Sword went out to sea,
But Ursula's was russet brown:
For the mist we could not see
The scarlet roofs of the good town,
When the Sword went out to sea.

Green holly in Alicia's hand,
When the Sword went out to sea;
With sere oak leaves did Ursula stand;
Oh! yet alas for me!
I did but bear a peeled white wand,
When the Sword went out to sea.

Oh, russet brown and scarlet bright,
When the Sword went out to sea,
My sisters wore; I wore but white;
Red, brown, and white, are three;
Three damozels; each had a knight,
When the Sword went out to sea.

Sir Robert shouted loud and said,
When the Sword went out to sea,
"Alicia, while I see thy head,
What shall I bring for thee?"
"Oh, my sweet Lord, a ruby red."
The Sword went out to sea.

Sir Miles said, while the sails hung down,
When the Sword went out to sea,
"Oh, Ursula! while I see the town,
What shall I bring for thee?"
"Dear knight, bring back a falcon brown":
The Sword went out to sea.

But my Roland, no word he said,
When the Sword went out to sea,
But only turned away his head;
A quick shriek came from me:
"Come back, dear lord, to your white maid!"
The Sword went out to sea.

The hot sun bit the garden beds
When the Sword came back from sea;
Beneath an apple tree our heads
Stretched out toward the sea;
Gray gleamed the thirsty castle-leads,
When the Sword came back from sea.

Lord Robert brought a ruby red,
When the Sword came back from sea;
He kissed Alicia on the head:
"I am come back to thee;
'Tis time, sweet love, that we were wed,
Now the Sword is back from sea!"

Sir Miles he bore a falcon brown,
When the Sword came back from sea;
His arms went round tall Ursula's gown:
"What joy, O love, but thee?
Let us be wed in the good town,
Now the Sword is back from sea!"

My heart grew sick, no more afraid,
When the Sword came back from sea;
Upon the deck a tall white maid
Sat on Lord Roland's knee;
His chin was pressed upon her head,
When the Sword came back from sea!

1858

THE BLUE CLOSET [1]

The Damozels

Lady Alice, lady Louise,
Between the wash of the tumbling seas
We are ready to sing, if so ye please:
So lay your long hands on the keys;
Sing, *"Laudate pueri."* [2]

[1] Written for a picture (a water-color) by Dante Gabriel Rossetti. The romantic theme, the medieval remoteness, the color and sound, the sharpness of detail with the vagueness of general outline and setting, are all in the early pre-Raphaelite manner.

[2] "Praise ye, youths." The beginnings of the so-called Irish version of the familiar hymn, *Te Deum Laudamus.*

And ever the great bell overhead
Boomed in the wind a knell for the dead,
Though no one tolled it, a knell for the dead.

Lady Louise

Sister, let the measure swell
Not too loud; for you sing not well
If you drown the faint boom of the bell;
He is weary, so am I.

And ever the chevron[1] *overhead*
Flapped on the banner of the dead;
(Was he asleep, or was he dead?)

Lady Alice

Alice the Queen, and Louise the Queen,
Two damozels wearing purple and green,
Four lone ladies dwelling here
From day to day and year to year;
And there is none to let us go,
To break the locks of the doors below,
Or shovel away the heaped-up snow;
And when we die no man will know
That we are dead; but they give us leave,
Once every year on Christmas-eve,
To sing in the Closet Blue one song;
And we should be so long, so long,
If we dared, in singing; for dream on dream,
They float on in happy stream;
Float from the gold strings, float from the keys,
Float from the opened lips of Louise;
But, alas! the sea-salt oozes through
The chinks of the tiles of the Closet Blue;

And ever the great bell overhead
Booms in the wind a knell for the dead,
The wind plays on it a knell for the dead.

They Sing All Together

How long ago was it, how long ago,
He came to this tower with hands full of snow?
"Kneel down, O love Louise, kneel down!" he said,
And sprinkled the dusty snow over my head.

He watched the snow melting, it ran through my hair,
Ran over my shoulders, white shoulders and bare.

"I cannot weep for thee, poor love Louise,
For my tears are all hidden deep under the seas;
In a gold and blue casket she keeps all my tears,
But my eyes are no longer blue, as in old years;
"Yea, they grow gray with time, grow small and dry,
I am so feeble now, would I might die."

And in truth the great bell overhead
Left off his pealing for the dead,
Perchance, because the wind was dead.

Will he come back again, or is he dead?
Oh! is he sleeping, my scarf round his head?

Or did they strangle him as he lay there,
With the long scarlet scarf I used to wear?

Only I pray thee, Lord, let him come here!
Both his soul and his body to me are most dear.

Dear Lord, that loves me, I wait to receive
Either body or spirit this wild Christmas-eve.

Through the floor shot up a lily red,
With a patch of earth from the land of the dead,
For he was strong in the land of the dead.

What matter that his cheeks were pale,
His kind, kissed lips all gray?
"O love Louise, have you waited long?"
"O my lord Arthur, yea."

What if his hair that brushed her cheek
Was stiff with frozen rime?
His eyes were grown quite blue again,
As in the happy time.

"O love Louise, this is the key
Of the happy, golden land!
O sisters, cross the bridge with me,
My eyes are full of sand.
What matter that I cannot see,
If ye take me by the hand?"

And ever the great bell overhead,
And the tumbling seas mourned for the dead;
For their song ceased, and they were dead!
1858

From THE EARTHLY PARADISE

An Apology

Of Heaven or Hell I have no power to sing,
I cannot ease the burden of your fears,
Or make quick-coming death a little thing,
Or bring again the pleasure of past years,
Nor for my words shall ye forget your tears,
Or hope again for aught that I can say,
The idle singer of an empty day.

[1] a V-shaped device in heraldry

But rather, when aweary of your mirth,
From full hearts still unsatisfied ye sigh,
And, feeling kindly unto all the earth,
Grudge every minute as it passes by,
Made the more mindful that the sweet days die—
Remember me a little then I pray,
The idle singer of an empty day.

The heavy trouble, the bewildering care
That weighs us down who live and earn our bread,
These idle verses have no power to bear;
So let me sing of names rememberèd,
Because they, living not, can ne'er be dead,
Or long time take their memory quite away
From us poor singers of an empty day.

Dreamer of dreams, born out of my due time,
Why should I strive to set the crooked straight?
Let it suffice me that my murmuring rime
Beats with light wing against the ivory gate,[1]
Telling a tale not too importunate
To those who in the sleepy region stay,
Lulled by the singer of an empty day.

Folk say, a wizard to a northern king
At Christmas-tide such wondrous things did show
That through one window men beheld the spring,
And through another saw the summer glow,
And through a third the fruited vines a-row,
While still, unheard, but in its wonted way,
Piped the drear wind of that December day.

So with this Earthly Paradise it is,
If ye will read aright, and pardon me,
Who strive to build a shadowy isle of bliss
Midmost the beating of the steely sea,
Where tossed about all hearts of men must be;
Whose ravening monsters mighty men shall slay,
Not the poor singer of an empty day.

1868

From LOVE IS ENOUGH

Song for Music

Love is enough: though the world be a-waning,
And the woods have no voice but the voice of complaining,
Though the sky be too dark for dim eyes to discover
The gold-cups and daisies fair blooming there-under,
Though the hills be held shadows, and the sea a dark wonder,
And this day draw a veil over all deeds passed over,
Yet their hands shall not tremble, their feet shall not falter,
The void shall not weary, the fear shall not alter
These lips and these eyes of the loved and the lover.

1872

[1] According to Greek legend, false dreams come through the gate of ivory, true dreams through the gate of horn.

From SIGURD THE VOLSUNG[2]

Of the Passing Away of Brynhild

Once more on the morrow-morning fair shineth the glorious sun,
And the Niblung children labor on a deed that shall be done;
For out in the people's meadows they raise a bale[3] on high,
The oak and the ash together, and thereon shall the Mighty lie;
Nor gold nor steel shall be lacking, nor savor of sweet spice,
Nor cloths in the Southlands woven, nor webs of untold price.
The work grows, toil is as nothing; long blasts of the mighty horn
From the topmost tower out-wailing o'er the woeful world are borne.

But Brynhild lay in her chamber, and her women went and came,
And they feared and trembled before her, and none spake Sigurd's name;
But whiles[4] they deemed her weeping, and whiles they deemed indeed

[2] The *Volsunga Saga* is an older, Norse version of the legend which appears in German literature as the *Nibelungenlied*, and which has been made familiar in modern times by Wagner's opera cycle *Der Ring des Nibelungen*. It is the Teutonic race epic. Sigurd (Siegfried, in the German version) is the grandson of Volsung, who was a descendant of Odin. Brynhild was originally a Valkyrie, one of Odin's "Choosers of the Slain," maidens who rode on white cloud-horses and visited battlefields to select heroes for Odin's great hall, Valhalla. Sigurd wakened Brynhild from an enchanted sleep to the doom of mortal life and love, and they plighted troth. But their love was thwarted at the court of the children of Giuki, the Niblung princes, Gunnar, Hogni, and Guttorm, and their sister Gudrun. Through the witchcraft of Grimhild, Gudrun's mother, Sigurd is made to lose all memory of Brynhild and to marry Gudrun. Moreover, he is made to assist in bringing about the marriage of Brynhild to Gunnar. Later, as a result of rivalry, Guttorm surprises and slays Sigurd, but is himself slain by Sigurd's sword, the "Wrath." Then follows the portion of the tale here given—the pathetic story of the means taken by Brynhild to rejoin Sigurd. Morris's metrical rendering of the entire legend extends to about ten thousand lines.

[3] funeral pile [4] at times

That she spake, if they might but hearken, but no words their ears might heed;
Till at last she spake out clearly: "I know not what ye would;
For ye come and go in my chamber, and ye seem of wavering mood
To thrust me on, or to stay me; to help my heart in woe,
Or to bid my days of sorrow midst nameless folly go."

None answered the word of Brynhild, none knew of her intent;
But she spake: "Bid hither Gunnar, lest the sun sink o'er the bent,[1]
And leave the words unspoken I yet have will to speak."

Then her maidens go from before her, and that lord of war they seek,
And he stands by the bed of Brynhild and strives to entreat and beseech,
But her eyes gaze awfully on him, and his lips may learn no speech.
And she saith: "I slept in the morning, or I dreamed in the waking-hour,
And my dream was of thee, O Gunnar, and the bed in thy kingly bower,
And the house that I blessed in my sorrow, and cursed in my sorrow and shame,
The gates of an ancient people, the towers of a mighty name;
King, cold was the hall I have dwelt in, and no brand burned on the hearth;
Dead-cold was thy bed, O Gunnar, and thy land was parched with dearth.
But I saw a great King riding, and a master of the harp,
And he rode amidst of the foemen, and the swords were bitter-sharp,
But his hand in the hand-gyves smote not, and his feet in the fetters were fast,
While many a word of mocking at his speechless face was cast.[2]

"Then I heard a voice in the world: 'O woe for the broken troth,
And the heavy Need of the Niblungs,[3] and the Sorrow of Odin the Goth!'[4]
Then I saw the halls of the strangers, and the hills, and the dark-blue sea,
Nor knew of their names and their nations, for earth was afar from me,
But brother rose up against brother, and blood swam over the board,
And women smote and spared not, and the fire was master and lord.
Then, then was the moonless mid-mirk, and I woke to the day and the deed—
The deed that earth shall name not, the day of its bitterest need.
Many words have I said in my life-days, and little more shall I say;
Ye have heard the dream of a woman, deal with it as ye may;
For meseems the world-ways sunder, and the dusk and the dark is mine,
Till I come to the hall of Freyia,[5] where the deeds of the mighty shall shine."

So hearkened Gunnar the Niblung, that her words he understood,
And he knew she was set on the death-stroke, and he deemed it nothing good;
But he said: "I have hearkened, and heeded thy death and mine in thy words:
I have done the deed and abide it, and my face shall laugh on the swords.
But thee, woman, I bid thee abide here till thy grief of soul abate;
Meseems nought lowly nor shameful shall be the Niblung fate;
And here shalt thou rule and be mighty, and be Queen of the measureless Gold[6]
And abase the Kings and upraise them; and anew shall thy fame be told,
And as fair shall thy glory blossom as the fresh fields under the spring."

Then he casteth his arms about her, and hot is the heart of the King.
For the glory of Queen Brynhild and the hope of her days of gain,
And he clean forgetteth Sigurd and the foster-brother slain;
But she shrank aback from before him, and cried: "Woe worth the while[7]
For the thoughts ye drive back on me, and the memory of your guile!
The Kings of Earth were gathered, the wise of men were met;
On the death of a woman's pleasure their glorious hearts were set,[8]

[1] heath, field
[2] a prophecy of Gunnar's fate at the hands of Atli, the eastern King, who afterward married Gudrun
[3] that is, their time of need, when punishment began to overtake them
[4] the sorrows of the race of Odin
[5] the goddess of love
[6] The Niblungs' hoard, won from the Dwarfs, or smiths, who dwelt in caves; the curse on this treasure brought sorrow to the winners.
[7] woe betide the time
[8] when Sigurd, disguised as Gunnar, walked through the flame and won Brynhild for Gunnar

And I was alone amidst them—ah, hold thy peace hereof!
Lest the thought of the bitterest hours this little hour should move."

He rose abashed from before her, and yet he lingered there;
Then she said: "O King of the Niblungs, what noise do I hearken and hear?
Why ring the axes and hammers, while feet of men go past,
And shields from the walls are shaken, and swords on the pavement cast,
And the door of the treasure is opened, and the horn cries loud and long,
And the feet of the Niblung children to the people's meadows throng?"

His face was troubled before her, and again she spake and said:
"Meseemeth this is the hour when men array the dead;
Wilt thou tell me tidings, Gunnar, that the children of thy folk
Pile up the bale for Guttorm, and the hand that smote the stroke?"

He said: "It is not so, Brynhild; for that Giuki's son [1] was burned
When the moon of the middle heaven last night toward dawning turned."

They looked on each other and spake not; but Gunnar gat him gone,
And came to his brother Hogni, the wise-heart Giuki's son,
And spake: "Thou art wise, O Hogni; go in to Brynhild the Queen,
And stay her swift departing; or the last of her days hath she seen."

"It is nought, thy word," said Hogni; "wilt thou bring dead men aback,
Or the souls of kings departed midst the battle and the wrack?
Yet this shall be easier to thee than the turning Brynhild's heart;
She came to dwell among us, but in us she had no part;
Let her go her ways from the Niblungs, with her hand in Sigurd's hand.
Will the grass grow up henceforward where her feet have trodden the land?"

"O evil day!" said Gunnar, "when my queen must perish and die!"

[1] Guttorm

"Such oft betide," saith Hogni, "as the lives of men flit by;
But the evil day is a day, and on each day groweth a deed,
And a thing that never dieth; and the fateful tale shall speed.
Lo, now, let us harden our hearts and set our brows as the brass,
Lest men say it, 'They loathed the evil and they brought the evil to pass.'"

So they spake, and their hearts were heavy, and they longed for the morrow morn,
And the morrow of tomorrow, and the new day yet to be born.

But Brynhild cried to her maidens: "Now open ark and chest,
And draw forth queenly raiment of the loveliest and the best;
Red rings that the Dwarf-lords fashioned, fair cloths that Queens have sewed,
To array the bride for the Mighty, and the traveler for the road."

They wept as they wrought her bidding and did on her goodliest gear;
But she laughed 'mid the dainty linen, and the gold rings fashioned fair;
She arose from the bed of the Niblungs, and her face no more was wan;
As a star in the dawn-tide heavens, 'mid the dusky house she shone;
And they that stood about her, their hearts were raised aloft
Amid their fear and wonder. Then she spake them kind and soft:

"Now give me the sword, O maidens, wherewith I sheared the wind
When the Kings of Earth were gathered to know the Chooser's mind." [2]

All sheathed the maidens brought it, and feared the hidden blade,
But the naked blue-white edges across her knees she laid,
And spake: "The heaped-up riches, the gear my fathers left,
All dear-bought woven wonders, all rings from battle reft,
All goods of men desired, now strew them on the floor,
And so share among you, maidens, the gifts of Brynhild's store."

[2] See introductory note, p. 753.

They brought them 'mid their weeping, but none put forth a hand
To take that wealth desired, the spoils of many a land.
There they stand and weep before her, and some are moved to speech,
And they cast their arms about her and strive with her and beseech
That she look on her loved-ones' sorrow and the glory of the day.
It was nought; she scarce might see them, and she put their hands away,
And she said: "Peace, ye that love me! and take the gifts and the gold
In remembrance of my fathers and the faithful deeds of old."
Then she spake: "Where now is Gunnar, that I may speak with him?
For new things are mine eyes beholding and the Niblung house grows dim,
And new sounds gather about me, that may hinder me to speak
When the breath is near to flitting, and the voice is waxen weak."

Then upright by the bed of the Niblungs for a moment doth she stand,
And the blade flasheth bright in the chamber, but no more they hinder her hand
Than if a god were smiting to rend the world in two;
Then dulled are the glittering edges, and the bitter point cleaves through
The breast of the all-wise Brynhild, and her feet from the pavement fail,
And the sigh of her heart is hearkened 'mid the hush of the maidens' wail.
Chill, deep is the fear upon them, but they bring her aback to the bed,
And her hand is yet on the hilts, and sidelong droopeth her head.

Then there cometh a cry from withoutward, and Gunnar's hurrying feet
Are swift on the kingly threshold, and Brynhild's blood they meet.
Low down o'er the bed he hangeth and hearkeneth for her word,
And her heavy lids are opened to look on the Niblung lord,
And she saith: "I pray thee a prayer, the last word in the world I speak,
That ye bear me forth to Sigurd, and the hand my hand would seek;
The bale for the dead is builded, it is wrought full wide on the plain,
It is raised for Earth's best Helper, and thereon is room for twain.
Ye have hung the shields about it, and the Southland hangings spread;
There lay me adown by Sigurd and my head beside his head;
But ere ye leave us sleeping draw his Wrath from out the sheath,
And lay that Light of the Branstock[1] and the blade that frighted death
Betwixt my side and Sigurd's, as it lay that while agone,
When once in one bed together we twain were laid alone:
How then when the flames flare upward may I be left behind?
How then may the road he wendeth be hard for my feet to find?
How then in the gates of Valhall may the door of the gleaming ring
Clash to on the heel of Sigurd, as I follow on my king?"

Then she raised herself on her elbow, but again her eyelids sank,
And the wound by the sword-edge whispered, as her heart from the iron shrank,
And she moaned: "O lives of man-folk, for unrest all overlong
By the Father were ye fashioned; and what hope amendeth wrong?
Now at last, O my beloved, all is gone; none else is near,
Through the ages of all ages, never sundered, shall we wear."

Scarce more than a sigh was the word, as back on the bed she fell,
Nor was there need in the chamber of the passing of Brynhild to tell;
And no more their lamentation might the maidens hold aback,
But the sound of their bitter mourning was as if red-handed wrack
Ran wild in the Burg of the Niblungs, and the fire were master of all.

Then the voice of Gunnar, the war-king, cried out o'er the weeping hall:
"Wail on, O women forsaken, for the mightiest woman born!

[1] Another name for Sigurd's sword; the Branstock was a great oak tree about which was built the ancestral home of the Volsungs. The sword, sent by Odin, was drawn from the Branstock by Sigurd's father. It was later broken into pieces, but reforged as Bram, or the Wrath of Sigurd.

Now the hearth is cold and joyless, and the waste bed lieth forlorn.
Wail on, but amid your weeping lay hand to the glorious dead,
That not alone for an hour may lie Queen Brynhild's head:
For here have been heavy tidings, and the Mightiest under shield
Is laid on the bale high-builded in the Niblungs' hallowed field.
Fare forth! for he abideth, and we do All-father wrong
If the shining Valhall's pavement await their feet o'erlong."

Then they took the body of Brynhild in the raiment that she wore,
And out through the gate of the Niblungs the holy corpse they bore,
And thence forth to the mead of the people, and the high-built, shielded bale:
Then afresh in the open meadows breaks forth the women's wail
When they see the bed of Sigurd and the glittering of his gear;
And fresh is the wail of the people as Brynhild draweth anear,
And the tidings go before her that for twain the bale is built,
That for twain is the oak-wood shielded and the pleasant odors spilt.

There is peace on the bale of Sigurd, and the Gods look down from on high,
And they see the lids of the Volsung close shut against the sky,
As he lies with his shield beside him in the hauberk all of gold,
That has not its like in the heavens, nor has earth of its fellow told;
And forth from the Helm of Aweing [1] are the sunbeams flashing wide,
And the sheathèd Wrath of Sigurd lies still by his mighty side.
Then cometh an elder of days, a man of the ancient times,
Who is long past sorrow and joy, and the steep of the bale he climbs;
And he kneeleth down by Sigurd, and bareth the Wrath to the sun
That the beams are gathered about it, and from hilt to blood-point run,
And wide o'er the plain of the Niblungs doth the Light of the Branstock glare,
Till the wondering mountain-shepherds on that star of noontide stare,
And fear for many an evil; but the ancient man stands still
With the war-flame on his shoulder, nor thinks of good or of ill,
Till the feet of Brynhild's bearers on the topmost bale are laid,
And her bed is dight [2] by Sigurd's; then he sinks the pale white blade
And lays it 'twixt the sleepers, and leaves them there alone—
He, the last that shall ever behold them—and his days are well-nigh done.

Then is silence over the plain; in the noon shine the torches pale,
As the best of the Niblung Earl-folk [3] bear fire to the builded bale.
Then a wind in the west ariseth, and the white flames leap on high,
And with one voice crieth the people a great and mighty cry,
And men cast up hands to the Heavens, and pray without a word,
As they that have seen God's visage, and the voice of the Father have heard.

They are gone—the lovely, the mighty, the hope of the ancient Earth:
It shall labor and bear the burden as before that day of their birth;
It shall groan in its blind abiding for the day that Sigurd hath sped,
And the hour that Brynhild hath hastened, and the dawn that waketh the dead;
It shall yearn, and be oft-times holpen, and forget their deeds no more,
Till the new sun beams on Baldur, and the happy sealess shore. [4]

1876

THE VOICE OF TOIL [5]

I heard men saying, Leave hope and praying,
All days shall be as all have been;
Today and tomorrow bring fear and sorrow,
The never-ending toil between.

When Earth was younger mid toil and hunger,
In hope we strove, and our hands were strong;

[1] Helm of Dread, won by slaying the dragon Fafnir

[2] prepared

[3] the nobles, or warriors, as opposed to the churls

[4] alluding to the new heaven that is to arise after the Twilight of the Gods, when Baldur the Good shall be released from Hel and reign in the seats of the old gods

[5] This poem, now printed in Morris's *Poems by the Way*, was first published in a pamphlet called *Chants for Socialists*. "The Cause" mentioned in the last stanza is of course socialism, in which Morris was much interested.

Then great men led us, with words they fed us,
And bade us right the earthly wrong.

Go read in story their deeds and glory,
Their names amidst the nameless dead;
Turn then from lying to us slow-dying
In that good world to which they led;

Where fast and faster our iron master,
The thing we made, forever drives,
Bids us grind treasure and fashion pleasure
For other hopes and other lives.

Where home is a hovel and dull we grovel,
Forgetting that the world is fair;
Where no babe we cherish, lest its very soul
 perish;
Where mirth is crime, and love a snare.

Who now shall lead us, what god shall heed us
As we lie in the hell our hands have won?
For us are no rulers but fools and befoolers,
The great are fallen, the wise men gone.

I heard men saying, Leave tears and praying,
The sharp knife heedeth not the sheep;
Are we not stronger than the rich and the
 wronger,
When day breaks over dreams and sleep?

Come, shoulder to shoulder ere the world
 grows older!
Help lies in naught but thee and me;
Hope is before us, the long years that bore us
Bore leaders more than men may be.

Let dead hearts tarry and trade and marry,
And trembling nurse their dreams of mirth,
While we the living our lives are giving
To bring the bright new world to birth.

Come, shoulder to shoulder ere earth grows
 older!
The Cause spreads over land and sea;
Now the world shaketh, and fear awaketh,
And joy at last for thee and me.

1885

ALGERNON CHARLES SWINBURNE 1837-1909

Swinburne, last of the major Victorian poets, son of an English admiral, was London-born. Although his forbears were inclined to deeds rather than books, he was bookish from the first. At Oxford, where he was conspicuous for eccentricities and liberal opinions, he made important friendships, and on quitting the university he became intimate with the Burne-Jones and Rossetti group. Habits of dissipation aggravated a nervous tendency to epilepsy, and at length his health became so precarious that Mr. Theodore Watts-Dunton took him to his home at Putney in the London suburbs, where he lived and worked for years.

Swinburne's long life was devoted to literature. *Atalanta in Calydon,* 1864, first gave him standing; *Poems and Ballads* (first series, 1866), *Songs before Sunrise,* 1871, *Tristram of Lyonesse,* 1882, represent his lyrics and romances, *Marino Faliero* and *Locrine* his later dramas; and *Essays and Studies,* 1885, show him an appreciative and scholarly critic.

Exuberance of figure and diction, sweeping eloquence, astonishing skill and abundance in metrical forms, and a dream-like atmosphere are the chief characteristics of Swinburne's work. Without being repetitious he is diffuse, and an exotic, hothouse air pervades many of his lyrics. The sensuous effect of meter, melody, and imagery is, by most critics, thought more characteristic of him than penetrating ideas. Pantheism, hero-worship, freedom, republicanism, the sea, the laudation of Man, are among his favorite themes.

Comp. Works, ed. Sir E. Grosse, 20 vols., 1926.

Biographies: Gosse, 1912; Nicholson (EML), 1926. Criticism: Lowell, Payne, Woodberry; see also, "On Swinburne," W. R. Benét, *Sat. Rev. Lit.* 2:801-2; P. Colum, *New Rep.* 16:101-3; A. Symons, *Fortn.* 107:795-804, same, *Liv. Age* 293: 666-73; A. Noyes, "Swinburne and Conventional Criticism," *Liv. Age* 327:378.

From ATALANTA IN CALYDON
CHORUS

When the hounds of spring are on winter's
 traces,
 The mother of months [1] in meadow or plain
Fills the shadows and windy places
 With lisp of leaves and ripple of rain;
And the brown bright nightingale amorous
Is half assuaged for Itylus, [2]
For the Thracian ships and the foreign faces,
 The tongueless vigil, and all the pain.

Come with bows bent and with emptying of
 quivers,
 Maiden most perfect, lady of light,
With a noise of winds and many rivers,
 With a clamor of waters, and with might;
Bind on thy sandals, O thou most fleet,
Over the splendor and speed of thy feet;
For the faint east quickens, the wan west
 shivers,
 Round the feet of the day and the feet of
 the night.

[1] Artemis, or Diana, the goddess of the moon; also the goddess of the hunt—see next stanza. Compare Shelley's *Prometheus Unbound,* IV, 207

[2] alluding to the old Thracian legend of Philomela and Procne

Where shall we find her, how shall we sing to
her,
Fold our hands round her knees, and cling?
Oh, that man's heart were as fire and could
spring to her,
Fire, or the strength of the streams that
spring!
For the stars and the winds are unto her
As raiment, as songs of the harp-player;
For the risen stars and the fallen cling to her,
And the southwest wind and the west wind
sing.

For winter's rains and ruins are over,
And all the season of snows and sins;
The days dividing lover and lover,
The light that loses, the night that wins;
And time remembered is grief forgotten,
And frosts are slain and flowers begotten,
And in green underwood and cover
Blossom by blossom the spring begins.

The full streams feed on flower of rushes,
Ripe grasses trammel a traveling foot,
The faint, fresh flame of the young year
flushes
From leaf to flower and flower to fruit;
And fruit and leaf are as gold and fire,
And the oat is heard above the lyre,[1]
And the hoofèd heel of a satyr crushes
The chestnut-husk at the chestnut-root.

And Pan by noon and Bacchus by night,
Fleeter of foot than the fleet-foot kid,
Follows with dancing and fills with delight
The Maenad and the Bassarid;[2]
And soft as lips that laugh and hide,
The laughing leaves of the trees divide,
And screen from seeing and leave in sight
The god pursuing, the maiden hid.

The ivy falls with the Bacchanal's hair
Over her eyebrows hiding her eyes;
The wild vine slipping down leaves bare
Her bright breast shortening into sighs;
The wild vine slips with the weight of its
leaves,
But the berried ivy catches and cleaves
To the limbs that glitter, the feet that scare
The wolf that follows, the fawn that flies.

1864 1865

[1] That is, pastoral out-of-door music takes the place of indoor festal song; Pan supplants Apollo. An oat is a shepherd's pipe made of an oat stem.

[2] names for bacchanals, or frenzied votaries of Bacchus

A LEAVE-TAKING

Let us go hence, my songs; she will not hear.
Let us go hence together without fear;
Keep silence now, for singing-time is over,
And over all old things and all things dear.
She loves not you nor me as all we love her.
Yea, though we sang as angels in her ear,
She would not hear.

Let us rise up and part; she will not know.
Let us go seaward as the great winds go,
Full of blown sand and foam; what help is
here?
There is no help, for all these things are so,
And all the world is bitter as a tear;
And how these things are, though ye strove to
show,
She would not know.

Let us go home and hence; she will not weep.
We gave love many dreams and days to keep,
Flowers without scent, and fruits that would
not grow,
Saying, "If thou wilt, thrust in thy sickle and
reap."
All is reaped now; no grass is left to mow;
And we that sowed, though all we fell on
sleep,
She would not weep.

Let us go hence and rest; she will not love.
She shall not hear us if we sing hereof,
Nor see love's ways, how sore they are and
steep.
Come hence, let be, lie still; it is enough.
Love is a barren sea, bitter and deep;
And though she saw all heaven in flower above,
She would not love.

Let us give up, go down; she will not care.
Though all the stars made gold of all the air,
And the sea moving saw before it move
One moon-flower making all the foam-flowers
fair,
Though all those waves went over us, and drove
Deep down the stifling lips and drowning hair,
She would not care.

Let us go hence, go hence; she will not see.
Sing all once more together; surely she,
She, too, remembering days and words that
were,
Will turn a little toward us, sighing; but we,
We are hence, we are gone, as though we had
not been there.
Nay, and though all men seeing had pity on me,
She would not see.

1866

HYMN TO PROSERPINE [1]

(After the Proclamation in Rome of the Christian Faith)

Vicisti, Galilaee

I have lived long enough, having seen one thing, that love hath an end;
Goddess and maiden and queen, be near me now and befriend.
Thou art more than the day or the morrow, the seasons that laugh or that weep;
For these give joy and sorrow; but thou, Proserpina, sleep.
Sweet is the treading of wine, and sweet the feet of the dove;
But a goodlier gift is thine than foam of the grapes or love.
Yea, is not even Apollo, with hair and harpstring of gold,
A bitter God to follow, a beautiful God to behold?
I am sick of singing; the bays burn deep and chafe; I am fain
To rest a little from praise and grievous pleasure and pain.
For the Gods we know not of, who give us our daily breath,
We know they are cruel as love or life, and lovely as death.
O Gods dethroned and deceased, cast forth, wiped out in a day!
From your wrath is the world released, redeemed from your chains, men say.
New Gods are crowned in the city, their flowers have broken your rods;
They are merciful, clothed with pity, the young, compassionate Gods.
But for me their new device is barren, the days are bare;
Things long past over suffice, and men forgotten that were.
Time and the Gods are at strife; ye dwell in the midst thereof,
Draining a little life from the barren breasts of love.
I say to you, cease, take rest; yea, I say to you all, be at peace,
Till the bitter milk of her breast and the barren bosom shall cease.
Wilt thou yet take all, Galilean? But these thou shalt not take,
The laurel, the palms, and the paean, the breasts of the nymphs in the brake;
Breasts more soft than a dove's, that tremble with tenderer breath;
And all the wings of the Loves, and all the joy before death;
All the feet of the hours that sound as a single lyre,
Dropped and deep in the flowers, with strings that flicker like fire.
More than these wilt thou give, things fairer than all these things?
Nay, for a little we live, and life hath mutable wings.
A little while and we die; shall life not thrive as it may?
For no man under the sky lives twice, outliving his day.
And grief is a grievous thing, and a man hath enough of his tears:
Why should he labor and bring fresh grief to blacken his years?
Thou hast conquered, O pale Galilean; the world has grown gray from thy breath;
We have drunken of things Lethean, and fed on the fullness of death.
Laurel is green for a season, and love is sweet for a day;
But love grows bitter with treason, and laurel outlives not May.
Sleep, shall we sleep after all? For the world is not sweet in the end;
For the old faiths loosen and fall, the new years ruin and rend.
Fate is a sea without shore, and the soul is a rock that abides;
But her ears are vexed with the roar and her face with the foam of the tides.
O lips that the live blood faints in, the leavings of racks and rods!
O ghastly glories of saints, dead limbs of gibbeted Gods!
Though all men abase them before you in spirit, and all knees bend,
I kneel not, neither adore you, but standing, look to the end.
All delicate days and pleasant, all spirits and sorrows are cast
Far out with the foam of the present that sweeps to the surf of the past;
Where beyond the extreme sea-wall, and between the remote sea-gates,
Waste water washes, and tall ships founder, and deep death waits:

[1] Proserpine, or Proserpina, was the Roman goddess of death and the underworld. The Latin motto set before this poem means "Thou hast conquered, Galilean." The words are traditionally ascribed to the dying Emperor Julian—Julian "the apostate," who had been brought up as a Christian but who reverted to paganism after his accession to the throne. The poem attempts to portray the sentiment of expiring paganism; Swinburne called it "the death-song of spiritual decadence."

Where, mighty with deepening sides, clad about
with the seas as with wings,
And impelled of invisible tides, and fulfilled
of unspeakable things,
White-eyed and poisonous-finned, shark-toothed
and serpentine-curled,
Rolls, under the whitening wind of the future,
the wave of the world.
The depths stand naked in sunder behind it,
the storms flee away;
In the hollow before it the thunder is taken
and snared as a prey;
In its sides is the north wind bound; and its
salt is of all men's tears;
With light of ruin, and sound of changes, and
pulse of years;
With travail of day after day, and with trouble
of hour upon hour;
And bitter as blood is the spray; and the
crests are as fangs that devour:
And its vapor and storm of its stream as the
sighing of spirits to be;
And its noise as the noise in a dream; and its
depth as the roots of the sea:
And the height of its heads as the height of the
utmost stars of the air;
And the ends of the earth at the might thereof
tremble, and time is made bare.
Will ye bridle the deep sea with reins, will ye
chasten the high sea with rods?
Will ye take her to chain her with chains, who
is older than all ye Gods?
All ye as a wind shall go by, as a fire shall ye
pass and be past;
Ye are Gods, and behold ye shall die, and the
waves be upon you at last.
In the darkness of time, in the deeps of the
years, in the changes of things,
Ye shall sleep as a slain man sleeps, and the
world shall forget you for kings.
Though the feet of thine high priests tread
where thy lords and our forefathers trod,
Though these that were Gods are dead, and
thou being dead art a God,
Though before thee the throned Cytherean be
fallen, and hidden her head,
Yet thy kingdom shall pass, Galilean, thy dead
shall go down to thee dead.
Of the maiden thy mother, men sing as a goddess with grace clad around;
Thou art throned where another was king;
where another was queen she is crowned.
Yea, once we had sight of another; but now
she is queen, say these.
Not as thine, not as thine was our mother, a
blossom of flowering seas,[1]
Clothed round with the world's desire as with
raiment, and fair as the foam,
And fleeter than kindled fire, and a goddess
and mother of Rome.
For thine came pale and a maiden, and sister
to sorrow; but ours,
Her deep hair heavily laden with odor and
color of flowers,
White rose of the rose-white water, a silver
splendor, a flame,
Bent down unto us that besought her, and earth
grew sweet with her name.
For thine came weeping, a slave among slaves,
and rejected; but she
Came flushed from the full-flushed wave, and
imperial, her foot on the sea,
And the wonderful waters knew her, the winds
and the viewless ways,
And the roses grew rosier, and bluer the sea-
blue stream of the bays.
Ye are fallen, our lords, by what token? We
wist that ye should not fall.
Ye were all so fair that are broken; and one
more fair than ye all.
But I turn to her still, having seen she shall
surely abide in the end;
Goddess and maiden and queen, be near me
now and befriend.
O daughter of earth, of my mother, her crown
and blossom of birth,
I am also, I also, thy brother; I go as I came
unto earth.
In the night where thine eyes are as moons are
in heaven, the night where thou art,
Where the silence is more than all tunes, where
sleep overflows from the heart,
Where the poppies are sweet as the rose in our
world, and the red rose is white,
And the wind falls faint as it blows with the
fume of the flowers of the night,
And the murmur of spirits that sleep in the
shadow of Gods from afar
Grows dim in thine ears and deep as the deep
dim soul of a star,
In the sweet low light of thy face, under heav-
ens untrod by the sun,
Let my soul with their souls find place, and
forget what is done and undone.
Thou are more than the Gods who number
the days of our temporal breath;
For these give labor and slumber; but thou,
Proserpina, death.
Therefore now at thy feet I abide for a season
in silence. I know
I shall die as my fathers died, and sleep as
they sleep; even so.

[1] Venus, born of the foam

For the glass of the years is brittle wherein we gaze for a span;
A little soul for a little bears up this corpse which is man.[1]
So long I endure, no longer; and laugh not again, neither weep.
For there is no God found stronger than death; and death is a sleep.

1866

PRELUDE TO SONGS BEFORE SUNRISE[2]

Between the green bud and the red
Youth sat and sang by Time, and shed
 From eyes and tresses flowers and tears,
 From heart and spirit hopes and fears,
Upon the hollow stream whose bed
 Is channeled by the foamless years;
And with the white the gold-haired head
 Mixed running locks, and in Time's ears
Youth's dreams hung singing, and Time's truth
Was half not harsh in the ears of Youth.

Between the bud and the blown flower
Youth talked with joy and grief an hour,
 With footless joy and wingless grief
 And twin-born faith and disbelief
Who share the seasons to devour;
 And long ere these made up their sheaf
Felt the winds round him shake and shower
 The rose-red and the blood-red leaf,
Delight whose germ grew never grain,
And passion dyed in its own pain.

Then he stood up, and trod to dust
Fear and desire, mistrust and trust,
 And dreams of bitter sleep and sweet,
 And bound for sandals on his feet
Knowledge and patience of what must
 And what things may be, in the heat
And cold of years that rot and rust
 And alter; and his spirit's meat
Was freedom, and his staff was wrought
Of strength, and his cloak woven of thought.

For what has he whose will sees clear
To do with doubt and faith and fear,
 Swift hopes and slow despondencies?
 His heart is equal with the sea's
And with the sea-wind's, and his ear
 Is level to the speech of these,
And his soul communes and takes cheer
 With the actual earth's equalities,
Air, light, and night, hills, winds, and streams,
And seeks not strength from strengthless dreams.

His soul is even with the sun
Whose spirit and whose eyes are one,
 Who seeks not stars by day nor light
 And heavy heat of day by night.
Him can no God cast down, whom none
 Can lift in hope beyond the height
Of faith and nature and things done
 By the calm rule of might and right
That bids men be and bear and do,
And die beneath blind skies or blue.

To him the lights of even and morn
Speak no vain things of love or scorn,
 Fancies and passions miscreate
 By man in things dispassionate.
Nor holds he fellowship forlorn
 With souls that pray and hope and hate,
And doubt they had better not been born,
 And fain would lure or scare off fate
And charm their doomsman from their doom
And make fear dig its own false tomb.

He builds not half of doubts and half
Of dreams his own soul's cenotaph,
 Whence hopes and fears with helpless eyes,
 Wrapped loose in cast-off cerecloths, rise
And dance and wring their hands and laugh,
 And weep thin tears and sigh light sighs,
And without living lips would quaff
 The living spring in man that lies,
And drain his soul of faith and strength
It might have lived on a life's length.

He hath given himself and hath not sold
To God for heaven or man for gold,
 Or grief for comfort that it gives,
 Or joy for grief's restoratives.
He hath given himself to time, whose fold
 Shuts in the mortal flock that lives
On its plain pasture's heat and cold
 And the equal year's alternatives.
Earth, heaven, and time, death, life, and he,
Endure while they shall be to be.

"Yet between death and life are hours
To flush with love and hide in flowers;
 What profit save in these?" men cry;
 "Ah, see, between soft earth and sky,
What only good things here are ours!"

[1] adapted from Epictetus
[2] Swinburne's *Songs Before Sunrise,* published in 1871, and dedicated to Joseph Mazzini, the Italian patriot, is a noteworthy contribution to the poetry of political and religious freedom. Many of the poems were inspired by the long struggle for a free and united Italy. The partial union of Italy, effected in 1861, was completed by the occupation of Rome in 1870, but the government was monarchical, and not republican, as the more ardent revolutionists had hoped.

They say, "What better wouldst thou try,
What sweeter sing of? Or what powers
Serve, that will give thee ere thou die
More joy to sing and be less sad,
More heart to play and grow more glad?"

Play then and sing; we, too, have played,
We likewise, in that subtle shade.
We, too, have twisted through our hair
Such tendrils as the wild Loves wear,
And heard what mirth the Maenads [1] made,
Till the wind blew our garlands bare
And left their roses disarrayed,
And smote the summer with strange air,
And disengirdled and discrowned
The limbs and locks that vine-wreaths bound.

We, too, have tracked by star-proof trees
The tempest of the Thyiades [1]
Scare the loud night on hills that hid
The blood-feasts of the Bassarid, [1]
Heard their song's iron cadences
Fright the wolf hungering from the kid,
Outroar the lion-throated seas,
Outchide the north wind if it chid,
And hush the torrent-tongued ravines
With thunders of their tambourines.

But the fierce flute whose notes acclaim
Dim goddesses of fiery fame,
Cymbal and clamorous kettledrum,
Timbrels and tabrets, all are dumb
That turned the high chill air to flame;
The singing tongues of fire are numb
That called on Cotys [2] by her name
Edonian, till they felt her come
And maddened, and her mystic face
Lightened along the streams of Thrace.

For Pleasure slumberless and pale,
And Passion with rejected veil,
Pass, and the tempest-footed throng
Of hours that follow them with song
Till their feet flag and voices fail,
And lips that were so loud so long
Learn silence, or a wearier wail;
So keen is change, and time so strong,
To weave the robes of life and rend
And weave again till life have end.

But weak is change, but strengthless time,
To take the light from heaven, or climb
The hills of heaven with wasting feet.
Songs they can stop that earth found meet,
But the stars keep their ageless rime;

[1] ancient names of votaries of Bacchus
[2] an Edonian, or Thracian, divinity, worshiped with licentious revelry

Flowers they can slay that spring thought
sweet,
But the stars keep their spring sublime,
Passions and pleasures can defeat,
Actions and agonies control,
And life and death, but not the soul.

Because man's soul is man's God still,
What wind soever waft his will
Across the waves of day and night
To port or shipwreck, left or right,
By shores and shoals of good and ill;
And still its flame at mainmast height
Through the rent air that foam flakes fill
Sustains the indomitable light
Whence only man hath strength to steer
Or helm to handle without fear.

Save his own soul's light overhead,
None leads him, and none ever led,
Across birth's hidden harbor-bar,
Past youth where shoreward shallows are,
Through age that drives on toward the red
Vast void of sunset hailed from far,
To the equal waters of the dead;
Save his own soul he hath no star,
And sinks, except his own soul guide,
Helmless in middle turn of tide.

No blast of air or fire of sun
Puts out the light whereby we run
With girdled loins our lamplit race, [3]
And each from each takes heart of grace
And spirit till his turn be done,
And light of face from each man's face
In whom the light of trust is one;
Since only souls that keep their place
By their own light, and watch things roll,
And stand, have light for any soul.

A little time we gain from time
To set our seasons in some chime,
For harsh or sweet or loud or low,
With seasons played out long ago
And souls that in their time and prime
Took part with summer or with snow,
Lived abject lives out or sublime,
And had their chance of seed to sow
For service or disservice done
To those days dead and this their son.

A little time that we may fill
Or with such good works or such ill
As loose the bonds or make them strong
Wherein all manhood suffers wrong.
By rose-hung river and light-foot rill

[3] An allusion to the ancient torch race; see note 2, p. 823.

There are who rest not; who think long
Till they discern as from a hill
At the sun's hour of morning song,
Known of souls only, and those souls free,
The sacred spaces of the sea.

1871

LINES ON THE MONUMENT OF GIUSEPPE MAZZINI [1]

Italia, mother of the souls of men,
Mother divine,
Of all that served thee best with sword or pen,
All sons of thine,

Thou knowest that here the likeness of the best
Before thee stands:
The head most high, the heart found faithfullest,
The purest hands.
Above the fume and foam of time that flits,
The soul, we know,
Now sits on high where Alighieri sits
With Angelo.

Not his own heavenly tongue hath heavenly speech
Enough to say
What this man was, whose praise no thought may reach,
No words can weigh.

Since man's first mother brought to mortal birth
Her first-born son,
Such grace befell not ever man on earth
As crowns this One.

Of God nor man was ever this thing said:
That he could give
Life back to her who gave him, whence his dead
Mother might live.

But this man found his mother dead and slain,
With fast-sealed eyes,
And bade the dead rise up and live again,
And she did rise;

And all the world was bright with her through him:
But dark with strife,
Like heaven's own sun that storming clouds bedim,
Was all his life.

Life and the clouds are vanished; hate and fear
Have had their span
Of time to hurt and are not: he is here,
The sun-like man.

City superb, that hadst Columbus first
For sovereign son,
Be prouder that thy breast hath later nurst
This mightier One.

Glory be his forever, while his land
Lives and is free,
As with controlling breath and sovereign hand
He bade her be.

Earth shows to heaven the names by thousands told
That crown her fame,
But highest of all that heaven and earth behold,
Mazzini's name.

1884

THE PILGRIMS [2]

Who is your lady of love, O ye that pass
Singing? And is it for sorrow of that which was
That ye sing sadly, or dream of what shall be?
For gladly at once and sadly it seems ye sing.
—Our lady of love by you is unbeholden;
For hands she hath none, nor eyes, nor lips, nor golden
Treasure of hair, nor face nor form; but we
That love, we know her more fair than anything.

—Is she a queen, having great gifts to give?
—Yea, these: that whoso hath seen her shall not live
Except he serve her sorrowing, with strange pain,
Travail and bloodshedding and bitterer tears;
And when she bids die he shall surely die.
And he shall leave all things under the sky,
And go forth naked under sun and rain,
And work and wait and watch out all his years.

—Hath she on earth no place of habitation?
—Age to age calling, nation answering nation,
Cries out, Where is she? and there is none to say;
For if she be not in the spirit of men,

[1] Joseph Mazzini, the Italian patriot, died in 1872. A monument was erected to him at Genoa (Genoa "La Superba"), where there is also a monument to Columbus. Alighieri (line 11) is Dante, Angelo is Michelangelo.

[2] The poem is in the form of a dialogue, as indicated by the dashes—a speech and a reply in each stanza. For form, compare with it Tennyson's "The Two Voices"; for thought, Wordsworth's "Ode to Duty," Tennyson's "Wages," and Browning's "Rabbi Ben Ezra."

For if in the inward soul she hath no place,
In vain they cry unto her, seeking her face,
In vain their mouths make much of her; for they
Cry with vain tongues, till the heart lives again.

—O ye that follow, and have ye no repentance?
For on your brows is written a mortal sentence,
An hieroglyph of sorrow, a fiery sign,
That in your lives ye shall not pause or rest,
Nor have the sure, sweet, common love, nor keep
Friends and safe days, nor joy of life nor sleep.
—These have we not, who have one thing, the divine
Face and clear eyes of faith and fruitful breast.

—And ye shall die before your thrones be won.
—Yea, and the changed world and the liberal sun
Shall move and shine without us, and we lie
Dead; but if she, too, move on earth, and live,
But if the old world with all the old irons rent
Laugh and give thanks, shall we not be content?
Nay, we shall rather live, we shall not die,
Life being so little, and death so good to give.

—And these men shall forget you.—Yea, but we
Shall be a part of the earth and the ancient sea,
And heaven-high air august, and awful fire,
And all things good; and no man's heart shall beat
But somewhat in it of our blood once shed
Shall quiver and quicken, as now in us the dead
Blood of men slain and the old same life's desire
Plants in their fiery footprints our fresh feet.

—But ye that might be clothed with all things pleasant,
Ye are foolish that put off the fair, soft present,
That clothe yourselves with the cold future air;
When mother and father, and tender sister and brother
And the old, live love that was shall be as ye,
Dust, and no fruit of loving life shall be.
—She shall be yet who is more than all these were,
Than sister or wife or father unto us or mother.

—Is this worth life, is this, to win for wages?
Lo, the dead mouths of the awful gray-grown ages,
The venerable, in the past that is their prison,
In the outer darkness, in the unopening grave,
Laugh, knowing how many as ye now say have said,
How many, and all are fallen, are fallen and dead.
Shall ye dead rise, and these dead have not risen?
—Not we but she who is tender, and swift to save.

—Are ye not weary and faint not by the way,
Seeing night by night devoured of day by day,
Seeing hour by hour consumed in sleepless fire?
Sleepless; and ye, too, when shall ye, too, sleep?
—We are weary in heart and head, in hands and feet,
And surely more than all things sleep were sweet—
Than all things save the inexorable desire
Which whoso knoweth shall neither faint nor weep.

—Is this so sweet that one were fain to follow?
Is this so sure where all men's hopes are hollow,
Even this your dream, that by much tribulation
Ye shall make whole flawed hearts, and bowed necks straight?
—Nay, though our life were blind, our death were fruitless,
Not therefore were the whole world's high hope rootless;
But man to man, nation would turn to nation,
And the old life live, and the old great word be great.

—Pass on, then, and pass by us, and let us be,
For what light think ye after life to see?
And if the world fare better will ye know?
And if man triumph who shall seek you and say?
—Enough of light is this for one life's span,
That all men born are mortal, but not man;
And we men bring death lives by night to sow,
That men may reap and eat and live by day.

1871

A FORSAKEN GARDEN

In a coign of the cliff between lowland and highland,
At the sea-down's edge between windward and lee,
Walled round with rocks as an inland island,
The ghost of a garden fronts the sea.

A girdle of brushwood and thorn incloses
The steep square slope of the blossomless bed
Where the weeds that grew green from the grave of its roses
Now lie dead.

The fields fall southward, abrupt and broken,
To the low last edge of the long lone land.
If a step should sound or a word be spoken,
Would a ghost not rise at the strange guest's hand?
So long have the gray bare walks lain guestless,
Through branches and briars if a man make way,
He shall find no life but the sea wind's, restless
Night and day.

The dense hard passage is blind and stifled
That crawls by a track none turn to climb
To the straight waste place that the years have rifled
Of all but the thorns that are touched not of time.
The thorns he spares when the rose is taken;
The rocks are left when he wastes the plain;
The wind that wanders, the weeds wind-shaken,
These remain.

Not a flower to be pressed of the foot that falls not;
As the heart of a dead man the seed plots are dry;
From the thicket of thorns whence the nightingale calls not,
Could she call, there were never a rose to reply.
Over the meadows that blossom and wither,
Rings but the note of a sea-bird's song.
Only the sun and the rain come hither
All year long.

The sun burns sere, and the rain dishevels
One gaunt bleak blossom of scentless breath.
Only the wind here hovers and revels
In a round where life seems barren as death.
Here there was laughing of old, there was weeping,
Haply, of lovers none ever will know,
Whose eyes went seaward a hundred, sleeping
Years ago.

Heart handfast in heart as they stood, "Look thither,"
Did he whisper? "Look forth from the flowers to the sea;
For the foam-flowers endure when the rose-blossoms wither,
And men that love lightly may die—But we?"
And the same wind sang, and the same waves whitened,
And or ever the garden's last petals were shed,
In the lips that had whispered, the eyes that had lightened,
Love was dead.

Or they loved their life through, and then went whither?
And were one to the end—but what end who knows?
Love deep as the sea as a rose must wither,
As the rose-red seaweed that mocks the rose.
Shall the dead take thought for the dead to love them?
What love was ever as deep as a grave?
They are loveless now as the grass above them
Or the wave.

All are at one now, roses and lovers,
Not known of the cliffs and the fields and the sea.
Not a breath of the time that has been hovers
In the air now soft with a summer to be.
Not a breath shall there sweeten the seasons hereafter
Of the flowers or the lovers that laugh now or weep,
When, as they that are free now of weeping and laughter,
We shall sleep.

Here death may deal not again forever;
Here change may come not till all change end.
From the graves they have made they shall rise up never,
Who have left naught living to ravage and rend.
Earth, stones, and thorns of the wild ground growing,
While the sun and the rain live, these shall be;
Till a last wind's breath upon all these blowing
Roll the sea.

Till the slow sea rise and the sheer cliff crumble,
Till terrace and meadow the deep gulfs drink,
Till the strength of the waves of the high tides humble
The fields that lessen, the rocks that shrink,
Here now in his triumph where all things falter,

Stretched out on the spoils that his own hand
spread,
As a god self-slain on his own strange altar,
Death lies dead.

1876 1878

A BALLAD OF DREAMLAND

I hid my heart in a nest of roses,
Out of the sun's way, hidden apart;
In a softer bed than the soft white snow's is,
Under the roses I hid my heart.
Why should it sleep not? Why should it start,
When never a leaf of the rose tree stirred?
What made sleep flutter his wings and part?
Only the song of a secret bird.

Lie still, I said, for the wind's wing closes,
And mild leaves muffle the keen sun's dart;
Lie still, for the wind on the warm sea dozes,
And the wind is unquieter yet than thou art.
Does a thought in thee still as a thorn's
wound smart?
Does the fang still fret thee of hope deferred?
What bids the lids of thy sleep dispart?
Only the song of a secret bird.

The green land's name that a charm incloses,
It never was writ in the traveler's chart,
And sweet on its trees as the fruit that grows is,
It never was sold in the merchant's mart.
The swallows of dreams through its dim
fields dart,
And sleep's are the tunes in its tree tops heard;
No hound's note wakens the wildwood hart,
Only the song of a secret bird.

ENVOI [1]

In the world of dreams I have chosen my part,
To sleep for a season and hear no word
Of true love's truth or of light love's art,
Only the song of a secret bird.

1878

UPON A CHILD

Of such is the kingdom of heaven.
No glory that ever was shed
From the crowning star of the seven
That crown the north world's head,

No word that ever was spoken
Of human or godlike tongue,
Gave ever such godlike token
Since human harps were strung.

No sign that ever was given
To faithful or faithless eyes
Showed ever beyond clouds riven
So clear a Paradise.

Earth's creeds may be seventy times seven
And blood have defiled each creed:
If of such be the kingdom of heaven,
It must be heaven indeed.

1882

A CHILD'S LAUGHTER

All the bells of heaven may ring,
All the birds of heaven may sing,
All the wells on earth may spring,
All the winds on earth may bring
All sweet sounds together;
Sweeter far than all things heard,
Hand of harper, tone of bird,
Sound of woods at sundawn stirred,
Welling water's winsome word,
Wind in warm, wan weather,

One thing yet there is, that none
Hearing ere its chime be done
Knows not well the sweetest one
Heard of man beneath the sun,
Hoped in heaven hereafter;
Soft and strong and loud and light,
Very sound of very light
Heard from morning's rosiest height,
When the soul of all delight
Fills a child's clear laughter.

Golden bells of welcome rolled
Never forth such notes, nor told
Hours so blithe in tones so bold,
As the radiant mouth of gold
Here that rings forth heaven.
If the golden-crested wren
Were a nightingale—why, then
Something seen and heard of men
Might be half as sweet as when
Laughs a child of seven.

1882

A BABY'S DEATH [2]

I

A little soul scarce fledged for earth
Takes wing with heaven again for goal
Even while we hailed as fresh from birth
A little soul.

[1] *L'envoi*, or "the despatch," was the name formerly given to the closing lines of a *ballade*, often containing an address to a prince, patron, or friend; see "The Compleynt of Chaucer to his Purse," p. 68. In modern imitations, this address may be only a formula and is frequently omitted, the *envoi* being merely a summary, or an appended stanza completing the metrical scheme.

[2] From *A Century of Roundels. Of the poem* here given in part there are seven sections, each in the form of a roundel with regularly recurring refrain. The last three sections, however, vary in length of line, and being of a personal nature detract from the universal appeal of the first four.

Our thoughts ring sad as bells that toll,
Not knowing beyond this blind world's girth
What things are writ in heaven's full scroll.

Our fruitfulness is there but dearth,
And all things held in time's control
Seem there, perchance, ill dreams, not worth
A little soul.

II

The little feet that never trod
Earth, never strayed in field or street,
What hand leads upward back to God
The little feet?

A rose in June's most honied heat,
When life makes keen the kindling sod,
Was not so soft and warm and sweet.

Their pilgrimage's period
A few, swift moons have seen complete
Since mother's hands first clasped and shod
The little feet.

III

The little hands that never sought
Earth's prizes, worthless all as sands,
What gift has death, God's servant, brought
The little hands?

We ask: but love's self silent stands,
Love, that lends eyes and wings to thought
To search where death's dim heaven expands.

Ere this, perchance, though love knew nought,
Flowers fill them, grown in lovelier lands,
Where hands of guiding angels caught
The little hands.

IV

The little eyes that never knew
Light other than of dawning skies,
What new life now lights up anew
The little eyes?

Who knows but on their sleep may rise
Such light as never heaven let through
To lighten earth from Paradise?

No storm, we know, may change the blue
Soft heaven that haply death descries;
No tears, like these in ours, bedew
The little eyes.

1883

From TRISTRAM OF LYONESSE[1]

Prelude. Tristram and Iseult

Love, that is first and last of all things made,
The light that has the living world for shade,
The spirit that for temporal veil has on
The souls of all men woven in unison,
One fiery raiment with all lives inwrought
And lights of sunny and starry deed and thought,
And always through new act and passion new
Shines the divine same body and beauty through,
The body spiritual of fire and light
That is to worldly noon as noon to night;
Love, that is flesh upon the spirit of man
And spirit within the flesh whence breath began;
Love, that keeps all the choir of lives in chime;
Love, that is blood within the veins of time;
That wrought the whole world without stroke of hand,
Shaping the breadth of sea, the length of land,
And with the pulse and motion of his breath
Through the great heart of the earth strikes life and death,
The sweet twain chords that make the sweet tune live
Through day and night of things alternative,
Through silence and through sound of stress and strife,
And ebb and flow of dying death and life;
Love, that sounds loud or light in all men's ears,
Whence all men's eyes take fire from sparks of tears,
That binds on all men's feet or chains or wings;
Love, that is root and fruit of terrene things;
Love, that the whole world's waters shall not drown,
The whole world's fiery forces not burn down;
Love, that what time his own hands guard his head
The whole world's wrath and strength shall not strike dead;
Love, that if once his own hands make his grave

[1] In the long lyrical epic thus named, Swinburne tells again the story of Tristram and Iseult, which shares with that of Siegfried and Brunhild the distinction of being one of the greatest love stories of the world. "The world of Swinburne," says Professor Woodberry, "is well symbolized by that Zodiac of the burning signs of love that he named in the prelude to *Tristram of Lyonesse*—the signs of Helen, Hero, Alcyone, Iseult, Rosamond, Dido, Juliet, Cleopatra, Francesca, Thisbe, Angelica, Guenevere; under the heavens of these starry names the poet moves in his place apart, and sees his visions of woe and wrath, and weaves his dream of the loves and the fates of men."

The whole world's pity and sorrow shall not save;
Love, that for very life shall not be sold,
Nor bought nor bound with iron nor with gold;
So strong that heaven, could love bid heaven farewell,
Would turn to fruitless and unflowering hell;
So sweet that hell, to hell could love be given,
Would turn to splendid and sonorous heaven;
Love that is fire within thee and light above,
And lives by grace of nothing but of love;
Through many and lovely thoughts and much desire
Led these twain to the life of tears and fire;
Through many and lovely days and much delight
Led these twain to the lifeless life of night.
Yea, but what then? Albeit all this were thus,
And soul smote soul and left it ruinous,
And love led love as eyeless men lead men,
Through chance by chance to deathward—ah, what then?
Hath love not likewise led them farther yet,
Out through the years where memories rise and set,
Some large as suns, some moon-like warm and pale,
Some starry-sighted, some through clouds that sail
Seen as red flame through spectral float of fume,
Each with the blush of its own special bloom
On the fair face of its own colored light,
Distinguishable in all the host of night,
Divisible from all the radiant rest
And separable in splendor? Hath the best
Light of love's all, of all that burn and move,
A better heaven than heaven is? Hath not love
Made for all these their sweet particular air
To shine in, their own beams and names to bear,
Their ways to wander and their wards to keep,
Till story and song and glory and all things sleep?
Hath he not plucked from death of lovers dead
Their musical soft memories, and kept red
The rose of their remembrance in men's eyes,
The sunsets of their stories in his skies,
The blush of their dead blood in lips that speak
Of their dead lives, and in the listener's cheek
That trembles with the kindling pity lit
In gracious hearts for some sweet fever-fit,
A fiery pity enkindled of pure thought
By tales that make their honey out of nought,
The faithless faith that lives without belief
Its light life through, the griefless ghost of grief?
Yea, as warm night refashions the sere blood
In storm-struck petal or in sun-struck bud,
With tender hours and tempering dew to cure
The hunger and thirst of day's distemperature
And ravin of the dry discoloring hours,
Hath he not bid relume their flameless flowers
With summer fire and heat of lamping song
And bid the short-lived things, long dead, live long,
And thought remake their wan funereal fames,
And the sweet, shining signs of women's names,
That mark the months out and the weeks anew
He moves in changeless change of seasons through
To fill the days up of his dateless year,
Flame from Queen Helen to Queen Guenevere?
For first of all the sphery signs whereby
Love severs light from darkness, and most high,
In the white front of January there glows
The rose-red sign of Helen like a rose:[1]
And gold-eyed as the shore-flower shelterless
Whereon the sharp-breathed sea blows bitterness,
A storm-star that the seafarers of love
Strain their wind-wearied eyes for glimpses of,
Shoots keen through February's gray frost and damp
The lamp-like star of Hero for a lamp;
The star that Marlowe[2] sang into our skies
With mouth of gold, and morning in his eyes;
And in clear March across the rough blue sea
The signal sapphire of Alcyone[3]
Makes bright the blown brows of the wind-foot year;
And shining like a sunbeam-smitten tear
Full ere it fall, the fair next sign in sight
Burns opal-wise with April-colored light
When air is quick with song and rain and flame,
My birth-month star that in love's heaven hath name
Iseult,[4] a light of blossom and beam and shower,
My singing sign that makes the song-tree flower;
Next like a pale and burning pearl beyond
The rose-white sphere of flower-named Rosamond[5]
Signs the sweet head of Maytime; and for June
Flares like an angered and storm-reddening moon
Her signal sphere, whose Carthaginian pyre

[1] Homer: *The Iliad*
[2] in his *Hero and Leander*
[3] Ovid: *Metamorphoses*, xi
[4] Her story has been told by Malory, Tennyson (*Idylls of the King*, "The Last Tournament"), Arnold, Wagner, etc.
[5] The "Fair Rosamond" of Henry II; see Scott's *The Talisman* and *Woodstock*.

Shadowed her traitor's flying sail with fire;[1]
Next, glittering as the wine-bright jacinth-stone,
A star south-risen that first to music shone,
The keen girl-star of golden Juliet [2] bears
Light northward to the month whose forehead wears
Her name for flower upon it, and his trees
Mix their deep English song with Veronese;
And like an awful sovereign chrysolite
Burning, the supreme fire that blinds the night,
The hot gold head of Venus kissed by Mars,
A sun-flower among small sphered flowers of stars,
The light of Cleopatra [3] fills and burns
The hollow of heaven whence ardent August yearns;
And fixed and shining as the sister-shed,
Sweet tears for Phaethon disorbed and dead, [4]
The pale bright autumn's amber-colored sphere,
That through September sees the saddening year
As love sees change through sorrow, hath to name
Francesca's; and the star that watches flame
The embers of the harvest overgone
Is Thisbe's, slain of love in Babylon, [5]
Set in the golden girdle of sweet signs
A blood-bright ruby; last, save one light, shines
An eastern wonder of sphery chrysopras,
The star that made men mad, Angelica's; [6]
And latest named and lordliest, with a sound
Of swords and harps in heaven that ring it round,
Last love-light and last love-song of the year's,
Gleams like a glorious emerald Guenevere's. [7]
These are the signs wherethrough the year sees move,
Full of the sun, the sun-god which is love,
A fiery body blood-red from the heart
Outward, with fire-white wings made wide apart,
That close not and unclose not, but upright
Steered without wind by their own light and might,
Sweep through the flameless fire of air that rings
From heaven to heaven with thunder of wheels and wings
And antiphones of motion-molded rime
Through spaces out of space and timeless time.
  So shine above dead chance and conquered change
The spherèd signs, and leave without their range
Doubt and desire, and hope with fear for wife,
Pale pains, and pleasures long worn out of life.
Yea, even the shadows of them spiritless,
Through the dim door of sleep that seem to press,
Forms without form, a piteous people and blind,
Men and no men, whose lamentable kind
The shadow of death and shadow of life compel
Through semblances of heaven and false-faced hell,
Through dreams of light and dreams of darkness tost
On waves innavigable, are these so lost?
Shapes that wax pale and shift in swift strange wise,
Void faces with unspeculative eyes,
Dim things that gaze and glare, dead mouths that move,
Featureless heads discrowned of hate and love,
Mockeries and masks of motion and mute breath,
Leavings of life, the superflux of death—
If these things and no more than these things be
Left when man ends or changes, who can see?
Or who can say with what more subtle sense
Their subtler natures taste in air less dense
A life less thick and palpable than ours,
Warmed with faint fires and sweetened with dead flowers
And measured by low music? How time fares
In that wan, time-forgotten world of theirs,
Their pale poor world too deep for sun or star
To live in, where the eyes of Helen are,
And hers [8] who made as God's own eyes to shine
The eyes that met them of the Florentine,
Wherein the godhead thence transfigured lit
All time for all men with the shadow of it;
Ah, and these too felt on them as God's grace
The pity and glory of this man's breathing face;
For these too, these my lovers, these my twain,
Saw Dante, [9] saw God visible by pain,
With lips that thundered and with feet that trod
Before men's eyes incognizable God;

[1] Vergil: *Aeneid,* iv
[2] Shakespeare: *Romeo and Juliet*
[3] Shakespeare: *Antony and Cleopatra*
[4] Alluding to the story that after Phaethon's fatal fall with the chariot of the sun, his sisters, the Heliades, mourned for him until they were changed into poplars and their tears into amber. The story of Paolo and Francesca is immortalized in Dante's *Inferno.*
[5] Chaucer: *Legend of Good Women,* p. 65
[6] Boiardo: *Orlando Innamorato;* Ariosto: *Orlando Furioso;* Angelica's coquetry drove Orlando mad.
[7] Cf. Malory, Tennyson, etc.
[8] Dante's Beatrice
[9] *Inferno,* v, 7

Saw love and wrath and light and night and fire
Live with one life and at one mouth respire,
And in one golden sound their whole soul heard
Sounding, one sweet immitigable word.
  They have the night, who had like us the day;[1]
We, whom day binds, shall have the night as they.
We, from the fetters of the light unbound,
Healed of our wound of living, shall sleep sound.
All gifts but one the jealous God may keep
From our soul's longing, one he cannot—sleep.
This, though he grudge all other grace to prayer,
This grace his closed hand cannot choose but spare.
This, though his ear be sealed to all that live,
Be it lightly given or loathly, God must give.
We, as the men whose name on earth is none,
We too shall surely pass out of the sun;
Out of the sound and eyeless light of things,
Wide as the stretch of life's time-wandering wings,
Wide as the naked world and shadowless,
And long-lived as the world's own weariness.
Us too, when all the fires of time are cold,
The heights shall hide us and the depths shall hold.
Us too, when all the tears of time are dry,
The night shall lighten from her tearless eye.
Blind is the day and eyeless all its light,
But the large unbewildered eye of night
Hath sense and speculation; and the sheer,
Limitless length of lifeless life and clear,
The timeless space wherein the brief worlds move
Clothed with light life and fruitful with light love,
With hopes that threaten, and with fears that cease,
Past fear and hope, hath in it only peace.
  Yet of these lives inlaid with hopes and fears,
Spun fine as fire and jeweled thick with tears,
These lives made out of loves that long since were,
Lives wrought as ours of earth and burning air,
Fugitive flame, and water of secret springs,
And clothed with joys and sorrows as with wings,

[1] In this passage, with its rapt contemplation and solemn music, Swinburne has surely attained to that "high seriousness" which Matthew Arnold regarded as the mark of the greatest poetry. A portion of it reads not unlike an expansion of *Paradise Lost,* Book II, lines 149, 150, p. 270.

Some yet are good, if aught be good, to save
Some while from washing wreck and wrecking wave.
Was such not theirs, the twain I take, and give
Out of my life to make their dead life live
Some days of mine, and blow my living breath
Between dead lips forgotten even of death?
So many and many ere me have given my twain
Love and live song and honey-hearted pain,
Whose root is sweetness and whose fruit is sweet,
So many and with such joy have tracked their feet,
What should I do to follow? Yet I, too,
I have the heart to follow, many or few
Be the feet gone before me; for the way,
Rose-red with remnant roses of the day
Westward, and eastward white with stars that break,
Between the green and foam is fair to take
For any sail the sea wind steers for me
From morning into morning, sea to sea.

1871 *1882*

WALTER PATER 1839-1894

Pater was born in London and, like Morris, had looked forward to the English Church as a career; but about the time when he received his degree from Oxford and became a fellow of Brasenose, he abandoned this idea and gave himself to the appreciation of literature and art. He remained a fellow at Oxford, where he died.

The art of the Renaissance appealed strongly to him and in the study of it he spent many years, publishing in 1873 his *Studies in the Renaissance.* Pater held to the "humanities as opposed to the expediencies." In his view, life is but a passing thing which affords, as its best gift, the enjoyment of beauty. This idea he developed in *Marius the Epicurean,* 1885, a book that presents the nobler aspects of ancient epicureanism. His literary essays are found in *Appreciations,* 1889.

Pater was a leader among the self-conscious stylists of the end of the century. His style is one of highly-wrought beauty, full of rhythm and melody, producing many of the effects of poetry. It seeks perfection of word and phrase, delicate shades of meaning, and subtleties of suggestion. It is as far as possible from straightforward narrative like Macaulay's and is in strongest contrast with Carlyle's rough and earnest manner. Although many readers find him too painstaking for spontaneity, Pater is important for his serious presentation of the best aspects of the aesthetic movement of the late nineteenth century.

Biography: A. C. Benson (EML). Criticism: G. Bradford, "Naturalist of Souls"; More (Shel. 8); "Pater the Humanist," A. Ralli, *No. Am.* 201: 217-22; "On re-reading Walter Pater," R. Le Gallienne, *No. Am.* 195:214-224.

THE CHILD IN THE HOUSE [1]

As Florian Deleal walked, one hot afternoon, he overtook by the wayside a poor aged man, and, as he seemed weary with the road, helped him on with the burden which he carried, a certain distance. And as the man told his story, it chanced that he named the place, a little place in the neighborhood of a great city, where Florian had passed his earliest years, but which he had never since seen, and, the story told, [2] went forward on his journey comforted. And that night, like a reward for his pity, a dream of that place came to Florian, a dream which did for him the office of the finer sort of memory, bringing its object to mind with a great clearness, yet, as sometimes happens in dreams, raised a little above itself, and above ordinary retrospect. The true aspect of the place, especially of the house there in which he had lived as a child, the fashion of its doors, its hearths, its windows, the very scent upon the air of it, was with him in sleep for a season; only, with tints more musically [3] blent on wall and floor, and some finer light and shadow running in and out along its curves and angles, and with all its little carvings daintier. He awoke with a sigh at the thought of almost thirty years which lay between him and that place, yet with a flutter of pleasure still within him at the fair light, as if it were a smile, upon it. And it happened that this accident of his dream was just the thing needed for the beginning of a certain design he then had in view, the noting, namely, of some things in the story of his spirit—in that process of brain-building by which we are, each one of us, what we are. With the image of the place so clear and favorable upon him, he fell to thinking of himself therein, and how his thoughts had grown up to him. In that half-spiritualized house he could watch the better, over again, the gradual expansion of the soul which had come to be there—of which indeed, through the law which makes the material objects about them so large an element in children's lives, it had actually become a part; inward and outward being woven through and through each other into one inextricable texture—half, tint and trace and accident of homely color and form, from the wood and the bricks; half, mere [4] soul-stuff, floated thither from who knows how far. In the house and garden of his dream he saw a child moving, and could divide the main streams at least of the winds that had played on him, and study so the first stage in that mental journey.

The *old house,* as when Florian talked of it afterwards he always called it, (as all children do, who can recollect a change of home, soon enough but not too soon to mark a period in their lives) really was an old house; and an element of French descent in its inmates—descent from Watteau, the old court-painter, [5] one of whose gallant pieces still hung in one of the rooms—might explain, together with some other things, a noticeable trimness and comely whiteness about everything there—the curtains, the couches, the paint on the walls with which the light and shadow played so delicately; might explain also the tolerance of the great poplar in the garden, a tree most often despised by English people, but which French people love, having observed a certain fresh way its leaves have of dealing with the wind, making it sound, in never so slight a stirring of the air, like running water.

The old-fashioned, low wainscoting went round the rooms, and up the staircase with carved balusters and shadowy angles, landing halfway up at a broad window, with a swallow's nest below the sill, and the blossom of an old pear tree showing across it in late April, against the blue, below which the perfumed juice of the find of fallen fruit in autumn was so fresh. At the next turning came the closet which held on its deep shelves the best china. Little angel faces and reedy flutings stood out round the fireplace of the children's room. And on the top of the house, above the large attic, where the white mice ran in the twilight—an infinite, unexplored wonderland of childish treasures, glass beads, empty scent-bottles still sweet, thrum of colored silks, among its lumber—a flat space of roof, railed round, gave a view of the neighboring steeples; for the house, as I said, stood near a great city, which sent up heavenward, over the twisting weather-vanes, not seldom, its beds of rolling cloud and smoke, touched with storm or sunshine. But the child of whom I am writing did not hate the fog, because of the crimson lights which fell from it sometimes upon the chim-

[1] When originally published in 1878 this essay was called an "Imaginary Portrait," though it is doubtless in some measure autobiographical. As an account of the development of an extremely sensitive and impressionable youth, it holds a unique place in our literature.

[2] Pater's fondness for participles partakes rather more of Latin than of English style. Note, too, the difficulty of resuming, in the close of this sentence, the grammatical subject of the beginning.

[3] harmoniously

[4] pure, unmixed

[5] There may have been some family connection between Pater and Jean Baptiste Pater, a French painter of Watteau's time.

neys, and the whites which gleamed through its openings, on summer mornings, on turret or pavement. For it is false to suppose that a child's sense of beauty is dependent on any choiceness or special fineness, in the objects which present themselves to it, though this indeed comes to be the rule with most of us in later life; earlier, in some degree, we see inwardly; and the child finds for itself, and with unstinted delight, a difference for the sense, in those whites and reds through the smoke on very homely buildings, and in the gold of the dandelions at the roadside, just beyond the houses, where not a handful of earth is virgin and untouched, in the lack of better ministries to its desire of beauty.[1]

This house then stood not far beyond the gloom and rumors of the town, among high garden-walls, bright all summer-time with goldenrod, and brown-and-golden wallflower—*Flos Parietis,* as the children's Latin-reading father taught them to call it, while he was with them. Tracing back the threads of his complex spiritual habit, as he was used in after years to do, Florian found that he owed to the place many tones of sentiment afterwards customary with him, certain inward lights under which things most naturally presented themselves to him. The coming and going of travelers to the town along the way, the shadow of the streets, the sudden breath of the neighboring gardens, the singular brightness of bright weather there, its singular darknesses which linked themselves in his mind to certain engraved illustrations in the old big Bible at home, the coolness of the dark, cavernous shops round the great church, with its giddy winding stair up to the pigeons and the bells—a citadel of peace in the heart of the trouble—all this acted on his childish fancy, so that ever afterwards the like aspects and incidents never failed to throw him into a well-recognized, imaginative mood, seeming actually to have become a part of the texture of his mind. Also, Florian could trace home to this point a pervading preference in himself for a kind of comeliness and dignity, an *urbanity* literally, in modes of life, which he connected with the pale people of towns, and which made him susceptible to a kind of exquisite satisfaction in the trimness and well-considered grace of certain things and persons he afterwards met with, here and there, in his way through the world.

[1] This last clause is to be attached to the subject, "child." Pater's sentences often wind thus, by a devious route, to an unexpected end.

So the child of whom I am writing lived on there quietly; things without thus ministering to him, as he sat daily at the window with the bird cage hanging below it, and his mother taught him to read, wondering at the ease with which he learned, and at the quickness of his memory. The perfume of the little flowers of the lime tree fell through the air upon them like rain; while time seemed to move ever more slowly to the murmur of the bees in it, till it almost stood still on June afternoons. How insignificant, at the moment, seem the influences of the sensible things which are tossed and fall and lie about us, so, or so, in the environment of early childhood. How indelibly, as we afterwards discover, they affect us; with what capricious attractions and associations they figure themselves on the white paper,[2] the smooth wax, of our ingenuous souls, as "with lead in the rock forever,"[3] giving form and feature, and as it were assigned house-room in our memory, to early experiences of feeling and thought, which abide with us ever afterwards, thus, and not otherwise. The realities and passions, the rumors of the greater world without, steal in upon us, each by its own special little passageway, through the wall of custom about us; and never afterwards quite detach themselves from this or that accident, or trick, in the mode of their first entrance to us. Our susceptibilities, the discovery of our powers, manifold experiences—our various experiences of the coming and going of bodily pain, for instance—belong to this or the other well-remembered place in the material habitation—that little white room with the window across which the heavy blossoms could beat so peevishly in the wind, with just that particular catch or throb, such a sense of teasing in it, on gusty mornings; and the early habitation thus gradually becomes a sort of material shrine or sanctuary of sentiment; a system of visible symbolism interweaves itself through all our thoughts and passions; and irresistibly, little shapes, voices, accidents—the angle at which the sun in the morning fell on the pillow—become parts of the great chain wherewith we are bound.

Thus far, for Florian, what all this had determined was a peculiarly strong sense of home—so forcible a motive with all of us—prompting to us our customary love of the earth, and

[2] Referring to Locke's familiar figure for the state of mind at birth (Locke believed it a blank: compare Wordsworth's belief, *Ode,* p. 461); the next figure is derived from the ancient practice of writing on tablets of wax.

[3] *Job,* xix, 24

the larger part of our fear of death, that revulsion we have from it, as from something strange, untried, unfriendly; though life-long imprisonment, they tell you, and final banishment from home is a thing bitterer still; the looking forward to but a short space, a mere childish *goûter* [1] and dessert of it, before the end, being so great a resource of effort to pilgrims and wayfarers, and the soldier in distant quarters, and lending, in lack of that, some power of solace to the thought of sleep in the home churchyard, at least—dead cheek by dead cheek, and with the rain soaking in upon one from above.

So powerful is this instinct, and yet accidents like those I have been speaking of so mechanically determine it; its essence being indeed the early familiar, as constituting our ideal, or typical conception, of rest and security. Out of so many possible conditions, just this for you and that for me, brings ever the unmistakable realization of the delightful *chez soi;* [2] this for the Englishman, for me and you, with the closely-drawn white curtain and the shaded lamp; that, quite other, for the wandering Arab, who folds his tent every morning, and makes his sleeping-place among haunted ruins, or in old tombs.

With Florian then the sense of home became singularly intense, his good fortune being that the special character of his home was in itself so essentially homelike. As after many wanderings I have come to fancy that some parts of Surrey and Kent are, for Englishmen, the true landscape, true home-counties, by right, partly, of a certain earthy warmth in the yellow of the sand below their gorse bushes and of a certain gray-blue mist after rain, in the hollows of the hills there, welcome to fatigued eyes, and never seen farther south; so I think that the sort of house I have described, with precisely those proportions of red brick and green, and with a just perceptible monotony in the subdued order of it, for its distinguishing note is, for Englishmen at least, typically homelike. And so for Florian that general human instinct was reinforced by this special homelikeness in the place his wandering soul had happened to light on, as, in the second degree, its body and earthly tabernacle; the sense of harmony between his soul and its physical environment became, for a time at least, like perfectly played music, and the life led there singularly tranquil and filled with a curious sense of self-possession. The love of security, of an habitually undisputed standing-ground or sleeping-place, came to count for much in the generation and correcting of his thoughts, and afterwards as a salutary principle of restraint in all his wanderings of spirit. The wistful yearning toward home, in absence from it, as the shadows of evening deepened, and he followed in thought what was doing there from hour to hour, interpreted to him much of a yearning and regret he experienced afterwards, toward he knew not what, out of strange ways of feeling and thought in which, from time to time, his spirit found itself alone; and in the tears shed in such absences there seemed always to be some soul-subduing foretaste of what his last tears might be.

[1] a slight repast, a taste [2] at home

And the sense of security could hardly have been deeper, the quiet of the child's soul being one with the quiet of its home, a place "inclosed" and "sealed." But upon this assured place, upon the child's assured soul which resembled it, there came floating in from the larger world without, as at windows left ajar unknowingly, or over the high garden walls, two streams of impressions, the sentiments of beauty and pain—recognitions of the visible, tangible, audible loveliness of things, as a very real and somewhat tyrannous element in them—and of the sorrow of the world, of grown people and children and animals, as a thing not to be put by in them. From this point he could trace two predominant processes of mental change in him—the growth of an almost diseased sensibility to the spectacle of suffering, and, parallel with this, the rapid growth of a certain capacity of fascination by bright color and choice form—the sweet curvings, for instance, of the lips of those who seemed to him comely persons, modulated in such delicate unison to the things they said or sang,—marking early the activity in him of a more than customary sensuousness, "the lust of the eye," as the Preacher says, [3] which might lead him, one day, how far! Could he have foreseen the weariness of the way! In music sometimes the two sorts of impressions came together, and he would weep, to the surprise of older people. Tears of joy too the child knew, also to older people's surprise; real tears, once, of relief from long-strung, childish expectation, when he found returned at evening, with new roses in her cheeks, the little sister who had been to a place where there was a wood, and brought back for him a treasure of fallen acorns, and black crow's feathers, and his peace at finding her again near him mingled all night with some

[3] The Preacher is Ecclesiastes, but the phrase "lust of the eyes" is in *1 John,* ii, 16.

intimate sense of the distant forest, the rumor of its breezes, with the glossy blackbirds aslant and the branches lifted in them, and of the perfect nicety of the little cups that fell. So those two elementary apprehensions of the tenderness and of the color in things grew apace in him, and were seen by him afterwards to send their roots back into the beginnings of life. Let me note first some of the occasions of his recognition of the element of pain in things—incidents, now and again, which seemed suddenly to awake in him the whole force of that sentiment which Goethe has called the *Weltschmerz,* [1] and in which the concentrated sorrow of the world seemed suddenly to lie heavy upon him. A book lay in an old bookcase, of which he cared to remember one picture—a woman sitting, with hands bound behind her, the dress, the cap, the hair, folded with a simplicity which touched him strangely, as if not by her own hands, but with some ambiguous care at the hands of others—Queen Marie Antoinette, on her way to execution—we all remember David's [2] drawing, meant merely to make her ridiculous. The face that had been so high had learned to be mute and resistless; but out of its very resistlessness, seemed now to call on men to have pity, and forbear; and he took note of that, as he closed the book, as a thing to look at again, if he should at any time find himself tempted to be cruel. Again, he would never quite forget the appeal in the small sister's face, in the garden under the lilacs, terrified at a spider lighted on her sleeve. He could trace back to the look then noted a certain mercy he conceived always for people in fear, even of little things, which seemed to make him, though but for a moment, capable of almost any sacrifice of himself. Impressible, susceptible persons, indeed, who had had their sorrows, lived about him; and this sensibility was due in part to the tacit influence of their presence, enforcing upon him habitually the fact that there are those who pass their days, as a matter of course, in a sort of "going quietly." Most poignantly of all he could recall, in unfading, minutest circumstance, the cry on the stair, sounding bitterly through the house, and struck into his soul forever, of an aged woman, his father's sister, come now to announce his death in distant India; how it seemed to make the aged woman like a child again; and, he knew not why, but this fancy was full of pity to him. There were the little sorrows of the dumb animals, too—of the white angora, with a dark tail like an ermine's, and a face like a flower, who fell into a lingering sickness, and became quite delicately human in its valetudinarianism, and came to have a hundred different expressions of voice—how it grew worse and worse, till it began to feel the light too much for it, and at last, after one wild morning of pain, the little soul flickered away from the body, quite worn to death already, and now but feebly retaining it.

So he wanted another pet; and as there were starlings about the place, which could be taught to speak, one of them was caught, and he meant to treat it kindly; but in the night its young ones could be heard crying after it, and the responsive cry of the mother bird toward them; and at last, with the first light, though not till after some debate with himself, he went down and opened the cage, and saw a sharp bound of the prisoner up to her nestlings; and therewith came the sense of remorse,—that he, too, was become an accomplice in moving, to the limit of his small power, the springs and handles of that great machine in things, constructed so ingeniously to play pain-fugues on the delicate nerve-work of living creatures.

I have remarked how, in the process of our brain-building, as the house of thought in which we live gets itself together, like some airy bird's nest of floating thistledown and chance straws, compact at last, little accidents have their consequence; and thus it happened that, as he walked one evening, a garden gate, usually closed, stood open; and lo! within, a great red hawthorn in full flower, embossing heavily the bleached and twisted trunk and branches, so aged that there were but few green leaves thereon—a plumage of tender, crimson fire out of the heart of the dry wood. The perfume of the tree had now and again reached him, in the currents of the wind, over the wall, and he had wondered what might be behind it, and was now allowed to fill his arms with the flowers—flowers enough for all the old blue-china pots along the chimney piece, making *fête* in the children's room. Was it some periodic moment in the expansion of soul within him, or mere trick of heat in the heavily-laden, summer air? But the beauty of the thing struck home to him feverishly; and in dreams all night he loitered along a magic roadway of crimson flowers, which seemed to open ruddily in thick, fresh masses about his feet, and fill softly all the little hollows in the banks on either side. Always afterwards, summer by summer, as the flowers came on, the blossom of the red hawthorn still seemed to him absolutely

[1] world-sorrow
[2] Jacques Louis David, court painter to Louis XVI and to Napoleon

the reddest of all things; and the goodly crimson, still alive in the works of old Venetian masters or old Flemish tapestries, called out always from afar the recollection of the flame in those perishing little petals, as it pulsed gradually out of them, kept long in the drawers of an old cabinet. Also then, for the first time, he seemed to experience a passionateness in his relation to fair outward objects, an inexplicable excitement in their presence, which disturbed him, and from which he half longed to be free. A touch of regret or desire mingled all night with the remembered presence of the red flowers, and their perfume in the darkness about him; and the longing for some undivined, entire possession of them was the beginning of a revelation to him, growing ever clearer with the coming of the gracious summer guise of fields and trees and persons in each succeeding year, of a certain, at times seemingly exclusive, predominance in his interests, of beautiful physical things, a kind of tyranny of the senses over him.

In later years he came upon philosophies which occupied him much in the estimate of the proportion of the sensuous and the ideal elements in human knowledge, the relative parts they bear in it; and, in his intellectual scheme, was led to assign very little to the abstract thought, and much to its sensible vehicle or occasion. Such metaphysical speculation did but reinforce what was instinctive in his way of receiving the world, and for him, everywhere, that sensible vehicle or occasion became, perhaps only too surely, the necessary concomitant of any perception of things, real enough to be of any weight or reckoning, in his house of thought. There were times when he could think of the necessity he was under of associating all thoughts to touch and sight, as a sympathetic link between himself and actual, feeling, living objects; a protest in favor of real men and women against mere gray, unreal abstractions; and he remembered gratefully how the Christian religion, hardly less than the religion of the ancient Greeks, translating so much of its spiritual verity into things that may be seen, condescends in part to sanction this infirmity, if so it be, of our human existence, wherein the world of sense is so much with us, [1] and welcomed this thought as a kind of keeper and sentinel over his soul therein. But certainly he came more and more to be unable to care for or think of soul but as in an actual body, or of any world but that wherein are water and trees, and where men and women look, so or so, and press actual hands. It was the trick even his pity learned, fastening those who suffered in anywise to his affections by a kind of sensible attachments. He would think of Julian, fallen into incurable sickness, as spoiled in the sweet blossom of his skin like pale amber, and his honey-like hair; of Cecil, early dead, as cut off from the lilies, from golden summer days, from women's voices; and then what comforted him a little was the thought of the turning of the child's flesh to violets in the turf above him. And thinking of the very poor, it was not the things which most men care most for that he yearned to give them; but fairer roses, perhaps, and power to taste quite as they will, at their ease and not task-burdened, a certain desirable, clear light in the new morning, through which sometimes he had noticed them, quite unconscious of it, on their way to their early toil.

So he yielded himself to these things, to be played upon by them like a musical instrument, and began to note with deepening watchfulness, but always with some puzzled, unutterable longing in his enjoyment, the phases of the seasons and of the growing or waning day, down even to the shadowy changes wrought on bare wall or ceiling—the light cast up from the snow, bringing out their darkest angles; the brown light in the cloud, which meant rain; that almost too austere clearness, in the protracted light of the lengthing day, before warm weather began, as if it lingered but to make a severer workday, with the schoolbooks opened earlier and later; that beam of June sunshine, at last, as he lay awake before the time, a way of gold dust across the darkness; all the humming, the freshness, the perfume of the garden seemed to lie upon it—and coming in one afternoon in September, along the red gravel walk, to look for a basket of yellow crab apples left in the cool, old parlor, he remembered it the more, and how the colors struck upon him, because a wasp on one bitten apple stung him, and he felt the passion of sudden, severe pain. For this too brought its curious reflections; and, in relief from it, he would wonder over it—how it had then been with him—puzzled at the depth of the charm or spell over him, which lay, for a little while at least, in the mere absence of pain; once, especially, when an older boy taught him to make flowers of sealing wax, and he had burnt his hand badly at the lighted taper, and been unable to sleep. He remembered that also afterwards, as a sort of typical thing—a white vision of heat about him, clinging closely, through the languid scent of the ointments put upon the place to make it well.

Also, as he felt this pressure upon him of

[1] See Wordsworth's sonnet, p. 464.

the sensible world, then, as often afterwards, there would come another sort of curious questioning how the last impressions of eye and ear might happen to him, how they would find him—the scent of the last flower, the soft yellowness of the last morning, the last recognition of some object of affection, hand or voice; it could not be but that the latest look of the eyes, before their final closing, would be strangely vivid; one would go with the hot tears, the cry, the touch of the wistful bystander, impressed how deeply on one! Or would it be, perhaps, a mere frail retiring of all things, great or little, away from one, into a level distance?

For with this desire of physical beauty mingled itself early the fear of death—the fear of death intensified by the desire of beauty. Hitherto he had never gazed upon dead faces, as sometimes, afterwards, at the *Morgue* in Paris, or in that fair cemetery at Munich, where all the dead must go and lie in state before burial, behind glass windows, among the flowers and incense and holy candles—the aged clergy with their sacred ornaments, the young men in their dancing shoes and spotless white linen—after which visits, those waxen, resistless faces would always live with him for many days, making the broadest sunshine sickly. The child had heard indeed of the death of his father, and how, in the Indian station, a fever had taken him, so that though not in action he had yet died as a soldier; and hearing of the "resurrection of the just,"[1] he could think of him as still abroad in the world, somehow, for his protection—a grand, though perhaps rather terrible figure, in beautiful soldier's things, like the figure in the picture of Joshua's Vision in the Bible[2]—and of that, round which the mourners moved so softly, and afterwards with such solemn singing, as but a worn-out garment left at a deserted lodging. So it was, until on a summer day he walked with his mother through a fair churchyard. In a bright dress he rambled among the graves, in the gay weather, and so came, in one corner, upon an open grave for a child—a dark space on the brilliant grass—the black mold lying heaped up round it, weighing down the little jeweled branches of the dwarf rosebushes in flower. And therewith came, full-grown, never wholly to leave him, with the certainty that even children do sometimes die, the physical horror of death, with its wholly selfish recoil from the association of lower forms of life, and the suffocating weight above. No benign grave figure in beautiful soldier's things any longer abroad in the world for his protection! only a few poor, piteous bones; and above them, possibly, a certain sort of figure he hoped not to see. For sitting one day in the garden below an open window, he heard people talking, and could not but listen, how, in a sleepless hour, a sick woman had seen one of the dead sitting beside her, come to call her hence; and from the broken talk evolved with much clearness the notion that not all those dead people had really departed to the churchyard, nor were quite so motionless as they looked, but led a secret, half-fugitive life in their old homes, quite free by night, though sometimes visible in the day, dodging from room to room, with no great goodwill toward those who shared the place with them. All night the figure sat beside him in the reveries of his broken sleep, and was not quite gone in the morning—an odd, irreconcilable new member of the household making the sweet familiar chambers unfriendly and suspect by its uncertain presence. He could have hated the dead he had pitied so, for being thus. Afterwards he came to think of those poor, home-returning ghosts, which all men have fancied to themselves—the *revenants*—pathetically, as crying, or beating with vain hands at the doors, as the wind came, their cries distinguishable in it as a wilder inner note. But, always making death more unfamiliar still, that old experience would ever, from time to time, return to him; even in the living he sometimes caught its likeness; at any time or place, in a moment, the faint atmosphere of the chamber of death would be breathed around him, and the image with the bound chin, the quaint smile, the straight, stiff feet, shed itself across the air upon the bright carpet, amid the gayest company, or happiest communing with himself.

To most children the somber questionings to which impressions like these attach themselves, if they come at all, are actually suggested by religious books, which therefore they often regard with much secret distaste, and dismiss, as far as possible, from their habitual thoughts as a too depressing element in life. To Florian such impressions, these misgivings as to the ultimate tendency of the years, of the relationship between life and death, had been suggested spontaneously in the natural course of his mental growth by a strong innate sense for the soberer tones in things, further strengthened by actual circumstances; and religious sentiment, that system of biblical ideas in which he had been brought up, presented itself to him as a thing that might soften and dignify, and light up as with a "lively hope,"[3]

[1] *Luke*, xiv, 14
[2] *Joshua*, v, 13
[3] *1 Peter*, i, 3

a melancholy already deeply settled in him. So he yielded himself easily to religious impressions, and with a kind of mystical appetite for sacred things; the more as they came to him through a saintly person who loved him tenderly, and believed that this early preoccupation with them already marked the child out for a saint. He began to love, for their own sakes, church lights, holy days, all that belonged to the comely order of the sanctuary, the secrets of its white linen, and holy vessels, and fonts of pure water; and its hieratic purity and simplicity became the type of something he desired always to have about him in actual life. He pored over the pictures in religious books, and knew by heart the exact mode in which the wrestling angel grasped Jacob, how Jacob looked in his mysterious sleep, how the bells and pomegranates were attached to the hem of Aaron's vestment, sounding sweetly as he glided over the turf of the holy place. [1] His way of conceiving religion came then to be in effect what it ever afterwards remained—a sacred history indeed, but still more a sacred ideal, a transcendent version or representation, under intenser and more expressive light and shade, of human life and its familiar or exceptional incidents, birth, death, marriage, youth, age, tears, joy, rest, sleep, waking—a mirror, toward which men might turn away their eyes from vanity and dullness, and see themselves therein as angels, with their daily meat and drink, even, become a kind of sacred transaction—a complementary strain or burden, applied to our everyday existence, whereby the stray snatches of music in it reset themselves, and fall into the scheme of some higher and more consistent harmony. A place adumbrated itself in his thoughts, wherein those sacred personalities, which are at once the reflex and the pattern of our nobler phases of life, housed themselves; and this region in his intellectual scheme all subsequent experience did but tend still further to realize and define. Some ideal, hieratic persons he would always need to occupy it and keep a warmth there. And he could hardly understand those who felt no such need at all, finding themselves quite happy without such heavenly companionship, and sacred double of their life, beside them.

Thus a constant substitution of the typical for the actual took place in his thoughts. Angels might be met by the way, under English elm or beech tree; mere messengers seemed like angels, bound on celestial errands; a deep mysticity brooded over real meetings and partings; marriages were made in heaven; and deaths also, with hands of angels thereupon, to bear soul and body quietly asunder, each to its appointed rest. All the acts and accidents of daily life borrowed a sacred color and significance; the very colors of things became themselves weighty with meanings like the sacred stuffs of Moses' tabernacle, [2] full of penitence or peace. Sentiment, congruous in the first instance only with those divine transactions, the deep, effusive unction of the house of Bethany, [3] was assumed as the due attitude for the reception of our everyday existence; and for a time he walked through the world in a sustained, not unpleasurable awe, generated by the habitual recognition, beside every circumstance and event of life, of its celestial correspondent.

Sensibility—the desire of physical beauty—a strange, biblical awe, which made any reference to the unseen act on him like solemn music—these qualities the child took away with him when, at about the age of twelve years, he left the old house, and was taken to live in another place. He had never left home before, and, anticipating much from this change, had long dreamed over it, jealously counting the days till the time fixed for departure should come; had been a little careless about others even, in his strong desire for it—when Lewis fell sick, for instance, and they must wait still two days longer. At last the morning came, very fine; and all things—the very pavement with its dust, at the roadside—seemed to have a white, pearl-like luster in them. They were to travel by a favorite road on which he had often walked a certain distance, and on one of those two prisoner days, when Lewis was sick, had walked farther than ever before, in his great desire to reach the new place. They had started and gone a little way when a pet bird was found to have been left behind, and must even now—so it presented itself to him—have already all the appealing fierceness and wild self-pity at heart of one left by others to perish of hunger in a closed house; and he returned to fetch it, himself in hardly less stormy distress. But as he passed in search of it from room to room, lying so pale, with a look of meekness in their denudation, and at last through that little, stripped white room, the aspect of the place touched him like the

[1] *Genesis,* xxxii, 24; xxviii, 11; *Exodus,* xxviii, 33-35

[2] *Exodus,* xxvi

[3] The house of Simon the leper, where the woman poured the box of ointment on Jesus' head—a "deep, effusive unction"; see *Matthew,* xxvi, 7.

face of one dead; and a clinging back toward it came over him, so intense that he knew it would last long, and spoiling all his pleasure in the realization of a thing so eagerly anticipated. And so, with the bird found, but himself in an agony of homesickness, thus capriciously sprung up within him, he was driven quickly away, far into the rural distance, so fondly speculated on, of that favorite country road.

1878

ROBERT LOUIS STEVENSON
1850-1894

Stevenson, much beloved child of the closing years of the nineteenth century, was the son of a prominent Scotch engineer and builder of lighthouses. He was born in Edinburgh, attended the university, and for a while planned to follow the footsteps of his father. But he turned to law, and then to literature. From young manhood he fought a valiant battle against consumption, holding off the immediate effects of the disease by an outdoor life which included boating on the canals of Belgium and France, camping in California, and residence on the Riviera, in the Adirondacks, and finally in Samoa, where he died.

Stevenson brought back into fiction a vigorous romance that had been all but extinguished in the realistic and philosophical novels of his day. Adventure once more came to its own, as in the days of Scott; in *Treasure Island, Kidnapped, The Master of Ballantrae,* produced between 1886 and 1889, and in *Weir of Hermiston,* 1896, he shows an increasing skill in the treatment of a serious plot and in the delineation of character. His essays, narratives of personal adventure, and verse, were produced after 1881. Stevenson acquired a workmanlike style only after prolonged apprenticeship when, as he says, he "played the sedulous ape" to many authors. In narrative and essay, Stevenson's style is an example of that easy prose which rarely intrudes upon the consciousness of the reader once fallen under its spell. Some feel that his style is excessively "mannered," but even they can find little fault with the spirit that animates the essays and is more than a little reminiscent of Charles Lamb.

Biography: G. Balfour, 2 vols. 1901. Criticism: W. Raleigh, *Robert Louis Stevenson,* 1905; Stephen Lang; "New Views of Stevenson," C. S. Northrup, *Dial* 59:561-4; "R. L. Stevenson's Contribution to Literature and Life," L. M. Watt, *Scrib.* 68:641-53; "The Stevenson Myth," G. S. Hellman, *Cent.* 105:240-52.

EL DORADO[1]

It seems as if a great deal were attainable in a world where there are so many marriages and decisive battles, and where we all, at certain hours of the day, and with great gusto and despatch, stow a portion of victuals finally and irretrievably into the bag which contains us. And it would seem also, on a hasty view, that the attainment of as much as possible was the one goal of man's contentious life. And yet, as regards the spirit, this is but a semblance. We live in an ascending scale when we live happily, one thing leading to another in an endless series. There is always a new horizon for onward-looking men,[2] and although we dwell on a small planet, immersed in petty business and not enduring beyond a brief period of years, we are so constituted that our hopes are inaccessible, like stars, and the term of hoping is prolonged until the term of life. To be truly happy is a question of how we begin and not of how we end, of what we want and not of what we have. An aspiration is a joy forever,[3] a possession as solid as a landed estate, a fortune which we can never exhaust and which gives us year by year a revenue of pleasurable activity. To have many of these is to be spiritually rich. Life is only a very dull and ill-directed theater unless we have some interests in the piece; and to those who have neither art nor science, the world is a mere arrangement of colors, or a rough footway where they may very well break their shins. It is in virtue of his own desires and curiosities that any man continues to exist with even patience, that he is charmed by the look of things and people, and that he wakens every morning with a renewed appetite for work and pleasure. Desire and curiosity are the two eyes through which he sees the world in the most enchanted colors; it is they that make women beautiful or fossils interesting: and the man may squander his estate and come to beggary, but if he keeps these two amulets he is still rich in the possibilities of pleasure. Suppose he could take one meal so compact and comprehensive that he should never hunger any more; suppose him, at a glance, to take in all the features of the world and allay the desire for knowledge; suppose him to do the like in any province of experience—would not that man be in a poor way for amusement ever after?

One who goes touring on foot with a single

[1] Spanish: The Gilded, or Golden. The name was originally given to a fabulous king of a wealthy city supposed to exist somewhere in South America, the object of much search in the 16th century. It was later applied to the city, and has now become a name for the object of any visionary quest. The essay is from *Virginibus Puerisque,* 1881, and is reprinted, along with the selections that follow, by permission of Messrs. Charles Scribner's Sons, who hold the copyright.

[2] Cf. Tennyson's famous figure, *Ulysses,* 19-21, p. 622.

[3] echoed from Keats's *Endymion,* 1

volume in his knapsack reads with circumspection, pausing often to reflect, and often laying the book down to contemplate the landscape or the prints in the inn parlor; for he fears to come to an end of his entertainment, and be left companionless on the last stages of his journey. A young fellow recently finished the works of Thomas Carlyle, winding up, if we remember aright, with the ten notebooks upon Frederick the Great. "What!" cried the young fellow, in consternation, "is there no more Carlyle? Am I left to the daily papers?" A more celebrated instance is that of Alexander, who wept bitterly because he had no more worlds to subdue. And when Gibbon had finished the *Decline and Fall,* [1] he had only a few moments of joy; and it was with a "sober melancholy" that he parted from his labors.

Happily we all shoot at the moon with ineffectual arrows; our hopes are set on inaccessible El Dorado; we come to an end of nothing here below. Interests are only plucked up to sow themselves again, like mustard. You would think, when the child was born, there would be an end to trouble; and yet it is only the beginning of fresh anxieties; and when you have seen it through its teething and its education, and at last its marriage, alas! it is only to have new fears, new, quivering sensibilities, with every day; and the health of your children's children grows as touching a concern as that of your own. Again, when you have married your wife, you would think you were got upon a hilltop, and might begin to go downward by an easy slope. But you have only ended courting to begin marriage. Falling in love and winning love are often difficult tasks to overbearing and rebellious spirits; but to keep in love is also a business of some importance, to which both man and wife must bring kindness and goodwill. The true love story commences at the altar, when there lies before the married pair a most beautiful contest of wisdom and generosity, and a life-long struggle toward an unattainable ideal. Unattainable? Aye, surely unattainable, from the very fact that they are two instead of one.

"Of making books there is no end," complained the Preacher; [2] and did not perceive how highly he was praising letters as an occupation. There is no end, indeed, to making books or experiments, or to travel, or to gathering wealth. Problem gives rise to problem. We may study for ever, and we are never as learned as we would. We have never made a statue worthy of our dreams. And when we have discovered a continent, or crossed a chain of mountains, it is only to find another ocean or another plain upon the farther side. In the infinite universe there is room for our swiftest diligence and to spare. It is not like the works of Carlyle, which can be read to an end. Even in a corner of it, in a private park, or in the neighborhood of a single hamlet, the weather and the seasons keep so deftly changing that although we walk there for a lifetime there will be always something new to startle and delight us.

There is only one wish realizable on the earth; only one thing that can be perfectly attained—death. And from a variety of circumstances we have no one to tell us whether it be worth attaining.

A strange picture we make on our way to our chimaeras, ceaselessly marching, grudging ourselves the time for rest; indefatigable, adventurous pioneers. It is true that we shall never reach the goal; it is even more than probable that there is no such place; and if we lived for centuries and were endowed with the powers of a god, we should find ourselves not much nearer what we wanted at the end. O toiling hands of mortals! O unwearied feet, traveling ye know not whither! Soon, soon, it seems to you, you must come forth on some conspicuous hilltop, and but a little way farther, against the setting sun, descry the spires of El Dorado. Little do ye know your own blessedness; for to travel hopefully is a better thing than to arrive, and the true success is to labor.

1881

[1] a twenty-four years' labor

[2] *Ecclesiastes,* xii, 12

THE MAROON [3]

Of the beauties of Anaho books might be written. I remember waking about three, to find the air temperate and scented. The long swell brimmed into the bay, and seemed to fill it full and then subside. Gently, deeply, and silently the *Casco* rolled; only at times a block [4] piped like a bird. Oceanward, the heaven was bright with stars and the sea with their reflections. If I looked to that side, I might have sung with the Hawaiian poet:

Ua maomao ka lani, ua kahaea luna,
Ua pipi ka maka o ka hoku.
(The heavens were fair, they stretched above,
Many were the eyes of the stars.)

[3] A maroon is one who has been "marooned," or abandoned on an island. This chapter is taken from *In the South Seas,* 1891. Stevenson made a cruise among the South Sea Islands in the yacht *Casco* in 1888. Anaho is a native village of Nuka-hiva. Kanaka, properly a Sandwich-Islander, is a general name for a South Sea Islander or his speech.

[4] pulley

And then I turned shoreward, and high squalls were overhead; the mountains loomed up black; and I could have fancied I had slipped ten thousand miles away and was anchored in a Highland loch; that when the day came, it would show pine, and heather, and green fern, and roofs of turf sending up the smoke of peats; and the alien speech that should next greet my ears must be Gaelic, not Kanaka.

And day, when it came, brought other sights and thoughts. I have watched the morning break in many quarters of the world; it has been certainly one of the chief joys of my existence, and the dawn that I saw with most emotion shone upon the bay of Anaho. The mountains abruptly overhang the port with every variety of surface and of inclination, lawn, and cliff, and forest. Not one of these but wore its proper tint of saffron, of sulphur, of the clove, and of the rose. The luster was like that of satin; on the lighter hues there seemed to float an efflorescence; a solemn bloom appeared on the more dark. The light itself was the ordinary light of morning, colorless and clean; and on this ground of jewels, penciled out the least detail of drawing. Meanwhile, around the hamlet, under the palms, where the blue shadow lingered, the red coals of coco-husk and the light trails of smoke betrayed the awakening business of the day; along the beach men and women, lads and lasses, were returning from the bath in bright raiment, red and blue and green, such as we delighted to see in the colored little pictures of our childhood; and presently the sun had cleared the eastern hill, and the glow of the day was over all.

The glow continued and increased, the business, from the main part, ceased before it had begun. Twice in the day there was a certain stir of shepherding along the seaward hills. At times a canoe went out to fish. At times a woman or two languidly filled a basket in the cotton patch. At times a pipe would sound out of the shadow of a house, ringing the changes on its three notes, with an effect like *Que le jour me dure*[1] repeated endlessly. Or at times, across a corner of the bay, two natives might communicate in the Marquesan manner with conventional whistlings. All else was sleep and silence. The surf broke and shone around the shores; a species of black crane fished in the broken water; the black pigs were continually galloping by on some affair; but the people might never have awaked, or they might all be dead.

[1] "How heavy hangs the day on me!"

My favorite haunt was opposite the hamlet, where was a landing in a cove under a lianaed[2] cliff. The beach was lined with palms and a tree called the purao, something between the fig and mulberry in growth, and bearing a flower like a great, yellow poppy with a maroon heart. In places rocks encroached upon the sand; the beach would be all submerged; and the surf would bubble warmly as high as to my knees, and play with coconut husks as our more homely ocean plays with wreck and wrack and bottles. As the reflux drew down, marvels of color and design streamed between my feet; which I would grasp at, miss, or seize—now to find them what they promised, shells to grace a cabinet or be set in gold upon a lady's finger; now to catch only *maya*[3] of colored sand, pounded fragments and pebbles, that, as soon as they were dry, became as dull and homely as the flints upon a garden path. I have toiled at this childish pleasure for hours in the strong sun, conscious of my incurable ignorance; but too keenly pleased to be ashamed. Meanwhile, the blackbird (or his tropical understudy) would be fluting in the thickets overhead.

A little farther, in the turn of the bay, a streamlet trickled in the bottom of a den,[4] thence spilling down a stair of rock into the sea. The draught of air drew down under the foliage in the very bottom of the den, which was a perfect arbor for coolness. In front it stood open on the blue bay and the *Casco* lying there under her awning and her cheerful colors. Overhead was a thatch of puraos, and over these again palms brandished their bright fans, as I have seen a conjurer make himself a halo out of naked swords. For in this spot, over a neck of low land at the foot of the mountains, the trade wind streams into Anaho Bay in a flood of almost constant volume and velocity, and of a heavenly coolness.

It chanced one day that I was ashore in the cove with Mrs. Stevenson and the ship's cook. Except for the *Casco* lying outside, and a crane or two, and the ever-busy wind and sea, the face of the world was of a prehistoric emptiness; life appeared to stand stockstill, and the sense of isolation was profound and refreshing. On a sudden, the trade wind, coming in a gust over the isthmus, struck and scattered the fans of the palms above the den; and, behold! in

[2] covered with lianas, or tropical vines
[3] illusion (Hindu philosophy)
[4] glen, dingle

two of the tops there sat a native, motionless as an idol, and watching us, you would have said, without a wink. The next moment the tree closed, and the glimpse was gone. This discovery of human presences latent overhead in a place where we had supposed ourselves alone, the immobility of our treetop spies, and the thought that perhaps at all hours we were similarly supervised, struck us with a chill. Talk languished on the beach. As for the cook (whose conscience was not clear), he never afterwards set foot on shore, and twice, when the *Casco* appeared to be driving on the rocks, it was amusing to observe that man's alacrity; death, he was persuaded, awaiting him upon the beach. It was more than a year later, in the Gilberts, that the explanation dawned upon myself. The natives were drawing palm-tree wine, a thing forbidden by law; and when the wind thus suddenly revealed them, they were doubtless more troubled than ourselves.

At the top of the den there dwelt an old, melancholy, grizzled man of the name of Tari (Charlie) Coffin. He was a native of Oahu, in the Sandwich Islands; and had gone to sea in his youth in the American whalers; a circumstance to which he owed his name, his English, his down-east twang, and the misfortune of his innocent life. For one captain, sailing out of New Bedford, carried him to Nuka-hiva and marooned him there among the cannibals. The motive for this act was inconceivably small; poor Tari's wages, which were thus economized, would scarce have shook the credit of the New Bedford owners. And the act itself was simply murder. Tari's life must have hung in the beginning by a hair. In the grief and terror of that time, it is not unlikely he went mad, an infirmity to which he was still liable; or perhaps a child may have taken a fancy to him and ordained him to be spared. He escaped at least alive, married in the island, and when I knew him was a widower with a married son and a granddaughter. But the thought of Oahu haunted him; its praise was forever on his lips; he beheld it, looking back, as a place of ceaseless feasting, song, and dance; and in his dreams I dare say he revisits it with joy. I wonder what he would think if he could be carried there indeed, and see the modern town of Honolulu brisk with traffic, and the palace with its guards, and the great hotel, and Mr. Berger's band with their uniforms and outlandish instruments; or what he would think to see the brown faces grown so few and the white so many; and his father's land sold for planting sugar, and his father's house quite perished, or perhaps the last of them struck leprous and immured between the surf and the cliffs on Molokai.[1] So simply, even in South Sea Islands, and so sadly, the changes come.

Tari was poor, and poorly lodged. His house was a wooden frame, run up by Europeans; it was indeed his official residence, for Tari was the shepherd of the promontory sheep. I can give a perfect inventory of its contents—three kegs, a tin biscuit-box, an iron sauce-pan, several coco-shell cups, a lantern, and three bottles, probably containing oil; while the clothes of the family and a few mats were thrown across the open rafters. Upon my first meeting with this exile he had conceived for me one of the baseless, island friendships, and given me nuts to drink, and carried me up the den "to see my house"—the only entertainment that he had to offer. He liked the "Amelican," he said, and the "Inglisman," but the "Flessman" was his abhorrence; and he was careful to explain that if he had thought us "Fless," we should have had none of his nuts, and never a sight of his house. His distaste for the French I can partly understand, but not at all his toleration of the Anglo-Saxon. The next day he brought me a pig, and some days later one of our party going ashore found him in act to bring a second. We were still strange to the islands; we were pained by the poor man's generosity, which he could ill afford; and by a natural enough but quite unpardonable blunder, we refused the pig. Had Tari been a Marquesan we should have seen him no more; being what he was, the most mild long-suffering, melancholy man, he took a revenge a hundred times more painful. Scarce had the canoe with the nine villagers put off from their farewell[2] before the *Casco* was boarded from the other side. It was Tari; coming thus late because he had no canoe of his own, and had found it hard to borrow one; coming thus solitary (as indeed we always saw him) because he was a stranger in the land, and the dreariest of company. The rest of my family basely fled from the encounter. I must receive our injured friend alone; and the interview must have lasted hard upon an hour, for he was loath to tear himself away. "You go 'way. I see you no more—no, sir!" he lamented; and then looking about him with rueful admiration, "This goodee ship!—no, sir!—

[1] an island on which the lepers are isolated, a little to the southeast of Oahu

[2] farewell visit mentioned in a preceding chapter

ROBERT LOUIS STEVENSON

goodee ship!" he would exclaim; the "no, sir," thrown out sharply through the nose upon a rising inflection, an echo from New Bedford and the fallacious whaler. From these expressions of grief and praise, he would return continually to the case of the rejected pig. "I like give plesent all the same you," he complained; "only got pig—you no take him!" he was a poor man; he had no choice of gifts; he had only a pig, he repeated; and I had refused it. I have rarely been more wretched than to see him sitting there, so old, so gray, so poor, so hardly fortuned, of so rueful a countenance, and to appreciate, with growing keeness, the affront which I had so innocently dealt him; but it was one of those cases in which speech is vain.

Tari's son was smiling and inert; his daughter-in-law, a girl of sixteen, pretty, gentle, and grave, more intelligent than most Anaho women, and with a fair share of French; his grandchild, a mite of a creature at the breast. I went up the den one day when Tari was from home, and found the son making a cotton sack, and madame suckling mademoiselle. When I had sat down with them on the floor, the girl began to question me about England; which I tried to describe, piling the pan and the coco shells one upon another to represent the houses, and explaining, as best I was able, and by word and gesture, the over-population, the hunger, and the perpetual toil. *"Pas de cocotiers? pas de popoi?"* [1] she asked. I told her it was too cold, and went through an elaborate performance, shutting out draughts, and crouching over an imaginary fire, to make sure she understood. But she understood right well; remarked it must be bad for the health, and sat a while gravely reflecting on that picture of unwonted sorrows. I am sure it roused her pity, for it struck in her another thought always uppermost in the Marquesan bosom; and she began with a smiling sadness, and looking on me out of melancholy eyes, to lament the decease of her own people. *"Ici pas de Kanaques,"* [2] said she; and taking the baby from her breast, she held it out to me with both her hands. "*Tenez* [3]—a little baby like this; then dead. All the Kanaques die. Then no more." The smile, and this instancing by the girl-mother of her own tiny flesh and blood, affected me strangely; they spoke of so tranquil a despair. Meanwhile the husband smilingly made his sack; and the unconscious babe struggled to reach a pot of raspberry jam, friendship's offering, which I had just brought up the den; and in a perspective of centuries I saw their case as ours, death coming in like a tide, and the day already numbered when there should be no more Beretani, [4] and no more of any race whatever, and (what oddly touched me) no more literary works and no more readers.

1891

[1] No coco-palms? no bread-fruit trees?
[2] Here no more Kanakas! [3] See here!

THE VAGABOND

(To an Air by Schubert)

Give to me the life I love,
  Let the lave [5] go by me,
Give the jolly heaven above
  And the byway nigh me.
Bed in the bush with stars to see,
  Bread I dip in the river —
There's the life for a man like me,
  There's the life forever.

Let the blow fall soon or late,
  Let what will be o'er me;
Give the face of earth around
  And the road before me.
Wealth I seek not, hope nor love,
  Nor a friend to know me;
All I seek the heaven above
  And the road below me.

Or let autumn fall on me
  Where afield I linger,
Silencing the bird on tree,
  Biting the blue finger;
White as meal the frosty field—
  Warm the fireside haven—
Not to autumn will I yield,
  Not to winter even!

Let the blow fall soon or late,
  Let what will be o'er me;
Give the face of earth around,
  And the road before me.
Wealth I ask not, hope nor love,
  Nor a friend to know me.
All I ask the heaven above,
  And the road below me.

c. 1888 1895

[4] I. e. Britannia, Britons; the language of the Kanakas being so largely vocalic, they find it difficult to pronounce two consonants in succession without interposing a vowel.
[5] the leave, the rest; a familiar word in Burns

THE MORNING DRUM-CALL ON MY EAGER EAR

The morning drum-call on my eager ear
Thrills unforgotten yet; the morning dew
Lies yet undried along my field of noon.
But now I pause at whiles in what I do,
And count the bell, and tremble lest I hear
(My work untrimmed) the sunset gun too soon.

c. 1888 1895

EVENSONG

The embers of the day are red
Beyond the murky hill.
The kitchen smokes: the bed
In the darkling house is spread;
The great sky darkens overhead,
And the great woods are shrill.
So far have I been led,
Lord, by Thy will:
So far I have followed, Lord, and wondered still.

The breeze from the embalmèd land
Blows sudden toward the shore,
And claps my cottage door.
I hear the signal, Lord—I understand.
The night at Thy command
Comes. I will eat and sleep and will not question more.

after 1890 1895

REQUIEM

Under the wide and starry sky,
Dig the grave and let me lie.
Glad did I live and gladly die,
And I laid me down with a will.

This be the verse you grave for me:
Here he lies where he longed to be;
Home is the sailor, home from sea,
And the hunter home from the hill.

1884 1887

THE POST-VICTORIAN PERIOD AND THE EARLY TWENTIETH CENTURY

THOUGH Queen Victoria died in 1901, the Victorian Age is generally considered as ending about 1890. In the last decade of the century, many of the active forces that had made notable the previous age, such as its optimism and its adherence to social convention, were dying out and leaving merely their influence behind. The last ten years of the century might be called a period of transition during which certain new tendencies, destined to supersede the old but for a time existing side by side with them, were making themselves felt. Some of the literary movements of the last forty years may be traced to a feeling of revolt against prevailing exaggerations. Among them are a sharper realism as a reaction from Victorian romanticism and sentimentality; free verse, voicing a protest against a too rigid adherence to poetic rules and forms; the cult of beauty substituted by Wilde and his followers for what they thought the petty code of conventional morality; the social satire of Shaw and Wells directed against smug hypocrisy. Some of the new tendencies are the results of social and political developments: with the expansion of the Empire came Kipling and the Anglo-Indian literature; closer intercourse with the Orient excited an interest in Japanese and Chinese verse forms. Perhaps the greatest differences between the present age and the Victorian lie in the ever-widening field of literary adventure: Barrie, using the life and customs of his native country as his material, created the "Kailyard School" which depicted in the vernacular, Scotch domestic life; Masefield and Gibson have developed, on levels never explored before, appealing themes for literature in the spiritual value of the lives of toilers; other authors, working for a revival of Celtic literature, produced an Irish School represented by such men as Yeats and Synge; the World War resulted in a flood of war lyrics.

It is difficult to foresee whither modern literature is tending, but the earlier decades of the twentieth century have shown it still gathering new harvests from new fields, demanding the right to throw off all shackles, and insisting on truth and individualism at all costs. As the end of the third decade of the twentieth century approaches, it appears that the reaction against the Victorian is somewhat spent.

SIR JAMES MATTHEW BARRIE
1860-

Barrie is such a notability in the fields of both fiction and drama that there is much difference of opinion as to which is his forte. The same qualities of humor, pathos, and romance appear in both types, in both he uses the Scotch vernacular, and sometimes his successful dramas are based on his earlier fiction. He was born in the little Scotch town of Kirriemuir, and much of his early life there is reproduced in *Auld Licht Idylls,* 1888, *A Window in Thrums,* 1889, and *Margaret Ogilvy,* 1896. He attended Dumfries Academy and Edinburgh University, and then became a journalist in Nottingham, later moving to London, where he contributed to several well-known periodicals. He was knighted in 1913.

His first long novel, *The Little Minister,* 1891, he dramatized in 1897 to show how the dramatizing of a novel should be done. *Sentimental Tommy,* 1896, for which R. L. Stevenson is supposed to be the boy model, is considered by many to be his best piece of fiction. By 1895 he had scored a success with his first notable play, *The Professor's Love Story;* and from 1900 on he wrote almost exclusively for the stage. Barrie bases many of his plays on incidents in real life (*The Little Minister*). *What Every Woman Knows* represents romance against a background of fancy; and *A Kiss for Cinderella* is placed in an improbable dream world. His best loved character, Peter Pan, comes from a realm unknown to time and space; and in his person unites the Puck of fairy tales with the qualities of eternal childhood.

Biography: Thomas Moult, 1928. Criticism: J. A. Hamerton, *J. M. Barrie and his Books,* 1902; Howe; Scott; Phelps (EMD); also *No. Am.* 212:829-43; Chevalley; Chubb; W. P. Eaton, "Dramatist and Dreamer," *Bookm.* 48:765-8; "Myself in Dumfries," *Liv. Age* 324:159-65; "Myself and my Island," *Liv. Age* 314:163-6.

From MARGARET OGILVY [1]

How My Mother Got Her Soft Face

On the day I was born we bought six hair-bottomed chairs, and in our little house it was an event, the first great victory in a woman's long campaign; how they had been labored for, the pound-note and the thirty threepenny bits they cost, what anxiety there was about the purchase, the show they made in possession of the west room, my father's unnatural coolness when he brought them in (but his face was white)—I so often heard the tale afterwards and shared as boy and man in so many similar triumphs, that the coming of the chairs seems to be something I remember, as if I had jumped out of bed on that first day, and run ben [2] to see how they looked. I am sure my mother's feet were ettling [3] to be ben long before they could be trusted, and that the moment after she was left alone with me she was discovered barefooted in the west room, doctoring a scar (which she had been the first to detect) on one of the chairs, or sitting on them regally or withdrawing and re-opening the door suddenly to take the six by surprise. And then, I think, a shawl was flung over her (it is strange to me to think it was not I who ran after her with the shawl), and she was escorted sternly back to bed and reminded that she had promised not to budge, to which her reply was probably that she had been gone but an instant, and the implication that therefore she had not been gone at all. Thus was one little bit of her revealed to me at once: I wonder if I took note of it. Neighbors came in to see the boy and the chairs. I wonder if she deceived me when she affected to think that there were others like us, or whether I saw through her from the first, she was so easily seen through. When she seemed to agree with them that it would be impossible to give me a college education, was I so easily taken in, or did I know already what ambitions burned behind that dear face? when they spoke of the chairs as the goal quickly reached, was I such a newcomer that her timid lips must say "They are but a beginning" before I heard the words? And when we were left together, did I laugh at the great things that were in her mind, or had she to whisper them to me first, and then did I put my arm round her and tell her that I would help? Thus it was for such a long time, it is strange to me to feel that it was not so from the beginning.

It is all guess-work for six years, and she whom I see in them is the woman who came suddenly into view when they were at an end. Her timid lips I have said, but they were not timid then, and when I knew her the timid lips had come. The soft face—they say the face was not so soft then. The shawl that was flung over her—we had not begun to hunt her with a shawl, nor to make our bodies a screen between her and the draughts, nor to creep into her room a score of times in the night to stand looking at

[1] From *Margaret Ogilvy* by Sir James Barrie, with the permission of Charles Scribner's Sons, publishers.

[2] Here "into the parlor"; the Scotch word means "in or into an inner part of the house."

[3] eager

her as she slept. We did not see her becoming little then, nor sharply turn our heads when she said wonderingly how small her arms had grown. In her happiest moments —and never was a happier woman—her mouth did not of a sudden begin to twitch, and tears to lie on the mute blue eyes in which I have read all I know and would ever care to write. For when you looked into my mother's eyes you knew, as if He had told you, why God sent her into the world—it was to open the minds of all who looked to beautiful thoughts. And that is the beginning and end of literature. Those eyes that I cannot see until I was six years old have guided me through life, and I pray God they may remain my only earthly judge to the last. They were never more my guide than when I helped to put her to earth, not whimpering because my mother had been taken away after seventy-six glorious years of life, but exulting in her even at the grave.

She had a son who was far away at school. I remember very little about him, only that he was a merry-faced boy who ran like a squirrel up a tree and shook the cherries into my lap. When he was thirteen and I was half his age, the terrible news came, and I have been told the face of my mother was awful in its calmness as she set off to get between Death and her boy. We trooped with her down the brae[1] to the wooden station, and I think I was envying her the journey in the mysterious wagons; I know we played around her, proud of our right to be there, but I do not recall it, I only speak from hearsay. Her ticket was taken, she had bidden us good-bye with that fighting face which I cannot see, and then my father came out of the telegraph office and said huskily "He's gone!" Then we turned very quietly and went home again up the little brae. But I speak from hearsay no longer; I knew my mother forever now.

That is how she got her soft face and her pathetic ways and her large charity, and why other mothers ran to her when they had lost a child. "Dinna greet, poor Janet," she would say to them, and they would answer, "Ah, Margaret, but you're greeting yoursel." Margaret Ogilvy had been her maiden name, and after the Scotch custom she was still Margaret Ogilvy to her old friends. Margaret Ogilvy, I loved to name her. Often when I was a boy, "Margaret Oglivy, are you there?" I would call up the stair.

[1] hill

She was always delicate from that hour, and for many months she was very ill. I have heard that the first thing she expressed a wish to see was the christening robe, and she looked long at it and then turned her face to the wall. That was what made me as a boy think of it always as the robe in which he was christened, but I knew later that we had all been christened in it, from the oldest of the family to the youngest, between whom stood twenty years. Hundreds of other children were christened in it also, such robes being then a rare possession, and the lending of ours among my mother's glories. It was carried carefully from house to house, as if it were itself a child; my mother made much of it, smoothed it out, petted it, smiled to it before putting it into the arms of those to whom it was being lent; she was in our pew to see it borne magnificently (something inside it now) down the aisle to the pulpit side, when a stir of expectancy went through the church and we kicked each other's feet beneath the book-board but were reverent in the face; and however the child might behave, laughing brazenly or skirling[2] to its mother's shame, and whatever the father as he held it up might do, look doited[3] probably and bow at the wrong time, the christening robe of long experience helped them through. And when it was brought back to her she took it in her arms as softly as if it might be asleep, and unconsciously pressed it to her breast: there was never anything in the house that spoke to her quite so eloquently as that little white robe; it was the one of her children that always remained a baby. And she had not made it herself, which was the most wonderful thing about it to me, for she seemed to have made all other things. All the clothes in the house were of her making, and you don't know her in the least if you think they were out of the fashion; she turned them and made them new again, she beat them and made them new again, and then she coaxed them into being new again just for the last time, she let them out and took them in and put on new braid, and added a piece up the back, and thus they passed from one member of the family to another until they reached the youngest, and even when we were done with them they reappeared as something else. In the fashion! I must come back to this. Never was a woman with such an eye for it. She had

[2] screaming
[3] stupid

no fashion-plates; she did not need them. The minister's wife (a cloak), the banker's daughters (the new sleeve)—they had but to pass our window once, and the scalp, so to speak, was in my mother's hands. Observe her rushing, scissors in hand, thread in mouth, to the drawers where her daughters' Sabbath clothes were kept. Or go to church next Sunday, and watch a certain family filing in, the boy lifting his legs high to show off his new boots, but all the others demure, especially the timid, unobservant looking little woman in the rear of them. If you were the minister's wife that day or the banker's daughters you would have got a shock. But she bought the christening robe, and when I used to ask why, she would beam and look conscious, and say she wanted to be extravagant once. And she told me, still smiling, that the more a woman was given to stitching and making things for herself, the greater was her passionate desire now and again to rush to the shops and "be foolish." The christening robe with its pathetic frills is over half a century old now, and has begun to droop a little, like a daisy whose time is past, but it is as fondly kept together as ever: I saw it in use again only the other day.

My mother lay in bed with the christening robe beside her, and I peeped in many times at the door and then went to the stair and sat on it and sobbed. I know not if it was that first day, or many days afterwards, that there came to me my sister, the daughter my mother loved the best, yes, more I am sure even than she loved me, whose great glory she has been since I was six years old. This sister, who was then passing out of her teens, came to me with a very anxious face and wringing her hands, and she told me to go ben to my mother and say to her that she still had another boy. I went ben excitedly, but the room was dark, and when I heard the door shut and no sound come from the bed I was afraid, and I stood still. I suppose I was breathing hard, or perhaps I was crying, for after a time I heard a listless voice that had never been listless before say, "Is that you?" I think the tone hurt me, for I made no answer, and then the voice said more anxiously, "Is that you?" again. I thought it was the dead boy she was speaking to, and I said in a little lonely voice, "No, it's no him, it's just me." Then I heard a cry, and my mother turned in bed, and though it was dark I knew that she was holding out her arms.

After that I sat a great deal in her bed trying to make her forget him, which was my crafty way of playing physician, and if I saw any one out of doors do something that made the others laugh I immediately hastened to that dark room and did it before her. I suppose I was an odd little figure; I have been told that my anxiety to brighten her gave my face a strained look and put a tremor into the joke (I would stand on my head in the bed, my feet against the wall, and then cry excitedly, "Are you laughing, mother?") —and perhaps what made her laugh was something I was unconscious of, but she did laugh suddenly now and then, whereupon I screamed exultantly to that dear sister, who was ever in waiting, to come and see the sight, but by the time she came the soft face was wet again. Thus I was deprived of some of my glory, and I remember once only making her laugh before witnesses. I kept a record of her laughs on a piece of paper, a stroke for each, and it was my custom to show this proudly to the doctor every morning. There were five strokes the first time I slipped it into his hand, and when their meaning was explained to him, he laughed so boisterously that I cried, "I wish that was one of hers!" Then he was sympathetic, and asked me if my mother had seen the paper yet, and when I shook my head he said that if I showed it to her now and told her that these were her five laughs he thought I might win another. I had less confidence, but he was the mysterious man whom you ran for in the dead of night (you flung sand at his window to waken him, and if it was only toothache he extracted the tooth through the open window, but when it was something sterner he was with you in the dark square at once, like a man who slept in his topcoat), so I did as he bade me, and not only did she laugh then but again when I put the laugh down, so that though it was really one laugh with a tear in the middle I counted it as two.

It was doubtless that same sister who told me not to sulk when my mother lay thinking of him, but to try instead to get her to talk about him. I did not see how this could make her the merry mother she used to be, but I was told that if I could not do it nobody could, and this made me eager to begin. At first, they say, I was often jealous, stopping her fond memories with the cry, "Do you mind nothing about me?" but that did not last; its place was taken by an intense desire (again, I think my sister must have breathed it into life) to become so like him that even my mother should not see the difference, and many and artful were the questions I put to that end. Then I practiced in secret, but after a whole week had passed I was still rather like myself. He had such a cheery way of whistling, she had told me, it had always brightened her at her work to hear him whistling, and when he whistled he stood with his legs apart, and his hands in the pockets of his knickerbockers. I decided to trust to this, so one day after I had learned his whistle (every boy of enterprise invents a whistle of his own) from boys who had been his comrades, I secretly put on a suit of his clothes, dark gray they were, with little spots, and they fitted me many years afterwards, and thus disguised I slipped, unknown to the others, into my mother's room. Quaking, I doubt not, yet so pleased, I stood still until she saw me, and then—how it must have hurt her! "Listen!" I cried in a glow of triumph, and I stretched my legs wide apart and plunged my hands into the pockets of my knickerbockers, and began to whistle.

She lived twenty-nine years after his death, such active years until toward the end, that you never knew where she was unless you took hold of her, and though she was frail henceforth and ever growing frailer, her housekeeping again became famous, so that brides called as a matter of course to watch her ca'ming [1] and sanding [2] and stitching; there are old people still, one or two, to tell with wonder in their eyes how she could bake twenty-four bannocks [3] in the hour, and not a chip in one of them. And how many she gave away, how much she gave away of all she had, and what pretty ways she had of giving it! Her face beamed and rippled with mirth as before, and her laugh, that I had tried so hard to force, came running home again. I have heard no such laugh as hers save from merry children; the laughter of most of us ages, and wears out with the body, but hers remained gleeful to the last, as if it were born afresh every morning. There was always something of the child in her, and her laugh was its voice, as eloquent of the past to me as was the christening robe to her. But I had not made her forget the bit of her that was dead; in those nine and twenty years he was not removed one day farther from her. Many a time she fell asleep speaking to him, and even while she slept her lips moved and she smiled as if he had come back to her, and when she woke he might vanish so suddenly that she started up bewildered and looked about her, and then said slowly, "My David's dead!" or perhaps he remained long enough to whisper why he must leave her now, and then she lay silent with filmy eyes. When I became a man and he was still a boy of thirteen, I wrote a little paper called "Dead this Twenty Years," which was about a similar tragedy in another woman's life, and it is the only thing I have written that she never spoke about, not even to that daughter she loved the best. No one ever spoke of it to her, or asked her if she had read it: one does not ask a mother if she knows that there is a little coffin in the house. She read many times the book in which it is printed, but when she came to that chapter she would put her hands to her heart or even over her ears.

1896

[1] scouring the stone doorstep
[2] the floor
[3] a kind of oatmeal or barley cake, baked on a griddle

ARTHUR O'SHAUGHNESSY
1844-1881

O'Shaughnessy, whose life was cut short just as he began to show what he might have achieved was a poet of very uneven quality, but one whose best work merits remembrance. He was born in London, was educated privately, and at seventeen procured the position of transcriber in the library of the British Museum. Promoted two years later to the department of natural history, he became such an authority in icthyology that his death was considered a loss to science.

His real interest, however, was in literature. In 1870 his first book of verse, *An Epic of Women,* surprised the literary world. *Lays of France,* 1872, and *Music and Moonlight,* 1874, followed. *Songs of a Worker,* 1881, was published after his death. A spirit of mild melancholy pervades O'Shaughnessy's work. His best poetry has been compared by H. Manners Chichester to Chopin's music, dreamy, sometimes weird, with original, delicious, inexhaustible melody; Palgrave speaks of his "exquisite tenderness of touch." O'Shaughnessy's ability to draw detailed word pictures, and to enrich his poetry by connotive, as well as musical words, gives his work a resemblance to that of Rossetti, Morris, and Swinburne.

Biography and criticism: L. C. Moulton, *Arthur O'Shaughnessy; His Life and Work, with Selections from his Poems,* 1894; *Athen.* 1881, Feb. 5: 196; "Arthur O'Shaughnessy's Poems," *Contemp.* 126:125-8.

SONG[1]

I made another garden, yea,
  For my new love;
I left the dead rose where it lay,
  And set the new above.
Why did the summer not begin?
  Why did my heart not haste?
My old love came and walked therein,
  And laid the garden waste.

She entered with her weary smile,
  Just as of old;
She looked around a little while,
  And shivered at the cold.
Her passing touch was death to all,
  Her passing look a blight:
She made the white rose-petals fall,
  And turned the red rose white.

Her pale robe, clinging to the grass,
  Seemed like a snake
That bit the grass and ground, alas!
  And a sad trail did make.
She went up slowly to the gate;
  And there, just as of yore,
She turned back at the last to wait,
  And say farewell once more.

1874

ODE[1]

We are the music makers,
  And we are the dreamers of dreams,
Wandering by lone sea-breakers,
  And sitting by desolate streams;—
World-losers and world-forsakers,
  On whom the pale moon gleams:
Yet we are the movers and shakers
  Of the world forever, it seems.

With wonderful deathless ditties
We build up the world's great cities,
  And out of a fabulous story
  We fashion an empire's glory:
One man with a dream, at pleasure,
  Shall go forth and conquer a crown;
And three with a new song's measure
  Can trample a kingdom down.

We, in the ages lying
  In the buried past of the earth,
Built Nineveh with our sighing,
  And Babel itself in our mirth;
And o'erthrew them with prophesying
  To the old of the new world's worth;
For each age is a dream that is dying,
  Or one that is coming to birth.

A breath of our inspiration
Is the life of each generation;
  A wondrous thing of our dreaming
  Unearthly, impossible seeming—
The soldier, the king, and the peasant
  Are working together in one,
Till our dream shall become their present,
  And their work in the world be done.

They had no vision amazing
Of the goodly house they are raising;
  They had no divine foreshowing
  Of the land to which they are going:
But on one man's soul it hath broken,
  A light that doth not depart;
And his look, or a word he hath spoken,
  Wrought flame in another man's heart.

And therefore today is thrilling
With a past day's late fulfilling;
  And the multitudes are enlisted
  In the faith that their fathers resisted,
And, scorning the dream of tomorrow,
  Are bringing to pass, as they may,
In the world, for its joy or its sorrow,
  The dream that was scorned yesterday.

But we, with our dreaming and singing,
  Ceaseless and sorrowless we!
The glory about us clinging
  Of the glorious futures we see,
Our souls with high music ringing:
  O men! It must ever be
That we dwell, in our dreaming and singing,
  A little apart from ye.

For we are afar with the dawning
  And the suns that are not yet high,
And out of the infinite morning
  Intrepid you hear us cry—
How, spite of your human scorning,
  Once more God's future draws nigh,
And already goes forth the warning
  That ye of the past must die.

Great hail! we cry to the comers
  From the dazzling unknown shore;
Bring us hither your sun and your summers,
  And renew our world as of yore;
You shall teach us your song's new numbers,
  And things that we dreamed not before:
Yea, in spite of a dreamer who slumbers,
  And a singer who sings no more.

1874

[1] Through the courtesy of Chatto and Windus, London, publishers.

OSCAR WILDE 1856-1900

The greatest wit among English dramatists at the end of the nineteenth century was Oscar Wilde, son of Sir William Wilde, an eminent Anglo-Irish medical scientist. He was born in Dublin, and was educated at Trinity College there, and at Oxford. During his student days at Magdalen College he took up some of the ideas of Ruskin and Morris, and soon after entered upon an individual propaganda for the aesthetic. Abundant egotism and love for both public and social notoriety made him proof against the storm of ridicule that arose, mostly from those whom he despised, the middle-class masses. They flocked to hear him lecture, in colorful costume, upon the principles of aestheticism. Wilde's typical witticisms were paradoxical retorts that still further served to alienate his critics and advertise himself, his "cult," and his clothes.

The Picture of Dorian Gray, a novel, 1891, brought him much notoriety. *Lady Windermere's Fan*, 1892, *The Importance of Being Earnest*, 1895, and other comedies attacked both the shams and the well-tried institutions of society by inuendo and witty epigram, a method of attack that lacked the courage of direct opposition. In the midst of the success of these plays, Wilde was convicted of an offense against public morals and was imprisoned for two years. When he was released, he went to France, where he died.

His poems were collected in 1902. In 1898 was published *The Ballad of Reading Gaol*, to some degree based upon his own prison experiences, one of the most graphic of modern English ballads. Its debt to *The Ancient Mariner* is easy to perceive and a likeness to passages in *A Shropshire Lad* (page 827) has been pointed out.

Biography and criticism: A. Gide, *Oscar Wilde*. With introd. note and bibliog. by Stuart Mason, 1905; R. T. Hopkins, *Oscar Wilde, A Study of the Man and His Work*, 1913; A. Ransome, *Oscar Wilde, A Critical Study*, 1913; Frank Harris, *Oscar Wilde, His Life and Confessions*, 1916; Jackson, Kennedy, Howe, Chevalley; E. T. Raymond, "Oscar Wilde: a Portrait of the Nineties," *Liv. Age* 308:536; see also *Liv. Age* 326:597-8; *Nation* 120:6; *Cur. Opin*. 61:194-5; 63:119; 64:350-1; *Bookm*. 43:576-8.

From THE BALLAD OF READING GAOL [1]

I

He did not wear his scarlet coat,
  For blood and wine are red,
And blood and wine were on his hands
  When they found him with the dead,
The poor dead woman whom he loved,
  And murdered in her bed.

He walked amongst the Trial Men
  In a suit of shabby gray;
A cricket cap was on his head,
  And his step seemed light and gay;
But I never saw a man who looked
  So wistfully at the day.

I never saw a man who looked
  With such a wistful eye
Upon that little tent of blue
  Which prisoners call the sky,
And at every drifting cloud that went
  With sails of silver by.

I walked, with other souls in pain,
  Within another ring,
And was wondering if the man had done
  A great or little thing,
When a voice behind me whispered low,
  "That fellow's got to swing."

Dear Christ! the very prison walls
  Suddenly seemed to reel,
And the sky above my head became
  Like a casque of scorching steel;
And, though I was a soul in pain,
  My pain I could not feel.

. . . .

V

I know not whether Laws be right
  Or whether Laws be wrong;
All that we know who lie in gaol
  Is that the wall is strong;
And that each day is like a year,
  A year whose days are long.

But this I know, that every Law
  That men have made for Man,
Since first Man took his brother's life,
  And the sad world began,
But straws [2] the wheat and saves the chaff
  With a most evil fan.

This too I know—and wise it were
  If each could know the same—
That every prison that men build
  Is built with bricks of shame,
And bound with bars lest Christ should see
  How men their brothers maim.

With bars they blur the gracious moon,
  And blind the goodly sun:
And they do well to hide their Hell,
  For in it things are done
That Son of God nor son of Man
  Ever should look upon!

The vilest deeds like poison weeds
  Bloom well in prison-air:

[1] From *The Ballad of Reading Gaol* by Oscar Wilde. By permission of Messrs. Methuen & Company, Ltd.

[2] strews, scatters

It is only what is good in Man
  That wastes and withers there:
Pale Anguish keeps the heavy gate,
  And the Warder is Despair.

For they starve the little frightened child
  Till it weeps both night and day:
And they scourge the weak, and flog the fool,
  And gibe the old and gray,
And some grow mad, and all grow bad,
  And none a word may say.

Each narrow cell in which we dwell
  Is a foul and dark latrine,
And the fetid breath of living Death
  Chokes up each grated screen,
And all, but Lust, is turned to dust
  In Humanity's machine.

The brackish water that we drink
  Creeps with a loathsome slime,
And the bitter bread they weigh in scales
  Is full of chalk and lime,
And Sleep will not lie down, but walks
  Wild-eyed, and cries to Time.

But though lean Hunger and green Thirst
  Like asp with adder fight,
We have little care of prison fare,
  For what chills and kills outright
Is that every stone one lifts by day
  Becomes one's heart by night.

With midnight always in one's heart,
  And twilight in one's cell,
We turn the crank, or tear the rope, [1]
  Each in his separate Hell,
And the silence is more awful far
  Than the sound of a brazen bell.

And never a human voice comes near
  To speak a gentle word:
And the eye that watches through the door
  Is pitiless and hard:
And by all forgot, we rot and rot,
  With soul and body marred.

And thus we rust Life's iron chain
  Degraded and alone:
And some men curse, and some men weep,
  And some men make no moan:
But God's eternal Laws are kind
  And break the heart of stone.

And every human heart that breaks,
  In prison-cell or yard,
Is as that broken box that gave
  Its treasure to the Lord,
And filled the unclean leper's house
  With the scent of costliest nard. [2]

Ah! Happy they whose hearts can break
  And peace of pardon win!
How else may man make straight his plan
  And cleanse his soul from Sin?
How else but through a broken heart
  May Lord Christ enter in?

And he of the swollen purple throat,
  And the stark and staring eyes,
Waits for the holy hands that took
  The Thief to Paradise; [3]
And a broken and a contrite heart
  The Lord will not despise. [4]

The man in red who reads the Law
  Gave him three weeks of life,
Three little weeks in which to heal
  His soul of his soul's strife,
And cleanse from every blot of blood
  The hand that held the knife.

And with tears of blood he cleansed the hand,
  The hand that held the steel:
For only blood can wipe out blood,
  And only tears can heal:
And the crimson stain that was of Cain
  Became Christ's snow-white seal.

VI

In Reading gaol by Reading town
  There is a pit of shame,
And in it lies a wretched man
  Eaten by teeth of flame,
In a burning winding-sheet he lies,
  And his grave has got no name.

And there, till Christ call forth the dead
  In silence let him lie;
No need to waste the foolish tear,
  Or heave the windy sigh:
The man had killed the thing he loved,
  And so he had to die.

And all men kill the thing they love,
  By all let this be heard,
Some do it with a bitter look,
  Some with a flattering word,
The coward does it with a kiss,
  The brave man with a sword!

1897-8 1898

[1] Picking rope to make oakum was prison work.

[2] Ointment of spikenard; see *John* xii, 3.

[3] *Luke* xxiii, 43

[4] *Psalms* li, 17

GEORGE MEREDITH 1828-1909

George Meredith, one of the foremost novelists of the nineteenth century, was born at Portsmouth, where his father was engaged in trade. After schooling at home and in Germany, he was apprenticed to a lawyer. Literature, however, drew him, and he began his literary career as a journalist, becoming at length reader of manuscripts for a London publishing house, which he served for more than thirty years. While in the midst of this occupation he began and continued writing prose and poetry, almost unheeded. Although a contemporary of Thackeray and Dickens, he obtained no general recognition until about 1890, and was never popular. The span of his writing is almost sixty years, from *Poems,* 1851, to *Last Poems,* 1909.

His fiction began with *The Ordeal of Richard Feverel,* 1859, and included some fifteen major novels. Perhaps the best known of these are *Rhoda Fleming,* 1865, *Beauchamp's Career,* 1865, *The Egoist,* 1879, *Diana of the Crossways,* 1885, and *The Amazing Marriage,* 1895. His novels typify the tendency of late nineteenth century authors to emphasize the intellectual rather than the emotional elements of plot and character. They see man as a creature being shaped (it may be against his will or without his knowledge) by education and society; particularly molded by that social force which Meredith calls the "Comic Spirit." This is the guide that enables man to regard himself as the best product, so far, in the universe, and one capable of improvement. Meredith's poetry is less consistently intellectual than his prose, and often expresses a romantic conception of love that is little in evidence in his fiction.

Biography: J. M. Barrie, 1909 (1914); J. B. Priestley, 1926 (EML). Criticism: R. Le Gallienne, *George Meredith: Some Characteristics,* 1890; M. Sturge Henderson, *George Meredith: Novelist, Poet, Reformer,* 1908; More (Shel. 2), Lang (EL), Brownell, Phelps (EN), Follett, Scott, Cunliffe, Chevalley; G. Turquet-Milnes, "Meredith and the Cosmic Spirit," *Contemp.* 127:500-8; J. L. Lowes, "Two Readings of Earth," *Yale R.* ns 15:515-39; J. Moffat, "Dickens and Meredith," *Liv. Age* 316:38-45; M. Armstrong, "The Poetry of George Meredith," *No. Am.* 213:354-61; J. L. Lowes, "An Unacknowledged Imagist," *Nation* 102:217-9.

From THE ORDEAL OF RICHARD FEVEREL [1]

Telling Austin he would be back in a few minutes, he sallied into the air, and walked on and on. "A father!" he kept repeating to himself: "a child!" And though he knew it not, he was striking the key-notes of Nature. But he did know of a singular harmony that suddenly burst over his whole being.

[1] By permission of Messrs. Charles Scribner's Sons, New York.

The moon was surpassingly bright: the summer air heavy and still. He left the high road and pierced into the forest. His walk was rapid: the leaves on the trees brushed his cheeks; the dead leaves heaped in the dells noised to his feet. Something of a religious joy—a strange sacred pleasure—was in him. By degrees it wore; he remembered himself: and now he was possessed by a proportionate anguish. A father! he dared never see his child. And he had no longer his phantasies to fall upon. He was utterly bare to his sin. In his troubled mind it seemed to him that Clare looked down on him—Clare who saw him as he was; and that to her eyes it would be infamy for him to go and print his kiss upon his child. Then came stern efforts to command his misery and make the nerves of his face iron.

By the log of an ancient tree half buried in dead leaves of past summers, beside a brook, he halted as one who had reached his journey's end. There he discovered he had a companion in Lady Judith's little dog. He gave the friendly animal a pat of recognition, and both were silent in the forest-silence.

It was impossible for Richard to return; his heart was surcharged. He must advance, and on he footed, the little dog following.

An oppressive slumber hung about the forest-branches. In the dells and on the heights was the same dead heat. Here where the brook tinkled it was no cool-lipped sound, but metallic, and without the spirit of water. Yonder in a space of moonlight on lush grass, the beams were as white fire to sight and feeling. No haze spread around. The valleys were clear, defined to the shadows of their verges; the distances sharply distinct, and with the colors of day but slightly softened. Richard beheld a roe moving across a slope of sward far out of rifle-mark. The breathless silence was significant, yet the moon shone in a broad blue heaven. Tongue out of mouth trotted the little dog after him; couched panting when he stopped an instant; rose weariedly when he started afresh. Now and then a large white night-moth flitted through the dusk of the forest.

On a barren corner of the wooded highland looking inland stood gray topless ruins set in nettles and rank grass-blades. Richard mechanically sat down on the crumbling flints to rest, and listened to the panting of the dog. Sprinkled at his feet were emerald lights:

hundreds of glowworms studded the dark dry ground.

He sat and eyed them, thinking not at all. His energies were expended in action. He sat as a part of the ruins, and the moon turned his shadow Westward from the South. Overhead, as she declined, long ripples of silver cloud were imperceptibly stealing toward her. They were the van of a tempest. He did not observe them or the leaves beginning to chatter. When he again pursued his course with his face to the Rhine, a huge mountain appeared to rise sheer over him, and he had it in his mind to scale it. He got no nearer to the base of it for all his vigorous outstepping. The ground began to dip; he lost sight of the sky. Then heavy thunder-drops struck his cheek, the leaves were singing, the earth breathed, it was black before him and behind. All at once the thunder spoke. The mountain he had marked was bursting over him.

Up started the whole forest in violet fire. He saw the country at the foot of the hills to the bounding Rhine gleam, quiver, extinguished. Then there were pauses; and the lightning seemed as the eye of heaven, and the thunder as the tongue of heaven, each alternately addressing him; filling him with awful rapture. Alone there—sole human creature among the grandeurs and mysteries of storm—he felt the representative of his kind, and his spirit rose, and marched, and exulted, let it be glory, let it be ruin! Lower down the lightened abysses of air rolled the wrathful crash: then white thrusts of light were darted from the sky, and great curving ferns, seen steadfast in pallor a second, were supernaturally agitated, and vanished. Then a shrill song roused in the leaves and the herbage. Prolonged and louder it sounded, as deeper and heavier the deluge pressed. A mighty force of water satisfied the desire of the earth. Even in this, drenched as he was by the first outpouring, Richard had a savage pleasure. Keeping in motion, he was scarcely conscious of the wet, and the grateful breath of the weeds was refreshing. Suddenly he stopped short, lifting a curious nostril. He fancied he smelt meadow-sweet. He had never seen the flower in Rhineland—never thought of it; and it would hardly be met with in a forest. He was sure he smelt it fresh in dews. His little companion wagged a miserable wet tail some way in advance. He went on slowly, thinking indistinctly. After two or three steps he stooped and stretched out his hand to feel for the flower, having, he knew not why, a strong wish to verify its growth there. Groping about, his hand encountered something warm that started at his touch, and he, with the instinct we have, seized it, and lifted it to look at it. The creature was very small, evidently quite young. Richard's eyes, now accustomed to the darkness, were able to discern it for what it was, a tiny leveret, and he supposed that the dog had probably frightened its dam just before he found it. He put the little thing on one hand in his breast, and stepped out rapidly as before.

The rain was now steady; from every tree a fountain poured. So cool and easy had his mind become that he was speculating on what kind of shelter the birds could find, and how the butterflies and moths saved their colored wings from washing. Folded close they might hang under a leaf, he thought. Lovingly he looked into the dripping darkness of the coverts on each side, as one of their children. He was next musing on a strange sensation he experienced. It ran up one arm with an indescribable thrill, but communicated nothing to his heart. It was purely physical, ceased for a time, and recommenced, till he had it all through his blood, wonderfully thrilling. He grew aware that the little thing he carried in his breast was licking his hand there. The small rough tongue going over and over the palm of his hand produced the strange sensation he felt. Now that he knew the cause, the marvel ended; but now that he knew the cause, his heart was touched and made more of it. The gentle scraping continued without intermission as on he walked. What did it say to him? Human tongue could not have said so much just then.

A pale gray light on the skirts of the flying tempest displayed the dawn. Richard was walking hurriedly. The green drenched weeds lay all about in his path, bent thick, and the forest drooped glimmeringly. Impelled as a man who feels a revelation mounting obscurely to his brain, Richard was passing one of those little forest-chapels, hung with votive wreaths, where the peasant halts to kneel and pray. Cold, still, in the twilight it stood, raindrops pattering round it. He looked within, and saw the Virgin holding her Child. He moved by. But not many steps had he gone ere his strength went out of him, and he shuddered. What was it? He asked not. He was in other hands. Vivid as lightning the Spirit of Life illumined him. He felt in his heart the cry of his child, his darling's touch.

With shut eyes he saw them both. They drew him from the depths; they led him a blind and tottering man. And as they led him he had a sense of purification so sweet he shuddered again and again.

When he looked out from his trance on the breathing world, the small birds hopped and chirped: warm fresh sunlight was over all the hills. He was on the edge of the forest, entering a plain clothed with ripe corn under a spacious morning sky.

1859

JUGGLING JERRY[1]

I

Pitch here the tent, while the old horse grazes:
  By the old hedge-side we'll halt a stage.
It's nigh my last above the daisies:
  My next leaf'll be man's blank page.
Yes, my old girl! and it's no use crying:
  Juggler, constable, king, must bow.
One that outjuggles all's been spying
  Long to have me, and he has me now.

II

We've traveled times to this old common:
  Often we've hung our pots in the gorse.
We've had a stirring life, old woman,
  You, and I, and the old gray horse.
Races, and fairs, and royal occasions,
  Found us coming to their call:
Now they'll miss us at our stations:
  There's a Juggler outjuggles all!

III

Up goes the lark, as if all were jolly!
  Over the duck-pond the willow shakes.
Easy to think that grieving's folly,
  When the hand's firm as driven stakes!
Aye, when we're strong, and braced, and manful,
  Life's a sweet fiddle: but we're a batch
Born to become the Great Juggler's han'ful:
  Balls he shies up, and is safe to catch.

IV

Here's where the lads of the village cricket:
  I was a lad not wide from here:
Couldn't I whip off the bail from the wicket!
  Like an old world those days appear!
Donkey, sheep, geese, and thatched ale-house
  —I know them!
  They are old friends of my halts, and seem,
Somehow, as if kind thanks I owe them:
  Juggling don't hinder the heart's esteem.

V

Juggling's no sin, for we must have victual:
  Nature allows us to bait for the fool.
Holding one's own makes us juggle no little;
  But, to increase it, hard juggling's the rule.
You that are sneering at my profession,
  Haven't you juggled a vast amount?
There's the Prime Minister, in one Session,
  Juggles more games than my sins'll count.

VI

I've murdered insects with mock thunder:
  Conscience, for that, in men don't quail.
I've made bread from the bump of wonder:[2]
  That's my business, and there's my tale.
Fashion and rank all praised the professor:
  Aye! and I've had my smile from the Queen:
Bravo, Jerry! she meant: God bless her!
  Ain't this a sermon on that scene?

VII

I've studied men from my topsy-turvy
  Close, and, I reckon, rather true.
Some are fine fellows: some, right scurvy:
  Most, a dash between the two.
But it's a woman, old girl, that makes me
  Think more kindly of the race:
And it's a woman, old girl, that shakes me
  When the Great Juggler I must face.

VIII

We two were married, due and legal:
  Honest we've lived since we've been one.
Lord! I could then jump like an eagle:
  You danced bright as a bit o' the sun.
Birds in a May-bush we were! right merry!
  All night we kiss'd, we juggled all day.
Joy was the heart of Juggling Jerry!
Now from his old girl he's juggled away.

IX

It's past parsons to console us:
  No, nor no doctor fetch for me:
I can die without my bolus;[3]
  Two of a trade, lass, never agree!
Parson and Doctor!—don't they love rarely
  Fighting the devil in other men's fields!
Stand up yourself and match him fairly:
  Then see how the rascal yields!

X

I, lass, have lived no gipsy, flaunting
  Finery while his poor helpmate grubs:

[1] From *The Poetical Works of George Meredith*, copyright, 1912, by permission of Charles Scribner's Sons, publishers.

[2] earned his living by appealing to the curiosity of people

[3] a large pill, as for a horse

Coin I've stored, and you won't be wanting:
 You shan't beg from the troughs and tubs.
Nobly you've stuck to me, though in his kitchen
 Many a Marquis would hail you Cook!
Palaces you could have ruled and grown rich in,
 But your old Jerry you never forsook.

XI

Hand up the chirper![1] ripe ale winks in it;
 Let's have comfort and be at peace.
Once a stout draught made me light as a linnet.
 Cheer up! the Lord must have his lease.
May be—for none see in that black hollow—
 It's just a place where we're held in pawn,
And, when the Great Juggler makes as to swallow,
 It's just the sword-trick—I ain't quite gone!

XII

Yonder came smells of the gorse, so nutty,
 Gold-like and warm: it's the prime of May.
Better than mortar, brick and putty,
 Is God's house on a blowing day.
Lean me more up the mound; now I feel it:
 All the old heath-smells! Ain't it strange?
There's the world laughing, as if to conceal it,
 But He's by us, juggling the change.

XIII

I mind it well, by the sea-beach lying,
 Once—it's long gone—when two gulls we beheld,
Which, as the moon got up, were flying
 Down a big wave that sparked and swelled.
Crack, went a gun: one fell: the second
 Wheeled round him twice, and was off for new luck:
There in the dark her white wing beckoned:—
 Drop me a kiss—I'm the bird dead-struck!

1859

LUCIFER IN STARLIGHT[2]

On a starred night Prince Lucifer uprose.
Tired of his dark dominion swung the fiend
Above the rolling ball in cloud part screened,
Where sinners hugged their specter of repose.
Poor prey to his hot fit of pride were those.
And now upon his western wing he leaned,
Now his huge bulk o'er Afric's sands careened,
Now the black planet shadowed Arctic snows.
Soaring through wider zones that pricked his scars
With memory of the old revolt from Awe,[3]
He reached the middle height, and at the stars,
Which are the brain of heaven, he looked, and sank.
Around the ancient track marched, rank on rank,
The army of unalterable law.

1883

THOMAS HARDY 1840-1928

Like Meredith, Hardy ranks among the great representatives of two types of literature in both the Victorian and the post-Victorian periods. After producing a series of great novels in the Victorian Era, Hardy, at the age of eighty-eight, was one of the most notable poets of the twentieth century. This meant a return to his earlier medium, for he wrote verse from 1860 to 1870, abandoned it in the latter year for fiction, but in *Wessex Poems,* 1898, turned again to poetry. His poems of war and patriotism are among the finest inspired by the World War. *Collected Poems,* second edition, 1923, illustrates well the wide and interesting variety of his verse.

He was born in Dorsetshire, was educated in local schools, and took up the profession of architecture. But literature proving a stronger attraction, he finally devoted himself to writing, producing a long series of novels of notable merit for their dank realism *Under the Greenwood Tree,* 1872, is "a rural painting of the Dutch School." In his tales of the Wessex scene and rural life, Hardy has preserved aspects of England now rapidly disappearing. *The Return of the Native,* 1878, and *Tess of the D'Urbervilles,* 1891, contain Hardy's most arresting characters; women of passion and will, whose hopeless struggle against inevitable defeat only intensifies the bitterness of their failure.

In *The Dynasts,* 1904-1908, is Hardy's monumental example of sustained pessimism. He uses the Napoleonic wars as a background for his drama of the implacable forces that rule the world. Battle clouds veil the arbiters of fortune, whose hidden purposes are revealed in national calamities, where individual tragedy is submerged in universal misery. Man's fortitude in facing the conditions of his life, and the benefit that the reader gains from regarding a universe indifferent, if not actually unfriendly to man, explain Hardy's definition of pessimism as "'questionings' in the exploration of reality, and the first step toward the soul's betterment, and the body's also."

Biography and criticism: L. P. Johnson, *The Art of Thomas Hardy,* 1894; L. Abercrombie, *Thomas Hardy, a Critical Study,* 1912; J. W. Beach, *The Technique of Thomas Hardy,* 1922;

[1] cheering cup
[2] From *The Poetical Works of George Meredith,* copyright, 1912, by permission of Charles Scribner's Sons, publishers.

[3] The scars formerly received by Lucifer during "the old revolt from Awe" were those of his battle with the angels and his fall through the regions of air with his rebel hosts.—Trevelyan.

Follett; Freeman; Cunliffe; Phelps; Chevalley; Monro; W. M. Parker, "The Genius of Thomas Hardy," *19th Cent.* 88:63-71; J. L. Lowes, "Two Readings of Earth," *Yale R.* ns 15:515-39 (interesting comparison of Hardy and Meredith); G. M. Harper, "Hardy, Hudson, Housman," *Scrib.* 78: 151-7; J. M. Hone, "The Poetry of Thomas Hardy," *Liv. Age* 313:52-7; H. Lea, *Thomas Hardy's Wessex* (an indispensable guide).

From THE RETURN OF THE NATIVE [1]

I

A Face on Which Time Makes but Little Impression

A Saturday afternoon in November was approaching the time of twilight, and the vast tract of uninclosed wild known as Egdon Heath embrowned itself moment by moment. Overhead the hollow stretch of whitish cloud shutting out the sky was as a tent which had the whole heath for its floor.

The heaven being spread with this pallid screen and the earth with the darkest vegetation, their meeting-line at the horizon was clearly marked. In such contrast the heath wore the appearance of an installment of night which had taken up its place before its astronomical hour was come: darkness had to a great extent arrived hereon, while day stood distinct in the sky. Looking upwards, a furze-cutter would have been inclined to continue work; looking down, he would have decided to finish his faggot and go home. The distant rims of the world and of the firmament seemed to be a division in time no less than a division in matter. The face of the heath by its mere complexion added half an hour to evening; it could in like manner retard the dawn, sadden noon, anticipate the frowning storms scarcely generated, and intensify the opacity of a moonless midnight to a cause of shaking and dread.

In fact, precisely at this transitional point of its nightly roll into darkness the great and particular glory of the Egdon waste began, and nobody could be said to understand the heath who had not been there at such a time. It could best be felt when it could not clearly be seen, its complete effect and explanation lying in this and the succeeding hours before the next dawn: then, and only then, did it tell its true tale. The spot was, indeed, a near relation of night, and when night showed itself an apparent tendency to gravitate together could be perceived in its shades and the scene. The somber stretch of rounds and hollows seemed to rise and meet the evening gloom in pure sympathy, the heath exhaling darkness as rapidly as the heavens precipitated it. And so the obscurity in the air and the obscurity in the land closed together in a black fraternization toward which each advanced half-way.

The place became full of a watchful intentness now; for when other things sank brooding to sleep the heath appeared slowly to awake and listen. Every night its Titanic form seemed to await something; but it had waited thus, unmoved, during so many centuries, through the crises of so many things, that it could only be imagined to await one last crisis—the final overthrow.

. . . .

To recline on a stump of thorn in the central valley of Egdon, between afternoon and night, as now, where the eye could reach nothing of the world outside the summits and shoulders of heathland which filled the whole circumference of its glance, and to know that everything around and underneath had been from prehistoric times as unaltered as the stars overhead, gave ballast to the mind adrift on change, and harassed by the irrepressible New. The great inviolate place had an ancient permanence which the sea cannot claim. Who can say of a particular sea that it is old? Distilled by the sun, kneaded by the moon, it is renewed in a year, in a day, or in an hour. The sea changed, the fields changed, the rivers, the villages, and the people changed, yet Egdon remained. Those surfaces were neither so steep as to be destructible by weather, nor so flat as to be the victims of floods and deposits. With the exception of an aged highway, and a still more aged barrow [2] presently to be referred to—themselves almost crystalized to natural products by long continuance—even the trifling irregularities were not caused by pickaxe, plough, or spade, but remained as the very finger-touches of the last geological change.

The above-mentioned highway traversed the lower levels of the heath, from one horizon to another. In many portions of its course it overlaid an old vicinal [3] way, which branched from the great Western road of the Romans, the Via Iceniana, or Ikenild Street, hard by. On the evening under consideration it would have been noticed that, though the gloom had increased sufficiently to confuse the minor

[1] From *The Return of the Native* by Thomas Hardy. By permission of the author and Messrs. Harper & Brothers, publishers.

[2] a large prehistoric burial mound

[3] neighboring

features of the heath, the white surface of the road remained almost as clear as ever.

II

Humanity Appears Upon the Scene, Hand in Hand With Trouble

. . . The scene before the reddleman's [1] eyes was a gradual series of ascents from the level of the road backward into the heart of the heath. It embraced hillocks, pits, ridges, acclivities, one behind the other, till all was finished by a high hill cutting against the still light sky. The traveler's eye hovered about these things for a time, and finally settled upon one noteworthy object up there. It was a barrow. This bossy projection of earth above its natural level occupied the loftiest ground of the loneliest height that the heath contained. Although from the vale it appeared but as a wart on an Atlantean brow, its actual bulk was great. It formed the pole and axis of this heathery world.

As the resting man looked at the barrow he became aware that its summit, hitherto the highest object in the whole prospect round, was surmounted by something higher. It rose from the semi-globular mound like a spike from a helmet. The first instinct of an imaginative stranger might have been to suppose it the person of the one of the Celts who built the barrow, so far had all of modern date withdrawn from the scene. It seemed a sort of last man among them, musing for a moment before dropping into eternal night with the rest of his race.

There the form stood, motionless as the hill beneath. Above the plain rose the hill, above the hill rose the barrow, and above the barrow rose the figure. Above the figure was nothing that could be mapped elsewhere than on a celestial globe.

Such a perfect, delicate, and necessary finish did the figure give to the dark pile of hills that it seemed to be the only obvious justification of their outline. Without it, there was the dome without the lantern; with it the architectural demands of the mass were satisfied. The scene was strangely homogeneous. The vale, the upland, the barrow, and the figure above it amounted only to unity. Looking at this or that member of the group was not observing a complete thing, but a fraction of a thing.

The form was so much like an organic part of the entire motionless structure that to see it move would have impressed the mind as a strange phenomenon. Immobility being the chief characteristic of that whole which the person formed portion of, the discontinuance of immobility in any quarter suggested confusion.

Yet that is what happened. The figure perceptibly gave up its fixity, shifted a step or two, and turned round. As if alarmed, it descended on the right side of the barrow, with the glide of a water-drop down a bud, and then vanished. The movement had been sufficient to show more clearly the characteristics of the figure, and that it was a woman's.

The reason of her sudden displacement now appeared. With her dropping out of sight on the right side, a newcomer, bearing a burden, protruded into the sky on the left side, ascended the tumulus, and deposited the burden on the top. A second followed, then a third, a fourth, a fifth, and ultimately the whole barrow was peopled with burdened figures.

The only intelligible meaning in this sky-backed pantomime of silhouettes was that the woman had no relation to the forms who had taken her place, was sedulously avoiding these, and had come thither for another object than theirs. The imagination of the observer clung by preference to that vanished, solitary figure, as to something more interesting, more important, more likely to have a history worth knowing than these newcomers, and unconsciously regarded them as intruders. But they remained, and established themselves; and the lonely person who hitherto had been queen of the solitude did not at present seem likely to return.

III

The Custom of the Country

Had a looker-on been posted in the immediate vicinity of the barrow, he would have learned that these persons were boys and men of the neighboring hamlets. Each, as he ascended the barrow, had been heavily laden with furze-faggots, carried upon the shoulder by means of a long stake sharpened at each end for impaling them easily—two in front and two behind. They came from a part of the heath a quarter of a mile to the rear, where furze almost exclusively prevailed as a product.

Every individual was so involved in furze by his method of carrying the faggots that he

[1] or raddleman, a dealer in raddle, a red paint used for marking sheep

appeared like a bush on legs till he had thrown them down. The party had marched in trail, like a traveling flock of sheep; that is to say, the strongest first, the weak and young behind.

The loads were all laid together, and a pyramid of furze thirty feet in circumference now occupied the crown of the tumulus, which was known as Rainbarrow for many miles round. Some made themselves busy with matches, and in selecting the driest tufts of furze, others in loosening the bramble bonds which held the faggots together. Others, again, while this was in progress, lifted their eyes and swept the vast expanse of country commanded by their position, now lying nearly obliterated by shade. In the valleys of the heath nothing save its own wild face was visible at any time of day; but this spot commanded a horizon enclosing a tract of far extent, and in many cases lying beyond the heath country. None of its features could be seen now, but the whole made itself felt as a vague stretch of remoteness.

While the men and lads were building the pile, a change took place in the mass of shade which denoted the distant landscape. Red suns and tufts of fire one by one began to arise, flecking the whole country round. They were the bonfires of other parishes and hamlets that were engaged in the same sort of commemoration. Some were distant, and stood in a dense atmosphere, so that bundles of pale strawlike beams radiated around them in the shape of a fan. Some were large and near, glowing scarlet-red from the shade, like wounds in a black hide. Some were Maenades,[1] with winy faces and blown hair. These tinctured the silent bosom of the clouds above them and lit up their ephemeral caves, which seemed thenceforth to become scalding caldrons. Perhaps as many as thirty bonfires could be counted within the whole bounds of the district; and as the hour may be told on a clockface when the figures themselves are invisible, so did the men recognize the locality of each fire by its angle and direction, though nothing of the scenery could be viewed.

The first tall flame from Rainbarrow sprang into the sky, attracting all eyes that had been fixed on the distant conflagrations back to their own attempt in the same kind. The cheerful blaze streaked the inner surface of the human circle—now increased by other stragglers, male and female—with its own gold livery, and even overlaid the dark turf around with a lively luminousness, which softened off into obscurity where the barrow rounded downward out of sight. It showed the barrow to be the segment of a globe, as perfect as on the day when it was thrown up, even the little ditch remaining from which the earth was dug. Not a plough had ever disturbed a grain of that stubborn soil. In the heath's barrenness to the farmer lay its fertility to the historian. There had been no obliteration, because there had been no tending.

It was as if the bonfire-makers were standing in some radiant upper story of the world, detached from and independent of the dark stretches below. The heath down there was now a vast abyss, and no longer a continuation of what they stood on; for their eyes, adapted to the blaze, could see nothing of the deeps beyond its influence. Occasionally, it is true, a more vigorous flare than usual from their faggots sent darting lights like aids-de-camp down the inclines to some distant bush, pool, or patch of white sand, kindling these to replies of the same color, till all was lost in the darkness again. Then the whole black phenomenon beneath represented Limbo[2] as viewed from the brink by the sublime Florentine in his vision, and the muttered articulations of the wind in the hollows were as complaints and petitions from the "souls of mighty worth" suspended therein.

It was as if these men and boys had suddenly dived into past ages, and fetched therefrom an hour and deed which had before been familiar with this spot. The ashes of the original British pyre which blazed from that summit lay fresh and undisturbed in the barrow beneath their tread. The flames from the funeral piles long ago kindled there had shone down upon the lowlands as these were shining now. Festival fires to Thor[3] and Woden[4] had followed on the same ground and duly had their day. Indeed, it is pretty well known that such blazes as this the heathmen were now enjoying are rather the lineal descendants from jumbled Druidical[5] rites and Saxon ceremonies than the invention of popular feeling about Gunpowder Plot.[6]

[1] Bacchantes, female followers of Bacchus, god of wine

[2] in Dante's *Inferno,* Canto IV, the abode of the souls of high-minded leaders of mankind, such as Moses, Homer, Socrates, Plato, who died before the birth of Christ

[3] Norse god of thunder, for whom Thursday is named

[4] or Odin, Norse supreme god, for whom Wednesday is named

[5] The Druids were the priests among the early Celts.

[6] Bonfires still celebrate the failure of Guy Fawkes to blow up the king (James VI) and Parliament, Nov. 5, 1605.

Moreover to light a fire is the instinctive and resistant act of man when, at the winter ingress, the curfew is sounded throughout Nature. It indicates a spontaneous, Promethean [1] rebelliousness against the fiat that this recurrent season shall bring foul times, cold darkness, misery and death. Black chaos comes, and the fettered gods of the earth say, Let there be light.

The brilliant lights and sooty shades which struggled upon the skin and clothes of the persons standing round caused their lineaments and general contours to be drawn with Dureresque [2] vigor and dash. Yet the permanent moral expression of each face it was impossible to discover, for as the nimble flames towered, nodded, and swooped through the surrounding air, the blots of shade and flakes of light upon the countenances of the group changed shape and position endlessly. All was unstable; quivering as leaves, evanescent as lightning. Shadowy eye-sockets, deep as those of a death's head, suddenly turned into pits of luster; a lantern-jaw was cavernous, then it was shining; wrinkles were emphasized to ravines, or obliterated entirely by a changed ray. Nostrils were dark wells; sinews in old necks were gilt moldings; things with no particular polish on them were glazed; bright objects, such as the tip of a furze-hook one of the men carried, were as glass; eyeballs glowed like little lanterns. Those whom Nature had depicted as merely quaint became grotesque, the grotesque became preternatural; for all was in extremity.

Hence it may be that the face of an old man, who had like others been called to the heights by the rising flames, was not really the mere nose and chin that it appeared to be, but an appreciable quantity of human countenance. He stood complacently sunning himself in the heat. With a speäker, or stake, he tossed the outlying scraps of fuel into the conflagration, looking at the midst of the pile, occasionally lifting his eyes to measure the height of the flame, or to follow the great sparks which rose with it and sailed away into darkness. The beaming sight, and the penetrating warmth, seemed to breed in him a cumulative cheerfulness, which soon amounted to delight. With his stick in his hand he began to jig a private minuet, a bunch of copper seals shining and swinging like a pendulum from under his waistcoat: he also began to sing, in the voice of a bee up a flue—

"The king′ call'd down′ his no-bles all′,
By one′, by two′, by three′;
Earl Mar′-shal, I'll′ go shrive′ the queen′,
And thou′ shalt wend′ with me′.

A boon′, a boon′, quoth Earl Mar-shal′,
And fell′ on his bend′-ded knee′,
That what′-so-e'er′ the queen′ shall say′,
No harm′ there-of′ may be′."

Want of breath prevented a continuance of the song; and the breakdown attracted the attention of a firm-standing man of middle age, who kept each corner of his crescent-shaped mouth rigorously drawn back into his cheek, as if to do away with any suspicion of mirthfulness which might erroneously have attached to him.

"A fair stave, Grandfer Cantle; but I'm afeared 'tis too much for the moldy weasand [3] of such a old man as you," he said to the wrinkled reveler. "Dostn't wish th' wast three sixes again, Grandfer, as you was when you first learnt to sing it?' "

"Hey?" said Grandfer Cantle, stopping in his dance.

"Dostn't wish was young again, I say? There's a hole in thy poor bellows nowadays seemingly."

"But there's good art in me. If I couldn't make a little wind go a long ways I should seem no younger than the most aged man, should I, Timothy?"

"And how about the new-married folks down there at the Quiet Woman Inn?" the other inquired, pointing toward a dim light in the direction of the distant highway, but considerably apart from where the reddleman was at that moment resting. "What's the rights of the matter about 'em? You ought to know, being an understanding man."

"But a little rakish, hey? I own to it. Master Cantle is that, or he's nothing. Yet 'tis a gay fault, neighbor Fairway, that age will cure."

"I heard that they were coming home tonight. By this time they must have come. What besides?"

"The next thing is for us to go and wish 'em joy, I suppose?"

"Well, no."

"No? Now, I thought we must. *I* must, or

[1] Prometheus, the mythological Titan who stole fire from heaven and gave it to man

[2] Albrecht Durer, 1471-1528, was a German painter noted for the wonderful effects of light and shade in his pictures.

[3] windpipe

'twould be very unlike me—the first in every spree that's going!

'Do thou' put on' a fri'-ar's coat',
And I'll' put on' a-no'-ther,
And we' will to' Queen Ele'-anor go',
Like Fri'-ar and' his bro'-ther.'

I met Mis'ess Yeobright, the young bride's aunt, last night, and she told me that her son Clym was coming home a' Christmas. Wonderful clever, 'a believe—ah, I should like to have all that's under that young man's hair. Well, then, I spoke to her in my well-known merry way, and she said, 'Oh, that what's shaped so venerable should talk like a fool!'—that's what she said to me. I don't care for her, be jowned[1] if I do, and so I told her. 'Be jowned if I care for 'ee,' I said. I had her there—hey?"

"I rather think she had you," said Fairway.

"No," said Grandfer Cantle, his countenance slightly flagging. " 'Tisn't so bad as that with me?"

"Seemingly 'tis; however, is it because of the wedding that Clym is coming home a' Christmas—to make a new arrangement because his mother is now left in the house alone?"

"Yes, yes—that's it. But, Timothy, hearken to me," said the Grandfer earnestly. "Though known as such a joker, I be an understanding man if you catch me serious, and I am serious now. I can tell 'ee lots about the married couple. Yes, this morning at six o'clock they went up the country to do the job, and neither vell[2] nor mark have been seen of 'em since, though I reckon that this afternoon has brought 'em home again, man and woman—wife, that is. Isn't it spoke like a man, Timothy, and wasn't Mis'ess Yeobright wrong about me?"

"Yes, it will do. I didn't know the two had walked together since last fall, when her mother forbade the banns. How long has this new set-to been in mangling[3] then? Do you know, Humphrey?"

"Yes, how long?" said Grandfer Cantle smartly, likewise turning to Humphrey. "I ask that question."

"Ever since her aunt altered her mind, and said she might hae the man after all," replied Humphrey, without removing his eyes from the fire. He was a somewhat solemn young fellow, and carried the hook and leather gloves of a furze-cutter, his legs, by reason of that occupation, being sheathed in bulging leggings as stiff as the Philistine's[4] greaves of brass. "That's why they went away to be married, I count. You see, after kicking up such a nunny-watch[5] and forbidding the banns 'twould have made Mis'ess Yeobright seem foolish-like to have a banging wedding in the same parish all as if she'd never gainsaid it."

"Exactly—seem foolish-like; and that's very bad for the poor things that be so, though I only guess as much, to be sure," said Grandfer Cantle, still strenuously preserving a sensible bearing and mien.

"Ah, well, I was at church that day," said Fairway, "which was a very curious thing to happen."

"If 'twasn't my name's Simple," said the Grandfer emphatically. "I ha'n't been there to-year; and now the winter is a'coming on I wont say I shall."

"I ha'n't been these three years," said Humphrey; "for I'm so dead sleepy of a Sunday; and 'tis so terrible far to get there; and when you do get there 'tis such a mortal poor chance that you'll be chose for up above, when so many bain't, that I bide at home and don't go at all."

"I not only happened to be there," said Fairway, with a fresh collection of emphasis, "but I was sitting in the same pew as Mis'ess Yeobright. And though you may not see it as such, it fairly made my blood run cold to hear her. Yes, it is a curious thing; but it made my blood run cold, for I was close at her elbow." The speaker looked round upon the bystanders, now drawing closer to hear him, with his lips gathered tighter than ever in the rigorousness of his descriptive moderation.

" 'Tis a serious job to have things happen to 'ee there," said a woman behind.

" 'Ye are to declare it,' wez the parson's words," Fairway continued. "And then up stood a woman at my side—a-touching of me. 'Well, be damned if there isn't Mis'ess Yeobright a-standing up,' I said to myself. Yes, neighbors, though I was in the temple of prayer that's what I said. 'Tis against my conscience to curse and swear in company, and I hope any woman here will overlook it.

[1] a dialect expression, equivalent to "I'll be struck (punished)"
[2] fell, a skin or hide
[3] This evidently means "going on"; the origin of the word is obscure.
[4] Goliath; see *1 Sam.* xvii, 6.
[5] or ninny-watch, a commotion

Still what I did say I did say, and 'twould be a lie if I didn't own it."

"So 'twould, neighbor Fairway."

"'Be damned if there isn't Mis'ess Yeobright a-standing up,' I said," the narrator repeated, giving out the bad word with the same passionless severity of face as before, which proved how entirely necessity and not gusto had to do with the iteration. "And the next thing I heard was, 'I forbid the banns,' from her. 'I'll speak to you after the service,' said the parson, in quite a homely way—yes, turning all at once into a common man no holier than you or I. Ah, her face was pale! Maybe you can call to mind that monument in church—the cross-legged soldier that have had his nose knocked away by the school-children? Well, he would about have matched that woman's face, when she said, 'I forbid the banns.'"

1876 1878

THE DARKLING THRUSH [1]

I leant upon a coppice gate
  When Frost was specter-gray,
And Winter's dregs made desolate
  The weakening eye of day.
And tangled bine [2]-stems scored the sky
  Like strings from broken lyres,
And all mankind that haunted nigh
  Had sought their household fires.

The land's sharp features seemed to be
  The Century's corpse outleant,
His crypt the cloudy canopy,
  The wind his death-lament.
The ancient pulse of germ and birth
  Was shrunken hard and dry,
And every spirit upon earth
  Seemed fervorless as I.

At once a voice arose among
  The bleak twigs overhead
In a full-hearted evensong
  Of joy illimited; [3]
An aged thrush, frail, gaunt, and small,
  In blast-beruffled plume,
Had chosen thus to fling his soul
  Upon the growing gloom.

So little cause for carolings
  Of such ecstatic sound
Was written on terrestrial things
  Afar or nigh around,
That I could think there trembled through
  His happy good-night air
Some blessed Hope, whereof he knew
  And I was unaware.

December, 1900 1900

[1] From *Poems Past and Present.* By permission of the author, Macmillan & Co., Ltd., London, and The Macmillan Company, New York.

[2] woodbine

[3] unlimited

THE MAN HE KILLED [4]

"Had he and I but met
  By some old ancient inn,
We should have sat us down to wet
  Right many a nipperkin! [5]

"But ranged as infantry,
  And staring face to face,
I shot at him as he at me,
  And killed him in his place.

"I shot him dead because—
  Because he was my foe,
Just so: my foe of course he was;
  That's clear enough; although

"He thought he'd 'list, perhaps
  Off-hand like—just as I—
Was out of work—had sold his traps—
  No other reason why.

"Yes; quaint and curious war is!
  You shoot a fellow down
You'd treat if met where any bar is,
  Or help to half-a-crown."

1902 1902

"AH, ARE YOU DIGGING ON MY GRAVE?" [6]

"Ah, are you digging on my grave
  My loved one?—planting rue?"
—"No: yesterday he went to wed
One of the brightest wealth has bred.
'It cannot hurt her now,' he said,
  'That I should not be true.'"

"Then who is digging on my grave?
  My nearest dearest kin?"
—"Ah, no; they sit and think, 'What use!
What good will planting flowers produce?
No tendance of her mound can loose
  Her spirit from Death's gin." [7]

[4] From *Time's Laughingstocks.* By permission of the author, Macmillan & Co., Ltd., London, and The Macmillan Company, New York.

[5] a cup containing about half a pint

[6] From *Satires of Circumstance.* By permission of the author, Macmillan & Co., Ltd., London, and The Macmillan Company, New York.

[7] trap

"But some one digs upon my grave?
  My enemy?—prodding sly?"
—"Nay: when she heard you had passed the
    Gate
That shuts on all flesh soon or late,
She thought you no more worth her hate,
  And cares not where you lie."

"Then, who is digging on my grave?
  Say—since I have not guessed!"
—"Oh, it is I, my mistress dear,
Your little dog, who still lives near,
And much I hope my movements here
  Have not disturbed your rest?"

"Ah, yes! *You* dig upon my grave . . .
  Why flashed it not on me
That one true heart was left behind!
What feeling do we ever find
To equal among human kind
  A dog's fidelity!"

"Mistress, I dug upon your grave
  To bury a bone, in case
I should be hungry near this spot
When passing on my daily trot.
I am sorry, but I quite forgot
  It was your resting-place."

1914

WEATHERS [1]

I

This is the weather the cuckoo likes,
    And so do I;
When showers betumble the chestnut spikes,
    And nestlings fly;
And the little brown nightingale bills his best,
They sit outside at "The Travelers' Rest,"
And maids come forth sprig-muslin dressed,
And citizens dream of the south and west,
    And so do I.

II

This is the weather the shepherd shuns,
    And so do I;
When beeches drip in browns and duns,
    And thresh, and ply;
And hill-hid tides throb, throe on throe,
And meadow rivulets overflow,
And drops on gate-bars hang in a row,
And rooks in families homeward go,
    And so do I.

1922

[1] Reprinted from *Late Lyrics* by permission of the author, Macmillan & Co., Ltd., London, and The Macmillan Company, New York.

HENRY AUSTIN DOBSON
1840-1921

Dobson was the son of a Plymouth civil engineer. After training in public and private schools in England and Germany, he entered the employ of the Board of Trade, and remained in its service for forty-five years. During most of this time he made literature his avocation. It is with poetic form that his name is most often connected, for he was prominent in bringing into modern English verse French metrical forms such as the ballade, rondeau, rondel, and villanelle. Though the forms are artificial and foreign, he has so molded the English language to them, so suited the idea to the form, that in them his ideas find spontaneous expression. In his volumes of poetry, *Vignettes in Rime,* 1873, *Proverbs in Porcelain,* 1877, and *Old-World Idylls,* 1883, he has expressed in contemporary terms the spirit of the eighteenth century intellect and wit. It was with that age that he was most familiar, and his critical writings upon it are among his most valuable contributions to the study of literature.

Complete Poetical Works, 1923.

Criticism: A. Noyes, *Modern Poetry,* writes convincingly of Mr. Dobson's work; same, *Liv. Age* 321:959-65; E. Gosse, *Quar.* 237:53-67, a personal account of the poet's life and aim; S. M. Ellis, *Fortn.* 116:640-50; *Outl.* 129:84-5.

"URCEUS EXIT" [2, 3]

I intended an Ode,
  And it turned to a Sonnet.
It began *à la mode,*
I intended an Ode;
But Rose crossed the road
  In her latest new bonnet;
I intended an Ode;
  And it turned to a Sonnet.

1874

FAREWELL, RENOWN! [3]

Farewell, Renown! Too fleeting flower,
That grows a year to last an hour;—
  Prize of the race's dust and heat,
  Too often trodden under feet,—
Why should I court your "barren dower?"

[2] "Amphora coepit Institui: currente rota cur urceus exit?" (Horace, *Ars Poetica, 22.*) "It was a wine jar that was to be molded: as the wheel runs round, why does it turn out a pitcher?" Translated by Wickham. The poem is an example of the triolet, a stanza of 8 lines with one rime in lines 2, 6, and 8, and another in the other lines, with certain repetitions of the first and second lines.

[3] From *Complete Poetical Works,* by permission of Mr. A. T. A. Dobson (as acting for the Trustees) and Mr. Humphrey Milford, London, publisher.

Nay;—had I Dryden's [1] angry power,—
The thews of Ben, [1]—the wind of Gower, [1]—
Not less my voice should still repeat,
"Farewell, Renown!"

Farewell!—Because the Muses' bower
Is filled with rival brows that lower;—
Because, howe'er his pipe be sweet,
The Bard, that "pays" must please the street;—
But most . . . because the grapes are sour,—
Farewell, Renown!

1876

IN AFTER DAYS [2]

In after days when grasses high
O'er-top the stone where I shall lie,
Though ill or well the world adjust
My slender claim to honored dust,
I shall not question or reply.

I shall not see the morning sky;
I shall not hear the night wind sigh;
I shall be mute, as all men must
In after days!

But yet, now living, fain were I
That some one then should testify,
Saying—"He held his pen in trust
To Art, not serving shame or lust."
Will none?—Then let my memory die
In after days!

1884

FOR A CHARITY ANNUAL [2]

In Angel-Court the sunless air
Grows faint and sick; to left and right
The cowering houses shrink from sight,
Huddled and hopeless, eyeless, bare.

Misnamed, you say? For surely rare
Must be the angel-shapes that light
In Angel-Court!

Nay! the Eternities are there.
Death at the doorway stands to smite;
Life in its garrets leaps to flight;
And Love has climbed that crumbling stair
In Angel-Court.

1901

[1] John Dryden, the poet and dramatist, noted as a satirist on p. 303; Ben Jonson, the dramatist, physically and mentally powerful, see p. 209; John Gower, 1325?-1408, a poet noted for his lengthy, dull poems.

[2] From *Complete Poetical Works,* by permission of Mr. A. T. A. Dobson (as acting for the Trustees) and Mr. Humphrey Milford, London, publisher.

SIR EDMUND GOSSE
1849-1928

The father of Sir Edmund was a well-known naturalist. The son, however, showed so great a taste for literature that at eighteen he was an assistant in the department of printed books in the British Museum. He was also translator to the Board of Trade, librarian to the House of Lords, and lecturer in English literature at Cambridge and in the United States. He was knighted in 1925.

He did valuable work in making foreign literature known to English readers especially through his *Northern Studies,* 1879, and his translations of Ibsen. He became one of the foremost critics of English literature, especially seventeenth century writers. He compiled several histories of English literature, and wrote an important *Life of Swinburne,* 1917. In his *Critical Kit-Kats* (Collected Essays, 5 vols. 1914), Gosse anticipated the modern type of biography. *Father and Son,* 1907, is an intimate study of his childhood. His poetry, belonging to his earlier work, *On Viol and Flute,* 1873, and included in his *Collected Poems,* 1911, is characteristic of the last century. His technique is excellent, expressing many moods.

Criticism: J. Drinkwater, "Poetry of Edmund Gosse," *Bookm.* 63:536-7; L. Binyon, "Edmund Gosse," *Liv. Age* 306:59-61; W. Tittle, "Portraits in Pencil and Pen," *Cent.* 108:500-4; S. T. Williams, "Two Victorian Boyhoods," *No. Am.* 213:819-26.

LYING IN THE GRASS [3]

TO THOMAS HARDY

Between two russet tufts of summer grass,
I watch the world through hot air as through glass,
And by my face sweet lights and colors pass.

Before me, dark against the fading sky,
I watch three mowers mowing, as I lie:
With brawny arms they sweep in harmony.

Brown English faces by the sun burnt red,
Rich glowing color on bare throat and head,
My heart would leap to watch them, were I dead!

And in my strong young living as I lie,
I seem to move with them in harmony,—
A fourth is mowing, and that fourth am I.

The music of the scythes that glide and leap,
The young men whistling as their great arms sweep,
And all the perfume and sweet sense of sleep,

[3] From *The Collected Poems of Edmund Gosse* by permission of the author, of William Heinemann, Ltd., London, and of Charles Scribner's Sons, New York.

The weary butterflies that droop their wings,
The dreamy nightingale that hardly sings,
And all the lassitude of happy things,

Is mingling with the warm and pulsing blood
That gushes through my veins a languid flood
And feeds my spirit as the sap a bud.

Behind the mowers, on the amber air,
A dark-green beech-wood rises, still and fair,
A white path winding up it like a stair.

And see that girl, with pitcher on her head,
And clean white apron on her gown of red,—
Her even-song of love is but half-said:

She waits the youngest mower. Now he goes;
Her cheeks are redder than a wild blush-rose;
They climb up where the deepest shadows close.

But though they pass and vanish, I am there;
I watch his rough hands meet beneath her hair,
Their broken speech sounds sweet to me like prayer.

Ah! now the rosy children come to play,
And romp and struggle with the new-mown hay;
Their clear high voices sound from far away.

They know so little why the world is sad,
They dig themselves warm graves and yet are glad;
Their muffled screams and laughter make me mad!

I long to go and play among them there;
Unseen, like wind, to take them by the hair,
And gently make their rosy cheeks more fair.

The happy children! full of frank surprise,
And sudden whims and innocent ecstasies;
What godhead sparkles from their liquid eyes!

No wonder round those urns of mingled clays
That Tuscan [1] potters fashioned in old days,
And colored like the torrid earth ablaze,

We find the little gods and loves portrayed,
Through ancient forests wandering undismayed,
Or gathered, whispering, in some pleasant glade.

[1] of Tuscany, a province of Italy

They knew, as I do now, what keen delight
A strong man feels to watch the tender flight
Of little children playing in his sight.

I do not hunger for a well-stored mind,
I only wish to live my life, and find
My heart in unison with all mankind.

My life is like the single dewy star
That trembles on the horizon's primrose-bar,—
A microcosm [2] where all things living are.

And if, among the noiseless grasses, Death
Should come behind and take away my breath,
I should not rise as one who sorroweth;

For I should pass, but all the world would be
Full of desire and young delight and glee,
And why should men be sad through loss of me?

The light is dying; in the silver blue
The young moon shines from her bright window through:
The mowers are all gone, and I go too.

1872 *1873*

WITH A COPY OF HERRICK [3]

Fresh with all airs of woodland brooks
And scents of showers,
Take to your haunt of holy books
This saint of flowers.

When meadows burn with budding May, [4]
And heaven is blue,
Before his shrine our prayers we say,—
Saint Robin [5] true.

Love crowned with thorns is on his staff,—
Thorns of sweet-brier;
His benediction is a laugh,
Birds are his choir.

His sacred robe of white and red
Unction [6] distills;
He hath a nimbus round his head
Of daffodils.

1883 *1885*

[2] man as representing the great world in miniature
[3] From *The Collected Poems of Edmund Gosse,* by permission of the author, of William Heinemann, Ltd., London, and of Charles Scribner's Sons, New York.
[4] hawthorn
[5] See p. 244; Robin is a nickname for Robert.
[6] consecration

EPILOGUE [1]

If thou disdain the sacred muse,
  Beware lest Nature, past recall,
Indignant at that crime, refuse
  Thee entrance to her audience-hall,
  Beware lest sea, and sky, and all
That bears reflection of her face
  Be blotted with a hueless pall
Of unillumined commonplace.

The moving heavens, in rhythmic time,
  Roll, if thou watch them or refrain;
The waves upon the shore in rime
  Beat, heedless of thy loss or gain;
  Not they, but thou, hast lived in vain,
If thou art deaf and blind and dumb,
  Parched in the heart of morning rain,
And on the flaming altar numb.

Ah! desolate hour when that shall be,
  When dew and sunlight, rain and wind,
Shall seem but trivial things to thee,
  Unloved, unheeded, undivined;
  Nay, rather let that morning find
Thy molten soul exhaled and gone,
  Than in a living death resigned
So darkly still to labor on.

1873 1873

WILLIAM ERNEST HENLEY
1849-1903

It is impossible to consider Henley without thinking of his picturesque and pathetic qualities. His vitality, his zest for life, and tenacity of purpose, have been embodied in the unforgettable personality of Long John Silver, the crippled pirate in Stevenson's *Treasure Island.* He was born in Gloucester, and apart from a little schooling there, was self-educated, being an insatiable reader. At twenty-three he had lost one leg by tuberculosis, and the other was threatened. He made his way, penniless, to Professor Lister of Edinburgh, who saved the leg. During the two years he spent in the hospital Henley studied languages, wrote verse, and gained the friendship of "R.L.S." (see "Apparition," p. 807).

Returning to London he devoted himself to journalism until his *Book of Verse,* 1888, drew the attention of the literary world. He edited various well-known periodicals, and was a force in the London world of letters until his death, being perhaps the most gifted and influential of the critics of his generation.

As Professor Phelps points out, Henley "was an Elizabethan in the spaciousness of his mind, in his robust salt-water breeziness, in his hearty, spontaneous singing, and in his deification of the human will." His peculiar literary gift was that of portraiture. It is visible in his best prose work (essays on Burns, Byron, Disraeli, and others), as well as his poetry. The gallery of portraits contained in ***In Hospital,*** 1888, and ***London Voluntaries,*** 1893, exhibits his skill in swift characterization.

Biography: L. C. Cornford, *William Ernest Henley,* 1913. Criticism: Noyes, Phelps (EP); *Athen.* 1903, 2:92-3, sketch of life; S. Low, "Some Memories and Impressions," *Liv. Age* 239: 150-8.

BEFORE [2]

Behold me waiting—waiting for the knife.
A little while, and at a leap I storm
The thick, sweet mystery of chloroform,
The drunken dark, the little death-in-life.
The gods are good to me: I have no wife,
No innocent child, to think of as I near
The fateful minute; nothing all-too dear
Unmans me for my bout of passive strife.
Yet am I tremulous and a trifle sick,
And, face to face with chance, I shrink a little:
My hopes are strong, my will is something weak.
Here comes the basket? [3] Thank you. I am ready.
But, gentlemen my porters, life is brittle:
You carry Caesar and his fortunes—steady!

1873-5 1888

CLINICAL [2]

Hist? . . . .
Through the corridor's echoes, [4]
Louder and nearer
Comes a great shuffling of feet.
Quick, every one of you,
Straight your quilts, and be decent!
Here's the Professor. [5]

In he comes first
With the bright look we know,
From the broad, white brows the kind eyes
Soothing yet nerving you. Here at his elbow,
White-capped, white-aproned, the Nurse,
Towel on arm and her inkstand
Fretful with quills.
Here in the ruck, anyhow,
Surging along,
Louts, duffers, exquisites, students, and prigs—

[1] From *The Collected Poems of Edmund Gosse,* by permission of the author, of William Heinemann, Ltd., London, and of Charles Scribner's Sons, New York.

[2] From *Poems.* By permission of Macmillan & Co., Ltd., London, and Charles Scribner's Sons, New York.

[3] stretcher

[4] The scene is the Infirmary at Edinburgh.

[5] Sir Joseph Lister, 1827-1912, famous English surgeon, pioneer in antiseptic surgery

Whiskers and foreheads, scarf-pins and spectacles—
Hustles the Class! And they ring themselves
Round the first bed, where the Chief
(His dressers and clerks at attention),
Bends in inspection already.

So shows the ring
Seen from behind round a conjurer
Doing his pitch [1] in the street.
High shoulders, low shoulders, broad shoulders, narrow ones,
Round, square, and angular, serry and shove;
While from within a voice,
Gravely and weightily fluent,
Sounds; and then ceases; and suddenly
(Look at the stress of the shoulders!)
Out of a quiver of silence,
Over the hiss of the spray,
Comes a low cry, and the sound
Of breath quick intaken through teeth
Clenched in resolve. And the Master
Breaks from the crowd, and goes,
Wiping his hands,
To the next bed, with his pupils
Flocking and whispering behind him.

Now one can see.
Case Number One
Sits (rather pale) with his bedclothes
Stripped up, and showing his foot
(Alas for God's Image!)
Swaddled in wet, white lint
Brilliantly hideous with red.

1873-5 1888

APPARITION [2]

Thin-legged, thin-chested, slight unspeakably, [3]
Neat-footed and weak-fingered: in his face—
Lean, large-boned, curved of beak, and touched with race,
Bold-lipped, rich-tinted, mutable as the sea,
The brown eyes radiant with vivacity—
There shines a brilliant and romantic grace,
A spirit intense and rare, with trace on trace
Of passion and impudence and energy.
Valiant in velvet, light in ragged luck,
Most vain, most generous, sternly critical,
Buffoon and poet, lover and sensualist:
A deal of Ariel, just a streak of Puck,
Much Antony, of Hamlet most of all,
And something of the Shorter-Catechist. [4]

1873-5 1888

[1] set of tricks
[2] From *Poems.* By permission of Macmillan & Co., Ltd., London, and Charles Scribner's Sons, New York.
[3] This verse describes Robert Louis Stevenson, who befriended Henley while in the Infirmary.
[4] i.e., a Scotch Presbyterian

INVICTUS [2]

I.M. [5]
R. T. Hamilton Bruce
(1846-1899)

Out of the night that covers me,
  Black as the Pit from pole to pole,
I thank whatever gods may be
  For my unconquerable soul.

In the fell clutch of circumstance
  I have not winced nor cried aloud.
Under the bludgeonings of chance
  My head is bloody, but unbowed.

Beyond this place of wrath and tears
  Looms but the Horror of the shade,
And yet the menace of the years
  Finds, and shall find, me unafraid.

It matters not how strait the gate,
  How charged with punishments the scroll,
I am the master of my fate:
  I am the captain of my soul.

1875 1898

I.M.
MARGARITAE SORORI [2, 6]

(1886)

A late lark twitters from the quiet skies;
And from the west,
Where the sun, his day's work ended,
Lingers as in content,
There falls on the old, gray city
An influence luminous and serene,
A shining peace.

The smoke ascends
In a rosy-and-golden haze. The spires
Shine, and are changed. In the valley
Shadows rise. The lark sings on. The sun,
Closing his benediction,
Sinks, and the darkening air
Thrills with a sense of the triumphing night—
Night with her train of stars
And her great gift of sleep.

So be my passing!
My task accomplished and the long day done,
My wages taken, and in my heart
Some late lark singing,
Let me gathered to the quiet west,
The sundown splendid and serene,
Death.

1876 1898

[5] In memoriam: *invictus* means unconquered.
[6] To Sister Margaret; the reference is uncertain.

JOHN DAVIDSON
1857-1909

The career of Davidson, son of a Scotch minister, was a struggle from beginning to end. He left school at thirteen to work, teaching or acting as clerk for a livelihood until 1890. Then, going to London, he took up journalism and the profession of literature, leading a pathetic existence darkened by the tragedy of illness and poverty, and the spiritual conflict that led him to reject the religion of his fathers. The last years of his life were spent at Penzance, where he lived on a small Civil List pension, eked out by a meager income from his writings. Fear of cancer haunted him, and he is supposed to have taken his own life. Davidson's early work, consisting of dramas and novels, though brilliant, was unsuccessful. His true means of expression was poetry, and it was with *Fleet Street Eclogues*, 1893, that he won his first reputation. *Ballads and Songs,* 1894, forms the highwater mark of his poetry; in these poems, occasionally sordid in subject, are found passages of unexpected beauty. Davidson's imaginative work lacks the conviction of his realistic poems in which he often advocates revolt. A deep love of nature, and a ready sympathy give his verse more substance than is found in the work of many of his minor contemporaries.

Criticism: Jackson; Kennedy; Hayim Fineman, *John Davidson, a Study of the Relation of his Ideas to his Poetry,* 1916; Filson Young, "The New Poetry," *Fortn.* 85:136-52; P. Colum, "The Poet of Armageddon," *New Repub.* 13:310-2; M. Bronner, "John Davidson; Poet of Anarchy," *Forum* 44:305-20.

A BALLAD OF HEAVEN [1]

He wrought at one great work for years;
  The world passed by with lofty look:
Sometimes his eyes were dashed with tears;
  Sometimes his lips with laughter shook.

His wife and child went clothed in rags,
  And in a windy garret starved:
He trod his measures on the flags,
  And high on heaven his music carved.

Wistful he grew but never feared;
  For always on the midnight skies
His rich orchestral score appeared
  In stars and zones and galaxies.

He thought to copy down his score:
  The moonlight was his lamp: he said,
"Listen, my love"; but on the floor
  His wife and child were lying dead.

Her hollow eyes were open wide;
  He deemed she heard with special zest:
Her death's-head infant coldly eyed
  The desert of her shrunken breast.

"Listen, my love: my work is done;
  I tremble as I touch the page
To sign the sentence of the sun
  And crown the great eternal age.

"The slow adagio [2] begins;
  The winding-sheets are raveled out
That swathe the minds of men, the sins
  That wrap their rotting souls about.

"The dead are heralded along;
  With silver trumps and golden drums,
And flutes and oboes, keen and strong,
  My brave andante [3] singing comes.

"Then like a python's sumptuous dress
  The frame of things is cast away,
And out of Time's obscure distress,
  The thundering scherzo [4] crashes Day.

"For three great orchestras I hope
  My mighty music shall be scored:
On three high hills they shall have scope
  With heaven's vault for a sounding-board.

"Sleep well, love; let your eyelids fall;
  Cover the child; goodnight, and if . . .
What? Speak . . . the traitorous end of all!
  Both . . . cold and hungry . . . cold and
    stiff!

"But no, God means us well, I trust:
  Dear ones, be happy, hope is nigh:
We are too young to fall to dust,
  And too unsatisfied to die."

He lifted up against his breast
  The woman's body stark and wan;
And to her withered bosom pressed
  The little skin-clad skeleton.

"You see you are alive," he cried.
  He rocked them gently to and fro.
"No, no, my love, you have not died;
  Nor you, my little fellow; no."

Long in his arms he strained his dead
  And crooned an antique lullaby;
Then laid them on the lowly bed,
  And broke down with a doleful cry.

[1] Used by permission of Dodd, Mead & Company, Inc.

[2] a slow movement in a musical composition
[3] a stately movement, moderately flowing
[4] a gay movement in music

"The love, the hope, the blood, the brain,
Of her and me, the budding life,
And my great music—all in vain!
My unscored work, my child, my wife!

"We drop into oblivion,
And nourish some suburban sod:
My work, this woman, this my son,
Are now no more: there is no God.

"The world's a dustbin; we are due,
And death's cart waits: be life accurst!"
He stumbled down beside the two,
And clasping them, his great heart burst.

Straightway he stood at heaven's gate,
Abashed and trembling for his sin:
I trow he had not long to wait,
For God came out and led him in.

And then there ran a radiant pair,
Ruddy with haste and eager-eyed
To meet him first upon the stair—
His wife and child beatified.

They clad him in a robe of light,
And gave him heavenly food to eat;
Great seraphs praised him to the height,
Archangels sat about his feet.

God, smiling, took him by the hand,
And led him to the brink of heaven;
He saw where systems whirling stand,
Where galaxies like snow are driven.

Dead silence reigned; a shudder ran
Through space; Time furled his wearied wings;
A slow adagio then began
Sweetly resolving [1] troubled things.

The dead were heralded along:
As if with drums and trumps of flame,
And flutes and oboes keen and strong,
A brave andante singing came.

Then like a python's sumptuous dress
The frame of things was cast away,
And out of Time's obscure distress
The conquering scherzo thundered Day.

He doubted; but God said "Even so;
Nothing is lost that's wrought with tears:
The music that you made below
Is now the music of the spheres."

1894

[1] in music, harmonizing

GEORGE GISSING
1857-1903

Gissing, the "historian of the middle classes," was born at Wakefield, and was well educated at a Quaker boarding-school and at Owen's College, Manchester. Although he showed unusual literary ability, the early part of his life was very much a hand-to-mouth existence, mainly in London, though for a time he was in America, teaching, and in Jena, Germany, studying. Later in life, when more prosperous, he spent much time on the Continent, where he wrote *By the Ionian Sea,* 1901, a series of autobiographical sketches.

His first novel appeared in 1878, but it was not until the publication of *Demos,* 1886, that his work attracted attention. *New Grub Street,* 1891, is possibly the best example of his quality and power. Most of Gissing's writings are influenced by, if not directly founded upon, personal experiences. *The Private Papers of Henry Ryecroft,* though charming and delicate in expression, have an undeniably acrid flavor. It is easy to infer from them that the hardness of Gissing's early struggles had somewhat embittered his nature. There is little glow in any of his work, for his scenes and characters are often depressing; but he was honest and self-reliant. "He cared always and only for truth."—Constable, *Sat. R.*

Biography and criticism: F. A. Swinnerton, *George Gissing: a Critical Study,* 1923; Cunliffe; More (Shel. 5); Follett; Chevalley; Kennedy; T. Seccombe, Introd. essay to Gissing's *House of Cobwebs,* 1906; G. A. Stearns, "George Gissing in America," *Bookm.* 63:683-6 V. Woolf, "George Gissing," *New Repub.* 50:49-50; A. Harrison, "Sign-Posts of Fiction," *Contemp.* 128:82-9; E. B. Osborn, "A Dismal Dickens," *Liv. Age* 315:361-3; S. Alden, "George Gissing, Humanist," *No. Am.* 216:364-77.

From THE PRIVATE PAPERS OF HENRY RYECROFT [2]

Spring

I

For more than a week my pen has lain untouched. I have written nothing for seven whole days, not even a letter. Except during one or two bouts of illness such a thing never happened in my life before. In my life; the life, that is, which had to be supported by anxious toil; the life which was not lived for living's sake, as all life should be, but under the goad of fear. The earning of money should be a means to an end; for more than thirty years—I began to support myself at sixteen—I had to regard it as the end itself.

[2] Reprinted by kind permission of Mr. A. C. Gissing.

I could imagine that my old penholder feels reproachfully toward me. Has it not served me well? Why do I, in my happiness, let it lie there neglected, gathering dust? The same penholder that has lain against my forefinger day after day, for—how many years? Twenty at least; I remember buying it at a shop in Tottenham Court Road. By the same token I bought that day a paper-weight, which cost me a whole shilling—an extravagance which made me tremble. The penholder shone with its new varnish, now it is plain brown wood from end to end. On my forefinger it has made a callosity.

Old companion, yet old enemy! How many a time have I taken it up, loathing the necessity, heavy in head and heart, my hand shaking, my eyes sick-dazzled! How I dreaded the white page I had to follow with ink! Above all, on days such as this, when the blue eyes of Spring laughed from between rosy clouds, when the sunlight shimmered upon my table and made me long, long all but to madness, for the scent of the flowering earth, for the green of hillside larches, for the singing of the skylark above the downs. There was a time—it seems further away than childhood—when I took up my pen with eagerness; if my hand trembled it was with hope. But a hope that fooled me, for never a page of my writing deserved to live. I can say that now without bitterness. It was youthful error, and only the force of circumstance prolonged it. The world has done me no injustice; thank Heaven I have grown wise enough not to rail at it for this! And why should any man who writes, even if he writes things immortal, nurse anger at the world's neglect? Who asked him to publish? Who promised him a hearing? Who has broken faith with him? If my shoemaker turn me out an excellent pair of boots, and I, in some mood of cantankerous unreason, throw them back upon his hands, the man has just cause of complaint. But your poem, your novel, who bargained with you for it? If it is honest journeywork, yet lacks purchasers, at most you may call yourself a hapless tradesman. If it come from on high, with what decency do you fret and fume because it is not paid for in heavy cash? For the work of man's mind there is one test, and one alone, the judgment of generations yet unborn. If you have written a great book, the world to come will know of it. But you don't care for posthumous glory. You want to enjoy fame in a comfortable armchair. Ah, that is quite another thing. Have the courage of your desire. Admit yourself a merchant, and protest to gods and men that the merchandise you offer is of better quality than much which sells for a high price. You may be right, and indeed it is hard upon you that Fashion does not turn to your stall.

II

The exquisite quiet of this room! I have been sitting in utter idleness, watching the sky, viewing the shape of golden sunlight upon the carpet, which changes as the minutes pass, letting my eye wander from one framed print to another, and along the ranks of my beloved books. Within the house nothing stirs. In the garden I can hear singing of birds, I can hear the rustle of their wings. And thus, if it please me, I may sit all day long, and into the profounder quiet of the night.

My house is perfect. By great good fortune I have found a housekeeper no less to my mind, a low-voiced, light-footed woman of discreet age, strong and deft enough to render me all the service I require, and not afraid of solitude. She rises very early. By my breakfast-time there remains little to be done under the roof save dressing of meals. Very rarely do I hear even a clink of crockery; never the closing of a door or window. Oh, blessed silence!

There is not the remotest possibility of any one's calling upon me, and that I should call upon any one else is a thing undreamed of. I owe a letter to a friend; perhaps I shall write it before bedtime; perhaps I shall leave it till tomorrow morning. A letter of friendship should never be written save when the spirit prompts. I have not yet looked at the newspaper. Generally I leave it till I come back tired from my walk; it amuses me then to see what the noisy world is doing, what new self-torments men have discovered, what new forms of vain toil, what new occasions of peril and of strife. I grudge to give the first freshness of the morning mind to things so sad and foolish.

My house is perfect. Just large enough to allow the grace of order in domestic circumstance; just that superfluity of intramural space, to lack which is to be less than at one's ease. The fabric is sound; the work in wood and plaster tells of a more leisurely and a more honest age than ours. The stairs do not creak under my step; I am waylaid by no unkindly draught; I can open or close a window without muscle-ache. As to such trifles as the tint and device of wall-paper, I confess my indifference; be the walls only unobtrusive, and I am satisfied. The first thing in one's home is comfort; let beauty of detail be added if one has the means, the patience, the eye.

To me, this little book-room is beautiful, and chiefly because it is home. Through the greater part of life I was homeless. Many places have I inhabited, some of which my soul loathed, and some which pleased me well; but never till now with that sense of security which makes a home. At any moment I might have been driven forth by evil hap, by nagging necessity. For all that time did I say within myself: Some day, perchance, I shall have a home; yet the "perchance" had more and more of emphasis as life went on, and at the moment when fate was secretly smiling on me, I had all but abandoned hope, I have my home at last. When I place a new volume on my shelves, I say: Stand there whilst I have eyes to see you; and a joyous tremor thrills me. This house is mine on a lease of a score of years. So long I certainly shall not live; but, if I did, even so long should I have the wherewithal to pay my rent and buy my food.

I think with compassion of the unhappy mortals for whom no such sun will ever rise. I should like to add to the Litany a new petition: "For all inhabitants of great towns, and especially for all such as dwell in lodgings, boarding-houses, flats, or any other sordid substitute for Home which need or foolishness may have contrived."

In vain I have pondered the Stoic virtues. I know that it is folly to fret about the spot of one's abode on this little earth.

> All places that the eye of heaven visits
> Are to the wise man ports and happy havens.

But I have always worshiped wisdom afar off. In the sonorous period of the philosopher, in the golden measure of the poet, I find it of all things lovely. To its possession I shall never attain. What will it serve me to pretend a virtue of which I am incapable? To me the place and manner of my abode is of supreme import; let it be confessed, and there an end of it. I am no cosmopolite. Were I to think that I should die away from England, the thought would be dreadful to me. And in England, this is the dwelling of my choice; this is my home.

III

I am no botanist, but I have long found pleasure in herb-gathering. I love to come upon a plant which is unknown to me, to identify it with the help of my book, to greet it by name when next it shines beside my path. If the plant be rare, its discovery gives me joy. Nature, the great Artist, makes her common flowers in the common view; no word in human language can express the marvel and the loveliness even of what we call the vulgarest weed, but these are fashioned under the gaze of every passer-by. The rare flower is shaped apart, in places secret, in the Artist's subtler mood; to find it is to enjoy the sense of admission to a holier precinct. Even in my gladness I am awed.

Today I have walked far, and at the end of my walk I found the little white-flowered woodruff. It grew in a copse of young ash. When I had looked long at the flower, I delighted myself with the grace of the slim trees about it—their shining smoothness, their olive hue. Hard by stood a bush of wych elm;[1] its tettered[2] bark, overlined as if with the character of some unknown tongue, made the young ashes yet more beautiful.

It matters not how long I wander. There is no task to bring me back; no one will be vexed or uneasy, linger I ever so late. Spring is shining upon these lanes and meadows; I feel as if I must follow every winding track that opens by my way. Spring has restored to me something of the long-forgotten vigor of youth; I walk without weariness; I sing to myself like a boy, and the song is one I knew in boyhood.

That reminds me of an incident. Near a hamlet, in a lonely spot by a woodside, I came upon a little lad of perhaps ten years old, who, his head hidden in his arms against a tree trunk, was crying bitterly. I asked him what was the matter, and, after a little trouble—he was better than a mere bumpkin—I learned that, having been sent with sixpence to pay a debt, he had lost the money. The poor little fellow was in a state of mind which in a grave man would be called the anguish of despair; he must have been crying for a long time; every muscle of his face quivered as if under torture, his limbs shook; his eyes, his voice, uttered such misery as only the vilest criminal should be made to suffer. And it was because he had lost sixpence!

[1] elm of Northern Europe
[2] rough, as though from skin disease

I could have shed tears with him—tears of pity and of rage at all this spectacle implied. On a day of indescribable glory, when earth and heaven shed benedictions upon the soul of man, a child, whose nature would have bidden him rejoice as only childhood may, wept his heart out because his hand had dropped a sixpenny piece! The loss was a very serious one, and he knew it; he was less afraid to face his parents, than overcome by misery at the thought of the harm he had done them. Sixpence dropped by the wayside, and a whole family made wretched! What are the due descriptive terms for a state of "civilization" in which such a thing as this is possible? I put my hand into my pocket, and wrought sixpennyworth of miracle.

It took me half an hour to recover my quiet mind. After all, it is as idle to rage against man's fatuity as to hope that he will ever be less a fool. For me, the great thing was my sixpenny miracle. Why, I have known the day when it would have been beyond my power altogether, or else would have cost me a meal. Wherefore, let me be glad again and thankful.

Summer

XXVII

Today I have read *The Tempest*. It is perhaps the play that I love best, and, because I seem to myself to know it so well, I commonly pass it over in opening the book. Yet, as always in regard to Shakespeare, having read it once more, I find that my knowledge was less complete than I supposed. So it would be, live as long as one might; so it would ever be, whilst one had strength to turn the pages and a mind left to read them.

I like to believe that this was the poet's last work, that he wrote it in his home at Stratford, walking day by day in the fields which had taught his boyhood to love rural England. It is ripe fruit of the supreme imagination, perfect craft of the master hand. For a man whose life's business it has been to study the English tongue, what joy can equal that of marking the happy ease wherewith Shakespeare surpasses, in mere command of words, every achievement of those even who, apart from him, are great? I could fancy that, in *The Tempest,* he wrought with a peculiar consciousness of this power, smiling as the word of inimitable felicity, the phrase of incomparable cadence, was whispered to him by the Ariel that was his genius. He seems to sport with language, to amuse himself with new discovery of its resources. From king to beggar, men of every rank and every order of mind have spoken with his lips; he has uttered the lore of fairyland; now it pleases him to create a being neither man nor fairy, a something between brute and human nature, and to endow its purposes with words. These words, how they smack of the moist and spawning earth, of the life of creatures that cannot rise above the soil! We do not think of it enough; we stint our wonder because we fall short in appreciation. A miracle is worked before us, and we scarce give heed; it has become familiar to our minds as any other of nature's marvels, which we rarely pause to reflect upon. *The Tempest* contains the noblest meditative passage in all the plays; that which embodies Shakespeare's final view of life, and is the inevitable quotation of all who would sum the teachings of philosophy. It contains his most exquisite lyrics, his tenderest love passages, and one glimpse of fairyland which—I cannot but think—outshines the utmost beauty of *A Midsummer Night's Dream:* Prospero's farewell to the "elves of hills, brooks, standing lakes, and groves." Again a miracle; these are things which cannot be staled by repetition. Come to them often as you will, they are ever fresh as though new minted from the brain of the poet. Being perfect, they can never droop under that satiety which arises from the perception of fault; their virtue can never be so entirely savored as to leave no pungency of gusto for the next approach.

Among the many reasons which make me glad to have been born in England, one of the first is that I read Shakespeare in my mother tongue. If I try to imagine myself as one who cannot know him face to face, who hears him only speaking from afar, and that in accents which only through the laboring intelligence can touch the living soul, there comes upon me a sense of chill discouragement, of dreary deprivation. I am wont to think that I can read Homer, and, assuredly, if any man enjoys him, it is I; but can I for a moment dream that Homer yields me all his music, that his word is to me as to him who walked by the Hellenic shore when Hellas lived? I know that there reaches me across the vast of time no more than a faint and broken echo; I know that it would be fainter still, but for its blending with those memories of youth which are as a glimmer of the world's primeval glory. Let every land have joy of its poet; for the poet is the land itself, all its greatness and its sweetness, all that incommunicable heritage for which men live and die. As I close the book, love and reverence possess me. Whether does my full heart turn to the great Enchanter, or to the Island upon which he has laid his spell? I know not. I cannot think of them apart. In the love and reverence awakened by that voice of voices, Shakespeare and England are but one.

1900 1903

WILLIAM HENRY HUDSON
1841-1922

For a picture of the early life of Hudson, naturalist and writer, one should turn to *Far Away and Long Ago,* 1918; this book is crowded with memories of his youthful adventures and his studies of human beings, animals, and plants. Hudson was born near Buenos Aires and lived on the pampas until he was twenty-nine. The rest of his life he spent in England, most of it in poverty and ill health. In 1901 he was granted a Civil List pension, which he voluntarily resigned when his writings brought financial success. For the most part he wandered through the southern countries of England "one among the rare itinerants who have revealed the beauty of this country by their affectionate art," (E. Rhys) though at intervals he lived in London, where he had many friends among the men of letters, and where he died.

His numerous writings, through all of which runs personal experience, include studies of bird life that rank Hudson high as an ornithologist; adventures, romantic novels, and short stories of South America: *The Purple Land,* 1885; *Green Mansions,* 1904; and essays of miscellaneous observations of English country life: *Afoot in England, A Shepherd's Life,* 1910; *A Hind in Richmond Park,* 1922, and others. As a writer and a naturalist he is a link in the chain joining White of Selborne and William Beebe.

Collected Works, 24 vols. 1923. Biography: M. Roberts, *W. H. Hudson,* 1924; T. J. Massingham, *Untrodden Ways,* 1923. Criticism: E. Garnett, *Friday Nights;* H. J. Massingham, "The Art of W. H. Hudson," *Liv. Age* 315:51-3; R. Curle, "W. H. Hudson," *Fortn.* 118:612-19, interesting personal reminiscences; E. Rhys, "A Rare Traveler," *19th Cent.* 88:72-8; G. M. Harper, "Hardy, Hudson, Housman," *Scrib.* 78:151-7; C. S. Evans, "The Writings of W. H. Hudson," *Bookm.* 52:18-21.

From A NATURALIST IN LA PLATA [1]

. . . .

My last case—the last, that is, of the few I have selected—relates to a singular variation in the human species. On this occasion I was again traveling alone in a strange district on the southern frontier of Buenos Aires. On a bitterly cold midwinter day, shortly before noon, I arrived, stiff and tired, at one of those pilgrims' rests on the pampas—a wayside *pulperia,* or public house, where the traveler can procure anything he may require or desire, from a tumbler of Brazilian rum to make glad his heart, to a poncho, or cloak of blue cloth with fluffy scarlet lining, to keep him warm o' nights; and, to speed him on his way, a pair of cast-iron spurs weighing six pounds avoirdupois, with rowels eight inches in diameter, manufactured in this island [2] for the use of barbarous men beyond the sea. The wretched mud-and-grass building was surrounded by a foss [3] crossed by a plank drawbridge; outside of the the enclosure twelve or fourteen saddled horses were standing, and from the loud noise of talk and laughter in the bar I conjectured that a goodly company of rough frontiersmen were already making merry at that early hour. It was necessary for me to go in among them to see the proprietor of the place and ask permission to visit his kitchen in order to make myself a "tin of coffee," that being the refreshment I felt inclined for. When I went in and made my salutation, one man wheeled round square before me, stared straight into my eyes, and in an exceedingly high-pitched reedy or screechy voice and a sing-song tone returned my "good-morning," and bade me call for the liquid I loved best at his expense. I declined with thanks, and in accordance with gaucho [4] etiquette added that I was prepared to pay for his liquor. It was then for him to say that he had already been served and so let the matter drop, but he did not do so: he screamed out in his wild animal voice that he would take gin. I paid for his drink, and would, I think, have felt greatly surprised at his strange insolent behavior, so unlike that of the usually courteous gaucho, but this thing affected me not at all, so profoundly had his singular appearance and voice impressed me; and for the rest of the time I remained in the place I continued to watch him narrowly. Professor Huxley has somewhere said, "A variation frequently occurs, but those who notice it take no care about noting down the particulars." That is not a failing of mine, and this is what I noted down while the man's appearance was still fresh in memory. He was about five feet

[1] From *A Naturalist in La Plata* by W. H. Hudson. Published by E. P. Dutton & Co.; used by permission.

[2] England

[3] ditch

[4] a native of the pampas, of mixed Spanish and Indian descent, often a cowboy

eleven inches in height—very tall for a gaucho—straight and athletic, with exceedingly broad shoulders, which made his round head look small; long arms and huge hands. The round flat face, coarse black hair, swarthy reddish color, and smooth hairless cheeks seemed to show that he had more Indian than Spanish blood in him, while his round black eyes were even more like those of a rapacious animal in expression than in the pure-blooded Indian. He also had the Indian or half-breed's moustache, when that natural ornament is permitted to grow, and which is composed of thick bristles standing out like a cat's whiskers. The mouth was the marvelous feature, for it was twice the size of an average mouth, and the two lips were alike in thickness. This mouth did not smile, but snarled, both when he spoke and when he should have smiled; and when he snarled the whole of his teeth and a part of the gums were displayed. The teeth were not as in other human beings—incisors, canines, and molars: they were all exactly alike, above and below, each tooth a gleaming white triangle, broad at the gum where it touched its companion teeth, and with a point sharp as the sharpest-pointed dagger. They were like the teeth of a shark or crocodile. I noticed that when he showed them, which was very often, they were not set together as in dogs, weasels, and other savage snarling animals, but apart, showing the whole terrible serration in the huge red mouth.

After getting his gin he joined in the boisterous conversation with the others, and this gave me an opportunity of studying his face for several minutes, all the time with a curious feeling that I had put myself into a cage with a savage animal of horrible aspect, whose instincts were utterly unknown to me, and were probably not very pleasant. It was interesting to note that whenever one of the others addressed him directly, or turned to him when speaking, it was with a curious expression, not of fear, but partly amusement and partly something else which I could not fathom. Now, one might think that this was natural enough purely on account of the man's extraordinary appearance. I do not think that a sufficient explanation; for however strange a man's appearance may be, his intimate friends and associates soon lose all sense of wonder at his strangeness, and even forget that he is unlike others. My belief is that this curiosity, or whatever it was they showed in their faces, was due to something in his character—a mental strangeness, showing itself at unexpected times, and which might flash out at any moment to amuse or astonish them. There was certainly a correspondence between the snarling action of the mouth and the dangerous form of the teeth, perfect as that in any snarling animal; and such animals, it should be remembered, snarl not only when angry and threatening, but in their playful moods as well. Other and more important correspondences or correlations might have existed; and the voice was certainly unlike any human voice I have ever heard, whether in white, red, or black man. But the time I had for observation was short, the conversation revealed nothing further, and by-and-by I went away in search of the odorous kitchen, where there would be hot water for coffee, or at all events cold water and a kettle, and materials for making a fire—to wit, bones of dead cattle, "buffalo chips," and rancid fat.

I have never been worried with the wish or ambition to be a head-hunter in the Dyak[1] sense, but on this one occasion I did wish that it had been possible, without violating any law, or doing anything to a fellow creature which I should not like done to myself, to have obtained possession of this man's head, with its set of unique and terrible teeth. For how, in the name of Evolution, did he come by them, and by other physical peculiarities—the snarling habit and that high-pitched animal voice, for instance—which made him a being different from others—one separate and far apart? Was he, so admirably formed, so complete and well-balanced, merely a freak of nature, to use an old-fashioned phrase—a sport, or spontaneous individual variation—an experiment for a new human type, imagined by Nature in some past period, inconceivably long ago, but which she had only now, too late, found time to carry out? Or rather was he like that little hairy maiden exhibited not long ago in London, a reproduction of the past, the mystery called reversion—a something in the life of a species like memory in the life of an individual, the memory which suddenly brings back to the old man's mind the image of his childhood? For no dream-monster in human form ever appeared to me with so strange and terrible a face; and this was no dream but sober fact, for I saw and spoke with this man; and unless cold steel has given him his quietus, or his own horse has crushed him, or a mad bull gored him—all natural forms of

[1] one of the aboriginal natives of Borneo who make war in order to procure the heads of enemies as trophies

death in that wild land—he is probably still living and in the prime of life, and perhaps at this very moment drinking gin at some astonished traveler's expense at that very bar where I met him. The old Palaeolithic [1] man, judging from the few remains we have of him, must have had an unspeakably savage and, to our way of thinking, repulsive and horrible aspect, with his villainous low receding forehead, broad nose, great projecting upper jaw, and retreating chin; to meet such a man face to face in Piccadilly [2] would frighten a nervous person of the present time. But his teeth were not unlike our own, only very much larger and more powerful, and well adapted to their work of masticating the flesh, underdone and possibly raw, of mammoth and rhinoceros. If, then, this living man recalls a type of the past, it is of a remoter past, a more primitive man, the volume of whose history is missing from the geological record. To speculate on such a subject seems idle and useless; and when I coveted possession of that head it was not because I thought that it might lead to any fresh discovery. A lower motive inspired the feeling. I wished for it only that I might bring it over the sea, to drop it like a new apple of discord, [3] suited to the spirit of the times, among the anthropologists and evolutionists generally of this old and learned world. Inscribed, of course, "To the most learned," but giving no locality and no particulars. I wished to do that for the pleasure—not a very noble kind of pleasure, I allow—of witnessing from some safe hiding-place the stupendous strife that would have ensued—a battle more furious, lasting, and fatal to many a brave knight of biology, than was ever yet fought over any bone or bony fragment or fabric ever picked up, including the celebrated cranium of the Neanderthal. [4]

1892

FRANCIS THOMPSON
1859-1907

The tragic life of Francis Thompson parallels in several details that of De Quincey. He was born in Lancashire, and after a childhood spent in much reading, chiefly of poetry, began preparation for the Roman Catholic priesthood. Proving unfit, he tried medicine. Again failing, he suffered a nervous breakdown, turned to opium for relief and made his way to London. In his poverty he left manuscripts of his verse at magazine offices; and at length some poems, after lying for months unread, interested an editor, Wilfrid Meynell. He managed to trace the vagrant author, printed the poems, and public recognition followed. Mr. and Mrs. Meynell befriended the poet and encouraged his talent until his death, hastened by the hardships he had undergone.

Thompson's poems, appearing in three small volumes (*Poems,* 1893; *Sister Songs,* 1895; *New Poems,* 1897) cover only about ten years. His prose, much of it written at the same time, continued during another decade. As a poet Thompson was a nineteenth-century descendant of the mystics of the seventeenth century, Crashaw, Vaughan, and Herbert; yet he was strongly individual. He was spontaneous; and though at times lacking restraint, he was deeply sincere. He had not the constructive faculty of Milton, or the lyric grace of Shelley, but like them he loved beauty: the beauty of nature, of children and all innocent creatures so filled him that in his poetry there was no room for his own misfortune.

The Works of Francis Thompson, ed. W. Meynell, 3 vols. 1913. Biography: E. Meynell, 1913. Criticism: Phelps (EP); More (Shel. 7); *Nation* 87:486-9; Freeman; Jackson; Kennedy; M. Bronner, "Francis Thompson: an Appraisement," *Ind.* 64:98-102; "Francis Thompson," *Liv. Age* 259:306-9; W. Meynell, "Mr. Francis Thompson," *Liv. Age* 255:804-8; C. Gauss, "The Poetry of Francis Thompson," *Nation* 85:513-4; K. Tynan, "Francis Thompson," *Liv. Age* 298-630-2; *Lit. Dig.* 58:36-7, Aug. 3 '18.

THE HOUND OF HEAVEN [5]

I fled Him, down the nights and down the days;
I fled Him, down the arches of the years;
I fled Him, down the labyrinthine ways
Of my own mind; and in the mist of tears
I hid from Him, and under running laughter,
Up vistaed hopes I sped;
And shot, precipitated
Adown Titanic glooms of chasmed fears,
From those strong Feet that followed, followed after.
But with unhurrying chase,
And unperturbèd pace,
Deliberate speed, majestic instancy,
They beat—and a Voice beat
More instant [6] than the Feet—
"All things betray thee, who betrayest Me."
I pleaded, outlaw-wise,
By many a hearted casement, curtained red,
Trellised with intertwining charities;
(For, though I knew His love Who followèd,
Yet was I sore adread

[1] the earliest known age of human culture, that of unpolished stone weapons
[2] a famous street in London
[3] The original apple of discord, inscribed "To the most beautiful"; see Tennyson's Oenone, p. 598.
[4] A skull found with other parts of a prehistoric skeleton at Neanderthal in the Rhine Valley in 1856; it has given rise to much scientific controversy over its place among human or sub-human remains.

[5] Used by the kind permission of Mr. Wilfrid Meynell.
[6] urgent

Lest, having Him, I must have naught beside)
But, if one little casement parted wide,
The gust of His approach would clash it to.
Fear wist [1] not to evade, as Love wist to pursue.
Across the margent of the world I fled,
And troubled the gold gateways of the stars,
Smiting for shelter on their clangèd bars;
Fretted to dulcet jars [2]
And silvern chatter the pale ports [3] o' the moon.
I said to dawn: Be sudden—to eve: Be soon;
With thy young skyey blossoms heap me over
From this tremendous Lover!
Float thy vague veil about me, lest He see!
I tempted all His servitors, but to find
My own betrayal in their constancy,
In faith to Him their fickleness to me,
Their traitorous trueness, and their loyal deceit.
To all swift things for swiftness did I sue;
Clung to the whistling mane of every wind.
But whether they swept, smoothly fleet,
The long savannahs [4] of the blue;
Or whether, Thunder-driven,
They clanged his chariot 'thwart a heaven,
Plashy with flying lightnings round the spurn o' their feet:—
Fear wist not to evade as Love wist to pursue.
Still with unhurrying chase,
And unperturbèd pace,
Deliberate speed, majestic instancy,
Came on the following Feet,
And a Voice above their beat—
"Naught shelters thee, who wilt not shelter Me."

I sought no more that, after which I strayed,
In face of man or maid;
But still within the little children's eyes
Seems something, something that replies,
They at least are for me, surely for me!
I turned me to them very wistfully;
But just as their young eyes grew sudden fair
With dawning answers there,
Their angel plucked them from me by the hair.
"Come then, ye other children, Nature's—share
With me" (said I) "your delicate fellowship;
Let me greet you lip to lip,
Let me twine with you caresses,
Wantoning

[1] knew
[2] jarrings
[3] gates
[4] plains

With our Lady-Mother's vagrant tresses,
Banqueting
With her in her wind-walled palace,
Underneath her azured daïs,
Quaffing, as your taintless way is,
From a chalice
Lucent-weeping out of the dayspring."
So it was done:
I in their delicate fellowship was one—
Drew the bolt of Nature's secrecies.
I knew all the swift importings
Of the willful face of skies;
I knew how the clouds arise
Spumèd of the wild sea-snortings;
All that's born or dies
Rose and drooped with—made them shapers
Of mine own moods, or wailful or divine—
With them joyed and was bereaven. [5]
I was heavy with the even,
When she lit her glimmering tapers
Round the day's dead sanctities.
I laughed in the morning's eyes.
I triumphed and I saddened with all weather,
Heaven and I wept together,
And its sweet tears were salt with mortal mine; [6]
Against the red throb of its sunset-heart
I laid my own to beat,
And share commingling heat;
But not by that, by that, was eased my human smart.
In vain my tears were wet on Heaven's gray cheek.
For ah! we know not what each other says,
These things and I; in sound *I* speak—
Their sound is but their stir, they speak by silences.
Nature, poor stepdame, cannot slake my drouth;
Let her, if she would owe [7] me,
Drop yon blue bosom-veil of sky, and show me
The breasts o' her tenderness:
Never did any milk of hers once bless
My thirsting mouth.
Nigh and nigh draws the chase,
With unperturbèd pace,
Deliberate speed, majestic instancy,
And past those noisèd Feet
A voice comes yet more fleet—
"Lo! naught contents thee, who content'st not Me."
Naked I wait Thy love's uplifted stroke!

[5] "Bereaved" or "bereft" are the usual forms.
[6] mine which were mortal
[7] own

My harness piece by piece Thou hast hewn from me,
And smitten me to my knee;
I am defenseless utterly.
I slept, methinks, and woke,
And, slowly gazing, find me stripped in sleep.
In the rash lustihead of my young powers,
I shook the pillaring hours [1]
And pulled my life upon me; grimed with smears,
I stand among the dust o' the mounded years—
My mangled youth lies dead beneath the heap.
My days have crackled and gone up in smoke,
Have puffed and burst as sun-starts on a stream.
Yea, faileth now even dream
The dreamer, and the lute the lutanist;
Even the linked fantasies, in whose blossomy twist
I swung the earth a trinket at my wrist,
Are yielding; cords of all too weak account
For earth with heavy griefs so overplussed.
Ah! is Thy love indeed
A weed, albeit an amaranthine [2] weed,
Suffering no flowers except its own to mount?
Ah! must—
Designer infinite!—
Ah! must Thou char [3] the wood ere Thou canst limn [3] with it?
My freshness spent its wavering shower i' the dust;
And now my heart is as a broken fount,
Wherein tear-drippings stagnate, spilt down ever
From the dank thoughts that shiver
Upon the sighful branches of my mind.
Such is; what is to be?
The pulp so bitter, how shall taste the rind?
I dimly guess what Time in mists confounds; [4]
Yet ever and anon a trumpet sounds
From the hid battlements of Eternity,
Those shaken mists a space unsettle, then
Round the half-glimpsèd turrets slowly wash again;
But not ere him who summoneth
I first have seen, enwound
With glooming robes purpureal, cypress-crowned;
His name I know, and what his trumpet saith.
Whether man's heart or life it be which yields
Thee harvest, must Thy harvest fields
Be dunged with rotten death?
Now of that long pursuit

[1] a reference to Samson, *Judges* xxvi, 26-30
[2] unfading
[3] a reference to sketching with charcoal
[4] hides

Comes on at hand the bruit; [5]
That Voice is round me like a bursting sea:
"And is thy earth so marred,
Shattered in shard [6] on shard?
Lo, all things fly thee, for thou fliest Me!

"Strange, piteous, futile thing!
Wherefore should any set thee love apart?
Seeing none but I makes much of naught"
(He said),
"And human love needs human meriting:
How hast thou merited—
Of all man's clotted clay the dingiest clot?
Alack, thou knowest not
How little worthy of any love thou art!
Whom wilt thou find to love ignoble thee,
Save Me, save only Me?
All which I took from thee I did but take,
Not for thy harms,
But just that thou might'st seek it in My arms.
All which thy child's mistake
Fancies as lost, I have stored for thee at home:
Rise, clasp My hand, and come."

Halts by me that footfall:
Is my gloom, after all,
Shade of His hand, outstretched caressingly?
"Ah, fondest, [7] blindest, weakest,
I am He Whom thou seekest!
Thou dravest love from thee, who dravest Me."

c.1890 1893

TO A SNOWFLAKE [8]

What heart could have thought you?—
Past our devisal
(O filigree petal!)
Fashioned so purely,
Fragilely, surely,
From what Paradisal
Imagineless metal,
Too costly for cost?
Who hammered you, wrought you,
From argentine [9] vapor?—
"God was my shaper.
Passing surmisal,
He hammered, He wrought me,
From curled silver vapor,

[5] noise
[6] fragment
[7] (in Elizabethan sense) most foolish
[8] Used by kind permission of Mr. Wilfrid Meynell.
[9] silvery

To lust [1] of His mind:—
Thou could'st not have thought me!
So purely, so palely,
Tinily, surely,
Mightily, frailly,
Insculped and embossed,
With His hammer of wind,
And His graver [2] of frost."

"IN NO STRANGE LAND" [3]

"The Kingdom of God is Within You."

O world invisible, we view thee:
O world intangible, we touch thee:
O world unknowable, we know thee:
Inapprehensible, we clutch thee!

Does the fish soar to find the ocean,
The eagle plunge to find the air—
That we ask of the stars in motion
If they have rumor of thee there?

Not where the wheeling systems darken,
And our benumbed conceiving soars—
The drift of pinions, would we harken,
Beats at our own clay-shuttered doors.

The angels keep their ancient places—
Turn but a stone, and start a wing!
'Tis ye, 'tis your estrangèd faces
That miss the many-splendored thing.

But (when so sad thou canst not sadder)
Cry;—and upon thy so sore loss
Shall shine the traffic of Jacob's ladder [4]
Pitched betwixt Heaven and Charing Cross. [5]

Yea, in the night, my Soul, my daughter,
Cry—clinging Heaven by the hems;
And lo, Christ walking on the water
Not of Genesareth, [6] but Thames!

1908

(MRS.) ALICE MEYNELL
1850-1922

"There feeling stills her breathing with her hand,
And Dream from Melancholy part wrests the wand;
And in the contemplation of those eyes,
Passionless passion, wild tranquilities."

So Francis Thompson wrote of his close friend and benefactress. The critics of Mrs. Meynell, also, have borne testimony to her rare personality, and have emphasized the quality of her work rather than the details of her life. She was born in London. Her father, a man of leisure, devoted himself to the education of his two daughters, Alice and Elizabeth, and much of her life was spent in Italy. In 1877 she married Wilfrid Meynell, journalist and author, and their home became a center for gifted contemporaries such as seldom came together elsewhere. Henley, Meredith, Ruskin, Rossetti, Browning, Chesterton not only were her warmest friends, but valued her work for its spiritual quality.

Her first collection, *Preludes,* appeared in 1875; her *Last Poems* in 1923. About 1893 she began to produce essays (*The Rhythm of Life,* 1893, *The Color of Life,* 1896) that equal her poetry in merit and might be called prose poems. The quality and content of Mrs. Meynell's work make her a transitional writer: in form she belongs with her generation; in sensitiveness and introspection she anticipates the next. In fervor of spirit, her poetry, like that of Francis Thompson, has much in common with that of Crashaw, Herbert, and other seventeenth century mystics. "In prose and verse alike she was . . . . a spiritual romantic."—Garvin.

Criticism: Scott; Noyes; J. L. Garvin, "Alice Meynell," *Liv. Age* 316:103-8; S. G. Ford, "Mrs. Meynell," *Liv. Age* 288:483-6; E. H. Moorhouse, "The Flower of the Mind: Alice Meynell and her Work," *Fortn.* 119:64-73; A. K. Tuell, "Mrs. Meynell: a Study," *Atlan.* 131:229-39.

RENOUNCEMENT [7]

I must not think of thee; and, tired yet strong,
I shun the thought that lurks in all delight—
The thought of thee—and in the blue Heaven's height,
And in the sweetest passage of a song.

O just beyond the fairest thoughts that throng
This breast, the thought of thee waits, hidden yet bright;
But it must never, never come in sight;
I must stop short of thee the whole day long.

But when sleep comes to close each difficult day,
When night gives pause to the long watch I keep,
And all my bonds I needs must loose apart,

Must doff my will as raiment laid away,—
With the first dream that comes with the first sleep
I run, I run, I am gathered to thy heart.

1893

[1] desire [2] engraving tool
[3] By kind permission of Mr. Wilfrid Meynell.
[4] See *Genesis* xxviii, 12. [5] in London
[6] Lake of Galilee in Palestine; see *Matt.* xiv, 25.

[7] From *The Poems of Alice Meynell,* comp. ed., 1923. By the kind permission of Mr. Wilfrid Meynell.

THE SHEPHERDESS [1]

She walks—the lady of my delight—
  A shepherdess of sheep.
Her flocks are thoughts. She keeps them white;
  She guards them from the steep;
She feeds them on the fragrant height,
  And folds them in for sleep.

She roams maternal hills and bright,
  Dark valleys safe and deep.
Into that tender breast at night
  The chastest stars may peep.
She walks—the lady of my delight—
  A shepherdess of sheep.

She holds her little thoughts in sight,
  Though gay they run and leap.
She is so circumspect and right;
  She has her soul to keep.
She walks—the lady of my delight—
  A shepherdess of sheep.

1913

A THRUSH BEFORE DAWN [1]

A voice peals in this end of night
  A phrase of notes resembling stars,
Single and spiritual notes of light.
  What call they at my window-bars?
    The South, the past, the day to be,
    An ancient infelicity.

Darkling, deliberate, what sings
  This wonderful one, alone, at peace?
What wilder things than song, what things
  Sweeter than youth, clearer than Greece,
    Dearer than Italy, untold
    Delight, and freshness centuries old?

And first first-loves, a multitude,
  The exaltation of their pain;
Ancestral childhood long renewed;
  And midnights of invisible rain;
    And gardens, gardens, night and day,
    Gardens and childhood all the way.

What Middle Ages passionate,
O passionate voice! What distant bells
Lodged in the hills, what palace state
  Illyrian! For it speaks, it tells,
    Without desire, without dismay,
    Some morrow and some yesterday.

All-natural things! But more—Whence came
  This yet remoter mystery?
How do these starry notes proclaim
  A graver still divinity?
    This hope, this sanctity of fear?
    O innocent throat! O human ear!

1914

[1] From *The Poems of Alice Meynell*, comp. ed., 1923. By the kind permission of Mr. Wilfrid Meynell.

RUDYARD KIPLING 1865-

Kipling was born in India, and thither, after some ten years in England for education, he returned at the age of seventeen to take up journalism. By 1886 he was becoming known as a writer, and *Plain Tales From the Hills* was published in 1888. The following year he went to England (see *Letters of Marque* and *From Sea to Sea*) and settled in London, where he continued to write. From 1892 to 1896 he was living in Brattleboro, Vermont, producing there his tale of Newfoundland fishermen, *Captains Courageous.* Again in 1900 his life in England was interrupted by his activities as war correspondent during the Boer War. He was awarded the Nobel Prize for Literature in 1907.

Kipling's individuality is known throughout the English-speaking world; he is famous as the poet of British imperialism, a cause reflected in much of his recent prose; and his powers of narration have given him high rank among short-story writers. Some of his most delightful stories in the field of English history are found in *Puck of Pook's Hill,* a collection of pseudo-autobiographical tales told by representatives of many periods in the country's annals. His work dealing with the military and official life on the Indian frontier (*Soldiers Three, Barrack-Room Ballads, Under the Deodars, Departmental Ditties, Kim, Jungle Books,* and others) is rich in local color. His prose style is marked by sustained vigor—is never mechanical, dull, or monotonous. In poetry, his primitive rhythms are perfectly suited to his subjects, and the beat of the tom-tom and clash of cymbals join in the glorification of Tommy Atkins and the British Empire.

Works: Inclusive Edition, 1885-1918.

Helpful: Arley Munson, *Kipling's India,* 1915.

Biography: Charles E. Norton, "Rudyard Kipling, a Biographical Sketch," (in *Plain Tales From the Hills*). Criticism: R. Hopkins, *Rudyard Kipling, A Literary Appreciation,* 1916; W. M. Hart, *Kipling the Story-Teller,* 1918; More (Shel. 2); Lang (EL); Phelps (EP); Chubb; Scott; Cunliffe; Jackson; Chevalley; Chavrillon; Cooper; Monro; E. Shanks, "Rudyard Kipling," *Liv. Age* 316:410-17; F. A. Waterhouse, "The Literary Fortunes of Kipling," *Yale R.* ns. 10:817-31; K. F. Gerould, "The Remarkable Rightness of Rudyard Kipling," *Atlan.* 123:12-21; R. T. Hopkins, "Rudyard Kipling in his own country," *Liv. Age* 323:342-4; "The Accuracy of Kipling," *Liv. Age* 326:71-2.

RECESSIONAL [1]

(1897)

God of our fathers, known of old,
Lord of our far-flung battle-line,
Beneath whose awful Hand we hold
Dominion over palm and pine [2]—
Lord God of Hosts, be with us yet,
Lest we forget—lest we forget!

The tumult and the shouting dies;
The captains and the kings depart;
Still stands Thine ancient sacrifice,
An humble and a contrite heart. [3]
Lord God of Hosts, be with us yet,
Lest we forget—lest we forget!

Far-called, our navies melt away;
On dune and headland sinks the fire:
Lo, all our pomp of yesterday
Is one with Nineveh and Tyre! [4]
Judge of the Nations, spare us yet,
Lest we forget—lest we forget!

If, drunk with sight of power, we loose
Wild tongues that have not Thee in awe,
Such boastings as the Gentiles [5] use,
Or lesser breeds without the Law—
Lord God of Hosts, be with us yet,
Lest we forget—lest we forget!

For heathen heart that puts her trust
In reeking tube and iron shard, [6]
All valiant dust that builds on dust,
And guarding, calls not Thee to guard,
For frantic boast and foolish word—
Thy mercy on Thy People, Lord!

1897 1903

THE BALLAD OF EAST AND WEST [7]

Oh, East is East, and West is West, and never the twain shall meet,
Till Earth and Sky stand presently at God's great Judgment Seat;
But there is neither East nor West, Border, nor Breed, nor Birth,
When two strong men stand face to face, tho' they come from the ends of the earth!

Kamal is out with twenty men to raise the Border side,
And he has lifted the Colonel's mare that is the Colonel's pride;
He has lifted her out of the stable-door between the dawn and the day,
And turned the calkins [8] upon her feet, and ridden her far away.
Then up and spoke the Colonel's son that led a troop of the Guides:
"Is there never a man of all my men can say where Kamal hides?"
Then up and spoke Mohammed Khan, the son of the Ressaldar: [9]
"If ye know the track of the morning-mist, ye know where his pickets are.
"At dusk he harries the Abazai [10]—at dawn he is into Bonair,
"But he must go by Fort Bukloh to his own place to fare,
"So if ye gallop to Fort Bukloh as fast as a bird can fly,
"By the favor of God ye may cut him off ere he win to the Tongue of Jagai,
"But if he be past the Tongue of Jagai, right swiftly turn ye then,
"For the length and the breadth of that grisly plain is sown with Kamal's men.
"There is rock to the left, and rock to the right, and low lean thorn between,
"And ye may hear a breech-bolt snick where never a man is seen."
The Colonel's son has taken a horse, and a raw rough dun was he,
With the mouth of a bell and the heart of Hell, and the head of the gallows-tree.
The Colonel's son to the Fort has won, they bid him stay to eat—
Who rides at the tail of a Border thief, he sits not long at his meat.
He's up and away from Fort Bukloh as fast as he can fly,
Till he was aware of his father's mare in the gut of the Tongue of Jagai,
Till he was aware of his father's mare with Kamal upon her back,
And when he could spy the white of her eye, he made the pistol crack.

[1] From *The Five Nations,* copyright 1903, by permission of the author and Doubleday, Page & Company, publishers.
[2] a reference to the fact that England's colonies cover wide regions of the world
[3] *Psalms* li, 17
[4] ancient cities of Assyria and Phoenicia
[5] figuratively; any foreign or alien races
[6] cannon and shrapnel
[7] From *Barrack-Room Ballads,* copyright 1892, by permission of the author and Doubleday, Page & Company, publishers.
[8] metal points on horse-shoes to prevent slipping
[9] native commander of a troop of native cavalry
[10] Apparently this and the names that follow are fictitious names for places in the Northwest Frontier Province; the background of the tale is Fort Jumrud on the Frontier, guarding the Khyber Pass into Afghanistan. This frontier region is the scene of many of Kipling's poems and tales: "The Man Who Would be King," "Wee Willie Winkie," "The Drums of the Fore and Aft," "The Man Who Was," "In the House of Suddhoo," parts of *Stalky and Co.,* and others.

He has fired once, he has fired twice, but the whistling ball went wide.
"Ye shoot like a soldier," Kamal said. "Show now if ye can ride."
It's up and over the Tongue of Jagai, as blown dust-devils go,
The dun he fled like a stag of ten,[1] but the mare like a barren doe.
The dun he leaned against the bit and slugged his head above,
But the red mare played with the snaffle-bars, as a maiden plays with a glove.
There was rock to the left and rock to the right, and low lean thorn between,
And thrice he heard a breech-bolt snick tho' never a man was seen.
They have ridden the low moon out of the sky, their hoofs drum up the dawn,
The dun he went like a wounded bull, but the mare like a new-roused fawn.
The dun he fell at a water-course—in a woeful heap fell he,
And Kamal has turned the red mare back, and pulled the rider free.
He has knocked the pistol out of his hand—small room was there to strive,
" 'Twas only by favor of mine," quoth he, "ye rode so long alive:
"There was not a rock for twenty mile, there was not a clump of tree,
"But covered a man of my own men with his rifle cocked on his knee.
"If I had raised my bridle-hand, as I have held it low,
"The little jackals that flee so fast were feasting all in a row:
"If I had bowed my head on my breast, as I have held it high,
"The kite that whistles above us now were gorged till she could not fly."
Lightly answered the Colonel's son: "Do good to bird and beast,
"But count who come for the broken meats before thou makest a feast.
"If there should follow a thousand swords to carry my bones away,
"Belike the price of a jackal's meal were more than a thief could pay.
"They will feed their horse on the standing crop, their men on the garnered grain,
"The thatch of the byres[2] will serve their fires when all the cattle are slain.
"But if thou thinkest the price be fair—thy brethren wait to sup,
"The hound is kin to the jackal-spawn—howl, dog, and call them up!
"And if thou thinkest the price be high, in steer and gear and stack,
"Give me my father's mare again, and I'll fight my own way back!"
Kamal has gripped him by the hand and set him upon his feet.
"No talk shall be of dogs," he said, "when wolf and gray wolf meet.
"May I eat dirt if thou hast hurt of me in deed or breath;
"What dam of lances brought thee forth to jest at the dawn with Death?"
Lightly answered the Colonel's son: "I hold by the blood of my clan:
"Take up the mare for my father's gift—by God, she has carried a man!"
The red mare ran to the Colonel's son, and nuzzled against his breast;
"We be two strong men," said Kamal then, "but she loveth the younger best.
"So she shall go with a litter's dower, my turquoise-studded rein,
"My broidered saddle and saddle-cloth, and silver stirrups twain."
The Colonel's son a pistol drew, and held it muzzle-end,
"Ye have taken the one from a foe," said he; "will ye take the mate from a friend?"
"A gift for a gift," said Kamal straight; "a limb for the risk of a limb.
"Thy father has sent his son to me, I'll send my son to him!"
With that he whistled his only son, that dropped from a mountain-crest—
He trod the ling[3] like a buck in spring, and he looked like a lance in rest.
"Now here is thy master," Kamal said, "who leads a troop of the Guides,
"And thou must ride at his left side as shield on shoulder rides.
"Till Death or I cut loose the tie, at camp and board and bed,
"Thy life is his—thy fate it is to guard him with thy head.
"So, thou must eat the White Queen's meat, and all her foes are thine,
"And thou must harry thy father's hold for the peace of the Border-line,
"And thou must make a trooper tough and hack thy way to power—
"Belike they will raise thee to Ressaldar when I am hanged in Peshawur."
They have looked each other between the eyes, and there they found no fault,

[1] ten points on his antlers [2] cattle-sheds (stables)

[3] heather

They have taken the Oath of the Brother-in-Blood on leavened bread and salt:
They have taken the Oath of the Brother-in-Blood on fire and fresh-cut sod,
On the hilt and the haft of the Khyber[1] knife, and the Wondrous Names of God.
The Colonel's son he rides the mare and Kamal's boy the dun,
And two have come back to Fort Bukloh where there went forth but one.
And when they drew to the Quarter-Guard, full twenty swords flew clear—
There was not a man but carried his feud with the blood of the mountaineer.
"Ha' done! ha' done!" said the Colonel's son. "Put up the steel at your sides!
"Last night ye had struck at a Border thief—tonight 'tis a man of the Guides!"

Oh, East is East, and West is West, and never the twain shall meet,
Till Earth and Sky stand presently at God's great Judgment Seat;
But there is neither East nor West, Border, nor Breed, nor Birth,
When two strong men stand face to face, tho' they come from the ends of the earth.

1889 1892-99

THE BALLAD OF THE "BOLIVAR"[2]

Seven men from all the world back to Docks again,
Rolling down the Ratcliffe Road drunk and raising Cain:
Give the girls another drink 'fore we sign away—
We that took the "Bolivar" out across the Bay![3]

We put out from Sunderland[4] loaded down with rails;
We put back to Sunderland 'cause our cargo shifted;
We put out from Sunderland—met the winter gales—
Seven days and seven nights to the Start[5] we drifted.

Racketing her rivets loose, smokestack white as snow,
All the coals adrift adeck, half the rails below,
Leaking like a lobster-pot, steering like a dray—
Out we took the *Bolivar*, out across the Bay!

One by one the Lights came up, winked and let us by;
Mile by mile we waddled on, coal and fo'c'sle short;
Met a blow that laid us down, heard a bulkhead fly;
Left The Wolf behind us with a two-foot list to port.

Trailing like a wounded duck, working out her soul;
Clanging like a smithy-shop after every roll;
Just a funnel and a mast lurching through the spray—
So we threshed the *Bolivar* out across the Bay!

Felt her hog[6] and felt her sag, betted when she'd break;
Wondered every time she raced[7] if she'd stand the shock;
Heard the seas like drunken men pounding at her strake;[8]
Hoped the Lord 'ud keep his thumb on the plummer-block.[9]

Banged against the iron decks, bilges[10] choked with coal;
Flayed and frozen foot and hand, sick of heart and soul;
'Last we prayed she'd buck herself into Judgment Day—
Hi! we cursed the *Bolivar* knocking round the Bay!

Oh! her nose flung up to sky, groaning to be still—
Up and down and back we went, never time for breath;
Then the money's paid at Lloyd's[11] caught her by the heel,
And the stars ran round and round dancin' at our death!

Aching for an hour's sleep, dozing off between;
Heard the rotten rivets draw when she took it green;

[1] a tribe in Afghanistan
[2] From *Barrack-Room Ballads,* copyright 1892, by permission of the author and Doubleday, Page & Company, publishers.
[3] of Biscay
[4] in Durham, a county in the north of England
[5] or Start Point, a headland and lighthouse of Scotland, in the Orkneys
[6] hump up from strain
[7] i.e., the engine ran too fast when the propeller was out of the water
[8] a line of planks on the side of a ship
[9] propeller-shaft bearing
[10] the space next the keelson in the bottom of a ship
[11] a firm dealing in marine insurance

Watched the compass chase its tail like a cat at play—
That was on the *Bolivar*, south across the Bay.

Once we saw between the squalls, lyin' head to swell—
Mad with work and weariness, wishin' they was we—
Some damned Liner's lights go by like a grand hotel;
Cheered her from the *Bolivar*, swampin' in the sea.

Then a grayback cleared us out, then the skipper laughed;
"Boys, the wheel has gone to Hell—rig the winches aft!
"Yoke the kicking rudder-head—get her under way!"
So we steered her, pulley-haul, out across the Bay!

Just a pack o' rotten plates puttied up with tar,
In we came, an' time enough, 'cross Bilbao[1] Bar.
Overloaded, undermanned, meant to founder, we
Euchred God Almighty's storm, bluffed the Eternal Sea!

Seven men from all the world back to town again,
Rollin' down the Ratcliffe Road drunk and raising Cain:
Seven men from out of Hell. Ain't the owners gay,
'Cause we took the "Bolivar" safe across the Bay?

1890 1892-1899

[1] a seaport in Spain

SIR HENRY JOHN NEWBOLT 1862-

Newbolt stands next to Kipling as a writer of patriotic poetry of the simple rather unintellectual type, and like him is a singer of England's imperialism. He is the son of a vicar, was born at Bilton, and was educated at Clifton College and Oxford. After his Oxford days, he read for the bar, practicing until 1899, when he turned to literature and for five years edited the *Monthly Review*. Newbolt was knighted in 1915; during the Great War he held important positions in the British Admiralty, and in 1923 was appointed Official Naval Historian.

It was with his sea ballads, *Admirals All,* 1897, that he won literary reputation and it is in work of this type that he excels. *The Island Race,* 1898, and *Drake's Drum and Other Sea Songs,* 1914, contain poems that are stirring, dramatic, vivid, with a fine feeling for action. They form a sincere tribute to the men who have defended England through the centuries. Besides writing several novels, which are not equal to his poetry, and a *Naval History of the War,* 1920, Sir Henry has published a critical volume, *A New Study of English Poetry,* 1917, and a volume entitled *Poetry and Time,* 1919.

Criticism: "Recent Poetry," *Edin. R.* 210:378-99 (396-7).

VITAÏ LAMPADA[2, 5]

There's a breathless hush in the Close[3] to-night—
Ten to make and the match to win—
A bumping pitch[4] and a blinding light,
An hour to play and the last man in.
And it's not for the sake of a ribboned coat,
Or the selfish hope of a season's fame,
But his Captain's hand on his shoulder smote—
"Play up! play up! and play the game!"

The sand of the desert is sodden red—
Red with the wreck of a square that broke;
The Gatling's jammed and the Colonel dead,
And the regiment blind with dust and smoke.
The river of death has brimmed his banks,
And England's far, and Honor a name,
But the voice of a schoolboy rallies the ranks:
"Play up! play up! and play the game!"

This is the word that year by year,
While in her place the School is set,
Every one of her sons must hear,
And none that hears it dare forget.
This they all with a joyful mind
Bear through life like a torch in flame,
And falling fling to the host behind—
"Play up! play up! and play the game!"

1892 1892

DRAKE'S DRUM[5]

Drake[6] he's in his hammock an' a thousand mile away,
(Capten, art tha sleepin' there below?),

[2] "The torch (or lamp) of life." The reference is to the annual torch-races of the ancient Greeks—somewhat like relay races.

[3] athletic field

[4] a cricket term

[5] From *Poems: New and Old* by Sir Henry Newboldt, published by Mr. John Murray, London. By permission of the author. The dialect of "Drake's Drum" is that of Devonshire.

[6] Sir Francis Drake, 1540?-1596

Slung atween the round shot in Nombre Dios Bay,[1]
  An' dreamin' arl the time o' Plymouth Hoe.[2]
Yarnder lumes the Island, yarnder lie the ships,
  Wi' sailor lads a-dancin' heel-an'-toe,
An' the shore-lights flashin', an' the night-tide dashin',
  He sees et arl so plainly as he saw et long ago.

Drake he was a Devon man, an' rüled the Devon seas,
  (Capten, art tha sleepin' there below?),
Rovin' tho' his death fell, he went wi' heart at ease,
  An' dreamin' arl the time o' Plymouth Hoe.
"Take my drum to England, hang et by the shore,
  Strike et when your powder's runnin' low;
If the Dons[3] sight Devon, I'll quit the port o' Heaven,
  An' drum them up the Channel as we drummed them long ago."[4]

Drake he's in his hammock till the great Armadas[5] come,
  (Capten, art tha sleepin' there below?),
Slung atween the round shot, listenin' for the drum,
  An' dreamin' arl the time o' Plymouth Hoe.
Call him on the deep sea, call him up the Sound,
  Call him when ye sail to meet the foe;
Where the old trade's plyin' an' the old flag flyin'
  They shall find him ware an' wakin', as they found him long ago!

1895 1895

HE FELL AMONG THIEVES[6]

"Ye have robbed," said he, "ye have slaughtered and made an end,
  Take your ill-got plunder, and bury the dead:
What will ye more of your guest and sometime friend?"
  "Blood for our blood," they said.

He laughed: "If one may settle the score for five,
  I am ready; but let the reckoning stand till day:
I have loved the sunlight as dearly as any alive."
  "You shall die at dawn," said they.

He flung his empty revolver down the slope,
  He climbed alone to the Eastward edge of the trees;
All night long in a dream untroubled of hope
  He brooded, clasping his knees.

He did not hear the monotonous roar that fills
  The ravine where the Yassin[7] river sullenly flows;
He did not see the starlight on the Laspur[7] hills,
  Or the far Afghan snows.

He saw the April noon on his books aglow,
  The wistaria trailing in at the window side;
He heard his father's voice from the terrace below
  Calling him down to ride.

He saw the gray little church across the park,
  The mounds that hide the loved and honored dead;
The Norman arch,[8] the chancel softly dark,
  The brasses[9] black and red.

He saw the School Close, sunny and green,
  The runner beside him, the stand by the parapet wall,
The distant tape, and the crowd roaring between
  His own name over all.

He saw the dark wainscot and timbered roof,
  The long tables, and the faces merry and keen;
The College Eight and their trainer dining aloof,
  The Dons[10] on the dais serene.
He watched the liner's stem ploughing the foam,
  He felt her trembling speed and the thrash of her screw;

[1] in the West Indies, where Drake was buried
[2] a cliff near Plymouth, the home of Drake
[3] Spaniards
[4] A reference to the defeat of the Spanish Armada, 1588; see Froude's description, p. 694.
[5] fleets of armed ships
[6] From *Poems: New and Old* by Sir Henry Newbolt, published by Mr. John Murray, London. By permission of the author.
[7] on the border of northwest India
[8] Romanesque architecture was introduced by the Normans into England.
[9] memorial tablets
[10] In English universities the Dons (college and university teachers) dine on a raised platform in the public dining hall.

He heard her passengers' voices talking of home,
He saw the flag she flew.

And now it was dawn. He rose strong on his feet,
And strode to his ruined camp below the wood;
He drank the breath of the morning cool and sweet;
His murderers round him stood.

Light on the Laspur hills was broadening fast,
The blood-red snow-peaks chilled to a dazzling white:
He turned, and saw the golden circle at last,
Cut by the Eastern height.

"O glorious Life, Who dwellest in earth and sun,
I have lived, I praise and adore Thee."
A sword swept.
Over the pass the voices one by one
Faded, and the hill slept.

1897 1897

ROBERT (SEYMOUR) BRIDGES 1844-

After receiving his education at Eton and Oxford and traveling on the Continent, Bridges studied medicine and practiced in London, where he was connected with the Children's and the Great Northern hospitals until he retired in 1882 to devote himself to literature. He is the author of many plays, poems, and studies in versification and metrics. *The Necessity of Poetry,* 1918, contains much interesting material on poetic diction and forms, and the nature of English prosody.

His work was slow in attracting attention but its artistic finish and practically flawless technique had gained due recognition by 1913 when he was appointed to succeed Alfred Austin in the laureateship. In 1924 he was a university lecturer at Ann Arbor, Michigan. His art is best revealed in his lyric poetry, particularly in his sonnet sequence, *The Growth of Love,* 1889, and his *Shorter Poems,* 1890. His best short poems show unusual variety in form and meter, picturesque realism, and scholarly culture. The strong graphic quality that characterizes Dr. Bridges's poetry is achieved by a skillful use of light and color, which compensates, in part, for the limited range of his work.

Collected Poetical Works, 1913.

Criticism: T. H. Warren, *Robert Bridges, Poet Laureate,* 1913; F. and E. B. Young, *Robert Bridges: a Critical Study,* 1914; E. Dowden, *New Studies in Literature,* 1895; Freeman; Monro; L. Binyon, "Robert Bridges and the Poetic Art," *Liv. Age* 299:155-60; P. Colum, "Robert Bridges and Thomas Hardy," *New Rep.* 12:47-9; Y. Noguchi, "Robert Bridges; a Japanese Impression of the Poet Laureate," *Nation* 101:465-6.

A PASSER-BY[1]

Whither, O splendid ship, thy white sails crowding,
Leaning across the bosom of the urgent West,
That fearest nor sea rising, nor sky clouding,
Whither away, fair rover, and what thy quest?
Ah! soon, when Winter has all our vales oppressed,
When skies are cold and misty, and hail is hurling,
Wilt thóu glide on the blue Pacific, or rest
In a summer haven asleep, thy white sails furling.

I there before thee, in the country that well thou knowest,
Already arrived am inhaling the odorous air:
I watch thee enter unerringly where thou goest,
And anchor queen of the strange shipping there,
Thy sails for awnings spread, thy masts bare:
Nor is aught from the foaming reef to the snowcapped, grandest
Peak, that is over the feathery palms more fair
Than thou, so upright, so stately, and still thou standest.

And yet, O splendid ship, unhailed and nameless,
I know not if, aiming a fancy, I rightly divine
That thou hast a purpose joyful, a courage blameless,
Thy port assured in a happier land than mine.
But for all I have given thee, beauty enough is thine,
As thou, aslant with trim tackle and shrouding,
From the proud nostril curve of a prow's line
In the offing scatterest foam, thy white sails crowding.

1879

[1] From *Poetical Works,* vol. II. By permission of the author and Mr. John Murray, publisher.

LONDON SNOW[1]

When men were all asleep the snow came flying,
In large white flakes falling on the city brown,
Stealthily and perpetually settling and loosely lying,
  Hushing the latest traffic of the drowsy town;
Deadening, muffling, stifling its murmurs failing;
Lazily and incessantly floating down and down:
  Silently sifting and veiling road, roof and railing;
Hiding difference, making unevenness even,
Into angles and crevices softly drifting and sailing.
  All night it fell, and when full inches seven
It lay in the depth of its uncompacted lightness,
The clouds blew off from a high and frosty heaven;
  And all woke earlier for the unaccustomed brightness
Of the winter dawning, the strange unheavenly glare:
The eye marveled—marveled at the dazzling whiteness;
  The ear harkened to the stillness of the solemn air;
No sound of wheel rumbling nor of foot falling,
And the busy morning cries came thin and spare.
  Then boys I heard, as they went to school, calling,
They gathered up the crystal manna to freeze
Their tongues with tasting, their hands with snowballing;
  Or rioted in a drift, plunging up to the knees;
Or peering up from under the white-mossed wonder,
"Oh, look at the trees!" they cried, "Oh, look at the trees!"
  With lessened load a few carts creak and blunder,
Following along the white deserted way,
A country company long dispersed asunder:
  When now already the sun, in pale display
Standing by Paul's[2] high dome, spread forth below
His sparkling beams, and awoke the stir of the day.
  For now doors open, and war is waged with the snow;
And trains of somber men, past tale of number,
Tread long brown paths, as toward their toil they go:
  But even for them awhile no cares encumber
Their minds diverted; the daily word is unspoken,
The daily thoughts of labor and sorrow slumber
At the sight of the beauty that greets them, for the charm they have broken.

1880

NORTH WIND IN OCTOBER[1, 3]

In the golden glade the chestnuts are fallen all;
From the sered boughs of the oak the acorns fall:
The beech scatters her ruddy fire;
The lime hath stripped to the cold,
And standeth naked above her yellow attire:
The larch thinneth her spire
To lay the ways of the wood with cloth of gold.

  Out of the golden-green and white
Of the brake[4] the fir trees stand upright
In the forest of flame, and wave aloft
To the blue of heaven their blue-green tuftings soft.

  But swiftly in shuddering gloom the splendors fail,
As the harrying Northwind beareth
A cloud of skirmishing hail
The grieved woodland to smite:
In a hurricane through the trees he teareth,
Raking the boughs and the leaves rending,
And whistleth to the descending
Blows of his icy flail.
Gold and snow he mixeth in spite,
And whirleth afar; as away on his winnowing flight
He passeth, and all again for awhile is bright.

1893

"SPRING GOETH ALL IN WHITE"[1]

Spring goeth all in white,
Crowned with milk-white may:
In fleecy flocks of light
O'er heaven the white clouds stray:

  White butterflies in the air;
White daisies prank[5] the ground:
The cherry and hoary pear
Scatter their snow around.

1890

[1] By permission of the author and Mr. John Murray, publisher.
[2] St. Paul's Cathedral
[3] Cf. Shelley's "Ode to the West Wind," p. 516.
[4] tall ferns
[5] adorn

ALFRED EDWARD HOUSMAN
1859-

Housman received his master's degree at St. John's College, Oxford. For awhile he was in the British Patent Office, was later a professor of Latin at University College, London, and now holds a like position at Cambridge, where he is also a Fellow of Trinity College. It is somewhat rare that one who has spent his life in lecturing, in editing classic authors, and in contributing to philological journals, should write poetry of the utmost simplicity depicting the life and thoughts of men of the soil. The *Shropshire Lad,* 1896, in its direct realism of treatment is prophetic of modern poetry. With one other book, *Last Poems,* 1922, it comprises the poetical works of Mr. Housman.

Of Housman and Hardy, Mr. Phelps says (*The Advance of English Poetry in the Twentieth Century*) that their poems express not merely their view of life but their "faith in the healing power of the bitter herb of pessimism." See headnote to Thomas Hardy, page 796.

See Monro; Wilkinson; H. S. Gorman, *Outl.* 133:35-6; F. L. Lucas, *Liv. Age* 319:419-23; H. Jackson, *Liv. Age* 302:728-31; G. M. Harper, *Scrib.* 78:151-57.

From A SHROPSHIRE LAD[1]

II
LOVELIEST OF TREES

Loveliest of trees, the cherry now
Is hung with bloom along the bough,
And stands about the woodland ride[2]
Wearing white for Eastertide.

Now, of my threescore years and ten,
Twenty will not come again,
And take from seventy springs a score,
It only leaves me fifty more.

And since to look at things in bloom
Fifty springs are little room,
About the woodlands I will go
To see the cherry hung with snow.

1896

IV
REVEILLE

Wake: the silver dusk returning
  Up the beach of darkness brims,
And the ship of sunrise burning
  Strands upon the eastern rims.

Wake: the vaulted shadow shatters,
  Trampled to the floor it spanned,
And the tent of night in tatters
  Straws[3] the sky-pavilioned land.

Up, lad, up, 'tis late for lying:
  Hear the drums of morning play;
Hark, the empty highways crying
  "Who'll beyond the hills away?"

Towns and countries woo together,
  Forelands beacon,[4] belfries call;
Never lad that trod on leather
  Lived to feast his heart with all.

Up, lad: thews[5] that lie and cumber
  Sunlit pallets never thrive;
Morns abed and daylight slumber
  Were not meant for man alive.

Clay lies still, but blood's a rover;
  Breath's a ware that will not keep.
Up, lad: when the journey's over
  There'll be time enough to sleep.

1896

IX
"ON MOONLIT HEATH"

On moonlit heath and lonesome bank
  The sheep beside me graze;
And yon the gallows used to clank
  Fast by the four crossways.

A careless shepherd once would keep
  The flocks by moonlight there,[6]
And high amongst the glimmering sheep
  The dead man stood on air.

They hang us now in Shrewsbury jail:
  The whistles blow forlorn,
And trains all night groan on the rail
  To men that die at morn.

There sleeps in Shrewsbury jail tonight,
  Or wakes, as may betide,
A better lad, if things went right,
  Than most that sleep outside.

And naked to the hangman's noose
  The morning clocks will ring
A neck God made for other use
  Than strangling in a string.

And sharp the link of life will snap,
  And dead on air will stand
Heels that held up as straight a chap
  As treads upon the land.

[1] By the kind permission of the author.
[2] road, especially as a place for riding

[3] strews
[4] signal, beckon
[5] muscles
[6] Hanging in chains was called "keeping sheep by moonlight."—Shropshire Lad

So here I'll watch the night and wait
  To see the morning shine,
When he will hear the stroke of eight
  And not the stroke of nine;

And wish my friend as sound a sleep
  As lads I did not know,
That shepherded the moonlit sheep
  A hundred years ago.

1896

XXI

BREDON [1] HILL

In summertime on Bredon
  The bells they sound so clear;
Round both the shires they ring them
  In steeples far and near,
  A happy noise to hear.

Here of a Sunday morning
  My love and I would lie,
And see the colored counties,
  And hear the larks so high
  About us in the sky.

The bells would ring to call her
  In valleys miles away:
"Come all to church, good people;
  Good people, come and pray."
  But here my love would stay.

And I would turn and answer
  Among the springing thyme,
"Oh, peal upon our wedding,
  And we will hear the chime,
  And come to church in time."

But when the snows at Christmas
  On Bredon top were strown,
My love rose up so early
  And stole out unbeknown
  And went to church alone.

They tolled the one bell only,
  Groom there was none to see,
The mourners followed after,
  And so to church went she,
  And would not wait for me.

The bells they sound on Bredon,
  And still the steeples hum.
"Come all to church, good people"—
  Oh, noisy bells, be dumb;
  I hear you, I will come.

1896

[1] pronounced Breedon—Shropshire Lad

ALFRED NOYES 1880-

Alfred Noyes, critic, essayist, teacher, born in Staffordshire, published his first book of verse, *The Loom of Years,* in 1902. He was then at Exeter College, Oxford, where he was something of an athlete. He has been a constant producer of poetry, with sixteen volumes to his credit, besides his *Collected Poems* in three volumes, 1913 and 1920. He has also written plays, essays, and a biography of William Morris. He is now (1928) engaged in writing a poetic trilogy, *The Torch-Bearers,* designed to tell the progress of scientific discovery. Two volumes have already appeared.

Mr. Noyes stands somewhat apart from other poets of his own generation in the fact that both in his poetical technique and in his outlook on society and social forces he holds to the manner of the nineteenth century. He has, for example, little patience with "free verse," for he feels that it is used chiefly by those who have not disciplined themselves to writing in regular forms. In this respect he has little in common with such poets as Monro and D. H. Lawrence. He is a wholesome optimist with faith that there is a sane order in the universe. His attitude toward the poetry of today may be found in his *Some Aspects of Modern Poetry,* 1924.

Criticism: His contribution to poetry is summed up by Phelps (EP); for interesting criticism see "Who is Alfred Noyes," *Cath. World* 97:289-303; G. Thomas, "Alfred Noyes," *Liv. Age* 285:742-7; Wilkinson; adverse, Munro.

THE BARREL-ORGAN [2]

There's a barrel-organ caroling across a golden street
  In the City as the sun sinks low;
And the music's not immortal; but the world has made it sweet
  And fulfilled it with the sunset glow;
And it pulses through the pleasures of the City and the pain
  That surround the singing organ like a large eternal light;
And they've given it a glory and a part to play again
  In the Symphony that rules the day and night.

And now it's marching onward through the realms of old romance,
  And trolling out a fond familiar tune,
And now it's roaring cannon down to fight the king of France,
  And now it's prattling softly to the moon,

[2] Reprinted by permission from *Collected Poems,* Volume I, by Alfred Noyes, copyright, 1906, by Frederick A. Stokes Company.

And all around the organ there's a sea without a shore
Of human joys and wonders and regrets;
To remember and to recompense the music evermore
For what the cold machinery forgets. . . . .

Yes, as the music changes,
Like a prismatic glass,
It takes the light and ranges
Through all the moods that pass;
Dissects the common carnival
Of passions and regrets,
And gives the world a glimpse of all
The colors it forgets.

And there *La Traviata* [1] sighs
Another sadder song;
And there *Il Trovatore* [1] cries
A tale of deeper wrong;
And bolder knights to battle go
With sword and shield and lance,
Than ever here on earth below
Have whirled into—*a dance!*—
Go down to Kew [2] in lilac-time, in lilac-time, in lilac-time;
Go down to Kew in lilac-time (it isn't far from London!)
And you shall wander hand in hand with love in summer's wonderland;
Go down to Kew in Lilac-time (it isn't far from London!)

The cherry-trees are seas of bloom and soft perfume and sweet perfume,
The cherry-trees are seas of bloom (and oh, so near to London!)
And there they say, when dawn is high and all the world's a blaze of sky
The cuckoo, though he's very shy, will sing a song for London.

The Dorian nightingale is rare and yet they say you'll hear him there
At Kew, at Kew in lilac-time (and oh, so near to London!)
The linnet and the throstle, too, and after dark the long halloo
And golden-eyed *tu-whit, tu-whoo* of owls that ogle London.

For Noah hardly knew a bird of any kind that isn't heard
At Kew, at Kew in lilac-time (and oh, so near to London!)
And when the rose begins to pout and all the chestnut spires are out
You'll hear the rest without a doubt, all chorusing for London:—

Come down to Kew in lilac-time, in lilac-time, in lilac-time;
Come down to Kew in lilac-time (it isn't far from London!)
And you shall wander hand in hand with love in summer's wonderland;
Come down to Kew in lilac-time (it isn't far from London!)

And then the troubadour begins to thrill the golden street,
In the City as the sun sinks low;
And in all the gaudy busses there are scores of weary feet
Marking time, sweet time, with a dull mechanic beat,
And a thousand hearts are plunging to a love they'll never meet,
Through the meadows of the sunset, through the poppies and the wheat,
In the land where the dead dreams go.

Verdi, Verdi, when you wrote *Il Trovatore* did you dream
Of the City when the sun sinks low,
Of the organ and the monkey and the many-colored stream
On the Piccadilly pavement, of the myriad eyes that seem
To be litten [3] for a moment with a wild Italian gleam
As *A che la morte* [4] parodies the world's eternal theme
And pulses with the sunset-glow?

There's a thief, perhaps, that listens with a face of frozen stone
In the City as the sun sinks low;
There's a portly man of business with a balance of his own,
There's a clerk and there's a butcher of a soft reposeful tone,
And they're all of them returning to the heavens they have known;
They are crammed and jammed in busses and—they're each of them alone
In the land where the dead dreams go.

[1] opera by Verdi, Italian composer, 1813-1901
[2] a famous botanical garden in Surrey, near London
[3] unusual form of the past participle "lighted"
[4] the beginning of an aria in the fourth act of *Il Trovatore*

There's a very modish woman and her smile is very bland
In the City as the sun sinks low;
And her hansom jingles onward, but her little jeweled hand
Is clenched a little tighter and she cannot understand
What she wants or why she wanders to that undiscovered land,
For the parties there are not at all the sort of thing she planned,
In the land where the dead dreams go.

There's a rowing man that listens and his heart is crying out
In the City as the sun sinks low;
For the barge,[1] the eight, the Isis,[2] and the coach's whoop and shout,
For the minute-gun, the counting and the long disheveled rout,
For the howl along the tow-path and a fate that's still in doubt,
For a roughened oar to handle and a race to think about
In the land where the dead dreams go.

There's a laborer that listens to the voices of the dead
In the City as the sun sinks low;
And his hand begins to tremble and his face to smolder red
As he sees a loafer watching him and—there he turns his head
And stares into the sunset where his April love is fled,
For he hears her softly singing and his lonely soul is led
Through the land where the dead dreams go.

There's an old and haggard demi-rep, it's ringing in her ears,
In the City as the sun sinks low;
With the wild and empty sorrow of the love that blights and sears,
Oh, and if she hurries onward, then be sure, be sure she hears,
Hears and bears the bitter burden of the unforgotten years,
And her laugh's a little harsher and her eyes are brimmed with tears
For the land where the dead dreams go.

There's a barrel-organ caroling across a golden street
In the City as the sun sinks low;

[1] a large flat-bottomed boat used for training
[2] the upper part of the Thames by Oxford

Though the music's only Verdi there's a world to make it sweet
Just as yonder yellow sunset where the earth and heaven meet
Mellows all the sooty City! Hark, a hundred thousand feet
Are marching on to glory through the poppies and the wheat
In the land where the dead dreams go.

So it's Jeremiah, Jeremiah,
What have you to say
When you meet the garland girls
Tripping on their way?

All around my gala hat
I wear a wreath of roses
(A long and lonely year it is
I've waited for the May!)
If any one should ask you,
The reason why I wear it is—
My own love, my true love
Is coming home today.

And it's buy a bunch of violets for the lady
(*It's lilac-time in London; it's lilac-time in London!*)
Buy a bunch of violets for the lady;
While the sky burns blue above:

On the other side the street you'll find it shady
(*It's lilac-time in London; it's lilac-time in London!*)
But buy a bunch of violets for the lady,
And tell her she's your own true love.

There's a barrel-organ caroling across a golden street
In the City as the sun sinks glittering and slow;
And the music's not immortal; but the world has made it sweet
And enriched it with the harmonies that make a song complete
In the deeper heavens of music where the night and morning meet,
As it dies into the sunset glow;
And it pulses through the pleasures of the City and the pain
That surround the singing organ like a large eternal light,
And they've given it a glory and a part to play again
In the Symphony that rules the day and night.

And there, as the music changes,
The song runs round again,
Once more it turns and ranges
Through all its joy and pain,
Dissects the common carnival
Of passions and regrets;
And the wheeling world remembers all
The wheeling song forgets.

Once more *La Traviata* sighs
Another sadder song:
Once more *Il Trovatore* cries
A tale of deeper wrong;
Once more the knights to battle go
With sword and shield and lance
Till once, once more, the shattered foe
Has whirled into—*a dance!*

Come down to Kew in lilac-time, in lilac-time, in lilac-time;
Come down to Kew in lilac-time (it isn't far from London!)
And you shall wander hand in hand with Love in summer's wonderland,
Come down to Kew in lilac-time (it isn't far from London!)

1904

THE HIGHWAYMAN [1]

Part One

I

The wind was a torrent of darkness among the gusty trees,
The moon was a ghostly galleon tossed upon cloudy seas,
The road was a ribbon of moonlight over the purple moor,
And the highwayman came riding—
Riding—riding—
The highwayman came riding, up to the old inn-door.

II

He'd a French cocked-hat on his forehead, a bunch of lace at his chin,
A coat of the claret velvet, and breeches of brown doe-skin;
They fitted with never a wrinkle: his boots were up to the thigh!
And he rode with a jeweled twinkle,
His pistol butts a-twinkle,
His rapier hilt a-twinkle, under the jeweled sky.

III

Over the cobbles he clattered and clashed in the dark inn-yard,
And he tapped with his whip on the shutters, but all was locked and barred;
He whistled a tune to the window, and who should be waiting there
But the landlord's black-eyed daughter,
Bess, the landlord's daughter,
Plaiting a dark red love-knot into her long black hair.

IV

And dark in the dark old inn-yard a stable wicket creaked
Where Tim the ostler listened; his face was white and peaked;
His eyes were hollows of madness, his hair like moldy hay,
But he loved the landlord's daughter,
The landlord's red-lipped daughter,
Dumb as a dog he listened, and he hear the robber say—

V

"One kiss, my bonny sweetheart, I'm after a prize tonight,
But I shall be back with the yellow gold before the morning light;
Yet, if they press me sharply, and harry me through the day,
Then look for me by moonlight,
Watch for me by moonlight,
I'll come to thee by moonlight, though hell should bar the way."

VI

He rose upright in the stirrups; he scarce could reach her hand,
But she loosened her hair i' the casement! His face burnt like a brand
As the black cascade of perfume came tumbling over his breast;
And he kissed its waves in the moonlight,
(Oh, sweet black waves in the moonlight!)
Then he tugged at his rein in the moonlight, and galloped away to the West.

Part Two

I

He did not come in the dawning; he did not come at noon;
And out o' the tawny sunset, before the rise o' the moon,
When the road was a gipsy's ribbon, looping the purple moor,

[1] Reprinted by permission from *Collected Poems*, Volume 1, by Alfred Noyes, copyright, 1906, by Frederick A. Stokes Company.

A red-coat troop came marching—
Marching—marching—
King George's men came marching, up to the old inn-door.

II

They said no word to the landlord, they drank his ale instead,
But they gagged his daughter and bound her to the foot of her narrow bed;
Two of them knelt at her casement, with muskets at their side!
There was death at every window;
And hell at one dark window;
For Bess could see, through her casement, the road that *he* would ride.

III

They had tied her up to attention, with many a sniggering jest;
They had bound a musket beside her, with the barrel beneath her breast!
"Now keep good watch!" and they kissed her.
She heard the dead man say—
Look for me by moonlight;
Watch for me by moonlight;
I'll come to thee by moonlight, though hell should bar the way!

IV

She twisted her hands behind her; but all the knots held good!
She writhed her hands till her fingers were wet with sweat or blood!
They stretched and strained in the darkness, and the hours crawled by like years,
Till, now, on the stroke of midnight,
Cold, on the stroke of midnight,
The tip of one finger touched it! The trigger at least was hers!

V

The tip of one finger touched it; she strove no more for the rest!
Up, she stood to attention, with the barrel beneath her breast,
She would not risk their hearing: she would not strive again;
For the road lay bare in the moonlight;
Blank and bare in the moonlight;
And the blood of her veins in the moonlight throbbed to her love's refrain.

VI

Tlot-tlot; tlot-tlot! Had they heard it? The horse-hoofs ringing clear;
Tlot-tlot, tlot-tlot, in the distance? Were they deaf that they did not hear?
Down the ribbon of moonlight, over the brow of the hill,
The highwayman came riding,
Riding, riding!
The red-coats looked to their priming! She stood up, straight and still!

VII

Tlot-tlot, in the frosty silence! *Tlot-tlot,* in the echoing night!
Nearer he came and nearer! Her face was like a light!
Her eyes grew wide for a moment; she drew one last deep breath,
Then her finger moved in the moonlight,
Her musket shattered the moonlight,
Shattered her breast in the moonlight and warned him—with her death.

VIII

He turned; he spurred to the West; he did not know who stood
Bowed, with her head o'er the musket, drenched with her own red blood!
Not till the dawn he heard it, and his face grew gray to hear
How Bess, the landlord's daughter,
The landlord's black-eyed daughter,
Had watched for her love in the moonlight, and died in the darkness there.

IX

Back, he spurred like a madman, shrieking a curse to the sky,
With the white road smoking behind him, and his rapier brandished high!
Blood-red were his spurs i' the golden noon; wine-red was his velvet coat;
When they shot him down on the highway,
Down like a dog on the highway,
And he lay in his blood on the highway, with the bunch of lace at his throat.

. . . .

X

And still of a winter's night, they say, when the wind is in the trees,
When the moon is a ghostly galleon tossed upon cloudy seas,
When the road is a ribbon of moonlight over the purple moor,
A highwayman comes riding—
Riding—riding—
A highwayman comes riding, up to the old inn-door.

XI

Over the cobbles he clatters and clangs in the
dark inn-yard;
And he taps with his whip on the shutters, but
all is locked and barred;
He whistles a tune to the window, and who
should be waiting there
But the landlord's black-eyed daughter,
Bess, the landlord's daughter,
Plaiting a dark red love-knot into her long
black hair.

1906

JOSEPH CONRAD 1856-1924

Joseph Conrad is of especial interest in the field of English literature for his romantic career and his high rank as a novelist achieved in a language foreign to him. He was born in Poland; after the death of his father and mother in exile, he was taken by an uncle and educated at the Gymnasium of Cracow, but was seized with the strange ambition to become a British sailor. He first joined the French mercantile marine in 1874. Three years later he shipped before the mast on a British vessel, worked his way up to the rank of master by 1884, and in 1894 left the sea to settle down in Kent and devote the rest of his life to literature.

His various ships, his voyages to Borneo, the Congo, and other tropical regions, and the characters he met live again for us in his writings, two of which, *The Mirror of the Sea,* 1906, and *A Personal Record,* 1912, are autobiographic. His first novel, *Almayer's Folly,* was begun in 1889 during a long voyage and finished in 1894. In *The Nigger of the Narcissus,* 1897, Conrad showed his ability in turning to account his wide experiences at sea by expressing with untrammeled vigor the relations existing, as he felt, between man and the inimical forces of nature. In "The Heart of Darkness" (*Youth,* 1902) Conrad makes one feel the compelling power of a tropical forest; *Typhoon,* 1903, is an example of his acute observation of the sea in all its aspects; its description of an ocean storm is almost unique as a masterful expression of the primal moods of the tempest.

Conrad's novels are, first of all, studies of character under the strain of unusual circumstances; they concern man's reaction to external crises that are less important in themselves than the personal crises that they precipitate. *Lord Jim* is typical of Conrad's pre-occupation with character portrayal. It illustrates his general contention that the ultimate test of character is loyalty to the principles or persons that have been admittedly the best influences in a man's life. The objective development of Conrad's plots parallels his treatment of the conflict in man's own spirit; for against a strange background of mystery and adventure his characters are clearly portrayed by his account of their struggles with themselves.

Works: Concord edition, 25 volumes, 1923.

Biography: G. J. Aubry, *The Life and Letters of Joseph Conrad,* 2 volumes, 1927; F. M. Ford, *Joseph Conrad, a Personal Remembrance,* 1924; R. Curle, *Joseph Conrad, a Study,* 1914. Criticism: Phelps (EN); Follett; Chevalley; Chubb; Drew; Freeman; Garnett; Cooper; J. Galsworthy, "Reminiscences of Conrad," *Scrib.* 77:3-10; R. Curle, "Conrad in the East," *Yale R.* ns 12:497-508; "Personality," *Edin. R.* 241:126-38; T. Moult, "Life and Work of Joseph Conrad," *Yale R.* ns 14:295-308; G. J. Jean-Aubry, "Joseph Conrad in the Heart of Darkness," *Bookm.* 63:429-35; *Fortn.* 122:303-13; M. Armstrong, "Joseph Conrad," *Liv. Age* 320:512-16; G. Overton, *Bookm.* 57:275-84.

THE MIRROR OF THE SEA [1]

XXXVI Initiation

The love that is given to ships is profoundly different from the love men feel for every other work of their hands—the love they bear to their houses, for instance—because it is untainted by the pride of possession. The pride of skill, the pride of responsibility, the pride of endurance there may be, but otherwise it is a disinterested sentiment. No seaman ever cherished a ship, even if she belonged to him, merely because of the profit she put in his pocket. No one, I think, ever did; for a shipowner, even of the best, has always been outside the pale of that sentiment embracing in a feeling of intimate, equal fellowship the ship and the man, backing each other against the implacable, if sometimes dissembled, hostility of their world of waters. The sea—this truth must be confessed—has no generosity. No display of manly qualities—courage, hardihood, endurance, faithfulness—has ever been known to touch its irresponsible consciousness of power. The ocean has the conscienceless temper of a savage autocrat spoiled by much adulation. He cannot brook the slightest appearance of defiance, and has remained the irreconcilable enemy of ships and men ever since ships and men had the unheard-of audacity to go afloat together in the face of his frown. From that day he has gone on swallowing up fleets and men without his resentment being glutted by the number of victims—by so many wrecked ships and wrecked lives. Today, as ever, he is ready to beguile and betray, to smash and to drown the incorrigible optimism of men who, backed by the fidelity of ships, are trying to wrest from him the fortune of

[1] From *The Mirror of the Sea* by Joseph Conrad, published by Doubleday, Doran and Company, Inc., and reprinted by special permission of James B. Pinker and Son, agents for the Conrad estate.

their house, the dominion of their world, or only a dole of food for their hunger. If not always in the hot mood to smash, he is always stealthily ready for a drowning. The most amazing wonder of the deep is its unfathomable cruelty.

I felt its dread for the first time in mid-Atlantic one day, many years ago, when we took off the crew of a Danish brig homeward bound from the West Indies. A thin, silvery mist softened the calm and majestic splendor of light without shadows—seemed to render the sky less remote and the ocean less immense. It was one of the days, when the might of the sea appears indeed lovable, like the nature of a strong man in moments of quiet intimacy. At sunrise we had made out a black speck to the westward, apparently suspended high up in the void behind a stirring, shimmering veil of silvery blue gauze that seemed at times to stir and float in the breeze which fanned us slowly along. The peace of that enchanting forenoon was so profound, so untroubled, that it seemed that every word pronounced loudly on our deck would penetrate to the very heart of that infinite mystery born from the conjunction of water and sky. We did not raise our voices. "A water-logged derelict, I think, sir," said the second officer, quietly, coming down from aloft with the binoculars in their case slung across his shoulders; and our captain, without a word, signed to the helmsman to steer for the black speck. Presently we made out a low, jagged stump sticking up forward—all that remained of her departed masts.

The captain was expatiating in a low conversational tone to the chief mate upon the danger of these derelicts, and upon his dread of coming upon them at night, when suddenly a man forward screamed out, "There's people on board of her, sir! I see them!" in a most extraordinary voice—a voice never heard before in our ship; the amazing voice of a stranger. It gave the signal for a sudden tumult of shouts. The watch below ran up the forecastle head in a body, the cook dashed out of the galley. Everybody saw the poor fellows now. There they were! And all at once our ship, which had the well-earned name of being without a rival for speed in light winds, seemed to us to have lost the power of motion, as if the sea, becoming viscous, had clung to her sides. And yet she moved. Immensity, the inseparable companion of a ship's life, chose that day to breathe upon her as gently as a sleeping child. The clamor of our excitement had died out, and our living ship, famous for never losing steerage-way [1] as long as there was air enough to float a feather, stole, without a ripple, silent and white as a ghost, toward her mutilated and wounded sister, come upon at the point of death in the sunlit haze of a calm day at sea.

With the binoculars glued to his eyes, the captain said in a quavering tone: "They are waving to us with something aft there." He put down the glasses on the skylight brusquely, and began to walk about the poop. "A shirt or a flag," he ejaculated, irritably. "Can't make it out . . . . Some damn rag or other!" He took a few more turns on the poop, glancing down over the rail now and then to see how fast we were moving. His nervous footsteps rang sharply in the quiet of the ship, where the other men, all looking the same way, had forgotten themselves in a staring immobility. "This will never do!" he cried out, suddenly. "Lower the boats at once! Down with them!"

Before I jumped into mine he took me aside, as being an inexperienced junior, for a word of warning:

"You look out as you come alongside that she doesn't take you down with her. You understand?"

He murmured this confidentially, so that none of the men at the falls [2] should overhear and I was shocked. "Heavens! as if in such an emergency one stopped to think of danger!" I exclaimed to myself mentally, in scorn of such cold-blooded caution.

It takes many lessons to make a real seaman, and I got my rebuke at once. My experienced commander seemed in one searching glance to read my thoughts on my ingenuous face.

"What you're going for is to save life, not to drown your boat's crew for nothing," he growled, severely, in my ear. But as we shoved off he leaned over and cried out: "It all rests on the power of your arms, men. Give way for life!"

We made a race of it, and I would never have believed that a common boat's crew of a merchantman could keep up so much determined fierceness in the regular swing of their stroke. What our captain had clearly perceived before we left had become plain to all of us since. The issue of our enterprise hung a hair above that abyss of waters which will not give up its dead till the Day of Judgment. It was a race of two ship's boats

[1] never failing to turn with the rudder
[2] tackle used to raise or lower the ship's boats

matched against Death for a prize of nine men's lives, and Death had a long start. We saw the crew of the brig from afar working at the pumps—still pumping on that wreck, which already had settled so far down that the gentle, low swell, over which our boats rose and fell easily without a check to their speed, welling up almost level with her head-rails, [1] plucked at the ends of broken gear swinging desolately under her naked bowsprit.

We could not, in all conscience, have picked out a better day for our regatta had we had the free choice of all the days that ever dawned upon the lonely struggles and solitary agonies of ships since the Norse rovers first steered to the westward against the run of Atlantic waves. It was a very good race. At the finish there was not an oar's length between the first and second boat, with Death coming in a good third on the top of the very next smooth swell, for all one knew to the contrary. The scuppers [2] of the brig gurgled softly all together when the water rising against her sides subsided sleepily with a low wash, as if playing about an immovable rock. Her bulwarks were gone fore and aft, and one saw her bare deck low-lying like a raft and swept clean of boats, spars, houses—of everything except the ringbolts and the heads of the pumps. I had one dismal glimpse of it as I braced myself up to receive upon my breast the last man to leave her, the captain, who literally let himself fall into my arms.

It had been a weirdly silent rescue—a rescue without a hail, without a single uttered word, without a gesture or a sign, without a conscious exchange of glances. Up to the very last moment those on board stuck to their pumps, which spouted two clear streams of water upon their bare feet. Their brown skin showed through the rents of their shirts; and the two small bunches of half-naked, tattered men went on bowing from the waist to each other in their back-breaking labor, up and down, absorbed, with no time for a glance over the shoulder at the help that was coming to them. As we dashed, unregarded, alongside, a voice let out one, only one hoarse howl of command, and then, just as they stood, without caps, with the salt drying gray in the wrinkles and folds of their hairy, haggard faces, blinking stupidly at us their red eyelids, they made a bolt away from the handles, tottering and jostling against each other, and positively flung themselves over upon our very heads. The clatter they made tumbling into the boats had an extraordinarily destructive effect upon the illusion of tragic dignity our self-esteem had thrown over the contests of mankind with the sea. On that exquisite day of gentle breathing peace and veiled sunshine perished my romantic love to what men's imagination had proclaimed the most august aspect of Nature. The cynical indifference of the sea to the merits of human suffering and courage, laid bare in this ridiculous, panic-tainted performance extorted from the dire extremity of nine good and honorable seamen, revolted me. I saw the duplicity of the sea's most tender mood. It was so because it could not help itself, but the awed respect of the early days was gone. I felt ready to smile bitterly at its enchanting charm and glare viciously at its furies. In a moment, before we shoved off, I had looked coolly at the life of my choice. Its illusions were gone, but its fascination remained. I had become a seaman at last.

We pulled hard for a quarter of an hour, then laid on our oars waiting for our ship. She was coming down on us with swelling sails, looking delicately tall and exquisitely noble through the mist. The captain of the brig, who sat in the stern sheets by my side with his face in his hands, raised his head and began to speak with a sort of somber volubility. They had lost their masts and sprung a leak in a hurricane; drifted for weeks, always at the pumps, met more bad weather; the ships they sighted failed to make them out, the leak gained upon them slowly, and the seas had left them nothing to make a raft of. It was very hard to see ship after ship pass by at a distance, "as if everybody had agreed that we must be left to drown," he added. But they went on trying to keep the brig afloat as long as possible, and working the pumps constantly on insufficient food, mostly raw, till "yesterday evening," he continued, monotonously, "just as the sun went down, the men's hearts broke."

He made an almost imperceptible pause here, and went on again with exactly the same intonation:

"They told me the brig could not be saved, and they thought they had done enough for themselves. I said nothing to that. It was true. It was no mutiny. I had nothing to say to them. They lay about aft all night, as still as so many dead men. I did not lie down. I kept a lookout. When the first light came

[1] the elliptical rails at the head of a ship
[2] openings at the level of the deck to let off water

I saw your ship at once. I waited for more light; the breeze began to fail on my face. Then I shouted out as loud as I was able, 'Look at that ship' but only two men got up very slowly and came to me. At first only we three stood alone, for a long time, watching you coming down to us, and feeling the breeze drop to a calm almost; but afterwards others, too, rose, one after another, and by and by I had all my crew behind me. I turned round and said to them that they could see the ship was coming our way, but in this small breeze she might come too late after all, unless we turned to and tried to keep the brig afloat long enough to give you time to save us all. I spoke like that to them, and then I gave the command to man the pumps."

He gave the command, and gave the example, too, by going himself to the handles, but it seems that these men did actually hang back for a moment, looking at each other dubiously before they followed him. "He! he! he!" He broke out into a most unexpected imbecile, pathetic, nervous little giggle. "Their hearts were broken so! They had been played with too long," he explained, apologetically, lowering his eyes, and became silent.

Twenty-five years is a long time—a quarter of a century is a dim and distant past; but to this day I remember the dark-brown feet, hands, and faces of two of these men whose hearts had been broken by the sea. They were lying very still on their sides on the bottom boards between the thwarts, curled up like dogs. My boat's crew, leaning over the loom [1] of their oars, stared and listened as if at the play. The master of the brig looked up suddenly to ask me what day it was.

They had lost the date. When I told him it was Sunday, the 22nd, he frowned, making some mental calculation, then nodded twice sadly to himself, staring at nothing.

His aspect was miserably unkempt and wildly sorrowful. Had it not been for the unquenchable candor of his blue eyes, whose unhappy, tired glance every moment sought his abandoned, sinking brig, as if it could find rest nowhere else, he would have appeared mad. But he was too simple to go mad, too simple with that manly simplicity which alone can bear men unscathed in mind and body through an encounter with the deadly playfulness of the sea or with its less abominable fury.

Neither angry, nor playful, nor smiling, it enveloped our distant ship growing bigger as she neared us, our boats with the rescued men and the dismantled hull of the brig we were leaving behind, in the large and placid embrace of its quietness, half lost in the fair haze, as if in a dream of infinite and tender clemency. There was no frown, no wrinkle on its face, not a ripple. And the run of the slight swell was so smooth that it resembled the graceful undulation of a piece of shimmering gray silk shot with gleams of green. We pulled an easy stroke; but when the master of the brig, after a glance over his shoulder, stood up with a low exclamation, my men feathered their oars instinctively, without an order, and the boat lost her way. [2]

He was steadying himself on my shoulder with a strong grip, while his other arm, flung up rigidly, pointed a denunciatory finger at the immense tranquility of the ocean. After his first exclamation, which stopped the swing of our oars, he made no sound, but his whole attitude seemed to cry out an indignant "Behold!" . . . . I could not imagine what vision of evil had come to him. I was startled, and the amazing energy of his immobilized gesture made my heart beat faster with the anticipation of something monstrous and unsuspected. The stillness around us became crushing.

For a moment the succession of silky undulations ran on innocently. I saw each of them swell up the misty line of the horizon, far, far away beyond the derelict brig, and the next moment, with a slight friendly toss of our boat, it had passed under us and was gone. The lulling cadence of the rise and fall, the invariable gentleness of this irresistible force, the great charm of the deep waters, warmed my breast deliciously, like the subtle poison of a love-potion. But all this lasted only a few soothing seconds before I jumped up, too, making the boat roll like the veriest land-lubber.

Something startling, mysterious, hastily confused was taking place. I watched it with incredulous and fascinated awe, as one watches the confused, swift movements of some deed of violence done in the dark. As if at a given signal, the run of the smooth undulations seemed checked suddenly around the brig. By a strange optical delusion the whole sea appeared to rise upon her in one overwhelming heave of its silky surface where in one spot a smother of foam broke out ferociously. And

[1] the part of the oar inboard from the rowlock

[2] lost headway

then the effort subsided. It was all over, and the smooth swell ran on as before from the horizon in uninterrupted cadence of motion, passing under us with a slight friendly toss of our boat. Far away, where the brig had been, an angry white stain undulating on the surface of steely-gray waters, shot with gleams of green, diminished swiftly without a hiss, like a patch of pure snow melting in the sun. And the great stillness after this initiation into the sea's implacable hate seemed full of dread thoughts and shadows of disaster.

"Gone!" ejaculated from the depths of his chest my bowman in a final tone. He spat in his hands, and took a better grip on his oar. The captain of the brig lowered his rigid arm slowly, and looked at our faces in a solemnly conscious silence, which called upon us to share in his simple-minded, marveling awe. All at once he sat down by my side, and leaned forward earnestly at my boat's crew, who, swinging together in a long, easy stroke, kept their eyes fixed upon him faithfully.

"No ship could have done so well," he addressed them, firmly, after a moment of strained silence, during which he seemed with trembling lips to seek for words fit to bear such high testimony. "She was small, but she was good. I had no anxiety. She was strong. Last voyage I had my wife and two children in her. No other ship could have stood so long the weather she had to live through for days and days before we got dismasted a fortnight ago. She was fairly worn out, and that's all. You may believe me. She lasted under us for days and days, but she could not last forever. It was long enough. I am glad it is over. No better ship was ever left to sink at sea on such a day as this."

He was competent to pronounce the funeral oration of a ship, this son of ancient sea-folk, whose national existence, so little stained by the excesses of manly virtues, had demanded nothing but the merest foothold from the earth. By the merits of his sea-wise forefathers and by the artlessness of his heart, he was made fit to deliver this excellent discourse. There was nothing wanting in its orderly arrangement—neither piety nor faith, nor the tribute of praise due to the worthy dead, with the edifying recital of their achievement. She had lived, he had loved her; she had suffered, and he was glad she was at rest. It was an excellent discourse. And it was orthodox, too, in its fidelity to the cardinal article of a seaman's faith, of which it was a single-minded confession. "Ships are all right." They are. They who live with the sea have got to hold by that creed first and last; and it came to me, as I glanced at him sideways, that some men were not altogether unworthy in honor and conscience to pronounce the funeral eulogium of a ship's constancy in life and death.

After this, sitting by my side with his loosely clasped hands hanging between his knees, he uttered no word, made no movement till the shadow of our ship's sails fell on the boat, when, at the loud cheer greeting the return of the victors with their prize, he lifted up his troubled face with a faint smile of pathetic indulgence. This smile of the worthy descendant of the most ancient sea-folk whose audacity and hardihood had left no trace of greatness and glory upon the waters, completed the cycle of my initiation. There was an infinite depth of hereditary wisdom in its pitying sadness. It made the hearty bursts of cheering sound like a childish noise of triumph. Our crew shouted with immense confidence—honest souls! As if anybody could ever make sure of having prevailed against the sea, which has betrayed so many ships of great "name," so many proud men, so many towering ambitions of fame, power, wealth, greatness!

As I brought the boat under the falls my captain, in high good humor, leaned over, spreading his red and freckled elbows on the rail, and called down to me sarcastically out of the depths of his cynic philosopher's beard:

"So you have brought the boat back after all, have you?"

Sarcasm was "his way," and the most that can be said for it is that it was natural. This did not make it lovable. But it is decorous and expedient to fall in with one's commander's way. "Yes. I brought the boat back all right, sir," I answered. And the good man believed me. It was not for him to discern upon me the marks of my recent initiation. And yet I was not exactly the same youngster who had taken the boat away—all impatience for a race against Death, with the prize of nine men's lives at the end.

Already I looked with other eyes upon the sea. I knew it capable of betraying the generous ardor of youth as implacably as, indifferent to evil and good, it would have betrayed the basest greed or the noblest heroism. My conception of its magnanimous greatness was gone. And I looked upon the true sea—the sea that plays with men till their hearts are broken, and wears stout ships to death. Nothing can touch the brooding bitterness of its soul. Open to all and faithful to none, it exercises its fascination for the undoing of the best. To love it is not well. It knows no bond of plighted troth, no fidelity to misfortune, to long companionship, to long devotion. The promise it holds out perpetually is very great; but the only secret of its possession is strength, strength—the jealous, sleepless strength of a man guarding a coveted treasure within his gates.

1905

JOHN MASEFIELD 1874-

Since Masefield has been very reticent about the details of his life, only a few main statements concerning him are reliable. We know that he ran away to sea from his home in Ledbury, in Western England. He shipped before the mast, and in an adventurous career engaged in many occupations and tramped through far countries. As he himself says, he was in Yonkers in 1896 when he made the acquaintance of Chaucer and awoke to "a new world of wonder and delight. . . . After that Sunday afternoon I read many poets . . . . and wrote many imitations of them." Returning to England, he wrote little for a few years, but early in the twentieth century his work began to appear with regularity.

Masefield's growing reputation as one of the foremost English poets of the day is based chiefly upon his long narrative poems, the best of which are *The Everlasting Mercy,* 1911; *The Widow in the Bye Street,* 1912; *Dauber, The Daffodil Fields,* 1913; and *Reynard the Fox,* 1919, which should be read with Chaucer's *Nun's Priest's Tale* in mind. He has also produced novels (*Captain Margaret,* 1908; *Sard Harker,* 1924, and others); dramas (*The Tragedy of Nan,* 1909; *Pompey the Great,* 1910; *The Faithful,* 1915); critical work (*Shakespeare,* 1911); histories (*Sea Life in Nelson's Time,* 1905; *Gallipoli,* 1916); and has edited much.

It is not surprising, considering his first inspiration, that Masefield should, among recent poets, be the one most closely akin to Chaucer; from him he has even borrowed a beautiful metrical form, the rime royal,[1] for *Dauber.* Since the death of Joseph Conrad he is probably the greatest living author using the sea as a background. All that he has written testifies to his intimate knowledge of ships and the sea, men, books, and cities, to a sympathy for the toilers that reminds one of Wilfrid Gibson. His method[2] as a whole is a wise application of the principles laid down by Wordsworth in the preface to *Lyrical Ballads.* In Masefield's estimation, moreover, poetry at its best heals; it is as he says in the preface to his *Collected Poems,* "inspiration enough and school enough and star enough to urge and guide in any night of the soul, however wayless from our blindness or black from our passions and our follies."

Poems and Plays, 2 Vols., 1921. (Preface autobiographical.)

Criticism: W. H. Hamilton, *John Masefield, a Critical Study,* 1922; Phelps (EP); Sturgeon; Scott; G. H. Campbell, "John Masefield of the Present Day," *Bookm.* 52:445-50; M. Bronner, "Masefield, Seaman-author," por. *Bookm.* 33:584-91; O. W. Firkins, "Mr. Masefield's Poetry," *Nation* 108:389-90; J. G. Fletcher, "John Masefield: a Study," *No. Am.* 212:548-51; A. H. Thorndike, "The Great Tradition," *Dial* 66:118-21; G. Dearmer, "Strength and Weakness of Mr. Masefield," *Fortn.* 120:345-52.

SEA FEVER [3]

I must go down to the seas again, to the lonely sea and the sky,
And all I ask is a tall ship and a star to steer her by;
And the wheel's kick and the wind's song and the white sail's shaking,
And a gray mist on the sea's face, and a gray dawn breaking.

I must go down to the seas again, for the call of the running tide
Is a wild call and a clear call that may not be denied;
And all I ask is a windy day with the white clouds flying,
And the flung spray and the blown spume,[4] and the sea-gulls crying.

I must go down to the seas again, to the vagrant gypsy life,
To the gull's way and the whale's way where the wind's like a whetted knife;
And all I ask is a merry yarn from a laughing fellow-rover,
And quiet sleep and a sweet dream when the long trick's[5] over.

1901 1902

TEWKESBURY ROAD [3]

It is good to be out on the road, and going one knows not where,
Going through meadow and village, one knows not whither nor why;

[1] a stanza of seven decasyllabic lines, rimed *ababbcc*—used by Chaucer in *Troilus and Cressida* and *The Prioress's Tale*

[2] "to choose incidents and situations from common life, and to relate or describe them, ... in a selection of language really used by men, and at the same time to throw over them a coloring of the imagination whereby ordinary things should be presented to the mind in an unusual aspect . . . ." —Preface to *Lyrical Ballads*

[3] From *The Collected Poems* of John Masefield. Reprinted by permission of the author.

[4] foam

[5] "the ordinary two-hour spell at the wheel or on the lookout"—Masefield's note

Through the gray light drift of the dust, in the keen cool rush of the air,
Under the flying white clouds, and the broad blue lift of the sky.

And to halt at the chattering brook, in the tall green fern at the brink
Where the harebell grows, and the gorse, and the foxgloves purple and white;
Where the shy-eyed delicate deer troop down to the brook to drink
When the stars are mellow and large at the coming on of the night.

Oh, to feel the beat of the rain, and the homely smell of the earth,
Is a tune for the blood to jig to, a joy past power of words;
And the blessed green comely meadows are all a-ripple with mirth
At the noise of the lambs at play and the dear wild cry of the birds.

1902

CARGOES[1]

Quinquireme[2] of Nineveh from distant Ophir[3]
Rowing home to haven in sunny Palestine,
With a cargo of ivory,
And apes and peacocks,
Sandalwood, cedarwood, and sweet white wine.

Stately Spanish galleon coming from the Isthmus,
Dipping through the Tropics by the palm-green shores,
With a cargo of diamonds,
Emeralds, amethysts,
Topazes, and cinnamon, and gold moidores.[4]

Dirty British coaster with a salt-caked smoke stack,
Butting through the Channel in the mad March days,
With a cargo of Tyne coal,
Road-rails, pig-lead,
Firewood, ironware, and cheap tin trays.

1912

THE "WANDERER"[1]

All day they loitered by the resting ships,
Telling their beauties over, taking stock;
At night the verdict left my messmates' lips,
"The *Wanderer* is the finest ship in dock."

I had not seen her, but a friend, since drowned,
Drew her, with painted ports, low, lovely, lean,
Saying, "The *Wanderer*,[5] clipper, outward bound,
The loveliest ship my eyes have ever seen—

"Perhaps tomorrow you will see her sail.
She sails at sunrise": but the morrow showed
No *Wanderer* setting forth for me to hail;
Far down the stream men pointed where she rode,

Rode the great trackway to the sea, dim, dim,
Already gone before the stars were gone.
I saw her at the sea-line's smoky rim
Grow swiftly vaguer as they towed her on.

Soon even her masts were hidden in the haze
Beyond the city; she was on her course
To trample billows for a hundred days;
That afternoon the norther gathered force,

Blowing a small snow from a point of east.[6]
"Oh, fair for her," we said, "to take her south."
And in our spirits, as the wind increased,
We saw her there, beyond the river mouth,

Setting her side-lights in the wildering dark,
To glint upon mad water, while the gale
Roared like a battle, snapping like a shark,
And drunken seamen struggle with the sail.

While with sick hearts her mates put out of mind
Their little children left astern, ashore,
And the gale's gathering made the darkness blind,
Water and air one intermingled roar.

Then we forgot her, for the fiddlers played,
Dancing and singing held our merry crew;
The old ship moaned a little as she swayed.
It blew all night, oh, bitter hard it blew!

So that at midnight I was called on deck
To keep an anchor-watch; I heard the sea
Roar past in white procession filled with wreck;
Intense bright frosty stars burned over me,

[1] From *The Collected Poems* of John Masefield. Reprinted by permission of the author.
[2] a galley with five banks of oars
[3] ancient country of unknown location, rich in gold
[4] a former Portuguese coin, worth about 8 dollars
[5] "I wrote the poem, 'The Wanderer,' about a beautiful but unlucky ship which I had seen years before in the Mersey. *The Wanderer* stays in my mind as one of the loveliest things ever made by men. She is still freshly remembered in Liverpool, and many men who sailed in her must still be alive. She was run down and sunk (I believe in daylight) in the Elbe near Hamburg about 1897."
[6] almost directly east

And the Greek brig beside us dipped and dipped,
White to the muzzle like a half-tide rock,
Drowned to the mainmast with the seas she shipped,
Her cable-swivels clanged at every shock.

And like a never-dying force, the wind
Roared till we shouted with it, roared until
Its last vitality of wrath was thinned,
Had beat its fury breathless and was still.

By dawn the gale had dwindled into flaw,[1]
A glorious morning followed: with my friend
I climbed the fo'c's'le-head to see; we saw
The waters hurrying shoreward without end.

Haze blotted out the river's lowest reach;
Out of the gloom the steamers, passing by,
Called with their sirens, hooting their sea-speech;
Out of the dimness others made reply.

And as we watched, there came a rush of feet
Charging the fo'c's'le till the hatchway shook.
Men all about us thrust their way, or beat,
Crying, "The *Wanderer!* Down the river! Look!"

I looked with them toward the dimness; there
Gleamed like a spirit striding out of night,
A full-rigged ship unutterably fair,
Her masts like trees in winter, frosty-bright.

Foam trembled at her bows like wisps of wool;
She trembled as she towed. I had not dreamed
That work of man could be so beautiful,
In its own presence and in what it seemed.

"So, she is putting back again," I said.
"How white with frost her yards are on the fore."
One of the men about me answer made,
"That is not frost, but all her sails are tore,

"Torn into tatters, youngster, in the gale;
Her best foul-weather suit gone." It was true,
Her masts were white with rags of tattered sail
Many as gannets[2] when the fish are due.

Beauty in desolation was her pride,
Her crowned array a glory that had been;
She faltered tow'rd us like a swan that died,
But although ruined she was still a queen.

[1] sudden gusts
[2] large seabirds

"Put back with all her sails gone," went the word;
Then, from her signals flying, rumor ran,
"The sea that stove her boats in killed her third;[3]
She has been gutted and has lost a man."

So, as though stepping to a funeral march,
She passed defeated homeward whence she came,
Ragged with tattered canvas white as starch,
A wild bird that misfortune had made tame.

She was refitted soon; another took
The dead man's office; then the singers hove
Her capstan till the snapping hawsers shook;
Out, with a bubble at her bows, she drove.

Again they towed her seaward, and again
We, watching, praised her beauty, praised her trim,
Saw her fair house-flag[4] flutter at the main,
And slowly saunter seaward, dwindling dim;

And wished her well, and wondered, as she died,
How, when her canvas had been sheeted home,
Her quivering length would sweep into her stride,
Making the greenness milky with her foam.

But when we rose next morning, we discerned
Her beauty once again a shattered thing;
Towing to dock the *Wanderer* returned,
A wounded sea-bird with a broken wing.

A spar was gone, her rigging's disarray
Told of a worse disaster than the last;
Like draggled hair disheveled hung the stay,
Drooping and beating on the broken mast.

Half-mast upon her flagstaff hung her flag;
Word went among us how the broken spar
Had gored her captain like an angry stag,
And killed her mate a half-day from the bar.

She passed to dock upon the top of the flood.
An old man near me shook his head and swore:
"Like a bad woman, she has tasted blood—
There'll be no trusting in her any more."

We thought it truth, and when we saw her there
Lying in dock, beyond, across the stream,

[3] third mate
[4] a small flag bearing the emblem of the ship's owners

We would forget that we had called her fair,
We thought her murderess and the past a dream.

And when she sailed again, we watched in awe,
Wondering what bloody act her beauty planned,
What evil lurked behind the thing we saw,
What strength was there that thus annulled man's hand,

How next its triumph would compel man's will
Into compliance with external Fate,
How next the powers would use her to work ill
On suffering men; we had not long to wait.

For soon the outcry of derision rose,
"Here comes the *Wanderer!*" the expected cry.
Guessing the cause, our mockings joined with those
Yelled from the shipping as they towed her by.

She passed us close, her seamen paid no heed
To what was called: they stood, a sullen group,
Smoking and spitting, careless of her need,
Mocking the orders given from the poop.

Her mates and boys were working her; we stared.
What was the reason of this strange return,
This third annulling of the thing prepared?
No outward evil could our eyes discern.

Only like one who having formed a plan
Beyond the pitch of common minds, she sailed,
Mocked and deserted by the common man,
Made half divine to me for having failed.

We learned the reason soon; below the town
A stay had parted like a snapping reed,
"Warning," the men thought, "not to take her down."
They took the omen, they would not proceed.

Days passed before another crew would sign.
The *Wanderer* lay in dock alone, unmanned,
Feared as a thing possessed by powers malign,
Bound under curses not to leave the land.

But under passing Time fear passes too;
That terror passed, the sailors' hearts grew bold.
We learned in time that she had found a crew
And was bound out and southward as of old.

And in contempt we thought, "A little while
Will bring her back again, dismantled, spoiled.
It is herself; she cannot change her style;
She has the habit now of being foiled."

So when a ship appeared among the haze,
We thought, "The *Wanderer* back again"; but no,
No *Wanderer* showed for many, many days,
Her passing lights made other waters glow.

But we would often think and talk of her,
Tell newer hands her story, wondering, then,
Upon what ocean she was *Wanderer,*
Bound to the cities built by foreign men.

And one by one our little conclave thinned,
Passed into ships and sailed and so away,
To drown in some great roaring of the wind,
Wanderers themselves, unhappy fortune's prey.

And Time went by me making memory dim,
Yet still I wondered if the *Wanderer* fared
Still pointing to the unreached ocean's rim,
Brightening the water where her breast was bared.

And much in ports abroad I eyed the ships,
Hoping to see her well-remembered form
Come with a curl of bubbles at her lips
Bright to her berth, the sovereign of the storm.

I never did, and many years went by,
Then, near a Southern port, one Christmas Eve,
I watched a gale go roaring through the sky,
Making the caldrons of the clouds upheave.

Then the wrack [1] tattered and the stars appeared,
Millions of stars that seemed to speak in fire;
A byre [2] cock cried aloud that morning neared,
The swinging wind-vane flashed upon the spire.

And soon men looked upon a glittering earth,
Intensely sparkling like a world new-born;
Only to look was spiritual birth,
So bright the raindrops ran along the thorn.

So bright they were, that one could almost pass
Beyond their twinkling to the source, and know
The glory pushing in the blade of grass,
That hidden soul which makes the flowers grow.

[1] thin flying clouds
[2] stable (farm yard)

That soul was there apparent, not revealed,
Unearthly meanings covered every tree,
That wet grass grew in an immortal field,
Those waters fed some never-wrinkled sea.

The scarlet berries in the hedge stood out
Like revelations but the tongue unknown;
Even in the brooks a joy was quick: the trout
Rushed in a dumbness dumb to me alone.

All of the valley was aloud with brooks;
I walked the morning, breasting up the fells,
Taking again lost childhood from the rooks,
Whose cawing came above the Christmas bells.

I had not walked that glittering world before,
But up the hill a prompting came to me,
"This line of upland runs along the shore:
Beyond the hedgegrow I shall see the sea."

And on the instant from beyond away
That long familiar sound, a ship's bell, broke
The hush below me in the unseen bay.
Old memories came: that inner prompting
    spoke.

And bright above the hedge a seagull's wings
Flashed and were steady upon empty air.
"A Power unseen," I cried, "prepares these
    things;
Those are her bells, the *Wanderer* is there."

So hurrying to the hedge and looking down,
I saw a mighty bay's wind-crinkled blue
Ruffling the image of a tranquil town,
With lapsing waters glittering as they grew.

And near me in the road the shipping swung,
So stately and so still in such great peace
That like to drooping crests their colors hung,
Only their shadows trembled without cease.

I did but glance upon those anchored ships.
Even as my thought had told, I saw her plain;
Tense, like a supple athlete with lean hips,
Swiftness at pause, the *Wanderer* come
    again—

Come as of old a queen, untouched by Time,
Resting the beauty that no seas could tire,
Sparkling, as though the midnight's rain were
    rime,
Like a man's thought transfigured into fire.

And as I looked, one of her men began
To sing some simple tune of Christmas day;
Among her crew the song spread, man to man,
Until the singing rang across the bay;

And soon in other anchored ships the men
Joined in the singing with clear throats, until
The farm-boy heard it up the windy glen,
Above the noise of sheep-bells on the hill.

Over the water came the lifted song—
Blind pieces in a mighty game we swing;
Life's battle is a conquest for the strong;
The meaning shows in the defeated thing.

1913 1913

JOHN MILLINGTON SYNGE
1871-1909

Synge's childhood was spent near Dublin rambling over the Wicklow Hills. This trained his powers of observation, and perhaps fixed a habit of wandering, for after a college career marked by real genius in mastering ancient and modern languages and music, a nomadic life on the Continent is the main feature in Synge's career up to 1899. In Paris in that year Mr. Yeats discovered him, "a drifting silent man full of hidden passion," and advised him to go to the Aran Islands for material never before turned to literary account.

From that time on Synge spent a good part of each year sharing the life of the islanders, absorbing impressions of the people and the country, until he was able to reproduce the life, the richly imaginative dialect, and the environment of this people, much as Pierre Loti described the fisherfolk of Iceland. *The Aran Islands,* 1907, is an objective study rich in dramatic interest from which he drew six plays, including *Riders to the Sea,* 1904, *The Well of the Saints,* and *The Playboy of the Western World,* 1907, which, though in prose, are among the most highly poetic writings of modern times.

Like Wordsworth, Synge believed that poetry dealt too much with abstractions, that it should occupy itself with the realities of life, even though brutal, and that a living and beautiful speech was necessary to clothe these realities. It is not surprising, then, to find that his work possesses four great qualities: the faculty of dramatic visualization, reverence for reality, poetry in concept and thought, and the unexpected in style—a style, S. P. Sherman points out, as patiently and cunningly wrought as Pater's.

Works, 4 volumes, 1910.

Biography and criticism: W. B. Yeats, *Synge and the Ireland of his Time,* 1912; also *Forum* 46:179-200; P. P. Howe, *J. M. Synge, a Critical Study,* 1912; Maurice Bourgeois, *J. M. Synge and the Irish Literary Theater,* 1913 (detailed account of life and works); J. Masefield, *Recent Prose,* "John M. Synge," 1924; J. Thornung, *J. M. Synge,* 1921; Ervine; Phelps (EP.); also *Bookm.* 47:63-6; D. Figgis, "The Art of J. M. Synge," *Fortn.* 96:1056-68; *Forum* 47:55-70; S. P. Sherman, "John Synge," *Nation* 95:608-11; C. A. Bennett, "The Plays of J. M. Synge," *Yale R.* ns 1:192-205; J. Masefield, "Reminiscences of Synge," *Contemp.* 99:470-8.

From *THE ARAN ISLANDS* [1]

Part I

. . . . . .

A week of sweeping fogs has passed over and given me a strange sense of exile and desolation. I walk round the island nearly every day, yet I can see nothing anywhere but a mass of wet rocks, a strip of surf, and then a tumult of waves.

The salty limestone has grown black with the water that is dripping on it, and wherever I turn there is the same gray obsession twining and wreathing itself among the narrow fields, and the same wail from the wind that shrieks and whistles in the loose rubble [2] of the walls.

At first the people do not give much attention to the wilderness that is round them, but after a few days their voices sink in the kitchen, and their endless talk of pigs and cattle falls to the whisper of men who are telling stories in a haunted house.

The rain continues; but this evening a number of young men were in the kitchen mending their nets, and the bottle of poteen [3] was drawn from its hiding-place.

One cannot think of these people drinking wine on the summit of this crumbling precipice; but their gray poteen, which brings a shock of joy to the blood, seems predestined to keep sanity in men who live forgotten in these worlds of mist.

I sat in the kitchen part of the evening to feel the gayety that was rising, and when I came into my own room after dark, one of the sons came in every time the bottle made its round, to pour me out my share.

It has cleared, and the sun is shining with a luminous warmth that makes the whole island glisten with the splendor of a gem, and fills the sea and sky with a radiance of blue light.

I have come out to lie on the rocks, where I have the black edge of the north island in front of me, Galway Bay, too blue almost to look at, on my right, the Atlantic on my left, a perpendicular cliff under my ankles, and over me innumerable gulls that chase each other in a white cirrus [4] of wings.

A nest of hooded crows is somewhere near me, and one of the old birds is trying to drive me away by letting itself fall like stone every few moments, from about forty yards above me to within reach of my hand.

Gannets are passing up and down above the sound, swooping at times after a mackerel, and farther off I can see the whole fleet of hookers coming out from Kilronan for a night's fishing in the deep water to the west.

As I lie here hour after hour, I seem to enter into the wild pastimes of the cliff, and to become a companion of the cormorants and crows.

Many of the birds display themselves before me with the vanity of barbarians, forming in strange evolutions as long as I am in sight, and returning to their ledge of rock when I am gone. Some are wonderfully expert, and cut graceful figures for an inconceivable time without a flap of their wings, growing so absorbed in their own dexterity that they often collide with one another in their flight, an incident always followed by a wild outburst of abuse. Their language is easier than Gaelic, [5] and I seem to understand the greater part of their cries, though I am not able to answer. There is one plaintive note which they take up in the middle of their usual babble with extraordinary effect, and pass on from one to another along the cliff with a sort of an inarticulate wail, as if they remembered for an instant the horror of the mist.

On the low sheets of rock to the east I can see a number of red and gray figures hurrying about their work. The continual passing in this island between the misery of last night and the splendor of today seems to create an affinity between the moods of these people and the moods of varying rapture and dismay that are frequent in artists, and in certain forms of alienation. [6] Yet it is only in the intonation of a few sentences or some old fragment of melody that I catch the real spirit of the island, for in general the men sit together and talk with endless iteration of the tides and fish, and of the price of kelp in Connemara.

. . . . . .

[1] By permission of John W. Luce and Company, Boston, publishers.

There are three islands: Aranmore, the north island, about nine miles long; Inishmaan, the middle island, about three miles and a half across, and nearly round in form; and the south island, Inishere—in Irish, east island—like the middle island but slightly smaller. They lie about thirty miles from Galway, up the center of the bay, but they are not far from the cliffs of County Clare, on the south, or from the corner of Connemara on the north. Kilronan [is] the principal village on Aranmore.—Synge, Introduction to *The Aran Islands*

[2] coarse masonry

[3] illicitly distilled whiskey

[4] white, filmy cloud

[5] native language of the Scottish highlanders and Irish

[6] insanity

Part II

. . . .

There has been a storm for the last twenty-four hours, and I have been wandering on the cliffs till my hair is stiff with salt. Immense masses of spray were flying up from the base of the cliff, and were caught at times by the wind and whirled away to fall at some distance from the shore. When one of these happened to fall on me, I had to crouch down for an instant, wrapped and blinded by a white hail of foam.

The waves were so enormous that when I saw one more than usually large coming toward me, I turned instinctively to hide myself, as one blinks when struck upon the eyes.

After a few hours the mind grows bewildered with the endless change and struggle of the sea, and an utter despondency replaces the first moment of exhilaration.

At the southwest corner of the island I came upon a number of people gathering the seaweed that is now thick upon the rocks. It was raked from the surf by men, and then carried up to the brow of the cliff by a party of young girls.

In addition to their ordinary clothing these girls wore a raw sheepskin on their shoulders, to catch the oozing sea-water, and they looked strangely wild and seal-like with the salt caked upon their lips and wreaths of seaweed in their hair.

For the rest of my walk I saw no living thing but one flock of curlews, and a few pipits hiding among the stones.

About the sunset the clouds broke and the storm turned to a hurricane. Bars of purple cloud stretched across the sound where immense waves were rolling from the west, wreathed with snowy phantasies of spray. Then there was the bay full of green delirium, and the Twelve Pins[1] touched with mauve and scarlet in the east.

The suggestion from this world of inarticulate power was immense, and now at midnight, when the wind is abating, I am still trembling and flushed with exultation.

. . . .

I am in the north island again, looking out with a singular sensation to the cliffs across the sound. It is hard to believe that those hovels I can just see in the south are filled with people whose lives have the strange quality that is found in the oldest poetry and legend. Compared with them the falling off that has come with the increased prosperity of this island is full of discouragement. The charm which the people over there share with the birds and flowers has been replaced here by the anxiety of men who are eager for gain. The eyes and expressions are different, though the faces are the same, and even the children here seem to have an indefinable modern quality that is absent from the men of Inishmaan.

My voyage from the middle island was wild. The morning was so stormy, that in ordinary circumstances I would not have attempted the passage, but as I had arranged to travel with a curagh[2] that was coming over for the Parish Priest—who is to hold stations[3] on Inishmaan—I did not like to draw back.

I went out in the morning and walked up to the cliffs as usual. Several men I fell in with shook their heads when I told them I was going away, and said they doubted if a curagh could cross the sound with the sea that was in it.

When I went back to the cottage I found the Curate had just come across from the south island, and had had a worse passage than any he had yet experienced.

The tide was to turn at two o'clock, and after that it was thought the sea would be calmer, as the wind and the waves would be running from the same point. We sat about in the kitchen all the morning, with men coming in every few minutes to give their opinion whether the passage should be attempted, and at what points the sea was likely to be at its worst.

At last it was decided we should go, and I started for the pier in a wild shower of rain with the wind howling in the walls. The schoolmaster and a priest who was to have gone with me came out as I was passing through the village and advised me not to make the passage; but my crew had gone on toward the sea, and I thought it better to go after them. The eldest son of the family was coming with me, and I considered that the old man, who knew the waves better than I did, would not send out his son if there was more than reasonable danger.

I found my crew waiting for me under a high wall below the village, and we went on together. The island had never seemed so desolate. Looking out over the black limestone

[1] peaks of Bennebeola, a mountain group in Galway

[2] or coracle, a small, almost circular boat of woven wicker covered with hide, leather, or canvas

[3] church services representing the successive stages of Christ's Passion

through the driving rain to the gulf of struggling waves, an indescribable feeling of dejection came over me.

The old man gave me his view of the use of fear.

"A man who is not afraid of the sea will soon be drownded," he said, "for he will be going out on a day he shouldn't. But we do be afraid of the sea, and we do only be drownded now and again."

A little crowd of neighbors had collected lower down to see me off, and as we crossed the sandhills we had to shout to each other to be heard above the wind.

The crew carried down the curagh and then stood under the lee of the pier tying on their hats with string and drawing on their oilskins.

They tested the braces of the oars, and the oarpins, and everything in the curagh with a care I had not yet seen them give to anything, then my bag was lifted in, and we were ready. Besides the four men of the crew a man was going with us who wanted a passage to this island. As he was scrambling into the bow, an old man stood forward from the crowd.

"Don't take that man with you," he said. "Last week they were taking him to Clare and the whole of them were near drownded. Another day he went to Inisheer and they broke three ribs of the curagh, and they coming back. There is not the like of him for ill-luck in the three islands."

"The divil choke your old gob," said the man, "you will be talking."

We set off. It was a four-oared curagh, and I was given the last seat so as to leave the stern for the man who was steering with an oar, worked at right angles to the others by an extra thole-pin [1] in the stern gunnel.

When we had gone about a hundred yards they ran up a bit of a sail in the bow, and the pace became extraordinarily rapid.

The shower had passed over and the wind had fallen; but large, magnificently brilliant waves were rolling down on us at right angles to our course.

Every instant the steersman whirled us round with a sudden stroke of his oar, the prow reared up and then fell into the next furrow with a crash, throwing up masses of spray. As it did so, the stern in its turn was thrown up, and both the steersman, who let go his oar and clung with both hands to the gunnel, and myself, were lifted high up above the sea.

[1] a wooden or metal pin set in the gunnel (edge) of a boat to serve as fulcrum for the oar

The wave passed, we regained our course and rowed violently for a few yards, when the same maneuver had to be repeated. As we worked out into the sound we began to meet another class of waves, that could be seen for some distance towering above the rest.

When one of these came in sight, the first effort was to get beyond its reach. The steersman began crying out in Gaelic, "Siubhal, siubhal," ("Run, run"), and sometimes, when the mass was gliding toward us with horrible speed, his voice rose to a shriek. Then the rowers themselves took up the cry, and the curagh seemed to leap and quiver with the frantic terror of a beast till the wave passed behind it or fell with a crash beside the stern.

It was in this racing with the waves that our chief danger lay. If the wave could be avoided, it was better to do so; but if it overtook us while we were trying to escape, and caught us on the broadside, our destruction was certain. I could see the steersman quivering with the excitement of his task, for any error in his judgment would have swamped us.

We had one narrow escape. A wave appeared high above the rest, and there was the usual moment of intense exertion. It was of no use, and in an instant the wave seemed to be hurling itself upon us. With a yell of rage the steersman struggled with his oar to bring our prow to meet it. He had almost succeeded, when there was a crash and rush of water round us. I felt as if I had been struck upon the back with knotted ropes. White foam gurgled round my knees and eyes. The curagh reared up, swaying and trembling for a moment, and then fell safely into the furrow.

This was our worst moment, though more than once, when several waves came so closely together that we had no time to regain control of the curagh between them, we had some dangerous work. Our lives depended upon the skill and courage of the men, as the life of the rider or swimmer is often in his own hands, and the excitement of the struggle was too great to allow time for fear.

I enjoyed the passage. Down in this shallow trough of canvas that bent and trembled with the motion of the men, I had a far more intimate feeling of the glory and power of the waves than I have ever known in a steamer.

. . . .

Part IV

. . . .

This evening the old man told me a story he had heard long ago on the mainland:—

There was a young woman, he said, and she had a child. In a little time the woman died and they buried her the day after. That night another woman—a woman of the family—was sitting by the fire with the child on her lap, giving milk to it out of a cup. Then the woman they were after burying opened the door, and came into the house. She went over to the fire, and she took a stool and sat down before the other woman. Then she put out her hand and took the child on her lap, and gave it her breast. After that she put the child in the cradle and went over to the dresser and took milk and potatoes off it, and ate them. Then she went out. The other woman was frightened, and she told the man of the house when he came back, and two young men. They said they would be there the next night, and if she came back they would catch hold of her. She came the next night and gave the child her breast, and when she got up to go to the dresser, the man of the house caught hold of her, but he fell down on the floor. Then the two young men caught hold of her and they held her. She told them she was away with the fairies, and they could not keep her that night, though she was eating no food with the fairies, the way she might be able to come back to her child. Then she told them they would all be leaving that part of the country on the Oidhche Shamhna,[1] and that there would be four or five hundred of them riding on horses, and herself would be on a gray horse, riding behind a young man. And she told them to go down to a bridge they would be crossing that night, and to wait at the head of it, and when she would be coming up she would slow the horse and they would be able to throw something on her and on the young man, and they would fall over on the ground and be saved.

She went away then, and on the Oidhche Shamhna the men went down and got her back. She had four children after that, and in the end she died.

It was not herself they buried at all the first time, but some old thing the fairies put in her place.

The young man[2] has been buried, and his funeral was one of the strangest scenes I have met with. People could be seen going down to his house from early in the day, yet when I went there with the old man about the middle of the afternoon, the coffin was still lying in front of the door, with the men and women of the family standing round beating it, and keening[3] over it, in a great crowd of people. A little later every one knelt down and a last prayer was said. Then the cousins of the dead man got ready two oars and some pieces of rope—the men of his own family seemed too broken with grief to know what they were doing—the coffin was tied up, and the procession began. The old women walked close behind the coffin, and I happened to take a place just after them, among the first of the men. The rough lane to the graveyard slopes away toward the east, and the crowd of women going down before me in their red dresses, cloaked with red petticoats, with the waistband that is held round the head just seen from behind, had a strange effect, to which the white coffin and the unity of color gave a nearly cloistral quietness.

This time the graveyard was filled with withered grass and bracken[4] instead of the early ferns that were to be seen everywhere at the other funeral I have spoken of, and the grief of the people was of a different kind, as they had come to bury a young man who had died in his first manhood, instead of an old woman of eighty. For this reason the keen lost a part of its formal nature, and was recited as the expression of intense personal grief by the young men and women of the man's own family.

When the coffin had been laid down near the grave that was to be opened, two long switches were cut out from the brambles among the rocks, and the length and breadth of the coffin were marked on them. Then the men began their work, clearing off stones and thin layers of earth, and breaking up an old coffin that was in the place into which the new one had to be lowered. When a number of blackened boards and pieces of bone had been thrown up with the clay, a skull was lifted out and placed upon a gravestone. Immediately the old woman, the mother of the dead man, took it up in her hands, and carried it away by herself. Then she sat down and put it in her lap—it was the skull of her own

[1] the night of the Feast of All-Souls
[2] He had been drowned a few weeks before.

[3] wailing a dirge
[4] large fern

mother—and began keening and shrieking over it with the wildest lamentation.

As the pile of moldering clay got higher beside the grave a heavy smell began to rise from it, and the men hurried with their work, measuring the hole repeatedly with the two rods of bramble. When it was nearly deep enough the old woman got up and came back to the coffin, and began to beat on it, holding the skull in her left hand. This last moment of grief was the most terrible of all. The young women were nearly lying among the stones, worn out with their passion of grief, yet raising themselves every few moments to beat with magnificent gestures on the boards of the coffin. The young men were worn out also, and their voices cracked continually in the wail of the keen.

When everything was ready the sheet was unpinned from the coffin, and it was lowered into its place. Then an old man took a wooden vessel with holy water in it, and a wisp of bracken, and the people crowded round him while he splashed the water over them. They seemed eager to get as much of it as possible, more than one old woman crying out with a humorous voice—"Tabhair dham braon eile, a Mhourteen" ("Give me another drop, Martin").

When the grave was half filled in, I wandered round toward the north, watching two seals that were chasing each other near the surf. I reached the Sandy Head as the light began to fail, and found some of the men I knew best fishing there with a sort of dragnet. It is a tedious process, and I sat for a long time on the sand watching the net being put out, and then drawn in again by eight men working together with a slow rhythmical movement.

As they talked to me and gave me a little poteen and a little bread when they thought I was hungry, I could not help feeling that I was talking with men who were under a judgment of death. I knew that every one of them would be drowned in the sea in a few years and battered naked on the rocks, or would die in his own cottage and be buried with another fearful scene in the graveyard I had come from.

1907

WILLIAM BUTLER YEATS
1865-

Born at Sandymount, Dublin, son of an Irish painter, Yeats spent his childhood at Sligo, in the wildest part of western Ireland, feeding his mind upon the quaint fairy tales and legends of the Irish peasantry, many of which he later edited. He studied painting, but before long he found himself absorbed in the movement to make the intellectual life of Ireland free from any impeding British influence and an expression of the native Celtic genius. He then began to write, and became one of the founders of the Irish National Theater.

Yeats, called by "A.E." the finest artist in Irish literature, continues to be an important figure in the Irish Free State, for his services both to national literature and to economic and political life. As a leader of the Celtic revival he was largely responsible for the recognition of Gaelic as an official language and for the recent growth of a strong national poetry expressing in simple English the peculiar native charm of Irish folk lore and mythology. In addition to his achievements in poetry, prose, and drama, for which he was awarded the Nobel Prize in 1923 for literature, Mr. Yeats is prominent for his political activities and, since 1922, as a senator of the Free State, he has been able to influence Irish national culture by his services to education.

His work shows traces of many influences: Celtic legend, Oriental tales, French symbolism, Blake. It may be divided into miscellaneous prose, best represented by *Celtic Twilight,* 1893; lyrical poetry, of which the best is in *Wind Among the Reeds,* 1899, and *The Wild Swans at Coole,* 1919; and poetic dramas, *The Countess Kathleen,* 1892, *The Land of Heart's Desire,* 1894, *Deirdre,* 1907.

Biography: W. B. Yeats, *Reveries Over Childhood and Youth,* 1916; Forrest Reid, 1915; J. M. Hone, 1916; Criticism: Ervine; Untermeyer; Phelps (EP); Kennedy; Monro; G. W. Russell ("A.E."), "Yeats's Early Poems," *Liv. Age* 327: 464-6; J. Eglington, "Yeats and his Story," *Dial* 80:357-66; L. Jones, "The Later Poetry of W. B. Yeats," *No. Am.* 219:499-506; H. S. Gorman, "The Later Mr. Yeats," *Outl.* 130:655-6.

THE LAKE ISLE OF INNISFREE [1]

I will arise and go now, and go to Innisfree,
And a small cabin build there, of clay and wattles [2] made;
Nine bean rows will I have there, a hive for the honey bee,
And live alone in the bee-loud glade.

And I shall have some peace there, for peace comes dropping slow,
Dropping from the veils of the morning to where the cricket sings;
There midnight's all a glimmer, and noon a purple glow,
And evening full of the linnet's wings.

[1] From William Butler Yeats's *Poetical Works,* Vol. I, copyright, 1917, by permission of The Macmillan Company, publishers.

[2] woven twigs

I will arise and go now, for always night and day
I hear lake water lapping with low sounds by the shore;
While I stand on the roadway, or on the pavements gray,
I hear it in the deep heart's core.

1892

THE WILD SWANS AT COOLE[1]

The trees are in their autumn beauty,
The woodland paths are dry,
Under the October twilight the water
Mirrors a still sky;
Upon the brimming water among the stones
Are nine and fifty swans.

The nineteenth Autumn has come upon me
Since I first made my count;
I saw, before I had well finished,
All suddenly mount
And scatter wheeling in great broken rings
Upon their clamorous wings.

I have looked upon those brilliant creatures,
And now my heart is sore.
All's changed since I, hearing at twilight,
The first time on this shore,
The bell-beat of their wings above my head,
Trod with a lighter tread.

Unwearied still, lover by lover,
They paddle in the cold,
Companionable streams or climb the air;
Their hearts have not grown old;
Passion or conquest, wander where they will,
Attend upon them still.

But now they drift on the still water
Mysterious, beautiful;
Among what rushes will they build,
By what lake's edge or pool
Delight men's eyes, when I awake some day
To find they have flown away?

1917

FRANCIS E. LEDWIDGE
1891-1917

According to his own charming and rather naïve account of his childhood in Ireland, "the poet of the blackbird" came of a family of soldiers and poets. His father died when the boy was but two; gradually the elder children went away from home, and Francis, left with his mother, received his education at the National School. As a child he preferred lonely, imaginative wanderings to games with companions, and began writing at an early age. Leaving school at fourteen and apprenticed to a Dublin grocer, he ran away from "brick horizons" back to the farm home, where he read in a wide range from Chaucer to Swinburne, and thirsted for travel and adventure. In 1912 he was discovered by Lord Dunsany, under whose sponsorship were published his first poems, *Songs of the Fields*, 1914, followed by *Songs of Peace*, 1916, and *Last Songs*, 1917, written at the front in the World War. Ledwidge enlisted in Dunsany's company, saw active service on several fronts, and fell in Flanders.

It is not as a background for man, but as man's chief joy that Ledwidge sees nature. He sees it as one whose daily life is spent in the fields and between the hawthorn hedgerows. It is the fresh, unconventional phrasing in which he describes unaccustomed things that gives his work charm, and also the spontaneous, artless nature of his imagination.

Criticism: J. Drinkwater, "Poetry of Francis Ledwidge, *Edin. R.* 228:180-9; same, *Liv. Age* 298:601-7; K. Tynan, "Francis Ledwidge," *Cath. World* 106:185-95; D. Gordon, "Francis Ledwidge," *Nation* 107:446-7; L. Chase, "Francis Ledwidge," *Liv. Age* 306:304-9; same, *Cent.* 95: 386-91; P. Colum, "Francis Ledwidge and his Poetry," *Liv. Age* 323:339-41.

JUNE[2]

Broom out the floor now, lay the fender by,
And plant this bee-sucked bough of woodbine there,
And let the window down. The butterfly
Floats in upon the sunbeam, and the fair
Tanned face of June, the nomad gipsy, laughs
Above her widespread wares, the while she tells
The farmers' fortunes in the fields, and quaffs
The water from the spider-peopled wells.

The hedges are all drowned in green grass seas,
And bobbing poppies flare like Elmor's light,[3]
While siren-like the pollen-stainéd bees
Drone in the clover depths. And up the height
The cuckoo's voice is hoarse and broke[4] with joy,
And on the lowland crops the crows make raid,
Nor fear the clappers of the farmer's boy,
Who sleeps, like drunken Noah, in the shade.

[1] From William Butler Yeats's *The Wild Swans at Coole*, copyright, 1918. By permission of The Macmillan Company, publishers.

[2] From *Songs of the Fields*, 1915. Reprinted by permission of Lord Dunsany.

[3] St. Elmo's fire, or light; a flamelike appearance sometimes seen during a storm, especially at mastheads and yardarms; see Ariel's description, *Tempest* I, ii, 193-201, p. 185.

[4] old and dialectic form of past participle

And loop this red rose in that hazel ring
That snares your little ear, for June is short
And we must joy in it and dance and sing,
And from her bounty draw her rosy worth.
Aye! soon the swallows will be flying south,
The wind wheel north to gather in the snow,
Even the roses spilt on youth's red mouth
Will soon blow down the road all roses go.

1915

THOUGHTS AT THE TRYSTING STILE [1]

Come, May, and hang a white flag on each thorn, [2]
Make truce with earth and heaven; the April child
Now hides her sulky face deep in the morn
Of your new flowers by the water wild
And in the ripples of the rising grass,
And rushes bent to let the south wind pass
On with her tumult of swift nomad wings,
And broken domes of downy dandelion.
Only in spasms now the blackbird sings.
The hour is all a-dream.

Nets of woodbine
Throw woven shadows over dreaming flowers,
And dreaming, a bee-luring lily bends
Its tender bell where blue dyke-water cowers
Thro' briars, and folded ferns, and gripping ends
Of wild convolvulus. [3]

The lark's sky-way
Is desolate.

I watch an apple-spray
Beckon across a wall as if it knew
I wait the calling of the orchard maid.

Inly I feel that she will come in blue,
With yellow on her hair, and two curls strayed
Out of her comb's loose stocks, and I shall steal
Behind and lay my hands upon her eyes,
"Look not, but be my Psyche!"

And her peal
Of laughter will ring far, and as she tries
For freedom I will call her names of flowers
That climb up walls; then thro' the twilight hours
We'll talk about the loves of ancient queens,
And kisses like wasp-honey, false and sweet,
And how we are entangled in love's snares
Like wind-looped flowers.

1915

[1] From *Songs of the Fields*, 1915. Reprinted by permission of Lord Dunsany.
[2] hawthorn, or blackthorn, bearing white blossoms
[3] a wild flower like the morning-glory

A TWILIGHT IN MIDDLE MARCH [1]

Within the oak a throb of pigeon wings
Fell silent, and gray twilight hushed the fold, [4]
And spiders' hammocks swung on half-oped things
That shook like foreigners upon our cold.
A gipsy lit a fire and made a sound
Of moving tins, and from an oblong moon
The river seemed to gush across the ground
To the cracked meter of a marching tune.

And then three syllables of melody
Dropped from a blackbird's flute, and died apart
Far in the dewy dark. No more but three,
Yet sweeter music never touched a heart
'Neath the blue domes of London. Flute and reed,
Suggesting feelings of the solitude
When will was all the Delphi I would heed, [5]
Lost like a wind within a summer wood
From little knowledge where great sorrows brood.

1915

THE LOST ONES [1]

Somewhere is music from the linnets' bills,
And thro' the sunny flowers the bee-wings drone,
And white bells of convolvulus on hills
Of quiet May make silent ringing, blown
Hither and thither by the wind of showers,
And somewhere all the wandering birds have flown;
And the brown breath of Autumn chills the flowers.

But where are all the loves of long ago?
Oh, little twilight ship blown up the tide,
Where are the faces laughing in the glow
Of morning years, the lost ones scattered wide?
Give me your hand, O brother, let us go
Crying about the dark for those who died.

1915

WINIFRED M. LETTS 1882-

One of the contemporary writers of Ireland, where she was born, educated, and still lives, Miss Letts has contributed to various periodicals, and produced poems, novels, books for children, and two dramas, performed at the Abbey Theater, Dublin. Among her volumes of poetry are: *Songs from Leinster*, 1913; *Hallowe'en*, 1916; *The Spires of Oxford*, 1917; and *More Songs from Leinster*, 1926. Her poems reveal a sincere response to the appealing charm and beauty of her country; and

[4] sheepfold
[5] The oracle at Delphi revealed its will to devotees; here, "my will was my sole guide."

reproduce the characteristic mingling of humor and sadness found in the everyday life of the simple people about her, toilers of the city, fisher-folk, peasants, young and old, drab or picturesque. Her war lyrics are full of the pathos of youth gallantly meeting the nation's call to arms.

THE SPIRES OF OXFORD [1]

(As seen from the train)

I saw the spires of Oxford
  As I was passing by,
The gray spires of Oxford
  Against a pearl-gray sky.
My heart was with the Oxford men
  Who went abroad to die.

The years go fast in Oxford,
  The golden years and gay,
The hoary Colleges look down
  On careless boys at play.
But when the bugles sounded war
  They put their games away.

They left the peaceful river,
  The cricket-field, the quad, [2]
The shaven lawns of Oxford
  To seek a bloody sod—
They gave their merry youth away
  For country and for God.

God rest you happy, gentlemen,
  Who laid your good lives down,
Who took the khaki and the gun
  Instead of cap and gown.
God bring you to a fairer place
  Than even Oxford town.

1915

THE CONNAUGHT RANGERS [1]

I saw the Connaught Rangers when they were passing by,
On a spring day, a good day, with gold rifts in the sky.
Themselves were marching steadily along the Liffey quay [3]
An' I see the young proud look of them as if it were today!
The bright lads, the right lads, I have them in my mind,
With the green flags on their bayonets all fluttering in the wind.

A last look at old Ireland, a last good-bye maybe,
Then the gray sea, the wide sea, my grief upon the sea!
And when will they come home, says I, when will they see once more
The dear blue hills of Wicklow and Wexford's dim gray shore?
The brave lads of Ireland, no better lads you'll find,
With the green flags on their bayonets all fluttering in the wind!

Three years have passed since that spring day, sad years for them and me.
Green graves there are in Serbia and in Galipoli.
And many who went by that day along the muddy street
Will never hear the roadway ring to their triumphant feet.
But they march before Him, God's welcome will be kind,
And the green flags on their bayonets will flutter in the wind.

1918

[1] By permission from *The Spires of Oxford and Other Poems,* by W. M. Letts. London: John Murray. New York: E. P. Dutton & Company.
[2] a four-square enclosure surrounded by college buildings
[3] masonry embankment of the river Liffey at Dublin

JAMES STEPHENS 1882-

George Moore tells us that Stephens was "a poor boy without education or a penny, who had wandered all over Ireland, and would have lost his life in Belfast from hunger had it not been for a charitable apple-woman." In some way the boy picked up an education, and managed to find work in a lawyer's office, where he was discovered by "A.E." (See page 851.) As an ardent nationalist, he has worked for the establishment of the Irish Free State. He is an authority on Gaelic art, and is now assistant curator in the Dublin National Gallery.

He has produced several volumes of verse (*The Hill of Vision,* 1912, *Songs from the Clay,* 1915, *Collected Poems,* 1926). His fiction includes *The Crock of Gold, The Charwoman's Daughter,* 1912, *The Demi-Gods,* 1914, and *Irish Fairy Tales,* 1920. Despite the faults of technique that most critics find in Stephens's verse, his poetry is impressive in the unerringness of its descriptions and characterizations. His characters and pictures generally show the seamy side of life, but he treats his subjects with strength and with a sympathy devoid of sentimentality. His approach to profound themes sometimes savors of cynicism and swagger.

Criticism: Boyd; Phelps (EP); Wilkinson; Sturgeon; *Bookm.* 39:493-4; S. Gwynn, "Making of a Poet," *19th Cent.* 67:68-71; *Liv. Age* 265: 487-8; R. Shafer, "James Stephens and the Poetry of the Day," *Forum* 50:560-9; W. A. Bradley, "James Stephens: Appreciation," *Bookm.* 41:20-2; E. Mason, "Personality of Mr. James Stephens," *Liv. Age* 305:540-3; J. Gollomb, "Here are Ladies in Paris," *Bookm.* 59:715-20, a personal sketch.

HATE [1]

My enemy came nigh;
And I
Stared fiercely in his face:
My lips went writhing back in a grimace,
And stern I watched him from a narrowed eye:

Then, as I turned away,
My enemy,
That bitter-heart, and savage, said to me:

—Some day, when this is past;
When all the arrows that we have are cast;
We may ask one another why we hate?
And fail to find a story to relate:
It may seem to us, then, a mystery
That we could hate each other—
Thus said he; and did not turn away;
Waiting to hear what I might have to say!

But I fled quickly: fearing, if I stayed,
I might have kissed him, as I would a maid.

1909

TO THE FOUR COURTS, PLEASE [1]

The driver rubbed at his nettly chin
With a huge, loose forefinger, crooked and black,
And his wobbly violet lips sucked in,
And puffed out again and hung down slack:
One fang shone through his lop-sided smile,
In his little pouched eye flickered years of guile.

And the horse, poor beast, it was ribbed and forked,
And its ears hung down, and its eyes were old,
And its knees were knuckly, and as we talked
It swung the stiff neck that could scarcely hold
Its big, skinny head up—then I stepped in,
And the driver climbed to his seat with a grin.

God help the horse, and the driver, too,
And the people and beast who have never a friend!
For the driver easily might have been you,
And the horse be me by a different end!
And nobody knows how their days may cease;
And the poor, when they're old, have little of peace!

1909

[1] From *Collected Poems* by James Stephens. By permission of The Macmillan Company, publishers.

"A.E." (GEORGE WILLIAM RUSSELL) 1867-

"A.E.," Irish painter, essayist, and publicist, was born at Lurgan, County Armagh, Ireland, and received his education in Irish schools. He has worked actively for the political independence of Ireland, passionately protesting against its exploitation by an alien race. For many years he has given himself without stint to bettering the industrial, especially the agricultural, conditions of his country, to its artistic development, and to its political and social unity north and south. "My conscience would not let me have peace," he says, "unless I worked with Irishmen at the reconstruction of Irish life." He believes that the true course of Irish development lies in going back, in spirit, by slow degrees, toward the primitive Celtic genius and nurturing a civilization as separate and distinct "as the Japanese."

Since 1904 he has published many volumes of poetry full of the traditions and mythology of the Celtic race and reflecting much of the pathos and melancholy of the Celtic spirit. In his *Collected Poems*, 1926, he has included those pieces which he ranks as those written in the moments of surest inspiration. The most characteristic of these express that mood in which nature, in a moment of spiritual exaltation, becomes the pathway to the infinite. "The universe," he says, "exists for the purposes of the soul." This is why he is termed a mystic. His expression of this idea should be compared with that of Wordsworth in "Lines Written in Early Spring," p. 452. The wide range of his interests and much of the variety of his imagination may be seen in his essays and tales, *Imaginations and Reveries*, 1915.

Biography: D. Figgis, *"A.E.," a Study of a Man and a Nation*, 1916. Criticism: Ervine; also *No. Am.* 212:238-49; Phelps (EP); R. C. Field, "The Opinions of 'A.E.'" *Cent.* 103:2-9; "The Spiritual Leader of New Ireland," *Cur. Opin.* 72:74-77.

A SUMMER NIGHT [2]

Her mist of primroses within her breast
Twilight hath folded up, and o'er the west,
Seeking remoter valleys long hath gone,
Not yet hath come her sister of the dawn.
Silence and coolness now the earth enfold,
Jewels of glittering green, long mists of gold,
Hazes of nebulous silver veil the height,
And shake in tremors through the shadowy night.
Heard through the stillness, as in whispered words,
The wandering God-guided wings of birds
Ruffle the dark. The little lives that lie
Deep hid in grass join in a long-drawn sigh

[2] From *Collected Poems by "A.E."* By permission of The Macmillan Company, publishers.

More softly still; and unheard through the blue
The falling of innumerable dew,
Lifts with gray fingers all the leaves that lay
Burned in the heat of the consuming day.
The lawns and lakes lie in this night of love,
Admitted to the majesty above.
Earth with the starry company hath part;
The waters hold all heaven within their heart,
And glimmer o'er with wave-lips everywhere
Lifted to meet the angel lips of air.
The many homes of men shine near and far,
Peace-laden as the tender evening star,
The late home-coming folk anticipate
Their rest beyond the passing of the gate,
And tread with sleep-filled hearts and drowsy feet.
Oh, far away and wonderful and sweet
All this, all this. But far too many things
Obscuring, as a cloud of seraph wings
Blinding the seeker for the Lord behind,
I fall away in weariness of mind.
And think how far apart are I and you,
Beloved, from those spirit children who
Felt but one single Being long ago,
Whispering in gentleness and leaning low
Out of its majesty, as child to child.
I think upon it all with heart grown wild.
Hearing no voice, howe'er my spirit broods,
No whisper from the dense infinitudes,
This world of myriad things whose distance awes.
Ah me; how innocent our childhood was!

1903

PROMISE [1]

Be not so desolate
Because thy dreams have flown
And the hall of the heart is empty
And silent as stone,
As age left by children
Sad and alone.

Those delicate children,
Thy dreams, still endure.
All pure and lovely things
Wend to the Pure.
Sigh not: unto the fold
Their way was sure.

Thy gentlest dreams, thy frailest,
Even those that were
Born and lost in a heart-beat,
Shall meet thee there.
They are become immortal
In shining air.

The unattainable beauty
The thought of which was pain,
That flickered in eyes and on lips
And vanished again:
That fugitive beauty
Thou shalt attain.

Those lights innumerable
That led thee on and on,
The Masque of Time ended,
Shall glow into one.
It shall be with thee forever,
Thy travel done.

1924

[1] From *Collected Poems by "A.E."* By permission of The Macmillan Company, publishers.

LORD DUNSANY 1878-

Lord Dunsany is said by his friends to have his creative power completely in control. He spends the greater part of his time in physical activity, including big-game hunting and sports; but when he will he commands his marvelous imagination, and at a sitting can write a one-act play. Though an Irishman, he was born in London, attended Eton and Sandhurst, and succeeded his father in 1899 in an English title. He is devoted to sports, served in the Boer War, and the World War, and since 1909, when *The Glittering Gate* was presented in Dublin, has been known as a playwright and writer of tales.

Dunsany has the power of leading the reader into a world made in likeness of our own, yet one in which men, women, and beasts are imbued with the vague splendors that belonged to the Golden Age or the Twilight of the Gods. As a creator in the realm of the non-earthly he is often compared with Poe, but his imagination is less somber. "He is, in fact, the foremost myth-maker, with Shelley as his nearest but far-away rival."—Shepard.

Biography: E. H. Bierstadt, *Dunsany the Dramatist,* 1919. Criticism: G. W. Russell, "A Maker of Mythologies," *Liv. Age* 329:464-6; C. E. Lawrence, "Lord Dunsany: a Modern Dreamer," *Liv. Age* 310:531-3; O. Shepard, "Lord Dunsany—Mythmaker," *Scrib.* 69:595-9; E. G. Boyd, "Lord Dunsany, Dreamer," *Forum* 57:497-508, excellent critical appraisal of works.

THE LORD OF CITIES [2]

I came one day upon a road that wandered so aimlessly that it was suited to my mood, so I followed it, and it led me presently among deep woods. Somewhere in the midst of them Autumn held his court, sitting wreathed with gorgeous garlands; and it was the day before his annual festival of the Dance of Leaves, the courtly festival upon which hungry Winter rushes mob-like, and there arise the furious cries of the North Wind

[2] From *The Sword of Welleran.* Reprinted by permission of the author.

triumphing, and all the splendor and grace of the woods is gone, and Autumn flees away, discrowned and forgotten, and never again returns. Other Autumns arise, other Autumns, and fall before other Winters. A road led away to the left, but my road went straight on. The road to the left had a trodden appearance; there were wheel tracks on it, and it seemed the correct way to take. It looked as if no one could have any business with the road that led straight on and up the hill. Therefore I went straight on and up the hill; and here and there on the road grew blades of grass undisturbed in the repose and hush that the road had earned from going up and down the world; for you can go by this road, as you can go by all roads, to London, to Lincoln, to the North of Scotland, to the West of Wales, and to Wrellisford, where roads end. Presently the woods ended, and I came to the open fields and at the same moment to the top of the hill, and saw the high places of Somerset and the downs[1] of Wilts[2] spread out along the horizon. Suddenly I saw underneath me the village of Wrellisford, with no sound in its street but the voice of the Wrellis roaring as he tumbled over a weir above the village. So I followed my road down over the crest of the hill, and the road became more languid as I descended, and less and less concerned with the cares of a highway. Here a spring broke out in the middle of it, and here another. The road never heeded. A stream ran right across it, still it straggled on. Suddenly it gave up the minimum property that a road should possess, and, renouncing its connection with High Streets, its lineage of Piccadilly, shrank to one side and became an unpretentious footpath. Then it led me to the old bridge over the stream, and thus I came to Wrellisford, and found after traveling in many lands a village with no wheel tracks in its street. On the other side of the bridge, my friend the road struggled a few yards up a grassy slope, and there ceased. Over all the village hung a great stillness, with the roar of the Wrellis cutting right across it, and there came occasionally the bark of a dog that kept watch over the broken stillness and over the sanctity of that untraveled road. That terrible and wasting fever that, unlike so many plagues, comes not from the East but from the West, the fever of hurry, had not come here—only the Wrellis hurried on his eternal quest, but it was a calm and placid hurry that gave one time for song. It was in the early afternoon, and nobody was about. Either they worked beyond the mysterious valley that nursed Wrellisford and hid it from the world, or else they secluded themselves within their old-time houses that were roofed with tiles of stone. I sat down upon the old stone bridge and watched the Wrellis, who seemed to me to be the only traveler that came from far away into this village where roads end, and passed on beyond it. And yet the Wrellis comes singing out of eternity, and tarries for a very little while in the village where roads end, and passes on into eternity again; and so surely do all that dwell in Wrellisford. I wondered as I leaned upon the bridge in what place the Wrellis would first find the sea, whether as he wound idly through meadows on his long quest he would suddenly behold him, and, leaping down over some rocky cliff, take to him at once the message of the hills. Or whether, widening slowly into some grand and tidal estuary, he would take his waste of waters to the sea and the might of the river should meet with the might of the waves, like to two Emperors clad in gleaming mail meeting midway between two hosts of war; and the little Wrellis would become a haven for returning ships and a setting-out place for adventurous men.

A little beyond the bridge there stood an old mill with a ruined roof, and a small branch of the Wrellis rushed through its emptiness shouting, like a boy playing alone in a corridor of some desolate house. The mill-wheel was gone, but there lay there still great bars and wheels and cogs, the bones of some dead industry. I know not what industry was once lord in that house, I know not what retinue of workers mourns him now; I only know who is lord there today in all those empty chambers. For as soon as I entered, I saw a whole wall draped with his marvelous black tapestry, without price because inimitable and too delicate to pass from hand to hand among merchants. I looked at the wonderful complexity of its infinite threads, my finger sank into it for more than an inch without feeling the touch; so black it was and so carefully wrought, somberly covering the whole of the wall, that it might have been worked to commemorate the deaths of all that ever lived there, as indeed it was. I looked through a hole in the wall into an inner chamber where a worn-out driving band went among many wheels, and there this priceless inimitable stuff not merely clothed the walls but hung from

[1] treeless chalk uplands along the south coast of England

[2] Wiltshire, a county in the south of England

bars and ceiling in beautiful draperies, in marvelous festoons. Nothing was ugly in this desolate house, for the busy artist's soul of its present lord had beautified everything in its desolation. It was the unmistakable work of the spider, in whose house I was, and the house was utterly desolate but for him, and silent but for the roar of the Wrellis and the shout of the little stream. Then I turned homeward; and as I went up and over the hill and lost the sight of the village, I saw the road whiten and harden and gradually broaden out till the tracks of wheels appeared; and it went afar to take the young men of Wrellisford into the wide ways of the earth—to the new West and the mysterious East, and into the troubled South.

And that night, when the house was still and sleep was far off, hushing hamlets and giving ease to cities, my fancy wandered up that aimless road and came suddenly to Wrellisford. And it seemed to me that the traveling of so many people for so many years between Wrellisford and John o' Groat's,[1] talking to one another as they went or muttering alone, had given the road a voice. And it seemed to me that night that the road spoke to the river by the Wrellisford bridge, speaking with the voice of many pilgrims. And the road said to the river: "I rest here. How is it with you?"

And the river, who is always speaking, said: "I rest nowhere from doing the Work of the World. I carry the murmur of inner lands to the sea, and to the abysses voices of the hills."

"It is I," said the road, "that do the Work of the World, and take from city to city the rumor of each. There is nothing higher than Man and the making of cities. What do you do for Man?"

And the river said: "Beauty and song are higher than Man. I carry the news seaward of the first song of the thrush after the furious retreat of winter northward, and the first timid anemone learns from me that she is safe and that spring has truly come. Oh, but the song of all the birds in spring is more beautiful than Man, and the first coming of the hyacinth more delectable than his face! When spring is fallen upon the days of summer, I carry away with mournful joy at night petal by petal the rhododendron's bloom. No lit[2] procession of purple kings is nigh so fair as that. No beautiful death of well-beloved men hath such a glory of forlorness. And I bear far away the pink and white petals of the apple-blossom's youth when the laborious time comes for his work in the world and for the bearing of apples. And I am robed each day and every night anew with the beauty of Heaven, and I make lovely visions of the trees. But Man! What is Man? In the ancient parliament of the elder hills, when the gray ones speak together, they say naught of Man, but concern themselves only with their brethren the stars. Or when they wrap themselves in purple cloaks at evening, they lament some old irreparable wrong, or, uttering some mountain hymn, all mourn the set of sun."

"Your beauty," said the road, "and the beauty of the sky, and of the rhododendron blossom and of spring, live only in the mind of Man, and except in the mind of Man the mountains have no voices. Nothing is beautiful that has not been seen by Man's eye. Or if your rhododendron blossom was beautiful for a moment, it soon withered and was drowned, and spring soon passes away; beauty can only live on in the mind of Man. I bring thought into the mind of Man swiftly from distant places every day. I know the Telegraph—I know him well; he and I have walked for hundreds of miles together. There is no work in the world except for Man and the making of his cities. I take wares to and fro from city to city."

"My little stream in the field there," said the river, "used to make wares in that house for a while once."

"Ah," said the road, "I remember, but I brought cheaper ones from distant cities. Nothing is of any importance but making cities for Man."

"I know so little about him," said the river, "but I have a great deal of work to do—I have all this water to send down to the sea; and then tomorrow or next day all the leaves of Autumn will be coming this way. It will be very beautiful. The sea is a very, very wonderful place. I know all about it; I have heard shepherd boys singing of it, and sometimes before a storm the gulls come up. It is a place all blue and shining and full of pearls, and has in it coral islands and isles of spice, and storms and galleons and the bones of Drake. The sea is much greater than Man. When I come to the sea, he will know that I have worked well for him. But I must hurry, for I have much to do. This bridge delays me a little; some day I will carry it away."

[1] the most northerly point of Scotland
[2] torch-lit

"Oh, you must not do that," said the road.

"Oh, not for a long time," said the river. "Some centuries perhaps—and I have much to do besides. There is my song to sing, for instance, and that alone is more beautiful than any noise that Man makes."

"All work is for Man," said the road, "and for the building of cities. There is no beauty or romance or mystery in the sea except for the men that sail abroad upon it, and for those that stay at home and dream of them. As for your song, it rings night and morning, year in, year out, in the ears of men that are born in Wrellisford; at night it is part of their dreams, at morning it is the voice of day, and so it becomes part of their souls. But the song is not beautiful in itself. I take these men with your song in their souls up over the edge of the valley and a long way off beyond, and I am a strong and dusty road up there, and they go with your song in their souls and turn it into music and gladden cities. But nothing is the Work of the World except work for Man."

"I wish I was quite sure about the Work of the World," said the stream; "I wish I knew for certain for whom we work. I feel almost sure that it is for the sea. He is very great and beautiful. I think that there can be no greater master than the sea. I think that some day he may be so full of romance and mystery and sound of sheep bells and murmur of mist-hidden hills, which we streams shall have brought him, that there will be no more music or beauty left in the world, and all the world will end; and perhaps the streams shall gather at the last, we all together, to the sea. Or perhaps the sea will give us at the last unto each one his own again, giving back all that he has garnered in the years—the little petals of the apple-blossom and the mourned ones of the rhododendron, and our old visions of the trees and sky; so many memories have left the hills. But who may say? For who knows the tides of the sea?"

"Be sure that it is all for Man," said the road. "For Man and the making of cities."

Something had come near on utterly silent feet.

"Peace, peace!" it said. "You disturb the queenly night, who, having come into this valley, is a guest in my dark halls. Let us have an end to this discussion."

It was the spider who spoke.

"The Work of the World is the making of cities and palaces. But it is not for man. What is Man? He only prepares my cities for me, and mellows them. All his works are ugly, his richest tapestries are coarse and clumsy. He is a noisy idler, He only protects me from mine enemy the wind; and the beautiful work in my cities, the curving outlines and the delicate weavings, is all mine. Ten years to a hundred it takes to build a city, for five or six hundred more it mellows, and is prepared for me; then I inhabit it, and hide away all that is ugly, and draw beautiful lines about it to and fro. There is nothing so beautiful as cities and palaces; they are the loveliest places in the world, because they are the stillest, and so most like the stars. They are noisy at first, for a little, before I come to them; they have ugly corners not yet rounded off, and coarse tapestries, and then they become ready for me and my exquisite work, and are quite silent and beautiful.[1] And there I entertain the regal nights when they come there jeweled with stars, and all their train of silence, and regale them with costly dust. Already nods, in a city that I wot of, a lonely sentinel whose lords are dead, who grows too old and sleepy to drive away the gathering silence that infests the streets; tomorrow I go to see if he be still at his post. For me Babylon was built, and rocky Tyre; and still men build my cities! All the Work of the World is the making of cities, and all of them I inherit."

1908

DEATH AND ODYSSEUS[2]

In the Olympian courts Love laughed at Death, because he was unsightly, and because She couldn't help it, and because he never did anything worth doing, and because She would.

And Death hated being laughed at, and used to brood apart thinking only of his wrongs and of what he could do to end this intolerable treatment.

But one day Death appeared in the courts with an air and They all noticed it. "What are you up to now?" said Love. And Death with some solemnity said to Her: "I am going to frighten Odysseus"; and drawing about him his gray traveler's cloak went out through the windy door with his jowl turned earthwards.

And he came soon to Ithaca and the hall that Athene knew, and opened the door and saw there famous Odysseus, with his white locks, bending close over the fire, trying to warm his hands.

[1] Cf. *Proverbs,* xxx, 28: "The spider taketh hold with her hands, and is in kings' palaces."

[2] From *Fifty One Tales.* By permission of and special arrangement with the author.

And the wind through the open door blew bitterly on Odysseus.

And Death came up behind him, and suddenly shouted.

And Odysseus went on warming his pale hands.

Then Death came close and began to mouth at him. After a while Odysseus turned and spoke. And "Well, old servant," he said, "have your masters been kind to you since I made you work for me round Ilion?"

And Death for some while stood mute, for he thought of the laughter of Love.

Then "Come now," said Odysseus, "lend me your shoulder," and he leaning heavily on that bony joint, they went together through the open door.

1915

WALTER DE LA MARE 1873-

Mr. de la Mare in his poetry combines the charm of folklore and mythology with a realistic presentation of detail that marks his work as distinctly of the twentieth century. His treatment of old themes in a modern manner, and of modern subjects in a manner reminiscent of earlier poets, is so individual that his work has been slow to gain wide-spread popularity; although his exact and rather daring experiments in rime and rhythm have won him the admiration of his fellow writers.

De la Mare is of Huguenot descent. He was born at Charlton, Kent, and educated at St. Paul's Cathedral Choir School. From 1889 to 1908 he was connected with the Anglo-American Oil Company. Then he received a grant from the Privy Purse that enabled him to devote himself exclusively to literary work. Though best known for his verse, he has written critical articles, tales, and novels. Of the latter *The Memoirs of a Midget,* 1921, shows his prose at its best. *The Listeners,* 1912, *Peacock Pie,* 1913, and *Motley,* 1918, brought him forward in the field of poetry. Some of de la Mare's most successful poems are those written for children; they possess much of the charm and gayety found in Stevenson's *Child's Garden of Verses.* Even these lack a certain earthly quality that would identify them with daily life, and are characterized by a gentle detachment that shows Mr. de la Mare's preference for the shadow rather than the substance. Yet we follow him gladly into his world of quietude where we willingly surrender to his fancy.

Biography and criticism: R. L. Mégroz, ***Walter de la Mare,*** 1924; S. P. Sherman, "Walter de la Mare" (in *The Main Stream,* 1927); Phelps (EP); Sturgeon; Monro; F. L. Lucas, "The Poetry of Walter de la Mare," *Liv. Age* 316:301-3; A. Lothian, "Walter de la Mare," *No. Am.* 216:663-72. For a discussion of *Memoirs of a Midget,* see Joseph Collins, *Taking the Literary Pulse.*

MACBETH[1]

Rose, like dim battlements, the hills and reared
Steep crags into the fading primrose sky;
But in the desolate valleys fell small rain,
Mingled with drifting cloud. I saw one come,
Like the fierce passion of that vacant place,
His face turned glittering to the evening sky;
His eyes, like gray despair, fixed satelessly[2]
On the still, rainy turrets of the storm;
And all his armor in a haze of blue.
He held no sword, bare was his hand and clenched,
As if to hide the inextinguishable blood
Murder had painted there. And his wild mouth
Seemed spouting echoes of deluded thoughts.
Around his head, like vipers all distort,
His locks shook, heavy-laden, at each stride.
If fire may burn invisible to the eye;
Oh, if despair strive everlastingly;
Then haunted here the creature of despair,
Fanning and fanning flame to lick upon
A soul still childish in a blackened hell.

1906

NOD[1]

Softly along the road of evening,
  In a twilight dim with rose,
Wrinkled with age, and drenched with dew,
  Old Nod, the shepherd, goes.

His drowsy flock streams on before him,
  Their fleeces charged with gold,
To where the sun's last beam leans low
  On Nod the shepherd's fold.

The hedge is quick[3] and green with brier,
  From their sand the conies[4] creep;
And all the birds that fly in heaven
  Flock singing home to sleep.

His lambs outnumber a noon's roses,
  Yet, when night's shadows fall,
His blind old sheep-dog, Slumber-soon,
  Misses not one of all.

His are the quiet steeps of dreamland,
  The waters of no-more-pain,
His ram's bell rings 'neath an arch of stars,
  "Rest, rest, and rest again."

1912

[1] From *Collected Poems,* Volume 1. By permission of the author, and Henry Holt and Company, publishers.
[2] without surfeit
[3] alive
[4] rabbits

OLD SUSAN [1]

When Susan's work was done, she would sit,
With one fat guttering candle lit,
And window open wide to win
The sweet night air to enter in.
There with a thumb to keep her place,
She would read, with stern and wrinkled face,
Her mild eyes gliding very slow
Across the letters to and fro,
While wagged the guttering candle flame
In the wind that through the window came.
And sometimes in the silence she
Would mumble a sentence audibly,
Or shake her head as if to say,
"You silly souls, to act this way!"
And never a sound from night I would hear,
Unless some far-off cock crowed clear;
Or her old shuffling thumb should turn
Another page; and rapt and stern,
Through her great glasses bent on me,
She would glance into reality;
And shake her round old silvery head,
With—"You!—I thought you was in bed!"—
Only to tilt her book again,
And rooted in Romance remain.

1912

SILVER [1]

Slowly, silently, now the moon
Walks the night in her silver shoon;
This way, and that, she peers, and sees
Silver fruit upon silver trees;
One by one the casements catch
Her beams beneath the silvery thatch;
Crouched in his kennel, like a log,
With paws of silver sleeps the dog;
From their shadowy cote the white breasts peep
Of doves in a silver-feathered sleep;
A harvest mouse goes scampering by,
With silver claws, and silver eye;
And moveless fish in the water gleam,
By silver reeds in a silver stream.

1913

THE SUNKEN GARDEN [1]

Speak not—whisper not;
Here bloweth thyme and bergamot;
Softly on the evening hour,
Secret herbs their spices shower.
Dark-spiked rosemary and myrrh,
Lean-stalked, purple lavender;
Hides within her bosom, too,
All her sorrows, bitter rue.
Breathe not—trespass not;
Of this green and darkling spot,
Latticed from the moon's beams,
Perchance a distant dreamer dreams;
Perchance upon its darkening air,
The unseen ghosts of children fare,
Faintly swinging, sway and sweep,
Like lovely sea-flowers in its deep;
While, unmoved, to watch and ward,
Amid its gloomed and daisied sward,
Stands with bowed and dewy head
That one little leaden Lad.

1918

[1] From *Collected Poems*, Volume 2, by permission of the author and Henry Holt and Company, publishers.

HERBERT GEORGE WELLS
1866-

Like Shaw, Wells disapproves highly of our present civilization; he has diagnosed its diseases brilliantly, and suggested more remedies than perhaps anyone else. His influence on younger contemporaries has been as strong as that of Ruskin and Carlyle on rising authors of their day. He advances his destructive comments with an engaging sincerity and kindliness. His generosity may be partly due to the fact that his chief criticism is directed toward the species, not the individual.

As a young man he was successively, clerk, grammar-school teacher, student of science, tutor, lecturer, and journalist; he finally settled down in London in 1893 to the career of a writer. His work falls into divisions illustrating different phases of his development. First came fantastic stories and romances based on modern scientific speculation, such as *The Time Machine,* 1895. Realistic novels followed, such as *Love and Mr. Lewisham,* 1900; *Kipps,* 1915. *Tono Bungay* and *Anne Veronica,* 1909, stand out in this group for lightness of touch, humor, and character portrayal. *The World of William Clissold,* 1926, is the psychological study of a business man, though some readers believe that William Clissold bears a strong autobiographical resemblance to his creator. The broad field of politics and economics is the background for many of Mr. Wells's novels and he incorporates in much of his work discussions of modern woman, marriage, education, religion. *The Outline of History,* 1920, is a fascinating account of the biological, social, and political history of the race to the present day.

Biography: J. D. Beresford, 1915; E. Guyot, 1920; I. J. C. Brown, 1923. Criticism: V. W. Brooks, *The World of H. G. Wells,* 1915; Drew; Cunliffe; Chevalley; Follett; Freeman; Scott; Phelps (EN); also *Bookm.* 43:409-10; Ervine; H. E. L. Mellersh, "Shaw, Wells, and Creative Evolution," *Fortn.* 125:178-88; S. P. Sherman, "H. G. Wells and the Victorians," *Nation* 100:558-61; J. H. Holmes, "H. G. Wells, Novelist and Prophet," *Bookm.* 43:507-14; W. H. Jones, "Message of Mr. H. G. Wells," *Liv. Age* 286:281-90; A. Guerard, "'The New History': H. G. Wells and Voltaire," *Scrib.* 76:476-84.

From MEN LIKE GODS [1]

[Mr. Barnstaple, an English gentleman starting out alone on a few days' rest tour, is motoring quietly along an English country road when something happens—a shock, a little dizziness—and he finds himself on a new road where two automobiles that had passed his roadster just a few minutes before have come to a stop. They have all been "rotated" from our universe "into the planet Utopia," at the time in close contact with the Earth. The Utopian scientists who made the experiment are therefore not so much surprised at the outcome as they are curious about their visitors. The selection following indicates some of the chief features in the state of human civilization reached in Wells's ideal world, where speech has been replaced by thought transference. The names of the Earthlings can readily be distinguished from those of the Utopians. A comparison with More, *Utopia,* p. 117, is of interest.]

BOOK THE SECOND

CHAPTER THE FIRST

1

The shadow of the great epidemic in Utopia fell upon our little band of Earthlings in the second day after their irruption. [2] For more than twenty centuries the Utopians had had the completest freedom from infections and contagious diseases of all sorts. Not only had the graver epidemic fevers and all sorts of skin diseases gone out of the lives of animals and men, but all the minor infections of colds, coughs, influenzas, and the like had also been mastered and ended. By isolation, [3] by the control of carriers, and so forth, the fatal germs had been cornered and obliged to die out.

And there had followed a corresponding change in the Utopian physiology. Secretions and reactions that had given the body resisting power to infection had diminished; the energy that produced them had been withdrawn to other more serviceable applications. The Utopian physiology, relieved of these merely defensive necessities, had simplified itself and become more direct and efficient. This cleaning up of infections was such ancient history in Utopia that only those who specialized in the history of pathology understood anything of the miseries mankind had suffered under from this source, and even these specialists do not seem to have had any idea how far the race had lost its former resistance to infection. The first person to think of this lost resisting power seems to have been Mr. Rupert Catskill. Mr. Barnstaple recalled that when they had met early on the first morning of their stay in the Conference Gardens, [4] he had been hinting that Nature was in some unexplained way on the side of the Earthlings.

If making them obnoxious was being on their side then certainly Nature was on their side. By the evening of the second day after their arrival nearly everybody who had been in contact with the Earthlings, with the exception of Lychnis, Serpentine, and three or four others who had retained something of their ancestral anti-toxins, was in a fever with cough, cold, sore throat, aching bones, headache, and such physical depression and misery as Utopia had not known for twenty centuries. The first inhabitant of Utopia to die was that leopard which had sniffed at Mr. Rupert Catskill on his first arrival. It was found unaccountably dead on the second morning after that encounter. In the afternoon of the same day one of the girls who had helped Lady Stella to unpack her bags sickened suddenly and died. . . . .

Utopia was even less prepared for the coming of these disease germs than for the coming of the Earthlings who brought them. The monstrous multitude of general and fever hospitals, doctors, drug shops, and so forth that had existed in the last Age of Confusion had long since passed out of memory; there was a surgical service for accidents and a watch kept upon the health of the young, and there were places of rest at which those who were extremely old were assisted, but there remained scarcely anything of hygienic organization that had formerly struggled against disease. Abruptly the Utopian intelligence had to take up again a tangle of problems long since solved and set aside, to improvise forgotten apparatus and organizations for disinfection and treatment, and to return to all the disciplines of the war against diseases that had marked an epoch in its history twenty centuries before. In one respect indeed that war had left Utopia with certain permanent advantages. Nearly all the insect disease carriers had been exterminated, and rats and mice and the untidier sorts of small bird had passed out of the problem of sanitation. That set very definite limits to the spread of the new infections and to the nature of the infections

[1] By permission of and special arrangement with the author.
[2] breaking in
[3] quarantine
[4] an assembly place for the Utopians

that could be spread. It enabled the Earthlings only to communicate such ailments as could be breathed across an interval, or conveyed by a contaminating touch. Though not one of them was ailing at all, it became clear that some one among them had brought latent measles into the Utopian universe, and that three or four of them had liberated a long suppressed influenza. Themselves too tough to suffer, they remained at the focus of these two epidemics, while their victims coughed and sneezed and kissed and whispered them about the Utopian planet. It was not until the afternoon of the second day after the irruption that Utopia realized what had happened, and set itself to deal with this relapse into barbaric solicitudes.

. . . .

BOOK THE THIRD

CHAPTER THE SECOND

3

[Mr. Barnstaple has made the acquaintance of Crystal, a lad of thirteen.]

Crystal was still of an age to be proud of his *savoir faire*.[1] He showed Mr. Barnstaple his books and told him of his tutors and exercises.

Utopia still made use of printed books; books were still the simplest, clearest way of bringing statements before a tranquil mind. Crystal's books were very beautifully bound in flexible leather that his mother had tooled for him very prettily, and they were made of hand-made paper. The lettering was some fluent phonetic script that Mr. Barnstaple could not understand. It reminded him of Arabic; and frequent sketches, outline maps, and diagrams were interpolated. Crystal was advised in his holiday reading by a tutor for whom he prepared a sort of exercise report, and he supplemented his reading by visits to museums; but there was no educational museum convenient in the Valley of Peace for Mr. Barnstaple to visit.

Crystal had passed out of the opening stage of education which was carried on, he said, upon large educational estates given up wholly to the lives of children. Education up to eleven or twelve seemed to be much more carefully watched and guarded and taken care of in Utopia than upon Earth. Shocks to the imagination, fear and evil suggestions were warded off as carefully as were infection and physical disaster; by eight or nine the foundations of a Utopian character were surely laid, habits of cleanliness, truth, candor and helpfulness, confidence in the world, fearlessness and a sense of belonging to the great purpose of the race.

Only after nine or ten did the child go outside the garden of its early growth and begin to see the ordinary ways of the world. Until that age the care of the children was largely in the hands of the nurses and teachers, but after that time the parents became more of a factor than they had been in a youngster's life. It was always a custom for the parents of a child to be near and to see that child in its nursery days, but just when earthly parents tended to separate from their children as they went away to school or went into business, Utopian parentage grew to be something closer. There was an idea in Utopia that between parent and child there was a necessary temperamental sympathy; children looked forward to the friendship and company of their parents, and parents looked forward to the interest of their children's adolescence, and though a parent had practically no power over a son or daughter, he or she took naturally the position of advocate, adviser, and sympathetic friend. The friendship was all the closer because of that lack of power, and all the easier because age for age the Utopians were so much younger and fresher-minded than Earthlings. Crystal it seemed had a very great passion for his mother. He was very proud of his father, who was a wonderful painter and designer; but it was his mother who possessed the boy's heart.

On his second walk with Mr. Barnstaple he said he was going to hear from his mother, and Mr. Barnstaple was shown the equivalent of correspondence in Utopia. Crystal carried a little bundle of wires and light rods; and presently coming to a place where a pillar stood in the midst of a lawn he spread this affair out like a long cat's cradle and tapped a little stud in the pillar with a key that he carried on a light gold chain around his neck. Then he took up a receiver attached to his apparatus, and spoke aloud and listened and presently heard a voice.

It was a very pleasant woman's voice; it talked to Crystal for a time without interruption, and then Crystal talked back, and afterwards there were other voices, some of which Crystal answered and some which he heard without replying. Then he gathered up his apparatus again.

This Mr. Barnstaple learned was the Utopian equivalent of letter and telephone. For in Utopia, except by previous arrangement,

[1] ability

people do not talk together on the telephone. A message is sent to the station of the district in which the recipient is known to be, and it there waits until he chooses to tap his accumulated messages. And any that one wishes to repeat can be repeated. Then he talks back to the senders and dispatches any other messages he wishes. The transmission is wireless. The little pillars supply electric power for transmission or for any other purpose the Utopians require. For example, the gardeners resort to them to run their mowers and diggers and rakes and rollers.

. . . .

CHAPTER THE THIRD

1

The man to whom Mr. Barnstaple, after due inquiries, went to talk was named Sungold. He was probably very old, because there were lines of age about his eyes and over his fine brow. He was a ruddy man, bearded with an auburn beard that had streaks of white, and his eyes were brown and nimble under his thick eyebrows. His hair had thinned but little and flowed back like a mane, but its copper-red color had gone. He sat at a table with papers spread before him, making manuscript notes. He smiled at Mr. Barnstaple, for he had been expecting him, and indicated a seat for him with his stout and freckled hand. Then he waited smilingly for Mr. Barnstaple to begin.

"This world is one triumph of the desire for order and beauty in men's minds," said Mr. Barnstaple. "But it will not tolerate one useless soul in it. Everyone is actively happy. Everyone but myself . . . . I belong nowhere. I have nothing to do. And no one—is related to me."

Sungold moved his head slightly to show that he understood.

"It is hard for an Earthling, with an earthly want of training, to fall into any place here. Into any usual work or any usual relationship. One is—a stranger . . . . But it is still harder to have no place at all. In the new work, of which I am told you know most of anyone and are indeed the center and regulator, it has occurred to me that I might be of some use, that I might, indeed, be as good as a Utopian . . . . If so, I want to be of use. You may want some one just to risk death—to take the danger of going into some strange place—someone who desires to serve Utopia—and who need not have skill or knowledge—or be a beautiful or able person?"

Mr. Barnstaple stopped short.

Sungold conveyed the completest understanding of all that was in Mr. Barnstaple's mind.

Mr. Barnstaple sat interrogative while for a time Sungold thought.[1]

Then words and phrases began to string themselves together in Mr. Barnstaple's mind.

Sungold wondered if Mr. Barnstaple understood either the extent or the limitations of the great discoveries that were now being made in Utopia. Utopia, he said, was passing into a phase of intense intellectual exaltation. New powers and possibilities intoxicated the imagination of the race, and it was indeed inconceivable that an unteachable and perplexed Earthling could be anything but distressed and uncomfortable amidst the vast strange activities that must now begin. Even many of their own people, the more backward Utopians, were disturbed. For centuries Utopian philosophers and experimentalists had been criticizing, revising, and reconstructing their former instinctive and traditional ideas of space and time, of form and substance, and now very rapidly the new ways of thinking were becoming clear and simple and bearing fruit in surprisingly practical applications. The limitations of space which had seemed forever insurmountable were breaking down; they were breaking down in a strange and perplexing way but they were breaking down. It was now theoretically possible, it was rapidly becoming practicably possible, to pass from the planet Utopia to which the race had hitherto been confined, to other points in the universe of origin, that is to say to remote planets and distant stars. . . . That was the gist of the present situation.

"I cannot imagine that," said Mr. Barnstaple.

"You cannot imagine it," Sungold agreed, quite cordially. "But it is so. A hundred years ago it was inconceivable—here."

"Do you get there by some sort of backstairs in another dimension?" said Mr. Barnstaple.

Sungold considered this guess. It was a grotesque image, he said, but from the point of view of an Earthling it would serve. That conveyed something of its quality. But it was so much more wonderful. . . . .

"A new and astounding phase has begun for life here. We learned long ago the chief secrets of happiness upon this planet. Life is good in this world. You find it good? . . . For thousands of years yet it will be our

[1] The Utopians communicated by means of thought-suggestion, not speech.

fastness and our home. But the wind of a new adventure blows through our life. All this world is in a mood like striking camp in the winter quarters when spring approaches."

He leaned over his papers toward Mr. Barnstaple, and held up a finger and spoke audible words as if to make his meaning plainer. It seemed to Mr. Barnstaple that each word translated itself into English as he spoke it. At any rate Mr. Barnstaple understood. "The collision of our planet Utopia with your planet Earth was a very curious accident, but an unimportant accident, in this story. I want you to understand that. Your universe and ours are two out of a great number of gravitation-time universes, which are translated together through the inexhaustible infinitude of God. They are similar throughout, but they are identical in nothing. Your planet and ours happen to be side by side, so to speak, but they are not traveling at exactly the same pace nor in a strictly parallel direction. They will drift apart again and follow their several destinies. When Arden and Greenlake made their experiment the chances of hitting anything in your universe were infinitely remote. They had disregarded it, they were merely rotating some of our matter out of and then back into our universe. You fell into us—as amazingly for us as for you. The importance of our discoveries for us lies in our own universe and not in yours. We do not want to come into your universe nor have more of your world come into ours. You are too like us, and you are too dark and troubled and diseased—you are too contagious—and we, we cannot help you because we are not gods but men.

Mr. Barnstaple nodded.

"What could Utopians do with the men of Earth? We have no strong instinct in us to teach or dominate other adults. That has been bred out of us by long centuries of equality and free coöperation. And you would be too numerous for us to teach and much of your population would be grown up and set in bad habits. Your stupidities would get in our way, your quarrels and jealousies and traditions, your flags and religions, and all your embodied spites and suppressions, would hamper us in everything we should want to do. We should be impatient with you, unjust, overbearing. You are too like us for us to be patient with your failures. It would be hard to remember constantly how ill-bred you were. In Utopia we found out long ago that no race of human beings was sufficiently great, subtle, and powerful to think and act for any other race. Perhaps already you are finding out the same thing on Earth as your races come into closer contact. And much more would this be true betwen Utopia and Earth. From what I know of your people and their ignorance and obstinacies it is clear that our people would despise you; and contempt is the cause of all injustice. We might end by exterminating you. . . . . But why should we make that possible? . . . . We must leave you alone. We cannot trust ourselves with you. . . . . . Believe me, this is the only reasonable course for us."

Mr. Barnstaple assented silently.

"You and I—two individuals—can be friends and understand."

"What you say is true," said Mr. Barnstaple. "It is true. But it grieves me it is true . . . . Greatly . . . . Nevertheless, I gather, I at least may be of service in Utopia?"

"You can."

"How?"

"By returning to your own world."

Mr. Barnstaple thought for some moments. It was what he had feared. But he had offered himself. "I will do that."

"By attempting to return, I should say. There is risk. You may be killed."

"I must take that."

"We want to verify all the data we have of the relations of our universe to yours. We want to reverse the experiment of Arden and Greenlake and see if we can return a living being to your world. We are almost certain now that we can do so. And that human being must care for us enough and care for his own world enough to go back and give us a sign that he has got there."

Mr. Barnstaple spoke huskily. "I can do that."

"We can put you into that machine of yours and into the clothes that you wore. You can be made again exactly as you left your world."

"Exactly. I understand."

"And because your world is vile and contentious and yet has some strangely able brains in it, here and there, we do not want your people to know of us, living so close to you—for we shall be close to you yet for some hundreds of years at least—we do not want them to know for fear that they should come here presently, led by some poor silly genius of a scientific man, come in their greedy, foolish, breeding swarms, hammering at our doors, threatening our lives, and spoiling our high adventures, and so have to be beaten off and killed like an invasion of rats or parasites."

"Yes," said Mr. Barnstaple. "Before men can come to Utopia, they must learn the way here. Utopia, I see, is only a home for those who have learned the way."

He paused and answered some of his own thoughts. "When I have returned," he said, "shall I begin to forget Utopia?"

Sungold smiled and said nothing.

"All my days the nostalgia of Utopia will distress me."

"And uphold you."

"I shall take up my earthly life at the point where I laid it down, but—on Earth—I shall be a Utopian. For I feel that having offered my service and had it accepted, I am no longer an outcast in Utopia. I belong . . . . "

"Remember you may be killed. You may die in the trial."

"As it may happen."

"Well—Brother!"

The friendly paw took Mr. Barnstaple's and pressed it and the deep eyes smiled.

. . . .

5

They took Mr. Barnstaple back by aeroplane to the point upon the glassy road where he had first come into Utopia. Lychnis came with him and Crystal, who was curious to see what would be done.

A group of twenty or thirty people, including Sungold, awaited him. The ruined laboratory of Arden and Greenlake had been replaced by fresh buildings, and there were additional erections on the further side of the road; but Mr. Barnstaple could recognize quite clearly the place where Mr. Catskill had faced the leopard and where Mr. Burleigh had accosted him. Several new kinds of flowers were now out, but the blue blossoms that had charmed him on arrival still prevailed. His old car, the Yellow Peril, looking now the clumsiest piece of ironmongery conceivable, stood in the road. He went and examined it. It seemed to be in perfect order; it had been carefully oiled and the petrol tank was full.

In a little pavilion were his bag and all his earthly clothes. They were very clean, and they had been folded and pressed, and he put them on. His shirt seemed tight across his chest, and his collar decidedly tight, and his coat cut him a little under the arms. Perhaps these garments had shrunken when they were disinfected. He packed his bag and Crystal put it in the car for him.

Sungold explained very simply all that Mr. Barnstaple had to do. Across the road, close by the restored laboratory, stretched a line as thin as gossamer. "Steer your car to that and break it," he said. "That is all you have to do. Then take this red flower and put it down exactly where your wheel tracks show that you have entered your own world."

Mr. Barnstaple was left beside the car. The Utopians went back twenty or thirty yards and stood in a circle about him. For a few moments everyone was still.

6

Mr. Barnstaple got into his car, started his engine, let it throb for a minute and then put in the clutch. The yellow car began to move toward the line of gossamer. He made a gesture with one hand which Lychnis answered. Sungold and others of the Utopians also made friendly movements. But Crystal was watching too intently for any gesture.

"Good-bye, Crystal!" cried Mr. Barnstaple, and the boy responded with a start.

Mr. Barnstaple accelerated, set his teeth and, in spite of his will to keep them open, shut his eyes as he touched the gossamer line. Came that sense again of unendurable tension and that sound like the snapping of a bowstring. He had an irresistible impulse to stop—go back. He took his foot from the accelerator, and the car seemed to fall a foot or so and stopped so heavily and suddenly that he was jerked forward against the steering wheel. The oppression lifted. He opened his eyes and looked about him.

The car was standing in a field from which the hay had recently been carried. He was tilted on one side because of a roll in the ground. A hedge in which there was an open black gate separated this hayfield from the high road. Close at hand was a board advertisement of some Maidenhead[1] hotel. On the far side of the road were level fields against a background of low wooded hills. Away to the left was a little inn. He turned his head and saw Windsor Castle in the remote distance rising above poplar-studded meadows. It was not, as his Utopians had promised him, the exact spot of his departure from our Earth, but it was certainly less than a hundred yards away.

. . . .

. . . . He must do as he was told. He walked back along the track of his car to its beginning, stood for a moment hesitating, tore a single petal from that glowing bloom, and then laid down the rest of the great flower carefully in the very center of his track. The petal he put in his pocket. . . . .

[1] a town about 25 miles west of London

Something happened very quickly. It was as if a hand appeared for a moment and took the flower. In a moment it had gone. A little eddy of dust swirled and drifted and sank. . . . .

It was the end.

. . . .

1922

GEORGE BERNARD SHAW
1856-

The social criticism which Mr. Wells expresses in his novels, Mr. Shaw has put into dramatic form. His mightiest weapon is his wit, and with this two-edged sword he can more than hold his own against any living English author. His comedies arouse mirth, not only by their cleverly constructed plots, but also by the verbal fireworks of the characters, in whose words Shaw advances his criticism of the state, the home, organized religion, formal education; and through whom he advocates reforms of every kind. Chief among these reforms is a plan for outlawing war. In the following selection he makes plain his view of the unreasoning and savage force that man unleashes on the world when he assists in or advocates war. His scathing denunciation of militarism is based upon his observation of Europe before and after the World War. Although this view is not the opinion of the majority, it is typically Shavian, and is held by many thinking people. In his plays, prefaces, and essays, Shaw endeavors always to portray the "normal man," who, by his practical intelligence contrasts strongly with the "fuddle-headed, average man," lost in a haze of sentimentality and romanticism.

Shaw was born in Dublin, was educated at Wesley College, and in 1876 went to London, where he endured nine years of poverty, writing five novels which publishers consistently rejected. He joined the socialists, his fortune turned, his novels were published, he became a dramatic, musical, and literary critic, and rose rapidly to fame. Between 1893 and 1926 he wrote thirty-four plays, by far his best work. Many of these have wide popularity as stage productions, but the pith of them often lies in the prefaces, which cannot be ignored if one is to know and judge Shaw as a whole. His earlier plays appeared in two collections: *Plays, Pleasant and Unpleasant,* 1898; *Three Plays for Puritans,* 1900. Among the many others are *Man and Superman,* 1903; *Heartbreak House,* 1919; *Back to Methusalah,* 1921; *Saint Joan,* 1923.

Biography: Holbrook Jackson, 1907; G. K. Chesterton, 1910; J. S. Collins, 1925. Criticism: G. K. Chesterton, *Heretics,* 1905; Phelps (MD); Ervine; Scott; Cunliffe; Follett; Kennedy; Freeman; Chubb; S. Desmond, "Dunsany, Yeats, and Shaw," *Bookm.* 58:260-6; C. Van Doren, "Mark Twain and Bernard Shaw," *Cent.* 109:705-10; E. E. Slosson, "A New Shaw," *Ind.* 86:135-8; W. Archer, "Psychology of G. B. S.," *Liv. Age* 324: 206-9.

From PREFACE to *HEARTBREAK HOUSE* [1]

THE RABID WATCHDOGS OF LIBERTY

Not content with these rancorous abuses of the existing law, the war maniacs made a frantic rush to abolish all constitutional guarantees of liberty and well-being. The ordinary law was superseded by Acts under which newspapers were seized and their printing machinery destroyed by simple police raids *à la Russe,* [2] and persons arrested and shot without any pretense of trial by jury or publicity of procedure or evidence. Though it was urgently necessary that production should be increased by the most scientific organization and economy of labor, and though no fact was better established than that excessive duration and intensity of toil reduces production heavily instead of increasing it, the factory laws were suspended, and men and women recklessly over-worked until the loss of their efficiency became too glaring to be ignored. Remonstrances and warnings were met either with an accusation of pro-Germanism or the formula, "Remember that we are at war now." I have said that men assumed that war had reversed the order of nature, and that all was lost unless we did the exact opposite of everything we had found necessary and beneficial in peace. But the truth was worse than that. The war did not change men's minds in any such impossible way. What really happened was that the impact of physical death and destruction, the one reality that every fool can understand, tore off the masks of education, art, science, and religion from our ignorance and barbarism, and left us glorying grotesquely in the license suddenly accorded to our vilest passions and most abject terrors. Ever since Thucydides wrote history, it has been on record that when the angel of death sounds his trumpet the pretenses of civilization are blown from men's heads into the mud like hats in a gust of wind. But when this scripture was fulfilled among us, the shock was not the less appalling because a few students of Greek history were not surprised by it. Indeed these students threw themselves into the orgy as shamelessly as the illiterate. The Christian priest joining in the war dance with-

[1] Reprinted by the courtesy of the author.
[2] in the manner of the despotic Russian Government

out even throwing off his cassock first, and the respectable school governor expelling the German professor with insult and bodily violence, and declaring that no English child should ever again be taught the language of Luther and Goethe, were kept in countenance by the most impudent repudiations of every decency of civilization and every lesson of political experience on the part of the very persons who, as university professors, historians, philosophers, and men of science, were the accredited custodians of culture. It was crudely natural, and perhaps necessary for recruiting purposes, that German militarism and German dynastic ambition should be painted by journalists and recruiters in black and red as European dangers (as in fact they are), leaving it to be inferred that our own militarism and our own political constitution are millennially democratic (which they certainly are not); but when it came to frantic denunciations of German chemistry, German biology, German poetry, German music, German literature, German philosophy, and even German engineering, as malignant abominations standing toward British and French chemistry and so forth in the relation of heaven to hell, it was clear that the utterers of such barbarous ravings had never really understood or cared for the arts and sciences they professed and were profaning, and were only the appallingly degenerate descendants of the men of the seventeenth and eighteenth centuries who, recognizing no national frontiers in the great realm of the human mind, kept the European comity of that realm loftily and even ostentatiously above the rancors of the battle-field. Tearing the Garter [1] from the Kaiser's leg, striking the German dukes from the roll of our peerage, changing the King's illustrious and historically appropriate surname [2] (for the war was the old war of Guelph against Ghibelline, [3] with the Kaiser as Arch-Ghibelline) to that of a traditionless locality. One felt that the figure of St. George and the Dragon on our coinage should be replaced by that of the soldier driving his spear through Archimedes. [4]

[1] The Kaiser had been invested with the English Order of the Garter.

[2] In 1917 the royal house of England, known as the house of Saxe-Coburg-Gotha, was proclaimed the house of Windsor.

[3] rival Tuscan families that kept Florence in a state of civil war that sometimes embroiled all Italy

[4] a Greek physicist, 287-212 B.C., killed at the fall of Syracuse by Roman soldiers tempted by the glitter of his instruments

THE SUFFERINGS OF THE SANE

The mental distress of living amid the obscene din of all these carmagnoles and corobberies [5] was not the only burden that lay on sane people during the war. There was also the emotional strain, complicated by the offended economic sense, produced by the casualty lists. The stupid, the selfish, the narrow-minded, the callous, and unimaginative were spared a great deal. "Blood and destruction shall be so in use that mothers shall but smile when they behold their infants quartered by the hands of war," was a Shakespearean prophecy that very nearly came true; for when nearly every house had a slaughtered son to mourn, we should all have gone quite out of our senses if we had taken our own and our friend's bereavements at their peace value. It became necessary to give them a false value; to proclaim the young life worthily and gloriously sacrificed to redeem the liberty of mankind, instead of to expiate the heedlessness and folly of their fathers, and expiate it in vain. We had even to assume that the parents and not the children had made the sacrifice, until at last the comic papers were driven to satirize fat old men, sitting comfortably in club chairs, and boasting of the sons they had "given" to their country.

No one grudged these anodynes to acute personal grief; but they only embittered those who knew that the young men were having their teeth set on edge because their parents had eaten sour political grapes. [6] Then think of the young men themselves! Many of them had no illusions about the policy that led to the war: they went clear-sighted to a horribly repugnant duty. Men essentially gentle and essentially wise, with really valuable work in hand, laid it down voluntarily and spent months of forming fours in the barrack yard, and stabbing sacks of straw in the public eye, so that they might go out to kill and maim men as gentle as themselves. These men, who were perhaps, as a class, our most efficient soldiers, were not duped for a moment by the hypocritical melodrama that consoled and stimulated the others. They left their creative work to drudge at destruction, exactly as they would have left it to take their turn at the pumps in a sinking ship. They did not, like some of the conscientious objectors, hold back because the ship had been neglected by

[5] Carmagnoles were frenzied dances by the lowest classes in France, celebrating the Revolution, 1789. Corobberies, or corroborees, are dances of the Australian aborigines.

[6] See *Ezekiel*, xviii, 2.

its officers and scuttled by its wreckers. The ship had to be saved, even if Newton had to leave his fluxions and Michael Angelo [1] his marbles to save it; so they threw away the tools of their beneficent and ennobling trades, and took up the blood-stained bayonet and the murderous bomb, forcing themselves to pervert their divine instinct for perfect artistic execution to the effective handling of these diabolical things, and their economic faculty for organization to the contriving of ruin and slaughter. For it gave an ironic edge to their tragedy that the very talents they were forced to prostitute made the prostitution not only effective, but even interesting; so that some of them were rapidly promoted, and found themselves actually becoming artists in war, with a growing relish for it, like Napoleon and all the other scourges of mankind, in spite of themselves. For many of them there was not even this consolation. They "stuck it," and hated it, to the end.

THE NEXT PHASE

The present situation will not last. Although the newspaper I read at breakfast this morning before writing these words contains a calculation that no less than twenty-three wars are at present being waged to confirm peace, England is no longer in khaki; and a violent reaction is setting in. We have been torn from the fool's paradise and thrust upon the sternest realities and necessities until we have lost both faith in and patience with romantic pretenses that have no root either in reality or necessity. It seems only the other day that a millionaire was a man with £50,000 a year. Today, when he has paid income tax and super tax, and insured his life for the amount of his death duties, he is lucky if his net income is £10,000, though his nominal property remains the same. And this is the result of a Budget which is called "a respite for the rich." At the other end of the scale millions of persons have had regular incomes for the first time in their lives; and their men have been regularly clothed, fed, lodged, and taught to make up their minds that certain things have to be done, also for the first time in their lives. Hundreds of thousands of women have been taken out of their domestic cages and tasted both discipline and independence. The thoughtless and snobbish middle classes have been pulled up short by the very unpleasant experience of being ruined to an unprecedented extent. We have all had a tremendous jolt; and although the widespread notion that the shock of the war would automatically make a new heaven and a new earth, and that the dog would never go back to his vomit nor the sow to her wallowing in the mire, is already seen to be a delusion, yet we are far more conscious of our condition than we were, and far less disposed to submit to it. Revolution, lately only a sensational chapter in history or a demagogic claptrap, is now a possibility so imminent that hardly by trying to suppress it in other countries by arms and defamation, and calling the process anti-Bolshevism, can our Government stave it off at home.

Perhaps the most tragic figure of the day is the American President who was once a historian. In those days it became his task to tell us how, after that great war in America which was more clearly than any other war of our time a war for an idea, the conquerors, confronted with a heroic task of reconstruction, turned recreat, and spent fifteen years in abusing their victory under cover of pretending to accomplish the task they were doing what they could to make impossible. Alas! Hegel [2] was right when he said that we learn from history that men never learn anything from history. With what anguish of mind the President sees that we, the new conquerors, forgetting everything we professed to fight for, are sitting down with watering mouths to a good square meal of ten years revenge upon and humiliation of our prostrate foe, can only be guessed by those who know, as he does, how hopeless is remonstrance, and how happy Lincoln was in perishing from the earth before his inspired messages became scraps of paper. He knows well that from the Peace Conference will come, in spite of his utmost, no edict on which he will be able, like Lincoln, to invoke "the considerate judgment of mankind, and the gracious favor of Almighty God." He led his people to destroy the militarism of Zabern; [3] and the army they rescued is busy in Cologne imprisoning every German who does not salute a British officer; whilst the Government at home, asked whether it approves, replies that it does not propose even to discontinue this Zabernism when the Peace is concluded, but in effect looks forward to making Germans salute British of-

[1] Isaac Newton invented the mathematical theory of fluxions; Michael Angelo was the greatest sculptor of the Italian Renaissance.

[2] a German philosopher, 1770-1831

[3] A city in Alsace where in 1913 citizens were mistreated by the German garrison; the incident became of national importance and universal interest.

ficers until the end of the world. That is what war makes of men and women. It will wear off; and the worst it threatens is already proving impracticable; but before the humble and contrite heart ceases to be despised, the President and I, being of the same age, will be dotards. In the meantime there is, for him, another history to write; for me, another comedy to stage. Perhaps, after all, that is what wars are for, and what historians and playwrights are for. If men will not learn until their lessons are written in blood, why, blood they must have, their own for preference.

1919, revised 1927 1919

RUPERT BROOKE
1887-1915

All who knew Rupert Brooke and his work cannot but regret that a life of such rich promise and great personal charm should have been cut short. He was born and educated at Rugby, where his father was a master, and at Cambridge, where he took honors in classics, going then to Germany and Italy to study. After his election to a fellowship at King's College in 1913, he spent a year in traveling through the United States and Canada to the South Seas. At the outbreak of the World War he enlisted in the navy, was present at the fall of Antwerp, and died at Lemnos on his way to Gallipoli, 1915.

His work, though limited (*John Webster,* 1916; *Letters from America,* 1916; *Collected Poems* with Memoir, 1918), shows wide intelligence, and power of poetic imagination. Brooke's acute sense perception and immediate response to everything that was living or beautiful made his poems a record of his personality. In his revolt against nineteenth century romanticism he affected an exaggerated realism, but this was merely a phase in his development. His sonnet "The Soldier" is often classed with Masefield's "August 1914" and Seeger's "I Have a Rendezvous with Death" as among the best poetry produced by the World War.

Biography: Introd. and biog. note, *Collected Poems,* 1916; E. Marsh, *Rupert Brooke, a Memoir,* 1918, interesting personal data. Criticism: Phelps (EP); Sturgeon; Scott; Wilkinson (NR), the enthusiasm of two contemporaries: J. Drinkwater, "Rupert Brooke," *Forum* 54:677-87, and S. J. Ervine, *No. Am.* 202:432-40 should be offset by a recent estimate: "The 'Paling of Rupert Brooke,'" *Lit. Dig.* 86:28-9 S 12 '25, an interesting comparison with Sassoon.

THE SOLDIER [1]

If I should die, think only this of me:
That there's some corner of a foreign field
That is for ever England. There shall be
In that rich earth a richer dust concealed;
A dust whom England bore, shaped, made aware,
Gave, once, her flowers to love, her ways to roam,
A body of England's, breathing English air,
Washed by the rivers, blest by suns of home.

And think, this heart, all evil shed away,
A pulse in the eternal mind, no less
Gives somewhere back the thoughts by England given;
Her sights and sounds; dreams happy as her day;
And laughter, learned of friends; and gentleness,
In heart at peace, under an English heaven.

1914 1915

THE DEAD [1]

Blow out, you bugles, over the rich Dead!
There's none of these so lonely and poor of old,
But, dying, has made us rarer gifts than gold.
These laid the world away; poured out the red
Sweet wine of youth; gave up the years to be
Of work and joy, and that unhoped serene,
That men call age; and those who would have been,
Their sons, they gave, their immortality.

Blow, bugles, blow! They brought us, for our dearth,
Holiness, lacked so long, and Love, and Pain.
Honor has come back, as a king, to earth,
And paid his subjects with a royal wage;
And Nobleness walks in our ways again;
And we have come into our heritage.

1914 1915

THE GREAT LOVER [1]

I have been so great a lover: filled my days
So proudly with the splendor of Love's praise,
The pain, the calm, and the astonishment,
Desire illimitable, and still content,
And all dear names men use, to cheat despair,
For the perplexed and viewless streams that bear
Our hearts at random down the dark of life.
Now, ere the unthinking silence on that strife
Steals down, I would cheat drowsy Death so far,
My night shall be remembered for a star
That outshone all the suns of all men's days.
Shall I not crown them with immortal praise
Whom I have loved, who have given me, dared with me

[1] From *The Collected Poems of Rupert Brooke.* Used by permission of Dodd, Mead & Company, Inc.

High secrets, and in darkness knelt to see
The inenarrable[1] godhead of delight?
Love is a flame;—we have beaconed the world's night.
A city:—and we have built it, these and I.
An emperor:—we have taught the world to die.
So, for their sakes I loved, ere I go hence,
And the high cause of Love's magnificence,
And to keep loyalties young, I'll write those names
Golden for ever, eagles, crying flames,
And set them as a banner, that men may know,
To dare the generations, burn, and blow
Out on the wind of Time, shining and streaming. . . . .

These I have loved:
White plates and cups, clean-gleaming,
Ringed with blue lines; and feathery, faery dust;
Wet roofs, beneath the lamp-light; the strong crust
Of friendly bread; and many-tasting food;
Rainbows; and the blue bitter smoke of wood;
And radiant raindrops couching in cool flowers;
And flowers themselves, that sway through sunny hours,
Dreaming of moths that drink them under the moon;
Then, the cool kindliness of sheets, that soon
Smooth away trouble; and the rough male kiss
Of blankets; grainy wood; live hair that is
Shining and free; blue-massing clouds; the keen
Unpassioned beauty of a great machine;
The benison of hot water; furs to touch;
The good smell of old clothes; and other such—
The comfortable smell of friendly fingers,[2]
Hair's fragrance, and the musty reek that lingers
About dead leaves and last year's ferns. . . . .
Dear names,
And thousand other throng to me! Royal flames;
Sweet water's dimpling laugh from tap or spring;
Holes in the ground; and voices that do sing;
Voices in laughter, too; and body's pain,
Soon turned to peace; and the deep-panting train;
Firm sands; the little dulling edge of foam
That browns and dwindles as the wave goes home;
And washen stones, gay for an hour; the cold
Graveness of iron; moist black earthen mold;
Sleep; and high places; footprints in the dew;
And oaks; and brown horse-chestnuts, glossy-new;
And new-peeled sticks; and shining pools on grass;—
All these have been my loves. And these shall pass,
Whatever passes not, in the great hour,
Nor all my passion, all my prayers, have power
To hold them with me through the gate of Death.
They'll play deserter, turn with the traitor breath,
Break the high bond we made, and sell Love's trust
And sacramental covenant to the dust.[3]
—Oh, never a doubt but, somewhere, I shall wake,
And give what's left of love again, and make
New friends, now strangers. . . . .
But the best I've known,
Stays here, and changes, breaks, grows old, is blown
About the winds of the world, and fades from brains
Of living men, and dies.
Nothing remains.
O dear my loves, O faithless, once again
This one last gift I give: that after men
Shall know, and later lovers, far-removed,
Praise you, "All these were lovely"; say, "He loved."

Mataiea, 1914 1915

[1] indescribable

[2] "When asked *whose* fingers, he said his nurse's; and admitted that it might have been the soap."—Marsh

[3] Note the same idea in the allegory of *Everyman*, p. 93.

SIEGFRIED LORRAINE SASSOON 1886-

The coming of the World War found Mr. Sassoon living the life of a country gentleman—a graduate of Oxford, a master of fox hounds, and a writer of conventional poems printed for his own pleasure. Little is known of him. He was in three battles in France, and one in Palestine, and came home captain of the Welsh Fusiliers.

It is the horror of war that fills Sassoon's most characteristic verse—*The Old Huntsman,* 1917; *Counter-Attack,* 1918; *Picture-Show,* 1920. "Let no one ever," he says, "from henceforth say a word in any way countenancing war . . . . its spiritual disasters far outweigh any of its advantages."

Criticism of Sassoon's poetry is to be found in *Lit. Dig.* 60:30-31, Feb. 1, '19; *Touchstone,* 7: 142-5, 247-48; also in the introduction to *Counter-Attack,* New York, 1918; Monro; Wilkinson (NV).

A WORKING PARTY [1]

Three hours ago he blundered up the trench,
Sliding and poising, groping with his boots;
Sometimes he tripped and lurched against the walls
With hands that pawed the sodden bags of chalk.
He couldn't see the man who walked in front;
Only he heard the drum and rattle of feet
Stepping along the trench-boards—often splashing
Wretchedly where the sludge was ankle-deep.

Voices would grunt, "Keep to your right—make way!"
When squeezing past the men from the front-line:
White faces peered, puffing a point of red;
Candles and braziers glinted through the chinks
And curtain-flaps of dug-outs; then the gloom
Swallowed his sense of sight; he stooped and swore
Because a sagging wire had caught his neck.
A flare went up; the shining whiteness spread
And flickered upward, showing nimble rats,
And mounds of glimmering sand-bags, bleached with rain;
Then the slow, silver moment died in dark.
The wind came posting by with chilly gusts
And buffeting at corners, piping thin
And dreary through the crannies; rifle-shots
Would split and crack and sing along the night,
And shells came calmly through the drizzling air
To burst with hollow bang below the hill.

Three hours ago he stumbled up the trench;
Now he will never walk that road again:
He must be carried back, a jolting lump
Beyond all need of tenderness and care;
A nine-stone [2] corpse with nothing more to do.
He was a young man with a meager wife
And two pale children in a Midland town;
He showed the photograph to all his mates;
And they considered him a decent chap
Who did his work and hadn't much to say,
And always laughed at other people's jokes
Because he hadn't any of his own.

That night, when he was busy at his job
Of piling bags along the parapet,
He thought how slow time went, stamping his feet,
And blowing on his fingers, pinched with cold.
He thought of getting back by half-past twelve,
And tot of rum to send him warm to sleep
In draughty dug-out frowsty [3] with the fumes
Of coke, and full of snoring, weary men.

He pushed another bag along the top,
Craning his body outward; then a flare
Gave one white glimpse of No Man's Land and wire;
And as he dropped his head the instant split
His startled life with lead, and all went out.

1916 1917

THE DEATH-BED [1]

He drowsed and was aware of silence heaped
Round him, unshaken as the steadfast walls;
Aqueous like floating rays of amber light,
Soaring and quivering in the wings of sleep—
Silence and safety; and his mortal shore
Lipped by the inward, moonless waves of death.

Someone was holding water to his mouth.
He swallowed, unresisting; moaned and dropped
Through crimson gloom to darkness; and forgot
The opiate throb and ache that was his wound.
Water—calm, sliding green above the weir;
Water—a sky-lit alley for his boat,
Bird-voiced, and bordered with reflected flowers
And shaken hues of summer: drifting down,
He dipped contented oars, and sighed, and slept.

Night, with a gust of wind, was in the ward,
Blowing the curtain to a glimmering curve.
Night. He was blind; he could not see the stars
Glinting among the wraiths of wandering cloud;
Queer blots of color, purple, scarlet, green,
Flickered and faded in his drowning eyes.

Rain; he could hear it rustling through the dark;
Fragrance and passionless music woven as one;
Warm rain on drooping roses; pattering showers
That soak the woods; not the harsh rain that sweeps
Behind the thunder, but a trickling peace
Gently and slowly washing life away.

. . . .

[1] By permission from *The Old Huntsman* by Siegfried Sassoon. Copyright by E. P. Dutton & Company.

[2] About 126 pounds; a stone is an English unit of weight equal to 14 pounds.

[3] stuffy

He stirred, shifting his body; then the pain
Leaped like a prowling beast, and gripped and tore
His groping dreams with grinding claws and fangs.
But someone was beside him; soon he lay
Shuddering because that evil thing had passed.
And death, who'd stepped toward him, paused and stared.

1916 1918

COUNTER-ATTACK [1]

We'd gained our first objective hours before
While dawn broke like a face with blinking eyes,
Pallid, unshaved and thirsty, blind with smoke.
Things seemed all right at first. We held their line,
With bombers posted, Lewis guns well placed,
And clink of shovels deepening the shallow trench.

The place was rotten with dead; green clumsy legs
High-booted, sprawled and groveled along the saps; [2]
And trunks, face downward, in the sucking mud,
Wallowed like trodden sand-bags loosely filled;
And naked sodden buttocks, mats of hair,
Bulged, clotted heads slept in the plastering slime.
And then the rain began,—the jolly old rain!

A yawning soldier knelt against the bank,
Staring across the morning blear with fog;
He wondered when the Allemands [3] would get busy;
And then, of course, they started with five-nines [4]
Traversing, [5] sure as fate, and never a dud. [6]
Mute in the clamor of shells he watched them burst
Spouting dark earth and wire with gusts from hell,
While posturing giants dissolved in drifts of smoke.
He crouched and flinched, dizzy with galloping fear,
Sick for escape,—loathing the strangled horror
And butchered, frantic gestures of the dead.

An officer came blundering down the trench:
"Stand-to and man the fire-step!" On he went. . . .
Gasping and bawling, "Fire-step . . . counter-attack!"

Then the haze lifted. Bombing on the right
Down the old sap: machine-guns on the left;
And stumbling figures looming out in front.
"O Christ, they're coming at us!" Bullets spat,
And he remembered his rifle . . . rapid fire . . .
And started blazing wildly . . . then a bang
Crumpled and spun him sideways, knocked him out
To grunt and wriggle: none heeded him; he choked
And fought the flapping veils of smothering gloom,
Lost in a blurred confusion of yells and groans . . .
Down, and down, and down, he sank and drowned,
Bleeding to death. The counter-attack had failed.

1917 1918

[1] By permission from *Counter-Attack and Other Poems* by Siegfried Sassoon. Copyright by E. P. Dutton & Company.
[2] covered trench
[3] a familiar term for Germans
[4] a term denoting the size of the shell
[5] swinging the muzzle of the gun from side to side in order to scatter the shells as widely as possible
[6] unexploded shell

THE REAR-GUARD [1]

(Hindenburg Line, April, 1917)

Groping along the tunnel, step by step,
He winked his prying torch with patching glare
From side to side, and sniffed the unwholesome air.

Tins, boxes, bottles, shapes too vague to know,
A mirror smashed, the mattress from a bed;
And he, exploring fifty feet below
The rosy gloom of battle overhead.

Tripping, he grabbed the wall; saw some one lie
Humped at his feet half-hidden by a rug,
And stooped to give the sleeper's arm a tug.
"I'm looking for headquarters." No reply.
"God blast your neck!" (For days he'd no sleep.)
"Get up and guide me through this stinking place."
Savage, he kicked a soft, unanswering heap,
And flashed his beam across the livid face
Terribly glaring up, whose eyes yet wore
Agony dying hard ten days before;
And fists of fingers clutched a blackening wound.

Alone he staggered on until he found
Dawn's ghost that filtered down a shafted stair
To the dazed, muttering creatures underground
Who hear the boom of shells in muffled sound.
At last, with sweat of horror in his hair,
He climbed through darkness to the twilight air,
Unloading hell behind him step by step.

1917 1918

AFTERMATH [1]

Have you forgotten yet? . . .
For the world's events have rumbled on, since those gagged days,
Like traffic checked a while at the crossing of city ways:
And the haunted gap in your mind has filled with thoughts that flow
Like clouds in the lit heavens of life; and you're a man reprieved to go,
Taking your peaceful share of Time, with joy to spare.
But the past is just the same—and War's a bloody game. . . .
Have you forgotten yet? . . .
Look down, and swear by the slain of the War that you'll never forget.

Do you remember the dark months you held the sector at Mametz—
The nights you watched and wired and dug and piled sandbags on parapets?
Do you remember the rats; and the stench
Of corpses rotting in front of the front-line trench—
And dawn coming, dirty-white, and chill with a hopeless rain?
Do you ever stop and ask, "Is it all going to happen again?"

Do you remember that hour of din before the attack—
And the anger, the blind compassion that seized and shook you then
As you peered at the doomed and haggard faces of your men?
Do you remember the stretcher-cases lurching back
With dying eyes and lolling heads, those ashen-gray
Masks of the lads who once were keen and kind and gay?

Have you forgotten yet? . . .
Look up, and swear by the green of the Spring that you'll never forget!

1919 1920

[1] By permission from *Picture-Show* by Siegfried Sassoon. Copyright by E. P. Dutton & Co.

WILFRID WILSON GIBSON
1880-

Mr. Gibson finds in the lives and experiences of toilers in our own industrial age the material for his best poetry. He was born in an industrial district at Hexam, Northumberland, has spent years in London, and now lives in Wales. His first poems, in regular form and upon conventional themes, soon gave place to those of less regular form based upon the lives of men and women of the mines, furnaces, shops, lighthouses, and fire stations. An important division of his work concerns the experiences of these same toilers flung into the horror of the trenches. In none of his poems does he preach or exhort; with simple, stern realism he pictures the emotions of the living cogs of the industrial mechanism, or the bits of human refuse it has flung aside. His verse is characteristically a short, unrimed, or even irregular line; sometimes it borrows the terse, unlettered speech of the workers who tell the tales.

Much of Mr. Gibson's poetry appears in the best periodicals. Excellent criticism, placing him among his contemporaries is found in Phelps (EP); same, *Bookm.* 46:563-68. Other helpful criticisms are those of Monro; Sturgeon, Wilkinson, W. A. Bradley, *Dial* 62:223-6; and Padric Colum, *New Repub.* 13: Sup. 10-12, Nov. 17, Part 2.

PROEM from FIRES [2]

Snug in my easy chair,
I stirred the fire to flame.
Fantastically fair,
The flickering fancies came,
Born of heart's desire:
Amber woodland streaming;
Topaz islands dreaming;
Sunset-cities gleaming,
Spire on burning spire;
Ruddy-windowed taverns;
Sunshine-spilling wines;
Crystal-lighted caverns
Of Golconda's [3] mines;
Summers, unreturning;
Passion's crater yearning;
Troy, the ever-burning;
Shelley's lustral [4] pyre;
Dragon-eyes, unsleeping;
Witches' cauldrons leaping;
Golden galleys sweeping
Out from sea-walled Tyre:
Fancies, fugitive and fair,
Flashed with singing through the air;

[2] From *Collected Poems* by Wilfrid Gibson. By permission of the author and The Macmillan Co., publishers.
[3] in India; formerly a famous diamond depot
[4] used for purification; Shelley was drowned off the coast of Italy, and his body was afterwards burned on the seashore.

Till, dazzled by the drowsy glare,
I shut my eyes to heat and light;
And saw, in sudden night,
Crouched in the dripping dark,
With steaming shoulders stark,
The man who hews the coal to feed my fire.

1912 1913

From BATTLE [1]

Hit

Out of the sparkling sea
I drew my tingling body clear, and lay
On a low ledge the livelong summer day,
Basking, and watching lazily
White sails in Falmouth Bay. [2]

My body seemed to burn
Salt in the sun that drenched it through and
through,
Till every particle glowed clean and new
And slowly seemed to turn
To lucent amber in a world of blue. . . . .

I felt a sudden wrench—
A trickle of warm blood—
And found that I was sprawling in the mud
Among the dead men in the trench.

1914-15 1915

JOHN COLLINGS SQUIRE
1884-

Mr. Squire, a native of Plymouth, received his early training at Blundell's School, Tiverton (where John Ridd, in Blackmore's *Lorna Doone,* was also a pupil), and then attended Cambridge. Afterwards he engaged in publishing and journalism, and became editor of the *New Statesman.* In 1919 he founded *The London Mercury,* which he later edited, a monthly periodical devoted to literature and the arts, and notable for its criticism of contemporary English letters.

Squire's work includes volumes of clever parodies, *Steps to Parnassus,* 1913, *Tricks of the Trade,* 1917; *Poems,* First and Second Series, 1919, 1920. His most important essays and literary criticisms written under the *nom de plume* "Solomon Eagle," were collected in *Books in General,* 1919. The intellect rather than the emotions dominates Mr. Squire's verse; his attitude toward life is critical, questioning. His verse is usually simple and conventional in form.

Criticism: Monro; E. Shanks, "English Lyrist," *Dial* 68:126-30; "J. C. Squire, A Poet of the Moon," *Athen.* 1920, 2:169-70.

[1] From *Collected Poems* by Wilfrid Gibson. By permission of the author and The Macmillan Co., publishers.
[2] off the coast of Cornwall

THE THREE HILLS [3]

There were three hills that stood alone
With woods about their feet.
They dreamed quiet when the sun shone
And whispered when the rain beat.

They wore all three their coronals [4]
Till men with houses came
And scored their heads with pits and walls
And thought the hills were tame.

Red and white when day shines bright
They hide the green for miles,
Where are the old hills gone? At night
The moon looks down and smiles.

She sees the captors small and weak,
She knows the prisoners strong,
She hears the patient hills that speak:
"Brothers, it is not long;

"Brothers, we stood when they were not
Ten thousand summers past.
Brothers, when they are clean forgot
We shall outlive the last;

"One shall die and one shall flee,
With terror in his train,
And earth shall eat the stones, and we
Shall be alone again."

1911 1919

THE MARCH [3]

I heard a voice that cried, "Make way for
those who died!"
And all the colored crowd like ghosts at morning fled;
And down the waiting road, rank after rank
there strode,
In mute and measured march, a hundred thousand dead.

A hundred thousand dead, with firm and noiseless tread,
All shadowy-gray yet solid, with faces gray
and ghast,
And by the house they went, and all their
brows were bent
Straight forward; and they passed, and passed,
and passed, and passed.

But Oh, there came a place, and Oh, there came
a face,
That clenched my heart to see it, and sudden
turned my way;
And in the Face that turned I saw two eyes
that burned,

[3] From *Poems,* First Series, by John C. Squire, copyright, 1919. George H. Doran Co., publishers.
[4] crowns

Never-forgotten eyes, and they had things to say.

Like desolate stars they shone one moment, and were gone,
And I sank down and put my arms across my head,
And felt them moving past, nor looked to see the last,
In steady silent march, our hundred thousand dead.

1916 1916

A DOG'S DEATH [1]

The loose earth falls in the grave like a peaceful regular breathing;
Too like, for I was deceived a moment by the sound:
It has covered the heap of bracken that the gardener laid above him;
Quiet the spade swings: there we have now his mound.

A patch of fresh earth on the floor of the wood's renewing chamber:
All around is grass and moss and the hyacinth's dark green sprouts:
And oaks are above that were old when his fiftieth sire was a puppy:
And far away in the garden I hear the children's shouts.

Their joy is remote as a dream. It is strange how we buy our sorrow
For the touch of perishing things, idly, with open eyes;
How we give our hearts to brutes that will die in a few seasons,
Nor trouble what we do when we do it; nor would have it otherwise.

1918 1920

WILLIAM HENRY DAVIES
1871-

Mr. Davies was born on the Welsh Border, at Newport in Monmouthshire. As the leader of a "gang" of boys he was officially chastized by the town authorities, but he seems to have had otherwise no formal education unless exception can be made of an apprenticeship to a picture-frame maker. When this was finished he crossed to America, became a tramp, and for several years roamed by land and sea, as he tells in his *Autobiography of a Super-Tramp,* 1908. After losing a leg under a train in Canada, he returned to England and began to write. On a legacy of eight shillings a week, supplemented at times by begging, he lived for two or three years in London lodging houses. At length, after failing at dramatic work he published at his own expense a volume of poems. His sending a copy to Mr. G. B. Shaw, who wrote an appreciative and cordial review, was the beginning of his recognition as a poet. Since then he has published some fifteen small volumes of verse and has twice made collected editions of his work. He now lives at Osted in Surrey.

Mr. Davies says that for thirty-four years he has been a poet, meaning that for that time he has looked at life poetically. In many of Mr. Davies's lyrics one may hear a note of naïveté, excited by a childlike delight in some aspect of nature such as is sometimes heard in the Elizabethan lyrics.

Criticism: Sturgeon; Phelps (EP); Cunliffe; Monro; Wilkinson (NV); G. H. Dillon, "Mr. Davies's Poetry," *Poetry* 27:44-8; T. Moult, "W. H. Davies, a Tramp Poet," *Liv. Age* 311:798-801; very interesting; see also *Cur. Lit.* 45:294-6; *19th Cent.* 67:71-8; same, *Liv. Age* 265:488-93; *No. Am.* 198:379-82.

CLOUDS [2]

My Fancy loves to play with Clouds
That hour by hour can change Heaven's face;
For I am sure of my delight,
In green or stony place.

Sometimes they on tall mountains pile
Mountains of silver, twice as high;
And then they break and lie like rocks
All over the wide sky.

And then I see flocks very fair;
And sometimes, near their fleeces white,
Are small, black lambs that soon will grow
And hide their mothers quite.

Sometimes, like little fishes, they
Are all one size, and one great shoal;
Sometimes they like big sailing ships
Across the blue sky roll.

Sometimes I see small Cloudlets tow
Big, heavy Clouds across those skies—
Like little Ants that carry off
Dead moths ten times their size.

Sometimes I see at morn bright Clouds
That stand so still, they make me stare;
It seems as they had trained all night
To make no motion there.

1910

[1] From *Poems,* Second Series, by John C. Squire, copyright, 1920, George H. Doran Co., publishers.

[2] From *The Collected Poems of William H. Davies.* By permission of the author and Jonathan Cape, Ltd., London, publishers.

DAYS TOO SHORT [1]

When Primroses are out in Spring
And small, blue violets come between;
When merry birds sing on boughs green,
And rills, as soon as born, must sing;

When butterflies will make side-leaps,
As though escaped from Nature's hand
Ere perfect quite; and bees will stand
Upon their heads in fragrant deeps;

When small clouds are so silvery white
Each seems a broken rimmèd moon—
When such things are, this world too soon,
For me, doth wear the veil of Night.

1911

IN MAY [1]

Yes, I will spend the livelong day
With Nature in this month of May;
And sit beneath the trees, and share
My bread with birds whose homes are there;
While cows lie down to eat, and sheep
Stand to their necks in grass so deep;
While birds do sing with all their might,
As though they felt the earth in flight.
This is the hour I dreamed of, when
I sat surrounded by poor men;
And thought of how the Arab sat
Alone at evening, gazing at
The stars that bubbled in clear skies;

And of young dreamers, when their eyes
Enjoyed methought a precious boon
In the adventures of the Moon
Whose light, behind the Clouds' dark bars,
Searched for her stolen flocks of stars.
When I, hemmed in by wrecks of men,
Thought of some lonely cottage then,
Full of sweet books; and miles of sea,
With passing ships, in front of me;
And having, on the other hand,
A flowery, green, bird-singing land.

1911

DREAMS OF THE SEA [1, 2]

I know not why I yearn for thee again,
To sail once more upon thy fickle flood;
I'll hear thy waves wash under my death-bed,
Thy salt is lodged forever in my blood.

Yet I have seen thee lash the vessel's sides
In fury, with thy many tailed whip;
And I have seen thee, too, like Galilee,
When Jesus walked in peace to Simon's ship. [3]

And I have seen thy gentle breeze as soft
As summer's, when it makes the cornfields run;
And I have seen thy rude and lusty gale
Make ships show half their bellies to the sun.

Thou knowest the way to tame the wildest life,
Thou knowest the way to bend the great and proud:
I think of that Armada whose puffed sails,
Greedy and large, came swallowing every cloud.

But I have seen the sea-boy, young and drowned,
Lying on shore and, by thy cruel hand,
A seaweed beard was on his tender chin,
His heaven-blue eyes were filled with common sand.

And yet, for all, I yearn for thee again,
To sail once more upon thy fickle flood;
I'll hear thy waves wash under my death-bed,
Thy salt is lodged forever in my blood.

1913

[1] From *The Collected Poems of William H. Davies.* By permission of the author and Jonathan Cape, Ltd., London, publishers.
[2] Cf. Conrad's *The Mirror of the Sea,* p. 833.
[3] *Matt.* xiv, 22-32

KATHERINE MANSFIELD
1888-1923

The life of Katherine Mansfield was a pathetic but courageous struggle, first, to gain recognition, then to preserve health after she had reached success. She was a daughter of Sir Harold Beauchamp of Wellington, New Zealand, and passed her childhood in Karori, a pupil in the little village school. At thirteen she was sent to Queen's College, London, for five years. Inspired by the intellectual and artistic life of the city she felt that a return to New Zealand would be exile, and preferred to remain in London on a meager allowance, which she supplemented by traveling with small opera companies while trying to get her writing accepted. *In a German Pension,* 1911, brought her temporary success. "Prelude," however, which shows that she had reached her goal in technique, was at first considered a failure.

In 1919 her brilliant work as reviewer and critic became widely known and approved; *Bliss,* 1920, and *The Garden Party,* 1922, established her as the foremost English short-story writer of her generation. But the hardships she suffered during the bombardment of Paris in 1918 brought on tuberculosis, and the last three years of her life she spent in a losing fight with death.

The usual absence of plot in Miss Mansfield's stories is more than compensated for by carefully selected pictures and incidents. By an accumulation of detail she emphasizes the salient traits of her characters. But such is her skill that it is not until her stories are analyzed that the reader becomes conscious of the perfect technique by which apparently irrelevant details are woven into a significant whole.

Criticism: "Katherine Mansfield's Hold on Literary Immortality," *Cur. Opin.* 74:436; J. M. Murry, "Katherine Mansfield," *Lit. R.* 3:461-2; R. Littell, "Katherine Mansfield," *New Repub.* 34: 22; "Greatest Short-story Writer," *Lit. Dig.* 76: 32-3, Mar. 17 '23; M. Armstrong, "The Art of Katherine Mansfield," *Fortn.* 119:484-90, delightful appreciation; G. Z. Brown, "Katherine Mansfield's Quest," *Bookm.* 61:687-91, vivid, readable.

AN IDEAL FAMILY [1]

That evening for the first time in his life, as he pressed through the swing door and descended the three broad steps to the pavement, old Mr. Neave felt he was too old for the spring. Spring—warm eager, restless—was there, waiting for him in the golden light, ready in front of everybody to run up, to blow in his white beard, to drag sweetly on his arm. And he couldn't meet her, no; he couldn't square up once more and stride off, jaunty as a young man. He was tired and, although the late sun was still shining, curiously cold, with a numbed feeling all over. Quite suddenly he hadn't the energy, he hadn't the heart to stand this gayety and bright movement any longer; it confused him. He wanted to stand still, to wave it away with his stick, to say, "Be off with you!" Suddenly it was a terrible effort to greet as usual—tipping his wide-awake with his stick—all the people whom he knew, the friends, acquaintances, shopkeepers, postmen, drivers. But the gay glance that went with the gesture, the kindly twinkle that seemed to say, "I'm a match and more for any of you"—that old Mr. Neave could not manage at all. He stumped along, lifting his knees high as if he were walking through air that had somehow grown heavy and solid like water. And the homeward-going crowd hurried by, the trams clanked, the light carts clattered, the big swinging cabs bowled along with that reckless, defiant indifference that one knows only in dreams. . . .

It had been a day like other days at the office. Nothing special had happened. Harold hadn't come back from lunch until close on four. Where had he been? What had he been up to? He wasn't going to let his father know. Old Mr. Neave had happened to be in the vestibule, saying good-bye to a caller, when Harold sauntered in, perfectly turned out as usual, cool, suave, smiling that peculiar little half-smile that women found so fascinating.

Ah, Harold was too handsome, too handsome by far; that had been the trouble all along. No man had a right to such eyes, such lashes, and such lips; it was uncanny. As for his mother, his sisters, and the servants, it was not too much to say they made a young god of him; they worshiped Harold, they forgave him everything; and he had needed some forgiving ever since the time when he was thirteen and he had stolen his mother's purse, taken the money, and hidden the purse in the cook's bedroom. Old Mr. Neave struck sharply with his stick upon the pavement edge. But it wasn't only his family who spoiled Harold, he reflected, it was everybody; he had only to look and to smile, and down they went before him. So perhaps it wasn't to be wondered at that he expected the office to carry on the tradition. H'm, h'm! But it couldn't be done. No business—not even a successful, established, big-paying concern—could be played with. A man had either to put his whole heart and soul into it, or it went all to pieces before his eyes. . .

And then Charlotte and the girls were always at him to make the whole thing over to Harold, to retire, and to spend his time enjoying himself. Enjoying himself! Old Mr. Neave stopped dead under a group of ancient cabbage palms outside the Government buildings! Enjoying himself! The wind of evening shook the dark leaves to a thin airy cackle. Sitting at home, twiddling his thumbs, conscious all the while that his life's work was slipping away, dissolving, disappearing through Harold's fine fingers, while Harold smiled. . .

"Why will you be so unreasonable, father? There's absolutely no need for you to go to the office. It only makes it very awkward for us when people persist in saying how tired you're looking. Here's this huge house and garden. Surely you could be happy in—in—appreciating it for a change. Or you could take up some hobby."

And Lola the baby had chimed in loftily, "All men ought to have hobbies. It makes life impossible if they haven't."

Well, well! He couldn't help a grim smile as painfully he began to climb the hill that led into Harcourt Avenue. Where would Lola and her sisters and Charlotte be if he'd gone in for hobbies, he's like to know? Hobbies couldn't pay for the town house and the sea-

[1] Reprinted from *The Garden Party and Other Stories* by Katherine Mansfield, by permission of and special arrangement with Alfred A. Knopf, Inc., authorized publisher.

side bungalow, and their horses, and their golf, and the sixty-guinea gramophone in the music-room for them to dance to. Not that he grudged them these things. No, they were smart, good-looking girls, and Charlotte was a remarkable woman; it was natural for them to be in the swim. As a matter of fact, no other house in the town was as popular as theirs; no other family entertained so much. And how many times old Mr. Neave, pushing the cigar box across the smoking-room table, had listened to praises of his wife, his girls, of himself even.

"You're an ideal family, sir, an ideal family. It's like something one reads about or sees on the stage."

"That's all right, my boy," old Mr. Neave would reply. "Try one of those; I think you'll like them. And if you care to smoke in the garden, you'll find the girls on the lawn, I dare say."

That was why the girls had never married, so people said. They could have married anybody. But they had too good a time at home. They were too happy together, the girls and Charlotte. H'm, h'm! Well, well! Perhaps so. . . . .

By this time he had walked the length of fashionable Harcourt Avenue; he had reached the corner house, their house. The carriage gates were pushed back; there were fresh marks of wheels on the drive. And then he faced the big white-painted house, with its wide-open windows, its tulle curtains floating outwards, its blue jars of hyacinths on the broad sills. On either side of the carriage porch their hydrangeas—famous in the town—were coming into flower; the pinkish, bluish masses of flower lay like light among the spreading leaves. And somehow, it seemed to old Mr. Neave that the house and the flowers, and even the fresh marks on the drive, were saying, "There is young life here. There are girls—"

The hall, as always, was dusky with wraps, parasols, gloves, piled on the oak chests. From the music-room sounded the piano, quick, loud and impatient. Through the drawing-room door that was ajar voices floated.

"And were there ices?" came from Charlotte. Then the creak, creak of her rocker.

"Ices!" cried Ethel. "My dear mother, you never saw such ices. Only two kinds. And one a common little strawberry shop ice, in a sopping wet frill."

"The food was altogether too appalling," came from Marion.

"Still, it's rather early for ices," said Charlotte easily.

"But why, if one has them at all . . . " began Ethel.

"Oh, quite so, darling," crooned Charlotte.

Suddenly the music-room door opened and Lola dashed out. She started, she nearly screamed, at the sight of old Mr. Neave.

"Gracious, father! What a fright you gave me! Have you just come home? Why isn't Charles here to help you off with your coat?"

Her cheeks were crimson from playing, her eyes glittered, the hair fell over her forehead. And she breathed as though she had come running through the dark and was frightened. Old Mr. Neave stared at his youngest daughter; he felt he had never seen her before. So that was Lola, was it? But she seemed to have forgotten her father; it was not for him that she was waiting there. Now she put the tip of her crumpled handkerchief between her teeth and tugged at it angrily. The telephone rang. A-ah! Lola gave a cry like a sob and dashed past him. The door of the telephone-room slammed, and at the same moment Charlotte called, "It that you, father?"

"You're tired again," said Charlotte reproachfully, and she stopped the rocker and offered him her warm plum-like cheek. Bright-haired Ethel pecked his beard; Marion's lips brushed his ear.

"Did you walk back, father?" asked Charlotte.

"Yes, I walked home," said old Mr. Neave, and he sank into one of the immense drawing-room chairs.

"But why didn't you take a cab?" said Ethel. "There are hundreds of cabs about at that time."

"My dear Ethel," cried Marion, "if father prefers to tire himself out, I really don't see what business of ours it is to interfere."

"Children, children?" coaxed Charlotte.

But Marion wouldn't be stopped. "No, mother, you spoil father, and it's not right. You ought to be stricter with him. He's very naughty." She laughed her hard, bright laugh and patted her hair in a mirror. Strange! When she was a little girl she had such a soft, hesitating voice; she had even stuttered, and now, whatever she said—even if it was only "Jam, please, father"—it rang out as though she were on the stage.

"Did Harold leave the office before you, dear?" asked Charlotte, beginning to rock again.

"I'm not sure," said old Mr. Neave. "I'm not sure. I didn't see him after four o'clock."

"He said—" began Charlotte.

But at that moment Ethel, who was twitching over the leaves of some paper or other, ran to her mother and sank down beside her chair.

"There, you see," she cried. "That's what I mean, mummy. Yellow, with touches of silver. Don't you agree?"

"Give it to me, love," said Charlotte. She fumbled for her tortoise-shell spectacles and put them on, gave the page a little dab with her plump small fingers, and pursed up her lips. "Very sweet!" she crooned vaguely. She looked at Ethel over her spectacles. "But I shouldn't have the train."

"Not the train?" wailed Ethel tragically. "But the train's the whole point."

"Here, mother, let me decide." Marion snatched the paper playfully from Charlotte. "I agree with mother," she cried triumphantly. "The train overweights it."

Old Mr. Neave, forgotten, sank into the broad lap of his chair, and, dozing, heard them as though he dreamed. There was no doubt about it, he was tired out; he had lost his hold. Even Charlotte and the girls were too much for him tonight. They were too . . . too. . . . But all his drowsing brain could think of was—too *rich* for him. And somewhere at the back of everything he was watching a little withered ancient man climbing up endless flights of stairs. Who was he?

"I shan't dress tonight," he muttered.

"What do you say, father?"

"Eh, what, what?" Old Mr. Neave woke with a start and stared across at them. "I shan't dress tonight," he repeated.

"But, father, we've got Lucile coming, and Henry Davenport, and Mrs. Teddie Walker."

"It will look so *very* out of the picture."

"Don't you feel well, dear?"

"You needn't make any effort. What is Charles *for?*"

"But if you're really not up to it," Charlotte wavered.

"Very well! Very well!" Old Mr. Neave got up and went to join that little old climbing fellow just as far as his dressing-room. . . . .

There young Charles was waiting for him. Carefully, as though everything depended on it, he was tucking a towel round the hot-water can. Young Charles had been a favorite of his ever since as a little red-faced boy he had come into the house to look after the fires. Old Mr. Neave lowered himself into the cane lounge by the window, stretched out his legs, and made his little evening joke. "Dress him up, Charles!" And Charles, breathing intensely and frowning, bent forward to take the pin out of his tie.

H'm, h'm! Well, well! It was pleasant by the open window, very pleasant—a fine mild evening. They were cutting the grass on the tennis court below; he heard the soft churr of the mower. Soon the girls would begin their tennis parties again. And at the thought he seemed to hear Marion's voice ring out, "Good for you, partner. . . . Oh, *played,* partner. . . . Oh, *very* nice indeed." Then Charlotte calling from the veranda, "Where is Harold?" And Ethel, "He's certainly not here, mother." And Charlotte's vague, "He said—"

Old Mr. Neave sighed, got up, and putting one hand under his beard, he took the comb from young Charles, and carefully combed the white beard over. Charles gave him a folded handkerchief, his watch and seals, and spectacle case.

"That will do, my lad." The door shut, he sank back, he was alone. . . . .

And now that little ancient fellow was climbing down endess flights that led to a glittering, gay dining-room. What legs he had! They were like a spider's—thin, withered.

"You're an ideal family, sir, an ideal family."

But if that were true, why didn't Charlotte or the girls stop him? Why was he all alone, climbing up and down? Where was Harold? Ah, it was no good expecting anything from Harold. Down, down went the little old spider, and then, to his horror, old Mr. Neave saw him slip past the dining-room and make for the porch, the dark drive, the carriage gates, the office. Stop him, stop him, somebody!

Old Mr. Neave started up. It was dark in his dressing-room; the window shone pale. How long had he been asleep? He listened, and through the big, airy, darkened house there floated far-away voices, far-away sounds. Perhaps, he thought vaguely, he had been asleep for a long time. He'd been forgotten. What had all this to do with him—this house and Charlotte, the girls and Harold—what did he know about them? They were strangers to him. Life had passed him by. Charlotte was not his wife. His wife!

. . . . A dark porch, half hidden by a passion-vine, that drooped sorrowful, mournful, as though it understood. Small, warm arms were round his neck. A face, little and pale, lifted to his, and a voice breathed, "Good-by, my treasure."

My treasure! "Good-by, my treasure!" Which of them had spoken? Why had they said good-by? There had been some terrible mistake. *She* was his wife, that little pale girl, and all the rest of his life had been a dream.

Then the door opened, and young Charles, standing in the light, put his hands by his side and shouted like a young soldier. "Dinner is on the table, sir!"

"I'm coming, I'm coming," said old Mr. Neave.

1922

GILES LYTTON STRACHEY 1880-

Mr. Strachey, son of Sir Richard Strachey, an eminent administrator of Indian affairs, received his education chiefly at Cambridge. He now lives in London. His attitude and methods have brought new life into the art of biography. He assumes the air of the detached and somewhat amused observer who watches, without too much enthusiasm, the play of life before him, quite in contrast with the attitude of Carlyle in *Heroes and Hero-Worship,* or *The French Revolution.*

A little of perverseness and paradox, perhaps, and a good deal of sly humor determine just what things Mr. Strachey will exhibit as the real traits of his characters.

His success lies in the wit, irony, and sometimes even ridicule with which he makes his portraits unforgettable. These pictures are not always accurate, and not always just: for Mr. Strachey sometimes draws too heavily upon an active imagination in setting forth the details of a situation; and certain limitations of sympathy make it impossible for him to estimate justly characters ruled more by emotion than by intellect. His sense of justice, however, prevents him from going far astray. His method is that of the skillful novelist, awakening and fulfilling anticipation, seizing upon dramatic moments, and preserving in his narrative all the interests of the plot. Since he takes the somewhat iconoclastic view of the present generation, and knows thoroughly Victorian society, he delights in exhibiting the solemnities of the past as one might in sportive mood comment upon the "portraits" in an album of daguerrotypes. *Eminent Victorians,* 1918, and his *Queen Victoria,* 1921, are his best-known works.

Criticism: Collins; Prince D. S. Mirsky, "Mr. Lytton Strachey," *Liv. Age* 318:126-31; E. Muir, "Lytton Strachey," *Nation* 120:658-60; see also *Lit. Dig.* 87:30, Dec. 12, '25; "The Bitter, Brilliant Briton who has Revived the Art of Biography," *Cur. Opin.* 65:182-3; "Is there a Menace of Literary Prussianism," *Cur. Lit.* 65:253.

From QUEEN VICTORIA [1]

Chapter II

IV

King William [2] could not away with [3] his sister-in-law, [4] and the Duchess [4] fully returned his antipathy. Without considerable tact and considerable forbearance their relative positions were well calculated to cause ill feeling; and there was very little tact in the composition of the Duchess, and no forbearance at all in that of his Majesty. A bursting, bubbling old gentleman, with quarter-deck gestures, round rolling eyes, and a head like a pineapple, his sudden elevation to the throne after fifty-six years of utter insignificance had almost sent him crazy. His natural exuberance completely got the better of him; he rushed about doing preposterous things in an extraordinary manner, spreading amusement and terror in every direction, and talking all the time. His tongue was decidedly Hanoverian, [5] with its repetitions, its catchwords—"That's quite another thing! That's quite another thing!"—its rattling indomitability, its loud indiscreetness. His speeches, made repeatedly at the most inopportune junctures, and filled pell-mell with all the fancies and furies that happened at the moment to be whisking about in his head, were the consternation of Ministers. He was one part blackguard, people said, and three parts buffoon; but those who knew him better could not help liking him—he meant well; and he was really good-humored and kind-hearted, if you took him the right way. If you took him the wrong way, however, you must look out for squalls, as the Duchess of Kent discovered.

. . . . .

Shortly afterwards King Leopold [6] came to England himself, and his reception was as cold at Windsor as it was warm at Kensington. "To hear dear Uncle speak on any sub-

[1] By permission. Reprinted from *Queen Victoria* by Lytton Strachey. Copyright, 1921, by Harcourt, Brace and Company, Inc. Throughout *Queen Victoria,* Mr. Strachey refers to the authorities on which his statements are based, consisting mostly of letters, diaries, and memoirs. References to them are omitted here.

[2] William IV, King of England 1830-1837, Victoria's uncle

[3] endure

[4] Duchess of York, mother of Princess Victoria afterwards queen

[5] The Hanoverian kings began with George I, who succeeded Queen Anne in 1714. He was Elector of Hanover, and through his mother, Elizabeth, youngest daughter of James I, was heir to the English throne; William IV was his great-grandson.

[6] King of the Belgians, 1831-1865, Victoria's favorite uncle, who had great influence over her

ject," the Princess wrote in her diary, "is like reading a highly instructive book; his conversation is so enlightened, so clear. He is universally admitted to be one of the first politicians now extant. He speaks so mildly, yet firmly and impartially, about politics. Uncle tells me "that Belgium is quite a pattern for its organization, its industry, and prosperity; the finances are in the greatest perfection. Uncle is so beloved and revered by his Belgian subjects, that it must be a great compensation for all his extreme trouble." But her other uncle by no means shared her sentiments. He could not, he said, put up with a water-drinker; and King Leopold would touch no wine. "What's that you're drinking sir?" he asked him one day at dinner. "Water, sir." "Why don't you drink wine? I never allow anybody to drink water at my table."

It was clear that before very long there would be a great explosion; and in the hot days of August it came. The Duchess and the Princess had gone down to stay at Windsor for the King's birthday party, and the King himself, who was in London for the day to prorogue[1] Parliament, paid a visit at Kensington Palace in their absence. There he found that the Duchess had just appropriated, against his express orders, a suite of seventeen apartments for her own use. He was extremely angry, and, when he returned to Windsor, after greeting the Princess with affection, he publicly rebuked the Duchess for what she had done. But this was little to what followed. On the next day was the birthday banquet; there were a hundred guests; the Duchess of Kent sat on the King's right hand, and the Princess Victoria opposite. At the end of the dinner, in reply to the toast of the King's health, he rose, and, in a long, loud, passionate speech, poured out the vials of his wrath upon the Duchess. She had, he declared, insulted him—grossly and continually; she had kept the Princess away from him in the most improper manner; she was surrounded by evil advisers, and was incompetent to act with propriety in the high station which she filled; but he would bear it no longer; he would have her to know he was King; he was determined that his authority should be respected; henceforth the Princess should attend at every Court function with the utmost regularity; and he hoped to God that his life might be spared for six months longer, so that the calamity of a regency might be avoided, and the functions of the Crown pass directly to the heiress-presumptive instead of into the hands of the "person now near him," upon whose conduct and capacity no reliance whatever could be placed. The flood of vituperation rushed on for what seemed an interminable period, while the Queen blushed scarlet, the Princess burst into tears, and the hundred guests sat aghast. The Duchess said not a word until the tirade was over and the company had retired; then in a tornado of rage and mortification, she called for her carriage and announced her immediate return to Kensington. It was only with the utmost difficulty that some show of a reconciliation was patched up, and the outraged lady was prevailed upon to put off her departure till the morrow.

. . . .

V

The King had prayed that he might live till his niece was of age; and a few days before her eighteenth birthday—the date of her legal majority—a sudden attack of illness very nearly carried him off. He recovered, however, and the Princess was able to go through her birthday festivities—a state ball and a drawing-room[2]—with unperturbed enjoyment. "Count Zichy," she noted in her diary, "is very good-looking in uniform, but not in plain clothes. Count Waldstein looks remarkably well in his pretty Hungarian uniform." With the latter young gentleman she wished to dance, but there was an insurmountable difficulty. "He could not dance quadrilles, and, as in my station I unfortunately cannot valse and galop, I could not dance with him." Her birthday present from the King was of a pleasing nature, but it led to a painful domestic scene. In spite of the anger of her Belgian uncle, she had remained upon good terms with her English one. He had always been very kind to her, and the fact that he had quarreled with her mother did not appear to be a reason for disliking him. He was, she said, "odd, very odd and singular," but "his intentions were often ill interpreted." He now wrote her a letter, offering her an allowance of £10,000 a year, which he proposed should be at her own disposal, and independent of her mother. Lord Conyngham, the Lord Chamberlain, was instructed to deliver the letter into the Princess's own hands. When he arrived at Kensington, he was ushered into the presence of the Duchess and the Princess, and, when he produced

[1] dismiss for a while

[2] formal Court reception

the letter, the Duchess put out her hand to take it. Lord Conyngham begged her Royal Highness's pardon, and repeated the King's commands. Thereupon the Duchess drew back, and the Princess took the letter. She immediately wrote to her uncle, accepting his kind proposal. The Duchess was much displeased; £4,000 a year, she said, would be quite enough for Victoria; as for the remaining £6,000, it would be only proper that she should have that herself.

King William had thrown off his illness, and returned to his normal life. Once more the royal circle at Windsor—their Majesties, the elder Princesses, and some unfortunate Ambassadress or Minister's wife—might be seen ranged for hours round a mahogany table, while the Queen netted a purse, and the King slept, occasionally waking from his slumbers to observe "Exactly so, ma'am, exactly so!" But this recovery was of short duration. The old man suddenly collapsed; with no specific symptoms besides an extreme weakness, he yet showed no power of rallying; and it was clear to everyone that his death was now close at hand.

All eyes, all thoughts, turned toward the Princess Victoria; but she still remained, shut away in the seclusion of Kensington, a small, unknown figure, lost in the large shadow of her mother's domination. The preceding year had in fact been an important one in her development. The soft tendrils of her mind had for the first time begun to stretch out toward unchildish things. In this King Leopold encouraged her. After his return to Brussels, he had resumed his correspondence in a more serious strain; he discussed the details of foreign politics; he laid down the duties of kingship; he pointed out the iniquitous foolishness of the newspaper press. On the latter subject, indeed, he wrote with some asperity. "If all the editors," he said, "of the papers in the countries where the liberty of the press exists were to be assembled, we should have a *crew* to which you would *not* confide a dog that you would value, still less your honor and reputation." On the functions of a monarch, his views were unexceptionable. "The business of the highest in a State," he wrote, "is certainly, in my opinion, to act with great impartiality and a spirit of justice for the good of all." At the same time the Princess's tastes were opening out. Though she was still passionately devoted to riding and dancing, she now began to have a genuine love of music as well, and to drink in the roulades and arias of the Italian opera with high enthusiasm. She even enjoyed reading poetry—at any rate, the poetry of Sir Walter Scott.

When King Leopold learned that King William's death was approaching, he wrote several long letters of excellent advice to his niece. "In every letter I shall write to you," he said, "I mean to repeat to you, as a *fundamental rule, to be courageous, firm, and honest, as you have been till now.*" For the rest, in the crisis that was approaching, she was not to be alarmed, but to trust in her "good natural sense and the *truth*" of her character; she was to do nothing in a hurry; to hurt no one's *amour-propre,*[1] and to continue her confidence in the Whig[2] administration. Not content with letters, however, King Leopold determined that the Princess should not lack personal guidance, and sent over to her aid the trusted friend whom, twenty years before, he had taken to his heart by the death-bed at Claremont.[3] Thus, once again, as if in accordance with some preordained destiny, the figure of Stockmar is discernible—inevitably present at a momentous hour.

On June 18, the King was visibly sinking. The Archbishop of Canterbury was by his side, with all the comforts of the church. Nor did the holy words fall upon a rebellious spirit; for many years his Majesty had been a devout believer. "When I was a young man," he once explained at a public banquet, "as well as I can remember, I believed in nothing but pleasure and folly—nothing at all. But when I went to sea, got into a gale, and saw the wonders of the mighty deep, then I believed; and I have been a sincere Christian ever since." It was the anniversary of the Battle of Waterloo, and the dying man remembered it. He should be glad to live, he said, over that day; he would never see another sunset. "I hope your Majesty may live to see many," said Dr. Chambers. "Oh! that's quite another thing, that's quite another thing," was the answer. One other sunset he did live to see; and he died in the early hours of the following morning. It was June 20, 1837.

When all was over, the Archbishop and the Lord Chamberlain ordered a carriage, and drove post-haste from Windsor to Kensington. They arrived at the Palace at five o'clock, and it was only with considerable difficulty that they gained admittance. At six the Duchess

[1] self-esteem
[2] liberal
[3] After the death of Leopold's wife, the Princess Charlotte, at Claremont, her physician, Dr. Stockmar, had been a confidential adviser of the King.

woke up her daughter, and told her that the Archbishop of Canterbury and Lord Conyngham were there, and wished to see her. She got out of bed, put on her dressing-gown, and went, alone, into the room where the messengers were standing. Lord Conyngham fell on his knees, and officially announced the death of the King; the Archbishop added some personal details. Looking at the bending, murmuring dignitaries before her, she knew that she was Queen of England. "Since it has pleased Providence," she wrote that day in her journal, "to place me in this station, I shall do my utmost to fulfill my duty toward my country; I am very young, and perhaps in many, though not in all things, inexperienced, but I am sure that very few have more real good will and more real desire to do what is fit and right than I have." But there was scant time for resolutions and reflections. At once, affairs were thick upon her. Stockmar came to breakfast, and gave some good advice. She wrote a letter to her uncle Leopold, and a hurried note to her sister Feodora. A letter came from the Prime Minister, Lord Melbourne, announcing his approaching arrival. He came at nine, in full court dress, and kissed her hand. She saw him alone, and repeated to him the lesson which, no doubt, the faithful Stockmar had taught her at breakfast, "It has long been my intention to retain your Lordship and the rest of the present Ministry at the head of affairs"; whereupon Lord Melbourne again kissed her hand and shortly after left her. She then wrote a letter of condolence to Queen Adelaide. At eleven, Lord Melbourne came again; and at half past eleven she went downstairs into the red saloon to hold her first Council. The great assembly of lords and notables, bishops, generals, and Ministers of State, saw the doors thrown open and a very short, very slim girl in deep plain mourning come into the room alone and move forward to her seat with extraordinary dignity and grace; they saw a countenance, not beautiful, but prepossessing—fair hair, blue prominent eyes, a small curved nose, an open mouth revealing the upper teeth, a tiny chin, a clear complexion, and, over all, the strangely mingled signs of innocence, of gravity, of youth, and of composure; they heard a high unwavering voice reading aloud with perfect clarity; and then, the ceremony over, they saw the small figure rise and, with the same consummate grace, the same amazing dignity, pass out from among them, as she had come in, alone.

RALPH HODGSON
1872-

Little is publicly known of the life and experiences of Mr. Hodgson. He was born in the north of England and now lives in London. A thin volume would hold all Mr. Hodgson's work, yet his few poems are of a high level, and it is doubtful if any of his contemporaries can show in their work so large a proportion of notable verse as he can. His poetry has the qualities of the imagistic school, (See note under D. H. Lawrence, p. 881.) vividness, exactness, brilliancy of picture. Some critics have likened his work to Blake's; but the similarity is only that of a first impression, for Hodgson's poetry has no quality of mysticism but is based upon external fact.

Criticism is to be found in Phelps (EP); Sturgeon; Monro; Wilkinson; also see J. G. Fletcher, *Dial* 63:50-52; *Liv. Age* 287:611-15; Conrad Akien, *Dial* 63:150-152; E. V. Lucas, *Nation* 99: 341-3; W. H. Chesson, *19th Cent.* 88:54-62.

BABYLON [1]

If you could bring her glories back!
You gentle sirs who sift the dust
And burrow in the mold and must
Of Babylon for bric-a-brac;
Who catalogue and pigeon-hole
The faded splendors of her soul
And put her greatness under glass—
If you could bring her past to pass!

If you could bring her dead to life!
The soldier lad; the market wife;
Madam buying fowls from her;
Tip, the butcher's bandy cur;
Workmen carting bricks and clay;
Babel passing to and fro
On the business of a day
Gone three thousand years ago—
That you cannot; then be done,
Put the goblet down again,
Let the broken arch remain,
Leave the dead men's dust alone—

Is it nothing how she lies,
This old mother of you all,
You great cities proud and tall
Towering to a hundred skies
Round a world she never knew,
Is it nothing, this, to you?
Must the ghoulish work go on
Till her very floors are gone?
While there's still a brick to save
Drive these people from her grave!

[1] From *Poems* by Ralph Hodgson, 1917. By permission of The Macmillan Company, publishers.

The Jewish seer when he cried
Woe to Babel's lust and pride
Saw the foxes at her gates;
Once again the wild thing waits.
Then leave her in her last decay
A house of owls, a foxes' den;
The desert that till yesterday
Hid her from the eyes of men
In its proper time and way
Will take her to itself again.

before 1914

STUPIDITY STREET [1]

I saw with open eyes
Singing birds sweet
Sold in the shops
For the people to eat,
Sold in the shops of
Stupidity Street.

I saw in vision
The worm in the wheat,
And in the shops nothing
For people to eat;
Nothing for sale in
Stupidity Street.

before 1914

DAVID HERBERT LAWRENCE
1885-

D. H. Lawrence, pronounced by Edward Garnett, the English critic, to be "one of the most interesting and uncompromising literary forces of the recent years," was born, the son of a coal miner, on the border between Nottinghamshire and Derbyshire. He won a scholarship in the Nottingham High School and at sixteen entered upon a career of teaching, carrying on his own studies at the same time. This occupation led him to London, where he followed it until the success of his novels allowed him to give it up. He has produced several volumes of verse (*Amores,* 1916; *Look! We Have Come Through!,* 1918; *New Poems,* 1920); novels (*Sons and Lovers,* 1913, "an epic of family life in a colliery district," largely biographical; *The Plumed Serpent,* 1926, and others); short stories, essays, a drama, translations, and psychoanalytical studies. As a poet he belongs to the Imagist School. [2]

Both his poems and his novels are characterized by a reveling in emotions and sense perceptions that resembles the manner of Keats.

Criticism: Phelps (EP), E. Garnett, *Friday Nights,* ser. 1; same, *Dial* 61:377-81; L. Untermeyer, "D. H. Lawrence," *New Repub.* 23:314-15; *Cur. Opin.* 72:248-50; M. Lesemann, "D. H. Lawrence in New Mexico," *Bookm.* 59:29-32, interesting personal recollections; R. Aldington, "D. H. Lawrence as Poet," *Sat. R. Lit.* 2:749-50; E. Muir, "D. H. Lawrence," *Nation* 120:148-50.

A BABY ASLEEP AFTER PAIN [3]

As a drenched drowned bee
Hangs numb and heavy from a bending flower,
So clings to me
My baby, her brown hair brushed with wet tears
And laid against her cheek;
Her soft white legs hanging heavily over my arm,
Swinging heavily to my movement as I walk.
My sleeping baby hangs upon my life,
Like a burden she hangs on me
She has always seemed so light,
But now she is wet with tears and numb with pain.
Even her floating hair sinks heavily,
Reaching downward;
As the wings of a drenched, drowned bee
Are a heaviness, and a weariness.

1911

SERVICE OF ALL THE DEAD [4]

Between the avenue of cypresses
All in their scarlet capes and surplices
Of linen, go the chaunting choristers,
The priests in gold and black, the villagers.

And all along the path to the cemetery
The round dark heads of men crowd silently;
And black-scarfed faces of women-folk wistfully
Watch at the banner of death, and the mystery.

And at the foot of a grave a father stands
With sunken head, and forgotten, folded hands;
And at the foot of a grave a mother kneels
With pale shut face, nor neither hears nor feels

The coming of the chaunting choristers
Between the avenue of cypresses,
The silence of the many villagers,
The candle-flames beside the surplices.

1915

[1] From *Poems* by Ralph Hodgson, 1917. By permission of The Macmillan Company, publishers.

[2] Imagists was the name adopted by certain poets who believed that a poem should present an image, or a series of related images, conveyed in rhythms suggestive of a mood. In the opinion of many critics Amy Lowell stood at the head of the group. The members formulated certain principles which they considered essential to all great poetry: poetry should use the language of common speech, and the *exact* word, allow absolute freedom in the choice of subject, be hard and clear, never blurred nor indefinite, and show concentration as its essence.

[3] From *Love Poems and Others.* By permission of the author and Curtis Brown, Ltd., publishers.

[4] From *Amores.* By permission of the author and Curtis Brown, Ltd., publishers.

GREEN [1]

The dawn was apple-green,
The sky was green wine held up in the sun,
The moon was a golden petal between.

She opened her eyes, and green
They shone, clear like flowers undone
For the first time, now for the first time seen.

1916

GILBERT KEITH CHESTERTON
1874-

A Londoner, educated at St. Paul's School and the Slade School of Art, Chesterton early found his field to be literature, and has made a name for himself as journalist, essayist, novelist, critic, and poet. As a critic and essayist his emotions rule his intellect. His rapid intuitions and over-indulgence in paradox often lead him to statements that are smart rather than sound. He is possibly best known for his essays—*Heretics,* 1905, *Orthodoxy,* 1908, *Tremendous Trifles,* 1909, for example. These essays cover deep problems of life as well as mere trifles; but his work includes also critical studies of Dickens, Browning, Victorian literature; grotesque, fantastic romances, such as *Napoleon of Notting Hill,* 1904; detective stories, *The Innocence of Father Brown,* 1911; short stories; and an operatic extravaganza, *The Flying Inn,* 1914. His verse, as individual as his prose, is characterized by the same startling and arresting qualities. The first volume, *The Wild Knight,* appeared in 1900; in *The Ballad of the White Horse,* 1911, he has achieved the vigor and simplicity of the true folk poetry.

Criticism: Anon., *G. K. Chesterton: a Criticism,* 1908; J. West, *Gilbert K. Chesterton, a Critical Study,* 1916; E. E. Slosson, *Six Major Prophets,* 1917; Scott; Ervine; Monro; Wilkinson; F. Lefèvre, "An Hour with G. K. Chesterton," *Liv. Age* 325:523-9; E. E. Slosson, "The Poet Chesterton," *Ind.* 88:349-52; S. G. Ford, "G. K. C. as Poet: an Appreciation," *Liv. Age* 288:314-16; J. C. Squire, "Mr. Chesterton as a Poet," *Liv. Age* 285:805-8; E. T. Raymond, "G. K. Chesterton, a Study," *Liv. Age* 301:162-5; see also E. C. Marsh, *Forum* 40:394-400; O. W. Firkins, *Forum* 48:597-607.

ELEGY IN A COUNTRY CHURCHYARD [2]

The men that worked for England
They have their graves at home;
And bees and birds of England
About the cross can roam.

But they that fought for England,
Following a falling star,
Alas, alas, for England,
They have their graves afar.

And they that rule in England
In stately conclave met
Alas, alas, for England,
They have no graves as yet.

THE DONKEY [3]

When fishes flew and forests walked
And figs grew upon thorn,
Some moment when the moon was blood,
Then surely I was born;

With monstrous head and sickening cry
And ears like errant wings,
The devil's walking parody
On all four-footed things.

The tattered outlaw of the earth,
Of ancient crooked will;
Starve, scourge, deride me; I am dumb,
I keep my secret still.

Fools! For I also had my hour;
One far fierce hour and sweet:
There was a shout about my ears,
And palms before my feet! [4]

THE IRISHMAN [5]

The other day I went to see the Irish plays, recently acted by real Irishmen—peasants and poor folk—under the inspiration of Lady Gregory [6] and Mr. W. B. Yeats. Over and above the excellence of the acting and the abstract merit of the plays (both of which were considerable), there emerged the strange and ironic interest which has been the source of so much fun and sin and sorrow—the interest of the Irishman in England. Since we have sinned by creating the Stage Irishman, it is fitting enough that we should all be rebuked by Irishmen on the stage. We have all seen some obvious Englishman performing a Paddy.

[1] From *Look! We Have Come Through!* By permission of the author and Curtis Brown, Ltd., publishers.

[2] From *The Ballad of St. Barbara* by G. K. Chesterton. Used by permission of the author and Dodd, Mead and Company, Inc.

[3] From *The Wild Knight* by G. K. Chesterton. Used by permission of the author and Dodd, Mead and Company, Inc.

[4] *Matt.* xxi, 1-8; *John* xii, 12-15

[5] From *The Uses of Diversity,* by G. K. Chesterton. Used by permission of the author and Dodd, Mead and Company, Inc.

[6] An Irish playwright, one of the supporters of Yeats (see p. 847) in founding the Irish Literary Theater, established in Dublin to encourage the national drama; at first actors were brought from London, but in 1902 the acting was taken over by Irish players, and in 1904 the Society came into possession of the famous Abbey Theater, since the center of Irish playwriting.

It was, perhaps, a just punishment to see an obvious Paddy performing the comic and contemptible part of an English gentleman. I have now seen both, and I can lay my hand on my heart (though my knowledge of physiology is shaky about its position) and declare that the Irish English gentleman was an even more abject and crawling figure than the English Irish servant. The Comic Irishman in the English plays was at least given credit for a kind of chaotic courage. The Comic Englishman in the Irish plays was represented not only as a fool, but as a nervous fool; fussy and spasmodic prig, who could not be loved either for strength or weakness. But all this only illustrates the fundamental fact that both the national views are wrong; both the versions are perversions. The rollicking Irishman and the priggish Englishman are alike the mere myths generated by a misunderstanding. It would be rather nearer the truth if we spoke of the rollicking Englishman and the priggish Irishman. But even that would be wrong too.

Unless people are near in soul they had better not be near in neighborhood. The Bible tells us to love our neighbors, and also to love our enemies; probably because they are generally the same people. And there is a real human reason for this. You think of a remote man merely as a man; that is, you think of him in the right way. Suppose I say to you suddenly—"Oblige me by brooding on the soul of the man who lives at 351 High Street, Islington." Perhaps (now I come to think of it) you *are* the man who lives at 351 High Street, Islington. In that case substitute some other unknown address and pursue the intellectual sport. Now you will probably be broadly right about the man in Islington whom you have never seen or heard of, because you will begin at the right end—the human end. The man in Islington is at least a man. The soul of the man in Islington is certainly a soul. He also has been bewildered and broadened by youth; he also has been tortured and intoxicated by love; he also is sublimely doubtful about death. You can think about the soul of that nameless man who is a mere number in Islington High Street. But you do not think about the soul of your next-door neighbor. He is not a man; he is an environment. He is the barking of a dog; he is the noise of a pianola; he is a dispute about a party wall; he is drains that are worse than yours, or roses that are better than yours. Now, all these are the wrong ends of a man; and a man, like many other things in this world, such as a cat-o-nine-tails, has a large number of wrong ends, and only one right one. These adjuncts are all tails, so to speak. A dog is a sort of curly tail to a man; a substitute for that which man so tragically lost at an early stage of evolution. And though I would rather myself go about trailing a dog behind me than tugging a pianola or towing a rose-garden, yet this is a matter of taste, and they are all alike appendages or things dependent upon man. But besides his twenty tails, every man really has a head, a center of identity, a soul. And the head of a man is even harder to find than the head of a Skye terrier, for the man has nine hundred and ninety-nine wrong ends instead of one. It is no question of getting hold of the sow by the right ear; it is a question of getting hold of the hedgehog by the right quill, of the bird by the right feather, of the forest by the right leaf. If we have never known the forest we shall know at least that it is a forest, a thing grown grandly out of the earth; we shall realize the roots toiling in the terrestial darkness, the trunks reared in the sylvan twilight.

But to find the forest is to find the fringe of the forest. To approach it from without is to see its mere accidental outline ragged against the sky. It is to come close enough to be superficial. The remote man, therefore, may stand for manhood; for the glory of birth or the dignity of death. But it is difficult to get Mr. Brown next door (with whom you have quarreled about the creepers) to stand for these things in any satisfactorily symbolic attitude. You do not feel the glory of his birth; you are more likely to hint heatedly at its ingloriousness. You do not, on purple and silver evenings, dwell on the dignity and quietude of his death; you think of it, if at all, rather as sudden. And the same is true of historical separation and proximity. I look forward to the same death as a Chinaman; barring one or two Chinese tortures, perhaps. I look back to the same babyhood as an ancient Phoenician; unless, indeed, it were one of that special Confirmation class of Sunday-school babies who were passed through the fire to Moloch. But these distant or antique terrors seem merely tied on to the life: they are not part of its texture. Babylonian mothers (however they yielded to etiquette) probably loved their children; and Chinamen unquestionably reverenced their dead. It is far different when two peoples are close enough to each other to mistake all the acts and gestures of everyday life. It is far different when the Baptist baker in Islington thinks of Irish infancy, passed amid Popish priests and impossible fairies. It is far different when the tramp from Tipperary thinks of Irish death, coming often in dying hamlets, in distant colonies, in English prisons, or on English gibbets. There childhood and death have lost all their reconciling qualities; the very details of them do not unite, but divide. Hence England and Ireland see the facts of each other without guessing the meaning of the facts. For instance, we may see the fact that an Irish housewife is careless. But we fancy falsely that this is because she is scatter-brained; whereas it is, on the contrary, because she is concentrated—on religion, or conspiracy, or tea. You may call her inefficient, but you certainly must not call her weak. In the same way, the Irish see the fact that the Englishman is unsociable; they do not see the reason, which is that he is romantic.

This seems to me the real value of such striking national sketches as those by Lady Gregory and Mr. Synge,[1] which I saw last week. Here is a case where mere accidental realism, the thing written on the spot, the "slice of life," may, for once in a way, do some good. All the signals, all the flags, all the declaratory externals of Ireland we are almost certain to mistake. If the Irishman speaks to us, we are sure to misunderstand him. But if we hear the Irishman talking to himself, it may begin to dawn on us that he is a man.

1921

HAROLD MONRO 1879-

For some years Mr. Monro has been interested in bringing poetry before the general public in various ways, since, as he says, he is an "author, publisher, editor, and bookseller." He was born in Brussels, and educated at Cambridge. In 1912 he founded in London the Poetry Bookshop, which has become a well-known literary center selling only works of poetry, the drama, and literature on these subjects.

His own work, which includes *Children of Love,* 1915, *Strange Meetings,* 1917, and *Real Property,* 1922, shows a steady development in power and in technical skill. Like other poets of the modern school, Monro is most at home in a world half fancy, half actuality. But when writing of rural England he is quick to recognize a single essential aspect of his subject and develop it in a style singularly free from monotonous regularity, and animated by whimsical humor and imagination.

Criticism: Sturgeon; C. Aiken, "Three English Poets," *Dial,* 63:150-2.

[1] see p. 842.

REAL PROPERTY[2]

Tell me about that harvest field.
Oh! Fifty acres of living bread.
The color has painted itself in my heart.
The form is patterned in my head.

So now I take it everywhere;
See it whenever I look round;
Hear it growing through every sound,
Know exactly the sound it makes—
Remembering, as one must all day,
Under the pavement the live earth aches.

Trees are at the farther end,
Limes[3] all full of the mumbling bee:
So there must be a harvest field
Whenever one thinks of a linden tree.

A hedge is about it, very tall,
Hazy and cool, and breathing sweet,
Round paradise is such a wall
And all the day, in such a way,
In paradise the wild birds call.

You only need to close your eyes
And go within your secret mind,
And you'll be into paradise:

I've learned quite easily to find
Some linden trees and drowsy bees,
A tall sweet hedge with the corn behind.

I will not have that harvest mown:
I'll keep the corn[4] and leave the bread.
I've bought that field; it's now my own:
I've fifty acres in my head.
I take it as a dream to bed.
I carry it about all day. . . .

Sometimes when I have found a friend
I give a blade of corn away.

1919 *1922*

FROM AN OLD HOUSE[2]

I

In lonely silence
Of windless country
I think of those
In far London
Who move in lamplight.

[2] The poems by Mr. Monro are from *Real Property,* The Poetry Bookshop, London. Reprinted by permission of the author.

[3] linden trees, basswood [4] grain, wheat

Hark!—the shuffle
Of groping feet.
No—the branches
Keen at the window.

II

I heard the latch:
You have gone perhaps
To buy food in the town.

It must have been that,
By the way the old house
Becomes suddenly quiet
Like a dog awaiting
Its absent master.

III

Look! Look!
Those are the fields
Of Paradise . . . .

—What can you mean?
That is the pasture,
The pond, the cattle,
(Grazing by moonlight),
Of my old tenant,
Mister Brown.

IV

The moonlight, it was blowing in waves
Tonight when I crossed the fields:
I waited below by the hedge.

My breath was caught up by the wind;
I stood and expected to drown.

Curling across the green,
It folded me up:
I swam to the land,
Came back to the house,
In the shelter of trees,
To the safety of you.

1921 *1922*

DOG[1]

O little friend, your nose is ready; you sniff,
Asking for that expected walk,
(Your nostrils full of the happy rabbit-whiff)
And almost talk.

And so the moment becomes a moving force;
Coats glide down from their pegs in the humble dark;
You scamper the stairs,
Your body informed[2] with the scent and the track and the mark
Of stoats and weasels, moles and badgers and hares.

We are going *Out*. You know the pitch of the word,
Probing the tone of thought as it comes through fog
And reaches by devious means (half-smelled, half-heard)
The four-legged brain of a walk-ecstatic dog.

Out through the garden your head is already low.
You are going your walk, you know,
And your limbs will draw
Joy from the earth through the touch of your padded paw.

Now, sending a little look to us behind,
Who follow slowly the track of your lovely play,
You fetch our bodies forward away from mind
Into the light and fun of your useless day.

. . . .

Thus, for your walk, we took ourselves, and went
Out by the hedge, and tree, to the open ground.
You ran, in delightful strata of wafted scent,
Over the hill without seeing the view;
Beauty is hinted through primitive smells to you:
And that ultimate Beauty you track is but rarely found.

. . . .

Home . . . . and further joy will be waiting there:
Supper full of the lovely taste of bone.
You lift up your nose again, and sniff, and stare
For the rapture known
Of the quick wild gorge of food, then the still lie-down;
While your people will talk above you in the light
Of candles, and your dreams will merge and drown
Into the bed-delicious hours of night.

1921 *1922*

THISTLEDOWN[1]

This might have been a place for sleep
But, as from that small hollow there
Hosts of bright thistledown begin
Their dazzling journey through the air,
An idle man can only stare.

[1] The poems by Mr. Monro are from *Real Property*, The Poetry Bookshop, London. Reprinted by permission of the author.
[2] inspired, animated

They grip their withered edge of stalk
In brief excitement for the wind;
They hold a breathless final talk,
And when their filmy cables part
One almost hears a little cry.

Some cling together while they wait
And droop and gaze and hesitate,
But others leap along the sky,
Or circle round and calmly choose
The gust they know they ought to use.

While some in loving pairs will glide,
Or watch the others as they pass,
Or rest on flowers in the grass,
Or circle through the shining day
Like silvery butterflies at play.

Some catch themselves to every mound,
They lingeringly and slowly move
As if they knew the precious ground
Were opening for their fertile love;
They almost try to dig, they need
So much to plant their thistle-seed.

1919 1922

MAN CARRYING BALE [1]

The tough hand closes gently on the load;
  Out of the mind, a voice
Calls "Lift!" and the arms, remembering well
    their work,
  Lengthen and pause for help.
Then a slow ripple flows along the body,
While all the muscles call to one another:
  "Lift!" and the bulging bale
  Floats like a butterfly in June.

So moved the earliest carrier of bales,
  And the same watchful sun
Glowed through his body feeding it with light.
  So will the last one move,
And halt, and dip his head, and lay his load
Down, and the muscles will relax and trem-
    ble . . . .
  Earth, you designed your man
Beautiful both in labor, and repose.

1921 1922

JOHN DRINKWATER
1882-

Since Drinkwater's father was a theatrical manager it is not surprising to learn that the son gave up the insurance business after twelve years to become the manager of the famous Birmingham Repertory Theater, renowned for the high standard of the plays it produces. He was born at Leytonstone, Essex, was educated at the Oxford High School, and is now widely known as poet, playwright, and critic. In his volumes of verse from *Poems,* 1903, to *Collected Poems,* 1923, can be traced a distinct advance in melody and in command of thought and language. His poetry is intellectual and meditative, distinguished, as St. John Ervine says, by a "high sincerity, a love of simple beauty and good purpose and fine character, and a deep regard for the dignity of his craft." He says that he sings of immemorial things—earth, love, pity for and pride in men and women.

Probably his best known productions are his dramas, especially *Abraham Lincoln,* 1918, based on Lord Charnwood's excellent *Life of Lincoln.* Drinkwater has taken a national figure and made it into one of universal appeal without sacrificing its local characteristics. Among his critical studies those on William Morris, 1912, and Swinburne, 1913, two poets to whom he owed much, were outstanding. In 1925, appeared *The Pilgrim of Eternity: Byron—a Conflict,* a biography in the most modern biographical style, which now ranks as his most important prose work.

Collected Plays, 2 volumes, 1925 (valuable preface).

Criticism: Phelps (EP); Monro; Wilkinson (NV); M. Bronner, "An Appreciation," *Bookm.* 41:446-52; St. J. Ervine, "John Drinkwater," *No. Am.* 210:824-36; (contains biography); "John Drinkwater's *Mary Stuart,*" *Liv. Age* 309:423-5; M. J. Moses, *"Abraham Lincoln," Bookm.* 50:551-5.

[1] The poems by Mr. Monro are from *Real Property,* The Poetry Bookshop, London. Reprinted by permission of the author.

SUNRISE ON RYDAL WATER [2]

To E. de S.

Come down at dawn from windless hills
  Into the valley of the lake,
Where yet a larger quiet fills
  The hour, and mist and water make
With rocks and reeds and island boughs
  One silence and one element,
Where wonder goes surely as once
  It went
    By Galilean prows.

Moveless the water and the mist,
  Moveless the secret air above,
Hushed, as upon some happy tryst
  The poised expectancy of love;
What spirit is it that adores
  What mighty presence yet unseen?
What consummation works apace
  Between
    These rapt enchanted shores?

[2] From *Alton Pools,* 1916, by John Drinkwater, with the permission of the author and Houghton Mifflin Company, authorized publishers.

Never did virgin beauty wake
  Devouter to the bridal feast
Than moves this hour upon the lake
  In adoration to the east.
Here is the bride a god may know,
  The primal will, the young consent,
Till surely upon the appointed mood
  Intent
    The god shall leap—and lo,

Over the lake's end strikes the sun—
  White, flameless fire; some purity
Thrilling the mist, a splendor won
  Out of the world's heart. Let there be
Thoughts, and atonements, and desires;
  Proud limbs, and undeliberate tongue;
Where now we move with mortal care
  Among
    Immortal dews and fires.

So the old mating goes apace,
  Wind with the sea, and blood with thought,
Lover with lover; and the grace
  Of understanding comes unsought
When stars into the twilight steer,
  Or thrushes build among the may,
Or wonder moves between the hills,
  And day
    Comes up on Rydal mere.[1]

1915

SYMBOLS[2]

I saw a history in a poet's song,
In a river-reach and a gallows-hill,
In a bridal bed, and a secret wrong,
In a crown of thorns: in a daffodil.

I imagined measureless time in a day,
And starry space in a wagon-road,
And the treasure of all good harvests lay
In the single seed that the sower sowed.

My garden-wind had driven and havened again
All ships that ever had gone to sea,
And I saw the glory of all dead men
In the shadow that went by the side of me.

1917

JOHN GALSWORTHY
1867-

John Galsworthy was born at Coombe, in Surrey, though the ancestral home of his family is Devon. He attended Harrow, and Oxford, where he took honors in law. Although he was admitted to the bar in 1890, he was under no necessity of practicing, and went on long tours and voyages to all parts of the world, on one of which he traveled for some weeks with the Polish master of a sailing ship, the then unknown Joseph Conrad.

During the thirty years that Galsworthy has been writing, he has produced some twenty novels and as many plays, besides poems and essays.

His novel sequence, the *Forsyte Saga,* 1922-1928, includes, in its first series, three novels: *A Man of Property, In Chancery, To Let;* and two stories, "Indian Summer of a Forsyte," and "Awakening." In this remarkable series he chronicles the establishment of the Forsyte family and fortune, and the interwoven lives of the individual members of the clan, Soames Forsyte, as the epitome of his class, figures most prominently in the early group, and links it with the second series, post-war novels and stories: *The White Monkey,* 1924; *The Silver Spoon,* 1926; "Two Interludes," 1927, and *Swan Song,* 1928. It is necessary to read the "saga" series in the order indicated if one would appreciate fully Mr. Galsworthy's development of the life of a family and its individuals, in the changing England of which he writes with understanding ironic sympathy.

Of his plays, *Justice* and *Strife* are well known. In such collections as *The Inn of Tranquility* and *Caravan,* 1925, his essays and short stories are seen at their best.

Galsworthy is a searching though gentle critic of our own times. He sees society in its entirety as a chaos and individuals engaged in much that is futile and unwise, pathetically unskillful in exerting the forbearance and charity that would solve many of its difficulties. He is, however, quite as much an artist as a reformer, and never vociferates or harangues. Whether in poetry or essays or fiction his work is always that of an exceedingly refined and sensitive spirit. Mr. Galsworthy understands and interprets the soul of the upper-class Englishman, and speaks for him much as Masefield speaks for the lower classes.

Criticism: Phelps (EN; MD) Follett; Howe; Cunliffe; Overton; Chevalley; Ervine, *Some Impressions,* also *No. Am.* 213:371-84; Chubb; D. Martin, "Mr. Galsworthy as Artist and Reformer," *Yale R.* ns 14:126-39; E. Shanks, "Mr. John Galsworthy," *Liv. Age* 319:604-8; A. W. Tilby, "Epic of Property," *Edin. R.* 241:271-85; H. and W. Follett, "Galsworthy," *Atlan.* 118:757-67; L. C. Willcox, "John Galsworthy," *No. Am.* 202:889-98.

RIDING IN MIST[3]

Wet and hot, having her winter coat, the mare exactly matched the drenched fox-colored beech-leaf drifts. As was her wont on such misty days, she danced along with head held high, her neck a little arched, her ears

[1] a lake in Westmoreland
[2] From *Poems 1908-14,* by John Drinkwater, with the permission of the author and Houghton Mifflin Company, authorized publishers.
[3] From *The Inn of Tranquility.* By permission of the author, and of William Heinemann, Ltd., London, and Charles Scribner's Sons, New York, publishers.

pricked, pretending that things were not what they seemed, and now and then vigorously trying to leave me planted on the air. Stones which had rolled out the lane banks were her especial goblins, for one such had maltreated her nerves before she came into this ball-room world, and she had not forgotten.

There was no wind that day. On the beech-trees were still just enough of coppery leaves to look like fires lighted high-up to air the eeriness; but most of the twigs, pearled with water, were patterned very naked against universal gray. Berries were few, except the pink spindle one, so far the most beautiful, of which there were more than Earth generally vouchsafes. There was no sound in the deep lanes, none of that sweet, overhead sighing of yesterday at the same hour, but there was a quality of silence—a dumb mist murmuration. We passed a tree with a proud pigeon sitting on its top spire, quite too heavy for the twig delicacy below; undisturbed by the mare's hoofs or the creaking of saddle leather, he let us pass, absorbed in his world of tranquil turtledoves. The mist had thickened to a white, infinitesimal rain-dust, and in it the trees began to look strange, as though they had lost one another. The world seemed inhabited only by quick, soundless wraiths as one trotted past.

Close to a farm-house the mare stood still with that extreme suddenness peculiar to her at times, and four black pigs scuttled by and at once became white air. By now we were both hot and inclined to cling closely together and take liberties with each other; I telling her about her nature, name, and appearance, together with comments on her manners; and she giving forth that stertorous, sweet snuffle, which begins under the star on her forehead. On such days she did not sneeze, reserving those expressions of her joy for sunny days and the crisp winds. At a forking of the ways we came suddenly on one gray and three brown ponies, who shied round and flung away in front of us, a vision of pretty heads and haunches tangled in the thin lane, till, conscious that they were beyond their beat, they faced the bank and, one by one, scrambled over to join the other ghosts out on the dim common.

Dipping down now over the road, we passed hounds going home. Pied, dumb-footed shapes, padding along in that soft-eyed, remote world of theirs, with a tall riding splash of red in front, and a tall splash of riding red behind. Then through a gate we came on to the moor, amongst whitened furze. The mist thickened. A curlew was whistling on its invisible way, far up; and that wistful, wild calling seemed the very voice of the day. Keeping in view the glint of the road, we galloped; rejoicing, both of us, to be free of the jog-jog of the lanes.

And first the voice of the curlew died; then the glint of the road vanished; and we were quite alone. Even the furze was gone; no shape of anything left, only the black, peaty ground, and the thickening mist. We might as well have been that lonely bird crossing up there in the blind white nothingness, like a human spirit wandering on the undiscovered moor of its own future.

The mare jumped a pile of stones, which appeared, as it were, after we had passed over; and it came into my mind that, if we happened to strike one of the old quarry pits, we should infallibly be killed. Somehow, there was pleasure in this thought, that we might, or might not, strike that old quarry pit. The blood in us being hot, we had pure joy in charging its white, impalpable solidity, which made way, and at once closed in behind us. There was great fun in this yard-by-yard discovery that we were not yet dead, this flying, shelterless challenge to whatever might lie out there, five yards in front. We felt supremely above the wish to know that our necks were safe; we were happy, panting in the vapor that beat against our faces from the sheer speed of our galloping. Suddenly the ground grew lumpy and made up-hill. The mare slackened pace; we stopped. Before us, behind, to right and left, white vapor. No sky, no distance, barely the earth. No wind in our faces, no wind anywhere. At first we just got our breath, thought nothing, talked a little. Then came a chillness, a faint clutching over the heart. The mare snuffled; we turned and made down-hill. And still the mist thickened, and seemed to darken ever so little; we went slowly, suddenly doubtful of all that was in front. There came into our minds visions, so distant in that darkening vapor, of a warm stall and manger of oats; of tea and a log fire. The mist seemed to have fingers now, long, dark-white, crawling fingers; it seemed, too to have in its sheer silence a sort of muttered menace, a shuddery lurkingness, as if from out of it that spirit of the unknown, which in hot blood we had just now so gleefully mocked, were creeping up at us, intent on its vengeance. Since the ground no longer sloped, we could not go down-hill; there were no means left of telling in what direction we were moving, and we stopped to listen. There was no sound, not one tiny noise of water, wind in trees, or man; not even of birds or the moor ponies. And the mist darkened. The mare reached her head down and walked on, smelling at the heather; every time she sniffed, one's heart quivered, hoping she had found the way. She threw up her head, snorted, and stood still; and there passed just in front of us a pony and her foal, shapes of scampering dusk, whisked like blurred shadows across a sheet. Hoof-silent in the long heather—as ever were visiting ghosts—they were gone in a flash. The mare plunged forward, following. But, in the feel of her gallop, and the feel of my heart, there was no more that ecstasy of facing the unknown; there was only the cold, hasty dread of loneliness. Far asunder as the poles were those two sensations, evoked by this same motion. The mare swerved violently and stopped. There, passing within three yards, *from the same direction as before,* the soundless shapes of the pony and her foal flew by again, more intangibly, less dusky now against the darker screen. Were we, then, to be haunted by those bewildering uncanny ones, flitting past ever from the same direction? This time the mare did not follow, but stood still; knowing as well as I that direction was quite lost. Soon, with a whimper, she picked her way on again, smelling at the heather. And the mist darkened.

Then, out of the heart of that dusky whiteness, came a tiny sound; we stood, not breathing, turning our heads. I could see the mare's eye fixed and straining at the vapor. The tiny sound grew till it became the muttering of wheels. The mare dashed forward. The muttering ceased untimely; but she did not stop; turning abruptly to the left, she slid, scrambled, and dropped into a trot. The mist seemed whiter below us; we were on the road. And involuntarily there came from me a sound not quite a shout, not quite an oath. I saw the mare's eye turn back, faintly derisive, as who should say: Alone I did it! Then slowly, comfortably, a little ashamed, we jogged on, in the mood of men and horses when danger is over. So pleasant it seemed now, in one short half-hour, to have passed through the circle-swing of the emotions, from the ecstasy of hot recklessness to the clutching of chill fear. But the meeting-point of those two sensations we had left out there on the mysterious moor! Why, at one moment, had we thought it finer than anything on earth to risk the breaking of our necks; and the next, shuddered at being lost in the darkening mist with winter night fast coming on?

And very luxuriously we turned once more into the lanes, enjoying the past, scenting the future. Close to home, the first little eddy of wind stirred, and the song of dripping twigs began; an owl hooted, honey-soft, in the fog. We came on two farm hands mending the lane at the turn of the avenue, and, curled on the top of the bank, their cosy red collie pup, waiting for them to finish work for the day. He raised his sharp nose and looked at us dewily. We turned down, padding softly in the wet fox-red drifts under the beech-trees, whereon the last leaves still flickered out in the darkening whiteness, that now seemed so little eerie. We passed the gray-green skeleton of the farm-yard gate. A hen ran across us, clucking, into the dusk. The mare drew her long, home-coming snuffle, and stood still.

1910 *1912*

THE RECRUIT [1]

Several times since that fateful fourth of August he had said: "I sh'll 'ave to go."

And the farmer and his wife would look at him, he with a sort of amusement, she with a queer compassion in her heart, and one or the other would reply smiling: "That's all right, Tom; there's plenty Germans yet. Yu wait a bit."

His mother, too, who came daily from the lonely cottage in the little combe [2] on the very edge of the big hill to work in the kitchen and farm dairy, would turn her dark, taciturn head, with still plentiful black hair, toward his face, which for all its tan was so weirdly reminiscent of a withered baby, pinkish and light-lashed with forelock and fair hair thin and rumpled, and small blue eyes; and she would mutter:

"Don't yu never fret, boy. They'll come for 'ee fast enough when they want 'ee." No one, least of all perhaps his mother, could take quite seriously that little square, short-footed man, born when she was just seventeen. Sure of work because he was first-rate with every kind of beast, he was not yet looked on as being quite "all there." He could neither read nor write, had scarcely ever been outside the parish, and then only in a shandrydan [3] on a

[1] From *Tatterdemalion.* By permission of the author, and of William Heinemann, Ltd., London, and Charles Scribner's Sons, New York, publishers.
[2] hollow
[3] a light cart or gig

club treat, and knew no more of the world than the native of a small South Sea Island. His life from school age on had been passed, year in, year out, from dawn till dark, with the cattle and their calves, the sheep, the horses and the wild moor ponies; except when hay or corn harvest, or any exceptionally exacting festival absorbed him for the moment. From shyness he never went into the bar of the inn, and so had missed the greater part of village education. He could, of course, read no papers; a map was to him but a mystic mass of marks and colors; he had never seen the sea, never a ship; no water broader than the parish streams; until the war had never met anything more like a soldier than the constable of the neighboring village. But he had once seen a Royal Marine in uniform. What sort of creatures these Germans were to him, who knows? They were cruel—he had grasped that. Something noxious, perhaps, like the adders whose backs he broke with his stick; something dangerous, like the chained dog at Shapton Farm, or the bull at Vannacombe. When the war first broke out, and they had called the younger blacksmith (a reservist and noted village marksman) back to his regiment, the little cowman had smiled and said: "Wait till regiment gets to front; Fred'll soon shoot 'em up."

But weeks and months went by, and it was always the Germans, the Germans; Fred had clearly not yet shot them up. And now one and now another went off from the village, and two from the farm itself; and the great Fred returned slightly injured for a few weeks' rest, and, full of whiskey from morning till night, made the village ring; and finally went off again in a mood of manifest reluctance. All this weighed dumbly on the mind of the little cowman, the more heavily that because of his inarticulate shyness he could never talk that weight away, nor could anyone by talk relieve him, no premises [1] of knowledge or vision being there. From sheer physical contagion he felt the grizzly menace in the air, and a sense of being left behind when others were going to meet that menace with their fists, as it were. There was something proud and sturdy in the little man, even in the look of him, for all that he was "poor old Tom," who brought a smile to the lips of all. He was passionate, too, if rubbed up the wrong way; but it needed the malevolence and ingenuity of human beings to annoy him—with his beasts he never lost his temper, so that they had perfect confidence in him. He resembled herdsmen of the Alps, whom one may see in dumb communion with their creatures up in those high solitudes; for he too dwelt in a high solitude cut off from real followship with men and women by lack of knowledge, and by the supercilious pity in them. Living in such a remote world his talk—when he did say something—had ever the surprising quality attaching to the thoughts of those by whom the normal proportions of things are quite unknown. His short square figure, hatless and rarely coated in any weather, dotting from foot to foot, a bit of stick in one hand and often a straw in the mouth—he did not smoke—was familiar in the yard where he turned the handle of the separator, or in the fields and cowsheds, from daybreak to dusk, save for the hours of dinner and tea, which he ate in the farm kitchen, making sparse and surprising comments. To his peculiar whistles and calls the cattle and calves, for all their rumination and stubborn shyness, were amazingly responsive. It was a pretty sight to see them pushing against each other round him—for, after all, he was as much the source of their persistence, [2] especially through the scanty winter months, as a mother starling to her unfledged young.

When the Government issued their request to householders to return the names of those of military age ready to serve if called on, he heard of it, and stopped munching to say in his abrupt fashion: "I'll go—fight the Germans." But the farmer did not put his name down, saying to his wife:

"Poor old Tom! 'Twidden [3] be 'ardly fair —they'd be makin' game of 'un."

And his wife, her eyes shining with motherliness, answered: "Poor lad, he's not fit-like."

The months went on—winter passing to spring, and the slow decking of the trees and fields began with leaves and flowers, with butterflies and the songs of birds. How far the little cowman would notice such a thing as that no one could ever have said, devoid as he was of the vocabulary of beauty, but like all the world his heart must have felt warmer and lighter under his old waistcoat, and perhaps more than most hearts, for he could often be seen standing stockstill in the fields, his browning face turned to the sun.

Less and less he heard talk of Germans—dogged acceptance of the state of war having settled on that far countryside—the beggars were not beaten and killed off yet, but they

[1] foundation

[2] existence

[3] it wouldn't (Devonshire dialect)

would be in good time. It was unpleasant to think of them more than could be helped. Once in a way a youth went off and " 'listed," but, though the parish had given more perhaps than the average, a good few of military age still clung to life as they had known it. Then some bright spirit conceived the notion that a county regiment should march through the remoter districts to rouse them up.

The cuckoo had been singing five days; the lanes and fields, the woods and the village green were as Joseph's coat, so varied and so bright the foliage, from golden oak-buds to the brilliant little lime-tree leaves, the feathery green shoots of larches, and the already darkening bunches of the sycamores. The earth was dry—no rain for a fortnight—when the cars containing the brown-clad men and a recruiting band drew up before the inn. Here were clustered the farmers, the innkeeper, the gray-haired postman; by the church gate and before the schoolyard were knots of girls and children, schoolmistress, schoolmaster, parson; and down on the lower green a group of likely youths, an old laborer or two, and apart from human beings, as was his wont, the little cowman in brown corduroys tied below the knee and an old waistcoat, the sleeves of his blue shirt dotted with pink rolled up to the elbows of his brown arms; so he stood, his brown neck and shaven-looking head quite bare, with his bit of stick wedged between his waist and the ground, staring with all his light-lashed water-blue eyes under the thatch of his forelock.

The speeches rolled forth glib; the khaki-clad men drank their second fill that morning of coffee and cider; the little cowman stood straight and still, his head drawn back. Two figures—officers, men who had been at the front—detached themselves and came toward the group of likely youths. These wavered a little, were silent, sniggered, stood their ground—the khaki-clad figures passed among them. Hackneyed words, jests, the touch of flattery changing swiftly to chaff—all the customary performance, hollow and pathetic; and then the two figures re-emerged, their hands clenched, their eyes shifting here and there, their lips drawn back in fixed smiles. They had failed and were trying to hide it. They must not show contempt—the young slackers might yet come in when the band played.

The cars were filled again, the band struck up: "It's a long, long way to Tipperary."

And at the edge of the green, within two yards of the car's dusty passage, the little cowman stood apart and stared. His face was red. Behind him they were cheering—the parson and farmers, schoolchildren, girls, even the group of youths. He alone did not cheer, but his face grew still more red. When the dust above the road and the distant blare of "Tipperary" had dispersed and died he walked back to the farm, dotting from one to other of his short feet. All that afternoon and evening he spoke no word; but that flush seemed to have settled in his face for good and all. He milked some cows, but forgot to bring the pails up. Two of his precious cows he left unmilked till their distressful lowing caused the farmer's wife to go down and see. There he was, standing against a gate moving his brown neck from side to side like an animal in pain, oblivious, seemingly, of everything. She spoke to him:

"What's matter, Tom?" All he could answer was:

"I'se goin,' I'se goin'." She milked the cows herself.

For the next three days he could settle to nothing, leaving his jobs half done, speaking to no one save to say:

"I'se goin'; I'se got to go." Even the beasts looked at him surprised.

On the Saturday the farmer, having consulted with his wife, said quietly:

"Well, Tom, ef yu want to go, yu shall. I'll drive 'ee down Monday. Us won't du nothin' to keep yu back."

The little cowman nodded. But he was restless as ever all through that Sunday, eating nothing.

On Monday morning, arrayed in his best clothes, he got into the dogcart. There, without good-bye to anyone, not even to his beasts, he sat staring straight before him, square, and jolting up and down beside the farmer, who turned on him now and then a dubious, almost anxious eye.

So they drove the eleven miles to the recruiting station. He got down, entered, the farmer with him.

"Well, my lad," they asked him, "what d'you want to join?"

"Royal Marines."

It was a shock, coming from the short, square figure of such an obvious landsman. The farmer took him by the arm.

"Why, yu'm a Devon man, Tom; better take county regiment. An't they gude enough for yu?"

Shaking his head he answered: "Royal Marines."

Was it the glamour of the words or the Royal Marine he had once seen that moved him to wish to join that outlandish corps? They took him to the recruiting station for the Royal Marines.

Stretching up his short square body and blowing out his cheeks to increase his height, he was put before the reading board. His eyes were splendid; little that passed in hedgerows, or the heavens, in woods, or on the hillsides, could escape them. They asked him to read the print.

Staring, he answered: "L."

"No, my lad, you're guessing."

"L."

The farmer plucked at the recruiting officer's sleeve, his face was twitching, and he whispered hoarsely:

"'E don't know 'is alphabet."

The officer turned and contemplated that short square figure with the browned face so reminiscent of a whithered baby, and the little blue eyes staring out under the dusty forelock. Then he grunted, and going up to him, laid a hand on his shoulder.

"*Your* heart's all right, my lad, but you can't pass."

The little cowman looked at him, turned, and went straight out. An hour later he sat again beside the farmer on the way home, staring before him and jolting up and down.

"They won't get me," he said suddenly: "I can fight, but I'se not goin'." A fire of resentment seemed to have been lit within him. That evening he ate his tea, and next day settled down again among his beasts. But whenever, now, the war was mentioned he would look up with his puckered smile which seemed to have in it a resentful amusement, and say:

"They ain't got me yet."

His dumb sacrifice passing their comprehension had been rejected—or so it seemed to him. He could not understand why they had spurned him—he was as good as they! His pride was hurt. No! They should not get him now!

1917 **1920**

APPENDIX

KEY TO THE ABBREVIATIONS USED IN THE HEADNOTES THROUGHOUT THE TEXT OF THE VOLUME

Atlan.	*The Atlantic Monthly,* Boston
Bookm.	*The Bookman,* New York
Cath. World	*The Catholic World,* New York
Cent.	*The Century Magazine,* New York
Contemp.	*The Contemporary Review,* London
Edin. Rev.	*The Edinburgh Review,* London and New York
Fortn.	*The Fortnightly Review,* London and New York
Forum	*The Forum,* New York
Harp.	*Harpers Magazine,* New York
Ind.	*The Independent,* New York
Lit. Dig.	*The Literary Digest,* New York
Lit. R.	*The Literary Review of the New York Evening Post,* New York
Liv. Age	*The Living Age,* Boston
New Rep.	*The New Republic,* New York
19th Cent.	*The Nineteenth Century,* London
No. Am.	*The North American Review,* New York
Outl.	*The Outlook,* New York
Poetry	*Poetry,* Chicago
Quart. / *Quart. R.*	*The Quarterly Review,* London and New York
Sat. Rev. of Lit.	*The Saturday Review of Literature,* New York
Scrib. M.	*Scribner's Magazine,* New York

The following abbreviations are used to identify more quickly certain volumes or series of volumes:

AMB	*Among My Books,* J. R. Lowell
DLAE / Eliz. L.	*Lectures on the Dramatic Literature of the Age of Elizabeth,* W. Hazlitt
EML	*English Men of Letters* [Series]
EP	*The Advance of English Poetry in the Twentieth Century,* W. L. Phelps
GE	*Great Englishmen of the Sixteenth Century,* Sidney Lee
GW	*Great Writers,* G. E. Woodberry
LE	*Literary Essays,* G. E. Woodberry
HHW	*Heroes and Hero-Worship,* T. Carlyle
OED	*The Old English Dramatists,* J. R. Lowell
Shel.	*Shelburne Essays* [Numbered in series], P. E. More
SPP	*Studies in Prose and Poetry,* A. C. Swinburne
TS / T & S	*Transcripts and Studies,* E. Dowden
Ward E P	*English Poets,* T. H. Ward

1. The headnotes under each author throughout the volume contain references to books, magazine articles, and critical essays, or chapters in books.

2. When, in the headnotes, a single critic is mentioned, e.g., Arnold, Lowell, not followed by the title of a book, the student may locate the criticism desired by looking under the critic's name in the list of MISCELLANEOUS CRITICAL WORKS at the beginning of the Bibliography.

3. Additional references may be found under the title of GENERAL BIBLIOGRAPHY, and also in the works concerning the period to which the author belongs.

4. Many references to books and biographical and critical articles concerning authors will be found in the bibliographical sections of the *Cambridge History of English Literature.* (See page 899.)

5. Special attention is called to articles in the *Encyclopedia Britannica* and the *Dictionary of National Biography.*

BIBLIOGRAPHY

MISCELLANEOUS CRITICAL WORKS

Arnold, Matthew *Essays in Criticism, Second Series*—New York, Macmillan, 1905
Milton Keats Byron Gray Wordsworth Shelley

Boyd, Ernest *Ireland's Literary Renaissance*—New York, A. A. Knopf, 1923
Synge Stephens "A.E." Yeats

Bradford, Gamaliel *Bare Souls*—New York, Harper & Brothers, 1924
Gray Cowper Lamb Keats Fitzgerald
A Naturalist of Souls—New York, Dodd, Mead & Co., 1917
Pater Donne

Brownell, William C. *Victorian Prose Masters*—New York, Scribner's Sons, 1901
Thackeray Carlyle Arnold Ruskin Meredith

Carlyle, Thomas *Critical and Miscellaneous Essays*—London, Chapman & Hall, 1888
Johnson Burns Boswell's Life of Johnson Scott
On Heroes, Hero-Worship, and the Heroic in History—New York & London, Longmans, Green & Co., 1906
Shakespeare Johnson Burns Swift

Chevalley, Abel *The Modern English Novel*—New York, A. A. Knopf, 1925
Kipling Meredith Wells Wilde Galsworthy Gissing Conrad Stephens Barrie Hardy

Chevrillon, André *Three Studies in English Literature*—London, W. Heinemann, 1923
Shakespeare Galsworthy Kipling

Chubb, E. W. *Stories of Authors, British and American*—New York, Macmillan, 1926
Sidney Gibbon Landor Lamb Byron Macaulay The Brownings Thackeray Kipling Barrie Shakespeare Johnson Burns Shelley Leigh Hunt Dickens Tennyson Conrad Shaw Milton Gray Coleridge Keats De Quincey Cowper Carlyle Scott Galsworthy Ruskin Stevenson Huxley

Coleridge, Samuel Taylor *Literary Criticism*—London, Oxford University Press, 1908
Wordsworth Shakespeare Swift Milton

Collins, Joseph *The Doctor Looks at Literature*—New York, George H. Doran, 1923
Mansfield Lawrence Strachey

Cooper, F. T. *Some English Story Tellers*—New York, Henry Holt & Co., 1912
Conrad Kipling Galsworthy

Cunliffe, J. W. *English Literature During the Last Half Century*—New York, Macmillan, 1919
Meredith Conrad Hardy Wells Stevenson Galsworthy Gissing Shaw Kipling

Dowden, Edward *Transcripts and Studies*—London, K. Paul, Trench, Trübner & Co., 1888
Carlyle Browning Shelley Shakespeare Wordsworth Marlowe Spenser Milton
Puritan and Anglican—London, K. Paul, Trench, Trübner & Co., 1901
Vaughan Milton Bunyan
Studies in Literature—London, K. Paul, Trench, Trübner & Co., 1889
Wordsworth Landor Tennyson Browning

Drew, Elizabeth A. *The Modern Novel*—London, J. Cape, Ltd., 1926
Galsworthy Wells Conrad

Ervine, St. J. *Some Impressions of My Elders*—New York, Macmillan, 1922
"A.E." Chesterton Galsworthy Shaw Wells Yeats Synge

Follett, Helen Thomas, and Wilson *Some Modern Novelists*—New York, Holt, 1918
Gissing Meredith Hardy Wells Galsworthy Conrad

Freeman, John *The Moderns: Essays in Literary Criticism*—New York, T. Y. Crowell, 1917
Shaw Wells Hardy Conrad Thompson Bridges

Garnett, Edward *Friday Nights: Literary Criticisms & Appreciations. 1st Series*—London, J. Cage, 1922
Hudson Conrad Lawrence

Harrison, Frederic *Studies in Early Victorian Literature*—London, E. Arnold, 1906
Carlyle Macaulay Thackeray Dickens
Tennyson, Ruskin, Mill, and other Literary Estimates—New York, Macmillan, 1900
Tennyson Ruskin Arnold Lamb Keats Gibbon Froude

Hazlitt, William *Lectures on the English Poets and Comic Writers*—London, J. M. Dent, 1902
Chaucer Pope Spenser Thomson Shakespeare Cowper Milton Gray Dryden Swift Collins Chatterton Burns Gay
Spirit of the Age—London, J. M. Dent, 1902
Coleridge Crabbe Scott Moore Byron Leigh Hunt Southey Elia Wordsworth
Lectures on the Dramatic Literature of the Age of Elizabeth—London, J. M. Dent, 1902
Marlowe Daniel Sidney Bacon Jonson Drayton Beaumont and Fletcher

Howe, P. P. *Dramatic Portraits*—London, M. Secker, 1913
Wilde Barrie Galsworthy

JACKSON, HOLBROOK *The Eighteen Nineties*—London, G. Richards, 1923
Wilde Thompson Davidson Kipling

JOHNSON, SAMUEL *Lives of the English Poets*—London, G. Bell & Sons
Milton Pope Gray Addison Gay Thomson Waller Prior Swift Collins Shakespeare Dryden

KENNEDY, J. M. *English Literature, 1880-1885*—Boston, Small, Maynard & Co., 1913
Wilde Shaw Wells Gissing Yeats Davidson Thompson

LANG, ANDREW *Essays in Little*—London, New York, Scribners, 1901
Stevenson Kipling Thackeray Dickens Scott Bunyan
Letters to Dead Authors—London, Longmans, Green & Co., 1896
Thackeray Scott Dickens Shelley Pope Burns Walton Byron Mandeville

LEE, SIR SIDNEY *Great Englishmen of the Sixteenth Century*—New York, C. Scribner's Sons, 1904
More Shakespeare Raleigh Sidney Spenser Bacon

LOWELL, JAMES RUSSELL *Among My Books*—Boston, Houghton Mifflin Co., 1898
Dryden Shakespeare
Old English Dramatists—Boston, Houghton Mifflin Co., 1892
Marlowe Beaumont and Fletcher
My Study Windows—Boston, James R. Osgood & Co., 1874
Carlyle Swinburne Chaucer Pope
Latest Literary Essays and Addresses—Boston, Houghton Mifflin Co., 1892
Walton Landor

MACAULAY, THOMAS BABINGTON *Critical, Historical, and Miscellaneous Essays*—Boston, Houghton Mifflin Co., 1886
Milton Thackeray Bunyan Southey Bacon Goldsmith Byron Addison Johnson Dryden Leigh Hunt Boswell's Johnson

MASSON, DAVID *Essays Biographical and Critical: Chiefly on the English Poets*—Cambridge, Macmillan, 1856
Shakespeare Wordsworth Milton De Quincey Dryden Swift Chatterton

MONRO, HAROLD *Some Contemporary Poets*—London, L. Parsons, 1920
Bridges Masefield Sassoon Hardy Davies de la Mare Yeats Chesterton Kipling Hodgson Squire Mrs. Meynell Drinkwater Housman Gibson Noyes

MORE, PAUL ELMER *Shelburne Essays*—New York, G. P. Putnam, 1904
1. Carlyle Yeats
2. Shakespeare Lamb Kipling Fitzgerald Crabbe Meredith
3. Byron Cowper Ch. Rossetti Browning
4. Herbert Keats Lamb Blake
5. Dickens Gissing J. Thomson
6. Bunyan
7. Shelley Wordsworth Hood Tennyson Morris Fr. Thompson
8. Newman Huxley Pater
9. Beaumont and Fletcher Swift Pope Gray

NOYES, ALFRED *Some Aspects of Modern Poetry*—New York, Stokes Co., 1924
Mrs. Meynell Shakespeare Shelley Swinburne Henley Dobson Wordsworth Stevenson Tennyson

PAYNE, WILLIAM MORTON *The Greater English Poets of the Nineteenth Century*—New York, Holt, 1909
Keats Landor Morris Shelley Browning Swinburne Byron Tennyson Coleridge Arnold Wordsworth Rossetti

PHELPS, WILLIAM LYON *Essays on Books*—New York, Macmillan, 1914
Dickens Carlyle Marlowe Herrick
Advance of English Poetry in the Twentieth Century—New York, Dodd, Mead & Co., 1919
Henley Masefield D. H. Lawrence "A.E." Thompson Gibson Drinkwater Stephens Hardy Hodgson Dunsany Kipling Brooke Davies Noyes de la Mare Yeats Housman Synge
Advance of the English Novel—New York, Dodd, Mead & Co., 1916
Defoe Barrie Meredith Wells Hardy Conrad Galsworthy
Essays on Modern Dramatists—New York, Macmillan, 1921
Barrie Galsworthy Shaw

ROSSETTI, WILLIAM MICHAEL *Lives of Famous Poets*—London, Ward, Locke & Co., 1878
Chaucer Spenser Shakespeare Milton Dryden Pope Thomson Gray Goldsmith Cowper Burns Arnold Wordsworth Piers Plowman

SAINTSBURY, GEORGE *Essays in English Literature*—New York, Scribner's Sons, 1895
1st series Crabbe Moore Leigh Hunt De Quincey Praed
2d series Southey Landor Hood Campbell Scott Coleridge

SCHOFIELD, WILLIAM HENRY *Chivalry in English Literature*—Cambridge, Harvard University, 1912
Chaucer Malory Spenser Shakespeare

SCOTT, DIXON *Men of Letters*—New York, George H. Doran Co., 1923
Shaw Mrs. Meynell Kipling Brooke Barrie Meredith Wells Chesterton Masefield

STEPHEN, LESLIE *Studies of a Biographer*—London, Duckworth & Co., 1898
Johnson Scott Browning Shakespeare Gibbon Arnold Ruskin Southey Wordsworth Tennyson Huxley Milton Froude Stevenson
Hours in a Library—New York, G. P. Putnam's Sons, 1894
1. Defoe Pope De Quincey
2. Johnson Crabbe

3. Cowper Wordsworth Macaulay Shelley
4. Gray Carlyle Coleridge

STEVENSON, ROBERT LOUIS *Familiar Studies of Men and Books*—New York, Charles Scribner's Sons, 1906
Burns Pepys

STURGEON, MARY C. *Studies of Contemporary Poets*—London, G. G. Harrap & Co., 1916
Brooke Masefield Davies Monro de la Mare Stephens Gibson Hodgson

SWINBURNE, ALGERNON CHARLES *Studies in Prose and Poetry*—London, Chatto & Windus, 1897
Scott Herrick Beaumont and Fletcher Tennyson
Miscellanies—London, Chatto & Windus, 1895
Collins Tennyson Wordsworth Dryden Byron Lamb Landor Keats

THACKERAY, WILLIAM MAKEPEACE *The English Humorists of the Eighteenth Century*—Boston, Estes & Lauriat, 1896
Swift Addison Steele Prior Gay Pope Goldsmith

WILKINSON, MARGUERITE *New Voices*—New York, Macmillan, 1919
Brooke Gibson Meynell Chesterton Hardy Noyes Davies Hodgson Sassoon de la Mare Housman Stephens Drinkwater Kipling Yeats Dunsany Masefield

WOODBERRY, GEORGE EDWARD *Makers of Literature*—New York, Macmillan, 1900
Shelley Landor Browning Byron Arnold Coleridge
Literary Essays—New York, Harcourt, Brace, 1920
Crabbe Coleridge Swinburne Landor Shelley Keats Byron Scott Milton Browning Shakespeare Arnold
Great Writers—New York, The McClure Co., 1907
Scott Milton Shakespeare

GENERAL BIBLIOGRAPHY

Books Treating All, or a Large Part of, the History of English Literature, Including the Historical and Social Background.

Cambridge History of English Literature, ed. by A. W. Ward and A. R. Waller, 14 vols.—New York and London, G. P. Putnam, 1907-1927. (Comprehensive. Bibliographies for each chapter, and an index of the whole)

Dictionary of National Biography, 63 vols. Two supplements

Encyclopedia Britannica, 31 vols.

Everyman's Dictionary of English Literature, 1 vol.—London and New York, J. M. Dent & Co.

Boynton, Percy H. *London in English Literature*—Chicago, University of Chicago Press, 1914

Literature, 2 vols.—New York, Holt, 1889-96

Literature, 2 vol.—New York, Holt, 1889-96

Brooke, Stopford A. *English Literature*—New York, Macmillan, 1901

Cheyney, Edward Potts *A Short History of England,* Rev. Ed.—Boston, Ginn & Co., 1919

Coulton, G. G. *Chaucer and His England*—London, Methuen, 1908

Courthope, W. J. *A History of English Poetry,* 6 vols.—New York, Macmillan, 1895-1910

Cousin, John W. *A Short Biographical Dictionary of English Literature*—London, J. M. Dent, 1910

Garnett, R. and Gosse, Sir E. *English Literature, an Illustrated Record,* 4 vols.—New York, Macmillan, 1903-04

Gautier, Leon *Chivalry*—New York, G. Routledge, 1891

Gosse, Sir Edmund William *A Short History of Modern English Literature*—New York, D. Appleton, 1900

Green, J. R. *A Short History of the English People*—New York, American Book Co., 1919

Greenough, James B. and Kittredge, G. L. *Words and their Ways in English Speech*—New York, Macmillan, 1901

Grierson, J. C. *The Background of English Literature*—New York, Holt, 1926

Hall, Hubert *Court Life Under the Plantagenets*—London, S. Sonnenschein & Co., 1890

Haughton, Thomas *The Student's Summary of the Principal Events in English History*—London, Bell, 1897

Hulme, Edward Maslin *A History of the British People*—New York. The Century Co. 1924

Jusserand, J. J. *English Wayfaring Life in the Middle Ages*—London, T. F. Unwin, 1890

Jusserand, J. J. *Histoire Littéraire du Peuple Anglais,* Translated by F. Didot, 3 vols.—New York, Putnam, 1895-99

Mitchell, Donald Grant *English Lands, Letters, and Kings*—New York, Scribner, 1907

Montgomery, David Henry *The Leading Facts of English History*—Boston, Ginn, 1912

Moody, W. V. and Lovett, R. M. *History of English Literature*—New York, Scribner, 1902

Morley, Henry *English Writers; an Attempt Toward a History of English Literature,* 2 vols.—New York, Cassell & Co., 1887-95

Ryland, Frederick *Chronological Outlines of English Literature*—London, Macmillan, 1903

Saintsbury, George E. *A Short History of English Literature*—New York, Macmillan, 1898

Scudder, Vida D. *Social Ideals in English Letters*—Boston, Houghton Mifflin Co., 1898

Stow, John *Survey of London*—New York, Routledge & Sons, 1890

Taine, H. A. *History of English Literature,* Translated by H. Van Laun, 4 vols.—New York, Henry Holt, 1900

Traill, Henry Duff *Social England,* 6 vols.—New York, Putnam, 1894-1902

THE EARLY PERIOD

Brooke, Stopford A. *A History of Early English Literature . . . . to King Alfred,* 2 vols.—London, Macmillan, 1892

Chambers, E. K., ed. *Early English Lyrics*—London, Sidgwick and Jackson, 1911

Gummere, F. B. *The Old English Ballads*—Athenaeum Press Series, 1911

Henderson, T. F. *The Ballad in Literature*—New York, Putnam, 1912

Kittredge, G. L. and Sargent, Helen C. *English and Scotch Popular Ballads,* 1 vol.—Boston, Houghton Mifflin, 1904

Pancoast, Henry S., ed. *Early English Poems*—New York, Holt, 1907

Pound, Louise *Poetic Origins and the Ballad*—New York, Macmillan, 1921

Snell, Frederick John *The Age of Transition, 1400-1500*—London, G. Bell, 1905

Spence, Lewis *A Dictionary of Medieval Romance and Romance Writers*—London, G. Routledge, 1913

THE FIFTEENTH AND SIXTEENTH CENTURIES

Ault, Norman *Elizabethan Lyrics*—London, Longmans, Green & Co., 1925

Berdan, John M. *Early Tudor Poetry, 1485-1547. Studies in Tudor Literature*—New York, Macmillan, 1920

Carpenter, F. I. *English Lyric Poetry, 1500-1700*—London, Blackie and Son, 1897

Chambers, E.K. *The Elizabethan Stage, 1558-1616*, 4 vols.—Oxford, Clarendon Press, 1923

Lee, Sidney *Great Englishmen of the Sixteenth Century*—New York, Scribner, 1904

Matthews, Brander *Development of the Drama*—New York, Scribner, 1903

Padelford, F. M. *Early Sixteenth Century Lyrics*—New York, D. C. Heath, 1907

Pollard, Alfred E. *English Miracle Plays, Moralities, and Interludes*—Oxford, Clarendon Press, 1923

Saintsbury, George E. *The Flourishing of Romance and the Use of Allegory*—New York, Scribner, 1897

Schelling, F. E. *English Drama*—London, J. M. Dent, 1914

The English Lyric—Boston, Houghton Mifflin, 1913

A Book of Elizabethan Lyrics—Boston, Ginn, 1893

Stobart, John C. *The Age of Spenser*—London, E. Arnold, 1906

[Various Writers] *An Account of the Life and Manners of Shakespeare's Age*, 2 vols.—London, Oxford Press, 1916

THE SEVENTEENTH CENTURY

Chambers, E. K. *The Elizabethan Stage, 1558*, 4 vols.—Oxford, Clarendon Press, 1923

Gosse, Sir Edmund *Seventeenth Century Studies*—London, K. Paul, Trench, and Co., 1883

Masterman, J. H. B. *The Age of Milton*—London, Bell, 1911

Nettleton, G. H. *The English Drama of the Restoration and Eighteenth Century (1642-1780)*—New York, Macmillan, 1914

Schelling, Felix E., ed. *A Book of Seventeenth Century Lyrics*—Boston, Ginn, 1899

Schelling, Felix E. *Elizabethan Drama, 1558-1642*, 2 vols.—Boston, Houghton, 1908

Wendell, Barrett *The Temper of the Seventeenth Century in English Literature*—New York, Scribner, 1904

THE EIGHTEENTH CENTURY

Cross, W. L. *The Development of the English Novel*—New York, Macmillan, 1899

Dennis, John *The Age of Pope*—London, Bell, 1894

Dobson, Austin *Eighteenth Century Vignettes*, three series, three volumes—New York, Dodd, Mead & Co., 1892-1896

Elton, Oliver *A Survey of English Literature, 1780-1830*, 2 vols.—L. E. Arnold, 1912

Gosse, Sir Edmund *A History of Eighteenth Century Literature, 1660-1780*—New York, Macmillan, 1889

Parry, T. S. *English Literature in the Eighteenth Century*—New York, Harper, 1883

Phelps, W. L. *Beginnings of the English Romantic Movement. A Study of Eighteenth Century Literature*—Boston, Ginn, 1893

Roscoe, E. S. *The English Scene in the Eighteenth Century*—New York, Putnam, 1912

Seccombe, Thomas *The Age of Johnson, 1748-1798*—New York, Macmillan, 1900

Stephen, Sir Leslie *English Literature and Society in the Eighteenth Century*—London, Duckworth, 1904

Stephen, Sir Leslie *History of English Thought in the Eighteenth Century*—London, Smith, Elder & Co., 3d ed., 1902

Symonds, Arthur *The Romantic Movement in English Poetry*—New York, E. P. Dutton & Co., 1907

Tinker, C. B. *The Salon and English Letters*—New York, Macmillan, 1915 [Society and literature of the age of Johnson]

Tuckerman, Bayard *History of Prose Fiction From Sir T. Malory to George Eliot*—New York, Putnam, 1899

Walpole, Horace *Letters* [Several editions]

THE NINETEENTH CENTURY

Bagehot, W. *Physics and Politics*—New York, Appleton, 1904

Beers, Henry A. *A History of English Romanticism in the Nineteenth Century*—New York, Holt, 1918

Chesterton, G. K. *The Victorian Age in English Literature*—London, Williams and Norgate, 1927

Cunliffe, J. W. *English Literature During the Last Half Century*—New York, Macmillan, 1918

Elton, Oliver *A Survey of English Literature, 1830-1880*, 2 vols.—New York, Macmillan, 1920

Fyvie, John *Some Literary Eccentricities*—London, Constable, 1906

Herford, C. H. *The Age of Wordsworth*—London, Bell, 1897

Miles, Alfred Henry *The Poets and Poetry of the Nineteenth Century*—New York, Dutton, 1905-7

Naar, Harks Gerrit de *A History of Modern English Romanticism*—London, Milford, 1924

Saintsbury, George *A History of Nineteenth Century Romanticism*—London, Macmillan, 1896

Walker, Hugh *The Age of Tennyson*—London, Bell, 1904

The Literature of the Victorian Era, Cambridge, The University Press, 1910

Williams, Stanley T. *Studies in Victorian Literature*—New York, Dutton, 1923

THE TWENTIETH CENTURY

Canby, H. S. *The Short Story in English*—New York, Holt, 1909

The Study of the Short Story—New York, Holt, 1913

DICKINSON, THOMAS H. *The Contemporary Drama in England*—Boston, Little Brown, 1917

GUEDALLA, PHILIP *A Gallery*—New York, Putnam, 1924

HARRIS, FRANK *Contemporary Portraits*—New York, Kennerley, 1915

MANLY, J. M. and RICKERT, EDITH *Contemporary British Literature*—New York, Harcourt, 1921 [Bibliographic and study outlines]

SHERMAN, STUART P. *On Contemporary Literature*—New York, Holt, 1917

VAN DOREN, C. and VAN DOREN, M. *American and British Literature since 1890*—New York, Century Co., 1925

WILKINSON, MARGUERITE *Contemporary Poetry*—New York, Macmillan, 1924

WILLIAMS, HAROLD *Modern English Writers*—New York, Knopf, 1919

COLLECTIONS

ARBER, EDWARD, ed. *British Anthologies* [Five volumes through the nineteenth century]—New York, H. Frowde, 1899-1901

BRONSON, W. C. *English Poems*, 4 vols. 1907-10—Chicago, University of Chicago Press

CHALMERS, ALEXANDER, ed. *The Works of the English Poets from Chaucer to Cowper*—21 vols., London, J. Johnson, 1810

CRAIK, SIR HENRY *English Prose Selections*, 4 vols., New York, Macmillan, 1893, 1900

PALGRAVE, FRANCIS T., ed. *The Golden Treasury of Lyrical Poems*—New York, Macmillan, 1901

QUILLER-COUCH, SIR ARTHUR T., ed. *The Oxford Book of English Ballads*, 1910 *The Oxford Book of English Verse*, 1900 *The Oxford Book of Victorian Verse*, 1914 *The Oxford Book of English Prose*, 1925—Oxford, The University Press

STEDMAN, EDMUND C., ed. *A Victorian Anthology, 1837-1895*—Boston, Houghton Mifflin Co., 1895

STEVENSON, BURTON E., ed. *The Home Book of Verse, American and English*, 1923 *The Home Book of Modern Verse*, 1925—New York, Holt

WARD, THOMAS H., ed *The English Poets*, 5 vols.—New York, Macmillan, 1902-20

WOODS, GEORGE B., ed. *English Poetry and Prose of the Romantic Movement*—Chicago, Scott Foresman, 1916

BIOGRAPHICAL SERIES

English Men of Letters Series Ed. by John Morley—New York, Harper and Brothers, 1879, contains biographies of:

Addison	(W. J. Courthorpe)
Arnold	(H. Paul)
Bacon	(R. W. Church)
Blake	(O. Burdett)
*Boswell	(G. Scott)
Browning	(G. K. Chesterton)
Bunyan	(J. A. Froude)
Burke	(J. Morley)
Burns	(J. C. Shairp)
Byron	(J. Nichol)
Carlyle	(J. Nichol)
Chaucer	(A. W. Ward)
Coleridge	(H. D. Traill)
Cowper	(Godwin Smith)
Crabbe	(A. Ainger)
Defoe	(W. Minto)
De Quincey	(D. Masson)
Dickens	(A. W. Ward)
*Dickens	(J. C. Squire)
Dryden	(L. Stephens)
Fitzgerald	(A. C. Benson)
Gibbon	(J. C. Morison)
Goldsmith	(W. Black)
Gray	(E. W. Gosse)
Hazlitt	(A. Birrell)
Johnson	(L. Stephen)
Jonson	(G. G. Smith)
Keats	(S. Colvin)
Lamb	(A. Ainger)
Landor	(S. Colvin)
Macaulay	(J. C. Morison)
Marvell	(A. Birrell)
Meredith	(J. B. Priestley)
Milton	(M. Pattison)
Morris	(A. Noyes)
Pater	(A. C. Benson)
*Pepys	(A. Ponsonby)
Pope	(L. Stephen)
Rossetti, D. G.	(A. C. Benson)
Ruskin	(F. Harrison)
Scott	(R. H. Hutton)
Shakespeare	(W. Raleigh)
Shelley	(J. A. Symonds)
Sidney	(J. A. Symonds)
Southey	(E. Dowden)
Spenser	(R. W. Church)
Sterne	(H. D. Traill)
*Stevenson	(R. Lynd)
Swift	(L. Stephen)
Swinburne	(H. G. Nicholson)
Tennyson	(A. Lyall)
Thackeray	(A. Trollope)
Thomson	(G. C. Macaulay)
*Wilde	(H. C. Harwood)
Wordsworth	(F. W. Myers)

(* Soon to appear)

Great Writers Series Ed. by E. S. Robertson—London, W. Scott, contains biographies of:

Browning	(W. Sharp)
Bunyan	(E. Venables)
Burns	(J. S. Blackie)
Byron	(Noel and Venables)
Carlyle	(R. Garnett)
Coleridge	(T. Hall Caine)
Crabbe	(T. E. Kebbel)
Dickens	(F. T. Marzials)
Goldsmith	(A. Dobson)
L. Hunt	(Cosmo Monkhouse)

Johnson	(F. Grant)
Keats	(W. M. Rossetti)
Milton	(R. Garnett)
Rossetti	(J. Knight)
Ruskin	(Ashmore Wingate)
Scott	(C. D. Yonge)
Shelley	(W. Sharp)
Tennyson	(A. Turnbull)
Thackeray	(Merivale and Marzials)

Handbooks of English Literature—London, G. Bell and Sons

Age of Alfred, 664-1154 (Snell)
Age of Chaucer, 1346-1400 (Snell)
Age of Transition, 1400-1580, 2 vols. (Snell)
Age of Shakespeare, 1579-1631, 2 vols. (Th. Seccombe and J. W. Allen)
Age of Milton, 1632-1660 (J. H. B. Masterman)
Age of Dryden, 1660-1700 (R. Garnett)
Age of Pope, 1700-1774 (John Dennis)
Age of Johnson, 1744-1798 (Thomas Seccombe)
Age of Wordsworth, 1798-1832 (C. H. Herford)
Age of Tennyson, 1830-1870 (Hugh Walker)

How to Know the Authors Series Ed. Will D. Howe—Indianapolis, Bobbs-Merrill Co.

Arnold	(S. P. Sherman)
Browning	(W. L. Phelps)
Burns	(W. A. Nielson)
Carlyle	(B. Perry)
Dickens	(R. Burton)
Defoe	(W. P. Trent)
Stevenson	(R. A. Rice)
Tennyson	(R. M. Alden)
Wordsworth	(C. T. Winchester)

Lives of Great Writers Series ed. Tudor Jenks—New York, A. S. Barnes

In the Days of—
Chaucer
Shakespeare
Milton
Goldsmith
Scott

IMPORTANT PERIODICALS

The Atlantic Monthly Boston
The Bookman New York
The Bookman London
The Dial New York
Harpers Magazine New York
The Living Age Boston
The Nation New York
The New York Times Book Review New York
The Nineteenth Century London
The North American Review New York
Poetry Chicago
The Saturday Review of Literature ed. H. S. Canby New York
The Saturday Review of Literature, Politics, Science, and Art London
The Yale Review New Haven

THE STUDY OF POETRY

ALDEN, R. M. *Introduction to Poetry*—New York, Holt, 1909
English Verse—New York, Holt, 1903
GUMMERE, F. B. *A Handbook of Poetics*—Boston, Ginn, 1885
JOHNSON, C. F. *Forms of English Poetry*—New York, Am. Book Co., 1904

CHRONOLOGY

ENGLISH LITERATURE: SOCIAL AND HISTORICAL BACKGROUND

[Julius Caesar invades Great Britain, 55 B.C. Constantine establishes Christianity in Rome, A.D. 395. Roman Empire divided, 395. Roman legions leave England, Rome sacked, 410. Angles, Saxons, Jutes begin invasion of and settlement in Great Britain about 450; movement complete about 600. Christianity introduced about 597. THE MIDDLE AGES (Fall of Rome, 476, to Fall of Constantinople, 1453): Continental Europe subject to vast changes in government and institutions. The age of Feudalism and Chivalry. Church fosters and spreads learning, preserves it throughout barbarian invasions. England, geographically favored, comparatively undisturbed.]

TEUTONIC ENGLAND

600-800

[England divided into small tribal and local kingdoms: Kent, Mercia, Wessex, East Anglia, Northumbria]

627 Conversion of Edwin of Northumbria

634 *Koran*

711 Arab conquest of Spain

778 Battle of Roncesvalles, source of heroic legends and songs

793–878 Danes invade and overrun England for a century and destroy Northumbrian culture and literature

[Literature derived from the Continent, the work of gleemen writing in the Northumbrian dialect, dominant till 850; later preserved in Wessex dialect, dominant after 880]

Beowulf
Widsith
Fight at Finnesburg
Battle of Maldon
The Wanderer
Deor's Lament
} Pagan with some Christian elements

Religious writings (Christian)
Caedmon (fl. 670): *Paraphrase of Scriptures*
Bede: *Ecclesiastical History* (in Latin), finished 731
Cynewulf (fl. 750): *Riddles, Elene, Christ*

800-1000

800 Charlemagne, Emperor, international hero, center of romantic cycle of legends

829 England united under Egbert: small kingdoms merged into kingdom of Wessex

871 Alfred the Great, King of England; stays the invasions of the Danes

878 Peace of Wedmore: [Danes share the country, finally absorbed; a period of general awakening and progress; growth of patriotism; establishing of legal codes; founding of schools and churches; encouraging of education; West-Saxon becomes dominant dialect into which is translated previous Northumbrian literature]

850–60 *Anglo-Saxon Chronicle* begun, and extended backward

Alfred's translations:
Orosius; Bede; Boethius; Gregory; *Ohthere's Narrative*

937 Battle of Brunanburh

937 "Battle of Brunanburh" inserted in *Anglo-Saxon Chronicle*

960 Dunstan Archbishop of Canterbury

Chronicle continued

1000

THE NORMAN INVASION

1066 Battle of Hastings. King Harold killed; William, Duke of Normandy, becomes king

[Establishment of French customs, as strong social force; introduction of feudalism; prevalence of chivalry; the era of the troubadours]

[Norman-French becomes the language of the court: growth of language, enriched by French terms, chivalry, fashion, law]

1087 William II

1096 First Crusade

[Contact with the Orient]

1100

1100 Henry I

1135 Stephen

c. 1140 *Nibelungenlied*

1147 Geoffrey of Monmouth: ***Historia Britonum Regum*** [Written in Latin; creation of Arthur as national hero]

1154 Henry II

[Old English dying out. Peterborough version of *English Chronicle* ends 1154. Many histories and chronicles in Latin and French]

1170 Murder of Thomas à Becket

1170–80 Miracle Plays in London

1179–1241 Prose Edda

[Beginning of drama—in churches under supervision of clergy]

1187 Saracens take Jerusalem

[Stories of the Holy Grail in French]

1189 Richard I
Third Crusade

Robin Hood ballads take form

1199 John

1200

1203 Murder of Arthur

1204 End of French political influence

1205 Layamon: *Brut*
[Arthurian legend in English]

1215 Magna Charta

[Crumbling of feudal and beginning of modern political system; people gaining sense of independence; genesis of Parliament and of universities; towns as industrial centers; establishment of gilds]

1216 Henry III

1272 Edward I

1294 First alliance of France and Scotland against England

1295 Final organization of English Parliament

1296 War with Scotland and France

1307 Edward II

[c. 1307 Dante begins *Divina Commedia;* Italian language fixed; Italian influence first reaches England]

1314 Battle of Bannockburn

1327 Edward III

1337 Beginning of Hundred Years' War (1337-1453)
[Outburst of national energy; patriotism urging England to conquest and commercial progress; decay of feudalism; decay of Church as social factor; rise of House of Commons; growth of universities and craft gilds; interest in sciences; foreign travel]

1346 Battle of Crécy
[Victory of man-at-arms and cross-bow; chivalry doomed]

[English language conquering; interest in folk poetry—ballad literature, metrical romances, miracle plays, all in English]

c. 1215–20 Orm: *Ormulum*

c. 1225 *Ancren Riwle*

c. 1250 *Cuckoo Song*
Nicholas of Guildford: *The Owl and the Nightingale*

Song of Horn

1270–80 *Havelock the Dane*
Guy of Warwick
Floriz and Blanchefleur

1300

1303 Robert Manning: *Handlyng Synne*
Amis and Amiloun
Horn Childe

1320–5 *Cursor Mundi*

1332? Langland born

[Period of stagnation in literature; drama taken over by gilds]

1340 Chaucer born

1349 Black Death
[Paralyzes England; want and suffering; scarcity of labor gives power to laboring classes; period of social criticism; Wyclif and Lollards; beginning of Puritanism, first hint of Reformation]

Before 1350 *Chester Miracle Plays*

1350 Boccaccio: *Decameron*
[Petrarch flourishing; Renaissance in Italy]

c. 1360 *The Pearl*
Sir Gawayne and the Green Knight
Cleanness
Patience

1356 Battle of Poitiers

1362–3 Langland: *Piers Plowman* (*A* text)
[Social and religious satire]
Harrowing of Hell (Miracle Play)

1370–1440 Chaucer: Poems and tales show medieval and modern elements; establishment of the Midland dialect (that of London, the center of the intellectual, commercial, and social life of England) as the national language; an influence enhanced by Wyclif's Bible, strengthened by Caxton's printing press; grammatical forms simplified, inflections weakened

1377 Richard II
Wyclif before the Bishop of London

1380 Wyclif's Bible

1381 Wat Tyler's Rebellion (Peasant Revolt)
[A social revolt against oppression of the poor]

1388 Battle of Otterburn (Chevy Chase)

1393 Gower: *Confessio Amantis*
[Gower writing in Latin, French, English; typical of condition of literature]

1399 Henry IV

1400

1400 Death of Chaucer

c. 1400 Mandeville's *Travels* (printed)

1413 Henry V

1415 Battle of Agincourt

c. 1415 Lydgate: *Troy Book*

c. 1420 Lydgate: *Romance of Thebes*
Towneley Mystery Plays
[Folk drama; a new form beginning]

1422 Henry VI

1429 Joan of Arc

c. 1450 Ballads
[Period of activity in folk poetry, especially in the north of England and the Scottish border; literature otherwise dormant]

1453 End of Hundred Years' War
[Loss of France]

Fall of Constantinople
[Greek culture takes refuge in Italy; civilization of East moves west; beginning of Renaissance; interest in classical literature and culture]

1455 Gutenberg's Bible
First battle of the Wars of the Roses
[Internal strife in England—York and Lancaster; growth in power of Parliament]

1461 Edward IV

1470 Malory: *Morte Darthur*
[Looks back at a dying age]

1474 Caxton: *Histories of Troy*

1476? Caxton sets up his printing press in Westminster
[Spread of learning, education, and common literary language; modern world at hand]

1483 Richard III

END OF MEDIEVALISM

1485 Henry VII
[End of Middle Ages; beginning of modern England; new class of nobility; voyages of discovery; opening up of New World]

1486 Bartholomeo Diaz rounds Cape of Good Hope

1492 Columbus discovers America

1497 Cabot discovers American mainland

1498 Vasco de Gama discovers sea route to India

1500

1509 Henry VIII

1510 Erasmus and Colet teaching Greek at Cambridge arouse English enthusiasm in Renaissance
[Revived life in universities]

1515 Wolsey Cardinal and Lord Chancellor

1516 More: *Utopia*
[First of the ideal reconstructions of society in English literature]

1517 Reformation flourishes under Luther in Germany; introduces new ideas into Europe

1521 Luther before the Diet of Worms
[Organized opposition to Rome begins]

1523 Lord Berners: ***Translation of Froissart***

1529 Fall of Wolsey
[Ends the English Church of the Middle Ages; signs of active Reformation]

1531 Sir T. Elyot: *The Governor*
[Moral philosophy]
[Reformation and renaissance in various branches of literature—experiments in poetry, drama, prose; study of foreign languages, imitation of foreign literature]

1532 Heywood: *Plays*

1534 Act of Supremacy
[England renounces Church of Rome; Church of England established; monasticism suppressed; redistribution of land and wealth; rise of middle classes; interest in social problems; growth of education; sea commerce; exploration.]

1534 Tyndale: *New Testament*

1535 Coverdale: *Bible*

1538 English Bible introduced into churches
[Fires zeal of the Protestants]

1543 Copernicus
[Heliocentric discoveries vastly enlarge conception of universe]

1544 Ascham: *Toxophilus*

1547 Edward VI

1549 *English Book of Common Prayer* in use

1550

1553 Mary
[Catholic reaction; social misery]

1557 *Tottel's Miscellany*
[First printed collection of verse, begins new era of English poetry]
Wyatt; Surrey; purveyors of Renaissance and Italian literature to England

1558 Elizabeth
[Religious struggles between Protestants and Catholics; rivalry with Spain for possessions in New World; attempts at colonization; foreign trade and travel; zeal for education; Elizabeth studies Greek]

[Golden Age of English literary production begins; drama, poetry, pamphlets, pastoral novels, social sketches; imitation of foreign models; translations; experimentation with meter and diction; poor prose; good verse]

1559 *Mirror for Magistrates*

1560 *Gammer Gurton's Needle*
[Popular comedy]

1561 *Gorboduc* (acted)
[First "regular" English tragedy; in imitation of Senecan tragedy]

1562 Sir John Hawkins begins slave trade with Africa

1563 Foxe: *Acts and Monuments (Book of Martyrs)*

1566 Udall: *Ralph Roister Doister*
[First "regular" English comedy, modeled on Terence; unities; acts and scenes]

1570 Ascham: *Schoolmaster*

1572 Massacre of St. Bartholomew
[Many Huguenots seek refuge in England, later in English colonies]

1577 Drake sails for the Pacific

1577 Holinshed: *Chronicle*
[Source for some of Shakespeare's plays]

1579 Gosson: *School of Abuse*
[Social satire]
Lyly: *Euphues, Anatomy of Wit*
North: Translation of Plutarch's *Lives*
[A source book for Shakespeare]
Spenser: *Shepheardes Calender*

1580 Lyly: *Euphues and his England*

1581 Sidney: *Apology for Poetry*

1584-5 Raleigh colonizes Virginia (colony fails)

1584 Peele: *Arraignment of Paris*
Lyly: *Alexander and Campaspe*

1586 Battle of Zutphen; death of Sidney

1587 Mary Queen of Scots executed

1588 Defeat of the Armada
[Secures England supremacy of the sea and frees her from fear of invasion; establishes Protestantism; strengthens national spirit; growth in population and prosperity; maritime and colonial expansion]

1588 *Martin Marprelate Tracts*
[Issued in spite of law strictly licensing press, and allowing printing only in London, Oxford, and Cambridge; begins century of struggle for free press]

1589 Hakluyt: *Voyages and Discoveries*
[Romance of travel and adventure; one of many similar compilations]

1590-1600

1590-1600 First great decade of Elizabethan Literature

1590 Lodge: *Rosalind*
Marlowe: *Tamburlaine*
Sidney: *Arcadia*
Spenser: *Fairy Queen,* I-III

1598 Edict of Nantes (France), first recognition of religious toleration by a great country

SHAKESPEARE'S FIRST PERIOD [Spontaneous, unrestrained]

1590 *A Midsummer Night's Dream*
Two Gentlemen of Verona

1591 *Romeo and Juliet*
Sidney: *Astrophel and Stella*

1592 *Venus and Adonis*
Sonnets (written ?)
Marlowe: *Edward II*

1593 *King Richard II*

1594 *King Richard III*
Lucrece

SHAKESPEARE'S SECOND PERIOD [Mastery of technique]

1595 *King John*
Sidney: *Apology for Poetry* (Criticism)
Spenser: *Colin Clout*
Spenser: *Amoretti*

1596 *The Merchant of Venice*
The Taming of the Shrew

Jonson: *Every Man in His Humor*
Spenser: *Fairy Queen*, IV-VI
Blackfriars Theater established

1597 1 *King Henry IV*
2 *King Henry IV*
Bacon: *Essays*

1598 Chapman: Translation of *Iliad* begun
The Merry Wives of Windsor
Much Ado About Nothing

1599 *King Henry V*
Spenser dies
Globe Theater built
Minor Dramatists of the decade: Lyly, Peele, Greene, Lodge, Nash, Kyd; Spanish influence on the drama

1600-1610

1601 Insurrection of Essex
[Fails; involves the death of some of Shakespeare's best friends]

1603 Death of Elizabeth
James I (VI of Scotland); Union of England and Scotland; Stuart dynasty; Divine

SHAKESPEARE'S SECOND PERIOD, Cont'd

1600 *As You Like It*

1601 *Twelfth Night*

SHAKESPEARE'S THIRD PERIOD [Darker comedies and tragedies]

Julius Caesar

1602 *Hamlet*

1603 *Measure for Measure*

Jonson: *Sejanus*

Right of Kings; conflict between King and Parliament, Church and State, Puritans and Cavaliers, ending in Civil War and execution of Charles I

1605 Gunpowder Plot

1607 Jamestown founded

1618 Beginning of Thirty Years' War; conflict between Protestants and Catholics on Continent

1620 Plymouth Colony founded
[First Puritan emigration to America]

1604 *Othello*

Marlowe: *Faustus*

1605 *Macbeth*

King Lear
Bacon: *Advancement of Learning*
[Impetus to scientific investigation]
Jonson: *Volpone*

1606 *Trolius and Cressida*
Antony and Cleopatra

1609 Dekker: *Gull's Hornbook*
[Social satire]

SHAKESPEARE'S FOURTH PERIOD [Milder view of life]

1610 *The Tempest*
Jonson: *The Alchemist*

c. 1610 Beaumont and Fletcher: *Knight of the Burning Pestle*
[Satire upon romance]
Minor Dramatists of the decade: Marston, Middleton, Heywood, Greene, Beaumont and Fletcher, Dekker, Webster

1611-1620

SHAKESPEARE'S FOURTH PERIOD, Cont'd

1611 *The Winter's Tale*
Authorized version of the Bible; greatly influential in fixing English vocabulary and grammatical forms

1612 Bacon: *Essays* (2d edition)

1613 Browne: *Britannia's Pastorals*
Wither: *Abuses Stript & Whipt*
[Puritan Satire]
Purchas: *Pilgrimage* (adventure)

1614 Raleigh: *History of the World*

1616 Chapman: Translation of *The Odyssey*
Webster: *Duchess of Malfi*
Beaumont and Shakespeare die

1620 Bacon: *Novum Organum*
[Treats the inductive method of logic, and stimulates the discovery of new truths in science]
Minor Poets: Drayton, Wither, Browne

1621-1630

1621 Impeachment of Bacon
Progress in science; theological controversies; political and philosophical writings; travels; sermons

1625 Charles I dissolves three Parliaments in succession; no Parliament 1629-40; Government expenses met by levied "ship money" and forced loans

1630 Massachusetts Bay Colony founded
[Puritanism established in Church and State in America]

1621 Burton: *Anatomy of Melancholy*

1622 *London Weekly Courant* (Newspaper)

1623 Massinger: *Duke of Milan*
SHAKESPEARE: FIRST FOLIO EDITION

1625 Bacon: *Essays* (Completed)

1626 Sandys: Translation of Ovid's *Metamorphoses*
[Heroic couplet appears in a popular work]

1627 Drayton: *Battle of Agincourt*

1630 Quarles: *Divine Poems* (Puritan verse)

1631-1640

1633 Laud, Archbishop of Canterbury, opposes Puritanism

1637 Trial of Hampden (For refusing to pay "ship money")

1638 Scotch Covenant to oppose Episcopacy

1640 "Long" Parliament meets [A Puritan parliament, sits twelve years]

[1640-1660 a time of confusion in literature as well as in society; an overlapping of the old and new; no dominant note]

1631 Herbert: *The Temple*
[Religious and devotional poetry, mysticism]

1634 Milton: *Comus*

1635 Quarles: *Emblems*

1638 Milton: *Lycidas*

1641-1650

1642 Outbreak of Civil War
Battle of Edgehill

1644 Battle of Marston Moor

1645 Battle of Naseby
[Parliamentary victories]

1646 Charles surrenders to the Scots

1642 Theaters closed

1644 Milton: *Areopagitica*
[Argument for freedom of the press]

1645 Waller: *Poems*
[Pseudo-classic; "refined" language; heroic couplets]

1646 Crashaw: *Steps to the Temple*
Vaughan: *Poems*
Suckling: *Fragmenta Aurea*
[Collected poems]

1648 Herrick: *Hesperides*
[Cavalier poetry, reminiscent of Elizabethan days]

1649 Execution of Charles I
Commonwealth

1649 Lovelace: *Lucasta*

1650 Taylor: *Holy Living*
Crashaw, Herbert, Vaughan, religious poets. Suckling, Herrick, Lovelace, amorous and "Cavalier" poets

1651-1660

1651 Taylor: *Holy Dying*
[Notable rhythmic prose]
Hobbes: *Leviathan*
[Reactionary; supports the divine right of kings]

1653 Cromwell, Protector

1653 Walton: *Complete Angler*

1656 Davenant: *Siege of Rhodes*
[First "heroic" play; theatrical performances resumed, but not publicly]

1658 Death of Cromwell

1658 Dryden: *Stanzas on Death of Cromwell*

1660 Restoration of Charles II

Royal Society chartered
[Experimentation and observation]

THE RESTORATION

Puritanism fails politically; personal will of sovereign temporarily restored; doctrine of "divine right" of kings asserts itself; lax morals, license becomes fashionable

The "Pseudo-Classic" Age begins; heroic couplet rules poetry for a century and a quarter; theaters reopen, "heroic" play in vogue, drama of manners increasingly corrupt

1661-1670

1661 Rule of Louis XIV, the "Great Monarch"

1663 Butler: *Hudibras*
[Satire on Puritans]
Dryden: *Wild Gallant*
[Comedy]
Dryden: *Rival Ladies*

1664 Waller: *Poems*

1665 War with the Dutch
The Great Plague

1666 Great Fire of London
Influence of great living French writers:

La Fontaine
Molière
Scudéry
Boileau

1666 Bunyan: *Grace Abounding*
[Religious]

1667 Dryden: *Essay on Dramatic Poesy*
[Criticism showing modern trend of thought]
Milton: *Paradise Lost*

1668 Mrs. Behn: *Oronoko*
[Beginning of modern novel]
Cowley: *Works*
[Contain many pseudo-Pindaric odes]

1670 Dryden: *Conquest of Granada*
[Notable "heroic" drama]
Walton: *Lives*
[A step toward modern biography]

1671-1680

1671 Duke of Buckingham: *Rehearsal*
[Dramatic satire]
Milton: *Paradise Regained*
" *Samson Agonistes*

1672 Dryden: *Marriage à la Mode*

1674 Milton dies

1675 Wycherley: *Country Life*
Dryden: *Aurengzebe*
[Last of Dryden's "heroic" plays]

1676 Etheredge: *Man of Mode*

1677 Wycherley: *Plain Dealer*

1678 Bunyan: *Pilgrim's Progress*
Dryden: *All for Love*
[Height of Dryden's drama]

THE AGE OF DRYDEN

1681-1690

In a reaction against internal political conflict, England seeks peace under the restored monarchy

1685 James II, a Catholic, ascends the throne; leagued with France; subsidized by Louis XIV; stands for personal rule
Protestant and Catholic influences in conflict in government and society

Monmouth's Rebellion
[A popular but ill-timed expression of Protestant sentiment]

In a reaction against Puritanism in its attempt to regulate conduct, literature becomes exotically and conspicuously lax

1680 Otway: *The Orphan*

1681 Dryden: *Absalom and Achitophel*
[Political satire]

1682 Otway: *Venice Preserved*
[Sentimental tragedy; blank verse; a return to the Elizabethan manner]
Dryden: *MacFlecknoe*
[Personal satire]
Dryden: *Religio Laici*
[Religious and controversial satire]

1687 Dryden: *The Hind and Panther*
[Religious and controversial satire]
Newton: *Principia*
[A fundamental work in mathematical physics]

"THE GLORIOUS REVOLUTION"

1688 James II abdicates; William III and Mary chosen sovereigns by Parliament; Protestant succession declared; ancient constitution affirmed; ancient rights restored. Parliament becomes the ruling power: end of fifty years' struggle between people and throne

1689 The Toleration Bill: Non-Conformists allowed freedom in religious practices, a share in official life

1690 The Battle of the Boyne
[James II defeated in attempting to regain the throne. England free from French threat of force for more than a century]

1690 Locke: *Essay Concerning the Human Understanding*
[Lasting contribution to modern philosophy]

A decade of advance in Science. Literature is characterized by satire growing out of political and religious controversy

1691-1700

1692 Freedom of the British Press established

1694 Bank of England founded
[A move toward sound finance]

1695 Congreve: *Love for Love*

1698 Vanbrugh: *The Provoked Wife*
Collier: *A Short View of the Immorality and Profaneness of the Stage*
[A reaction of public taste against vicious comedy]

1700 Congreve: *The Way of the World*
Dryden: *Fables*
Dryden dies

In this decade the cynical and licentious comedy of manners reached its height.

THE AGE OF QUEEN ANNE

1701-1710

1702 The War of the Spanish Succession
[England fights to prevent a union of Catholic monarchies]

An era of intense party strife. Whig against Tory

1701 Steele: *The Christian Hero*
Defoe: *The True-Born Englishman*

An era of prose which becomes influential through the free press, appealing to middle-class partisans. The age of political satire; pamphleteering

1702 Steele: *The Funeral*

1703 Steele: *The Lying Lover*

1704 Addison: *The Campaign*
[Political poetry]

Newton: *Optics*
[Discoveries in physics]

1706 Franklin born The European War drags on	
	1707 Prior: *Poems*
	1709 Pope: *Pastorals*
	Steele and Addison: *The Tatler*. Steele reaches some success in a reformed comedy. The periodical essay becomes established

THE AGE OF POPE

1711-1720

England's triumph in foreign war is followed by a long Whig régime in politics. Trade expands; foreign and colonial commerce flourishes. Party strife fierce	An age of prose. The periodical essay an influence in refining manners. Social and political satire of widening range in prose and verse, a reaction against the foolishness of war and the swaying of society by emotion. Reason is assumed to be the law of society and of literature. Pseudo-Classicism reaches its height in Pope. Literature of adventure and pseudo-adventure: Defoe, Swift
	1711 Pope: *Essay on Criticism* Steele and Addison: *Spectator*
	1712 Pope: *Rape of the Lock*
1713 Treaty of Utrecht closes eleven years of war	1713 Addison: *Cato* [Pseudo-classic drama at its best] Pope: *Ode for St. Cecilia's Day*
1714 Anne dies, last of Stuarts George I. Hanoverian dynasty. Democracy ascendant. Political power wholly in Parliament	1714 Gay: *Shepherd's Week* [Satiric, but pastoral] Steele: *The Lover*
1715 "Old Pretender," son of James I, tries, with help of Scots, to gain English throne	1715 Gay: *Poems* Pope: Translation of *The Iliad*
	1718 Prior: *Poems*
	1719 Defoe: *Robinson Crusoe* [Realistic romance; elementary form of novel] Watts: *Psalms* and *Hymns*
1720 South Sea Bubble	

1721-1730

1721 Walpole, Prime Minister Peace and political corruption	1721 Ramsay: *Poems*
	1722 Defoe: *Journal of the Plague Year* Steele: *The Conscious Lovers*
	1725 Pope: *Edition of Shakespeare*
	1726 Swift: *Gulliver's Travels* Thomson: *Seasons* (begun) [Forerunner of new treatment of Nature]

1727 George II

1727 Gay: *Fables*

1728 Gay· *Beggar's Opera*
Pope: *Dunciad*
[Personal satire]

1729 Gay: *Polly*
Swift: *Modest Proposal*
[Social satire]

1730 Pope, etc.: *Grub Street Journal*
The greatest decade of English satire

1731-1750

1731 Fielding: *Tragedy of Tom Thumb*
[The modern novel begun by Richardson and Fielding]
Lillo: *George Barnwell*
[Popular domestic tragedy]

1732 Pope: *Essay on Man*

1737 Shenstone: *Schoolmistress*

1738 Johnson: *London*

1740 Richardson: *Pamela*
[First novel of sentiment]

1741 Hume: *Essays Moral and Political*

1742 Fielding: *Joseph Andrews*
[Satire on Pamela]

Young: *Night Thoughts* } "graveyard"
1743 Blair: *The Grave* } poetry
Fielding: *Jonathan Wild*

1744 Pope dies

1745 The "Young Pretender," Charles Stuart, makes last attempt by his house to gain the English throne

1745 Swift dies

1746 Collins: *Odes*

1747 Gray: *Ode on Eton College*

1748 Richardson: *Clarissa Harlowe*
Smollett: *Roderick Random*
Thomson: *Castle of Indolence*
Wesley: *Hymns*

1749 Fielding: *Tom Jones*
[Fully developed realistic novel]

1750 Johnson: *Rambler*

1751-1760

1751 Fielding: *Amelia*
Gray: *Elegy*
Smollett: *Peregrine Pickle*

	1753 Hume: *Essays and Treatises* Richardson: *Sir Charles Grandison* Smollett: *Ferdinand, Count Fathom*

THE AGE OF JOHNSON

Party strife continues. The foundation of the British Empire in India, North America, and the Antipodes. Methodism fights against the lethargy of the English Church. Rumblings of political revolt	England much influenced by French rationalistic thought. Johnson a personal influence for conservatism in literary form and in thought. An age of prose. Reason has killed emotion; but Romantic dawn appears
	1754 Hume: *History of Great Britain*
	1755 Johnson: *Dictionary* [An epoch in English lexicography]
1756 Seven Years' War begins Black Hole of Calcutta	1756 J. Warton: *Essay on Pope* [Questions Pope's supremacy]
	1757 Gray: *Pindaric Odes* [Classic influence]
1759 Voltaire: *Candide* The Fall of Quebec	1759 Johnson: *Rasselas* Sterne: *Tristram Shandy*
1760 George III Rousseau: *Nouvelle Heloise*	1760 Goldsmith: *Citizen of the World*

1761-1770

1762 Rousseau: *Contrat Social* [Questions benefits of civilized society] Rousseau: *Émile* [Theories of education]	1762 Macpherson: *Poems of Ossian* [Romantic Celtic revival]
1763 Wilkes and No. 45 of North Briton [Radical]	1763 Lady M. W. Montagu: *Letters*
	1764 Goldsmith: *The Traveler* Walpole: *Castle of Otranto* [Gothic novel]
1765 Stamp Act for American Colonies Revolutionary ideas quicken in America and France Watt invents steam engine	1765 Percy: *Reliques of Ancient English Poetry* [Popular romanticism] Johnson: *Edition of Shakespeare*
	1766 Brooke: *The Fool of Quality* Goldsmith: *Vicar of Wakefield* [Domestic novel]
	1768 Goldsmith: *Good-Natured Man* Gray: *Poems* [Some show a romantic tendency] Sterne: *Sentimental Journey*
1770 Tax on tea resisted in America	1770 Goldsmith: *The Deserted Village*

1771-1780

	1771 Mackenzie: *Man of Feeling* [sentimental] Encyclopedia Britannica [1st edition] Smollett: *Humphrey Clinker*

	1772 *Morning Post* established
1773 Boston Tea Party	1773 Goldsmith: *She Stoops to Conquer* [Popular comedy of Manners]
1774 Goethe: *Sorrows of Werther* [German Romanticism]	1774 Burke: *Speech on American Taxation* Chesterfield: *Letters to his Son* Warton: *History of English Poetry*
1775 Battle of Lexington	1775 Burke: *Speech on Conciliation* Sheridan: *The Rivals* [Comedy of Manners]
1776 Jefferson writes *Declaration of Independence* [A world text for Democracy]	1776 Gibbon: *The Decline and Fall of the Roman Empire,* I Paine: *Common Sense* [Radical in politics] A. Smith: *Wealth of Nations* [Political science]
1777 Burgoyne surrenders at Saratoga	1777 Sheridan: *School for Scandal* [Comedy of Manners] Chatterton: *Poems* (romantic)
	1778 Burney: *Evelina*
	1779 Johnson: *Lives of the Poets* The Comedy of Manners reaches its height in this decade

1781-1790

1781 Cornwallis surrenders at Yorktown	
1782 Independence of America recognized	1782 Cowper: *Table Talk*
	1783 Crabbe: *The Village*
	1784 Beckford: *Vathek* [Romance and magic of the East] Johnson dies
	1785 Cowper: *The Task* *London Times* established
1786 Impeachment of Warren Hastings [England recognizes obligations to native races]	1786 Burns: *Poems* [Nature, sentiment, individual revolt]
	1787 Wesley: *Sermons*
1789 Fall of the Bastille [French Revolution begins]	1789 Blake: *Songs of Innocence* G. White: *Natural History of Selborne*
	1790 Burke: *Reflections on the Revolution in France* [Conservative reaction against upheaval in society]

THE AGE OF ROMANTICISM

1790-1832

Historical	Literary
Revolt against established authority. French Revolution. Danger of French invasion quiets democratic uprising in England. Society permeated by French skeptical philosophy and doctrinaire radicalism. Industrial revolution unsettles working classes	Literary convention discounted and flaunted. The infusion of emotion, feeling, variety into literature. A return to the emotional spirit of the Middle Ages, the spirit of wonder and awe; the use of medieval subjects in prose and poetry. The EXPRESSION OF THE EGO

1791-1800

1791	Representative government in Canada	1791	Boswell: *Life of Johnson* Paine: *Rights of Man* [Doctrinaire radicalism]
		1792	Paine: *The Age of Reason* [French skepticism]
1793	War renewed with France, continues until Waterloo	1793	Godwin: *Inquiry Concerning Political Justice* [Social revolt]
		1794	A. Radcliffe: *Mysteries of Udolpho* [Romantic Gothic novel]
		1795	Lewis: *The Monk* [Gothic novel]
		1796	Coleridge: *Poems*
1798	Battle of the Nile	1798	Cowper: *Poems* Wordsworth and Coleridge: *Lyrical Ballads* [The great landmark in the English romantic movement] Malthus: *Principles of Population* [Sociology]
1799	Napoleon First Consul	1799	H. More: *Modern Female Education*
		1800	M. Edgeworth: *Castle Rackrent* Wordsworth: *Lyrical Ballads* [Second edition, with notable preface advocating new principles in poetry]

1801-1810

		1801	Southey: *Thalaba*
		1802	M. Edgeworth: *Moral Tales* Scott: *Minstrelsy of the Scottish Border* [Old ballads] *Edinburgh Review* established [Whig, critical]
1803	Peace of Amiens; war soon renewed		
1804	Napoleon Emperor French plan to invade England		
1805	Battle of Trafalgar; French power at sea crushed	1805	Scott: *Lay of the Last Minstrel* [Metrical romance]

1807 Abolition of slave trade

1807 Byron: *Hours of Idleness*

1809 Byron: *English Bards and Scotch Reviewers*
[Literary satire]
M. Edgeworth: *Tales of Fashionable Life*

1810 Crabbe: *The Borough*
[Realistic]
J. Porter: *Scottish Chiefs*
[Popular romance]
Scott: *Lady of the Lake*
[Metrical romance]

1811-1820

1811 Austen: *Sense and Sensibility*

1812 War with America
Napoleon's Russian Campaign; disastrous to French military power

1812 Byron: *Childe Harold* I, II
[Romantic wandering and adventure]

1813 Battle of Leipzig

1813 Austen: *Pride and Prejudice*
Byron: *Bride of Abydos*
Shelley: *Queen Mab*
[Free thought in religion]
Southey: *Life of Nelson*

1814 First Locomotive

1814 Scott: *Waverley* novels begun
[Romantic fiction established]
Wordsworth: *Excursion*

1815 Battle of Waterloo
Napoleon banished, French imperial ambition checked for a century

1815–1832 A period of social and political upheaval and reform; the Industrial Revolution in full swing

1816 Byron: *Prisoner of Chillon*
Coleridge: *Christabel*
Shelley: *Alastor*
Scott: *Old Mortality*
Austen: *Emma*

1817 Byron: *Manfred*
[Emphasis on ego]
Coleridge: *Biographia Literaria*
Keats: *Poems*

Moore: *Lalla Rookh*
[Oriental romance]

1818 Byron: *Childe Harold* IV
Austen: *Northanger Abbey*
[Satire upon the Gothic Novel]
Keats: *Endymion*
Scott: *Rob Roy*
Scott: *Heart of Midlothian*

1819 Manchester riots

1819 Byron: *Don Juan* I, II
Scott: *Bride of Lammermoor*
Scott: *Legend of Montrose*
Shelley: *The Cenci*

History	Literature
1820 George IV England increases trade, applies science to life; develops the arts	1820 Keats: *Lamia, Isabella, Eve of St. Agnes, Hyperion* Lamb: *Essays of Elia* Scott: *Ivanhoe* Scott: *The Monastery* Shelley: *Prometheus Unbound* Wordsworth: *Sonnets on the River Duddon*
1821-1830	
	1821 Byron: *Cain* De Quincey: *Confessions* Hazlitt: *Table Talk* Mill: *Elements of Political Economy* Scott: *Kenilworth* Shelley: *Adonais*
	1824 Lamb: *Essays*, 2d series Landor: *Imaginary Conversations*
	1825 Macaulay: *Essay on Milton*
	1827 A. and C. Tennyson: *Poems by Two Brothers*
1830 William IV Liberal Revolutions in France and Belgium	1830 Moore: *Life of Byron* Tennyson: *Poems Chiefly Lyrical*
1831-1840	
1832 Reform Bill	
1833 Final abolition of slavery in British dominions	1833 E. B. Browning: *Pauline* Carlyle: *Sartor Resartus* Lamb: *Last Essays of Elia* Tennyson: *Poems*
1834 New Poor Law; system of national education begun	1834 Bulwer-Lytton: *Last Days of Pompeii* Dickens: *Sketches by Boz*
	1835 Browning: *Paracelsus* Coleridge: *Table Talk* Wordsworth: *Yarrow Revisited*
	1836 Marryat: *Midshipman Easy*
1837 Victoria	1837 Carlyle: *French Revolution* Dickens: *Oliver Twist* Lockhart: *Life of Scott* Thackeray: *Yellowplush Papers* E. B. Browning: *The Seraphin*
1838 Beginning of Chartist Movement	

THE VICTORIAN PERIOD

Intense social consciousness following previous period of intense individual consciousness; men of all countries seeking to adjust man's claims on society; Continental social revolutions; society increasingly complex in (1) changing social groupings (rise of middle classes) (2) industrial and commercial ex-

Literature obeying the social forces, examines the past to justify and correct the present, and to reap its benefits. Writers reach various and contradictory conclusions. Mill, Macaulay, and Darwin seek a mechanical adjustment of Man to Nature; the novelists and Browning reach an intensified realism;

pansion (3) scientific discovery. Facing these forces, progress seeks the best means of serving the human spirit	Carlyle, Ruskin, Arnold, and the Pre-Raphaelites urge the claims of the Spirit against mechanistic philosophy and increasing wealth. Tennyson and Morris reflect the reverence for the Past, and the spirit of Romanticism

1841-1850

1841 Free Trade agitation; partial free trade; abolition of corn laws; advocacy of socialism	1841 Carlyle: *Heroes and Hero-Worship* Dickens: *Barnaby Rudge* Macaulay: *Warren Hastings*
	1842 Browning: *Dramatic Lyrics* Macaulay: *Lays of Ancient Rome* Tennyson: *Poems*
	1843 Dickens: *Christmas Carol* Macaulay: *Essays* Ruskin: *Modern Painters*
	1844 E. B. Browning: *Poems*
1846 Liberalism favored by Pope Pius IX	1846 Dickens: *Dombey and Son*
	1847 C. Brontë: *Jane Eyre* Tennyson: *Princess* Thackeray: *Vanity Fair*
1848 End of Chartist Movement. Liberal revolutions in Europe	1848 Macaulay: *History of England* Mill: *Principles of Political Economy*
	1849 Ruskin: *Seven Lamps of Architecture*
	1850 Tennyson: *In Memoriam* Wordsworth: *Prelude*

1851-1860

	1851 E. B. Browning: *Casa Guidi Windows*
	1851 Ruskin: *Stones of Venice* Thackeray: *English Humorists*
	1852 Dickens: *Bleak House* Thackeray: *Henry Esmond*
1853 Crimean War	
	1854 Thackeray: *The Newcomes*
	1855 Browning: *Men and Women* Tennyson: *Maud*
	1856 E. B. Browning: *Aurora Leigh* Froude: *History of England* Thackeray: *The Four Georges*
1858 England crushes Sepoy rebellion in India	1858 Carlyle: *History of Frederick the Great* Tennyson: *Idylls of the King* [begun]
	1859 Darwin: *Origin of Species* Dickens: *Tale of Two Cities* Eliot: *Adam Bede* Fitzgerald: *Omar Khayyạm*

1860 French Constitution liberalized by Napoleon III

1861-1870

1861 Civil War in America; England wishes to intervene, but held back by middle classes

1861 Reade: *The Cloister and the Hearth*
Spencer: *Education*

1862 Hugo: *Les Miserables*

1862 Meredith: *Poems*
C. Rossetti: *Goblin Market*

1863 Eliot: *Romola*
Huxley: *Man's Place in Nature*

1864–9 Tolstoy: *War and Peace*

1864 Browning: *Dramatis Personae*
Newman: *Apologia Pro Vita Sua*
Swinburne: *Atalanta in Calydon*
Tennyson: *Enoch Arden*

1865 Arnold: *Essays in Criticism*
Meredith: *Rhoda Fleming*
Ruskin: *Sesame and Lilies*

1866 Gladstone's Reform Bill
Atlantic Cable

1866 Ruskin: *The Crown of Wild Olive*
Swinburne: *Poems and Ballads,* First Series

1867 Parliamentary Reform Bill greatly enlarging the franchise

1867 Arnold: *Study of Celtic Literature*

1868 Browning: *The Ring and the Book*
W. Morris: *Earthly Paradise*

1869 Arnold: *Culture and Anarchy*

1870 Huxley: *Lay Sermons*
Rossetti: *Poems*

1871-1880

1870–1871 Franco-Prussian War; unification of Germany

1871 Darwin: *Descent of Man*
Swinburne: *Songs before Sunrise*
Tennyson: *The Last Tournament*

1872 Hardy: *Under the Greenwood Tree*

1873 Arnold: *Literature and Dogma*
Pater: *Studies in the Renaissance*

1874 Green: *Short History of the English People*

1875 Browning: *Aristophanes' Apology*
Meredith: *Beauchamp's Career*

1876 Bell's Telephone

1876 Eliot: *Daniel Deronda*
Morris: *Sigurd the Volsung*
Spencer: *Principles of Sociology*

1877 Tolstoy: *Anna Karénina*

1877 Hardy: *Return of the Native*

1878 Arnold: *Mixed Essays*

1879 Browning: *Dramatic Idyls*
Meredith: *The Egoist*

1881-1890

1881 Ibsen: *Ghosts*

1881 Rossetti: *Ballads and Sonnets*
Stevenson: *Virginibus Puerisque*

1882 Froude: *Thomas Carlyle*
Stevenson: *Familiar Studies*
Swinburne: *Tristram of Lyonesse*

1883 Carlyle: *Correspondence with Emerson*
Stevenson: *Treasure Island*

1885 Death of Hugo
[Literature of India]

1885 Hudson: *The Purple Land*
Meredith: *Diana of the Crossways*
Pater: *Marius the Epicurean*

1886 Kipling: *Departmental Ditties*
Stevenson: *Kidnapped*
Tennyson: *Locksley Hall Sixty Years After*

1887 The Queen's Jubilee celebrating her fifty years upon the throne

1888 Barrie: *Auld Licht Idylls*
Kipling: *Plain Tales from the Hills*
Ward: *Robert Elsmere*

1889 Browning: *Asolando*
Death of Browning
Barrie: *Window in Thrums*
Pater: *Appreciations*
Stevenson: *Master of Ballantrae*

1890 Ibsen: *Hedda Gabler*
Tolstoy: *Kreutzer Sonata*

1890 Bridges: *Shorter Poems*
Barrie: *The Little Minister*

THE CONTEMPORARY PERIOD

Application of science to sanitation, medicine, arts; some diseases being stifled. Discoveries in science stimulating new inquiries and re-estimates in sociology and philosophy

A new era in literature; expression direct, realism intense; romanticism of great variety; little restraint in form or subject-matter. New fields of material constantly discovered

1891-1900

1890 Shaw: *Quintessence of Ibsenism*

1892 Hauptmann: *The Weavers*

1892 Kipling: *Barrack-Room Ballads*
Hardy: *Tess of the D'Urbervilles*
Tennyson: *Death of Oenone*
Zangwill: *Children of the Ghetto*
Death of Tennyson
Celtic Revival in Ireland

1893 Pinero: *The Second Mrs. Tanqueray*

1894 Kipling: *The Jungle Book*
G. Moore: *Esther Waters*

	1895 Barrie: *The Professor's Love Story* Conrad: *Almayer's Folly*
	1896 Barrie: *Sentimental Tommy* Hardy: *Jude the Obscure* Housman: *A Shropshire Lad*
1897 Second Victorian Jubilee 1897 Establishment of Wireless by Marconi	1897 Conrad: *Nigger of the Narcissus* Newbolt: *Admirals All*
1898 Spanish-American War, the United States a world power	1898 Hardy: *Wessex Poems* Shaw: *Plays Pleasant and Unpleasant* Wilde: *Ballad of Reading Gaol*
1899-1901 The Boer War; England modifies its colonial policy	1899 Irish Literary Theater
1899 The Hague Conference	
1900 The Boxer Rebellion	1900 Conrad: *Lord Jim*

1901-1910

1901 X-rays used in medicine and surgery Edward VII	1901 Kipling: *Kim* 1902 Masefield: *Salt-Water Ballads*
1903 Wright Brothers aeroplane	1903 Shaw: *Man and Superman* Barrie: *The Admirable Crichton* Conrad: *Typhoon*
1904 Russo-Japanese War, Russian power crumbling The automobile cheapened and made procurable by millions The motion picture brings cheap entertainment; diffuses knowledge	1904 Barrie: *Peter Pan* Lady Gregory: *Gods and Fighting Men* Hardy: *The Dynasts* I
	1905 Chesterton: *Heretics* Wells: *Kipps* Synge: *Riders to the Sea*
	1906 Galsworthy: *Man of Property* Noyes: *Drake*
1907 Bergson: *Creative Evolution*	1907 Synge: *Playboy of the Western World*
1908 Peary reaches the North Pole	1908 Barrie: *What Every Woman Knows*
	1909 Galsworthy: *Plays* Wells: *Tono Bungay*
1910 George V	1910 Galsworthy: *Justice* Gibson: *Daily Bread*

1911-1919

	1911 Masefield: *The Everlasting Mercy* Noyes: *Robin Hood*
1912 China a Republic	1912 Masefield: *The Widow in the Bye Street* de la Mare: *Collected Poems*

1913 Masefield: *Dauber; The Daffodil Fields*

1914–1918 The World War staggers civilization. Modern science furnishes high explosives, submarines, aeroplanes, tanks; military sanitation, motor transportation

1915 Brooke: *Poems*

1917 Hodgson: *Poems*

1918 Drinkwater: *Abraham Lincoln*
Gibson: *Hill-Tracks*

1919 The League of Nations
Atlantic ocean crossed by air

1920 Masefield: *Reynard the Fox*
Wells: *Outline of History*

Lawrence: *New Poems*

1921 Aeroplanes for discovery, exploration, pleasure, saving of life.

1924 Pacific ocean crossed by air; air mail and commercial routes established; great extension of radio communication

1928 Beginning of trans-Atlantic commercial air service

INDEX TO AUTHORS, TITLES, AND FIRST LINES